DODS

PARLIAMENTARY COMPANION

2021

189th year

ACKNOWLEDGEMENTS

Dods Parliamentary Companion published since 1832

Published by

Dods
Data and Reference Division
11th Floor
The Shard, 32 London Bridge Street
London SE1 9SG

Telephone: 020 7593 5500
E-mail: editor@dodsgroup.com
www.dodspeople.com

Editor: Elizabeth Newton
Deputy Editor: Imogen Spencer-Dale
Reference Data Manager: Tom Harris

Photo of Richard Drax MP © The Dorset Echo; photo of Baroness Young of Hornsey © Eamonn.McCabe@btinternet.com; photo of Lord Giddens © Nigel Stead/LSE; photo of Lord Tyler © Paul Heartfield; photo of Baroness Neuberger ©Derek Tamea; photo of Baroness Vadera © Charlie Bibby, FT. Contains Parliamentary photos licensed under the Open Parliament Licence v3.0.

No payment is either solicited or accepted for the inclusion of editorial entries in this publication. We reserve the right to include or eliminate listings and otherwise edit and present the data based on our direction and judgement. Every possible precaution has been taken to ensure that the information contained in this publication is accurate at the time of going to press and the publisher cannot accept any liability for errors or omissions, however caused. Inclusion in the publication does not imply endorsement by the editor or publisher. Errors brought to the attention of the publisher and verified to the satisfaction of the editor will be corrected in future publications.

Typesetting by Dataset Media Ltd
Printed in Great Britain by Short Run Press Ltd, Exeter, Devon

ISBN 978-1-908232-34-2 ISSN 0070-7007

CONTENTS

DEVOLVED PARLIAMENT AND ASSEMBLIES 1281

GOVERNMENT AND PUBLIC OFFICES 1379

EDITOR'S INTRODUCTION

The emergence and rapid spread of Covid-19 around the UK in 2020 led to a national lockdown and for politicians this meant the first ever virtual parliaments and voting.

Elections across the country were postponed until 2021, which means the London Assembly and Mayor, Police and Crime Commissioners and local council elections are due to take place on 6 May 2021, along with the Scottish and Welsh Parliaments.

In May Conor Burns resigned as Minister of State for International Trade and Ranil Jayawardena joined the Department for International Trade as a Parliamentary Under-Secretary of State. In September the Foreign and Commonwealth Office and Department for International Development were merged to form the Foreign, Commonwealth and Development Office. Also in September Simon Clarke resigned as Minister of State for Regional Growth and Local Government. Luke Hall replaced Clarke and in turn was replaced as Parliamentary Under-Secretary of State for Rough Sleeping by Kelly Tolhurst. In November Baroness Sugg resigned as Minister for Overseas Territories and Sustainable Development and Nadhim Zahawi was appointed a Parliamentary Under-Secretary of State in the Department of Health and Social Care in late November, taking on the responsibility for the Covid Vaccine Deployment. In January Alok Sharma left his role as Business Secretary of State to take on his role as President of the UK COP26 Climate Conference full time. He was replaced as Business Secretary by Kwasi Kwarteng.

In June the UK's chief Brexit negotiator David Frost was nominated for a life peerage. In late July 36 new life peerages were announced. Keith Stewart became a life peer in November, to replace Lord Keen of Elie as Advocate General for Scotland. In December 17 more new life peers were announced, including David Wolfson who was also appointed a Parliamentary Under-Secretary of State at the Ministry of Justice.

Following the election of Keir Starmer as the Leader of the Labour Party he made several changes to the frontbench, bringing Ed Miliband back as Shadow Business Secretary, naming Annelise Dodds as Shadow Chancellor and Nick Thomas-Symonds as Shadow Home Secretary. In June Rebecca Long Bailey was sacked as Shadow Secretary of State for Education and replaced by Kate Green.

In May Plaid Cymru withdrew the whip from Jonathan Edwards following his arrest on suspicion of assault. Claudia Webbe was suspended by Labour in September after being charged with harassment. Jeremy Corbyn was suspended by Labour in October over his reaction to the Equality and Human Rights Commission's report into anti-Semitism in the Labour Party, he was later reinstated to the party but not the Labour whip. Margaret Ferrier was suspended by the SNP in October after travelling to London with Covid symptoms and returning after receiving a positive test result.

In July, Jackson Carlaw resigned as Scottish Conservative leader after only six months and was replaced by Douglas Ross. Richard Leonard resigned as Scottish Labour Leader in January 2021.

The National Assembly of Wales is now officially known as the Welsh Parliament or Senedd Cymru; its members are no longer AMs but MSs.

Elizabeth Newton, *Editor,* February 2021

Public Legislation 2019-21

Dates are of Royal Assent

Agriculture Act 2020 (12 November 2020)
Birmingham Commonwealth Games Act 2020 (9 September 2020)
Business and Planning Act 2020 (24 July 2020)
Contingencies Fund Act 2020 (26 March 2020)
Coronavirus Act 2020 (26 March 2020)
Corporate Insolvency and Governance Act 2020 (26 June 2020)
Direct Payments to Farmers (Legislative Continuity) Act 2020 (31 January 2020)
Divorce, Dissolution and Separation Act 2020 (26 June 2020)
European Union (Future Relationship) Act 2020 (31 December 2020)
European Union (Withdrawal Agreement) Act 2020 (31 January 2020)
Extradition (Provisional Arrest) Act 2020 (12 November 2020)
Finance Act 2020 (27 July 2020)
Fisheries Act 2020 (25 November 2020)
Immigration and Social Security Co-ordination (EU Withdrawal) Act 2020 (12 November 2020)
Medicines and Medical Devices Act 2021 (12 February 2021)
NHS Funding Act 2020 (17 March 2020)
Parliamentary Constituencies Act 2020 (15 December 2020)
Pension Schemes Act 2021 (12 February 2021)
Prisoners (Disclosure of Information About Victims) Act 2020 (12 November 2020)
Private International Law (Implementation of Agreements) Act 2020 (15 December 2020)
Sentencing (Pre-consolidation Amendments) Act 2020 (10 June 2020)
Sentencing Act 2020 (12 November 2020)
Social Security (Up-rating of Benefits) Act 2020 (24 November 2020)
Stamp Duty Land Tax (Temporary Relief) Act 2020 (24 July 2020)
Supply and Appropriation (Anticipation and Adjustments) Act 2020 (2 April 2020)
Supply and Appropriation (Main Estimates) Act 2020 (24 July 2020)
Taxation (Post-transition Period) Act 2020 (18 December 2020)
Terrorist Offenders (Restriction of Early Release) Act 2020 (27 February 2020)
Trade (Disclosure of Information) Act 2020 (18 December 2020)
United Kingdom Internal Market Act 2020 (18 December 2020)
Windrush Compensation Scheme (Expenditure) Act 2020 (10 June 2020)

Source:
https://bills.parliament.uk

Related Politicians

The following lists those who are related and are current members of UK and European legislatures.

Baroness Blake of Leeds and Olivia Blake MP
Mother and daughter

Baroness Bonham-Carter of Yarnbury and Lord Razzall
Partners

Lord Boswell of Aynho and Victoria Prentis MP
Father and daughter

Sir Peter Bottomley MP and Baroness Bottomley of Nettlestone
Spouses

Lord Chadlington and Lord Deben
Siblings

Baroness Chapman of Darlington and Nick Smith MP
Spouses

Jon Cruddas MP and Baroness Healy of Primrose Hill
Spouses

John Cryer MP and Ellie Reeves MP
Spouses

John Cryer MP and Rachel Reeves MP
Siblings-in-law

Alun Davies MS and Anna McMorrin MP
Partners

Philip Davies MP and Esther McVey MP
Spouses

Spouses Lord Deben and Lord Chadlington
Siblings

Lord Denham and Lord Redesdale
Cousins

Caroline Dinenage MP and Lord Lancaster of Kimbolton
Spouses

Diane Dodds MLA and Lord Dodds of Duncairn
Spouses

Spouses Jack Dromey MP and Harriet Harman MP
Spouses

Dame Angela Eagle MP and Maria Eagle MP
Twins

Baroness Eccles of Moulton and Viscount Eccles
Spouses

Annabelle Ewing MSP and Fergus Ewing MSP
Siblings

Kenneth Gibson MSP and Patricia Gibson MP
Spouses

Colm Gildernew MLA and Michelle Gildernew MP
Siblings

Viscount Hailsham and Baroness Hogg
Spouses

Baroness Harding of Winscombe and John Penrose MP
Spouses

Harriet Harman MP and Jack Dromey MP
Spouses

Baroness Healy of Primrose Hill and Jon Cruddas MP
Spouses

Baroness Hodgson of Abinger and Lord Hodgson of Astley Abbotts
Spouses

Baroness Hogg and Viscount Hailsham
Spouses

Stewart Hosie MP and Shona Robison MSP
Former Spouses

Lord Hoyle and Sir Lindsay Hoyle MP
Father and son

Bernard Jenkin MP and Baroness Jenkin of Kennington
Spouses

Andrea Jenkyns MP and Jack Lopresti MP
Spouses

Baroness Kennedy of Cradley and Lord Kennedy of Southwark
Spouses

Lord Kinnock and Baroness Kinnock of Holyhead
Spouses

Lord Kinnock, Baroness Kinnock of Holyhead and Stephen Kinnock MP
Parents and son

Lord Layard and Baroness Meacher
Spouses

Jack Lopresti MP and Andrea Jenkyns MP
Spouses

Baroness McDonagh and Siobhain McDonagh MP
Siblings

Anna McMorrin MP and Alun Davies AM
Partners

Esther McVey MP and Philip Davies MP
Spouses

Alex Maskey MLA and Paul Maskey MP
Siblings

Baroness Meacher and Lord Layard
Spouses

David Mundell MP and Oliver Mundell MSP
Father and son

Baroness Neuberger and Lord Neuberger of Abbotsbury
Siblings-in-law

Kate Osamor MP and Baroness Osamor
Daughter and mother

John Penrose MP and Baroness Harding of Winscombe
Spouses

Victoria Prentis MP and Lord Boswell of Aynho
Daughter and father

Lord Razzall and Baroness Bonham-Carter of Yarnbury
Partners

Lord Redesdale and Lord Denham
Cousins

Ellie Reeves MP and John Cryer MP
Spouses

Ellie Reeves MP and Rachel Reeves MP
Siblings

Rachel Reeves MP and John Cryer MP
Siblings-in-law

Lord Sainsbury of Preston Candover and Lord Sainsbury of Turville
Cousins

Nick Smith MP and Baroness Chapman of Darlington
Spouses

Lord Thomas of Gresford and Baroness Walmsley
Spouses

Tom Tugendhat MP and Lord Tugendhat
Nephew and uncle

Baroness Walmsley and Lord Thomas of Gresford
Spouses

Parliaments of the 20th and 21st centuries

Assembled		Dissolved		Length	Ministries	Took Office	
VICTORIA				yrs. m. d.			
3 Dec	1900	8 Jan	1906	5 1 5	{ Salisbury (Con)	6 Dec	1900
					Balfour (Con)	12 July	1902
EDWARD VII							
13 Feb	1906	10 Jan	1910	3 10 28	{ C. Bannerman (Lib)	5 Dec	1905
					Asquith (Lib)	5 April	1908
15 Feb	1910	28 Nov	1910	9 13	Asquith (Lib)	15 Feb	1910
GEORGE V							
31 Jan	1911	25 Nov	1918	7 9 25	{ Asquith (Lib)	25 May	1915
4 Feb	1919	25 Oct	1922	3 8 21	Lloyd George (Lib)	6 Dec	1916
					Coalition		
20 Nov	1922	16 Nov	1923	11 27	A. Bonar Law (Con)	23 Oct	1922
8 Jan	1924	9 Oct	1924	9 1	J. R. MacDonald (Lab)	22 Jan	1924
2 Dec	1924	10 May	1929	4 5 8	S. Baldwin (Con)	4 Nov	1924
25 June	1929	7 Oct	1931	2 3 12	J. R. MacDonald (Lab)	5 June	1929
					{ J. R. MacDonald	24 August	1931
3 Nov	1931	25 Oct	1935	3 11 22	(Nat. Govt.)		
					S. Baldwin		
26 Nov	1935				S. Baldwin (Nat. Govt.)	7 June	1935
EDWARD VIII					N. Chamberlain (Nat. Govt.)	28 May	1937
GEORGE VI		15 June	1945	9 6 20	W. Churchill (Nat. Govt.)	10 May	1940
1 Aug	1945	3 Feb	1950	4 6 2	C. R. Attlee (Lab)	26 July	1945
1 Mar	1950	5 Oct	1951	1 7 4	C. R. Attlee (Lab)	25 Feb	1950
31 Oct	1951	6 May	1955	3 6 6	{ W. Churchill (Con)	26 Oct	1951
					A. Eden (Con)		
ELIZABETH II					A. Eden (Con)	6 April	1955
7 June	1955	18 Sept	1959	4 3 11	{ H. Macmillan (Con)	10 Jan	1957
					H. Macmillan (Con)	9 Oct	1959
20 Oct	1959	25 Sept	1964	4 11 5	A. Douglas-Home (Con)	9 Oct	1963
27 Oct	1964	10 Mar	1966	1 4 11	{ H. Wilson (Lab)	16 Oct	1964
18 Apr	1966	29 May	1970	4 1 11	H. Wilson (Lab)	1 April	1966
29 June	1970	8 Feb	1974	3 7 10	E. R. G. Heath (Con)	19 June	1970
6 Mar	1974	20 Sept	1974	6 14	H. Wilson (Lab) (Minority Govt.)	4 Mar	1974
22 Oct	1974	7 April	1979	4 5 15	{ H. Wilson (Lab)	11 Oct	1974
					J. Callaghan (Lab)	5 April	1976
9 May	1979	13 May	1983	4 0 4	Mrs M. Thatcher (Con)	3 May	1979
15 June	1983	18 May	1987	3 11 3	Mrs M. Thatcher (Con)	9 June	1983
17 June	1987	16 Mar	1992	4 8 28	{ Mrs M. Thatcher (Con)	11 June	1987
					J. Major (Con)	28 Nov	1990
27 April	1992	8 April	1997	4 11 19	J. Major (Con)	10 April	1992
7 May	1997	14 May	2001	4 0 7	T. Blair (Lab)	1 May	1997
20 June	2001	11 April	2005	3 9 22	T. Blair (Lab)	7 June	2001
17 May	2005	8 April	2010	4 10 22	{ T. Blair (Lab)	5 May	2005
					G. Brown (Lab)	27 June	2007
13 May	2010	30 Mar	2015	4 10 18	D. Cameron (Con) (Coalition Govt.)	11 May	2010
18 May	2015	3 May	2017	1 11 15	{ D. Cameron (Con)	7 May	2015
					T. May (Con)	13 July	2016
13 June	2017	6 Nov	2019	2 4 24	{ T. May (Con)	8 June	2017
					B. Johnson (Con)	24 July	2019
17 Dec	2019				B. Johnson (Con)	12 Dec	2019

Size of the House of Commons since 1801

With the Union of Great Britain and Ireland in 1801 the number of members of Parliament was fixed at 658. In 1885 the total was increased to 670, and by the Act of 1918 to 707. With the creation of the Irish Free State in 1922, the Irish representation was reduced to 13 members from Ulster, making the membership of the House of Commons 615. In 1945, owing to the division of large constituencies, the number was increased by 25 to 640. Under the Act of 1948 the number was decreased to 625. Orders passed in 1954 and 1955 increased the number to 630. As the result of redistribution and boundary changes, the total number of MPs elected at the 1979 general election was 635. The House of Commons (Redistribution of Seats) Act 1979 and the Boundary Commission reports of 1983 resulted in an increase of 15 seats after the 1983 election to 650 members. At the 1992 election, 651 Members were elected, an extra seat having been created for Milton Keynes. Reports from the Boundary Commission caused an increase to 659 at the 1997 election. The fifth Periodical Review of Westminster constituencies cut the number of seats to 646 at the 2005 general election, with Scotland losing 13 seats as a result of previous over representation and the creation of the Scottish Parliament. The changes to the boundaries in England, Wales and Northern Ireland came into effect at the 2010 election, increasing the number of seats to 650.

General Election Majorities since the Reform Act

(NB *In certain cases, such as the election of* 1910, *the Government Party had a working arrangement with other parties, which ensured them a majority in the House*)

Year	Party	Majority
1832	Lib	300
1835	Lib	108
1837	Lib	40
1841	Con	78
1847	Lib	2
1852	Con	8
1857	Lib	92
1859	Lib	40
1865	Lib	62
1868	Lib	106
1874	Con	52
1880	Lib	176
1885	Lib	No majority
1886	Unionist	120
1892	Lib	No majority
1895	Unionist	152
1900	Unionist	135
1906	Lib	130
1910	(Jan) Lib	No majority
1910	(Dec) Lib	No majority
1918	Coalition	249
1922	Con	75
1923	Con	No majority
1924	Con	223
1929	Lab	No majority
1931	Nat Govt	493
1935	Nat Govt	249
1945	Lab	146
1950	Lab	5
1951	Con	17
1955	Con	58
1959	Con	100
1964	Lab	4
1966	Lab	96
1970	Con	30
1974	(Feb) Lab	No majority
1974	(Oct) Lab	3
(3 over all parties, 42 over Cons)		
1979	Con	43
1983	Con	144
1987	Con	101
1992	Con	21
1997	Lab	177
2001	Lab	165
2005	Lab	66
2010	Con/Lib Dem coalition	83
2015	Con	12
2017	Con	No majority
2019	Con	81

Long Parliaments

The longest lived Parliaments in English history have been the Elizabethan Parliament of 1572–83, the Long Parliament of 1640–53, and the Cavalier Parliament of 1661–79. The First World War Parliament met on 31 January 1911, and was dissolved on 25 November 1918. That of the Second met 26 November 1935, and was dissolved 15 June 1945.

Prime Ministers since 1721

1721–42	Sir Robert Walpole (Whig)
1742–43	Spencer Compton (Whig)
1743–54	Henry Pelham (Whig)
1754–56	Duke of Newcastle (Whig)
1756–57	Duke of Devonshire (Whig)
1757–62	Duke of Newcastle (Whig)
1762–63	Earl of Bute (Tory)
1763–65	George Grenville (Whig)
1765–66	Marquess of Rockingham (Whig)
1766–67	William Pitt (the Elder) (Whig)
1767–70	Duke of Grafton (Whig)
1770–82	Lord North (Tory)
1782	Marquess of Rockingham (Whig)
1782–83	Earl of Shelburne (Whig)
1783	Duke of Portland (Coalition)
1783–1801	William Pitt (the Younger) (Tory)
1801–04	Henry Addington (Tory)
1804–06	William Pitt (the Younger) (Tory)
1806–07	Lord Grenville (Whig)
1807–09	Duke of Portland (Tory)
1809–12	Spencer Perceval (Tory)
1812–27	Earl of Liverpool (Tory)
1827	George Canning (Tory)
1827–28	Viscount Goderich (Tory)
1828–30	Duke of Wellington (Tory)
1830–34	Earl Grey (Whig)
1834	Viscount Melbourne (Whig)
1834–35	Sir Robert Peel (Tory)
1835–41	Viscount Melbourne (Whig)
1841–46	Sir Robert Peel (Tory)
1846–52	Lord John Russell (Whig)
1852	Earl of Derby (Con)
1852–55	Earl of Aberdeen (Lib) (Coalition)
1855–58	Viscount Palmerston (Lib)
1858–59	Earl of Derby (Con)
1859–65	Viscount Palmerston (Lib)
1865–66	Earl Russell (Lib)
1866–68	Earl of Derby (Con)
1868	Benjamin Disraeli (Con)
1868–74	William Gladstone (Lib)
1874–80	Benjamin Disraeli (Con)
1880–85	William Gladstone (Lib)
1885–86	Marquess of Salisbury (Con)
1886	William Gladstone (Lib)
1886–92	Marquess of Salisbury (Con)
1892–94	William Gladstone (Lib)
1894–95	Earl of Rosebery (Lib)
1895–1902	Marquess of Salisbury (Con)
1902–05	Arthur Balfour (Con)
1905–08	Sir Henry Campbell-Bannerman (Lib)
1908–16	Herbert Asquith (Lib)
1916–22	David Lloyd George (Lib) (Coalition)
1922–23	Andrew Bonar Law (Con)
1923–24	Stanley Baldwin (Con)
1924	Ramsay MacDonald (Lab)
1924–29	Stanley Baldwin (Con)
1929–35	Ramsay MacDonald (Lab)
1935–37	Stanley Baldwin (Con) (Nat Govt)
1937–40	Neville Chamberlain (Con) (Nat Govt)
1940–45	Winston Churchill (Con) (Coalition)
1945–51	Clement Attlee (Lab)
1951–55	Winston Churchill (Con)
1955–57	Sir Anthony Eden (Con)
1957–63	Harold Macmillan (Con)
1963–64	Sir Alec Douglas-Home (Con)
1964–70	Harold Wilson (Lab)
1970–74	Edward Heath (Con)
1974–76	Harold Wilson (Lab)
1976–79	James Callaghan (Lab)
1979–90	Margaret Thatcher (Con)
1990–97	John Major (Con)
1997–2007	Tony Blair (Lab)
2007–10	Gordon Brown (Lab)
2010–16	David Cameron (Con) (Coalition 2010-15)
2016–19	Theresa May (Con)
2019–	Boris Johnson (Con)

The Government

The Cabinet

Prime Minister, First Lord of the Treasury and Minister for the Civil Service, and Minister for the Union	**Boris Johnson** MP
Chancellor of the Exchequer	**Rishi Sunak** MP
First Secretary of State, Secretary of State for Foreign, Commonwealth and Development Affairs	**Dominic Raab** MP
Secretary of State for the Home Department	**Priti Patel** MP
Chancellor of the Duchy of Lancaster and Minister for the Cabinet Office	**Michael Gove** MP
Lord Chancellor and Secretary of State for Justice	**Robert Buckland** QC MP
Secretary of State for Defence	**Ben Wallace** MP
Secretary of State for Health and Social Care	**Matt Hancock** MP
President of the UN COP26 Climate Conference	**Alok Sharma** MP
Secretary of State for Business, Energy and Industrial Strategy	**Kwasi Kwarteng** MP
Secretary of State for International Trade; President of the Board of Trade; Minister for Women and Equalities	**Elizabeth Truss** MP
Secretary of State for Work and Pensions	Dr **Therese Coffey** MP
Secretary of State for Education	**Gavin Williamson** CBE MP
Secretary of State for Environment, Food and Rural Affairs	**George Eustice** MP
Secretary of State for Housing, Communities and Local Government	**Robert Jenrick** MP
Secretary of State for Transport	**Grant Shapps** MP
Secretary of State for Northern Ireland	**Brandon Lewis** CBE MP
Secretary of State for Scotland	**Alister Jack** MP
Secretary of State for Wales	**Simon Hart** MP
Leader of the House of Lords and Lord Privy Seal	**Baroness Evans of Bowes Park**
Secretary of State for Digital, Culture, Media and Sport	**Oliver Dowden** CBE MP
Minister without portfolio and Chairman, Conservative Party	**Amanda Milling** MP

Also attending Cabinet

Chief Secretary to the Treasury	**Stephen Barclay** MP
Leader of the House of Commons; Lord President of the Council	**Jacob Rees-Mogg** MP
Chief Whip; Parliamentary Secretary to the Treasury	**Mark Spencer** MP
Attorney General	**Suella Braverman** QC MP

Departmental Ministers

Department for Business, Energy and Industrial Strategy

Secretary of State for Business, Energy and Industrial Strategy	Rt Hon **Kwasi Kwarteng** MP
Ministers of State	Rt Hon **Anne-Marie Trevelyan** MP
	Lord Grimstone of Boscobel
Parliamentary Under-Secretaries of State	**Nadhim Zahawi** MP
	Amanda Solloway MP
	Paul Scully MP
	Lord Callanan

Cabinet Office

Chancellor of the Duchy of Lancaster and Minister for the Cabinet Office	Rt Hon **Michael Gove** MP
Paymaster General	Rt Hon **Penny Mordaunt** MP
Ministers of State	**Chloe Smith** MP
	Lord Agnew of Oulton DL
	Lord True CBE
Minister without portfolio	Rt Hon **Amanda Milling** MP
Parliamentary Secretaries	**Julia Lopez** MP
	Johnny Mercer MP
President of the UN COP26 Climate Conference	Rt Hon **Alok Sharma** MP

Ministry of Defence

Secretary of State for Defence	Rt Hon **Ben Wallace** MP
Ministers of State	**Jeremy Quin** MP
	Baroness Goldie DL
Parliamentary Under-Secretaries of State	**James Heappey** MP
	Johnny Mercer MP

Department for Digital, Culture, Media and Sport

Secretary of State for Digital, Culture, Media and Sport	Rt Hon **Oliver Dowden** CBE MP
Ministers of State	**Caroline Dinenage** MP
	Rt Hon **John Whittingdale** OBE MP
Parliamentary Under-Secretaries of State	**Matt Warman** MP
	Nigel Huddleston MP
	Baroness Barran MBE

Department for Education

Secretary of State for Education	Rt Hon **Gavin Williamson** CBE MP
Ministers of State	**Michelle Donelan** MP
	Rt Hon **Nick Gibb** MP
Parliamentary Under-Secretaries of State	**Gillian Keegan** MP
	Vicky Ford MP
	Baroness Berridge

Department for Environment, Food and Rural Affairs

Secretary of State for Environment, Food and Rural Affairs	Rt Hon **George Eustice** MP
Minister of State	Rt Hon **Lord Goldsmith of Richmond Park**
Parliamentary Under-Secretaries of State	**Rebecca Pow** MP
	Lord Gardiner of Kimble
	Victoria Prentis MP

Foreign, Commonwealth and Development Office

First Secretary of State, Secretary of State for Foreign, Commonwealth and Development Affairs (Foreign Secretary)	Rt Hon **Dominic Raab** MP
Ministers of State	Rt Hon **James Cleverly** MP
	Rt Hon **Lord Goldsmith of Richmond Park**
	Nigel Adams MP
	Lord Ahmad of Wimbledon
Parliamentary Under-Secretaries of State	**James Duddridge** MP
	Wendy Morton MP

Department of Health and Social Care

Secretary of State for Health and Social Care	Rt Hon **Matt Hancock** MP
Ministers of State	**Edward Argar** MP
	Helen Whately MP
	Nadine Dorries MP
Parliamentary Under-Secretaries of State	**Jo Churchill** MP
	Lord Bethell
	Nadhim Zahawi MP

Home Office

Secretary of State for the Home Department (Home Secretary)	Rt Hon **Priti Patel** MP
Ministers of State	Rt Hon **James Brokenshire** MP
	Kit Malthouse MP
	Baroness Williams of Trafford
	Lord Greenhalgh
Parliamentary Under-Secretaries of State	**Victoria Atkins** MP
	Kevin Foster MP
	Chris Philp MP

Ministry of Housing, Communities and Local Government

Secretary of State for Housing, Communities and Local Government	Rt Hon **Robert Jenrick** MP
Ministers of State	Rt Hon **Christopher Pincher** MP
	Luke Hall MP
	Lord Greenhalgh
Parliamentary Under-Secretary of State	**Eddie Hughes** MP

Department for International Trade

Secretary of State for International Trade; President of the Board of Trade; Minister for Women and Equalities	Rt Hon **Elizabeth Truss** MP
Ministers of State	Rt Hon **Greg Hands** MP
	Lord Grimstone of Boscobel
Parliamentary Under-Secretaries of State	**Graham Stuart** MP
	Ranil Jayawardena MP

Ministry of Justice

Lord Chancellor and Secretary of State for Justice	Rt Hon **Robert Buckland** QC MP
Ministers of State	**Lucy Frazer** QC MP
	Kit Malthouse MP
Parliamentary Under-Secretaries of State	**Alex Chalk** MP
	Chris Philp MP
	Lord Wolfson of Tredegar QC

Law Officers

Attorney General	Rt Hon **Suella Braverman** QC MP
Solicitor General	Rt Hon **Michael Ellis** QC MP
Advocate General for Scotland	**Lord Stewart of Dirleton** QC

Office of the Leader of the House of Commons

Leader of the House of Commons	Rt Hon **Jacob Rees-Mogg** MP

Office of the Leader of the House of Lords

Leader of the House of Lords	Rt Hon **Baroness Evans of Bowes Park**
Deputy Leader	Rt Hon **Earl Howe**

Northern Ireland Office

Secretary of State for Northern Ireland	Rt Hon **Brandon Lewis** CBE MP
Minister of State	**Robin Walker** MP

Office of the Secretary of State for Scotland

Secretary of State for Scotland	Rt Hon **Alister Jack** MP
Parliamentary Under-Secretaries of State	**Iain Stewart** MP
	David Duguid MP

Department for Transport

Secretary of State for Transport	Rt Hon **Grant Shapps** MP
Ministers of State	**Andrew Stephenson** MP
	Chris Heaton-Harris MP
Parliamentary Under-Secretaries of State	**Rachel Maclean** MP
	Robert Courts MP
	Baroness Vere of Norbiton

HM Treasury

Chancellor of the Exchequer	Rt Hon **Rishi Sunak** MP
Chief Secretary to the Treasury	Rt Hon **Stephen Barclay** MP
Financial Secretary	Rt Hon **Jesse Norman** MP
Minister of State	**Lord Agnew of Oulton** DL
Economic Secretary	**John Glen** MP
Exchequer Secretary	**Kemi Badenoch** MP

Office of the Secretary of State for Wales

Secretary of State for Wales	Rt Hon **Simon Hart** MP
Parliamentary Under-Secretary of State	**David Davies** MP

Department for Work and Pensions

Secretary of State for Work and Pensions	Rt Hon Dr **Therese Coffey** MP
Minister of State	**Justin Tomlinson** MP
Parliamentary Under-Secretaries of State	**Mims Davies** MP
	Guy Opperman MP
	Will Quince MP
	Baroness Stedman-Scott OBE

Government Whips

Commons

Chief Whip

Parliamentary Secretary to the Treasury	Rt Hon **Mark Spencer** MP

Deputy Chief Whip

Treasurer of HM Household	**Stuart Andrew** MP

Whips

Comptroller of HM Household	**Mike Freer** MP
Vice-Chamberlain of HM Household	**Marcus Jones** MP

Lord Commissioner of HM Treasury	**James Morris** MP **Rebecca Harris** MP **David Rutley** MP **Maggie Throup** MP **Michael Tomlinson** MP **David Duguid** MP
Assistant Whips	**Scott Mann** MP **Leo Docherty** MP **David Davies** MP **Alex Chalk** MP **Tom Pursglove** MP **Maria Caulfield** MP **Nigel Huddleston** MP

Lords

Chief Whip	
Captain of the Honourable Corps of the Gentlemen-at-Arms	Rt Hon **Lord Ashton of Hyde**
Deputy Chief Whip	
Captain of the Queen's Bodyguard of the Yeomen of the Guard	**Earl of Courtown**
Whips	
Baronesses in Waiting	**Baroness Scott of Bybrook** OBE **Baroness Bloomfield of Hinton Waldrist** **Baroness Penn**
Lords in Waiting	**Lord Parkinson of Whitley Bay** **Viscount Younger of Leckie**

Government Spokespeople in the Lords

Leader of the House of Lords and Lord Privy Seal	Rt Hon **Baroness Evans of Bowes Park**
Deputy Leader of the House of Lords	Rt Hon **Earl Howe**
Business, Energy and Industrial Strategy	**Lord Callanan**
Business, Energy and Industrial Strategy	**Lord Grimstone of Boscobel**
Cabinet Office	**Lord True** CBE
Cabinet Office	**Lord Agnew of Oulton** DL
Defence	**Baroness Goldie** DL
Digital, Culture, Media and Sport	**Baroness Barran** MBE
Education	**Baroness Berridge**
Environment, Food and Rural Affairs	**Lord Gardiner of Kimble**
Environment, Food and Rural Affairs	Rt Hon **Lord Goldsmith of Richmond Park**
Foreign, Commonwealth and Development Office	**Lord Ahmad of Wimbledon**
Foreign, Commonwealth and Development Office	Rt Hon **Lord Goldsmith of Richmond Park**
Health and Social Care	**Lord Bethell**
Home Office	**Baroness Williams of Trafford**
Home Office	**Lord Greenhalgh**
Housing, Communities and Local Government	**Lord Greenhalgh**
International Trade	**Lord Grimstone of Boscobel**
Justice	**Lord Wolfson of Tredegar** QC
Law Officers	**Lord Stewart of Dirleton** QC
Northern Ireland	**Viscount Younger of Leckie**
Scotland	**Viscount Younger of Leckie**
Transport	**Baroness Vere of Norbiton**
HM Treasury	**Lord Agnew of Oulton** DL
Wales	**Baroness Bloomfield of Hinton Waldrist**
Women and Equalities	**Baroness Berridge**
Work and Pensions	**Baroness Stedman-Scott** OBE

Alphabetical list of Ministers and Whips

ADAMS, Nigel	Minister of State for Asia, Foreign, Commonwealth and Development Office
AGNEW OF OULTON, Lord	Minister of State for Efficiency and Transformation and Government Spokesperson, Cabinet Office and HM Treasury
AHMAD OF WIMBLEDON, Lord	Minister of State for South Asia and the Commonwealth and Government Spokesperson, Foreign, Commonwealth and Development Office; Prime Minister's Special Representative on Preventing Sexual Violence in Conflict
ANDREW, Stuart	Deputy Chief Whip (Treasurer of HM Household)
ARGAR, Edward	Minister of State for Health, Department of Health and Social Care
ASHTON OF HYDE, Rt Hon Lord	Lords Chief Whip (Captain of the Honourable Corps of the Gentlemen-at-Arms)
ATKINS, Victoria	Parliamentary Under-Secretary of State for Safeguarding, Home Office
BADENOCH, Kemi	Exchequer Secretary, HM Treasury and Minister for Equalities, Government Equalities Office
BARCLAY, Rt Hon Stephen	Chief Secretary to the Treasury, HM Treasury
BARRAN, Baroness	Parliamentary Under-Secretary of State for Civil Society and Government Spokesperson, Department for Digital, Culture, Media and Sport
BERRIDGE, Baroness	Parliamentary Under-Secretary of State for the School System and Government Spokesperson, Department for Education and Minister for Women and Government Spokesperson, Government Equalities Office
BETHELL, Lord	Parliamentary Under-Secretary of State for Innovation and Government Spokesperson, Department of Health and Social Care
BLOOMFIELD OF HINTON WALDRIST, Baroness	Government Spokesperson, Wales Office; Government Whip (Baroness in Waiting)
BRAVERMAN, Rt Hon Suella	Attorney General
BROKENSHIRE, Rt Hon James	Minister of State for Security, Home Office
BUCKLAND, Rt Hon Robert	Lord Chancellor and Secretary of State for Justice
CALLANAN, Lord	Parliamentary Under-Secretary of State (Minister for Climate Change and Corporate Responsibility) and Government Spokesperson, Department for Business, Energy and Industrial Strategy
CAULFIELD, Maria	Assistant Government Whip
CHALK, Alex	Parliamentary Under-Secretary of State, Ministry of Justice; Assistant Government Whip
CHURCHILL, Jo	Parliamentary Under-Secretary of State for Prevention, Public Health and Primary Care, Department of Health and Social Care
CLEVERLY, Rt Hon James	Minister of State for Middle East and North Africa, Foreign, Commonwealth and Development Office
COFFEY, Rt Hon Dr Therese	Secretary of State for Work and Pensions
COURTOWN, Earl of	Lords Deputy Chief Whip (Captain of the Queen's Bodyguard of the Yeomen of the Guard)
COURTS, Robert	Parliamentary Under-Secretary of State, Department for Transport

DAVIES, David	Parliamentary Under-Secretary of State, Wales Office; Assistant Government Whip
DAVIES, Mims	Parliamentary Under-Secretary of State for Employment, Department for Work and Pensions
DINENAGE, Caroline	Minister of State for Digital and Culture, Department for Digital, Culture, Media and Sport
DOCHERTY, Leo	Assistant Government Whip
DONELAN, Michelle	Minister of State for Universities, Department for Education
DORRIES, Nadine	Minister of State for Patient Safety, Suicide Prevention and Mental Health, Department of Health and Social Care
DOWDEN, Rt Hon Oliver	Secretary of State for Digital, Culture, Media and Sport
DUDDRIDGE, James	Parliamentary Under-Secretary of State (Minister for Africa), Foreign, Commonwealth and Development Office
DUGUID, David	Parliamentary Under-Secretary of State, Scotland Office; Government Whip (Lord Commissioner of HM Treasury)
ELLIS, Rt Hon Michael	Solicitor General
EUSTICE, Rt Hon George	Secretary of State for Environment, Food and Rural Affairs
EVANS OF BOWES PARK, Rt Hon Baroness	Leader of the House of Lords and Lord Privy Seal
FORD, Vicky	Parliamentary Under-Secretary of State for Children and Families, Department for Education
FOSTER, Kevin	Parliamentary Under-Secretary of State for Future Borders and Immigration, Home Office
FRAZER, Lucy	Minister of State, Ministry of Justice
FREER, Mike	Government Whip (Comptroller of HM Household)
GARDINER OF KIMBLE, Lord	Parliamentary Under-Secretary of State for Rural Affairs and Biosecurity and Government Spokesperson, Department for Environment, Food and Rural Affairs
GIBB, Rt Hon Nick	Minister of State for School Standards, Department for Education
GLEN, John	Economic Secretary (Minister for the City of London), HM Treasury
GOLDIE, Baroness	Minister of State and Government Spokesperson, Ministry of Defence
GOLDSMITH OF RICHMOND PARK, Rt Hon Lord	Minister of State for the Pacific and Environment and Government Spokesperson, Foreign, Commonwealth and Development Office and Department for Environment, Food and Rural Affairs
GOVE, Rt Hon Michael	Chancellor of the Duchy of Lancaster and Minister for the Cabinet Office
GREENHALGH, Lord	Minister of State for Building Safety and Communities and Government Spokesperson, Ministry of Housing, Communities and Local Government and Home Office
GRIMSTONE OF BOSCOBEL, Lord	Minister of State for Investment and Government Spokesperson, Department for International Trade and Department for Business, Energy and Industrial Strategy

HALL, Luke	Minister of State for Regional Growth and Local Government, Ministry of Housing, Communities and Local Government
HANCOCK, Rt Hon Matt	Secretary of State for Health and Social Care
HANDS, Rt Hon Greg	Minister of State for Trade Policy, Department for International Trade
HARRIS, Rebecca	Government Whip (Lord Commissioner of HM Treasury)
HART, Rt Hon Simon	Secretary of State for Wales
HEAPPEY, James	Parliamentary Under-Secretary of State (Minister for the Armed Forces), Ministry of Defence
HEATON-HARRIS, Chris	Minister of State, Department for Transport
HOWE, Rt Hon Earl	Deputy Leader of the House of Lords
HUDDLESTON, Nigel	Parliamentary Under-Secretary of State for Sport, Tourism and Heritage, Department for Digital, Culture, Media and Sport; Assistant Government Whip
HUGHES, Eddie	Parliamentary Under-Secretary of State for Rough Sleeping and Housing, Ministry of Housing, Communities and Local Government
JACK, Rt Hon Alister	Secretary of State for Scotland
JAYAWARDENA, Ranil	Parliamentary Under-Secretary of State, Department for International Trade
JENRICK, Rt Hon Robert	Secretary of State for Housing, Communities and Local Government
JOHNSON, Rt Hon Boris	Prime Minister, First Lord of the Treasury and Minister for the Civil Service, and Minister for the Union
JONES, Marcus	Government Whip (Vice-Chamberlain of HM Household)
KEEGAN, Gillian	Parliamentary Under-Secretary of State for Apprenticeships and Skills, Department for Education
KWARTENG, Rt Hon Kwasi	Secretary of State for Business, Energy and Industrial Strategy
LEWIS, Rt Hon Brandon	Secretary of State for Northern Ireland
LOPEZ, Julia	Parliamentary Secretary, Cabinet Office
MACLEAN, Rachel	Parliamentary Under-Secretary of State, Department for Transport
MALTHOUSE, Kit	Minister of State for Crime and Policing, Home Office and Ministry of Justice
MANN, Scott	Government Whip (Lord Commissioner of HM Treasury)
MERCER, Johnny	Parliamentary Under-Secretary of State (Minister for Defence People and Veterans), Ministry of Defence and Cabinet Office
MILLING, Rt Hon Amanda	Minister without Portfolio, Cabinet Office; Chairman, Conservative Party
MORDAUNT, Rt Hon Penny	Paymaster General, Cabinet Office
MORRIS, James	Government Whip, Lord Commissioner of HM Treasury
MORTON, Wendy	Parliamentary Under-Secretary of State (Minister for the European Neighbourhood and Americas), Foreign, Commonwealth and Development Office
NORMAN, Rt Hon Jesse	Financial Secretary, HM Treasury
OPPERMAN, Guy	Parliamentary Under-Secretary of State for Pensions and Financial Inclusion, Department for Work and Pensions
PARKINSON OF WHITLEY BAY, Lord	Government Whip, Lord in Waiting
PATEL, Rt Hon Priti	Home Secretary

PENN, Baroness	Government Whip (Baroness in Waiting)
PHILP, Chris	Parliamentary Under-Secretary of State for Immigration Compliance and the Courts, Home Office and Ministry of Justice
PINCHER, Rt Hon Christopher	Minister of State for Housing, Ministry of Housing, Communities and Local Government
POW, Rebecca	Parliamentary Under-Secretary of State, Department for Environment, Food and Rural Affairs
PRENTIS, Victoria	Parliamentary Under-Secretary of State, Department for Environment, Food and Rural Affairs
PURSGLOVE, Tom	Assistant Government Whip
QUIN, Jeremy	Minister of State (Minister for Defence Procurement), Ministry of Defence
QUINCE, Will	Parliamentary Under-Secretary of State for Welfare Delivery, Department for Work and Pensions
RAAB, Rt Hon Dominic	First Secretary of State and Foreign Secretary
REES-MOGG, Rt Hon Jacob	Leader of the House of Commons; Lord President of the Council
RUTLEY, David	Government Whip (Lord Commissioner of HM Treasury)
SCOTT OF BYBROOK, Baroness	Government Whip, Baroness in Waiting
SCULLY, Paul	Parliamentary Under-Secretary of State (Minister for Small Business, Consumers and Labour Markets), Department for Business, Energy and Industrial Strategy and Minister for London
SHAPPS, Rt Hon Grant	Secretary of State for Transport
SHARMA, Rt Hon Alok	President of the UN COP26 Climate Conference
SMITH, Chloe	Minister of State for the Constitution and Devolution, Cabinet Office
SOLLOWAY, Amanda	Parliamentary Under-Secretary of State (Minister for Science, Research and Innovation), Department for Business, Energy and Industrial Strategy
SPENCER, Rt Hon Mark	Chief Whip, Parliamentary Secretary to the Treasury
STEDMAN-SCOTT, Baroness	Parliamentary Under-Secretary of State and Government Spokesperson, Department for Work and Pensions
STEPHENSON, Andrew	Minister of State, Department for Transport
STEWART, Iain	Parliamentary Under-Secretary of State (Minister for Scotland), Scotland Office
STEWART OF DIRLETON, Lord	Advocate General for Scotland and Government Spokesperson, Law Officers
STUART, Graham	Parliamentary Under-Secretary of State (Minister for Exports), Department for International Trade
SUNAK, Rt Hon Rishi	Chancellor of the Exchequer
THROUP, Maggie	Government Whip (Lord Commissioner of HM Treasury)
TOMLINSON, Justin	Minister of State for Disabled People, Health and Work, Department for Work and Pensions
TOMLINSON, Michael	Government Whip, Lord Commissioner of HM Treasury
TREVELYAN, Rt Hon Anne-Marie	Minister of State for Business, Energy and Clean Growth, Department for Business, Energy and Industrial Strategy
TRUE, Lord	Minister of State and Government Spokesperson, Cabinet Office
TRUSS, Rt Hon Elizabeth	Secretary of State for International Trade; President of the Board of Trade; Minister for Women and Equalities

VERE OF NORBITON, Baroness	Parliamentary Under-Secretary of State and Government Spokesperson, Department for Transport
WALKER, Robin	Minister of State, Northern Ireland Office
WALLACE, Rt Hon Ben	Secretary of State for Defence
WARMAN, Matt	Parliamentary Under-Secretary of State for Digital Infrastructure, Department for Digital, Culture, Media and Sport
WHATELY, Helen	Minister of State for Care, Department of Health and Social Care
WHITTINGDALE, Rt Hon John	Minister of State for Media and Data, Department for Digital, Culture, Media and Sport
WILLIAMS OF TRAFFORD, Baroness	Minister of State and Government Spokesperson, Home Office
WILLIAMSON, Rt Hon Gavin	Secretary of State for Education
WOLFSON OF TREDEGAR, Lord	Parliamentary Under-Secretary of State and Government Spokesperson, Ministry of Justice
YOUNGER OF LECKIE, Viscount	Government Spokesperson, Scotland Office and Northern Ireland Office; Government Whip (Lord in Waiting)
ZAHAWI, Nadhim	Parliamentary Under-Secretary of State, Department for Business, Energy and Industrial Strategy and Parliamentary Under-Secretary of State for COVID Vaccine Deployment, Department of Health and Social Care

Ministerial Responsibilities and Staff

Prime Minister's Office

10 Downing Street, London SW1A 2AA
020 7930 4433
Website: www.gov.uk/number10 Twitter: @10DowningStreet

Prime Minister, First Lord of the Treasury and Minister for the Civil Service, and Minister for the Union
Rt Hon **Boris Johnson** MP

Leader of Her Majesty's Government; responsible for the policy and decisions of the government; oversees the operation of the Civil Service and government agencies; chooses members of the government; principal government figure in the House of Commons; ensures that all of government is acting on behalf of the entire United Kingdom: England, Northern Ireland, Scotland, and Wales.

Parliamentary Private Secretaries	Dr Alex Burghart MP	020 7219 1613
	Email: alex.burghart.mp@parliament.uk	
	Trudy Harrison MP	020 7219 4002
	Email: trudy.harrison.mp@parliament.uk	
Principal Private Secretary	Martin Reynolds CMG	
Deputy Principal Private Secretary	Stuart Glassborow	
Chief of Staff (Political)	Dan Rosenfield	
Chief Strategic Adviser (Political)	Lord Udny-Lister	
Deputy Chiefs of Staff (Political)	Henry Cook	
	Katie Lam	
Private Secretaries to the Prime Minister		
(Public Services)	Imran Shafi	
(Justice and Home Affairs)	Gemma Ungoad-Thomas	
(Economic Affairs)	Emily Beynon	
(Foreign Affairs)	William Gelling OBE	
Speech Writers	Tim Kiddell CBE	
	David Blair	
Prime Minister's Official Spokesperson	Max Blain	
Director of Communications (Political)	James Slack CBE	
Head of Research and Messaging (Political)	Declan Lyons	
Director of Policy (Political)	Munira Mirza	
Deputy Director, Head of Policy Unit	Patrick Curry	
Prime Minister's Representative on Brexit and International Policy (Political)	Lord Frost CMG	

Department for Business, Energy and Industrial Strategy

1 Victoria Street, London SW1H 0ET
020 7215 5000
Email: enquiries@beis.gov.uk (Please note: see Private Secretary for Minister's email)
Website: www.gov.uk/beis Twitter: @beisgovuk

Secretary of State for Business, Energy and Industrial Strategy Rt Hon **Kwasi Kwarteng** MP

Developing and delivering a comprehensive industrial strategy and leading the government's relationship with business; ensuring that the country has secure energy supplies that are reliable, affordable and clean; ensuring the UK remains at the leading edge of science, research and innovation; tackling climate change.

Parliamentary Private Secretaries

Secretary of State	Jo Gideon MP Email: jo.gideon.mp@parliament.uk	020 7219 8131
Ministerial Team	Mark Fletcher MP Email: mark.fletcher.mp@parliament.uk	020 7219 3662
Senior Private Secretary, Special Adviser's Office	Eleanor Potter Email: spads.office@beis.gov.uk	020 7215 6629
Principal Private Secretary	Jacqui Ward Email: secretary.state@beis.gov.uk	020 7215 5621

Minister of State for Business, Energy and Clean Growth Rt Hon **Anne-Marie Trevelyan** MP

Carbon budgets; green finance; energy efficiency and heat, including fuel poverty; clean heat; low carbon generation; energy retail markets; oil and gas, including shale gas; security of supply; electricity and gas wholesale markets and networks; international energy; EU energy and climate; energy security, including resilience and emergency planning; sectoral lead: nuclear, construction.

Senior Private Secretary	Theo Walsingham Email: minister.trevelyan@beis.gov.uk	020 7215 0967

Minister of State for Investment **Lord Grimstone of Boscobel**

(jointly with Department for International Trade) Advanced manufacturing, automotive, defence, infrastructure, materials, including steel; professional and business services; rail supply chain.

Senior Private Secretary	Frances Knight Email: grimstone@trade.gov.uk	020 7008 8147

Parliamentary Under-Secretary of State (Minister for Business and Industry) **Nadhim Zahawi** MP

(jointly with Department of Health and Social Care) Vaccine Taskforce (VTF); national security and investment; sectoral lead: life sciences.

Senior Private Secretary	Lizzie Hatfield Email: minister.zahawi@beis.gov.uk	020 7215 0971

Parliamentary Under-Secretary of State (Minister for Science, Research and Innovation) **Amanda Solloway** MP

Science and research; innovation; industrial strategy delivery; sectoral lead: intellectual property, maritime, space, technology.

Senior Private Secretary	Rosie Perkins Email: minister.solloway@beis.gov.uk	020 7215 5568

Parliamentary Under-Secretary of State (Minister for Small Business, Consumers and Labour Markets); Minister for London **Paul Scully** MP

Small business and enterprise, including access to finance; consumer and competition, including competition law; labour markets; postal affairs; sector lead: retail, aerospace.

Senior Private Secretary	To be appointed Email: minister.scully@beis.gov.uk	020 7215 5933

Parliamentary Under-Secretary of State (Minister for Climate Change and Corporate Responsibility) **Lord Callanan**

Lords lead on all BEIS issues; corporate governance; insolvency; HM Land Registry; Ordnance Survey; better regulation and regulatory reform; international climate change, including International Climate Fund; climate science and innovation; smart meters and smart systems.

Senior Private Secretary	Jennie Cartwright Email: minister.callanan@beis.gov.uk	020 7215 6011
Head of Parliamentary Unit	Helen Chapman Email: parliamentary.unit@beis.gov.uk	020 7215 6630

Cabinet Office

70 Whitehall, London SW1A 2AS
020 7276 1234
Email: publiccorrespondence@cabinetoffice.gov.uk
(Please note: see Private Secretary for Minister's email) Website: www.gov.uk/cabinet-office
Twitter: @cabinetofficeuk

Chancellor of the Duchy of Lancaster and Minister for the Cabinet Office Rt Hon **Michael Gove** MP

Oversight of all Cabinet Office policy and appointments; oversight of transition period activity and our future relations with the EU; oversight of constitutional policy and enhancement, defending democracy and electoral law; oversight of devolution issues and strengthening the Union; leading cross-government and public sector transformation and efficiency; oversight of cross-government work on veterans' issues; oversight of Cabinet Office responsibilities on National Security and resilience and the Civil Contingencies Secretariat, including COVID-19; supporting the co-ordination of the cross-government and the devolution aspects of the response to COVID-19.

Parliamentary Private Secretaries		
Chancellor of the Duchy of Lancaster	Kevin Hollinrake MP Email: kevin.hollinrake.mp@parliament.uk	020 7219 4746
Ministerial Team	Jane Hunt MP Email: jane.hunt.mp@parliament.uk	020 7219 8647
Special Advisers	Henry Newman Charlie Rowley Josh Grimstone	
Private Secretary to the Special Adviser Team	Berenice Burnett Email: psspecialadvisers@cabinetoffice.gov.uk	07712 546086
Principal Private Secretary	William Burgon Email: psmichaelgove@cabinetoffice.gov.uk	07515 356575
Deputy Principal Private Secretary	Ellie de la Bedoyere Email: psmichaelgove@cabinetoffice.gov.uk	07720 641972

Paymaster General Rt Hon **Penny Mordaunt** MP

Supporting the Chancellor of the Duchy of Lancaster in co-ordinating the transition to our future relations with the EU; supporting the Chancellor of the Duchy of Lancaster on devolution issues relating to our future relationship with the EU and international trade; supporting the Chancellor of the Duchy of Lancaster on civil contingencies issues, including COVID-19, cyber security, joint funds, Official Development Assistance (ODA) and the global goals; government inquiries: Infected Blood.

Head of Office	Alwyn Spencer Email: pspennymordaunt@cabinetoffice.gov.uk	020 7276 6312
Senior Private Secretary	Geraint Thomas Email: pspennymordaunt@cabinetoffice.gov.uk	07712 546084

Minister of State for the Constitution and Devolution **Chloe Smith** MP

Supporting the Chancellor of the Duchy of Lancaster on constitutional policy and enhancement; defending democracy and electoral law; supporting the Chancellor of the Duchy of Lancaster on driving the government's devolution agenda; supporting the Chancellor of the Duchy of Lancaster to strengthen the Union.

Head of Office | Rebecca Cowper | 020 7271 6869
Email: pschloesmith@cabinetoffice.gov.uk

Minister of State for Efficiency and Transformation **Lord Agnew of Oulton** DL

(jointly with HM Treasury) Supporting the Chancellor of the Duchy of Lancaster and the Chief Secretary to the Treasury to deliver cross-government efficiency and public sector transformation improvements, including public value and planning and performance, supporting the Chancellor of the Duchy of Lancaster on cross-government functions and controls, including public bodies and Cabinet Office domestic, supporting procurement and other government functional activity relating to COVID-19.

Head of Office | Louis Reynolds | 07864 605617
Email: pslordagnew@cabinetoffice.gov.uk

Minister of State **Lord True** CBE

Leading on all Cabinet Office business in the Lords, including the Cabinet Office legislation programme in the Lords; supporting the Chancellor of the Duchy of Lancaster in co-ordinating the transition to our future relations with the EU; supporting the Chancellor of the Duchy of Lancaster on constitutional policy and enhancement.

Head of Office | Alex Pack | 07746 142726
Email: pslordtrue@cabinetoffice.gov.uk

Minister without portfolio (Conservative Party Chair) Rt Hon **Amanda Milling** MP

Attends Cabinet and several committees.

Parliamentary Private Secretary | Peter Gibson MP | 020 7219 3077
Email: peter.gibson.mp@parliament.uk
Special Adviser | Emily Maister
Private Secretary | Francesca Clark | 07749 386181
Email: psamandamilling@cabinetoffice.gov.uk

Parliamentary Secretary **Julia Lopez** MP

Supporting the Chancellor of the Duchy of Lancaster and Minister of State for Efficiency and Transformation to deliver cross-government efficiency and public sector transformation; supporting the Chancellor of the Duchy of Lancaster in co-ordinating the transition to our future relations with the EU; supporting Cabinet Office primary legislation in the Commons and the Cabinet Office secondary legislation programme; oversight of Cabinet Office corporate activity, including staff within the Equalities Hub (responsibility for equalities policy sits with Minister for Women and Equalities, Minister for Women, Minister for Equalities and Minister for Disabled People).

Head of Office | Emily Dick-Cleland | 020 7276 2482
Email: psjulialopez@cabinetoffice.gov.uk

Parliamentary Secretary (Minister for Defence People and Veterans) **Johnny Mercer** MP

(jointly with Ministry of Defence) Civilian and service personnel policy; armed forces pay, pensions and compensation; Armed Forces Covenant; welfare and service families; veterans, including resettlement, transition, defence charities and Ministerial Covenant and Veterans Board, and Office of Veteran Affairs; legacy issues and non-operational public inquiries and inquests; mental health; People programme (Flexible Engagement Strategy, Future Accommodation Model and Enterprise Approach); estates service family accommodation policy and engagement with welfare.

Private Secretary | Dale Kernohan | 020 7218 7116
Email: mindpv-privateoffice@mod.gov.uk

President of the UN COP26 Climate Conference Rt Hon **Alok Sharma** MP

Special Adviser | Alex Hitchcock

Private Secretary	To be appointed Email: cop26@cabinetoffice.gov.uk	
Head of Parliamentary and Correspondence Team	Alex Badrick Email: alex.badrick@cabinetoffice.gov.uk	020 7276 1208
Parliamentary Clerk	Ellie Markham Email: parliamentary.branch@cabinetoffice.gov.uk	020 7276 7561

Ministry of Defence

Floor 5, Main Building, Whitehall, London SW1A 2HB
020 7218 9000
Email: All Ministers' correspondence to parlibranch-mincorrespondence@mod.gov.uk/ defencesecretary-group@mod.gov.uk Website: www.gov.uk/mod Twitter: @DefenceHQ

Secretary of State for Defence Rt Hon **Ben Wallace** MP

Strategic operations and operational strategy, including membership of the National Security Council; defence planning, programme and resource allocation; strategic international partnerships: US, France, Germany, Saudi Arabia and the Gulf, NATO; nuclear operations, policy and organisations; strategic communications.

Parliamentary Private Secretaries		
Secretary of State	Jack Brereton MP Email: jack.brereton.mp@parliament.uk	020 7219 4460
Ministerial Team	Natalie Elphicke OBE MP Email: natalie.elphicke.mp@parliament.uk	020 7219 7052
Special Advisers	Peter Quentin Lucia Hodgson Daisy Peck	

Minister of State (Minister for Defence Procurement) **Jeremy Quin** MP

Delivery of the Equipment Plan; nuclear enterprise; defence exports; innovation; defence science and technology, including Dstl; information computer technology; Single Source Regulations Office (SSRO); DIO estates and investment; environment and sustainability; Defence Supply Chain and Defence Estate monitoring, engagement and resilience in the context of COVID-19.

Minister of State **Baroness Goldie** DL

Spokesperson in the House of Lords on all defence matters; corporate governance, including transformation programme, single departmental plan, risk reporting and health, safety and security; future relations with European Union; engagement with retired senior Defence personnel and wider opinion formers; arms control and counter-proliferation, including export licensing and chemical and biological weapons; community engagement; equality, diversity and inclusion; UK Hydrographic Office; Statutory Instrument programme; Australia, Asia and Far East defence engagement; Defence Fire and Rescue; Scotland, Wales and Northern Ireland devolved authorities; ship wrecks, museums and heritage; commemorations, ceremonial duties, medallic recognition and protocol policy; casework; Ministry of Defence Police.

Parliamentary Under-Secretary of State (Minister for the Armed Forces) **James Heappey** MP

Operations and operational legal policy; Brexit no deal planning; force generation, including exercises; military recruitment and retention policy (regulars and reserves); cyber; Permanent Joint Operating bases; international defence engagement strategy; lead for defence engagement in Africa and Latin America; human security; operational public inquiries, inquests; youth and cadets.

Parliamentary Under-Secretary of State (Minister for Defence People and Veterans) **Johnny Mercer** MP

(jointly with Cabinet Office) Civilian and service personnel policy; armed forces pay, pensions and compensation; Armed Forces Covenant; welfare and service families; veterans, including resettlement, transition, defence charities and Ministerial Covenant and Veterans Board, and Office of

Veterans' Affairs; legacy issues and non-operational public inquiries and inquests; mental health; People programme (Flexible Engagement Strategy, Future Accommodation Model and Enterprise Approach); estates service family accommodation policy and engagement with welfare.

Department for Digital, Culture, Media and Sport

Fourth Floor, 100 Parliament Street, London SW1A 2BQ
020 7211 6000
Email: enquiries@dcms.gov.uk/
[firstname.surname]@dcms.gov.uk (Please note: see Private Secretary for Minister's email)
Website: www.gov.uk/dcms Twitter: @DCMS

Secretary of State for Digital, Culture, Media and Sport Rt Hon **Oliver Dowden** CBE MP

Overall responsibility for strategy and policy across the department; management of the UK transition for the department; arts and culture; broadcasting; creative industries; Creative Industries Council; cultural property, heritage and historic environment; Cultural Renewal Taskforce; culture, sports and arts sector recovery from COVID-19; gambling and racing; libraries; media ownership and mergers; museums and galleries; National Lottery; sport; telecommunications and online; tourism.

Parliamentary Private Secretaries

Secretary of State	John Lamont MP Email: john.lamont.mp@parliament.uk	020 7219 1557
Ministerial Team	Alicia Kearns MP Email: alicia.kearns.mp@parliament.uk	020 7219 3000
Special Advisers	Lucy Noakes Email: special.advisers@dcms.gov.uk Mike Crowhurst Email: special.advisers@dcms.gov.uk	
Principal Private Secretary	Scott Bailey Email: secretary.statesoffice@dcms.gov.uk	

Minister of State for Digital and Culture **Caroline Dinenage** MP

Online harms and security; digital and tech policy, including digital skills; creative industries; arts and libraries; museums and cultural property; Festival 2022; COVID-19 sector recovery.

Private Secretary	Alex Ratcliffe Email: ps.dinenage@dcms.gov.uk

Minister of State for Media and Data Rt Hon **John Whittingdale** OBE MP

Media; data; future relations with the EU; international strategy, including oversight of trade negotiations; public appointments; National Archives; culture, sports and arts sector recovery from COVID-19.

Private Secretary	Ellen Bloss Email: ps.whittingdale@dcms.gov.uk

Parliamentary Under-Secretary of State for Digital Infrastructure **Matt Warman** MP

Broadband Delivery UK (BDUK); gigabit delivery programme; mobile coverage; telecoms supply chain; cyber security.

Private Secretary	John Peart Email: ps.warman@dcms.gov.uk

Parliamentary Under-Secretary of State for Sport, Tourism and Heritage **Nigel Huddleston** MP

Sport; heritage; tourism; gambling; lotteries; Commonwealth Games; Secondary Legislation; culture, sports and arts sector recovery from COVID-19.

Private Secretary	Tom Pudlo Email: ps.huddleston@dcms.gov.uk

Parliamentary Under-Secretary of State for Civil Society and Lords Minister **Baroness Barran** MBE

Civil society; youth and social action; Government Inclusive Economy Unit; loneliness; ceremonials; all DCMS business in the House of Lords; culture, sports and arts sector recovery from COVID-19.

Private Secretary	Matt Hiorns Email: dcmslordsminister@dcms.gov.uk
Parliamentary Clerk	To be appointed Email: parliamentarybranch@dcms.gov.uk

Department for Education

Sanctuary Buildings, Great Smith Street, London SW1P 3BT
0370 000 2288 (Public Communications Unit) Fax: 0161-600 1332
Email: sec-of-state.ps@education.gov.uk (Please note: see Private Secretary for Minister's email)
www.gov.uk/contact-dfe Website: www.gov.uk/dfe Twitter: @educationgovuk

Secretary of State for Education Rt Hon **Gavin Williamson** CBE MP

All the Department's policies, including: early years, children's social care, teacher recruitment and retention, school curriculum, school improvement, academies and free schools, further education, apprenticeships and skills, higher education, oversight of the departmental coronavirus (COVID-19) response.

Parliamentary Private Secretary to the Secretary of State	Angela Richardson MP 020 7219 5851 Email: angela.richardson.mp@parliament.uk
Special Advisers	Iain Mansfield Email: advisers.ps@education.gov.uk Angus Walker Email: advisers.ps@education.gov.uk
Principal Private Secretary	Hollie Godsmark
Deputy Principal Private Secretaries	Emma Hockley Juliette Cammaerts
Senior Private Secretaries	Gladys Mugugu Charlotte Hogg Gurveer Dhama
Private Secretaries	Natasha Lee Jakob Dowse Elena Gillies Email: sec-of-state.ps@education.gov.uk
Diary Managers	Sam Cox Zach Lloyd Email: sec-of-state-diary.ps@education.gov.uk
Private Secretary to Special Advisers	Chloe Paraskeva Email: advisers.ps@education.gov.uk

Minister of State for Universities **Michelle Donelan** MP

Strategy for post-16 education (jointly with Parliamentary-Under Secretary of State for Apprenticeships and Skills); universities and higher education reform; higher education student finance, including the Student Loans Company; widening participation in higher education; quality of higher education and Teaching Excellence Framework; international education strategy, including education exports international students and technology in education (Edtech); Opportunity Areas programme; coronavirus (COVID-19) response for universities and higher education institutions.

Senior Private Secretary	Martina Residenti Email: universities.ps@education.gov.uk

Minister of State for School Standards Rt Hon **Nick Gibb** MP

Recruitment and retention of teachers and school leaders, including initial teacher training, qualifications and professional development; supporting a high-quality teaching profession and reducing teacher workload; Teaching Regulation Agency; admissions and school transport; school revenue funding, including national funding formula for schools; curriculum and qualifications, including links with Ofqual; Standards and Testing Agency and primary assessment; school accountability and inspection, including links with Ofsted; support for raising school standards; school sport; pupil premium; relationships, sex and health education, and personal, social, health and economic education; behaviour and attendance and exclusions; early education curriculum and teaching quality; coronavirus (COVID-19) response for schools.

Senior Private Secretary	Harriette Cradock Email: gibb.ps@education.gov.uk

Parliamentary Under-Secretary of State for Apprenticeships and Skills **Gillian Keegan** MP

Strategy for post-16 education (jointly with Minister of State for Universities); technical education and skills, including T Levels and qualifications review; apprenticeships including traineeships; further education workforce; further education provider market, including quality and improvement and further education efficiency; adult education, including National Retraining Scheme and basic skills; Institutes of Technology and National Colleges; reducing the number of young people who are not in education, employment or training; careers education, information and guidance, including the Careers and Enterprise Company; coronavirus (COVID-19) response for further education services.

Senior Private Secretary	Dominic McDonagh Email: keegan.ps@education.gov.uk

Parliamentary Under-Secretary of State for Children and Families **Vicky Ford** MP

Children's social care, including system and funding, workforce, child protection, children in care, adoption, care leavers and local authority performance; special educational needs, including high needs funding; early years policy and childcare, including funding, providers, workforce, children's centres, home learning environment and childcare entitlements; alternative provision; disadvantage and social mobility, including links to the Social Mobility Commission; school food, including free school meals; children and young people's mental health, online safety and preventing bullying in schools; policy to protect against serious violence; coronavirus (COVID-19) response for children's services and childcare.

Senior Private Secretary	Sean Hilditch Email: ford.ps@education.gov.uk

Parliamentary Under-Secretary of State for the School System; Minister for Women **Baroness Berridge**

Free schools, university technical colleges and studio schools; academies and multi-academy trusts, including governance; faith schools; independent schools; home education and supplementary schools; intervention in underperforming schools, including trust capacity funds; school capital investment, including pupil place planning, new school places and school condition; counter-extremism and integration in schools; safeguarding in schools and post-16 settings; school efficiency; departmental efficiency and commercial.

Senior Private Secretary	Jon Bennett Email: berridge.ps@education.gov.uk
Parliamentary Clerk	Amy Ross Email: team.parliamentary@education.gov.uk

Department for Environment, Food and Rural Affairs

Fourth Floor, Seacole Building, 2 Marsham Street, London SW1P 4DF
0345 933 5577
Email: defra.helpline@defra.gov.uk/

[firstname.surname]@defra.gov.uk (Please note: see Private Secretary for Minister's email)
Website: www.gov.uk/defra Twitter: @DefraGovUK

Secretary of State for Environment, Food and Rural Affairs Rt Hon **George Eustice** MP

Oversight of Defra's COVID-19 response; departmental administration; emergencies; EU and international relations and oversight trade mandates and post-transition delivery and policy programme; general licencing; senior appointments.

Parliamentary Private Secretaries		
Secretary of State	Damien Moore MP	020 7219 4684
	Email: damien.moore.mp@parliament.uk	
Ministerial Team	Fay Jones MP	020 7219 3000
	Email: fay.jones.mp@parliament.uk	
Special Advisers	Sara Rajeswaran	020 8026 2809/020 8415 2941
	Email: ps.advisers@defra.gov.uk	
	Emma Pryor	020 8026 2809/020 8415 2941
	Email: ps.advisers@defra.gov.uk	
Principal Private Secretary	Georgina Collins OBE	020 8225 6945
	Email: secretary.state@defra.gov.uk	

Minister of State for the Pacific and Environment Rt Hon **Lord Goldsmith of Richmond Park**

(jointly with Foreign, Commonwealth and Development Office) Ocean and Blue Belt; international environment, climate, biodiversity; forestry and biodiversity; illegal wildlife trade; animal welfare, on farm and companion animals; conservation; COP26 (United Nations Climate Change Conference) nature; International Whaling Commission; Overseas Territories environment; agri-food trade; trade standards; Environment Bill in the House of Lords.

Private Secretary	James Wheatley	020 8720 2347
	Email: ps.zac.goldsmith@defra.gov.uk	

Parliamentary Under-Secretary of State **Rebecca Pow** MP

COVID-19 issues related to waste and water; domestic natural environment, including biodiversity, marine, net gain, wildlife, pollinators; 25 Year Environment Plan; Environment Bill; climate change adaptation, land use and Defra input to net zero; floods, water and emergencies; environmental management and regulation, including resources and waste, air quality and chemicals; commercial projects, including Covent Garden Market and waste Private Finance Initiative (PFI) projects; lead for Environment Agency and Natural England; Commons Minister for rural affairs, landscape and international environment.

Private Secretary	Hannah Sampson	020 8565 4488
	Email: ps.rebecca.pow@defra.gov.uk	

Parliamentary Under-Secretary of State for Rural Affairs and Biosecurity **Lord Gardiner of Kimble**

All Defra parliamentary business in the House of Lords; rural affairs; countryside and access; biosecurity; endemic and exotic animal diseases; plant and tree health; invasive non-native species; landscape; national pollinator strategy.

Private Secretary	Adam Diep	020 8225 6962
	Email: ps.lord.gardiner@defra.gov.uk	

Parliamentary Under-Secretary of State **Victoria Prentis** MP

COVID-19 issues related to food for the vulnerable, farming and fisheries and Fisheries Bill; farming, including Agriculture Bill, Environmental Land Management, Common Agricultural Policy and pesticides; food, including the National Food Strategy, production, growth, skills and apprenticeships; science and innovation, including GMOs and gene editing; better regulation and the department's secondary legislation programme; transition period activity, leading to our future relations with the EU; lead for Rural Payments Agency (RPA), Agriculture and Horticulture Development Board

(AHDB), FERA Science, Centre for Environment, Fisheries and Aquaculture Science (Cefas), Marine Management Organisation (MMO).

Private Secretary	Helena Jones Email: ps.victoria.prentis@defra.gov.uk	020 8225 8948
Parliamentary Clerk	Deirdre Kennedy MBE Email: parliament.cabinet@defra.gov.uk	020 8026 3042

Foreign, Commonwealth and Development Office

King Charles Street, London SW1A 2AH
020 7008 5000
Email: fcdo.correspondence@fcdo.gov.uk (Please note: see Private Secretary for Minister's email)
Website: www.gov.uk/fcdo Twitter: @FCDOGovUK

First Secretary of State, Secretary of State for Foreign, Commonwealth and Development Affairs (Foreign Secretary) Rt Hon **Dominic Raab** MP

Strategy Directorate; national security; intelligence; honours; Europe; all major spending decisions, and overall delivery and management of the 0.7% of Gross National Income spending for Official Development Assistance (ODA); working with and supporting international partners on the global response to COVID-19.

Parliamentary Private Secretaries		
Foreign Secretary	Gareth Johnson MP Email: gareth.johnson.mp@parliament.uk	020 7219 7047
Ministerial Team	Joy Morrissey MP Email: joy.morrissey.mp@parliament.uk	020 7219 6453
Special Advisers	Beth Armstrong Email: pospads@fcdo.gov.uk	020 7008 2312
	Simon Finkelstein Email: pospads@fcdo.gov.uk	020 7008 2312
	Robert Oxley Email: pospads@fcdo.gov.uk	020 7008 2312
	William Sweet Email: pospads@fcdo.gov.uk	020 7008 2312
Principal Private Secretary	Susannah Goshko Email: private.office@fcdo.gov.uk	020 7008 1500

Minister of State for Middle East and North Africa Rt Hon **James Cleverly** MP

Middle East and North Africa; conflict, humanitarian issues, human security; CHASE (Conflict, Humanitarian and Security Department); Stabilisation Unit; defence and international security; Organisation for Security and Cooperation in Europe (OCSE) and Council of Europe; Conflict, Stability and Security Fund (CSSF); safeguarding; counter terrorism.

Private Secretary	Ian Allison Email: psministercleverlyaction@fcdo.gov.uk	020 7008 2090

Minister of State for the Pacific and Environment Rt Hon **Lord Goldsmith of Richmond Park**

(jointly with Department for Environment, Food and Rural Affairs) Ocean and Blue Belt; international environment, climate, biodiversity; forestry and biodiversity; illegal wildlife trade; Pacific region.

Private Secretary	James Wheatley Email: ps.zac.goldsmith@defra.gov.uk	020 8720 2347

Minister of State for Asia **Nigel Adams** MP

East Asia and South East Asia; economic diplomacy; trade, including Trade for Development; Economics Unit; Prosperity Fund; communications; soft power, including British Council, BBC

World Service and scholarships; third-country agreements; consular; global Travel Advice; repatriations policy and operations related to COVID-19; parliamentary relations.

Private Secretary	Charlotte Jago Email: psadams@fcdo.gov.uk	020 7008 6194

Minister of State for South Asia and the Commonwealth **Lord Ahmad of Wimbledon**

South Asia; Commonwealth; UN and multilateral; governance and democracy; open societies and anti-corruption; human rights, including Preventing Sexual Violence in Conflict Initiative (PSVI); treaty policy and practice; sanctions; departmental operations: human resources and estates; COVID-19 HR issues; multilateral duties to the UN and the Commonwealth related to COVID-19; Prime Minister's Special Representative on Preventing Sexual Violence in Conflict.

On a temporary basis also responsible for: Overseas Territories, excluding Gibraltar and the Falkland Islands, and Polar Regions; Caribbean; global partnerships and Sustainable Development Goals; departmental operations: finance and Protocol.

Private Secretary	Laura Dunbar-Brooks Email: psministerahmadaction@fcdo.gov.uk	020 7008 2356

Parliamentary Under-Secretary of State (Minister for Africa) **James Duddridge** MP

Sub-Saharan Africa; economic development; oversight of international financial institutions; CDC (UK government's development finance institution); research and evidence; medical procurement; wider supply chains.

Private Secretary	Nicola Crissell Email: psduddridge@fcdo.gov.uk	07471 711090

Parliamentary Under-Secretary of State (Minister for the European Neighbourhood and Americas)
Wendy Morton MP

East and South-East Europe; Central Asia; Americas; health, global health security, neglected tropical diseases; water and sanitation; nutrition; global health, including global work on COVID-19 vaccines; therapeutics and diagnostics, and multilateral health organisations, including WHO; Global Fund, GAVI (the Vaccine Alliance); cruises and contact with the cruise ship industry.

On a temporary basis also responsible for: inclusive societies (LGBT, civil society, disability, ageing, social protection, Leave No One Behind); children, youth and education, including girls' education; gender equality, and sexual and reproductive health and rights.

Private Secretary	Daniel Cartridge Email: psmorton@fcdo.gov.uk	020 7008 8412

Parliamentary Under-Secretary of State (Minister for the Overseas Territories and Sustainable Development)
To be appointed

Overseas Territories (except Falklands and Gibraltar) and Polar Regions; Caribbean; children, youth and education, including girls' education; gender equality and sexual and reproductive health and rights; inclusive societies (LGBT, civil society, disability, ageing, social protection, Leave No One Behind); global partnerships and sustainable development goals; departmental operations: finance and protocol; Prime Minister's Special Envoy for Girls' Education.

Private Secretary	Ruth Turner	07824 836339
Parliamentary Clerk	Nat Dawbarn Email: prd.actioninfo@fcdo.gov.uk	020 7008 4005

Department of Health and Social Care

39 Victoria Street, London SW1H 0EU
020 7210 4850
Email: [firstname.surname]@dhsc.gov.uk (Please note: see Private Secretary for Minister's email)
Website: www.gov.uk/dhsc Twitter: @DHSCgovuk

Secretary of State for Health and Social Care Rt Hon **Matt Hancock** MP

Business and policies of the Department, including financial control; oversight of all NHS delivery and performance; workforce; technology; prevention.

Parliamentary Private Secretaries

Secretary of State	Steve Double MP Email: steve.double.mp@parliament.uk	020 7219 4408
Ministerial Team	Virginia Crosbie MP Email: virginia.crosbie.mp@parliament.uk	020 7219 4091
Special Advisers	Allan Nixon Email: specialadvisors@dhsc.gov.uk	020 7210 5945
	Emma Dean Email: specialadvisors@dhsc.gov.uk	020 7210 5945
	Beatrice Timpson Email: specialadvisors@dhsc.gov.uk	020 7210 5945
	Damon Poole Email: specialadvisors@dhsc.gov.uk	020 7210 5945
Principal Private Secretary	Natasha Price Email: mb-sofs@dhsc.gov.uk	020 7210 5875

Minister of State for Health **Edward Argar** MP

COVID-19: NHS resilience (acute capacity), supply (ventilators); NHS operational performance; Long Term Plan Bill; finance, efficiency and commercial; NHS capital, land and estates; transformation; NHS England mandate; devolved administrations, Crown Dependencies and Overseas Territories; secondary legislation; departmental management; EU future relationship and trade; sponsorship of NHSE, NHSI.

Senior Private Secretary	Vincent Noone Email: mshealth@dhsc.gov.uk	020 7210 4988

Minister of State for Care **Helen Whately** MP

COVID-19: social care resilience, NHS workforce, test and trace: Joint Biosecurity Centre; adult social care; health/care integration; workforce; dementia, disabilities and long-term conditions; abortion; NHS Continuing Healthcare; sponsorship of HEE.

Senior Private Secretary	Abigail Johnson Email: msc@dhsc.gov.uk	020 7972 4203

Minister of State for Patient Safety, Suicide Prevention and Mental Health **Nadine Dorries** MP

COVID-19: test and trace: contain framework, social distancing; mental health; suicide prevention and crisis prevention; offender health; vulnerable groups; patient safety; women's health strategy; maternity care; inquiries; patient experience; cosmetic regulation; armed forces' and veterans' health; sponsorship of NHS Resolution and CQC.

Senior Private Secretary	Charlotte Kume-Holland Email: mspsm@dhsc.gov.uk	020 7972 2848

Parliamentary Under-Secretary of State for Prevention, Public Health and Primary Care **Jo Churchill** MP

COVID-19: supply (PPE), shielding and vulnerable groups, vaccine deployment; health improvement; health inequalities; prevention; primary care; gender identity services; major diseases; community health; lead minister for crisis response; sponsorship of PHE and FSA.

Senior Private Secretary	Luke Blakeley Email: psp@dhsc.gov.uk	020 7210 5119

Parliamentary Under-Secretary of State for Innovation **Lord Bethell**

COVID-19: supply (medicines and testing), treatments and vaccines, long-term health impacts, test and trace: testing, trace, technology; life sciences; medicines; research; health protection; anti-microbial resistance; global health security; international diplomacy and relations; data and technology; rare diseases; NHS security management, including cyber security; blood and transplants and organ donation; sponsorship of: NHS Blood and Transplant, Human Tissue Authority, Human Fertilisation and Embryology Authority, Medicines and Healthcare Products Regulatory Agency, National Institute for Health and Care Excellence, NHS Digital, Health Research Authority, NHSX, NHS Business Services Authority, NHS Counter Fraud Authority and National Institute of Health Protection; National Institute for Health Research.

Senior Private Secretary	Eloise Kohler Email: pslords@dhsc.gov.uk	020 7972 4568

Parliamentary Under-Secretary of State for COVID Vaccine Deployment **Nadhim Zahawi** MP

(jointly with Department for Business, Energy and Industrial Strategy) COVID vaccine deployment.

Parliamentary Clerk	Claire Reading Email: claire.reading@dhsc.gov.uk	020 7210 5808

Home Office

Peel Building, 2 Marsham Street, London SW1P 4DF
020 7035 4848
Email: public.enquiries@homeoffice.gov.uk (Please note: see Private Secretary for Minister's email)
Website: www.gov.uk/home-office Twitter: @ukhomeoffice

Secretary of State for the Home Department (Home Secretary) Rt Hon **Priti Patel** MP

Overarching responsibility for the departmental portfolio and oversight of the ministerial team; Cabinet; National Security Council (NSC); public appointments; oversight of the Security Service; overall responsibility for the Home Office response to COVID-19, including health measures at the border and police powers to enforce lockdown.

Parliamentary Private Secretaries		
Home Secretary	Mike Wood MP Email: mike.wood.mp@parliament.uk	020 7219 6982
Ministerial Team	Andrew Lewer MBE MP Email: andrew.lewer.mp@parliament.uk	020 7219 3870
Special Advisers	Charlotte Miller Email: specialadvisers@homeoffice.gov.uk	020 7035 0196
	Hannah Guerin Email: specialadvisers@homeoffice.gov.uk	020 7035 0196
	Harry Methley Email: specialadvisers@homeoffice.gov.uk	020 7035 0196
Principal Private Secretary	Rosalind Campion Email: ministers.ho@homeoffice.gov.uk	020 7035 8813

Minister of State for Security Rt Hon **James Brokenshire** MP

Counter terrorism – prepare, prevent, pursue, protect; serious and organised crime; cybercrime; economic crime; hostile state activity; extradition; royal and VIP protection; online harms; Common

Travel Area; aviation and maritime security; Commons lead on transition period (named EU Exit Operations board deputy); Grenfell; flooding/hurricane/natural disaster relief; functioning of the domestic national security system during COVID-19: MI5, Counter Terrorism Policing (CTP); functioning of the serious and organised crime system during COVID-19: National Crime Agency (NCA), Cyber; ensuring COVID-19 regulations continue to consider security (crowded places, insider threat, data retention extension); oversight of fraud during COVID-19.

Private Secretary	Anne-Marie Bunting	020 7035 4414
	Email: securityminister@homeoffice.gov.uk	

Minister of State for Crime and Policing **Kit Malthouse** MP

(jointly with Ministry of Justice) Policing; crime; county lines; criminal justice system; acquisitive crime; public protection and protests; undercover policing; Her Majesty's Inspectorate of Constabulary and Fire and Rescue Services (HMICFRS); police technology; police powers; facial recognition; major events; football policing; flooding, hurricane and natural disaster relief; reoffending; unauthorised encampments; firearms; serious violence; drugs and alcohol; police powers to enforce lockdown and social distancing measures.

Private Secretary	Rosemarie Little	07786 424299
	Email: ministerforpolicingandfire@homeoffice.gov.uk ps.kitmalthouse@justice.gov.uk	

Minister of State (Lords) **Baroness Williams of Trafford**

Overall corporate lead, including Spending Review and Budget; data and identity; enablers; digital and technology, including the emergency services network; public appointments; sponsorship unit; countering extremism; hate crime; forensic science and DNA.

Private Secretary	Una Dumigan	020 7035 8798
	Email: una.dumigan@homeoffice.gov.uk	

Minister of State for Building Safety and Communities **Lord Greenhalgh**

(jointly with Ministry for Housing, Communities and Local Government) Building Safety Programme; Grenfell recovery and public inquiry; Resilience and Emergencies Minister, including transformation and non-Covid/transition winter response (eg flooding); leasehold and freehold abuses; faith; communities; Holocaust Memorial; fire and rescue services; fire and building safety.

Private Secretary	Uroosa Syed	030 3444 0000
	Email: stephen.greenhalgh@communities.gov.uk	

Parliamentary Under-Secretary of State for Safeguarding **Victoria Atkins** MP

Modern slavery and national referral mechanism; domestic abuse; violence against women and girls, including female genital mutilation (FGM) and forced marriage; early youth intervention on serious violence; Disclosure and Barring Service (DBS); victims; child sexual abuse and exploitation; Independent Inquiry into Child Sexual Abuse; Gangmasters and Labour Abuse Authority; sexual violence, including the rape review; anti-social behavior; prostitution; stalking; online internet safety/WeProtect; victims of terrorism; Security Industry Authority; safeguarding and DBS checks for COVID volunteers and community groups.

Private Secretary	Richard Alexander	020 7035 0037
	Email: ministerforsafeguarding@homeoffice.gov.uk	

Parliamentary Under-Secretary of State for Future Borders and Immigration **Kevin Foster** MP

Design and implementation of the UK's points-based system; design and implementation of digital and secure borders, including Electronic Travel Authorities; counting in and counting out; current and future visa system including fees; global visa operations; net migration; immigration rules; immigration system simplification; exit checks; Immigration Bill; EU Settlement Scheme; immigration casework; nationality; sponsorship of UK Visas and Immigration (UKVI), Her Majesty's

Passport Office (HMPO) and Borders, Immigration and Citizenship System (BICS) policy directorates; border health measures (cross-government policy, DfT lead).

Private Secretary	Joanna Kitson	020 7035 8774
	Email: ministerforimmigration@homeoffice.gov.uk	

Parliamentary Under-Secretary of State for Immigration Compliance and the Courts **Chris Philp** MP

(jointly with Ministry of Justice) Access to work, benefits and services; detention; returns; foreign national offenders; illegal immigration strategy; overseas development aid; Immigration Enforcement; asylum; resettlement; casework; animals (illegal wildlife trade); sponsorship of Border Force and Immigration Enforcement directorates; supporting Lords Minister on corporate affairs, including the Spending Review and Budget; COVID-19 impacts on business as usual function of asylum and returns systems, detention and Border Force.

Private Secretary	Rebecca Fynn	020 3334 0288
	Email: immigrationminister@homeoffice.gov.uk	
	ps.chrisphilp@justice.gov.uk	
Parliamentary Clerk	Mirsada Dema	07384 455301
	Email: parliamentaryteam@homeoffice.gov.uk	

Ministry of Housing, Communities and Local Government

Fry Building, 2 Marsham Street, London SW1P 4DF
030 3444 0000
Email: [firstname.lastname]@communities.gov.uk
(Please note: see Private Secretary for Minister's email) Website: www.gov.uk/mhclg
Twitter: @mhclg

Secretary of State for Housing, Communities and Local Government Rt Hon **Robert Jenrick** MP

Overall leadership and strategic direction of the department; Midlands Engine Champion; Chair of Grenfell Ministerial Recovery Group.

Parliamentary Private Secretaries		
Secretary of State	Andrea Jenkyns MP	020 7219 5798
	Email: andrea.jenkyns.mp@parliament.uk	
Ministerial Team	Jacob Young MP	020 7219 3936
	Email: jacob.young.mp@parliament.uk	
(with responsibility for ending rough sleeping)	Adam Holloway MP	020 7219 8402
		Fax: 020 7219 2871
	Email: hollowaya@parliament.uk	
Special Advisers	Olivia Oates	030 3444 0000
	Email: psadvisers@communities.gov.uk	
	Thomas Kennedy	030 3444 0000
	Email: psadvisers@communities.gov.uk	
	Jack Lewy	030 3444 0000
	Email: psadvisers@communities.gov.uk	
Principal Private Secretary	Jamie Cowling	030 3444 0000
	Email: robert.jenrick@communities.gov.uk	

Minister of State for Housing Rt Hon **Christopher Pincher** MP

Home ownership; housing strategy; housing delivery; Homes England Stewardship; Affordable Housing Programme; Design and Building Better; planning reform; Commons Minister on Building Safety; winter preparedness (transition and Covid, including Deputy at XO and Covid-O); Project Speed; Ox-Cam; homebuying and selling; Voluntary Right to Buy; private rented sector; planning casework.

Private Secretary	Thomas Lambert	030 3444 0000
	Email: chris.pincher@communities.gov.uk	

Minister of State for Regional Growth and Local Government **Luke Hall** MP

Local government engagement, policy and finance; devolution and Devolution White Paper; levelling up; high streets; climate change; UK Shared Prosperity Fund; Mayoral Combined Authorities; pan-regional growth bodies; local digital; freeports; planning casework.

Private Secretary	Sarah Morgan Email: luke.hall@communities.gov.uk	030 3444 0000

Minister of State for Building Safety and Communities **Lord Greenhalgh**

(jointly with Home Office) Building Safety Programme; Grenfell recovery and public inquiry; Resilience and Emergencies Minister, including transformation and non-Covid/Transition winter response (eg flooding); leasehold and freehold abuses; faith; communities; Holocaust Memorial; fire and rescue services; fire and building safety.

Private Secretary	Uroosa Syed Email: stephen.greenhalgh@communities.gov.uk	030 3444 0000

Parliamentary Under-Secretary of State for Rough Sleeping and Housing **Eddie Hughes** MP

Homelessness and rough sleeping; supported housing; New Homes Ombudsman and redress; support for Housing Minister on private rented sector; Troubled Families; domestic abuse; social housing white paper; community assets; Departmental SI Minister; corporate matters.

Private Secretary	Ben Glassman Email: eddie.hughes@communities.gov.uk	030 3444 0000
Parliamentary Clerk	Paul B Smith Email: parliamentary@communities.gov.uk	030 3444 0000

Department for International Trade

King Charles Street, London SW1A 2AH
020 7215 5000
Email: enquiries@trade.gov.uk (Please note: see Private Secretary for Minister's email)
Website: www.gov.uk/dit Twitter: @tradegovuk/GEOgovuk

Government Equalities Office, Sanctuary Buildings, 16-20 Great Smith Street, London SW1P 3BT
0300 020 0229
Email: geo.correspondence@geo.gov.uk Website: www.gov.uk/geo

Secretary of State for International Trade; President of the Board of Trade; Minister for Women and Equalities Rt Hon **Elizabeth Truss** MP

Overall responsibility for the business of the department, including the running of the department and its finances; leading the UK's role in championing free trade through securing new free trade agreements, developing a new UK global tariff policy and reforming the WTO; upgrading the UK's export performance by increasing the number of exporters and the value of exports; increasing the amount and value of FDI into the UK; overall responsibility for developing an equalities policy that it is based on individual autonomy and dignity; promoting equality of opportunity for everyone.

Parliamentary Private Secretaries		
Secretary of State	Saqib Bhatti MP Email: saqib.bhatti@parliament.uk	020 7219 3423
Ministerial Team	Suzanne Webb MP Email: suzanne.webb.mp@parliament.uk	020 7219 3000
Special Advisers	Sophie Jarvis Email: spadtruss@trade.gov.uk Adam Jones Email: spadtruss@trade.gov.uk	
Principal Private Secretary	Matthew Grainger Email: truss@trade.gov.uk	

Deputy Principal Private Secretary Aaron Downey
Email: truss@trade.gov.uk

Senior Private Secretary Hamed Kamal
Email: truss@trade.gov.uk

Private Secretary (GEO) Ieuan Willox
Email: ieuan.willox2@trade.gov.uk

Minister of State for Trade Policy Rt Hon **Greg Hands** MP

Securing new free trade agreements with the US, Australia, New Zealand and Japan; engaging with the devolved administrations; trade for development; Official Development Assistance (ODA); engagement with the WTO; tariff policy.

Senior Private Secretary Grace McDonagh
Email: hands@trade.gov.uk

Minister of State for Investment **Lord Grimstone of Boscobel**

(jointly with Department for Business, Energy and Industrial Strategy) Developing a new investment strategy; promoting all forms of investment; leading on the strategic relationship management programme cross-Whitehall; global marketing to attract investment; managing business investor relations; covering departmental business in the House of Lords; increasing foreign direct investment (FDI) and portfolio investment into the UK; promoting and supporting outward direct investment (ODI).

Senior Private Secretary Frances Knight 020 7008 8147
Email: grimstone@trade.gov.uk

Parliamentary Under-Secretary of State (Minister for Exports) **Graham Stuart** MP

Export policy and promotion; UK Export Finance; UK Defence and Security Exports; climate change and COP26; GREAT campaign; trade missions; global events; investment policy in the House of Commons.

Senior Private Secretary James McMeekin
Email: stuart@trade.gov.uk

Parliamentary Under-Secretary of State (Minister for International Trade) **Ranil Jayawardena** MP

Future free trade agreements; trade agreement continuity; export controls; tackling barriers to market access; trade remedies; trade dialogues; joint economic and trade committees.

Senior Private Secretary Marcus Belli
Email: jayawardena@trade.gov.uk

Parliamentary Clerk Rachel Williams
Email: parly.unit@trade.gov.uk

Ministry of Justice

102 Petty France, London SW1H 9AJ
020 3334 3555 Fax: 020 3334 4455
Email: general.queries@justice.gov.uk/
[firstname.surname]@justice.gov.uk (Please note: see Private Secretary for Minister's email)
Website: www.gov.uk/moj Twitter: @MoJGovUK

Lord Chancellor and Secretary of State for Justice Rt Hon **Robert Buckland** QC MP

Oversight of all portfolios and Ministry of Justice strategy; oversight of international business and future relations with the EU; resourcing of the department; functions of the Lord Chancellor; judicial policy, including pay, pensions and diversity; corporate services; oversight of departmental COVID-19 response supported by other ministers according to portfolio.

Parliamentary Private Secretaries

Lord Chancellor and Secretary of State	Chris Clarkson MP Email: chris.clarkson.mp@parliament.uk	020 7219 4405
Ministerial Team	Julie Marson MP Email: julie.marson.mp@parliament.uk	020 7219 2429
Special Advisers	Alex Wild Email: advisers@justice.gov.uk Ben Jafari Email: advisers@justice.gov.uk	
Principal Private Secretary	Jack Cole Email: ps.lordchancellor@justice.gov.uk	020 3334 3720

Minister of State for Prisons and Probation **Lucy Frazer** QC MP

Prison operations, policy, reform and industrial relations; probation services, policy, reform and industrial relations; public protection, including Parole Board, Imprisonment for Public Protection and Serious Further Offences; offender health; female offenders; transgender offenders; veteran offenders; foreign national offenders (joint work with the Parliamentary Under-Secretary of State for Immigration Compliance and the Courts); offender rehabilitation and release; reducing reoffending (joint work with the Minister of State for Crime and Policing); Extremism, Release On Temporary License and Home Detention Curfew; electronic monitoring (joint work with the Minister of State for Crime and Policing); youth justice; supporting Global Britain and the promotion of legal services.

Private Secretary	Nathaniel Bellio Email: ps.lucyfrazer@justice.gov.uk

Minister of State for Crime and Policing **Kit Malthouse** MP

(jointly with Home Office) Cross-cutting criminal justice system issues; rape review; cross-criminal justice system demand; swift justice with knife crime focus; reducing reoffending (joint work with the Minister of State for Prisons and Probation); support on criminal justice board and Prime Minister's Crime and Justice Taskforce; electronic monitoring (joint work with the Minister of State for Prisons and Probation); drugs and alcohol; joint Spending Review bids.

Private Secretary	Rosemarie Little Email: ps.kitmalthouse@justice.gov.uk ministerforpolicingandfire@homeoffice.gov.uk

Parliamentary Under-Secretary of State **Alex Chalk** MP

Family law and justice; domestic abuse and violence (MoJ lead); legal aid; legal support; victims; mental capacity and Office of the Public Guardian; race disparity in the justice system; coroners, burials, inquests and inquiries, probate; miscarriages of justice; criminal law; human rights; administrative justice; lawfare; devolved administrations and devolution; Independent Monitoring Authority; Shadow Commons Minister for the Lords Minister's portfolio; supporting the Secretary of State on international business and future relationship with the EU.

Private Secretary	Rob Ryan Email: ps.alexchalk@justice.gov.uk

Parliamentary Under-Secretary of State for Immigration Compliance and the Courts **Chris Philp** MP

(jointly with Home Office) Foreign national offenders and removing barriers to removal (joint work with the Minister of State for Prisons and Probation); court and tribunal services and reform; court and tribunal fees; sentencing; supporting the Secretary of State on departmental finance.

Private Secretary	Rebecca Fynn Email: ps.chrisphilp@justice.gov.uk immigrationminister@homeoffice.gov.uk

Parliamentary Under-Secretary of State **Lord Wolfson of Tredegar** QC

Departmental business in the Lords; civil law and justice; legal services worldwide; relationship with the legal profession; Global Britain; Crown Dependencies.

Assistant Private Secretary	Molly Stacey Email: molly.stacey@justice.gov.uk
Head of Parliament and Legislation	Sarah Mahony Email: sarah.mahony@justice.gov.uk
Head of Parliamentary Branch and Parliamentary Clerk	Samuel Talalay Email: samuel.talalay@justice.gov.uk

Law Officers

Attorney General's Office, 102 Petty France, London SW1H 9EA
020 7271 2492
Email: correspondence@attorneygeneral.gov.uk/privateoffice@attorneygeneral.gov.uk
Website: www.gov.uk/ago Twitter: @attorneygeneral

Office of the Advocate General for Scotland, Dover House, 66 Whitehall, London SW1A 2AU
020 7270 6720
Email: privateoffice@advocategeneral.gov.uk/[firstname.surname]@advocategeneral.gov.uk
Website: www.gov.uk/oag

Attorney General Rt Hon **Suella Braverman** QC MP

Overall responsibility for the work of the Attorney General's Office and superintended Departments (Government Legal Department, Crown Prosecution Service, Serious Fraud Office and HM Crown Prosecution Service Inspectorate); specific statutory duty to superintend the discharge of duties by the Director of Public Prosecutions (who heads the Crown Prosecution Service) and the Director of the Serious Fraud Office; non-statutory general oversight of the Services Prosecuting Authority and government prosecuting departments; Government's principal legal adviser dealing with (amongst others) questions of international law, human rights, devolution and COVID-19 issues; public interest functions, for example, reference of unduly lenient sentences to the Court of Appeal, bringing proceedings for contempt of court and intervention in certain proceedings to protect charities; questions of law arising on Bills and with issues of legal policy; legal aspects of all major international and domestic litigation involving the Government, including matters related to future relations with the EU.

Parliamentary Private Secretary	Alberto Costa MP Email: alberto.costa.mp@parliament.uk	020 7219 4936
Special Adviser	Chris Jenkins	

Solicitor General Rt Hon **Michael Ellis** QC MP

Deputising for the Attorney General and responsible for such matters as the Attorney General delegates; providing support to the Attorney General in their superintendence of the Government Legal Department, Crown Prosecution Service, HM Crown Prosecution Service Inspectorate and Serious Fraud Office; providing support to the Attorney General on civil litigation and advice on civil law matters and on the public interest function.

Advocate General for Scotland **Lord Stewart of Dirleton** QC

The Advocate General for Scotland is a Minister of the Crown and is one of the three UK Law Officers. Along with the Attorney General and the Solicitor General for England and Wales, the Advocate General provides legal advice to all UK Government departments on a wide range of issues including human rights, European and constitutional law. The Advocate General is also the UK Government's principal legal adviser on Scots law and its senior representative within the Scottish legal community. The Advocate General is the Minister responsible to the UK Parliament for the Office of the Advocate General.

Private Secretary	Nathan Lappin Email: privateoffice@advocategeneral.gov.uk	020 7270 6720

Office of the Leader of the House of Commons

Room 4, House of Commons, London SW1A 0AA
020 7276 1005
Email: commonsleader@cabinetoffice.gov.uk
Website: www.gov.uk/government/organisations/the-office-of-the-leader-of-the-house-of-commons
Twitter: @CommonsLeader

Leader of the House of Commons; Lord President of the Council Rt Hon **Jacob Rees-Mogg** MP

Government's Legislative Programme; managing the business of the House; Government's representative in the House (House of Commons Commission); House of Commons representative in Government; House of Commons reform and related issues.

Parliamentary Private Secretary	Lucy Allan MP Email: lucy.allan.mp@parliament.uk	020 7219 4815
Special Adviser	Fred De Fossard Email: fred.defossard@cabinetoffice.go.uk	
Head of Office	Rob Foot Email: commonsleader@cabinetoffice.gov.uk	020 7276 1005

Office of the Leader of the House of Lords

House of Lords, London SW1A 0PW
020 7219 3200 Fax: 020 7219 5251
Email: psleaderofthelords@cabinetoffice.gov.uk/psdeputyleaderofthelords@cabinetoffice.gov.uk
Website: www.gov.uk/government/organisations/office-of-the-leader-of-the-house-of-lords

Leader of the House of Lords and Lord Privy Seal Rt Hon **Baroness Evans of Bowes Park**

Principal responsibility for the strategic management and delivery of the Government's legislative programme in the Lords; leading Government benches in the House of Lords; conduct of Government business in the Lords (together with the Lords Chief Whip); repeating in the Lords statements made by the Prime Minister in the Commons; giving guidance to the House on matters of order and procedure; Chair, Board of Trustees for Chevening.

Parliamentary Private Secretary	Jonathan Gullis MP Email: jonathan.gullis.mp@parliament.uk	020 7219 6837
Special Advisers	Annabelle Eyre Email: annabelle.eyre@cabinetoffice.gov.uk	020 7219 1046
	Hannah Ellis Email: hannah.ellis@cabinetoffice.gov.uk	
	Yasmin Kalhori Email: yasmin.kalhori@cabinetoffice.gov.uk	
Principal Private Secretary	Victoria Warren Email: victoria.warren@cabinetoffice.gov.uk	020 7219 1113
Private Secretary	Philip Lloyd Email: philip.lloyd@cabinetoffice.gov.uk	020 7219 6782

Deputy Leader of the House of Lords Rt Hon **Earl Howe**

Support the House of Lords in its job of questioning government ministers, improving legislation and debating topics of national significance.

Private Secretary	Johnny Bland Email: psdeputyleaderofthelords@cabinetoffice.gov.uk	020 7219 8075

Northern Ireland Office

1 Horse Guards Road, London SW1A 2HQ
020 7210 6455 (London)
Email: sos.lewis@nio.gov.uk (Please note: see Private Secretary for Minister's email)
Website: www.gov.uk/nio Twitter: @NIOgov

Secretary of State for Northern Ireland Rt Hon **Brandon Lewis** CBE MP

Overall responsibility for all aspects of the department's work; political stability and relations with the Northern Ireland Executive; national security and counter-terrorism; implementation of the Stormont House and Fresh Start Agreements, including legacy of the past; representing Northern Ireland in the Cabinet on EU exit, including new economic opportunities; international interest in Northern Ireland, including relations with the Irish government.

Parliamentary Private Secretary	Sarah Dines MP Email: sarah.dines.mp@parliament.uk	020 7219 6660
Special Advisers	Amy Fisher Email: spads.ps@nio.gov.uk	
	Oliver Legard Email: spads.ps@nio.gov.uk	
	Isabel Bruce Email: spads.ps@nio.gov.uk	
Private Secretary	Kathryn Evans Email: sos.lewis@nio.gov.uk	020 7210 6455

Minister of State **Robin Walker** MP

Supporting the passage of the Withdrawal Agreement Bill and the Armed Forces Covenant through Parliament; strengthening the Union, City Deals and the Shared Prosperity Fund; promotion of the economy; relations with the business sector.

Private Secretary	Peter White Email: min.walker@nio.gov.uk	020 7210 0819
Parliamentary Clerk	Louise Newby Email: parly.section@nio.gov.uk	020 7210 6575

Office of the Secretary of State for Scotland

Dover House, 66 Whitehall, London SW1A 2AU
020 7270 6741 Fax: 020 7270 6815
Email: secretaryofstate@scotlandoffice.gov.uk/
[firstname.surname]@scotlandoffice.gov.uk (Please note: see Private Secretary for Minister's email)
Website: www.gov.uk/scotland-office Twitter: @UKGovScotland

Secretary of State for Scotland Rt Hon **Alister Jack** MP

Overall responsibility for: Union, including Union strategy, UK Government in Scotland, Dunlop Review, Intergovernmental Relations Review, UK Shared Prosperity Fund; EU Exit, including No deal preparations, Common frameworks and internal market; investment and infrastructure, including City and Growth Deals (Stirling and Clacks, Edinburgh, Glasgow, Ayrshire, Falkirk, Moray); immigration; Constitution, including Scotland Act Orders, Scotland Act 2016; business, infrastructure and economy, including rural economy, security and defence; international, including trade, international development; culture.

Parliamentary Private Secretary	Ruth Edwards MP Email: ruth.edwards.mp@parliament.uk	020 7219 3549
Special Advisers	John Cooper Email: sospecialadvisers@scotlandoffice.gov.uk	020 7270 6814
	Magnus Gardham Email: sospecialadvisers@scotlandoffice.gov.uk	020 7270 6814

	Geoff Mawdsley Email: sospecialadvisers@scotlandoffice.gov.uk	020 7270 6814
Principal Private Secretary	Victoria Jones Email: secretaryofstate@scotlandoffice.gov.uk	020 7270 6741
Senior Private Secretary	Jethro House Email: secretaryofstate@scotlandoffice.gov.uk	020 7270 6741
Private Secretary	Natalie Golding Email: secretaryofstate@scotlandoffice.gov.uk	020 7270 6741
Diary Secretary	Rebecca Tremlett Email: secretaryofstate@scotlandoffice.gov.uk	020 7270 6741

Parliamentary Under-Secretary of State (Minister for Scotland) **Iain Stewart** MP

Strengthening the Union; energy, including: oil and gas, renewables; business and economy, including: agriculture and fisheries, food and drink, manufacturing, retail and tourism, financial services; investment and infrastructure, including: City Region and Growth Deals, industrial strategy, digital and connectivity, transport and aviation; higher education and academia; security and defence; sport.

Parliamentary Under-Secretary of State **David Duguid** MP

Strengthening the Union; energy, including oil and gas, renewables; investment and infrastructure, including City Region and Growth Deals; business and the economy, including agriculture and fisheries.

Private Secretary to Parliamentary Under-Secretaries of State	Sam Gold Email: pusos@scotlandoffice.gov.uk	020 7270 6816
Assistant Private Secretary to Parliamentary Under-Secretaries of State	Rachel Stonebridge Email: pusos@scotlandoffice.gov.uk	020 7270 6816
Diary Secretary to Parliamentary Under-Secretaries of State	Oluwafemi Ekolie Email: pusos@scotlandoffice.gov.uk	020 7270 6816
Parliamentary Clerk	Louise Newby Email: parly.section@nio.gov.uk	020 7210 6575

Department for Transport

Great Minster House, 33 Horseferry Road, London SW1P 4DR
0300 330 3000
Email: pocorrespondence@dft.gov.uk/
[firstname.surname]@dft.gov.uk (Please note: see Private Secretary for Minister's email)
Website: www.gov.uk/dft Twitter: @transportgovuk

Secretary of State for Transport Rt Hon **Grant Shapps** MP

Overall responsibility for policies of the Department for Transport; cabinet responsibility for the Northern Powerhouse; oversight of departmental COVID-19 responsibilities.

Parliamentary Private Secretaries		
Secretary of State	Laura Trott MBE MP Email: laura.trott.mp@parliament.uk	020 7219 4964
Ministerial Team	Gagan Mohindra MP Email: gagan.mohindra.mp@parliament.uk	020 7219 3000
Special Advisers	Neil Tweedie Email: dftspecialadvisers@dft.gov.uk Meera Vadher Email: dftspecialadvisers@dft.gov.uk	
Principal Private Secretary	Rupesh Mehta Email: transportsecretary@dft.gov.uk	020 7944 4394

Minister of State **Andrew Stephenson** MP

HS2; Northern Powerhouse Rail; Transpennine route upgrade; skills.

Private Secretary	Abigail Bennetton Email: andrew.stephenson_mp@dft.gov.uk	020 7944 4407

Minister of State **Chris Heaton-Harris** MP

Rail, Crossrail and Crossrail 2; East West Rail; cycling and walking; accessibility; corporate.

Private Secretary	Toby Fountain Email: chris.heatonharris_mp@dft.gov.uk	020 7944 8695

Parliamentary Under-Secretary of State **Rachel Maclean** MP

Future of transport, including future of freight; environment, including transport decarbonization; transition period activity and future relations with the EU; international, exports and inward investment; space; secondary legislation.

Private Secretary	Thomas Ashe Email: rachel.maclean_mp@dft.gov.uk	020 7944 4491

Parliamentary Under-Secretary of State **Robert Courts** MP

Aviation; maritime; security and civil contingencies.

Private Secretary	Joshua Crossley Email: robert.courts_mp@dft.gov.uk	020 7944 2637

Parliamentary Under-Secretary of State **Baroness Vere of Norbiton**

Roads, including Highways England; motoring agencies (DVSA, DVLA, VCA); buses and taxis; light rail, including tram, underground and metro systems; devolution, including union connectivity and London transport.

Private Secretary	Beth Newing Email: baroness.vere_puss@dft.gov.uk	020 7944 4124
Parliamentary Clerk	James Langston Email: james.langston@dft.gov.uk	020 7944 4472

HM Treasury

1 Horse Guards Road, London SW1A 2HQ
020 7270 4558 Fax: 020 7270 4861
Email: public.enquiries@hmtreasury.gov.uk/
[firstname.surname]@hmtreasury.gov.uk (Please note: see Private Secretary for Minister's email)
Website: www.gov.uk/hm-treasury Twitter: @hmtreasury

Chancellor of the Exchequer Rt Hon **Rishi Sunak** MP

Overall responsibility for the work of the Treasury; fiscal policy, including the presenting of the annual Budget; monetary policy, setting inflation targets; ministerial arrangements (in his role as Second Lord of the Treasury); overall responsibility for the Treasury's response to COVID-19.

Parliamentary Private Secretary to the Chancellor of the Exchequer	James Cartlidge MP Email: james.cartlidge.mp@parliament.uk	020 7219 4875
Parliamentary Private Secretary to Ministerial Team	Claire Coutinho MP Email: claire.coutinho.mp@parliament.uk	020 7219 5972
Special Advisers		
Joint No10/HMT Economic Unit	Liam Booth-Smith Michael Webb Douglas McNeill	

	Nerissa Chesterfield
	Cass Horowitz
	Rupert Yorke
	Lisa Lovering
Principal Private Secretary	Elizabeth Perelman
	Email: action.chancellors@hmtreasury.gov.uk

Chief Secretary to the Treasury Rt Hon **Stephen Barclay** MP

Public expenditure, including spending reviews and strategic planning, in-year spending control, public sector pay and pensions, including the state pension, Annually Managed Expenditure (AME) and welfare reform, efficiency and value for money in public service, procurement, capital investment, infrastructure spending, housing and planning, spending issues related to trade, transport policy, including HS2, Crossrail 2, Roads, Network Rail, Oxford/Cambridge corridor, Treasury interest in devolution to Scotland, Wales and Northern Ireland; women in the economy; childcare policy, including tax free childcare; tax credits policy; labour market policy, housing and planning, freeports.

Parliamentary Private Secretary	Craig Williams MP	020 7219 3000
	Email: craig.williams.mp@parliament.uk	
Special Adviser	Aled Maclean-Jones	
Private Secretary	Elkie Symes	
	Email: action.cst@hmtreasury.gov.uk	

Financial Secretary Rt Hon **Jesse Norman** MP

Strategic oversight of the UK tax system, including direct, indirect, business, property and personal taxation; corporate and small business taxation; European and international tax issues; customs policy; Value Added Tax (VAT); infrastructure policy (National Infrastructure Strategy, National Infrastructure Commission, and joint responsibility with Cabinet Office for the Infrastructure and Projects Authority); Departmental Minister for HM Revenue and Customs and Valuation Office Agency; HMRC planning and delivery of the UK's future partnership with the EU; overall responsibility for the Finance Bill; Government Actuary's Department; parliamentary deputy on public spending issues.

Private Secretary	Laura Oakley
	Email: action.fst@hmtreasury.gov.uk

Minister of State for Efficiency and Transformation **Lord Agnew of Oulton** DL

(jointly with Cabinet Office) Supporting the Chancellor of the Duchy of Lancaster and the Chief Secretary to the Treasury to deliver cross-government efficiency and public sector transformation improvements, including public value and planning and performance, supporting the Chancellor of the Duchy of Lancaster on cross-government functions and controls, including public bodies and Cabinet Office domestic, supporting procurement and other government functional activity relating to COVID-19.

Private Secretary	Louis Reynolds
	Email: pslordagnew@cabinetoffice.gov.uk

Economic Secretary (Minister for the City of London) **John Glen** MP

Banking and financial services reform and regulation, financial stability, including relationship with the PRA; financial conduct, including relationship with the FCA; relationships with other financial services regulatory bodies; EU exit financial services; City competitiveness, including Financial Services Trade and Investment Board; retail financial services, including banking competition, consumer finance, financial advice and capability; bank lending, access to finance and payment systems; global financial partnerships; green finance, Islamic finance, fintech; financial services taxation, including bank levy, bank corporation tax surcharge, IPT; personal savings tax and pensions tax policy; insurance; asset management; Women in Finance Charter; sponsorship of UKFI and state owned financial assets: RBS, UKAR; sponsorship of UKGI and sale of government non-financial assets; illicit finance, financial sanctions and anti-money laundering; financial inclusion (lead on the government's financial inclusion agenda); Equitable Life; foreign exchange reserves and debt management policy, NS&I and Debt Management Office; parliamentary deputy on economy issues; Royal Mint.

Private Secretary	Sophie Fry Email: est.action@hmtreasury.gov.uk

Exchequer Secretary; Minister for Equalities **Kemi Badenoch** MP

UK growth and productivity, including: regional devolution, City deals, Northern Powerhouse, Midlands Engine, Ox-Cam Arc, place based economic strategy, better regulation and competition policy, R&D and science policy, skills, migration, National Retraining Scheme and apprenticeship levy, digital, fibre and mobile, implementation of the Rose Review, corporate governance, Patient Capital Review implementation, Small Business Policy (including prompt payments and FSB stakeholder engagement), Crown Estate and the Royal Household, Overseas territories and Crown dependencies, promoting UK as a destination for FDI (non-FS), Departmental minister for HM Treasury Group, supporting tax legislation in Parliament; energy infrastructure, energy, environment and climate policy, including the net zero review into the costs of decarbonization, new nuclear, roll out of green infrastructure, consumer bills vs tax, energy and environment taxes (including plastics taxation and carbon taxes), transport taxation (including vehicle taxes and future strategy and air passenger duty), North Sea oil, gas and shipping; in addition to supporting tax legislation in Parliament, the XST leads on the following indirect taxes: excise duties (alcohol, tobacco and gambling), including excise fraud and law enforcement, soft drink industry levy, charities, the voluntary sector and gift aid.

Private Secretary	Annie Leigh Email: action.xst@hmtreasury.gov.uk
Parliamentary Clerk	Simon Turrell Email: simon.turrell@hmtreasury.gov.uk

Office of the Secretary of State for Wales

Gwydyr House, Whitehall, London SW1A 2NP
020 7270 0534
Email: correspondence@ukgovwales.gov.uk (Please note: see Private Secretary for Minister's email)
Website: www.gov.uk/wales Twitter: @UKGovWales

Secretary of State for Wales Rt Hon **Simon Hart** MP

Fiscal; constitutional and electoral issues; EU exit; international trade; energy and climate change; broadcasting; steel; defence; public appointments; foreign affairs; agriculture; justice; third sector; economy; home affairs; digital infrastructure; tourism, heritage and culture.

Parliamentary Private Secretary	Sarah Atherton MP Email: sarah.atherton.mp@parliament.uk	020 7219 4885
Special Advisers	Jack Sellers Email: jack.sellers@ukgovwales.gov.uk Olivia Williams	07971 490154
Principal Private Secretary	Sarah Jennings Email: secretary.state@ukgovwales.gov.uk	07811 732894
Private Secretary	Josh Harris Email: secretary.state@ukgovwales.gov.uk	07776 227246

Parliamentary Under-Secretary of State **David Davies** MP

Cardiff City Deal; Swansea City Deal; North Wales Growth Deal; Mid Wales Growth Deal; Western Gateway; rail; road; air; Welsh language; health; education; local government; sport.

Private Secretary	Calum Taylor Email: ukg.ministers@ukgovwales.gov.uk	07977 220837

Parliamentary Clerk	Louise Newby Email: parly.section@nio.gov.uk	07554 115063

Department for Work and Pensions

Caxton House, Tothill Street, London SW1H 9DA
020 7340 4000
Email: ministers@dwp.gov.uk (Please note: see Private Secretary for Minister's email)
Website: www.gov.uk/dwp Twitter: @DWP

Secretary of State for Work and Pensions Rt Hon Dr **Therese Coffey** MP

Overall responsibility for the business of the department; responsibility for departmental expenditure and departmental management; responsible for the department's overall response to COVID-19.

Parliamentary Private Secretaries		
Secretary of State	Bim Afolami MP Email: bim.afolami.mp@parliament.uk	020 7219 3000
Ministerial Team	Flick Drummond MP Email: flick.drummond.mp@parliament.uk	020 7219 8018
Special Advisers		
(Media)	Rhiannon Padley Jessica Prestidge Ed Winfield	
(Disability)	Jean-Andre Prager	
Private Secretary to Special Advisers	Rachel Eckersley Email: special-advisers@dwp.gov.uk	020 3267 5001
Principal Private Secretary	Ellie Nicholson Email: secretaryofstate@dwp.gov.uk	020 3267 5007

Minister of State for Disabled People, Health and Work **Justin Tomlinson** MP

Responsible for the departmental strategy on disability and disability employment; cross-government responsibility for disabled people; Employment and Support Allowance, Personal Independence Payment, Disability Living Allowance and elements of Universal Credit that relate to disabled people, including Severe Disability Premium; EU Exit oversight; work and health strategy, including sponsorship of the joint Department for Work and Pensions/Department of Health and Social Care Work and Health Unit; disability benefit reform; devolution framework; Carer's Allowance; motability and arms-length compensation schemes.

Private Secretary	Zoe Garrett Email: minister.disabledpeople@dwp.gov.uk	020 3267 5040

Parliamentary Under-Secretary of State for Employment **Mims Davies** MP

Responsible for departmental strategy on the labour market, unemployment and in work progression, with a focus on under-represented groups, young people and skills; in-work conditionality, including sanctions; international labour market policy (International Labour Organization, G20, Employment, Social Policy, Health and Consumer Affairs Council); European Social Fund and UK Shared Prosperity Fund; work services and Jobcentre Plus partnership working; Jobcentre Plus campaigns; Jobseeker's Allowance, Income Support; People and Location Programme; Youth Employment Programme; Flexible Support Fund; labour market interventions for self-employment, including New Enterprise Allowance and future offer and Minimum Income Floor; benefit cap; Health and Safety Executive.

Private Secretary	Emma Luxford Email: minister.employment@dwp.gov.uk	020 3267 5019

Parliamentary Under-Secretary of State for Pensions and Financial Inclusion **Guy Opperman** MP

Pensioner benefits, including new State Pension, Winter Fuel Payments, Pension Credit and Attendance Allowance; private and occupational pensions, including regulatory powers and National Employment Savings Trust (NEST); automatic enrolment into a workplace pension; oversight of arms-length bodies, including Pensions Regulator, Pension Protection Fund, Financial Assistance Scheme and Pensions Ombudsman; financial guidance, budgeting, saving and debt, including Money and Pensions Service and Financial Inclusion Policy Forum; methods of payment and Post Office card accounts; EU Exit preparation relevant to pensions; cross-DWP spokesperson – shadowing Lords.

Private Secretary	Lauren Thomas Email: minister.pensions@dwp.gov.uk	020 3267 5027

Parliamentary Under-Secretary of State for Welfare Delivery **Will Quince** MP

Overall management and delivery of Universal Credit; support for disadvantaged groups in Universal Credit, including care leavers, prison leavers, survivors of domestic abuse, people with drug or alcohol dependency, rough sleepers and those who are facing homelessness; housing policy and housing benefit delivery; 'Help to Claim' service; poverty and food banks; benefit up-rating; military covenant; fraud, error and debt.

Private Secretary	Aysha Ali Email: minister.welfaredelivery@dwp.gov.uk	020 7867 3104

Parliamentary Under-Secretary of State (Lords) **Baroness Stedman-Scott** OBE

Departmental spokesperson in the Lords; child maintenance; family test; parental conflict; legislation and statutory instruments strategy; Social Security Advisory Committee (SSAC) relationship management; Social Fund (Cold Weather Payments, Sure Start Maternity grants, Funeral Expenses Payment scheme and Budgeting loans); bereavement benefits; supported accommodation; Support for Mortgage Interest; maternity benefits; departmental planning and performance management, including oversight of the single departmental plan, including tracking progress against manifesto commitments, other external reporting and governance requirements; departmental business, including oversight of departmental capability in commercial and digital affairs, commercial contracting policy, transparency and data-sharing issues, research and trialling; Office for Nuclear Regulation.

Private Secretary	Vanessa Drury Email: minister.lords@dwp.gov.uk	020 3267 5035
Parliamentary Clerk	Howard Sargent Email: howard.sargent@dwp.gov.uk	020 3267 5159

Ministerial Committees of the Cabinet

Climate Action Implementation Committee
Chair: President of the UN COP26 Climate Conference

Climate Action Strategy Committee
Chair: Prime Minister, First Lord of the Treasury and Minister for the Civil Service

Covid-19 Operations Committee
Chair: Chancellor of the Duchy of Lancaster and Minister for the Cabinet Office

Covid-19 Strategy Committee
Chair: Prime Minister, First Lord of the Treasury and Minister for the Civil Service

Crime and Justice Task Force
Chair: Prime Minister, First Lord of the Treasury and Minister for the Civil Service
Deputy chair: Secretary of State for the Home Department

Domestic and Economic Strategy Committee
Chair: Prime Minister, First Lord of the Treasury and Minister for the Civil Service

Domestic and Economy Implementation Committee
Chair: Chancellor of the Exchequer

Economic Operations Committee
Chair: Chancellor of the Exchequer

EU Exit Operations Committee
Chair: Chancellor of the Duchy of Lancaster and Minister for the Cabinet Office

EU Exit Strategy Committee
Chair: Prime Minister, First Lord of the Treasury and Minister for the Civil Service

National Security Council
Chair: Prime Minister, First Lord of the Treasury and Minister for the Civil Service

NSC (Nuclear Deterrence and Security) Sub-committee
Chair: Prime Minister, First Lord of the Treasury and Minister for the Civil Service

National Space Council
Chair: Prime Minister, First Lord of the Treasury and Minister for the Civil Service
Deputy chair: First Secretary of State and Secretary of State for Foreign, Commonwealth and Development Affairs

Parliamentary Business and Legislation Committee
Chair: Leader of the House of Commons; Lord President of the Council

Union Policy Implementation Committee
Chair: Chancellor of the Duchy of Lancaster and Minister for the Cabinet Office

Parliamentary Private Secretaries

Prime Minister's Office

Boris Johnson, Prime Minister	Alex Burghart 020 7219 1613 Email: alex.burghart.mp@parliament.uk Trudy Harrison 020 7219 4002 Email: trudy.harrison.mp@parliament.uk

Business, Energy and Industrial Strategy

Kwasi Kwarteng, Secretary of State	Jo Gideon 020 7219 8131 Email: jo.gideon.mp@parliament.uk
Ministerial Team	Mark Fletcher 020 7219 3662 Email: mark.fletcher.mp@parliament.uk

Cabinet Office

Michael Gove, Chancellor of the Duchy of Lancaster	Kevin Hollinrake 020 7219 4746 Email: kevin.hollinrake.mp@parliament.uk
Ministerial Team	Jane Hunt 020 7219 8647 Email: jane.hunt.mp@parliament.uk
Amanda Milling, Minister without portfolio	Peter Gibson 020 7219 3077 Email: peter.gibson.mp@parliament.uk

Defence

Ben Wallace, Secretary of State	Jack Brereton 020 7219 4460 Email: jack.brereton.mp@parliament.uk
Ministerial Team	Natalie Elphicke 020 7219 7052 Email: natalie.elphicke.mp@parliament.uk

Digital, Culture, Media and Sport

Oliver Dowden, Secretary of State	John Lamont 020 7219 1557 Email: john.lamont.mp@parliament.uk
Ministerial Team	Alicia Kearns 020 7219 3000 Email: alicia.kearns.mp@parliament.uk

Education

Gavin Williamson, Secretary of State	Angela Richardson 020 7219 5851 Email: angela.richardson.mp@parliament.uk

Environment, Food and Rural Affairs

George Eustice, Secretary of State — Damien Moore
020 7219 4684
Email: damien.moore.mp@parliament.uk

Ministerial Team — Fay Jones
020 7219 3000
Email: fay.jones.mp@parliament.uk

Foreign, Commonwealth and Development Office

Dominic Raab, Foreign Secretary — Gareth Johnson
020 7219 7047
Email: gareth.johnson.mp@parliament.uk

Ministerial Team — Joy Morrissey
020 7219 6453
Email: joy.morrissey.mp@parliament.uk

Health and Social Care

Matt Hancock, Secretary of State — Steve Double
020 7219 4408
Email: steve.double.mp@parliament.uk

Ministerial Team — Virginia Crosbie
020 7219 4091
Email: virginia.crosbie.mp@parliament.uk

Home Office

Priti Patel, Home Secretary — Mike Wood
020 7219 6982
Email: mike.wood.mp@parliament.uk

Ministerial Team — Andrew Lewer
020 7219 3870
Email: andrew.lewer.mp@parliament.uk

Housing, Communities and Local Government

Robert Jenrick, Secretary of State — Andrea Jenkyns
020 7219 5798
Email: andrea.jenkyns.mp@parliament.uk

Ministerial Team — Jacob Young
020 7219 3936
Email: jacob.young.mp@parliament.uk

(with responsibility for ending rough sleeping) — Adam Holloway
020 7219 8402 Fax: 020 7219 2871
Email: hollowaya@parliament.uk

International Trade

Elizabeth Truss, Secretary of State — Saqib Bhatti
020 7219 3423
Email: saqib.bhatti@parliament.uk

Justice

Robert Buckland, Lord Chancellor and Secretary of State	Chris Clarkson 020 7219 4405 Email: chris.clarkson.mp@parliament.uk
Ministerial Team	Julie Marson 020 7219 2429 Email: julie.marson.mp@parliament.uk

Law Officers

Suella Braverman, Attorney General	Alberto Costa 020 7219 4936 Email: alberto.costa.mp@parliament.uk

House of Commons

Jacob Rees-Mogg, Leader of the House of Commons	Lucy Allan 020 7219 4815 Email: lucy.allan.mp@parliament.uk

House of Lords

Baroness Evans of Bowes Park, Leader of the House of Lords	Jonathan Gullis 020 7219 6837 Email: jonathan.gullis.mp@parliament.uk

Northern Ireland

Brandon Lewis, Secretary of State	Sarah Dines 020 7219 6660 Email: sarah.dines.mp@parliament.uk

Scotland

Alister Jack, Secretary of State	Ruth Edwards 020 7219 3549 Email: ruth.edwards.mp@parliament.uk

Transport

Grant Shapps, Secretary of State	Laura Trott 020 7219 4964 Email: laura.trott.mp@parliament.uk
Ministerial Team	Gagan Mohindra 020 7219 3000 Email: gagan.mohindra.mp@parliament.uk

HM Treasury

Rishi Sunak, Chancellor of the Exchequer	James Cartlidge 020 7219 4875 Email: james.cartlidge.mp@parliament.uk
Ministerial Team	Claire Coutinho 020 7219 5972 Email: claire.coutinho.mp@parliament.uk

Stephen Barclay, Chief Secretary to the Treasury

Craig Williams
020 7219 3000
Email: craig.williams.mp@parliament.uk

Wales

Simon Hart, Secretary of State

Sarah Atherton
020 7219 4885
Email: sarah.atherton.mp@parliament.uk

Work and Pensions

Therese Coffey, Secretary of State

Bim Afolami
020 7219 3000
Email: bim.afolami.mp@parliament.uk

Special Advisers

Prime Minister's Office

Boris Johnson, Prime Minister	Dan Rosenfield Lord Udny-Lister Henry Cook Katie Lam James Slack Declan Lyons Munira Mirza Lord Frost

Cabinet Office

Michael Gove, Chancellor of the Duchy of Lancaster	Henry Newman Charlie Rowley Josh Grimstone 07712 546086 Email: psspecialadvisers@cabinetoffice.gov.uk
Alok Sharma, President of the UN COP26 Climate Conference	Alex Hitchcock
Amanda Milling, Minister without portfolio	Emily Maister

Defence

Ben Wallace, Secretary of State	Peter Quentin Lucia Hodgson

Digital, Culture, Media and Sport

Oliver Dowden, Secretary of State	Lucy Noakes Email: special.advisers@dcms.gov.uk Mike Crowhurst Email: special.advisers@dcms.gov.uk

Education

Gavin Williamson, Secretary of State	Iain Mansfield Email: advisers.ps@education.gov.uk

Environment, Food and Rural Affairs

George Eustice, Secretary of State	Emma Pryor 020 8026 2809/020 8415 2941 Email: ps.advisers@defra.gov.uk Sara Rajeswaran 020 8026 2809/020 8415 2941 Email: ps.advisers@defra.gov.uk

Foreign, Commonwealth and Development Office

Dominic Raab, First Secretary of State

Beth Armstrong
020 7008 2312
Email: pospads@fcdo.gov.uk
William Sweet
020 8871 6000
Email: wsweet@wandsworth.gov.uk
Robert Oxley
020 7008 2312
Email: pospads@fcdo.gov.uk
Simon Finkelstein
020 7008 2312
Email: pospads@fcdo.gov.uk

Health and Social Care

Matt Hancock, Secretary of State

Allan Nixon
020 7210 5945
Email: specialadvisors@dhsc.gov.uk
Emma Dean
020 7210 5945
Email: specialadvisors@dhsc.gov.uk
Damon Poole
020 7210 5945
Email: specialadvisors@dhsc.gov.uk

Home Office

Priti Patel, Secretary of State

Hannah Guerin
020 7035 0196
Email: specialadvisers@homeoffice.gov.uk
Charlotte Miller
020 7035 0196
Email: specialadvisers@homeoffice.gov.uk
Harry Methley
020 7035 0196
Email: specialadvisers@homeoffice.gov.uk

Housing, Communities and Local Government

Robert Jenrick, Secretary of State

Olivia Oates
030 3444 0000
Email: psadvisers@communities.gov.uk
Thomas Kennedy
030 3444 0000
Email: psadvisers@communities.gov.uk
Jack Lewy
030 3444 0000
Email: psadvisers@communities.gov.uk

International Trade

Elizabeth Truss, Secretary of State

Adam Jones
Email: spadtruss@trade.gov.uk
Sophie Jarvis
Email: spadtruss@trade.gov.uk

Justice

Robert Buckland, Lord Chancellor

Alex Wild
Email: advisers@justice.gov.uk
Ben Jafari
Email: advisers@justice.gov.uk

Law Officers

Suella Braverman, Attorney General

Chris Jenkins

House of Commons

Jacob Rees-Mogg, Leader of the House of Commons

Fred De Fossard
Email: fred.defossard@cabinetoffice.go.uk

House of Lords

Baroness Evans of Bowes Park, Leader of the House of Lords

Hannah Ellis
Email: hannah.ellis@cabinetoffice.gov.uk
Annabelle Eyre
020 7219 1046
Email: annabelle.eyre@cabinetoffice.gov.uk
Yasmin Kalhori
Email: yasmin.kalhori@cabinetoffice.gov.uk

Northern Ireland

Brandon Lewis, Secretary of State

Amy Fisher
Email: spads.ps@nio.gov.uk
Oliver Legard
Email: spads.ps@nio.gov.uk
Isabel Bruce
Email: spads.ps@nio.gov.uk

Scotland

Alister Jack, Secretary of State

John Cooper
020 7270 6814
Email: sospecialadvisers@scotlandoffice.gov.uk
Magnus Gardham
020 7270 6814
Email: sospecialadvisers@scotlandoffice.gov.uk
Geoff Mawdsley
020 7270 6814
Email: sospecialadvisers@scotlandoffice.gov.uk

Transport

Grant Shapps, Secretary of State

Neil Tweedie
Email: dftspecialadvisers@dft.gov.uk
Meera Vadher
Email: dftspecialadvisers@dft.gov.uk

HM Treasury

Rishi Sunak, Chancellor of the Exchequer	Lisa Lovering Douglas McNeill Rupert Yorke Liam Booth-Smith Nerissa Chesterfield Michael Webb Cass Horowitz
Stephen Barclay, Chief Secretary to the Treasury	Aled Maclean-Jones

Wales

Simon Hart, Secretary of State	Jack Sellers 07971 490154 Email: jack.sellers@ukgovwales.gov.uk

Work and Pensions

Therese Coffey, Secretary of State	Rhiannon Padley Jessica Prestidge Ed Winfield Jean-Andre Prager 020 3267 5001 Email: special-advisers@dwp.gov.uk

The Opposition

Labour (official opposition)

Shadow Cabinet

Leader of the Opposition	Rt Hon Sir **Keir Starmer** KCB QC MP
Deputy Leader, National Campaign Co-ordinator and Chair of the Labour Party; Shadow First Secretary of State	**Angela Rayner** MP
Shadow Chancellor of the Exchequer	**Anneliese Dodds** MP
Shadow Secretary of State for Foreign and Commonwealth Affairs (Shadow Foreign Secretary)	**Lisa Nandy** MP
Shadow Secretary of State for the Home Department (Shadow Home Secretary)	**Nick Thomas-Symonds** MP
Shadow Chancellor of the Duchy of Lancaster	**Rachel Reeves** MP
Shadow Secretary of State for Justice	Rt Hon **David Lammy** MP
Shadow Secretary of State for Defence	Rt Hon **John Healey** MP
Shadow Secretary of State for Business, Energy and Industrial Strategy	Rt Hon **Ed Miliband** MP
Shadow Secretary of State for International Trade	Rt Hon **Emily Thornberry** MP
Shadow Secretary of State for Work and Pensions	**Jonathan Reynolds** MP
Shadow Secretary of State for Health and Social Care	**Jon Ashworth** MP
Shadow Secretary of State for Education	**Kate Green** OBE MP
Shadow Secretary of State for Digital, Culture, Media and Sport	**Jo Stevens** MP
Shadow Chief Secretary to the Treasury	**Bridget Phillipson** MP
Shadow Secretary of State for Environment, Food and Rural Affairs	**Luke Pollard** MP
Shadow Secretary of State for Communities and Local Government	**Steve Reed** OBE MP
Shadow Secretary of State for Housing	**Thangam Debbonaire** MP
Shadow Secretary of State for Transport	**Jim McMahon** OBE MP
Shadow Secretary of State for International Development	**Preet Kaur Gill** MP
Shadow Secretary of State for Northern Ireland	**Louise Haigh** MP
Shadow Secretary of State for Scotland	**Ian Murray** MP
Shadow Secretary of State for Wales	**Nia Griffith** MP
Shadow Secretary of State for Women and Equalities	**Marsha De Cordova** MP
Shadow Secretary of State for Employment Rights and Protections	**Andy McDonald** MP
Shadow Minister for Mental Health	Dr **Rosena Allin-Khan** MP
Shadow Minister for Young People and Democracy	**Cat Smith** MP
Shadow Attorney General	Rt Hon **Lord Falconer of Thoroton** QC
Shadow Leader of the House of Commons	Rt Hon **Valerie Vaz** MP
Opposition Chief Whip	Rt Hon **Nick Brown** MP
Shadow Leader of the House of Lords	Rt Hon **Baroness Smith of Basildon**

Shadow Chief Whip in the House of Lords	Rt Hon **Lord McAvoy**

Shadow Ministers

Leader's Office	
Leader of the Opposition	Rt Hon Sir **Keir Starmer** KCB QC MP
Deputy Leader's Office	
Deputy Leader	**Angela Rayner** MP
Business, Energy and Industrial Strategy	
Shadow Secretary of State	Rt Hon **Ed Miliband** MP
Shadow Ministers	**Chi Onwurah** MP
	Matthew Pennycook MP
	Lucy Powell MP
	Dr **Alan Whitehead** MP
Lords Spokespeople	Rt Hon **Lord Bassam of Brighton**
	Lord Grantchester
	Baroness Hayter of Kentish Town
Cabinet Office	
Shadow Chancellor of the Duchy of Lancaster	**Rachel Reeves** MP
Shadow Ministers	**Cat Smith** MP
	Jack Dromey MP
	Fleur Anderson MP
Lords Spokespeople	Rt Hon **Baroness Smith of Basildon**
	Baroness Hayter of Kentish Town
Communities and Local Government	
Shadow Secretary of State	**Steve Reed** OBE MP
Shadow Ministers	**Kate Hollern** MP
	Naz Shah MP
	Mike Amesbury MP
Lords Spokesperson	**Lord Kennedy of Southwark**
Defence	
Shadow Secretary of State	Rt Hon **John Healey** MP
Shadow Ministers	**Sharon Hodgson** MP
	Stephen Morgan MP
	Khalid Mahmood MP
Lords Spokesperson	**Lord Tunnicliffe** CBE
Digital, Culture, Media and Sport	
Shadow Secretary of State	**Jo Stevens** MP
Shadow Ministers	**Rachael Maskell** MP
	Alison McGovern MP
	Chris Matheson MP
	Chi Onwurah MP
	Alex Sobel MP
Lords Spokespeople	Rt Hon **Lord Bassam of Brighton**
	Baroness Hayter of Kentish Town
Education	
Shadow Secretary of State	**Kate Green** OBE MP
Shadow Ministers	**Wes Streeting** MP
	Emma Hardy MP
	Toby Perkins MP
	Tulip Siddiq MP
Lords Spokespeople	Rt Hon **Lord Bassam of Brighton**
	Lord Watson of Invergowrie

Employment Rights and Protections	
Shadow Secretary of State	**Andy McDonald** MP
Shadow Minister	**Imran Hussain** MP
Environment, Food and Rural Affairs	
Shadow Secretary of State	**Luke Pollard** MP
Shadow Ministers	**Stephanie Peacock** MP
	Ruth Jones MP
	Daniel Zeichner MP
Lords Spokespeople	**Baroness Jones of Whitchurch**
	Lord Grantchester
	Baroness Hayman of Ullock
Foreign Affairs	
Shadow Foreign Secretary	**Lisa Nandy** MP
Shadow Ministers	**Wayne David** MP
	Stephen Doughty MP
	Stephen Kinnock MP
	Catherine West MP
	Fabian Hamilton MP
Lords Spokesperson	**Lord Collins of Highbury**
Health and Social Care	
Shadow Secretary of State	**Jon Ashworth** MP
Shadow Ministers	Dr **Rosena Allin-Khan** MP
	Liz Kendall MP
	Justin Madders MP
	Alex Norris MP
Lords Spokespeople	**Baroness Thornton**
	Baroness Wheeler MBE
Home Office	
Shadow Home Secretary	**Nick Thomas-Symonds** MP
Shadow Ministers	**Bambos Charalambous** MP
	Sarah Jones MP
	Holly Lynch MP
	Conor McGinn MP
	Jess Phillips MP
Lords Spokespeople	**Lord Rosser**
	Lord Kennedy of Southwark
Housing	
Shadow Secretary of State	**Thangam Debbonaire** MP
Shadow Minister	**Mike Amesbury** MP
Lords Spokesperson	**Lord Kennedy of Southwark**
International Development	
Shadow Secretary of State	**Preet Kaur Gill** MP
Shadow Ministers	**Stephen Doughty** MP
	Anna McMorrin MP
	Yasmin Qureshi MP
Lords Spokesperson	**Lord Collins of Highbury**
International Trade	
Shadow Secretary of State	Rt Hon **Emily Thornberry** MP
Shadow Ministers	**Bill Esterson** MP
	Gareth Thomas MP
Lords Spokespeople	Rt Hon **Lord Bassam of Brighton**
	Lord Grantchester
	Baroness Hayter of Kentish Town

Justice	
Shadow Secretary of State	Rt Hon **David Lammy** MP
Shadow Ministers	**Lyn Brown** MP
	Alex Cunningham MP
	Dr **Peter Kyle** MP
	Karl Turner MP
Lords Spokespeople	Rt Hon **Lord Falconer of Thoroton** QC
	Lord Ponsonby of Shulbrede
Law Officers	
Shadow Attorney General	Rt Hon **Lord Falconer of Thoroton** QC
Shadow Solicitor General	**Ellie Reeves** MP
Shadow Advocate General for Scotland	**Lord Davidson of Glen Clova** QC
Leader of the House of Commons	
Shadow Leader	Rt Hon **Valerie Vaz** MP
Shadow Deputy Leader	**Afzal Khan** CBE MP
Leader of the House of Lords	
Shadow Leader	Rt Hon **Baroness Smith of Basildon**
Shadow Deputy Leader	**Baroness Hayter of Kentish Town**
Northern Ireland	
Shadow Secretary of State	**Louise Haigh** MP
Shadow Minister	**Karin Smyth** MP
Lords Spokesperson	Rt Hon **Baroness Smith of Basildon**
Scotland	
Shadow Secretary of State	**Ian Murray** MP
Shadow Minister	**Chris Elmore** MP
Lords Spokesperson	**Lord Davidson of Glen Clova** QC
Transport	
Shadow Secretary of State	**Jim McMahon** OBE MP
Shadow Ministers	**Kerry McCarthy** MP
	Tanmanjeet Singh Dhesi MP
	Mike Kane MP
	Sam Tarry MP
Lords Spokespeople	**Lord Rosser**
	Lord Tunnicliffe CBE
Treasury	
Shadow Chancellor of the Exchequer	**Anneliese Dodds** MP
Shadow Chief Secretary	**Bridget Phillipson** MP
Shadow Financial Secretary	**James Murray** MP
Shadow Economic Secretary	Rt Hon **Pat McFadden** MP
Shadow Exchequer Secretary	**Abena Oppong-Asare** MP
Lords Spokesperson	**Lord Tunnicliffe** CBE
Wales	
Shadow Secretary of State	**Nia Griffith** MP
Shadow Minister	**Gerald Jones** MP
Lords Spokesperson	**Baroness Hayter of Kentish Town**
Women and Equalities	
Shadow Secretary of State	**Marsha De Cordova** MP
Shadow Ministers	**Gill Furniss** MP
	Charlotte Nichols MP
Lords Spokesperson	**Baroness Wilcox of Newport**

Work and Pensions

Shadow Secretary of State	**Jonathan Reynolds** MP
Shadow Ministers	**Matt Rodda** MP **Vicky Foxcroft** MP **Seema Malhotra** MP **Karen Buck** MP
Lords Spokesperson	**Baroness Sherlock** OBE

Opposition Commons Whips

Chief Whip	Rt Hon **Nick Brown** MP
Deputy Chief Whip	Rt Hon Sir **Alan Campbell** MP
Pairing Whip	Rt Hon **Mark Tami** MP
Senior Whips	**Jessica Morden** MP **Chris Elmore** MP **Colleen Fletcher** MP **Jeff Smith** MP **Liz Twist** MP
Whips	**Bambos Charalambous** MP **Mary Glindon** MP **Marie Rimmer** CBE MP **Matt Western** MP **Gill Furniss** MP **Feryal Clark** MP

Opposition Lords Spokespeople

Leader of the Opposition	Rt Hon **Baroness Smith of Basildon**
Deputy Leader of the Opposition	**Baroness Hayter of Kentish Town**
Business, Energy and Industrial Strategy and International Trade	Rt Hon **Lord Bassam of Brighton**
	Baroness Hayter of Kentish Town
(Energy)	**Lord Grantchester**
Cabinet Office, Constitutional and Devolved Issues	Rt Hon **Baroness Smith of Basildon**
	Baroness Hayter of Kentish Town
Communities and Local Government and Housing	**Lord Kennedy of Southwark**
Defence	**Lord Tunnicliffe** CBE
Digital, Culture, Media and Sport	Rt Hon **Lord Bassam of Brighton**
	Baroness Hayter of Kentish Town
Education	Rt Hon **Lord Bassam of Brighton**
	Lord Watson of Invergowrie
Environment, Food and Rural Affairs	**Lord Grantchester**
	Baroness Jones of Whitchurch
	Baroness Hayman of Ullock
Foreign and Commonwealth Office	**Lord Collins of Highbury**
Health and Social Care	**Baroness Thornton**
	Baroness Wheeler MBE
Home Office	**Lord Rosser**
	Lord Kennedy of Southwark
International Development	**Lord Collins of Highbury**

Justice	Rt Hon **Lord Falconer of Thoroton** QC
	Lord Ponsonby of Shulbrede
Law Officers	Rt Hon **Lord Falconer of Thoroton** QC
	Lord Davidson of Glen Clova QC
Northern Ireland	Rt Hon **Baroness Smith of Basildon**
Scotland	**Lord Davidson of Glen Clova** QC
Transport	**Lord Rosser**
	Lord Tunnicliffe CBE
Treasury	**Lord Tunnicliffe** CBE
Wales	**Baroness Hayter of Kentish Town**
Women and Equalities	**Baroness Wilcox of Newport**
Work and Pensions	**Baroness Sherlock** OBE

Opposition Lords Whips

Chief Whip	Rt Hon **Lord McAvoy**
Deputy Chief Whips	**Lord Tunnicliffe** CBE **Baroness Wheeler** MBE
Whips	**Lord Kennedy of Southwark** **Lord Collins of Highbury** **Lord Lennie** **Lord Grantchester** **Baroness Wilcox of Newport** **Baroness Hayman of Ullock**

Scottish National Party

Frontbench

Westminster Group Leader	Rt Hon **Ian Blackford** MP
Deputy Group Leader; Shadow Minister for Women and Equalities	**Kirsten Oswald** MP
Chief Whip	**Patrick Grady** MP
Shadow Chancellor of the Exchequer	**Alison Thewliss** MP
Shadow Secretary of State for Foreign, Commonwealth and Development Office (Shadow Foreign Secretary)	**Alyn Smith** MP
Shadow Secretary of State for the Home Department (Shadow Home Secretary) and for Justice	**Stuart C McDonald** QC MP
Shadow Secretary of State for Health and Social Care; Shadow Minister for Europe	Dr **Philippa Whitford** MP
Shadow Secretary of State for International Trade	**Drew Hendry** MP
Shadow Secretary of State for Business, Energy and Industrial Strategy	**Stephen Flynn** MP
Shadow Secretary of State for Work and Pensions	**David Linden** MP
Shadow Secretary of State for Defence	**Stewart Malcolm McDonald** MP
Shadow Secretary of State for Scotland	**Mhairi Black** MP
Shadow Secretary of State for Justice and Immigration	**Anne McLaughlin** MP
Shadow Secretary of State for Housing, Communities and Local Government	**Patricia Gibson** MP
Shadow Secretary of State for Culture, Media and Sport	**John Nicolson** MP
Shadow Attorney General	**Angela Crawley** MP

Shadow Secretary of State for Transport	**Gavin Newlands** MP
Shadow Secretary of State for Education; Shadow Minister for Armed Forces and Veterans	**Carol Monaghan** MP
Spokesperson for International Development	**Chris Law** MP
Shadow Secretary of State for Environment, Food and Rural Affairs	**Deidre Brock** MP
Shadow Secretary of State for Northern Ireland and Welsh Affairs	**Richard Thomson** MP
Shadow Chancellor of the Duchy of Lancaster and Minister for the Cabinet Office	**Stewart Hosie** MP
Shadow Leader of the House of Commons	**Peter Wishart** MP
Shadow Minister for Women and Equalities	**Anne McLaughlin** MP
Shadow Minister for Energy and Climate Change	**Alan Brown** MP

Spokespeople

Scotland in the World

Co-ordinator	**Drew Hendry** MP
Spokesperson for Defence and Procurement	**Angela Crawley** MP
Spokesperson for Defence and Foreign Affairs	**Martin Docherty-Hughes** MP
Spokesperson for Human Rights and Conflict Resolution	**Brendan O'Hara** MP
Team Members, Foreign Affairs	**Allan Dorans** MP
	Hannah Bardell MP
Team Member, Defence	**Dave Doogan** MP

Finance and Economy

Co-ordinator	**Alison Thewliss** MP
Shadow Chief Secretary to the Treasury	**Peter Grant** MP
Spokesperson for Infrastructure and Manufacturing	**Ronnie Cowan** MP
Spokesperson for Small Business and Innovation	**Douglas Chapman** MP
Spokesperson for Consumer Affairs	**Patricia Gibson** MP
Spokesperson for Industries Future/Blockchain	**Martin Docherty-Hughes** MP
Shadow Financial Secretary	**Richard Thomson** MP
Team Member, Economy	**Kirsty Blackman** MP

Inclusion and Wellbeing

Co-ordinator	**Neil Gray** MP
Spokesperson for Vaccines	**Neale Hanvey** MP
Spokesperson for Sport	**Gavin Newlands** MP
Spokesperson for Pensions and Intergenerational Fairness	**Amy Callaghan** MP
Spokesperson for Fair Work and Employment	**Chris Stephens** MP
Spokesperson for Disabilities	**Marion Fellows** MP
Spokesperson for Mental Health	Dr **Lisa Cameron** MP
Spokesperson for Public Health and Primary Care	**Martyn Day** MP

Constitution and Human Rights

Co-ordinator	**Stewart Hosie** MP
Spokesperson for Constitutional Affairs	**Tommy Sheppard** MP
Spokesperson for Environment	**John McNally** MP
Team Members, Agriculture and Rural Affairs	**Dave Doogan** MP

	Steven Bonnar MP

Whips

Chief Whip	**Patrick Grady** MP
Deputy Whips	**Owen Thompson** MP
	Marion Fellows MP

Liberal Democrats

Leader	Rt Hon Sir **Ed Davey** MP
Deputy Leader; Spokesperson for Education	**Daisy Cooper** MP
Spokesperson for Home Affairs; Political and Constitutional Reform; Northern Ireland	Rt Hon **Alistair Carmichael** MP
Chief Whip; Spokesperson for Scotland; Wales; Work and Pensions	**Wendy Chamberlain** MP
Spokesperson for Housing, Communities and Local Government; Food and Rural Affairs	**Tim Farron** MP
Spokesperson for Climate Emergency and Energy; Justice; Women and Equalities; Shadow Leader of the House	**Wera Hobhouse** MP
Spokesperson for Treasury	**Christine Jardine** MP
Spokesperson for Foreign Affairs and International Development	**Layla Moran** MP
Spokesperson for Business; Trade; Transport	**Sarah Olney** MP
Spokesperson for Defence; Digital, Culture, Media and Sport	**Jamie Stone** MP
Spokesperson for Health, Wellbeing and Social Care	**Munira Wilson** MP

Lords Spokespeople

Leader	Rt Hon **Lord Newby** OBE
Deputy Leader	Rt Hon **Lord Dholakia** OBE DL
Deputy Leader	**Baroness Walmsley**
Africa	**Lord Chidgey**
Business, Enterprise and Industrial Strategy	**Lord Fox**
Cabinet Office	Rt Hon **Lord Wallace of Saltaire**
Communities and Local Government	**Baroness Pinnock**
Defence	**Baroness Smith of Newnham**
Digital	**Lord Clement-Jones** CBE
Digital, Culture, Media and Sport	**Baroness Bonham-Carter of Yarnbury**
Education	**Lord Storey** CBE
Energy and Climate Change	**Lord Oates**
Environment, Food and Rural Affairs	**Baroness Bakewell of Hardington Mandeville** MBE
Equality	**Baroness Hussein-Ece** OBE
Existing European Union	**Baroness Ludford**
Foreign and Commonwealth Affairs	Rt Hon **Baroness Northover**
Health	**Baroness Brinton**
Home Affairs	**Lord Paddick**
Housing	**Baroness Grender** MBE
Immigration	**Baroness Hamwee**

International Development	**Baroness Sheehan**
International Trade	**Lord Purvis of Tweed**
Justice	**Lord Marks of Henley-on-Thames** QC
Law Officers (Shadow Attorney General)	**Lord Thomas of Gresford** OBE QC
Mental Health	**Baroness Tyler of Enfield**
Northern Ireland	**Baroness Suttie**
Rehabilitation and Probation	**Lord German** OBE
Scotland	Rt Hon **Lord Bruce of Bennachie**
Sport	**Lord Addington**
Transport	**Baroness Randerson**
Treasury	Rt Hon **Baroness Kramer**
Voluntary Sector and LGBT Equality	**Baroness Barker**
Wales	**Baroness Humphreys**
Work and Pensions	**Baroness Janke**

Lords Whips

Chief Whip	**Lord Stoneham of Droxford**
Deputy Chief Whip	**Baroness Humphreys**
Deputy Chief Whip	**Baroness Thornhill** MBE
Whip	**Baroness Harris of Richmond** DL
Whip	**Baroness Janke**
Whip	**Baroness Pinnock**
Whip	**Lord Shipley** OBE
Whip	**Lord Storey** CBE
Leader of the House of Lords	Rt Hon **Lord Newby** OBE

Plaid Cymru (The Party of Wales)

Parliamentary Group Leader; Attorney General; Business, Energy and Industrial Strategy; Home Affairs; Justice; Transport; Women and Equalities	Rt Hon **Liz Saville Roberts** MP
Cabinet Office; Defence; Foreign Affairs; International Development; International Trade; Work and Pensions; Chief Whip	**Hywel Williams** MP
Constitution and Welsh Affairs; Digital, Culture, Media and Sport; Education; Environment, Food and Rural Affairs; Health and Social Care; Housing, Communities and Local Government; Treasury	**Ben Lake** MP

Crossbench

Convenor	Rt Hon **Lord Judge**

Salaried Parliamentarians

The Independent Parliamentary Standards Authority (IPSA) was created in 2009 and has two roles – to regulate the expenses system and to administer and pay MPs' expenses and salaries.

Most Members of the House of Lords do not receive a salary for carrying out their Parliamentary duties. They may claim a flat rate attendance allowance of £162 or £323.

	Annual salary from 1 April 2020 (£)
Member of Parliament	81,932

With effect from 1 April each year, starting with 1 April 2016, the MP salary will be adjusted by the rate of annual change in public sector average earnings.

If an MP holds office, as listed below, they are entitled to receive an additional annual salary.

Office	**As of 1 April 2020 Annual salary (£)**
Prime Minister	79,936

	Salary if a member of the House of Commons (£)	Salary if a member of the House of Lords (no parliamentary salary) (£)
Chancellor of the Exchequer	71,673	
Chancellor of the Duchy of Lancaster and Minister for the Cabinet Office	71,673	
Secretary of State	71,673	
Lord Chancellor	71,673	
Leader of the House of Lords and Lord Privy Seal		105,216
Attorney General	99,732	
Solicitor General	61,696	
Advocate General for Scotland		95,549
Leader of the House of Commons; Lord President of the Council	34,367	
Chief Secretary to the Treasury	34,367	
Financial Secretary	34,367	
Minister of State	34,367	82,153
Parliamentary Secretary	24,678	71,551
Parliamentary Under-Secretary of State	24,678	71,551
Economic Secretary	24,678	
Exchequer Secretary	24,678	
Parliamentary Secretary to the Treasury (Chief Whip)	34,367	
Government Deputy Chief Whip	34,367	
Government Whip	20,043	
Assistant Government Whip	20,043	
Government Lords Chief Whip		82,153
Government Lords Deputy Chief Whip		71,551
Lord/Baroness in Waiting		66,163
Leader of the Opposition	65,171	
Opposition Chief Whip	34,087	
Opposition Deputy Chief Whip	19,880	
Opposition Assistant Whip	19,880	
Speaker	78,258	104,360
Chairman of Ways and Means	42,157	
First Deputy Chairman of Ways and Means	37,051	
Second Deputy Chairman of Ways and Means	37,051	
Chairman of Committees (Senior Deputy Speaker)		84,524
Principal Deputy Chairman of Committees		79,076
Commons Select Committee Chair	16,422	
Member of Panel of Chairs	16,422	

The number of paid Ministerial posts is limited to 109. The Government may appoint additional Ministers; however, these will be unpaid appointments.

MP ALLOWANCES

For the full guide see:
https://www.ipsaonline.org.uk/guidance/reports-and-budgeting

Accommodation

MPs can claim for accommodation costs either in London or their constituency (but not both), with the exception of those with London area constituencies. Eligible MPs can claim for accommodation in one of two ways: a rental property and associated costs or associated costs only, if they own the property.

The annual London rental accommodation budget is £23,010 for 2020-21.

MPs can claim for budget uplifts for their dependants at a rate of £5,435 per dependant per financial year.

London area MPs can claim a London Area Living Payment (LALP) to help cover the additional costs of living and travelling in London. Non-London area MPs who do not claim accommodation costs can claim the £4,090 LALP instead.

The annual budget limit for MPs to claim for associated costs, if they own their home, is £5,410 for 2020-21.

Office costs

To maintain a constituency office and provide surgeries London area MPs may claim up to £28,800 and Non-London area MPs up to £25,910 for 2020-21.

Staffing costs

The annual staffing budget is £188,860 for London area MPs and £177,550 for non-London area MPs for 2020-21.

Starting-up budget

Start-up expenditure is available for MPs elected to Parliament for the first time. The budget is set at £6,000 and lasts for 365 days from the day after the MP is elected.

Winding-up budget

The winding-up budget for London area MPs is £57,150 and for non-London area MPs it is £53,950.

When MPs leave Parliament, their staff have to be made redundant. Staff redundancy costs are met from a contingency fund.

Other assistance

Disability assistance and security assistance may be claimed by any MP if they are necessary for MPs to carry out their parliamentary functions.

MPs can apply for contingency funding to deal with exceptional and unpredictable circumstances.

Parliamentary Contributory Pension Fund

Benefits provided are on a 'career average revalued earnings' (CARE) basis.

The accrual rate is 1/51st of pensionable earnings, revalued annually in line with the Consumer Prices Index (CPI).

There is now one level of pension contribution for all members: current estimate is 11.09 per cent of pay, but the rate paid will vary in line with the costs of the Scheme. Normal pension age is linked to state pension age.

If an MP was aged 55 or over on 1 April 2013, and re-elected in 2015, they will stay in the previous final salary scheme for as long as you remain an MP.

If an MP was aged between 51 years six months and 55 years on 1 April 2013, and re-elected in 2015, they can choose either to stay in the previous final salary scheme for a limited period before transferring, or to transfer to the new CARE scheme.

If an MP was younger than 51 years and six months on 1 April 2013, and re-elected in 2015, they will automatically move into the new CARE scheme for future service.

Ministerial Pension Scheme

The accrual rate is 1.775 per cent of pensionable earnings (about 1/56).

The member pension contribution rate is 11.1 per cent.

Normal pension age is linked to state pension age.

Severance pay

Ministers and other paid office holders (with the exception of the Prime Minister and Commons Speaker) are entitled to a severance payment of one-quarter of their final Ministerial salary when they leave office for whatever reason.

Severance payments under £30,000 are tax and National Insurance exempt.

HOUSE OF COMMONS

PARLIAMENT

HOUSE OF COMMONS

London SW1A 0AA 020 7219 3000 Enquiry service 020 7219 4272
Website: www.parliament.uk Twitter: @HouseofCommons/@HoCPress

Bulk correspondence to MPs may be delivered to Derby Gate at the Palace of Westminster, but must be stamped or franked or accompanied by a cheque for second-class postage made out to Post Office Counters. A single letter petitioning an individual MP can be delivered without postage payment by hand when the House is sitting.

SPEAKER AND DEPUTY SPEAKERS

The Speaker is the presiding officer of the Commons, whose main responsibility is to maintain order in debates and apply the rules and traditions of the House. The Chairman of Ways and Means is the principal deputy speaker. By tradition, the Speaker, once elected, renounces party allegiance for the remainder of his or her career.

The Speaker: Rt Hon Sir **Lindsay Hoyle** MP
Chairman of Ways and Means: Rt Hon Dame **Eleanor Laing** DBE MP (Con)
First Deputy Chairman of Ways and Means and Deputy Speaker:
Rt Hon Dame **Rosie Winterton** DBE MP (Lab)
Second Deputy Chairman of Ways and Means and Deputy Speaker: **Nigel Evans** MP (Con)

Speaker's Secretary: **Helen Wood** 020 7219 4111 Email: woodhe@parliament.uk
Speaker's Chaplain: Rev **Tricia Hillas** 020 7219 3768 Email: hillast@parliament.uk

HOUSE OF COMMONS COMMISSION/MEMBERS ESTIMATE COMMITTEE

The House of Commons Commission is responsible for the management of the House, including the employment of its staff and the provision of services by the departments of the House.

Chair: Rt Hon Sir **Lindsay Hoyle** MP (Speaker)
Members:
Rt Hon **Jacob Rees-Mogg** MP (Con)
Rt Hon **Valerie Vaz** MP (Lab)
Sir **Charles Walker** KBE MP (Con)
Rt Hon Dame **Rosie Winterton** DBE MP (Lab)
Pete Wishart MP (SNP)
Dr **John Benger**
Ian Ailles
Jane McCall
Dr **Rima Makarem**

Secretary: **Marianne Cwynarski** 020 7219 8135 Email: hoccommission@parliament.uk

Members (MPs)

State of the Parties (February 2021)

Conservative	365
Labour (includes Labour/Co-operative)	200
Scottish National Party	47
Liberal Democrat	11
Democratic Unionist Party	8
Sinn Féin	7
Independent	4
Plaid Cymru	3
Social Democratic and Labour Party	2
Alliance Party of Northern Ireland	1
Green Party	1
The Speaker	1
	650 seats

Changes since 2019 General Election

CHANGE OF PARTY

Jonathan Edwards	Carmarthen East and Dinefwr	Plaid Cymru Whip suspended May 2020, now Independent
Claudia Webbe	Leicester East	Labour Whip suspended September 2020, now Independent
Jeremy Corbyn	Islington North	Labour Whip suspended October 2020, now Independent
Margaret Ferrier	Rutherglen and Hamilton West	SNP Whip suspended October 2020, now Independent

MPs' BIOGRAPHIES

LABOUR

ABBOTT, DIANE

Hackney North and Stoke Newington *(Majority 33,188)*

Diane Julie Abbott. Born 27 September 1953; Daughter of late Reginald Abbott, welder, and late Julie Abbott, psychiatric nurse; Married David Thompson 1991 (divorced 1993) (1 son).

Education: Harrow County Girls' Grammar School; Newnham College, Cambridge (BA history 1976).

Non-political career: Administration trainee, Home Office 1976-78; Race relations officer, National Council for Civil Liberties 1978-80; Journalist: Thames Television 1980-82, TV AM 1982-84, Freelance 1984-85; Principal press officer, Lambeth Council 1986-87. Equality officer, ACTT 1985-86; Member, RMT Parliamentary Campaigning Group 2002-.

Political career: Member for Hackney North and Stoke Newington 1987-2010, for Hackney North and Stoke Newington (revised boundary) since 6 May 2010 general election; Shadow Minister for Public Health 2010-13; Shadow Secretary of State for: International Development 2015-16, Health 2016, Home Department (Shadow Home Secretary) 2016-20. *Select committees:* Member: Treasury and Civil Service 1989-97, Foreign Affairs 1997-2001, Home Affairs 2020-. Labour Party: Member, National Executive Committee 1994-97, 2019-20, Contested Labour leadership 2010. *Councils and public bodies:* Westminster City Councillor 1982-86; Former member, advisory cabinet for women and equality, Greater London Assembly.

Political interests: Small businesses, education; Africa, Jamaica.

Other: Founder, Black Women Mean Business 1992-; London Schools and the Black Child; *Spectator* Speech of the Year 2008; PC 2017.

Recreations: Reading, cinema.

Rt Hon Diane Abbott MP, House of Commons, London SW1A 0AA
Tel: 020 7219 4426 *Fax:* 020 7219 4964 *Email:* diane.abbott.office@parliament.uk
Constituency: No constituency office
Website: www.dianeabbott.org.uk *Twitter:* @HackneyAbbott

LABOUR

ABRAHAMS, DEBBIE

Oldham East and Saddleworth *(Majority 1,499)*

Deborah Angela Elspeth Marie Abrahams. Born 15 September 1960; Married John Abrahams (2 daughters).

Education: Bolton Institute of Technology; Salford University (BA biochemistry and physiology 1984); Liverpool University (MS health and education 1994); Conversational French.

Non-political career: Community worker, charity, Wythenshawe; Head of healthy cities, Knowsley Council 1992-2000; Senior research fellow, IMPACT, University of London 2000-06; Director, International Health Impact Assessment Consortium, Liverpool University 2006-10. Member, Unison.

Political career: Contested Colne Valley 2010 general election. Member for Oldham East and Saddleworth since 13 January 2011 by-election; PPS to Andy Burnham as Shadow Secretary of State for Health 2011-15; Shadow Minister for Work and Pensions 2015-16; Shadow Secretary of State for Work and Pensions 2016-18. *Select committees:* Member, Work and Pensions 2011-15, 2020-. Chair, PLP Departmental Group for Health and Social Services 2011-15. Member, Labour National Policy Forum and Joint Policy Committee. *Councils and public bodies:* Board member, Bury and Rochdale Health Authority 1998-2002; Chair, Rochdale Primary Care NHS Trust 2002-06; School governor.

Political interests: Health, education, child protection, welfare, employment, inequality; Bangladesh, Kashmir, Pakistan.

Other: Co-operative Society; Former Chair, North West Action on Smoking and Health; Fellow, Faculty of Public Health. Hon. President, Greater Manchester and High Peak Ramblers Association.

Recreations: Running, gardening, film.

Debbie Abrahams MP, House of Commons, London SW1A 0AA
Tel: 020 7219 1041 *Fax:* 020 7219 2405 *Email:* abrahamsd@parliament.uk
Constituency: 9 Church Lane, Oldham OL1 3AN
Tel: 0161-624 4248 Website: debbieabrahams.org.uk *Twitter:* @debbie_abrahams

CONSERVATIVE

ADAMS, NIGEL

Selby and Ainsty *(Majority 20,137)*

Minister of State for Asia, Foreign, Commonwealth and Development Office

Born 30 November 1966; Son of Derek Adams, school caretaker, and late Isabella Adams, home help; Married Claire Robson 1992 (1 son 3 daughters).

Education: Selby High School; French, Spanish.

Non-political career: Managing director, Advanced Digital Telecom Ltd 1993-2000; Commercial director, Yorkshire Tourist Board 2005-06; Chairman: NGC Networks Ltd 2006-18, NGC Network Services Ltd 2007-18. Member, Armed Forces Parliamentary Scheme (RAF) 2012-.

Political career: Contested Rossendale and Darwen 2005 general election. Member for Selby and Ainsty since 6 May 2010 general election; PPS to Leaders of the House of Lords and Chancellors of the Duchy of Lancaster: Lord Strathclyde 2010-13, Lord Hill of Oareford 2013-14; Assistant Government Whip 2017-18, 2018-19; Government Whip (Lord Commissioner of HM Treasury) 2018; Parliamentary Under-Secretary of State: Ministry of Housing, Communities and Local Government 2018, Wales Office 2018-19; Minister of State for: Sport, Media and Creative Industries, Department for Digital, Culture, Media and Sport 2019-20, Asia: Foreign and Commonwealth Office and Department for International Development 2020, Foreign, Commonwealth and Development Office 2020-. *Select committees:* Member: Environment, Food and Rural Affairs 2010, Culture, Media and Sport 2015-17. Deputy regional chair, Yorkshire and Humber Conservatives 2001-03; President, Selby Conservative Association 2002-04; Board member, North of England Conservative Party 2002-03; President, Conservatives at Work 2012-13; Member, Number 10 Policy Advisory Board (Economic Affairs). *Councils and public bodies:* Governor: Camblesforth Primary School, Selby 2002-04, Selby High School 2007-.

Political interests: Energy, culture, media and sport, business, environment, food and rural affairs.

Other: Member, Yorkshire County Cricket Club Members' Committee 2004-05; Patron, Selby Hands of Hope Charity. Carlton Club, Selby Conservative Club; Member: Yorkshire County Cricket Club, Hovingham Cricket Club, House of Lords and House of Commons Cricket Club.

Recreations: Cricket, golf, football, theatre, shooting.

Nigel Adams MP, House of Commons, London SW1A 0AA
Tel: 020 7219 7141 *Email:* nigel.adams.mp@parliament.uk
Constituency: 17 High Street, Tadcaster, North Yorkshire LS24 9AP
Tel: 01937 838088 Website: www.selbyandainsty.com *Twitter:* @nadams

CONSERVATIVE

AFOLAMI, BIM

Hitchin and Harpenden *(Majority 6,895)*

PPS to Therese Coffey as Secretary of State for Work and Pensions

Abimbola Afolami. Born 11 February 1986; Married Hetti (3 sons).

Education: Bishopsgate School; Eton; University College, Oxford (BA modern history 2007) (Vice-president, Oxford Union).

Non-political career: Political adviser to George Osborne; Corporate lawyer: Freshfields Bruckhaus Deringer 2009-12, Simpson Thacher & Bartlett 2012-15; Senior executive, HSBC 2015-17.

Political career: Contested Lewisham Deptford 2015 general election. Member for Hitchin and Harpenden since 8 June 2017; Team PPS, Department for Transport 2018-19; PPS to: Penny Mordaunt as Secretary of State for International Development and Minister for Women and Equalities 2019, Rory Stewart as Secretary of State for International Development 2019, Elizabeth Truss as Secretary of State for International Trade and President of the Board of Trade

2019, Therese Coffey as Secretary of State for Work and Pensions 2020-. *Select committees:* Member: Public Accounts 2017-18, Regulatory Reform 2017-19, Joint Committee on Consolidation, &c, Bills 2018-19.

Other: Secretary, Bow Publications Ltd 2008-09; Member, Programme Committee, Ditchley Foundation; Fellow, Royal Society of Arts.

Recreations: Playing cricket, reading history books, *The Archers*, supporter of Northampton Saints RUFC and Arsenal FC.

Bim Afolami MP, House of Commons, London SW1A 0AA
Tel: 020 7219 3000 *Email:* bim.afolami.mp@parliament.uk
Constituency: PO Box 1241, Harpenden AL1 9JF
Tel: 01582 310160 Website: www.bimafolami.co.uk *Twitter:* @BimAfolami

CONSERVATIVE

AFRIYIE, ADAM

Windsor *(Majority 20,079)*

Born 4 August 1965; Married Tracy-Jane Newall 2005 (3 sons 1 daughter 1 stepson).

Education: Addey and Stanhope School, New Cross; Imperial College (Wye), London (BSc agricultural economics 1987).

Non-political career: Managing director (now non-executive chair), Connect Support Services 1993-2016; Chair, DeHavilland Information Services 1998-2005; Board member, Policy Exchange 2003-05; Non-executive chair: Axonn Ltd 2005-, Castleford Media 2010-.

Political career: Member for Windsor 2005-10, for Windsor (revised boundary) since 6 May 2010 general election; Shadow Minister for: Innovation, Universities and Skills 2007-09, Innovation and Science 2009-10; Chair, Parliamentary Office of Science and Technology (POST) 2010-; Trade Envoy to: Ghana 2016-, Guinea 2017-. *Select committees:* Member: Science and Technology/Innovation, Universities and Skills 2005-07, Children, Schools and Families 2007-09; Chair, Members' Expenses 2011-15. Chair, Tonbridge Edenbridge and Malling Association constituency branch 1999-2004; President, Conservative Technology Forum 2010-; Founding Member, Conservatives for Britain 2015-16. *Councils and public bodies:* Governor, Museum of London 1999-2005.

Political interests: Mental health, financial technology, simpler tax and benefits system, public policy, innovation and science.

Other: Chair (London region): Business for Sterling 1999-2004, No to the Euro campaign 2001-04; Trustee, Museum in Docklands 2003-05; Young Enterprise (North Berkshire): Chair 2005-07, Patron 2008-; Sebastian's Action Trust. Windsor and Eton Society.

Publications: The Forgotten (2016).

Recreations: Distance running.

Adam Afriyie MP, House of Commons, London SW1A 0AA
Tel: 020 7219 8023 *Email:* adam.afriyie.mp@parliament.uk
Constituency: No constituency office
Website: www.adamafriyie.org *Twitter:* @AdamAfriyie

CONSERVATIVE

AHMAD KHAN, IMRAN

Wakefield *(Majority 3,358)*

Imran Nasir Ahmad Khan. Born 6 September 1973; Son of late Dr Saeed Ahmad Khan and Selma M Khan (née Susan Reynolds).

Education: Silcoates School; Pushkin State Russian Language Institute (Diploma Russian language 1993); King's College London (AKC theology 1996, BA war studies 1996); Russian.

Non-political career: Campaign Co-Ordinator, Ontario provisional elections 1989; Special Adviser to President Shushkevich of Belarus, Supreme Court, Minsk 1992-93; President, King's College London Conservative Students Association 1993; Special Adviser on Terrorism and the Muslim World, Ministry of Foreign Affairs, Ottawa, Canada 2002; Co-Founder and Director, DarkBlack Limited 1998-2003; Director of Business Development, Strategic Communications Laboratories 2003-04; Director of Communications and Strategy, Syrian Media Centre 2004-05; Head of Policy and Business Development, Novoe Limited 2005-07; Founder and President: Transnational Crisis Project 2007-16, Pakhtoonkhwa Arts and Culture Project 2010-15;

Founder and Executive Director, Xain Research and Communication Ltd 2010-16; Special Assistant, Political Affairs, United Nations 2017-18; Senior Consultant, M&C Saatchi London 2019.

Political career: Member for Wakefield since 12 December 2019. *Select committees:* Member, Backbench Business 2021-. Vice-chair, Gormersal Conservative Association.

Political interests: Northern Powerhouse, jobs and investment, equality; Africa, Asia, Middle East, former Soviet Union.

Other: Humanity First, Help for Heroes.

Imran Ahmad Khan MP, House of Commons, London SW1A 0AA
Tel: 020 7219 3000 *Email:* imran.mp@parliament.uk
Constituency: No constituency office publicised
Website: www.imranahmadkhan.org.uk *Twitter:* @imranahmadkhan

CONSERVATIVE

AIKEN, NICKIE

Cities of London and Westminster *(Majority 3,953)*

Nicola Jane Aiken. Born 4 February 1969; Married Alex (2 children).

Education: The Mary Erskine School for Girls, Edinburgh; Radyr Comprehensive, Cardiff; Exeter University (BA sociology 1991).

Non-political career: Press office, Welsh Conservative Party; Head of PR, Bradford & Bingley 2001-09; Self-employed crisis management trainer 2009-; Associate director, Liquid PR 2011-15.

Political career: Member for Cities of London and Westminster since 12 December 2019; Team PPS, Ministry of Housing, Communities and Local Government 2020. *Select committees:* Member: Women and Equalities 2020, Backbench Business 2020. Vice-chair, Women, Conservative Party. *Councils and public bodies:* Westminster City Council: Cabinet Member for: Councillor 2006-, Children, Young People and Community Protection 2010-13, Community Protection, Premises and Parking 2013-15, Public Protection 2015-19, Conservative Group Leader 2016-20, Council Leader 2017-20; London Councils: Shadow Lead for Crime and Policing 2018-20, Leader for Education and Children Services 2018-20; Member, Association of Local Conservative Councillors; Board member: Children and Family Court Advisory and Support Service (Cafcass), Royal Parks 2017-20.

Political interests: Rough sleeping, women's and girls' rights, securing education for girls to at least aged 12 in developing countries, preventing sexual violence in conflict; Africa, USA.

Nickie Aiken MP, House of Commons, London SW1A 0AA
Tel: 020 7219 4553 *Email:* nickie.aiken.mp@parliament.uk
Constituency: 90 Ebury Street, London SW1W 9QD
Website: www.nickieaiken.org.uk *Twitter:* @twocitiesnickie

CONSERVATIVE

ALDOUS, PETER

Waveney *(Majority 18,002)*

Peter James Guy Aldous. Born 26 August 1961; Single.

Education: Harrow School; Reading University (BSc land management 1982).

Non-political career: Chartered surveyor, private practice, Norwich and Ipswich 1983-2010.

Political career: Contested Waveney 2005 general election. Member for Waveney since 6 May 2010 general election. *Select committees:* Member: Environmental Audit 2010-17, Joint Committee on the Draft Registration of Overseas Entities Bill 2019. Member, Conservative Party 1998-. *Councils and public bodies:* Councillor, Waveney District Council 1999-2002; Suffolk County Council: Councillor 2001-05, Deputy Leader, Conservative Group 2002-05.

Political interests: East Anglian fishing, local infrastructure projects, offshore renewables, town planning and urban regeneration, north sea oil and gas, support for the disadvantaged.

Other: Beccles Conservative Club, Farmers' Club.

Recreations: Squash, Ipswich Town FC, horse racing, cricket.

Peter Aldous MP, House of Commons, London SW1A 0AA
Tel: 020 7219 7182 *Email:* peter.aldous.mp@parliament.uk
Constituency: The Kirkley Centre, 154 London Road South, Lowestoft, Suffolk NR33 0AZ
Tel: 01502 586568 Website: www.peteraldous.com *Twitter:* @peter_aldous

LABOUR

ALI, RUSHANARA

Bethnal Green and Bow *(Majority 37,524)*

Born 14 March 1975.

Education: Mulberry School; Tower Hamlets College; Oxford University (BA philosophy, politics and economics 1997); Bengali.

Non-political career: Research assistant to Lord Young of Dartington 1997; Parliamentary assistant to Oona King MP; Research fellow, Institute for Public Policy Research 1999-2001: Seconded to Foreign and Commonwealth Office 2001-02; Communities Directorate, Home Office 2002-05; Associate director, Young Foundation 2005-10.

Political career: Member for Bethnal Green and Bow since 6 May 2010 general election; Shadow Minister for: International Development 2010-13, Education 2013-14; Trade Envoy to Bangladesh 2016-. *Select committees:* Member: Treasury 2014-15, 2017-, Energy and Climate Change 2015-16, Communities and Local Government 2016-17, Treasury Sub-committee 2017-19, Panel of Chairs 2020-. *Councils and public bodies:* Governor, Tower Hamlets College.

Political interests: Education and young people, economic affairs, foreign affairs, housing.

Other: Former Commissioner, London Child Poverty Commission; Former chair, Tower Hamlets Summer University; Former trustee, Paul Hamlyn Foundation; Former member, Tate Britain Council; Westminster Foundation for Democracy: Governor, Vice-chair of board 2018-; Chair, UpRising.

Publications: Sinking and Swimming: Understanding Britain's Unmet Needs; Parties for the Public Good; Life begins at 60: what kind of NHS after 2008?; Turning the Corner: Beyond incarceration and re-offending; Charm Offensive: Cultivating Civility in 21st Century Britain; Our House? Race and Representation in British Politics (with Colm O'Cinneide, IPPR); Stuck on London's hard shoulder: Social needs in a fast moving city; Cohesive Communities; Seeing the wood for the trees – The evolving landscape for neighbourhood arrangements; Social Silicon Valleys; Cities in Transition: Global exchange forum report; Taking the lead: Youth leadership in theory and practice; Social Innovation: what it is, why it matters, how it can be accelerated; In and out of sync: The challenge of growing social innovations.

Rushanara Ali MP, House of Commons, London SW1A 0AA
Tel: 020 7219 7200 *Email:* rushanara.ali.mp@parliament.uk
Constituency: No constituency office publicised
Email: rushanara@rushanaraali.org Website: www.rushanaraali.org *Twitter:* @rushanaraali

LABOUR

ALI, TAHIR

Birmingham, Hall Green *(Majority 28,508)*

Born 1971.

Non-political career: Former Royal Mail worker. Midlands Political Officer, Communication Workers Union.

Political career: Member for Birmingham, Hall Green since 12 December 2019. *Select committees:* Member, European Scrutiny 2020-. *Councils and public bodies:* Councillor, Birmingham City Council 1999-.

Tahir Ali MP, House of Commons, London SW1A 0AA
Tel: 020 7219 6901 *Email:* tahir.ali.mp@parliament.uk
Constituency: No constituency office publicised
Twitter: @TahirAliMP

CONSERVATIVE

ALLAN, LUCY

Telford *(Majority 10,941)*

PPS to Jacob Rees-Mogg as Leader of the House of Commons and Lord President of the Council

Born 2 October 1964; Married Robin (1 son).

Education: Durham University (anthropology); Kingston Law School (Masters employment law); French.

Non-political career: PWC 1987-97; Head of Investment Trusts, Gartmore 1997-2004; UBS Warburg 2004; Owner/Director, Workplace Law 2004-11; Judicial Office Holder, Ministry of Justice 2010-13; Campaign Director, Lobby Family Rights 2011-13.

Political career: Member for Telford since 7 May 2015 general election; PPS to Jacob Rees-Mogg as Leader of the House of Commons and Lord President of the Council 2020-. *Select committees:* Member: Education 2015-19, Education, Skills and the Economy Sub-committee 2016-17, Women and Equalities 2017. Member, management committee, Wandsworth Conservatives; Deputy chair, Putney Conservatives 2007-09. *Councils and public bodies:* Councillor, Wandsworth Council 2006-12; Non-executive director, Wandsworth NHS.

Political interests: Family rights, children in care, broadband, rail links, child protection; Middle East.

Other: Trustee, Women's Aid; ICAEW; ICSA.

Lucy Allan MP, House of Commons, London SW1A 0AA
Tel: 020 7219 4815 *Email:* lucy.allan.mp@parliament.uk
Constituency: Suite 1 Preston House, Hawksworth Road, Central Park, Telford TF2 9TU
Tel: 01952 290039 Website: www.lucyallan.com *Twitter:* @lucyallan

LABOUR

ALLIN-KHAN, ROSENA

Tooting *(Majority 14,307)*

Shadow Minister for Mental Health

Rosena Chantelle Allin-Khan. Born 1 January 1977; Married Tudor (2 daughters).

Education: Brunel University (BSC medical biochemistry); Cambridge University (medicine): Scholarship: Cancer research, USA, Peace-keeping and conflict-resolution, Switzerland; Polish, Urdu.

Non-political career: NHS doctor 2005-: Royal London Hospital, Homerton Hospital, A&E department, St George's Hospital; Emergency humanitarian assistance, Palestinian refugees in Lebanese camps and with victims of flooding in Pakistan.

Political career: Member for Tooting since 16 June 2016 by-election; Shadow Minister for: Culture, Media and Sport/Digital, Culture, Media and Sport (Sport) 2016-19, Mental Health 2020-. *Councils and public bodies:* Wandsworth Council: Councillor 2014-18, Deputy leader, Labour group.

Other: Balham Boxing Club.

Recreations: Boxing.

Dr Rosena Allin-Khan MP, House of Commons, London SW1A 0AA
Tel: 020 7219 3000 *Email:* rosena.allinkhan.mp@parliament.uk
Constituency: No constituency office publicised
Tel: 020 3621 2509 *Email:* rosena@drrosena.co.uk Website: www.drrosena.co.uk
Twitter: @DrRosena

LABOUR

AMESBURY, MIKE

Weaver Vale *(Majority 562)*

Shadow Minister for Housing and Planning

Michael Lee Amesbury. Born 6 May 1969; Married Amanda 2006 (1 son).

Education: Castleford High School; Bradford University (BA social science); University of Central England (Postgraduate qualification careers guidance and education).

Non-political career: Careers adviser 2002-08; Parliamentary Adviser to Angela Rayner as Shadow Secretary of State for Education 2015-17; Stakeholder Manager to Andy Burnham, Metro Mayoral election campaign.

Political career: Member for Weaver Vale since 8 June 2017; PPS to Debbie Abrahams as Shadow Secretary of State for Work and Pensions 2018; Shadow Minister for: Work and Pensions (Employment) 2018-20, Communities and Local Government (Housing and Planning) 2020-. *Select committees:* Member, Communities and Local Government/Housing, Communities and Local Government 2017-18. *Councils and public bodies:* Manchester City Council: Councillor 2006-17, Executive Member for Culture and Leisure 2008-17; Vice-President, Local Government Association 2018-.

Mike Amesbury MP, House of Commons, London SW1A 0AA
Tel: 020 7219 2072 *Email:* mike.amesbury.mp@parliament.uk
Constituency: Suite 4, Second Floor, Halton 5 Office Centre, Northway, Halton Lea Runcorn WA7 2HF
Tel: 01928 620061 *Twitter:* @MikeAmesburyMP

CONSERVATIVE

AMESS, DAVID

Southend West *(Majority 14,459)*

David Anthony Andrew Amess. Born 26 March 1952; Son of late James Amess and late Maud Amess; Married Julia Arnold 1983 (1 son 4 daughters).

Education: St Bonaventure's Grammar School, Forest Gate, London; Bournemouth College of Technology (BSc economics and government 1974).

Non-political career: Teacher, St John Baptist Junior School, Bethnal Green, London 1970-71; Underwriter, Leslie Godwin Agency 1974-76; Accountancy Personnel 1976-79; Senior Consultant, Executemps Company Agency 1979-81; AA Recruitment Co 1981-87; Chair and Chief Executive: Accountancy Solutions 1987-90, Accountancy Group 1990-96; Parliamentary adviser to Caravan Club -2019.

Political career: Contested Newham North West 1979 general election. Member for Basildon 1983-97, for Southend West 1997-2010, for Southend West (revised boundary) since 6 May 2010 general election; PPS to: Parliamentary Under-Secretaries of State, DHSS: Edwina Currie 1987-88, Lord Skelmersdale 1988, to Michael Portillo: as Minister of State: Department of Transport 1988-90, Department of Environment 1990-92, as Chief Secretary to the Treasury 1992-94, as Secretary of State: for Employment 1994-95, for Defence 1995-97; Contested Deputy Speaker election 2013; Member, House of Commons Fire Safety Committee 2018-. *Select committees:* Member: Broadcasting 1994-97, Health 1998-2007, Chairmen's Panel/ Panel of Chairs 2001-, Backbench Business 2012-15, Administration 2015-19. Chair, Conservative Party Committee on Health 1999; Vice-chair, Conservative Party Committee on Health and Social Services 2001; Member, Executive, 1922 Committee 2004-12. Hon. Secretary, Conservative Friends of Israel 1998-. *Councils and public bodies:* Councillor, London Borough of Redbridge Council 1982-86.

Political interests: Health, education, transport, environment, pro-life movement, animal welfare, foreign affairs; Asia, Far East, Indian Ocean countries, Middle East, Pacific Basin, USA.

Other: Member, Executive Committee, Commonwealth Parliamentary Association United Kingdom 2020-; Founder Member, Wallenberg Appeal Foundation 1996; Industry and Parliament Trust: Fellow, Chair, Fellowship Committee 2007-17, Chair, Board of Trustees 2014-17; Chair, 1912 Club 1996-; Fairhaven Hospices, Salvation Army, RSPCA, Southend Fund, Mencap, Age UK, Dogs Trust; Freedom, City of London; Charity Champion awards: Animal Welfare and Environment Champion 2011, Outstanding Achievement (with Stephen Pound MP and Bob Russell MP) 2012; Knighted 2015.

Publications: The Road to Basildon (1993); The Basildon Experience (1995); Basildon 1992: Against All Odds! (2012); Party of Opportunity (2014); Party of Opportunity, The Second Edition (2015); Ayes & Ears: A Survivor's Guide to Westminster (2020).

Recreations: Socialising, reading, writing, sports, modern music, keeping animals, gardening, travel, history.

Sir David Amess MP, House of Commons, London SW1A 0AA
Tel: 020 7219 3452 *Fax:* 020 7219 2245 *Email:* amessd@parliament.uk
Constituency: Iveagh Hall, 67 Leigh Road, Leigh-on-Sea, Essex SS9 1JW
Tel: 01702 472391 *Email:* swca@tory.org Website: www.davidamess.co.uk
Twitter: @amessd_southend

LABOUR

ANDERSON, FLEUR

Putney *(Majority 4,774)*

Shadow Minister for Cabinet Office

Born 6 February 1971; 4 children.

Education: York University (BA politics 1993); Open University (MSc development management 2010).

Non-political career: Campaign Team Administrator, Christian Aid 1994-97; Head of World Action Methodist Church 1997-99; Head of Bosnia Country Office, Christian Aid 1999-2000; Cafod: Head of Campaigns 2001-02, Advcacy Strategy Manager 2003-06; Freelance Consultant in Kenya 2008-10; CBO Capacity Building Trainer in Nairobi 2009-10; International Campaign Coordinator 2010-12; Global Head of Campaigns, WaterAid 2012-16; Head of Community Services, Katherine Low Settlement 2016-20.

Political career: Member for Putney since 12 December 2019; PPS to Preet Kaur Gill as Shadow Secretary of State for International Development 2020-21; Shadow Minister for Cabinet Office 2021-. *Select committees:* Member: Education 2020, 2020-, Ecclesiastical Committee 2020-. Chair, PLP Departmental Group for Communities and Local Government 2020-. *Councils and public bodies:* Wandsworth Borough Council: Councillor 2014-, Spokesperson for Community Services and the Environment 2015-18, Deputy Leader, Labour Group 2016-18; School Governor, St Anselm's School.

Political interests: NHS, Brexit, climate emergency, housing, international development.

Other: Co-founder, Wandsworth Welcomes Refugees.

Fleur Anderson MP, House of Commons, London SW1A 0AA
Tel: 020 7219 3348 *Email:* fleur.anderson.mp@parliament.uk
Constituency: 35 Felsham Road, London SW15 1AY
Website: fleuranderson.co.uk *Twitter:* @PutneyFleur

CONSERVATIVE

ANDERSON, LEE

Ashfield *(Majority 5,733)*

Married Sinead.

Education: Ashfield School.

Non-political career: Miner: Sutton Colliery, Welbeck Colliery; Ashfield and Broxtowe Citizens Advice Bureau; Various homeless shelters; Office of Gloria De Piero MP -2018.

Political career: Member for Ashfield since 12 December 2019. *Select committees:* Member, Future Relationship with the European Union 2020-21. *Councils and public bodies:* Councillor, Ashfield District Council 2015-19.

Lee Anderson MP, House of Commons, London SW1A 0AA
Tel: 020 7219 3000 *Email:* lee.anderson.mp@parliament.uk
Constituency: 70-78 High Pavement, Sutton-in-Ashfield NG17 4FY
Tel: 01623 550604 Website: www.leeanderson.org.uk

CONSERVATIVE

ANDERSON, STUART

Wolverhampton South West *(Majority 1,661)*

Stuart Paul Anderson. Born 17 July 1976; Married (5 children).

Education: Leicester University (Foundation Degree security and risk management 2004; MSc security and risk management 2008); Buckinghamshire Chilterns University College (Foundation Degree protective security management 2008).

Non-political career: Soldier, British Army 1993-2001; Freelance security professional at risk management companies 2001-05; Managing director, Anubis Associates 2005-13; Chief executive, eTravelSafety 2013-.

Political career: Member for Wolverhampton South West since 12 December 2019. *Select committees:* Member, Defence 2020-. Chair, Hereford City Conservative Branch 2016-18; Hereford and South Herefordshire Conservative Association: Deputy Chair (Membership) 2016-18, Deputy Chair (Political) 2018-19. *Councils and public bodies:* Councillor, Herefordshire Council 2017-19.

Other: Member, UK delegation, NATO Parliamentary Assembly 2020-.

Stuart Anderson MP, House of Commons, London SW1A 0AA
Tel: 020 7219 4396 *Email:* stuart.anderson.mp@parliament.uk
Constituency: 35 Chapel Ash, Wolverhampton WV3 0UF
Tel: 01902 680549 Website: www.stuartanderson.org.uk *Twitter:* @Stuart4WolvesSW

CONSERVATIVE

ANDREW, STUART

Pudsey *(Majority 3,517)*

Deputy Chief Whip (Treasurer of HM Household)

Stuart James Andrew. Born 25 November 1971; Son of James Andrew and Maureen Andrew; Partner.

Education: Ysgol David Hughes, Menai Bridge; Welsh.

Non-political career: British Heart Foundation -1998; Fundraiser, Hope House Children's Hospice 1998-2000; Head of fundraising, East Lancashire Hospice 2000-03; Fundraising manager, Martin House Children's Hospice 2003-10.

Political career: Contested Wrexham 1997 general election. Member for Pudsey since 6 May 2010 general election; PPS: to Francis Maude as Minister for the Cabinet Office and Paymaster General 2012-15, to Patrick McLoughlin: as Secretary of State for Transport 2015-16, as Chancellor of the Duchy of Lancaster, Cabinet Office 2016-17; Assistant Government Whip 2017-18; Parliamentary Under-Secretary of State: Wales Office 2018, for Defence Procurement, Ministry of Defence 2018-19; Government Whip (Vice-Chamberlain of HM Household) 2019-20; Deputy Chief Whip (Treasurer of HM Household) 2020-. *Select committees:* Member: Welsh Affairs 2010-12, Selection 2020-. Vice-chairman (Cities), Conservative Party 2016-17. *Councils and public bodies:* Councillor, Leeds City Council 2003-10.

Political interests: Special needs education, transport, planning, charities, health; Commonwealth, USA.

Other: Chair, Yeadon Project; Member, Institute of Fundraising.

Recreations: Walking the Yorkshire Dales, attending the gym.

Stuart Andrew MP, House of Commons, London SW1A 0AA
Tel: 020 7219 7130 *Email:* stuart.andrew.mp@parliament.uk
Constituency: 94a Town Street, Horsforth, Leeds, West Yorkshire LS18 4AP
Tel: 0113-258 5615 Website: www.stuartandrew.org.uk *Twitter:* @StuartAndrew

CONSERVATIVE

ANSELL, CAROLINE

Eastbourne *(Majority 4,331)*

Caroline Julie Porte Ansell. Born 12 January 1971; Married Nicholas Ansell (3 sons).

Education: Beresford House School; Royal Holloway, University of London (BA French); MEd 2001.

Non-political career: Teacher; Ofsted School Inspector.

Political career: Member for Eastbourne 2015-17. Contested Eastbourne 2017 general election. Member for Eastbourne since 12 December 2019; PPS to George Eustice as Secretary of State for Environment, Food and Rural Affairs 2020. *Select committees:* Member: Environmental Audit 2015-17, Ecclesiastical Committee 2015-17, Northern Ireland Affairs 2020-21. Chairman, Conservative Backbench Policy Committee on Education 2016-17. Member: Conservative Councillors Association, Conservative Christian Fellowship. *Councils and public bodies:* Eastbourne Borough Council: Councillor 2012-15, 2019-, Shadow Cabinet Portfolio Holder for Tourism; Governor: Langney Primary School, College Central.

Political interests: Transport, NHS, education.

Other: Member, Association of Christian Teachers; Patron, Motivational Preparation College for Training.

Caroline Ansell MP, House of Commons, London SW1A 0AA
Tel: 020 7219 3000 *Email:* caroline.ansell.mp@parliament.uk
Constituency: Eastbourne Town Hall, Grove Road, Eastbourne BN21 4TX
Tel: 01323 409000 Website: carolineansell.co.uk *Twitter:* @Caroline_Ansell

LABOUR

ANTONIAZZI, TONIA

Gower *(Majority 1,837)*

Antonia Louise Antoniazzi. Born 5 October 1971; Divorced (1 son).

Education: St John Lloyd School; Gower College, Swansea; Exeter University (French and Italian); Cardiff University (PGCE).

Non-political career: Welsh Women's rugby player; Head of languages, Bryngwyn School; Leader of Learning for Foundation, Education through Regional Working (ERW).

Political career: Member for Gower since 8 June 2017; PPS: to Shadow Secretary of State for Northern Ireland: Owen Smith 2017-18, Tony Lloyd 2018, to Christina Rees as Shadow Secretary of State for Wales 2018, to Jonathan Reynolds as Shadow Secretary of State for Work and Pensions 2020. *Select committees:* Member: Welsh Affairs 2017-, Women and Equalities 2017-19, Petitions 2020-. Chair, PLP Departmental Group for Employment Rights and Protection 2020-. Contested Mid and West Wales region 2016 National Assembly for Wales election.

Other: UK Delegation to Parliamentary Assembly, Council of Europe: Substitute member 2020, Member 2020-.

Tonia Antoniazzi MP, House of Commons, London SW1A 0AA
Tel: 020 7219 1199 *Email:* tonia.antoniazzi.mp@parliament.uk
Constituency: Ty Newydd Community Centre, 17 West Street, Gorseinon, Swansea SA4 4AA
Tel: 01792 899025 Website: www.toniaantoniazzi.co.uk *Twitter:* @ToniaAntoniazzi

CONSERVATIVE

ARGAR, EDWARD

Charnwood *(Majority 22,397)*

Minister of State for Health, Department of Health and Social Care

Edward John Comport Argar. Born 9 December 1977.

Education: Harvey Grammar School, Folkestone; Oriel College, Oxford (BA modern history 2000, MA; Masters 2001); French, German.

Non-political career: Political adviser to Michael Ancram MP as Shadow Foreign Secretary 2001-05; Management consultant: Hedra plc 2005-08, Mouchel 2008-11; Head of Public Affairs in UK and Europe, Serco 2011-14.

Political career: Contested Oxford East 2010 general election. Member for Charnwood since 7 May 2015 general election; Team PPS, Department for Education 2016-17; PPS: to Patrick McLoughlin as Chancellor of the Duchy of Lancaster and Conservative Party Chair 2017-18, to

Amber Rudd as Home Secretary and Minister for Women and Equalities 2018, to Sajid Javid as Home Secretary 2018; Parliamentary Under-Secretary of State, Ministry of Justice 2018-19; Minister of State for Health, Department of Health and Social Care 2019-. *Select committees:* Member, Procedure 2015-16. *Councils and public bodies:* Westminster City Council: Councillor 2006-15, Cabinet Member for: Health and Adult Services 2008-10, City Management, Transport and Infrastructure 2010-15; Vice-chair, Health and Adult Social Care Forum, London Councils 2008-10; School governor 2004-15; Board member, NHS trust 2008-10.

Political interests: Foreign policy, rural affairs, health and social care, particularly dementia care, justice policy; France, Oman, Norway, USA, Yemen.

Other: RNLI, Alzheimer's Society.

Recreations: Travel, reading, skiing, gardening, cricket, tennis.

Edward Argar MP, House of Commons, London SW1A 0AA
Tel: 020 7219 8140 *Email:* edward.argar.mp@parliament.uk
Constituency: Suite 26, Unit 3, Q-Estate, 1487 Melton Road, Queniborough, Leicestershire LE7 3FP
Tel: 0116-269 3789 Website: www.edwardargar.org.uk

LABOUR/ CO-OPERATIVE

ASHWORTH, JON

Leicester South *(Majority 22,675)*

Shadow Secretary of State for Health and Social Care

Jonathan Michael Graham Ashworth. Born 14 October 1978; Married Emilie Oldknow (2 daughters).

Education: Philips High School, Bury; Bury College; Durham University (BA politics and philosophy 2000).

Non-political career: Special adviser to Chief Secretaries to the Treasury 2004-07: Paul Boateng 2004-05, Des Browne 2005-06, Stephen Timms 2006-07; Deputy Political Secretary to Gordon Brown as Prime Minister 2007-10; Political Secretary to Harriet Harman as Acting Leader of the Opposition 2010; Head of party relations to Ed Miliband as Leader of the Opposition 2010-11. Member: Unite, GMB.

Political career: Member for Leicester South since 6 May 2011 by-election; Opposition Whip 2011-13; Shadow Minister for Cabinet Office 2013-15; Shadow Minister without Portfolio (attending Shadow Cabinet) 2015-16; Shadow Secretary of State for Health/Health and Social Care 2016-. Labour Party: Political research officer 2001, Economics and welfare policy officer 2002-04, Member, National Executive Committee 2013-16, Campaign Deputy, General Election Strategy 2014-15; Member, Co-operative Party.

Political interests: Health, economy, foreign affairs, international development; Australia, Bangladesh, India, Italy, Middle East, Myanmar, Pakistan, Palestine, Somalia, Syria, USA.

Other: National Association for Children of Alcoholics. Saffron Lane Working Men's Club.

Recreations: Reading, cinema, boxing fan, music.

Jon Ashworth MP, House of Commons, London SW1A 0AA
Tel: 020 7219 0517 *Email:* jon.ashworth.mp@parliament.uk
Constituency: Tenth Floor, 60 Charles Street, Leicester, Leicestershire LE1 1FB
Tel: 0116-251 1927 Website: www.jonashworth.org *Twitter:* @JonAshworth

CONSERVATIVE

ATHERTON, SARAH

Wrexham *(Majority 2,131)*

PPS to Simon Hart as Secretary of State for Wales

Sarah Elizabeth Atherton. Born 15 November 1967; Married Nick (1 son from previous relationship).

Non-political career: District Nurse, NHS; Social Worker, Flintshire County Council; Owner, micro-brewery. Army Intelligence Corps.

Political career: Member for Wrexham since 12 December 2019; PPS to Simon Hart as Secretary of State for Wales 2020-. *Select committees:* Member, Defence 2020-. Contested Alyn and Deeside constituency National Assembly for Wales 2018 by-election. *Councils and public bodies:* Councillor, Gresford Community Council 2017-.

Political interests: Dementia, ex-service personnel, homelessness.

Other: Trustee, Gresford and District War Memorial Trust.

Sarah Atherton MP, House of Commons, London SW1A 0AA
Tel: 020 7219 4885 *Email:* sarah.atherton.mp@parliament.uk
Constituency: 65 Regent Street, Wrexham LL11 1PF
Tel: 01978 291742 Website: www.sarahatherton.org.uk *Twitter:* @AthertonNWales

CONSERVATIVE

ATKINS, VICTORIA

Louth and Horncastle *(Majority 28,868)*

Parliamentary Under-Secretary of State for Safeguarding, Home Office

Victoria Mary Atkins. Born 22 March 1976; Married Paul (1 son).

Education: Cambridge University (law).

Non-political career: Called to the Bar, Middle Temple 1998; Barrister, specialising in serious organised crime, fraud and regulatory crime.

Political career: Member for Louth and Horncastle since 7 May 2015 general election; PPS to: Brandon Lewis as Minister of State for Policing and the Fire Service, Home Office 2016-17, Baroness Evans of Bowes Park as Leader of the House of Lords and Lord Privy Seal 2017; Parliamentary Under-Secretary of State for Crime, Safeguarding and Vulnerability/Safeguarding, Home Office 2017-; Minister for Women, Government Equalities Office 2018-20. *Select committees:* Member: Home Affairs 2015-16, Joint Committee on the Draft Investigatory Powers Bill 2015-16. Contested Gloucestershire 2012 Police and Crime Commissioner election.

Political interests: Home affairs, agriculture, defence, education.

Other: Associate Member, MCC.

Recreations: Going to concerts, travelling, horse riding.

Victoria Atkins MP, House of Commons, London SW1A 0AA
Tel: 020 7219 5897
Constituency: No constituency office publicised
Tel: 01507 527017 *Email:* victoria@victoriaatkins.org.uk Website: www.victoriaatkins.org.uk

CONSERVATIVE

BACON, GARETH

Orpington *(Majority 22,378)*

Gareth Andrew Bacon. Born 7 April 1972; Married Cheryl (1 daughter).

Education: St. Mary and St. Josephs RC Secondary School, Sidcup; Kent University (BA politics and government 1996; MA European politics and democracy 1997).

Non-political career: Manager, Public and Not For Profit Division, Martin Ward Anderson 2004-10; Director, Public and Not-For-Profit Division, Randstad Financial and Professional 2010-12; Head of Finance and Accountancy, Eligis Select Ltd 2012-13; Associate Director, Operations, Hanami International 2017-18.

Political career: Member for Orpington since 12 December 2019; Chair: London Fire and Emergency Planning Authority 2015-16, London Local Resilience Forum 2015-16; Leader, Conservative Group on the Assembly 2016-19; Conservative Spokesperson for: Budget and Oversight 2016-18, Financial Issues 2018-20. *Select committees:* Member: Public Accounts 2020-, Backbench Business 2020-. AM for Londonwide region 2008-16 and for Bexley and Bromley constituency since 5 May 2016: Leader, Conservative Group on the Assembly 2015-20; Chair, Budget Committee 2016-20; Conservative Spokesperson for: Budget and Oversight 2016-18, Financial Issues 2018-20. *Councils and public bodies:* London Fire and Emergency Planning Authority: Member 2010-18, Chair 2015-16; London Borough of Bexley Council: Councillor 1998-2020, Vice-chair, Town Planning Committee 1998-2002, Deputy Mayor 2001-02 Shadow Cabinet Spokesman for Environment, Transport and Regeneration 2003-06, Cabinet Member for the Environment 2006-14, Cabinet Member for Finance and Corporate Services/Deputy Leader 2014-15.

Political interests: Local government, town planning, green belt protection, policing, fire, transport, finance/economy, the Union.

Other: Carlton Club; Sidcup Rugby Club; Bexley Lawn Tennis and Squash Club.

Recreations: Rugby, tennis, squash, Manchester United, military history, gardening.

Gareth Bacon MP, House of Commons, London SW1A 0AA
Tel: 020 7219 6806 *Email:* gareth.bacon.mp@parliament.uk
Constituency: Orpington Conservative Association, 6 Sevenoaks Road, Orpington BR6 9JJ
Tel: 01689 820347 *Email:* garethbacon.orpington@gmail.com Website: www.garethbacon.com
Twitter: @GarethBaconMP

CONSERVATIVE

BACON, RICHARD

South Norfolk *(Majority 21,275)*

Richard Michael Bacon. Born 3 December 1962; Married Catherine White 2019 (2 sons from a previous marriage).

Education: King's School, Worcester; London School of Economics (BSc (Econ) politics and economics 1986); German.

Non-political career: Investment banker, Barclays de Zoete Wedd 1986-89; Financial journalist, Euromoney Publications plc 1993-94; Deputy director, Management Consultancies Association 1994-96; Brunswick Public Relations 1996-99; Founder, English Word Factory 1999-.

Political career: Contested Vauxhall 1997 general election. Member for South Norfolk 2001-10, for South Norfolk (revised boundary) since 6 May 2010 general election; Member, Public Accounts Commission 2005-. *Select committees:* Public Accounts: Member 2001-17, Deputy Chair 2010-17; Member: European Scrutiny 2003-07, Unopposed Bills (Panel) 2010-15, International Development 2020-, Work of the Independent Commission for Aid Impact Sub-committee 2020-. Chair, Hammersmith Conservative Association 1995-96; Co-founder, Geneva Conservative general election voluntary agency 2000.

Political interests: Housing, public expenditure, education, health, agriculture, Europe.

Other: Member, UK Delegation to Parliamentary Assembly, Council of Europe 2020-; Ambassador, Right to Build Task Force; Backbencher of the Year, House Magazine Awards 2006; Outstanding Parliamentarian of the Year, ConservativeHome Awards 2006; Parliamentarian of the Year, The Spectator magazine awards 2006; Parliamentarian of the Year, Political Studies Association Awards 2006; Commons Select Committee Member of the Year, House Magazine Awards 2012; Parliamentarian of the Year, The Spectator Magazine Awards 2013.

Publications: Co-author, Conundrum: Why every government gets things wrong and what we can do about it (2013).

Recreations: Music, reading, modern painting.

Richard Bacon MP, House of Commons, London SW1A 0AA
Tel: 020 7219 8301 *Email:* richardbaconmp@parliament.uk
Constituency: Pretoria House, Ipswich Road, Long Stratton, Norwich, Norfolk NR15 2TA
Tel: 01508 530040/01508 532222 *Email:* sally.culling@parliament.uk
Website: www.richardbacon.org.uk *Twitter:* @richardbaconmp

CONSERVATIVE

BADENOCH, KEMI

Saffron Walden *(Majority 27,594)*

Exchequer Secretary, HM Treasury and Minister for Equalities, Government Equalities Office

Olukemi Olufunto Badenoch. Born January 1980; Daughter of Prof Feyi Adegoke and Dr Femi Adegoke; Married (2 daughters 1 son).

Education: International School of Lagos; Sussex University (MEng systems engineering 2003); University of London (LLB 2009).

Non-political career: Associate Director, Coutts 2008-15; Head of Digital, *The Spectator* 2015-16.

Political career: Contested (as Kemi Adegoke) Dulwich and West Norwood 2010 general election. Member for Saffron Walden since 8 June 2017; Parliamentary Under-Secretary of State for Children and Families, Department for Education 2019-20 (on maternity leave September 2019-February 2020); Exchequer Secretary, HM Treasury 2020-; Minister for Equalities, Government Equalities Office 2020-. *Select committees:* Member: Justice 2017-19, Standing Orders 2017-, Public Accounts 2020-. Member, Executive, 1922 Committee 2017-19; Chairman, Conservative Backbench Policy Committee on Justice 2017-19. AM (replacement) for Londonwide region 2015-17: Conservative Spokesperson on: Policing and Crime 2015-16, Economy 2016-17. Project Leader, Global Poverty Policy Group 2006-07; Deputy Chair, South London Area Conservatives 2014-; Vice-chairman, Candidates, Conservative Party 2018-19.

Political interests: Policing, crime, economy, housing, transport, international development; India, Nigeria, USA.

Other: Member: British Computer Society, Women's Engineering Society.

Recreations: Chess and poker player, reading.

Kemi Badenoch MP, House of Commons, London SW1A 0AA
Tel: 020 7219 1943 *Email:* kemi.badenoch.mp@parliament.uk
Constituency: The Old Armoury, 3 Museum Street, Saffron Walden, Essex CB10 1JN
Website: kemibadenoch.org.uk *Twitter:* @KemiBadenoch

CONSERVATIVE

BAILEY, SHAUN

West Bromwich West *(Majority 3,799)*

Shaun Stephen Bailey. Born 22 July 1992.

Education: Burton Borough School; Idsall School; University of Wales, Aberystwyth (LLB law with French 2014); University of the West of England (LLM advanced legal practice); French, Welsh.

Non-political career: Legal Team Assistant, Hazlewoods 2015-16; Equilaw: Administration Assistant 2016, Paralegal 2016-17; Paralegal, Shakespeare Martineau: Remortgage and Volume Conveyancing 2017, Commercial Property 2017-18; Central Legal Team, Barclays: Paralegal, Legal Copy Clearance 2018-19, Trainee Solicitor 2019-.

Political career: Member for West Bromwich West since 12 December 2019. *Select committees:* Member: Work and Pensions 2020-, Public Accounts 2020-. *Councils and public bodies:* Councillor, Chetwynd Aston and Woodcote Parish Council 2019-.

Shaun Bailey MP, House of Commons, London SW1A 0AA
Tel: 020 7219 3982 *Email:* shaun.bailey.mp@parliament.uk
Constituency: 290 Whitehall Road, Great Bridge, Tipton DY4 7EX
Tel: 0121-389 4419 *Email:* shaun@shaunbailey.org.uk Website: www.shaunbailey.org.uk
Twitter: @Shaun4WBW

CONSERVATIVE

BAILLIE, SIOBHAN

Stroud *(Majority 3,840)*

Siobhan Kathleen Baillie. Born September 1981; Married Kristian Tiggle 2018 (1 daughter).

Non-political career: Legal Secretary; Legal Assistant; Family Law Solicitor; Head of Policy and Communications, OnePlusOne 2017-19.

Political career: Contested Bermondsey and Old Southwark 2017 general election. Member for Stroud since 12 December 2019; Team PPS, Ministry of Justice 2020. *Select committees:* Member, Work and Pensions 2020-. *Councils and public bodies:* Councillor, Camden Council 2014-18; School Governor, Fitzjohn's Primary School.

Siobhan Baillie MP, House of Commons, London SW1A 0AA
Tel: 020 7219 4920 *Email:* siobhan.baillie.mp@parliament.uk
Constituency: 3 King Street, Stroud, Gloucestershire GL5 3DA
Website: www.siobhanbaillie.org.uk *Twitter:* @Siobhan_Baillie

CONSERVATIVE

BAKER, DUNCAN

North Norfolk *(Majority 14,395)*

Duncan Charles Baker. Born 15 November 1979; Married Nina (2 daughters).

Education: Gresham's School, Holt; Nottingham Trent University (BA business studies 2002).

Non-political career: Auditor, Baker Tilly International 2002-06; Audit Senior, Grant Thornton LLP 2006-07; Finance Manager, Archant 2007-08; Finance Director, CT Baker Ltd 2008-.

Political career: Member for North Norfolk since 12 December 2019. *Select committees:* Member: Environmental Audit 2020-, Joint Committee on Consolidation, &c, Bills 2020-. *Councils and public bodies:* Holt Town Council: Councillor 2009-, Mayor; North Norfolk District Council: Councillor 2017-, Leader of the Opposition 2019-.

Political interests: Investment, business, family values.

Other: Member, UK Delegation to Parliamentary Assembly, Council of Europe 2020-; Treasurer, Holt Youth Centre 2015-; Chair, Holt 1940's Weekend and Owl Trail Project; ICAEW.

Recreations: Family time, tennis, golf, walks.

Duncan Baker MP, House of Commons, London SW1A 0AA
Tel: 020 7219 3000 *Email:* duncan.baker.mp@parliament.uk
Constituency: Tudor House, Grammar School Road, North Walsham NR28 9JH
Tel: 01692 557140 *Email:* duncan@duncanbaker.org.uk Website: www.duncanbaker.org.uk
Twitter: @duncancbaker

CONSERVATIVE

BAKER, STEVE

Wycombe *(Majority 4,214)*

Steven John Baker. Born 6 June 1971; Married Beth 1996 (no children).

Education: Poltair Comprehensive School, St Austell; St Austell Sixth Form College; Southampton University (BEng aerospace systems engineering 1992); St Cross College, Oxford (MSc computer science 2000).

Non-political career: Head of consulting and product manager, DecisionSoft Ltd, Oxford 2000-01; Principal, Ambriel Consulting Ltd 2001-10; Chief technology officer, BASDA Ltd, Great Missenden 2002-07; Product development director, Core Filing Ltd, Oxford 2005-06; Chief architect, global financing and asset servicing platforms, Lehman Brothers, London 2006-08; Corporate affairs director, Cobden Centre 2009-10; Ambriel Consulting. Engineer officer, Royal Air Force 1989-99.

Political career: Member for Wycombe since 6 May 2010 general election; Parliamentary Under-Secretary of State, Department for Exiting the European Union 2017-18. *Select committees:* Member: Transport 2010-13, Treasury 2014-17, 2018-, Standing Orders 2015-17, Treasury Sub-committee 2018-19. Chair, Conservative Party Committee for Public Services 2011-15; Member, Executive, 1922 Committee 2012-17, 2020-. Chairman, Conservatives for Britain 2015-16; European Research Group: Chairman 2016-17, 2019-20, Deputy chairman 2018-19.

Political interests: Enterprise, economics, money and banking, health, education, liberty, foreign affairs, defence; Kashmir, Pakistan.

Other: Associate consultant, Centre for Social Justice 2008-10; Member: Speen Baptist Church, Campaign committee, Vote Leave 2016; Chartered aerospace engineer, Royal Aeronautical Society 1999; Member, Institute of Directors; Volunteer, Wycombe Winter Night Shelter 2008-09. Royal Air Force Club.

Recreations: Skydiving, motorcycling, photography, sailing.

Steve Baker MP, House of Commons, London SW1A 0AA
Tel: 020 7219 3547 *Email:* steve.baker.mp@parliament.uk
Constituency: 150a West Wycombe Road, High Wycombe, Buckinghamshire HP12 3AE
Tel: 01494 448408 *Email:* sue.hynard@parliament.uk Website: www.stevebaker.info
Twitter: @SteveBakerHW

CONSERVATIVE

BALDWIN, HARRIETT

West Worcestershire *(Majority 24,499)*

Harriett Mary Morison Baldwin. Born 2 May 1960; Daughter of Anthony Eggleston OBE and late Jane Eggleston, née Buxton; Married James Stanley Baldwin 2004 (1 son from previous marriage 2 stepdaughters).

Education: Friends' School, Saffron Walden; Marlborough College; Lady Margaret Hall, Oxford (MA French and Russian 1982); McGill University, Montreal, Canada (MBA international finance 1985); French, Russian.

Non-political career: Graduate Trainee, Security Pacific National Bank 1982-83; Treasury Analyst, Hewlett-Packard Canada 1985-86; JP Morgan 1986-2008: Various roles/investor 1986-98, Head of Currency Management, Asset Management Division 1998-2006, Managing Director 1998-2008, Senior Adviser -2008. Armed Forces RAF Parliamentary Scheme.

Political career: Contested Stockton North 2005 general election. Member for West Worcestershire since 6 May 2010 general election; PPS to Minister of State for Employment, Department for Work and Pensions: Mark Hoban 2012-13, Esther McVey 2013-14; Assistant Government Whip 2014; Government Whip 2014-15; Economic Secretary (Minister for the City of London), HM Treasury 2015-16; Parliamentary Under-Secretary of State (Defence Procurement), Ministry of Defence 2016-18; Minister of State: for Africa, Foreign and Commonwealth Office 2018-19, Department for International Development 2018-19. *Select committees:* Member: Work and Pensions 2010-12, Joint Committee on the Draft Care and Support Bill 2013, Administration 2014, Public Accounts 2015-16, Treasury 2020-, Finance 2020-.

Political interests: Pensions, economics, social enterprise, financial literacy, micro-finance, welfare reform, global education; Cyprus, Russia, Sudan.

Other: Member: NATO Parliamentary Assembly 2010-14, 2020-, Executive Committee, Commonwealth Parliamentary Association United Kingdom 2020-; Chair, British Group Inter-Parliamentary Union 2020-; Founding Co-chair, International Parliamentary Network for Education; Vice-chair, Social Investment Business 2008-12; Centre for Social Justice, Camfed, Opportunity International, Save the Children, Plan International; Merchant Taylors; Freedom, City of London. Carlton Club.

Publications: Author: Leviathan Is Still At Large (Centre for Policy Studies, 2002), Social Enterprise Zones (Conservative Policy Review, 2007), Growth, Growth, Growth, (Centre for Policy Studies, 2011), Iron Ladies (Demos, 2012).

Recreations: Canal boats, swimming, walking, cycling.

Harriett Baldwin MP, House of Commons, London SW1A 0AA
Tel: 020 7219 5487 *Fax:* 020 7219 5151 *Email:* harriett.baldwin.mp@parliament.uk
Constituency: Malvern Hills Science Park, Geraldine Road, Malvern, Worcestershire WR14 3SZ
Tel: 01684 585165 Website: www.harriettbaldwin.com *Twitter:* @hbaldwin

CONSERVATIVE

BARCLAY, STEPHEN

North East Cambridgeshire *(Majority 29,993)*

Chief Secretary to the Treasury, HM Treasury

Stephen Paul Barclay. Born 30 June 1972; Married Karen.

Education: King Edward VII School, Lancashire; Peterhouse, Cambridge (BA history 1994, MA); College of Law, Chester (1996).

Non-political career: Trainee solicitor, Lawrence Graham Solicitors 1996-98; Company lawyer, Axa Insurance 1998-2001; Financial Services Authority 2002-06; Barclays Retail Bank 2006-10: Director of regulatory affairs 2006-08, Head of anti-money laundering and sanctions 2008-10. 2nd Lieutenant, Royal Regiment of Fusiliers 1991.

Political career: Contested Manchester Blackley 1997 and Lancaster and Wyre 2001 general elections. Member for North East Cambridgeshire since 6 May 2010 general election; Assistant Government Whip 2015-16; Government Whip (Lord Commissioner of HM Treasury) 2016-17; Economic Secretary, HM Treasury 2017-18; Minister of State for Health, Department of Health and Social Care 2018; Secretary of State for Exiting the European Union 2018-20; Chief Secretary to the Treasury, HM Treasury 2020-. *Select committees:* Member, Public Accounts 2010-14. Member, Conservative Party 1994-.

Other: PC 2018.

Recreations: Rugby, skydiving.

Rt Hon Stephen Barclay MP, House of Commons, London SW1A 0AA
Tel: 020 7219 7117 *Email:* stephen.barclay.mp@parliament.uk
Constituency: MJS House, Wisbech Road, March, Cambridgeshire PE15 0BA
Tel: 01354 656635 Website: www.stevebarclay.net *Twitter:* @SteveBarclay

SCOTTISH NATIONAL PARTY

BARDELL, HANNAH

Livingston *(Majority 13,435)*

SNP Foreign Affairs Team Member

Hannah Mary Bardell. Born 1 June 1983.

Education: Broxburn Academy; Stirling University (film, media, politics and English 2005).

Non-political career: STV, Glasgow; Producer and presenter, SNPtv online; Researcher/assistant producer, GMTV 2005-07; Assistant to Ian Hudghton MEP; Office Manager to Alex Salmond MSP 2007-10; Protocol executive and events manager, American Consulate, Edinburgh 2010-12; Communications manager, Subsea 7 2012; Head of communications and marketing (UK, Africa and Norway), Stork Technical Services 2013-15.

Political career: Member for Livingston since 7 May 2015 general election; SNP: Spokesperson for: Fair Work and Employment 2015, Business, Innovation and Skills 2015-16, Business and Economy Engagement 2016-17, Trade and Investment 2017-18, Culture, Digital, Media and Sport 2018-19, SNP Foreign Affairs Team Member 2020-, International Development Team Member 2020-21. *Select committees:* Member: Speaker's Advisory Committee on Works of Art 2017-19, Panel of Chairs 2020-.

Political interests: Anti-trident, anti-austerity, anti-privatisation, deaths abroad, consular services and assistance, LGBT rights, Primodos campaign.

Other: Member, UK Delegation, Parliamentary Assembly of the Council of Europe 2017-; Member: Policy Committee, Grampian Chamber of Commerce, Business for Scotland; Aberdeen Performing Arts Development Committee; Pushkin Prize winner for creative writing.

Recreations: Guitar, singing, creative writing, arts, musical theatre, watching sports, surfing, golf.

Hannah Bardell MP, House of Commons, London SW1A 0AA
Tel: 020 7219 5907 *Email:* hannah.bardell.mp@parliament.uk
Constituency: No constituency office
Tel: 01506 462004 Website: hannahbardellmp.scot *Twitter:* @HannahB4LiviMP

LABOUR

BARKER, PAULA

Liverpool Wavertree *(Majority 27,085)*

Born 9 May 1972.

Non-political career: North West Regional Convenor, Unison; Unison Branch Secretary, Halton Borough Council.

Political career: Member for Liverpool Wavertree since 12 December 2019. *Select committees:* Member, Justice 2020-.

Political interests: Green space development, council housing, jobs, care workers.

Paula Barker MP, House of Commons, London SW1A 0AA
Tel: 020 7219 3000 *Email:* paula.barker.mp@parliament.uk
Constituency: 108 Prescot Road, Liverpool L7 0JA
Twitter: @PaulaBarkerMP

CONSERVATIVE

BARON, JOHN

Basildon and Billericay *(Majority 20,412)*

John Charles Baron. Born 21 June 1959; Son of Raymond Baron and Kathleen Baron, née Whittlestone; Married Thalia Mayson, née Laird 1992 (2 daughters).

Education: Attended various state and grammar schools, finishing Sixth Form at Queen's College, Taunton, Somerset; Jesus College, Cambridge (BA history and economics 1982); Royal Military College Sandhurst (1984); Limited German and Farsi.

Non-political career: Director: Henderson Private Investors Ltd 1987-99, Rothschild Asset Management 1999-2001. Captain Royal Regiment of Fusiliers 1984-87.

Political career: Contested Basildon 1997 general election. Member for Billericay 2001-10, for Basildon and Billericay since 6 May 2010 general election; Shadow Minister for: Health 2002-03 (resigned over Iraq War), Health 2003-07; Opposition Whip 2007-10. *Select committees:* Member: Education and Skills 2001-02, Foreign Affairs 2010-17.

Political interests: Foreign affairs, economy, civil liberties, defence, cancer, British Council.

Other: Chair, The Fun Walk Trust; Director, Equi Ltd; Member, Chartered Institute for Securities and Investment (MCSI); Supports numerous charities courtesy of Investors Chronicle column/other donations; Northern Ireland and UN Medals. Harlequins Rugby Club.

Publications: Regular column for *Financial Times*'s Investors Chronicle; Co-author, The Future of Conservatism: Values Revisited (Biteback, 2011); The FT Guide to Investment Trusts (Pearson, 2013); Time to Recognise the Danger (RUSI, 2015); Hard Choices: Britain's Foreign Policy for a Dangerous World (Politeia, 2017).

Recreations: Walking, financial journalism, gardening, theatre, film.

John Baron MP, House of Commons, London SW1A 0AA
Tel: 020 7219 8138 *Fax:* 020 7219 1743 *Email:* baronj@parliament.uk
Constituency: Suites 2 and 3, Bowden Terminal, Luckyn Lane, Basildon, Essex SS14 3AX
Tel: 01268 520765 Website: www.johnbaron.co.uk

CONSERVATIVE

BAYNES, SIMON

Clwyd South *(Majority 1,239)*

Simon Robert Maurice Baynes. Born 21 April 1960; Son of Lt. Col Sir John and Lady Shirley Baynes; Married Margaret Anne Mary Boag 1992 (2 daughters).

Education: Shrewsbury School; Magdalene College, Cambridge (BA history 1982) (President Cambridge Union 1982); French, Spanish.

Non-political career: Partner, Cazenove & Co/JP Morgan Cazenove 1982-2006; Research Analyst, Spanish market, General Sales, European markets, Head, Latin American Department, Deputy Head, European equity capital markets, Ran Simon Baynes Books and Music, Shrewsbury 2008-13; Author, 2013-19.

Political career: Contested Montgomeryshire 2005, Dwyfor Meirionnydd 2010 and Clwyd South 2017 general elections. Member for Clwyd South since 12 December 2019. *Select committees:* Member: Welsh Affairs 2020-, Joint Committee on Consolidation, &c, Bills 2020-, Speaker's Advisory Committee on Works of Art 2020-. Contested Dwyfor Meirionnydd constituency 2011 and Clwyd South constituency 2016 National Assembly for Wales elections. Chair, Cambridge University Conservative Association 1982; Vice-chair, Vauxhall Conservative Association 1990-93; Deputy Chair, Welsh Conservatives 2008-11, 2019-20; Montgomeryshire Conservative Association: Chair 2018-19; President 2011-14; Deputy Chair, Clwyd South Conservative Association 2017-18. *Councils and public bodies:* Governor: Ysgol Pennant Penybontfawr, Powys 2008-12, Moreton Hall School, Shropshire 2015-18, Llanfyllin High School 2017-19; Powys County Council: Councillor 2008-12, Joint Leader, Conservative group; Councillor, Llanfyllin Town Council 2013-19; Mayor of Llanfyllin 2018-19.

Political interests: Affordable housing, elderly care, small business and shops, Europe, heritage and culture, rural affairs, youth issues; Continental Europe.

Other: Chair: Hartfield Village Hall, East Sussex 2003-06, North Powys Youth Music Trust 2005-12, Welsh Historic Gardens Trust 2016-19, Holroyd Community Theatre 2018-19; Trustee: Llanfyllin Workhouse 2005-12; Mid Wales Opera 2011-19, Llangollen International Musical Eisteddfod 2016-19; Fellow, Securities Institute; Founder and Trustee: Concertina Charitable Trust 1998-, Bodfach Charitable Trust 2008-; MA (Cantab); Choral Exhibitioner, Magdalene College, Cambridge; Dunster History Essay Prize, Magdalene College, Cambridge. Carlton Club.

Publications: Lake Vyrnwy – The Story of a Sporting Hotel (Quiller, 2019); The Forgotten Country House – Rise and Fall of Roundway Park (Quiller, 2019).

Recreations: Gardening, heritage, collecting memorabilia, playing piano and organ.

Simon Baynes MP, House of Commons, London SW1A 0AA
Tel: 020 7219 3709 *Email:* simon.baynes.mp@parliament.uk
Constituency: Unit 13, Big Padlock Business Centre, Vauxhall Business Park, Ruabon, Wrexham LL14 6HA
Tel: 01978 810319 Website: www.simonbaynes.co.uk *Twitter:* @baynes_simon

LABOUR

BECKETT, MARGARET

Derby South *(Majority 6,019)*

Margaret Mary Beckett. Born 15 January 1943; Daughter of late Cyril Jackson, carpenter, and Winifred Jackson, teacher; Married Lionel (Leo) Beckett 1979 (2 stepsons).

Education: Notre Dame High School, Manchester and Norwich; Manchester College of Science and Technology; John Dalton Polytechnic.

Non-political career: Student apprentice in metallurgy, AEI Manchester 1961-66; Experimental officer, Department of Metallurgy, Manchester University 1966-70; Industrial policy researcher, Labour Party 1970-74; Political adviser, Ministry of Overseas Development 1974; Principal researcher, Granada Television 1979-83. Member: Transport and General Workers' Union 1964-, National Union of Journalists.

Political career: Contested (as Margaret Jackson) Lincoln February 1974 general election. Member for Lincoln October 1974-79. Contested Lincoln 1979 general election. Member (as Margaret Beckett) for Derby South 1983-2010, for Derby South (revised boundary) since 6 May 2010 general election; PPS to Judith Hart as Minister of Overseas Development 1974-75; Assistant Government Whip 1975-76; Parliamentary Under-Secretary of State, Department of Education and Science 1976-79; Shadow Minister, Social Security 1984-89; Shadow Chief Secretary to the Treasury 1989-92; Shadow Leader, House of Commons 1992-94; Deputy Leader, Labour Party and Opposition 1992-94; Leader of Opposition May-July 1994; Shadow Secretary of State for Health 1994-95; Shadow President of the Board of Trade 1995-97; President of the Board of Trade 1997-98; Secretary of State for Trade and Industry 1997-98; President of the Council and Leader of the House of Commons 1998-2001; Secretary of State for: Environment, Food and Rural Affairs 2001-06, Foreign and Commonwealth Affairs (Foreign Secretary) 2006-07; Minister for Housing and Planning (attending Cabinet), Department for Communities and Local Government 2008-09; Chair Intelligence and Security Committee 2008-10; Contested Speaker election 2009. *Select committees:* Chair: Modernisation of the House of Commons 1998-2001; Joint Committee on National Security Strategy 2010-. Labour Party: Member 1963-, Secretary, Trades Council and Labour Party, Swinton and Pendlebury 1968-70, National Executive Committee: Member 1980-81, 1985-86, 1988-97, 2011-, Chair 2020-, Member: Tribune Group, Socialist Education Committee, Labour Women's Action Committee, Socialist Environment and Resources Association, Chair, Environment, Energy and Culture Policy Commission. *Councils and public bodies:* Member, Committee on Standards in Public Life 2010-.

Political interests: Industry, climate change, nuclear disarmament.

Other: Member: Amnesty International, Anti-Apartheid Movement, Fabian Society, Global Zero, Top Level Group on Nuclear non-proliferation; Hon. DUniv, Derby University; PC 1993; DBE 2013.

Publications: The Need For Consumer Protection (1972); The National Enterprise Board; The Nationalisation of Shipbuilding, Ship Repair and Marine Engineering; Renewing the NHS (1995); Vision for Growth – A New Industrial Strategy for Britain (1996).

Recreations: Cooking, reading, caravanning.

Rt Hon Dame Margaret Beckett DBE MP, House of Commons, London SW1A 0AA
Tel: 020 7219 5135 (casework) *Fax:* 020 7219 4780 *Email:* margaret.beckett.mp@parliament.uk
Constituency: No constituency office publicised
Tel: 01332 345636 *Email:* james@derbylabourparty.co.uk

SINN FÉIN

BEGLEY, ÓRFHLAITH

West Tyrone *(Majority 7,478)*

Órfhlaith Acife Begley. Born 19 December 1991; Daughter of Seán Begley.

Education: Queen's University, Belfast (law and politics).

Political career: MP for West Tyrone since 3 May 2018 by-election.

Órfhlaith Begley MP, House of Commons, London SW1A 0AA
Tel: 020 7219 3000 *Email:* orfhlaith.begley.mp@parliament.uk
Constituency: No constituency office publicised
Email: orfhlaith.begley@sinnfein.ie *Twitter:* @OrfhlaithBegley

LABOUR

BEGUM, APSANA

Poplar and Limehouse *(Majority 28,904)*

Born May 1990.

Education: Mulberry School for Girls; Queen Mary, University of London.

Non-political career: Unite; UNISON.

Political career: Member for Poplar and Limehouse since 12 December 2019. *Select committees:* Member, Education 2020-. Secretary, Tower Hamlets Labour Party 2017-.

Political interests: Public services, inequalities.

Apsana Begum MP, House of Commons, London SW1A 0AA
Tel: 020 7219 6826 *Email:* apsana.begum.mp@parliament.uk
Constituency: No constituency office publicised
Website: apsanabegum.com *Twitter:* @ApsanaBegumMP

CONSERVATIVE

BELL, AARON

Newcastle-under-Lyme *(Majority 7,446)*

Aaron Stuart Bell. Born 25 February 1980; Married Emily (3 children).

Education: St Olave's Grammar School, Orpington; Episcopal High School, Virginia, USA; St John's College, Oxford (MA Philosophy, Politics and Economics 2001).

Non-political career: Graduate scheme and various roles, Ladbrokes 2003-06; Trading Development Manager, Bet365 2006-19; Investor, DivideBuy 2015-.

Political career: Contested Don Valley 2017 general election. Member for Newcastle-under-Lyme since 12 December 2019. *Select committees:* Member: Science and Technology 2020-, Procedure 2020-, Joint Committee on Fixed-Term Parliaments Act 2020-. East Staffordshire Conservative Association: Treasurer 2016-19, Deputy Chair 2019-20. *Councils and public bodies:* Former School Governor. Newcastle-under-Lyme Town Deal Board.

Political interests: Regeneration, science and technology, NHS, town centres, taxation reform.

Recreations: Sport, especially cricket, quizzing.

Aaron Bell MP, House of Commons, London SW1A 0AA
Tel: 020 7219 5610 *Email:* aaron.bell.mp@parliament.uk
Constituency: 3 Queens Parade, Newcastle-under-Lyme ST5 1RW
Tel: 01782 308102 Website: www.aaronbell.org.uk *Twitter:* @AaronBell4NUL

LABOUR

BENN, HILARY

Leeds Central *(Majority 19,270)*

Hilary James Wedgwood Benn. Born 26 November 1953; Son of late Tony Benn (MP for Bristol South East 1950-61, 1963-83 and Chesterfield 1984-2001) and late Caroline Middleton De Camp; Married Rosalind Retey 1973 (died 1979); married Sally Clark 1982 (3 sons 1 daughter).

Education: Holland Park Comprehensive School; Sussex University (BA Russian and East European studies 1974).

Non-political career: Research officer and latterly head of policy and communications, MSF 1975-97; Special adviser to David Blunkett as Secretary of State for Education and Employment 1997-99. Member, Unite.

Political career: Contested Ealing North 1983 and 1987 general elections. Member for Leeds Central 10 June 1999 by-election to 2010, for Leeds Central (revised boundary) since 6 May 2010 general election; Parliamentary Under-Secretary of State: Department for International Development 2001-02, Home Office (Community and Custodial Provision) 2002-03; Department for International Development: Minister of State 2003, Secretary of State 2003-07; Secretary of State for Environment, Food and Rural Affairs 2007-10; Shadow Secretary of State for Environment, Food and Rural Affairs 2010; Shadow Leader of the House of Commons 2010-11; Member: House of Commons Commission 2010-11, Speaker's Committee for the Independent Parliamentary Standards Authority 2011-12; Shadow Secretary of State for: Communities and Local Government 2011-15, Foreign and Commonwealth Affairs (Shadow Foreign Secretary) 2015-16. *Select committees:* Member: Environment, Transport and Regional Affairs 1999-2001, Environment, Transport and Regional Affairs (Environment Sub-committee) 1999-2001; Chair, Exiting the European Union/Future Relationship with the European Union 2016-21; Member, Liaison 2016-. Joint vice-chair, PLP Departmental Committee for Education and Employment 2000-01. Member: Labour Party Society – Stronger, Safer Communities Policy Commission as DCLG Shadow Secretary of State 2011-15, Labour Party Britain in the World Policy Commission as Shadow Foreign Secretary 2015-16. *Councils and public bodies:* London Borough of Ealing: Councillor 1979-99, Deputy Leader 1986-90, Chair, Education Committee 1986-90; Member, Association of Metropolitan Authorities Education Committee 1986-90; Chair, Association of London Authorities Education Committee 1989-90.

Political interests: European Union, foreign affairs, international development, home affairs, education, employment, trade unions, environment, urban policy, climate change; Democratic Republic of the Congo, European Union, Sudan, USA.

Other: Minister of the Year *House Magazine* 2006, 2007; Politicians' Politician Channel 4 2006; Parliamentarian of the Year, League Against Cruel Sports 2011; Spectator Parliamentarian of the Year 2016; PC 2003.

Publications: Contributor: Beyond 2002: Long-term policies for Labour (Profile Books, 1999), The Forces of Conservatism (IPPR, 1999), Men who made Labour (Routledge, 2006), Politics for a New Generation (IPPR, 2007), The End of the Peer Show: Responses to the Draft Bill on Lords Reform (2011).

Recreations: Watching sport, gardening.

Rt Hon Hilary Benn MP, House of Commons, London SW1A 0AA
Tel: 020 7219 5770 *Email:* hilary.benn.mp@parliament.uk
Constituency: Unity Business Centre, 26 Roundhay Road, Leeds, West Yorkshire LS7 1AB
Tel: 0113-244 1097 *Email:* boxj@parliament.uk Website: www.hilarybennmp.com
Twitter: @HilaryBennMP

CONSERVATIVE

BENTON, SCOTT

Blackpool South *(Majority 3,690)*

Scott Lloyd Benton. Born 1 July 1987; Single.

Education: Rastrick High School; Nottingham University (BA theology 2009, MA theology 2010).

Non-political career: Former primary school teacher; Parliamentary Assistant to Craig Whittaker MP 2013-19.

Political career: Contest Huddersfield 2017 general election. Member for Blackpool South since 12 December 2019. *Select committees:* Member, Northern Ireland Affairs 2020-. Contested Strangford 2017 Northern Ireland Assembly election. Deputy Chair: Calder Valley Conservative Association, 2012-16, Halifax Conservative Association 2015-16; Member, Conservative Friends of Israel. *Councils and public bodies:* Calderdale Council: Councillor 2011-, Deputy Leader of the Council 2014-15, Leader, Conservative group 2016-.

Political interests: Foreign policy, defence, local government; Israel, Middle East, USA.

Other: Member: Society for the Protection of the Unborn Child, Christian Institute.

Recreations: Football.

Scott Benton MP, House of Commons, London SW1A 0AA
Tel: 020 7219 3000 *Email:* scott.benton.mp@parliament.uk
Constituency: Lancaster House, Amy Johnson Way, Blackpool FY4 2RP
Tel: 01253 361350 Website: www.scottbenton.org.uk *Twitter:* @ScottBentonMP

CONSERVATIVE

BERESFORD, PAUL

Mole Valley *(Majority 12,041)*

Alexander Paul Beresford. Born 6 April 1946; Son of Raymond and Joan Beresford; Married Julie Haynes (3 sons 1 daughter).

Education: Waimea College, New Zealand; Otago University, Dunedin, New Zealand (BDS 1970).

Non-political career: Dental surgeon, Beresford Dental Practice. Member, National Farmers' Union.

Political career: Member for Croydon Central 1992-97, for Mole Valley 1997-2010, for Mole Valley (revised boundary) since 6 May 2010 general election; Parliamentary Under-Secretary of State, Department of the Environment 1994-97; Member, House of Commons Commission 2010-19; Board Member, Parliamentary Office of Science and Technology (POST) 2015-16. *Select committees:* Member: Education 1992-94, Procedure 1997-2001, Environment, Transport and Regional Affairs 2000-01, Environment, Transport and Regional Affairs (Environment Sub-Committee) 2001, Environment, Transport and Regional Affairs (Transport Sub-Committee) 2001, Transport, Local Government and the Regions 2001-02, Transport, Local Government and the Regions (Urban Affairs Sub-Committee) 2001-02, ODPM/ Communities and Local Government 2002-10, ODPM/Communities and Local Government (Urban Affairs Sub-Committee) 2003-05, Finance and Services 2010-15, Standards and Privileges 2010-13, Joint Committee on Security 2010-15, Standards 2013-17, Privileges 2013-17, Liaison 2015-19; Chair, Administration 2015-19. 1922 Committee: Secretary 2002-06, Member, Executive 2006-07. *Councils and public bodies:* London Borough of Wandsworth: Councillor 1978-94, Leader 1983-92.

Political interests: Inner cities, housing, education, health; Australia, Fiji, New Zealand, Samoa.

Other: Fellow, Industry and Parliament Trust 2002; British Dental Association; British Academy/Cosmetic Dentistry; British Endodontic Society; Kt 1990.

Recreations: DIY, reading.

Sir Paul Beresford MP, House of Commons, London SW1A 0AA
Tel: 020 7219 5018 *Email:* annie.winsbury@parliament.uk
Constituency: 212 Barnett Wood Lane, Ashtead, Surrey KT21 2DB
Tel: 01306 883312 *Email:* office@molevalleyconservatives.org.uk
Website: www.molevalleyconservatives.org.uk

CONSERVATIVE

BERRY, JAKE

Rossendale and Darwen *(Majority 9,522)*

James Jacob Gilchrist Berry. Born 29 December 1978; Married Charlotte 2009 (divorced 2016); Partner Alice Robinson (1 son).

Education: Liverpool College; Sheffield University (BA law 2000); Chester College (law finals).

Non-political career: Property lawyer, Halliwells LLP.

Political career: Member for Rossendale and Darwen since 6 May 2010 general election; PPS: to Grant Shapps: as Minister of State for Housing and Local Government 2010-12, as Minister without Portfolio, Cabinet Office and Chairman Conservative Party 2012-15, to Greg Hands as Chief Secretary to the Treasury 2015-16; Parliamentary Under-Secretary of State (Minister for the Northern Powerhouse and Local Growth): Department for Communities and Local Government/Ministry of Housing, Communities and Local Government 2017-19, Department for Business, Energy and Industrial Strategy 2019; Minister of State for the Northern Powerhouse and Local Growth: Cabinet Office 2019-20, Ministry of Housing, Communities and Local Government (also attending Cabinet) 2019-20. *Select committees:* Member, Finance 2015-17. Member, Number 10 Policy Advisory Board (Housing, Transport and Environment).

Other: Legal Consultant, Squire Patton Boggs 2014-15, 2020-; Legal Equity Partner, Unlimited Green Energy LLP 2020-; PC 2019.

Recreations: Walking, water-skiing.

Rt Hon Jake Berry MP, House of Commons, London SW1A 0AA
Tel: 020 7219 7214 *Email:* jake.berry.mp@parliament.uk
Constituency: Cheadle House, 8 Kay Street, Rawtenstall, Rossendale BB4 7LS
Tel: 01706 215547 Website: www.jakeberry.org *Twitter:* @JakeBerry

LABOUR

BETTS, CLIVE

Sheffield South East *(Majority 4,289)*

Chair, Select Committee on Housing, Communities and Local Government

Clive James Charles Betts. Born 13 January 1950; Son of late Harold and Nellie Betts; Civil partner James Thomas 2011.

Education: King Edward VII School, Sheffield; Pembroke College, Cambridge (BA economics and politics 1971).

Non-political career: Economist, Trades Union Congress 1971-73; Local government economist: Derbyshire County Council 1973-74, South Yorkshire County Council 1974-86, Rotherham Borough Council 1986-91. Member, TGWU.

Political career: Contested Sheffield Hallam October 1974 and Louth 1979 general elections. Member for Sheffield Attercliffe 1992-2010, for Sheffield South East since 6 May 2010 general election; Opposition Whip 1996-97; Assistant Government Whip 1997-98; Government Whip 1998-2001. *Select committees:* Member: Treasury 1996-97, Selection 1997-2001, Transport, Local Government and the Regions 2001-02, Transport, Local Government and the Regions (Urban Affairs Sub-committee) 2001-02, ODPM/Communities and Local Government 2002-10, ODPM/Communities and Local Government (Urban Affairs Sub-committee) 2003-05, Finance and Services 2005-10, 2010-15, Chairmen's Panel/Panel of Chairs 2009-, Yorkshire and the Humber 2009-10, Reform of the House of Commons 2009-10; Chair, Communities and Local Government/Housing, Communities and Local Government 2010-; Member: Liaison 2010-, National Policy Statements Sub-committee 2010-15, 2017-19, Finance 2015-. Member, Labour Leader's Campaign Team, with responsibility for Environment and Local Government 1995-96; Patron, LGBT Labour. *Councils and public bodies:* Sheffield City Council: Councillor 1976-92, Chair: Housing Committee 1980-86, Finance Committee 1986-88, Leader 1987-92; Vice-chair, Association of Metropolitan Authorities 1988-91; Chair, South Yorkshire Pensions Authority 1989-92; Vice-President, Local Government Association 2010-.

Political interests: Local and regional government, housing, planning, regeneration, transport; Bosnia, Iran, Middle East, Netherlands, Portugal, Serbia, Ukraine.

Other: Trustee, Parliamentary Pension Scheme; Fellow, Industry and Parliament Trust 1997; President, South East Sheffield Citizens' Advice Bureau 1998-.

Recreations: Supporting Sheffield Wednesday FC, playing squash, cricket, walking, real ale, scuba diving.

Clive Betts MP, House of Commons, London SW1A 0AA
Tel: 020 7219 5114 *Email:* officeofclivebettsmp@parliament.uk
Constituency: PO Box 6031, Sheffield, South Yorkshire S12 9EQ
Tel: 0114-275 7788 Website: clivebettsmp.wordpress.com

CONSERVATIVE

BHATTI, SAQIB

Meriden *(Majority 22,836)*

PPS to Elizabeth Truss as Secretary of State for International Trade, President of the Board of Trade and Minister for Women and Equalities

Mohammad Saqib Bhatti. Born 18 June 1985.

Education: King Edward VI School for Boys; London School of Economics and Political Science (LLB law 2007).

Non-political career: Assistant manager, Deloitte 2007-10; Associate and director, Younis Bhatti & Company Ltd 2011-; Senior policy adviser, Alliance of Conservatives and Reformists in Europe 2016-19.

Political career: Member for Meriden since 12 December 2019; PPS to Elizabeth Truss as Secretary of State for International Trade, President of the Board of Trade and Minister for Women and Equalities 2020-. *Councils and public bodies:* Director: Greater Birmingham and Solihull Local Enterprise Partnership 2015-, Broad Street Business Improvement District 2013-; Greater Birmingham Chambers of Commerce: Vice-President 2017-18, President 2018-.

Political interests: Education, investment, jobs, green belt.

Other: Substitute Member, UK Delegation to Parliamentary Assembly, Council of Europe 2020-; Vice-President, Institute of Asian Businesses 2011-13; Lunar Society 2012-16: Executive Committee Member, Chair of Membership Committee; Asian Business Chamber of Commerce: President 2014-18, Honorary Chair 2018-; Co-Secretary-General, Muslims for Britain 2016; Board Member, West Midlands Reserve Forces and Cadets Association; Institute of Chartered Accountants in England and Wales; Honorary Doctorate, Aston University.

Recreations: Horse riding, hockey.

Saqib Bhatti MP, House of Commons, London SW1A 0AA
Tel: 020 7219 3423 *Email:* saqib.bhatti@parliament.uk
Constituency: 631 Warwick Road, Solihull B91 1AR
Tel: 0121-711 7029 Website: www.saqibbhatti.org.uk *Twitter:* @bhatti_saqib

SCOTTISH NATIONAL PARTY

BLACK, MHAIRI

Paisley and Renfrewshire South *(Majority 10,679)*

SNP Shadow Secretary of State for Scotland

Born 12 September 1994.

Education: Lourdes Secondary School; Glasgow University (BA politics and public policy 2015).

Political career: Member for Paisley and Renfrewshire South since 7 May 2015 general election; SNP: Spokesperson for: Pensions 2017-19, Youth Affairs 2017-18, Women and Equalities 2018-19, Disabilities 2018-19, Shadow Secretary of State for Scotland 2020-. *Select committees:* Member: Work and Pensions 2015-17, Scottish Affairs 2020-. Member, SNP 2011-.

Political interests: Social justice, powers for Scotland.

Other: Volunteer, Oxfam; Women Against State Pension Inequality (WASPI).

Recreations: Football, Partick Thistle FC supporter.

Mhairi Black MP, House of Commons, London SW1A 0AA
Tel: 020 7219 5558 *Email:* mhairi.black.mp@parliament.uk
Constituency: 9 Wellmeadow Street, Paisley PA1 2EF
Tel: 0141-571 4370 Website: mhairiblack.scot *Twitter:* @MhairiBlack

SCOTTISH NATIONAL PARTY

BLACKFORD, IAN

Ross, Skye and Lochaber *(Majority 9,443)*

Leader, SNP Westminster Group

Born 14 May 1961; Married Ann.

Non-political career: Director, UBS Philips and Drew 1989-93; Managing director: Natwest Markets 1993-96, Deutsche Bank 1999-2002, First Seer 2003-; Investor relations, CSM 2005-12; Commsworld: Non-executive director 2006-15, Chair 2015-; Golden Charter Trust: Non-executive director 2008-15, Chair 2015-.

Political career: Contested Ayr 1997 general election and Paisley South November 1997 by-election. Member for Ross, Skye and Lochaber since 7 May 2015 general election; SNP: Spokesperson for Pensions 2015-17, Leader, Westminster Group 2017-; Member, Intelligence and Security Committee 2017-19. *Select committees:* Member, Petitions 2015-16. Scottish National Party: Member 1970s-, Member, National Executive Committee, National treasurer.

Political interests: Connectivity, both digital and transport, anti-austerity.

Other: Chair, North West Skye Recreational Association; Director, Cuillin FM; Non-executive director: Edinburgh Bicycle Cooperative 2008-13, New City Agenda 2017; PC 2017.

Recreations: Hibernian FC supporter.

Rt Hon Ian Blackford MP, House of Commons, London SW1A 0AA
Tel: 020 7219 3494 *Email:* ian.blackford.mp@parliament.uk
Constituency: 29 High Street, Dingwall IV15 9RU
Tel: 01349 866397
Mamore House, The Parade, Fort William PH33 6BA
Tel: 01397 700030 Website: www.ianblackford.scot *Twitter:* @Ianblackford_MP

CONSERVATIVE

BLACKMAN, BOB

Harrow East *(Majority 8,170)*

Robert John Blackman. Born 26 April 1956; Son of Robert Blackman and Winifred Blackman; Married Nicola 1988 (no children).

Education: Preston Manor High School; Liverpool University (BSc physics and maths 1978) (Union President 1978-79).

Non-political career: Sales, Unisys 1979-90; British Telecom 1991-2010: Sales Manager 1991-95, Sales Tutor, Training College 1995-98, Regulatory Compliance Manager 1998-2010. Member, Connect.

Political career: Contested Brent South 1992, Bedford 1997 and Brent North 2005 general elections. Member for Harrow East since 6 May 2010 general election. *Select committees:* Member: Communities and Local Government/Housing, Communities and Local Government 2010-, Backbench Business 2012-, Procedure 2015-19. Secretary, 1922 Committee 2015-; Chairman, Conservative Backbench Policy Committee on Foreign Affairs 2017-19. AM for Brent and Harrow constituency, London Assembly 2004-08. Vice-chair: National Association of Conservative Graduates 1981-87, Brent South Conservative Association 1986-87; Chair, Brent South Conservative Association 1987-90; Board member, Conservative Party 2020-. *Councils and public bodies:* London Borough of Brent Council: Councillor 1986-2010, Conservative Group Leader 1990-2010, Council Leader 1991-96, Deputy Council Leader 2006-10; Governor: Preston Manor High School, Wembley Primary School; Vice-President, Local Government Association 2016-.

Political interests: Local government, science, communications, sport, public expenditure, housing, housing benefit reform and welfare reform; Azerbaijan, Bangladesh, Brazil, India, Iran, Israel, Italy, Nepal, Sri Lanka, USA.

Other: Member: Executive Committee, Commonwealth Parliamentary Association UK 2015-16, 2018-, Executive Committee, British Group, Inter- Parliamentary Union 2015-; St Luke's Hospice, Cancer Research; Padma Shri 2020.

Recreations: Tottenham Hotspur FC, bridge, chess, reading, cricket.

Bob Blackman MP, House of Commons, London SW1A 0AA
Tel: 020 7219 7082 *Email:* bob.blackman.mp@parliament.uk
Constituency: 209 Headstone Lane, Harrow HA2 6ND
Tel: 020 8421 3323 Website: www.bobblackman.org.uk *Twitter:* @BobBlackman

SCOTTISH NATIONAL PARTY

BLACKMAN, KIRSTY

Aberdeen North *(Majority 12,670)*

SNP Economy Team Member

Kirsty Ann Blackman. Born 20 March 1986; Married Luke (2 children).

Education: Robert Gordon's College, Aberdeen; Aberdeen University (medicine) (did not complete degree); Open University (mathematics).

Non-political career: Former parliamentary assistant to Nigel Don MSP, Brian Adam MSP and Mark McDonald MSP.

Political career: Member for Aberdeen North since 7 May 2015 general election; SNP Spokesperson for: House of Lords 2015-17, Economy 2017-19; Deputy Leader, SNP Westminster Group 2017-20; SNP Economy Team Member 2021-; Member: Speaker's Committee on the Electoral Commission 2017-19, Speaker's Committee for the Independent Parliamentary Standards Authority 2017-19. *Select committees:* Member: Scottish Affairs 2015-16, European Statutory Instruments 2018-, Procedure 2019-. *Councils and public bodies:* Aberdeen City Council: Councillor 2007-15, Convener, SNP Group 2009-15.

Political interests: Welfare, anti-trident.

Other: Trustee: Aberdeen International Football Festival -2012; Aberdeen Endowment Trust 2007-15; Director, Aberdeen Exhibition and Conference Centre -2013; Representative, Epilepsy Association of Scotland. Granite City Wanderers Hockey Club 2006-11.

Kirsty Blackman MP, House of Commons, London SW1A 0AA
Tel: 020 7219 8791 *Email:* kirsty.blackman.mp@parliament.uk
Constituency: 46 John Street, Aberdeen, Aberdeenshire AB25 1LL
Tel: 01224 633285 *Twitter:* @KirstySNP

LABOUR

BLAKE, OLIVIA

Sheffield, Hallam *(Majority 712)*

Olivia Frances Blake Dagnall. Born 10 March 1990; Daughter of Judith Blake, Leader of Leeds Council, now Baroness Blake of Leeds (qv); Married Lewis Dagnall.

Education: Sheffield University (biomedical science).

Non-political career: GMB.

Political career: Member for Sheffield, Hallam since 12 December 2019; PPS to: Jo Stevens as Shadow Secretary of State for Digital, Culture, Media and Sport 2020, Ian Murray as Shadow Secretary of State for Scotland 2020. *Select committees:* Member, Public Accounts 2020-. *Councils and public bodies:* Non-Executive Director, Sheffield Health and Social Care Trust; Sheffield City Council: Councillor 2014-20, Cabinet Member for Finance, Deputy Leader of the Council.

Political interests: Public services, climate change, Brexit.

Olivia Blake MP, House of Commons, London SW1A 0AA
Tel: 020 7219 3552 *Email:* olivia.blake.mp@parliament.uk
Constituency: No constituency office publicised
Website: www.oliviablake.org.uk *Twitter:* @_OliviaBlake

LABOUR

BLOMFIELD, PAUL

Sheffield Central *(Majority 27,273)*

Paul Christopher Blomfield. Born 25 August 1953; Son of Henry and Mabel Blomfield; Married Linda McAvan 2000 (1 son from previous marriage).

Education: Abbeydale Boys Grammar School, Sheffield; Tadcaster Grammar School; St John's College, York (theology); Teacher training (CertEd 1976).

Non-political career: Sheffield University 1978-2010: Various posts 1978-2003, General manager, Students' Union 2003-10. Member, National Executive Committee and Vice-President, National Union of Students 1976-78; Former branch secretary, Unison; Member: Amicus/Unite, GMB.

Political career: Member for Sheffield Central since 6 May 2010 general election; PPS to Hilary Benn: as Shadow Leader of the House of Commons 2010-11, as Shadow Secretary of State for Communities and Local Government 2011-15, as Shadow Foreign Secretary 2015-16; Shadow Minister for: Exiting the European Union 2016-20, Cabinet Office and International Trade (Brexit and EU Negotiations) 2020. *Select committees:* Member: Business, Innovation and Skills 2010-16, Joint Committee on Able Marine Energy Park Development Consent Order 2014 2014-15, Education, Skills and the Economy Sub-committee 2015-16. Chair, Labour for Democracy 2012-. Member: Co-operative Party, Labour Party 1978-; Chair, Sheffield Labour Party 1993-2008. *Councils and public bodies:* Governor, Sheffield City Polytechnic 1982-92; Sheffield City Trust: Board member 1994-2008, Chair 1997-2008.

Political interests: Universities, education, skills, housing, voluntary and community sector, financial inclusion, small businesses; Southern Africa, Burma, Kashmir, Palestine, Somaliland.

Other: Executive committee, Anti-Apartheid Movement 1978-94; Former executive member, Sheffield Race Equality Council.

Recreations: Walking, cycling, Sheffield United FC season ticket holder.

Paul Blomfield MP, House of Commons, London SW1A 0AA
Tel: 020 7219 7142 *Email:* paul.blomfield.mp@parliament.uk
Constituency: Unit 4, Edmund Road Business Centre, 135 Edmund Road, Sheffield S2 4ED
Tel: 0114-272 2882 Website: www.paulblomfield.co.uk *Twitter:* @paulblomfieldmp

CONSERVATIVE

BLUNT, CRISPIN

Reigate *(Majority 18,310)*

Crispin Jeremy Rupert Blunt. Born 15 July 1960; Son of late Major-General Peter and Adrienne Blunt; Married Victoria Jenkins 1990 (separated) (1 son 1 daughter).

Education: Wellington College, Berkshire; Royal Military Academy, Sandhurst (commissioned 1980); University College, Durham University (BA politics 1984); Cranfield Institute of Technology (MBA 1991).

Non-political career: District agent, Forum of Private Business 1991-92; Political consultant, Politics International 1993; Special adviser to Malcolm Rifkind MP: as Secretary of State for Defence 1993-95, as Foreign Secretary 1995-97; Non-executive director, Social Investment Business Group 2013-17. Army Officer 1979-90; Regimental duty 13th/18th Royal Hussars (QMO) in England, Germany and Cyprus.

Political career: Contested West Bromwich East 1992 general election. Member for Reigate 1997-2010, for Reigate (revised boundary) since 6 May 2010 general election; Opposition Spokesperson for Northern Ireland 2001-02; Shadow Minister for Trade and Industry 2002-03; Opposition Whip 2004-09; Shadow Minister for National Security 2009-10; Parliamentary Under-Secretary of State, Ministry of Justice 2010-12. *Select committees:* Member: Defence 1997-2000, 2003-04, Environment, Transport and Regional Affairs 2000-01, Environment, Transport and Regional Affairs (Environment Sub-Committee) 2000-01, Finance and Services 2005-09, Joint Committee on Voting Eligibilty (Prisoners) Bill 2013, Liaison 2015-17; Chair, Foreign Affairs 2015-17; Member: Joint Committee on the National Security Strategy 2015-17, Arms Export Controls 2016-17. Executive member, 1922 Committee 2000-01; Treasurer, Conservative Parliamentary Friends of India 2001-06; Conservative Middle East Council: Chair 2003-08, Vice-chair 2017-; Founder and Chair, Conservative Drug Policy Reform Group 2019-.

Political interests: Defence, foreign affairs, environment, energy, justice, drug policy; Middle East, India, USA.

Other: Reigate Priory Cricket, MCC; House of Lords and House of Commons Cricket Club.

Recreations: Cricket, skiing, gardening.

Crispin Blunt MP, House of Commons, London SW1A 0AA
Tel: 020 7219 2254 *Fax:* 020 7219 3373 *Email:* crispinbluntmp@parliament.uk
Constituency: Skinner House, 38-40 Bell Street, Reigate, Surrey RH2 7BA
Tel: 01737 222756 Website: www.blunt4reigate.com *Twitter:* @CrispinBlunt

CONSERVATIVE

BONE, PETER

Wellingborough *(Majority 18,540)*

Peter William Bone. Born 19 October 1952; Son of late William and Marjorie Bone; Married Jeanette Sweeney 1981 (2 sons 1 daughter).

Education: Stewards Comprehensive School, Harlow, Essex; Westcliff High School for Boys, Essex.

Non-political career: Financial director, Essex Electronics and Precision Engineering Group 1977-83; Press secretary to Paul Channon MP 1982-84; Chief executive, High Tech Electronics Company 1983-90; Managing director: Palm Travel (West) Ltd 1990-, AJWB Travel Ltd.

Political career: Contested Islwyn 1992, Pudsey 1997 and Wellingborough 2001 general elections. Member for Wellingborough 2005-10, for Wellingborough (revised boundary) since 6 May 2010 general election. *Select committees:* Member: Joint Committee on Statutory Instruments and Commons Committee on Statutory Instruments 2005-10, Trade and Industry 2005-07, Health 2007-10, Backbench Business 2010-12, 2015-16, Chairmen's Panel/Panel of Chairs 2010-, Exiting the European Union/Future Relationship with the European Union 2017-21, Procedure 2017-19. Member, Executive, 1922 Committee 2007-12. Contested Mid and West Wales 1994 European Parliament election. Deputy chair, Southend West Conservative Association 1977-84; Member, National Union Executive Committee 1993-96; Founding Member: All Wales Conservative Policy Group (think tank), Conservatives for Britain 2015-16. *Councils and public bodies:* Councillor, Southend-on-Sea Borough Council 1977-86; Former member, Southern Airport Management Committee.

Political interests: European Union parliamentary reform, human trafficking.

Other: Secretary, Parliament First; Founding member, Grassroots Out 2015-16; Fellow, Institute of Chartered Accountants of England and Wales 1976. Wellingborough Golf Club; Wellingborough Old Grammarians.

Publications: Contributor: *Daily Telegraph*, *The Times*, *Daily Express*, *Western Mail*; Numerous TV appearances and radio interviews.

Recreations: Running marathons for charity, cricket.

Peter Bone MP, House of Commons, London SW1A 0AA
Tel: 020 7219 8496 *Fax:* 020 7219 0301 *Email:* bonep@parliament.uk
Constituency: 42 Midland Road, Wellingborough, Northamptonshire NN8 1LU
Tel: 01933 279343 *Twitter:* @PeterBoneUK

SCOTTISH NATIONAL PARTY

BONNAR, STEVEN

Coatbridge, Chryston and Bellshill *(Majority 5,624)*

SNP Agriculture and Rural Affairs Team Member

Education: Cardinal Newman High.

Non-political career: Loss Prevention Manager, BHS 2000-03; Loss Prevention Supervisor, Debenhams 2003-11; Internal Auditor, John Lewis Partnership 2011-15.

Political career: Member for Coatbridge, Chryston and Bellshill since 12 December 2019; SNP Environment, Food and Rural Affairs/Agriculture and Rural Affairs Team Member 2020-. *Councils and public bodies:* Councillor, North Lanarkshire Council 2015-.

Steven Bonnar MP, House of Commons, London SW1A 0AA
Tel: 020 7219 3000 *Email:* steven.bonnar.mp@parliament.uk
Constituency: Municipal Buildings, Kildonan Street, Coatbridge ML5 3BT
Tel: 01236 429939 Website: www.stevenbonnar.scot *Twitter:* @StevenBonnarSNP

CONSERVATIVE

BOTTOMLEY, PETER

Worthing West *(Majority 14,823)*

Peter James Bottomley. Born 30 July 1944; Son of Sir James Bottomley KCMG, HM Diplomatic Service, and Barbara Bottomley, social worker; Married Virginia Garnett 1967 (MP for South West Surrey 1984-2005 as Virginia Bottomley, now Baroness Bottomley of Nettlestone (qv)) (1 son 2 daughters).

Education: Comprehensive school, Washington DC; Westminster School, London; Trinity College, Cambridge (BA economics 1966, MA).

Non-political career: Industrial sales, industrial relations, industrial economics. Former member, TGWU.

Political career: Contested Greenwich, Woolwich West February and October 1974 general elections. Member for Greenwich, Woolwich West 1975 by-election to 1983, for Eltham 1983-97, for Worthing West 1997-2010, for Worthing West (revised boundary) since 6 May 2010 general election; PPS to: Cranley Onslow as Minister of State, Foreign and Commonwealth Office 1982-83, Norman Fowler as Secretary of State for Health and Social Security 1983-84; Parliamentary Under-Secretary of State: Department of Employment 1984-86, Department of Transport (Minister for Roads and Traffic) 1986-89, Northern Ireland Office (Agriculture, Environment) 1989-90; PPS to Peter Brooke as Secretary of State for Northern Ireland 1990; Father of the House 2019-. *Select committees:* Member: Standards and Privileges 1997-2002, Unopposed Bills (Panel) 1997-2015, Ecclesiastical Committee 2002-, Constitutional Affairs 2003-05, Joint Committee on the Draft Defamation Bill 2011, High Speed Rail (London-West Midlands) Bill 2014-16. President, Conservative Trade Unionists 1978-80; Founding member, Conservatives for Reform in Europe 2016.

Political interests: Southern Africa, El Salvador, USA.

Other: Member, UK Delegation: NATO Parliamentary Assembly, Organisation for Security and Co-operation in Europe Parliamentary Assembly; Trustee, Christian Aid 1978-84; Chair: Family Forum 1980-82, Church of England Children's Society 1982-84; Member, Council of Nacro 1997-2003; Fellow, Industry and Parliament Trust; Trustee, Dr Busby's Trustees (Willen) Main Charity; Court Member, Drapers' Company; Former Fellow, Institute of Personnel Management; Fellow, Institute of Road Safety Officers; Gold Medal, Institute of the Motor Industry 1988; Kt 2011. Former Parliamentary swimming and occasional dinghy sailing champion.

Recreations: Children, canoeing.

Sir Peter Bottomley MP, House of Commons, London SW1A 0AA
Tel: 020 7219 5060 *Fax:* 020 7219 1212 *Email:* bottomleyp@parliament.uk
Constituency: No constituency office publicised
Website: www.sirpeterbottomley.com

CONSERVATIVE

BOWIE, ANDREW West Aberdeenshire and Kincardine *(Majority 843)*

Andrew Campbell Bowie. Born 28 May 1987; Son of Donald Bowie and Karen Bowie (née Campbell); Married Madeleine (née Clarke) 2015.

Education: Inverurie Academy; Britannia Royal Naval College Dartmouth; Aberdeen University (MA history and politics 2013).

Non-political career: Junior Warfare Officer, Royal Navy 2007-10; Military Projects Co-ordinator, Divex 2013; North Scotland Campaign Manager, Conservative Party 2014-15; Parliamentary Assistant and Rural Affairs Policy Adviser to Ian Duncan MEP 2015-16; Head of Office to Liam Kerr MSP 2016-17. Midshipman/Sub Lieutenant, Royal Navy Feb 2007-10.

Political career: Member for West Aberdeenshire and Kincardine since 8 June 2017; Team PPS, Department for Digital, Culture, Media and Sport 2018; PPS to Theresa May as Prime Minister 2019. *Select committees:* Member: Work and Pensions 2017-18, Scottish Affairs 2020-. Vice-chairman, Conservative Party 2019-.

Political interests: Digital, culture, media, sport, Scotland, devolution, foreign affairs, defence, democratisation; France, Sweden, USA.

Other: Britannia Association; Carlton Club.

Recreations: Aberdeen Football Club Season ticket holder, hill walking, running.

Andrew Bowie MP, House of Commons, London SW1A 0AA
Tel: 020 7219 2791 *Email:* andrew.bowie.mp@parliament.uk
Constituency: Unit 6, 75 Highstreet, Banchory AB31 5TJ
Tel: 01330 705013 Website: www.andrewbowie.org.uk *Twitter:* @AndrewBowie_MP

LABOUR/
CO-OPERATIVE

BRABIN, TRACY Batley and Spen *(Majority 3,525)*

Tracy Lynn Brabin. Born 9 May 1961; Married Richard Platt 2005 (2 daughters).

Education: Loughborough University (BA drama); London College of Printing (MA screenwriting 2000).

Non-political career: Actress and screenwriter, Origin Films 2000-2012; Actress: David Pugh (theatre company) 2012-14, ITV 2014, Derby Playhouse 2014; Writer: Tracy Beaker, BBC 2004-06, Shameless, Channel Four 2010, Rollem 2014-, Noon Vision 2015, LAMDA 2015, Bob&Co 2015-.

Political career: Member for Batley and Spen since 20 October 2016 by-election; Shadow Minister for Education (Early Years) 2017-20; Shadow Secretary of State for Digital, Culture, Media and Sport 2020; Shadow Minister for Digital, Culture, Media and Sport (Cultural Industries) 2020. *Select committees:* Member, Women and Equalities 2016-17.

Other: Trustee, Harinder Veriah Trust.

Tracy Brabin MP, House of Commons, London SW1A 0AA
Tel: 020 7219 4594 *Email:* tracy.brabin.mp@parliament.uk
Constituency: 286 Oxford Road, Gomersal BD19 4PY
Tel: 01924 900036 Website: tracybrabinmp.com *Twitter:* @TracyBrabin

CONSERVATIVE

BRADLEY, BEN

Mansfield *(Majority 16,306)*

Benjamin David Bradley. Born 11 December 1989; Married Shanade 2015 (2 sons).

Education: Derby Grammar School; Mill Hill School; Bath University (sports science) (did not complete degree); Nottingham Trent University (BA politics 2013).

Non-political career: Administrator, Open University 2008-11; Landscape gardener 2009-10; Store assistant, Aldi 2011-12; Associate consultant, accountancy and finance, Hays 2013; Office of Mark Spencer MP: Campaign manager 2013-15, Constituency office manager 2015-17; Representing Nick Boles MP and Grantham and Stamford Constituency 2016-17.

Political career: Member for Mansfield since 8 June 2017; Team PPS, Ministry of Housing, Communities and Local Government 2019-20, PPS to Alok Sharma as Secretary of State for Business, Energy and Industrial Strategy 2020. *Select committees:* Member: Education 2018-19, Regulatory Reform 2018-19. Chair, Conservative Backbench Policy Committee on Digital, Culture, Media and Sport 2017-18. Hucknall Conservatives: Deputy Chair 2012-14, Chair 2016-17; Deputy Chair, Sherwood Constituency Conservative Association 2016-17; Vice-chair, Youth, Conservative Party 2018. *Councils and public bodies:* Ashfield District Council: Councillor 2015-17, Leader, Conservative Group 2015-17; Governor, Holgate Academy 2016-17; Councillor, Nottingham County Council 2017-.

Political interests: Education, young people, coalfield regeneration, sports, high streets.

Ben Bradley MP, House of Commons, London SW1A 0AA
Tel: 020 7219 3594 *Email:* ben.bradley.mp@parliament.uk
Constituency: 36 Church Street, Mansfield, Nottinghamshire NG18 1AE
Tel: 01623 372016 Website: www.benbradleymp.com *Twitter:* @BBradley_Mans

CONSERVATIVE

BRADLEY, KAREN

Staffordshire Moorlands *(Majority 16,428)*

Chair, Select Committee on Procedure

Karen Anne Bradley. Born 12 March 1970; Married Neil Bradley 2001 (2 sons).

Education: Buxton Girls School, Buxton; Imperial College, London (BSc mathematics 1991).

Non-political career: Student accountant, then manager, Deloittes 1991-98; Senior manager, KPMG 1998-2004, 2007-14; Self-employed economic and fiscal adviser.

Political career: Contested Manchester Withington 2005 general election. Member for Staffordshire Moorlands since 6 May 2010 general election; Assistant Government Whip 2012-13; Government Whip (Lord Commissioner of HM Treasury) 2013-14; Home Office: Parliamentary Under-Secretary of State: (Modern Slavery and Organised Crime) 2014-15, (Preventing Abuse and Exploitation) 2015-16, (Crime) 2016; Secretary of State for: Culture, Media and Sport 2016-18, Digital 2017-18, Northern Ireland 2018-19. *Select committees:* Member, Work and Pensions 2010-12; Procedure: Member 2011-12, Chair 2020-; Member: Administration 2012-14, Liaison 2020-. Secretary, 1922 Committee 2012.

Political interests: Economy, rural affairs, home affairs, childcare.

Other: Patron, Foxlowe Arts Centre, Leek; Trustee, Human Trafficking Foundation 2020-; Associate, Institute Chartered Accountants in England and Wales 1994; Member, Chartered Institute of Taxation 1995; Royal British Legion; PC 2016.

Recreations: Walking, cooking.

Rt Hon Karen Bradley MP, House of Commons, London SW1A 0AA
Tel: 020 7219 7215 *Email:* karen.bradley.mp@parliament.uk
Constituency: Unit 24, The Smithfield Centre, Haywood Street, Leek, Staffordshire ST13 5JW
Tel: 01538 382421 Website: www.karenbradley.co.uk

House of Commons MPs' Biographies

LABOUR

BRADSHAW, BEN

Exeter *(Majority 10,403)*

Benjamin Peter James Bradshaw. Born 30 August 1960; Son of late Canon Peter Bradshaw and late Daphne Bradshaw, teacher; Civil partner Neal Dalgleish 2006.

Education: Thorpe St Andrew School, Norwich; Sussex University (BA German 1982); Freiburg University, Germany; German, Italian.

Non-political career: BBC 1986-97: Reporter and presenter 1986-97, Berlin correspondent during fall of Berlin Wall 1989-91, Reporter *World At One* and *World This Weekend*, Radio 4 1991-97. Member: NUJ, GMB, USDAW.

Political career: Member for Exeter 1997-2010, for Exeter (revised boundary) since 6 May 2010 general election; Introduced Pesticides Act (Private Member's Bill) 1998; PPS to John Denham as Minister of State, Department of Health 2000-01; Parliamentary Under-Secretary of State, Foreign and Commonwealth Office 2001-02; Parliamentary Secretary, Privy Council Office 2002-03; Department for Environment, Food and Rural Affairs 2003-07: Parliamentary Under-Secretary of State 2003-06, Minister of State (MoS) 2006-07; MoS for Health Services, Department of Health 2007-09; Minister for the South West 2007-09; Secretary of State for Culture, Media and Sport 2009-10; Shadow Secretary of State for Culture, Olympics, Media and Sport 2010. *Select committees:* Member: European Scrutiny 1998-2001, Ecclesiastical Committee 2010-, Joint Committee on Privacy and Injunctions 2011-12, Culture, Media and Sport 2012-15, Health/Health and Social Care 2015-19. Labour Movement for Europe; Member: Labour Campaign for Electoral Reform, SERA, Christian Socialist Movement/ Christians on the Left; Contested Labour deputy leadership election 2015; Patron, LGBT Labour.

Political interests: Foreign affairs, environment, transport, modernisation of Parliament; Europe – particularly Germany and Italy, USA.

Other: Trustee, Terrence Higgins Trust 2011-; Member, Advisory Board, Humboldt University, Berlin; Honorary fellowship, Humboldt University, Berlin; Consumer Journalist of the Year, Argos 1989; Journalist of the Year, Anglo-German Foundation 1990; News Reporter award, Sony 1993; Politician of the Year, Stonewall awards 2009; PC 2009. Whipton Labour Club.

Publications: Numerous for the BBC on domestic and foreign affairs.

Recreations: Cycling, walking, cooking, music, ashtanga yoga.

Rt Hon Ben Bradshaw MP, House of Commons, London SW1A 0AA
Tel: 020 7219 6597 *Fax:* 020 7219 0950 *Email:* ben.bradshaw.mp@parliament.uk
Constituency: Labour HQ, 26b Clifton Hill, Exeter, Devon EX1 2DJ
Tel: 01392 424464 Website: www.benbradshaw.co.uk *Twitter:* @BenPBradshaw

CONSERVATIVE

BRADY, GRAHAM

Altrincham and Sale West *(Majority 6,139)*

Graham Stuart Brady. Born 20 May 1967; Son of John Brady, accountant, and Maureen Brady, née Birch, medical secretary; Married Victoria Lowther 1992 (1 son 1 daughter).

Education: Altrincham Grammar School; Durham University (BA law 1989).

Non-political career: Shandwick plc 1989-90; Assistant director of publications, Centre for Policy Studies 1990-92; Public affairs director, The Waterfront Partnership 1992-97.

Political career: Member for Altrincham and Sale West 1997-2010, for Altrincham and Sale West (revised boundary) since 6 May 2010 general election; PPS to Michael Ancram as Conservative Party Chairman 1999-2000; Opposition Whip 2000; Opposition Spokesperson for: Employment 2000-01, Schools 2001-03; PPS to Michael Howard as Leader of the Opposition 2003-04; Shadow Minister for Europe 2004-07. *Select committees:* Member: Education and Employment 1997-2001, Education and Employment (Employment Sub-Committee) 1997-2001, Office of the Deputy Prime Minister 2004-05, Office of the Deputy Prime Minister (Urban Affairs Sub-Committee) 2004-05, Treasury 2007-10, Reform of the House of Commons 2009-10, Chairmen's Panel/Panel of Chairs 2009-. Joint Secretary, Conservative Party Committee for Education and Employment 1997-2000; 1922 Committee: Member, executive 1998-2000, 2007-10, Chairman 2010-May 2019, September 2019-. Chair, Durham University Conservative Association 1987-88; National Union Executive Committee 1988; Chair, Northern Area Conservative Collegiate Forum 1987-89; Vice-chair, East

Berkshire Conservative Association 1993-95; Council Member, AECR 2015-. *Councils and public bodies:* Independent governor and member, audit committee, Manchester Metropolitan University 2008-11.

Political interests: Education, health, Europe; Commonwealth, Far East, British Overseas Territories.

Other: Vice-Patron, Friends of Rosie (research into children's cancer); Vice-President, Altrincham Chamber of Trade Commerce and Industry 1997-; Patron, Family Contact Line/ Counselling and Family Centre; Governor, Westminster Foundation for Democracy 2009-10; Panellist, Medical Practitioners Tribunal Service 2010-; Founding supporter, Change Britain 2016-; Stockdales, Genie Networks, Counselling and Family Centre, Friends of Rosie; Freeman, Burgess of Altrincham 2016; Honorary Doctor of Social Science, Bolton University 2018; Backbencher of the Year, *Spectator*/Threadneedle award 2010; Kt 2018. Carlton Club.

Publications: Towards an Employees' Charter – and Away From Collective Bargaining (Centre for Policy Studies, 1991); The Future of Conservatism: Values Revisited (Biteback, 2010); Editor, *House Magazine* 2017-.

Recreations: Family, gardening, reading.

Sir Graham Brady MP, House of Commons, London SW1A 0AA
Tel: 020 7219 1260 *Fax:* 020 7219 1649 *Email:* altsale@parliament.uk
Constituency: Altrincham and Sale West Conservative Association, Office 70, Atlantic Business Centre, Atlantic Street, Altrincham WA14 5NQ
Tel: 0161-904 8828 *Email:* office@altsale.org Website: www.grahambrady.co.uk
Twitter: @SirGrahamBrady

House of Commons MPs' Biographies

SINN FÉIN

BRADY, MICKEY

Newry and Armagh *(Majority 9,287)*

Michael Brady. Born 7 October 1950.

Non-political career: Project manager and worker, Newry Welfare Rights Centre.

Political career: Member for Newry and Armagh since 7 May 2015 general election. MLA for Newry and Armagh 7 March 2007 to 5 June 2015: Sinn Féin Spokesperson for: Benefits, Older People, Welfare. Social Development: Member 2007-11, Deputy Chair 2011-15; Member: Public Accounts 2007-08, Draft Sexual Offences (NI) Order 2007-08, Procedures 2008-11, Standards and Privileges 2010-11, Health, Social Services and Public Safety 2010-15, Conformity with Equality Requirements, Welfare Reform Bill 2012-13. *Councils and public bodies:* Governor, St Coleman's Abbey Primary School, Newry.

Other: Non-executive member, Committee of the Confederation of Community Groups, Newry.

Mickey Brady MP, House of Commons, London SW1A 0AA
Tel: 020 7219 5775 *Email:* mickey.brady.mp@parliament.uk
Constituency: c/o Newry Sinn Féin Office, 1 Kilmorey Terrace, Newry BT35 8DW
Tel: 028 3026 1693 Website: newryarmaghsinnfein.com *Twitter:* @MickeyBradySF

CONSERVATIVE

BRAVERMAN, SUELLA

Fareham *(Majority 26,086)*

Attorney General

Sue-Ellen Cassiana Braverman. Born 3 April 1980; Daughter of Chris and Uma Fernandes; Née Fernandes. Married Rael Braverman 2018 (1 son, expecting second child early 2021).

Education: Heathfield School, Pinner; Queens' College, Cambridge (MA law 2002); Universite de Paris I, Pantheon-Sorbonne (LLM); Admitted to the New York Bar 2006; French.

Non-political career: Called to the Bar, Middle Temple 2005; Barrister, No 5 Chambers, London, specialising in planning, public and judicial review 2005-15; Treasury Counsel Panel 2010-15.

Political career: Contested Leicester East 2005 general election. Member for Fareham since 7 May 2015 general election; Team PPS, HM Treasury 2017-18; Parliamentary Under-Secretary of State, Department for Exiting the European Union 2018; Attorney General 2020-. *Select committees:* Member: Education 2015-17, Joint Committee on the Draft Investigatory Powers

Bill 2015-16, Education, Skills and the Economy Sub-committee 2015-16. Contested Londonwide region 2012 London Assembly election. *Councils and public bodies:* Michaela Community School, Brent: Co-founder and Chair of Governors 2014-17, Governor 2017-18.

Political interests: Education, social mobility, local investment.

Other: Council of Europe UK Delegation: Committee for Legal Affairs and Human Rights; Chair, European Research Group 2017-18; Bar Counsel of England and Wales; New York State Bar; Co-founder and chair, Africa Justice Foundation 2010-14; Middle Temple Scholarship, Bar Vocational Course 2004; Pegasus Scholarship 2010; PC 2020.

Recreations: Cinema, theatre, camping.

Rt Hon Suella Braverman QC MP, House of Commons, London SW1A 0AA
Tel: 020 7219 8191 *Email:* suella.braverman.mp@parliament.uk
Constituency: 14 East Street, Fareham, Hampshire PO16 0BN
Tel: 01329 233573 *Email:* suella@suellabraverman.co.uk Website: www.suellabraverman.co.uk
Twitter: @SuellaBraverman

LABOUR

BRENNAN, KEVIN

Cardiff West *(Majority 10,986)*

Kevin Denis Brennan. Born 16 October 1959; Son of late Michael Brennan, steelworker, and Beryl Brennan, née Evans, school cook/cleaner; Married Amy Wack 1988 (1 daughter).

Education: St Alban's RC Comprehensive, Pontypool; Pembroke College, Oxford (BA philosophy, politics and economics 1982) (President Oxford Union 1982); University College of Wales, Cardiff (PGCE history 1985); Glamorgan University (MSc education management 1992); Welsh.

Non-political career: News editor, volunteer organiser, Cwmbran Community Press 1982-84; Head of economics and business studies, Radyr Comprehensive School 1985-94; Research officer to Rhodri Morgan MP 1995-99; Special adviser to Rhodri Morgan as First Minister, National Assembly for Wales 2000-01. Member: NUT 1984-94, TGWU/Unite 1995-, Musicians' Union 2003-.

Political career: Member for Cardiff West 2001-10, for Cardiff West (revised boundary) since 6 May 2010 general election; PPS to Alan Milburn as Chancellor of the Duchy of Lancaster 2004-05; Assistant Government Whip 2005-06; Government Whip 2006-07; Parliamentary Under-Secretary of State, Department for Children, Schools and Families 2007-08; Parliamentary Secretary, Cabinet Office 2008-09; Minister of State (Further Education, Skills, Apprenticeships and Consumer Affairs), Departments for Business, Innovation and Skills and Children, Schools and Families 2009-10; Shadow Minister for: Business, Innovation and Skills 2010, 2015-16, Education 2010-15; Culture, Media and Sport/Digital, Culture, Media and Sport: Shadow Minister for Arts and Heritage 2016-20, Deputy Shadow Secretary of State 2016-20. *Select committees:* Member: Public Administration 2001-05, 2010-11, Digital, Culture, Media and Sport 2020-. Chair, PLP Department Group for Northern Ireland 2020-. Chair, Cardiff West CLP 1998-2000; Member, Labour Campaign Electoral Reform. *Councils and public bodies:* Cardiff City Council: Councillor, Chair: Finance Committee 1993-96, Economic Scrutiny Committee 1999-2001.

Political interests: Economy, constitutional affairs, creative industries, education; Ireland, USA.

Other: Member, Fabian Society; Chair, Yes for Wales Cardiff 1997; Member, Bevan Foundation.

Recreations: Rugby, golf, reading, cricket, music, member parliamentary rock band 'MP4'.

Kevin Brennan MP, House of Commons, London SW1A 0AA
Tel: 020 7219 8156 *Email:* brennank@parliament.uk
Constituency: 395 Cowbridge Road East, Canton, Cardiff, South Glamorgan CF5 1JG
Tel: 029 2022 3207 Website: www.kevinbrennan.co.uk *Twitter:* @KevinBrennanMP

CONSERVATIVE

BRERETON, JACK

Stoke-on-Trent South *(Majority 11,271)*

PPS to Ben Wallace as Secretary of State for Defence

Jack Edgar Brereton. Born 3 May 1991; Married Laura (1 son).

Education: Keele University (politics); University College London.

Non-political career: Election consultancy; Parliamentary Assistant to Karen Bradley MP.

Political career: Contested Stoke-on-Trent Central 2017 by-election. Member for Stoke-on-Trent South since 8 June 2017; Member, Public Accounts Commission 2017-; Team PPS, Department for Education 2018-19; PPS to: Steve Barclay as Secretary of State for Exiting the European Union 2019-20, Ben Wallace as Secretary of State for Defence 2020-. *Select committees:* Member: Work and Pensions 2017-18, Transport 2018-19, Procedure 2020-. Chairman, Conservative Backbench Policy Committee on Transport 2017-19. Area Chairman, Conservative Future, Staffordshire Conservatives; Treasurer, Stoke-on-Trent Conservative Federation; Member, Conservative Councillors Association. *Councils and public bodies:* Stoke-on-Trent City Council: Councillor 2011-19, Deputy Leader, Conservative Group, Cabinet Member for Regeneration, Transport and Heritage.

Other: Member, National Trust; Director, Stoke-on-Trent Regeneration Ltd.

Jack Brereton MP, House of Commons, London SW1A 0AA
Tel: 020 7219 4460 *Email:* jack.brereton.mp@parliament.uk
Constituency: 69 The Strand, Longton, Stoke-on-Trent, Staffordshire ST3 2NS
Tel: 01782 922525 Website: www.jackbrereton.co.uk

CONSERVATIVE

BRIDGEN, ANDREW

North West Leicestershire *(Majority 20,400)*

Andrew James Bridgen. Born 28 October 1964; Son of Alan and Ann Bridgen; Married Jacqueline Cremin 2000 (2 sons) (divorced); married Nevena Pavlovic 2017 (1 son).

Education: Pingle School, Swadlincote; Nottingham University (BSc biological sciences 1986); CPC road haulage operations 1991; French, German.

Non-political career: AB Produce plc (market gardening business): Managing director 1988-2010, Non-executive chairman -2014. Royal Marine officer training.

Political career: Member for North West Leicestershire since 6 May 2010 general election. *Select committees:* Regulatory Reform: Member 2010-15, 2017-19, Chair 2015-17; Member: Joint Committee on Draft Deregulation Bill 2013, Liaison 2015-17. Member, North West Leicestershire Conservative Association; Founding Member, Conservatives for Britain 2015-16. *Councils and public bodies:* Business member, East Midlands Regional Assembly 1999-2000.

Political interests: Business and enterprise, civil liberties, law and order, armed force, transport, environment, food and rural affairs; Italy, Serbia, Syria, USA, Uzbekistan.

Other: Member, British-Irish Parliamentary Assembly 2015-20; Regional committee member: Business for Sterling, The 'No' Campaign; Institute of Directors: Member 1992-, Regional chair 1999-2003; Christians Against Poverty, Hospice Hope, National Forest, Action Deafness. Ivanhoe Club Ashby, Carlton Club; Burton Rugby Club.

Recreations: Military history, skiing, fishing, driving, reading, country pursuits.

Andrew Bridgen MP, House of Commons, London SW1A 0AA
Tel: 020 7219 7238 *Fax:* 020 7219 6819 *Email:* andrew.bridgen.mp@parliament.uk
Constituency: Unit 10, The Courtyard, Whitwick Business Park, Coalville, Leicestershire LE67 4JP
Website: www.andrewbridgen.com *Twitter:* @Abridgen

CONSERVATIVE

BRINE, STEVE

Winchester *(Majority 985)*

Stephen Charles Brine. Born 28 January 1974; Married Susie (1 daughter 1 son).

Education: Bohunt Comprehensive School; Highbury College, Portsmouth; Liverpool Hope University (BA history 2006) (Student Union President).

Non-political career: Journalist: BBC Radio, WGN Radio, Chicago USA; Former director, Azalea Group (public relations and marketing firm).

Political career: Member for Winchester since 6 May 2010 general election; PPS to: Mike Penning as Minister of State for: Disabled People, Department for Work and Pensions 2013-14, Policing, Criminal Justice and Victims, Home Office and Ministry of Justice 2014-15, Jeremy Hunt as Secretary of State for Health 2015-16; Assistant Government Whip 2016-17; Parliamentary Under-Secretary of State for Public Health and Primary Care, Department of Health/Department of Health and Social Care 2017-19. *Select committees:* Member: Justice 2011-14, Joint Committee on Voting Eligibilty (Prisoners) Bill 2013, Digital, Culture, Media and Sport 2020-. Conservative Party whip removed September-October 2019.

Political interests: NHS, media, planning and development, justice, environment; Italy, USA.

Other: Member, Executive Committee, Commonwealth Parliamentary Association United Kingdom 2020-. Liphook Golf Club, Hampshire.

Recreations: Football, skiing, tennis, golf, live music.

Steve Brine MP, House of Commons, London SW1A 0AA
Tel: 020 7219 7189 *Email:* steve.brine.mp@parliament.uk
Constituency: No constituency office publicised
Website: www.stevebrine.com *Twitter:* @BrineMP

CONSERVATIVE

BRISTOW, PAUL

Peterborough *(Majority 2,580)*

Born 27 March 1979; Partner Sara (2 daughters).

Education: Sir Harry Smith Community College, Whittlesey; Lancaster University (history 2000).

Non-political career: Research assistant to Richard Spring MP 2003-05; Account manager, Morgan Allen Moore 2005-07; Director of research and consulting services, BIBA Medical 2007-10; Managing director, PB Consulting 2010-19.

Political career: Contested Middlesbrough South and East Cleveland 2010 general election and Peterborough 2019 by-election. Member for Peterborough since 12 December 2019. *Select committees:* Member, Health and Social Care 2020-. Chair, Conservative Future 2003-05; Associate member, Conservative Way Forward. *Councils and public bodies:* London Borough of Hammersmith and Fulham Council: Councillor 2006-10, Cabinet Member for Residents' Services 2007-10; Governor, Bayonne Nursery 2005-15.

Political interests: Health, foreign affairs; Commonwealth, Kashmir, UK Overseas Territories.

Other: Chair: Association of Professional Political Consultants 2017-19, PRCA Public Affairs Board 2019.

Recreations: Travel, football, cricket.

Paul Bristow MP, House of Commons, London SW1A 0AA
Tel: 020 7219 3690 *Email:* paul.bristow.mp@parliament.uk
Constituency: 193 Dogsthorpe Road, Peterborough PE1 3AT
Tel: 01733 343190 Website: www.paulbristow.org.uk *Twitter:* @paulbristow79

CONSERVATIVE

BRITCLIFFE, SARA

Hyndburn *(Majority 2,951)*

Sara Alice Kroeger Britcliffe. Born 21 February 1995.

Education: St Christopher's High School; Manchester University (German and Spanish 2018).

Non-political career: Manager, Hurns Bread Basket 2017-18.

Political career: Member for Hyndburn since 12 December 2019. *Select committees:* Member, Women and Equalities 2020-. *Councils and public bodies:* Hyndburn Borough Council: Mayoress 2017-18, Councillor 2018-.

Sara Britcliffe MP, House of Commons, London SW1A 0AA
Tel: 020 7219 4836 *Email:* sara.britcliffe.mp@parliament.uk
Constituency: 14 Broadway, Accrington BB5 1HZ
Tel: 01254 230441 Website: www.sarabritcliffe.org.uk *Twitter:* @SarBritcliffeMP

SCOTTISH NATIONAL PARTY

BROCK, DEIDRE

Edinburgh North and Leith *(Majority 12,808)*

SNP Shadow Secretary of State for Environment, Food and Rural Affairs

Deidre Leanne Brock. Born 8 December 1961; Partner Dougie (2 daughters).

Education: John Curtin University, Australia (English); WA Academy of Performing Arts, Australia (acting).

Non-political career: Actress; Parliamentary assistant to Rob Gibson MSP.

Political career: Member for Edinburgh North and Leith since 7 May 2015 general election; Member, Public Accounts Commission 2015-16; SNP: Spokesperson for: Devolved Government Relations 2015-18, Northern Ireland 2017-18, Fair Work and Employment 2017-18, Spokesperson/Shadow Secretary of State for: Environment, Food and Rural Affairs 2018-. *Select committees:* Member: Public Accounts 2015-16, Scottish Affairs 2016-. *Councils and public bodies:* City of Edinburgh Council: Councillor 2007-15, Former Deputy Lord Provost.

Political interests: Women in politics, job creation, public services.

Other: Member: British-Irish Parliamentary Assembly 2015-18, UK delegation, Parliamentary Assembly of the Organisation for Security and Co-operation in Europe 2020-; Board member, Edinburgh International Festival Council; Director, Centre for the Moving Image; Creative Edinburgh.

Recreations: Theatre, netball, cinema, traditional Scottish music and arts.

Deidre Brock MP, House of Commons, London SW1A 0AA
Tel: 020 7219 6647 *Email:* deidre.brock.mp@parliament.uk
Constituency: 166 Great Junction Street, Edinburgh EH6 5LJ
Tel: 0131-555 7009 *Twitter:* @DeidreBrock

CONSERVATIVE

BROKENSHIRE, JAMES

Old Bexley and Sidcup *(Majority 18,952)*

Minister of State for Security, Home Office

James Peter Brokenshire. Born 8 January 1968; Son of Joan and Peter Brokenshire; Married Cathrine Anne Mamelok 1999 (2 daughters 1 son).

Education: Davenant Foundation Grammar School; Cambridge Centre for Sixth Form Studies; Exeter University (LLB 1990).

Non-political career: Trainee, solicitor, then partner, Jones Day Gouldens Solicitors 1991-2005.

Political career: Member for Hornchurch 2005-10, for Old Bexley and Sidcup since 6 May 2010 general election; Shadow Minister for Home Affairs 2006-10; Home Office: Parliamentary Under-Secretary of State (Minister for Crime Prevention) 2010-11, Parliamentary Under-Secretary of State for: Crime and Security 2011-14, Security 2014, Minister of State for: Security 2014-15, 2020- (on leave January 2021-), Immigration 2014-16; Secretary of State for: Northern Ireland 2016-18, Housing, Communities and Local Government 2018-19. *Select committees:* Member, Constitutional Affairs 2005-06.

Political interests: Health, housing and regeneration, law and order.

Other: Patron, Bexley Borough Neighbourhood Watch Association; Vice-president: Bexleyheath and District Club for the Disabled, Sidcup and Footscray Branch, Royal British Legion; PC 2015.

Recreations: Community radio, watching cricket, hill-walking.

Rt Hon James Brokenshire MP, House of Commons, London SW1A 0AA
Tel: 020 7219 8400 *Fax:* 020 7219 2043 *Email:* james.brokenshire.mp@parliament.uk
Constituency: 19 Station Road, Sidcup, Kent DA15 7EB
Tel: 020 8302 7352 Website: www.jamesbrokenshire.com *Twitter:* @Jbrokenshire

SCOTTISH NATIONAL PARTY

BROWN, ALAN

Kilmarnock and Loudoun *(Majority 12,659)*

SNP Shadow Minister for Energy and Climate Change

Born 12 August 1970; Son of Eric and Irene Brown; Married Cyndi (2 sons).

Education: Loudoun Academy; Glasgow University (civil engineering 1993).

Non-political career: Civil engineer, private and public sector for 21 years; Principal engineer.

Political career: Member for Kilmarnock and Loudoun since 7 May 2015 general election; SNP Spokesperson for: Transport and Energy 2017-19, Infrastructure 2017-18, Energy and Climate Change 2020-. *Select committees:* Member: European Scrutiny 2016-17, Environment, Food and Rural Affairs 2017-19, Business, Energy and Industrial Strategy 2020-. *Councils and public bodies:* East Ayrshire Council: Councillor 2007-15, Spokesperson for: Planning, Housing, Strategic Planning and Resources.

Political interests: Infrastructure, NHS, energy, environment; Palestine.

Other: Trustee and Director, Newmilns Snow and Sports Complex; Fellow, Institution of Civil Engineers.

Recreations: Attending Kilmarnock FC matches, walking, camping, cooking.

Alan Brown MP, House of Commons, London SW1A 0AA
Tel: 020 7219 6093 *Email:* alan.brown.mp@parliament.uk
Constituency: 31a Titchfield Street, Kilmarnock KA1 1QW
Tel: 01563 501412/01563 501411 Website: www.alanbrownmp.scot *Twitter:* @AlanBrownSNP

LABOUR

BROWN, LYN

West Ham *(Majority 32,388)*

Shadow Minister for Prisons and Probation

Lyn Carol Brown. Born 13 April 1960; Daughter of Joseph and Iris Brown; Married John Cullen 2008.

Education: Plashet Comprehensive School; Whitelands College, Roehampton (BA English and religious studies 1982).

Non-political career: Residential social worker, London Borough of Ealing Council 1984-85; Newham Voluntary Agencies, Newham 1985-87; London Borough of Waltham Forest Council 1988-2005. Member, Unison.

Political career: Contested Wanstead and Woodford general election 1992. Member for West Ham 2005-10, for West Ham (revised boundary) since 6 May 2010 general election; PPS to: Phil Woolas as Minister of State, Department for Communities and Local Government 2006-07, John Denham as Secretary of State for Innovation, Universities and Skills 2007-09; Assistant Government Whip 2009-10; Opposition Whip 2010-13; Shadow Minister for: Communities and Fire 2013-15, Home Office 2015-16, 2016-17, Treasury 2018-20, Justice (Prisons and Probation) 2020-. *Select committees:* Member, ODPM/Communities and Local Government 2005-07. Member, Co-operative Party. *Councils and public bodies:* London Borough of Newham: Councillor 1988-2005, Chair, Direct Services Organisation 1989-90, Chair, Leisure 1992-2002, Cabinet Member for Culture and Community 2002-05; Founder Member and Chair, London Library Development Agency 1999-2006; Chair: Cultural Services Executive, Local Government Association 2000-03, Culture and Tourism Panel, Association of London

Government 2002-05; Member: London Regional Sports Board -2007, London Arts Board -2007, Museums, Libraries and Archives Council, London -2007: Judge, Golden Dagger Award 2005-07.

Political interests: Poverty, housing, libraries, local government, sexual and reproductive health, foreign affairs; Africa, Bangladesh, China, Pakistan.

Other: Member, Fabian Society.

Recreations: Walking, reading, relaxing with friends.

Lyn Brown MP, House of Commons, London SW1A 0AA
Tel: 020 7219 6999 *Email:* brownl@parliament.uk
Constituency: No constituency office publicised
Email: lyn@lynbrown.org.uk Website: www.lynbrown.org.uk *Twitter:* @lynbrownmp

LABOUR

BROWN, NICK

Newcastle upon Tyne East *(Majority 15,463)*

Opposition Chief Whip

Nicholas Hugh Brown. Born 13 June 1950.

Education: Tunbridge Wells Technical High School; Manchester University (BA 1971).

Non-political career: Proctor and Gamble advertising department. Legal adviser for northern region, GMBATU 1978-83.

Political career: Member for Newcastle upon Tyne East 1983-97, for Newcastle upon Tyne East and Wallsend 1997-2010, for Newcastle upon Tyne East since 6 May 2010 general election; Opposition Frontbench Spokesperson for: Legal Affairs 1985-92, Treasury and Economic Affairs 1988-94; Deputy to Margaret Beckett as Shadow Leader of the Commons 1992-94; Opposition Spokesperson for Health 1994-95; Opposition Deputy Chief Whip 1995-97; Government Chief Whip 1997-98; Minister of Agriculture, Fisheries and Food 1998-2001; Minister of State for Work, Department of Work and Pensions 2001-03; Deputy Government Chief Whip 2007-08; Minister for the North East 2007-10; Government Chief Whip 2008-10; Shadow Parliamentary Secretary to the Treasury and Opposition Chief Whip 2010; Member: Speaker's Committee for the Independent Parliamentary Standards Authority 2010-17, House of Commons Commission 2015-16, Public Accounts Commission 2015-; Opposition Chief Whip 2016-; Member, Parliamentary and Political Service Honours Committee 2016-. *Select committees:* Member: Broadcasting 1994-95, Selection 1996-97, 2007-08, Administration 2007-09, Joint Committees on the: Draft Financial Services Bill 2011-12, Draft Communications Data Bill 2012-13; Chair, Finance 2015-16; Member, Liaison 2015-16. Patron, LGBT Labour; Ex-officio member, National Executive Committee, Labour Party 2016-. *Councils and public bodies:* Councillor, Newcastle upon Tyne City Council 1980-83.

Political interests: Australia, China, European Union, Ireland, Japan, New Zealand, Singapore, USA.

Other: Trustee, Biscuit Factory Foundation 2011-; Non-executive director, Mariinksky Theatre Trust 2012-; Freedom, City of Newcastle 2001; PC 1997.

Rt Hon Nick Brown MP, House of Commons, London SW1A 0AA
Tel: 020 7219 6814 *Email:* nickbrownmp@parliament.uk
Constituency: Lifton House, Eslington Road, Jesmond, Tyne and Wear NE2 4SP
Tel: 0191-249 8403 Website: www.nickbrownmp.com

CONSERVATIVE

BROWNE, ANTHONY

South Cambridgeshire *(Majority 2,904)*

Anthony Howe Browne. Born 19 January 1967; Married.

Education: Perse School; Hills Road Sixth Form College; Cambridge University (BA mathematics 1988).

Non-political career: Economics Correspondent, Business Reporter, Assistant Producer, BBC 1993-98; Economics Correspondent, Health Editor and Environment Correspondent, *The Observer* 1998-2002; Chief Political Correspondent, Brussels Correspondent, *The Times* 2002-07; Director, Policy Exchange 2007-08; Policy Director for Economic Development,

Mayor of London 2008-11; Head of Government Relations for Europe, Middle East and Africa, Morgan Stanley 2012; Columnist, CityAM 2011-13; Chief Executive, British Bankers' Association 2012-17.

Political career: Member for South Cambridgeshire since 12 December 2019. *Select committees:* Member, Treasury 2020-. Deputy chair (Political), Hornsey and Wood Green Conservative Association 2019. *Councils and public bodies:* Chair, Regulatory Policy Committee 2018-19.

Political interests: Environment, public transport, education, life sciences, AI; Canada, Europe.

Other: Board member, TheCityUK 2009-17; Entrepreneur-in-Residence, Techstars 2018; Co-founder and adviser, HomeOwners Alliance 2018-; Board adviser: Courtsdesk 2017-, Blockchain 2018-, Habito 2018-; Non-executive director: Coconut 2018-, AuditXPRT 2018-, Wayhome 2018- Board adviser: Iwoca 2019-, Hastee Pay 2019-.

Publications: The Euro – Should Britain Join: Yes or No? (Icon Books, 2001) NHS Reform: Towards Consensus? (Adam Smith Institute, 2002); Do We Need Mass Immigration? (Civitas, 2002); The Retreat of Reason – Political Correctness and the Corruption of Public Debate in Modern Britain (Civitas, 2006); Contributor Contemporary Social Evils (Joseph Rowntree Foundation, 2009); The Case for European Localism, with Mats Persson [33] (Open Europe, 2011).

Recreations: Walking, climbing, skiing.

Anthony Browne MP, House of Commons, London SW1A 0AA
Tel: 020 7219 8089 *Email:* anthony.browne.mp@parliament.uk
Constituency: Broadway House, 149-151 St Neots Road, Hardwick CB23 7QJ
Tel: 01223 603677 Website: www.anthonybrowne.org *Twitter:* @ab4scambs

CONSERVATIVE

BRUCE, FIONA

Congleton *(Majority 18,561)*

Fiona Claire Bruce. Born 26 March 1957; Married Richard (2 sons).

Education: Burnley High School; Howell's School, Llandaff; Manchester University; Chester Law College; Qualified solicitor 1981.

Non-political career: Senior partner, Fiona Bruce & Co LLP.

Political career: Contested Warrington South 2005 general election. Member for Congleton since 6 May 2010 general election; Prime Minister's Special Envoy for Freedom of Religion or Belief 2020-. *Select committees:* Member: Scottish Affairs 2010-13, International Development 2012-17, Joint Committee on the Draft Modern Slavery Bill 2014, Joint Committee on Human Rights 2015-, Ecclesiastical Committee 2015-; Chair, Work of the Independent Commission for Aid Impact Sub-committee 2015-17; Member, Backbench Business 2020-21. Chair, Conservative Human Rights Commission 2012-. *Councils and public bodies:* Warrington Borough Council: Councillor 2004-10, Executive Member for Money and Finance 2006-10; Former school governor.

Political interests: Small business, family, community, international aid and development, human rights; North Korea, Rwanda, Tanzania.

Other: Board Member, Evangelical Alliance 2015–; Lay Canon, Chester Cathedral 2018-; Member: Law Society, Specialist Society of Trusts and Estate Practitioners; The Prison Fellowship, Lawyers Christian Fellowship; National Winner, Women into Business Award 2005.

Publications: Co-author: There is such a thing as society (Politicos, 2002), Freedom, Responsibility and the State: Curbing Over-Mighty Government (Politeia, 2012).

Recreations: Family, countryside, theatre.

Fiona Bruce MP, House of Commons, London SW1A 0AA
Tel: 020 7219 2969 *Email:* fiona.bruce.mp@parliament.uk
Constituency: Riverside, Mountbatten Way, Congleton, Cheshire CW12 IDY
Tel: 01260 274044 Website: www.fionabruce.org.uk

LABOUR

BRYANT, CHRIS

Rhondda *(Majority 11,440)*

Chair, Select Committees on Standards and on Privileges

Christopher John Bryant. Born 11 January 1962; Son of Rees Bryant and Anne Bryant, née Goodwin; Civil partner Jared Cranney 2010.

Education: Cheltenham College; Mansfield College, Oxford (BA English 1983, MA); Ripon College, Cuddesdon (MA CertTheol 1986); French, Spanish.

Non-political career: Church of England: Ordained Deacon 1986, Priest 1987; Curate, All Saints High Wycombe 1986-89; Diocesan youth chaplain, Diocese of Peterborough 1989-91; Local government development officer, Labour Party 1993-94; London manager, Common Purpose 1994-96; Freelance author 1996-98; Head of European Affairs, BBC 1998-2000. Member: GMB 1991-94, MSF 1994-.

Political career: Contested Wycombe 1997 general election. Member for Rhondda since 7 June 2001 general election; PPS to: Lord Falconer of Thoroton as Lord Chancellor 2005-06, Harriet Harman as Leader of the House of Commons 2007-08; Deputy Leader of the House of Commons 2008-09; Parliamentary Under-Secretary of State, Foreign and Commonwealth Office 2009-10; Shadow Minister for: Foreign and Commonwealth Office 2010, Justice (Political and Constitutional Reform) 2010-11; Shadow Minister for: Immigration 2011-13, Work and Pensions 2013-14, Arts 2014-15; Shadow Secretary of State for Culture, Media and Sport 2015; Shadow Leader of the House of Commons 2015-16; Member: House of Commons Commission 2015-16, Speaker's Committee for the Independent Parliamentary Standards Authority 2015-20. *Select committees:* Member: Culture, Media and Sport 2001-05, Joint Committee on House of Lords Reform 2002-10, Public Accounts 2007, Modernisation of the House of Commons 2007-10, Joint Committee on the Palace of Westminster 2015-16, Foreign Affairs 2017-, Liaison 2017-19, 2020-; Chair, Finance 2017-19; Lay Member, Speaker's Advisory Committee on Works of Art 2019; Chair: Standards 2020-, Privileges 2020-; Member: Speaker's Committee for the Independent Parliamentary Standards Authority 2020-, Joint Committee on Fixed-Term Parliaments Act 2020-. Agent, Holborn and St Pancras Labour Party 1991-93; Chair, Christian Socialist Movement 1993-98; Labour Movement for Europe: Chair 2002-07, Vice-chair 2007-; Patron, LGBT Labour. *Councils and public bodies:* London Borough of Hackney: Councillor 1993-98, Chief Whip 1994-95.

Political interests: Wales, European affairs, broadcasting, information economy; Latin America, Spain.

Other: Associate, National Youth Theatre of Great Britain; Campaigner of the Year, *Wales Yearbook* awards 2011; Politician of the Year, Stonewall awards 2011. Ferndale RFC.

Publications: Reclaiming The Ground (Hodder and Stoughton, 1993); John Smith: An Appreciation (Hodder and Stoughton, 1994); Possible Dreams (Hodder and Stoughton, 1995); Stafford Cripps: The First Modern Chancellor (Hodder and Stoughton, 1997); Glenda Jackson: The Biography (HarperCollins, 1999).

Recreations: Swimming, theatre.

Chris Bryant MP, House of Commons, London SW1A 0AA
Tel: 020 7219 8315 *Fax:* 020 7219 1792 *Email:* bryantc@parliament.uk
Constituency: Oxford House, Dunraven Street, Tonypandy, Mid Glamorgan CF40 1AU
Tel: 01443 442521 Website: www.chrisbryantmp.org.uk *Twitter:* @RhonddaBryant

CONSERVATIVE

BUCHAN, FELICITY

Kensington *(Majority 150)*

Felicity Christiana Buchan.

Education: Fraserburgh Academy; Christ Church, Oxford (law).

Political career: Contested South Down 2015 and South Shields 2017 general elections. Member for Kensington since 12 December 2019. *Select committees:* Member: Treasury 2020-, Finance 2020-. *Councils and public bodies:* Chair of governors, Bousfield Primary School.

Felicity Buchan MP, House of Commons, London SW1A 0AA
Tel: 020 7219 6732 *Email:* felicity.buchan.mp@parliament.uk
Constituency: No constituency office publicised
Email: felicity@felicitybuchan.com Website: www.felicitybuchan.com
Twitter: @FelicityBuchan

House of Commons MPs' Biographies

LABOUR

BUCK, KAREN

Westminster North *(Majority 10,759)*

Shadow Minister for Social Security

Karen Patricia Buck. Born 30 August 1958; Married Barrie Taylor (1 son).

Education: Chelmsford High School; London School of Economics (BSc Econ; MSc Econ; MA social policy and administration).

Non-political career: Research and development worker, Outset (charity specialising in employment for disabled people) 1979-83; London Borough of Hackney: Specialist officer developing services/employment for disabled people 1983-86, Public health officer 1986-87. Member, TGWU.

Political career: Member for Regent's Park and Kensington North 1997-2010, for Westminster North since 6 May 2010 general election; Parliamentary Under-Secretary of State, Department for Transport 2005-06; Parliamentary assistant to Tony McNulty as Minister for London 2008-10; Shadow Minister for: Welfare Reform 2010-11, Education 2011-13; PPS to Leader of the Opposition: Ed Miliband 2013-15, Harriet Harman 2015; Shadow Minister for Social Security 2020-. *Select committees:* Member: Social Security 1997-2001, Selection 1999-2001, Work and Pensions 2001-05, 2010, Home Affairs 2006-09, Home Affairs Sub-Committee 2008-09, Children, Schools and Families 2009-10; Chair, London 2009-10; Member: Work and Pensions 2015-17, Joint Committee on Human Rights 2015-, Panel of Chairs 2015-, Court of Referees 2016-17. Chair: PLP London Regional Group 1999-2010, PLP Department Group for Housing 2020-. Labour Party: Policy Directorate (Health) 1987-92, Campaign Strategy Co-ordinator 1992-99. *Councils and public bodies:* Councillor, Westminster City Council 1990-97.

Political interests: Housing, urban regeneration, health care, welfare, children, child poverty, environment and climate change.

Other: EveryChild, Amnesty; MP of the Year, Women in Public Life Awards 2007.

Recreations: Music: rock, soul, jazz, opera.

Karen Buck MP, House of Commons, London SW1A 0AA
Tel: 020 7219 3000 *Fax:* 020 7219 3664 *Email:* buckk@parliament.uk
Constituency: Westminster North Labour Party, 4G Shirland Mews, London W9 3DY
Tel: 020 8968 7999/020 8968 7888 Website: www.karenbuck.org.uk *Twitter:* @KarenPBuckMP

CONSERVATIVE

BUCKLAND, ROBERT

South Swindon *(Majority 6,625)*

Lord Chancellor and Secretary of State for Justice

Robert James Buckland. Born 22 September 1968; Son of Roger and Barbara Buckland.

Education: St Michael's School, Bryn, Llanelli; Hatfield College, Durham (BA law 1990); Inns of Court School of Law 1991.

Non-political career: Called to the Bar 1991; Barrister, Wales and Chester circuit 1992-: Iscoed Chambers, Swansea -1999, 30 Park Place, Cardiff 1999-2007, Apex Chambers 2007-, Recorder of Crown Court 2009-; Bencher, Inner Temple.

Political career: Contested Islwyn 1995 by-election, Preseli Pembrokeshire 1997 and South Swindon 2005 general elections. Member for South Swindon since 6 May 2010 general election; Solicitor General 2014-19; Ministry of Justice: Minister of State 2019, Lord Chancellor and Secretary of State for Justice 2019-. *Select committees:* Member, Justice 2010-13; Member Joint Committees on: Statutory Instruments 2010-14, Consolidation, Etc, Bills 2010-14; Member: Works of Art 2011-12, Joint Committee on Privacy and Injunctions 2011-12, Standards 2013-14, Privileges 2013-14, Joint Committee on Human Rights 2013-15, Justice 2014. Secretary, 1922 Committee 2012-14; Chair, Conservative Party Committee for Home Affairs and Constitution 2014. Society of Conservative Lawyers: Member 1990-, Chair, Executive Committee 2013-; Constituency chair, Conservative Party: Llanelli 1993-96, Swansea West 1999-2000; Tory Reform Group: Board Member 2000-03, Vice-President; Conservative Group for Europe: Member 2002-, Vice-president 2012-; Conservative Foreign Affairs Forum 2006-; Chair, Conservative Human Rights Commission 2011-. *Councils and public bodies:* Councillor, Dyfed County Council 1993-96.

Political interests: Criminal justice, constitutional affairs, foreign affairs, education; South and East Asia, Europe, Israel, Middle East, North Africa, Russia.

Other: Patron: Swindon Threshold (homelessness charity), Hop Skip and Jump, Swindon Calm, Greatwood; Member, Criminal Bar Association; Bencher, Inner Temple; Llanelli Crossroads Scheme; PC 2019. The Garrick; Patron, Llanelli Conservative Club; Swindon Conservative Club; Glamorgan County Cricket Club; Crawshays Welsh RFC.

Recreations: Music, wine, family, church architecture, watching rugby, football and cricket.

Rt Hon Robert Buckland QC MP, House of Commons, London SW1A 0AA
Tel: 020 7219 7168 *Fax:* 020 7219 4849 *Email:* robert.buckland.mp@parliament.uk
Constituency: 29b Wood Street, Swindon SN1 4AN
Tel: 01793 533393 Website: www.robertbuckland.co.uk *Twitter:* @robertbuckland

CONSERVATIVE

BURGHART, ALEX

Brentwood and Ongar *(Majority 29,065)*

PPS to Boris Johnson as Prime Minister

Michael Alex Burghart. Born 7 September 1977; Married Hermione Eyre 2011 (2 daughters).

Education: Millfield School; Christ Church College, Oxford (MA modern history 1999 MSt modern history 2001); King's College London (PhD 2007).

Non-political career: Researcher and history tutor, King's College London 2001-08; Adviser to Tim Loughton as Shadow Minister for Children and Young People 2008-10; Policy adviser (Munro Review of Children Protection), Department for Education 2010-11; Director of Policy, Centre for Social Justice 2012-16; Director of Strategy, Office of the Children's Commissioner 2016; Special Adviser, Number 10 Policy Unit 2016-17.

Political career: Contested Islington North 2015 general election. Member for Brentwood and Ongar since 8 June 2017; PPS to: Geoffrey Cox as Attorney General 2018-19, Boris Johnson as Prime Minister 2019-. *Select committees:* Member: Work and Pensions 2017-19, Standing Orders 2017-, Joint Committee on Human Rights 2017-18.

Other: Board Member, Yarlington Housing Group 2015-17.

Dr Alex Burghart MP, House of Commons, London SW1A 0AA
Tel: 020 7219 1613 *Email:* alex.burghart.mp@parliament.uk
Constituency: No constituency office publicised
Email: burgharta2@parliament.uk Website: www.alexburghart.org.uk *Twitter:* @alexburghart

LABOUR

BURGON, RICHARD

Leeds East *(Majority 5,531)*

Born 19 September 1980; Son of Terence and Mary Burgon.

Education: Cardinal Heenan RC High School; St. John Fisher/St. Aidan's Associated Sixth Form; St John's College, Cambridge (English literature 2002); Leeds Metropolitan University (Graduate Diploma In Law 2003); York College of Law (LPC 2004).

Non-political career: Trainee Solicitor 2004-06; Admitted solicitor 2006; Trade Union Lawyer, Thompsons Solicitors, Leeds 2004-15. Unite the Union; BFAWU; GMB.

Political career: Member for Leeds East since 7 May 2015 general election; Shadow Economic Secretary 2015-16; Shadow Lord Chancellor and Shadow Secretary of State for Justice 2016-20. *Select committees:* Member: Justice 2015, 2020-, Joint Committee on Consolidation, &c, Bills 2020-.

Political interests: Employment law, workers' rights, trade unions, the economy, housing, NHS, foreign policy, civil liberties; Latin America, USA.

Other: Member: East Leeds History and Archaeology Society, Leeds United Supporters' Trust, Woodland Trust.

Recreations: Music, reading, Leeds United, walking.

Richard Burgon MP, House of Commons, London SW1A 0AA
Tel: 020 7219 5980 *Email:* richard.burgon.mp@parliament.uk
Constituency: Former Presbytery of Our Lady of Good Counsel, Rosgill Drive, Leeds, West

Yorkshire LS14 6QY
Tel: 0113-232 3266 *Email:* richard@richardburgon.com Website: www.richardburgon.com
Twitter: @RichardBurgon

CONSERVATIVE

BURNS, CONOR

Bournemouth West *(Majority 10,150)*

Born 24 September 1972; Son of Thomas Burns and Kathleen Burns, née Kennedy; Single.

Education: St Columba's College, St Albans; Southampton University (BA modern history and politics with philosophy 1994).

Non-political career: Director, Policy Research Centre for Business Ltd 1997; Company secretary, DeHavilland Global Knowledge Distribution plc 1998; Sales director, insurance company; Associate director, PLMR 2008-10; Consultant to Trant Engineering.

Political career: Contested Eastleigh 2001 and 2005 general elections. Member for Bournemouth West since 6 May 2010 general election; PPS to: Hugo Swire as Minister of State, Northern Ireland Office 2010-11, Owen Paterson as Secretary of State for Northern Ireland 2011-12, David Gauke as Financial Secretary, HM Treasury 2015-16, Greg Clark as Secretary of State for Business, Energy and Industrial Strategy 2016-17, Boris Johnson as Foreign Secretary 2017-18; Minister of State for Trade Policy, Department for International Trade 2019-20. *Select committees:* Member: Education 2010, Culture, Media and Sport 2012-15, Administration 2014-15. Member, Executive, 1922 Committee 2014-15. Chair: Southampton University Conservative Association 1992-93, Wessex Area Conservative Students 1993-94. *Councils and public bodies:* Southampton City Council: Councillor 1999-2002, Housing and urban regeneration spokesperson 1999, Education and employment spokesperson 1999, Conservative group leader 2001-02.

Political interests: Mental health, foreign affairs, Northern Ireland, education; China, Latin America, Middle East, USA.

Other: Member, British-Irish Parliamentary Assembly 2017; Management team, Homestart; PC 2019.

Recreations: Swimming, snooker, cooking, collecting political biographies.

Rt Hon Conor Burns MP, House of Commons, London SW1A 0AA
Tel: 020 7219 7021 *Email:* conor.burns.mp@parliament.uk
Constituency: 3 Lorne Park Road, Bournemouth, Dorset BH1 1AH
Tel: 01202 553330 Website: www.conorburns.com *Twitter:* @ConorBurnsUK

LABOUR

BUTLER, DAWN

Brent Central *(Majority 20,870)*

Dawn Petula Butler. Born 3 November 1969; Daughter of Milo and Ambrozene Butler.

Education: Tom Hood Senior High School, Waltham Forest, London; Waltham Forest College; British Sign Language.

Non-political career: Computer programmer, Johnson Matthey 1989-92; Executive officer, Job Centre 1993-96; Recruitment officer and black women's officer, Public and Commercial Services Union 1996-97; GMB 1997-2005: Regional equality officer and regional race officer 1997-2003, National officer 2003-05. Member: GMB, Amicus, Unite.

Political career: Member for Brent South 2005-10. Contested Brent Central 2010 general election. Member for Brent Central since 7 May 2015 general election; PPS to Jane Kennedy as Minister of State, Department of Health 2005-06; Assistant Government Whip 2008-09; Parliamentary Secretary (Minister for Young Citizens and Youth Engagement), Cabinet Office 2009-10; Shadow Minister for Diverse Communities (attends Shadow Cabinet) 2016-17, 2017; Shadow Secretary of State for Women and Equalities 2017-20. *Select committees:* Member: Modernisation of the House of Commons 2005-10, Children, Schools and Families 2007-09, Education 2020, Science and Technology 2020-. Chair, PLP Departmental Group for Women 2015-16. Vice-chair, Labour Friends of India 2006. *Councils and public bodies:* Magistrate (Lay Judge) 2013-15.

Political interests: Poverty, unemployment, crime, children's welfare, equality, employment rights, youth, environment, legal aid; Jamaica.

Other: Member, UK delegation, Parliamentary Assembly of the Council of Europe 2016; Executive Member, Race Equality In Newham 2000-03; Vice-chair, Patient and Public Involvement in Health 2002-05; Chair, Greater London Authority London Black Women's Council 2000-05; Executive member, Black Public Sector Workers GLA think tank 2000-05; Patron: Black Women's Mental Health Project 2006, West Indian Self Effort 2006-; Associate, Westminster Abbey Institute; *New Statesman* Most Promising Feminist Under 35 (2002); Patron's Award, Black Women in Business Awards (2007); MP of the Year Award, Women in Public Life Awards (2009); Community Award, Jamaica National (2009).

Recreations: Salsa dancing.

Dawn Butler MP, House of Commons, London SW1A 0AA
Tel: 020 7219 8591 *Email:* dawn.butler.mp@parliament.uk
Constituency: 156 High Road, Willesden, London NW10 2PB
Tel: 020 8451 6560 Website: www.dawnbutler.org.uk *Twitter:* @DawnButlerBrent

CONSERVATIVE

BUTLER, ROB

Aylesbury *(Majority 17,373)*

Robert Butler. Born June 1967.

Education: Bicester School; Sheffield University (French and economics 1989); French.

Non-political career: Presenter-Reporter, BBC News 1989-96; Newscaster, ITN 1996-2004; Presenter, Channel 5 1997-2004; Senior Trainer and Consultant, BBC World Service Trust 2005-08; Owner, Butler Corporate Communications and Media Ltd 2005-.

Political career: Member for Aylesbury since 12 December 2019. *Select committees:* Member, Justice 2020-. *Councils and public bodies:* Board Member, Ministry of Justice: Youth Justice Board 2013-17, Youth Custody Improvement Board 2016-17, The Sentencing Council 2018-19; Non-executive Director, Her Majesty's Prison and Probation Service 2018-19; Magistrate.

Recreations: Walking, cycling, travelling.

Rob Butler MP, House of Commons, London SW1A 0AA
Tel: 020 7219 3000 *Email:* rob.butler.mp@parliament.uk
Constituency: 100 Walton Street, Aylesbury, Buckinghamshire HP21 7QP
Tel: 01296 587001 Website: www.robbutler.org.uk *Twitter:* @RobBAylesbury

LABOUR

BYRNE, IAN

Liverpool West Derby *(Majority 29,984)*

Ian Robert Byrne. Married Debbie (3 children).

Education: Open University (BA history).

Non-political career: Printer; Taxi Driver; Office of Dan Carden MP. Unite.

Political career: Member for Liverpool West Derby since 12 December 2019. *Select committees:* Member: Housing, Communities and Local Government 2020-, Environment, Food and Rural Affairs 2020-. *Councils and public bodies:* Councillor, Liverpool City Council 2018-.

Political interests: Education, food banks.

Other: Co-founder, Fans Supporting Foodbanks 2015-.

Ian Byrne MP, House of Commons, London SW1A 0AA
Tel: 020 7219 3000 *Email:* ian.byrne.mp@parliament.uk
Constituency: No constituency office publicised
Twitter: @IanByrneMP

LABOUR

BYRNE, LIAM

Birmingham, Hodge Hill *(Majority 28,655)*

Liam Dominic Byrne. Born 2 October 1970; Married Sarah Harnett 1998 (2 sons 1 daughter).

Education: Burnt Mill Comprehensive, Harlow, Essex; Manchester University (BA politics and modern history); Harvard Business School, USA (Fulbright Scholar MBA).

Non-political career: Andersen Consulting 1993-96; Leader of Labour Party's Office 1996-97; N M Rothschild 1997-99; Co-founder eGS Group Ltd 2000-04. Member: National Council, NUS, Unite.

Political career: Member for Birmingham Hodge Hill 15 July 2004 by-election to 2010, for Birmingham, Hodge Hill (revised boundary) since 6 May 2010 general election; Parliamentary Under-Secretary of State, Department of Health (Care Services) 2005-06; Minister of State, Home Office 2006-08 (Policing, Security and Community Safety 2006, Citizenship, Immigration and Nationality 2006-07, Borders and Immigration 2007-08); Minister for the West Midlands 2007-08; Minister of State, HM Treasury 2008; Minister for the Cabinet Office; Chancellor of the Duchy of Lancaster (attending Cabinet) 2008-09; Chair, Council of Regional Ministers 2008-10; Chief Secretary to the Treasury 2009-10; Shadow Chief Secretary to the Treasury 2010; Shadow Minister for the Cabinet Office 2010-11; Shadow Secretary of State for Work and Pensions 2011-13; Shadow Minister for: Education (Higher Education) 2013-15, Digital, Culture, Media and Sport (Digital Economy) 2017-20. *Select committees:* Member: European Scrutiny 2005-10, European Standing B 2005-06, International Trade 2016-17. Adviser 1997 general election campaign; Policy Review Co-ordinator, Labour Party 2011-12.

Political interests: Anti-social behaviour, drugs, social policy, welfare reform, youth policy; Kashmir.

Other: Member, UK Delegation, Parliamentary Assembly of the Council of Europe 2017-18; Fellow, Social Market Foundation; Member: Christian Socialist Movement, Fabian Society; PC 2008.

Publications: Local Government transformed (1996); Information Age Government (1997); Cities of Enterprise, New Strategies for Full Employment (2002); A Chance to Serve? (Progress, 2002); Britain in 2020 (2003); The Fate We're In (Progress, 2003); Reinventing Government Again (2004); The Left's Agenda for Science (2004); Why Labour Won: Lessons from 2005 (Fabian Society, 2005); Powered by Politics: Reforming Parties from the Inside (2005); Power to the People, Next Steps for New Labour (Progress); From Free Movement to Fair Movement: The Immigration Debate in the UK (in Rethinking Immigration and Integration: A New Centre-Left Agenda) (Policy Network, 2007); From Choice to Control: Empowering Public Services (in Public Matters: The Renewal of the Public Realm) (2007); A Common Place (Fabian Society, 2007); Contributor, The Purple Book (Progress, 2011); Turning to Face the East (Guardian Books, 2013); Dragons: Ten Entrepreneurs Who Built Britain (Head of Zeus, 2016); Black Flag Down: Counter-extremism, Defeating ISIS and Winning the Battle of Ideas (Biteback Publishing, 2016).

Recreations: Running, music, family.

Rt Hon Liam Byrne MP, House of Commons, London SW1A 0AA
Tel: 020 7219 6953 *Fax:* 020 7219 1431 *Email:* byrnel@parliament.uk
Constituency: No constituency office publicised
Tel: 0121-789 7287 Website: www.liambyrne.co.uk *Twitter:* @LiamByrneMP

LABOUR

CADBURY, RUTH

Brentford and Isleworth *(Majority 10,514)*

PPS to: David Lammy as Shadow Secretary of State for Justice and to Lord Falconer of Thoroton as Shadow Attorney General

Ruth Margaret Cadbury. Born 14 May 1959; Married Nick Gash (2 sons).

Education: Mount School, York; Bournville FE College; Salford University (BA 1981).

Non-political career: Planning Adviser, Planning Aid for London 1989-96; Policy Planner, Richmond upon Thames Council 1996-2001; Freelance Consultant 2006-10.

Political career: Member for Brentford and Isleworth since 7 May 2015 general election; Shadow Minister for Housing 2016-17; PPS to: David Lammy as Shadow Secretary of State for Justice 2020-, Lord Falconer of Thoroton as Shadow Attorney General 2020-. *Select committees:* Member: Women and Equalities 2015-17, Justice 2017-18, Transport 2018-.

Councils and public bodies: London Borough of Hounslow Council: Councillor 1986-94, 1998-2015, Deputy Leader of Council 2010-12, Cabinet Member for Regeneration and Economic Development and Financial Inclusion 2010-13.

Other: Trustee, Barrow Cadbury Trust -2015; Freedom, London Borough of Hounslow.

Ruth Cadbury MP, House of Commons, London SW1A 0AA
Tel: 020 7219 8590 *Email:* ruthcadburymp@parliament.uk
Constituency: No constituency office publicised
Tel: 020 8581 3646 *Email:* ruth@ruthcadbury.org.uk Website: www.ruthcadburymp.co.uk
Twitter: @RuthCadbury

CONSERVATIVE

CAIRNS, ALUN

Vale of Glamorgan *(Majority 3,562)*

Alun Hugh Cairns. Born 30 July 1970; Son of Hugh Cairns, retired, and Margaret Cairns; Married Emma Turner 1996 (1 son).

Education: Ysgol Gyfun Ddwyieithog Ystalyfera; University of Wales (MBA 2001); Welsh.

Non-political career: Lloyd's Bank Group 1989-99: Business development consultant 1992-98, Field manager 1998-99. Board Member, Reserve and Cadet Forces in Wales.

Political career: Contested Gower 1997 and Vale of Glamorgan 2005 general elections. Member for Vale of Glamorgan since 6 May 2010 general election; Government Whip (Lord Commissioner of HM Treasury) 2014-16; Wales Office: Parliamentary Under-Secretary of State 2014-16, Secretary of State for Wales 2016-19. *Select committees:* Member: Welsh Affairs 2010-11, Public Administration 2011-14. Contested Bridgend constituency 1999 and 2003 National Assembly for Wales elections. AM for South Wales West region 1999-2011: Welsh Conservative: Spokesperson for: Economic Development 1999-2000, Economic Development and Europe 2000-03, Economic Development and Transport 2003-07; Chair, Committee on Finance 2007-08; Shadow Minister for: Education and Lifelong Learning 2007-08, Local Government 2008-09, Heritage 2009-10; Spokesperson for the Economy 2009-10; Shadow Chief Whip and Business Manager 2009-10. Member: Vale of Glamorgan Conservative Association, Swansea West Conservative Association 1987-; Deputy Chair, Welsh Young Conservatives 1995-96; Chaired one of William Hague's Policy Advisory Groups 1996-97; Conservative Economic Spokesperson in Wales 1997-98; Regional Policy co-ordinator, South Wales West 1998-99; Member, Number 10 Policy Advisory Board 2013-14. *Councils and public bodies:* Member, UK Board of Trade 2017-19.

Political interests: Economy, trade and industry, special educational needs, culture, media and sport, defence; North and South America, South East Asia, Australasia.

Other: Member, UK delegation, NATO Parliamentary Assembly 2020-; Trustee, Ocean Water Sports Trust, Vale of Glamorgan; Adviser, BBI Group 2020-; Senior Adviser to the Board, Veezu Ltd 2020-; Motor Neurone Disease Association, Children with Special Needs, MIND in the Vale, Royal British Legion, RAF Association, Alzheimer's Society, Alzheimer's Research UK, Guide Dogs, NSPCC, Heads Together, Age Connects, Breast Cancer Now, Brain Tumour Charity, Macmillan Cancer Care, People's Dispensary for Sick Animals (PDSA), Ty Hapus, Marie Curie, RNLI Barry Dock, Age Connects Holton Road; PC 2016.

Recreations: Running, computing, skiing, gardening, shooting, squash.

Rt Hon Alun Cairns MP, House of Commons, London SW1A 0AA
Tel: 020 7219 7175 *Email:* alun.cairns.mp@parliament.uk
Constituency: Unit 6, BSC 2, Hood Road, Barry CF62 5QL
Tel: 01446 748657 Website: www.aluncairns.com *Twitter:* @AlunCairns

SCOTTISH NATIONAL PARTY

CALLAGHAN, AMY

East Dunbartonshire *(Majority 149)*

SNP Spokesperson for Pensions and Intergenerational Fairness

Born 21 May.

Education: Strathclyde University (BA politics 2015).

Non-political career: Personal support assistant, Strathclyde University 2014-15; Scottish Parliament: Parliamentary assistant to Aileen McLeod MSP 2015-16, Senior Caseworker 2016-18, Office manager to Rona Mackay MSP 2018-.

Political career: Member for East Dunbartonshire since 12 December 2019; SNP Spokesperson for Pensions and Intergenerational Fairness 2020-. *Select committees:* Member, Health and Social Care 2020.

Amy Callaghan MP, House of Commons, London SW1A 0AA
Tel: 020 7219 3000 *Email:* amy.callaghan.mp@parliament.uk
Constituency: No constituency office publicised
Twitter: @AmyCallaghanSNP

SCOTTISH NATIONAL PARTY

CAMERON, LISA

East Kilbride, Strathaven and Lesmahagow *(Majority 13,322)*

SNP Spokesperson for Mental Health

Born 8 April 1972; Married Mark Horsham (2 daughters).

Education: Duncanrig Secondary; Strathclyde University (MA psychology); Stirling University (MSc psychology and health); Glasgow University (DClinPsy).

Non-political career: NHS Greater Glasgow 1999-2001; Clinical psychologist, NHS Lanarkshire 2001-04; Consultant clinical psychologist, State Hospital 2004-06; Consultant forensic and clinical psychologist, NHS Greater Glasgow and Clyde 2006-; Psychological Services Scotland Ltd 2015-. Member, Unite.

Political career: Member for East Kilbride, Strathaven and Lesmahagow since 7 May 2015 general election; SNP Spokesperson for: Climate Justice 2015-17, Mental Health 2017-; Member, Commons Reference Group on Representation and Inclusion 2017-19. *Select committees:* Member: International Development 2015-17, Work of the Independent Commission for Aid Impact Sub-committee 2016-17, Health/Health and Social Care 2017-19, Ecclesiastical Committee 2020-.

Political interests: NHS, job creation, infrastructure, fairer society, disability, animal welfare, mental health.

Other: Member, Executive Committee, Commonwealth Parliamentary Association United Kingdom 2020-; Director, UK Japan 21C Group 2016-; Trustee, Industry and Parliament Trust.

Dr Lisa Cameron MP, House of Commons, London SW1A 0AA
Tel: 020 7219 6855 *Email:* lisa.cameron.mp@parliament.uk
Constituency: MP's Office, Civic Centre, Andrew Street, East Kilbride G74 1AB
Tel: 01355 587430
32 Waterside Street, Strathaven ML10 6AW
Tel: 01357 520879 *Twitter:* @DrLisaCameronMP

LABOUR

CAMPBELL, ALAN

Tynemouth *(Majority 4,857)*

Opposition Deputy Chief Whip

Born 8 July 1957; Son of Albert Campbell and Marian Campbell, née Hewitt; Married Jayne Lamont 1991 (1 son 1 daughter).

Education: Blackfyne Secondary School, Consett; Lancaster University (BA politics 1978); Leeds University (PGCE 1979); Newcastle Polytechnic (MA history 1984); French (basic).

Non-political career: Whitley Bay High School 1980-89; Hirst High School, Ashington, Northumberland: Teacher 1989-97, Head of sixth form, Head of department.

Political career: Member for Tynemouth 1997-2010, for Tynemouth (revised boundary) since 6 May 2010 general election; PPS to: Lord Macdonald of Tradeston as Minister for the Cabinet Office and Chancellor of the Duchy of Lancaster 2001-03, Adam Ingram as Minister of State, Ministry of Defence 2003-05; Assistant Government Whip 2005-06; Government Whip 2006-08; Parliamentary Under-Secretary of State (Crime Reduction), Home Office 2008-10; Shadow Minister for Home Office 2010; Opposition Deputy Chief Whip 2010-. *Select committees:* Member: Public Accounts 1997-2001, Armed Forces Bill 2005-06, Selection 2006-08, 2010-, Joint Committee on Security 2010-15. Hon. Secretary and Hon. Treasurer, Northern Group of Labour MPs 1999-2005.

Political interests: Crime and policing, fishing, seaside and coastal regeneration; Colombia, Falkland Islands.

Other: PC 2014; Kt 2019.

Recreations: Family.

Rt Hon Sir Alan Campbell MP, House of Commons, London SW1A 0AA
Tel: 020 7219 3000 *Email:* alan.campbell.mp@parliament.uk
Constituency: 99 Howard Street, North Shields, Tyne and Wear NE30 1NA
Tel: 0191-257 1927 Website: www.alancampbellmp.co.uk *Twitter:* @alancampbellmp

DEMOCRATIC UNIONIST PARTY

CAMPBELL, GREGORY

East Londonderry *(Majority 9,607)*

DUP Spokesperson for International Development and Cabinet Office

Gregory Lloyd Campbell. Born 15 February 1953; Son of James Campbell and Martha Joyce, née Robinson; Married Frances Patterson 1979 (1 son 3 daughters).

Education: Londonderry Technical College; Magee College (Extra-Mural Certificate political studies 1982).

Non-political career: Civil servant 1972-82, 1986-94; Self-employed (set up publishing company) 1994-99; Director, Causeway Press.

Political career: Contested Foyle 1983, 1987, 1992 and East Londonderry 1997 general elections. Member for East Londonderry 2001-10, for East Londonderry (revised boundary) since 6 May 2010 general election; DUP Spokesperson for: Defence 2005-07, Culture, Media and Sport/Culture, Olympics, Media and Sport 2005-12, Work and Pensions 2007-09, 2009-10, Transport 2009, International Development 2010-, Cabinet Office 2012-. *Select committees:* Member: Transport, Local Government and the Regions 2001-02, Transport, Local Government and the Regions (Transport Sub-Committee) 2001-02, Transport 2002-04, Northern Ireland Affairs 2004-09, 2016-. Member: Northern Ireland Assembly 1982-86, Northern Ireland Forum for Political Dialogue 1996-98; MLA for East Londonderry 1998-2011, and for East Londonderry (revised boundary) 2011-16: Minister for Regional Development 2000-01, Chair, Committee on Social Development 2007-08, Minister of Culture, Arts and Leisure 2008-09. DUP: Security Spokesman 1994; Treasurer; Senior Party Officer. *Councils and public bodies:* Councillor, Londonderry City Council 1981-2011.

Political interests: Economic development, tourism, employment, enterprise, trade and industry.

Other: Member, British-Irish Parliamentary Assembly 2020-.

Publications: Discrimination: The Truth (1987); Discrimination: Where Now? (1993); Ulster's Verdict on the Joint Declaration (1994); Working Toward 2000 (1998).

Recreations: Football, music, reading.

Gregory Campbell MP, House of Commons, London SW1A 0AA
Tel: 020 7219 8495 *Fax:* 020 7219 1953 *Email:* fieldingm@parliament.uk
Constituency: 25 Bushmills Road, Coleraine, Co Londonderry BT52 2BP
Tel: 028 7032 7327 *Email:* dupcoleraine@parliament.uk

LABOUR

CARDEN, DAN

Liverpool Walton *(Majority 30,520)*

Daniel Joseph Carden. Born 28 October 1986.

Education: St Edward's College, Liverpool; London School of Economics (international relations).

Non-political career: Parliamentary Researcher; Aide to Unite General Secretary Len McCluskey. Unite the Union.

Political career: Member for Liverpool Walton since 8 June 2017; PPS to Rebecca Long-Bailey as Shadow Secretary of State for Business, Energy and Industrial Strategy 2017-18; Shadow Minister for International Development 2018; Shadow Secretary of State for International Development 2018-20; Shadow Minister for Treasury (Shadow Financial Secretary) 2020. *Select committees:* Member: Procedure 2017-19, Joint Committee on Statutory Instruments 2017-19.

Dan Carden MP, House of Commons, London SW1A 0AA
Tel: 020 7219 2673 *Email:* dan.carden.mp@parliament.uk
Constituency: 66 Priory Road, Anfield, Liverpool L4 2RZ
Tel: 0151-284 1160 Website: www.66prioryroad.co.uk *Twitter:* @DanCardenMP

LIBERAL DEMOCRAT

CARMICHAEL, ALISTAIR

Orkney and Shetland *(Majority 2,507)*

Liberal Democrat Spokesperson for Home Affairs, Political and Constitutional Reform and Northern Ireland

Alexander Morrison Carmichael. Born 15 July 1965; Son of Alexander Carmichael, farmer, and Mina Carmichael, née McKay; Married Kathryn Jane Eastham 1987 (2 sons).

Education: Islay High School, Argyll; Aberdeen University (LLB Scots law 1992; Dip LP 1993); French, German.

Non-political career: Hotel manager 1984-89; Procurator fiscal depute, Procurator Fiscal Service 1993-96; Solicitor, private practice 1996-2001.

Political career: Contested Paisley South 1987 general election. Member for Orkney and Shetland since 7 June 2001 general election; Scottish Liberal Democrat Spokesperson on the Energy Review 2001-02; Liberal Democrat: Deputy Spokesperson for: Northern Ireland 2002-05, Home Affairs 2004-06, Shadow Secretary of State for: Transport 2006-07, Northern Ireland and Scotland 2007-08, 2008-10; Deputy Chief Whip (Comptroller of HM Household) 2010-13; Member, Parliamentary and Political Service Honours Committee 2012-13; Secretary of State for Scotland 2013-15; Liberal Democrat: Spokesperson for Home Affairs 2015-16, 2020-, Shadow First Secretary of State 2016-17, Chief Whip 2017-20, Shadow Secretary of State/Spokesperson for Northern Ireland 2017-19, 2020-, Spokesperson for: Environment, Food and Rural Affairs 2019, Foreign Affairs 2019-20, Exiting the European Union 2019-20, Political and Constitutional Reform 2020-. *Select committees:* Member: Scottish Affairs 2001-05, 2008-10 International Development 2001-02, Public Accounts 2005-06, Joint Committee on Consolidation, Etc, Bills 2008-10, Members' Allowances 2009-10, Joint Committee on Security 2010-13, Energy and Climate Change 2015-16, Exiting the European Union 2016-17. Liberal Democrat: Member, Federal Policy Committee 2004-, Deputy Leader, Scottish Liberal Democrats 2012-.

Political interests: Transport, agriculture, fishing industry, criminal justice, energy, human rights, connectivity; Burma, Palestine/Israel, Uzbekistan.

Other: Member, British-Irish Parliamentary Assembly 2020-; Amnesty International; Elder, Church of Scotland 1995-; Director, Solicitors Will Aid (Scotland) Ltd; Patron, Hong Kong Watch 2019-; RNLI, Amicus Lime; PC 2011.

Recreations: Amateur dramatics, music.

Rt Hon Alistair Carmichael MP, House of Commons, London SW1A 0AA
Tel: 020 7219 8181 *Email:* carmichaela@parliament.uk
Constituency: Orkney: 14 Palace Road, Kirkwall, Orkney KW15 1PA
Tel: 01856 876541
Shetland: 171 Commercial Street, Lerwick, Shetland ZE1 0EN
Tel: 01595 690044 Website: www.alistaircarmichael.co.uk *Twitter:* @amcarmichaelMP

CONSERVATIVE

CARTER, ANDY

Warrington South *(Majority 2,010)*

Andrew John Carter. Born January 1974; Married Aggie (1 son).

Education: Worksop College, Nottinghamshire; De Montfort University (BA economics 1995); Wharton Business School, Pennsylvania University (AMP strategy 2011).

Non-political career: Radio journalist; Managing director: Trax FM, Linc FM Group 1995-2000, Radio Investments 2000-02, Guardian Media Group, Cardiff 2003-08; Group managing director, Real and Smooth Ltd 2010-14; Managing director, Shoebridge 2014-.

Political career: Member for Warrington South since 12 December 2019. *Select committees:* Member: Privileges 2020-, Standards 2020-. Deputy chair, Warrington Conservative Association. *Councils and public bodies:* Councillor, Lymm Parish Council 2018-; Trustee, TBAP Multi Academy Trust; Magistrate, Merseyside Bench.

Recreations: Watching both cricket and football.

Andy Carter MP, House of Commons, London SW1A 0AA
Tel: 020 7219 6867 *Email:* andy.carter.mp@parliament.uk
Constituency: Conservative House, 1 Stafford Road, Warrington WA4 6RP
Tel: 01925 231267 Website: www.andycarter.org.uk *Twitter:* @MrAndy_Carter

CONSERVATIVE

CARTLIDGE, JAMES

South Suffolk *(Majority 22,897)*

PPS to Rishi Sunak as Chancellor of the Exchequer

James Roger Cartlidge. Born 30 April 1974; Married Emily (daughter of Sir Gerald Howarth, MP 1983-92, 1997-2017) (4 children).

Education: Queen Elizabeth Boys' School, Barnet; Manchester University (BA economics 1996); Middlesex University (MSc computing 1997).

Non-political career: Researcher: House of Commons, Conservative Research Department; Freelance Journalist; Founder and Director, Share to Buy Ltd 2004-15.

Political career: Contested Lewisham Deptford 2005 general election. Member for South Suffolk since 7 May 2015 general election; Member, Public Accounts Commission 2015-17; Team PPS, Department of Health 2017-18; PPS: to Secretary of State for Health and Social Care: Jeremy Hunt 2018, Matt Hancock 2018, to Jeremy Hunt as Foreign Secretary 2018-19, to Ben Wallace as Secretary of State for Defence 2019-20, to Rishi Sunak as Chancellor of the Exchequer 2020-. *Select committees:* Member, Work and Pensions 2016-17. Vice-chairman, Lewisham Deptford Conservative Association; Founding member, Conservatives for Reform in Europe 2016. *Councils and public bodies:* Councillor, Babergh District Council 2013-15.

Political interests: Housing, economy, employee share ownership, rural services, welfare reform; Hungary, Romania.

Other: St Mungos Broadway.

Recreations: Football, cricket, drummer.

James Cartlidge MP, House of Commons, London SW1A 0AA
Tel: 020 7219 4875 *Email:* james.cartlidge.mp@parliament.uk
Constituency: No constituency office publicised
Website: www.jamescartlidge.com *Twitter:* @jc4southsuffolk

CONSERVATIVE

CASH, BILL

Stone *(Majority 19,945)*

Chair, Select Committee on European Scrutiny

William Nigel Paul Cash. Born 10 May 1940; Son of late Paul Cash MC (killed in action 1944) and Moyra Roberts, née Morrison; Married Bridget Lee 1965 (2 sons 1 daughter).

Education: Stonyhurst College, Clitheroe, Lancashire; Lincoln College, Oxford (MA history); French.

Non-political career: Solicitor 1967-: Solicitor, William Cash & Company 1979-.

Political career: Member for Stafford 1984 by-election to 1997, for Stone 1997-2010, for Stone (revised boundary) since 6 May 2010 general election; Shadow Attorney General and Shadow Secretary of State for Constitutional Affairs 2001-03. *Select committees:* European Scrutiny: Member 1998-2010, Chair 2010-; Member: Joint Committee on Consolidation, Etc, Bills 2005-10, Liaison 2010-, Joint Committee on Parliamentary Privilege 2013. Conservative Backbench Committee for European Affairs: Chair 1989-91, Joint vice-chair 1997-. Vice-President, Conservatives for Britain 2015-16.

Political interests: European Union, trade and industry, media, small businesses, heritage, debt relief; East Africa, Far East, Europe, Malaysia.

Other: Founder and Chair, European Foundation 1993-; Vice-President, Conservative Small Business Bureau 1986-2000; Spectator Parliamentary Campaigner of the Year 1991; Kt 2014; KM (Knight of Malta). Beefsteak Club, Carlton Club, Vincent's Club Oxford, Garrick Club; Free Foresters Cricket Club.

Publications: Against a Federal Europe (1991); Europe – The Crunch (1992); AEA – The Associated European Area (2000); John Bright: Statesman, Orator, Agitator (I.B.Tauris, 2011); From Brussels With Love (Duckworth New Academia, 2016).

Recreations: Local history, cricket, jazz.

Sir Bill Cash MP, House of Commons, London SW1A 0AA
Tel: 020 7219 6330 *Email:* cashw@parliament.uk
Constituency: 50 High Street, Stone, Staffordshire ST15 8AU
Tel: 01785 811000 *Email:* office@stoneconservatives.co.uk *Twitter:* @BillCashMP

CONSERVATIVE

CATES, MIRIAM

Penistone and Stocksbridge *(Majority 7,210)*

Miriam Joy Cates. Born 23 August 1982; Married (3 children).

Education: Oxford University (BA genetics); Sheffield Hallam University (PGCE).

Non-political career: Teacher; Owner and Finance Director, Redemption Media.

Political career: Member for Penistone and Stocksbridge since 12 December 2019. *Select committees:* Member, Ecclesiastical Committee 2020-. *Councils and public bodies:* Parish Councillor, Bradfield Parish Council 2015-.

Miriam Cates MP, House of Commons, London SW1A 0AA
Tel: 020 7219 3000 *Email:* miriam.cates.mp@parliament.uk
Constituency: 2 Maria House, 3 Fox Valley Way, Stocksbridge, Sheffield S36 2AA
Tel: 0114-288 3034 Website: miriamcates.org.uk

CONSERVATIVE

CAULFIELD, MARIA

Lewes *(Majority 2,457)*

Assistant Government Whip

Maria Colette Caulfield. Born 6 August 1973; Partner Steve Bell.

Education: La Retraite High School, Clapham; RGN Dip adult nursing 1994; BSc cancer care 1996; MSc cancer care 2003.

Non-political career: Registered nurse, Royal Marsden Hospital 2004-.

Political career: Contested Caerphilly 2010 general election. Member for Lewes since 7 May 2015 general election; Apprenticeship Ambassador 2017-; PPS to Grant Shapps as Secretary of State for Transport 2019; Assistant Government Whip 2019-. *Select committees:* Member: Women and Equalities 2015-17, Exiting the European Union 2016-17, Northern Ireland Affairs 2017-18, 2018-19, Joint Committee on Statutory Instruments 2019. Chairman, Conservative Backbench Policy Committee on Health 2015-17. Member, Conservative Councillors Association; Vice-chairman, Women, Conservative Party 2018. *Councils and public bodies:* Brighton and Hove City Council: Councillor 2007-11, Cabinet Member for Housing 2007-11; Vice-President, Local Government Association 2018-19.

Political interests: NHS, housing and homelessness, rural issues and farming.

Other: Member, British-Irish Parliamentary Assembly 2017-18; Owner and shareholder, Lewes Football Club; Member, Nursing and Midwifery Council 1994-; Trustee, BHT Sussex 2013-.

Maria Caulfield MP, House of Commons, London SW1A 0AA
Tel: 020 7219 5946 *Email:* maria.caulfield.mp@parliament.uk
Constituency: Unit 6 Villandry, West Quay, Newhaven, East Sussex BN9 9GB
Website: www.mariacaulfield.co.uk *Twitter:* @mariacaulfield

CONSERVATIVE

CHALK, ALEX

Cheltenham *(Majority 981)*

Parliamentary Under-Secretary of State, Ministry of Justice; Assistant Government Whip

Alexander John Gervase Chalk. Born 8 August 1976; Married Sarah 2011 (3 children).

Education: Winchester College; Magdalen College, Oxford (BA history 1998); City University (Graduate Diploma law 2000); Inns of Court School of Law (Bar Vocational Course 2001); Conversational French and Russian.

Non-political career: Called to the Bar, Middle Temple 2001; Barrister, 6KBW College Hill 2004-.

Political career: Member for Cheltenham since 7 May 2015 general election; Team PPS, Department for Education 2018; PPS to: Matt Hancock as Secretary of State for Health and Social Care 2018-19, Penny Mordaunt as Secretary of State for Defence and Minister for Women and Equalities 2019, Dominic Raab as First Secretary of State and Foreign Secretary 2019-20; Assistant Government Whip 2020-; Parliamentary Under-Secretary of State, Ministry of Justice 2020-. *Select committees:* Member, Justice 2015-19. *Councils and public bodies:* Councillor, Hammersmith and Fulham Council 2006-14.

Other: Substitute Member, UK Delegation to Parliamentary Assembly of Council of Europe 2017-18; Member, South Eastern Circuit; Member, Criminal Bar Association.

Alex Chalk MP, House of Commons, London SW1A 0AA
Tel: 020 7219 8087 *Email:* alex.chalk.mp@parliament.uk
Constituency: 2 Henrietta Street, Cheltenham, Gloucestershire GL50 4AA
Tel: 01242 210473 Website: www.alexchalk.com *Twitter:* @AlexChalkChelt

LIBERAL DEMOCRAT

CHAMBERLAIN, WENDY

North East Fife *(Majority 1,316)*

Liberal Democrat Chief Whip; Spokesperson for Scotland, Wales and Work and Pensions

Wendy Anne Chamberlain. Born 2 December 1976; Married (2 children).

Education: Greenock Academy; Edinburgh University (MA English language and literature 1998); Carnegie College (CMI executive diploma management 2009).

Non-political career: Lothian and Borders Police: Police Officer 1999-2005, Investors in People Coordinator 2005-07; Part-time Communications Lecturer, Carnegie College 2006-07; Business Support Manager, Association of Chief Police Officers in Scotland 2007-10; Business Management Unit Project Officer, Scottish Police Services Authority 2010-11; Scottish Regional Employment and Training Manager, Right Management 2013-15; Diageo: Capability Development Manager 2015-18, Capability Specialist 2018-19.

Political career: Contested Stirling 2017 general election. Member for North East Fife since 12 December 2019; Liberal Democrat: Spokesperson for: Political and Constitutional Reform 2019-20, Scotland 2019-, Wales 2019-, Northern Ireland 2019-20, International Development 2019-20, Work and Pensions 2020-, Chief Whip 2020-. *Select committees:* Member, Scottish Affairs 2020-.

Political interests: Education, NHS, mental health.

Other: Board Member, Camanachd Association 2017-.

Wendy Chamberlain MP, House of Commons, London SW1A 0AA
Tel: 020 7219 4409 *Email:* wendy.chamberlain.mp@parliament.uk
Constituency: Unit G3, Granary Business Centre, Coal Road, Cupar, Fife KY15 5YQ
Tel: 01334 656361 *Twitter:* @wendychambLD

LABOUR

CHAMPION, SARAH

Rotherham *(Majority 3,121)*

Chair, Select Committee on International Development

Sarah Deborah Champion. Born 10 July 1969; Daughter of Ronald Champion and Mary Champion, née Biggs; Divorced.

Education: Prince William Comprehensive School, Oundle; Sheffield University (BA psychology 1991); Derby University (PG Cert; Diploma psychodynamic counselling).

Non-political career: Arts centre manager, Rotherham Metropolitan Borough Council 1992-94; Arts development officer, Ashfield Metropolitan Borough Council 1994-96; Chief executive officer: Chinese Arts Centre, Manchester 1996-2008, Bluebell Wood Children's Hospice, Dinnington 2008-12. Member, Community.

Political career: Member for Rotherham since 29 November 2012 by-election; Shadow Minister for Preventing Abuse and Domestic Violence 2015-June 2016, July 2016; Shadow Secretary of State for Women and Equalities 2016-17. *Select committees:* Member: Transport 2012-15, Environment, Food and Rural Affairs 2015, Administration 2017-19, Public Administration and Constitutional Affairs 2018, Women and Equalities 2018-19; Chair, International Development 2020-; Member: Liaison 2020-, Work of the Independent Commission for Aid Impact Sub-committee 2020-, Joint Committee on the National Security Strategy 2020-, Speaker's Advisory Committee on Works of Art 2020-, Arms Export Controls 2020-.

Political interests: Welfare, health, education, social care, defence, economy, manufacturing, justice; China, East Asia, Kashmir, Palestine, South East Asia, Sri Lanka, USA.

Other: Member, Executive Committee, Commonwealth Parliamentary Association United Kingdom 2020-; Various national and constituency based charities; Youth Friendly MP Award.

Publications: Representing the People (1999); Made in China (2001); Vital: International Live Artists of Chinese Descent (2008).

Recreations: Endurance horse riding, gardening, food, travel, film.

Sarah Champion MP, House of Commons, London SW1A 0AA
Tel: 020 7219 5942/2645 *Email:* sarah.champion.mp@parliament.uk
Constituency: Unit 35, Moorgate Crofts Business Centre, South Grove, Rotherham S60 2DH
Tel: 01709 331035/01709 331036 Website: www.sarahchampionmp.com
Twitter: @sarahchampionMP

SCOTTISH NATIONAL PARTY

CHAPMAN, DOUGLAS

Dunfermline and West Fife *(Majority 10,699)*

SNP Spokesperson for Small Business and Innovation

Born 5 January 1955; Married (2 children).

Education: W Calder High School; Napier College.

Non-political career: TSB Scotland: Branch banking, Personnel management; Gleneagles Hotel; Fife Enterprise; Researcher to Bruce Crawford MSP 1999-2005.

Political career: Contested Dunfermline and West Fife 2005 and Kirkcaldy and Cowdenbeath 2010 general elections. Member for Dunfermline and West Fife since 7 May 2015 general election; SNP Spokesperson for: Defence Procurement 2017-19, Nuclear Disarmament 2018-19; Member, Public Accounts Commission 2018-20; SNP Spokesperson for Small Business and Innovation 2020-. *Select committees:* Member: Defence 2015-17, Arms Export Controls 2016-17, Standards 2017-19, Privileges 2017-19, European Scrutiny 2017-18, Regulatory Reform 2017-19, Public Accounts 2018-19. Contested Mid Scotland and Fife region (6) 2011 Scottish Parliament election. Campaign manager, SNP 2006-07. *Councils and public bodies:* Fife Council: Councillor 1997-98, 2007-15, Chair, Education and Children's Services Committee 2007-12.

Political interests: Defence procurement, nuclear disarmament.

Other: Member: UK delegation, NATO Parliamentary Assembly 2017-20, Executive Committee, British-American Parliamentary Group.

Douglas Chapman MP, House of Commons, London SW1A 0AA
Tel: 020 7219 6888 *Email:* douglas.chapman.mp@parliament.uk
Constituency: 16 Cromarty Campus, Rosyth Europarc, Rosyth KY11 2WX
Tel: 01383 324775 Website: douglaschapman.scot *Twitter:* @DougChapmanSNP

LABOUR

CHARALAMBOUS, BAMBOS

Enfield Southgate *(Majority 4,450)*

Shadow Minister for Crime Reduction and Courts; Opposition Whip

Charalambos Charalambous. Born 2 December 1967.

Education: Chace School, Enfield; Liverpool Polytechnic (LLB 1990); London South Bank University (Postgraduate Diploma in Legal Practice 1996); Greek.

Non-political career: Trainee solicitor/outdoor clerk, Saunders & Co 1994-97; Housing caseworker, Hodge, Jones & Allen 1998; Solicitor, housing litigation team, London Borough of Hackney Council 1998-2017. Member: GMB 1994-, Unison 2009-.

Political career: Contested Epping Forest 2005 and Enfield Southgate 2010 and 2015 general elections. Member for Enfield Southgate since 8 June 2017; PPS to Rebecca Long-Bailey as Shadow Secretary of State for Business, Energy and Industrial Strategy 2018; Opposition Whip 2018-; Shadow Minister for: Justice 2020, Home Office (Crime Reduction and Courts) 2020-. *Select committees:* Member: Justice 2017-19, Procedure 2017-, Finance 2019. *Councils and public bodies:* London Borough of Enfield Council: Councillor 1994-2018, Cabinet member for Leisure, Culture, Localism and Young People; Governor, Eversley Primary School 1993-2014.

Political interests: Culture, law and order, justice, local government, child poverty, education, end-of-life care, climate change, international aid; Cyprus, Middle East.

Other: Member: Amnesty International 1996-, Fabian Society 2003-; Member, Law Society; Chair, Enfield Law Centre 2002-.

Recreations: Reading, travel, the arts, cinema, sport, walking.

Bambos Charalambous MP, House of Commons, London SW1A 0AA
Tel: 020 7219 3460 *Email:* bambos.charalambous.mp@parliament.uk
Constituency: 472 Green Lanes, London N13 5PA
Tel: 020 8882 0088 Website: www.bambos.org.uk *Twitter:* @Bambos_MP

SCOTTISH NATIONAL PARTY

CHERRY, JOANNA

Edinburgh South West *(Majority 11,982)*

Joanna Catherine Cherry. Born 18 March 1966.

Education: Holy Cross School, Edinburgh; St Margaret's Convent School for Girls, Edinburgh; Edinburgh University (LLB 1988; LLM 1989; DipLP 1990); French.

Non-political career: Called to the Bar 1995; Standing Junior Counsel, Scottish Government 2003-09; Advocate Depute 2008-11; National Sex Crimes Unit, Crown Office; QC, Faculty of Advocates 2009-.

Political career: Member for Edinburgh South West since 7 May 2015 general election; SNP: Spokesperson for Home Affairs/SNP Shadow Home Secretary 2015-21, Spokesperson/Shadow Secretary of State for Justice 2015-21. *Select committees:* Member: Exiting the European Union/Future Relationship with the European Union 2016-21, Joint Committee on Human Rights 2017-. Member, SNP 2008-; Co-founder, Lawyers for Yes; Elected Member, Parliamentarian – National Executive Committee 2020-.

Political interests: Prorogation of Parliament 2019.

Other: Pro bono work: Women's Aid, Rape Crisis; Non-practising member, Faculty of Advocates; Honorary Bencher, Middle Temple.

Publications: Co-author, Mental Health and Scots Law in Practice.

Joanna Cherry QC MP, House of Commons, London SW1A 0AA
Tel: 020 7219 6646 *Email:* joanna.cherry.mp@parliament.uk
Constituency: 139 Dundee Street, Edinburgh EH11 1BP
Tel: 0131-600 0156 Website: www.joannacherry.scot *Twitter:* @joannaccherry

CONSERVATIVE

CHISHTI, REHMAN

Gillingham and Rainham *(Majority 15,119)*

Atta-Ur-Rehman Chishti. Born 4 October 1978.

Education: Fort Luton High School for Boys; Chatham Grammar School for Girls; University of Wales, Aberystwyth (law 2000); Inns of Court School of Law (Bar Vocational Course; Postgraduate Diploma law 2001); Urdu.

Non-political career: Special adviser to Benazir Bhutto 1999-2007; Called to the Bar, Lincoln's Inn 2001; Barrister, Goldsmith Chambers, London 2003-09; Special adviser to Francis Maude MP as Chair of Conservative Party 2006-07; Adviser to King Faisal Center for Research and Islamic Studies 2016-.

Political career: Contested (Labour) Horsham 2005 general election. Member for Gillingham and Rainham since 6 May 2010 general election; PPS to: Nick Gibb as Minister of State for School Reform, Department for Education 2014-15, Jeremy Wright as Attorney General 2015-16; Trade Envoy to Pakistan 2017-18; Prime Minister's Special Envoy for Freedom of Religion or Belief 2019-20. *Select committees:* Member: Joint Committee on Human Rights 2010-14, Joint Committee on the Draft Defamation Bill 2011, Justice 2012-15, Backbench Business 2017, Petitions 2017-18, Home Affairs 2017-19. Vice-chairman, Communities, Conservative Party 2018. *Councils and public bodies:* Medway Council: Councillor 2003-, Cabinet Member for Community Safety and Enforcement 2007-10; Governor, Chatham Grammar School for Girls 2001-12.

Political interests: Law and order, criminal justice system, foreign affairs, NHS; Asia, Central America, Middle East, Pakistan, Saudi Arabia, South America, USA.

Other: Bar Council of England and Wales.

Recreations: Cricket, running, reading, squash, tennis.

Rehman Chishti MP, House of Commons, London SW1A 0AA
Tel: 020 7219 7075 *Email:* rehman.chishti.mp@parliament.uk
Constituency: Gillingham and Rainham Conservatives, Burden House, 200a Canterbury Street, Gillingham, Kent ME7 5XG
Tel: 01634 570118 Website: www.rehmanchishti.com *Twitter:* @Rehman_Chishti

CONSERVATIVE

CHOPE, CHRISTOPHER

Christchurch *(Majority 24,617)*

Christopher Robert Chope. Born 19 May 1947; Son of late Judge Robert Chope and Pamela Chope, née Durell; Married Christine Hutchinson 1987 (1 son 1 daughter).

Education: St Andrew's School, Eastbourne; Marlborough College; St Andrew's University (LLB 1970).

Non-political career: Barrister, Inner Temple 1972; Consultant, Ernst and Young 1992-98.

Political career: Member for Southampton Itchen 1983-92. Contested Southampton Itchen 1992 general elecion. Member for Christchurch 1997-2010, for Christchurch (revised boundary) since 6 May 2010 general election; PPS to Peter Brooke as Minister of State, HM Treasury 1986; Parliamentary Under-Secretary of State: Department of the Environment 1986-90, Department of Transport (Minister for Roads and Traffic) 1990-92; Opposition Spokesperson for: the Environment, Transport and the Regions 1997-98, Trade and Industry 1998-99, the Treasury 2001-02; Shadow Minister for: Transport 2002-03, Environment and Transport 2003-05. *Select committees:* Member: Trade and Industry 1999-2002, Chairmen's Panel/Panel of Chairs 2005-, Procedure 2005-10, 2016-, Administration 2006-10, Political and Constitutional Reform 2010-15, Standards 2013-19, Privileges 2013-19, Justice 2013-15, Scottish Affairs 2015-17, Communities and Local Government 2017, Exiting the European Union/Future Relationship with the European Union 2017-21, Home Affairs 2017-19, Environmental Audit 2020-. Joint Secretary, Conservative Backbench Environmental Committee 1983-86; 1922 Committee: Executive member 2001-05, 2005-06, Secretary 2006-12. Member, Executive Committee, Society of Conservative Lawyers 1983-86; Vice-chair, Conservative Party 1997-98; Founding Member, Conservatives for Britain 2015-16. *Councils and public bodies:* London Borough Wandsworth Council: Councillor 1974-83, Council Leader 1979-83; Member: Health and Safety Commission 1992-97, Local Government Commission for England 1994-95.

Other: Member, Parliamentary Delegation to Council of Europe -2015: Chair: Migration and Refugees Committee 2011-12, Legal Affairs and Human Rights Committee 2012-; Substitute Member, UK Delegation to Parliamentary Assembly of Council of Europe 2017-; Fellow, Industry and Parliament Trust 2001; OBE 1982; Kt 2018.

Sir Christopher Chope OBE MP, House of Commons, London SW1A 0AA
Tel: 020 7219 5808 *Email:* chopec@parliament.uk
Constituency: 37 Bargates, Christchurch, Dorset BH23 1QD
Tel: 01425 541087 Website: www.chrischope.com

CONSERVATIVE

CHURCHILL, JO

Bury St Edmunds *(Majority 24,988)*

Parliamentary Under-Secretary of State for Prevention, Public Health and Primary Care, Department of Health and Social Care

Johanna Peta Churchill. Born 18 March 1964; Daughter of G R Wuidart; Married (4 daughters).

Education: Dame Alice Harpur School, Bedford; BSc business and psychology; MSc business and occupational psychology.

Non-political career: Financial and operational director, SLS Ltd 1998-2015.

Political career: Member for Bury St Edmunds since 7 May 2015 general election; PPS to: Mike Penning as Minister of State for the Armed Forces, Ministry of Defence 2016-17, Jeremy Hunt as Secretary of State for Health/Health and Social Care 2017-18; Assistant Government Whip 2018-19; Parliamentary Under-Secretary of State for Prevention, Public Health and Primary Care, Department of Health and Social Care 2019-. *Select committees:* Member: Women and Equalities 2015-17, Environmental Audit 2015-16. Founding member, Conservatives for Reform in Europe 2016. *Councils and public bodies:* Lincolnshire County Council: Councillor 2013-15, Executive Support Councillor, Economic and Environmental Portfolio; School governor.

Political interests: Health, business, agritech, life sciences, education.

Other: Member, Executive Committee, Commonwealth Parliamentary Association UK 2016-17; Member: Lincolnshire Economic Action Partnership, Lincolnshire Forum for Agriculture and Horticulture, Breakthrough National Advisory Group; Breakthrough Breast Cancer.

Recreations: Skiing, walking, gardening.

Jo Churchill MP, House of Commons, London SW1A 0AA
Tel: 020 7219 8487 *Email:* jo.churchill.mp@parliament.uk
Constituency: 10 Hatter Street, Bury St Edmunds, Suffolk IP33 1LZ
Tel: 01284 752311 *Email:* lesley.canham@parliament.uk Website: www.jochurchill.org.uk
Twitter: @Jochurchill4

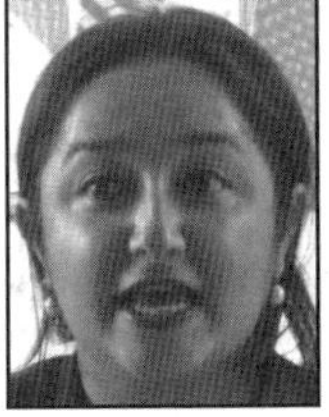

LABOUR

CLARK, FERYAL

Enfield North *(Majority 6,492)*

Opposition Whip

Feryal Demirci Clark. Married Andrew.

Education: Exeter University (bioinformatics).

Non-political career: Diagnostic Biochemistry, University College Hospital 2006-09; Diagnostic Virology, Barts and The London NHS Trust 2009-10. Unison.

Political career: Member for Enfield North since 12 December 2019; PPS to: Steve Reed as Shadow Secretary of State for Communities and Local Government 2020, Thangam Debbonaire as Shadow Secretary of State for Housing 2020; Opposition Whip 2020-. *Select committees:* Member, Environmental Audit 2020-. *Councils and public bodies:* Hackney Council: Councillor 2006-, Cabinet Member for Neighbourhoods, Cabinet Member for Health, Social Care, Leisure and Parks, Deputy Mayor; Member, London Waste Authority Recycling Board.

Other: Member, UK delegation, NATO Parliamentary Assembly 2020-; Association of Labour Councillors.

Feryal Clark MP, House of Commons, London SW1A 0AA
Tel: 020 7219 6607 *Email:* feryal.clark.mp@parliament.uk
Constituency: 542 Hertford Road, Enfield Lock, Enfield EN3 5ST
Tel: 020 8804 4543 Website: www.feryalclark.co.uk *Twitter:* @FeryalClark

CONSERVATIVE

CLARK, GREG

Tunbridge Wells *(Majority 14,645)*

Chair, Select Committee on Science and Technology

Gregory David Clark. Born 28 August 1967; Son of John and Patricia Clark; Married Helen Fillingham 1999 (2 daughters 1 son).

Education: St Peter's Comprehensive, Middlesbrough; Magdalene College, Cambridge (BA economics 1989, MA); London School of Economics (PhD 1992).

Non-political career: Consultant, Boston Consulting Group 1991-94; Teaching and research, LSE and Open University Business School 1994-96; Commercial Policy, BBC: Chief adviser 1997-99, Controller 1999-2001; Special adviser to Ian Lang as Secretary of State for Trade and Industry 1996-97; Director of Policy, Conservative Party 2001-05.

Political career: Member for Tunbridge Wells 2005-10, for Tunbridge Wells (revised boundary) since 6 May 2010 general election; Shadow Minister for: Charities, Voluntary Bodies and Social Enterprise 2006-07, Cabinet Office 2007-08; Shadow Secretary of State for Energy and Climate Change 2008-10; Minister of State for: Decentralisation, Department for Communities and Local Government 2010-11, Cities, Departments for Communities and Local Government and Business, Innovation and Skills 2011, Decentralisation and Cities, Departments for Business, Innovation and Skills and Communities and Local Government 2011-12; Financial Secretary, HM Treasury 2012-13; Minister of State for: Cities and Constitution, Cabinet Office 2013-14, Universities, Science and Cities, Department for Business, Innovation and Skills and Cabinet Office 2014-15; Secretary of State for: Communities and Local Government 2015-16, Business, Energy and Industrial Strategy 2016-19; Board Member, Parliamentary Office of Science and Technology (POST) 2020-. *Select committees:* Member: Public Accounts 2005-07, Liaison 2020-; Chair, Science and Technology 2020-. Conservative Party whip removed September-October 2019. *Councils and public bodies:* Councillor, Westminster City Council 2002-05.

Political interests: Economics, poverty, welfare reform, transport, health, housing development, energy and climate change.

Other: President: Tunbridge Wells Constitutional Club, Hawkhurst Community Hospital League of Friends; Vice-president: Tunbridge Wells Rugby Football Club, Tunbridge Wells Cricket Club; Patron: Institute of Economic Development, Tunbridge Wells Mental Health Resource Centre, Royal Tunbridge Wells Orpheus Male Voice Choir, Hospice in the Weald, Friends of Grosvenor and Hilbert Park; Vice-patron, Brains Matter; Honorary Member, Tunbridge Wells Rotary Club; Honorary Fellow, Nuffield College, Oxford; PC 2010.

Rt Hon Greg Clark MP, House of Commons, London SW1A 0AA
Tel: 020 7219 6977 *Email:* greg.clark.mp@parliament.uk
Constituency: No constituency office publicised
Tel: 01892 519854 Website: www.gregclark.org *Twitter:* @GregClarkMP

CONSERVATIVE

CLARKE, SIMON

Middlesbrough South and East Cleveland *(Majority 11,626)*

Simon Richard Clarke. Born 28 September 1984; Married Hannah 2012 (1 son).

Education: Yarm School, Yarm, Stockton on Tees; University College, Oxford (MA modern history 2006); Oxford Brookes University (Graduate Diploma law 2007); BPP Law School (LPC 2008); French.

Non-political career: Trainee Solicitor, Slaughter and May 2008-10; Senior Parliamentary Assistant to Dominic Raab MP 2010-13; Senior Policy Adviser to Graham Stuart MP 2013-17.

Political career: Contested Middlesbrough 2015 general election. Member for Middlesbrough South and East Cleveland since 8 June 2017; Exchequer Secretary, HM Treasury 2019-20; Minister of State for Regional Growth and Local Government, Ministry of Housing,

Communities and Local Government 2020; Member, Speaker's Committee on the Electoral Commission 2020. *Select committees:* Member: Regulatory Reform 2017-19, Treasury 2018-19, Treasury Sub-committee 2018-19.

Political interests: Industrial strategy, economics, energy, education, transport, foreign affairs; China, Iran, Pakistan, Russia.

Recreations: Middlesbrough FC supporter.

Simon Clarke MP, House of Commons, London SW1A 0AA
Tel: 020 7219 2674 *Email:* simon.clarke.mp@parliament.uk
Constituency: 11 Rectory Lane, Guisborough TS14 7DJ
Tel: 01287 204709 *Email:* simonclarkecasework@gmail.com
Website: www.simon-clarke.org.uk *Twitter:* @SimonClarkeMP

CONSERVATIVE

CLARKE, THEO

Stafford *(Majority 14,377)*

Theodora Roosevelt Clarke. Born August 1985; Daughter of Theresa and Sir Toby Clarke.

Education: Downe House; Newcastle University (BA English literature, politics and history of art 2007); Courtault Institute of Art (MA history of art 2008).

Non-political career: Head of Programmes, Sales and Business Development, Lifestep Futures Ltd 2009-13; Curatorial Department of Photography, Museum of Modern Art, New York 2010; Youth Organiser, No to AV 2010-11; Team Leader, Project Umubano 2011-12; Founder and Editor, Russian Art and Culture online magazine 2011-; Coalition for Global Prosperity: Founder 2017-, Chief Executive 2017-19.

Political career: Contested Bristol East 2015 and 2017 general elections. Member for Stafford since 12 December 2019; Trade Envoy to Kenya 2020-. *Select committees:* Chair, Work of the Independent Commission for Aid Impact Sub-committee 2020-; Member: International Development 2020-, Speaker's Advisory Committee on Works of Art 2020-, Women and Equalities 2020-, Arms Export Controls 2020-. Director of Communications, Conservative Women's Organisation 2011-13; Vice-chair, Cities of London and Westminster Conservatives 2013-14; Director, Conservative Friends of International Development 2016-.

Political interests: Foreign affairs, international development.

Other: Co-founder, Association of Women in the Arts 2016-.

Theo Clarke MP, House of Commons, London SW1A 0AA
Tel: 020 7219 3000 *Email:* theo.clarke.mp@parliament.uk
Constituency: No constituency office publicised
Tel: 01785 245444 Website: www.theo-clarke.org.uk *Twitter:* @theodoraclarke

CONSERVATIVE

CLARKE-SMITH, BRENDAN

Bassetlaw *(Majority 14,013)*

Born 17 August 1980; Married Andra (1 son).

Education: Harry Carlton Comprehensive School; South Nottingham College; Nottingham Trent University (BA politics 2001); Bishop Grosserteste College (PGCE religious education (secondary) 2008); Gothenburg University (MSc European studies 2013).

Non-political career: Teacher; Head of Royal School in Transylvania.

Political career: Member for Bassetlaw since 12 December 2019. *Select committees:* Member: Housing, Communities and Local Government 2020-, International Development 2020-. Contested East Midlands region 2014 and 2019 European Parliament elections. *Councils and public bodies:* Councillor: Nottingham City Council 2003-11, Newark and Sherwood District Council 2019-.

Political interests: Brexit, NHS, education.

Brendan Clarke-Smith MP, House of Commons, London SW1A 0AA
Tel: 020 7219 3000 *Email:* brendan.clarkesmith.mp@parliament.uk
Constituency: 16 Bridge Place, Worksop S80 1JS
Tel: 01909 738956 Website: www.brendanclarkesmith.com *Twitter:* @Bren4Bassetlaw

CONSERVATIVE

CLARKSON, CHRIS

Heywood and Middleton *(Majority 663)*

PPS to Robert Buckland as Lord Chancellor and Secretary of State for Justice

Christopher Mark Clarkson. Born 12 November 1982; Son of Terrence Clarkson and Alison Parker; Single.

Education: St Wilfrids Church of England GM School; Dundee University (LLB 2005); German, French, Dutch, Japanese.

Non-political career: Corporate Development Manager, IRIS Legal 2007-10; Corporate Development Consultant, Virgin 2010-19.

Political career: Contested Wallasey 2015 and Heywood and Middleton 2017 general elections. Member for Heywood and Middleton since 12 December 2019; PPS to Robert Buckland as Lord Chancellor and Secretary of State for Justice 2020-. *Select committees:* Member: Regulatory Reform 2020-, Science and Technology 2020-. *Councils and public bodies:* Salford City Council: Councillor 2011-19, Opposition Spokesperson for Finance 2015-18.

Political interests: Planning and development issues, rural affairs, law and order, utility and fuel pricing, tax reform, local government finance, electoral reform.

Other: Member: Countryside Alliance, Mensa. St James' Club (Manchester), Carlton Club.

Recreations: Cooking, running.

Chris Clarkson MP, House of Commons, London SW1A 0AA
Tel: 020 7219 4405 *Email:* chris.clarkson.mp@parliament.uk
Constituency: 83 Manchester Street, Heywood OL10 1PB
Tel: 01706 538262 Website: www.chrisclarkson.org.uk *Twitter:* @ChrisClarksonMP

CONSERVATIVE

CLEVERLY, JAMES

Braintree *(Majority 24,673)*

Minister of State for Middle East and North Africa, Foreign, Commonwealth and Development Office

James Spencer Cleverly. Born 4 September 1969; Married Susannah 2000 (2 sons).

Education: Colfe's School for Boys; University of West London (Degree business).

Non-political career: Sales manager, VNU 1996-2002; International advertising manager, Informa 2002-04; Group advertising manager, Crimson Publishing 2005-06; Online commercial manager, Caspian Publishing 2006-07; Director, Port & Fire Media 2007-11. Lt Colonel, Territorial Army: Commanding officer, 266 (Para) Battery Royal Artillery (Volunteers) 2003-05.

Political career: Contested Lewisham East 2005 general election. Member for Braintree since 7 May 2015 general election; PPS to Brandon Lewis as Minister of State for Immigration, Home Office 2017-18; Parliamentary Under-Secretary of State, Department for Exiting the European Union 2019; Minister without Portfolio, Cabinet Office 2019-20; Minister of State for Middle East and North Africa: Foreign and Commonwealth Office and Department for International Development 2020, Foreign, Commonwealth and Development Office 2020-. *Select committees:* Member: Joint Committee on Consolidation, &c, Bills 2015-19, International Trade 2016-17. Member, Executive, 1922 Committee 2015-17. London Assembly: AM for Bexley and Bromley constituency 2008-16, Youth Ambassador to Mayor of London -2010, Conservative Spokesperson for Environment, Chair: London Waste and Recycling Board 2010-12, London Fire and Emergency Planning Authority 2012-15, London Local Resilience Forum 2012-15. Founding Member, Conservatives for Britain 2015-16; Convenor, Free Enterprise Group 2015-18; Conservative Party: Deputy Chairman 2018-19, Chairman 2019-20.

Political interests: Local business, technology, trade out of poverty, international trade.

Other: President, Bromley District Scouts; Ulysses Trust; Freedom, City of London; Territorial Decoration (TD); PC 2019.

Rt Hon James Cleverly MP, House of Commons, London SW1A 0AA
Tel: 020 7219 8593 *Email:* james.cleverly.mp@parliament.uk
Constituency: No constituency office publicised
Website: www.cleverly4braintree.com *Twitter:* @JamesCleverly

CONSERVATIVE

CLIFTON-BROWN, GEOFFREY

The Cotswolds *(Majority 20,214)*

Geoffrey Robert Clifton-Brown. Born 23 March 1953; Son of Robert Clifton-Brown and late Elizabeth Clifton-Brown; Married Alexandra Peto-Shepherd 1979 (divorced 2003) (1 son 1 daughter).

Education: Eton College; Royal Agricultural College, Cirencester (ARICS); French.

Non-political career: Graduate Estate Surveyor, Property Services Agency, Dorchester 1975; Investment Surveyor, Jones Lang Wootton 1975-79; Managing Director, own farming business in Norfolk 1979-.

Political career: Member for Cirencester and Tewkesbury 1992-97, for Cotswold 1997-2010, for The Cotswolds since 6 May 2010 general election; PPS to Douglas Hogg as Minister of Agriculture, Fisheries and Food 1995-97; Opposition Whip 1999-2001; Opposition Spokesperson for: Environment, Food and Rural Affairs 2001, Transport, Local Government and the Regions 2001-02; Shadow Minister for: Local Government 2002-03, Local and Devolved Government 2003-04; Opposition Whip 2004-05; Assistant Chief Whip 2005; Shadow Minister for: Foreign Affairs 2005-07, Trade 2007, 2009-10, International Development 2007-10. *Select committees:* Member: Public Accounts 1997-99, 2017-, Broadcasting 2000-01, Administration 2001, 2010-11, Finance and Services 2005-15; Selection: Member 2005-06, Chair 2010-15; Member: Liaison 2010-15, High Speed Rail (London-West Midlands) Bill 2015-16, Finance 2015-19, 2020-. 1922 Committee: Member, Executive 2015-16, Treasurer 2016-. Conservative Party: Chair: North Norfolk Constituency Association 1986-91, International Office 2010-15, Vice-chair (international affairs) 2010-15, Board Member 2015-19.

Political interests: Economy, taxation, foreign affairs, environment, agriculture; Brazil, China, India.

Other: Fellow, Industry and Parliament Trust 1996; Armed Forces Parliamentary Fellowship 1997; Fellow, Royal Institute of Chartered Surveyors (FRICS) 2002; Liveryman, Worshipful Company of Farmers; Freedom, City of London; Fellow: Royal Institute of Chartered Surveyors, Royal Agricultural University; Kt 2018. Farmers' Club.

Publications: Privatisation of the State Pension – Secure Funded Provision For All (Bow Group, 1996).

Recreations: Fishing, other rural pursuits.

Sir Geoffrey Clifton-Brown MP, House of Commons, London SW1A 0AA
Tel: 020 7219 5147 *Fax:* 020 7219 2550 *Email:* cliftonbrowng@parliament.uk
Constituency: Gloucestershire Conservative Association Office, 1143 Regent Court, Gloucester Business Park, Gloucester, Gloucestershire GL3 4AD
Tel: 01452 371630 *Email:* info@gloucestershireconservatives.com
Website: www.cliftonbrown.co.uk

CONSERVATIVE

COFFEY, THERESE

Suffolk Coastal *(Majority 20,533)*

Secretary of State for Work and Pensions

Therese Anne Coffey. Born 18 November 1971; Daughter of late Tom Coffey and Sally Coffey.

Education: St Mary's College, Rhos-on-Sea; St Mary's College, Crosby; St Edward's College, Liverpool; University College, London (BSc 1993; PhD chemistry 1997).

Non-political career: Chartered management accountant, Mars UK Ltd 1997-2007; Finance director, Mars Drinks UK 2007-09; Property finance manager, BBC 2009-10.

Political career: Contested Wrexham 2005 general election. Member for Suffolk Coastal since 6 May 2010 general election; Board member, Parliamentary Office of Science and Technology (POST) -2014; PPS to Michael Fallon as Minister of State for: Business and Enterprise, Department for Business, Innovation and Skills 2012-13, Energy, Department of Energy and Climate Change 2013-14, Business and Energy, Department for Business, Innovation and Skills

2013-14; Assistant Government Whip 2014-15; Parliamentary Secretary (Deputy Leader of the House of Commons) 2015-16; Department for Environment, Food and Rural Affairs: Parliamentary Under-Secretary of State for: Environment 2016, 2017-19, Rural Life Opportunities 2016-17, Minister of State 2019; Secretary of State for Work and Pensions 2019-. *Select committees:* Member: Culture, Media and Sport 2010-12, Environmental Audit 2016-19. Contested South East 2004 and 2009 European Parliament elections. Member, Conservative Party 1988-; National deputy chair, Conservative Students 1993-94; Chair, North West Hampshire Conservatives 2006-09; Deputy regional chair, South East 2009; Former member, Conservative Way Forward. *Councils and public bodies:* Councillor, Whitchurch Town Council 1999-2003.

Political interests: Rural affairs, enterprise, energy; EU, Latin America.

Other: Member, CAMRA; Patron: East Coast Hospice, Suffolk Coast Rural Responders, Friends of St Mary's College, Crosby; Life Vice-president, Suffolk Agricultural Association; Member, National Trust; Chair, Suffolk Coast Energy Delivery Board; Water Aid, Dogs Trust; PC 2019.

Recreations: Watching football, gardening, music.

Rt Hon Dr Therese Coffey MP, House of Commons, London SW1A 0AA
Tel: 020 7219 7164 *Email:* therese.coffey.mp@parliament.uk
Constituency: No constituency office publicised
Website: www.theresecoffey.co.uk *Twitter:* @theresecoffey

CONSERVATIVE

COLBURN, ELLIOT

Carshalton and Wallington *(Majority 629)*

Born 6 August 1992; Engaged to Jed Dwight.

Education: Carshalton Boys Sports College; Aberystwyth University (BA law with politics 2013; MA postcolonial politics 2015).

Non-political career: CCS-Collect: Client Services Officer 2011-13, Quality and Compliance Officer 2013-14; Parliamentary Assistant to Paul Scully MP 2015-18; Public Affairs Officer, South West London Health and Care Partnership 2018-19.

Political career: Member for Carshalton and Wallington since 12 December 2019. *Select committees:* Member: Petitions 2020-, Joint Committee on Consolidation, &c, Bills 2020-, Women and Equalities 2020-. *Councils and public bodies:* Councillor, Sutton Council 2018-.

Political interests: Public transport, hospitals.

Other: Trustee, Community Action Sutton 2017-18; Scout Leader, 6th Carshalton Scout Group.

Elliot Colburn MP, House of Commons, London SW1A 0AA
Tel: 020 7219 5862 *Email:* elliot.colburn.mp@parliament.uk
Constituency: No constituency office publicised
Website: www.elliotcolburn.co.uk *Twitter:* @ElliotColburn

CONSERVATIVE

COLLINS, DAMIAN

Folkestone and Hythe *(Majority 21,337)*

Damian Noel Thomas Collins. Born 4 February 1974; Married Sarah Richardson 2004 (1 daughter 1 son).

Education: St Mary's High School, Herefordshire; Belmont Abbey School, Herefordshire; St Benet's Hall, Oxford (BA modern history 1996).

Non-political career: Desk Officer, Conservative Party Research Department 1996-98; Press Officer, Conservative Party Press Office 1998-99; Director, M&C Saatchi 1999-2008; Senior Counsel, Lexington Communications 2008-10.

Political career: Contested Northampton North 2005 general election. Member for Folkestone and Hythe since 6 May 2010 general election; PPS to: Theresa Villers as Secretary of State for Northern Ireland 2012-14, Philip Hammond as Foreign Secretary 2014-15. *Select committees:* Culture, Media and Sport/Digital, Culture, Media and Sport: Member 2010-12, 2015-16, Chair 2016-19; Member: Joint Committee on Consolidation, Etc, Bills 2010-15, Liaison 2016-19. President, Oxford University Conservative Association 1995; Vice-chair, Conservative Party (with responsibility for candidates) 2016-18.

Political interests: Digital and technology policy and regulation, sports governance, social impact of culture and the arts, media and broadcasting, nuclear power, economic regeneration, border security.

Other: Political Officer, Bow Group 2003-04; Member, Advisory Board, Author's Licensing and Collecting Society 2015-; Partner, Infotagion LLP 2019-; Board Member, Center for Countering Digital Hate 2020-; Trustee, Shepway Sports Trust; Folkestone Stop Short Project, Folkestone Youth Project. MCC; Lord's Taverners Club.

Publications: Contributer, Conservative Revival (Politicos, 2006); The New Blue (Social Market Foundation, 2008); Contributor: Britain Beyond Brexit (The Centre for Policy Studies); The Prime Ministers (Hodder & Stoughton, 2020).

Recreations: Sport (football, cricket, rugby union).

Damian Collins MP, House of Commons, London SW1A 0AA
Tel: 020 7219 7072 *Email:* damian.collins.mp@parliament.uk
Constituency: 4 West Cliff Gardens, Folkestone, Kent CT20 1SP
Tel: 01303 253524 *Email:* office@fhconservatives.org.uk Website: www.damiancollins.com
Twitter: @DamianCollins

LIBERAL DEMOCRAT

COOPER, DAISY

St Albans *(Majority 6,293)*

Deputy Leader, Liberal Democrats and Spokesperson for Education

Born 29 October 1981; Married.

Education: Leeds University (LLB 2002); Nottingham University (LLM public international law 2004); Foundation Certificate psychotherapy and counselling.

Non-political career: Project Officer, UN reform, Commonwealth Policy Studies Unit 2004-06; Commonwealth Secretariat: Strategic Planning Officer 2006-10, Consultant to Commonwealth Eminent Persons Group 2010-11; Director, Commonwealth Advisory Bureau 2011-13; Stakeholder manager, Voluntary Service Overseas 2013; Joint Executive Director, Hacked Off 2013-17; Executive Director of Campaigns, More United 2017-19.

Political career: Contested Suffolk Coastal 2010, Mid Sussex 2015 and St Albans 2017 general elections. Member for St Albans since 12 December 2019; Liberal Democrat Spokesperson for: Justice 2019-20, Digital, Culture, Media and Sport 2019-20, Education 2020-. Liberal Democrats: Contested 2014 President election, Deputy Leader 2020-; Campaign director to Jo Swinson, Liberal Democrat Leadership campaign 2019. *Councils and public bodies:* Councillor, Lewes District Council 2015-16.

Political interests: Education, taxation of pubs, commuter services, long-term conditions and disability rights, media reform, international affairs.

Recreations: Playing piano and violin, live music, ballet.

Daisy Cooper MP, House of Commons, London SW1A 0AA
Tel: 020 7219 8568 *Email:* daisy.cooper.mp@parliament.uk
Constituency: No constituency office publicised
Tel: 01727 519900 Website: www.daisycooper.org.uk *Twitter:* @libdemdaisy

LABOUR

COOPER, ROSIE

West Lancashire *(Majority 8,336)*

Rosemary Elizabeth Cooper. Born 5 September 1950; Daughter of William and Rose Cooper; Single.

Education: Bellerive Convent Grammar School; Liverpool University.

Non-political career: Concept Design Partnership & W Cooper Limited 1973-80; The Littlewoods Organisation 1980-2001: Merchandiser 1980-92, Public relations manager 1994-95, Group corporate communications manager 1995-2000, Seconded as project manager for government task force on equal pay 1999-2001. Member, USDAW.

Political career: Contested (Liberal) Liverpool Garston 1983 general election, Knowsley North 1986 by-election and (Liberal/Alliance) 1987 general election, and (Liberal Democrat) Liverpool Broadgreen 1992 general election. Member (Labour) for West Lancashire since 5 May 2005 general election; PPS to: Lord Rooker as Minister of State, Department for Environment, Food and Rural Affairs 2006-07, Ben Bradshaw: as Minister of State, Department for Health

2007-09, as Secretary of State for Culture, Media and Sport 2009-10. *Select committees:* Member: European Scrutiny 2005-06, Northern Ireland Affairs 2005-10, Justice 2007-08, 2010, North West 2009-10, Health 2010-15, Administration 2010-12, Unnopposed Bills (Panel) 2013-15, Health/Health and Social Care 2016-. Hon. Secretary, PLP Departmental Committee for Northern Ireland 2005-10. Contested North West region 2004 European Parliament election. Member: Liberal Party/Liberal Democrats 1966-99, Labour Party 1999-. *Councils and public bodies:* Liverpool City Council (Liberal/Liberal Democrat 1973-99, Labour 1999-2000): Councillor 1973-2000, Lord Mayor 1992-93, Labour spokesperson for housing 1999-2000, Honorary Alderman 2011; Member and vice-chair, Liverpool Health Authority 1994-96; Chair, Liverpool Women's Hospital NHS Foundation Trust 1996-2005.

Political interests: Health, disability equality, housing, social care, transport; Dominican Republic, Haiti, Ireland, Northern Ireland, USA.

Other: Member, British-Irish Parliamentary Assembly; Director, Merseyside Centre for Deaf People 1973-2004; Cosmopolitan Housing Association 1994-2011; Trustee, Roy Castle Lung Cancer Foundation.

Recreations: Theatre, music, cinema, community affairs, tennis.

Rosie Cooper MP, House of Commons, London SW1A 0AA
Tel: 020 7219 3000
Constituency: Suite 108, Malthouse Business Centre, 48 Southport Road, Ormskirk, Lancashire L39 1QR
Tel: 01695 570094 *Email:* rosie@rosiecooper.net Website: www.rosiecooper.net
Twitter: @rosie4westlancs

LABOUR

COOPER, YVETTE Normanton, Pontefract and Castleford *(Majority 1,276)*

Chair, Select Committee on Home Affairs

Born 20 March 1969; Daughter of Tony Cooper, former leader Engineers and Managers Association, and June Cooper; Married Ed Balls 1998 (MP for Normanton 2005-10 and Morley and Outwood 2010-15) (2 daughters 1 son).

Education: Eggars Comprehensive; Balliol College, Oxford (BA philosophy, politics and economics 1990); Harvard University (Kennedy Scholar 1991); London School of Economics (MSc economics 1995).

Non-political career: Economic researcher for John Smith MP 1990-92; Domestic policy specialist, Bill Clinton presidential campaign 1992; Policy adviser to Labour Treasury teams 1992-94; Economic columnist/Leader writer, *The Independent* 1995-97. Member: TGWU, GMB.

Political career: Member for Pontefract and Castleford 1997-2010, for Normanton, Pontefract and Castleford since 6 May 2010 general election; Parliamentary Under-Secretary of State, Department of Health (Public Health) 1999-2002; Parliamentary Secretary, Lord Chancellor's Department 2002-03; Office of the Deputy Prime Minister/Department for Communities and Local Government 2003-08: Parliamentary Under-Secretary of State 2003-05, Minister of State (Minister for Housing and Planning) 2005-07, Minister for Housing (attending cabinet) 2007-08; Chief Secretary to the Treasury 2008-09; Secretary of State for Work and Pensions 2009-10; Shadow Secretary of State for: Work and Pensions 2010, Foreign and Commonwealth Affairs (Shadow Foreign Secretary) 2010-11; Shadow Minister for Women and Equalities 2010-13; Shadow Secretary of State for Home Department (Shadow Home Secretary) 2011-15. *Select committees:* Member: Education and Employment 1997-99, Education and Employment (Employment Sub-Committee) 1997-99; Chair, Home Affairs 2016-; Member: Liaison 2016-, Joint Committee on the National Security Strategy 2016-. Member, Society – Stronger, Safer Communities Policy Commission; Contested Labour leadership election 2015; Chair, Labour's Refugee Taskforce 2015-.

Political interests: Unemployment, coal industry, poverty, equal opportunities; USA.

Other: PC 2007.

Rt Hon Yvette Cooper MP, House of Commons, London SW1A 0AA
Tel: 020 7219 5080 *Email:* coopery@parliament.uk
Constituency: Queen's Mill, 1 Aire Street, Castleford WF10 1JL
Tel: 01977 553388 Website: www.yvettecooper.com *Twitter:* @YvetteCooperMP

INDEPENDENT

CORBYN, JEREMY

Islington North *(Majority 26,188)*

Jeremy Bernard Corbyn. Born 26 May 1949; Son of David Corbyn and Naomi Corbyn; Married Laura Alvarez 2015 (3 sons from previous marriage).

Education: Adams Grammar School, Newport, Shropshire; Spanish.

Non-political career: Official: National Union of Tailor and Garment Workers (NUTGW), Amalgamated Union of Engineering Workers (AUEW); Full-time organiser, National Union of Public Employees (NUPE) 1975-83. NUPE sponsored MP; Member, RMT Parliamentary Campaigning Group 2002-.

Political career: Member for Islington North since 9 June 1983 general election; Leader of the Opposition 2015-20. *Select committees:* Member: Social Security 1991-97, London 2009-10, Justice 2011-15. Member, Socialist Campaign Group; Labour Party: Leader 2015-20, Suspended October-November 2020, PLP Whip withdrawn October 2020-. *Councils and public bodies:* Councillor, Haringey Borough Council 1974-84: Chair: Community Development 1975-78, Public Works 1978-79, Planning 1980-81.

Political interests: People of Islington, Stop the War, Liberation, welfare state, NHS, socialism, human rights, anti-racism, anti-imperialism and internationalism, transport safety, environment; Africa, Chagos Islands, Middle East, Latin America.

Other: Member, Executive Committee, Inter-Parliamentary Union, British Group; Substitute Member, UK Delegation to Parliamentary Assembly, Council of Europe 2020-; Vice-president, Campaign for Nuclear Disarmament; PC 2015.

Recreations: Running, railways.

Rt Hon Jeremy Corbyn MP, House of Commons, London SW1A 0AA
Tel: 020 7219 3000 *Email:* jeremy.corbyn.mp@parliament.uk
Constituency: 86 Durham Road, London N7 7DU
Tel: 020 7561 7488 Website: www.jeremycorbyn.org.uk *Twitter:* @jeremycorbyn

CONSERVATIVE

COSTA, ALBERTO

South Leicestershire *(Majority 24,004)*

PPS to Suella Braverman as Attorney General

Alberto Castrenze Costa. Born 13 November 1971; Married Maria (1 daughter 1 son).

Education: Glasgow University (MA; LLB) (President SRC 1995-96); Strathclyde University (Postgraduate Diploma legal practice); English law conversion course.

Non-political career: Solicitor, Glasgow, Edinburgh and Aberdeen; International lawyer, commercial law firm, London; Solicitor, HM Treasury; Associate: Bellenden Public Affairs, Brizmo Public Affairs; Consultant solicitor, Nicholas Woolf and Co Solicitors 2015-.

Political career: Contested Angus 2010 general election. Member for South Leicestershire since 7 May 2015 general election; PPS to: David Mundell as Secretary of State for Scotland 2017-19, Suella Braverman as Attorney General 2020-. *Select committees:* Member: Justice 2015-17, Privileges 2020-, Standards 2020-, Scottish Affairs 2020-. Trustee, Islington Conservative Association.

Political interests: Dementia care, local business, education.

Other: Secretary, Montrose and District Round Table; Associate member, Chartered Institute of Arbitrators; Member: Law Society of England and Wales, Law Society of Scotland; Director, Furniture Recycling Project Angus.

Recreations: Cooking.

Alberto Costa MP, House of Commons, London SW1A 0AA
Tel: 020 7219 4936 *Email:* alberto.costa.mp@parliament.uk
Constituency: Unit 3, 8a Lutterworth Road, Blaby, Leicestershire LE8 4DN
Tel: 0116-278 1924 Website: www.albertocosta.org.uk *Twitter:* @AlbertoCostaMP

CONSERVATIVE

COURTS, ROBERT

Witney *(Majority 15,177)*

Parliamentary Under-Secretary of State, Department for Transport

Robert Alexander Courts. Born 21 October 1978; Married Kathryn (1 son).

Education: Berkhamsted School; Sheffield University (law).

Non-political career: Called to the Bar, Lincolns' Inn 2003; Barrister, 3 Paper Buildings 2003-; Crown Law Office, New Zealand.

Political career: Member for Witney since 20 October 2016 by-election; Team PPS, Foreign and Commonwealth Office 2018; PPS to: Theresa Villiers as Secretary of State for Environment, Food and Rural Affairs 2019-20, Grant Shapps as Secretary of State for Transport 2020; Parliamentary Under-Secretary of State, Department for Transport 2020-. *Select committees:* Member: Backbench Business 2017-18, Transport 2018-19, Justice 2019, International Trade 2020. Member, Conservative Party 1998-; Chairman, Conservative Future, Meriden; Member, Society of Conservative Lawyers. *Councils and public bodies:* West Oxfordshire District Council: Councillor 2014-17, Deputy Leader and Cabinet Member for Communities and Housing.

Other: Speaker, Thames Valley and Chiltern Air Ambulance Trust 2013-; Member, Federation of Small Businesses; Committee member, Churchill Centre (UK); Member: Personal Injury Bar Association, Criminal Bar Association; Supporter: RAFBF, Combat Stress, Help for Heroes; Pegasus Scholarship to Wellington, New Zealand 2009.

Recreations: Hiking, cycling, playing guitar.

Robert Courts MP, House of Commons, London SW1A 0AA
Tel: 020 7219 5638 *Email:* robert.courts.mp@parliament.uk
Constituency: 58-60 High Street, Witney OX28 6HJ
Tel: 01993 225020 *Email:* robert@robertcourts.co.uk Website: www.robertcourts.co.uk
Twitter: @robertcourts

CONSERVATIVE

COUTINHO, CLAIRE

East Surrey *(Majority 24,040)*

Team PPS, HM Treasury

Claire Coryl Julia Coutinho. Born July 1985.

Education: James Alleyn's Girls' School; Oxford University (MA maths and philosophy 2008).

Non-political career: Associate, Merill Lynch 2008-12; Centre for Social Justice 2013-15; Programme Director, Housing and Finance Institute 2015-17; Corporate Responsibility Manager for Education, KPMG 2017-18; Special Adviser 2017-19: 10 Downing Street, HM Treasury.

Political career: Member for East Surrey since 12 December 2019; Team PPS, HM Treasury 2020-.

Other: Co-Founder, The Novel Diner 2012-14; Organiser, Tomax Talks; Age UK, Jo Cox Foundation.

Claire Coutinho MP, House of Commons, London SW1A 0AA
Tel: 020 7219 5972 *Email:* claire.coutinho.mp@parliament.uk
Constituency: No constituency office publicised
Website: www.clairecoutinho.com *Twitter:* @ClaireCoutinho

SCOTTISH NATIONAL PARTY

COWAN, RONNIE

Inverclyde *(Majority 7,512)*

SNP Spokesperson for Infrastructure and Manufacturing

Ronald Jack Cowan. Born 6 September 1959; Son of late James Cowan and May Piggott; 3 children.

Education: Greenock Academy.

Non-political career: Computer Software Consultant; IT Manager; Director, Ronnie Cowan Solutions Ltd 2001-15.

Political career: Member for Inverclyde since 7 May 2015 general election; SNP Spokesperson for: Infrastructure 2018-, Manufacturing 2021-. *Select committees:* Member: Public Administration and Constitutional Affairs 2015-, Transport 2017-19.

Political interests: Scotland's independence, inclusive society, universal basic income, anti-trident, renewables, addressing gambling related harm, drugs policy reform.

Other: Leader, Yes Inverclyde -2014; Marie Curie; Fellow, RSA. Greenock Wanderers Rugby Football Club.

Recreations: Music, art, rugby union.

Ronnie Cowan MP, House of Commons, London SW1A 0AA
Tel: 020 7219 6122 *Email:* ronnie.cowan.mp@parliament.uk
Constituency: 20 Crawfurd Street, Greenock, Inverclyde PA15 1LJ
Tel: 01475 721877 Website: www.ronniecowan.com *Twitter:* @ronniecowan

CONSERVATIVE

COX, GEOFFREY

Torridge and West Devon *(Majority 24,992)*

Charles Geoffrey Cox. Born 30 April 1960; Son of Michael and Diane Cox; Married Patricia Macdonald 1985 (1 daughter 2 sons).

Education: King's College, Taunton; Downing College, Cambridge (BA English and law 1981).

Non-political career: Barrister 1982-; Co-Founder and Head of Thomas More Chambers 1992; Standing Counsel to Mauritius, 1996-2000; QC, 2003. Member, National Farmers' Union.

Political career: Contested Torridge and West Devon 2001 general election. Member for Torridge and West Devon 2005-10, for Torridge and West Devon (revised boundary) since 6 May 2010 general election; Attorney General 2018-20. *Select committees:* Member: Environment, Food and Rural Affairs 2006-10, Standards and Privileges 2010-13, Standards 2013-15, Privileges 2013-15.

Political interests: Agriculture, education, defence, legal and constitutional issues; Mauritius.

Other: Consultant Global Counsel, Withersworldwide LLP 2020-; PC 2018; Kt 2021.

Recreations: Reading, walking dogs, swimming, countryside.

Rt Hon Sir Geoffrey Cox QC MP, House of Commons, London SW1A 0AA
Tel: 020 7219 4719 *Email:* coxg@parliament.uk
Constituency: First Floor, Lockyer House, Paddons Row, Tavistock, Devon PL19 0HF
Tel: 01822 612925 Website: www.geoffreycox.co.uk *Twitter:* @Geoffrey_Cox

LABOUR

COYLE, NEIL

Bermondsey and Old Southwark *(Majority 16,126)*

Born 30 December 1978; Son of Alan Coyle and Mary Coyle, née Wesson; Married Sarah 2014 (1 daughter).

Education: Hull University (2001).

Non-political career: Disability Rights Commission 2003-07; Head of Policy, National Centre for Independent Living 2007-09; Director of Policy, Disability Alliance 2009-12; Director of Policy and Campaigns, DRUK 2012-13.

Political career: Member for Bermondsey and Old Southwark since 7 May 2015 general election; PPS to Chris Bryant as Shadow Leader of the House of Commons 2015-16. *Select committees:* Member: Work and Pensions 2016-, Foreign Affairs 2020-, Committees on Arms

Export Controls 2020-. Chair, PLP Department Group for Work and Pensions 2020-. *Councils and public bodies:* London Borough of Southwark Council: Councillor 2010-16, Deputy Cabinet Member 2011-13.

Political interests: Disability, welfare, social security, social care, local government.

Other: Board Member, Tower Hamlets Advocacy Network and Community Support; Pecan (charity).

Neil Coyle MP, House of Commons, London SW1A 0AA
Tel: 020 7219 8733 *Email:* neil.coyle.mp@parliament.uk
Constituency: 149-151 Jamaica Road, London SE16 4SH
Tel: 020 7232 4640 (11am-3pm) Website: neilcoyle.laboursites.org *Twitter:* @coyleneil

CONSERVATIVE

CRABB, STEPHEN

Preseli Pembrokeshire *(Majority 5,062)*

Chair, Select Committee on Welsh Affairs

Born 20 January 1973; Married Béatrice Monnier 1996 (1 son 1 daughter).

Education: Tasker Milward VC School, Haverfordwest; Bristol University (BSc politics 1995); London Business School (MBA 2004); French.

Non-political career: Research assistant to Andrew Rowe MP 1995-96; Parliamentary affairs officer, National Council for Voluntary Youth Services 1996-98; Policy and campaign manager, London Chamber of Commerce 1998-2002; Self-employed marketing consultant 2002-05.

Political career: Contested Preseli Pembrokeshire 2001 general election. Member for Preseli Pembrokeshire 2005-10, for Preseli Pembrokeshire (revised boundary) since 6 May 2010 general election; Assistant Government Whip 2010-12; Parliamentary Under-Secretary of State, Wales Office 2012-14; Government Whip 2012-14; Secretary of State for: Wales 2014-16, Work and Pensions 2016. *Select committees:* Welsh Affairs: Member 2005-07, Chair 2020-; Member: International Development 2007-09, Treasury 2008-09, Exiting the European Union 2017-19, Liaison 2020-. Chair, North Southwark and Bermondsey Conservative Association 1998-2000; Conservative Party: Chair, Human Rights Commission 2007-09, Leader, Social Action Project in Rwanda and Sierra Leone: "Project Umubano" 2010-13.

Political interests: Welfare reform, energy, trade and industry, farming and international development; Africa, France, India, Middle East, USA.

Other: Patron, Haverfordwest Mencap 2005-; PC 2014. Balfour Conservative Club; Haverfordwest County AFC.

Recreations: Rugby, long distance running, cooking, family.

Rt Hon Stephen Crabb MP, House of Commons, London SW1A 0AA
Tel: 020 7219 0907 *Email:* stephen.crabb.mp@parliament.uk
Constituency: Suite 1, 20 Upper Market Street, Haverfordwest, Pembrokeshire SA61 1QA
Tel: 01437 767555 Website: www.stephencrabb.com *Twitter:* @SCrabbPembs

SCOTTISH NATIONAL PARTY

CRAWLEY, ANGELA

Lanark and Hamilton East *(Majority 5,187)*

SNP Shadow Attorney General and Spokesperson for Defence and Procurement

Born 3 June 1987.

Education: John Ogilvie High School; Stirling University (BA politics 2009); Glasgow University (LLB 2015).

Non-political career: Parliamentary Assistant to Bruce Crawford MSP and Clare Adamson MSP 2011-13; Legal assistant, Aamer Anwar & Co 2014.

Political career: Member for Lanark and Hamilton East since 7 May 2015 general election; SNP: Spokesperson for: Equalities, Women and Children/Women and Equalities 2015-19, Family Support 2017-18, Housing 2017-18, Child Maintenance 2017-18, Disabilities 2017-19, Pensions 2018-19, Shadow Minister for Defence and Procurement 2020-, Shadow Attorney General 2021-. *Select committees:* Member: Women and Equalities 2015-, Health and Social

Care 2019. National Convener, Young Scots for Independence; Member, National Executive Committee, Scottish National Party. *Councils and public bodies:* Councillor, South Lanarkshire Council 2012-15.

Political interests: Equal rights, social justice.

Other: Member, UK delegation, NATO Parliamentary Assembly 2020-.

Angela Crawley MP, House of Commons, London SW1A 0AA
Tel: 020 7219 6044 *Email:* angela.crawley.mp@parliament.uk
Constituency: Brandon Gate, 1 Leechlee Road, Hamilton ML3 0XB
Tel: 01698 200065 Website: angelacrawleymp.com *Twitter:* @AngelaCrawley30

LABOUR/
CO-OPERATIVE

CREASY, STELLA

Walthamstow *(Majority 30,862)*

Stella Judith Creasy. Born 5 April 1977; Partner (1 daughter, expecting second child).

Education: Colchester County High School; Magdalene College, Cambridge (psychology); London School of Economics (PhD psychology).

Non-political career: Researcher to Douglas Alexander MP, Charles Clarke MP and Ross Cranston MP; Deputy director, Involve; Head of campaigns, Scout Association. Member, Unite.

Political career: Member for Walthamstow since 6 May 2010 general election; Member, Public Accounts Commission 2011-15; PPS to Andy Burnham as Shadow Secretary of State for Education 2011; Shadow Minister for: Crime Prevention 2011-13, Business, Innovation and Skills 2013-15. *Select committees:* Member: Public Accounts 2010-11, Science and Technology 2015-17. Member: SERA, Labour Women's Network, Co-operative Party; Contested Labour deputy leadership election 2015. *Councils and public bodies:* Waltham Forest Council: Councillor 2002-05, Former Deputy Mayor, Interim mayor 2003.

Other: UK Delegation to Parliamentary Assembly, Council of Europe: Substitute Member 2017-19, Member 2020; Fabian Society; Campaigner of the Year, *Spectator* awards 2011; Campaign of the Year, *PoliticsHome* awards 2012.

Recreations: Indie music, American TV crime drama, cake, pub quizzes.

Dr Stella Creasy MP, House of Commons, London SW1A 0AA
Tel: 020 7219 6980
Constituency: Walthamstow Labour Party, 23 Orford Road, Walthamstow, London E17 9NL
Tel: 020 8521 1223 *Email:* stella@workingforwalthamstow.org.uk
Website: www.working4walthamstow.co.uk *Twitter:* @stellacreasy

CONSERVATIVE

CROSBIE, VIRGINIA

Ynys Môn *(Majority 1,968)*

Team PPS, Department of Health and Social Care

Virginia Ann Crosbie. Married (3 children).

Education: Queen Mary University, London (microbiology); Westminster University (Diploma management studies).

Non-political career: Dolphin Trainer, Terry Nutkin; GlaxoWelllcome; Pharmaceutical Analyst: UBS, HSBC; Maths Teacher, Masbro Adult Community Centre; Governor: Hammersmith Academy, Ark Brunel Academy; Director, Women2win 2015-.

Political career: Contested Rhondda 2017 general election. Member for Ynys Môn since 12 December 2019; Team PPS, Department of Health and Social Care 2020-. *Select committees:* Member: Women and Equalities 2020, Welsh Affairs 2020-. Deputy Chair Political, Kensington, Chelsea and Fulham Conservative Association.

Virginia Crosbie MP, House of Commons, London SW1A 0AA
Tel: 020 7219 4091 *Email:* virginia.crosbie.mp@parliament.uk
Constituency: 19 Stanley Street, Holyhead, Ynys Môn LL65 1HG
Tel: 01407 644645 Website: www.virginiacrosbie.co.uk *Twitter:* @VirginiaCrosbie

CONSERVATIVE

CROUCH, TRACEY

Chatham and Aylesford *(Majority 18,540)*

Tracey Elizabeth Anne Crouch. Born 24 July 1975; Partner Steve (1 son).

Education: Folkestone Grammar School for Girls; Hull University (BA law and politics 1996).

Non-political career: Researcher to Michael Howard MP 1996-98; Public affairs manager, Harcourt 1998-2000; Senior public affairs manager, Westminster Strategy 2000-03; Chief of staff to: Damian Green MP 2003, David Davis MP 2003-05; Norwich Union/Aviva 2005-10: Senior political adviser 2005-07, Head of public affairs 2007-10; Senior adviser, The Playbook 2019-.

Political career: Member for Chatham and Aylesford since 6 May 2010 general election; Member, Speaker's Committee on the Electoral Commission 2013-15; Parliamentary Under-Secretary of State for: Sport, Tourism and Heritage, Department for Culture, Media and Sport 2015-17 (on maternity leave January-July 2016), Sport and Civil Society, Department for Digital, Culture, Media and Sport 2017-18. *Select committees:* Member: Culture, Media and Sport 2012-15, Political and Constitutional Reform 2013-15. Member, Executive, 1922 Committee 2010-12. Member, Conservative Co-operative Movement.

Political interests: Sport and wellbeing, health and social care, mental health, constitutional affairs, older people's issues.

Other: Member, UK Delegation, Organisation for Security and Co-operation in Europe Parliamentary Assembly 2011-13; Honorary Member, Royal Engineers; Independent Chair, Medway Council's Physical Disability Partnership Board; President, RSPCA Medway; Vice-president, Campaign to Protect Rural England (Kent Branch); Patron: National Osteoporosis Society (Medway), Peter's Place, Halpern Charitable Foundation, Blenheim CDP; Member, World Anti-Doping Agency Foundation Board 2016-17; Senior Independent Director, Parkour UK 2019-; Founding Trustee, Made By Sport 2019-. FA coaching level 1 2006; Manager, Meridian Girls FC.

Recreations: Sport, music, reading.

Tracey Crouch MP, House of Commons, London SW1A 0AA
Tel: 020 7219 7203 *Email:* tracey.crouch.mp@parliament.uk
Constituency: 6-8 Revenge Road, Lordswood, Chatham, Kent ME5 8UD
Tel: 01634 673180 Website: www.traceycrouch.org *Twitter:* @tracey_crouch

LABOUR

CRUDDAS, JON

Dagenham and Rainham *(Majority 293)*

Jonathan Cruddas. Born 7 April 1962; Son of John Cruddas, sailor, and Pat Cruddas, housewife; Married Anna Healy 1992, now Baroness Healy of Primrose Hill (qv) (1 son).

Education: Oaklands RC Comprehensive, Portsmouth; Warwick University 1981-88 (BSc economics; MA industrial relations; PhD industrial and business studies); Visiting fellow, University of Wisconsin, USA 1987-88.

Non-political career: Policy officer, Labour Party Policy Directorate 1989-94; Chief assistant to General Secretary, Labour Party 1994-97; Deputy political secretary, Prime Minister's political office, Downing Street 1997-2001. TGWU 1989-2001: Branch secretary 1992-94.

Political career: Member for Dagenham 2001-10, for Dagenham and Rainham since 6 May 2010 general election. *Select committees:* Member: Public Accounts 2003-05, European Scrutiny 2020-, Scottish Affairs 2020-. Hon. Secretary, PLP London Regional Group 2005-10. Policy Review Co-ordinator, Labour Party 2012-15.

Political interests: Labour law, industrial economy, economic regeneration, housing, the far right, community cohesion.

Other: Dagenham Working Men's Club, Dagenham Royal Naval Association; White Hart Dagenham Angling Society.

Recreations: Golf, angling.

Jon Cruddas MP, House of Commons, London SW1A 0AA
Tel: 020 7219 8161 *Fax:* 020 7219 1756 *Email:* cruddasj@parliament.uk
Constituency: 598 Rainham Road South, Dagenham RM10 8YP
Tel: 020 8984 7854 *Email:* mullanem@parliament.uk Website: www.joncruddas.org.uk
Twitter: @JonCruddas_1

LABOUR

CRYER, JOHN

Leyton and Wanstead *(Majority 20,808)*

John Robert Cryer. Born 11 April 1964; Son of late Bob Cryer (MP for Keighley 1974-83 and Bradford South 1987-94) and Ann Cryer, née Place (MP for Keighley 1997-2010); Married Narinder Bains 1994 (divorced 2011) (2 sons 1 daughter); married Ellie Reeves 2012 (MP for Lewisham West and Penge) (1 son).

Education: Oakbank School, Keighley; Hatfield Polytechnic (BA literature and history 1985); London College of Printing (Postgraduate Certificate print journalism 1988).

Non-political career: Journalist: *Tribune* 1992-96, *Morning Star* 1989-92; Freelance journalist, 1992-97: *Labour Briefing* (editor), *Guardian*, *GPMU Journal*, *T&G Record*; Lloyd's of London Publications; Trade Union Officer: ASLEF 2005-06, Unite 2006-10. Member: TGWU 1986-, NUJ 1988-, UCATT 1997-.

Political career: Member for Hornchurch 1997-2005. Contested Hornchurch 2005 general election. Member for Leyton and Wanstead since 6 May 2010 general election. *Select committees:* Member: Deregulation and Regulatory Reform 1997-2002, Treasury 2010-11, Justice 2014-15, Administration 2015-. Member, Labour Party Departmental Committees for: Education and Employment 1997-2001, Parliamentary Affairs 1997-2001, Trade and Industry 1997-2001; Member, PLP Committee 2003-05, 2010-; Secretary, Labour Against the European Superstate 2004-05; Contested PLP chairman election 2012; Chair: Labour for a Referendum, Parliamentary Labour Party 2015-. Member, Executive, Labour Euro Safeguards Committee; Press officer, Defend Clause Four Campaign 1995; Member, Co-operative Party; Secretary, Labour Against the Euro; Vice-chair, PLP 2013-14; Ex-officio member, National Executive Committee, Labour Party 2015-.

Political interests: Employment, social security, education, further education, European Union, health, economic policy, industry, energy policy, transport; Australia, India, USA.

Other: Member: CND, Amnesty International, Transport on Water, Tibet Support Group, Keighley and Worth Valley Railway, RAF Hornchurch Association; Member, British Board of Boxing Control 1997-99; Founder and Chair, Socialist Education Associations 2010-18; First Step Nursery Hornchurch, St Francis Hospice Havering, Child Poverty Action Group, St Francis Foundation for Animal Welfare, Islamic Relief, East Africa Flood Apeal, Leyton Royal British Legion, Carefree Kids Waltham Forest, Box4Life Leyton, Recovery Resoucres, Foundation Leytonstone. Member: House of Commons Cricket Club, House of Commons Rugby Club, House of Commons Boxing Club.

Publications: Co-author with Ann Cryer, Boldness be my Friend: Remembering Bob Cryer MP (1996); Many articles mainly in political publications.

Recreations: Swimming, reading, sport, old cars, cinema, cycling, triathlons.

John Cryer MP, House of Commons, London SW1A 0AA
Tel: 020 7219 7100 *Email:* john.cryer.mp@parliament.uk
Constituency: 6 Gainsborough Road, Leytonstone, London E11 1HR
Tel: 020 8989 5249 Website: www.johncryermp.co.uk *Twitter:* @JohnCryerMP

LABOUR

CUMMINS, JUDITH

Bradford South *(Majority 2,346)*

Judith Mary Cummins. Born 26 June 1967; Married Mark (2 children).

Education: Ruskin College; Leeds University.

Non-political career: Benefits adviser; Low Pay Unit. Member: GMB, Unison.

Political career: Member for Bradford South since 7 May 2015 general election; Opposition Whip 2015-18; Shadow Minister for International Trade 2018-20. *Select committees:* Member: Armed Forces Bill 2015 2015-16, Standing Orders 2017-, Panel of Chairs 2020-, Business, Energy and Industrial Strategy 2020-. Chair, PLP Departmental Group for Future Relationship with the European Union 2020-. *Councils and public bodies:* Former Councillor: Bradford District Council, Leeds City Council 2012-16; West Yorkshire Fire and Rescue Authority: Member, Chair, Audit Committee.

Judith Cummins MP, House of Commons, London SW1A 0AA
Tel: 020 7219 8607 *Email:* judith.cummins.mp@parliament.uk
Constituency: 26-28 Church Bank, Bradford BD1 4DZ
Tel: 01274 924280 Website: www.judithcummins.org.uk *Twitter:* @JudithCummins

LABOUR

CUNNINGHAM, ALEX

Stockton North *(Majority 1,027)*

Shadow Minister for Courts and Sentencing

Alexander Cunningham. Born 1 May 1955; Son of John and Jean Cunningham; Married Evaline 1977 (2 sons).

Education: Branksome Comprehensive, Darlington; Queen Elizabeth Sixth Form; Darlington College of Technology (NCTJ certificate journalism 1976).

Non-political career: Journalist: *Darlington and Stockton Times* 1974-76, *The Mail*, Hartlepool 1976-77, Radio Tees 1977-79, Radio Clyde 1979, *Evening Gazette* 1979-84; Public relations officer, British Gas 1984-89; Transco: Communications adviser 1995-2000, Head of communications 2000-02; Managing director, Tees Valley Communicators Ltd 2002-10. National Union of Journalists: Member 1974-80, Father of Chapel 1977-79; Member, National Union of Public Employees/Unison 1980-.

Political career: Member for Stockton North since 6 May 2010 general election; PPS to: Sadiq Khan as Shadow Lord Chancellor and Secretary of State for Justice 2011-15, Lord Falconer as Shadow Lord Chancellor and Secretary of State for Justice 2015; Shadow Minister for: Environment, Food and Rural Affairs 2015-16, Work and Pensions (Pensions) 2016-17, Housing 2019, Justice (Courts and Sentencing) 2020-. *Select committees:* Member: Work and Pensions 2010-11, Armed Forces Bill 2011, Education 2011-15, Environmental Audit 2019. Stockton North CLP: Press officer 1984-2010, Vice-chair, secretary 1985-95, Chair 1995-2000; Member, Co-operative Party 1985-. *Councils and public bodies:* Cleveland County Council: Councillor 1989-96, Vice-chair, Education Committee 1990-96, Chair, Standing Advisory Council for Religious Education 1989-96; Stockton Borough Council: Councillor 1999-2010, Cabinet Member for Children and Young People 2000-10; Chair, Stockton Children's Trust; Board member, Arts Council England North East 2002-08; Board member and chair, North East Libraries and Archives Council (later MLA North East) 2003-09; Council member, Museums, Libraries and Archives Council 2008-09; Non-executive director, North Tees and Hartlepool NHS Trust 2008-10; Board member, One North East Regional Development Agency 2008-10; Hon Alderman, Stockton on Tees Borough Council 2015.

Political interests: Children's services, education, health, leisure, culture, energy, carers, poverty, pensions; France, Palestine.

Other: Member, Socialist Education Association 1984-; Eastern Ravens Trust, Awayout, Daisychain, Justice First. Patron, Stockton Rugby Club.

Recreations: Sport, reading, travel.

Alex Cunningham MP, House of Commons, London SW1A 0AA
Tel: 020 7219 7157 *Email:* alex.cunningham.mp@parliament.uk
Constituency: Unit 144, Stockton Business Centre, 70-74 Brunswick Street, Stockton on Tees TS18 1DW
Tel: 01642 345291 Website: www.alexcunninghammp.com *Twitter:* @ACunninghamMP

LABOUR

DABY, JANET

Lewisham East *(Majority 17,008)*

Janet Jessica Daby. Born 15 December 1970; Married.

Education: Blackheath Blue Coat School; Greenwich Community College; Brunel University (BSc hons sociology and applied social studies with a social work diploma 1995); London School of Economics (MSc criminal justice policy 2016).

Non-political career: Lambeth Social Services -2002; Fostering Manager, Outcomes First Group (Previously Hillcrest Foster care) 2002-12; Independent Social Work Consultant 2012-18. Unison.

Political career: MP for Lewisham East since 14 June 2018 by-election; Shadow Minister for Faiths: Communities and Local Government team 2020, Women and Equalities team 2020. *Select committees:* Member: Justice 2018-19, Home Affairs 2019-20. Labour Group Secretary 2010-12; BAME officer, Lewisham East 2011-13. *Councils and public bodies:* Lewisham Council: Councillor 2010-19, Cabinet Member for Community Safety 2012-18, Nominated Deputy Mayor 2018; Local Government Association: Board member 2014-18, Peer mentor 2016-18.

Political interests: Poverty, crime, children and young people; Guyana, Jamaica.

Other: Member, board of directors, Phoenix Community Housing 2011-16; Chair and Director, Whitefoot and Downham Communty Food Plus Project 2013-18; Stephen Lawrence Work in the Community Award 2014.

Janet Daby MP, House of Commons, London SW1A 0AA
Tel: 020 7219 7565 *Email:* janet.daby.mp@parliament.uk
Constituency: No constituency office publicised
Tel: 020 8461 4733 Website: www.janetdaby.org *Twitter:* @JanetDaby

CONSERVATIVE

DALY, JAMES

Bury North *(Majority 105)*

James Barry Daly. Married Joanne (2 sons).

Education: Qualified Solicitor 2001; Higher Court Advocacy qualification 2011.

Non-political career: Partner, Crompton Halliwell Solicitors 2012-.

Political career: Contested Bolton North East 2015 general election, Oldham West and Royton 2015 by-election and Bolton North East 2017 general election. Member for Bury North since 12 December 2019. *Select committees:* Member, Justice 2020-. Member: Conservative Councillors Association, Bury North Conservative Party. *Councils and public bodies:* Bury Council: Councillor 2012-, Leader, Conservative Group 2017-; Governor: Hoyle Nursery School, Springside Primary School.

Other: Member, National Trust; Member, Law Society.

Recreations: Real ale, cricket, golf.

James Daly MP, House of Commons, London SW1A 0AA
Tel: 020 7219 3000 *Email:* james.daly.mp@parliament.uk
Constituency: 60 Bolton Street, Bury BL9 0LL
Tel: 0161-546 0161 Website: www.jamesdaly.org.uk *Twitter:* @JamesDalyMP

LIBERAL DEMOCRAT

DAVEY, ED

Kingston and Surbiton *(Majority 10,489)*

Leader, Liberal Democrats

Edward Jonathon Davey. Born 25 December 1965; Son of late John Davey, solicitor, and late Nina Davey, née Stanbrook, teacher; Married Emily Gasson 2005 (1 son 1 daughter).

Education: Nottingham High School; Jesus College, Oxford (BA philosophy, politics and economics 1988); Birkbeck College, London (MSc economics 1993).

Non-political career: Senior economics adviser to Liberal Democrat MPs 1989-93; Management consultant, Omega Partners 1993-97; Director, Omega Partners Postal 1996-97; Renewable Energy Consultant, Herbert Smith 2015-; Chair, Mongoose Energy.

Political career: Member for Kingston and Surbiton 1997-2010, for Kingston and Surbiton (revised boundary) 2010-15. Contested Kingston and Surbiton 2015 general election. Member for Kingston and Surbiton since 8 June 2017; Liberal Democrat: London Whip 1997-2000, Spokesperson for: the Treasury (Public Spending and Taxation) 1997-99, Economy 1999-2001, London 2000-03, Shadow Chief Secretary to the Treasury 2001-02, Spokesperson for Office of the Deputy Prime Minister 2002-05, Shadow Secretary of State for: Education and Skills 2005-06, Trade and Industry 2006, Chief of Staff to Sir Menzies Campbell as Leader of the Liberal Democrats 2006-07, Shadow Secretary of State for Foreign and Commonwealth Affairs 2007-10; Parliamentary Under-Secretary of State (Minister for Employment Relations, Consumer and Postal Affairs), Department for Business, Innovation and Skills 2010-12; Secretary of State for Energy and Climate Change 2012-15; Liberal Democrat: Shadow Home Secretary/Spokesperson for Home Affairs 2017-19, Shadow Chancellor of the Exchequer 2019, Shadow Secretary of State for Business, Energy and Industrial Strategy 2019, Spokesperson for Economy and Social Justice 2019-20. *Select committees:* Member: Procedure 1997-2000, Treasury 1999-2001, Treasury (Treasury Sub-Committee) 1999-2001. Liberal Democrats: Chair, Costing Group (costing all policies for manifesto) 1992 and 1997 general elections, Member: Federal Policy Committee 1994-95, Policy Group (Economics, Tax and Benefits and Transport), Association of Liberal Democrat Councillors, Chair, Campaigns and Communications Committee 2006-09, Contested 2019 leadership contest, Deputy leader 2019, Acting Leader 2019-20, Leader 2020-.

Political interests: Taxation, economics, internet, employment, environment, modernisation of Parliament; Latin America.

Other: Patron: Jigsaw, Kingston Special Needs Project; Goodwill Ambassador for Children of Peace; Trustee, Kidsout; Love Kingston; Member, advisory board: Next Energy Capital, Grantham Research Institute; Chair, Fit for the Future; Royal Humane Society Honourable Testimonial; Chief Constable, London Transport Police Commendation 1994; Royal Humane Society 1994; Double Act of the Year (with John Hayes MP), *Spectator* awards 2012; PC 2012; Kt 2016.

Publications: Making MPs Work for our Money: Reforming Budget Scrutiny (Centre for Reform), 2000.

Recreations: Music, walking, swimming.

Rt Hon Sir Ed Davey MP, House of Commons, London SW1A 0AA
Tel: 020 7219 4530 *Email:* edward.davey.mp@parliament.uk
Constituency: 21 Berrylands Road, Surbiton KT5 8QX
Tel: 020 8288 2736 Website: www.eddavey.org *Twitter:* @EdwardJDavey

LABOUR

DAVID, WAYNE

Caerphilly *(Majority 6,833)*

Shadow Minister for Middle East and North Africa

Born 1 July 1957; Son of David Haydn David, teacher, and Edna David, née Jones, housewife; Married Catherine Thomas 1991 (divorced 2007); married Jayne Edwards 2016.

Education: Cynffig Comprehensive School, Kenfig Hill, Mid Glamorgan; University College, Cardiff (BA history and Welsh history 1979; PGCE further education 1983); University College, Swansea (economic history research 1979-82).

Non-political career: History teacher, Brynteg Comprehensive School 1983-85; Tutor organiser, Workers' Educational Association South Wales District 1985-89; Policy adviser, youth policy, Wales Youth Agency 1999-2001. Member: MSF 1983-2004, AEEU 1998-2004, Amicus 2004-07, Unite 2007-.

Political career: Member for Caerphilly 2001-10, for Caerphilly (revised boundary) since 6 May 2010 general election; Team PPS, Ministry of Defence 2005; PPS to Adam Ingram as Minister of State, Ministry of Defence 2005-06; Assistant Government Whip 2007-08; Parliamentary Under-Secretary of State, Wales Office 2008-10; Shadow Minister for: Wales 2010, Europe 2010-11, Justice (Political and Constitutional Reform) 2011-13; PPS to Leader of the Opposition: Ed Miliband 2013-15, Harriet Harman 2015; Shadow Minister for: Justice 2015-16, Cabinet Office 2015-16, Scotland 2015-16, Armed Forces and Defence Procurement 2016-19, Foreign and Commonwealth Office (Middle East and North Africa) 2020-. *Select committees:* Member: European Scrutiny 2001-07, Standards and Privileges 2004-05, Joint Committee on Conventions 2006, Welsh Affairs 2007, Defence 2020. Honorary Secretary PLP: Departmental Committee for Work and Pensions 2002-08, Welsh Regional Group 2003-07. European Parliament: MEP for South Wales 1989-94, for South Wales Central 1994-99: Vice-president, Socialist Group 1994-98, Leader, European Parliamentary Labour Party 1994-98; Contested Rhondda constituency 1999 National Assembly for Wales election. Ex-officio member, NEC, Labour Party 1994-98. *Councils and public bodies:* Cefn Cribwr Community Council: Councillor 1985-91, Chair 1986-87.

Political interests: European affairs, economy, education, devolution, constitution, foreign affairs; Belgium, Bulgaria, Poland, Vietnam.

Other: Vice-president, Cardiff UN Association 1989-; Member, Executive Committee, British Group of the Inter-Parliamentary Union 2017-; President: Aber Valley Male Voice Choir 2001-, Council for Wales of Voluntary Youth Services 2002-, Caerphilly Local History Society 2006-, Labour Heritage 2015-; Bedwas, Trethomas and Machen Brass Band 2019-; Fellow, Cardiff University 1995. Bargoed Labour Club.

Publications: Contributor, The Future of Europe, Problems and Issues for the 21st Century (1996); Remaining True: Biography of Ness Edwards (2006); Morgan Jones – Man of Conscience (2019).

Recreations: Music, playing the oboe.

Wayne David MP, House of Commons, London SW1A 0AA
Tel: 020 7219 8152 *Fax:* 020 7219 1751 *Email:* wayne.david.mp@parliament.uk
Constituency: BTM Community Council Offices, Newport Road, Bedwas, Caerphilly CF83 8YB
Tel: 029 2088 1061 *Email:* thomasta@parliament.uk Website: www.waynedavid.co.uk
Twitter: @WayneDavid_MP

CONSERVATIVE

DAVIES, DAVID

Monmouth *(Majority 9,982)*

Parliamentary Under-Secretary of State, Wales Office; Assistant Government Whip

David Thomas Charles Davies. Born 27 June 1970; Son of Peter and Kathleen Davies; Married Aliz Harnisfoger 2003 (2 daughters 1 son).

Education: Bassaleg Comprehensive, Newport; HGV class one; German, Hungarian, Welsh.

Non-political career: British Steel Corporation 1988-89; Casual work in Australia 1989-91; Manager, Burrow Heath Ltd (forwarder and tea importers) 1991-99; Special Constable, British Transport Police 2006-15. Served as a gunner with 104 Air Defence Regiment, Territorial Army, Raglan Barracks, Newport.

Political career: Contested Bridgend 1997 general election. Member for Monmouth since 5 May 2005 general election; Parliamentary Under-Secretary of State, Wales Office 2019-; Assistant Government Whip 2019-. *Select committees:* Welsh Affairs: Member 2005-10, Chair 2010-19; Member: Home Affairs 2007-10, Home Affairs Sub-Committee 2008-09, Liaison 2010-19, National Policy Statements Sub-committee 2010-15, 2017-19. Chairman, Conservative Backbench Policy Committee on Welsh Affairs 2017-19. National Assembly for Wales: AM for Monmouth constituency 1999-2007: Deputy Leader/Business Secretary 1999; Chief Whip 1999-2001. Organiser for anti-Assembly 'No' Campaign 1997; Campaign manager for Rod Richards as leader of Welsh Conservative Party 1998.

Political interests: Policing, climate change, Middle East; China, Cuba, Germany, Hungary.

Other: UK delegation, Parliamentary Assembly of the Council of Europe: Member, Substitute member; Honorary Member: Rotary Club of Usk and District, Institution of Royal Engineers; Former President, Welsh Amateur Boxing Association; Honorary Vice-President, Monmouthshire and District National Eisteddfod 2016; Combat Stress, The Richard Hunt Foundation, Chepstow Mencap. Chepstow Conservative Club, Abergavenny Conservative Club, Usk Conservative Club, Monmouth Conservative Club; Torfaen Warriors Boxing Club; Chepstow Amateur Boxing Club.

Recreations: Family, running, surfing, history, boxing.

David Davies MP, House of Commons, London SW1A 0AA
Tel: 020 7219 8360 *Email:* david.davies.mp@parliament.uk
Constituency: The Grange, 16 Maryport Street, Usk, Monmouthshire NP15 1AB
Tel: 01291 672817 Website: www.david-davies.org.uk *Twitter:* @davidtcdavies

CONSERVATIVE

DAVIES, GARETH

Grantham and Stamford *(Majority 26,003)*

Gareth Mark Davies. Born 31 March 1984; Married Laura 2019.

Education: Nottingham University (BA politics); John F Kennedy School of Government, Harvard University (MPA).

Non-political career: Columbia Threadneedle Investments 2006-: Head of Global Strategic Relations, Head of Responsible Investment Solutions, Trustee, Columbia Threadneedle Foundation.

Political career: Contested Doncaster Central 2010 and Leeds Central 2017 general elections. Member for Grantham and Stamford since 12 December 2019. *Select committees:* Member, Finance 2020-. Conservative Policy Forum Ambassador for UK Social Enterprises.

Gareth Davies MP, House of Commons, London SW1A 0AA
Tel: 020 7219 3443 *Email:* gareth.davies.mp@parliament.uk
Constituency: Office 1, The Old National School, 62 North Street, Bourne PE10 9AJ
Tel: 01778 421498 Website: www.garethdavies.co.uk *Twitter:* @GarethDavies_MP

LABOUR/
CO-OPERATIVE

DAVIES, GERAINT

Swansea West *(Majority 8,116)*

Geraint Richard Davies. Born 3 May 1960; Son of David Davies, civil servant, and Betty Davies; Married Dr Vanessa Fry 1991 (3 daughters).

Education: Llanishen Comprehensive, Cardiff; JCR President, Jesus College, Oxford (BA philosophy, politics and economics 1982).

Non-political career: Sales and marketing trainee; Group product manager, Unilever 1982-88; Marketing manager, Colgate Palmolive Ltd 1988-89; Managing director, Pure Crete Ltd 1989-97; Chair, Flood Risk Management Wales, Environment Agency 2005-10. Member, GMB.

Political career: Contested Croydon South 1987 and Croydon Central 1992 general elections. Member for Croydon Central 1997-2005. Contested Croydon Central 2005 general election. Member for Swansea West since 6 May 2010 general election; Team PPS, Department for Constitutional Affairs 2003-05. *Select committees:* Member: Public Accounts 1997-2003, Welsh Affairs 2010-15, 2017-, Standing Orders 2011-17, Unopposed Bills (Panel) 2011-15, European Scrutiny 2013-17, 2017-19, Panel of Chairs 2015-, Environmental Audit 2015-19, European Statutory Instruments 2020-, Environment, Food and Rural Affairs 2020-. Chair, PLP Departmental Committee for Environment, Transport and the Regions 1997-2004; Member, PLP Departmental Committees for: National Heritage/Culture, Media and Sport 1997-98, Trade and Industry 1997-2001, Treasury 1998-2001; Vice-chair, PLP Departmental: Committee for Transport 2004-05, Group for Justice 2010-15. Chair, Labour Finance and Industry Group 1998-2005; Member, Co-operative Party. *Councils and public bodies:* Councillor, Croydon Council 1986-97: Chair, Housing Committee 1994-96, Council Leader 1996-97; Governor, Dylan Thomas Community School.

Political interests: Treasury, trade and industry, housing, children's issues, transport, environment, human rights, equality; Crete, Wales.

Other: Member, UK delegation, Parliamentary Assembly of the Council of Europe 2015-17; NSPCC, Amnesty International, WWF (UK); Royal Humane Society Award for saving a man's life.

Recreations: Family, singing.

Geraint Davies MP, House of Commons, London SW1A 0AA
Tel: 020 7219 1540 *Email:* geraint.davies.mp@parliament.uk
Constituency: 32 Walter Road, Swansea SA1 5NW
Tel: 01792 475943 Website: www.geraintdavies.org.uk *Twitter:* @GeraintDaviesMP

CONSERVATIVE

DAVIES, JAMES

Vale of Clwyd *(Majority 1,827)*

James Michael Davies. Born 27 February 1980; Son of Michael and Belinda Davies; Married Nina 2012 (2 sons).

Education: King's School, Chester; Christ's College, Cambridge (MB BChir 2004; MA 2005); A-Level Spanish.

Non-political career: Trainee doctor, Glan Clwyd Hospital 2004-05; Senior house officer, Countess of Chester Hospital 2005-07; GP: City Walls Medical Centre 2007-08, Boughton Medical Group 2008-15.

Political career: Member for Vale of Clwyd 2015-17. Contested Vale of Clwyd 2017 general election. Member for Vale of Clwyd since 12 December 2019. *Select committees:* Member: Health 2015-17, Welsh Affairs 2015-17, Joint Committee on Statutory Instruments 2020-, Health and Social Care 2020-. Member, Executive, 1922 Committee 2016-17, 2020-. Contested North Wales region (5) 2007 National Assembly for Wales election. Former Deputy Chair (Political), Vale of Clwyd Conservative Association. *Councils and public bodies:* Councillor: Prestatyn Town Council 2004-15, Denbighshire County Council 2004-15.

Political interests: Health, transport, Welsh and constitutional affairs, life chances.

Other: Member, British Medical Association; MRCGP 2008. Carlton Club.

Recreations: Travelling, walking, languages, DIY, local community regeneration, real ale, dining out, skiing.

Dr James Davies MP, House of Commons, London SW1A 0AA
Tel: 020 7219 4606 *Email:* james.davies.mp@parliament.uk
Constituency: 198 High Street, Prestatyn, Denbighshire LL19 9BP
Tel: 01745 888920 Website: www.jamesdavies.org.uk *Twitter:* @JamesDavies

CONSERVATIVE

DAVIES, MIMS

Mid Sussex *(Majority 18,197)*

Parliamentary Under-Secretary of State for Employment, Department for Work and Pensions

Miriam Jane Alice Davies. Born 2 June 1975; Married (2 children).

Education: Croydon Collyers Sixth Form College, Horsham; Swansea University (BA politics and international relations).

Non-political career: Local radio presenter, reporter and producer; Road safety communications officer.

Political career: Member for Eastleigh 2015-19, and for Mid Sussex since 12 December 2019; PPS to: Matt Hancock as Minister of State for Digital and Culture, Department for Culture, Media and Sport 2016-17, Sajid Javid as Secretary of State for Communities and Local Government 2017-18; Member, Commons Reference Group on Representation and Inclusion 2017-18; Assistant Government Whip 2018; Parliamentary Under-Secretary of State: Wales Office 2018, for Sport and Civil Society, Department for Digital, Culture, Media and Sport 2018-19, for Employment, Department for Work and Pensions 2019-. *Select committees:* Member: Women and Equalities 2015-16, Joint Committee on Consolidation, &c, Bills 2015-18. Chairman, Conservative Backbench Policy Committee on Culture, Media and Sport 2015-16. Chair, Southern Region, Conservative Women's Organisation. *Councils and public bodies:* Councillor: Haywards Heath Town Council, Mid Sussex District Council 2011-15.

Political interests: Carers, sports, equalities, women's rights, transport, road quality and safety.

Other: Haywards Heath Harriers.

Recreations: Running.

Mims Davies MP, House of Commons, London SW1A 0AA
Tel: 020 7219 6853 *Email:* mims.davies.mp@parliament.uk
Constituency: Suite B, KBF House, 55 Victoria Road, Burgess Hill, West Sussex RH15 9LH
Tel: 01444 616061 Website: www.mimsdavies.org.uk *Twitter:* @mimsdavies

CONSERVATIVE

DAVIES, PHILIP

Shipley *(Majority 6,242)*

Philip Andrew Davies. Born 5 January 1972; Son of Peter Davies and Marilyn Lifsey; Married Deborah Hemsley 1994 (divorced) (2 sons); married Esther McVey (qv) 2020 (MP for Tatton).

Education: Old Swinford Hospital School, Stourbridge; Huddersfield University (BA historical and political studies 1993).

Non-political career: Asda Stores: Management training scheme 1995-97, Deputy customer services manager 1997, Customer relations manager 1997-98, Call centre manager 1998-99, Customer service project manager 2000-04, Senior marketing manager 2004-05.

Political career: Contested Colne Valley 2001 general election. Member for Shipley 2005-10, for Shipley (revised boundary) since 6 May 2010 general election. *Select committees:* Member: Culture, Media and Sport 2006-15, Modernisation of the House 2007-10, Backbench Business 2010-12, Chairmen's Panel/Panel of Chairs 2010-, Joint Committee on Privacy and Injunctions 2011-12, Justice 2015-17, Women and Equalities 2016-19, Digital, Culture, Media and Sport 2019-20. Member, Executive, 1922 Committee 2006-12.

Political interests: Law and order, Europe, education; USA.

Other: Readers' Representative of the Year, *Spectator* awards 2011; Parliamentarians of the Year, *Spectator* awards 2013; Champion Award, Internet Telephony Services Providers' Association 2015.

Recreations: Horseracing, cricket, football, rugby league.

House of Commons MPs' Biographies

Philip Davies MP, House of Commons, London SW1A 0AA
Tel: 020 7219 8264 *Email:* daviesp@parliament.uk
Constituency: First Floor, 3 Manor Lane, Shipley BD18 3EA
Tel: 01274 592248 *Email:* deborah.davies@parliament.uk Website: www.philip-davies.org.uk
Twitter: @PhilipDaviesUK

LABOUR

DAVIES-JONES, ALEX

Pontypridd *(Majority 5,887)*

PPS to Rachel Reeves as Shadow Chancellor of the Duchy of Lancaster and Shadow Minister for the Cabinet Office and to Nia Griffith as Shadow Secretary of State for Wales

Alexandra Mary Davies-Jones. Born 5 April 1989; Daughter of Mary and Austin Davies; Married Andrew (1 son 2 stepsons).

Education: Tonyrefail Comprehensive School; Cardiff University (LLB law and politics 2010); Conversational Welsh and French.

Non-political career: Researcher and Caseworker to Owen Smith MP 2012-13; Research, Press and Policy Officer to Mick Antoniw AM 2012-13; Press and Communications Officer, RICS 2013-15; Dwr Cymru Welsh Water: Regional Communications Manager 2015-19, Community Engagement Manager 2019. Air Cadet. Unite the Union.

Political career: Member for Pontypridd since 12 December 2019; PPS to: Jim McMahon as Shadow Secretary of State for Transport 2020, Nia Griffith as Shadow Secretary of State for Wales 2020-, Rachel Reeves as Shadow Chancellor of the Duchy of Lancaster and Shadow Minister for the Cabinet Office 2020-. *Select committees:* Member: Women and Equalities 2020-, Digital, Culture, Media and Sport 2020-. Pontypridd CLP: Women's Officer, Youth Officer, Unite the Union Representative. *Councils and public bodies:* Governor: Tonyrefail Primary School 2012-14, Cwmlai Primary School 2013-, Tonyrefail Community School 2017-, Williamstown Primary School 2017-; Councillor: Tonyrefail Community Council 2012-, Rhondda Cynon Taf County Borough Council 2017-.

Political interests: Women's pensions, austerity, maternity rights, infant feeding, musical education, water; Europe, Wales.

Other: CIPR; WaterAid, Jo's Cervical Cancer Trust. Captain, Women's Darts Team.

Recreations: Singing, rugby, reading.

Alex Davies-Jones MP, House of Commons, London SW1A 0AA
Tel: 020 7219 4981 *Email:* alex.daviesjones.mp@parliament.uk
Constituency: 10 Market Street, Pontypridd CF37 2ST
Website: www.alexdaviesjones.com *Twitter:* @AlexDaviesJones

CONSERVATIVE

DAVIS, DAVID

Haltemprice and Howden *(Majority 20,329)*

David Michael Davis. Born 23 December 1948; Son of late Ronald and Elizabeth Davis; Married Doreen Cook 1973 (1 son 2 daughters).

Education: Bec Grammar School; Warwick University (BSc molecular science, computing science 1971); London Business School (MSc business studies 1973); Harvard Business School (AMP 1985).

Non-political career: Joined Tate & Lyle 1974; Finance director, Manbré & Garton 1976-80; Managing director, Tate & Lyle Transport 1980-82; President, Redpath-Labatt joint venture 1982-84; Tate & Lyle 1984-87: Strategic planning director 1984-87, Non-executive director 1987-90.

Political career: Member for Boothferry 1987-97, for Haltemprice and Howden from 1997 to 18 June 2008 and 11 July 2008 by-election to 2010, for Haltemprice and Howden (revised boundary) since 6 May 2010 general election; PPS to Francis Maude as Financial Secretary to Treasury 1988-90; Assistant Government Whip 1990-93; Parliamentary Secretary, Office of Public Service and Science 1993-94; Minister of State, Foreign and Commonwealth Office 1994-97; Shadow Deputy Prime Minister with responsibility for the Cabinet Office 2002-03; Shadow Secretary of State for Home, Constitutional and Legal Affairs 2003-04; Shadow Home Secretary 2003-08; Secretary of State for Exiting the European Union 2016-18. *Select* *committees:* Chair, Public Accounts 1997-2001; Member, Liaison 1998-2001. Conservative Party: Contested Party leadership 2001, 2005, Chairman 2001-02, Member, Policy Board 2001-03.

Political interests: Health, law and order, industry, agriculture.

Other: Trustee, Special Air Services Association; Board member, Mansfelder Kupfer Und Messing 2018-19; External Adviser, JC Bamford Excavators Ltd 2019-20; Member, advisory board, THI Investments UK 2019-; Chair, supervisory board, Kohlgartenstrabe 15 Verwaltungs AG 2019-; PC 1997.

Publications: How to Turn Round a Company (1988); The BBC Viewer's Guide to Parliament (1989); Co-author, The Future of Conservatism: Values Revisited (Biteback, 2011).

Recreations: Mountaineering, flying light aircraft, writing.

Rt Hon David Davis MP, House of Commons, London SW1A 0AA
Tel: 020 7219 5900 *Email:* david.davis.mp@parliament.uk
Constituency: No constituency office
Website: www.daviddavismp.com *Twitter:* @DavidDavisMP

CONSERVATIVE

DAVISON, DEHENNA

Bishop Auckland *(Majority 7,962)*

Dehenna Sheridan Davison. Born 27 July 1993; Separated.

Education: Sheffield High School 2004-11; Hull University (BA British politics and legislative studies 2016; MA international politics 2018).

Non-political career: Junior Secretary (university placement), Houses of Parliament 2013-14; Political Researcher, Hull Conservative Group 2014-; Duty Manager, Grainger Games 2015-18; Customer Service Officer, Hull City Council 2018-19; Research and Development Technical Analyst, LUMO 2019-.

Political career: Contested Kingston-Upon-Hull North 2015 and Sedgefield 2017 general elections. Member for Bishop Auckland since 12 December 2019. *Select committees:* Member, Home Affairs 2020-.

Recreations: Walking the dog, running, virtual reality and video gaming.

Dehenna Davison MP, House of Commons, London SW1A 0AA
Tel: 020 7219 3000 *Email:* dehenna.davison.mp@parliament.uk
Constituency: 16 Tenters Street, Bishop Auckland DL14 7AD
Tel: 01388 342022 Website: www.dehennadavison.com *Twitter:* @DehennaDavison

SCOTTISH NATIONAL PARTY

DAY, MARTYN

Linlithgow and East Falkirk *(Majority 11,266)*

SNP Spokesperson for Public Health and Primary Care

Born 26 March 1971; Son of Margaret Grant and Ronald Day; Divorced, Partner Nidhin Chand.

Education: Linlithgow Academy.

Non-political career: Former bank worker.

Political career: Member for Linlithgow and East Falkirk since 7 May 2015 general election; Member, Public Accounts Commission 2017-18; SNP Spokesperson for Public Health and Primary Care 2020-. *Select committees:* Member: Administration 2015-17, Petitions 2016-, Public Accounts 2017-18, European Scrutiny 2018-19. Election agent 1999-2015. *Councils and public bodies:* West Lothian Council: Councillor 1999-2015, Portfolio holder for Development and Transport.

Political interests: Anti-austerity, anti-Trident; India.

Other: Member: National Association of Councillors -2015, West Lothian Economic Partnership Forum -2015.

Recreations: Reading, listening to music.

Martyn Day MP, House of Commons, London SW1A 0AA
Tel: 020 7219 5930 *Email:* martyn.day.mp@parliament.uk
Constituency: 62 Hopetoun Street, Bathgate, West Lothian EH48 4PD
Tel: 01506 654415 Website: www.martynday.scot *Twitter:* @MartynDaySNP

LABOUR

DEBBONAIRE, THANGAM

Bristol West *(Majority 28,219)*

Shadow Secretary of State for Housing

Thangam Elizabeth Rachel Debbonaire. Born 3 August 1966; Daughter of late Prabhu Singh, musician, and Eleanor James, musician and teacher; Married Kevin Walton.

Education: Chetham's Music School; Bradford Girls' Grammar School; Bristol University (MSc management, development and social responsibility 1995); Associate, Royal College of Music 1997; Arabic (intermediate level).

Non-political career: Freelance classical cellist 1976–2000; National Children's Officer, Women's Aid Federation England 1991-98; Director and lead independent practitioner, Domestic Violence Responses 1997-2015; Respect: Accreditation Officer 2006-08, Research Manager 2008-15; Perpetrator Group Worker, Domestic Violence Intervention Project 2008-10. Member: Musicians' Union 1984-2000, Unison (and predecessor union) 1991-.

Political career: Member for Bristol West since 7 May 2015 general election; Shadow Minister for Culture, Media and Sport 2016; Opposition Whip 2016-20; Board Member, Parliamentary Office of Science and Technology (POST) 2018-; Shadow Minister for Exiting the European Union 2020; Shadow Secretary of State for Housing 2020-. Member, South West Regional Labour Party Board 2016. *Councils and public bodies:* Governor, Glenfrome Primary School, Bristol 2011-15.

Political interests: Housing, refugees, autism, violence against women, science and research, climate change and the environment, arts, European Union; Countries in the Horn of Africa, Middle East, Indian sub-continent.

Publications: Numerous articles on domestic violence.

Recreations: Playing the cello.

Thangam Debbonaire MP, House of Commons, London SW1A 0AA
Tel: 020 7219 0974 *Email:* thangam.debbonaire.mp@parliament.uk
Constituency: 16-18 King Square, Bristol BS2 8AZ
Tel: 0117-379 0980 Website: www.debbonaire.co.uk *Twitter:* @ThangamMP

LABOUR

DE CORDOVA, MARSHA

Battersea *(Majority 5,668)*

Shadow Secretary of State for Women and Equalities

Marsha Chantol De Cordova. Born 23 January 1976.

Education: London South Bank University (law).

Non-political career: Action for Blind People: Welfare rights officer 2005-07, Service Development Manager 2007-10, Policy and Development Manager 2010-12; Welfare Benefit Specialist, Turn2us 2013-14; Thomas Pocklington Trust: Development Manager 2014-15, Engagement and Advocacy Director 2016-17; Chief Executive, South East London Vision 2015-16. Member, Unite.

Political career: Member for Battersea since 8 June 2017; PPS to Debbie Abrahams as Shadow Secretary of State for Work and Pensions 2017; Shadow Minister for Work and Pensions (Disabled People) 2017-20; Shadow Secretary of State for Women and Equalities 2020-. *Select committees:* Member, Work and Pensions 2017. Equality and Inclusion Lead (reporting to Angela Rayner as Party Chair), Labour Party 2020-. *Councils and public bodies:* Councillor, London Borough of Lambeth Council 2014-18.

Political interests: Disability, human rights, welfare reform, poverty, employment.

Marsha De Cordova MP, House of Commons, London SW1A 0AA
Tel: 020 7924 1973 *Email:* marsha.decordova.mp@parliament.uk
Constituency: No constituency office publicised
Tel: 020 7924 1973 Website: marshadecordova.co.uk *Twitter:* @Marshadecordova

LABOUR

DHESI, TANMANJEET SINGH

Slough *(Majority 13,640)*

Shadow Minister for Railways

Born 17 August 1978; Married Manveen 2005 (2 sons).

Education: Sir Joseph Williamson's Mathematical (Grammar) School; Gravesend Grammar School; University College London (mathematics with management studies); Keble College, Oxford (applied statistics); Fitzwilliam College, Cambridge (MPhil history of politics and history of South Asia); Punjabi, Hindi, Urdu, French, German, Italian, Latin.

Non-political career: Family construction business: Worked in a number of entry level roles, including handyman, scabbler, core driller and general labourer, Site Foreman, Site Manager, Project Manager, Project Director; Director, DGP Logistics plc, Edinburgh 2005-11; Consultant, DGP Logistics.

Political career: Contested Gravesham 2015 general election. Member for Slough since 8 June 2017; PPS to Jeremy Corbyn as Leader of the Opposition 2020; Shadow Minister for Transport (Railways) 2020-. *Select committees:* Member: Housing, Communities and Local Government 2018-19, Defence 2020. Chair, Gravesham Constituency Labour Party. *Councils and public bodies:* Gravesham Council: Councillor 2007-15, Mayor 2011, Cabinet Member, Business and Communities 2012-15; Councillor, Kent County Council 2017-.

Other: Member, UK Delegation to the NATO Parliamentary Assembly 2019-; President, Gatka Federation.

Tanmanjeet Singh Dhesi MP, House of Commons, London SW1A 0AA
Tel: 020 7219 1946 *Email:* tan.dhesi.mp@parliament.uk
Constituency: 52 Chalvey High Street, Slough SL1 2SQ
Tel: 01753 518161 Website: www.tsdhesi.com *Twitter:* @TanDhesi

CONSERVATIVE

DINENAGE, CAROLINE

Gosport *(Majority 23,278)*

Minister of State for Digital and Culture, Department for Digital, Culture, Media and Sport

Caroline Julia Dinenage. Born 28 October 1971; Daughter of Fred Dinenage, tv presenter; Married Carlos (divorced) (2 sons); married Mark Lancaster 2014 (MP for Milton Keynes North 2010-19, now Lord Lancaster of Kimbolton (qv)).

Education: Wykeham House, Fareham; Oaklands RC Comprehensive, Waterlooville; University of Wales, Swansea (BA English and politics); French.

Non-political career: Director, Recognition Express. Graduate, Armed Forces Parliamentary Scheme.

Political career: Contested Portsmouth South 2005 general election. Member for Gosport since 6 May 2010 general election; PPS to Nicky Morgan as Secretary of State for Education and Minister for Women and Equalities 2014-15; Parliamentary Under-Secretary of State: for Women, Equalities and Family Justice, Ministry of Justice and Department for Education 2015-16, for Women, Equalities and Early Years, Department for Education 2016-17, for Family Support, Housing and Child Maintenance, Department for Work and Pensions 2017-18; Minister of State: for Care, Department of Health and Social Care 2018-20, for Digital and Culture, Department for Digital, Culture, Media and Sport 2020-. *Select committees:* Member: Science and Technology 2012-13, Business, Innovation and Skills 2012-15. *Councils and public bodies:* Councillor, Winchester District Council 1998-2003.

Political interests: Defence, business and industry, education and skills, culture, media, women and equalities; China, Falkland Islands, Gibraltar, Hong Kong, India.

Other: Member, NATO Parliamentary Assembly -2015.

Caroline Dinenage MP, House of Commons, London SW1A 0AA
Tel: 020 7219 0231 *Email:* caroline.dinenage.mp@parliament.uk
Constituency: 167 Stoke Road, Gosport, Hampshire PO12 1SE
Tel: 023 9252 2121 Website: www.caroline4gosport.co.uk *Twitter:* @cj_dinenage

CONSERVATIVE

DINES, SARAH

Derbyshire Dales *(Majority 17,381)*

PPS to Brandon Lewis as Secretary of State for Northern Ireland

Sarah Elizabeth Dines. 4 sons.

Education: Brunel University (1987); Inns of Court School of Law (1988).

Non-political career: Barrister: 1 Gray's Inn Square, 3PB Barristers.

Political career: Contested East Belfast 1997 general election. Member for Derbyshire Dales since 12 December 2019; PPS to Brandon Lewis as Secretary of State for Northern Ireland 2020-. *Select committees:* Member, Justice 2020-.

Political interests: Digital connectivity, green belt development.

Other: Member, British-Irish Parliamentary Assembly 2020-; Member: Family Law Bar Association, The British Academy of Forensic Sciences.

Sarah Dines MP, House of Commons, London SW1A 0AA
Tel: 020 7219 6660 *Email:* sarah.dines.mp@parliament.uk
Constituency: No constituency office publicised
Tel: 01629 57205 *Email:* dinesforderbyshiredales@gmail.com Website: www.sarahdines.org.uk
Twitter: @Dines4Dales

CONSERVATIVE

DJANOGLY, JONATHAN

Huntingdon *(Majority 19,383)*

Jonathan Simon Djanogly. Born 3 June 1965; Son of Sir Harry Djanogly CBE and late Carol Djanogly; Married Rebecca Silk 1991 (1 son 1 daughter).

Education: University College School, London; Oxford Polytechnic (BA law and politics 1987); Guildford College of Law (law finals 1988); ICAEW (corporate finance qualification).

Non-political career: Partner: SJ Berwin LLP Solicitors 1988-2009, Mail order retail business 1994-2002.

Political career: Contested Oxford East 1997 general election. Member for Huntingdon 2001-10, for Huntingdon (revised boundary) since 6 May 2010 general election; Shadow Minister for Home, Constitutional and Legal Affairs 2004-05; Shadow Solicitor General 2005-10; Shadow Minister for Trade and Industry/Business, Enterprise and Regulatory Reform/ Business, Innovation and Skills 2005-10 (Corporate Governance 2006-09, Business 2009-10); Parliamentary Under-Secretary of State, Ministry of Justice 2010-12. *Select committees:* Member: Trade and Industry 2001-05, Joint Committee on Statutory Instruments 2001-02, Exiting the European Union 2017-19, Speaker's Advisory Committee on Works of Art 2017-19. *Councils and public bodies:* Councillor, Westminster City Council 1994-2001.

Political interests: Small businesses, trade, environment, rural affairs, transport, planning, justice.

Other: Chairman: Pembroke VCT plc 2013-, Task Force Europe, British-Swiss Chamber of Commerce 2015-, British Shooting Sports Council 2017-; Law Society.

Recreations: Sport, arts, theatre, reading histories and biographies, Britain's countryside and heritage.

Jonathan Djanogly MP, House of Commons, London SW1A 0AA
Tel: 020 7219 2367 *Email:* jonathan.djanogly.mp@parliament.uk
Constituency: HCCA, Centenary House, St Mary's Street, Huntingdon, Cambridgeshire PE29 3PE
Tel: 01480 453062 *Email:* admin@huntscca.co.uk Website: www.jonathandjanogly.com
Twitter: @JDjanogly

CONSERVATIVE

DOCHERTY, LEO

Aldershot *(Majority 16,698)*

Assistant Government Whip

Born 4 October 1976; Married Lucy (2 children).

Education: School of Oriental and African Studies (2000); Royal Military Academy, Sandhurst (2001).

Non-political career: Editor and publisher, Steppe Magazine Ltd; Director, Conservative Middle East Council 2010-17. Soldier, 1st Battalion Scots Guards (operational tours in Iraq and Afghanistan) 2001-07.

Political career: Contested Caerphilly 2015 general election. Member for Aldershot since 8 June 2017; Team PPS, Ministry of Housing, Communities and Local Government 2018-19; PPS to Jeremy Wright as Secretary of State for Digital, Culture, Media and Sport 2019; Assistant Government Whip 2019-. *Select committees:* Member: Defence 2017-19, Arms Export Controls 2017-19. Vice-chairman, Conservative Middle East Council. *Councils and public bodies:* Councillor, South Oxfordshire District Council 2011-15.

Other: Council Member, Chatham House.

Publications: Desert of Death: A Soldier's Journey from Iraq to Afghanistan (2007).

Leo Docherty MP, House of Commons, London SW1A 0AA
Tel: 020 7219 1833 *Email:* leo.docherty.mp@parliament.uk
Constituency: 147 Victoria Road, Aldershot GU11 1JW
Tel: 01252 377567 Website: www.leodocherty.org.uk *Twitter:* @LeoDochertyUK

SCOTTISH NATIONAL PARTY

DOCHERTY-HUGHES, MARTIN

West Dunbartonshire *(Majority 9,553)*

SNP Spokesperson for Industries Future and Blockchain Technology and for Defence and Foreign Affairs

Martin John Docherty-Hughes. Born 21 January 1971; Son of Patrick Anthony Docherty and Eleanor Docherty (née Logan); Married.

Education: Saint Columba High Clydebank; GCFT (HND business administration 1997); Essex University (BA politics 2004); Glasgow School of Art (MPhil).

Non-political career: Policy and research, West Dunbartonshire Community and Volunteering Services; National policy adviser, Volunteer Scotland 2014-15.

Political career: Member for West Dunbartonshire since 7 May 2015 general election; SNP Spokesperson for: Voluntary Sector 2016-17, Industries for the Future/Industries Future 2017-, Blockchain Technology 2018-; PPS to Ian Blackford as SNP Westminster Group Leader 2020-21; SNP Defence and Foreign Affairs Team Member 2020-21, Spokesperson for Defence and Foreign Affairs 2021-. *Select committees:* Member: Defence 2017-, Committees on Arms Export Controls 2020-. Scottish National Party: Member 1991-, Former Secretary and Chair, Clydebank SNP, Secretary, Clydebank and Milngavie Constituency, Chair, West Dunbartonshire Liaison Committee. *Councils and public bodies:* Councillor: Clydebank District Council 1992-96, Glasgow City Council 2012-15, Bailie City of Glasgow 2012-15.

Political interests: Scottish independence, child poverty, anti-austerity, disability, technology, defence; Brazil, Denmark, Estonia, Ireland, Latvia, Lithuania, Russia, Ukraine, Venezuela.

Other: Member, UK delegation to NATO Parliamentary Assembly 2015-17.

Martin Docherty-Hughes MP, House of Commons, London SW1A 0AA
Tel: 020 7219 4609 *Email:* martin.docherty.mp@parliament.uk
Constituency: Titan Enterprise Centre, Suite 1-11, 1 Aurora Avenue, 1 Queens Quay, Clydebank, Dunbartonshire G81 1BF
Tel: 0141-952 2988 Website: www.martindocherty.scot *Twitter:* @MartinJDocherty

LABOUR/ CO-OPERATIVE

DODDS, ANNELIESE

Oxford East *(Majority 17,832)*

Shadow Chancellor of the Exchequer

Anneliese Jane Dodds. Born 16 March 1978; Partner Ed (1 son 1 daughter).

Education: Robert Gordon's College, Aberdeen; St Hilda's College, Oxford (BA politics, philosophy and economics 2001) (Oxford Union President 1999-2000); Edinburgh University (Masters social policy 2002); London School of Economics (PhD 2006); French.

Non-political career: Economic and Social Research Council postdoctoral fellow, Department of Government, London School of Economics 2006; Public policy lecturer, King's College London 2007-10; Lecturer and Senior Lecturer in Public Policy, Sociology and Public Policy Group, Aston University 2010-14. Member: Universities and College Union 2003-, Unite 2006-.

Political career: Contested Billericay 2005 and Reading East 2010 general elections. Member for Oxford East since 8 June 2017; Shadow Minister for Treasury (Shadow Financial Secretary) 2017-20; Shadow Chancellor of the Exchequer 2020-. MEP for South East 2014-17. Member: Labour Party 1996-, Co-op Party.

Political interests: Economy, public policy, health.

Other: Member, Higher Education Academy; Volunteer, Oxfam; Member, Political Studies Association 2002-; Research associate, Centre for Analysis of Risk and Regulation, London School of Economics.

Publications: The Growth of Agencies in Britain and France: EduFrance – transferred from Britain, or an indigenous creation? (2004); The Politicisation of Trade in Health and Education Services: Black and White Divisions Over a 'Grey Area', Scottish Affairs (2004); The spread of evaluation in international higher education – a uniform phenomenon? (2005); The Core Executive's Approach to Regulation: From 'Better Regulation' to 'Risk-Tolerant Deregulation', Social Policy and Administration (2006); How does globalization interact with higher education? – The continuing lack of consensus, Comparative Education (2008); Families 'at risk' and the Family Nurse Partnership: The intrusion of risk into social exclusion policy, Journal of Social Policy (2009); Liberalization and the public sector: the pre-eminent role of governments in the 'sale' of higher education abroad, Public Administration (2009); The British higher education funding debate: the perils of 'talking economics', London Review of Education (2011); Logics, Thresholds, Strategic Power, and the Promotion of Liberalisation by Governments: A Case Study from British Higher Education, Public Policy and Administration (2011); Comparative Public Policy (2012); Co-author: Can incident reporting improve safety? Healthcare practitioners' views of the effectiveness of incident reporting, (International Journal for Quality in Health Care); Understanding institutional conversion: the case of the National Reporting and Learning System (Journal of Public Policy); Accountability, organisational learning and risks to patient safety in England: conflict or compromise?; Top-down or bottom up: the real choice for public services? The Journal of Poverty and Social Justice; The challenge of improving patient safety in primary care, British Journal of General Practice (2009); The Future of Public Administration, Special edition of the journal Public Policy and Administration, and Introduction to Public Administration in an Age of Austerity: The Future of the Discipline within the special edition (2012).

Recreations: Cycling, travelling.

Anneliese Dodds MP, House of Commons, London SW1A 0AA
Tel: 020 7219 2705 *Email:* anneliese.dodds.mp@parliament.uk
Constituency: Unit A, Bishop Mews, Transport Way, Oxford OX4 6HD
Tel: 01865 595790 *Email:* anneliese.dodds.casework@parliament.uk
Website: www.anneliesedodds.org.uk *Twitter:* @AnnelieseDodds

DEMOCRATIC UNIONIST PARTY

DONALDSON, JEFFREY

Lagan Valley *(Majority 6,499)*

Leader, DUP Parliamentary Group; Spokesperson for Business in the House of Commons

Jeffrey Mark Donaldson. Born 7 December 1962; Son of late James and Sarah Anne Donaldson; Married Eleanor Cousins 1987 (2 daughters).

Education: Kilkeel High School; Castlereagh College (Diploma electrical engineering 1982); French.

Non-political career: Agent to Enoch Powell MP 1983-84; Personal assistant to Sir James Molyneaux MP 1984-85; Partner, financial services and estate agency business 1986-96. Ulster Defence Regiment 1980-85. Former member, AEEU.

Political career: Member for Lagan Valley 1997-2010, for Lagan Valley (revised boundary) since 6 May 2010 general election; Ulster Unionist Spokesperson for: Trade and Industry 1997-2000, Environment, Transport and the Regions 2000-01, Treasury 2001-02, Transport, Local Government and the Regions 2001-02, Work and Pensions 2001-03, Defence 2002-03, Trade and Industry 2002-03; DUP Spokesperson for: Education 2004-05, Defence 2004-05, 2007-17, Transport 2005-07, 2009-10, International Development 2005-07, Home Office 2007-10, Equality 2010-12, Energy and Climate Change 2010-15, Business in the House of Commons 2015-; DUP Chief Whip 2015-19; Trade Envoy to Egypt 2015-; Leader, DUP Parliamentary Group 2019-. *Select committees:* Member: Northern Ireland Affairs 1997-2000, Environment, Transport and Regional Affairs 2000-01, Environment, Transport and Regional Affairs (Transport Sub-Committee) 2000-01, Regulatory Reform 2001-05, Joint Committee on Statutory Instruments 2001-06, Transport 2004-07, 2009-10, Defence 2010-15, Arms Export Controls 2011-12, 2013-15. Member: Northern Ireland Assembly (UUP) 1985-86, Northern Ireland Forum 1996-98; MLA for Lagan Valley 2003-10 (UUP November 2003 to 15 January 2004, DUP 15 January 2004 to 2010): Junior Minister, Office of the First Minister and Deputy First Minister 2008-09; Chair, Assembly Committee on Assembly and Executive Review 2007-08. Ulster Unionist Council: Honorary Secretary 1988-2000, Vice-president 2000-03; Resigned from UUP 15 January 2004; Democratic Unionist Party: Joined 15 January 2004, Party officer 2004-. *Councils and public bodies:* Alderman, Lisburn City Council 2005-10; Member, Northern Ireland Policing Board 2007-08.

Political interests: Christian values, constitution, transport, defence, international development; Cyprus, Ethiopia, Israel, Moldova, Northern Ireland, South Africa, USA.

Other: Member: UK delegation, Parliamentary Assembly of the Council of Europe 2015-, British-Irish Parliamentary Assembly 2015-20, UK delegation, NATO Parliamentary Assembly 2020-; Member: Presbyterian Church, Loyal Orange Order, Constitutional Monarchy Association, Regimental Association of the Ulster Defence Regiment; Trustee, Royal Ulster Rifles Association; Chairman, Causeway Institute for Peace-building and Conflict Resolution; Governor, Westminster Foundation for Democracy; Care and Tear Fund; PC 2007; Kt 2016.

Recreations: Hill-walking, reading, local history, church.

Rt Hon Sir Jeffrey Donaldson MP, House of Commons, London SW1A 0AA
Tel: 020 7219 3407 *Fax:* 020 7219 2347 *Email:* jeffrey.donaldson.mp@parliament.uk
Constituency: The Old Town Hall, 29 Castle Street, Lisburn, Co Antrim BT27 4DH
Tel: 028 9266 8001 *Email:* jeffreydonaldsonmp@laganvalley.net
Website: www.jeffreydonaldson.org *Twitter:* @J_Donaldson_MP

CONSERVATIVE

DONELAN, MICHELLE

Chippenham *(Majority 11,288)*

Minister of State for Universities, Department for Education

Michelle Emma May Elizabeth Donelan. Born 8 April 1984; Daughter of Michael and Kathryn Donelan.

Education: The County High School, Leftwich; York University (BA history and politics).

Non-political career: Marketing, Pacific Magazines, Sydney, Australia 2006-07; Senior partnership marketing, AETN UK 2007-10; International marketing communications manager, WWE 2010-14.

Political career: Contested Wentworth and Dearne 2010 general election. Member for Chippenham since 7 May 2015 general election; PPS to: Jeremy Wright as Attorney General 2017-18, Liam Fox as Secretary of State for International Trade and President of the Board of Trade 2018; Assistant Government Whip 2018-19; Government Whip (Lord Commissioner of HM Treasury) 2019-20; Department for Education: Parliamentary Under-Secretary of State for Children and Families (maternity cover for Kemi Badenoch MP) September 2019-February 2020, Minister of State for Universities 2020-. *Select committees:* Member: Education 2015-18, Education, Skills and the Economy Sub-committee 2015-17, Petitions 2017-19. Press and media development officer, Conservative Future 2009-.

Political interests: Asia Pacific, Oceania.

Recreations: Travel, history, culture.

Michelle Donelan MP, House of Commons, London SW1A 0AA
Tel: 020 7219 4451 *Email:* michelle.donelan.mp@parliament.uk
Constituency: 61 New Road, Chippenham, Wiltshire SN15 1ES
Tel: 01249 704465 *Email:* michelle@michelledonelan.com Website: michelledonelan.co.uk
Twitter: @michelledonelan

SCOTTISH NATIONAL PARTY

DOOGAN, DAVE

Angus *(Majority 3,795)*

SNP Agriculture and Rural Affairs and Defence Teams Member

David Michael Doogan. Born 4 March 1973; Son of James Doogan and Annie Doogan (née Walsh); Married (2 children).

Education: Dundee University (MA politics and international relations 2011).

Non-political career: Aircraft engineer; Commercial Manager, Ministry of Defence; Groundworker; FE College Technician Taxi Driver; Parliamentary Caseworker to John Swinney MSP; Self-employed Landscaping Contractor 2016-19.

Political career: Member for Angus since 12 December 2019; SNP Spokesperson for/Team Member, Agriculture and Rural Affairs 2020-, Defence Team Member 2020-; SNP Spokesperson for Manufacturing 2020-21; *Select committees:* Member, Environment, Food and Rural Affairs 2020-. Contested Mid Scotland and Fife region 2016 Scottish Parliament election. Convener, Perthshire South and Kinross-shire Constituency 2012-19. *Councils and public bodies:* Perth and Kinross Council: Councillor 2012-20, Group Leader 2017-19; Non-executive member, NHS Tayside Board 2012-17.

Political interests: Scottish independence, Celtic nations, defence, international relations, global trade; British Isles, European Union, Scandinavia.

Dave Doogan MP, House of Commons, London SW1A 0AA
Tel: 020 7219 3000 *Email:* dave.doogan.mp@parliament.uk
Constituency: No constituency office publicised
Tel: 01241 815330 Website: davedoogan.scot *Twitter:* @DaveDooganSNP

SCOTTISH NATIONAL PARTY

DORANS, ALLAN

Ayr, Carrick and Cumnock *(Majority 2,329)*

SNP Foreign Affairs Team Member

Allan Hopkins Dorans. Born 30 July 1955; Son of Peter and Agnes Dorans; Married Maureen Lilian (née Beeson) 1979.

Education: Carrick Academy; University of the West of Scotland (Diploma public service leadership).

Non-political career: Personnel and Training Executive, the Rank Organisation; Metropolitan Police, rising to the rank of Detective Inspector.

Political career: Member for Ayr, Carrick and Cumnock since 12 December 2019; SNP Foreign Affairs Team Member 2020-. *Select committees:* Member, European Scrutiny 2020-. Convener, Ayr West SNP Branch 2014-17. *Councils and public bodies:* South Ayrshire Council: Councillor 2012-17, Leader, SNP group 2014-17.

Political interests: Scottish independence; India, Ireland, USA.

Other: Open University: Chartered Member of the Institute of Human Resource Management, Chartered Member of the Institute of Management.

Allan Dorans MP, House of Commons, London SW1A 0AA
Tel: 020 7219 5965 *Email:* allan.dorans.mp@parliament.uk
Constituency: Office 1, 6 Alloway Place, Ayr KA7 2AA
Tel: 01292 848102 *Twitter:* @allandoranssnp

CONSERVATIVE

DORRIES, NADINE

Mid Bedfordshire *(Majority 24,664)*

Minister of State for Patient Safety, Suicide Prevention and Mental Health, Department of Health and Social Care

Nadine Vanessa Dorries. Born 21 May 1957; Daughter of Sylvia and George Bargery; 3 daughters.

Education: Halewood Grange Comprehensive, Liverpool; Warrington District School of Nursing.

Non-political career: Former nurse; Businesswoman; Director, BUPA; Adviser to Oliver Letwin MP 2002-05.

Political career: Contested Hazel Grove 2001 general election (as Nadine Bargery). Member for Mid Bedfordshire 2005-10, for Mid Bedfordshire (revised boundary) since 6 May 2010 general election; Contested Deputy Speaker election 2013; Department of Health and Social Care: Parliamentary Under-Secretary of State for Patient Safety, Suicide Prevention and Mental Health 2019-20, Minister of State for Patient Safety, Suicide Prevention and Mental Health 2020-. *Select committees:* Member: Education and Skills 2005-06, Science and Technology 2007, Innovation, Universities[, Science] and Skills/Science and Technology 2007-10, Energy and Climate Change 2009-10, Health 2010-11, Chairmen's Panel/Panel of Chairs 2010-19. Conservative Whip suspended November 2012-May 2013; Founding member, Conservatives for Britain 2015-16.

Political interests: Law and order, social structure, health, rural affairs; Angola, Zambia.

Publications: The Four Streets (2014); Hide Her Name (2015); Ruby Flynn (2015); The Ballymara Road (2016); The Angels of Lovely Lane (2016); The Children of Lovely Lane (2016).

Recreations: Family, friends, walking, reading, dogs.

Nadine Dorries MP, House of Commons, London SW1A 0AA
Tel: 020 7219 5928 *Fax:* 020 7219 6428 *Email:* dorriesn@parliament.uk
Constituency: No constituency office publicised
Website: www.dorries.org *Twitter:* @NadineDorries

CONSERVATIVE

DOUBLE, STEVE

St Austell and Newquay *(Majority 16,526)*

PPS to Matt Hancock as Secretary of State for Health and Social Care

Stephen Daniel Double. Born 19 December 1966; Son of Donald and Heather Double; Married Anne 1986 (2 sons).

Education: Poltair School, St Austell; BTEC Diploma business studies 1987.

Non-political career: Barclay Bank 1983-92; Church Pastor 1992-2002; Director: Bay Director Media 2001-15, Phoenix Corporate Ltd 2011-15.

Political career: Member for St Austell and Newquay since 7 May 2015 general election; Department of Health and Social Care: Team PPS 2019-20, PPS to Matt Hancock as Secretary of State for Health and Social Care 2020-. *Select committees:* Member: Petitions 2015-20, European Scrutiny 2016-19, Transport 2017-19. Founding member, Conservatives for Britain 2015-16. *Councils and public bodies:* St Austell Town Council 2009-16; Councillor, Cornwall Council 2009-13; Mayor, St Austell 2013-14.

Political interests: Transport, tourism, space, business, environment, hospitality, food and drink; Hong Kong, Israel, Kenya, Tanzania.

Other: Substitute Member, UK Delegation to Parliamentary Assembly, Council of Europe 2018-.

House of Commons MPs' Biographies

Steve Double MP, House of Commons, London SW1A 0AA
Tel: 020 7219 4408 *Email:* steve.double.mp@parliament.uk
Constituency: Unit 1, Bucklers Lane, Holmbush, St Austell, Cornwall PL25 3JN
Tel: 01726 829379 *Email:* office@stevedouble.org.uk Website: www.stevedouble.org.uk
Twitter: @stevedouble

LABOUR/
CO-OPERATIVE

DOUGHTY, STEPHEN

Cardiff South and Penarth *(Majority 12,737)*

Shadow Minister for Africa

Stephen John Doughty. Born 15 April 1980; Single.

Education: Llantwit Major Comprehensive School, Vale of Glamorgan; Lester B Pearson United World College, Victoria, Canada; Corpus Christi College, Oxford (BA 2001); St Andrews University (MLitt 2003); Royal College of Defence Studies (RCDS(s) 2018); French, Welsh (basic).

Non-political career: Policy and Campaigns Adviser, World Vision 2004-06; Head, UK and EU Government Relations, Oxfam 2006-09; Special Adviser to Douglas Alexander as Secretary of State for International Development 2009-10; Head: Health and Education Campaign, Oxfam International 2010-11, Oxfam Cymru 2011-12. Member, GMB.

Political career: Member for Cardiff South and Penarth since 15 November 2012 by-election; PPS to Rachel Reeves as Shadow Chief Secretary to the Treasury 2013; Opposition Whip 2013-15; Shadow Minister for: Trade, Industry, Industrial Relations, Business, Innovation and Skills 2015, Foreign and Commonwealth Office 2015-16, Foreign and Commonwealth Office and International Development (Africa) 2020-. *Select committees:* Member: Welsh Affairs 2012-15, International Development 2016-17, Arms Export Controls 2016-17, Independent Commission for Aid Impact Sub-committee 2016-17, Home Affairs 2017-20. Member: Labour Party, Co-operative Party; Patron, LGBT Labour.

Political interests: Economy, home affairs, foreign affairs, defence, international development, climate change, equalities; Afghanistan, Africa, Argentina, Bangladesh, Canada, EU, India, Israel, Pakistan, Palestine, Somaliland, Syria, USA, Yemen.

Other: Member, British-Irish Parliamentary Assembly 2020-; Christians on the Left.

Recreations: Cardiff City FC, Welsh rugby union, singing, surfing, sailing, walking.

Stephen Doughty MP, House of Commons, London SW1A 0AA
Tel: 020 7219 5348 *Email:* stephen.doughty.mp@parliament.uk
Constituency: Regus House, Falcon Drive, Cardiff Bay CF10 4RU
Tel: 029 2267 7904 Website: stephendoughty.wales *Twitter:* @SDoughtyMP

LABOUR

DOWD, PETER

Bootle *(Majority 34,556)*

Peter Christopher Dowd. Born 20 June 1957.

Education: Hugh Baird College, Liverpool; Liverpool University; Lancaster University.

Non-political career: Head of care delivery frameworks, 5 Boroughs NHS Partnership Trust.

Political career: Member for Bootle since 7 May 2015 general election; Shadow Financial Secretary 2016-17; Shadow Chief Secretary to the Treasury 2017-20. *Select committees:* Member, Panel of Chairs 2020-. Agent to Joe Benton MP. *Councils and public bodies:* Councillor, Merseyside County Council 1981-86; Sefton Council: Councillor 1991-, Leader, Labour Group 2008-15, Leader of the Council 2011-15; Former chair, Merseyside Fire and Rescue Service.

Political interests: Health.

Peter Dowd MP, House of Commons, London SW1A 0AA
Tel: 020 7219 8671 *Email:* peter.dowd.mp@parliament.uk
Constituency: Opportunities House, 270 Marsh Lane, Bootle L20 5BW
Tel: 0151-933 8432 Website: www.peterdowd.com *Twitter:* @Peter_Dowd

CONSERVATIVE

DOWDEN, OLIVER

Hertsmere *(Majority 21,313)*

Secretary of State for Digital, Culture, Media and Sport

Oliver James Dowden. Born 1 August 1978; Married Blythe (2 children).

Education: Parmiter's School, Watford; Trinity College, Cambridge (BA law); College of London (Legal Practice Course).

Non-political career: Conservative Research Department 2004-07; Hill and Knowlton 2007-09; Conservative Campaign Headquarters 2009-10; Prime Minister's Office: Special Adviser to David Cameron as Prime Minister 2010-12, Deputy Chief of Staff 2012-14, Senior Adviser to David Cameron as Prime Minister 2014-15; Consultant, Policy Exchange 2014-; Policy adviser, Caxton Europe Asset Management 2015-; Political adviser, Association of Independent Professionals and the Self Employed 2015-.

Political career: Member for Hertsmere since 7 May 2015 general election; PPS to Secretary of State for Defence: Michael Fallon 2017, Gavin Williamson 2017-18; Cabinet Office: Parliamentary Secretary (Minister for Implementation) 2018-19, Minister for the Cabinet Office; Paymaster General (also attending Cabinet) 2019-20; Member, Speaker's Committee on the Electoral Commission 2020; Secretary of State for Digital, Culture, Media and Sport 2020-. *Select committees:* Member: Public Administration and Constitutional Affairs 2015-16, Petitions 2015-17.

Political interests: Immigration, welfare, health, criminal justice, education; Canada, India, Israel, Japan.

Other: Conservative Friends of Israel; UK-Japan 21st Century Group -2018; Trustee, Law Family Education Trust 2016-; CBE 2015; PC 2019.

Rt Hon Oliver Dowden CBE MP, House of Commons, London SW1A 0AA
Tel: 020 7219 3415 *Email:* oliver.dowden.mp@parliament.uk
Constituency: 104 High Street, London Colney, Hertfordshire AL2 1QL
Tel: 01727 828221 *Email:* oliver@oliverdowden.com Website: www.oliverdowden.com
Twitter: @OliverDowden

CONSERVATIVE

DOYLE-PRICE, JACKIE

Thurrock *(Majority 11,482)*

Jacqueline Doyle-Price. Born 5 August 1969; Daughter of Brian and Kathleen Doyle-Price; Partner Mark Coxshall.

Education: Notre Dame RC, Sheffield; Durham University (BA economics and politics 1991).

Non-political career: Administrative officer, South Yorkshire Police 1992; Parliamentary officer, City of London Corporation 1993-2000; Assistant private secretary to Rt Hon the Lord Mayor of the City of London 2000-05; Associate, Financial Services Authority 2005.

Political career: Contested Sheffield Hillsborough 2005 general election. Member for Thurrock since 6 May 2010 general election; Assistant Government Whip 2015-17; Parliamentary Under-Secretary of State: (Care and Mental Health), Department of Health 2017-18, for Mental Health, Inequalities and Suicide Prevention, Department of Health and Social Care 2018-19. *Select committees:* Member: Public Accounts 2010-14, Selection 2015-17, Regulatory Reform 2020-, Public Administration and Constitutional Affairs 2020-, Joint Committee on Fixed-Term Parliaments Act 2020-. Treasurer, National Association of Conservative Graduates 1994-97; Chair, Lewisham Deptford Constituency Association 1997-98; Constituency officer, Greenwich and Woolwich Conservatives 2006-07.

Political interests: Welfare, foreign affairs, vocational education, financial services, transport; Bosnia and Herzegovina, Croatia, Serbia.

Other: Patron, Thurrock Male Voice Choir; Member, Tilbury Cruise Terminal and Railway Station Trust; Freedom, City of London. Grays Conservative Club, RAFA Club, Grays Club.

Recreations: Theatre, reading, film, watching soaps.

Jackie Doyle-Price MP, House of Commons, London SW1A 0AA
Tel: 020 7219 7171 *Fax:* 020 7219 4924 *Email:* jackie.doyleprice.mp@parliament.uk
Constituency: 2 Orsett Business Centre, Stanford Road, Grays, Essex RM16 3BX
Tel: 01375 802029 Website: www.jackiedoyleprice.com *Twitter:* @JackieDP

CONSERVATIVE

DRAX, RICHARD

South Dorset *(Majority 17,153)*

Richard Grosvenor Plunkett-Ernle-Erle Drax. Born 29 January 1958; Divorced Zara (2 daughters 2 sons); married Elsebet.

Education: Harrow School; Royal Agricultural College, Cirencester (Diploma of Membership rural land management 1990); Westminster Press (Diploma journalism 1995).

Non-political career: Journalist: *Yorkshire Evening Press* 1991-96, *TyneTees, Calendar, Daily Telegraph* 1996-97; Journalist/Reporter, *BBC South Today, BBC Solent* 1997-2006. Officer, Coldstream Guards 1978-87.

Political career: Member for South Dorset since 6 May 2010 general election. *Select committees:* Member: Environment, Food and Rural Affairs 2010-15, European Scrutiny 2015-, Defence 2020-.

Political interests: Defence.

Other: Patron, Cherry Tree Nursery 2006.

Recreations: Sailing, golf, skiing.

Richard Drax MP, House of Commons, London SW1A 0AA
Tel: 020 7219 7051 *Email:* richard.drax.mp@parliament.uk
Constituency: SDCA, Chesil House, Dorset Green Innovation Park, Winfrith Newburgh, Dorchester, Dorset DT2 8ZB
Tel: 01929 462803 Websites: www.southdorsetconservatives.com/www.richarddrax.com

LABOUR

DROMEY, JACK

Birmingham, Erdington *(Majority 3,601)*

Shadow Minister for Cabinet Office

John Eugene Joseph Dromey. Born 29 September 1948; Married Harriet Harman (qv) 1982 (MP for Camberwell and Peckham) (2 sons 1 daughter).

Education: Cardinal Vaughan Grammar School; French.

Non-political career: Secretary: South East Regional Council, TUC, Brent Trades Council 1976-78; Transport and General Workers' Union 1978-2003: Has served at all levels of the union from district officer to national organiser, Deputy general secretary 2003-08; Deputy general secretary, Unite 2008-10. Chair for 15 years, Joint Industrial Council, Ministry of Defence.

Political career: Member for Birmingham, Erdington since 6 May 2010 general election; Shadow Minister for: Communities and Local Government 2010-13, Home Office 2013-16, Business, Energy and Industrial Strategy (Labour) 2016-17, Work and Pensions (Pensions) 2018-21, Cabinet Office 2021-. *Select committees:* Member: Business, Innovation and Skills 2010-11, Regulatory Reform 2010-15. Chair, PLP Departmental Group for Business, Innovation and Skills 2010. Treasurer, Labour Party 2004-10. *Councils and public bodies:* Founder member, Greater London Enterprise Board.

Political interests: Workers' rights (including equalities and the Vulnerable Workers' Agenda), manufacturing, housing, transport, international development (including supply chain ethical trading).

Other: Global Organising Alliance; Former executive council member and chair, National Council for Civil Liberties.

Recreations: Music, gym, walking, family.

Jack Dromey MP, House of Commons, London SW1A 0AA
Tel: 020 7219 0903 *Email:* jack.dromey.mp@parliament.uk
Constituency: 77 Mason Road, Birmingham, West Midlands B24 9EH
Tel: 0121-350 6077 *Twitter:* @JackDromeyMP

CONSERVATIVE

DRUMMOND, FLICK

Meon Valley *(Majority 23,555)*

Team PPS, Department for Work and Pensions

Felicia Jane Beatrix Drummond. Born 16 June 1962; Daughter of George Anthony Shepherd CMG, diplomat, and Sarah Shepherd; Married Hereward Drummond 1987 (2 sons 2 daughters).

Education: Roedean School; Goldaming Sixth Form College; Hull University (BA South East Asian studies 1983); Insurance exams 1985; Southampton University (MSc global politics and international relations 2007).

Non-political career: Insurance broker, Porchester Group, London 1983-86; Lay school inspector, OFSTED 1994-99. Part-time soldier, Intelligence Corps, Territorial Army 1985-88.

Political career: Contested Southampton Itchen 2005 and Portsmouth South 2010 general elections. Member for Portsmouth South 2015-17. Contested Portsmouth South 2017 general election. Member for Meon Valley since 12 December 2019; PPS to Anne-Marie Trevelyan as Secretary of State for International Development 2020; Team PPS, Department for Work and Pensions 2020-. *Select committees:* Member: Women and Equalities 2015-17, European Statutory Instruments 2020-. Winchester Conservatives 1993-2007: Campaign Director 2006; Corporate Director, Conservative Middle East Council 2010-11; Deputy Chairman, Political, Portsmouth South Conservative Association 2011-13; Director, Conservative Policy Forum 2018-20. *Councils and public bodies:* Chair, acute group, Community Health Council, Winchester 1991-99; Councillor, Winchester City Council 1996-99; Board of Governors, Milton Park Primary School: Member 2008-15, Chair 2010-14; Board member, Salterns Academy Trust 2017-.

Political interests: Foreign affairs, defence, education; Commonwealth, Middle East, South Asia, South East Asia.

Other: Member, Executive Committee, Commonwealth Parliamentary Association UK 2016-17; Editor of report and Clerk, Social Workers' Commission 2007; Honorary vice-president, Society of Maritime Industries 2016-17. Member, Pompey Supporters Trust.

Publications: No More Blame Game – The Future of Children's Social Workers, Conservative Party Commission on Social Workers (2007); Coastal Communities chapter in Beyond Brexit (2019).

Recreations: Travel, walking, sport, family.

Flick Drummond MP, House of Commons, London SW1A 0AA
Tel: 020 7219 8018 *Email:* flick.drummond.mp@parliament.uk
Constituency: Manor Farm, Itchen Stoke, Alresford SO24 0QT
Tel: 01962 679920 Website: www.flickdrummond.com *Twitter:* @FlickD

CONSERVATIVE

DUDDRIDGE, JAMES

Rochford and Southend East *(Majority 12,286)*

Parliamentary Under-Secretary of State (Minister for Africa), Foreign, Commonwealth and Development Office

James Philip Duddridge. Born 26 August 1971; Son of Philip and Jenny Duddridge; Married Kathryn (Katy) Thompson 2004 (2 sons 1 daughter).

Education: Crestwood School, Eastleigh, Hampshire; Huddersfield New College; Wells Blue School; Essex University (BA government 1993); French.

Non-political career: Research assistant to Bernard Jenkin MP 1991-93; Retail and merchant banking, Barclays Bank 1993-2002: Barclays Bank of Swaziland 1995-96, Barclays Bank Head Office 1996, Sales director, Banque Belgolaise, Ivory Coast 1997-98, National sales manager, Barclays 1998-2001, Service delivery director, Barclays Bank Botswana 2001-02; Account director and consultant, YouGov 2000-05; Director, Okavango Ltd 2002-05; Adviser: Brand Communications Group 2017-18, TLG Capital Investments Ltd 2017-.

Political career: Contested Rother Valley 2001 general election. Member for Rochford and Southend East 2005-10, for Rochford and Southend East (revised boundary) since 6 May 2010 general election; Opposition Whip 2008-10; Government Whip 2010-12; Parliamentary Under-Secretary of State: Foreign and Commonwealth Office 2014-16, Department for Exiting the European Union 2019-20; Parliamentary Under-Secretary of State (Minister for Africa): Department for International Development and Foreign and Commonwealth office 2020,

Foreign, Commonwealth and Development Office 2020-. *Select committees:* Member: Environment, Food and Rural Affairs 2005-07, International Development 2006-08, 2017-18, Strategic Export Controls (Quadripartite Committee)/Arms Export Controls 2007-08; Chair, Regulatory Reform 2012-14; Member: Liaison 2013-14, Joint Committee on Draft Deregulation Bill 2013, Procedures 2016-17, Work of the Independent Commission for Aid Impact Sub-committee 2017-18; Chair, High Speed Rail (West Midlands – Crewe) Bill 2018-19. Member, Executive, 1922 Committee 2013-14. Chair, Wells Young Conservatives 1989-91; Campaigns department, Conservative Central Office 1989-91; Chair, Essex University Conservative Students 1990-91; General election campaign manager to Stephen Shakespeare, Colchester 1997; Adviser, Lady Miller Postal Services Bill 1999; Executive committee member, Conservative Way Forward 2000-01.

Political interests: African politics, pensions; Botswana, Ivory Coast, South Africa, Swaziland, Zimbabwe.

Other: Member, Executive Committee, British Group Inter-Parliamentary Union 2005-06; Chair, Executive Committee, Commonwealth Parliamentary Association United Kingdom 2017-19; Student representative, Huddersfield Police Forum 1987-88; Member, Bow Group 1999-; Speaker, Westminster Foundation for Democracy 2003-04; Member, Chartered Institute of Bankers 1993-2002; Associate member, Market Research Society 2003-05.

Recreations: Running, cycling, Southampton FC, Southend United FC.

James Duddridge MP, House of Commons, London SW1A 0AA
Tel: 020 7219 4830 *Email:* james.duddridge.mp@parliament.uk
Constituency: No constituency office
Email: james@jamesduddridge.com Website: www.jamesduddridge.com
Twitter: @JamesDuddridge

LABOUR

DUFFIELD, ROSIE

Canterbury *(Majority 1,836)*

Rosemary Clare Duffield. Born 8 June 1971.

Non-political career: Teaching Assistant; Political satire writer/comedian. Member: Unison, DGMB, CWU.

Political career: Member for Canterbury since 8 June 2017; PPS to Dawn Butler as Shadow Secretary of State for Women and Equalities 2018; Opposition Whip 2020. *Select committees:* Member: Women and Equalities 2017-18, 2020, Work and Pensions 2018-19, Environment, Food and Rural Affairs 2020-. Chair, PLP Department Group for Women 2020-. Canterbury Labour Party Branch: Chair 2013-17, Women's Officer 2015-17.

Political interests: Early education, animal rights, healthcare, social care, equalities, LGBTQ+, equal opportunities, post-partum healthcare, air pollution, social housing.

Other: Canterbury Action Network; Amnesty International Canterbury Branch; 50:50 Parliament.

Rosie Duffield MP, House of Commons, London SW1A 0AA
Tel: 020 7219 1183 *Email:* rosie.duffield.mp@parliament.uk
Constituency: 27 Castle Street, Canterbury CT1 2PX
Tel: 01227 467888 *Email:* enquiries@rosieduffieldmp.co.uk
Website: www.rosieduffieldmp.co.uk *Twitter:* @RosieDuffield1

CONSERVATIVE

DUGUID, DAVID

Banff and Buchan *(Majority 4,118)*

Parliamentary Under-Secretary of State, Scotland Office; Government Whip (Lord Commissioner of HM Treasury)

David James Duguid. Born 8 October 1970; Son of Norman Morrison Jane Anne Duguid (née Barron); Married Raziya Gasimova 2010 (1 son 1 daughter).

Education: Banff Academy; Robert Gordon University (HND chemistry 1991); Russian, Spanish.

Non-political career: Chemical Sales/Service Engineer, Servo Oilfield Chemicals 1992-93; Production Chemist, SGS 1993-2001; BP: Production Efficiency Engineer/Operationss Excellence Coach 2001-03, Integrity Management/Process Safety Engineer 2003-06, Common

Process/Continuous Improvement Coach 2006-11; Project Manager (Management Consulting/ Change Management), Hitachi Consulting 2011-16; Managing Director, D&R Duguid Ltd 2016-.

Political career: Member for Banff and Buchan since 8 June 2017; Team PPS: Department of Health and Social Care 2019, Department for Business, Energy and Industrial Strategy 2019; PPS to Elizabeth Truss as Secretary of State for International Trade, President of the Board of Trade and Minister for Women and Equalities 2020; Parliamentary Under-Secretary of State, Scotland Office 2020-; Government Whip (Lord Commissioner of HM Treasury) 2020-. *Select committees:* Member, Scottish Affairs 2017-20.

Political interests: Fisheries, agriculture, food and drink production, energy industry, Scottish tourism, Scottish development/regeneration, rural economy, infrastructure and connectivity, exiting the EU with the best deal for Banff and Buchan; Angola, Azerbaijan, Canada, Denmark, Venezuela.

Other: Member: Institute of Asset Management, Institute of Engineering and Technology'; Member, Institute of Engineering and Technology; Cancer Research, Breast Cancer Now, Parkinsons UK, RNLI.

Recreations: Playing guitar.

David Duguid MP, House of Commons, London SW1A 0AA
Tel: 020 7219 2819 *Email:* david.duguid.mp@parliament.uk
Constituency: Suite 6, 8 Low Street, Banff AB45 1AS
Tel: 01261 818744 Website: www.davidduguid.com *Twitter:* @david_duguid

CONSERVATIVE

DUNCAN SMITH, IAIN

Chingford and Woodford Green *(Majority 1,262)*

George Iain Duncan Smith. Born 9 April 1954; Son of late Group Captain W. G. G. Duncan Smith DSO DFC, and late Pamela Duncan Smith, née Summers; Married Hon. Elizabeth Fremantle 1982 (2 sons 2 daughters).

Education: HMS Conway (Cadet School); Universita per Stranieri, Perugia, Italy; RMA Sandhurst; Dunchurch College of Management; Italian.

Non-political career: GEC Marconi 1981-88; Director: Bellwinch Property 1988-89, Publishing Director Jane's Information Group 1989-92. Commissioned, Scots Guards 1975-81; Active service in: Northern Ireland 1976, Rhodesia/Zimbabwe 1979-80; ADC to Major-General Sir John Acland, KCB, CBE, Commander of Commonwealth Monitoring Force in Zimbabwe 1979-81.

Political career: Contested Bradford West 1987 general election. Member for Chingford 1992-97, for Chingford and Woodford Green 1997-2010, for Chingford and Woodford Green (revised boundary) since 6 May 2010 general election; Shadow Secretary of State for: Social Security 1997-99, Defence 1999-2001; Leader of the Opposition 2001-03; Secretary of State for Work and Pensions 2010-16. *Select committees:* Member: Health 1993-95, Administration 1993-97, Standards and Privileges 1995-97. Joint Secretary, Conservative Parliamentary Committees on: Foreign Affairs 1992-97, Defence 1995-96; Former vice-chair, European Affairs Committee; Chair, Conservative Party Committee for Social Security 1997-99. Vice-chair, Fulham Conservative Association 1991; Chair, Conservative Policy Board 2001-03; Leader, Conservative Party 2001-03.

Political interests: Finance, small businesses, transport, defence, environment, social policy.

Other: Member, Employment, Social Affairs, Health and Consumer Affairs Council, Council of the European Union 2010-16; Founder and Patron, Centre for Social Justice 2004-; Patron, Haven House Childrens Hospice; Trustee, Whitefields School Community Trust; Member, Campaign committee, Vote Leave 2016; Haven House Foundation, Whitefields Community Trust; Freedom, City of London 1993; Commons Minister of the Year, *House Magazine* awards 2011; PC 2001; Kt 2020. Buck's Club 1919, Pratt's Club.

Publications: Co-author, Who Benefits? Reinventing Social Security; Game, Set and Match? (Maastricht); Facing the Future (Defence and Foreign and Commonwealth Affairs); 1994 and Beyond; A Response to Chancellor Kohl; A Race Against Time, Europe's growing vulnerability to missile attack (2002); The Devil's Tune (Robson Books, 2003).

Recreations: Cricket, rugby, tennis, sport in general, painting, theatre, family, shooting, fishing.

Rt Hon Sir Iain Duncan Smith MP, House of Commons, London SW1A 0AA
Tel: 020 7219 2667 *Email:* iain.duncansmith.mp@parliament.uk
Constituency: 105c Station Road, Chingford, London E4 7BU
Tel: 020 8524 4344 Website: www.iainduncansmith.org.uk *Twitter:* @MPIainDS

CONSERVATIVE

DUNNE, PHILIP

Ludlow *(Majority 23,648)*

Chair, Select Committee on Environmental Audit

Philip Martin Dunne. Born 14 August 1958; Son of Sir Thomas Dunne KG and Henrietta Dunne, née Crawley; Married Domenica Fraser 1989 (2 sons 2 daughters).

Education: Eton College; Keble College, Oxford (BA philosophy, politics and economics 1980, MA).

Non-political career: Graduate trainee to senior manager, S G Warburg & Co Ltd 1980-88; Partner, Gatley Farms 1987-; Ottakar's plc: Co-founder director (non-executive) 1987-2006, Chair (non-executive) 1998-2006; Director of corporate development, James Gulliver Associates 1988-90; Partner, Phoenix Securities and successor 1991-2001; Managing director, Donaldson, Lufkin and Jenette 1997-2001; Chair (non-executive), Baronsmead VCT 4 plc 2001-10; Director, Ruffer Investment Management Limited and Ruffer LLP 2002-09 (non-executive 2005-09); Non-executive Director, Reaction Engines Ltd 2020-. Member, NFU 1987-.

Political career: Member for Ludlow since 5 May 2005 general election; Opposition Whip 2008-10; Assistant Government Whip 2010-12; Ministry of Defence: Parliamentary Under-Secretary of State (Defence Equipment, Support and Technology) 2012-15, Minister of State for Defence Procurement 2015-16; Minister of State for Health, Department of Health 2016-18. *Select committees:* Member: Work and Pensions 2005-06, Public Accounts 2006-09; Treasury 2007-08, European Statutory Instruments 2018-; Environmental Audit: Member 2018-19, Chair 2020-; Member, Liaison 2020-. Deputy chair, International Office and Conservatives Abroad, Conservative Party 2008-10. *Councils and public bodies:* South Shropshire District Council: Councillor 2001-07, Conservative group leader 2003-05.

Political interests: Agriculture, business (especially small business), defence, economy, financial services, health, international affairs, local government; Hong Kong, Middle East, USA.

Other: Non-executive director, Juvenile Diabetes Research Foundation 1998-2005; Director, Moor Park Charitable Trust 2001-07; Governor, Westminster Foundation for Democracy 2008-10; Member, Country Land and Business Association; Trustee: Henry Hewes Almshouse, MA Walker Charitable Trust; President, Three Counties Agricultural Society 2016; Commissioner, Commonwealth War Graves Commission 2019-; Deputy Chair, Defence Growth Partnership 2019-; PC 2019. White's Club; Church Stretton Golf Club.

Recreations: Country sports, skiing, travel.

Rt Hon Philip Dunne MP, House of Commons, London SW1A 0AA
Tel: 020 7219 2388 *Email:* philip.dunne.mp@parliament.uk
Constituency: 54 Broad Street, Ludlow, Shropshire SY8 1GP
Tel: 01584 872187 Website: www.philipdunne.com *Twitter:* @Dunne4Ludlow

LABOUR

EAGLE, ANGELA

Wallasey *(Majority 18,322)*

Born 17 February 1961; Daughter of André Eagle, printworker, and late Shirley Eagle, dressmaker; Civil partner Maria Exall 2008.

Education: Formby High School; St John's College, Oxford (BA philosophy, politics and economics 1983).

Non-political career: Researcher, then national press officer, COHSE 1984-92. Member: COHSE, National Union of Journalists, Unison.

Political career: Member for Wallasey 1992-2010, for Wallasey (revised boundary) since 6 May 2010 general election; Opposition Whip 1996-97; Parliamentary Under-Secretary of State: Department of the Environment, Transport and the Regions (Minister for Green Issues and Regeneration) 1997-98, Department of Social Security 1998-2001, Home Office 2001-02; Exchequer Secretary, HM Treasury 2007-09; Minister of State (Minister for Pensions and the

Ageing Society), Department for Work and Pensions 2009-10; Shadow Minister for Treasury 2010; Shadow Chief Secretary to the Treasury 2010-11; Shadow Leader of the House of Commons 2011-15; Member: House of Commons Commission 2011-15, Speaker's Committee for the Independent Parliamentary Standards Authority 2012-15; Shadow First Secretary of State and Secretary of State for Business, Innovation and Skills 2015-16. *Select committees:* Member: Public Accounts 1995-97, 2002-03, 2007-09, Treasury 2003-07, 2020-, Treasury (Treasury Sub-Committee) 2003-10, Joint Committee on the Palace of Westminster 2015, European Statutory Instruments 2018-19, Procedure 2020-, Panel of Chairs 2020-, Joint Committee on Fixed-Term Parliaments Act 2020-. Chair, PLP Department Group for Treasury 2020-. Active at branch, women's section, general committee levels in Crosby Constituency 1978-80; Chair: Oxford University Fabian Club 1980-83, National Conference of Labour Women 1991; Vice-chair, PLP 2005-; Member, Labour Party NEC 2005-16; Chair, National Policy Forum 2012-16; Contested Labour deputy leadership election 2015; Patron, LGBT Labour.

Political interests: Economic policy, NHS, politics of sport.

Other: Member, British Film Institute; DBE 2021.

Publications: Columnist and regular contributor to Tribune; Co-author, The New Serfdom (Biteback Publishing, 2018).

Recreations: Chess, cricket, cinema.

Dame Angela Eagle DBE MP, House of Commons, London SW1A 0AA
Tel: 020 7219 5057 *Email:* eaglea@parliament.uk
Constituency: Sherlock House, 6 Manor Road, Liscard, Wallasey, Wirral CH45 4JB
Tel: 0151-637 1979 Website: www.angelaeagle.co.uk *Twitter:* @angelaeagle

LABOUR

EAGLE, MARIA

Garston and Halewood *(Majority 31,624)*

Born 17 February 1961; Daughter of André Eagle, printworker, and late Shirley Eagle, dressmaker.

Education: Formby High School; Pembroke College, Oxford (BA philosophy, politics and economics 1983); College of Law, London (Common Professional Exam, Law Society Finals 1990).

Non-political career: Voluntary sector 1983-90; Articles of clerkship, Brian Thompson & Partners, Liverpool 1990-92; Goldsmith Williams, Liverpool 1992-95; Senior Solicitor, Steven Irving & Co, Liverpool 1994-97. Member, GMB.

Political career: Contested Crosby 1992 general election. Member for Liverpool Garston 1997-2010, for Garston and Halewood since 6 May 2010 general election; PPS to John Hutton as Minister of State, Department of Health 1999-2001; Parliamentary Under-Secretary of State: Department for Work and Pensions (Minister for Disabled People) 2001-05, Department for Education and Skills 2005-06 (Minister for Children and Families 2005-06, for Young People 2006), Northern Ireland Office 2006-07; Ministry of Justice 2007-10: Parliamentary Under-Secretary of State 2007-09, Minister of State 2009-10; Government Equalities Office 2008-10: Parliamentary Under-Secretary of State 2008-09, Minister of State (Deputy Minister for Women and Equality) 2009-10; Shadow Solicitor General 2010; Shadow Minister for Justice 2010; Shadow Secretary of State for: Transport 2010-13, Environment, Food and Rural Affairs 2013-15, Defence 2015-16, Culture, Media and Sport 2016. *Select committees:* Member: Public Accounts 1997-99, Justice 2020-, Joint Committee on Consolidation, &c, Bills 2020-, Joint Committee on Fixed-Term Parliaments Act 2020-. Chair, PLP Department Group for Justice 2020-. Campaigns organiser and press officer, Merseyside West Euro CLP 1983-84; CLP secretary, press officer and political education officer 1983-85; Campaigns organiser, Crosby 1993-96; Member, Economy – Living Standards and Sustainability Policy Commission.

Political interests: Transport, housing, employment; Australia, Nicaragua, USA.

Other: Fellow, Industry and Parliament Trust 2001. Played cricket for Lancashire as a Junior; Played chess for England and Lancashire.

Publications: Co-author, High Time or High Tide for Labour Women.

Recreations: Cinema, chess, cricket.

Maria Eagle MP, House of Commons, London SW1A 0AA
Tel: 020 7219 0551 *Email:* eaglem@parliament.uk
Constituency: Unit House, Speke Boulevard, Liverpool, Merseyside L24 9HZ
Tel: 0151-448 1167 Website: www.mariaeagle.co.uk *Twitter:* @Meaglemp

SOCIAL DEMOCRATIC AND LABOUR PARTY

EASTWOOD, COLUM

Foyle *(Majority 17,110)*

Leader, Social Democratic and Labour Party

Colum Paul Eastwood. Born 30 April 1983; Married Rachael Parkes (1 daughter).

Education: St Columb's College; Liverpool University (Latin American studies – did not finish degree).

Political career: Member for Foyle since 12 December 2019. *Select committees:* Member: Justice 2011-12, Office of the First Minister and Deputy First Minister 2011-13, Standards and Privileges 2012-16, Environment 2012-15, Conformity with Equality Requirements, Welfare Reform Bill 2012-13, Education 2014-17; Chair, Communities 2016-17; Member, Chairpersons' Liaison Group 2016-17. MLA for Foyle 2011 to 2020: Assembly Private Secretary to Alex Attwood as Minister of Environment 2011-13, SDLP Spokesperson for: Office of the First Minister and Deputy First Minister 2011-13, Environment 2013-17, Climate Change 2014-17, Chair, Assembly Committee on Communities 2016-17; Contested Northern Ireland region 2019 European Parliament election. Leader, Social Democratic and Labour Party 2015-. *Councils and public bodies:* Derry City Council: Councillor 2005-11, Mayor 2010-11; Board member, City of Derry Airport -2011.

Other: Trustee, Bloody Sunday Trust.

Recreations: Music, Derry City FC.

Colum Eastwood MP, House of Commons, London SW1A 0AA
Tel: 020 7219 3000 *Email:* colum.eastwood.mp@parliament.uk
Constituency: 34 Great James Street, Derry BT48 7DB
Tel: 028 7135 0045 *Twitter:* @columeastwood

CONSERVATIVE

EASTWOOD, MARK

Dewsbury *(Majority 1,561)*

Mark Simon Eastwood. Married (2 children).

Political career: Member for Dewsbury since 12 December 2019. *Select committees:* Member: Regulatory Reform 2020-, Future Relationship with the European Union 2020-21. Chair, Dewsbury County Conservative Association 2016-19.

Political interests: Local businesses, housing, green belt.

Other: Yorkshire and Humber Representative, Conservative Workers and Trade Unionists.

Mark Eastwood MP, House of Commons, London SW1A 0AA
Tel: 020 7219 3000 *Email:* mark.eastwood.mp@parliament.uk
Constituency: 5 Northgate, Shepley, Dewsbury, West Yorkshire WF13 1DS
Tel: 01924 939007 Website: www.markeastwood.org.uk *Twitter:* @mark4dewsbury

INDEPENDENT

EDWARDS, JONATHAN

Carmarthen East and Dinefwr *(Majority 1,809)*

David Jonathan Edwards. Born 26 April 1976; Married Emma Edwards (2012).

Education: Ysgol Gymraeg Rhydaman; Ysgol Gyfun Maes yr Yrfa; University of Wales, Aberystwyth (history and politics); Postgraduate Degree international history; Welsh.

Non-political career: Chief of staff to Rhodri Glyn Thomas AM and Adam Price MP; National Campaigns Directorate, Plaid Cymru 2005-07; Citizens Advice Cymru 2007-10.

Political career: Member for Carmarthen East and Dinefwr since 6 May 2010 general election; Plaid Cymru: Spokesperson for: Business, Innovation and Skills 2010-16, Communities and Local Government 2010-15, Culture, Olympics, Media and Sport 2010-15, Transport 2010-20, Treasury 2010-20, Foreign Intervention 2015-16, Leader, Parliamentary group 2015, Spokesperson for: Exiting the European Union 2016-17, International Trade 2016-17, Whip 2017-20, Spokesperson for: Foreign Affairs 2017-20, Defence 2017-20, International

Development 2017-20. *Select committees:* Member: Welsh Affairs 2010-13, 2014-15, 2019, Exiting the European Union 2016-17. Plaid Cymru Whip suspended May 2020. *Councils and public bodies:* Councillor, Carmarthen Town Council; Sheriff of Carmarthen Town.

Political interests: Social justice, foreign affairs.

Other: Penygroes cricket team.

Recreations: Cricket, Swansea City FC.

Jonathan Edwards MP, House of Commons, London SW1A 0AA
Tel: 020 7219 3000 *Email:* jonathan.edwards.mp@parliament.uk
Constituency: 30 Parc Hafan, Newcastle Emlyn, Carmarthenshire SA38 9AR
Tel: 01239 712952 Website: www.carmarthenshiresvoice.org.uk *Twitter:* @JonathanPlaid

CONSERVATIVE

EDWARDS, RUTH

Rushcliffe *(Majority 7,643)*

PPS to Alister Jack as Secretary of State for Scotland

Ruth Rosamond Edwards. Born 11 May 1984; Daughter of Christopher Davis, retired engineer, and Nelly Davis, retired parish worker; Married Owen Edwards.

Education: Clifton High School; London School of Theology (BA theological studies 2007); Bristol University (MSc international development and security 2008).

Non-political career: Parliamentary Researcher to Crispin Blunt 2009-10; Strategy Consultant, Deloitte 2010-12; Specialist to the Home Affairs Select Committee 2012-13; Crime and Justice Research Fellow, Policy Exchange 2013; Head of Programme Cyber, Justice and National Security 2013-15; Head of Commercial Strategy and Public Policy, BT Security 2015-19.

Political career: Contested Ceredigion 2017 general election. Member for Rushcliffe since 12 December 2019; PPS to Alister Jack as Secretary of State for Scotland 2020-. *Select committees:* Member, Home Affairs 2020-. Campaign Organiser, Charlotte Leslie Bristol North West election campaign 2014-15.

Political interests: Environment and climate change, cyber security, digital economy, rural issues.

Other: ISG Paragon Woman in Technology award.

Recreations: Reading, scuba diving, alpaca wrangling, tea and cake consumption, travel, gardening, rounding up our escaped chickens.

Ruth Edwards MP, House of Commons, London SW1A 0AA
Tel: 020 7219 3549 *Email:* ruth.edwards.mp@parliament.uk
Constituency: Rushcliffe House, 17-19 Rectory Road, West Bridgford NG2 6BE
Website: www.ruthedwards.org.uk *Twitter:* @RuthEdwardsMP

LABOUR

EFFORD, CLIVE

Eltham *(Majority 3,197)*

Clive Stanley Efford. Born 10 July 1958; Son of Stanley Efford, retired civil servant, and Mary Efford, née Caldwell; Married Gillian Vallins 1981 (3 daughters).

Education: Walworth Comprehensive School; Southwark Further Education College.

Non-political career: Youth and community worker assistant to warden, Pembroke College Mission 1976; Partner family-owned jewellery and watch repair business 1981-85; Taxi driver 1987-97. Member, T&GWU: Member, Passenger Transport Committee of T&G; Represented T&G on London Taxi Board; Member, GMB.

Political career: Contested Eltham 1992 general election. Member for Eltham 1997-2010, for Eltham (revised boundary) since 6 May 2010 general election; Presented two bills in Parliament on energy efficiency and energy conservation; Assistant to Tony McNulty as Minister for London 2008-10; PPS to Ministers of State, Department for Communities and Local Government: Margaret Beckett 2008-09, John Healey 2009; Shadow Minister for: Home Office 2010-11, Culture, Media and Sport 2011-16; Member, Public Accounts Commission 2017-. *Select committees:* Member: Procedure 1997-2001, Standing Orders 1999-2000, Transport 2002-09, 2016-17, London 2009-10, Communities and Local Government 2010-11, Digital, Culture, Media and Sport 2018-, Panel of Chairs 2020-. London Group of Labour MPs: Vice-chair 2001-07, Chair 2010-; Hon. Secretary, PLP Departmental Committee for Transport 2006-10. Member, Labour Friends of India. *Councils and public bodies:* London Borough of

Greenwich: Councillor 1986-98, Chair: Social Services 1989-90, Health and Environment 1992-96, Secretary Labour Group 1986-87, Chief Whip Labour Group 1990-92; Chair, Eltham area planning and transport committee 1992-97.

Political interests: Welfare state, health, transport, education, environment, local and regional government, energy conservation, energy efficiency, energy from waste, waste management, recycling, social housing.

Other: Chair of trustees, Samuel Montagu Youth Club; Trustee, Greenwich Community College Trust. Eltham Hill CIU Club.

Recreations: Football (FA Preliminary Coachers Club).

Clive Efford MP, House of Commons, London SW1A 0AA
Tel: 020 7219 4057 *Email:* effordc@parliament.uk
Constituency: 132 Westmount Road, Eltham, London SE9 1UT
Tel: 020 8850 5744 *Email:* clive@cliveefford.org.uk Website: www.cliveefford.org.uk
Twitter: @Cliveefford

LABOUR

ELLIOTT, JULIE

Sunderland Central *(Majority 2,964)*

Born 29 July 1963; Daughter of late Laura Smith and late Harold Smith; 4 children.

Education: Seaham Northlea Comprehensive; Newcastle Polytechnic (Degree government and public policy).

Non-political career: Organiser, Labour Party 1993-98; Regional officer, National Asthma Campaign 1998-99; Political officer, GMB 1999-2010. Former secretary and treasurer, Northern Trade Union Liaison Organisation.

Political career: Member for Sunderland Central since 6 May 2010 general election; PPS to Caroline Flint as Shadow Secretary of State for: Communities and Local Government 2010-11, Energy and Climate Change 2011-13; Shadow Minister for Energy and Climate Change 2013-15. *Select committees:* Member: European Scrutiny 2010-15, Business, Innovation and Skills 2011-13, Culture, Media and Sport/Digital, Culture, Media and Sport 2015-, Regulatory Reform 2017-, Panel of Chairs 2020-. Chair, PLP Departmental Group for: Housing and Planning 2015-17, International Development 2020-. Member, Labour Party 1984-; Agent, Tynemouth 1997 general election; Former chair, Labour North Board. *Councils and public bodies:* Former governor and chair, Whitburn Comprehensive School.

Political interests: Employment and skills, regeneration, health inequalities, education.

Other: Treasurer, Executive Committee, Commonwealth Parliamentary Association United Kingdom 2020-; Vice-chair, Progress 2012-.

Recreations: Walking, baking, Rugby Union.

Julie Elliott MP, House of Commons, London SW1A 0AA
Tel: 020 7219 7165 *Fax:* 020 7219 4597 *Email:* julie.elliott.mp@parliament.uk
Constituency: Suite 204, The Place, Athenaeum Street, Sunderland SR1 1QX
Tel: 0191-565 5327 Website: www.julie4sunderland.co.uk *Twitter:* @JulieElliottMP

CONSERVATIVE

ELLIS, MICHAEL

Northampton North *(Majority 5,507)*

Solicitor General

Michael Tyrone Ellis. Born 13 October 1967.

Education: Wellingborough School, Northamptonshire; Buckingham University (LLB 1993); Inns of Court School of Law (Bar Vocational Course 1993).

Non-political career: Called to the Bar, Middle Temple 1993; Barrister, Clarendon Chambers, Northampton 1993-2010.

Political career: Member for Northampton North since 6 May 2010 general election; PPS to Theresa May as Home Secretary 2015-16; Deputy Leader of the House of Commons 2016-18; Assistant Government Whip 2016-17; Parliamentary Under-Secretary of State for Arts, Heritage and Tourism, Department for Digital, Culture, Media and Sport 2018-19; Minister of State, Department for Transport 2019; Solicitor General 2019-. *Select committees:* Member: Joint Committee on Statutory Instruments 2010-15, Home Affairs 2011-15, Unopposed Bills (Panel)

2011-15, Joint Committee on the Draft Communications Data Bill 2012-13. Parliamentary Adviser to Lord Feldman of Elstree as Chair of the Conservative Party 2012-15. *Councils and public bodies:* Councillor, Northamptonshire County Council 1997-2001.

Political interests: Justice, home affairs, constitution, foreign affairs, arts, heritage and tourism; Israel, USA.

Other: President, Commonwealth Jewish Council 2012-14; PC 2019. Carlton Club.

Recreations: Gym, theatre.

Rt Hon Michael Ellis QC MP, House of Commons, London SW1A 0AA
Tel: 020 7219 7220 *Email:* michael.ellis.mp@parliament.uk
Constituency: 78 St George's Avenue, Northampton, Northamptonshire NN2 6JF
Tel: 01604 210707 Website: www.michaelellis.co.uk *Twitter:* @Michael_Ellis1

CONSERVATIVE

ELLWOOD, TOBIAS

Bournemouth East *(Majority 8,806)*

Chair, Select Committee on Defence

Tobias Martin Ellwood. Born 12 August 1966; Son of Peter and Dr Caroline Ellwood; Married Hannah Ryan 2005 (2 sons).

Education: Vienna International School, Austria; Loughborough University of Technology (BA design and technology 1990) (Student Union President); City University Business School (MBA 1998); Kennedy School of Government, Harvard University, USA (Senior Executive Course national and international studies 2009); German.

Non-political career: Army officer, Royal Green Jackets 1991-96, served in Northern Ireland, Cyprus, Kuwait, Germany, Gibraltar and Bosnia; Researcher to Tom King MP 1996-97; Senior business development manager: London Stock Exchange 1998-2002, Allen and Overy 2002-04. Member, British Reserve Forces.

Political career: Contested Worsley 2001 general election. Member for Bournemouth East 2005-10, for Bournemouth East (revised boundary) since 6 May 2010 general election; Opposition Whip 2005-07; Shadow Minister for Culture, Media and Sport 2007-10; PPS to: Liam Fox as Secretary of State for Defence 2010-11, David Lidington as Minister of State, Foreign and Commonwealth Office 2011-13, Jeremy Hunt as Secretary of State for Health 2013-14; Parliamentary Adviser to the Prime Minister for the NATO Summit 2014; Parliamentary Under-Secretary of State: Foreign and Commonwealth Office 2014-17 (Minister for Middle East and Africa 2016-17), Ministry of Defence 2017-19. *Select committees:* Member: Environmental Audit 2005-06, Armed Forces Bill 2011, Liaison 2020-, Joint Committee on the National Security Strategy 2020-, Committees on Arms Export Controls 2020-; Chair, Defence 2020-. Chair, Conservative Insight 2000; Branch chair, South West Hertfordshire Conservative Association 1998-2003; Vice-chair, Conservative Middle East Council 2010-. *Councils and public bodies:* Councillor: Aldbury Parish Council 1996-99, Dacorum Borough Council 1999-2003; Governor, Queen's Park Infant School, Bournemouth.

Political interests: Defence, education, environment, tourism, space industry; Afghanistan, Iraq, Middle East, USA, Yemen.

Other: Member, UK Delegation to NATO Parliamentary Assembly 2014-15; CBI London Council 2000; Treasurer, Bow Group 2000; Member, Atlantic Council; Patron: Caring Canines, Crumbs Café, Aleevee8, Springbourne Family Centre, ME Support Group; PC 2017.

Publications: Post Conflict Reconstruction – Bridging the Gap Between Military and Civilian Affairs on the Modern Battlefield (2009); Time to Change the Clocks – Arguing the Case for Moving Our Clocks Forward (2010); Upgrading UK Influence in the European Union – A Strategy to Improve Upstreasm Scrutiny of EU Legislation (2012); Stabilizing Afghanistan – Proposals for Improving Security, Governance and Aid/Economic Development (Atlantic Council, 2013); Leveraging UK Carrier Capability (RUSI, 2013); Improving Efficiency, Interoperability and Resilience of our Blue Light Services (Henry Jackson Society, 2013).

Recreations: Volleyball, windsurfing, saxophone, theatre.

Rt Hon Tobias Ellwood MP, House of Commons, London SW1A 0AA
Tel: 020 7219 6459 *Email:* tobias.ellwood.mp@parliament.uk
Constituency: Bournemouth East Conservative Association, Haviland Road West, Boscombe,

Bournemouth, Dorset BH1 4JW
Tel: 01202 801990 *Email:* bournemoutheastconservatives@gmail.com
Website: www.tobiasellwood.com *Twitter:* @Tobias_Ellwood

LABOUR

ELMORE, CHRIS

Ogmore *(Majority 7,805)*

Shadow Minister for Scotland; Senior Opposition Whip

Christopher Philip James Elmore. Born 23 December 1983.

Education: Cardiff Metropolitan University (BA history and culture 2005).

Non-political career: Trainee butcher; Worked in further education. Member, GMB.

Political career: Contested Vale of Glamorgan 2015 general election. Member for Ogmore since 5 May 2016 by-election; Opposition Whip 2016-20; Shadow Minister for Scotland 2020-; Senior Opposition Whip 2020-. *Select committees:* Member: Justice 2016, Welsh Affairs 2016-17, Procedure 2017-, Joint Committee on Consolidation, &c, Bills 2017-20, Foreign Affairs 2020, Standards 2020-, Privileges 2020-. Member, Co-operative Party. *Councils and public bodies:* Vale of Glamorgan Council: Councillor 2008-17, Youth Champion for the Vale of Glamorgan 2010-11, Cabinet Member for Children's Services and Schools 2012-16; Governor: Holton Primary School 2008-16, Cardiff and Vale College 2009-16; Independent member, Cardiff and Vale University Health Board 2009-16; Governor, Barry Comprehensive School 2012-16.

Political interests: Pensions, industry, trade, children and young people, voter engagement; China, France, Ireland, USA.

Other: Member, Executive Committee, Commonwealth Parliamentary Association United Kingdom 2020-; Board Member, Barry YMCA Hub.

Recreations: Walking, listening to music, watching sport, reading autobiographies.

Chris Elmore MP, House of Commons, London SW1A 0AA
Tel: 020 7219 1165 *Email:* chris.elmore.mp@parliament.uk
Constituency: 44a Penybont Road, Pencoed CF35 5RA
Tel: 01656 860034 Website: www.chriselmore.co.uk *Twitter:* @CPJElmore

CONSERVATIVE

ELPHICKE, NATALIE

Dover *(Majority 12,278)*

Team PPS, Ministry of Defence

Natalie Cecilia Elphicke. Born November 1970; Married Charlie Elphicke, former MP for Dover (separated) (2 children).

Education: Kent University.

Non-political career: Partner: Denton Wilde Sapte, Addleshaw Goddard, Stephenson Harwood 2009-13; Co-founder and Chair, Million Homes, Million Lives 2013-16 Chief Executive, Housing and Finance Institute 2015-19.

Political career: Member for Dover since 12 December 2019; Team PPS: Ministry of Housing, Communities and Local Government 2020, Ministry of Defence 2020-. *Councils and public bodies:* Co-chair and Independent Adviser, Local Authority Housing Supply Review 2014-15; Non-executive director, Student Loans Company 2016-19; Independent member, Departmental Audit and Risk Assurance Committee, Department for Education 2017-19.

Political interests: Housing, Brexit, jobs.

Other: Founder, Dover People's Port Trust; Principality Building Society 2012-18: Chair, Board's Risk Committee, Non-executive director; Volunteer, Dover Winter Night Shelter; OBE 2015.

Natalie Elphicke OBE MP, House of Commons, London SW1A 0AA
Tel: 020 7219 7052 *Email:* natalie.elphicke.mp@parliament.uk
Constituency: 54 The Strand, Walmer, Deal CT14 7DP
Tel: 01304 379669 Website: natalieelphicke.com *Twitter:* @NatalieElphicke

LABOUR/ CO-OPERATIVE

ESHALOMI, FLORENCE

Vauxhall *(Majority 19,612)*

Born 18 September 1980; Married Matthew (1 daughter 1 son).

Education: Bishop Thomas Grant Secondary School; St Francis Xavier Sixth Form College; Middlesex University (BA political and international studies with law).

Non-political career: Public Affairs Manager, Runnymede Trust 2013-14; Account Manager, Four Communications 2014-16.

Political career: Member for Vauxhall since 12 December 2019; Opposition Whip 2020. *Select committees:* Member, Future Relationship with the European Union 2020-21. AM for Lambeth and Southwark since 5 May 2016: Labour Spokesperson on Transport 2016-20. Labour Party Regional Organiser, 2005 general election. *Councils and public bodies:* London Borough of Lambeth Council: Councillor 2006-18, Cabinet Member for Culture, Sport and 2012 Olympics 2010-12, Deputy Cabinet Member for Tackling Violent Youth Crime 2012-13, Deputy Cabinet Member for Housing 2013-14.

Florence Eshalomi MP, House of Commons, London SW1A 0AA
Tel: 020 7219 6552 *Email:* florence.eshalomi.mp@parliament.uk
Constituency: Flat 8, 2 Kennington Lane, London SE11 4FA
Website: www.florence4vauxhall.org.uk *Twitter:* @FloEshalomi

LABOUR

ESTERSON, BILL

Sefton Central *(Majority 15,122)*

Shadow Minister for International Trade

William Roffen Esterson. Born 27 October 1966; Son of Derek and Joyce Esterson; Married Caroline (1 son 1 daughter).

Education: Rochester Mathematical School; Leeds University (BSc maths and philosophy 1990); French, German.

Non-political career: Director, training consultancy 1995-2010. Member: Unite, USDAW.

Political career: Member for Sefton Central since 6 May 2010 general election; PPS to Stephen Twigg as Shadow Secretary of State for Education 2011-13; Shadow Minister for: Business, Innovation and Skills 2015-16, Business, Energy and Industrial Strategy 2016-20, International Trade 2016-. *Select committees:* Member: Environment, Food and Rural Affairs 2010-11, Education 2010-15, Joint Committee on the Draft House of Lords Reform Bill 2011-12, Unopposed Bills (Panel) 2011-15, Communities and Local Government 2011-13, Joint Committee on the Rookery South (Resource Recovery Facility) Order 2012-13, Treasury 2015. Chair, PLP Departmental Group for Education 2010-12. *Councils and public bodies:* Medway Council: Councillor 1995-2010, Labour Spokesperson for Children's Services.

Political interests: Children's service, fetal alcohol spectrum disorders.

Other: Formby Hockey Club.

Recreations: Playing hockey and cricket.

Bill Esterson MP, House of Commons, London SW1A 0AA
Tel: 020 7219 0463 *Email:* bill.esterson.mp@parliament.uk
Constituency: Office 19, Space Solutions Business Centre, Sefton Lane Industrial Estate, Sefton Lane, Liverpool L31 8BX
Tel: 0151-531 8433 *Email:* bill.esterson@gmail.com *Twitter:* @Bill_Esterson

CONSERVATIVE

EUSTICE, GEORGE

Camborne and Redruth *(Majority 8,700)*

Secretary of State for Environment, Food and Rural Affairs

Charles George Eustice. Born 28 September 1971; Son of Paul Eustice and Adele Eustice; Married Katy Taylor-Richards 2013.

Education: Truro Cathedral School; Truro School; Cornwall College, Pool; Writtle College, Chelmsford (commercial horticulture 1993).

Non-political career: Trevaskis Fruit Farm 1993-99; Campaign director, anti-Euro 'No Campaign' 1999-2003; Conservative Party: Deputy Press Secretary to Conservative Leader Michael Howard 2003-05; Press Secretary to Conservative Leader David Cameron 2005-07; External relations co-ordinator, Conservative HQ 2008-09; Associate director, Portland PR 2009-10.

Political career: Member for Camborne and Redruth since 6 May 2010 general election; Department for Environment, Food and Rural Affairs: Parliamentary Under-Secretary of State (Farming, Food and Marine Environment) 2013-15, Minister of State for Farming, Food and the Marine Environment 2015-16, Minister of State for Agriculture, Fisheries and Food 2016-19, Minister of State 2019-20, Secretary of State for Environment, Food and Rural Affairs 2020-. *Select committees:* Member: Environment, Food and Rural Affairs 2010-13, Joint Committee on Privacy and Injunctions 2011-12. Member, Executive, 1922 Committee 2012-13. Contested South West region (UKIP) 1999 European Parliament election. Member: UKIP 1998-99, Conservative Party 2003-; Member, Number 10 Policy Advisory Board April-October 2013.

Political interests: Farming, environment, Europe, economic regeneration.

Other: Redruth 2000; MS Society; PC 2020. Hayle RFC; Camborne RFC; Cornwall Athletic Club.

Publications: Columnist, *PR Week* 2012-13.

Rt Hon George Eustice MP, House of Commons, London SW1A 0AA
Tel: 020 7219 7032 *Email:* george.eustice.mp@parliament.uk
Constituency: 13 Commercial Street, Camborne, Cornwall TR14 8JZ
Tel: 01209 713355 *Email:* camborneredruthconservatives@googlemail.com
Websites: www.camborneredruthconservatives.com/www.georgeeustice.org.uk

LABOUR/ CO-OPERATIVE

EVANS, CHRIS

Islwyn *(Majority 5,464)*

PPS to John Healey as Shadow Secretary of State for Defence

Christopher James Evans. Born 17 June 1977; Son of late Michael Evans and Lynne Evans; Married Julia Ockenden 2013.

Education: Porth County Comprehensive; Pontypridd College; Trinity College, Carmarthen (BA history).

Non-political career: Manager, bookmaker 1998-2001; Lloyds TSB Bank plc 2001-03; Marketing, Glamorgan University 2003-04; Official, Union of Finance Staff 2004-06; Parliamentary researcher to Don Touhig MP 2006-10. Member, Unite.

Political career: Contested Cheltenham 2005 general election. Member for Islwyn since 6 May 2010 general election; PPS: to Chris Leslie: as Shadow Chief Secretary to the Treasury 2013-15, as Shadow Chancellor 2015, to John Healey as Shadow Secretary of State for Defence 2020-. *Select committees:* Member: Justice 2010-12, Joint Committees on: the Draft Defamation Bill 2011, the Draft Enhanced Terrorism Prevention and Investigation Measures Bill 2012-13; Member: Environmental Audit 2012-14, Public Accounts 2015-19, Public Administration and Constitutional Affairs 2020, Petitions 2020-, Speaker's Advisory Committee on Works of Art 2020-. Member, Co-operative Party.

Political interests: Justice, finance, welfare; China, France, Germany, Greece, USA.

Other: Member, Fabian Society; Hon. Fellow. University of Wales Trinity St David.

Publications: Fearless Freddie: The Life and Times of Freddie Mills (2017).

Recreations: Watching sports, running, reading.

Chris Evans MP, House of Commons, London SW1A 0AA
Tel: 020 7219 7091 *Email:* chris.evans.mp@parliament.uk
Constituency: 6 Woodfieldside Business Park, Penmaen Road, Pontllanfraith, Blackwood, Gwent NP12 2DG
Tel: 01495 231990 Website: www.chrisevansmp.com *Twitter:* @Chris_EvansMP

CONSERVATIVE

EVANS, LUKE

Bosworth *(Majority 26,278)*

Luke Morgan Evans. Born 10 January 1983; Married Charlie.

Education: Birmingham University (medicine 2007).

Non-political career: Anatomy Lecturer, Birmingham University; General Practitioner, NHS 2013-.

Political career: Contested Birmingham, Edgbaston 2015 general election. Member for Bosworth since 12 December 2019. *Select committees:* Member, Health and Social Care 2020-. *Councils and public bodies:* School Governor.

Recreations: Rugby, singing, debating.

Dr Luke Evans MP, House of Commons, London SW1A 0AA
Tel: 020 7219 3000 *Email:* luke.evans.mp@parliament.uk
Constituency: 10a Priory Walk, Hinckley LE10 1HU
Tel: 01455 635741 Website: www.drlukeevans.org.uk *Twitter:* @drlukeevans

CONSERVATIVE

EVANS, NIGEL

Ribble Valley *(Majority 18,439)*

Second Deputy Chairman of Ways and Means and Deputy Speaker

Nigel Martin Evans. Born 10 November 1957; Son of late Albert Evans and Betty Evans; Single.

Education: Dynevor School, Swansea; University College of Wales, Swansea (BA politics 1979); French, Russian (poor).

Non-political career: Management family retail newsagent and convenience store 1979-90; Worked on three US presidential elections in New York, Florida and California.

Political career: Contested Swansea West 1987 general election and Pontypridd 1989 and Ribble Valley 1991 by-elections. Member for Ribble Valley 1992-2010, for Ribble Valley (revised boundary) since 6 May 2010 general election; PPS: to David Hunt: as Secretary of State for Employment 1993-94, as Chancellor of the Duchy of Lancaster 1994-95, to Tony Baldry as Minister of State, Ministry of Agriculture, Fisheries and Food 1995-96, to William Hague as Secretary of State for Wales 1996-97; Opposition Spokesperson for: Scotland and Wales 1997-99, Wales 1999-2001; Shadow Secretary of State for Wales 2001-03; First Deputy Chairman, Ways and Means and Deputy Speaker 2010-13; Second Deputy Chairman of Ways and Means and Deputy Speaker 2020-. *Select committees:* Member: Welsh Affairs 2003-05, Trade and Industry 2003-05, Culture, Media and Sport 2005-09, International Development 2009-10, 2015-19; Chairmen's Panel/Panel of Chairs: Member 2009-10, 2015-, Ex-officio member 2010-13; Member: Public Administration 2014-15, Backbench Business 2014-15, Administration 2014-15, Northern Ireland Affairs 2015-16, Arms Export Controls 2016-19, Court of Referees 2016-17, Work of the Independent Commission for Aid Impact Sub-committee 2016-19, International Trade 2016-19. 1922 Committee: Member, Executive 2014-15, Secretary 2015-20. Chair, Conservative Welsh Parliamentary Candidates Policy Group 1990; President, Conservative North West Parliamentary Candidates Group 1991; North West Conservative MPs: Secretary 1992-97, Chair 2014; Vice-chair, Conservative Party: (Wales) 1999-2001, (Conservatives Abroad) 2004-05; Resigned Conservative Party whip September 2013-April 2014; Founding member, Conservatives for Britain 2015-16. *Councils and public bodies:* West Glamorgan County Council: Councillor 1985-91, Deputy Leader, Conservative Group 1990-91.

Political interests: Education, small businesses, US elections, local and regional government, defence, agriculture, international politics, European affairs, telecommunications, space; Australia, Bahrain, Caribbean, Egypt, Europe, Far East, Gibraltar, India, USA.

Other: British Group, Inter-Parliamentary Union: Treasurer 2005-08, Vice-chair 2008-10, Chair 2015-18; Executive Committee, Commonwealth Parliamentary Association (United Kingdom branch): Member 2005-17, Hon Treasurer 2010, Vice-chair 2017-19; Member: Council of Europe 2006, Western European Union 2006-; UK chair, Technological and Aerospace committee; Member, UK delegation, Parliamentary Assembly of the Council of Europe 2015-; British-Irish Parliamentary Assembly: Member 2015-17, Vice-chair 2017-20; Fellow, Industry and Parliament Trust 1998; Adviser, Arensky Chamber Orchestra; Hon. President, British Youth Council; Macmillan Cancer Support; Hon. LLD Swansea University 2012. Carlton Club, CountryClubuk, Royal Automobile Club, Groucho Club.

Recreations: Tennis, swimming, running, theatre, cinema, arts, music.

Nigel Evans MP, House of Commons, London SW1A 0AA
Tel: 020 7219 6939 *Email:* nigel.evans.mp@parliament.uk
Constituency: 9 Railway View, Clitheroe, Lancashire BB7 2HA
Tel: 01200 425939 Website: www.nigel-evans.org.uk *Twitter:* @nigelmp

CONSERVATIVE

EVENNETT, DAVID

Bexleyheath and Crayford *(Majority 13,103)*

David Anthony Evennett. Born 3 June 1949; Son of late Norman Evennett and late Irene Evennett, née Turner; Married Marilyn Smith 1975 (2 sons).

Education: Buckhurst Hill County High School; London School of Economics (BSc Econ economics 1971; MSc Econ politics 1972).

Non-political career: Schoolmaster, Ilford County High School 1972-74; Marine insurance broker, Lloyds 1974-81; Member, Lloyds 1976-92; Director, Lloyds Underwriting Agency 1982-91; Commercial liaison manager, Bexley College 1997-2001; Consultant, J&H Marsh and McLennan (UK) then Marsh (UK) Ltd 1998-2000; Freelance lecturer 2001-05.

Political career: Contested Hackney South and Shoreditch 1979 general election. Member for Erith and Crayford 1983-97. Contested Bexleyheath and Crayford 1997 and 2001 general elections. Member for Bexleyheath and Crayford since 5 May 2005 general election; PPS to: Baroness Blatch as Minister of State for Education 1992-93, John Redwood as Secretary of State for Wales 1993-95, Baroness Blatch and David Maclean as Ministers of State, Home Office 1995-96, Gillian Shephard as Secretary of State for Education and Employment 1996-97; Opposition Whip 2005-09; Shadow Minister for: Innovation, Universities and Skills 2009, Universities and Skills 2009-10; PPS to Michael Gove as Secretary of State for Education 2010-12; Government Whip (Lord Commissioner of HM Treasury) 2012-18; Parliamentary Under-Secretary of State for Sport, Tourism and Heritage January-July 2016 (maternity cover for Tracey Crouch MP). *Select committees:* Member: Education, Science and the Arts 1986-92, Education and Skills 2005-06, Selection 2012-18, Administration 2013-15, Procedure 2018-19, European Statutory Instruments 2018-. Vice-chairman, Conservative Party 2019-. *Councils and public bodies:* Councillor, London Borough of Redbridge 1974-78.

Political interests: Education, economy, transport, London, heritage, tourism; Australia, Canada, Italy, New Zealand, USA.

Other: Patron: Townley, Grammar School for Girls, Friends of Christchurch Bexleyheath; Vice-president, Bexleyheath and District Club for the Disabled; Member, National Trust; PC 2015; Kt 2018. Bexleyheath Conservative Club.

Recreations: Travel, reading, cinema, family, music.

Rt Hon Sir David Evennett MP, House of Commons, London SW1A 0AA
Tel: 020 7219 8403 *Email:* david.evennett.mp@parliament.uk
Constituency: 17 Church Road, Bexleyheath, Kent DA7 4DD
Websites: www.bexleyheathandcrayford.com/davidevennett.wordpress.com
Twitter: @davidevennett

CONSERVATIVE

EVERITT, BEN

Milton Keynes North *(Majority 6,255)*

Benjamin William Everitt. Married Emma (3 children).

Education: Kings Grantham; Durham University (BSc education 2001).

Non-political career: Farmer, Lincolnshire 1996-2002; Transport Planner, Christian Salvesen 2002-03; Assistant Programme Manager, Department for Transport 2002-04; Policy Adviser, Office of the Deputy Prime Minister 2004-06; Consultant, Hornagold and Hills/Mouchel Parkman 2006-09; Senior Consultant, Deloitte 2009-12; ICAEW: Manager, Strategy and Risk 2012-15, Head of Strategy 2015-19.

Political career: Member for Milton Keynes North since 12 December 2019. *Select committees:* Member, Housing, Communities and Local Government 2020-. Chair, Streatham Conservatives 2011-13. *Councils and public bodies:* Chair, St Leonards Safer Neighbourhoods Panel 2009-13; Councillor, Aylesbury Vale District Council 2015-.

Political interests: Business, green belt.

Ben Everitt MP, House of Commons, London SW1A 0AA
Tel: 020 7219 5898 *Email:* ben.everitt.mp@parliament.uk
Constituency: Suite 102, Milton Keynes Business Centre, Foxhunter Drive, Linford Wood MK14 6GD
Tel: 01908 686830 Website: www.beneveritt.com *Twitter:* @Ben_Everitt

CONSERVATIVE

FABRICANT, MICHAEL

Lichfield *(Majority 23,638)*

Michael Louis David Fabricant. Born 12 June 1950; Son of late Isaac Fabricant and Helena Fabricant, née Freed; Single.

Education: Brighton, Hove and Sussex Grammar School, Brighton; Loughborough University (BSc economics and law 1973); Sussex University (MSc systems and econometrics 1974); Oxford University/London University/University of Southern California, Los Angeles, USA (PhD econometrics and economic forecasting 1975-78); Dutch, French, German, Hebrew (basic), Russian (basic).

Non-political career: Staff, then freelance radio broadcaster and journalist 1968-80; Economist and founder director, leading broadcast and communications group, manufacturing and commissioning electronics equipment to radio stations to 48 countries 1980-91; Adviser, Home Office on broadcasting matters; Adviser to foreign governments on establishment and management of radio stations, including Russian Federation 1980-91; Has lived and worked extensively in Europe, Africa, the Far East, former Soviet Union, and USA.

Political career: Contested South Shields 1987 general election. Member for Mid Staffordshire 1992-97, for Lichfield 1997-2010, for Lichfield (revised boundary) since 6 May 2010 general election; Presented Bills to strengthen economic and political ties between UK, USA, Canada, Australia and New Zealand; Promoted legislation to encourage flying of Union Flag and to force Government to undertake and publish regular financial cost-benefit analyses of Britain's membership of European Union; PPS to Michael Jack as Financial Secretary to the Treasury 1996-97; Shadow Minister for: Trade and Industry 2003, Economic Affairs 2003-05; Opposition Whip 2005-10; Government Whip 2010-12. *Select committees:* Member: Culture, Media and Sport 1997-99, 2001-05, Home Affairs 1999-2001, Catering 1999-2001, Liaison 2001-03; Chair, Information 2001-03; Member: Finance and Services 2001-04, Administration 2009-10, 2014-, Selection 2010-12. Member, Executive, 1922 Committee 2001-03. Chair, Brighton Pavilion Conservative Association 1985-88; Member, Conservative Way Forward; Associate member, European Research Group; Member, Conservative Against a Federal Europe; Chair, Conservative Friends of America 2007-10; Vice-chairman (parliamentary campaigning), Conservative Party 2012-14.

Political interests: Broadcasting and media, business, defence, engineering, enterprise, exports, foreign affairs, heritage, industry, inland waterways, international aid and development, international trade, internet, manufacturing, police and security issues, science and technology, technology, telecommunications, trade and industry; Australia, Eastern Europe, Middle East, USA, Wales.

Other: Member: Inter-Parliamentary Union, Commonwealth Parliamentary Association; Member: Council, Institution of Electrical Engineers 1996-2000, Senate, Engineering Council 1996-2002; Director, Engineering and Technology Board 2002-06; Cancer Research; CEng; FIET; FRSA. Blacks (Dean Street, London), Crows Nest (St John's, Newfoundland, Canada), Rottingdean Club (Sussex).

Publications: Regular articles in *The Daily Telegraph* and *The Guardian*.

Recreations: Reading, music, fell-walking, skiing and listening to the omnibus edition of *The Archers*.

Michael Fabricant MP, House of Commons, London SW1A 0AA
Tel: 020 7219 5022 *Email:* michael.fabricant.mp@parliament.uk
Constituency: No constituency office publicised
Tel: 01543 419650 Website: www.michael.fabricant.mp.co.uk *Twitter:* @Mike_Fabricant

CONSERVATIVE

FARRIS, LAURA

Newbury *(Majority 16,047)*

Laura Rose Farris. Daughter of Michael McNair-Wilson (MP for Newbury 1974-92); Married (2 children).

Education: Oxford University (MA philosophy, politics, economics).

Non-political career: Barrister.

Political career: Contested Leyton and Wansted 2017 general election. Member for Newbury since 12 December 2019. *Select committees:* Member, Home Affairs 2020-.

Political interests: Home affairs, justice, employment, environment and equalities.

Laura Farris MP, House of Commons, London SW1A 0AA
Tel: 020 7219 4829 *Email:* laura.farris.mp@parliament.uk
Constituency: Park Street Offices, Park Street, Newbury RG14 1EA
Tel: 01635 551070 Website: www.laurafarris.org.uk *Twitter:* @Laura__Farris

LIBERAL DEMOCRAT

FARRON, TIM

Westmorland and Lonsdale *(Majority 1,934)*

Liberal Democrat Spokesperson for Housing, Communities and Local Government and Food and Rural Affairs

Timothy James Farron. Born 27 May 1970; Son of Chris Farron and late Susan Farron, née Trenchard; Married Rosie Cantley 2000 (2 daughters 2 sons).

Education: Lostock Hall High School, Preston, Lancashire; Runshaw Tertiary College, Leyland; Newcastle University (BA politics 1991).

Non-political career: Lancaster University: Adult education officer 1992-96, Student support officer 1996-98, Faculty administrator 1998-2002; Head of faculty administration, St Martin's College (Ambleside, Lancaster, Carlisle) 2002-05. Association of University Teachers 1995-.

Political career: Contested North West Durham 1992, South Ribble 1997 and Westmorland and Lonsdale 2001 general elections. Member for Westmorland and Lonsdale 2005-10, for Westmorland and Lonsdale (revised boundary) since 6 May 2010 general election; Liberal Democrat: Spokesperson for Youth Affairs 2005-06, PPS to Sir Menzies Campbell as Leader of the Liberal Democrats 2006-07, Shadow Minister for: Home Affairs 2007, Countryside 2007-08, Shadow Secretary of State/Spokesperson for Environment, Food and Rural Affairs 2008-10, 2017-19; North of England 2017-20, Work and Pensions 2019, Housing, Communities and Local Government 2019-, Food and Rural Affairs 2019-. *Select committees:* Member: Education and Skills 2005-06, Environmental Audit 2006-07, European Scrutiny 2010-13. Chair, Liberal Democrat Policy Committee on International Affairs 2010-11. Contested North West England 1999 European Parliament election. Liberal Democrats: President 2010-14, Member, Manifesto Working Group 2013-15, Leader 2015-17. *Councils and public bodies:* Councillor: Lancashire County Council 1993-2000, South Ribble Borough Council 1995-99, South Lakeland District Council 2004-08; Vice-president, Local Government Association 2017-.

Political interests: Education, rural affairs, youth work, health, crime and policing, social care.

Other: Member, Amnesty International 1993-. President Kendal and South Westmorland Liberal Club.

Recreations: Fell-walking, running, cycling, football, watching Blackburn Rovers FC, music.

Tim Farron MP, House of Commons, London SW1A 0AA
Tel: 020 7219 8498 *Fax:* 020 7219 2810 *Email:* farront@parliament.uk
Constituency: Acland House, Yard 2, Stricklandgate, Kendal, Cumbria LA9 4ND
Tel: 01539 723403 *Email:* tim@timfarron.co.uk Website: www.timfarron.co.uk
Twitter: @timfarron

ALLIANCE PARTY OF NORTHERN IRELAND

FARRY, STEPHEN

North Down *(Majority 2,968)*

Stephen Anthony Farry. Born 22 April 1971; Son of Vincent Farry and Margaret Farry, née Greer; Married Dr Wendy Farry.

Education: Our Lady and St Patrick's College, Belfast; Queen's University, Belfast (BSSc politics 1992; PhD international relations 2000).

Non-political career: Consultant trainer, National Democratic Institute for International Affairs, Croatia and Bosnia 1996-2000; Director, Bangor and Holywood Town Centre Management Ltd; Member, Northern Ireland Community Relations Council 2007-; Director, Lagan Print Ltd.

Political career: Contested Fermanagh and South Tyrone 1997 and North Down 2010 general elections. Member for North Down since 12 December 2019. Member, Northern Ireland Affairs 2020-. MLA for North Down 7 March 2007 to 19 December 2019: Alliance Party Spokesperson for: Finance and Personnel 2007-11, Justice and Human Rights 2007-11, First Minister and Deputy First Minister 2010-11; Minister for Employment and Learning 2011-16; Alliance Party Spokesperson for: Economy and Finance 2016-17, Exiting the European Union 2016-17. Alliance Party: Party Organiser 1997-2000, Policy Officer 2000, General Secretary 2000-07, Deputy Leader 2016-. *Councils and public bodies:* North Down Borough Council: Councillor 1993-2011, Leader, Alliance Group 1995-2011, Chair, Queen's Parade and Upper Main Street Working Group 1999-2007, Deputy Mayor 2002-03, Mayor 2007-08; Governor, Priory Integrated College, Holywood; Member, Northern Ireland Policing Board 2016-.

Political interests: Environment, finance, transport, urban regeneration; USA.

Other: Member: Liberal International, Academic council, United Nations System; Senior Fellow, United States Institute of Peace 2005-06.

Dr Stephen Farry MP, House of Commons, London SW1A 0AA
Tel: 020 7219 3000 *Email:* stephen.farry.mp@parliament.uk
Constituency: 58 Abbey Street, Bangor BT20 4JB
Tel: 028 9185 9475 *Email:* stephen.farry@alliancepartyni.org *Twitter:* @StephenFarryMP

CONSERVATIVE

FELL, SIMON

Barrow and Furness *(Majority 5,789)*

Simon Richard James Fell. Born 9 February 1981; Married Pippa (1 daughter 1 son).

Education: Stonyhurst College, Lancashire; Warwick University (BA English literature 2003).

Non-political career: Director, Irton-Fell Consultants 2006-08; Regulatory Affairs Manager, Hutchison H3g 2008-11; Cifas: Assistant Director, Strategy and Policy 2011-19, Director of External Relations 2019.

Political career: Contested Barrow and Furness 2015 and 2017 general elections. Member for Barrow and Furness since 12 December 2019. *Select committees:* Member, Home Affairs 2020-.

Political interests: Home affairs, defence, technology, social enterprise; China, USA.

Recreations: Running, cycling, reading.

Simon Fell MP, House of Commons, London SW1A 0AA
Tel: 020 7219 3000 *Email:* simon.fell.mp@parliament.uk
Constituency: 132 Cavendish Street, Barrow-in-Furness LA14 1DJ
Tel: 01229 314220 Website: www.simonfell.org *Twitter:* @simonfell

SCOTTISH NATIONAL PARTY

FELLOWS, MARION

Motherwell and Wishaw *(Majority 6,268)*

SNP Deputy Whip; SNP Spokesperson for Disabilities

Born 5 May 1949; Widowed.

Education: Heriot Watt University (BA accountancy and finance).

Non-political career: Accountant; Business Studies Lecturer, West Lothian College. Member, EIS.

Political career: Contested Motherwell and Wishaw 2010 general election. Member for Motherwell and Wishaw since 7 May 2015 general election; SNP: Deputy Whip 2015-, Spokesperson for: Small Business, Enterprise and Innovation 2017-19, Disabilities 2020-; Member, Speaker's Committee for the Independent Parliamentary Standards Authority 2020-.

Select committees: Member: Education 2015-19, Education, Skills and the Economy Sub-committee 2016-17, Administration 2018-. Contested Motherwell and Wishaw constituency 2007 Scottish Parliament election. *Councils and public bodies:* Councillor, North Lanarkshire Council 2012-15.

Political interests: Scottish independence; Child Maintenance Service and social security; protecting the Post Office network and other public services; cystic fibrosis; autism.

Recreations: Knitting, spending time with family.

Marion Fellows MP, House of Commons, London SW1A 0AA
Tel: 020 7219 5784 *Email:* marion.fellows.mp@parliament.uk
Constituency: Dalziel Building, 7 Scott Street, Motherwell, North Yorkshire ML1 1PN
Tel: 01698 337191 Website: marionfellows.scot *Twitter:* @marionfellows

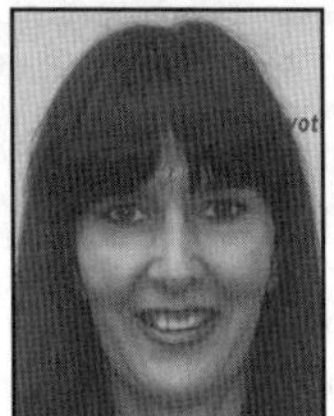

INDEPENDENT

FERRIER, MARGARET Rutherglen and Hamilton West *(Majority 5,230)*

Born 10 September 1960; 1 daughter.

Education: Holyrood Secondary School.

Non-political career: Commercial sales supervisor, Terex Equipment.

Political career: Member for Rutherglen and Hamilton West 2015-17. Contested Rutherglen and Hamilton West 2017 general election. Member for Rutherglen and Hamilton West since 12 December 2019; SNP Spokesperson for: Scotland Office 2015-17, Manufacturing 2020. *Select committees:* Member: Scottish Affairs 2015-17, European Scrutiny 2020-. Member, SNP National Council 2016-20; SNP Whip suspended October 2020-. *Councils and public bodies:* Councillor, Halfway Community Council.

Political interests: Equality, human rights.

Other: Member: Amnesty International, Scottish CND; Volunteer, Citizens Advice Bureau.

Margaret Ferrier MP, House of Commons, London SW1A 0AA
Tel: 020 7219 3272 *Email:* margaret.ferrier.mp@parliament.uk
Constituency: 43 Farmeloan Road, Rutherglen, Glasgow G73 1DN
Tel: 020 3545 2491 Website: margaretferriermp.scot *Twitter:* @MargaretFerrier

SINN FÉIN

FINUCANE, JOHN Belfast North *(Majority 1,943)*

Born March 1980; Son of Pat and Geraldine Finucane.

Education: Dundee University (law and history 2002).

Non-political career: Paralegal, Madden and Finucane; Solicitor, Kevin Winters and Company; Partner, Finucane Toner Ltd.

Political career: Contested Belfast North 2017 general election. Member for Belfast North since 12 December 2019.

John Finucane MP, House of Commons, London SW1A 0AA
Tel: 020 7219 3000 *Email:* john.finucane.mp@parliament.uk
Constituency: 7 Altantic Avenue, Belfast BT7 2HN
Tel: 028 9050 0890 *Twitter:* @johnfinucane

LABOUR

FLETCHER, COLLEEN Coventry North East *(Majority 7,692)*

Senior Opposition Whip

Colleen Margaret Fletcher. Born 23 November 1954; Daughter of Dot and Bill Dalton; Married (2 sons).

Education: Lyng Hall Comprehensive School; Henley College.

Non-political career: GEC, Coventry; Home Care Assistant, Coventry City Council; Customer Services Officer, Orbit Housing Group.

Political career: Member for Coventry North East since 7 May 2015 general election; PPS to Kerry McCarthy as Secretary of State for Environment, Food and Rural Affairs 2016; Opposition Whip 2017-20; Senior Opposition Whip 2020-. *Select committees:* Member,

Administration 2017-. Member, National Policy Forum; Officer, West Midlands Regional Board. *Councils and public bodies:* Coventry City Council: Councillor 1992-2000, 2002-04, 2011-15, Former Cabinet Member for Community Safety, Chair: Labour Group, Scrutiny Co-ordination.

Colleen Fletcher MP, House of Commons, London SW1A 0AA
Tel: 020 7219 8036 *Email:* colleen.fletcher.mp@parliament.uk
Constituency: Unite House, Short Street, Coventry, Warwickshire CV1 2LS
Tel: 024 7663 0700 Website: colleenfletchermp.wordpress.com

CONSERVATIVE

FLETCHER, KATHERINE

South Ribble *(Majority 11,199)*

Born 18 February 1976; Daughter of Alan Fletcher and Elaine Fletcher (née Turner).

Education: Altrincham Girls Grammar School; Nottingham University (BSc biology 1997).

Non-political career: Consultant: IT Consultancy – Xayce Consulting Corporation 1997-2001, Gemini Consulting (Cap Gemini Ernst Young) Management consultancy 2001-05; Head of Fulfilment Operations, LTSB Business Banking 2006-07; Field Guide (Safari Ranger), Mpumalanga, South Africa 2008; LBG SME Banking Division: PMI Integration Director 2009, Head of Strategy 2010-12; Owner, BritishOriginals 2012-19; Strategy Lead, Northern Powerhouse Partnership (six months setup) 2017.

Political career: Contested Ellesmere Port and Neston 2015 general election. Member for South Ribble since 12 December 2019; Prime Minister's Trade Envoy to Mozambique 2020-. *Select committees:* Member: Science and Technology 2020-, Petitions 2020-. Conservative Party: Member 2013-, Deputy chair, Northwest Region 2018-19.

Political interests: Northern Powerhouse, supporting small businesses – especially to export, environment, STEM innovation research and development; North of England.

Recreations: Mountain biking and walking in the Peak District, Lake District and North Wales, birdwatching, Manchester United FC season ticket holder.

Katherine Fletcher MP, House of Commons, London SW1A 0AA
Tel: 020 7219 4622 *Email:* katherine.fletcher.mp@parliament.uk
Constituency: First Floor, Leyland Conservative Club, 67-69 Towngate, Leyland PR25 2LR
Website: www.katherinefletcher.uk *Twitter:* @K_Fletcher_MP

CONSERVATIVE

FLETCHER, MARK

Bolsover *(Majority 5,299)*

Team PPS, Department for Business, Energy and Industrial Strategy

Mark Peter Fletcher. Born 29 September 1985; Son of Peter John Hannington and Catherine Mary Fletcher; Married Will Knock 2016.

Education: Ridgewood School; Danum School Technology College; Jesus College, Cambridge (land economy 2007) (President, Cambridge University Students' Union 2007-09).

Non-political career: Campaign Manager and Parliamentary Assistant to George Freeman 2009-11; Chief of Staff to Lord Popat 2011-17; Director of Communications, Synergix Health 2018; Freelance Author, E1 Communications 2018-.

Political career: Contested Doncaster North 2015 and Stockton North 2017 general elections. Member for Bolsover since 12 December 2019; Team PPS, Department for Business, Energy and Industrial Strategy 2020-. *Select committees:* Member: Future Relationship with the European Union 2020, Privileges 2020-, Standards 2020-. Acting Director, Conservative Friends of India 2011-12; Chair, Poplar and Limehouse Conservative Party 2017-18. *Councils and public bodies:* Chair of Governors, Hartley Primary School 2011-15.

Political interests: Brexit, crime, NHS, housing, employment; East Africa, India.

Mark Fletcher MP, House of Commons, London SW1A 0AA
Tel: 020 7219 3662 *Email:* mark.fletcher.mp@parliament.uk
Constituency: Unit 1, Church View, Chesterfield S45 9HA
Website: www.mark-fletcher.org.uk

CONSERVATIVE

FLETCHER, NICK

Don Valley *(Majority 3,630)*

Nicholas Anthony Fletcher. Born July 1972.

Education: Armthorpe Comprehensive School; DMIHE (HNC electrical electronic engineering 1992).

Non-political career: Electrician, RFS Engineering Ltd 1988-94; Director, Analogue Electrics Ltd 1994-.

Political career: Member for Don Valley since 12 December 2019. *Select committees:* Member, Petitions 2020-. Chair, Doncaster Conservative Federation.

Other: Director, Doncaster Chamber of Commerce.

Nick Fletcher MP, House of Commons, London SW1A 0AA
Tel: 020 7219 5192 *Email:* nick.fletcher.mp@parliament.uk
Constituency: S4 Heyford House, Doncaster Sheffield Airport, First Avenue, Doncaster DN9 3RH
Tel: 01302 579020 Website: www.nickfletcher.org.uk *Twitter:* @NickFletcherMP

SCOTTISH NATIONAL PARTY

FLYNN, STEPHEN

Aberdeen South *(Majority 3,990)*

SNP Shadow Secretary of State for Business, Energy and Industrial Strategy

Stephen Mark Flynn. Born 13 October 1988; Partner.

Non-political career: Parliamentary Assistant to Callum McCaig MP 2015-17; Part-time Office Manager to Maureen Watt MSP.

Political career: Member for Aberdeen South since 12 December 2019; SNP Shadow Financial Secretary 2020-21, Shadow Secretary of State for Business, Energy and Industrial Strategy 2021-. *Councils and public bodies:* Aberdeen City Council: Councillor 2015-20, SNP Group Leader 2016-20.

Political interests: Independence, European Union.

Stephen Flynn MP, House of Commons, London SW1A 0AA
Tel: 020 7219 5151 *Email:* stephen.flynn.mp@parliament.uk
Constituency: 1 Pitstruan Place, Aberdeen AB10 6PQ
Tel: 01224 213114 *Twitter:* @StephenFlynnSNP

CONSERVATIVE

FORD, VICKY

Chelmsford *(Majority 17,621)*

Parliamentary Under-Secretary of State for Children and Families, Department for Education

Victoria Grace Ford. Born 21 September 1967; Married Hugo Edward Rawlinson Ford 1996 (1 daughter 2 sons).

Education: St Paul's School, London; Marlborough College, Wiltshire; Trinity College, Cambridge (BA economics 1989, MA).

Non-political career: Vice-president, loans, JP Morgan, London 1988-2000; Managing director, loans, Bear Stearns International, London 2001-03.

Political career: Contested Birmingham Northfield 2005 general election. Member for Chelmsford since 8 June 2017; Team PPS, Foreign and Commonwealth Office 2018-19; PPS to Alok Sharma as Secretary of State for International Development 2019-20; Parliamentary Under-Secretary of State for Children and Families, Department for Education 2020-. *Select committees:* Member: Science and Technology 2017-20, Women and Equalities 2018-20, European Statutory Instruments 2018-20. Chairman, Conservative Backbench Policy Committee on Exiting the European Union 2017-19. MEP for Eastern 2009-17: Chair, Internal Market and Consumer Protection Committee 2014-17. Deputy chair: South East Cambridgeshire Conservative Association 2004-08, Cambridgeshire and Bedfordshire Conservatives 2005-07. *Councils and public bodies:* Member, South Cambridgeshire district council 2006-08.

Political interests: Finance, health, family, education, environment.

Other: Substitute Member, UK Delegation to Parliamentary Assembly of Council of Europe 2018-19; Chair, Abington Pre-school; Treasurer, Akiki.

Recreations: Fly fishing, gardening, singing.

Vicky Ford MP, House of Commons, London SW1A 0AA
Tel: 020 7219 0138 *Email:* vicky.ford.mp@parliament.uk
Constituency: 88 Rectory Lane, Chelmsford CM1 1RF
Tel: 01245 352872 Website: www.vickyford.uk *Twitter:* @vickyford

CONSERVATIVE

FOSTER, KEVIN

Torbay *(Majority 17,749)*

Parliamentary Under-Secretary of State for Future Borders and Immigration, Home Office

Kevin John Foster. Born 31 December 1978; Son of Michael and Linda Foster; Married Hazel 2017.

Education: Hele's School, Plymouth; Warwick University (LLB 2000; LLM international economic law 2001); Bar Vocational Course 2002.

Non-political career: Called to the Bar 2002; Assistant to Philip Bradbourn MEP 2002-03; Criminal defence paralegal, Birmingham 2003-04.

Political career: Contested Coventry South 2010 general election. Member for Torbay since 7 May 2015 general election; Team PPS, Department for Communities and Local Government 2017-18; PPS to David Lidington as Minister for the Cabinet Office and Chancellor of the Duchy of Lancaster 2018-19; Parliamentary Under-Secretary of State, Wales Office 2019; Assistant Government Whip 2019; Interim Parliamentary Secretary (Minister for the Constitution), Cabinet Office (maternity cover for Chloe Smith MP) April-October 2019; Parliamentary Under-Secretary of State for Immigration/Future Borders and Immigration, Home Office 2019-. *Select committees:* Member: Public Accounts 2015-17, Ecclesiastical Committee 2015-19, Backbench Business 2015-17. Chairman, Conservative Backbench Policy Committee on Northern Ireland 2015-17. Member, Conservative Party 1995-; President, Warwick University Conservative Association 1998. *Councils and public bodies:* Coventry City Council: Councillor 2002-14, Deputy Leader of Council 2008-10, Council Leader 2011-13.

Other: Trustee, Coventry Law Centre; Director, Whitley Community Centre.

Recreations: Coventry City FC, Torquay United, military history.

Kevin Foster MP, House of Commons, London SW1A 0AA
Tel: 020 7219 4711 *Email:* kevin.foster.mp@parliament.uk
Constituency: 5-7 East Street, Torquay TQ2 5SD
Tel: 01803 214989 *Email:* kevin@kevinjfoster.com Website: www.kevinjfoster.com
Twitter: @kevin_j_foster

LABOUR

FOVARGUE, YVONNE

Makerfield *(Majority 4,740)*

Yvonne Helen Fovargue. Born 29 November 1956; Daughter of late Kenneth Gibbon and late Irene Gibbon; Married Paul Kenny 2009 (1 daughter).

Education: Sale Girls Grammar School; Leeds University (BA English 1978); Manchester City College (PGCE English and religious studies 1979); NVQ strategic management level 5 2003.

Non-political career: Housing department, Manchester City Council: Housing information manager 1979-82, Estate manager 1982-86; Newton le Willows Citizens Advice Bureau/St Helen's District Citizens Advice Bureau: Manager 1986-92, Chief executive 1992-2010. Member 1979-: NALGO, NUPE, ASTMS, Amicus, Unite, USDAW.

Political career: Member for Makerfield since 6 May 2010 general election; Opposition Whip 2011-13; Shadow Minister for: Transport 2013, Defence 2013-14, 2015, Education 2014-15, Business, Innovation and Skills 2015-16, Local Government 2017-19. *Select committees:* Member: Health 2010-11, Joint Committee on Consolidation, Etc, Bills 2010-15, Selection 2012-13, Procedure 2014-17, Panel of Chairs 2020-. Vice-chair, PLP Departmental Group for Work and Pensions 2010-15; Chair, PLP Departmental Group for Cabinet Office 2020-. Vice-chair, Warrington South CLP 2008-10. *Councils and public bodies:* Councillor, Warrington Borough Council 2004-10.

Political interests: Third sector, consumer credit and debt, employment law, health, legal aid.

Other: Member, Mensa; Trustee and board member, St Helens CVS 2001-10.

Recreations: Reading, theatre, music.

Yvonne Fovargue MP, House of Commons, London SW1A 0AA
Tel: 020 7219 3000 *Email:* yvonne.fovargue.mp@parliament.uk
Constituency: Wigan Investment Centre, Waterside Drive, Wigan WN3 5BA
Tel: 01942 824029 Website: www.yvonnefovargue.com *Twitter:* @Y_FovargueMP

CONSERVATIVE

FOX, LIAM

North Somerset *(Majority 17,536)*

Born 22 September 1961; Son of William Fox, teacher, and Catherine Fox; Married Jesme Baird 2005.

Education: St Bride's High School, East Kilbride; Glasgow University (MB, ChB 1983; MROGP 1989).

Non-political career: General practitioner, Beaconsfield, Buckinghamshire and Nailsea, North Somerset; Divisional surgeon, St John's Ambulance, Buckinghamshire. Civilian Army Medical Officer.

Political career: Contested Roxburgh and Berwickshire 1987 general election. Member for Woodspring 1992-2010, for North Somerset since 6 May 2010 general election; PPS to Michael Howard as Home Secretary 1993-94; Assistant Government Whip 1994-95; Government Whip 1995-96; Parliamentary Under-Secretary of State, Foreign and Commonwealth Office 1996-97; Opposition Spokesperson for: Constitutional Affairs, Scotland and Wales 1997-99; Member Shadow Cabinet 1998-2010: Shadow Secretary of State for Health 1999-2003, Shadow Foreign Secretary 2005, Shadow Secretary of State for Defence 2005-10; Secretary of State for: Defence 2010-11, International Trade 2016-19; President of the Board of Trade 2016-19. *Select committees:* Member, Scottish Affairs 1992-93. Chair, Conservative Health/Social Services Policy Committee 2001-05. Chair, West of Scotland Young Conservatives 1983; National vice-chair, Scottish Young Conservatives 1983-84; Secretary, West Country Conservative Members' Committee 1992-93; Chair, Conservative Party 2003-05; Contested Conservative Party leadership 2005; Chair, South West Conservative MPs' Group 2015-; Vice-President, Conservatives for Britain 2015-16.

Political interests: Health, mental health, economic policy, foreign affairs, defence; USA.

Other: President, Glasgow University Club 1982-83; Guest of US State Department, involving study of drug abuse problems in USA, and Republican Party campaigning techniques 1985; Member: Central Committee, Families for Defence 1987-89, Campaign committee, Vote Leave 2016; Founder, Give Us Time 2012-; World Debating Competition, Toronto (Individual speaking prize) 1982; Best Speaker's Trophy, Glasgow University 1983; PC 2010.

Publications: Making Unionism Positive (1988); Rising Tides (2013).

Recreations: Tennis, swimming, cinema, theatre.

Rt Hon Dr Liam Fox MP, House of Commons, London SW1A 0AA
Tel: 020 7219 4198 *Email:* ione.douglas@parliament.uk
Constituency: No constituency office publicised
Website: www.liamfox.co.uk *Twitter:* @LiamFox

LABOUR

FOXCROFT, VICKY

Lewisham Deptford *(Majority 32,913)*

Shadow Minister for Disability

Victoria Jane Foxcroft. Born 9 March 1977.

Education: De Montfort University (BA 2000); French.

Non-political career: Research officer, AEEU 2002-05; Political officer, Amicus 2005-09; Finance sector officer, Unite 2009-15. Member: Unite, GMB.

Political career: Member for Lewisham Deptford since 7 May 2015 general election; Opposition Whip 2015-19; Shadow Minister for: Digital, Culture, Media and Sport (Civil Society) 2019-20, Work and Pensions (Disability) 2020-. *Select committees:* Member, Joint

Committee on Statutory Instruments 2016-19. Chair, Labour Students; Member: National Policy Forum, Labour Party; Co-operative Party. *Councils and public bodies:* Lewisham Council: Councillor 2010-14, Chair, Labour Group.

Political interests: Youth violence reduction, youth affairs, housing.

Vicky Foxcroft MP, House of Commons, London SW1A 0AA
Tel: 020 7219 5934 *Email:* vicky.foxcroft.mp@parliament.uk
Constituency: 82 Tanners Hill, Deptford, London SE8 4PN
Tel: 020 8469 4638 Website: www.vickyfoxcroft.org.uk *Twitter:* @vickyfoxcroft

LABOUR

FOY, MARY

City of Durham *(Majority 5,025)*

Mary Kelly Foy. Born 27 February 1968; Married Paul (3 children).

Education: Social sciences.

Non-political career: Development Worker, Durham City District CVS; Senior Parliamentary Assistant to Stephen Hepburn MP. Unite; Unison.

Political career: Member for City of Durham since 12 December 2019; PPS to: Andrew Gwynne as Shadow Secretary of State for Communities and Local Government 2020, Andy McDonald as Shadow Secretary of State for Employment Rights and Protections 2020. *Select committees:* Member, Northern Ireland Affairs 2020-. Regional Representative, Labour National Policy Forum; Chair, Blaydon Constituency Labour Party. *Councils and public bodies:* Gateshead Council: Councillor 2006-, Cabinet Member for Health and Wellbeing; Governor: St Joseph's School, Birtley, Birtley East Primary School; Director, Northern IT Research Ltd.

Other: Movement of Christian Workers.

Mary Foy MP, House of Commons, London SW1A 0AA
Tel: 020 7219 3000 *Email:* mary.foy.mp@parliament.uk
Constituency: Miners Hall, 8 Flass Street, Durham DH1 4BE
Tel: 0191-374 1915 Website: maryfoy.org.uk *Twitter:* @marykfoy

CONSERVATIVE

FRANCOIS, MARK

Rayleigh and Wickford *(Majority 31,000)*

Mark Gino Francois. Born 14 August 1965; Son of Reginald Francois, engineer, and Anna Francois, née Carloni, cook; Married Karen Thomas 2000 (divorced 2006).

Education: St Nicholas Comprehensive School, Basildon; Bristol University (BA history 1986); King's College, London (MA war studies 1987).

Non-political career: Management trainee, Lloyds Bank 1987; Market Access International (public affairs consultancy) 1988-95: Consultant, Director; Public affairs consultant, Francois Associates 1996-2001. TA 1983-89, Commissioned 1985.

Political career: Contested Brent East 1997 general election. Member for Rayleigh 2001-10, for Rayleigh and Wickford since 6 May 2010 general election; Opposition Whip 2002-04; Shadow Economic Secretary 2004-05; Shadow Paymaster General 2005-07; Shadow Minister for Europe 2007-10; Government Whip (Vice-Chamberlain of HM Household) 2010-12; Ministry of Defence: Minister of State for: Defence Personnel, Welfare and Veterans 2012-13, the Armed Forces 2013-15; Minister of State for Communities and Resilience (Minister for Portsmouth), Department for Communities and Local Government 2015-16; Member, Speaker's Committee on the Electoral Commission 2015-16; Chair, Review into the use of Reserves in the Army 2016-. *Select committees:* Member: Environmental Audit 2001-05, European Standing Committee A 2002-05, Selection 2010-12, Administration 2010-12, Armed Forces Bill 2011, Defence 2017-. *Councils and public bodies:* Councillor, Basildon District Council 1991-95.

Political interests: Defence, local and regional government, housing, environment.

Other: Member, Royal United Services Institute for Defence Studies 1991-; President: Friends of Holy Trinity Church, Rayleigh 2002-, Rayleigh Division, St John Ambulance 2002-; Patron, Rayleigh Branch of Royal British Legion 2002-; President: Rayleigh Brass Band 2006-, Wyvern Community Transport 2008-; Patron, Rayleigh Bowls Club 2011-; National Patron, Cruse Bereavement Care -2019; Member, Worshipful Company of Wheelwrights 2003-; Freedom, City of London 2004; PC 2010. Carlton Club, Rayleigh Conservative Club.

Recreations: Reading, sports, military history, travel.

Rt Hon Mark Francois MP, House of Commons, London SW1A 0AA
Tel: 020 7219 8287 *Email:* mark.francois.mp@parliament.uk
Constituency: 25 Bellingham Lane, Rayleigh, Essex SS6 7ED
Tel: 01268 742044 Website: www.markfrancois.com

CONSERVATIVE

FRAZER, LUCY

South East Cambridgeshire *(Majority 11,490)*

Minister of State, Ministry of Justice

Lucy Claire Frazer. Born 17 May 1972; Married David Leigh 2002 (2 children).

Education: Leeds Girls' High School; Newnham College, Cambridge (BA law 1994) (President, Cambridge Union Society 1993).

Non-political career: Called to the Bar, Middle Temple 1996; Barrister, specialising in commercial law, South Square, Gray's Inn 1998-2015; QC 2013.

Political career: Member for South East Cambridgeshire since 7 May 2015 general election; PPS to: Ben Gummer as Minister for the Cabinet Office and Paymaster General 2016-17, David Lidington as Lord Chancellor and Secretary of State for Justice 2017-18; Ministry of Justice: Parliamentary Under-Secretary of State 2018-19, Minister of State 2019-; Solicitor General 2019. *Select committees:* Member: Education 2015-17, Education, Skills and the Economy Sub-committee 2015-16.

Lucy Frazer QC MP, House of Commons, London SW1A 0AA
Tel: 020 7219 5082 *Email:* lucy.frazer.mp@parliament.uk
Constituency: No constituency office publicised
Website: www.lucyfrazer.org.uk *Twitter:* @lucyfrazermp

CONSERVATIVE

FREEMAN, GEORGE

Mid Norfolk *(Majority 22,594)*

George William Freeman. Born 12 July 1967; Son of Arthur Freeman, National Hunt jockey and trainer, and Joanna Philipson; Married Eleanor Holmes (1 son 1 daughter).

Education: Radley College, Oxfordshire; Girton College, Cambridge (BA geography 1989); French.

Non-political career: Parliamentary officer, National Farmers Union 1990-92; Founder, The Local Identity Agency 1992-97; Director, Early Stage Ventures, Merlin Ventures 1997-2001; Chief executive officer, Amedis Pharmaceuticals 2001-03; Director, 4D Biomedical 2003-11; Adviser to Norwich Research Park Venture Fund 2007-10; Non-executive director, Elsoms Seeds Ltd.

Political career: Contested Stevenage 2005 general election. Member for Mid Norfolk since 6 May 2010 general election; PPS to Gregory Barker as Minister of State for Climate Change, Department of Energy and Climate Change 2010-12; Adviser on Life Sciences to David Willetts as Minister of State for Universities and Science 2011-13; Trade Envoy to the Philippines 2014; Parliamentary Under-Secretary of State (Life Sciences), Department for Business, Innovation and Skills and Department of Health 2014-16; Chair, Prime Minister's Policy Board 2016-17; Minister of State, Department for Transport 2019-20. *Select committees:* Member, Communities and Local Government 2010. Founding member, 2020 group 2011-14; Chair, Conservative Policy Forum 2016-. *Councils and public bodies:* Governor, Bevington Primary School 1995-96; Board member, Greater Cambridge Partnership 2005-10.

Political interests: Constitution, crime, civil society, localism, rural economy, universities and innovation, biotechnology, healthcare reform; France, USA.

Other: Co-founder, Businesswise Learn to Earn 1995-97; Trustee, Cambridge Union Society 2005-09. Norfolk Club; Rob Roy Boat Club.

Recreations: Sailing, horseracing, hill-walking, rowing.

George Freeman MP, House of Commons, London SW1A 0AA
Tel: 020 7219 6502 *Email:* george.freeman.mp@parliament.uk
Constituency: 8 Damgate Street, Wymondham, Norfolk NR18 0BQ
Tel: 01953 600617 Website: www.georgefreeman.co.uk *Twitter:* @GeorgeFreemanMP

CONSERVATIVE

FREER, MIKE

Finchley and Golders Green *(Majority 6,562)*

Government Whip (Comptroller of HM Household)

Michael Whitney Freer. Born 29 May 1960; Married Angelo Crolla 2015.

Education: Chadderton Grammar School, Manchester; St Aidan's School, Carlisle.

Non-political career: Retail catering industry; Retail gaming industry; Relationship director, Barclays Bank plc; Self-employed consultant.

Political career: Contested Harrow West 2005 general election. Member for Finchley and Golders Green since 6 May 2010 general election; PPS: to Department for Communities and Local Government ministerial team 2013-14, to Nick Boles as Minister of State for Skills and Equalities, Department for Business, Innovation and Skills and Department for Education 2014, to Chris Grayling: as Leader of the House of Commons and Lord President of the Council 2015-16, as Secretary of State for Transport 2016-17; Assistant Government Whip 2017-18; Government Whip: (Lord Commissioner of HM Treasury) 2018-19, (Comptroller of HM Household) 2019-. *Select committees:* Member: Communities and Local Government 2010-11, Scottish Affairs 2010-13, Work and Pensions 2013, Selection 2020-. Conservative Friends of Cyprus; Conservative Friends of Israel; Friend of British-Asian Conservative Link; Conservative Muslim Forum. *Councils and public bodies:* London Borough of Barnet Council: Councillor 1990-94, 2001-10, Council Leader 2006-09; Non-executive director, London Development Agency 2008-10; Vice-President, Local Government Association 2011-.

Political interests: Breast cancer screening, local government funding, local government reform, dementia, reducing cost of central government; Cyprus, Israel, Middle East, USA.

Other: Member, Friends of Windsor Open Space; Chair, Barnet Multi-faith Forum.

Recreations: Cycling, reading.

Mike Freer MP, House of Commons, London SW1A 0AA
Tel: 020 7219 7071 *Fax:* 020 7219 2211 *Email:* mike.freer.mp@parliament.uk
Constituency: 212 Ballards Lane, Finchley, London N3 2LX
Tel: 020 8445 5875 Website: www.mikefreer.com

CONSERVATIVE

FULLER, RICHARD

North East Bedfordshire *(Majority 24,283)*

Richard Quentin Fuller. Born 30 May 1962.

Education: Bedford Modern School; Oxford University (BA philosophy, politics and economics 1981); Harvard Business School (MBA 1987).

Non-political career: Partner: LEK Consulting, Investcorp Technology Ventures.

Political career: Contested Bedford 2005 general election. Member for Bedford 2010-17. Contested Bedford 2017 general election. Member for North East Bedfordshire since 12 December 2019. *Select committees:* Member: Regulatory Reform 2012-17, Business, Innovation and Skills 2015-16, Business, Energy and Industrial Strategy 2016-17, 2020-. Chair, Oxford University Conservative Association 1983; National chair, Young Conservatives 1985-87; Patron, Tory Reform Group.

Political interests: Social enterprise, entrepreneurship, small business, education, economic development in West Africa; Bangladesh, South Korea, Nigeria, USA.

Other: President, Bedfordshire Blue Raiders (American football).

Richard Fuller MP, House of Commons, London SW1A 0AA
Tel: 020 7219 8602 *Email:* richard.fuller.mp@parliament.uk
Constituency: Biggleswade Conservative Club, St Andrews Street, Biggleswade, Bedfordshire SG18 8BA
Tel: 01767 313385 Website: www.richardfuller.co.uk

LABOUR

FURNISS, GILL

Sheffield, Brightside and Hillsborough *(Majority 12,274)*

Shadow Minister for Women and Equalities; Opposition Whip

Gillian Furniss. Born 14 March 1957; Married Harry Harpham (died 2016) (MP for Sheffield, Brightside and Hillsborough 2015-16).

Education: Chaucer Comprehensive, Sheffield; Leeds Metropolitan University (BA library and information studies 1998).

Non-political career: Librarian, Firth Park, Parson Cross and Burngreave libraries, Sheffield College 1973-2000; Medical Records Clerk, Northern General Hospital 2008-15; Councillor, Sheffield City Council 1999-2016; Researcher to Harry Harpham MP 2015-16. GMB, Unite.

Political career: Contested Sheffield Hallam 2001 general election. Member for Sheffield, Brightside and Hillsborough since 5 May 2016 by-election; Shadow Minister for: Steel, Postal Affairs Royal Mail, Consumer Protection and Pubs 2016-20, Women and Equalities 2020-; Opposition Whip 2020-. *Select committees:* Member, Women and Equalities 2016. *Councils and public bodies:* Sheffield City Council: Councillor 1999-2016, Former Cabinet Member for: Planning, Regeneration, Libraries, Parks, Waste management.

Political interests: Industrial strategy, climate change, women and equalities, health; Qatar, USA.

Other: Ambassador, Hallam FM's Cash for Kids.

Gill Furniss MP, House of Commons, London SW1A 0AA
Tel: 020 7219 0364 *Email:* gill.furniss.mp@parliament.uk
Constituency: Shirecliffe Community Centre, 349 Shirecliffe Road, Sheffield S5 8XJ
Tel: 0114-234 9079 Website: gillfurnissmp.wordpress.com *Twitter:* @GillFurnissMP

CONSERVATIVE

FYSH, MARCUS

Yeovil *(Majority 16,181)*

Marcus John Hudson Fysh. Born 8 November 1970; Married Jenny 2011 (1 daughter).

Education: Oxford University (literature).

Non-political career: Mercury Asset Management 1993-2003; Set up own business in: Australia and India, Healthcare research.

Political career: Member for Yeovil since 7 May 2015 general election. *Select committees:* Member: Standing Orders 2015-17, Public Administration and Constitutional Affairs 2016-19, International Trade 2016-19, European Scrutiny 2017-, Arms Export Controls 2017-19. *Councils and public bodies:* Councillor: South Somerset District Council 2011-15, Somerset County Council 2013-17.

Political interests: Infrastructure, rail and road transport, healthcare, education, housing.

Other: Member, UK delegation, Parliamentary Assembly of the Organisation for Security and Co-operation in Europe.

Recreations: Cinema, playing cricket and tennis, spending time with family.

Marcus Fysh MP, House of Commons, London SW1A 0AA
Tel: 020 7219 4527 *Email:* marcus.fysh.mp@parliament.uk
Constituency: 21-22 High Street, Yeovil BA20 1RF
Tel: 01935 314321 *Email:* marcus@marcusfysh.org.uk Website: www.marcusfysh.org.uk
Twitter: @MarcusFysh

CONSERVATIVE

GALE, ROGER

North Thanet *(Majority 17,189)*

Roger James Gale. Born 20 August 1943; Son of Richard Gale, solicitor, and Phyllis Gale, née Rowell; Married Wendy Bowman 1964 (divorced 1967); married Susan Sampson 1971 (divorced 1980) (1 daughter); married Susan Marks 1980 (2 sons).

Education: Thomas Hardye School, Dorchester; Guildhall School of Music and Drama (LGSM&D 1963); French (working).

Non-political career: Freelance broadcaster 1963-; Programme director, Radio Scotland 1965; Personal assistant to general manager, Universal Films 1971-72; Freelance reporter, BBC Radio London 1972-73; Producer: Radio 1 *Newsbeat*, BBC Radio 4 *Today* 1973-76; Director, BBC Children's Television 1976-79; Senior producer, Children's Television, Thames TV; Editor, Teenage Unit; Producer special projects, Thames TV 1979-83. Advanced post-graduate, Parliament and Armed Forces Scheme. Member: National Union of Journalists -2005, Equity, BECTU -2005.

Political career: Contested Birmingham Northfield 1982 by-election. Member for North Thanet 1983-2010, for North Thanet (revised boundary) since 6 May 2010 general election; PPS to Ministers of State for the Armed Forces: Archibald Hamilton 1992-93, Jeremy Hanley 1993-94; Temporary Deputy Speaker May-June 2015. *Select committees:* Member: Home Affairs 1990-92, Broadcasting 1997-2005, Chairmen's Panel/Panel of Chairs 1997-, Procedure 2007-15, Ecclesiastical Committee 2015-, Court of Referees 2016-17. Vice-chair, Conservative Party Committee for Culture, Media and Sport (Media) 1997-2001. President, Conservative Animal Welfare; Vice-chair: Holborn and St Pancras Conservative Association 1971-72, Conservative Party 2001-03. *Councils and public bodies:* Special constable, British Transport Police 2004-07.

Political interests: Animal welfare, media, broadcasting, tourism, leisure industry; Cyprus, Europe, Russia, Tunisia, Ukraine.

Other: Delegate: Council of Europe 1987-89, 2011-15, Western European Union 1987-89; International Election Observer: Armenia, Botswana, Gambia, Georgia, Ghana, Kenya, Macedonia, Mongolia, Mozambique, South Africa, Ukraine, Tunisia; Parliamentary Assembly of the Council of Europe: Leader, UK Delegation 2015-20, Interim President July-September 2017, Senior Vice-President 2015-20; Member, Baltic Plus Group 2018–; Vice-President, St John (Kent); President, Herne Bay Air Cadets; Hon Member, British Veterinary Association; Lord's Taverners; Fellow, Industry and Parliament Trust; Chair, Try Angle Awards Foundation; Patron, Animals Worldwide; Former Chair and Trustee, Society for the Protection of Animals Abroad; Royal College of Defence Studies; Dogs Trust, Animal Health Trust, Scouts, St John Ambulance, RNLI, Animals Worldwide; Freedom: City of London, City of Morphou (Cyprus); LGSMD; RSPCA Richard Martin Award for Outstanding Contribution to Animal Welfare; Kt 2012; PC 2019. Farmers' Club; Royal Temple Yacht.

Recreations: Swimming, sailing.

Rt Hon Sir Roger Gale MP, House of Commons, London SW1A 0AA
Tel: 020 7219 4087 *Email:* galerj@parliament.uk
Constituency: The Old Forge, 215a Canterbury Road, Birchington, Kent CT7 9AH
Tel: 01843 848588 (am) *Email:* suzy@galemail.com Website: www.rogergale.com
Twitter: @SirRogerGale

LABOUR

GARDINER, BARRY

Brent North *(Majority 8,079)*

Barry Strachan Gardiner. Born 10 March 1957; Son of late John Flannegan Gardiner, general manager Kelvin Hall, and late Sylvia Strachan, doctor; Married Caroline Smith 1979 (3 sons 1 daughter).

Education: Haileybury College, Hertford; St Andrews University (MA philosophy 1983); Harvard University (JF Kennedy Scholarship 1984); Cambridge University (research 1984-87); French, Russian.

Non-political career: Partner, Mediterranean Average Adjusting Co 1987-97; Occasional lecturer, Academy of National Economy, Moscow, Russia 1992-96. Member: MSF, GMB.

Political career: Member for Brent North 1997-2010, for Brent North (revised boundary) since 6 May 2010 general election; PPS to Beverley Hughes as Minister of State, Home Office 2002-04; Parliamentary Under-Secretary of State: Northern Ireland Office 2004-05, Department of Trade and Industry 2005-06, Minister for Biodiversity, Landscape and Rural

House of Commons MPs' Biographies

Affairs, Department for Environment, Food and Rural Affairs 2006-07; Prime Minister's Special Envoy for Forestry 2007-08; PPS to Lord Mandelson as Secretary of State for Business, Enterprise and Regulatory Reform/Business, Innovation and Skills 2009-10; Leader of the Opposition's Special Envoy for Climate Change and the Environment 2011-15; Shadow Minister for: Natural Environment and Fisheries 2013-15, Water 2015, Energy and Climate Change 2015-16; Shadow Secretary of State for International Trade 2016-20; Shadow Minister for International Climate Change 2016-20. *Select committees:* Member: Procedure 1997-2001, Broadcasting 1998-2001, Public Accounts 1999-2002, Joint Committee on Consolidation of Bills Etc 2001-10, Energy and Climate Change 2010-13, Environment, Food and Rural Affairs 2011-13, 2020-, Environmental Audit 2020-, Public Accounts 2020-. Chair, PLP Departmental Committee for Culture, Media and Sport 2002-04; Vice-chair, PLP Departmental: Committee for the Treasury 2002-04, Group for Energy and Climate Change 2010-15; Chair, PLP Departmental Group for Environment, Food and Rural Affairs 2010-13. Member, Labour Finance and Industry Group; Former vice-chair, Labour Friends of Israel; Chair, Labour Friends of India 1999-2002, 2008-. *Councils and public bodies:* Cambridge City Council: Councillor 1988-94, Chair of Finance, Mayor 1992-93.

Political interests: Chinese community in the UK, economic policy, trade and industry, education, foreign affairs, environment, climate change, India-UK relations; Brazil, China, India, Russia, Sri Lanka.

Other: Former Chair of the Board, GLOBE International Ltd (Global Legislators Organisation); Fellow, Linnean Society; Director, GLOBE International 2016-; Associate, Chartered Insurance Institute; Move It!, Fryent Country Park; Member, Shipwrights' Company; Freedom, City of London; Environmental Parliamentarian of the Year 2013.

Publications: Articles on: International trade, Brexit, shipping and maritime affairs, energy policy and the environment, science, nature and climate change, Political philosophy in *Philosophical Quarterly.*

Recreations: Walking, music, reading philosophy, bird-watching, singing, opera.

Barry Gardiner MP, House of Commons, London SW1A 0AA
Tel: 020 7219 4046 *Fax:* 020 7219 2495 *Email:* barry.gardiner.mp@parliament.uk
Constituency: No constituency office
Website: www.barrygardiner.com *Twitter:* @BarryGardiner

CONSERVATIVE

GARNIER, MARK

Wyre Forest *(Majority 21,413)*

Chair, Committees on Arms Export Controls

Mark Robert Timothy Garnier. Born 26 February 1963; Son of late Peter Garnier, motoring writer, and Patricia Garnier, née Dowden, journalist; Married Caroline Joyce 2001 (2 sons 1 daughter).

Education: Charterhouse, Surrey.

Non-political career: Manager, Swiss Bank Corporation 1982-89; Managing director, South China Securities (UK) Ltd 1989-95; Executive director, Daiwa Europe Ltd 1995-96; Executive, LCF Edmond de Rothschild Securities 1996-97; Executive director, Bear Stearns 1998; Self-employed hedge fund adviser 1999-2005; Partner, CGR Capital LLP 2006-09; Senior partner, Severn Capital LLP 2009-.

Political career: Contested Wyre Forest 2005 general election. Member for Wyre Forest since 6 May 2010 general election; Trade Envoy to Burma, Brunei and Thailand 2016; Parliamentary Under-Secretary of State, Department for International Trade 2016-18 (covering Investment September 2017-January 2018); Trade Envoy to Brunei, Myanmar and Thailand 2020-. *Select committees:* Member: Treasury 2010-16, Parliamentary Commission on Banking Standards 2012-13, Finance 2015-16, European Statutory Instruments 2020, Regulatory Reform 2020-, International Trade 2020-; Chair, Committees on Arms Export Controls 2020-. Deputy chair (membership), Forest of Dean Conservative Association 2003-04; Founding member, Conservatives for Reform in Europe 2016. *Councils and public bodies:* Councillor, Forest of Dean District Council 2003-07; Member, Financial Services Trade and Investment Board 2016-.

Political interests: Economic issues, banking and financial regulation reform, financial education, tourism, European Union; China and emerging Asia, Middle East.

Other: Member, Steering Board, Kidderminster College; Fellow, Chartered Institute for Securities and Investment; Chairman, Investment Committee, Coachmakers of London; Court assistant, Worshipful Company of Coachmakers and Coach Harness Makers of London; Freedom, City of London; Royal Society of Arts. Royal Automobile Club, Carlton Club; North London Rifle Club.

Recreations: Historic aviation, historic motorsport, full-bore target rifle, shooting, fishing, photography, writing, skiing, squash.

Mark Garnier MP, House of Commons, London SW1A 0AA
Tel: 020 7219 7198 *Email:* mark.garnier.mp@parliament.uk
Constituency: 9a Lower Mill Street, Kidderminster, Worcestershire DY11 6UU
Tel: 01562 746771 Website: www.markgarnier.co.uk *Twitter:* @Mark4wyreForest

CONSERVATIVE

GHANI, NUSRAT

Wealden *(Majority 25,655)*

Nusrat Munir Ul-Ghani. Born 1 September 1972; Married.

Education: Bordesley Green Girls School; University of Central England; Leeds University (Masters international relations); Urdu, Hindi, Punjabi.

Non-political career: Age Concern; Breakthrough Breast Cancer; Clerk to All-Party Parliamentary Group on Breast Cancer; BBC World Service Trust.

Political career: Contested Birmingham, Ladywood 2010 general election. Member for Wealden since 7 May 2015 general election; Team PPS, Home Office 2017-18; Member, Speaker's Committee on the Electoral Commission 2017-18; Parliamentary Under-Secretary of State, Department for Transport 2018-20; Assistant Government Whip 2018-19; Government Whip (Lord Commissioner of HM Treasury) 2019. *Select committees:* Member: Home Affairs 2015-17, Armed Forces Bill 2015 2015-16, Foreign Affairs 2017-18, Arms Export Controls 2017-18, Business, Energy and Industrial Strategy 2020-, Panel of Chairs 2020-. Deputy chair, Brentford and Isleworth Conservative Association; Parliamentary Liaison Officer, Conservative Rural Affairs Group 2016-.

Political interests: Agriculture and farming, security and defence, education and life chances.

Other: Member: Executive Committee, Commonwealth Parliamentary Association United Kingdom 2017-18, UK delegation, NATO Parliamentary Assembly 2020-; Non-executive chair, Artemis Technologies 2020-; Supporter: AgeUK, Breakthrough Breast Cancer, Refuge, RNIB, British Heart Foundation, Prostate Cancer UK, Médecins Sans Frontières/Doctors Without Borders.

Nusrat Ghani MP, House of Commons, London SW1A 0AA
Tel: 020 7219 4619 *Email:* nusrat.ghani.mp@parliament.uk
Constituency: No constituency office publicised
Website: www.nusghani.org.uk *Twitter:* @Nus_Ghani

CONSERVATIVE

GIBB, NICK

Bognor Regis and Littlehampton *(Majority 22,503)*

Minister of State for School Standards, Department for Education

Nicolas John Gibb. Born 3 September 1960; Son of late John Gibb, civil engineer, and Eileen Gibb, schoolteacher; Married Michael Simmonds 2015.

Education: Maidstone Boys' Grammar School, Kent; Roundhay School, Leeds; Thornes House School, Wakefield; Durham University (BA law 1981).

Non-political career: Chartered accountant, specialising in taxation, KPMG, London 1984-97.

Political career: Contested Stoke-on-Trent Central 1992 general election and Rotherham 1994 by-election. Member for Bognor Regis and Littlehampton 1997-2010, for Bognor Regis and Littlehampton (revised boundary) since 6 May 2010 general election; Opposition Spokesperson for: the Treasury December 1998-99, Trade and Industry 1999-2001, Transport, Local Government and the Regions 2001; Shadow Minister for: Education and for Young People 2005, Schools 2005-10; Department for Education: Minister of State for: Schools 2010-12, 2015-16, School Reform 2014-15, School Standards 2016-, Minister for Equalities 2017-18. *Select committees:* Member: Social Security 1997-98, Treasury 1998, Treasury (Treasury

Sub-Committee) 1998, Public Accounts 2001-03, Education and Skills 2003-05; Chair, Joint Committee on Voting Eligibilty (Prisoners) Bill 2013. Member, Number 10 Policy Advisory Board 2013-14.

Political interests: Economics, taxation, education, social security; Israel, USA.

Other: Patron: Bognor Regis Shopmobility, Arun Community Transport, Littlehampton, Sammy Community Transport, Bognor Regis, Arun Sports Association for the Disabled, Littlehampton Sailing and Motorboat Club, West Sussex South Motor Neurone Disease Association, St Barnabas House Hospice, Worthing; Fellow, Institute of Chartered Accountants in England and Wales; PC 2016.

Recreations: Long-distance running, skiing.

Rt Hon Nick Gibb MP, House of Commons, London SW1A 0AA
Tel: 020 7219 6374 *Email:* gibbn@parliament.uk
Constituency: 2 Flansham Business Centre, Hoe Lane, Bognor Regis, West Sussex PO22 8NJ
Tel: 01243 587016/01243 585506 Website: www.nickgibb.org.uk *Twitter:* @NickGibbUK

SCOTTISH NATIONAL PARTY

GIBSON, PATRICIA

North Ayrshire and Arran *(Majority 8,521)*

SNP Shadow Secretary of State for Housing, Communities and Local Government and Spokesperson for Consumer Affairs

Born 12 May 1968; Née Duffy. Married Kenneth Gibson 2007 (MSP for Cunninghame North).

Education: Glasgow University (BA English and politics 1991).

Non-political career: English teacher for 20 years, Glasgow, Lanarkshire and East Renfrewshire; Parliamentary adviser to Kenneth Gibson MSP.

Political career: Contested North Ayrshire and Arran 2010 general election. Member for North Ayrshire and Arran since 7 May 2015 general election; SNP Spokesperson for Consumer Affairs 2017-, SNP Shadow Secretary of State for Housing, Communities and Local Government 2021-. *Select committees:* Member: Procedure 2015-17, Backbench Business 2017-. *Councils and public bodies:* Glasgow City Council: Councillor 2007-12, SNP Spokesperson for Education.

Political interests: Anti-austerity, anti-Trident, Scottish home rule.

Other: Member, General Teaching Council.

Patricia Gibson MP, House of Commons, London SW1A 0AA
Tel: 020 7219 5748 *Email:* patricia.gibson.mp@parliament.uk
Constituency: 78 Princes Street, Ardrossan, North Ayrshire KA22 8DF
Tel: 01294 603774 Website: www.patriciagibson.org *Twitter:* @PGibsonSNP

CONSERVATIVE

GIBSON, PETER

Darlington *(Majority 3,294)*

PPS to Amanda Milling as Minister without Portfolio and Conservative Party Chair

Peter Alexander Gibson. Born 22 May 1975; Son of Anita (community NHS midwife) and Alexander Gibson (shipwright); Civil Partnered Gareth Wedgwood Dadd 2008.

Education: Huntcliff School, Saltburn; Sir William Turner Sixth Form College, Redcar; Newcastle University (LLB 1997); University of Law (Postgraduate Diploma legal practice 2000).

Non-political career: Claims technician, Iron Trades Insurance Company 1998; Solicitor, Corries Solicitors 1998-2005; Minster Law: Solicitor 2005-06, Project Manager 2006; Managing Director and Principal Solicitor, Coles Solicitors 2006-; Managing Director, Kingly Solicitors 2019-.

Political career: Contested Redcar 2017 general election. Member for Darlington since 12 December 2019; PPS to Amanda Milling as Minister without Portfolio and Conservative Party Chair 2020-. *Select committees:* Member: Women and Equalities 2020-, Joint Committee on Fixed-Term Parliaments Act 2020-. Chair, Young Conservatives Langbaurgh 1992-95.

Political interests: Hospices, social care, heritage, railways, equality, LGBT issues, defence, architecture; Australia, India, Israel, Spain, USA.

Other: Member, Board of Trustees: Herriot Hospice Homecare 2011-, Newcastle University Students' Union 2012-18, St Michael's Hospice 2019-; Honorary Life Membership, Newcastle University Students Union; Law Society; Association of Personal Injury Lawyers (Emeritus); Thormanby United Charities; Harrogate and District Hospice; Terrence Higgins Trust; Stroke Association; Paul Harris Fellowship, Rotary. Member: Northallerton Mowbray Rotary Club, Easingwold and District Cinematographer Appreciation Society; Aldwark Manor.

Recreations: Dog walking, swimming, walking.

Peter Gibson MP, House of Commons, London SW1A 0AA
Tel: 020 7219 3077 *Email:* peter.gibson.mp@parliament.uk
Constituency: 34 Duke Street, Darlington DL3 7AQ
Tel: 01325 711711 Website: www.petergibson.org *Twitter:* @Gibbo4Darlo

CONSERVATIVE

GIDEON, JO

Stoke-on-Trent Central *(Majority 670)*

PPS to Kwasi Kwarteng as Secretary of State for Business, Energy and Industrial Strategy

Joanna Mary Gideon. Born 7 November 1952; Divorced.

Education: Stourbridge County High School; Lancaster University (Germany, French, Sociology 1973); Sheffield University (German 1975); Birmingham University (BA German 1984); French, German.

Non-political career: Sales Office Manager, Wilkhahn Ltd 1989-91; Founder and Managing Director, Papeterie Ltd 1991-2001; Head of Commercial Enterprise, Canterbury Christ Church University 2002-06; Chief Executive, The Knowledge Hive 2005-; Chair, Academy for Chief Executives 2007-09; Operations Director, Executives Association of Great Britain 2008-10; Director of Fundraising, The ELLA Foundation 2009-11; Co-founder, Futures for Heroes 2012-14; Business Partnerships Manager, Innovation and Enterprise Service, Bedfordshire University 2017; Office of Damian Green MP.

Political career: Contested Scunthorpe 2015 and Great Grimsby 2017 general elections. Member for Stoke-on-Trent Central since 12 December 2019; Department for Business, Energy and Industrial Strategy: Team PPS 2020, PPS to Secretary of State: Alok Sharma 2020-21, Kwasi Kwarteng 2021-. *Councils and public bodies:* Councillor: Thanet District Council 2003-15, Ashford Borough Council 2019-20.

Political interests: Business and enterprise, levelling-up, transport, education and skills, health, police, climate change; Commonwealth, Japan, Middle East, USA.

Other: Business Champion, Myddfai Trading Company Village SOS Programme 2010-11; Fellow, Royal Society of Arts 2005-.

Jo Gideon MP, House of Commons, London SW1A 0AA
Tel: 020 7219 8131 *Email:* jo.gideon.mp@parliament.uk
Constituency: Suite 8, The Forecourt, 12 Albion Street, Hanley, Stoke-on-Trent ST1 1QH
Tel: 01782 497379 Website: jogideon.org *Twitter:* @jogideon

SINN FÉIN

GILDERNEW, MICHELLE

Fermanagh and South Tyrone *(Majority 57)*

Michelle Angela Grainne Gildernew. Born 28 March 1970; Married Jimmy Taggert (2 sons 1 daughter).

Education: St Catherine's College, Armagh; Ulster University, Coleraine.

Non-political career: Sinn Féin: Press officer 1997, Head of London office 1997-98.

Political career: Member for Fermanagh and South Tyrone 2001-15. Contested Fermanagh and South Tyrone 2015 general election. Member for Fermanagh and South Tyrone since 8 June 2017. MLA for Fermanagh and South Tyrone 1998-2012, 2016-17: Sinn Féin Spokesperson for: Social Development, Women's issues, Member, Preparation for Government Committee 2006-07, Minister of Agriculture and Rural Development 2007-11, Sinn Féin Spokesperson for Health 2011-12. Member, Sinn Féin Inter-Party talks team.

Political interests: Housing, rural affairs, education.

Other: Aghaloo GFC.

Michelle Gildernew MP, House of Commons, London SW1A 0AA
Tel: 020 7219 3000 *Email:* michelle.gildernew.mp@parliament.uk
Constituency: 89 Main Street, Clogher, Co Tyrone BT76 0AA
Tel: 028 8556 9250 *Twitter:* @gildernewm

LABOUR/
CO-OPERATIVE

GILL, PREET KAUR

Birmingham, Edgbaston *(Majority 5,614)*

Shadow Secretary of State for International Development

Born 21 November 1972; Married Sureash Singh Chopra 2009 (2 daughters).

Education: University of East London (Degree sociology and social work).

Non-political career: Team manager, Children Young People and Families Directorate, Birmingham City Council 2000-17. Member, Unison.

Political career: Member for Birmingham, Edgbaston since 8 June 2017; Shadow Minister for International Development 2018-20; Shadow Secretary of State for International Development 2020-. *Select committees:* Member, Home Affairs 2017-18. Parliamentary Group, Co-operative Party: Vice-chair -2020, Chair 2020-. *Councils and public bodies:* Sandwell Council: Councillor 2012-18, Cabinet Member for Public Health and Protection 2016-17; Member, West Midlands Combined Authority; Vice-President, Local Government Association 2018-.

Other: Non-executive Director, Spring Social Housing Board; Bank Inspector, Care Quality Commission; Vice-chair, West Midlands Race and Equality Board; Member: Sikh Network, Jo Cox Women In Leadership; Trustee, The Albion Foundation.

Preet Kaur Gill MP, House of Commons, London SW1A 0AA
Tel: 020 7219 2879 *Email:* preet.gill.mp@parliament.uk
Constituency: No constituency office publicised
Tel: 0121-392 8426 Website: www.preetkaurgill.com *Twitter:* @PreetKGillMP

CONSERVATIVE

GILLAN, CHERYL

Chesham and Amersham *(Majority 16,223)*

Cheryl Elise Kendall Gillan. Born 21 April 1952; Daughter of late Major Adam Gillan, company director, and late Mona Gillan; Married John 'Jack' Leeming 1985 (died 2019).

Education: Cheltenham Ladies' College; College of Law; Chartered Institute of Marketing; French.

Non-political career: International Management Group 1977-84; Director, British Film Year 1984-86; Senior marketing consultant, Ernst and Young 1986-91; Marketing director, Kidsons Impey 1991-93; Consultant, PKF 1999-2005.

Political career: Member for Chesham and Amersham 1992-2010, for Chesham and Amersham (revised boundary) since 6 May 2010 general election; PPS to Viscount Cranborne as Leader of the House of Lords and Lord Privy Seal 1994-95; Parliamentary Under-Secretary of State, Department of Education and Employment 1995-97; Shadow Minister for: Trade and Industry 1997-98, Foreign and Commonwealth Affairs 1998-2001, International Development 1998-2001; Opposition Whip 2001-03; Shadow Minister for Home Affairs 2003-05; Shadow Secretary of State for Wales 2005-10; Secretary of State for Wales 2010-12; Member, Speaker's Committee for the Independent Parliamentary Standards Authority 2015-. *Select committees:* Member: Science and Technology 1992-95, Procedure 1994-95, Public Accounts 2003-04, Public Administration 2014-15, Public Administration and Constitutional Affairs 2015-19, Panel of Chairs 2015-, Public Accounts 2020-. 1922 Committee: Vice-chairman 2015-, Acting Co-chairman June-September 2019; Chairman, Conservative Backbench Policy Committee on Business, Innovation and Skills 2015-17. Contested Greater Manchester Central 1989 European Parliament election. Board member, Conservative Party 2018-.

Political interests: Industry, space, international affairs, defence, education, employment; China, Commonwealth, Europe, Hungary, Japan, Pacific Rim, Poland, former Soviet Union, USA.

Other: Member, Executive Committee, Commonwealth Parliamentary Association (CPA) UK Branch 1998-2001: UK Representative British Islands and Mediterranean region 1999-2004, International treasurer 2004-06; Member, NATO Parliamentary Assembly 2003-05; Council of Europe: Member, UK delegation, Parliamentary Assembly 2012-15, 2016-, Vice-President, European Conservative Group 2016-; Chairman, Bow Group 1987-88; Trustee: Parliamentary

Choir 2012-18, House of Commons Members Fund 2016-; Fellow, Chartered Institute of Marketing; Member, Worshipful Company of Marketors; Freedom, City of London; MP of the Year, *Wales Yearbook* awards 2011; PC 2010; DBE 2018. Royal Automobile Club.

Recreations: Golf, music, gardening.

Rt Hon Dame Cheryl Gillan DBE MP, House of Commons, London SW1A 0AA
Tel: 020 7219 4061 *Email:* cheryl.gillan.mp@parliament.uk
Constituency: 7a Hill Avenue, Amersham, Buckinghamshire HP6 5BD
Tel: 01494 721577 *Email:* shawmj@parliament.uk Website: www.cherylgillan.co.uk
Twitter: @CherylGillan

DEMOCRATIC UNIONIST PARTY

GIRVAN, PAUL

South Antrim *(Majority 2,689)*

DUP Spokesperson for Education and Transport

William Paul Girvan. Born 6 July 1963; Son of William and Annie Girvan; Married Mandy Girvan (1 son 1 daughter).

Education: Ballyclare Secondary School; Newtownabbey Technical College; Ulster University.

Non-political career: Director, Grow South Antrim Ltd 2009-15.

Political career: Member for South Antrim since 8 June 2017; DUP Spokesperson for Education and Transport 2017-. *Select committees:* Member: Transport 2017-19, International Trade 2020-. MLA for South Antrim 2003-07, (replacement) 1 July 2010 to 2011, and for South Antrim (revised boundary) 2011-17: Assembly Private Secretary to Peter Robinson as First Minister 2011-15. *Councils and public bodies:* Newtownabbey Borough Council: Councillor 1997-2013, Deputy Mayor 2001-02, Mayor 2002-03, 2003-04; Member: Newtownabbey District Policing Board, Metropolitan Area Plan Advisory Team; Governor, Ballyclare Secondary School.

Political interests: Israel, USA.

Other: Director, Ballyclare Community Concerns; Member, Orange Institution; Chest Heart and Stroke; Action Cancer.

Recreations: Fishing, motorsport, athletics.

Paul Girvan MP, House of Commons, London SW1A 0AA
Tel: 020 7219 3987 *Email:* paul.girvan.mp@parliament.uk
Constituency: 29a The Square, Ballyclare BT39 9BB
Tel: 028 9334 0111 *Twitter:* @PaulGirvanMP

CONSERVATIVE

GLEN, JOHN

Salisbury *(Majority 19,736)*

Economic Secretary (Minister for the City of London), HM Treasury

John Philip Glen. Born 1 April 1974; Son of Philip Glen, nursery man, and Thalia Glen, hairdresser; Married Emma O'Brien 2008 (1 stepson 1 stepdaughter).

Education: King Edward's School, Bath; Mansfield College, Oxford (BA modern history 1996 (JCR President); Judge Institute, Cambridge (MBA 2003); Royal College of Defence Studies, King's College London (MA International Security and Strategy 2015).

Non-political career: Parliamentary researcher to Michael Bates MP and Gary Streeter MP 1996-97; Strategy consultant, Andersen Consulting 1997-2004: Head of political section, Office of William Hague MP as Leader of the Opposition (on secondment) 2000-01; Research Department, Conservative Party: Deputy director 2004-05, Director 2005-06; Senior adviser to global head of strategy, Accenture 2006-10; Director, Walton Bates 2007-11.

Political career: Contested Plymouth Devonport 2001 general election. Member for Salisbury since 6 May 2010 general election; PPS: to Eric Pickles: as Secretary of State for Communities and Local Government 2012-15, as Minister for Faith 2014-15, to Sajid Javid as Secretary of State for Business, Innovation and Skills and President of the Board of Trade 2015-16, to Philip Hammond as Chancellor of the Exchequer 2016-17; Parliamentary Under-Secretary of State for Arts, Heritage and Tourism, Department for Digital, Culture, Media and Sport 2017-18; Economic Secretary (Minister for the City of London), HM Treasury 2018-. *Select committees:* Member: Defence 2010-12, Arms Export Controls 2010-12, Work and Pensions 2015-16.

Member, Number 10 Policy Advisory Board (Home Affairs and Constitution) 2014-15; Parliamentary Chair, Conservative Christian Fellowship 2015-17. *Councils and public bodies:* JP, Westminster 2006-12.

Political interests: Policy development, youth issues, armed forces, foreign affairs, education, health; Maldives, Uganda, USA.

Other: Board member, Centre for Policy Studies 2009-10. Pratts.

Recreations: Church, family, eating out, friends.

John Glen MP, House of Commons, London SW1A 0AA
Tel: 020 7219 2675 *Fax:* 020 7219 3951 *Email:* john.glen.mp@parliament.uk
Constituency: The Morrison Hall, 12 Brown Street, Salisbury, Wiltshire SP1 1HE
Tel: 01722 323050 Website: www.johnglen.org.uk *Twitter:* @JohnGlenUK

LABOUR

GLINDON, MARY

North Tyneside *(Majority 9,561)*

Opposition Whip

Mary Theresa Glindon. Born 13 January 1957; Daughter of Margaret and Cecil Mulgrove; Married Raymond Glindon 2000 (1 daughter 1 stepson 1 stepdaughter).

Education: Sacred Heart Grammar School, Fenham, Newcastle upon Tyne; Newcastle upon Tyne Polytechnic (BSc sociology 1979).

Non-political career: Clerical officer, civil service 1980-85; Administrator, local government 1987-88; Administrator/community development/manager, Centre for Unemployment 1988-2004; Administrator, NHS call centre 2005; Trainee dispenser, NHS 2005-06; Travel sales adviser, call centre 2006; Sales assistant, department store 2006-08; Administration officer, Department for Work and Pensions and Child Maintenance and Enforcement Commission 2008-10. Member: North Tyneside Trades Union Council, GMB.

Political career: Member for North Tyneside since 6 May 2010 general election; Shadow Minister for Farming and Rural Communities 2016-17; Opposition Whip 2020-. *Select committees:* Member: Environment, Food and Rural Affairs 2010-15, 2020, Unopposed Bills (Panel) 2011-15, Communities and Local Government 2013-15, Transport 2015-16. Member, Labour Party 1990-; Former constituency chair and vice-chair -2010. *Councils and public bodies:* Councillor, North Tyneside Council 1995-2010; Deputy Mayor 1998-99, Mayor 1999-2000.

Political interests: Employment, housing, health, environment, older people's issues; Middle East.

Other: Founding member and treasurer, Battle Hill Community Development Project 1983-; Kettlewell Education Trust; YMCA, Scouts.

Recreations: Travel, history, walking.

Mary Glindon MP, House of Commons, London SW1A 0AA
Tel: 020 7219 3000 *Fax:* 020 7219 3272 *Email:* mary.glindon.mp@parliament.uk
Constituency: Swans Centre For Innovation, Station Road, Wallsend NE28 6HJ
Tel: 0191-234 2493 *Email:* mary.glindon@maryglindonmp.co.uk
Websites: www.northtynesidelabour.co.uk/www.maryglindonmp.co.uk *Twitter:* @GlindonMary

CONSERVATIVE

GOODWILL, ROBERT

Scarborough and Whitby *(Majority 10,270)*

Born 31 December 1956; Son of Robert Goodwill and Joan Goodwill; Married Maureen Short 1987 (2 sons 1 daughter).

Education: Bootham School, York; Newcastle University (BSc agriculture 1979); French, German.

Non-political career: Farmer 1979-; Director, Mowthorpe (UK) Ltd. Member, then branch chairman, National Farmers Union.

Political career: Contested Redcar 1992 and North West Leicestershire 1997 general elections. Member for Scarborough and Whitby since 5 May 2005 general election; Opposition Whip 2006-07; Shadow Minister for Transport 2007-10; Assistant Government Whip 2010-12; Government Whip (Lord Commissioner of HM Treasury) 2012-13; Department for Transport: Parliamentary Under-Secretary of State 2013-15, Minister of State 2015-16; Flooding envoy for Yorkshire 2016-; Minister of State for: Immigration, Home Office 2016-17, Children and Families, Department for Education 2017-18; Minister of State for Agriculture, Fisheries and Food, Department for Environment, Food and Rural Affairs 2019. *Select committees:* Member: Transport 2005-06, Environmental Audit 2018-19, 2020-, Northern Ireland Affairs 2018-19, 2020-, Joint Committee on Fixed-Term Parliaments Act 2020-. European Parliament: Contested Cleveland and Richmond 1994 and Yorkshire (South) 1998 elections; MEP for Yorkshire and the Humber 1999-2004: Deputy Conservative leader 2003-04.

Political interests: Agriculture, fisheries, environment, transport; Belarus, Moldova, Ukraine.

Other: Substitute Member, UK Delegation to Parliamentary Assembly of Council of Europe 2018-19; Patron, National Traction Engine Trust; PC 2018. Farmers' Club.

Recreations: Steam ploughing, travel.

Rt Hon Robert Goodwill MP, House of Commons, London SW1A 0AA
Tel: 020 7219 8268 *Email:* robert.goodwill.mp@parliament.uk
Constituency: 6 Albemarle Crescent, Scarborough, North Yorkshire YO11 1XS
Tel: 01723 365656 Website: www.robertgoodwill.co.uk

CONSERVATIVE

GOVE, MICHAEL

Surrey Heath *(Majority 18,349)*

Chancellor of the Duchy of Lancaster and Minister for the Cabinet Office

Michael Andrew Gove. Born 26 August 1967; Son of Ernest and Christine Gove; Married Sarah Vine 2001 (1 daughter 1 son).

Education: Robert Gordon's College, Aberdeen; Lady Margaret Hall, Oxford (BA English 1988).

Non-political career: Reporter, *Press and Journal*, Aberdeen 1989; Researcher/reporter, Scottish Television 1990-91; Reporter, BBC News and Current Affairs 1991-96; *The Times*: Writer and editor 1996-2005, Writer 2005-. National Union of Journalists 1989-.

Political career: Member for Surrey Heath since 5 May 2005 general election; Shadow Minister for Housing 2005-07; Shadow Secretary of State for Children, Schools and Families 2007-10; Secretary of State for Education 2010-14; Parliamentary Secretary to the Treasury; Chief Whip 2014-15; Member, Parliamentary and Political Service Honours Committee 2014-15; Lord Chancellor and Secretary of State for Justice 2015-16; Secretary of State for Environment, Food and Rural Affairs 2017-19; Cabinet Office: Chancellor of the Duchy of Lancaster 2019-, Minister for the Cabinet Office 2020-; Member, Speaker's Committee on the Electoral Commission 2020-. *Select committees:* Member: European Scrutiny 2005-07, Exiting the European Union 2016-17.

Political interests: Education, crime, terrorism; Canada, Colombia, Germany, Indonesia, Iraq, Ireland, Israel, Italy, Jordan, Poland, Vietnam.

Other: Member, Education, Youth, Culture and Sport Council, Council of the European Union 2010-14; Chair, Policy Exchange 2003-05; President, Industry and Parliament Trust 2015-16; Co-convenor, Campaign Committee, Vote Leave 2016; Founding supporter, Change Britain 2016-; Public speaker, London Speaker Bureau and Chartwell Speakers 2016-; Member, Advisory Board, Red Tape Initiative 2017; Minister of the Year, *Spectator* awards 2011; PC 2010. Garrick Club.

Publications: Michael Portillo – The Future of the Right (Fourth Estate, 1995); The Price of Peace (CPS, 2000); Celsius 7/7 (Weidenfeld-Nicolson, 2005).

Rt Hon Michael Gove MP, House of Commons, London SW1A 0AA
Tel: 020 7219 3000 *Fax:* 020 7219 4829 *Email:* michael.gove.mp@parliament.uk
Constituency: Curzon House, Church Road, Windlesham, Surrey GU20 6BH
Tel: 01276 472468 *Email:* office@shca.org.uk Website: www.michaelgove.com
Twitter: @michaelgove

SCOTTISH NATIONAL PARTY

GRADY, PATRICK

Glasgow North *(Majority 5,601)*

SNP Chief Whip

Patrick John Grady. Born 5 February 1980.

Education: Inverness Royal Academy; Strathclyde University (BA history 2000).

Non-political career: President, University of Strathclyde Students' Association 2001-02; Scottish Catholic International Aid Fund: Campaigns officer 2002-04, Advocacy Manager 2011-15; Countryside Campaigns Manager, Ramblers' Association 2005-07; Parliamentary Assistant to Jamie Hepburn MSP and Aileen Campbell MSP 2007-11.

Political career: Contested Glasgow North 2010 general election. Member for Glasgow North since 7 May 2015 general election; SNP: Spokesperson for International Development 2015-17, Chief Whip 2017-. *Select committees:* Member: Procedure 2015-17, Selection 2017-20, Joint Committee on Statutory Instruments 2017-19, Joint Committee on Consolidation, &c, Bills 2017-19, Administration 2017-18, European Statutory Instruments 2018-19. National Secretary, Federation of Student Nationalists 2000-01; Convener, Glasgow Kelvin Constituency Association 2008-11, SNP National Secretary 2012-16.

Political interests: International development, international relations, climate change, transport, arts and creative industries, youth empowerment.

Other: Member, Executive Committee, Commonwealth Parliamentary Association United Kingdom 2015-17; Governor, Westminster Foundation for Democracy.

Recreations: Swimming, hill-walking, reading, music.

Patrick Grady MP, House of Commons, London SW1A 0AA
Tel: 020 7219 6398 *Email:* patrick.grady.mp@parliament.uk
Constituency: Suite 1, Firhill Business Centre, 76 Firhill Road, Glasgow G20 7BA
Tel: 0141-946 3062 Website: www.patrickgrady.scot *Twitter:* @GradySNP

CONSERVATIVE

GRAHAM, RICHARD

Gloucester *(Majority 10,277)*

Richard Michael John Ogilvie Graham. Born 4 April 1958; Married Anthea 1989 (1 daughter 2 sons).

Education: Christ Church College, Oxford (BA history 1979); Certificate Investment Management (IMC) 1998; Bahasa Indonesia, Mandarin, Cantonese, French, Malay, Swahili, Tagalog.

Non-political career: Airline Manager, Cathay Pacific Airways and John Swire & Sons 1980-86; Diplomat, HM Diplomatic Service 1986-92: First Secretary: British High Commission, Nairobi, British Embassy, Beijing 1989-92; Trade Commissioner, China, HM Consul, Macau; Investment manager 1992-2009: Director, Greater China Fund Inc 1994-2004, Baring Asset Management: Director 1995-2010, Head of Institutional and International Business. Cadet Pilot, Oxford University Air Squadron RAFVR 1977-78.

Political career: Member for Gloucester since 6 May 2010 general election; PPS to: Lord Howell of Guildford as Minister of State and Government Spokesperson, Foreign and Commonwealth Office 2010-12, Hugo Swire as Minister of State, Foreign and Commonwealth Office 2012-14; Trade Envoy to: Indonesia 2012-, ASEAN Economic Community 2015-, Philippines and Malaysia 2016-. *Select committees:* Member: Work and Pensions 2010, 2015-17, Exiting the European Union 2017-19, Joint Committee on the National Security Strategy 2020-. Chairman, Conservative Backbench Policy Committee on Foreign and Commonwealth 2015-17. Contested South West England 2004 European Parliament election. Elected Member, Conservative Party Board 2020-. *Councils and public bodies:* Cotswold District Council: Councillor 2003-07, Chair, Overview and Scrutiny Committee.

Political interests: Keep calm and carry on regenerating.

Other: Chair, British Chamber of Commerce, Shanghai; Vice-chair, Board of Airline Representatives in the Philippines; Former member, executive council, China-Britain Business Council; Chair, Pensions Group, International Financial Services Ltd, London; Director, Great Britain China Centre 2010-18; Chair, Westminster Foundation for Democracy 2018-; Chair and Trustee, Gloucester History Trust; Trustee, Parliamentary Contributory Pension Fund. Gloucester Cricket Club; Marylebone Cricket Club; Lords and Commons Cricket Club.

Recreations: Cricket, squash, tennis, walking, heritage.

Richard Graham MP, House of Commons, London SW1A 0AA
Tel: 020 7219 7077 *Email:* richard.graham.mp@parliament.uk
Constituency: Second Floor, St Peters House, 2 College Street, Gloucester, Gloucestershire GL1 2NE
Tel: 01452 501167 Website: www.richardgraham.org *Twitter:* @RichardGrahamUK

CONSERVATIVE

GRANT, HELEN

Maidstone and The Weald *(Majority 21,772)*

Born 28 September 1961; Daughter of Dr Gladys Spedding and Dr Julius Okuboye, both retired; Married Simon Grant 1991 (2 sons).

Education: St Aidans Comprehensive School, Carlisle; Trinity Comprehensive School, Carlisle; Hull University (LLB 1982); College of Law, Guildford (Solicitors Finals 1984).

Non-political career: Articled clerk, Cartmell Mawson & Maine, Carlisle 1985-87; Assistant solicitor, Hempsons, London 1987-88; Fayers & Co, London: Associate solicitor 1988-92, Equity partner 1992-94; Maternity sabbatical 1994-95; Consultant solicitor, T G Baynes & Co, Kent 1995-96; Senior partner/owner, Grants Solicitors LLP 1996-2013.

Political career: Member for Maidstone and The Weald since 6 May 2010 general election; Parliamentary Under-Secretary of State: (Women and Equalities), Department for Culture, Media and Sport and Ministry of Justice 2012-13, (Minister for Victims and the Courts), Ministry of Justice 2012-13, Department for Culture, Media and Sport: (Sport and Tourism) 2013-15, (Equalities) 2013-14; Trade Envoy to Nigeria 2020-; UK's Special Envoy on Girls' Education 2021-. *Select committees:* Member: Justice 2010-11, International Development 2015-16, Arms Export Controls 2016, Work of the Independent Commission for Aid Impact Sub-committee 2015-16. Member, Labour Party 2004-05; Conservative Party: Member 2006-, Deputy Chair, diversity group, Croydon Central and Croydon South Conservative Federation 2006-08, Special adviser to Oliver Letwin MP as Chair of Party Policy Review 2006-10; Member: Social Mobility Task Force 2007-08, Society of Conservative Lawyers, Conservative Party: Vice-chairman (Communities) 2018-19, Vice-chairman 2019-. *Councils and public bodies:* Non-executive director, Croydon NHS Primary Care Trust 2005-07; Chair, Apprenticeship Diversity Champions Network 2017-.

Political interests: Justice, business and enterprise, women, children and families, social mobility, sport, tourism, gambling, First World War commemorations, international development, equalities; Chagos Islands/Diego Garcia, India, Maldives, Nigeria, Sri Lanka, USA.

Other: Hon Vice-president, MENCAP Trust, Maidstone; Co-president, Maidstone Operatic Society; Centre for Social Justice: Member, Family Division Policy Group 2006-08, Member, Family Law Reform Commission 2007-08; President, Maidstone Museums Foundation 2008-17; Patron, Women in Racing 2015-; Trustee: Human Trafficking Foundation 2016-18, Social Mobility Foundation 2016-; Non-executive director, Cell Therapy Limited 2017-18; Law Society: Member 1985-2013, Resolution 1997-2010, Family Law Panel 2000-12, Equalities and Diversities Committee 2008-09; National Osteoporosis Society Maidstone, Advocacy After Fatal Domestic Abuse; Asian Voice Minister of the Year 2014.

Publications: State of the Nation/Fractured Families (Centre for Social Justice, 2006); Breakthrough Britain (Centre for Social Justice, 2007); Every Family Matters (Centre for Social Justice, 2009).

Recreations: Tennis, movies, family life, sporting events.

Helen Grant MP, House of Commons, London SW1A 0AA
Tel: 020 7219 7107 *Email:* helen.grant.mp@parliament.uk
Constituency: First Floor, 109/111 Week Street, Maidstone, Kent ME14 1RB
Website: www.helengrant.org *Twitter:* @HelenGrantMP

SCOTTISH NATIONAL PARTY

GRANT, PETER

Glenrothes *(Majority 11,757)*

SNP Shadow Chief Secretary to the Treasury

Born 12 October 1960; Married Fiona 1984.

Education: Glasgow University.

Non-political career: Physics teacher in Lanarkshire and Fife; Accountant; Senior local government and NHS finance roles.

Political career: Contested Glenrothes 6 November 2008 by-election. Member for Glenrothes since 7 May 2015 general election; SNP: Spokesperson for: Europe 2017-18, Exiting the European Union 2018-19, Shadow Chief Secretary to the Treasury 2020-; Member, Public Accounts Commission 2020-. *Select committees:* Member: European Scrutiny 2015-16, Joint Committee on Consolidation, &c, Bills 2015-17, Exiting the European Union 2016-19, Public Accounts 2020-. Scottish National Party: Member 1987-, SNP Westminster Parliamentary Group Treasurer 2016-. *Councils and public bodies:* Fife Council: Councillor 1992-2015, Council Leader 2007-12, SNP Group Leader 2007-15.

Political interests: Welfare, anti-austerity, child poverty.

Other: Member, UK Delegation, Organisation for Security and Co-operation in Europe Parliamentary Assembly 2015-19; Member, Chartered Institute of Public Finance and Accountancy. Member, Leslie Bowling Club.

Recreations: Traditional Scottish music, bowls.

Peter Grant MP, House of Commons, London SW1A 0AA
Tel: 020 7219 6340 *Email:* peter.grant.mp@parliament.uk
Constituency: Castleblair Business Centre, Fullerton Road, Glenrothes KY7 5QR
Tel: 01592 759335 Website: www.petergrant.scot *Twitter:* @PeterGrantMP

CONSERVATIVE

GRAY, JAMES

North Wiltshire *(Majority 17,626)*

James Whiteside Gray. Born 7 November 1954; Son of late Very Revd John R. Gray, Moderator of General Assembly of Church of Scotland, and Dr Sheila Gray; Married Sarah Ann Beale 1980 (divorced) (2 sons 1 daughter); married Mrs Philippa Mayo 2009 (1 stepson 2 stepdaughters).

Education: Glasgow High School; Glasgow University (MA history 1975); Christ Church, Oxford (history thesis 1975-77); French.

Non-political career: Management trainee, P&O 1977-78; Anderson Hughes & Co Ltd (Shipbrokers) 1978-84; Baltic Exchange: Member 1978-91, Pro Bono Member 1997-; Managing director, GNI Freight Futures Ltd, Senior Manager, GNI Ltd (Futures Brokers) 1984-92; Special adviser to Secretaries of State for Environment: Michael Howard MP 1992-93, John Gummer MP 1993-95; Director, Westminster Strategy 1995-96. Honourable Artillery Company (TA) 1978-84; Armed Forces Parliamentary Scheme (Army): Member 1998, Post-Graduate Scheme 2000, Chair 2013-; Member, HAC Court of Assistants 2002-07; Royal College of Defence Studies 2003. Union of Country Sports Workers.

Political career: Contested Ross, Cromarty and Skye 1992 general election. Member for North Wiltshire 1997-2010, for North Wiltshire (revised boundary) since 6 May 2010 general election; Opposition Whip 2000-01; Opposition Spokesman for Defence 2001-02; Shadow Minister for: Environment, Food and Rural Affairs 2002-03, Environment and Transport 2003-05; Shadow Secretary of State for Scotland May 2005. *Select committees:* Member: Environment, Transport and Regional Affairs 1997-2000, Broadcasting 2001-03, Regulatory Reform 2005-10, Environment, Food and Rural Affairs 2007-10, Chairmen's Panel/Panel of Chairs 2010-, Finance and Services 2010-13, Procedure 2010-15, 2020-, Defence 2013-17, Arms Export Controls 2014-15, Administration 2015-17, Joint Committee on the National Security Strategy 2017-19, Environmental Audit 2018-19. Chairman: Conservative Rural Affairs Group 2003-04, Conservative Backbench Policy Committee on Defence 2018-19. Deputy Chair, Wandsworth Tooting Conservative Association 1994-96; Board Member, Conservative Party South West 2010-.

Political interests: Countryside, agriculture, defence, environment, foreign affairs, polar affairs; Afghanistan, America, Arctic, Antarctica, China, Mongolia, Nepal, Russia, Sri Lanka.

Other: Parliamentary delegate to Council of Europe and Western European Union 2007-10; Member, UK delegation to NATO Parliamentary Assembly 2015-19; Vice-president, HAC Saddle Club; Former president: North Wiltshire Multiple Sclerosis Society, Association of British Riding Schools; Younger Brother, Trinity House; Fellow, Royal Geographical Society; Member, Honourable Artillery Company; Freedom, City of London 1978; Visiting Parliamentary Fellow, St Anthony's College, Oxford. President, Chippenham Constitutional Club 2000-, Wootton Bassett Conservative Club, Pratt's Club; Member, Avon Vale Foxhounds.

Publications: Financial Risk Management in the Shipping Industry (1985); Futures and Options for Shipping (1987) (Lloyds of London Book Prize winner); Shipping Futures (1990); Crown v Parliament: Who decides on Going to War (2003); Poles Apart (2013); Who Takes Britain to War? (2014); Full English Brexit (2018).

Recreations: Riding horses, heritage and local history.

James Gray MP, House of Commons, London SW1A 0AA
Tel: 020 7219 6237 *Email:* jamesgraymp@parliament.uk
Constituency: No constituency office publicised
Twitter: @Jgray

SCOTTISH NATIONAL PARTY

GRAY, NEIL

Airdrie and Shotts *(Majority 5,201)*

Co-ordinator, SNP Inclusion and Wellbeing Policy Group

Neil Charles Gray. Born 16 March 1986; Married (1 daughter 1 son).

Education: Kirkwall Grammar School; Stirling University (BA politics and journalism 2008).

Non-political career: Represented Scotland in 400m athletics; Contract producer and reporter, BBC Radio Orkney 2003-08; Press and research intern, SNP Press Office 2008; Office of Alex Neil MSP 2008-15: Constituency office manager 2011-15.

Political career: Member for Airdrie and Shotts since 7 May 2015 general election; SNP: Spokesperson for: Fair Work and Employment 2015-17, Social Justice 2017-18, Spokesperson/Shadow Secretary of State for Work and Pensions 2018-21, Co-ordinator, SNP Inclusion and Wellbeing Policy Group 2021-. *Select committees:* Member: Joint Committee on the Palace of Westminster 2015-16, Finance 2015-19, Joint Committee on the Draft Parliamentary Buildings (Restoration and Renewal) Bill 2018-19. *Councils and public bodies:* Board member, Shadow Sponsor Body for the Houses of Parliament Restoration and Renewal Programme 2018-20.

Recreations: Running (completed an ultra marathon in 2013).

Neil Gray MP, House of Commons, London SW1A 0AA
Tel: 020 7219 8787 *Email:* neil.gray.mp@parliament.uk
Constituency: Office 15, Airdrie Business Centre, 1 Chapel Lane, Airdrie ML6 6GX
Tel: 01236 439630
Shotts Healthy Living Centre, Kirk Road, Shotts ML7 5ET
Tel: 01501 821821 *Twitter:* @neilgraysnp

CONSERVATIVE

GRAYLING, CHRIS

Epsom and Ewell *(Majority 17,873)*

Christopher Stephen Grayling. Born 1 April 1962; Son of John and Elizabeth Grayling; Married Susan Dillistone 1987 (1 son 1 daughter).

Education: Royal Grammar School, High Wycombe; Sidney Sussex College, Cambridge (BA history 1984); French.

Non-political career: BBC News: Trainee 1985-86, Producer 1986-88; Programme editor, *Business Daily*, Channel 4 1988-91; Business development manager, BBC Select 1991-93; Director: Charterhouse Prods Ltd 1993, Workhouse Ltd 1993-95, SSVC Group 1995-97; Change consultant and European marketing director, Burson Marsteller 1997-2001.

Political career: Contested Warrington South 1997 general election. Member for Epsom and Ewell 2001-10, for Epsom and Ewell (revised boundary) since 6 May 2010 general election; Opposition Whip 2002; Shadow Spokesperson for Health 2002-03; Shadow Minister for: Public Services, Health and Education 2003-04, Higher Education 2004-05, Health 2005; Shadow Leader of the House of Commons 2005; Member, House of Commons Commission 2005, 2015-16; Shadow Secretary of State for: Transport 2005-07, Work and Pensions

2007-09; Shadow Home Secretary 2009-10; Minister of State for Employment, Department for Work and Pensions 2010-12; Lord Chancellor and Secretary of State for Justice 2012-15; Leader of the House of Commons 2015-16; Lord President of the Council 2015-16; Member: Public Accounts Commission 2015-16, Speaker's Committee on the Electoral Commission 2015, Speaker's Committee for the Independent Parliamentary Standards Authority 2015-16; Secretary of State for Transport 2016-19; Member, Intelligence and Security Committee of Parliament 2020. *Select committees:* Member: Transport, Local Government and the Regions 2001-02, Transport, Local Government and the Regions (Transport Sub-Committee) 2001-02, Transport, Local Government and the Regions (Urban Affairs Sub-Committee) 2001-02, Transport 2002, Modernisation of the House of Commons 2005-06; Joint Committee on the Palace of Westminster: Member 2015, Chair 2015-16. *Councils and public bodies:* Councillor, London Borough of Merton 1998-2002.

Political interests: Transport, welfare reform, pensions, home affairs.

Other: Member, Corporation of Merton College 1999-2001; Chair, Epsom Victim Support 2001-07; President, Industry and Parliament Trust 2012-15; Member, Campaign committee, Vote Leave 2016; Patron: Forces Childrens Trust, Nork Music in the Park; Strategic Adviser to the Board, Hutchison Ports Europe 2020-; PC 2010.

Publications: The Bridgwater Heritage (1983); A Land Fit for Heroes (1985); Co-author, Just Another Star? (1987).

Recreations: Golf, cricket, football.

Rt Hon Chris Grayling MP, House of Commons, London SW1A 0AA
Tel: 020 7219 8194 *Email:* chris.grayling.mp@parliament.uk
Constituency: PO Box 164, Ashtead, Surrey KT21 9BS
Tel: 01372 271036 Website: www.chrisgrayling.net

CONSERVATIVE

GREEN, CHRIS

Bolton West *(Majority 8,855)*

Christopher James Green. Born 12 August 1973.

Political career: Contested Manchester Withington 2010 general election. Member for Bolton West since 7 May 2015 general election; Team PPS: Department for Transport 2018, Department for Education 2019; PPS to Baroness Evans of Bowes Park as Leader of the House of Lords and Lord Privy Seal 2020. *Select committees:* Member: Science and Technology 2015-17, Work and Pensions 2017-18, Home Affairs 2018-19.

Political interests: Investment in science and manufacturing, education, infrastructure, transport, apprenticeships, Brexit, technology, welfare, health.

Chris Green MP, House of Commons, London SW1A 0AA
Tel: 020 7219 8685 *Email:* chris.green.mp@parliament.uk
Constituency: 15 Market Street, Westhoughton BL5 3AH
Tel: 01942 409132 *Email:* chris@chris-green.org.uk Website: www.chris-green.org.uk
Twitter: @CGreenUK

CONSERVATIVE

GREEN, DAMIAN

Ashford *(Majority 24,029)*

Damian Howard Green. Born 17 January 1956; Son of late Howard Green and late Audrey Green; Married Alicia Collinson 1988 (2 daughters).

Education: Reading School; Balliol College, Oxford (BA philosophy, politics and economics 1977, MA) (President, Oxford Union 1977); French.

Non-political career: Financial journalist, BBC Radio 1978-82; *Channel 4 News*: Business producer 1982-84, Business editor 1985-87; News editor, business news, *The Times* 1984-85; Programme presenter and city editor, *Business Daily* 1987-92; Special adviser, Prime Minister's Policy Unit 1992-94; Self-employed public affairs consultant 1995-97.

Political career: Contested Brent East 1992 general election. Member for Ashford 1997-2010, for Ashford (revised boundary) since 6 May 2010 general election; Opposition Spokesperson for: Education and Employment 1998-99, Environment 1999-2001; Shadow Secretary of State for: Education and Skills 2001-03, Transport 2003-04; Shadow Minister for Immigration 2005-10; Minister of State for: Immigration, Home Office 2010-12, Policing, Criminal Justice and Victims, Home Office and Ministry of Justice 2012-14; Secretary of State for Work and Pensions 2016-17; First Secretary of State and Minister for the Cabinet Office 2017. *Select* *committees:* Member: Culture, Media and Sport 1997-98, Procedure 1997-98, Home Affairs 2004-05, Treasury 2005-06, European Scrutiny 2015-16, Joint Committee on the National Security Strategy 2015-16, Digital, Culture, Media and Sport 2020-. Chairman, Conservative Education Policy Committee 2001-03; Member, Executive, 1922 Committee 2004-05, 2014-15; Chairman, Conservative Backbench Policy Committee on Education 2015-16. Vice-President, Tory Reform Group 1997-; Chair: Conservative Parliamentary Mainstream Group 2003-10, European Mainstream 2014-16.

Political interests: Economic policy, foreign affairs, media, education, employment, rural affairs; France, Georgia, Italy, Moldova.

Other: President, Find a Voice; Trustee, Godinton House Preservation Trust; Board member, Britain Stronger in Europe 2015-16; PC 2012.

Publications: ITN Budget Fact Book (1984, 1985, 1986); A Better BBC (1990); The Cross-Media Revolution (1995); Communities in the Countryside (1996); Regulating the Media in the Digital Age (1997); 21st Century Conservatism (1998); The Four Failures of the New Deal (1999); Better Learning (2002); More than Markets (2003); Co-author, Controlling Economic Migration (2006); Fixing the Care Crisis (2019).

Recreations: Football, cricket, opera, cinema.

Rt Hon Damian Green MP, House of Commons, London SW1A 0AA
Tel: 020 7219 3911 *Email:* damian.green.mp@parliament.uk
Constituency: c/o Hardy House, The Street, Bethersden, Ashford, Kent TN26 3AG
Tel: 01233 820911 *Email:* ashfordconservatives@btconnect.com
Website: www.damiangreen.co.uk *Twitter:* @DamianGreen

House of Commons MPs' Biographies

LABOUR

GREEN, KATE

Stretford and Urmston *(Majority 16,417)*

Shadow Secretary of State for Education

Katherine Anne Green. Born 2 May 1960; Divorced.

Education: Currie High School; Edinburgh University (LLB 1982).

Non-political career: Various roles, Barclays Bank 1982-97; Whitehall and Industry Group (on secondment), Home Office 1997-99; Director, National Council for One Parent Families 2000-04; Chief executive, Child Poverty Action Group 2004-09. Member: Unite 2000-, GMB 2009-, USDAW 2009-.

Political career: Contested Cities of London and Westminster 1997 general election. Member for Stretford and Urmston since 6 May 2010 general election; Shadow Minister for: Equalities Office 2011-13, Disabled People 2013-15, Women and Equalities (attending Shadow Cabinet) 2015-16; Member, Speaker's Committee for the Independent Parliamentary Standards Authority 2018-20; Shadow Minister for Work and Pensions (Child Poverty Strategy) 2020; Shadow Secretary of State for Education 2020-. *Select committees:* Member: Work and Pensions 2010-11, European Scrutiny 2016-19, Justice 2016-17; Privileges: Member 2017-18, Chair 2018-20; Standards: Member 2017-18, Chair 2018-20; Member: Home Affairs 2018-19, Liaison 2018-20. Chair, PLP Departmental Group for Women 2011. Member, Labour Party 1990-; Chair, Owen Smith's Labour leadership campaign 2016. *Councils and public bodies:* Magistrate, City of London 1993-2009; Member, National Employment Panel 2001-07; Member, then Chair, London Child Poverty Commission 2006-09; Member, Greater Manchester Poverty Commission 2011-.

Political interests: Employment, exclusion, poverty, criminal justice; United Kingdom.

Other: Trustee: Avenues Youth Project 1998-2003, End Child Poverty 2000-09, Family and Parenting Institute 2000-07, Institute for Fiscal Studies 2006-09; Member, Fawcett Society 2006-; Trustee, Friends Provident Foundation 2007-09; Fabian Society: Member 2009-, Chair 2016-; Trustee, Webb Memorial Trust 2010-; Freedom, City of London; OBE 2005.

Kate Green OBE MP, House of Commons, London SW1A 0AA
Tel: 020 7219 7162 *Fax:* 020 7219 4561 *Email:* kate.green.mp@parliament.uk
Constituency: Stretford Public Hall, Chester Road, Stretford M32 0LG
Tel: 0161-749 9120 Website: www.kategreen.org *Twitter:* @KateGreenSU

LABOUR

GREENWOOD, LILIAN

Nottingham South *(Majority 12,568)*

Chair, Select Committee on Finance

Lilian Rachel Greenwood. Born 26 March 1966; Daughter of Harry Greenwood, lecturer, and Patricia Greenwood, typist; Married Ravi Subramanian 2008 (3 daughters).

Education: Canon Slade, Bolton; St Catharine's College, Cambridge (BA economics and social and political science 1987); Southbank University, London (MSc sociology and social policy 1991).

Non-political career: Research officer: Local Authority Conditions of Service Advisory Board 1988-89, Civil and Public Services Association 1989-92; Trade union organiser, latterly regional head of campaigns and policy, Unison 1992-2010. Member: NALGO 1988-89, GMB 1989-92, NUPE/Unison 1992-.

Political career: Member for Nottingham South since 6 May 2010 general election; Opposition Assistant Whip 2010-11; Shadow Minister for Transport 2011-15; Shadow Secretary of State for Transport 2015-16. *Select committees:* Transport: Member 2010, Chair 2017-19; Member: Regulatory Reform 2010-15, Education 2016-17, Liaison 2017-19, 2020-, National Policy Statements Sub-committee 2017-19, Transport 2020-; Chair, Finance 2020-; Member, Parliamentary Works Estimates Commission 2020-. Chair, PLP Department Group for Transport 2020-. Member, Co-operative Party.

Political interests: Transport, employment rights, pensions; Kashmir.

Other: Member: Fabian Society, Compass 2007-. Holme Pierrepont Running Club.

Recreations: Running, walking, cinema, reading.

Lilian Greenwood MP, House of Commons, London SW1A 0AA
Tel: 020 7219 7122 *Email:* lilian.greenwood.mp@parliament.uk
Constituency: First Floor, 12 Regent Street, Nottingham, Nottinghamshire NG1 5BQ
Tel: 0115-711 7000 Website: www.liliangreenwood.co.uk *Twitter:* @LilianGreenwood

LABOUR

GREENWOOD, MARGARET

Wirral West *(Majority 3,003)*

Born 14 March 1959.

Non-political career: Former English teacher in secondary schools, FE colleges and adult education centres, Liverpool and Wirral; Travel writer; Web consultant. Unite.

Political career: Member for Wirral West since 7 May 2015 general election; PPS to Owen Smith as Shadow Secretary of State for Work and Pensions 2015-16; Shadow Minister for Work and Pensions (Employment and Inequalities) 2016-18; Shadow Secretary of State for Work and Pensions 2018-20; Shadow Minister for Education (Schools) 2020. *Select committees:* Member, Environmental Audit 2015-16.

Other: Founding member, Defend our NHS.

Recreations: Hill-walking, theatre, music, painting.

Margaret Greenwood MP, House of Commons, London SW1A 0AA
Tel: 020 7219 4608 *Email:* margaret.greenwood.mp@parliament.uk
Constituency: Hilbre House, 35a Market Street, Hoylake, Wirral CH47 2BG
Tel: 0151-792 3416 Website: www.margaretgreenwood.org.uk *Twitter:* @MGreenwoodWW

CONSERVATIVE

GRIFFITH, ANDREW

Arundel and South Downs *(Majority 22,521)*

Andrew John Griffith. Born 23 February 1971; Married Barbara Tippett 1997 (1 son 1 daughter).

Education: St Mary's and St Joseph's RC School, Sidcup, Kent; Nottingham University (BA law 1992).

Non-political career: Corporate Finance Manager, Price Waterhouse Coopers 1992-96; Investment Banker, N M Rothschild and Sons Ltd 1996-99; Sky: Executive 1999-2008, Chief Financial Officer 2008-16, Chief Operating Officer 2016-19; Chief Business Adviser (Political) to Boris Johnson as Prime Minister 2019.

Political career: Contested Corby 2001 and 2005 general elections. Member for Arundel and South Downs since 12 December 2019; UK Net Zero Business Champion 2020-. *Select committees:* Member: Procedure 2020-21, Science and Technology 2020-. Chair: Nottingham University Conservative Association 1991-92, Greater London Young Conservatives 1994-95; National Chair, Young Conservatives 1997-98; Member, National Union Executive Committee 1996-98.

Political interests: Ageing and care and respect for the elderly, automotive industry and electric vehicles/green mobility, aviation and aerospace, broadband and telecommunications, broadcasting and media, business, enterprise and industrial strategy, countryside and rural affairs, Dark Skies campaign, farming, government, internet and e-commerce, rural economy, rural transport, science and technology.

Other: Non-executive Director, Just Eat 2014-19; ICAEW 1996; Patron, Science Museum.

Andrew Griffith MP, House of Commons, London SW1A 0AA
Tel: 020 7219 4557 *Email:* andrew.griffith.mp@parliament.uk
Constituency: No constituency office publicised
Email: andrew@griffithmp.com Website: www.andrewgriffithmp.com *Twitter:* @griffitha

LABOUR

GRIFFITH, NIA

Llanelli *(Majority 4,670)*

Shadow Secretary of State for Wales

Nia Rhiannon Griffith. Born 4 December 1956; Daughter of Prof T Gwynfor Griffith, professor of Italian and member of Gorsedd of Bards, and Dr Rhiannon Griffith, née Howell, medical doctor; Married Richard Leggett 1982 (divorced) (no children).

Education: Newland High School, Hull; Somerville College, Oxford (BA modern languages 1979); University College of North Wales, Bangor (PGCE 1980); French, Italian, Spanish, Welsh.

Non-political career: Language teacher 1980-92, 1997-2005; Education adviser 1992-97, Estyn schools inspector 1992-97; Head of modern languages, Morriston Comprehensive School, Swansea 1997-2005; Chair, Carmarthenshire Youth Project 1998-2005. National Union of Teachers; USDAW.

Political career: Member for Llanelli since 5 May 2005 general election; PPS: at Department for Environment, Food and Rural Affairs 2007-08, to Harriet Harman: as Minister for Women and Equality 2008-10, as Acting Leader of the Opposition 2010; Shadow Minister for: Business, Innovation and Skills 2010-11, Wales 2011-15; Shadow Secretary of State for: Wales 2015-16, 2020-, Defence 2016-20. *Select committees:* Member: European Scrutiny 2005-07, 2010-15, Welsh Affairs 2005-10, 2011-15, Joint Committee on Human Rights 2006-07, Joint Committee on the Draft Climate Change Bill 2007. Chair: PLP Welsh Regional Group 2007-08, PLP Departmental Group for Environment, Food and Rural Affairs 2010; Vice-chair, PLP Departmental Group for Energy and Climate Change 2010. Secretary, Carmarthenshire County Labour Party 1994-99, 2004-05; Chair, Carmarthen West and South Pembrokeshire CLP 1999-2000; Patron, LGBT Labour. *Councils and public bodies:* Carmarthen Town Council: Councillor 1987-99, Sheriff 1997, Deputy mayor 1998.

Political interests: Defence, environment, Europe, industry, energy, equalities; France, Italy, Spain.

Publications: Co-author Ciao BK3 Italian textbook (Nelson, 1990); 100 ideas for teaching languages (Continuum Press, 2005).

Recreations: Arts, European cinema, music, cycling.

Nia Griffith MP, House of Commons, London SW1A 0AA
Tel: 020 7219 3410 *Email:* nia.griffith.mp@parliament.uk
Constituency: 43 Pottery Street, Llanelli SA15 1SU
Tel: 01554 756374 Website: niagriffith.org.uk *Twitter:* @NiaGriffithMP

CONSERVATIVE

GRIFFITHS, KATE
Burton *(Majority 14,496)*

Kate Elizabeth Griffiths. Married Andrew Griffiths, former MP for Burton (divorced) (1 daughter).

Education: Derby High School; Exeter University (classics).

Non-political career: Corporate Hospitality Co-ordinator, Burton Albion Football Club.

Political career: Member for Burton since 12 December 2019.

Political interests: NHS, domestic abuse, high street regeneration.

Kate Griffiths MP, House of Commons, London SW1A 0AA
Tel: 020 7219 3000 *Email:* kate.griffiths.mp@parliament.uk
Constituency: 9 St Paul's Square, Burton upon Trent DE14 2EF
Tel: 01283 384026 Website: www.kategriffiths.org.uk

CONSERVATIVE

GRUNDY, JAMES
Leigh *(Majority 1,965)*

James Nelson Grundy. Born 8 December .

Education: Lowton High School; University of Central Lancashire.

Political career: Contested Leigh 2017 general election. Member for Leigh since 12 December 2019. *Select committees:* Member, European Statutory Instruments 2020-. *Councils and public bodies:* Councillor: Wigan Council 2008-, Greater Manchester Combined Authority 2016-; Member, Greater Manchester Transport Authority.

Political interests: Brexit, police, regeneration, green belt.

James Grundy MP, House of Commons, London SW1A 0AA
Tel: 020 7219 3602 *Email:* james.grundy.mp@parliament.uk
Constituency: 37-39 Lord Street, Leigh WN7 1BY
Tel: 01942 857326 Website: www.jamesgrundy.org.uk

CONSERVATIVE

GULLIS, JONATHAN
Stoke-on-Trent North *(Majority 6,286)*

PPS to Baroness Evans of Bowes Park as Leader of the House of Lords and Lord Privy Seal

Jonathan Edward Gullis. Born 9 January 1990; Married Amy (divorced); partner Nkita (1 daughter).

Non-political career: Teacher 2012-. NASUWT.

Political career: Contested Washington and Sunderland West 2017 general election. Member for Stoke-on-Trent North since 12 December 2019; PPS to Baroness Evans of Bowes Park as Leader of the House of Lords and Lord Privy Seal 2020-. *Select committees:* Member: Education 2020-, Petitions 2020-. Deputy Chair, Stratford-on-Avon Conservative Association; Secretary, Conservative Education Society.

Political interests: Education, health, housing, business.

Jonathan Gullis MP, House of Commons, London SW1A 0AA
Tel: 020 7219 6837 *Email:* jonathan.gullis.mp@parliament.uk
Constituency: 93 High Street, Tunstall, Stoke-on-Trent ST6 5TA
Tel: 01782 497199 Website: www.jonathangullis.com *Twitter:* @JEGullis

GWYNNE, ANDREW

Denton and Reddish *(Majority 6,175)*

LABOUR

Andrew John Gwynne. Born 4 June 1974; Son of Richard John Gwynne and Margaret Gwynne, née Ridgway; Married Allison Dennis 2003 (2 sons 1 daughter).

Education: Egerton Park Community High School, Denton; North East Wales Institute of Higher Education, Wrexham (HND business and finance 1995); Salford University (BA politics and contemporary history 1998).

Non-political career: Assistant to European Declarative System (EDS) programme manager, ICL 1990-92; National Computing Centre, Y2K team 1999-2000; Researcher for Andrew Bennett MP 2000-05; European co-ordinator for Arlene McCarthy MEP 2000-01. Member, Unite (formerly AEEU and Amicus) 2000-.

Political career: Member for Denton and Reddish 2005-10, for Denton and Reddish (revised boundary) since 6 May 2010 general election; PPS to: Baroness Scotland of Asthal as Minister of State, Home Office 2005-07, Jacqui Smith as Home Secretary 2007-09, Ed Balls as Secretary of State for Children, Schools and Families 2009-10; Shadow Minister for: Transport 2010-11, Health 2011-16 (Public Health 2015-16); Shadow Minister without Portfolio (attends Shadow Cabinet) 2016-17; National Elections and Campaign Co-ordinator/National Campaign Co-ordinator 2017-20; Shadow Secretary of State for Communities and Local Government 2017-20. *Select committees:* Member: Procedure 2005-10, Court of Referees 2007-10, Home Affairs 2020-. PLP North West Regional Group: Vice-chair 2008-09, Chair 2009-11; Chair, PLP Departmental Group for Business, Energy and Industrial Strategy 2020-. Chair, Denton and Reddish Constituency Labour Party 1998-2004; Member, Co-operative Party 2000-; Member, Christian Socialist Movement/Christians on the Left 2000-; Chair, Labour Friends of Israel 2007-10; Campaign manager to Andy Burnham MP, Labour's mayoral candidate in Greater Manchester 2016-17. *Councils and public bodies:* Tameside MBC: Councillor 1996-2008, Chair: Denton and Audenshaw District Assembly 1998-2001, Resources and community services scrutiny panel 2003-04.

Political interests: Education and skills, regeneration, local government, environment, transport; China, Commonwealth, India, Israel/Palestinian Authority, Latin America, USA.

Other: Member, UK delegation, Parliamentary Assembly of the Organisation for Security and Co-operation in Europe 2020-; Patron: Tameside and Stockport Homestart, Friends of Dukinfield Old Hall Chapel, Keep Our NHS Public, Friends of Real Lancashire; President: Denton and Audenshaw Carnival Association, Denton Brass; Honorary Member, XX The Lancashire Fusiliers; Vice President, RSPCA Tameside and Glossop Branch; Honorary President, Denton Park Social Bowling Club; Director, Great Britain-China Centre. Denton Labour Club, Stockport Labour Club.

Recreations: Reading, computing, history, family.

Andrew Gwynne MP, House of Commons, London SW1A 0AA
Tel: 020 7219 4708 *Fax:* 020 7219 4548 *Email:* gwynnea@parliament.uk
Constituency: Town Hall, Market Street, Denton, Greater Manchester M34 2AP
Tel: 0161-320 1504 Website: www.andrewgwynne.co.uk *Twitter:* @GwynneMP

HAIGH, LOUISE

Sheffield Heeley *(Majority 8,520)*

LABOUR

Shadow Secretary of State for Northern Ireland

Louise Margaret Haigh. Born 22 July 1987.

Education: Sheffield High School; Nottingham University (politics and economics); Birkbeck School of Law (LLM).

Non-political career: Ant Marketing; Corporate governance policy manager, Aviva Insurance; Parliamentary researcher to Lisa Nandy MP; Youth service training manager, Nottingham Council. Member: Unite, GMB.

Political career: Member for Sheffield Heeley since 7 May 2015 general election; Shadow Minister for: Cabinet Office 2015-16, Culture, Media and Sport (Digital Economy) 2016-17, Home Office (Policing and Crime) 2017-20; Shadow Secretary of State for Northern Ireland 2020-.

Political interests: Financial services, investment, education; Kashmir, Palestine, South Africa.

Louise Haigh MP, House of Commons, London SW1A 0AA
Tel: 020 7219 5255 *Email:* louise.haigh.mp@parliament.uk
Constituency: 63 Chesterfield Road, Sheffield S8 0RL
Tel: 0114-250 8113 Website: www.louisehaigh.org.uk *Twitter:* @LouHaigh

CONSERVATIVE

HALFON, ROBERT

Harlow *(Majority 14,063)*

Chair, Select Committee on Education

Robert Henry Halfon. Born 22 March 1969; Son of Clement and Jenny Halfon; Partner Vanda Colombo.

Education: Highgate School, London; Exeter University (BA politics 1991; MA Russian and East European politics 1992).

Non-political career: Parliamentary researcher to a number of Conservative MPs; Head of Research, Market Access Ltd 1994-98; Policy Analyst, APCO UK 1998-2000; Political Director, Renewing One Nation, Conservative Central Office 2000-01; Chief of Staff to Oliver Letwin MP 2001-05; Political Director/Consultant, Conservative Friends of Israel 2005-10; Self-employed Consultant 2005-10. Member, Prospect.

Political career: Contested Harlow 2001 and 2005 general elections. Member for Harlow since 6 May 2010 general election; PPS to George Osborne as Chancellor of the Exchequer 2014-15; Minister without Portfolio, Cabinet Office 2015-16; Minister of State, Department for Education 2016-17. *Select committees:* Member, Public Administration 2010-14; Chair, Education 2017-; Member, Liaison 2017-. 1922 Committee: Member, Executive 2010-14, 2020-, Member, Sub-committee for Campaigning. Chair: Western Area Conservative Students 1987-90, Exeter University Conservative Association 1989-90; Deputy Chair: Vauxhall Conservative Association 1998-2000, Conservative Party 2015-16. *Councils and public bodies:* Councillor, Roydon Parish Council 2005-11.

Political interests: Apprenticeships, skills, community cohesion, education, housing, information technology, literacy, mobile technology, social action, terrorism, trade unions, fuel duty, NHS hospital parking charges; Eastern Europe, Iraq (Kurdistan region), Israel.

Other: Member, Advisory Board, Centre for Social Justice; Great Parndon Community Association President, St Johns Ambulance, Harlow; Honorary President, Union Blue; Patron: Harlow Homestart, St Clare's Hospice, Harlow; Trustee, Parndon Mill, Harlow; Harlow Employability, Heart4Harlow, Princess Alexandra NHS Hospital Trust, Harlow Stroke Support Rehab Centre; Freedom, Clockmakers' Company 2018; Doctor Honoris Causa; University of Craiova, Romania 2018; National Conservative Excellence Award for Social Action 2008; *The Spectator* Campaigning MP of the Year Award 2013; *The House Magazine* Transport Campaigner of the Year, Dods Parliamentary Awards 2014; PC 2015. Harlow Royal British Legion.

Publications: Retreat or Reform (Institute for European Defence and Strategic Studies, 1994); Corporate Irresponsibility (Social Affairs Unit, 1998); Numerous articles in various publications and written chapters for: Encyclopaedia of Soviet Union and Eastern Europe (by Bogdan Szajkowski, 1994), From the Ashes... The Future of the Conservative Party (Bow Group, 2005), The Last Moral Force, The New Blue (Social Market Foundation, 2008), Stop the Union Bashing – Why Conservatives Should Embrace the Trade Union Movement (Demos, 2012).

Recreations: Chelsea FC, countryside, horology, travelling, mobile technology.

Rt Hon Robert Halfon MP, House of Commons, London SW1A 0AA
Tel: 020 7219 7223
Constituency: Harlow Enterprise Hub, Kao-Hockham Building, Edinburgh Way, Harlow, Essex CM20 2NQ
Tel: 01279 311451 *Email:* halfon4harlow@roberthalfon.com Website: www.roberthalfon.com
Twitter: @halfon4harlowMP

CONSERVATIVE

HALL, LUKE

Thornbury and Yate *(Majority 12,369)*

Minister of State for Regional Growth and Local Government, Ministry of Housing, Communities and Local Government

Luke Anthony Hall. Born 8 July 1986; Married Roisin Cabry 2016.

Non-political career: Store Manager, Lidl, Yate; South West area manager, Farmfoods -2015.

Political career: Member for Thornbury and Yate since 7 May 2015 general election; Team PPS, Department for Education 2017-18; PPS to: Baroness Evans of Bowes Park as Leader of the House of Lords and Lord Privy Seal 2018, Brandon Lewis as Minister without portfolio and Conservative Party Chair, Cabinet Office 2018-19; Member, Speaker's Committee on the Electoral Commission 2019, 2020-; Ministry of Housing, Communities and Local Government: Parliamentary Under-Secretary of State: Local Government and Homelessness 2019-20, Rough Sleeping and Housing 2020, Minister of State for Regional Growth and Local Government 2020-. *Select committees:* Member: Environmental Audit 2015-17, Work and Pensions 2016-17, Petitions 2016-17, 2018-19. Constituency chair, South Gloucestershire; Deputy chair, Bristol and South Gloucestershire Conservatives; Vice-chair, Candidates, Conservative Party 2019-.

Other: Has held an amateur boxing licence.

Luke Hall MP, House of Commons, London SW1A 0AA
Tel: 020 7219 4741 *Email:* luke.hall.mp@parliament.uk
Constituency: 26 High Street, Chipping Sodbury, Gloucestershire BS35 6AH
Tel: 01454 311267 *Email:* luke@lukehall.org.uk Website: www.lukehall.org.uk
Twitter: @LukeHall

LABOUR

HAMILTON, FABIAN

Leeds North East *(Majority 17,089)*

Shadow Minister for Peace and Disarmament

Fabian Uziell-Hamilton. Born 12 April 1955; Son of late Mario Uziell-Hamilton, solicitor, and late Adrianne Uziell-Hamilton (Her Honour Judge Adrianne Uziell-Hamilton); Married Rosemary Ratcliffe 1980 (1 son 2 daughters).

Education: Brentwood School, Essex; York University (BA social sciences 1977); French.

Non-political career: Taxi driver 1978-79; Graphic designer 1979-94; Consultant and dealer, Apple Macintosh computer systems 1994-97. Member: SLADE 1978-82, NGA 1982-91, GPMU 1991-2005, Amicus 2005-07, Unite 2007-14, GMB 2014-.

Political career: Contested Leeds North East 1992 general election. Member for Leeds North East 1997-2010, for Leeds North East (revised boundary) since 6 May 2010 general election; PPS to Rachel Reeves as Shadow Chief Secretary to the Treasury 2012-13; Shadow Minister for Foreign and Commonwealth Office 2016; Shadow Minister for Peace and Disarmament: Foreign and Commonwealth Office 2016-, Defence 2016-20. *Select committees:* Member: Administration 1997-2001, Foreign Affairs 2001-10, Quadripartite (Committees on Strategic Export Controls)/Arms Export Controls 2006-10, Political and Constitutional Reform 2010-15, Joint Committee on National Security Strategy 2010-15, International Development 2013-16, Arms Exports Controls 2013-15, Panel of Chairs 2015-16. Vice-chair, PLP Departmental Group for Home Affairs 2010-15. Member, Co-operative Party 1981-; Member, Labour Friends of Israel 1997-. *Councils and public bodies:* Councillor, Leeds City Council 1987-98: Chair: Race Equality Committee 1988-94, Economic Development Committee 1994-96, Education Committee 1996-97.

Political interests: Education, transport, small businesses, anti-racism, international development, alternative fuels, foreign affairs, holocaust education, prison health, hospices and palliative care; Southern Africa, Caribbean, Cyprus, Europe, Iceland, Indian sub-continent, Iran, Japan, Jordan, Kashmir, Korea, Middle East, Morocco, Russia, Tibet, Turkey.

Other: Treasurer, Inter-Parliamentary Union, British Group 2013-16; Member: Fabian Society 1990-, Jewish Labour Movement; St Gemmas Hospice, Childline, Practical Actions, Refugee Education, Training and Advisory Service, St George's Crypt Leeds, Polycycstic Kidney Disease, UNICEF, Funzi and Bodo Trust, Heart Research UK, Donisthorpe Hall.

Recreations: Film, opera, cycling, computers, photography.

Fabian Hamilton MP, House of Commons, London SW1A 0AA
Tel: 020 7219 2788 *Fax:* 020 7219 5540 *Email:* fabian.hamilton.mp@parliament.uk
Constituency: 147a Easterly Road, Leeds, West Yorkshire LS8 2RY
Tel: 0113-249 6600 Website: www.leedsne.co.uk *Twitter:* @FabianLeedsNE

CONSERVATIVE

HAMMOND, STEPHEN

Wimbledon *(Majority 628)*

Stephen William Hammond. Born 4 February 1962; Son of Bryan Hammond and Janice Hammond; Married Sally Brodie 1991 (1 daughter).

Education: King Edward VI School, Southampton; Richard Hale School, Hertford; Queen Mary College, London University (BSc Econ 1982).

Non-political career: Trainee analyst, Reed Stenhouse Investment Services 1983-85; Fund manager, Canada Life 1987-88; Stockbroker, UBS Philips and Drew 1987-91; Director: UK equities, Dresdner Kleinwort Benson Securities 1991-98, Pan European research, Commerzbank Securities 1998-2001; Adviser: Inmarsat 2014-, Confederation of Passenger Transport 2016-.

Political career: Contested North Warwickshire 1997 and Wimbledon 2001 general elections. Member for Wimbledon since 5 May 2005 general election; Shadow Minister for Transport 2005-10; PPS to Eric Pickles as Secretary of State for Communities and Local Government 2010-12; Parliamentary Under-Secretary of State, Department for Transport 2012-14; Minister of State for Health, Department of Health and Social Care 2018-19. *Select committees:* Member: Regulatory Reform 2005-08, Public Accounts 2014-15, Treasury 2015-18, Joint Committee on Statutory Instruments 2015-17, Treasury Sub-committee 2017-18. Conservative Party: Chair, Stevenage Conservatives 1991-94, Member, Executive, Eastern Area 1992-94, Chair, Wimbledon Conservative Association 2001-03, Member, 2020 Group, Founding member, Conservatives for Reform in Europe 2016, Vice-chairman 2017; Conservative Party whip removed September-October 2019. *Councils and public bodies:* Merton Borough Council: Councillor 2002-06, Environment spokesman 2002-04, Deputy group leader 2004-06.

Political interests: Economics, financial affairs, transport, foreign affairs; China, EU, India, Portugal, Sri Lanka, USA.

Other: Member, Executive Committee, Commonwealth Parliamentary Association UK 2016-17; Wimbledon Society; Director (unpaid), South Coast Regeneration and Investment Property 2017-; Associate, Society of Investment Analysts 1985; Macmillan Cancer Support. Royal Wimbledon Golf Club; Wimbledon Hockey Club.

Recreations: Reading, sport, relaxing with family, cooking.

Stephen Hammond MP, House of Commons, London SW1A 0AA
Tel: 020 7219 3401 *Email:* hammondsp@parliament.uk
Constituency: Wimbledon Conservative Association, c/o 1 Summerstown, London SW17 0BQ
Tel: 020 8944 2905 *Email:* stephen@stephenhammond.net Website: stephenhammond.net
Twitter: @S_Hammond

CONSERVATIVE

HANCOCK, MATT

West Suffolk *(Majority 23,194)*

Secretary of State for Health and Social Care

Matthew John David Hancock. Born 2 October 1978; Married Martha 2006 (2 sons 1 daughter).

Education: King's School, Chester; West Cheshire College; Exeter College, Oxford (BA politics, philosophy and economics 1999); Christ College, Cambridge (Master's economics 2003).

Non-political career: Border Business Systems, Farndon; Economist, Bank of England 2000-05; Chief of staff to George Osborne MP 2005-10.

Political career: Member for West Suffolk since 6 May 2010 general election; Departments for Business, Innovation and Skills and Education: Parliamentary Under-Secretary of State 2012-13, Minister of State for Skills and Enterprise 2013-14; Minister of State for: Business and Enterprise and Minister for Portsmouth, Department for Business, Innovation and Skills 2014-15, Energy, Department of Energy and Climate Change 2014-15; Minister for the Cabinet Office; Paymaster General (also attending Cabinet) 2015-16; Minister of State for Digital and Culture, Department for Culture, Media and Sport 2016-17; Department for Digital, Culture,

Media and Sport: Minister of State for Digital 2017-18, Secretary of State for: Digital, Culture, Media and Sport 2018, Health and Social Care 2018-. *Select committees:* Member: Public Accounts 2010-12, Standards and Privileges 2010-12. Member, Conservative Party 1999-.

Political interests: India, Japan, UK, USA.

Other: Cancer Research UK, Racing Welfare, St Nicholas Hospice, Injured Jockeys Fund; PC 2014. Jockey Club.

Publications: Various Bank of England publications; Master of Nothing (with Nadim Zahawi MP) 2011.

Recreations: Walking, cooking, cricket, horse racing.

Rt Hon Matt Hancock MP, House of Commons, London SW1A 0AA
Tel: 020 7219 7186 *Email:* matt.hancock.mp@parliament.uk
Constituency: 1 Park Farm Cottage, Fornham St Genevieve, Exning, Bury St Edmunds, Suffolk IP28 6TS
Tel: 01284 701807 *Email:* matt@matt-hancock.com Website: www.matt-hancock.com
Twitter: @MattHancock

CONSERVATIVE

HANDS, GREG

Chelsea and Fulham *(Majority 11,241)*

Minister of State for Trade Policy, Department for International Trade

Gregory William Hands. Born 14 November 1965; Son of Edward and Mavis Hands; Married Irina Hundt 2005 (1 daughter 1 son).

Education: Dr Challoner's Grammar School, Amersham; Robinson College, Cambridge (BA modern history 1989); Czech, French, German.

Non-political career: Banker 1989-97; Political consultant, BNP Paribas UK 2018-.

Political career: Member for Hammersmith and Fulham 2005-10, for Chelsea and Fulham since 6 May 2010 general election; Shadow Minister for the Treasury 2009-10; PPS to George Osborne as Chancellor of the Exchequer 2010-11; Assistant Government Whip 2011-13; Deputy Chief Whip (Treasurer of HM Household) 2013-15; Chief Secretary to the Treasury 2015-16; Department for International Trade: Minister of State for: Trade and Investment 2016-17, Trade Policy 2017-18, 2020-; Minister for London 2017-18. *Select committees:* Member: ODPM/Communities and Local Government 2006-08, European Scrutiny 2007-10, Communities and Local Government 2009-10, Selection 2013-15; Chair, Joint Committee on Security 2013-15. *Councils and public bodies:* Hammersmith and Fulham Borough Council: Councillor 1998-2006: Leader, Conservative group 1999-2003; Prison visitor, HMP Wormwood Scrubs 2002-04.

Political interests: Finance, foreign affairs, housing, local government; Central and Eastern Europe, Germany, Ireland, North Korea, Russia and ex-USSR.

Other: Trustee, Brunswick Club for Young People 2003-; Co-Patron, Fulham Boys School; PC 2014. Carlton Club.

Recreations: Playing and watching football, local history, British, German and Soviet history, photography.

Rt Hon Greg Hands MP, House of Commons, London SW1A 0AA
Tel: 020 7219 5448 *Email:* handsg@parliament.uk
Constituency: No constituency office publicised
Website: www.greghands.com *Twitter:* @greghands

SOCIAL DEMOCRATIC AND LABOUR PARTY

HANNA, CLAIRE

Belfast South *(Majority 15,401)*

Claire Aisling Hanna. Born 19 June 1980; Married Donal (3 daughters).

Education: Rathmore; Open University (BA international relations); Queen's University Belfast (MA law and governance).

Non-political career: Policy Officer, overseas development agency.

Political career: Contested Strangford 2010 general election. Member for Belfast South since 12 December 2019; SDLP Spokesperson for: Finance 2016-17, Brexit 2018-19. *Select committees:* Member, Northern Ireland Affairs 2020-. MLA (replacement) for South Belfast since 29 June 2015: SDLP Spokesperson for: Finance 2016-17, Brexit 2018-19. Former international secretary, Social Democratic and Labour Party. *Councils and public bodies:* Councillor, Belfast City Council 2011-15.

Political interests: Sustainability, economy, promoting a genuinely shared future, arts, Brexit.

Claire Hanna MP, House of Commons, London SW1A 0AA
Tel: 020 7219 3000 *Email:* claire.hanna.mp@parliament.uk
Constituency: 1 Rushfield Avenue, Belfast BT7 3FP
Tel: 028 9099 6066 Website: clairehanna.org *Twitter:* @ClaireHanna

SCOTTISH NATIONAL PARTY

HANVEY, NEALE

Kirkcaldy and Cowdenbeath *(Majority 1,243)*

SNP Spokesperson for Vaccines

James Neale Hanvey.

Education: Dundee University (RMN); Napier University (RGN); London South Bank University (DipHE); City University (MSc 2003).

Non-political career: University College London Hospitals NHS Foundation Trust: Teenage Cancer Trust Unit Charge Nurse 1998-2002, Senior Nurse, Oncology 2002-05; Divisional Nurse Director, Royal Marsden NHS Foundation Trust 2005-10; Freelance Videographer 2017-19.

Political career: Member for Kirkcaldy and Cowdenbeath since 12 December 2019; SNP Health Team Member 2020-21, Spokesperson for Vaccines 2021-. *Select committees:* Member, Health and Social Care 2020-. Contested Mid Scotland and Fife region 2016 Scottish Parliament election. Suspended by SNP November 2019-May 2020. *Councils and public bodies:* Fife Council: Councillor 2012-17, Leader, SNP group 2017.

Neale Hanvey MP, House of Commons, London SW1A 0AA
Tel: 020 7219 6877 *Email:* neale.hanvey.mp@parliament.uk
Constituency: Unit 1, 206-210 High Street, Kirkcaldy KY1 1JT
Tel: 01592 210088 *Twitter:* @JNHanvey

LABOUR

HARDY, EMMA

Kingston upon Hull West and Hessle *(Majority 2,856)*

Shadow Minister for Further Education and Universities

Emma Ann Hardy. Born 17 July 1979; 2 daughters.

Education: Wyke Sixth Form College; Liverpool University (BA politics 2001); Leeds University (PGCE 2003).

Non-political career: Teacher: North East Lincolnshire Council 2003-05, East Riding of Yorkshire Council 2004-11; Organiser, National Union of Teachers Midland Region 2015-17.

Political career: Member for Kingston upon Hull West and Hessle since 8 June 2017; PPS to Keir Starmer as Shadow Secretary of State for Exiting the European Union 2017-19; Shadow Minister for Education (Further Education and Universities) 2020-. *Select committees:* Member, Education 2017-19. Labour Party: Branch secretary 2010, National Policy Forum Representative 2015-, CLP Women's Officer 2016-. *Councils and public bodies:* Councillor, Hessle Town Council 2015-17.

Political interests: Education, NHS, environment.

Other: Patron: STAND, Articulacy.

Emma Hardy MP, House of Commons, London SW1A 0AA
Tel: 020 7219 5256 *Email:* emma.hardy.mp@parliament.uk
Constituency: The Octagon, Walker Street, Hull HU3 2RA
Tel: 01482 219211 *Email:* contact@emmahardy.org.uk Website: www.emmahardy.org.uk
Twitter: @EmmaHardyMP

LABOUR

HARMAN, HARRIET

Camberwell and Peckham *(Majority 33,780)*

Chair, Joint Committee on Human Rights

Harriet Ruth Harman. Born 30 July 1950; Daughter of late John Bishop Harman and Anna Harman; Married Jack Dromey (qv) 1982 (MP for Birmingham Erdington) (2 sons 1 daughter).

Education: St Paul's Girls' School, London; York University (BA politics 1978).

Non-political career: Legal officer, National Council for Civil Liberties 1978-82; QC 2001. Member, Unite (TGWU sector).

Political career: Member for Peckham 1982 by-election to 1997, for Camberwell and Peckham 1997-2010, for Camberwell and Peckham (revised boundary) since 6 May 2010 general election; Member, Public Accounts Commission; Shadow Minister, Social Services 1984, 1985-87; Spokesperson for Health 1987-92; Shadow Chief Secretary to the Treasury 1992-94; Shadow Secretary of State for: Employment 1994-95, Health 1995-96, Social Security 1996-97; Secretary of State for Social Security and Minister for Women 1997-98; Solicitor General 2001-05; Minister of State, Department for Constitutional Affairs/Ministry of Justice 2005-07; Leader of the House of Commons and Lord Privy Seal 2007-10; Ex-officio member House of Commons Commission 2007-10; Minister for Women and Equality 2007-10; Member Speaker's Committee for the Independent Parliamentary Standards Authority 2009-10; Acting Leader of the Opposition 2010, 2015; Deputy Leader of the Opposition/Shadow Deputy Prime Minister 2010-15; Shadow Secretary of State for: International Development 2010-11, Culture, Media and Sport 2011-15. *Select committees:* Chair: Modernisation of the House of Commons 2007-10; Joint Committee on Human Rights 2015-; Member, Liaison 2015-. Labour Party: Member, National Executive Committee 1993-98, Deputy Leader 2007-15, Chair 2007-15, Acting Leader 2010, 2015. *Councils and public bodies:* Chair, Childcare Commission 1999-2001.

Political interests: Women, social services, provision for under-fives, law, domestic violence, civil liberties.

Other: PC 1997.

Publications: A Woman's Work (Allen Lane, 2017).

Rt Hon Harriet Harman QC MP, House of Commons, London SW1A 0AA
Tel: 020 7219 4218 *Fax:* 020 7219 4877 *Email:* harriet.harman.mp@parliament.uk
Constituency: No constituency office
Website: www.harrietharman.org *Twitter:* @HarrietHarman

CONSERVATIVE

HARPER, MARK

Forest of Dean *(Majority 15,869)*

Mark James Harper. Born 26 February 1970; Son of James and Jane Harper; Married Margaret Whelan 1999.

Education: Headlands School, Swindon, Wiltshire; Swindon College; Brasenose College, Oxford (BA philosophy, politics and economics 1991).

Non-political career: Auditor, KPMG 1991-95; Intel Corporation (UK) Ltd: Senior finance analyst 1995-97, Finance manager 1997-2000, Operations manager 2000-02; Owned accountancy practice 2002-05; Senior adviser, DWF LLP 2017-19.

Political career: Contested Forest of Dean 2001 general election. Member for Forest of Dean since 5 May 2005 general election; Shadow Minister for: Defence 2005-07, Work and Pensions (Disabled People) 2007-10; Parliamentary Secretary (Minister for Political and Constitutional Reform), Cabinet Office 2010-12; Minister of State for: Immigration, Home Office 2012-14, Disabled People, Department for Work and Pensions 2014-15; Chief Whip; Parliamentary Secretary to the Treasury 2015-16; Member, Parliamentary and Political Service Honours

Committee 2015-16. *Select committees:* Member: Administration 2005-06, 2014, Work and Pensions 2009. South Swindon Conservative Association: Treasurer 1993-98, Deputy chair 1998.

Political interests: Education, special needs education, law and order, health, defence; Israel, Turkey, USA.

Other: ACA 1995; PC 2015.

Recreations: Walking the dogs, travel, cinema.

Rt Hon Mark Harper MP, House of Commons, London SW1A 0AA
Tel: 020 7219 5056 *Fax:* 020 7219 0937 *Email:* mark.harper.mp@parliament.uk
Constituency: 35 High Street, Cinderford, Gloucestershire GL14 2SL
Tel: 01594 823482 Website: www.markharper.org *Twitter:* @Mark_J_Harper

LABOUR

HARRIS, CAROLYN

Swansea East *(Majority 7,970)*

Deputy Leader, Welsh Labour; PPS to Keir Starmer as Leader of the Opposition

Born 18 September 1960; Daughter of Don and Pauline Marvelley; 3 sons (1 deceased).

Education: Swansea University (BSc social history 1998).

Non-political career: Project Manager, Guiding Hands Charity 1998-2000; Wales Regional Director, Community Logistics 2000-03; Wales Regional Manager, Children's Cancer Charity 2003-05; Senior Parliamentary Assistant/Constituency Manager to Siân James MP 2005-15. GMB; Unison; Unite; Usdaw.

Political career: Member for Swansea East since 7 May 2015 general election; Shadow Minister for: Home Office 2016-17, 2018-20, Women and Equalities 2017-20; PPS to Keir Starmer as Leader of the Opposition 2020-. *Select committees:* Member: Welsh Affairs 2015-16, Environmental Audit 2015-16. Deputy Leader, Welsh Labour 2018-.

Political interests: Support for the beauty and wellbeing sector, home electrical safety, gambling related harm, children's funeral fund.

Other: Trustee, Unity Trust Wales; Vice-President, Chartered Institute for Trading Standards; Campaigning MP of the Year, Mirror Politics 2016 Welsh Labour Campaign of the Year 2016; Backbencher of the Year, PSA 2019.

Carolyn Harris MP, House of Commons, London SW1A 0AA
Tel: 020 7219 4316 *Email:* carolyn.harris.mp@parliament.uk
Constituency: 485 Llangyfelach Road, Brynhyfryd, Swansea SA5 9EA
Tel: 01792 462054 Website: www.carolynharris.org.uk
Twitter: @carolynharris24/@WelshLabDeputy

CONSERVATIVE

HARRIS, REBECCA

Castle Point *(Majority 26,634)*

Government Whip (Lord Commissioner of HM Treasury)

Rebecca Elizabeth Scott Harris. Born 22 December 1967; Daughter of Philip and Louise Harris; Married Frank Skelton 1999 (1 son).

Non-political career: Marketing director, Philimore and Co (publisher) 1997-2007; Campaign officer, Conservative Research Department 1998-2001; Special adviser to Tim Yeo MP 2003-10.

Political career: Member for Castle Point since 6 May 2010 general election; PPS to: Theresa Villiers as Secretary of State for Northern Ireland 2015-16, Sajid Javid as Secretary of State for Communities and Local Government 2016-17; Assistant Government Whip 2017-18; Government Whip (Lord Commissioner of HM Treasury) 2018-. *Select committees:* Member: Business, Innovation and Skills 2010-15, Joint Committee on the Draft Enhanced Terrorism Prevention and Investigation Measures Bill 2012-13, Regulatory Reform 2012-17, Selection 2019-. Conservative Party: Campaign co-ordinator, Campaign HQ 2000-01, North West London area officer 2007-08, Vice-chairman (Youth) 2013-. *Councils and public bodies:* Chichester District Council: Councillor 1999-2003, Deputy chair, scrutiny committee 1999-2003.

Political interests: Small business, education and skills, planning.

Other: Patron: Cascade Foundation, Danny Green Foundation, Mickey Payne Foundation, Careers Choices. Hadleigh Conservative Club, Canvey Island Conservative Club, Benfleet Conservative Club.

Recreations: Gardening, walking.

Rebecca Harris MP, House of Commons, London SW1A 0AA
Tel: 020 7219 7206 *Email:* rebecca.harris.mp@parliament.uk
Constituency: c/o Castle Point Conservatives, Bernard Braine House, 8 Green Road, Benfleet, Essex SS7 5JT
Tel: 01268 792992 *Email:* office@castlepointconservatives.com
Websites: www.castlepointconservatives.com/www.rebeccaharris.org
Twitter: @RebeccaHarrisMP

CONSERVATIVE

HARRISON, TRUDY

Copeland *(Majority 5,842)*

PPS to Boris Johnson as Prime Minister

Trudy Lynne Harrison. Born 19 April 1976; Married Keith (4 daughters).

Education: Salford University (FdSc sustainable communities 2013).

Non-political career: Technical clerk, Sellafield Ltd 1993-98; Owner/Director, Sunny Days (childcare business) 2002-06; Copeland Borough Council: Locality officer 2010-13, Community regeneration officer 2013; Project manager, Wellbank Project 2013-17; Programme manager, Bootle2020 2014-17.

Political career: Member for Copeland since 23 February 2017 by-election; Apprenticeship Ambassador 2017-; Team PPS: Ministry of Defence 2018-19, Department for Transport 2019; PPS: to Secretary of State for Education: Damian Hinds 2019, Gavin Williamson 2019, to Boris Johnson as Prime Minister 2019-. *Select committees:* Member: Education 2017-19, European Statutory Instruments 2018-19. *Councils and public bodies:* Chair of governors, Captain Shaw's CoE Primary School 2003-; Parish Councillor, Bootle Parish Council; Chair, Apprenticeship Delivery Board 2017-.

Other: Director, Pub at Millstones Ltd.

Trudy Harrison MP, House of Commons, London SW1A 0AA
Tel: 020 7219 4002 *Email:* trudy.harrison.mp@parliament.uk
Constituency: Main Street, Bootle, Millom, Cumbria LA19 5TF
Tel: 01229 718333 *Email:* trudy@trudyharrison.co.uk Website: www.trudyharrison.co.uk

CONSERVATIVE

HART, SALLY-ANN

Hastings and Rye *(Majority 4,043)*

Born 6 March 1968; Married (3 children).

Education: Kings College London (BA geography 1989); College of Law, Lancaster Gate (CPE/LSF 1992).

Non-political career: Assistant Solicitor, Theodore Goddard; Corporate Solicitor, Hallett & Co; Magistrate, Hastings 2005-; Governor: ARK Little Ridge, ARK Blacklands, ARK Castledown.

Political career: Contested North West Durham 2017 general election. Member for Hastings and Rye since 12 December 2019. *Select committees:* Member: Future Relationship with the European Union 2020-21, Scottish Affairs 2020-, Speaker's Advisory Committee on Works of Art 2020-. *Councils and public bodies:* Councillor, Rother District Council 2015-.

Sally-Ann Hart MP, House of Commons, London SW1A 0AA
Tel: 020 7219 5726 *Email:* sallyann.hart.mp@parliament.uk
Constituency: Swallow House, Theaklen Drive, St Leonard-on-sea TN38 9AZ
Tel: 01424 716756 Website: www.sallyannhart.org.uk *Twitter:* @SallyAnn1066

CONSERVATIVE

HART, SIMON Carmarthen West and South Pembrokeshire *(Majority 7,745)*

Secretary of State for Wales

Simon Anthony Hart. Born 15 August 1963; Married Abigail Holland 1998 (1 son 1 daughter).

Education: Radley College, Oxfordshire; Royal Agriculture College, Cirencester (Diploma rural estate management 1984).

Non-political career: Chartered surveyor, Knight, Frank & Rutley 1986-88; Associated to sole principal, Llewellyn Humphreys 1988-98; Associate land agent, Balfour, Burd & Benson 1998-99; Countryside Alliance 1999-2010: Campaigns director 1999-2003, Chief executive 2003-10, Outdoor education consultant -2015, Chair 2015-19. Territorial Army.

Political career: Member for Carmarthen West and South Pembrokeshire since 6 May 2010 general election; Trade Envoy to Panama, Costa Rica and Dominican Republic 2017-19; Parliamentary Secretary (Minister for Implementation), Cabinet Office 2019; Secretary of State for Wales 2019-. *Select committees:* Member: Political and Constitutional Reform 2010-13, Welsh Affairs 2012-15, Environment, Food and Rural Affairs 2015-17, Environment, Food and Rural Affairs Sub-committee 2015-17, Digital, Culture, Media and Sport 2017-19, Standards 2017, Privileges 2017. Member, Executive, 1922 Committee 2012-16. Founding member, Conservatives for Reform in Europe 2016. *Councils and public bodies:* Member, Committee on Standards in Public Life 2017-19.

Political interests: Rural affairs, small business; Falkland Islands.

Other: Member, UK Delegation, Organisation for Security and Co-operation in Europe Parliamentary Assembly 2016-17; Associate, Royal Institute of Chartered Surveyors 1985; PC 2019. Cresselly Cricket Club.

Recreations: Cricket, all aspects of country sports.

Rt Hon Simon Hart MP, House of Commons, London SW1A 0AA
Tel: 020 7219 3000 *Email:* simon.hart.mp@parliament.uk
Constituency: 15 St John Street, Whitland, Carmarthenshire SA34 0AN
Tel: 01994 242002 Website: www.simon-hart.com *Twitter:* @Simonhartmp

LABOUR

HAYES, HELEN Dulwich and West Norwood *(Majority 27,310)*

Helen Elizabeth Hayes. Born 8 August 1974; Married (2 daughters).

Education: Ormskirk Grammar School 1985-92; Balliol College, Oxford (BA politics, philosophy and economics 1996); London School of Economics (MSc social policy and administration 1997).

Non-political career: Joint Managing Director, Urban Practitioners Ltd 1998-2011 Partner, Allies and Morrison 2011-15. Member, GMB.

Political career: Member for Dulwich and West Norwood since 7 May 2015 general election; Opposition Whip 2020; Shadow Minister for Cabinet Office 2020. *Select committees:* Member, Communities and Local Government/Housing, Communities and Local Government 2015-19. Chair, PLP Departmental Groups for Housing and Planning 2019. *Councils and public bodies:* Councillor, Southwark Council 2010-16; Vice-President, Local Government Association 2018-.

Political interests: NHS, local government, housing, planning, climate change, human rights, international development, arts and culture, mental health, autism and learning disabilities.

Other: Member: Amnesty International, Fabian Society, Friends of Dulwich Picture Gallery, Friends of Kingswood House, Tate; Chartered member, Royal Town Planning Institute; Academician, Academy of Urbanism.

Helen Hayes MP, House of Commons, London SW1A 0AA
Tel: 020 7219 6971 *Email:* helen.hayes.mp@parliament.uk
Constituency: No constituency office publicised
Website: www.helenhayes.org.uk *Twitter:* @helenhayes_

CONSERVATIVE

HAYES, JOHN

South Holland and The Deepings *(Majority 30,838)*

John Henry Hayes. Born 23 June 1958; Son of late Henry Hayes and Lily Hayes; Married Susan Hopewell 1997 (2 sons).

Education: Colfe's Grammar School, London; Nottingham University (BA politics 1980; PGCE history/English 1982); Some Italian and Spanish.

Non-political career: Data Base Ltd IT company 1983-99: Director 1986-97, Non-executive director 1997-99; Associate professor, American University in London 2005-10. Associate member, Association of Teachers and Lecturers.

Political career: Contested Derbyshire North East 1987 and 1992 general elections. Member for South Holland and The Deepings 1997-2010, for South Holland and The Deepings (revised boundary) since 6 May 2010 general election; Shadow Minister for Schools 2000-01; Opposition Pairing Whip 2001-02; Shadow Minister for: Agriculture, Fisheries and Food 2002-03, Local and Devolved Government (Housing and Planning) 2003-05, Transport 2005, Vocational Education 2005-09, Lifelong Learning, Further and Higher Education 2009, Universities and Skills 2009-10; Minister of State for: Further Education, Skills and Lifelong Learning, Departments for Business, Innovation and Skills and Education 2010-12, Energy, Department of Energy and Climate Change 2012-13; Minister without Portfolio, Cabinet Office 2013-14; Senior Parliamentary Adviser to the Prime Minister 2013-15; Minister of State: Department for Transport 2014-15, 2016-18 (for Transport Legislation and Maritime 2017-18), for Security, Home Office 2015-16; Member, Intelligence and Security Committee of Parliament 2020-. *Select committees:* Member: Agriculture 1997-99, Education and Employment 1998-99,1999-2000, Education and Employment (Education Sub-Committee) 1999-2000, Selection 2001-02, Administration 2001-02. Joint vice-chair, Conservative Party Committee for Education and Employment 1997-99; Conservative Party Committee for Agriculture, Fisheries and Food: Joint secretary 1998-99, Secretary 1999-2000. Former chair, Young Conservatives; Vice-chair: Conservatives Against Federal Europe, Conservative Party 1999-2000; Member, 1992 Group; Joint chair, Cornerstone Group 2004-. *Councils and public bodies:* Councillor, Nottinghamshire County Council 1985-98.

Political interests: Education, elections and campaigning, political ideas and philosophy, local government, agriculture, commerce and industry, energy, welfare of elderly and disabled people; England, Italy, Spain, USA.

Other: Countryside member, NFU; Countryside Alliance; SPUC; Patron, Headway Cambridgeshire; Chair, British Caribbean Association 2009-; President: Spalding Parkinson Society, Sneath's Mill; Patron: Headway, Cambridgeshire, Lincolnshire Brain Tumour Support Group, Holbeach Community Vehicle, Spalding Transport Forum; Headway, various local charities in South Lincolnshire; Charity Champion award 2008; Double Act of the Year (with Ed Davey MP), *Spectator* awards 2012; *The House Magazine*: Commons Minister of the Year, Dods Parliamentary Awards 2012, Environmental Campaigner of the Year, Dods Parliamentary Awards 2014; PC 2013; CBE 2016; Kt 2018. Carlton Club, Spalding Club, Spalding Gentlemen's Society.

Publications: Representing Rural Britain – Blair's Bogus Claim (Conservative Policy Forum, 2000); Answer the Question: Prime Ministerial Accountability and the Rule of Parliament (Politica, 2000); Tony B. Liar (Conservative Party, 2001); The Right to Own: Conservative Action on Housing (Conservative Party, 2004); The Right Homes in the Right Places (Conservative Party, 2005); Being Conservative: A Cornerstone of Policies to Revive Tory Britain (Cornerstone Group, 2005); Towards a Virtuous Circle of Learning (NIACE, 2006); Towards a Gold Standard for Craft, Guaranteeing Professional Apprenticeships (Centre for Policy Studies, 2007); From Social Engineering to Social Aspiration: Strategies to Broaden Access to Higher Education (UALL/Birkbeck, 2008).

Recreations: The arts (particularly English painting, poetry and prose), good food and wine, many sports (including boxing), studying the past, gardening, making jam, antiques, architecture and aesthetics.

Rt Hon Sir John Hayes CBE MP, House of Commons, London SW1A 0AA
Tel: 020 7219 1389 *Fax:* 020 7219 2273 *Email:* hayesj@parliament.uk
Constituency: 24-25 Westlode Street, Spalding, Lincolnshire PE11 2AF
Tel: 01775 711534 *Email:* davieshm@parliament.uk

SINN FÉIN

HAZZARD, CHRIS

South Down *(Majority 1,620)*

Christopher John Hazzard. Born 20 August 1984; Son of Brian Hazzard and Teresa Hazzard, née McManus; Married Lisa.

Education: Our Lady and St Patrick's College, Belfast; Queen's University, Belfast (BA history and politics 2006; MA Irish politics 2008; PhD political philosophy).

Non-political career: Press officer, Sinn Féin.

Political career: Contested South Down 2015 general election. Member for South Down since 8 June 2017; Sinn Féin Spokesperson for: Environment 2012, Education 2012-16, Victims and Truth 2014-16; Minister for Infrastructure 2016-. MLA (replacement) for South Down 2012-17: Sinn Féin Spokesperson for: Environment 2012, Education 2012-16, Victims and Truth 2014-16; Minister for Infrastructure 2016-17.

Chris Hazzard MP, House of Commons, London SW1A 0AA
Tel: 020 7219 4004 *Email:* chris.hazzard.mp@parliament.uk
Constituency: 2 Circular Road, Castlewellan, Co Down BT31 9ED
Tel: 028 4377 0185 *Email:* southdownmp@gmail.com *Twitter:* @chrishazzardsf

CONSERVATIVE

HEALD, OLIVER

North East Hertfordshire *(Majority 18,189)*

Born 15 December 1954; Son of late J A Heald, chartered engineer, and late Joyce Heald, née Pemberton, teacher; Married Christine Whittle 1979 (1 son 2 daughters).

Education: Reading School; Pembroke College, Cambridge (MA law 1976); French, German.

Non-political career: Barrister, Middle Temple 1977-; Bencher 2013; QC.

Political career: Contested Southwark and Bermondsey 1987 general election. Member for North Hertfordshire 1992-97, for North East Hertfordshire 1997-2010, for North East Hertfordshire (revised boundary) since 6 May 2010 general election; PPS to: Sir Peter Lloyd as Minister of State, Home Office 1994, William Waldegrave as Minister of Agriculture, Fisheries and Food 1994-95; Sponsored Private Member's Bill: Insurance Companies (Reserves) Act 1995; Parliamentary Under-Secretary of State, Department of Social Security 1995-97; Opposition Whip 1997-2000; Opposition Spokesperson for: Home Affairs 2000-01, Health 2001-02; Shadow Minister for Work and Pensions 2002-03; Shadow Leader of the House 2003-05; Member House of Commons' Commission 2003-05; Shadow Secretary of State for Constitutional Affairs 2004-07; Shadow Chancellor of the Duchy of Lancaster 2005-07; Solicitor General 2012-14; Minister of State for Courts and Justice, Ministry of Justice 2016-17. *Select committees:* Member: Administration 1998-2000, Modernisation of the House of Commons 2003-05, Work and Pensions 2007-12, Selection 2009-10, Standards and Privileges 2010-12, Ecclesiastical Committee 2010-12, Joint Committee on the Draft House of Lords Reform Bill 2011-12, House of Commons Governance 2014-15, Regulatory Reform 2020-. Chair, North Hertfordshire Conservative Association 1984-86; Southwark and Bermondsey Conservative Association: President 1993-98, 2012-, Patron 1998-12; Chairman: Executive Society of Conservative Lawyers 2008-12, Executive Parliamentary Resources Unit; Founding member, Conservatives for Reform in Europe 2016. *Councils and public bodies:* Member, Committee on Standards in Public Life 2008-12; DFID Steering Group on Aid Worker ID 2019-.

Political interests: Industrial relations, environment, law and order, pensions.

Other: Member, Council of Europe 2008-12; Chair, PRU 2010-12; British Commissioner, Oxfam Independent Commission on Sexual Misconduct, Accountability and Culture Change 2018-1; Conservative Environment Network 2017-; Kt 2014; PC 2016.

Publications: Co-author, Auditing the New Deal: What Figures for the Future (Politeia, 2004); A Reformed Second Chamber: Building a Better House (Society of Conservative Lawyers, 2012); Co-author, An Executive Decision: Parliamentary Approval of Armed Forces in Conflict (Society of Conservative Lawyers, 2018).

Recreations: Sport, family.

Rt Hon Sir Oliver Heald QC MP, House of Commons, London SW1A 0AA
Tel: 020 7219 6354 *Email:* oliver.heald.mp@parliament.uk
Constituency: No constituency office publicised
Tel: 01462 486074 Website: www.oliverhealdmp.com *Twitter:* @OliverHealdUK

LABOUR

HEALEY, JOHN

Wentworth and Dearne *(Majority 2,165)*

Shadow Secretary of State for Defence

Born 13 February 1960; Son of Aidan Healey, prison service, and Jean Healey, teacher; Married Jackie Bate 1993 (1 son).

Education: Lady Lumley's Comprehensive School, Pickering; St Peter's School, York; Christ's College, Cambridge (Scholar; BA 1982).

Non-political career: Journalist/deputy editor, *House Magazine* 1983-84; Disability campaigner for three national charities 1984-90; Tutor, Open University Business School 1989-92; Campaigns manager, Issue Communications 1990-92; Head of communications, MSF Union 1992-94; Campaigns and communications director, Trades Union Congress 1994-97. Member, GMB.

Political career: Contested Ryedale 1992 general election. Member for Wentworth 1997-2010, for Wentworth and Dearne since 6 May 2010 general election; PPS to Gordon Brown as Chancellor of the Exchequer 1999-2001; Parliamentary Under-Secretary of State, Department for Education and Skills (Adult Skills) 2001-02; HM Treasury 2002-07: Economic Secretary 2002-05, Financial Secretary 2005-07; Minister of State, Department for Communities and Local Government 2007-10: Minister for Local Government 2007-09, Minister for Housing (attending Cabinet) 2009-10; Member Speaker's Committee on the Electoral Commission -2009; Shadow Minister for Housing 2010; Shadow Secretary of State for Health 2010-11; Shadow Minister for Housing and Planning (attending Shadow Cabinet) 2015-16; Shadow Secretary of State for: Housing 2016-20, Defence 2020-. *Select committees:* Member: Education and Employment 1997-99, Education and Employment (Employment Sub-Committee) 1997-99, Public Accounts 2005-07, Joint Committee on Tax Law Rewrite Bills 2005-09. Member, Labour Party National Executive Committee 2014-15. *Councils and public bodies:* Vice-President, Local Government Association 2010-11, 2017-.

Political interests: Employment, trade unions, economy, tax, industrial relations, disability, local and regional government; Australia, USA.

Other: Group Board member, Incommunities Housing Association 2013-15; Rotherham Hospice; *The House Magazine* Dods Parliamentary Awards 2014: Constituency Campaigner of the Year, Written Contribution of the Year; PC 2008.

Recreations: Family.

Rt Hon John Healey MP, House of Commons, London SW1A 0AA
Tel: 020 7219 6359 *Email:* john.healey.mp@parliament.uk
Constituency: 79 High Street, Wath-upon-Dearne, Rotherham, South Yorkshire S63 7QB
Tel: 01709 875943 Website: www.johnhealeymp.co.uk *Twitter:* @JohnHealey_MP

CONSERVATIVE

HEAPPEY, JAMES

Wells *(Majority 9,991)*

Parliamentary Under-Secretary of State (Minister for the Armed Forces), Ministry of Defence

James Stephen Heappey. Born 30 January 1981; Married Kate (2 children).

Education: Queen Elizabeth's Hospital School, Bristol; Birmingham University (BA political science 2003).

Non-political career: British Army: Operations in: Kabul 2005, Northern Ireland 2006, Basra 2007, Sangin, Helmand Province 2009, Executive Office, Army General Staff, Ministry of Defence, London; Parliamentary researcher to Liam Fox MP; Self-employed project manager, specialising in business risk and resilience. Lieutenant, Royal Gloucestershire, Berkshire and Wiltshire Regiment 2004-06; Captain, the Major, The Rifles 2007-12.

Political career: Member for Wells since 7 May 2015 general election; PPS to: Chris Grayling as Secretary of State for Transport 2017-19, Boris Johnson as Prime Minister 2019; Parliamentary Under-Secretary of State, Ministry of Defence: (Defence Procurement) 2019-20, (Minister for the Armed Forces) 2020-. *Select committees:* Member, Energy and Climate Change 2015-16. Chairman, Conservative Backbench Policy Committee on Business, Energy and Industrial Strategy 2017-19.

Political interests: Rural affairs, tourism, digital economy, environment, energy, skills.

House of Commons MPs' Biographies

Recreations: Rugby, golf, tennis, cooking.

James Heappey MP, House of Commons, London SW1A 0AA
Tel: 020 7219 4289 *Email:* james.heappey.mp@parliament.uk
Constituency: 10 Broad Street, Wookey Hole Road, Wells, Somerset BA5 2DN
Tel: 01749 343255 Website: www.jamesheappey.org.uk *Twitter:* @JSHeappey

CONSERVATIVE

HEATON-HARRIS, CHRIS

Daventry *(Majority 26,080)*

Minister of State, Department for Transport

Christopher Heaton-Harris. Born 28 November 1967; Son of David and Ann Heaton-Harris; Married Jayne Carlow 1990 (2 daughters).

Education: Tiffin Grammar School for Boys, Kingston-upon-Thames, Surrey.

Non-political career: Various positions, What 4 Ltd (wholesale fresh produce company) 1989-99; Owner, Whistle Blower Ltd 2009-10.

Political career: Contested Leicester South 1997 general election and 2004 by-election. Member for Daventry since 6 May 2010 general election; Assistant Government Whip 2016-17; Government Whip: Vice-Chamberlain of HM Household 2017-18, Comptroller of HM Household 2018; Parliamentary Under-Secretary of State, Department for Exiting the European Union 2018-19; Minister of State, Department for Transport 2019-. *Select committees:* Member: Public Accounts 2010-15, European Scrutiny 2010-15, Selection 2018. European Parliament: MEP for East Midlands 1999-2009: Founder member, Campaign for Parliamentary Reform 2001, Chief Whip, EP Conservatives 2001-04.

Political interests: EU renegotiations, Europe, energy policy, sport, education, disabilities, special olympics, health, neonatal care, selective dorsal rhizotomy; Kenya, Uganda, USA.

Other: Member, Executive Committee, Inter-Parliamentary Union, British Group 2010-12; President, Sports Intergroup 2002-09; Chair, Friends of Football 2003-06; Patron, UKAN2.

Recreations: Football referee, sport.

Chris Heaton-Harris MP, House of Commons, London SW1A 0AA
Tel: 020 7219 7048 *Fax:* 020 7219 1375 *Email:* chris.heatonharris.mp@parliament.uk
Constituency: 78 St George's Avenue, Northampton, Northamptonshire NN2 6JF
Tel: 01604 859721 *Email:* agent@wnc.uk.com Websites: www.daventryconservatives.com/ www.heatonharris.com *Twitter:* @chhcalling

CONSERVATIVE

HENDERSON, GORDON

Sittingbourne and Sheppey *(Majority 24,479)*

Gordon Leonard Henderson. Born 27 January 1948; Son of William and Shirley Henderson; Married Louise Crowder 1993 (1 son 2 daughters).

Education: Fort Luton High School for Boys; Rochester Mathematical School.

Non-political career: Manager, Woolworths 1964-79; Self-employed Restaurateur 1979-83; Senior Contracts Officer, GEC Marconi Avionics 1983-93; Operations Manager, Beams UK 1993-2007; Management Consultant 2008-10.

Political career: Contested Luton South 2001 and Sittingbourne and Sheppey 2005 general elections. Member for Sittingbourne and Sheppey since 6 May 2010 general election. *Select committees:* Member, Regulatory Reform 2010-15. Member: Conservative Party, Conservative Friends of Israel. *Councils and public bodies:* Deputy leader, Conservative group, Swale Borough Council 1986-90, 1991-95; Member, Kent Police Authority 1989-93; Councillor, Kent County Council 1989-93.

Political interests: Law and order, defence, business; Southern Africa, India, Israel.

Other: Director, Halfway Conservative Hall Ltd 1989-; Chair: Litter Angels Ltd 2007-, Sheppey Natural Burial Ground Ltd 2019-; Freedom Centre, Demelza House Children's Hospice, Litter Angels. Sheerness Conservative Club.

Publications: The Almost Twins and the Litter Angel (2014); Pigeon Pie and Other Tasty Pieces (2014); Operation Seal Island (2016); The Mandela Project (2018).

Recreations: Reading, writing, football.

Gordon Henderson MP, House of Commons, London SW1A 0AA
Tel: 020 7219 7144 *Email:* gordon.henderson.mp@parliament.uk
Constituency: Top Floor, Unit 10, Periwinkle Court Business Centre, Milton Regis, Sittingbourne, Kent ME10 2JZ
Tel: 01795 423199 *Email:* jess.mcmahon@parliament.uk
Website: www.gordonhendersonmp.org.uk

LABOUR/ CO-OPERATIVE

HENDRICK, MARK

Preston *(Majority 12,146)*

Mark Phillip Hendrick. Born 2 November 1958; Son of Brian Hendrick, timber worker, and Jennifer Hendrick, née Chapman, clerk/typist; Married Yu Yannan 2008.

Education: Salford Grammar School; Liverpool Polytechnic (BSc electrical and electronic engineering 1982); Manchester University (MSc computer science 1985, CertEd 1992); Volkshochschule, Hanau, Germany ('Zertifikat Deutsch als Fremdsprache'); CEng; German (fluent).

Non-political career: Student engineer, Ministry of Defence 1979; Work student, AEG Telefunken 1981; Science and Engineering Research Council 1982-84, 1985-88; Lecturer in electronics and software design, Stockport college 1990-94. GMB, USDAW, Unite.

Political career: Member for Preston 23 November 2000 by-election to 2010, for Preston (revised boundary) since 6 May 2010 general election; PPS: to Margaret Beckett: as Secretary of State for Environment, Food and Rural Affairs 2003-06, as Foreign Secretary 2006-07, to Jack Straw as Lord Chancellor and Secretary of State for Justice 2007-08, to Ivan Lewis as Minister of State, Foreign and Commonwealth Office 2009-10; Opposition Whip 2010-12. *Select committees:* Member: European Scrutiny 2001-04, International Development 2009-10, Foreign Affairs 2012-17, High Speed Rail (London-West Midlands) Bill 2015-16, International Trade 2018-, Panel of Chairs 2020-, Committees on Arms Export Controls 2020-. European Parliament: MEP for Lancashire Central 1994-99. Chair, Eccles CLP 1990-94; Member, Preston and District Co-operative Party 1994-; Chair, Labour/Co-operative Parliamentary Group 2005-06. *Councils and public bodies:* Salford City Council: Councillor 1987-95, Representative as an alternate director, Manchester Airport plc 1987-94.

Political interests: Foreign affairs, defence, European affairs, economic and industrial affairs, international development; China, Germany, Hungary, Japan, Poland, USA.

Other: Member, UK Delegation, Organisation for Security and Co-operation in Europe Parliamentary Assembly 2017-19; RSPCA, CAFOD; Kt 2018. Deepdale Labour Club; Penwortham Sports and Social, Lonsdale Sports and Social.

Publications: Changing States: A Labour Agenda for Europe (Mandarin Paperbacks, 1996); The euro and Co-operative Enterprise: Co-operating with the euro (Co-operative Press Ltd, 1998).

Recreations: Football, boxing, chess, travel, foreign languages.

Sir Mark Hendrick MP, House of Commons, London SW1A 0AA
Tel: 020 7219 4791 *Email:* mark.hendrick.mp@parliament.uk
Constituency: PTMC, Marsh Lane, Preston, Lancashire PR1 8UQ
Tel: 01772 883575 *Email:* warhurste@parliament.uk Website: www.prestonmp.co.uk
Twitter: @MpHendrick

SCOTTISH NATIONAL PARTY

HENDRY, DREW

Inverness, Nairn, Badenoch and Strathspey *(Majority 10,440)*

SNP Shadow Secretary of State for International Trade

Andrew Egan Henderson Hendry. Born 31 May 1964; Married Jackie (4 children).

Non-political career: Director: Electrolux, AEG; Teclan Ltd: Founder 1999-, Honorary Chairman.

Political career: Member for Inverness, Nairn, Badenoch and Strathspey since 7 May 2015 general election; SNP: Spokesperson for Transport 2015-17, Spokesperson/Shadow Secretary of State for Business, Energy and Industrial Strategy 2017-21, Shadow Secretary of State for International Trade 2021-; Suspended from House of Commons 16 December 2020-12 January 2021. *Select committees:* Member, Business, Energy and Industrial Strategy 2017-19. Contested Scotland region 2009 European Parliament election and Highlands and Islands region (9) 2011

House of Commons MPs' Biographies

Scottish Parliament election. Vice-convener, Dingwall and District SNP; Member, SNP CND. *Councils and public bodies:* Highland Council: Councillor 2007-15, Chair, Planning Environment and Development Committee, SNP Group: Finance Spokesperson, Leader 2011-15, Leader of the Council 2012-15.

Political interests: Scottish home rule.

Other: Vice-President, Conference of Maritime Peripheral Regions 2012-; Honorary Consul to Embassy of Romania 2012-.

Recreations: Football, swimming.

Drew Hendry MP, House of Commons, London SW1A 0AA
Tel: 020 7219 6118 *Email:* drew.hendry.mp@parliament.uk
Constituency: 79 Kenneth Street, Inverness IV3 5QQ
Tel: 01463 611024 Website: www.drewhendrymp.scot *Twitter:* @drewhendrySNP

CONSERVATIVE

HENRY, DARREN

Broxtowe *(Majority 5,331)*

Darren George Henry. Born August 1968; Married Caroline (twin children).

Education: Lincoln University (BSc logistics management 2016).

Non-political career: Royal Air Force: Squadron Leader 1987-2013, Community Support Officer 2010-12; Programme Manager, Carillion plc 2014; General Manager, Harvest Fine Foods Ltd 2014-15.

Political career: Contested Wolverhampton North East 2015 general election. Member for Broxtowe since 12 December 2019; Trade Envoy to the Caribbean (with focus on 12 Commonwealth countries) 2020-. Chair, Wiltshire Conservative Area Council. *Councils and public bodies:* Governor, St Edmund's Girls School, Salisbury 2014-15; Councillor: Shrewton Parish Council 2015-19, Wiltshire Council 2017-20.

Other: Volunteers Co-ordinator, Shrewton Youth Club 2015-.

Recreations: Rugby Union referee 2013-.

Darren Henry MP, House of Commons, London SW1A 0AA
Tel: 020 7219 5198 *Email:* darren.henry.mp@parliament.uk
Constituency: 168 Derby Road, Stapleford, Nottingham NG9 7AY
Website: www.darrenhenry.org.uk *Twitter:* @DarrenG_Henry

CONSERVATIVE

HIGGINBOTHAM, ANTONY

Burnley *(Majority 1,352)*

Born 16 December 1989; Son of Julie Acton and Christopher Higginbotham; Single.

Education: Haslingden High School and Sixth Form; Hull University (BA British politics and legislative studies 2012); City University London (Graduate Diploma law 2014).

Non-political career: Researcher to John Baron MP 2010-11; Analyst, Association of Foreign Banks 2014-15; Senior Associate, Bank of Toyko-Mitsubishi UFJ 2015; Regulatory Liaison Manager, NatWest 2015-19. Lancashire's Army Cadet Force.

Political career: Member for Burnley since 12 December 2019. *Select committees:* Member, Future Relationship with the European Union 2020-21. Greenwich Conservative Federation: Deputy Chair, Membership and Finance 2017-19, Branch Chair Greenwich North 2017.

Political interests: Brexit, public services, Northern Powerhouse, NHS, international trade, foreign and defence, Global Britain; China, European Union, Israel, Middle East, Russia, USA.

Other: Mentor, Trailblazers 2015-17; Management Committee, Newhaven Pupil Newhaven Referral Unit 2016-17.

Recreations: Running.

Antony Higginbotham MP, House of Commons, London SW1A 0AA
Tel: 020 7219 3981 *Email:* antony.higginbotham.mp@parliament.uk
Constituency: 1 Nicholas Street, Burnley BB11 2AQ
Tel: 01282 969377 Website: www.antonyhig.co.uk *Twitter:* @antony_hig

LABOUR

HILL, MIKE

Hartlepool *(Majority 3,595)*

Michael Robert Hill. Born 12 May 1963; Married Glynis (2 sons).

Education: Lancaster University (BA drama and theatre arts).

Non-political career: Regional Organiser, Unison -2017. Political lead officer, Unison Northern Region; Secretary, Trade Union and Labour Party Liaison Organisation; Former branch secretary, Rochdale Branch, Unison.

Political career: Contested Richmond (Yorkshire) 2015 general election. Member for Hartlepool since 8 June 2017. *Select committees:* Member: Petitions 2017-, Treasury 2020-. Vice-chair, Labour North; Member, Co-operative Party; Labour Party whip and membership suspended September-October 2019.

Mike Hill MP, House of Commons, London SW1A 0AA
Tel: 020 7219 2543 *Email:* mike.hill.mp@parliament.uk
Constituency: 23 South Road, Hartlepool TS26 9HD
Tel: 01429 290168 *Twitter:* @MikeHillMP

LABOUR/ CO-OPERATIVE

HILLIER, MEG

Hackney South and Shoreditch *(Majority 33,985)*

Chair, Select Committee on Public Accounts

Margaret Olivia Hillier. Born 14 February 1969.

Education: Portsmouth High School; St Hilda's College, Oxford (MA philosophy, politics and economics 1990); City University, London (Diploma newspaper journalism 1991).

Non-political career: Reporter, *South Yorkshire Times* 1991; Petty officer, P&O European Ferries 1992; Public relations officer, Newlon Housing Group 1993; *Housing Today*: Reporter 1994-95, Features editor 1995-98; Freelance journalist 1998-2000. Member, Unite.

Political career: Member for Hackney South and Shoreditch 2005-10, for Hackney South and Shoreditch (revised boundary) since 6 May 2010 general election; PPS to Ruth Kelly as Secretary of State for Communities and Local Government 2006-07; Parliamentary Under-Secretary of State, Home Office 2007-10; Shadow Minister for Home Office 2010; Shadow Secretary of State for Energy and Climate Change 2010-11; Ex-officio member, Public Accounts Commission 2015-. *Select committees:* Member, Northern Ireland Affairs 2005-06; Public Accounts: Member 2011-15, Chair 2015-; Member: Liaison 2015-, Joint Committee on the Draft Parliamentary Buildings (Restoration and Renewal) Bill 2018-19. AM for North East constituency, London Assembly 2000-04. Co-operative Party: Member, Chair, parliamentary group 2010-11. *Councils and public bodies:* London Borough of Islington: Councillor 1994-2002, Chair, Neighbourhood Services Committee 1995-97, Mayor 1998-99; Board member, Transport for London 2004-05.

Political interests: Hackney.

Other: Member, Fabian Society; Trustee, War Memorials Trust 2001-15.

Meg Hillier MP, House of Commons, London SW1A 0AA
Tel: 020 7219 5325 *Fax:* 020 7219 8768 *Email:* meghilliermp@parliament.uk
Constituency: No constituency office
Website: meghillier.com *Twitter:* @Meg_HillierMP

CONSERVATIVE

HINDS, DAMIAN

East Hampshire *(Majority 19,696)*

Damian Patrick George Hinds. Born 27 November 1969; Son of Frank Hinds and Bebe Hinds; Married Jacqui Morel 2007 (2 daughters 1 son).

Education: St Ambrose Grammar, Altrincham; Trinity College, Oxford (BA philosophy, politics and economics 1992).

Non-political career: Research analyst, Mercer Management Consulting 1992-95; Various marketing and commercial management roles, Holiday Inn/Bass plc 1995-2003; Freelance adviser to the hotel trade 2003-05, 2007-10; Strategy director, Greene King plc 2005-07.

Political career: Contested Stretford and Urmston 2005 general election. Member for East Hampshire since 6 May 2010 general election; PPS to Mark Francois as Minister of State for: Defence Personnel, Welfare and Veterans, Ministry of Defence 2012-13, the Armed Forces,

Ministry of Defence 2013-14; Assistant Government Whip 2014-15; Exchequer Secretary, HM Treasury 2015-16; Minister of State for Employment, Department for Work and Pensions 2016-18; Secretary of State for Education 2018-19. *Select committees:* Member: Education 2010-12, Digital, Culture, Media and Sport 2020-. *Councils and public bodies:* Board member, Shadow Sponsor Body for the Houses of Parliament Restoration and Renewal Programme 2020-.

Political interests: Social mobility, education, welfare, affordable credit, financial inclusion.

Other: Chairman, Bow Group 2001-02; Volunteer, The Prince's Trust 2002-08; PC 2018.

Publications: Co-author, Power to the People (Bow Group, 1998); Editor, The Ideas Book 2000 (Bow Group, 1999); Co-editor, Go Zones: Policies for the Places Politics Forgot (Bow Group, 2004); Co-author, Seven Key Truths About Social Mobility (APPG report on Social Mobility, 2012); Contributor, Unlocking Local Leadership on Climate Change (Green Alliance, 2012).

Recreations: Music.

Rt Hon Damian Hinds MP, House of Commons, London SW1A 0AA
Tel: 020 7219 7057 *Email:* damian.hinds.mp@parliament.uk
Constituency: 14a Butts Road, Alton, Hampshire GU34 1ND
Tel: 01420 84122 Website: www.damianhinds.com *Twitter:* @DamianHinds

CONSERVATIVE

HOARE, SIMON

North Dorset *(Majority 24,301)*

Chair, Select Committee on Northern Ireland Affairs

Simon James Hoare. Born 28 June 1969; Son of Maria and late Colin Hoare; Married Kate 2000 (3 daughters).

Education: Bishop Hannon School, Fairwater; Oxford University (BA modern history 1990).

Non-political career: Managing Director, Community Connect 2002-15.

Political career: Contested Cardiff West 1997 and Cardiff South and Penarth 2010 general elections. Member for North Dorset since 7 May 2015 general election; PPS to George Eustice as Minister of State for Agriculture, Fisheries and Food, Department for Environment, Food and Rural Affairs 2016-17; Team PPS, Home Office 2017-18; PPS to: Damian Hinds as Secretary of State for Education 2018, Sajid Javid as Home Secretary 2018-19. *Select committees:* Member: Procedure 2015-16, Regulatory Reform 2015-19, Speaker's Advisory Committee on Works of Art 2015-18, Welsh Affairs 2017-18, Liaison 2019-; Chair, Northern Ireland Affairs 2019-. Former vice-chair, Wales Young Conservatives. *Councils and public bodies:* West Oxfordshire District Council: Councillor 2004-15, Cabinet Member for Resources and Asset Management 2007-15; Councillor, Oxfordshire County Council 2013-15; Vice-President, Local Government Association 2018-.

Political interests: Housing, planning, regeneration, farming, education.

Other: Member, Tory Reform Group; Vice-President, Local Government Association 2017-. Garrick Club; North Dorset Rugby Football Club, Newport (Pembs) Boat Club.

Recreations: Gardening, cooking, walking, family, messing about in boats.

Simon Hoare MP, House of Commons, London SW1A 0AA
Tel: 020 7219 5697 *Email:* simon.hoare.mp@parliament.uk
Constituency: The Stables, Whitecliff Gardens, Blandford Forum, Dorset DT11 7BU
Tel: 01258 452585 *Email:* diana.mogg@parliament.uk Websites: www.ndca.org.uk/ www.simonhoare.org.uk *Twitter:* @Simon4NDorset

LIBERAL DEMOCRAT

HOBHOUSE, WERA

Bath *(Majority 12,322)*

Liberal Democrat Spokesperson for Climate Emergency and Energy, Justice and Women and Equalities; Shadow Leader of the House

Wera Benedicta Hobhouse. Born 8 February 1960; Married William 1989 (2 daughters 2 sons).

Education: Münster University, Germany (history and fine arts 1987); École des Beaux Arts, Paris, France (art 1989); Masters history and fine art (Berlin, Germany).

Non-political career: Radio journalist, Germany; Member, Bluecoat Artists, Liverpool (opened a commercial modern art gallery); Foreign Language Teacher, Audenshaw School; Secretary, Composite Textiles Ltd 2007-17.

Political career: Contested Heywood and Middleton 2010 and North East Somerset 2015 general elections. Member for Bath since 8 June 2017; Liberal Democrat: Shadow Secretary of State/Spokesperson for: Communities and Local Government 2017-19, Refugees 2017, Commons Spokesperson for Justice 2019, Spokesperson/Shadow Secretary of State for Environment and Climate Change 2019; Shadow Secretary of State/Spokesperson for: Climate Emergency 2019-20, 2021-, Environment and Food 2019, Transport 2019, Energy 2019-20, 2021-, Environment 2019-20, Justice 2020-, Women and Equalities 2020-, Shadow Leader of the House 2020-. *Select committees:* Member, Exiting the European Union 2017-19. *Councils and public bodies:* Rochdale Council: Councillor 2004-14 (Con 2004-05, Lib Dem 2005-14), Cabinet member for Environment 2006-09, Chair, Health Scrutiny Committee 2009-10, Liberal Democrat Group Leader -2012; Vice-president, Local Government Association 2017-.

Political interests: Waste management, recycling, contaminated land regulations, green agenda.

Other: Trustee, Norden Community Trust; Patron, Bath Festivals.

Wera Hobhouse MP, House of Commons, London SW1A 0AA
Tel: 020 7219 2093 *Email:* wera.hobhouse.mp@parliament.uk
Constituency: 31 James Street West, Bath BA1 2BT
Tel: 01225 307024 *Email:* office@werahobhouse.co.uk Website: www.werahobhouse.co.uk
Twitter: @Wera_Hobhouse

LABOUR

HODGE, MARGARET

Barking *(Majority 15,427)*

Margaret Eve Hodge. Born 8 September 1944; Daughter of Hans and Lisbeth Oppenheimer; Married Andrew Watson 1968 (divorced 1978) (1 son 1 daughter); married Henry Hodge 1978 (later Mr Justice Hodge) (died 2009) (2 daughters).

Education: Bromley High School; Oxford High School; London School of Economics (BSc economics 1966); German, French, Italian.

Non-political career: Teaching and market research 1966-73; Senior consultant, Price Waterhouse 1992-94. Member, Unison.

Political career: Member for Barking 1994 by-election to 2010, for Barking (revised boundary) since 6 May 2010 general election; Parliamentary Under-Secretary of State, Department for Education and Employment (Employment and Equal Opportunities) 1998-2001; Minister of State: Department for Education and Skills 2001-05: (Lifelong Learning and Higher Education 2001-03, Lifelong Learning, Further and Higher Education 2003, Children, Young People and Families 2003-05), Department for Work and Pensions (Employment and Welfare Reform) 2005-06, Department of Trade and Industry (Industry and the Regions) 2006-07, Department for Culture, Media and Sport 2007-08, 2009-10 (Culture, Creative Industries and Tourism 2007-08, Culture and Tourism 2009-10); Shadow Minister for Culture, Media and Sport 2010; Chair, Public Accounts Commission 2010-15; Member, Commons Reference Group on Representation and Inclusion 2017-19. *Select committees:* Member: Education and Employment 1996-97, Deregulation 1996-97, Liaison 1997-98, 2010-15; Chair: Education and Employment (Education Sub-Committee) 1997-98, Public Accounts 2010-15. Progress; Member, Labour Party Local Government Committee 1983-92; Chair, London Group of Labour MPs 1995-98; Labour Women's Network; Chair, Fabian Executive Committee 1997-98. *Councils and public bodies:* London Borough of Islington: Councillor 1973-94, Chair, Housing Committee 1975-79, Leader 1982-92; Chair, Association of London Authorities 1984-92; Member, Home Office Advisory Committee on Race Relations 1988-92.

Political interests: Education, economy, local and regional government, housing, inner cities, democratic reform, London government, tax, fighting racism in all of its forms; Nepal.

Other: Director: University College, Middlesex Hospitals; Governor, London School of Economics 1990-2001; Vice-chair, AMA 1991-92; Fellow, Industry and Parliament Trust 1996; Member, advisory board, GovernUp; Visiting Professor, King's College London 2015-; Chair, board of directors, Theatre Royal Stratford East 2015-; Member, Editorial Board, Political Quarterly 2015-; Visiting Fellow of Practice, Blavatnik School of Government, Oxford University 2016-19; Chair, Fawcett Society's Local Government Commission 2016-18; Governor, Westminster Foundation for Democracy 2017-; Board Member, Social Market Foundation 2018-; Chair of Council, Royal Holloway, University of London 2019-; Freedom, City of London; Hon. Fellow, University of North London; Hon. DCL, City University 1993; Hon. Degree, University of South Wales 2014; Inquisitor of the Year, *Spectator* awards 2012, Parliamentarian of the Year Award, Political Studies Association 2012; *The House Magazine* Select Committee Member of the Year, Dods Parliamentary Awards 2014; Tax Personality of the Year Award, Taxation Awards 2014; Speech of the Year, Spectator awards 2019; MBE 1978; PC 2003; DBE 2015.

Publications: Quality, Equality and Democracy; Beyond the Town Hall; Fabian pamphlet on London Government, Not Just the Flower Show; Called to Account: How Corporate Bad Behaviour and Government Waste Combine to Cost us Millions (2016).

Recreations: Family, opera, piano, travel, cooking.

Rt Hon Dame Margaret Hodge DBE MP, House of Commons, London SW1A 0AA
Tel: 020 7219 6666 *Email:* hodgem@parliament.uk
Constituency: Barking Learning Centre, 2 Town Square, Barking, London IG11 7NB
Tel: 020 8594 1333 *Email:* margarethodge@hotmail.co.uk
Website: www.margarethodgemp.com *Twitter:* @margarethodge

LABOUR

HODGSON, SHARON Washington and Sunderland West *(Majority 3,723)*

Shadow Minister for Veterans

Born 1 April 1966; Daughter of Joan Cohen, née Wilson; Married Alan Hodgson 1990 (1 son 1 daughter).

Education: Heathfield Senior High School, Gateshead; Newcastle College (HEFC English 1997); TUC, National Education Centre (Open College Network Diploma Labour Party organising 2000).

Non-political career: Team Valley Trading Estate, Gateshead: Payroll/account clerk, Tyneside Safety Glass 1982-88, Payroll administrator, Burgess Microswitch 1992-94; Personnel, Northern Rock Building Society, Gosforth 1988-92; Charity administrator, The Total Learning Challenge (educational charity), Newcastle 1998-99; Regional organiser, Labour North 1999-2000; Constituency organiser, Mitcham and Morden CLP 2000-02; Labour link co-ordinator, London, Unison 2002-05. Member: GMB 1999-2007, Unite 2007-, CWU 2008-.

Political career: Member for Gateshead East and Washington West 2005-10, for Washington and Sunderland West since 6 May 2010 general election; PPS to: Liam Byrne as Minister of State, Home Office 2006-07, Bob Ainsworth as Minister of State, Ministry of Defence 2007-08, Dawn Primarolo as Minister of State, Department of Health 2008-09; Sponsored Special Educational Needs (Information) Act 2008; Assistant Government Whip 2009-10; Opposition Whip 2010; Shadow Minister for: Education 2010-13, 2015, Women and Equalities Office 2013-15, Children 2015-16, Health (Public Health) 2016-20, Defence (Veterans) 2020-. *Select committees:* Member: Regulatory Reform 2005-10, European Scrutiny 2006, Court of Referees 2007-10, Children, Schools and Families 2007-10, North East 2009-10, Ecclesiastical Committee 2010-15. Hon. Secretary, PLP Departmental Committee for the Treasury 2006-10; Chair, PLP Northern Group 2015-16. Women's officer, Tyne Bridge CLP 1998-2000; Constituency secretary, Mitcham and Morden CLP 2002-05.

Political interests: North/South divide, employment (especially youth and green jobs), education (especially special educational needs), health (especially cancer issues), child poverty, fuel poverty, free school meals, childcare and early intervention, equality, women's issues, consumer protection (especially secondary ticketing), basketball; Cambodia, China, Japan, New Zealand, Pakistan, Singapore, South Africa, Sri Lanka, USA.

Other: Member: Fabian Society 2004-, Christian Socialist Movement 2005-; Board Member, Basketball Foundation.

Recreations: Reading, cinema, cooking, shopping, travel, family.

Sharon Hodgson MP, House of Commons, London SW1A 0AA
Tel: 020 7219 5160 *Fax:* 020 7219 4493 *Email:* sharon.hodgson.mp@parliament.uk
Constituency: Suites 1 and 1a, Vermont House, Concord, Washington, Tyne and Wear NE37 2SQ
Tel: 0191-417 2000 Website: www.sharonhodgson.org *Twitter:* @SharonHodgsonMP

CONSERVATIVE

HOLDEN, RICHARD

North West Durham *(Majority 1,144)*

Richard John Holden. Born 11 March 1985.

Education: London School of Economics and Political Science (BSc government and history 2007).

Non-political career: Conservative Party: Data Administrator 2007-08, Media Monitoring Officer 2008, Duty Press Officer 2008-10, Political Press Adviser 2010-12, Deputy Head of Press 2012-15; Special Adviser: to the Leader and Chief Whip, House of Lords 2015-16, to the Secretary of State for Defence 2016-17, to the Department for Transport 2018-19, to the Department for Education 2019-.

Political career: Contested Preston 2015 general election. Member for North West Durham since 12 December 2019. *Select committees:* Member: Public Accounts 2020-, European Statutory Instruments 2020-.

Richard Holden MP, House of Commons, London SW1A 0AA
Tel: 020 7219 3059 *Email:* richard.holden.mp@parliament.uk
Constituency: 25-27 Medomsley Road, Consett DH8 5HE
Tel: 01207 500944 Website: www.richardholden.org.uk *Twitter:* @RicHolden

House of Commons MPs' Biographies

LABOUR

HOLLERN, KATE

Blackburn *(Majority 18,304)*

Shadow Minister for Local Government

Catherine Malloy Hollern. Born 12 April 1955; 2 daughters.

Non-political career: Work study manager, Newman's Footwear; Contracts manager, Blackburn College.

Political career: Member for Blackburn since 7 May 2015 general election; PPS to Maria Eagle as Shadow Secretary of State for Defence 2015-16; Shadow Minister for: Defence 2016, Communities and Local Government 2016-17; PPS to Jeremy Corbyn as Leader of the Opposition 2017-19; Shadow Minister for Communities and Local Government (Local Government) 2020-. *Select committees:* Member: Education 2015-16, Armed Forces Bill 2015 2015-16, Education, Skills and the Economy Sub-committee 2015-16, Procedure 2020. *Councils and public bodies:* Blackburn with Darwen Council: Councillor -2015, Leader, Labour group 2004-15, Council Leader 2004-07, 2010-15.

Kate Hollern MP, House of Commons, London SW1A 0AA
Tel: 020 7219 8692 *Email:* kate.hollern.mp@parliament.uk
Constituency: Richmond Chambers, Richmond Terrace, Blackburn, Lancashire BB1 7AS
Tel: 01254 52317 *Twitter:* @Kate_HollernMP

CONSERVATIVE

HOLLINRAKE, KEVIN

Thirsk and Malton *(Majority 25,154)*

PPS to Michael Gove as Chancellor of the Duchy of Lancaster

Kevin Paul Hollinrake. Born 28 September 1963; Married Nicola Sara Thompson 1994 (1 son 3 daughters).

Education: Easingwold School; Sheffield Polytechnic (physics 1982).

Non-political career: Hunters Property Group Ltd: Managing Director 1992-2015, Chair 2015-.

Political career: Member for Thirsk and Malton since 7 May 2015 general election; PPS to: David Lidington as Leader of the House of Commons and Lord President of the Council 2016-17, Michael Gove as Secretary of State for Environment, Food and Rural Affairs 2017-19, Michael Gove as Chancellor of the Duchy of Lancaster 2019-. *Select committees:* Member:

Communities and Local Government/Housing, Communities and Local Government 2015-19, Armed Forces Bill 2015 2015-16. Treasurer, Conservative Friends of Bangladesh; Founding member, Conservatives for Reform in Europe 2016.

Political interests: Business, housing, banking, poverty, economy, social care.

Other: Member: NAEA 1990, Institute of Directors 2006.

Recreations: Golf, cricket, rugby union, reading.

Kevin Hollinrake MP, House of Commons, London SW1A 0AA
Tel: 020 7219 4746 *Email:* kevin.hollinrake.mp@parliament.uk
Constituency: 109 Town Street, Old Malton YO17 7HD
Tel: 01347 666880 Website: www.kevinhollinrake.org.uk *Twitter:* @kevinhollinrake

CONSERVATIVE

HOLLOBONE, PHILIP

Kettering *(Majority 16,765)*

Philip Thomas Hollobone. Born 7 November 1964; Son of Thomas and Patricia Hollobone.

Education: Dulwich College, London; Lady Margaret Hall, Oxford University (BA modern history and economics 1987, MA).

Non-political career: Industry research analyst 1987-2003. Soldier and paratrooper, Territorial Army 1984-93.

Political career: Contested Lewisham East 1997 and Kettering 2001 general elections. Member for Kettering 2005-10, for Kettering (revised boundary) since 6 May 2010 general election. *Select committees:* Member: Crossrail Bill 2006-07, Transport 2006-10, Backbench Business 2010-12, 2015-16, Chairmen's Panel/Panel of Chairs 2010-. Chair, Bromley and Chislehurst Conservative Association 1999; Deputy Chair, Kettering Constituency Conservative Association 2002-14, 2017-. *Councils and public bodies:* Councillor: London Borough of Bromley 1990-94, Kettering Borough Council 2003-.

Other: Special Constable, British Transport Police 2008-15.

Philip Hollobone MP, House of Commons, London SW1A 0AA
Tel: 020 7219 8373 *Fax:* 020 7219 8802 *Email:* philip.hollobone.mp@parliament.uk
Constituency: No constituency office publicised

CONSERVATIVE

HOLLOWAY, ADAM

Gravesham *(Majority 15,581)*

PPS (with responsibility for ending rough sleeping), Ministry of Housing, Communities and Local Government

Adam James Harold Holloway. Born 29 July 1965; Single.

Education: Cranleigh School, Surrey; Magdalene College, Cambridge (MA); Imperial College, London (MBA 1998); Royal Military Academy Sandhurst (Commissioned 1987).

Non-political career: Presenter: World in Action, Granada TV 1992-93; Senior reporter: ITN 1993-97, *Tonight with Trevor McDonald* 2000-01, Contributions to ITN/Sky News, Iraq War 2003. Commissioned, Grenadier Guards 1987-92.

Political career: Member for Gravesham since 5 May 2005 general election; PPS: to David Lidington as Minister of State, Foreign and Commonwealth Office 2010-11, (with responsibility for ending rough sleeping), Ministry of Housing, Communities and Local Government 2020-. *Select committees:* Member: Defence 2006-10, 2012-14, Arms Export Controls 2009-11, Public Administration 2014-15, Foreign Affairs 2015-17, Public Administration and Constitutional Affairs 2016, Science and Technology 2017-18, Home Affairs 2020-. Chairman, Conservative Backbench Policy Committees on: Defence 2017-18, Home Affairs 2017-19. Deputy chairman, Conservative Middle East Council 2010-; Founding member, Conservatives for Britain 2015-16.

Political interests: Constituents, defence, foreign, crime.

Other: Trustee: Christian Aid 1997-2001, Map Action 2002-10; Former Parliamentary Chair, Council for Arab British Understanding; Backbencher of the Year, *Spectator* awards 2011. Gravesend Conservative Club, Northfleet Conservative Club, Pratt's Club.

Publications: In Blood Stepp'd in Too Far: Towards a realistic policy for Afghanistan (Centre for Policy Studies, 2009); The Failure of British Political and Military Leadership in Basra (First Defence, 2010).

Adam Holloway MP, House of Commons, London SW1A 0AA
Tel: 020 7219 8402 *Fax:* 020 7219 2871 *Email:* hollowaya@parliament.uk
Constituency: No constituency office
Website: www.adamholloway.co.uk

CONSERVATIVE

HOLMES, PAUL

Eastleigh *(Majority 15,607)*

Paul John Holmes. Born 25 August 1988.

Education: Kelsey Park Sports College; Southampton University (BSc politics and international relations 2009).

Non-political career: Senior Parliamentary Adviser to Stephen Hammond MP 2011-15; Account Manager, Portland 2015-16; Special Adviser to: Patrick McLoughlin as Chancellor of the Duchy of Lancaster 2016-17, Damian Green as First Secretary of State, Minister for the Cabinet Office 2017, Damian Hinds as Secretary of State for Education 2018; Head of Public Affairs, Clarion Housing Group 2018-19.

Political career: Contested Mitcham and Morden 2015 and Southampton Test 2017 general elections. Member for Eastleigh since 12 December 2019. *Select committees:* Member: Joint Committee on Statutory Instruments 2020-, Housing, Communities and Local Government 2020-. *Councils and public bodies:* Southampton City Council: Councillor 2008-12, Cabinet Member for Children's Services and Learning 2009-11.

Paul Holmes MP, House of Commons, London SW1A 0AA
Tel: 020 7219 5484 *Email:* paul.holmes.mp@parliament.uk
Constituency: 46 Leigh Road, Eastleigh SO50 9DT
Tel: 023 8254 2205 Website: www.voteholmes.co.uk *Twitter:* @pauljholmes

LABOUR

HOPKINS, RACHEL

Luton South *(Majority 8,756)*

Rachel Louise Hopkins. Born 30 December 1972; Daughter of Kelvin Hopkins, MP for Luton North 1997-2019; Partner Iain.

Education: Denbigh High School; Luton Sixth Form College; Leicester University (BA French and politics 1994); Bedfordshire University (MSc human resource management 2012).

Non-political career: Customer service centre, TSB bank; Review Manager, Electoral Commission 2001-03; Conduct Team Leader, General Social Care Council 2003; Senior Team Member, Accreditation, Training and Development Agency for Schools 2004-05; Special Project Officer, Programme Management Office, Bedfordshire University 2005-07; Human Fertilisation and Embryology Authority: Policy Manager 2007-08, Programme Office Manager 2008-09, HR Manager 2009-10, Head of Human Resources 2010-17.

Political career: Member for Luton South since 12 December 2019; PPS to: Richard Burgon as Shadow Lord Chancellor and Secretary of State for Justice 2020, Marsha De Cordova as Shadow Secretary of State for Women and Equalities 2020. *Select committees:* Member: Public Administration and Constitutional Affairs 2020-, Housing, Communities and Local Government 2020-. *Councils and public bodies:* Luton Borough Council: Councillor 2011-, Executive portfolio holder for Commissioning and Public Health; Governor, Luton Sixth Form College 2014-.

Rachel Hopkins MP, House of Commons, London SW1A 0AA
Tel: 020 7219 8424 *Email:* rachel.hopkins.mp@parliament.uk
Constituency: 3 Union Street, Luton LU1 3AN
Website: www.rachelhopkins.org *Twitter:* @rach_hopkins

SCOTTISH NATIONAL PARTY

HOSIE, STEWART

Dundee East *(Majority 13,375)*

SNP Shadow Chancellor of the Duchy of Lancaster and Minister for the Cabinet Office

Born 3 January 1963; Son of R A Hosie, architectural ironmonger, and E A Hosie, bookkeeper; Married Shona Robison 1997, MSP for Dundee City East (1 daughter) (divorced).

Education: Carnoustie High School; Bell Street Tech (HD computer studies 1981); Dundee College of Technology 1981.

Non-political career: Group IS manager, MIH 1988-93; Systems analyst, various organisations 1993-96; Year 2000/EMU project manager, Stakis plc/Hilton 1996-2000; Various project management posts 2000-05. Member, MSF 1992.

Political career: Contested Kirkcaldy 1992 and 1997 general elections. Member for Dundee East since 5 May 2005 general election; SNP: Spokesperson for: Treasury 2005-15, Women 2005-07, Home Affairs 2005-07, Economy 2005-07, 2015-17, Deputy Leader, Westminster Group 2007-17, Chief Whip 2007-13; Member, House of Commons Commission 2015-19; SNP Spokesperson/Shadow Secretary of State for International Trade 2018-21, Shadow Chancellor of the Duchy of Lancaster and Minister for the Cabinet Office 2021-; Member, Intelligence and Security Committee 2019, 2020-. *Select committees:* Member: Treasury 2010-15, 2017-19, Panel of Chairs 2017-, Treasury Sub-committee 2017-19. Contested Kirkcaldy constituency 1999 Scottish Parliament election. Scottish National Party: Youth convener 1986-89, National secretary 1999-2003, Organisation convener 2003-05, Deputy leader 2014-16.

Political interests: Economic development, job creation.

Other: Endorsed by the Save the Scottish Regiments Campaign.

Recreations: Football, hill-walking, rugby.

Stewart Hosie MP, House of Commons, London SW1A 0AA
Tel: 020 7219 8164 *Fax:* 020 7219 6716 *Email:* stewart.hosie.mp@parliament.uk
Constituency: 8 Old Glamis Road, Dundee DD3 8HP
Tel: 01382 623200 *Email:* stewart@stewarthosie.com
95 High Street, Carnoustie, Angus DD7 9EA
Tel: 01241 856489 Website: www.stewarthosie.com *Twitter:* @StewartHosieSNP

LABOUR

HOWARTH, GEORGE

Knowsley *(Majority 39,942)*

George Edward Howarth. Born 29 June 1949; Son of late George Howarth and Eleanor Howarth; Married Julie Rodgers 1977 (2 sons 1 daughter).

Education: Schools in Huyton; Liverpool Polytechnic (BA social sciences 1977).

Non-political career: Engineering apprentice 1966-70; Engineer 1970-75; Teacher 1977-82; Co-operative Development Services 1980-82; Chief executive, Wales Co-operative Centre 1982-86. Member, Unite.

Political career: Member for Knowsley North 13 November 1986 by-election to 1997, for Knowsley North and Sefton East 1997-2010, for Knowsley since 6 May 2010 general election; Opposition Spokesperson for: the Environment 1989-92, Environmental Protection 1993-94, Home Affairs 1994-97; Parliamentary Under-Secretary of State: Home Office 1997-99, Northern Ireland Office 1999-2001; Member, Intelligence and Security Committee 2008-16; Temporary Deputy Speaker May-June 2015. *Select committees:* Member: Public Accounts 2002-03, Modernisation of the House of Commons 2005-10; Chair, Armed Forces Bill 2005-06; Member: Joint Committee on Conventions 2006, Chairmen's Panel/Panel of Chairs 2009-, Finance and Services 2012-15. Labour Party: Chair, Knowsley South 1981-85, Secretary, Knowsley Borough District 1977-80, Member: North West Region Executive 1981-84, National Executive Committee October 2016-. *Councils and public bodies:* Councillor, Huyton Urban District Council 1971-75; Knowsley Borough Council: Councillor 1975-86, Deputy Leader 1982-83.

Political interests: Housing, environment, crime, disorder; Middle East, South Africa.

Other: Chair, Knowsley Skills Academy; PC 2005; Kt 2019.

Recreations: Coarse fishing, family, reading.

Rt Hon Sir George Howarth MP, House of Commons, London SW1A 0AA
Tel: 020 7219 6902 *Fax:* 020 7219 0495 *Email:* george.howarth.mp@parliament.uk
Constituency: Lathom House, North Mersey Business Centre, Woodward Road, Kirkby, Merseyside L33 7UY
Tel: 0151-546 9918 Website: www.georgehowarth.org.uk

CONSERVATIVE

HOWELL, JOHN

Henley *(Majority 14,053)*

John Michael Howell. Born 27 July 1955; Son of Alexander and Gladys Howell; Married Alison Parker 1987 (dissolved 2020) (1 son 2 daughters).

Education: Battersea Grammar School, London; Edinburgh University (MA archaeology 1978); St John's College, Oxford (DPhil prehistoric archaeology 1981); French, Russian.

Non-political career: Ernst & Young 1987-96; Business presenter, BBC World Service Television 1996-97; Director: Fifth World Productions Ltd 1996-2003, Media Presentation Consultants Ltd 2005-08.

Political career: Member for Henley 26 June 2008 by-election to 2010, for Henley (revised boundary) since 6 May 2010 general election; PPS: to Greg Clark as Minister of State for Decentralisation 2010-11, to Leaders of the House of Commons and Lords Privy Seal: Sir George Young 2010-12, Andrew Lansley 2012-14; Trade Envoy to Nigeria 2016-20; Government's Neighbourhood Planning Champion; Team PPS, Ministry of Housing, Communities and Local Government 2019. *Select committees:* Member: Work and Pensions 2009-10, Justice 2014-, Armed Forces Bill 2015 2015-16. Member, Executive, 1922 Committee 2014-15; Chairman, Conservative Backbench Policy Committee on Communities and Local Government 2015-19. Treasurer, European Conservative and Democratic Alliance 2019-. *Councils and public bodies:* Oxfordshire County Council: Councillor 2004-09, Cabinet Member for Change Management 2005-08; Vice-President, Local Government Association 2010-11.

Political interests: Rural issues, social policy, local government, foreign affairs, planning, environment; Central and Eastern Europe, Israel, Nigeria, South Asia.

Other: UK delegation, Parliamentary Assembly of the Council of Europe: Member 2015-21, Leader 2021-; Trustee, Holocaust Memorial Day Trust; Chair, Industry and Parliament Trust Board of Trustees 2020-; Associate, Chartered Institute of Arbitrators; Fellow: Royal Geographic Society, Society of Antiquaries; OBE 2000. Leander Club Henley.

Publications: Neolithic Northern France (1983); Understanding Eastern Europe: the context of change (1994).

Recreations: Music, theatre.

Dr John Howell OBE MP, House of Commons, London SW1A 0AA
Tel: 020 7219 6676 *Email:* howelljm@parliament.uk
Constituency: PO Box 84, Watlington, Oxfordshire OX49 5XD
Tel: 01491 613088 Website: www.johnhowell.org.uk *Twitter:* @JHowellUK

CONSERVATIVE

HOWELL, PAUL

Sedgefield *(Majority 4,513)*

Born January 1960.

Non-political career: Private Landlord; Governor, West Park Academy.

Political career: Contested Houghton and Sunderland South 2017 general election. Member for Sedgefield since 12 December 2019. *Select committees:* Member, Business, Energy and Industrial Strategy 2020-.

Other: Bishop Auckland Rotary Club; Darlington Freemasons.

Paul Howell MP, House of Commons, London SW1A 0AA
Tel: 020 7219 6385 *Email:* paul.howell.mp@parliament.uk
Constituency: No constituency office publicised
Twitter: @PaulHowellMP

THE SPEAKER

HOYLE, LINDSAY

Chorley *(Majority 17,392)*

Speaker

Lindsay Harvey Hoyle. Born 10 June 1957; Son of Doug Hoyle (MP for Nelson and Colne October 1974-79, Warrington 1981-83 and Warrington North 1983-97, now Lord Hoyle (qv)) and late Pauline Hoyle; Married Lynda Fowler (divorced 1982); married Catherine Swindley (1 daughter 1 daughter deceased).

Education: Lords College, Bolton; Horwich FE; Bolton TIC (City & Guilds Construction).

Non-political career: Honorary Colonel, 3 Medical Regiment. Member, Unite.

Political career: Member for Chorley 1997-2010, for Chorley (revised boundary) since 6 May 2010 general election [Lab 1997-2019, Speaker since 2019]; Parliamentary assistant to Beverley Hughes as Minister for the North West 2008-10; Chairman, Ways and Means and Deputy Speaker 2010-19; Speaker 2019-; Chair: Consultative Panel on Parliamentary Security 2015-20, House of Commons Commission 2019-, Speaker's Committee for the Independent Parliamentary Standards Authority 2020-, Speaker's Committee on the Electoral Commission 2020-. *Select committees:* Member: Catering 1997-2005, Trade and Industry/Business, Enterprise and Regulatory Reform/Business and Enterprise/Business, Innovation and Skills 1998-2010, European Scrutiny 2005-10, Quadripartite (Committees on Strategic Export Controls) 2006-07; Member, Finance and Services 2010-18; Panel of Chairs: Ex-officio member 2010-19 Member 2013-15, Chair 2015-19, Member, Finance 2015-19; Chair, Court of Referees 2016-17. Joint vice-chair, PLP Departmental Committee for Defence 1997-2001. *Councils and public bodies:* Councillor, Adlington Town Council 1980-98; Chorley Borough Council: Councillor 1980-98, Chair, Economic Development and Deputy Leader 1994-97, Mayor of Chorley 1997-98; Chairman (ex-officio): Boundary Commission for England 2019- Boundary Commission for Scotland 2019-, Boundary Commission for Wales 2019-, Boundary Commission for Northern Ireland 2019-.

Political interests: Trade and industry, sport, defence, small businesses, agriculture; British Overseas Territories, Commonwealth Countries.

Other: President, Commonwealth Parliamentary Association (UK Branch) 2019-; Hon. President, Inter-Parliamentary Union, British Group 2019-; Armed Forces Parliamentary Scheme (Royal Marines) 1998-; President, Chorley Mencap; Trustee, History of Parliament Trust; President, Industry and Parliament Trust 2019-; Juvenile Diabetes Research Foundation; Inspire Youth Zone Chorley; Chorley Pals Memorial; Patchwork Foundation; Chancellor, Gibraltar University; PC 2013; Kt 2018. Member: Adlington Cricket Club, Chorley Cricket Club.

Recreations: Cricket, Rugby League, football.

Rt Hon Sir Lindsay Hoyle MP, House of Commons, London SW1A 0AA
Tel: 020 7219 3515 *Email:* speakersoffice@parliament.uk
Constituency: 35-39 Market Street, Chorley, Lancashire PR7 2SW
Tel: 01257 271555 *Email:* goreb@parliament.uk Website: lindsayhoylemp.strikingly.com
Twitter: @LindsayHoyle_MP

CONSERVATIVE

HUDDLESTON, NIGEL

Mid Worcestershire *(Majority 28,018)*

Parliamentary Under-Secretary of State for Sport, Tourism and Heritage, Department for Digital, Culture, Media and Sport; Assistant Government Whip

Nigel Paul Huddleston. Born 13 October 1970; Son of Alan Huddleston, factory worker, and Pauline Huddleston, secretary, sales representative and supermarket checkout operator; Married Melissa Peters 1999 (1 son 1 daughter).

Education: Robert Pattinson Comprehensive School, North Hykeham; Oxford University (BA philosophy, politics and economics 1992) (Vice-President Student Union 1992-93); Anderson Business School, University of California, Los Angeles, USA (MBA 1998).

Non-political career: Management consultant: Arthur Andersen Business Consulting 1993-2002, Deloitte Strategy Consulting 2002-10; Industry Head for Travel, Google 2010-15.

Political career: Contested Luton South 2010 general election. Member for Mid Worcestershire since 7 May 2015 general election; Department for Digital, Culture, Media and Sport: Team PPS 2017-18, PPS to Secretary of State for Digital, Culture, Media and Sport: Matt Hancock 2018, Jeremy Wright 2018-19, Parliamentary Under-Secretary of State for Sport, Tourism and Heritage 2020-; Assistant Government Whip 2019-. *Select committees:* Member, Culture, Media and Sport 2015-17. Board Member, Tory Reform Group 2010-15; Founding Member, Conservatives for Reform in Europe 2016; Vice-chairman, Youth, Conservative Party 2019. *Councils and public bodies:* Councillor, St Albans City and District Council 2011-14.

Political interests: Business (especially digital sector and the internet), travel and tourism, education; UAE, USA.

Other: Member, National Trust; Chair, Democracy Forum -2017; Freedom, City of Lincoln 1996.

Recreations: Travel, spending time with his children.

Nigel Huddleston MP, House of Commons, London SW1A 0AA
Tel: 020 7219 5814 *Email:* nigel.huddleston.mp@parliament.uk
Constituency: No constituency office
Website: www.nigelhuddleston.com *Twitter:* @HuddlestonNigel

CONSERVATIVE

HUDSON, NEIL

Penrith and The Border *(Majority 18,519)*

Neil Peter Hammerton Hudson. Married (2 children).

Education: Cambridge University Veterinary School (MA 1994); Sydney University (Diploma veterinary clinical studies 1995); Edinburgh University (PhD grass sickness and equine gastroenterology, Residency equine internal medicine, Certificate equine internal medicine, RCVS Diploma equine internal medicine 2006).

Non-political career: Veterinary Surgeon; Edinburgh University Veterinary School: Lecturer, Equine Medicine, Director of Undergraduate Admissions, Senior Veterinary Clinical Lecturer, Programme Director, Equine Science Postgraduate Programme.

Political career: Contested Newcastle upon Tyne North 2005 and Edinburgh South 2010 general elections. Member for Penrith and The Border since 12 December 2019. *Select committees:* Member, Environment, Food and Rural Affairs 2020-.

Political interests: Health, education, science, rural affairs.

Other: Higher Education Academy: Senior Fellow 2015, Principal Fellow 2019; Fellow, Royal College of Veterinary Surgeons 2018.

Recreations: Cricket, music, theatre.

Dr Neil Hudson MP, House of Commons, London SW1A 0AA
Tel: 020 7219 3000 *Email:* neil.hudson.mp@parliament.uk
Constituency: No constituency office publicised
Tel: 01768 484114 Website: www.neilhudson.org.uk *Twitter:* @DrNeilHudson

CONSERVATIVE

HUGHES, EDDIE

Walsall North *(Majority 11,965)*

Parliamentary Under-Secretary of State for Rough Sleeping and Housing, Ministry of Housing, Communities and Local Government

Edmund Francis Hughes. Born 3 October 1968; Married Clare (2 children).

Education: Handsworth Grammar School; Glamorgan University (BSc civil engineering).

Non-political career: YMCA Birmingham: Director of Development and Asset Management 2014-17, Assistant Chief Executive 2017.

Political career: Contested Birmingham Hall Green 2005 general election. Member for Walsall North since 8 June 2017; Team PPS: Ministry of Housing, Communities and Local Government 2018, Department for Exiting the European Union 2018-19; PPS to Brandon Lewis as Minister of State for Security and Economic Crime and Deputy Minister for Brexit, Home Office 2019-20; Assistant Government Whip 2020-21; Parliamentary Under-Secretary of State for Rough Sleeping and Housing, Ministry of Housing, Communities and Local Government 2021-.

Select committees: Member: Women and Equalities 2017-20, Joint Committee on Consolidation, &c, Bills 2017-20. *Councils and public bodies:* Councillor, Walsall Council 1999-2018; Governor, St Anne's School, Streetly.

Political interests: Brexit, crime.

Other: whg Housing Association: Board member 2012-16, Chairperson 2016-; Member, Barr Beacon Trust; Chartered member, Chartered Institute of Building (CIOB) 2011-; Trustee, Walsall Wood Allotment Charity.

Eddie Hughes MP, House of Commons, London SW1A 0AA
Tel: 020 7219 6315 *Email:* eddie.hughes.mp@parliament.uk
Constituency: 74b Park Road, Bloxwich, Walsall WS3 3SW
Tel: 01922 477877 *Email:* eddie@eddiehughes.co.uk Website: www.eddiehughes.co.uk
Twitter: @EddieHughes4WN

CONSERVATIVE

HUNT, JANE

Loughborough *(Majority 7,169)*

Team PPS, Cabinet Office

Jane Marion Hunt. Born 4 June 1966; Married Tim (2 children).

Non-political career: Sales Manager; Civil Servant; Charity Worker; Caseworker to Nicky Morgan MP.

Political career: Contested Leicester East 2010 general election, Leicester South 2011 by-election and Nottingham South 2015 and 2017 general elections. Member for Loughborough since 12 December 2019; Team PPS, Cabinet Office 2020-. Loughborough Constituency Conservative Association; Member, Executive Council, Leicester Conservatives. *Councils and public bodies:* Charnwood Borough Council: Councillor 2003-, Lead Member for Housing and Regulatory Services, Lead Member for Planning, Inward Investment and Tourism Strategy; Former school governor.

Political interests: Education.

Other: President, Loughborough Ladies Circle; Trustee: Loughborough Welfare Trust, Clarke and Somerville Foundation.

Jane Hunt MP, House of Commons, London SW1A 0AA
Tel: 020 7219 8647 *Email:* jane.hunt.mp@parliament.uk
Constituency: 18 Pinfold Gate, Loughborough LE11 1BE
Tel: 01509 262723 Website: www.janehunt.uk *Twitter:* @JaneMHunt

CONSERVATIVE

HUNT, JEREMY

South West Surrey *(Majority 8,817)*

Chair, Select Committee on Health and Social Care

Jeremy Richard Streynsham Hunt. Born 1 November 1966; Son of late Admiral Sir Nicholas Hunt and Meriel Hunt; Married Lucia Guo 2009 (1 son 2 daughters).

Education: Charterhouse, Surrey; Magdalen College, Oxford (BA philosophy, politics and economics 1988, MA); French, Japanese.

Non-political career: Management consultant, Outram Cullinan and Co 1988-89; English teacher, Japan 1990-91; Founder and managing director, Hotcourses Ltd 1991-2005.

Political career: Member for South West Surrey 2005-10, for South West Surrey (revised boundary) since 6 May 2010 general election; Shadow Minister for Disabled People 2005-07; Shadow Secretary of State for Culture, Media and Sport 2007-10; Secretary of State for: Culture, Olympics, Media and Sport 2010-12, Health 2012-18, Social Care 2018, Foreign and Commonwealth Affairs (Foreign Secretary) 2018-19. *Select committees:* Member: International Development 2005-06, Liaison 2020-; Chair, Health and Social Care 2020-. *Councils and public bodies:* Ex-officio member, Olympic Board -2012.

Political interests: Education, international development, philanthropy; Africa, Japan.

Other: Member, Education, Youth, Culture and Sport Council, Council of the European Union 2010-12; Founder and trustee, Hotcourses Foundation 2004-; Patron: Haselmere Museum, Meath Art Trust, Brightwells Gostry Community Centre, COINS Foundation, Undershaw School, DFN Project Search; Trustee and Chair, Patient Safety Watch 2019-; Board Representative, Soak and Sleep 2020-; PC 2010.

Recreations: Latin music and dance.

Rt Hon Jeremy Hunt MP, House of Commons, London SW1A 0AA
Tel: 020 7219 6813 *Email:* huntj@parliament.uk
Constituency: South West Surrey Conservative Association, 2 Royal Parade, Tilford Road, Hindhead, Surrey GU26 6TD
Tel: 01428 609416 Website: www.jeremyhunt.org *Twitter:* @Jeremy_Hunt

CONSERVATIVE

HUNT, TOM

Ipswich *(Majority 5,479)*

Thomas Patrick Hunt.

Education: The King's school, Ely; Hills Road Sixth Form College; Manchester University (BA politics and modern history 2010); Oxford University (MSc Russian, Central European, East European and Eurasian studies 2011).

Non-political career: Senior Parliamentary Assistant to Oliver Dowden MP 2015-16; Media Relations Manager, Countryside Alliance 2016-17; Chief of Staff, Cambridgeshire and Peterborough Combined Authority 2017-19.

Political career: Contested Doncaster Central 2017 general election. Member for Ipswich since 12 December 2019. *Select committees:* Member: Petitions 2020-, Education 2020-. Contested Eastern region 2014 European Parliament election. *Councils and public bodies:* Councillor, East Cambridgeshire District Council 2011-17.

Tom Hunt MP, House of Commons, London SW1A 0AA
Tel: 020 7219 4013 *Email:* tom.hunt.mp@parliament.uk
Constituency: No constituency office publicised
Tel: 01473 599155 Website: www.tom4ipswich.com *Twitter:* @tomhunt1988

LABOUR

HUQ, RUPA

Ealing Central and Acton *(Majority 13,300)*

Rupa Asha Huq. Born 2 April 1972; 1 son.

Education: Notting Hill and Ealing High School; Newnham College, Cambridge (BA social and political sciences 1993); University of East London (PhD cultural studies thesis on youth culture 1999).

Non-political career: Assistant to Carole Tongue MEP 1996; Lecturer, School of Education, Manchester University 1998-2004; Senior Lecturer in sociology, Kingston University 2004-15.

Political career: Contested Chesham and Amersham 2005 general election. Member for Ealing Central and Acton since 7 May 2015 general election; Shadow Minister for Home Office 2016-17. *Select committees:* Member: Regulatory Reform 2015-17, Justice 2015-16, Public Administration and Constitutional Affairs 2017-19, Future Relationship with the European Union 2020-21, Panel of Chairs 2020-. Contested North West region 2004 European Parliament election. Member, Labour Party 1991-. *Councils and public bodies:* Deputy Mayoress of Ealing 2010-11.

Other: Member, UK delegation, Parliamentary Assembly of the Organisation for Security and Co-operation in Europe 2020-.

Dr Rupa Huq MP, House of Commons, London SW1A 0AA
Tel: 020 7219 6865 *Email:* rupa.huq.mp@parliament.uk
Constituency: No constituency office
Website: www.rupahuq.co.uk *Twitter:* @RupaHuq

LABOUR

HUSSAIN, IMRAN

Bradford East *(Majority 18,144)*

Shadow Minister for Employment Rights and Protections

Born 7 June 1978; Married (2 children).

Education: Rhodesway High School; Huddersfield University (LLB).

Non-political career: Called to the Bar, Lincoln's Inn 2003; Barrister, Altaf Solicitors, Bradford. Member, Unite.

Political career: Contested Bradford West 29 March 2012 by-election. Member for Bradford East since 7 May 2015 general election; PPS to Diane Abbott as Shadow Secretary of State for International Development 2015-16; Shadow Minister for: International Development 2016-17, Justice 2017-20, Employment Rights and Protections 2020-. *Select committees:* Member: Regulatory Reform 2015-17, Joint Committee on Consolidation, &c, Bills 2015-20. Member, Labour Party 1995-; Chair, Bradford West Labour Party. *Councils and public bodies:* Bradford Metropolitan Borough Council: Councillor 2002-, Deputy Leader 2010-15, Portfolio Holder for Safer And Stronger Communities; Governor, Lilycroft Primary School; Chair, Safer Communities Partnership Board; Local Authority Commission on Asylum and Migration; Member, Stronger Communities Partnership Executive Board.

Other: Alternate member, EU Committee of the Regions 2015-; Bradford Centre Regeneration Company.

Imran Hussain MP, House of Commons, London SW1A 0AA
Tel: 020 7219 8636 *Email:* imran.hussain.mp@parliament.uk
Constituency: Karmand Community Centre, Barkerend Road, Bradford, West Yorkshire BD3 9EP
Tel: 01274 231527 Website: imranhussain.laboursites.org *Twitter:* @Imran_HussainMP

CONSERVATIVE

JACK, ALISTER

Dumfries and Galloway *(Majority 1,805)*

Secretary of State for Scotland

Alister William Jack. Born 7 July 1963; Married Ann 1987 (1 son 2 daughters).

Education: Glenalmond College; Heriot-Watt University.

Non-political career: Knight Frank and Rutley; Director, Field & Lawn 1986-2017; Managing director, Aardvark Self-Storage 1995-2002; Partner, Courance Farms and Dairy 2003-; Director, Armadillo Self-Storage 2003-08; Chair, Edinburgh Self-Storage 2006-17; Director, Alligator Self-Storage 2008-14; Chair: Galloway Woodlands 2012-17 Fulling Mill Ltd 2013-19. Member, Queen's Bodyguard for Scotland (Royal Company of Archers) 2007-.

Political career: Contested Tweeddale, Ettrick and Lauderdale 1997 general election. Member for Dumfries and Galloway since 8 June 2017; PPS to Baroness Evans of Bowes Park as Leader of the House of Lords and Lord Privy Seal 2018-19; Assistant Government Whip 2019; Government Whip (Lord Commissioner of HM Treasury) 2019; Secretary of State for Scotland 2019-. *Select committees:* Member: Treasury 2017-18, Treasury Sub-committee 2017-18. Scottish Conservatives: Vice-chair 1997-2001, Spokesperson for Industry and Economy 1996-99. *Councils and public bodies:* DL, Dumfries.

Other: Non-executive director, James Gordon (Agricultural Engineers) 2003-08; Chair: River Annan Fishery Board and Trust 2013-, Fisheries Management Scotland 2016-18; Non-executive director, Atlantic Salmon Trust 2016-; PC 2019.

Rt Hon Alister Jack MP, House of Commons, London SW1A 0AA
Tel: 020 7219 2994 *Email:* alister.jack.mp@parliament.uk
Constituency: 20 Academy Street, Dumfries DG1 1BY
Tel: 01387 216109 Website: www.alisterjack.co.uk *Twitter:* @ScotSecofState

LIBERAL DEMOCRAT

JARDINE, CHRISTINE

Edinburgh West *(Majority 3,769)*

Liberal Democrat Spokesperson for Treasury

Christine Anne Jardine. Born 24 November 1960; Married Calum Macdonald 1987 (died 2017) (1 daughter).

Education: Braidfield High School; Glasgow University (MA modern history and politics 1982); NCTJ (Proficiency Certificate 1985).

Non-political career: Editor, *Deeside Piper*; Senior production journalist, BBC Scotland, Aberdeen 1991-97; Tutor/lecturer in journalism, Strathclyde University 1997-2002; Editor, Scotland, Press Association 2002-04; Freelance consultant 2004-09; Project manager, international programme, TRC Media 2009-11; Scotland media adviser, 10 Downing Street 2011-12; Media consultant and political commentator, Scottish Liberal Democrats 2012-17.

Political career: Contested Gordon 2015 general election. Member for Edinburgh West since 8 June 2017; Liberal Democrat: Shadow Secretary of State for Culture, Media and Sport 2017, Spokesperson for: Scotland 2017-19, Work and Pensions 2019, Commons Spokesperson for Culture, Media and Sport 2019, Shadow Secretary of State/Spokesperson for: Home Office 2019-20, Justice 2019, Women and Equalities 2019-20, Deputy Chief Whip 2019, Spokesperson for: Treasury 2020-, Brexit 2020, Europe 2020, Trade 2020-21. *Select committees:* Member, Scottish Affairs 2017-19. Contested Inverness and Nairn constituency 2011 Scottish Parliament election, Aberdeen Donside constituency 2013 Scottish Parliament by-election and Aberdeenshire East constituency 2016 Scottish Parliament election.

Christine Jardine MP, House of Commons, London SW1A 0AA
Tel: 020 7219 1701 *Email:* christine.jardine.mp@parliament.uk
Constituency: 125a St John's Road, Edinburgh EH12 7SB
Tel: 0131-285 5972 Website: www.christinejardine.com *Twitter:* @cajardineMP

House of Commons MPs' Biographies

LABOUR

JARVIS, DAN

Barnsley Central *(Majority 3,571)*

Daniel Owen Woolgar Jarvis. Born 30 November 1972; Married Caroline (died 2010) (1 son 1 daughter); Married Rachel 2013 (1 daughter).

Education: Rushcliffe Comprehensive, Nottingham; Aberystwyth University (international politics and strategic studies); Royal Military Academy, Sandhurst.

Non-political career: Major, The Parachute Regiment 1996-2011. Member: Unite, Unison.

Political career: Member for Barnsley Central since 3 March 2011 by-election; Shadow Minister for: Culture, Media and Sport 2011-13, Justice 2013-15, Foreign and Commonwealth Office 2015. *Select committees:* Member: Business, Innovation and Skills 2011, Joint Committee on the National Security Strategy 2017-19. Chair, PLP Departmental Group for Business, Innovation and Skills 2011. Opposition Lead, First World War Centenary 2012-18. *Councils and public bodies:* Mayor, Sheffield City Region Combined Authority 2018-.

Political interests: Britain's role in the world, defence, security and international development, the environment (tree planting), child poverty, education and skills, cancer, organ donation, fuel poverty, culture, heritage, sport and the countryside, devolution, transport, the North; Afghanistan, Nepal, Pakistan.

Other: Honorary Patron, Barnsley Youth Choir; Trustee, Barnsley TUC; Board Member, Transport for the North; MBE (mil) 2011. Barnsley Harriers; Vice-president, Kexborough Cricket Club.

Publications: Why Vote Labour (Biteback, 2015); Long Way Home: Love, life, death, and everything in between (Little, Brown, 2020).

Recreations: Parliamentary Mountaineering Group; London Marathon (completed seven times).

Dan Jarvis MBE MP, House of Commons, London SW1A 0AA
Tel: 020 7219 1082 *Email:* dan.jarvis.mp@parliament.uk
Constituency: Corporate Mailroom, PO Box 634, Barnsley, South Yorkshire S70 9GG
Tel: 01226 787893 Website: www.danjarvis.org *Twitter:* @DanJarvisMP/@SCR_Mayor

CONSERVATIVE

JAVID, SAJID

Bromsgrove *(Majority 23,106)*

Born 5 December 1969; Married Laura (4 children).

Education: Downend School, Bristol; Filton Technical College, Bristol; Exeter University (BA economics and politics 1991); Punjabi, Urdu.

Non-political career: Chase Manhattan Bank: Associate and Analyst 1991-95, Vice-president 1995-2000; Deutsche Bank AG: Director 2000-04, Managing director 2004-09; Board member, Deutsche Bank International (Asia) Ltd 2007-09.

Political career: Member for Bromsgrove since 6 May 2010 general election; PPS to: John Hayes as Minister of State for Further Education, Skills and Lifelong Learning 2010-11, George Osborne as Chancellor of the Exchequer 2011-12; HM Treasury: Economic Secretary 2012-13, Financial Secretary 2013-14; Secretary of State for Culture, Media and Sport 2014-15; Minister for Equalities 2014; Secretary of State for: Business, Innovation and Skills and President of the Board of Trade 2015-16, Communities and Local Government/Housing, Communities and Local Government 2016-18, Home Department (Home Secretary) 2018-19; Chancellor of the Exchequer 2019-20. *Select committees:* Member, Work and Pensions 2010; Ex-officio Member, Public Accounts 2012-13. *Councils and public bodies:* Governor, Normand Croft Community School 2004-05.

Political interests: Civil liberties, free enterprise, defence, welfare policy.

Other: Trustee, London Early Years Foundation 2009-12; Senior Fellow, Harvard Kennedy School, Mossavar-Rahmani Centre, Harvard University 2020-; Senior Adviser, JP Morgan Chase & Co 2020-; PC 2014.

Publications: Contributor, There is Such a Thing as Society (2002).

Recreations: Gym, running, hiking, cricket.

Rt Hon Sajid Javid MP, House of Commons, London SW1A 0AA
Tel: 020 7219 7027 *Email:* sajid.javid.mp@parliament.uk
Constituency: 18 High Street, Bromsgrove B61 8HQ
Tel: 01527 872135 Website: www.sajidjavid.com *Twitter:* @SajidJavid

CONSERVATIVE

JAYAWARDENA, RANIL

North East Hampshire *(Majority 20,211)*

Parliamentary Under-Secretary of State, Department for International Trade

Ranil Malcolm Jayawardena. Born 3 September 1986; Son of Nalin Jayawardena JP, chartered accountant, and Indira, née Daas; Married Alison Lyn Roberts 2011 (2 daughters).

Education: Robert May's School, Odiham; Alton College; London School of Economics; Royal College of Defence Studies; French.

Non-political career: Crown Golf 2003-07; Lloyds Banking Group: Wholesale Banking 2008-10, Group Executive Functions 2010-15; SEEK Group 2017-20; TrustMark 2018-20; Great Western Railway 2019-20.

Political career: Member for North East Hampshire since 7 May 2015 general election; Prime Minister's Trade Envoy to Sri Lanka 2018-19; Team PPS: Department for Work and Pensions 2018, Ministry of Justice 2018; Parliamentary Under-Secretary of State, Department for International Trade 2020-. *Select committees:* Member: Home Affairs 2015-17, International Trade 2016-19, Procedure 2017-19, Arms Export Controls 2017-19, Panel of Chairs 2020. Contested North Wales region (5) 2011 National Assembly for Wales election. North East Hampshire Conservatives: Member 2003-, Deputy Chair 2009-12; Deputy Chair, South East England Conservatives 2010-12; Conservative Party: Vice-chair 2019-20, Deputy Chair 2020-. *Councils and public bodies:* Basingstoke and Deane Borough Council: Councillor 2008-15, Cabinet Member for Finance and Property 2011-12, Cabinet Member for Strategy 2012-15, Deputy Leader of Council 2012-15.

Political interests: The family, economy, law and order, criminal justice, education, infrastructure, constitution, environment and endangered species; Commonwealth, USA.

Other: Freeman, City of London; FRSA. RAF Club; MCC.

Recreations: Watching cricket and tennis, walks in the local area, shooting, golf, board games, theatre, film, local history.

Ranil Jayawardena MP, House of Commons, London SW1A 0AA
Tel: 020 7219 3637 *Email:* ranil.jayawardena.mp@parliament.uk
Constituency: The Office of Ranil Jayawardena MP, The Bur, Odiham, Hampshire RG29 1NB
Tel: 01256 702468 *Email:* email@ranil.uk Website: www.ranil.uk *Twitter:* @ranil

CONSERVATIVE

JENKIN, BERNARD

Harwich and North Essex *(Majority 20,182)*

Chair, Select Committee on Liaison

Bernard Christison Jenkin. Born 9 April 1959; Son of late Patrick Jenkin (MP for Wanstead and Woodford 1964-87, later Lord Jenkin of Roding) and Alison Graham; Married Anne Strutt 1988 (now Baroness Jenkin of Kennington (qv)) (2 sons).

Education: Highgate School, London; William Ellis School, London; Corpus Christi College, Cambridge (BA English literature 1982) (President, Cambridge Union Society 1982); French (conversational).

Non-political career: Ford Motor Co Ltd 1983-86; Venture capital manager, 3i plc 1986-88; Manager, Legal and General Ventures Ltd 1989-92; Adviser, Legal and General Group plc 1992-95.

Political career: Contested Glasgow Central 1987 general election. Member for North Colchester 1992-97, for North Essex 1997-2010, for Harwich and North Essex since 6 May 2010 general election; PPS to Michael Forsyth as Secretary of State for Scotland 1995-97; Opposition Spokesperson for: Constitutional Affairs, Scotland and Wales 1997-98, Environment, Transport and the Regions (Roads and Environment) 1998; Shadow Minister for Transport 1998-2001; Member, Shadow Cabinet 1999-2003; Shadow Secretary of State for: Defence 2001-03, The Regions 2003-05; Shadow Minister for Energy 2005; Member, Speaker's Committee on the Electoral Commission 2015-19. *Select committees:* Member: European Standing Committee B 1992-97, Social Security 1993-97, Defence 2006-10, Arms Export Controls 2008-10; Chair, Public Administration 2010-15; Member: Liaison 2010-19, Unopposed Bills (Panel) 2010-15, Joint Committees on: Parliamentary Privilege 2013, Draft Protection of Charities Bill 2014-15; Chair: Public Administration and Constitutional Affairs 2015-19, Joint Committee on Draft Health Service Safety Investigations Bill 2018; Member: Public Accounts 2020-, Privileges 2020-, Standards 2020-; Chair, Liaison 2020-. Conservative Backbench Committees: Vice-chair, Smaller Businesses 1992-95, Secretary, Foreign Affairs 1994-95; Member, Executive, 1922 Committee 2010-. Deputy chair (candidates), Conservative Party 2005-06; Vice-President, Conservatives for Britain 2015-16. *Councils and public bodies:* Governor, Central Foundation Girls' School 1985-89.

Political interests: Economic policy, trade, European Union, defence, foreign affairs, good governance, the Civil Service; Afghanistan, Chile, France, Georgia, Germany, India, Iraq, New Zealand, Pakistan, Russia, Singapore, USA.

Other: Governor, London Goodenough Trust for Overseas Graduates 1992-2001; Council member, St Paul's Cathedral 2006-; Vice-President, Combat Stress 2009-; Vice-chair and trustee, Parliament Choir; Board member, Vote Leave 2016; Action Aid, BASC, National Trust, British Paralympic Association, Students Partnership Worldwide; Kt 2018. Colchester Conservative Constitutional Club.

Publications: Maastricht: Game Set and Match? (1993); Who Benefits: Reinventing Social Security (1993); A Conservative Europe: 1994 and beyond (1994); Fairer Business Rates (1996); A Defence Policy for the UK: Matching Commitments and Resources (2007).

Recreations: Sailing, music (especially opera), fishing, family, DIY.

Sir Bernard Jenkin MP, House of Commons, London SW1A 0AA
Tel: 020 7219 4029 *Fax:* 020 7219 5963 *Email:* bernard.jenkin.mp@parliament.uk
Constituency: Harwich and North Essex Conservatives Association, Unit C2, East Gores Farm, Salmons Lane, Coggeshall, Colchester, Essex CO6 1RZ
Email: info@hneca.co.uk Website: www.bernardjenkin.com *Twitter:* @bernardjenkin

CONSERVATIVE

JENKINSON, MARK

Workington *(Majority 4,176)*

Mark Ian Jenkinson. Born 28 January 1982; Married Dawn (4 children).

Education: St Joseph's RC Secondary School; West Cumbria College (ONC electrical and electronics engineering 2001).

Non-political career: M&E Project Engineer, P J Donnelly Ltd 2009-12; Operations Technician, PX Group 2012-14; Lead Technical Author (CE&I), Costain Oil, Gas & Process 2014-17; Technical Author: Cavendish Nuclear 2017, Jacobs 2017-; Director, Jolievue Holdings 2017-.

Political career: Contested (UKIP) Workington 2015 general election. Member for Workington since 12 December 2019. *Select committees:* Member, Business, Energy and Industrial Strategy 2020-. Chair, West Cumbria branch, UK Independence Party 2012-15; Member, Conservative Party 2016-. *Councils and public bodies:* Allerdale Borough Council: Councillor 2015-, Deputy Leader of the Council 2019-; Councillor, Seaton Parish Council 2015-.

Other: Member, Seaton Rangers Amateur Rugby League Football Club Foundation.

Mark Jenkinson MP, House of Commons, London SW1A 0AA
Tel: 020 7219 3000 *Email:* mark.jenkinson.mp@parliament.uk
Constituency: 104 Senhouse Street, Maryport CA15 6BS
Tel: 01900 876189 *Email:* office@mark-jenkinson.co.uk Website: www.mark-jenkinson.co.uk
Twitter: @markjenkinsonmp

CONSERVATIVE

JENKYNS, ANDREA

Morley and Outwood *(Majority 11,267)*

PPS to Robert Jenrick as Secretary of State for Housing, Communities and Local Government

Andrea Marie Jenkyns. Born 16 June 1974; Married Jack Lopresti 2017 (qv) (MP for Filton and Bradley Stoke) (1 son).

Education: Open University (Diploma economics 2013); Lincoln University (BA international relations and politics 2014).

Non-political career: International business development manager, executive management training company; Music tutor, teaching in three secondary schools.

Political career: Member for Morley and Outwood since 7 May 2015 general election; Ministry of Housing, Communities and Local Government: Team PPS 2018, PPS to Robert Jenrick as Secretary of State 2020-; Member, Speaker's Committee on the Electoral Commission 2018-19. *Select committees:* Member: Health 2015-17, Exiting the European Union 2016-19, European Scrutiny 2020-. *Councils and public bodies:* Councillor, Lincolnshire County Council 2009-13.

Other: Trustee and regional representative, MRSA Action UK 2012-.

Recreations: Soprano singer and songwriter.

Andrea Jenkyns MP, House of Commons, London SW1A 0AA
Tel: 020 7219 5798 *Email:* andrea.jenkyns.mp@parliament.uk
Constituency: 62 Queen Street, Morley, West Yorkshire LS27 9BP
Tel: 0113-345 0380/0113-345 2530
581a Leeds Road, Outwood WF1 2JL
Tel: 01924 695655 Website: www.andreajenkyns.co.uk *Twitter:* @andreajenkyns

CONSERVATIVE

JENRICK, ROBERT

Newark *(Majority 21,816)*

Secretary of State for Housing, Communities and Local Government

Robert Edward Jenrick. Born 9 January 1982; Married Michal Berkner (3 daughters).

Education: Wolverhampton Grammar School; St John's College, Cambridge (BA history); Pennsylvania University, Philadelphia, USA (Thouron Fellowship politics); College of Law, Birmingham (law).

Non-political career: Solicitor: Skadden Arps, Sullivan & Cromwell; Senior Executive and International Managing Director, Christie's.

Political career: Contested Newcastle-under-Lyme 2010 general election. Member for Newark since 5 June 2014 by-election; PPS: to Amber Rudd: as Energy Minister 2014-15, as Home Secretary 2017-18; to Lord Chancellor and Secretary of State for Justice: Michael Gove 2015-16, Elizabeth Truss 2016-17; Exchequer Secretary, HM Treasury 2018-19; Secretary of State for Housing, Communities and Local Government 2019-. *Select committees:* Member: Health 2014-15, Public Accounts 2018-19. Conservative Party: Member 1998-, Chair, North Herefordshire Conservative Association, Member, Conservative Party Board 2017-18.

Other: PC 2019.

Rt Hon Robert Jenrick MP, House of Commons, London SW1A 0AA
Tel: 020 7219 7335 *Email:* robert.jenrick.mp@parliament.uk
Constituency: 29a London Road, Newark, Nottinghamshire NG24 1TN
Tel: 01636 612837 *Email:* graysj@parliament.uk Website: robertjenrick.com
Twitter: @RobertJenrick

CONSERVATIVE

JOHNSON, BORIS

Uxbridge and South Ruislip *(Majority 7,210)*

Prime Minister, First Lord of the Treasury and Minister for the Civil Service, and Minister for the Union

Alexander Boris de Pfeffel Johnson. Born 19 June 1964; Son of Stanley Patrick Johnson and Charlotte Johnson, neé Fawcett; Married Marina Wheeler 1993 (later QC) (separated) (2 sons 2 daughters); engaged to Carrie Symonds (1 son).

Education: Eton College (King's Scholar); Balliol College, Oxford (Brackenbury Scholar in classics) (BA literae humaniores 1987).

Non-political career: Trainee reporter: *The Times*, *Wolverhampton Express*, *Star* 1987-88; *Daily Telegraph*: Leader and feature writer 1988-89, EC correspondent Brussels 1989-94, Assistant editor 1994-99; Political columnist, *Spectator* 1994-95; Chief political commentator, *Daily Telegraph*; Editor, *Spectator* 1999-2005.

Political career: Contested Clwyd South 1997 general election. Member for Henley 7 June 2001 to 4 June 2008, for Uxbridge and South Ruislip since 7 May 2015 general election; Shadow Minister for: the Arts 2004, Higher Education 2005-07; Secretary of State for Foreign and Commonwealth Affairs (Foreign Secretary) 2016-18; Prime Minister, First Lord of the Treasury and Minister for the Civil Service 2019-; Minister for the Union 2019-. Mayor of London 2008-16. Conservative Party: Vice-chairman (Campaigning) 2003-04, Member, political cabinet 2015-16, Leader 2019-.

Other: Patron, Downside UP Moscow; Member, Campaign Committee, Vote Leave 2016; President, Anglo Turkish Society; Patron: Iris Project, Classics for All, Faiths Forum; Honorary Ambassador, KP24 Foundation; Honorary Member, Battle of Britain Historical Society; Honorary Fellow, Royal Institute of British Architects; *What the Papers Say* Political Commentator of the Year 1997; Pagan Federation of Great Britain National Journalist of the Year 1998; Editors' Editor of the Year 2003; British Press Awards Columnist of the Year 2004; Channel 4 News Biggest Impression in Politics 2004, 2005; *What the Papers Say* Columnist of the Year 2005; PC 2016. Beefsteak Club.

Publications: Numerous radio and television broadcasts and publications; Friends, Voters, Countrymen (2001); Lend Me Your Ears (2004); Seventy Two Virgins; Dream of Rome (2006, 2007); Have I Got Views For You (2006); Life in the Fast Lane (2007); Perils of the Pushy Parent (2007); Johnson's Life of London (2011); The Churchill Factor (2015).

Recreations: Painting, poetry, tennis, skiing, rugby, cricket, cycling.

Rt Hon Boris Johnson MP, House of Commons, London SW1A 0AA
Tel: 020 7219 4682 *Email:* boris.johnson.mp@parliament.uk
Constituency: No constituency office publicised
Website: www.gov.uk/number10 *Twitter:* @BorisJohnson

CONSERVATIVE

JOHNSON, CAROLINE

Sleaford and North Hykeham *(Majority 32,565)*

Caroline Elizabeth Johnson. Born 31 December 1977; Married Nik (2 daughters 1 son).

Education: Nunthorpe Comprehensive School; Gordonstoun; Newcastle University (MBBS 2001).

Non-political career: Consultant Paediatrician, Peterborough City Hospital, North West Anglia NHS Foundation Trust.

Political career: Contested Scunthorpe 2010 general election. Member for Sleaford and North Hykeham since 8 December 2016 by-election; Team PPS: HM Treasury 2018, Department for International Trade 2018-19. *Select committees:* Member: Environment, Food and Rural Affairs 2017-19, Health 2017-18, Education 2020-. Conservative Party: Deputy Regional Chairman, Political (East Midlands) 2011-14, Vice-chairman 2019-.

Political interests: Health, education, children, agriculture, defence.

Other: Member: RCPCH, British Medical Association.

Dr Caroline Johnson MP, House of Commons, London SW1A 0AA
Tel: 020 7219 5381 *Email:* caroline.johnson.mp@parliament.uk
Constituency: 5&6 White Hart Mews, Sleaford, Lincolnshire NG34 7RY
Tel: 01529 306721 Website: www.carolinejohnson.co.uk *Twitter:* @drcarolinej

LABOUR

JOHNSON, DIANA

Kingston upon Hull North *(Majority 7,593)*

Diana Ruth Johnson. Born 25 July 1966; Daughter of late Eric and Ruth Johnson; Partner Kevin Morton.

Education: Sir John Deane's Sixth Form College, Cheshire; Northwich County Grammar School for Girls, Cheshire; Queen Mary College, London University (LLB 1989); Council for Legal Education (law finals 1991).

Non-political career: Volunteer/locum lawyer, Tower Hamlets Law Centre 1991-94; Employment, immigration and education lawyer, North Lewisham Law Centre 1995-99; Employment lawyer, Paddington Law Centre 1999-2002; National Officer, FDA Trade Union 2002-03. Member: Unite, Unison.

Political career: Contested Brentwood and Ongar 2001 general election. Member for Hull North 2005-10, for Kingston upon Hull North since 6 May 2010 general election; PPS to Stephen Timms: as Minister of State, Department for Work and Pensions 2005-06, as Chief Secretary to the Treasury 2006-07; Assistant Government Whip 2007-09; Parliamentary Under-Secretary of State for Schools, Department for Children, Schools and Families 2009-10; Shadow Minister for: Health 2010, Home Office 2010-11, Crime and Security 2011-15, Foreign and Commonwealth Office 2015-16; Member, Intelligence and Security Committee of Parliament 2020-. *Select committees:* Member: Public Accounts 2005, Health/Health and Social Care 2017-19, Joint Committee on Draft Health Service Safety Investigations Bill 2018, Joint Committee on the Draft Domestic Abuse Bill 2019, Home Affairs 2020-. Chair, PLP Departmental Group for: Communities and Local Government 2017-19, Home Affairs 2020-. AM for Londonwide region, London Assembly 2003-04. Member: Co-operative Party, Labour Women's Network. *Councils and public bodies:* London Borough of Tower Hamlets: Councillor 1994-2002, Chair: Social services 1997-2000, Social services and health scrutiny panel 2000-02; Legal visiting member, Mental Health Act Commission 1995-98; Member, Metropolitan Police Authority 2003-04; Non-executive director: Newham Healthcare Trust 1998-2001, Tower Hamlets PCT 2001-05; Vice-President, Local Government Association 2018-.

Political interests: Employment rights, health, education, animal welfare, policing; Colombia, Denmark, Jordan.

Other: Member, UK Delegation, Organisation for Security and Co-operation in Europe Parliamentary Assembly 2017-19; Vice-chair, British Group Inter-Parliamentary Union 2020-; Member: Fawcett Society, Amnesty International, Fabian Society; Commissioner, Commonwealth War Graves Commission 2019-; DBE 2020.

Recreations: Cinema, theatre, Hull City FC.

Dame Diana Johnson DBE MP, House of Commons, London SW1A 0AA
Tel: 020 7219 5647 *Fax:* 020 7219 0959 *Email:* johnsond@parliament.uk
Constituency: The Avenues Centre, Rooms 0-031 - 0-035, Park Avenue, Hull HU5 4DA
Tel: 01482 319135 *Email:* johnsond@parliament.uk Website: www.dianajohnson.co.uk
Twitter: @DianaJohnsonMP

CONSERVATIVE

JOHNSON, GARETH

Dartford *(Majority 19,160)*

PPS to Dominic Raab as First Secretary of State and Foreign Secretary

Gareth Alan Johnson. Born 12 October 1969; Son of Alan Johnson, retired milkman, and Ruth Johnson; Married Wendy Morris 1997 (1 son 1 daughter).

Education: Dartford Grammar School; University of the West of England (Postgraduate Diploma law); College of Law (legal practice course 1995).

Non-political career: Legal adviser, Magistrates Court Service 1988-98; Solicitor, Gary Jacobs Mehta & Co 1997-2002; Assistant solicitor, then solicitor, Thomas Boyd Whyte 2002-16.

Political career: Contested Lewisham West 2001 and Dartford 2005 general elections. Member for Dartford since 6 May 2010 general election; PPS: to David Gauke as Financial Secretary, HM Treasury 2014-15, to Matthew Hancock as Minister for the Cabinet Office and Paymaster General 2015-16, to Secretary of State for Exiting the European Union: David Davis 2017-18, Dominic Raab 2018; Assistant Government Whip 2018-19; PPS to Dominic Raab as First Secretary of State and Foreign Secretary: Foreign and Commonwealth Office 2020, Foreign, Commonwealth and Development Office 2020-. *Select committees:* Member: Science and Technology 2012, Justice 2013-14, Joint Committee on Human Rights 2014-15. *Councils and public bodies:* London Borough of Bexley Council: Councillor 1998-2002, Cabinet Member for Policy and Resources 1998-2002; Governor, Dartford Grammar Girls School.

Political interests: Home affairs, environment; USA.

Other: Member, Executive Committee, Inter-Parliamentary Union, British Group; Leader, UK delegation, Parliamentary Assembly of the Organisation for Security and Co-operation in Europe 2020-; Member, Law Society. Dartford Conservative Club.

Recreations: Cricket, rugby.

Gareth Johnson MP, House of Commons, London SW1A 0AA
Tel: 020 7219 7047 *Email:* gareth.johnson.mp@parliament.uk
Constituency: Dartford Civic Offices, Home Gardens, Dartford, Kent DA1 1DR
Tel: 01322 225958 Website: www.garethjohnsondartford.co.uk

LABOUR

JOHNSON, KIM

Liverpool Riverside *(Majority 37,043)*

Kim Marie Johnson. Born August 1960.

Non-political career: Surestart project and childcare strategy, Department for Education and Skills; Creative Diversity Manager, Liverpool Capital of Culture 2005-08. Unison: North West Regional Representative, Deputy Chair, National Black Members Committee 2017-18.

Political career: Member for Liverpool Riverside since 12 December 2019; PPS to Angela Rayner as Shadow First Secretary of State 2020. *Select committees:* Member: Women and Equalities 2020-, Education 2020-, Speaker's Advisory Committee on Works of Art 2020-. Black Members Officer, Riverside CLP.

Other: Chair, Squash Liverpool; Former Board Member, 20 Stories High Theatre.

Kim Johnson MP, House of Commons, London SW1A 0AA
Tel: 020 7219 3000 *Email:* kim.johnson.mp@parliament.uk
Constituency: No constituency office publicised
Twitter: @KimJohnsonMP

House of Commons MPs' Biographies

CONSERVATIVE

JOHNSTON, DAVID

Wantage *(Majority 12,653)*

David Mervyn Johnston. Born 27 November 1981.

Education: Tom Hood Comprehensive; Sir George Monoux Sixth Form College.

Non-political career: Co-ordinator, Oxford Access Scheme 2003-06; Director, Future 2006-09; Chief Executive, Social Mobility Foundation 2009-19.

Political career: Member for Wantage since 12 December 2019. *Select committees:* Member, Education 2020-. *Councils and public bodies:* Commissioner, Social Mobility Commission 2012-17; Governor: Pimlico Academy 2008-17, Sir George Monoux Sixth Form College 2008-16.

Political interests: Social mobility, education, academies.

Other: Director, Future Academies 2014-17; OBE 2018.

David Johnston OBE MP, House of Commons, London SW1A 0AA
Tel: 020 7219 6350 *Email:* david.johnston.mp@parliament.uk
Constituency: No constituency office publicised
Website: www.david-johnston.org.uk *Twitter:* @david4wantage

CONSERVATIVE

JONES, ANDREW

Harrogate and Knaresborough *(Majority 9,675)*

Chair, Select Committee on European Statutory Instruments

Andrew Hanson Jones. Born 28 November 1963; Single.

Education: Bradford Grammar School; Leeds University (BA English 1985).

Non-political career: Kingfisher plc; Going Places plc; Marketing Store; M&C Saatchi; Bettys and Taylors of Harrogate.

Political career: Contested Harrogate and Knaresborough 2001 general election. Member for Harrogate and Knaresborough since 6 May 2010 general election; PPS to: Mark Prisk as Minister of State for Business and Enterprise 2010-11, Justine Greening as Secretary of State for Transport 2011-12, Andrew Mitchell as Parliamentary Secretary to the Treasury and Chief Whip September-October 2012, Department of Health ministerial team 2013-14, Jeremy Hunt as Secretary of State for Health 2014-15; Apprenticeship Ambassador in Parliament 2014-15; Parliamentary Under-Secretary of State, Department for Transport 2015-17, 2018-19; Exchequer Secretary, HM Treasury 2017-18. *Select committees:* Member: Regulatory Reform 2010-15, Public Accounts 2017-18, Liaison 2020-; Chair, European Statutory Instruments 2020-. Conservative Party: Member 1987-, Vice-chairman, Business Engagement 2018. *Councils and public bodies:* Harrogate Borough Council: Councillor 2003-11, Cabinet Member, Resources 2006-10.

Political interests: Transport, renewable energy.

Other: Chair, Bow Group 1998-99; Patron: Harrogate Gateway FC, Mad4Football, Tewit Youth Band, Harrogate. Member, Yorkshire County Cricket Club.

Recreations: Cricket, walking, music.

Andrew Jones MP, House of Commons, London SW1A 0AA
Tel: 020 7219 3000 *Email:* andrew.jones.mp@parliament.uk
Constituency: 57 East Parade, Harrogate, North Yorkshire HG1 5LQ
Tel: 01423 529614 Website: www.andrewjonesmp.co.uk *Twitter:* @AJonesMP

LABOUR

JONES, DARREN

Bristol North West *(Majority 5,692)*

Chair, Select Committee on Business, Energy and Industrial Strategy

Darren Paul Jones. Born 13 November 1986; Married Lucy Symons 2017 (2 daughters).

Education: Portway Community School; Plymouth University (BSc human biosciences 2008) (President, Students' Union 2008-09); Chartered Management Institute (Certificate leadership and management 2010); University of West of England (Graduate Diploma law 2010); Bristol College of Law (LPC legal practice 2011).

Non-political career: Clinical Auditor, NHS 2002-11; Technology, media and communications solicitor, Bond Dickinson LLP 2009-16; Legal Counsel, British Telecommunications plc 2015-17. Member, Unite.

Political career: Contested Torridge and West Devon 2010 and Bristol North West 2015 general elections. Member for Bristol North West since 8 June 2017; PPS to: David Lammy as Shadow Secretary of State for Justice 2020, Lord Falconer of Thoroton as Shadow Attorney General 2020. *Select committees:* Member: Science and Technology 2017-, European Scrutiny 2017-19, Joint Committee on the National Security Strategy 2020-, Liaison 2020-; Chair, Business, Energy and Industrial Strategy 2020-. Chair, PLP Departmental Group for Digital, Culture, Media and Sport 2020-. Member, Labour Party 2003-; President, Plymouth Labour Students 2006-08; Member, National Policy Forum, Labour Students; Youth and students officer, Plymouth Sutton and Devonport CLP; South West NEC representative, Co-operative Party (youth) 2008-09. *Councils and public bodies:* Governor: Plymouth University Students' Union 2008-09, Avon Primary School 2009-11, Plymouth NHS Foundation Trust 2009, Hannah More Primary School 2012-13; Chair, Institute of AI 2019-; Programme Committee Member, Ditchely 2020-.

Political interests: Technology, business, climate change, national security; Australia, China, EU, India, USA.

Other: Director, Shirehampton Community Action Forum; Trustee, North Bristol Advice Centre; Chair of Policy and Current Affairs, Bristol Junior Chamber of Commerce; Business Mentor, Prince's Trust; Associate, Chartered Management Institute; Henacre Charitable Trust.

Darren Jones MP, House of Commons, London SW1A 0AA
Tel: 020 7219 5225 *Email:* darren.jones.mp@parliament.uk
Constituency: No constituency office publicised
Tel: 0117-959 6545 Website: darren-jones.co.uk *Twitter:* @darrenpjones

CONSERVATIVE

JONES, DAVID

Clwyd West *(Majority 6,747)*

David Ian Jones. Born 22 March 1952; Son of late Bryn Jones and Elspeth Jones, née Savage-Williams; Married Sara Tudor 1982 (2 sons).

Education: Ruabon Grammar School, Wrexham; University College London (LLB 1973); Chester College of Law; French, Welsh.

Non-political career: Senior partner, David Jones & Company, Llandudno 1985-2005; Director, David Jones (Solicitors) Ltd.

Political career: Contested Conwy 1997 and City of Chester 2001 general elections. Member for Clwyd West 2005-10, for Clwyd West (revised boundary) since 6 May 2010 general election; Shadow Minister for Wales 2006-10; Wales Office: Parliamentary Under-Secretary of State 2010-12, Secretary of State for Wales 2012-14; Minister of State, Department for Exiting the European Union 2016-17. *Select committees:* Member: Welsh Affairs 2005-10, Public Administration and Constitutional Affairs 2015-16, 2017-, European Scrutiny 2017-, Joint Committee on Draft Health Service Safety Investigations Bill 2018, Joint Committee on the Draft Parliamentary Buildings (Restoration and Renewal) Bill 2018-19. Contested North Wales region 1999 National Assembly for Wales election. AM (replacement) for North Wales 2002-03. Chair, Conwy Conservative Association 1998-99; Patron, Chinese Conservative Group; Vice-President, Conservatives for Britain 2015-16.

Political interests: Law and order, constitution, Welsh affairs, countryside; ASEAN, China, Middle East.

Other: Member, UK Delegation, Organisation for Security and Co-operation in Europe Parliamentary Assembly 2015-16, 2017-; Honorary Life Fellow, Cancer Research UK; Honorary Member, Colwyn Bay Rotary Club; Ambassador, Girlguiding; Member, Law Society; PC 2012.

Recreations: Travel.

Rt Hon David Jones MP, House of Commons, London SW1A 0AA
Tel: 020 7219 8070 *Email:* katharine.huggins@parliament.uk
Constituency: First Floor, 27 Princes Drive, Colwyn Bay LL29 8HT
Tel: 01492 535845 Website: www.davidjonesmp.co.uk *Twitter:* @DavidJonesMP

CONSERVATIVE

JONES, FAY

Brecon and Radnorshire *(Majority 7,131)*

Team PPS, Department for Environment, Food and Rural Affairs

Fay Alicia Jones. Partner Tim.

Education: King's College London (French 2008); French.

Non-political career: Senior Research and Project Officer, Household of TRH The Prince of Wales and The Duchess of Cornwall 2009-13; National Farmers' Union: Government and Parliamentary Affairs Adviser 2013-14, European Parliamentary and Communications Adviser 2014-17, External Affairs Manager 2017; Grayling: Head of Wales 2017-19, Head of Wales/ Senior Account Director 2019.

Political career: Member for Brecon and Radnorshire since 12 December 2019; Team PPS, Department for Environment, Food and Rural Affairs 2020-. *Select committees:* Member, Northern Ireland Affairs 2021-. Contested Wales region 2019 European Parliament election.

Recreations: Cycling, running, cooking.

Fay Jones MP, House of Commons, London SW1A 0AA
Tel: 020 7219 3000 *Email:* fay.jones.mp@parliament.uk
Constituency: Leamington House, Temple Street, Llandrindod Wells, Powys LD1 5DU
Website: www.fayjones.org.uk *Twitter:* @JonesyFay

LABOUR

JONES, GERALD

Merthyr Tydfil and Rhymney *(Majority 10,606)*

Shadow Minister for Wales

Born 21 August 1970; Partner Tyrone Powell.

Education: Bedwellty Comprehensive School; Ysrad Mynach College.

Non-political career: Grant Liaison Officer, Cardiff County Council 1990-2000; Development Officer, Gwent Association of Voluntary Organisations 2001-05, 2009-15. Member, GMB.

Political career: Member for Merthyr Tydfil and Rhymney since 7 May 2015 general election; PPS to: Nia Griffith as Shadow Secretary of State for Wales 2015-16, Emily Thornbury as Shadow Secretary of State for Defence 2015-16; Shadow Minister for: Wales 2016-17, 2020-, Defence 2017-20. *Select committees:* Member: Public Administration and Constitutional Affairs 2015-17, Welsh Affairs 2015-16. Patron, LGBT Labour; Election Agent, Merthyr Tydfil and Rhymney Labour Party 2003–14; Chair, Merthyr Tydfil and Rhymney Labour Party 2008–12. *Councils and public bodies:* Caerphilly County Borough Council: Councillor 1995-2015, Cabinet Member for Policy and Resources 2004-08, Deputy Leader of the Council 2004-08, 2012-15, Cabinet Member for Housing 2012-15, Anti-poverty Champion.

Political interests: Cost of living, job creation, regeneration, home affairs, defence, welfare.

Gerald Jones MP, House of Commons, London SW1A 0AA
Tel: 020 7219 5874 *Email:* gerald.jones.mp@parliament.uk
Constituency: Oldway House, Castle Street, Merthyr Tydfil, Mid Glamorgan CF47 8UX
Tel: 01685 383739 Website: www.geraldjones.co.uk *Twitter:* @GeraldJonesLAB

LABOUR

JONES, KEVAN

North Durham *(Majority 4,742)*

Kevan David Jones. Born 25 April 1964.

Education: Portland Comprehensive, Worksop, Nottinghamshire; Newcastle upon Tyne Polytechnic (BA government and public policy 1985); University of Southern Maine, USA.

Non-political career: Parliamentary assistant to Nick Brown MP 1985-89; GMB: Political officer 1989-2001, Regional organiser 1992-99, Senior organiser 1999-2001. Member, GMB.

Political career: Member for North Durham 2001-10, for North Durham (revised boundary) since 6 May 2010 general election; Parliamentary Under-Secretary of State (Minister for Veterans), Ministry of Defence 2008-10; Shadow Minister for Defence 2010-15; Member, Intelligence and Security Committee 2017-19, 2020-. *Select committees:* Member: Defence 2001-09, Armed Forces Bill 2005-06, 2011, Administration 2005-09, 2010-13, Armed Forces Bill 2015 2015-16, Regulatory Reform 2017-, Defence 2020-, Procedure 2020-. Member PLP Parliamentary Affairs Committee 2006-. Northern Region Labour Party: Chair 1998-2000, Vice-chair 2000-. *Councils and public bodies:* Newcastle City Council: Councillor 1990-2001, Chair, Public Health 1993-97, Chief Whip 1994-2000, Chair, Development and Transport 1997-2001.

Political interests: Regeneration, transport, employment, regional policy, local and regional government, defence, mental health; Afghanistan, Iraq, Poland, UAE, USA.

Other: Member, UK Delegation, NATO Parliamentary Assembly 2017-; Patron, Chester Le Street Mind 2001-; Speech of the Year (with Charles Walker MP), *Spectator* awards 2012; Opposition Frontbencher of the Year, *House Magazine* awards 2012; PC 2018. Sacriston Working Men's Club.

Recreations: Golf.

Rt Hon Kevan Jones MP, House of Commons, London SW1A 0AA
Tel: 020 7219 8219 *Fax:* 020 7219 1759 *Email:* kevanjonesmp@parliament.uk
Constituency: Fulforth Centre, Front Street, Sacriston, Co Durham DH7 6JT
Tel: 0191-371 8834 Website: www.kevanjonesmp.org.uk *Twitter:* @KevanJonesMP

CONSERVATIVE

JONES, MARCUS

Nuneaton *(Majority 13,144)*

Government Whip (Vice-Chamberlain of HM Household)

Marcus Charles Jones. Born 5 April 1974; Son of Brian Jones, signwriter, and Jean Jones, legal cashier; Married Suzanne 2004 (1 son 1 daughter).

Education: St Thomas More School, Nuneaton; King Edward VI College.

Non-political career: Conveyancing manager, Tustain Jones & Co. Solicitors 1999-2010.

Political career: Member for Nuneaton since 6 May 2010 general election; PPS to Sajid Javid: as Financial Secretary, HM Treasury 2013-14, as Secretary of State for Culture, Media and Sport 2014-15; Parliamentary Under-Secretary of State (Minister for Local Government), Department for Communities and Local Government 2015-18; Member, Speaker's Committee on the Electoral Commission 2017-18; Assistant Government Whip 2019-20; Government Whip (Vice-Chamberlain of HM Household) 2020-. *Select committees:* Member: Backbench Business 2012-13, Administration 2012-15. Vice-chairman, Local Government, Conservative Party 2018-19. *Councils and public bodies:* Nuneaton and Bedworth Borough Council: Councillor 2005-10, Leader, Conservative group 2006-09, Council Leader 2008-09; Vice-President, Local Government Association 2018-19.

Political interests: Economy, business and skills, local government.

Recreations: Family, watching Coventry City FC, angling.

Marcus Jones MP, House of Commons, London SW1A 0AA
Tel: 020 7219 7123 *Fax:* 020 7219 3483 *Email:* marcus.jones.mp@parliament.uk
Constituency: 13-17 Hollybush House, Bond Gate, Nuneaton, Warwickshire CV11 4AR
Tel: 024 7634 8482 Website: www.marcusjones.org.uk *Twitter:* @Marcus4Nuneaton

LABOUR

JONES, RUTH

Newport West *(Majority 902)*

Shadow Minister for Natural Environment and Air Quality

Ruth Lorraine Jones. Born 23 April 1962; Daughter of Hazel and Keith Jones; Married (2 children).

Education: Duffyrn School; Cardiff University (Diploma physiotherapy 1983, MA education 1997).

Non-political career: NHS Physiotherapist 1983-2016; Senior Negotiating Officer for the Chartered Society of Physiotherapy 2016-19; Physiotherapy Manager, Aneurin Bevan University Health Board, for Children and Adults with a Learning Disability. Steward, Chartered Society of Physiotherapy 1987-2009; President, Wales TUC 2007-08; GMB.

Political career: Contested Monmouth 2015 and 2017 general elections. Member for Newport West since 4 April 2019 by-election; Shadow Minister for Fisheries 2020; PPS to: Luke Pollard as Shadow Secretary of State for Environment, Food and Rural Affairs 2020, Louise Haigh as Shadow Secretary of State for Northern Ireland 2020; Shadow Minister for Environment, Food and Rural Affairs (Natural Environment and Air Quality) 2020-. *Select committees:* Member: Environmental Audit 2019, Business, Energy and Industrial Strategy 2020, Welsh Affairs 2020-. Contested South Wales East region 2016 National Assembly for Wales election. Member, Labour Party 1999-; Chair, Constituency Labour Party 2016-17; Women's Officer 2017-19.

Political interests: NHS, social justice; Wales.

Other: Member, UK Delegation to Parliamentary Assembly, Council of Europe 2020-; Eden Gate, Cancer Research UK, Amnesty International; Fellow, Chartered Society of Physiotherapy.

Recreations: Singing, keep fit, church.

Ruth Jones MP, House of Commons, London SW1A 0AA
Tel: 020 7219 3000 *Email:* ruth.jones.mp@parliament.uk
Constituency: 25-26 Gold Tops, Newport NP20 4PG
Tel: 01633 256268 Website: www.ruthjones.wales *Twitter:* @RuthNewportWest

LABOUR

JONES, SARAH

Croydon Central *(Majority 5,949)*

Shadow Minister for Policing and the Fire Service

Sarah Ann Jones. Born 20 December 1972; Married Ian Lloyd (3 sons including twins 1 daughter).

Education: Old Palace School; Durham University (BA history 1995).

Non-political career: Researcher to Mo Mowlam MP 1996-97; Public affairs and campaigns manager, Shelter UK 2000-04; Deputy director of communications, NHS Confederation 2004-08; Deputy director, Government Olympic Communications 2008-13; Acting director of campaigns and policy, Bond 2013; Director, Lloyd-Jones Communications 2013-16; Strategic communications adviser, Cambridge University Hospital NHS Foundation Trust 2013-14; Consultant, Inc London 2014-15; Senior consultant, Quiller Consultants 2016-17.

Political career: Contested Croydon Central 2015 general election. Member for Croydon Central since 8 June 2017; PPS to John Healey as Shadow Secretary of State for Housing 2018; Shadow Minister for: Housing 2018-20, Home Office (Policing and the Fire Service) 2020-. *Select committees:* Member, Home Affairs 2017-18. *Councils and public bodies:* Governor, Wolsey Junior School.

Other: Non-executive director, Wandle Housing Association 2013-17.

Sarah Jones MP, House of Commons, London SW1A 0AA
Tel: 020 7219 2963 *Email:* sarah.jones.mp@parliament.uk
Constituency: 43 Blackhorse Lane, Croydon CR0 6RT
Tel: 020 8191 7066 Website: www.sarah-jones.org *Twitter:* @laboursj

CONSERVATIVE

JUPP, SIMON

East Devon *(Majority 6,708)*

Simon James Jupp. Born 8 September 1985.

Non-political career: Radio presenter, Radio Exe and Radio Plymouth; Reporter, ITV and BBC radio; Manager, BBC Radio Solent; Special Adviser to: Tim Bowles as Mayor of the West of England, West of England Combined Authority 2018-19, Dominic Raab as Foreign Secretary and First Secretary of State 2019.

Political career: Member for East Devon since 12 December 2019. *Select committees:* Member: Transport 2020-, Joint Committee on Consolidation, &c, Bills 2020-.

Recreations: Walking.

Simon Jupp MP, House of Commons, London SW1A 0AA
Tel: 020 7219 2639 *Email:* simon.jupp.mp@parliament.uk
Constituency: Mamhead View, Exmouth, Devon EX8 1DU
Tel: 01395 542750 Website: www.simonjupp.org.uk *Twitter:* @simonjamesjupp

LABOUR

KANE, MIKE

Wythenshawe and Sale East *(Majority 10,396)*

Shadow Minister for Aviation and Maritime

Michael Joseph Patrick Kane. Born 9 January 1969; Married Sandra Bracegirdle.

Education: St Paul's School, Newall Green.

Non-political career: Teacher, Springfield Primary School, Sale 2000-08; Parliamentary manager to: James Purnell MP 2008-10, Jonathan Reynolds MP 2010-11; Senior Executive Assistant to Kieran Quinn as Executive Leader, Tameside Council 2011-14; Acting Chief Executive, Movement for Change 2014. Member: Community, Unite.

Political career: Member for Wythenshawe and Sale East since 13 February 2014 by-election; Shadow Minister for: International Development 2015-16, Education (Schools) 2016-20, Transport (Aviation and Maritime) 2020-. *Select committees:* Member: Environmental Audit 2014-15, Treasury 2014-15. Former parliamentary agent to Jonathan Reynolds MP. *Councils and public bodies:* Manchester City Council: Former Councillor, Former executive member for Art and Leisure.

Political interests: Chagos Islands, Ireland.

Recreations: Season ticket holder at Manchester City FC, plays flute and bagpipes.

Mike Kane MP, House of Commons, London SW1A 0AA
Tel: 020 7219 7524 *Email:* mike.kane.mp@parliament.uk
Constituency: Unit A, Etrop Court, Wythenshawe, Greater Manchester M22 5RG
Tel: 0161-499 7900 Website: www.mikekane.org *Twitter:* @MikeKaneMP

CONSERVATIVE

KAWCZYNSKI, DANIEL

Shrewsbury and Atcham *(Majority 11,217)*

Daniel Robert Kawczynski. Born 24 January 1972; Son of Leonard and Halina Kawczynski; Married Kate Lumb 2000 (divorced) (1 daughter).

Education: St George's College, Weybridge; Stirling University (BA business studies with French 1994); French, Polish.

Non-political career: Sales account manager telecommunications: BT, Cable & Wireless, Xerox 1994-2004; Owner/joint manager, equestrian centre and livery stables.

Political career: Contested Ealing Southall 2001 general election. Member for Shrewsbury and Atcham since 5 May 2005 general election; PPS to: Jim Paice as Minister of State for Agriculture and Food 2010-12, Richard Benyon as Parliamentary Under-Secretary of State (Natural Environment and Fisheries), Department for Environment, Food and Rural Affairs 2010-12, David Jones as Secretary of State for Wales 2012-14; Trade Envoy to Mongolia 2020-. *Select committees:* Member: Environment, Food and Rural Affairs 2005-07, Justice 2007-09, International Development 2008-10, Foreign Affairs 2015-17, Housing, Communities and Local Government 2020, Speaker's Advisory Committee on Works of Art 2020-21. Chairman, Stirling University Conservative Association 1991-93.

Political interests: Agriculture, foreign affairs, trade, foreign relations; Libya, Mauritania, Saudi Arabia.

Other: Member, UK Delegation, Organisation for Security and Co-operation in Europe Parliamentary Assembly 2014-; Hon. President, Shrewsbury Parkinson's Society; Fight for Sight.

Publications: Seeking Gadhafi (2010).

Recreations: Golf, vegetable and fruit growing.

Daniel Kawczynski MP, House of Commons, London SW1A 0AA
Tel: 020 7219 6249 *Fax:* 020 7219 1047 *Email:* kawczynskid@parliament.uk
Constituency: Flat 1, 17 Meadow Terrace, Shrewsbury, Shropshire SY1 1PE
Tel: 01743 233646 Website: www.daniel4shrewsbury.co.uk *Twitter:* @DKShrewsbury

CONSERVATIVE

KEARNS, ALICIA

Rutland and Melton *(Majority 26,924)*

Team PPS, Department for Digital, Culture, Media and Sport

Alicia Alexandra Martha Kearns. Born 11 November; Married 2017 (2 children).

Education: Impington Village College; Fitzwilliam College, Cambridge (social and political sciences 2006); German.

Non-political career: Account Executive, Munro and Forster 2009-10; Consultant, Grayling 2010-12; Press Secretary to Victims' Minister 2012-13; Head, Ministry of Defence Scottish Referendum Campaign 2013-14; Press Secretary to Secretary of State for Defence, NATO Summit 2014; Cross-Government Lead, Counter Daesh, Syria and Iraq Effort 2014-16; Director, Global Influence 2016-17; Freelance Counter-terrorism and Counter-threats Consultant 2017-.

Political career: Contested Mitcham and Morden 2017 general election. Member for Rutland and Melton since 12 December 2019; Team PPS, Department for Digital, Culture, Media and Sport 2020-. *Select committees:* Member: Foreign Affairs 2020-, Joint Committee on the National Security Strategy 2020-. Deputy Chair, East of England Conservative Women's Party.

Political interests: Foreign affairs, national security, agriculture, children and young people, geographically protected foods; CANZUK, Middle East, specifically Jordan, Kurdistan, Iraq and Syria, Western Balkans, specifically Bosnia and Herzegovina, UK Overseas Territories, specifically Turks and Caicos, Africa, specifically Commonwealth Nations.

Other: Independent Visitor, Jigsaw4u 2015-; Volunteer, Lighthouse Relief 2016.

Publications: Contributor, Countering Online Propaganda and Extremism: The Dark Side of Digital Diplomacy (2018).

Alicia Kearns MP, House of Commons, London SW1A 0AA
Tel: 020 7219 3000 *Email:* alicia.kearns.mp@parliament.uk
Constituency: 33 High Street, Melton Mowbray LE13 0TR
Tel: 01664 411211 Website: www.aliciakearns.com *Twitter:* @aliciakearns

CONSERVATIVE

KEEGAN, GILLIAN

Chichester *(Majority 21,490)*

Parliamentary Under-Secretary of State for Apprenticeships and Skills, Department for Education

Born March 1968; Daughter of Duncan and Jacqueline Gibson; Married Michael (2 stepsons).

Education: St Augustine of Canterbury Comprehensive School, Huyton; Liverpool John Moores University (BA business studies 1990); London Business School Sloan Fellowship (MSc leadership and strategy 2010); Intermediate Spanish.

Non-political career: Delco Electronics (subsidiary of General Motors): Apprentice including degree sponsorship 1984-89, Buyer 1989-91; National Westminster Bank plc: Senior Buyer, Technology 1992, IT Procurement Manager 1993-96; Mondex International Ltd (subsidiary of MasterCard International): Head of Strategic Alliances and Partnerships 1996-99, Commercial Director 1999-2001; Amadeus IT Group: Director, Business Travel 2001-02, Group Director, Global Customer Group 2002-07, Group Vice-president, Multinational Customer Group 2007-09; Executive Vice-president and Chief Marketing Officer, Travelport 2011-12.

Political career: Contested St Helens South and Whiston 2015 general election. Member for Chichester since 8 June 2017; Team PPS, HM Treasury 2018-19; PPS to: Gavin Williamson as Secretary of State for Defence 2019, Sajid Javid as Home Secretary 2019, Matt Hancock as Secretary of State for Health and Social Care 2019-20; MP Apprenticeship Ambassador 2019; Parliamentary Under-Secretary of State for Apprenticeships and Skills, Department for Education 2020-. *Select committees:* Member: Public Accounts 2017-18, Standing Orders 2017-20, Joint Committee on the Draft Domestic Abuse Bill 2019-20. Director, Women2Win 2015-17. *Councils and public bodies:* Chichester District Council: Councillor 2014-18, Cabinet Member for Commercial Services 2015-17; Governor, Western Sussex Hospitals NHS Trust 2015-17; Vice-President, Local Government Association 2018-.

Other: Patron, Chichester Lunch Club. Women's Parliamentary Football Team.

Gillian Keegan MP, House of Commons, London SW1A 0AA
Tel: 020 7219 1193 *Email:* gillian.keegan.mp@parliament.uk
Constituency: St John's House, St John's Street, Chichester PO19 1UU
Website: www.gilliankeegan.com *Twitter:* @GillianKeegan

LABOUR

KEELEY, BARBARA

Worsley and Eccles South *(Majority 3,219)*

Barbara Mary Keeley. Born 26 March 1952; Daughter of Edward and Joan Keeley; Married Colin Huggett 1985.

Education: Mount St Mary's College, Leeds; Salford University (BSc politics and contemporary history 1994).

Non-political career: IBM UK Limited: Systems programmer 1983, Field systems engineer 1983-87, Field systems engineering manager 1987-89; Consultant and adviser in community regeneration 1989-94, 1995-2001; Area manager, Business in the Community North West 1994-95; Consultant, Princess Royal Trust for Carers 2001-05; Research on policy issues related to primary health care for Princess Royal Trust 2003-05. Member, GMB.

Political career: Member for Worsley 2005-10, for Worsley and Eccles South since 6 May 2010 general election; PPS: to Jim Murphy: as Parliamentary Secretary, Cabinet Office 2006, as Minister of State, Department for Work and Pensions 2006-07, to Harriet Harman as Minister for Women 2007-08; Assistant Government Whip 2008-09; Deputy Leader of the House of Commons 2009-10; Shadow Deputy Leader of the House of Commons 2010; Shadow Minister for: Health 2010, 2015-16, Communities and Local Government 2010-11; PPS to Ed Balls as Shadow Chancellor of the Exchequer 2011-15; Shadow Financial Secretary 2015; Shadow Minister for Mental Health and Social Care (attends Shadow Cabinet) 2016-20. *Select committees:* Member: Constitutional Affairs 2005-06, Finance and Services 2006-10, Health 2011-15, Joint Committee on the Draft Care and Support Bill 2013, Health and Social Care 2020-, Speaker's Advisory Committee on Works of Art 2020-. PLP Departmental Group for Women: Hon Secretary 2006-07, Chair 2007-08, Vice-chair 2015-19. *Councils and public bodies:* Trafford Borough Council: Councillor 1995-2004, Vice-chair, social services 1995-97, Cabinet member 1997-99, 2000-04; Director, Trafford's pathfinder Children's Trust 2002-04.

Political interests: Health and social care, carers, mental health, women in sport; European Union.

Other: Member: Amnesty International, Fabian Society.

Publications: Co-author: Carers Speak Out (2002), Primary Carers (2003).

Recreations: Jogging, swimming, live music.

Barbara Keeley MP, House of Commons, London SW1A 0AA
Tel: 020 7219 8025 *Email:* barbara.keeley.mp@parliament.uk
Constituency: First Floor, 37 Manchester Road, Walkden, Greater Manchester M28 3NS
Tel: 0161-799 4159 Website: www.barbarakeeley.co.uk *Twitter:* @KeeleyMP

LABOUR

KENDALL, LIZ

Leicester West *(Majority 4,212)*

Shadow Minister for Social Care

Elizabeth Louise Kendall. Born 11 June 1971.

Education: Watford Grammar School for Girls; Cambridge University (history).

Non-political career: Special adviser to Harriet Harman MP: as Shadow Secretary of State for Social Security 1996-97, as Secretary of State for Social Security and Minister for Women 1997-98; Research fellow, King's Fund; Associate director, health, social care and children's early years, Institute for Public Policy Research; Director, Maternity Alliance; Special adviser to Patricia Hewitt MP as Secretary of State for: Trade and Industry and Minister for Women and Equality 2004-05, Health 2005-07; Director, Ambulance Service Network 2007-09. Member, Unite.

Political career: Member for Leicester West since 6 May 2010 general election; Shadow Minister for: Health 2010-15, Care and Older People 2011-15, Health and Social Care (Social Care) 2020-. *Select committees:* Member: Education 2010, Communities and Local Government 2015-16, Science and Technology 2018-19, Treasury 2020. Chair, PLP Departmental Group for Education 2010. Member: Labour Party 1992-, Co-operative Party, Society – Health and Care Policy Commission; Contested Labour leadership election 2015.

Political interests: Employment, care for the elderly, early years services, NHS.

Other: Member, Fabian Society; Vice-chair, Progress.

Publications: Contributor, The Purple Book (Progress, 2011).

Liz Kendall MP, House of Commons, London SW1A 0AA
Tel: 020 7219 3000 *Email:* liz.kendall.mp@parliament.uk
Constituency: Westend Neighbourhood Centre, Andrewes Street, Leicester LE3 5PA
Tel: 0116-204 4980 Website: lizkendall.org *Twitter:* @leicesterliz

LABOUR

KHAN, AFZAL

Manchester Gorton *(Majority 30,339)*

Shadow Deputy Leader of the Leader of the House of Commons

Mohammed Afzal Khan. Born 5 April 1958; Married Shkeela (2 daughters 1 son).

Education: Abraham Moss College; Manchester Metropolitan University (BA law 1992); Urdu, Panjabi, Hindi.

Non-political career: Labourer in cotton mill; Bus driver; Police Officer, Greater Manchester Police; Senior Partner, HSK Solicitors; Founder and Partner, Khan Solicitors 2005-09; Partner, Mellor & Jackson Solicitors 2009-18. Member: GMB, Unite.

Political career: Member for Manchester Gorton since 8 June 2017; Shadow Minister for: Home Office (Immigration) 2017-20, Foreign and Commonwealth Office 2020; Shadow Deputy Leader of the Leader of the House of Commons 2020-. MEP for North West 2014-17. Member, Labour Party 2000-; Member, Labour Movement for Europe; Co-founder, Black and Minority Ethic Forum. *Councils and public bodies:* Councillor, Manchester City Council 2000-15; Lord Mayor of Manchester 2005-06.

Political interests: Poverty and inequality, racism and islamophobia, international affairs, young people; China, Kashmir, Morocco, Pakistan, Palestine, Qatar, Saudi Arabia, Turkey.

Other: Former Trustee, British Red Cross; Vice-president, World Mayors for Peace 2005-06; Honorary Doctorate: Government College University, Lahore (philosophy), Mirpur University of Science and Technology (law); Mayor of the Year, Co-op Bank Award; CBE 2008; Sitara-i-Quaid-i-Azam Pakistan 2018.

Afzal Khan CBE MP, House of Commons, London SW1A 0AA
Tel: 020 7219 3570 *Email:* afzal.khan.mp@parliament.uk
Constituency: BMHC, College Road, Whalley Range M16 8BP
Tel: 0161-226 5546 Website: www.afzalkhan.org.uk *Twitter:* @Afzal4Gorton

LABOUR

KINNOCK, STEPHEN

Aberavon *(Majority 10,490)*

Shadow Minister for Asia and Pacific

Stephen Nathan Kinnock. Born 1 January 1970; Son of Neil Kinnock (MP for Bedwellty 1970-83 and Islwyn 1983-95, Labour Party Leader 1983-92, European Commissioner 1995-2004, now Lord Kinnock (qv)) and Glenys Kinnock (MEP for South East Wales 1994-99 and Wales region 1999-2009, now Baroness Kinnock of Holyhead (qv)); Married Helle Thorning-Schmidt 1996 (former Prime Minister of Denmark) (2 daughters).

Education: Drayton Manor Comprehensive School; Cambridge University (BA modern languages 1992); College of Europe, Bruges (MA European studies 1993); French, Spanish, Russian, Danish.

Non-political career: Research Assistant, European Parliament 1993-94; Consultant, Lancashire Enterprises, Brussels 1994-96; British Council Brussels: Manager 1996-2001, Director 2001-04; Director, British Council: St Petersburg, Russia 2005-08, Sierra Leone 2008-09; Director for Europe and Central Asia, World Economic Forum, Geneva 2009-12; Managing Director, UK office, Xynteo 2012-15. Community Union; Unison.

Political career: Member for Aberavon since 7 May 2015 general election; PPS to Angela Eagle as Shadow First Secretary of State and Secretary of State for Business, Innovation and Skills 2015-16; Shadow Minister for Foreign and Commonwealth Office (Asia and Pacific) 2020-. *Select committees:* Member: European Scrutiny 2015-, Welsh Affairs 2016-17, 2017-18, Exiting the European Union/Future Relationship with the European Union 2017-21, European Statutory Instruments 2020-. Chair, Labour Business Parliamentary Group.

Political interests: Workers' rights, employers' responsibility, European Union, steel, industrial strategy, electoral reform, renewable energy, sustainable economic growth; European Union, Palestine, Russia, Wales.

Other: Member, Advisory Board, Social Market Foundation 2016-; Trustee, Radix 2016-; Patron, No Offence! 2014-15. Parliamentary football team.

Publications: A New Nation: building a United Kingdom of purpose, patriotism and resilience; Labour and Business: partners for a new kind of growth; Co-Editor, Spirit of Britain, Purpose of Labour (2018).

Recreations: Rugby, football.

Stephen Kinnock MP, House of Commons, London SW1A 0AA
Tel: 020 7219 8801 *Email:* stephen.kinnock.mp@parliament.uk
Constituency: Unit 2, Water Street Business Centre, Water Street, Port Talbot, West Glamorgan SA12 6LF
Tel: 01639 897660 Website: www.stephenkinnock.co.uk *Twitter:* @Skinnock

CONSERVATIVE

KNIGHT, GREG

East Yorkshire *(Majority 22,787)*

Gregory Knight. Born 4 April 1949; Son of Albert Knight, company director, and Isabel Knight, née Bell; Married Janet Knight.

Education: Alderman Newton's Grammar School, Leicester; College of Law, London; College of Law, Guildford (solicitor 1973).

Non-political career: Solicitor 1973-89, 1997-2001; Business consultant 1997-2001.

Political career: Member for Derby North 1983-97. Contested Derby North 1997 general election. Member for Yorkshire East 2001-10, for East Yorkshire (revised boundary) since 6 May 2010 general election; PPS to David Mellor as Minister of State: Foreign and Commonwealth Office 1987-88, Department of Health 1988-89; Assistant Government Whip 1989-90; Government Whip 1990-93; Government Deputy Chief Whip 1993-96; Minister of State, Department of Trade and Industry 1996-97; Deputy Shadow Leader of the House 2002-03; Shadow Minister for: Culture, Media and Sport 2003, Environment and Transport 2003-05, Transport 2005; Government Whip (Vice-Chamberlain of HM Household) 2012-13. *Select committees:* Member: Broadcasting 1993-96, Finance and Services 1993-96, 2013-15, Modernisation of the House of Commons 2001-03, 2005-10, Procedure: Member 2005, Chair 2005-12; Member: Liaison 2006-12, Administration 2006-10, 2020-, Standards and Privileges 2009-10, Reform of the House of Commons 2009-10, Joint Committee on the Draft Detention of Terrorist Suspects (Temporary Extension) Bills 2011. Chair, Leicester and Leicestershire

Young Conservatives 1972-73; Vice-chair, Conservative Parliamentary Candidates Association 1997-2001. *Councils and public bodies:* Councillor: Leicester City Council 1976-79, Leicestershire County Council 1977-83.

Political interests: Consumer issues, information technology, music, arts, home affairs; USA.

Other: British-American Parliamentary Group: Executive Committee Member 2001-08, Treasurer 2008-; The Law Society; PC 1995; Kt 2013. Bridlington Conservative Club.

Publications: Co-author, Westminster Words (1988); Honourable Insults (1990); Parliamentary Sauce (1993); Right Honourable Insults (1998); Naughty Graffiti (2005); Dishonourable Insults (2011).

Recreations: Classic and vintage cars, music, member parliamentary rock band 'MP4'.

Rt Hon Sir Greg Knight MP, House of Commons, London SW1A 0AA
Tel: 020 7219 4077 *Email:* sothcottt@parliament.uk
Constituency: 18 Exchange Street, Driffield, East Yorkshire YO25 6LJ
Tel: 01377 812123 Website: www.gregknight.com *Twitter:* @GregKnight

CONSERVATIVE

KNIGHT, JULIAN

Solihull *(Majority 21,273)*

Chair, Select Committee on Digital, Culture, Media and Sport

Julian Carlton Knight. Born 5 January 1972; Married Philippa.

Education: Chester Catholic High School; Hull University (BA history 1994).

Non-political career: Published author; Consumer journalist, BBC News; Money and property editor, *Independent*.

Political career: Member for Solihull since 7 May 2015 general election; Member, Public Accounts Commission 2017-20; Trade Envoy for Mongolia 2018-19; Team PPS: Ministry of Justice 2018, Department for Work and Pensions 2018-19, HM Treasury 2019. *Select committees:* Member, Communities and Local Government 2015-17; Culture, Media and Sport/ Digital, Culture, Media and Sport: Member 2016-19, Chair 2020-; Member, Liaison 2020-. *Councils and public bodies:* Public Accounts Commission.

Political interests: Fraud, homelessness, financial education for young people; Cyprus, Malta, West Indies.

Other: Organisation for Security and Cooperation in Europe; Marie Curie, Troop Aid; Professional Journalist of the Year 2006. Lions Club.

Publications: British Politics for Dummies; The British Citizenship Test for Dummies; Wills, Probate, and Inheritance Tax for Dummies; Retiring Wealthy for Dummies; Cricket for Dummies; The Royal Wedding for Dummies.

Recreations: Cycling.

Julian Knight MP, House of Commons, London SW1A 0AA
Tel: 020 7219 3577 *Email:* julian.knight.mp@parliament.uk
Constituency: 631 Warwick Road, Solihull, West Midlands B91 1AR
Tel: 0121-709 0458 Website: www.julianknight.org.uk *Twitter:* @julianknight15

CONSERVATIVE

KRUGER, DANNY

Devizes *(Majority 23,993)*

Daniel Rayne Kruger. Born 23 October 1974; Son of Prue Leith and late Rayne Kruger; Married Emma.

Education: Eton College; Edinburgh University (MA history 1997); Oxford University (DPhil history 2000).

Non-political career: Director of Research, Centre for Policy Studies 2001-03; Policy Adviser, Conservative Party 2003-05; Chief Leader-Writer, The Daily Telegraph 2005-06; Special Adviser (Chief Speechwriter) to David Cameron as Leader of the Opposition 2006-08; Founder and Chief Executive: Only Connect 2008-15, West London Zone 2014-16; Senior Fellow, Legatum Institute 2017-18; Expert Adviser, Department for Digital, Culture, Media and Sport 2018-19; Political Secretary to Boris Johnson as Prime Minister 2019.

Political career: Member for Devizes since 12 December 2019.

Other: MBE 2017.

Danny Kruger MBE MP, House of Commons, London SW1A 0AA
Tel: 020 7219 7050 *Email:* danny.kruger.mp@parliament.uk
Constituency: Renelec House, 46 New Park Street, Devizes SN10 1DT
Tel: 01380 729358 Website: www.dannykruger.org.uk *Twitter:* @danny__kruger

CONSERVATIVE

KWARTENG, KWASI

Spelthorne *(Majority 18,393)*

Secretary of State for Business, Energy and Industrial Strategy

Kwasi Alfred Addo Kwarteng. Born 26 May 1975; Son of Alfred Kwasi Kwarteng, economist, and Charlotte Kwarteng, barrister; Single.

Education: Eton College (King's Scholar; Newcastle Scholar); Trinity College, Cambridge (BA classics and history 1996, MA; PhD British history 2000); Kennedy Scholar, Harvard University, USA 1997; Birkbeck College, London (Postgraduate Certificate economics 2000); Certificate investment management 2005; Arabic (basic), French, German, Italian.

Non-political career: Financial analyst: Investment banking 2000-04, Fund management 2004-06; Freelance journalist and author 2006-.

Political career: Contested Brent East 2005 general election. Member for Spelthorne since 6 May 2010 general election; PPS: to Leader of the House of Lords and Lord Privy Seal: Baroness Stowell of Beeston 2015-16, Baroness Evans of Bowes Park 2016-17; to Philip Hammond as Chancellor of the Exchequer 2017-18; Parliamentary Under-Secretary of State, Department for Exiting the European Union 2018-19; Department for Business, Energy and Industrial Strategy: Minister of State for Business, Energy and Clean Growth 2019-21, Secretary of State for Business, Energy and Industrial Strategy 2021-. *Select committees:* Member: Transport 2010-13, Work and Pensions 2013-15, Finance 2015-17, Public Accounts 2016-17.

Political interests: Economy and finance, transport; Africa, Middle East.

Other: Chair, Bow Group 2005-06; Trustee, History of Parliament Trust; PC 2019.

Publications: Author: Ghosts of Empire (Bloomsbury, 2011), Gridlock Nation (Biteback, 2011); Co-author: (with Chris Skidmore MP), After the Coalition (Biteback, 2011), (with Priti Patel MP, Dominic Raab MP, Chris Skidmore MP and Elizabeth Truss MP) Britannia Unchained: Global Lessons for Growth and Prosperity (Palgrave Macmillan, 2012).

Recreations: Music, foreign languages, travel.

Rt Hon Kwasi Kwarteng MP, House of Commons, London SW1A 0AA
Tel: 020 7219 4017 *Fax:* 020 7219 5852 *Email:* kwasi.kwarteng.mp@parliament.uk
Constituency: 13 Station Approach, Ashford, Middlesex TW15 2GH
Email: office@spelthorneconservatives.org.uk Website: www.kwasi4spelthorne.org.uk
Twitter: @KwasiKwarteng

LABOUR

KYLE, PETER

Hove *(Majority 17,044)*

Shadow Minister for Victims and Youth Justice

Peter John Kyle. Born 9 September 1970.

Education: Sussex University (BA geography, international development and environmental studies 1999; DPhil community economic development 2003).

Non-political career: Body Shop/Children on the Edge 1989-96: Aid worker, Eastern Europe and the Balkans; Fat Sand Production: Founder 2003-06, Non-executive director 2013-; Special adviser to Hilary Armstrong as Minister for the Cabinet Office and Social Exclusion and Chancellor of the Duchy of Lancaster 2006-07; Deputy chief executive, ACEVO 2007-13; Non-executive director, CAF Bank Ltd 2011-; Chief executive, Working For Youth 2013-15.

Political career: Member for Hove since 7 May 2015 general election; Shadow Minister for Justice (Victims and Youth Justice) 2020-. *Select committees:* Member: Business, Innovation and Skills 2015-16, Business, Energy and Industrial Strategy 2016-20. Chair, PLP Departmental

Group for Business, Innovation and Skills/Business, Energy and Industrial Strategy 2015-19. Patron, LGBT Labour. *Councils and public bodies:* Governor, Portslade Aldridge Community College; Chair of governors, Brighton Aldridge Community College.

Dr Peter Kyle MP, House of Commons, London SW1A 0AA
Tel: 020 7219 6133 *Email:* peter.kyle.mp@parliament.uk
Constituency: 99 Church Road, Hove, East Sussex BN3 2BA
Tel: 01273 933380 *Email:* hove.portslade@parliament.uk Website: www.peterkyle.co.uk
Twitter: @peterkyle

House of Commons MPs' Biographies

CONSERVATIVE

LAING, ELEANOR

Epping Forest *(Majority 22,173)*

Chairman, Ways and Means and Deputy Speaker

Eleanor Fulton Laing. Born 1 February 1958; Daughter of late Matthew Pritchard and Betty Pritchard, née McFarlane; Married Alan Laing 1983 (divorced 2003) (1 son).

Education: St Columba's School, Kilmacolm, Renfrewshire; Edinburgh University (BA 1982; LLB) (First woman Union President); French.

Non-political career: Practised law in Edinburgh, City of London and industry 1983-89; Special adviser to John MacGregor MP: as Secretary of State for Education 1989-90, as Leader of the House of Commons 1990-92, as Secretary of State for Transport 1992-94.

Political career: Contested Paisley North 1987 general election. Member for Epping Forest 1997-2010, for Epping Forest (revised boundary) since 6 May 2010 general election; Opposition Whip 1999-2000; Opposition Spokesperson for: Constitutional Affairs and Scotland 2000-01, Education and Skills 2001-03; Shadow Minister for: Children 2003, Women 2004-07; Shadow Secretary of State for Scotland 2005; Shadow Minister for: Women and Equality 2005-07, Justice 2007-10; Special Representative to Gibraltar 2010-; Member: Speakers' Working Group on All-Party Groups 2011-12, Speaker's Committee on the Electoral Commission 2012-13; First Deputy Chairman, Ways and Means and Deputy Speaker 2013-19; Chairman, Ways and Means and Deputy Speaker 2020-. *Select committees:* Member: Education and Employment 1997-98, Education and Employment (Employment Sub-committee) 1997-98, Environment, Transport and Regional Affairs 1998-99, Environment, Transport and Regional Affairs (Transport Sub-committee) 1998-99, Office of the Deputy Prime Minister 2004-05, Office of the Deputy Prime Minister (Urban Affairs Sub-committee) 2004-05, Political and Constitutional Reform 2010-13, Joint Committee on Human Rights 2010, Joint Committee on the Draft House of Lords Reform Bill 2011-12, Joint Committee on Parliamentary Privilege 2013, Scottish Affairs 2013, Panel of Chairs 2013-19, Court of Referees 2016-17; Chair, Panel of Chairs 2019-; Member: Finance 2020-, Parliamentary Works Estimates Commission 2020-. Chair, Conservative Party Committee for Home Affairs and Constitution -2013. Chairman, Society of Conservative Lawyers.

Political interests: Education, transport, economic policy, constitution, devolution; Australia, Gibraltar, New Zealand, Uganda, USA.

Other: PC 2017; DBE 2018.

Recreations: Theatre, music, golf.

Rt Hon Dame Eleanor Laing DBE MP, House of Commons, London SW1A 0AA
Tel: 020 7219 2086 *Email:* eleanor.laing.mp@parliament.uk
Constituency: Thatcher House, 4 Meadow Road, Loughton, Essex IG10 4HX
Tel: 020 8508 6608 Website: www.eleanorlaing.com *Twitter:* @eleanor4epping

PLAID CYMRU

LAKE, BEN

Ceredigion *(Majority 6,329)*

Plaid Cymru Spokesperson for Constitutional and Welsh Affairs, Digital, Culture, Media and Sport, Education, Environment, Food and Rural Affairs, Health and Social Care, Housing, Communities and Local Government and Treasury

Ben Morgan Lake. Born 22 January 1993.

Education: Lampeter Comprehensive School; Trinity College, Oxford (BA history and politics 2014; MSt modern European and British history 2015); Welsh.

Non-political career: Press Officer and Caseworker to Elin Jones AM; Research Officer, Plaid Cymru Group in National Assembly for Wales.

Political career: Member for Ceredigion since 8 June 2017; Plaid Cymru Spokesperson for: Education 2017-, Health/Health and Social Care 2017-, Communities and Local Government/ Housing, Communities and Local Government 2017-, Constitutional and Welsh Affairs 2017-, Culture, Media and Sport/Digital, Culture, Media and Sport 2017-, Environment, Food and Rural Affairs 2020-, Treasury 2020-. *Select committees:* Member, Welsh Affairs 2017-. *Councils and public bodies:* Vice-President, Local Government Association 2019-.

Political interests: Rural economy and rural development, youth engagement, sustainable development, education, health.

Other: Lampeter RFC, Lampeter AFC.

Ben Lake MP, House of Commons, London SW1A 0AA
Tel: 020 7219 3000 *Email:* ben.lake.mp@parliament.uk
Constituency: Bryndulais, 67 Bridge Street, Lampeter, Ceredigion SA48 7AB
Tel: 01570 940333 *Twitter:* @BenMLake

LABOUR

LAMMY, DAVID

Tottenham *(Majority 30,175)*

Shadow Secretary of State for Justice

David Lindon Lammy. Born 19 July 1972; Son of Rosalind Lammy, council officer; Married Nicola Green 2005 (3 children).

Education: The King's School, Peterborough; School of Oriental and African Studies, London University (LLB 1993); Harvard Law School, USA (LLM 1997).

Non-political career: Barrister, 3 Serjeants Inn, Philip Naughton QC 1994-96; Attorney, Howard Rice Nemerovsky Canada Falk & Rabkin 1997-98; Barrister, D J Freeman 1998-2000. Member: Amicus branch of Unite, Unison, Co-op.

Political career: Member for Tottenham since 22 June 2000 by-election; PPS to Estelle Morris as Secretary of State for Education and Skills 2001-02; Parliamentary Under-Secretary of State: Department of Health 2002-03, Department for Constitutional Affairs 2003-05, Department for Culture, Media and Sport 2005-07, Department for Innovation, Universities and Skills (DIUS) (Skills) 2007-08; Minister of State (Higher Education and Intellectual Property) DIUS/ Department for Business, Innovation and Skills 2008-10; Shadow Minister for Higher Education 2010; Chair, Lammy Review Leading (review of the treatment of, and outcomes for, Black, Asian and Minority Ethnic individuals in the Criminal Justice System) 2016-; Shadow Secretary of State for Justice 2020-. *Select committees:* Member: Public Administration 2001, Procedure 2001, Ecclesiastical Committee 2010-, Speaker's Advisory Committee on Works of Art 2011-19, Joint Committee on the Draft Defamation Bill 2011, European Scrutiny 2020-. AM for Londonwide region, London Assembly 2000. Member: Society of Labour Lawyers, Christian Socialist Movement. *Councils and public bodies:* Member, Archbishops' Council 1999-2002.

Political interests: Health, Treasury (regeneration), arts and culture, education, international development, gambling, race and poverty, sport; Africa, Latin America, Caribbean, USA.

Other: ActionAid: Trustee 2000-06, Honorary Ambassador 2006-; Patron: Peace Alliance, boys2MEN, Haringey Shed, Oxford Access Scheme, Into University, London Nightline; Honorary president, Haringey Borough Swimming Club; Honorary vice-president, Haringey Advisory Group on Alcohol; President, Tottenham Community Festival; Ovarian Cancer Action; Member, Fabian Society; Council Member, National Youth Theatre; Fawcett Society;

Non-practicing Barrister Associate Tenant, Doughty Street Chambers; Co-founder, Tottenham Youth Fund; Envoy Extraordinaire, University of Guyana; Fellow: Birkbeck, University of London, City Lit; Honorary Doctorate of Law, University of East London 2004; Visiting Professor of Practice, London School of Economics; Professor of Practice, SOAS Law; GQ's and the Political Studies Association's Politician of the Year 2018; PC 2008. Honourable Society of Lincoln's Inn.

Publications: Leading Together (2002); Out of the Ashes (2011).

Recreations: Film, live music, Tottenham Hotspur FC.

Rt Hon David Lammy MP, House of Commons, London SW1A 0AA
Tel: 020 7219 0899 *Fax:* 020 7219 0357 *Email:* lammyd@parliament.uk
Constituency: No constituency office
Website: www.davidlammy.co.uk *Twitter:* @DavidLammy

CONSERVATIVE

LAMONT, JOHN

Berwickshire, Roxburgh and Selkirk *(Majority 5,148)*

PPS to Oliver Dowden as Secretary of State for Digital, Culture, Media and Sport

John Robert Lamont. Born 15 April 1976; Son of Robert Lamont, farmer, and Elizabeth Lamont, née Wilson, teacher.

Education: Kilwinning Academy, Ayrshire; Glasgow University (LLB law 1998); College of Law, Chester (CPD 1999; LPC 2000; qualified solicitor 2002).

Non-political career: Freshfields, London 2000-04: Trainee solicitor 2000-02, Assistant 2002-03; Associate, Bristows, London 2003-05; Solicitor, Brodies, Edinburgh 2005-07.

Political career: Contested Berwickshire, Roxburgh and Selkirk 2005, 2010 and 2015 general elections. Member for Berwickshire, Roxburgh and Selkirk since 8 June 2017; Department for Digital, Culture, Media and Sport: Team PPS 2019, PPS to Secretary of State: Nicky Morgan [Baroness Morgan of Cotes] 2019-20, Oliver Dowden 2020-. *Select committees:* Member: Scottish Affairs 2017-, Joint Committee on Statutory Instruments 2017-. Member, Executive, 1922 Committee 2017-20; Chairman, Conservative Backbench Policy Committee on Scottish Affairs 2017-20. MSP for Roxburgh and Berwickshire constituency 2007-11, and for Ettrick, Roxburgh and Berwickshire constituency 2011-17: Scottish Conservatives: Shadow Minister for Community Safety 2007-10, Shadow Cabinet Secretary for Justice 2010-11, Spokesperson for Justice 2011, Chief Whip 2011-17, Business Manager 2011-17; Member: Scottish Parliamentary Bureau 2011-17, Scottish Commission for Public Audit 2016-17. Member, Conservative Friends of Israel 2011-; National co-ordinator, Conservative Friends of the Union 2012-.

Political interests: Rural affairs, tourism, farming, justice, digital infrastructure; Israel, Taiwan, USA.

Other: Member: East of Scotland Rail Action Group 2005-, Scottish Athletics 2008-, Borders Sport and Leisure Trust 2010-; Trustee, St Abbs Lifeboat Trust; Member, Law Society of England and Wales 2002-; Patron, Borders Osteoporosis Society; College of Law prize for excellence 2002; City of London Company law prize (nominated) 2002. Borders Triathlon Club.

Recreations: Cycling, running, swimming, competing in triathlons.

John Lamont MP, House of Commons, London SW1A 0AA
Tel: 020 7219 1557 *Email:* john.lamont.mp@parliament.uk
Constituency: 25 High Street, Hawick TD9 9BU
Tel: 01450 375948 Website: www.johnlamont.org *Twitter:* @john2win

CONSERVATIVE

LARGAN, ROBERT

High Peak *(Majority 590)*

Born 29 May 1987.

Education: Philips High School, Whitfield, Manchester; Manchester University (BA economic and social studies); German.

Non-political career: Equity Capital Markets Manager, Deloitte; Finance Manager, Marks and Spencer.

Political career: Contested Bury South 2017 general election. Member for High Peak since 12 December 2019. *Select committees:* Member, Transport 2020-. *Councils and public bodies:* Councillor, Hammersmith and Fulham Council 2014-17; School governor 2009-13.

Political interests: Rail and road investment, NHS, finance; Iran, Israel, Oman, South Africa, Syria.

Other: ACA, Institute of Chartered Accountants for England and Wales.

Recreations: Walking, cooking, reading, watching football and rugby.

Robert Largan MP, House of Commons, London SW1A 0AA
Tel: 020 7219 3000 *Email:* robert.largan.mp@parliament.uk
Constituency: 18 Market Street, Whaley Bridge SK23 7LP
Tel: 01663 769779 *Email:* mail@robertlargan.co.uk Website: www.robertlargan.co.uk
Twitter: @robertlargan

CONSERVATIVE

LATHAM, PAULINE

Mid Derbyshire *(Majority 15,385)*

Pauline Elizabeth Latham. Born 4 February 1948; Married Derek Latham 1968 (1 daughter 2 sons).

Education: Bramcote Hills Technical Grammar School.

Non-political career: Proprietor, Humble Pie 1976-87; Director, Michael St Development 1982-95; Founder Member and Chair, Grant Maintained Schools Advisory Committee -2004.

Political career: Contested Broxtowe 2001 general election. Member for Mid Derbyshire since 6 May 2010 general election; PPS to: Hugo Swire as Minister of State, Foreign and Commonwealth Office 2015-16, Alan Duncan as Minister of State for Europe and the Americas, Foreign and Commonwealth Office 2016-17; Trade Envoy to Kenya 2018-20; Prime Minister's Ambassador for Performing Arts 2018-. *Select committees:* Member: International Development 2010-, Work of the Independent Commission for Aid Impact Sub-committee 2017-19, Administration 2017-, Arms Export Controls 2017-19, Joint Committee on Human Rights 2020-. Secretary, 1922 Sub-committee on Foreign Affairs, Defence and International Development; 1922 Committee: Member, Executive 2017-20, Secretary 2020-. Contested East Midlands 1999 and 2004 European Parliament elections. *Councils and public bodies:* Councillor: Derbyshire County Council 1987-2002, Derby City Council 1992-96, 1998-2010; Mayor of Derby 2007-08; Governor and chair of governors, Ecclesbourne School.

Political interests: International development, health (cancer and type 1 diabetes), marriage law reform (age of marriage, marriage ceremonies), rare diseases (aortic dissection, malaria); Africa.

Other: Commonwealth Parliamentary Association (UK Branch): Vice-chair 2011-14, Member, Executive Committee 2014-15; Board member, WE Charity 2013-; Patron, Women's Work; Director, Furthest from the Sea 2017-; Trustee, Industry and Parliament Trust; OBE 1995. Carlton Club.

Recreations: Horse riding, walking, travel.

Pauline Latham OBE MP, House of Commons, London SW1A 0AA
Tel: 020 7219 7110 *Email:* pauline.latham.mp@parliament.uk
Constituency: The Old Station, Station Road, Spondon, Derby, Derbyshire DE21 7NE
Tel: 01332 676679 Website: www.paulinelatham.co.uk *Twitter:* @Pauline_Latham

LABOUR

LAVERY, IAN

Wansbeck *(Majority 814)*

Born 6 January 1963; Son of John Lavery, miner, and Patricia Lavery; Married Hilary (2 sons).

Education: Ashington High School; New College, Durham (HNC mining engineering).

Non-political career: Miner, National Coal Board: Lynemouth Colliery 1980, Ellington Colliery 1980-92; National Union of Mine Workers: General Secretary, Northumberland Area 1992-2002, National President 2002-10. National Union of Mineworkers: Member 1980-, Representative, Ellington Colliery 1986-92; Member, Unite.

Political career: Member for Wansbeck since 6 May 2010 general election; PPS to Harriet Harman: as Deputy Leader and Chair, Labour Party; Deputy Leader of the Opposition; Shadow Secretary of State for International Development 2010-11, as Shadow Deputy Prime Minister, Chair, Labour Party, and Shadow Secretary of State for Culture, Media and Sport 2011-12; Shadow Minister for Cabinet Office 2015-16; Shadow Minister for the Cabinet Office (attends Shadow Cabinet) 2016-17; National Elections and Campaign Co-ordinator/National Campaign Co-ordinator 2016-20. *Select committees:* Member: Northern Ireland Affairs 2010-11, Regulatory Reform 2010-15, Energy and Climate Change 2010-15, Joint Committee on Draft Deregulation Bill 2013. Labour Party: Member, Ashington Town branch, Executive committee member, Wansbeck CLP, Chair, Trade Union Group of MPs, Party Chair 2017-20. *Councils and public bodies:* Former councillor, Wansbeck District Council.

Political interests: Local regeneration, employment, energy, climate change, poverty, internationalism, sport, foreign and Commonwealth affairs.

Other: International Energy Miners Organisation; Chair: Ashington Community Football Club -2018, Hirst Welfare Centre, Ashington Group – The Pitmen Painters; Trustee: Northumberland Aged Miners Homes Association, North East Area Miners Trust, Woodhorn Museum, North East CISWO Trust.

Recreations: History, walking, horse and greyhound racing, Newcastle United FC, all sports.

Ian Lavery MP, House of Commons, London SW1A 0AA
Tel: 020 7219 7177 *Email:* ian.lavery.mp@parliament.uk
Constituency: 7 Esther Court, Wansbeck Business Park, Ashington, Northumberland NE63 8AP
Tel: 01670 852494 Website: www.ianlavery.co.uk *Twitter:* @IanLaveryMP

SCOTTISH NATIONAL PARTY

LAW, CHRIS

Dundee West *(Majority 12,259)*

SNP Shadow Spokesperson for International Development

Christopher Murray Alexander Law. Born 21 October 1969.

Education: Dundee College of Further Education (C&G catering); St Andrews University (cultural and social anthropology; Postgraduate Diploma IT).

Non-political career: French chef; Founder and expedition leader, Freewheeling Travels 1997-; Founder, director and writer, Freewheeling Films 2003-; Founder and director, The Mortgage Doctor 2007-.

Political career: Member for Dundee West since 7 May 2015 general election; SNP: Spokesperson for Climate Justice 2017-18, Spokesperson/Shadow Secretary of State for International Development 2017-. *Select committees:* Member: Scottish Affairs 2015-17, International Development 2017-, Work of the Independent Commission for Aid Impact Sub-committee 2017-, Arms Export Controls 2017-19, 2020-.

Political interests: Disability benefits, welfare.

Other: Member, Executive Committee, Commonwealth Parliamentary Association (UK Branch) 2017-19; Founder and campaigner, Spirit of Independence 2014.

Chris Law MP, House of Commons, London SW1A 0AA
Tel: 020 7219 6917 *Email:* chris.law.mp@parliament.uk
Constituency: 2 Marshall Street, Lochee, Dundee DD2 3BR
Tel: 01382 848906 Website: chrislaw.scot *Twitter:* @ChrisLawSNP

CONSERVATIVE

LEADSOM, ANDREA

South Northamptonshire *(Majority 27,761)*

Andrea Jacqueline Leadsom. Born 13 May 1963; Daughter of Judy Crompton and Richard Salmon; Married Ben Leadsom 1993 (2 sons 1 daughter).

Education: Tonbridge Girls Grammar; Warwick University (political science 1984); French.

Non-political career: Various roles, BZW 1987-93; Financial institutions director, Barclays Bank 1991-97; Managing director, De Putron (funds management) 1997-99; Head of corporate governance, Invesco Perpetual 1999-2009.

Political career: Contested Knowsley South 2005 general election. Member for South Northamptonshire since 6 May 2010 general election; Economic Secretary (Minister for the City of London), HM Treasury 2014-15; Minister of State, Department of Energy and Climate Change 2015-16; Secretary of State for Environment, Food and Rural Affairs 2016-17; Leader of the House of Commons and Lord President of the Council (also attending Cabinet) 2017-19; Member: House of Commons Commission 2017-19, Speaker's Committee for the Independent Parliamentary Standards Authority 2017-19; Ex-officio member, Public Accounts Commission 2017-19; Chair, Ministerial Group on Family Support from Conception to the Age of Two 2018-19; Secretary of State for Business, Energy and Industrial Strategy 2019-20. *Select committees:* Member: Treasury 2010-14, Public Accounts 2014-15. Member, Number 10 Policy Advisory Board 2013-14. *Councils and public bodies:* Councillor, South Oxfordshire District Council 2003-07.

Political interests: Economy, early years development, bank reform, energy and the green economy.

Other: Oxford Parent Infant Project: Chair 2001-09, Patron; Patron: Northamptonshire Parent Infant Project, PIP UK, PSP Association; Member, Campaign committee, Vote Leave 2016; Newcomer of the Year, *Spectator* awards 2012; PC 2016.

Rt Hon Andrea Leadsom MP, House of Commons, London SW1A 0AA
Tel: 020 7219 7149 *Fax:* 020 7219 4045 *Email:* andrea.leadsom.mp@parliament.uk
Constituency: 4a Victoria House, 138 Watling Street East, Towcester NN12 6BT
Tel: 01327 353124 Website: www.andrealeadsom.com *Twitter:* @andrealeadsom

CONSERVATIVE

LEIGH, EDWARD

Gainsborough *(Majority 22,967)*

Chair, Public Accounts Commission

Edward Julian Egerton Leigh. Born 20 July 1950; Son of late Sir Neville Leigh, former Clerk to the Privy Council; Married Mary Goodman 1984 (3 sons 3 daughters).

Education: Oratory School, Reading, Berkshire; French Lycee, London; Durham University (BA history 1972) (Union President); French.

Non-political career: Member, Conservative Research Department 1973-75; Principal correspondence secretary to Margaret Thatcher as Leader of the Opposition 1976-77; Barrister, Inner Temple 1977-.

Political career: Contested Teesside, Middlesbrough October 1974 general election. Member for Gainsborough and Horncastle 1983-97, for Gainsborough 1997-2010, for Gainsborough (revised boundary) since 6 May 2010 general election; PPS to John Patten as Minister of State, Home Office 1990; Parliamentary Under-Secretary of State, Department of Trade and Industry 1990-93; Public Accounts Commission: Member -2010, 2015-20, Chair 2011-15, 2020-Financial Adviser to the Treasury 2010-11. *Select committees:* Member, Social Security 1997-2000; Public Accounts: Member 2000-01, Chair 2001-10; Member: Liaison 2001-10, Chairmen's Panel/Panel of Chairs 2010-, Members' Expenses 2011-15, Procedure 2015-17, 2018-19, Court of Referees 2016-17, International Trade 2016-17, Joint Committee on the Draft Parliamentary Buildings (Restoration and Renewal) Bill 2018-19, Joint Committee on the National Security Strategy 2020-. Vice-chair, Conservative Party Committees for: Foreign and Commonwealth Affairs 1997-2001, Social Security 1997-2001; Chair, Conservative Party Committee for Foreign Affairs, Defence and International Development -2015. Member, governing council, Conservative Christian Fellowship; Chair, Cornerstone Group 2004-. *Councils and public bodies:* Councillor: Richmond Borough Council 1974-78, GLC 1977-81; Chair, National Council for Civil Defence 1979-83; Director, Coalition For Peace Through Security 1981-83.

Political interests: Defence, foreign affairs, agriculture, families.

Other: Member, UK Delegation, Parliamentary Assembly of the Council of Europe -2015, 2017-; Fellow, Industry and Parliament Trust 1983; Veteran Member, Honourable Artillery Company; President, Catholic Union of Great Britain; CAFOD, Malteser International, Order of Malta Volunteers; Fellow Institute of Arbitrators 1999-; Knight of Honour and Devotion Sovereign Military Order of Malta; Kt 2013; Officier, Légion d'honneur 2015; PC 2019.

Publications: Right Thinking (1982); Onwards from Bruges (1989); Choice and Responsibility – The Enabling State (1990); The Nation that Forgot God (2009); Monastery of the Mind (2012).

Recreations: Walking, reading, swimming.

Rt Hon Sir Edward Leigh MP, House of Commons, London SW1A 0AA
Tel: 020 7219 6480 *Email:* edward.leigh.mp@parliament.uk
Constituency: No constituency office publicised
Website: www.edwardleigh.org.uk *Twitter:* @EdwardLeighMP

CONSERVATIVE

LEVY, IAN

Blyth Valley *(Majority 712)*

Born 14 February 1966; Married Maureen (1 daughter).

Education: Blyth Ridley High School.

Non-political career: Mental Health Nursing Assistant, St Nicholas Hospital, Newcastle upon Tyne.

Political career: Contested Blyth Valley 2017 general election. Member for Blyth Valley since 12 December 2019. *Select committees:* Member: Environmental Audit 2020-, Housing, Communities and Local Government 2020-.

Ian Levy MP, House of Commons, London SW1A 0AA
Tel: 020 7219 3000 *Email:* ian.levy.mp@parliament.uk
Constituency: Blyth Workspace, Commissioners Quay, Quay Road, Blyth NE24 3AG
Tel: 01670 338435 Website: www.ianlevy.org.uk

LABOUR

LEWELL-BUCK, EMMA

South Shields *(Majority 9,585)*

Emma Louise Lewell-Buck. Born 8 November 1978; Daughter of Linda and David Lewell; Married Simon Buck.

Education: St Joseph's Comprehensive; Northumbria University (BA politics and media studies); Durham University (MSW social work).

Non-political career: Child Protection Social Worker; Cleaner; Bar Worker; Waitress; Salesperson; Shop Assistant; Call Centre Worker; Play Worker. Member, GMB.

Political career: Member for South Shields since 2 May 2013 by-election; PPS to: Ivan Lewis as Shadow Secretary of State for Northern Ireland 2013-15, Andy Burnham as Shadow Home Secretary 2015-16; Shadow Minister for: Communities and Local Government 2016, Children and Families 2016-19. *Select committees:* Member: Environment, Food and Rural Affairs 2013-15, Joint Committee on the Draft Protection of Charities Bill 2014-15, Work and Pensions 2015-16, Defence 2020-, Committees on Arms Export Controls 2020-. Member, Co-operative. *Councils and public bodies:* South Tyneside Council: Councillor 2004-13, Lead Member for Adult Social Care and Support Services.

Political interests: Child protection, children's and adults' social care, welfare, food poverty, homelessness.

Other: Member, Dyspraxia Foundation; Trustee, Feeding Britain charity; Asian Voice's Labour Backbencher of the Year 2015; Dyspraxia Foundation's Mary Colley Award for raising awareness of Dyspraxia 2014; Top 50 Influential Neurodivergent Women 2019.

Emma Lewell-Buck MP, House of Commons, London SW1A 0AA
Tel: 020 7219 4468 *Email:* emma.lewell-buck.mp@parliament.uk
Constituency: 19 Westoe Road, South Shields NE33 4LS
Tel: 0191-427 1240 *Twitter:* @EmmaLewellBuck

CONSERVATIVE

LEWER, ANDREW

Northampton South *(Majority 4,697)*

Team PPS, Home Office

Andrew Iain Lewer. Born 18 July 1971; Married Gabriela 2005 (1 son).

Education: Queen Elizabeth's Grammar School, Ashbourne; Newcastle University (BA history 1992); Downing College, Cambridge.

Non-political career: Sales and marketing manager, Landmark Publishing.

Political career: Member for Northampton South since 8 June 2017; PPS to: Julian Smith as Secretary of State for Northern Ireland 2019-20, Alun Cairns as Secretary of State for Wales 2019, Simon Hart as Secretary of State for Wales 2019-20; Team PPS, Home Office 2020-. *Select committees:* Member: Communities and Local Government/Housing, Communities and Local Government 2017-19, European Scrutiny 2017-19. MEP for East Midlands 2014-17. *Councils and public bodies:* Councillor, Derbyshire Dales District Council 2003-14; Derbyshire County Council: Councillor 2005-14, Leader, Conservative group 2007-14, Leader of the Council 2009-13; Governor, Derby University 2009-; Local Government Association: Deputy Chair 2011-14, Vice-president 2017-.

Political interests: Regional policy.

Other: UK Delegate, EU Committee of the Regions; Director: Derbyshire Historic Buildings Trust 2003-, Foundation for European Reform 2015-; MBE 2014.

Andrew Lewer MBE MP, House of Commons, London SW1A 0AA
Tel: 020 7219 3870 *Email:* andrew.lewer.mp@parliament.uk
Constituency: White Lodge, 42 Billing Road, Northampton NN1 5DA
Tel: 01604 978080 Website: www.andrewlewer.com *Twitter:* @ALewerMBE

CONSERVATIVE

LEWIS, BRANDON

Great Yarmouth *(Majority 17,663)*

Secretary of State for Northern Ireland

Brandon Kenneth Lewis. Born 20 June 1971; Son of Jack and Lynn Lewis; Married Justine Rappolt 1999 (1 son 1 daughter).

Education: Forest School, Snaresbrook; Buckingham University (BSc economics 1993; LLB 1996); King's College, London (LLM commercial law 1998); Inns of Court, School of Law (Bar Vocational Course).

Non-political career: Director: Woodlands Schools Ltd 2001-12, i5 Consulting Ltd -2010.

Political career: Contested Sherwood 2001 general election. Member for Great Yarmouth since 6 May 2010 general election; Department for Communities and Local Government: Parliamentary Under-Secretary of State 2012-14, Minister of State for Housing and Planning 2014-16; Member Speaker's Committee on the Electoral Commission 2013-15; Minister of State, Home Office: for Policing and the Fire Service 2016-17, for Immigration (also attending Cabinet) 2017-18; Minister without Portfolio, Cabinet Office 2018-19; Minister of State for Security and Economic Crime; Deputy Minister for Brexit, Home Office (also attending Cabinet) 2019-20; Secretary of State for Northern Ireland 2020-. *Select committees:* Member: Regulatory Reform 2010-12, Work and Pensions 2010-12. Chairman, Conservative Party 2018-. *Councils and public bodies:* Brentwood Borough Council: Councillor 1998-2009, Leader 2004-09; Associate Governor, Great Yarmouth College; Governor, Felsted School.

Political interests: Tourism, local government, coastal erosion, business, transport; Italy, USA.

Other: Council Member, Buckingham University; Member, Lords Taverner's; Trustee, British Triathlon Trust; Patron, East Coast Hospice; Member, Institute of Directors 2001-07; PC 2016; CBE 2019. Carlton Club.

Recreations: Running, cycling, swimming, reading.

Rt Hon Brandon Lewis CBE MP, House of Commons, London SW1A 0AA
Tel: 020 7219 7231 *Email:* brandon.lewis.mp@parliament.uk
Constituency: 20 Church Plain, Great Yarmouth, Norfolk NR30 1NE
Tel: 01493 854550 *Email:* office@brandonlewis.co Website: www.brandonlewis.co
Twitter: @BrandonLewis

LABOUR

LEWIS, CLIVE

Norwich South *(Majority 12,760)*

Clive Anthony Lewis. Born 11 September 1971; Married Kate Steel 2017 (1 daughter).

Education: Bradford University (BSc economics 1993) (Student Union president).

Non-political career: Vice-president, National Union of Students; BBC: News trainee, TV news reporter, Eastern region's chief political reporter. Former Territorial Army reservist, served a tour of duty in Afghanistan 2009.

Political career: Member for Norwich South since 7 May 2015 general election; Shadow Minister for Energy and Climate Change 2015-16; Shadow Secretary of State for: Defence 2016, Business, Energy and Industrial Strategy 2016-17, Shadow Minister for Treasury (Shadow Exchequer Secretary) 2018-20. *Select committees:* Member: Public Accounts 2015, Science and Technology 2017-18. *Councils and public bodies:* Associate governor, Thorpe St Andrew School.

Political interests: Social justice, climate change, economics, humanism, progressive alliance, education (academisation), human rights, military personnel, fair banking.

Recreations: Norwich City FC Season ticket holder.

Clive Lewis MP, House of Commons, London SW1A 0AA
Tel: 020 7219 5593 *Email:* clive.lewis.mp@parliament.uk
Constituency: 20 Bank Plain, Norwich, Norfolk NR2 4SF
Tel: 01603 510755 Website: www.clivelewis.org *Twitter:* @labourlewis

CONSERVATIVE

LEWIS, JULIAN

New Forest East *(Majority 25,251)*

Chair, Intelligence and Security Committee of Parliament

Julian Murray Lewis. Born 26 September 1951; Son of late Samuel Lewis and late Hilda Lewis.

Education: Dynevor School, Swansea; Balliol College, Oxford (BA philosophy and politics, MA 1977); St Antony's College, Oxford (DPhil strategic studies 1981); Doctoral research (strategic studies) 1975-77, 1978-81.

Non-political career: Secretary, Campaign for Representative Democracy 1977-78; Research Director and Director, Coalition for Peace Through Security 1981-85; Director, Policy Research Associates 1985-; Deputy director, Conservative Research Department 1990-96; Visiting Senior Research Fellow, Centre for Defence Studies, Department of War Studies, King's College, London 2010-. Seaman, HM Royal Naval Reserve 1979-82.

Political career: Contested Swansea West 1983 general election. Member for New Forest East 1997-2010, for New Forest East (revised boundary) since 6 May 2010 general election; Opposition Whip 2001-02; Shadow Minister for: Defence 2002-04, 2005-10, the Cabinet Office 2004-05; Intelligence and Security Committee: Member 2010-15, Chair 2020-. *Select committees:* Member, Welsh Affairs 1998-2001; Defence: Member 2000-01, 2014-15, Chair 2015-19; Member: Arms Export Controls 2014-15, 2016-17, Liaison 2015-19, Joint Committee on the National Security Strategy 2015-19. Secretary, Conservative Parliamentary Defence Committee 1997-2001; Vice-chair, Conservative Parliamentary Committees for: European Affairs 2000-01, Foreign and Commonwealth Affairs 2000-01; Member Executive, 1922 Committee 2001. Treasurer, Oxford University Conservative Association 1971; Vice-President, Conservatives for Britain 2015-16; Conservative whip withdrawn July-December 2020.

Political interests: Defence, security, foreign affairs, European affairs; Western Europe, Central and Eastern Europe, Russia.

Other: Secretary, Oxford Union 1972; Joint organiser of campaign against militant infiltration of the Labour Party 1977-78; Patron, Pilgrim Bandits; Honorary Professor, Strategy and Security Institute, Exeter University; Trench Gascoigne prize winner RUSI 2005, 2007; Royal College of Defence Studies prize winner 2006; PC 2015. Athenæum, Totton Conservative Club; President, Calshot Association.

Publications: Changing Direction: British Military Planning for Post-War Strategic Defence 1942-1947 (1988, 2003, 2008); Who's Left? An Index of Labour MPs and Left-Wing Causes 1985-1992 (1992); Labour's CND Cover-Up (1992); The Liberal Democrats: The Character of Their Politics (1993); What's Liberal? Liberal Democrat Quotations and Facts (1996); Racing Ace – The Fights and Flights of 'Kink' Kinkead DSO, DSC*, DFC* (2011).

Recreations: History, fiction, films, music, photography.

Rt Hon Dr Julian Lewis MP, House of Commons, London SW1A 0AA
Tel: 020 7219 4179
Constituency: 3 The Parade, Southampton Road, Cadnam, Hampshire SO40 2NG
Tel: 023 8081 4817 Website: www.julianlewis.net

CONSERVATIVE

LIDDELL-GRAINGER, IAN

Bridgwater and West Somerset *(Majority 24,439)*

Ian Richard Peregrine Liddell-Grainger. Born 23 February 1959; Son of late David Liddell-Grainger, farmer, and Ann Grainger; Married Jill Nesbitt 1985 (1 son 2 daughters).

Education: Millfield School, Somerset; South of Scotland Agricultural College, Edinburgh (National Certificate agriculture 1978).

Non-political career: Family farm, Berwickshire 1980-85; Managing director, property management and development companies group 1985-2000. Major Fusiliers TA.

Political career: Contested Torridge and Devon West 1997 general election. Member for Bridgwater 2001-10, for Bridgwater and West Somerset since 6 May 2010 general election. *Select committees:* Member: Public Administration 2001-10, Scottish Affairs 2002-05, Environment, Food and Rural Affairs 2003-05, Crossrail Bill 2006-07, Environmental Audit 2007-10, Joint Committee on Statutory Instruments 2010-17, Works of Art 2011-17, Business, Energy and Industrial Strategy 2017-19, International Development 2020-. Contested Tyne and Wear 1994 European Parliament election. Member, Conservative Agricultural Forum 1992-97; President, Tyne Bridge Conservative Association 1993-96. *Councils and public bodies:* Councillor: Tynedale District Council 1989-95, Northern Area Council 1992-95.

Political interests: Business, economy, defence, rural affairs, farming, taxation, education, health, energy; Africa especially South Africa, China, Hong Kong, Singapore, Switzerland, USA, Vietnam.

Other: Executive Committee, Commonwealth Parliamentary Association UK: Member -2015, 2017-19, Chair 2015-17, 2020-; Inter-Parliamentary Union, British Group: Member, Executive Committee, Vice-chair 2014-17, 2018-; Parliamentary Assembly of the Council of Europe: Member, UK delegation 2010-, Leader, Conservative Grouping for the Council 2016-; British Isles and Mediterranean Region Representative, International Commonwealth Parliamentary Association 2020-; England Branch Executive Member and CPA Executive Committee Member, Commonwealth Parliamentary Association 2020-; RNLI, Macmillan Cancer Support, Help for Heroes, Royal British Legion, Brainwave.

Recreations: Walking, travel, family, gardening, vigorous debate.

Ian Liddell-Grainger MP, House of Commons, London SW1A 0AA
Tel: 020 7219 8149 *Email:* ianlg@parliament.uk
Constituency: 16 Northgate, Bridgwater, Somerset TA6 3EU
Tel: 01278 458383 Website: www.liddellgrainger.org.uk

SCOTTISH NATIONAL PARTY

LINDEN, DAVID

Glasgow East *(Majority 5,566)*

SNP Shadow Secretary of State for Work and Pensions

David Melvyn Linden. Born 14 May 1990; Married Roslyn (1 son 1 daughter).

Education: Bannerman High School; Modern Apprenticeship (business administration).

Non-political career: Underwriter, Access Loans and Mortgages; Loan Officer, Glasgow Credit Union; Constituency Caseworker to John Mason MP; SNP campaigns and research in Holyrood, Brussels and Westminster; Office Manager to Alison Thewliss MP 2015-17.

Political career: Member for Glasgow East since 8 June 2017; SNP: Deputy Whip 2017-19, Shadow Secretary of State for Housing, Communities and Local Government 2020-21, Shadow Secretary of State for Work and Pensions 2021-. *Select committees:* Member: Procedure 2017-19, Standing Orders 2017-, Joint Committee on Fixed-Term Parliaments Act 2020-.

Political interests: Social security, housing, equal pay, gambling proliferation, inequality.

Other: Member: Bellahouston Road Runners, Airdrieonians Supporters Trust.

Recreations: Badminton, football, angling.

David Linden MP, House of Commons, London SW1A 0AA
Tel: 020 7219 1801 *Email:* david.linden.mp@parliament.uk
Constituency: Suite 6, Academy House, 1346 Shettleston Road, Shettleston, Glasgow G32 9AT
Tel: 0141-778 1177 Website: www.davidlinden.scot *Twitter:* @davidlinden

LABOUR

LLOYD, TONY

Rochdale *(Majority 9,668)*

Anthony Joseph Lloyd. Born 25 February 1950; Son of late Sydney Lloyd, lithographic printer, and Ciceley Lloyd, administrative officer; Married Judith Tear 1974 (separated) (1 son 3 daughters).

Education: Stretford Grammar School; Nottingham University (BSc maths); Manchester Business School (Diploma business administration).

Non-political career: Business administration lecturer, Salford University 1979-83. GMB; Unite.

Political career: Member for Stretford 1983-97, for Manchester Central 1997-2010, for Manchester Central (revised boundary) 2010-12, and for Rochdale since 8 June 2017; Opposition Whip 1986-87; Opposition Spokesperson for: Transport 1988-89, Employment 1988-92, 1993-94, Education 1992-94, The Environment and London 1994-95, Foreign and Commonwealth Affairs 1995-97; Minister of State, Foreign and Commonwealth Office 1997-99; Shadow Minister for Housing 2017-18; Shadow Secretary of State for: Northern Ireland 2018-20, Scotland 2019-20. *Select committees:* Member: Social Services 1983-84, Home Affairs 1984-86, North West 2009-10, European Scrutiny 2010-11. Chair, Parliamentary Labour Party 2006-12. Police and Crime Commissioner for Greater Manchester 2012-17. *Councils and public bodies:* Councillor, Trafford District Council 1979-84; Interim Mayor of Greater Manchester 2015-17.

Political interests: Civil liberties, global security and disarmament, community relations, employment and industrial policy, human rights, overseas aid and development, international relations.

Other: Leader, UK Delegation to Parliamentary Assembly of: Council of Europe/Western European Union 2000-07, OSCE 2005-10; Member: Executive Committee, Inter-Parliamentary Union, British Group, UK Delegation to Parliamentary Assembly, Council of Europe 2020-; Visiting fellow, St Antony's College, Oxford.

Tony Lloyd MP, House of Commons, London SW1A 0AA
Tel: 020 7219 3000 *Email:* tony.lloyd.mp@parliament.uk
Constituency: 23 The Wheatsheaf, Baillie Street, Rochdale OL16 1JZ
Tel: 01706 356542 Website: tonylloyd.org.uk *Twitter:* @tony4rochdale

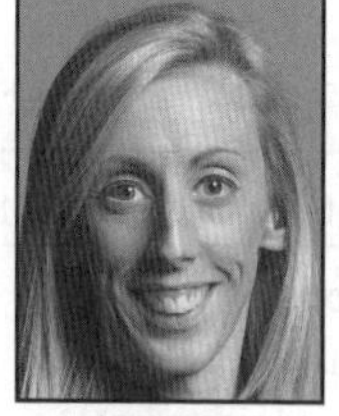

DEMOCRATIC UNIONIST PARTY

LOCKHART, CARLA

Upper Bann *(Majority 8,210)*

Carla Rebecca Lockhart. Born 28 February 1985; Married Rodney Condell 2011.

Education: Aughnacloy High School; Armagh Tech; Ulster University (BA business administration and management 2007).

Non-political career: Political Researcher to Stephen Moutray MLA, Lurgan DUP Advice Centre.

Political career: Member for Upper Bann since 12 December 2019. MLA for Upper Bann 5 May 2016 to 7 January 2020: Member, Assembly Committees on: Education 2016, Public Accounts 2016-17. Campaign manager to David Simpson MP 2015, 2017. *Councils and public bodies:* Craigavon Borough Council: Councillor 2005-15, Lord Mayor 2012-13; Armagh Banbridge Craigavon District Council: Councillor 2015-16, DUP Group Leader 2015-16; President, Northern Ireland Local Government Association; Governor, Lurgan Junior High and Magheralin Primary.

Other: Member, Royal British Legion.

Carla Lockhart MP, House of Commons, London SW1A 0AA
Tel: 020 7219 3000 *Email:* carla.lockhart.mp@parliament.uk
Constituency: 31 High Street, Lurgan, Craigavon BT66 8AU
Tel: 028 3831 0088 *Twitter:* @carlalockhart

CONSERVATIVE

LODER, CHRIS

West Dorset *(Majority 14,106)*

Christopher Lionel John Loder. Born 5 September 1981.

Education: Gryphon School, Sherborne; Warwick Business School (Postgraduate Diploma strategic leadership 2012).

Non-political career: Train Services Manager, Great Western Railway 2003-05; Performance Manager, Arriva Trains 2005-07; Operations Manager, c2c 2007-09; Deutsche Bahn: Deputy Operations Director (Chiltern) 2009-10, Head of UK Planning and Access 2010-12; Deputy Operations Director, Abellio Greater Anglia 2012; South Western Railway: Head of Business Projects 2012-15, Head of Service and Pricing Strategy 2015-19, Head of Waterloo Upgrade Programme 2017, Head of New Trains 2019.

Political career: Member for West Dorset since 12 December 2019. *Select committees:* Member, Transport 2020-. West Dorset Conservative Party: Vice-chair 2014-16, Chair 2016-19; Chair, Dorset Conservatives 2018-. *Councils and public bodies:* Councillor, West Dorset District Council 2013-15.

Other: Trustee, Southwark Cathedral 2008-12; South East Area Chair, Institution of Railway Operators 2011-13; Freedom, City of London.

Recreations: Travelling, classical music.

Chris Loder MP, House of Commons, London SW1A 0AA
Tel: 020 7219 3912 *Email:* chris.loder.mp@parliament.uk
Constituency: 9 Challacombe Square, Poundbury, Dorset DT1 3SX
Tel: 01305 818446 *Email:* hello@chrisloder.co.uk Website: www.chrisloder.co.uk
Twitter: @chrisloder

CONSERVATIVE

LOGAN, MARK

Bolton North East *(Majority 378)*

Mark Rory Logan.

Education: Queen's University Belfast (LLB law 2006); Shanghai Jiao Tong University (Mandarin 2008); Peking University (Mandarin 2009); School of Oriental and African Studies, University of London (2010); London School of Economics and Political Science (MSc comparative politics 2010); Chartered Institute of Public Relations (Diploma public relations 2015); Oxford University (MSc Chinese studies 2017); Mandarin.

Non-political career: Field Manager, Democratic National Committee 2006; Olympic Attache, Ministry of Foreign Affairs 2008; Director of International Marketing Communications, EBF 2010-12; Head of Communications and Chief Spokesperson in Shanghai, Foreign and Commonwealth Office 2012-16; Head of Global Communications, General Manager International Affairs and Assistant President, Sanpower Group in Nanjing, 2016-18; Founder and Managing Director, Oxford PR 2016-.

Political career: Contested East Antrim 2017 general election. Member for Bolton North East since 12 December 2019. *Select committees:* Member, Science and Technology 2020-. Contested South Antrim 2017 Northern Ireland Assembly election.

Political interests: NHS, education, law and order.

Other: Member, British-Irish Parliamentary Assembly 2020-.

Mark Logan MP, House of Commons, London SW1A 0AA
Tel: 020 7219 6435 *Email:* mark.logan.mp@parliament.uk
Constituency: 501 Tonge Moor Road, Bolton BL2 3BG
Website: www.marklogan.org.uk

LABOUR

LONG BAILEY, REBECCA
Salford and Eccles *(Majority 16,327)*

Born 22 September 1979; Married Stephen (1 son).

Education: Manchester Metropolitan University (politics and sociology).

Non-political career: Solicitor: Halliwells 2003-07, Hill Dickinson LLP 2007-15.

Political career: Member for Salford and Eccles since 7 May 2015 general election; Shadow Exchequer Secretary 2015-16; Shadow Chief Secretary to the Treasury 2016-17; Shadow Secretary of State for: Business, Energy and Industrial Strategy 2017-20, Education 2020. Member, Labour Party NEC 2015-20.

Rebecca Long Bailey MP, House of Commons, London SW1A 0AA
Tel: 020 7219 5275 *Email:* rebecca.longbailey.mp@parliament.uk
Constituency: 191 Langworthy Road, Salford M6 5PW
Tel: 0161-425 3738 Website: www.rebeccalongbailey.com *Twitter:* @RLong_Bailey

CONSERVATIVE

LONGHI, MARCO
Dudley North *(Majority 11,533)*

Born 22 April 1967; Son of Antonio and Josephine Longhi; Married Andrea (2 daughters).

Education: Istituto Tecnico Aeronautico F. De Pinedo (aeronautical engineering 1986); Manchester University (BEng civil engineering 1990); Warwick University Business School (MBA 1994); Italian, Portuguese.

Non-political career: Senior Field Engineer Brasil, Schlumberger Wireline and Testing 1990-93; Country Manager, Chesterton International 1994-98; Managing Director, Rubicon House Ltd. 1999-2005; Owner, Value Management Company LLP 2006-09; Director, Marco Longhi Ltd 2009-13; Managing Director, Justmove Lettings Ltd 2011-.

Political career: Contested Dudley South 2005 general election. Member for Dudley North since 12 December 2019. *Select committees:* Member: Environmental Audit 2020-, European Scrutiny 2020-. *Councils and public bodies:* Walsall Council: Councillor 1999-, Mayor 2017-19, Cabinet Member for Public Health; Inspector, Audit Commission 2005-12; Lead Member for Finance and Capital Programme, West Midlands Integrated Transport Authority 2005-09; Non-executive Director: Walsall Hospitals Trust 2006-10, Mersey Care NHS Trust 2012-13.

Political interests: Brownfield sites, knife crime, mental health; Brazil, Italy.

Other: Trustee: Walsall Wood Allotment Charity, WPH Counselling and Education Service Charity.

Marco Longhi MP, House of Commons, London SW1A 0AA
Tel: 020 7219 8598 *Email:* marco.longhi.mp@parliament.uk
Constituency: The White House, 10 Ednam Road, Dudley DY1 1JX
Tel: 01384 314001 Website: www.marcolonghi.org.uk *Twitter:* @marcolonghi4dn

CONSERVATIVE

LOPEZ, JULIA
Hornchurch and Upminster *(Majority 23,308)*

Parliamentary Secretary, Cabinet Office

Julia Louise Lopez. Born 4 June 1984; Née Dockerill. Married 2017 (1 daughter).

Education: Herts and Essex High School; Queens' College, Cambridge (MA social and political science 2005).

Non-political career: Chief of Staff to Mark Field MP 2006-17; Freelance writer 2013-.

Political career: Member for Hornchurch and Upminster since 8 June 2017; Parliamentary Secretary, Cabinet Office 2020-. *Select committees:* Member: International Trade 2017-19, Joint Committee on Statutory Instruments 2018-19, European Statutory Instruments 2018-19. *Councils and public bodies:* Councillor, London Borough of Tower Hamlets Council 2014-18; Vice-President, Local Government Association 2018-.

Other: Trustee, Inspire Malawi 2015-.

Publications: Co-author, The Best of Times and Between the Crashes.

Julia Lopez MP, House of Commons, London SW1A 0AA
Tel: 020 7219 2631 *Email:* julia.lopez.mp@parliament.uk
Constituency: The Coach House, 133 Hall Lane, Upminster RM14 1AL
Tel: 01708 226126 Website: www.julialopez.co.uk *Twitter:* @JuliaLopezMP

CONSERVATIVE

LOPRESTI, JACK

Filton and Bradley Stoke *(Majority 5,646)*

Giacomo Lopresti. Born 23 August 1969; Son of Grace Ann and Domenico Lopresti; Married Lucy Cope 1992 (divorced 2016) (2 sons 1 daughter); married Andrea Jenkyns 2017 (qv) (MP for Morley and Outwood) (1 son).

Education: Brislington Secondary School.

Non-political career: Estate agent 1998-2001; Independent mortgage broker 2001-05; Regional development manager, Treasurer's Department, Conservative Party 2005-07. GVA; Gunner, 266 Battery, Royal Artillery; Served with 29 Commando Regiment RA in Helmand Province, Afghanistan 2008-09.

Political career: Contested Bristol East 2001 general election. Member for Filton and Bradley Stoke since 6 May 2010 general election; PPS to Desmond Swayne as Minister of State, Department for International Development 2014-15; Team PPS, Ministry of Defence 2018; PPS to Steve Barclay as Secretary of State for Exiting the European Union 2018-19. *Select committees:* Member: Northern Ireland Affairs 2010-18, Armed Forces Bill 2011; Chair, Armed Forces Bill 2015 2015-16; Member: Defence 2016-17, Welsh Affairs 2018-19. Chair, Conservative Backbench Policy Committee on Defence 2015-17, 2020-. Contested South West region 2004 European Parliament election. *Councils and public bodies:* Councillor, Bristol City Council 1999-2007.

Political interests: Defence, security, foreign affairs; Afghanistan, Iraq, Israel, USA.

Other: Member: British-Irish Parliamentary Assembly 2015-20, UK delegation to NATO Parliamentary Assembly 2015-18; Member: International Churchill Society, General George Patton Historical Society; RUSI. Military and Naval Club.

Recreations: Running half-marathons.

Jack Lopresti MP, House of Commons, London SW1A 0AA
Tel: 020 7219 7070 *Email:* jack.lopresti.mp@parliament.uk
Constituency: Office 29, The South Block, The Courtyard, Woodlands, Bradley Stoke, Gloucestershire BS32 4NH
Tel: 01454 617783 Website: www.jacklopresti.com *Twitter:* @JackLopresti

CONSERVATIVE

LORD, JONATHAN

Woking *(Majority 9,767)*

Jonathan George Caladine Lord. Born 17 September 1962; Son of late His Honour John Lord and Ann Lord, née Caladine; Married Caroline Commander 2000 (1 son 1 daughter).

Education: Shrewsbury School; Kent School, Connecticut, USA; Merton College, Oxford (BA modern history 1985, MA).

Non-political career: Bates Dorland; AP Lintas; Ogilvy and Mather; Director, Saatchi & Saatchi 1998-2000; Marketing consultant.

Political career: Contested Oldham West and Royton 1997 general election. Member for Woking since 6 May 2010 general election; Sponsored: Sports Ground Safety Authority Act 2011, Citizenship (Armed Forces) Act 2014. President, Oxford University Conservative Association 1983; Campaign manager to Anne Milton MP 2005 general election; Chairman, Guildford Conservative Association 2006-10; Deputy chairman, Surrey Area Conservatives 2007-09. *Councils and public bodies:* Westminster City Council: Councillor 1994-2002, Council Deputy Leader 1998-2000; Councillor, Surrey County Council 2009-11.

Political interests: Culture, media and sport, business, health, education; Egypt, France, Germany, Italy, Spain, USA.

Other: Patron, Home-Start, Runnymede and Woking.

Recreations: Cricket, theatre, walking.

Jonathan Lord MP, House of Commons, London SW1A 0AA
Tel: 020 7219 6913 *Email:* jonathan.lord.mp@parliament.uk
Constituency: Woking Conservatives, Churchill House, Chobham Road, Woking, Surrey GU21 4AA
Website: www.jonathanlord.co.uk *Twitter:* @JonathanLord

CONSERVATIVE

LOUGHTON, TIM

East Worthing and Shoreham *(Majority 7,474)*

Timothy Paul Loughton. Born 30 May 1962; Son of Reverend Michael Loughton and Pamela Loughton; Married Elizabeth MacLauchlan 1992 (1 son 2 daughters).

Education: The Priory School, Lewes; Warwick University (BA classical civilisation 1983); Clare College, Cambridge (Mesopotamian archaeology 1984).

Non-political career: Montagu Loebl Stanley/Flemings London: Fund Manager 1984-, Director 1992-2000. Formerly BIFU.

Political career: Contested Sheffield Brightside 1992 general election. Member for East Worthing and Shoreham 1997-2010, for East Worthing and Shoreham (revised boundary) since 6 May 2010 general election; Opposition Spokesman for: Regeneration, Poverty, Regions, Housing 2000-01, Health 2001-03; Shadow Minister for: Health 2003-07, Children 2003-10; Children's Bill 2004; Childcare Bill 2006; Adoption and Children Bill 2006; Mental Health Bill 2007; Children and Young Person's Bill 2008; Children, Schools and Families Bill 2010; Parliamentary Under-Secretary of State for Children and Families, Department for Education 2010-12; Trade Envoy to Mozambique and Democratic Republic of Congo 2018-19. *Select committees:* Member: Environmental Audit 1997-2001, European Standing committee C 1999-2001, Home Affairs 2014-. Chairman, Lewes Young Conservatives 1978; Vice-chairman: Sussex Young Conservatives 1979, Lewes Constituency Conservative Association 1979-81, South East Area Young Conservatives 1980-82; Secretary, Warwick University Conservative Association 1981-82; Member, Cambridge University Conservative Association 1983-84; Vice-chairman, Battersea Conservative Association 1990-93; Member, London Area Conservative Executive Committee 1993-96; Chairman, Conservative Disability Group 1998-2006; President, Shoreham Conservative Club. *Councils and public bodies:* Governor, Battersea Technology College; Governor and Chairman, Finance Committee, Latchmere Primary School, Battersea; Local Authority appointee, Wandsworth Community Health Council; Vice-chair, Wandsworth Alcohol Group; Member, Wandsworth Health Authority Substance Misuse Committee; Vice-President, Local Government Association 2018-.

Political interests: Finance, foreign affairs, home affairs, education (special needs), environmental taxation, environment and housing, disability, animal welfare, health, children's issues; Indian sub-continent, Latin America, Middle East.

Other: Member: CPA, IPU, British-American Parliamentary Group; Non-executive director, Netlink 1996-99; Member, Securities and Futures Association Working Party on Training; Chair, PIP UK charity trustees (Parent and Infant Partnership); Patron: Positive For Youth Awards, Fatherhood Institute, Grandparents' Association, St Barnabas Hospice, Worthing, Electric Storm Youth, Canadian Roots UK, Guild Care, Worthing, Social Worker of the Year Award, EYE Project, CHAT; Ambassador, Ambition; President: Southwick Camera Club, Lancing Art Club; Member: Sussex Archaeological Society, South Downs Society, Friends of British Museum, Shoreham Society, Southwick Society, Court of Sussex University; Global Change Ambassador, Round Table Global; Member, Securities Institute MSi; St Barnabas Hospice, Ropetackle Centre Trust, Adur Special Needs Project, Guildcare Worthing; MSi(Dip); Society of Antiquaries 2015. President, Shoreham Conservative Club; Patron, Worthing Hockey Club; Captain, Lords and Commons Hockey Team; President, Adur Athletic Football Club; Member: Commons and Lords Ski team, Commons and Lords Tennis team.

Recreations: Archaeology, Sussex Downs, wine, travel, hockey, tennis, skiing.

Tim Loughton MP, House of Commons, London SW1A 0AA
Tel: 020 7219 4471 *Fax:* 020 7219 0461 *Email:* loughtont@parliament.uk
Constituency: 88a High Street, Shoreham by Sea, West Sussex BN43 5DB
Tel: 01273 757182 *Email:* office@eastworthingandshoreham.org.uk
Website: www.timloughton.com *Twitter:* @timloughton

House of Commons MPs' Biographies

GREEN PARTY

LUCAS, CAROLINE

Brighton Pavilion *(Majority 19,940)*

Caroline Patricia Lucas. Born 9 December 1960; Married Richard Savage 1991 (2 sons).

Education: Malvern Girls' College; Exeter University (BA English literature 1983; PhD English and women's studies 1989); Kansas University, USA (Scholarship 1983-84); Journalism (Diploma 1987); French.

Non-political career: Oxfam: Press officer 1989-91, Communications officer, Asia desk 1991-94, Policy adviser on trade and environment 1994-97, Team leader, Trade and investment, Policy department 1998-99; Policy adviser on trade and investment, Department for International Development 1997-98; Author.

Political career: Contested Oxford East 1992 general election. Member for Brighton Pavilion since 6 May 2010 general election. *Select committees:* Member, Environmental Audit 2010-. European Parliament: MEP for South East 1999-2010: Intergroup on the Welfare and Conservation of Animals: Vice-president 2004-09, President 2009-10. Green Party: National Press Officer 1987-89, Co-chair, Party Council 1989-90, Member, Regional Council 1997-99, Leader 2008-12, Co-leader 2016-18. *Councils and public bodies:* Councillor, Oxfordshire County Council 1993-97; Vice-president, Local Government Association 2017-.

Political interests: Animal welfare, environment, social justice, green economy, climate change, drugs policy, equalities and human rights; Burma, Palestine.

Other: Vice-President, Stop the War Coalition -2015; Member, National Council, Campaign for Nuclear Disarmament; Board Member, International Forum on Globalisation; Matron, Women's Environmental Network; Board Member, Britain Stronger in Europe 2015-16; Vice-President, RSPCA; Michael Kay Award for Animal Welfare 2006; Michael Kay Award for Services to European Animal Welfare, RSPCA 2006; *Observer* Ethical Politician of the Year 2007, 2009, 2010; MP of the Year, Women in Public Life Awards 2011.

Publications: Co-author, Writing for Women (Oxford University Press, 1989); Reforming World Trade (Oxfam, 1996); Co-author: With Ruth Mayne: Global Trade and the Rise of New Social Issues (Routledge, 1999), Watchful in Seattle: WTO Threats to Public Services, Food and the Environment (1999); With Mike Woodin: The Euro or a Sustainable Future for Britain (2000); With Colin Hines: From Seattle to Nice: Challenging the Free Trade Agenda at the Heart of Enlargement (2000), Stopping the Great Food Swap: Relocalising Europe's Food Supply (2001); With Mike Woodin: Green Alternatives to Globalisation: A Manifesto (Pluto, 2004); Author, Honourable Friends?: Parliament and the Fight for Change (Portobello Books, 2015); Co-author, with Lisa Nandy MP and Chris Bowers, The Alternative: Towards a New Progressive Politics (Biteback, 2016).

Recreations: Gardening, country walks.

Dr Caroline Lucas MP, House of Commons, London SW1A 0AA
Tel: 020 7219 7025 *Email:* caroline.lucas.mp@parliament.uk
Constituency: Werks Central, 15-17 Middle Street, Brighton, East Sussex BN1 1AL
Tel: 01273 201130 *Email:* brightonoffice@parliament.uk Website: www.carolinelucas.com
Twitter: @CarolineLucas

LABOUR

LYNCH, HOLLY

Halifax *(Majority 2,569)*

Shadow Minister for Immigration

Holly Jamie Walker-Lynch. Born 8 October 1986; Daughter of James Lynch and Diane Lynch, née Brophy; Married Chris Walker 2014 (1 son).

Education: Brighouse High School; Lancaster University (history and politics).

Non-political career: Matrix Technology Solutions; Communications officer to Linda McAvan MEP. Member, GMB.

Political career: Member for Halifax since 7 May 2015 general election; Opposition Whip 2015-16; Shadow Minister for: Environment, Food and Rural Affairs (Flooding and Coastal Communities) 2017-18, Home Office (Immigration) 2020-. *Select committees:* Member: Environmental Audit 2015, Procedure 2016-17, Women and Equalities 2017, Home Affairs 2020.

Political interests: Policing, international development.

Other: Grassroots Diplomat Award 2016.

House of Commons MPs' Biographies

Holly Lynch MP, House of Commons, London SW1A 0AA
Tel: 020 7219 6277 *Email:* holly.lynch.mp@parliament.uk
Constituency: Elsie Whiteley Innovation Centre, Hopwood Lane, Halifax, West Yorkshire HX1 5ER
Tel: 01422 399515/01422 399516 Website: www.hollylynch.org.uk *Twitter:* @HollyLynch5

SCOTTISH NATIONAL PARTY

MACASKILL, KENNY

East Lothian *(Majority 3,886)*

Kenneth Wright MacAskill. Born 28 April 1958; Married Susan (2 sons from previous marriage).

Education: Linlithgow Academy; Edinburgh University (LLB).

Non-political career: Senior partner, Edinburgh Law firm 1984-2000; Director, Legal Services Agency.

Political career: Contested Livingston 1983 and 1987 and Linlithgow 1992 and 1997 general elections. Member for East Lothian since 12 December 2019; SNP Justice Team Member 2020-21. *Select committees:* Member, Justice 2020-. Contested Edinburgh East and Musselburgh constituency 1999 and 2003 Scottish Parliament elections. MSP for Lothians region 1999-2007, and for Edinburgh East and Musselburgh constituency 2007-11, and for Edinburgh Eastern constituency 2011-16: Scottish National Party (SNP): Convener, Parliamentary Committee on Subordinate Legislation 1999-2001; Member, Parliamentary Committee on Transport and the Environment 1999-2000; SNP Shadow Minister for: Transport and the Environment 1999-2000, Enterprise and Lifelong Learning 2000-01, Tourism, Transport and Telecommunications 2001-04; Member: Parliamentary Committee on Enterprise and Lifelong Learning 2001-02, Scottish Parliamentary Standards Commissioner Bill 2002; Deputy Convener, Parliamentary Committee on Audit 2003-04; SNP Shadow Minister for Justice 2004-07; Member: Parliamentary Committee on Baird Trust Reorganisation Bill 2005, Scottish Parliamentary Corporate Body 2006-07; Deputy Convener, Justice 2 Sub-committee 2006; Cabinet Secretary for Justice 2007-14; Member, Parliamentary Committee on Public Petitions 2014-16. Scottish National Party: Vice-convener, policy, Spokesperson for Poll Tax, National treasurer 2000-01.

Other: Free Spirit Award 2004; Herald Politician of the Year Awards; Legal Personality of the Year, Law Awards of Scotland 2008.

Publications: Co-author, Global Scots (Luath Press, 2005); Co-editor, Wherever the Saltire Flies (Luath Press, 2006); Author: The Lockerbie Bombing: The Search for Justice (Biteback Publishing, 2016), Jimmy Reid: A Scottish Political Journey (Biteback Publishing, 2017), Glasgow 1919: The Rise of Red Clydeside (Biteback Publishing, 2019); Radical Scotland: Uncovering Scotland's radical history – from the French Revolutionary era to the 1820 Rising (Biteback Publishing, 2020).

Recreations: Reading, football.

Kenny MacAskill MP, House of Commons, London SW1A 0AA
Tel: 020 7219 3000 *Email:* kenny.macaskill.mp@parliament.uk
Constituency: 37 Sidegate, Haddington EH41 4BU
Tel: 01620 829513 Website: www.kennymacaskillmp.scot *Twitter:* @KennyMacAskill

LABOUR

MCCABE, STEVE

Birmingham, Selly Oak *(Majority 12,414)*

Stephen James McCabe. Born 4 August 1955; Son of James and Margaret McCabe; Married Lorraine Lea Clendon 1991 (divorced) (1 son 1 daughter).

Education: Port Glasgow, Senior Secondary; Moray House College, Edinburgh (Diploma social studies 1977; Certificate Qualification Social Work 1977); Bradford University (MA social work 1986).

Non-political career: Social work with young offenders 1977-85; Lecturer in social work, North East Worcestershire College 1989-91; Part-time researcher, British Association of Social Workers 1989-91; Part-time child protection social worker 1989-91; Central Council for Education in Social Work 1991-97. Member: MSF, Unite; Shop steward, NALGO 1978-82.

Political career: Member for Birmingham Hall Green 1997-2010, for Birmingham, Selly Oak since 6 May 2010 general election; PPS to Charles Clarke: as Secretary of State for Education and Skills 2003-04, as Home Secretary 2004-05; Assistant Government Whip 2006-07;

Government Whip 2007-10; Opposition Whip 2010; Shadow Minister for Education 2013-15. *Select committees:* Member: Deregulation 1997-99, Northern Ireland Affairs 1998-2003, Joint Committee on House of Lords Reform 2003-10, Home Affairs 2005-06, 2010-13, Panel of Chairs 2015-, Work and Pensions 2015-. Chair, PLP Departmental Group for Home Affairs 2006, 2010-13, 2015-19. Chair, Labour Friends of Israel 2019-. *Councils and public bodies:* Birmingham City Council: Councillor 1990-98, Chair, Transportation Committee 1993-96.

Political interests: Community care, transport, economic issues, police and security issues.

Other: Local cricket club.

Recreations: Reading, football, hill-walking.

Steve McCabe MP, House of Commons, London SW1A 0AA
Tel: 020 7219 3509 *Email:* mccabes@parliament.uk
Constituency: No constituency office publicised
Tel: 0121-443 3878 Website: stevemccabe.org *Twitter:* @steve_mccabe

LABOUR

MCCARTHY, KERRY

Bristol East *(Majority 10,794)*

Shadow Minister for Green Transport

Kerry Gillian McCarthy. Born 26 March 1965; Daughter of Oliver Haughney and Sheila Rix; Single.

Education: Denbigh High School, Luton; Luton Sixth Form College; Liverpool University (BA Russian, politics and linguistics 1986); Law Society (CPE and final solicitors examinations 1992).

Non-political career: Legal assistant, South Bedfordshire Magistrates Court 1986-88; Litigation assistant, Neves Solicitors, Luton 1988-89; Trainee solicitor, Wilde Sapte 1992-94; Legal manager, Abbey National Treasury Services 1994-96; Senior counsel, debt markets, Merrill Lynch Europe plc 1996-99; Lawyer, Labour Party 2001; Regional director, Britain in Europe campaign 2002-04; Head of public policy, Waterfront Partnership 2004-05. Member: TGWU 1994-2007, Unite 2007-.

Political career: Member for Bristol East 2005-10, for Bristol East (revised boundary) since 6 May 2010 general election; PPS to: Rosie Winterton as Minister of State, Department of Health 2007, Douglas Alexander as Secretary of State for International Development 2007-09; Assistant Government Whip 2009-10; Shadow Minister for Work and Pensions 2010; Opposition Whip 2010; Shadow Economic Secretary 2010-11; Shadow Minister for Foreign and Commonwealth Office 2011-15; Shadow Secretary of State for Environment, Food and Rural Affairs 2015-16; Shadow Minister for Transport (Green Transport) 2020-. *Select committees:* Member: Treasury 2005-07, South West 2009-10, Environmental Audit 2016-20, Environment, Food and Rural Affairs 2016-17, 2017-19, Petitions 2020. Chair, PLP South West Regional Group 2007-09. Luton North CLP: Chair 1994-96, Secretary 1996-99; National Policy Forum 1998-2005; Economic Policy Commission 1998-2005. *Councils and public bodies:* Luton Borough Council: Councillor 1995-96, 1999-2003, Chair of housing and cabinet member 1999-2001; Director, London Luton Airport 1999-2003.

Political interests: Environment, food policy, poverty, foreign affairs; Central America, Jordan, Russia, Somaliland/Somalia, Tibet.

Other: UK delegation, Parliamentary Assembly of the Council of Europe: Substitute Member 2016-17, Member 2017-; Member, Labour Animal Welfare Society; Patron: FoodCycle, Music Venue Trust, Attitude is Everything; Honorary Associate, National Secular Society; Member, The Law Society 1994-99.

Recreations: Travel, scuba diving, music.

Kerry McCarthy MP, House of Commons, London SW1A 0AA
Tel: 020 7219 4510 *Email:* kerry.mccarthy.mp@parliament.uk
Constituency: No constituency office publicised
Tel: 0117-939 9901 Website: www.kerrymccarthy.org *Twitter:* @kerryMP

CONSERVATIVE

MCCARTNEY, JASON

Colne Valley *(Majority 5,103)*

Jason Alexander McCartney. Born 29 January 1968; Divorced (2 daughters).

Education: Lancaster Royal Grammar School; RAF College, Cranwell (officer training 1988); Leeds Trinity (Postgraduate Diploma broadcast journalism 1997).

Non-political career: RAF Officer 1988-1997; Journalist, BBC Radio 1997-98; Broadcast Journalist, ITV Yorkshire 1998-2007; Senior Lecturer: Broadcast Journalism, Leeds Trinity 2007-08, Journalism, Leeds Metropolitan University 2008-10; Head of Public Affairs, Huddersfield University 2017-19. Officer, Royal Air Force 1988-97. National Union of Journalists: Former member, Father of Chapel, ITV Yorkshire 2005-07.

Political career: Member for Colne Valley 2010-17. Contested Colne Valley 2017 general election. Member for Colne Valley since 12 December 2019. *Select committees:* Member: Transport 2013-15, Culture, Media and Sport 2015-17. Member, Executive, 1922 Committee 2013-17, 2020-. Founding member, Conservatives for Britain 2015-16.

Political interests: Mental health, education, armed forces, crime, broadcasting, sport, pensions, transport, planning; Kurdistan region of Iraq, Kashmir, Pakistan.

Other: Member: UK Delegation to NATO Parliamentary Assembly 2010-17, NATO Defence and Security Committee; Royal British Legion; Honorary President, RAFA, Huddersfield 2010-; Huddersfield Town Supporters' Trust; Director, fairandfunky CIC; Kirkwood Hospice, Forget Me Not Children's Hospice. RAF Club; Yorkshire County Cricket Club.

Publications: Co-author, Freedom, Responsibility and the State: Curbing Over-Mighty Government (Politeia, 2012).

Recreations: Cricket, tennis, Huddersfield Town FC, running (London Marathons and Great North Run), days out with my daughters.

Jason McCartney MP, House of Commons, London SW1A 0AA
Tel: 020 7219 4403 *Email:* jason.mccartney.mp@parliament.uk
Constituency: 2a Marsh, Honley, Holmfirth HD9 6AQ
Tel: 01484 443975 Website: www.jasonmccartney.com *Twitter:* @JasonMcCartney

CONSERVATIVE

MCCARTNEY, KARL

Lincoln *(Majority 3,514)*

Karl Ian McCartney. Born 25 October 1968; Son of John McCartney and Brenda McCartney, neé Weir; Married Cordelia Pyne 1999 (2 sons).

Education: Birkenhead School for Boys; Neston High School; Willink School, Burghfield Common; St David's University College (BA geography 1991) (Student Union President 1991-92); Kingston University Business School (MBA 1998); French, Welsh (basic).

Non-political career: Various Part-Time roles 1980-92; Logistics Analyst, Hasbro UK 1992-93; Agent and Researcher, Conservative Central Office 1993-96; Corporate Affairs, Corporation of London 1996-2001; Director, MLSystems Ltd (Consultancy) 2000-; Public relations manager, Norton Rose 2001; London Communications Agency 2002-03; Strategic Rail Authority 2003-05; Transport for London 2005-07; Campaign Director, Sir Keith Park Memorial Campaign 2007-10. Armed Forces Parliamentary Scheme (RAF) 2011; Combined Cadet Force School (RAF).

Political career: Contested Lincoln 2005 general election. Member for Lincoln 2010-17. Contested Lincoln 2017 general election. Member for Lincoln since 12 December 2019; Member, Speaker's Committee on the Electoral Commission 2020-. *Select committees:* Member: Unopposed Bills (Panel) 2011-15, Transport 2012-17, 2020-, Exiting the European Union 2016-17. Member, Executive, 1922 Committee 2012-17, 2020-. Agent and Researcher: Mitcham and Morden Conservative Association 1993-95, Dover and Deal Conservative Association 1995; Various Officer roles in Kent Area Executive, Tonbridge and Malling Conservative Association 1996-2004; Chair, Lincolnshire Area 2007-10. *Councils and public bodies:* Wrotham Parish Council 1999-2004; Magistrate: Dartford and Gravesham 1999-2002, Maidstone 2002-04, Lincoln 2004-10; Upper Witham Internal Drainage Board 2007-11; Witham Third District Internal Drainage Board 2008-11; Member, Court: Lincoln University 2011-, Hull University 2011-.

Political interests: Small business, education, sport, transport, military matters, crime and the judiciary; The Commonwealth, England, Italy, New Zealand, Northern Ireland, Scotland, Wales.

Other: Board member, Servol 1997-98; Adviser, Prince's Youth Business Trust 1997-2001; Trustee, Friends of Wrotham St Georges 1999-; Former Patron: St John's Ambulance, YMCA, MND Lincolnshire; MISM 1994-, AMBA 1997-, MIPR 1998-; High Hopes, Nomad Trust Lincoln, Cooke & Connell Lincoln, Bomber Command Memorial Campaign, St Barnardos Lincolnshire, LIVES; Freedom, City of London 1999. UK Parliament FC Ex Westminster Wanderers (legends) Football Club; Ex Westminster Lobbyists XV; The Fighting Pilgrims, SDUC Oldboys XI; Houses of Parliament Football, Rugby, Cricket, Shooting, Hockey and Ski/ Snowboarding Teams.

Recreations: Football, rugby union, rugby league, cricket, snowboarding, croquet, cooking, golf, hill-walking, classic cars, shooting.

Karl McCartney MP, House of Commons, London SW1A 0AA
Tel: 020 7219 7221 *Email:* karl.mccartney.mp@parliament.uk
Constituency: 1b Farrier Road, Lincoln LN6 3RU
Website: www.karlmccartney.co.uk *Twitter:* @karlmccartney

LABOUR

MCDONAGH, SIOBHAIN

Mitcham and Morden *(Majority 16,482)*

Siobhain Ann McDonagh. Born 20 February 1960; Daughter of Breda McDonagh, née Doogue, psychiatric nurse, and Cumin McDonagh, building labourer; Single (no children).

Education: Holy Cross Convent, New Malden; Essex University (BA government 1981).

Non-political career: Clerical officer, DHSS 1981-83; Housing benefits assistant 1983-84; Receptionist, Homeless Persons Unit, London Borough of Wandsworth 1984-86; Housing adviser 1986-88; Development co-ordinator, Battersea Church Housing Trust 1988-97. Member, GMB.

Political career: Contested Mitcham and Morden 1987 and 1992 general elections. Member for Mitcham and Morden 1997-2010, for Mitcham and Morden (revised boundary) since 6 May 2010 general election; PPS to John Reid: as Secretary of State for Defence 2005-06, as Home Secretary 2006-07; Assistant Government Whip 2007-08. *Select committees:* Member: Social Security 1997-98, Health 2000-05, Unopposed Bills (Panel) 2004-15, London 2009-10, Education 2012-15, Women and Equalities 2015-16, Panel of Chairs 2017-, Treasury 2020-. *Councils and public bodies:* Councillor, London Borough of Merton 1982-97: Chair, Housing Committee 1990-95.

Political interests: Health, housing, quality of life, welfare reform.

Other: Member: South Mitcham Community Centre, Colliers Wood Community Centre, Grenfell Housing Association, Merton MIND; Vice-President, QUIT (smoking cessation charity); Trustee, Mitcham Garden Village.

Recreations: Travel, friends, music.

Siobhain McDonagh MP, House of Commons, London SW1A 0AA
Tel: 020 7219 4678 *Email:* mcdonaghs@parliament.uk
Constituency: 1 Crown Road, Morden SM4 5DD
Tel: 020 8542 4835 Website: www.siobhainmcdonagh.org.uk *Twitter:* @Siobhain_Mc

LABOUR

MCDONALD, ANDY

Middlesbrough *(Majority 8,395)*

Shadow Secretary of State for Employment Rights and Protections

Andrew Joseph McDonald. Born 8 March 1958; Married Sally (children).

Non-political career: Head of office and senior serious injury solicitor, Thompsons Solicitors, Middlesbrough.

Political career: Member for Middlesbrough since 29 November 2012 by-election; PPS to: Chuka Umunna as Shadow Secretary of State for Business, Innovation and Skills 2013-15, John McDonnell as Shadow Chancellor of the Exchequer 2015-16; Shadow Minister for Transport 2016; Shadow Secretary of State for: Transport 2016-20, Employment Rights and Protections 2020-. *Select committees:* Member, Justice 2012-15, 2015-16. *Councils and public bodies:* Councillor, Middlesbrough Council 1995-99; Governor: Abingdon Primary School 1995-2010, Middlesbrough College 2012-.

Other: Former chair, Davison Trust, Middlesbrough; Chair, Teeside branch, Headway; Former chair and secretary, Military Special Interest Group, Association of Personal Injury Lawyers.

Recreations: Singing, playing the piano, going to Middlesbrough FC matches.

Andy McDonald MP, House of Commons, London SW1A 0AA
Tel: 020 7219 4995 *Email:* andy.mcdonald.mp@parliament.uk
Constituency: Unit 4, Broadcasting House, Newport Road, Middlesbrough, North Yorkshire TS1 5JA
Tel: 01642 246574 *Email:* andy.mcdonald.2nd@parliament.uk
Website: www.andymcdonaldmp.org *Twitter:* @AndyMcDonaldMP

SCOTTISH NATIONAL PARTY

MCDONALD, STEWART MALCOLM Glasgow South *(Majority 9,005)*

SNP Shadow Secretary of State for Defence

Born 24 August 1986.

Education: Govan High School.

Non-political career: Tour guide, Canary Islands, Spain; Caseworker to James Dornan MSP.

Political career: Member for Glasgow South since 7 May 2015 general election; SNP Spokesperson/Shadow Secretary of State for Defence 2017-. *Select committees:* Member: Transport 2015-17, Standards 2019, Privileges 2019, Foreign Affairs 2020-.

Political interests: Poverty, inequality, creating job opportunities, young people.

Stewart Malcolm McDonald MP, House of Commons, London SW1A 0AA
Tel: 020 7219 6388 *Email:* stewart.mcdonald.mp@parliament.uk
Constituency: Suite 5, City Wall House, 32 Eastwood Avenue, Glasgow G41 3NS
Tel: 0141-632 5043 Website: www.stewartmcdonald.scot *Twitter:* @StewartMcDonald

SCOTTISH NATIONAL PARTY

MCDONALD, STUART C Cumbernauld, Kilsyth and Kirkintilloch East *(Majority 12,976)*

SNP Shadow Home Secretary

Stuart Campbell McDonald. Born 2 May 1978.

Education: Kilsyth Academy; Edinburgh University (LLB Scots law 2000; Diploma legal practice 2001).

Non-political career: Trainee Solicitor, Simpson and Marwick 2001-03; Solicitor: NHS National Services Scotland 2003-05, Immigration Advisory Service 2005-09; Parliamentary Researcher to Shirley-Anne Somerville MSP and Jim Eadie MSP 2009-13, Senior Researcher, Yes Scotland 2013-14; Parliamentary and public affairs officer, Coalition for Racial Equality and Rights -2015. Member, Unite.

Political career: Member for Cumbernauld, Kilsyth and Kirkintilloch East since 7 May 2015 general election; SNP: Spokesperson/Shadow Minister for Immigration 2015-21, Spokesperson for Asylum and Border Control 2015-18, Shadow Attorney General 2020-21, Shadow Home Secretary 2021-. *Select committees:* Member: Home Affairs 2015-, Joint Committee on the Draft Investigatory Powers Bill 2015-16.

Political interests: Anti-fracking, poverty, job creation.

Recreations: Sport, especially football, music, reading.

Stuart C McDonald MP, House of Commons, London SW1A 0AA
Tel: 020 7219 7758 *Email:* stuart.mcdonald.mp@parliament.uk
Constituency: Suite 1, Lennox House, Lennox Road, Cumbernauld G67 1LL
Tel: 01236 453969 Website: www.stuartmcdonaldmp.co.uk *Twitter:* @Stuart_McDonald

LABOUR

MCDONNELL, JOHN

Hayes and Harlington *(Majority 9,261)*

John Martin McDonnell. Born 8 September 1951; Son of late Robert and Elsie McDonnell; Married Marilyn Cooper 1971 (divorced 1987) (2 daughters); married Cynthia Pinto 1995 (1 son).

Education: Great Yarmouth Grammar School; Burnley Technical College; Brunel University (BSc government and politics); Birkbeck College, London University (MSc politics and sociology); French.

Non-political career: Shopfloor production worker 1968-73; Assistant head, social insurance department, National Union of Mineworkers 1977-78; Researcher, TUC 1978-82; Head of policy unit, London Borough of Camden 1985-87; Chief Executive: Association of London Authorities 1987-95, Association of London Government 1995-97. Former shop steward, Unison; Co-ordinator, RMT Parliamentary Group 2002-; Chair, Bakers and Allied Workers Union Parliamentary Group; PCS Parliamentary Group: Chair -2016, Honorary life chair 2015-; Member: Justice Trade Unions Group, ASLEF Parliamentary Group; Secretary: FBU Group, NUJ Group, Justice Unions Group.

Political career: Contested Hayes and Harlington 1992 general election. Member for Hayes and Harlington 1997-2010, for Hayes and Harlington (revised boundary) since 6 May 2010 general election; Shadow Chancellor of the Exchequer 2015-20. *Select committees:* Member: Deregulation and Regulatory Reform 1999-2002, Unopposed Bills (Panel) 1999-2004, Justice 2013-15. Member, Labour Party: Committee on Ireland, CND; Chair: Labour Representation Committee, Socialist Campaign Group of MPs; Member, Unison Group. *Councils and public bodies:* Councillor, GLC 1981-86: Chair, Finance Committee 1982-85, Deputy Leader 1984-85.

Political interests: Economics, local and regional government, Irish affairs, environment, aviation, public administration; Gambia, Iran, Ireland, Kenya, Lango, Nullo Mountains, Punjab, Somalia, Tanzania.

Other: Chair: Britain and Ireland Human Rights Centre, Hands Off Venezuela Group, Hands Off People of Iran; Treasurer Liberation; Chair, Friends of Lake Farm Country Park; Member: Friends of Ireland – Coalition in support of Belfast Agreement, London Wildlife Trust, Hayes Irish Society, Hayes and Harlington History Society, Hayes and Harlington Community Development Forum, Hayes and Harlington Canal Society; Harlington Hospice; PC 2016. Hayes and Harlington Working Men's Club; Hillingdon Outdoor Activities Centre; Wayfarer Sailing Association; Vice-president, Hayes Football Club; Patron, Hayes Cricket Club.

Publications: Editor, Labour Herald; Another World is Possible: a manifesto for 21st century socialism.

Recreations: Sailing, football refereeing, cycling, gardening, theatre, cinema.

Rt Hon John McDonnell MP, House of Commons, London SW1A 0AA
Tel: 020 7219 4100 *Email:* mcdonnellj@parliament.uk
Constituency: Pump Lane, Hayes, Middlesex UB3 3NB
Tel: 020 8569 0010 Website: www.john-mcdonnell.net *Twitter:* @johnmcdonnellMP

LABOUR

MCFADDEN, PAT

Wolverhampton South East *(Majority 1,235)*

Shadow Economic Secretary

Patrick Bosco McFadden. Born 26 March 1965; Son of James and Annie McFadden; Married (1 son 1 daughter).

Education: Holyrood Secondary School, Glasgow; Edinburgh University (MA politics 1988).

Non-political career: Adviser to Donald Dewar MP as Scottish Affairs Spokesperson 1988-93; Speechwriter and policy adviser to John Smith MP as Labour Party Leader 1993; Policy adviser to Tony Blair MP as Labour Party Leader and political secretary to him as Prime Minister 1994-2005. Member, Community.

Political career: Member for Wolverhampton South East 2005-10, for Wolverhampton South East (revised boundary) since 6 May 2010 general election; Parliamentary Secretary, Cabinet Office 2006-07; Minister of State (Employment Relations and Postal Affairs 2007-09), Department for Business, Enterprise and Regulatory Reform/Business, Innovation and Skills 2007-10 (attending Cabinet 2009-10); Shadow Secretary of State for Business, Innovation and

Skills 2010; Shadow Minister for: Foreign and Commonwealth Office (Europe) 2014-16, Treasury (Shadow Economic Secretary) 2020-. *Select committees:* Member: Treasury 2011-14, Parliamentary Commission on Banking Standards 2012-13, Exiting the European Union 2016-19, Business, Energy and Industrial Strategy 2020, Panel of Chairs 2020. Chair, PLP Departmental Groups for Foreign Affairs 2019. Chair, PLP Labour In group 2016.

Other: PC 2008.

Recreations: Reading, sport.

Rt Hon Pat McFadden MP, House of Commons, London SW1A 0AA
Tel: 020 7219 4036 *Email:* mcfaddenp@parliament.uk
Constituency: Crescent House, Broad Street, Bilston, West Midlands WV14 0BZ
Tel: 01902 405762 Website: www.patmcfadden.com *Twitter:* @patmcfaddenmp

LABOUR

MCGINN, CONOR

St Helens North *(Majority 12,209)*

Shadow Minister for Security

Conor Patrick McGinn. Born 31 July 1984; Married Kate 2009 (1 son 1 daughter).

Education: St Paul's High School, Bessbrook; London Metropolitan University (BA history, politics and Irish studies).

Non-political career: Immigrant counselling and psychotherapy; Political Adviser to Vernon Coaker MP as Shadow Secretary of State for Northern Ireland and for Defence.

Political career: Member for St Helens North since 7 May 2015 general election; Opposition Whip 2015-16, 2020; Shadow Minister for Home Office (Security) 2020-. *Select committees:* Member: Defence 2015, Northern Ireland Affairs 2017-20, Joint Committee on Consolidation, &c, Bills 2017-20, Regulatory Reform 2017-, Foreign Affairs 2019. Chair, PLP Departmental Groups for Northern Ireland 2017-19. Labour Party: Honorary President, Socialist Societies, Member (Socialist Societies), National Executive Committee 2011-15; Political Secretary, National Union of Labour and Socialist Clubs. *Councils and public bodies:* School governor 2005-12; Governor, NHS trust 2011-15.

Political interests: Defence, home affairs; Australia, Brazil, Ireland, South Africa, USA.

Other: Member, British-Irish Parliamentary Assembly 2015-; Alternate Member, UK Delegation, Organisation for Security and Co-operation in Europe Parliamentary Assembly 2016-17; Substitute Member, UK Delegation to Parliamentary Assembly of Council of Europe 2017-; Member, Gaelic Athletic Association. Ulster Reform Club.

Conor McGinn MP, House of Commons, London SW1A 0AA
Tel: 020 7219 4367 *Email:* conor.mcginn.mp@parliament.uk
Constituency: Westway House, Bridge Street, Newton Le Willows WA12 9QT
Tel: 01744 21336 Website: www.conormcginn.co.uk *Twitter:* @ConorMcGinn

LABOUR

MCGOVERN, ALISON

Wirral South *(Majority 6,105)*

Shadow Minister for Culture and Sport

Born 30 December 1980; Daughter of Mike McGovern, British Rail telecoms engineer, and Ann McGovern, nurse; Married Ashwin Kumar (1 daughter).

Education: Wirral Grammar School; University College, London (BA philosophy); Birkbeck College London (Post Grad Cert economics).

Non-political career: Researcher, House of Commons 2002-06; Public affairs manager: Network Rail 2006-08, The Art Fund 2008-09, Creativity, Culture and Education 2009. Member, Unite.

Political career: Member for Wirral South since 6 May 2010 general election; PPS to Gordon Brown MP 2010-13; Opposition Whip 2013; Shadow Minister for: International Development 2013-14, Children and Families 2014-15; Shadow Economic Secretary 2015; Shadow Minister for Digital, Culture, Media and Sport (Culture and Sport) 2020-. *Select committees:* Member, International Development 2010-13; Works of Art: Member 2011-16, Chair 2016-19;

Member: Treasury 2017-20, Treasury Sub-committee 2017-19. *Councils and public bodies:* London Borough of Southwark Council: Councillor 2006-10, Deputy Leader, Labour group -2010.

Political interests: International development, employment, economy, arts and culture, regeneration; Africa, India.

Other: Trustee, South London Gallery 2006-10; Progress: Vice-chair 2012-15, Chair 2015-16.

Publications: The Real Life State (Fabian); Co-editor, Politics of Solutions (Progress); Contributor: Wirral News, Progress Online, Fabian Society.

Alison McGovern MP, House of Commons, London SW1A 0AA
Tel: 020 7219 7190 *Email:* alison.mcgovern.mp@parliament.uk
Constituency: 99 New Chester Road, New Ferry, Wirral, Merseyside CH62 4RA
Tel: 0151-645 6590 *Email:* alison@alisonmcgovern.org.uk
Website: www.alisonmcgovern.org.uk *Twitter:* @Alison_McGovern

CONSERVATIVE

MACKINLAY, CRAIG

South Thanet *(Majority 10,587)*

Born 7 October 1966; Son of Colin and Margaret Mackinlay; Married Katalin 2011 (1 daughter).

Education: Rainham Mark Grammar School, Kent; Birmingham University (BSc zoology and comparative physiology); Hungarian.

Non-political career: Assistant manager, Robson Rhodes Chartered Accountants 1989-93; Partner, Beak Kemmenoe Chartered Accountants and Chartered Tax Advisers 2011-. Parliamentary Armed Forces Scheme 2016-17.

Political career: Contested Gillingham (Ind) 1992, Gillingham (UKIP) 1997, Totnes 2001, Gillingham 2005 general elections. Member (Con) for South Thanet since 7 May 2015 general election; Member, Speaker's Committee on the Electoral Commission 2020-. *Select committees:* Member: Work and Pensions 2015-17, European Scrutiny 2015-17, Exiting the European Union 2016-19, European Scrutiny 2020-, Public Accounts 2020-. Contested (Con) Kent Police and Crime Commissioner 2012 election. UK Independence Party: Founding Member 1993, Acting Leader 1997, Deputy Leader 1997-2000; Member, Conservative Party 2005-; Founding member, Conservatives for Britain 2015-16. *Councils and public bodies:* Councillor, Medway Council 2007-15.

Political interests: Taxation, pensions, European Union, live animal exports, tobacco, fishing, energy, aviation; Hungary, USA.

Other: Trustee, Chatham Historic Dockyard Trust 2007-; Vice-chair, Foord Almshouses, Rochester 2007-; Institute of Chartered Accountants in England and Wales; Chartered Institute of Taxation; Chatham Historic Dockyard Trust, The Foord Alsmshouses Rochester; Freedom, City of London. Carlton Club, Castle Club; Royal Temple Yacht Club, Ramsgate.

Recreations: Sailing.

Craig Mackinlay MP, House of Commons, London SW1A 0AA
Tel: 020 7219 4442 *Email:* craig.mackinlay.mp@parliament.uk
Constituency: 4 The Broadway, Broadstairs, Kent CT10 2AD
Tel: 01843 603242 Website: www.craigmackinlay.com *Twitter:* @cmackinlay

LABOUR

MCKINNELL, CATHERINE

Newcastle upon Tyne North *(Majority 5,765)*

Chair, Select Committee on Petitions

Born 8 June 1976; Daughter of John and Agnes Grady; Married Rhys (3 children).

Education: Sacred Heart Comprehensive School, Fenham, Newcastle upon Tyne; Edinburgh University (MA politics and history 2000); Northumbria University (Postgraduate Diploma law and common professional examination 2002); Italian.

Non-political career: Employment solicitor, Newcastle. Member, GMB.

Political career: Member for Newcastle upon Tyne North since 6 May 2010 general election; Shadow Solicitor General 2010-11; Shadow Minister for Education 2011-12; Shadow Exchequer Secretary 2012-13, 2015; Shadow Economic Secretary 2013-15; Shadow Attorney General 2015-16. *Select committees:* Member: Political and Constitutional Reform 2010, Education 2016-17, Education, Skills and the Economy Sub-committee 2016-17, Petitions

2016-17, 2017-; Treasury 2017-19, Member: Treasury Sub-committee 2017-19, Liaison 2020-; Chair, Petitions 2020-. Chair, PLP Department Group for International Trade 2016-19; Member, PLP Parliamentary Committee 2017-; Chair, PLP Department Group for Foreign Affairs 2020-. Chair, Northern Group of Labour MPs 2017-18. *Councils and public bodies:* Vice-President, Local Government Association 2016-.

Political interests: Regional development, manufacturing, economy, women and children, international development, justice and legal aid, apprenticeships; Italy.

Other: Northumbrian Association; Tyneside Irish Centre; MS Society, CAFOD, Together for Short Lives. British Military Fitness.

Recreations: Swimming, travel.

Catherine McKinnell MP, House of Commons, London SW1A 0AA
Tel: 020 7219 2231 *Email:* catherine.mckinnell.mp@parliament.uk
Constituency: No constituency office publicised
Tel: 0191-229 0352 Website: www.catherinemckinnellmp.co.uk *Twitter:* @CatMcKinnell

CONSERVATIVE

MACKRORY, CHERILYN

Truro and Falmouth *(Majority 4,561)*

Born 5 June 1976; Married Nick (1 daughter).

Non-political career: IT Project Manager; Sales and Business Development Manager, Spiezia Organics; Caseworker for: Scott Mann MP, Steve Double MP.

Political career: Member for Truro and Falmouth since 12 December 2019. *Select committees:* Member, Environmental Audit 2020-. *Councils and public bodies:* Councillor, Cornwall Council 2017-20.

Political interests: NHS, education, policing, environment, recycling.

Other: Substitute Member, UK Delegation to Parliamentary Assembly of Council of Europe 2021-.

Cherilyn Mackrory MP, House of Commons, London SW1A 0AA
Tel: 020 7219 3713 *Email:* cherilyn.mackrory.mp@parliament.uk
Constituency: Lemon Chapel, William Street, Truro TR1 2ED
Tel: 01872 229698 Website: www.cherilynmackrory.org.uk *Twitter:* @thisischerilyn

SCOTTISH NATIONAL PARTY

MCLAUGHLIN, ANNE

Glasgow North East *(Majority 2,548)*

SNP Shadow Secretary of State for Justice and Immigration

Elizabeth Anne McLaughlin. Born 8 March 1966; Daughter of John Robert (Bobby) McLaughlin and Elizabeth Fulton McLaughlin, née Purdie.

Education: Port Glasgow High School; Royal Scottish Academy of Music and Drama, Glasgow University (BA dramatic studies); Scots, learning Spanish.

Non-political career: Tenth Anniversary Co-ordinator, Sense Scotland 1994-96; Scottish Fundraising Manager, Imperial Cancer Research Fund 1996-2000; Staff Fundraiser, Scottish Power 2000-01; Managing Director, Business for Scotland 2001-02; Internal Communications Executive, SNP 2002-06; Political Adviser to Aileen Campbell MSP 2007-08; Communications Consultant (based in Sri Lanka), Challenges Worldwide, Edinburgh 2008; Parliamentary Researcher to Bob Doris MSP 2008-09; Independent Consultant 2017-19.

Political career: Contested Glasgow Rutherglen 2001 general election and Inverclyde 30 June 2011 by-election. Member for Glasgow North East 2015-17. Contested Glasgow North East 2017 general election. Member for Glasgow North East since 12 December 2019; SNP: Spokesperson for Civil Liberties 2015-17, Shadow Minister for Women and Equalities 2020-21, Shadow Secretary of State for Justice and Immigration 2021-. *Select committees:* Member: Privileges 2020-, Standards 2020-. Contested Glasgow Rutherglen constituency 2003 and Glasgow Springburn constituency 2007 Scottish Parliament elections. MSP (replacement) for Glasgow region 12 February 2009 to 2011. Contested Glasgow region 2011 Scottish Parliament election. Member, Scottish National Party 1977-82, 1988-; Convener: Springburn SNP 2007-09, Glasgow Regional Association 2007-; Elected member, SNP National Council 2007-; Member, SNP National Disciplinary Committee 2007-; Campaign co-ordinator, Glasgow East by-election 2008.

Political interests: Racial equality, mental health, homelessness, international development, welfare rights, independence; Scotland, Sri Lanka.

Publications: Editor, Tall Tales, Short Stories (Sense Scotland, 1996).

Recreations: Singing, walking, swimming, music, writing, reading, blogging, travel, languages, people watching.

Anne McLaughlin MP, House of Commons, London SW1A 0AA
Tel: 020 7219 6484 *Email:* anne.mclaughlin.mp@parliament.uk
Constituency: Springburn Old Library and Museum, 179 Ayr Street, Glasgow G21 4BW
Twitter: @AnneMcLaughlin

CONSERVATIVE

MACLEAN, RACHEL

Redditch *(Majority 16,036)*

Parliamentary Under-Secretary of State, Department for Transport

Rachel Helen Maclean. Born 3 October 1965; Married David 1992 (1 daughter 3 sons).

Education: Tudor Grange School; Solihull Sixth Form College; St Hugh's College, Oxford (BA experimental psychology); Aston University (MSc work and organisational psychology 2006).

Non-political career: International Officer, HSBC 1989-92; Head of Direct Sales, Computer Manuals Ltd 1992-94; Sales and Editorial Manager, Wrox Press Ltd 1994-99; Part-time Post-Natal Teacher, National Childbirth Trust 2000-02; Director of Organisation Development and Human Resources, Packt Publishing 2005-13; Managing Director, ImPackt Publishing 2012-13; Founder and Director, Skilled and Ready 2012-; Head of HR and Organisation Development, Hollywood Monster 2015-16; Co-Founder and COO, Air 2016-17. Armed Forces Parliamentary Scheme.

Political career: Contested Birmingham, Northfield 2015 general election. Member for Redditch since 8 June 2017; Home Office: Team PPS 2018-19, PPS to: Caroline Nokes as Minister of State for Immigration 2018-19, Amber Rudd as Secretary of State for Work and Pensions and Minister for Women and Equalities 2019, Sajid Javid as Chancellor of the Exchequer 2019-20; Parliamentary Under-Secretary of State, Department for Transport 2020-. *Select committees:* Member, Business, Energy and Industrial Strategy 2017-18. Co-chair, Andy Street West Midlands Mayoral Campaign 2016. *Councils and public bodies:* Governor, King Edwards Camp Hill School for Boys 2010-14.

Political interests: Business, entrepreneurs, small business, apprenticeships, technology, health.

Other: Sunday School teacher; Scout Association: Beaver Scout Leader 2004-06, Cub Scout Leader 2006-12, Assistant District Commissioner 2011-13; Managing Director, Skills for Birmingham; Ambassador, LoveBrum 2015-; Member, Regional Council, CBI West Midlands 2015-; Sprint Pirates 2016-; National Childbirth Trust; Founder, Skilled and Ready.

Recreations: Spending time with family, jogging, long distance walking holidays.

Rachel Maclean MP, House of Commons, London SW1A 0AA
Tel: 020 7219 1848 *Email:* rachel.maclean.mp@parliament.uk
Constituency: Grosvenor House, Prospect Hill, Redditch B97 4DL
Tel: 01527 591334 Website: www.rachelmaclean.uk *Twitter:* @redditchrachel

LABOUR/
CO-OPERATIVE

MCMAHON, JIM

Oldham West and Royton *(Majority 11,127)*

Shadow Secretary of State for Transport

James McMahon. Born 7 July 1980; Son of William McMahon, truck driver, and Alice O'Rourke; Partner Charlene (2 sons).

Education: Oldham College.

Non-political career: Manchester University 1997-2004: Apprentice technician, Senior technician; Programme co-ordinator, Groundwork Trust, Wythenshawe and South Manchester; Town centre manager, Middleton. Member, GMB.

Political career: Member for Oldham West and Royton since 3 December 2015 by-election; PPS to Tom Watson as Deputy Leader, Labour Party, Party Chair and Shadow Minister for the Cabinet Office 2016; Shadow Minister for Communities and Local Government: (Local Government and Devolution) 2016-17, (Local Government Devolution and Finance) 2017-20;

Shadow Secretary of State for Transport 2020-. *Select committees:* Member, Communities and Local Government 2016. Leader, Labour Group, Local Government Association 2014-15; Member, National Executive Committee, Labour Party 2014-15, 2020-; Co-operative Party: Chair, Parliamentary Group 2018-20, Chair 2020-. *Councils and public bodies:* Oldham Council: Councillor 2003-17, Leader of the Opposition 2008-11, Leader of the Council 2011-16; Representative: Greater Manchester Combined Authority, Association of Greater Manchester Authorities, Police and Crime Panel 2011-16; Vice-president, Local Government Association 2017-.

Political interests: Finance, local government, English devolution, regeneration/urban renewal.

Other: Fellow, British American Project 2010-; Co-operative Council Innovation Network; Patron, Oldham Cancer Support; Fellow, Royal Society of Arts 2014; Honorary fellowship, University Campus Oldham 2014; Council Leader of the Year, C'llr Achievement Awards; Youth Champion, British Youth Council Awards; OBE 2015.

Jim McMahon OBE MP, House of Commons, London SW1A 0AA
Tel: 020 7219 6039 *Email:* jim.mcmahon.mp@parliament.uk
Constituency: Textile House, 108 Union Street, Oldham OL1 1DU
Tel: 0161-652 8485 Website: www.jimmcmahon.co.uk *Twitter:* @JimfromOldham

LABOUR

MCMORRIN, ANNA

Cardiff North *(Majority 6,982)*

Shadow Minister for International Development

Anna Rhiannon McMorrin. Born September 1971; Partner Alun Davies (AM for Blaenau Gwent) (2 daughters).

Education: Brecon High School; Southampton University (BA French and politics 1994); Cardiff University (Postgraduate Diploma journalim 1997); French, Spanish, Welsh learner.

Non-political career: Communications Officer, Labour Party 1997; Account Director: Political Intelligence 1997-99, Hill and Knowlton 1999-2001; Consultant 2001-06; Campaigns and Communications Officer, Friends of the Earth Cymru 2006-08; Specialist Policy Adviser to Minister for Natural Resources, Welsh Government 2008-14; Head of Welsh Office, Invicta Public Affairs 2016-17; Director, Llais Ltd 2016-. Member: Unison, GMB.

Political career: Member for Cardiff North since 8 June 2017; PPS to Barry Gardiner as Shadow Secretary of State for International Trade 2017-18; Shadow Minister for International Development 2020-. *Select committees:* Member: Environmental Audit 2017-19, Welsh Affairs 2017-20, Business, Energy and Industrial Strategy 2020. Contested South Wales Central region 2016 National Assembly for Wales election. Member: LGBT Labour, Labour Women's Network, Co-operative Party.

Political interests: Climate change, energy, sustainable development, economy, Brexit, international trade, tackling poverty, dementia, mental health, workers' rights, Welsh affairs.

Anna McMorrin MP, House of Commons, London SW1A 0AA
Tel: 020 7219 4307 *Email:* anna.mcmorrin.mp@parliament.uk
Constituency: 2 Codas House, 52-60 Merthyr Road, Cardiff CF14 1DJ
Tel: 029 2062 4440 Website: www.annamcmorrin.co.uk *Twitter:* @annamcmorrin

SCOTTISH NATIONAL PARTY

MCNALLY, JOHN

Falkirk *(Majority 14,948)*

SNP Spokesperson for Environment

John Joseph McNally. Born 1 February 1951; Married Sandra (1 son 1 daughter).

Education: St Modan's High School.

Non-political career: Self-employed hairdresser/barber, The Barber Shop 1970s-.

Political career: Contested Falkirk 2010 general election. Member for Falkirk since 7 May 2015 general election; SNP Spokesperson for Environment 2017-. *Select committees:* Member, Environmental Audit 2015-. Honorary President, Denny Branch, SNP. *Councils and public bodies:* Councillor, Falkirk Council 2005-15.

Political interests: Scottish independence.

Other: Local football coach.

John McNally MP, House of Commons, London SW1A 0AA
Tel: 020 7219 6525 *Email:* john.mcnally.mp@parliament.uk
Constituency: 16 Vicar Street, Falkirk FK1 1JL
Tel: 01324 628001 *Twitter:* @JohnMcNallySNP

SCOTTISH NATIONAL PARTY

MACNEIL, ANGUS

Na h-Eileanan An Iar *(Majority 2,438)*

Chair, Select Committee on International Trade

Angus Brendan MacNeil. Born 21 July 1970; Son of Iain MacNeil, postman and crofter, and late Clare MacNeil, district nurse; Married Jane (3 daughters) (separated).

Education: Castlebay Secondary School, Isle of Barra; Nicolson Institute, Stornoway, Isle of Lewis; Strathclyde University (BEng civil engineering 1992); Jordanhill College (PGCE primary teaching and bilingualism 1996); Gaelic, Irish gaelic.

Non-political career: Civil engineer, Lilley Construction Ltd, Edinburgh 1992-93; Radio reporter, BBC, Inverness 1993-95; Primary teacher, Salen Primary School, Mull 1996-98; Gaelic development officer, Lochaber 1998-99; Education lecturer (part-time), Inverness College.

Political career: Contested Inverness East, Nairn and Lochaber 2001 general election. Member for Na h-Eileanan An Iar since 5 May 2005 general election; SNP: Spokesperson for: Transport 2005-15, Environment 2005-07, Tourism 2005-15, Fishing 2005-10, Food and Rural Affairs 2005-10, Work and Pensions 2007-08, Scotland Office 2008-15, Deputy Prime Minister's Portfolio 2013-15, Environment and Rural Affairs 2017-18, Trade Team Member 2020-21. *Select committees:* Member: Scottish Affairs 2005-09, Liaison 2015-, Joint Committee on the National Security Strategy 2015-; Chair: Energy and Climate Change 2015-16, International Trade 2016-. Convener, Lochaber branch, SNP 1999.

Political interests: Economics of small states; Faroe Islands, Iceland, Norway.

Other: Amnesty International, VSO.

Recreations: Football, sailing, fishing.

Angus MacNeil MP, House of Commons, London SW1A 0AA
Tel: 020 7219 8476 *Fax:* 020 7219 6111 *Email:* macneila@parliament.uk
Constituency: 31 Bayhead Street, Stornoway, Isle of Lewis, Outer Hebrides HS1 2DU
Tel: 01851 702272 *Email:* macdonaldrm@parliament.uk Website: angusmacneilsnp.com
Twitter: @AngusMacNeilSNP

CONSERVATIVE

MCPARTLAND, STEPHEN

Stevenage *(Majority 8,562)*

Chair, Select Committee on Regulatory Reform

Stephen Anthony McPartland. Born 9 August 1976; Married Emma.

Education: Liverpool College; Liverpool University (BA history 1997); Liverpool John Moores University (MSc technology management 1998).

Non-political career: Agent, North East Hertfordshire Conservative Association 2001-08; Membership director, British American Business (American Chamber of Commerce) 2008-10.

Political career: Member for Stevenage since 6 May 2010 general election; Board Member, Parliamentary Office of Science and Technology (POST) 2013-19; PPS to Lord Livingston of Parkhead as Minister of State for Trade and Investment, Department for Business, Innovation and Skills and Foreign and Commonwealth Office 2014-15. *Select committees:* Member: Science and Technology 2011-12, Finance 2017-19, Liaison 2017-; Regulatory Reform: Member 2017, Chair 2017-. Founding member, Conservatives for Britain 2015-16.

Political interests: Healthcare (particularly cancer treatment and respiratory diseases), education, satellite technology, international trade, policing, addiction treatment, urban regeneration, government procurement of IT projects; China, India, UK, USA.

Other: Non-executive director, Furniture Village Ltd 2014-; Asthma UK, The Living Room, Turn the Tide.

Recreations: Reading, keeping fit, cinema.

Stephen McPartland MP, House of Commons, London SW1A 0AA
Tel: 020 7219 7156 *Email:* stephen.mcpartland.mp@parliament.uk
Constituency: No constituency office publicised
Website: www.stephenmcpartland.co.uk *Twitter:* @SMcPartland

CONSERVATIVE

MCVEY, ESTHER

Tatton *(Majority 17,387)*

Esther Louise McVey. Born 24 October 1967; Daughter of James and Barbara McVey; Married Philip Davies (qv) 2020 (MP for Shipley).

Education: Belvedere School, Liverpool; Queen Mary and Westfield, London (LLB 1990); City University, London (Postgraduate Course radio journalism 1991); John Moore's University, Liverpool (MSc corporate governance 2009, winner North of England Excellence Award).

Non-political career: Presenter: CBBC, BBC 1 1991, BBC Radio 5 1992, *Reportage*, BBC 2 1993, Live TV and Meridian TV 1994, Living TV 1995, *How Do They Do That?*, BBC 1 1996, *Nothing but the Truth*, Channel 4 1997, *5's Company*, Channel 5 1995, *GMTV*, ITV 1999, BBC 1 2000, Director, JG McVey & Co Ltd 2000-06; Managing director, Making It (UK) Ltd 2002-10; Founder, Winning Women 2003-10.

Political career: Contested Wirral West 2005 general election. MP for Wirral West 2010-15. Contested Wirral West 2015 general election. Member for Tatton since 8 June 2017; PPS to Chris Grayling as Minister of State for Employment 2010-12; Parliamentary Under-Secretary of State (Minister for Disabled People), Department for Work and Pensions 2012-13; Minister of State for Employment, Department for Work and Pensions 2013-15; Deputy Chief Whip (Treasurer of HM Household) 2017-18; Secretary of State for Work and Pensions 2018; Minister of State for Housing, Ministry of Housing, Communities and Local Government (also attending Cabinet) 2019-20. *Select committees:* Member: Home Affairs 2017, Selection 2017-18, Panel of Chairs 2020-. *Councils and public bodies:* Chair, British Transport Police Authority 2015-17.

Political interests: Law and order and sentencing, transport, education, city regeneration.

Other: Board member: Madeleine McCann Fund 2007-08, North West Women's Enterprise Forum 2008-10; Patron: Wirral Holistic Therapeutic Cancer Care, Full of Life (charity); Ambassador, Action Medical Research; Member, NCH; Director, LYJ Ltd; Trustee, "If Chloe Can" (charity); PC 2014.

Recreations: Theatre, cinema, walking.

Rt Hon Esther McVey MP, House of Commons, London SW1A 0AA
Tel: 020 7219 3226 *Email:* officeofesthermcveymp@parliament.uk
Constituency: 84 Chapel Lane, Wilmslow SK9 5JH
Tel: 01625 529922 Website: www.esthermcvey.com *Twitter:* @EstherMcVey1

LABOUR

MADDERS, JUSTIN

Ellesmere Port and Neston *(Majority 8,764)*

Shadow Minister for Secondary Care, Workforce and Patient Health

Justin Piers Richard Madders. Born 22 November 1972; Married (3 children).

Education: Sheffield University.

Non-political career: Solicitor. Member, Unite.

Political career: Contested Tatton 2005 general election. Member for Ellesmere Port and Neston since 7 May 2015 general election; Shadow Minister for: Health 2015-19, Business, Energy and Industrial Strategy (Labour) (maternity cover for Laura Pidcock MP) 2018, Health and Social Care (Secondary Care, Workforce and Patient Health) 2020-. *Select committees:* Member, Petitions 2015. Member, Co-operative Party. *Councils and public bodies:* Ellesmere Port and Neston Borough Council: Councillor 1998-2009, Leader 2007-09; Cheshire West and Chester Council: Councillor 2009-15, Leader of the Opposition 2011-14.

Other: Member, Fabian Society; Member: RSPB, Cheshire Wildlife.

Recreations: Football.

Justin Madders MP, House of Commons, London SW1A 0AA
Tel: 020 7219 6584 *Email:* justin.madders.mp@parliament.uk
Constituency: 23 Whitby Road, Ellesmere Port, Cheshire CH65 8AA
Tel: 0151-355 2365 Website: www.justinmadders.com *Twitter:* @justinmadders

LABOUR

MAHMOOD, KHALID

Birmingham, Perry Barr *(Majority 15,317)*

Shadow Minister for Defence Procurement

Born 13 July 1961.

Non-political career: Former engineer. Member, AEEU; Former adviser, Danish International Trade Union.

Political career: Member for Birmingham Perry Barr 2001-10, for Birmingham, Perry Bar (revised boundary) since 6 May 2010 general election; PPS to Tony McNulty as Minister of State: Department for Transport 2004-05, Home Office 2005-06; Shadow Minister for: Foreign and Commonwealth Office 2016-20, Defence (Procurement) 2020-. *Select committees:* Member: Broadcasting 2001-05, Home Affairs 2009-10. Local Constituency Labour Party: Secretary, Vice-chair; Member: Socialist Health Association, Socialist Education Association; Labour Finance and Industry Group: National member, Midlands branch executive member. *Councils and public bodies:* Birmingham City Council 1990-93: Councillor, Chair Race Relations.

Political interests: Community relations, British industry, international trade, terrorism.

Other: Substitute Member, UK delegation, Parliamentary Assembly of the Council of Europe -2016; Honorary Associate, Council of Europe 2018; Adviser to President of Olympic Council Asia; Member, governing body: Neighbourhood forum, South Birmingham CHC.

Khalid Mahmood MP, House of Commons, London SW1A 0AA
Tel: 020 7219 8141 *Fax:* 020 7219 1745 *Email:* mahmoodk@parliament.uk
Constituency: 18 Heathfield Road, Handsworth, Birmingham, West Midlands B19 1HB
Tel: 0121-356 8268 *Twitter:* @khalid4pb

LABOUR

MAHMOOD, SHABANA

Birmingham, Ladywood *(Majority 28,582)*

Born 17 September 1980; Daughter of Zubaida and Mahmood Ahmed.

Education: Small Heath School, Birmingham; King Edward VI Camp Hill School for Girls; Lincoln College, Oxford (BA law 2002); Inns of Court School of Law (Bar Vocational Course 2003); Mirpuri and Urdu (fluent), French (basic).

Non-political career: Barrister: 12 King's Bench Walk 2003-04, Berrymans Lace Mawer 2004-07.

Political career: Member for Birmingham, Ladywood since 6 May 2010 general election; Shadow Minister for: Home Office 2010-11, Business, Innovation and Skills (Higher Education) 2011-13, Business, Innovation and Skills (Universities and Science) 2013; Shadow Exchequer Secretary 2013-15; Shadow Chief Secretary to the Treasury 2015. *Select committees:* Member: Work and Pensions 2010, Joint Committee on the Draft Investigatory Powers Bill 2015-16, International Trade 2016-17, Public Accounts 2017-. Chair, PLP Departmental Group for Justice 2015-17. Labour Party: Member, National Executive Committee 2016-, Vice-chair, National Policy Forum.

Other: Substitute Member, UK Delegation to Parliamentary Assembly of Council of Europe 2017-19; St. Basil's, Birmingham.

Shabana Mahmood MP, House of Commons, London SW1A 0AA
Tel: 020 7219 7818 *Email:* shabana.mahmood.mp@parliament.uk
Constituency: No constituency office publicised
Tel: 0121-661 9440 Website: www.shabanamahmood.org *Twitter:* @shabanamahmood

House of Commons MPs' Biographies

CONSERVATIVE

MAK, ALAN

Havant *(Majority 21,792)*

Born 19 November 1983.

Education: St Peter's School, York; Peterhouse College, Cambridge (BA law 2005, MA); Oxford Institute of Legal Practice (Postgraduate Diploma 2006).

Non-political career: Solicitor, Clifford Chance LLP; Small business owner and investor; Non-executive board member, Havas Worldwide Group UK; Judge, Wayra UnLtd; Management committee, Enterprise Forum. Armed Forces Parliamentary Scheme Graduate 2015-16.

Political career: Member for Havant since 7 May 2015 general election; Team PPS, Ministry of Justice 2017-18; PPS to: Greg Clark as Secretary of State for Business, Energy and Industrial Strategy 2018-19, Robert Jenrick as Secretary of State for Housing, Communities and Local Government 2019-20; Member, Public Accounts Commission 2020-. *Select committees:* Member: Procedure 2015-16, Joint Committee on Fixed-Term Parliaments Act 2020-. Chairman, Conservative Backbench Policy Committee on International Trade 2017-19. *Councils and public bodies:* Governor, primary school 2008-15.

Political interests: Economy, business, education, defence, foreign policy, social mobility; China, Europe, Israel, South Africa, USA.

Other: Young Global Shaper, World Economic Forum; Former President and Trustee, Magic Breakfast; Founder and President, British Legion's Young Professionals' Branch; Member, Speakers for Schools; Advisory Board Member and Ambassador, One Young World; Former Alumni Advisory Board, Cambridge University; Fellow, Royal Society of Arts; Member, Law Society of England and Wales; Royal British Legion; Freedom, City of London. Vice-President: Havant Rugby Club, Havant and Waterlooville Football Club; President, Havant Borough Sports Association.

Publications: Next Generation Vision for Financial Services.

Recreations: Playing and watching sports, spending time with family, films, travel.

Alan Mak MP, House of Commons, London SW1A 0AA
Tel: 020 7219 6266 *Email:* alan.mak.mp@parliament.uk
Constituency: 1 Hermitage Park, Harts Farm Way, Havant, Hampshire PO9 1FA
Tel: 023 9421 2298 Website: www.alanmak.org.uk *Twitter:* @AlanMakMP

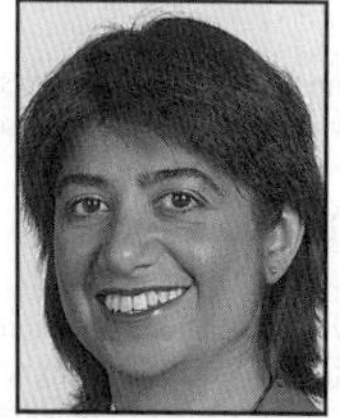

LABOUR/
CO-OPERATIVE

MALHOTRA, SEEMA

Feltham and Heston *(Majority 7,859)*

Shadow Minister for Employment

Seema Malhotra-Saluja. Born 7 August 1972; Daughter of Sushil Kumar Malhotra, retired engineer and small businessman, and Usha Malhotra, retired teacher; Married Sushil Saluja 2005.

Education: Green School, Isleworth; Warwick University (politics and philosophy 1994) (scholarship, University of Massachusetts, Amhurst, USA 1992-93); Aston University (business IT 1995); German (some), Hindi, Punjabi.

Non-political career: Management consultant, Accenture 1995-2003; Senior manager, PriceWaterhouseCoopers 2003-07; Consultant 2004-05; Adviser: to Liam Byrne MP: as Minister for the West Midlands 2007-08, as Chair of the Council of Regional Ministers 2008-09, to Ian Austin MP as Minister for the West Midlands 2008-09; Adviser to the video games industry on child safety agenda 2008; Programme leader, cross-government programme to increase diversity in public appointments 2009-10; Political adviser to Harriet Harman MP as Acting Leader of the Opposition May-October 2010; Strategic programme adviser, UKIE May-November 2011. Unite: Member, Chair, South Thames Community Branch 2007-11.

Political career: Member for Feltham and Heston since 15 December 2011 by-election; PPS to Yvette Cooper as Shadow Secretary of State for Home Department (Home Secretary); Shadow Minister for Women and Equalities 2012; Opposition Whip 2013-14; Shadow Minister for Preventing Violence Against Women and Girls 2014-15; Shadow Chief Secretary to the Treasury 2015-16; Member, Commons Reference Group on Representation and Inclusion 2017-19; Shadow Minister for Work and Pensions (Employment) 2020-. *Select committees:*

Member: Justice 2012-13, Exiting the European Union/Future Relationship with the European Union 2016-21, Panel of Chairs 2020. Chair, PLP Departmental Group for Business, Innovation and Skills 2012-14. Member, Co-operative Party.

Political interests: Business and entrepreneurship, civil and criminal justice, public administration, youth offending, apprenticeships, aviation, gender and equalities, British-American relations, policing, women offenders, community banking, women and business, diversity on public boards; China, India, Middle East.

Other: Chair, Young Fabians 1999-2000; Fabian Society: Executive member 2000-, Chair 2005-06, 2015-16; Founder and director, Fabian Women's Network 2005-; Fellow, British American Project; Trustee, Swanswell 2011-; Fellow, Royal Society of Arts; Shortlisted, Asian Women of Achievement awards 2006.

Publications: Contributor: Dictionary of Labour Biography (Politico's, 2001), From the Workhouse to Welfare (Fabian Society and Webb Memorial Trust, 2009).

Recreations: Running, cinema, music, gardening, playing the guitar.

Seema Malhotra MP, House of Commons, London SW1A 0AA
Tel: 020 7219 8957 *Email:* seema.malhotra.mp@parliament.uk
Constituency: No constituency office publicised
Website: www.seemamalhotra.com *Twitter:* @SeemaMalhotra1

CONSERVATIVE

MALTHOUSE, KIT

North West Hampshire *(Majority 26,308)*

Minister of State for Crime and Policing, Home Office and Ministry of Justice

Christopher Laurie Malthouse. Born 27 October 1966; Married (3 children).

Education: Liverpool College; Newcastle University (politics and economics 1989).

Non-political career: Trainee accountant, Deloitte & Touche, London 1990-94; Finance director, Cannock Investments Ltd 1994-2001; Chair and founder, County Finance Group 2001-.

Political career: Member for North West Hampshire since 7 May 2015 general election; Parliamentary Under-Secretary of State for Family Support, Housing and Child Maintenance, Department for Work and Pensions 2018; Minister of State: for Housing, Ministry of Housing, Communities and Local Government 2018-19, for Crime, Policing and the Fire Service, Home Office 2019-20, Minister of State for Crime and Policing: Home Office 2020-, Ministry of Justice 2020-. *Select committees:* Member: Armed Forces Bill 2015 2015-16, Treasury 2016-18, Treasury Sub-committee 2017-18. London Assembly: AM for West Central constituency 2008-16, Deputy Mayor of London for: Policing and Crime 2008-12, Business and Enterprise 2012-15. *Councils and public bodies:* Westminster City Council: Councillor 1998-2006, Deputy Leader of the Council, Cabinet Member for Finance.

Other: Vice-chair, London Enterprise Panel; Chair, London and Partners.

Publications: Features editor, *The Courier.*

Recreations: Gardening, reading, writing, watching modern dance.

Kit Malthouse MP, House of Commons, London SW1A 0AA
Tel: 020 7219 5605 *Email:* kit.malthouse.mp@parliament.uk
Constituency: 2 Church Close, Andover, Hampshire SP10 1DP
Tel: 01264 401401 Website: kitmalthouse.com *Twitter:* @kitmalthouse

CONSERVATIVE

MANGNALL, ANTHONY

Totnes *(Majority 12,724)*

Anthony James Holland Mangnall. Born 8 December 1989; Son of Carola and Col Nick Mangnall OBE.

Education: Shrewsbury School; Exeter University (BA historical, political and sociological studies 2012).

Non-political career: Shepherd, Lochbuie Estate 2009; Parliamentary Researcher to William Hague MP 2011-12; Broker: Braemar ACM Shipbroking, 2012-14, Poten & Partners 2014-16; Senior Adviser to Lord William Hague of Richmond 2016-18; Special Adviser to Alun Cairns as Secretary of State for Wales 2018-19.

Political career: Contested Warley 2017 general election. Member for Totnes since 12 December 2019. *Select committees:* Member: Regulatory Reform 2020-, Procedure 2020, International Trade 2020-. Former Chair, South West Wiltshire Conservatives.

Political interests: Environment, local community, international trade and development, Prevention of Sexual Violence in Conflict Initiative, foreign policy, digital connectivity, human rights, climate change, transport connectivity; Africa, Europe, Far East.

Other: Gender Action for Peace and Security, The Fund for Refugees, Pete's Dragons, Young Devon; Merchant Taylors; Freedom, City of London.

Recreations: Kite surfing, wild swimming, fishing, cycling.

Anthony Mangnall MP, House of Commons, London SW1A 0AA
Tel: 020 7219 5579 *Email:* anthony.mangnall.mp@parliament.uk
Constituency: Conservative Club, Station Road, Totnes TQ9 5HW
Tel: 01803 868378 Website: www.anthonymangnall.co.uk *Twitter:* @AnthonyMangnal1

CONSERVATIVE

MANN, SCOTT

North Cornwall *(Majority 14,752)*

Government Whip (Lord Commissioner of HM Treasury)

Scott Leslie Mann. Born 24 June 1977; Divorced (1 daughter).

Education: Wadebridge Boys' School.

Non-political career: Gardener; Butcher; Postman, Royal Mail 1995-2015.

Political career: Member for North Cornwall since 7 May 2015 general election; Team PPS: Department for Transport 2017-18, HM Treasury 2018; PPS to: Therese Coffey as Secretary of State for Work and Pensions 2019, Gavin Williamson as Secretary of State for Education 2020-21; Government Whip (Lord Commissioner of HM Treasury) 2021-. *Select committees:* Member: Environmental Audit 2016-17, Joint Committee on Human Rights 2019. Founding member, Conservatives for Britain 2015-16. *Councils and public bodies:* Cornwall Council: Councillor 2009-16, Deputy leader, Conservative group -2012.

Recreations: Darts, fly-fishing.

Scott Mann MP, House of Commons, London SW1A 0AA
Tel: 020 7219 5744 *Email:* scott.mann.mp@parliament.uk
Constituency: Market House Arcade, 10 Fore Street, Bodmin, Cornwall PL31 2JA
Tel: 01208 74337 Website: www.scottmann.org.uk *Twitter:* @scottmann4NC

CONSERVATIVE

MARSON, JULIE

Hertford and Stortford *(Majority 19,620)*

Team PPS, Ministry of Justice

Born March 1965; Married (1 son).

Education: Grammar school; Downing College, Cambridge (modern history).

Non-political career: International banker.

Political career: Contested Dagenham and Rainham 2015 and 2017 general elections. Member for Hertford and Stortford since 12 December 2019; Team PPS, Ministry of Justice 2020-. *Select committees:* Member, Treasury 2020-. Contested South East 2014 European Parliament election. *Councils and public bodies:* Councillor, Thanet District Council 2011-15; Local magistrate.

Political interests: Education, healthcare, job prospects, housing.

Other: Vice-chair, British-Irish Parliamentary Assembly 2020-.

Julie Marson MP, House of Commons, London SW1A 0AA
Tel: 020 7219 2429 *Email:* julie.marson.mp@parliament.uk
Constituency: GF04 Harlow Enterprise Hub, Kao Hockham Building, Edinburgh Way, Harlow CM20 2NQ
Tel: 01279 312197 Website: www.juliemarson.org.uk *Twitter:* @JulieMarsonMP

LABOUR/ CO-OPERATIVE

MASKELL, RACHAEL

York Central *(Majority 13,545)*

Shadow Minister for Voluntary Sector and Charities

Rachael Helen Maskell. Born 5 July 1972.

Education: Highcliffe Comprehensive School; University of East Anglia (BSc physiotherapy 1994).

Non-political career: NHS Care Worker; Physiotherapist, NHS 1994-2015; Unite: National Officer Equalities, Voluntary and Community Sector, Head of Health 2003-15. Unite; GMB.

Political career: Member for York Central since 7 May 2015 general election; Shadow Minister for Defence 2015-16; Shadow Secretary of State for Environment, Food and Rural Affairs 2016-17; Shadow Minister for Transport (Rail) 2017-20; Shadow Secretary of State for Employment Rights 2020; Shadow Minister for Digital, Culture, Media and Sport (Voluntary Sector and Charities) 2020-. *Select committees:* Member: Health 2015, Ecclesiastical Committee 2015-. Labour Party NEC.

Political interests: Ageing and older people, health and social care, substance abuse, mental health and wellbeing, adoption, flooding, environment, stress and wellbeing at work, sport, health, housing, local economy.

Rachael Maskell MP, House of Commons, London SW1A 0AA
Tel: 020 7219 4525 *Email:* rachael.maskell.mp@parliament.uk
Constituency: 59 Holgate Road, York YO24 4AA
Tel: 01904 623713 Website: www.rachaelmaskell.com *Twitter:* @rachaelmaskell

SINN FÉIN

MASKEY, PAUL

Belfast West *(Majority 14,672)*

Paul John Maskey. Born 10 June 1967; Son of Alex and Teresa Maskey; Married Patricia (2 children).

Education: Edmund Rice College; Irish.

Non-political career: Development co-ordinator, Fáilte Feirste Thiar (tourism development agency in West Belfast).

Political career: Member for Belfast West since 9 June 2011 by-election. Northern Ireland Assembly: MLA for Belfast West 2007-11, and for Belfast West (revised boundary) 2011-12: Deputy chair, Enterprise, Trade and Investment Committee 2007-08, Chair, Public Accounts Committee 2008-12; Sinn Féin: Deputy Whip, Spokesperson for: Public Accounts, Governance 2011-12. *Councils and public bodies:* Belfast City Council: Councillor 2001-09, Leader, Sinn Féin Group -2009.

Political interests: Poverty; Basque Country, Italy.

Other: Board member: Upper Andersonstown Community Forum, Greater Andersonstown Neighbourhood Partnership.

Recreations: Walking, five-a-side football.

Paul Maskey MP, House of Commons, London SW1A 0AA
Tel: 020 7219 3000 *Email:* paul.maskey.mp@parliament.uk
Constituency: Unit 29 Kennedy Centre, 564-568 Bóthar na bhFál, Béal Feirste BT11 9AE
Tel: 028 9620 6402 *Email:* westbelfastmp@sinnfein.ie Website: www.sinnfeinbelfast.com
Twitter: @PaulMaskeyMP

LABOUR

MATHESON, CHRIS

City of Chester *(Majority 6,164)*

Shadow Minister for Media

Christian John Patrick Matheson. Born 2 January 1968; Married Katherine (2 daughters).

Education: Manchester Grammar School; London School of Economics (Degree).

Non-political career: Manager, electricity industry; Industrial officer, Unite. Member: Unite, GMB.

Political career: Member for City of Chester since 7 May 2015 general election; PPS to John Healey as Shadow Secretary of State for Housing 2017-18; Shadow Minister for Cabinet Office 2018-20; Member, Speaker's Committee on the Electoral Commission 2020-; Shadow Minister for Digital, Culture, Media and Sport (Media) 2020-. *Select committees:* Member, Culture, Media and Sport/Digital, Culture, Media and Sport 2015-18.

Political interests: Argentina, Colombia, Latin America.

Chris Matheson MP, House of Commons, London SW1A 0AA
Tel: 020 7219 8078 *Email:* chris.matheson.mp@parliament.uk
Constituency: Robinson House, 25 Castle Street, Chester, Cheshire CH1 2DS
Tel: 01244 343214 *Email:* chris@chrismatheson.co.uk Website: www.chrismatheson.co.uk
Twitter: @chrisM4Chester

CONSERVATIVE

MAY, THERESA

Maidenhead *(Majority 18,846)*

Theresa Mary May. Born 1 October 1956; Daughter of late Rev Hubert and Zaidee Brasier; Married Philip May 1980.

Education: Wheatley Park Comprehensive School, Holton, Oxfordshire; St Hugh's College, Oxford (BA geography 1977, MA); French (basic).

Non-political career: Various posts latterly senior adviser, international affairs, Association for Payment Clearing Services 1985-97.

Political career: Contested North West Durham 1992 general election and Barking 1994 by-election. Member for Maidenhead 1997-2010, for Maidenhead (revised boundary) since 6 May 2010 general election; Opposition Spokesperson for Education and Employment (schools, disabled people and women) 1998-99; Member Shadow Cabinet 1999-2010: Spokesperson for Women's Issues 1999-2001, Shadow Secretary of State for: Education and Employment 1999-2001, Transport, Local Government and the Regions 2001-02, Transport 2002, Environment and Transport 2003-04, the Family 2004-05, Culture, Media and Sport 2005; Shadow Leader of the House of Commons 2005-09; Member, House of Commons Commission 2005-09; Shadow Minister for Women 2007-10; Shadow Secretary of State for Work and Pensions 2009-10; Secretary of State for the Home Department (Home Secretary) 2010-16; Minister for Women and Equalities 2010-12; Prime Minister, First Lord of the Treasury and Minister for the Civil Service 2016-19. *Select committees:* Member: Education and Employment 1997-98, Education and Employment (Education Sub-Committee) 1997-99, Modernisation of the House of Commons 2006-10. Joint secretary, Conservative Party Committee for Home Affairs 1997-98; Chair, Conservative Transport/Local Government/Planning Policy Committee 2001-02. Conservative Party: Chair, Conservative Disability Group 1997-98, Party Chair 2002-03, Leader 2016-June 2019, Acting Leader June-July 2019; Patron, Conservative Alumni; President, Conservatives Abroad. *Councils and public bodies:* Councillor, London Borough of Merton 1986-94.

Other: Chair of the Branch, Commonwealth Parliamentary Association (UK Branch) 2016-19; President, British Group, Inter-Parliamentary Union; Chairman, British-American Parliamentary Group; Advisory Board Member, Renewal; Fellow, Royal Geographical Society; Honorary member, Rotary Club of Eastbourne; Joint Patron, St Andrew's Church building appeal, Sonning; Vice-president, Littlewick Green Show Society; Ambassador, Juvenile Diabetes Research Foundation 2020-; Honorary Fellow, Chartered Institute of Marketing; Member, Worshipful Company of Marketors; *Spectator* awards: Double Act of the Year (with Kenneth Clarke MP) 2011, Minister of the Year 2012; PC 2003. Member, Maidenhead Conservative Club; President, United & Cecil Club; Member, Leander Club; President, Wargrave Girls Football Club; Honorary President, Lords and Commons Tennis Club; Honorary member: Maidenhead Golf Club, Ellesborough Golf Club.

Recreations: Walking, cooking.

Rt Hon Theresa May MP, House of Commons, London SW1A 0AA
Tel: 020 7219 5206 *Email:* mayt@parliament.uk
Constituency: c/o Maidenhead Conservative Association, 2 Castle End Farm, Ruscombe, Berkshire RG10 9XQ
Website: www.tmay.co.uk *Twitter:* @theresa_may

CONSERVATIVE

MAYHEW, JEROME

Broadland *(Majority 21,861)*

Jerome Patrick Burke Mayhew. Born 11 April 1970; Son of late Patrick Mayhew (MP for Tunbridge Wells 1974-97, Lord Mayhew of Twysden) and Jean Gurney; Married Kate Wallis 2001 (2 daughters 1 son).

Education: Edinburgh University (MA politics 1993); Inns of Court School of Law (1995); Cranfield School of Management (BGP business growth 2011).

Non-political career: Barrister, Temple Garden Chambers 1995–2006; Adventure Forest Ltd t/a Go Ape!: Director of Business Development and Risk 2006-09, Managing Director 2009-19.

Political career: Member for Broadland since 12 December 2019. *Select committees:* Member, Environmental Audit 2020-.

Other: Cranfield School of Management Entrepreneur Alumnus of the Year 2014.

Recreations: Sailing.

Jerome Mayhew MP, House of Commons, London SW1A 0AA
Tel: 020 7219 4733 *Email:* jerome.mayhew.mp@parliament.uk
Constituency: The Old Smithy, Church Farm, Attlebridge, Norwich, Norfolk NR9 5ST
Website: www.jeromemayhew.org.uk *Twitter:* @JeromeMayhew

CONSERVATIVE

MAYNARD, PAUL

Blackpool North and Cleveleys *(Majority 8,596)*

Paul Christopher Maynard. Born 16 December 1975.

Education: St Ambrose College, Altrincham; University College, Oxford (BA modern history 1997); French, German.

Non-political career: Researcher, Hodgart Temporal 1997-99; Health policy officer, Conservative Party 1999-2002; Head of home affairs, Conservative Research Department 2001-02; Senior researcher, Reform 2003; Special adviser to Dr Liam Fox MP 2003-07.

Political career: Contested Twickenham 2005 general election. Member for Blackpool North and Cleveleys since 6 May 2010 general election; PPS: to Oliver Letwin: as Minister for Government Policy, Cabinet Office 2012-14, as Chancellor of the Duchy of Lancaster 2014, to Nick Boles as Minister of State for Skills and Equalities, Departments for Business, Innovation and Skills and for Education 2014-15, to Amber Rudd as Secretary of State for Energy and Climate Change 2015-16; Parliamentary Under-Secretary of State, Department for Transport 2016-18 (for Rail, Accessibility and HS2 2017-18); Government Whip (Lord Commissioner of HM Treasury) 2018-19; Parliamentary Under-Secretary of State: Ministry of Justice 2019, Department for Transport 2019-20. *Select committees:* Member: Transport 2010-12, Work and Pensions 2014-15. Vice-chair, Weaver Vale Conservative Association 1997-99.

Political interests: Education, social policy; Australia, Bosnia and Herzegovina, Germany, Moldova.

Other: Patron, Blackpool and District Choral Society; Society Champion, Charity Champion awards 2012.

Paul Maynard MP, House of Commons, London SW1A 0AA
Tel: 020 7219 7017 *Email:* paul.maynard.mp@parliament.uk
Constituency: Room 11, Blackpool Technology Management Centre, Faraday Way, Blackpool, Lancashire FY2 0JW
Tel: 01253 473071 Website: paulmaynard.co.uk *Twitter:* @PaulMaynardUK

House of Commons MPs' Biographies

LABOUR

MEARNS, IAN

Gateshead *(Majority 7,200)*

Chair, Select Committee on Backbench Business

James Ian Mearns. Born 21 April 1957; Son of James Mearns and Agnes Mearns, née Watson; Partner Anne (1 son 1 daughter from previous marriage).

Education: St Mary's Technical School, Newcastle upon Tyne.

Non-political career: Northern Gas 1974-85. Member: Unite, Unison.

Political career: Member for Gateshead since 6 May 2010 general election; PPS to Ivan Lewis as Shadow Secretary of State for International Development 2011-13. *Select committees:* Member, Education 2010-; Backbench Business: Member 2010-15, Chair 2015-; Member: High Speed Rail (London-West Midlands) Bill 2014-15, Liaison 2015-, Education, Skills and the Economy Sub-committee 2015-17. Chair, PLP Departmental Group for: Communities and Local Government 2011-15, Education 2020-. *Councils and public bodies:* Gateshead Council: Councillor 1983-2010, Cabinet Member for: Education 1993-2002, Lifelong Learning, Adult Social Care, Jobs and Employment; Council Deputy Leader 2002-10; Local Government Association: Council representative, Vice-President 2010-; Member: Association of North East Councils, North East Regional Authority; Former chair of governors: Kelvin Grove Primary School, Gateshead, Thomas Hepburn Community Comprehensive, Felling.

Political interests: Education, local government, regional development, health, transport; Kurdistan (Iraq).

Other: Patron, Redheugh Boys Club; President, Trinity Community Association, Gateshead; Honorary Member, Royal Engineers; Trustee, Industry and Parliament Trust 2015-. Saltwell Social Club, Gateshead Corporation, Tyneside Irish Centre, Parliamentary Sports and Social Club.

Recreations: Sports – football, cricket.

Ian Mearns MP, House of Commons, London SW1A 0AA
Tel: 020 7219 7074 *Email:* ian.mearns.mp@parliament.uk
Constituency: 12 Regent Terrace, Gateshead NE8 1LU
Tel: 0191-477 0651 Website: www.ianmearns.org.uk *Twitter:* @IanMearnsMP

CONSERVATIVE

MENZIES, MARK

Fylde *(Majority 16,611)*

Mark Andrew Menzies. Born 18 May 1971; Single (no children).

Education: Keil School, Dumbarton; Glasgow University (MA economic and social history 1994).

Non-political career: Graduate trainee, Marks & Spencer 1994-95; Marketing executive, Asda supermarkets 1995-2008; Senior marketing executive, Morrisons supermarkets 2008-10.

Political career: Contested Glasgow Govan 2001 and Selby 2005 general elections. Member for Fylde since 6 May 2010 general election; PPS to: Charles Hendry as Minister of State, Department of Energy and Climate Change 2010-12, Mark Prisk as Minister of State for Housing, Department for Communities and Local Government 2012-13, Alan Duncan as Minister of State, Department for International Development 2013-14; Trade Envoy to: Colombia, Chile and Peru 2017-, Argentina 2018-. *Select committees:* Member: Scottish Affairs 2010, 2014-15, Joint Committee on the Draft Protection of Charities Bill 2014-15, Transport 2015-17, Finance 2016-19, Regulatory Reform 2017, International Development 2018-19, Work of the Independent Commission for Aid Impact Sub-committee 2018-19, Joint Committee on the Draft Registration of Overseas Entities Bill 2019, International Trade 2020-, Committees on Arms Export Controls 2020-. Member, Conservative Party 1987-.

Political interests: Dementia, defence, energy, transport and infrastructure, farming, food retailing; Australia, Middle East, South America, USA.

Other: Member, British-Irish Parliamentary Assembly 2020-; Social innovation marketing award, IGD/Unilever 2007.

Recreations: Skiing, walking, film.

Mark Menzies MP, House of Commons, London SW1A 0AA
Tel: 020 7219 7073 *Fax:* 020 7219 2235 *Email:* mark.menzies.mp@parliament.uk
Constituency: No constituency office publicised
Tel: 01253 739848 Website: www.markmenzies.org.uk

CONSERVATIVE

MERCER, JOHNNY

Plymouth, Moor View *(Majority 12,897)*

Parliamentary Under-Secretary of State (Minister for Defence People and Veterans), Ministry of Defence and Cabinet Office

John Luther Mercer. Born 17 August 1981; Married Felicity Cornelius (3 daughters).

Education: Royal Military Academy, Sandhurst (2002).

Non-political career: British Army, serving at tactical and strategic level, including three combat tours of Afghanistan 2002-14.

Political career: Member for Plymouth, Moor View since 7 May 2015 general election; Parliamentary Under-Secretary of State (Minister for Defence People and Veterans): Ministry of Defence 2019-, Cabinet Office 2019-. *Select committees:* Member: Defence 2015-19, Health/ Health and Social Care 2017-19.

Political interests: Veterans, mental health, inequality, transport.

Publications: We Were Warriors (2017).

Johnny Mercer MP, House of Commons, London SW1A 0AA
Tel: 020 7219 2648 *Email:* johnny.mercer.mp@parliament.uk
Constituency: No constituency office publicised
Tel: 01752 876979 *Email:* johnny@johnnyforplymouth.co.uk
Website: www.johnnyforplymouth.co.uk *Twitter:* @JohnnyMercerUK

CONSERVATIVE

MERRIMAN, HUW

Bexhill and Battle *(Majority 26,059)*

Chair, Select Committee on Transport

Huw William Merriman. Born 13 July 1973.

Education: Buckingham Secondary School; Aylesbury College; Durham University (LLB 1995); Inns of Court School of Law.

Non-political career: Called to the Bar, Inner Temple 1997.

Political career: Member for Bexhill and Battle since 7 May 2015 general election; Department for Work and Pensions: Team PPS 2017-18, PPS to Esther McVey as Secretary of State 2018; HM Treasury: Team PPS 2018, PPS to Philip Hammond as Chancellor of the Exchequer 2018-19. *Select committees:* Transport: Member 2015-19, Chair 2020-; Member: Procedures 2016-17, Liaison 2020-. *Councils and public bodies:* Councillor, Wealden District Council 2007-15.

Political interests: Transport, education, health, social, economic policy, international development; Ireland.

Other: Member: Parliamentary Delegation to Council of Europe -2017, Legal and Human Rights Committee; Trustee and manager, Accra Crawford Youth Charity, Brixton 1998-2003.

Recreations: Cooking, sport, gardening.

Huw Merriman MP, House of Commons, London SW1A 0AA
Tel: 020 7219 1852 *Email:* huw.merriman.mp@parliament.uk
Constituency: 29-31 Sea Road, Bexhill on Sea, East Sussex TN40 1EE
Tel: 01424 736861 Website: www.huwmerriman.org.uk *Twitter:* @HuwMerriman

CONSERVATIVE

METCALFE, STEPHEN South Basildon and East Thurrock *(Majority 19,922)*

Stephen James Metcalfe. Born 9 January 1966; Son of late David Metcalfe and Valerie Metcalfe; Married Angela Giblett 1988 (1 son 1 daughter).

Education: Loughton School; Buckhurst Hill County High School.

Non-political career: Order Clerk, Burrup Mathison, London 1985-86; Metloc Printers Ltd (family business): Sales Executive 1986-87, Studio Manager 1987-92, Director 1992-2011.

Political career: Contested Ilford South 2005 general election. Member for South Basildon and East Thurrock since 6 May 2010 general election; PPS to: Chris Grayling as Lord Chancellor and Secretary of State for Justice 2014-15, Nick Gibb as Minister of State for Schools, Department for Education 2015-16, Edward Timpson as Minister of State for Children and Families, Department for Education 2015-16; Board Member, Parliamentary Office of Science and Technology 2016-19; Apprenticeship Ambassador 2017-; Government Envoy for the Year of Engineering 2017-. *Select committees:* Science and Technology: Member 2010-15, 2017-19, Chair 2016-17; Member, Liaison 2016-17. Deputy chairman, Essex Area Conservatives 2002-06; Member: Conservative Friends of Israel 2006-, Conservative Christian Fellowship 2006-. *Councils and public bodies:* Epping Forest District Council: Customer service e-government and ICT 2003-06, Customer service including waste management portfolio holder 2006-07.

Political interests: Economy, small business, foreign policy, science and technology, education; Africa, China, Japan, Middle East, USA.

Other: Founder, Wasters Wine Society; President, Northlands Park Community Centre, Basildon 2008-. United and Cecil Club; Woodford Rugby Club.

Recreations: Theatre, wine tasting, travel.

Stephen Metcalfe MP, House of Commons, London SW1A 0AA
Tel: 020 7219 7009 *Email:* stephen.metcalfe.mp@parliament.uk
Constituency: South Basildon and East Thurrock Conservatives, 2 Orsett Business Centre, Stanford Road, Grays, Essex RM16 1BX
Tel: 01268 200430 Website: www.stephenmetcalfe.org.uk *Twitter:* @Metcalfe_SBET

LABOUR

MILIBAND, ED Doncaster North *(Majority 2,370)*

Shadow Secretary of State for Business, Energy and Industrial Strategy

Edward Samuel Miliband. Born 24 December 1969; Son of Ralph Miliband and Marion Miliband, née Kozak; Married Justine Thornton 2011 (later High Court Judge) (2 sons).

Education: Corpus Christi College, Oxford (BA philosophy, politics and economics); London School of Economics (MSc Econ).

Non-political career: Television journalist; Speechwriter and researcher to: Harriet Harman MP 1993, Gordon Brown MP as Shadow Chancellor of the Exchequer 1994-97; HM Treasury: Special adviser to Gordon Brown MP as Chancellor of the Exchequer 1997-2002, Chair, Council of Economic Advisers 2004-05; Fellow and lecturer in government, Harvard University 2002-04. Member, TGWU/USDAW.

Political career: Member for Doncaster North 2005-10, for Doncaster North (revised boundary) since 6 May 2010 general election; Parliamentary Secretary, Cabinet Office 2006-07; Minister for the Cabinet Office; Chancellor of the Duchy of Lancaster 2007-08; Secretary of State for Energy and Climate Change 2008-10; Shadow Secretary of State for Energy and Climate Change 2010; Leader of the Opposition 2010-15; Shadow Secretary of State for Business, Energy and Industrial Strategy 2020-. Leader, Labour Party 2010-15.

Other: PC 2007.

Publications: Contributor, The Purple Book (Progress, 2011).

Rt Hon Ed Miliband MP, House of Commons, London SW1A 0AA
Tel: 020 7219 7318 *Email:* ed.miliband.mp@parliament.uk
Constituency: No constituency office publicised
Tel: 01302 875462 Website: www.edmiliband.org.uk *Twitter:* @Ed_Miliband

CONSERVATIVE

MILLAR, ROBIN

Aberconwy *(Majority 2,034)*

Robin John Millar. Born October 1968; Married Bonny.

Education: Manchester University (BEng civil engineering 1991).

Non-political career: Director, Millar Consulting 2000-19; Strategic director, British Veterinary Nursing Association 2017-.

Political career: Contested Arfon 2010 general election. Member for Aberconwy since 12 December 2019. *Select committees:* Member, Welsh Affairs 2020-. Director, Conservative Christian Fellowship 2009-. *Councils and public bodies:* Forest Heath District Council: Councillor 1999-2019, Deputy Leader and Portfolio Holder for Families and Community 2011-19; Mayor of Newmarket 2003-04; Councillor, West Suffolk Council 2019-; Suffolk County Council: Councillor 2016-, Cabinet Member for Families and Communities and Passenger Transport 2017-18.

Other: Trustee, Relate 2003-; Fellow, Centre for Social Justice 2012-16. Chair, Newmarket Cycling and Triathlon Club.

Recreations: Football, tennis.

Robin Millar MP, House of Commons, London SW1A 0AA
Tel: 020 7219 3000 *Email:* robin.millar.mp@parliament.uk
Constituency: 4 Brunswick House, Riverside Business Park, Conwy LL32 8UB
Tel: 01492 583094 Website: www.robin-millar.org.uk *Twitter:* @RobinMillarMP

CONSERVATIVE

MILLER, MARIA

Basingstoke *(Majority 14,198)*

Maria Frances Lewis Miller. Born 26 March 1964; Daughter of John and June Lewis; Married Iain Miller 1990 (1 daughter 2 sons).

Education: Brynteg Comprehensive, Bridgend; London School of Economics (BSc economics 1985).

Non-political career: Advertising executive, Grey Advertising Ltd 1985-90; Marketing manager, Texaco 1990-94; Company director: Grey Advertising Ltd 1995-99, The Rowland Company/PR21 1999-2003.

Political career: Contested Wolverhampton North East 2001 general election. Member for Basingstoke 2005-10, for Basingstoke (revised boundary) since 6 May 2010 general election; Shadow Minister for: Education 2005-06, Family Welfare, including Child Support Agency 2006-07, Families 2007-10; Parliamentary Under-Secretary of State (Minister for Disabled People), Department for Work and Pensions 2010-12; Secretary of State for Culture, Media and Sport 2012-14; Minister for Women and Equalities 2012-14; Member, Commons Reference Group on Representation and Inclusion 2017-18. *Select committees:* Member: Trade and Industry 2005-06, Children, Schools and Families 2007, Liaison 2015-19; Chair: Women and Equalities 2015-19, Joint Committee on the Draft Domestic Abuse Bill 2019, Member: Administration 2020-, Panel of Chairs 2020-, Joint Committee on Fixed-Term Parliaments Act 2020-. Chairman, Conservative Backbench Policy Committee on Women and Equalities 2017-19. President, Wolverhampton North East Conservative Association 2001-07; Chair, Wimbledon Conservative Association 2002-03.

Political interests: Housing, education, media, UK and international women and equality issues, infrastructure provision, online crime; Belarus, Canada, Nepal, Turkey.

Other: Executive Committee, Commonwealth Parliamentary Association United Kingdom: Member 2017-19, Vice-chair 2020-; Governor, Westminster Foundation for Democracy 2020-; Trustee, Belarus Free Theatre; Rising Star, *House Magazine* awards 2012; Pink News MP of the Year 2015; PC 2012.

Recreations: Cycling.

Rt Hon Maria Miller MP, House of Commons, London SW1A 0AA
Tel: 020 7219 5749 *Email:* maria.miller.mp@parliament.uk
Constituency: No constituency office publicised
Website: www.maria4basingstoke.co.uk *Twitter:* @MariaMillerUK

CONSERVATIVE

MILLING, AMANDA

Cannock Chase *(Majority 19,879)*

Minister without Portfolio, Cabinet Office; Chairman, Conservative Party

Amanda Anne Milling. Born 12 March 1975; Daughter of Humphrey and Patricia Milling; Divorced.

Education: Moreton Hall; University College London (BSc economics and statistics 1997).

Non-political career: Researcher, SWI Research 1997-99; Director: Quaestor 1999-2009, Optimisa Research Ltd 2010-14.

Political career: Member for Cannock Chase since 7 May 2015 general election; PPS to Baroness Anelay of St Johns as Minister of State for the Commonwealth and the UN: Foreign and Commonwealth Office 2016-17; Team PPS, Foreign and Commonwealth Office 2017-18; Assistant Government Whip 2018-19; Deputy Chief Whip (Treasurer of HM Household) 2019-20; Minister without Portfolio, Cabinet Office 2020-. *Select committees:* Member: Business, Innovation and Skills 2015-16, Joint Committee on Consolidation, &c, Bills 2015-18, Education, Skills and the Economy Sub-committee 2015-17, Arms Export Controls 2016, Business, Energy and Industrial Strategy 2016-17, Selection 2019-20. Deputy Chair, Rossendale and Darwen Conservative Association 2012-14; Chairman, Conservative Party 2020-. *Councils and public bodies:* Councillor, Rossendale Borough Council 2009-14; Governor, Helmshore Primary School.

Political interests: Business and skills, economy, education and young people.

Other: PC 2020.

Recreations: Running.

Rt Hon Amanda Milling MP, House of Commons, London SW1A 0AA
Tel: 020 7219 8356 *Email:* amanda.milling.mp@parliament.uk
Constituency: 11a Market Street, Hednesford, Cannock, Staffordshire WS11 1AY
Tel: 01543 877142 Website: www.amandamilling.com *Twitter:* @amandamilling

CONSERVATIVE

MILLS, NIGEL

Amber Valley *(Majority 16,886)*

Nigel John Mills. Born 28 October 1974; Married Alice 2013.

Education: Loughborough Grammar School; Newcastle University (classics 1996).

Non-political career: Accountant: PriceWaterhouseCoopers 1996-2008, Deloitte LLP 2008-10.

Political career: Member for Amber Valley since 6 May 2010 general election. *Select committees:* Member: Administration 2010-17, Northern Ireland Affairs 2011-19, Work and Pensions 2012-15, 2018-, Public Accounts 2015-18, 2018-19, Backbench Business 2018-, Future Relationship with the European Union 2020-21, Procedure 2020-. Chairman, Conservative Backbench Policy Committee on Work and Pensions 2015-19. Deputy chair, Amber Valley Conservative Association. *Councils and public bodies:* Amber Valley Borough Council: Councillor 2004-11, Chair, scrutiny committee; Councillor, Heanor and Loscoe Town Council 2007-11.

Political interests: Employment, crime, anti-social behaviour, education, taxation.

Other: Member: British-Irish Parliamentary Assembly 2015-, UK delegation, Parliamentary Assembly of the Organisation for Security and Co-operation in Europe; Institute of Chartered Accountants in England and Wales.

Recreations: Sport.

Nigel Mills MP, House of Commons, London SW1A 0AA
Tel: 020 7219 7233 *Email:* nigel.mills.mp@parliament.uk
Constituency: Unicorn House, Wellington Street, Ripley, Derbyshire DE5 3EH
Tel: 01773 744341 *Email:* nigel@nigelmillsmp.com Website: www.nigelmillsmp.com
Twitter: @nigelmills

House of Commons MPs' Biographies

LABOUR

MISHRA, NAVENDU

Stockport *(Majority 10,039)*

Navendu Prabhat Mishra.

Non-political career: John Lewis Partnership.

Political career: Contested Hazel Grove 2017 general election. Member for Stockport since 12 December 2019; PPS to Angela Rayner: as Shadow Secretary of State for Education 2020, as Labour Party Chair 2020. *Select committees:* Member: International Development 2020-, Public Administration and Constitutional Affairs 2020-, Arms Export Controls 2020-. Member, Division III, National Executive Committee, Labour Party 2018-19; Founder, Stockport Momentum.

Political interests: Inequalities, health, housing.

Navendu Mishra MP, House of Commons, London SW1A 0AA
Tel: 020 7219 3000 *Email:* navendu.mishra.mp@parliament.uk
Constituency: No constituency office publicised
Email: team@navendumishra.co.uk Website: www.navendumishra.co.uk *Twitter:* @navpmishra

CONSERVATIVE

MITCHELL, ANDREW

Sutton Coldfield *(Majority 19,272)*

Andrew John Bower Mitchell. Born 23 March 1956; Son of Sir David Mitchell (MP for Basingstoke 1964-83 and North West Hampshire 1983-97) and Pamela Mitchell; Married Sharon Bennet 1985 (2 daughters).

Education: Rugby School; Jesus College, Cambridge (MA history 1978) (Union President 1978); French.

Non-political career: International and Corporate Finance, Lazard Brothers and Company Ltd 1979-87; Lazard Brothers: Consultant 1987-92, Director 1997-2009; Director: Miller Insurance Group 1997-2001, Financial Dynamics Holdings 1997-2002; Senior Strategy Adviser: Boots 1997-2000, Andersen Consulting/Accenture 1997-2009; Director, Commer Group 1998-2002; Supervisory Board Member, The Foundation 1999-2009, 2013-16; Senior Adviser: Montrose Associates 2015-, Investec 2015-, EY 2016-. UN Peacekeeping Forces Cyprus: 1st Royal Tank Regiment (SSLC).

Political career: Contested Sunderland South 1983 general election. Member for Gedling 1987-97. Contested Gedling 1997 general election. Member for Sutton Coldfield 2001-10, for Sutton Coldfield (revised boundary) since 6 May 2010 general election; PPS to: William Waldegrave as Minister of State, Foreign and Commonwealth Office 1988-90, John Wakeham as Secretary of State for Energy 1990-92; Assistant Government Whip 1992-93; Government Whip 1993-95; Parliamentary Under-Secretary of State, Department of Social Security 1995-97; Shadow Minister for: Economic Affairs 2003-04, Home Affairs 2004-05; Shadow Secretary of State for International Development 2005-10; Secretary of State for International Development 2010-12; Chief Whip; Parliamentary Secretary to the Treasury September-October 2012; Member, Parliamentary and Political Service Honours Committee September-October 2012. *Select committees:* Member: Work and Pensions 2001-03, Modernisation of the House of Commons 2002-04, Parliamentary and Political Service Honours Committee 2012-13. Chair, Cambridge University Conservative Association 1977; Secretary, One Nation Group of Conservative MPs 1989-92, 2005-; Vice-chair, Conservative Party (candidates) 1992-93; Founder, Conservative Friends of International Development; Founder and Leader, Project Umubano 2007-17.

Political interests: International development, health, defence, economy, foreign policy; Africa, Far East, USA.

Other: Council SOS SAHEL 1992-2010; English Speaking Union Council International Debate Council 1998-2010; Council of management, GAP 1999-2006; Alexandra Rose Charity: Vice-chair 1999-2010, Trustee 2010-; Liveryman, Vintners' Company; Freedom, City of London; Senior Research Fellow, Centre for Rising Powers, Cambridge University; Senior Research Associate, Jesus College, Cambridge; Birmingham University: Honorary Professor, College of Social Sciences, Advisory Board Member, Institute for Global Innovation; Strategy Advisory Committee Member, Oxford Centre for Islamic Studies; UN Military Medal 1978; PC 2010. Chair, Coningsby Club 1984-85.

Recreations: Music, cycling, skiing, walking.

Rt Hon Andrew Mitchell MP, House of Commons, London SW1A 0AA
Tel: 020 7219 8516 *Email:* andrew.mitchell.mp@parliament.uk
Constituency: Sutton Coldfield Conservative Association, 36 High Street, Sutton Coldfield, West Midlands B72 1UP
Tel: 0121-321 3113 Website: www.andrew-mitchell-mp.co.uk

CONSERVATIVE

MOHINDRA, GAGAN

South West Hertfordshire *(Majority 14,408)*

Team PPS, Department for Transport

Born April 1978; Married.

Education: King's College, London (BSc mathematics 1999).

Non-political career: Equity research, Deutsche Bank; Founder, thisisfurniture.com; Chief financial officer, Chromex Group; Self-employed businessman.

Political career: Contested North Tyneside 2010 general election. Member for South West Hertfordshire since 12 December 2019; Team PPS, Department for Transport 2020-. *Select committees:* Member: Public Accounts 2020, Speaker's Advisory Committee on Works of Art 2021-. Member, Executive, 1922 Committee 2020. Essex Conservative Party: Deputy Chair 2015-18, Chair 2018-; Chair, Epping Forest Conservative Association 2015-18; Conservative Friends of India. *Councils and public bodies:* Epping Forest Council: Councillor 2006-, Business Support Services Portfolio Holder; Essex County Council: Councillor 2017-, Deputy Portfolio Holder for Economic Growth, Infrastructure, Skills and the Digital Economy 2017-18, Portfolio Holder for Economic Development 2018-19, Cabinet Member for Finance, Property and Housing 2019-; Former Chair of Governors, Epping Forest College; Board Member, West Essex Clinical Commissioning Group.

Other: Member, UK Delegation to Parliamentary Assembly, Council of Europe 2020-.

Recreations: Football, skiing, reading.

Gagan Mohindra MP, House of Commons, London SW1A 0AA
Tel: 020 7219 3000 *Email:* gagan.mohindra.mp@parliament.uk
Constituency: No constituency office publicised
Website: www.gaganmohindra.org.uk *Twitter:* @gaganmohindra

SINN FÉIN

MOLLOY, FRANCIE

Mid Ulster *(Majority 9,537)*

Francis Joseph Molloy. Born 16 December 1950; Son of late Arthur Molloy and Annie, née Daly; Married Ann Mulgrew 1971 (2 sons 2 daughters).

Education: St Patrick's Intermediate, Dungannon; FELDEN Government Training Centre (engineering 1967); Ulster University; Newry Further Education College (Foundation Studies humanities).

Non-political career: Trainee fitter welder, Feldon GTC 1966-67; Fitter/welder/sales, Ulster Plant (later Powerscreen) 1967-74; Self-employed welder/light engineer 1978-81. Former member, AEWU.

Political career: Member for Mid Ulster since 7 March 2013 by-election. Contested Northern Ireland region 1994 European Parliament election; Member: Northern Ireland Forum for Political Dialogue 1996, Sinn Féin Talks Team, Castle Buildings Talks 1997-98; MLA for Mid Ulster 1998-2013: Chair Assembly Committee on Finance and Personnel 1999-2002, Deputy Speaker 2006-11, Sinn Féin Spokesperson for: Victims, Families and Poverty 2011-12; Principal Deputy Speaker 2011-13; Sinn Féin Spokesperson for Environment 2012-13. *Councils and public bodies:* Councillor 1985-2011: Dungannon District Council, Dungannon and South Tyrone Borough Council, Mayor 2001, 2005, Deputy mayor 2003.

Political interests: Housing, rural affairs, Lough Neagh, engineering skills development; South Africa.

Other: Member, EU Committee of the Regions 2010-13. Clonmore Robert Emmetts Gaelic FC.

Recreations: Painting, art, mainly water colour, organic gardening, Spanish civil war.

Francie Molloy MP, House of Commons, London SW1A 0AA
Tel: 020 7219 3000 *Email:* francie.molloy.mp@parliament.uk
Constituency: 30f Fairhill Road, Cookstown BT80 8AG
Tel: 028 8676 5850 *Twitter:* @FrancieMolloy

SCOTTISH NATIONAL PARTY

MONAGHAN, CAROL

Glasgow North West *(Majority 8,359)*

SNP Shadow Secretary of State for Education; Shadow Minister for Armed Forces and Veterans

Carol Frances Monaghan. Born 2 August 1972; Married Feargal Dalton (1 son 2 daughters).

Education: Strathclyde University (BSc laser physics and optoelectronics 1993); PGCE physics and maths.

Non-political career: Hyndland Secondary School: Head of Physics, Head of Science; Lecturer, Glasgow University; Consultant, SQA.

Political career: Member for Glasgow North West since 7 May 2015 general election; Board member, Parliamentary Office of Science and Technology 2015-17; SNP: Spokesperson for Public Services 2015-17, Spokesperson/Shadow Secretary of State for Education 2015-, Spokesperson for Veterans and Armed Forces/Shadow Minister for Military Personnel/Armed Forces and Veterans 2017-. *Select committees:* Member, Science and Technology 2015-17, 2017-.

Carol Monaghan MP, House of Commons, London SW1A 0AA
Tel: 020 7219 6396 *Email:* carol.monaghan.mp@parliament.uk
Constituency: 500 Dumbarton Road, Glasgow G11 6SL
Tel: 0141-337 2211 Website: www.carol.monaghan.scot *Twitter:* @CMonaghanSNP

CONSERVATIVE

MOORE, DAMIEN

Southport *(Majority 4,147)*

PPS to George Eustice as Secretary of State for Environment, Food and Rural Affairs

Born 26 April 1980.

Education: University of Central Lancashire (BA history 2005).

Non-political career: Retail manager, ASDA.

Political career: Contested Southport 2015 general election. Member for Southport since 8 June 2017; PPS to: Oliver Dowden as Minister for the Cabinet Office and Paymaster General 2019-20, Amanda Milling as Minister without Portfolio and Conservative Party Chair 2020, George Eustice as Secretary of State for Environment, Food and Rural Affairs 2020-; Trade Envoy to Tunisia and Libya 2020-. *Select committees:* Member: Petitions 2017-19, Science and Technology 2018-19. Chair, Lancashire Conservatives. *Councils and public bodies:* Preston City Council: Councillor 2012-18, Deputy Leader, Conservative group.

Political interests: Belgium, Luxembourg, Spain, Tunisia.

Other: SSAFA.

Damien Moore MP, House of Commons, London SW1A 0AA
Tel: 020 7219 4684 *Email:* damien.moore.mp@parliament.uk
Constituency: 4 Post Office Avenue, Southport PR9 0US
Tel: 01704 500577 Website: www.damienmooremp.com *Twitter:* @Moore4Southport

House of Commons MPs' Biographies

CONSERVATIVE

MOORE, ROBBIE

Keighley *(Majority 2,218)*

Robert Peter Moore. Born 28 November 1984.

Education: Newcastle University (BA architecture 2007); University College of Estate Management (PgDipSurv rural surveying 2011).

Non-political career: Architectural assistant, IDPartnership Group 2007-08; George F White: Rural Surveyor 2009-17 Associate 2017-18; Nuffield Farming Scholar, Nuffield Farming Scholarships Trust 2015-17; Director, Brockthorpe Consultancy 2018-.

Political career: Member for Keighley since 12 December 2019. *Select committees:* Member, Environment, Food and Rural Affairs 2020-. Contested Northumbria Police and Crime Commissioner 2019 by-election. *Councils and public bodies:* Councillor: Alnwick Town Council, Northumberland County Council.

Other: Fellow, Central Association of Agricultural Valuers; Member, Royal Institution of Chartered Surveyors.

Robbie Moore MP, House of Commons, London SW1A 0AA
Tel: 020 7219 3000 *Email:* robbie.moore.mp@parliament.uk
Constituency: Shan House, 80-86 North Street, Keighley BD21 3AG
Tel: 01535 600538 Website: www.robbiemoore.org.uk *Twitter:* @_RobbieMoore

LIBERAL DEMOCRAT

MORAN, LAYLA

Oxford West and Abingdon *(Majority 8,943)*

Liberal Democrat Spokesperson for Foreign Affairs and International Development

Layla Michelle Moran. Born 12 September 1982.

Education: Imperial College London (BSc physics 2003); Brunel University (PCGE 2006); UCL (MA comparative education 2008); French, Spanish, Arabic, Greek.

Non-political career: Maths and Physics Teacher, International School of Brussels 2003-07; Physics Teacher, Southbank International School 2007-13; Academic Development Manager, Oxford Study Courses Ltd 2008-17.

Political career: Contested Battersea 2010 and Oxford West and Abingdon 2015 general elections. Member for Oxford West and Abingdon since 8 June 2017; Liberal Democrat: Shadow Secretary of State/Spokesperson for: Science 2017-19, Young People 2017, Shadow Secretary of State/Spokesperson for Education 2017-20, Shadow Secretary of State for Digital, Culture, Media and Sport 2019, Spokesperson for Foreign Affairs and International Development 2020-. *Select committees:* Member, Public Accounts 2017-19. Contested West Central constituency 2012 GLA election. *Councils and public bodies:* Vice-President, Local Government Association 2018-.

Political interests: Education, sustainable transport, homelessness, Hong Kong, human rights, Uyghurs and China, international development, coronavirus, heritage and planning; China, Europe, Hong Kong, North America.

Other: Member, Executive Committee, Commonwealth Parliamentary Association United Kingdom 2020-.

Layla Moran MP, House of Commons, London SW1A 0AA
Tel: 020 7219 3905 *Email:* layla.moran.mp@parliament.uk
Constituency: Unit C5, Grange Court, Abingdon Science Park, Barton Lane, Abingdon OX14 3NB
Tel: 01235 522535 Website: www.laylamoran.com *Twitter:* @laylamoran

CONSERVATIVE

MORDAUNT, PENNY

Portsmouth North *(Majority 15,780)*

Paymaster General, Cabinet Office

Penelope Mary Mordaunt. Born 4 March 1973; Daughter of John Mordaunt and Jennifer Snowden.

Education: Oaklands RC Comprehensive School, Waterlooville; Reading University (philosophy) (President Students' Union).

Non-political career: Magician's assistant to Will Ayling, President of Magic Circle; Head of foreign press, George W Bush's presidential campaign 2000; Former communications director: London Borough of Kensington and Chelsea Council, Freight Transport Association, National Lottery; Director of strategy, policy and partnerships, Diabetes UK; Associate, Hanover. Royal Navy Reservist on List 6 2015-.

Political career: Contested Portsmouth North 2005 general election. Member for Portsmouth North since 6 May 2010 general election; PPS to Philip Hammond as Secretary of State for Defence 2013-14; Parliamentary Under-Secretary of State, Department for Communities and Local Government 2014-15; Minister of State for: the Armed Forces, Ministry of Defence 2015-16, Disabled People, Health and Work, Department for Work and Pensions 2016-17; Secretary of State for International Development 2017-19; Minister for Women and Equalities 2018-19; Secretary of State for Defence 2019; Paymaster General, Cabinet Office 2020-. *Select committees:* Member: European Scrutiny 2010-13, Defence 2010-13, Arms Export Controls 2011-13, Joint Committee on Privacy and Injunctions 2011-12. Member, Executive, 1922 Committee 2012-13. *Councils and public bodies:* Commissioner, Commission on Assisted Dying 2010-12.

Political interests: Care and quality of life for the elderly, healthcare, defence, the arts, space; India, USA.

Other: British Astronomical Association; Trustee, Wymering Manor Trust; Patron: Enable Ability, Portsmouth, The Victoria Cross; Speech of the Year, *Spectator* awards 2014; PC 2017.

Recreations: Painting, astronomy, Burmese cats.

Rt Hon Penny Mordaunt MP, House of Commons, London SW1A 0AA
Tel: 020 7219 3000 *Email:* penny.mordaunt.mp@parliament.uk
Constituency: Ground Floor, 1000 Lakeside, North Harbour, Portsmouth, Hampshire PO6 3EN
Tel: 023 9237 5377 Website: www.pennymordaunt.com *Twitter:* @PennyMordaunt

LABOUR

MORDEN, JESSICA

Newport East *(Majority 1,992)*

Senior Opposition Whip (Shadow Vice-Chamberlain of HM Household); Chair, Joint Committee on Statutory Instruments

Jessica Elizabeth Morden. Born 29 May 1968; Daughter of Mick and Margaret Morden; Partner Sion Ffrancon Jones (1 daughter 1 son).

Education: Croesyceiliog Comprehensive School; Birmingham University (BA history 1989).

Non-political career: Labour Party organiser; Political assistant to Llew Smith MEP; Constituency assistant to Huw Edwards MP; General Secretary, Welsh Labour Party 1999-2005. Member, GMB.

Political career: Member for Newport East since 5 May 2005 general election; PPS: to Secretaries of State for Wales: Peter Hain 2007-08, 2009-10, Paul Murphy 2008-09; to Shadow Secretaries of State for Wales: Peter Hain 2011-12, Owen Smith 2012-15; Opposition Whip 2015-20; Member, Speaker's Committee on the Electoral Commission 2015-19; Senior Opposition Whip (Shadow Vice-Chamberlain of HM Household) 2020-. *Select committees:* Member: Constitutional Affairs/Justice 2005-10, Modernisation of the House of Commons 2005-06, Welsh Affairs 2005-07, 2010-15, Standing Orders 2015-, Selection 2016-, Administration 2017-, Liaison 2018-19, 2020-; Chair, Joint Committee on Statutory Instruments 2018-.

Political interests: Anti-social behaviour, electoral issues, police, children, steel industry.

Recreations: Cinema, gym.

Jessica Morden MP, House of Commons, London SW1A 0AA
Tel: 020 7219 6213 *Fax:* 020 7219 6196 *Email:* jessica.morden.mp@parliament.uk
Constituency: Room 2, Seventh Floor, Clarence House, Clarence Place, Newport, Gwent NP19 7AA
Tel: 01633 841725 Website: www.jessicamorden.com *Twitter:* @jessicamordenmp

LABOUR

MORGAN, STEPHEN

Portsmouth South *(Majority 5,363)*

Shadow Minister for the Armed Forces

Stephen James Morgan. Born 17 January 1981.

Education: Priory School, Southsea; Portsmouth College, Baffins; Bristol University (BA politics and sociology); Goldsmiths College, University of London (MA politics).

Non-political career: Portsmouth City Council: Strategy adviser, Chief Executive's Office 2003-06, Projects manager 2006-08; Head of Community Engagement, Royal Borough of Kensington and Chelsea Council 2008-15; Chief Executive, Basingstoke Voluntary Action 2015-17. GMB.

Political career: Member for Portsmouth South since 8 June 2017; PPS to Andrew Gwynne as Shadow Secretary of State for Communities and Local Government and National Campaign Co-ordinator 2017-19; Shadow Minister for: Communities and Local Government (Communities) 2019-20, Defence: (Defence Procurement) 2020, (Armed Forces) 2020-. *Select committees:* Member, Public Accounts 2017-19. *Councils and public bodies:* Portsmouth City Council: Councillor 2016-, Leader, Labour group.

Political interests: Education, crime and policing, defence, local government, health and social care, the environment.

Stephen Morgan MP, House of Commons, London SW1A 0AA
Tel: 020 7219 3906 *Email:* stephen.morgan.mp@parliament.uk
Constituency: 72 Albert Road, Southsea PO5 2SL
Tel: 023 9229 1088 Website: www.stephenjmorgan.org *Twitter:* @StephenMorganMP

CONSERVATIVE

MORRIS, ANNE MARIE

Newton Abbot *(Majority 17,501)*

Born 5 July 1957; Daughter of Margaret Agg and late John Backes.

Education: Bryanston School, Dorset; Hertford College, Oxford (BA jurisprudence 1980); College of Law, London (Law Society finals 1981); Open University (MBA 1997); Harvard University (leadership programme 2004); School of Coaching, Strathclyde University (Diploma executive coaching 2007); French.

Non-political career: Trainee solicitor, Withers, London 1981-83; Corporate finance lawyer, Norton Rose, London 1983-85; Corporate commercial banking lawyer, Crossman Block, London 1985; Asset finance lawyer, Sinclair Roche & Temerley, Singapore 1986-88; Allen & Overy, London: Corporate finance lawyer 1988-90, Head of education and training 1990-93; Director of professional and business development, Baker & McKenzie 1993-95; Director of marketing and business development, Simmons & Simmons 1995-97; Marketing director, tax and legal services, PricewaterhouseCoopers 1997-99; Global marketing director: Ernst & Young 1999-2002, Linklaters 2002-05; Director, Manteion Ltd.

Political career: Member for Newton Abbot since 6 May 2010 general election; PPS to: Nick Boles as Minister of State for Skills, Department for Business, Innovation and Skills and Department for Education 2015-16, Jo Johnson as Minister of State for Universities and Science, Department for Business, Innovation and Skills 2015-16. *Select committees:* Member: Work and Pensions 2012-15, Public Accounts 2016-17, 2018-19, Health and Social Care 2019, European Scrutiny 2020-. Conservative Whip suspended July-December 2017. *Councils and public bodies:* Councillor, West Sussex County Council 2005-07; Associate Governor, Rydon Primary School, Kingsteignton; Governor, Newton Abbot College.

Political interests: Micro and small businesses, health and the NHS, social care, the elderly, education, vocational training and apprenticeships, life sciences, pharmaceuticals.

Other: Director: LawWorks, Small Business Bureau; Member: Devon and Cornwall Board, Institute of Directors 2001-, Federation of Small Businesses; Fellow, Chartered Institute of Marketing 2002; Member: Law Society of England and Wales, European Mentoring and Coaching Council; Dame Hannah Roger Trust at Seale-Hayne.

Recreations: Horse riding, dog walking.

Anne Marie Morris MP, House of Commons, London SW1A 0AA
Tel: 020 7219 8928 *Fax:* 020 7219 6578 *Email:* annemarie.morris.mp@parliament.uk
Constituency: 2 Salisbury House, Salisbury Road, Newton Abbot, Devon TQ12 2DF
Tel: 01626 368277 *Email:* annemarie@annemariemorris.co.uk
Website: www.annemariemorris.co.uk *Twitter:* @AnneMarieMorris

CONSERVATIVE

MORRIS, DAVID

Morecambe and Lunesdale *(Majority 6,354)*

David Thomas Morris. Born 3 January 1966; Son of Lieutenant Commander Alan Morris, retired Royal Navy, and Vera Morris; Divorced (2 sons); married Emma 2019.

Education: St Andrews School, Bahamas; Lowton High School.

Non-political career: Song writer and session guitar player, music industry; Former managing director, David Morris Hairdressing; Commercial property investor, northern England. Honorary Lieutenant Commander, Royal Navy (Armed Forces Parliamentary Scheme).

Political career: Contested Blackpool South 2001 and Carmarthen West and South Pembrokeshire 2005 general elections. Member for Morecambe and Lunesdale since 6 May 2010 general election; Self-Employment Ambassador 2014-; PPS: to Secretaries of State for Wales: Stephen Crabb 2014-16, Alun Cairns 2016, to David Mundell as Secretary of State for Scotland 2016-17, to James Brokenshire as Secretary of State for Northern Ireland 2017-18, to Caroline Nokes as Minister of State for Immigration, Home Office 2018, to Damian Hinds as Secretary of State for Education 2018-19, to James Brokenshire as Secretary of State for Housing, Communities and Local Government 2019. *Select committees:* Member: Science and Technology 2010-12, 2012-14, Administration 2012-14, Political and Constitutional Reform 2014-15, 2017-19. Member, Executive, 1922 Committee 2020-. Chair, Conservative Friends of Nuclear Energy; Board member, Conservative Party 2020-.

Political interests: Nuclear energy, small business, maritime affairs; Bahamas, Hong Kong.

Other: Member, British-Irish Parliamentary Assembly 2017-20; Government-appointed member, National Hairdressing Council.

Recreations: Playing and collecting guitars, classic cars.

David Morris MP, House of Commons, London SW1A 0AA
Tel: 020 7219 7234 *Email:* david.morris.mp@parliament.uk
Constituency: Office 204, Riverway House, Morecambe Road, Lancaster, Lancashire LA1 2RX
Tel: 01524 841225 Website: www.davidmorris.org.uk *Twitter:* @davidmorrisml

LABOUR

MORRIS, GRAHAME

Easington *(Majority 6,581)*

Grahame Mark Morris. Born 13 March 1961; Son of late Richard Morris, colliery electrician, and Constance Morris, pit canteen worker; Married Michelle Hughes 1986 (2 sons).

Education: Peterlee Howletch Secondary School; Newcastle College (BTEC Ordinary National Certificate); Newcastle Polytechnic (BTEC Higher National Certificate medical laboratory sciences).

Non-political career: Medical laboratory scientific officer, Sunderland Royal Infirmary 1980-87; Researcher and constituency caseworker to John Cummings MP 1987-2010. Member, Unite.

Political career: Member for Easington since 6 May 2010 general election; PPS to: Meg Hillier as Shadow Secretary of State for Energy and Climate Change 2010-11, Rachel Reeves as Shadow Chief Secretary to the Treasury 2011-12; Opposition Whip 2015-16; Shadow Secretary of State for Communities and Local Government and for Housing; Shadow Minister for the Constitutional Convention 2016. *Select committees:* Member: Health 2010-15, Joint Committee on the Draft Care and Support Bill 2013, Unopposed Bills (Panel) 2013-15, Joint Committee on Consolidation, &c, Bills 2015-20, Transport 2018-. Member, Labour Party

1976-; Secretary, Easington Constituency Labour Party 1996-2006. *Councils and public bodies:* Councillor, Easington District Council 1987-2003; Non-executive director, City Hospitals Sunderland NHS Trust 1997-2005.

Political interests: NHS, local government, economic regeneration, public health, housing; China, Cuba, Venezuela.

Other: Haswell and District Mencap, Easington Riding for the Disabled, World Vision, Shelter, Dogs Trust. Peterlee Labour Club, Easington Colliery Workingmen's Club CIU, Southside Social Club Easington Village.

Grahame Morris MP, House of Commons, London SW1A 0AA
Tel: 020 7219 1283 *Email:* grahame.morris.mp@parliament.uk
Constituency: Seaton Holme, Hall Walks, Easington, Co Durham SR8 3BS
Tel: 0191-527 9091 Website: www.grahamemorrismp.co.uk *Twitter:* @grahamemorris

CONSERVATIVE

MORRIS, JAMES

Halesowen and Rowley Regis *(Majority 12,074)*

Government Whip, Lord Commissioner of HM Treasury

James George Morris. Born 4 February 1967; Married Anna Mellitt (1 son 1 daughter).

Education: Nottingham High School; Birmingham University (English literature); Oxford University (Postgraduate research); Cranfield School Management (MBA).

Non-political career: Managing director: 1996-2001, Vice-Versa Ltd 2001-06; Director, Mind the Gap 2003-08; Chief executive officer, Localis 2008-10.

Political career: Member for Halesowen and Rowley Regis since 6 May 2010 general election; PPS to: Esther McVey as Minister of State for Employment, Department for Work and Pensions 2014-15, David Lidington as Minister of State for Europe, Foreign and Commonwealth Office 2015-16, Jeremy Hunt as Secretary of State for Health 2016-17, Damian Green as First Secretary of State and Minister for the Cabinet Office 2017; Assistant Government Whip 2019-20; Government Whip, Lord Commissioner of HM Treasury 2020-. *Select committees:* Member: Communities and Local Government 2010-14, Selection 2020-. Vice-chairman, Training and Development, Conservative Party 2018-19.

Political interests: Localism, local government, foreign affairs.

Publications: Change Starts Small (2004); Big Ideas (2008); Million Vote Mandate (2008); Can Localism Deliver? (2009); The Bottom Line (2009); For Good Measure (2010); Co-author, Freedom, Responsibility and the State: Curbing Over-Mighty Government (Politeia, 2012).

Recreations: Cricket, family, theatre, music.

James Morris MP, House of Commons, London SW1A 0AA
Tel: 020 7219 8715 *Fax:* 020 7219 1429 *Email:* james.morris.mp@parliament.uk
Constituency: Trinity Point, New Road, Halesowen, West Midlands B63 3HY
Tel: 0121-550 6777 *Email:* hadleys@parliament.uk Website: www.jamesmorris.co.uk
Twitter: @JamesMorris

CONSERVATIVE

MORRISSEY, JOY

Beaconsfield *(Majority 15,712)*

Team PPS, Foreign, Commonwealth and Development Office

Joy Inboden Morrissey. Born 30 January 1981; Married William (1 daughter).

Education: International relations and Chinese; London School of Economics (Masters); Chinese, Albanian.

Non-political career: Stage and film actress; Producer; Parliamentary Assistant to: Angie Bray MP, Will Quince MP; Centre for Social Justice 2016-.

Political career: Contested Ealing Central and Acton 2017 general election. Member for Beaconsfield since 12 December 2019; Team PPS: Foreign and Commonwealth Office 2020, Foreign, Commonwealth and Development Office 2020-. Contested London-wide region 2016 Greater London Assembly elections. *Councils and public bodies:* Ealing Council: Councillor 2014-20, Shadow Portfolio Holder for Health and Adult Social Service.

Other: LSE Court of Governors.

Joy Morrissey MP, House of Commons, London SW1A 0AA
Tel: 020 7219 6453 *Email:* joy.morrissey.mp@parliament.uk
Constituency: Disraeli House, 12 Aylesbury End, Beaconsfield HP9 1LW
Tel: 01494 977505 Website: www.joymorrissey.uk *Twitter:* @joymorrissey

CONSERVATIVE

MORTON, WENDY

Aldridge-Brownhills *(Majority 19,836)*

Parliamentary Under-Secretary of State (Minister for the European Neighbourhood and Americas), Foreign, Commonwealth and Development Office

Born 9 November 1967; Daughter of Thomas and Edna Hunter; Married David Morton 1990.

Education: Wensleydale Comprehensive School, Leyburn; Open University (Diploma German; MBA); German.

Non-political career: Executive officer, HM Diplomatic Services, London 1987-89; Sales, marketing and business administration 1989-2015; Director, DM Electronics Ltd 1991-.

Political career: Contested Newcastle upon Tyne Central 2005 and Tynemouth 2010 general elections. Member for Aldridge-Brownhills since 7 May 2015 general election; PPS: to Jo Johnson as Minister of State for Universities, Science, Research and Innovation, Department for Business, Energy and Industrial Strategy 2016-17, to Priti Patel as Secretary of State for International Development 2017; Assistant Government Whip 2018-19; Parliamentary Under-Secretary of State, Ministry of Justice 2019-20; Parliamentary Under-Secretary of State (Minister for the European Neighbourhood and Americas): Foreign and Commonwealth Office and Department for International Development 2020, Foreign, Commonwealth and Development Office 2020-. *Select committees:* Member: International Development 2015-17, Regulatory Reform 2015-17, Arms Export Controls 2016-17, Backbench Business 2016. Chair, Richmond Conservative Association 2012-14; Vice-chair (Social Action), Conservative Party 2013-14. *Councils and public bodies:* Councillor, Richmondshire District Council 2002-06.

Political interests: EU referendum, communities, local business, local environment, business, enterprise.

Other: Volunteer, Project Umubano. Rotary Club.

Recreations: Running, cooking.

Wendy Morton MP, House of Commons, London SW1A 0AA
Tel: 020 7219 8784 *Email:* wendy.morton.mp@parliament.uk
Constituency: 82 Walsall Road, Aldridge, Walsall WS9 0JW
Tel: 01922 452228 Website: wendymorton.co.uk *Twitter:* @morton_wendy

CONSERVATIVE

MULLAN, KIERAN

Crewe and Nantwich *(Majority 8,508)*

Kieran John Mullan. Born June 1984.

Non-political career: A&E Doctor; Volunteer, Special Constable 2014-18; Founder and CEO, ValueYou 2014-.

Political career: Contested Birmingham Hodge Hill 2015 and Wolverhampton South East 2017 general elections. Member for Crewe and Nantwich since 12 December 2019. *Select committees:* Member, Justice 2020-.

Political interests: NHS, social care, schools funding including special needs.

Dr Kieran Mullan MP, House of Commons, London SW1A 0AA
Tel: 020 7219 6819 *Email:* kieran.mullan.mp@parliament.uk
Constituency: 249 Edleston Road, Crewe CW2 7EA
Tel: 020 3882 1829 Website: www.drkieranmullan.org.uk *Twitter:* @KieranMullanUK

House of Commons MPs' Biographies

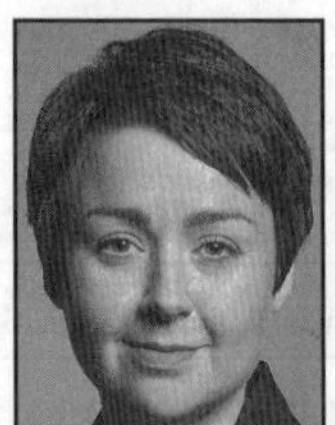

CONSERVATIVE

MUMBY-CROFT, HOLLY

Scunthorpe *(Majority 6,451)*

Married Paul (1 daughter).

Education: Sir John Nelthorpe School, Brigg; Brigg Sixth Form College; Lincoln University (English and history).

Political career: Contested Scunthorpe 2017 general election. Member for Scunthorpe since 12 December 2019. *Councils and public bodies:* North Lincolnshire Council: Councillor 2015-, Lead Member for Young People and Skills.

Holly Mumby-Croft MP, House of Commons, London SW1A 0AA
Tel: 020 7219 3000 *Email:* holly.mumbycroft.mp@parliament.uk
Constituency: Ground Floor, 45 Oswald Road, Scunthorpe DN15 7PN
Tel: 0161-818 9390 Website: www.hollymumbycroft.org.uk

CONSERVATIVE

MUNDELL, DAVID

Dumfriesshire, Clydesdale and Tweeddale *(Majority 3,781)*

David Gordon Mundell. Born 27 May 1962; Son of Dorah Mundell, hotelier; Married Lynda Carmichael 1987 (divorced) (2 sons 1 daughter).

Education: Lockerbie Academy; Edinburgh University (LLB 1984); Strathclyde University Business School (MBA 1991); French, German.

Non-political career: Solicitor, Maxwell Waddell 1987-89; Corporate lawyer, Biggart Baillie & Gifford, Glasgow 1989-91; BT Scotland: Group legal adviser 1991-98, Head of national affairs 1998-99.

Political career: Member for Dumfriesshire, Clydesdale and Tweeddale since 5 May 2005 general election; Shadow Secretary of State for Scotland 2005-10; Parliamentary Under-Secretary of State, Scotland Office 2010-15; Secretary of State for Scotland 2015-19. *Select committees:* Member: Scottish Affairs 2005-10, Public Administration and Constitutional Affairs 2020-, Panel of Chairs 2020-. Contested Dumfries constituency 1999 and 2003 Scottish Parliament elections. MSP for South of Scotland region 1999-2005. Chair, Scottish Conservative and Unionist Party 1007-09, 2011-14. *Councils and public bodies:* Councillor: Annandale and Eskdale District Council 1984-86, Dumfries and Galloway Council 1986-87.

Political interests: Scotland, rural affairs, LGBT+, Nutrition for Growth; Commonwealth, South America, USA.

Other: Member, Executive Committee, Commonwealth Parliamentary Association United Kingdom 2020-; Trustee, Lockerbie Trust; Law Society of Scotland 1986-; Society of Writers to Her Majesty's Signet; PC 2010.

Rt Hon David Mundell MP, House of Commons, London SW1A 0AA
Tel: 020 7219 4895 *Email:* david.mundell.mp@parliament.uk
Constituency: Monro House, Duncan Drive, Moffat, Dumfriesshire DG10 9JW
Tel: 01683 222746 *Email:* david@davidmundell.com Website: www.davidmundell.com
Twitter: @DavidMundellDCT

LABOUR

MURRAY, IAN

Edinburgh South *(Majority 11,095)*

Shadow Secretary of State for Scotland

Born 10 August 1976; Son of Lena Murray and late James Brownlie Murray; Partner Mariam (1 daughter).

Education: Wester Hailes Education Centre; Edinburgh University (MA social policy and law 1997).

Non-political career: Royal Blind Asylum 1996-97; Aegon UK 1998-99; Operations director, Internet TV station 1999-2001; Director, 100mph Events Ltd 2001-; Partner, Alibi Bars 2005-11. Member: USDAW, Community.

Political career: Member for Edinburgh South since 6 May 2010 general election; PPS to Ivan Lewis as Shadow Secretary of State for Culture, Media and Sport 2010-11; Shadow Minister for: Business, Innovation and Skills 2011-13, Trade and Investment 2013-15; Shadow Secretary of State for Scotland 2015-16, 2020-; Member, Public Accounts Commission

2015-17. *Select committees:* Member: Environmental Audit 2010-12, Business, Innovation and Skills 2010-11, Arms Export Controls 2010-12, Scottish Affairs 2016-17, Foreign Affairs 2016-20. Vice-chair, PLP Departmental Group for Culture, Olympics, Media and Sport 2010-11. Member: Labour Party, Co-operative Party; Campaign manager, Edinburgh Pentlands, 2001 general election; Westminster Spokesperson for Scottish Labour, Scottish Shadow Cabinet 2016-17. *Councils and public bodies:* Councillor, Edinburgh City Council 2003-10.

Political interests: Education, services for disabled people, social justice, equal opportunities, environment, conservation, business; South America, Middle East, Nepal, USA.

Other: UK Delegation, Parliamentary Assembly of the Council of Europe: Substitute Member 2016-17, Member 2018-; Executive Committee, Commonwealth Parliamentary Association United Kingdom: Member 2017-19, Vice-chair 2020-; More United; Open Britain; People's Vote Campaign; Member, Fabian Society; Trustee, Great War Memorial Committee; McCrae's Battalion Trust 2007-; Fellow, Industry and Parliament Trust 2011-15; Chair, Foundation of Hearts 2013-15; Director, Heart of Midlothian Football Club plc 2014-15; Scottish Labour for the Single Market and Customs Union 2016-19; Labour for the Single Market and Customs Union 2017-19; Supporter: Care for the Wild, Amnesty International.

Publications: This is our story: How the supporters kept their Hearts beating (2019).

Recreations: Sport, reading, cooking, cycling.

Ian Murray MP, House of Commons, London SW1A 0AA
Tel: 020 7219 7064 *Email:* ian.murray.mp@parliament.uk
Constituency: 31 Minto Street, Edinburgh EH9 2BT
Tel: 0131-662 4520 Website: www.ianmurraymp.com *Twitter:* @ianmurraymp

LABOUR/ CO-OPERATIVE

MURRAY, JAMES

Ealing North *(Majority 12,269)*

Shadow Financial Secretary

James Stewart Murray. Born 13 July 1983.

Education: Oxford University (politics, philosophy and economics).

Non-political career: Management Consultant; Parliamentary Aide to Emily Thornberry MP; Deputy Mayor for Housing, London Assembly 2016-19.

Political career: Member for Ealing North since 12 December 2019; Opposition Whip 2020; Shadow Minister for Treasury (Shadow Financial Secretary) 2020-. *Select committees:* Member, Health and Social Care 2020. *Councils and public bodies:* Islington Council: Councillor 2006-16, Executive Member for Housing and Development.

Political interests: Housing.

James Murray MP, House of Commons, London SW1A 0AA
Tel: 020 7219 3931 *Email:* james.murray.mp@parliament.uk
Constituency: No constituency office publicised
Website: www.jamesmurray.org *Twitter:* @jamesmurray_ldn

CONSERVATIVE

MURRAY, SHERYLL

South East Cornwall *(Majority 20,971)*

Born 4 February 1956; Married Neil (died 2011) (1 son 1 daughter); Married Bob Davidson 2019.

Education: Torpoint Comprehensive School.

Non-political career: Insurance and NHS.

Political career: Member for South East Cornwall since 6 May 2010 general election; PPS: to Ed Vaizey as Minister of State for Culture and the Digital Economy, Departments for Business, Innovation and Skills and for Culture, Media and Sport 2015-16, to Andrea Leadsom: as Minister of State, Department of Energy and Climate Change 2015-16, as Secretary of State for Environment, Food and Rural Affairs 2016-17. *Select committees:* Member: Environmental Audit 2010-12, Environment, Food and Rural Affairs 2012-15, 2017-, High Speed Rail (West Midlands – Crewe) Bill 2018-19, Panel of Chairs 2020-. Member, Executive, 1922 Committee 2012-15, 2017-. *Councils and public bodies:* Former councillor, Cornwall County Council; Caradon District Council: Councillor, Leader, Conservative group.

Political interests: Environment, tourism, Royal Navy; America, Middle East, UK.

Other: President, Palace of Westminster Lions Club 2014-; Fishermen's Mission; Animal Welfare Champion, Charity Champion awards 2012.

Recreations: Formula 1.

Sheryll Murray MP, House of Commons, London SW1A 0AA
Tel: 020 7219 3000 *Email:* sheryll.murray.mp@parliament.uk
Constituency: The Parade, Liskeard, Cornwall PL14 6AF
Tel: 01579 344428 *Email:* sheryll@sheryllmurray.com Website: www.sheryllmurray.com
Twitter: @sheryllmurray

CONSERVATIVE

MURRISON, ANDREW

South West Wiltshire *(Majority 21,630)*

Andrew William Murrison. Born 24 April 1961; Son of William Murrison and Marion Murrison, née Horn; Married Jennifer Munden 1994 (5 daughters).

Education: Harwich High School; The Harwich School; Bristol University (MB CHB 1984; MD 1995); Cambridge University (DPH medicine 1996); French.

Non-political career: Principal medical officer, HM Naval Base Portsmouth 1996-99; Staff officer, Commander-In-Chief Fleet 1999-2000; Locum consultant occupational physician, Gloucestershire Royal Hospital and GP 2000-01. Surgeon Commander Royal Navy 1981-2000; Royal Naval Reserve 2000-: Served in Iraq (Operation Telic II) 2003.

Political career: Member for Westbury 2001-10, for South West Wiltshire since 6 May 2010 general election; Shadow Minister for: Public Services, Health and Education 2003-04, Health 2004-07, Defence 2007-10; PPS to Andrew Lansley as Secretary of State for Health 2010-12; Prime Minister's Special Representative for the Centenary Commemoration of the First World War 2011-14; Parliamentary Under-Secretary of State (International Security Strategy), Ministry of Defence 2012-14; Parliamentary Under-Secretary of State, Northern Ireland Office 2014-15; Trade Envoy to: Morocco 2016-19, 2020-, Tunisia 2016-19; Minister of State: for the Middle East and North Africa, Foreign and Commonwealth Office 2019-20, Department for International Development 2019-20. *Select committees:* Member: Science and Technology 2001-05, Joint Committee on the Draft Investigatory Powers Bill 2015-16, Joint Committee on the National Security Strategy 2015-17, Liaison 2017-19; Chair, Northern Ireland Affairs 2017-19.

Political interests: Health, defence; Morocco, Iraq.

Other: Royal British Legion; Gilbert Blane Medal 1994; PC 2019. Warminster Conservative Club, Royal British Legion Warminster Branch, Vice-president, Trowbridge White Ensign Association, Westbury Lions Club.

Publications: Tommy This an' Tommy That: The Military Covenant (Biteback, 2011).

Recreations: Sailing, skiing.

Rt Hon Dr Andrew Murrison MP, House of Commons, London SW1A 0AA
Tel: 020 7219 8337 *Email:* murrisona@parliament.uk
Constituency: Suite 1, Holloway House, Epsom Square, White Horse Business Park, Trowbridge, Wiltshire BA14 0XG
Tel: 01225 358584 *Email:* packerj@parliament.uk Website: www.andrewmurrison.co.uk
Twitter: @AWMurrison

LABOUR

NANDY, LISA

Wigan *(Majority 6,728)*

Shadow Foreign Secretary

Lisa Eva Nandy. Born 9 August 1979; Daughter of Dipak Nandy, academic and founding director of the Runnymede Trust, and Luise Nandy, television producer.

Education: Parrs Wood Comprehensive School, Manchester; Holy Cross Sixth Form College, Bury; Newcastle University (BA politics 2001); Birkbeck University, London (MSc government, policy and politics 2005).

Non-political career: Parliamentary Assistant to Neil Gerrard MP 2001-03; Policy Researcher, Refugee Children and Families, Centrepoint 2003-05; Policy Adviser, Children's Society 2005-10. Member: Unite, CWU.

Political career: Member for Wigan since 6 May 2010 general election; PPS to Tessa Jowell as Shadow Minister for London and the Olympics 2011-12; Shadow Minister for: Children and Families 2012-13, Cabinet Office 2013-15; Shadow Secretary of State for: Energy and Climate Change 2015-16, Foreign and Commonwealth Affairs (Shadow Foreign Secretary) 2020-. *Select committees:* Member, Education 2010-12. Vice-chair, PLP Departmental Group for Communities and Local Government 2010-11. Member, Wigan Labour Party; Chair, Labour Friends of Palestine and the Middle East. *Councils and public bodies:* London Borough of Hammersmith and Fulham Council: Councillor 2006-10, Shadow Cabinet Member for Housing and Regeneration; Governor, Brackenbury Primary School.

Political interests: Children, poverty, low pay, towns; Palestine.

Other: Director, Lyric Theatre, Hammersmith 2006-10; Member, Amnesty International; Director, Centre for Towns 2017-.

Publications: Author: Waiting in Line: Young Refugees in the Labour Market (Centrepoint, 2003), Bed and Breakfast: Unfit Housing for Young People (Centrepoint, 2005), Co-author, with: Nicola Clarke, Living on the Edge of Despair (The Children's Society, 2008); Caroline Lucas MP and Chris Bowers, The Alternative: Towards a New Progressive Politics (Biteback, 2016).

Recreations: Rugby league, theatre and the arts.

Lisa Nandy MP, House of Commons, London SW1A 0AA
Tel: 020 7219 7188 *Fax:* 020 7219 5152 *Email:* lisa.nandy.mp@parliament.uk
Constituency: Room S46, Second Floor, Wigan Investment Centre, Waterside Drive, Wigan WN3 5BA
Tel: 01942 242047 Website: www.lisanandy.co.uk *Twitter:* @lisanandy

CONSERVATIVE

NEILL, ROBERT

Bromley and Chislehurst *(Majority 10,891)*

Chair, Select Committee on Justice

Robert James Macgillivray Neill. Born 24 June 1952; Son of John Neill and Elsie Neill, née Coombs; Married Daphne White 2009 (dissolved 2015).

Education: Abbs Cross School, Havering; London School of Economics (LLB 1973); French.

Non-political career: Trainee dealer, London Stock Exchange 1974; Barrister in private practice (specialising in criminal law) 1975-2006; Called to the Irish Bar 1990.

Political career: Contested Dagenham 1983 and 1987 general elections. Member for Bromley and Chislehurst 29 June 2006 by-election to 2010, for Bromley and Chislehusrt (revised boundary) since 6 May 2010 general election; Shadow Minister for Communities and Local Government 2007-10 (Local Government 2009-10); Parliamentary Under-Secretary of State, Department for Communities and Local Government 2010-12. *Select committees:* Member, Constitutional Affairs/Justice 2006-10; Justice: Member 2012-13, Chair 2015-; Member: Political and Constitutional Reform 2013-15, Liaison 2015-, Joint Committee on the National Security Strategy 2015-. Greater London Conservatives: Deputy chairman 1993-96, Chair 1996-99; Conservative Party: Deputy chairman (local government) 2008-10, Vice-chairman (local government) 2012-; Founding member, Conservatives for Reform in Europe 2016. *Councils and public bodies:* London Borough of Havering: Councillor 1974-90, Chief whip and chairman of Environment and Social Services Committees; GLC Councillor for Romford 1985-86; Leader, London Fire and Civil Defence Authority 1985-87; Greater London Authority: Member 2000-08, Leader, Conservative group 2000-02; Non-executive board director, North East London Strategic Health Authority 2002-06; Board member, London Regional Arts Council 2003-07.

Political interests: Policing and criminal justice, local government, environment, arts; France, Hungary, Ireland, Italy, Spain, Switzerland.

Other: Member: EU Committee of the Regions 2002-08, Parliamentary Assembly, Council of Europe 2012-; Member: Royal Opera House Trust, Friends of English National Opera; Kt 2020. Carlton Club.

Recreations: Theatre, travel, opera, sailing.

Sir Robert Neill MP, House of Commons, London SW1A 0AA
Tel: 020 7219 8169 *Fax:* 020 7219 8089 *Email:* bob.neill.mp@parliament.uk
Constituency: Bromley and Chislehurst Conservative Association, The Coach House, 1a Queens

Road, Chislehurst, Kent BR7 5AZ
Tel: 020 8295 2639 *Email:* office@bromleyconservatives.co.uk Website: www.bobneill.org.uk
Twitter: @neill_bob

SCOTTISH NATIONAL PARTY

NEWLANDS, GAVIN

Paisley and Renfrewshire North *(Majority 11,902)*

SNP Shadow Secretary of State for Transport and Spokesperson for Sport

Gavin Andrew Stuart Newlands. Born 2 February 1980; Son of Gordon and Isabel Newlands; Married Lynn (2 daughters).

Education: Trinity High School, Renfrew.

Non-political career: Business analyst.

Political career: Member for Paisley and Renfrewshire North since 7 May 2015 general election; SNP: Spokesperson for: Sport 2016-19, 2021-, Northern Ireland and Wales 2018-19, Shadow Secretary of State for Transport 2020-. *Select committees:* Member: Backbench Business 2015-17, Justice 2017-19, Transport 2020-. Fundraiser, Renfrew and Gallowhill SNP. *Councils and public bodies:* Councillor: Renfrew Community Council, Maryhill Community Council.

Political interests: Independence, carers, welfare, Scotland's constitution, CND; Nordic countries, USA.

Other: Member, British-Irish Parliamentary Assembly 2018-20; Brightest Star, Educate the Kids. Paisley Rugby Club: Member, Management Committee, Captain.

Recreations: Sports.

Gavin Newlands MP, House of Commons, London SW1A 0AA
Tel: 020 7219 5583 *Email:* gavin.newlands.mp@parliament.uk
Constituency: 6 Porterfield Road, Renfrew, Renfrewshire PA4 8HG
Tel: 0141-378 0600/0141-378 0601 Website: www.gavinnewlands.scot
Twitter: @GavNewlandsSNP

LABOUR

NICHOLS, CHARLOTTE

Warrington North *(Majority 1,509)*

Shadow Minister for Women and Equalities

Charlotte Louise Nichols. Born 6 April 1991.

Education: Liverpool University (2013).

Non-political career: Usdaw 2013-18; Industrial policy officer, GMB 2018-19.

Political career: Member for Warrington North since 12 December 2019; PPS to: Tracy Brabin as Shadow Secretary of State for Digital, Culture, Media and Sport 2020, Emily Thornberry as Shadow Secretary of State for International Trade 2020, Louise Haigh as Shadow Secretary of State for Northern Ireland 2020; Shadow Minister for Women and Equalities 2020-. *Select committees:* Member: European Statutory Instruments 2020-, European Scrutiny 2020-, Business, Energy and Industrial Strategy 2020-. Women's Officer, Young Labour.

Political interests: Workers' rights, Brexit, NHS, green new deal.

Charlotte Nichols MP, House of Commons, London SW1A 0AA
Tel: 020 7219 3000 *Email:* charlotte.nichols.mp@parliament.uk
Constituency: Orford Jubilee Neighbourhood Hub, Jubilee Way, Warrington WA2 8HE
Website: charlottenicholsmp.com *Twitter:* @charlotte2153

CONSERVATIVE

NICI, LIA

Great Grimsby *(Majority 7,331)*

Lia Nici-Townend. Born 1 August 1969; Married Dave Townend.

Non-political career: Grimsby Institute: Head of Media 2005-09, Creative and Media Business Manager 2009-11; Station Manager and Executive Producer, Estuary TV 2011-18; Self-employer TV Producer 2018-.

Political career: Contested Kingston upon Hull North 2017 general election. Member for Great Grimsby since 12 December 2019. *Select committees:* Member, Backbench Business 2020-. *Councils and public bodies:* Councillor, North East Lincolnshire Council 2018-.

Political interests: NHS, Brexit, policing.

Lia Nici MP, House of Commons, London SW1A 0AA
Tel: 020 7219 6196 *Email:* lia.nici.mp@parliament.uk
Constituency: Unit M03-05, The Hub @ Freeman Street Market, Nelson Street, Grimsby DN32 7DS
Website: www.lianici.org.uk *Twitter:* @lia_nici

SCOTTISH NATIONAL PARTY

NICOLSON, JOHN

Ochil and South Perthshire *(Majority 4,498)*

SNP Shadow Secretary of State for Culture, Media and Sport

John MacKenzie Nicolson. Born 23 June 1961.

Education: Glasgow University (MA); Harvard University, USA (Kennedy Scholarship and Harkness Fellowship).

Non-political career: Speechwriter, Senator Moynihan, US Senate 1985-87; Journalist and broadcaster 1987-2015: Presenter, *Open to Question*, BBC Scotland, Political correspondent, *On the Record*, London, BBC: Reporter: *Newsnight*, *Panorama*, *Public Eye*, Presenter: *BBC Breakfast*, *BBC News 24*.

Political career: Member for East Dunbartonshire 2015-17. Contested East Dunbartonshire 2017 general election. Member for Ochil and South Perthshire since 12 December 2019; SNP: Spokesperson for Culture, Media and Sport 2015-17, Shadow Secretary of State for Culture, Media and Sport 2020-. *Select committees:* Member: Culture, Media and Sport 2015-17, Works of Art 2015-17, Digital, Culture, Media and Sport 2020-.

Other: Scottish and World Student debating champion.

John Nicolson MP, House of Commons, London SW1A 0AA
Tel: 020 7219 3000 *Email:* john.nicolson.mp@parliament.uk
Constituency: 38 Primrose Street, Alloa, Clackmannanshire FK10 1JG
Tel: 01259 211615 Website: johnnicolson.scot *Twitter:* @MrJohnNicolson

CONSERVATIVE

NOKES, CAROLINE

Romsey and Southampton North *(Majority 10,872)*

Chair, Select Committee on Women and Equalities

Caroline Fiona Ellen Nokes. Born 26 June 1972; Daughter of Roy Perry (MEP for Wight and Hampshire South 1994-99 and South East region 1999-2004) and Veronica Haswell; 1 daughter.

Education: La Sagesse Convent, Romsey; Peter Symonds' College, Winchester; Sussex University (BA government and politics 1994); French.

Non-political career: Political researcher to Roy Perry MEP 1994-2004; Consultant, Euro/Arab affairs 2004; Chief executive, National Pony Society 2008-09.

Political career: Contested Southampton Itchen 2001 and Romsey 2005 general elections. Member for Romsey and Southampton North since 6 May 2010 general election; PPS to: Mark Harper as Minister of State for Disabled People, Department for Work and Pensions 2014-15, Robert Goodwill as Minister of State, Department for Transport 2016; Parliamentary Under-Secretary of State for Welfare Delivery, Department for Work and Pensions 2016-17; Parliamentary Secretary (Minister for Government Resilience and Efficiency), Cabinet Office 2017-18; Minister of State for Immigration, Home Office 2018-19. *Select committees:* Member, Environmental Audit 2010-15; Speaker's Advisory Committee on Works of Art: Member 2011-15, 2020-, Chair 2015-16; Member, Education 2014-16; Chair, Women and Equalities

2020-; Member: Panel of Chairs 2020-, Liaison 2020-. Conservative Party whip removed September-October 2019. *Councils and public bodies:* Test Valley Borough Council: Councillor 1999-2011, Leisure portfolio holder 2001-10; Governor, Eastleigh College.

Political interests: Agriculture, sport, environment, education.

Other: Member, UK Delegation, Organisation for Security and Co-operation in Europe Parliamentary Assembly 2015-16; Vice-president, Romsey Hospital Appeal 2001; Trustee, World Horse Welfare 2015-; PC 2018.

Recreations: Riding.

Rt Hon Caroline Nokes MP, House of Commons, London SW1A 0AA
Tel: 020 7219 1468 *Email:* caroline.nokes.mp@parliament.uk
Constituency: Room 4, 13 Market Place, Romsey, Hampshire SO51 8NA
Tel: 01794 521155 Website: www.carolinenokes.com *Twitter:* @carolinenokes

CONSERVATIVE

NORMAN, JESSE

Hereford and South Herefordshire *(Majority 19,686)*

Financial Secretary, HM Treasury

Alexander Jesse Norman. Born 23 June 1962; Married Kate 1992 (2 sons 1 daughter).

Education: Merton College, Oxford (BA classics 1985); University College, London (MPhil philosophy 1999; PhD 2003).

Non-political career: Project director, educational charity, eastern Europe 1988-91; Director, BZW (Barclays de Zoete Wedd) 1991-97; Teaching fellow and lecturer, University College, London 1999-2003; Conservative Research Department 2004-05; Policy adviser to: George Osborne as Shadow Chancellor of the Exchequer 2005, Philip Hammond as Shadow Secretary of State for Work and Pensions 2005-07; Executive director, Policy Exchange 2005-06.

Political career: Member for Hereford and South Herefordshire since 6 May 2010 general election; Parliamentary Under-Secretary of State (Minister for Energy and Industry), Department for Business, Energy and Industrial Strategy 2016-17; Department for Transport: Parliamentary Under-Secretary of State 2017-18, Minister of State 2018-19; HM Treasury: Financial Secretary 2019-, Paymaster General 2019. *Select committees:* Member: Treasury 2010-15, Joint Committees on: Consolidation, Etc, Bills 2010-15, the Draft Enhanced Terrorism Prevention and Investigation Measures Bill 2012-13; House of Commons Governance 2014-15, Liaison 2015-16; Chair, Culture, Media and Sport 2015-16. Chair, Conservative Co-operative Movement 2007-15; Member, 10 Downing Street Policy Advisory Board April-September 2013. *Councils and public bodies:* Former school governor.

Political interests: Big Society, economy, public services, PFI, human rights.

Other: Founder, schoolsfirst.org.uk; Former Board Member, Roundhouse; Former Director, Hay Festival of Literature and the Arts; Vice-President: Ross-on-Wye Horticultural Society, Herefordshire and Gloucestershire Canal Trust, Hereford Musical Theatre Company; Patron: Kindle Centre, Hereford City, Friends of St Mary's, Ross-on-Wye, Herefordshire Mind, Hereford Music Pool, Riding for the Disabled, Herefordshire, St Martin's Church Roof Appeal, Hereford, Yeleni Trust Cancer Care; Vice-president, Westfields Football Club; New Model Institute in Technology and Engineering, Hereford; Honorary Fellow, University College London 2005-10; Visiting Fellow, All Souls College, Oxford 2016-17; Distinguished Fellow, PM Glynn Institute, ACU; Fellow, Royal Historical Society; Parliamentarian of the Year, *Spectator* awards 2012; Commons Backbencher of the Year, *House Magazine* awards 2012; Winner (non-fiction), Parliamentary Book Awards 2018; PC 2019.

Publications: Author: The Achievements of Michael Oakeshott (Gerald Duckworth & Co, 1993), After Euclid (University of Chicago Press, 2005), Compassionate Conservatism (Policy Exchange, 2006); From Here to Fraternity (Centre Forum, 2007); Compassionate Economics (Policy Exchange, 2008); Churchill's Legacy (Liberty, 2009); The Big Society (University of Buckingham Press, 2010) Edmund Burke: Philosopher, Politician, Prophet (William Collins, 2013); Adam Smith: What He Thought, and Why it Matters (Allen Lane, 2018).

Recreations: Music, sports, theatre, hill-walking.

Rt Hon Jesse Norman MP, House of Commons, London SW1A 0AA
Tel: 020 7219 7084 *Email:* jesse.norman.mp@parliament.uk
Constituency: Suite 2a, Penn House, Broad Street, Hereford, Herefordshire HR4 9AP
Tel: 01432 276422 Websites: www.jesse4hereford.com/www.jessenorman.com
Twitter: @jesse_norman

LABOUR/
CO-OPERATIVE

NORRIS, ALEX

Nottingham North *(Majority 4,490)*

Shadow Minister for Public Health and Patient Safety

Alexander James Jordan Norris. Born 4 February 1984; Married Emma 2017.

Education: Manchester Grammar School; Nottingham University (BA history and politics).

Non-political career: Trade Union Representative, GMB and Co-Operative; Area organiser, Unison 2015-17.

Political career: Member for Nottingham North since 8 June 2017; PPS to Jon Ashworth as Shadow Secretary of State for Health/Health and Social Care 2017-19; Opposition Whip 2019-20; Shadow Minister for: International Development 2019-20, Health and Social Care (Public Health and Patient Safety) 2020-. *Select committees:* Member: Home Affairs 2018-19, Joint Committee on the Draft Domestic Abuse Bill 2019, Procedure 2020. Former Secretary, East Midlands Regional Co-operative Party. *Councils and public bodies:* Nottingham City Council: Councillor 2011-17, Cabinet Member for Area Working, Cleansing and Community Safety; Chair of governors, Rosslyn Park Primary School.

Other: Member, Society of Union Employees.

Recreations: Running, Manchester City FC supporter.

Alex Norris MP, House of Commons, London SW1A 0AA
Tel: 020 7219 3899 *Email:* alex.norris.mp@parliament.uk
Constituency: No constituency office publicised
Tel: 0115-975 2377 Website: alexnorrismp.co.uk *Twitter:* @AlexNorrisNN

CONSERVATIVE

O'BRIEN, NEIL

Harborough *(Majority 17,278)*

Neil John O'Brien. Born 6 November 1978; Married Jemma 2012 (2 children).

Education: Greenhead College, Huddersfield; Christ Church, Oxford (BA politics, philosophy and economics 2000).

Non-political career: Director: Open Europe 2005-08, Policy Exchange 2008-12; Special Adviser: HM Treasury 2013-16, Prime Minister's Office 2016-17.

Political career: Member for Harborough since 8 June 2017; Team PPS, Department for Business, Energy and Industrial Strategy 2018-19; PPS to Robert Buckland as Lord Chancellor and Secretary of State for Justice 2019-20. *Select committees:* Member: Science and Technology 2017-19, Standing Orders 2017-. Vice-chair, Conservative Party 2020-. *Councils and public bodies:* Vice-President, Local Government Association 2018-.

Other: OBE 2016.

Neil O'Brien OBE MP, House of Commons, London SW1A 0AA
Tel: 020 7219 1802 *Email:* neil.obrien.mp@parliament.uk
Constituency: 24 Nelson Street, Market Harborough LE16 9AY
Tel: 01858 464146 *Email:* office@harboroughconservatives.com
Website: www.neilobrien.org.uk *Twitter:* @neildotobrien

CONSERVATIVE

OFFORD, MATTHEW

Hendon *(Majority 4,230)*

Matthew James Offord. Born 3 September 1969; Married Claire Rowles 2010.

Education: Amery Hill School, Alton; Nottingham Trent University (BA photography 1992); Lancaster University (MA environment, culture and society 2000); King's College London (PhD rural governance and economic redevelopment).

Non-political career: Media analyst, Medialink Communications 1995-96; Political adviser: Conservative Central Office 1996-97, Local Government Association 1997; Political analyst, BBC 2001-10.

Political career: Contested Barnsley East and Mexborough 2001 general election. Member for Hendon since 6 May 2010 general election; PPS to George Eustice as Minister of State for Farming, Food and the Marine Environment, Department for Environment, Food and Rural Affairs 2015-16. *Select committees:* Member: Environmental Audit 2012-15, 2016-, Joint Committee on Able Marine Energy Park Development Consent Order 2014 2014-15. Chair, Hendon Conservative Association 2004-. *Councils and public bodies:* London Borough of Barnet Council: Councillor 2002-10, Council deputy leader 2006-09, Former cabinet member for: Environment and Transport, Community Safety, Community Engagement.

Political interests: Sub-Saharan Africa, Cyprus, Israel, Middle East, Sri Lanka.

Other: Fellow, Royal Geographical Society; Member, Association of European Parliamentarians for Africa. Welsh Harp's Seahorse Sailing Club.

Recreations: Sailing, scuba diving.

Dr Matthew Offord MP, House of Commons, London SW1A 0AA
Tel: 020 7219 7083 *Email:* matthew.offord.mp@parliament.uk
Constituency: 120 Bunns Lane, Mill Hill, London NW7 2AS
Tel: 020 3114 2131 Website: www.matthewofford.co.uk *Twitter:* @Offord4Hendon

SCOTTISH NATIONAL PARTY

O'HARA, BRENDAN

Argyll and Bute *(Majority 4,110)*

SNP Spokesperson for Human Rights and Conflict Resolution

Born 27 April 1963; Married Catherine (2 daughters).

Education: St Andrew's, Carntyne; Strathclyde University (economic history and modern history 1992).

Non-political career: Glasgow District Council; Television producer, credits include: *Comedy Connections* and *Movie Connections*, BBC, *The Football Years*, STV, *Scotland's Greatest Album*, STV, *Road To Referendum*, STV, Sky Sports.

Political career: Contested Springburn 1987 and Glasgow Central 1992 general elections. Member for Argyll and Bute since 7 May 2015 general election; SNP: Spokesperson for: Defence 2015-17, Culture and Media 2017-18, Inclusive Society 2018-21, Human Rights and Conflict Resolution 2021-. *Select committees:* Member, Digital, Culture, Media and Sport 2017-19.

Political interests: Rural issues, transport.

Other: Member, UK delegation, Parliamentary Assembly of the Organisation for Security and Co-operation in Europe 2020-.

Brendan O'Hara MP, House of Commons, London SW1A 0AA
Tel: 020 7219 8783 *Email:* brendan.ohara.mp@parliament.uk
Constituency: 8 Colquhoun Square, Helensburgh G84 8AD
Tel: 01436 670587 Website: www.brendanoharamp.scot *Twitter:* @BrendanOHaraMP

LIBERAL DEMOCRAT

OLNEY, SARAH

Richmond Park *(Majority 7,766)*

Liberal Democrat Spokesperson for Business, Trade and Transport

Sarah Jane Olney. Born 11 January 1977; Married Ben (1 daughter 1 son).

Education: All Hallows Comprehensive School, Surrey; King's College London (English literature 1998).

Non-political career: Events Planning Manager, Barclays 2004-06; Account Manager, Arts and Business 2006-08; Chief Financial Officer: Distilled Ltd 2008-14, SCi Sales Group 2014-15; Assistant Finance Manager, National Physical Laboratory 2015-16; Financial Accountant, Historic Royal Palaces 2018-19.

Political career: Member for Richmond Park 1 December 2016 by-election to 2017. Contested Richmond Park 2017 general election. Member for Richmond Park since 12 December 2019; Liberal Democrat Spokesperson for: Business 2019-, Trade 2019-20, 2021-, Transport 2020-, Climate Emergency 2020-21, Energy 2020-21. *Select committees:* Member, Public Accounts 2020-.

Political interests: Business, trade, transport, climate change.

Other: Association of Chartered and Certified Accountants.

Sarah Olney MP, House of Commons, London SW1A 0AA
Tel: 020 7219 4821 *Email:* sarah.olney.mp@parliament.uk
Constituency: 108 South Worple Way, East Sheen SW14 8TN
Tel: 020 8876 2986 *Email:* office@saraholneymp.org.uk Website: www.saraholneymp.org.uk
Twitter: @sarahjolney1

LABOUR

ONWURAH, CHI

Newcastle upon Tyne Central *(Majority 12,278)*

Shadow Minister for Science, Research and Digital

Chinyelu Susan Onwurah. Born 12 April 1965; Daughter of Kathleen Onwurah, née Roche, and Dr Moses Onwurah.

Education: Kenton School; Imperial College, London (BEng electrical engineering 1987); Manchester Business School (MBA 2002); French.

Non-political career: Nortel 1987-95; Cable & Wireless 1995-99; Director of product strategy, Global Telesystems UK 1999-2000; Director of market development, Teligent 2000-01; Partner, Hammatan Ventures 2001-04; Head of telecoms technology, OFCOM 2004-10. Member, Unite.

Political career: Member for Newcastle upon Tyne Central since 6 May 2010 general election; Shadow Minister for Business, Innovation and Skills (Innovation, Science and Digital Infrastructure) 2010-13; Board member, Parliamentary Office of Science and Technology (POST); Shadow Minister for: Cabinet Office 2013-15, Business, Innovation and Skills 2015-16, Culture, Media and Sport 2015-16, Industrial Strategy 2016-20, Business, Energy and Industrial Strategy and Digital, Culture, Media and Sport (Science, Research and Digital) 2020-. *Select committees:* Member: Business, Innovation and Skills 2010, Science and Technology 2020. Member, Labour Party 1981-.

Political interests: Education, technology, manufacturing, international development, trade, social mobility; China, France, Nigeria, South Africa.

Other: Board member, Franco-British Council; Former national executive member, Anti-Apartheid Movement; Member, Chatham House; Open University Business School; Honorary Vice-president, Action for South Africa (ACTSA) 2015-; Institute of Engineering Technology; Action for South Africa; Fellow: Institute of Engineering and Technology, City and Guilds Institute.

Recreations: Reading, music, country walks.

Chi Onwurah MP, House of Commons, London SW1A 0AA
Tel: 020 7219 7114 *Email:* chi.onwurah.mp@parliament.uk
Constituency: Suite 24, 7-15 Pink Lane, Newcastle upon Tyne, Tyne and Wear NE1 5DW
Tel: 0191-232 5838 *Email:* carol.stanners@parliament.uk Website: www.chionwurahmp.com
Twitter: @ChiOnwurah

House of Commons MPs' Biographies

CONSERVATIVE

OPPERMAN, GUY

Hexham *(Majority 10,549)*

Parliamentary Under-Secretary of State for Pensions and Financial Inclusion, Department for Work and Pensions

Guy Thomas Opperman. Born 18 May 1965; Son of Michael and Julie Opperman; Married Flora (née Coleman).

Education: Harrow School; Lille University, France (Diploma 1984); Buckingham University (LLB 1987); Bar Vocational Course 1989; French.

Non-political career: Farmer near Arusha, Tanzania 1987-88; Director, TD Chrome Ltd (family engineering business) (unpaid) -2009; Called to the Bar, Middle Temple 1989; Barrister, 3 Paper Buildings 1991-2010; Adviser to Michael Ancram as Shadow Secretary of State for Foreign and Commonwealth Affairs (unpaid) 2001-03.

Political career: Contested North Swindon 1997 and Caernarfon 2005 general elections. Member for Hexham since 6 May 2010 general election; PPS to: Mark Harper as Minister of State for Immigration, Home Office 2012-14, James Brokenshire as Minister of State for Security and Immigration, Home Office 2014-15; Assistant Government Whip 2015-16; Government Whip (Lord Commissioner of HM Treasury) 2016-17; Parliamentary Under-Secretary of State for Pensions and Financial Inclusion, Department for Work and Pensions 2017-. *Councils and public bodies:* Councillor, Marlborough, Wiltshire 1995-99.

Political interests: Prison reform and sentencing, health, fuel poverty, tourism, apprenticeships and youth training, equal pay, Northumberland; Falkland Islands, India, Syria.

Other: Member: Countryside Alliance, Prudhoe Allotments; Co-founder, Tynedale Community Bank; Help for Heroes, Injured Jockeys Fund, Save the Children, Tynedale Hospice at Home, Children with Leukaemia, Great North Air Ambulance Service; Bar Pro Bono Award for Services to Victim Support 2007; Pro Bono Champion Award for Services to Pro Bono and local community hospital campaign 2009. Albert Edward Club, Hexham.

Publications: 150 journalist articles; Author, Doing Time: Prisons in the 21st Century (Bretwalda Books, 2012).

Recreations: Cricket, amateur steeplechase jockey.

Guy Opperman MP, House of Commons, London SW1A 0AA
Tel: 020 7219 1925 *Email:* guy.opperman.mp@parliament.uk
Constituency: Suite 2, St Matthews House, Hexham, Northumberland NE46 3PU
Tel: 01434 239205 Websites: www.guyopperman.co.uk/www.guyopperman.blogspot.com
Twitter: @GuyOpperman

LABOUR

OPPONG-ASARE, ABENA

Erith and Thamesmead *(Majority 3,758)*

Shadow Exchequer Secretary

Born 8 February.

Education: Kent University (BA politics with international relations 2004; LLM international law with international relations 2005).

Non-political career: Complaint's Officer, Children's Trust, Hammersmith and Fulham Council 2006; House of Commons: Parliamentary assistant 2006, Constituency Liaison Officer for Minister of State, Department of Energy and Climate Change 2007-10, Independent adviser to Shadow Minister for Preventing Violence Against Women and Girls 2015, Member, Race Equality Advisory Group 2016-17; Researcher and Office Manager (maternity cover), BLF, London 2006-07; Researcher, Imported Food Division, Food Standards Agency 2007; Research Support Officer/Research Policy Lead on Equalities, Greater London Authority 2010-18; Grenfell Community Liaison Manager (on secondment from Greater London Authority) 2017.

Political career: Member for Erith and Thamesmead since 12 December 2019; PPS to: Luke Pollard as Shadow Secretary of State for Environment, Food and Rural Affairs 2020, Anneliese Dodds as Shadow Chancellor of the Exchequer 2020, Bridget Phillipson as Shadow Chief Secretary to the Treasury 2020; Shadow Minister for Treasury (Shadow Exchequer Secretary) 2020-. *Select committees:* Member, Housing, Communities and Local Government 2020-.

Executive Committee Member, Labour Women's Network 2017-. *Councils and public bodies:* Bexley Council: Councillor 2014-18, Deputy Leader of the Opposition 2014-16, Shadow Cabinet Member for Education 2014-16.

Other: Member, UK delegation, NATO Parliamentary Assembly 2020-; Head of Policy, Research and Stakeholder Relations, Fabian Women's Network 2013-17.

Abena Oppong-Asare MP, House of Commons, London SW1A 0AA
Tel: 020 7219 3000 *Email:* abena.oppongasare.mp@parliament.uk
Constituency: 315 Bexley Road, Erith DA8 3HB
Website: www.abenaoppongasare.com *Twitter:* @abenaopp

LABOUR/ CO-OPERATIVE

OSAMOR, KATE

Edmonton *(Majority 16,015)*

Kate Ofunne Osamor. Born 15 August 1968; Daughter of Martha Osamor (now Baroness Osamor (qv)); 1 son.

Education: Fortismere School; University of East London (BA third world studies and international development 2006).

Non-political career: Executive assistant, Camidoc GP Out Of Hours 2002-10; Practice Manager: Sterndale Surgery, Hammersmith 2012-13, Park Lodge Medical Centre, Enfield 2013-15. Unite the Union.

Political career: Member for Edmonton since 7 May 2015 general election; PPS to Jeremy Corbyn as Leader of the Opposition 2015-16; Shadow Minister for Women and Equalities Office 2016; Shadow Secretary of State for International Development 2016-18. *Select committees:* Member: Education 2015-16, Petitions 2015-16, Joint Committee on Consolidation, &c, Bills 2015-17, International Development 2020-, Work of the Independent Commission for Aid Impact Sub-committee 2020-, Arms Export Controls 2020-. Member, Labour: BAME 2012-13, National Executive Committee 2014-15, 2016-18.

Other: Member, UK delegation, Parliamentary Assembly of the Council of Europe 2015-16.

Kate Osamor MP, House of Commons, London SW1A 0AA
Tel: 020 7219 6602 *Email:* kate.osamor.mp@parliament.uk
Constituency: 37 Market Square, Edmonton Green Shopping Centre, London N9 0TZ
Tel: 020 8803 0574 *Email:* edmontonconstituency@parliament.uk
Website: www.kateosamor.co.uk *Twitter:* @KateOsamor

LABOUR

OSBORNE, KATE

Jarrow *(Majority 7,120)*

Katharine Helen Brooks-Osborne.

Education: Sudbury Upper School, Suffolk.

Non-political career: Unite National Trade Union Representative, Royal Mail 1994-; Registered foster carer. Member, executive council, Unite.

Political career: Member for Jarrow since 12 December 2019; PPS to Diane Abbott as Shadow Home Secretary 2020. *Select committees:* Member, Women and Equalities 2020-. Union representative, national constitutional committee, Labour Party. *Councils and public bodies:* Councillor, North Tyneside Council 2014-.

Other: Member, Amnesty International.

Kate Osborne MP, House of Commons, London SW1A 0AA
Tel: 020 7219 3000 *Email:* kate.osborne.mp@parliament.uk
Constituency: The Clervaux Exchange, Clervaux Terrace, Jarrow NE32 5UP
Tel: 0191-466 1509 *Twitter:* @KateOsborneMP

SCOTTISH NATIONAL PARTY

OSWALD, KIRSTEN

East Renfrewshire *(Majority 5,426)*

Deputy Leader, SNP Westminster Group and Shadow Minister for Women and Equalities

Kirsten Frances Oswald. Born 21 December 1972; Married (2 sons).

Education: Carnoustie High School; Glasgow University (MA history 2005).

Non-political career: Human Resources, Motherwell College 1998-2002; Head of Human Resources, South Lanarkshire College 2002-15.

Political career: Member for East Renfrewshire 2015-17. Contested East Renfrewshire 2017 general election. Member for East Renfrewshire since 12 December 2019; SNP: Spokesperson for Armed Forces and Veterans 2015-17, Shadow Secretary of State for Northern Ireland and Wales 2020-21, Spokesperson for Work, Pensions and Inclusion 2020-21; Deputy Leader, Westminster Group 2020-, Shadow Minister for Women and Equalities 2021-. *Select committees:* Member, Armed Forces Bill 2015 2015-16. SNP: Member 2014-, Member, Eastwood branch, Group Executive Member 2015-, Business Convener 2018-. *Councils and public bodies:* Community councillor.

Political interests: Equalities, engagement.

Other: Member, British-Irish Parliamentary Assembly 2020-; Committee Member, Women for Independence East Renfrewshire -2014.

Recreations: Sports fan.

Kirsten Oswald MP, House of Commons, London SW1A 0AA
Tel: 020 7219 3000 *Email:* kirsten.oswald.mp@parliament.uk
Constituency: Spiersbridge House, 1 Spiersbridge Way, Thornliebank G46 8NG
Tel: 0141-648 8822 Website: www.kirstenoswaldmp.scot *Twitter:* @kirstenoswald

LABOUR

OWATEMI, TAIWO

Coventry North West *(Majority 208)*

PPS to Nick Thomas-Symonds as Shadow Home Secretary

Education: Kent University (MSc pharmacy).

Non-political career: Senior Oncology Pharmacist.

Political career: Member for Coventry North West since 12 December 2019; PPS to Nick Thomas-Symonds as Shadow Home Secretary 2020-. *Select committees:* Member: Health and Social Care 2020-, International Trade 2020-.

Political interests: Future of the NHS, ending the housing crisis, tackling knife crime.

Taiwo Owatemi MP, House of Commons, London SW1A 0AA
Tel: 020 7219 5842 *Email:* taiwo.owatemi.mp@parliament.uk
Constituency: No constituency office publicised
Tel: 024 7625 7870 *Twitter:* @TaiwoOwatemi

LABOUR

OWEN, SARAH

Luton North *(Majority 9,247)*

Sarah Mei Li Owen. 1 daughter.

Education: The Grove; Sussex University (BA international relations; MA human rights).

Non-political career: Healthcare Assistant, Conquest Hospital; Emergency Planning Department, London Fire Brigade; Political Assistant, Brighton and Hove City Council; Political Adviser to Lord Sugar. Representative, GMB.

Political career: Contested Hastings and Rye 2015 general election. Member for Luton North since 12 December 2019; PPS to: Lisa Nandy as Shadow Foreign Secretary 2020, Rachel Reeves as Shadow Chancellor of the Duchy of Lancaster 2020. *Select committees:* Member, Health and Social Care 2020-. Chair, PLP Department Group for Health 2020-. Chair, Chinese For Labour; Member, National Executive Committee, Labour -2019.

Sarah Owen MP, House of Commons, London SW1A 0AA
Tel: 020 7219 8434 *Email:* sarah.owen.mp@parliament.uk
Constituency: 3 Union Street, Luton LU1 3AN
Tel: 01582 488208 Website: sarahleeowen.wixsite.com/sarah-owen *Twitter:* @SarahOwen_

DEMOCRATIC UNIONIST PARTY

PAISLEY, IAN

North Antrim *(Majority 12,721)*

DUP Spokesperson for Culture, Media and Sport and Communities and Local Government

Ian Richard Kyle Paisley. Born 12 December 1966; Son of late Ian Paisley (MP for North Antrim 1970-85 and 1986-2010, MEP for Northern Ireland 1979-2004, MLA for North Antrim 1998-2011, later Lord Bannside) and Eileen Paisley, née Cassells (now Baroness Paisley of St George's); Married Fiona Currie 1990 (2 daughters 2 sons).

Education: Shaftesbury House College; Methodist College, Belfast; Queen's University, Belfast (BA modern history 1989; MSc Irish politics 1992).

Non-political career: Researcher, author and political assistant.

Political career: Member for North Antrim since 6 May 2010 general election; DUP Spokesperson for: Work and Pensions 2010-15, Environment, Food and Rural Affairs 2010-15, Culture, Media and Sport 2015-, Communities and Local Government 2015-, Energy and Climate Change 2015-17; Suspended from House of Commons September-October 2018. *Select committees:* Member: Northern Ireland Affairs 2010-16, 2017-, House of Commons Governance 2014-15, Joint Committee on the Palace of Westminster 2015-16, Panel of Chairs 2016-. Member Northern Ireland Forum for Political Dialogue 1996-98; MLA for North Antrim 1998-2010: Member, Preparation for Government Committee 2006-07; Junior Minister, Office of First and Deputy First Minister 2007-08; Chair, Agriculture and Rural Development Committee 2009-10. DUP membership suspended July-September 2018. *Councils and public bodies:* Lay visitor, Police Holding Centres for the Police Authority 1996-2001; Member, Northern Ireland Policing Board 2001-07, 2008-10.

Political interests: Justice, Europe, agriculture, policing, foreign policy; Africa, China, Middle East, USA.

Other: Member: Executive Committee: Inter-Parliamentary Union, British Group 2012-14, Commonwealth Parliamentary Association UK 2015-16, 2017-19, UK Delegation to Parliamentary Assembly, Council of Europe 2020-; British Motorcycle Federation; Fellow, University of Maryland School of Leadership, Washington DC, USA; Royal Humane Society for Life Saving 1999.

Publications: Reasonable Doubt – The Case for the UDR4; Echoes; Peace Deal; Ian Paisley – A Life in Photographs.

Recreations: Rugby, reading, motor racing, collector of 19th century cartoons and political caricatures, motorcycling.

Ian Paisley MP, House of Commons, London SW1A 0AA
Tel: 020 7219 7116 *Fax:* 020 7219 2996 *Email:* ian.paisley.mp@parliament.uk
Constituency: 9-11 Church Street, Ballymena, Co Antrim BT43 6DD
Tel: 028 2564 1421 *Email:* info@ianpaisleymp.co.uk Website: www.ianpaisleymp.co.uk

CONSERVATIVE

PARISH, NEIL

Tiverton and Honiton *(Majority 24,239)*

Chair, Select Committee on Environment, Food and Rural Affairs

Neil Quentin Gordon Parish. Born 26 May 1956; Married Sue Edwards 1981 (1 son 1 daughter).

Education: Brymore School; Taunton College.

Non-political career: Former farmer and businessman.

Political career: Contested Torfaen 1997 general election. Member for Tiverton and Honiton since 6 May 2010 general election; PPS to John Hayes as Minister of State, Department for Transport 2014-15. *Select committees:* Environment, Food and Rural Affairs: Member 2010-15, Chair 2015-; Chair, Environment, Food and Rural Affairs Sub-committee 2015-17; Member: Liaison 2015-, National Policy Statements Sub-committee 2017-19. Chair, Conservative Party Committee for Environment -2015. MEP for South West 1999-2009: Conservative agriculture spokesperson, President, Animal Welfare Intergroup, Chair: Australia and New Zealand Delegation 2004-07, Agriculture and Rural Development Committee 2007-09. Chair, Bridgwater Conservative Assocation 1997-99; Founding member, Conservatives for Reform in Europe 2016. *Councils and public bodies:* Sedgemoor District Council: Councillor 1983-95, Deputy Leader 1989-95; Councillor, Somerset County Council 1989-93.

Political interests: Regional policy, animal welfare, agriculture; China, Israel, Slovenia, Zimbabwe.

Other: Election monitor, Zimbabwe 2000; Founding supporter, Change Britain 2016-; Brains Trust.

Recreations: Swimming, music, country life, debating.

Neil Parish MP, House of Commons, London SW1A 0AA
Tel: 020 7219 7172 *Fax:* 020 7219 5005 *Email:* neil.parish.mp@parliament.uk
Constituency: No constituency office publicised
Website: www.neilparish.co.uk *Twitter:* @neil_parish

CONSERVATIVE

PATEL, PRITI

Witham *(Majority 24,082)*

Home Secretary

Priti Sushil Patel. Born 29 March 1972; Married Alex Sawyer.

Education: Watford Grammar School for Girls; Keele University (BA economics 1994); Essex University (Diploma British government and politics 1995).

Non-political career: Corporate communications.

Political career: Contested Nottingham North 2005 general election. Member for Witham since 6 May 2010 general election; Prime Minister's Indian Diaspora Champion 2013-; Exchequer Secretary, HM Treasury 2014-15; Minister of State for Employment, Department for Work and Pensions 2015-16; Secretary of State for: International Development 2016-17, Home Department (Home Secretary) 2019-. *Select committees:* Member: Members' Expenses 2011-15, Public Administration 2011-14, Joint Committee on Draft Deregulation Bill 2013, Foreign Affairs 2018-19, Arms Export Controls 2018-19. Member, Executive, 1922 Committee 2010-14. Elected Member, Conservative Party Board 2010-14; Member, Number 10 Policy Advisory Board 2013-14.

Political interests: Trade, business, the economy, Europe, law and order, immigration; Africa, Asia, India, Middle East.

Other: Member, Campaign committee, Vote Leave 2016; Vice-president, CHAPS; Patron, Dancing Giraffe; Honorary member, Holdfast Credit Union Ltd; Trustee, Crossroads Care Braintree District and Chelmsford; Crossroads Care Braintree and Witham, Brainwave Witham, Homestart Witham, Royal British Legion Witham; PC 2015.

Publications: Co-author (with Kwasi Kwarteng MP, Dominic Raab MP, Chris Skidmore MP and Elizabeth Truss MP), Britannia Unchained: Global Lessons for Growth and Prosperity (Palgrave Macmillan, 2012).

Recreations: Horse racing, cricket, travel, music.

Rt Hon Priti Patel MP, House of Commons, London SW1A 0AA
Tel: 020 7219 3528 *Fax:* 020 7219 5192 *Email:* withammp@parliament.uk
Constituency: No constituency office publicised
Website: www.priti4witham.co.uk *Twitter:* @pritipatel

CONSERVATIVE

PATERSON, OWEN

North Shropshire *(Majority 22,949)*

Owen William Paterson. Born 24 June 1956; Son of late Alfred and Cynthia Paterson; Married Hon Rose Ridley 1980 (died 2020) (2 sons 1 daughter).

Education: Radley College, Oxfordshire; Corpus Christi College, Cambridge (MA history 1978); French, German.

Non-political career: British Leather Co Ltd: Sales director 1985-93, Managing director 1993-99; Consultant: Randox Laboratories Ltd 2015-, Lynn's Country Foods Ltd 2016-.

Political career: Contested Wrexham 1992 general election. Member for North Shropshire since 1 May 1997 general election; Opposition Whip 2000-01; PPS to Iain Duncan Smith as Leader of the Opposition 2001-03; Shadow Minister for: Environment, Food and Rural Affairs 2003-05, Transport 2005-07; Shadow Secretary of State for Northern Ireland 2007-10; Secretary of State for: Northern Ireland 2010-12, Environment, Food and Rural Affairs 2012-14. *Select committees:* Member: Welsh Affairs 1997-2001, European Standing Committee A 1998-2001, Welsh Grand Committee 1998-2000, European Scrutiny 1999-2000, Agriculture 2000-01. Conservative Party Committees: Joint Vice-chair, Environment, Transport and Regions 1999-2001, Joint Secretary, European Affairs 1999-2001, Secretary, Foreign and Commonwealth Affairs 1999-2001. Member: 92 Group 1997-, Conservative Friends of Israel 1997-, Conservative Way Forward 1997-, Conservative 2000 1997-; Vice-President, Conservatives Against a Federal Europe 1998-2001, Member: No Turning Back Group 1998-, Executive, 1922 Committee 2000; Vice-President, Conservatives for Britain 2015-16.

Political interests: Trade, industry, agriculture, foreign affairs, economy, social justice, Northern Ireland; China, Western and Eastern Europe, India, USA.

Other: President, Cotance (European Tanners' Confederation) 1996-98; Member: Inter-Parliamentary Union 1997-, Commonwealth Parliamentary Association 1997-; Member, Advisory Board, European Foundation 1998-; Director, Orthopaedic Institute Ltd, Oswestry; Member, Countryside Alliance; Royal Irish Regiment Benevolent Fund, Midlands Centre for Spinal Injuries, Ellesmere Community Care Centre Trust; Liveryman, Leathersellers' Company; PC 2010. Patron, Oswestry Cricket Club; Member, Shropshire Cricket Club.

Rt Hon Owen Paterson MP, House of Commons, London SW1A 0AA
Tel: 020 7219 5185 *Fax:* 020 7219 3955 *Email:* patersono@parliament.uk
Constituency: No constituency office publicised
Tel: 01978 710073 *Email:* rose@repaterson.co.uk Website: www.owenpaterson.org
Twitter: @OwenPaterson

CONSERVATIVE

PAWSEY, MARK

Rugby *(Majority 13,447)*

Mark Julian Francis Pawsey. Born 16 January 1957; Son of James Pawsey (MP for Rugby 1979-83 and Rugby and Kenilworth 1983-97) and Cynthia Pawsey; Married Tracy Harris 1984 (2 sons 2 daughters).

Education: Lawrence Sheriff Grammar School, Rugby; Reading University (estate management 1978); French.

Non-political career: Trainee Surveyor, Strutt and Parker 1978-79; Account Manager, Autobar Vending Supplies Ltd 1979-82; Managing Director, Central Catering Supplies Ltd 1982-2008. Member, Armed Forces Parliamentary Scheme.

Political career: Contested Nuneaton 2005 general election. Member for Rugby since 6 May 2010 general election; PPS: to Anna Soubry as Minister of State: for Defence Personnel, Welfare and Veterans, Ministry of Defence 2014-15, for Small Business, Industry and Enterprise, Department for Business, Innovation and Skills 2015-16, to Damian Green as Secretary of State for Work and Pensions 2016-17. *Select committees:* Member: Communities and Local Government 2010-15, Business, Energy and Industrial Strategy 2017-, Joint Committee on the Draft Registration of Overseas Entities Bill 2019. Member, Executive, 1922 Committee 2017-. *Councils and public bodies:* Councillor, Rugby Borough Council 2002-07; Vice-President, Local Government Association 2018-.

Political interests: Planning, environment, local government, trade, vaping, business and industrial strategy; China, India, Middle East, Pakistan, Rwanda.

Other: Parkinson's UK, Air Ambulance, DeafKidz International, Friends of the Hospital of St Cross (Rugby), Haemochromatosis UK; FSB Member of Parliament Small Business Friendly Award 2014, 2015. Chairman, Commons and Lords RFC; Old Laurentian RFC.

Recreations: Village life, rugby, wine appreciation.

Mark Pawsey MP, House of Commons, London SW1A 0AA
Tel: 020 7219 7136 *Email:* mark.pawsey.mp@parliament.uk
Constituency: Albert Buildings, 2 Castle Mews, Rugby CV21 2XL
Tel: 01788 579499 Website: www.markpawsey.org.uk *Twitter:* @markpawsey

LABOUR

PEACOCK, STEPHANIE

Barnsley East *(Majority 3,217)*

Shadow Minister for Flooding

Stephanie Louise Peacock. Born 19 December 1986.

Education: Queen Mary, University of London (BA modern and contemporary history 2010); Canterbury Christ Church University (PGCE 2011); Institute of Education, University of London (MA 2013).

Non-political career: Parliamentary Assistant to Sylvia Heal MP 2005-10; Secondary school history and politics teacher 2010-12; Trade union training officer, Usdaw 2012-13; Regional political officer, GMB 2013-17.

Political career: Contested Halesowen and Rowley Regis 2015 general election. Member for Barnsley East since 8 June 2017; Opposition Whip 2018-19; Shadow Minister for: Cabinet Office 2020, Shadow Minister for Environment, Food and Rural Affairs (Flooding) 2020-. *Select committees:* Member: Science and Technology 2017, International Trade 2017-18, Women and Equalities 2019, Northern Ireland Affairs 2020-. Labour Party: Member, NEC, West Midlands representative, National Policy Forum.

Political interests: Education, worker's rights.

Stephanie Peacock MP, House of Commons, London SW1A 0AA
Tel: 020 7219 4129 *Email:* stephanie.peacock.mp@parliament.uk
Constituency: West Bank House, West Street, Hoyland, Barnsley S74 9EE
Tel: 01226 743483 Website: www.stephaniepeacock.org.uk *Twitter:* @Steph_Peacock

CONSERVATIVE

PENNING, MIKE

Hemel Hempstead *(Majority 14,563)*

Michael Allan Penning. Born 28 September 1957; Son of Freda and Brian Penning; Married Angela Louden 1988 (2 daughters).

Education: Appleton Comprehensive School, Benfleet, Essex; King Edmund Comprehensive School, Rochford, Essex.

Non-political career: Soldier, Grenadier Guards 1974-80; Royal Army Medical Corps (RAMC) 1980-81; Fire Officer, Essex Fire and Rescue Services 1982-88; Freelance Political Journalist, Express Newspapers and News International 1988-92; Politics and Journalism Lecturer, UK and USA 1992-2005; Journalist and Media Adviser to six Shadow Cabinet members 1996-2004; Head of News and Media, Conservative Central Office 2000-04; Director, MA Penning Ltd. Member, FBU 1982-.

Political career: Contested Thurrock 2001 general election. Member for Hemel Hempstead 2005-10, for Hemel Hempstead (revised boundary) since 6 May 2010 general election; Shadow Minister for Health 2007-10; Parliamentary Under-Secretary of State, Department for Transport 2010-12; Minister of State, Northern Ireland Office 2012-13; Minister for Disabled People, Department for Work and Pensions 2013-14; Minister of State for: Policing, Crime, Criminal Justice and Victims 2014-16, Fire 2016; Chair, Inter-Ministerial Group on Anti-Corruption 2015-16; Minister of State for the Armed Forces, Ministry of Defence 2016-17. *Select committees:* Member, Health 2005-07. Member, Executive, 1922 Committee 2006-07. Director, Conservatives Against a Federal Europe 1995; General election campaign manager, Rochford and Southend East 1997.

Political interests: Constitution, single currency (against), health, home affairs, defence; Gibraltar.

Other: British Legion; Patron: St Francis Hospice, Ian Rennie Grove Hospice, Paper Trail Heritage Fire Brigade, Herts Hearing Advisory Service; Trustee, Snowbility; GSM (Northern Ireland); PC 2014; Kt 2017. President, Hemel Hempstead Town Football Club.

Recreations: Rugby union, football, coarse fishing, golf.

Rt Hon Sir Mike Penning MP, House of Commons, London SW1A 0AA
Tel: 020 7219 3000 *Email:* mike.penning.mp@parliament.uk
Constituency: The Bury, Queensway, Hemel Hempstead, Hertfordshire HP1 1HR
Tel: 01442 251126 Website: www.penning4hemel.com

LABOUR

PENNYCOOK, MATTHEW

Greenwich and Woolwich *(Majority 18,464)*

Shadow Minister for Climate Change

Matthew Thomas Pennycook. Born 29 October 1982; Married Joanna Otterburn (1 son 1 daughter).

Education: London School of Economics (history and international relations); Balliol College, Oxford (MPhil international relations).

Non-political career: Child Poverty Action Group; Fair Pay Network; Senior Research and Policy Analyst, Resolution Foundation 2012-14. Member: GMB, Unite.

Political career: Member for Greenwich and Woolwich since 7 May 2015 general election; PPS to John Healey as Shadow Minister for Housing and Planning 2015-16; Shadow Minister for: Exiting the European Union 2016-19, Business, Energy and Industrial Strategy (Climate Change) 2020-. *Select committees:* Member: Energy and Climate Change 2015-16, Future Relationship with the European Union 2020. *Councils and public bodies:* Councillor, Greenwich Council 2010-15; Former governor, James Wolfe Primary School.

Other: Member, Advisory Board, Living Wage Foundation; Trustee, Greenwich Housing Rights.

Matthew Pennycook MP, House of Commons, London SW1A 0AA
Tel: 020 7219 6280 *Email:* matthew.pennycook.mp@parliament.uk
Constituency: No constituency office
Email: matthew@matthewpennycook.com Website: www.matthewpennycook.com
Twitter: @mtpennycook

CONSERVATIVE

PENROSE, JOHN

Weston-Super-Mare *(Majority 17,121)*

John David Penrose. Born 22 June 1964; Son of late David Penrose and Anna Penrose, now Lawrie; Married Diana (Dido) Harding 1995, now Baroness Harding of Winscombe (qv) (2 daughters).

Education: Ipswich School, Suffolk; Downing College, Cambridge (BA law 1986); Columbia University, USA (MBA 1991); French, German.

Non-political career: RiskMmanager, JP Morgan 1986-90; Management Consultant, McKinsey and Company 1992-94; Commercial Director, academic books division, Thomson Publishing 1995-96; Managing Director, schools publishing, Europe, Pearson plc 1996-2000; Director, Credit Market Analysis 2001–03; Chair, Logotron Ltd 2001-08.

Political career: Contested Ealing Southall 1997 and Weston-Super-Mare 2001 general elections. Member for Weston-Super-Mare 2005-10, for Weston-Super-Mare (revised boundary) since 6 May 2010 general election; PPS to Oliver Letwin as Chair, Conservative Policy Review 2006-09; Shadow Minister for: Business, Enterprise and Regulatory Reform 2009, Business 2009-10; Parliamentary Under-Secretary of State (Minister for Tourism and Heritage), Department for Culture, Media and Sport 2010-12; Assistant Government Whip 2013-14; Government Whip (Lord Commissioner of HM Treasury) 2014-16; Parliamentary Secretary, Cabinet Office 2015-16; PM's Anti-Corruption Champion 2017-; Minister of State, Northern Ireland Office 2018-19. *Select committees:* Member: Work and Pensions 2005-09, Regulatory Reform 2009-10, Administration 2012-13, Selection 2014-15. Treasurer, Leyton and Wanstead Conservative Association 1993-95; Member, Conservative Party Policy Board; Chair, Conservative Policy Forum. *Councils and public bodies:* Leading review exploring how to bolster UK competition policy 2020-.

Political interests: Drug addiction, pensions, environment, education, international development.

Other: Research secretary, Bow Group 1998-99; President, Weston Abbeyfields Nursing (charity); Member, Priory Multi-Academy Trust 2015-. President Weston Conservative Club, President Weston Constitutional Club.

Publications: Members' Rights (The Bow Group, 1997); Better Regulation (Conservative Party, 2009); UK Tourism Policy (UK Government, 2010); We Deserve Better: replacing failed economic regulators with consumer reforms (2013); The Great Rebalancing: a UK Sovereign Wealth Fund (2017) A Shining City Upon A Hill: rebooting capitalism for the many not the few (2018).

Recreations: Fishing, beekeeping.

John Penrose MP, House of Commons, London SW1A 0AA
Tel: 020 7219 5310 *Email:* penrosej@parliament.uk
Constituency: 24-26 Alexandra Parade, Weston-Super-Mare, Somerset BS23 1QX
Tel: 01934 613841 *Email:* john@johnpenrose.org Website: www.johnpenrose.org
Twitter: @JohnPenroseNews

CONSERVATIVE

PERCY, ANDREW

Brigg and Goole *(Majority 21,941)*

Andrew Theakstone Percy. Born 18 September 1977.

Education: York University.

Non-political career: History teacher; MP's researcher; Part-time primary teacher. Member, NASUWT.

Political career: Contested Normanton 2005 general election. Member for Brigg and Goole since 6 May 2010 general election; Trade Envoy to Canada 2016-19; Parliamentary Under-Secretary of State (Minister for the Northern Powerhouse), Department for Communities and Local Government 2016-17. *Select committees:* Member: Procedure 2010-11, Regulatory Reform 2010-17, Standing Orders 2011-15, Northern Ireland Affairs 2012-15, Health 2012-16, Panel of Chairs 2015-16. *Councils and public bodies:* Governor, Goole Academy; Assistant Governor, Bricknell Primary School.

Political interests: Education; Canada, Commonwealth, Far East, Israel, USA.

Other: Member, Executive Committee, Commonwealth Parliamentary Association UK 2015-16; Supporter: Countryside Alliance, Campaign Against Political Correctness; Patron: Save a Child's Heart UK, St Mary's Community Charity, Goole; Ambassador, White Ribbon Campaign; Chair: Imagination Library Goole and Snaith, Imagination Library North Lincolnshire; Community First Responder, Yorkshire Ambulance Service; Chair: Ancholme Flood Strategy Board, Brigg 2020, Humber Flood Strategy Steering Group; President, Northern Association of Drainage Authorities; Member, advisory board, GEX Management 2017-.

Andrew Percy MP, House of Commons, London SW1A 0AA
Tel: 020 7219 7208 *Email:* andrew.percy.mp@parliament.uk
Constituency: 81-83 Pasture Road, Goole, East Yorkshire DN14 6BP
Tel: 01405 767969 *Email:* brigg.goole@gmail.com
2 Morley's Yard, Old Courts Road, Brigg, North Lincolnshire DN20 8JD
Tel: 01652 650094 Website: www.andrewpercy.org

LABOUR

PERKINS, TOBY

Chesterfield *(Majority 1,451)*

Shadow Minister for Apprenticeships and Lifelong Learning

Matthew Toby Perkins. Born 12 August 1970; Son of V.F Perkins and late Teresa Perkins, both university lecturers; Married Susan Francis 1996 (1 son 1daughter).

Education: Trinity School, Leamington Spa; Silverdale School, Sheffield.

Non-political career: Telephone sales, CCS Media 1991-95; Recruitment consultant/area manager, Prime Time Recruitment 1995-2002; Business owner, Club Rugby (internet sports firm) 2005-. Member, Amicus/Unite 2005-.

Political career: Member for Chesterfield since 6 May 2010 general election; Shadow Minister for: Education 2010-11, Business, Innovation and Skills 2011-15, Defence 2015-16, Education (Apprenticeships and Lifelong Learning) 2020-. *Select committees:* Member: Communities and Local Government 2010, Joint Committee on Statutory Instruments 2010-15, International Trade 2016-17, Home Affairs 2019, Environment, Food and Rural Affairs 2020. Chair, PLP Departmental Group for Communities and Local Government 2010-11. Member: Labour Party, Co-operative Party; Campaign Deputy, General Election Strategy 2014-15. *Councils and public bodies:* Councillor, Chesterfield Borough Council 2003-11; Director, Families First Nursery 2007-11.

Political interests: Sport and youth involvement, small businesses, crime, jobs and regeneration.

Other: Founder, Chesterfield Flood Victims Appeal 2007-09; Vice-chair, Progress 2012-. Former player, Chesterfield Rugby Club; Coach, Sheffield Tigers Rugby Club.

Recreations: Rugby (qualified coach).

Toby Perkins MP, House of Commons, London SW1A 0AA
Tel: 020 7219 2320 *Email:* toby.perkins.mp@parliament.uk
Constituency: 113 Saltergate, Chesterfield, Derbyshire S40 1NF
Tel: 01246 386286 Website: www.tobyperkins.org.uk *Twitter:* @tobyperkinsmp

LABOUR

PHILLIPS, JESS

Birmingham, Yardley *(Majority 10,659)*

Shadow Minister for Domestic Violence and Safeguarding

Jessica Rose Phillips. Born 9 October 1981; Married Tom Phillips (2 sons).

Education: Leeds University (BA economic and social history/social policy 2003); Institute of Local Government, Birmingham University (PGD public sector management 2013).

Non-political career: Project/event manager, Health Links 2008-10; Business development manager, Sandwell Women's Aid 2010-15.

Political career: Member for Birmingham, Yardley since 7 May 2015 general election; PPS to Lucy Powell as Shadow Secretary of State for Education 2015-16; Member, Commons Reference Group on Representation and Inclusion 2017-19; Shadow Minister for Home Office (Domestic Violence and Safeguarding) 2020-. *Select committees:* Member: Women and Equalities 2015-19, Backbench Business 2015-19. PLP Departmental Group for Women: Chair 2016-19, Vice-chair 2020-. *Councils and public bodies:* Victims Champion for Birmingham 2011; Councillor, Birmingham City Council 2012-16.

Other: Vice-President, Chartered Institute for Trading Standards 2017-.

Publications: Everywoman: One Woman's Truth About Speaking the Truth (Penguin, 2017).

Jess Phillips MP, House of Commons, London SW1A 0AA
Tel: 020 7219 8703 *Email:* jess.phillips.mp@parliament.uk
Constituency: 64 Yardley Road, Acocks Green, West Midlands B27 6LG
Tel: 0121-708 2412 Website: www.jessphillips.net *Twitter:* @jessphillips

LABOUR

PHILLIPSON, BRIDGET

Houghton and Sunderland South *(Majority 3,115)*

Shadow Chief Secretary to the Treasury

Bridget Maeve Phillipson. Born 19 December 1983; Daughter of Clare Phillipson; Married Lawrence Dimery 2009 (1 daughter 1 son).

Education: St Robert of Newminster School and Sixth Form College, Washington; Hertford College, Oxford (MA modern history 2005); French, Spanish.

Non-political career: Sunderland City Council 2005-07; Women's refuge manager, Wearside Women in Need 2007-10. Member, GMB 2005-.

Political career: Member for Houghton and Sunderland South since 6 May 2010 general election; Member, Speaker's Committee on the Electoral Commission 2010-20; PPS to Jim Murphy as Shadow Secretary of State for Defence 2010-13; Opposition Whip 2013-15; Shadow Chief Secretary to the Treasury 2020-. *Select committees:* Member: Home Affairs 2010-13, Procedure 2010-11, Public Accounts 2015-20, Standards 2017-20, Privileges

2017-20, European Statutory Instruments 2018-19. Labour Party: Member 1998-, Chair, Oxford University Labour Club -2003, National Policy Forum: North East representative 2002-05, PLP Representative and Vice-chair 2013-15.

Political interests: Economy, jobs, skills, infrastructure.

Other: Member, British-Irish Parliamentary Assembly 2020-.

Recreations: Running, reading, history, music.

Bridget Phillipson MP, House of Commons, London SW1A 0AA
Tel: 020 7219 7087 *Fax:* 020 7219 2419 *Email:* bridget.phillipson.mp@parliament.uk
Constituency: 106 Newbottle Street, Houghton le Spring, Tyne and Wear DH4 4AJ
Tel: 0191-584 4317 *Email:* bridget@bridgetphillipson.co.uk
Website: www.bridgetphillipson.com *Twitter:* @bphillipsonmp

CONSERVATIVE

PHILP, CHRIS

Croydon South *(Majority 12,339)*

Parliamentary Under-Secretary of State for Immigration Compliance and the Courts, Home Office and Ministry of Justice

Chris Ian Brian Mynitt Philp. Born 6 July 1976; Son of Dr Brian Philp MBE, Director of Kent Archaeological Rescue Unit; Married Elizabeth (twin son and daughter).

Education: St Olave's Grammar School, Orpington; University College, Oxford (physics 1998).

Non-political career: McKinsey & Co; Owner, distribution company; Property Investment manager; Director, BP Balkans Pluto (Cyprus) Ltd.

Political career: Contested Hampstead and Kilburn 2010 general election. Member for Croydon South since 7 May 2015 general election; Team PPS, HM Treasury 2017-18; PPS: to Secretary of State for Housing, Communities and Local Government: Sajid Javid 2018, James Brokenshire 2018, to Sajid Javid as Chancellor of the Exchequer 2019; Minister for London 2019-20; Parliamentary Under-Secretary of State, Ministry of Justice 2019-20; Parliamentary Under-Secretary of State for Immigration Compliance and the Courts: Home Office 2020-, Ministry of Justice 2020-. *Select committees:* Member, Treasury 2015-17. Co-ordinator, Conservative No2AV Campaign, London; Conservative National No2AV Spokesperson; National Conservatives Treasurers team; Vice-chairman, Policy, Conservative Party 2018-19. *Councils and public bodies:* Councillor, London Borough of Camden Council 2006-10.

Political interests: Economy, creating jobs, state education, housing, road and rail transport.

Other: Former chair, Bow Group; Founder, Next Big Thing 2009-; London's Emerging Entrepreneur, Ernst and Young/*The Times* 2003.

Recreations: Horse riding, skiing, running, football.

Chris Philp MP, House of Commons, London SW1A 0AA
Tel: 020 7219 8026 *Email:* chris.philp.mp@parliament.uk
Constituency: c/o Croydon Conservative Association, 36 Brighton Road, Purley, Surrey CR8 2LG
Tel: 020 8660 0491 Websites: www.croydonconservatives.com/www.chrisphilp.com
Twitter: @CPhilpOfficial

CONSERVATIVE

PINCHER, CHRISTOPHER

Tamworth *(Majority 19,634)*

Minister of State for Housing, Ministry of Housing, Communities and Local Government

Christopher John Pincher. Born 24 September 1969; Son of John Pincher and Sandra Pincher; Single.

Education: Ounsdale School, Staffordshire; London School of Economics (BSc (Econ) government and history 1991).

Non-political career: Manager, Accenture 1993-2010.

Political career: Contested Warley 1997 and Tamworth 2005 general elections. Member for Tamworth since 6 May 2010 general election; PPS to Philip Hammond as Foreign Secretary 2015-16; Assistant Government Whip 2016-17; Government Whip (Comptroller of HM

Household) 2017; Deputy Chief Whip (Treasurer of HM Household) 2018-19; Minister of State for: Europe and the Americas, Foreign and Commonwealth Office 2019-20, Housing, Ministry of Housing, Communities and Local Government 2020-. *Select committees:* Member: Energy and Climate Change 2010-15, Armed Forces Bill 2011, Standing Orders 2011-15, Regulatory Reform 2015-16, Selection 2017, 2018-19. 1922 Committee: Member, Executive 2014, Secretary 2014-15. Member, Conservative Party 1987-; Treasurer, Conservative Friends of Azerbaijan.

Political interests: Home affairs, defence, education, energy; Azerbaijan, Middle East, Latvia, Russia, USA.

Other: Macmillan Cancer Support, Tamworth in the Community; PC 2018. Travellers' Club.

Recreations: Literature and biographies, golf, the turf, history, Formula 1, horse racing.

Rt Hon Christopher Pincher MP, House of Commons, London SW1A 0AA
Tel: 020 7219 7169 *Email:* christopher.pincher.mp@parliament.uk
Constituency: The White House, 93 Lichfield Street, Tamworth, Staffordshire B79 7QF
Tel: 01827 312778 Website: www.christopherpincher.com *Twitter:* @ChrisPincher

LABOUR/ CO-OPERATIVE

POLLARD, LUKE

Plymouth, Sutton and Devonport *(Majority 4,757)*

Shadow Secretary of State for Environment, Food and Rural Affairs

Luke Jonathan Pollard. Born 10 April 1980; Partner Sydney Robertson.

Education: Tavistock College, Tavistock; Christleton High School, Chester; Exeter University (BA politics 2001) (President, Students' Union); German.

Non-political career: Studio Manager, Carlton (ITV) 2002-03 Researcher to David Jamieson MP and George Foulkes MP 2003-05; Account Director, Edelman 2005-09; ABTA – The Travel Association: Head of Public Affairs 2009-13, Head of European Development 2013-14; Director, Field Consulting UK 2015-17. Member: GMB, Unite (TGWU section) 2003-.

Political career: Contested South West Devon 2010 and Plymouth, Sutton and Devonport 2015 general elections. Member for Plymouth, Sutton and Devonport since 8 June 2017; PPS to Sue Hayman as Shadow Secretary of State for Environment, Food and Rural Affairs 2017-18; Shadow Minister for Environment, Food and Rural Affairs (Fishing, Flooding and Water) 2018-20; Shadow Secretary of State for Environment, Food and Rural Affairs 2020-. *Select committees:* Member, Transport 2017-18. Campaign Co-ordinator, Plymouth Sutton and Devonport Labour Party, 2010-15, 2016-17; Member: Co-operative Party 2007-, SERA (Labour's Environment Campaign). *Councils and public bodies:* Governor, Millbank Primary School 2008-13.

Political interests: Defence, transport, health, education, housing, fishing, environment, climate change.

Other: Member: Fabian Society 2003-, Campaign for Real Ale 2005-, Plymouth Argyle Supporters Trust 2010-, Plymouth Energy Community and PEC Renewables 2014-, Nudge Community Builders 2018-. House of Lords and Commons Hockey Club.

Recreations: Hockey, football (Plymouth Argyle supporter), running, wild swimming.

Luke Pollard MP, House of Commons, London SW1A 0AA
Tel: 020 7219 2749 *Email:* luke.pollard.mp@parliament.uk
Constituency: 13 Frankfort Gate, Plymouth PL1 1QA
Tel: 01752 717255 Website: www.lukepollard.org *Twitter:* @lukepollard

CONSERVATIVE

POULTER, DAN

Central Suffolk and North Ipswich *(Majority 23,391)*

Daniel Leonard James Poulter. Born 30 October 1978.

Education: Bristol University (LLB); Guys and St Thomas' School of Medicine (MBBS); King's College, London (AKC).

Non-political career: Speciality registrar, obstetrics and gynaecology 2008-10; NHS doctor 2010-; Visiting Professor, King's College London 2016-.

Political career: Member for Central Suffolk and North Ipswich since 6 May 2010 general election; Parliamentary Under-Secretary of State, Department of Health 2012-15. *Select committees:* Member: Health 2011-12, Joint Committee on the Draft House of Lords Reform Bill 2011-12, Scottish Affairs 2015-17, Energy and Climate Change 2015-16, Backbench Business 2016-17, Public Administration and Constitutional Affairs 2016-17, Environmental Audit 2017-19, International Development 2020-, Work of the Independent Commission for Aid Impact Sub-committee 2020-. *Councils and public bodies:* Councillor, Hastings Borough Council 2006-07; Deputy Leader, Reigate and Banstead Council 2008-10.

Political interests: Health, global health, mental health, rural affairs, pensions, older people, voluntary sector, overseas development, energy and climate change; Australasia, Caribbean.

Other: Member, British Medical Association -2012, 2015-; Help for Heroes, Set up medical and lifestyle advice clinics for homeless, raised money for victims of domestic violence, St Elizabeth Hospice Ipswich. Guy's Hospital Rugby Club.

Publications: Published author in field of women's health.

Recreations: Cricket, rugby, golf.

Dr Dan Poulter MP, House of Commons, London SW1A 0AA
Tel: 020 7219 7038 *Fax:* 020 7219 1192 *Email:* daniel.poulter.mp@parliament.uk
Constituency: The Technology Cenre, Station Road, Framlingham, Suffolk IP13 9EZ
Tel: 01728 726588 Website: www.drdanielpoulter.com

CONSERVATIVE

POW, REBECCA

Taunton Deane *(Majority 11,700)*

Parliamentary Under-Secretary of State, Department for Environment, Food and Rural Affairs

Rebecca Faye Pow. Born 10 October 1960; Married Charles Clark (died 2019) (3 children).

Education: Wye College; Imperial College, London (BSc rural environment studies 1982).

Non-political career: Set up PR and communications business, Pow Productions 1988-; Reporter, BBC, ITV and Channel 4, specialising in the environment, farming and gardening 1989-2005; National Farmers Union.

Political career: Member for Taunton Deane since 7 May 2015 general election; PPS to Gavin Barwell as Minister of State for Housing and Planning and Minister for London, Department for Communities and Local Government 2016-17; Team PPS, Department for Environment, Food and Rural Affairs 2017-18; PPS to Secretary of State for Work and Pensions: Esther McVey 2018, Amber Rudd 2018-19; Parliamentary Under-Secretary of State: for Arts, Heritage and Tourism, Department for Digital, Culture, Media and Sport 2019, Department for Environment, Food and Rural Affairs 2019-. *Select committees:* Member: Environment, Food and Rural Affairs 2015-17, Environmental Audit 2015-16, Environment, Food and Rural Affairs Sub-committee 2016-17, Digital, Culture, Media and Sport 2017-19. Chairman, Conservative Backbench Policy Committee on Environment, Food and Rural Affairs 2016-17. Parliamentary Liaison Officer, Conservative Rural Affairs Group 2016-. *Councils and public bodies:* Former school governor; Councillor, Stoke St Mary Parish Council.

Other: Trustee, Somerset Wildlife Trust.

Rebecca Pow MP, House of Commons, London SW1A 0AA
Tel: 020 7219 4831 *Email:* rebecca.pow.mp@parliament.uk
Constituency: The Great Western Hotel, Station Approach, Taunton TA1 1QW
Tel: 01823 443062 Website: www.rebeccapow.org.uk *Twitter:* @pow_rebecca

LABOUR/
CO-OPERATIVE

POWELL, LUCY

Manchester Central *(Majority 29,089)*

Shadow Minister for Business and Consumers

Lucy Maria Powell. Born 10 October 1974; Married James (1 daughter 1 son 1 stepson).

Education: Parrs Wood High School, Manchester; Xaverian Sixth Form; Oxford University (BSc chemistry); King's College, London.

Non-political career: Labour Party, London, general election campaign 1997; Parliamentary assistant to Beverley Hughes MP; Director, Britain in Europe; Project manager, National Endowment for Science, Technology and the Arts (NESTA) 2007-10; Deputy chief of staff to Ed Miliband MP as Labour Party Leader 2010-12. Member, Unite.

Political career: Contested Manchester Withington 2010 general election. Member for Manchester Central since 15 November 2012 by-election; Shadow Minister for: Childcare and Children 2013-14, the Cabinet Office 2014-15; Shadow Secretary of State for Education 2015-16; Shadow Minister for Business, Energy and Industrial (Business and Consumers) 2020-. *Select committees:* Member: Transport 2012-13, Education 2017-20. Chair, PLP Departmental Group for: Communities and Local Government 2017, Education 2017-19. Member, Co-operative Party; Campaign manager to Ed Miliband MP, Labour Party Leadership Campaign 2010; Vice-chair, General Election Campaign (Operations) 2014-15.

Political interests: Education, health, environment, foreign policy, regeneration, economic development, innovation and skills.

Recreations: Manchester City FC.

Lucy Powell MP, House of Commons, London SW1A 0AA
Tel: 020 7219 4402 *Email:* lucy.powell.mp@parliament.uk
Constituency: No constituency office publicised
Tel: 0161-232 0872 *Email:* contact@lucypowell.org.uk *Twitter:* @LucyMPowell

CONSERVATIVE

PRENTIS, VICTORIA

Banbury *(Majority 16,813)*

Parliamentary Under-Secretary of State, Department for Environment, Food and Rural Affairs

Victoria Mary Boswell Prentis. Born 24 March 1971; Daughter of Timothy Boswell (MP for Daventry 1987-2010, now Lord Boswell of Aynho (qv)) and late Helen Delahay, née Rees; Married Sebastian Prentis 1996 (2 daughters 1 son deceased).

Education: Malvern St James Girls' School; University of London (BA English literature 1992); Downing College, Cambridge (MA law 1994); French, German.

Non-political career: Called to the Bar, Middle Temple 1995; Government Legal Service 1997-2014.

Political career: Member for Banbury since 7 May 2015 general election; PPS: to John Hayes as Minister of State, Department for Transport 2016-17, to Leader of the House of Commons and Lord President of the Council: Andrea Leadsom 2017-19, Mel Stride 2019, to Geoffrey Cox as Attorney General 2019-20; Parliamentary Under-Secretary of State, Department for Environment, Food and Rural Affairs 2020-. *Select committees:* Member: Justice 2015-19, Joint Committee on Statutory Instruments 2015-17; Lay Member, Speaker's Advisory Committee on Works of Art 2019. Founding member, Conservatives for Reform in Europe 2016; Chair, Society of Conservative Lawyers Executive Committee.

Political interests: Maternal health, aspirations and education, human rights, justice, especially prison reform, early years, transport; China, France, Germany, Morocco, Russia.

Other: Director, Transport Sense; Member, Benefactors' Board, Oxford Children's Hospital Trust; Hands Up Foundation (Singing for Syrians). Carlton Club, Farmers' Club.

Recreations: Cider making, cooking, detective fiction, charitable fundraising.

Victoria Prentis MP, House of Commons, London SW1A 0AA
Tel: 020 7219 8756 *Email:* victoria.prentis.mp@parliament.uk
Constituency: Orchard House, Hopcraft Lane, Deddington OX15 0TD
Tel: 01869 233685 Website: www.victoriaprentis.com *Twitter:* @VictoriaPrentis

CONSERVATIVE

PRITCHARD, MARK

The Wrekin *(Majority 18,726)*

Mark Andrew Pritchard. Born 22 November 1966; Son of late Frank Pritchard and Romona Pritchard; Divorced 2013.

Education: St Owen's School, Hereford; Afan Comprehensive School, Cymmer, Glamorgan; Aylestone School, Hereford; Regents Theological College; London Guildhall University (MA marketing management; Postgraduate Diploma marketing); Buckingham University (MA international diplomacy).

Non-political career: Parliamentary researcher 1993-05; Director and founder 1998-2007: Pritchard Communications Ltd, Next Steps Market Research Ltd.

Political career: Contested Warley 2001 general election. Member for The Wrekin 2005-10, for The Wrekin (revised boundary) since 6 May 2010 general election; Trade Envoy to Georgia and Armenia 2017-19; Member, Intelligence and Security Committee of Parliament 2020-. *Select committees:* Member: Environmental Audit 2005-07, Work and Pensions 2006-09, Welsh Affairs 2007-10, Transport 2009-10, Joint Committee on National Security Strategy 2010-15, International Development 2012-13, Panel of Chairs 2012-, Joint Committee on Human Rights 2015-17, Northern Ireland Affairs 2016-17. Joint secretary, Conservative Parliamentary: Defence Committee -2005, Foreign Affairs Committee -2005; Secretary, 1922 Committee 2010-12. National Board Member, Conservative Councillors Association 2002; Conservative Party Human Rights Commission 2006-; Deputy Chair, International Office, Conservative Party 2010-12. *Councils and public bodies:* Councillor, Harrow Council 1993-94; Woking Borough Council: Councillor 2000-03, Chair, Economic Committee.

Political interests: Defence, cyber-security, homeland security, foreign relations, counter-terrorism, animal welfare and conservation; Africa, Latin America, ASEAN region, India, Israel, USA.

Other: UK Chair, Parliamentarians for Global Action; Member, Executive Committee: Commonwealth Parliamentary Association, Inter-Parliamentary Union; British-American Parliamentary Group: Executive Member, Vice-chair 2010-; Member, UK Parliamentary Delegation to NATO 2010-; Vice-chair, Inter-Parliamentary Union, British Group 2010-11; Member: British-Irish Parliamentary Assembly 2013-18, UK Delegation, Parliamentary Assembly of the Council of Europe 2015-17; Leader, UK Delegation, Organisation for Security and Co-operation in Europe Parliamentary Assembly 2017-19; Bow Group Council 1994; Member, Miniature Schnauzer Club of Great Britain; Oliver Twist Club; Founder, The Music Charity; Member: Chartered Institute of Marketing, Institute of Public Relations, Market Research Society; Great Ormond Street Children's Hospital, Various orphanage charities, Hereford Cathedral Perpetual Trust. Carlton Club.

Recreations: Walking, skiing, writing, animal welfare, tennis, writing comedy.

Mark Pritchard MP, House of Commons, London SW1A 0AA
Tel: 020 7219 8494 *Fax:* 020 7219 5969 *Email:* pritchardm@parliament.uk
Constituency: 25 Church Street, Wellington, Shropshire TF1 1DG
Tel: 01952 256080 Website: www.markpritchard.com *Twitter:* @MPritchardUK

CONSERVATIVE

PURSGLOVE, TOM

Corby *(Majority 10,268)*

Assistant Government Whip

Thomas Christopher John Pursglove. Born 5 November 1988.

Education: Sir Christopher Hatton School, Wellingborough; Queen Mary College, University of London (BA politics 2010).

Non-political career: Parliamentary Assistant to Chris Heaton-Harris MP 2010-15; Former Director, Together Against Wind Ltd.

Political career: Member for Corby since 7 May 2015 general election; PPS to: Robert Goodwill as Minister of State for Immigration, Home Office 2016-17, Liam Fox as Secretary of State for International Trade and President of the Board of Trade 2017-18, Sajid Javid as Home Secretary 2018; Assistant Government Whip 2019-. Deputy Chair, Political, Wellingborough Conservative Association 2011-14; Founding member, Conservatives for Britain 2015-16; Vice-chair, Youth, Conservative Party 2018-19. *Councils and public bodies:* Councillor, Wellingborough Borough Council 2007-15.

Political interests: Brexit, home affairs, constitutional matters, industry, housing and planning, sport; Australia, USA, New Zealand.

Other: Co-founder, Grassroots Out Ltd 2015-16; Crazy Hats, Cransley Hospice, Care after Combat, Corby Mind. Wellingborough Old Grammarians Cricket Club; Wellingborough Golf Club.

Recreations: Cricket (playing and ECB qualified umpire), golf, running, general fitness.

Tom Pursglove MP, House of Commons, London SW1A 0AA
Tel: 020 7219 8043 *Email:* tom.pursglove.mp@parliament.uk
Constituency: No constituency office publicised
Website: www.votepursglove.co.uk *Twitter:* @VotePursglove

CONSERVATIVE

QUIN, JEREMY

Horsham *(Majority 21,127)*

Minister of State (Minister for Defence Procurement), Ministry of Defence

Jeremy Mark Quin. Born 24 September 1968; Son of the Revd David Quin and late Elizabeth Quin; Married Joanna.

Education: St Albans School; Hertford College, Oxford (modern history 1990).

Non-political career: NatWest Securities/BT Alex Brown 1990-2000; Deutsche Bank: Managing Director: Corporate Finance (Global Consumer Group) 2001-08, UK Corporate Finance/Regional Management 2009-15; Senior corporate finance adviser, HM Treasury 2008-09.

Political career: Contested Meirionnydd Nant Conwy 1997 general election. Member for Horsham since 7 May 2015 general election; Department for Exiting the European Union: PPS to David Jones as Minister of State 2016-17, Team PPS 2017-18, PPS to David Davis as Secretary of State 2018; Assistant Government Whip 2018; Government Whip: (Lord Commissioner of HM Treasury) 2018-19, (Comptroller of HM Household) 2019; Parliamentary Secretary (Minister for Implementation), Cabinet Office 2019-20; Minister of State (Minister for Defence Procurement), Ministry of Defence 2020-. *Select committees:* Member: Work and Pensions 2015-16, Regulatory Reform 2015-18, Selection 2019-20. Chair, Buckingham Constituency Conservative Association 2010-13; Deputy Chair, Oxfordshire and Buckinghamshire Conservatives 2013-15. *Councils and public bodies:* Member, Financial Inclusion Commission 2017-.

Political interests: Treasury/economic affairs, welfare, financial inclusion; China, India.

Jeremy Quin MP, House of Commons, London SW1A 0AA
Tel: 020 7219 6341 *Email:* jeremy.quin.mp@parliament.uk
Constituency: Gough House, Madeira Avenue, Horsham, West Sussex RH12 1AB
Tel: 01403 210600 Website: www.jeremyquin.com

CONSERVATIVE

QUINCE, WILL

Colchester *(Majority 9,423)*

Parliamentary Under-Secretary of State for Welfare Delivery, Department for Work and Pensions

William James Quince. Born 27 December 1982; Married Elinor Hart (1 daughter).

Education: Windsor Boys' School; University of Wales, Aberystwyth (LLB 2005) (Deputy President Student's Union); University of West of England, Bristol (Postgraduate Diploma legal practice 2012).

Non-political career: Marketing developing executive, Concur Technologies 2005-06; Britvic plc: Customer development executive 2006-07, Customer development manager 2007-09, Customer development manager, branded restuarants 2008-10; Trainee solicitor, Asher Prior Bates 2010-13; Solicitor, Thompson Smith and Puxon Solicitors 2013-15. Armed Forces Parliamentary Scheme.

Political career: Contested Colchester 2010 general election. Member for Colchester since 7 May 2015 general election; Team PPS, Cabinet Office 2017-18; Member, Commons Reference Group on Representation and Inclusion 2017-18; PPS to Gavin Williamson as Secretary of State for Defence 2018; Department for Work and Pensions: Parliamentary Under-Secretary of State for: Family Support, Housing and Child Maintenance 2019, Welfare Delivery 2019-. *Select committees:* Member: Transport 2015-17, Home Affairs 2017-18. Member, national executive, Conservative Future 2003-04. *Councils and public bodies:* East Hertfordshire District Council: Councillor 2007-09, Chair, Environmental Scrutiny Committee; Councillor, Colchester Borough Council 2011-16.

Political interests: Health, transport, justice, voluntary sector; China.

Other: Member, Bow Group 2007-; Trustee, Grassroots–Colchester and Tendring Community Trust; Law Society.

Will Quince MP, House of Commons, London SW1A 0AA
Tel: 020 7219 8049 *Email:* will.quince.mp@parliament.uk
Constituency: 37 Layer Road, Colchester, Essex CO2 7JW
Tel: 01206 545990 Website: www.willquince.com *Twitter:* @willquince

LABOUR

QURESHI, YASMIN

Bolton South East *(Majority 7,598)*

Shadow Minister for International Development

Born 5 July 1963; Daughter of Mohammad Qureshi, civil engineer, and Sakina Beg, primary school teacher; Married Nadeem Ashraf Butt 2008.

Education: Westfield School; South Bank Polytechnic, London (BA law 1984); Council of Legal Education (Barrister Exams 1985); University College, London (Masters law); Punjabi, Urdu.

Non-political career: Called to the Bar, Lincoln's Inn 1985; Barrister 1987-: Crown prosecutor, Crown Prosecution Service 1987-2000, 2004-08; United Nations Mission in Kosovo, Judicial Affairs Department Co-ordinator, Criminal Law Unit 2000-01, Department director 2001-02; Human rights adviser to Ken Livingstone as Mayor of London 2004-08; Barrister: 2 Kings Bench Walk Chambers, London 2004-08, Kenworthy's Chambers 2008-. Member: First Division Association, USDAW, GMB.

Political career: Contested Brent East 2005 general election. Member for Bolton South East since 6 May 2010 general election; Shadow Minister for: Justice 2016-20, International Development 2020-. *Select committees:* Member: Justice 2010-15, Political and Constitutional Reform 2011, Joint Committee on Privacy and Injunctions 2011-12, Home Affairs 2013-15, High Speed Rail (London-West Midlands) Bill 2014-15, Foreign Affairs 2015-16. Vice-chair, PLP Departmental Group for Women 2013-. Watford CLP, Labour Party: Secretary, Treasurer, Regional delegate to area, Delegate to Labour group.

Political interests: Crime, education, young people.

Other: Former chair, Human Rights and Civil Liberties Working Group, Association of Muslim Lawyers; Former president, Pakistan Club (UK); British Institute of Human Rights; Society of Labour Lawyers; Fabian Society: Member, Former chair, Watford and District branch; Voluntary legal work for the Free Representation Unit. Bolton Labour Socialist Club.

Recreations: Reading.

Yasmin Qureshi MP, House of Commons, London SW1A 0AA
Tel: 020 7219 7019 *Fax:* 020 7219 0595 *Email:* yasmin.qureshi.mp@parliament.uk
Constituency: c/o Bolton Labour Party, 60 St Georges Road, Bolton, Lancashire BL1 2DD
Tel: 01204 371202 Website: www.yasminqureshi.org.uk *Twitter:* @YasminQureshiMP

CONSERVATIVE

RAAB, DOMINIC

Esher and Walton *(Majority 2,743)*

First Secretary of State and Foreign Secretary

Dominic Rennie Raab. Born 25 February 1974; Married Erika (2 sons).

Education: Dr Challoner's Grammar School, Amersham; Lady Margaret Hall, Oxford (law); Jesus College, Cambridge (Master's law).

Non-political career: Lawyer, Linklaters; Foreign and Commonwealth Office 2000-06: British Embassy, The Hague 2003-06; Chief of staff to: David Davis MP 2006-08, Dominic Grieve MP 2008-10.

Political career: Member for Esher and Walton since 6 May 2010 general election; Ministry of Justice: Parliamentary Under-Secretary of State for Human Rights 2015-16, Minister of State 2017-18; Minister of State for Housing and Planning, Ministry of Housing, Communities and Local Government 2018; Secretary of State for: Exiting the European Union 2018, Foreign and Commonwealth Affairs/Foreign, Commonwealth and Development Affairs (Foreign Secretary) 2019-; First Secretary of State 2019-. *Select committees:* Member: Joint Committee on Human Rights 2010-13, Education 2013-15, Exiting the European Union 2016-17.

Political interests: Civil liberties, human rights, industrial relations, economy; Far East, Latin America, Middle East.

Other: Member, Campaign committee, Vote Leave 2016; Founding supporter, Change Britain 2016-; Member, advisory board, Reliance ACSN Ltd 2017-; Member, Law Society; Esher Neighbourhood Fund; Clive Parry Prize for international law; Newcomer of the Year, *Spectator* awards 2011; PC 2018.

Publications: Author, The Assault on Liberty (Fourth Estate, 2009); Co-author (with Kwasi Kwarteng MP, Priti Patel MP, Chris Skidmore MP and Elizabeth Truss MP), Britannia Unchained: Global Lessons for Growth and Prosperity (Palgrave Macmillan, 2012).

Recreations: Travel, boxing, theatre.

Rt Hon Dominic Raab MP, House of Commons, London SW1A 0AA
Tel: 020 7219 7069 *Email:* dominic.raab.mp@parliament.uk
Constituency: No constituency office publicised
Website: www.dominicraab.com *Twitter:* @DominicRaab

CONSERVATIVE

RANDALL, TOM

Gedling *(Majority 679)*

Thomas William Randall.

Education: Redhill School; Oxford University (law).

Non-political career: Solicitor.

Political career: Member for Gedling since 12 December 2019. *Select committees:* Member, Public Administration and Constitutional Affairs 2020-.

Tom Randall MP, House of Commons, London SW1A 0AA
Tel: 020 7219 6613 *Email:* tom.randall.mp@parliament.uk
Constituency: 28a High Street, Arnold NG5 7DZ
Tel: 0115-648 0754 Website: www.tomforgedling.com *Twitter:* @Tom_Randall

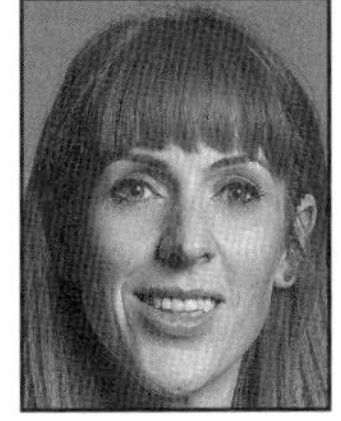

LABOUR

RAYNER, ANGELA

Ashton under Lyne *(Majority 4,263)*

Deputy Leader, National Campaign Co-ordinator and Chair, Labour Party; Shadow First Secretary of State

Born 28 March 1980; Married Mark (3 children).

Education: Avondale High School.

Non-political career: Care assistant for the elderly 1998-2005; Trade union official, Unison. Unison: Secretary, Stockton branch, Lay official, North West region 2002-15.

Political career: Member for Ashton under Lyne since 7 May 2015 general election; Opposition Whip 2015-16; Shadow Minister for Work and Pensions 2016; Shadow Secretary of State for Education 2016-20; Shadow Minister for Women and Equalities 2016; Deputy Leader of the Opposition and Shadow First Secretary of State 2020-. *Select committees:* Member, Communities and Local Government 2015. Labour Party: Deputy Leader 2020-, Chair 2020-, National Campaign Co-ordinator 2020-. *Councils and public bodies:* Vice-president, Local Government Association 2017-.

Recreations: Running.

Angela Rayner MP, House of Commons, London SW1A 0AA
Tel: 020 7219 8782 *Email:* angela.rayner.mp@parliament.uk
Constituency: Ashton Market Hall, Market Street, Ashton OL6 7JU
Tel: 0161-342 5800 *Email:* angela@angelarayner.com Website: www.angelarayner.co.uk
Twitter: @AngelaRayner

CONSERVATIVE

REDWOOD, JOHN

Wokingham *(Majority 7,383)*

John Alan Redwood. Born 15 June 1951; Son of William Redwood and Amy Redwood, née Champion; Married Gail Chippington 1974 (divorced 2004) (1 son 1 daughter).

Education: Kent College, Canterbury; Magdalen College, Oxford (BA modern history 1971, MA); St Antony's College, Oxford (DPhil modern history 1975); French, Spanish.

Non-political career: Fellow, All Souls College, Oxford 1972-87, 2003-05, 2007-; Tutor and lecturer 1972-73; Investment analyst, Robert Fleming & Co. 1974-77; N. M. Rothschild: Bank clerk 1977-78, Manager 1978-79, Assistant director 1979-80, Director, investment division 1980-83, Overseas corporate finance director and head of international (non-UK) privatisation 1986-87; Head, Prime Minister's policy unit 1983-85; Norcros plc: Director 1985-89, Chair 1987-89; Chair, Hare Hatch Holdings 1999-2008; Visiting professor, Middlesex University Business School 2000-16; Chair, Concentric plc 2003-08; Non-executive chair, Evercore Pan-Asset Management Ltd 2008-09.

Political career: Contested Southwark Peckham 1981 by-election. Member for Wokingham 1987-2010, for Wokingham (revised boundary) since 6 May 2010 general election; Department of Trade and Industry: Parliamentary Under-Secretary of State for Corporate Affairs 1989-90, Minister of State 1990-92; Minister for Local Government 1992-93; Secretary of State for Wales 1993-95; Member Shadow Cabinet 1997-2000, 2004-05: Shadow Secretary of State for: Trade and Industry 1997-99, Environment, Transport and the Regions 1999-2000, Deregulation 2004-05. Chair, Conservative Party Committees on: Trade and Industry 1997-99, Environment, Transport and the Regions 1999-2000, Economic Affairs 2010-15, Treasury 2015-19. Contested Conservative Party leadership election 1995, 1997; Chair: No Turning Back Group 2001-, Policy Review on Economic Competitiveness 2005-10; Vice-President, Conservatives for Britain 2015-16. *Councils and public bodies:* Councillor, Oxfordshire County Council 1973-77; Governor, Oxford Polytechnic 1973-77.

Political interests: Popular capitalism, European affairs, constitution, Euro, transport, economy; China, India, USA.

Other: Member, Level 6 Investment Qualification with Distinction 2012, Chartered Institute for Securities and Investment; Various local and educational charities; Chartered Fellow, CISI; Honorary Visiting Professor, Middlesex; PC 1993; Kt 2019. All Souls Cricket.

Publications: Reason, Ridicule and Religion (Thames & Hudson, 1976); Public Enterprise in Crisis (Blackwell, 1980); Going for Broke (Blackwell, 1984); Popular Capitalism (Routledge, 1987); The Global Marketplace (HarperCollins, 1993); Our Currency, Our Country (Penguin, 1997); Several books and articles, especially on wider ownership and popular capitalism; The Death of Britain (Macmillan, 1999); Stars and Strife (Macmillan, 2001); Just Say No (Politicos, 2001); Third Way Which Way? (Middlesex, 2002); Singing the Blues (Politicos, 2004); Superpower Struggles (Palgrave, 2005); I Want To Make A Difference, But I Don't Like Politics (Politicos, 2006); After the Credit Crisis (Middlesex, 2009); We Don't Believe You (Bite sized books, 2019).

Recreations: Village cricket, water sports.

Rt Hon Sir John Redwood MP, House of Commons, London SW1A 0AA
Tel: 020 7219 4205 *Fax:* 020 7219 0377 *Email:* john.redwood.mp@parliament.uk
Constituency: 30 Rose Street, Wokingham, Berkshire RG40 1XU
Tel: 0118-304 0200 *Email:* office@wokinghamconservatives.org.uk
Website: www.johnredwoodsdiary.com *Twitter:* @JohnRedwood

LABOUR/
CO-OPERATIVE

REED, STEVE

Croydon North *(Majority 24,673)*

Shadow Secretary of State for Communities and Local Government

Stephen Mark Ward Reed. Born 12 November 1963.

Education: Sheffield University (English language and literature).

Non-political career: Educational publishing: Routledge, Chapman & Hall, Thomson. Member: Unite, GMB.

Political career: Member for Croydon North since 29 November 2012 by-election; Shadow Minister for: Home Office 2013-15, Communities and Local Government 2015, Local Government 2015-16, Culture, Media and Sport/Digital, Culture, Media and Sport (Civil

Society) 2016-19, Education (Children and Families) 2019-20; Shadow Secretary of State for Communities and Local Government 2020-. *Select committees:* Member, Public Administration 2012-13. Chair, PLP Departmental Group for Education 2013. Member: Labour Party, Co-operative Party; Patron, LGBT Labour. *Councils and public bodies:* London Borough of Lambeth Council: Councillor 1998-12, Leader 2006-12; Member, London Enterprise Panel 2012-13; Vice-president, Local Government Association.

Other: Fellow, Royal Society for the Encouragement of Arts, Manufactures and Commerce; OBE 2013.

Recreations: Cycling, camping, walking, cookery.

Steve Reed OBE MP, House of Commons, London SW1A 0AA
Tel: 020 7219 7297 *Email:* steve.reed.mp@parliament.uk
Constituency: 908 London Road, Thornton Heath CR7 7PE
Tel: 020 8665 1214 Website: www.stevereedmp.co.uk *Twitter:* @SteveReedMP

LABOUR/ CO-OPERATIVE

REES, CHRISTINA

Neath *(Majority 5,637)*

Christina Elizabeth Rees. Born 21 February 1954; Married Ronald Davies 1981 (divorced 2000) (MP for Caerphilly 1983-2001) (1 daughter).

Education: Cynffig Comprehensive School; University of Wales (LLB 1995).

Non-political career: Auditor, South Glamorgan County Council 1979-84; Constituency secretary 1984-96; Called to the Bar 1996; Barrister, 30 Park Place, Cardiff 1997-98; Development officer and national coach, National Governing Body, Squash in Wales 2003-15.

Political career: Member for Neath since 7 May 2015 general election; PPS to Lord Falconer of Thoroton as Shadow Lord Chancellor and Secretary of State for Justice 2015-16; Shadow Minister for Justice Jan-June 2016, October 2016-17; Shadow Secretary of State for Wales 2017-20. *Select committees:* Member: Justice 2015, Welsh Affairs 2015-16, Joint Committee on Consolidation, &c, Bills 2020-, Panel of Chairs 2020-. Contested Arfon constituency 2011 National Assembly for Wales election and Wales region 2014 European Parliament election. *Councils and public bodies:* Councillor: Mid Glamorgan Council 1988-95, Bridgend Country Borough Council 2012-15, Porthcawl Town Council 2012-15.

Other: Member, UK delegation, Parliamentary Assembly of the Council of Europe 2015-16; Sport Wales National Coach of the Year Award 2008.

Christina Rees MP, House of Commons, London SW1A 0AA
Tel: 020 7219 5783 *Email:* christina.rees.mp@parliament.uk
Constituency: 39 Windsor Road, Neath, West Glamorgan SA11 1NB
Tel: 01639 630152 Website: www.christinarees.org *Twitter:* @Rees4Neath

CONSERVATIVE

REES-MOGG, JACOB

North East Somerset *(Majority 14,729)*

Leader of the House of Commons; Lord President of the Council

Jacob William Rees-Mogg. Born 24 May 1969; Son of late William Rees-Mogg, later Lord Rees-Mogg, and Gillian Rees-Mogg, née Morris; Married Helena de Chair 2007 (5 sons 1 daughter).

Education: Eton College; Trinity College, Oxford (BA history).

Non-political career: *Daily Telegraph* 1989; Conservative Central Office Research Department 1990; J. Rothschild 1991-93; Director: Lloyd George Management 1993-2007, Somerset Capital Management 2007-19.

Political career: Contested Central Fife 1997 and the Wrekin 2001 general elections. Member for North East Somerset since 6 May 2010 general election; Leader of the House of Commons; Lord President of the Council 2019-; Member: House of Commons Commission 2019-, Speaker's Committee for the Independent Parliamentary Standards Authority 2019-, Public Accounts Commission 2019-. *Select committees:* Member: Procedure 2010-15, European Scrutiny 2010-17, Works of Art 2013-15, House of Commons Governance 2014-15, Treasury 2015-17, Joint Committee on the Palace of Westminster 2015-16, Exiting the European Union 2017-19. President, Oxford University Conservative Association 1990; Cities of London and Westminster Conservative Association: Treasurer 1997-2000, Chair 2003-06; Trustee, Conservative Agents' Superannuation Fund.

Political interests: Treasury, Europe (Eurosceptic); China, Far East, India.

Other: Trustee: Mitsubishi UFJ Trust Oxford Foundation, Oxford Literary and Debating Union Trust; Chair, European Research Group 2018-; PC 2019.

Publications: Co-author, Freedom, Responsibility and the State: Curbing Over-Mighty Government (Politeia, 2012); The Victorians: Twelve Titans who Forged Britain (WH Allen, 2019).

Recreations: History, cricket.

Rt Hon Jacob Rees-Mogg MP, House of Commons, London SW1A 0AA
Tel: 020 7219 7118 *Email:* jacob.reesmogg.mp@parliament.uk
Constituency: North East Somerset Conservative Association, Rear of 16 High Street, Keynsham, Bristol BS31 1DQ
Tel: 0117-987 2313 *Email:* jacob@northeastsomersetconservatives.co.uk
Websites: www.northeastsomersetconservatives.co.uk/www.jacobreesmogg.com
Twitter: @Jacob_Rees_Mogg

LABOUR

REEVES, ELLIE

Lewisham West and Penge *(Majority 21,543)*

Shadow Solicitor General

Eleanor Claire Reeves. Born 11 December 1980; Married John Cryer 2012 (MP for Leyton and Wanstead) (2 sons).

Education: Cator Park Secondary School; Oxford University (law).

Non-political career: Barrister 2004-17. GMB.

Political career: Member for Lewisham West and Penge since 8 June 2017; PPS to Kate Osamor as Shadow Secretary of State for International Development 2018; Shadow Solicitor General 2020-. *Select committees:* Member, Justice 2017-20. Chair, PLP Departmental Group for Justice 2017-19. Labour Party: Member, National Executive Committee 2006-16, Vice-chair, London Labour Party 2016-19.

Political interests: Justice, workplace rights, housing, democracy, mental health, education, maternity rights.

Ellie Reeves MP, House of Commons, London SW1A 0AA
Tel: 020 7219 2589 *Email:* ellie.reeves.mp@parliament.uk
Constituency: 43 Sunderland Road, Forest Hill, London SE23 2PS
Website: www.elliereeves.com *Twitter:* @elliereeves

LABOUR

REEVES, RACHEL

Leeds West *(Majority 10,564)*

Shadow Chancellor of the Duchy of Lancaster

Rachel Jane Reeves. Born 13 February 1979; Daughter of Graham and Sally Reeves, both teachers; Married Dr Nicholas Joicey 2010 (1 daughter 1 son).

Education: Cator Park School; New College, Oxford (BA philosophy, politics and economics 2000); London School of Economics (MSc economics 2004).

Non-political career: Economist: Bank of England 2000-02; British Embassy, Washington DC 2002-03; Bank of England 2004-06, Halifax Bank of Scotland 2006-10. Amicus/MSF/Unite: Member 1998-; Youth representative, Southern Region 1999-2000, Political representative, Southern Region 2001-02, National political committee 2004-06, Yorkshire political committee 2006-.

Political career: Contested Bromley and Chislehurst 2005 general election and 2006 by-election. Member for Leeds West since 6 May 2010 general election; Shadow Minister for Work and Pensions (Pensions) 2010-11; Shadow Chief Secretary to the Treasury 2011-13; Shadow Secretary of State for Work and Pensions 2013-15; Shadow Chancellor of the Duchy of Lancaster 2020-. *Select committees:* Member: Business, Innovation and Skills 2010, Treasury 2015-17, Liaison 2017-20; Chair, Business, Energy and Industrial Strategy 2017-20; Member, Joint Committee on the National Security Strategy 2017-19. Vice-chair, PLP Departmental

Group for Transport 2010-14. Member, Economy – Work and Business Policy Commission; Labour Friends of Israel. *Councils and public bodies:* Governor: Kirkstall Valley Primary School 2006-10, West Leeds High School 2007-09.

Political interests: Economy, education; China, Japan, USA.

Other: Amnesty International 1996-; Fawcett Society 1998-; Fabian Society 1998-; Board: Leeds Healthy Living Network 2008-, Bramley and Rodley Community Action 2008-10; Patron: Bramley Elderly Action 2010-, June Hancock Mesothelioma Research Fund; Chair, Jo Cox Commission on Loneliness; Trustee, Bramley and Rodley Community Action 2008-.

Publications: How do Financial Markets React to Central Bank Communication? (Journal of Political Economy, 2006); Why Vote Labour? (2010); Contributor, The Purple Book (Progress, 2011); Alice in Westminster: The Political Life of Alice Bacon (I B Tauris, 2016).

Recreations: Tennis, swimming, cycling, reading.

Rachel Reeves MP, House of Commons, London SW1A 0AA
Tel: 020 7219 2898 *Email:* rachel.reeves.mp@parliament.uk
Constituency: 8a Bramley Shopping Centre, Bramley, Leeds, West Yorkshire LS13 2ET
Tel: 0113-255 2311 *Email:* rreevesmp@gmail.com Website: www.rachelreevesmp.co.uk
Twitter: @RachelReevesMP

LABOUR/ CO-OPERATIVE

REYNOLDS, JONATHAN

Stalybridge and Hyde *(Majority 2,946)*

Shadow Secretary of State for Work and Pensions

Jonathan Neil Reynolds. Born 28 August 1980; Son of Keith Reynolds, fireman, and Judith Reynolds, civil servant; Married Claire (3 sons 1 daughter).

Education: Houghton Kepier Comprehensive School; Sunderland City College; Manchester University (BA politics and modern history 2001); BPP Law School, Manchester (2009).

Non-political career: Parliamentary Assistant 2003-07; Trainee Solicitor, Addleshaw Goddard LLP 2007-10. Honorary Army, Major, Armed Forces Parliamentary Scheme 2010-11. Member: Unite, USDAW.

Political career: Member for Stalybridge and Hyde since 6 May 2010 general election; Opposition Assistant Whip 2010-11; PPS to Ed Miliband as Leader of the Opposition 2011-13; Shadow Minister for: Energy and Climate Change 2013-15, Transport (Rail) 2015-16; Shadow Economic Secretary to the Treasury (City Minister) 2016-20; Shadow Secretary of State for Work and Pensions 2020-. *Select committees:* Member: Science and Technology 2010-12, Finance and Services 2010-12, Business, Innovation and Skills 2016, Education, Skills and the Economy Sub-committee 2016, Ecclesiastical Committee 2017-19. Member: National Executive Committee, Labour Party 2003-05, 2020-, Co-operative Party; Labour Friends of Israel, Fabian Society Democratic Reform. *Councils and public bodies:* Tameside Council: Councillor 2007-11, Cabinet Secretary Without Portfolio (Policy and Corporate Performance).

Political interests: Transport, economy, financial services, manufacturing, autism, devolution; China, Germany, Middle East, USA.

Other: Chair, Christians on the Left 2016-; National Autistic Society; LLD, BPP University.

Recreations: Football, history, music, gardening.

Jonathan Reynolds MP, House of Commons, London SW1A 0AA
Tel: 020 7219 7155 *Email:* jonathan.reynolds.mp@parliament.uk
Constituency: Hyde Town Hall, Market Street, Hyde, Greater Manchester SK14 1AL
Tel: 0161-367 8077 *Email:* jonathan@jonathanreynolds.org.uk
Website: www.jonathanreynolds.org.uk *Twitter:* @jreynoldsmp

LABOUR

RIBEIRO-ADDY, BELL

Streatham *(Majority 17,690)*

Bellavia Janet Ribeiro-Addy. Born 1 March.

Education: Bradford University (BSc biomedical sciences with ethics and philosophy of science 2006); Queen Mary, University of London (MA medical law and ethics); BPP Law School (Graduate Diploma law 2015).

Non-political career: Events Co-ordinator, Kanu Nwankwo Heart Foundation 2000-02; Race Relations officer, Bradford University Students Union 2004-06; Campaign Co-ordinator and Administrator, National Assembly Against Racism 2007-08; National Black Students' Officer, National Union of Students 2008-10; Campaigns Officer, Palestine Solidarity Campaign Ltd 2010-11; Office of Diane Abbott MP: Parliamentary Assistant 2012-15, Political Adviser 2015-16, Chief of Staff 2016-19. Branch Secretary, Unite.

Political career: Member for Streatham since 12 December 2019; Shadow Minister for Home Office (Immigration) 2020. *Select committees:* Member, Women and Equalities 2020-. Co-ordinator, Diane4Leader Campaign 2010. *Councils and public bodies:* Governor, St Gabriel's College 2018-.

Political interests: NHS, education, Palestine, social housing, immigration.

Other: Amnesty International UK Campaigns and Impact Sub-committee: Government Relations and Advocacy.

Bell Ribeiro-Addy MP, House of Commons, London SW1A 0AA
Tel: 020 7219 6695 *Email:* bell.ribeiroaddy.mp@parliament.uk
Constituency: No constituency office publicised
Website: bellribeiroaddy.com *Twitter:* @BellRibeiroAddy

CONSERVATIVE

RICHARDS, NICOLA

West Bromwich East *(Majority 1,593)*

Nicola Faye Richards.

Education: The Kingswinford School; King Edward VI College Stourbridge; Birmingham University (BA political science 2016).

Non-political career: Temporary Sales Assistant, Next Group PLC 2011; Sales Assistant, Halfords 2012-13; Constituency Caseworker for Chris Kelly MP 2013-15; Parliamentary Assistant for Mike Wood MP 2015; Caseworker and Communications Officer for Margot James MP 2016-17; Midlands External Affairs Manager, The Jewish Leadership Council 2017; Public Affairs Officer, Holocaust Educational Trust 2017-18; Content Creator for Andy Street, Mayor of the West Midlands 2018-.

Political career: Member for West Bromwich East since 12 December 2019. *Select committees:* Member: Future Relationship with the European Union 2020-21, Women and Equalities 2020-. Member, Executive, 1922 Committee 2020-. Chair, Black Country Young Conservatives 2015-; Deputy Chair Political, Dudley South Conservatives 2018-. *Councils and public bodies:* Councillor, Dudley Council 2015-.

Nicola Richards MP, House of Commons, London SW1A 0AA
Tel: 020 7219 6945 *Email:* nicola.richards.mp@parliament.uk
Constituency: No constituency office publicised
Tel: 0121-553 6897 Website: www.nicolarichards.org.uk *Twitter:* @Nicola4WBE

CONSERVATIVE

RICHARDSON, ANGELA

Guildford *(Majority 3,337)*

PPS to Gavin Williamson as Secretary of State for Education

Angela Joy Richardson. Married Jeremy (3 children).

Non-political career: Numerous roles inkling Reconciliations Manager, Fund Management Supervisor, Settlements Officer Derivatives and Fixed Income, Bankers Trust NZ Limited 1994-99; Transitions Manager/Fund Managers Assistant, Schroders 1999-2000; PFI Administrator, AXA Investment Managers 2001-02.

Political career: Member for Guildford since 12 December 2019; Department for Education: Team PPS 2020-21, PPS to Gavin Williamson as Secretary of State 2021-. Conservative Party: Member 2016-, Voluntary Campaign Assistant 2016-17, Voluntary Campaign Manager

2017-18; National officer, Conservative Women's Organisation 2017-18; Guildford Conservative Association: Deputy Chairman, Fundraising and Membership 2017-18, Deputy Chairman, Political 2018-19. *Councils and public bodies:* Governor, Wey House School 2017-18; Vice-chair, Cranleigh Parish Council 2017-.

Other: Various roles including singer, actor, director, producer and vocal coach, Ewhurst Players 2012-. Chair, 1867 Patrons Club 2017-.

Angela Richardson MP, House of Commons, London SW1A 0AA
Tel: 020 7219 5851 *Email:* angela.richardson.mp@parliament.uk
Constituency: No constituency office publicised
Website: www.angelarichardson.uk *Twitter:* @AJRichardsonMP

LABOUR

RIMMER, MARIE

St Helens South and Whiston *(Majority 19,122)*

Opposition Whip

Marie Elizabeth Rimmer. Born 27 April 1947.

Non-political career: Pilkington Glass 1962-99: Statistics and accounts, Procurement/buyer of engineering equipment for glass production lines, Health and safety adviser in float glass manufacturing. Member, Unite.

Political career: Member for St Helens South and Whiston since 7 May 2015 general election; Shadow Minister for Disabled People 2017; Opposition Whip 2020-. *Select committees:* Member, Justice 2015-17, 2018-20. *Councils and public bodies:* St Helens Council: Councillor 1978-2016, Council Leader 1985-93, 1999-2013.

Other: Trustee, Hope Centre, St Helens.

Marie Rimmer CBE MP, House of Commons, London SW1A 0AA
Tel: 020 7219 4847 *Email:* marie.rimmer.mp@parliament.uk
Constituency: Century House, Hardshaw Street, St Helens WA10 1QU
Tel: 01744 752075 Website: www.marierimmer.co.uk *Twitter:* @MarieRimmer

CONSERVATIVE

ROBERTS, ROB

Delyn *(Majority 865)*

Robert Joseph Roberts. Married (1 daughter).

Education: Certificate mortgage advice and practice; Certificate regulated customer care and financial planning; IFS (Advanced Certificate mortgage advice and practise issues); Chartered Insurance Institute (Diploma financial planning); French, Welsh.

Non-political career: Independent Financial Advisor and Manager, Chesterton Grant 2003-09; Head of Mortgage Services, LIFT-Financial Ltd 2009-11; Wealth Planner, Sanlam 2011-15; Co-Founder and Director of Financial Planning, A Transparent Financial Solution Lrd 2015-18; Financial Planner, The Chester Partnership Ltd 2018-.

Political career: Member for Delyn since 12 December 2019. *Select committees:* Member: Welsh Affairs 2020-, Procedure 2020.

Rob Roberts MP, House of Commons, London SW1A 0AA
Tel: 020 7219 4901 *Email:* rob.roberts.mp@parliament.uk
Constituency: 8 Chester Street, Mold CH7 1EG
Tel: 01352 710232 Website: www.rjroberts.co.uk *Twitter:* @RobDelyn

CONSERVATIVE

ROBERTSON, LAURENCE

Tewkesbury *(Majority 22,410)*

Laurence Anthony Robertson. Born 29 March 1958; Son of James Robertson, former colliery electrician, and late Jean Robertson, née Larkin; Married Susan Lees 1989 (marriage dissolved) (2 stepdaughters); married Anne Marie, née Adams 2015.

Education: St James' Church of England Secondary School; Farnworth Grammar School; Bolton Institute of Higher Education (Diploma management services 1979).

Non-political career: Warehouse assistant 1976-77; Work study engineer 1977-83; Industrial management consultant 1983-89; Factory owner 1987-88; Charity fundraising, public relations and special events consultant 1988-.

Political career: Contested Makerfield 1987 and Ashfield 1992 general elections. Member for Tewkesbury 1997-2010, for Tewkesbury (revised boundary) since 6 May 2010 general election; Opposition Whip 2001-03; Shadow Minister for: Trade and Industry 2003, Economic Affairs 2003-05, Northern Ireland 2005-10; Trade Envoy to Angola and Zambia 2021-. *Select committees:* Member: Environmental Audit 1997-99, Joint Committee on Consolidation of Bills Etc 1997-2001, Social Security 1999-2001, European Scrutiny 1999-2002, Education and Skills 2001, Liaison 2010-17; Chair, Northern Ireland Affairs 2010-17; Member, Panel of Chairs 2017-. Chairman, Conservative Backbench Policy Committee on Northern Ireland 2017-19. Vice-chair, Association of Conservative Clubs 1997-2000; Chair, Westminster Africa Business Group 2001-.

Political interests: International development, constitutional affairs, countryside, Northern Ireland; Africa, particularly Ethiopia, UK, USA.

Other: Co-chairman, British-Irish Parliamentary Association 2011-17; Member, Executive Committee, Commonwealth Parliamentary Association UK 2015-17, 2018-19; Fellow, Industry and Parliament Trust 2001; Overseas aid charities, charities linked to horse racing.

Publications: Europe: The Case Against Integration (1991); The Right Way Ahead (1995).

Recreations: Horses and horseracing, golf, other sports (completed six marathons), reading, writing, countryside.

Laurence Robertson MP, House of Commons, London SW1A 0AA
Tel: 020 7219 4196 *Fax:* 020 7219 2325 *Email:* robertsonl@parliament.uk
Constituency: 22 High Street, Tewkesbury, Gloucestershire GL20 5AL
Tel: 01684 291640 Website: www.laurencerobertson.org.uk *Twitter:* @lrobertsonTewks

DEMOCRATIC UNIONIST PARTY

ROBINSON, GAVIN

Belfast East *(Majority 1,819)*

DUP Spokesman for Defence and Home Affairs

Gavin James Robinson. Born 22 November 1984; Married Lindsay (1 son).

Education: Greenwood, Strandtown and Grosvenor Grammar school; Ulster University (law); Queens University Belfast (MA politics).

Non-political career: Barrister 2007-11; Special Adviser to Peter Robinson MLA as First Minister 2011.

Political career: Member for Belfast East since 7 May 2015 general election; DUP Spokesperson for: Justice 2015-17, Home Affairs 2015-, Human Rights 2015-17, Defence 2017-. *Select committees:* Member: Northern Ireland Affairs 2015-16, Ecclesiastical Committee 2015-19, Defence 2016-, Arms Export Controls 2017-19. *Councils and public bodies:* Belfast City Council: Councillor 2010-15, Lord Mayor 2012-13, Alderman 2012-15.

Political interests: Economy, benefits, schools, healthcare.

Other: Ulster Orchestra Board; World Police and Fire Games; Board member: iESE, Craigavon House Preservation Trust.

Recreations: Art, sport.

Gavin Robinson MP, House of Commons, London SW1A 0AA
Tel: 020 7219 3000 *Email:* gavin.robinson.mp@parliament.uk
Constituency: Strandtown Hall, 96 Belmont Avenue, Belfast BT4 3DE
Tel: 028 9047 3111 *Twitter:* @GRobinsonDUP

CONSERVATIVE

ROBINSON, MARY

Cheadle *(Majority 2,336)*

Mary Josephine Robinson. Born 23 August 1955; Married Stephen (4 children).

Education: Degree law.

Non-political career: Founder, Robinson Rose Accountants -2008; Mary Felicity Design.

Political career: Member for Cheadle since 7 May 2015 general election; Team PPS, Department for Business, Energy and Industrial Strategy 2018. *Select committees:* Member: Communities and Local Government/Housing, Communities and Local Government 2015-,

Administration 2017-19, European Statutory Instruments 2018-. Chair, South Ribble Conservative Association. *Councils and public bodies:* Councillor, South Ribble Borough Council -2013; School governor.

Other: Member, Healthwatch Stockport.

Mary Robinson MP, House of Commons, London SW1A 0AA
Tel: 020 7219 8091 *Email:* mary.robinson.mp@parliament.uk
Constituency: 8a Station Road, Cheadle Hulme, Cheadle SK8 5AE
Tel: 0161-672 6855 Website: www.mary-robinson.org.uk *Twitter:* @MaryRobinson01

LABOUR

RODDA, MATT

Reading East *(Majority 5,924)*

Shadow Minister for Pensions

Matthew Richard Allen Rodda. Born 15 December 1966; Married Sarah (2 children).

Education: Sussex University.

Non-political career: Journalist: *Coventry Telegraph*, *The Independent*; Civil Servant, Department for Education; Educational Charity Project Manager. Usdaw, GMB.

Political career: Contested East Surrey 2010 and Reading East 2015 general elections. Member for Reading East since 8 June 2017; PPS to Andy McDonald as Shadow Secretary of State for Transport 2017-18; Shadow Minister for: Local Transport 2018-21, Work and Pensions (Pensions) 2021-. *Councils and public bodies:* Councillor, Reading Borough Council 2011-18.

Political interests: Europe, education, environment, housing, planning, heritage.

Matt Rodda MP, House of Commons, London SW1A 0AA
Tel: 020 7219 3980 *Email:* matt.rodda.mp@parliament.uk
Constituency: No constituency office publicised
Tel: 0118-206 2966 *Email:* mattroddampcasework@parliament.uk Website: www.mattrodda.net
Twitter: @MattRodda

CONSERVATIVE

ROSINDELL, ANDREW

Romford *(Majority 17,893)*

Andrew Richard Rosindell. Born 17 March 1966; Son of Frederick Rosindell, tailor, and Eileen Clark, pianist; Single.

Education: Marshalls Park Comprehensive School, Romford.

Non-political career: Central Press Features London 1984-86; Freelance journalist 1986-97; Parliamentary researcher to Vivian Bendall MP 1986-97; Director and international director, European Foundation 1997-2001. Armed Forces Parliamentary Scheme: Royal Marines 2002-03, RAF 2004-06, Army 2009-13.

Political career: Contested Glasgow Provan 1992 and Thurrock 1997 general elections. Member for Romford 2001-10, for Romford (revised boundary) since 6 May 2010 general election; Opposition Whip 2005-07; Shadow Minister for Home Affairs (Animal Welfare) 2007-10; Trade Envoy to Tanzania 2018-. *Select committees:* Member: Regulatory Reform 2001-05, Joint Committee on Statutory Instruments 2002-03, Constitutional Affairs 2004-05, Foreign Affairs 2010-, Panel of Chairs 2010-. Member, National Union Executive Committee, Conservative Party 1986-88, 1992-94; Chairman, Greater London Young Conservatives 1987-88; International secretary, Young Conservatives United Kingdom 1991-98; Chairman: National Young Conservatives 1993-94, Romford Conservative Association 1998-2001, Conservative Friends of Gibraltar 2002-; Member, Conservative Christian Fellowship; Vice-chair (campaigning), Conservative Party 2004-05; Chairman, Conservative Friends of Australia and New Zealand 2010-; Founding member, Conservatives for Britain 2015-16. *Councils and public bodies:* London Borough of Havering: Councillor 1990-2002, Alderman 2007-; Chairman, North Romford Community Area Forum 1998-2002.

Political interests: Foreign and international relations, European affairs, law and order, defence, local and regional government, animal welfare; Australia, British Overseas Territories and Crown Dependencies, Canada, Eastern Europe, Gulf States, Liechtenstein, New Zealand, Nordic countries, Switzerland, USA.

Other: Chairman, European Young Conservatives 1993-97; Executive member, International Democrat Union 1994-2002; Chair, International Young Democrat Union 1998-2002; Executive Committee, Commonwealth Parliamentary Association: Member 2010-15, 2017-, Vice-chair 2015-17; Member, Executive Committee, Inter-Parliamentary Union, British Group 2010-; British-Irish Parliamentary Assembly: Vice-chair 2015-17, Chair 2017-; Member, UK delegation to NATO Parliamentary Assembly 2015-19; Westminster Foundation for Democracy: Governor 2010, Board Member 2010-19; Fellow, Industry and Parliament Trust; Freedom, City of London. Romford Conservative and Constitutional Club, Royal Air Forces Association, Romford Royal British Legion Club.

Publications: Co-author, Defending Our Great Heritage (1993).

Recreations: Staffordshire bull terrier named Buster, travel, philately, history.

Andrew Rosindell MP, House of Commons, London SW1A 0AA
Tel: 020 7219 8475 *Email:* andrew.rosindell.mp@parliament.uk
Constituency: Margaret Thatcher House, 85 Western Road, Romford RM1 3LS
Tel: 01708 766700/01708 761583 *Email:* andrew@rosindell.com Website: www.rosindell.com
Twitter: @AndrewRosindell

CONSERVATIVE

ROSS, DOUGLAS

Moray *(Majority 513)*

Leader, Scottish Conservative and Unionist Party

Douglas Gordon Ross. Born 27 January 1983; Son of Alexander and Lesley Ross; Married Krystle Bentley 2015 (1 son).

Education: Forres Academy; Scottish Agricultural College, Ayr (BTech agriculture 2004).

Non-political career: Dairy farm worker 2004-07; Parliamentary Assistant to MSP 2007-16.

Political career: Contested Moray 2010 and 2015 general elections. Member for Moray since 8 June 2017; Team PPS, Department for Transport 2019; Scotland Office: PPS to Alister Jack as Secretary of State for Scotland 2019, Parliamentary Under-Secretary of State 2019-20; Government Whip (Lord Commissioner of HM Treasury) 2019-20. *Select committees:* Member: Home Affairs 2017-19, Scottish Affairs 2020-, Procedure 2020-. Contested Moray constituency 2011 and 2016 Scottish Parliament elections. MSP for Highlands and Islands region 2016 to 11 June 2017: Shadow Cabinet Secretary for Justice 2016-17. Leader, Scottish Conservative and Unionist Party 2020-. *Councils and public bodies:* Councillor, Moray Council 2001-17.

Recreations: Scottish FA qualified referee.

Douglas Ross MP, House of Commons, London SW1A 0AA
Tel: 020 7219 6510 *Email:* douglas.ross.mp@parliament.uk
Constituency: 63 High Street, Forres, Moray IV36 1PB
Tel: 01309 679253 Website: www.douglasross.org.uk *Twitter:* @douglas4moray

CONSERVATIVE

ROWLEY, LEE

North East Derbyshire *(Majority 12,876)*

Lee Benjamin Rowley. Born 11 September 1980; Son of Linda Rowley, teacher, and Malcolm Rowley, milkman.

Education: St Mary's High School, Chesterfield; Lincoln College, Oxford (BA modern history 2002); Manchester University (MA history 2004).

Non-political career: Senior Energy Analyst, H Clarkson & Co 2004-07; Strategy Analyst, Barclays 2007-08; Senior Consultant, Santander 2008-11; Manager, KPMG 2011-12; Santander: Senior Manager Corporate Change 2012-14, Head of Risk Change Management and Processes 2014-17; Head of Change and Portfolio, Co-op Insurance 2017.

Political career: Contested Bolsover 2010 and North East Derbyshire 2015 general elections. Member for North East Derbyshire since 8 June 2017; Team PPS, HM Treasury 2019-20. *Select committees:* Member: Joint Committee on Statutory Instruments 2017-18, Public Accounts 2018-19. Deputy Chair, Conservative Party 2020-. *Councils and public bodies:* Councillor, City of Westminster Council 2006-14.

Political interests: Housing and planning, economy, finance, transport, energy, artificial intelligence; Australia, USA.

Recreations: Travel, local history, fitness.

Lee Rowley MP, House of Commons, London SW1A 0AA
Tel: 020 7219 4197 *Email:* lee.rowley.mp@parliament.uk
Constituency: Eckington Business Centre, 42 Market Street, Eckington, Derbyshire S21 4JH
Tel: 01246 439222
128 High Street, Clay Cross S45 9EG
Tel: 01246 439222 Website: www.lee4ned.com *Twitter:* @Lee4NED

CONSERVATIVE

RUSSELL, DEAN

Watford *(Majority 4,433)*

Born 1976; Married (with children).

Education: De Montfort University (BSc physics and business studies 1998; MPhil physics/material science 2001).

Non-political career: Consultant, Bluewave 2001-02; Project manager, Reading Room 2002-3; Head of web division, 2B Group 2003-04; Client services director, iConcertina Creative 2003-07; Head of digital marketing, Precedent Communications 2007-10; Head of digital practice, Fleishman-Hillard 2010-12; LEWIS PR: Digital marketing director 2012-14, Creative strategy director 2014-15; Founder and CEO, epifny consulting 2016-.

Political career: Contested Luton North 2015 and Luton South 2017 general elections. Member for Watford since 12 December 2019. *Select committees:* Member: Health and Social Care 2020-, Joint Committee on Human Rights 2020-, Speaker's Advisory Committee on Works of Art 2020-. *Councils and public bodies:* Councillor, St Albans District Council 2010-13.

Dean Russell MP, House of Commons, London SW1A 0AA
Tel: 020 7219 3000 *Email:* dean.russell.mp@parliament.uk
Constituency: The Wenta Business Centre, Colne Way, Watford, Hertfordshire WD24 7ND
Tel: 01923 296790 Website: www.deanrussell.co.uk *Twitter:* @dean4watford

LABOUR/ CO-OPERATIVE

RUSSELL-MOYLE, LLOYD

Brighton Kemptown *(Majority 8,061)*

Born 14 September 1986.

Education: Priory School, Lewes; Sussex Downs College; Bradford University (BA peace studies 2012); Sussex University (LLM international law 2016).

Non-political career: Union Secretary/Treasurer, Bradford University 2007-09; Consultant, United Nations 2015. Member: GMB, Unite.

Political career: Contested Lewes 2015 general election. Member for Brighton Kemptown since 8 June 2017; PPS to Richard Burgon as Shadow Lord Chancellor and Secretary of State for Justice 2017-20; Shadow Minister for: Foreign and Commonwealth Office 2020, Shadow Minister for Environment, Food and Rural Affairs (Natural Environment and Air Quality) 2020. *Select committees:* Member: International Development 2017-19, Work of the Independent Commission for Aid Impact Sub-committee 2017-19, Arms Export Controls 2017-19, Joint Committee on the Draft Registration of Overseas Entities Bill 2019, Public Administration and Constitutional Affairs 2020-, International Trade 2020-. Chair, Brighton and Hove Labour Party 2016-; Member: LGBT Labour, Labour Campaign for International Development. *Councils and public bodies:* Councillor, Brighton and Hove City Council 2016-17.

Other: Young trainer and consultant, National Youth Agency 2003-06; Woodcraft Folk: Member, General Council 2004-13, Chair 2009-12; British Youth Council: Trustee 2006-07, Vice-chair (participation and development) 2007-08; European Volunteer, International Falcon Movement 2010-11; European Youth Forum: Board member 2011-14, Vice-president 2012-14; Member: Campaign for Nuclear Disarmament, Royal Society of Arts, British Humanist Association; Trustee, Graham's Gift; Chair, Children and Youth International; Trustee, Crew Club; Sussex University Branch, University and College Union.

Lloyd Russell-Moyle MP, House of Commons, London SW1A 0AA
Tel: 020 7219 2280 *Email:* lloyd.russellmoyle.mp@parliament.uk
Constituency: 11 Hunns Mere Way, Woodingdean BN2 6AH
Tel: 01273 550121 *Email:* lloyd@russell-moyle.co.uk Website: russell-moyle.co.uk
Twitter: @lloyd_rm

House of Commons MPs' Biographies

CONSERVATIVE

RUTLEY, DAVID

Macclesfield *(Majority 10,711)*

Government Whip (Lord Commissioner of HM Treasury)

David Henry Rutley. Born 7 March 1961; Son of John Rutley and Birthe Anderson; Married Rachel (4 children).

Education: The Priory School, Lewes; London School of Economics (BSc (Econ) 1985); Harvard Business School (MBA 1989).

Non-political career: Business development director, PepsiCo International 1991-94; Special adviser 1994-96: Cabinet Office, Ministry of Agriculture, HM Treasury; Director of business effectiveness, Safeway Stores 1996-2000; ASDA stores 2000-05: Director of Financial Services, Director of E-commerce; Sales and marketing director, Halifax General Insurance 2005-07; Barclays Bank 2008-10: Business consultant 2008-09, Marketing director 2009-10.

Political career: Contested St Albans 1997 general election. Member for Macclesfield since 6 May 2010 general election; PPS: to Damian Green as Minister of State: for Immigration, Home Office 2010-12, for Policing, Criminal Justice and Victims, Home Office and Ministry of Justice 2012-14, to David Lidington as Minister of State for Europe, Foreign and Commonwealth Office 2014-15, to Secretary of State for Work and Pensions: Iain Duncan Smith 2015-16, Stephen Crabb 2016, to Amber Rudd as Home Secretary 2016-17; Government Whip (Lord Commissioner of HM Treasury) 2017-; Department for Environment, Food and Rural Affairs: Interim Parliamentary Under Secretary of State for Environment May-July 2018, Parliamentary Under-Secretary of State for Food and Animal Welfare 2018-19. *Select committees:* Member, Treasury 2010.

Political interests: Economy, business, home affairs, rural issues, community groups; China, Denmark, Slovenia, USA.

Other: Trustee, Kids Count 1988; Member: British Mountaineering Council, RSPB, National Trust; Many charities in Macclesfield including: NSPCC (East Cheshire Branch), East Cheshire Hospice, Macclesfield Silk Museum Trust, Just Drop In, Macclesfield Community Garden Centre, Poynton Royal British Legion Concert Band.

Recreations: Spending time with family, walking and climbing in the Peak District, mountaineering, fishing, ornithology.

David Rutley MP, House of Commons, London SW1A 0AA
Tel: 020 7219 7106 *Email:* david.rutley.mp@parliament.uk
Constituency: c/o Macclesfield Conservative Association, West Bank Road, Macclesfield, Cheshire SK10 3BT
Tel: 01625 422848 Websites: www.macclesfieldconservatives.org.uk/www.davidrutley.org.uk
Twitter: @DavidRutley

CONSERVATIVE

SAMBROOK, GARY

Birmingham, Northfield *(Majority 1,640)*

Gary William Sambrook. Born 25 June 1989.

Education: The College High School; Birmingham City University (BA human resources management and public relations 2012).

Non-political career: Human Resources Assistant 2012-13; Campaign Manager, Conservative Party 2013-15; Parliamentary Assistant to James Morris MP 2015-19.

Political career: Member for Birmingham, Northfield since 12 December 2019. *Select committees:* Member: Future Relationship with the European Union 2020-21, Regulatory Reform 2020-, Procedure 2020, Ecclesiastical Committee 2020-. Member, Executive, 1922 Committee 2020-. *Councils and public bodies:* Birmingham City Council: Councillor 2014-, Shadow Cabinet Member for Homes and Neighbourhoods.

Political interests: Education, housing, regeneration.

Other: Trustee: Kingstanding Regeneration Trust, Birmingham YMCA, The Rep Theatre.

Gary Sambrook MP, House of Commons, London SW1A 0AA
Tel: 020 7219 3000 *Email:* gary.sambrook.mp@parliament.uk
Constituency: Longbridge Place, 23 Ambassador Avenue, Longbridge, Birmingham B31 2GZ
Tel: 0121-472 0740 *Email:* northfield@garysambrook.co.uk Website: www.garysambrook.co.uk
Twitter: @GarySambrook89

PLAID CYMRU

SAVILLE ROBERTS, LIZ

Dwyfor Meirionnydd *(Majority 4,740)*

Plaid Cymru Parliamentary Group Leader; Spokesperson for Attorney General, Business, Energy and Industrial Strategy, Home Affairs, Justice, Transport and Women and Equalities

Elizabeth Saville Roberts. Born 16 December 1964; Married Dewi Wyn Roberts 1994 (twin daughters).

Education: Blackheath High School; Avery Hill College, Eltham; Aberystwyth University (BA Celtic studies 1987); WJEC Postgraduate Certificate (1988); National Council for Training of Journalists (1992); PGCE (1996); Welsh, Irish, French, some Russian.

Non-political career: Secretary, Russian and French departments, Queen Mary College, London 1988-89; Staff reporter, Retail Journalist 1989-90; News Reporter 1990-93: *Holyhead and Anglesey Mail*, *Caernarfon Herald*, *Herald Môn*, *Herald Cymraeg*; Lecturer, Manager and Director, Coleg Meirion-Dwyfor/Grwp Llandrillo Menai 1993-2014. Member, UCAC (Welsh teachers' union) 1993-.

Political career: Member for Dwyfor Meirionnydd since 7 May 2015 general election; Plaid Cymru: Spokesperson for: Home Affairs 2015-, Education 2015-17, Health 2015-16, Environment, Food and Rural Affairs 2015-17, Women and Equalities 2015-, Communities and Local Government 2015-17, Energy and Natural Resources 2015-16, Business, Energy and Industrial Strategy 2016-, Justice 2016-, Constitutional Affairs 2016-17, Parliamentary Group Leader 2017-, Spokesperson for: Attorney General 2020-, Transport 2020-. *Select committees:* Member: Welsh Affairs 2015-17, 2017-19, Joint Committee on the Draft Domestic Abuse Bill 2019. Contested North Wales region 2003, Mid and West Wales (4) region 2007 and North Wales (4) region 2011 National Assembly for Wales elections. *Councils and public bodies:* Councillor, Gwynedd Council 2004-15; Vice-president, Local Government Association 2017-.

Political interests: Economic development of Wales, rural affairs, social justice, sustainability; Wales.

Other: Member, Amnesty 2008-; Trustee, Canolfan Iaith Nant Gwrtheyrn -2016; PC 2019. Barddas, Cymdeithas Hanes Uwchgwyrfai, Cymdeithas Marchogaeth Llyn Club.

Recreations: Horse riding, hill-walking, agricultural shows, languages, folk music, poetry and eisteddfodau.

Rt Hon Liz Saville Roberts MP, House of Commons, London SW1A 0AA
Tel: 020 7219 6876 *Email:* liz.savilleroberts.mp@parliament.uk
Constituency: Angorfa, Heol Meurig, Dolgellau, Gwynedd LL40 1LN
Tel: 01341 422661 *Twitter:* @LSRPlaid

CONSERVATIVE

SAXBY, SELAINE

North Devon *(Majority 14,813)*

Selaine Rachel Saxby. Born 25 November 1970; Single.

Education: Cambridge University (MA mathematics and management studies 1992); Exeter University (PGCE mathematics 2017).

Non-political career: Founder and Owner, LessBounce.com 2000-16; Chief of Staff to Ben Howlett MP 2015-17; Owner, Selaine Saxby Business Support 2017-18; Teacher and PGCE, Bideford College 2018-19. NASUWT.

Political career: Contested Llanelli 2015 general election. Member for North Devon since 12 December 2019. *Select committees:* Member, Work and Pensions 2020-. *Councils and public bodies:* Councillor, North Devon Council 2019-.

Political interests: Rural disconnect, broadband, health, transport, fisheries.

Other: Delivery Partner, Nordic Walking UK; The Calvert Trust Exmoor. Torridge Gig Rowing.

Recreations: Nordic walking, gig rowing.

Selaine Saxby MP, House of Commons, London SW1A 0AA
Tel: 020 7219 5952 *Email:* selaine.saxby.mp@parliament.uk
Constituency: Church House, Church Lane, Barnstaple EX31 1DE
Tel: 01271 327990 Website: www.selainesaxby.org.uk *Twitter:* @SelaineSaxby

CONSERVATIVE

SCULLY, PAUL

Sutton and Cheam *(Majority 8,351)*

Parliamentary Under-Secretary of State (Minister for Small Business, Consumers and Labour Markets), Department for Business, Energy and Industrial Strategy and Minister for London

Paul Stuart Scully. Born 29 April 1968; Married Emma Scully.

Education: Bedford School; Reading University (chemistry and food science).

Non-political career: Parliamentary Assistant to Alok Sharma MP 2010-12; Partner, Nudge Factory Ltd 2011-.

Political career: Member for Sutton and Cheam since 7 May 2015 general election; Trade Envoy to Burma, Brunei and Thailand 2017-20; PPS to Baroness Evans of Bowes Park as Leader of the House of Lords and Lord Privy Seal 2017-18; Parliamentary Under-Secretary of State (Minister for Small Business, Consumers and Labour Markets), Department for Business, Energy and Industrial Strategy 2020-; Minister for London 2020-. *Select committees:* Member: Petitions 2015-20, Standing Orders 2015-17, International Development 2016-20; Work of the Independent Commission for Aid Impact Sub-committee: Member 2016-17, Chair 2017-20. Member, Conservative Party's Project Maja and Project Shapla; Conservative Party: Vice-chairman, London -2019, Deputy Chairman 2019-20. *Councils and public bodies:* Sutton Borough Council: Councillor -2010, Former Leader of the Opposition; Governor, Manor Park Primary School.

Political interests: Small business, local government, education, international development, human rights; Bangladesh, Burma, India, Israel, Saudi Arabia, Sri Lanka.

Paul Scully MP, House of Commons, London SW1A 0AA
Tel: 020 7219 4837 *Email:* paul.scully.mp@parliament.uk
Constituency: Donnington House, 2a Sutton Court Road, Sutton SM1 4SY
Tel: 020 8661 9900 *Email:* info@scully.org.uk Website: www.scully.org.uk *Twitter:* @scullyp

CONSERVATIVE

SEELY, BOB

Isle of Wight *(Majority 23,737)*

Robert William Henry Seely. Born 1 June 1966; Son of late Richard Seely and late Helga Seely; Divorced.

Education: Harrow School; Birkbeck University (MA); Oxford University (Research Associate, Changing Character of War Programme); Russian.

Non-political career: Journalist 1990-2000: *The Times* Kiev Correspondent, *Washington Post* Kiev Special Correspondent, Associated Press London; Adviser, CCHQ 2000-05; Public relations team, MTV 2005-08. Mobilised or on FTRS 2008-17.

Political career: Contested Broxtowe 2005 general election. Member for Isle of Wight since 8 June 2017; Team PPS: Department for Environment, Food and Rural Affairs 2019, Ministry of Defence 2019-20. *Select committees:* Member: Foreign Affairs 2018-, Arms Export Controls 2018-19. *Councils and public bodies:* Councillor, Isle of Wight Council 2013-17.

Political interests: The Isle of Wight, UK Islands, overseas policy: foreign, defence and aid, housing and land use, education; States of the former Soviet Union, the Middle East.

Other: Military MBE 2016. Island Sailing Club, Yarmouth Sailing Club.

Publications: Russo-Chechen Conflict 1800-2000: A Deadly Embrace (2001, 2004); Co-Author, War and Humanitarian Action in Chechnya (2002).

Bob Seely MBE MP, House of Commons, London SW1A 0AA
Tel: 020 7219 1840 *Email:* bob.seely.mp@parliament.uk
Constituency: Northwood House, Ward Avenue, Cowes PO31 8AZ
Tel: 01983 220220 Website: www.bobseely.org.uk *Twitter:* @iowbobseely

CONSERVATIVE

SELOUS, ANDREW

South West Bedfordshire *(Majority 18,583)*

Andrew Edmund Armstrong Selous. Born 27 April 1962; Son of Commander Gerald Selous and Miranda Selous, née Casey; Married Harriet Marston 1993 (3 daughters).

Education: Eton College; London School of Economics (BSc (Econ) industry and trade 1984); French, German.

Non-political career: Director, CNS Electronics Ltd 1988-94; Underwriter, Great Lakes Re (UK) plc 1991-2001. TA officer, Honourable Artillery Company, Royal Regiment of Fusiliers 1981-94.

Political career: Contested Sunderland North 1997 general election. Member for South West Bedfordshire since 7 June 2001 general election; PPS to Michael Ancram as Shadow Foreign Secretary 2004; Opposition Whip 2004-06; Shadow Minister for Work and Pensions 2006-10; PPS to Iain Duncan Smith as Secretary of State for Work and Pensions 2010-14; Assistant Government Whip 2014-16; Ministry of Justice: Parliamentary Under-Secretary of State: (Minister for Prisons, Probation and Rehabilitation) 2014-15, for Prisons, Probation, Rehabilitation and Sentencing 2015-16; Trade Envoy to South Africa 2017-; Second Church Estates Commissioner 2020-. *Select committees:* Member: Work and Pensions 2001-05, Ecclesiastical Committee 2010-14, 2020-, Health/Health and Social Care 2016-19, Joint Committee on Draft Health Service Safety Investigation Bill 2018, European Statutory Instruments 2018-19. Chair: Conservative Christian Fellowship 2001-06, Social Justice Caucus. *Councils and public bodies:* Vice-President, Local Government Association 2019-.

Political interests: Trade and industry, families, defence, homelessness, environment, sustainable aviation and child health and nutrition; Australia, Nicaragua, USA.

Other: Parkinsons UK, Homestart, Leighton Linslade Homeless, Brain Tumour Action; ACII 1993; Chartered Insurer 1998. Leighton Buzzard Conservative Club, Dunstable Conservative Club.

Recreations: Family, walking, tennis, bridge.

Andrew Selous MP, House of Commons, London SW1A 0AA
Tel: 020 7219 8134 *Fax:* 020 7219 1741 *Email:* andrew.selous.mp@parliament.uk
Constituency: Rooms 26/27, Wentworth House, 83 High Street North, Dunstable, Bedfordshire LU6 1JJ
Tel: 01582 662821 Website: www.andrewselous.org.uk *Twitter:* @AndrewSelous

LABOUR

SHAH, NAZ

Bradford West *(Majority 27,019)*

Shadow Minister for Community Cohesion

Naseem Akhter Shah. Born 13 November 1973; 1 daughter 2 sons.

Education: Urdu, Punjabi.

Non-political career: Social worker, Bradford Council 1998-99; Senior advocate, Bradnet 2000-03; Commissioner, Bradford and Airedale Primary Care Trust 2003-07; Programme director, Local Government Yorkshire and Humber 2009-10; Chief executive, Monster Fun and Listers Ladies Gym 2010-13.

Political career: Member for Bradford West since 7 May 2015 general election; PPS to John McDonnell as Shadow Chancellor of the Exchequer 2016; Shadow Minister for: Women and Equalities 2018-20, Communities and Local Government (Community Cohesion) 2020-. *Select committees:* Member, Home Affairs 2015-18. Suspended from Labour Party April-July 2016. *Councils and public bodies:* Executive board member, Nashayman Housing Association 2001-03.

Other: Chair, Sharing Voices Bradford 2012-15; Emma Humphries Memorial Prize (1999).

Naz Shah MP, House of Commons, London SW1A 0AA
Tel: 020 7219 8603 *Email:* naz.shah.mp@parliament.uk
Constituency: West Riding House, 41 Cheapside, Bradford, West Yorkshire BD1 4HR
Tel: 01274 725171 *Twitter:* @NazShahBfd

DEMOCRATIC UNIONIST PARTY

SHANNON, JIM

Strangford *(Majority 7,071)*

DUP Spokesperson for Human Rights and Health

Richard James Shannon. Born 25 March 1955; Son of Richard and Moira Shannon, both retired; Married Sandra George 1987 (3 sons).

Education: Coleraine Academical Institution (1971); Ulster-Scots.

Non-political career: Self-employed pork retailer 1985-. Ulster Defence Regiment 1973-75, 1976-77; Royal Artillery, TA 1977-88. Member: Mid Ards Branch, Ulster Farmers' Union, TGWU 1976-85.

Political career: Member for Strangford since 6 May 2010 general election; DUP Spokesperson for: Health 2010-, Transport 2010-17, Equality 2012-17, Human Rights 2012-15, 2017-. *Select committees:* Member: Defence 2015-16, Arms Export Controls 2016-17, Northern Ireland Affairs 2016-19, Ecclesiastical Committee 2020-. Member Northern Ireland Forum for Political Dialogue 1996-98; MLA for Strangford 1998-2010. *Councils and public bodies:* Ards Borough Council: Councillor 1985-2010, Mayor 1991-92.

Political interests: Farming, fishing, environment, Ulster-Scots; Scotland, USA.

Other: Secretary, Loyal Orange Institution, Kircubbin LOL 1900; Registrar, Royal Black Perceptory Ballywater No 675; Comber, Apprentice Boys of Derry; Member: British Association Shooting and Conservation, Countryside Alliance NI, Royal British Legion, Greyabbey Branch, National Trust; NSPCC, Action Cancer; General Service Medal, Ulster Defence Regiment. Carrowdore Shooting Club.

Recreations: Fieldsports, football.

Jim Shannon MP, House of Commons, London SW1A 0AA
Tel: 020 7219 7160 *Fax:* 020 7219 2347 *Email:* jim.shannon.mp@parliament.uk
Constituency: 34a Frances Street, Newtownards, Co Down BT23 7DN
Tel: 028 9182 7990 *Twitter:* @JimShannonMP

CONSERVATIVE

SHAPPS, GRANT

Welwyn Hatfield *(Majority 10,955)*

Secretary of State for Transport

Born 14 September 1968; Son of Tony and Beryl Shapps; Married Belinda Goldstone 1997 (1 son twin son and daughter).

Education: Watford Boys' Grammar School; Cassio College, Watford (OND business and finance 1987); Manchester Polytechnic (HND business and finance 1989).

Non-political career: Sales executive, Nashua Gestetner 1989-90; Printhouse Corporation: Founder 1990-, Chairman 2000-; Adviser, Avanti Communications Group 2017-.

Political career: Contested North Southwark and Bermondsey 1997 and Welwyn Hatfield 2001 general elections. Member for Welwyn Hatfield since 5 May 2005 general election; Shadow Minister for Housing (attending Shadow Cabinet) 2007-10; Minister of State for Housing and Local Government, Department for Communities and Local Government 2010-12; Member Speaker's Committee on the Electoral Commission 2010-12; Minister without Portfolio, Cabinet Office 2012-15; Minister of State: Department for International Development 2015, Foreign and Commonwealth Office 2015; Secretary of State for Transport 2019-. *Select committees:* Member, Public Administration 2005-07. Branch chair, Barnhill, Brent North 1995-99; Member: Conservative Friends of Israel 1995, Selsdon Group 1996, Conservative Foreign Affairs Forum 1996; Vice-President, North Southwark and Bermondsey Association 1997; Conservative Party: Vice-chair (Campaigning) 2005-09, Chairman 2012-15.

Political interests: Health, education, home affairs, foreign affairs.

Other: Isabel Hospice, Resolve, Hertfordshire Action on Disability, Mixed Group; MP Contribution to Central Lobby, *PoliticsHome* awards 2012; PC 2010.

Rt Hon Grant Shapps MP, House of Commons, London SW1A 0AA
Tel: 020 7219 8497 *Email:* shappsg@parliament.uk
Constituency: Welwyn Hatfield Conservative Association, Maynard House, The Common, Hatfield, Hertfordshire AL10 0NF
Tel: 01707 262632 Website: www.shapps.com *Twitter:* @grantshapps

CONSERVATIVE

SHARMA, ALOK

Reading West *(Majority 4,117)*

President of the UN COP26 Climate Conference

Alok Kumar Sharma. Born 7 September 1967; Married (2 daughters).

Education: Blue Coat School, Reading; Salford University (BSc applied physics with electronics 1988); Institute of Chartered Accountants in England and Wales (ACA 1991).

Non-political career: Chartered accountant; Accountancy and corporate finance advicer.

Political career: Member for Reading West since 6 May 2010 general election; PPS to: Mark Hoban as Financial Secretary 2010-12, Oliver Letwin as Chancellor of the Duchy of Lancaster 2015-16; Parliamentary Under-Secretary of State (Minister for Asia and the Pacific), Foreign and Commonwealth Office 2016-17; Minister of State for: Housing and Planning, Department for Communities and Local Government 2017-18, Employment, Department for Work and Pensions 2018-19; Secretary of State for: International Development 2019-20, Business, Energy and Industrial Strategy 2020-21; President of the UN COP26 Climate Conference (attends Cabinet) 2020-. *Select committees:* Member: Science and Technology 2010-11, Treasury 2014-15. Conservative Party: Member 1978-, Vice-chairman (BME communities); Chair, Conservative Friends of India.

Political interests: Trade, industry, finance; India, Pakistan, Sweden.

Other: Former chair, economic affairs committee, Bow Group; Patron: Wren Free School, Bengali Cultural Society of Reading; Member, Institute of Chartered Accountants in England and Wales; PC 2019.

Rt Hon Alok Sharma MP, House of Commons, London SW1A 0AA
Tel: 020 7219 7131 *Email:* alok.sharma.mp@parliament.uk
Constituency: 16c Upton Road, Tilehurst, Reading, Berkshire RG30 4BJ
Tel: 0118-941 3803 Website: www.aloksharma.co.uk *Twitter:* @AlokSharma_RDG

LABOUR

SHARMA, VIRENDRA

Ealing Southall *(Majority 16,084)*

Virendra Kumar Sharma. Born 5 April 1947; Married Nirmala (1 son 1 daughter).

Education: London School of Economics (MA 1979); Punjabi, Hindi, Urdu.

Non-political career: Day services manager, London Borough of Hillingdon 1996-2007. Member, TGWU/Unite.

Political career: Member for Ealing Southall 17 July 2007 by-election to 2010, for Ealing Southall (revised boundary) since 6 May 2010 general election; PPS to Phil Woolas as Minister of State, Home Office and HM Treasury 2008-09. *Select committees:* Member: Joint Committee on Human Rights 2007-10, 2010-15, Justice 2007-09, International Development 2009-10, 2015-, Health 2010-15, Arms Export Controls 2016-17, Work of the Independent Commission for Aid Impact Sub-committee 2017-19, Panel of Chairs 2017-. Labour Party National Ethnic Minorities Officer 1986-92. *Councils and public bodies:* Councillor, London Borough of Ealing 1982-2010: Former Mayor.

Political interests: Health, international development, human rights; Bangladesh, Canada, Cyprus, India, Mauritius, Nepal, Pakistan, Sri Lanka, USA.

Other: Member, UK delegation, Parliamentary Assembly, Council of Europe 2016-; Member, Indian Workers Association; Age UK.

Virendra Sharma MP, House of Commons, London SW1A 0AA
Tel: 020 7219 6080 *Fax:* 020 7219 3969 *Email:* sharmav@parliament.uk
Constituency: 112a The Green, Southall, Middlesex UB2 4BQ
Tel: 020 8571 1003 Website: www.virendrasharma.com *Twitter:* @VirendraSharma

LABOUR/
CO-OPERATIVE

SHEERMAN, BARRY

Huddersfield *(Majority 4,937)*

Barry John Sheerman. Born 17 August 1940; Son of late Albert Sheerman and Florence Sheerman, née Pike; Married Pamela Brenchley 1965 (1 son 3 daughters).

Education: Hampton Grammar School; Kingston Technical College (economics and politics); London School of Economics (BSc economics 1965); London University (MSc political sociology 1967); French.

Non-political career: Lecturer, University College of Wales, Swansea 1966-79. Member: AUT, Amicus.

Political career: Contested Taunton October 1974 general election. Member for Huddersfield East 1979-83, for Huddersfield 1983-2010, for Huddersfield (revised boundary) since 6 May 2010 general election; Opposition Spokesperson for: Employment and Education 1983-88, Home Affairs 1988-92, Disabled People's Rights 1992-94; Chair, Cross-Party Advisory Group on Preparation for EMU; Vice-chair, Joint Pre-Legislative Committee Investigating the Financial Services and Markets Bill; Chair, Cross-Party Advisory Group to Chancellor of the Exchequer on European Economic Reform. *Select committees:* Chair, Education and Employment (Education Sub-committee) 1999-2001; Member: Liaison 1999-2010, Education and Employment (Employment Sub-committee) 2000-01; Chair, Education and Skills/Children, Schools and Families 2001-10; Member: Liaison (Liaison Sub-committee) 2002-10, Future Relationship with the European Union 2020-21. Chair, PLP Departmental Group for Environment, Food and Rural Affairs 2015-. Member, Co-operative Party; Chair, Labour Forum for Criminal Justice. *Councils and public bodies:* Councillor, Loughor and Lliw Valley Unitary District Council 1972-79; Emeritus Governor, London School of Economics 1995-.

Political interests: Trade, industry, finance, further education, education, economy, social enterprise and entrepreneurship; European Union, Kenya, South America, USA.

Other: World Bank Business Partnership for Development Global Road Safety Partnership (GRSP); Chair: Parliamentary Advisory Council on Transport Safety 1981-, National Educational Research and Development Trust; Fellow, Industry and Parliament Trust 1982, 1996; Chair: Urban Mines 1995-, Networking for Industry/Policy Connect 1995-2017, Schools to Work; Director and trustee, National Children's Centre; Chair: John Clare Education and Environment Trust 2004-, Sutton Trust Education Advisory Group 2015-; National Children's Centre, John Clare Trust, Dominic Rogers Trust; FRSA, FRGS, City and Guilds Institute; Two honorary doctorates. Member, Royal Commonwealth Club.

Publications: Co-author, Harold Laski: A Life on the Left (1993).

Recreations: Walking, biography, films, social entrepreneurship.

Barry Sheerman MP, House of Commons, London SW1A 0AA
Tel: 020 7219 5037 *Fax:* 020 7219 2404 *Email:* sheermanb@parliament.uk
Constituency: Office F18, The Media Centre, 7 Northumberland Street, Huddersfield, West Yorkshire HD1 1RL
Tel: 01484 487970 Website: barrysheerman.co.uk *Twitter:* @BarrySheerman

CONSERVATIVE

SHELBROOKE, ALEC

Elmet and Rothwell *(Majority 17,353)*

Alec Edward Shelbrooke. Born 10 January 1976; Son of Cllr Derek Shelbrooke and Patricia Shelbrooke JP, both retired teachers; Married Susan Shelbrooke.

Education: St George's CoE Comprehensive School, Gravesend; Brunel University (BSc mechanical engineering 1998).

Non-political career: Project Manager, Leeds University 1999-2010. Member, MSF/Unite 1999-2010.

Political career: Contested Wakefield 2005 general election. Member for Elmet and Rothwell since 6 May 2010 general election; PPS to: Theresa Villiers as Minister of State, Department for Transport 2010-12, Mike Penning as Minister of State, Northern Ireland Office 2012-13, Hugo Swire as Minister of State, Foreign and Commonwealth Office 2014-15, Priti Patel as Minister of State for Employment, Department for Work and Pensions 2015-16. *Select committees:* Member: Backbench Business 2013-14, Communities and Local Government 2014-15, European Scrutiny 2015-16. Member, Executive, 1922 Committee 2016-20. Conservative Party: Deputy chair, Elmet Conservative Association 2001-04, Vice-chairman, International 2017-. *Councils and public bodies:* Councillor, Leeds City Council 2004-10.

Political interests: Foreign affairs, transport, welfare, international aid; Middle East, USA.

Other: UK delegation to NATO Parliamentary Assembly: Member 2015-20, Leader 2020-; Member: Institute of Mechanical Engineers 1994-, Association of Project Managers 2001-11; Martin House, Lee's Smile; PC 2019. Carlton Club.

Recreations: Football, motor racing, cricket, music, reading.

Rt Hon Alec Shelbrooke MP, House of Commons, London SW1A 0AA
Tel: 020 7219 3000 *Email:* alec.shelbrooke.mp@parliament.uk
Constituency: First Floor, 43 Market Place, Wetherby, Leeds, West Yorkshire LS22 6LN
Tel: 01937 589002 Website: www.alecshelbrooke.co.uk *Twitter:* @AlecShelbrooke

SCOTTISH NATIONAL PARTY

SHEPPARD, TOMMY

Edinburgh East *(Majority 10,417)*

SNP Spokesperson for Constitutional Affairs

Born 6 March 1959; Partner Kate.

Education: Aberdeen University (Degree sociology and politics 1982).

Non-political career: Vice-president, National Union of Students; Public Relations; Founder, Stand Comedy Club 1995-.

Political career: Contested (Labour) Bury St Edmunds 1992 general election. Member (SNP) for Edinburgh East since 7 May 2015 general election; SNP: Spokesperson for: Cabinet Office 2015-19, House of Lords 2017-19, Scotland Office 2017-19, Shadow Leader of the House of Commons 2020-21, Spokesperson for Constitutional Affairs 2021-. *Select committees:* Member: Standards 2015-17, Privileges 2015-17, Scottish Affairs 2017-19, Finance 2020-. Assistant general secretary, Labour Party 1993-96. *Councils and public bodies:* Former Labour Councillor, London Borough of Hackney Council; Board member, Shadow Sponsor Body for the Houses of Parliament Restoration and Renewal Programme 2020-.

Other: Substitute Member, UK Delegation to Parliamentary Assembly of Council of Europe 2017-; Member, national council, Scottish Independence Convention.

Tommy Sheppard MP, House of Commons, London SW1A 0AA
Tel: 020 7219 6653 *Email:* tommy.sheppard.mp@parliament.uk
Constituency: 94 Portobello High Street, Portobello, Edinburgh EH15 1AN
Tel: 0131-661 8023 Website: tommysheppardmp.scot *Twitter:* @TommySheppard

LABOUR

SIDDIQ, TULIP

Hampstead and Kilburn *(Majority 14,188)*

Shadow Minister for Children and Early Years

Tulip Rizwana Siddiq. Born 16 September 1982; Married Chris Percy 2013 (1 daughter 1 son).

Education: University College London (BA); King's College London (MA); University of London, Birkbeck (MSc).

Non-political career: Policy adviser to Dame Tessa Jowell MP; Researcher: Philip Gould Association, Greater London Authority; Caseworker for Harry Cohen MP. Member, Unite.

Political career: Member for Hampstead and Kilburn since 7 May 2015 general election; PPS to Michael Dugher as Shadow Secretary of State for Culture, Media and Sport 2015-16; Shadow Minister for Education: (Early Years) 2016-17, (Children and Early Years) 2020-. *Select committees:* Member: Women and Equalities 2015, 2017-18, 2018-19, Public Administration and Constitutional Affairs 2018-19. Member, Co-operative Party; Labour Party: Deputy field director to Ed Miliband MP, 2010 Leadership campaign, Parliamentary Lead (Party Development) (reporting to Angela Rayner as Party Chair) 2020-. *Councils and public bodies:* Camden Council: Councillor 2010-14, Cabinet Member for Culture and Communities 2010-14; Governor: Richard Cobden Primary School, Working Men's College, Camden and Islington NHS Trust.

Other: Member, Royal Society of Arts; Chair: Camden Library Network, Camden Faith Leaders' Forum.

Tulip Siddiq MP, House of Commons, London SW1A 0AA
Tel: 020 7219 6276 *Email:* tulip.siddiq.mp@parliament.uk
Constituency: 21 Winchester Road, London NW3 3NR
Tel: 020 8127 5525 *Email:* tulip@tulipsiddiq.com Website: www.tulipsiddiq.com
Twitter: @TulipSiddiq

CONSERVATIVE

SIMMONDS, DAVID

Ruislip, Northwood and Pinner *(Majority 16,394)*

David Timothy Simmonds. Married (2 children).

Education: Durham University (BA politics, economics and management); Birkbeck College, London (Postgraduate Certificate elected member development); Chartered Institute of Insurers (Certificate financial planning 1997); French.

Non-political career: Graduate Trainee, Eagle Star 1997; Financial Adviser: Lloyds TSB, HSBC.

Political career: Contested Caerphilly 2001 and Erewash 2005 general elections. Member for Ruislip, Northwood and Pinner since 12 December 2019. *Select committees:* Member: Education 2020-, Finance 2020-. Treasurer, Conservative Councillors Association 2011-15, 2016-19. *Councils and public bodies:* Hillingdon Council: Councillor 1998-, Deputy Leader of the Council 2002-20, Lead on Education and Children's Services; Non-executive Director, NHS Hillingdon; Magistrate; Vice-president, Local Government Association 2020-.

Political interests: Education, teachers, children, immigration and asylum.

Other: Founding Member and Chair, Education Employers' Organisation for Europe; Leader of the Conservative Group: Education Commission EU Committee of the Regions; EU Committee of the Regions 2018-20, Congress of the Council of Europe 2019-; Local Government Association: Chair, Children and Young People Board 2011-15, Chair, Improvement and Innovation Board 2015-16, Chair, Asylum and Refugee Task Group; Deputy Chair, National Conservative Councillors' Association; Trustee, Early Intervention Foundation; Chair, National Employers Organisation for Schoolteachers 2013-18; School Support Staff Negotiating Body; Joint Negotiating Committee for Youth Workers; Hon Fellow, Birkbeck College, London; CBE 2015.

Recreations: Family, two cats, travel, collections of tennis shoes and 20th Century British prints.

David Simmonds CBE MP, House of Commons, London SW1A 0AA
Tel: 020 7219 6578 *Email:* david.simmonds.mp@parliament.uk
Constituency: 10 Village Way, Pinner HA5 5AF
Tel: 01923 822876 Website: www.davidsimmonds.org.uk *Twitter:* @DSimmonds_RNP

CONSERVATIVE

SKIDMORE, CHRIS

Kingswood *(Majority 11,220)*

Christopher James Skidmore. Born 17 May 1981; Married Lydia (1 son 2 daughters).

Education: Bristol Grammar School; Oxford University (history).

Non-political career: *Western Daily Press*; *People* magazine; Researcher, *Great Tales of English History*; University tutor, Bristol University; Author.

Political career: Member for Kingswood since 6 May 2010 general election; PPS to George Osborne as First Secretary of State and Chancellor of the Exchequer 2015-16; Parliamentary Secretary (Minister for the Constitution), Cabinet Office 2016-18; Minister of State for Universities, Science, Research and Innovation, Department for Business, Energy and Industrial Strategy and Department for Education 2018-19, 2019-20; Interim Minister of State for Energy and Clean Growth, Department for Business, Energy and Industrial Strategy (covering Claire Perry MP taking a temporary leave of absence) May-July 2019; Minister of State, for Health, Department of Health and Social Care 2019. *Select committees:* Member: Health 2010-13, Education 2012-14. Conservative Party: Member 1996-, Adviser on education, Director, Public Services Improvement Group; Number 10 Policy Advisory Board: Member (Public Services and Family), Vice-chair, Policy 2018.

Political interests: Health, education, social care, disability.

Other: Chair, Bow Group; Fellow, Royal Society of Arts; Chair, advisory board and trustee, The UPP Foundation 2020-; Fellow, Royal Historical Society; PC 2019.

Publications: Author: Edward VI: The Lost King of England (Weidenfeld, 2007), Death and the Virgin (Weidenfeld, 2010); Co-author: (with Kwasi Kwarteng MP) After the Coalition (BiteBack, 2011), (with Kwasi Kwarteng MP, Priti Patel MP, Dominic Raab MP and Elizabeth Truss MP) Britannia Unchained: Global Lessons for Growth and Prosperity (Palgrave Macmillan, 2012); Death and the Virgin Queen (St Martin's Griffin, 2012); Bosworth: The Birth of the Tudors (Weidenfeld and Nicolson, 2013); The Rise of the Tudors: The Family That Changed English History (St Martin's Griffin 2015); Richard III: Brother, Protector, King (W&N, 2017).

Rt Hon Chris Skidmore MP, House of Commons, London SW1A 0AA
Tel: 020 7219 7094 *Email:* chris.skidmore.mp@parliament.uk
Constituency: 60 High Street, Hanham BS15 3DR
Tel: 0117-908 1524 Website: www.chrisskidmore.com *Twitter:* @CSkidmoreUK

LABOUR

SLAUGHTER, ANDY

Hammersmith *(Majority 17,847)*

Andrew Francis Slaughter. Born 29 September 1960; Son of Alfred Slaughter and Marie Slaughter; Single.

Education: Latymer Upper School, London; Exeter University (BA English 1982); Qualified as a Barrister 1993.

Non-political career: Barrister, specialising in housing and personal injury law 1993-. Member: GMB, Unite.

Political career: Contested Uxbridge 1997 by-election. Member for Ealing, Acton and Shepherd's Bush 2005-10, for Hammersmith since 6 May 2010 general election; PPS to: Stephen Ladyman as Minister of State, Department for Transport 2005-07, Lord Jones of Birmingham as Minister of State, Foreign and Commonwealth Office and Department for Business, Enterprise and Regulatory Reform 2007-08, Lord Malloch-Brown as Minister of State, Foreign and Commonwealth Office 2007-09; Shadow Minister for: Justice 2010-16, Housing 2016-17, London 2016-17. *Select committees:* Member: Regulatory Reform 2005-07, Children, Schools and Families 2007-09, Court of Referees 2007-10, Communities and Local Government 2009-10, London 2009-10, Joint Committee on Human Rights 2010, Justice 2019-, Joint Committee on Consolidation, &c, Bills 2020-. Vice-chair, PLP London Regional Group 2007-. *Councils and public bodies:* Governor, William Morris Sixth Form 1994-; London Borough of Hammersmith and Fulham: Councillor 1986-2006, Council leader 1996-2005.

Political interests: International affairs, housing, education, health, transport; Bahrain, Caribbean, Egypt, Middle East, Palestine, Spain, Tunisia.

Other: Management committee, Hammersmith and Fulham Community Law Centre 1990-.

Andy Slaughter MP, House of Commons, London SW1A 0AA
Tel: 020 7219 4990 *Email:* andy.slaughter.mp@parliament.uk
Constituency: 28 Greyhound Road, London W6 8NX
Tel: 020 7610 1950 *Email:* andy@andyslaughter.com Website: www.andyslaughter.co.uk
Twitter: @hammersmithandy

SCOTTISH NATIONAL PARTY

SMITH, ALYN

Stirling *(Majority 9,254)*

SNP Shadow Foreign Secretary

Alyn Edward Smith. Born 15 September 1973.

Education: The International School, Riyadh, Saudi Arabia; Hutchesons' Grammar School, Glasgow; Leeds University (LLB law and European law 1994); College of Europe, Warsaw University (MA advanced central European and European Union studies 1995); Nottingham Law School (legal practice 1996).

Non-political career: Solicitor: Clifford Chance, London 1999, Anderson Strathern, Edinburgh 2000-02; Adviser: Shadow Scottish Fisheries Minister 2002-03, SNP group, Scottish Parliament 2003-04.

Political career: Contested Edinburgh West 2001 general election. Member for Stirling since 12 December 2019; SNP Shadow Foreign Secretary 2020-. Contested Edinburgh West constituency 2003 Scottish Parliament election; MEP for Scotland region 2004-19: First vice-president,

Greens/EFA Group 2019. Member, Member: Regional Development Committee 2004-07, Switzerland, Iceland, Norway and EEA Delegation 2004-09, Agriculture and Rural Development Committee 2007-14, Arab Peninsula Delegation 2009-19, Financial, Economic and Social Crisis Special Committee 2009-11, Foreign Affairs Committee 2014-17, Iraq Delegation 2014-19, Foreign Affairs Committee 2017-19; Kazakhstan, Kyrgyzstan, Uzbekistan, Tajikistan, Turkmenistan and Mongolia Delegation 2019-; Substitute: Industry, Research and Energy Committee 2004-09, 2012-17, Policy challenges and budgetary means of the enlarged Union 2007-2013 Temporary Committee 2004-05, Culture and Education Committee 2009-12, Constitutional Affairs Committee 2009-12, Switzerland, Iceland, Norway and EEA Delegation 2009-14, Agriculture and Rural Development Committee 2014-17, 2019, Civil Liberties, Justice and Home Affairs Committee 2017-18. SNP National Executive Committee; SNP Policy Convener.

Political interests: European Union, agriculture, foreign affairs, animal welfare; Arabian peninsula, EEA and EFTA countries, Sub-Saharan Africa, stateless European nations.

Other: Honorary vice-president, Scottish Society for the Prevention of Cruelty to Animals; Trustee, LGBT Youth Scotland 2012-.

Alyn Smith MP, House of Commons, London SW1A 0AA
Tel: 020 7219 3000 *Email:* alyn.smith.mp@parliament.uk
Constituency: 16 Stirling Enterprise Park, Stirling FK7 7RP
Tel: 01786 471899 Website: alynsmith.scot *Twitter:* @alynsmith

LABOUR

SMITH, CAT

Lancaster and Fleetwood *(Majority 2,380)*

Shadow Minister for Young People and Democracy

Catherine Jane Smith. Born 16 June 1985; 1 son.

Education: Parkview School, Barrow-in-Furness; Barrow Sixth Form College; Lancaster University (BA gender and sociology 2006).

Non-political career: Campaign and policy officer, British Association of Social Workers 2011-15.

Political career: Contested Wyre and Preston North 2010 general election. Member for Lancaster and Fleetwood since 7 May 2015 general election; Shadow Minister for: Women and Equalities Office 2015-16, Young People and Voter Engagement/Democracy (attends Shadow Cabinet) 2016-; Shadow Deputy Leader of the House of Commons 2016-17; Shadow Minister for Transport 2017-18; Member, Speaker's Committee on the Electoral Commission 2020-. *Select committees:* Member, Women and Equalities 2015. Patron, LGBT Labour.

Other: Former chair, Compass Youth Organising Committee; Trustee, Empowerment (formed by merger of Lancaster and Blackpool Women's Aids).

Cat Smith MP, House of Commons, London SW1A 0AA
Tel: 020 7219 6001 *Email:* cat.smith.mp@parliament.uk
Constituency: 50 Lord Street, Fleetwood FY7 6DT
Website: www.catsmith.co.uk *Twitter:* @CatSmithMP

CONSERVATIVE

SMITH, CHLOE

Norwich North *(Majority 4,738)*

Minister of State for the Constitution and Devolution, Cabinet Office

Chloe Rebecca Smith. Born 17 May 1982; Daughter of David Smith, furniture designer and maker, and Claire Smith, teacher; Married Sandy McFadzean (1 son 1 daughter).

Education: Methwold High School, Norfolk; Swaffham Sixth Form College, Norfolk; York University (BA English literature 2004); French.

Non-political career: Business consultant, Deloitte 2004-09.

Political career: Member for Norwich North 23 July 2009 by-election to 2010, for Norwich North (revised boundary) since 6 May 2010 general election; Assistant Government Whip 2010-11, 2017-18; Economic Secretary, HM Treasury 2011-12; Cabinet Office: Parliamentary Secretary: (Minister for Political and Constitutional Reform) 2012-13, (Minister for the Constitution) 2018-20 (on maternity leave April-October 2019), Minister of State for the Constitution and Devolution 2020-; Parliamentary Adviser to Lord Feldman as Chairman,

Conservative and Unionist Party 2015-16; Parliamentary Under-Secretary of State, Northern Ireland Office 2017-18. *Select committees:* Member: Work and Pensions 2009-10, Public Accounts 2011-12, Transport 2013-15. Member: Conservative Friends of Israel 2001-, Conservative Party Implementation Team 2008-09, Tory Reform Group 2009-; Conservative Party: Board member 2015-17, Member, Organisational Review Panel 2015-17. *Councils and public bodies:* Governor, Heartsease Primary School, Norwich 2010-12; Member: Hellesdon High School Academy Trust/Wesum Trust 2012-, Advisory Board, Norwich Business School.

Political interests: Transport, skills, youth engagement, work and pensions, modern slavery, public services, efficiency, electoral engagement.

Other: Patron, YMCA Norfolk 2009-; Honorary Vice-President, Norfolk and Norwich Novi Sad Association 2009-; Patron, Blue Ribbon Foundation; Chair, National Youth Agency's Commission into Young People and Enterprise 2014-15; Commissioner, Industry and Parliament Trust's Youth Skills Commission 2014-15; Patron: Eating Matters, Surviving Together; Trustee, Chill4Us; Youth Friendly MP, Youth Employment UK 2014; Business Driver, Grassroots Diplomat Initiative 2014.

Recreations: Arts, including theatre and drawing; sports, including cycling, badminton.

Chloe Smith MP, House of Commons, London SW1A 0AA
Tel: 020 7219 8449
Constituency: No constituency office publicised
Tel: 01603 414756 *Email:* chloe@chloesmith.org.uk Website: www.chloesmith.org.uk
Twitter: @NorwichChloe

SMITH, GREG

Buckingham *(Majority 20,411)*

CONSERVATIVE

Gregory David Smith. Born 3 March 1979; Married Annalise (2 sons).

Education: Birmingham University (BA political science 2001).

Political career: Contested Hayes and Harlington 2017 general election. Member for Buckingham since 12 December 2019. *Select committees:* Member: European Scrutiny 2020-, Transport 2020-. South East Regional Co-ordinator, Boris Johnson 2019 leadership campaign. *Councils and public bodies:* Hammersmith and Fulham Council: Councillor 2006-18, Deputy Leader, Leader of the Opposition.

Other: Trustee, Riverside Studios 2008-; Board Member, Lyric Theatre Hammersmith 2010-12; Culture, Tourism and Sport Board Member, Local Government Association 2014-17.

Recreations: Watching Formula 1, helping on family farm.

Greg Smith MP, House of Commons, London SW1A 0AA
Tel: 020 7219 4287 *Email:* greg.smith.mp@parliament.uk
Constituency: 34 Buckingham Road, Winslow MK18 3DY
Tel: 01296 714240 Website: www.gregsmith.co.uk *Twitter:* @gregsmith_uk

SMITH, HENRY

Crawley *(Majority 8,360)*

CONSERVATIVE

Henry Edward Millar Smith. Born 14 May 1969; Son of late John Smith and late Josephine Smith; Married Jennifer Ricks 1994 (divorced 2015) (1 son 1 daughter 1 son deceased).

Education: Frensham Heights, Farnham; University College London (BA philosophy 1991).

Political career: Contested Crawley 2001 and 2005 general elections. Member for Crawley since 6 May 2010 general election; PPS to: Greg Clark as Secretary of State for Communities and Local Government 2015-16, Justine Greening as Secretary of State for Education and Minister for Women and Equalities 2016-17. *Select committees:* Member: European Scrutiny 2010-15, International Development 2017-19, Work of the Independent Commission for Aid Impact Sub-committee 2017-19, Arms Export Controls 2017-19, Foreign Affairs 2020-. Founding member, Conservatives for Britain 2015-16. *Councils and public bodies:* West Sussex County Council: Councillor 1997-2010, Council leader 2003-10; Councillor, Crawley Borough Council 2002-04; Vice-President, Local Government Association 2011-15.

Political interests: Local government, foreign policy; British Overseas Territories, USA.

Other: Parliamentary Champion, Bloodwise Supporter Awards 2020. Flag Institute.

Publications: Co-author, Direct Democracy: An Agenda for a New Model Party (2005); The Hidden Cancer – The Need to Improve Blood Cancer Care (2018); Putting Patients at the Heart of Artificial Intelligence (2019).

Recreations: Vexillology, skiing.

Henry Smith MP, House of Commons, London SW1A 0AA
Tel: 020 7219 7043 *Email:* henry.smith.mp@parliament.uk
Constituency: Crawley Business Centre, Stephenson Way, Three Bridges, Crawley, West Sussex RH10 1TN
Tel: 01293 934554 *Email:* steve.aldridge@parliament.uk Website: www.henrysmith.info
Twitter: @HenrySmithUK

LABOUR

SMITH, JEFF

Manchester Withington *(Majority 27,905)*

Senior Opposition Whip

Jeffrey Smith. Born 26 January 1963; Son of Alan and Deirdre Smith; Unmarried.

Education: Manchester Grammar School; Manchester University (BA economics).

Non-political career: Self-employed event manager and DJ 1985-2011. Member, USDAW.

Political career: Member for Manchester Withington since 7 May 2015 general election; Opposition Whip 2015-20; Senior Opposition Whip 2020-. *Select committees:* Member, Environmental Audit 2015. Former Chair, Secretary and Agent, Withington CLP; Member, Co-operative Party. *Councils and public bodies:* Manchester City Council: Councillor 1997-2015, Executive Member for: Children's Services, Finance, Housing and Regeneration.

Other: Former Board Member, Southway Housing Trust; Former Governor: Parrs Wood High School, Old Moat School, Mauldeth Road Primary.

Jeff Smith MP, House of Commons, London SW1A 0AA
Tel: 020 7219 5878 *Email:* jeff.smith.mp@parliament.uk
Constituency: Unit 1, Withington Fire Station, 505-507 Wilmslow Road, Withington, Manchster M20 4AW
Tel: 0161-445 0678 Website: jeffsmithmp.com *Twitter:* @JeffSmithetc

CONSERVATIVE

SMITH, JULIAN

Skipton and Ripon *(Majority 23,694)*

Julian Richard Smith. Born 30 August 1971; Married Amanda.

Education: Balfron High School; Millfield School, Somerset; Birmingham University (BA English and history 1993); French.

Non-political career: Squash Coach, Perpignan; The Bird Moore Partnership 1994-99; Arq International Ltd, London: Founder and Managing Director 1999-2010, Non-executive Director 2010-11.

Political career: Member for Skipton and Ripon since 6 May 2010 general election; PPS to: Alan Duncan as Minister of State, Department for International Development 2010-12, Justine Greening as Secretary of State for International Development 2012-15; Assistant Government Whip 2015-16; Government Whip (Vice-Chamberlain of HM Household) 2016-17; Deputy Chief Whip (Treasurer of HM Household) 2017; Chief Whip, Parliamentary Secretary to the Treasury 2017-19; Member, Parliamentary and Political Service Honours Committee 2017-19; Secretary of State for Northern Ireland 2019-20. *Select committees:* Member: Scottish Affairs 2010, Selection 2015-17. Deputy chair, Bethnal Green and Bow Conservatives 2008-09.

Political interests: Business, education, welfare, universities and skills, agriculture.

Other: External Adviser, Ryse Hydrogen 2020-; PC 2017; CBE 2019. Junior international squash player.

Recreations: Violin and piano.

Rt Hon Julian Smith CBE MP, House of Commons, London SW1A 0AA
Tel: 020 7219 7145 *Email:* julian.smith.mp@parliament.uk
Constituency: No constituency office
Website: www.juliansmith.org.uk *Twitter:* @JulianSmithUK

LABOUR

SMITH, NICK

Blaenau Gwent *(Majority 8,647)*

Nicholas Desmond John Smith. Born 14 January 1960; Son of William and Alma Smith; Married (2 daughters); married Jenny Chapman, now Baroness Chapman of Darlington (qv) 2014 (MP for Darlington 2010-19).

Education: Tredegar Comprehensive School; Coventry University (BA history, politics and international relations 1981); Birkbeck College, London (MSc economic change 1991).

Non-political career: Constituency organiser to Frank Dobson MP 1989-91; Organiser, Wales Labour Party 1991-93; Head of membership development, Labour Party 1993-98; Consultant, international campaigning 1998-2000; Campaign manager, public policy, NSPCC 2000-04; Secretary general, European Parliamentary Labour Party 2005-06; Director, policy and partnerships, Royal College of Speech and Language Therapists 2006-10. Member: AEEU, Transport and General Workers' Union, GMB, Community, Unite.

Political career: Member for Blaenau Gwent since 6 May 2010 general election; PPS to Douglas Alexander as Shadow Secretary of State for: Work and Pensions 2010-11, Foreign and Commonwealth Office 2011-15; Shadow Minister for Environment, Food and Rural Affairs 2015-16; Opposition Whip 2016-19. *Select committees:* Member: Public Accounts 2010-15, 2020-, Procedure 2017-19, Standing Orders 2017-. Election agent to Emily Thornberry MP 2005. *Councils and public bodies:* London Borough of Camden Council: Former councillor, Member, then Executive Member for Education 2003-05.

Political interests: Economic development, health, children; China, India, Nepal, USA.

Other: Member, UK Delegation, Organisation for Security and Co-operation in Europe Parliamentary Assembly 2020-; Member: Aneurin Bevan Society, Tribune, Fabian Society; Fellow, Royal Geographical Society.

Recreations: Hiking, singing, reading, chess.

Nick Smith MP, House of Commons, London SW1A 0AA
Tel: 020 7219 7018 *Email:* nick.smith.mp@parliament.uk
Constituency: 23 Beaufort Street, Brynmawr, Blaenau Gwent, Gwent NP23 4AQ
Tel: 01495 313167 Website: www.nick-smith.net *Twitter:* @BlaenauGwentMP

CONSERVATIVE

SMITH, ROYSTON

Southampton Itchen *(Majority 4,498)*

Royston Matthew Smith. Born 13 May 1964.

Education: Bitterne Park Secondary School; Royal Air Force School of Technical Training (aeronautical engineering 1980).

Non-political career: Aeronautical engineer: Royal Air Force 1980-90, British Airways 1990-2006.

Political career: Contested Southampton Itchen 2010 general election. Member for Southampton Itchen since 7 May 2015 general election. *Select committees:* Member: Work and Pensions 2016-17, Foreign Affairs 2017-, Arms Export Controls 2017-18. *Councils and public bodies:* Southampton City Council: Councillor 2000-15, Deputy Leader; Vice-chair, Hampshire Fire and Rescue Authority 2000-15.

Political interests: Economic development, defence.

Other: Member, UK Delegation, Organisation for Security and Co-operation in Europe Parliamentary Assembly 2015-; Director, Blue Lamp Trust; Member, Institute of British Engineers.

Recreations: Walking, climbing, tennis, gym.

Royston Smith MP, House of Commons, London SW1A 0AA
Tel: 020 7219 5226 *Email:* royston.smith.mp@parliament.uk
Constituency: 70 Dean Road, Bitterne, Southampton SO18 6AN
Tel: 023 8047 3309 *Email:* royston@roystonsmith.co.uk Website: www.roystonsmith.co.uk
Twitter: @Royston_Smith

LABOUR

SMYTH, KARIN

Bristol South *(Majority 9,859)*

Shadow Minister for Northern Ireland

Karin Marguerite Smyth. Born 8 September 1964; Married (3 children).

Education: Bishopshalt School; University of East Anglia (Degree economics and social studies 1988); Bath University (MBA 1995).

Non-political career: NHS Management 1988-97; Political Assistant to Valerie Davey MP 1997-2001; Non-executive director, Bristol North PCT 2002-06; Independent Project and Interim Manager 2008-10; Locality Manager, South Bristol Consortium 2010-15. Managers in Partnership.

Political career: Member for Bristol South since 7 May 2015 general election; PPS to: Heidi Alexander as Shadow Secretary of State for Health 2015-16, Keir Starmer as Shadow Secretary of State for Exiting the European Union 2016-17; Shadow Deputy Leader of House of Commons 2017-18; Shadow Minister for Northern Ireland 2018-. *Select committees:* Member: Public Accounts 2015-17, Public Administration and Constitutional Affairs 2020-, Northern Ireland Affairs 2020. Member, Labour Party 1985-. *Councils and public bodies:* School governor; Non-executive director, NHS Trust.

Political interests: Post-16 education and training; health and social care; trailer safety; Ireland, USA.

Other: Vice-chair, British-Irish Parliamentary Association 2017-.

Karin Smyth MP, House of Commons, London SW1A 0AA
Email: karin.smyth.mp@parliament.uk
Constituency: No constituency office publicised
Tel: 0117-953 3575 Website: karinsmyth.com *Twitter:* @karinsmyth

LABOUR/ CO-OPERATIVE

SOBEL, ALEX

Leeds North West *(Majority 10,749)*

Shadow Minister for Tourism and Heritage

Alexander David Sobel. Born 26 April 1975; Married Susan (2 sons).

Education: Leeds University (BSc information systems 1997) (Finance Officer, Leeds University Union 1997-98).

Non-political career: Community relations officer, Leeds University 2000-01; Community participation co-ordinator, Leeds Voice 2001-03; Senior development officer, Bradford University 2004-06; Development manager, UnLtd 2006-08; Centre manager, Urban Biz 2008-09; General manager, Social Enterprise Yorkshire and the Humber 2009-17.

Political career: Contested Beaconsfield 2005 and Leeds North West 2015 general elections. Member for Leeds North West since 8 June 2017; PPS to Emily Thornberry as Shadow Foreign Secretary 2019; Shadow Minister for Digital, Culture, Media and Sport (Tourism and Heritage) 2020-. *Select committees:* Member: Backbench Business 2017-19, Environmental Audit 2017-. Member, Labour Party 1997-; Regional organiser, Yorkshire and Humber, Ed Miliband's Leadership campaign 2010; Operations manager, Labour Yes to Fairer Votes 2011. *Councils and public bodies:* Councillor, Leeds City Council 2012-18.

Other: Treasurer, British Group Inter-Parliamentary Union 2020-.

Alex Sobel MP, House of Commons, London SW1A 0AA
Tel: 020 7219 8295 *Email:* alex.sobel.mp@parliament.uk
Constituency: No constituency office publicised
Tel: 0113-898 0969 Website: alexsobel.co.uk *Twitter:* @alexsobel

House of Commons MPs' Biographies

CONSERVATIVE

SOLLOWAY, AMANDA

Derby North *(Majority 2,540)*

Parliamentary Under-Secretary of State (Minister for Science, Research and Innovation), Department for Business, Energy and Industrial Strategy

Amanda Jane Solloway. Born 6 June 1961; Married (2 children).

Education: Bramcote Hills Grammar School.

Non-political career: Head of training and development, Baird Clothing 1998-2009; Consultant 2006-15.

Political career: Member for Derby North 2015-17. Contested Derby North 2017 general election. Member for Derby North since 12 December 2019; PPS to Rory Stewart as Minister of State, Department for International Development 2016-17; Parliamentary Under-Secretary of State (Minister for Science, Research and Innovation), Department for Business, Energy and Industrial Strategy 2020-. *Select committees:* Member: Business, Innovation and Skills 2015-16, Joint Committee on Human Rights 2015-17, Education, Skills and the Economy Sub-committee 2015-16 Joint Committee on Consolidation, &c, Bills 2015-17, Business, Energy and Industrial Strategy 2016-17, European Statutory Instruments 2020. *Councils and public bodies:* Councillor, Ockbrook and Borrowash Parish Council 2011; School governor.

Political interests: Small businesses, local environment, waste collection.

Other: Board Member: National Skills Academy for Retail, Aim Awards; Counsellor, Victim Support 2007; Mentor: Prince's Trust, YMCA Derbyshire; Volunteer: Project Umbano 2011, Girl Guides; Fellow member, Chartered Institute of Personnel and Development.

Amanda Solloway MP, House of Commons, London SW1A 0AA
Tel: 020 7219 6089 *Email:* amanda.solloway.mp@parliament.uk
Constituency: 13 Darley Street, Derby DE22 1DX
Tel: 01332 504159 Website: www.amandasolloway.org.uk *Twitter:* @ASollowayUK

LABOUR

SPELLAR, JOHN

Warley *(Majority 11,511)*

John Francis Spellar. Born 5 August 1947; Son of late William Spellar and Phyllis Spellar; Married Anne Wilmot 1981 (died 2003) (1 daughter).

Education: Dulwich College, London; St Edmund's Hall, Oxford (BA philosophy, politics and economics 1969).

Non-political career: Electrical, Electronic, Telecommunication and Plumbing Union: Research officer 1969-76, National officer 1976-92.

Political career: Contested Bromley 1970 general election. Member for Birmingham Northfield 28 October 1982 by-election to June 1983. Contested Birmingham Northfield 1983 and 1987 general elections. Member for Warley West 1992-97, for Warley 1997-2010, for Warley (revised boundary) since 6 May 2010 general election; Opposition Whip 1992-94; Opposition Spokesperson for: Northern Ireland 1994-95, Defence, Disarmament and Arms Control 1995-97; Ministry of Defence: Parliamentary Under-Secretary of State 1997-99, Minister of State for the Armed Forces 1999-2001; Minister for Transport: Department of Transport, Local Government and the Regions 2001-02, Department for Transport 2002-03; Minister of State, Northern Ireland Office 2003-05; Government Whip 2008-10; Opposition Deputy Chief Whip 2010; Shadow Minister for Foreign and Commonwealth Office 2010-15. *Select committees:* Member: Joint Committee on Conventions 2006, Finance and Services 2009-10, Selection 2010, Joint Committee on Security 2010, Administration 2010-13, Defence 2015-, Arms Export Controls 2016-17, 2020-, Joint Committee on Fixed-Term Parliaments Act 2020-.

Political interests: Energy, electronics industry, motor industry, construction industry, defence; Australia, Israel, USA.

Other: Member, Executive Committee: Commonwealth Parliamentary Association UK 2015-17, NATO Parliamentary Assembly 2017-; PC 2001. Rowley Regis and Blackheath Labour Club, Brand Hall Labour Club.

Recreations: Gardening.

Rt Hon John Spellar MP, House of Commons, London SW1A 0AA
Tel: 020 7219 0674 *Fax:* 020 7219 2113 *Email:* john.spellar.mp@parliament.uk
Constituency: Brandhall Labour Club, Tame Road, Oldbury, West Midlands B68 0JT
Tel: 0121-423 2933 *Email:* colyerl@parliament.uk Website: www.johnspellar.org.uk
Twitter: @spellar

CONSERVATIVE

SPENCER, BEN

Runnymede and Weybridge *(Majority 18,270)*

Benjamin Walter Jack Spencer. Born 11 December 1981; Married (2 children).

Non-political career: Junior doctor (psychiatry registrar), King's College Hospital and Maudsley Hospital.

Political career: Contested Camberwell and Peckham 2017 general election. Member for Runnymede and Weybridge since 12 December 2019. *Select committees:* Member, Work and Pensions 2020-. Chair, London South East Area Conservatives 2017-; Vice-chair, Conservative Health.

Political interests: NHS, mental health.

Dr Ben Spencer MP, House of Commons, London SW1A 0AA
Tel: 020 7219 6783 *Email:* ben.spencer.mp@parliament.uk
Constituency: No constituency office publicised
Website: www.drbenspencer.org.uk *Twitter:* @DrBenSpencer

CONSERVATIVE

SPENCER, MARK

Sherwood *(Majority 16,186)*

Chief Whip, Parliamentary Secretary to the Treasury

Mark Steven Spencer. Born 20 January 1970; Son of Cyril and Dorothy Spencer; Married Claire (1 son 1 daughter).

Education: Colonel Frank Seeley School, Calverton; Shuttleworth Agricultural College, Bedfordshire (farming course; National Certificate agriculture).

Non-political career: Farmer; Proprietor: Spring Lane Farm Shop, Floralands Garden Village, Lambley.

Political career: Member for Sherwood since 6 May 2010 general election; PPS to: Baroness Stowell of Beeston as Leader of the House of Lords and Lord Privy Seal 2014-15, Elizabeth Truss as Secretary of State for Environment, Food and Rural Affairs 2015-16; Assistant Government Whip 2016-17; Government Whip: Lord Commissioner of HM Treasury 2017-18, Vice-Chamberlain of HM Household 2018, Comptroller of HM Household 2018-19, Chief Whip, Parliamentary Secretary to the Treasury 2019-; Member, Parliamentary and Political Service Honours Committee 2019-. *Select committees:* Member: Environmental Audit 2010-15, Backbench Business 2013, Environment, Food and Rural Affairs 2013-15, Selection 2017-19. *Councils and public bodies:* Councillor, Gedling District Council 2003-11; Nottinghamshire County Council: Councillor 2005-13, Shadow Spokesperson for Community Safety and Partnerships 2006-13; Member, East Midlands Regional Assembly 2009-10.

Political interests: Rural affairs, education, health, employment, business; UK.

Other: Chair, National Federation of Young Farmers' Clubs 2000; Royal Agricultural Society of England: Trustee, Associate 2005, Honorary show director 2007-09, Fellow 2010; Trustee, Core Centre, Calverton; Council member, Royal Agricultural Society; Nottingham Breast Institute, NORSACA; Fellow, Royal Agricultural Societies; PC 2019.

Recreations: Family, farming, socialising.

Rt Hon Mark Spencer MP, House of Commons, London SW1A 0AA
Tel: 020 7219 7143 *Email:* mark.spencer.mp@parliament.uk
Constituency: Sherwood Constituency Office, Room 3, Under One Roof, 3a Vine Terrace, Hucknall, Nottingham, Nottinghamshire NG15 7HN
Tel: 0115-968 1186 Website: www.markspencer.org.uk *Twitter:* @mark_spencer

CONSERVATIVE

STAFFORD, ALEXANDER

Rother Valley *(Majority 6,318)*

Alexander Paul Thomas Stafford. Born 19 July 1987; Son of James and Theresa Stafford; Married Natalie (1 daughter).

Education: St Benedict's, Ealing; St Benet's Hall, Oxford (BA history 2008).

Non-political career: Political Secretary to Andrew Rosindell MP 2008-12; Senior Researcher to Owen Paterson MP 2008-12; Account Manager, MHP Communications 2012-14; Senior Account Manager: Fleishman Hillard 2014-15, Instinctif Partners 2015; Freelance Communications Consultant 2016; Acting Head of Media/Senior Media Manager, WWF 2016-18; External Relations Adviser, Shell 2019.

Political career: Member for Rother Valley since 12 December 2019. *Select committees:* Member: Business, Energy and Industrial Strategy 2020-, Joint Committee on Fixed-Term Parliaments Act 2020-. *Councils and public bodies:* Ealing Borough Council: Councillor 2014-20, Shadow Cabinet Member for Business and Community.

Political interests: Energy, climate change, business, environment, foreign affairs.

Alexander Stafford MP, House of Commons, London SW1A 0AA
Tel: 020 7219 6376 *Email:* alexander.stafford.mp@parliament.uk
Constituency: 39 Laughton Road, Dinnington, South Yorkshire S25 2PN
Tel: 01909 494952 Website: www.alexanderstafford.org.uk *Twitter:* @Alex_Stafford

LABOUR

STARMER, KEIR

Holborn and St Pancras *(Majority 27,763)*

Leader, Labour Party; Leader of the Opposition

Born 2 September 1962; Married Victoria (1 son 1 daughter).

Education: Reigate Grammar School; Leeds University (LLB); Oxford University (BCL).

Non-political career: Called to the Bar 1987; Legal officer, Liberty -1990; Doughty Street Chambers: Barrister 1990-2008, Associate tenant 2015-; QC 2002; Consultant, Association of Chief Police Officers; Human rights adviser, Northern Ireland Policing Board 2003-07; Director of Public Prosecutions and Head of the Crown Prosecution Service 2008-13.

Political career: Member for Holborn and St Pancras since 7 May 2015 general election; Shadow Minister for Home Office 2015-16; Shadow Secretary of State for Exiting the European Union 2016-20; Leader of the Opposition 2020-. *Select committees:* Member, Home Affairs 2015. Leader, Labour Party 2020-. *Councils and public bodies:* Member: Sentencing Guidelines Council 2008-10, Sentencing Council 2010-13.

Other: Chair, advisory board, Kids Company taskforce 'See the child, change the system' -2015; Member, advisory board, Youth Justice Legal Centre; Advisory board, Leeds University Law Faculty; Director, Death Penalty Project; Member, advisory board, European Institute, University College, London 2015-; Patron, Sante Refugee Mental Health Project 2015-; Fellow, Human Rights Centre, Essex University; Honorary doctorate: Leeds University, Essex University, University of East London, London School of Economics; KCB 2014; PC 2017.

Publications: The Three Pillars of Liberty: Political Rights and Freedoms in the UK (Routledge); European Human Rights Law (LAG); Human Rights Manual for Africa (BIICL).

Recreations: Playing football, Arsenal FC.

Rt Hon Sir Keir Starmer KCB QC MP, House of Commons, London SW1A 0AA
Tel: 020 7219 6234 *Email:* keir.starmer.mp@parliament.uk
Constituency: 7-9 Crowndale Road, London NW1 1TU
Tel: 020 7388 7862 *Email:* keir.starmer.constituency@parliament.uk
Website: www.keirstarmer.com *Twitter:* @Keir_Starmer

SCOTTISH NATIONAL PARTY

STEPHENS, CHRIS

Glasgow South West *(Majority 4,900)*

SNP Spokesperson for Fair Work and Employment

Christopher Charles Stephens. Born 20 March 1973; Married Aileen Colleran.

Education: Trinity High School.

Non-political career: Strathclyde Regional Council/Glasgow City Council: Senior Unison activist and lead negotiator. Member, Unison; Chair, PCS Parliamentary Group 2016-.

Political career: Contested Hamilton North and Bellshill 2001 and Glasgow South West 2010 general elections. Member for Glasgow South West since 7 May 2015 general election; SNP Spokesperson for: Trade Unions and Workers' Rights 2017-18, Fair Work and Employment 2018-. *Select committees:* Member: European Scrutiny 2017, Work and Pensions 2017-. Contested Glasgow Pollock constituency 2007 and 2011 Scottish Parliament elections. Member, SNP National Executive Committee; Convener, Glasgow Pollock Constituency Association; Secretary, SNP Trade Union Group.

Political interests: Equal pay, disability discrimination, pensions, social justice, Scottish independence.

Recreations: Partick Thistle FC supporter.

Chris Stephens MP, House of Commons, London SW1A 0AA
Tel: 020 7219 6381 *Email:* chris.stephens.mp@parliament.uk
Constituency: 1612-1614 Paisley Road West, Glasgow G52 3QN
Tel: 0141-883 0875 Website: www.chrisstephens.scot *Twitter:* @ChrisStephens

CONSERVATIVE

STEPHENSON, ANDREW

Pendle *(Majority 6,186)*

Minister of State, Department for Transport

Andrew George Stephenson. Born 17 February 1981; Son of Malcolm Stephenson and Ann Stephenson.

Education: Poynton County High School; Royal Holloway, University of London (BSc business management 2002).

Non-political career: Partner, Stephenson and Threader Insurances 2002-10.

Political career: Member for Pendle since 6 May 2010 general election; PPS to: Robert Halfon as Minister without portfolio, Cabinet Office 2015-16, Mike Penning as Minister for Policing, Fire and Criminal Justice and Victims, Home Office and Ministry of Justice 2015-16, John Hayes as Minister for Security, Home Office 2015-16, Boris Johnson as Foreign Secretary 2016-17; Assistant Government Whip 2017-18; Government Whip: Lord Commissioner of HM Treasury 2018, Vice-Chamberlain of HM Household 2018-19; Parliamentary Under-Secretary of State (Minister for Business and Industry), Department for Business, Energy and Industrial Strategy 2019; Minister of State: for Africa, Foreign and Commonwealth Office 2019-20, Department for International Development 2019-20, Department for Transport 2020-. *Select committees:* Member, Selection 2018-19. Chair, Royal Holloway Conservative Students 2000-02; National Deputy Chair, Conservative Future 2001-02; Area Officer, Cheshire & the Wirral Area Management Executive 2005-07; Chair, Tatton Conservative Association 2006-07; Vice-chair, Conservative Party (Youth) 2010-13; Parliamentary Co-Chair, Conservative Friends of Pakistan 2012-; Member, Conservative Trade Unionists Advisory Panel 2015-16; Copeland By-Election Campaign Coordinator 2017; Vice President, Conservative Friends of Bangladesh 2018-. *Councils and public bodies:* Macclesfield Borough Council: Councillor 2003-07, Chair, Housing Policy Development Committee 2005-07; School Governor, Whitefield Infant School (Nelson) 2009-' Crown Estate Paving Commissioner 2018-19.

Political interests: Foreign affairs, health, small business, apprenticeships, economy, manufacturing, aerospace, domestic violence, democracy and elections, dementia, community cohesion, charities and volunteering, enterprise, employment, engineering, home affairs, NHS, Northern Ireland, tourism; America, Bangladesh, Canada, China, Commonwealth, Kashmir, Middle East, Montenegro, Pakistan, Saudi Arabia, Sierra Leone.

Other: Vice-President, Trawden Agricultural Show 2007-; Member, Friends of the Pendle Hippodrome Theatre 2008-; Patron, SELRAP (Skipton East Lancashire Railway Action Partnership) 2010-20; President: Nelson Brass Band 2010-13, North East Lancashire Ramblers

2014-16; Executive Committee Member, John Adams Society 2012-19; Member, Pendle Vision Board 2012-; Community First Responder, North West Ambulance Service 2014-; Life Member: Friends of Pendle Heritage 2016-, Bancroft Mill Engine Trust 2018-. Colne Legion, Earby Conservative Club, Barnoldswick Conservative Club; Honorary Vice-president, Pendle Phoenix RUFC 2011-17; Member, House of Commons Tug of War Team 2010-14, 2018.

Recreations: Manchester City FC, walking, food and drink.

Andrew Stephenson MP, House of Commons, London SW1A 0AA
Tel: 020 7219 7222 *Email:* andrew.stephenson.mp@parliament.uk
Constituency: 9 Cross Street, Nelson, Lancashire BB9 7EN
Tel: 01282 614748 Websites: www.pendleconservatives.com/www.andrewstephenson.org.uk
Twitter: @Andrew4Pendle

LABOUR

STEVENS, JO

Cardiff Central *(Majority 17,179)*

Shadow Secretary of State for Digital, Culture, Media and Sport

Joanna Meriel Stevens. Born 6 September 1966.

Education: Ysgol Uwchradd Argoed; Elfed High School; Manchester University (Degree law 1988); Manchester Polytechnic (Law Society Professional Examination 1989).

Non-political career: Solicitor and Director, Thompsons Solicitors LLP 1989-2015. Member: GMB, Unison, Usdaw.

Political career: Member for Cardiff Central since 7 May 2015 general election; PPS to Tom Watson as Deputy Leader, Labour Party, Party Chair and Shadow Minister for the Cabinet Office 2015-16; Shadow Solicitor General and Shadow Minister for Justice 2016; Shadow Secretary of State for: Wales 2016-17, Digital, Culture, Media and Sport 2020-. *Select committees:* Member: Business, Innovation and Skills 2015-16, Standards 2015-16, Privileges 2015-16, Justice 2017, Digital, Culture, Media and Sport 2017-20, European Statutory Instruments 2018-. Member, Co-operative Party; Vice-chair, Welsh Parliamentary Labour Party; Secretary, Trade Union Group of MPs; Co-chair, Parliamentary Friends of Colombia; Executive Committee Member, Society of Labour Lawyers; Member, National Executive Committee, Labour Party 2020-.

Political interests: Digital, culture, media and sport, civil and criminal justice, employment rights; Colombia.

Other: Member: Justice for Colombia, Fabian Society, Haldane Society of Socialist Lawyers, Cardiff City Supporters' Trust, CF10 Rugby Trust; Member, Law Society of England and Wales; Show Racism the Red Card. Member: Glamorgan County Cricket Club, Surrey County Cricket Club.

Recreations: Football (Cardiff City FC), cricket (Glamorgan County Cricket Club member), rugby, darts, theatre, music.

Jo Stevens MP, House of Commons, London SW1A 0AA
Tel: 020 7219 8290 *Email:* jo.stevens.mp@parliament.uk
Constituency: 116 Albany Road, Cardiff, South Glamorgan CF24 3RU
Tel: 029 2132 9736 Website: www.jostevens.co.uk *Twitter:* @JoStevensLabour

CONSERVATIVE

STEVENSON, JANE

Wolverhampton North East *(Majority 4,080)*

Jane Fiona Catherine Stevenson. Born 18 February 1971.

Education: Wolverhampton Girls' High School; Guildhall School of Music and Drama (AGSM post-graduate opera course).

Non-political career: Self-employed.

Political career: Member for Wolverhampton North East since 12 December 2019. *Select committees:* Member: Future Relationship with the European Union 2020-21, Joint Committee on Consolidation, &c, Bills 2020-. *Councils and public bodies:* Councillor, City of Wolverhampton Council 2018-20.

Political interests: Apprenticeships, high street regeneration, arts, music, fire safety.

Jane Stevenson MP, House of Commons, London SW1A 0AA
Tel: 020 7219 3846 *Email:* jane.stevenson.mp@parliament.uk
Constituency: 4 Raynor Parade, Raynor Road, Wolverhampton WV10 9QY
Tel: 01902 722026 Website: www.janestevenson.com *Twitter:* @Jane_Stevenson_

CONSERVATIVE

STEVENSON, JOHN

Carlisle *(Majority 8,319)*

Andrew John Stevenson. Born 4 July 1963; Married Tracy Nixon 2013.

Education: Aberdeen Grammar School; Dundee University (BA history and politics); College of Law, Chester.

Non-political career: Trainee solicitor, Dickinson Dees, Newcastle upon Tyne 1990; Solicitor, now partner, Bendles, Carlisle.

Political career: Member for Carlisle since 6 May 2010 general election; Borderlands Deal Champion 2018-. *Select committees:* Member: Joint Committee on the Draft House of Lords Reform Bill 2011-12, Communities and Local Government 2012-15, Scottish Affairs 2015-17, Public Administration and Constitutional Affairs 2016-17, 2020-, Standards 2017-19, Privileges 2017-19. Member, Executive, 1922 Committee 2017-20. Chair: Carlisle Conservative Association, Penrith and the Border Conservative Association, North Cumbria Conservatives. *Councils and public bodies:* Councillor, Carlisle City Council 1999-2010.

Political interests: Israel.

Other: Member, Law Society; Eden Valley Hospice. Committee member, Chatsworth Tennis Club.

Publications: Co-author, Freedom, Responsibility and the State: Curbing Over-Mighty Government (Politeia, 2012).

Recreations: Golf, running, sport.

John Stevenson MP, House of Commons, London SW1A 0AA
Tel: 020 7219 3000 *Email:* john.stevenson.mp@parliament.uk
Constituency: 2 Currie Street, Carlisle, Cumbria CA1 1HH
Tel: 01228 550684 *Email:* office@johnstevensonmp.co.uk
Website: www.johnstevensonmp.co.uk *Twitter:* @John4Carlisle

CONSERVATIVE

STEWART, BOB

Beckenham *(Majority 14,258)*

Robert Alexander Stewart. Born 7 July 1949; Son of Jock Stewart MC and Joan Stewart; Married Claire Podbielski 1994 (4 children 2 children from first marriage).

Education: Chigwell School; Royal Military Academy Sandhurst 1969; Wales University (international politics 1977); Army Staff College 1980-81; Joint Services Staff College 1987-88.

Non-political career: Regular officer (infantry officer-colonel) British Army, Cheshire Regiment 1969-96: Served in Northern Ireland, British UN Commander, Bosnia 1992-93, Policy chief, Supreme HQ Allied Powers Europe, Belgium -1996; Senior consultant, Hill & Knowlton 1997-98; Managing director, WorldSpace 1999-2001; Freelance writer and lecturer 2002-.

Political career: Member for Beckenham since 6 May 2010 general election; Member, Intelligence and Security Committee of Parliament 2020-. *Select committees:* Member: Defence 2010-17, Arms Export Controls 2011-14, Northern Ireland Affairs 2016-, Joint Committee on the National Security Strategy 2020-.

Political interests: Defence, veteran service personnel, disabled children; Eastern Europe, Middle East, Northern Ireland.

Other: Member, UK Delegation to: Organisation for Security and Co-operation in Europe Parliamentary Assembly, NATO Parliamentary Assembly 2015-; President, Action for Armed Forces; Vice-president, UKNDA; Patron, ELIFAR; DSO 1993. Army and Navy Club.

Publications: Broken Lives (1993); Leadership Under Pressure (2009).

Bob Stewart MP, House of Commons, London SW1A 0AA
Tel: 020 7219 7011 *Email:* bob.stewart.mp@parliament.uk
Constituency: No constituency office
Website: www.bobstewart.org.uk

CONSERVATIVE

STEWART, IAIN

Milton Keynes South *(Majority 6,944)*

Parliamentary Under-Secretary of State (Minister for Scotland), Scotland Office

Iain Aitken Stewart. Born 18 September 1972; Son of James Stewart and Leila Stewart.

Education: Hutchesons' Grammar School, Glasgow; Exeter University (BA politics 1993); Chartered Management Institute (Diploma management 2006).

Non-political career: Trainee Chartered Accountant, Coopers and Lybrand 1993-94; Head of Research, Scottish Conservative Party 1994-98; Parliamentary Resources Unit, House of Commons: Deputy Director 1998-2001, Director 2001-06; Associate, Odgers Berndtson 2006-10.

Political career: Contested Milton Keynes South West 2001 and 2005 general elections. Member for Milton Keynes South since 6 May 2010 general election; PPS to: Patrick McLoughlin as Secretary of State for Transport 2013-15, David Mundell as Secretary of State for Scotland 2015-16, Liam Fox as Secretary of State for International Trade and President of the Board of Trade 2016-17; Cambridge-Milton Keynes-Oxford Corridor Champion 2017-; Assistant Government Whip 2018-19; Government Whip (Lord Commissioner of HM Treasury) 2019-20; Parliamentary Under-Secretary of State (Minister for Scotland), Scotland Office 2020-. *Select committees:* Member: Transport 2010-13, 2015-18, Selection 2019-20. Chairman, Conservative Backbench Policy Committee on Transport 2015-16. Contested Glasgow Rutherglen constituency 1999 Scottish Parliament election. *Councils and public bodies:* Councillor, Shenley Brook End and Tattenhoe Parish Council 2005-11.

Political interests: Constitution, economy, transport, energy security, education.

Other: Founder member, Atlantic Bridge 1999; Patron, Milton Keynes City Orchestra. Bletchley Conservative Club, President, Stony Stratford Conservative 2007-.

Publications: It's Our Money! Who Spends it? (London Scottish Tory Club, 2004) The Scottish Constitution – In Search of a New Settlement (Policy Institute, 2007).

Recreations: Opera, good food, wine and whisky, gym, running marathons.

Iain Stewart MP, House of Commons, London SW1A 0AA
Tel: 020 7219 7230 *Email:* iain.stewart.mp@parliament.uk
Constituency: Suite 102, Milton Keynes Business Centre, Foxhunter Drive, Linford Wood, Buckinghamshire MK14 6GD
Tel: 01908 686830 Website: www.iainstewart.org.uk *Twitter:* @iainastewart

LIBERAL DEMOCRAT

STONE, JAMIE

Caithness, Sutherland and Easter Ross *(Majority 204)*

Liberal Democrat Spokesperson for Defence and Digital, Culture, Media and Sport

James Hume Walter Miéville Stone. Born 16 June 1954; Son of late Edward Reginald Stone, farmer, and Susannah Gladys, née Waddell-Dudley, company director; Married Flora Armstrong 1981 (1 son 2 daughters).

Education: Tain Royal Academy; Gordonstoun School; St Andrews University (MA history and geology 1977); French, Italian.

Non-political career: Cleaner/kitchen porter, Grandmet 1977; English teacher, Catania, Sicily 1977-78; Fish gutting, Faroe Islands 1978; Stores clerk, Wimpey 1979-81; Site administrator, Bechtel Great Britain Ltd 1981-84; Administrative manager, Odfjell Drilling (UK) Ltd 1984-86; Director, Highland Fine Cheeses Ltd 1986-94; Freelance newspaper columnist and broadcaster 1990-. Territorial Army 1979-80.

Political career: Member for Caithness, Sutherland and Easter Ross since 8 June 2017; Liberal Democrat: Shadow Secretary of State for Scotland 2017, 2019, Spokesperson for Armed Forces 2017-19, Shadow Secretary of State/Spokesperson for Defence 2019-, Spokesperson for Digital, Culture, Media and Sport 2020-. *Select committees:* Member, Scottish Affairs 2019. MSP for Caithness, Sutherland and Easter Ross constituency 1999-2011; Contested Caithness, Sutherland and Ross constituency and the Highlands and Islands region 2016 Scottish Parliament election; Spokesperson for: Highlands and Islands and Fisheries 2000-01, Equal Opportunities 2001, Fisheries 2001-02, Finance 2002-03, Enterprise, Lifelong Learning and Tourism 2003-05, Justice 2005, Enterprise and Lifelong Learning (including Tourism) 2005-07; Shadow Minister for Public Health 2007-08; Deputy Spokesperson on Health 2008-11. Chair, Ross, Cromarty and Skye Scottish Liberal Democrats 1992-93. *Councils and public bodies:* Councillor, Ross and Cromarty District Council 1986-96; Chair, Tain Community Council 1983-84; Councillor, Highland Council 1995-99, 2012-17.

Political interests: France, Germany, Italy, Poland.

Other: Trustee, Tain Museum Trust 1992-; Member, Cromarty Firth Port Authority 1998-2000; Director, Grey Coast Theatre 2000-; FRSA. New (Edinburgh), Armagh (Armagh City).

Recreations: Singing, gardening, golf, reading, classical music.

Jamie Stone MP, House of Commons, London SW1A 0AA
Tel: 020 7219 1654 *Email:* jamie.stone.mp@parliament.uk
Constituency: Hillview, Market Street, Tain, Ross Shire IV19 1AR
Tel: 01862 892726 Website: www.jamiestone.org.uk *Twitter:* @Jamie4North

STREETER, GARY

South West Devon *(Majority 21,430)*

CONSERVATIVE

Gary Nicholas Streeter. Born 2 October 1955; Son of Kenneth Streeter, farmer, and Shirley Streeter; Married Janet Stevens 1978 (1 son 1 daughter).

Education: Tiverton Grammar School; King's College, London (LLB 1977).

Non-political career: Solicitor; Partner, specialising in company and employment law, Foot and Bowden, Plymouth 1984-98.

Political career: Member for Plymouth Sutton 1992-97, for South West Devon 1997-2010, for South West Devon (revised boundary) since 6 May 2010 general election; PPS to: Sir Derek Spencer as Solicitor General 1993-95, Sir Nicholas Lyell as Attorney General 1994-95; Assistant Government Whip 1995-96; Parliamentary Secretary, Lord Chancellor's Department 1996-97; Opposition Spokesperson for: Foreign Affairs 1997-98, Europe 1997-98; Shadow Secretary of State for International Development 1998-2001; Shadow Minister for Foreign Affairs 2003-04; Member, Speaker's Committee on the Electoral Commission 2010-17; Contested Deputy Speaker election 2013. *Select committees:* Member: Office of the Deputy Prime Minister 2002-04, Office of the Deputy Prime Minister (Urban Affairs Sub-Committee) 2003-04, Home Affairs 2005-10, Chairmen's Panel/Panel of Chairs 2009-, Joint Committee on Security 2010-15, Ecclesiastical Committee 2010-17, Court of Referees 2016-17, Standards 2017-19, Privileges 2017-19. Chair, board of directors, governing council, Conservative Christian Fellowship; Conservative Party: Vice-chair 2001-02 Chair: Human Rights Commission 2005-07, International Office 2005-08; Founding member, Conservatives for Reform in Europe 2016. *Councils and public bodies:* Plymouth City Council: Councillor 1986-92, Chair, Housing Committee 1989-91.

Political interests: Law and order, family moral and social affairs, developing world; Middle East, North Korea.

Other: Chair: Westminster Foundation for Democracy 2010-, Christians in Parliament 2010-; Kt 2019.

Recreations: Watching cricket and rugby, family.

Sir Gary Streeter MP, House of Commons, London SW1A 0AA
Tel: 020 7219 5033 *Fax:* 020 7219 2414 *Email:* deans@parliament.uk
Constituency: No constituency office publicised
Tel: 01752 335666 *Email:* deans@parliament.uk Website: www.garystreeter.co.uk
Twitter: @garystreeterSWD

LABOUR

STREETING, WES

Ilford North *(Majority 5,218)*

Shadow Minister for Schools

Wesley Paul William Streeting. Born 21 January 1983; Son of Mark Streeting, car salesman, and Corrina, cleaner and shopworker; Engaged to Joseph Dancey.

Education: Westminster City School; Selwyn College, Cambridge (BA history 2004) (President Students' Union 2004-05); Limited French.

Non-political career: National Union of Students: National executive member 2005-06, Vice-President (Education) 2006-08, National President 2008-10; Membership assistant, Progress 2005-06; Chief Executive, Helena Kennedy Foundation 2010-12; Member, Widening Participation Strategic Advisory Committee, Higher Education Funding Council of England 2011-14; Head of Education, Stonewall 2012-13; Self-employed campaigns consultant 2014-16. Member: Community, Unison, GMB.

Political career: Member for Ilford North since 7 May 2015 general election; Shadow Minister for: Treasury (Shadow Exchequer Secretary) 2020, Education (Schools) 2020-. *Select committees:* Member: Treasury 2015-19, Treasury Sub-committee 2017-19, Future Relationship with the European Union 2020-21. Chair, PLP Departmental Groups for Treasury 2019. National Committee, Labour Students 2006-10; Member, Co-operative Party 2006-; Patron, LGBT Labour 2006-; Chair, London Group of Labour MPs 2016-; Member, London Regional Board 2016-20. *Councils and public bodies:* London Borough of Redbridge Council: Councillor 2010-18, Deputy Leader of the Opposition 2011-14, Deputy Leader of Council and Cabinet Member for Health and Wellbeing 2014-15; Governor, Grove Primary School 2011-15; Vice-president, Local Government Association 2015-.

Political interests: Economic policy, financial services, social justice, schools, further education, higher education, foreign policy, local government, London, taxi and private hire industry; Australia, Bangladesh, China, European Union, France, India, Israel and the Occupied Palestine Territories, New Zealand, Pakistan, Sri Lanka, USA.

Other: Member, Progress 2000-; Fellow, RSA 2008-; Commissioner, HIV Commission 2019-20; The Fabian Society: Executive Committee 2019-, Vice-chair 2020-; Shelter, Great Ormond Street Hospital, Holocaust Educational Trust.

Recreations: Reading, walking, arts, film.

Wes Streeting MP, House of Commons, London SW1A 0AA
Tel: 020 7219 6132 *Email:* wes.streeting.mp@parliament.uk
Constituency: 12a Highview Parade, Woodford Avenue, Ilford IG4 5EP
Tel: 020 3475 7901 *Email:* wes@redbridgelabour.org.uk Website: www.wesstreeting.org
Twitter: @wesstreeting

CONSERVATIVE

STRIDE, MEL

Central Devon *(Majority 17,721)*

Chair, Select Committee on Treasury

Melvyn John Stride. Born 30 September 1961; Son of Mel Stride and Barbara Stride; Married Michelle King Hughes 2006 (3 daughters).

Education: Portsmouth Grammar School; St Edmund Hall, Oxford (BA politics, philosophy and economics 1984) (President, Oxford Union 1984).

Non-political career: Founder and ex-director, Venture Marketing Group 1987-2007. Member, Amicus 2006-10.

Political career: Member for Central Devon since 6 May 2010 general election; PPS to John Hayes as Minister: of State for Further Education, Skills and Lifelong Learning 2011-12, of State for Energy, Department of Energy and Climate Change 2012-13, without Portfolio, Cabinet Office 2013-14; Assistant Government Whip 2014-15; Government Whip: (Lord Commissioner of HM Treasury) 2015-16, (Comptroller of HM Household) 2016-17; Financial Secretary; Paymaster General, HM Treasury 2017-19; Leader of the House of Commons; Lord President of the Council 2019; Member: House of Commons Commission 2019, Public Accounts Commission 2019, Speaker's Committee for the Independent Parliamentary Standards Authority 2019. *Select committees:* Member, Northern Ireland Affairs 2010-11; Chair, Treasury

2019-; Member, Liaison 2019-. Oxford University Conservative Association: Member 1981-84, President 1982. *Councils and public bodies:* Community Governor, Okehampton College.

Political interests: Economy, education, welfare reform, social justice; USA.

Other: Oxford Union Society: Member 1981-, President 1984; Pilot's licence 1990; Registered blue badge guide 2005; Commission for Social Justice Working Group 2006-07; President, Tarka Railway Association; Member, Association of Professional Tourist Guides 2006; Guide of the Year 2005; PC 2017.

Recreations: History, walking, spending time with family.

Rt Hon Mel Stride MP, House of Commons, London SW1A 0AA
Tel: 020 7219 7037 *Email:* mel.stride.mp@parliament.uk
Constituency: 2a Manaton Court, Manaton Close, Matford Business Park, Exeter, Devon EX2 8PF
Tel: 01392 823306 Website: www.melstridemp.com *Twitter:* @MelJStride

LABOUR

STRINGER, GRAHAM

Blackley and Broughton *(Majority 14,402)*

Graham Eric Stringer. Born 17 February 1950; Son of late Albert Stringer, railway clerk, and late Brenda Stringer, shop assistant; Married Kathryn Carr 1999 (1 son 1 stepson 1 stepdaughter).

Education: Moston Brook High School; Sheffield University (BSc chemistry 1971).

Non-political career: Analytical chemist; Chair of Board, Manchester Airport plc 1996-97. Branch officer and shop steward, MSF; Member, Amicus/Unite.

Political career: Member for Manchester Blackley 1997-2010, for Blackley and Broughton since 6 May 2010 general election; Parliamentary Secretary, Cabinet Office 1999-2001; Government Whip 2001-02. *Select committees:* Member: Environment, Transport and Regional Affairs 1997-99, Environment, Transport and Regional Affairs (Transport Sub-Committee) 1997-99, Transport 2002-10, 2011-19, Modernisation of the House of Commons 2006, Science and Technology 2006-07, 2010-, Innovation, Universities[, Science] and Skills 2007-10, Justice 2013-14, Energy and Climate Change 2013-15, Panel of Chairs 2015-, European Scrutiny 2015-17, Foreign Affairs 2020-. Vice-chair, PLP Departmental Committee for Transport 2006-10. Chair, Labour Leave 2016. *Councils and public bodies:* Manchester City Council: Councillor 1979-98, Leader 1984-96.

Political interests: Urban regeneration, House of Lords reform, revitalising local democracy, aviation and airports, bus regulation, science policy, justice policy.

Other: Trustee, Global Warming Policy Foundation; Vote Leave: Board member 2016, Member, Campaign Committee 2016; Founding supporter, Change Britain 2016-; Hon. RNCM. Member: Manchester Tennis and Racquet Club, Cheetham Hill Cricket Club.

Recreations: Real tennis, squash.

Graham Stringer MP, House of Commons, London SW1A 0AA
Tel: 020 7219 5235 *Email:* graham.stringer.mp@parliament.uk
Constituency: North Manchester Sixth Form College, Rochdale Road, Manchester M9 4AF
Tel: 0161-202 6600

CONSERVATIVE

STUART, GRAHAM

Beverley and Holderness *(Majority 20,448)*

Parliamentary Under-Secretary of State (Minister for Exports), Department for International Trade

Graham Charles Stuart. Born 12 March 1962; Son of late Dr Peter Stuart and Joan Stuart; Married Anne Crawshaw 1989 (2 daughters).

Education: Glenalmond College, Perthshire; Selwyn College, Cambridge (law/philosophy 1985).

Non-political career: Sole proprietor, Go Enterprises 1984-2010; Director, CSL Publishing Ltd 1987-.

Political career: Contested Cambridge 2001 general election. Member for Beverley and Holderness 2005-10, for Beverley and Holderness (revised boundary) since 6 May 2010 general election; Assistant Government Whip 2016-18; Parliamentary Under-Secretary of State, Department for International Trade: (Minister for Investment) 2018-20, (Minister for Exports) 2020-. *Select committees:* Member: Environmental Audit 2006-10, Joint Committee on the Draft Climate Change Bill 2007, Education and Skills/Children, Schools and Families 2007-10; Chair, Education 2010-15; Member, Liaison 2010-15. Chairman, Cambridge University Conservative Association 1985; Board member, Conservative Party 2006-10. *Councils and public bodies:* Cambridge City Council: Councillor 1998-2004, Leader, Conservative Group 2000-04.

Political interests: Education, older people, mental health, welfare, economics, rural funding, climate change; China, Latin America.

Other: Chair: CHANT (Community Hospitals Acting Nationally Together) 2005-10, East Riding Health Action Group 2007-09, Globe International 2007-16, Rural Fair Share Campaign -2011; Vice-chair, f40 Group 2015-16; Vice-president: Northern branch, Association of Drainage Authorities, Beverley and District Civic Society; Member, River Hull Board 2016-18.

Recreations: Sailing, cricket, motor cycling, triathlon.

Graham Stuart MP, House of Commons, London SW1A 0AA
Tel: 020 7219 6925 *Email:* graham.stuart.mp@parliament.uk
Constituency: 9 Cross Street, Beverley, East Yorkshire HU17 9AX
Tel: 01482 679687 Website: www.grahamstuart.com *Twitter:* @grahamstuart

CONSERVATIVE

STURDY, JULIAN

York Outer *(Majority 9,985)*

Julian Charles Sturdy. Born 3 June 1971; Son of Robert Sturdy, MEP for Cambridgeshire 1994-99 and Eastern region 1999-2014, and Elizabeth Hommes; Married Victoria (1 son 1 daughter).

Education: Harper Adams University (agriculture).

Non-political career: Farming and property business.

Political career: Contested Scunthorpe 2005 general election. Member for York Outer since 6 May 2010 general election; PPS to: Simon Burns as Minister of State, Department for Transport 2012-13, Department for Transport ministerial team 2013-14, Brandon Lewis as Minister of State, Department for Communities and Local Government 2014-15. *Select committees:* Member: Transport 2010-12, Energy and Climate Change 2015-16, Standing Orders 2015-17, Joint Committee on Consolidation, &c, Bills 2015-, Environment, Food and Rural Affairs 2017-. *Councils and public bodies:* Councillor, Harrogate Borough Council 2002-07; Governor, educational foundation of local school.

Other: Director, Harrogate District Community Transport.

Julian Sturdy MP, House of Commons, London SW1A 0AA
Tel: 020 7219 7199 *Email:* julian.sturdy.mp@parliament.uk
Constituency: 1 Ash Street, Poppleton Road, York, North Yorkshire YO26 4UR
Tel: 01904 784847 Website: www.juliansturdy.co.uk *Twitter:* @JulianSturdy

LABOUR

SULTANA, ZARAH

Coventry South *(Majority 401)*

Born 31 October 1993.

Education: Birmingham University.

Non-political career: Member, Unite the Union.

Political career: Member for Coventry South since 12 December 2019; PPS to Dan Carden as Acting Shadow Secretary of State for International Development 2020. *Select committees:* Member: Science and Technology 2020-, Business, Energy and Industrial Strategy 2020-.

Other: Board member, Albany Theatre Trust 2020-.

Zarah Sultana MP, House of Commons, London SW1A 0AA
Tel: 020 7219 3000 *Email:* zarah.sultana.mp@parliament.uk
Constituency: No constituency office publicised
Website: zarahsultana.com *Twitter:* @zarahsultana

CONSERVATIVE

SUNAK, RISHI

Richmond (Yorkshire) *(Majority 27,210)*

Chancellor of the Exchequer

Born 12 May 1980; Married Akshatha Murthy 2009 (2 daughters).

Education: Winchester College; Oxford University (BA philosophy, politics and economics 2001); Stanford University (Fulbright Scholar, MBA 2006).

Non-political career: Principal Investment Area, Goldman Sachs; The Children's Investment Fund; Theleme Fund; Head of Black and Minority Ethnic (BME) Research Unit, Policy Exchange; Catamaran Ventures UK.

Political career: Member for Richmond (Yorkshire) since 7 May 2015 general election; Team PPS, Department for Business, Energy and Industrial Strategy 2017-18; Parliamentary Under-Secretary of State (Minister for Local Government), Ministry of Housing, Communities and Local Government 2018-19; Member, Speaker's Committee on the Electoral Commission 2018-19; HM Treasury: Chief Secretary to the Treasury 2019-20, Chancellor of the Exchequer 2020-. *Select committees:* Member, Environment, Food and Rural Affairs 2015-17.

Political interests: Rural affairs, economy and enterprise, defence; India, USA.

Other: PC 2019.

Recreations: Southampton FC supporter, Yorkshire County Cricket Club supporter.

Rt Hon Rishi Sunak MP, House of Commons, London SW1A 0AA
Tel: 020 7219 5437 *Email:* rishi.sunak.mp@parliament.uk
Constituency: Unit 1, Omega Business Village, Northallerton, North Yorkshire DL6 2NJ
Tel: 01609 765330 Website: www.rishisunak.com *Twitter:* @RishiSunak

CONSERVATIVE

SUNDERLAND, JAMES

Bracknell *(Majority 19,829)*

Born 6 June 1970; Married.

Education: Royal Grammar School, Guildford; Birmingham University (BA 1992); Royal Military Academy, Sandhurst (1993); Defence Academy (2011) Kings College London (MA 2011); French.

Non-political career: British Army 1993-2019 including: Worldwide appointments at Regimental Duty and Staff, Military Assistant to Deputy Commander Joint Operations, Deputy Chief of Staff, 101 Logistic Brigade, Commanding Officer, 27 Regiment Royal Logistic Corps; Commander, Army Engagement Group.

Political career: Member for Bracknell since 12 December 2019. *Select committees:* Member, Procedure 2020-. Member: Aldershot Conservative Association, Bracknell Conservative Association. *Councils and public bodies:* School Governor.

Political interests: Defence, armed forces, education (including SEN), homelessness, global Britain, international trade, British history and values, parliamentary procedure and process, law and order, Brexit; Africa, India, Middle East, Overseas Territories.

Other: Motorsport Bodies; Charity Trustee. Carlton Club; Sutton and Cheam Motor Club; Southern Car Club.

Recreations: Motorsport, football, golf, cricket.

James Sunderland MP, House of Commons, London SW1A 0AA
Tel: 020 7219 5032 *Email:* james.sunderland.mp@parliament.uk
Constituency: 10 Milbanke Court, Milbanke Way, Bracknell RG12 1RP
Tel: 01344 481900 Website: www.jamessunderland.org.uk *Twitter:* @JamesSunderl

CONSERVATIVE

SWAYNE, DESMOND

New Forest West *(Majority 24,403)*

Desmond Angus Swayne. Born 20 August 1956; Son of George Swayne and Elisabeth Swayne, née Gibson; Married Moira Teek 1987 (1 son 2 daughters).

Education: Bedford School; St Mary's College, St Andrews University (MA theology 1980); Spanish and French (rusty).

Non-political career: Schoolmaster, A-level economics: Charterhouse 1980-81, Wrekin College 1982-87; Risk management systems manager, Royal Bank of Scotland 1988-96. Major, Territorial Army.

Political career: Contested Pontypridd 1987 and West Bromwich West 1992 general elections. Member for New Forest West 1997-2010, for New Forest West (revised boundary) since 6 May 2010 general election; Opposition Whip 2002-03; Opposition Spokesperson for: Health 2001, Defence 2001-02; Shadow Minister for: International Affairs 2003-04, Northern Ireland 2004; PPS to: Michael Howard as Leader of the Opposition 2004-05, David Cameron: as Leader of the Opposition 2005-10, as Prime Minister 2010-12; Government Whip 2012-13; Government Whip (Vice-Chamberlain of HM Household) 2013-14; Minister of State, Department for International Development 2014-16; Member, Speaker's Committee for the Independent Parliamentary Standards Authority 2020-. *Select committees:* Member: Scottish Affairs 1997-2001, Social Security 1999-2001, Procedure 2002-05, Defence 2005-06, Ecclesiastical Committee 2005-10, 2017-, Administration 2012-13, International Trade 2016-17, Northern Ireland Affairs 2019, Work and Pensions 2020-.

Other: Member, Countryside Alliance; TD; PC 2011; Kt 2016. Cavalry and Guards Club; Serpentine Swimming Club.

Recreations: Territorial Army.

Rt Hon Sir Desmond Swayne TD MP, House of Commons, London SW1A 0AA
Tel: 020 7219 4886 *Fax:* 020 7219 0901 *Email:* swayned@parliament.uk
Constituency: 4 Cliff Crescent, Marine Drive, Barton-on-Sea, New Milton, Hampshire BH25 7EB
Tel: 01425 629844 *Email:* desmondswayne@hotmail.com
Website: www.desmondswaynemp.com *Twitter:* @desmondswayne

CONSERVATIVE

SYMS, ROBERT

Poole *(Majority 19,116)*

Robert Andrew Raymond Syms. Born 15 August 1956; Son of Raymond Syms, builder, and Mary Syms, teacher; Married Nicola Guy 1991 (divorced 1999); married Fiona Mellersh 2000 (divorced 2009) (1 daughter 1 son).

Education: Colston's School, Bristol.

Non-political career: Director, family building, plant hire and property group, Chippenham, Wiltshire 1978-.

Political career: Contested Walsall North 1992 general election. Member for Poole 1997-2010, for Poole (revised boundary) since 6 May 2010 general election; PPS to Michael Ancram as Chair Conservative Party 1999-2000; Opposition Spokesperson for Environment, Transport and Regions 1999-2001; Opposition Whip 2003; Shadow Minister for: Local and Devolved Government Affairs 2003-05, Local Government 2005-07; Assistant Government Whip 2012-13; Government Whip (Lord Commissioner of HM Treasury) 2016-17. *Select committees:* Member: Health 1997-2000, 2007-10, Procedure 1998-99, Transport 2002-03, Liaison 2010-13; Chair, Regulatory Reform 2010-12; Member: Joint Committee on the Draft Detention of Terrorist Suspects (Temporary Extension) Bills 2011, Administration 2013-14, 2016-17, Finance and Services 2013-15, Standing Orders 2014-15; Chair, High Speed Rail (London-West Midlands) Bill 2014-16; Member: Finance 2017-20, Joint Committee on Statutory Instruments 2017-. Joint Vice-chair, Conservative Party Committee for Constitutional Affairs, Scotland and Wales 1997-99. North Wiltshire Conservative Association: Treasurer 1982-84, Deputy chair 1983-84, Chair 1984-86; Vice-chair, Conservative Party 2001-03. *Councils and public bodies:* Councillor: North Wiltshire District Council 1983-87, Wiltshire County Council 1985-97; Member, Wessex Regional Health Authority 1988-90; Board member, Shadow Sponsor Body for the Houses of Parliament Restoration and Renewal Programme 2020-.

Political interests: Economic policy, constitution, local and regional government; USA, most of English speaking world.

House of Commons MPs' Biographies

Other: Member: North Wiltshire Enterprise Agency 1986-90, Calne Development Project Trust 1986-97; Fellow, Chartered Institute of Building; Kt 2017.

Recreations: Reading, music.

Sir Robert Syms MP, House of Commons, London SW1A 0AA
Tel: 020 7219 4601 *Fax:* 020 7219 6867 *Email:* symsr@parliament.uk
Constituency: Poole Conservative Association, 38 Sandbanks Road, Poole, Dorset BH14 8BX
Tel: 01202 739922 *Email:* symsr@pooleconservatives.org
Website: www.pooleconservatives.org *Twitter:* @RobertSyms

LABOUR

TAMI, MARK

Alyn and Deeside *(Majority 213)*

Opposition Pairing Whip

Mark Richard Tami. Born 3 October 1962; Son of Michael Tami and Patricia Tami; Married Sally Ann Daniels 1994 (2 sons).

Education: Enfield Grammar School; Swansea University (BA history 1985).

Non-political career: AEEU: Head of research and communications 1992-99, Head of policy 1999-2001. Member: AEEU/Amicus 1986-, TUC General Council 1999-2001.

Political career: Member for Alyn and Deeside since 7 June 2001 general election; PPS to John Healey as Financial Secretary to the Treasury 2005-06; Assistant Government Whip 2007-10; Opposition Whip 2010-11; Opposition Assistant Chief Whip 2011-20; Opposition Pairing Whip 2020-. *Select committees:* Member: Northern Ireland Affairs 2001-05, European Standing Committee B 2003-05, Joint Committee on Tax Law Rewrite Bills 2005-07, Joint Committee on Human Rights 2007, Selection 2010-, Works of Art 2011-12, Joint Committee on Security 2011-15, Administration 2012-, Joint Committee on the Palace of Westminster 2015-16, Finance 2017-, Joint Committee on the Draft Parliamentary Buildings (Restoration and Renewal) Bill 2018-19. Vice-chair PLP Welsh Regional Group 2005-07. Treasurer, Labour Friends of Australia.

Political interests: Manufacturing, aerospace, animal welfare.

Other: PC 2018. Glamorgan County Cricket.

Recreations: Football (Norwich City FC), cricket, fishing, antiques.

Rt Hon Mark Tami MP, House of Commons, London SW1A 0AA
Tel: 020 7219 8174 *Email:* tamim@parliament.uk
Constituency: 70 High Street, Connah's Quay, Flintshire CH5 4DD
Tel: 01244 819854 Website: www.marktami.co.uk *Twitter:* @MarkTamiMP

LABOUR

TARRY, SAM

Ilford South *(Majority 24,101)*

Shadow Minister for Buses and Local Transport

Samuel Peter Tarry. Born August 1982; Married Julia Fozard 2016.

Non-political career: Researcher in local and regional governance, Office of the Deputy Prime Minister; Executive Officer, Home Office: International Police Assistance Section, National Offender Management/National Probation Directorate; Events and Local Campaigns Officer, UnlockDemocracy; Campaign Organiser, Hope not Hate; Political officer, TSSA Union. Vice-chair, GMB Young London 2007-09.

Political career: Member for Ilford South since 12 December 2019; PPS to Ed Miliband as Shadow Secretary of State for Business, Energy and Industrial Strategy 2021; Shadow Minister for Transport (Buses and Local Transport) 2021-. *Select committees:* Member, Transport 2020-. Labour Party: Anti-racism officer, London Young Labour, National chair, Young Labour 2009-11, Campaign director to Jeremy Corbyn, 2015 and 2016 Leadership campaigns, Chair, Angela Rayner's Deputy Leadership campaign 2020, Parliamentary Lead (Campaigns and Organisation) (reporting to Angela Rayber as Party Chair) 2020-. *Councils and public bodies:* Councillor, Barking and Dagenham Council 2010-18.

Other: Member, National Steering Committee, Stop the War Coalition 2004-08; President and chair, Centre for Labour and Social Studies.

Sam Tarry MP, House of Commons, London SW1A 0AA
Tel: 020 7219 6807 *Email:* sam.tarry.mp@parliament.uk
Constituency: 6 Mildmay Road, Ilford, Essex IG1 1DTT
Tel: 020 8478 6781 *Twitter:* @SamTarry

SCOTTISH NATIONAL PARTY

THEWLISS, ALISON

Glasgow Central *(Majority 6,474)*

SNP Shadow Chancellor of the Exchequer

Alison Emily Thewliss. Born 13 September 1982; Married (2 children).

Education: Aberdeen University (politics and international relations 2004).

Non-political career: Part-time parliamentary assistant to Bill Kidd MSP.

Political career: Member for Glasgow Central since 7 May 2015 general election; SNP: Spokesperson for: Cities 2015-18, Treasury (Shadow Chief Secretary to the Treasury) 2017-19, Housing and Local Government 2018-19, Shadow Chancellor of the Exchequer 2020-. *Select committees:* Member: Communities and Local Government 2015-17, Procedure 2017-19, Joint Committee on the Draft Registration of Overseas Entities Bill 2019, Treasury 2019-. National Convener, Young Scots for Independence 2006-08. *Councils and public bodies:* Glasgow City Council: Councillor 2007-15, SNP Spokesperson for Land and Environmental Services.

Political interests: Local government, democracy, anti-nuclear weapons.

Other: Member, Scottish CND; Best Scot at Westminster, Herald Scottish Politician of the Year 2017.

Alison Thewliss MP, House of Commons, London SW1A 0AA
Tel: 020 7219 6447 *Email:* alison.thewliss.mp@parliament.uk
Constituency: 33 London Road, Glasgow G1 5NW
Tel: 0141-552 7117 Website: www.alisonthewliss.scot *Twitter:* @alisonthewliss

CONSERVATIVE

THOMAS, DEREK

St Ives *(Majority 4,284)*

Derek Gordon Thomas. Born 20 July 1972; Married 1998 (2 sons).

Education: Camborne Comprehensive.

Non-political career: Cornish mason (including apprenticeship), Trethowan Builders, West Cornwall 1988-93; Outreach worker, Church of England, Wallington 1993-96; Youth and community manager, Methodist Church, Penzance 1996-99; Self-employed craftsman 1999-2002; Former Community development manager, Mustard Seed Helston; Businessman.

Political career: Contested St Ives 2010 general election. Member for St Ives since 7 May 2015 general election. *Select committees:* Member: Science and Technology 2015-17, Health and Social Care 2018-19, Work and Pensions 2018-19, Environmental Audit 2019, Environment, Food and Rural Affairs 2020-. Deputy chair (political), St Ives Conservative Association. *Councils and public bodies:* Penwith District Council: Councillor 2005-09, Chair, Overview and Scrutiny 2007-09, Champion, Children and Young People 2006-09.

Political interests: Health, education.

Recreations: Sport, sea kayaking.

Derek Thomas MP, House of Commons, London SW1A 0AA
Tel: 020 7219 4435 *Email:* derek.thomas.mp@parliament.uk
Constituency: Wharfside Shopping Centre, Wharf Road, Penzance, Cornwall TR18 2GB
Tel: 01736 363038 Website: derekthomas.org *Twitter:* @DerekThomasUK

LABOUR/ CO-OPERATIVE

THOMAS, GARETH

Harrow West *(Majority 8,692)*

Shadow Minister for International Trade

Gareth Richard Thomas. Born 15 July 1967.

Education: Hatch End High School; Lowlands College; University College of Wales, Aberystwyth (BSc (Econ) politics 1988); Greenwich University (PGCE 1992); King's College, London (MA imperial and Commonwealth studies 1996).

Non-political career: Teacher. Member, Amicus.

Political career: Member for Harrow West 1997-2010, for Harrow West (revised boundary) since 6 May 2010 general election; PPS to Charles Clarke: as Minister of State, Home Office 1999-2001, as Minister without Portfolio and Party Chair 2001-02, as Secretary of State for Education and Skills 2002-03; Sponsored Private Member's Bill, Industrial and Provident Societies Act 2002; Parliamentary Under-Secretary of State: Department for International Development 2003-08, Department for Business, Enterprise and Regulatory Reform (Trade and Consumer Affairs) 2007-08; Minister of State (Trade, Investment and Consumer Affairs/Trade, Development and Consumer Affairs), Departments for: Business, Enterprise and Regulatory Reform 2008-09, International Development 2008-10; Shadow Minister for: International Development 2010, Treasury 2010, Business, Innovation and Skills 2010-11, Cabinet Office 2011-13; Shadow Deputy Minister for London 2013; Shadow Minister for Foreign and Commonwealth Office: Europe 2013-14, North Africa and Middle East 2014-15; Shadow Minister for: Communities and Local Government 2016-17, International Trade 2020-. *Select committees:* Member: Environmental Audit 1997-99, International Trade 2019-20. Vice-chair, PLP Departmental Committee for Culture, Media and Sport 2000-04; Hon. Secretary, PLP Departmental Committee for Trade and Industry 2000-04. Member, SERA; Chair, Co-operative Party 2000-19. *Councils and public bodies:* London Borough of Harrow: Councillor 1990-97, Labour Group Whip 1996; Vice-chair, Association of Local Government Social Services Committee.

Political interests: Energy, mutuals, health, environment; Europe, India, Norway, Pakistan, Sri Lanka.

Other: Member, Fabian Society; Fellow, Industry and Parliament Trust 2003. Pinner United Services Club.

Publications: At the Energy Crossroads Policies for a Low Carbon Economy (Fabian Society, 2001); From Margins to Mainstream – Making Social Responsibility Part of Corporate Culture (2002).

Recreations: Running, rugby union.

Gareth Thomas MP, House of Commons, London SW1A 0AA
Tel: 020 7219 4243 *Email:* gareth.thomas.mp@parliament.uk
Constituency: 132 Blenheim Road, West Harrow, Middlesex HA2 7AA
Tel: 020 8861 6300 Website: gareththomas.org.uk *Twitter:* @GarethThomasMP

LABOUR

THOMAS-SYMONDS, NICK

Torfaen *(Majority 3,742)*

Shadow Home Secretary

Nicklaus Thomas-Symonds. Born 26 May 1980; Married Rebecca (2 daughters 1 son).

Education: St Alban's RC High School, Pontypool; Oxford University (BA politics, philosophy and economics 2001); Glamorgan University (DipLaw); Cardiff University (BVC).

Non-political career: Lecturer, Oxford University 2002-15; Called to the Bar, Lincoln's Inn 2004; Practising Barrister: 33 Park Place 2004–08, Civitas Law 2008-15. Unite.

Political career: Member for Torfaen since 7 May 2015 general election; Shadow Minister for Pensions 2015-16, Shadow Minister for Employment 2016; Shadow Solicitor General 2016-20; Shadow Minister for Security 2017-20; Shadow Minister for Wales 2020; Shadow Secretary of State for the Home Department (Shadow Home Secretary) 2020-. *Select committees:* Member, Justice 2015. Secretary, Torfaen CLP 2009-15.

Political interests: Home affairs, health, work and pensions, historical matters, archiving issues, legal issues, industrial heritage; France.

Other: Fellow, Royal Historical Society 2012. President, Blaenavon Blues FC.

Publications: Attlee: A Life in Politics (2010); Nye: The Political Life of Aneurin Bevan (2014).

Recreations: Reading, jogging, most sports, Liverpool FC.

Nick Thomas-Symonds MP, House of Commons, London SW1A 0AA
Tel: 020 7219 4294 *Email:* nick.thomassymonds.mp@parliament.uk
Constituency: 73 Upper Trosnant Street, Pontypool, Torfaen NP4 8AU
Tel: 01495 740498 Website: www.nickthomassymonds.uk *Twitter:* @NickTorfaen

SCOTTISH NATIONAL PARTY

THOMPSON, OWEN

Midlothian *(Majority 5,705)*

SNP Deputy Whip

Owen George Thompson. Born 17 March 1978.

Education: Beeslack High School; Napier University (BA accounting and finance 2001).

Non-political career: Various positions in financial services industry 2001-07; Assistant to Rob Gibson MSP 2007-11; Assistant to Clare Adamson MSP 2011-15; Chief of Staff to Peter Grant MP 2017-18; Director, Owen Thompson Consulting 2017-.

Political career: Member for Midlothian 2015-17. Contested Midlothian 2017 general election. Member for Midlothian since 12 December 2019; SNP Deputy Whip 2015-17, 2020-; Member, Speaker's Committee on the Electoral Commission 2020-. *Select committees:* Member: Selection 2015-17, 2020-, Joint Committee on Statutory Instruments 2020-, European Statutory Instruments 2020-, Procedure 2020-, Joint Committee on Consolidation, &c, Bills 2020-. Scottish National Party: NEC member 2010-14, Local government convener 2011-14. *Councils and public bodies:* Midlothian Council: Councillor 2005-15, Leader 2013-15, Former Cabinet Member for Planning, Housing and Community Safety.

Political interests: Community empowerment, supporting the vulnerable, Scottish independence.

Other: Chair, Midlothian Community Planning Partnership 2012-15.

Recreations: Football, tough mudder, craft beer.

Owen Thompson MP, House of Commons, London SW1A 0AA
Tel: 020 7219 3000 *Email:* owen.thompson.mp@parliament.uk
Constituency: 106 High Street, Dalkeith, Midlothian EH22 1HZ
Tel: 0131-285 8283 Website: www.owenthompson.scot *Twitter:* @OwenThompson

SCOTTISH NATIONAL PARTY

THOMSON, RICHARD

Gordon *(Majority 819)*

SNP Shadow Secretary of State for Northern Ireland and Wales and Shadow Financial Secretary

Richard Gordon Thomson. Born 16 June 1976; Partner Eilidh (2 daughters).

Education: Tynecastle High School, Edinburgh; Stirling University (BA history and politics 1998).

Non-political career: Clerk, Bank of Scotland 1998-99; Scottish Widows: Assistant Customer Relations Manager 1999-2001, Corporate Account Manager 2001-04; Head of Campaign Unit, SNP HQ 2004-05; Senior Researcher to Stewart Hosie MP and Shona Robinson MSP 2005-07; Head of Research, SNP Westminster Group 2007-08; Parliamentary Assistant to Alex Salmond MSP 2008-11; Reporter and Columnist, *Ellon Times* and *Inverurie Herald* 2011-12.

Political career: Contested Tweeddale, Ettrick and Lauderdale 2001 and Gordon 2010 general election. Member for Gordon since 12 December 2019; SNP Spokesperson for Business and Industry 2020-, Shadow Secretary of State for Northern Ireland and Wales 2021-, Shadow Financial Secretary 2021-. *Councils and public bodies:* Aberdeenshire Council: Councillor 2012-, SNP Group Leader 2015-, Co-Leader of the Council 2015-17, Opposition Leader 2017-.

Political interests: Business, economics, transport, constitution; Canada, European Union, EFTA, USA.

Recreations: Music, family.

Richard Thomson MP, House of Commons, London SW1A 0AA
Tel: 020 7219 3843 *Email:* richard.thomson.mp@parliament.uk
Constituency: Unit F6, Enterprise Centre, Aberdeen Energy Park, Exploration Drive, Aberdeen AB23 8GX
Tel: 020 3545 2236 *Twitter:* @RThomsonMP

LABOUR

THORNBERRY, EMILY

Islington South and Finsbury *(Majority 17,328)*

Shadow Secretary of State for International Trade

Emily Anne Thornberry. Born 27 July 1960; Daughter of late Sallie Thornberry and late Cedric Thornberry; Married Christopher Nugee 1992 (1 daughter 2 sons).

Education: Church of England Secondary Modern, Guildford; Burlington Danes, Shepherd's Bush, London; Kent University, Canterbury (BA law 1982).

Non-political career: Member, Mike Mansfield's Chambers: Tooks Court 1985. Member, Unite (TGWU sector) 1985-.

Political career: Member for Islington South and Finsbury since 5 May 2005 general election; PPS to Joan Ruddock as Minister of State, Department of Energy and Climate Change 2009-10; Shadow Minister for: Energy and Climate Change 2010, Health 2010-11; Shadow Attorney General 2011-14; Shadow Minister for Employment 2015-16; Shadow Secretary of State for: Defence 2016, Foreign and Commonwealth Affairs (Shadow Foreign Secretary) 2016-20, Exiting the European Union 2016, International Trade 2020-. *Select committees:* Member: Environmental Audit 2005-07, Joint Committee on the Draft Legal Services Bill 2006, Communities and Local Government 2006-09, Health 2015.

Political interests: Housing, environment, poverty, equality; Middle East.

Other: Society of Labour Lawyers 1983; Friends of the Earth 1990; Fawcett Society; Fabian Society; PC 2017.

Recreations: Family, cycling, travel.

Rt Hon Emily Thornberry MP, House of Commons, London SW1A 0AA
Tel: 020 7219 5676 *Fax:* 020 7219 5955 *Email:* emily.thornberry.mp@parliament.uk
Constituency: 65 Barnsbury Street, Islington, London N1 1EJ
Tel: 020 7697 9307 Website: www.emilythornberry.com *Twitter:* @emilythornberry

CONSERVATIVE

THROUP, MAGGIE

Erewash *(Majority 10,606)*

Government Whip (Lord Commissioner of HM Treasury)

Margaret Ann Throup. Born 27 January 1957; Divorced.

Education: Bradford Girls' Grammar School; Manchester University (BSc biology 1978); Diploma marketing 1987; Fellowship biomedical sciences 1980.

Non-political career: Medical laboratory scientist, Calderdale Health Authority 1978-85; Nycomed (UK) Ltd: Sales executive 1985-86, Product manager 1986-90, Sales and marketing manager 1990-93, Business development manager 1993-96; Director, Maggie Throup Marketing Ltd 1996-.

Political career: Contested Colne Valley 2005 and Solihull 2010 general elections. Member for Erewash since 7 May 2015 general election; Board Member, Parliamentary Office of Science and Technology Board 2018-19; Department of Health and Social Care: Team PPS 2018-19, PPS to Matt Hancock as Secretary of State for Health and Social Care 2019; Government Whip (Lord Commissioner of HM Treasury) 2019-. *Select committees:* Member: Scottish Affairs 2015-16, Health 2015-18. Chairman, Conservative Backbench Policy Committee on Health 2017-19.

Political interests: Healthcare, small business, environment; Rwanda.

Other: Substitute Member, UK Delegation to Parliamentary Assembly of Council of Europe 2017-18; Trustee, Industry and Parliament Trust 2017-19; Fellow, Institute of Biomedical Sciences 1978-85; Chartered Institute of Marketing 1987-96; Trustee: Solihull Community Foundation 2003-, Solihull Carers Centre 2007-.

Recreations: Skiing, sailing, walking.

Maggie Throup MP, House of Commons, London SW1A 0AA
Tel: 020 7219 6571 *Email:* maggie.throup.mp@parliament.uk
Constituency: Unit 2, The Old Co-op, South Street, Ilkeston, Derbyshire DE7 5SG
Tel: 0115-930 0521 Website: www.maggiethroup.com *Twitter:* @maggie_erewash

LABOUR

TIMMS, STEPHEN

East Ham *(Majority 33,176)*

Chair, Select Committee on Work and Pensions

Stephen Creswell Timms. Born 29 July 1955; Son of late Ronald Timms, engineer, and Margaret Timms, retired school teacher; Married Hui-Leng Lim 1986.

Education: Farnborough Grammar School, Hampshire; Emmanuel College, Cambridge (MA mathematics 1977; MPhil operational research 1978); German.

Non-political career: Computer and telecommunications industry; Logica Ltd 1978-86; Ovum Ltd 1986-94. Member: Unite, GMB.

Political career: Member for Newham North East from 9 June 1994 by-election to 1997, for East Ham 1997-2010, for East Ham (revised boundary) since 6 May 2010 general election; PPS to Andrew Smith as Minister of State, Department for Education and Employment 1997-98; Joint PPS to Mo Mowlam as Secretary of State for Northern Ireland 1998; Department of Social Security 1998-99: Parliamentary Under-Secretary of State 1998-99, Minister of State 1999; Financial Secretary, HM Treasury 1999-2001, 2004-05, 2008-10; Minister of State: Department for Education and Skills (School Standards) 2001-02, Department of Trade and Industry (Energy, E-Commerce and Postal Services) 2002-04, Department for Work and Pensions (Pensions Reform) 2005-06; Chief Secretary to the Treasury 2006-07; Minister of State: Department for Business, Enterprise and Regulatory Reform (Competitiveness) 2007-08, Department for Work and Pensions 2008; Parliamentary Under-Secretary of State, Department for Business, Innovation and Skills (Digital Britain) 2009-10; Shadow Financial Secretary 2010; Shadow Minister for: Business, Innovation and Skills 2010, Employment 2010-15. *Select committees:* Member: Treasury 1996-97, Public Accounts 2004-05, Joint Committee on Tax Law Rewrite Bills 2009-10, Education 2016, Education, Skills and the Economy Sub-committee 2016, Exiting the European Union 2016-19, Liaison 2020-, Ecclesiastical Committee 2020-; Chair, Work and Pensions 2020-. Chair, PLP Departmental Group for Work and Pensions 2015-19. Christian Socialist Movement/Christians on the Left: Joint Vice-chair 1995-98, Chair 2012-16; Labour Party Faith Envoy 2007-. *Councils and public bodies:* London Borough of Newham: Councillor 1984-97, Leader of the Council 1990-94; Board Member, East London Partnership (now East London Business Alliance) 1990-2006; Stratford Development Partnership 1992-94.

Political interests: Economic policy, urban regeneration, telecommunications, employment, Christian socialism; Germany, Singapore.

Other: Fellow, Industry and Parliament Trust 1997; Trustee, Traidcraft Foundation 2011-; Honorary doctorate; PC 2006.

Publications: Broadband Communications: The Commercial Impact (1987).

Recreations: Cycling, walking.

Rt Hon Stephen Timms MP, House of Commons, London SW1A 0AA
Tel: 020 7219 4000 *Fax:* 020 7219 2949 *Email:* stephen.timms.mp@parliament.uk
Constituency: No constituency office
Email: stephen@stephentimms.org.uk Website: www.stephentimms.org.uk
Twitter: @stephenctimms

House of Commons MPs' Biographies

CONSERVATIVE

TIMPSON, EDWARD

Eddisbury *(Majority 18,443)*

Anthony Edward Timpson. Born 26 December 1973; Son of John Timpson and Alexandra Timpson; Married Julia Still 2002 (1 son 3 daughters).

Education: Uppingham School, Rutland; Durham University (BA politics 1996); Law conversion; College of Law, London (LLB 1997).

Non-political career: Called to the Bar 1999; Non-practising family law barrister; Member, Inner Temple; Door tenant, Linenhall Chambers, Chester.

Political career: Member for Crewe and Nantwich 22 May 2008 by-election to 2010, for Crewe and Nantwich (revised boundary) 2010-17. Contested Crewe and Nantwich 2017 general election. Member for Eddisbury since 12 December 2019; PPS to Theresa May as Home Secretary 2010-12; Department for Education: Parliamentary Under-Secretary of State for Children and Families 2012-15, Minister of State for: Children and Families 2015-16, Vulnerable Children and Families 2016-17. *Select committees:* Member: Children, Schools and Families 2008-10, Joint Committee on Human Rights 2008-10. Campaign co-ordinator, Eddisbury Conservative Association 2006-07; Vice-president, Conservative Friends of Poland. *Councils and public bodies:* Chair: Children and Family Court Advisory and Support Service 2018-19, Child Safeguarding Practice Review Panel 2019-20.

Political interests: Crime, family, education, children in care, fostering and adoption.

Other: Vice-president, Acton Amateur Operatic Society; Honorary Vice-president, Crewe Amateur Musicals Society; Patron: Holly Holy Day Society, Home Start (Cheshire), Leighton Academy year 5 peer mentoring group, Support Community Business, One in Eleven' Charity; Honorary member: Crewe Rotary Club, Royal British Legion, Crewe Alexandra Supporters Club; Member, Worshipful Company of Pattenmakers; Freeman, City of London; *The House Magazine* Minister of the Year, Dods Parliamentary Awards 2014; CBE 2018.

Recreations: Marathons, travel, writing, cricket, football.

Edward Timpson CBE MP, House of Commons, London SW1A 0AA
Tel: 020 7219 3000 *Email:* edward.timpson.mp@parliament.uk
Constituency: 58a High Street, Tarporley, Cheshire CW6 0AG
Tel: 01829 733385 Website: www.edwardtimpson.com *Twitter:* @edwardtimpson

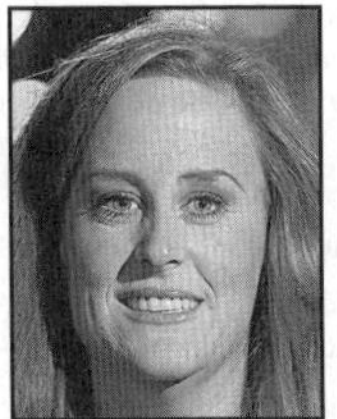

CONSERVATIVE

TOLHURST, KELLY

Rochester and Strood *(Majority 17,072)*

Kelly Jane Tolhurst. Born 23 August 1978; Daughter of Morris and Christine Tolhurst.

Education: Chapter High School; Italian.

Non-political career: Account Manager, New Zealand Farmers 1996-99; Sales and Marketing Director, Masion Mer Seafood 1999-2001; Business Development Manager, Lactalis UK 2001-02; Director, Skipper (UK) Ltd 2002-; Yacht Surveyor, Tolhurst Associated 2008; Contact Supervisor, Supported Fostering Services 2007-15.

Political career: Contested Rochester and Strood 20 November 2014 by-election. Member for Rochester and Strood since 7 May 2015 general election; PPS to: Priti Patel as Secretary of State for International Development 2016-17, Greg Clark as Secretary of State for Business, Energy and Industrial Strategy 2017-18; Assistant Government Whip 2018; Parliamentary Under-Secretary of State: (Minister for Small Business, Consumers and Corporate Responsibility), Department for Business, Energy and Industrial Strategy 2018-20, Department for Transport 2020, for Rough Sleeping and Housing, Ministry of Housing, Communities and Local Government 2020-21. *Select committees:* Member: Business, Innovation and Skills 2015-16, European Scrutiny 2015-16, Business, Energy and Industrial Strategy 2016-17. *Councils and public bodies:* Medway Council: Councillor 2011-18, Portfolio Holder for Educational Improvement 2013-15.

Other: Trustee, Chatham Maritime Trust; Trustee and Director, Action for Borstal Community Project; Association of Dunkirk Little Ships; International Institute of Marine Surveyors; British Marine Federation; RSPB. Medway Yacht Club.

Kelly Tolhurst MP, House of Commons, London SW1A 0AA
Tel: 020 7219 5387 *Email:* kelly.tolhurst.mp@parliament.uk
Constituency: No constituency office publicised
Tel: 01634 840411 Website: www.kelly4rochesterandstrood.com *Twitter:* @KellyTolhurst

House of Commons
MPs' Biographies

CONSERVATIVE

TOMLINSON, JUSTIN

North Swindon *(Majority 16,171)*

Minister of State for Disabled People, Health and Work, Department for Work and Pensions

Justin Paul Tomlinson. Born 5 November 1976; Son of Vera and Paul Tomlinson; Married Katherine Bennett 2018 (1 daughter).

Education: Harry Cheshire High School, Kidderminster; Oxford Brookes University (BA business 1999).

Non-political career: Sales and marketing manager, First Leisure 1999-2000; Marketing executive, Point to Point Ltd 2000; Director, TB Marketing Solutions Ltd 2000-10.

Political career: Contested North Swindon 2005 general election. Member for North Swindon since 6 May 2010 general election; PPS to Ed Vaizey as Minister of State for Culture and the Digital Economy, Departments for Business, Innovation and Skills and Culture, Media and Sport 2014-15; Department for Work and Pensions: Parliamentary Under-Secretary of State: for Disabled People 2015-16, for Family Support, Housing and Child Maintenance 2018-19, Minister of State for Disabled People, Health and Work 2019-. *Select committees:* Member: Joint Committee on Consolidation, Etc, Bills 2010-15, Unopposed Bills (Panel) 2011-15, Public Accounts 2012-14, Work and Pensions 2018. Chair, Oxford Brookes University Conservative Students' Association 1995-99; Deputy Chair, North Swindon Conservative Association 2000-04; National Chair, Conservative Future 2002-03; Small Business Ambassador – South West. *Councils and public bodies:* Swindon Borough Council: Councillor 2000-10, Cabinet member 2003-08.

Political interests: Sport, business, financial education, disability, local government, housing and development, consumer issues, retail, young entrepreneurs.

Other: Swindon Supermarine; Kidderminster Harriers; Blackburn Rovers.

Recreations: Football, cricket, cinema, video games.

Justin Tomlinson MP, House of Commons, London SW1A 0AA
Tel: 020 7219 7167 *Email:* justin.tomlinson.mp@parliament.uk
Constituency: First Floor, Customer Service Hub, Orbital Shopping Park, Swindon SN25 4AN
Tel: 01793 533393 Website: www.justintomlinson.com *Twitter:* @JustinTomlinson

CONSERVATIVE

TOMLINSON, MICHAEL

Mid Dorset and North Poole *(Majority 14,898)*

Government Whip, Lord Commissioner of HM Treasury

Michael James Tomlinson-Mynors. Born 1 October 1977; Married Frances Mynors 2000 (3 children).

Education: University of London (BA classics).

Non-political career: Called to the Bar, Middle Temple 2002; Barrister, specialising in housing and property related work, 3PB.

Political career: Member for Mid Dorset and North Poole since 7 May 2015 general election; Team PPS, Department for International Development 2017-18; PPS to: Penny Mordaunt as Secretary of State for International Development and Minister for Women and Equalities 2018, Dominic Raab as Secretary of State for Exiting the European Union 2018, Jacob Rees-Mogg as Leader of the House of Commons and Lord President of the Council 2019-20; Government Whip, Lord Commissioner of HM Treasury 2020-. *Select committees:* Member, European Scrutiny 2016-19. Deputy chair, political, Mid Dorset and North Poole Conservative Association; Campaign manager to Nick King, 2010 general election.

Other: Member: Poole Hockey Club, Hamworthy Cricket Club.

Recreations: Spending time with family, walking, playing sport.

Michael Tomlinson MP, House of Commons, London SW1A 0AA
Tel: 020 7219 5844 *Email:* michael.tomlinson.mp@parliament.uk
Constituency: The Office, Race Farm, Huntick Road, Lytchett Matravers, Poole BH16 6BB
Tel: 01202 624216 Website: www.michaeltomlinson.org.uk *Twitter:* @Michael4MDNP

CONSERVATIVE

TRACEY, CRAIG

North Warwickshire *(Majority 17,956)*

Craig Paul Tracey. Born 21 August 1974; Married Karen 2014.

Education: Framwellgate Moor Comprehensive School.

Non-political career: Senior Partner, Dunelm Insurance Brokers, Lichfield 1996-2015; Director, Politically Correct 2014-.

Political career: Member for North Warwickshire since 7 May 2015 general election; Team PPS: Department for International Development 2018, Department for Environment, Food and Rural Affairs 2018-19; PPS to Andrea Leadsom as Secretary of State for Business, Energy and Industrial Strategy 2019-20. *Select committees:* Member: Business, Innovation and Skills 2015-16, Education, Skills and the Economy Sub-committee 2015-16, Business, Energy and Industrial Strategy 2016-17. Former chair, North Warwickshire Conservative Association; West Midlands Co-ordinator, Conservative Voice 2012-.

Other: Member, UK Delegation, Organisation for Security and Co-operation in Europe Parliamentary Assembly 2016-; Founder trustee, Lichfield Garrick Theatre 2012-; Board member, Southern Staffordshire Employment and Skills Board 2014-.

Craig Tracey MP, House of Commons, London SW1A 0AA
Tel: 020 7219 5646 *Email:* craig.tracey.mp@parliament.uk
Constituency: 76 Station Street, Atherstone, Warwickshire CV9 1BU
Tel: 01827 715243 Website: www.craigtracey.co.uk *Twitter:* @craig4nwarks

CONSERVATIVE

TREVELYAN, ANNE-MARIE

Berwick-upon-Tweed *(Majority 14,835)*

Minister of State for Business, Energy and Clean Growth, Department for Business, Energy and Industrial Strategy

Anne-Marie Belinda Trevelyan. Born 6 April 1969; Married John Trevelyan 1998 (1 daughter 1 son).

Education: St Pauls Girls School, London; Oxford Polytechnic (mathematics 1990); ACA 1993; French.

Non-political career: PricewaterhouseCoopers, London 1990-94; European financial controller, Blenheim Exhibitions, London 1994-97; Corporate finance, PricewaterhouseCoopers, Newcastle 1997-99; Self-employed consultant 1999-2008.

Political career: Contested Berwick-upon-Tweed 2010 general election. Member for Berwick-upon-Tweed since 7 May 2015 general election; Team PPS: Ministry of Defence 2017-18, Department for Education 2018; Ministry of Defence: Parliamentary Under-Secretary of State (Defence Procurement) 2019, Minister of State for the Armed Forces 2019-20; Secretary of State for International Development 2020; UK International Champion on Adaptation and Resilience, COP26 Presidency 2020-; Minister of State for Business, Energy and Clean Growth, Department for Business, Energy and Industrial Strategy 2021-. *Select committees:* Member, Public Accounts 2015-17, 2018-19. Founding member, Conservatives for Britain 2015-16.

Political interests: Education, health, finance.

Other: Member, UK Delegation, Organisation for Security and Co-operation in Europe Parliamentary Assembly 2015-17; Board member, Vote Leave 2016; Treasurer, Action Research Medical 1997-2006; PC 2020. Carlton Club.

Recreations: Tennis, reading, cooking for friends.

Rt Hon Anne-Marie Trevelyan MP, House of Commons, London SW1A 0AA
Tel: 020 7219 4437 *Email:* annemarie.trevelyan.mp@parliament.uk
Constituency: 21a The Hotspur, Bondgate Without, Alnwick, Northumberland NE66 1PR
Tel: 01665 517512 *Email:* trevelyanoffice@gmail.com Website: www.teamtrevelyan.co.uk
Twitter: @annietrev

LABOUR

TRICKETT, JON

Hemsworth *(Majority 1,180)*

Jon Hedley Trickett. Born 2 July 1950; Son of Laurence and Rose Trickett; Married Sarah Balfour 1993 (1 son 2 daughters).

Education: Roundhay School, Leeds; Hull University (BA politics); Leeds University (MA political sociology); French.

Non-political career: Plumber/builder 1974-86. Member: GMB, RMT Parliamentary Campaigning Group 2002-.

Political career: Member for Hemsworth 1 February 1996 by-election to 2010, for Hemsworth (revised boundary) since 6 May 2010 general election; PPS: to Peter Mandelson: as Minister without Portfolio 1997-98, as Secretary of State for Trade and Industry July-December 1998; to Gordon Brown as Prime Minister 2008-10; Shadow Minister of State for Cabinet Office 2010-11; Shadow Minister for the Cabinet Office 2011-13, 2017-20; Shadow Minister without Portfolio 2013-15; Shadow Secretary of State for Communities and Local Government 2015-16; Shadow Minister for the Constitutional Convention 2015-16; Shadow Secretary of State for Business, Innovation and Skills/Business and Industrial Strategy 2016; Shadow Lord President of the Council 2016-20; National Elections and Campaigns Co-ordinator 2016-17; Leading the Shadow Cabinet's work on preparation for Government 2017-20. *Select committees:* Member: Unopposed Bills (Panel) 1997-2013, Education and Employment 2001, Education and Employment (Employment Sub-Committee) 2001, Public Accounts 2001-06, Public Administration 2010. Secretary PLP Departmental Committee for Health and Social Services 2005-08. Labour Party: Deputy Chair 2013-15, Senior Adviser, Office of the Leader 2014-15, Election co-ordinator 2015-20, Member, NEC 2016-20. *Councils and public bodies:* Leeds City Council: Councillor 1984-96, Leader of the Council 1989-96.

Political interests: Economic policy, finance, industry, sport; Middle East, France, USA.

Other: Member: British Cycling Federation, West Riding Sailing Club; Hon Life Member, Cyclists' Touring Club.

Recreations: Cycle racing, windsurfing.

Jon Trickett MP, House of Commons, London SW1A 0AA
Tel: 020 7219 5074 *Fax:* 020 7219 2133 *Email:* jon.trickett.mp@parliament.uk
Constituency: Ground Floor, Moorthorpe Railway Station, Barnsley Road, South Kirkby WF9 3AT
Tel: 01977 655695 *Email:* jtrickett@jontrickett.org.uk Website: www.jontrickett.org.uk
Twitter: @jon_trickett

CONSERVATIVE

TROTT, LAURA

Sevenoaks *(Majority 20,818)*

PPS to Grant Shapps as Secretary of State for Transport

Born 7 December 1984; Married (1 daughter twin sons).

Education: Oxford University (BA history and economics).

Non-political career: Strategy consultant, Booz & Company 2007-09; Political adviser, Conservative Party 2009-10; Special adviser to Francis Maude MP as Minister for the Cabinet Office 2010-12; Political adviser: Head of Education and Family Policy, Number 10 Policy Unit 2012-15, Director of Strategic Communications, 10 Downing Street 2015-16; Partner, Portland Communications 2017-19.

Political career: Member for Sevenoaks since 12 December 2019; Department for Transport: Team PPS 2020, PPS to Grant Shapps as Secretary of State 2020-. *Select committees:* Member, Health and Social Care 2020-. *Councils and public bodies:* Councillor, Camden Council.

Other: Patron, Ormiston Trust; MBE 2016.

Laura Trott MBE MP, House of Commons, London SW1A 0AA
Tel: 020 7219 4964 *Email:* laura.trott.mp@parliament.uk
Constituency: No constituency office publicised
Website: www.lauratrott.org.uk

CONSERVATIVE

TRUSS, ELIZABETH

South West Norfolk *(Majority 26,195)*

Secretary of State for International Trade; President of the Board of Trade; Minister for Women and Equalities

Elizabeth Mary Truss. Born 26 July 1975; Daughter of John Truss and Priscilla Truss; Married Hugh O'Leary 2000 (2 daughters).

Education: Roundhay School, Leeds; Merton College, Oxford (BA philosophy, politics and economics 1996).

Non-political career: Commercial analyst, Shell International 1996-2000; Director, financial analysis, Cable and Wireless 2000-05; Managing director, political division, Communication Group 2006-07; Deputy director, Reform 2007-09.

Political career: Contested Hemsworth 2001 and Calder Valley 2005 general elections. Member for South West Norfolk since 6 May 2010 general election; Parliamentary Under-Secretary of State, Department for Education 2012-14; Secretary of State for Environment, Food and Rural Affairs 2014-16; Lord Chancellor and Secretary of State for Justice 2016-17; Chief Secretary to the Treasury 2017-19; Secretary of State for International Trade; President of the Board of Trade 2019-; Minister for Women and Equalities 2019-. *Select committees:* Member, Justice 2010-12. Member, Conservative Party 1996-; Chair, Lewisham Deptford Conservative Association 1998-2000. *Councils and public bodies:* Councillor, London Borough of Greenwich Council 2006-10.

Political interests: Economy, education, environment, food.

Other: President, Industry and Parliament Trust 2016-17; Member, Chartered Institute of Management Accountants; Minister to Watch, *Spectator* awards 2012; PC 2014.

Publications: Co-author (with Kwasi Kwarteng MP, Priti Patel MP, Dominic Raab MP and Chris Skidmore MP), Britannia Unchained: Global Lessons for Growth and Prosperity (Palgrave Macmillan, 2012).

Recreations: Film, food, design.

Rt Hon Elizabeth Truss MP, House of Commons, London SW1A 0AA
Tel: 020 7219 7151 *Email:* elizabeth.truss.mp@parliament.uk
Constituency: No constituency office publicised
Tel: 01842 766155 Website: www.elizabethtruss.com *Twitter:* @trussliz

CONSERVATIVE

TUGENDHAT, TOM

Tonbridge and Malling *(Majority 26,941)*

Chair, Select Committee on Foreign Affairs

Thomas Georg John Tugendhat. Born 27 June 1973; Son of Michael and Blandine Tugendhat; Married Anissia Morel 2013 (1 son, 1 daughter).

Education: St Paul's School, London; Bristol University (BA theology and religious studies 1995); Cambridge University (MPhil Islamic studies 1996); French, Italian, Arabic, Pashto, Dari.

Non-political career: Journalist 1997-99; Management consultant, First Consulting 1999-2000; Energy analyst, Bloomberg 2000-03; Military Services Overseas 2003-09; Foreign and Commonwealth Office: Adviser to: the National Security Adviser of Afghanistan 2005-06, the Governor of Helmand 2006-07; Military Assistant to the Chief of Defence Staff, Ministry of Defence 2010-13. Commissioned Territorial Army Officer 2003; British Army: Army officer 2003, 2007-09, Army Strategy Team 2009-10.

Political career: Member for Tonbridge and Malling since 7 May 2015 general election. *Select committees:* Member: Public Administration and Constitutional Affairs 2015-16, Joint Committee on Consolidation, &c, Bills 2015-17, Speaker's Advisory Committee on Works of Art 2016-19, Liaison 2017-, Joint Committee on the National Security Strategy 2017-; Chair, Foreign Affairs 2017-; Member, Committees on Arms Export Controls 2020-.

Political interests: Localism, business, economic development, defence, foreign affairs; North Africa, Southern Africa, West Africa, Central Asia, Europe, Middle East, USA.

Other: MBE (Military) 2010. Special Forces Club.

Recreations: Walking, conversation, family.

Tom Tugendhat MBE MP, House of Commons, London SW1A 0AA
Tel: 020 7219 3000 *Email:* tom.tugendhat.mp@parliament.uk
Constituency: 130 Vale Road, Tonbridge, Kent TN9 1SP
Tel: 01732 441563 Website: www.tomtugendhat.org.uk *Twitter:* @TomTugendhat

LABOUR

TURNER, KARL

Kingston upon Hull East *(Majority 1,239)*

Shadow Minister for Legal Aid

Born 15 April 1971; Son of Ken Turner, trade unionist, and Pat Turner; Married Leanne (1 daughter).

Education: Bransholme High School; Hull College; Hull University (law 2004).

Non-political career: Youth training scheme, Hull City Council; Self-employed antiques dealer; Called to the Bar, Middle Temple 2005; Barrister: Max Gold Partnership, Hull 2005-09, Wilberforce Chambers, Hull 2009-10. Member: Unison, GMB.

Political career: Member for Kingston upon Hull East since 6 May 2010 general election; Opposition Whip 2013-15, 2016-17; Shadow Solicitor General 2014-16; Shadow Minister for Justice (Legal Aid) 2015-16; Shadow Attorney General 2016; Shadow Minister for: Transport (Shipping, Aviation and Road Safety) 2017-20, Justice (Legal Aid) 2020-. *Select committees:* Member: Justice 2010-13, Home Affairs 2012-13, Regulatory Reform 2017-.

Political interests: Justice, jobs, welfare, home affairs, animal welfare; Sri Lanka.

Karl Turner MP, House of Commons, London SW1A 0AA
Tel: 020 7219 7088 *Email:* karl.turner.mp@parliament.uk
Constituency: 430 Holderness Road, Hull, East Yorkshire HU9 3DW
Tel: 01482 781019 Website: www.karlturnermp.org.uk *Twitter:* @KarlTurnerMP

LABOUR

TWIGG, DEREK

Halton *(Majority 18,975)*

John Derek Twigg. Born 9 July 1959; Son of Kenneth and Irene Twigg; Married Mary Cassidy 1988 (1 son 1 daughter).

Education: Bankfield High School, Widnes; Halton College of Further Education (1978).

Non-political career: Civil servant, Department for Education and Employment 1975-96. Member, GMB.

Political career: Member for Halton 1997-2010, for Halton (revised boundary) since 6 May 2010 general election; PPS: to Helen Liddell as Minister of State: Department of the Environment, Transport and the Regions 1999, Department of Trade and Industry 1999-2001, to Stephen Byers as Secretary of State for Transport, Local Government and the Regions 2001-02; Assistant Government Whip 2002-03, Government Whip 2003-04; Parliamentary Under-Secretary of State: Department for Education and Skills 2004-05, Department for Transport 2005-06; Parliamentary Under-Secretary of State (Minister for Veterans), Ministry of Defence 2006-08; Shadow Minister for Health 2010-11. *Select committees:* Member: Public Accounts 1998-99, Children, Schools and Families 2009-10, Joint Committee on Voting Eligibilty (Prisoners) Bill 2013, Defence 2013-15, Arms Export Controls 2014, Liaison 2015-18; Chair, Joint Committee on Statutory Instruments 2015-18; Member: Defence 2020-, Panel of Chairs 2020-. Chair, PLP Departmental Group for Defence 2020-. *Councils and public bodies:* Councillor: Cheshire County Council 1981-85, Halton Borough Council 1983-97.

Political interests: Economy, education, health and poverty, defence; Greece.

Recreations: Various sporting activities, hill-walking, military history.

Derek Twigg MP, House of Commons, London SW1A 0AA
Tel: 020 7219 1039 *Email:* derek.twigg.mp@parliament.uk
Constituency: Bridge Buisness Centre, Suite E, Cheshire House, Gorsey Lane, Widnes, Cheshire WA8 0RP
Tel: 0151-424 7030 Website: www.derektwigg.org *Twitter:* @DerekTwiggMP

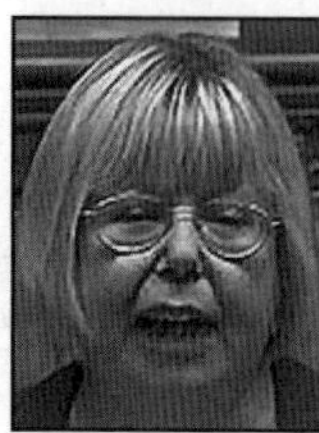

LABOUR

TWIST, LIZ

Blaydon *(Majority 5,531)*

Senior Opposition Whip

Mary Elizabeth Twist. Born July 1956; Married Charles (died 2000).

Non-political career: Constituency Staff Member to Dave Anderson MP; Regional Head of Health, Unison. Unison.

Political career: Member for Blaydon since 8 June 2017; Opposition Whip 2019-20; Senior Opposition Whip 2020-. *Select committees:* Member: Communities and Local Government/ Housing, Communities and Local Government 2017-19, Petitions 2017-19, European Statutory Instruments 2018-, Standards 2019, Privileges 2019, Joint Committee on Statutory Instruments 2020-, Procedure 2020-, Scottish Affairs 2020-. *Councils and public bodies:* Gateshead Council: Councillor 2012-18, Cabinet Member for Housing.

Other: Listener, Tyneside Samaritans.

Liz Twist MP, House of Commons, London SW1A 0AA
Tel: 020 7219 2221 *Email:* liz.twist.mp@parliament.uk
Constituency: St Cuthbert's Community Hall, Shibdon Road, Blaydon NE21 5PT
Tel: 0191-414 2488 Website: liztwist.co.uk *Twitter:* @LizTwistMP

CONSERVATIVE

VARA, SHAILESH

North West Cambridgeshire *(Majority 25,983)*

Shailesh Lakhman Vara. Born 4 September 1960; Son of Lakhman Arjan Vara and Savita, née Gadher; Married Beverley Fear 2002 (2 sons).

Education: Aylesbury Grammar School; Brunel University (LLB).

Non-political career: Articled: Richards Butler 1988-90 (in Hong Kong 1989-90), Solicitor: Crossman Block 1991-92, Payne Hicks Beach 1992-93, CMS Cameron McKenna 1994-2001.

Political career: Contested Birmingham Ladywood 1997 and Northampton South 2001 general elections. Member for North West Cambridgeshire 2005-10, for North West Cambridgeshire (revised boundary) since 6 May 2010 general election; Shadow Deputy Leader of the House 2006-10; Assistant Government Whip 2010-12; Parliamentary Under-Secretary of State: for the Courts and Legal Aid, Ministry of Justice 2013-16, Department for Work and Pensions 2015-16; Northern Ireland Office: Parliamentary Under-Secretary of State 2018, Minister of State 2018. *Select committees:* Member: Environment, Food and Rural Affairs 2005-06, Administration 2010-11, Finance and Services 2011-13, Environmental Audit 2020, Joint Committee on Fixed-Term Parliaments Act 2020-. Society of Conservative Lawyers: Treasurer 2001-04, Vice-chair, Executive Committee 2006-09; Vice-chair, Conservative Party 2001-05; Chair, Conservative Parliamentary Friends of India 2008-10.

Other: Member, Executive Committee, Commonwealth Parliamentary Association United Kingdom 2017-18; Ambassador for Breast Cancer Now 2017-; RNIB (Royal National Institute for the Blind) Champion 2020; Hon. Fellow, Brunel University 2010-; Pravasi Bharatiya Samman, Indian Government 2014. Vice-president, Huntingdonshire County Cricket Club 2007-.

Recreations: Cricket, theatre, taekwondo.

Shailesh Vara MP, House of Commons, London SW1A 0AA
Tel: 020 7219 6050 *Email:* shailesh.vara.mp@parliament.uk
Constituency: North West Cambridgeshire Conservative Association, The Old Barn, Hawthorn Farm, Ashton, Cambridgeshire PE9 3BA
Tel: 01780 781224 *Email:* chantel.saunders@parliament.uk Website: www.shaileshvara.com
Twitter: @ShaileshVara

LABOUR

VAZ, VALERIE

Walsall South *(Majority 3,456)*

Shadow Leader of the House of Commons

Valerie Carol Marian Vaz. Born 7 December 1954; Daughter of late Merlyn Verona Vaz, teacher, and late Anthony Xavier Vaz, personnel manager; Married Paul Townsend 1992 (1 daughter).

Education: Twickenham County Grammar School; Bedford College, London University (BSc biochemistry 1978); Sidney Sussex College, Cambridge (Research animal nutrition 1978-79); College of Law, London (CPE 1981; SFE 1982); French (basic).

Non-political career: Trainee solicitor, Herbert Smith; Lawyer: London Borough of Brent, London Borough of Hammersmith and Fulham; Presenter, Network East, BBC; Townsend Vaz Solicitors; Deputy district judge (part-time), Midlands and Oxford Circuits; Solicitor, Government Legal Service, Treasury Solicitors Department 2001-10; On secondment, Ministry of Justice 2008-09. Member, USDAW.

Political career: Contested Twickenham 1987 general election. Member for Walsall South since 6 May 2010 general election; Shadow Leader of the House of Commons 2016-; Member: House of Commons Commission 2016-, Speaker's Committee for the Independent Parliamentary Standards Authority 2017-. *Select committees:* Member: Health 2010-15, Regulatory Reform 2010-15, House of Commons Governance 2014-15, Panel of Chairs 2015-16, Science and Technology 2015-16, Environment, Food and Rural Affairs 2016. Vice-chair, PLP Departmental Group for Business, Innovation and Skills 2010-14. Contested East Midlands 1999 European Parliament election. Vice-chair, PLP 2010-16. *Councils and public bodies:* London Borough of Ealing Council: Councillor 1986-90, Deputy Council Leader 1988-89; Member, Ealing Health Authority 1986-89; School governor 1986-90.

Political interests: Health, science and technology, legal and constitutional affairs, music; South Asia, Burma, Yemen.

Other: Member, Executive Committee, Commonwealth Parliamentary Association UK 2015-19; Member, National Trust; Friend: Kew Gardens, New Art Gallery Walsall; Law Society; Association of Women Solicitors; PC 2019.

Publications: Author, Obesity and Diabetes Programmes in England: Capturing the State of Play (2011); Instruments on Planes (compiled and prepared with the Incorporated Society of Musicians) (2012); Author, The Use of Higher Rate Telephone Numbers by Government Departments (2014).

Recreations: Music – playing piano, gardening, walking.

Rt Hon Valerie Vaz MP, House of Commons, London SW1A 0AA
Tel: 020 7219 2237 *Email:* valerie.vaz.mp@parliament.uk
Constituency: 16a Lichfield Street, Walsall WS1 1TJ
Tel: 01922 635835 Website: www.valerievazmp.co.uk *Twitter:* @Valerie_VazMP

CONSERVATIVE

VICKERS, MARTIN

Cleethorpes *(Majority 21,418)*

Martin John Vickers. Born 13 September 1950; Son of Norman and Winifred Vickers, née Watson; Married Ann 1981 (1 daughter).

Education: Havelock School; Grimsby College; Lincoln University (BA politics 2004).

Non-political career: Printing industry; Retail industry.

Political career: Contested Cleethorpes 2005 general election. Member for Cleethorpes since 6 May 2010 general election; Trade Envoy to the Western Balkans (covering Albania, Bosnia and Herzegovina, Kosovo, Montenegro, North Macedonia and Serbia) 2020-. *Select committees:* Member: Procedure 2012-15, Transport 2013-18, Health and Social Care 2018-19, Ecclesiastical Committee 2019-, International Trade 2020-. Constituency agent to Edward Leigh MP 1994-2010. *Councils and public bodies:* Councillor, Great Grimsby Borough Council 1980-94; North East Lincolnshire Council: Councillor 1999-2011, Cabinet Member for Environmental Services 2003-08.

Political interests: Constitution, local government, regeneration issues, energy policy, transport, international trade; Azerbaijan, British Overseas Territories, Taiwan, Uzbekistan, USA,Western Balkans.

Other: UK Delegation to Parliamentary Assembly of Council of Europe: Substitute Member 2018-21, Member 2021-.

Publications: Contributor: Freedom, Responsibility and the State: Curbing Over-Mighty Government (Politeia, 2012), Unlocking Local Leadership on Climate Change (Green Alliance, 2012).

Recreations: Reading, football, cricket, travel, railways, music, religion.

Martin Vickers MP, House of Commons, London SW1A 0AA
Tel: 020 7219 7212 *Email:* martin.vickers.mp@parliament.uk
Constituency: 62 St Peter's Avenue, Cleethorpes, North East Lincolnshire DN35 8HP
Tel: 01472 603554 *Email:* mvickersmp@gmail.com Website: www.martinvickers.org.uk
Twitter: @MartinVickers

CONSERVATIVE

VICKERS, MATT

Stockton South *(Majority 5,260)*

Matthew Alexander Vickers. Born 24 September 1983.

Education: Teesside University (BA business management 2005; LLB law 2013; LLM law 2017); University of Law (MSc law and business 2019).

Non-political career: Trainee Solicitor, Coles Solicitors 2019-.

Political career: Member for Stockton South since 12 December 2019. *Select committees:* Member, Future Relationship with the European Union 2020-21. Contested Cleveland police and crime commissioner election 2016. Constituency Agent, Richmond (Yorks) 2008-. *Councils and public bodies:* Councillor, Stockton-on-Tees Borough Council 2015-.

Matt Vickers MP, House of Commons, London SW1A 0AA
Tel: 020 7219 3723 *Email:* matt.vickers.mp@parliament.uk
Constituency: No constituency office publicised
Tel: 01642 956526 Website: www.mattvickers.co.uk *Twitter:* @Matt_VickersMP

CONSERVATIVE

VILLIERS, THERESA

Chipping Barnet *(Majority 1,212)*

Theresa Anne Villiers. Born 5 March 1968; Daughter of Virginia Villiers and late George Villiers; Married Sean Wilken 1999 (divorced).

Education: Francis Holland School, London; Bristol University (LLB 1990); Jesus College, Oxford (BCL 1991); Inns of Court School of Law (1992).

Non-political career: Barrister Lincoln's Inn 1994-95; Lecturer in law King's College, London University 1995-99.

Political career: Member for Chipping Barnet 2005-10, for Chipping Barnet (revised boundary) since 6 May 2010 general election; Shadow Chief Secretary to the Treasury 2005-07; Shadow Secretary of State for Transport 2007-10; Minister of State, Department for Transport 2010-12; Secretary of State for: Northern Ireland 2012-16, Environment, Food and Rural Affairs 2019-20; Member, Intelligence and Security Committee of Parliament 2020-. *Select committees:* Member: Environmental Audit 2005-06, Joint Committee on the National Security Strategy 2016-19, Petitions 2020-. European Parliament: MEP for London 1999-2005: Deputy leader, Conservatives group 2001-02.

Political interests: Economic policy, business, transport, animal welfare, financial services, environment; Cyprus, Israel.

Other: President: Friends of Barnet Hospital, Barnet Borough Talking Newspapers, Barnet Old People's Welfare; Member: Campaign committee, Vote Leave 2016, Board Member, Red Tape Initiative 2017-; North London Hospice, Cherry Lodge Cancer Care; Freedom, City of London; PC 2010. Middlesex County Cricket Club.

Publications: European Tax harmonisation: The Impending Threat; Co-author, Waiver, Variation and Estoppel (Chancery Wiley Law Publications, 1998).

Recreations: Cycling.

Rt Hon Theresa Villiers MP, House of Commons, London SW1A 0AA
Tel: 020 7219 3000
Constituency: 163 High Street, Barnet, Hertfordshire EN5 5SU
Tel: 020 8449 7345 *Email:* theresa@theresavilliers.co.uk Website: www.theresavilliers.co.uk

CONSERVATIVE

WAKEFORD, CHRISTIAN

Bury South *(Majority 402)*

Born 9 November; Married Alexandra 2016.

Education: Colne Park High School; Nelson and Colne College; Lancaster University (BA politics 2007); Open University (BSc chemistry 2014).

Non-political career: Indirect Account Manager, Daisy plc 2009-13; Caseworker to Andrew Stephenson MP 2015-16.

Political career: Member for Bury South since 12 December 2019. *Select committees:* Member, Education 2020-. Chair, Lancashire Area Conservatives 2016-. *Councils and public bodies:* Councillor: Lancashire County Council 2013-, Pendle Borough Council 2015-; Governor, Colne Park High School 2009-17.

Political interests: Crime, economy, employment.

Recreations: Rugby, real ale.

Christian Wakeford MP, House of Commons, London SW1A 0AA
Tel: 020 7219 6437 *Email:* christian.wakeford.mp@parliament.uk
Constituency: 11 Deansgate, Radcliffe, Manchester 26 2SH
Tel: 0161-533 0801 Website: www.christianwakeford.org.uk *Twitter:* @Christian4BuryS

CONSERVATIVE

WALKER, CHARLES

Broxbourne *(Majority 19,807)*

Charles Ashley Rupert Walker. Born 11 September 1967; Son of Carola Chataway, née Ashton, and late Timothy Walker; Married Fiona Newman 1995 (1 daughter 2 sons).

Education: American School of London; University of Oregon, USA (BSc politics and American history 1990).

Non-political career: Communications director, CSG (Corporate Services Group) plc 1997-2001; Director: Blue Arrow Ltd 1999-2001, LSM Processing Ltd 2002-04, Debitwise 2004. Member, Amicus.

Political career: Contested Ealing North 2001 general election. Member for Broxbourne since 5 May 2005 general election; Member: Speaker's Committee for the Independent Parliamentary Standards Authority 2010-, House of Commons Commission 2020-. *Select committees:* Member: Scottish Affairs 2005-10, Public Administration 2007-11, Chairmen's Panel/Panel of Chairs 2010-, Standing Orders 2011-15; Chair, Prodecure 2012-19; Member, Liaison 2012-19, 2020-; Chair, Administration 2020-. 1922 Committee: Member, Executive 2006-10, 2014-15, Vice-chairman 2010-14, 2015-; Chairman, Conservative Backbench Policy Committee on Scotland 2015-17. Vice-chair: Lewisham East Conservatives 1992-93, Battersea Conservatives 2002-03; Member, Conservative Party Board 2010-19. *Councils and public bodies:* Councillor, Wandsworth Borough Council 2002-06; Vice-President, Local Government Association 2010-.

Political interests: Employment, taxation, the economy, mental health.

Other: Patron, Isabelle Hospice; *Spectator* awards: Speech of the Year 2011, Speech of the Year (with Kevan Jones MP) 2012; Best Contribution to the *House Magazine*, *House Magazine* awards 2012; OBE 2015; KBE 2019.

Recreations: Fishing, watching cricket.

Sir Charles Walker KBE MP, House of Commons, London SW1A 0AA
Tel: 020 7219 0338 *Fax:* 020 7219 0505 *Email:* charles.walker.mp@parliament.uk
Constituency: Ambition Broxbourne Business Centre (Unit 16), Pindar Road, Hoddesdon, Hertfordshire EN11 0FJ
Tel: 01992 479972 *Email:* office@broxbourneconservatives.com
Website: www.charleswalker.org.uk *Twitter:* @CharlesWalkerMP

CONSERVATIVE

WALKER, ROBIN

Worcester *(Majority 6,758)*

Minister of State, Northern Ireland Office

Robin Caspar Walker. Born 12 April 1978; Son of late Peter Walker (MP for Worcester 1961-92, later Lord Walker of Worcester) and Tessa Pout; Married Charlotte Keenan 2011.

Education: St Paul's School, London; Balliol College, Oxford (BA ancient and modern history 2000).

Non-political career: Intern, Office of the chairman of the House Ways and Means Committee, Washington DC September 2000; Chief executive, Property Map Ltd 2000-01; Research executive, i-Search Ltd 2001-03; Finsbury Group (Financial Communications): Executive 2003-04, Senior executive 2004-06, Associate partner 2006-09, Partner 2009-10. Member, Armed Forces Parliamentary Scheme (RAF).

Political career: Member for Worcester since 6 May 2010 general election; PPS to: Andrew Robathan as Minister of State, Northern Ireland Office 2013-14, Elizabeth Truss as Secretary of State for Environment, Food and Rural Affairs 2014-15, Nicky Morgan as Secretary of State for Education and Minister for Women and Equalities 2015-16; Parliamentary Under-Secretary of State: Department for Exiting the European Union 2016-19, Scotland Office 2019; Northern Ireland Office: Parliamentary Under-Secretary of State 2019-20, Minister of State 2020-. *Select committees:* Member: Welsh Affairs 2011-12, Business, Innovation and Skills 2012-15, Arms Export Controls 2013, Administration 2015-16. Volunteer assistant to: Stephen Dorrell MP, 1997 general election campaign, Worcester Conservative Association, 2001 general election campaign; Press officer to Oliver Letwin MP, 2005 general election; Member: Conservative Middle East Council, Tory Reform Group.

Political interests: Education, health, police, foreign affairs, defence, business; Canada, India, Italy, Latin America, Middle East, South Africa, USA, Zambia.

Other: Commonwealth Parliamentary Association; Inter-Parliamentary Union; Member, British-Irish Parliamentary Assembly 2015-17; Member, TRG 1997-; Honorary Board Member, Worcester Live; St Richard's Hospice Worcester, New Hope Worcester, Acorns Children's Hospice. Carlton Club; Worcester County Cricket Club; Worcester Warriors RFC.

Recreations: Walking, reading, travel, writing, watching cricket and rugby.

Robin Walker MP, House of Commons, London SW1A 0AA
Tel: 020 7219 7196 *Email:* robin.walker.mp@parliament.uk
Constituency: Office of Robin Walker MP, Guildhall, High Street, Worcester WR1 2EY
Tel: 01905 22401 Website: www.walker4worcester.com *Twitter:* @WalkerWorcester

CONSERVATIVE

WALLACE, BEN

Wyre and Preston North *(Majority 16,781)*

Secretary of State for Defence

Robert Ben Lobban Wallace. Born 15 May 1970; Married Liza Cooke 2001 (2 sons 1 daughter).

Education: Millfield School, Somerset; Royal Military Academy, Sandhurst (Commission 1991); French, German.

Non-political career: Ski instructor, Austrian National Ski School 1988-89; EU and overseas director, Qinetiq 2003-05. Army officer, Scots Guards 1991-98: Mentioned in Despatches 1992, Service in Northern Ireland, Central America, Cyprus, Germany; Intelligence 1994-95.

Political career: Member for Lancaster and Wyre 2005-10, for Wyre and Preston North since 6 May 2010 general election; Shadow Minister for Scotland 2007-10; PPS to Kenneth Clarke: as Lord Chancellor and Secretary of State for Justice 2010-12, as Minister without portfolio, Cabinet Office 2012-14; Assistant Government Whip 2014-15; Parliamentary Under-Secretary of State, Northern Ireland Office 2015-16; Home Office: Minister of State for: Security 2016-19, Economic Crime 2017-19; Secretary of State for Defence 2019-. *Select committees:* Member: Scottish Affairs 2005-10, Administration 2014-15. Contested West Aberdeenshire and Kincardine constituency 1999 Scottish Parliament election. MSP for North East Scotland region 1999-2003: Scottish Conservative Spokesperson for Health.

Political interests: Foreign policy, intelligence, defence, home affairs, health, security, sport; Iran, Italy, Middle East, Romania, Russia, USA.

Other: Member, Queen's Bodyguard of Scotland, Royal Archers 2007-; President, Lancashire branch, Scots Guards Association; PC 2017. Lancashire Cricket.

Recreations: Sailing, skiing, racing, motorsport.

Rt Hon Ben Wallace MP, House of Commons, London SW1A 0AA
Tel: 020 7219 5804 *Email:* wallaceb@parliament.uk
Constituency: Great Eccleston Village Centre, 59 High Street, Great Eccleston, Lancashire PR3 0YB
Tel: 01995 672977 Website: www.benwallace.org.uk *Twitter:* @BWallaceMP

CONSERVATIVE

WALLIS, JAMIE

Bridgend *(Majority 1,157)*

Jamie Hamilton Wallis. Born 2 June 1984; Married (2 daughters).

Education: Oxford University (MChem chemistry); Wales University (PhD planetary astronomy and science).

Non-political career: Managing Director, UK DIgital Solutions; Owner and Managing Director, Fields Associates.

Political career: Contested Ogmore 2017 general election. Member for Bridgend since 12 December 2019. *Select committees:* Member: Future Relationship with the European Union 2020-21, Welsh Affairs 2020-. Contested Ogmore constituency 2016 National Assembly for Wales election. Deputy Chair: Welsh Conservatives, South Wales West Conservatives. *Councils and public bodies:* Councillor: Pencoed Town Council, Cowbridge Town Council.

Political interests: Welsh affairs, orderly departure from the European Union.

Dr Jamie Wallis MP, House of Commons, London SW1A 0AA
Tel: 020 7219 6762 *Email:* jamie.wallis.mp@parliament.uk
Constituency: 2 Park Street, Bridgend CF31 4AU
Tel: 01656 330142 Website: www.jamiewallisbridgend.com *Twitter:* @JamieWallisMP

CONSERVATIVE

WARBURTON, DAVID

Somerton and Frome *(Majority 19,213)*

David John Warburton. Born 28 October 1965; Son of John and Erica Warburton; Married Harriet (1 daughter 1 son).

Education: Reading School; Waingel's College; Royal College of Music (Masters classical music composition and piano 1994); King's College London (Doctorate studies 1995).

Non-political career: Pianist, London hotels and restaurants 1987-95; Shop Assistant, Our Price Records, King's Road and Selfridges London 1992-94; Cleaner, delivery van driver, sandwich seller office-to-office, carpet cleaner 1993-96; Teacher: Junior department, Royal College of Music 1995-98, Hurlingham and Chelsea School, London 1995-98; Founder, Chief Executive and Chair: The Music Solution Ltd/Pitch Entertainment Group Ltd 1999-2008, Oflang Partners LLP and Oflang Ltd 2008-15; Co-founder, MyHigh.St Ltd 2012-15; Forex Trader 2007-12; Non-executive Chair, Vouch/Triple C Consulting 2018-19; Advisory Board, Inspiring Interns 2018-.

Political career: Member for Somerton and Frome since 7 May 2015 general election; Team PPS: Department for Education 2018, Department for International Development 2018-19. *Select committees:* Member, European Scrutiny 2016-19. Wells Conservative Associations 2009-12: Treasurer, Deputy Chair. *Councils and public bodies:* Member, British-American Parliamentary Group.

Political interests: Business, education, arts, culture and media, rural affairs, foreign affairs, environment; India, Japan, USA.

Other: Member: Mensa 1993-, Royal Bath and West Society, Mendip Decorative and Fine Arts Society, Rectory Society, Bow Group, Arts Theatre Club, English Speaking Union, Taxpayers' Alliance, National Trust, Campaign to Protect Rural England, Frome Festival, Frome Society for Local Study, Somerset Historic Buildings Preservation Trust; Member, capital executive committee and commercial working group, Shakespeare Globe Trust 2007-09; Founder, The Pulse 2008-11; Volunteer business mentor, Working Knowledge Group 2011-13; Volunteer advocate, Age UK Somerset 2012-13; Trustee, Ups and Downs Southwest; Member, Conservative Environment Network; Board Trustee and Chair, Development Board, National Youth Orchestra; Board Trustee: Music for Youth, British Youth Music Theatre; Royal Society of Arts; Arts and Culture Fellowship, Arts Council England; Elgar Memorial Prize; United Music Publishers Prize; Octavia Scholarship; Ralph Vaughan Williams Trust Scholarship; Major van Someron Godfrey Prize; Sir Richard Stapley Educational Trust Scholarship; Dartington International Scholarship. Carlton Club; East India Club.

Recreations: Occasional organist at two Somerset churches on the Mendips, keen reader, particularly history, music, politics and finance.

David Warburton MP, House of Commons, London SW1A 0AA
Tel: 020 7219 5229 *Email:* david.warburton.mp@parliament.uk
Constituency: Unit G9, Woodside Court, Dairy House Yard, Sparkford BA22 7LH
Tel: 01373 580500 Website: www.davidwarburton.org.uk *Twitter:* @DJWarburton

CONSERVATIVE

WARMAN, MATT

Boston and Skegness *(Majority 25,621)*

Parliamentary Under-Secretary of State for Digital Infrastructure, Department for Digital, Culture, Media and Sport

Matthew Robert Warman. Born 1 September 1981; Married Rachel.

Education: Salcombe Preparatory School; Haberdashers' Aske's Boys School; Durham University (BA English literature 2004).

Non-political career: Telegraph Media Group: Journalist 1999-15, Writer 2004-09, Consumer Technology Editor 2008-13, Technology Editor (Head of Technology) 2013-15.

Political career: Member for Boston and Skegness since 7 May 2015 general election; Board Member, Parliamentary Office of Science and Technology (POST) 2015-19; PPS to Karen Bradley as Secretary of State for: Digital, Culture, Media and Sport 2017-18, Northern Ireland 2018-19; Assistant Government Whip 2019; Parliamentary Under-Secretary of State for Digital and Broadband/for Digital Infrastructure, Department for Digital, Culture, Media and Sport 2019-. *Select committees:* Member: Science and Technology 2015-17, Joint Committee on the Draft Investigatory Powers Bill 2015-16. Parliamentary Under-Secretary of State, Department for Digital, Culture, Media and Sport 2019-.

Matt Warman MP, House of Commons, London SW1A 0AA
Tel: 020 7219 8643 *Email:* matt.warman.mp@parliament.uk
Constituency: 63 Wide Bargate, Boston, Lincolnshire PE21 6SG
Tel: 01205 809110 Website: www.mattwarman.co.uk *Twitter:* @mattwarman

CONSERVATIVE

WATLING, GILES

Clacton *(Majority 24,702)*

Giles Francis Watling. Born 18 February 1953; Son of late Jack Watling and late Patricia Hicks; Married Vanda 1979 (twin daughters).

Education: Forest School, Snaresbrooke.

Non-political career: Actor, in shows including: *Gideon's Way* 1964-67, *How's Your Father* 1979-80, *You're Only Young Twice*, *Keep It In The Family*, *Allo Allo*, *Bread* 1988-91, *Upstairs Downstairs*, *Grange Hill*, *Melissa*, *The Tutankhamun Conspiracy* 2001; Producer and director.

Political career: Contested Clacton 2014 by-election and 2015 general election. Member for Clacton since 8 June 2017. *Select committees:* Member: Digital, Culture, Media and Sport 2017-, Administration 2020-. *Councils and public bodies:* Tendring District Council: Councillor 2007-, Chair, Education and Skills Committee.

Other: Trustee, Patricia Watling Trust; Vice-chair, Royal Theatrical Fund; Variety Club's BBC TV Personality of the Year award (1988). Essex Junior Champion Archer.

Recreations: Sailing, horse-riding, scuba-diving.

Giles Watling MP, House of Commons, London SW1A 0AA
Tel: 020 7219 0795 *Email:* giles.watling.mp@parliament.uk
Constituency: 84 Station Road, Clacton-on-Sea CO15 1SP
Tel: 01255 473748 Website: www.gileswatling.co.uk *Twitter:* @GilesWatling

CONSERVATIVE

WEBB, SUZANNE

Stourbridge *(Majority 13,571)*

Team PPS, Department for International Trade

Born 1966.

Non-political career: Senior leadership roles at a global logistics company.

Political career: Member for Stourbridge since 12 December 2019; Team PPS, Department for International Trade 2020-. *Select committees:* Member: Procedure 2020-, Joint Committee on Consolidation, &c, Bills 2020-. Chair, West Midlands Region Conservative Party. *Councils and public bodies:* Councillor, Birmingham City Council 2018-.

Other: Spokesperson, Project Fields.

Suzanne Webb MP, House of Commons, London SW1A 0AA
Tel: 020 7219 3000 *Email:* suzanne.webb.mp@parliament.uk
Constituency: 1a Worcester Street, Stourbridge DY8 1AH
Tel: 01384 370574 Website: www.suzannewebb.org.uk *Twitter:* @Q66Suzi

INDEPENDENT

WEBBE, CLAUDIA

Leicester East *(Majority 6,019)*

Claudia Naomi Webbe. Born 8 March.

Education: London University (MSc race and ethnic relations).

Non-political career: Chair, Operation Trident Independent Advisory Group 2008-13; Adviser, to Ken Livingstone as Mayor of London 2000, 2004.

Political career: Member for Leicester East since 12 December 2019; PPS to Margaret Greenwood as Shadow Secretary of State for Work and Pensions 2020. *Select committees:* Member: Environmental Audit 2020-, Backbench Business 2020-, Foreign Affairs 2020-, Committees on Arms Export Controls 2020-. Member, National Executive Committee, Labour Party 2016-19; Labour Whip suspended September 2020-. *Councils and public bodies:* Councillor, Islington London Borough Council 2010-.

Claudia Webbe MP, House of Commons, London SW1A 0AA
Tel: 020 7219 3000 *Email:* claudia.webbe.mp@parliament.uk
Constituency: 218 Uppingham Road, Leicester LE5 0QG
Tel: 0800 799 9870 Website: www.claudiawebbe.org *Twitter:* @ClaudiaWebbe

LABOUR

WEST, CATHERINE

Hornsey and Wood Green *(Majority 19,242)*

Shadow Minister for Europe and Americas

Catherine Elizabeth West. Born 14 September 1966; Married (2 children).

Education: Degree social science and languages; School of Oriental and African Studies (Masters Chinese studies 2004); French, Italian, German, Mandarin.

Non-political career: Teacher of English as a second language, Nanjing, China 1996-97; Caseworker to David Lammy MP 2000-03; Publisher; Local government social worker with asylum seekers. Member: Unite, GMB.

Political career: Member for Hornsey and Wood Green since 7 May 2015 general election; Shadow Minister for: Foreign and Commonwealth Office 2015-17, Digital, Culture, Media and Sport (Sport) 2020, Foreign and Commonwealth Office (Europe and Americas) 2020-. *Select committees:* Member: International Trade 2017-19, Arms Export Controls 2017-19, Foreign Affairs 2019. *Councils and public bodies:* London Borough of Islington Council: Councillor 2000-14, Leader of the Opposition 2004-10, Leader of the Council 2010-13; Chair, London Councils Transport and Environment Committee 2010-14; Vice-president, Local Government Association.

Political interests: Housing infrastructure, economy, health, communities, human rights, affordable housing, local government, hospitals, GP provision, mental health, living wage, legal aid, London, education, climate change; Algeria, Australia, Bangladesh, China, Cyprus, Greece, Somalia, Turkey.

Other: Fabian Society; Local Authority Leader of the Year, Local Government Information Unit 2013.

Recreations: Walking, cycling, swimming.

Catherine West MP, House of Commons, London SW1A 0AA
Tel: 020 7219 6141 *Email:* catherine.west.mp@parliament.uk
Constituency: No constituency office publicised
Website: www.catherinewest.org.uk *Twitter:* @CatherineWest1

LABOUR

WESTERN, MATT

Warwick and Leamington *(Majority 789)*

Opposition Whip

Matthew Raymond Western. Born November 1962; Married Rebecca Earle.

Education: St Albans School; Bristol University (BSc geography 1984).

Non-political career: Peugeot Motor Company: Fleet Sales Manager 1992-95, Advertising and Media Manager 1997-2002, Manager International Communications Strategy 2002-03, Regional Manager 2003-04, Purchasing Manager 2004-08; Owner, Oxygency 2008-.

Political career: Member for Warwick and Leamington since 8 June 2017; Opposition Whip 2020-. *Select committees:* Member: International Trade 2017-20, Communities and Local Government/Housing, Communities and Local Government 2018-19. *Councils and public bodies:* Councillor, Warwickshire County Council 2013-18.

Political interests: Housing, transport, education.

Recreations: Cycling.

Matt Western MP, House of Commons, London SW1A 0AA
Tel: 020 7219 2051 *Email:* matt.western.mp@parliament.uk
Constituency: Town Hall, Parade, Leamington Spa CV32 4AT
Tel: 01926 882006 Website: www.mattwestern.org *Twitter:* @MattWestern_

CONSERVATIVE

WHATELY, HELEN

Faversham and Mid Kent *(Majority 21,976)*

Minister of State for Care, Department of Health and Social Care

Helen Olivia Bicknell Whately. Born 23 June 1976; Married Marcus Whately 2005 (3 children).

Education: Woldingham School; Westminster School (sixth form); Lady Margaret Hall, Oxford (BA philosophy, politics and economics 1998).

Non-political career: Consultant, PricewaterhouseCoopers 1998-2001; AOL Europe: Senior analyst 2001-02, Manager 2003-05, Senior manager 2005-06; Adviser on media/new media to Hugo Swire MP as Shadow Secretary of State for Culture, Media and Sport 2006-07; Consultant, McKinsey & Co 2007-15.

Political career: Contested Kingston and Surbiton 2010 general election. Member for Faversham and Mid Kent since 7 May 2015 general election; PPS to: Greg Hands as Minister of State for Trade and Investment, Department for International Trade 2016-17, Justine Greening as Secretary of State for Education and Minister for Women and Equalities 2017-18, Brandon Lewis as Minister without portfolio and Conservative Party Chair, Cabinet Office 2018; Parliamentary Under-Secretary of State for Arts, Heritage and Tourism, Department for Digital, Culture, Media and Sport 2019-20; Minister of State for Care, Department of Health and Social Care 2020-. *Select committees:* Member: Health 2015-17, Standing Orders 2015-17, Joint Committee on the Draft Domestic Abuse Bill 2019. Conservative Party: Vice-chairman, Women 2018-19, Deputy Chairman 2019.

Political interests: Housing, NHS.

Recreations: Riding, running, skiing.

Helen Whately MP, House of Commons, London SW1A 0AA
Tel: 020 7219 6472 *Email:* helen.whately.mp@parliament.uk
Constituency: No constituency office publicised
Website: www.helenwhately.co.uk *Twitter:* @helen_whately

House of Commons
MPs' Biographies

CONSERVATIVE

WHEELER, HEATHER

South Derbyshire *(Majority 19,335)*

Heather Kay Wheeler. Born 14 May 1959; Daughter of Mr C.P.C. Wilkinson, retired civil servant, and Mrs F.M. Wilkinson, retired primary teacher; Married Bob Wheeler 1986 (died 2018) (1 daughter).

Education: Grey Coat Hospital Secondary School, London.

Non-political career: Manager, Rics Ins Brokers 1979-87; Company secretary and director, Bretby Inns Ltd 1997-2006; Professional indemnity insurance broker, Lloyd's.

Political career: Contested Coventry South 2001 and 2005 general elections. Member for South Derbyshire since 6 May 2010 general election; PPS to: Jeremy Wright as Attorney General 2014-15, John Whittingdale as Secretary of State for Culture, Media and Sport 2015-16; Assistant Government Whip 2016-17; Government Whip (Lord Commissioner of HM Treasury) 2017-18; Parliamentary Under-Secretary of State: (Minister for Housing and Homelessness), Ministry of Housing, Communities and Local Government 2018-19, (Minister for Asia and the Pacific), Foreign and Commonwealth Office 2019-20; Trade Envoy to Cambodia, Laos and Vietnam 2020-. *Select committees:* Member: Standards and Privileges 2010-13, Communities and Local Government 2011-15, Standards 2013-14, Privileges 2013-14, European Scrutiny 2015-16, Digital, Culture, Media and Sport 2020-. Member, Executive, 1922 Committee 2012-14. Various posts, Putney and South Derbyshire Conservative Association 1976-99. *Councils and public bodies:* Councillor, London Borough of Wandsworth Council 1982-86; South Derbyshire District Council: Councillor 1995-2011, Leader, Conservative group 2002-10, Council Leader 2007-10; Vice-President, Local Government Association 2011-16.

Political interests: Affordable housing, economic regeneration; China, Japan, Taiwan.

Other: Member, UK delegation, NATO Parliamentary Assembly 2020-; Trustee, Industry and Parliament Trust; Patron, Leaside Singers; Association of Chartered Insurance Institute 1985.

Recreations: Watching sport, DIY, the Archers.

Heather Wheeler MP, House of Commons, London SW1A 0AA
Tel: 020 7219 1184 *Email:* heather.wheeler.mp@parliament.uk
Constituency: Room 1/24, Repton House, Bretby Business Park, Bretby, Derbyshire DE15 0YZ
Tel: 01283 225365 *Email:* heather@heatherwheeler.org.uk Website: www.heatherwheeler.org.uk
Twitter: @HeatherWheeler

LABOUR

WHITEHEAD, ALAN

Southampton Test *(Majority 6,213)*

Shadow Minister for Green New Deal and Energy

Alan Patrick Vincent Whitehead. Born 15 September 1950; Married Sophie Wronska 1979 (1 son 1 daughter).

Education: Isleworth Grammar School, Middlesex; Southampton University (BA politics and philosophy 1973; PhD political science 1976); French.

Non-political career: Outset: Deputy director 1976-79, Director 1979-83; Director, BIIT 1983-92; Professor of public policy, Southampton Institute 1992-97. Member, Unison (formerly NUPE).

Political career: Contested Southampton Test 1983, 1987 and 1992 general elections. Member for Southampton Test 1997-2010, for Southampton Test (revised boundary) since 6 May 2010 general election; Joint PPS to David Blunkett as Secretary of State for Education and Employment 1999-2000; PPS to Baroness Blackstone as Minister for Education and Employment 1999-2001; Parliamentary Under-Secretary of State, Department for Transport, Local Government and the Regions 2001-02; Shadow Minister for Energy and Climate Change 2015-16, 2016-20; Board Member, Parliamentary Office of Science and Technology (POST) 2015-; Business, Energy and Industrial Strategy: Waste and Recycling 2020, Green New Deal and Energy 2020-. *Select committees:* Member: Environment, Transport and Regional Affairs 1997-99, Environment, Transport and Regional Affairs (Environment Sub-committee) 1997-99, Constitutional Affairs/Justice 2003-10, Standards and Privileges 2005-13, Joint Committee on the Draft Climate Change Bill 2007, Energy and Climate Change 2009-15 Environmental Audit 2010-15, 2016, Standards 2013-15, Privileges 2013-15. Chair: PLP Departmental Committee for Local Government 1998-2001, PLP Departmental Group for Energy and Climate Change 2010-15; Vice-chair, PLP Departmental Group for Environment, Food and Rural

Affairs 2010-15. Member, Labour Party National Policy Forum 1999-2001, 2010-; Chair, Manifesto Group Local Government 2007-; Sustainable Communities Policy Commission, National Policy Forum. *Councils and public bodies:* Southampton City Council: Councillor 1980-92, Leader 1984-92.

Political interests: Environment, local and regional government, higher education, education, constitution, transport, energy; France, Lithuania, Poland.

Other: Director/board member: Southampton Environment Centre, Third Age Centre, Southampton; Visiting professor, Southampton Institute 1997-.

Recreations: Football (playing and watching), writing, tennis.

Dr Alan Whitehead MP, House of Commons, London SW1A 0AA
Tel: 020 7219 5517 *Fax:* 020 7219 0918 *Email:* whiteheada@parliament.uk
Constituency: Unit 39, Basepoint Centres, Anderson's Road, Southampton SO14 5FE
Tel: 023 8068 2086 Website: alan-whitehead.org.uk *Twitter:* @alanwhiteheadmp

SCOTTISH NATIONAL PARTY

WHITFORD, PHILIPPA

Central Ayrshire *(Majority 5,304)*

SNP Shadow Secretary of State for Health and Social Care and Shadow Minister for Europe

Born 24 December 1958; Married Hans 1987 (1 son).

Education: Glasgow University (MB ChB 1982; MD 1991); German.

Non-political career: Medical volunteer in Gaza and Lebanon 1991-93; Senior registrar, Aberdeen Royal Infirmary 1994-96; Consultant breast surgeon, Crosshouse Hospital 1996-2014; Lead Clinician: Ayrshire and Arran Health Board 1996-2010, West of Scotland Managed Clinical Network 2006-09; Locum consultant breast cancer surgeon, Ayrshire and Arran Health Board 2015-.

Political career: Member for Central Ayrshire since 7 May 2015 general election; SNP: Spokesperson for Health 2015-18, Spokesperson/Shadow Secretary of State for Health and Social Care 2018-, Spokesperson/Shadow Minister for Europe 2020-. *Select committees:* Member: Health 2015-17, European Scrutiny 2017-, Joint Committee on Draft Health Service Safety Investigations Bill 2018, Health and Social Care 2019, Future Relationship with the European Union 2020-21.

Political interests: NHS, breast cancer, Trident, Brexit, universal credit separate payments. EU citizens' rights, vaccinations, health; Palestine.

Other: Chair, breast cancer project groups, Clinical Standards Board for Scotland.

Dr Philippa Whitford MP, House of Commons, London SW1A 0AA
Tel: 020 7219 8158 *Email:* philippa.whitford.mp@parliament.uk
Constituency: 14 Eglinton Street, Irvine KA12 8AS
Tel: 01294 311160 Website: whitford.scot *Twitter:* @Dr_PhilippaW

LABOUR

WHITLEY, MICK

Birkenhead *(Majority 17,705)*

Michael Whitley.

Education: St Hughes Secondary.

Non-political career: Merchant Navy; Vauxhall Cars: Shop Steward, Trade Union Convenor; Regional Co-ordinator, Transport and General Workers Union/Unite 2010-13; North West Regional Secretary, Unite 2013-17. Unite.

Political career: Member for Birkenhead since 12 December 2019. *Select committees:* Member, International Trade 2020-. Chair, PLP Department Group for International Trade 2020-.

Mick Whitley MP, House of Commons, London SW1A 0AA
Tel: 020 7219 3000 *Email:* mick.whitley.mp@parliament.uk
Constituency: The Lauries Centre, 142 Claughton Road, Birkenhead CH41 6EY
Tel: 0151-650 5494 Website: www.mickwhitleyforbirkenhead.com *Twitter:* @MickWhitleyMP

CONSERVATIVE

WHITTAKER, CRAIG

Calder Valley *(Majority 5,774)*

Born 30 August 1962; Son of late Frank Whittaker and Marjorie Whittaker; Married (1 son 2 daughters).

Education: Belmont High School, New South Wales, Australia; Tighes Hill College, New South Wales, Australia.

Non-political career: Director, Kezdem PTY Ltd, New South Wales, Australia 1991; Branch manager, Wilkinsons Home and Garden Stores 1992-98; General manager, PC World Dixons Store Group 1998-2009. Armed Forces Parliamentary Scheme 2010-11.

Political career: Member for Calder Valley since 6 May 2010 general election; PPS to: James Brokenshire as Minister for Immigration, Home Office 2015-16, Karen Bradley as Secretary of State for Culture, Media and Sport 2016-17; Assistant Government Whip 2017-18; Government Whip: (Lord Commissioner of HM Treasury) 2018-19, (Vice-Chamberlain of HM Household) 2019. *Select committees:* Member: Education 2010-15, Unopposed Bills (Panel) 2011-15, Joint Committee on the Draft Communications Data Bill 2012-13, Joint Committee on Able Marine Energy Park Development Consent Order 2014 2014-15, Selection 2018-19, Joint Committee on Fixed-Term Parliaments Act 2020-. Constituency agent 2005 general election; Chair, Calder Valley Conservative Association 2005-06; Founding member, Conservatives for Reform in Europe 2016. *Councils and public bodies:* Councillor, Heptonstall Parish Council 1998-2003; Calderdale Metropolitan Borough Council: Councillor 2003-04, 2007-11, Cabinet member, Children and Young Peoples Services 2007-10.

Political interests: Education, children, aged care; Australia, Kenya, New Zealand, Tanzania.

Other: Member, Executive Committee, Commonwealth Parliamentary Association (UK Branch) 2014-15; Treasurer, Heptonstall Festival Committee 1996-2000; TLC (Together for Looked-After Children): Chair 2010-, President.

Publications: Co-author, Freedom, Responsibility and the State: Curbing Over-Mighty Government (Politeia, 2012).

Recreations: Sailing, reading.

Craig Whittaker MP, House of Commons, London SW1A 0AA
Tel: 020 7219 7031 *Email:* craig.whittaker.mp@parliament.uk
Constituency: Ground Floor, Right Wing, The Old Council Offices, Lawson Road, Brighouse HD6 1NY
Tel: 01484 711260 Website: www.craigwhittaker.org.uk *Twitter:* @CWhittaker_MP

CONSERVATIVE

WHITTINGDALE, JOHN

Maldon *(Majority 30,041)*

Minister of State for Media and Data, Department for Digital, Culture, Media and Sport

John Flasby Lawrance Whittingdale. Born 16 October 1959; Son of late John Whittingdale and Margaret Whittingdale; Married Ancilla Murfitt 1990 (divorced 2008) (1 son 1 daughter).

Education: Winchester College; University College, London (BSc economics 1982).

Non-political career: Head of Political Section, Conservative Research Department 1982-84; Special Sdviser to Secretaries of State for Trade and Industry 1984-87: Norman Tebbit MP, Leon Brittan MP and Paul Channon MP; Manager, N M Rothschild & Sons 1987; Political Secretary to Margaret Thatcher MP as Prime Minister 1988-90; Private Secretary to Margaret Thatcher MP 1990-92.

Political career: Member for South Colchester and Maldon 1992-97, for Maldon and Chelmsford East 1997-2010, for Maldon since 6 May 2010 general election; PPS to Eric Forth as Minister of State for: Education 1994-95, Education and Employment 1994-96; Opposition Whip 1997-98; Opposition Spokesperson for the Treasury 1998-99; PPS to William Hague as Leader of Opposition 1999-2001; Shadow Secretary of State for: Trade and Industry 2001-02, Culture, Media and Sport 2002-03, 2004-05, Agriculture, Fisheries and Food 2003-04; Secretary of State for Culture, Media and Sport 2015-16; Minister of State for Media and Data, Department for Digital, Culture, Media and Sport 2020-. *Select committees:* Member: Health 1993-97, Information 1997-98, Trade and Industry 2001; Chair, Culture, Media and Sport 2005-15; Member, Liaison 2005-15; Joint Committee on Privacy and Injunctions: Member 2011, Chair 2011-12; Member, Exiting the European Union 2016-20. 1922 Committee:

Member, Executive 2005-06, Vice-chair 2006-15. Member: 92 Group, No Turning Back Group; Member: Executive, Conservative Way Forward 2005-10, Conservative Party Board 2006-10. *Councils and public bodies:* Trustee, Royal Albert Hall Council 2018-20.

Political interests: Broadcasting and media, digital technology, foreign affairs and security; Armenia, China, Georgia, Israel, Japan, Korea, Malaysia, Russia, Ukraine, USA.

Other: Inter-Parliamentary Union, British Group: Member, Executive Committee 2010-15, 2016-20, Vice-chair 2017-18, Chair 2018-20; Member, UK Delegation, Organisation for Security and Co-operation in Europe Parliamentary Assembly 2017-20; Fellow: Industry and Parliament Trust 1996, Royal Society of Arts 2008-; Council Member, Freedom Association 2008-15; Member, Campaign committee, Vote Leave 2016; Consultant, Authors Licensing and Collecting Society 2017-20; Member, advisory board, SWNS Media Group 2017-20; Fellow, Royal Society of Arts 2008; Inquisitor of the Year, *The Spectator* awards 2011; OBE 1990; PC 2015; Order of Merit (Ukraine) 2019. Essex Club; Captain, House of Commons Rifle Team 2010-15.

Publications: New Policies for the Media (1995).

Recreations: Cinema, music.

Rt Hon John Whittingdale OBE MP, House of Commons, London SW1A 0AA
Tel: 020 7219 3557 *Fax:* 020 7219 2522 *Email:* john.whittingdale.mp@parliament.uk
Constituency: 19 High Street, Maldon, Essex CM9 5PE
Tel: 01621 855663 *Email:* m.c.c.a@btconnect.com Website: www.johnwhittingdale.org.uk
Twitter: @Jwhittingdale

LABOUR

WHITTOME, NADIA

Nottingham East *(Majority 17,393)*

Nadia Edith Whittome. Born 29 August 1996.

Education: West Bridgford School; Bilborough College; New College Nottingham (access to law); Nottingham University (LLB – left university before graduating); French, German.

Non-political career: Care assistant, ExtraCare Charitable Trust 2017-18; BME Network General Secretary, Nottingham University Students' Union 2018-; Communities Inc: Hate Crime Project Worker and Trainer 2018-19, Activities Co-ordinator 2019-. GMB.

Political career: Member for Nottingham East since 12 December 2019; PPS to Jon Ashworth as Shadow Secretary of State for Health and Social Care 2020. *Select committees:* Member, Environmental Audit 2020-. National Committee Member: Labour for a Socialist Europe 2019-, Labour Campaign for Free Movement 2019-.

Political interests: Climate policy, immigration policy, improving workers' rights and combatting poverty.

Other: National Committee Member: Labour for a Socialist Europe 2019, Labour Campaign for Free Movement 2019, Another Europe Is Possible 2018-19.

Nadia Whittome MP, House of Commons, London SW1A 0AA
Tel: 020 7219 3000 *Email:* nadia.whittome.mp@parliament.uk
Constituency: No constituency office publicised
Website: nadiawhittome.org *Twitter:* @NadiaWhittomeMP

CONSERVATIVE

WIGGIN, BILL

North Herefordshire *(Majority 24,856)*

Chair, Select Committee on Selection

William David Wiggin. Born 4 June 1966; Son of Sir Jerry Wiggin (MP for Weston-super-Mare 1969-97) and Mrs Rosie Dale Harris; Married Camilla Chilvers 1999 (2 sons 1 daughter).

Education: Eton College; University College of North Wales (BA economics 1988).

Non-political career: Trader, UBS 1991-93; Associate director, currency options sales, Dresdner Kleinwort Benson 1994-98; Manager, structured products, Commerzbank 1998-2001; Managing director, Emerging Asset Management Ltd 2015-.

Political career: Contested Burnley 1997 general election. Member for Leominster 2001-10, for North Herefordshire since 6 May 2010 general election; Shadow Minister for Environment, Food and Rural Affairs 2003, 2005-09; Shadow Secretary of State for Wales 2003-05; Opposition Whip 2009-10; Assistant Government Whip 2010-12. *Select committees:* Member:

Welsh Affairs 2001-03, Transport, Local Government and the Regions 2001-02, Environment, Food and Rural Affairs 2002-05, Liaison 2015-; Chair, Selection 2015-; Member, High Speed Rail (West Midlands – Crewe) Bill 2018-19. Secretary, Conservative Agricultural/Rural Affairs Policy Committee 2001-03; Member, Executive, 1922 Committee 2002-03, 2015-20. Contested North West region 1999 European Parliament election. Vice-chair, Hammersmith and Fulham Conservative Association 1995-97. *Councils and public bodies:* Governor, Hammersmith and West London College 1995-98.

Political interests: Defence, agriculture, Treasury, environment.

Other: Trustee, Violet Eveson Charitable Trust; Non-executive director: Philip T English International Financial Services Ltd, Allpay Ltd; Goldsmiths' Company; Freedom, City of London. Hurlingham Club, Annabel's Club, Pratt's Club, Rankin Club.

Recreations: Motorcycles, country sports, Hereford cattle.

Bill Wiggin MP, House of Commons, London SW1A 0AA
Tel: 020 7219 8175 *Fax:* 020 7219 1893 *Email:* bill.wiggin.mp@parliament.uk
Constituency: North Herefordshire Conservative Association Office, 8 Corn Square, Leominster, Herefordshire HR6 8LR
Tel: 01568 612565 Website: billwiggin.wordpress.com

CONSERVATIVE

WILD, JAMES

North West Norfolk *(Majority 19,922)*

James Oliver Wild. Born 5 January 1977; Married Natalie Evans 2010, now Baroness Evans of Bowes Park.

Education: Norwich School; Queen Mary, University of London (BA politics 1998).

Non-political career: Head of information and research, The Communication Group 1999-2001; Business policy adviser, Conservative Party Research Department 2000-01; Senior accounts executive, Politics Direct 2001-03; Public affairs manager, T-Mobile UK 2005-09; Account director, Hanover 2009-12; Special adviser to Michael Fallon: Department for Business, Innovation and Skills 2012-14, Department for Energy and Climate Change 2013-14, as Secretary of State for Defence 2014-17; Special adviser: to David Lidington as Chancellor of the Duchy of Lancaster and Minister for the Cabinet Office 2018-19, to Boris Johnson as Prime Minister 2019.

Political career: Contested North Norfolk 2017 general election. Member for North West Norfolk since 12 December 2019. *Select committees:* Member, Public Accounts 2020-.

James Wild MP, House of Commons, London SW1A 0AA
Tel: 020 7219 6968 *Email:* james.wild.mp@parliament.uk
Constituency: 202/3, 27-28 Tuesday Market Place, King's Lynn PE30 1JJ
Website: www.jameswild.org.uk *Twitter:* @jamesowild

CONSERVATIVE

WILLIAMS, CRAIG

Montgomeryshire *(Majority 12,138)*

PPS to Stephen Barclay as Chief Secretary to the Treasury

Alun Craig Williams. Born 7 June 1985; Married Clare (1 son).

Non-political career: Researcher to Nicholas Bourne AM as Leader of the Welsh Conservatives; Policy Adviser to Byron Davies AM; Director, Cardiff Bus 2011-15; Special Adviser, Department for Exiting the European Union 2019.

Political career: Contested Cardiff South and Penarth 15 November 2012 by-election. Member for Cardiff North 2015-17. Contested Cardiff North 2017 general election. Member for Montgomeryshire since 12 December 2019; PPS to Chief Secretary to the Treasury: David Gauke 2016-17, Stephen Barclay 2020-. *Select committees:* Member: Work and Pensions 2015-16, Welsh Affairs 2015-17, Scottish Affairs 2017, European Statutory Instruments 2020-, International Trade 2020-. Contested Cardiff West constituency 2007 and 2011 National Assembly for Wales elections. Chair, South Wales Central Conservatives; Founding member, Conservatives for Reform in Europe 2016. *Councils and public bodies:* Cardiff City Council: Councillor 2008-15, Chair, Economy and Culture Committee; Governor: Pentyrch Primary School, Radyr Comprehensive.

Recreations: Real ale, rugby.

Craig Williams MP, House of Commons, London SW1A 0AA
Tel: 020 7219 3000 *Email:* craig.williams.mp@parliament.uk
Constituency: 20 High Street, Welshpool, Powys SY21 7JP
Tel: 01938 552315 Website: www.craig-williams.org.uk *Twitter:* @craig4monty

PLAID CYMRU

WILLIAMS, HYWEL

Arfon *(Majority 2,781)*

Plaid Cymru Spokesperson for Cabinet Office, Defence, Foreign Affairs, International Development, International Trade, Work and Pensions; Chief Whip

Born 14 May 1953; Son of Robert Williams and Jennie Page Williams, shopkeepers; Divorced (3 daughters); married Dr Myfanwy Davies 2010 (1 son 1 daughter).

Education: Glan y Môr School, Pwllheli; University of Wales: Cardiff (BSc psychology 1974), Bangor (CQSW social work 1979); Welsh.

Non-political career: Social Worker: Mid Glamorgan County Council 1974-76, Gwynedd County Council 1976-84; North Wales Social Work Practice Centre, University of Wales, Bangor 1985-94: Project Worker 1985-94, Head of Centre 1991-94; Freelance Lecturer, Consultant and Author social work and social policy 1994-2001. Member: NALGO 1974-84, NUPE 1974-84, UCAC 1984-94.

Political career: Member for Caernarfon 2001-10, for Arfon since 6 May 2010 general election; Plaid Cymru Spokesperson for: Work and Pensions 2001-, Health 2001-15, 2016-17, Disability 2001-05, International Development 2004-17, 2020-, Culture, Media and Sport 2005-06, 2015-17, Education and Skills/Children, Schools and Families 2005-10, Treasury 2006-07, Defence 2007-09, 2015-17, 2020-, Transport 2007-09, Cabinet Office 2010-15, 2016-, Energy and Climate Change 2010-14, Education 2010-15, Foreign and Commonwealth Office 2015-17, Europe 2015-16, Leader, Parliamentary Group 2015-17, Spokesperson for: Exiting the European Union 2017-20, International Trade 2017-, Foreign Affairs 2020-, Chief Whip 2020-. *Select committees:* Member: European Standing Committee B 2002-04, Welsh Affairs 2004-05, 2014, Chairmen's Panel/Panel of Chairs 2005-15, Science and Technology 2012-14; Works of Art: Member 2012-19, Chair 2020-; Member, Exiting the European Union 2017-19. Contested Clwyd South constituency 1999 National Assembly for Wales election. Plaid Cymru: Policy developer (social security and policy for older people) 1999-2001, Policy cabinet 1999-2001.

Political interests: Social affairs, social security, social work, language issues, international development; France, Turkey.

Publications: Geirfa Gwaith Cymdeithasol/A Social Work Vocabulary (University of Wales Press, 1988); General editor Geirfa Gwaith Plant/Child Care Terms (UWP, 1993); Gwaith Cymdeithasol a'r Iaith Gymraeg/Social Work and the Welsh Language (UWP/CCETSW); Llawlyfr Hyfforddi a Hyfforddwyr/An Index of Trainers and Training (AGWC, 1994); Gofal – Pecyn Adnoddau a Hyfforddi Gofal yn y Gymuned yng Nghymru/A Training and Resource Pack for Community Care in Wales (CCETSW Cymru, 1998).

Recreations: Reading, walking, cooking.

Hywel Williams MP, House of Commons, London SW1A 0AA
Tel: 020 7219 8150 *Email:* hywel.williams.mp@parliament.uk
Constituency: 8 Castle Street, Caernarfon, Gwynedd LL55 1SE
Tel: 01286 672076
70 High Street, Bangor, Gwynedd LL57 1NR
Tel: 01248 372948 *Twitter:* @HywelPlaidCymru

CONSERVATIVE

WILLIAMSON, GAVIN

South Staffordshire *(Majority 28,250)*

Secretary of State for Education

Gavin Alexander Williamson. Born 25 June 1976; Married Joanne (2 daughters).

Education: Raincliffe Comprehensive School; Bradford University (BSc social sciences 1997).

Non-political career: Businessman; Managing director, architecture design company; Ran and owned a pottery company.

Political career: Contested Blackpool North and Fleetwood 2005 general election. Member for South Staffordshire since 6 May 2010 general election; PPS to Hugo Swire as Minister of State, Northern Ireland Office 2011-12; Acting PPS to Owen Paterson as Secretary of State for Northern Ireland July-September 2012; PPS: to Patrick McLoughlin as Secretary of State for Transport 2012-13, to David Cameron as Prime Minister 2013-16; Chief Whip; Parliamentary Secretary to the Treasury 2016-17; Member Parliamentary and Political Service Honours Committee 2016-17; Secretary of State for: Defence 2017-19, Education 2019-. *Select committees:* Member, Northern Ireland Affairs 2010-11. Former chair, Conservative Students; Deputy chair, Staffordshire Conservatives; Chair, Stoke-on-Trent Conservative Association; Vice-chair, Derbyshire Dales Conservative Association. *Councils and public bodies:* Councillor, North Yorkshire County Council 2001-05; Governor, St Thomas More RC Primary School.

Political interests: Manufacturing and industry, design, Ministry of Defence, Commonwealth affairs, green belt, fair funding for schools; China, Japan, Korea, Sierra Leone.

Other: Member, British Irish Parliamentary Assembly; Executive member, Commonwealth Parliamentary Association; Patron: South Staffordshire Community and Voluntary Action, World Owl Trust; PC 2015; CBE 2016.

Recreations: Pottery, time with family, books, architecture, cars.

Rt Hon Gavin Williamson CBE MP, House of Commons, London SW1A 0AA
Tel: 020 7219 7245 *Email:* gavin.williamson.mp@parliament.uk
Constituency: Jubilee House, 59 Wolverhampton Road, Codsall, South Staffordshire, Staffordshire WV8 1PL
Tel: 01902 846616 *Email:* gavin@gavinwilliamson.org Website: www.gavinwilliamson.org
Twitter: @GavinWilliamson

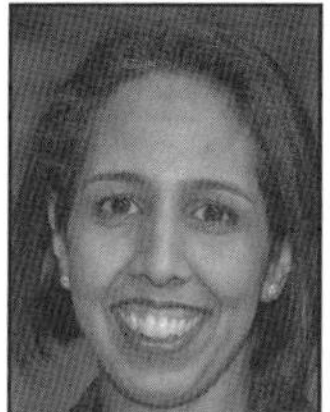

LIBERAL DEMOCRAT

WILSON, MUNIRA

Twickenham *(Majority 14,121)*

Liberal Democrat Spokesperson for Health, Wellbeing and Social Care

Born 26 April 1978; Married Michael 2007 (2 children).

Education: Henrietta Barnett School, London; Cambridge University (BA modern and medieval languages 2000); French, German.

Non-political career: Trainee Tax Consultant, Ernst & Young 2001-04; Campaign Organiser to Sue Doughty MP 2004-05; Parliamentary Researcher to Nick Clegg MP 2006; Public Affairs Officer, Save the Children 2006-08; Public Relations and Public Affairs Manager, Beating Bowel Cancer 2008-09; Novartis: Government and Corporate Affairs Manager 2009-11, Senior Government Affairs Manager 2011-12, National Specialised Commissioning and Patient Access manager 2012-13, Head of Government Affairs 2013-15; Strategic Account Manager, NHS Digital 2015-16; Corporate Affairs Director, Merck Group 2016-.

Political career: Contested Feltham and Heston 2010 general election. Member for Twickenham since 12 December 2019; Liberal Democrat Spokesperson for: Health, Wellbeing and Social Care 2019-, Transport 2019-20. *Councils and public bodies:* Councillor, London Borough of Richmond upon Thames Council 2006-10.

Political interests: Heathrow expansion, climate emergency, mental health provision for young people, local rail services, education.

Other: Member: Liberty, HACAN ClearSkies, Twickenham Society.

Munira Wilson MP, House of Commons, London SW1A 0AA
Tel: 020 7219 6474 *Email:* munira.wilson.mp@parliament.uk
Constituency: 49 Church Lane, Teddington TW11 8PA
Tel: 020 8977 0606 Website: www.munira.org.uk *Twitter:* @munirawilson

DEMOCRATIC UNIONIST PARTY

WILSON, SAMMY

East Antrim *(Majority 6,706)*

DUP Chief Whip; Spokesperson for Exiting the European Union, Treasury and Work and Pensions

Samuel Wilson. Born 4 April 1953; Son of Alexander and Mary Wilson.

Education: Methodist College, Belfast; Queen's University, Belfast (BA economics and politics 1975); Stranmillis College, Belfast (DipEd 1976).

Non-political career: Head of economics, Grosvenor Grammar School, Belfast 1975-83.

Political career: Contested Strangford 1992 and East Antrim 2001 general elections. Member for East Antrim 2005-10, for East Antrim (revised boundary) since 6 May 2010 general election; DUP: Spokesperson for: Education and Skills 2003-07, Housing 2005-07, Communities and Local Government 2007-09, Children, Schools and Families 2007-10, Innovation, Universities and Skills 2007-09, Treasury 2009-, Education 2010-12, 2015-17, Work and Pensions 2015-, Exiting the European Union 2017-, Chief Whip 2019-. *Select committees:* Member: Northern Ireland Affairs 2005-09, Transport 2009, Exiting the European Union 2016-19. Northern Ireland Assembly: Member Northern Ireland Forum for Political Dialogue 1996, MLA for Belfast East 1998-2003, for East Antrim 2003-11, and for East Antrim (revised boundary) 2011 to 29 July 2015: Education Committee: Deputy chair 1999-2003, Chair 2007-08; Minister of: Environment 2008-09, Finance and Personnel 2009-13. DUP press officer 1982-96. *Councils and public bodies:* East Belfast City Council: Councillor 1981-2010, Lord Mayor 1986-87, 2000-01; Member, Northern Ireland Policing Board 2001-06.

Political interests: Social issues, policing, education; America, China.

Other: PC 2017.

Publications: The Carson Trail (1982); The Unionist Case – The Forum Report Answered (1984); Data Response Questions in Economics (1995).

Recreations: Gardening, motorbikes.

Rt Hon Sammy Wilson MP, House of Commons, London SW1A 0AA
Tel: 020 7219 8523 *Fax:* 020 7219 3671 *Email:* barronj@parliament.uk
Constituency: East Antrim DUP, 116 Main Street, Larne, Co Antrim BT40 1RG
Tel: 028 2826 7722 *Twitter:* @eastantrimmp

LABOUR

WINTER, BETH

Cynon Valley *(Majority 8,822)*

Bethan Winter.

Education: Bristol University (BSc social policy; MA housing studies 1999); Swansea University (PhD 2017).

Non-political career: Research Assistant, Swansea University Centre for Social Work and Social Care Research 2008-10; Centre for Innovative Ageing 2010; Policy and Communications Officer, University and College Union Wales.

Political career: Member for Cynon Valley since 12 December 2019; PPS to: Rachael Maskell as Shadow Secretary of State for Employment Rights 2020, Rachel Reeves as Shadow Chancellor of the Duchy of Lancaster 2020. *Select committees:* Member, Welsh Affairs 2020-.

Dr Beth Winter MP, House of Commons, London SW1A 0AA
Tel: 020 7219 3000 *Email:* beth.winter.mp@parliament.uk
Constituency: No constituency office publicised
Tel: 01685 243166 *Twitter:* @BethWinterMP

House of Commons MPs' Biographies

LABOUR

WINTERTON, ROSIE

Doncaster Central *(Majority 2,278)*

First Deputy Chairman, Ways and Means and Deputy Speaker

Rosalie Winterton. Born 10 August 1958; Daughter of late Gordon and Valerie Winterton, teachers.

Education: Doncaster Grammar School; Hull University (BA history 1979).

Non-political career: Constituency personal assistant to John Prescott MP 1980-86; Parliamentary officer: Southwark Council 1986-88, Royal College of Nursing 1988-90; Managing director, Connect Public Affairs 1990-94; Head of private office, John Prescott MP as Deputy Leader of Labour Party 1994-97. Member, Armed Forces Parliamentary Scheme. Transport and General Workers' Union: Branch officer 1998-99, Chair, Parliamentary Group 1998-99; Member, Unite.

Political career: Member for Doncaster Central 1997-2010, for Doncaster Central (revised boundary) since 6 May 2010 general election; Parliamentary Secretary, Lord Chancellor's Department 2001-03; Minister of State: Department of Health 2003-07, Department for Transport 2007-08; Minister for Yorkshire and the Humber 2008-10; Minister of State: (Pensions and the Ageing Society), Department for Work and Pensions 2008-09, (Regional Economic Development and Co-ordination) Departments for Business, Innovation and Skills and for Communities and Local Government 2009-10; Member, Speaker's Committee on the Electoral Commission 2009-10; Shadow Leader of the House of Commons and Lord Privy Seal 2010; Shadow Minister for Women 2010; Member: House of Commons Commission 2010, 2016-, Speaker's Committee for the Independent Parliamentary Standards Authority 2010-11; Opposition Chief Whip 2010-16; Member, Parliamentary and Political Service Honours Committee 2012-16; Second Deputy Chairman of Ways and Means and Deputy Speaker 2017-19; First Deputy Chairman, Ways and Means and Deputy Speaker 2020-. *Select committees:* Member: Transport Bill January 2000, Finance Bill April 2000, Liaison 2016-17; Finance: Chair 2016-17, Member 2020-; Member, Panel of Chairs 2017-. Led Labour Party's work on the Boundary Review 2015-16; Labour Party envoy to the Party of European Socialists 2016-.

Political interests: Regional policy, employment, transport, housing, home affairs.

Other: Member, UK delegation, Parliamentary Assembly of the Council of Europe 2016-17; Member, Amnesty International; Patron: Doncaster Housing for Young People (DHYP), Darts Doncaster Community Arts, South Yorkshire Centre for Inclusive Living (SYCIL), Doncaster Cancer Detection Trust (DCDT), Doncaster Mencap; PC 2006; DBE 2016. Intake Social Club, Doncaster Catholic Club; Green Wyvern Sailing Club.

Recreations: Sailing, reading.

Rt Hon Dame Rosie Winterton DBE MP, House of Commons, London SW1A 0AA
Tel: 020 7219 3000 *Email:* rosie.winterton.mp@parliament.uk
Constituency: Doncaster Trades, 19 South Mall, Frenchgate, Doncaster, South Yorkshire DN1 1LL
Tel: 01302 326297 Website: www.rosiewinterton.co.uk

SCOTTISH NATIONAL PARTY

WISHART, PETE

Perth and North Perthshire *(Majority 7,550)*

Chair, Select Committee on Scottish Affairs; SNP Shadow Leader of the House of Commons

Peter Wishart. Born 9 March 1962; Son of late Alex Wishart, former dockyard worker, and Nan Irvine, retired teacher; Married Carrie Lindsay 1990 (separated 2003) (1 son).

Education: Queen Anne High School, Dunfermline; Moray House College of Education (Dip CommEd 1984).

Non-political career: Musician, Big Country 1981; Community worker, Central Region 1984-85; Musician, Runrig 1985-2001. Member, Musicians' Union 1985-.

Political career: Member for North Tayside 2001-05, for Perth and North Perthshire since 5 May 2005 general election; SNP: Chief Whip 2001-07, 2013-15, Spokesperson for: Transport 2001-05, Rural Affairs 2001-05, Culture, Media and Sport 2001-15, Constitution 2005-07, 2012-15, 2017-19, Overseas Aid 2005-07, Home Affairs 2007-15, Justice 2007-15, International Development 2007-10, Shadow Leader of the House of Commons 2015-19;

Member: Speaker's Committee on the Electoral Commission 2015-17, Speaker's Committee for the Independent Parliamentary Standards Authority 2015-17; SNP MP Group Secretary 2017-; Member, House of Commons Commission 2019-; SNP Shadow Chancellor of the Duchy of Lancaster and Minister for the Cabinet Office 2020-21, Shadow Leader of the House of Commons 2021-. *Select committees:* Member: Catering 2004-05, Administration 2005-08; Scottish Affairs: Member 2009-10, Chair 2015-; Member: Works of Art 2011-12, Liaison 2015-. SNP: Member: National Council 1997-, NEC 1999-2006, Executive vice-convener, fundraising 1999-2001, Group executive member 2015-.

Political interests: Arts and culture, international development, justice and equality; Southern Africa, Germany, Scandinavia.

Other: Member, Executive Committee, Commonwealth Parliamentary Association (UK Branch) 2014-15; Director, Fast Forward Positive Lifestyle 1992-2001; Campaign Committee, Scotland Against Drugs 1997-99.

Recreations: Music, hill-walking, travel, member parliamentary rockband 'MP4'.

Pete Wishart MP, House of Commons, London SW1A 0AA
Tel: 020 7219 8303 *Email:* pete.wishart.mp@parliament.uk
Constituency: 17-19 Leslie Street, Blairgowrie, Perthshire PH10 6AH
Tel: 01250 876576
63 Glasgow Road, Perth, Perthshire PH2 0PE
Tel: 01738 639598 Website: www.petewishartmp.com *Twitter:* @PeteWishart

CONSERVATIVE

WOOD, MIKE

Dudley South *(Majority 15,565)*

PPS to Priti Patel as Home Secretary

Michael Jon Wood. Born 17 March 1976; Married Laura (1 daughter 1 son).

Education: Old Swinford Hospital School; University of Wales, Aberystwyth (BScEcon economics and law 1997); Cardiff University (Postgraduate Diploma Bar Vocational Course 1999).

Non-political career: Assistant to Earl of Stockton MEP, Brussels 1999-2002; Policy adviser, internal market legislation and environmental regulation, European Parliament 2002-06; Senior researcher, JDS Associates 2006-08; Constituency organiser, Stourbridge, Halesowen and Rowley Regis 2009-10; Caseworker to Andrew Griffiths MP 2010-11; Parliamentary assistant to James Morris MP 2011-14.

Political career: Member for Dudley South since 7 May 2015 general election; Department for International Trade: Team PPS 2017-18, PPS to: Liam Fox as Secretary of State for International Trade and President of the Board of Trade 2018-19, Priti Patel as Home Secretary 2019-. *Select committees:* Member, European Scrutiny 2016-17. *Councils and public bodies:* Dudley Metropolitan Borough Council: Councillor 2014-16, Spokesperson for Finance; School governor.

Other: Member, UK delegation, Parliamentary Assembly of the: Council of Europe 2015-17, Organisation for Security and Co-operation in Europe 2020-.

Mike Wood MP, House of Commons, London SW1A 0AA
Tel: 020 7219 6982 *Email:* mike.wood.mp@parliament.uk
Constituency: 111a High Street, Wordsley, Stourbridge DY8 5QR
Tel: 01384 913123 *Email:* mike@mikewood.mp Website: www.mikewood.mp
Twitter: @mikejwood

CONSERVATIVE

WRAGG, WILLIAM

Hazel Grove *(Majority 4,423)*

Chair, Select Committee on Public Administration and Constitutional Affairs

William Peter Wragg. Born 11 December 1987.

Education: Poynton High School; Manchester University (BA history 2010); Liverpool John Moores University (PGCE 2013).

Non-political career: Teacher: Hulme Hall Grammer School, 2011-12, St Mary's CofE Primary School 2012-14. Member, Association of Teachers and Lecturers.

Political career: Member for Hazel Grove since 7 May 2015 general election; Member, Speaker's Committee on the Electoral Commission 2020-. *Select committees:* Member: Education 2016-19, Backbench Business 2016-19, Education, Skills and the Economy Sub-committee 2016, Finance 2017-18, Procedure 2017-19, 2021-, Liaison 2020-; Chair, Public Administration and Constitutional Affairs 2020-. Member, Executive, 1922 Committee 2016-; Chairman, Conservative Backbench Policy Committee on Education 2017-19. Member, Conservative Councillors Association 2011-15; Founding Member, Conservatives for Britain 2015-16. *Councils and public bodies:* Councillor, Stockport Council 2011-15; Governor, Hazel Grove Primary School 2008-15.

Other: Hazel Grove Conservative Club.

William Wragg MP, House of Commons, London SW1A 0AA
Tel: 020 7219 6258
Constituency: 13 Stockport Road, Marple, Stockport SK6 6BD
Tel: 0161-427 0660 *Email:* william@williamwragg.org.uk Website: www.williamwragg.org.uk
Twitter: @William_Wragg

CONSERVATIVE

WRIGHT, JEREMY

Kenilworth and Southam *(Majority 20,353)*

Jeremy Paul Wright. Born 24 October 1972; Son of John and Audrey Wright; Married Yvonne Salter 1998 (1 daughter 1 son).

Education: Taunton School, Somerset; Trinity School, New York City, USA; Exeter University (LLB 1995); Inns of Court School of Law (Bar Vocational Course 1996).

Non-political career: Barrister, specialising in criminal law 1996-; Called to the Bar of Northern Ireland 2016.

Political career: Member for Rugby and Kenilworth 2005-10, for Kenilworth and Southam since 6 May 2010 general election; Opposition Whip 2007-10; Government Whip 2010-12; Parliamentary Under-Secretary of State (Minister for Prisons and Rehabilitation), Ministry of Justice 2012-14; Attorney General 2014-18; Secretary of State for Digital, Culture, Media and Sport 2018-19. *Select committees:* Member, Constitutional Affairs 2005-07. Chair, Warwick and Leamington Conservative Association 2002-03. *Councils and public bodies:* Member, Committee on Standards in Public Life 2019-.

Political interests: Criminal justice, education, foreign affairs, dementia; USA.

Other: PC 2014.

Recreations: Travel, golf, James Bond films.

Rt Hon Jeremy Wright QC MP, House of Commons, London SW1A 0AA
Tel: 020 7219 2008 *Email:* jeremy.wright.mp@parliament.uk
Constituency: Jubilee House, Smalley Place, Kenilworth, Warwickshire CV8 1QG
Tel: 01926 853650 *Email:* jeremy@jeremywright.org.uk Website: www.jeremywright.org.uk

LABOUR

YASIN, MOHAMMAD

Bedford *(Majority 145)*

Born 15 October 1971; Married Shakila (4 children).

Education: Degree College Mirpur (BCom commerce).

Non-political career: Taxi driver (Milton Keynes area).

Political career: Member for Bedford since 8 June 2017. *Select committees:* Member, Housing, Communities and Local Government 2019-. *Councils and public bodies:* Bedford Borough Council: Councillor 2006-, Speaker, Portfolio Holder for Adult Services and Housing -2017.

Other: Trustee: Bedford Freemen's Common Charity, Bedford Tree Fund, Mayor of Bedford's Charity.

Mohammad Yasin MP, House of Commons, London SW1A 0AA
Tel: 020 7219 1513 *Email:* mohammad.yasin.mp@parliament.uk
Constituency: 2a Duke Street, Bedford MK40 3HR
Tel: 01234 346525 *Email:* office@mohammadyasin.org Website: mohammadyasin.org
Twitter: @YasinForBedford

CONSERVATIVE

YOUNG, JACOB

Redcar *(Majority 3,527)*

Team PPS, Ministry of Housing, Communities and Local Government

Born 2 February 1993.

Education: Redcar and Cleveland College; Macmillan Academy; Teeside University (HNC chemical engineering 2014).

Non-political career: Advanced Apprentice, The TTE Technical Training Group 2010-14; Process Operator, Chemoxy International Ltd 2012-14; Lead Technician, Petrochemicals 2014-19.

Political career: Contested Redcar 2015 and Middlesbrough 2017 general elections. Member for Redcar since 12 December 2019; Team PPS, Ministry of Housing, Communities and Local Government 2020-. *Select committees:* Member, European Statutory Instruments 2020-. *Councils and public bodies:* Councillor, Middlesbrough Council 2017-19.

Jacob Young MP, House of Commons, London SW1A 0AA
Tel: 020 7219 3936 *Email:* jacob.young.mp@parliament.uk
Constituency: Churchill House, 118 High Street, Redcar TS10 3DH
Tel: 01642 432588 *Email:* office@jacobyoung.org.uk Website: www.jacobyoung.org.uk
Twitter: @JacobYoungMP

CONSERVATIVE

ZAHAWI, NADHIM

Stratford-on-Avon *(Majority 19,972)*

Parliamentary Under-Secretary of State, Department for Business, Energy and Industrial Strategy and Parliamentary Under-Secretary of State for COVID Vaccine Deployment, Department of Health and Social Care

Born 2 June 1967; Married Lana (2 sons 1 daughter).

Education: King's College School, Wimbledon; University College, London (BSc chemical engineering).

Non-political career: European marketing director, Smith and Brooks Ltd; Co-founder and chief executive officer, YouGov 2000-10; Chief strategy officer, Gulf Keystone Petroleum 2015-17.

Political career: Contested Erith and Thamesmead 1997 general election. Member for Stratford-on-Avon since 6 May 2010 general election; Prime Minister's Adviser on Apprentices 2015-18; Parliamentary Under-Secretary of State: for Children and Families, Department for Education 2018-19, Department for Business, Energy and Industrial Strategy 2019-, for COVID Vaccine Deployment, Department of Health and Social Care 2020-. *Select committees:* Member: Business, Innovation and Skills 2010-15, Arms Export Controls 2010-15, Joint Committee on Privacy and Injunctions 2011-12, Foreign Affairs 2014-18, Speaker's Advisory Committee on Works of Art 2015-18. Founding member, 2020 group 2011-; Member, Number

10 Policy Advisory Board (Economic Affairs); Founding member, Conservatives for Reform in Europe 2016. *Councils and public bodies:* Councillor, London Borough of Wandsworth Council 1994-2006; Governor: Chartfield Delicate School 2002-04, Brandlehow Primary School.

Political interests: Business, foreign affairs; Middle East.

Other: Chair: Police Consultative Committee, Putney, Apprenticeship Delivery Board 2015-16; Patron, Peace One Day.

Recreations: Horseriding and show jumping.

Nadhim Zahawi MP, House of Commons, London SW1A 0AA
Tel: 020 7219 7159 *Fax:* 020 7219 4462 *Email:* nadhim.zahawi.mp@parliament.uk
Constituency: First Floor, 3 Trinity Street, Stratford-upon-Avon, Warwickshire CV37 6BL
Tel: 01789 264362 *Email:* nadhim@zahawi.com Website: www.zahawi.com
Twitter: @nadhimzahawi

LABOUR

ZEICHNER, DANIEL

Cambridge *(Majority 9,639)*

Shadow Minister for Food, Farming and Fisheries

Daniel Stephen Zeichner. Born 9 November 1956; Partner Barbara.

Education: King's College, Cambridge (history).

Non-political career: Computer programmer, Perkins Engines, Peterborough; Red and Green Nurseries 1983-91; Parliamentary assistant to MP 1992-97; Assistant to MEP 1995-99; National political officer, Unison 2002-15.

Political career: Contested Mid Norfolk 2005 and Cambridge 2010 general elections. Member for Cambridge since 7 May 2015 general election; Shadow Minister for: Transport 2015-17, Environment, Food and Rural Affairs (Food, Farming and Fisheries) 2020-. *Select committees:* Member: Science and Technology 2015, Transport 2017-19, Petitions 2018-19. Chair, PLP Departmental Groups for Transport 2019. Member: National Policy Forum, SERA. *Councils and public bodies:* Councillor, South Norfolk Council 1995-2003.

Recreations: Cycling, walking, music, international cinema, gardening.

Daniel Zeichner MP, House of Commons, London SW1A 0AA
Tel: 020 7219 8462 *Email:* daniel.zeichner.mp@parliament.uk
Constituency: Alex Wood Hall, Norfolk Street, Cambridge CB1 2LD
Tel: 01223 500515 *Email:* daniel@danielzeichner.co.uk Website: www.danielzeichner.co.uk
Twitter: @DanielZeichner

MPs' Political Interests

For precise details of individuals' stated interests, see relevant biography. The interests listed are supplied by MPs themselves.

Animals

See also:
- Animal health
- Animal rights and welfare

Benefits

See also:
- Benefits payment systems

Business and industry

See also:
- Business
- Economics and finance
- Economy
- Enterprise
- Finance
- Financial services
- Personal finance
- Tax
- Trade

Children and Families

See also:
- Childcare
- Children
- Family

Communities, planning and local government

See also:
- Communities
- Construction industry
- Housing
- Local government
- Planning
- Urban renewal

Culture, media and sport

See also:
- Alcohol licensing
- Architecture
- Arts
- Broadcasting
- Creative industries
- Culture
- Culture, Media and Sport
- Gambling and lotteries
- Heritage
- Media
- Music
- Tourism

Defence and security

See also:
- Armed Forces
- Defence
- Security

Disability

See also:
- Disability equality
- Disability rights
- Disabled children
- Learning disabilities

Education and skills

See also:
- Education
- Further and higher education
- Schools
- Skills
- Student finance

Employment and welfare

See also:
- Employment
- Employment Law
- Employment rights
- Equal opportunities and diversity
- Unemployment and jobseeking
- Welfare

Energy and Utilities

See also:
- Electricity
- Energy
- Energy Industry
- Energy Security
- Energy sources
- Telecommunications

Environment, agriculture and rural affairs

See also:
- Agriculture
- Countryside
- Environment
- Farming
- Fisheries
- Recycling
- Rural affairs
- Rural communities
- Sustainable development
- Waste management

European affairs

See also:
- European Union
- Internal Market
- Justice and Home Affairs
- Regional policy

Government, politics and public administration

See also:
Civil Service
Constitutional Affairs
Democracy and elections
Ireland
Public administration
Scotland

Health, wellbeing and care

See also:
Addiction
Care
Cosmetic surgery
Food and drink
Health
Mental health
National Health Service

Home affairs

See also:
Charities and volunteers
Consumer affairs
Counter-terrorism
Crime
Human rights
Immigration and nationality
Justice system
Law
Police
Prisons
Security
Sentencing
Social affairs
Social inclusion
Social justice
Youth justice

Information and communication

See also:
Communications
Information and communication technology
Intellectual property

International affairs

See also:
Foreign policy
International development and aid
Terrorism
Third World

Religion

See also:
Church Affairs

Science, technology and research

See also:
Biotechnology
Engineering
Research and development
Science
Technology

Transport

See also:
Aviation
Infrastructure
Road safety
Road transport

Abortion

David Amess	*Con*	p70

Academies

David Johnston	*Con*	p234
Clive Lewis	*Lab*	p254

Addiction

Stephen McPartland	*Con*	p273

Adoption

Rachael Maskell	*Lab/Co-op*	p279
Edward Timpson	*Con*	p368

Affordable housing

Catherine West	*Lab*	p381
Heather Wheeler	*Con*	p383

Agriculture

Nigel Adams	*Con*	p65
Victoria Atkins	*Con*	p75
Richard Bacon	*Con*	p76
Alistair Carmichael	*Lib Dem*	p112
Geoffrey Clifton-Brown	*Con*	p123
Geoffrey Cox	*Con*	p129
David Davis	*Con*	p140
David Duguid	*Con*	p154
Philip Dunne	*Con*	p156
Nigel Evans	*Con*	p165
Nusrat Ghani	*Con*	p181
Robert Goodwill	*Con*	p186
James Gray	*Con*	p190
John Hayes	*Con*	p207
Lindsay Hoyle	*Speaker*	p222
Caroline Johnson	*Con*	p232
Daniel Kawczynski	*Con*	p239
Alicia Kearns	*Con*	p240
Edward Leigh	*Con*	p251
Caroline Nokes	*Con*	p301
Ian Paisley	*DUP*	p309
Neil Parish	*Con*	p309
Owen Paterson	*Con*	p311
Luke Pollard	*Lab/Co-op*	p317
Alyn Smith	*SNP*	p343
Julian Smith	*Con*	p346
Bill Wiggin	*Con*	p386

Airports

Graham Stringer	*Lab*	p358
Munira Wilson	*Lib Dem*	p389

Alcoholism

Bill Esterson	*Lab*	p163

Alternative fuels

Fabian Hamilton	*Lab*	p199

Animal health

Craig Mackinlay	*Con*	p269

Animal rights and welfare

David Amess	*Con*	p70
Lisa Cameron	*SNP*	p110
Rosie Duffield	*Lab*	p154
Roger Gale	*Con*	p179
Diana Johnson	*Lab*	p232
Tim Loughton	*Con*	p260
Caroline Lucas	*Green*	p261
Neil Parish	*Con*	p309
Mark Pritchard	*Con*	p320
Andrew Rosindell	*Con*	p331
Alyn Smith	*SNP*	p343
Karl Turner	*Lab*	p373
Theresa Villiers	*Con*	p376

Anti-social behaviour

Liam Byrne	*Lab*	p108
Nigel Mills	*Con*	p286
Jessica Morden	*Lab*	p291

Apprenticeships

Chris Green	*Con*	p192
Robert Halfon	*Con*	p198
Catherine McKinnell	*Lab*	p269
Rachel Maclean	*Con*	p271
Seema Malhotra	*Lab/Co-op*	p276
Anne Marie Morris	*Con*	p292
Guy Opperman	*Con*	p306
Andrew Stephenson	*Con*	p352
Jane Stevenson	*Con*	p353

Architecture

Peter Gibson	*Con*	p182

Armed Forces

Andrew Bridgen	*Con*	p97
John Glen	*Con*	p185
Clive Lewis	*Lab*	p254
Jason McCartney	*Con*	p264
Karl McCartney	*Con*	p264
James Sunderland	*Con*	p360

Arts

Damian Collins	*Con*	p124
Thangam Debbonaire	*Lab*	p142
Michael Ellis	*Con*	p160
Patrick Grady	*SNP*	p188
Claire Hanna	*SDLP*	p202
Helen Hayes	*Lab*	p206
Greg Knight	*Con*	p243
David Lammy	*Lab*	p247
Alison McGovern	*Lab*	p268
Robert Neill	*Con*	p299
Jane Stevenson	*Con*	p353
David Warburton	*Con*	p379
Pete Wishart	*SNP*	p391

Asylum

David Simmonds	*Con*	p342

Autism

Thangam Debbonaire	*Lab*	p142
Marion Fellows	*SNP*	p169
Helen Hayes	*Lab*	p206
Jonathan Reynolds	*Lab/Co-op*	p327

Aviation

Andrew Griffith	*Con*	p194
John McDonnell	*Lab*	p267
Craig Mackinlay	*Con*	p269
Seema Malhotra	*Lab/Co-op*	p276
Andrew Selous	*Con*	p337
Andrew Stephenson	*Con*	p352
Graham Stringer	*Lab*	p358

Banking and finance

Steve Baker	*Con*	p78
Mark Garnier	*Con*	p180
Kevin Hollinrake	*Con*	p217

Banking services

Clive Lewis	*Lab*	p254

Benefits

Gavin Robinson	*DUP*	p330

Benefits payment systems

Adam Afriyie	*Con*	p66

Big Society

Jesse Norman	*Con*	p302

Biodiversity

Rachael Maskell	*Lab/Co-op*	p279

Biotechnology

George Freeman	*Con*	p176

Breast cancer

Philippa Whitford	*SNP*	p384

Breast cancer screening

Mike Freer	*Con*	p177

Broadband

Lucy Allan	*Con*	p69
Andrew Griffith	*Con*	p194
Selaine Saxby	*Con*	p335

Broadcasting

Chris Bryant	*Lab*	p103
Damian Collins	*Con*	p124

Michael Fabricant	*Con*	p167
Roger Gale	*Con*	p179
Andrew Griffith	*Con*	p194
Jason McCartney	*Con*	p264
Alison McGovern	*Lab*	p268
John Whittingdale	*Con*	p385

Brownfield development

Marco Longhi	*Con*	p258

Buses

Graham Stringer	*Lab*	p358

Business

Nigel Adams	*Con*	p65
Duncan Baker	*Con*	p78
Andrew Bridgen	*Con*	p97
Jo Churchill	*Con*	p119
James Cleverly	*Con*	p122
Alberto Costa	*Con*	p127
Caroline Dinenage	*Con*	p143
Steve Double	*Con*	p149
Ben Everitt	*Con*	p166
Michael Fabricant	*Con*	p167
Jo Gideon	*Con*	p183
Helen Grant	*Con*	p189
Andrew Griffith	*Con*	p194
Jonathan Gullis	*Con*	p196
Gordon Henderson	*Con*	p210
Kevin Hollinrake	*Con*	p217
Nigel Huddleston	*Con*	p222
Darren Jones	*Lab*	p235
Marcus Jones	*Con*	p237
Brandon Lewis	*Con*	p253
Ian Liddell-Grainger	*Con*	p255
Jonathan Lord	*Con*	p259
Rachel Maclean	*Con*	p271
Alan Mak	*Con*	p276
Seema Malhotra	*Lab/Co-op*	p276
Wendy Morton	*Con*	p295
Ian Murray	*Lab*	p296
Sarah Olney	*Lib Dem*	p305
Priti Patel	*Con*	p310
David Rutley	*Con*	p334
Julian Smith	*Con*	p346
Mark Spencer	*Con*	p350
Alexander Stafford	*Con*	p351
Richard Thomson	*SNP*	p365
Justin Tomlinson	*Con*	p369
Tom Tugendhat	*Con*	p372
Theresa Villiers	*Con*	p376
Robin Walker	*Con*	p378
David Warburton	*Con*	p379
Nadhim Zahawi	*Con*	p394

Business and industry

Caroline Dinenage	*Con*	p143
Chris Elmore	*Lab*	p162
Michael Fabricant	*Con*	p167
Nia Griffith	*Lab*	p195
John Hayes	*Con*	p207
Lindsay Hoyle	*Speaker*	p222
Khalid Mahmood	*Lab*	p275
Owen Paterson	*Con*	p311
Mark Pawsey	*Con*	p311
Dominic Raab	*Con*	p322
Andrew Selous	*Con*	p337
Alok Sharma	*Con*	p339
Barry Sheerman	*Lab/Co-op*	p340
Jon Trickett	*Lab*	p371
Gavin Williamson	*Con*	p389

Cancer

John Baron	*Con*	p81
Sharon Hodgson	*Lab*	p216
Dan Jarvis	*Lab*	p227
Pauline Latham	*Con*	p249
Stephen McPartland	*Con*	p273

Care

Sarah Champion	*Lab*	p116
Rosie Cooper	*Lab*	p125
John Cryer	*Lab*	p133
Tim Farron	*Lib Dem*	p168
Peter Gibson	*Con*	p182
Emma Lewell-Buck	*Lab*	p252
Rachael Maskell	*Lab/Co-op*	p279
Kieran Mullan	*Con*	p295
Chris Skidmore	*Con*	p342
Maggie Throup	*Con*	p366

Care for the disabled

Mims Davies	*Con*	p139
Dan Jarvis	*Lab*	p227

Care for the elderly

Simon Baynes	*Con*	p81
Mims Davies	*Con*	p139
Mary Glindon	*Lab*	p186
Andrew Griffith	*Con*	p194
Dan Jarvis	*Lab*	p227
Liz Kendall	*Lab*	p242
Rachael Maskell	*Lab/Co-op*	p279
Penny Mordaunt	*Con*	p291
Anne Marie Morris	*Con*	p292
Dan Poulter	*Con*	p318
Graham Stuart	*Con*	p358
Craig Whittaker	*Con*	p385

Carer's allowance

Gavin Newlands	*SNP*	p300

Charities and volunteers

Stuart Andrew	*Con*	p72
Paul Blomfield	*Lab*	p89
Yvonne Fovargue	*Lab*	p173
Jeremy Hunt	*Con*	p224
Dan Poulter	*Con*	p318
Will Quince	*Con*	p321

Constitutional Affairs

Kevin Brennan	*Lab*	p96
Robert Buckland	*Con*	p104
Tracey Crouch	*Con*	p132
Wayne David	*Lab*	p136
James Davies	*Con*	p138
Jeffrey Donaldson	*DUP*	p147
Michael Ellis	*Con*	p160
George Freeman	*Con*	p176
David Jones	*Con*	p235
Eleanor Laing	*Con*	p246
Mike Penning	*Con*	p312
Tom Pursglove	*Con*	p320
John Redwood	*Con*	p324
Laurence Robertson	*Con*	p329
Iain Stewart	*Con*	p355
Robert Syms	*Con*	p361
Richard Thomson	*SNP*	p365
Valerie Vaz	*Lab*	p375
Martin Vickers	*Con*	p375
Alan Whitehead	*Lab*	p383

Constitutional reform

Geoffrey Cox	*Con*	p129
Ranil Jayawardena	*Con*	p228

Construction industry

John Spellar	*Lab*	p349

Consumer affairs

Greg Knight	*Con*	p243
Justin Tomlinson	*Con*	p369

Consumer debt

Yvonne Fovargue	*Lab*	p173

Consumer rights

Sharon Hodgson	*Lab*	p216

Council and social housing

Paula Barker	*Lab*	p80
Bell Ribeiro-Addy	*Lab*	p328

Counter-terrorism

Mark Pritchard	*Con*	p320

Countryside

James Gray	*Con*	p190
Dan Jarvis	*Lab*	p227
David Jones	*Con*	p235
Laurence Robertson	*Con*	p329

Creative industries

Kevin Brennan	*Lab*	p96
Patrick Grady	*SNP*	p188

Crime

Kemi Badenoch	*Con*	p76
Dawn Butler	*Lab*	p106
Alan Campbell	*Lab*	p110
Janet Daby	*Lab*	p134
Tim Farron	*Lib Dem*	p168
Mark Fletcher	*Con*	p171
George Freeman	*Con*	p176
Michael Gove	*Con*	p187
Adam Holloway	*Con*	p218
George Howarth	*Lab*	p220
Marco Longhi	*Con*	p258
Jason McCartney	*Con*	p264
Karl McCartney	*Con*	p264
Maria Miller	*Con*	p285
Nigel Mills	*Con*	p286
Stephen Morgan	*Lab*	p292
Taiwo Owatemi	*Lab*	p308
Toby Perkins	*Lab*	p314
Yasmin Qureshi	*Lab*	p322
Edward Timpson	*Con*	p368
Christian Wakeford	*Con*	p377

Culture

Nigel Adams	*Con*	p65
Bambos Charalambous	*Lab*	p117
Damian Collins	*Con*	p124
Alex Cunningham	*Lab*	p134
Caroline Dinenage	*Con*	p143
Helen Hayes	*Lab*	p206
Dan Jarvis	*Lab*	p227
David Lammy	*Lab*	p247
Jonathan Lord	*Con*	p259
Alison McGovern	*Lab*	p268
Jo Stevens	*Lab*	p353
David Warburton	*Con*	p379
Pete Wishart	*SNP*	p391

Culture, Media and Sport

Nigel Adams	*Con*	p65
Andrew Bowie	*Con*	p92
Alun Cairns	*Con*	p109
Jonathan Lord	*Con*	p259

Cystic fibrosis

Marion Fellows	*SNP*	p169

Debt advice

Bill Cash	*Con*	p113

Defence

Victoria Atkins	*Con*	p75
Steve Baker	*Con*	p78
John Baron	*Con*	p81
Scott Benton	*Con*	p84
Crispin Blunt	*Con*	p90
Andrew Bowie	*Con*	p92
Alun Cairns	*Con*	p109
Sarah Champion	*Lab*	p116
Douglas Chapman	*SNP*	p116
Geoffrey Cox	*Con*	p129
Caroline Dinenage	*Con*	p143
Martin Docherty-Hughes	*SNP*	p145
Jeffrey Donaldson	*DUP*	p147
Dave Doogan	*SNP*	p148

Stephen Doughty	*Lab/Co-op*	p150
Richard Drax	*Con*	p152
Flick Drummond	*Con*	p153
Iain Duncan Smith	*Con*	p155
Tobias Ellwood	*Con*	p161
Nigel Evans	*Con*	p165
Michael Fabricant	*Con*	p167
Simon Fell	*Con*	p169
Liam Fox	*Con*	p174
Mark Francois	*Con*	p175
Nusrat Ghani	*Con*	p181
Peter Gibson	*Con*	p182
Cheryl Gillan	*Con*	p184
James Gray	*Con*	p190
Nia Griffith	*Lab*	p195
Mark Harper	*Con*	p203
Chris Heaton-Harris	*Con*	p210
Gordon Henderson	*Con*	p210
Mark Hendrick	*Lab/Co-op*	p211
Antony Higginbotham	*Con*	p212
Adam Holloway	*Con*	p218
Lindsay Hoyle	*Speaker*	p222
Dan Jarvis	*Lab*	p227
Sajid Javid	*Con*	p228
Bernard Jenkin	*Con*	p229
Caroline Johnson	*Con*	p232
Gerald Jones	*Lab*	p236
Kevan Jones	*Lab*	p237
Edward Leigh	*Con*	p251
Julian Lewis	*Con*	p254
Ian Liddell-Grainger	*Con*	p255
Jack Lopresti	*Con*	p259
Conor McGinn	*Lab*	p268
Alan Mak	*Con*	p276
Mark Menzies	*Con*	p282
Andrew Mitchell	*Con*	p287
Stephen Morgan	*Lab*	p292
Andrew Murrison	*Con*	p298
Mike Penning	*Con*	p312
Christopher Pincher	*Con*	p316
Luke Pollard	*Lab/Co-op*	p317
Mark Pritchard	*Con*	p320
Andrew Rosindell	*Con*	p331
Bob Seely	*Con*	p336
Andrew Selous	*Con*	p337
Royston Smith	*Con*	p347
John Spellar	*Lab*	p349
Bob Stewart	*Con*	p354
Rishi Sunak	*Con*	p360
James Sunderland	*Con*	p360
Tom Tugendhat	*Con*	p372
Derek Twigg	*Lab*	p373
Robin Walker	*Con*	p378
Ben Wallace	*Con*	p378
Bill Wiggin	*Con*	p386
Gavin Williamson	*Con*	p389

Dementia

Edward Argar	*Con*	p73
Sarah Atherton	*Con*	p74
Alberto Costa	*Con*	p127
Mike Freer	*Con*	p177
Anna McMorrin	*Lab*	p272
Mark Menzies	*Con*	p282
Andrew Stephenson	*Con*	p352
Jeremy Wright	*Con*	p393

Democracy and elections

Andrew Bowie	*Con*	p92
John Hayes	*Con*	p207
Ellie Reeves	*Lab*	p326
Andrew Stephenson	*Con*	p352
Alison Thewliss	*SNP*	p363

Devolved government

Andrew Bowie	*Con*	p92
Dan Jarvis	*Lab*	p227
Jonathan Reynolds	*Lab/Co-op*	p327

Diabetes

Pauline Latham	*Con*	p249

Disability

Lisa Cameron	*SNP*	p110
Rosie Cooper	*Lab*	p125
Neil Coyle	*Lab*	p129
Marsha De Cordova	*Lab*	p142
Martin Docherty-Hughes	*SNP*	p145
John Hayes	*Con*	p207
John Healey	*Lab*	p209
Chris Heaton-Harris	*Con*	p210
Tim Loughton	*Con*	p260
Chris Skidmore	*Con*	p342
Owen Thompson	*SNP*	p365
Justin Tomlinson	*Con*	p369

Disability rights

Daisy Cooper	*Lib Dem*	p125
Chris Law	*SNP*	p250

Disabled children

Bob Stewart	*Con*	p354

Doctors

Catherine West	*Lab*	p381

Domestic violence

Thangam Debbonaire	*Lab*	p142
Kate Griffiths	*Con*	p196
Harriet Harman	*Lab*	p203
Andrew Stephenson	*Con*	p352

Drugs use and abuse

Crispin Blunt	*Con*	p90
Liam Byrne	*Lab*	p108
Ronnie Cowan	*SNP*	p129
Rachael Maskell	*Lab/Co-op*	p279

Economic development

Gregory Campbell	*DUP*	p111
Stewart Hosie	*SNP*	p220
Lucy Powell	*Lab/Co-op*	p319
Nick Smith	*Lab*	p347
Royston Smith	*Con*	p347
Tom Tugendhat	*Con*	p372

Economics and finance

Simon Clarke	*Con*	p120
John Cryer	*Lab*	p133
Stephen Hammond	*Con*	p200
Clive Lewis	*Lab*	p254
John McDonnell	*Lab*	p267
Huw Merriman	*Con*	p283
Graham Stuart	*Con*	p358
Richard Thomson	*SNP*	p365

Economy

Jon Ashworth	*Lab/Co-op*	p74
Gareth Bacon	*Con*	p75
Kemi Badenoch	*Con*	p76
Steve Baker	*Con*	p78
Harriett Baldwin	*Con*	p79
John Baron	*Con*	p81
Karen Bradley	*Con*	p93
Kevin Brennan	*Lab*	p96
Richard Burgon	*Lab*	p105
Alun Cairns	*Con*	p109
James Cartlidge	*Con*	p113
Sarah Champion	*Lab*	p116
Greg Clark	*Con*	p120
Geoffrey Clifton-Brown	*Con*	p123
Jon Cruddas	*Lab*	p132
John Cryer	*Lab*	p133
Wayne David	*Lab*	p136
Geraint Davies	*Lab/Co-op*	p138
Anneliese Dodds	*Lab/Co-op*	p146
Stephen Doughty	*Lab/Co-op*	p150
Philip Dunne	*Con*	p156
Angela Eagle	*Lab*	p156
David Evennett	*Con*	p166
Liam Fox	*Con*	p174
Barry Gardiner	*Lab*	p179
Mark Garnier	*Con*	p180
Nick Gibb	*Con*	p181
Claire Hanna	*SDLP*	p202
John Healey	*Lab*	p209
Mark Hendrick	*Lab/Co-op*	p211
Margaret Hodge	*Lab*	p215
Kevin Hollinrake	*Con*	p217
Ranil Jayawardena	*Con*	p228
Bernard Jenkin	*Con*	p229
Marcus Jones	*Con*	p237
Stephen Kinnock	*Lab*	p243
Kwasi Kwarteng	*Con*	p245
Eleanor Laing	*Con*	p246
David Lammy	*Lab*	p247
Andrea Leadsom	*Con*	p251
Ian Liddell-Grainger	*Con*	p255
Steve McCabe	*Lab*	p262
Alison McGovern	*Lab*	p268
Catherine McKinnell	*Lab*	p269
Anna McMorrin	*Lab*	p272
Alan Mak	*Con*	p276
Stephen Metcalfe	*Con*	p284
Andrew Mitchell	*Con*	p287
Grahame Morris	*Lab*	p293
Jesse Norman	*Con*	p302
Priti Patel	*Con*	p310
Owen Paterson	*Con*	p311
Bridget Phillipson	*Lab*	p315
Chris Philp	*Con*	p316
Jeremy Quin	*Con*	p321
Dominic Raab	*Con*	p322
John Redwood	*Con*	p324
Rachel Reeves	*Lab*	p326
Jonathan Reynolds	*Lab/Co-op*	p327
Gavin Robinson	*DUP*	p330
Lee Rowley	*Con*	p332
David Rutley	*Con*	p334
Barry Sheerman	*Lab/Co-op*	p340
Andrew Stephenson	*Con*	p352
Iain Stewart	*Con*	p355
Wes Streeting	*Lab*	p357
Mel Stride	*Con*	p357
Rishi Sunak	*Con*	p360
Robert Syms	*Con*	p361
Stephen Timms	*Lab*	p367
Jon Trickett	*Lab*	p371
Elizabeth Truss	*Con*	p372
Derek Twigg	*Lab*	p373
Theresa Villiers	*Con*	p376
Christian Wakeford	*Con*	p377
Charles Walker	*Con*	p377
Catherine West	*Lab*	p381
Heather Wheeler	*Con*	p383
Bill Wiggin	*Con*	p386

Education

Diane Abbott	*Lab*	p64
Debbie Abrahams	*Lab*	p64
Nigel Adams	*Con*	p65
Nickie Aiken	*Con*	p67
Rushanara Ali	*Lab*	p68
David Amess	*Con*	p70
Caroline Ansell	*Con*	p73
Victoria Atkins	*Con*	p75
Richard Bacon	*Con*	p76
Steve Baker	*Con*	p78
Harriett Baldwin	*Con*	p79
Hilary Benn	*Lab*	p83
Paul Beresford	*Con*	p85
Saqib Bhatti	*Con*	p86

Paul Blomfield	*Lab*	p89	Sharon Hodgson	*Lab*	p216
Ben Bradley	*Con*	p93	Nigel Huddleston	*Con*	p222
Graham Brady	*Con*	p94	Neil Hudson	*Con*	p223
Suella Braverman	*Con*	p95	Jane Hunt	*Con*	p224
Kevin Brennan	*Lab*	p96	Jeremy Hunt	*Con*	p224
Anthony Browne	*Con*	p101	Ranil Jayawardena	*Con*	p228
Robert Buckland	*Con*	p104	Caroline Johnson	*Con*	p232
Conor Burns	*Con*	p106	Diana Johnson	*Lab*	p232
Ian Byrne	*Lab*	p107	David Johnston	*Con*	p234
Wendy Chamberlain	*Lib Dem*	p115	Eleanor Laing	*Con*	p246
Sarah Champion	*Lab*	p116	Ben Lake	*PlC*	p247
Bambos Charalambous	*Lab*	p117	David Lammy	*Lab*	p247
Simon Clarke	*Con*	p120	Clive Lewis	*Lab*	p254
Brendan Clarke-Smith	*Con*	p121	Ian Liddell-Grainger	*Con*	p255
Daisy Cooper	*Lib Dem*	p125	Mark Logan	*Con*	p257
Alberto Costa	*Con*	p127	Jonathan Lord	*Con*	p259
Geoffrey Cox	*Con*	p129	Tim Loughton	*Con*	p260
John Cryer	*Lab*	p133	Jason McCartney	*Con*	p264
Alex Cunningham	*Lab*	p134	Karl McCartney	*Con*	p264
Wayne David	*Lab*	p136	Cherilyn Mackrory	*Con*	p270
Philip Davies	*Con*	p139	Esther McVey	*Con*	p274
Caroline Dinenage	*Con*	p143	Alan Mak	*Con*	p276
Oliver Dowden	*Con*	p151	Julie Marson	*Con*	p278
Jackie Doyle-Price	*Con*	p151	Paul Maynard	*Con*	p281
Flick Drummond	*Con*	p153	Ian Mearns	*Lab*	p282
Rosie Duffield	*Lab*	p154	Huw Merriman	*Con*	p283
Clive Efford	*Lab*	p159	Stephen Metcalfe	*Con*	p284
Julie Elliott	*Lab*	p160	Maria Miller	*Con*	p285
Tobias Ellwood	*Con*	p161	Nigel Mills	*Con*	p286
Nigel Evans	*Con*	p165	Layla Moran	*Lib Dem*	p290
David Evennett	*Con*	p166	Stephen Morgan	*Lab*	p292
Tim Farron	*Lib Dem*	p168	Anne Marie Morris	*Con*	p292
Richard Fuller	*Con*	p177	Ian Murray	*Lab*	p296
Marcus Fysh	*Con*	p178	Caroline Nokes	*Con*	p301
Barry Gardiner	*Lab*	p179	Chi Onwurah	*Lab*	p305
Nusrat Ghani	*Con*	p181	Stephanie Peacock	*Lab*	p312
Nick Gibb	*Con*	p181	John Penrose	*Con*	p313
Jo Gideon	*Con*	p183	Andrew Percy	*Con*	p314
Michelle Gildernew	*Sinn Féin*	p183	Christopher Pincher	*Con*	p316
Cheryl Gillan	*Con*	p184	Luke Pollard	*Lab/Co-op*	p317
John Glen	*Con*	p185	Lucy Powell	*Lab/Co-op*	p319
Michael Gove	*Con*	p187	Victoria Prentis	*Con*	p319
Chris Green	*Con*	p192	Yasmin Qureshi	*Lab*	p322
Damian Green	*Con*	p192	Ellie Reeves	*Lab*	p326
Jonathan Gullis	*Con*	p196	Rachel Reeves	*Lab*	p326
Andrew Gwynne	*Lab*	p197	Bell Ribeiro-Addy	*Lab*	p328
Louise Haigh	*Lab*	p197	Matt Rodda	*Lab*	p331
Robert Halfon	*Con*	p198	Paul Scully	*Con*	p336
Fabian Hamilton	*Lab*	p199	Bob Seely	*Con*	p336
Emma Hardy	*Lab*	p202	Grant Shapps	*Con*	p338
Mark Harper	*Con*	p203	Barry Sheerman	*Lab/Co-op*	p340
Rebecca Harris	*Con*	p204	David Simmonds	*Con*	p342
John Hayes	*Con*	p207	Chris Skidmore	*Con*	p342
Chris Heaton-Harris	*Con*	p210	Andy Slaughter	*Lab*	p343
Damian Hinds	*Con*	p213	Julian Smith	*Con*	p346
Simon Hoare	*Con*	p214	Mark Spencer	*Con*	p350
Margaret Hodge	*Lab*	p215	Iain Stewart	*Con*	p355

Mel Stride	*Con*	p357
Graham Stuart	*Con*	p358
Derek Thomas	*Con*	p363
Edward Timpson	*Con*	p368
Anne-Marie Trevelyan	*Con*	p370
Elizabeth Truss	*Con*	p372
Derek Twigg	*Lab*	p373
Robin Walker	*Con*	p378
David Warburton	*Con*	p379
Catherine West	*Lab*	p381
Matt Western	*Lab*	p382
Alan Whitehead	*Lab*	p383
Craig Whittaker	*Con*	p385
Gavin Williamson	*Con*	p389
Munira Wilson	*Lib Dem*	p389
Sammy Wilson	*DUP*	p390
Jeremy Wright	*Con*	p393

Education and skills

Diane Abbott	*Lab*	p64
Vicky Ford	*Con*	p172
Andrew Gwynne	*Lab*	p197
Rebecca Harris	*Con*	p204
Dan Jarvis	*Lab*	p227

Electoral reform

Chris Clarkson	*Con*	p122
Stephen Kinnock	*Lab*	p243

Electoral services

Chloe Smith	*Con*	p344

Electricity

Carolyn Harris	*Lab*	p204

Employment

Debbie Abrahams	*Lab*	p64
Imran Ahmad Khan	*Con*	p66
Paula Barker	*Lab*	p80
Hilary Benn	*Lab*	p83
Saqib Bhatti	*Con*	p86
Deidre Brock	*SNP*	p99
Gregory Campbell	*DUP*	p111
John Cryer	*Lab*	p133
Ed Davey	*Lib Dem*	p135
Marsha De Cordova	*Lab*	p142
Maria Eagle	*Lab*	p157
Julie Elliott	*Lab*	p160
Natalie Elphicke	*Con*	p162
Mark Fletcher	*Con*	p171
Cheryl Gillan	*Con*	p184
Mary Glindon	*Lab*	p186
Damian Green	*Con*	p192
Kate Green	*Lab*	p193
John Healey	*Lab*	p209
Margaret Hodge	*Lab*	p215
Sharon Hodgson	*Lab*	p216
Gerald Jones	*Lab*	p236
Kevan Jones	*Lab*	p237
Liz Kendall	*Lab*	p242
Ian Lavery	*Lab*	p250
Alison McGovern	*Lab*	p268
Julie Marson	*Con*	p278
Nigel Mills	*Con*	p286
Bridget Phillipson	*Lab*	p315
Chloe Smith	*Con*	p344
Mark Spencer	*Con*	p350
Andrew Stephenson	*Con*	p352
Nick Thomas-Symonds	*Lab*	p364
Stephen Timms	*Lab*	p367
Karl Turner	*Lab*	p373
Christian Wakeford	*Con*	p377
Charles Walker	*Con*	p377
Rosie Winterton	*Lab*	p391

Employment and welfare

Gerald Jones	*Lab*	p236
Rachael Maskell	*Lab/Co-op*	p279
Chloe Smith	*Con*	p344

Employment Law

Richard Burgon	*Lab*	p105
Yvonne Fovargue	*Lab*	p173

Employment rights

Dawn Butler	*Lab*	p106
Lilian Greenwood	*Lab*	p194
Diana Johnson	*Lab*	p232
Stephen Kinnock	*Lab*	p243
Charlotte Nichols	*Lab*	p300
Jo Stevens	*Lab*	p353
Nadia Whittome	*Lab*	p386

Energy

Nigel Adams	*Con*	p65
Crispin Blunt	*Con*	p90
Alan Brown	*SNP*	p100
Alistair Carmichael	*Lib Dem*	p112
Greg Clark	*Con*	p120
Simon Clarke	*Con*	p120
Therese Coffey	*Con*	p123
Stephen Crabb	*Con*	p130
John Cryer	*Lab*	p133
Alex Cunningham	*Lab*	p134
Clive Efford	*Lab*	p159
Nia Griffith	*Lab*	p195
John Hayes	*Con*	p207
James Heappey	*Con*	p209
Chris Heaton-Harris	*Con*	p210
Ian Lavery	*Lab*	p250
Andrea Leadsom	*Con*	p251
Ian Liddell-Grainger	*Con*	p255
Craig Mackinlay	*Con*	p269
Anna McMorrin	*Lab*	p272
Mark Menzies	*Con*	p282
Christopher Pincher	*Con*	p316
Dan Poulter	*Con*	p318
Tom Pursglove	*Con*	p320

Deidre Brock *SNP* p99
Dawn Butler *Lab* p106
Lisa Cameron *SNP* p110
Rosie Cooper *Lab* p125
Yvette Cooper *Lab* p126
Ronnie Cowan *SNP* p129
Angela Crawley *SNP* p130
Geraint Davies *Lab/Co-op* p138
James Davies *Con* p138
Mims Davies *Con* p139
Caroline Dinenage *Con* p143
Stephen Doughty *Lab/Co-op* p150
Rosie Duffield *Lab* p154
Laura Farris *Con* p168
Margaret Ferrier *Ind* p170
Gill Furniss *Lab* p178
Nusrat Ghani *Con* p181
Peter Gibson *Con* p182
Helen Grant *Con* p189
Nia Griffith *Lab* p195
Harriet Harman *Lab* p203
Sharon Hodgson *Lab* p216
David Linden *SNP* p255
Caroline Lucas *Green* p261
Stewart Malcolm McDonald *SNP* p266
Seema Malhotra *Lab/Co-op* p276
Johnny Mercer *Con* p283
Maria Miller *Con* p285
Navendu Mishra *Lab* p287
David Mundell *Con* p296
Ian Murray *Lab* p296
Kirsten Oswald *SNP* p308
Victoria Prentis *Con* p319
Emily Thornberry *Lab* p366
Pete Wishart *SNP* p391

Equal pay

David Linden *SNP* p255
Guy Opperman *Con* p306

European affairs

Richard Bacon *Con* p76
Simon Baynes *Con* p81
Graham Brady *Con* p94
Chris Bryant *Lab* p103
Wayne David *Lab* p136
Philip Davies *Con* p139
George Eustice *Con* p163
Nigel Evans *Con* p165
Mark Hendrick *Lab/Co-op* p211
Julian Lewis *Con* p254
Ian Paisley *DUP* p309
Priti Patel *Con* p310
John Redwood *Con* p324
Matt Rodda *Lab* p331
Andrew Rosindell *Con* p331

European Union

Hilary Benn *Lab* p83
Olivia Blake *Lab* p89
Bill Cash *Con* p113
John Cryer *Lab* p133
Thangam Debbonaire *Lab* p142
David Duguid *Con* p154
Natalie Elphicke *Con* p162
Stephen Flynn *SNP* p172
Mark Garnier *Con* p180
Nia Griffith *Lab* p195
Claire Hanna *SDLP* p202
Chris Heaton-Harris *Con* p210
Bernard Jenkin *Con* p229
Stephen Kinnock *Lab* p243
Craig Mackinlay *Con* p269
Wendy Morton *Con* p295
Tom Pursglove *Con* p320
Alyn Smith *SNP* p343
Jamie Wallis *Con* p379

Exports

Michael Fabricant *Con* p167

Family

Lucy Allan *Con* p69
Fiona Bruce *Con* p102
Edward Leigh *Con* p251
Andrew Selous *Con* p337
Gary Streeter *Con* p356
Edward Timpson *Con* p368

Farming

Maria Caulfield *Con* p114
Stephen Crabb *Con* p130
George Eustice *Con* p163
Nusrat Ghani *Con* p181
Andrew Griffith *Con* p194
Simon Hoare *Con* p214
John Lamont *Con* p248
Ian Liddell-Grainger *Con* p255
Mark Menzies *Con* p282
Jim Shannon *DUP* p338

Finance

Gareth Bacon *Con* p75
Harriett Baldwin *Con* p79
John Cryer *Lab* p133
Iain Duncan Smith *Con* p155
Chris Evans *Lab/Co-op* p164
Stephen Farry *APNI* p169
Greg Hands *Con* p201
Kwasi Kwarteng *Con* p245
Robert Largan *Con* p249
Tim Loughton *Con* p260
Jim McMahon *Lab/Co-op* p271
Lee Rowley *Con* p332
Alok Sharma *Con* p339

Analysis of MPs
House of Commons

Carolyn Harris	*Lab*	p204
David Lammy	*Lab*	p247
David Linden	*SNP*	p255

Government

Andrew Griffith	*Con*	p194

Green belts

Gareth Bacon	*Con*	p75
Paula Barker	*Lab*	p80
Saqib Bhatti	*Con*	p86
Sarah Dines	*Con*	p144
Mark Eastwood	*Con*	p158
Ben Everitt	*Con*	p166
James Grundy	*Con*	p196
Gavin Williamson	*Con*	p389

Greenbelt development

Wendy Morton	*Con*	p295

Health

Debbie Abrahams	*Lab*	p64
David Amess	*Con*	p70
Stuart Andrew	*Con*	p72
Edward Argar	*Con*	p73
Jon Ashworth	*Lab/Co-op*	p74
Richard Bacon	*Con*	p76
Steve Baker	*Con*	p78
Paul Beresford	*Con*	p85
Graham Brady	*Con*	p94
Paul Bristow	*Con*	p98
James Brokenshire	*Con*	p99
Karen Buck	*Lab*	p104
Sarah Champion	*Lab*	p116
Jo Churchill	*Con*	p119
Greg Clark	*Con*	p120
Rosie Cooper	*Lab*	p125
Tracey Crouch	*Con*	p132
John Cryer	*Lab*	p133
Alex Cunningham	*Lab*	p134
James Davies	*Con*	p138
David Davis	*Con*	p140
Anneliese Dodds	*Lab/Co-op*	p146
Nadine Dorries	*Con*	p149
Peter Dowd	*Lab*	p150
Oliver Dowden	*Con*	p151
Rosie Duffield	*Lab*	p154
Philip Dunne	*Con*	p156
Clive Efford	*Lab*	p159
Julie Elliott	*Lab*	p160
Tim Farron	*Lib Dem*	p168
Yvonne Fovargue	*Lab*	p173
Liam Fox	*Con*	p174
George Freeman	*Con*	p176
Gill Furniss	*Lab*	p178
Marcus Fysh	*Con*	p178
Jo Gideon	*Con*	p183
John Glen	*Con*	p185
Mary Glindon	*Lab*	p186
Chris Green	*Con*	p192
Jonathan Gullis	*Con*	p196
Mark Harper	*Con*	p203
Chris Heaton-Harris	*Con*	p210
Sharon Hodgson	*Lab*	p216
Neil Hudson	*Con*	p223
Caroline Johnson	*Con*	p232
Diana Johnson	*Lab*	p232
Barbara Keeley	*Lab*	p241
Ben Lake	*PlC*	p247
David Lammy	*Lab*	p247
Pauline Latham	*Con*	p249
Emma Lewell-Buck	*Lab*	p252
Ian Liddell-Grainger	*Con*	p255
Jonathan Lord	*Con*	p259
Tim Loughton	*Con*	p260
Siobhain McDonagh	*Lab*	p265
Rachel Maclean	*Con*	p271
Stephen McPartland	*Con*	p273
Julie Marson	*Con*	p278
Rachael Maskell	*Lab/Co-op*	p279
Ian Mearns	*Lab*	p282
Huw Merriman	*Con*	p283
Navendu Mishra	*Lab*	p287
Andrew Mitchell	*Con*	p287
Stephen Morgan	*Lab*	p292
Anne Marie Morris	*Con*	p292
Grahame Morris	*Lab*	p293
Andrew Murrison	*Con*	p298
Guy Opperman	*Con*	p306
Mike Penning	*Con*	p312
Luke Pollard	*Lab/Co-op*	p317
Dan Poulter	*Con*	p318
Lucy Powell	*Lab/Co-op*	p319
Will Quince	*Con*	p321
Gavin Robinson	*DUP*	p330
Selaine Saxby	*Con*	p335
Grant Shapps	*Con*	p338
Virendra Sharma	*Lab*	p339
Chris Skidmore	*Con*	p342
Andy Slaughter	*Lab*	p343
Nick Smith	*Lab*	p347
Karin Smyth	*Lab*	p348
Mark Spencer	*Con*	p350
Andrew Stephenson	*Con*	p352
Derek Thomas	*Con*	p363
Gareth Thomas	*Lab/Co-op*	p364
Nick Thomas-Symonds	*Lab*	p364
Maggie Throup	*Con*	p366
Anne-Marie Trevelyan	*Con*	p370
Derek Twigg	*Lab*	p373
Valerie Vaz	*Lab*	p375
Robin Walker	*Con*	p378
Ben Wallace	*Con*	p378
Catherine West	*Lab*	p381
Philippa Whitford	*SNP*	p384

Heritage

Simon Baynes	*Con*	p81
Bill Cash	*Con*	p113
Michael Ellis	*Con*	p160
David Evennett	*Con*	p166
Michael Fabricant	*Con*	p167
Peter Gibson	*Con*	p182
Dan Jarvis	*Lab*	p227
Layla Moran	*Lib Dem*	p290
Matt Rodda	*Lab*	p331

Home affairs

Victoria Atkins	*Con*	p75
Hilary Benn	*Lab*	p83
Karen Bradley	*Con*	p93
Stephen Doughty	*Lab/Co-op*	p150
Michael Ellis	*Con*	p160
Laura Farris	*Con*	p168
Simon Fell	*Con*	p169
Chris Grayling	*Con*	p191
Gareth Johnson	*Con*	p233
Greg Knight	*Con*	p243
Tim Loughton	*Con*	p260
Conor McGinn	*Lab*	p268
Mike Penning	*Con*	p312
Christopher Pincher	*Con*	p316
Tom Pursglove	*Con*	p320
Will Quince	*Con*	p321
David Rutley	*Con*	p334
Grant Shapps	*Con*	p338
Andrew Stephenson	*Con*	p352
Nick Thomas-Symonds	*Lab*	p364
Karl Turner	*Lab*	p373
Ben Wallace	*Con*	p378
Rosie Winterton	*Lab*	p391

Homelessness

Nickie Aiken	*Con*	p67
Sarah Atherton	*Con*	p74
Maria Caulfield	*Con*	p114
Emma Lewell-Buck	*Lab*	p252
Anne McLaughlin	*SNP*	p270
Layla Moran	*Lib Dem*	p290
Andrew Selous	*Con*	p337

Hospices

Peter Gibson	*Con*	p182
Fabian Hamilton	*Lab*	p199

Hospitals

Elliot Colburn	*Con*	p124
Catherine West	*Lab*	p381

Housing

Rushanara Ali	*Lab*	p68
Fleur Anderson	*Lab*	p71
Richard Bacon	*Con*	p76
Kemi Badenoch	*Con*	p76
Simon Baynes	*Con*	p81
Paul Beresford	*Con*	p85
Clive Betts	*Lab*	p86
Bob Blackman	*Con*	p88
Paul Blomfield	*Lab*	p89
James Brokenshire	*Con*	p99
Lyn Brown	*Lab*	p100
Karen Buck	*Lab*	p104
Richard Burgon	*Lab*	p105
James Cartlidge	*Con*	p113
Maria Caulfield	*Con*	p114
Greg Clark	*Con*	p120
Rosie Cooper	*Lab*	p125
Jon Cruddas	*Lab*	p132
Geraint Davies	*Lab/Co-op*	p138
Thangam Debbonaire	*Lab*	p142
Jack Dromey	*Lab*	p152
Maria Eagle	*Lab*	p157
Mark Eastwood	*Con*	p158
Clive Efford	*Lab*	p159
Natalie Elphicke	*Con*	p162
Mark Fletcher	*Con*	p171
Vicky Foxcroft	*Lab*	p174
Mark Francois	*Con*	p175
Marcus Fysh	*Con*	p178
Michelle Gildernew	*Sinn Féin*	p183
Mary Glindon	*Lab*	p186
Jonathan Gullis	*Con*	p196
Robert Halfon	*Con*	p198
Greg Hands	*Con*	p201
Helen Hayes	*Lab*	p206
Simon Hoare	*Con*	p214
Margaret Hodge	*Lab*	p215
Kevin Hollinrake	*Con*	p217
George Howarth	*Lab*	p220
David Linden	*SNP*	p255
Tim Loughton	*Con*	p260
Siobhain McDonagh	*Lab*	p265
Julie Marson	*Con*	p278
Rachael Maskell	*Lab/Co-op*	p279
Maria Miller	*Con*	p285
Navendu Mishra	*Lab*	p287
Francie Molloy	*Sinn Féin*	p288
Grahame Morris	*Lab*	p293
James Murray	*Lab/Co-op*	p297
Taiwo Owatemi	*Lab*	p308
Chris Philp	*Con*	p316
Luke Pollard	*Lab/Co-op*	p317
Tom Pursglove	*Con*	p320
Ellie Reeves	*Lab*	p326
Matt Rodda	*Lab*	p331
Lee Rowley	*Con*	p332
Bob Seely	*Con*	p336
Andy Slaughter	*Lab*	p343
Emily Thornberry	*Lab*	p366
Justin Tomlinson	*Con*	p369
Catherine West	*Lab*	p381
Matt Western	*Lab*	p382

Helen Whately	*Con*	p382
Rosie Winterton	*Lab*	p391

Human rights

Steve Baker	*Con*	p78
John Baron	*Con*	p81
Andrew Bridgen	*Con*	p97
Fiona Bruce	*Con*	p102
Alistair Carmichael	*Lib Dem*	p112
Jeremy Corbyn	*Ind*	p127
Geraint Davies	*Lab/Co-op*	p138
Marsha De Cordova	*Lab*	p142
Margaret Ferrier	*Ind*	p170
Harriet Harman	*Lab*	p203
Helen Hayes	*Lab*	p206
Sajid Javid	*Con*	p228
Clive Lewis	*Lab*	p254
Caroline Lucas	*Green*	p261
Anthony Mangnall	*Con*	p278
Layla Moran	*Lib Dem*	p290
Jesse Norman	*Con*	p302
Victoria Prentis	*Con*	p319
Dominic Raab	*Con*	p322
Paul Scully	*Con*	p336
Virendra Sharma	*Lab*	p339
Catherine West	*Lab*	p381

Immigration and nationality

Oliver Dowden	*Con*	p151
Priti Patel	*Con*	p310
Bell Ribeiro-Addy	*Lab*	p328
David Simmonds	*Con*	p342
Nadia Whittome	*Lab*	p386

Information and communication technology

Greg Knight	*Con*	p243

Infrastructure

Peter Aldous	*Con*	p67
Alan Brown	*SNP*	p100
Lisa Cameron	*SNP*	p110
David Duguid	*Con*	p154
Marcus Fysh	*Con*	p178
Chris Green	*Con*	p192
Ranil Jayawardena	*Con*	p228
Mark Menzies	*Con*	p282
Maria Miller	*Con*	p285
Bridget Phillipson	*Lab*	p315

Intellectual property

David Lammy	*Lab*	p247

Intelligence Services

Ben Wallace	*Con*	p378

International affairs

Hilary Benn	*Lab*	p83
Andrew Bowie	*Con*	p92
Theo Clarke	*Con*	p121
Daisy Cooper	*Lib Dem*	p125
Jeremy Corbyn	*Ind*	p127
Wayne David	*Lab*	p136
Dave Doogan	*SNP*	p148
Philip Dunne	*Con*	p156
Cheryl Gillan	*Con*	p184
Patrick Grady	*SNP*	p188
Fabian Hamilton	*Lab*	p199
Stephen Hammond	*Con*	p200
Dan Jarvis	*Lab*	p227
Alicia Kearns	*Con*	p240
Afzal Khan	*Lab*	p242
Jack Lopresti	*Con*	p259
Kerry McCarthy	*Lab*	p263
Andrew Mitchell	*Con*	p287
Andrew Rosindell	*Con*	p331
Grant Shapps	*Con*	p338
Alec Shelbrooke	*Con*	p340
Andy Slaughter	*Lab*	p343
Robin Walker	*Con*	p378
John Whittingdale	*Con*	p385

International development and aid

Fleur Anderson	*Lab*	p71
Jon Ashworth	*Lab/Co-op*	p74
Kemi Badenoch	*Con*	p76
Hilary Benn	*Lab*	p83
Fiona Bruce	*Con*	p102
Theo Clarke	*Con*	p121
Stephen Crabb	*Con*	p130
Jeffrey Donaldson	*DUP*	p147
Stephen Doughty	*Lab/Co-op*	p150
Jack Dromey	*Lab*	p152
Michael Fabricant	*Con*	p167
Richard Fuller	*Con*	p177
Patrick Grady	*SNP*	p188
Helen Grant	*Con*	p189
Fabian Hamilton	*Lab*	p199
Helen Hayes	*Lab*	p206
Mark Hendrick	*Lab/Co-op*	p211
Jeremy Hunt	*Con*	p224
Dan Jarvis	*Lab*	p227
David Lammy	*Lab*	p247
Pauline Latham	*Con*	p249
Holly Lynch	*Lab*	p261
Alison McGovern	*Lab*	p268
Catherine McKinnell	*Lab*	p269
Anne McLaughlin	*SNP*	p270
Anthony Mangnall	*Con*	p278
Huw Merriman	*Con*	p283
Layla Moran	*Lib Dem*	p290
Chi Onwurah	*Lab*	p305
John Penrose	*Con*	p313
Dan Poulter	*Con*	p318
Laurence Robertson	*Con*	p329
Paul Scully	*Con*	p336
Bob Seely	*Con*	p336
Virendra Sharma	*Lab*	p339

Alec Shelbrooke	*Con*	p340
Hywel Williams	*PlC*	p388
Pete Wishart	*SNP*	p391

International Development and Humanitarian Aid

Bambos Charalambous	*Lab*	p117

Internet

Ed Davey	*Lib Dem*	p135
Michael Fabricant	*Con*	p167
Andrew Griffith	*Con*	p194
Nigel Huddleston	*Con*	p222

Investment

Imran Ahmad Khan	*Con*	p66
Duncan Baker	*Con*	p78
Saqib Bhatti	*Con*	p86
Louise Haigh	*Lab*	p197

Job vacancies

Lisa Cameron	*SNP*	p110
Stewart Hosie	*SNP*	p220
Stewart Malcolm McDonald	*SNP*	p266
Toby Perkins	*Lab*	p314

Justice and Home Affairs

Bambos Charalambous	*Lab*	p117
Laura Farris	*Con*	p168
John Lamont	*Con*	p248
Will Quince	*Con*	p321

Justice system

Edward Argar	*Con*	p73
Crispin Blunt	*Con*	p90
Steve Brine	*Con*	p98
Robert Buckland	*Con*	p104
Alistair Carmichael	*Lib Dem*	p112
Sarah Champion	*Lab*	p116
Rehman Chishti	*Con*	p118
Jonathan Djanogly	*Con*	p144
Michael Ellis	*Con*	p160
Chris Evans	*Lab/Co-op*	p164
Helen Grant	*Con*	p189
Ranil Jayawardena	*Con*	p228
Catherine McKinnell	*Lab*	p269
Seema Malhotra	*Lab/Co-op*	p276
Robert Neill	*Con*	p299
Ian Paisley	*DUP*	p309
Victoria Prentis	*Con*	p319
Will Quince	*Con*	p321
Ellie Reeves	*Lab*	p326
Jo Stevens	*Lab*	p353
Graham Stringer	*Lab*	p358
Karl Turner	*Lab*	p373
Pete Wishart	*SNP*	p391
Jeremy Wright	*Con*	p393

Law

Oliver Dowden	*Con*	p151
Harriet Harman	*Lab*	p203

Law and order

Andrew Bridgen	*Con*	p97
James Brokenshire	*Con*	p99
Bambos Charalambous	*Lab*	p117
Rehman Chishti	*Con*	p118
Chris Clarkson	*Con*	p122
Philip Davies	*Con*	p139
David Davis	*Con*	p140
Nadine Dorries	*Con*	p149
Mark Harper	*Con*	p203
Oliver Heald	*Con*	p208
Gordon Henderson	*Con*	p210
Ranil Jayawardena	*Con*	p228
David Jones	*Con*	p235
Mark Logan	*Con*	p257
Priti Patel	*Con*	p310
Andrew Rosindell	*Con*	p331
Gary Streeter	*Con*	p356

Learning disabilities

Stuart Andrew	*Con*	p72
Alun Cairns	*Con*	p109
Helen Hayes	*Lab*	p206

Legal affairs

Geoffrey Cox	*Con*	p129
Valerie Vaz	*Lab*	p375

Legal aid

Dawn Butler	*Lab*	p106
Yvonne Fovargue	*Lab*	p173
Catherine McKinnell	*Lab*	p269
Catherine West	*Lab*	p381

Leisure centres

Roger Gale	*Con*	p179

Libraries

Lyn Brown	*Lab*	p100

Light pollution

Andrew Griffith	*Con*	p194

Local elections

Graham Stringer	*Lab*	p358

Local government

Gareth Bacon	*Con*	p75
Scott Benton	*Con*	p84
Clive Betts	*Lab*	p86
Bob Blackman	*Con*	p88
Lyn Brown	*Lab*	p100
Bambos Charalambous	*Lab*	p117
Neil Coyle	*Lab*	p129
Philip Dunne	*Con*	p156
Clive Efford	*Lab*	p159
Nigel Evans	*Con*	p165
Mark Francois	*Con*	p175
Mike Freer	*Con*	p177
Andrew Gwynne	*Lab*	p197
Greg Hands	*Con*	p201

Helen Hayes	*Lab*	p206
John Hayes	*Con*	p207
John Howell	*Con*	p221
Marcus Jones	*Con*	p237
Brandon Lewis	*Con*	p253
Jim McMahon	*Lab/Co-op*	p271
Ian Mearns	*Lab*	p282
Stephen Morgan	*Lab*	p292
Grahame Morris	*Lab*	p293
James Morris	*Con*	p294
Robert Neill	*Con*	p299
Mark Pawsey	*Con*	p311
Andrew Rosindell	*Con*	p331
Paul Scully	*Con*	p336
Henry Smith	*Con*	p345
Wes Streeting	*Lab*	p357
Alison Thewliss	*SNP*	p363
Justin Tomlinson	*Con*	p369
Martin Vickers	*Con*	p375
Catherine West	*Lab*	p381
Alan Whitehead	*Lab*	p383

Local government funding

Chris Clarkson	*Con*	p122
Mike Freer	*Con*	p177

Local government reform

Mike Freer	*Con*	p177

London economy

David Evennett	*Con*	p166
Catherine West	*Lab*	p381

Manufacturing

Sarah Champion	*Lab*	p116
Jack Dromey	*Lab*	p152
Michael Fabricant	*Con*	p167
Chris Green	*Con*	p192
Catherine McKinnell	*Lab*	p269
Chi Onwurah	*Lab*	p305
Jonathan Reynolds	*Lab/Co-op*	p327
Andrew Stephenson	*Con*	p352
Mark Tami	*Lab*	p362
Gavin Williamson	*Con*	p389

Marriage and Co-Habiting

Pauline Latham	*Con*	p249

Maternity rights

Alex Davies-Jones	*Lab*	p140
Ellie Reeves	*Lab*	p326

Maternity services

Alex Davies-Jones	*Lab*	p140
Victoria Prentis	*Con*	p319

Media

Nigel Adams	*Con*	p65
Steve Brine	*Con*	p98
Bill Cash	*Con*	p113
Damian Collins	*Con*	p124
Caroline Dinenage	*Con*	p143
Michael Fabricant	*Con*	p167
Roger Gale	*Con*	p179
Andrew Griffith	*Con*	p194
Jonathan Lord	*Con*	p259
Maria Miller	*Con*	p285
Jo Stevens	*Lab*	p353
David Warburton	*Con*	p379
John Whittingdale	*Con*	p385

Media and regulatory policy

Daisy Cooper	*Lib Dem*	p125

Mental health

Adam Afriyie	*Con*	p66
Conor Burns	*Con*	p106
Lisa Cameron	*SNP*	p110
Wendy Chamberlain	*Lib Dem*	p115
Tracey Crouch	*Con*	p132
Liam Fox	*Con*	p174
Helen Hayes	*Lab*	p206
Kevan Jones	*Lab*	p237
Barbara Keeley	*Lab*	p241
Marco Longhi	*Con*	p258
Jason McCartney	*Con*	p264
Anne McLaughlin	*SNP*	p270
Anna McMorrin	*Lab*	p272
Rachael Maskell	*Lab/Co-op*	p279
Johnny Mercer	*Con*	p283
Dan Poulter	*Con*	p318
Ellie Reeves	*Lab*	p326
Ben Spencer	*Con*	p350
Graham Stuart	*Con*	p358
Charles Walker	*Con*	p377
Catherine West	*Lab*	p381
Munira Wilson	*Lib Dem*	p389

Mental health support

Conor Burns	*Con*	p106

Motor industry

John Spellar	*Lab*	p349

Music

Greg Knight	*Con*	p243
Jane Stevenson	*Con*	p353
Valerie Vaz	*Lab*	p375

National Health Service

Fleur Anderson	*Lab*	p71
Caroline Ansell	*Con*	p73
Apsana Begum	*Lab*	p83
Aaron Bell	*Con*	p83
Steve Brine	*Con*	p98
Alan Brown	*SNP*	p100
Richard Burgon	*Lab*	p105
Lisa Cameron	*SNP*	p110
Maria Caulfield	*Con*	p114
Wendy Chamberlain	*Lib Dem*	p115
Rehman Chishti	*Con*	p118

Poverty

Lyn Brown	*Lab*	p100
Dawn Butler	*Lab*	p106
Greg Clark	*Con*	p120
Yvette Cooper	*Lab*	p126
Alex Cunningham	*Lab*	p134
Janet Daby	*Lab*	p134
Marsha De Cordova	*Lab*	p142
Martin Docherty-Hughes	*SNP*	p145
Kate Green	*Lab*	p193
Kevin Hollinrake	*Con*	p217
Afzal Khan	*Lab*	p242
Ian Lavery	*Lab*	p250
Kerry McCarthy	*Lab*	p263
Stewart Malcolm McDonald	*SNP*	p266
Stuart C McDonald	*SNP*	p266
Anna McMorrin	*Lab*	p272
Paul Maskey	*Sinn Féin*	p279
Lisa Nandy	*Lab*	p298
Emily Thornberry	*Lab*	p366
Derek Twigg	*Lab*	p373
Nadia Whittome	*Lab*	p386

Pregnancy

Hannah Bardell	*SNP*	p80
Bill Esterson	*Lab*	p163
Chris Heaton-Harris	*Con*	p210

Prison health

Fabian Hamilton	*Lab*	p199

Prison reform

Guy Opperman	*Con*	p306
Victoria Prentis	*Con*	p319

Procurement

Stephen McPartland	*Con*	p273

Public administration

John McDonnell	*Lab*	p267
Seema Malhotra	*Lab/Co-op*	p276

Public services

Adam Afriyie	*Con*	p66
Apsana Begum	*Lab*	p83
Olivia Blake	*Lab*	p89
Deidre Brock	*SNP*	p99
Marion Fellows	*SNP*	p169
Antony Higginbotham	*Con*	p212
Jesse Norman	*Con*	p302
Chloe Smith	*Con*	p344

Public transport

Anthony Browne	*Con*	p101
Elliot Colburn	*Con*	p124

Pubs and Clubs

Daisy Cooper	*Lib Dem*	p125

Racial discrimination

Jeremy Corbyn	*Ind*	p127
Anne McLaughlin	*SNP*	p270

Rail transport

Lucy Allan	*Con*	p69
Marcus Fysh	*Con*	p178
Peter Gibson	*Con*	p182
Robert Largan	*Con*	p249
Chris Philp	*Con*	p316
Munira Wilson	*Lib Dem*	p389

Recycling

Clive Efford	*Lab*	p159
Cherilyn Mackrory	*Con*	p270

Refugees and asylum seekers

Thangam Debbonaire	*Lab*	p142

Regeneration

Aaron Bell	*Con*	p83
Clive Betts	*Lab*	p86
James Brokenshire	*Con*	p99
Alan Campbell	*Lab*	p110
Damian Collins	*Con*	p124
Julie Elliott	*Lab*	p160
George Eustice	*Con*	p163
Kate Griffiths	*Con*	p196
James Grundy	*Con*	p196
Andrew Gwynne	*Lab*	p197
Simon Hoare	*Con*	p214
Gerald Jones	*Lab*	p236
Kevan Jones	*Lab*	p237
Alison McGovern	*Lab*	p268
Jim McMahon	*Lab/Co-op*	p271
Toby Perkins	*Lab*	p314
Lucy Powell	*Lab/Co-op*	p319
Jane Stevenson	*Con*	p353

Regional policy

Neil Parish	*Con*	p309
Rosie Winterton	*Lab*	p391

Renewables

Peter Aldous	*Con*	p67
Ronnie Cowan	*SNP*	p129
Andrew Jones	*Con*	p234
Stephen Kinnock	*Lab*	p243

Research and development

Thangam Debbonaire	*Lab*	p142
Vicky Ford	*Con*	p172
Stephen Metcalfe	*Con*	p284
Valerie Vaz	*Lab*	p375

Retail industry

Justin Tomlinson	*Con*	p369

Road accidents

Mims Davies	*Con*	p139

Road building

Mims Davies	*Con*	p139
Marcus Fysh	*Con*	p178

Road safety

Mims Davies	*Con*	p139

Road transport

Chris Philp	*Con*	p316

Roads and highways

Robert Largan	*Con*	p249

Royal Navy

Sheryll Murray	*Con*	p297

Rural affairs

Nigel Adams	*Con*	p65
Edward Argar	*Con*	p73
Simon Baynes	*Con*	p81
Karen Bradley	*Con*	p93
Andrew Bridgen	*Con*	p97
James Cartlidge	*Con*	p113
Maria Caulfield	*Con*	p114
Chris Clarkson	*Con*	p122
Therese Coffey	*Con*	p123
Jonathan Djanogly	*Con*	p144
Nadine Dorries	*Con*	p149
Ruth Edwards	*Con*	p159
Tim Farron	*Lib Dem*	p168
Michelle Gildernew	*Sinn Féin*	p183
Damian Green	*Con*	p192
Andrew Griffith	*Con*	p194
Simon Hart	*Con*	p206
James Heappey	*Con*	p209
John Howell	*Con*	p221
Neil Hudson	*Con*	p223
John Lamont	*Con*	p248
Ian Liddell-Grainger	*Con*	p255
Francie Molloy	*Sinn Féin*	p288
David Mundell	*Con*	p296
Brendan O'Hara	*SNP*	p304
Dan Poulter	*Con*	p318
David Rutley	*Con*	p334
Liz Saville Roberts	*PlC*	p335
Selaine Saxby	*Con*	p335
Mark Spencer	*Con*	p350
Rishi Sunak	*Con*	p360
David Warburton	*Con*	p379

Rural economy

David Duguid	*Con*	p154
George Freeman	*Con*	p176
Andrew Griffith	*Con*	p194
Ben Lake	*PlC*	p247
Graham Stuart	*Con*	p358

Rural transport

Andrew Griffith	*Con*	p194

School finance

Kieran Mullan	*Con*	p295

School meals

Sharon Hodgson	*Lab*	p216

Schools

Gavin Robinson	*DUP*	p330
Wes Streeting	*Lab*	p357

Science

Adam Afriyie	*Con*	p66
Aaron Bell	*Con*	p83
Bob Blackman	*Con*	p88
Thangam Debbonaire	*Lab*	p142
Michael Fabricant	*Con*	p167
Chris Green	*Con*	p192
Andrew Griffith	*Con*	p194
Neil Hudson	*Con*	p223
Stephen Metcalfe	*Con*	p284
Graham Stringer	*Lab*	p358
Valerie Vaz	*Lab*	p375

Science, technology and research

Katherine Fletcher	*Con*	p171
Stephen Metcalfe	*Con*	p284
Valerie Vaz	*Lab*	p375

Scotland

Andrew Bowie	*Con*	p92
David Duguid	*Con*	p154
David Mundell	*Con*	p296

Scotland economy

David Duguid	*Con*	p154

Scottish Government

Gavin Newlands	*SNP*	p300

Scottish independence

Mhairi Black	*SNP*	p87
Ronnie Cowan	*SNP*	p129
Martin Docherty-Hughes	*SNP*	p145
Dave Doogan	*SNP*	p148
Allan Dorans	*SNP*	p148
Marion Fellows	*SNP*	p169
Stephen Flynn	*SNP*	p172
Patricia Gibson	*SNP*	p182
Drew Hendry	*SNP*	p211
Anne McLaughlin	*SNP*	p270
Gavin Newlands	*SNP*	p300
Owen Thompson	*SNP*	p365

Security

Michael Fabricant	*Con*	p167
Nusrat Ghani	*Con*	p181
Dan Jarvis	*Lab*	p227
Julian Lewis	*Con*	p254
Jack Lopresti	*Con*	p259
Steve McCabe	*Lab*	p262
Ben Wallace	*Con*	p378
John Whittingdale	*Con*	p385

Sentencing

Guy Opperman	*Con*	p306

Skills

Diane Abbott	*Lab*	p64
Nigel Adams	*Con*	p65
Paul Blomfield	*Lab*	p89
Caroline Dinenage	*Con*	p143
Julie Elliott	*Lab*	p160
Jo Gideon	*Con*	p183
Andrew Gwynne	*Lab*	p197
Rebecca Harris	*Con*	p204
James Heappey	*Con*	p209
Marcus Jones	*Con*	p237
Bridget Phillipson	*Lab*	p315
Lucy Powell	*Lab/Co-op*	p319
Chloe Smith	*Con*	p344
Julian Smith	*Con*	p346

Small businesses

Diane Abbott	*Lab*	p64
Simon Baynes	*Con*	p81
Paul Blomfield	*Lab*	p89
Fiona Bruce	*Con*	p102
Bill Cash	*Con*	p113
Jonathan Djanogly	*Con*	p144
Iain Duncan Smith	*Con*	p155
Philip Dunne	*Con*	p156
Mark Eastwood	*Con*	p158
Nigel Evans	*Con*	p165
Katherine Fletcher	*Con*	p171
Richard Fuller	*Con*	p177
Fabian Hamilton	*Lab*	p199
Rebecca Harris	*Con*	p204
Simon Hart	*Con*	p206
Lindsay Hoyle	*Speaker*	p222
Karl McCartney	*Con*	p264
Rachel Maclean	*Con*	p271
Stephen Metcalfe	*Con*	p284
Anne Marie Morris	*Con*	p292
David Morris	*Con*	p293
Toby Perkins	*Lab*	p314
Paul Scully	*Con*	p336
Amanda Solloway	*Con*	p349
Andrew Stephenson	*Con*	p352
Maggie Throup	*Con*	p366

Social affairs

Liam Byrne	*Lab*	p108
Iain Duncan Smith	*Con*	p155
Paul Maynard	*Con*	p281
Huw Merriman	*Con*	p283
Gary Streeter	*Con*	p356
Sammy Wilson	*DUP*	p390

Social inclusion

Nadine Dorries	*Con*	p149
Damian Hinds	*Con*	p213
David Johnston	*Con*	p234
Chi Onwurah	*Lab*	p305

Social justice

Mhairi Black	*SNP*	p87
Suella Braverman	*Con*	p95
Angela Crawley	*SNP*	p130
Jonathan Edwards	*Ind*	p158
Ruth Jones	*Lab*	p238
Clive Lewis	*Lab*	p254
Caroline Lucas	*Green*	p261
Alan Mak	*Con*	p276
Ian Murray	*Lab*	p296
Owen Paterson	*Con*	p311
Liz Saville Roberts	*PlC*	p335
Wes Streeting	*Lab*	p357
Mel Stride	*Con*	p357

Social workers

Neil Coyle	*Lab*	p129
Tracey Crouch	*Con*	p132
Alex Cunningham	*Lab*	p134
Rosie Duffield	*Lab*	p154
Anne Marie Morris	*Con*	p292
Hywel Williams	*PlC*	p388

Socialism

Jeremy Corbyn	*Ind*	p127

Special schools

Stuart Andrew	*Con*	p72
Alun Cairns	*Con*	p109

Sport

Nigel Adams	*Con*	p65
Bob Blackman	*Con*	p88
Ben Bradley	*Con*	p93
Damian Collins	*Con*	p124
Tracey Crouch	*Con*	p132
Mims Davies	*Con*	p139
Angela Eagle	*Lab*	p156
Helen Grant	*Con*	p189
Chris Heaton-Harris	*Con*	p210
Sharon Hodgson	*Lab*	p216
Lindsay Hoyle	*Speaker*	p222
Dan Jarvis	*Lab*	p227
Barbara Keeley	*Lab*	p241
David Lammy	*Lab*	p247
Ian Lavery	*Lab*	p250
Jonathan Lord	*Con*	p259
Jason McCartney	*Con*	p264
Karl McCartney	*Con*	p264
Rachael Maskell	*Lab/Co-op*	p279
Caroline Nokes	*Con*	p301
Toby Perkins	*Lab*	p314
Tom Pursglove	*Con*	p320
Jo Stevens	*Lab*	p353
Justin Tomlinson	*Con*	p369
Jon Trickett	*Lab*	p371
Ben Wallace	*Con*	p378

Jack Dromey	*Lab*	p152
Robert Halfon	*Con*	p198
John Healey	*Lab*	p209

Transport

David Amess	*Con*	p70
Stuart Andrew	*Con*	p72
Caroline Ansell	*Con*	p73
Gareth Bacon	*Con*	p75
Kemi Badenoch	*Con*	p76
Clive Betts	*Lab*	p86
Ian Blackford	*SNP*	p87
Ben Bradshaw	*Lab*	p94
Andrew Bridgen	*Con*	p97
Alistair Carmichael	*Lib Dem*	p112
Greg Clark	*Con*	p120
Simon Clarke	*Con*	p120
Rosie Cooper	*Lab*	p125
Jeremy Corbyn	*Ind*	p127
John Cryer	*Lab*	p133
Geraint Davies	*Lab/Co-op*	p138
James Davies	*Con*	p138
Jonathan Djanogly	*Con*	p144
Jeffrey Donaldson	*DUP*	p147
Steve Double	*Con*	p149
Jackie Doyle-Price	*Con*	p151
Jack Dromey	*Lab*	p152
Iain Duncan Smith	*Con*	p155
Maria Eagle	*Lab*	p157
Clive Efford	*Lab*	p159
David Evennett	*Con*	p166
Stephen Farry	*APNI*	p169
Jo Gideon	*Con*	p183
Robert Goodwill	*Con*	p186
Patrick Grady	*SNP*	p188
Chris Grayling	*Con*	p191
Chris Green	*Con*	p192
Lilian Greenwood	*Lab*	p194
Andrew Gwynne	*Lab*	p197
Fabian Hamilton	*Lab*	p199
Stephen Hammond	*Con*	p200
Dan Jarvis	*Lab*	p227
Andrew Jones	*Con*	p234
Kevan Jones	*Lab*	p237
Kwasi Kwarteng	*Con*	p245
Eleanor Laing	*Con*	p246
Brandon Lewis	*Con*	p253
Steve McCabe	*Lab*	p262
Jason McCartney	*Con*	p264
Karl McCartney	*Con*	p264
Esther McVey	*Con*	p274
Anthony Mangnall	*Con*	p278
Ian Mearns	*Lab*	p282
Mark Menzies	*Con*	p282
Johnny Mercer	*Con*	p283
Huw Merriman	*Con*	p283
Layla Moran	*Lib Dem*	p290
Brendan O'Hara	*SNP*	p304
Sarah Olney	*Lib Dem*	p305
Luke Pollard	*Lab/Co-op*	p317
Victoria Prentis	*Con*	p319
Will Quince	*Con*	p321
John Redwood	*Con*	p324
Jonathan Reynolds	*Lab/Co-op*	p327
Lee Rowley	*Con*	p332
Selaine Saxby	*Con*	p335
Alec Shelbrooke	*Con*	p340
Andy Slaughter	*Lab*	p343
Chloe Smith	*Con*	p344
Iain Stewart	*Con*	p355
Richard Thomson	*SNP*	p365
Martin Vickers	*Con*	p375
Theresa Villiers	*Con*	p376
Matt Western	*Lab*	p382
Alan Whitehead	*Lab*	p383
Rosie Winterton	*Lab*	p391

Unemployment and jobseeking

Dawn Butler	*Lab*	p106
Yvette Cooper	*Lab*	p126
Stuart C McDonald	*SNP*	p266

Urban renewal

Peter Aldous	*Con*	p67
Stephen McPartland	*Con*	p273
Graham Stringer	*Lab*	p358

Utility bills

Chris Clarkson	*Con*	p122

Veterans

Sarah Atherton	*Con*	p74
Johnny Mercer	*Con*	p283
Bob Stewart	*Con*	p354

Wales economy

Liz Saville Roberts	*PlC*	p335

Waste collection

Amanda Solloway	*Con*	p349

Waste management

Clive Efford	*Lab*	p159

Water

Alex Davies-Jones	*Lab*	p140

Welfare

Debbie Abrahams	*Lab*	p64
Edward Argar	*Con*	p73
Harriett Baldwin	*Con*	p79
Bob Blackman	*Con*	p88
Kirsty Blackman	*SNP*	p88
Karen Buck	*Lab*	p104
Liam Byrne	*Lab*	p108
James Cartlidge	*Con*	p113
Sarah Champion	*Lab*	p116
Greg Clark	*Con*	p120
Rosie Cooper	*Lab*	p125

Jeremy Corbyn	*Ind*	p127
Neil Coyle	*Lab*	p129
Stephen Crabb	*Con*	p130
Marsha De Cordova	*Lab*	p142
Oliver Dowden	*Con*	p151
Jackie Doyle-Price	*Con*	p151
Clive Efford	*Lab*	p159
Chris Evans	*Lab/Co-op*	p164
Peter Grant	*SNP*	p190
Chris Grayling	*Con*	p191
Chris Green	*Con*	p192
Damian Hinds	*Con*	p213
Sajid Javid	*Con*	p228
Gerald Jones	*Lab*	p236
Chris Law	*SNP*	p250
Emma Lewell-Buck	*Lab*	p252
Siobhain McDonagh	*Lab*	p265
Anne McLaughlin	*SNP*	p270
Gavin Newlands	*SNP*	p300
Jeremy Quin	*Con*	p321
Alec Shelbrooke	*Con*	p340
Chloe Smith	*Con*	p344
Julian Smith	*Con*	p346
Karin Smyth	*Lab*	p348
Mel Stride	*Con*	p357
Graham Stuart	*Con*	p358
Karl Turner	*Lab*	p373

Welsh Government

James Davies	*Con*	p138

Youth justice

Vicky Foxcroft	*Lab*	p174
Seema Malhotra	*Lab/Co-op*	p276

Youth services

Simon Baynes	*Con*	p81
Liam Byrne	*Lab*	p108
Janet Daby	*Lab*	p134
John Glen	*Con*	p185
Patrick Grady	*SNP*	p188

Youth training schemes

Guy Opperman	*Con*	p306

MPs' Countries of Interest

For precise details of individuals' stated interests, see relevant biography. The interests listed are supplied by MPs themselves.

Afghanistan

Stephen Doughty	*Lab/Co-op*	p150
Tobias Ellwood	*Con*	p161
James Gray	*Con*	p190
Dan Jarvis	*Lab*	p227
Bernard Jenkin	*Con*	p229
Kevan Jones	*Lab*	p237
Jack Lopresti	*Con*	p259

Algeria

Catherine West	*Lab*	p381

Angola

Nadine Dorries	*Con*	p149
David Duguid	*Con*	p154

Antarctica

James Gray	*Con*	p190

Argentina

Stephen Doughty	*Lab/Co-op*	p150
Chris Matheson	*Lab*	p280
Mark Menzies	*Con*	p282

Armenia

John Whittingdale	*Con*	p385

Australia

Jon Ashworth	*Lab/Co-op*	p74
Paul Beresford	*Con*	p85
Nick Brown	*Lab*	p101
John Cryer	*Lab*	p133
Maria Eagle	*Lab*	p157
Nigel Evans	*Con*	p165
David Evennett	*Con*	p166
Michael Fabricant	*Con*	p167
Peter Gibson	*Con*	p182
John Healey	*Lab*	p209
Darren Jones	*Lab*	p235
Eleanor Laing	*Con*	p246
Conor McGinn	*Lab*	p268
Paul Maynard	*Con*	p281
Mark Menzies	*Con*	p282
Tom Pursglove	*Con*	p320
Andrew Rosindell	*Con*	p331
Lee Rowley	*Con*	p332
Andrew Selous	*Con*	p337
John Spellar	*Lab*	p349
Wes Streeting	*Lab*	p357
Catherine West	*Lab*	p381
Craig Whittaker	*Con*	p385

Azerbaijan

Bob Blackman	*Con*	p88
David Duguid	*Con*	p154
Christopher Pincher	*Con*	p316
Martin Vickers	*Con*	p375

Bahamas

David Morris	*Con*	p293

Bahrain

Nigel Evans	*Con*	p165
Andy Slaughter	*Lab*	p343

Bangladesh

Debbie Abrahams	*Lab*	p64
Jon Ashworth	*Lab/Co-op*	p74
Bob Blackman	*Con*	p88
Lyn Brown	*Lab*	p100
Stephen Doughty	*Lab/Co-op*	p150
Richard Fuller	*Con*	p177
Paul Scully	*Con*	p336
Virendra Sharma	*Lab*	p339
Andrew Stephenson	*Con*	p352
Catherine West	*Lab*	p381

Belarus

Robert Goodwill	*Con*	p186
Maria Miller	*Con*	p285

Belgium

Wayne David	*Lab*	p136
Damien Moore	*Con*	p289

Bosnia/Herzegovina

Clive Betts	*Lab*	p86
Jackie Doyle-Price	*Con*	p151
Alicia Kearns	*Con*	p240
Paul Maynard	*Con*	p281
Andrew Stephenson	*Con*	p352

Botswana

James Duddridge	*Con*	p153

Brazil

Bob Blackman	*Con*	p88
Geoffrey Clifton-Brown	*Con*	p123
Martin Docherty-Hughes	*SNP*	p145
Barry Gardiner	*Lab*	p179
Marco Longhi	*Con*	p258
Conor McGinn	*Lab*	p268

Bulgaria

Wayne David	*Lab*	p136

Burma (Myanmar)

Paul Blomfield	*Lab*	p89
Alistair Carmichael	*Lib Dem*	p112
Caroline Lucas	*Green*	p261
Paul Scully	*Con*	p336
Valerie Vaz	*Lab*	p375

Cambodia

Sharon Hodgson	*Lab*	p216

Canada

Anthony Browne	*Con*	p101
Stephen Doughty	*Lab/Co-op*	p150
Oliver Dowden	*Con*	p151
David Duguid	*Con*	p154
David Evennett	*Con*	p166
Michael Gove	*Con*	p187
Maria Miller	*Con*	p285
Andrew Percy	*Con*	p314
Andrew Rosindell	*Con*	p331
Virendra Sharma	*Lab*	p339
Andrew Stephenson	*Con*	p352
Richard Thomson	*SNP*	p365
Robin Walker	*Con*	p378

Chile

Bernard Jenkin	*Con*	p229

China

Lyn Brown	*Lab*	p100
Nick Brown	*Lab*	p101
Conor Burns	*Con*	p106
Sarah Champion	*Lab*	p116
Simon Clarke	*Con*	p120
Geoffrey Clifton-Brown	*Con*	p123
David Davies	*Con*	p137
Caroline Dinenage	*Con*	p143
Chris Evans	*Lab/Co-op*	p164
Simon Fell	*Con*	p169
Barry Gardiner	*Lab*	p179
Mark Garnier	*Con*	p180
Cheryl Gillan	*Con*	p184
James Gray	*Con*	p190
Andrew Gwynne	*Lab*	p197
Stephen Hammond	*Con*	p200
Mark Hendrick	*Lab/Co-op*	p211
Antony Higginbotham	*Con*	p212
Sharon Hodgson	*Lab*	p216
Darren Jones	*Lab*	p235
David Jones	*Con*	p235
Afzal Khan	*Lab*	p242
Ian Liddell-Grainger	*Con*	p255
Stephen McPartland	*Con*	p273
Alan Mak	*Con*	p276
Seema Malhotra	*Lab/Co-op*	p276
Stephen Metcalfe	*Con*	p284
Layla Moran	*Lib Dem*	p290
Grahame Morris	*Lab*	p293
Chi Onwurah	*Lab*	p305
Ian Paisley	*DUP*	p309
Neil Parish	*Con*	p309
Owen Paterson	*Con*	p311
Mark Pawsey	*Con*	p311
Victoria Prentis	*Con*	p319
Jeremy Quin	*Con*	p321
Will Quince	*Con*	p321
John Redwood	*Con*	p324
Jacob Rees-Mogg	*Con*	p325
Rachel Reeves	*Lab*	p326
Jonathan Reynolds	*Lab/Co-op*	p327
David Rutley	*Con*	p334
Nick Smith	*Lab*	p347
Andrew Stephenson	*Con*	p352
Wes Streeting	*Lab*	p357
Graham Stuart	*Con*	p358
Catherine West	*Lab*	p381
Heather Wheeler	*Con*	p383
John Whittingdale	*Con*	p385
Gavin Williamson	*Con*	p389
Sammy Wilson	*DUP*	p390

Colombia

Alan Campbell	*Lab*	p110
Michael Gove	*Con*	p187
Diana Johnson	*Lab*	p232
Chris Matheson	*Lab*	p280
Lisa Nandy	*Lab*	p298
Jo Stevens	*Lab*	p353

Croatia

Jackie Doyle-Price	*Con*	p151

Cuba

David Davies	*Con*	p137
Grahame Morris	*Lab*	p293
Wes Streeting	*Lab*	p357

Cyprus

Harriett Baldwin	*Con*	p79
Bambos Charalambous	*Lab*	p117
Jeffrey Donaldson	*DUP*	p147
Mike Freer	*Con*	p177
Roger Gale	*Con*	p179
Fabian Hamilton	*Lab*	p199
Julian Knight	*Con*	p244
Matthew Offord	*Con*	p304
Virendra Sharma	*Lab*	p339
Theresa Villiers	*Con*	p376
Catherine West	*Lab*	p381

Democratic Republic of Congo

Hilary Benn	*Lab*	p83

Denmark

Martin Docherty-Hughes	*SNP*	p145
David Duguid	*Con*	p154
Diana Johnson	*Lab*	p232
David Rutley	*Con*	p334

Dominican Republic

Rosie Cooper	*Lab*	p125

Egypt

Nigel Evans	*Con*	p165
Jonathan Lord	*Con*	p259
Andy Slaughter	*Lab*	p343

El Salvador

Peter Bottomley	*Con*	p91

Estonia

Martin Docherty-Hughes	*SNP*	p145

Ethiopia

Jeffrey Donaldson	*DUP*	p147
Laurence Robertson	*Con*	p329

Falkland Islands

Alan Campbell	*Lab*	p110
Caroline Dinenage	*Con*	p143
Simon Hart	*Con*	p206
Lindsay Hoyle	*Speaker*	p222
Guy Opperman	*Con*	p306

Faroe Islands

Angus MacNeil	*SNP*	p273

Fiji

Paul Beresford	*Con*	p85

France

Edward Argar	*Con*	p73
Andrew Bowie	*Con*	p92
Stephen Crabb	*Con*	p130
Alex Cunningham	*Lab*	p134
Chris Elmore	*Lab*	p162
Chris Evans	*Lab/Co-op*	p164
George Freeman	*Con*	p176
Damian Green	*Con*	p192
Nia Griffith	*Lab*	p195
Bernard Jenkin	*Con*	p229
Jonathan Lord	*Con*	p259
Robert Neill	*Con*	p299
Chi Onwurah	*Lab*	p305
Victoria Prentis	*Con*	p319
Jamie Stone	*Lib Dem*	p355
Wes Streeting	*Lab*	p357
Nick Thomas-Symonds	*Lab*	p364
Jon Trickett	*Lab*	p371
Alan Whitehead	*Lab*	p383
Hywel Williams	*PlC*	p388

Gambia

John McDonnell	*Lab*	p267

Georgia

Damian Green	*Con*	p192
Bernard Jenkin	*Con*	p229
John Whittingdale	*Con*	p385

Germany

Ben Bradshaw	*Lab*	p94
David Davies	*Con*	p137
Chris Evans	*Lab/Co-op*	p164
Michael Gove	*Con*	p187
Greg Hands	*Con*	p201
Mark Hendrick	*Lab/Co-op*	p211
Bernard Jenkin	*Con*	p229
Jonathan Lord	*Con*	p259
Paul Maynard	*Con*	p281
Victoria Prentis	*Con*	p319
Jonathan Reynolds	*Lab/Co-op*	p327
Jamie Stone	*Lib Dem*	p355
Stephen Timms	*Lab*	p367
Pete Wishart	*SNP*	p391

Ghana

Adam Afriyie	*Con*	p66

Gibraltar

Caroline Dinenage	*Con*	p143
Nigel Evans	*Con*	p165
Lindsay Hoyle	*Speaker*	p222
Eleanor Laing	*Con*	p246
Mike Penning	*Con*	p312

Greece

Chris Elmore	*Lab*	p162
Chris Evans	*Lab/Co-op*	p164
Derek Twigg	*Lab*	p373
Catherine West	*Lab*	p381

Guinea

Adam Afriyie	*Con*	p66

Guyana

Janet Daby	*Lab*	p134

Haiti

Rosie Cooper	*Lab*	p125

Hong Kong

Caroline Dinenage	*Con*	p143
Steve Double	*Con*	p149
Philip Dunne	*Con*	p156
Ian Liddell-Grainger	*Con*	p255
Layla Moran	*Lib Dem*	p290
David Morris	*Con*	p293

Hungary

James Cartlidge	*Con*	p113
David Davies	*Con*	p137
Cheryl Gillan	*Con*	p184
Mark Hendrick	*Lab/Co-op*	p211
Craig Mackinlay	*Con*	p269
Robert Neill	*Con*	p299

Iceland

Fabian Hamilton	*Lab*	p199
Angus MacNeil	*SNP*	p273

India

Jon Ashworth	*Lab/Co-op*	p74
Kemi Badenoch	*Con*	p76
Bob Blackman	*Con*	p88
Crispin Blunt	*Con*	p90
Geoffrey Clifton-Brown	*Con*	p123
Stephen Crabb	*Con*	p130
John Cryer	*Lab*	p133
Martyn Day	*SNP*	p141
Caroline Dinenage	*Con*	p143
Allan Dorans	*SNP*	p148
Stephen Doughty	*Lab/Co-op*	p150

Andrew Bridgen	*Con*	p97
Steve Brine	*Con*	p98
David Evennett	*Con*	p166
Michael Gove	*Con*	p187
Damian Green	*Con*	p192
Nia Griffith	*Lab*	p195
John Hayes	*Con*	p207
Brandon Lewis	*Con*	p253
Marco Longhi	*Con*	p258
Jonathan Lord	*Con*	p259
Karl McCartney	*Con*	p264
Catherine McKinnell	*Lab*	p269
Paul Maskey	*Sinn Féin*	p279
Robert Neill	*Con*	p299
Jamie Stone	*Lib Dem*	p355
Robin Walker	*Con*	p378
Ben Wallace	*Con*	p378

Jamaica

Diane Abbott	*Lab*	p64
Dawn Butler	*Lab*	p106
Janet Daby	*Lab*	p134

Japan

Nick Brown	*Lab*	p101
Oliver Dowden	*Con*	p151
Jo Gideon	*Con*	p183
Cheryl Gillan	*Con*	p184
Fabian Hamilton	*Lab*	p199
Matt Hancock	*Con*	p200
Mark Hendrick	*Lab/Co-op*	p211
Sharon Hodgson	*Lab*	p216
Jeremy Hunt	*Con*	p224
Stephen Metcalfe	*Con*	p284
Rachel Reeves	*Lab*	p326
David Warburton	*Con*	p379
Heather Wheeler	*Con*	p383
John Whittingdale	*Con*	p385
Gavin Williamson	*Con*	p389

Jordan

Michael Gove	*Con*	p187
Fabian Hamilton	*Lab*	p199
Diana Johnson	*Lab*	p232
Alicia Kearns	*Con*	p240

Kenya

Steve Double	*Con*	p149
Chris Heaton-Harris	*Con*	p210
John McDonnell	*Lab*	p267
Barry Sheerman	*Lab/Co-op*	p340
Craig Whittaker	*Con*	p385

Korea, North

Fiona Bruce	*Con*	p102
Richard Fuller	*Con*	p177
Fabian Hamilton	*Lab*	p199
Greg Hands	*Con*	p201
Gary Streeter	*Con*	p356
John Whittingdale	*Con*	p385
Gavin Williamson	*Con*	p389

Korea, South

Fabian Hamilton	*Lab*	p199
John Whittingdale	*Con*	p385
Gavin Williamson	*Con*	p389

Latvia

Martin Docherty-Hughes	*SNP*	p145
Christopher Pincher	*Con*	p316

Libya

Daniel Kawczynski	*Con*	p239

Liechtenstein

Andrew Rosindell	*Con*	p331

Lithuania

Martin Docherty-Hughes	*SNP*	p145
Alan Whitehead	*Lab*	p383

Luxembourg

Damien Moore	*Con*	p289

Malaysia

Bill Cash	*Con*	p113
John Whittingdale	*Con*	p385

Maldives

John Glen	*Con*	p185
Helen Grant	*Con*	p189

Malta

Douglas Chapman	*SNP*	p116
Julian Knight	*Con*	p244

Mauritania

Daniel Kawczynski	*Con*	p239

Mauritius

Geoffrey Cox	*Con*	p129
Virendra Sharma	*Lab*	p339

Moldova

Jeffrey Donaldson	*DUP*	p147
Robert Goodwill	*Con*	p186
Damian Green	*Con*	p192
Paul Maynard	*Con*	p281

Mongolia

James Gray	*Con*	p190

Montenegro

Andrew Stephenson	*Con*	p352

Morocco

Fabian Hamilton	*Lab*	p199
Afzal Khan	*Lab*	p242
Andrew Murrison	*Con*	p298
Victoria Prentis	*Con*	p319

Myanmar (Burma)

Jon Ashworth	*Lab/Co-op*	p74

Nepal

Bob Blackman *Con* p88
James Gray *Con* p190
Margaret Hodge *Lab* p215
Dan Jarvis *Lab* p227
Maria Miller *Con* p285
Ian Murray *Lab* p296
Virendra Sharma *Lab* p339
Nick Smith *Lab* p347

Netherlands

Clive Betts *Lab* p86

New Zealand

Paul Beresford *Con* p85
Nick Brown *Lab* p101
David Evennett *Con* p166
Sharon Hodgson *Lab* p216
Bernard Jenkin *Con* p229
Eleanor Laing *Con* p246
Karl McCartney *Con* p264
Tom Pursglove *Con* p320
Andrew Rosindell *Con* p331
Wes Streeting *Lab* p357
Craig Whittaker *Con* p385

Nicaragua

Maria Eagle *Lab* p157
Andrew Selous *Con* p337

Nigeria

Kemi Badenoch *Con* p76
Richard Fuller *Con* p177
Helen Grant *Con* p189
John Howell *Con* p221
Chi Onwurah *Lab* p305

Norway

Edward Argar *Con* p73
Angus MacNeil *SNP* p273
Gareth Thomas *Lab/Co-op* p364

Oman

Edward Argar *Con* p73
Robert Largan *Con* p249

Pakistan

Debbie Abrahams *Lab* p64
Jon Ashworth *Lab/Co-op* p74
Steve Baker *Con* p78
Lyn Brown *Lab* p100
Rehman Chishti *Con* p118
Simon Clarke *Con* p120
Stephen Doughty *Lab/Co-op* p150
Sharon Hodgson *Lab* p216
Dan Jarvis *Lab* p227
Bernard Jenkin *Con* p229
Afzal Khan *Lab* p242
Jason McCartney *Con* p264
Mark Pawsey *Con* p311
Alok Sharma *Con* p339
Virendra Sharma *Lab* p339
Andrew Stephenson *Con* p352
Gareth Thomas *Lab/Co-op* p364

Poland

Wayne David *Lab* p136
Cheryl Gillan *Con* p184
Michael Gove *Con* p187
Mark Hendrick *Lab/Co-op* p211
Kevan Jones *Lab* p237
Jamie Stone *Lib Dem* p355
Alan Whitehead *Lab* p383

Portugal

Clive Betts *Lab* p86
Stephen Hammond *Con* p200

Qatar

Gill Furniss *Lab* p178
Afzal Khan *Lab* p242

Romania

James Cartlidge *Con* p113
Ben Wallace *Con* p378

Russia

Harriett Baldwin *Con* p79
Robert Buckland *Con* p104
Simon Clarke *Con* p120
Martin Docherty-Hughes *SNP* p145
Barry Gardiner *Lab* p179
James Gray *Con* p190
Fabian Hamilton *Lab* p199
Greg Hands *Con* p201
Antony Higginbotham *Con* p212
Bernard Jenkin *Con* p229
Stephen Kinnock *Lab* p243
Julian Lewis *Con* p254
Kerry McCarthy *Lab* p263
Christopher Pincher *Con* p316
Victoria Prentis *Con* p319
Ben Wallace *Con* p378
John Whittingdale *Con* p385

Rwanda

Fiona Bruce *Con* p102
Mark Pawsey *Con* p311
Maggie Throup *Con* p366

Samoa

Paul Beresford *Con* p85

Saudi Arabia

Rehman Chishti *Con* p118
Daniel Kawczynski *Con* p239
Afzal Khan *Lab* p242
Karl McCartney *Con* p264
Paul Scully *Con* p336
Andrew Stephenson *Con* p352

Scotland

Karl McCartney	*Con*	p264
Jim Shannon	*DUP*	p338

Serbia

Clive Betts	*Lab*	p86
Andrew Bridgen	*Con*	p97
Jackie Doyle-Price	*Con*	p151

Sierra Leone

Andrew Stephenson	*Con*	p352
Gavin Williamson	*Con*	p389

Singapore

Nick Brown	*Lab*	p101
Sharon Hodgson	*Lab*	p216
Bernard Jenkin	*Con*	p229
Ian Liddell-Grainger	*Con*	p255
Stephen Timms	*Lab*	p367

Slovenia

Neil Parish	*Con*	p309
David Rutley	*Con*	p334

Somalia

Jon Ashworth	*Lab/Co-op*	p74
Paul Blomfield	*Lab*	p89
Stephen Doughty	*Lab/Co-op*	p150
Kerry McCarthy	*Lab*	p263
John McDonnell	*Lab*	p267
Catherine West	*Lab*	p381

South Africa

Caroline Dinenage	*Con*	p143
Jeffrey Donaldson	*DUP*	p147
James Duddridge	*Con*	p153
Louise Haigh	*Lab*	p197
Sharon Hodgson	*Lab*	p216
George Howarth	*Lab*	p220
Robert Largan	*Con*	p249
Ian Liddell-Grainger	*Con*	p255
Conor McGinn	*Lab*	p268
Alan Mak	*Con*	p276
Francie Molloy	*Sinn Féin*	p288
Chi Onwurah	*Lab*	p305
Robin Walker	*Con*	p378

Spain

Chris Bryant	*Lab*	p103
Peter Gibson	*Con*	p182
Nia Griffith	*Lab*	p195
John Hayes	*Con*	p207
Jonathan Lord	*Con*	p259
Damien Moore	*Con*	p289
Robert Neill	*Con*	p299
Andy Slaughter	*Lab*	p343

Sri Lanka

Bob Blackman	*Con*	p88
Sarah Champion	*Lab*	p116
Barry Gardiner	*Lab*	p179
Helen Grant	*Con*	p189
James Gray	*Con*	p190
Stephen Hammond	*Con*	p200
Sharon Hodgson	*Lab*	p216
Matthew Offord	*Con*	p304
Paul Scully	*Con*	p336
Virendra Sharma	*Lab*	p339
Gareth Thomas	*Lab/Co-op*	p364
Karl Turner	*Lab*	p373

Sudan

Harriett Baldwin	*Con*	p79
Hilary Benn	*Lab*	p83

Swaziland

James Duddridge	*Con*	p153

Sweden

Andrew Bowie	*Con*	p92
Alok Sharma	*Con*	p339

Switzerland

Ian Liddell-Grainger	*Con*	p255
Robert Neill	*Con*	p299
Andrew Rosindell	*Con*	p331

Syria

Jon Ashworth	*Lab/Co-op*	p74
Andrew Bridgen	*Con*	p97
Stephen Doughty	*Lab/Co-op*	p150
Alicia Kearns	*Con*	p240
Robert Largan	*Con*	p249
Guy Opperman	*Con*	p306

Taiwan

John Lamont	*Con*	p248
Martin Vickers	*Con*	p375
Heather Wheeler	*Con*	p383

Tanzania

Fiona Bruce	*Con*	p102
Steve Double	*Con*	p149
David Linden	*SNP*	p255
John McDonnell	*Lab*	p267
Craig Whittaker	*Con*	p385

Tunisia

Roger Gale	*Con*	p179
Damien Moore	*Con*	p289
Andy Slaughter	*Lab*	p343

Turkey

Fabian Hamilton	*Lab*	p199
Mark Harper	*Con*	p203
Afzal Khan	*Lab*	p242
Maria Miller	*Con*	p285
Jonathan Reynolds	*Lab/Co-op*	p327
Catherine West	*Lab*	p381
Hywel Williams	*PlC*	p388

Turks & Caicos Isl.

Alicia Kearns	*Con*	p240

Gavin Newlands	*SNP*	p300
Ian Paisley	*DUP*	p309
Owen Paterson	*Con*	p311
Andrew Percy	*Con*	p314
Christopher Pincher	*Con*	p316
Mark Pritchard	*Con*	p320
Tom Pursglove	*Con*	p320
John Redwood	*Con*	p324
Rachel Reeves	*Lab*	p326
Jonathan Reynolds	*Lab/Co-op*	p327
Jonathan Reynolds	*Lab/Co-op*	p327
Laurence Robertson	*Con*	p329
Andrew Rosindell	*Con*	p331
Lee Rowley	*Con*	p332
David Rutley	*Con*	p334
Andrew Selous	*Con*	p337
Jim Shannon	*DUP*	p338
Virendra Sharma	*Lab*	p339
Barry Sheerman	*Lab/Co-op*	p340
Alec Shelbrooke	*Con*	p340
Henry Smith	*Con*	p345
Nick Smith	*Lab*	p347
Karin Smyth	*Lab*	p348
John Spellar	*Lab*	p349
Andrew Stephenson	*Con*	p352
Wes Streeting	*Lab*	p357
Mel Stride	*Con*	p357
Rishi Sunak	*Con*	p360
Robert Syms	*Con*	p361
Richard Thomson	*SNP*	p365
Jon Trickett	*Lab*	p371
Tom Tugendhat	*Con*	p372
Martin Vickers	*Con*	p375
Robin Walker	*Con*	p378
Ben Wallace	*Con*	p378
David Warburton	*Con*	p379
John Whittingdale	*Con*	p385
Sammy Wilson	*DUP*	p390
Jeremy Wright	*Con*	p393

Uzbekistan

Andrew Bridgen	*Con*	p97
Alistair Carmichael	*Lib Dem*	p112
Martin Vickers	*Con*	p375

Venezuela

Martin Docherty-Hughes	*SNP*	p145
David Duguid	*Con*	p154
Grahame Morris	*Lab*	p293

Vietnam

Wayne David	*Lab*	p136
Michael Gove	*Con*	p187
Ian Liddell-Grainger	*Con*	p255

Wales

Geraint Davies	*Lab/Co-op*	p138
Alex Davies-Jones	*Lab*	p140
Michael Fabricant	*Con*	p167
Ruth Jones	*Lab*	p238
Stephen Kinnock	*Lab*	p243
Karl McCartney	*Con*	p264
Liz Saville Roberts	*PlC*	p335
Jamie Wallis	*Con*	p379

Yemen

Edward Argar	*Con*	p73
Douglas Chapman	*SNP*	p116
Stephen Doughty	*Lab/Co-op*	p150
Tobias Ellwood	*Con*	p161
Valerie Vaz	*Lab*	p375

Zambia

Nadine Dorries	*Con*	p149
Robin Walker	*Con*	p378

Zimbabwe

James Duddridge	*Con*	p153
David Linden	*SNP*	p255
Neil Parish	*Con*	p309

MPs by UK Regions

England

Eastern

Basildon and Billericay	John Baron	Con
South Basildon and East Thurrock	Stephen Metcalfe	Con
Bedford	Mohammad Yasin	Lab
Mid Bedfordshire	Nadine Dorries	Con
North East Bedfordshire	Richard Fuller	Con
South West Bedfordshire	Andrew Selous	Con
Braintree	James Cleverly	Con
Brentwood and Ongar	Alex Burghart	Con
Broadland	Jerome Mayhew	Con
Broxbourne	Charles Walker	Con
Bury St Edmunds	Jo Churchill	Con
Cambridge	Daniel Zeichner	Lab
North East Cambridgeshire	Stephen Barclay	Con
North West Cambridgeshire	Shailesh Vara	Con
South Cambridgeshire	Anthony Browne	Con
South East Cambridgeshire	Lucy Frazer	Con
Castle Point	Rebecca Harris	Con
Chelmsford	Vicky Ford	Con
Clacton	Giles Watling	Con
Colchester	Will Quince	Con
Epping Forest	Eleanor Laing	Con
Great Yarmouth	Brandon Lewis	Con
Harlow	Robert Halfon	Con
Harwich and North Essex	Bernard Jenkin	Con
Hemel Hempstead	Mike Penning	Con
Hertford and Stortford	Julie Marson	Con
North East Hertfordshire	Oliver Heald	Con
South West Hertfordshire	Gagan Mohindra	Con
Hertsmere	Oliver Dowden	Con
Hitchin and Harpenden	Bim Afolami	Con
Huntingdon	Jonathan Djanogly	Con
Ipswich	Tom Hunt	Con
Luton North	Sarah Owen	Lab
Luton South	Rachel Hopkins	Lab
Maldon	John Whittingdale	Con
Mid Norfolk	George Freeman	Con
North Norfolk	Duncan Baker	Con
North West Norfolk	James Wild	Con
South Norfolk	Richard Bacon	Con
South West Norfolk	Elizabeth Truss	Con
Norwich North	Chloe Smith	Con
Norwich South	Clive Lewis	Lab
Peterborough	Paul Bristow	Con
Rayleigh and Wickford	Mark Francois	Con
Rochford and Southend East	James Duddridge	Con
Saffron Walden	Kemi Badenoch	Con
St Albans	Daisy Cooper	Lib Dem
Southend West	David Amess	Con
Stevenage	Stephen McPartland	Con
Central Suffolk and North Ipswich	Dan Poulter	Con
Suffolk Coastal	Therese Coffey	Con
South Suffolk	James Cartlidge	Con

West Suffolk	Matt Hancock	Con
Thurrock	Jackie Doyle-Price	Con
Watford	Dean Russell	Con
Waveney	Peter Aldous	Con
Welwyn Hatfield	Grant Shapps	Con
Witham	Priti Patel	Con

East Midlands

Amber Valley	Nigel Mills	Con
Ashfield	Lee Anderson	Con
Bassetlaw	Brendan Clarke-Smith	Con
Bolsover	Mark Fletcher	Con
Boston and Skegness	Matt Warman	Con
Bosworth	Luke Evans	Con
Broxtowe	Darren Henry	Con
Charnwood	Edward Argar	Con
Chesterfield	Toby Perkins	Lab
Corby	Tom Pursglove	Con
Daventry	Chris Heaton-Harris	Con
Derby North	Amanda Solloway	Con
Derby South	Margaret Beckett	Lab
Derbyshire Dales	Sarah Dines	Con
Mid Derbyshire	Pauline Latham	Con
North East Derbyshire	Lee Rowley	Con
South Derbyshire	Heather Wheeler	Con
Erewash	Maggie Throup	Con
Gainsborough	Edward Leigh	Con
Gedling	Tom Randall	Con
Grantham and Stamford	Gareth Davies	Con
Harborough	Neil O'Brien	Con
High Peak	Robert Largan	Con
Kettering	Philip Hollobone	Con
Leicester East	Claudia Webbe	Ind*
Leicester South	Jon Ashworth	Lab/Co-op
Leicester West	Liz Kendall	Lab
North West Leicestershire	Andrew Bridgen	Con
South Leicestershire	Alberto Costa	Con
Lincoln	Karl McCartney	Con
Loughborough	Jane Hunt	Con
Louth and Horncastle	Victoria Atkins	Con
Mansfield	Ben Bradley	Con
Newark	Robert Jenrick	Con
Northampton North	Michael Ellis	Con
Northampton South	Andrew Lewer	Con
South Northamptonshire	Andrea Leadsom	Con
Nottingham East	Nadia Whittome	Lab
Nottingham North	Alex Norris	Lab/Co-op
Nottingham South	Lilian Greenwood	Lab
Rushcliffe	Ruth Edwards	Con
Rutland and Melton	Alicia Kearns	Con
Sherwood	Mark Spencer	Con
Sleaford and North Hykeham	Caroline Johnson	Con
South Holland and The Deepings	John Hayes	Con
Wellingborough	Peter Bone	Con

*Elected as Labour

London

Constituency	MP	Party
Barking	Margaret Hodge	Lab
Battersea	Marsha De Cordova	Lab
Beckenham	Bob Stewart	Con
Bermondsey and Old Southwark	Neil Coyle	Lab
Bethnal Green and Bow	Rushanara Ali	Lab
Old Bexley and Sidcup	James Brokenshire	Con
Bexleyheath and Crayford	David Evennett	Con
Brent Central	Dawn Butler	Lab
Brent North	Barry Gardiner	Lab
Brentford and Isleworth	Ruth Cadbury	Lab
Bromley and Chislehurst	Robert Neill	Con
Camberwell and Peckham	Harriet Harman	Lab
Carshalton and Wallington	Elliot Colburn	Con
Chelsea and Fulham	Greg Hands	Con
Chingford and Woodford Green	Iain Duncan Smith	Con
Chipping Barnet	Theresa Villiers	Con
Croydon Central	Sarah Jones	Lab
Croydon North	Steve Reed	Lab/Co-op
Croydon South	Chris Philp	Con
Dagenham and Rainham	Jon Cruddas	Lab
Dulwich and West Norwood	Helen Hayes	Lab
Ealing Central and Acton	Rupa Huq	Lab
Ealing North	James Murray	Lab/Co-op
Ealing Southall	Virendra Sharma	Lab
East Ham	Stephen Timms	Lab
Edmonton	Kate Osamor	Lab/Co-op
Eltham	Clive Efford	Lab
Enfield North	Feryal Clark	Lab
Enfield Southgate	Bambos Charalambous	Lab
Erith and Thamesmead	Abena Oppong-Asare	Lab
Feltham and Heston	Seema Malhotra	Lab/Co-op
Finchley and Golders Green	Mike Freer	Con
Greenwich and Woolwich	Matthew Pennycook	Lab
Hackney North and Stoke Newington	Diane Abbott	Lab
Hackney South and Shoreditch	Meg Hillier	Lab/Co-op
Hammersmith	Andy Slaughter	Lab
Hampstead and Kilburn	Tulip Siddiq	Lab
Harrow East	Bob Blackman	Con
Harrow West	Gareth Thomas	Lab/Co-op
Hayes and Harlington	John McDonnell	Lab
Hendon	Matthew Offord	Con
Holborn and St Pancras	Keir Starmer	Lab
Hornchurch and Upminster	Julia Lopez	Con
Hornsey and Wood Green	Catherine West	Lab
Ilford North	Wes Streeting	Lab
Ilford South	Sam Tarry	Lab
Islington North	Jeremy Corbyn	Ind*
Islington South and Finsbury	Emily Thornberry	Lab
Kensington	Felicity Buchan	Con
Kingston and Surbiton	Ed Davey	Lib Dem
Lewisham Deptford	Vicky Foxcroft	Lab
Lewisham East	Janet Daby	Lab
Lewisham West and Penge	Ellie Reeves	Lab
Leyton and Wanstead	John Cryer	Lab

*Elected as Labour

Cities of London and Westminster	Nickie Aiken	Con
Mitcham and Morden	Siobhain McDonagh	Lab
Orpington	Gareth Bacon	Con
Poplar and Limehouse	Apsana Begum	Lab
Putney	Fleur Anderson	Lab
Richmond Park	Sarah Olney	Lib Dem
Romford	Andrew Rosindell	Con
Ruislip, Northwood and Pinner	David Simmonds	Con
Streatham	Bell Ribeiro-Addy	Lab
Sutton and Cheam	Paul Scully	Con
Tooting	Rosena Allin-Khan	Lab
Tottenham	David Lammy	Lab
Twickenham	Munira Wilson	Lib Dem
Uxbridge and South Ruislip	Boris Johnson	Con
Vauxhall	Florence Eshalomi	Lab/Co-op
Walthamstow	Stella Creasy	Lab/Co-op
West Ham	Lyn Brown	Lab
Westminster North	Karen Buck	Lab
Wimbledon	Stephen Hammond	Con

North East

Berwick-upon-Tweed	Anne-Marie Trevelyan	Con
Bishop Auckland	Dehenna Davison	Con
Blaydon	Liz Twist	Lab
Blyth Valley	Ian Levy	Con
Darlington	Peter Gibson	Con
City of Durham	Mary Foy	Lab
North Durham	Kevan Jones	Lab
North West Durham	Richard Holden	Con
Easington	Grahame Morris	Lab
Gateshead	Ian Mearns	Lab
Hartlepool	Mike Hill	Lab
Hexham	Guy Opperman	Con
Houghton and Sunderland South	Bridget Phillipson	Lab
Jarrow	Kate Osborne	Lab
Middlesbrough	Andy McDonald	Lab
Middlesbrough South and East Cleveland	Simon Clarke	Con
Newcastle upon Tyne Central	Chi Onwurah	Lab
Newcastle upon Tyne East	Nick Brown	Lab
Newcastle upon Tyne North	Catherine McKinnell	Lab
Redcar	Jacob Young	Con
Sedgefield	Paul Howell	Con
South Shields	Emma Lewell-Buck	Lab
Stockton North	Alex Cunningham	Lab
Stockton South	Matt Vickers	Con
Sunderland Central	Julie Elliott	Lab
Tynemouth	Alan Campbell	Lab
North Tyneside	Mary Glindon	Lab
Wansbeck	Ian Lavery	Lab
Washington and Sunderland West	Sharon Hodgson	Lab

North West

Altrincham and Sale West	Graham Brady	Con
Ashton under Lyne	Angela Rayner	Lab
Barrow and Furness	Simon Fell	Con
Birkenhead	Mick Whitley	Lab
Blackburn	Kate Hollern	Lab

Blackley and Broughton	Graham Stringer	Lab
Blackpool North and Cleveleys	Paul Maynard	Con
Blackpool South	Scott Benton	Con
Bolton North East	Mark Logan	Con
Bolton South East	Yasmin Qureshi	Lab
Bolton West	Chris Green	Con
Bootle	Peter Dowd	Lab
Burnley	Antony Higginbotham	Con
Bury North	James Daly	Con
Bury South	Christian Wakeford	Con
Carlisle	John Stevenson	Con
Cheadle	Mary Robinson	Con
City of Chester	Chris Matheson	Lab
Chorley	Lindsay Hoyle	Speaker
Congleton	Fiona Bruce	Con
Copeland	Trudy Harrison	Con
Crewe and Nantwich	Kieran Mullan	Con
Denton and Reddish	Andrew Gwynne	Lab
Eddisbury	Edward Timpson	Con
Ellesmere Port and Neston	Justin Madders	Lab
Fylde	Mark Menzies	Con
Garston and Halewood	Maria Eagle	Lab
Halton	Derek Twigg	Lab
Hazel Grove	William Wragg	Con
Heywood and Middleton	Chris Clarkson	Con
Hyndburn	Sara Britcliffe	Con
Knowsley	George Howarth	Lab
West Lancashire	Rosie Cooper	Lab
Lancaster and Fleetwood	Cat Smith	Lab
Leigh	James Grundy	Con
Liverpool Riverside	Kim Johnson	Lab
Liverpool Walton	Dan Carden	Lab
Liverpool Wavertree	Paula Barker	Lab
Liverpool West Derby	Ian Byrne	Lab
Macclesfield	David Rutley	Con
Makerfield	Yvonne Fovargue	Lab
Manchester Central	Lucy Powell	Lab/Co-op
Manchester Gorton	Afzal Khan	Lab
Manchester Withington	Jeff Smith	Lab
Morecambe and Lunesdale	David Morris	Con
Oldham East and Saddleworth	Debbie Abrahams	Lab
Oldham West and Royton	Jim McMahon	Lab/Co-op
Pendle	Andrew Stephenson	Con
Penrith and The Border	Neil Hudson	Con
Preston	Mark Hendrick	Lab/Co-op
South Ribble	Katherine Fletcher	Con
Ribble Valley	Nigel Evans	Con
Rochdale	Tony Lloyd	Lab
Rossendale and Darwen	Jake Berry	Con
St Helens North	Conor McGinn	Lab
St Helens South and Whiston	Marie Rimmer	Lab
Salford and Eccles	Rebecca Long Bailey	Lab
Sefton Central	Bill Esterson	Lab
Southport	Damien Moore	Con
Stalybridge and Hyde	Jonathan Reynolds	Lab/Co-op
Stockport	Navendu Mishra	Lab
Stretford and Urmston	Kate Green	Lab

Tatton	Esther McVey	Con
Wallasey	Angela Eagle	Lab
Warrington North	Charlotte Nichols	Lab
Warrington South	Andy Carter	Con
Weaver Vale	Mike Amesbury	Lab
Westmorland and Lonsdale	Tim Farron	Lib Dem
Wigan	Lisa Nandy	Lab
Wirral South	Alison McGovern	Lab
Wirral West	Margaret Greenwood	Lab
Workington	Mark Jenkinson	Con
Worsley and Eccles South	Barbara Keeley	Lab
Wyre and Preston North	Ben Wallace	Con
Wythenshawe and Sale East	Mike Kane	Lab

South East

Aldershot	Leo Docherty	Con
Arundel and South Downs	Andrew Griffith	Con
Ashford	Damian Green	Con
Aylesbury	Rob Butler	Con
Banbury	Victoria Prentis	Con
Basingstoke	Maria Miller	Con
Beaconsfield	Joy Morrissey	Con
Bexhill and Battle	Huw Merriman	Con
Bognor Regis and Littlehampton	Nick Gibb	Con
Bracknell	James Sunderland	Con
Brighton Kemptown	Lloyd Russell-Moyle	Lab/Co-op
Brighton Pavilion	Caroline Lucas	Green
Buckingham	Greg Smith	Con
Canterbury	Rosie Duffield	Lab
Chatham and Aylesford	Tracey Crouch	Con
Chesham and Amersham	Cheryl Gillan	Con
Chichester	Gillian Keegan	Con
Crawley	Henry Smith	Con
Dartford	Gareth Johnson	Con
Dover	Natalie Elphicke	Con
Eastbourne	Caroline Ansell	Con
Eastleigh	Paul Holmes	Con
Epsom and Ewell	Chris Grayling	Con
Esher and Walton	Dominic Raab	Con
Fareham	Suella Braverman	Con
Faversham and Mid Kent	Helen Whately	Con
Folkestone and Hythe	Damian Collins	Con
Gillingham and Rainham	Rehman Chishti	Con
Gosport	Caroline Dinenage	Con
Gravesham	Adam Holloway	Con
Guildford	Angela Richardson	Con
East Hampshire	Damian Hinds	Con
North East Hampshire	Ranil Jayawardena	Con
North West Hampshire	Kit Malthouse	Con
Hastings and Rye	Sally-Ann Hart	Con
Havant	Alan Mak	Con
Henley	John Howell	Con
Horsham	Jeremy Quin	Con
Hove	Peter Kyle	Lab
Isle of Wight	Bob Seely	Con
Lewes	Maria Caulfield	Con
Maidenhead	Theresa May	Con

Maidstone and The Weald	Helen Grant	Con
Meon Valley	Flick Drummond	Con
Milton Keynes North	Ben Everitt	Con
Milton Keynes South	Iain Stewart	Con
Mole Valley	Paul Beresford	Con
New Forest East	Julian Lewis	Con
New Forest West	Desmond Swayne	Con
Newbury	Laura Farris	Con
Oxford East	Anneliese Dodds	Lab/Co-op
Oxford West and Abingdon	Layla Moran	Lib Dem
Portsmouth North	Penny Mordaunt	Con
Portsmouth South	Stephen Morgan	Lab
Reading East	Matt Rodda	Lab
Reading West	Alok Sharma	Con
Reigate	Crispin Blunt	Con
Rochester and Strood	Kelly Tolhurst	Con
Romsey and Southampton North	Caroline Nokes	Con
Runnymede and Weybridge	Ben Spencer	Con
Sevenoaks	Laura Trott	Con
Sittingbourne and Sheppey	Gordon Henderson	Con
Slough	Tanmanjeet Singh Dhesi	Lab
Southampton Itchen	Royston Smith	Con
Southampton Test	Alan Whitehead	Lab
Spelthorne	Kwasi Kwarteng	Con
East Surrey	Claire Coutinho	Con
Surrey Heath	Michael Gove	Con
South West Surrey	Jeremy Hunt	Con
Mid Sussex	Mims Davies	Con
North Thanet	Roger Gale	Con
South Thanet	Craig Mackinlay	Con
Tonbridge and Malling	Tom Tugendhat	Con
Tunbridge Wells	Greg Clark	Con
Wantage	David Johnston	Con
Wealden	Nusrat Ghani	Con
Winchester	Steve Brine	Con
Windsor	Adam Afriyie	Con
Witney	Robert Courts	Con
Woking	Jonathan Lord	Con
Wokingham	John Redwood	Con
East Worthing and Shoreham	Tim Loughton	Con
Worthing West	Peter Bottomley	Con
Wycombe	Steve Baker	Con

South West

Bath	Wera Hobhouse	Lib Dem
Bournemouth East	Tobias Ellwood	Con
Bournemouth West	Conor Burns	Con
Bridgwater and West Somerset	Ian Liddell-Grainger	Con
Bristol East	Kerry McCarthy	Lab
Bristol North West	Darren Jones	Lab
Bristol South	Karin Smyth	Lab
Bristol West	Thangam Debbonaire	Lab
Camborne and Redruth	George Eustice	Con
Cheltenham	Alex Chalk	Con
Chippenham	Michelle Donelan	Con
Christchurch	Christopher Chope	Con
North Cornwall	Scott Mann	Con

South East Cornwall	Sheryll Murray	Con
The Cotswolds	Geoffrey Clifton-Brown	Con
Devizes	Danny Kruger	Con
Central Devon	Mel Stride	Con
East Devon	Simon Jupp	Con
North Devon	Selaine Saxby	Con
South West Devon	Gary Streeter	Con
Mid Dorset and North Poole	Michael Tomlinson	Con
North Dorset	Simon Hoare	Con
South Dorset	Richard Drax	Con
West Dorset	Chris Loder	Con
Exeter	Ben Bradshaw	Lab
Filton and Bradley Stoke	Jack Lopresti	Con
Forest of Dean	Mark Harper	Con
Gloucester	Richard Graham	Con
Kingswood	Chris Skidmore	Con
Newton Abbot	Anne Marie Morris	Con
Plymouth, Moor View	Johnny Mercer	Con
Plymouth, Sutton and Devonport	Luke Pollard	Lab/Co-op
Poole	Robert Syms	Con
St Austell and Newquay	Steve Double	Con
St Ives	Derek Thomas	Con
Salisbury	John Glen	Con
North Somerset	Liam Fox	Con
North East Somerset	Jacob Rees-Mogg	Con
Somerton and Frome	David Warburton	Con
Stroud	Siobhan Baillie	Con
North Swindon	Justin Tomlinson	Con
South Swindon	Robert Buckland	Con
Taunton Deane	Rebecca Pow	Con
Tewkesbury	Laurence Robertson	Con
Thornbury and Yate	Luke Hall	Con
Tiverton and Honiton	Neil Parish	Con
Torbay	Kevin Foster	Con
Torridge and West Devon	Geoffrey Cox	Con
Totnes	Anthony Mangnall	Con
Truro and Falmouth	Cherilyn Mackrory	Con
Wells	James Heappey	Con
Weston-Super-Mare	John Penrose	Con
North Wiltshire	James Gray	Con
South West Wiltshire	Andrew Murrison	Con
Yeovil	Marcus Fysh	Con

West Midlands

Aldridge-Brownhills	Wendy Morton	Con
Birmingham, Edgbaston	Preet Kaur Gill	Lab/Co-op
Birmingham, Erdington	Jack Dromey	Lab
Birmingham, Hall Green	Tahir Ali	Lab
Birmingham, Hodge Hill	Liam Byrne	Lab
Birmingham, Ladywood	Shabana Mahmood	Lab
Birmingham, Northfield	Gary Sambrook	Con
Birmingham, Perry Barr	Khalid Mahmood	Lab
Birmingham, Selly Oak	Steve McCabe	Lab
Birmingham, Yardley	Jess Phillips	Lab
Bromsgrove	Sajid Javid	Con
Burton	Kate Griffiths	Con
Cannock Chase	Amanda Milling	Con

Coventry North East	Colleen Fletcher	Lab
Coventry North West	Taiwo Owatemi	Lab
Coventry South	Zarah Sultana	Lab
Dudley North	Marco Longhi	Con
Dudley South	Mike Wood	Con
Halesowen and Rowley Regis	James Morris	Con
Hereford and South Herefordshire	Jesse Norman	Con
North Herefordshire	Bill Wiggin	Con
Kenilworth and Southam	Jeremy Wright	Con
Lichfield	Michael Fabricant	Con
Ludlow	Philip Dunne	Con
Meriden	Saqib Bhatti	Con
Newcastle-under-Lyme	Aaron Bell	Con
Nuneaton	Marcus Jones	Con
Redditch	Rachel Maclean	Con
Rugby	Mark Pawsey	Con
Shrewsbury and Atcham	Daniel Kawczynski	Con
North Shropshire	Owen Paterson	Con
Solihull	Julian Knight	Con
Stafford	Theo Clarke	Con
Staffordshire Moorlands	Karen Bradley	Con
South Staffordshire	Gavin Williamson	Con
Stoke-on-Trent Central	Jo Gideon	Con
Stoke-on-Trent North	Jonathan Gullis	Con
Stoke-on-Trent South	Jack Brereton	Con
Stone	Bill Cash	Con
Stourbridge	Suzanne Webb	Con
Stratford-on-Avon	Nadhim Zahawi	Con
Sutton Coldfield	Andrew Mitchell	Con
Tamworth	Christopher Pincher	Con
Telford	Lucy Allan	Con
Walsall North	Eddie Hughes	Con
Walsall South	Valerie Vaz	Lab
Warley	John Spellar	Lab
Warwick and Leamington	Matt Western	Lab
North Warwickshire	Craig Tracey	Con
West Bromwich East	Nicola Richards	Con
West Bromwich West	Shaun Bailey	Con
Wolverhampton North East	Jane Stevenson	Con
Wolverhampton South East	Pat McFadden	Lab
Wolverhampton South West	Stuart Anderson	Con
Worcester	Robin Walker	Con
Mid Worcestershire	Nigel Huddleston	Con
West Worcestershire	Harriett Baldwin	Con
The Wrekin	Mark Pritchard	Con
Wyre Forest	Mark Garnier	Con

Yorkshire and Humberside

Barnsley Central	Dan Jarvis	Lab
Barnsley East	Stephanie Peacock	Lab
Batley and Spen	Tracy Brabin	Lab/Co-op
Beverley and Holderness	Graham Stuart	Con
Bradford East	Imran Hussain	Lab
Bradford South	Judith Cummins	Lab
Bradford West	Naz Shah	Lab
Brigg and Goole	Andrew Percy	Con
Calder Valley	Craig Whittaker	Con

Cleethorpes	Martin Vickers	Con
Colne Valley	Jason McCartney	Con
Dewsbury	Mark Eastwood	Con
Don Valley	Nick Fletcher	Con
Doncaster Central	Rosie Winterton	Lab
Doncaster North	Ed Miliband	Lab
Elmet and Rothwell	Alec Shelbrooke	Con
Great Grimsby	Lia Nici	Con
Halifax	Holly Lynch	Lab
Haltemprice and Howden	David Davis	Con
Harrogate and Knaresborough	Andrew Jones	Con
Hemsworth	Jon Trickett	Lab
Huddersfield	Barry Sheerman	Lab/Co-op
Kingston upon Hull East	Karl Turner	Lab
Kingston upon Hull North	Diana Johnson	Lab
Kingston upon Hull West and Hessle	Emma Hardy	Lab
Keighley	Robbie Moore	Con
Leeds Central	Hilary Benn	Lab
Leeds East	Richard Burgon	Lab
Leeds North East	Fabian Hamilton	Lab
Leeds North West	Alex Sobel	Lab/Co-op
Leeds West	Rachel Reeves	Lab
Morley and Outwood	Andrea Jenkyns	Con
Normanton, Pontefract and Castleford	Yvette Cooper	Lab
Penistone and Stocksbridge	Miriam Cates	Con
Pudsey	Stuart Andrew	Con
Richmond (Yorkshire)	Rishi Sunak	Con
Rother Valley	Alexander Stafford	Con
Rotherham	Sarah Champion	Lab
Scarborough and Whitby	Robert Goodwill	Con
Scunthorpe	Holly Mumby-Croft	Con
Selby and Ainsty	Nigel Adams	Con
Sheffield, Brightside and Hillsborough	Gill Furniss	Lab
Sheffield Central	Paul Blomfield	Lab
Sheffield, Hallam	Olivia Blake	Lab
Sheffield Heeley	Louise Haigh	Lab
Sheffield South East	Clive Betts	Lab
Shipley	Philip Davies	Con
Skipton and Ripon	Julian Smith	Con
Thirsk and Malton	Kevin Hollinrake	Con
Wakefield	Imran Ahmad Khan	Con
Wentworth and Dearne	John Healey	Lab
York Central	Rachael Maskell	Lab/Co-op
York Outer	Julian Sturdy	Con
East Yorkshire	Greg Knight	Con

Northern Ireland

East Antrim	Sammy Wilson	DUP
North Antrim	Ian Paisley	DUP
South Antrim	Paul Girvan	DUP
Belfast East	Gavin Robinson	DUP
Belfast North	John Finucane	Sinn Féin
Belfast South	Claire Hanna	SDLP
Belfast West	Paul Maskey	Sinn Féin
North Down	Stephen Farry	APNI
South Down	Chris Hazzard	Sinn Féin

Fermanagh and South Tyrone	Michelle Gildernew	Sinn Féin
Foyle	Colum Eastwood	SDLP
Lagan Valley	Jeffrey Donaldson	DUP
East Londonderry	Gregory Campbell	DUP
Newry and Armagh	Mickey Brady	Sinn Féin
Strangford	Jim Shannon	DUP
West Tyrone	Órfhlaith Begley	Sinn Féin
Mid Ulster	Francie Molloy	Sinn Féin
Upper Bann	Carla Lockhart	DUP

Scotland

Aberdeen North	Kirsty Blackman	SNP
Aberdeen South	Stephen Flynn	SNP
West Aberdeenshire and Kincardine	Andrew Bowie	Con
Airdrie and Shotts	Neil Gray	SNP
Angus	Dave Doogan	SNP
Argyll and Bute	Brendan O'Hara	SNP
Ayr, Carrick and Cumnock	Allan Dorans	SNP
Central Ayrshire	Philippa Whitford	SNP
North Ayrshire and Arran	Patricia Gibson	SNP
Banff and Buchan	David Duguid	Con
Berwickshire, Roxburgh and Selkirk	John Lamont	Con
Caithness, Sutherland and Easter Ross	Jamie Stone	Lib Dem
Coatbridge, Chryston and Bellshill	Steven Bonnar	SNP
Cumbernauld, Kilsyth and Kirkintilloch East	Stuart C McDonald	SNP
Dumfries and Galloway	Alister Jack	Con
Dumfriesshire, Clydesdale and Tweeddale	David Mundell	Con
East Dunbartonshire	Amy Callaghan	SNP
West Dunbartonshire	Martin Docherty-Hughes	SNP
Dundee East	Stewart Hosie	SNP
Dundee West	Chris Law	SNP
Dunfermline and West Fife	Douglas Chapman	SNP
East Kilbride, Strathaven and Lesmahagow	Lisa Cameron	SNP
Edinburgh East	Tommy Sheppard	SNP
Edinburgh North and Leith	Deidre Brock	SNP
Edinburgh South	Ian Murray	Lab
Edinburgh South West	Joanna Cherry	SNP
Edinburgh West	Christine Jardine	Lib Dem
Falkirk	John McNally	SNP
North East Fife	Wendy Chamberlain	Lib Dem
Glasgow Central	Alison Thewliss	SNP
Glasgow East	David Linden	SNP
Glasgow North	Patrick Grady	SNP
Glasgow North East	Anne McLaughlin	SNP
Glasgow North West	Carol Monaghan	SNP
Glasgow South	Stewart Malcolm McDonald	SNP
Glasgow South West	Chris Stephens	SNP
Glenrothes	Peter Grant	SNP
Gordon	Richard Thomson	SNP
Inverclyde	Ronnie Cowan	SNP
Inverness, Nairn, Badenoch and Strathspey	Drew Hendry	SNP
Kilmarnock and Loudoun	Alan Brown	SNP
Kirkcaldy and Cowdenbeath	Neale Hanvey	SNP

Lanark and Hamilton East	Angela Crawley	SNP
Linlithgow and East Falkirk	Martyn Day	SNP
Livingston	Hannah Bardell	SNP
East Lothian	Kenny MacAskill	SNP
Midlothian	Owen Thompson	SNP
Moray	Douglas Ross	Con
Motherwell and Wishaw	Marion Fellows	SNP
Na h-Eileanan An Iar	Angus MacNeil	SNP
Ochil and South Perthshire	John Nicolson	SNP
Orkney and Shetland	Alistair Carmichael	Lib Dem
Paisley and Renfrewshire North	Gavin Newlands	SNP
Paisley and Renfrewshire South	Mhairi Black	SNP
Perth and North Perthshire	Pete Wishart	SNP
East Renfrewshire	Kirsten Oswald	SNP
Ross, Skye and Lochaber	Ian Blackford	SNP
Rutherglen and Hamilton West	Margaret Ferrier	Ind*
Stirling	Alyn Smith	SNP

Wales

Aberavon	Stephen Kinnock	Lab
Aberconwy	Robin Millar	Con
Alyn and Deeside	Mark Tami	Lab
Arfon	Hywel Williams	PlC
Blaenau Gwent	Nick Smith	Lab
Brecon and Radnorshire	Fay Jones	Con
Bridgend	Jamie Wallis	Con
Caerphilly	Wayne David	Lab
Cardiff Central	Jo Stevens	Lab
Cardiff North	Anna McMorrin	Lab
Cardiff South and Penarth	Stephen Doughty	Lab/Co-op
Cardiff West	Kevin Brennan	Lab
Carmarthen East and Dinefwr	Jonathan Edwards	Ind†
Carmarthen West and South Pembrokeshire	Simon Hart	Con
Ceredigion	Ben Lake	PlC
Clwyd South	Simon Baynes	Con
Vale of Clwyd	James Davies	Con
Clwyd West	David Jones	Con
Cynon Valley	Beth Winter	Lab
Delyn	Rob Roberts	Con
Dwyfor Meirionnydd	Liz Saville Roberts	PlC
Vale of Glamorgan	Alun Cairns	Con
Gower	Tonia Antoniazzi	Lab
Islwyn	Chris Evans	Lab/Co-op
Llanelli	Nia Griffith	Lab
Merthyr Tydfil and Rhymney	Gerald Jones	Lab
Monmouth	David Davies	Con
Montgomeryshire	Craig Williams	Con
Neath	Christina Rees	Lab/Co-op
Newport East	Jessica Morden	Lab
Newport West	Ruth Jones	Lab
Ogmore	Chris Elmore	Lab
Pontypridd	Alex Davies-Jones	Lab
Preseli Pembrokeshire	Stephen Crabb	Con

*Elected as Scottish National Party
†Elected as Plaid Cymru

Analysis of MPs
House of Commons

Rhondda	Chris Bryant	Lab
Swansea East	Carolyn Harris	Lab
Swansea West	Geraint Davies	Lab/Co-op
Torfaen	Nick Thomas-Symonds	Lab
Wrexham	Sarah Atherton	Con
Ynys Môn	Virginia Crosbie	Con

Constituencies, MPs and Majorities

ENGLAND	533
SCOTLAND	59
WALES	40
NORTHERN IRELAND	18
	TOTAL 650

England

			Majority	*%*
Aldershot	Leo Docherty	Con	16,698	34.66
Aldridge-Brownhills	Wendy Morton	Con	19,836	50.23
Altrincham and Sale West	Graham Brady	Con	6,139	11.17
Amber Valley	Nigel Mills	Con	16,886	36.93
Arundel and South Downs	Andrew Griffith	Con	22,521	36.5
Ashfield	Lee Anderson	Con	5,733	11.68
Ashford	Damian Green	Con	24,029	39.82
Ashton under Lyne	Angela Rayner	Lab	4,263	11.01
Aylesbury	Rob Butler	Con	17,373	28.55
Banbury	Victoria Prentis	Con	16,813	26.57
Barking	Margaret Hodge	Lab	15,427	34.57
Barnsley Central	Dan Jarvis	Lab	3,571	9.65
Barnsley East	Stephanie Peacock	Lab	3,217	8.43
Barrow and Furness	Simon Fell	Con	5,789	12.54
Basildon and Billericay	John Baron	Con	20,412	46.06
South Basildon and East Thurrock	Stephen Metcalfe	Con	19,922	43.79
Basingstoke	Maria Miller	Con	14,198	25.83
Bassetlaw	Brendan Clarke-Smith	Con	14,013	27.45
Bath	Wera Hobhouse	Lib Dem	12,322	23.55
Batley and Spen	Tracy Brabin	Lab/Co-op	3,525	6.65
Battersea	Marsha De Cordova	Lab	5,668	9.43
Beaconsfield	Joy Morrissey	Con	15,712	27.07
Beckenham	Bob Stewart	Con	14,258	28.07
Bedford	Mohammad Yasin	Lab	145	0.31
Mid Bedfordshire	Nadine Dorries	Con	24,664	37.98
North East Bedfordshire	Richard Fuller	Con	24,283	37.23
South West Bedfordshire	Andrew Selous	Con	18,583	34.7
Bermondsey and Old Southwark	Neil Coyle	Lab	16,126	27.4
Berwick-upon-Tweed	Anne-Marie Trevelyan	Con	14,835	35.08
Bethnal Green and Bow	Rushanara Ali	Lab	37,524	61.72
Beverley and Holderness	Graham Stuart	Con	20,448	38.01
Bexhill and Battle	Huw Merriman	Con	26,059	43.84
Old Bexley and Sidcup	James Brokenshire	Con	18,952	40.86
Bexleyheath and Crayford	David Evennett	Con	13,103	30.18
Birkenhead	Mick Whitley	Lab	17,705	41.76
Birmingham, Edgbaston	Preet Kaur Gill	Lab/Co-op	5,614	13.22
Birmingham, Erdington	Jack Dromey	Lab	3,601	10.2
Birmingham, Hall Green	Tahir Ali	Lab	28,508	53.7
Birmingham, Hodge Hill	Liam Byrne	Lab	28,655	63.49
Birmingham, Ladywood	Shabana Mahmood	Lab	28,582	67.62
Birmingham, Northfield	Gary Sambrook	Con	1,640	3.79
Birmingham, Perry Barr	Khalid Mahmood	Lab	15,317	36.24
Birmingham, Selly Oak	Steve McCabe	Lab	12,414	25.01

			Majority	%
Birmingham, Yardley	Jess Phillips	Lab	10,659	24.91
Bishop Auckland	Dehenna Davison	Con	7,962	17.72
Blackburn	Kate Hollern	Lab	18,304	40.82
Blackley and Broughton	Graham Stringer	Lab	14,402	37.16
Blackpool North and Cleveleys	Paul Maynard	Con	8,596	22.08
Blackpool South	Scott Benton	Con	3,690	11.24
Blaydon	Liz Twist	Lab	5,531	12.08
Blyth Valley	Ian Levy	Con	712	1.74
Bognor Regis and Littlehampton	Nick Gibb	Con	22,503	43.75
Bolsover	Mark Fletcher	Con	5,299	11.5
Bolton North East	Mark Logan	Con	378	0.87
Bolton South East	Yasmin Qureshi	Lab	7,598	18.66
Bolton West	Chris Green	Con	8,855	17.9
Bootle	Peter Dowd	Lab	34,556	70.06
Boston and Skegness	Matt Warman	Con	25,621	61.19
Bosworth	Luke Evans	Con	26,278	46.37
Bournemouth East	Tobias Ellwood	Con	8,806	17.8
Bournemouth West	Conor Burns	Con	10,150	21.98
Bracknell	James Sunderland	Con	19,829	36.34
Bradford East	Imran Hussain	Lab	18,144	40.98
Bradford South	Judith Cummins	Lab	2,346	5.89
Bradford West	Naz Shah	Lab	27,019	60.86
Braintree	James Cleverly	Con	24,673	48.61
Brent Central	Dawn Butler	Lab	20,870	42.28
Brent North	Barry Gardiner	Lab	8,079	15.51
Brentford and Isleworth	Ruth Cadbury	Lab	10,514	17.98
Brentwood and Ongar	Alex Burghart	Con	29,065	54.65
Bridgwater and West Somerset	Ian Liddell-Grainger	Con	24,439	42.19
Brigg and Goole	Andrew Percy	Con	21,941	50.35
Brighton Kemptown	Lloyd Russell-Moyle	Lab/Co-op	8,061	16.56
Brighton Pavilion	Caroline Lucas	Green	19,940	34.29
Bristol East	Kerry McCarthy	Lab	10,794	20.63
Bristol North West	Darren Jones	Lab	5,692	10.15
Bristol South	Karin Smyth	Lab	9,859	17.8
Bristol West	Thangam Debbonaire	Lab	28,219	37.19
Broadland	Jerome Mayhew	Con	21,861	38.24
Bromley and Chislehurst	Robert Neill	Con	10,891	23.8
Bromsgrove	Sajid Javid	Con	23,106	42.37
Broxbourne	Charles Walker	Con	19,807	42.21
Broxtowe	Darren Henry	Con	5,331	9.61
Buckingham	Greg Smith	Con	20,411	32.04
Burnley	Antony Higginbotham	Con	1,352	3.46
Burton	Kate Griffiths	Con	14,496	29.61
Bury North	James Daly	Con	105	0.22
Bury South	Christian Wakeford	Con	402	0.8
Bury St Edmunds	Jo Churchill	Con	24,988	40.14
Calder Valley	Craig Whittaker	Con	5,774	9.94
Camberwell and Peckham	Harriet Harman	Lab	33,780	59.54
Camborne and Redruth	George Eustice	Con	8,700	17.21
Cambridge	Daniel Zeichner	Lab	9,639	17.89
North East Cambridgeshire	Stephen Barclay	Con	29,993	56.37
North West Cambridgeshire	Shailesh Vara	Con	25,983	40.07
South Cambridgeshire	Anthony Browne	Con	2,904	4.32
South East Cambridgeshire	Lucy Frazer	Con	11,490	17.78
Cannock Chase	Amanda Milling	Con	19,879	42.71
Canterbury	Rosie Duffield	Lab	1,836	3.04

			Majority	%
Carlisle	John Stevenson	Con	8,319	19.32
Carshalton and Wallington	Elliot Colburn	Con	629	1.28
Castle Point	Rebecca Harris	Con	26,634	59.75
Charnwood	Edward Argar	Con	22,397	40.26
Chatham and Aylesford	Tracey Crouch	Con	18,540	42.62
Cheadle	Mary Robinson	Con	2,336	4.16
Chelmsford	Vicky Ford	Con	17,621	30.73
Chelsea and Fulham	Greg Hands	Con	11,241	23.93
Cheltenham	Alex Chalk	Con	981	1.65
Chesham and Amersham	Cheryl Gillan	Con	16,223	28.98
City of Chester	Chris Matheson	Lab	6,164	11.27
Chesterfield	Toby Perkins	Lab	1,451	3.2
Chichester	Gillian Keegan	Con	21,490	34.95
Chingford and Woodford Green	Iain Duncan Smith	Con	1,262	2.59
Chippenham	Michelle Donelan	Con	11,288	19.66
Chipping Barnet	Theresa Villiers	Con	1,212	2.1
Chorley	Lindsay Hoyle	Speaker	17,392	42.24
Christchurch	Christopher Chope	Con	24,617	47.12
Clacton	Giles Watling	Con	24,702	56.63
Cleethorpes	Martin Vickers	Con	21,418	46
Colchester	Will Quince	Con	9,423	17.59
Colne Valley	Jason McCartney	Con	5,103	8.35
Congleton	Fiona Bruce	Con	18,561	32.32
Copeland	Trudy Harrison	Con	5,842	13.68
Corby	Tom Pursglove	Con	10,268	16.9
North Cornwall	Scott Mann	Con	14,752	28.41
South East Cornwall	Sheryll Murray	Con	20,971	38.92
The Cotswolds	Geoffrey Clifton-Brown	Con	20,214	32.9
Coventry North East	Colleen Fletcher	Lab	7,692	17.26
Coventry North West	Taiwo Owatemi	Lab	208	0.43
Coventry South	Zarah Sultana	Lab	401	0.89
Crawley	Henry Smith	Con	8,360	16.69
Crewe and Nantwich	Kieran Mullan	Con	8,508	15.71
Croydon Central	Sarah Jones	Lab	5,949	10.98
Croydon North	Steve Reed	Lab/Co-op	24,673	44.24
Croydon South	Chris Philp	Con	12,339	20.71
Dagenham and Rainham	Jon Cruddas	Lab	293	0.67
Darlington	Peter Gibson	Con	3,294	7.56
Dartford	Gareth Johnson	Con	19,160	35.28
Daventry	Chris Heaton-Harris	Con	26,080	45.24
Denton and Reddish	Andrew Gwynne	Lab	6,175	15.96
Derby North	Amanda Solloway	Con	2,540	5.39
Derby South	Margaret Beckett	Lab	6,019	14.13
Derbyshire Dales	Sarah Dines	Con	17,381	34.6
Mid Derbyshire	Pauline Latham	Con	15,385	31.05
North East Derbyshire	Lee Rowley	Con	12,876	26.07
South Derbyshire	Heather Wheeler	Con	19,335	35.93
Devizes	Danny Kruger	Con	23,993	46.84
Central Devon	Mel Stride	Con	17,721	30.33
East Devon	Simon Jupp	Con	6,708	10.44
North Devon	Selaine Saxby	Con	14,813	26.57
South West Devon	Gary Streeter	Con	21,430	39.95
Dewsbury	Mark Eastwood	Con	1,561	2.75
Don Valley	Nick Fletcher	Con	3,630	7.97
Doncaster Central	Rosie Winterton	Lab	2,278	5.46

			Majority	%
Doncaster North	Ed Miliband	Lab	2,370	5.81
Mid Dorset and North Poole	Michael Tomlinson	Con	14,898	30.35
North Dorset	Simon Hoare	Con	24,301	43.11
South Dorset	Richard Drax	Con	17,153	33.47
West Dorset	Chris Loder	Con	14,106	23.06
Dover	Natalie Elphicke	Con	12,278	24.11
Dudley North	Marco Longhi	Con	11,533	31.31
Dudley South	Mike Wood	Con	15,565	42.37
Dulwich and West Norwood	Helen Hayes	Lab	27,310	48.76
City of Durham	Mary Foy	Lab	5,025	10.25
North Durham	Kevan Jones	Lab	4,742	11.21
North West Durham	Richard Holden	Con	1,144	2.39
Ealing Central and Acton	Rupa Huq	Lab	13,300	24.2
Ealing North	James Murray	Lab/Co-op	12,269	24.66
Ealing Southall	Virendra Sharma	Lab	16,084	37.92
Easington	Grahame Morris	Lab	6,581	18.96
East Ham	Stephen Timms	Lab	33,176	60.54
Eastbourne	Caroline Ansell	Con	4,331	7.84
Eastleigh	Paul Holmes	Con	15,607	26.38
Eddisbury	Edward Timpson	Con	18,443	34.72
Edmonton	Kate Osamor	Lab/Co-op	16,015	39.41
Ellesmere Port and Neston	Justin Madders	Lab	8,764	17.93
Elmet and Rothwell	Alec Shelbrooke	Con	17,353	29.71
Eltham	Clive Efford	Lab	3,197	7.3
Enfield North	Feryal Clark	Lab	6,492	14.33
Enfield Southgate	Bambos Charalambous	Lab	4,450	9.36
Epping Forest	Eleanor Laing	Con	22,173	43.87
Epsom and Ewell	Chris Grayling	Con	17,873	29.94
Erewash	Maggie Throup	Con	10,606	21.65
Erith and Thamesmead	Abena Oppong-Asare	Lab	3,758	9.06
Esher and Walton	Dominic Raab	Con	2,743	4.34
Exeter	Ben Bradshaw	Lab	10,403	18.44
Fareham	Suella Braverman	Con	26,086	45.34
Faversham and Mid Kent	Helen Whately	Con	21,976	43.45
Feltham and Heston	Seema Malhotra	Lab/Co-op	7,859	16.39
Filton and Bradley Stoke	Jack Lopresti	Con	5,646	10.47
Finchley and Golders Green	Mike Freer	Con	6,562	11.86
Folkestone and Hythe	Damian Collins	Con	21,337	36
Forest of Dean	Mark Harper	Con	15,869	30.69
Fylde	Mark Menzies	Con	16,611	35.48
Gainsborough	Edward Leigh	Con	22,967	44.77
Garston and Halewood	Maria Eagle	Lab	31,624	59.14
Gateshead	Ian Mearns	Lab	7,200	18.77
Gedling	Tom Randall	Con	679	1.36
Gillingham and Rainham	Rehman Chishti	Con	15,119	32.8
Gloucester	Richard Graham	Con	10,277	19.04
Gosport	Caroline Dinenage	Con	23,278	47.82
Grantham and Stamford	Gareth Davies	Con	26,003	46.18
Gravesham	Adam Holloway	Con	15,581	32.64
Great Grimsby	Lia Nici	Con	7,331	48.85
Great Yarmouth	Brandon Lewis	Con	17,663	40.49
Greenwich and Woolwich	Matthew Pennycook	Lab	18,464	34.65
Guildford	Angela Richardson	Con	3,337	5.67
Hackney North and Stoke Newington	Diane Abbott	Lab	33,188	58.11
Hackney South and Shoreditch	Meg Hillier	Lab/Co-op	33,985	62.22
Halesowen and Rowley Regis	James Morris	Con	12,074	28.42

			Majority	*%*
Halifax	Holly Lynch	Lab	2,569	5.51
Haltemprice and Howden	David Davis	Con	20,329	40.64
Halton	Derek Twigg	Lab	18,975	40.94
Hammersmith	Andy Slaughter	Lab	17,847	34.22
East Hampshire	Damian Hinds	Con	19,696	34.5
North East Hampshire	Ranil Jayawardena	Con	20,211	34
North West Hampshire	Kit Malthouse	Con	26,308	44.45
Hampstead and Kilburn	Tulip Siddiq	Lab	14,188	24.62
Harborough	Neil O'Brien	Con	17,278	30.03
Harlow	Robert Halfon	Con	14,063	32.26
Harrogate and Knaresborough	Andrew Jones	Con	9,675	16.94
Harrow East	Bob Blackman	Con	8,170	16.43
Harrow West	Gareth Thomas	Lab/Co-op	8,692	18.08
Hartlepool	Mike Hill	Lab	3,595	8.74
Harwich and North Essex	Bernard Jenkin	Con	20,182	38.72
Hastings and Rye	Sally-Ann Hart	Con	4,043	7.41
Havant	Alan Mak	Con	21,792	47.42
Hayes and Harlington	John McDonnell	Lab	9,261	21
Hazel Grove	William Wragg	Con	4,423	9.95
Hemel Hempstead	Mike Penning	Con	14,563	28.29
Hemsworth	Jon Trickett	Lab	1,180	2.68
Hendon	Matthew Offord	Con	4,230	7.66
Henley	John Howell	Con	14,053	23.8
Hereford and South Herefordshire	Jesse Norman	Con	19,686	39.49
North Herefordshire	Bill Wiggin	Con	24,856	48.44
Hertford and Stortford	Julie Marson	Con	19,620	32.52
North East Hertfordshire	Oliver Heald	Con	18,189	32.71
South West Hertfordshire	Gagan Mohindra	Con	14,408	23.44
Hertsmere	Oliver Dowden	Con	21,313	40.62
Hexham	Guy Opperman	Con	10,549	22.77
Heywood and Middleton	Chris Clarkson	Con	663	1.39
High Peak	Robert Largan	Con	590	1.09
Hitchin and Harpenden	Bim Afolami	Con	6,895	11.66
Holborn and St Pancras	Keir Starmer	Lab	27,763	48.73
Hornchurch and Upminster	Julia Lopez	Con	23,308	42.98
Hornsey and Wood Green	Catherine West	Lab	19,242	31.39
Horsham	Jeremy Quin	Con	21,127	33.25
Houghton and Sunderland South	Bridget Phillipson	Lab	3,115	7.8
Hove	Peter Kyle	Lab	17,044	30.14
Huddersfield	Barry Sheerman	Lab/Co-op	4,937	11.73
Kingston upon Hull East	Karl Turner	Lab	1,239	3.81
Kingston upon Hull North	Diana Johnson	Lab	7,593	22.13
Kingston upon Hull West and Hessle	Emma Hardy	Lab	2,856	8.94
Huntingdon	Jonathan Djanogly	Con	19,383	32.62
Hyndburn	Sara Britcliffe	Con	2,951	6.94
Ilford North	Wes Streeting	Lab	5,218	10.39
Ilford South	Sam Tarry	Lab	24,101	44.92
Ipswich	Tom Hunt	Con	5,479	11.03
Isle of Wight	Bob Seely	Con	23,737	31.78
Islington North	Jeremy Corbyn	Ind*	26,188	48.47
Islington South and Finsbury	Emily Thornberry	Lab	17,328	36.11
Jarrow	Kate Osborne	Lab	7,120	17.44
Keighley	Robbie Moore	Con	2,218	4.19
Kenilworth and Southam	Jeremy Wright	Con	20,353	38.54

*Elected as Labour

			Majority	*%*
Kensington	Felicity Buchan	Con	150	0.34
Kettering	Philip Hollobone	Con	16,765	33.86
Kingston and Surbiton	Ed Davey	Lib Dem	10,489	17.2
Kingswood	Chris Skidmore	Con	11,220	22.69
Knowsley	George Howarth	Lab	39,942	72.53
West Lancashire	Rosie Cooper	Lab	8,336	15.78
Lancaster and Fleetwood	Cat Smith	Lab	2,380	5.25
Leeds Central	Hilary Benn	Lab	19,270	38.97
Leeds East	Richard Burgon	Lab	5,531	14.12
Leeds North East	Fabian Hamilton	Lab	17,089	33.49
Leeds North West	Alex Sobel	Lab/Co-op	10,749	21.75
Leeds West	Rachel Reeves	Lab	10,564	26.15
Leicester East	Claudia Webbe	Ind*	6,019	12.12
Leicester South	Jon Ashworth	Lab/Co-op	22,675	45.04
Leicester West	Liz Kendall	Lab	4,212	12.06
North West Leicestershire	Andrew Bridgen	Con	20,400	38.01
South Leicestershire	Alberto Costa	Con	24,004	41.55
Leigh	James Grundy	Con	1,965	4.17
Lewes	Maria Caulfield	Con	2,457	4.47
Lewisham Deptford	Vicky Foxcroft	Lab	32,913	59.19
Lewisham East	Janet Daby	Lab	17,008	37.83
Lewisham West and Penge	Ellie Reeves	Lab	21,543	41.2
Leyton and Wanstead	John Cryer	Lab	20,808	46.53
Lichfield	Michael Fabricant	Con	23,638	43.59
Lincoln	Karl McCartney	Con	3,514	6.92
Liverpool Riverside	Kim Johnson	Lab	37,043	69.85
Liverpool Walton	Dan Carden	Lab	30,520	74.47
Liverpool Wavertree	Paula Barker	Lab	27,085	62.24
Liverpool West Derby	Ian Byrne	Lab	29,984	68.02
Cities of London and Westminster	Nickie Aiken	Con	3,953	9.22
Loughborough	Jane Hunt	Con	7,169	13.07
Louth and Horncastle	Victoria Atkins	Con	28,868	54.86
Ludlow	Philip Dunne	Con	23,648	46.84
Luton North	Sarah Owen	Lab	9,247	21.63
Luton South	Rachel Hopkins	Lab	8,756	20.73
Macclesfield	David Rutley	Con	10,711	19.8
Maidenhead	Theresa May	Con	18,846	33.2
Maidstone and The Weald	Helen Grant	Con	21,772	41.92
Makerfield	Yvonne Fovargue	Lab	4,740	10.67
Maldon	John Whittingdale	Con	30,041	59.32
Manchester Central	Lucy Powell	Lab/Co-op	29,089	55.43
Manchester Gorton	Afzal Khan	Lab	30,339	67.88
Manchester Withington	Jeff Smith	Lab	27,905	52.48
Mansfield	Ben Bradley	Con	16,306	32.99
Meon Valley	Flick Drummond	Con	23,555	42.8
Meriden	Saqib Bhatti	Con	22,836	41.98
Middlesbrough	Andy McDonald	Lab	8,395	24.56
Middlesbrough South and East Cleveland	Simon Clarke	Con	11,626	24.22
Milton Keynes North	Ben Everitt	Con	6,255	9.96
Milton Keynes South	Iain Stewart	Con	6,944	10.82
Mitcham and Morden	Siobhain McDonagh	Lab	16,482	35.95
Mole Valley	Paul Beresford	Con	12,041	21.01
Morecambe and Lunesdale	David Morris	Con	6,354	13.98

*Elected as Labour

			Majority	*%*
Morley and Outwood	Andrea Jenkyns	Con	11,267	21.62
New Forest East	Julian Lewis	Con	25,251	49.54
New Forest West	Desmond Swayne	Con	24,403	48.27
Newark	Robert Jenrick	Con	21,816	39.65
Newbury	Laura Farris	Con	16,047	26.66
Newcastle-under-Lyme	Aaron Bell	Con	7,446	16.59
Newcastle upon Tyne Central	Chi Onwurah	Lab	12,278	32.64
Newcastle upon Tyne East	Nick Brown	Lab	15,463	35.47
Newcastle upon Tyne North	Catherine McKinnell	Lab	5,765	12.24
Newton Abbot	Anne Marie Morris	Con	17,501	33.18
Mid Norfolk	George Freeman	Con	22,594	39.97
North Norfolk	Duncan Baker	Con	14,395	28.23
North West Norfolk	James Wild	Con	19,922	42.57
South Norfolk	Richard Bacon	Con	21,275	33.89
South West Norfolk	Elizabeth Truss	Con	26,195	50.72
Normanton, Pontefract and Castleford	Yvette Cooper	Lab	1,276	2.64
Northampton North	Michael Ellis	Con	5,507	13.89
Northampton South	Andrew Lewer	Con	4,697	11.47
South Northamptonshire	Andrea Leadsom	Con	27,761	41.33
Norwich North	Chloe Smith	Con	4,738	10.21
Norwich South	Clive Lewis	Lab	12,760	24.69
Nottingham East	Nadia Whittome	Lab	17,393	43.33
Nottingham North	Alex Norris	Lab/Co-op	4,490	12.68
Nottingham South	Lilian Greenwood	Lab	12,568	26.01
Nuneaton	Marcus Jones	Con	13,144	28.95
Oldham East and Saddleworth	Debbie Abrahams	Lab	1,499	3.24
Oldham West and Royton	Jim McMahon	Lab/Co-op	11,127	24.98
Orpington	Gareth Bacon	Con	22,378	45.68
Oxford East	Anneliese Dodds	Lab/Co-op	17,832	35.97
Oxford West and Abingdon	Layla Moran	Lib Dem	8,943	15.14
Pendle	Andrew Stephenson	Con	6,186	13.86
Penistone and Stocksbridge	Miriam Cates	Con	7,210	14.52
Penrith and The Border	Neil Hudson	Con	18,519	38.55
Peterborough	Paul Bristow	Con	2,580	5.39
Plymouth, Moor View	Johnny Mercer	Con	12,897	29.02
Plymouth, Sutton and Devonport	Luke Pollard	Lab/Co-op	4,757	8.92
Poole	Robert Syms	Con	19,116	37.76
Poplar and Limehouse	Apsana Begum	Lab	28,904	46.96
Portsmouth North	Penny Mordaunt	Con	15,780	34.26
Portsmouth South	Stephen Morgan	Lab	5,363	11.27
Preston	Mark Hendrick	Lab/Co-op	12,146	35.84
Pudsey	Stuart Andrew	Con	3,517	6.47
Putney	Fleur Anderson	Lab	4,774	9.44
Rayleigh and Wickford	Mark Francois	Con	31,000	56.17
Reading East	Matt Rodda	Lab	5,924	10.57
Reading West	Alok Sharma	Con	4,117	8.14
Redcar	Jacob Young	Con	3,527	8.62
Redditch	Rachel Maclean	Con	16,036	36.21
Reigate	Crispin Blunt	Con	18,310	34.3
South Ribble	Katherine Fletcher	Con	11,199	20.74
Ribble Valley	Nigel Evans	Con	18,439	33.2
Richmond Park	Sarah Olney	Lib Dem	7,766	11.9
Richmond (Yorkshire)	Rishi Sunak	Con	27,210	46.99
Rochdale	Tony Lloyd	Lab	9,668	20.31
Rochester and Strood	Kelly Tolhurst	Con	17,072	32.76
Rochford and Southend East	James Duddridge	Con	12,286	26.53

			Majority	%
Romford	Andrew Rosindell	Con	17,893	37.69
Romsey and Southampton North	Caroline Nokes	Con	10,872	21.08
Rossendale and Darwen	Jake Berry	Con	9,522	19.41
Rother Valley	Alexander Stafford	Con	6,318	12.94
Rotherham	Sarah Champion	Lab	3,121	8.73
Rugby	Mark Pawsey	Con	13,447	26.34
Ruislip, Northwood and Pinner	David Simmonds	Con	16,394	30.88
Runnymede and Weybridge	Ben Spencer	Con	18,270	34.17
Rushcliffe	Ruth Edwards	Con	7,643	12.58
Rutland and Melton	Alicia Kearns	Con	26,924	45.98
Saffron Walden	Kemi Badenoch	Con	27,594	43.52
St Albans	Daisy Cooper	Lib Dem	6,293	10.89
St Austell and Newquay	Steve Double	Con	16,526	29.56
St Helens North	Conor McGinn	Lab	12,209	25.58
St Helens South and Whiston	Marie Rimmer	Lab	19,122	37.96
St Ives	Derek Thomas	Con	4,284	8.31
Salford and Eccles	Rebecca Long Bailey	Lab	16,327	32.14
Salisbury	John Glen	Con	19,736	36.62
Scarborough and Whitby	Robert Goodwill	Con	10,270	20.57
Scunthorpe	Holly Mumby-Croft	Con	6,451	17.05
Sedgefield	Paul Howell	Con	4,513	10.83
Sefton Central	Bill Esterson	Lab	15,122	29.63
Selby and Ainsty	Nigel Adams	Con	20,137	35.57
Sevenoaks	Laura Trott	Con	20,818	40.66
Sheffield, Brightside and Hillsborough	Gill Furniss	Lab	12,274	30.9
Sheffield Central	Paul Blomfield	Lab	27,273	53.32
Sheffield, Hallam	Olivia Blake	Lab	712	1.25
Sheffield Heeley	Louise Haigh	Lab	8,520	19.89
Sheffield South East	Clive Betts	Lab	4,289	10.18
Sherwood	Mark Spencer	Con	16,186	30.6
Shipley	Philip Davies	Con	6,242	11.5
Shrewsbury and Atcham	Daniel Kawczynski	Con	11,217	18.92
North Shropshire	Owen Paterson	Con	22,949	40.46
Sittingbourne and Sheppey	Gordon Henderson	Con	24,479	47.53
Skipton and Ripon	Julian Smith	Con	23,694	40.18
Sleaford and North Hykeham	Caroline Johnson	Con	32,565	48.76
Slough	Tanmanjeet Singh Dhesi	Lab	13,640	26.64
Solihull	Julian Knight	Con	21,273	38.29
North Somerset	Liam Fox	Con	17,536	28.15
North East Somerset	Jacob Rees-Mogg	Con	14,729	26.08
Somerton and Frome	David Warburton	Con	19,213	29.5
South Holland and The Deepings	John Hayes	Con	30,838	62.45
South Shields	Emma Lewell-Buck	Lab	9,585	25.25
Southampton Itchen	Royston Smith	Con	4,498	9.46
Southampton Test	Alan Whitehead	Lab	6,213	13.77
Southend West	David Amess	Con	14,459	30.9
Southport	Damien Moore	Con	4,147	8.57
Spelthorne	Kwasi Kwarteng	Con	18,393	36.95
Stafford	Theo Clarke	Con	14,377	28
Staffordshire Moorlands	Karen Bradley	Con	16,428	37.48
South Staffordshire	Gavin Williamson	Con	28,250	56.2
Stalybridge and Hyde	Jonathan Reynolds	Lab/Co-op	2,946	6.93
Stevenage	Stephen McPartland	Con	8,562	17.88
Stockport	Navendu Mishra	Lab	10,039	23.98
Stockton North	Alex Cunningham	Lab	1,027	2.49

			Majority	*%*
Stockton South	Matt Vickers	Con	5,260	9.57
Stoke-on-Trent Central	Jo Gideon	Con	670	2.08
Stoke-on-Trent North	Jonathan Gullis	Con	6,286	15.63
Stoke-on-Trent South	Jack Brereton	Con	11,271	28.34
Stone	Bill Cash	Con	19,945	39.84
Stourbridge	Suzanne Webb	Con	13,571	29.61
Stratford-on-Avon	Nadhim Zahawi	Con	19,972	36.1
Streatham	Bell Ribeiro-Addy	Lab	17,690	31.2
Stretford and Urmston	Kate Green	Lab	16,417	32.69
Stroud	Siobhan Baillie	Con	3,840	5.81
Central Suffolk and North Ipswich	Dan Poulter	Con	23,391	41.38
Suffolk Coastal	Therese Coffey	Con	20,533	35.09
South Suffolk	James Cartlidge	Con	22,897	42.59
West Suffolk	Matt Hancock	Con	23,194	44.8
Sunderland Central	Julie Elliott	Lab	2,964	6.8
East Surrey	Claire Coutinho	Con	24,040	40.12
Surrey Heath	Michael Gove	Con	18,349	31.16
South West Surrey	Jeremy Hunt	Con	8,817	14.52
Mid Sussex	Mims Davies	Con	18,197	28.89
Sutton and Cheam	Paul Scully	Con	8,351	16.47
Sutton Coldfield	Andrew Mitchell	Con	19,272	36.61
North Swindon	Justin Tomlinson	Con	16,171	29.23
South Swindon	Robert Buckland	Con	6,625	12.99
Tamworth	Christopher Pincher	Con	19,634	42.49
Tatton	Esther McVey	Con	17,387	35.38
Taunton Deane	Rebecca Pow	Con	11,700	18.3
Telford	Lucy Allan	Con	10,941	25.42
Tewkesbury	Laurence Robertson	Con	22,410	36.5
North Thanet	Roger Gale	Con	17,189	35.49
South Thanet	Craig Mackinlay	Con	10,587	21.84
Thirsk and Malton	Kevin Hollinrake	Con	25,154	44.26
Thornbury and Yate	Luke Hall	Con	12,369	23.56
Thurrock	Jackie Doyle-Price	Con	11,482	24.12
Tiverton and Honiton	Neil Parish	Con	24,239	40.49
Tonbridge and Malling	Tom Tugendhat	Con	26,941	47.01
Tooting	Rosena Allin-Khan	Lab	14,307	24.39
Torbay	Kevin Foster	Con	17,749	35.1
Torridge and West Devon	Geoffrey Cox	Con	24,992	41.68
Totnes	Anthony Mangnall	Con	12,724	24.29
Tottenham	David Lammy	Lab	30,175	64.12
Truro and Falmouth	Cherilyn Mackrory	Con	4,561	7.68
Tunbridge Wells	Greg Clark	Con	14,645	26.64
Twickenham	Munira Wilson	Lib Dem	14,121	21.81
Tynemouth	Alan Campbell	Lab	4,857	8.64
North Tyneside	Mary Glindon	Lab	9,561	18.9
Uxbridge and South Ruislip	Boris Johnson	Con	7,210	14.93
Vauxhall	Florence Eshalomi	Lab/Co-op	19,612	34.67
Wakefield	Imran Ahmad Khan	Con	3,358	7.44
Wallasey	Angela Eagle	Lab	18,322	39.32
Walsall North	Eddie Hughes	Con	11,965	32.62
Walsall South	Valerie Vaz	Lab	3,456	8.12
Walthamstow	Stella Creasy	Lab/Co-op	30,862	63.58
Wansbeck	Ian Lavery	Lab	814	2
Wantage	David Johnston	Con	12,653	18.75
Warley	John Spellar	Lab	11,511	30.79
Warrington North	Charlotte Nichols	Lab	1,509	3.22

			Majority	%
Warrington South	Andy Carter	Con	2,010	3.24
Warwick and Leamington	Matt Western	Lab	789	1.45
North Warwickshire	Craig Tracey	Con	17,956	38.96
Washington and Sunderland West	Sharon Hodgson	Lab	3,723	9.9
Watford	Dean Russell	Con	4,433	7.6
Waveney	Peter Aldous	Con	18,002	35.09
Wealden	Nusrat Ghani	Con	25,655	41.87
Weaver Vale	Mike Amesbury	Lab	562	1.11
Wellingborough	Peter Bone	Con	18,540	35.55
Wells	James Heappey	Con	9,991	16.16
Welwyn Hatfield	Grant Shapps	Con	10,955	20.95
Wentworth and Dearne	John Healey	Lab	2,165	5.19
West Bromwich East	Nicola Richards	Con	1,593	4.42
West Bromwich West	Shaun Bailey	Con	3,799	11
West Ham	Lyn Brown	Lab	32,388	53.61
Westminster North	Karen Buck	Lab	10,759	25
Westmorland and Lonsdale	Tim Farron	Lib Dem	1,934	3.66
Weston-Super-Mare	John Penrose	Con	17,121	30.64
Wigan	Lisa Nandy	Lab	6,728	14.89
North Wiltshire	James Gray	Con	17,626	32.06
South West Wiltshire	Andrew Murrison	Con	21,630	39.23
Wimbledon	Stephen Hammond	Con	628	1.18
Winchester	Steve Brine	Con	985	1.67
Windsor	Adam Afriyie	Con	20,079	37.22
Wirral South	Alison McGovern	Lab	6,105	13.98
Wirral West	Margaret Greenwood	Lab	3,003	6.98
Witham	Priti Patel	Con	24,082	48.6
Witney	Robert Courts	Con	15,177	24.6
Woking	Jonathan Lord	Con	9,767	18.05
Wokingham	John Redwood	Con	7,383	11.87
Wolverhampton North East	Jane Stevenson	Con	4,080	11.87
Wolverhampton South East	Pat McFadden	Lab	1,235	3.68
Wolverhampton South West	Stuart Anderson	Con	1,661	4.02
Worcester	Robin Walker	Con	6,758	13.23
Mid Worcestershire	Nigel Huddleston	Con	28,018	49.74
West Worcestershire	Harriett Baldwin	Con	24,499	42.37
Workington	Mark Jenkinson	Con	4,176	10.02
Worsley and Eccles South	Barbara Keeley	Lab	3,219	7.18
East Worthing and Shoreham	Tim Loughton	Con	7,474	14.02
Worthing West	Peter Bottomley	Con	14,823	26.99
The Wrekin	Mark Pritchard	Con	18,726	38.15
Wycombe	Steve Baker	Con	4,214	7.67
Wyre and Preston North	Ben Wallace	Con	16,781	31.59
Wyre Forest	Mark Garnier	Con	21,413	42.14
Wythenshawe and Sale East	Mike Kane	Lab	10,396	23.16
Yeovil	Marcus Fysh	Con	16,181	27.24
York Central	Rachael Maskell	Lab/Co-op	13,545	27.25
York Outer	Julian Sturdy	Con	9,985	17.97
East Yorkshire	Greg Knight	Con	22,787	43.02

Scotland

			Majority	%
Aberdeen North	Kirsty Blackman	SNP	12,670	33.8
Aberdeen South	Stephen Flynn	SNP	3,990	8.72
West Aberdeenshire and Kincardine	Andrew Bowie	Con	843	1.58
Airdrie and Shotts	Neil Gray	SNP	5,201	13.05

			Majority	*%*
Angus	Dave Doogan	SNP	3,795	8.77
Argyll and Bute	Brendan O'Hara	SNP	4,110	8.53
Ayr, Carrick and Cumnock	Allan Dorans	SNP	2,329	4.98
Central Ayrshire	Philippa Whitford	SNP	5,304	11.37
North Ayrshire and Arran	Patricia Gibson	SNP	8,521	17.65
Banff and Buchan	David Duguid	Con	4,118	9.72
Berwickshire, Roxburgh and Selkirk	John Lamont	Con	5,148	9.66
Caithness, Sutherland and Easter Ross	Jamie Stone	Lib Dem	204	0.65
Coatbridge, Chryston and Bellshill	Steven Bonnar	SNP	5,624	11.63
Cumbernauld, Kilsyth and Kirkintilloch East	Stuart C McDonald	SNP	12,976	28.31
Dumfries and Galloway	Alister Jack	Con	1,805	3.5
Dumfriesshire, Clydesdale and Tweeddale	David Mundell	Con	3,781	7.67
East Dunbartonshire	Amy Callaghan	SNP	149	0.28
West Dunbartonshire	Martin Docherty-Hughes	SNP	9,553	21.11
Dundee East	Stewart Hosie	SNP	13,375	29.45
Dundee West	Chris Law	SNP	12,259	29.42
Dunfermline and West Fife	Douglas Chapman	SNP	10,699	19.96
East Kilbride, Strathaven and Lesmahagow	Lisa Cameron	SNP	13,322	23.48
Edinburgh East	Tommy Sheppard	SNP	10,417	21.72
Edinburgh North and Leith	Deidre Brock	SNP	12,808	21.54
Edinburgh South	Ian Murray	Lab	11,095	22.25
Edinburgh South West	Joanna Cherry	SNP	11,982	22.94
Edinburgh West	Christine Jardine	Lib Dem	3,769	6.9
Falkirk	John McNally	SNP	14,948	26.65
North East Fife	Wendy Chamberlain	Lib Dem	1,316	2.86
Glasgow Central	Alison Thewliss	SNP	6,474	16.08
Glasgow East	David Linden	SNP	5,566	14.43
Glasgow North	Patrick Grady	SNP	5,601	15.44
Glasgow North East	Anne McLaughlin	SNP	2,548	7.49
Glasgow North West	Carol Monaghan	SNP	8,359	20.94
Glasgow South	Stewart Malcolm McDonald	SNP	9,005	18.95
Glasgow South West	Chris Stephens	SNP	4,900	13.27
Glenrothes	Peter Grant	SNP	11,757	28.25
Gordon	Richard Thomson	SNP	819	1.46
Inverclyde	Ronnie Cowan	SNP	7,512	18.77
Inverness, Nairn, Badenoch and Strathspey	Drew Hendry	SNP	10,440	19.01
Kilmarnock and Loudoun	Alan Brown	SNP	12,659	26.5
Kirkcaldy and Cowdenbeath	Neale Hanvey	SNP	1,243	2.64
Lanark and Hamilton East	Angela Crawley	SNP	5,187	9.75
Linlithgow and East Falkirk	Martyn Day	SNP	11,266	19.46
Livingston	Hannah Bardell	SNP	13,435	24.54
East Lothian	Kenny MacAskill	SNP	3,886	6.63
Midlothian	Owen Thompson	SNP	5,705	11.8
Moray	Douglas Ross	Con	513	1.05
Motherwell and Wishaw	Marion Fellows	SNP	6,268	14.08
Na h-Eileanan An Iar	Angus MacNeil	SNP	2,438	16.77
Ochil and South Perthshire	John Nicolson	SNP	4,498	7.76
Orkney and Shetland	Alistair Carmichael	Lib Dem	2,507	10.79
Paisley and Renfrewshire North	Gavin Newlands	SNP	11,902	23.88
Paisley and Renfrewshire South	Mhairi Black	SNP	10,679	24.71

			Majority	%
Perth and North Perthshire	Pete Wishart	SNP	7,550	13.93
East Renfrewshire	Kirsten Oswald	SNP	5,426	9.77
Ross, Skye and Lochaber	Ian Blackford	SNP	9,443	23.64
Rutherglen and Hamilton West	Margaret Ferrier	Ind*	5,230	9.7
Stirling	Alyn Smith	SNP	9,254	17.55

Wales

			Majority	%
Aberavon	Stephen Kinnock	Lab	10,490	33.11
Aberconwy	Robin Millar	Con	2,034	6.36
Alyn and Deeside	Mark Tami	Lab	213	0.49
Arfon	Hywel Williams	PlC	2,781	9.54
Blaenau Gwent	Nick Smith	Lab	8,647	28.54
Brecon and Radnorshire	Fay Jones	Con	7,131	17.21
Bridgend	Jamie Wallis	Con	1,157	2.73
Caerphilly	Wayne David	Lab	6,833	16.97
Cardiff Central	Jo Stevens	Lab	17,179	40.88
Cardiff North	Anna McMorrin	Lab	6,982	13.23
Cardiff South and Penarth	Stephen Doughty	Lab/Co-op	12,737	25.1
Cardiff West	Kevin Brennan	Lab	10,986	23.72
Carmarthen East and Dinefwr	Jonathan Edwards	Ind†	1,809	4.37
Carmarthen West and South Pembrokeshire	Simon Hart	Con	7,745	18.33
Ceredigion	Ben Lake	PlC	6,329	15.74
Clwyd South	Simon Baynes	Con	1,239	3.4
Vale of Clwyd	James Davies	Con	1,827	4.9
Clwyd West	David Jones	Con	6,747	16.72
Cynon Valley	Beth Winter	Lab	8,822	29.08
Delyn	Rob Roberts	Con	865	2.25
Dwyfor Meirionnydd	Liz Saville Roberts	PlC	4,740	15.77
Vale of Glamorgan	Alun Cairns	Con	3,562	6.46
Gower	Tonia Antoniazzi	Lab	1,837	4.12
Islwyn	Chris Evans	Lab/Co-op	5,464	15.84
Llanelli	Nia Griffith	Lab	4,670	12.17
Merthyr Tydfil and Rhymney	Gerald Jones	Lab	10,606	32.81
Monmouth	David Davies	Con	9,982	19.82
Montgomeryshire	Craig Williams	Con	12,138	84.25
Neath	Christina Rees	Lab/Co-op	5,637	15.29
Newport East	Jessica Morden	Lab	1,992	5.48
Newport West	Ruth Jones	Lab	902	2.07
Ogmore	Chris Elmore	Lab	7,805	21.99
Pontypridd	Alex Davies-Jones	Lab	5,887	15.07
Preseli Pembrokeshire	Stephen Crabb	Con	5,062	11.89
Rhondda	Chris Bryant	Lab	11,440	38.49
Swansea East	Carolyn Harris	Lab	7,970	23.69
Swansea West	Geraint Davies	Lab/Co-op	8,116	22.57
Torfaen	Nick Thomas-Symonds	Lab	3,742	10.03
Wrexham	Sarah Atherton	Con	2,131	6.34
Ynys Môn	Virginia Crosbie	Con	1,968	5.37

Northern Ireland

			Majority	%
East Antrim	Sammy Wilson	DUP	6,706	17.92

*Elected as Scottish National Party
†Elected as Plaid Cymru

Analysis of MPs House of Commons

			Majority	%
North Antrim	Ian Paisley	DUP	12,721	28.68
South Antrim	Paul Girvan	DUP	2,689	6.23
Belfast East	Gavin Robinson	DUP	1,819	4.27
Belfast North	John Finucane	Sinn Féin	1,943	3.93
Belfast South	Claire Hanna	SDLP	15,401	32.41
Belfast West	Paul Maskey	Sinn Féin	14,672	37.63
North Down	Stephen Farry	APNI	2,968	7.27
South Down	Chris Hazzard	Sinn Féin	1,620	3.24
Fermanagh and South Tyrone	Michelle Gildernew	Sinn Féin	57	0.11
Foyle	Colum Eastwood	SDLP	17,110	36.12
Lagan Valley	Jeffrey Donaldson	DUP	6,499	14.26
East Londonderry	Gregory Campbell	DUP	9,607	24.32
Newry and Armagh	Mickey Brady	Sinn Féin	9,287	18.17
Strangford	Jim Shannon	DUP	7,071	18.78
West Tyrone	Órfhlaith Begley	Sinn Féin	7,478	18.16
Mid Ulster	Francie Molloy	Sinn Féin	9,537	21.21
Upper Bann	Carla Lockhart	DUP	8,210	16.31

2019 GENERAL ELECTION

New MPs (155)

Imran Ahmad Khan	Con	Wakefield
Nickie Aiken	Con	Cities of London and Westminster
Tahir Ali	Lab	Birmingham, Hall Green
Fleur Anderson	Lab	Putney
Lee Anderson	Con	Ashfield
Stuart Anderson	Con	Wolverhampton South West
Caroline Ansell*	Con	Eastbourne
Sarah Atherton	Con	Wrexham
Gareth Bacon	Con	Orpington
Shaun Bailey	Con	West Bromwich West
Siobhan Baillie	Con	Bermondsey and Old Southwark
Duncan Baker	Con	North Norfolk
Paula Barker	Lab	Liverpool Wavertree
Simon Baynes	Con	Clwyd South
Apsana Begum	Lab	Poplar and Limehouse
Aaron Bell	Con	Don Valley
Scott Benton	Con	Blackpool South
Saqib Bhatti	Con	Meriden
Olivia Blake	Lab	Sheffield, Hallam
Steven Bonnar	SNP	Coatbridge, Chryston and Bellshill
Paul Bristow	Con	Middlesbrough South and East Cleveland
Sara Britcliffe	Con	Hyndburn
Anthony Browne	Con	South Cambridgeshire
Felicity Buchan	Con	Kensington
Rob Butler	Con	Aylesbury
Ian Byrne	Lab	Liverpool West Derby
Amy Callaghan	SNP	East Dunbartonshire
Andy Carter	Con	Warrington South
Miriam Cates	Con	Penistone and Stocksbridge
Wendy Chamberlain	Lib Dem	North East Fife
Feryal Clark	Lab	Enfield North
Theo Clarke	Con	Bristol East
Brendan Clarke-Smith	Con	Bassetlaw

*MP in previous Parliament

Chris Clarkson	Con	Heywood and Middleton
Elliot Colburn	Con	Carshalton and Wallington
Daisy Cooper	Lib Dem	Mid Sussex
Claire Coutinho	Con	East Surrey
Virginia Crosbie	Con	Ynys Môn
James Daly	Con	Bolton North East
Gareth Davies	Con	Doncaster Central
James Davies*	Con	Vale of Clwyd
Alex Davies-Jones	Lab	Pontypridd
Dehenna Davison	Con	Bishop Auckland
Sarah Dines	Con	Derbyshire Dales
Dave Doogan	SNP	Angus
Allan Dorans	SNP	Ayr, Carrick and Cumnock
Flick Drummond*	Con	Meon Valley
Colum Eastwood	SDLP	Foyle
Mark Eastwood	Con	Dewsbury
Ruth Edwards	Con	Rushcliffe
Natalie Elphicke	Con	Dover
Florence Eshalomi	Lab/Co-op	Vauxhall
Luke Evans	Con	Birmingham, Edgbaston
Ben Everitt	Con	Milton Keynes North
Laura Farris	Con	Leyton and Wanstead
Stephen Farry	APNI	North Down
Simon Fell	Con	Barrow and Furness
Margaret Ferrier*	Ind	Rutherglen and Hamilton West
John Finucane	Sinn Féin	Belfast North
Katherine Fletcher	Con	Ellesmere Port and Neston
Mark Fletcher	Con	Bolsover
Nick Fletcher	Con	Don Valley
Stephen Flynn	SNP	Aberdeen South
Mary Foy	Lab	City of Durham
Richard Fuller*	Con	Bedford
Peter Gibson	Con	Darlington
Jo Gideon	Con	Great Grimsby
Andrew Griffith	Con	Arundel and South Downs
Kate Griffiths	Con	Burton
James Grundy	Con	Leigh
Jonathan Gullis	Con	Stoke-on-Trent North
Claire Hanna	SDLP	Strangford
Neale Hanvey	SNP	Kirkcaldy and Cowdenbeath
Sally-Ann Hart	Con	Hastings and Rye
Darren Henry	Con	Broxtowe
Antony Higginbotham	Con	Burnley
Richard Holden	Con	North West Durham
Paul Holmes	Con	Eastleigh
Rachel Hopkins	Lab	Luton South
Paul Howell	Con	Houghton and Sunderland South
Neil Hudson	Con	Edinburgh South
Jane Hunt	Con	Leicester East
Tom Hunt	Con	Doncaster Central
Mark Jenkinson	Con	Workington
Kim Johnson	Lab	Liverpool Riverside
David Johnston	Con	Wantage
Fay Jones	Con	Brecon and Radnorshire
Simon Jupp	Con	East Devon

*MP in previous Parliament

Alicia Kearns	Con	Mitcham and Morden
Danny Kruger	Con	Devizes
Robert Largan	Con	Bury South
Ian Levy	Con	Blyth Valley
Carla Lockhart	DUP	Upper Bann
Chris Loder	Con	West Dorset
Mark Logan	Con	Bolton North East
Marco Longhi	Con	Dudley North
Kenny MacAskill	SNP	East Lothian
Jason McCartney*	Con	Colne Valley
Karl McCartney*	Con	Lincoln
Cherilyn Mackrory	Con	Truro and Falmouth
Anne McLaughlin*	SNP	Glasgow North East
Anthony Mangnall	Con	Totnes
Julie Marson	Con	Dagenham and Rainham
Jerome Mayhew	Con	Broadland
Robin Millar	Con	Aberconwy
Navendu Mishra	Lab	Hazel Grove
Gagan Mohindra	Con	North Tyneside
Robbie Moore	Con	Keighley
Joy Morrissey	Con	Beaconsfield
Kieran Mullan	Con	Birmingham, Hodge Hill
Holly Mumby-Croft	Con	Scunthorpe
James Murray	Lab/Co-op	Ealing North
Charlotte Nichols	Lab	Warrington North
Lia Nici	Con	Great Grimsby
John Nicolson*	SNP	East Dunbartonshire
Sarah Olney*	Lib Dem	Richmond Park
Abena Oppong-Asare	Lab	Erith and Thamesmead
Kate Osborne	Lab	Jarrow
Kirsten Oswald*	SNP	East Renfrewshire
Taiwo Owatemi	Lab	Coventry North West
Sarah Owen	Lab	Hastings and Rye
Tom Randall	Con	Gedling
Bell Ribeiro-Addy	Lab	Streatham
Nicola Richards	Con	West Bromwich East
Angela Richardson	Con	Guildford
Rob Roberts	Con	Delyn
Dean Russell	Con	Luton North
Gary Sambrook	Con	Birmingham, Northfield
Selaine Saxby	Con	North Devon
David Simmonds	Con	Ruislip, Northwood and Pinner
Alyn Smith	SNP	Stirling
Greg Smith	Con	Buckingham
Amanda Solloway*	Con	Derby North
Ben Spencer	Con	Camberwell and Peckham
Alexander Stafford	Con	Rother Valley
Jane Stevenson	Con	Wolverhampton North East
Zarah Sultana	Lab	Coventry South
James Sunderland	Con	Bracknell
Sam Tarry	Lab	Ilford South
Owen Thompson*	SNP	Midlothian
Richard Thomson	SNP	Gordon
Edward Timpson*	Con	Crewe and Nantwich
Laura Trott	Con	Sevenoaks

*MP in previous Parliament

Matt Vickers	Con	Stockton South
Christian Wakeford	Con	Bury South
Jamie Wallis	Con	Bridgend
Suzanne Webb	Con	Stourbridge
Claudia Webbe	Ind	Leicester East
Mick Whitley	Lab	Birkenhead
Nadia Whittome	Lab	Nottingham East
James Wild	Con	North Norfolk
Craig Williams*	Con	Cardiff North
Munira Wilson	Lib Dem	Feltham and Heston
Beth Winter	Lab	Cynon Valley
Jacob Young	Con	Middlesbrough

*MP in previous Parliament

Most Vulnerable Constituencies

Constituencies have been classed as vulnerable if their majority is less than 15 per cent following the 2019 general election.

				Majority	*%*
1	Fermanagh and South Tyrone	Michelle Gildernew	Sinn Féin	57	0.11
2	Bury North	James Daly	Con	105	0.22
3	Bedford	Mohammad Yasin	Lab	145	0.31
4	East Dunbartonshire	Amy Callaghan	SNP	149	0.28
5	Kensington	Felicity Buchan	Con	150	0.34
6	Caithness, Sutherland and Easter Ross	Jamie Stone	Lib Dem	204	0.65
7	Coventry North West	Taiwo Owatemi	Lab	208	0.43
8	Alyn and Deeside	Mark Tami	Lab	213	0.49
9	Dagenham and Rainham	Jon Cruddas	Lab	293	0.67
10	Bolton North East	Mark Logan	Con	378	0.87
11	Coventry South	Zarah Sultana	Lab	401	0.89
12	Bury South	Christian Wakeford	Con	402	0.8
13	Moray	Douglas Ross	Con	513	1.05
14	Weaver Vale	Mike Amesbury	Lab	562	1.11
15	High Peak	Robert Largan	Con	590	1.09
16	Wimbledon	Stephen Hammond	Con	628	1.18
17	Carshalton and Wallington	Elliot Colburn	Con	629	1.28
18	Heywood and Middleton	Chris Clarkson	Con	663	1.39
19	Stoke-on-Trent Central	Jo Gideon	Con	670	2.08
20	Gedling	Tom Randall	Con	679	1.36
21	Blyth Valley	Ian Levy	Con	712	1.74
22	Sheffield, Hallam	Olivia Blake	Lab	712	1.25
23	Warwick and Leamington	Matt Western	Lab	789	1.45
24	Wansbeck	Ian Lavery	Lab	814	2
25	Gordon	Richard Thomson	SNP	819	1.46
26	West Aberdeenshire and Kincardine	Andrew Bowie	Con	843	1.58
27	Delyn	Rob Roberts	Con	865	2.25
28	Newport West	Ruth Jones	Lab	902	2.07
29	Cheltenham	Alex Chalk	Con	981	1.65
30	Winchester	Steve Brine	Con	985	1.67
31	Stockton North	Alex Cunningham	Lab	1,027	2.49
32	North West Durham	Richard Holden	Con	1,144	2.39
33	Bridgend	Jamie Wallis	Con	1,157	2.73
34	Hemsworth	Jon Trickett	Lab	1,180	2.68
35	Chipping Barnet	Theresa Villiers	Con	1,212	2.1
36	Wolverhampton South East	Pat McFadden	Lab	1,235	3.68
37	Kingston upon Hull East	Karl Turner	Lab	1,239	3.81
38	Clwyd South	Simon Baynes	Con	1,239	3.4
39	Kirkcaldy and Cowdenbeath	Neale Hanvey	SNP	1,243	2.64
40	Chingford and Woodford Green	Iain Duncan Smith	Con	1,262	2.59
41	Normanton, Pontefract and Castleford	Yvette Cooper	Lab	1,276	2.64
42	North East Fife	Wendy Chamberlain	Lib Dem	1,316	2.86
43	Burnley	Antony Higginbotham	Con	1,352	3.46
44	Chesterfield	Toby Perkins	Lab	1,451	3.2
45	Oldham East and Saddleworth	Debbie Abrahams	Lab	1,499	3.24
46	Warrington North	Charlotte Nichols	Lab	1,509	3.22
47	Dewsbury	Mark Eastwood	Con	1,561	2.75
48	West Bromwich East	Nicola Richards	Con	1,593	4.42
49	South Down	Chris Hazzard	Sinn Féin	1,620	3.24

				Majority	*%*
50	Birmingham, Northfield	Gary Sambrook	Con	1,640	3.79
51	Wolverhampton South West	Stuart Anderson	Con	1,661	4.02
52	Dumfries and Galloway	Alister Jack	Con	1,805	3.5
53	Carmarthen East and Dinefwr	Jonathan Edwards	Ind*	1,809	4.37
54	Belfast East	Gavin Robinson	DUP	1,819	4.27
55	Vale of Clwyd	James Davies	Con	1,827	4.9
56	Canterbury	Rosie Duffield	Lab	1,836	3.04
57	Gower	Tonia Antoniazzi	Lab	1,837	4.12
58	Westmorland and Lonsdale	Tim Farron	Lib Dem	1,934	3.66
59	Belfast North	John Finucane	Sinn Féin	1,943	3.93
60	Leigh	James Grundy	Con	1,965	4.17
61	Ynys Môn	Virginia Crosbie	Con	1,968	5.37
62	Newport East	Jessica Morden	Lab	1,992	5.48
63	Warrington South	Andy Carter	Con	2,010	3.24
64	Aberconwy	Robin Millar	Con	2,034	6.36
65	Wrexham	Sarah Atherton	Con	2,131	6.34
66	Wentworth and Dearne	John Healey	Lab	2,165	5.19
67	Keighley	Robbie Moore	Con	2,218	4.19
68	Doncaster Central	Rosie Winterton	Lab	2,278	5.46
69	Ayr, Carrick and Cumnock	Allan Dorans	SNP	2,329	4.98
70	Cheadle	Mary Robinson	Con	2,336	4.16
71	Bradford South	Judith Cummins	Lab	2,346	5.89
72	Doncaster North	Ed Miliband	Lab	2,370	5.81
73	Lancaster and Fleetwood	Cat Smith	Lab	2,380	5.25
74	Lewes	Maria Caulfield	Con	2,457	4.47
75	Orkney and Shetland	Alistair Carmichael	Lib Dem	2,507	10.79
76	Derby North	Amanda Solloway	Con	2,540	5.39
77	Glasgow North East	Anne McLaughlin	SNP	2,548	7.49
78	Halifax	Holly Lynch	Lab	2,569	5.51
79	Peterborough	Paul Bristow	Con	2,580	5.39
80	South Antrim	Paul Girvan	DUP	2,689	6.23
81	Esher and Walton	Dominic Raab	Con	2,743	4.34
82	Arfon	Hywel Williams	PlC	2,781	9.54
83	Kingston upon Hull West and Hessle	Emma Hardy	Lab	2,856	8.94
84	South Cambridgeshire	Anthony Browne	Con	2,904	4.32
85	Stalybridge and Hyde	Jonathan Reynolds	Lab/Co-op	2,946	6.93
86	Hyndburn	Sara Britcliffe	Con	2,951	6.94
87	Sunderland Central	Julie Elliott	Lab	2,964	6.8
88	North Down	Stephen Farry	APNI	2,968	7.27
89	Wirral West	Margaret Greenwood	Lab	3,003	6.98
90	Houghton and Sunderland South	Bridget Phillipson	Lab	3,115	7.8
91	Rotherham	Sarah Champion	Lab	3,121	8.73
92	Eltham	Clive Efford	Lab	3,197	7.3
93	Barnsley East	Stephanie Peacock	Lab	3,217	8.43
94	Worsley and Eccles South	Barbara Keeley	Lab	3,219	7.18
95	Darlington	Peter Gibson	Con	3,294	7.56
96	Guildford	Angela Richardson	Con	3,337	5.67
97	Wakefield	Imran Ahmad Khan	Con	3,358	7.44
98	Walsall South	Valerie Vaz	Lab	3,456	8.12
99	Lincoln	Karl McCartney	Con	3,514	6.92
100	Pudsey	Stuart Andrew	Con	3,517	6.47
101	Batley and Spen	Tracy Brabin	Lab/Co-op	3,525	6.65
102	Redcar	Jacob Young	Con	3,527	8.62

*Elected as Plaid Cymru

				Majority	%
103	Vale of Glamorgan	Alun Cairns	Con	3,562	6.46
104	Barnsley Central	Dan Jarvis	Lab	3,571	9.65
105	Hartlepool	Mike Hill	Lab	3,595	8.74
106	Birmingham, Erdington	Jack Dromey	Lab	3,601	10.2
107	Don Valley	Nick Fletcher	Con	3,630	7.97
108	Blackpool South	Scott Benton	Con	3,690	11.24
109	Washington and Sunderland West	Sharon Hodgson	Lab	3,723	9.9
110	Torfaen	Nick Thomas-Symonds	Lab	3,742	10.03
111	Erith and Thamesmead	Abena Oppong-Asare	Lab	3,758	9.06
112	Edinburgh West	Christine Jardine	Lib Dem	3,769	6.9
113	Dumfriesshire, Clydesdale and Tweeddale	David Mundell	Con	3,781	7.67
114	Angus	Dave Doogan	SNP	3,795	8.77
115	West Bromwich West	Shaun Bailey	Con	3,799	11
116	Stroud	Siobhan Baillie	Con	3,840	5.81
117	East Lothian	Kenny MacAskill	SNP	3,886	6.63
118	Cities of London and Westminster	Nickie Aiken	Con	3,953	9.22
119	Aberdeen South	Stephen Flynn	SNP	3,990	8.72
120	Hastings and Rye	Sally-Ann Hart	Con	4,043	7.41
121	Wolverhampton North East	Jane Stevenson	Con	4,080	11.87
122	Argyll and Bute	Brendan O'Hara	SNP	4,110	8.53
123	Reading West	Alok Sharma	Con	4,117	8.14
124	Banff and Buchan	David Duguid	Con	4,118	9.72
125	Southport	Damien Moore	Con	4,147	8.57
126	Workington	Mark Jenkinson	Con	4,176	10.02
127	Leicester West	Liz Kendall	Lab	4,212	12.06
128	Wycombe	Steve Baker	Con	4,214	7.67
129	Hendon	Matthew Offord	Con	4,230	7.66
130	Ashton under Lyne	Angela Rayner	Lab	4,263	11.01
131	St Ives	Derek Thomas	Con	4,284	8.31
132	Sheffield South East	Clive Betts	Lab	4,289	10.18
133	Eastbourne	Caroline Ansell	Con	4,331	7.84
134	Hazel Grove	William Wragg	Con	4,423	9.95
135	Watford	Dean Russell	Con	4,433	7.6
136	Enfield Southgate	Bambos Charalambous	Lab	4,450	9.36
137	Nottingham North	Alex Norris	Lab/Co-op	4,490	12.68
138	Ochil and South Perthshire	John Nicolson	SNP	4,498	7.76
139	Southampton Itchen	Royston Smith	Con	4,498	9.46
140	Sedgefield	Paul Howell	Con	4,513	10.83
141	Truro and Falmouth	Cherilyn Mackrory	Con	4,561	7.68
142	Llanelli	Nia Griffith	Lab	4,670	12.17
143	Northampton South	Andrew Lewer	Con	4,697	11.47
144	Norwich North	Chloe Smith	Con	4,738	10.21
145	Makerfield	Yvonne Fovargue	Lab	4,740	10.67
146	North Durham	Kevan Jones	Lab	4,742	11.21
147	Plymouth, Sutton and Devonport	Luke Pollard	Lab/Co-op	4,757	8.92
148	Putney	Fleur Anderson	Lab	4,774	9.44
149	Tynemouth	Alan Campbell	Lab	4,857	8.64
150	Glasgow South West	Chris Stephens	SNP	4,900	13.27
151	Huddersfield	Barry Sheerman	Lab/Co-op	4,937	11.73
152	City of Durham	Mary Foy	Lab	5,025	10.25
153	Preseli Pembrokeshire	Stephen Crabb	Con	5,062	11.89
154	Colne Valley	Jason McCartney	Con	5,103	8.35

				Majority	%
155	Berwickshire, Roxburgh and Selkirk	John Lamont	Con	5,148	9.66
156	Lanark and Hamilton East	Angela Crawley	SNP	5,187	9.75
157	Airdrie and Shotts	Neil Gray	SNP	5,201	13.05
158	Ilford North	Wes Streeting	Lab	5,218	10.39
159	Rutherglen and Hamilton West	Margaret Ferrier	Ind*	5,230	9.7
160	Stockton South	Matt Vickers	Con	5,260	9.57
161	Bolsover	Mark Fletcher	Con	5,299	11.5
162	Central Ayrshire	Philippa Whitford	SNP	5,304	11.37
163	Broxtowe	Darren Henry	Con	5,331	9.61
164	Portsmouth South	Stephen Morgan	Lab	5,363	11.27
165	East Renfrewshire	Kirsten Oswald	SNP	5,426	9.77
166	Ipswich	Tom Hunt	Con	5,479	11.03
167	Northampton North	Michael Ellis	Con	5,507	13.89
168	Blaydon	Liz Twist	Lab	5,531	12.08
169	Leeds East	Richard Burgon	Lab	5,531	14.12
170	Glasgow East	David Linden	SNP	5,566	14.43
171	Birmingham, Edgbaston	Preet Kaur Gill	Lab/Co-op	5,614	13.22
172	Coatbridge, Chryston and Bellshill	Steven Bonnar	SNP	5,624	11.63
173	Filton and Bradley Stoke	Jack Lopresti	Con	5,646	10.47
174	Battersea	Marsha De Cordova	Lab	5,668	9.43
175	Bristol North West	Darren Jones	Lab	5,692	10.15
176	Midlothian	Owen Thompson	SNP	5,705	11.8
177	Ashfield	Lee Anderson	Con	5,733	11.68
178	Newcastle upon Tyne North	Catherine McKinnell	Lab	5,765	12.24
179	Calder Valley	Craig Whittaker	Con	5,774	9.94
180	Barrow and Furness	Simon Fell	Con	5,789	12.54
181	Copeland	Trudy Harrison	Con	5,842	13.68
182	Reading East	Matt Rodda	Lab	5,924	10.57
183	Croydon Central	Sarah Jones	Lab	5,949	10.98
184	Derby South	Margaret Beckett	Lab	6,019	14.13
185	Leicester East	Claudia Webbe	Ind†	6,019	12.12
186	Wirral South	Alison McGovern	Lab	6,105	13.98
187	Altrincham and Sale West	Graham Brady	Con	6,139	11.17
188	City of Chester	Chris Matheson	Lab	6,164	11.27
189	Pendle	Andrew Stephenson	Con	6,186	13.86
190	Southampton Test	Alan Whitehead	Lab	6,213	13.77
191	Shipley	Philip Davies	Con	6,242	11.5
192	Milton Keynes North	Ben Everitt	Con	6,255	9.96
193	Motherwell and Wishaw	Marion Fellows	SNP	6,268	14.08
194	St Albans	Daisy Cooper	Lib Dem	6,293	10.89
195	Rother Valley	Alexander Stafford	Con	6,318	12.94
196	Morecambe and Lunesdale	David Morris	Con	6,354	13.98
197	Enfield North	Feryal Clark	Lab	6,492	14.33
198	Lagan Valley	Jeffrey Donaldson	DUP	6,499	14.26
199	Finchley and Golders Green	Mike Freer	Con	6,562	11.86
200	South Swindon	Robert Buckland	Con	6,625	12.99
201	East Devon	Simon Jupp	Con	6,708	10.44
202	Wigan	Lisa Nandy	Lab	6,728	14.89
203	Worcester	Robin Walker	Con	6,758	13.23
204	Hitchin and Harpenden	Bim Afolami	Con	6,895	11.66
205	Milton Keynes South	Iain Stewart	Con	6,944	10.82

*Elected as Scottish National Party
†Elected as Labour

				Majority	%
206	Cardiff North	Anna McMorrin	Lab	6,982	13.23
207	Loughborough	Jane Hunt	Con	7,169	13.07
208	Penistone and Stocksbridge	Miriam Cates	Con	7,210	14.52
209	Uxbridge and South Ruislip	Boris Johnson	Con	7,210	14.93
210	Wokingham	John Redwood	Con	7,383	11.87
211	East Worthing and Shoreham	Tim Loughton	Con	7,474	14.02
212	Perth and North Perthshire	Pete Wishart	SNP	7,550	13.93
213	Rushcliffe	Ruth Edwards	Con	7,643	12.58
214	Richmond Park	Sarah Olney	Lib Dem	7,766	11.9
215	South West Surrey	Jeremy Hunt	Con	8,817	14.52

50 Safest Constituencies

50 safest constituencies are calculated on the 2019 General Election.

				Majority	%
1	Knowsley	George Howarth	Lab	39,942	72.53
2	Bethnal Green and Bow	Rushanara Ali	Lab	37,524	61.72
3	Liverpool Riverside	Kim Johnson	Lab	37,043	69.85
4	Bootle	Peter Dowd	Lab	34,556	70.06
5	Hackney South and Shoreditch	Meg Hillier	Lab/Co-op	33,985	62.22
6	Camberwell and Peckham	Harriet Harman	Lab	33,780	59.54
7	Hackney North and Stoke Newington	Diane Abbott	Lab	33,188	58.11
8	East Ham	Stephen Timms	Lab	33,176	60.54
9	Lewisham Deptford	Vicky Foxcroft	Lab	32,913	59.19
10	Sleaford and North Hykeham	Caroline Johnson	Con	32,565	48.76
11	West Ham	Lyn Brown	Lab	32,388	53.61
12	Garston and Halewood	Maria Eagle	Lab	31,624	59.14
13	Rayleigh and Wickford	Mark Francois	Con	31,000	56.17
14	Walthamstow	Stella Creasy	Lab/Co-op	30,862	63.58
15	South Holland and The Deepings	John Hayes	Con	30,838	62.45
16	Liverpool Walton	Dan Carden	Lab	30,520	74.47
17	Manchester Gorton	Afzal Khan	Lab	30,339	67.88
18	Tottenham	David Lammy	Lab	30,175	64.12
19	Maldon	John Whittingdale	Con	30,041	59.32
20	North East Cambridgeshire	Stephen Barclay	Con	29,993	56.37
21	Liverpool West Derby	Ian Byrne	Lab	29,984	68.02
22	Manchester Central	Lucy Powell	Lab/Co-op	29,089	55.43
23	Brentwood and Ongar	Alex Burghart	Con	29,065	54.65
24	Poplar and Limehouse	Apsana Begum	Lab	28,904	46.96
25	Louth and Horncastle	Victoria Atkins	Con	28,868	54.86
26	Birmingham, Hodge Hill	Liam Byrne	Lab	28,655	63.49
27	Birmingham, Ladywood	Shabana Mahmood	Lab	28,582	67.62
28	Birmingham, Hall Green	Tahir Ali	Lab	28,508	53.70
29	South Staffordshire	Gavin Williamson	Con	28,250	56.20
30	Bristol West	Thangam Debbonaire	Lab	28,219	37.19
31	Mid Worcestershire	Nigel Huddleston	Con	28,018	49.74
32	Manchester Withington	Jeff Smith	Lab	27,905	52.48
33	Holborn and St Pancras	Keir Starmer	Lab	27,763	48.73
34	South Northamptonshire	Andrea Leadsom	Con	27,761	41.33
35	Saffron Walden	Kemi Badenoch	Con	27,594	43.52
36	Dulwich and West Norwood	Helen Hayes	Lab	27,310	48.76
37	Sheffield Central	Paul Blomfield	Lab	27,273	53.32
38	Richmond (Yorkshire)	Rishi Sunak	Con	27,210	46.99
39	Liverpool Wavertree	Paula Barker	Lab	27,085	62.24
40	Bradford West	Naz Shah	Lab	27,019	60.86

				Majority	%
41	Tonbridge and Malling	Tom Tugendhat	Con	26,941	47.01
42	Rutland and Melton	Alicia Kearns	Con	26,924	45.98
43	Castle Point	Rebecca Harris	Con	26,634	59.75
44	North West Hampshire	Kit Malthouse	Con	26,308	44.45
45	Bosworth	Luke Evans	Con	26,278	46.37
46	South West Norfolk	Elizabeth Truss	Con	26,195	50.72
47	Islington North	Jeremy Corbyn	Ind*	26,188	48.47
48	Fareham	Suella Braverman	Con	26,086	45.34
49	Daventry	Chris Heaton-Harris	Con	26,080	45.24
50	Bexhill and Battle	Huw Merriman	Con	26,059	43.84

*Elected as Labour

Women MPs 1945–2019 general elections

	Conservative	*Labour**	*Liberal/ Liberal Democrat*	*SNP†*	*Others*	*Total*
1945	1	21	1	–	1	24
1950	6	14	1	–	0	21
1951	6	11	0	–	0	17
1955	10	14	0	–	0	24
1959	12	13	0	–	0	25
1964	11	18	0	–	0	29
1966	7	19	0	–	0	26
1970	15	10	0	–	1	25
1974 (Feb)	9	13	0	–	1	23
1974 (Oct)	7	18	0	–	2	27
1979	8	11	0	–	0	19
1983	13	10	0	–	0	23
1987	17	21	2	–	1	41
1992	20	37	2	–	1	60
1997	13	101	3	–	3	120
2001	14	95	5	–	4	118
2005	17	98	9	–	3	128
2010	49	81	7	1	5	143
2015	68	99	0	19	5	191
2017	66	119	4	12	7	208
2019	87	104	7	16	6	220

* Includes Labour/Co-operative
† SNP have been included in the analysis since the 2010 General Election

WOMEN MPs (220)

ABBOTT Diane	*Lab*	Hackney North and Stoke Newington
ABRAHAMS Debbie	*Lab*	Oldham East and Saddleworth
AIKEN Nickie	*Con*	Cities of London and Westminster
ALI Rushanara	*Lab*	Bethnal Green and Bow
ALLAN Lucy	*Con*	Telford
ALLIN-KHAN Rosena	*Lab*	Tooting
ANDERSON Fleur	*Lab*	Putney
ANSELL Caroline	*Con*	Eastbourne
ANTONIAZZI Tonia	*Lab*	Gower
ATHERTON Sarah	*Con*	Wrexham
ATKINS Victoria	*Con*	Louth and Horncastle
BADENOCH Kemi	*Con*	Saffron Walden
BAILLIE Siobhan	*Con*	Stroud
BALDWIN Harriett	*Con*	West Worcestershire
BARDELL Hannah	*SNP*	Livingston
BARKER Paula	*Lab*	Liverpool Wavertree
BECKETT Margaret	*Lab*	Derby South
BEGLEY Órfhlaith	*Sinn Féin*	West Tyrone
BEGUM Apsana	*Lab*	Poplar and Limehouse
BLACK Mhairi	*SNP*	Paisley and Renfrewshire South
BLACKMAN Kirsty	*SNP*	Aberdeen North
BLAKE Olivia	*Lab*	Sheffield, Hallam
BRABIN Tracy	*Lab/Co-op*	Batley and Spen
BRADLEY Karen	*Con*	Staffordshire Moorlands
BRAVERMAN Suella	*Con*	Fareham
BRITCLIFFE Sara	*Con*	Hyndburn

BROCK Deidre	*SNP*	Edinburgh North and Leith
BROWN Lyn	*Lab*	West Ham
BRUCE Fiona	*Con*	Congleton
BUCHAN Felicity	*Con*	Kensington
BUCK Karen	*Lab*	Westminster North
BUTLER Dawn	*Lab*	Brent Central
CADBURY Ruth	*Lab*	Brentford and Isleworth
CALLAGHAN Amy	*SNP*	East Dunbartonshire
CAMERON Lisa	*SNP*	East Kilbride, Strathaven and Lesmahagow
CATES Miriam	*Con*	Penistone and Stocksbridge
CAULFIELD Maria	*Con*	Lewes
CHAMBERLAIN Wendy	*Lib Dem*	North East Fife
CHAMPION Sarah	*Lab*	Rotherham
CHERRY Joanna	*SNP*	Edinburgh South West
CHURCHILL Jo	*Con*	Bury St Edmunds
CLARK Feryal	*Lab*	Enfield North
CLARKE Theo	*Con*	Stafford
COFFEY Therese	*Con*	Suffolk Coastal
COOPER Daisy	*Lib Dem*	St Albans
COOPER Rosie	*Lab*	West Lancashire
COOPER Yvette	*Lab*	Normanton, Pontefract and Castleford
COUTINHO Claire	*Con*	East Surrey
CRAWLEY Angela	*SNP*	Lanark and Hamilton East
CREASY Stella	*Lab/Co-op*	Walthamstow
CROSBIE Virginia	*Con*	Ynys Môn
CROUCH Tracey	*Con*	Chatham and Aylesford
CUMMINS Judith	*Lab*	Bradford South
DABY Janet	*Lab*	Lewisham East
DAVIES Mims	*Con*	Mid Sussex
DAVIES-JONES Alex	*Lab*	Pontypridd
DAVISON Dehenna	*Con*	Bishop Auckland
DEBBONAIRE Thangam	*Lab*	Bristol West
DE CORDOVA Marsha	*Lab*	Battersea
DINENAGE Caroline	*Con*	Gosport
DINES Sarah	*Con*	Derbyshire Dales
DODDS Anneliese	*Lab/Co-op*	Oxford East
DONELAN Michelle	*Con*	Chippenham
DORRIES Nadine	*Con*	Mid Bedfordshire
DOYLE-PRICE Jackie	*Con*	Thurrock
DRUMMOND Flick	*Con*	Meon Valley
DUFFIELD Rosie	*Lab*	Canterbury
EAGLE Angela	*Lab*	Wallasey
EAGLE Maria	*Lab*	Garston and Halewood
EDWARDS Ruth	*Con*	Rushcliffe
ELLIOTT Julie	*Lab*	Sunderland Central
ELPHICKE Natalie	*Con*	Dover
ESHALOMI Florence	*Lab/Co-op*	Vauxhall
FARRIS Laura	*Con*	Newbury
FELLOWS Marion	*SNP*	Motherwell and Wishaw
FERRIER Margaret	*Ind**	Rutherglen and Hamilton West
FLETCHER Colleen	*Lab*	Coventry North East
FLETCHER Katherine	*Con*	South Ribble
FORD Vicky	*Con*	Chelmsford
FOVARGUE Yvonne	*Lab*	Makerfield
FOXCROFT Vicky	*Lab*	Lewisham Deptford

*Elected as Scottish National Party

FOY Mary	*Lab*	City of Durham
FRAZER Lucy	*Con*	South East Cambridgeshire
FURNISS Gill	*Lab*	Sheffield, Brightside and Hillsborough
GHANI Nusrat	*Con*	Wealden
GIBSON Patricia	*SNP*	North Ayrshire and Arran
GIDEON Jo	*Con*	Stoke-on-Trent Central
GILDERNEW Michelle	*Sinn Féin*	Fermanagh and South Tyrone
GILL Preet Kaur	*Lab/Co-op*	Birmingham, Edgbaston
GILLAN Cheryl	*Con*	Chesham and Amersham
GLINDON Mary	*Lab*	North Tyneside
GRANT Helen	*Con*	Maidstone and The Weald
GREEN Kate	*Lab*	Stretford and Urmston
GREENWOOD Lilian	*Lab*	Nottingham South
GREENWOOD Margaret	*Lab*	Wirral West
GRIFFITH Nia	*Lab*	Llanelli
GRIFFITHS Kate	*Con*	Burton
HAIGH Louise	*Lab*	Sheffield Heeley
HANNA Claire	*SDLP*	Belfast South
HARDY Emma	*Lab*	Kingston upon Hull West and Hessle
HARMAN Harriet	*Lab*	Camberwell and Peckham
HARRIS Carolyn	*Lab*	Swansea East
HARRIS Rebecca	*Con*	Castle Point
HARRISON Trudy	*Con*	Copeland
HART Sally-Ann	*Con*	Hastings and Rye
HAYES Helen	*Lab*	Dulwich and West Norwood
HILLIER Meg	*Lab/Co-op*	Hackney South and Shoreditch
HOBHOUSE Wera	*Lib Dem*	Bath
HODGE Margaret	*Lab*	Barking
HODGSON Sharon	*Lab*	Washington and Sunderland West
HOLLERN Kate	*Lab*	Blackburn
HOPKINS Rachel	*Lab*	Luton South
HUNT Jane	*Con*	Loughborough
HUQ Rupa	*Lab*	Ealing Central and Acton
JARDINE Christine	*Lib Dem*	Edinburgh West
JENKYNS Andrea	*Con*	Morley and Outwood
JOHNSON Caroline	*Con*	Sleaford and North Hykeham
JOHNSON Diana	*Lab*	Kingston upon Hull North
JOHNSON Kim	*Lab*	Liverpool Riverside
JONES Fay	*Con*	Brecon and Radnorshire
JONES Ruth	*Lab*	Newport West
JONES Sarah	*Lab*	Croydon Central
KEARNS Alicia	*Con*	Rutland and Melton
KEEGAN Gillian	*Con*	Chichester
KEELEY Barbara	*Lab*	Worsley and Eccles South
KENDALL Liz	*Lab*	Leicester West
LAING Eleanor	*Con*	Epping Forest
LATHAM Pauline	*Con*	Mid Derbyshire
LEADSOM Andrea	*Con*	South Northamptonshire
LEWELL-BUCK Emma	*Lab*	South Shields
LOCKHART Carla	*DUP*	Upper Bann
LONG BAILEY Rebecca	*Lab*	Salford and Eccles
LOPEZ Julia	*Con*	Hornchurch and Upminster
LUCAS Caroline	*Green*	Brighton Pavilion
LYNCH Holly	*Lab*	Halifax
MCCARTHY Kerry	*Lab*	Bristol East
MCDONAGH Siobhain	*Lab*	Mitcham and Morden
MCGOVERN Alison	*Lab*	Wirral South

MCKINNELL Catherine	*Lab*	Newcastle upon Tyne North
MACKRORY Cherilyn	*Con*	Truro and Falmouth
MCLAUGHLIN Anne	*SNP*	Glasgow North East
MACLEAN Rachel	*Con*	Redditch
MCMORRIN Anna	*Lab*	Cardiff North
MCVEY Esther	*Con*	Tatton
MAHMOOD Shabana	*Lab*	Birmingham, Ladywood
MALHOTRA Seema	*Lab/Co-op*	Feltham and Heston
MARSON Julie	*Con*	Hertford and Stortford
MASKELL Rachael	*Lab/Co-op*	York Central
MAY Theresa	*Con*	Maidenhead
MILLER Maria	*Con*	Basingstoke
MILLING Amanda	*Con*	Cannock Chase
MONAGHAN Carol	*SNP*	Glasgow North West
MORAN Layla	*Lib Dem*	Oxford West and Abingdon
MORDAUNT Penny	*Con*	Portsmouth North
MORDEN Jessica	*Lab*	Newport East
MORRIS Anne Marie	*Con*	Newton Abbot
MORRISSEY Joy	*Con*	Beaconsfield
MORTON Wendy	*Con*	Aldridge-Brownhills
MUMBY-CROFT Holly	*Con*	Scunthorpe
MURRAY Sheryll	*Con*	South East Cornwall
NANDY Lisa	*Lab*	Wigan
NICHOLS Charlotte	*Lab*	Warrington North
NICI Lia	*Con*	Great Grimsby
NOKES Caroline	*Con*	Romsey and Southampton North
OLNEY Sarah	*Lib Dem*	Richmond Park
ONWURAH Chi	*Lab*	Newcastle upon Tyne Central
OPPONG-ASARE Abena	*Lab*	Erith and Thamesmead
OSAMOR Kate	*Lab/Co-op*	Edmonton
OSBORNE Kate	*Lab*	Jarrow
OSWALD Kirsten	*SNP*	East Renfrewshire
OWATEMI Taiwo	*Lab*	Coventry North West
OWEN Sarah	*Lab*	Luton North
PATEL Priti	*Con*	Witham
PEACOCK Stephanie	*Lab*	Barnsley East
PHILLIPS Jess	*Lab*	Birmingham, Yardley
PHILLIPSON Bridget	*Lab*	Houghton and Sunderland South
POW Rebecca	*Con*	Taunton Deane
POWELL Lucy	*Lab/Co-op*	Manchester Central
PRENTIS Victoria	*Con*	Banbury
QURESHI Yasmin	*Lab*	Bolton South East
RAYNER Angela	*Lab*	Ashton under Lyne
REES Christina	*Lab/Co-op*	Neath
REEVES Ellie	*Lab*	Lewisham West and Penge
REEVES Rachel	*Lab*	Leeds West
RIBEIRO-ADDY Bell	*Lab*	Streatham
RICHARDS Nicola	*Con*	West Bromwich East
RICHARDSON Angela	*Con*	Guildford
RIMMER Marie	*Lab*	St Helens South and Whiston
ROBINSON Mary	*Con*	Cheadle
SAVILLE ROBERTS Liz	*PlC*	Dwyfor Meirionnydd
SAXBY Selaine	*Con*	North Devon
SHAH Naz	*Lab*	Bradford West
SIDDIQ Tulip	*Lab*	Hampstead and Kilburn
SMITH Cat	*Lab*	Lancaster and Fleetwood
SMITH Chloe	*Con*	Norwich North

SMYTH Karin	*Lab*	Bristol South
SOLLOWAY Amanda	*Con*	Derby North
STEVENS Jo	*Lab*	Cardiff Central
STEVENSON Jane	*Con*	Wolverhampton North East
SULTANA Zarah	*Lab*	Coventry South
THEWLISS Alison	*SNP*	Glasgow Central
THORNBERRY Emily	*Lab*	Islington South and Finsbury
THROUP Maggie	*Con*	Erewash
TOLHURST Kelly	*Con*	Rochester and Strood
TREVELYAN Anne-Marie	*Con*	Berwick-upon-Tweed
TROTT Laura	*Con*	Sevenoaks
TRUSS Elizabeth	*Con*	South West Norfolk
TWIST Liz	*Lab*	Blaydon
VAZ Valerie	*Lab*	Walsall South
VILLIERS Theresa	*Con*	Chipping Barnet
WEBB Suzanne	*Con*	Stourbridge
WEBBE Claudia	*Ind**	Leicester East
WEST Catherine	*Lab*	Hornsey and Wood Green
WHATELY Helen	*Con*	Faversham and Mid Kent
WHEELER Heather	*Con*	South Derbyshire
WHITFORD Philippa	*SNP*	Central Ayrshire
WHITTOME Nadia	*Lab*	Nottingham East
WILSON Munira	*Lib Dem*	Twickenham
WINTER Beth	*Lab*	Cynon Valley
WINTERTON Rosie	*Lab*	Doncaster Central

*Elected as Labour

MPs by Age

(Ages as at 1 February 2021)

	Conservative	%	*Labour*	%	*SNP*	%	*Other*	%	*Total*	%
Under 30	6	1.7	3	1.6	1	2.3	2	5.4	12	2.0
30–39	50	14.6	20	10.5	8	18.2	6	16.2	84	13.7
40–49	102	29.7	54	28.4	12	27.3	7	18.9	175	28.5
50–59	118	34.4	51	26.8	14	31.8	9	24.3	192	31.3
60–69	53	15.5	46	24.2	7	15.9	10	27.0	116	18.9
70–79	13	3.8	15	7.9	2	4.5	3	8.1	33	5.4
Over 80	1	0.3	1	0.5	0	0.0	0	0.0	2	0.3
	343		190		44		37		614*	
Average age	**50.5**		**52.7**		**49.7**		**51.8**			

*The average age has been calculated on supplied dates of birth only.

MPs who have not supplied date of birth

Lee Anderson (Con)
Steven Bonnar (SNP)
Felicity Buchan (Con)
Ian Byrne (Lab)
Amy Callaghan (SNP)
Feryal Clark (Lab)
Virginia Crosbie (Con)
James Daly (Con)
Sarah Dines (Con)
Mark Eastwood (Con)
Ben Everitt (Con)
Laura Farris (Con)
Kate Griffiths (Con)
James Grundy (Con)
Neale Hanvey (SNP)
Neil Hudson (Con)
Tom Hunt (Con)
Fay Jones (Con)
Alicia Kearns (Con)
Mark Logan (Con)
Navendu Mishra (Lab)
Holly Mumby-Croft (Con)
Abena Oppong-Asare (Lab)
Kate Osborne (Lab)
Taiwo Owatemi (Lab)
Sarah Owen (Lab)
Tom Randall (Con)
Bell Ribeiro-Addy (Lab)
Nicola Richards (Con)
Angela Richardson (Con)
Rob Roberts (Con)
David Simmonds (Con)
Christian Wakeford (Con)
Claudia Webbe (Ind)
Mick Whitley (Lab)
Beth Winter (Lab)

Nadia Whittome	24	*Lab*
Sara Britcliffe	25	*Con*
Mhairi Black	26	*SNP*
Dehenna Davison	27	*Con*
Zarah Sultana	27	*Lab*
Jacob Young	27	*Con*
Shaun Bailey	28	*Con*
Elliot Colburn	28	*Con*
Ben Lake	28	*PlC*
Órfhlaith Begley	29	*Sinn Féin*
Jack Brereton	29	*Con*
Charlotte Nichols	29	*Lab*
Apsana Begum	30	*Lab*
Olivia Blake	30	*Lab*
David Linden	30	*SNP*
Ben Bradley	31	*Con*
Alex Davies-Jones	31	*Lab*
Jonathan Gullis	31	*Con*
Antony Higginbotham	31	*Con*
Anthony Mangnall	31	*Con*
Gary Sambrook	31	*Con*
Stephen Flynn	32	*SNP*
Paul Holmes	32	*Con*
Tom Pursglove	32	*Con*
Scott Benton	33	*Con*
Andrew Bowie	33	*Con*
Angela Crawley	33	*SNP*
Louise Haigh	33	*Lab*
Robert Largan	33	*Con*
Alexander Stafford	33	*Con*
William Wragg	33	*Con*
Bim Afolami	34	*Con*
Kirsty Blackman	34	*SNP*
Dan Carden	34	*Lab*
Neil Gray	34	*SNP*
Luke Hall	34	*Con*
Ranil Jayawardena	34	*Con*
Darren Jones	34	*Lab*
Holly Lynch	34	*Lab*
	34	*SNP*

Stewart Malcolm McDonald		
Stephanie Peacock	34	*Lab*
Lloyd Russell-Moyle	34	*Lab/Co-op*
Saqib Bhatti	35	*Con*
Theo Clarke	35	*Con*
Claire Coutinho	35	*Con*
Mark Fletcher	35	*Con*
Richard Holden	35	*Con*
Simon Jupp	35	*Con*
Carla Lockhart	35	*DUP*
Cat Smith	35	*Lab*
Craig Williams	35	*Con*
Simon Clarke	36	*Con*
Gareth Davies	36	*Con*
Michelle Donelan	36	*Con*
Ruth Edwards	36	*Con*
Chris Hazzard	36	*Sinn Féin*
Julia Lopez	36	*Con*
Conor McGinn	36	*Lab*
Robbie Moore	36	*Con*
Kieran Mullan	36	*Con*
Alex Norris	36	*Lab/Co-op*
Gavin Robinson	36	*DUP*
Laura Trott	36	*Con*
Jamie Wallis	36	*Con*
Hannah Bardell	37	*SNP*
Colum Eastwood	37	*SDLP*
Chris Elmore	37	*Lab*
Alan Mak	37	*Con*
James Murray	37	*Lab/Co-op*
Bridget Phillipson	37	*Lab*
Matt Vickers	37	*Con*
Miriam Cates	38	*Con*
Chris Clarkson	38	*Con*
Luke Evans	38	*Con*
Layla Moran	38	*Lib Dem*
Matthew Pennycook	38	*Lab*
Will Quince	38	*Con*
Douglas Ross	38	*Con*
Tulip Siddiq	38	*Lab*
Chloe Smith	38	*Con*
Wes Streeting	38	*Lab*
Sam Tarry	38	*Lab*
Alison Thewliss	38	*SNP*
Siobhan Baillie	39	*Con*
Daisy Cooper	39	*Lib Dem*
Simon Fell	39	*Con*
Mark Jenkinson	39	*Con*
Robert Jenrick	39	*Con*
David Johnston	39	*Con*
Chris Loder	39	*Con*
Johnny Mercer	39	*Con*
Jess Phillips	39	*Lab*
Chris Skidmore	39	*Con*
Ben Spencer	39	*Con*
Andrew Stephenson	39	*Con*
Matt Warman	39	*Con*
Aaron Bell	40	*Con*
Suella Braverman	40	*Con*
Richard Burgon	40	*Lab*
Brendan Clarke-Smith	40	*Con*
James Davies	40	*Con*
Stephen Doughty	40	*Lab/Co-op*
Florence Eshalomi	40	*Lab/Co-op*
John Finucane	40	*Sinn Féin*
Patrick Grady	40	*SNP*
Claire Hanna	40	*SDLP*
James Heappey	40	*Con*
Alison McGovern	40	*Lab*
Jim McMahon	40	*Lab/Co-op*
Shabana Mahmood	40	*Lab*
Damien Moore	40	*Con*
Stephen Morgan	40	*Lab*
Joy Morrissey	40	*Con*
Gavin Newlands	40	*SNP*
Luke Pollard	40	*Lab/Co-op*
Angela Rayner	40	*Lab*
Ellie Reeves	40	*Lab*
Jonathan Reynolds	40	*Lab/Co-op*
Lee Rowley	40	*Con*
Rishi Sunak	40	*Con*
Nick Thomas-Symonds	40	*Lab*
Kemi Badenoch	41	*Con*
Duncan Baker	41	*Con*
Paul Bristow	41	*Con*
Emma Hardy	41	*Lab*
Rebecca Long Bailey	41	*Lab*
Lisa Nandy	41	*Lab*
Rachel Reeves	41	*Lab*
Greg Smith	41	*Con*
Jon Ashworth	42	*Lab/Co-op*
Jake Berry	42	*Con*
Rehman Chishti	42	*Con*
Robert Courts	42	*Con*
Neil Coyle	42	*Lab*
Tanmanjeet Singh Dhesi	42	*Lab*
Anneliese Dodds	42	*Lab/Co-op*
Oliver Dowden	42	*Con*
Kevin Foster	42	*Con*
Matt Hancock	42	*Con*
Imran Hussain	42	*Lab*
Emma Lewell-Buck	42	*Lab*
Stuart C McDonald	42	*SNP*
Gagan Mohindra	42	*Con*
Neil O'Brien	42	*Con*
Dan Poulter	42	*Con*
Owen Thompson	42	*SNP*
Kelly Tolhurst	42	*Con*
Robin Walker	42	*Con*
Munira Wilson	42	*Lib Dem*
Edward Argar	43	*Con*
Alex Burghart	43	*Con*
Stella Creasy	43	*Lab/Co-op*

Chris Evans	43	*Lab/Co-op*
Vicky Foxcroft	43	*Lab*
Caroline Johnson	43	*Con*
Scott Mann	43	*Con*
Andrew Percy	43	*Con*
Michael Tomlinson	43	*Con*
Rosena Allin-Khan	44	*Lab*
Stuart Anderson	44	*Con*
Victoria Atkins	44	*Con*
Alex Chalk	44	*Con*
Wendy Chamberlain	44	*Lib Dem*
Leo Docherty	44	*Con*
Jonathan Edwards	44	*Ind*
Katherine Fletcher	44	*Con*
Trudy Harrison	44	*Con*
John Lamont	44	*Con*
Catherine McKinnell	44	*Lab*
Cherilyn Mackrory	44	*Con*
Stephen McPartland	44	*Con*
Ian Murray	44	*Lab*
Sarah Olney	44	*Lib Dem*
Chris Philp	44	*Con*
Dean Russell	44/45	*Con*
Richard Thomson	44	*SNP*
Justin Tomlinson	44	*Con*
Helen Whately	44	*Con*
James Wild	44	*Con*
Gavin Williamson	44	*Con*
Mike Wood	44	*Con*
Rushanara Ali	45	*Lab*
Tracey Crouch	45	*Con*
Mims Davies	45	*Con*
Marsha De Cordova	45	*Lab*
Peter Gibson	45	*Con*
Kwasi Kwarteng	45	*Con*
Paul Maynard	45	*Con*
Amanda Milling	45	*Con*
Alec Shelbrooke	45	*Con*
Alex Sobel	45	*Lab/Co-op*
Elizabeth Truss	45	*Con*
James Cartlidge	46	*Con*
Damian Collins	46	*Con*
John Glen	46	*Con*
Andrew Gwynne	46	*Lab*
Helen Hayes	46	*Lab*
Andrea Jenkyns	46	*Con*
Marcus Jones	46	*Con*
Danny Kruger	46	*Con*
Nigel Mills	46	*Con*
Lucy Powell	46	*Lab/Co-op*
Dominic Raab	46	*Con*
Craig Tracey	46	*Con*
Imran Ahmad Khan	47	*Con*
Steve Brine	47	*Con*
Andy Carter	47	*Con*
Maria Caulfield	47	*Con*
Dave Doogan	47	*SNP*
Chris Green	47	*Con*
Huw Merriman	47	*Con*
Penny Mordaunt	47	*Con*
Naz Shah	47	*Lab*
Alyn Smith	47	*SNP*
Chris Stephens	47	*SNP*
Edward Timpson	47	*Con*
Tom Tugendhat	47	*Con*
Gareth Bacon	48	*Con*
Stephen Barclay	48	*Con*
Paula Barker	48	*Lab*
Conor Burns	48	*Con*
Lisa Cameron	48	*SNP*
Stephen Crabb	48	*Con*
Nick Fletcher	48	*Con*
Lucy Frazer	48	*Con*
Nusrat Ghani	48	*Con*
Preet Kaur Gill	48	*Lab/Co-op*
Rachel Hopkins	48	*Lab*
Rupa Huq	48	*Lab*
Dan Jarvis	48	*Lab*
Sarah Jones	48	*Lab*
David Lammy	48	*Lab*
Justin Madders	48	*Lab*
Seema Malhotra	48	*Lab/Co-op*
Rachael Maskell	48	*Lab/Co-op*
Carol Monaghan	48	*SNP*
Caroline Nokes	48	*Con*
Kirsten Oswald	48	*SNP*
Priti Patel	48	*Con*
Iain Stewart	48	*Con*
Derek Thomas	48	*Con*
Jeremy Wright	48	*Con*
Tahir Ali	49/50	*Lab*
Fleur Anderson	49	*Lab*
Stuart Andrew	49	*Con*
Tonia Antoniazzi	49	*Lab*
Steve Baker	49	*Con*
Therese Coffey	49	*Con*
Alberto Costa	49	*Con*
Philip Davies	49	*Con*
Martyn Day	49	*SNP*
Caroline Dinenage	49	*Con*
James Duddridge	49	*Con*
Rosie Duffield	49	*Lab*
George Eustice	49	*Con*
Stephen Farry	49	*APNI*
Andrew Griffith	49	*Con*
Daniel Kawczynski	49	*Con*
Liz Kendall	49	*Lab*
Julian Knight	49	*Con*
Andrew Lewer	49	*Con*
Brandon Lewis	49	*Con*
Clive Lewis	49	*Lab*
Anna McMorrin	49	*Lab*
Mark Menzies	49	*Con*
Victoria Prentis	49	*Con*

Julian Smith	49	*Con*
Jane Stevenson	49	*Con*
Julian Sturdy	49	*Con*
Karl Turner	49	*Lab*
Mohammad Yasin	49	*Lab*
Caroline Ansell	50	*Con*
Karen Bradley	50	*Con*
Alan Brown	50	*SNP*
Liam Byrne	50	*Lab*
Alun Cairns	50	*Con*
Janet Daby	50	*Lab*
David Davies	50	*Con*
Martin Docherty-Hughes	50	*SNP*
David Duguid	50	*Con*
Natalie Elphicke	50	*Con*
Tim Farron	50	*Lib Dem*
Marcus Fysh	50	*Con*
Michelle Gildernew	50	*Sinn Féin*
Mark Harper	50	*Con*
Nigel Huddleston	50	*Con*
Gerald Jones	50	*Lab*
Peter Kyle	50	*Lab*
Angus MacNeil	50	*SNP*
Jerome Mayhew	50	*Con*
Toby Perkins	50	*Lab*
Selaine Saxby	50	*Con*
James Sunderland	50	*Con*
Ben Wallace	50	*Con*
Nickie Aiken	51	*Con*
Mike Amesbury	51	*Lab*
Dawn Butler	51	*Lab*
Sarah Champion	51	*Lab*
James Cleverly	51	*Con*
Yvette Cooper	51	*Lab*
Jackie Doyle-Price	51	*Con*
Robert Halfon	51	*Con*
Meg Hillier	51	*Lab/Co-op*
Damian Hinds	51	*Con*
Simon Hoare	51	*Con*
Sajid Javid	51	*Con*
Gareth Johnson	51	*Con*
Stephen Kinnock	51	*Lab*
Chris Law	51	*SNP*
Jack Lopresti	51	*Con*
Ed Miliband	51	*Lab*
Lia Nici	51	*Con*
Matthew Offord	51	*Con*
Christopher Pincher	51	*Con*
Jacob Rees-Mogg	51	*Con*
Henry Smith	51	*Con*
Mark Spencer	51	*Con*
Anne-Marie Trevelyan	51	*Con*
Robert Buckland	52	*Con*
Mary Foy	52	*Lab*
Patricia Gibson	52	*SNP*
Sally-Ann Hart	52	*Con*
Darren Henry	52	*Con*
Eddie Hughes	52	*Con*
Mike Kane	52	*Lab*
Gillian Keegan	52	*Con*
Karl McCartney	52	*Con*
Robin Millar	52	*Con*
Jessica Morden	52	*Lab*
Kate Osamor	52	*Lab/Co-op*
Jeremy Quin	52	*Con*
Paul Scully	52	*Con*
Grant Shapps	52	*Con*
Theresa Villiers	52	*Con*
Sarah Atherton	53	*Con*
Graham Brady	53	*Con*
James Brokenshire	53	*Con*
Rob Butler	53	*Con*
Bambos Charalambous	53	*Lab*
Greg Clark	53	*Con*
Judith Cummins	53	*Lab*
Michael Ellis	53	*Con*
Vicky Ford	53	*Con*
George Freeman	53	*Con*
Michael Gove	53	*Con*
Rebecca Harris	53	*Con*
Chris Heaton-Harris	53	*Con*
Marco Longhi	53	*Con*
Jason McCartney	53	*Con*
Esther McVey	53	*Con*
Paul Maskey	53	*Sinn Féin*
Chris Matheson	53	*Lab*
James Morris	53	*Con*
Wendy Morton	53	*Con*
Alok Sharma	53	*Con*
Gareth Thomas	53	*Lab/Co-op*
Charles Walker	53	*Con*
Nadhim Zahawi	53	*Con*
Nigel Adams	54	*Con*
Anthony Browne	54	*Con*
Joanna Cherry	54	*SNP*
Thangam Debbonaire	54	*Lab*
Steve Double	54	*Con*
Tobias Ellwood	54	*Con*
Bill Esterson	54	*Lab*
Lilian Greenwood	54	*Lab*
Sharon Hodgson	54	*Lab*
Jane Hunt	54	*Con*
Jeremy Hunt	54	*Con*
Diana Johnson	54	*Lab*
Ian Levy	54	*Con*
Craig Mackinlay	54	*Con*
Anne McLaughlin	54	*SNP*
Kit Malthouse	54	*Con*
Ian Paisley	54	*DUP*
Mark Pritchard	54	*Con*
Matt Rodda	54	*Lab*
Andrew Rosindell	54	*Con*
Bob Seely	54	*Con*
Jo Stevens	54	*Lab*

Suzanne Webb	54/55	*Con*	David Mundell	58	*Con*
Catherine West	54	*Lab*	Jesse Norman	58	*Con*
Bill Wiggin	54	*Con*	Andrew Selous	58	*Con*
Adam Afriyie	55	*Con*	Jeff Smith	58	*Lab*
Alistair Carmichael	55	*Lib Dem*	Keir Starmer	58	*Lab*
Ed Davey	55	*Lib Dem*	Graham Stuart	58	*Con*
Jonathan Djanogly	55	*Con*	Mark Tami	58	*Lab*
Mark Francois	55	*Con*	Matt Western	58	*Lab*
Greg Hands	55	*Con*	Craig Whittaker	58	*Con*
Adam Holloway	55	*Con*	Pete Wishart	58	*SNP*
Kerry McCarthy	55	*Lab*	Peter Aldous	59	*Con*
Pat McFadden	55	*Lab*	Ian Blackford	59	*SNP*
Rachel Maclean	55	*Con*	Tracy Brabin	59	*Lab/Co-op*
Julie Marson	55	*Con*	Deidre Brock	59	*SNP*
Stephen Metcalfe	55	*Con*	Chris Bryant	59	*Lab*
David Morris	55	*Con*	Angela Eagle	59	*Lab*
Chi Onwurah	55	*Lab*	Maria Eagle	59	*Lab*
Guy Opperman	55	*Con*	Liam Fox	59	*Con*
David Warburton	55	*Con*	Helen Grant	59	*Con*
Lucy Allan	56	*Con*	Khalid Mahmood	59	*Lab*
Andrew Bridgen	56	*Con*	Grahame Morris	59	*Lab*
Jo Churchill	56	*Con*	Andrew Murrison	59	*Con*
John Cryer	56	*Lab*	John Nicolson	59	*SNP*
Drew Hendry	56	*SNP*	David Rutley	59	*Con*
Philip Hollobone	56	*Con*	Amanda Solloway	59	*Con*
Boris Johnson	56	*Con*	Mel Stride	59	*Con*
Kevan Jones	56	*Lab*	Debbie Abrahams	60	*Lab*
Maria Miller	56	*Con*	Harriett Baldwin	60	*Con*
John Penrose	56	*Con*	Simon Baynes	60	*Con*
Liz Saville Roberts	56	*PlC*	Crispin Blunt	60	*Con*
Royston Smith	56	*Con*	Ben Bradshaw	60	*Lab*
Karin Smyth	56	*Lab*	Lyn Brown	60	*Lab*
Julie Elliott	57	*Lab*	Geoffrey Cox	60	*Con*
Mark Garnier	57	*Con*	Geraint Davies	60	*Lab/Co-op*
Paul Girvan	57	*DUP*	Margaret Ferrier	60	*Ind*
Simon Hart	57	*Con*	Mike Freer	60	*Con*
Mike Hill	57	*Lab*	Nick Gibb	60	*Con*
Kevin Hollinrake	57	*Con*	Peter Grant	60	*SNP*
Alister Jack	57	*Con*	Kate Green	60	*Lab*
Andrew Jones	57	*Con*	Carolyn Harris	60	*Lab*
Andrea Leadsom	57	*Con*	John Healey	60	*Lab*
Brendan O'Hara	57	*SNP*	Wera Hobhouse	60	*Lib Dem*
Yasmin Qureshi	57	*Lab*	Christine Jardine	60	*Lib Dem*
Steve Reed	57	*Lab/Co-op*	Kim Johnson	60	*Lab*
John Stevenson	57	*Con*	Caroline Lucas	60	*Green*
Richard Bacon	58	*Con*	Siobhain McDonagh	60	*Lab*
Jon Cruddas	58	*Lab*	Rebecca Pow	60	*Con*
Jeffrey Donaldson	58	*DUP*	Andy Slaughter	60	*Lab*
Flick Drummond	58	*Con*	Emily Thornberry	60	*Lab*
Richard Fuller	58	*Con*	Shailesh Vara	60	*Con*
Chris Grayling	58	*Con*	John Baron	61	*Con*
Stephen Hammond	58	*Con*	Kevin Brennan	61	*Lab*
Stewart Hosie	58	*SNP*	Ruth Cadbury	61	*Lab*
Ruth Jones	58	*Lab*	Ronnie Cowan	61	*SNP*
Ian Lavery	58	*Lab*	Margaret Greenwood	61	*Lab*
Jonathan Lord	58	*Con*	Paul Howell	61	*Con*
Tim Loughton	58	*Con*	Bernard Jenkin	61	*Con*

Ian Liddell-Grainger	61	*Con*
Tommy Sheppard	61	*SNP*
Nick Smith	61	*Lab*
Derek Twigg	61	*Lab*
Heather Wheeler	61	*Con*
John Whittingdale	61	*Con*
Karen Buck	62	*Lab*
Philip Dunne	62	*Con*
Clive Efford	62	*Lab*
Richard Graham	62	*Con*
John Hayes	62	*Con*
Mark Hendrick	62	*Lab/Co-op*
Afzal Khan	62	*Lab*
Kenny MacAskill	62	*SNP*
Andy McDonald	62	*Lab*
Laurence Robertson	62	*Con*
Philippa Whitford	62	*SNP*
Rosie Winterton	62	*Lab*
Fiona Bruce	63	*Con*
Alan Campbell	63	*Lab*
Wayne David	63	*Lab*
Nadine Dorries	63	*Con*
Peter Dowd	63	*Lab*
Richard Drax	63	*Con*
Nigel Evans	63	*Con*
Gill Furniss	63	*Lab*
Barry Gardiner	63	*Lab*
Lindsay Hoyle	63	*Speaker*
Eleanor Laing	63	*Con*
Ian Mearns	63	*Lab*
Anne Marie Morris	63	*Con*
Mike Penning	63	*Con*
Bob Blackman	64	*Con*
Yvonne Fovargue	64	*Lab*
Mary Glindon	64	*Lab*
Robert Goodwill	64	*Con*
Nia Griffith	64	*Lab*
Theresa May	64	*Con*
Andrew Mitchell	64	*Con*
Sheryll Murray	64	*Con*
Neil Parish	64	*Con*
Owen Paterson	64	*Con*
Mark Pawsey	64	*Con*
Desmond Swayne	64	*Con*
Robert Syms	64	*Con*
Maggie Throup	64	*Con*
Liz Twist	64	*Lab*
Daniel Zeichner	64	*Lab*
Alex Cunningham	65	*Lab*
Allan Dorans	65	*SNP*
Damian Green	65	*Con*
Fabian Hamilton	65	*Lab*
Kate Hollern	65	*Lab*
John Howell	65	*Con*
Steve McCabe	65	*Lab*
Mary Robinson	65	*Con*
Jim Shannon	65	*DUP*
Gary Streeter	65	*Con*
Stephen Timms	65	*Lab*
Douglas Chapman	66	*SNP*
Iain Duncan Smith	66	*Con*
Colleen Fletcher	66	*Lab*
James Gray	66	*Con*
Oliver Heald	66	*Con*
Christina Rees	66	*Lab/Co-op*
Jamie Stone	66	*Lib Dem*
Valerie Vaz	66	*Lab*
Diane Abbott	67	*Lab*
Hilary Benn	67	*Lab*
Paul Blomfield	67	*Lab*
Gregory Campbell	67	*DUP*
Geoffrey Clifton-Brown	67	*Con*
Giles Watling	67	*Con*
Hywel Williams	67	*PlC*
Sammy Wilson	67	*DUP*
David Amess	68	*Con*
Peter Bone	68	*Con*
Jo Gideon	68	*Con*
Cheryl Gillan	68	*Con*
David Jones	68	*Con*
Barbara Keeley	68	*Lab*
Robert Neill	68	*Con*
Julian Lewis	69	*Con*
John McDonnell	69	*Lab*
John Redwood	69	*Con*
Mickey Brady	70	*Sinn Féin*
Nick Brown	70	*Lab*
Rosie Cooper	70	*Lab*
Michael Fabricant	70	*Con*
Harriet Harman	70	*Lab*
Edward Leigh	70	*Con*
Tony Lloyd	70	*Lab*
John McNally	70	*SNP*
Francie Molloy	70	*Sinn Féin*
Graham Stringer	70	*Lab*
Jon Trickett	70	*Lab*
Martin Vickers	70	*Con*
Alan Whitehead	70	*Lab*
Clive Betts	71	*Lab*
Jeremy Corbyn	71	*Ind*
David Evennett	71	*Con*
Marion Fellows	71	*SNP*
George Howarth	71	*Lab*
Greg Knight	71	*Con*
Bob Stewart	71	*Con*
David Davis	72	*Con*
Jack Dromey	72	*Lab*
Pauline Latham	72	*Con*
Christopher Chope	73	*Con*
Gordon Henderson	73	*Con*
Marie Rimmer	73	*Lab*
Virendra Sharma	73	*Lab*
John Spellar	73	*Lab*
Paul Beresford	74	*Con*

Peter Bottomley	76	*Con*	Bill Cash	80	*Con*
Margaret Hodge	76	*Lab*	Barry Sheerman	80	*Lab/Co-op*
Roger Gale	77	*Con*			
Margaret Beckett	78	*Lab*			

MPs by Party

Conservative

ADAMS Nigel
AFOLAMI Bim
AFRIYIE Adam
AHMAD KHAN Imran
AIKEN Nickie
ALDOUS Peter
ALLAN Lucy
AMESS David
ANDERSON Lee
ANDERSON Stuart
ANDREW Stuart
ANSELL Caroline
ARGAR Edward
ATHERTON Sarah
ATKINS Victoria
BACON Gareth
BACON Richard
BADENOCH Kemi
BAILEY Shaun
BAILLIE Siobhan
BAKER Duncan
BAKER Steve
BALDWIN Harriett
BARCLAY Stephen
BARON John
BAYNES Simon
BELL Aaron
BENTON Scott
BERESFORD Paul
BERRY Jake
BHATTI Saqib
BLACKMAN Bob
BLUNT Crispin
BONE Peter
BOTTOMLEY Peter
BOWIE Andrew
BRADLEY Ben
BRADLEY Karen
BRADY Graham
BRAVERMAN Suella
BRERETON Jack
BRIDGEN Andrew
BRINE Steve
BRISTOW Paul
BRITCLIFFE Sara
BROKENSHIRE James
BROWNE Anthony
BRUCE Fiona
BUCHAN Felicity
BUCKLAND Robert
BURGHART Alex
BURNS Conor
BUTLER Rob
CAIRNS Alun
CARTER Andy
CARTLIDGE James
CASH Bill
CATES Miriam
CAULFIELD Maria
CHALK Alex
CHISHTI Rehman
CHOPE Christopher
CHURCHILL Jo
CLARK Greg
CLARKE Simon
CLARKE Theo
CLARKE-SMITH Brendan
CLARKSON Chris
CLEVERLY James
CLIFTON-BROWN Geoffrey
COFFEY Therese
COLBURN Elliot
COLLINS Damian
COSTA Alberto
COURTS Robert
COUTINHO Claire
COX Geoffrey
CRABB Stephen
CROSBIE Virginia
CROUCH Tracey
DALY James
DAVIES David
DAVIES Gareth
DAVIES James
DAVIES Mims
DAVIES Philip
DAVIS David
DAVISON Dehenna
DINENAGE Caroline
DINES Sarah
DJANOGLY Jonathan
DOCHERTY Leo
DONELAN Michelle
DORRIES Nadine
DOUBLE Steve
DOWDEN Oliver
DOYLE-PRICE Jackie
DRAX Richard
DRUMMOND Flick
DUDDRIDGE James
DUGUID David
DUNCAN SMITH Iain
DUNNE Philip
EASTWOOD Mark
EDWARDS Ruth
ELLIS Michael
ELLWOOD Tobias
ELPHICKE Natalie
EUSTICE George
EVANS Luke
EVANS Nigel
EVENNETT David
EVERITT Ben
FABRICANT Michael
FARRIS Laura
FELL Simon
FLETCHER Katherine
FLETCHER Mark
FLETCHER Nick
FORD Vicky
FOSTER Kevin
FOX Liam
FRANCOIS Mark
FRAZER Lucy
FREEMAN George
FREER Mike
FULLER Richard
FYSH Marcus
GALE Roger
GARNIER Mark
GHANI Nusrat
GIBB Nick
GIBSON Peter
GIDEON Jo
GILLAN Cheryl
GLEN John
GOODWILL Robert
GOVE Michael
GRAHAM Richard
GRANT Helen
GRAY James
GRAYLING Chris
GREEN Chris
GREEN Damian
GRIFFITH Andrew
GRIFFITHS Kate
GRUNDY James
GULLIS Jonathan
HALFON Robert
HALL Luke
HAMMOND Stephen
HANCOCK Matt
HANDS Greg
HARPER Mark
HARRIS Rebecca
HARRISON Trudy
HART Sally-Ann
HART Simon
HAYES John

HEALD Oliver
HEAPPEY James
HEATON-HARRIS Chris
HENDERSON Gordon
HENRY Darren
HIGGINBOTHAM Antony
HINDS Damian
HOARE Simon
HOLDEN Richard
HOLLINRAKE Kevin
HOLLOBONE Philip
HOLLOWAY Adam
HOLMES Paul
HOWELL John
HOWELL Paul
HUDDLESTON Nigel
HUDSON Neil
HUGHES Eddie
HUNT Jane
HUNT Jeremy
HUNT Tom
JACK Alister
JAVID Sajid
JAYAWARDENA Ranil
JENKIN Bernard
JENKINSON Mark
JENKYNS Andrea
JENRICK Robert
JOHNSON Boris
JOHNSON Caroline
JOHNSON Gareth
JOHNSTON David
JONES Andrew
JONES David
JONES Fay
JONES Marcus
JUPP Simon
KAWCZYNSKI Daniel
KEARNS Alicia
KEEGAN Gillian
KNIGHT Greg
KNIGHT Julian
KRUGER Danny
KWARTENG Kwasi
LAING Eleanor
LAMONT John
LARGAN Robert
LATHAM Pauline
LEADSOM Andrea
LEIGH Edward
LEVY Ian
LEWER Andrew
LEWIS Brandon
LEWIS Julian
LIDDELL-GRAINGER Ian
LODER Chris
LOGAN Mark

LONGHI Marco
LOPEZ Julia
LOPRESTI Jack
LORD Jonathan
LOUGHTON Tim
MCCARTNEY Jason
MCCARTNEY Karl
MACKINLAY Craig
MACKRORY Cherilyn
MACLEAN Rachel
MCPARTLAND Stephen
MCVEY Esther
MAK Alan
MALTHOUSE Kit
MANGNALL Anthony
MANN Scott
MARSON Julie
MAY Theresa
MAYHEW Jerome
MAYNARD Paul
MENZIES Mark
MERCER Johnny
MERRIMAN Huw
METCALFE Stephen
MILLAR Robin
MILLER Maria
MILLING Amanda
MILLS Nigel
MITCHELL Andrew
MOHINDRA Gagan
MOORE Damien
MOORE Robbie
MORDAUNT Penny
MORRIS Anne Marie
MORRIS David
MORRIS James
MORRISSEY Joy
MORTON Wendy
MULLAN Kieran
MUMBY-CROFT Holly
MUNDELL David
MURRAY Sheryll
MURRISON Andrew
NEILL Robert
NICI Lia
NOKES Caroline
NORMAN Jesse
O'BRIEN Neil
OFFORD Matthew
OPPERMAN Guy
PARISH Neil
PATEL Priti
PATERSON Owen
PAWSEY Mark
PENNING Mike
PENROSE John
PERCY Andrew

PHILP Chris
PINCHER Christopher
POULTER Dan
POW Rebecca
PRENTIS Victoria
PRITCHARD Mark
PURSGLOVE Tom
QUIN Jeremy
QUINCE Will
RAAB Dominic
RANDALL Tom
REDWOOD John
REES-MOGG Jacob
RICHARDS Nicola
RICHARDSON Angela
ROBERTS Rob
ROBERTSON Laurence
ROBINSON Mary
ROSINDELL Andrew
ROSS Douglas
ROWLEY Lee
RUSSELL Dean
RUTLEY David
SAMBROOK Gary
SAXBY Selaine
SCULLY Paul
SEELY Bob
SELOUS Andrew
SHAPPS Grant
SHARMA Alok
SHELBROOKE Alec
SIMMONDS David
SKIDMORE Chris
SMITH Chloe
SMITH Greg
SMITH Henry
SMITH Julian
SMITH Royston
SOLLOWAY Amanda
SPENCER Ben
SPENCER Mark
STAFFORD Alexander
STEPHENSON Andrew
STEVENSON Jane
STEVENSON John
STEWART Bob
STEWART Iain
STREETER Gary
STRIDE Mel
STUART Graham
STURDY Julian
SUNAK Rishi
SUNDERLAND James
SWAYNE Desmond
SYMS Robert
THOMAS Derek
THROUP Maggie

TIMPSON Edward
TOLHURST Kelly
TOMLINSON Justin
TOMLINSON Michael
TRACEY Craig
TREVELYAN Anne-Marie
TROTT Laura
TRUSS Elizabeth
TUGENDHAT Tom
VARA Shailesh
VICKERS Martin
VICKERS Matt
VILLIERS Theresa
WAKEFORD Christian
WALKER Charles
WALKER Robin
WALLACE Ben
WALLIS Jamie
WARBURTON David
WARMAN Matt
WATLING Giles
WEBB Suzanne
WHATELY Helen
WHEELER Heather
WHITTAKER Craig
WHITTINGDALE John
WIGGIN Bill
WILD James
WILLIAMS Craig
WILLIAMSON Gavin
WOOD Mike
WRAGG William
WRIGHT Jeremy
YOUNG Jacob
ZAHAWI Nadhim

Labour

ABBOTT Diane
ABRAHAMS Debbie
ALI Rushanara
ALI Tahir
ALLIN-KHAN Rosena
AMESBURY Mike
ANDERSON Fleur
ANTONIAZZI Tonia
BARKER Paula
BECKETT Margaret
BEGUM Apsana
BENN Hilary
BETTS Clive
BLAKE Olivia
BLOMFIELD Paul
BRADSHAW Ben
BRENNAN Kevin
BROWN Lyn
BROWN Nick
BRYANT Chris
BUCK Karen
BURGON Richard
BUTLER Dawn
BYRNE Ian
BYRNE Liam
CADBURY Ruth
CAMPBELL Alan
CARDEN Dan
CHAMPION Sarah
CHARALAMBOUS Bambos
CLARK Feryal
COOPER Rosie
COOPER Yvette
COYLE Neil
CRUDDAS Jon
CRYER John
CUMMINS Judith
CUNNINGHAM Alex
DABY Janet
DAVID Wayne
DAVIES-JONES Alex
DEBBONAIRE Thangam
DE CORDOVA Marsha
DHESI Tanmanjeet Singh
DOWD Peter
DROMEY Jack
DUFFIELD Rosie
EAGLE Angela
EAGLE Maria
EFFORD Clive
ELLIOTT Julie
ELMORE Chris
ESTERSON Bill
FLETCHER Colleen
FOVARGUE Yvonne
FOXCROFT Vicky
FOY Mary
FURNISS Gill
GARDINER Barry
GLINDON Mary
GREEN Kate
GREENWOOD Lilian
GREENWOOD Margaret
GRIFFITH Nia
GWYNNE Andrew
HAIGH Louise
HAMILTON Fabian
HARDY Emma
HARMAN Harriet
HARRIS Carolyn
HAYES Helen
HEALEY John
HILL Mike
HODGE Margaret
HODGSON Sharon
HOLLERN Kate
HOPKINS Rachel
HOWARTH George
HUQ Rupa
HUSSAIN Imran
JARVIS Dan
JOHNSON Diana
JOHNSON Kim
JONES Darren
JONES Gerald
JONES Kevan
JONES Ruth
JONES Sarah
KANE Mike
KEELEY Barbara
KENDALL Liz
KHAN Afzal
KINNOCK Stephen
KYLE Peter
LAMMY David
LAVERY Ian
LEWELL-BUCK Emma
LEWIS Clive
LLOYD Tony
LONG BAILEY Rebecca
LYNCH Holly
MCCABE Steve
MCCARTHY Kerry
MCDONAGH Siobhain
MCDONALD Andy
MCDONNELL John
MCFADDEN Pat
MCGINN Conor
MCGOVERN Alison
MCKINNELL Catherine
MCMORRIN Anna
MADDERS Justin
MAHMOOD Khalid
MAHMOOD Shabana
MATHESON Chris
MEARNS Ian
MILIBAND Ed
MISHRA Navendu
MORDEN Jessica
MORGAN Stephen
MORRIS Grahame
MURRAY Ian
NANDY Lisa
NICHOLS Charlotte
ONWURAH Chi
OPPONG-ASARE Abena
OSBORNE Kate
OWATEMI Taiwo
OWEN Sarah

PEACOCK Stephanie
PENNYCOOK Matthew
PERKINS Toby
PHILLIPS Jess
PHILLIPSON Bridget
QURESHI Yasmin
RAYNER Angela
REEVES Ellie
REEVES Rachel
RIBEIRO-ADDY Bell
RIMMER Marie
RODDA Matt
SHAH Naz
SHARMA Virendra
SIDDIQ Tulip
SLAUGHTER Andy
SMITH Cat
SMITH Jeff
SMITH Nick
SMYTH Karin
SPELLAR John
STARMER Keir
STEVENS Jo
STREETING Wes
STRINGER Graham
SULTANA Zarah
TAMI Mark
TARRY Sam
THOMAS-SYMONDS Nick
THORNBERRY Emily
TIMMS Stephen
TRICKETT Jon
TURNER Karl
TWIGG Derek
TWIST Liz
VAZ Valerie
WEST Catherine
WESTERN Matt
WHITEHEAD Alan
WHITLEY Mick
WHITTOME Nadia
WINTER Beth
WINTERTON Rosie
YASIN Mohammad
ZEICHNER Daniel

Scottish National Party

BARDELL Hannah
BLACK Mhairi
BLACKFORD Ian
BLACKMAN Kirsty
BONNAR Steven
BROCK Deidre
BROWN Alan
CALLAGHAN Amy
CAMERON Lisa
CHAPMAN Douglas
CHERRY Joanna
COWAN Ronnie
CRAWLEY Angela
DAY Martyn
DOCHERTY-HUGHES Martin
DOOGAN Dave
DORANS Allan
FELLOWS Marion
FLYNN Stephen
GIBSON Patricia
GRADY Patrick
GRANT Peter
GRAY Neil
HANVEY Neale
HENDRY Drew
HOSIE Stewart
LAW Chris
LINDEN David
MACASKILL Kenny
MCDONALD Stewart Malcolm
MCDONALD Stuart C
MCLAUGHLIN Anne
MCNALLY John
MACNEIL Angus
MONAGHAN Carol
NEWLANDS Gavin
NICOLSON John
O'HARA Brendan
OSWALD Kirsten
SHEPPARD Tommy
SMITH Alyn
STEPHENS Chris
THEWLISS Alison
THOMPSON Owen
THOMSON Richard
WHITFORD Philippa
WISHART Pete

Labour/Co-operative

ASHWORTH Jon
BRABIN Tracy
CREASY Stella
DAVIES Geraint
DODDS Anneliese
DOUGHTY Stephen
ESHALOMI Florence
EVANS Chris
GILL Preet Kaur
HENDRICK Mark
HILLIER Meg
MCMAHON Jim
MALHOTRA Seema
MASKELL Rachael
MURRAY James
NORRIS Alex
OSAMOR Kate
POLLARD Luke
POWELL Lucy
REED Steve
REES Christina
REYNOLDS Jonathan
RUSSELL-MOYLE Lloyd
SHEERMAN Barry
SOBEL Alex
THOMAS Gareth

Liberal Democrat

CARMICHAEL Alistair
CHAMBERLAIN Wendy
COOPER Daisy
DAVEY Ed
FARRON Tim
HOBHOUSE Wera
JARDINE Christine
MORAN Layla
OLNEY Sarah
STONE Jamie
WILSON Munira

Democratic Unionist Party

CAMPBELL Gregory
DONALDSON Jeffrey
GIRVAN Paul
LOCKHART Carla
PAISLEY Ian
ROBINSON Gavin
SHANNON Jim
WILSON Sammy

Sinn Féin

BEGLEY Órfhlaith
BRADY Mickey
FINUCANE John
GILDERNEW Michelle
HAZZARD Chris
MASKEY Paul
MOLLOY Francie

Independent

CORBYN Jeremy
EDWARDS Jonathan
FERRIER Margaret
WEBBE Claudia

Plaid Cymru

LAKE Ben
SAVILLE ROBERTS Liz
WILLIAMS Hywel

Social Democratic and Labour Party

EASTWOOD Colum
HANNA Claire

Alliance Party of Northern Ireland

FARRY Stephen

Green Party

LUCAS Caroline

The Speaker

HOYLE Lindsay

Select Committees

Each Department of State is shadowed by a Select Committee. In addition to these departmentally related select committees there are committees with responsibilities cutting across government departments (Public Accounts, Public Administration and Constitutional Affairs, Environmental Audit, Human Rights, Statutory Instruments, European Scrutiny, Regulatory Reform, etc.) and a number of committees which concern themselves with the running of the House.

Departmental Committees

Committees on Arms Export Controls

The Committees on Arms Export Controls consist of four select committees meeting concurrently: Defence; Foreign Affairs; International Development; and International Trade. All members of the four committees can attend; the committees have designated the following members to attend meetings of the Committees on Arms Export Controls.

Tel: 020 7219 2567
Email: caeccom@parliament.uk
committees.parliament.uk/committee/15/committees-on-arms-export-controls-formerly-quadripartite-committee
Twitter: @CommonsCAEC

Mark Garnier (Chair) *Con*
International Development:
Sarah Champion *Lab*
Theo Clarke *Con*
Foreign Affairs:
Neil Coyle *Lab*
Defence:
Martin Docherty-Hughes *SNP*
Tobias Ellwood *Con*
International Trade:
Sir Mark Hendrick *Lab/Co-op*
International Development:
Chris Law *SNP*
Defence:
Emma Lewell-Buck *Lab*
International Trade:
Mark Menzies *Con*
International Development:
Navendu Mishra *Lab*
Kate Osamor *Lab/Co-op*
Defence:
John Spellar *Lab*
Foreign Affairs:
Tom Tugendhat *Con*
Claudia Webbe *Ind*

Staff: Simon Fiander (Clerk), Ian Thomson (Committee Specialist), George Perry (Senior Media Officer), Carolyn Bowes (Committee Assistant)

Business, Energy and Industrial Strategy

Tel: 020 7219 4494
Email: beiscom@parliament.uk
www.parliament.uk/beis
Twitter: @CommonsBEIS

Darren Jones (Chair) *Lab*
Alan Brown *SNP*
Judith Cummins *Lab*
Richard Fuller *Con*
Nusrat Ghani *Con*
Paul Howell *Con*
Mark Jenkinson *Con*
Charlotte Nichols *Lab*
Mark Pawsey *Con*
Alexander Stafford *Con*
Zarah Sultana *Lab*

Staff: Rebecca Davies (Clerk), Alison Groves (Second Clerk), Ian Cruse, Becky Mawhood, Ashleigh Morris (Committee Specialists), Gary Calder (Media Officer), James McQuade (Senior Committee Assistant), Matthew Eaton (Committee Assistant)

Defence

All members also meet as the Defence Sub-committee.

Tel: 020 7219 5745
Email: defcom@parliament.uk
www.parliament.uk/defcom
Twitter: @CommonsDefence

Tobias Ellwood (Chair) *Con*
Stuart Anderson *Con*
Sarah Atherton *Con*
Martin Docherty-Hughes *SNP*
Richard Drax *Con*
Mark Francois *Con*
Kevan Jones *Lab*
Emma Lewell-Buck *Lab*
Gavin Robinson *DUP*
John Spellar *Lab*
Derek Twigg *Lab*

Staff: Mark Etherton (Clerk), Matthew Congreve (Second Clerk), Ian Thomson, Lauren Twort, George Woodhams (Committee Specialists), Joe Williams (Media Officer), Sarah Williams (Senior Committee Assistant), Arvind Gunnoo (Committee Assistant)

Digital, Culture, Media and Sport

All members also meet as the Sub-committee on Online Harms and Disinformation.

Tel: 020 7219 6188
Email: cmscom@parliament.uk
committees.parliament.uk/committee/378/digital-culture-media-and-sport
Twitter: @CommonsDCMS

Julian Knight (Chair)	*Con*
Kevin Brennan	*Lab*
Steve Brine	*Con*
Alex Davies-Jones	*Lab*
Clive Efford	*Lab*
Julie Elliott	*Lab*
Damian Green	*Con*
Damian Hinds	*Con*
John Nicolson	*SNP*
Giles Watling	*Con*
Heather Wheeler	*Con*

Staff: Chloe Challender (Clerk), Charlotte Swift (Second Clerk), Conor Durham, Lois Jeary (Committee Specialists), Anne Peacock (Senior Media and Communications Officer), Andy Boyd (Senior Committee Assistant), Keely Bishop (Committee Assistant)

Education

Tel: 020 7219 2370
Email: educom@parliament.uk
committees.parliament.uk/committee/203/education-committee Twitter: @CommonsEd

Robert Halfon (Chair)	*Con*
Fleur Anderson	*Lab*
Apsana Begum	*Lab*
Jonathan Gullis	*Con*
Tom Hunt	*Con*
Dr Caroline Johnson	*Con*
Kim Johnson	*Lab*
David Johnston	*Con*
Ian Mearns	*Lab*
David Simmonds	*Con*
Christian Wakeford	*Con*

Staff: Michael Everett (Clerk), Daniel Schlappa (Assistant Clerk), Chloë Cockett, Vanessa Donhowe, Rosemary Hill (Committee Specialists), Oliver Florence (Senior Media Officer), Natalie Flanagan (Senior Committee Assistant), Olivia Cormack (Committee Assistant)

Environment, Food and Rural Affairs

Tel: 020 7219 1119
Email: efracom@parliament.uk
committees.parliament.uk/committee/52/environment-food-and-rural-affairs-committee
Twitter: @CommonsEFRA

Neil Parish (Chair)	*Con*
Ian Byrne	*Lab*
Geraint Davies	*Lab/Co-op*
Dave Doogan	*SNP*
Rosie Duffield	*Lab*
Barry Gardiner	*Lab*
Dr Neil Hudson	*Con*
Robbie Moore	*Con*
Sheryll Murray	*Con*
Julian Sturdy	*Con*
Derek Thomas	*Con*

Staff: Ian Bradshaw (Clerk), Xameerah Malik (Senior Committee Specialist), Jonathan Finlay, Andy French (Committee Specialists), Joe Williams (Media Officer), Beth Goodwin (Senior Committee Assistant), Ian Blair, Annabel Russell (Committee Assistants)

Foreign Affairs

Tel: 020 7219 6106
Email: fac@parliament.uk
committees.parliament.uk/committee/78/foreign-affairs-committee
Twitter: @CommonsForeign

Tom Tugendhat (Chair)	*Con*
Chris Bryant	*Lab*
Neil Coyle	*Lab*
Alicia Kearns	*Con*
Stewart Malcolm McDonald	*SNP*
Andrew Rosindell	*Con*
Bob Seely	*Con*
Henry Smith	*Con*
Royston Smith	*Con*
Graham Stringer	*Lab*
Claudia Webbe	*Ind*

Staff: Chris Shaw (Clerk), Lauren Boyer (Second Clerk), Ashlee Godwin, Areilla Huff (Senior Committee Specialists), James Hockaday, James Jennion, Emma Makey, Hannah Stone, Nicholas Wade (Committee Specialists), Joe Williams (Media and Communications Manager), Toni McAndrew-Noon (Media and Communications Officer), Clare Genis (Senior Committee Assistant), Ed Hamill (Committee Assistant)

Health and Social Care

Tel: 020 7219 6182
Email: hsccom@parliament.uk
committees.parliament.uk/committee/81/health-and-social-care-committee
Twitter: @CommonsHealth

Jeremy Hunt (Chair)	*Con*
Paul Bristow	*Con*
Rosie Cooper	*Lab*

Dr James Davies *Con*
Dr Luke Evans *Con*
Neale Hanvey *SNP*
Barbara Keeley *Lab*
Taiwo Owatemi *Lab*
Sarah Owen *Lab*
Dean Russell *Con*
Laura Trott *Con*

Staff: Huw Yardley (Clerk), Previn Desai (Second Clerk), Laura Daniels (Senior Committee Specialist), Rosemary Hill (Committee Specialist), Charlie Bell (Clinical Fellow), Joe Williams (Senior Media and Communications Officer), James McQuade (Senior Committee Assistant), Sandy Gill (Committee Assistant)

Home Affairs

Tel: 020 7219 6856
Email: homeaffcom@parliament.uk
committees.parliament.uk/committee/83/home-affairs-committee
Twitter: @CommonsHomeAffs

Yvette Cooper (Chair) *Lab*
Diane Abbott *Lab*
Dehenna Davison *Con*
Ruth Edwards *Con*
Laura Farris *Con*
Simon Fell *Con*
Andrew Gwynne *Lab*
Adam Holloway *Con*
Dame Diana Johnson *Lab*
Tim Loughton *Con*
Stuart C McDonald *SNP*

Staff: Elizabeth Hunt (Clerk), Dominic Stockbridge (Second Clerk), Simon Armitage, Penny McLean (Committee Specialists), Chloë Cockett (Senior Specialist), George Perry (Senior Media and Communications Officer), Paul Simpkin (Senior Committee Assistant), Melissa Bailey (Committee Assistant)

Housing, Communities and Local Government

Tel: 020 7219 5364
Email: hclgcom@parliament.uk
committees.parliament.uk/committee/17/housing-communities-and-local-government-committee Twitter: @CommonsHCLG

Clive Betts (Chair) *Lab*
Bob Blackman *Con*
Ian Byrne *Lab*
Brendan Clarke-Smith *Con*
Ben Everitt *Con*
Paul Holmes *Con*
Rachel Hopkins *Lab*
Ian Levy *Con*
Abena Oppong-Asare *Lab*
Mary Robinson *Con*
Mohammad Yasin *Lab*

Staff: Mike Winter (Clerk), Jack Dent (Second Clerk), Edward Hicks, Nick Taylor (Committee Specialists), George Perry (Media Officer), Eldon Gallagher (Committee Support Assistant)

International Development

Tel: 020 7219 1223
Email: indcom@parliament.uk
committees.parliament.uk/committee/98/international-development-committee
Twitter: @CommonsIDC

Sarah Champion (Chair) *Lab*
Richard Bacon *Con*
Theo Clarke *Con*
Brendan Clarke-Smith *Con*
Pauline Latham *Con*
Chris Law *SNP*
Ian Liddell-Grainger *Con*
Navendu Mishra *Lab*
Kate Osamor *Lab/Co-op*
Dr Dan Poulter *Con*
Virendra Sharma *Lab*

Staff: Fergus Reid (Clerk), Jeanne Delebarre (Second Clerk), Alison Pickard, Kenneth Foreman (Committee Specialists), Jack Tennant (Assistant Inquiry Manager), Chloe Jago (Senior Media Officer), Leo Oliveira (Senior Committee Assistant), Paul Hampson, Rowena Macdonald (Committee Assistants)

Work of the Independent Commission for Aid Impact Sub-committee

Tel: 020 7219 1223
Email: jagoc@parliament.uk

Theo Clarke (Chair) *Con*
Richard Bacon *Con*
Sarah Champion *Lab*
Chris Law *SNP*
Kate Osamor *Lab/Co-op*
Dr Dan Poulter *Con*

Staff: Jeanne Delebarre (Second Clerk), Paul Hampson (Committee Assistant)

International Trade

Email: tradecom@parliament.uk
committees.parliament.uk/committee/367/international-trade-committee
Twitter: @CommonsIntTrade

Angus MacNeil (Chair) *SNP*
Mark Garnier *Con*
Paul Girvan *DUP*

Sir Mark Hendrick	*Lab/Co-op*
Anthony Mangnall	*Con*
Mark Menzies	*Con*
Taiwo Owatemi	*Lab*
Lloyd Russell-Moyle	*Lab/Co-op*
Martin Vickers	*Con*
Mick Whitley	*Lab*
Craig Williams	*Con*

Staff: Joanna Welham (Clerk), Sean Kinsey (Second Clerk), Anna Sydorak-Tomczyk, Anna Sydorak-Tomczyk, David Turner (Committee Specialists), Ben Shave (Media Officer), Hannah Barlow, Matthew Chappell (Committee Assistants)

Justice

Tel: 020 7219 8196
Email: justicecom@parliament.uk
committees.parliament.uk/committee/102/justice-committee Twitter: @CommonsJustice

Sir Robert Neill (Chair)	*Con*
Paula Barker	*Lab*
Richard Burgon	*Lab*
Rob Butler	*Con*
James Daly	*Con*
Sarah Dines	*Con*
Maria Eagle	*Lab*
Dr John Howell	*Con*
Kenny MacAskill	*SNP*
Dr Kieran Mullan	*Con*
Andy Slaughter	*Lab*

Staff: David Weir (Clerk), Holly Tremain (Committee Specialist), Nony Ardill (Legal Specialist), Liz Parratt (Media Officer), Christine Randall (Senior Committee Assistant), Su Panchanathan (Committee Assistant)

Northern Ireland Affairs

Tel: 020 7219 2173
Email: northircom@parliament.uk
committees.parliament.uk/committee/120/northern-ireland-affairs-committee
Twitter: @CommonsNIAC

Simon Hoare (Chair)	*Con*
Scott Benton	*Con*
Gregory Campbell	*DUP*
Dr Stephen Farry	*APNI*
Mary Foy	*Lab*
Robert Goodwill	*Con*
Claire Hanna	*SDLP*
Fay Jones	*Con*
Ian Paisley	*DUP*
Stephanie Peacock	*Lab*
Bob Stewart	*Con*

Staff: Nick Beech (Clerk), Mems Ayinla (Second Clerk), Simon Horswell, George James, Sam Nariani (Committee Specialists), Chloe Smith (Inquiry Manager), Zoë Grünewald (Media Officer), John Hitchcock (Senior Committee Assistant), Kelly Tunnicliffe (Committee Assistant)

Science and Technology

Tel: 020 7219 2793
Email: scitechcom@parliament.uk
committees.parliament.uk/committee/135/science-and-technology-committee-commons
Twitter: @CommonsSTC

Greg Clark (Chair)	*Con*
Aaron Bell	*Con*
Dawn Butler	*Lab*
Chris Clarkson	*Con*
Katherine Fletcher	*Con*
Andrew Griffith	*Con*
Darren Jones	*Lab*
Mark Logan	*Con*
Carol Monaghan	*SNP*
Graham Stringer	*Lab*
Zarah Sultana	*Lab*

Staff: Danielle Nash (Clerk), Masrur Ahmed (Second Clerk), Harry Beeson, Christopher Brown, James Chandler (Committee Specialists), Emily Pritchard (Media Officer), Sonia Draper (Senior Committee Assistant), Emma Dobrzynski (Committee Assistant)

Scottish Affairs

Tel: 020 7219 8204
Email: scotaffcom@parliament.uk
committees.parliament.uk/committee/136/scottish-affairs-committee
Twitter: @CommonsScotAffs

Pete Wishart (Chair)	*SNP*
Mhairi Black	*SNP*
Andrew Bowie	*Con*
Deidre Brock	*SNP*
Wendy Chamberlain	*Lib Dem*
Alberto Costa	*Con*
Jon Cruddas	*Lab*
Sally-Ann Hart	*Con*
John Lamont	*Con*
Douglas Ross	*Con*
Liz Twist	*Lab*

Staff: Leoni Kurt (Clerk), Samir Amar Setti (Second Clerk), Simon Horswell, Ben Rayner (Committee Specialists), Tim West (Senior Media and Communications Officer), Abi Samuels (Senior Committee Assistant), Robert McQuade (Committee Assistant)

Transport
Tel: 020 7219 7570
Email: transcom@parliament.uk
committees.parliament.uk/committee/153/transport-committee Twitter: @CommonsTrans

Huw Merriman (Chair) *Con*
Ruth Cadbury *Lab*
Lilian Greenwood *Lab*
Simon Jupp *Con*
Robert Largan *Con*
Chris Loder *Con*
Karl McCartney *Con*
Grahame Morris *Lab*
Gavin Newlands *SNP*
Greg Smith *Con*
Sam Tarry *Lab*

Staff: Marek Kubala (Clerk), Robi Quigley (Assistant Clerk), Nerys Davies, Lewis Pickett (Committee Specialists), Estelle Currie (Media Officer), Deborah Courtney (Senior Committee Assistant), Michelle Owens (Committee Assistant)

Treasury
Tel: 020 7219 5769
Email: treascom@parliament.uk
committees.parliament.uk/committee/158/treasury-committee
Twitter: @CommonsTreasury

Mel Stride (Chair) *Con*
Rushanara Ali *Lab*
Steve Baker *Con*
Harriett Baldwin *Con*
Anthony Browne *Con*
Felicity Buchan *Con*
Dame Angela Eagle *Lab*
Mike Hill *Lab*
Siobhain McDonagh *Lab*
Julie Marson *Con*
Alison Thewliss *SNP*

Staff: Gosia McBride (Clerk), Gail Bartlett (Second Clerk), Adam Wales (Chief Policy Adviser), Marcus Wilton, Dan Lee, Aruni Muthumala (Senior Economists), Matt Panteli (Senior Media and Policy Officer), Maciej Wenerski (Senior Committee Assistant), Baris Tufekci (Committee Assistant)

Welsh Affairs
Tel: 020 7219 0316
Email: welshcom@parliament.uk
committees.parliament.uk/committee/162/welsh-affairs-committee
Twitter: @CommonsWelshAff

Stephen Crabb (Chair) *Con*
Tonia Antoniazzi *Lab*
Simon Baynes *Con*
Virginia Crosbie *Con*
Geraint Davies *Lab/Co-op*
Ruth Jones *Lab*
Ben Lake *PlC*
Robin Millar *Con*
Rob Roberts *Con*
Dr Jamie Wallis *Con*
Dr Beth Winter *Lab*

Staff: Adam Evans (Clerk), Mems Ayinla (Second Clerk), Rhiannon Williams, Simon Horswell (Committee Specialists), Zoë Grünewald (Media Officer), Louise Glen (Senior Committee Assistant), Kelly Tunnicliffe (Committee Assistant)

Women and Equalities
Tel: 020 7219 5113
Email: womeqcom@parliament.uk
committees.parliament.uk/committee/328/women-and-equalities-committee
Twitter: @Commonswomequ

Caroline Nokes (Chair) *Con*
Sara Britcliffe *Con*
Theo Clarke *Con*
Elliot Colburn *Con*
Angela Crawley *SNP*
Alex Davies-Jones *Lab*
Peter Gibson *Con*
Kim Johnson *Lab*
Kate Osborne *Lab*
Bell Ribeiro-Addy *Lab*
Nicola Richards *Con*

Staff: Jyoti Chandola (Clerk), Radhika Handa (Second Clerk), Tansy Hutchinson, Shai Jacobs, Mariam Keating (Committee Specialists), Liz Parratt (Media Officer), Ellie Goodchild (Senior Committee Assistant), Mandy Sullivan (Committee Assistant)

Work and Pensions
Tel: 020 7219 8976
Email: workpencom@parliament.uk
committees.parliament.uk/committee/164/work-and-pensions-committee
Twitter: @CommonsWorkPen

Stephen Timms (Chair) *Lab*
Debbie Abrahams *Lab*
Shaun Bailey *Con*
Siobhan Baillie *Con*
Neil Coyle *Lab*
Steve McCabe *Lab*
Nigel Mills *Con*
Selaine Saxby *Con*
Dr Ben Spencer *Con*
Chris Stephens *SNP*

Sir Desmond Swayne *Con*

Staff: Anne-Marie Griffiths (Clerk), Libby McEnhill, James Mirza Davies (Senior Committee Specialists), Aisling Munnelly (Assistant Policy Analyst), Oliver Florence (Senior Media and Communications Officer), Esther Goosey (Senior Committee Assistant), Michelle Garratty (Committee Assistant)

Joint Committees

See Lords and Commons Joint Select Committees on p1164

Other Committees

Environmental Audit

Tel: 020 7219 8890
Email: eacom@parliament.uk
committees.parliament.uk/committee/62/environmental-audit-committee
Twitter: @Commonseac

Philip Dunne (Chair) *Con*
Duncan Baker *Con*
Sir Christopher Chope *Con*
Feryal Clark *Lab*
Barry Gardiner *Lab*
Robert Goodwill *Con*
Ian Levy *Con*
Marco Longhi *Con*
Dr Caroline Lucas *Green*
Cherilyn Mackrory *Con*
John McNally *SNP*
Jerome Mayhew *Con*
Dr Matthew Offord *Con*
Alex Sobel *Lab/Co-op*
Claudia Webbe *Ind*
Nadia Whittome *Lab*

Staff: Martyn Atkins (Clerk), Leoni Kurt (Second Clerk), Ruth Cahir, Laura Grant, Laura Scott (Committee Specialists), Anne Peacock (Senior Media and Communications Officer), Jonathan Wright (Senior Committee Assistant), Katie Gibbs (Committee Assistant)

European Scrutiny

Tel: 020 7219 3292
Email: escom@parliament.uk
committees.parliament.uk/committee/69/european-scrutiny-committee
Twitter: @CommonsEU

Sir Bill Cash (Chair) *Con*
Tahir Ali *Lab*
Jon Cruddas *Lab*
Allan Dorans *SNP*
Richard Drax *Con*
Margaret Ferrier *Ind*
Marcus Fysh *Con*
Andrea Jenkyns *Con*
David Jones *Con*
Stephen Kinnock *Lab*
David Lammy *Lab*
Marco Longhi *Con*
Craig Mackinlay *Con*
Anne Marie Morris *Con*
Charlotte Nichols *Lab*
Greg Smith *Con*

Staff: Jessica Mulley (Clerk), Sibel Taner (Second Clerk), Ben Shave (Media and Communications Officer), Daniel Moeller (Senior Committee Assistant)

European Statutory Instruments

Tel: 020 7219 3000
Email: esic@parliament.uk
committees.parliament.uk/committee/393/european-statutory-instruments
Twitter: @CommonsESIC

Andrew Jones (Chair) *Con*
Kirsty Blackman *SNP*
Geraint Davies *Lab/Co-op*
Flick Drummond *Con*
Philip Dunne *Con*
Sir David Evennett *Con*
James Grundy *Con*
Richard Holden *Con*
Stephen Kinnock *Lab*
Charlotte Nichols *Lab*
Mary Robinson *Con*
Jo Stevens *Lab*
Owen Thompson *SNP*
Liz Twist *Lab*
Craig Williams *Con*
Jacob Young *Con*

Staff: Luanne Middleton (Clerk), Ben Shave (Media and Communications Officer)

Petitions

Tel: 020 7219 4887
Email: petitionscommittee@parliament.uk
committees.parliament.uk/committee/326/petitions-committee Twitter: @HoCpetitions

Catherine McKinnell (Chair) *Lab*
Tonia Antoniazzi *Lab*
Elliot Colburn *Con*
Martyn Day *SNP*
Chris Evans *Lab/Co-op*
Katherine Fletcher *Con*
Nick Fletcher *Con*
Jonathan Gullis *Con*
Mike Hill *Lab*

Tom Hunt	*Con*
Theresa Villiers	*Con*

Staff: Ben Sneddon (Clerk), Hannah Olbison (Senior Media Relations Officer)

Privileges
Tel: 020 7219 3259
Email: privileges@parliament.uk
committees.parliament.uk/committee/289/committee-on-privileges
Twitter: @HoCPrivileges

Chris Bryant (Chair)	*Lab*
Andy Carter	*Con*
Alberto Costa	*Con*
Chris Elmore	*Lab*
Mark Fletcher	*Con*
Sir Bernard Jenkin	*Con*
Anne McLaughlin	*SNP*

Staff: Robin James (Clerk), Medha Bhasin (Second Clerk), Paul Connolly (Media Officer), Jim Camp (Committee Assistant)

Procedure
Tel: 020 7219 3351 Fax: 020 7219 2269
Email: proccom@parliament.uk
committees.parliament.uk/committee/126/procedure-committee
Twitter: @commonsproccom

Karen Bradley (Chair)	*Con*
Aaron Bell	*Con*
Kirsty Blackman	*SNP*
Jack Brereton	*Con*
Bambos Charalambous	*Lab*
Sir Christopher Chope	*Con*
Dame Angela Eagle	*Lab*
Chris Elmore	*Lab*
James Gray	*Con*
Kevan Jones	*Lab*
Nigel Mills	*Con*
Douglas Ross	*Con*
James Sunderland	*Con*
Owen Thompson	*SNP*
Liz Twist	*Lab*
Suzanne Webb	*Con*
William Wragg	*Con*

Staff: Richard Ward (Clerk), Zoë Backhouse (Second Clerk), Paul Connolly (Media Officer), Jim Lawford (Committee Assistant)

Public Accounts
Tel: 020 7219 3273
Email: pubaccom@parliament.uk
committees.parliament.uk/committee/127/public-accounts-committee
Twitter: @CommonsPAC

Meg Hillier (Chair)	*Lab/Co-op*
Gareth Bacon	*Con*
Kemi Badenoch	*Con*
Shaun Bailey	*Con*
Olivia Blake	*Lab*
Sir Geoffrey Clifton-Brown	*Con*
Barry Gardiner	*Lab*
Dame Cheryl Gillan	*Con*
Peter Grant	*SNP*
Richard Holden	*Con*
Sir Bernard Jenkin	*Con*
Craig Mackinlay	*Con*
Shabana Mahmood	*Lab*
Sarah Olney	*Lib Dem*
Nick Smith	*Lab*
James Wild	*Con*

Staff: Richard Cooke (Clerk), Bradley Albrow (Second Clerk), Shai Jacobs (Chair), Jess Bridges Palmer (Senior Media and Communications Officer), Ameet Chudasama (Senior Committee Assistant), Hajera Begum (Committee Assistant)

Public Administration and Constitutional Affairs
Tel: 020 7219 3268
Email: pacac@parliament.uk
committees.parliament.uk/committee/327/public-administration-and-constitutional-affairs-committee Twitter: @CommonsPACAC

William Wragg (Chair)	*Con*
Ronnie Cowan	*SNP*
Jackie Doyle-Price	*Con*
Rachel Hopkins	*Lab*
David Jones	*Con*
Navendu Mishra	*Lab*
David Mundell	*Con*
Tom Randall	*Con*
Lloyd Russell-Moyle	*Lab/Co-op*
Karin Smyth	*Lab*
John Stevenson	*Con*

Staff: Sarah Rees (Clerk), Jonathan Whiffing, Sarah Ioannou (Second Clerks), Patrick Thomas, Phil Larkin (Committee Specialists), George Perry, Ben Shave (Media Officers), Gabrielle Hill (Senior Committee Assistant), Iwona Hankin (Committee Assistant)

Regulatory Reform
Tel: 020 7219 6352
Email: regrefcom@parliament.uk
committees.parliament.uk/committee/131/regulatory-reform

Stephen McPartland (Chair)	*Con*
Chris Clarkson	*Con*
Jackie Doyle-Price	*Con*
Mark Eastwood	*Con*

Julie Elliott	*Lab*
Mark Garnier	*Con*
Sir Oliver Heald	*Con*
Kevan Jones	*Lab*
Anthony Mangnall	*Con*
Gary Sambrook	*Con*
Karl Turner	*Lab*

Staff: Alison Groves (Clerk), Matthew Eaton (Committee Assistant)

Selection

To nominate or propose Members to serve on General and Select Committees of the House of Commons. The Committee's decisions are recorded in the Votes and Proceedings on a daily basis.

Tel: 020 7219 3123
committees.parliament.uk/committee/381/committee-of-selection

Bill Wiggin (Chair)	*Con*
Stuart Andrew	*Con*
Sir Alan Campbell	*Lab*
Mike Freer	*Con*
Rebecca Harris	*Con*
Jessica Morden	*Lab*
James Morris	*Con*
Mark Tami	*Lab*
Owen Thompson	*SNP*

Staff: Anwen Rees, Yohanna Sallberg (Clerks), Christine McGrane (Committee Assistant)

Standards

Tel: 020 7219 1493
Email: standards@parliament.uk
committees.parliament.uk/committee/290/committee-on-standards
Twitter: @HoCStandards

Chris Bryant (Chair)	*Lab*
Andy Carter	*Con*
Alberto Costa	*Con*
Chris Elmore	*Lab*
Mark Fletcher	*Con*
Sir Bernard Jenkin	*Con*
Anne McLaughlin	*SNP*

Lay Members:
Tammy Banks
Jane Burgess
Rita Dexter
Dr Arun Midha
Paul Thorogood

Staff: Robin James (Clerk), Medha Bhasin (Second Clerk), Maev MacCoille (Media Officer), Jim Camp (Committee Assistant)

Internal Committees

Administration

Tel: 020 7219 4151
Email: ac@parliament.uk
committees.parliament.uk/committee/2/administration-committee

Sir Charles Walker (Chair)	*Con*
John Cryer	*Lab*
Michael Fabricant	*Con*
Marion Fellows	*SNP*
Colleen Fletcher	*Lab*
Sir Greg Knight	*Con*
Pauline Latham	*Con*
Maria Miller	*Con*
Jessica Morden	*Lab*
Mark Tami	*Lab*
Giles Watling	*Con*

Staff: Kevin Candy (Clerk), Sean Harris (Senior Committee Assistant)

Backbench Business

The Committee gives an opportunity to backbench Members to bring forward debates of their choice.

Tel: 020 7219 3302
Email: bbcom@parliament.uk
www.parliament.uk/bbcom
Twitter: @CommonsBBCom

Ian Mearns (Chair)	*Lab*
Imran Ahmad Khan	*Con*
Gareth Bacon	*Con*
Bob Blackman	*Con*
Patricia Gibson	*SNP*
Nigel Mills	*Con*
Lia Nici	*Con*
Claudia Webbe	*Ind*

Staff: Sarah Hartwell-Naguib (Clerk), Gini Griffin, Catherine Meredith (Second Clerks), Lorcan O'Donoghue (Senior Media Relations Officer), Amira Shariif Ali (Committee Assistant)

Finance

Tel: 020 7219 3299
Email: financecommittee@parliament.uk
committees.parliament.uk/committee/325/finance-committee-commons

Lilian Greenwood (Chair)	*Lab*
Harriett Baldwin	*Con*
Clive Betts	*Lab*
Felicity Buchan	*Con*
Sir Geoffrey Clifton-Brown	*Con*
Gareth Davies	*Con*
Dame Eleanor Laing	*Con*
Tommy Sheppard	*SNP*
David Simmonds	*Con*

Mark Tami	*Lab*
Dame Rosie Winterton	*Lab*

Staff: Robert Cope (Clerk), Ronnie Jefferson (Committee Assistant)

Liaison

All members of the Liaison Committee are members of the Sub-committee on the effectiveness and influence of the select committee system.

Tel: 020 7219 5675
Email: liaisoncommittee@parliament.uk
committees.parliament.uk/committee/103/liaison-committee-commons

Sir Bernard Jenkin (Chair)	*Con*
Hilary Benn	*Lab*
Clive Betts	*Lab*
Karen Bradley	*Con*
Chris Bryant	*Lab*
Sir Bill Cash	*Con*
Sarah Champion	*Lab*
Greg Clark	*Con*
Yvette Cooper	*Lab*
Stephen Crabb	*Con*
Philip Dunne	*Con*
Tobias Ellwood	*Con*
Lilian Greenwood	*Lab*
Robert Halfon	*Con*
Harriet Harman	*Lab*
Meg Hillier	*Lab/Co-op*
Simon Hoare	*Con*
Jeremy Hunt	*Con*
Andrew Jones	*Con*
Darren Jones	*Lab*
Julian Knight	*Con*
Catherine McKinnell	*Lab*
Angus MacNeil	*SNP*
Stephen McPartland	*Con*
Ian Mearns	*Lab*
Huw Merriman	*Con*
Jessica Morden	*Lab*
Sir Robert Neill	*Con*
Caroline Nokes	*Con*
Neil Parish	*Con*
Mel Stride	*Con*
Stephen Timms	*Lab*
Tom Tugendhat	*Con*
Sir Charles Walker	*Con*
Bill Wiggin	*Con*
Pete Wishart	*SNP*
William Wragg	*Con*

Staff: David Slater (Clerk), Liz Parratt (Media Officer), Richard Dawson (Senior Committee Assistant)

Panel of Chairs

The Panel of Chairs comprises the Chairman of Ways and Means, the Deputy Chairmen of Ways and Means, and not fewer than ten Members nominated by the Speaker. Members of the Panel chair debates in Westminster Hall and act as the chairs of Public Bill Committees and other general committees. They may also act as temporary chairs of committees of the whole House when requested by the Chairman of Ways and Means.

Tel: 020 7219 3257
Email: pbohoc@parliament.uk
committees.parliament.uk/committee/11/panel-of-chairs

Dame Eleanor Laing (Chair)	*Con*
Rushanara Ali	*Lab*
Sir David Amess	*Con*
Hannah Bardell	*SNP*
Clive Betts	*Lab*
Peter Bone	*Con*
Sir Graham Brady	*Con*
Karen Buck	*Lab*
Sir Christopher Chope	*Con*
Judith Cummins	*Lab*
Geraint Davies	*Lab/Co-op*
Philip Davies	*Con*
Peter Dowd	*Lab*
Dame Angela Eagle	*Lab*
Clive Efford	*Lab*
Julie Elliott	*Lab*
Nigel Evans	*Con*
Yvonne Fovargue	*Lab*
Sir Roger Gale	*Con*
Nusrat Ghani	*Con*
Dame Cheryl Gillan	*Con*
James Gray	*Con*
Sir Mark Hendrick	*Lab/Co-op*
Philip Hollobone	*Con*
Stewart Hosie	*SNP*
Sir George Howarth	*Lab*
Dr Rupa Huq	*Lab*
Sir Edward Leigh	*Con*
Steve McCabe	*Lab*
Siobhain McDonagh	*Lab*
Esther McVey	*Con*
Maria Miller	*Con*
David Mundell	*Con*
Sheryll Murray	*Con*
Caroline Nokes	*Con*
Ian Paisley	*DUP*
Mark Pritchard	*Con*
Christina Rees	*Lab/Co-op*
Laurence Robertson	*Con*
Andrew Rosindell	*Con*
Virendra Sharma	*Lab*

Sir Gary Streeter	*Con*
Graham Stringer	*Lab*
Derek Twigg	*Lab*
Sir Charles Walker	*Con*
Dame Rosie Winterton	*Lab*

Staff: Colin Lee (Secretary)

Officers and Officials

GOVERNANCE AND STRATEGIC BUSINESS RESILIENCE

Email: governanceoffice@parliament.uk

Clerk of the House: Dr John Benger
Director-General of the House of Commons: Ian Ailles
Managing Director of Governance and Strategic Business Resilience: Marianne Cwynarski
Private Secretary to the Clerk: Hannah Bryce
Private Secretary to the Director-General: Emma Sawyer
Head of Internal Audit and Risk: Richard Stammers
Corporate Risk Management Facilitator: Rachel Harrison
Clerk of Domestic Committees: Robert Cope
Head of Parliamentary Safety: Marianne McDougall
Business Management Director: Vasilis Gialias
Director of Customer and Insight: David Newsome
Commons Restoration and Renewal Director: Charlotte Simmonds
Cultural Transformation Director: Sarah Petit

COMMUNICATIONS OFFICE

Tel: 020 7219 0969 (media general enquiries)/020 7219 7395 (media out of hours)/020 7219 4801 (central communications)
Email: communications@parliament.uk

Directors of Communications (job share): Alice Holmes 020 7219 7111, Clare Jennings 020 7219 7006
Deputy Directors: Sasha Fuller 020 7219 2967, Alex Noonoo 020 7219 0532
Head of Strategic Communications and Capability: David Rose 020 7219 4624
Head of Broadcast Relations: Alasdair Rendall 020 7219 0771

CHAMBER AND COMMITTEES TEAM

Clerk Assistant and Managing Director: Sarah Davies 020 7219 3311
PA to the Clerk Assistant: Charlotte Every 020 7219 8232
Head of Team Services: Edward Beale 020 7219 8428

Media and Communications Service (Select Committees)

Head: Liz Parratt 07917 488978 Email: parrattl@parliament.uk
Media and Communications Managers: Estelle Currie 07834 171965 Email: curriee@parliament.uk, Joe Williams 07546 517626 Email: williamsjb@parliament.uk
Senior Media and Communications Officers: Jess Bridges Palmer 07917 488489 Email: bridgespalmerj@parliament.uk, Gary Calder 07917 488622 Email: calderg@parliament.uk, Oliver Florence 07720 205645 Email: florenceo@parliament.uk, Zoë Grünewald 07565 202054 Email: grunewaldz@parliament.uk, Chloe Jago 07710 064583 Email: jagoc@parliament.uk, Matt Panteli 07720 205645 Email: pantelim@parliament.uk, Anne Peacock 07753 101607 Email: peacocka@parliament.uk, George Perry 07834 172099 Email: perryg@parliament.uk, Emily Pritchard 07734 974282 Email: pritcharde@parliament.uk, Ben Shave 07917 488183 Email: shaveb@parliament.uk, Tim West 07933 386949 Email: westtb@parliament.uk
Media and Communications Officers: Gina Degtyareva 07548 146012 Email: degtyarevae@parliament.uk, Mark Doyle 07842 601500 Email: doylem@parliament.uk, Nelson Idama 020 7219 6585 Email: idaman@parliament.uk, Toni McAndrew-Noon 07562 435286 Email: mcandrewnoona@parliament.uk

Overseas Office

Tel: 020 7219 3314
Email: overseasoffice@parliament.uk

Principal Clerk: Dr Lynn Gardner 020 7219 3314
Head of Parliamentary Assemblies Section: Nick Wright 020 7219 2611

Chamber Business Team
Strategic Director, Chamber Business Team: Matthew Hamlyn 020 7219 7379

Public Bill Office
Tel: 020 7219 6758/020 7219 3251
Email: pbohoc@parliament.uk

Clerk of Legislation: Liam Laurence Smyth 020 7219 3255
Clerk of Bills: Chris Stanton 020 7219 3257
Examiner of Petitions for Private Bills and Taxing Officer: Chris Stanton
Clerks: Joanna Dodd, Kenneth Fox, Kevin Maddison, Steven Mark, Adam Mellows Facer, Seb Newman, Rob Page, Anwen Rees, Yohanna Sallberg, Dr Sarah Thatcher, Huw Yardley
Business Manager (CBT): Julie Evans
Chamber Business Digital Systems Manager (CBT): Fliss Batty

Private Bill Office
Tel: 020 7219 6008/020 7219 4975
Email: prbohoc@parliament.uk

Clerk of Private Bills: Rob Page

Journal Office
Tel: 020 7219 3318/020 7219 3361
Email: journaloffice@parliament.uk

Clerk of the Journals: Eve Samson 020 7219 3278
Clerks: Martyn Atkins, Zoë Backhouse, Claire Cozens, Mike Hennessy, Sara Howe, Dr Robin James, Crispin Poyser, Stuart Ramsay, Peter Stam, Ben Street

Centre of Excellence for Procedural Practice
Tel: 020 7219 5495
Email: ppcoe@parliament.uk

Clerks: Sarah Heath, Libby Kurien, Richard Ward
Engagement and Communications Manager (CBT): Caitríona Ridout
Business Manager, Centre of Excellence: Julie Evans

Table Office
Tel: 020 7219 3302
Email: tableoffice@parliament.uk

Principal Clerk: Colin Lee
Clerks: Amelia Aspden, Chloe Challender, Nina Foster, Gini Griffin, Steve Habberley, Sarah Hartwell-Naguib, Phil Jones, Lydia Menzies, Catherine Meredith, Joseph Watt, Sîan Woodward
Business Manager (CBT): Anita Fuki

Vote Office
Tel: 020 7219 3631
Email: vote_office@parliament.uk

Deliverer of the Vote: Tom McVeagh 020 7219 4220
Print and Publications Enquiries Lead: Barry Underwood
Procedural Publishing Operations Lead: Stuart Miller
Business Manager and Contracts Lead: Kathy Barker

Committee Office
Tel: 020 7219 4300/020 7219 1366
Email: cocommunications@parliament.uk

Clerk of Committees: Tom Goldsmith 020 7219 3313
Principal Clerks: Dr Farrah Bhatti 020 7219 3728, Tom Healey 020 7219 0531, James Rhys 020 7219 6461
Head of Scrutiny Unit: David Lloyd 020 7219 8370
Programme Manager, CCT Communications Capability and Change:

Amanda Saunders 020 7219 3488
Head of Media and Communications (Select Committees): Liz Parratt 020 7219 1708
Head of Select Committee Online Services: Miranda Olivier-Wright 020 7219 7589

Official Report (Hansard)
Tel: 020 7219 4786/020 7219 5290
Email: hansardmes@parliament.uk Website: hansard.parliament.uk
Editor: Alex Newton 020 7219 3388
Deputy Editor: Jack Homer 020 7219 5291

Parliamentary Audio Visual
Parliamentary Press Gallery enquiries: 020 7219 4700
Tel: 020 7219 4975/020 7219 6758
Director: John Angeli 020 7219 5848
Deputy Director: Sally Freestone 020 7219 8634

Office of Speaker's Counsel
Reporting directly to the Clerk of the House
Speaker's Counsel: Saira Salimi 020 7219 3776 Email: salimis@parliament.uk
Deputy Speaker's Counsel: Helen Emes
Counsel for Domestic Legislation: Daniel Greenberg
Counsel for European Legislation: To be appointed
Counsel to the Joint Committee on Human Rights: Eleanor Hourigan

IN-HOUSE SERVICES AND ESTATES

Tel: 020 7219 6551
Email: inhouseservices@parliament.uk
Managing Director: Isabel Coman 020 7219 1471
Head of In-House Services and Estates Finance: Ebenezer Oduwole 020 7219 2873
Director of Operations: Jennifer Crook
Director of Capital Investment: Bev Weston 020 7219 3106
Director of Property, Planning and Design: Donald Grant 020 7219 3815
Business Management Director: Charissa Fiander 020 7219 6329
Director of PMO: Catherine Hallett

Serjeant at Arms Office
Tel: 020 7219 3030
Serjeant at Arms: Ugbana Oyet
Deputy Serjeant at Arms (Operations): Chris Rust
Principal Doorkeeper: Phil Howse

Parliamentary Maintenance Services Team
Tel: 020 7219 3202/020 7219 4747 (Parliamentary Maintenance Helpdesk)
Director of Parliamentary Maintenance Services: Tim Killip 020 7219 0737
Head of Maintenance Operations: Mike McCann 020 7219 6493
Reactive and Ceremonial Maintenance Manager: Steve Jaggs 020 7219 4762
Small Works Maintenance Manager: Len Thorogood 020 7219 4814
Contracts Manager: John Taylor 020 7219 4785

Catering Services
Tel: 020 7219 3686
Email: csfeedback@parliament.uk
Director of Catering Services: Richard Tapner-Evans 020 7219 3686
Executive Chef: Mark Hill 020 7219 1444

Decant Services

Decant Director: Dr Patsy Richards 020 7219 5594
Deputy Director (Business Change and Engagement): Emma Downing 020 7219 3813
Deputy Director (Building Services and Moves Readiness): Helen Spall 07562 465545

Customer Experience and Service Delivery

Tel: 020 7219 1319
Email: accommodationservices@parliament.uk

Director of Customer Experience and Service Delivery: James Turner 020 7219 3060
Head of Service Delivery: Simon Mansfield 020 7219 3799
Head of Access and Services: Andy Martin 020 7219 0145
Head of Accommodation: Dominic Bransden 020 7219 1795
Head of Customer Relationship Team: Caroline Nicholls 020 7219 3080
Parliamentary Logistics Manager: Wes Auvache 020 7219 7525
Parliamentary Facilities Performance and Contract Manager: Ryan Auvache 020 7219 5412
Parliamentary Contracts Manager (Service Delivery): Gary Malmstrom 020 7219 3664
Fire Safety Manager: John Bradbury 020 7219 8451

HR AND DIVERSITY

Tel: 020 7219 8001
Email: hrfinancecommunication@parliament.uk

Managing Director, HR and Diversity: Mandy Eddolls
Director of HR Operations: Markos Koumaditis
Acting Director of Members Services Team: Chris Sear
Director of Business Management: Della Herd

INDEPENDENT COMPLAINTS AND GRIEVANCE SCHEME

Email: icgs@parliament.uk

Director: Josephine Willows

FINANCE, PORTFOLIO AND PERFORMANCE

Tel: 020 7219 8001
Email: hrfinancecommunication@parliament.uk

Managing Director, Finance, Portfolio and Performance: Mostaque Ahmed
Director of Financial Management and Performance: Malin Eliasson
Head of Enterprise Portfolio Management Office: Jamie Williams
Head of Members' Hub: Gurpeet Bassi
Director of Business Management: Della Herd

PARLIAMENTARY DIGITAL SERVICE

Website: pds.blog.parliament.uk Twitter: @ParliDigital

Chief Information Officer and Managing Director: Tracey Jessup
Deputy Managing Director (Delivery): David Smith
Interim Deputy Managing Director (Strategy, Improvement and Innovation): Michael Ekpe
Director of Live Services: Rob Sanders
Director of Cyber Security: Mark Harbord
Director of Service Design: Rebecca Elton
Director of Resources: Tim Youngs
Director for R&R and Futures/Cyber Security Capability Programme: Steven Mark
Director of Software Engineering: Matt Stutely
Director of Digital Portfolio: Dan Cook
Director of PDS HR: Richard Shoreland

PARLIAMENTARY SECURITY DEPARTMENT

Email: psdenquiries@parliament.uk
Director of Security for Parliament: Alison Giles
Deputy Director of Security (Operations): Fay Tennet

PARTICIPATION TEAM

Managing Director: Dr Edge Watchorn
Director of Strategy: Matthew Ringer
Director of Visitor and Retail Services: Abigail Fox-Smith
Head of Audiences and Business Engagement: Amy Baxter
Head of Education and Engagement: David Clark
Head of Heritage Collections: Melissa Hamnett

House of Commons Enquiry Service

Tel: 020 7219 4272
Email: hcenquiries@parliament.uk Website: www.parliament.uk/hcio
Public Enquiries Manager: Fiona Green

Houses of Parliament Shop

Tel: 020 7219 3890
Email: shop@parliament.uk
Head of Retail Operations: Diana Christou
Senior Retail Operations Manager: Tamsin Swain

Heritage Collections and Curator's Office

Tel: 020 7219 3157
Email: curator@parliament.uk
Head of Heritage Collections and Curator of Works of Art: Melissa Hamnett 020 7219 2845
Deputy Curator of Works of Art and Head of Interpretation: Melanie Unwin 020 7219 3157
Assistant Curators: Emma Gormley 020 7219 0183, Sileas Wood 020 7219 3157
Collections Care Manager: Caroline Babington 020 7219 5069
Registrar of Collections: Natasha Walsh 020 7219 2812
Assistant Registrar: Anna Rowe 020 7219 4124
Keeper of Collections (Furniture and Decorative Arts): Mary-Jane Tsang 020 7219 4798
Conservation Manager (Furniture and Decorative Arts): Patrick Walsh 020 7219 5321

RESEARCH AND INFORMATION TEAM

House of Commons Librarian and Managing Director: Penny Young
Director of Library Services: Martin Reid
Director of Research: Edward Wood
Director of Strategy and Service Development: Bryn Morgan
Head of Parliamentary Office of Science and Technology: Dr Grant Hill-Cawthorne
Head of Information Rights and Information Security (IRIS): Victoria Payne
Head of Research Communications: Grace Rowley

House of Commons Library

Tel: 020 7219 3666
Email: hclibrary@parliament.uk Twitter: @commonslibrary
Acting Head of Operations and Engagement, House of Commons Library: Amina Gual

Research Sections

Tel: 020 7219 3666
Email: papers@parliament.uk
Head of Business and Transport Section: Oliver Bennett MBE
Library Clerks: Steve Browning, Daniel Ferguson, David Hirst, Antony Seely, Ali Shalchi,

Djuna Thurley
Head of Economic Policy and Statistics Section: Lorna Booth
Library Clerks: Philip Brien, Brigid Francis-Devine, Daniel Harari, Georgina Hutton, Ilze Jozepa, Matthew Keep, Andrew Powell, Dominic Webb
Head of Home Affairs Section: Douglas Pyper
Library Clerks: Jacqueline Beard, Jenny Brown, Lorraine Conway, Joanna Dawson, Catherine Fairbairn, Melanie Gower, Sally Lipscombe, Terry McGuinness, John Woodhouse
Head of International Affairs and Defence Section: Dr Anna Dickson
Library Clerks: Louisa Brooke-Holland, Dr Patrick Butchard, John Curtis, Dr Stefano Fella, Claire Mills, Ben Smith
Head of Parliament and Constitution Centre: Chris Rhodes
Library Clerks: Graeme Cowie, Neil Johnston, Richard Kelly, Dr Mark Sandford, Dr David Torrance
Head of Science and Environment Section: Edward Potton
Library Clerks: Dr Elena Ares, Bukky Balogun, Dr Sarah Barber, Sarah Coe, Jonathan Finlay, Gabrielle Garton Grimwood, Suzanna Hinson, Dr Elizabeth Rough, Louise Smith
Head of Social and General Statistics Section: Richard Cracknell
Library Clerks: Grahame Allen, Dr Carl Baker, Cassie Barton, Paul Bolton, Shadi Danechi, Noel Dempsey, Dr Rachael Harker, Rod McInnes, Georgina Sturge, Dr Elise Uberoi
Head of Social Policy Section: Wendy Wilson
Library Clerks: Hannah Cromarty, David Foster, Manjit Gheera, Francis Hobson, Susan Hubble, Steven Kennedy, Robert Long, Melissa Macdonald, Andrew Mackley, Elizabeth Parkin, Tom Powell, Nerys Roberts

Parliamentary Office of Science and Technology (POST)
Tel: 020 7219 2840
Email: post@parliament.uk Website: post.parliament.uk Twitter: @POST_UK
Head of POST: Dr Grant Hill-Cawthorne
Advisers: Dr Rowena Bermingham, Dr Sarah Bunn, Dr Lorna Christie, Dr Lydia Harriss, Dr Abbi Hobbs, Jack Miller, Dr Cristiana Vagnoni, Dr Jonathan Wentworth

Knowledge Exchange Unit
Lead: Dr Sarah Foxen
Managers: Naomi Saint, Dr Laura Webb

Parliamentary Office of Science and Technology Board
Chair: Adam Afriyie MP
Vice-chair: Professor Lord Winston
Head of POST: Dr Grant Hill-Cawthorne
Board Members: Greg Clark MP, Thangam Debbonaire MP, Professor Elizabeth Fisher, Lord Haskel, Paul Martynenko, Lord Oxburgh KBE, Lord Patel KT, Professor Sir Bernard Silverman, Professor Dame Sarah Whatmore, Dr Alan Whitehead MP

Associated Offices

Parliamentary Commissioner for Standards
Office of the Parliamentary Commissioner for Standards, House of Commons, London SW1A 0AA
Tel: 020 7219 3738
Email: standardscommissioner@parliament.uk Website: www.parliament.uk/pcs
Parliamentary Commissioner for Standards: Kathryn Stone OBE
Registrar of Members' Financial Interests: Heather Wood

Shadow Sponsor Body for the Restoration and Renewal Programme
Email: randrshadowsponsorbody@parliament.uk Website: restorationandrenewal.parliament.uk
Chair: Liz Peace CBE
Members: Lord Best OBE, Lord Carter of Coles, Lord Deighton KBE, Damian Hinds MP, Brigid Janssen, Marta Phillips OBE, Baroness Scott of Needham Market, Tommy Sheppard MP, Sir Robert Syms MP, Mark Tami MP, Dr Simon Thurley CBE, Simon Wright OBE

Chief Executive Designate: Sarah Johnson
Head of Secretariat: Michael Torrance

GENERAL ELECTION 2019

Electoral Information

The Fixed-Term Parliaments Act 2011 set the polling day of the first general election following its enactment as Thursday 7 May 2015, and set each subsequent parliamentary general election to the first Thursday in May in the fifth calendar year following the polling day the previous parliamentary general election fell on. There are two provisions that could be used to trigger an earlier election – a motion of no confidence is passed in Her Majesty's Government by a simple majority and 14 days elapses without the House passing a confidence motion in any new Government formed or a motion for a general election is agreed by two thirds of the total number of seats in the Commons including vacant seats (currently 434 out of 650). This second provision was used in 2017 to call an early general election, which took place on Thursday 8 June 2017.

Parliament dissolves at the beginning of the 25th working day before the polling day for the parliamentary general election. The last day for the delivery of nomination papers is the sixth day after the date of dissolution. The poll is held in every constituency on the 19th day after the last day for delivery of nomination papers.

In the case of a by-election, the last day for the delivery of nomination papers and the date the polling day takes place is fixed by the Returning Officer and are stated on the notice of election. There is a limit of £100,000 on the total amount that a candidate can spend on campaigning in the run-up to a parliamentary by-election.

In calculating election timetables Saturdays, Sundays, Christmas Eve, Christmas Day, Good Friday, bank holidays and days appointed for public thanksgiving or mourning are disregarded.

Parliamentary Franchise

A person resident in the United Kingdom is entitled to be entered on the register of electors if he or she is:

- resident in the constituency
- not subject to any legal incapacity to vote (age apart)
- a British or other qualifying Commonwealth citizen or a citizen of the Republic of Ireland
- is at least 18 years of age (or will become 18 during the currency of the register)
- applies to vote to the Registration Officer no later than 11 working days before polling day.

British citizens resident abroad may also register and vote in parliamentary elections for up to 15 years after leaving the UK. HM Forces can register while serving.

Since 1999 hereditary peers, who were previously barred from voting in general elections, have been allowed to do so if they no longer sit in the Lords.

Parliamentary Candidates

A candidate must be at least 18 years old and a citizen of the United Kingdom, Commonwealth or Republic of Ireland and have indefinite leave to remain in the UK.

Since 1999 hereditary peers who no longer sit in the House of Lords have been allowed to stand as candidates for the Commons.

Each candidate must deposit £500 with the Returning Officer at the time of nomination, refunded if elected, or polls over 5 per cent of votes cast.

Rules on candidate spending apply during the 'regulated period', this is made up of the Long campaign and Short campaign:

Long campaign – the fixed amount is £30,700 plus, 6p per registered parliamentary elector in a borough constituency, or 9p per registered parliamentary elector in a county constituency.

Short campaign – the fixed amount is £8,700 plus, 6p per registered parliamentary elector in a borough constituency, or 9p per registered parliamentary elector in a county constituency.

Number of Voters

In December 2020 there was a total of 47,558,400 names on the electoral registers for the United Kingdom.

England	39,860,400
Scotland	4,079,600
Wales	2,322,700
Northern Ireland	1,295,700

Parties with seats in the House of Commons

APNI	Alliance Party of Northern Ireland	**Lib Dem**	Liberal Democrat
Con	Conservative	**PlC**	Plaid Cymru
DUP	Democratic Unionist Party	**SDLP**	Social Democratic and Labour Party
Green	Green Party	**Sinn Féin**	Sinn Féin
Lab	Labour	**SNP**	Scottish National Party
Lab/Co-op	Labour/Co-operative	**Speaker**	The Speaker

Parties with candidates in the General Election

Advance Advance Together; **Aontú** Aontú; **APNI** Alliance Party of Northern Ireland; **Ashfield Ind** Ashfield Independents; **AWP** Animal Welfare Party; **B&P Ind** Burnley and Padiham Independent Party; **Best4Luton** Best For Luton Party; **BNP** British National Party; **BP** Brexit Party; **Bus-Pass** Bus-Pass Elvis Party; **CB** Crossbench; **Christian** Christian Party; **CMP** Citizens Movement Party; **Comm League** Communist League; **Comm United** Communities United Party; **Common People** Common People; **Con** Conservative; **CPA** Christian Peoples Alliance; **CRP** Constitution and Reform Party; **CumbriaFirst** Cumbria First; **CVP** Cynon Valley Party; **DUP** Democratic Unionist Party; **Eng Dem** English Democrats; **Green** Green Party; **Green Soc** Alliance for Green Socialism; **Gwlad** Gwlad Gwlad; **HWD Ind** Heavy Woollen District Independents; **IGC** The Independent Group for Change; **Ind** Independent; **Ind Net** Independent Network; **JACP** Justice and Anti-Corruption Party; **Lab** Labour; **Lab/Co-op** Labour/Co-operative; **Lib** Liberal Party; **Lib Dem** Liberal Democrat; **Libertarian** Libertarian Party; **Lincs Ind** Lincolnshire Independents; **Loony** Official Monster Raving Loony Party; **MK** Mebyon Kernow; **Motherworld** Motherworld Party; **NEP** North East Party; **Patria** Patria; **PBPA** People Before Profit Alliance; **Peace Party** Peace Party; **PFP** Psychedelic Future Party; **PlC** Plaid Cymru; **PO&S** Proud of Oldham & Saddleworth; **Reboot** Rebooting Democracy; **Renew** Renew; **SDLP** Social Democratic and Labour Party; **SDP** Social Democratic Party; **SEP** Socialist Equality Party; **SFP** Scottish Family Party; **Shropshire** Shropshire Party; **Sinn Féin** Sinn Féin; **SLP** Socialist Labour Party; **SNP** Scottish National Party; **SP** Socialist Party; **Space Navies** Space Navies Party; **Speaker** The Speaker; **TLW** Touch Love Worldwide; **UGP** Universal Good Party; **UKIP** UK Independence Party; **UUP** Ulster Unionist Party; **VAPP** Veterans and People's Party; **WEP** Women's Equality Party; **WRP** Workers Revolutionary Party; **Wycombe Ind** Wycombe Independents; **Yeshua** Yeshua; **YP** Yorkshire Party; **YPP** Young People's Party.

ABERAVON

		%	+/-%
Kinnock, S. Lab*	17,008	53.7	-14.3
Lang, C. Con	6,518	20.6	2.9
Davies, G. BP	3,108	9.8	
Hunt, N. PlC	2,711	8.6	0.3
Kingston-Jones, S. Lib Dem	1,072	3.4	1.6
Beany, C. Ind	731	2.3	
Finney, G. Green	450	1.4	
Lab majority	10,490	33.11	
Electorate	50,750		
Turnout	31,680	62.42	

Lab hold (8.59% from Lab to Con)

ABERDEEN NORTH

		%	+/-%
Blackman, K. SNP*	20,205	53.9	12.7
Houghton, R. Con	7,535	20.1	-2.6
Ali, N. Lab	4,939	13.2	-16.8
Davidson, I. Lib Dem	2,846	7.6	3.0
Leslie, S. BP	1,008	2.7	
Ingerson, G. Green	880	2.4	
SNP majority	12,670	33.8	
Electorate	62,489		
Turnout	37,485	59.99	

SNP hold (7.63% from Con to SNP)

ABERCONWY

		%	+/-%
Millar, R. Con	14,687	45.9	1.4
Owen, E. Lab	12,653	39.6	-3.0
Goodier, L. PlC	2,704	8.5	-1.4
Edwards, J. Lib Dem	1,821	5.7	2.8
Con majority	2,034	6.36	
Electorate	44,699		
Turnout	31,988	71.56	

Con hold (2.19% from Lab to Con)

ABERDEEN SOUTH

		%	+/-%
Flynn, S. SNP	20,388	44.6	13.1
Lumsden, D. Con	16,398	35.8	-6.2
Yuill, I. Lib Dem	5,018	11.0	5.1
Simpson, S. Lab	3,834	8.4	-12.1
SNP majority	3,990	8.72	
Electorate	65,719		
Turnout	45,769	69.64	

SNP gain (9.69% from Con to SNP)

General Election 2019

WEST ABERDEENSHIRE AND KINCARDINE

		%	+/-%
Bowie, A. Con*	22,752	42.6	-5.3
Mutch, F. SNP	21,909	41.0	8.6
Waddell, J. Lib Dem	6,253	11.7	3.1
Coffield, P. Lab	2,431	4.6	-6.5
Con majority	843	1.58	
Electorate	72,640		
Turnout	53,459	73.59	

Con hold (6.91% from Con to SNP)

AIRDRIE AND SHOTTS

		%	+/-%
Gray, N. SNP*	17,929	45.0	7.4
Mcfarlane, H. Lab	12,728	31.9	-5.1
Nolan, L. Con	7,011	17.6	-5.6
Crossman, W. Lib Dem	1,419	3.6	1.5
McGowan, R. Green	685	1.7	
SNP majority	5,201	13.05	
Electorate	64,011		
Turnout	39,863	62.28	

SNP hold (6.27% from Lab to SNP)

ALDERSHOT

		%	+/-%
Docherty, L. Con*	27,980	58.1	3.1
Kaye, H. Lab	11,282	23.4	-8.1
Hilliar, A. Lib Dem	6,920	14.4	7.0
Wallace, D. Green	1,750	3.6	1.4
Con majority	16,698	34.66	
Electorate	72,617		
Turnout	48,183	66.35	

Con hold (5.64% from Lab to Con)

ALDRIDGE-BROWNHILLS

		%	+/-%
Morton, W. Con*	27,850	70.5	5.3
Morgan, D. Lab	8,014	20.3	-9.5
Garrett, I. Lib Dem	2,371	6.0	2.7
McComish, B. Green	771	2.0	
Beech, M. Loony	336	0.9	-0.6
Con majority	19,836	50.23	
Electorate	60,138		
Turnout	39,494	65.67	

Con hold (7.38% from Lab to Con)

ALTRINCHAM AND SALE WEST

		%	+/-%
Brady, G. Con*	26,311	47.9	-3.0
Western, A. Lab	20,172	36.7	-2.0
Smith, A. Lib Dem	6,036	11.0	3.3
Coggins, G. Green	1,566	2.9	1.0
Taylor, N. Lib	454	0.8	0.3
Kiani, I. Ind	224	0.4	
Con majority	6,139	11.17	
Electorate	73,107		
Turnout	54,936	75.14	

Con hold (0.48% from Con to Lab)

ALYN AND DEESIDE

		%	+/-%
Tami, M. Lab*	18,271	42.4	-9.6
Sen, S. Con	18,058	41.9	1.6
Wall, S. BP	2,678	6.2	
Lalek, D. Lib Dem	2,548	5.9	3.5
Hills, S. PlC	1,453	3.4	0.8
Lab majority	213	0.49	
Electorate	62,789		
Turnout	43,129	68.69	

Lab hold (5.59% from Lab to Con)

AMBER VALLEY

		%	+/-%
Mills, N. Con*	29,096	63.6	7.2
Thompson, A. Lab	12,210	26.7	-11.6
Smith, K. Lib Dem	2,873	6.3	3.9
Pizzey, L. Green	1,388	3.0	1.6
Con majority	16,886	36.93	
Electorate	69,976		
Turnout	45,719	65.34	

Con hold (9.43% from Lab to Con)

ANGUS

		%	+/-%
Doogan, D. SNP	21,216	49.0	10.5
Hair, K. Con*	17,421	40.3	-4.8
Lawrie, B. Lib Dem	2,482	5.7	2.5
Miller, M. Lab	2,051	4.7	-8.3
SNP majority	3,795	8.77	
Electorate	63,952		
Turnout	43,262	67.65	

SNP gain (7.67% from Con to SNP)

EAST ANTRIM

		%	+/-%
Wilson, S. DUP*	16,871	45.1	-12.1
Donnelly, D. APNI	10,165	27.2	11.6
Aiken, S. UUP	5,475	14.6	2.8
McMullan, O. Sinn Féin	2,120	5.7	-3.6
Rankin, A. Con	1,043	2.8	0.3
Mulholland, A. SDLP	902	2.4	-0.9
Randle, P. Green	685	1.8	
DUP majority	6,706	17.92	
Electorate	64,830		
Turnout	37,431	57.74	

DUP hold (11.85% from DUP to APNI)

NORTH ANTRIM

		%	+/-%
Paisley, I. DUP*	20,860	47.0	-11.7
Swann, R. UUP	8,139	18.4	11.2
O'Lynn, P. APNI	6,231	14.1	8.4
McShane, C. Sinn Féin	5,632	12.7	-3.5
McKillop, M. SDLP	2,943	6.6	1.3
Palmer, S. Ind	246	0.6	
DUP majority	12,721	28.68	
Electorate	77,134		
Turnout	44,355	57.50	

DUP hold (11.43% from DUP to UUP)

SOUTH ANTRIM

		%	+/-%
Girvan, P. DUP*	15,149	35.1	-3.1
Kinahan, D. UUP	12,460	28.9	-1.9
Blair, J. APNI	8,190	19.0	11.6
Kearney, D. Sinn Féin	4,887	11.3	-6.7
Lynch, R. SDLP	2,288	5.3	-0.2
DUP majority	2,689	6.23	
Electorate	71,711		
Turnout	43,188	60.23	

DUP hold (0.59% from DUP to UUP)

ARFON

		%	+/-%
Williams, H. PlC*	13,134	45.0	4.3
Williams Roberts, S. Lab	10,353	35.5	-4.9
Daniels, G. Con	4,428	15.2	-1.1
Gribben, G. BP	1,159	4.0	
PlC majority	2,781	9.54	
Electorate	42,215		
Turnout	29,166	69.09	

PlC hold (4.6% from Lab to PlC)

ARGYLL AND BUTE

		%	+/-%
O'Hara, B. SNP*	21,040	43.7	7.7
Mulvaney, G. Con	16,930	35.1	1.9
Reid, A. Lib Dem	6,832	14.2	-4.0
Barnes, R. Lab	3,248	6.7	-5.8
SNP majority	4,110	8.53	
Electorate	66,525		
Turnout	48,192	72.44	

SNP hold (2.88% from Con to SNP)

ARUNDEL AND SOUTH DOWNS

		%	+/-%
Griffith, A. Con	35,566	57.4	-4.8
Bennett, A. Lib Dem	13,045	21.1	13.1
Sankey, B. Lab	9,722	15.7	-7.0
Thurston, I. Green	2,519	4.1	-0.2
Wheal, R. Ind	556	0.9	
Con majority	22,521	36.5	
Electorate	81,726		
Turnout	61,695	75.49	

Con hold (8.98% from Con to Lib Dem)

ASHFIELD

		%	+/-%
Anderson, L. Con	19,231	39.2	-2.5
Zadrozny, J. Ashfield Ind	13,498	27.5	18.3
Fleet, N. Lab	11,971	24.4	-18.2
Daubney, M. BP	2,501	5.1	
Wain, R. Lib Dem	1,105	2.3	0.3
Woods, R. Green	674	1.4	0.6
Con majority	5,733	11.68	
Electorate	78,204		
Turnout	49,098	62.78	

Con gain (10.39% from Lab to Con)

ASHFORD

		%	+/-%
Green, D. Con*	37,270	61.8	2.9
Farrell, D. Lab	13,241	21.9	-7.8
Gee-Turner, A. Lib Dem	6,048	10.0	4.9
Rossi, M. Green	2,638	4.4	2.0
De Sanvil, S. Ind	862	1.4	
Con majority	24,029	39.82	
Electorate	89,553		
Turnout	60,338	67.38	

Con hold (5.36% from Lab to Con)

ASHTON UNDER LYNE

		%	+/-%
Rayner, A. Lab*	18,544	47.9	-12.3
Costello, D. Con	14,281	36.9	5.0
Brocklehurst, D. BP	3,151	8.1	
Rice, G. Lib Dem	1,395	3.6	2.0
Huntbach, L. Green	1,208	3.1	1.8
Lab majority	4,263	11.01	
Electorate	67,978		
Turnout	38,704	56.94	

Lab hold (8.67% from Lab to Con)

AYLESBURY

		%	+/-%
Butler, R. Con	32,737	53.8	-1.1
Hind, L. Lab	15,364	25.3	-4.7
Lambert, S. Lib Dem	10,081	16.6	7.0
Simpson, C. Green	2,394	3.9	1.8
Con majority	17,373	28.55	
Electorate	86,665		
Turnout	60,855	70.22	

Con hold (1.84% from Lab to Con)

AYR, CARRICK AND CUMNOCK

		%	+/-%
Dorans, A. SNP	20,272	43.4	9.3
Dowey, M. Con	17,943	38.4	-1.7
Townson, D. Lab	6,219	13.3	-10.5
Bongard, H. Lib Dem	2,158	4.6	2.7
SNP majority	2,329	4.98	
Electorate	71,970		
Turnout	46,730	64.93	

SNP gain (5.49% from Con to SNP)

CENTRAL AYRSHIRE

		%	+/-%
Whitford, P. SNP*	21,486	46.1	8.9
Stillie, D. Con	16,182	34.7	0.4
McPhater, L. Lab	6,583	14.1	-11.9
Farthing-Sykes, E. Lib Dem	2,283	4.9	2.6
SNP majority	5,304	11.37	
Electorate	69,742		
Turnout	46,639	66.87	

SNP hold (4.28% from Con to SNP)

NORTH AYRSHIRE AND ARRAN

		%	+/-%
Gibson, P. SNP*	23,376	48.4	9.6
Rocks, D. Con	14,855	30.8	-0.4
Gilmore, C. Lab	6,702	13.9	-13.6
Young, L. Lib Dem	2,107	4.4	2.0
Nairn, D. Green	1,114	2.3	
SNP majority	8,521	17.65	
Electorate	73,534		
Turnout	48,269	65.64	

SNP hold (5.01% from Con to SNP)

BANBURY

		%	+/-%
Prentis, V. Con*	34,148	54.0	-0.2
Watson, S. Lab	17,335	27.4	-6.6
Bearder, T. Lib Dem	8,831	14.0	8.4
Middleton, I. Green	2,607	4.1	2.1
Con majority	16,813	26.57	
Electorate	90,116		
Turnout	63,276	70.22	

Con hold (3.24% from Lab to Con)

BANFF AND BUCHAN

		%	+/-%
Duguid, D. Con*	21,182	50.0	2.1
Robertson, P. SNP	17,064	40.3	1.2
Smith, A. Lib Dem	2,280	5.4	1.9
Balcombe, B. Lab	1,734	4.1	-5.4
Con majority	4,118	9.72	
Electorate	66,655		
Turnout	42,356	63.55	

Con hold (0.43% from SNP to Con)

BARKING

		%	+/-%
Hodge, M. Lab*	27,219	61.0	-6.6
Shaikh, T. Con	11,792	26.4	4.0
Batley, K. BP	3,186	7.1	
Haigh, A. Lib Dem	1,482	3.3	2.1
Butterfield, S. Green	820	1.8	0.3
Lab majority	15,427	34.57	
Electorate	77,953		
Turnout	44,619	57.24	

Lab hold (5.33% from Lab to Con)

BARNSLEY CENTRAL

		%	+/-%
Jarvis, D. Lab*	14,804	40.0	-23.8
Felton, V. BP	11,233	30.4	
Ahmed, I. Con	7,892	21.3	-2.8
Sapwell, W. Lib Dem	1,176	3.2	1.8
Heyes, T. Green	900	2.4	1.0
Williams, R. YP	710	1.9	
Wood, D. Ind	188	0.5	
Lab majority	3,571	9.65	
Electorate	65,277		
Turnout	37,008	56.69	

Lab hold (27.08% from Lab to BP)

BARNSLEY EAST

		%	+/-%
Peacock, S. Lab*	14,329	37.5	-21.9
Ferguson, J. BP	11,112	29.1	
Gregg, A. Con	10,377	27.2	0.3
Thornton, S. Lib Dem	1,330	3.5	1.6
Trotman, R. Green	922	2.4	
Lab majority	3,217	8.43	
Electorate	69,504		
Turnout	38,180	54.93	

Lab hold (25.49% from Lab to BP)

BARROW AND FURNESS

		%	+/-%
Fell, S. Con	23,876	51.7	4.8
Altree, C. Lab	18,087	39.2	-8.2
Birchall, L. Lib Dem	2,025	4.4	1.7
McGrath, G. BP	1,355	2.9	
Loynes, C. Green	703	1.5	0.7
Con majority	5,789	12.54	
Electorate	70,158		
Turnout	46,148	65.78	

Con gain (17.21% from Lab to Con)

BASILDON AND BILLERICAY

		%	+/-%
Baron, J. Con*	29,590	66.8	6.0
Gordon, A. Lab	9,178	20.7	-10.3
Sainsbury, E. Lib Dem	3,741	8.4	5.0
Goshawk, S. Green	1,395	3.2	
Breedon, S. SDP	224	0.5	
Con majority	20,412	46.06	
Electorate	69,906		
Turnout	44,313	63.39	

Con hold (8.16% from Lab to Con)

SOUTH BASILDON AND EAST THURROCK

		%	+/-%
Metcalfe, S. Con*	29,973	65.9	9.1
Ferguson, J. Lab	10,051	22.1	-10.4
Smith, K. Ind	3,316	7.3	
Bukola, M. Lib Dem	1,957	4.3	2.8
Con majority	19,922	43.79	
Electorate	74,441		
Turnout	45,495	61.12	

Con hold (9.72% from Lab to Con)

BASINGSTOKE

		%	+/-%
Miller, M. Con*	29,593	53.9	1.3
Marchant, K. Lab	15,395	28.0	-7.7
Mylvaganam, S. Lib Dem	6,841	12.5	6.4
Jenkin, J. Green	2,138	3.9	1.9
Stone, A. Ind	746	1.4	
Con majority	14,198	25.83	
Electorate	82,928		
Turnout	54,957	66.27	

Con hold (4.49% from Lab to Con)

BASSETLAW

		%	+/-%
Clarke-Smith, B. Con	28,078	55.0	11.7
Morrison, K. Lab	14,065	27.6	-25.0
Soloman, D. BP	5,366	10.5	
Tamblyn-Saville, H. Lib Dem	3,332	6.5	4.3
Con majority	14,013	27.45	
Electorate	80,024		
Turnout	51,052	63.80	

Con gain (18.37% from Lab to Con)

BATH

		%	+/-%
Hobhouse, W. Lib Dem*	28,419	54.3	7.2
Tall, A. Con	16,097	30.8	-4.9
Davies, M. Lab	6,639	12.7	-2.0
Ogunnusi, J. BP	642	1.2	
Blockhead, B. Ind	341	0.7	
Lib Dem majority	12,322	23.55	
Electorate	67,805		
Turnout	52,330	77.18	

Lib Dem hold (6.05% from Con to Lib Dem)

BATLEY AND SPEN

		%	+/-%
Brabin, T. Lab/Co-op*	22,594	42.6	-12.8
Brooks, M. Con	19,069	36.0	-2.8
Halloran, P. HWD Ind	6,432	12.1	
Lawson, J. Lib Dem	2,462	4.6	2.4
Minihan, C. BP	1,678	3.2	
Akram, T. Green	692	1.3	0.0
Lab/Co-op majority	3,525	6.65	
Electorate	79,558		
Turnout	53,031	66.66	

Lab/Co-op hold (4.99% from Lab to Con)

BATTERSEA

		%	+/-%
De Cordova, M. Lab*	27,290	45.4	-0.5
Caddy, K. Con	21,622	36.0	-5.5
Gitsham, M. Lib Dem	9,150	15.2	7.2
Davis, L. Green	1,529	2.5	1.0
Thomas, J. BP	386	0.6	
Lab majority	5,668	9.43	
Electorate	79,281		
Turnout	60,134	75.85	

Lab hold (2.52% from Con to Lab)

BEACONSFIELD

		%	+/-%
Morrissey, J. Con	32,477	56.0	-9.2
Grieve, D. Ind*	16,765	28.9	
Collins, A. Lab	5,756	9.9	-11.5
Hatch, Z. Green	2,033	3.5	1.0
Cleary, A. Ind	837	1.4	
Con majority	15,712	27.07	
Electorate	77,720		
Turnout	58,035	74.67	

Con hold (19.03% from Con to Ind)

BECKENHAM

		%	+/-%
Stewart, B. Con*	27,282	53.7	-5.4
Ahmad, M. Lab	13,024	25.6	-4.4
Ross, C. Lib Dem	8,194	16.1	8.3
Fabricant, R. Green	2,055	4.1	1.4
Con majority	14,258	28.07	
Electorate	68,662		
Turnout	50,791	73.97	

Con hold (0.52% from Con to Lab)

BEDFORD

		%	+/-%
Yasin, M. Lab*	20,491	43.2	-3.5
Henson, R. Con	20,346	42.9	-2.2
Vann, H. Lib Dem	4,608	9.7	3.9
Spurrell, A. Green	960	2.0	0.0
Bunker, C. BP	896	1.9	
Lab majority	145	0.31	
Electorate	71,581		
Turnout	47,441	66.28	

Lab hold (0.66% from Lab to Con)

MID BEDFORDSHIRE

		%	+/-%
Dorries, N. Con*	38,692	59.6	-1.9
Meades, R. Lab	14,028	21.6	-6.8
McGann, R. Lib Dem	8,171	12.6	6.6
Ellis, G. Green	2,478	3.8	1.0
Victor, A. Ind	812	1.3	
Kelly, A. Loony	536	0.8	-0.2
Con majority	24,664	37.98	
Electorate	87,795		
Turnout	64,942	73.97	

Con hold (2.42% from Lab to Con)

NORTH EAST BEDFORDSHIRE

		%	+/-%
Fuller, R. Con	38,443	59.0	-1.9
Vaughan, J. Lab	14,160	21.7	-6.7
Norton, D. Lib Dem	7,999	12.3	6.5
Zerny, A. Ind	2,525	3.9	
Fleming, P. Green	1,891	2.9	1.0
Con majority	24,283	37.23	
Electorate	90,678		
Turnout	65,218	71.92	

Con hold (2.41% from Lab to Con)

SOUTH WEST BEDFORDSHIRE

		%	+/-%
Selous, A. Con*	32,212	60.1	1.1
Anderson, C. Lab	13,629	25.5	-8.2
Matanle, E. Lib Dem	5,435	10.2	5.4
Waters, A. Green	2,031	3.8	2.1
Con majority	18,583	34.7	
Electorate	79,926		
Turnout	53,561	67.01	

Con hold (4.65% from Lab to Con)

BELFAST EAST

		%	+/-%
Robinson, G. DUP*	20,874	49.0	-6.7
Long, N. APNI	19,055	44.7	8.8
McClean, C. UUP	2,516	5.9	2.6
DUP majority	1,819	4.27	
Electorate	66,245		
Turnout	42,614	64.33	

DUP hold (7.73% from DUP to APNI)

BELFAST NORTH

		%	+/-%
Finucane, J. Sinn Féin	23,078	46.7	5.1
Dodds, N. DUP*	21,135	42.8	-3.3
McAllister, N. APNI	4,824	9.8	4.4
Sinn Féin majority	1,943	3.93	
Electorate	72,225		
Turnout	49,425	68.43	

Sinn Féin gain (4.23% from DUP to Sinn Féin)

BELFAST SOUTH

		%	+/-%
Hanna, C. SDLP	27,079	57.0	31.2
Little Pengelly, E. DUP*	11,678	24.6	-5.8
Bradshaw, P. APNI	6,786	14.3	-3.8
Henderson, M. UUP	1,259	2.7	-0.8
McHugh, C. Aontú	550	1.2	
SDLP majority	15,401	32.41	
Electorate	69,984		
Turnout	47,524	67.91	

SDLP gain (18.48% from DUP to SDLP)

BELFAST WEST

		%	+/-%
Maskey, P. Sinn Féin*	20,866	53.5	-12.9
Carroll, G. PBPA	6,194	15.9	5.8
McCoubrey, F. DUP	5,220	13.4	0.0
Doherty, P. SDLP	2,985	7.7	0.7
Higgins, D. APNI	1,882	4.8	3.0
Digney, M. Aontú	1,635	4.2	
Sinn Féin majority	14,672	37.63	
Electorate	65,644		
Turnout	38,988	59.39	

Sinn Féin hold (9.32% from Sinn Féin to PBPA)

BERMONDSEY AND OLD SOUTHWARK

		%	+/-%
Coyle, N. Lab*	31,723	53.9	0.8
Ali, H. Lib Dem	15,597	26.5	-4.5
Baker, A. Con	9,678	16.4	3.5
Matthews, A. BP	1,617	2.8	
Lab majority	16,126	27.4	
Electorate	88,971		
Turnout	58,861	66.16	

Lab hold (2.64% from Lib Dem to Lab)

BERWICKSHIRE, ROXBURGH AND SELKIRK

		%	+/-%
Lamont, J. Con*	25,747	48.3	-5.5
Kerr, C. SNP	20,599	38.6	5.9
Marr, J. Lib Dem	4,287	8.0	3.3
Davidson, I. Lab	2,513	4.7	-3.9
Con majority	5,148	9.66	
Electorate	74,518		
Turnout	53,316	71.55	

Con hold (5.72% from Con to SNP)

BERWICK-UPON-TWEED

		%	+/-%
Trevelyan, A. Con*	23,947	56.6	4.3
Williams, T. Lab	9,112	21.6	-3.0
Hancock, T. Lib Dem	7,656	18.1	-3.0
Stewart, T. Green	1,394	3.3	1.4
Con majority	14,835	35.08	
Electorate	60,907		
Turnout	42,287	69.43	

Con hold (3.62% from Lab to Con)

BETHNAL GREEN AND BOW

		%	+/-%
Ali, R. Lab*	44,052	72.5	1.0
Stovold, N. Con	6,528	10.7	-1.9
Babarinde, J. Lib Dem	5,892	9.7	4.7
Ali, S. Green	2,570	4.2	1.7
Axe, D. BP	1,081	1.8	
Hudson, V. AWP	439	0.7	
Lab majority	37,524	61.72	
Electorate	88,262		
Turnout	60,802	68.89	

Lab hold (1.41% from Con to Lab)

BEVERLEY AND HOLDERNESS

		%	+/-%
Stuart, G. Con*	33,250	61.8	3.6
Hopkins, C. Lab	12,802	23.8	-9.3
Healy, D. Lib Dem	4,671	8.7	3.7
Shead, A. YP	1,441	2.7	0.6
Pires, I. Green	1,378	2.6	1.3
Con majority	20,448	38.01	
Electorate	79,696		
Turnout	53,790	67.49	

Con hold (6.43% from Lab to Con)

BEXHILL AND BATTLE

		%	+/-%
Merriman, H. Con*	37,590	63.2	1.4
Bayliss, C. Lab	11,531	19.4	-5.3
Saunders, M. Lib Dem	7,280	12.3	4.7
Kent, J. Green	2,692	4.5	2.1
Con majority	26,059	43.84	
Electorate	81,963		
Turnout	59,445	72.53	

Con hold (3.32% from Lab to Con)

OLD BEXLEY AND SIDCUP

		%	+/-%
Brokenshire, J. Con*	29,786	64.2	2.9
Tingle, D. Lab	10,834	23.4	-5.9
Reynolds, S. Lib Dem	3,822	8.2	5.0
Browne, M. Green	1,477	3.2	1.5
Valinejad, C. CPA	226	0.5	0.3
Con majority	18,952	40.86	
Electorate	66,104		
Turnout	46,384	70.17	

Con hold (4.37% from Lab to Con)

BEXLEYHEATH AND CRAYFORD

		%	+/-%
Evennett, D. Con*	25,856	59.6	4.1
Day, A. Lab	12,753	29.4	-6.0
McBride, D. Lib Dem	2,819	6.5	3.8
Ball, A. Green	1,298	3.0	1.7
Moore, G. Eng Dem	520	1.2	
Con majority	13,103	30.18	
Electorate	65,466		
Turnout	43,413	66.31	

Con hold (5.07% from Lab to Con)

BIRKENHEAD

		%	+/-%
Whitley, M. Lab	24,990	58.9	-17.7
Field, F. CB*	7,285	17.2	
Rowles, C. Con	5,540	13.1	-5.3
Kelly, S. Lib Dem	1,620	3.8	1.3
Lythgoe, D. BP	1,489	3.5	
Cleary, P. Green	1,405	3.3	1.2
Lab majority	17,705	41.76	
Electorate	63,762		
Turnout	42,402	66.50	

Lab hold (17.46% from Lab to BSJP)

BIRMINGHAM, EDGBASTON

		%	+/-%
Gill, P. Lab/Co-op*	21,217	50.0	-5.2
Yip, A. Con	15,603	36.7	-2.6
Green, C. Lib Dem	3,349	7.9	4.3
Simpson, P. Green	1,112	2.6	1.3
Wilks, D. BP	1,047	2.5	
Lab/Co-op majority	5,614	13.22	
Electorate	68,828		
Turnout	42,477	61.71	

Lab/Co-op hold (1.3% from Lab to Con)

BIRMINGHAM, ERDINGTON

		%	+/-%
Dromey, J. Lab*	17,720	50.2	-7.6
Alden, R. Con	14,119	40.0	1.7
Garcarz, W. BP	1,441	4.1	
Holtom, A. Lib Dem	1,301	3.7	1.7
Grant, R. Green	648	1.8	0.2
Lab majority	3,601	10.2	
Electorate	66,148		
Turnout	35,321	53.40	

Lab hold (4.66% from Lab to Con)

BIRMINGHAM, HALL GREEN

		%	+/-%
Ali, T. Lab	35,889	67.6	-9.7
O'Donnell, P. Con	7,381	13.9	-1.1
Godsiff, R. Ind*	4,273	8.1	
Knowles, I. Lib Dem	3,673	6.9	1.2
Cuckston, R. BP	877	1.7	
Cox, P. Green	818	1.5	0.0
Lab majority	28,508	53.7	
Electorate	80,283		
Turnout	53,091	66.13	

Lab hold (4.3% from Lab to Con)

BIRMINGHAM, HODGE HILL

		%	+/-%
Byrne, L. Lab*	35,397	78.4	-2.3
Sidhu, A. Con	6,742	14.9	0.8
Dagnan, J. BP	1,519	3.4	
Rafiq, W. Lib Dem	760	1.7	-0.1
McKears, J. Green	328	0.7	-0.1
Johani, H. CPA	257	0.6	
Lab majority	28,655	63.49	
Electorate	78,295		
Turnout	45,134	57.65	

Lab hold (1.58% from Lab to Con)

BIRMINGHAM, LADYWOOD

		%	+/-%
Mahmood, S. Lab*	33,355	78.9	-3.5
Noone, M. Con	4,773	11.3	-1.9
Dargue, L. Lib Dem	2,228	5.3	2.5
Nettle, A. Green	931	2.2	0.9
Garcarz, A. BP	831	2.0	
Lab majority	28,582	67.62	
Electorate	74,912		
Turnout	42,271	56.43	

Lab hold (0.82% from Lab to Con)

BIRMINGHAM, NORTHFIELD

		%	+/-%
Sambrook, G. Con	19,957	46.2	3.6
Burden, R. Lab*	18,317	42.4	-10.7
Scott, J. Lib Dem	1,961	4.5	2.4
Rowe, K. BP	1,655	3.8	
Masters, E. Green	954	2.2	0.3
Lowry, K. UKIP	254	0.6	
Con majority	1,640	3.79	
Electorate	73,694		
Turnout	43,238	58.67	

Con gain (7.15% from Lab to Con)

BIRMINGHAM, PERRY BARR

		%	+/-%
Mahmood, K. Lab*	26,594	62.9	-4.9
Shamji, R. Con	11,277	26.7	0.3
Jerome, G. Lib Dem	1,901	4.5	2.1
Willcox, A. BP	1,382	3.3	
Dennis, K. Green	845	2.0	0.7
Braich, T. Yeshua	148	0.4	
Lab majority	15,317	36.24	
Electorate	72,006		
Turnout	42,262	58.69	

Lab hold (2.6% from Lab to Con)

BIRMINGHAM, SELLY OAK

		%	+/-%
McCabe, S. Lab*	27,714	55.8	-6.9
Campbell, H. Con	15,300	30.8	-1.0
Radcliffe, D. Lib Dem	3,169	6.4	3.0
Peacock, J. Green	1,848	3.7	1.9
Tawonezvi, J. BP	1,436	2.9	
Lab majority	12,414	25.01	
Electorate	82,665		
Turnout	49,627	60.03	

Lab hold (2.97% from Lab to Con)

BIRMINGHAM, YARDLEY

		%	+/-%
Phillips, J. Lab*	23,379	54.6	-2.3
Garrington, V. Con	12,720	29.7	10.0
Harmer, R. Lib Dem	3,754	8.8	-9.1
McKenna, M. BP	2,246	5.3	
Garghan, C. Green	579	1.4	0.7
Lab majority	10,659	24.91	
Electorate	74,704		
Turnout	42,785	57.27	

Lab hold (6.13% from Lab to Con)

BISHOP AUCKLAND

		%	+/-%
Davison, D. Con	24,067	53.6	6.7
Goodman, H. Lab*	16,105	35.8	-12.2
Brown, N. BP	2,500	5.6	
Georgeson, R. Lib Dem	2,133	4.8	2.0
Con majority	7,962	17.72	
Electorate	68,170		
Turnout	44,936	65.92	

Con gain (9.44% from Lab to Con)

BLACKBURN

		%	+/-%
Hollern, K. Lab*	29,040	64.8	-4.7
Gill, C. Con	10,736	23.9	-2.9
Moore, R. BP	2,770	6.2	
Waller-Slack, B. Lib Dem	1,130	2.5	1.0
Hossain, S. Green	741	1.7	
Shah, R. Ind	319	0.7	
Lab majority	18,304	40.82	
Electorate	71,234		
Turnout	44,845	62.95	

Lab hold (0.94% from Lab to Con)

BLACKLEY AND BROUGHTON

		%	+/-%
Stringer, G. Lab*	23,887	61.6	-8.6
Elias, A. Con	9,485	24.5	2.9
Buckley, J. BP	2,736	7.1	
Donaldson, I. Lib Dem	1,590	4.1	2.3
Jones, D. Green	920	2.4	1.2
Lab majority	14,402	37.16	
Electorate	73,372		
Turnout	38,760	52.83	

Lab hold (5.79% from Lab to Con)

BLACKPOOL NORTH AND CLEVELEYS

		%	+/-%
Maynard, P. Con*	22,364	57.4	8.1
Webb, C. Lab	13,768	35.4	-9.0
Close, S. Lib Dem	1,494	3.8	2.0
Royle, D. Green	735	1.9	1.0
Holden, N. Ind	443	1.1	
Con majority	8,596	22.08	
Electorate	63,692		
Turnout	38,934	61.13	

Con hold (8.58% from Lab to Con)

BLACKPOOL SOUTH

		%	+/-%
Benton, S. Con	16,247	49.5	6.5
Marsden, G. Lab*	12,557	38.2	-12.0
Brown, D. BP	2,009	6.1	
Greene, B. Lib Dem	1,008	3.1	1.3
Daniels, B. Green	563	1.7	0.7
Coleman, G. Ind	368	1.1	
Con majority	3,690	11.24	
Electorate	57,690		
Turnout	32,838	56.92	

Con gain (9.23% from Lab to Con)

BLAENAU GWENT

		%	+/-%
Smith, N. Lab*	14,862	49.0	-8.9
Taylor, R. BP	6,215	20.5	
Jones, L. Con	5,749	19.0	4.2
Griffiths, P. PlC	1,722	5.7	-15.5
Annett, C. Lib Dem	1,285	4.2	3.3
Priestnall, S. Green	386	1.3	
Lab majority	8,647	28.54	
Electorate	50,739		
Turnout	30,303	59.72	

Lab hold (14.71% from Lab to BP)

BLAYDON

		%	+/-%
Twist, L. Lab*	19,794	43.2	-12.8
Pepper, A. Con	14,263	31.1	3.1
Robinson, M. BP	5,833	12.7	
Anderson, V. Lib Dem	3,703	8.1	-1.0
Cadman, D. Green	1,279	2.8	1.6
King, K. Lib	615	1.3	
Marschild, L. Space Navies	118	0.3	0.1
Garrett, L. Ind	76	0.2	
Lab majority	5,531	12.08	
Electorate	67,853		
Turnout	45,802	67.50	

Lab hold (7.96% from Lab to Con)

BLYTH VALLEY

		%	+/-%
Levy, I. Con	17,440	42.6	5.3
Dungworth, S. Lab/Co-op	16,728	40.9	-15.0
Peart, M. BP	3,394	8.3	
Chapman, T. Lib Dem	2,151	5.3	0.7
Furness, D. Green	1,146	2.8	0.6
Con majority	712	1.74	
Electorate	65,305		
Turnout	40,953	62.71	

Con gain (10.17% from Lab to Con)

BOGNOR REGIS AND LITTLEHAMPTON

		%	+/-%
Gibb, N. Con*	32,521	63.2	4.4
Butcher, A. Lab	10,018	19.5	-5.4
Oppler, F. Lib Dem	5,645	11.0	4.5
Birch, C. Green	1,826	3.6	1.6
Kurten, D. UKIP	846	1.6	-2.0
Elston, A. Ind	367	0.7	
Con majority	22,503	43.75	
Electorate	77,446		
Turnout	51,431	66.41	

Con hold (4.87% from Lab to Con)

BOLSOVER

		%	+/-%
Fletcher, M. Con	21,791	47.3	6.7
Skinner, D. Lab*	16,492	35.8	-16.1
Harper, K. BP	4,151	9.0	
Hancock, D. Lib Dem	1,759	3.8	0.9
Kesteven, D. Green	758	1.6	
Walker, R. Ind	517	1.1	
Hoy, N. Ind	470	1.0	
Con majority	5,299	11.5	
Electorate	75,161		
Turnout	46,089	61.32	

Con gain (11.44% from Lab to Con)

BOLTON NORTH EAST

		%	+/-%
Logan, M. Con	19,759	45.3	3.1
Crausby, D. Lab*	19,381	44.4	-6.1
Jones, T. BP	1,880	4.3	
Fox, W. Lib Dem	1,847	4.2	1.3
Spencer, L. Green	689	1.6	0.8
Con majority	378	0.87	
Electorate	67,564		
Turnout	43,668	64.63	

Con gain (4.63% from Lab to Con)

BOLTON SOUTH EAST

		%	+/-%
Qureshi, Y. Lab*	21,516	52.9	-7.7
Lee, J. Con	13,918	34.2	4.6
Cunningham, M. BP	2,968	7.3	
Walsh, K. Lib Dem	1,411	3.5	1.6
Figgins, D. Green	791	1.9	0.7
Lab majority	7,598	18.66	
Electorate	69,163		
Turnout	40,715	58.87	

Lab hold (6.14% from Lab to Con)

BOLTON WEST

		%	+/-%
Green, C. Con*	27,255	55.1	7.3
Hilling, J. Lab	18,400	37.2	-8.8
Forrest, R. Lib Dem	2,704	5.5	2.6
Hayes, P. Green	939	1.9	
Con majority	8,855	17.9	
Electorate	73,191		
Turnout	49,461	67.58	

Con hold (8.04% from Lab to Con)

BOOTLE

		%	+/-%
Dowd, P. Lab*	39,066	79.2	-4.6
Onuluk, T. Con	4,510	9.1	-2.9
Knight, K. BP	2,610	5.3	
Hanson, R. Lib Dem	1,822	3.7	2.0
Carter, M. Green	1,166	2.4	1.0
Lab majority	34,556	70.06	
Electorate	74,832		
Turnout	49,323	65.91	

Lab hold (0.85% from Lab to Con)

BOSTON AND SKEGNESS

		%	+/-%
Warman, M. Con*	31,963	76.3	12.7
Cook, B. Lab	6,342	15.2	-9.8
Jones, H. Lib Dem	1,963	4.7	2.9
Watson, P. Ind	1,428	3.4	
Con majority	25,621	61.19	
Electorate	69,381		
Turnout	41,871	60.35	

Con hold (11.27% from Lab to Con)

BOSWORTH

		%	+/-%
Evans, L. Con	36,056	63.6	7.1
Middleton, R. Lab	9,778	17.3	-6.7
Mullaney, M. Lib Dem	9,096	16.1	-1.3
Gregg, M. Green	1,502	2.7	0.8
Con majority	26,278	46.37	
Electorate	81,542		
Turnout	56,666	69.49	

Con hold (6.9% from Lab to Con)

BOURNEMOUTH EAST

		%	+/-%
Ellwood, T. Con*	24,926	50.4	-1.4
Drew, C. Lab	16,120	32.6	-2.9
Dunn, P. Lib Dem	5,418	11.0	4.5
Keddie, A. Green	2,049	4.1	1.6
Aston, B. Ind	447	0.9	
Johnson, E. Ind	314	0.6	
Con majority	8,806	17.8	
Electorate	74,125		
Turnout	49,462	66.73	

Con hold (0.76% from Lab to Con)

BOURNEMOUTH WEST

		%	+/-%
Burns, C. Con*	24,550	53.2	-0.2
Stokes, D. Lab	14,400	31.2	-4.9
Nicholas, J. Lib Dem	4,931	10.7	4.1
Bull, S. Green	2,096	4.5	1.8
Con majority	10,150	21.98	
Electorate	74,205		
Turnout	46,188	62.24	

Con hold (2.35% from Lab to Con)

BRACKNELL

		%	+/-%
Sunderland, J. Con	31,894	58.5	-0.2
Bidwell, P. Lab	12,065	22.1	-8.0
Beheshtizadeh, K. Lib Dem	7,749	14.2	6.7
Florey, D. Green	2,089	3.8	
Barreto, O. Ind	553	1.0	0.2
Con majority	19,829	36.34	
Electorate	78,978		
Turnout	54,562	69.09	

Con hold (3.88% from Lab to Con)

BRADFORD EAST

		%	+/-%
Hussain, I. Lab*	27,825	62.9	-2.4
Kemkaran, L. Con	9,681	21.9	1.5
Sunderland, J. Lib Dem	3,316	7.5	5.7
Barras, J. BP	2,700	6.1	
Stanford, A. Green	662	1.5	0.9
Lab majority	18,144	40.98	
Electorate	73,206		
Turnout	44,275	60.48	

Lab hold (1.99% from Lab to Con)

BRADFORD SOUTH

		%	+/-%
Cummins, J. Lab*	18,390	46.2	-8.2
Sekhon, N. Con	16,044	40.3	2.2
Manik, K. BP	2,819	7.1	
Griffiths, A. Lib Dem	1,505	3.8	2.5
Edwards, M. Green	983	2.5	1.6
Lab majority	2,346	5.89	
Electorate	69,046		
Turnout	39,828	57.68	

Lab hold (5.21% from Lab to Con)

BRADFORD WEST

		%	+/-%
Shah, N. Lab*	33,736	76.0	11.6
Afzal, M. Con	6,717	15.1	-1.4
Hodgson, D. BP	1,556	3.5	
Christie, M. Lib Dem	1,349	3.0	1.5
Parkinson, D. Green	813	1.8	0.8
Bukhari, A. Ind	90	0.2	
Lab majority	27,019	60.86	
Electorate	70,694		
Turnout	44,395	62.80	

Lab hold (6.5% from Con to Lab)

BRAINTREE

		%	+/-%
Cleverly, J. Con*	34,112	67.2	4.5
Garfield, J. Lab	9,439	18.6	-9.0
Graham, D. Lib Dem	4,779	9.4	5.1
Beavis, J. Ind	1,488	2.9	
Mansell, D. Ind	420	0.8	
Dorkins, A. Ind	261	0.5	
Con majority	24,673	48.61	
Electorate	75,208		
Turnout	50,757	67.49	

Con hold (6.73% from Lab to Con)

BRECON AND RADNORSHIRE

		%	+/-%
Jones, F. Con	21,958	53.0	4.5
Dodds, J. Lib Dem	14,827	35.8	6.7
Davies, T. Lab	3,944	9.5	-8.2
The Pink, L. Loony	345	0.8	
Green, J. Christian	245	0.6	
Con majority	7,131	17.21	
Electorate	55,490		
Turnout	41,429	74.66	

Con hold (10.84% from Con to Lib Dem)

BRENT CENTRAL

		%	+/-%
Butler, D. Lab*	31,779	64.4	-8.4
Brescia, D. Con	10,909	22.1	2.7
Ungar, D. Lib Dem	4,844	9.8	5.0
Relton, W. Green	1,600	3.2	1.7
Lab majority	20,870	42.28	
Electorate	84,032		
Turnout	49,356	58.73	

Lab hold (5.52% from Lab to Con)

BRENT NORTH

		%	+/-%
Gardiner, B. Lab*	26,911	51.7	-11.0
Patel, A. Con	18,832	36.2	3.6
Lorber, P. Lib Dem	4,065	7.8	5.0
O'Brien, S. BP	951	1.8	
Rebbitt, S. Green	850	1.6	0.5
Coonan, N. Ind	169	0.3	
Jeffers, E. Ind	101	0.2	-0.2
Lab majority	8,079	15.51	
Electorate	83,788		
Turnout	52,078	62.15	

Lab hold (7.31% from Lab to Con)

BRENTFORD AND ISLEWORTH

		%	+/-%
Cadbury, R. Lab*	29,266	50.1	-7.2
Shah, S. Con	18,752	32.1	-5.5
Cross, H. Lib Dem	7,314	12.5	7.5
Goldsmith, D. Green	1,829	3.1	
O'Sullivan, L. BP	1,165	2.0	
Lab majority	10,514	17.98	
Electorate	85,775		
Turnout	58,471	68.17	

Lab hold (0.87% from Lab to Con)

BRENTWOOD AND ONGAR

		%	+/-%
Burghart, A. Con	36,308	68.3	2.6
Durose, O. Lab	7,243	13.6	-6.8
Kendall, D. Lib Dem	7,187	13.5	5.2
Jeater, P. Green	1,679	3.2	1.4
Tilbrook, R. Eng Dem	532	1.0	
Con majority	29,065	54.65	
Electorate	75,255		
Turnout	53,187	70.68	

Con hold (4.69% from Lab to Con)

BRIDGEND

		%	+/-%
Wallis, J. Con	18,193	43.0	9.6
Moon, M. Lab*	17,036	40.2	-2.3
Pratt, J. Lib Dem	2,368	5.6	3.8
Lewis, L. PlC	2,013	4.8	1.3
Morgan, R. BP	1,811	4.3	
Harris, A. Green	815	1.9	
Con majority	1,157	2.73	
Electorate	63,303		
Turnout	42,337	66.88	

Con gain (5.93% from Lab to Con)

BRIDGWATER AND WEST SOMERSET

		%	+/-%
Liddell-Grainger, I. Con*	35,827	61.8	6.9
Thornton, O. Lab	11,388	19.7	-8.9
Revans, B. Lib Dem	7,805	13.5	2.6
Ritchie, M. Green	1,877	3.2	1.4
Moussa, F. Lib	755	1.3	
Con majority	24,439	42.19	
Electorate	85,327		
Turnout	57,931	67.89	

Con hold (7.86% from Lab to Con)

BRIGG AND GOOLE

		%	+/-%
Percy, A. Con*	30,941	71.0	10.7
Khan, M. Lab	9,000	20.7	-12.3
Dobbie, D. Lib Dem	2,180	5.0	3.2
Baker, J. Green	1,281	2.9	1.7
Con majority	21,941	50.35	
Electorate	65,939		
Turnout	43,580	66.09	

Con hold (11.48% from Lab to Con)

BRIGHTON KEMPTOWN

		%	+/-%
Russell-Moyle, L. Lab/Co-op*	25,033	51.4	-6.7
Miller, J. Con	16,972	34.9	-3.3
Thomas, B. Lib Dem	2,964	6.1	3.1
Phillips, A. Green	2,237	4.6	
Cushway, G. BP	1,327	2.7	
Lab/Co-op majority	8,061	16.56	
Electorate	69,833		
Turnout	48,673	69.70	

Lab/Co-op hold (1.72% from Lab to Con)

BRIGHTON PAVILION

		%	+/-%
Lucas, C. Green*	33,151	57.0	4.9
Imanpour, A. Lab	13,211	22.7	-4.0
Hogan, E. Con	10,176	17.5	-1.7
Milton, R. BP	770	1.3	
Skwith, C. Loony	301	0.5	
Dobbs, B. Ind	212	0.4	
Furness, N. UKIP	177	0.3	-0.8
Green majority	19,940	34.29	
Electorate	79,057		
Turnout	58,156	73.56	

Green hold (4.44% from Lab to Green)

BRISTOL EAST

		%	+/-%
McCarthy, K. Lab*	27,717	53.0	-7.6
Codling, S. Con	16,923	32.4	-1.9
Coombes, N. Lib Dem	3,527	6.7	4.0
Connolly, C. Green	2,106	4.0	1.9
Page, T. BP	1,881	3.6	
Lab majority	10,794	20.63	
Electorate	73,867		
Turnout	52,311	70.82	

Lab hold (2.83% from Lab to Con)

BRISTOL NORTH WEST

		%	+/-%
Jones, D. Lab*	27,330	48.8	-1.8
Weston, M. Con	21,638	38.6	-3.2
Coleman, C. Lib Dem	4,940	8.8	3.6
Mack, H. Green	1,977	3.5	1.2
Lab majority	5,692	10.15	
Electorate	76,273		
Turnout	56,054	73.49	

Lab hold (0.69% from Con to Lab)

BRISTOL SOUTH

		%	+/-%
Smyth, K. Lab*	27,895	50.4	-9.6
Morgan, R. Con	18,036	32.6	2.0
Brown, A. Lib Dem	4,227	7.6	4.3
Dyer, T. Green	2,713	4.9	2.3
de Vito Boutin, R. BP	2,325	4.2	
Lab majority	9,859	17.8	
Electorate	84,079		
Turnout	55,377	65.86	

Lab hold (5.77% from Lab to Con)

BRISTOL WEST

		%	+/-%
Debbonaire, T. Lab*	47,028	62.0	-3.8
Denyer, C. Green	18,809	24.8	12.0
Aujla, S. Con	8,822	11.6	-2.1
Hipkiss, N. BP	869	1.2	
Lab majority	28,219	37.19	
Electorate	99,253		
Turnout	75,883	76.45	

Lab hold (7.88% from Lab to Green)

BROADLAND

		%	+/-%
Mayhew, J. Con	33,934	59.4	1.6
Barnard, J. Lab	12,073	21.1	-8.5
Goodwin, B. Lib Dem	9,195	16.1	8.2
Boswell, A. Green	1,412	2.5	0.8
Rous, S. UGP	363	0.6	
Con majority	21,861	38.24	
Electorate	78,151		
Turnout	57,174	73.16	

Con hold (5.02% from Lab to Con)

BROMLEY AND CHISLEHURST

		%	+/-%
Neill, R. Con*	23,958	52.4	-1.5
Wilkins, A. Lab	13,067	28.6	-4.8
Ireland, J. Lib Dem	6,621	14.5	7.3
Ion, M. Green	1,546	3.4	0.9
Amodu, Z. CPA	255	0.6	
Dialani, J. Renew	119	0.3	
Con majority	10,891	23.8	
Electorate	66,697		
Turnout	45,767	68.62	

Con hold (1.65% from Lab to Con)

BROMSGROVE

		%	+/-%
Javid, S. Con*	34,408	63.1	1.4
Shannon, R. Lab	11,302	20.7	-10.5
Nicholl, D. Lib Dem	6,779	12.4	7.8
White, K. Green	1,783	3.3	1.2
Con majority	23,106	42.37	
Electorate	75,078		
Turnout	54,532	72.63	

Con hold (5.91% from Lab to Con)

BROXBOURNE

		%	+/-%
Walker, C. Con*	30,631	65.3	3.3
Waters, S. Lab	10,824	23.1	-5.8
Bird, J. Lib Dem	3,970	8.5	5.4
Cox, N. Green	1,281	2.7	1.0
Con majority	19,807	42.21	
Electorate	73,182		
Turnout	46,920	64.11	

Con hold (4.52% from Lab to Con)

BROXTOWE

		%	+/-%
Henry, D. Con	26,602	48.0	1.2
Marshall, G. Lab	21,271	38.4	-6.9
Soubry, A. IGC	4,668	8.4	
Boettge, K. Green	1,806	3.3	2.0
Dalla Mura, A. Eng Dem	432	0.8	
Khong, T. Ind	321	0.6	
Bishop, D. Bus-Pass	172	0.3	
Con majority	5,331	9.61	
Electorate	73,052		
Turnout	55,445	75.90	

Con hold (4.03% from Lab to Con)

BUCKINGHAM

		%	+/-%
Smith, G. Con	37,035	58.1	
Dorrell, S. Lib Dem	16,624	26.1	
Morgan, D. Lab	7,638	12.0	
Bell, A. BP	1,286	2.0	
Thompson, N. Ind	681	1.1	
Vitiello, A. Eng Dem	194	0.3	
Con majority	20,411	32.04	
Electorate	83,146		
Turnout	63,699	76.61	

Con gain (16.02% from Con to Lib Dem)

BURNLEY

		%	+/-%
Higginbotham, A. Con	15,720	40.2	9.3
Cooper, J. Lab*	14,368	36.8	-9.9
Birtwistle, G. Lib Dem	3,501	9.0	-6.0
Scott, S. BP	3,362	8.6	
Briggs, C. B&P Ind	1,162	3.0	
Fisk, L. Green	739	1.9	0.8
Helsby Entwistle, K. Ind	132	0.3	
Con majority	1,352	3.46	
Electorate	64,345		
Turnout	39,075	60.73	

Con gain (9.61% from Lab to Con)

BURTON

		%	+/-%
Griffiths, K. Con	29,560	60.4	2.6
Walker, L. Lab	15,064	30.8	-7.0
Wain, A. Lib Dem	2,681	5.5	3.0
Copeland, K. Green	1,433	2.9	1.3
Con majority	14,496	29.61	
Electorate	75,036		
Turnout	48,950	65.24	

Con hold (4.78% from Lab to Con)

BURY NORTH

		%	+/-%
Daly, J. Con	21,660	46.1	1.8
Frith, J. Lab*	21,555	45.9	-7.5
Lloyd-Johnson, G. Lib Dem	1,584	3.4	1.5
McCarthy, A. BP	1,240	2.6	
Allen, C. Green	802	1.7	
Con majority	105	0.22	
Electorate	68,802		
Turnout	46,952	68.24	

Con gain (4.66% from Lab to Con)

BURY SOUTH

		%	+/-%
Wakeford, C. Con	22,034	43.7	2.3
Burke, L. Lab	21,632	42.9	-10.2
Kilpatrick, R. Lib Dem	2,315	4.6	2.5
Livesey, A. BP	1,672	3.3	
Lewis, I. Ind*	1,366	2.7	
Heath, G. Green	848	1.7	
Boyle, M. Ind	277	0.6	
Evans, G. WEP	130	0.3	
Con majority	402	0.8	
Electorate	75,152		
Turnout	50,377	67.03	

Con gain (6.24% from Lab to Con)

BURY ST EDMUNDS

		%	+/-%
Churchill, J. Con*	37,770	60.7	1.6
Waterman, C. Lab	12,782	20.5	-8.9
Geake, H. Green	9,711	15.6	11.4
Hopfensperger, P. Ind	1,694	2.7	
Con majority	24,988	40.14	
Electorate	89,644		
Turnout	62,245	69.44	

Con hold (5.28% from Lab to Con)

CAERPHILLY

		%	+/-%
David, W. Lab*	18,018	44.7	-9.6
Pratt, J. Con	11,185	27.8	2.6
Whittle, L. PlC	6,424	16.0	1.5
Gill, N. BP	4,490	11.2	
Lab majority	6,833	16.97	
Electorate	63,166		
Turnout	40,277	63.76	

Lab hold (6.11% from Lab to Con)

CAITHNESS, SUTHERLAND AND EASTER ROSS

		%	+/-%
Stone, J. Lib Dem*	11,705	37.1	1.4
Rosie, K. SNP	11,501	36.5	7.3
Sinclair, A. Con	5,176	16.4	-6.2
McDonald, C. Lab	1,936	6.1	-6.3
Skinner, S. BP	1,139	3.6	
Lib Dem majority	204	0.65	
Electorate	46,930		
Turnout	31,518	67.16	

Lib Dem hold (2.98% from Lib Dem to SNP)

CALDER VALLEY

		%	+/-%
Whittaker, C. Con*	29,981	51.6	5.6
Fenton-Glynn, J. Lab	24,207	41.7	-3.3
Bashir, J. Lib Dem	2,884	5.0	1.6
Phillips, R. Lib	721	1.2	
Con majority	5,774	9.94	
Electorate	79,287		
Turnout	58,066	73.24	

Con hold (4.45% from Lab to Con)

CAMBERWELL AND PECKHAM

		%	+/-%
Harman, H. Lab*	40,258	71.0	-6.5
Quentin, P. Con	6,478	11.4	-1.3
Ogiehor, J. Lib Dem	5,087	9.0	3.1
Sheppard, C. Green	3,501	6.2	3.4
Cass-Horne, J. BP	1,041	1.8	
Ogunleye, J. WRP	127	0.2	0.0
Lab majority	33,780	59.54	
Electorate	88,971		
Turnout	56,738	63.77	

Lab hold (2.6% from Lab to Con)

CAMBORNE AND REDRUTH

		%	+/-%
Eustice, G. Con*	26,764	53.0	5.6
Farmer, P. Lab	18,064	35.7	-8.4
Macdonald, F. Lib Dem	3,504	6.9	0.8
La Borde, K. Green	1,359	2.7	0.5
Holmes, P. Lib	676	1.3	
Con majority	8,700	17.21	
Electorate	70,250		
Turnout	50,542	71.95	

Con hold (6.98% from Lab to Con)

CAMBRIDGE

		%	+/-%
Zeichner, D. Lab*	25,776	47.8	-4.0
Cantrill, R. Lib Dem	16,137	29.9	0.7
Perrin, R. Con	8,342	15.5	-0.8
Caddick, J. Green	2,164	4.0	1.8
Dawe, P. BP	1,041	1.9	
Hurley, M. Ind	111	0.2	
Robins, J. SDP	91	0.2	
Garrett, K. Reboot	67	0.1	-0.1
Lab majority	9,639	17.89	
Electorate	79,951		
Turnout	53,891	67.41	

Lab hold (2.35% from Lab to Lib Dem)

NORTH EAST CAMBRIDGESHIRE

		%	+/-%
Barclay, S. Con*	38,423	72.2	7.9
Boyd, D. Lab	8,430	15.8	-8.7
Moss-Eccardt, R. Lib Dem	4,298	8.1	3.6
Johnson, R. Green	1,813	3.4	1.5
Con majority	29,993	56.37	
Electorate	83,713		
Turnout	53,203	63.55	

Con hold (8.26% from Lab to Con)

NORTH WEST CAMBRIDGESHIRE

		%	+/-%
Vara, S. Con*	40,307	62.2	3.6
Cordiner-Achenbach, C. Lab	14,324	22.1	-8.4
Smith, B. Lib Dem	6,881	10.6	5.7
Day, N. Green	3,021	4.7	2.7
Con majority	25,983	40.07	
Electorate	94,909		
Turnout	64,848	68.33	

Con hold (5.98% from Lab to Con)

SOUTH CAMBRIDGESHIRE

		%	+/-%
Browne, A. Con	31,015	46.1	-5.5
Sollom, I. Lib Dem	28,111	41.8	23.2
Greef, D. Lab	7,803	11.6	-15.6
Con majority	2,904	4.32	
Electorate	87,288		
Turnout	67,233	77.02	

Con hold (14.38% from Con to Lib Dem)

SOUTH EAST CAMBRIDGESHIRE

		%	+/-%
Frazer, L. Con*	32,187	49.8	-3.4
Heylings, P. Lib Dem	20,697	32.0	13.1
Bull, J. Lab	10,492	16.2	-11.4
Fordham, E. Ind	1,009	1.6	
Con majority	11,490	17.78	
Electorate	86,769		
Turnout	64,640	74.50	

Con hold (8.23% from Con to Lib Dem)

CANNOCK CHASE

		%	+/-%
Milling, A. Con*	31,636	68.0	13.1
Hobbs, A. Lab	11,757	25.3	-12.1
Woodhead, P. Green	2,920	6.3	4.6
Con majority	19,879	42.71	
Electorate	74,813		
Turnout	46,540	62.21	

Con hold (12.61% from Lab to Con)

CANTERBURY

		%	+/-%
Duffield, R. Lab*	29,018	48.1	3.2
Firth, A. Con	27,182	45.0	0.5
Malcomson, C. Lib Dem	3,408	5.7	-2.4
Gould, M. Ind	505	0.8	
Lab majority	1,836	3.04	
Electorate	80,203		
Turnout	60,353	75.25	

Lab hold (1.36% from Con to Lab)

CARDIFF CENTRAL

		%	+/-%
Stevens, J. Lab*	25,605	60.9	-1.4
Jenkins, M. Con	8,426	20.1	0.3
Molik, B. Lib Dem	6,298	15.0	1.6
Pearce, G. BP	1,006	2.4	
Caiach, S. Gwlad	280	0.7	
Kata, M. Ind	119	0.3	
Johnson, B. SP	88	0.2	
Lab majority	17,179	40.88	
Electorate	64,037		
Turnout	42,026	65.63	

Lab hold (0.82% from Lab to Con)

CARDIFF NORTH

		%	+/-%
McMorrin, A. Lab*	26,064	49.4	-0.6
Ali, M. Con	19,082	36.2	-5.9
Taylor, R. Lib Dem	3,580	6.8	3.5
Webb, S. PlC	1,606	3.0	-0.3
Butler, C. BP	1,311	2.5	
Cope, M. Green	820	1.6	
Jones, R. Ind	203	0.4	
Lab majority	6,982	13.23	
Electorate	68,438		
Turnout	52,777	77.12	

Lab hold (2.61% from Con to Lab)

CARDIFF SOUTH AND PENARTH

		%	+/-%
Doughty, S. Lab/Co-op*	27,382	54.0	-5.4
Broom, P. Con	14,645	28.9	-1.3
Schmeising, D. Lib Dem	2,985	5.9	3.1
Adam, N. PlC	2,386	4.7	0.5
Price, T. BP	1,999	3.9	
Barker, K. Green	1,182	2.3	1.3
Lab/Co-op majority	12,737	25.1	
Electorate	78,837		
Turnout	50,739	64.36	

Lab/Co-op hold (2.06% from Lab to Con)

CARDIFF WEST

		%	+/-%
Brennan, K. Lab*	23,908	51.6	-5.0
Webster, C. Con	12,922	27.9	-1.8
Clack, B. PlC	3,864	8.3	-1.1
Littlemore, C. Lib Dem	2,731	5.9	3.3
Mullins, N. BP	1,619	3.5	
Griffin, D. Green	1,133	2.5	
Lab majority	10,986	23.72	
Electorate	68,508		
Turnout	46,321	67.61	

Lab hold (1.58% from Lab to Con)

CARLISLE

		%	+/-%
Stevenson, J. Con*	23,659	54.9	5.2
Alcroft, R. Lab	15,340	35.6	-8.1
Aglionby, J. Lib Dem	2,829	6.6	3.7
Mills, F. UKIP	1,045	2.4	-0.9
Con majority	8,319	19.32	
Electorate	65,105		
Turnout	43,068	66.15	

Con hold (6.64% from Lab to Con)

CARMARTHEN EAST AND DINEFWR

		%	+/-%
Edwards, J. Ind*	15,939	38.5	-0.8
Hughes, H. Con	14,130	34.1	7.9
Carroll, M. Lab	8,622	20.8	-8.9
Prosser, P. BP	2,311	5.6	
PIC majority	1,809	4.37	
Electorate	57,419		
Turnout	41,417	72.13	

PIC hold (4.33% from PIC to Con)

CARMARTHEN WEST AND SOUTH PEMBROKESHIRE

		%	+/-%
Hart, S. Con*	22,183	52.5	5.7
Tierney, M. Lab	14,438	34.2	-5.2
Thomas, R. PIC	3,633	8.6	-0.7
Cameron, A. Lib Dem	1,860	4.4	2.1
Con majority	7,745	18.33	
Electorate	59,158		
Turnout	42,260	71.44	

Con hold (5.49% from Lab to Con)

CARSHALTON AND WALLINGTON

		%	+/-%
Colburn, E. Con	20,822	42.3	4.1
Brake, T. Lib Dem*	20,193	41.0	0.1
Wattoo, A. Lab	6,081	12.4	-6.1
Woudhuysen, J. BP	1,043	2.1	
Hague, T. Green	759	1.5	0.6
Dickenson, A. CPA	200	0.4	0.0
Con majority	629	1.28	
Electorate	72,941		
Turnout	49,223	67.48	

Con gain (1.99% from Lib Dem to Con)

CASTLE POINT

		%	+/-%
Harris, R. Con*	33,971	76.2	9.1
Curtis, K. Lab	7,337	16.7	-8.4
Howson, J. Lib Dem	2,969	6.7	4.4
Con majority	26,634	59.75	
Electorate	69,608		
Turnout	44,573	64.03	

Con hold (8.58% from Lab to Con)

CEREDIGION

		%	+/-%
Lake, B. PIC*	15,208	37.8	8.6
Jenner, A. Con	8,879	22.1	3.7
Williams, M. Lib Dem	6,975	17.3	-11.6
Mulholland, D. Lab	6,317	15.7	-4.4
James, G. BP	2,063	5.1	
Simpson, C. Green	663	1.7	
PIC majority	6,329	15.74	
Electorate	57,383		
Turnout	40,222	70.09	

PIC hold (2.45% from Con to PIC)

CHARNWOOD

		%	+/-%
Argar, E. Con*	35,121	63.1	0.4
Godden, G. Lab	12,724	22.9	-9.1
Tipton, K. Lib Dem	4,856	8.7	4.9
Needham, L. Green	2,664	4.8	2.8
Con majority	22,397	40.26	
Electorate	79,534		
Turnout	55,631	69.95	

Con hold (4.75% from Lab to Con)

CHATHAM AND AYLESFORD

		%	+/-%
Crouch, T. Con*	28,856	66.3	9.4
Maple, V. Lab	10,316	23.7	-9.9
Naghi, D. Lib Dem	2,866	6.6	4.1
Wilkinson, G. Green	1,090	2.5	1.2
Gibson, J. CPA	212	0.5	-0.1
Con majority	18,540	42.62	
Electorate	71,642		
Turnout	43,499	60.72	

Con hold (9.68% from Lab to Con)

CHEADLE

		%	+/-%
Robinson, M. Con*	25,694	45.8	1.3
Morrison, T. Lib Dem	23,358	41.6	5.4
Chauhan, Z. Lab	6,851	12.2	-6.8
Con majority	2,336	4.16	
Electorate	74,577		
Turnout	56,118	75.25	

Con hold (2.04% from Lab to Con)

CHELMSFORD

		%	+/-%
Ford, V. Con*	31,934	55.7	2.1
Goldman, M. Lib Dem	14,313	25.0	12.8
Richards, P. Lab	10,295	18.0	-11.8
Lawrence, M. Loony	580	1.0	
Con majority	17,621	30.73	
Electorate	80,394		
Turnout	57,346	71.33	

Con hold (5.36% from Con to Lib Dem)

CHELSEA AND FULHAM

		%	+/-%
Hands, G. Con*	23,345	49.7	-2.8
Horlick, N. Lib Dem	12,104	25.8	14.8
Uberoi, M. Lab	10,872	23.2	-10.0
Morland, S. AWP	500	1.1	
Con majority	11,241	23.93	
Electorate	67,110		
Turnout	46,971	69.99	

Con hold (8.81% from Con to Lib Dem)

CHELTENHAM

		%	+/-%
Chalk, A. Con*	28,486	47.9	1.3
Wilkinson, M. Lib Dem	27,505	46.2	4.1
Penny, G. Lab	2,921	4.9	-4.6
Ridgeon, G. Loony	445	0.8	
Con majority	981	1.65	
Electorate	81,044		
Turnout	59,510	73.43	

Con hold (1.43% from Con to Lib Dem)

CHESHAM AND AMERSHAM

		%	+/-%
Gillan, C. Con*	30,850	55.1	-5.4
Gallagher, D. Lib Dem	14,627	26.1	13.2
Turmaine, M. Lab	7,166	12.8	-7.7
Booth, A. Green	3,042	5.4	2.4
Con majority	16,223	28.98	
Electorate	72,542		
Turnout	55,974	77.16	

Con hold (9.29% from Con to Lib Dem)

CITY OF CHESTER

		%	+/-%
Matheson, C. Lab*	27,082	49.5	-7.1
George, S. Con	20,918	38.2	-2.2
Thompson, B. Lib Dem	3,734	6.8	4.1
Brown, N. Green	1,438	2.6	
Argyle, A. BP	1,388	2.5	
Lab majority	6,164	11.27	
Electorate	76,046		
Turnout	54,697	71.93	

Lab hold (2.48% from Lab to Con)

CHESTERFIELD

		%	+/-%
Perkins, T. Lab*	18,171	40.1	-14.6
Higgins, L. Con	16,720	36.9	2.2
Scotting, J. BP	4,771	10.5	
Coy, E. Lib Dem	3,985	8.8	3.4
Jackson, N. Green	1,148	2.5	0.9
Daramy, J. Ind	391	0.9	
Lab majority	1,451	3.2	
Electorate	71,034		
Turnout	45,322	63.80	

Lab hold (8.41% from Lab to Con)

CHICHESTER

		%	+/-%
Keegan, G. Con*	35,402	57.6	-2.4
O'Kelly, K. Lib Dem	13,912	22.6	11.4
Morton, J. Lab	9,069	14.8	-7.6
Barrie, H. Green	2,527	4.1	0.8
Brown, A. Libertarian	224	0.4	
Emerson, A. Patria	109	0.2	0.0
Con majority	21,490	34.95	
Electorate	85,499		
Turnout	61,494	71.92	

Con hold (6.91% from Con to Lib Dem)

CHINGFORD AND WOODFORD GREEN

		%	+/-%
Duncan Smith, I. Con*	23,481	48.2	-0.7
Shaheen, F. Lab	22,219	45.6	1.9
Seeff, G. Lib Dem	2,744	5.6	1.3
Con majority	1,262	2.59	
Electorate	65,393		
Turnout	48,679	74.44	

Con hold (1.29% from Con to Lab)

CHIPPENHAM

		%	+/-%
Donelan, M. Con*	30,994	54.0	-0.5
Belcher, H. Lib Dem	19,706	34.3	8.8
Anachury, M. Lab	6,399	11.1	-8.5
Con majority	11,288	19.66	
Electorate	77,221		
Turnout	57,420	74.36	

Con hold (4.67% from Con to Lib Dem)

CHIPPING BARNET

		%	+/-%
Villiers, T. Con*	25,745	44.6	-1.6
Whysall, E. Lab	24,533	42.5	-3.1
Parasram, I. Lib Dem	5,932	10.3	4.9
Bailey, G. Green	1,288	2.2	-0.3
Sheffield, J. Advance	71	0.1	
Con majority	1,212	2.1	
Electorate	79,960		
Turnout	57,762	72.24	

Con hold (0.74% from Lab to Con)

CHORLEY

		%	+/-%
Hoyle, L. Speaker*	26,831	65.2	
Brexit-Smith, M. Ind	9,439	22.9	
Melling, J. Green	3,600	8.7	7.8
Speaker majority	17,392	42.24	
Electorate	78,177		
Turnout	41,173	52.67	

Speaker gain (21.12% from Lab to Speaker)

CHRISTCHURCH

		%	+/-%
Chope, C. Con*	33,894	64.9	-4.5
Cox, M. Lib Dem	9,277	17.8	9.9
Dunne, A. Lab	6,568	12.6	-7.2
Rigby, C. Green	2,212	4.2	1.6
Con majority	24,617	47.12	
Electorate	71,520		
Turnout	52,248	73.05	

Con hold (7.17% from Con to Lib Dem)

CLACTON

		%	+/-%
Watling, G. Con*	31,438	72.1	10.9
Bonavia, K. Lab	6,736	15.4	-9.9
Robertson, C. Lib Dem	2,541	5.8	3.8
Southall, C. Green	1,225	2.8	1.2
Morgan, A. Ind	1,099	2.5	
Bennett, C. Ind	243	0.6	
Sexton, J. Loony	224	0.5	
Con majority	24,702	56.63	
Electorate	70,930		
Turnout	43,622	61.50	

Con hold (10.42% from Lab to Con)

CLEETHORPES

		%	+/-%
Vickers, M. Con*	31,969	68.7	11.6
James, R. Lab	10,551	22.7	-12.7
Horobin, R. Lib Dem	2,535	5.4	3.1
Shanahan, J. Green	1,284	2.8	1.8
Con majority	21,418	46	
Electorate	73,689		
Turnout	46,565	63.19	

Con hold (12.15% from Lab to Con)

CLWYD SOUTH

		%	+/-%
Baynes, S. Con	16,222	44.6	5.5
Jones, S. Lab*	14,983	41.1	-9.5
Allen, C. PlC	2,137	5.9	-0.2
Davies, C. Lib Dem	1,496	4.1	2.2
Adams, J. BP	1,468	4.0	
Con majority	1,239	3.4	
Electorate	53,919		
Turnout	36,416	67.54	

Con gain (7.51% from Lab to Con)

VALE OF CLWYD

		%	+/-%
Davies, J. Con	17,270	46.3	2.3
Ruane, C. Lab*	15,443	41.4	-8.7
Swingler, G. PlC	1,552	4.2	0.2
Dain, P. BP	1,477	4.0	
Scott, G. Lib Dem	1,471	3.9	2.2
Con majority	1,827	4.9	
Electorate	56,649		
Turnout	37,297	65.84	

Con gain (5.51% from Lab to Con)

CLWYD WEST

		%	+/-%
Jones, D. Con*	20,403	50.6	2.6
Thomas, J. Lab	13,656	33.8	-5.7
Williams, E. PlC	3,907	9.7	0.1
Wilkins, D. Lib Dem	2,237	5.5	2.9
Con majority	6,747	16.72	
Electorate	57,714		
Turnout	40,350	69.91	

Con hold (4.15% from Lab to Con)

COATBRIDGE, CHRYSTON AND BELLSHILL

		%	+/-%
Bonnar, S. SNP	22,680	46.9	7.9
Gaffney, H. Lab*	17,056	35.3	-7.3
Wilson, N. Con	6,113	12.7	-3.6
Stevens, D. Lib Dem	1,564	3.2	1.2
McAleer, P. Green	808	1.7	
SNP majority	5,624	11.63	
Electorate	72,943		
Turnout	48,342	66.27	

SNP gain (7.58% from Lab to SNP)

COLCHESTER

		%	+/-%
Quince, W. Con*	26,917	50.3	4.5
McKay, T. Lab	17,494	32.7	-2.5
Goss, M. Lib Dem	7,432	13.9	-3.1
Goacher, M. Green	1,530	2.9	1.3
Con majority	9,423	17.59	
Electorate	82,625		
Turnout	53,563	64.83	

Con hold (3.51% from Lab to Con)

COLNE VALLEY

		%	+/-%
McCartney, J. Con	29,482	48.2	2.2
Walker, T. Lab*	24,379	39.9	-7.7
Burke, C. Lib Dem	3,815	6.2	2.1
Harrison, S. BP	1,268	2.1	
Gould, D. Green	1,068	1.8	0.3
Aspinall, O. YP	548	0.9	
Roberts, M. UKIP	230	0.4	
Peel, C. Ind	102	0.2	
Con majority	5,103	8.35	
Electorate	84,174		
Turnout	61,120	72.61	

Con gain (4.93% from Lab to Con)

CONGLETON

		%	+/-%
Bruce, F. Con*	33,747	58.8	2.3
Dale, J. Lab	15,186	26.4	-7.7
Duffy, P. Lib Dem	6,026	10.5	5.3
McCarthy, R. Green	1,616	2.8	1.0
Smith, J. AWP	658	1.2	
Con majority	18,561	32.32	
Electorate	80,930		
Turnout	57,426	70.96	

Con hold (4.96% from Lab to Con)

COPELAND

		%	+/-%
Harrison, T. Con*	22,856	53.5	4.6
Lywood, T. Lab	17,014	39.9	-5.2
Studholme, J. Lib Dem	1,888	4.4	1.2
Lenox, J. Green	765	1.8	
Con majority	5,842	13.68	
Electorate	61,693		
Turnout	42,696	69.21	

Con hold (4.87% from Lab to Con)

CORBY

		%	+/-%
Pursglove, T. Con*	33,410	55.0	5.9
Miller, B. Lab	23,142	38.1	-6.6
Stanbra, C. Lib Dem	3,932	6.5	3.9
Con majority	10,268	16.9	
Electorate	86,153		
Turnout	60,749	70.51	

Con hold (6.22% from Lab to Con)

NORTH CORNWALL

		%	+/-%
Mann, S. Con*	30,671	59.1	8.5
Chambers, D. Lib Dem	15,919	30.7	-5.9
Bassett, J. Lab	4,516	8.7	-3.4
Liepins, E. Lib	572	1.1	
Con majority	14,752	28.41	
Electorate	69,935		
Turnout	51,934	74.26	

Con hold (7.16% from Lib Dem to Con)

SOUTH EAST CORNWALL

		%	+/-%
Murray, S. Con*	31,807	59.0	3.8
Derrick, G. Lab	10,836	20.1	-2.5
Martin, C. Lib Dem	8,650	16.1	-3.3
Green, M. Green	1,493	2.8	0.3
Latham, J. Lib	869	1.6	
Con majority	20,971	38.92	
Electorate	71,825		
Turnout	53,885	75.02	

Con hold (3.12% from Lab to Con)

THE COTSWOLDS

		%	+/-%
Clifton-Brown, G. Con*	35,484	57.8	-2.8
Webster, L. Lib Dem	15,270	24.9	8.6
Mackenzie, A. Lab	7,110	11.6	-6.3
Poole, S. Green	3,312	5.4	2.5
Con majority	20,214	32.9	
Electorate	81,939		
Turnout	61,441	74.98	

Con hold (5.66% from Con to Lib Dem)

COVENTRY NORTH EAST

		%	+/-%
Fletcher, C. Lab*	23,412	52.5	-10.7
Richards, S. Con	15,720	35.3	5.4
Sufyan, I. BP	2,110	4.7	
Proctor, N. Lib Dem	2,061	4.6	2.1
Handley, M. Green	1,141	2.6	1.5
Lab majority	7,692	17.26	
Electorate	76,001		
Turnout	44,571	58.65	

Lab hold (8.07% from Lab to Con)

COVENTRY NORTH WEST

		%	+/-%
Owatemi, T. Lab	20,918	43.7	-10.2
Golby, C. Con	20,710	43.3	6.6
Judge, G. Lib Dem	2,717	5.7	3.1
Richardson, J. BP	1,956	4.1	
Gray, S. Green	1,443	3.0	1.7
Lab majority	208	0.43	
Electorate	75,243		
Turnout	47,888	63.64	

Lab hold (8.38% from Lab to Con)

COVENTRY SOUTH

		%	+/-%
Sultana, Z. Lab	19,544	43.3	-11.7
Heaven, M. Con	19,143	42.4	4.3
Richmond, S. Lib Dem	3,398	7.5	4.7
Crocker, J. BP	1,432	3.2	
Finlayson, B. Green	1,092	2.4	1.1
Manning, E. Ind	435	1.0	
Lab majority	401	0.89	
Electorate	70,970		
Turnout	45,182	63.66	

Lab hold (7.99% from Lab to Con)

CRAWLEY

		%	+/-%
Smith, H. Con*	27,040	54.0	3.6
Lamb, P. Lab	18,680	37.3	-8.2
Yousuf, K. Lib Dem	2,728	5.5	1.7
Dickson, I. Green	1,451	2.9	
Con majority	8,360	16.69	
Electorate	74,207		
Turnout	50,092	67.50	

Con hold (5.91% from Lab to Con)

CREWE AND NANTWICH

		%	+/-%
Mullan, K. Con	28,704	53.0	6.1
Smith, L. Lab*	20,196	37.3	-9.7
Theobald, M. Lib Dem	2,618	4.8	2.4
Wood, M. BP	1,390	2.6	
Browne, T. Green	975	1.8	
Kinsman, A. Libertarian	149	0.3	
Con majority	8,508	15.71	
Electorate	80,321		
Turnout	54,155	67.42	

Con gain (7.9% from Lab to Con)

CROYDON CENTRAL

		%	+/-%
Jones, S. Lab*	27,124	49.9	-2.3
Creatura, M. Con	21,175	39.0	-3.4
Sprague, S. Lib Dem	3,532	6.5	4.6
Sutton, E. Green	1,215	2.2	1.2
Sonnex, P. BP	999	1.8	
Lab majority	5,949	10.98	
Electorate	81,407		
Turnout	54,180	66.55	

Lab hold (0.53% from Con to Lab)

CROYDON NORTH

		%	+/-%
Reed, S. Lab/Co-op*	36,495	65.4	-8.6
Ekekhomen, D. Con	11,822	21.2	1.4
Bonham, C. Lib Dem	4,476	8.0	5.3
Chance, R. Green	1,629	2.9	1.3
Ngwaba, C. BP	839	1.5	
Mitchell, C. CPA	348	0.6	
Lab/Co-op majority	24,673	44.24	
Electorate	88,468		
Turnout	55,776	63.05	

Lab/Co-op hold (4.96% from Lab to Con)

CROYDON SOUTH

		%	+/-%
Philp, C. Con*	30,985	52.0	-2.3
FitzRoy, O. Lab	18,646	31.3	-4.4
Jones, A. Lib Dem	7,503	12.6	6.8
Underwood, P. Green	1,782	3.0	1.2
Garner, K. UKIP	442	0.7	-1.1
Con majority	12,339	20.71	
Electorate	83,982		
Turnout	59,580	70.94	

Con hold (1.06% from Lab to Con)

CUMBERNAULD, KILSYTH AND KIRKINTILLOCH EAST

		%	+/-%
McDonald, S. SNP*	24,158	52.7	9.1
McPhilemy, J. Lab	11,182	24.4	-9.5
McCall, R. Con	7,380	16.1	-2.2
Murray, S. Lib Dem	2,966	6.5	3.7
SNP majority	12,976	28.31	
Electorate	66,079		
Turnout	45,829	69.35	

SNP hold (9.3% from Lab to SNP)

CYNON VALLEY

		%	+/-%
Winter, B. Lab	15,533	51.2	-9.7
Church, P. Con	6,711	22.1	2.8
Rees-Evans, R. BP	3,045	10.0	
Benney, G. PIC	2,562	8.5	-5.3
Chainey, A. CVP	1,322	4.4	
Bray, S. Lib Dem	949	3.1	1.3
McLean, I. SDP	114	0.4	
Lab majority	8,822	29.08	
Electorate	51,134		
Turnout	30,335	59.32	

Lab hold (6.23% from Lab to Con)

DAGENHAM AND RAINHAM

		%	+/-%
Cruddas, J. Lab*	19,468	44.4	-5.6
White, D. Con	19,175	43.7	3.9
Bewick, T. BP	2,887	6.6	
Fisk, S. Lib Dem	1,182	2.7	1.7
Minott, A. Green	602	1.4	0.2
Emin, R. Ind	212	0.5	
London, T. Ind	209	0.5	
Lab majority	293	0.67	
Electorate	71,045		
Turnout	43,862	61.74	

Lab hold (4.74% from Lab to Con)

DARLINGTON

		%	+/-%
Gibson, P. Con	20,901	48.0	4.8
Chapman, J. Lab*	17,607	40.4	-10.1
Curry, A. Lib Dem	2,097	4.8	2.5
Mawson, D. BP	1,544	3.5	
Snedker, M. Green	1,057	2.4	1.3
Black, M. Ind	292	0.7	
Con majority	3,294	7.56	
Electorate	66,397		
Turnout	43,579	65.63	

Con gain (7.44% from Lab to Con)

DARTFORD

		%	+/-%
Johnson, G. Con*	34,006	62.6	5.2
Gosine, S. Lab	14,846	27.3	-5.8
Marsh, K. Lib Dem	3,736	6.9	4.3
Lindop, M. Green	1,435	2.6	1.2
Con majority	19,160	35.28	
Electorate	82,209		
Turnout	54,303	66.05	

Con hold (5.51% from Lab to Con)

DAVENTRY

		%	+/-%
Heaton-Harris, C. Con*	37,055	64.3	0.7
Joyce, P. Lab	10,975	19.0	-5.6
Simpson, A. Lib Dem	7,032	12.2	5.0
Slater, C. Green	2,341	4.1	2.3
Con majority	26,080	45.24	
Electorate	77,423		
Turnout	57,649	74.46	

Con hold (3.13% from Lab to Con)

DELYN

		%	+/-%
Roberts, R. Con	16,756	43.6	2.2
Hanson, D. Lab*	15,891	41.3	-10.8
Parkhurst, A. Lib Dem	2,346	6.1	3.5
Williams, N. BP	1,971	5.1	
Rowlinson, P. PlC	1,406	3.7	-0.1
Con majority	865	2.25	
Electorate	54,560		
Turnout	38,475	70.52	

Con gain (6.5% from Lab to Con)

DENTON AND REDDISH

		%	+/-%
Gwynne, A. Lab*	19,317	49.9	-13.5
Bott, I. Con	13,142	34.0	6.0
Power, M. BP	3,039	7.9	
Hardwick, D. Lib Dem	1,642	4.2	2.1
Lawson, G. Green	1,124	2.9	1.7
Dave, F. Loony	324	0.8	0.3
Lab majority	6,175	15.96	
Electorate	66,234		
Turnout	38,694	58.42	

Lab hold (9.76% from Lab to Con)

DERBY NORTH

		%	+/-%
Solloway, A. Con	21,259	45.1	0.8
Tinley, T. Lab	18,719	39.7	-8.7
Webb, G. Lib Dem	3,450	7.3	2.7
Graves, A. BP	1,908	4.1	
Hitchcock, H. Green	1,046	2.2	
Williamson, C. Ind*	635	1.4	
Con majority	2,540	5.39	
Electorate	73,199		
Turnout	47,128	64.38	

Con gain (4.76% from Lab to Con)

DERBY SOUTH

		%	+/-%
Beckett, M. Lab*	21,690	50.9	-7.3
Barker, E. Con	15,671	36.8	3.4
Naitta, J. Lib Dem	2,621	6.2	3.4
Prosser, T. BP	2,480	5.8	
Lab majority	6,019	14.13	
Electorate	73,062		
Turnout	42,599	58.31	

Lab hold (5.32% from Lab to Con)

DERBYSHIRE DALES

		%	+/-%
Dines, S. Con	29,356	58.5	-1.4
Raw, C. Lab	11,975	23.8	-7.2
Court, R. Lib Dem	6,627	13.2	6.9
Buckler, M. Green	2,058	4.1	2.1
Con majority	17,381	34.6	
Electorate	65,080		
Turnout	50,227	77.18	

Con hold (2.9% from Lab to Con)

MID DERBYSHIRE

		%	+/-%
Latham, P. Con*	29,027	58.6	0.1
Monkman, E. Lab	13,642	27.5	-7.9
Dodds, F. Lib Dem	4,756	9.6	6.1
MacFarlane, S. Green	1,931	3.9	1.6
Con majority	15,385	31.05	
Electorate	67,442		
Turnout	49,553	73.47	

Con hold (4.03% from Lab to Con)

NORTH EAST DERBYSHIRE

		%	+/-%
Rowley, L. Con*	28,897	58.5	9.4
Peace, C. Lab	16,021	32.4	-11.0
Shipman, R. Lib Dem	3,021	6.1	3.4
Adlington Stringer, F. Green	1,278	2.6	1.2
Con majority	12,876	26.07	
Electorate	72,345		
Turnout	49,390	68.27	

Con hold (10.2% from Lab to Con)

SOUTH DERBYSHIRE

		%	+/-%
Wheeler, H. Con*	33,502	62.3	3.7
Pearson, R. Lab	14,167	26.3	-9.6
Johnson, L. Lib Dem	3,924	7.3	3.8
Baker, A. Green	1,788	3.3	1.6
Con majority	19,335	35.93	
Electorate	79,331		
Turnout	53,810	67.83	

Con hold (6.62% from Lab to Con)

DEVIZES

		%	+/-%
Kruger, D. Con	32,150	62.8	0.1
Waltham, J. Lib Dem	8,157	15.9	6.6
Scheider Ross, R. Lab	7,838	15.3	-5.6
Dawnay, E. Green	2,809	5.5	2.3
Con majority	23,993	46.84	
Electorate	73,372		
Turnout	51,223	69.81	

Con hold (3.25% from Con to Lib Dem)

CENTRAL DEVON

		%	+/-%
Stride, M. Con*	32,095	54.9	0.9
Robillard Webb, L. Lab	14,374	24.6	-2.3
Eden, A. Lib Dem	8,770	15.0	3.3
Williamson, A. Green	2,833	4.9	2.2
Con majority	17,721	30.33	
Electorate	74,296		
Turnout	58,419	78.63	

Con hold (1.64% from Lab to Con)

EAST DEVON

		%	+/-%
Jupp, S. Con	32,577	50.7	2.2
Wright, C. Ind	25,869	40.3	5.1
Wilson, D. Lab	2,870	4.5	-6.9
Rylance, E. Lib Dem	1,771	2.8	0.3
Gent, H. Green	711	1.1	
Faithfull, P. Ind	275	0.4	0.2
Con majority	6,708	10.44	
Electorate	87,168		
Turnout	64,223	73.68	

Con hold (1.43% from Con to Ind)

NORTH DEVON

		%	+/-%
Saxby, S. Con	31,479	56.5	10.7
White, A. Lib Dem	16,666	29.9	-8.1
O'Neill, F. Lab	5,097	9.1	-3.5
Mack, R. Green	1,759	3.2	1.8
Cotten, S. Ind	580	1.0	
Con majority	14,813	26.57	
Electorate	75,859		
Turnout	55,747	73.49	

Con hold (9.41% from Lib Dem to Con)

SOUTH WEST DEVON

		%	+/-%
Streeter, G. Con*	33,286	62.1	2.3
Beverly, A. Lab	11,856	22.1	-7.8
Davarian, S. Lib Dem	6,207	11.6	6.4
Poyser, I. Green	2,018	3.8	1.6
Con majority	21,430	39.95	
Electorate	72,535		
Turnout	53,642	73.95	

Con hold (5.04% from Lab to Con)

DEWSBURY

		%	+/-%
Eastwood, M. Con	26,179	46.2	1.2
Sherriff, P. Lab*	24,618	43.5	-7.4
Rossington, J. Lib Dem	2,406	4.3	2.1
James, P. BP	1,874	3.3	
Cope, S. Green	1,060	1.9	0.1
Stanton, S. Loony	252	0.4	
Con majority	1,561	2.75	
Electorate	81,253		
Turnout	56,661	69.73	

Con gain (4.31% from Lab to Con)

DON VALLEY

		%	+/-%
Fletcher, N. Con	19,609	43.1	1.5
Flint, C. Lab*	15,979	35.1	-17.7
Whitehurst, P. BP	6,247	13.7	
Alcock, M. Lib Dem	1,907	4.2	2.3
Needham, K. Green	872	1.9	
Holmes, C. YP	823	1.8	-1.7
Con majority	3,630	7.97	
Electorate	75,356		
Turnout	45,519	60.41	

Con gain (9.6% from Lab to Con)

DONCASTER CENTRAL

		%	+/-%
Winterton, R. Lab*	16,638	39.9	-17.8
Weeden-Sanz, R. Con	14,360	34.5	0.2
Duhre, S. BP	6,842	16.4	
Horton, P. Lib Dem	1,748	4.2	1.9
French, L. YP	1,012	2.4	-0.7
Sheridan, F. Green	981	2.4	
Lab majority	2,278	5.46	
Electorate	71,389		
Turnout	41,689	58.40	

Lab hold (9.01% from Lab to Con)

DONCASTER NORTH

		%	+/-%
Miliband, E. Lab*	15,740	38.6	-22.1
Sale, K. Con	13,370	32.8	5.2
Stewart, A. BP	8,294	20.3	
Otten, J. Lib Dem	1,476	3.6	2.0
Manion, S. YP	959	2.4	0.6
Calladine, F. Eng Dem	309	0.8	-0.1
Todd, E. Ind	220	0.5	-0.3
Bailey, W. Ind	188	0.5	-0.4
Wood, N. Ind	142	0.4	-0.5
Lab majority	2,370	5.81	
Electorate	72,362		
Turnout	40,793	56.37	

Lab hold (13.64% from Lab to Con)

MID DORSET AND NORTH POOLE

		%	+/-%
Tomlinson, M. Con*	29,548	60.2	1.1
Slade, V. Lib Dem	14,650	29.9	2.5
Oldale, J. Lab	3,402	6.9	-6.3
Carswell, N. Green	1,330	2.7	
Con majority	14,898	30.35	
Electorate	65,427		
Turnout	49,082	75.02	

Con hold (0.67% from Con to Lib Dem)

NORTH DORSET

		%	+/-%
Hoare, S. Con*	35,705	63.3	-1.4
Chadwick, D. Lib Dem	11,404	20.2	6.7
Osborne, P. Lab	6,737	12.0	-6.6
Huggins, K. Green	2,261	4.0	1.1
Con majority	24,301	43.11	
Electorate	75,956		
Turnout	56,370	74.21	

Con hold (4.04% from Con to Lib Dem)

SOUTH DORSET

		%	+/-%
Drax, R. Con*	30,024	58.6	2.6
Parkes, C. Lab	12,871	25.1	-8.4
Ireland, N. Lib Dem	5,432	10.6	4.7
Orrell, J. Green	2,246	4.4	
Green, J. Ind	485	1.0	
Con majority	17,153	33.47	
Electorate	73,809		
Turnout	51,242	69.43	

Con hold (5.49% from Lab to Con)

WEST DORSET

		%	+/-%
Loder, C. Con	33,589	54.9	-0.4
Morello, E. Lib Dem	19,483	31.9	8.4
Sorin, C. Lab	5,729	9.4	-8.9
Clayton, K. Green	2,124	3.5	0.7
Con majority	14,106	23.06	
Electorate	81,897		
Turnout	61,162	74.68	

Con hold (4.45% from Con to Lib Dem)

DOVER

		%	+/-%
Elphicke, N. Con	28,830	56.6	4.3
Cornell, C. Lab	16,552	32.5	-7.4
Dodds, S. Lib Dem	2,895	5.7	3.1
Sawbridge, B. Green	1,371	2.7	0.9
Sutton, N. Ind	916	1.8	
Morais, E. WEP	137	0.3	
Con majority	12,278	24.11	
Electorate	76,355		
Turnout	50,920	66.69	

Con hold (5.87% from Lab to Con)

NORTH DOWN

		%	+/-%
Farry, S. APNI	18,358	45.0	35.7
Easton, A. DUP	15,390	37.7	-0.3
Chambers, A. UUP	4,936	12.1	
Robinson, M. Con	1,959	4.8	2.4
APNI majority	2,968	7.27	
Electorate	67,099		
Turnout	40,815	60.83	

APNI gain (18.03% from Ind to APNI)

SOUTH DOWN

		%	+/-%
Hazzard, C. Sinn Féin*	16,137	32.3	-7.5
Savage, M. SDLP	14,517	29.1	-6.0
Hanna, G. DUP	7,619	15.3	-2.1
Brown, P. APNI	6,916	13.8	10.3
Macauley, J. UUP	3,307	6.6	2.7
Brady, P. Aontú	1,266	2.5	
Sinn Féin majority	1,620	3.24	
Electorate	79,175		
Turnout	49,971	63.11	

Sinn Féin hold (0.77% from Sinn Féin to SDLP)

DUDLEY NORTH

		%	+/-%
Longhi, M. Con	23,134	62.8	16.5
Dudley, M. Lab	11,601	31.5	-14.9
Flynn, I. Lib Dem	1,210	3.3	2.3
Harrison, M. Green	739	2.0	1.4
Con majority	11,533	31.31	
Electorate	62,102		
Turnout	36,840	59.32	

Con gain (15.68% from Lab to Con)

DUDLEY SOUTH

		%	+/-%
Wood, M. Con*	24,835	67.6	11.2
Caldicott, L. Lab	9,270	25.2	-11.0
Bramall, J. Lib Dem	1,608	4.4	2.8
Mohr, C. Green	863	2.4	1.4
Con majority	15,565	42.37	
Electorate	60,884		
Turnout	36,739	60.34	

Con hold (11.1% from Lab to Con)

DULWICH AND WEST NORWOOD

		%	+/-%
Hayes, H. Lab*	36,521	65.2	-4.2
Bartley, J. Green	9,211	16.4	13.9
Lyons, J. Con	9,160	16.4	-3.1
Stephenson, J. BP	571	1.0	
Hodgson, A. CPA	242	0.4	
Plume, J. UKIP	73	0.1	
Lab majority	27,310	48.76	
Electorate	80,331		
Turnout	56,014	69.73	

Lab hold (9.09% from Lab to Green)

DUMFRIES AND GALLOWAY

		%	+/-%
Jack, A. Con*	22,678	44.0	0.7
Arkless, R. SNP	20,873	40.5	8.2
Thompson, T. Lab	4,745	9.2	-11.7
Laurie, M. Lib Dem	3,133	6.1	3.7
Con majority	1,805	3.5	
Electorate	74,580		
Turnout	51,552	69.12	

Con hold (3.72% from Con to SNP)

DUMFRIESSHIRE, CLYDESDALE AND TWEEDDALE

		%	+/-%
Mundell, D. Con*	22,611	45.9	-3.5
Burgauer, A. SNP	18,830	38.2	8.1
Chisholm, N. Lab	4,172	8.5	-8.1
Ferry, J. Lib Dem	3,540	7.2	3.2
Con majority	3,781	7.67	
Electorate	68,330		
Turnout	49,295	72.14	

Con hold (5.8% from Con to SNP)

EAST DUNBARTONSHIRE

		%	+/-%
Callaghan, A. SNP	19,672	37.0	6.8
Swinson, J. Lib Dem*	19,523	36.8	-3.8
Gosal, P. Con	7,455	14.0	-0.5
McNally, C. Lab	4,839	9.1	-5.4
Scrimgeour, C. Green	916	1.7	
Dickson, R. Ind	221	0.4	
MacKay, M. UKIP	208	0.4	
McKechnie, L. SFP	197	0.4	
SNP majority	149	0.28	
Electorate	66,075		
Turnout	53,111	80.38	

SNP gain (5.29% from Lib Dem to SNP)

WEST DUNBARTONSHIRE

		%	+/-%
Docherty-Hughes, M. SNP*	22,396	49.5	6.7
Mitchell, J. Lab	12,843	28.4	-9.2
Mathieson, A. Con	6,436	14.2	-2.9
Lang, J. Lib Dem	1,890	4.2	1.9
Conolly, P. Green	867	1.9	
Muir, A. Ind	708	1.6	
SNP majority	9,553	21.11	
Electorate	66,517		
Turnout	45,244	68.02	

SNP hold (7.97% from Lab to SNP)

DUNDEE EAST

		%	+/-%
Hosie, S. SNP*	24,361	53.7	10.9
Scott, P. Con	10,986	24.2	-3.1
Garton, R. Lab	6,045	13.3	-12.7
Crichton, M. Lib Dem	3,573	7.9	4.1
Morton, G. Ind	312	0.7	
SNP majority	13,375	29.45	
Electorate	66,210		
Turnout	45,411	68.59	

SNP hold (7.01% from Con to SNP)

DUNDEE WEST

		%	+/-%
Law, C. SNP*	22,355	53.7	7.1
Malone, J. Lab	10,096	24.2	-8.7
White, T. Con	5,149	12.4	-3.8
Coleman, D. Lib Dem	2,468	5.9	2.9
Waiton, S. BP	1,271	3.1	
Arrey, Q. CPA	240	0.6	
SNP majority	12,259	29.42	
Electorate	64,431		
Turnout	41,671	64.68	

SNP hold (7.93% from Lab to SNP)

DUNFERMLINE AND WEST FIFE

		%	+/-%
Chapman, D. SNP*	23,727	44.3	8.8
Hilton, C. Lab/Co-op	13,028	24.3	-9.5
Benny, M. Con	11,207	20.9	-3.8
Bell, R. Lib Dem	4,262	8.0	2.0
Hall, M. Green	1,258	2.4	
SNP majority	10,699	19.96	
Electorate	76,652		
Turnout	53,612	69.94	

SNP hold (9.16% from Lab to SNP)

CITY OF DURHAM

		%	+/-%
Foy, M. Lab	20,531	41.9	-13.4
Morgan, W. Con	15,506	31.6	1.9
Hopgood, A. Lib Dem	7,935	16.2	6.3
Wright, L. BP	3,252	6.6	
Elmer, J. Green	1,635	3.3	1.7
Lab majority	5,025	10.25	
Electorate	71,271		
Turnout	49,034	68.80	

Lab hold (7.65% from Lab to Con)

NORTH DURHAM

		%	+/-%
Jones, K. Lab*	18,639	44.1	-15.7
Parson, E. Con	13,897	32.9	2.9
Telford, P. BP	4,693	11.1	
Martin, C. Lib Dem	2,879	6.8	2.2
Morse, D. Green	1,126	2.7	
Rollings, K. Ind	961	2.3	
Lab majority	4,742	11.21	
Electorate	66,796		
Turnout	42,302	63.33	

Lab hold (9.32% from Lab to Con)

NORTH WEST DURHAM

		%	+/-%
Holden, R. Con	19,990	41.8	7.4
Pidcock, L. Lab*	18,846	39.4	-13.3
Wolstenholme, J. BP	3,193	6.7	
Peacock, M. Lib Dem	2,831	5.9	-1.2
Stelling, W. Ind	1,216	2.5	
Sewell, D. Green	1,173	2.5	1.4
Lindsay, D. Ind	414	0.9	
Con majority	1,144	2.39	
Electorate	72,166		
Turnout	47,791	66.22	

Con gain (10.36% from Lab to Con)

DWYFOR MEIRIONNYDD

		%	+/-%
Saville Roberts, L. PlC*	14,447	48.1	3.1
Davies, T. Con	9,707	32.3	3.3
Hogg, G. Lab	3,998	13.3	-7.3
Hughes, L. BP	1,776	5.9	
PlC majority	4,740	15.77	
Electorate	44,362		
Turnout	30,056	67.75	

PlC hold (0.09% from PlC to Con)

EALING CENTRAL AND ACTON

		%	+/-%
Huq, R. Lab*	28,132	51.2	-8.3
Gallant, J. Con	14,832	27.0	-7.7
Badiani-Hamment, S. Lib Dem	9,444	17.2	11.6
Crossland, K. Green	1,735	3.2	
Alsoodani, S. BP	664	1.2	
Lab majority	13,300	24.2	
Electorate	75,510		
Turnout	54,969	72.80	

Lab hold (0.33% from Lab to Con)

EALING NORTH

		%	+/-%
Murray, J. Lab/Co-op	28,036	56.4	-9.4
Pickles, A. Con	15,767	31.7	3.3
Bewley, H. Lib Dem	4,370	8.8	6.4
Parker, J. Green	1,458	2.9	1.5
Lab/Co-op majority	12,269	24.66	
Electorate	74,473		
Turnout	49,755	66.81	

Lab/Co-op hold (6.37% from Lab to Con)

EALING SOUTHALL

		%	+/-%
Sharma, V. Lab*	25,678	60.5	-9.5
Bennett, T. Con	9,594	22.6	1.4
Mahmood, T. Lib Dem	3,933	9.3	5.1
Moore, D. Green	1,688	4.0	1.7
Beattie, R. BP	867	2.0	
Fernandes, S. CPA	287	0.7	
Zulkifal, H. WRP	170	0.4	-0.4
Lab majority	16,084	37.92	
Electorate	64,581		
Turnout	42,420	65.68	

Lab hold (5.42% from Lab to Con)

EASINGTON

		%	+/-%
Morris, G. Lab*	15,723	45.3	-18.3
Ambrosino, C. Con	9,142	26.3	3.7
Maughan, J. BP	6,744	19.4	
Haney, D. Lib Dem	1,526	4.4	3.1
McDonnell, S. NEP	1,448	4.2	-2.3
Lab majority	6,581	18.96	
Electorate	61,182		
Turnout	34,705	56.72	

Lab hold (10.97% from Lab to Con)

EAST HAM

		%	+/-%
Timms, S. Lab*	41,703	76.1	-6.9
Pattenden, S. Con	8,527	15.6	2.8
Fox, M. Lib Dem	2,158	3.9	2.8
Cuthbert, A. BP	1,107	2.0	
Spracklin, M. Green	883	1.6	0.8
Malik, K. Comm United	250	0.5	
Lab majority	33,176	60.54	
Electorate	88,319		
Turnout	54,802	62.05	

Lab hold (4.83% from Lab to Con)

EAST KILBRIDE, STRATHAVEN AND LESMAHAGOW

		%	+/-%
Cameron, L. SNP*	26,113	46.0	7.2
McAdams, M. Lab	12,791	22.5	-9.1
MacGregor, G. Con	11,961	21.1	-4.2
McRobert, E. Lib Dem	3,760	6.6	3.7
Bradley-Young, E. Green	1,153	2.0	
Mackay, D. UKIP	559	1.0	-0.2
SNP majority	13,322	23.48	
Electorate	81,224		
Turnout	56,747	69.86	

SNP hold (8.17% from Lab to SNP)

EASTBOURNE

		%	+/-%
Ansell, C. Con	26,951	48.8	4.8
Lloyd, S. Lib Dem*	22,620	40.9	-5.9
Lambert, J. Lab	3,848	7.0	-1.2
Gander, S. BP	1,530	2.8	
Pollock, K. Ind	185	0.3	
Con majority	4,331	7.84	
Electorate	79,307		
Turnout	55,255	69.67	

Con gain (5.32% from Lib Dem to Con)

EASTLEIGH

		%	+/-%
Holmes, P. Con	32,690	55.3	4.9
Murphy, L. Lib Dem	17,083	28.9	3.3
Jordan, S. Lab	7,559	12.8	-7.2
Meldrum, R. Green	1,639	2.8	1.5
Con majority	15,607	26.38	
Electorate	83,880		
Turnout	59,157	70.53	

Con hold (0.84% from Lab to Con)

EDDISBURY

		%	+/-%
Timpson, E. Con	30,095	56.7	-0.1
Savage, T. Lab	11,652	21.9	-11.6
Sandbach, A. Lib Dem*	9,582	18.0	12.6
Jewkes, L. Green	1,191	2.2	0.7
Allen, A. UKIP	451	0.9	-1.3
Con majority	18,443	34.72	
Electorate	74,549		
Turnout	53,114	71.25	

Con hold (5.75% from Lab to Con)

EDINBURGH EAST

		%	+/-%
Sheppard, T. SNP*	23,165	48.3	5.9
Gilmore, S. Lab	12,748	26.6	-8.0
Price, E. Con	6,549	13.7	-4.9
Reilly, J. Lib Dem	3,289	6.9	2.6
Miller, C. Green	2,064	4.3	
SNP majority	10,417	21.72	
Electorate	69,424		
Turnout	47,957	69.08	

SNP hold (6.94% from Lab to SNP)

EDINBURGH NORTH AND LEITH

		%	+/-%
Brock, D. SNP*	25,925	43.6	9.6
Munro, G. Lab/Co-op	13,117	22.1	-9.1
McGill, I. Con	11,000	18.5	-8.7
Wilson, B. Lib Dem	6,635	11.2	6.6
Burgess, S. Green	1,971	3.3	0.3
Speirs, R. BP	558	0.9	
Astbury, H. Renew	138	0.2	
SNP majority	12,808	21.54	
Electorate	81,336		
Turnout	59,449	73.09	

SNP hold (9.34% from Lab to SNP)

EDINBURGH SOUTH

		%	+/-%
Murray, I. Lab*	23,745	47.6	-7.2
MacDonald, C. SNP	12,650	25.4	2.9
Cook, N. Con	8,161	16.4	-3.3
Beal, A. Lib Dem	3,819	7.7	4.8
Nevens, K. Green	1,357	2.7	
Lab majority	11,095	22.25	
Electorate	66,188		
Turnout	49,854	75.32	

Lab hold (5.06% from Lab to SNP)

EDINBURGH SOUTH WEST

		%	+/-%
Cherry, J. SNP*	24,830	47.6	12.0
Laidlaw, C. Con	12,848	24.6	-8.7
Cooke, S. Lab	7,478	14.3	-12.4
Inglis, T. Lib Dem	4,971	9.5	5.2
Parker, B. Green	1,265	2.4	
Ballantine, D. BP	625	1.2	
Brown, M. SDP	114	0.2	
SNP majority	11,982	22.94	
Electorate	73,501		
Turnout	52,222	71.05	

SNP hold (10.37% from Con to SNP)

EDINBURGH WEST

		%	+/-%
Jardine, C. Lib Dem*	21,766	39.8	5.6
Masson, S. SNP	17,997	32.9	4.3
Hutchison, G. Con	9,283	17.0	-4.9
Bolton, C. Lab	4,460	8.2	-6.7
Gunn, E. Green	1,027	1.9	
Lib Dem majority	3,769	6.9	
Electorate	72,507		
Turnout	54,657	75.38	

Lib Dem hold (0.62% from SNP to Lib Dem)

EDMONTON

		%	+/-%
Osamor, K. Lab/Co-op*	26,217	64.5	-6.8
Hockney, J. Con	10,202	25.1	2.0
Schmitz, D. Lib Dem	2,145	5.3	3.3
Maydon, B. Green	862	2.1	0.7
Sehgal, S. BP	840	2.1	
Warsame, S. Ind	75	0.2	
Lab/Co-op majority	16,015	39.41	
Electorate	65,568		
Turnout	40,637	61.98	

Lab/Co-op hold (4.41% from Lab to Con)

ELLESMERE PORT AND NESTON

		%	+/-%
Madders, J. Lab*	26,001	53.2	-5.9
Rodwell, A. Con	17,237	35.3	-1.5
Gough, E. Lib Dem	2,406	4.9	3.2
Stevens, C. BP	2,138	4.4	
Copeman, C. Green	964	2.0	1.3
Lab majority	8,764	17.93	
Electorate	70,317		
Turnout	48,874	69.51	

Lab hold (2.2% from Lab to Con)

ELMET AND ROTHWELL

		%	+/-%
Shelbrooke, A. Con*	33,726	57.7	3.5
Nagle, D. Lab	16,373	28.0	-9.8
Golton, S. Lib Dem	5,155	8.8	4.5
Stables, P. Green	1,775	3.0	1.4
Clover, M. YP	1,196	2.1	0.3
Con majority	17,353	29.71	
Electorate	80,957		
Turnout	58,412	72.15	

Con hold (6.64% from Lab to Con)

ELTHAM

		%	+/-%
Efford, C. Lab*	20,550	46.9	-7.4
French, L. Con	17,353	39.6	-1.1
Hasted, C. Lib Dem	2,941	6.7	3.6
Kelleher, S. BP	1,523	3.5	
Stratford, M. Green	1,322	3.0	
Lab majority	3,197	7.3	
Electorate	64,086		
Turnout	43,803	68.35	

Lab hold (from Lab to Con)

ENFIELD NORTH

		%	+/-%
Clark, F. Lab	23,340	51.5	-6.4
Laban, J. Con	16,848	37.2	0.4
Russo, G. Lib Dem	2,950	6.5	4.4
Whittaker, I. Green	1,115	2.5	1.3
Ijeh, I. BP	797	1.8	
Lab majority	6,492	14.33	
Electorate	68,066		
Turnout	45,314	66.57	

Lab hold (3.36% from Lab to Con)

ENFIELD SOUTHGATE

		%	+/-%
Charalambous, B. Lab*	22,923	48.2	-3.3
Burrowes, D. Con	18,473	38.9	-3.7
Wilson, R. Lib Dem	4,344	9.1	5.2
Balnave, L. Green	1,042	2.2	0.6
Shah, P. BP	494	1.0	
Lab majority	4,450	9.36	
Electorate	65,055		
Turnout	47,530	73.06	

Lab hold (0.19% from Con to Lab)

EPPING FOREST

		%	+/-%
Laing, E. Con*	32,364	64.0	2.2
te Velde, V. Lab	10,191	20.2	-5.8
Whitehouse, J. Lib Dem	5,387	10.7	5.0
Neville, S. Green	1,975	3.9	1.5
Hall, T. YPP	181	0.4	0.1
Newham, J. SDP	170	0.3	-3.3
Con majority	22,173	43.87	
Electorate	74,304		
Turnout	50,537	68.01	

Con hold (4.02% from Lab to Con)

EPSOM AND EWELL

		%	+/-%
Grayling, C. Con*	31,819	53.3	-6.1
Gee, S. Lib Dem	13,946	23.4	10.9
Mayne, E. Lab	10,226	17.1	-7.8
Baker, J. Green	2,047	3.4	0.6
Woodbridge, C. Ind	1,413	2.4	
Con majority	17,873	29.94	
Electorate	81,138		
Turnout	59,705	73.58	

Con hold (8.5% from Con to Lib Dem)

EREWASH

		%	+/-%
Throup, M. Con*	27,560	56.3	4.3
Atkinson, C. Lab	16,954	34.6	-8.3
Archer, J. Lib Dem	2,487	5.1	2.6
Poland, B. Green	1,115	2.3	0.9
Ball, D. Ind	388	0.8	
Shaw, R. Ind	188	0.4	
Dunn, R. Ind	122	0.3	-0.8
Con majority	10,606	21.65	
Electorate	72,523		
Turnout	48,982	67.54	

Con hold (6.28% from Lab to Con)

ERITH AND THAMESMEAD

		%	+/-%
Oppong-Asare, A. Lab	19,882	47.9	-9.5
Robertson, J. Con	16,124	38.9	3.9
Bright, T. BP	2,246	5.4	
Webber, S. Lib Dem	1,984	4.8	3.1
Letsae, C. Green	876	2.1	1.0
Mitchell, R. CPA	272	0.7	0.1
Lab majority	3,758	9.06	
Electorate	65,399		
Turnout	41,499	63.46	

Lab hold (6.71% from Lab to Con)

ESHER AND WALTON

		%	+/-%
Raab, D. Con*	31,132	49.2	-9.3
Harding, M. Lib Dem	28,389	44.9	27.6
Ashurst, P. Lab	2,838	4.5	-15.2
Keens, K. Ind	347	0.6	
Badger, B. Loony	326	0.5	0.0
Taylor, K. Advance	52	0.1	
Con majority	2,743	4.34	
Electorate	81,184		
Turnout	63,247	77.91	

Con hold (18.46% from Con to Lib Dem)

EXETER

		%	+/-%
Bradshaw, B. Lab*	29,882	53.0	-8.8
Gray, J. Con	19,479	34.5	1.7
Levy, J. Green	4,838	8.6	6.7
Willis, L. BP	1,428	2.5	
Page, D. Ind	306	0.5	
Odgers, D. UKIP	259	0.5	
Lab majority	10,403	18.44	
Electorate	82,054		
Turnout	56,413	68.75	

Lab hold (5.29% from Lab to Con)

FALKIRK

		%	+/-%
McNally, J. SNP*	29,351	52.3	13.4
Munro, L. Con	14,403	25.7	-0.5
Ali, S. Lab	6,243	11.1	-18.6
Reid, A. Lib Dem	3,990	7.1	5.0
McLaughlin, T. Green	1,885	3.4	1.7
SNP majority	14,948	26.65	
Electorate	84,472		
Turnout	56,089	66.40	

SNP hold (6.95% from Con to SNP)

FAREHAM

		%	+/-%
Braverman, S. Con*	36,459	63.4	0.5
Randall, M. Lab	10,373	18.0	-7.1
Winnington, M. Lib Dem	8,006	13.9	7.1
Lyle, N. Green	2,412	4.2	1.9
Con majority	26,086	45.34	
Electorate	78,625		
Turnout	57,536	73.18	

Con hold (3.81% from Lab to Con)

FAVERSHAM AND MID KENT

		%	+/-%
Whately, H. Con*	31,864	63.0	2.0
Reeves, J. Lab	9,888	19.6	-6.5
Perkin, H. Lib Dem	6,170	12.2	5.7
Temple, H. Green	2,103	4.2	1.3
Butler, G. Ind	369	0.7	
Con majority	21,976	43.45	
Electorate	73,403		
Turnout	50,583	68.91	

Con hold (4.25% from Lab to Con)

FELTHAM AND HESTON

		%	+/-%
Malhotra, S. Lab/Co-op*	24,876	51.9	-9.2
Keep, J. Con	17,017	35.5	3.8
Malik, H. Lib Dem	3,127	6.5	3.9
Nelson, M. BP	1,658	3.5	
Firkins, T. Green	1,133	2.4	0.8
Lab/Co-op majority	7,859	16.39	
Electorate	80,934		
Turnout	47,957	59.25	

Lab/Co-op hold (6.49% from Lab to Con)

FERMANAGH AND SOUTH TYRONE

		%	+/-%
Gildernew, M. Sinn Féin*	21,986	43.0	-3.9
Elliott, T. UUP	21,929	42.9	-2.4
Gannon, A. SDLP	3,446	6.8	1.9
Beaumont, M. APNI	2,650	5.2	3.5
Wheeler, C. Ind	751	1.5	
Sinn Féin majority	57	0.11	
Electorate	72,848		
Turnout	51,086	70.13	

Sinn Féin hold (0.76% from Sinn Féin to UUP)

NORTH EAST FIFE

		%	+/-%
Chamberlain, W. Lib Dem	19,763	43.0	10.1
Gethins, S. SNP*	18,447	40.1	7.3
Miklinski, T. Con	5,961	13.0	-11.2
Haynes, W. Lab	1,707	3.7	-5.9
Lib Dem majority	1,316	2.86	
Electorate	60,905		
Turnout	46,018	75.56	

Lib Dem gain (1.43% from SNP to Lib Dem)

FILTON AND BRADLEY STOKE

		%	+/-%
Lopresti, J. Con*	26,293	48.7	-1.1
Threlfall, M. Lab	20,647	38.3	-3.3
Harris, L. Lib Dem	4,992	9.3	3.3
Vernon, J. Green	1,563	2.9	0.6
Hardwick, E. CMP	257	0.5	
Con majority	5,646	10.47	
Electorate	74,016		
Turnout	53,946	72.88	

Con hold (1.12% from Lab to Con)

FINCHLEY AND GOLDERS GREEN

		%	+/-%
Freer, M. Con*	24,162	43.7	-3.1
Berger, L. Lib Dem*	17,600	31.8	25.2
Houston, R. Lab	13,347	24.1	-19.5
Con majority	6,562	11.86	
Electorate	77,573		
Turnout	55,322	71.32	

Con hold (14.18% from Con to Lib Dem)

FOLKESTONE AND HYTHE

		%	+/-%
Collins, D. Con*	35,483	59.9	5.3
Davison, L. Lab	14,146	23.9	-4.6
Bishop, S. Lib Dem	5,755	9.7	2.6
Treloar, G. Green	2,706	4.6	0.3
Bolton, H. Ind	576	1.0	
Menniss, C. SDP	190	0.3	
Kapur, R. YPP	80	0.1	
Thomas, A. SP	69	0.1	
Con majority	21,337	36	
Electorate	88,272		
Turnout	59,265	67.14	

Con hold (4.93% from Lab to Con)

FOREST OF DEAN

		%	+/-%
Harper, M. Con*	30,680	59.3	5.2
Martin, D. Lab/Co-op	14,811	28.7	-7.2
McFarling, C. Green	4,681	9.1	6.7
Burrett, J. Ind	1,303	2.5	1.4
Con majority	15,869	30.69	
Electorate	71,438		
Turnout	51,705	72.38	

Con hold (6.18% from Lab to Con)

FOYLE

		%	+/-%
Eastwood, C. SDLP	26,881	56.8	
McCallion, E. Sinn Féin*	9,771	20.6	-18.9
Middleton, G. DUP	4,773	10.1	-6.0
McCloskey, A. Aontú	2,032	4.3	
Harkin, S. PBPA	1,332	2.8	-0.2
Ferguson, R. APNI	1,267	2.7	0.8
Guy, D. UUP	1,088	2.3	
SDLP majority	17,110	36.12	
Electorate	74,346		
Turnout	47,370	63.72	

SDLP gain (37.85% from Sinn Féin to SDLP)

FYLDE

		%	+/-%
Menzies, M. Con*	28,432	60.7	2.1
Mitchell, M. Lab	11,821	25.3	-8.1
Jewell, M. Lib Dem	3,748	8.0	3.0
Dowding, G. Green	1,731	3.7	1.0
Higgins, A. Ind	927	2.0	
Con majority	16,611	35.48	
Electorate	66,847		
Turnout	46,821	70.04	

Con hold (5.07% from Lab to Con)

GAINSBOROUGH

		%	+/-%
Leigh, E. Con*	33,893	66.1	4.4
Smith, P. Lab	10,926	21.3	-7.3
Rollings, L. Lib Dem	5,157	10.1	3.0
Cavill, M. Ind	1,070	2.1	
Con majority	22,967	44.77	
Electorate	76,343		
Turnout	51,305	67.20	

Con hold (5.88% from Lab to Con)

GARSTON AND HALEWOOD

		%	+/-%
Eagle, M. Lab*	38,578	72.1	-5.4
Novaky, N. Con	6,954	13.0	-4.6
Brown, K. Lib Dem	3,324	6.2	3.0
Fraser, J. BP	2,943	5.5	
Roberts, J. Green	1,183	2.2	0.8
Williams, H. Lib	344	0.6	
Lab majority	31,624	59.14	
Electorate	76,116		
Turnout	53,473	70.25	

Lab hold (0.38% from Lab to Con)

GATESHEAD

		%	+/-%
Mearns, I. Lab*	20,450	53.3	-11.7
MacBean, J. Con	13,250	34.5	10.7
Maughan, P. Lib Dem	2,792	7.3	3.2
Cabral, R. Green	1,653	4.3	2.9
Lab majority	7,200	18.77	
Electorate	64,449		
Turnout	38,366	59.53	

Lab hold (11.19% from Lab to Con)

GEDLING

		%	+/-%
Randall, T. Con	22,718	45.4	2.6
Coaker, V. Lab*	22,039	44.0	-7.9
Prabhakar, A. Lib Dem	2,279	4.6	2.5
Hunt, G. BP	1,820	3.6	
Norris, J. Green	1,097	2.2	1.2
Con majority	679	1.36	
Electorate	71,366		
Turnout	50,097	70.20	

Con gain (5.22% from Lab to Con)

GILLINGHAM AND RAINHAM

		%	+/-%
Chishti, R. Con*	28,173	61.1	5.8
Stamp, A. Lab	13,054	28.3	-7.8
Bullion, A. Lib Dem	2,503	5.4	2.6
Salomon, G. Green	1,043	2.3	1.2
McCulloch, R. UKIP	837	1.8	-2.5
Cook, P. Ind	229	0.5	
Peacock, R. CPA	119	0.3	
Con majority	15,119	32.8	
Electorate	73,549		
Turnout	46,096	62.67	

Con hold (6.77% from Lab to Con)

VALE OF GLAMORGAN

		%	+/-%
Cairns, A. Con*	27,305	49.6	2.1
Loveluck-Edwards, B. Lab	23,743	43.1	-0.3
Slaughter, A. Green	3,251	5.9	5.1
Williams, L. Gwlad	508	0.9	
Con majority	3,562	6.46	
Electorate	76,508		
Turnout	55,101	72.02	

Con hold (1.19% from Lab to Con)

GLASGOW CENTRAL

		%	+/-%
Thewliss, A. SNP*	19,750	49.1	4.5
Hameed, F. Lab	13,276	33.0	-5.3
Scarabello, F. Con	3,698	9.2	-4.7
Hoyle, E. Lib Dem	1,952	4.9	2.0
Gallagher, E. Green	1,429	3.6	
SNP majority	6,474	16.08	
Electorate	69,230		
Turnout	40,258	58.15	

SNP hold (4.9% from Lab to SNP)

GLASGOW EAST

		%	+/-%
Linden, D. SNP*	18,357	47.6	8.9
Watson, K. Lab	12,791	33.2	-5.4
Kerr, T. Con	5,709	14.8	-4.0
Harrison, J. Lib Dem	1,626	4.2	2.6
SNP majority	5,566	14.43	
Electorate	67,381		
Turnout	38,585	57.26	

SNP hold (7.11% from Lab to SNP)

GLASGOW NORTH

		%	+/-%
Grady, P. SNP*	16,982	46.8	9.3
Duncan-Glancy, P. Lab	11,381	31.4	-3.0
Curtis, T. Con	3,806	10.5	-4.2
Chamberlain, A. Lib Dem	2,394	6.6	3.2
MacGregor, C. Green	1,308	3.6	-6.1
Cocozza, D. BP	320	0.9	
SNP majority	5,601	15.44	
Electorate	57,130		
Turnout	36,275	63.50	

SNP hold (6.14% from Lab to SNP)

GLASGOW NORTH EAST

		%	+/-%
McLaughlin, A. SNP	15,911	46.7	4.7
Sweeney, P. Lab/Co-op*	13,363	39.3	-3.6
Bennie, L. Con	3,558	10.5	-2.5
Moohan, N. Lib Dem	1,093	3.2	1.2
SNP majority	2,548	7.49	
Electorate	61,075		
Turnout	34,041	55.74	

SNP gain (4.12% from Lab to SNP)

GLASGOW NORTH WEST

		%	+/-%
Monaghan, C. SNP*	19,678	49.3	6.9
Ferguson, P. Lab	11,319	28.4	-7.5
Aibinu, A. Con	6,022	15.1	-2.9
Speirs, J. Lib Dem	2,716	6.8	3.2
SNP majority	8,359	20.94	
Electorate	63,402		
Turnout	39,915	62.96	

SNP hold (7.18% from Lab to SNP)

GLASGOW SOUTH

		%	+/-%
McDonald, S. SNP*	22,829	48.0	7.0
Lamont, J. Lab/Co-op	13,824	29.1	-7.4
Thornton, K. Con	6,237	13.1	-5.9
Ford, C. Lib Dem	2,786	5.9	2.6
Hutchison, D. Green	1,251	2.6	
Raja, D. BP	516	1.1	
SNP majority	9,005	18.95	
Electorate	70,891		
Turnout	47,523	67.04	

SNP hold (7.21% from Lab to SNP)

GLASGOW SOUTH WEST

		%	+/-%
Stephens, C. SNP*	17,643	47.8	7.2
Kerr, M. Lab/Co-op	12,743	34.5	-5.9
Haddow, T. Con	4,224	11.4	-4.2
Denton-Cardew, B. Lib Dem	1,435	3.9	2.0
Brown, P. BP	802	2.2	
SNP majority	4,900	13.27	
Electorate	64,575		
Turnout	36,923	57.18	

SNP hold (6.55% from Lab to SNP)

GLENROTHES

		%	+/-%
Grant, P. SNP*	21,234	51.0	8.3
Egan, P. Lab	9,477	22.8	-11.9
Thomson, A. Con	6,920	16.6	-2.9
Liston, J. Lib Dem	2,639	6.3	3.4
Farrell, V. BP	1,276	3.1	
SNP majority	11,757	28.25	
Electorate	65,672		
Turnout	41,616	63.37	

SNP hold (10.09% from Lab to SNP)

GLOUCESTER

		%	+/-%
Graham, R. Con*	29,159	54.0	3.8
Boait, F. Lab/Co-op	18,882	35.0	-5.1
Trimnell, R. Lib Dem	4,338	8.0	3.0
Byfield, M. Green	1,385	2.6	1.2
Con majority	10,277	19.04	
Electorate	81,319		
Turnout	53,964	66.36	

Con hold (4.42% from Lab to Con)

GORDON

		%	+/-%
Thomson, R. SNP	23,885	42.6	6.8
Clark, C. Con*	23,066	41.1	0.5
Oates, J. Lib Dem	5,913	10.6	-1.0
Herbert, H. Lab	3,052	5.4	-6.4
SNP majority	819	1.46	
Electorate	79,629		
Turnout	56,064	70.41	

SNP gain (3.16% from Con to SNP)

GOSPORT

		%	+/-%
Dinenage, C. Con*	32,226	66.2	4.3
Chatwin, T. Lab	8,948	18.4	-8.8
Pepper, M. Lib Dem	5,473	11.2	6.5
Aspinall, Z. Green	1,806	3.7	1.6
Con majority	23,278	47.82	
Electorate	73,541		
Turnout	48,678	66.19	

Con hold (6.53% from Lab to Con)

GOWER

		%	+/-%
Antoniazzi, T. Lab*	20,208	45.3	-4.5
O'Brien, F. Con	18,371	41.2	-1.5
Davies, J. PlC	2,288	5.1	1.5
Bennett, S. Lib Dem	2,236	5.0	3.0
Ross, R. BP	1,379	3.1	
Lab majority	1,837	4.12	
Electorate	61,762		
Turnout	44,604	72.22	

Lab hold (1.53% from Lab to Con)

GRANTHAM AND STAMFORD

		%	+/-%
Davies, G. Con	36,794	65.3	3.5
Salt, K. Lab	10,791	19.2	-7.3
Bisnauthsing, H. Lib Dem	6,153	10.9	5.4
Gayfer, A. Green	2,265	4.0	2.6
Con majority	26,003	46.18	
Electorate	81,502		
Turnout	56,308	69.09	

Con hold (5.37% from Lab to Con)

GRAVESHAM

		%	+/-%
Holloway, A. Con*	29,580	62.0	6.5
Sullivan, L. Lab	13,999	29.3	-7.1
Obasi, U. Lib Dem	2,584	5.4	3.0
Gilligan, M. Green	1,397	2.9	1.5
Con majority	15,581	32.64	
Electorate	73,242		
Turnout	47,734	65.17	

Con hold (6.8% from Lab to Con)

GREAT GRIMSBY

		%	+/-%
Nici, L. Con	18,150	120.9	78.8
Onn, M. Lab*	10,819	72.1	22.8
Barker, C. BP	2,378	15.8	
Barfield, I. Lib Dem	1,070	7.1	4.5
Emmerson, L. Green	514	3.4	
Winn, N. Ind	156	1.0	
Con majority	7,331	48.85	
Electorate	61,409		
Turnout	15,008	24.44	

Con gain (28.03% from Lab to Con)

GREAT YARMOUTH

		%	+/-%
Lewis, B. Con*	28,593	65.5	11.7
Smith-Clare, M. Lab/Co-op	10,930	25.1	-10.9
Joyce, J. Lib Dem	1,661	3.8	1.6
Killett, A. Green	1,064	2.4	1.2
Harding, D. VAPP	631	1.5	
Myers, A. Ind	429	1.0	
McMahon-Morris, M. Ind	154	0.4	
Con majority	17,663	40.49	
Electorate	71,957		
Turnout	43,627	60.63	

Con hold (6.7% from Lab to Con)

GREENWICH AND WOOLWICH

		%	+/-%
Pennycook, M. Lab*	30,185	56.6	-7.6
Turrell, T. Con	11,721	22.0	-3.3
O'Connor, R. Lib Dem	7,253	13.6	6.5
Rance, V. Green	2,363	4.4	1.4
Trivedi, K. BP	1,228	2.3	
Odesanmi, E. CPA	245	0.5	
Gaikwad, S. Ind	125	0.2	
Lab majority	18,464	34.65	
Electorate	79,997		
Turnout	53,294	66.62	

Lab hold (from Lab to Con)

GUILDFORD

		%	+/-%
Richardson, A. Con	26,317	44.8	-9.7
Franklin, Z. Lib Dem	22,980	39.1	15.3
Rouse, A. Lab	4,515	7.7	-11.3
Milton, A. Ind*	4,356	7.4	
Hugh, J. Peace Party	483	0.8	0.5
Con majority	3,337	5.67	
Electorate	77,729		
Turnout	58,803	75.65	

Con hold (12.47% from Con to Lib Dem)

HACKNEY NORTH AND STOKE NEWINGTON

		%	+/-%
Abbott, D. Lab*	39,972	70.0	-4.8
Obese-Jecty, B. Con	6,784	11.9	-0.7
Armitage, A. Green	4,989	8.7	4.1
Mathis, B. Lib Dem	4,283	7.5	0.7
Ings, R. BP	609	1.1	
Ur-Rehman, H. Renew	151	0.3	
Lixenberg, L. Ind	76	0.1	
Lab majority	33,188	58.11	
Electorate	85,058		
Turnout	57,108	67.14	

Lab hold (2.05% from Lab to Con)

HACKNEY SOUTH AND SHOREDITCH

		%	+/-%
Hillier, M. Lab/Co-op*	39,884	73.0	-6.1
Beckett, M. Con	5,899	10.8	-0.1
Raval, D. Lib Dem	4,853	8.9	3.2
Scott, T. Green	2,948	5.4	2.7
Lloyd, R. BP	744	1.4	
Leff, J. WRP	111	0.2	0.1
Lab/Co-op majority	33,985	62.22	
Electorate	83,099		
Turnout	54,621	65.73	

Lab/Co-op hold (3.02% from Lab to Con)

HALESOWEN AND ROWLEY REGIS

		%	+/-%
Morris, J. Con*	25,607	60.3	8.5
Cooper, I. Lab	13,533	31.9	-8.1
Priest, R. Lib Dem	1,738	4.1	2.2
Windridge, J. Green	934	2.2	1.2
Cross, J. Ind	232	0.6	
Fleming, I. Ind	190	0.5	
Weller, T. Ind	111	0.3	-0.2
Con majority	12,074	28.42	
Electorate	68,436		
Turnout	42,477	62.07	

Con hold (8.31% from Lab to Con)

HALIFAX

		%	+/-%
Lynch, H. Lab*	21,496	46.1	-6.6
Ali, K. Con	18,927	40.6	-1.0
Wood, S. BP	2,813	6.0	
Baker, J. Lib Dem	2,276	4.9	2.7
Jessop, B. Green	946	2.0	
Lab majority	2,569	5.51	
Electorate	71,887		
Turnout	46,592	64.81	

Lab hold (2.8% from Lab to Con)

HALTEMPRICE AND HOWDEN

		%	+/-%
Davis, D. Con*	31,045	62.1	1.3
Ayre, G. Lab	10,716	21.4	-9.5
Johnson, L. Lib Dem	5,215	10.4	5.6
Stone, A. Green	1,764	3.5	2.2
Honnoraty, R. YP	1,039	2.1	0.3
Con majority	20,329	40.64	
Electorate	71,083		
Turnout	50,028	70.38	

Con hold (5.75% from Lab to Con)

HALTON

		%	+/-%
Twigg, D. Lab*	29,333	63.3	-9.5
Rowley, C. Con	10,358	22.4	0.8
Balfe, J. BP	3,730	8.1	
Gribbon, S. Lib Dem	1,800	3.9	2.1
O'Keefe, D. Green	982	2.1	
Lab majority	18,975	40.94	
Electorate	71,930		
Turnout	46,346	64.43	

Lab hold (5.14% from Lab to Con)

HAMMERSMITH

		%	+/-%
Slaughter, A. Lab*	30,074	57.7	-6.1
Wang, X. Con	12,227	23.4	-4.7
Venegas, J. Lib Dem	6,947	13.3	8.0
Horn, A. Green	1,744	3.3	1.8
Keyse, J. BP	974	1.9	
Lab majority	17,847	34.22	
Electorate	74,759		
Turnout	52,156	69.77	

Lab hold (0.69% from Lab to Con)

EAST HAMPSHIRE

		%	+/-%
Hinds, D. Con*	33,446	58.6	-4.9
Buxton, D. Lib Dem	13,750	24.1	9.0
Austin, G. Lab	6,287	11.0	-5.9
Parker, Z. Green	2,600	4.6	1.4
Makin, J. UKIP	616	1.1	
Trotter, E. JACP	196	0.3	-0.7
Con majority	19,696	34.5	
Electorate	76,478		
Turnout	57,094	74.65	

Con hold (6.92% from Con to Lib Dem)

NORTH EAST HAMPSHIRE

		%	+/-%
Jayawardena, R. Con*	35,280	59.4	-6.0
Cockarill, G. Lib Dem	15,069	25.4	13.3
Jones, B. Lab	5,760	9.7	-7.6
Walsh, C. Green	1,754	3.0	0.4
Durrant, T. Ind	831	1.4	
Hope, H. Loony	576	1.0	
Con majority	20,211	34	
Electorate	78,954		
Turnout	59,444	75.29	

Con hold (9.64% from Lab to Con)

NORTH WEST HAMPSHIRE

		%	+/-%
Malthouse, K. Con*	36,591	61.8	-0.1
Gregori, J. Lib Dem	10,283	17.4	7.7
Bell, L. Lab	9,327	15.8	-7.7
Mitchell, L. Green	2,717	4.6	2.3
Con majority	26,308	44.45	
Electorate	83,083		
Turnout	59,188	71.24	

Con hold (3.9% from Con to Lib Dem)

HAMPSTEAD AND KILBURN

		%	+/-%
Siddiq, T. Lab*	28,080	48.7	-10.1
Luk, J. Con	13,892	24.1	-8.2
Sanders, M. Lib Dem	13,121	22.8	15.8
Stansell, D. Green	1,608	2.8	1.5
Pointon, J. BP	684	1.2	
Lab majority	14,188	24.62	
Electorate	86,061		
Turnout	57,617	66.95	

Lab hold (0.97% from Lab to Con)

HARBOROUGH

		%	+/-%
O'Brien, N. Con*	31,698	55.1	2.9
Hibbert, C. Lab	14,420	25.1	-5.6
Haq, Z. Lib Dem	9,103	15.8	3.2
Woodiwiss, D. Green	1,709	3.0	1.1
Lambert, R. Ind	389	0.7	
Con majority	17,278	30.03	
Electorate	80,151		
Turnout	57,531	71.78	

Con hold (4.26% from Lab to Con)

HARLOW

		%	+/-%
Halfon, R. Con*	27,510	63.1	9.2
McAlpine, L. Lab	13,447	30.9	-7.4
Cane, C. Lib Dem	2,397	5.5	3.3
Con majority	14,063	32.26	
Electorate	68,078		
Turnout	43,590	64.03	

Con hold (8.31% from Lab to Con)

HARROGATE AND KNARESBOROUGH

		%	+/-%
Jones, A. Con*	29,962	52.5	-2.9
Rogerson, J. Lib Dem	20,287	35.5	12.1
Sewards, M. Lab	5,480	9.6	-10.4
George, K. YP	1,208	2.1	
Con majority	9,675	16.94	
Electorate	77,941		
Turnout	57,104	73.27	

Con hold (7.5% from Lib Dem to Con)

HARROW EAST

		%	+/-%
Blackman, B. Con*	26,935	54.2	4.9
Fitzpatrick, P. Lab	18,765	37.7	-8.1
Bernard, A. Lib Dem	3,791	7.6	4.5
Con majority	8,170	16.43	
Electorate	72,106		
Turnout	49,728	68.97	

Con hold (6.49% from Lab to Con)

HARROW WEST

		%	+/-%
Thomas, G. Lab/Co-op*	25,132	52.3	-8.4
Ali, A. Con	16,440	34.2	-0.1
Bornemann, L. Lib Dem	4,310	9.0	6.5
Langley, R. Green	1,109	2.3	1.0
Jones, R. BP	931	1.9	
Lab/Co-op majority	8,692	18.08	
Electorate	72,464		
Turnout	48,080	66.35	

Lab/Co-op hold (4.15% from Lab to Con)

HARTLEPOOL

		%	+/-%
Hill, M. Lab*	15,464	37.6	-14.8
Houghton, S. Con	11,869	28.8	-5.3
Tice, R. BP	10,603	25.8	
Hagon, A. Lib Dem	1,696	4.1	2.3
Bousfield, J. Ind	911	2.2	
Cranney, K. SLP	494	1.2	
Lab majority	3,595	8.74	
Electorate	70,855		
Turnout	41,156	58.08	

Lab hold (4.76% from Lab to Con)

HARWICH AND NORTH ESSEX

		%	+/-%
Jenkin, B. Con*	31,830	61.1	2.7
Rice, S. Lab	11,648	22.4	-8.0
Beckett, M. Lib Dem	5,866	11.3	5.8
Banks, P. Green	1,945	3.7	1.7
Francis, T. Ind	411	0.8	
Browning-Smith, R. Ind	263	0.5	
Con majority	20,182	38.72	
Electorate	74,153		
Turnout	52,125	70.29	

Con hold (5.35% from Lab to Con)

HASTINGS AND RYE

		%	+/-%
Hart, S. Con	26,896	49.3	2.5
Chowney, P. Lab	22,853	41.9	-4.3
Perry, N. Lib Dem	3,960	7.3	3.8
Crosland, P. Ind	565	1.0	
Con majority	4,043	7.41	
Electorate	80,524		
Turnout	54,536	67.73	

Con hold (3.39% from Lab to Con)

HAVANT

		%	+/-%
Mak, A. Con*	30,051	65.4	5.7
Knight, R. Lab	8,259	18.0	-7.3
Gray, P. Lib Dem	5,708	12.4	6.4
Colman, J. Green	1,597	3.5	1.1
Black, A. SDP	344	0.8	
Con majority	21,792	47.42	
Electorate	72,103		
Turnout	45,959	63.74	

Con hold (6.51% from Lab to Con)

HAYES AND HARLINGTON

		%	+/-%
McDonnell, J. Lab*	24,545	55.7	-10.7
Bridges, W. Con	15,284	34.7	6.1
Cunliffe, A. Lib Dem	1,947	4.4	3.2
Boparai, H. BP	1,292	2.9	
West, C. Green	739	1.7	0.5
Amadi, C. CPA	187	0.4	
Lab majority	9,261	21	
Electorate	72,357		
Turnout	44,102	60.95	

Lab hold (8.4% from Lab to Con)

HAZEL GROVE

		%	+/-%
Wragg, W. Con*	21,592	48.6	3.2
Smart, L. Lib Dem	17,169	38.6	5.8
Wilson, T. Lab	5,508	12.4	-8.0
Con majority	4,423	9.95	
Electorate	63,346		
Turnout	44,472	70.20	

Con hold (1.26% from Lib Dem to Con)

HEMEL HEMPSTEAD

		%	+/-%
Penning, M. Con*	28,968	56.3	1.5
Ahmed, N. Lab	14,405	28.0	-8.8
Barry, S. Lib Dem	6,317	12.3	6.1
Hassan, S. Green	1,581	3.1	1.1
Con majority	14,563	28.29	
Electorate	74,035		
Turnout	51,478	69.53	

Con hold (5.14% from Lab to Con)

HEMSWORTH

		%	+/-%
Trickett, J. Lab*	16,460	37.4	-18.5
Calland, L. Con	15,280	34.7	0.9
Ali, W. BP	5,930	13.5	
Womersley, I. Ind	2,458	5.6	
Monaghan, J. Lib Dem	1,734	3.9	2.0
Roberts, M. YP	964	2.2	-0.3
Morton, L. Green	916	2.1	
Wilks, P. Ind	165	0.4	
Lab majority	1,180	2.68	
Electorate	73,726		
Turnout	44,036	59.73	

Lab hold (9.71% from Lab to Con)

HENDON

		%	+/-%
Offord, M. Con*	26,878	48.7	0.7
Pinto-Duschinsky, D. Lab	22,648	41.0	-4.9
Enderby, C. Lib Dem	4,628	8.4	4.6
Vincent-Kirby, P. Green	921	1.7	0.6
Con majority	4,230	7.66	
Electorate	82,661		
Turnout	55,252	66.84	

Con hold (2.81% from Lab to Con)

HENLEY

		%	+/-%
Howell, J. Con*	32,189	54.5	-4.5
Coyle, L. Lib Dem	18,136	30.7	15.9
Marham, Z. Lab	5,698	9.7	-10.4
Robb, J. Green	2,736	4.6	1.4
Con majority	14,053	23.8	
Electorate	76,646		
Turnout	59,040	77.03	

Con hold (10.18% from Con to Lib Dem)

HEREFORD AND SOUTH HEREFORDSHIRE

		%	+/-%
Norman, J. Con*	30,390	61.0	7.5
Coda, A. Lab	10,704	21.5	-2.3
Hurds, L. Lib Dem	6,181	12.4	5.4
Toynbee, D. Green	2,371	4.8	2.4
Con majority	19,686	39.49	
Electorate	72,085		
Turnout	49,853	69.16	

Con hold (4.9% from Lab to Con)

NORTH HEREFORDSHIRE

		%	+/-%
Wiggin, B. Con*	32,158	62.7	0.9
Howells, P. Lib Dem	7,302	14.2	2.6
Wood, J. Lab	6,804	13.3	-5.6
Chowns, E. Green	4,769	9.3	3.8
Con majority	24,856	48.44	
Electorate	70,252		
Turnout	51,309	73.04	

Con hold (0.85% from Con to Lib Dem)

HERTFORD AND STORTFORD

		%	+/-%
Marson, J. Con	33,712	55.9	-4.2
Vince, C. Lab	14,092	23.4	-5.1
Lucas, C. Lib Dem	8,596	14.3	6.2
Downes, L. Green	2,705	4.5	1.5
Lindsay, C. UKIP	681	1.1	
Percival, B. Ind	308	0.5	
Con majority	19,620	32.52	
Electorate	81,765		
Turnout	60,323	73.78	

Con hold (0.47% from Lab to Con)

NORTH EAST HERTFORDSHIRE

		%	+/-%
Heald, O. Con*	31,293	56.3	-2.2
Green, K. Lab	13,104	23.6	-4.7
Finch, A. Lib Dem	8,563	15.4	7.7
Lee, T. Green	2,367	4.3	-1.1
Con majority	18,189	32.71	
Electorate	76,123		
Turnout	55,608	73.05	

Con hold (1.26% from Lab to Con)

SOUTH WEST HERTFORDSHIRE

		%	+/-%
Mohindra, G. Con	30,327	49.3	-8.4
Gauke, D. Ind*	15,919	25.9	
Aklakul, A. Lab	7,228	11.8	-13.9
Symington, S. Lib Dem	6,251	10.2	-1.5
Pashby, T. Green	1,466	2.4	-0.2
Con majority	14,408	23.44	
Electorate	80,449		
Turnout	61,468	76.41	

Con hold (17.17% from Con to Ind)

HERTSMERE

		%	+/-%
Dowden, O. Con*	32,651	62.2	1.3
Kal-Weiss, H. Lab	11,338	21.6	-7.0
Barrett, S. Lib Dem	6,561	12.5	7.2
Humphries, J. Green	1,653	3.2	1.3
Con majority	21,313	40.62	
Electorate	73,971		
Turnout	52,471	70.93	

Con hold (4.14% from Lab to Con)

HEXHAM

		%	+/-%
Opperman, G. Con*	25,152	54.3	0.3
Grennan, P. Lab	14,603	31.5	-2.5
Howse, S. Lib Dem	4,672	10.1	3.0
Morphet, N. Green	1,723	3.7	1.0
Con majority	10,549	22.77	
Electorate	62,195		
Turnout	46,330	74.49	

Con hold (1.42% from Lab to Con)

HEYWOOD AND MIDDLETON

		%	+/-%
Clarkson, C. Con	20,453	42.9	5.0
McInnes, L. Lab*	19,790	41.5	-11.7
Lambert, C. BP	3,952	8.3	
Smith, A. Lib Dem	2,073	4.4	2.2
Ainsworth-Barnes, N. Green	1,220	2.6	
Con majority	663	1.39	
Electorate	80,162		
Turnout	47,641	59.43	

Con gain (8.32% from Lab to Con)

HIGH PEAK

		%	+/-%
Largan, R. Con	24,844	45.7	0.5
George, R. Lab*	24,254	44.7	-4.9
Lomax, D. Lib Dem	2,750	5.1	0.1
Graves, A. BP	1,177	2.2	
Hodgetts-Haley, R. Green	1,148	2.1	
Con majority	590	1.09	
Electorate	74,265		
Turnout	54,314	73.14	

Con gain (2.69% from Lab to Con)

HITCHIN AND HARPENDEN

		%	+/-%
Afolami, B. Con*	27,719	46.9	-6.1
Collins, S. Lib Dem	20,824	35.2	24.6
Tart, K. Lab	9,959	16.8	-15.7
Cordle, S. CPA	268	0.5	0.0
Marshall, P. Advance	101	0.2	
Con majority	6,895	11.66	
Electorate	76,323		
Turnout	59,137	77.48	

Con hold (15.35% from Con to Lib Dem)

HOLBORN AND ST PANCRAS

		%	+/-%
Starmer, K. Lab*	36,641	64.3	-5.6
Hayward, A. Con	8,878	15.6	-2.7
Kirk, M. Lib Dem	7,314	12.8	6.1
de Keyser, K. Green	2,746	4.8	1.5
Birchwood, H. BP	1,032	1.8	
Bhatti, M. UKIP	138	0.2	-1.0
Scripps, T. SEP	37	0.1	
Lab majority	27,763	48.73	
Electorate	86,571		
Turnout	56,977	65.82	

Lab hold (1.42% from Lab to Con)

HORNCHURCH AND UPMINSTER

		%	+/-%
Lopez, J. Con*	35,495	65.5	5.4
Lawal, T. Lab	12,187	22.5	-6.1
Clarke, T. Lib Dem	3,862	7.1	4.7
Caton, P. Green	1,920	3.5	1.6
Furness, D. BNP	510	0.9	0.4
Con majority	23,308	42.98	
Electorate	80,765		
Turnout	54,227	67.14	

Con hold (5.72% from Lab to Con)

HORNSEY AND WOOD GREEN

		%	+/-%
West, C. Lab*	35,126	57.3	-7.9
Barnes, D. Lib Dem	15,884	25.9	9.9
McGuinness, E. Con	6,829	11.1	-3.7
Francis, J. Green	2,192	3.6	1.7
Corrigan, D. BP	763	1.2	
Spiby-Vann, H. CPA	211	0.3	0.2
Wakie, S. Ind	100	0.2	
Lab majority	19,242	31.39	
Electorate	81,814		
Turnout	61,302	74.93	

Lab hold (8.92% from Lab to Lib Dem)

HORSHAM

		%	+/-%
Quin, J. Con*	35,900	56.5	-3.0
Potter, L. Lib Dem	14,773	23.3	10.9
Jones, M. Lab	9,424	14.8	-6.8
Ross, C. Green	2,668	4.2	1.2
Duggan, J. Peace Party	477	0.8	0.3
Con majority	21,127	33.25	
Electorate	86,730		
Turnout	63,549	73.27	

Con hold (6.95% from Con to Lib Dem)

HOUGHTON AND SUNDERLAND SOUTH

		%	+/-%
Phillipson, B. Lab*	16,210	40.6	-18.8
Howarth, C. Con	13,095	32.8	3.1
Yuill, K. BP	6,165	15.4	
Edgeworth, P. Lib Dem	2,319	5.8	3.6
Bradley, R. Green	1,125	2.8	1.1
Elvin, R. UKIP	897	2.3	-3.5
Lab majority	3,115	7.8	
Electorate	68,835		
Turnout	39,940	58.02	

Lab hold (10.95% from Lab to Con)

HOVE

		%	+/-%
Kyle, P. Lab*	32,876	58.1	-5.9
Nemeth, R. Con	15,832	28.0	-3.5
Bass, B. Lib Dem	3,731	6.6	4.3
Sykes, O. Green	2,496	4.4	2.7
Hancock, A. BP	1,111	2.0	
Dixon, D. Loony	195	0.3	
Sabel, C. Ind	150	0.3	
Lab majority	17,044	30.14	
Electorate	74,313		
Turnout	56,542	76.09	

Lab hold (1.18% from Lab to Con)

HUDDERSFIELD

		%	+/-%
Sheerman, B. Lab/Co-op*	20,509	48.7	-11.5
Davy, K. Con	15,572	37.0	4.1
Wilkinson, J. Lib Dem	2,367	5.6	3.0
Cooper, A. Green	1,768	4.2	1.0
Hale, S. BP	1,666	4.0	
Lab/Co-op majority	4,937	11.73	
Electorate	65,525		
Turnout	42,098	64.25	

Lab/Co-op hold (7.8% from Lab to Con)

KINGSTON UPON HULL EAST

		%	+/-%
Turner, K. Lab*	12,713	39.1	-19.1
Storer, R. Con	11,474	35.3	5.4
Hall, M. BP	5,764	17.7	
Morgan, B. Lib Dem	1,707	5.2	1.8
Brown, J. Green	784	2.4	1.1
Lab majority	1,239	3.81	
Electorate	65,745		
Turnout	32,549	49.51	

Lab hold (12.26% from Lab to Con)

KINGSTON UPON HULL NORTH

		%	+/-%
Johnson, D. Lab*	17,033	49.6	-14.0
Whitbread, H. Con	9,440	27.5	2.3
Abram, D. BP	4,771	13.9	
Ross, M. Lib Dem	2,084	6.1	1.1
Howarth, R. Green	875	2.6	0.9
Lab majority	7,593	22.13	
Electorate	65,515		
Turnout	34,315	52.38	

Lab hold (8.19% from Lab to Con)

KINGSTON UPON HULL WEST AND HESSLE

		%	+/-%
Hardy, E. Lab*	13,384	41.9	-11.1
Bell, S. Con	10,528	33.0	3.2
Dewberry, M. BP	5,638	17.7	
Nolan, D. Lib Dem	1,756	5.5	-0.9
Lammiman, M. Green	560	1.8	0.8
Lab majority	2,856	8.94	
Electorate	60,192		
Turnout	31,946	53.07	

Lab hold (7.12% from Lab to Con)

HUNTINGDON

		%	+/-%
Djanogly, J. Con*	32,386	54.5	-0.5
Sweek, S. Lab	13,003	21.9	-8.9
Argent, M. Lib Dem	9,432	15.9	7.4
Laycock, D. Green	2,233	3.8	1.9
Bullen, P. Ind	1,789	3.0	
Varghese, T. Ind	304	0.5	
Con majority	19,383	32.62	
Electorate	84,657		
Turnout	59,413	70.18	

Con hold (4.22% from Lab to Con)

HYNDBURN

		%	+/-%
Britcliffe, S. Con	20,565	48.3	7.9
Jones, G. Lab*	17,614	41.4	-11.8
Butt, G. BP	2,156	5.1	
Waller-Slack, A. Lib Dem	1,226	2.9	1.1
Brockbank, K. Green	845	2.0	
Con majority	2,951	6.94	
Electorate	70,842		
Turnout	42,543	60.05	

Con gain (9.89% from Lab to Con)

ILFORD NORTH

		%	+/-%
Streeting, W. Lab*	25,323	50.4	-7.3
Berlin, H. Con	20,105	40.0	0.5
Johnson, M. Lib Dem	2,680	5.3	3.4
Anderson, N. BP	960	1.9	
Reynolds, D. Green	845	1.7	
Akhigbe, D. CPA	201	0.4	
Lab majority	5,218	10.39	
Electorate	72,973		
Turnout	50,231	68.84	

Lab hold (3.9% from Lab to Con)

ILFORD SOUTH

		%	+/-%
Tarry, S. Lab	35,085	65.4	-10.3
Azeem, A. Con	10,984	20.5	-0.4
Gapes, M. IGC*	3,891	7.3	
Holder, A. Lib Dem	1,795	3.4	2.0
Sharma, M. BP	1,008	1.9	
Warrington, R. Green	714	1.3	0.4
Lab majority	24,101	44.92	
Electorate	84,972		
Turnout	53,655	63.14	

Lab hold (32.91% from Lab to Con)

INVERCLYDE

		%	+/-%
Cowan, R. SNP*	19,295	48.2	9.8
McCluskey, M. Lab	11,783	29.4	-8.0
Malik, H. Con	6,265	15.7	-5.8
Stoyle, J. Lib Dem	2,560	6.4	3.9
SNP majority	7,512	18.77	
Electorate	60,622		
Turnout	40,028	66.03	

SNP hold (from Lab to SNP)

INVERNESS, NAIRN, BADENOCH AND STRATHSPEY

		%	+/-%
Hendry, D. SNP*	26,247	47.8	8.0
Fawcett, F. Con	15,807	28.8	-1.7
Rixson, D. Lib Dem	5,846	10.6	-1.6
Whyte, L. Lab	4,123	7.5	-8.7
Burgess, A. Green	1,709	3.1	
Durance, L. BP	1,078	2.0	
SNP majority	10,440	19.01	
Electorate	78,059		
Turnout	54,922	70.36	

SNP hold (4.85% from Con to SNP)

IPSWICH

		%	+/-%
Hunt, T. Con	24,952	50.2	4.6
Martin, S. Lab*	19,473	39.2	-8.1
Hyyrylainen-Trett, A. Lib Dem	2,439	4.9	2.6
Thomas, N. BP	1,432	2.9	
Broom, B. Green	1,283	2.6	0.9
Con majority	5,479	11.03	
Electorate	75,525		
Turnout	49,695	65.80	

Con gain (6.32% from Lab to Con)

ISLE OF WIGHT

		%	+/-%
Seely, B. Con*	41,815	56.0	4.8
Quigley, R. Lab	18,078	24.2	1.2
Lowthion, V. Green	11,338	15.2	-2.1
Feeney, C. Ind Net	1,542	2.1	
Love, K. Ind	874	1.2	
Pitcher, D. Ind	795	1.1	
Con majority	23,737	31.78	
Electorate	113,021		
Turnout	74,689	66.08	

Con hold (1.77% from Lab to Con)

ISLINGTON NORTH

		%	+/-%
Corbyn, J. Ind*	34,603	64.0	-8.8
Wakeling, N. Lib Dem	8,415	15.6	6.6
Clark, J. Con	5,483	10.2	-2.3
Russell, C. Green	4,326	8.0	4.0
David, Y. BP	742	1.4	
Brick, N. Loony	236	0.4	0.3
Lab majority	26,188	48.47	
Electorate	75,162		
Turnout	54,032	71.89	

Lab hold (7.68% from Lab to Con)

ISLINGTON SOUTH AND FINSBURY

		%	+/-%
Thornberry, E. Lab*	26,897	56.1	-6.6
Pothalingam, K. Lib Dem	9,569	19.9	7.9
Charalambous, J. Con	8,045	16.8	-3.8
Hussain, T. Green	1,987	4.1	1.7
Hannam, P. BP	1,136	2.4	
of Bunhill, L. Loony	182	0.4	
Lab majority	17,328	36.11	
Electorate	70,489		
Turnout	47,987	68.08	

Lab hold (from Lab to Lib Dem)

ISLWYN

		%	+/-%
Evans, C. Lab/Co-op*	15,356	44.5	-14.2
Chambers, G. Con	9,892	28.7	1.5
Wells, J. BP	4,834	14.0	
Hammond, Z. PlC	2,286	6.6	-0.9
Watkins, J. Lib Dem	1,313	3.8	1.9
Linstrum, C. Green	669	1.9	
Lab/Co-op majority	5,464	15.84	
Electorate	55,423		
Turnout	34,495	62.24	

Lab/Co-op hold (7.86% from Lab to Con)

JARROW

		%	+/-%
Osborne, K. Lab	18,363	45.0	-20.0
Oliver, N. Con	11,243	27.5	2.6
Monaghan, R. BP	4,122	10.1	
Robertson, J. Ind	2,991	7.3	
Wilkinson, D. Lib Dem	2,360	5.8	3.1
Paul Milne, J. Green	831	2.0	0.3
Sadler, S. Ind	614	1.5	
Conway, M. SDP	212	0.5	
Lab majority	7,120	17.44	
Electorate	65,103		
Turnout	40,827	62.71	

Lab hold (11.31% from Lab to Con)

KEIGHLEY

		%	+/-%
Moore, R. Con	25,298	47.8	1.9
Grogan, J. Lab*	23,080	43.7	-2.8
Franks, T. Lib Dem	2,573	4.9	2.5
Khan, W. BP	850	1.6	
Barton, M. YP	667	1.3	
Rose, M. SDP	132	0.3	
Con majority	2,218	4.19	
Electorate	72,778		
Turnout	52,876	72.65	

Con gain (2.33% from Lab to Con)

KENILWORTH AND SOUTHAM

		%	+/-%
Wright, J. Con*	30,351	57.5	-3.2
Dickson, R. Lib Dem	9,998	18.9	9.4
Tucker, A. Lab	9,440	17.9	-7.7
Firth, A. Green	2,351	4.5	2.3
Green, N. Loony	457	0.9	
Con majority	20,353	38.54	
Electorate	68,154		
Turnout	52,808	77.48	

Con hold (6.29% from Con to Lib Dem)

KENSINGTON

		%	+/-%
Buchan, F. Con	16,768	38.2	-3.8
Dent Coad, E. Lab*	16,618	37.9	-4.2
Gyimah, S. Lib Dem*	9,312	21.2	9.1
Lichtenstein, V. Green	535	1.2	-0.8
Aston Colquhoun, J. BP	384	0.9	
Phillips, R. CPA	70	0.2	
Gore, H. TLW	47	0.1	
Dore, S. WRP	28	0.1	
Con majority	150	0.34	
Electorate	64,609		
Turnout	43,854	67.88	

Con gain (0.2% from Lab to Con)

KETTERING

		%	+/-%
Hollobone, P. Con*	29,787	60.2	2.4
Pavitt, C. Lab	13,022	26.3	-10.2
Nelson, C. Lib Dem	3,367	6.8	3.5
Hakewill, J. Ind	1,642	3.3	
Wildman, J. Green	1,543	3.1	0.9
Con majority	16,765	33.86	
Electorate	73,164		
Turnout	49,516	67.68	

Con hold (6.27% from Lab to Con)

KILMARNOCK AND LOUDOUN

		%	+/-%
Brown, A. SNP*	24,216	50.7	8.4
Hollins-Martin, C. Con	11,557	24.2	-2.4
McGregor, K. Lab	9,009	18.9	-10.0
Thornley, E. Lib Dem	2,444	5.1	3.0
Johnstone, S. Libertarian	405	0.9	
SNP majority	12,659	26.5	
Electorate	74,517		
Turnout	47,769	64.10	

SNP hold (5.43% from Con to SNP)

KINGSTON AND SURBITON

		%	+/-%
Davey, E. Lib Dem*	31,103	51.0	6.3
Brandreth, A. Con	20,614	33.8	-4.2
Werner, L. Lab	6,528	10.7	-4.1
Sumner, S. Green	1,038	1.7	0.8
Holman, S. BP	788	1.3	
Giles, J. Ind	458	0.8	
Chinnery, J. Loony	193	0.3	0.1
Glencross, R. UKIP	124	0.2	-0.9
Lib Dem majority	10,489	17.2	
Electorate	81,975		
Turnout	60,981	74.39	

Lib Dem hold (5.29% from Con to Lib Dem)

KINGSWOOD

		%	+/-%
Skidmore, C. Con*	27,712	56.0	1.3
Bowden-Jones, N. Lab	16,492	33.3	-6.1
Romero, D. Lib Dem	3,421	6.9	3.3
Evans, J. Green	1,200	2.4	0.4
Cowell, A. AWP	489	1.0	
Con majority	11,220	22.69	
Electorate	68,972		
Turnout	49,459	71.71	

Con hold (3.67% from Lab to Con)

KIRKCALDY AND COWDENBEATH

		%	+/-%
Hanvey, N. SNP	16,568	35.3	
Laird, L. Lab*	15,325	32.6	-4.2
Leslie, K. Con	9,449	20.1	-3.2
Cole-Hamilton, G. Lib Dem	2,903	6.2	3.8
Rutherford, S. Green	1,628	3.5	
Mitch, W. BP	1,132	2.4	1.2
SNP majority	1,243	2.64	
Electorate	72,853		
Turnout	47,005	64.52	

SNP gain (1.61% from Lab to SNP)

KNOWSLEY

		%	+/-%
Howarth, G. Lab*	44,374	80.6	-4.7
Millns, R. Con	4,432	8.1	-1.2
McCollough, T. BP	3,348	6.1	
Woodruff, P. Green	1,262	2.3	1.4
Slupsky, J. Lib Dem	1,117	2.0	-0.1
Catesby, R. Lib	405	0.7	
Lab majority	39,942	72.53	
Electorate	84,082		
Turnout	55,071	65.50	

Lab hold (1.73% from Lab to Con)

LAGAN VALLEY

		%	+/-%
Donaldson, J. DUP*	19,586	43.0	-16.5
Eastwood, S. APNI	13,087	28.7	17.6
Butler, R. UUP	8,606	18.9	2.2
Haydock, A. SDLP	1,758	3.9	-3.7
McCleave, G. Sinn Féin	1,098	2.4	-1.1
Hynds, G. Con	955	2.1	1.1
Love, A. UKIP	315	0.7	
DUP majority	6,499	14.26	
Electorate	75,735		
Turnout	45,589	60.20	

DUP hold (17.04% from DUP to APNI)

LANARK AND HAMILTON EAST

		%	+/-%
Crawley, A. SNP*	22,243	41.8	9.3
Haslam, S. Con	17,056	32.1	0.0
Hilland, A. Lab	10,736	20.2	-11.7
Pickard, J. Lib Dem	3,037	5.7	3.3
SNP majority	5,187	9.75	
Electorate	77,659		
Turnout	53,201	68.51	

SNP hold (4.62% from Con to SNP)

WEST LANCASHIRE

		%	+/-%
Cooper, R. Lab*	27,458	52.0	-6.8
Gilmore, J. Con	19,122	36.2	-1.1
Thomson, S. Lib Dem	2,560	4.9	2.9
Stanton, M. BP	2,275	4.3	
Puddifer, J. Green	1,248	2.4	1.1
Lab majority	8,336	15.78	
Electorate	73,347		
Turnout	52,833	72.03	

Lab hold (2.84% from Lab to Con)

LANCASTER AND FLEETWOOD

		%	+/-%
Smith, C. Lab*	21,184	46.7	-8.3
Thistlethwaite, L. Con	18,804	41.5	0.9
Jackson, P. Lib Dem	2,018	4.5	1.9
Murray, L. BP	1,817	4.0	
Jackson, C. Green	1,396	3.1	1.4
Lab majority	2,380	5.25	
Electorate	70,059		
Turnout	45,347	64.73	

Lab hold (4.6% from Lab to Con)

LEEDS CENTRAL

		%	+/-%
Benn, H. Lab*	30,413	61.5	-8.5
Fortune, P. Con	11,143	22.5	2.1
Thomas, P. BP	2,999	6.1	
Holland, J. Lib Dem	2,343	4.7	2.5
Carlisle, E. Green	2,105	4.3	1.8
Clouston, W. SDP	281	0.6	
Lab majority	19,270	38.97	
Electorate	90,971		
Turnout	49,444	54.35	

Lab hold (5.31% from Lab to Con)

LEEDS EAST

		%	+/-%
Burgon, R. Lab*	19,464	49.7	-11.5
Mortimer, J. Con	13,933	35.6	5.1
Wass, S. BP	2,981	7.6	
Dresser, D. Lib Dem	1,796	4.6	2.8
Adris, S. Green	878	2.2	1.2
Lab majority	5,531	14.12	
Electorate	67,286		
Turnout	39,172	58.22	

Lab hold (8.3% from Lab to Con)

LEEDS NORTH EAST

		%	+/-%
Hamilton, F. Lab*	29,024	56.9	-6.1
Bashir, A. Con	11,935	23.4	-7.6
Hannah, J. Lib Dem	5,665	11.1	7.4
Hartshorne, R. Green	1,931	3.8	2.5
Iman, I. BP	1,769	3.5	
Foote, C. Green Soc	176	0.3	0.1
Lab majority	17,089	33.49	
Electorate	70,580		
Turnout	51,031	72.30	

Lab hold (0.75% from Con to Lab)

LEEDS NORTH WEST

		%	+/-%
Sobel, A. Lab/Co-op*	23,971	48.5	4.5
Harper, S. Con	13,222	26.8	7.1
Hussain, K. Lib Dem	9,397	19.0	-15.9
Hemingway, M. Green	1,389	2.8	1.6
Webber, G. BP	1,304	2.6	
Lab/Co-op majority	10,749	21.75	
Electorate	67,741		
Turnout	49,421	72.96	

Lab/Co-op hold (1.33% from Lab to Con)

LEEDS WEST

		%	+/-%
Reeves, R. Lab*	22,186	54.9	-9.0
Dormer, M. Con	11,622	28.8	2.7
Mars, P. BP	2,685	6.7	
Walker, D. Lib Dem	1,787	4.4	2.3
Smith, V. Green	1,274	3.2	0.7
Cowling, I. YP	650	1.6	0.7
Whetstone, D. SDP	46	0.1	
Davies, M. Green Soc	31	0.1	0.0
Lab majority	10,564	26.15	
Electorate	67,727		
Turnout	40,402	59.65	

Lab hold (5.8% from Lab to Con)

LEICESTER EAST

		%	+/-%
Webbe, C. Ind	25,090	50.5	-16.2
Dave, B. Con	19,071	38.4	14.3
Dave, N. Lib Dem	2,800	5.6	3.1
Baldwin, T. BP	1,243	2.5	
Wakley, M. Green	888	1.8	-0.2
Gogia, S. Ind	329	0.7	
Lab majority	6,019	12.12	
Electorate	78,433		
Turnout	49,680	63.34	

Lab hold (15.24% from Lab to Con)

LEICESTER SOUTH

		%	+/-%
Ashworth, J. Lab/Co-op*	33,606	66.8	-6.5
Neale, N. Con	10,931	21.7	0.2
Coghlan, C. Lib Dem	2,754	5.5	2.9
Lewis, M. Green	1,669	3.3	1.0
Potter, J. BP	1,187	2.4	
Lab/Co-op majority	22,675	45.04	
Electorate	77,708		
Turnout	50,339	64.78	

Lab/Co-op hold (3.38% from Lab to Con)

LEICESTER WEST

		%	+/-%
Kendall, L. Lab*	17,291	49.5	-11.1
Wright, A. Con	13,079	37.5	6.2
Bradwell, I. Lib Dem	1,808	5.2	3.1
Collier, J. BP	1,620	4.6	
Goddard, A. Green	977	2.8	1.2
Lab majority	4,212	12.06	
Electorate	64,940		
Turnout	34,926	53.78	

Lab hold (8.66% from Lab to Con)

NORTH WEST LEICESTERSHIRE

		%	+/-%
Bridgen, A. Con*	33,811	63.0	5.0
Eynon, T. Lab	13,411	25.0	-8.3
Hudson, G. Lib Dem	3,614	6.7	0.4
Benfield, C. Green	2,478	4.6	2.6
Nudd, E. Ind	367	0.7	
Liddicott, D. Libertarian	140	0.3	
Con majority	20,400	38.01	
Electorate	78,935		
Turnout	53,665	67.99	

Con hold (6.64% from Lab to Con)

SOUTH LEICESTERSHIRE

		%	+/-%
Costa, A. Con*	36,791	63.7	2.3
Koriya, T. Lab	12,787	22.1	-6.4
Knowles, P. Lib Dem	5,452	9.4	5.2
Cox, N. Green	2,439	4.2	2.3
Con majority	24,004	41.55	
Electorate	80,520		
Turnout	57,767	71.74	

Con hold (4.34% from Lab to Con)

LEIGH

		%	+/-%
Grundy, J. Con	21,266	45.1	9.4
Platt, J. Lab/Co-op*	19,301	40.9	-15.1
Melly, J. BP	3,161	6.7	
Clayton, M. Lib Dem	2,252	4.8	2.8
O'Bern, A. Ind	551	1.2	
Peters, L. UKIP	448	1.0	-5.0
Con majority	1,965	4.17	
Electorate	77,417		
Turnout	47,147	60.90	

Con gain (12.25% from Lab to Con)

LEWES

		%	+/-%
Caulfield, M. Con*	26,268	47.8	-1.6
Henman, O. Lib Dem	23,811	43.3	4.1
Chappell, K. Lab	3,206	5.8	-5.3
Denis, J. Green	1,453	2.6	
Cragg, P. Ind	113	0.2	
Con majority	2,457	4.47	
Electorate	71,503		
Turnout	54,995	76.91	

Con hold (2.84% from Con to Lib Dem)

LEWISHAM DEPTFORD

		%	+/-%
Foxcroft, V. Lab*	39,216	70.5	-6.2
Haran, G. Con	6,303	11.3	-2.3
Dean, B. Lib Dem	5,774	10.4	5.1
Carey Fuller, A. Green	3,085	5.6	2.6
Etienne, M. BP	789	1.4	
Bui, T. Ind	130	0.2	
Lloyd, J. Green Soc	71	0.1	
Lab majority	32,913	59.19	
Electorate	80,631		
Turnout	55,604	68.96	

Lab hold (1.95% from Lab to Con)

LEWISHAM EAST

		%	+/-%
Daby, J. Lab*	26,661	59.3	-8.5
Thurgood, S. Con	9,653	21.5	-1.5
Fatukasi, A. Lib Dem	5,039	11.2	6.8
Adoo-Kissi-Debrah, R. Green	1,706	3.8	2.1
Pollard, W. BP	1,234	2.8	
Martin, M. CPA	277	0.6	0.1
Barber, M. Ind	152	0.3	
Galloway, R. YPP	50	0.1	
Mighton, E. Ind	43	0.1	
Lab majority	17,008	37.83	
Electorate	67,857		
Turnout	44,954	66.25	

Lab hold (1.07% from Lab to Con)

LEWISHAM WEST AND PENGE

		%	+/-%
Reeves, E. Lab*	31,860	60.9	-5.4
Cuthbert, A. Con	10,317	19.7	-3.2
Feakes, A. Lib Dem	6,260	12.0	5.8
Braun, J. Green	2,390	4.6	2.4
Hambro, T. BP	1,060	2.0	
Hortense, K. CPA	213	0.4	-0.2
Lab majority	21,543	41.2	
Electorate	74,617		
Turnout	52,292	70.08	

Lab hold (1.11% from Lab to Con)

LEYTON AND WANSTEAD

		%	+/-%
Cryer, J. Lab*	28,836	64.5	-5.1
Khiljee, N. Con	8,028	18.0	-2.8
Sims, B. Lib Dem	4,666	10.4	4.0
Gunstock, A. Green	1,805	4.0	1.1
Jannaty, Z. BP	785	1.8	
Scott, H. Ind	427	1.0	
Lab majority	20,808	46.53	
Electorate	64,852		
Turnout	44,721	68.96	

Lab hold (1.14% from Lab to Con)

LICHFIELD

		%	+/-%
Fabricant, M. Con*	34,844	64.3	0.9
Robertson, D. Lab	11,206	20.7	-8.1
Ray, P. Lib Dem	5,632	10.4	5.4
Muckley, A. Green	1,743	3.2	0.6
Madden, J. Ind	568	1.1	
Con majority	23,638	43.59	
Electorate	76,616		
Turnout	54,233	70.79	

Con hold (4.49% from Lab to Con)

LINCOLN

		%	+/-%
McCartney, K. Con	24,267	47.8	3.1
Lee, K. Lab*	20,753	40.9	-6.9
Kenyon, C. Lib Dem	2,422	4.8	2.1
Horscroft, S. Green	1,195	2.4	1.2
Wilkes, R. BP	1,079	2.1	
Bradley, R. Ind	609	1.2	
Shaw, C. Lib	304	0.6	
Con majority	3,514	6.92	
Electorate	74,942		
Turnout	50,763	67.74	

Con gain (5.04% from Lab to Con)

LINLITHGOW AND EAST FALKIRK

		%	+/-%
Day, M. SNP*	25,551	44.1	7.9
Kennedy, C. Con	14,285	24.7	-4.4
Milne, W. Lab	10,517	18.2	-12.9
Pattle, S. Lib Dem	4,393	7.6	4.2
Bozza, M. BP	1,257	2.2	
Mackay, G. Green	1,184	2.1	
Tunnicliff, M. VAPP	588	1.0	
SNP majority	11,266	19.46	
Electorate	87,044		
Turnout	57,880	66.50	

SNP hold (6.1% from Con to SNP)

LIVERPOOL RIVERSIDE

		%	+/-%
Johnson, K. Lab	41,170	77.6	-6.6
Malkeson, S. Con	4,127	7.8	-1.9
Crone, T. Green	3,017	5.7	2.4
McAllister-Bell, R. Lib Dem	2,696	5.1	2.6
Leach, D. BP	1,779	3.4	
Lab majority	37,043	69.85	
Electorate	80,310		
Turnout	53,031	66.03	

Lab hold (39.76% from Lab to Con)

LIVERPOOL WALTON

		%	+/-%
Carden, D. Lab*	34,538	84.3	-1.2
Phillips, A. Con	4,018	9.8	1.2
Grant, T. Green	814	2.0	0.8
Newman, D. Lib Dem	756	1.8	0.3
Lake, B. Lib	660	1.6	
Lab majority	30,520	74.47	
Electorate	62,628		
Turnout	40,981	65.44	

Lab hold (1.24% from Lab to Con)

LIVERPOOL WAVERTREE

		%	+/-%
Barker, P. Lab	31,310	72.0	-7.4
Mulhern, C. Con	4,225	9.7	-2.3
Kemp, R. Lib Dem	4,055	9.3	2.8
Heatherington, A. BP	1,921	4.4	
Inckle, K. Green	1,365	3.1	1.8
Coyne, M. Lib	501	1.2	
Lab majority	27,085	62.24	
Electorate	63,458		
Turnout	43,518	68.58	

Lab hold (37.12% from Lab to Con)

LIVERPOOL WEST DERBY

		%	+/-%
Byrne, I. Lab	34,117	77.4	-5.2
Bradley, T. Con	4,133	9.4	-0.5
Pearson, R. BP	2,012	4.6	
Radford, S. Lib	1,826	4.1	-0.6
Parr, P. Lib Dem	1,296	2.9	1.7
Ward, W. Green	605	1.4	0.6
Lab majority	29,984	68.02	
Electorate	65,640		
Turnout	44,082	67.16	

Lab hold (2.34% from Lab to Con)

LIVINGSTON

		%	+/-%
Bardell, H. SNP*	25,617	46.8	6.8
Timson, D. Con	12,182	22.3	-2.1
Kane, C. Lab	11,915	21.8	-10.9
Dundas, C. Lib Dem	3,457	6.3	3.4
Glasgow, C. Green	1,421	2.6	
SNP majority	13,435	24.54	
Electorate	82,285		
Turnout	54,738	66.52	

SNP hold (4.44% from Con to SNP)

LLANELLI

		%	+/-%
Griffith, N. Lab*	16,125	42.0	-11.4
Reay, T. Con	11,455	29.8	6.2
Arthur, M. PlC	7,048	18.4	0.2
Boucher, S. BP	3,605	9.4	
Lab majority	4,670	12.17	
Electorate	60,518		
Turnout	38,385	63.43	

Lab hold (8.8% from Lab to Con)

CITIES OF LONDON AND WESTMINSTER

		%	+/-%
Aiken, N. Con	17,049	39.8	-6.6
Umunna, C. Lib Dem*	13,096	30.6	19.5
Nardell, G. Lab	11,624	27.1	-11.2
Polanski, Z. Green	728	1.7	-0.4
McLachlan, J. CPA	125	0.3	
van Heck, D. Lib	101	0.2	
Con majority	3,953	9.22	
Electorate	63,700		
Turnout	42,863	67.29	

Con hold (13.09% from Con to Lib Dem)

EAST LONDONDERRY

		%	+/-%
Campbell, G. DUP*	15,765	39.9	-7.9
Hunter, C. SDLP	6,158	15.6	4.9
Nicholl, D. Sinn Féin	6,128	15.5	-10.8
McCaw, C. APNI	5,921	15.0	8.8
Holmes, R. UUP	3,599	9.1	1.5
McNicholl, S. Aontú	1,731	4.4	
DUP majority	9,607	24.32	
Electorate	69,246		
Turnout	39,495	57.04	

DUP hold (6.37% from DUP to SDLP)

EAST LOTHIAN

		%	+/-%
MacAskill, K. SNP	21,156	36.1	5.6
Whitfield, M. Lab*	17,270	29.5	-6.6
Hoy, C. Con	15,523	26.5	-3.1
O'Riordan, R. Lib Dem	4,071	6.9	3.8
Sisson, D. UKIP	493	0.8	
SNP majority	3,886	6.63	
Electorate	81,600		
Turnout	58,627	71.85	

SNP gain (6.07% from Lab to SNP)

LOUGHBOROUGH

		%	+/-%
Hunt, J. Con	27,954	51.0	1.2
Brady, S. Lab	20,785	37.9	-4.0
Sharpe, I. Lib Dem	4,153	7.6	4.0
Walton, W. Green	1,504	2.7	1.0
Tea, Q. Ind	235	0.4	
Con majority	7,169	13.07	
Electorate	79,764		
Turnout	54,851	68.77	

Con hold (2.6% from Lab to Con)

LOUTH AND HORNCASTLE

		%	+/-%
Atkins, V. Con*	38,021	72.3	8.4
Green, E. Lab	9,153	17.4	-9.3
Pepper, R. Lib Dem	4,114	7.8	4.1
Arty-Pole, T. Loony	1,044	2.0	1.0
Con majority	28,868	54.86	
Electorate	79,634		
Turnout	52,618	66.07	

Con hold (8.85% from Lab to Con)

LUDLOW

		%	+/-%
Dunne, P. Con*	32,185	63.8	1.0
Kidd, H. Lib Dem	8,537	16.9	6.3
Sahota, K. Lab	7,591	15.0	-9.2
Wendt, H. Green	1,912	3.8	1.7
Con majority	23,648	46.84	
Electorate	69,444		
Turnout	50,484	72.70	

Con hold (2.62% from Con to Lib Dem)

LUTON NORTH

		%	+/-%
Owen, S. Lab	23,496	55.0	-8.7
Bains, J. Con	14,249	33.3	0.4
Jack, L. Lib Dem	2,063	4.8	3.1
Sharma, S. BP	1,215	2.8	
Hall, S. Green	771	1.8	0.4
Rehman, M. Ind	646	1.5	
Laidley, S. WEP	149	0.4	
Lab majority	9,247	21.63	
Electorate	68,185		
Turnout	42,744	62.69	

Lab hold (4.55% from Lab to Con)

LUTON SOUTH

		%	+/-%
Hopkins, R. Lab	21,787	51.6	-10.7
Akhtar, P. Con	13,031	30.9	-1.3
Shuker, G. Ind*	3,893	9.2	
Warren, G. BP	1,601	3.8	
Foley, B. Green	995	2.4	1.4
Ashraf, M. Ind	489	1.2	
French, J. Best4Luton	268	0.6	
Lab majority	8,756	20.73	
Electorate	69,338		
Turnout	42,239	60.92	

Lab hold (26.46% from Lab to Con)

MACCLESFIELD

		%	+/-%
Rutley, D. Con*	28,292	52.3	-0.2
Puttick, N. Lab	17,581	32.5	-4.2
Christian, N. Lib Dem	5,684	10.5	4.4
Booth, J. Green	2,310	4.3	2.0
Con majority	10,711	19.8	
Electorate	76,216		
Turnout	54,104	70.99	

Con hold (2% from Lab to Con)

MAIDENHEAD

		%	+/-%
May, T. Con*	32,620	57.5	-7.2
Reynolds, J. Lib Dem	13,774	24.3	13.1
McDonald, P. Lab	7,882	13.9	-5.4
Tomalin, E. Green	2,216	3.9	2.4
Con majority	18,846	33.2	
Electorate	76,668		
Turnout	56,770	74.05	

Con hold (10.12% from Con to Lib Dem)

MAIDSTONE AND THE WEALD

		%	+/-%
Grant, H. Con*	31,220	60.1	3.8
Wilkinson, D. Lab	9,448	18.2	-3.9
Willis, J. Lib Dem	8,482	16.3	0.0
Jeffery, S. Green	2,172	4.2	2.5
Kenward, Y. Ind	358	0.7	0.4
Con majority	21,772	41.92	
Electorate	76,109		
Turnout	51,941	68.25	

Con hold (3.86% from Lab to Con)

MAKERFIELD

		%	+/-%
Fovargue, Y. Lab*	19,954	44.9	-15.1
King, N. Con	15,214	34.3	3.0
Wright, R. BP	5,817	13.1	
Skipworth, J. Lib Dem	2,108	4.8	1.9
Shaw, S. Green	1,166	2.6	
Lab majority	4,740	10.67	
Electorate	74,190		
Turnout	44,420	59.87	

Lab hold (9.06% from Lab to Con)

MALDON

		%	+/-%
Whittingdale, J. Con*	36,304	71.7	3.9
Capper, S. Lab	6,263	12.4	-8.9
Baldy, C. Lib Dem	5,990	11.8	7.5
Band, J. Green	1,851	3.7	1.5
Con majority	30,041	59.32	
Electorate	72,438		
Turnout	50,644	69.91	

Con hold (6.37% from Lab to Con)

MANCHESTER CENTRAL

		%	+/-%
Powell, L. Lab/Co-op*	36,823	70.2	-7.0
Jaradat, S. Con	7,734	14.7	0.6
Bridges, J. Lib Dem	3,420	6.5	3.2
Chadwick, S. BP	2,335	4.5	
Horrocks, M. Green	1,870	3.6	1.9
Leech, D. SEP	107	0.2	
Lab/Co-op majority	29,089	55.43	
Electorate	92,247		
Turnout	52,482	56.89	

Lab/Co-op hold (3.82% from Lab to Con)

MANCHESTER GORTON

		%	+/-%
Khan, A. Lab*	34,583	77.4	1.3
Lowe, S. Con	4,244	9.5	2.2
Pearcey, J. Lib Dem	2,448	5.5	-0.1
Tyrrell, E. Green	1,697	3.8	1.6
Kaya, L. BP	1,573	3.5	
Lab majority	30,339	67.88	
Electorate	76,419		
Turnout	44,692	58.48	

Lab hold (0.48% from Lab to Con)

MANCHESTER WITHINGTON

		%	+/-%
Smith, J. Lab*	35,902	67.5	-4.0
Leech, J. Lib Dem	7,997	15.0	-0.9
Zhi, S. Con	5,820	10.9	0.7
Bannister, L. Green	1,968	3.7	2.1
Ward, S. BP	1,308	2.5	
Lab majority	27,905	52.48	
Electorate	76,530		
Turnout	53,176	69.48	

Lab hold (1.56% from Lab to Con)

MANSFIELD

		%	+/-%
Bradley, B. Con*	31,484	63.7	17.1
Ward, S. Lab	15,178	30.7	-13.7
Brown, S. Lib Dem	1,626	3.3	1.9
Pepper, S. Ind	527	1.1	
Harvey, S. Ind	458	0.9	
Con majority	16,306	32.99	
Electorate	77,131		
Turnout	49,430	64.09	

Con hold (15.44% from Lab to Con)

MEON VALLEY

		%	+/-%
Drummond, F. Con	35,271	64.1	-1.5
North, L. Lib Dem	11,716	21.3	10.4
Bunday, M. Lab	5,644	10.3	-8.0
Wallace, M. Green	2,198	4.0	1.6
Con majority	23,555	42.8	
Electorate	75,737		
Turnout	55,040	72.67	

Con hold (5.98% from Con to Lib Dem)

MERIDEN

		%	+/-%
Bhatti, S. Con	34,358	63.2	1.3
Beddis, T. Lab	11,522	21.2	-5.6
McCarthy, L. Lib Dem	5,614	10.3	5.5
Caudwell, S. Green	2,667	4.9	2.3
Con majority	22,836	41.98	
Electorate	85,368		
Turnout	54,397	63.72	

Con hold (3.46% from Lab to Con)

MERTHYR TYDFIL AND RHYMNEY

		%	+/-%
Jones, G. Lab*	16,913	52.3	-14.3
Jones, S. Con	6,307	19.5	1.4
Jones, C. BP	3,604	11.2	
Evans, M. PlC	2,446	7.6	-0.6
Hughes, D. Ind	1,860	5.8	
D'Cruz, B. Lib Dem	1,116	3.5	1.0
Lab majority	10,606	32.81	
Electorate	56,322		
Turnout	32,329	57.40	

Lab hold (7.89% from Lab to Con)

MIDDLESBROUGH

		%	+/-%
McDonald, A. Lab*	17,207	50.3	-15.2
Betson, R. Con	8,812	25.8	-0.9
High, A. Ind	4,548	13.3	
Clements, F. BP	2,168	6.3	
Crawford, T. Lib Dem	816	2.4	1.4
Alberti, H. Green	546	1.6	0.9
Lab majority	8,395	24.56	
Electorate	60,764		
Turnout	34,182	56.25	

Lab hold (7.16% from Lab to Con)

MIDDLESBROUGH SOUTH AND EAST CLEVELAND

		%	+/-%
Clarke, S. Con*	28,135	58.6	9.1
Dingsdale, L. Lab	16,509	34.4	-13.0
Joy, J. Lib Dem	1,953	4.1	1.2
Brown, S. Green	1,220	2.5	
Con majority	11,626	24.22	
Electorate	72,348		
Turnout	47,997	66.34	

Con hold (11.04% from Lab to Con)

MIDLOTHIAN

		%	+/-%
Thompson, O. SNP	20,033	41.4	7.1
Rowley, D. Lab*	14,328	29.6	-6.7
Fraser, R. Con	10,467	21.6	-3.8
Arrundale, S. Lib Dem	3,393	7.0	3.2
SNP majority	5,705	11.8	
Electorate	70,544		
Turnout	48,361	68.55	

SNP gain (6.88% from Lab to SNP)

MILTON KEYNES NORTH

		%	+/-%
Everitt, B. Con	30,938	49.3	1.9
Pullen, C. Lab	24,683	39.3	-5.0
Mir, A. Lib Dem	4,991	8.0	4.1
Rose, C. Green	1,931	3.1	1.4
Con majority	6,255	9.96	
Electorate	91,545		
Turnout	62,780	68.58	

Con hold (3.44% from Lab to Con)

MILTON KEYNES SOUTH

		%	+/-%
Stewart, I. Con*	32,011	49.9	2.5
O'Neill, H. Lab	25,067	39.1	-5.8
Ahsan, S. Lib Dem	4,688	7.3	4.4
Francis, A. Green	1,495	2.3	0.5
Fulton, S. Ind	539	0.8	
Ogba, M. CPA	207	0.3	
Con majority	6,944	10.82	
Electorate	96,363		
Turnout	64,188	66.61	

Con hold (18.29% from Lab to Con)

MITCHAM AND MORDEN

		%	+/-%
McDonagh, S. Lab*	27,964	61.0	-7.5
Williams, T. Con	11,482	25.1	0.9
Taylor, L. Lib Dem	3,717	8.1	5.0
Maddocks, J. BP	1,202	2.6	
Maslin, P. Green	1,160	2.5	1.2
Coke, D. CPA	216	0.5	0.0
Lab majority	16,482	35.95	
Electorate	70,021		
Turnout	45,845	65.47	

Lab hold (4.18% from Lab to Con)

MOLE VALLEY

		%	+/-%
Beresford, P. Con*	31,656	55.2	-6.5
Kennedy, P. Lib Dem	19,615	34.2	15.0
Bostock, B. Lab	2,965	5.2	-8.7
Scott-Conte, L. Green	1,874	3.3	0.7
Horsley, R. Ind	536	0.9	
Cox, G. UKIP	464	0.8	-1.6
Con majority	12,041	21.01	
Electorate	74,665		
Turnout	57,304	76.75	

Con hold (10.72% from Con to Lib Dem)

MONMOUTH

		%	+/-%
Davies, D. Con*	26,160	52.0	-1.1
Murphy, Y. Lab	16,178	32.1	-4.4
Willott, A. Lib Dem	4,909	9.8	5.6
Chandler, I. Green	1,353	2.7	0.8
Kocan, H. PlC	1,182	2.4	-0.3
Ford, M. Ind	435	0.9	
Con majority	9,982	19.82	
Electorate	67,098		
Turnout	50,353	75.04	

Con hold (1.67% from Lab to Con)

MONTGOMERYSHIRE

		%	+/-%
Williams, C. Con	20,020	139.0	87.3
Devani, K. Lib Dem	7,882	54.7	29.6
Duerden, K. Lab	5,585	38.8	22.9
Evans, G. Gwlad	727	5.1	
Con majority	12,138	84.25	
Electorate	48,997		
Turnout	14,407	29.40	

Con hold (28.85% from Lib Dem to Con)

MORAY

		%	+/-%
Ross, D. Con*	22,112	45.2	-2.3
Mitchell, L. SNP	21,599	44.2	5.4
Kirby, J. Lab	2,432	5.0	-6.0
Campbell Trevor, F. Lib Dem	2,269	4.6	2.4
Scorer, R. UKIP	413	0.8	
Con majority	513	1.05	
Electorate	71,035		
Turnout	48,917	68.86	

Con hold (3.84% from Con to SNP)

MORECAMBE AND LUNESDALE

		%	+/-%
Morris, D. Con*	23,925	52.6	5.0
Collinge, L. Lab	17,571	38.7	-5.9
Lambert, O. Lib Dem	2,328	5.1	1.4
Buckley, C. Green	938	2.1	1.0
Clifford, D. Ind	548	1.2	
Con majority	6,354	13.98	
Electorate	67,397		
Turnout	45,448	67.43	

Con hold (5.46% from Lab to Con)

MORLEY AND OUTWOOD

		%	+/-%
Jenkyns, A. Con*	29,424	56.5	5.9
Ferguson, D. Lab	18,157	34.8	-11.7
Dobson, C. Lib Dem	2,285	4.4	1.8
Bell, C. Green	1,107	2.1	
Woodlock, D. YP	957	1.8	
Con majority	11,267	21.62	
Electorate	78,803		
Turnout	52,121	66.14	

Con hold (8.81% from Lab to Con)

MOTHERWELL AND WISHAW

		%	+/-%
Fellows, M. SNP*	20,622	46.3	7.9
Feeney, A. Lab	14,354	32.3	-5.5
Gallacher, M. Con	7,150	16.1	-4.2
Wilson, C. Lib Dem	1,675	3.8	1.6
Wilson, N. UKIP	619	1.4	0.1
SNP majority	6,268	14.08	
Electorate	68,856		
Turnout	44,513	64.65	

SNP hold (6.66% from Lab to SNP)

NA H-EILEANAN AN IAR

		%	+/-%
MacNeil, A. SNP*	6,531	44.9	4.4
MacCorquodale, A. Lab	4,093	28.2	-5.6
Ross, J. Con	3,216	22.1	5.7
Mitchison, N. Lib Dem	637	4.4	2.7
SNP majority	2,438	16.77	
Electorate	21,106		
Turnout	14,542	68.90	

SNP hold (4.99% from Lab to SNP)

NEATH

		%	+/-%
Rees, C. Lab/Co-op*	15,920	43.2	-13.4
Burns, J. Con	10,283	27.9	4.2
Williams, D. PIC	4,495	12.2	-1.7
Briscoe, S. BP	3,184	8.6	
Kingston-Jones, A. Lib Dem	1,485	4.0	2.1
Lloyd, M. Green	728	2.0	
Rogers, P. Ind	594	1.6	
Williams, C. SDP	67	0.2	
Lab/Co-op majority	5,637	15.29	
Electorate	56,419		
Turnout	36,863	65.34	

Lab/Co-op hold (8.82% from Lab to Con)

NEW FOREST EAST

		%	+/-%
Lewis, J. Con*	32,769	64.3	1.8
Hope, J. Lab	7,518	14.8	-5.0
Johnston, B. Lib Dem	7,390	14.5	-0.6
Jolly, N. Green	2,434	4.8	2.3
Knight, A. AWP	675	1.3	
Con majority	25,251	49.54	
Electorate	73,549		
Turnout	50,975	69.31	

Con hold (3.41% from Lab to Con)

NEW FOREST WEST

		%	+/-%
Swayne, D. Con*	32,113	63.5	-3.2
Davies, J. Lib Dem	7,710	15.3	5.6
Graham, J. Lab	6,595	13.0	-6.6
Bubb, J. Green	3,888	7.7	4.8
Con majority	24,403	48.27	
Electorate	70,866		
Turnout	50,556	71.34	

Con hold (4.42% from Con to Lib Dem)

NEWARK

		%	+/-%
Jenrick, R. Con*	34,660	63.0	0.5
Baggaley, J. Lab	12,844	23.3	-6.3
Watts, D. Lib Dem	5,308	9.7	4.6
Henderson, J. Green	1,950	3.5	
Con majority	21,816	39.65	
Electorate	75,850		
Turnout	55,021	72.54	

Con hold (3.38% from Lab to Con)

NEWBURY

		%	+/-%
Farris, L. Con	34,431	57.2	-4.1
Dillon, L. Lib Dem	18,384	30.5	9.2
Wilder, J. Lab	4,404	7.3	-6.8
Masters, S. Green	2,454	4.1	1.6
Holden-Crowther, B. Ind	325	0.5	
Con majority	16,047	26.66	
Electorate	83,414		
Turnout	60,188	72.16	

Con hold (6.65% from Con to Lib Dem)

NEWCASTLE-UNDER-LYME

		%	+/-%
Bell, A. Con	23,485	52.3	4.4
Greatbatch, C. Lab	16,039	35.7	-12.3
Jones, N. Lib Dem	2,361	5.3	1.6
Cooper, J. BP	1,921	4.3	
Johnson, C. Green	933	2.1	
Con majority	7,446	16.59	
Electorate	68,211		
Turnout	44,879	65.79	

Con gain (8.33% from Lab to Con)

NEWCASTLE UPON TYNE CENTRAL

		%	+/-%
Onwurah, C. Lab*	21,568	57.3	-7.4
Payne, E. Con	9,290	24.7	0.1
Avaei, A. Lib Dem	2,709	7.2	2.3
Griffin, M. BP	2,542	6.8	
Pitman, T. Green	1,365	3.6	2.0
Lab majority	12,278	32.64	
Electorate	57,845		
Turnout	37,611	65.02	

Lab hold (3.77% from Lab to Con)

NEWCASTLE UPON TYNE EAST

		%	+/-%
Brown, N. Lab*	26,049	59.8	-7.7
Gwynn, R. Con	10,586	24.3	3.0
Taylor, W. Lib Dem	4,535	10.4	4.2
Hartley, N. Green	2,195	5.0	3.2
Lab majority	15,463	35.47	
Electorate	63,796		
Turnout	43,598	68.34	

Lab hold (5.35% from Lab to Con)

NEWCASTLE UPON TYNE NORTH

		%	+/-%
McKinnell, C. Lab*	21,354	45.3	-9.9
Lehain, M. Con	15,589	33.1	-0.8
Cott, N. Lib Dem	4,357	9.3	4.0
Ogden, R. BP	4,331	9.2	
Ford, A. Green	1,368	2.9	1.8
Lab majority	5,765	12.24	
Electorate	68,486		
Turnout	47,118	68.80	

Lab hold (4.59% from Lab to Con)

NEWPORT EAST

		%	+/-%
Morden, J. Lab*	16,125	44.4	-12.1
Brown, M. Con	14,133	38.9	4.2
Price, J. BP	2,454	6.8	
Hamilton, M. Lib Dem	2,121	5.8	3.2
Wixcey, C. PIC	872	2.4	0.0
Varley, P. Green	577	1.6	
Lab majority	1,992	5.48	
Electorate	58,554		
Turnout	36,362	62.10	

Lab hold (8.11% from Lab to Con)

NEWPORT WEST

		%	+/-%
Jones, R. Lab*	18,977	43.6	-8.7
Evans, M. Con	18,075	41.5	2.3
Jones, R. Lib Dem	2,565	5.9	3.7
Edwards, C. BP	1,727	4.0	
Clark, J. PIC	1,187	2.7	0.3
Womack, A. Green	902	2.1	0.9
Lab majority	902	2.07	
Electorate	66,657		
Turnout	43,563	65.35	

Lab hold (3.1% from Lab to Con)

NEWRY AND ARMAGH

		%	+/-%
Brady, M. Sinn Féin*	20,287	39.7	-7.9
Irwin, W. DUP	11,000	21.5	-2.9
Byrne, P. SDLP	9,449	18.5	1.7
Coade, J. APNI	4,211	8.2	5.9
Nicholson, S. UUP	4,204	8.2	0.0
Kelly, M. Aontú	1,628	3.2	
Sinn Féin majority	9,287	18.17	
Electorate	81,226		
Turnout	51,120	62.94	

Sinn Féin hold (2.5% from Sinn Féin to DUP)

NEWTON ABBOT

		%	+/-%
Morris, A. Con*	29,190	55.4	0.0
Wrigley, M. Lib Dem	11,689	22.2	1.7
Osben, J. Lab	9,329	17.7	-4.5
Debenham, M. Green	1,508	2.9	1.1
Halpin, D. Ind	840	1.6	
Con majority	17,501	33.18	
Electorate	72,529		
Turnout	52,738	72.71	

Con hold (0.82% from Con to Lib Dem)

MID NORFOLK

		%	+/-%
Freeman, G. Con*	35,051	62.0	3.1
Heald, A. Lab	12,457	22.0	-8.0
Aquarone, S. Lib Dem	7,739	13.7	8.6
O'Gorman, P. Ind	939	1.7	
Con majority	22,594	39.97	
Electorate	82,203		
Turnout	56,521	68.76	

Con hold (5.56% from Lab to Con)

NORTH NORFOLK

		%	+/-%
Baker, D. Con	29,792	58.4	16.8
Ward, K. Lib Dem	15,397	30.2	-18.1
Corlett, E. Lab	3,895	7.6	-2.3
Gwynne, H. BP	1,739	3.4	
Con majority	14,395	28.23	
Electorate	70,729		
Turnout	50,995	72.10	

Con gain (17.48% from Lib Dem to Con)

NORTH WEST NORFOLK

		%	+/-%
Wild, J. Con	30,627	65.4	5.3
Rust, J. Lab	10,705	22.9	-9.1
Colwell, R. Lib Dem	3,625	7.8	4.9
de Whalley, M. Green	1,645	3.5	1.8
Con majority	19,922	42.57	
Electorate	72,040		
Turnout	46,802	64.97	

Con hold (7.19% from Lab to Con)

SOUTH NORFOLK

		%	+/-%
Bacon, R. Con*	36,258	57.8	-0.3
Jones, B. Lab	14,983	23.9	-7.0
Brown, C. Lib Dem	8,744	13.9	5.7
Price, B. Green	2,499	4.0	1.4
Con majority	21,275	33.89	
Electorate	86,214		
Turnout	62,775	72.81	

Con hold (3.34% from Lab to Con)

SOUTH WEST NORFOLK

		%	+/-%
Truss, E. Con*	35,507	68.8	6.2
Blake, E. Lab	9,312	18.0	-9.7
Ratcliffe, J. Lib Dem	4,166	8.1	3.6
Devulapalli, P. Green	1,645	3.2	
of Outwell, E. Loony	836	1.6	
Con majority	26,195	50.72	
Electorate	78,384		
Turnout	51,650	65.89	

Con hold (7.95% from Lab to Con)

NORMANTON, PONTEFRACT AND CASTLEFORD

		%	+/-%
Cooper, Y. Lab*	18,297	37.8	-21.6
Lee, A. Con	17,021	35.2	5.2
Florence-Jukes, D. BP	8,032	16.6	
Gordon, T. Lib Dem	3,147	6.5	5.1
Walker, L. YP	1,762	3.6	0.7
Lab majority	1,276	2.64	
Electorate	84,527		
Turnout	48,386	57.24	

Lab hold (13.4% from Lab to Con)

NORTHAMPTON NORTH

		%	+/-%
Ellis, M. Con*	21,031	53.0	5.9
Keeble, S. Lab	15,524	39.1	-6.0
Sawyer, M. Lib Dem	2,031	5.1	2.6
Pate, K. Green	953	2.4	0.8
Con majority	5,507	13.89	
Electorate	58,768		
Turnout	39,659	67.48	

Con hold (5.95% from Lab to Con)

NORTHAMPTON SOUTH

		%	+/-%
Lewer, A. Con*	20,914	51.1	4.3
Eales, G. Lab	16,217	39.6	-4.4
Hope, J. Lib Dem	2,482	6.1	2.6
Mabbutt, S. Green	1,222	3.0	1.3
Con majority	4,697	11.47	
Electorate	62,163		
Turnout	40,957	65.89	

Con hold (4.32% from Lab to Con)

SOUTH NORTHAMPTONSHIRE

		%	+/-%
Leadsom, A. Con*	41,755	62.2	-0.2
Kitchen, G. Lab	13,994	20.8	-6.4
Lofts, C. Lib Dem	7,891	11.8	6.2
Donaldson, D. Green	2,634	3.9	1.8
Phillips, J. Ind	463	0.7	0.2
McCutcheon, S. Ind	171	0.3	
Con majority	27,761	41.33	
Electorate	90,842		
Turnout	67,174	73.95	

Con hold (3.13% from Lab to Con)

NORWICH NORTH

		%	+/-%
Smith, C. Con*	23,397	50.4	2.8
Davis, K. Lab	18,659	40.2	-6.3
Thomas, D. Lib Dem	2,663	5.7	2.5
Holmes, A. Green	1,078	2.3	0.6
Moreland, D. UKIP	488	1.1	
Con majority	4,738	10.21	
Electorate	67,172		
Turnout	46,412	69.09	

Con hold (4.56% from Lab to Con)

NORWICH SOUTH

		%	+/-%
Lewis, C. Lab*	27,766	53.7	-7.1
Spencer, M. Con	15,006	29.0	-1.5
Wright, J. Lib Dem	4,776	9.2	3.7
Rowett, C. Green	2,469	4.8	1.9
Gilchris, A. BP	1,656	3.2	
Lab majority	12,760	24.69	
Electorate	77,845		
Turnout	51,673	66.38	

Lab hold (2.8% from Lab to Con)

NOTTINGHAM EAST

		%	+/-%
Whittome, N. Lab	25,735	64.1	-7.1
Stapleton, V. Con	8,342	20.8	-0.8
Swift, R. Lib Dem	1,954	4.9	2.3
Leslie, C. IGC*	1,447	3.6	
Smith, D. BP	1,343	3.4	
Vacciana, M. Green	1,183	3.0	1.2
Lab majority	17,393	43.33	
Electorate	66,262		
Turnout	40,145	60.59	

Lab hold (32.46% from Lab to Con)

NOTTINGHAM NORTH

		%	+/-%
Norris, A. Lab/Co-op*	17,337	48.9	-11.2
Bestwick, S. Con	12,847	36.3	5.3
Carter, J. BP	2,686	7.6	
Morgan-Danvers, C. Lib Dem	1,582	4.5	2.7
Jones, G. Green	868	2.5	1.1
Lab/Co-op majority	4,490	12.68	
Electorate	66,495		
Turnout	35,423	53.27	

Lab/Co-op hold (8.2% from Lab to Con)

NOTTINGHAM SOUTH

		%	+/-%
Greenwood, L. Lab*	26,586	55.0	-7.2
Nykolyszyn, M. Con	14,018	29.0	-1.8
Holliday, B. Lib Dem	3,935	8.1	4.9
Lawson, J. BP	2,012	4.2	
Sutherland, C. Green	1,583	3.3	2.0
Lab majority	12,568	26.01	
Electorate	79,485		
Turnout	48,315	60.79	

Lab hold (2.7% from Lab to Con)

NUNEATON

		%	+/-%
Jones, M. Con*	27,390	60.3	8.8
Mayou, Z. Lab	14,246	31.4	-9.8
Brighton-Knight, R. Lib Dem	1,862	4.1	2.1
Kondakor, K. Green	1,692	3.7	2.1
Con majority	13,144	28.95	
Electorate	70,226		
Turnout	45,405	64.66	

Con hold (9.34% from Lab to Con)

OCHIL AND SOUTH PERTHSHIRE

		%	+/-%
Nicolson, J. SNP	26,882	46.4	11.2
Graham, L. Con*	22,384	38.6	-2.8
Robertson, L. Lab	4,961	8.6	-11.4
Stefanov, I. Lib Dem	3,204	5.5	2.3
Martin, S. UKIP	382	0.7	
SNP majority	4,498	7.76	
Electorate	78,776		
Turnout	57,944	73.56	

SNP gain (6.98% from Con to SNP)

OGMORE

		%	+/-%
Elmore, C. Lab*	17,602	49.6	-12.7
Vidal, S. Con	9,797	27.6	2.5
Roach, C. BP	2,991	8.4	
Fletcher, L. PlC	2,919	8.2	0.7
Davies, A. Lib Dem	1,460	4.1	2.5
Muller, T. Green	621	1.8	
Lab majority	7,805	21.99	
Electorate	57,581		
Turnout	35,486	61.63	

Lab hold (7.62% from Lab to Con)

OLDHAM EAST AND SADDLEWORTH

		%	+/-%
Abrahams, D. Lab*	20,088	43.4	-11.0
Lord, T. Con	18,589	40.2	3.2
Brierley, P. BP	2,980	6.4	
Al-Hamdani, S. Lib Dem	2,423	5.2	1.7
Errock, P. PO&S	1,073	2.3	
Olsen, W. Green	778	1.7	
Lindo, A. Ind	233	0.5	
Lab majority	1,499	3.24	
Electorate	72,120		
Turnout	46,287	64.18	

Lab hold (7.06% from Lab to Con)

OLDHAM WEST AND ROYTON

		%	+/-%
McMahon, J. Lab/Co-op*	24,579	55.2	-9.9
Finlayson, K. Con	13,452	30.2	2.6
Formby, H. BP	3,316	7.4	
Harkness, G. Lib Dem	1,484	3.3	1.3
Jerrome, D. Green	681	1.5	0.6
Cole, D. PO&S	533	1.7	
Prince, A. UKIP	389	0.9	-3.3
Lab/Co-op majority	11,127	24.98	
Electorate	72,999		
Turnout	44,551	61.03	

Lab/Co-op hold (6.25% from Lab to Con)

ORKNEY AND SHETLAND

		%	+/-%
Carmichael, A. Lib Dem*	10,381	44.7	-3.8
Leslie, R. SNP	7,874	33.9	4.9
Fairbairn, J. Con	2,287	9.8	1.2
Drake, C. Lab	1,550	6.7	-4.8
Smith, R. BP	900	3.9	
Barnard, D. Ind	168	0.7	
Lib Dem majority	2,507	10.79	
Electorate	34,211		
Turnout	23,240	67.93	

Lib Dem hold (4.39% from Lib Dem to SNP)

ORPINGTON

		%	+/-%
Bacon, G. Con	30,882	63.1	0.2
Jeal, S. Lab	8,504	17.4	-7.0
Tweddle, A. Lib Dem	7,552	15.4	8.9
Wheller, K. Green	1,783	3.6	1.5
Con majority	22,378	45.68	
Electorate	68,877		
Turnout	48,984	71.12	

Con hold (3.61% from Con to Lab)

OXFORD EAST

		%	+/-%
Dodds, A. Lab/Co-op*	28,135	56.8	-8.3
Staite, L. Con	10,303	20.8	-1.1
Fernie, A. Lib Dem	6,884	13.9	4.8
Williams, D. Green	2,392	4.8	1.5
Carter, R. BP	1,146	2.3	
Henwood, D. Ind	238	0.5	
Artwell, C. Ind	143	0.3	-0.2
Taylor, P. Ind	118	0.2	
Lab/Co-op majority	17,832	35.97	
Electorate	78,303		
Turnout	49,578	63.32	

Lab/Co-op hold (3.58% from Lab to Con)

OXFORD WEST AND ABINGDON

		%	+/-%
Moran, L. Lib Dem*	31,340	53.1	9.4
Fredrickson, J. Con	22,397	37.9	-4.4
Sourbut, R. Lab	4,258	7.2	-5.4
Wild, A. BP	829	1.4	
Lib Dem majority	8,943	15.14	
Electorate	76,951		
Turnout	59,062	76.75	

Lib Dem hold (6.9% from Con to Lib Dem)

PAISLEY AND RENFREWSHIRE NORTH

		%	+/-%
Newlands, G. SNP*	23,353	46.9	9.5
Taylor, A. Lab	11,451	23.0	-8.8
Pirone, J. Con	11,217	22.5	-5.0
Stalker, R. Lib Dem	3,661	7.4	4.2
SNP majority	11,902	23.88	
Electorate	72,007		
Turnout	49,835	69.21	

SNP hold (9.14% from Lab to SNP)

PAISLEY AND RENFREWSHIRE SOUTH

		%	+/-%
Black, M. SNP*	21,637	50.1	9.5
Ramage, M. Lab	10,958	25.4	-9.2
Dougan, M. Con	7,571	17.5	-1.9
Clark, J. Lib Dem	2,918	6.8	3.6
SNP majority	10,679	24.71	
Electorate	64,385		
Turnout	43,217	67.12	

SNP hold (9.32% from Lab to SNP)

PENDLE

		%	+/-%
Stephenson, A. Con*	24,076	53.9	5.0
Ali, A. Lab	17,890	40.1	-6.0
Lishman, G. Lib Dem	1,548	3.5	1.4
Hales, C. Green	678	1.5	0.4
Richardson, J. Ind	268	0.6	
Con majority	6,186	13.86	
Electorate	65,292		
Turnout	44,632	68.36	

Con hold (5.51% from Lab to Con)

PENISTONE AND STOCKSBRIDGE

		%	+/-%
Cates, M. Con	23,688	47.7	4.6
Johnson, F. Lab	16,478	33.2	-12.5
Kitching, H. Lib Dem	5,054	10.2	6.1
Booker, J. BP	4,300	8.7	
Con majority	7,210	14.52	
Electorate	70,925		
Turnout	49,669	70.03	

Con gain (8.58% from Lab to Con)

PENRITH AND THE BORDER

		%	+/-%
Hudson, N. Con	28,875	60.1	-0.2
Williams, S. Lab/Co-op	10,356	21.6	-4.6
Severn, M. Lib Dem	5,364	11.2	3.4
Ross, A. Green	2,159	4.5	2.3
Davies, J. CumbriaFirst	1,070	2.2	
Con majority	18,519	38.55	
Electorate	67,555		
Turnout	48,033	71.10	

Con hold (2.19% from Lab to Con)

PERTH AND NORTH PERTHSHIRE

		%	+/-%
Wishart, P. SNP*	27,362	50.5	8.3
Forbes, A. Con	19,812	36.6	-5.6
Barrett, P. Lib Dem	3,780	7.0	2.0
Bretherton, A. Lab	2,471	4.6	-5.8
Powell, S. BP	651	1.2	
SNP majority	7,550	13.93	
Electorate	72,600		
Turnout	54,187	74.64	

SNP hold (6.95% from Con to SNP)

PETERBOROUGH

		%	+/-%
Bristow, P. Con	22,334	46.6	0.0
Forbes, L. Lab*	19,754	41.2	-6.7
Sellick, B. Lib Dem	2,334	4.9	1.5
Greene, M. BP	2,127	4.4	
Wells, J. Green	728	1.5	-0.3
Ferguson, L. Ind	260	0.5	
Rogers, T. CPA	151	0.3	
Mr P, T. Loony	113	0.2	
Con majority	2,580	5.39	
Electorate	72,560		
Turnout	47,899	66.01	

Con gain (7.47% from Lab to Con)

PLYMOUTH, MOOR VIEW

		%	+/-%
Mercer, J. Con*	26,831	60.4	8.6
Holloway, C. Lab/Co-op	13,934	31.4	-9.4
Martin, S. Lib Dem	2,301	5.2	3.2
Melling Flavell, E. Green	1,173	2.6	1.5
Con majority	12,897	29.02	
Electorate	69,430		
Turnout	44,441	64.01	

Con hold (9% from Lab to Con)

PLYMOUTH, SUTTON AND DEVONPORT

		%	+/-%
Pollard, L. Lab/Co-op*	25,461	47.8	-5.4
Smith, R. Con	20,704	38.8	-1.1
Widdecombe, A. BP	2,909	5.5	
Reed, G. Lib Dem	2,545	4.8	2.3
Ellwood, J. Green	1,557	2.9	1.7
Lab/Co-op majority	4,757	8.92	
Electorate	77,852		
Turnout	53,317	68.49	

Lab/Co-op hold (2.18% from Lab to Con)

PONTYPRIDD

		%	+/-%
Davies-Jones, A. Lab	17,381	44.5	-10.8
Trask, S. Con	11,494	29.4	2.8
Elin, F. PlC	4,990	12.8	2.5
Bayliss, S. BP	2,917	7.5	
Powell, M. Ind	1,792	4.6	
Prior, S. Ind	337	0.9	
Bishop, J. Ind	149	0.4	
Lab majority	5,887	15.07	
Electorate	60,327		
Turnout	39,060	64.75	

Lab hold (6.78% from Lab to Con)

POOLE

		%	+/-%
Syms, R. Con*	29,599	58.5	0.7
Aitkenhead, S. Lab/Co-op	10,483	20.7	-8.7
Collins, V. Lib Dem	7,819	15.5	6.6
Harding-Rathbone, B. Green	1,702	3.4	0.8
Young, D. Ind	848	1.7	
Con majority	19,116	37.76	
Electorate	73,989		
Turnout	50,620	68.42	

Con hold (4.67% from Lab to Con)

POPLAR AND LIMEHOUSE

		%	+/-%
Begum, A. Lab	38,660	62.8	-4.1
Oke, S. Con	9,756	15.9	-4.2
Cregan, A. Lib Dem	8,832	14.4	7.7
Jameson, N. Green	2,159	3.5	1.8
Cui, C. BP	1,493	2.4	
Erlam, A. Ind	376	0.6	
Lab majority	28,904	46.96	
Electorate	91,836		
Turnout	61,553	67.02	

Lab hold (from Con to Lab)

PORTSMOUTH NORTH

		%	+/-%
Mordaunt, P. Con*	28,172	61.2	6.5
Martin, A. Lab	12,392	26.9	-6.7
Harrison, A. Lib Dem	3,419	7.4	1.9
Day, L. Green	1,304	2.8	1.2
Madgwick, G. Ind	623	1.4	
Con majority	15,780	34.26	
Electorate	71,299		
Turnout	46,055	64.59	

Con hold (6.59% from Lab to Con)

PORTSMOUTH SOUTH

		%	+/-%
Morgan, S. Lab*	23,068	48.5	7.5
Jones, D. Con	17,705	37.2	-0.3
Vernon-Jackson, G. Lib Dem	5,418	11.4	-5.9
Kennedy, J. BP	994	2.1	
George, S. JACP	240	0.5	
Lab majority	5,363	11.27	
Electorate	74,186		
Turnout	47,588	64.15	

Lab hold (3.9% from Con to Lab)

PRESELI PEMBROKESHIRE

		%	+/-%
Crabb, S. Con*	21,381	50.2	6.9
Thompson, P. Lab	16,319	38.3	-4.2
Tomos, C. PlC	2,776	6.5	0.1
Hughes, T. Lib Dem	1,943	4.6	1.9
Con majority	5,062	11.89	
Electorate	59,606		
Turnout	42,572	71.42	

Con hold (5.58% from Lab to Con)

PRESTON

		%	+/-%
Hendrick, M. Lab/Co-op*	20,870	61.6	-6.3
Scott, M. Con	8,724	25.7	1.9
Sherratt, R. BP	1,799	5.3	
Darby, N. Lib Dem	1,737	5.1	1.8
Welton, M. Green	660	2.0	1.0
Lab/Co-op majority	12,146	35.84	
Electorate	59,672		
Turnout	33,888	56.79	

Lab/Co-op hold (4.12% from Lab to Con)

PUDSEY

		%	+/-%
Andrew, S. Con*	26,453	48.7	1.4
Aitchison, J. Lab	22,936	42.2	-4.4
Dowling, I. Lib Dem	3,088	5.7	2.4
Daley, Q. Green	894	1.6	
Buxton, B. YP	844	1.6	-0.6
Con majority	3,517	6.47	
Electorate	73,212		
Turnout	54,357	74.25	

Con hold (2.93% from Lab to Con)

PUTNEY

		%	+/-%
Anderson, F. Lab	22,780	45.0	4.3
Sweet, W. Con	18,006	35.6	-8.4
Wixley, S. Lib Dem	8,548	16.9	5.3
McEntee, F. Green	1,133	2.2	-0.1
Lab majority	4,774	9.44	
Electorate	65,348		
Turnout	50,586	77.41	

Lab gain (6.37% from Con to Lab)

RAYLEIGH AND WICKFORD

		%	+/-%
Francois, M. Con*	39,864	72.2	5.6
Flack, D. Lab	8,864	16.1	-8.2
Tindall, R. Lib Dem	4,171	7.6	4.8
Thorogood, P. Green	2,002	3.6	1.7
Con majority	31,000	56.17	
Electorate	78,930		
Turnout	55,194	69.93	

Con hold (6.93% from Lab to Con)

READING EAST

		%	+/-%
Rodda, M. Lab*	27,102	48.4	-0.6
Morley, C. Con	21,178	37.8	-4.4
Shepherd-DuBey, I. Lib Dem	5,035	9.0	2.9
McElroy, D. Green	1,549	2.8	0.8
Feierstein, M. BP	852	1.5	
Awolola, Y. CPA	202	0.4	
Lab majority	5,924	10.57	
Electorate	77,152		
Turnout	56,055	72.66	

Lab hold (1.9% from Con to Lab)

READING WEST

		%	+/-%
Sharma, A. Con*	24,393	48.2	-0.5
Eden, R. Lab/Co-op	20,276	40.1	-3.1
O'Connell, M. Lib Dem	4,460	8.8	3.0
Whitham, J. Green	1,263	2.5	0.6
Con majority	4,117	8.14	
Electorate	74,137		
Turnout	50,572	68.21	

Con hold (1.3% from Lab to Con)

REDCAR

		%	+/-%
Young, J. Con	18,811	46.0	12.8
Turley, A. Lab/Co-op*	15,284	37.3	-18.1
Cummins, J. BP	2,915	7.1	
King, K. Lib Dem	2,018	4.9	-1.8
Wales, F. Ind	1,323	3.2	
McLaughlin, R. Green	491	1.2	
Con majority	3,527	8.62	
Electorate	65,864		
Turnout	40,937	62.15	

Con gain (15.43% from Lab to Con)

REDDITCH

		%	+/-%
Maclean, R. Con*	27,907	63.0	10.8
Jenkins, R. Lab	11,871	26.8	-9.2
Horton, B. Lib Dem	2,905	6.6	4.0
Davies, C. Green	1,384	3.1	2.3
Con majority	16,036	36.21	
Electorate	65,391		
Turnout	44,282	67.72	

Con hold (9.98% from Lab to Con)

REIGATE

		%	+/-%
Blunt, C. Con*	28,665	53.7	-3.5
Gregory, S. Lab	10,355	19.4	-5.2
Vincent, J. Lib Dem	10,320	19.3	8.4
Essex, J. Green	3,169	5.9	1.8
Searle, J. UKIP	647	1.2	-1.7
Con majority	18,310	34.3	
Electorate	74,930		
Turnout	53,387	71.25	

Con hold (0.84% from Lab to Con)

EAST RENFREWSHIRE

		%	+/-%
Oswald, K. SNP	24,877	44.8	13.6
Masterton, P. Con*	19,451	35.0	-4.9
Davidson, C. Lab	6,855	12.3	-14.3
McGlynn, A. Lib Dem	4,174	7.5	5.5
SNP majority	5,426	9.77	
Electorate	72,232		
Turnout	55,533	76.88	

SNP gain (9.27% from Con to SNP)

RHONDDA

		%	+/-%
Bryant, C. Lab*	16,115	54.2	-9.7
Jarvis, H. Con	4,675	15.7	5.6
Cennard, B. PlC	4,069	13.7	-8.6
Watkins, J. BP	3,733	12.6	
Berman, R. Lib Dem	612	2.1	1.2
Thomas, S. Green	438	1.5	
Lab majority	11,440	38.49	
Electorate	50,262		
Turnout	29,725	59.14	

Lab hold (7.68% from Lab to Con)

SOUTH RIBBLE

		%	+/-%
Fletcher, K. Con	30,028	55.6	2.9
Snape, K. Lab	18,829	34.9	-4.4
Barton, J. Lib Dem	3,720	6.9	3.1
Fewings, A. Green	1,207	2.2	1.3
Con majority	11,199	20.74	
Electorate	75,351		
Turnout	53,993	71.66	

Con hold (3.62% from Lab to Con)

RIBBLE VALLEY

		%	+/-%
Evans, N. Con*	33,346	60.0	2.4
Bridge, G. Lab	14,907	26.8	-7.0
Seddon, C. Lib Dem	4,776	8.6	2.7
Yates, P. Green	1,704	3.1	0.7
Johnson, T. Ind	551	1.0	
Con majority	18,439	33.2	
Electorate	79,247		
Turnout	55,544	70.09	

Con hold (4.68% from Lab to Con)

RICHMOND PARK

		%	+/-%
Olney, S. Lib Dem	34,559	53.0	8.0
Goldsmith, Z. Con*	26,793	41.1	-4.0
Keen, S. Lab	3,407	5.2	-3.9
Shah, C. Ind	247	0.4	
Usher, J. Ind	61	0.1	
Lib Dem majority	7,766	11.9	
Electorate	82,699		
Turnout	65,240	78.89	

Lib Dem gain (from Con to Lib Dem)

RICHMOND (YORKSHIRE)

		%	+/-%
Sunak, R. Con*	36,693	63.4	-0.4
Kirkwood, T. Lab	9,483	16.4	-7.0
Knowles, P. Lib Dem	6,989	12.1	6.2
Yorke, J. Green	2,500	4.3	1.3
Waterhouse, L. YP	1,077	1.9	-1.8
Jardine, N. Ind	961	1.7	
Con majority	27,210	46.99	
Electorate	82,569		
Turnout	57,906	70.13	

Con hold (3.28% from Lab to Con)

ROCHDALE

		%	+/-%
Lloyd, T. Lab*	24,475	51.4	-6.5
Shah, A. Con	14,807	31.1	2.8
Green, C. BP	3,867	8.1	
Kelly, A. Lib Dem	3,312	7.0	-1.1
Croke, S. Green	986	2.1	
Lab majority	9,668	20.31	
Electorate	78,909		
Turnout	47,609	60.33	

Lab hold (4.62% from Lab to Con)

ROCHESTER AND STROOD

		%	+/-%
Tolhurst, K. Con*	31,151	59.8	5.5
Murray, T. Lab	14,079	27.0	-9.0
Colley, G. Lib Dem	3,717	7.1	4.9
Hyner, S. Green	1,312	2.5	1.1
Freshwater, R. UKIP	1,080	2.1	-3.3
Spalding, C. Ind	587	1.1	
Con majority	17,072	32.76	
Electorate	82,056		
Turnout	52,113	63.51	

Con hold (7.23% from Lab to Con)

General Election 2019

ROCHFORD AND SOUTHEND EAST

		%	+/-%
Duddridge, J. Con*	27,063	58.4	9.8
Dalton, A. Lab	14,777	31.9	-5.0
Miller, K. Lib Dem	2,822	6.1	3.4
Kumar, N. Ind	1,107	2.4	
Pilley, J. PFP	367	0.8	
Con majority	12,286	26.53	
Electorate	75,624		
Turnout	46,316	61.25	

Con hold (7.41% from Lab to Con)

ROMFORD

		%	+/-%
Rosindell, A. Con*	30,494	64.2	5.0
Leatherbarrow, A. Lab	12,601	26.5	-5.2
Sanderson, I. Lib Dem	2,708	5.7	3.3
Hughes, D. Green	1,428	3.0	1.4
Con majority	17,893	37.69	
Electorate	72,350		
Turnout	47,471	65.61	

Con hold (5.09% from Lab to Con)

ROMSEY AND SOUTHAMPTON NORTH

		%	+/-%
Nokes, C. Con*	27,862	54.0	-3.0
Fletcher, C. Lib Dem	16,990	32.9	11.8
Ransom, M. Lab	5,898	11.4	-7.7
Bentley, G. UKIP	640	1.2	
Con majority	10,872	21.08	
Electorate	68,228		
Turnout	51,577	75.60	

Con hold (7.42% from Con to Lib Dem)

ROSS, SKYE AND LOCHABER

		%	+/-%
Blackford, I. SNP*	19,263	48.2	8.0
Harrow, C. Lib Dem	9,820	24.6	3.7
Berkenheger, G. Con	6,900	17.3	-7.6
Erskine, J. Lab	2,448	6.1	-6.1
Brownlie, K. BP	710	1.8	
Boyd, D. Christian	460	1.2	
Lucas, R. SFP	268	0.7	
SNP majority	9,443	23.64	
Electorate	54,230		
Turnout	39,949	73.67	

SNP hold (2.17% from Lib Dem to SNP)

ROSSENDALE AND DARWEN

		%	+/-%
Berry, J. Con*	27,570	56.2	5.5
Barnes, A. Lab	18,048	36.8	-7.5
Valentine, P. Lib Dem	2,011	4.1	1.0
Hall, S. Green	1,193	2.4	0.8
Con majority	9,522	19.41	
Electorate	72,770		
Turnout	49,053	67.41	

Con hold (6.51% from Lab to Con)

ROTHER VALLEY

		%	+/-%
Stafford, A. Con	21,970	45.0	4.8
Wilson, S. Lab	15,652	32.1	-16.0
Cowles, A. BP	6,264	12.8	
Taylor, C. Lib Dem	2,553	5.2	2.9
West, E. Green	1,219	2.5	0.8
Short, N. Ind	1,040	2.1	
Con majority	6,318	12.94	
Electorate	74,804		
Turnout	48,841	65.29	

Con gain (10.38% from Lab to Con)

ROTHERHAM

		%	+/-%
Champion, S. Lab*	14,736	41.2	-15.1
Hickton, G. Con	11,615	32.5	6.1
Hague, P. BP	6,125	17.1	
Carter, A. Lib Dem	2,090	5.9	1.2
Bannan, D. YP	1,085	3.0	-0.7
Lab majority	3,121	8.73	
Electorate	61,688		
Turnout	35,754	57.96	

Lab hold (10.62% from Lab to Con)

RUGBY

		%	+/-%
Pawsey, M. Con*	29,255	57.3	3.2
Bannigan, D. Lab	15,808	31.0	-7.2
Das Gupta, R. Lib Dem	4,207	8.2	2.7
Stevenson, R. Green	1,544	3.0	1.2
Con majority	13,447	26.34	
Electorate	72,292		
Turnout	51,046	70.61	

Con hold (5.2% from Lab to Con)

RUISLIP, NORTHWOOD AND PINNER

		%	+/-%
Simmonds, D. Con	29,391	55.4	-1.7
Assad, P. Lab	12,997	24.5	-6.5
Banks, J. Lib Dem	7,986	15.0	7.9
Green, S. Green	1,646	3.1	0.7
Amin, F. AWP	325	0.6	
Blackwell, T. Ind	295	0.6	
Wilson, J. Ind	264	0.5	
Con majority	16,394	30.88	
Electorate	72,816		
Turnout	53,092	72.91	

Con hold (2.39% from Lab to Con)

RUNNYMEDE AND WEYBRIDGE

		%	+/-%
Spencer, B. Con	29,262	54.7	-6.0
King, R. Lab	10,992	20.6	-5.3
O'Carroll, R. Lib Dem	9,236	17.3	10.0
Smith, B. Green	1,876	3.5	0.9
Mackay, S. Ind	777	1.5	
Rowland, L. Ind	670	1.3	
Wood, N. UKIP	476	0.9	-2.4
Con majority	18,270	34.17	
Electorate	77,196		
Turnout	53,473	69.27	

Con hold (0.36% from Con to Lab)

RUSHCLIFFE

		%	+/-%
Edwards, R. Con	28,765	47.4	-4.3
Pidgeon, C. Lab	21,122	34.8	-3.2
Billin, J. Lib Dem	9,600	15.8	11.1
Faithfull, M. UKIP	591	1.0	-1.6
Kirby, J. Ind	427	0.7	
Con majority	7,643	12.58	
Electorate	77,047		
Turnout	60,756	78.86	

Con hold (0.56% from Con to Lab)

RUTHERGLEN AND HAMILTON WEST

		%	+/-%
Ferrier, M. Ind	23,775	44.1	7.1
Killen, G. Lab/Co-op*	18,545	34.4	-3.1
Nailon, L. Con	8,054	14.9	-4.6
McGeever, M. Lib Dem	2,791	5.2	0.9
MacKay, J. UKIP	629	1.2	0.3
SNP majority	5,230	9.7	
Electorate	80,918		
Turnout	53,919	66.63	

SNP gain (5.12% from Lab to SNP)

RUTLAND AND MELTON

		%	+/-%
Kearns, A. Con	36,507	62.4	-0.3
Thomas, A. Lab	9,583	16.4	-6.3
Weaver, C. Lib Dem	7,970	13.6	5.5
McQuillan, A. Green	2,875	4.9	1.9
King, M. UKIP	917	1.6	-1.7
Watchorn, A. Ind	458	0.8	
Con majority	26,924	45.98	
Electorate	82,705		
Turnout	58,554	70.80	

Con hold (2.98% from Lab to Con)

SAFFRON WALDEN

		%	+/-%
Badenoch, K. Con*	39,714	62.6	1.1
Hibbs, M. Lib Dem	12,120	19.1	5.2
Van de Bilt, T. Lab	8,305	13.1	-7.6
Wing, C. Green	2,947	4.7	
Con majority	27,594	43.52	
Electorate	87,017		
Turnout	63,404	72.86	

Con hold (2.05% from Lab to Con)

ST ALBANS

		%	+/-%
Cooper, D. Lib Dem	28,867	50.0	17.7
Main, A. Con*	22,574	39.1	-3.9
Lury, R. Lab	5,000	8.7	-14.3
Grover, S. Green	1,004	1.7	0.3
Sherrington, J. Ind	154	0.3	
Lib Dem majority	6,293	10.89	
Electorate	73,727		
Turnout	57,772	78.36	

Lib Dem gain (10.8% from Con to Lib Dem)

ST AUSTELL AND NEWQUAY

		%	+/-%
Double, S. Con*	31,273	55.9	6.6
Owen, F. Lab	14,747	26.4	-2.5
Styles, T. Lib Dem	5,861	10.5	-10.9
Cole, D. MK	1,660	3.0	
Harker, C. Green	1,609	2.9	
Byrne, R. Lib	626	1.1	
Con majority	16,526	29.56	
Electorate	79,930		
Turnout	55,916	69.96	

Con hold (4.55% from Lab to Con)

ST HELENS NORTH

		%	+/-%
McGinn, C. Lab*	24,870	52.1	-11.5
Charles, J. Con	12,661	26.5	-0.5
Webster, M. BP	5,396	11.3	
Moloney, P. Lib Dem	2,668	5.6	3.0
van der Burg, D. Green	1,966	4.1	1.7
Lab majority	12,209	25.58	
Electorate	75,593		
Turnout	47,728	63.14	

Lab hold (5.51% from Lab to Con)

ST HELENS SOUTH AND WHISTON

		%	+/-%
Rimmer, M. Lab*	29,457	58.5	-9.3
Short, R. Con	10,299	20.5	-1.3
Oxley, D. BP	5,353	10.6	
Spencer, B. Lib Dem	2,882	5.7	1.8
Taylor, K. Green	2,249	4.5	1.8
Lab majority	19,122	37.96	
Electorate	79,058		
Turnout	50,369	63.71	

Lab hold (3.97% from Lab to Con)

ST IVES

		%	+/-%
Thomas, D. Con*	25,365	49.2	6.1
George, A. Lib Dem	21,085	40.9	-1.6
Bates, A. Lab	3,553	6.9	-7.3
Flindall, I. Green	964	1.9	
Smith, R. Lib	314	0.6	
Harris, J. Common People	132	0.3	
Con majority	4,284	8.31	
Electorate	68,795		
Turnout	51,524	74.89	

Con hold ()

SALFORD AND ECCLES

		%	+/-%
Long Bailey, R. Lab*	28,755	56.6	-8.7
Choudhary, A. Con	12,428	24.5	-0.8
Mickler, M. BP	4,290	8.4	
Overend, J. Lib Dem	3,099	6.1	3.4
Blears, B. Green	2,060	4.1	2.4
Lab majority	16,327	32.14	
Electorate	82,202		
Turnout	50,804	61.80	

Lab hold (3.97% from Lab to Con)

SALISBURY

		%	+/-%
Glen, J. Con*	30,280	56.2	-1.8
Charleston, V. Lib Dem	10,544	19.6	8.4
Corbin, T. Lab	9,675	18.0	-7.6
Page, R. Green	2,486	4.6	2.5
Pendragon, K. Ind	745	1.4	0.6
Con majority	19,736	36.62	
Electorate	74,556		
Turnout	53,898	72.29	

Con hold (5.07% from Con to Lib Dem)

SCARBOROUGH AND WHITBY

		%	+/-%
Goodwill, R. Con*	27,593	55.3	7.0
Fearnley, H. Lab	17,323	34.7	-6.8
Lockwood, G. Lib Dem	3,038	6.1	3.4
Derrick, L. YP	1,770	3.6	2.8
Con majority	10,270	20.57	
Electorate	74,404		
Turnout	49,921	67.09	

Con hold (6.89% from Lab to Con)

SCUNTHORPE

		%	+/-%
Mumby-Croft, H. Con	20,306	53.7	10.3
Dakin, N. Lab*	13,855	36.6	-15.3
Gorman, J. BP	2,044	5.4	
Downes, R. Lib Dem	875	2.3	0.9
Dennington, P. Green	670	1.8	
Con majority	6,451	17.05	
Electorate	61,955		
Turnout	37,834	61.07	

Con gain (12.78% from Lab to Con)

SEDGEFIELD

		%	+/-%
Howell, P. Con	19,609	47.1	8.3
Wilson, P. Lab*	15,096	36.2	-17.1
Bull, D. BP	3,518	8.4	
Welsh, D. Lib Dem	1,955	4.7	2.8
Furness, J. Green	994	2.4	0.7
Joyce, M. Ind	394	1.0	
Con majority	4,513	10.83	
Electorate	64,325		
Turnout	41,664	64.77	

Con gain (12.69% from Lab to Con)

SEFTON CENTRAL

		%	+/-%
Esterson, B. Lab*	29,254	57.3	-5.6
Mughal, W. Con	14,132	27.7	-5.3
Cawdron, K. Lib Dem	3,386	6.6	4.0
Lomas, P. BP	2,425	4.8	
Gibbon, A. Green	1,261	2.5	1.2
Preston, A. Lib	285	0.6	
Burns, C. Renew	137	0.3	
Lab majority	15,122	29.63	
Electorate	69,760		
Turnout	51,033	73.16	

Lab hold (0.14% from Lab to Con)

SELBY AND AINSTY

		%	+/-%
Adams, N. Con*	33,995	60.1	1.5
Rofidi, M. Lab	13,858	24.5	-9.6
Macy, K. Lib Dem	4,842	8.6	4.5
Jordan, M. YP	1,900	3.4	
Warneken, A. Green	1,823	3.2	
Con majority	20,137	35.57	
Electorate	78,398		
Turnout	56,609	72.21	

Con hold (5.54% from Lab to Con)

SEVENOAKS

		%	+/-%
Trott, L. Con	30,932	60.4	-3.1
Willis, G. Lib Dem	10,114	19.8	11.4
McCauley, S. Lab	6,946	13.6	-7.3
Wharton, P. Green	1,974	3.9	0.6
Furse, P. Ind	695	1.4	
Finch, S. Libertarian	295	0.6	
Con majority	20,818	40.66	
Electorate	71,757		
Turnout	51,200	71.35	

Con hold (7.28% from Con to Lib Dem)

SHEFFIELD, BRIGHTSIDE AND HILLSBOROUGH

		%	+/-%
Furniss, G. Lab*	22,369	56.3	-10.9
Westropp, H. Con	10,095	25.4	3.8
Johnson, J. BP	3,855	9.7	
Porter, S. Lib Dem	1,517	3.8	1.3
Gilligan Kubo, C. Green	1,179	3.0	1.2
Harper, S. UKIP	585	1.5	-4.8
Lab majority	12,274	30.9	
Electorate	69,333		
Turnout	39,722	57.29	

Lab hold (7.37% from Lab to Con)

SHEFFIELD CENTRAL

		%	+/-%
Blomfield, P. Lab*	33,968	66.4	-4.3
Silvester-Hall, J. Con	6,695	13.1	0.2
Teal, A. Green	4,570	8.9	0.9
Ross, C. Lib Dem	3,237	6.3	1.2
Ward, P. BP	1,969	3.9	
Carrington, J. YP	416	0.8	0.4
James, B. Ind	30	0.1	
Marsden, C. SEP	28	0.1	
Lab majority	27,273	53.32	
Electorate	89,849		
Turnout	51,146	56.92	

Lab hold (2.24% from Lab to Con)

SHEFFIELD, HALLAM

		%	+/-%
Blake, O. Lab	19,709	34.6	-3.8
Gordon, L. Lib Dem	18,997	33.3	-1.3
Walker, I. Con	14,696	25.8	2.0
Thomas, N. Green	1,630	2.9	1.4
McHale, T. BP	1,562	2.7	
Virgo, M. UKIP	168	0.3	-1.3
Aspden, E. Ind	123	0.2	
Lab majority	712	1.25	
Electorate	72,763		
Turnout	57,035	78.38	

Lab hold (1.24% from Lab to Lib Dem)

SHEFFIELD HEELEY

		%	+/-%
Haigh, L. Lab*	21,475	50.1	-9.7
Gregory, G. Con	12,955	30.3	1.6
Knowles, T. BP	3,538	8.3	
Clement-Jones, S. Lib Dem	2,916	6.8	2.3
Turpin, P. Green	1,811	4.2	2.1
Lab majority	8,520	19.89	
Electorate	66,940		
Turnout	42,827	63.98	

Lab hold (5.66% from Lab to Con)

SHEFFIELD SOUTH EAST

		%	+/-%
Betts, C. Lab*	19,359	45.9	-12.5
Bayliss, M. Con	15,070	35.8	4.4
Kus, K. BP	4,478	10.6	
Chowdhury, R. Lib Dem	2,125	5.0	1.8
Martin, A. YP	966	2.3	
Lab majority	4,289	10.18	
Electorate	67,832		
Turnout	42,144	62.13	

Lab hold (8.42% from Lab to Con)

SHERWOOD

		%	+/-%
Spencer, M. Con*	32,049	60.6	9.2
Hague, J. Lab	15,863	30.0	-11.7
Ball, T. Lib Dem	2,883	5.5	3.4
Cropper, E. Green	1,214	2.3	1.1
Rood, S. Ind	700	1.3	
Con majority	16,186	30.6	
Electorate	77,888		
Turnout	52,892	67.91	

Con hold (10.44% from Lab to Con)

SHIPLEY

		%	+/-%
Davies, P. Con*	27,437	50.6	-0.7
Pike, J. Lab	21,195	39.1	-3.4
Jones, C. Lib Dem	3,188	5.9	1.8
Hickson, C. Green	1,301	2.4	
Longhorn, D. YP	883	1.6	
Con majority	6,242	11.5	
Electorate	74,029		
Turnout	54,262	73.30	

Con hold (1.38% from Lab to Con)

SHREWSBURY AND ATCHAM

		%	+/-%
Kawczynski, D. Con*	31,021	52.3	2.5
Buckley, J. Lab	19,804	33.4	-5.1
Green, N. Lib Dem	5,906	10.0	2.7
Dean, J. Green	1,762	3.0	1.1
Locke, H. Ind	572	1.0	
Con majority	11,217	18.92	
Electorate	82,238		
Turnout	59,282	72.09	

Con hold (3.78% from Lab to Con)

NORTH SHROPSHIRE

		%	+/-%
Paterson, O. Con*	35,444	62.5	2.1
Currie, G. Lab	12,495	22.0	-9.0
Morgan, H. Lib Dem	5,643	10.0	4.7
Adams, J. Green	1,790	3.2	0.1
Jones, R. Shropshire	1,141	2.0	
Con majority	22,949	40.46	
Electorate	83,258		
Turnout	56,718	68.12	

Con hold (5.56% from Lab to Con)

SITTINGBOURNE AND SHEPPEY

		%	+/-%
Henderson, G. Con*	34,742	67.5	7.4
Johnson, C. Lab	10,263	19.9	-10.6
Martin, B. Lib Dem	3,213	6.2	3.5
Bonney, M. Ind	1,257	2.4	
Collins, S. Green	1,188	2.3	1.2
Young, M. Loony	404	0.8	
McCall, L. Ind	327	0.6	0.1
Con majority	24,479	47.53	
Electorate	83,917		
Turnout	51,497	61.37	

Con hold (8.99% from Lab to Con)

SKIPTON AND RIPON

		%	+/-%
Smith, J. Con*	34,919	59.2	-3.2
McDaid, B. Lab	11,225	19.0	-9.2
Murday, A. Lib Dem	8,701	14.8	
Brown, A. Green	2,748	4.7	-1.7
Render, J. YP	1,131	1.9	-0.7
Con majority	23,694	40.18	
Electorate	78,673		
Turnout	58,963	74.95	

Con hold (2.96% from Lab to Con)

SLEAFORD AND NORTH HYKEHAM

		%	+/-%
Johnson, C. Con*	44,683	66.9	2.8
Edwards-Shea, L. Lab	12,118	18.1	-7.7
Craven, O. Lib Dem	5,355	8.0	3.9
Overton, M. Lincs Ind	1,999	3.0	
Tooke, S. Green	1,742	2.6	1.1
Coram, C. Ind	657	1.0	
Con majority	32,565	48.76	
Electorate	94,761		
Turnout	66,790	70.48	

Con hold (5.24% from Lab to Con)

SLOUGH

		%	+/-%
Dhesi, T. Lab*	29,421	57.5	-5.3
Toor Gill, K. Con	15,781	30.8	-0.7
Chahal, A. Lib Dem	3,357	6.6	4.2
Gray-Fisk, D. BP	1,432	2.8	
Edmonds, J. Green	1,047	2.1	
Lab majority	13,640	26.64	
Electorate	73,102		
Turnout	51,193	70.03	

Lab hold (2.29% from Lab to Con)

SOLIHULL

		%	+/-%
Knight, J. Con*	32,309	58.2	0.2
Stephens, N. Lab/Co-op	11,036	19.9	-2.0
Adeyemo, A. Lib Dem	9,977	18.0	2.3
Sexton, R. Green	2,022	3.6	1.6
Con majority	21,273	38.29	
Electorate	78,760		
Turnout	55,553	70.53	

Con hold (1.06% from Lab to Con)

NORTH SOMERSET

		%	+/-%
Fox, L. Con*	32,801	52.7	-1.5
Young, H. Lab	15,265	24.5	-2.1
Cartman, A. Lib Dem	11,051	17.7	8.1
Neve, P. Green	2,938	4.7	1.5
Con majority	17,536	28.15	
Electorate	80,194		
Turnout	62,296	77.68	

Con hold (0.31% from Lab to Con)

NORTH EAST SOMERSET

		%	+/-%
Rees-Mogg, J. Con*	28,360	50.2	-3.3
Huband, M. Lab	13,631	24.1	-10.5
Coates, N. Lib Dem	12,422	22.0	13.8
Whitfield, F. Green	1,423	2.5	0.2
Hughes, S. Ind	472	0.8	-0.3
Con majority	14,729	26.08	
Electorate	73,692		
Turnout	56,477	76.64	

Con hold (3.59% from Lab to Con)

SOMERTON AND FROME

		%	+/-%
Warburton, D. Con*	36,230	55.6	-1.0
Boyden, A. Lib Dem	17,017	26.1	5.3
Dromgoole, S. Lab	8,354	12.8	-4.4
Dexter, A. Green	3,295	5.1	1.4
Con majority	19,213	29.5	
Electorate	85,866		
Turnout	65,121	75.84	

Con hold (3.15% from Con to Lib Dem)

SOUTH HOLLAND AND THE DEEPINGS

		%	+/-%
Hayes, J. Con*	37,338	75.6	5.8
Popple, M. Lab	6,500	13.2	-7.2
Kirby, D. Lib Dem	3,225	6.5	3.7
Blake, M. Green	1,613	3.3	1.5
Stringer, R. Ind	503	1.0	0.3
Con majority	30,838	62.45	
Electorate	75,975		
Turnout	49,381	65.00	

Con hold (6.53% from Lab to Con)

SOUTH SHIELDS

		%	+/-%
Lewell-Buck, E. Lab*	17,273	45.5	-15.9
Oviri, O. Con	7,688	20.3	-5.6
Thompson, G. BP	6,446	17.0	
Thompson, G. Ind	3,658	9.6	
Shepherd, B. Lib Dem	1,514	4.0	2.3
McKeown, S. Green	1,303	3.4	-0.1
Lab majority	9,585	25.25	
Electorate	62,793		
Turnout	37,962	60.46	

Lab hold (5.13% from Lab to Con)

SOUTHAMPTON ITCHEN

		%	+/-%
Smith, R. Con*	23,952	50.4	3.9
Letts, S. Lab	19,454	40.9	-5.5
Jarvis, L. Lib Dem	2,503	5.3	2.2
Sen-Chadun, O. Green	1,040	2.2	0.6
Rose, K. UKIP	472	1.0	-1.4
Con majority	4,498	9.46	
Electorate	72,299		
Turnout	47,558	65.78	

Con hold (4.69% from Lab to Con)

SOUTHAMPTON TEST

		%	+/-%
Whitehead, A. Lab*	22,256	49.3	-9.2
Galton, S. Con	16,043	35.6	1.5
Richards, J. Lib Dem	3,449	7.6	3.6
Crook, P. BP	1,591	3.5	
Barbour, K. Green	1,433	3.2	
Barry, K. Ind	222	0.5	
Lab majority	6,213	13.77	
Electorate	70,116		
Turnout	45,116	64.34	

Lab hold (5.35% from Lab to Con)

SOUTHEND WEST

		%	+/-%
Amess, D. Con*	27,555	58.9	3.8
Line, A. Lab	13,096	28.0	-6.0
Stimson, N. Lib Dem	5,312	11.4	6.9
Joseph, 7. Ind	574	1.2	0.8
Con majority	14,459	30.9	
Electorate	69,043		
Turnout	46,797	67.78	

Con hold (4.88% from Lab to Con)

SOUTHPORT

		%	+/-%
Moore, D. Con*	22,914	47.4	8.8
Savage, L. Lab	18,767	38.8	6.3
Wright, J. Lib Dem	6,499	13.4	-12.9
Con majority	4,147	8.57	
Electorate	70,837		
Turnout	48,370	68.28	

Con hold (1.25% from Lab to Con)

SPELTHORNE

		%	+/-%
Kwarteng, K. Con*	29,141	58.5	1.4
Mann, P. Lab	10,748	21.6	-8.8
Campanale, D. Lib Dem	7,499	15.1	9.6
Jacobs, P. Green	2,122	4.3	2.1
Con majority	18,393	36.95	
Electorate	70,929		
Turnout	49,783	70.19	

Con hold (5.11% from Lab to Con)

STAFFORD

		%	+/-%
Clarke, T. Con	29,992	58.4	3.8
Still, J. Lab	15,615	30.4	-9.4
Wagner, A. Lib Dem	3,175	6.2	3.2
Carter, E. Green	2,367	4.6	2.2
Con majority	14,377	28	
Electorate	72,572		
Turnout	51,342	70.75	

Con hold (6.58% from Lab to Con)

STAFFORDSHIRE MOORLANDS

		%	+/-%
Bradley, K. Con*	28,192	64.3	6.3
Price, D. Lab	11,764	26.8	-7.0
Gant, A. Lib Dem	2,469	5.6	2.3
Rouxel, D. Green	1,231	2.8	1.6
Con majority	16,428	37.48	
Electorate	65,485		
Turnout	43,829	66.93	

Con hold (6.64% from Lab to Con)

SOUTH STAFFORDSHIRE

		%	+/-%
Williamson, G. Con*	36,520	72.7	3.1
Freeman, A. Lab	8,270	16.5	-8.7
Fewtrell, C. Lib Dem	3,280	6.5	3.9
McIlvenna, C. Green	1,935	3.9	1.6
Con majority	28,250	56.2	
Electorate	73,668		
Turnout	50,264	68.23	

Con hold (5.95% from Lab to Con)

STALYBRIDGE AND HYDE

		%	+/-%
Reynolds, J. Lab/Co-op*	19,025	44.8	-12.3
Amjad, T. Con	16,079	37.8	-0.2
Newton, J. BP	3,591	8.5	
Dwan, J. Lib Dem	1,827	4.3	2.0
Wood, J. Green	1,411	3.3	1.0
Edge, J. Lib	435	1.0	
Lab/Co-op majority	2,946	6.93	
Electorate	73,064		
Turnout	42,511	58.18	

Lab/Co-op hold ()

STEVENAGE

		%	+/-%
McPartland, S. Con*	25,328	52.9	2.8
Borcherds, J. Lab	16,766	35.0	-8.3
Nash, L. Lib Dem	4,132	8.6	4.5
Snelling, V. Green	1,457	3.0	0.9
Con majority	8,562	17.88	
Electorate	71,562		
Turnout	47,880	66.91	

Con hold (5.52% from Lab to Con)

STIRLING

		%	+/-%
Smith, A. SNP	26,895	51.0	14.3
Kerr, S. Con*	17,641	33.5	-3.6
Ross, M. Lab	4,275	8.1	-14.0
Rehman, F. Lib Dem	2,867	5.4	2.0
Quinn, B. Green	942	1.8	
SNP majority	9,254	17.55	
Electorate	68,473		
Turnout	52,725	77.00	

SNP gain (8.93% from Con to SNP)

STOCKPORT

		%	+/-%
Mishra, N. Lab	21,695	51.8	-11.3
Imarni, I. Con	11,656	27.9	-0.5
Meikle, W. Lib Dem	5,043	12.1	7.8
Montague-Trenchard, L. BP	1,918	4.6	
Mellish, H. Green	1,403	3.4	1.9
Lab majority	10,039	23.98	
Electorate	65,391		
Turnout	41,860	64.01	

Lab hold (5.4% from Lab to Con)

STOCKTON NORTH

		%	+/-%
Cunningham, A. Lab*	17,728	43.0	-13.8
Jackson, S. Con	16,701	40.5	4.1
Walker, M. BP	3,907	9.5	
King, A. Lib Dem	1,631	4.0	2.4
Burdon, M. NEP	1,189	2.9	
Lab majority	1,027	2.49	
Electorate	66,649		
Turnout	41,272	61.92	

Lab hold (8.94% from Lab to Con)

STOCKTON SOUTH

		%	+/-%
Vickers, M. Con	27,764	50.5	3.8
Williams, P. Lab*	22,504	41.0	-7.5
Devlin, B. Lib Dem	2,338	4.3	2.5
Prescott, J. BP	2,196	4.0	
Con majority	5,260	9.57	
Electorate	76,870		
Turnout	54,944	71.48	

Con gain (5.61% from Lab to Con)

STOKE-ON-TRENT CENTRAL

		%	+/-%
Gideon, J. Con	14,557	45.3	5.6
Snell, G. Lab/Co-op*	13,887	43.2	-8.2
Mahmood, T. BP	1,691	5.3	
Pritchard, S. Lib Dem	1,116	3.5	1.4
Colclough, A. Green	819	2.6	1.4
Con majority	670	2.08	
Electorate	55,419		
Turnout	32,137	57.99	

Con gain (6.91% from Lab to Con)

STOKE-ON-TRENT NORTH

		%	+/-%
Gullis, J. Con	20,974	52.1	7.0
Smeeth, R. Lab*	14,688	36.5	-14.3
Watkin, R. BP	2,374	5.9	
Andras, P. Lib Dem	1,268	3.2	1.0
Borgars, A. Green	508	1.3	-0.4
Dilworth, M. Ind	322	0.8	
Con majority	6,286	15.63	
Electorate	84,348		
Turnout	40,230	47.70	

Con gain (10.63% from Lab to Con)

STOKE-ON-TRENT SOUTH

		%	+/-%
Brereton, J. Con*	24,632	61.9	13.0
McDonald, M. Lab	13,361	33.6	-13.8
Gordon, R. Lib Dem	1,611	4.1	2.1
Con majority	11,271	28.34	
Electorate	64,491		
Turnout	39,775	61.68	

Con hold (13.38% from Lab to Con)

STONE

		%	+/-%
Cash, B. Con*	31,687	63.3	0.2
Stubbs, M. Lab	11,742	23.5	-4.7
Sandiford, A. Lib Dem	4,412	8.8	4.4
Adamson, T. Green	2,002	4.0	2.6
Con majority	19,945	39.84	
Electorate	69,378		
Turnout	50,065	72.16	

Con hold (2.47% from Lab to Con)

STOURBRIDGE

		%	+/-%
Webb, S. Con	27,534	60.1	5.6
Lowe, P. Lab	13,963	30.5	-7.8
Bramall, C. Lib Dem	2,523	5.5	3.2
Mohr, A. Green	1,048	2.3	1.3
Hudson, A. Ind	621	1.4	
Con majority	13,571	29.61	
Electorate	70,160		
Turnout	45,831	65.32	

Con hold (6.7% from Lab to Con)

STRANGFORD

		%	+/-%
Shannon, J. DUP*	17,705	47.0	-14.9
Armstrong, K. APNI	10,634	28.2	13.6
Smith, P. UUP	4,023	10.7	-0.7
Boyle, J. SDLP	1,994	5.3	-0.9
Abraham, G. Con	1,476	3.9	2.6
Macartney, M. Green	790	2.1	0.5
Carlin, R. Sinn Féin	555	1.5	-1.3
Stephenson, R. UKIP	308	0.8	
DUP majority	7,071	18.78	
Electorate	66,928		
Turnout	37,660	56.27	

DUP hold (from DUP to APNI)

STRATFORD-ON-AVON

		%	+/-%
Zahawi, N. Con*	33,343	60.3	-2.4
Skinner, D. Lib Dem	13,371	24.2	12.3
Ling, F. Lab	6,222	11.3	-10.5
Passingham, D. Green	2,112	3.8	1.3
Con majority	19,972	36.1	
Electorate	74,037		
Turnout	55,321	74.72	

Con hold (7.38% from Con to Lib Dem)

STREATHAM

		%	+/-%
Ribeiro-Addy, B. Lab	30,976	54.6	-13.7
Thompson, H. Lib Dem	13,286	23.4	17.0
O'Broin, R. Con	9,060	16.0	-5.3
Ainslie, S. Green	2,567	4.5	1.5
Becker, P. BP	624	1.1	
Lab majority	17,690	31.2	
Electorate	84,783		
Turnout	56,691	66.87	

Lab hold (15.32% from Lab to Lib Dem)

STRETFORD AND URMSTON

		%	+/-%
Green, K. Lab*	30,195	60.1	-6.5
Mirza, M. Con	13,778	27.4	0.0
Fryer, A. Lib Dem	2,969	5.9	3.9
Powell, G. BP	1,768	3.5	
Leicester, J. Green	1,357	2.7	1.4
Lab majority	16,417	32.69	
Electorate	72,372		
Turnout	50,222	69.39	

Lab hold (3.25% from Lab to Con)

STROUD

		%	+/-%
Baillie, S. Con	31,582	47.8	1.9
Drew, D. Lab/Co-op*	27,742	42.0	-5.0
Scott Cato, M. Green	4,954	7.5	5.3
Latimer, L. BP	1,085	1.6	
Gogerly, G. Libertarian	567	0.9	
Con majority	3,840	5.81	
Electorate	84,537		
Turnout	66,115	78.21	

Con gain (3.45% from Lab to Con)

CENTRAL SUFFOLK AND NORTH IPSWICH

		%	+/-%
Poulter, D. Con	35,253	62.4	2.3
Bonner-Morgan, E. Lab	11,862	21.0	-8.7
Sandbach, J. Lib Dem	6,485	11.5	7.2
Pratt, D. Green	2,650	4.7	1.8
Con majority	23,391	41.38	
Electorate	80,037		
Turnout	56,524	70.62	

Con hold (5.52% from Lab to Con)

SUFFOLK COASTAL

		%	+/-%
Coffey, T. Con*	32,958	56.3	-1.5
Matthews, C. Lab	12,425	21.2	-9.1
Ewart, J. Lib Dem	8,719	14.9	8.0
Smith-Lyte, R. Green	2,713	4.6	1.6
Love, T. Ind	1,493	2.6	
Con majority	20,533	35.09	
Electorate	81,910		
Turnout	58,507	71.43	

Con hold (3.81% from Lab to Con)

SOUTH SUFFOLK

		%	+/-%
Cartlidge, J. Con*	33,270	61.9	1.5
Hughes, E. Lab	10,373	19.3	-8.5
Beavan, D. Lib Dem	6,702	12.5	6.7
Lindsay, R. Green	3,144	5.9	2.7
Con majority	22,897	42.59	
Electorate	76,201		
Turnout	53,766	70.56	

Con hold (4.97% from Lab to Con)

WEST SUFFOLK

		%	+/-%
Hancock, M. Con*	33,842	65.4	4.3
Unwin, C. Lab	10,648	20.6	-7.6
Tealby-Watson, E. Lib Dem	4,685	9.1	4.9
Allwright, D. Green	2,262	4.4	2.6
Con majority	23,194	44.8	
Electorate	80,193		
Turnout	51,773	64.56	

Con hold (5.95% from Lab to Con)

SUNDERLAND CENTRAL

		%	+/-%
Elliott, J. Lab*	18,336	42.1	-13.4
D'Silva, T. Con	15,372	35.3	1.9
Parikh, V. BP	5,047	11.6	
Hodson, N. Lib Dem	3,025	6.9	3.0
Featherstone, R. Green	1,212	2.8	1.2
McKenzie, D. Ind	484	1.1	
Lab majority	2,964	6.8	
Electorate	72,680		
Turnout	43,580	59.96	

Lab hold (7.66% from Lab to Con)

EAST SURREY

		%	+/-%
Coutinho, C. Con	35,624	59.5	-0.1
Ehmann, A. Lib Dem	11,584	19.3	8.9
Rehal, F. Lab	8,247	13.8	-5.5
Booton, J. Green	2,340	3.9	2.1
Windsor, H. Ind	1,374	2.3	
Hogbin, M. Loony	521	0.9	
Con majority	24,040	40.12	
Electorate	83,148		
Turnout	59,925	72.07	

Con hold (4.48% from Con to Lib Dem)

SURREY HEATH

		%	+/-%
Gove, M. Con*	34,358	58.3	-5.6
Pinkerton, A. Lib Dem	16,009	27.2	16.4
Mohanty, B. Lab	5,407	9.2	-11.8
Galliford, S. Green	2,252	3.8	-0.1
Roe, D. UKIP	628	1.1	
Con majority	18,349	31.16	
Electorate	81,439		
Turnout	58,891	72.31	

Con hold (10.99% from Con to Lib Dem)

SOUTH WEST SURREY

		%	+/-%
Hunt, J. Con*	32,191	53.0	-2.6
Follows, P. Lib Dem	23,374	38.5	28.7
Corry, T. Lab	4,775	7.9	-4.7
Con majority	8,817	14.52	
Electorate	79,096		
Turnout	60,714	76.76	

Con hold (15.62% from Con to Lib Dem)

MID SUSSEX

		%	+/-%
Davies, M. Con*	33,455	53.1	-3.7
Eggleston, R. Lib Dem	15,258	24.2	11.5
Bolton, G. Lab	11,218	17.8	-7.2
Nicholson, D. Green	2,234	3.6	1.0
Thunderclap, B. Loony	550	0.9	0.1
Mortensen, B. Advance	47	0.1	
Con majority	18,197	28.89	
Electorate	85,146		
Turnout	62,984	73.97	

Con hold (7.61% from Lib Dem to Con)

SUTTON AND CHEAM

		%	+/-%
Scully, P. Con*	25,235	49.8	-1.2
Bokhari, H. Lib Dem	16,884	33.3	6.7
Craven, B. Lab	7,200	14.2	-6.3
Jackson-Prior, C. Green	1,168	2.3	0.6
Con majority	8,351	16.47	
Electorate	71,779		
Turnout	50,698	70.63	

Con hold (3.95% from Lab to Con)

SUTTON COLDFIELD

		%	+/-%
Mitchell, A. Con*	31,604	60.0	-0.8
Knowles, D. Lab	12,332	23.4	-8.4
Wilkinson, J. Lib Dem	6,358	12.1	7.7
Auton, B. Green	2,031	3.9	2.0
Con majority	19,272	36.61	
Electorate	75,638		
Turnout	52,637	69.59	

Con hold (3.84% from Lab to Con)

SWANSEA EAST

		%	+/-%
Harris, C. Lab*	17,405	51.7	-11.6
Howard, D. Con	9,435	28.0	2.1
Willicombe, T. BP	2,842	8.5	
Havard, G. PIC	1,905	5.7	0.9
Hutchinson, C. Lib Dem	1,409	4.2	2.4
Evans, C. Green	583	1.7	0.7
Lab majority	7,970	23.69	
Electorate	58,450		
Turnout	33,645	57.56	

Lab hold (6.86% from Lab to Con)

SWANSEA WEST

		%	+/-%
Davies, G. Lab/Co-op	18,493	51.4	-8.2
Price, J. Con	10,377	28.9	-2.4
O'Carroll, M. Lib Dem	2,993	8.3	4.9
Williams, G. PIC	1,984	5.5	1.4
Hopkins, P. BP	1,983	5.5	
Lab/Co-op majority	8,116	22.57	
Electorate	57,078		
Turnout	35,967	63.01	

Lab/Co-op hold (from Lab to Con)

NORTH SWINDON

		%	+/-%
Tomlinson, J. Con*	32,584	58.9	5.4
Linnegar, K. Lab	16,413	29.7	-8.7
Critchlow, K. Lib Dem	4,408	8.0	4.4
Bentley, A. Green	1,710	3.1	1.5
Con majority	16,171	29.23	
Electorate	82,441		
Turnout	55,324	67.11	

Con hold (7.04% from Lab to Con)

SOUTH SWINDON

		%	+/-%
Buckland, R. Con*	26,536	52.0	3.7
Church, S. Lab/Co-op	19,911	39.1	-4.5
Pajak, S. Lib Dem	4,299	8.4	4.4
Con majority	6,625	12.99	
Electorate	73,118		
Turnout	50,993	69.74	

Con hold (4.1% from Lab to Con)

TAMWORTH

		%	+/-%
Pincher, C. Con*	30,542	66.1	5.3
Bain, C. Lab/Co-op	10,908	23.6	-11.1
Wheway, R. Lib Dem	2,426	5.3	1.1
Tilley, A. Green	935	2.0	
Bilcliff, R. UKIP	814	1.8	
Wright, J. Ind	431	0.9	
Con majority	19,634	42.49	
Electorate	72,544		
Turnout	46,210	63.70	

Con hold (8.19% from Lab to Con)

TATTON

		%	+/-%
McVey, E. Con*	28,277	57.5	-0.9
Weinberg, J. Lab	10,890	22.2	-6.2
Smith, J. Lib Dem	7,712	15.7	6.7
Hennerley, N. Green	2,088	4.3	2.2
Con majority	17,387	35.38	
Electorate	69,018		
Turnout	49,146	71.21	

Con hold (2.67% from Lab to Con)

TAUNTON DEANE

		%	+/-%
Pow, R. Con*	34,164	53.4	0.7
Amos, G. Lib Dem	22,464	35.1	7.5
Canham, L. Lab	4,715	7.4	-8.0
Hunt, J. Ind	2,390	3.7	
Con majority	11,700	18.3	
Electorate	88,676		
Turnout	63,925	72.09	

Con hold (3.43% from Con to Lib Dem)

TELFORD

		%	+/-%
Allan, L. Con*	25,546	59.3	10.8
Gilman, K. Lab	14,605	33.9	-13.0
Roberts, S. Lib Dem	2,674	6.2	4.1
Con majority	10,941	25.42	
Electorate	68,921		
Turnout	43,049	62.46	

Con hold (11.91% from Lab to Con)

TEWKESBURY

		%	+/-%
Robertson, L. Con*	35,728	58.2	-1.7
Hegenbarth, A. Lib Dem	13,318	21.7	8.2
Chaplin, L. Lab	9,310	15.2	-6.6
Cody, C. Green	2,784	4.5	1.9
Con majority	22,410	36.5	
Electorate	83,958		
Turnout	61,401	73.13	

Con hold (4.95% from Con to Lib Dem)

NORTH THANET

		%	+/-%
Gale, R. Con*	30,066	62.1	6.0
Jones, C. Lab	12,877	26.6	-7.3
Curwen, A. Lib Dem	3,439	7.1	3.8
Edwards, R. Green	1,796	3.7	2.0
Con majority	17,189	35.49	
Electorate	72,756		
Turnout	48,428	66.56	

Con hold (6.66% from Lab to Con)

SOUTH THANET

		%	+/-%
Mackinlay, C. Con*	27,084	55.9	5.2
Gordon-Nesbitt, R. Lab	16,497	34.0	-3.8
Pennington, M. Lib Dem	2,727	5.6	2.6
Wing, R. Green	1,949	4.0	2.4
Con majority	10,587	21.84	
Electorate	73,223		
Turnout	48,468	66.19	

Con hold (4.52% from Lab to Con)

THIRSK AND MALTON

		%	+/-%
Hollinrake, K. Con*	35,634	62.7	2.8
Yellen, D. Lab	10,480	18.4	-7.6
Keal, D. Lib Dem	6,774	11.9	5.0
Brampton, M. Green	2,263	4.0	2.0
Hall, J. YP	881	1.6	
Mullins, S. Ind	245	0.4	
Johnson, G. Ind	184	0.3	
Taylor, M. SDP	127	0.2	
Con majority	25,154	44.26	
Electorate	80,991		
Turnout	56,830	70.17	

Con hold (5.17% from Lab to Con)

THORNBURY AND YATE

		%	+/-%
Hall, L. Con*	30,202	57.5	2.4
Young, C. Lib Dem	17,833	34.0	2.6
Logan, R. Lab	4,208	8.0	-4.0
Con majority	12,369	23.56	
Electorate	69,492		
Turnout	52,497	75.54	

Con hold (0.1% from Con to Lib Dem)

THURROCK

		%	+/-%
Doyle-Price, J. Con*	27,795	58.4	19.0
Kent, J. Lab	16,313	34.3	-4.5
Stone, S. Lib Dem	1,510	3.2	1.6
Woollard, J. Ind	1,042	2.2	
Harvey, B. Green	807	1.7	
Con majority	11,482	24.12	
Electorate	79,659		
Turnout	47,606	59.76	

Con hold (11.72% from Lab to Con)

TIVERTON AND HONITON

		%	+/-%
Parish, N. Con*	35,893	60.0	-1.2
Pole, L. Lab	11,654	19.5	-7.6
Timperley, J. Lib Dem	8,807	14.7	6.7
Reed, C. Green	2,291	3.8	0.3
Dennis, M. UKIP	968	1.6	
Con majority	24,239	40.49	
Electorate	82,953		
Turnout	59,861	72.16	

Con hold (3.17% from Lab to Con)

TONBRIDGE AND MALLING

		%	+/-%
Tugendhat, T. Con*	35,784	62.4	-1.1
Morris, R. Lib Dem	8,843	15.4	8.8
Jones, D. Lab	8,286	14.5	-7.8
Clark, A. Green	4,090	7.1	3.0
Con majority	26,941	47.01	
Electorate	79,278		
Turnout	57,315	72.30	

Con hold (4.94% from Con to Lib Dem)

TOOTING

		%	+/-%
Allin-Khan, R. Lab*	30,811	52.5	-7.0
Briscoe, K. Con	16,504	28.1	-4.9
Glover, O. Lib Dem	8,305	14.2	8.9
Goodwin, G. Green	2,314	4.0	2.5
Shakir, A. BP	462	0.8	
Hubley, R. SDP	77	0.1	
Lab majority	14,307	24.39	
Electorate	76,937		
Turnout	58,650	76.23	

Lab hold (1.07% from Lab to Con)

TORBAY

		%	+/-%
Foster, K. Con*	29,863	59.1	6.1
Howgate, L. Lib Dem	12,114	24.0	-1.1
Middleditch, M. Lab	6,562	13.0	-5.2
Moss, S. Green	1,239	2.5	1.2
Channer, J. Ind	648	1.3	
Con majority	17,749	35.1	
Electorate	75,054		
Turnout	50,567	67.37	

Con hold (3.62% from Lib Dem to Con)

TORFAEN

		%	+/-%
Thomas-Symonds, N. Lab*	15,546	41.7	-15.8
Smith, G. Con	11,804	31.6	0.7
Thomas, D. BP	5,742	15.4	
Miller, J. Lib Dem	1,831	4.9	2.7
Bowler-Brown, M. PlC	1,441	3.9	-1.5
Heygate-Browne, A. Green	812	2.2	
Lab majority	3,742	10.03	
Electorate	62,330		
Turnout	37,302	59.85	

Lab hold (8.28% from Lab to Con)

TORRIDGE AND WEST DEVON

		%	+/-%
Cox, G. Con*	35,904	59.9	3.5
Chalmers, D. Lib Dem	10,912	18.2	0.6
Strode, S. Lab	10,290	17.2	-4.5
Jordan, C. Green	2,077	3.5	0.7
Wootton, B. Ind	547	0.9	
Con majority	24,992	41.68	
Electorate	80,403		
Turnout	59,963	74.58	

Con hold (1.48% from Lib Dem to Con)

TOTNES

		%	+/-%
Mangnall, A. Con	27,751	53.0	-0.6
Wollaston, S. Lib Dem*	15,027	28.7	15.9
Webberley, L. Lab	8,860	16.9	-9.9
Kitson, J. Ind	544	1.0	
Con majority	12,724	24.29	
Electorate	69,863		
Turnout	52,378	74.97	

Con hold (8.22% from Con to Lib Dem)

TOTTENHAM

		%	+/-%
Lammy, D. Lab*	35,621	75.7	-5.6
Newhall, J. Con	5,446	11.6	0.1
Palmer, T. Lib Dem	3,168	6.7	3.3
Chan, E. Green	1,873	4.0	1.4
Turay, A. BP	527	1.1	
Bence, A. SDP	91	0.2	
Sweeney, F. WRP	88	0.2	
Silberman, J. Comm League	42	0.1	
Lab majority	30,175	64.12	
Electorate	75,740		
Turnout	47,060	62.13	

Lab hold (2.88% from Lab to Con)

TRURO AND FALMOUTH

		%	+/-%
Mackrory, C. Con	27,237	45.9	1.6
Forbes, J. Lab	22,676	38.2	0.6
Gripper, R. Lib Dem	7,150	12.0	-2.9
Scott, T. Green	1,714	2.9	1.4
Nicholson, P. Lib	413	0.7	
Con majority	4,561	7.68	
Electorate	76,719		
Turnout	59,361	77.37	

Con hold (0.5% from Lab to Con)

TUNBRIDGE WELLS

		%	+/-%
Clark, G. Con*	30,119	54.8	-2.0
Chapelard, B. Lib Dem	15,474	28.2	18.3
Weiss, A. Lab	8,098	14.7	-11.8
Camp, C. Ind	488	0.9	
Peacock, N. Ind	471	0.9	
Con majority	14,645	26.64	
Electorate	74,823		
Turnout	54,971	73.47	

Con hold (10.16% from Con to Lib Dem)

TWICKENHAM

		%	+/-%
Wilson, M. Lib Dem	36,166	55.9	3.2
Grant, I. Con	22,045	34.1	-3.9
Walia, R. Lab	5,476	8.5	-0.7
Wells, S. BP	816	1.3	
Lib Dem majority	14,121	21.81	
Electorate	84,906		
Turnout	64,742	76.25	

Lib Dem hold (3.56% from Con to Lib Dem)

TYNEMOUTH

		%	+/-%
Campbell, A. Lab*	26,928	47.9	-9.0
Bartoli, L. Con	22,071	39.3	2.9
Appleby, J. Lib Dem	3,791	6.7	3.7
Punchard, E. BP	1,963	3.5	
Erskine, J. Green	1,281	2.3	1.2
Lab majority	4,857	8.64	
Electorate	77,261		
Turnout	56,213	72.76	

Lab hold (5.92% from Lab to Con)

NORTH TYNESIDE

		%	+/-%
Glindon, M. Lab*	25,051	49.5	-14.8
Carroll, D. Con	15,490	30.6	3.4
Husband, A. BP	5,254	10.4	
Boyle, C. Lib Dem	3,241	6.4	3.5
Buttery, J. Green	1,393	2.8	1.5
Lab majority	9,561	18.9	
Electorate	78,902		
Turnout	50,589	64.12	

Lab hold (9.1% from Lab to Con)

WEST TYRONE

		%	+/-%
Begley, Ó. Sinn Féin*	16,544	40.2	-10.3
Buchanan, T. DUP	9,066	22.0	-4.8
McCrossan, D. SDLP	7,330	17.8	4.9
Donnelly, S. APNI	3,979	9.7	7.4
McKane, A. UUP	2,774	6.7	1.6
Hope, J. Aontú	972	2.4	
Glass, S. Green	521	1.3	0.3
Sinn Féin majority	7,478	18.16	
Electorate	66,259		
Turnout	41,186	62.16	

Sinn Féin hold (2.18% from Sinn Féin to DUP)

MID ULSTER

		%	+/-%
Molloy, F. Sinn Féin*	20,473	45.5	-8.7
Buchanan, K. DUP	10,936	24.3	-2.4
Johnston, D. SDLP	6,384	14.2	4.5
Boyle, M. APNI	3,526	7.8	5.5
Richardson, N. UUP	2,611	5.8	-0.6
Rafferty, C. Ind	690	1.5	
Sinn Féin majority	9,537	21.21	
Electorate	70,449		
Turnout	44,968	63.83	

Sinn Féin hold (3.12% from Sinn Féin to DUP)

UPPER BANN

		%	+/-%
Lockhart, C. DUP	20,501	40.7	-2.7
O'Dowd, J. Sinn Féin	12,291	24.4	-3.4
Tennyson, E. APNI	6,433	12.8	8.3
Beattie, D. UUP	6,197	12.3	-3.1
Kelly, D. SDLP	4,623	9.2	0.6
DUP majority	8,210	16.31	
Electorate	82,887		
Turnout	50,348	60.74	

DUP hold (0.39% from Sinn Féin to DUP)

UXBRIDGE AND SOUTH RUISLIP

		%	+/-%
Johnson, B. Con*	25,351	52.5	1.8
Milani, A. Lab	18,141	37.6	-2.4
Humphreys, J. Lib Dem	3,026	6.3	2.4
Keir, M. Green	1,090	2.3	0.4
Courtenay, G. UKIP	283	0.6	-2.8
Buckethead, L. Loony	125	0.3	
Count Binface, . Ind	69	0.1	
Utting, A. Ind	44	0.1	
Yogenstein, Y. Ind	23	0.1	
Burke, N. Ind	22	0.1	
Smith, B. Ind	8	0.0	
Tobin, W. Ind	5	0.0	
Con majority	7,210	14.93	
Electorate	70,365		
Turnout	48,280	68.61	

Con hold (2.09% from Lab to Con)

VAUXHALL

		%	+/-%
Eshalomi, F. Lab/Co-op	31,615	70.9	13.7
Lewis, S. Lib Dem	12,003	26.9	6.4
Bool, S. Con	9,422	21.1	2.5
Bond, J. Green	2,516	5.7	3.6
McGuinness, A. BP	641	1.4	
Faissal, S. Ind	136	0.3	
Lab/Co-op majority	19,612	34.67	
Electorate	88,659		
Turnout	56,569	63.81	

Lab/Co-op hold (3.67% from Lab to Lib Dem)

WAKEFIELD

		%	+/-%
Ahmad Khan, I. Con	21,283	47.1	2.3
Creagh, M. Lab*	17,925	39.7	-9.9
Wiltshire, P. BP	2,725	6.0	
Needle, J. Lib Dem	1,772	3.9	1.9
Kett, R. YP	868	1.9	-0.6
Whyte, S. Ind	454	1.0	0.2
Con majority	3,358	7.44	
Electorate	70,192		
Turnout	45,164	64.34	

Con gain (6.06% from Lab to Con)

WALLASEY

		%	+/-%
Eagle, A. Lab*	29,901	64.2	-7.2
Baker, J. Con	11,579	24.9	1.7
York, M. BP	2,037	4.4	
Downie, V. Lib Dem	1,843	4.0	2.4
Clough, L. Green	1,132	2.4	1.1
Lab majority	18,322	39.32	
Electorate	66,310		
Turnout	46,594	70.27	

Lab hold (4.42% from Lab to Con)

WALSALL NORTH

		%	+/-%
Hughes, E. Con*	23,334	63.6	14.1
Ogilvie, G. Lab	11,369	31.0	-11.7
Gray, J. Lib Dem	1,236	3.4	1.8
Wilson, M. Green	617	1.7	
Con majority	11,965	32.62	
Electorate	67,177		
Turnout	36,681	54.60	

Con hold (12.91% from Lab to Con)

WALSALL SOUTH

		%	+/-%
Vaz, V. Lab*	20,872	49.0	-8.2
Bains, G. Con	17,416	40.9	3.8
Hughes, G. BP	1,660	3.9	
Harris, P. Lib Dem	1,602	3.8	2.4
Macefield, J. Green	634	1.5	
Mehboob, A. Ind	288	0.7	
Lab majority	3,456	8.12	
Electorate	68,024		
Turnout	42,587	62.61	

Lab hold (6.01% from Lab to Con)

WALTHAMSTOW

		%	+/-%
Creasy, S. Lab/Co-op*	36,784	75.8	-4.5
Adoh, S. Con	5,922	12.2	-1.8
Chadha Moynihan, M. Lib Dem	2,874	5.9	3.1
Johns, A. Green	1,733	3.6	1.1
Campbell, P. BP	768	1.6	
Longe, D. CPA	254	0.5	
Lab/Co-op majority	30,862	63.58	
Electorate	70,267		
Turnout	48,541	69.08	

Lab/Co-op hold (1.35% from Lab to Con)

WANSBECK

		%	+/-%
Lavery, I. Lab*	17,124	42.2	-15.1
Gebhard, J. Con	16,310	40.1	7.4
Webley, E. BP	3,141	7.7	
Psallidas, S. Lib Dem	2,539	6.3	1.5
Leyland, S. Green	1,217	3.0	1.3
Flynn, M. CPA	178	0.4	
Lab majority	814	2	
Electorate	64,094		
Turnout	40,628	63.39	

Lab hold (11.27% from Lab to Con)

WANTAGE

		%	+/-%
Johnston, D. Con	34,085	50.5	-3.6
Benwell, R. Lib Dem	21,432	31.8	17.3
Roberts, J. Lab	10,181	15.1	-11.7
Gray, M. Ind	1,475	2.2	
Con majority	12,653	18.75	
Electorate	90,867		
Turnout	67,479	74.26	

Con hold (10.41% from Con to Lib Dem)

WARLEY

		%	+/-%
Spellar, J. Lab*	21,901	58.6	-8.4
Kanneganti, C. Con	10,390	27.8	1.7
Cooper, M. BP	2,469	6.6	
Manley-Green, B. Lib Dem	1,588	4.3	2.3
Downs, K. Green	891	2.4	1.0
Lab majority	11,511	30.79	
Electorate	62,357		
Turnout	37,381	59.95	

Lab hold (5.04% from Lab to Con)

WARRINGTON NORTH

		%	+/-%
Nichols, C. Lab	20,611	44.0	-12.3
Maisey, W. Con	19,102	40.8	4.2
Crowther, D. Lib Dem	3,071	6.6	4.1
Babade, E. BP	2,626	5.6	
McAteer, L. Green	1,257	2.7	1.4
Lab majority	1,509	3.22	
Electorate	72,235		
Turnout	46,836	64.84	

Lab hold (8.24% from Lab to Con)

WARRINGTON SOUTH

		%	+/-%
Carter, A. Con	28,187	45.4	1.2
Rashid, F. Lab*	26,177	42.2	-6.1
Bate, R. Lib Dem	5,732	9.2	3.9
Aspinall, C. BP	1,635	2.6	
Hickson, K. SDP	168	0.3	
Con majority	2,010	3.24	
Electorate	86,015		
Turnout	62,086	72.18	

Con gain (3.68% from Lab to Con)

WARWICK AND LEAMINGTON

		%	+/-%
Western, M. Lab*	23,718	43.7	-2.9
Rankin, J. Con	22,929	42.2	-2.1
Adam, L. Lib Dem	4,995	9.2	4.0
Chilvers, J. Green	1,536	2.8	0.6
Griffiths, T. BP	807	1.5	
Dhillon, B. Ind	153	0.3	
Bennett, X. SDP	67	0.1	
Lab majority	789	1.45	
Electorate	76,362		
Turnout	54,333	71.15	

Lab hold (0.39% from Lab to Con)

NORTH WARWICKSHIRE

		%	+/-%
Tracey, C. Con*	30,249	65.6	8.9
Breeze, C. Lab/Co-op	12,293	26.7	-12.1
Whelan, R. Lib Dem	2,069	4.5	2.3
Platt, J. Green	1,303	2.8	0.8
Con majority	17,956	38.96	
Electorate	70,271		
Turnout	46,085	65.58	

Con hold (10.49% from Lab to Con)

WASHINGTON AND SUNDERLAND WEST

		%	+/-%
Hodgson, S. Lab*	15,941	42.4	-18.3
Allen, V. Con	12,218	32.5	3.7
Brown, H. BP	5,439	14.5	
West, C. Lib Dem	2,071	5.5	3.1
Chantkowski, M. Green	1,005	2.7	1.4
Jenkins, K. UKIP	839	2.2	-4.6
Lab majority	3,723	9.9	
Electorate	66,278		
Turnout	37,621	56.76	

Lab hold (10.98% from Lab to Con)

WATFORD

		%	+/-%
Russell, D. Con	26,421	45.3	-0.2
Ostrowski, C. Lab	21,988	37.7	-4.3
Stotesbury, I. Lib Dem	9,323	16.0	6.9
McGarrick, M. SDP	333	0.6	
Con majority	4,433	7.6	
Electorate	83,359		
Turnout	58,328	69.97	

Con hold (2.02% from Lab to Con)

WAVENEY

		%	+/-%
Aldous, P. Con*	31,778	61.9	7.6
Barker, S. Lab	13,776	26.9	-10.0
Brambley-Crawshaw, E. Green	2,727	5.3	2.8
Korfanty, H. Lib Dem	2,603	5.1	3.2
Brennan, D. CPA	245	0.5	
Con majority	18,002	35.09	
Electorate	82,791		
Turnout	51,304	61.97	

Con hold (8.81% from Lab to Con)

WEALDEN

		%	+/-%
Ghani, N. Con*	37,043	60.5	-0.7
Bowers, C. Lib Dem	11,388	18.6	8.2
Smith, A. Lab	9,377	15.3	-6.8
Taylor, G. Green	3,099	5.1	1.8
Con majority	25,655	41.87	
Electorate	82,998		
Turnout	61,272	73.82	

Con hold (4.44% from Con to Lib Dem)

WEAVER VALE

		%	+/-%
Amesbury, M. Lab*	22,772	44.8	-6.6
Wordsworth, A. Con	22,210	43.7	0.1
Parker, D. Lib Dem	3,300	6.5	3.3
Goulding, N. BP	1,380	2.7	
Bowers, P. Green	1,051	2.1	0.5
Lab majority	562	1.11	
Electorate	70,545		
Turnout	50,826	72.05	

Lab hold (3.32% from Lab to Con)

WELLINGBOROUGH

		%	+/-%
Bone, P. Con*	32,277	61.9	4.6
Watts, A. Lab	13,737	26.3	-7.6
Austin, S. Lib Dem	4,078	7.8	4.5
Turner-Hawes, M. Green	1,821	3.5	1.7
Con majority	18,540	35.55	
Electorate	80,765		
Turnout	52,148	64.57	

Con hold (6.1% from Lab to Con)

WELLS

		%	+/-%
Heappey, J. Con*	33,336	53.9	3.9
Munt, T. Lib Dem	23,345	37.8	0.2
McKenzie, K. Lab	4,304	7.0	-4.7
Dobbs, D. Ind	373	0.6	
Quatermass, S. Motherworld	270	0.4	
Con majority	9,991	16.16	
Electorate	84,124		
Turnout	61,844	73.52	

Con hold (1.86% from Lib Dem to Con)

WELWYN HATFIELD

		%	+/-%
Shapps, G. Con*	27,394	52.4	1.5
Newbigging, R. Lab	16,439	31.4	-5.3
Zukowskyj, P. Lib Dem	6,602	12.6	5.2
Sayers, O. Green	1,618	3.1	1.5
Con majority	10,955	20.95	
Electorate	74,892		
Turnout	52,279	69.81	

Con hold (3.36% from Lab to Con)

WENTWORTH AND DEARNE

		%	+/-%
Healey, J. Lab*	16,742	40.2	-24.4
Barley, E. Con	14,577	35.0	3.9
Cavell, S. BP	7,019	16.8	
Middleton, J. Lib Dem	1,705	4.1	0.4
Brown, L. YP	1,201	2.9	
Bettney, D. SDP	313	0.8	
Lab majority	2,165	5.19	
Electorate	74,536		
Turnout	41,684	55.92	

Lab hold (14.14% from Lab to Con)

WEST BROMWICH EAST

		%	+/-%
Richards, N. Con	16,804	46.6	8.5
Dogus, I. Lab	15,211	42.2	-15.6
Lucas, C. BP	1,475	4.1	
Graham, A. Lib Dem	1,313	3.6	2.1
Redding, M. Green	627	1.7	0.4
Galloway, G. Ind	489	1.4	0.5
Rankine, C. Yeshua	56	0.2	
Con majority	1,593	4.42	
Electorate	62,046		
Turnout	36,079	58.15	

Con gain (12.04% from Lab to Con)

WEST BROMWICH WEST

		%	+/-%
Bailey, S. Con	17,419	50.4	10.8
Cunningham, J. Lab	13,620	39.4	-12.5
D'Aulerio, F. BP	1,841	5.3	
Clucas, F. Lib Dem	915	2.7	1.7
Williams, K. Green	664	1.9	1.0
Con majority	3,799	11	
Electorate	64,517		
Turnout	34,543	53.54	

Con gain (11.67% from Lab to Con)

WEST HAM

		%	+/-%
Brown, L. Lab*	42,181	69.8	-6.7
Kumar, S. Con	9,793	16.2	0.1
O'Casey, E. Lib Dem	4,161	6.9	3.9
Keeling, D. Green	1,780	3.0	1.4
Stockdale, E. BP	1,679	2.8	
Jobson, P. CPA	463	0.8	0.2
Kamran, H. Comm United	143	0.2	
Lab majority	32,388	53.61	
Electorate	97,947		
Turnout	60,417	61.68	

Lab hold (3.39% from Lab to Con)

WESTMINSTER NORTH

		%	+/-%
Buck, K. Lab*	23,240	54.0	-5.7
Macfarlane, J. Con	12,481	29.0	-4.2
Lee, G. Lib Dem	5,593	13.0	7.8
Robinson, H. Green	1,064	2.5	1.1
Parvin, C. BP	418	1.0	
Fajardo, G. CPA	115	0.3	
Lab majority	10,759	25	
Electorate	65,519		
Turnout	43,044	65.70	

Lab hold (0.75% from Lab to Con)

WESTMORLAND AND LONSDALE

		%	+/-%
Farron, T. Lib Dem*	25,795	48.8	3.1
Airey, J. Con	23,861	45.2	0.9
Black, P. Lab	2,293	4.3	-4.9
Bolton, S. BP	763	1.4	
Lib Dem majority	1,934	3.66	
Electorate	67,789		
Turnout	52,853	77.97	

Lib Dem hold (1.08% from Con to Lib Dem)

WESTON-SUPER-MARE

		%	+/-%
Penrose, J. Con*	31,983	57.3	4.2
Taylor, T. Lab	14,862	26.6	-6.0
Keating, P. Lib Dem	6,935	12.4	3.3
Basu, S. Green	1,834	3.3	1.7
Con majority	17,121	30.64	
Electorate	82,526		
Turnout	55,869	67.70	

Con hold (5.12% from Lab to Con)

WIGAN

		%	+/-%
Nandy, L. Lab*	21,042	46.6	-15.5
Williams, A. Con	14,314	31.7	3.2
Malloy, W. BP	5,959	13.2	
Thomas, S. Lib Dem	2,428	5.4	3.5
Jacobs, P. Green	1,299	2.9	1.3
Lab majority	6,728	14.89	
Electorate	75,680		
Turnout	45,176	59.69	

Lab hold (9.37% from Lab to Con)

NORTH WILTSHIRE

		%	+/-%
Gray, J. Con*	32,373	58.9	-1.3
Mathew, B. Lib Dem	14,747	26.8	9.1
Fisher, J. Lab	5,699	10.4	-7.1
Jackson, B. Green	1,939	3.5	1.4
Con majority	17,626	32.06	
Electorate	73,280		
Turnout	54,974	75.02	

Con hold (5.23% from Con to Lib Dem)

SOUTH WEST WILTSHIRE

		%	+/-%
Murrison, A. Con*	33,038	59.9	0.1
Pomroy-Smith, E. Lab	11,408	20.7	-5.8
Nicholson, E. Lib Dem	8,015	14.5	4.8
Phillips, J. Green	2,434	4.4	1.8
Con majority	21,630	39.23	
Electorate	77,969		
Turnout	55,141	70.72	

Con hold (2.93% from Lab to Con)

WIMBLEDON

		%	+/-%
Hammond, S. Con*	20,373	38.3	-8.1
Kohler, P. Lib Dem	19,745	37.1	22.6
Schneider, J. Lab	12,543	23.6	-11.9
Hadley, G. Ind	366	0.7	
Con majority	628	1.18	
Electorate	68,240		
Turnout	53,244	78.02	

Con hold (15.36% from Con to Lib Dem)

WINCHESTER

		%	+/-%
Brine, S. Con*	28,430	48.1	-3.8
Ferguson, P. Lib Dem	27,445	46.4	12.0
Baker, G. Lab	2,723	4.6	-5.9
Skelton, T. JACP	292	0.5	0.2
Con majority	985	1.67	
Electorate	75,582		
Turnout	59,100	78.19	

Con hold (7.9% from Con to Lib Dem)

WINDSOR

		%	+/-%
Afriyie, A. Con*	31,501	58.4	-5.8
Tisi, J. Lib Dem	11,422	21.2	11.1
Shearman, P. Lab	8,147	15.1	-7.7
McKeown, F. Green	1,796	3.3	0.7
Buckley, D. Ind	508	0.9	
Da Costa, W. Ind	376	0.7	
Con majority	20,079	37.22	
Electorate	75,038		
Turnout	53,951	71.90	

Con hold (8.46% from Con to Lib Dem)

WIRRAL SOUTH

		%	+/-%
McGovern, A. Lab*	22,284	51.0	-6.1
Gardiner, S. Con	16,179	37.1	-1.7
Carubia, C. Lib Dem	2,917	6.7	3.8
Waring, M. BP	1,219	2.8	
Gorman, H. Green	948	2.2	1.2
Lab majority	6,105	13.98	
Electorate	57,280		
Turnout	43,659	76.22	

Lab hold (2.2% from Lab to Con)

WIRRAL WEST

		%	+/-%
Greenwood, M. Lab*	20,695	48.1	-6.1
Evans, L. Con	17,692	41.1	-0.9
Corkhill, A. Lib Dem	2,706	6.3	3.7
Coyne, J. Green	965	2.2	1.3
Kelly, J. BP	860	2.0	
Lab majority	3,003	6.98	
Electorate	55,550		
Turnout	43,025	77.45	

Lab hold (2.6% from Lab to Con)

WITHAM

		%	+/-%
Patel, P. Con*	32,876	66.4	2.2
Edobor, M. Lab	8,794	17.8	-8.6
North, S. Lib Dem	4,584	9.3	3.8
Abbott, J. Green	3,090	6.2	2.5
Con majority	24,082	48.6	
Electorate	70,402		
Turnout	49,553	70.39	

Con hold (5.43% from Lab to Con)

WITNEY

		%	+/-%
Courts, R. Con*	33,856	54.9	-0.6
Hoagland, C. Lib Dem	18,679	30.3	9.9
Bolger, R. Lab/Co-op	8,770	14.2	-6.4
Con majority	15,177	24.6	
Electorate	83,845		
Turnout	61,697	73.58	

Con hold (5.22% from Con to Lib Dem)

WOKING

		%	+/-%
Lord, J. Con*	26,396	48.8	-5.2
Forster, W. Lib Dem	16,629	30.7	13.2
Mitchell, G. Lab	8,827	16.3	-7.5
Walding, E. Green	1,485	2.7	0.8
De Leon, T. UKIP	600	1.1	-1.0
Con majority	9,767	18.05	
Electorate	75,424		
Turnout	54,114	71.75	

Con hold (9.21% from Lab to Con)

WOKINGHAM

		%	+/-%
Redwood, J. Con*	30,734	49.4	-7.1
Lee, P. Lib Dem	23,351	37.5	21.7
Medhurst, A. Lab	6,450	10.4	-14.7
Johannessen, M. Green	1,382	2.2	-0.1
Mullin, A. Advance	80	0.1	
Con majority	7,383	11.87	
Electorate	83,956		
Turnout	62,216	74.11	

Con hold (14.35% from Con to Lib Dem)

WOLVERHAMPTON NORTH EAST

		%	+/-%
Stevenson, J. Con	17,722	51.6	11.4
Reynolds, E. Lab*	13,642	39.7	-13.0
Khatri, V. BP	1,354	3.9	
Maxwell, R. Lib Dem	960	2.8	1.2
Cantrill, A. Green	603	1.8	0.4
Con majority	4,080	11.87	
Electorate	61,660		
Turnout	34,373	55.75	

Con gain (12.2% from Lab to Con)

WOLVERHAMPTON SOUTH EAST

		%	+/-%
McFadden, P. Lab*	15,522	46.3	-11.8
Ejaz, A. Con	14,287	42.6	7.9
Chaggar, R. BP	2,094	6.3	
Coleman-Taylor, R. Lib Dem	1,019	3.0	1.8
Gilbert, K. Green	521	1.6	0.4
Lab majority	1,235	3.68	
Electorate	62,883		
Turnout	33,521	53.31	

Lab hold (9.85% from Lab to Con)

WOLVERHAMPTON SOUTH WEST

		%	+/-%
Anderson, S. Con	19,864	48.1	4.1
Smith, E. Lab*	18,203	44.1	-5.1
Ricketts, B. Lib Dem	2,041	4.9	3.1
Grandison, L. BP	1,028	2.5	
Con majority	1,661	4.02	
Electorate	60,534		
Turnout	41,284	68.20	

Con gain (4.59% from Lab to Con)

WORCESTER

		%	+/-%
Walker, R. Con*	25,856	50.6	2.6
Denham, L. Lab	19,098	37.4	-5.8
Kearney, S. Lib Dem	3,666	7.2	3.8
Stephen, L. Green	1,694	3.3	1.0
Potter, M. Ind	584	1.1	
Con majority	6,758	13.23	
Electorate	73,485		
Turnout	51,072	69.50	

Con hold (4.19% from Lab to Con)

MID WORCESTERSHIRE

		%	+/-%
Huddleston, N. Con*	37,426	66.4	1.3
Russell, H. Lab	9,408	16.7	-6.2
Rowley, M. Lib Dem	6,474	11.5	5.2
Howarth, S. Green	2,177	3.9	1.4
Brockman, B. Loony	638	1.1	
Con majority	28,018	49.74	
Electorate	78,220		
Turnout	56,327	72.01	

Con hold (3.74% from Lab to Con)

WEST WORCESTERSHIRE

		%	+/-%
Baldwin, H. Con*	34,909	60.4	-1.0
Nielsen, B. Lib Dem	10,410	18.0	8.6
Charles, S. Lab	9,496	16.4	-7.2
Allen, M. Green	2,715	4.7	1.9
Con majority	24,499	42.37	
Electorate	76,241		
Turnout	57,826	75.85	

Con hold (4.79% from Con to Lib Dem)

WORKINGTON

		%	+/-%
Jenkinson, M. Con	20,488	49.1	7.5
Hayman, S. Lab*	16,312	39.1	-12.0
Walker, D. BP	1,749	4.2	
Hughes, N. Lib Dem	1,525	3.7	0.9
Cockburn, N. Ind	842	2.0	
Perry, J. Green	596	1.4	
Ivinson, R. Ind	87	0.2	-0.5
Con majority	4,176	10.02	
Electorate	61,372		
Turnout	41,692	67.93	

Con gain (9.71% from Lab to Con)

WORSLEY AND ECCLES SOUTH

		%	+/-%
Keeley, B. Lab*	20,446	45.6	-11.3
Saunders, A. Con	17,227	38.4	-0.2
Martin, S. BP	3,224	7.2	
Johnson-Tod, J. Lib Dem	2,510	5.6	3.2
Towers, D. Green	1,300	2.9	1.1
Lab majority	3,219	7.18	
Electorate	75,219		
Turnout	44,825	59.59	

Lab hold (5.57% from Lab to Con)

EAST WORTHING AND SHOREHAM

		%	+/-%
Loughton, T. Con*	27,107	50.8	2.0
O'Connor, L. Lab	19,633	36.8	-2.4
Ridely, A. Lib Dem	4,127	7.7	3.0
Groves Williams, L. Green	2,006	3.8	1.4
Cook, S. Ind	255	0.5	
Con majority	7,474	14.02	
Electorate	75,194		
Turnout	53,316	70.90	

Con hold (2.21% from Lab to Con)

WORTHING WEST

		%	+/-%
Bottomley, P. Con*	30,475	55.5	0.2
Cooper, B. Lab	15,652	28.5	-4.6
Bennett, J. Lib Dem	6,024	11.0	5.5
Paul, J. Green	2,008	3.7	0.7
Aherne, D. Ind	489	0.9	
Con majority	14,823	26.99	
Electorate	78,585		
Turnout	54,922	69.89	

Con hold (2.43% from Lab to Con)

THE WREKIN

		%	+/-%
Pritchard, M. Con*	31,029	63.2	7.9
Harrison, D. Lab	12,303	25.1	-11.0
Janke, T. Lib Dem	4,067	8.3	5.6
Dawes, T. Green	1,491	3.0	1.4
Con majority	18,726	38.15	
Electorate	70,693		
Turnout	49,084	69.43	

Con hold (9.44% from Lab to Con)

WREXHAM

		%	+/-%
Atherton, S. Con	15,199	45.2	1.7
Wimbury, M. Lab/Co-op	13,068	38.9	-9.9
Harper, C. PlC	2,151	6.4	1.4
Sly, T. Lib Dem	1,447	4.3	1.9
Berkely-Hurst, I. BP	1,222	3.6	
Rees, D. Green	445	1.3	
Con majority	2,131	6.34	
Electorate	49,737		
Turnout	33,602	67.56	

Con gain (5.78% from Lab to Con)

WYCOMBE

		%	+/-%
Baker, S. Con*	24,766	45.1	-4.8
Ahmed, K. Lab	20,552	37.4	-0.2
Brodelle, T. Lib Dem	6,543	11.9	4.2
Sims, P. Green	1,454	2.7	0.5
Wassell, J. Wycombe Ind	926	1.7	
Srao, V. UKIP	324	0.6	-1.7
Gemmells, E. Ind	191	0.4	
Con majority	4,214	7.67	
Electorate	78,093		
Turnout	54,924	70.33	

Con hold (2.3% from Lab to Con)

WYRE AND PRESTON NORTH

		%	+/-%
Wallace, B. Con*	31,589	59.5	1.3
Ainscough, J. Lab	14,808	27.9	-7.1
Potter, J. Lib Dem	4,463	8.4	3.6
Norbury, R. Green	1,729	3.3	1.4
Ragozzino, D. Ind	335	0.6	
Con majority	16,781	31.59	
Electorate	74,775		
Turnout	53,124	71.05	

Con hold (4.2% from Lab to Con)

WYRE FOREST

		%	+/-%
Garnier, M. Con*	32,960	64.9	6.6
Lunn, R. Lab	11,547	22.7	-9.5
Miah, S. Lib Dem	4,081	8.0	4.2
Davis, J. Green	1,973	3.9	1.9
Con majority	21,413	42.14	
Electorate	78,077		
Turnout	50,818	65.09	

Con hold (8.05% from Lab to Con)

WYTHENSHAWE AND SALE EAST

		%	+/-%
Kane, M. Lab*	23,855	53.2	-9.0
Harrop, P. Con	13,459	30.0	0.4
Lepori, S. Lib Dem	3,111	6.9	3.7
Fousert, J. BP	2,717	6.1	
Nunney, R. Green	1,559	3.5	2.2
Bellamy, C. Comm League	58	0.1	
Lab majority	10,396	23.16	
Electorate	76,313		
Turnout	44,884	58.82	

Lab hold (4.69% from Lab to Con)

YEOVIL

		%	+/-%
Fysh, M. Con*	34,588	58.2	3.8
Clark, M. Lib Dem	18,407	31.0	1.3
Ledlie, T. Lab	3,761	6.3	-6.1
Wood, D. Green	1,629	2.7	1.0
Capozzoli, T. Ind	689	1.2	
Fox, T. CRP	186	0.3	
Con majority	16,181	27.24	
Electorate	82,468		
Turnout	59,408	72.04	

Con hold (1.25% from Lib Dem to Con)

YNYS MÔN

		%	+/-%
Crosbie, V. Con	12,959	35.3	7.6
Roberts, M. Lab	10,991	30.0	-11.9
ap Dafydd, A. PlC	10,418	28.4	1.0
Jenner, H. BP	2,184	6.0	
Con majority	1,968	5.37	
Electorate	51,925		
Turnout	36,673	70.63	

Con gain (9.72% from Lab to Con)

YORK CENTRAL

		%	+/-%
Maskell, R. Lab/Co-op*	27,312	55.0	-10.0
Tate, F. Con	13,767	27.7	-2.4
Blanchard, J. Lib Dem	4,149	8.4	3.7
Franklin, T. Green	2,107	4.2	
Szkiler, N. BP	1,479	3.0	
Snedden, A. YP	557	1.1	
Dunn, A. SDP	134	0.3	
Lab/Co-op majority	13,545	27.25	
Electorate	74,899		
Turnout	49,703	66.36	

Lab/Co-op hold (3.8% from Lab to Con)

YORK OUTER

		%	+/-%
Sturdy, J. Con*	27,324	49.2	-1.8
Perrett, A. Lab	17,339	31.2	-5.4
Aspden, K. Lib Dem	9,992	18.0	7.7
Marmion, S. Ind	692	1.3	
Con majority	9,985	17.97	
Electorate	74,673		
Turnout	55,575	74.42	

Con hold (1.79% from Lab to Con)

EAST YORKSHIRE

		%	+/-%
Knight, G. Con*	33,988	64.2	6.0
Minnis, C. Lab	11,201	21.1	-9.3
Needham, D. Lib Dem	4,219	8.0	4.0
Norman, T. YP	1,686	3.2	1.3
Jackson, M. Green	1,675	3.2	1.4
Con majority	22,787	43.02	
Electorate	80,923		
Turnout	52,974	65.46	

Con hold (7.63% from Lab to Con)

State of the parties

	2019 General Election	*2017 General Election*
Conservative	365	317
Labour*	202	262
Scottish National Party	48	35
Liberal Democrat	11	12
Democratic Unionist Party	8	10
Sinn Féin	7	7
Plaid Cymru	4	4
Social Democratic and Labour Party	2	0
Alliance Party of Northern Ireland	1	0
Green Party	1	1
The Speaker	1	1
Independent	0	1
TOTAL	**650**	**650**

* Includes Labour/Co-operative MPs.

Share of the vote

	Total Seats	*Total Votes*	*% of Votes*
Con	365	13966418	43.6
Lab	200	10209358	31.9
Lib Dem	11	3696424	11.5
SNP	47	1218605	3.8
Green	1	866192	2.7
BP	0	644257	2.0
Ind	0	305893	1.0
DUP	8	244128	0.8
Sinn Féin	7	181853	0.6
PlC	3	137326	0.4
APNI	1	134115	0.4
SDLP	2	118737	0.4
UUP	0	93123	0.3
Speaker	1	26831	0.1
UKIP	0	22817	0.1
Other	0	148479	0.5
TOTAL	**646**	**32014556**	**100**

Share of the vote by region

England

Eastern

	Total Seats	*Total Votes*	*% of Votes*
Con	52	1754091	57.2
Lab	5	749906	24.4
Lib Dem	1	410849	13.4
Green	0	90965	3.0
Ind	0	43152	1.4
BP	0	11707	0.4
Loony	0	2289	0.1
UKIP	0	1169	0.0
SDP	0	818	0.0
CPA	0	664	0.0
VAPP	0	631	0.0
Eng Dem	0	532	0.0
PFP	0	367	0.0
UGP	0	363	0.0
Best4Luton	0	268	0.0

	Total Seats	*Total Votes*	*% of Votes*
YPP	0	181	0.0
WEP	0	149	0.0
Advance	0	101	0.0
Reboot	0	67	0.0
TOTAL	**58**	**3068269**	**100**

East Midlands

	Total Seats	*Total Votes*	*% of Votes*
Con	38	1280724	54.8
Lab	7	715885	30.6
Lib Dem	0	182665	7.8
Green	0	60067	2.6
Ind	0	38555	1.6
BP	0	35344	1.5
Ashfield Ind	0	13498	0.6
IGC	0	6115	0.3
Lincs Ind	0	1999	0.1
UKIP	0	1508	0.1
Loony	0	1044	0.0
Eng Dem	0	432	0.0
Lib	0	304	0.0
Bus-Pass	0	172	0.0
Libertarian	0	140	0.0
TOTAL	**45**	**2338452**	**100**

London

	Total Seats	*Total Votes*	*% of Votes*
Lab	48	1778207	47.2
Con	21	1205129	32.0
Lib Dem	3	562564	14.9
Green	0	115527	3.1
BP	0	51735	1.4
Ind	0	38796	1.0
CPA	0	4407	0.1
IGC	0	3891	0.1
AWP	0	1264	0.0
UKIP	0	1060	0.0
Loony	0	736	0.0
WRP	0	524	0.0
Eng Dem	0	520	0.0
BNP	0	510	0.0
Comm United	0	393	0.0
Renew	0	270	0.0
SDP	0	168	0.0
Lib	0	101	0.0
Advance	0	71	0.0
Green Soc	0	71	0.0
YPP	0	50	0.0
TLW	0	47	0.0
Comm League	0	42	0.0
SEP	0	37	0.0
TOTAL	**72**	**3766120**	**100**

North East

	Total Seats	*Total Votes*	*% of Votes*
Lab	19	532127	42.6
Con	10	478208	38.3
BP	0	100910	8.1
Lib Dem	0	85243	6.8

	Total Seats	Total Votes	% of Votes
Green	0	29732	2.4
Ind	0	17882	1.4
NEP	0	2637	0.2
UKIP	0	1736	0.1
Lib	0	615	0.0
SLP	0	494	0.0
SDP	0	212	0.0
CPA	0	178	0.0
Space Navies	0	118	0.0
TOTAL	**29**	**1250092**	**100**

North West

	Total Seats	Total Votes	% of Votes
Lab	41	1638258	46.5
Con	32	1321036	37.5
Lib Dem	1	277501	7.9
BP	0	136196	3.9
Green	0	86782	2.5
Speaker	1	26831	0.8
Ind	0	16910	0.5
CB	0	7285	0.2
Lib	0	4910	0.1
UKIP	0	2333	0.1
PO&S	0	1606	0.0
B&P Ind	0	1162	0.0
CumbriaFirst	0	1070	0.0
AWP	0	658	0.0
Loony	0	324	0.0
SDP	0	168	0.0
Libertarian	0	149	0.0
Renew	0	137	0.0
WEP	0	130	0.0
SEP	0	107	0.0
Comm League	0	58	0.0
TOTAL	**75**	**3523611**	**100**

South East

	Total Seats	Total Votes	% of Votes
Con	74	2512869	54.0
Lab	8	1029966	22.1
Lib Dem	1	848382	18.2
Green	1	183724	3.9
Ind	0	46845	1.0
BP	0	12868	0.3
UKIP	0	7807	0.2
Loony	0	2873	0.1
Ind Net	0	1542	0.0
Peace Party	0	960	0.0
Wycombe Ind	0	926	0.0
CPA	0	740	0.0
JACP	0	728	0.0
AWP	0	675	0.0
SDP	0	534	0.0
Libertarian	0	519	0.0
Eng Dem	0	194	0.0
Advance	0	179	0.0
WEP	0	137	0.0
Patria	0	109	0.0

	Total Seats	Total Votes	% of Votes
YPP	0	80	0.0
SP	0	69	0.0
TOTAL	**84**	**4652726**	**100**

South West

	Total Seats	Total Votes	% of Votes
Con	48	1612090	52.8
Lab	6	713226	23.4
Lib Dem	1	554504	18.2
Green	0	115021	3.8
Ind	0	38016	1.2
BP	0	11139	0.4
Lib	0	4225	0.1
MK	0	1660	0.1
UKIP	0	1227	0.0
Libertarian	0	567	0.0
AWP	0	489	0.0
Loony	0	445	0.0
Motherworld	0	270	0.0
CMP	0	257	0.0
CRP	0	186	0.0
Common People	0	132	0.0
TOTAL	**55**	**3053454**	**100**

West Midlands

	Total Seats	Total Votes	% of Votes
Con	44	1449289	53.4
Lab	15	918123	33.9
Lib Dem	0	213903	7.9
Green	0	80556	3.0
BP	0	36646	1.4
Ind	0	9269	0.3
Loony	0	1431	0.1
Shropshire	0	1141	0.0
UKIP	0	1068	0.0
CPA	0	257	0.0
Yeshua	0	204	0.0
SDP	0	67	0.0
TOTAL	**59**	**2711954**	**100**

Yorkshire and Humberside

	Total Seats	Total Votes	% of Votes
Con	26	1097376	43.1
Lab	28	989787	38.9
Lib Dem	0	205225	8.1
BP	0	150561	5.9
Green	0	57872	2.3
YP	0	29201	1.1
Ind	0	7438	0.3
HWD Ind	0	6432	0.3
SDP	0	1033	0.0
UKIP	0	983	0.0
Lib	0	721	0.0
Eng Dem	0	309	0.0
Loony	0	252	0.0
Green Soc	0	207	0.0
SEP	0	28	0.0
TOTAL	**54**	**2547425**	**100**

Nothern Ireland

	Total Seats	*Total Votes*	*% of Votes*
DUP	8	244128	30.6
Sinn Féin	7	181853	22.8
APNI	1	134115	16.8
SDLP	2	118737	14.9
UUP	0	93123	11.7
Aontú	0	9814	1.2
PBPA	0	7526	0.9
Con	0	5433	0.7
Green	0	1996	0.2
Ind	0	1687	0.2
UKIP	0	623	0.1
TOTAL	**18**	**799035**	**100**

Scotland

	Total Seats	*Total Votes*	*% of Votes*
SNP	47	1218605	44.2
Con	6	692939	25.1
Lab	1	511838	18.6
Lib Dem	4	263417	9.5
Green	0	28122	1.0
Ind	0	25184	0.9
BP	0	13243	0.5
UKIP	0	3303	0.1
VAPP	0	588	0.0
SFP	0	465	0.0
Christian	0	460	0.0
Libertarian	0	405	0.0
CPA	0	240	0.0
Renew	0	138	0.0
SDP	0	114	0.0
TOTAL	**58**	**2759061**	**100**

Wales

	Total Seats	*Total Votes*	*% of Votes*
Lab	22	632035	40.9
Con	14	557234	36.1
PlC	3	137326	8.9
Lib Dem	0	92171	6.0
BP	0	83908	5.4
Ind	0	22159	1.4
Green	0	15828	1.0
Gwlad	0	1515	0.1
CVP	0	1322	0.1
Loony	0	345	0.0
Christian	0	245	0.0
SDP	0	181	0.0
SP	0	88	0.0
TOTAL	**39**	**1544357**	**100**

Seats which changed parties

	2017	*2019*
Aberdeen South	Con	SNP
Angus	Con	SNP
Ashfield	Lab	Con
Ayr, Carrick and Cumnock	Con	SNP

	2017	2019
Barrow and Furness	Lab/Co-op	Con
Bassetlaw	Lab	Con
Belfast North	DUP	Sinn Féin
Belfast South	DUP	SDLP
Birmingham, Northfield	Lab	Con
Bishop Auckland	Lab	Con
Blackpool South	Lab	Con
Blyth Valley	Lab	Con
Bolsover	Lab	Con
Bolton North East	Lab	Con
Bridgend	Lab	Con
Buckingham	Speaker	Con
Burnley	Lab	Con
Bury North	Lab	Con
Bury South	Lab	Con
Carshalton and Wallington	Lib Dem	Con
Chorley	Lab	Speaker
Clwyd South	Lab	Con
Vale of Clwyd	Lab	Con
Coatbridge, Chryston and Bellshill	Lab	SNP
Colne Valley	Lab	Con
Crewe and Nantwich	Lab	Con
Darlington	Lab	Con
Delyn	Lab	Con
Derby North	Lab	Con
Dewsbury	Lab	Con
Don Valley	Lab	Con
North Down	Ind	APNI
Dudley North	Lab	Con
East Dunbartonshire	Lib Dem	SNP
North West Durham	Lab	Con
Eastbourne	Lib Dem	Con
North East Fife	SNP	Lib Dem
Foyle	Sinn Féin	SDLP
Gedling	Lab	Con
Glasgow North East	Lab/Co-op	SNP
Gordon	Con	SNP
Great Grimsby	Lab	Con
Heywood and Middleton	Lab	Con
High Peak	Lab	Con
Hyndburn	Lab	Con
Ipswich	Lab	Con
Keighley	Lab	Con
Kensington	Lab	Con
Kirkcaldy and Cowdenbeath	Lab	SNP
Leigh	Lab/Co-op	Con
Lincoln	Lab	Con
East Lothian	Lab	SNP
Midlothian	Lab	SNP
Newcastle-under-Lyme	Lab	Con
North Norfolk	Lib Dem	Con
Ochil and South Perthshire	Con	SNP
Penistone and Stocksbridge	Lab	Con
Peterborough	Lab	Con
Putney	Con	Lab
Redcar	Lab/Co-op	Con
East Renfrewshire	Con	SNP

	2017	*2019*
Richmond Park	Con	Lib Dem
Rother Valley	Lab	Con
Rutherglen and Hamilton West	Lab/Co-op	SNP
St Albans	Con	Lib Dem
Scunthorpe	Lab	Con
Sedgefield	Lab	Con
Stirling	Con	SNP
Stockton South	Lab	Con
Stoke-on-Trent Central	Lab/Co-op	Con
Stoke-on-Trent North	Lab	Con
Stroud	Lab/Co-op	Con
Wakefield	Lab	Con
Warrington South	Lab	Con
West Bromwich East	Lab	Con
West Bromwich West	Lab/Co-op	Con
Wolverhampton North East	Lab	Con
Wolverhampton South West	Lab	Con
Workington	Lab	Con
Wrexham	Lab	Con
Ynys Môn	Lab	Con

Results in vulnerable Conservative seats

	% majority 2017	*Result*	*Swing*
Aberconwy	1.97	Con Hold	2.19% from Lab to Con
Aberdeen South	10.67	SNP Gain	9.69% from Con to SNP
Altrincham and Sale West	12.14	Con Hold	0.48% from Con to Lab
Angus	6.57	SNP Gain	7.67% from Con to SNP
Ayr, Carrick and Cumnock	5.99	SNP Gain	5.49% from Con to SNP
Banff and Buchan	8.86	Con Hold	0.43% from SNP to Con
Blackpool North and Cleveleys	4.93	Con Hold	8.58% from Lab to Con
Bolton West	1.83	Con Hold	8.04% from Lab to Con
Broxtowe	1.55	Con Hold	4.03% from Lab to Con
Calder Valley	1.05	Con Hold	4.45% from Lab to Con
Camborne and Redruth	3.25	Con Hold	6.98% from Lab to Con
Carlisle	6.02	Con Hold	6.64% from Lab to Con
Carmarthen West and South Pembrokeshire	7.35	Con Hold	5.49% from Lab to Con
Cheadle	8.24	Con Hold	2.04% from Lab to Con
Cheltenham	4.5	Con Hold	1.43% from Con to Lib Dem
Chingford and Woodford Green	5.17	Con Hold	1.29% from Con to Lab
Chipping Barnet	0.63	Con Hold	0.74% from Lab to Con
Clwyd West	8.44	Con Hold	4.15% from Lab to Con
Colchester	10.58	Con Hold	3.51% from Lab to Con
Copeland	3.94	Con Hold	4.87% from Lab to Con
Corby	4.48	Con Hold	6.22% from Lab to Con
North Cornwall	14.1	Con Hold	7.16% from Lib Dem to Con
Crawley	4.87	Con Hold	5.91% from Lab to Con
North East Derbyshire	5.67	Con Hold	10.2% from Lab to Con
East Devon	13.3	Con Hold	1.43% from Con to Ind
North Devon	7.77	Con Hold	9.41% from Lib Dem to Con
Dover	12.37	Con Hold	5.87% from Lab to Con
Dumfries and Galloway	10.93	Con Hold	3.72% from Con to SNP
Erewash	9.09	Con Hold	6.28% from Lab to Con
Filton and Bradley Stoke	8.24	Con Hold	1.12% from Lab to Con
Finchley and Golders Green	3.15	Con Hold	14.18% from Con to Lib Dem
Vale of Glamorgan	4.07	Con Hold	1.19% from Lab to Con

	% majority 2017	*Result*	*Swing*
Gloucester	10.19	Con Hold	4.42% from Lab to Con
Gordon	4.85	SNP Gain	3.16% from Con to SNP
Halesowen and Rowley Regis	11.81	Con Hold	8.31% from Lab to Con
Harrow East	3.45	Con Hold	6.49% from Lab to Con
Hastings and Rye	0.63	Con Hold	3.39% from Lab to Con
Hazel Grove	12.46	Con Hold	1.26% from Lib Dem to Con
Hendon	2.05	Con Hold	2.81% from Lab to Con
Lewes	10.14	Con Hold	2.84% from Con to Lib Dem
Cities of London and Westminster	8.12	Con Hold	13.09% from Con to Lib Dem
Loughborough	7.87	Con Hold	2.6% from Lab to Con
Mansfield	2.1	Con Hold	15.44% from Lab to Con
Middlesbrough South and East Cleveland	2.14	Con Hold	11.04% from Lab to Con
Milton Keynes North	3.08	Con Hold	3.44% from Lab to Con
Milton Keynes South	2.57	Con Hold	18.29% from Lab to Con
Moray	8.73	Con Hold	3.84% from Con to SNP
Morecambe and Lunesdale	3.06	Con Hold	5.46% from Lab to Con
Morley and Outwood	4	Con Hold	8.81% from Lab to Con
Northampton North	2	Con Hold	5.95% from Lab to Con
Northampton South	2.82	Con Hold	4.32% from Lab to Con
Norwich North	1.1	Con Hold	4.56% from Lab to Con
Nuneaton	10.27	Con Hold	9.34% from Lab to Con
Ochil and South Perthshire	6.19	SNP Gain	6.98% from Con to SNP
Pendle	2.85	Con Hold	5.51% from Lab to Con
Plymouth, Moor View	11.03	Con Hold	9% from Lab to Con
Preseli Pembrokeshire	0.74	Con Hold	5.58% from Lab to Con
Pudsey	0.61	Con Hold	2.93% from Lab to Con
Putney	3.31	Lab Gain	6.37% from Con to Lab
Reading West	5.54	Con Hold	1.3% from Lab to Con
East Renfrewshire	8.76	SNP Gain	9.27% from Con to SNP
South Ribble	13.51	Con Hold	3.62% from Lab to Con
Richmond Park	0.07	Lib Dem Gain	% from Con to Lib Dem
Rochford and Southend East	11.72	Con Hold	7.41% from Lab to Con
Rossendale and Darwen	6.39	Con Hold	6.51% from Lab to Con
Rushcliffe	13.7	Con Hold	0.56% from Con to Lab
St Albans	10.69	Lib Dem Gain	10.8% from Con to Lib Dem
St Ives	0.61	Con Hold	3.85% from to
Scarborough and Whitby	6.8	Con Hold	6.89% from Lab to Con
Sherwood	9.72	Con Hold	10.44% from Lab to Con
Shipley	8.74	Con Hold	1.38% from Lab to Con
Shrewsbury and Atcham	11.36	Con Hold	3.78% from Lab to Con
Southampton Itchen	0.07	Con Hold	4.69% from Lab to Con
Southport	6.07	Con Hold	1.25% from Lab to Con
Stafford	14.85	Con Hold	6.58% from Lab to Con
Stevenage	6.84	Con Hold	5.52% from Lab to Con
Stirling	0.3	SNP Gain	8.93% from Con to SNP
Stoke-on-Trent South	1.59	Con Hold	13.38% from Lab to Con
South Swindon	4.8	Con Hold	4.1% from Lab to Con
Telford	1.61	Con Hold	11.91% from Lab to Con
South Thanet	12.81	Con Hold	4.52% from Lab to Con
Thurrock	0.68	Con Hold	11.72% from Lab to Con
Truro and Falmouth	6.69	Con Hold	0.5% from Lab to Con
Uxbridge and South Ruislip	10.76	Con Hold	2.09% from Lab to Con
Walsall North	6.81	Con Hold	12.91% from Lab to Con
Watford	3.56	Con Hold	2.02% from Lab to Con
Wells	12.43	Con Hold	1.86% from Lib Dem to Con

	% majority 2017	Result	Swing
Welwyn Hatfield	14.23	Con Hold	3.36% from Lab to Con
Wimbledon	10.88	Con Hold	15.36% from Con to Lib Dem
Worcester	4.87	Con Hold	4.19% from Lab to Con
East Worthing and Shoreham	9.6	Con Hold	2.21% from Lab to Con
Wycombe	12.26	Con Hold	2.3% from Lab to Con
York Outer	14.4	Con Hold	1.79% from Lab to Con

Results in vulnerable Labour seats

	% majority 2017	Result	Swing
Alyn and Deeside	11.67	Lab Hold	5.59% from Lab to Con
Ashfield	0.88	Con Gain	10.39% from Lab to Con
Bassetlaw	9.26	Con Gain	18.37% from Lab to Con
Battersea	4.38	Lab Hold	2.52% from Con to Lab
Bedford	1.62	Lab Hold	0.66% from Lab to Con
Birmingham, Northfield	10.49	Con Gain	7.15% from Lab to Con
Bishop Auckland	1.16	Con Gain	9.44% from Lab to Con
Blackpool South	7.21	Con Gain	9.23% from Lab to Con
Bolsover	11.34	Con Gain	11.44% from Lab to Con
Bolton North East	8.39	Con Gain	4.63% from Lab to Con
Bridgend	10.85	Con Gain	5.93% from Lab to Con
Bristol North West	8.78	Lab Hold	0.69% from Con to Lab
Bury North	9.1	Con Gain	4.66% from Lab to Con
Bury South	11.67	Con Gain	6.24% from Lab to Con
Canterbury	0.33	Lab Hold	1.36% from Con to Lab
Cardiff North	8.01	Lab Hold	2.61% from Con to Lab
Chorley	13.47	Speaker Gain	21.12% from Lab to Speaker
Clwyd South	11.61	Con Gain	7.51% from Lab to Con
Vale of Clwyd	6.14	Con Gain	5.51% from Lab to Con
Coatbridge, Chryston and Bellshill	3.52	SNP Gain	7.58% from Lab to SNP
Colne Valley	1.51	Con Gain	4.93% from Lab to Con
Crewe and Nantwich	0.09	Con Gain	7.9% from Lab to Con
Croydon Central	9.88	Lab Hold	0.53% from Con to Lab
Dagenham and Rainham	10.13	Lab Hold	4.74% from Lab to Con
Darlington	7.31	Con Gain	7.44% from Lab to Con
Delyn	10.74	Con Gain	6.5% from Lab to Con
Derby North	4.13	Con Gain	4.76% from Lab to Con
Dewsbury	5.86	Con Gain	4.31% from Lab to Con
Don Valley	11.22	Con Gain	9.6% from Lab to Con
Dudley North	0.06	Con Gain	15.68% from Lab to Con
Eltham	13.6	Lab Hold	% from Lab to Con
Enfield Southgate	8.98	Lab Hold	0.19% from Con to Lab
Gedling	9.07	Con Gain	5.22% from Lab to Con
Gower	7.16	Lab Hold	1.53% from Lab to Con
Great Grimsby	7.21	Con Gain	28.03% from Lab to Con
Halifax	11.11	Lab Hold	2.8% from Lab to Con
High Peak	4.3	Con Gain	2.69% from Lab to Con
Hyndburn	12.83	Con Gain	9.89% from Lab to Con
Ipswich	1.62	Con Gain	6.32% from Lab to Con
Keighley	0.46	Con Gain	2.33% from Lab to Con
Kensington	0.05	Con Gain	0.2% from Lab to Con
Kirkcaldy and Cowdenbeath	0.56	SNP Gain	1.61% from Lab to SNP
Lancaster and Fleetwood	14.45	Lab Hold	4.6% from Lab to Con
Lincoln	3.15	Con Gain	5.04% from Lab to Con
East Lothian	5.51	SNP Gain	6.07% from Lab to SNP
Midlothian	1.95	SNP Gain	6.88% from Lab to SNP

	% majority 2017	*Result*	*Swing*
Newcastle-under-Lyme	0.07	Con Gain	8.33% from Lab to Con
Newport West	13	Lab Hold	3.1% from Lab to Con
Penistone and Stocksbridge	2.65	Con Gain	8.58% from Lab to Con
Peterborough	1.27	Con Gain	7.47% from Lab to Con
Portsmouth South	3.48	Lab Hold	3.9% from Con to Lab
Reading East	6.77	Lab Hold	1.9% from Con to Lab
Rother Valley	7.83	Con Gain	10.38% from Lab to Con
Scunthorpe	8.52	Con Gain	12.78% from Lab to Con
Sedgefield	14.55	Con Gain	12.69% from Lab to Con
Sheffield, Hallam	3.72	Lab Hold	1.24% from Lab to Lib Dem
Stockton South	1.65	Con Gain	5.61% from Lab to Con
Stoke-on-Trent North	5.63	Con Gain	10.63% from Lab to Con
Wakefield	4.69	Con Gain	6.06% from Lab to Con
Warrington South	4.1	Con Gain	3.68% from Lab to Con
Warwick and Leamington	2.23	Lab Hold	0.39% from Lab to Con
Weaver Vale	7.74	Lab Hold	3.32% from Lab to Con
Wirral West	12.18	Lab Hold	2.6% from Lab to Con
Wolverhampton North East	12.53	Con Gain	12.2% from Lab to Con
Wolverhampton South West	5.15	Con Gain	4.59% from Lab to Con
Workington	9.41	Con Gain	9.71% from Lab to Con
Wrexham	5.21	Con Gain	5.78% from Lab to Con
Ynys Môn	14.06	Con Gain	9.72% from Lab to Con

Results in vulnerable Labour/Co-operative seats

	% majority 2017	*Result*	*Swing*
Barrow and Furness	0.44	Con Gain	17.21% from Lab to Con
Glasgow North East	0.76	SNP Gain	4.12% from Lab to SNP
Leeds North West	9.11	Lab/Co-op Hold	1.33% from Lab to Con
Plymouth, Sutton and Devonport	13.27	Lab/Co-op Hold	2.18% from Lab to Con
Rutherglen and Hamilton West	0.52	SNP Gain	5.12% from Lab to SNP
Stoke-on-Trent Central	11.73	Con Gain	6.91% from Lab to Con
Stroud	1.07	Con Gain	3.45% from Lab to Con
West Bromwich West	12.33	Con Gain	11.67% from Lab to Con

Results in vulnerable SNP seats

	% majority 2017	*Result*	*Swing*
Aberdeen North	11.24	SNP Hold	7.63% from Con to SNP
Airdrie and Shotts	0.51	SNP Hold	6.27% from Lab to SNP
Argyll and Bute	2.76	SNP Hold	2.88% from Con to SNP
Central Ayrshire	2.81	SNP Hold	4.28% from Con to SNP
North Ayrshire and Arran	7.65	SNP Hold	5.01% from Con to SNP
Cumbernauld, Kilsyth and Kirkintilloch East	9.72	SNP Hold	9.3% from Lab to SNP
West Dunbartonshire	5.18	SNP Hold	7.97% from Lab to SNP
Dundee West	13.57	SNP Hold	7.93% from Lab to SNP
Dunfermline and West Fife	1.65	SNP Hold	9.16% from Lab to SNP
East Kilbride, Strathaven and Lesmahagow	7.14	SNP Hold	8.17% from Lab to SNP
Edinburgh East	7.85	SNP Hold	6.94% from Lab to SNP
Edinburgh North and Leith	2.87	SNP Hold	9.34% from Lab to SNP
Edinburgh South West	2.22	SNP Hold	10.37% from Con to SNP
Falkirk	9.14	SNP Hold	6.95% from Con to SNP
North East Fife	0	Lib Dem Gain	1.43% from SNP to Lib Dem
Glasgow Central	6.28	SNP Hold	4.9% from Lab to SNP

	% majority 2017	*Result*	*Swing*
Glasgow East	0.21	SNP Hold	7.11% from Lab to SNP
Glasgow North	3.16	SNP Hold	6.14% from Lab to SNP
Glasgow North West	6.58	SNP Hold	7.18% from Lab to SNP
Glasgow South	4.54	SNP Hold	7.21% from Lab to SNP
Glasgow South West	0.17	SNP Hold	6.55% from Lab to SNP
Glenrothes	8.08	SNP Hold	10.09% from Lab to SNP
Inverclyde	0.98	SNP Hold	% from Lab to SNP
Inverness, Nairn, Badenoch and Strathspey	9.31	SNP Hold	4.85% from Con to SNP
Kilmarnock and Loudoun	13.46	SNP Hold	5.43% from Con to SNP
Lanark and Hamilton East	0.53	SNP Hold	4.62% from Con to SNP
Linlithgow and East Falkirk	5.2	SNP Hold	6.1% from Con to SNP
Livingston	7.37	SNP Hold	4.44% from Con to SNP
Motherwell and Wishaw	0.76	SNP Hold	6.66% from Lab to SNP
Na h-Eileanan An Iar	6.78	SNP Hold	4.99% from Lab to SNP
Paisley and Renfrewshire North	5.6	SNP Hold	9.14% from Lab to SNP
Paisley and Renfrewshire South	6.08	SNP Hold	9.32% from Lab to SNP
Perth and North Perthshire	0.04	SNP Hold	6.95% from Con to SNP

Results in vulnerable DUP seats

	% majority 2017	*Result*	*Swing*
South Antrim	7.41	DUP Hold	0.59% from DUP to UUP
Belfast North	4.51	Sinn Féin Gain	4.23% from DUP to Sinn Féin
Belfast South	4.55	SDLP Gain	18.48% from DUP to SDLP

Results in vulnerable Liberal Democrat seats

	% majority 2017	*Result*	*Swing*
Bath	11.46	Lib Dem Hold	6.05% from Con to Lib Dem
Caithness, Sutherland and Easter Ross	6.61	Lib Dem Hold	2.98% from Lib Dem to SNP
Carshalton and Wallington	2.69	Con Gain	1.99% from Lib Dem to Con
East Dunbartonshire	10.29	SNP Gain	5.29% from Lib Dem to SNP
Eastbourne	2.8	Con Gain	5.32% from Lib Dem to Con
Edinburgh West	5.65	Lib Dem Hold	0.62% from SNP to Lib Dem
Kingston and Surbiton	6.62	Lib Dem Hold	5.29% from Con to Lib Dem
North Norfolk	6.72	Con Gain	17.48% from Lib Dem to Con
Oxford West and Abingdon	1.36	Lib Dem Hold	6.9% from Con to Lib Dem
Twickenham	14.69	Lib Dem Hold	3.56% from Con to Lib Dem
Westmorland and Lonsdale	1.5	Lib Dem Hold	1.08% from Con to Lib Dem

Results in vulnerable PlC seats

	% majority 2017	*Result*	*Swing*
Arfon	0.33	PlC Hold	4.6% from Lab to PlC
Carmarthen East and Dinefwr	9.51	PlC Hold	4.33% from PlC to Con
Ceredigion	0.26	PlC Hold	2.45% from Con to PlC

Results in vulnerable Sinn Féin seats

	% majority 2017	*Result*	*Swing*
South Down	4.79	Sinn Féin Hold	0.77% from Sinn Féin to SDLP
Fermanagh and South Tyrone	1.63	Sinn Féin Hold	0.76% from Sinn Féin to UUP

	% majority 2017	*Result*	*Swing*
Foyle	0.37	SDLP Gain	37.85% from Sinn Féin to SDLP

New MPs (155)

* served in previous Parliaments.

AHMAD KHAN, Imran	Con	Wakefield
AIKEN, Nickie	Con	Cities of London and Westminster
ALI, Tahir	Lab	Birmingham, Hall Green
ANDERSON, Fleur	Lab	Putney
ANDERSON, Lee	Con	Ashfield
ANDERSON, Stuart	Con	Wolverhampton South West
ANSELL, Caroline*	Con	Eastbourne
ATHERTON, Sarah	Con	Wrexham
BACON, Gareth	Con	Orpington
BAILEY, Shaun	Con	West Bromwich West
BAILLIE, Siobhan	Con	Bermondsey and Old Southwark
BAKER, Duncan	Con	North Norfolk
BARKER, Paula	Lab	Liverpool Wavertree
BAYNES, Simon	Con	Clwyd South
BEGUM, Apsana	Lab	Poplar and Limehouse
BELL, Aaron	Con	Don Valley
BENTON, Scott	Con	Blackpool South
BHATTI, Saqib	Con	Meriden
BLAKE, Olivia	Lab	Sheffield, Hallam
BONNAR, Steven	SNP	Coatbridge, Chryston and Bellshill
BRISTOW, Paul	Con	Middlesbrough South and East Cleveland
BRITCLIFFE, Sara	Con	Hyndburn
BROWNE, Anthony	Con	South Cambridgeshire
BUCHAN, Felicity	Con	Kensington
BUTLER, Rob	Con	Aylesbury
BYRNE, Ian	Lab	Liverpool West Derby
CALLAGHAN, Amy	SNP	East Dunbartonshire
CARTER, Andy	Con	Warrington South
CATES, Miriam	Con	Penistone and Stocksbridge
CHAMBERLAIN, Wendy	Lib Dem	North East Fife
CLARK, Feryal	Lab	Enfield North
CLARKE, Theo	Con	Bristol East
CLARKE-SMITH, Brendan	Con	Bassetlaw
CLARKSON, Chris	Con	Heywood and Middleton
COLBURN, Elliot	Con	Carshalton and Wallington
COOPER, Daisy	Lib Dem	Mid Sussex
COUTINHO, Claire	Con	East Surrey
CROSBIE, Virginia	Con	Ynys Môn
DALY, James	Con	Bolton North East
DAVIES, Gareth	Con	Doncaster Central
DAVIES, James*	Con	Vale of Clwyd
DAVIES-JONES, Alex	Lab	Pontypridd
DAVISON, Dehenna	Con	Bishop Auckland
DINES, Sarah	Con	Derbyshire Dales
DOOGAN, Dave	SNP	Angus
DORANS, Allan	SNP	Ayr, Carrick and Cumnock
DRUMMOND, Flick*	Con	Meon Valley
EASTWOOD, Colum	SDLP	Foyle
EASTWOOD, Mark	Con	Dewsbury
EDWARDS, Ruth	Con	Rushcliffe
ELPHICKE, Natalie	Con	Dover
ESHALOMI, Florence	Lab/Co-op	Vauxhall
EVANS, Luke	Con	Birmingham, Edgbaston

EVERITT, Ben	Con	Milton Keynes North
FARRIS, Laura	Con	Leyton and Wanstead
FARRY, Stephen	APNI	North Down
FELL, Simon	Con	Barrow and Furness
FERRIER, Margaret*	Ind	Rutherglen and Hamilton West
FINUCANE, John	Sinn Féin	Belfast North
FLETCHER, Katherine	Con	Ellesmere Port and Neston
FLETCHER, Mark	Con	Bolsover
FLETCHER, Nick	Con	Don Valley
FLYNN, Stephen	SNP	Aberdeen South
FOY, Mary	Lab	City of Durham
FULLER, Richard*	Con	Bedford
GIBSON, Peter	Con	Darlington
GIDEON, Jo	Con	Great Grimsby
GRIFFITH, Andrew	Con	Arundel and South Downs
GRIFFITHS, Kate	Con	Burton
GRUNDY, James	Con	Leigh
GULLIS, Jonathan	Con	Stoke-on-Trent North
HANNA, Claire	SDLP	Strangford
HANVEY, Neale	SNP	Kirkcaldy and Cowdenbeath
HART, Sally-Ann	Con	Hastings and Rye
HENRY, Darren	Con	Broxtowe
HIGGINBOTHAM, Antony	Con	Burnley
HOLDEN, Richard	Con	North West Durham
HOLMES, Paul	Con	Eastleigh
HOPKINS, Rachel	Lab	Luton South
HOWELL, Paul	Con	Houghton and Sunderland South
HUDSON, Neil	Con	Edinburgh South
HUNT, Jane	Con	Leicester East
HUNT, Tom	Con	Doncaster Central
JENKINSON, Mark	Con	Workington
JOHNSON, Kim	Lab	Liverpool Riverside
JOHNSTON, David	Con	Wantage
JONES, Fay	Con	Brecon and Radnorshire
JUPP, Simon	Con	East Devon
KEARNS, Alicia	Con	Mitcham and Morden
KRUGER, Danny	Con	Devizes
LARGAN, Robert	Con	Bury South
LEVY, Ian	Con	Blyth Valley
LOCKHART, Carla	DUP	Upper Bann
LODER, Chris	Con	West Dorset
LOGAN, Mark	Con	Bolton North East
LONGHI, Marco	Con	Dudley North
MACASKILL, Kenny	SNP	East Lothian
MCCARTNEY, Jason*	Con	Colne Valley
MCCARTNEY, Karl*	Con	Lincoln
MACKRORY, Cherilyn	Con	Truro and Falmouth
MCLAUGHLIN, Anne*	SNP	Glasgow North East
MANGNALL, Anthony	Con	Totnes
MARSON, Julie	Con	Dagenham and Rainham
MAYHEW, Jerome	Con	Broadland
MILLAR, Robin	Con	Aberconwy
MISHRA, Navendu	Lab	Hazel Grove
MOHINDRA, Gagan	Con	North Tyneside
MOORE, Robbie	Con	Keighley
MORRISSEY, Joy	Con	Beaconsfield
MULLAN, Kieran	Con	Birmingham, Hodge Hill

MUMBY-CROFT, Holly	Con	Scunthorpe
MURRAY, James	Lab/Co-op	Ealing North
NICHOLS, Charlotte	Lab	Warrington North
NICI, Lia	Con	Great Grimsby
NICOLSON, John*	SNP	East Dunbartonshire
OLNEY, Sarah*	Lib Dem	Richmond Park
OPPONG-ASARE, Abena	Lab	Erith and Thamesmead
OSBORNE, Kate	Lab	Jarrow
OSWALD, Kirsten*	SNP	East Renfrewshire
OWATEMI, Taiwo	Lab	Coventry North West
OWEN, Sarah	Lab	Hastings and Rye
RANDALL, Tom	Con	Gedling
RIBEIRO-ADDY, Bell	Lab	Streatham
RICHARDS, Nicola	Con	West Bromwich East
RICHARDSON, Angela	Con	Guildford
ROBERTS, Rob	Con	Delyn
RUSSELL, Dean	Con	Luton North
SAMBROOK, Gary	Con	Birmingham, Northfield
SAXBY, Selaine	Con	North Devon
SIMMONDS, David	Con	Ruislip, Northwood and Pinner
SMITH, Alyn	SNP	Stirling
SMITH, Greg	Con	Buckingham
SOLLOWAY, Amanda*	Con	Derby North
SPENCER, Ben	Con	Camberwell and Peckham
STAFFORD, Alexander	Con	Rother Valley
STEVENSON, Jane	Con	Wolverhampton North East
SULTANA, Zarah	Lab	Coventry South
SUNDERLAND, James	Con	Bracknell
TARRY, Sam	Lab	Ilford South
THOMPSON, Owen*	SNP	Midlothian
THOMSON, Richard	SNP	Gordon
TIMPSON, Edward*	Con	Crewe and Nantwich
TROTT, Laura	Con	Sevenoaks
VICKERS, Matt	Con	Stockton South
WAKEFORD, Christian	Con	Bury South
WALLIS, Jamie	Con	Bridgend
WEBB, Suzanne	Con	Stourbridge
WEBBE, Claudia	Ind	Leicester East
WHITLEY, Mick	Lab	Birkenhead
WHITTOME, Nadia	Lab	Nottingham East
WILD, James	Con	North Norfolk
WILLIAMS, Craig*	Con	Cardiff North
WILSON, Munira	Lib Dem	Feltham and Heston
WINTER, Beth	Lab	Cynon Valley
YOUNG, Jacob	Con	Middlesbrough

Defeated MPs (79)

BERGER, Luciana	Lib Dem	Finchley and Golders Green
BRAKE, Tom	Lib Dem	Carshalton and Wallington
BURDEN, Richard	Lab	Birmingham, Northfield
CHAPMAN, Jenny	Lab	Darlington
CLARK, Colin	Con	Gordon
COAKER, Vernon	Lab	Gedling
COOPER, Julie	Lab	Burnley
CRAUSBY, David	Lab	Bolton North East
CREAGH, Mary	Lab	Wakefield

DAKIN, Nic	Lab	Scunthorpe
DENT COAD, Emma	Lab	Kensington
DODDS, Jane	Lib Dem	Brecon and Radnorshire
DODDS, Nigel	DUP	Belfast North
DREW, David	Lab/Co-op	Stroud
FIELD, Frank	CB	Birkenhead
FLINT, Caroline	Lab	Don Valley
FORBES, Lisa	Lab	Peterborough
FRITH, James	Lab	Bury North
GAFFNEY, Hugh	Lab	Coatbridge, Chryston and Bellshill
GAPES, Mike	IGC	Ilford South
GAUKE, David	Ind	South West Hertfordshire
GEORGE, Ruth	Lab	High Peak
GETHINS, Stephen	SNP	North East Fife
GODSIFF, Roger	Ind	Birmingham, Hall Green
GOLDSMITH, Zac	Con	Richmond Park
GOODMAN, Helen	Lab	Bishop Auckland
GRAHAM, Luke	Con	Ochil and South Perthshire
GRIEVE, Dominic	Ind	Beaconsfield
GROGAN, John	Lab	Keighley
GYIMAH, Sam	Lib Dem	East Surrey
HAIR, Kirstene	Con	Angus
HANSON, David	Lab	Delyn
HAYMAN, Sue	Lab	Halesowen and Rowley Regis
JONES, Graham	Lab	Hyndburn
JONES, Susan Elan	Lab	Clwyd South
KERR, Stephen	Con	Stirling
KILLEN, Ged	Lab/Co-op	Rutherglen and Hamilton West
LAIRD, Lesley	Lab	Kirkcaldy and Cowdenbeath
LEE, Karen	Lab	Lincoln
LEE, Phillip	Lib Dem	Bracknell
LESLIE, Chris	IGC	Nottingham East
LEWIS, Ivan	Ind	Bury South
LITTLE PENGELLY, Emma	DUP	Belfast South
LLOYD, Stephen	Lib Dem	Eastbourne
MCCALLION, Elisha	Sinn Féin	Foyle
MCINNES, Liz	Lab	Heywood and Middleton
MAIN, Anne	Con	St Albans
MARSDEN, Gordon	Lab	Blackpool South
MARTIN, Sandy	Lab	Ipswich
MASTERTON, Paul	Con	East Renfrewshire
MILTON, Anne	Ind	Guildford
MOON, Madeleine	Lab	Bridgend
ONN, Melanie	Lab	Great Grimsby
PIDCOCK, Laura	Lab	North West Durham
PLATT, Jo	Lab/Co-op	Leigh
RASHID, Faisal	Lab	Warrington South
REYNOLDS, Emma	Lab	Wolverhampton North East
ROWLEY, Danielle	Lab	Midlothian
RUANE, Chris	Lab	Vale of Clwyd
SANDBACH, Antoinette	Lib Dem	Eddisbury
SHERRIFF, Paula	Lab	Dewsbury
SHUKER, Gavin	Ind	Luton South
SKINNER, Dennis	Lab	Bolsover
SMEETH, Ruth	Lab	Burton
SMITH, Angela	Lib Dem	Altrincham and Sale West
SMITH, Eleanor	Lab	Wolverhampton South West

SMITH, Laura	Lab	Crewe and Nantwich
SNELL, Gareth	Lab/Co-op	Stoke-on-Trent Central
SOUBRY, Anna	IGC	Broxtowe
SWEENEY, Paul	Lab/Co-op	Glasgow North East
SWINSON, Jo	Lib Dem	East Dunbartonshire
TURLEY, Anna	Lab/Co-op	Redcar
UMUNNA, Chuka	Lib Dem	Cities of London and Westminster
WALKER, Thelma	Lab	Colne Valley
WHITFIELD, Martin	Lab	East Lothian
WILLIAMS, Paul	Lab	Stockton South
WILLIAMSON, Chris	Ind	Derby North
WILSON, Phil	Lab	Sedgefield
WOLLASTON, Sarah	Lib Dem	Totnes

Retired MPs (74)

ALLEN, Heidi	Lib Dem	South Cambridgeshire
AUSTIN, Ian	Lab	Dudley North
BAILEY, Adrian	Lab/Co-op	West Bromwich West
BARRON, Kevin	Lab	Rother Valley
BEBB, Guto	Ind	Aberconwy
BELLINGHAM, Henry	Con	North West Norfolk
BENYON, Richard	Con	Newbury
BLACKMAN-WOODS, Roberta	Lab	City of Durham
BOLES, Nick	Ind	Grantham and Stamford
BURT, Alistair	Con	North East Bedfordshire
CABLE, Vince	Lib Dem	Twickenham
CAMPBELL, Ronnie	Lab	Blyth Valley
CLARKE, Kenneth	Con	Rushcliffe
CLWYD, Ann	Lab	Cynon Valley
COFFEY, Ann	IGC	Stockport
CUNNINGHAM, Jim	Lab	Coventry South
DAVIES, Glyn	Con	Montgomeryshire
DE PIERO, Gloria	Lab	Ashfield
DUNCAN, Alan	Con	Rutland and Melton
ELLMAN, Louise	Ind	Liverpool Riverside
ELPHICKE, Charlie	Ind	Dover
FALLON, Michael	Con	Sevenoaks
FARRELLY, Paul	Lab	Newcastle-under-Lyme
FIELD, Mark	Con	Cities of London and Westminster
FITZPATRICK, Jim	Lab	Poplar and Limehouse
GRANT, Bill	Con	Ayr, Carrick and Cumnock
GREENING, Justine	Ind	Putney
GRIFFITHS, Andrew	Con	Burton
HAMMOND, Philip	Con	Runnymede and Weybridge
HARRINGTON, Richard	Con	Watford
HEATON-JONES, Peter	Con	North Devon
HEPBURN, Stephen	Ind	Jarrow
HERBERT, Nick	Con	Arundel and South Downs
HERMON, Sylvia	Ind	North Down
HOEY, Kate	Lab	Vauxhall
HOLLINGBERY, George	Con	Meon Valley
HOPKINS, Kelvin	Ind	Luton North
HURD, Nick	Con	Ruislip, Northwood and Pinner
JAMES, Margot	Con	Stourbridge
JOHNSON, Jo	Con	Orpington
JONES, Helen	Lab	Warrington North

KENNEDY, Seema	Con	Ashton under Lyne
LAMB, Norman	Lib Dem	North Norfolk
LANCASTER, Mark	Con	Milton Keynes North
LEFROY, Jeremy	Con	Stafford
LETWIN, Oliver	Ind	West Dorset
LIDINGTON, David	Con	Aylesbury
LUCAS, Ian C	Lab	Wrexham
MCLOUGHLIN, Patrick	Con	Derbyshire Dales
MORGAN, Nicky	Con	Loughborough
NEWTON, Sarah	Con	Truro and Falmouth
O'MARA, Jared	Ind	Sheffield, Hallam
OWEN, Albert	Lab	Ynys Môn
PEARCE, Teresa	Lab	Erith and Thamesmead
PERRY O'NEILL, Claire	Con	Devizes
POUND, Stephen	Lab	Ealing North
PRISK, Mark	Con	Hertford and Stortford
ROBINSON, Geoffrey	Lab	Coventry North West
RUDD, Amber	Ind	Hastings and Rye
RYAN, Joan	IGC	Enfield North
SIMPSON, David	DUP	Upper Bann
SIMPSON, Keith	Con	Broadland
SMITH, Owen	Lab	Pontypridd
SOAMES, Nicholas	Con	Mid Sussex
SPELMAN, Caroline	Con	Meriden
STEWART, Rory	Ind	Penrith and The Border
SWIRE, Hugo	Con	East Devon
THOMSON, Ross	Con	Aberdeen South
TREDINNICK, David	Con	Bosworth
TWIGG, Stephen	Lab/Co-op	Liverpool West Derby
VAIZEY, Ed	Con	Wantage
VAZ, Keith	Lab	Leicester East
WOODCOCK, John	Lab/Co-op	Barrow and Furness
WATSON, Tom	Lab	West Bromwich East

House of Lords

London SW1A 0PW 020 7219 8670 Enquiry service 020 7219 4272
Website: www.parliament.uk Twitter: @UKHouseofLords

Bulk correspondence to Members may be delivered to Derby Gate at the Palace of Westminster, but must be stamped or franked or accompanied by a cheque for second-class postage made out to Post Office Counters.

Membership

Since the passing of the House of Lords Act, 1999, the majority of members, around 700, are life peers. The minority of life peers who are Lords of Appeal in Ordinary became Justices of the Supreme Court of the United Kingdom from October 2009, forfeiting their right to participate in the Lords. The Archbishops of Canterbury and York and the Bishops of London, Durham and Winchester are ex-officio members of the Lords, while the remaining 21 Bishops who are members sit by rotation according to seniority; these are known as Lords Spiritual.

Ninety hereditary peers still sit by virtue of election by their fellow peers. In addition, some hereditary peers have been created life peers, of whom 11 remain.

There are two hereditary office holders who are members of the House under the House of Lords Act, 1999: the Duke of Norfolk as Earl Marshal, and the Marquess of Cholmondeley as Lord Great Chamberlain.

Speaker and Deputies

Lord Speaker

Lord Fowler

Deputy Speakers

Several Lords are appointed to act as Speaker of the House of Lords in the absence of the Lord Speaker. Last Commission: 29 November 2010.

Baroness Andrews (Lab)
Lord Brougham and Vaux (Con)
Lord Dear (CB)
Lord Faulkner of Worcester (Lab)
Baroness Finlay of Llandaff (CB)
Baroness Fookes (Con)
Baroness Garden of Frognal (Lib Dem)
Lord Geddes (Con)
Lord Haskel (Lab)
Baroness Henig (Lab)
Lord Lexden (Con)
Lord McAvoy (Lab/Co-op)
Baroness McIntosh of Hudnall (Lab)
Baroness Morris of Bolton (Con)
Baroness Newlove (Con)
Lord Palmer of Childs Hill (Lib Dem)
Baroness Pitkeathley (Lab)
Lord Rogan (UUP)
Viscount Simon (Lab)
Lord Stoneham of Droxford (Lib Dem)

Chairman and Deputy Chairmen

Lords are appointed by the House to fill the offices of Chairman and Principal Deputy Chairman of Committees. The Chairman [now known as Senior Deputy Speaker] is chairman *ex-officio* of all committees of the House.

Senior Deputy Speaker and Chairman of Committees: Lord McFall of Alcluith (NA)
Principal Deputy Chairman of Committees: Earl of Kinnoull (NA)
Deputy Chairmen: Lord Alderdice (Lib Dem)
Baroness Andrews (Lab)
Lord Ashton of Hyde (Con)
Baroness Barker (Lib Dem)
Lord Bates (Con)
Lord Brougham and Vaux (Con)
Lord Caine (Con)
Lord Dear (CB)
Lord Duncan of Springbank (Con)
Lord Faulkner of Worcester (Lab)
Baroness Finlay of Llandaff (CB)
Baroness Fookes (Con)
Baroness Garden of Frognal (Lib Dem)
Lord Geddes (Con)
Lord Haskel (Lab)
Baroness Healy of Primrose Hill (Lab)
Baroness Henig (Lab)
Lord Lexden (Con)
Lord McAvoy (Lab/Co-op)
Baroness McIntosh of Hudnall (Lab)
Lord McNicol of West Kilbride (Lab)
Baroness Morris of Bolton (Con)
Baroness Newlove (Con)
Lord Palmer of Childs Hill (Lib Dem)
Baroness Pitkeathley (Lab)
Lord Rogan (UUP)
Lord Russell of Liverpool (CB)
Viscount Simon (Lab)
Viscount Ullswater (Con)
Professor Baroness Watkins of Tavistock (CB)

House of Lords Commission

House of Lords, London SW1A 0PW
Tel: 020 7219 6644 Email: milnerp@parliament.uk
Website: www.parliament.uk/business/committees/committees-a-z/lords-select/house-of-lords-commission

Senior Committee to provide high-level strategic and political direction for the House of Lords.

Chair: Rt Hon **Lord Fowler** (Lord Speaker)
Members: Rt Hon **Baroness Evans of Bowes Park** (Con), **Lord German** OBE (Lib Dem), Rt Hon **Lord Hill of Oareford** CBE (Con), Rt Hon **Lord Judge** (CB), Rt Hon **Lord McFall of Alcluith** (Non-Affiliated), Rt Hon **Lord Newby** OBE (Lib Dem), Rt Hon **Baroness Smith of Basildon** (Lab/Co-op), Rt Hon **Lord Touhig** (Lab), **Lord Vaux of Harrowden** (CB)
External Member: **Matthew Duncan**
Clerk: **Patrick Milner**

House of Lords Appointments Commission

Room G/40, Ground Floor, 1 Horse Guards Road, London SW1A 2HQ
Tel: 020 7276 6794 Email: enquiry@lordsappointments.gov.uk
Website: lordsappointments.independent.gov.uk

The Appointments Commission is a non-statutory advisory non-departmental public body. It has two functions: to make recommendations for non-party-political peers and to vet for propriety nominations for peerages, including those from the political parties.

Chair: **Lord Bew** (CB)
Independent Members: Rt Rev and Rt Hon **Lord Chartres** GCVO (CB), **Fionnuala Jay-O'Boyle** CBE, **To be appointed**
Political Party Nominees: **Baroness Browning** (Con), Rt Hon **Lord Clark of Windermere** DL (Lab), **Baroness Parminter** (Lib Dem)
Secretary: **Alison Bennett**

Members (Peers)

Party Affiliation (February 2021)

Conservative	270
Crossbench	187
Labour	186*
Other	90†
Liberal Democrat	87
Democratic Unionist Party	5
Green Party	2
Ulster Unionist Party	2
Plaid Cymru	1
	830 seats

* Includes 12 Labour/Co-operative peers.
† Includes the Lord Speaker, Lords Spiritual, independents and peers who have not declared any party affiliation.

Summary (February 2021)

Life Peers	716
Hereditary Peers	88
Archbishops and Bishops	26

Changes since last edition

NEW MEMBERS

Bishop of Manchester (*NA*)	28 July 2020
Archbishop of York (*NA*)	28 July 2020
Lord Frost (*Con*)	12 August 2020
Lord Herbert of South Downs (*Con*)	1 September 2020
Lord Vaizey of Didcot (*Con*)	1 September 2020
Lord Austin of Dudley (*NA*)	2 September 2020
Lord Wharton of Yarm (*Con*)	2 September 2020
Baroness Clark of Kilwinning (*Lab*)	3 September 2020
Baroness Morrissey (*Con*)	3 September 2020
Lord Clarke of Nottingham (*Con*)	4 September 2020
Lord Walney (*NA*)	4 September 2020
Baroness Fullbrook (*Con*)	7 September 2020
Baroness Stuart of Edgbaston (*NA*)	7 September 2020
Lord McLoughlin (*Con*)	8 September 2020
Lord Sarfraz (*Con*)	8 September 2020
Baroness Hayman of Ullock (*Lab*)	9 September 2020
Lord Moylan (*Con*)	9 September 2020
Lord Botham (*CB*)	10 September 2020
Lord Sikka (*Lab*)	10 September 2020
Lord Field of Birkenhead (*CB*)	11 September 2020
Lord Sedwill (*CB*)	11 September 2020
Baroness Fox of Buckley (*NA*)	14 September 2020
Baroness Hoey (*NA*)	14 September 2020
Baroness Fleet (*Con*)	15 September 2020
Lord Sharpe of Epsom (*Con*)	15 September 2020
Lord Lancaster of Kimbolton (*Con*)	16 September 2020
Lord Mendoza (*Con*)	16 September 2020
Lord Moore of Etchingham (*NA*)	17 September 2020
Lord Spencer of Alresford (*Con*)	17 September 2020
Lord Davies of Brixton (*Lab*)	18 September 2020
Lord Dodds of Duncairn (*DUP*)	18 September 2020
Lord Hammond of Runnymede (*Con*)	30 September 2020
Baroness Shafik (*CB*)	30 September 2020
Lord Johnson of Marylebone (*Con*)	12 October 2020
Baroness Casey of Blackstock (*CB*)	30 October 2020
Lord Woodley (*Lab*)	2 November 2020
Lord Bellingham (*Con*)	5 November 2020
Lord Stewart of Dirleton (*Con*)	6 November 2020
Lord Udny-Lister (*Con*)	6 November 2020
Lord Lebedev (*CB*)	19 November 2020
Lord Etherton (*CB*)	23 December 2020
Lord Wolfson of Tredegar (*Con*)	30 December 2020
Lord Godson (*Con*)	25 January 2021
Lord Hannan of Kingsclere (*Con*)	25 January 2021
Lord Benyon (*Con*)	26 January 2021
Baroness Fraser of Craigmaddie (*Con*)	26 January 2021
Lord Cruddas (*Con*)	27 January 2021
Lord McDonald of Salford (*CB*)	27 January 2021
Lord Kamall (*Con*)	28 January 2021
Baroness Merron (*Lab*)	28 January 2021
Baroness Foster of Oxton (*Con*)	29 January 2021
Lord Parker of Minsmere (*CB*)	29 January 2021
Baroness Blake of Leeds (*Lab*)	1 February 2021
Baroness Chapman of Darlington (*Lab*)	1 February 2021

Lord Coaker (*Lab*)	3 February 2021
Lord Khan of Burnley (*Lab*)	4 February 2021

DEATHS

Lord Rea (*Lab*)	1 June 2020
Baroness Maddock (*Lib Dem*)	26 June 2020
Lord O'Neill of Clackmannan (*Lab*)	26 August 2020
Lord Shutt of Greetland (*Lib Dem*)	30 October 2020
Lord Sacks (*CB*)	7 November 2020
Lord Stoddart of Swindon (*Ind Lab*)	14 November 2020
Lord Kerr of Tonaghmore (*NA*)	1 December 2020

CHANGE OF PARTY

Lord Mitchell	Left Crossbench, now Labour
Lord Eatwell	Left Non-affiliated, now Labour
Lord Turnberg	Left Non-affiliated, now Labour
Baroness Kennedy of Cradley	Left Labour, now Non-Affiliated
Lord Triesman	Left Non-affiliated, now Labour
Duke of Wellington	Left Non-affiliated, now Crossbench
Baroness Falkner of Margravine	Left Non-affiliated, now Crossbench
Lord Holmes of Richmond	Left Non-affiliated, now Conservative
Lord Desai	Left Labour, now Non-Affiliated
Lord Bowness	Left Conservative, now Non-Affiliated
Lord Wallace of Tankerness	Left Liberal Democrats, now Non-Affiliated
Baroness Wheatcroft	Left Non-affiliated, now Crossbench

RETIREMENTS

Countess of Mar (*CB*)	1 May 2020
Baroness Byford (*Con*)	5 May 2020
Lord Cope of Berkeley (*Con*)	13 May 2020
Lord Woolmer of Leeds (*Lab*)	26 May 2020
Archbishop of York (*NA*)	7 June 2020
Baroness Howe of Idlicote (*CB*)	2 June 2020
Lord Luce (*CB*)	29 June 2020
Lord Morris of Handsworth (*Lab*)	21 July 2020
Baroness Hanham (*Con*)	22 July 2020
Lord Darling of Roulanish (*Lab*)	28 July 2020
Lord Jones of Birmingham (*CB*)	31 August 2020
Lord Williams of Oystermouth (*CB*)	31 August 2020
Lord Kirkwood of Kirkhope (*Lib Dem*)	2 September 2020
Lord Clarke of Stone-cum-Ebony (*CB*)	14 September 2020
Lord Freeman (*Con*)	1 October 2020
Lord Elton (*Con*)	29 October 2020
Lord Ahmed (*NA*)	14 November 2020
Lord Guthrie of Craigiebank (*CB*)	1 December 2020
Lord Haskins (*CB*)	1 December 2020
Baroness Wilcox (*Con*)	17 December 2020
Lord Cavendish of Furness (*Con*)	1 January 2021
Baroness Tonge (*NA*)	19 February 2021

PEERAGES PENDING	**BIOGRAPHIES**
Ruth Davidson (*Con*)	Page 700
John Sentamu (*CB*)	Page 992

Peers' Biographies

CROSSBENCH

ABERDARE, LORD

ABERDARE (5th Baron, UK), Alastair John Lyndhurst Bruce; cr. 1873. Born 2 May 1947; Son of Morys George Lyndhurst Bruce, 4th Baron Aberdare, and Sarah, née Dashwood; Married Elizabeth Foulkes 1971 (1 son 1 daughter).

Education: Eton College; Christ Church, Oxford (MA literae humaniores 1972); French.

Non-political career: IBM UK 1969-91; Partner, Bruce Naughton Wade (public affairs management consultants) 1991-99; Director: ProbusBNW Ltd (corporate reputation consultants) 1999-2009, WALTZ Programmes Ltd, learning to work 2009-12.

Political career: *House of Lords:* Elected hereditary peer 2009-. Member: Information 2012-15, Digital Skills 2014-15, EU Internal Market Sub-committee 2015-19, Highgate Cemetery Bill [HL] 2020-. *Other:* Trustee: National Botanic Garden of Wales 1994-2006, National Library of Wales 2012-; DL, Dyfed 2009.

Political interests: Arts, culture and heritage, education and skills, trade and technology, small businesses and entrepreneurship; China, Kenya, Russia, USA, Wales.

Other: Trustee, St John Cymru-Wales 2008-18; Vice-President, Public Monuments and Sculpture Association 2011-; Chair, Berlioz Society 2014-; Trustee, Stephen Dodgson Charitable Trust 2015-; Chair, Berlioz Sesquicentenary Committee 2017-; FRSA; FRGS; Hon Fellow, Cardiff University 2008; KStJ 2015. MCC.

Publications: Translator and Editor, Hector Berlioz: The Musical Madhouse (University of Rochester Press, 2003); Contributor: Berlioz: Scenes from the Life and Work (University of Rochester Press, 2008), The Cambridge Berlioz Encyclopedia (2017).

Recreations: Wales, classical music – especially Berlioz, crosswords, family.

The Lord Aberdare, House of Lords, London SW1A 0PW
Tel: 020 7219 6861 *Email:* aberdarea@parliament.uk
Email: alastair@aberdares.co.uk

LABOUR

ADAMS OF CRAIGIELEA, BARONESS

ADAMS OF CRAIGIELEA (Life Baroness), (Katherine Patricia) Irene Adams; cr 2005. Born 27 December 1947; Married Allen Adams 1968 (MP 1979-90, died 1990) (1 son 2 daughters).

Education: Stanley Green High School, Paisley.

Political career: *House of Commons:* MP (Labour) for Paisley North 29 November 1990 by-election to 2005. Member, Chairmen's Panel 1998-2005; Chair, Scottish Affairs 2001-05. *House of Lords:* Raised to the peerage as Baroness Adams of Craigielea, of Craigielea in Renfrewshire 2005. Member, Electoral Registration and Administration Act 2013 2019-. *Other:* Councillor: Paisley Town Council 1970, Renfrew District Council 1974-78, Strathclyde Regional Council 1979-84; JP.

Other: Member, UK delegation to NATO Parliamentary Assembly 2015-19.

Recreations: Reading, walking.

The Baroness Adams of Craigielea, House of Lords, London SW1A 0PW
Tel: 020 7219 6536

LIBERAL DEMOCRAT

ADDINGTON, LORD

Liberal Democrat Lords Spokesperson for Sport

ADDINGTON (6th Baron, UK), Dominic Bryce Hubbard; cr. 1887. Born 24 August 1963; Son of 5th Baron; Married Elizabeth Ann Morris 1999.

Education: The Hewett School, Norwich; Aberdeen University (MA history 1988).

Non-political career: Charity fundraiser and counsellor, Apex Trust 1991-94; Consultant, Milton Broadway, Events Company 1996-99; Chair, Microlink plc 2012-.

Political career: *House of Lords:* First entered House of Lords 1986; Liberal Democrat Spokesperson for: Work and Social Services/Pensions (Disability) 1994-2009, Culture, Media and Sport (Sport) 1995-2015; Elected hereditary peer 1999-; Liberal Democrat: Whip 2002-13, Deputy Chief Whip 2005-13, Spokesperson for: Defence 2007-10, Sport 2015, 2020-. Member: Merits of Statutory Instruments 2003-05, Procedure 2005-08, Hybrid Instruments 2011-, Olympic and Paralympic Legacy 2013-14, The Arctic 2014-15, EU Energy and Environment Sub-committee 2019-20, National Plan for Sport and Recreation 2020-.

Political interests: Education, prison reform, disabilities, sport.

Other: Vice-President: British Dyslexia Association, UK Sports Association (Sport for those with learning disabilities); President, Apex Trust; Patron: Cascade Foundation, X-Forces 2015-; Aberdeen University Student Hardship Fund. National Liberal Club; Lakenham Hewett Rugby Club; Playing Captain, Commons and Lords RFC.

Recreations: Rugby football, portrait painting.

The Lord Addington, House of Lords, London SW1A 0PW
Tel: 020 7219 4443 *Email:* addingtond@parliament.uk

CROSSBENCH

ADEBOWALE, LORD

ADEBOWALE (Life Baron), Victor Olufemi Adebowale; cr 2001. Born 21 July 1962; Son of Grace Adebowale and Ezekiel Adebowale; Married Tracey Jones (1 son 1 daughter).

Education: Thornes House School, Wakefield; Tavistock Institute (Postgraduate Diploma advanced organisational consulting); City University (MA advanced organisational consulting 2008).

Non-political career: Housing administration, London Borough of Newham 1983-86; Management posts, housing associations 1986-90; Director, alcohol recovery project 1990-95; Chief executive, Centre Point (youth social exclusion charity) 1995-2001; Member: Social Exclusion Unit Policy Action, National Employment Panel, New Deal Task Force 1997-2007; Chief executive, Turning Point 2001-; Visiting Professor, Lincoln University. Member, Unison.

Political career: *House of Lords:* Raised to the peerage as Baron Adebowale, of Thornes in the County of West Yorkshire 2001. *Other:* Commission Employment and Skills 2007; Board member, Audit Commission -2012; President, Community Practitioners' and Health Visitors' Association; Council member, Social Enterprise Coalition -2009; Non-executive director, NHS England; Vice-President, Local Government Association.

Political interests: Poverty, regeneration, arts; Italy, Nigeria, USA.

Other: Director: Leadership in Mind Ltd, THP Ltd, 360 action Ltd; Patron: Tomorrow's Project, Nursing Council on Alcohol, CARE International Foundation, National College for School Leadership, ROTA, International Philosophy and Psychiatry, Social Enterprise UK; Centre for Inclusion and Diversity, Bradford University, Equalities National Council; Urban Development (Music); Non-executive director, Co-op Board 2016-; Hon. Fellow, Royal College of Psychiatry; Chancellor, Lincoln University 2008-; Sunningdale fellow; Four honorary doctorates; Three honorary fellowships; Honorary degree, Nottingham University 2017; CBE 2000.

Recreations: Poetry writing, reading, music, kites.

The Lord Adebowale CBE, House of Lords, London SW1A 0PW
Tel: 020 7219 8704 *Email:* adebowalev@parliament.uk
Tel: 020 7481 7600 *Email:* victor@leadershipinmind.co.uk *Twitter:* @Voa1234

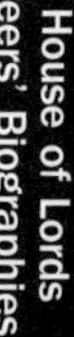

LABOUR

ADONIS, LORD

ADONIS (Life Baron), Andrew Adonis; cr 2005. Born 22 February 1963; Married Kathryn Davies 1994 (1 son 1 daughter) (divorced 2015).

Education: Kingham Hill School, Oxford; Keble College, Oxford (BA modern history 1984); Christ Church, Oxford (DPhil 1988).

Non-political career: Headquarters Secretariat, British Gas Corporation 1984-85; Nuffield College, Oxford: Research student 1985-86, Fellow, politics 1988-91; Journalist, *Financial Times* 1991-96: Political columnist, *Observer* 1996-98; Prime Minister's Policy Unit 1998-2005: Head of Policy 2001-03; Non-executive director, Dods Group plc 2011-17; Non-executive board member, HS2 Ltd 2015-17.

Political career: *House of Lords:* Raised to the peerage as Baron Adonis, of Camden Town in the London Borough of Camden 2005. Parliamentary Under-Secretary of State and Government Spokesperson for Department for Education and Skills/Children, Schools and Families (Schools and Learners) 2005-08; Department for Transport 2008-10: Minister of State and Government Spokesperson 2008-09, Secretary of State 2009-10; Opposition Spokesperson for Treasury 2012-15; Shadow Minister for the Treasury 2013-15. *Other:* Contested South West region 2019 European Parliament election. Adviser to Policy Review on Industrial Strategy, Labour Party 2012-15; Resigned Labour Party Whip October 2015-June 2017. Councillor, Oxford City Council 1987-91; Chair, National Infrastructure Commission 2015-17.

Other: Director, Institute for Government 2010-; Chair, Progress 2012-; Director, English National Ballet; Peer of the Year, Channel 4 Political awards 2009; PC 2009.

Publications: Parliament Today (1990); Making Aristocracy Work: The peerage and the political system in Britain 1884-1914 (1993); Co-Author, A Conservative Revolution?: The Thatcher-Reagan decade in perspective (1994); Failure in British Government: The politics of the poll tax (1994); A Class Act: the myth of Britain's classless society (1997); Co-editor, Roy Jenkins: a retrospective (2004); Contributor, The Purple Book (Progress, 2011); Education, Education, Education: Reforming England's schools (2012); Five Days in May: The Coalition and Beyond (Biteback, 2013); Half In, Half Out – Prime Ministers on Europe (Biteback, 2018); Saving Britain: How We Must Change to Prosper in Europe (Abacus, 2018).

Rt Hon the Lord Adonis, House of Lords, London SW1A 0PW
Tel: 020 7219 3000 *Email:* adonisa@parliament.uk Website: www.andrewadonistour.org
Twitter: @Andrew_Adonis

CROSSBENCH

AFSHAR, BARONESS

AFSHAR (Life Baroness), Haleh Afshar; cr 2007. Born 21 May 1944; Daughter of Pouran Afshar and Prof Hassan Afshar; Married Maurice, later Professor, Dodson 1974 (1 daughter 1 son).

Education: Ecole Jeanne d'Arc Theran, Iran; St Martin's School, Solihull; Davis College, Brighton; York University (BA social sciences 1967); Strasbourg University (Diploma comparative European Community law 1972); Department of Land Economy, Cambridge (PhD 1974); French, Persian.

Non-political career: Researcher, Rural Research Centre, Tehran; Journalist, *Kayhan International* daily newspaper, Tehran 1971-74; Lecturer in development, Bradford University 1976-85; York University 1985-: Deputy Director and Lecturer in health economics 1985-87, Department of Politics and Centre for Women's Studies 1987-: Professor 1999-, Emeritus Professor 2012; Visiting Professor, Strasbourg University International Faculty of Comparative Law 1986-; Founder Member, Women Living Under Muslim Laws 1987-; Visiting Professor, Women's studies, Strathclyde University 1993-98; Muslim Women's Network: Founder Member and Chair 2002-10, Honorary President 2010-. Member, AUT 1975-.

Political career: *House of Lords:* Raised to the peerage as Baroness Afshar, of Heslington in the County of North Yorkshire 2007. *Other:* Commissioner, UK Drug Policy Commission 2006-13; Member, Education Honours Committee 2007-13; Commissioner, National Commission for Women 2008-10.

Political interests: Islam, feminism; France, India, Iran, Middle East, North Africa.

Other: Member and various posts numerous organisations, concerned with women, particularly ethnic minority women, and education, including: Deputy chair, British Council's Gender and Development Task Force 2001-03, UN Associations' Services: Chair, board of trustees 2001-04, President 2004-; Fellow, Academy of Social Sciences; Political Studies Association; British Association for Middle Eastern Studies; Development Studies Association; Oxfam, NSPCC, Samaritans, Friends of the Earth, National Trust, Scope, Shelter, CAF/Mind, Cancer Research, Centrepoint, Camphill Village, Medecins sans Frontiers, Refugee Action, Action Aid; Fellow, Academy of Social Sciences 2009; Hon doctorate: Exeter University 2011, York St John University 2013; OBE 2005.

Publications: Books: (as Homa Omid) Islam and the Post-Revolutionary State in Iran (Macmillan, 1994), Islam and Feminisms, an Iranian case study (Macmillan, 1998), Co-author, Women in Later Life: Exploring Race and Ethnicity (Open University Press, 2008); Reports: 'Women and poverty' in Women and Development (International Development Committee, Seventh Report, 1999), Pamphlet, Democracy and Islam (Hansard Society, 2006); Edited volumes: Iran, A Revolution in Turmoil (Macmillan, l985, reprinted 1989), Women, Work and Ideology In The Third World (Tavistock, 1985), Women, State and Ideology (Macmillan, 1987), Co-editor, Women, Poverty and Ideology (Macmillan, 1989), Women Development and Survival in the Third World (Longman, 1991), Co-editor, Women and Adjustment Policies in The Third World (Macmillan, 1992), Women in the Middle East: Perceptions, Realities and Struggles for Liberation (Macmillan, 1993), Co-editor, The Dynamics of Race and Gender: some Feminist Interventions (Taylor and Francis 1994, reprinted 1995), Women and Politics in the Third World (Routledge, 1996), Co-editor, Empowering Women for Development (Booklinks Corporation, Hyderabad, 1997), Women and Empowerment, Illustrations from the Third World (Macmillan, 1998), Co-editor: Women and Globalization and Fragmentation in the Developing World (Macmillan, 1999), Development, Women, and War (Oxfam, 2004); Authored many papers in academic journals and contributed chapters to books, mainly on women, feminism, politics and Iran.

Recreations: Reading, opera.

The Baroness Afshar OBE, House of Lords, London SW1A 0PW
Tel: 020 7219 8530 *Email:* afsharh@parliament.uk
Department of Politics, York University, York YO10 5DD *Email:* haleh.afshar@york.ac.uk

CONSERVATIVE

AGNEW OF OULTON, LORD

Minister of State for Efficiency and Transformation and Government Spokesperson, Cabinet Office and HM Treasury

AGNEW OF OULTON (Life Baron), Theodore Thomas More Agnew; cr 2017. Born 17 January 1961; Married Clare (1 son 1 daughter).

Education: Rugby School.

Non-political career: Founder: Town & Country Assistance 1989-2002, WNS Global Services 2002-04, Somerton Capital LLP 2007-, Inspiration Trust 2012-.

Political career: *House of Lords:* Raised to the peerage as Baron Agnew of Oulton, of Oulton in the County of Norfolk 2017. Parliamentary Under-Secretary of State for the School System and Government Spokesperson, Department for Education 2017-20; Minister of State for Efficiency and Transformation and Government Spokesperson, Cabinet Office and HM Treasury 2020-. *Other:* Department for Education: Non-executive director 2010-15, Chair, Academies Board 2013-15; DL, Norfolk 2013-; Lead non-executive director, Ministry of Justice 2015-17.

Other: Trustee: Policy Exchange, Education Policy Institute; Vice-patron, Norfolk Community Foundation; Kt 2015. Cavalry and Guards Club.

The Lord Agnew of Oulton DL, House of Lords, London SW1A 0PW
Tel: 020 7219 3000

CONSERVATIVE

AHMAD OF WIMBLEDON, LORD

Minister of State for South Asia and the Commonwealth and Government Spokesperson, Foreign, Commonwealth and Development Office; Prime Minister's Special Representative on Preventing Sexual Violence in Conflict

AHMAD OF WIMBLEDON (Life Baron), Tariq Mahmood Ahmad; cr 2011. Born 3 April 1968; Son of Ch. Mansoor Ahmad and Amtul Matin Ahmad, nee Mir; Married Siddiquea Masud 2011 (2 sons 1 daughter).

Education: Rutlish School, London; London South Bank University/South Bank Polytechnic (BA business, corporate finance 1990); Chartered Institute of Bankers (ACIB 1995); Hindi, Punjabi, Urdu.

Non-political career: NatWest Group 1991-2000: Corporate Banking Executive 1991-94, Manager: Market Intelligence 1994-97, European Strategy 1997-99, Senior manager, Corporate Banking and Financial Markets 1999-2000; Alliance Bernstein: Vice-president, Marketing director 2000-04; Strategy and marketing director and head of Russia and CIS, Sucden Financial 2004-12.

Political career: *House of Commons:* Contested (Conservative) Croydon North 2005 general election. *House of Lords:* Raised to the peerage as Baron Ahmad of Wimbledon, of Wimbledon in the London Borough of Merton 2011. Party Whip 2012; Government Whip 2012-14; Department for Communities and Local Government: Government Spokesperson 2012-15, Parliamentary Under-Secretary of State 2014-15; Government Spokesperson for: International Development 2012-13, Justice 2012-14, Business, Innovation and Skills (Universities and Science) 2013-14, Home Office 2013-14; Parliamentary Under-Secretary of State and Government Spokesperson: Home Office 2015-16, Department for Transport 2015-17; Minister of State and Government Spokesperson, Foreign and Commonwealth Office: for the Commonwealth and the UN 2017-19, for the Commonwealth, the UN and South Asia 2019-20; Minister of State for South Asia and the Commonwealth: Foreign and Commonwealth Office and Department for International Development 2020, Foreign, Commonwealth and Development Office 2020-; Prime Minister's: Special Representative on Preventing Sexual Violence in Conflict 2017-, Special Envoy on Freedom of Religion or Belief 2018-19. Member, Inheritance and Trustees' Powers Bill 2013. *Other:* Deputy chairman, Wimbledon Conservative Association 1997-2002; Member, Conservative Friends of India 2003-; Vice-chairman (Cities), Conservative Party 2008-10; Parliamentary chairman, Conservative Friends of Pakistan 2011-. Member, Merton Racial Equality Council 1994-97; London Borough of Merton Council: Councillor 2002-12, Opposition Spokesperson on Environment and Regeneration 2002-06, Cabinet Member: Environment and Transport 2006-08, Community Safety and Engagement 2008-09; Governor, Wimbledon Park School 2003-06; Deputy chairman, London Councils Transport and Environment Committee 2006-08.

Political interests: Foreign affairs, EU, international development, city and financial affairs; Bangladesh, China, India, Indonesia, Israel, Middle East, Pakistan, Russia, USA.

Other: National Vice-president, AMYA-UK 2000-09; Patron: Humanity First, MDS UK Patient Support Group; Associate, Institute of Financial Services; Member, Institute of Directors; Associate, Chartered Institute of Bankers 1995; Conservative Friends of Bangladesh, Save the Children; Glory of India Award 2010.

Recreations: Gym, tennis, voluntary work.

The Lord Ahmad of Wimbledon, House of Lords, London SW1A 0PW
Tel: 020 7219 2807 *Email:* ahmadt@parliament.uk
Tel: 020 7219 6802 *Email:* anoomj@parliament.uk *Twitter:* @tariqahmadbt

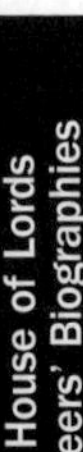

LIBERAL DEMOCRAT

ALDERDICE, LORD

ALDERDICE (Life Baron), John Thomas Alderdice; cr. 1996. Born 28 March 1955; Son of late Reverend David Alderdice and Helena Alderdice, née Shields; Married Joan Hill 1977 (2 sons 1 daughter).

Education: Ballymena Academy, County Antrim; Queen's University, Belfast (MB BCh BAO 1978); Royal College of Psychiatrists, London (MRCPsych 1982).

Non-political career: Consultant Psychiatrist in Psychotherapy, Belfast Health and Social Care Trust 1988-2010; Executive Medical Director, South and East Belfast Health and Social Services Trust 1993-97; President, ARTIS (Europe) Ltd 2009-; Oxford University: Senior Research Fellow, Harris Manchester College, Oxford 2012-, Research Affiliate, School of Anthropology and Museum Ethnography 2013-, Director, Centre for the Resolution of Intractable Conflict 2013-, Research Associate, Department of Politics and International Relations 2014-; Chair, Centre for Democracy and Peace Building 2014-19; Clinical Professor, Department of Psychiatry, Maryland University, USA 2016-.

Political career: *House of Commons:* Contested (Alliance) Belfast East 1987 and 1992 general elections. *House of Lords:* Raised to the peerage as Baron Alderdice, of Knock in the City of Belfast 1996. Convener of the Liberal Democrat Peers 2010-14; Liberal Democrat Spokesperson for: Health 2010, Northern Ireland 2015-16; Deputy Chairman of Committees 2020-. Member: Procedure 2003-05, House 2010-14, Liaison 2010-14, Mental Capacity Act 2005 2013-14, Administration and Works 2015-16, EU External Affairs Sub-committee 2019-20, EU International Agreements Sub-committee 2020, COVID-19 2020-. Chair, Liberal Democrat: Policy Committee on Health and Social Care 2010-11, Parliamentary Party Committee on Northern Ireland 2011-15. *Other:* Leader, Alliance Delegation, Forum for Peace and Reconciliation, Dublin Castle 1994-97; Member, Northern Ireland Forum 1996-98; Leader, Alliance Delegation to Northern Ireland Multiparty Talks 1996-98; Northern Ireland Assembly: MLA (Alliance) for Belfast East 1998-2004: Speaker 1998-2004; Contested European Parliament election 1989. Alliance Party: Executive Committee 1984-98: Chair, Policy Committee 1985-87; Party Vice-chair 1987, Party Leader 1987-98; European Liberal Democrat and Reform Party: Executive Committee 1987-2003, Treasurer 1995-99, Vice-President 1999-2003; Liberal International: Deputy President 2000-05, President 2005-09, Presidente D'Honneur 2015-. Councillor, Belfast City Council 1989-97; Member: Belfast Education and Library Board 1993-97, UK Committee on Standards in Public Life 2010-16.

Political interests: Northern Ireland, application of psychoanalysis and complexity science to fundamentalism, radicalisation, terrorism and violent political conflict resolution, theology, mental health, problems of indigenous peoples; Colombia, Middle East.

Other: Member, Commonwealth Parliamentary Association (President Northern Ireland Assembly Branch) 2000-04; Commissioner: Independent Monitoring Commission 2003-11, Commonwealth Commission on Respect and Understanding 2006-07; Patron, Northern Ireland Institute of Human Relations; President, Westminster Pastoral Foundation; Trustee, Ulster Museum 1993-97; Chair, World Education of Scientists Permanent Monitoring Panel on Motivations for Terrorism 2004-17; Vice-President, International Dialogue Initiative 2009-; Chair of trustees, National Liberal Club, London 2012-14; Freedom, City of Baltimore, USA 1991; FRCPsych 1997; Faculty of Medicine, Queen's University, Belfast: Hon. Lecturer 1991-99, Hon. Senior Lecturer 1999; Hon. Fellow, Royal College of Physicians of Ireland 1997; Hon. Professor, Faculty of Medicine, University of San Marcos, Peru 1999; Hon. Fellow, Royal College of Psychiatrists 2001; Hon. Affiliate, British Psychoanalytical Society 2001; Visiting Professor, Department of Psychiatry, University of Virginia, USA 2006-; Seven honorary doctorates; Galloway Medal (National Schizophrenia Fellowship, NI) 1987; John F Kennedy Profiles in Courage Award 1998; W Averell Harriman Democracy Award 1998; Silver Medal Congress of Peru 1999, 2004; Medal of Honour College of Medicine, Peru 1999; KCFO (Knight Commander Royal Order of Francis I) 2002; World Federation of Scientists Ettore Majorana Erice Prize 2005; International Psychoanalytic Association's 2005 Award for Extraordinarily Meritorious Service to Psychoanalysis; Prize for Freedom, Liberal International 2015; Global Thinkers Forum Award for Excellence in Promoting Peace and Collaboration, London 2016; Dr Whitney Holland Rose Memorial Award for Cultural Diversity in Psychiatry, University of Maryland and Sheppard Pratt Psychiatry Program 2017. National Liberal Club.

Publications: Various professional articles on eating disorders, psychotherapy and ethics, the psychology of fundamentalism, radicalisation and intractable conflict and terrorism, the problems of indigenous peoples, complexity theories, many political papers, articles and book chapters.

Recreations: Reading, music, gastronomy.

The Lord Alderdice, House of Lords, London SW1A 0PW
Tel: 020 7219 5050 *Email:* alderdicej@parliament.uk
Email: john.alderdice@hmc.ox.ac.uk Website: www.lordalderdice.com
Twitter: @AlderdiceLord

LIBERAL DEMOCRAT

ALLAN OF HALLAM, LORD

ALLAN OF HALLAM (Life Baron), Richard Beecroft Allan; cr 2010. Born 11 February 1966; Son of John Allan, retired, and Elizabeth Allan, doctor's receptionist; Married Louise Netley 1991 (1 daughter) (divorced).

Education: Oundle School, Northamptonshire; Pembroke College, Cambridge (BA archaeology and anthropology 1988); Bristol Polytechnic (MSc information technology 1990); French, Spanish.

Non-political career: Field archaeologist in: Britain, France and Netherlands 1984-85, Ecuador 1988-89; Computer manager: Avon FHSA 1991-95, FHS 1995-97; Director of government affairs, Europe, Cisco 2005-09; Director of policy, Europe, Facebook 2009-.

Political career: *House of Commons:* MP (Liberal Democrat) for Sheffield Hallam 1997-2005; Board member, Parliamentary Office of Science and Technology (POST) 1997-2001; Liberal Democrat Spokesperson for: Home and Legal Affairs (Community Relations and Urban Affairs) 1997-99, Education and Employment (Employment and Information Technology) 1999-2001, Trade and Industry (Information Technology) 2001-02, Cabinet Office (Information Technology) 2002-05. Member: Home Affairs 1997-98, Liaison 1998-2005, Finance and Services 1998-2001; Chair, Information 1998-2001; Member: Education and Employment 2000-01, Education and Employment (Employment Sub-Committee) 2001, Information 2001-05, Liaison (Liaison Sub-Committee) 2002-05, Public Accounts 2003-05. *House of Lords:* Raised to the peerage as Baron Allan of Hallam, of Ecclesall in the County of South Yorkshire 2010. *Other:* Avon County Council: Councillor 1993-95, Deputy Leader, Liberal Democrats group; Councillor, Bath City Council 1994-95.

Political interests: Information technology, heritage, home affairs, education; Kenya, Latin America especially Ecuador and Colombia, USA.

Other: Board member, Sheffield City Trust 1999-2005.

Recreations: Visiting sites of natural beauty and historical interest, walking.

The Lord Allan of Hallam, House of Lords, London SW1A 0PW
Tel: 020 7219 5353 *Email:* allanr@parliament.uk

LABOUR

ALLEN OF KENSINGTON, LORD

ALLEN OF KENSINGTON (Life Baron), Charles Lamb Allen; cr 2013. Born 4 January 1957; Son of John and Helen Allen.

Education: Bellshill Academy, Bellshill; Bell College, Hamilton.

Non-political career: Accountant, British Steel 1974-79; Deputy audit manager, Gallaghers plc 1979-82; Director, Management Services, Grandmet International Services Ltd 1982-85; Group managing director, Compass Vending, Grandmet Innovations Ltd 1986-87; Managing director, Compass Group Ltd 1988-91; Granada Group: Chief executive, Leisure Division 1991-92, Chief executive 1996-2000; Granada TV: Chief executive 1992-96, Chair 1996-2006; LWT: Chief executive 1994-96, Chair 1996-2006; Executive chair, Granada Media/Granada plc 2000–04; Chief executive, ITV plc 2004-06; Chief adviser, Home Office 2006-08.

Political career: *House of Lords:* Raised to the peerage as Baron Allen of Kensington, of Kensington in the Royal Borough of Kensington and Chelsea 2013. Member, Communications/Communications and Digital 2016-. *Other:* Chair, Labour Party management board; Patron, LGBT Labour.

Political interests: Business and the economy, humanitarian and development aid, culture, media and sport, third sector, home affairs; Europe, Middle East, USA.

Other: Chair: Granada Leisure and Services 1993-2000, Boxclever 1994-2000; GMTV: Deputy chair 1994-96, Chair 1996-2000; Vice-President, RTS 1996-2010; Member, International Academy of Television Arts and Sciences 1996; Deputy chair, Business in the Community 1997-2007; Chair: Tyne Tees TV 1997-2006, Yorkshire TV 1997-2006, Creative Industries Advisory Group 1999-2002; Non-executive director, Tesco plc 1999-2010; Chair: Anglia TV 2000-06, Meridian TV 2000-06, ITV Digital 2001-02; Chair: British Commonwealth Games 2000-02, Manchester 2002 Ltd 2000-02; Vice-chair, London 2012 Olympic Bid 2004-05; Director, London Organising Committee of the Olympic and Paralympic Games 2005-13; Member, Talent and Enterprise Taskforce Advisory Group 2006-08; Chair, Global Radio Group 2007-; Senior adviser, Goldman Sachs Equity Partners 2008-; Chair, Endemol 2008-14; Non-executive director, Virgin Media 2008-12; Get AS 2009-; EMI Music: Non-executive chair 2009-10, Executive chair 2010-11; Chair: 2 Sisters Food Group 2011-, Red Cross 2012-13, ISS A/S 2013; Advisory chair, Moelis and Company 2016-; ACMA; British Red Cross, Seagulls Reuse, Simon on the Streets, Gipton Together, Happy Faces in South Africa; Freedom, City of London; FRSA; FCMA 1989; Hon. doctor of Business Administration, Manchester Metropolitan University 1999; Hon. doctor of Letters, Salford University 2002; Hon. doctor of Education, Southampton Solent University 2006; CBE 2003; Kt 2012. Garrick Club, The Ivy Club.

Recreations: Walking, boating, travel.

The Lord Allen of Kensington CBE, House of Lords, London SW1A 0PW
Tel: 020 7219 5353 *Email:* charles.allen@parliament.uk
Global Radio, 30 Leicester Square, London WC2H 7LA *Tel:* 020 7766 6065
Email: charles.allen@global.com

LABOUR

ALLI, LORD

ALLI (Life Baron), Waheed Alli; cr. 1998. Born 16 November 1964; Partner.

Education: Norbury Manor School, south London; Stanley Technical High School.

Non-political career: Research Wootton Publications Ltd 1982-85; Head of investment research, Save and Prosper Investment 1985-88; United Trade Press Ltd 1988-91: Marketing director 1988-89, Publisher 1989-91; Management consultant, Bacon and Woodrow 1991-92; Managing director, Planet 24 Productions Ltd 1992-99; Director, Carlton Media Group 1999-2000; Non-executive director, ShineLimited 2000-; Chairman, Chorion plc 2002-11.

Political career: *House of Lords:* Raised to the peerage as Baron Alli, of Norbury in the London Borough of Croydon 1998. *Other:* Patron, LGBT Labour.

Other: Patron: Skillset (national training organisation for broadcast, film, video and multimedia), Family Planning Association, Naz Foundation, Albert Kennedy Trust; Director, Elton John Aids Foundation; Vice-President, Unicef UK; President, National Youth Theatre London Academy; Trustee: Crimestoppers -2016, Charlie Parsons Foundation.

The Lord Alli, House of Lords, London SW1A 0PW
Tel: 020 7219 8537 *Email:* alliw@parliament.uk

LIBERAL DEMOCRAT

ALLIANCE, LORD

ALLIANCE (Life Baron), David Alliance; cr. 2004. Born 15 June 1932; Son of Eliyahou Alliance and Ashouri Sarehi; Divorced (2 sons 1 daughter).

Education: Etahad School, Iran.

Non-political career: Chair, N Brown Group plc 1968-2012; Founder, Coats Viyella plc (now Coats plc) 1986: Group chief executive 1975-90, Chair 1989-99; Chair, Tootal Group 1991-99.

Political career: *House of Lords:* Raised to the peerage as Baron Alliance, of Manchester in the County of Greater Manchester 2004. *Other:* Board member, UK Holocaust Memorial Foundation 2015-.

Other: CBIM 1985; Three honorary doctorates; Two honorary fellowships; CBE 1984; Kt 1989.

Publications: Co-author, A Bazaar Life (autobiography) (The Robson Press, 2015).

Recreations: Art, persian poetry, music.

The Lord Alliance CBE, House of Lords, London SW1A 0PW
Tel: 020 7219 5353

CONSERVATIVE

ALTMANN, BARONESS

ALTMANN (Life Baroness), Rosalind Miriam Altmann; cr 2015. Born 8 April 1956; Daughter of Leo and Renate Altmann; Married Paul Richer (1 son 2 daughters).

Education: Henrietta Barnett Grammar School; University College London (BScEcon 1977); Harvard University, USA (Kennedy Scholarship economics and government 1978); London School of Economics (PhD economics of pensions and pensioner incomes 1981); French, German.

Non-political career: Fund Manager, Prudential Assurance 1981-84; Head, international equities, Chase Manhattan Bank 1984-89; Director: Rothschild Asset Management, Rothschild International Asset Management 1989-91, Natwest Investment Management 1991-93; Independent Consultant 1994-2010, 2013-15; Independent Policy Adviser on pensions, investments and savings to Number 10 Policy Unit 2000-05; Director-General, Saga Group 2010-13; Chair, Office of Public Guardian and Official Solicitor, Strategic Investment Board 2014-15; Adviser: SalaryFinance 2017-, Huntswood Group 2017–.

Political career: *House of Lords:* Raised to the peerage as Baroness Altmann, of Tottenham in the London Borough of Haringey 2015. Minister of State for Pensions and Government Spokesperson, Department for Work and Pensions 2015-16. *Other:* Conservative Group for Europe; Conservative Friends of Israel.

Political interests: Personal finance, consumer protection, pensions policy, social care policy, economic policy, financial markets, intergenerational equity, demographics, climate change, sustainable investment, Brexit; European Union.

Other: Chair, Investment Committee, London School of Economics 1988-2017; Governor: Nightingale House for the Elderly 1990-, Pensions Policy Institute 2001-15, 2017-; Trustee, Age Employment Network 2006-10; Non-executive director: Trafalgar House Trust 2006-10, 2013-15, Green Deal Finance Co 2014-15, IPSO 2014-15; Non-executive board member, Lord Chancellor's Strategic Investment Board 2014-15; Business Champion for Older Workers 2014-15; Non-executive chair, Pensionsync 2018-; Teenage Cancer Trust, Macmillan Cancer Research, Jewish Care, OneFamilyUK, Magen David Adom, Union of Jewish Students; Hon. DLitt, Westminster University 2010; Hon Doctor of Civil Law, Newcastle University 2015; Women in Public Life Award; Pensions Personality of the Year, Professional Pensions; Lifetime Achievement Award, Reward Strategy; CBE 2014.

Recreations: Swimming, walking.

The Baroness Altmann CBE, House of Lords, London SW1A 0PW
Tel: 020 7219 3000 *Email:* altmannr@parliament.uk Website: www.rosaltmann.com
Twitter: @rosaltmann

CROSSBENCH

ALTON OF LIVERPOOL, LORD

ALTON OF LIVERPOOL (Life Baron), David Patrick Paul Alton; cr. 1997. Born 15 March 1951; Son of late Frederick Alton, car worker, and Bridget Mulroe; Married Elizabeth Bell 1988 (3 sons 1 daughter).

Education: Edmund Campion School, Hornchurch; Christ's College, Liverpool (Teaching Certificate history and divinity 1972); Visiting Fellowship, Philosophy and Theology, St Andrew's University 1996-97.

Non-political career: Primary school teacher 1972-74, then with children with special needs 1974-79; Liverpool John Moores University: Professor of Citizenship 1997-2016, Director, Roscoe Foundation for Citizenship 1997-2016; Visiting Professor, Liverpool Hope University 2017-. Former member, National Union of Teachers.

Political career: *House of Commons:* Contested Liverpool Edge Hill February and October 1974 general elections. MP for Liverpool Edge Hill 1979-83, and for Liverpool Mossley Hill 1983-97 (Liberal 1979-88, Liberal Democrat 1988-97); Liberal Chief Whip 1985-87; Party Spokesperson on several portfolios. *House of Lords:* Raised to the peerage as Baron Alton of Liverpool, of Mossley Hill in the County of Merseyside 1997. Member, International Relations/ International Relations and Defence 2019-. *Other:* National President, National League of Young Liberals 1976; Chair: Liberal Policy Committee 1981-83, Candidates Committee 1984-87. Liverpool City Council: Councillor 1972-80, Chair, Housing Committee 1977, Deputy Leader of Council 1978; Merseyside County Council: Councillor 1973-77, Chief Whip (Liberal); Vice-President, Local Government Association 2010-.

Political interests: Pro-life, environment, housing, inner cities, refugees, human rights, freedom of religion or belief, Northern Ireland, citizenship; Burma, China, Congo, Egypt, Indian sub-continent, Iraq, Kenya, North Korea, Sudan, Syria, Tibet, Uganda.

Other: Member: Inter-Parliamentary Union, Commonwealth Parliamentary Association; Patron, vice-president, or chair of several charities, especially those concerned with human rights; Trustee: Chesterton Institute, Christian Heritage Centre, Arise Foundation; Patron: Save the Congo, Hong Kong Watch, Asylum Link, Merseyside, Karen Aid 2001-19; Member, Korean Sages international advisory group on North Korea; Vice-president: Liverpool School of Tropical Medicine, Crisis; Former Board Member, US Institute on Religion and Public Policy; Former Patron, Karen Aid 2001-19; Former Trustee ,Aid to the Church in Need 2014-19; Former Chair, Council for Education in the Commonwealth; Former Director and Chair, Merseyside Special Investment Fund and Banner Ethical Investment Fund; Founder, Liverpool John Moores Foundation for Citizenship and Roscoe Lectures; Life hospice for dying children, Zoe's Place, NSPCC, St Francis House, Jubilee Action, Jospice, CAFOD, Aid to the Church In Need; Hon. Professor, Yanbian University of Science and Technology, China 2012; Hon. Fellowship, Liverpool John Moores University 2016; Knights of St Columba Michael Bell award for services to the life cause 1997; Advocates International award for human rights work 2004; Mystery of Life award for human rights work 2009; 2014 Coptic Solidarity Leadership award presented at the US Congress; St. Thomas More Religious Freedom Award, presented in Rome, for work on Article 18 of the Universal declaration of Human Rights 2016; US State Department Award for work on freedom of religion or belief 2019; Knight of the Sacred Military Constantinian Order of St George 2002; Knight Commander Order of St Gregory 2008; Commander's Cross of the Order of Merit, Hungary 2017.

Publications: Author of numerous human rights reports for Jubilee Campaign of which he was a co-founder 1987-; What Kind of Country (1987); Whose Choice Anyway – the Right to Life (1988); Faith in Britain (1991); Signs of Contradiction (1996); Life After Death (1997); Citizen Virtues (1998); Citizen 2000 (2000); Pilgrim Ways (2001); Passion and Pain (2003); Abortion: Heart of the Matter (2005); Euthanasia: Heart of the Matter (2005); Building Bridges: Is There Hope for North Korea? (2013).

Recreations: Walking, reading, theatre, gardening, Liverpool FC supporter.

The Lord Alton of Liverpool, House of Lords, London SW1A 0PW
Tel: 020 7219 3551 *Email:* altond@parliament.uk Website: www.davidalton.net

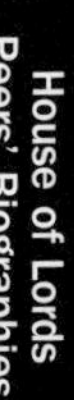

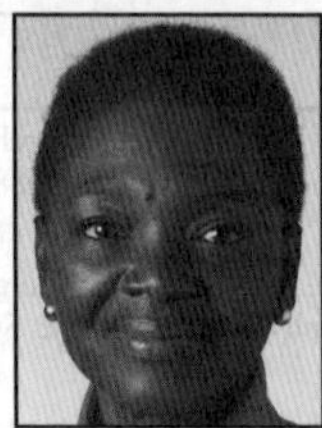

LABOUR

AMOS, BARONESS

AMOS (Life Baroness), Valerie Ann Amos; cr. 1997. Born 13 March 1954; Daughter of Michael and Eunice Amos.

Education: Townley Grammar School for Girls; Warwick University (BA sociology 1976); Birmingham University (MA cultural studies 1977); University of East Anglia (doctoral research).

Non-political career: London Boroughs of: Lambeth 1981-82, Camden 1983-85, Hackney 1985-89: Head of training, Head of management services; Chief executive, Equal Opportunities Commission 1989-94; Director, Amos Fraser Bernard 1995-98; Non-executive director: Travant Capital Partners 2007-09, Titanium Resources Group 2008-09; High Commissioner to Australia 2009-11; Under-Secretary-General, Office of the Co-ordination of Humanitarian Affairs, United Nations 2010-15; Director of SOAS, London University 2015-20.

Political career: *House of Lords:* Raised to the peerage as Baroness Amos, of Brondesbury in the London Borough of Brent 1997. Government Whip 1998-2001; Government Spokesperson for: Social Security 1998-2001, International Development 1998-2007, Women's Issues 1998-2001; Parliamentary Under-Secretary of State and Government Spokesperson, Foreign and Commonwealth Office 2001-03; Secretary of State for International Development 2003; Government Spokesperson for Northern Ireland Office 2003-05; Leader of the House of Lords and Lord President of the Council 2003-07; On leave of absence 2009-18. Member: Selection 2000-07, House 2003-07, Liaison 2003-07, Privileges 2003-07, Procedure 2003-07. *Other:* Council member, Institute of Employment Studies 1993-98; Chair, board of governors, Royal College of Nursing Institute 1994-98.

Political interests: Sub-Saharan Africa, Caribbean, China, India.

Other: Deputy chair, Runnymede Trust 1990-98; Trustee, Institute of Public Policy Research 1994-98; Non-executive director, UCLH Trust; Director, Hampstead Theatre 1995-98; Chair, Afiya Trust 1996-98; Trustee: VSO 1997-98, Project Hope 1997-98; Chair, Royal African Society 2008-09; Board member, Institute for Government; Amos Bursary; Honorary professorship; 12 honorary doctorates; Peer of the Year award, Women in Public Life Awards 2007; PC 2003; CH 2016.

Rt Hon the Baroness Amos CH, House of Lords, London SW1A 0PW
Tel: 020 7219 5353 *Email:* amosv@parliament.uk *Twitter:* @ValerieAmos

CROSSBENCH

ANDERSON OF IPSWICH, LORD

ANDERSON OF IPSWICH (Life Baron), David William Kinloch Anderson; cr 2018. Born 5 July 1961; Married Margaret Beeton 1989 (2 daughters).

Education: Eton College; New College, Oxford (ancient and modern history 1982); Downing College, Cambridge (law 1984); Inns of Court School of Law.

Non-political career: Called to the Bar, Middle Temple 1985; Covington & Burling, Washington DC 1985-86; Cabinet of Lord Cockfield, European Commission, Brussels 1987-88; Barrister, Brick Court Chambers 1988-; King's College London: Visiting Lecturer 1988-99, Visiting Professor 1999-; QC 1999; Recorder, South Eastern Circuit 2004-13; Bencher, Middle Temple 2007-; Independent Reviewer of Terrorism Legislation 2011-17; Judge of the Courts of Appeal of Jersey and Guernsey 2014-; Investigatory Powers Commissioner, Guernsey and Jersey 2017-.

Political career: *House of Lords:* Raised to the peerage as Baron Anderson of Ipswich, of Ipswich in the County of Suffolk 2018. Member: EU Justice Sub-committee 2019-20, EU Security and Justice Sub-committee 2020-.

Other: Chair, Inter Mediate 2019-; KBE 2018.

The Lord Anderson of Ipswich KBE QC, House of Lords, London SW1A 0PW
Tel: 020 7219 3000
Tel: 020 7379 3550 *Email:* david.anderson@brickcourt.co.uk Website: www.daqc.co.uk
Twitter: @bricksilk

LABOUR

ANDERSON OF SWANSEA, LORD

ANDERSON OF SWANSEA (Life Baron), Donald Anderson; cr 2005. Born 17 June 1939; Son of late David Anderson, fitter, and late Eva Anderson, née Mathias; Married Dr Dorothy Trotman 1963 (3 sons).

Education: Bishop Gore Grammar School, Swansea; University College of Wales, Swansea (BA modern history and politics 1960); Inns of Court School of Law 1966-69; French, German.

Non-political career: HM Diplomatic Service 1960-64; Lecturer in US and comparative government, University College of Wales, Swansea 1964-66; Director, Campaign for a Politcal Europe 1966-67; Called to the Bar, Inner Temple 1969-85; Barrister, South Eastern Circuit 1970-97. Former member: TGWU, NUR/RMT, AUT, FDA, FSBAA, Bar.

Political career: *House of Commons:* MP (Labour) for Monmouth 1966-70, for Swansea East October 1974-2005; PPS: to Minister of Defence (Administration) 1969-70, to Sam Silkin as Attorney General 1974-79; Opposition Frontbench Spokesperson for: Foreign and Commonwealth Affairs 1983-92, Defence, Disarmament and Arms Control 1993-94, Shadow Solicitor General 1994-96. Chair, Welsh Affairs 1981-83; Member, Chairman's Panel 1994-97; Chair, Foreign Affairs 1997-2005. *House of Lords:* Raised to the peerage as Baron Anderson of Swansea, of Swansea in the County of West Glamorgan 2005. Co-opted Member, EU Sub-committee C (Foreign Affairs, Defence and Development Policy) 2006-10; Member EU Sub-committee E: (Justice and Institutions) 2011-12, (Justice, Institutions and Consumer Protection) 2012-15; Member: EU Justice Sub-committee 2017-20, EU Security and Justice Sub-committee 2020-. Vice-chair, PLP Departmental Group for Foreign and Commonwealth Affairs 2010-15, 2018-. *Other:* Welsh Labour Group: Vice-chair 1969-70, Chair 1977-78. Councillor, Royal Borough of Kensington and Chelsea 1970-75; Vice-President, Institute of Environmental Health Officers 1984-95; DL, West Glamorgan 2006-15.

Political interests: Wales, foreign affairs, law, transport; Africa, particularly South Africa, Central Europe and Balkans, EU, France, Germany, Norway.

Other: Commonwealth Parliamentary Association (CPA) UK Branch: Member, Executive Committee 1983-2012, Vice-chair 1987-88, 2007-08, 2010-11, Treasurer 1990-93, Special Representative 1989-90, Chair 1997-2001; Co-founder and Senior Vice-President, Association of European Parliamentarians for Africa (AWEPA) (Southern) 1984-97; Inter-Parliamentary Union: Member, Executive 1983-2001, 2005-06, Vice-chair 1985-88,2016-17, Treasurer 1988-90, 1993-95; UK Delegation to North Atlantic Assembly: Member 1992-2005, Leader 1997-2001, Leader, Socialist Group 1997-2001; Organisation for Security and Co-operation in Europe: Member 1997-2001, Leader, UK delegation 1997-98; Executive Committee Member: British-American Parliamentary Group 2006-, UK Delegation to Council of Europe and WEU Assembly 2008-17; Former Chair, Middle East Sub-committee; Member: Political Committee -2016, Legal Affairs and Human Rights Committee 2016-; Vice-President, Committee for the selection of Judges to the European Court of Human Rights 2016-; Substitute Member, UK Delegation to Parliamentary Assembly of Council of Europe 2017-; Member, UK delegation, NATO Parliamentary Assembly 2020-; Former board member, World Vision; Former president, Swansea Association for the Single Homeless 1975-81; President, Gower Society 1976-78; Chair, Parliamentary Campaign for the Homeless and Rootless 1984-90; Chair: Parliamentary Christian Fellowship 1993-95, National Prayer Breakfast 1994, Anglo-Israel Association 2005-08; Board member, Mercy Ships 2005-12; President: Swansea Male Choir 1990-2007, Morriston Big Band; Patron, Morriston Ladies Choir; Vice-President, Morriston Orpheus Choir; Swansea Harriers; President: HAFOD Brotherhood, 32nd Rhyddings Scout Group; Vice-president: Morriston Rotary Club, Swansea Business Club; Churches in London and Swansea; Freedom: City and County of Swansea 2000, City of London 2006; Hon. Fellow, Swansea Metropolitan University 2005; Hon. Parliamentary Fellow, St Antony's College, Oxford 1999-2000; Honorary Fellow, Swansea University 1985-2000; Visiting Parliamentary Fellow, St Antony's College, Oxford 1999-2000; Honorary Fellow, Swansea Metropolitan University 2006; Commander's Cross, Order of Merit (Federal Republic of Germany) 1986; PC 2001; Medal of the Foreign Minister of Slovakia 2004; Chevalier de la Légion d'Honneur (France) 2005; Order of Merit of Republic of Hungary 2007. Bonymaen RFC; Ospreys RFC.

Recreations: Walking, church work.

Rt Hon the Lord Anderson of Swansea, House of Lords, London SW1A 0PW
Tel: 020 7219 2870 *Email:* trotmang@parliament.uk

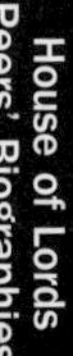

LABOUR

ANDREWS, BARONESS

Chair, Select Committee on Common Frameworks Scrutiny

ANDREWS (Life Baroness), Elizabeth Kay Andrews; cr. 2000. Born 16 May 1943; Married Professor Roy MacLeod 1970 (divorced 1992).

Education: Lewis School for Girls, Hengoed, Ystradmynach; University College of Wales, Aberystwyth (BA international politics 1964); Sussex University (MA political sociology 1966; DPhil history and social studies of science 1975).

Non-political career: Fellow, Science Policy Research Unit, Sussex University 1968-70; Parliamentary Clerk 1970-85; Policy adviser to Neil Kinnock MP as Leader of the Opposition 1985-92; Founder and director, Education Extra 1992-2002; Adviser on culture and heritage to the Welsh Government 2013-15.

Political career: *House of Lords:* Raised to the peerage as Baroness Andrews, of Southover in the County of East Sussex 2000. Government Whip 2002-05; Government Spokesperson for: Health 2002-05, Work and Pensions 2002-05, Education and Skills 2003-05, Parliamentary Under-Secretary of State and Government Spokesperson, Office of the Deputy Prime Minister/ Department for Communities and Local Government 2005-09; Deputy Chair of Committees 2012-, Deputy Speaker 2012, 2018-. Member: Delegated Powers and Regulatory Reform 2010-15, Leader's Group on the Working Practices of the House of Lords 2010-11, Joint Committee on the Draft House of Lords Reform Bill 2011-12, Mental Capacity Act 2005 2013-14, Joint Committee on the Draft Deregulation Bill 2013, Secondary Legislation Scrutiny 2014-17, Built Environment 2015-16, Joint Committee on Consolidation, &c, Bills 2015-, Delegated Powers and Regulatory Reform 2018-; Chair, Common Frameworks Scrutiny 2020-. *Other:* Deputy Chair and Trustee for Wales, National Heritage Memorial Fund/Heritage Lottery Fund.

Political interests: Education and social policy, international development, cultural policy, science policy, heritage, housing and planning; Latin America.

Other: Chair, English Heritage 2009-13; Trustee: Kids in Museums 2013-16, National Literacy Trust 2014-16; President, Friends of Lewes 2014; Trustee, National Museum of Wales 2015-; ContinYou; Hon. Fellow, Aberystwyth University; Hon. Doctor of Laws, Sussex University 2012; OBE 1998.

Publications: Articles and books on science and education policy, social policy and out of school learning; Extra Learning (Kogan Page, 2001).

Recreations: Music, mountains, museums.

The Baroness Andrews OBE, House of Lords, London SW1A 0PW
Tel: 020 7219 8656 *Email:* andrewsk@parliament.uk

CONSERVATIVE

ANELAY OF ST JOHNS, BARONESS

Chair, Select Committee on International Relations and Defence

ANELAY OF ST JOHNS (Life Baroness) Joyce Anne Anelay; cr. 1996. Born 17 July 1947; Daughter of late Stanley and Annette Clarke; Married Richard Anelay QC 1970.

Education: Enfield County School; Bristol University (BA history 1968); London University Institute of Education (CertEd 1969); Brunel University (MA public and social administration 1982).

Non-political career: History teacher, St David's School, Ashford, Middlesex 1969-74.

Political career: *House of Lords:* Raised to the peerage as Baroness Anelay of St Johns, of St Johns in the County of Surrey 1996. Opposition Whip 1997-98; Opposition Spokesperson for: Agriculture 1997-98, Social Security 1997-99, Home Affairs 1997-98, 2002-07, Culture, Media and Sport 1998-2002, Legal Affairs 2003-04, Opposition Chief Whip 2007-10; Deputy Speaker 2008-14; Deputy Chairman of Committees 2008-14; Government Chief Whip 2010-14; Minister of State and Government Spokesperson, Foreign and Commonwealth Office 2014-16 (also attending Cabinet 2014-16); Prime Minister's Special Representative on Preventing Sexual Violence in Conflict 2015-17; Acting Minister of State for Trade and Investment and Government Spokesperson, Department for Business, Innovation and Skills

2016; Minister of State for the Commonwealth and the UN and Government Spokesperson: Foreign and Commonwealth Office 2016-17, Department for International Development 2016; Minister of State and Government Spokesperson, Department for Exiting the European Union 2017. Member: Procedure 1997-2000, 2007-14, Selection 2007-14, Administration and Works 2007-14, Privileges/Privileges and Conduct 2007-14, Sub-committee on Leave of Absence 2011-13; International Relations/International Relations and Defence: Member 2018-19, Chair 2019-; Member, Conduct 2019-. *Other:* Chair, South East Area Conservative Women's Committee 1987-90; Member, National Union Executive Committee Conservative Party 1987-97, Vice-chair, South East Area Executive Committee 1990-93; Chair, Women's National Committee 1993-96; Vice-President, National Union 1996-97. Member, Social Security Appeal Tribunal 1983-96; JP, North West Surrey 1985-97; Member: Social Security Advisory Committee for Great Britain and Northern Ireland 1989-96, Women's National Commission 1991-94, Child Support Appeal Tribunal 1993-96; President, World Travel Market 2003-08.

Political interests: Foreign affairs, human rights.

Other: President, Woking Citizens' Advice Bureau 1996-2010; Trustee, UNICEF UK 2004-07; Patron: St John's Memorial Hall Appeal Fund, Talking about Cannabis; Trustee, 1949 Conservative and Unionist Trust; Hon. DSocSci, Brunel University 1997; OBE 1990; DBE 1995; PC 2009. Carlton Club; Woking Golf.

Recreations: Golf, reading.

Rt Hon the Baroness Anelay of St Johns DBE, House of Lords, London SW1A 0PW
Tel: 020 7219 5353 *Twitter:* @JoyceAnelay

CONSERVATIVE

ARBUTHNOT OF EDROM, LORD

Chair, Select Committee on Risk Assessment and Risk Planning

ARBUTHNOT OF EDROM (Life Baron), James Norwich Arbuthnot; cr 2015. Born 4 August 1952; Son of late Sir John Sinclair-Wemyss Arbuthnot (MP for Dover 1950-64) and Lady Arbuthnot; Married Emma Broadbent 1984 (1 son 3 daughters).

Education: Eton College; Trinity College, Cambridge (BA law 1974).

Non-political career: Called to the Bar: Inner Temple 1975, Lincoln's Inn 1977.

Political career: *House of Commons:* Contested Cynon Valley 1983 general election and 1984 by-election. MP (Conservative) for Wanstead and Woodford 1987-97, for North East Hampshire 1997-2010, for North East Hampshire (revised boundary) 2010-15; PPS to: Archie Hamilton as Minister of State for the Armed Forces 1988-90, Peter Lilley as Secretary of State for Trade and Industry 1990-92; Assistant Government Whip 1992-94; Parliamentary Under-Secretary of State, Department of Social Security 1994-95; Minister of State for Procurement, Ministry of Defence 1995-97; Member, Shadow Cabinet 1997-2001: Opposition Chief Whip 1997-2001; Member, Intelligence and Security Committee 2001-05; Shadow Secretary of State for Trade 2003-05; Shadow Minister for Trade 2005. Member, Joint Committee on House of Lords Reform 2002-03; Chair, Defence 2005-14; Member: Liaison 2005-14, Joint Committee on National Security Strategy 2010-14; Chair, Armed Forces Bill 2011. *House of Lords:* Raised to the peerage as Baron Arbuthnot of Edrom, of Edrom in the County of Berwick 2015. Member: EU Energy and Environment Sub-committee 2019-20, EU Security and Justice Sub-committee 2020-; Chair, Risk Assessment and Risk Planning 2020-. *Other:* Branch chair, Putney Conservative Association 1975-77; Joint deputy chair, Chelsea Conservative Association 1980-82; President, Cynon Valley Conservative Association 1983-92; Chairman, Conservative Friends of Israel 2005-13; President, North East Hampshire Conservative Association 2015-18. Councillor, Royal Borough of Kensington and Chelsea 1978-87.

Political interests: Defence, security, foreign affairs, law, taxation; Afghanistan, Australia, France, Germany, India, Israel, Italy, Pakistan, Russia, Spain, Taiwan, USA.

Other: Member, Advisory Board, Electric Infrastucture Security Council (USA); Fellow, Industry and Parliament Trust 1989; Chair (UK), UK-Spain Tertulias 2012-15; Senior associate fellow, RUSI 2014-; Chair: Nuffield Trust for the Forces of the Crown 2017-, Advisory Board, Thales (UK), NeuroBio Ltd; Director: SC Strategy Ltd, Astute Strategy Ltd, Gusbourne Estates Ltd; Adviser, Pure Storage Inc; Liveryman, Goldsmiths' Company; Freedom, City of London 1974-; PC 1998.

Recreations: Playing guitar, skiing, cooking.

Rt Hon the Lord Arbuthnot of Edrom, House of Lords, London SW1A 0PW
Tel: 020 7219 3000 *Email:* arbuthnotj@parliament.uk

NON-AFFILIATED

ARCHER OF WESTON-SUPER-MARE, LORD

ARCHER OF WESTON-SUPER-MARE (Life Baron), Jeffrey Howard Archer; cr. 1992. Born 15 April 1940; Son of late William and Lola Archer; Married Mary Doreen Weeden (later DBE) 1966 (2 sons).

Education: Wellington School, Somerset; Brasenose College, Oxford (Dip Ed 1963).

Non-political career: Athletics Blues 1963-65; Gymnastics Blue 1963; Represented Great Britain in athletics 1966; Author, playwright and amateur auctioneer.

Political career: *House of Commons:* MP (Conservative) for Louth 1969-74. Contested Louth February 1974 general election. *House of Lords:* Raised to the peerage as Baron Archer of Weston-super-Mare, of Mark in the County of Somerset 1992. *Other:* Deputy chair, Conservative Party 1985-86; President, Conservative Party London Clubs 1998-99. Councillor, Greater London Council 1966-70.

Political interests: Art, sport, 2012 Olympics; Australia, India, Kurdistan.

Other: The Archer Charitable Trust; Honorary Doctorate of Literature, Amity University Rajasthan, Jaipur. President, Somerset AAA 1973-99; Vice-President, Cambridge City RFU; President, World Snooker Association 1997-99.

Publications: Plays: Beyond Reasonable Doubt (1987), Exclusive (1990), The Accused (2000), Who Killed The Mayor (2018), The Confession (2018); Novels/short stories: Not a Penny More, Not a Penny Less (1975); Shall We Tell the President? (1977); Kane and Abel (1979); A Quiver Full of Arrows (short stories, 1980); The Prodigal Daughter (1982); First Among Equals (1984); A Matter of Honour (1986); A Twist in the Tale (short stories, 1988); As the Crow Flies (1991); Honour Among Thieves (1993); Twelve Red Herrings (short stories, 1994); The Fourth Estate (1996); Collected Short Stories (1997); The Eleventh Commandment (1998); To Cut a Long Story Short (short stories, 2000); A Prison Diary – Volume I: Hell (2002); Sons of Fortune (2003); A Prison Diary – Volume II: Purgatory (2003); A Prison Diary – Volume III: Heaven (2004); False Impression (2006); Cat O'Nine Tales (short stories, 2006); The Gospel According to Judas (2007); A Prisoner of Birth (2008); Paths of Glory (2009); Rewrite of Kane and Abel (2009); And Thereby Hangs a Tale (short stories, 2010); Only Time Will Tell (2011); The Sins of the Father (2012); Best Kept Secret (2013); Be Careful What You Wish For (2014); Mightier Than The Sword (2015); Cometh The Hour (2016); This Was A Man (2016); Tell Tale short stories (2017); Heads You Win (2018); Heads You Win (2018); Nothing Ventured (2019) Kane and Abel, 40th Anniversary Edition (2019).

Recreations: Theatre, cricket, auctioneering, art.

The Lord Archer of Weston-super-Mare, House of Lords, London SW1A 0PW
Tel: 020 7219 5353
The Penthouse, Peninsula Heights, 93 Albert Embankment, London SE1 7TY
Email: questions@jeffreyarcher.co.uk Website: www.jeffreyarcher.com
Twitter: @Jeffrey_Archer

LABOUR

ARMSTRONG OF HILL TOP, BARONESS

Chair, Select Committee on Public Services

ARMSTRONG OF HILL TOP (Life Baroness), Hilary Jane Armstrong; cr 2010. Born 30 November 1945; Daughter of late Ernest Armstrong (MP for Durham North West 1966-87) and Hannah Armstrong; Married Dr Paul Corrigan 1992.

Education: Monkwearmouth Comprehensive School, Sunderland; West Ham College of Technology (BSc sociology 1967); Birmingham University (Diploma social work 1970); Swahili (rusty).

Non-political career: VSO teaching in Kenya 1967-69; Social worker, Newcastle Social Services 1970-73; Community worker, Southwick Neighbourhood Action Project 1973-75; Lecturer in community and youth work, Sunderland Polytechnic 1975-86; Secretary/researcher for Ernest Armstrong MP 1986-87. Chair ASTMS Northern Division Council 1981-88.

Political career: *House of Commons:* MP (Labour) for North West Durham 1987-2010; Opposition Spokesperson for Education 1988-92; PPS to John Smith as Leader of the Opposition 1992-94; Opposition Spokesperson for: Treasury and Economic Affairs 1994-95, Environment and London 1995-97; Minister of State, Department of the Environment, Transport and the Regions 1997-2001; Government Chief Whip 2001-06; Minister for the Cabinet Office and Social Exclusion; Chancellor of the Duchy of Lancaster 2006-07. Member, Education 1998. Chair, PLP Northern Regional Group 2009-10. *House of Lords:* Raised to the peerage as Baroness Armstrong of Hill Top, of Crook in the County of Durham 2010. Member: Adoption Legislation 2012-13, Soft Power and the UK's Influence 2013-14, European Union 2015-19, EU External Affairs Sub-committee 2015-19, Joint Committee on the Draft Domestic Abuse Bill 2019, Social and Economic Impact of the Gambling Industry 2019-; Chair, Public Services 2020-. *Other:* Member, National Executive Committee, Labour Party 1992-94, 1996-2006. Councillor, Durham County Council 1985-88; Vice-chair, British Council 1994-97; Non-executive director, Co Durham and Darlington Foundation Hospital Trust 2010-11.

Political interests: Regional development, world development, education, environment, social exclusion and social enterprise; Central Africa, Kenya, South Africa, Tanzania, Uganda.

Other: NCH Action for Children: Member, NCH Board 1985-91, Vice-president 1991-97; Member, UNICEF National Committee 1995-97; Patron, Revolving Doors 2007-; Chair, Tony Blair Sports Foundation 2008-, Trustee, Africa Governance Initiative 2008-18, Board member, Emmaus 2008-11; The Cyrenians (Tyneside): Board member 2008-, Chair 2010-; Ambassador Action for Children 2008-; Board member, VSO International 2008-11; Chair, Community Energy Solutions 2009-13 Board member, VSO UK 2011-; Chair, VSO Federation Council 2011-; Honorary degree, Sunderland University; PC 1999.

Recreations: Theatre, reading, football.

Rt Hon the Baroness Armstrong of Hill Top, House of Lords, London SW1A 0PW
Tel: 020 7219 5353 *Email:* armstrongh@parliament.uk

ARRAN, EARL OF

CONSERVATIVE

ARRAN (9th Earl of, I), Arthur Desmond Colquhoun Gore; cr. 1762; 9th Viscount Sudley and Baron Saunders (I) 1758; 5th Baron Sudley (UK) 1884; 11th Bt of Castle Gore (I) 1662. Born 14 July 1938; Son of 8th Earl; Married Eleanor Van Cutsem 1974 (2 daughters).

Education: Eton College; Balliol College, Oxford (BA English literature 1960, MA).

Non-political career: Assistant manager, *Daily Mail* 1972-73; Managing director, Clark Nelson 1973-74; Assistant general manager, *Daily Express* and *Sunday Express* 1974; Director, Waterstone & Co Ltd 1984-87; Parliamentary consultant to the waste industry 1995-; Non-executive director: HMV (EMI) 1995-98, SWEL (the Economy and Inward Investment of the West Country), Bonham's (Auctioneers) 1998-2001, Weather World 2005-. Served Grenadier Guards, national service, commissioned 1958-60.

Political career: *House of Lords:* First entered House of Lords 1983. Sits as Baron Sudley; Government Whip 1987-89; Government Spokesperson for: Home Office, Department for Education and Science and Department of Health and Social Security 1987-89, Department of the Environment 1988-89; Parliamentary Under-Secretary of State: Ministry of Defence (Armed Forces) 1989-92, Northern Ireland Office 1992-94, Department of the Environment 1994; Government Deputy Chief Whip 1994-95; Elected hereditary peer 1999-. EU Sub-committee D (Environment and Agriculture): Member 2007-08, Co-opted member 2008-10; Member: EU Sub-committee D (Agriculture, Fisheries and Environment) 2010-12, Olympic and Paralympic Legacy 2013-14, Communications 2015-16, Natural Environment and Rural Communities Act 2006 2017-18.

Political interests: Media, charity, sport, foreign affairs.

Other: President, Children's Country Holidays Fund 1999; Trustee, Chelsea Physic Garden. Turf, Beefsteak, Pratt's.

Recreations: Tennis, golf, croquet, shooting, gardening.

The Earl of Arran, House of Lords, London SW1A 0PW
Tel: 020 7219 3000
Castle Hill Estate Office, Filleigh, Barnstaple EX32 0RH *Tel:* 01598 760336
Email: office@castlehill-devon.com

CONSERVATIVE

ASHTON OF HYDE, LORD

Lords Chief Whip (Captain of the Honourable Corps of the Gentlemen-at-Arms)

ASHTON OF HYDE (4th Baron, UK), Thomas Henry Ashton; cr. 1911. Born 18 July 1958; Son of late 3rd Baron and Pauline Trewlove Ashton, née Brackenbury; Married Emma Allinson 1987 (4 daughters).

Education: Eton College; Trinity College, Oxford (BA 1980, MA).

Non-political career: Barclays Bank 1981-82; CT Bowring Reinsurance Ltd 1982-90; Vice-President, Guy Carpenter & Company 1990-92; Director: C.T Bowring Reinsurance Ltd 1992-93, D.P Mann Ltd 1996-99; Faraday Underwriting Ltd: Director 1999-2013, Chief Executive Officer 2005-13; Faraday Reinsurance Company Ltd: Director 2002-13, Chief Executive Officer 2005-13; Council Member, Lloyd's 2010-13; Non-executive Director, Aegis Managing Agency Ltd 2014. Lieutenant: Royal Hussars, Royal Wessex Yeomanry.

Political career: *House of Lords:* Elected hereditary peer 2011-; Government Whip (Lord in Waiting) 2014-17; Government Spokesperson for: Business, Innovation and Skills 2014-15, Home Office 2014-16, Justice 2014-15, Defence 2015-16, Treasury 2015-16; Parliamentary Under-Secretary of State and Government Spokesperson, Department for Culture, Media and Sport/Digital, Culture, Media and Sport 2016-19; Lords Chief Whip (Captain of the Honourable Corps of the Gentlemen-at-Arms) 2019-; Deputy Chairman of Committees 2019-. Member: The Arctic 2014, Insurance Bill 2014-15, Services 2019-, Procedure/Procedure and Privileges 2019-, Selection 2019-.

Other: PC 2019.

Rt Hon the Lord Ashton of Hyde, House of Lords, London SW1A 0PW
Email: holgovernmentwhips@parliament.uk

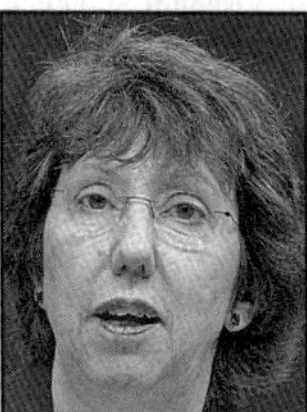

NON-AFFILIATED

ASHTON OF UPHOLLAND, BARONESS

ASHTON OF UPHOLLAND (Life Baroness), Catherine Margaret Ashton; cr 1999. Born 20 March 1956; Daughter of late Harold and Clare Ashton; Married Peter Kellner 1988 (1 son 1 daughter 1 stepson 2 stepdaughters).

Education: Upholland Grammar School; Bedford College, London University (BSc (Econ) 1977); French.

Non-political career: Administrative officer, CND 1977-79; The Coverdale Organisation 1979-81; Central Council for Education and Training in Social Work 1981-83; Director of community development and public affairs, Business in the Community 1983-89; Public policy adviser 1989-, seconded by London First to Home Office 1998-99; Director, Political Context 1996-98; Adviser, Lattice Foundation 2000-01; European Commission: Commissioner for Trade 2008-09, High Representative for Foreign Affairs and Security Policy, and Vice-President and External Relations Commissioner 2009-14; Chair, steering board, European Defence Agency 2009-14; Visiting Professor, King's College London; King of Arms of the Most Distinguished Order of St Michael and St George 2019-.

Political career: *House of Lords:* Raised to the peerage as Baroness Ashton of Upholland, of St Albans in the County of Hertfordshire 1999. Parliamentary Under-Secretary of State and Government Spokesperson, Department for Education and Skills 2001-04 (also Department for Work and Pensions 2002-04); Government Spokesperson for Children 2003-04; Parliamentary Under-Secretary of State and Government Spokesperson, Department for Constitutional Affairs/Ministry of Justice 2004-07; Leader of the House of Lords and Lord President of the Council 2007-08; Government Spokesperson for: Cabinet Office 2008, Equality 2008; On leave of absence 2008-15, March 2016-August 2019, December 2020-. Member: Selection 2007-08,

Liaison 2007-08, Privileges 2007-08, House 2007-08, Procedure 2007-08. *Other:* Chair, Hertfordshire Health Authority 1998-2001.

Other: Vice-president, National Council for One Parent Families 1998-2001; Trustee, Verulamium Museum 2000-; Chancellor, Warwick University 2017-; *House Magazine* Minister of the Year 2005; Channel 4 Peer of the Year 2005; Stonewall Politician of the Year 2006; PC 2006; GCMG 2015. Royal Commonwealth Society Club.

Rt Hon the Baroness Ashton of Upholland GCMG, House of Lords, London SW1A 0PW
Tel: 020 7219 5353

CONSERVATIVE

ASTOR, VISCOUNT

ASTOR (4th Viscount, UK), William Waldorf Astor; cr. 1917; 4th Baron Astor (UK) 1916. Born 27 December 1951; Son of 3rd Viscount and Hon. Sarah Norton, daughter of 6th Baron Grantley; Married Annabel Sheffield, née Jones 1976 (2 sons 1 daughter).

Education: Eton College.

Non-political career: Silvergate Media 2011-.

Political career: *House of Lords:* First entered House of Lords 1972; Government Whip 1990-93; Government Spokesperson for: Department of Environment 1990-91, Home Office 1991-92, Department of National Heritage 1992-93; Parliamentary Under-Secretary of State: Department of Social Security 1993-94, Department of National Heritage 1994-95; Opposition Spokesperson for: Home Office 1997-2001; Elected hereditary peer 1999-; Opposition Spokesperson for: Education and Employment 1999-2001, Transport, Local Government and the Regions 2001-02, Transport 2002-05, Culture, Media and Sport 2005-06.

Other: Trustee, Stanley Spencer Gallery, Cookham. White's Club.

The Viscount Astor, House of Lords, London SW1A 0PW
Tel: 020 7219 4139 *Email:* astorw@parliament.uk
44 Grosvenor Gardens Mews South, London SW1W 0LB

CONSERVATIVE

ASTOR OF HEVER, LORD

ASTOR OF HEVER (3rd Baron, UK), John Jacob Astor; cr. 1956. Born 16 June 1946; Son of 2nd Baron and late Lady Irene Haig; Married Fiona Harvey 1970 (divorced 1990) (3 daughters); married Hon. Elizabeth Mackintosh 1990 (1 son 1 daughter).

Education: Eton College; French.

Non-political career: Chair, Newwaves Solutions Ltd 2016-. Lieutenant, Life Guards 1966-70; Honorary Colonel 101 (City of London) Engineer Regiment 2005-10.

Political career: *House of Lords:* First entered House of Lords 1984; Opposition Whip 1998-2010; Elected hereditary peer 1999-; Opposition Spokesperson for: Defence 2003-10, Foreign and Commonwealth Office 2003-10, International Development 2003-10; Parliamentary Under-Secretary of State and Government Spokesperson, Ministry of Defence 2010-15; Government Whip 2010-11; Trade Envoy to: Kazakhstan 2015-17, Oman 2016-; Adviser on Oman to the Secretary of State for Defence 2016-. *Other:* Member of Executive, Association of Conservative Peers 1996-98; Conservative Middle East Council: Deputy Chair 2015-18, Honorary Vice-president 2018-. DL Kent 1996-.

Political interests: France, motorsport industry, defence; Belgium, France, USA.

Other: Trustee, Astor of Hever Trust 1986-; Chair, Council of the Order of St John for Kent 1987-97; Trustee: Astor Foundation 1988-2008, Rochester Cathedral Trust 1988-2010; Patron, Edenbridge Music and Arts Trust 1989-2010; Trustee, Canterbury Cathedral Trust 1992-2007; Patron, Kent Youth Trust 1994-2010; President: Earl Haig Branch, Royal British Legion 1994-2010, Motorsport Industry Association 1995-2010, RoSPA 1996-99, Eden Valley Museum Trust 1998-2010; Patron, Aquarian Opera 1999-2010; Royal British Legion, Kent 2002-07; President, Kent County Agricultural Society 2006-10; Patron, Conservatives in Paris; President: Tunbridge Wells International Music Festival 2009-10, Motorsport Industry Association 2016-; Member, Goldsmiths' Company; PC 2015. White's Club.

Rt Hon the Lord Astor of Hever DL, House of Lords, London SW1A 0PW
Tel: 020 7219 5475 *Email:* astorjj@parliament.uk

CONSERVATIVE

ATTLEE, EARL

ATTLEE (3rd Earl, UK), John Richard Attlee; cr. 1955; Viscount Prestwood. Born 3 October 1956; Son of 2nd Earl; Married Celia Plummer 1993 (divorced); married Terese Ahern 2008.

Education: Stowe School, Buckinghamshire.

Non-political career: Materials Management, Smith Industries; In-Country director (Rwanda), British Direct Aid 1995-96. Major, REME TA, All Arms Pool of Watchkeepers; Operation Lodestar 1997-98; Operation Telic (Iraq) 2003.

Political career: *House of Lords:* First entered House of Lords 1994; Opposition Whip 1997-99, 2002-05, 2007-10; Opposition Spokesperson for: Defence June-Oct 1997, 1998-2001, 2002-03, Transport 1997, 1999-2001, 2002-03, 2007-10, Northern Ireland 1997, 1998-99, Trade and Industry 1998-99; Elected hereditary peer 1999-; Opposition Spokesperson for: Energy 2003-04, Office of the Deputy Prime Minister 2004-05, Maritime and Shipping 2007-10; Government Whip 2010-14; Government Spokesperson for: International Development 2010, Northern Ireland 2010-14, Transport 2010-13, Communities and Local Government 2010-12, 2013-14, Home Office 2010-14, Wales 2012-14, Law Officers 2013-14, Scotland 2013-14, Immigration 2013-14. Member: Statutory Instruments Joint Committee 2007-08, Partnerships (Prosecution) (Scotland) Bill 2013, Administration and Works 2015-16, Services 2016-17.

Political interests: Overseas aid and development, engineering, defence, transport.

Other: Patron, Steamship Freshspring Society 2014-; President, Heavy Transport Association 1994-2008; TD.

Recreations: Restoration and operation of classic commericial and military vehicles.

The Earl Attlee TD, House of Lords, London SW1A 0PW
Tel: 020 7219 6071 *Email:* attleej@parliament.uk

NON-AFFILIATED

AUSTIN OF DUDLEY, LORD

AUSTIN OF DUDLEY (Life Baron), Ian Christopher Austin; cr 2020. Born 6 March 1965; Son of Alfred and Margaret Austin; Married Catherine Miles 1993 (2 sons 1 daughter).

Education: Dudley School; Essex University (BA government 1987).

Non-political career: Communications manager, Focus Housing 1989-94; Regional press officer, West Midlands Labour Party 1995-98; Deputy director of communications, Scottish Labour Party 1998-99; Special adviser to Gordon Brown as Chancellor of the Exchequer 1999-2005.

Political career: *House of Commons:* MP (Lab) for Dudley North 2005-10, for Dudley North (revised boundary) 2010-19; PPS to Gordon Brown: as Chancellor of the Exchequer 2007, as Prime Minister 2007-08; Assistant Government Whip 2008-09; Minister for the West Midlands 2008-10; Parliamentary Under-Secretary of State, Department for Communities and Local Government 2009-10; Shadow Minister for: Communities and Local Government 2010, Sports 2010-11, Work and Pensions 2011-13; Trade Envoy to Israel 2019. Member: Home Affairs 2013-15, Education 2015-17, Education, Skills and the Economy Sub-committee 2015-16, Foreign Affairs 2017-19, Panel of Chairs 2017-19. Chair, PLP Departmental Group for Education 2015-17. *House of Lords:* Raised to the peerage as Baron Austin of Dudley, of Dudley in the County of West Midlands 2020. Trade Envoy to Israel 2020-. *Other:* Member, Labour Party 1984-2019. Councillor, Dudley Borough Council 1991-95.

Political interests: Housing, education, manufacturing, foreign policy.

Other: Member, UK Delegation, Organisation for Security and Co-operation in Europe Parliamentary Assembly 2015-17.

Recreations: Football, cycling, reading.

The Lord Austin of Dudley, House of Lords, London SW1A 0PW
Tel: 020 7219 3000 *Twitter:* @LordIanAustin

LABOUR

BACH, LORD

BACH (Life Baron), William Stephen Goulden Bach; cr. 1998. Born 25 December 1946; Son of late Stephen Bach CBE and late Joan Bach; Married Caroline Jones 1984 (1 daughter and 2 children from previous marriage).

Education: Westminster School; New College, Oxford (BA English 1968).

Non-political career: Called to the Bar, Middle Temple 1972, Tenant Barristers' Chambers 1975-2000, Head of Chambers 1996-99; Served on a number of circuit and local court and bar committees over many years. Member, TGWU/Unite 1977-.

Political career: *House of Commons:* Contested (Labour) Gainsborough 1979 and Sherwood 1983 and 1987 general elections. *House of Lords:* Raised to the peerage as Baron Bach, of Lutterworth in the County of Leicestershire 1998. Government Whip 1999-2000, 2007-08; Government Spokesperson for: Home Office 1999-2000, Lord Chancellor's Department 1999-2000, Education and Employment 1999-2000; Parliamentary Secretary, Lord Chancellor's Department 2000-01; Parliamentary Under-Secretary of State (Minister for Defence Procurement) and Government Spokesperson, Ministry of Defence 2001-05; Parliamentary Under-Secretary of State and Government Spokesperson, Department for Environment, Food and Rural Affairs 2005-06; Government Spokesperson for: Business, Enterprise and Regulatory Reform 2007-08, Justice 2007-10, HM Treasury 2007-08, Foreign and Commonwealth Office 2008; Parliamentary Under-Secretary of State, Ministry of Justice 2008-10; Opposition Spokesperson for: Justice 2010-12, 2015-16, Foreign and Commonwealth Office 2013-15, Law Officers 2014-15; Shadow Attorney General 2014-15. Member: European Communities Sub-committee E (Laws and Institutions) 1998-99, Draft Legal Services Bill Joint Committee 2006; Co-opted Member, EU Sub-committee D (Environment and Agriculture) 2006-07. *Other:* Police and Crime Commissioner for Leicestershire 2016-. Society of Labour Lawyers: Executive committee member, Chair and co-founder, Society of Labour Lawyers, East Midlands; Elected member, Labour Party: National Policy Forum 1998-99, Economic Policy Commission 1998-99; Member, Co-operative Party; Chair: Harborough District Labour Party 1989-95, 2007-, Northants and Blaby Euro Constituency GC 1992-99, South Leicestershire CLP 2007-. Leicester City Council: Councillor 1976-87, Chief Whip, Labour Group 1981-83; Councillor, Lutterworth Town Council 1991-99; Mayor of Lutterworth 1993-94; Harborough District Council: Councillor 1995-99, Chair, Contracts Services Committee 1995-97; Chief Whip, Labour Group 1995-98.

Political interests: Crime and criminal justice, local government, sport, foreign affairs, defence and security, social welfare law; Latin America, Chile, India, Italy, Portugal, Spain, USA.

Other: Leicester University: Council member 1980-99, Court member 1980-; Member, Fabian Society; Vice-chair, Cotesbach Education Trust; Trustee, LawWorks; Patron, Coventry Law Centre; Honorary degree, Leicester University; Peer of the Year, *House Magazine* awards 2012. Leicestershire CCC; Founder Member and President, Walcote Cricket Club.

Recreations: Playing and watching football and cricket, supporting Leicester City FC, American crime writing.

The Lord Bach, House of Lords, London SW1A 0PW
Tel: 020 7219 6389 *Fax:* 020 7219 2146 *Email:* bachw@parliament.uk *Twitter:* @FightBach

CONSERVATIVE

BAKER OF DORKING, LORD

BAKER OF DORKING (Life Baron), Kenneth Wilfred Baker; cr. 1997. Born 3 November 1934; Son of late Wilfred Baker, OBE; Married Mary Gray-Muir 1963 (1 son 2 daughters).

Education: St Paul's School, London; Magdalen College, Oxford (BA history 1958) (Union Secretary 1958).

Non-political career: Non-executive director, Stanley Leisure plc (now called Genting UK) 2001-. National service 1953-55 (Lieutenant in Gunners).

Political career: *House of Commons:* Contested (Conservative) Poplar 1964 and Acton 1966 general elections. MP for Acton 1968-70, for St Marylebone 1970-83, for Mole Valley 1983-97; PPS to Minister of State, Department of Employment 1970-72; Parliamentary Secretary, Civil Service Department 1972-74; Minister of State for Industry and Information Technology 1981-84; Minister for Local Government 1984-85; Secretary of State for: Environment 1985-86, Education and Science 1986-89; Chancellor of the Duchy of Lancaster 1989-90; Home Secretary 1990-92. *House of Lords:* Raised to the peerage as Baron Baker of Dorking, of Iford in the County of East Sussex 1997. Chair, Information 2003-07; Member, House 2007-12. *Other:* Chairman, Conservative Party 1989-90; Hon. Life member, Tory Reform Group. Councillor, Twickenham Borough Council 1960-62.

Political interests: Education, history, information technology; UK.

Other: Chair: Hansard Society 1978-81, Museum of British History 1995-2005; President, Royal London Society for the Blind 2000-10; Trustee: Cartoon AG Trust 2003-, Booker Prize Foundation 2005-; President, Old Pauline Club 2007-09; Chair, Edge Foundation 2008-; Trustee, Baker Dearing Educational Trust 2003-; Cartoon Museum; City & Guilds Fellowship Diploma 2012; Hon degree, Richmond College, American University in London; Hon fellowship diploma, City and Guilds; Hon DSc, Aston University; Hon doctorate of education, Plymouth University; DLitt, Chester University; PC 1984; CH 1992. Athenæum, Garrick Club.

Publications: I Have No Gun But I Can Spit (1980); London Lines (1982); The Faber Book of English History in Verse (1988); Unauthorised Versions: Poems and their Parodies (1990); The Faber Book of Conservatism (1993); The Turbulent Years: My Life in Politics (1993); The Prime Ministers – An Irreverent Political History in Cartoons (1995); Kings and Queens: An Irreverent Cartoon History of the British Monarchy (1996); The Faber Book of War Poetry (1996); Children's English History in Verse (2000); The Faber Book of Landscape Poetry (2000); George IV: A Life in Caricature (2005); George III: A Life in Caricature (2007); GK Chesterton Poems (2007); George Washington's War in Contemporary Caricature and Print (2009); 14-18: A New Vision for Secondary Education (2013).

Recreations: Collecting books, collecting political cartoons.

Rt Hon the Lord Baker of Dorking CH, House of Lords, London SW1A 0PW
Tel: 020 7219 4434 *Email:* bakerk@parliament.uk

LABOUR

BAKEWELL, BARONESS

BAKEWELL (Life Baroness), Joan Dawson Bakewell; cr 2011. Born 16 April 1933; Daughter of John Rowlands and Rose Bland; Married Michael Bakewell 1955 (divorced 1972) (1 daughter 1 son); married Jack Emery (divorced 2001).

Education: Stockport High School for Girls; Newnham College, Cambridge (BA history and economics).

Non-political career: TV presenter: *Sunday Break* 1962, *Home at 4.30* 1964, *Meeting Point* 1964, *The Second Sex* 1964, *Late Night Line Up* 1965-72, *The Youthful Eye* 1968, *Moviemakers at the National Film Theatre* 1971, *Film 72* 1972, *Film 73* 1973, *For the Sake of Appearance, Where is Your God?, Who Cares?, and the Affirmative Way* (series) 1973, *Holiday* (series) 1974-78, *Thank You, Ron* (documentary) 1974, *What's it All About?* (series) 1974, *Fairest Fortune and Edinburgh Festival Report* 1974, *Time Running Out* (series) 1974, *The Shakespeare Business* (series) 1976, *The Brontë Business* (series) 1976, *Generation to Generation* (series) 1976, *Reports Action* (series) 1976-79, *My Dad with the Children* 1977, *Arts UK: OK?* 1980, *The Heart of the Matter* 1988-2000, *Travels with Persner* 1998, *My Generation* 2000, *Taboo* (series) 2001, Sky Arts 2013-; TV critic, *The Times* 1978-81; Radio presenter: *Away From it All* 1978-79, *PM* 1979-81, *Artist of the Week* 1998-2000, *Belief* 2001-, *Midsummer Sins* 2004, *There and Back* (play), *We Need to Talk About Death* 2016-; *Brontës:*

The Private Faces (theatre), Edinburgh Festival 1979; Arts correspondent, BBC 1981-87; Columnist, *Sunday Times* 1988-90; Chair, *The Brains Trust*, BBC 1998-2001; Columnist: *Guardian* 2003-05, *Independent* 2006-.

Political career: *House of Lords:* Raised to the peerage as Baroness Bakewell, of Stockport in the County of Greater Manchester 2011. Member: Communications 2012-15, Works of Art 2015-16, Lord Speaker's Advisory Panel on Works of Art 2017-19, Artificial Intelligence 2017-18, Intergenerational Fairness and Provision 2018, Regenerating Seaside Towns and Communities 2018-19.

Political interests: Women's rights, the elderly, the arts; Brazil, India, Turkey.

Other: President, Society of Arts Publicists 1984-90; Council member, Aldeburgh Foundation 1985-99; British Film Institute: Governor 1994-2003, Deputy chair 1997-99, Chair 1999-2003; Board member, Royal National Theatre 1996-2003; Chair: Shared Experience Theatre Co 2007-12, National Campaign on the Arts 2009-11; President, Birkbeck College 2013-; Breast Cancer Care, Women for Refugee Women, British Humanist Association, English Pen, Fawcett Society, Amnesty International; Hon. FRCA 1994; Newnham College, Cambridge: Associate 1980-91, Associate fellow 1984-87; Hon. Fellow, Royal Holloway and Bedford New College 1997; Hon. DLitt, Queen Margaret University College, Edinburgh 2005; Honorary professor, Department of Film and Media, Stirling University 2006-; Hon. DLitt: Chester 2007, University of Arts, London 2008, Staffordshire University 2009, Lancaster University 2010, Newcastle University 2011, Open University 2010, Essex University 2011, Manchester Metropolitan University 2013; Richard Dimbleby Award, BAFTA 1994; Journalist of the Year, Stonewall awards 2009; CBE 1999; DBE 2008.

Publications: Co-author, The New Priesthood: British Television Today (1970); A Fine and Private Place (1977); The Complete Traveller (1977); The Heart of Heart of the Matter (1996); The Centre of the Bed (autobiography, 2003); Belief (2005); The View from Here (2006); All the Nice Girls (2009); She's Leaving Home (2012); Stop the Clocks: Thoughts on What I Leave Behind (2017).

Recreations: Cinema, theatre, travel.

The Baroness Bakewell DBE, House of Lords, London SW1A 0PW
Tel: 020 7219 2921
Email: joanbakewell@googlemail.com Website: joanbakewell.com *Twitter:* @JDBakewell

LIBERAL DEMOCRAT

BAKEWELL OF HARDINGTON MANDEVILLE, BARONESS

Liberal Democrat Lords Spokesperson for Environment, Food and Rural Affairs

BAKEWELL OF HARDINGTON MANDEVILLE (Life Baroness), Catherine Mary Bakewell; cr 2013. Born 7 March 1949; Married David Bakewell 1979 (1 daughter 1 son).

Non-political career: Assistant to Leader of Liberal Democrats 1983-95, 1997-98.

Political career: *House of Lords:* Raised to the peerage as Baroness Bakewell of Hardington Mandeville, of Hardington Mandeville in the County of Somerset 2013. Liberal Democrat: Spokesperson for: Housing 2015, Communities and Local Government 2016, Shadow Secretary of State for Work and Pensions 2016-17, Lords Spokesperson for Environment, Food and Rural Affairs 2017-19, 2020-. Member, Personal Service Companies 2013-14; Alternate Member, Procedure 2014-17; Member: EU Energy and Environment Sub-committee 2015, Middle Level Bill 2018, Secondary Legislation Scrutiny 2019-. *Other:* Member, Liberal Party/ Liberal Democrats 1974-; Yeovil Liberal Democrats: Chair 2008-11, Vice-chair 2011-13. Somerset County Council: Councillor 1993-2013, Leader 2001-07; Member: Somerset Strategic Partnership 2013-16, County Council Network 2001-08, South West Regional Assembly; Non-executive director, South West Regional Development Agency 2004-12; Member: Councillors Commission 2007, Avon and Somerset Police Authority 2008-09; Councillor, South Somerset District Council 2009-; Governor, Yeovil College Corporation 2010-13; Member, Devon and Somerset Fire and Rescue Service 2012-13; Vice-president, Local Government Association 2017-.

Political interests: Local government, rural affairs and agriculture, housing, children and young people.

Other: Non-executive director, Somerset Rural Youth Project 1997-2009; Board member, Equality South West 2009-13; Chair, South Somerset Together 2013-16 Patron, South Somerset Mind 2015-; Vice-president, Local Education Authority 2017-; MBE 1999.

The Baroness Bakewell of Hardington Mandeville MBE, House of Lords, London SW1A 0PW
Tel: 020 7219 8310 *Email:* bakewellc@parliament.uk

CONSERVATIVE

BALFE, LORD

BALFE (Life Baron), Richard Andrew Balfe; cr 2013. Born 14 May 1944; Son of Dr Richard Balfe and Dorothy Balfe; Married Susan Jane Honeyford (2 sons 1 daughter).

Education: Brook Secondary Modern School, Sheffield; London School of Economics (BSc social policy and administration 1971); French.

Non-political career: Civil Servant: Crown Agents for Overseas Governments 1961-65, Foreign Office 1965-70 (1967-70 on sabbatical at LSE); Research Officer, Finer Committee on One Parent Families 1970-73; Political Secretary, Royal Arsenal Co-operative Society 1973-79; Director: Co-operative Wholesale Society 1978-80, Royal Arsenal Co-operative Society and associated companies 1987-96; Chair, Royal Arsenal Co-operative Society Political Purposes Committee 1981-97. 1st Battalion Irish Rifles (TA) 1961-1967. AUEW TASS/Unite.

Political career: *House of Commons:* Contested (Labour) Paddington South 1970 and Southwark and Bermondsey 1992 general elections. *House of Lords:* Raised to the peerage as Baron Balfe, of Dulwich in the London Borough of Southwark 2013. Member: European Union Sub-committee A (Economic and Financial Affairs) 2014-15, EU External Affairs Sub-Committee 2015-17, International Relations 2017-18. *Other:* European Parliament: MEP for: London South Inner 1979-99, London region 1999-2004: Quaestor 1994-2004, Member: PES bureau 1994-99, European Parliament Bureau 1994-2004. Labour Party 1963-64, 1967-2001: London Executive 1973-95, Chair, Policy Committee 1983-85, Labour Whip removed 2001; Conservative Party: Member 2002-, Envoy to the Trades Union Movement 2007-15. Greater London Council: Member for Southwark Dulwich 1973-77, Chair, Housing Development Committee 1975-77; Member, Court of Governors, London School of Economics 1973-91; Chair, Thamesmead New Town 1973-75.

Political interests: Defence, foreign policy, trade union affairs; Turkey, all EU countries, Commonwealth, USA.

Other: Member, European Economic and Social Committee 2012-13; Election Monitor in: Ukraine 2004, 2007, 2014, Turkey 2015; Substitute Member, UK Delegation to Parliamentary Assembly of Council of Europe 2016-; Member, Executive Committee, Fabian Society 1981-82; President, European Parliament Members Pension Fund 2004-; Chair, Anglia Community Leisure 2008-13; Director, CERN Pension Fund 2009-15; Trustee, Royal Statistical Society Pension Fund 2011-13; Vice-President, European Parliament Former Members' Association; Executive Committee Member, Global Democracy Initiative; Honorary President, British Dietetic Association; Member, CERN Actuarial and Technical Committee 2012-17; BALPA: Honorary Adviser 2015-17, Vice-President 2017-19, President 2019-; Fellow, Royal Statistical Society 1973-. Reform Club.

Recreations: Walking, reading, opera.

The Lord Balfe, House of Lords, London SW1A 0PW
Tel: 020 7219 8710 *Email:* richard.balfe@parliament.uk

CONSERVATIVE

BAMFORD, LORD

BAMFORD (Life Baron), Anthony Paul Bamford; cr 2013. Born 23 October 1945; Son of late Joseph Cyril Bamford CBE; Married Carole Gray Whitt 1974 (2 sons 1 daughter).

Education: Ampleforth College; Grenoble University.

Non-political career: Chair, J C Bamford Group/JCB 1975-; Director, Tarmac plc 1988-94.

Political career: *House of Lords:* Raised to the peerage as Baron Bamford, of Daylesford in the County of Gloucestershire and of Wootton in the County of Staffordshire 2013. *Other:* President, Burton on Trent Conservative Association 1987-90. Staffordshire: High Sheriff 1985-86, DL 1989.

Other: Member: President's committee, CBI 1986-88, Design Council 1987-89; President, Staffordshire Agricultural Society 1987-88; NSPCC; Hon. Fellow: City and Guilds Institute 1993, Chartered Society of Designers 1994; Fellow, Institute of Agricultural Engineers 2003; Hon. Fellow: Institution of Engineering Designers 2008, Royal Academy of Engineering 2014, Institution of Mechanical Engineers 2015; Hon. MA engineering, Birmingham University 1987; Hon. doctorate in science, Cranfield University 1994; Hon. degree of business administration, Robert Gordon University, Aberdeen 1996; Hon. doctorates in: Technology, Staffordshire University 1998, Technology, Loughborough University 2002, Science, Harper Adams University College 2010; Chevalier de l'Ordre National du Mérite, France 1989; Commendatore al merito della Republica Italiana 1995; Kt 1990.

Recreations: Farming, gardening.

The Lord Bamford, House of Lords, London SW1A 0PW
Tel: 020 7219 5353
J C Bamford Excavators Ltd, Rocester ST14 5JP *Tel:* 01889 590312
Email: jane.cornwall@jcb.com

LIBERAL DEMOCRAT

BARKER, BARONESS

Liberal Democrat Lords Spokesperson for Voluntary Sector and LGBT Equality

BARKER (Life Baroness); Elizabeth Jean Barker; cr. 1999. Born 31 January 1961; Married Caroline Downie 2016.

Education: Dalziel High School, Motherwell; Broadway School, Oldham; Southampton University (BSc (SocSci) psychology 1982).

Non-political career: Age Concern England 1982-2008: Project co-ordinator, Opportunities for Volunteering Programme 1983-88, Grants officer 1988-92, Field officer 1992-2008; Management consultant to Age Concern organisations; Director: Third Sector Business (management consultancy) 2008-17, B&W Consulting 2008-; Head of business development, SeeTheDifference.org 2010-11; Development Adviser, Charity Checkout 2014-.

Political career: *House of Lords:* Raised to the peerage as Baroness Barker, of Anagach in Highland 1999. Liberal Democrat Spokesperson for: Pensions 2000-02, Social Services 2000-04, Health 2004-10, Voluntary Sector and LGBT Equality 2015-; Deputy Chairman of Committees 2020-. Member: Mental Capacity Act 2005 2013-14, Joint Committee on the Draft Protection of Charities Bill 2014-15, Charities 2016-17, Citizenship and Civic Engagement 2017-18, Joint Committee on the Draft Registration of Overseas Entities Bill 2019. *Other:* Union of Liberal Students: Member 1979-83, Chair 1982-83; Member: Liberal Party National Executive 1982-83, Liberal Assembly Committee 1984-97; Liberal Democrats: Member, Federal Policy Committee 1997-2003, Chair, Federal Conference Committee 1997-2004, Member, Policy Working Groups on: Future of Social Services, Freedom and Fairness for Women, An Age of Opportunity, It's About Freedom, Member, Federal Executive 2004, Chair, Policy Working Groups on: Poverty and Inequality 2006-07, Future of the Voluntary Sector 2010-11. Vice-President, Local Government Association 2010-18.

Political interests: Health, social services, ageing, LGBT equality, equality for women and girls, social enterprise, HIV/AIDS; Balkans, India, Nigeria, South Africa.

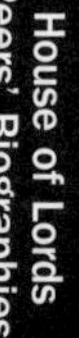

Other: Patron, Spare Tyre Theatre Company 2010-; Ambassador, Albert Kennedy Trust 2014-; Trustee, Andy Lawson Memorial Fund; Patron: Opening Doors London 2016-, East London Out Project 2019; Albert Kennedy Trust, East London Out Project, Opening Doors London, The Bike Project, Voluntary Service Overseas.

The Baroness Barker, House of Lords, London SW1A 0PW
Tel: 020 7219 2955 *Email:* barkere@parliament.uk *Twitter:* @LizBarkerLords

CONSERVATIVE

BARKER OF BATTLE, LORD

BARKER OF BATTLE (Life Baron), Gregory Leonard George Barker; cr 2015. Born 8 March 1966; Married Celeste Harrison 1992 (divorced 2008) (1 daughter 2 sons).

Education: Steyning Grammar School; Lancing College, West Sussex; Royal Holloway College, London University (BA modern history, economic history, politics 1987); London Business School (corporate finance programme 1992).

Non-political career: Researcher, Centre for Policy Studies 1987-89; Equity analyst, Gerrard Vivian Gray 1988-90; Director, International Pacific Securities 1990-97; Associate partner, Brunswick Group Ltd 1997-98; Head, investor communications, Siberian Oil Company 1998-2000; Director, Daric plc (Bartlett Merton) 1998-2001; Chair, London Sustainable Development Commission 2014-2016; Senior adviser, Powerhive Ltd 2015-; Independent Non-Executive Director and Chair, En+ Group plc -2017; Chair, Imprimatur Capital Limited -2017; Director, Quercus Investment Selection Limited 2017-.

Political career: *House of Commons:* Contested Eccles 1997 general election. MP (Conservative) for Bexhill and Battle 2001-10, for Bexhill and Battle (revised boundary) 2010-15; Opposition Whip 2003-05; Shadow Minister for: the Environment 2005-08, Climate Change 2008-10; Minister of State, Department of Energy and Climate Change 2010-14. Member: Environmental Audit 2001-05, 2007-10, Broadcasting 2003-05. *House of Lords:* Raised to the peerage as Baron Barker of Battle, of Battle in the County of East Sussex 2015. On leave of absence February 2019-. *Other:* Chair: Shoreham Young Conservatives 1982-83, Royal Holloway Conservative Society 1986-87; Vice-chair: Hammersmith Conservative Association 1993-95, Wandsworth and Tooting Conservative Association 1997-98; Founding Member, 2020 group 2011.

Political interests: Environment, education, overseas development; Australia, Germany, Russia, USA.

Other: Associate, Centre for Policy Studies 1988-89; Director of European Board, Environmental Defense Fund; Trustee: De La Warr Pavilion, Bexhill-on-Sea, The Climate Group; Honourable Artillery Company; PC 2012. Carlton Club.

Recreations: Skiing, hunting, horse racing, gardening.

Rt Hon the Lord Barker of Battle, House of Lords, London SW1A 0PW
Tel: 020 7219 3000
Email: office@gregorybarker.com *Twitter:* @GregBarkerUK

CONSERVATIVE

BARRAN, BARONESS

Parliamentary Under-Secretary of State for Civil Society and Government Spokesperson, Department for Digital, Culture, Media and Sport

BARRAN (Life Baroness), Diana Francesca Caroline Barran; cr 2018. Born 10 February 1959; Daughter of late Cosmo de Bosdari and Erica de Bosdari (née Lajta); Married Julian Barran 1986 (1 daughter, 3 sons).

Education: Benenden School, Kent; King's College, Cambridge (MA history 1980); French, Italian.

Non-political career: Analyst/Fund Manager, Morgan Grenfell Ltd 1980-83; Fund Manager Europe, Lombard Odier International 1983-85; Head of Research, Enskilda Securities 1985-90; Chief Executive, Enskilda Asset Management 1990-92; Founder and Chief Executive, Barran and Partners 1992-2000; Director of Research, Beaumont Capital 2001; Donor Adviser and

Head of Grant Development, New Philanthropy Capital 2001-04; Founder and Chief Executive, SafeLives (previously Coordinated Action Against Domestic Abuse) 2004-17.

Political career: *House of Lords:* Raised to the peerage as Baroness Barran, of Bathwick in the City of Bath 2018. Government Whip (Baroness in Waiting) 2018-19; Parliamentary Under-Secretary of State for Civil Society and Government Spokesperson, Department for Digital, Culture, Media and Sport 2019-.

Political interests: Asylum, immigration and nationality, communities and families, crime, civil law, justice and rights, child protection, domestic violence and abuse, social services – children and adults.

Other: Chair, Henry Smith Charity 2002-; Advisory board, Greenwood Place; Trustee, Comic Relief 2010-; Member: National Oversight Panel for Domestic Abuse 2014-17, HMIC Expert Panels on Child Abuse and Domestic Abuse 2014-17; Trustee, Royal Foundation 2018-; Beacon Prize for England (2007); MBE 2011.

Publications: Co-author: Charity Begins at Home – A guide for donors and philanthropists (NPC, 2003), Safety in Numbers – a multi site evaluation of independent domestic violence advisor services (2009).

Recreations: Yoga.

The Baroness Barran MBE, House of Lords, London SW1A 0PW
Tel: 020 7219 6328 *Email:* barrand@parliament.uk *Twitter:* @dianabarran

CONSERVATIVE

BARWELL, LORD

BARWELL (Life Baron), Gavin Laurence Barwell; cr 2019. Born 23 January 1972; Married Karen 2001 (3 sons).

Education: Trinity School, Croydon; Trinity College, Cambridge (BA natural sciences 1993).

Non-political career: Environment desk officer, Conservative Research Department 1993-95; Special adviser to John Gummer as Secretary of State for the Environment 1995-97; Press Officer, CCHQ May-October 1997, Head of Political Section, Conservative Research Department CCHQ 1997-98, Head of Local Government, Campaigning Department CCHQ 1998-2003, Chief Operating Officer, Conservative Party 2003-06; Political Consultant 2006-10; Chief of Staff to Theresa May as Prime Minister 2017-19.

Political career: *House of Commons:* MP for Croydon Central 2010-17. Contested Croydon Central 2017 general election; PPS to: Greg Clark as Minister of State for Decentralisation and Cities 2011-12, Michael Gove as Secretary of State for Education 2012-13; Assistant Government Whip 2013-14; Government Whip 2014-15; Deputy Chief Whip (Comptroller of HM Household) 2015-16; Minister of State for Housing and Planning and Minister for London, Department for Communities and Local Government 2016-17. Member: Science and Technology 2010-12, Joint Committee on the Draft House of Lords Reform Bill 2011-12. Member, Executive, 1922 Committee 2010-11. *House of Lords:* Raised to the peerage as Baron Barwell, of Croydon in the London Borough of Croydon 2019. *Other:* Croydon Council: Councillor 1998-2010, Chief Whip 2006-07, Cabinet Member for: Resources and Customer Services 2007-08, Community Safety and Cohesion 2008-10; Chair of governors, Trinity School of John Whitgift, Croydon; Vice-President, Local Government Association 2011-17.

Political interests: Education, housing, race, migration; India, USA.

Other: Strategic Adviser: Barratt Developments plc 2020-, PwC 2020-, Arcadis 2020-, Avonhurst 2020-; Non-executive director, Clarion Housing Group 2020-; PC 2017. Sanderstead Village Lawn Tennis Club.

Publications: How to Win a Marginal Seat: My Year Fighting for My Political Life (2016).

Recreations: Sport (particularly football and tennis), history, travel.

Rt Hon the Lord Barwell, House of Lords, London SW1A 0PW
Tel: 020 7219 3000 *Email:* barwellg@parliament.uk *Twitter:* @GavinBarwell

LABOUR/ CO-OPERATIVE

BASSAM OF BRIGHTON, LORD

Opposition Spokesperson for Education, Business, Energy and Industrial Strategy and International Trade and Digital, Culture, Media and Sport

BASSAM OF BRIGHTON (Life Baron), John Steven Bassam; cr. 1997. Born 11 June 1953; Son of late Sydney Stevens and Enid Bassam; Partner Jill Whittaker (1 son 2 daughters 1 son deceased).

Education: Clarton Secondary Modern School for Boys; Sussex University (BA history 1975); Kent University (MA social work 1979).

Non-political career: Social worker, East Sussex County Council 1976-77; Legal adviser, North Lewisham Law Centre 1979-83; Research officer, Camden Council 1983-84; Head of environmental health, Trading Standards AMA 1988-97; Consultant adviser, KPMG Capital 1997-99. Member, Unison.

Political career: *House of Commons:* Contested (Labour) Brighton Kemptown 1987 general election. *House of Lords:* Raised to the peerage as Baron Bassam of Brighton, of Brighton in the County of East Sussex 1997. Parliamentary Under-Secretary of State, Home Office 1999-2001; Government Spokesperson for: Home Office 1999-2008, Cabinet Office 2001-07; Government Whip 2001-08; Government Spokesperson for: Lord Chancellor's Department 2001-04, Office of the Deputy Prime Minister/Communities and Local Government 2002-04, 2005-07, 2008, Attorney General's Office 2005-08, Transport 2007-08, Culture, Media and Sport 2008; Government Chief Whip 2008-10; Deputy Speaker 2008-18; Deputy Chairman of Committees 2008-18; Opposition Chief Whip 2010-18; Opposition Spokesperson for: Education (Higher and Further Education) 2019-, Business, Energy and Industrial Strategy 2020-, International Trade 2020-, Digital, Culture, Media and Sport (Sport) 2020-. Member: Administration and Works 2008-12, 2015-16, Procedure 2008-18, Selection 2008-18, Privileges/Privileges and Conduct 2009-18, Sub-committee on Leave of Absence 2011-13, Services 2016-18; Chair, Regenerating Seaside Towns and Communities 2018-19; Member, Sentencing (Pre-consolidation Amendments) Bill 2019. *Other:* Brighton Borough Council: Councillor 1983-97, Leader 1987-96; Brighton and Hove Council: Councillor 1996-99, Leader 1996-99; Local Government Association: Head of Environmental Health and Consumer Issues 1997-99, Vice-president 2019-.

Political interests: Local government, housing, home affairs, culture, education, political strategy, environment; Australia, India, Spain, USA.

Other: Laura Martin Trust (homelessness charity); Fellow, Brighton College 2002; Alumni Fellow, Sussex University 2001; PC 2009. Preston Village Cricket Club, Hadlow Down and Moulscomb Wanderers Cricket Club.

Recreations: Cricket, walking, running.

Rt Hon the Lord Bassam of Brighton, House of Lords, London SW1A 0PW
Tel: 020 7219 4918 *Fax:* 020 7219 6837 *Email:* bassams@parliament.uk
Longstone, 25 Church Place, Brighton BN2 5JN *Tel:* 01273 609473 *Twitter:* @SteveTheQuip

CONSERVATIVE

BATES, LORD

BATES (Life Baron), Michael Walton Bates; cr 2008. Born 26 May 1961; Son of John MacLennan Bates and Ruth Bates, née Walton; Married Carole Whitfield 1983 (divorced 2008) (2 sons); married Xuelin 2012.

Education: Heathfield Senior High School, Gateshead; Gateshead College (Diploma business studies 1982); Saïd Business School, Oxford (MBA Wadham College 1998).

Non-political career: Trainee Salesman, Gresham Life Assurance 1983; Agency Inspector, Clerical Medical Investment Group 1983-87; Investment Adviser: Hogg Robinson (benefit consultants) 1986-87, Joseph Nelson (fund management) 1987-91; Assistant Director, Godwins (pension consultants and actuaries) 1991; Oxford Analytica International Group 1998-2007: Senior Vice-president 1998-99, Director of Consultancy and Research 1999-2005, Head of Operations 2004-05, Director 2004-06, Senior Adviser 2006-07; Managing Director, Walton Bates (management consultants) Ltd 2006-11; Non-executive Director, Vardy Group 2006-10;

Non-executive Chair: Scholes & Brown Asset Management 2008-11, 55 Plus Ltd 2010-11; Chair, International Property Awards 2013.

Political career: *House of Commons:* Contested Tynebridge 1987 general election and Langbaurgh 1991 by-election. MP (Conservative) for Langbaurgh 1992-97. Contested Middlesbrough South and Cleveland East 1997 general election; PPS to Ministers of State: Nicholas Scott, Department of Social Security 1992-93, Sir John Wheeler, Northern Ireland Office 1994; Assistant Government Whip 1994-95; Government Whip 1995-96; Paymaster General, Office of Public Services 1996-97. *House of Lords:* Raised to the peerage as Baron Bates, of Langbaurgh in the County of North Yorkshire 2008. Opposition Whip 2009-10; Opposition Spokesperson for: Cabinet Office 2009-10, Communities and Local Government 2009-10, Energy and Climate Change 2009, Children, Schools and Families 2009-10; Deputy Chairman of Committees 2013-14, 2020-; Government Whip 2013-14; Government Spokesperson for: Culture, Media and Sport (Broadcasting) 2013-14, International Development 2013-14, Work and Pensions 2013-14, Business, Innovation and Skills (Universities and Science) 2014; Home Office: Government Spokesperson 2014-16, Parliamentary Under-Secretary of State 2014-15, Minister of State 2015-16; Leave of absence April-September 2016; Minister of State and Government Spokesperson, Department for International Development 2016-19; Government Spokesperson, HM Treasury 2017-19; Trade Envoy to Ethiopia 2020-. Member: Leader's Group on the Working Practices of the House of Lords 2010-11, Partnerships (Prosecution) (Scotland) Bill 2013, Olympic and Paralympic Legacy 2013. *Other:* Young Conservatives: Member, National Advisory Committee 1984-87, Chair, Northern Area 1984-87; Deputy chair, Conservative Party 2007-10; Project director, Campaign North 2007-10.

Political interests: Education, foreign policy, sport for development and peace; Albania, Brazil, China, Croatia, Ethiopia, Greece, Japan, Korea, USA.

Other: Founder, Walk for Peace Foundation 2012-; Board Member, International Olympic Truce Foundation of the International Olympic Committee 2016-; Walking Ambassador, Northumberland County Council 2019-; Visiting Professor, Peking University 2019-; Fellow: Industry and Parliament Trust 1996, Caux Round Table 2001, Royal Geographical Society 2016; Open Fields Awards, Olympic Truce Foundation 2012; Order of Skanderbeg, Albania 2014; Ice-breaker Award, 48 Group Club 2015; Sense, Parliamentarian of the Year Award 2018; PC 2015.

Publications: Walk for Peace (2018); Walk your Dream (2019).

Recreations: Walking.

Rt Hon the Lord Bates, House of Lords, London SW1A 0PW
Tel: 020 7219 5353 *Email:* batesm@parliament.uk *Twitter:* @bateslord

LABOUR

BEECHAM, LORD

BEECHAM (Life Baron), Jeremy Hugh Beecham; cr 2010. Born 17 November 1944; Son of Lawrence Beecham and Florence Beecham; Married Brenda Woolf 1968 (died 2010) (1 son 1 daughter).

Education: Royal Grammar School, Newcastle upon Tyne; University College, Oxford (BA jurisprudence 1965, MA).

Non-political career: Solicitor 1968; Partner, Allan Henderson Beecham & Peacock/Beecham Peacock 1968-2002; Director, Northern Development Company 1986-91; Consultant, Beecham Peacock 2002-11.

Political career: *House of Commons:* Contested (Labour) Tynemouth 1970 general election. *House of Lords:* Raised to the peerage as Baron Beecham, of Benwell and Newcastle upon Tyne in the County of Tyne and Wear 2010. Opposition Spokesperson for: Communities and Local Government 2010-20, Health 2010-12, Justice 2012-20, Housing 2015-20. Member, Inheritance and Trustees' Powers Bill 2013. *Other:* Chair, Oxford University Labour Club 1964; Labour Party: Member: National Executive Committee/Shadow Cabinet Working Party on Future of Local Government 1984-87, Joint Policy Committee 1992-; National Executive Committee: Member 1998-2010, Chair 2005-06. Newcastle upon Tyne City Council: Councillor 1967-, Leader 1977-1994; Commissioner, English Heritage 1983-87; Association of Metropolitan Authorities: Deputy chair 1984-86, Vice-chair 1986-91, Chair 1991-97;

Vice-chair, Northern Regional Councils Association 1986-91; DL, Tyne and Wear 1995; Local Government Association: Chair 1995-2004, Vice-chair 2004-10, Vice-President 2010-.

Political interests: Local government, social policy, health, criminal justice, legal aid, regional policy, environment; Israel.

Other: President: Bura 1995-2009, Age Concern Newcastle 1995-2017, Newcastle Choral Society 1995; Vice-President, Newcastle CVS; Trustee, Trusthouse Charitable Foundation 1999-2012; Vice-President, Community Foundation 2000-; Member, advisory board, Harold Hartog School of Government, Tel Aviv 2005-; New Israel Fund: Vice-chair 2006-, Board member 2007-; Hon. Freedom, Newcastle upon Tyne 1995; Hon. Fellow, Northumbria University 1989; Hon. DCL, Newcastle University 1992; Kt 2004.

Recreations: Reading, music.

The Lord Beecham, House of Lords, London SW1A 0PW
Tel: 020 7219 8910 *Email:* beechamj@parliament.uk *Twitter:* @JeremyBeecham

LIBERAL DEMOCRAT

BEITH, LORD

BEITH (Life Baron), Alan James Beith; cr 2015. Born 20 April 1943; Son of late James Beith, foreman packer, and Joan Beith; Married Barbara Ward 1965 (died 1998) (1 son deceased 1 daughter); married Baroness Maddock 2001 (died 2020).

Education: King's School, Macclesfield; Balliol College, Oxford (BA philosophy, politics and economics 1964); Nuffield College, Oxford (BLitt, MA 1966); Welsh, French, Norwegian.

Non-political career: Politics lecturer, Newcastle University 1966-73. Member, Association of University Teachers.

Political career: *House of Commons:* Contested Berwick-upon-Tweed 1970 general election. MP for Berwick-upon-Tweed 8 November 1973 by-election to 2010, for Berwick-upon-Tweed (revised boundary) 2010-15 (Liberal 1973-83, Liberal/All 1983-88, Liberal Democrat 1988-2015); Chief Whip, Liberal Party 1976-87; Member House of Commons Commission 1979-97; Liberal Spokesperson for: Foreign Affairs 1985-87, Treasury 1987; SLD Spokesperson for Treasury 1988-89; Liberal Democrat Spokesperson for: Treasury 1989-94, Home Affairs 1994-95; Member, Intelligence and Security Committee 1994-2008; Liberal Democrat Spokesperson for: Police, Prison and Security Matters 1995-97, Home and Legal Affairs (Home Affairs) 1997-99; Contested Speaker election 2000, 2009; Member, Speaker's Committee on the Electoral Commission 2001-10; Deputy Chair, Review Committee of Privy Counsellors of the Anti-terrorism, Crime and Security Act 2002-04 Member, Advisory Group of Privy Counsellors on use of Intercept as Evidence 2007-12. Member: Procedure 2000-01; Liaison: Member 2003-10, Chair 2010-15; Chair, Constitutional Affairs/Justice 2003-15; Member: Liaison (Liaison Sub-Committee) 2006-10, Joint Committee on National Security Strategy 2010-15; Liaison (National Policy Statements Sub-committee): Member 2010-12, Chair 2012-15. *House of Lords:* Raised to the peerage as Baron Beith, of Berwick upon Tweed in the County of Northumberland 2015. Member: Constitution 2016-, Lord Speaker's Committee on the Size of the House 2016-, Joint Committee on Fixed-Term Parliaments Act 2020-. *Other:* Deputy Leader: Liberal Party 1985-88, Liberal Democrat Party 1993-2003. Councillor: Hexham RDC 1969-74, Tynedale DC 1974-75.

Political interests: Parliamentary and constitutional affairs, justice and the legal system, architectural and artistic heritage; Canada, Scandinavia, Zimbabwe.

Other: Local preacher, Methodist Church 1965-; Historic Chapels Trust: Trustee 1995-, Chair 2002-15, President 2015-; President, North of England Civic Trust 2005-; Member, Committee of Privy Councillors to Review Use of Intercept as Evidence 2008-14; Vice-President, Northumberland and Newcastle Society 2009-; Chair, Methodist Church Heritage Committee 2018-; Honorary Bencher, Middle Temple 2014-; Diabetes UK, Hospice Care North Northumberland; Honorary DCL: Newcastle University 1998, Northumbria University 2010; Honorary doctorate, Earlham College, Indiana 2013; PC 1992; Kt 2008. President, National Liberal Club 2009-, Athenæum, Northern Counties, Newcastle upon Tyne Club.

Publications: Co-author, Case for Liberal Party and Alliance (1983); Faith and Politics (1987); A View From the North (2008).

Recreations: Music, walking, boating.

Rt Hon the Lord Beith, House of Lords, London SW1A 0PW
Tel: 020 7219 3540
Email: beithalanj@gmail.com

CONSERVATIVE

BELLINGHAM, LORD

BELLINGHAM (Life Baron), Henry Campbell Bellingham; cr 2020. Born 29 March 1955; Married Emma Whiteley 1993 (1 son).

Education: Eton College; Magdalene College, Cambridge (BA law 1978, MA); Council of Legal Education 1978-79.

Non-political career: Barrister, Middle Temple 1978-87; Company Director and Business Consultant 1997-2001.

Political career: *House of Commons:* MP for Norfolk North West 1983-97. Contested Norfolk North West 1997 general election. MP for North West Norfolk 2001-10, for North West Norfolk (revised boundary) 2010-19; PPS to Malcolm Rifkind as Secretary of State for Transport and for Defence and as Foreign Secretary 1991-97; Shadow Minister for: Trade and Industry (Small Business and Enterprise) 2002-03, Economic Affairs (Small Business and Enterprise) 2003-05; Opposition Whip 2005-06; Shadow Minister for Constitutional Affairs/Justice 2006-10; Parliamentary Under-Secretary of State, Foreign and Commonwealth Office (Minister for Africa, UN and overseas territories) 2010-12; Contested Deputy Speaker election 2013; Trade Envoy to Libya 2018-19. Member: Environment 1988-90, Northern Ireland 2001-02, Trade and Industry 2002-03, High Speed Rail (London-West Midlands) Bill 2014-16, Panel of Chairs 2017-19. *House of Lords:* Raised to the peerage as Baron Bellingham, of Congham in the County of Norfolk 2020. *Other:* Chair: Conservative Council on Eastern Europe 1989-93, Policy Research Unit (PRU).

Political interests: Small businesses, agriculture, defence, Northern Ireland, foreign policy, legal services; Africa, Caribbean, Overseas Territories.

Other: Westminster Foundation for Democracy 2013-18; Non-executive director and chair, Developing Markets Associates 2013-; Non-executive chair, Pathfinder Minerals plc 2013-; Co-chair, Global Law Summit 2015; Non-executive chair, Clifton Africa 2018-; Kt 2016.

Recreations: Country sports, golf, cricket.

The Lord Bellingham, House of Lords, London SW1A 0PW
Tel: 020 7219 3000

LIBERAL DEMOCRAT

BENJAMIN, BARONESS

BENJAMIN (Life Baroness), Floella Karen Yunies Benjamin; cr 2010. Born 23 September 1949; Daughter of Roy and Veronica Benjamin; Married Keith Taylor 1980 (1 son 1 daughter).

Education: Penge Girls' School.

Non-political career: Chief Accountant's Office, Barclays Bank 1967-69; Founder, Crystalrowe Ltd 1987-; Actress: Appeared in a number of productions on the stage including: *Hair* 1970-72, *Jesus Christ Superstar* 1972-74, *Black Mikado* 1974-75, *The Husband-in-Law* 1976; Television appearances include: *Within These Walls* 1973-75, *Playschool* 1976-88, *PlayAway* 1976-82, *Angels* 1978-80, *Gentle Touch* 1980, *Bergerac* 1980, *Fast Forward* 1983-85, *Sarah Jane Adventures* 2007-10, *Mama Mirabelle's Home Movies* 2007-09, *Chuggington* 2010-13; *CBeebies Bedtime Stories* 2010-; Film appearances include: *Black Joy* 1977, *Run Fatboy Run* 2007, *Rendition* 2008; Floella Benjamin Productions Ltd: Founder 1987, Chief Executive 1998-2013, Chair 2002-12; Floella Food and Drink Ltd 2004-12. Equity.

Political career: *House of Lords:* Raised to the peerage as Baroness Benjamin, of Beckenham in the County of Kent 2010. Member: EU Sub-committee F (Home Affairs, Health and Education) 2013-15, Communications 2015-19, COVID-19 2020-. Chair, Liberal Democrat Parliamentary Party Committee on Culture, Media and Sport 2012. *Other:* Millenium Commission 1999-2004; Governor, Dulwich College 2001-11; Member, Content Board, Ofcom 2003-06; DL, Greater London 2008-; Chair of Governors, Isle of Sheppey Academy 2009-11; Chair, Windrush Commemoration Committee 2018-.

Political interests: Children and young people, media, culture and arts, sport, education, diversity, equality; All Caribbean countries, France, Ghana, South Korea, South Africa, USA.

Other: Patron, Sickle Cell Society 1985-; BAFTA: Council member 1990-2001, Vice-chair 1998-99, Chair, Television 1999-2000; President, Elizabeth R Commonwealth Broadcasting Fund 1995-2015; Governor: National Film and Television School 1995-2015, Commonwealth Institute 1998-2006; Vice-president, Barnardo's 2000-; President, Ramblers' Association 2008-10; Patron, British Association of Play Therapists 2009-; Trustee, Sparks 2009-13; Vice-president, Royal Television Society; Patron: Transplant Links 2013-, Finding Rhythms 2015-; President, Society of Women Writers & Journalists 2017-; Patron, Beating Bowel Cancer; NSPCC; Chancellor, Exeter University 2006-16; DLitt Exeter University; Doctor of Education, Yorl University of York; RTS award 2004; Special Lifetime Achievement award, BAFTA 2004; J.M. Barrie Award, Action for Children's Arts 2012; OBE 2001; DBE 2020.

Publications: Author of numerous children's books; Written over 25 books including: Autobiographies: Coming to England (1995), 20th Anniversary edition (2016); The Arms of Britannia (2010), Sea of Tears (2011); My Two Grandads (2011).

Recreations: Running, golf, singing, photography, walking, cooking.

The Baroness Benjamin DBE, House of Lords, London SW1A 0PW
Tel: 020 7219 8901 *Email:* benjaminf@parliament.uk Website: www.floellabenjamin.com
Twitter: @FloellaBenjamin

GREEN PARTY

BENNETT OF MANOR CASTLE, BARONESS

BENNETT OF MANOR CASTLE (Life Baroness), Natalie Louise Bennett; cr 2019. Born 10 February 1966.

Education: Sydney University (BAgrSC agricultural science); University of New England – Armidale (BA Asian studies); Leicester University (MA mass communications).

Non-political career: Journalist: *Bangkok Post* 1996-99, *The Times* 2000-04, *The Independent* 2004-05; Editor, *Guardian Weekly* 2007-12.

Political career: *House of Commons:* Contested Holborn and St Pancras 2010 and 2015 and Sheffield Central 2017 general elections. *House of Lords:* Raised to the peerage as Baroness Bennett of Manor Castle, of Camden in the London Borough of Camden 2019. *Other:* Green Party: Co-ordinator, Camden Greens, Founding chair, Women's Group, Internal communications co-ordinator 2007-10, Leader 2012-16. Governor, Netley Primary School 2008-16; Vice-President, Local Government Association 2020-.

Other: Trustee, Fawcett Society 2010-14.

The Baroness Bennett of Manor Castle, House of Lords, London SW1A 0PW
Tel: 020 7219 4406 *Email:* bennettn@parliament.uk Website: www.nataliebennett.org
Twitter: @natalieben

CONSERVATIVE

BENYON, LORD

BENYON (Life Baron), Richard Henry Ronald Benyon; cr 2021. Born 21 October 1960; Son of Sir William Benyon (MP for Buckingham 1970-83 and Milton Kenyes 1983-92) and Lady Benyon; Married Zoe Robinson 2004 (2 sons and 3 sons by previous marriage).

Education: Bradfield College, Reading; Royal Agricultural College (Diploma real estate management, land economy 1987); French, some Swahili.

Non-political career: Land agent chartered surveyor 1987-; Farmer 1990-; Chair, Rural and Urban Housing Business 2001-10; Director, Englefield Estate Trust Corporation Limited; Director and Chair, UK Water Partnership 2015-. Army officer, Royal Green Jackets 1980-85.

Political career: *House of Commons:* Contested Newbury 1997 and 2001 general elections. MP for Newbury 2005-10, for Newbury (revised boundary) 2010-19; Opposition Whip 2007-09; Shadow Minister for Environment, Food and Rural Affairs 2009-10; Parliamentary Under-Secretary of State, Department for Environment, Food and Rural Affairs 2010-13 (Natural Environment and Fisheries 2010-12, Natural Environment, Water and Rural Affairs 2012-13); Trade Envoy to: Mozambique and Democratic Republic of Congo 2016-17,

Ethiopia 2016-17; Member, Intelligence and Security Committee 2016-19. Member, Home Affairs 2005-07; *Ex-officio* Member, Environmental Audit 2010-13; Member: Defence 2014-16, Arms Export Controls 2014-15. *House of Lords:* Raised to the peerage as Baron Benyon, of Englefield in the Royal County of Berkshire 2021. *Other:* Founding member, Conservatives for Reform in Europe 2016; Conservative Party whip removed September-October 2019. Newbury District Council: Councillor 1991-95, Leader, Conservative group 1994-95.

Political interests: Rural matters, social affairs, defence, health, home affairs, environment, security; Africa, Middle East, Northern Ireland, Zimbabwe.

Other: UK delegation to NATO Parliamentary Assembly: Member 2014-15, Leader 2015-19; Founder patron, Help for Heroes; Vice-chair, Citizens Advice 1994-2000; Trustee: Plantlife, Game and Wildlife Conservation Trust; Member, Royal Institution of Chartered Surveyors; Berkshire Community Foundation; Fellow, Royal Agricultural Societies; PC 2017.

Publications: Blue Belt 2:0 (2017).

Recreations: Walking, shooting, fishing, cooking.

Rt Hon the Lord Benyon, House of Lords, London SW1A 0PW *Twitter:* @RichardHRBenyon

LABOUR

BERKELEY, LORD

BERKELEY (18th Baron, E), Anthony Fitzhardinge Gueterbock; cr. 1421; (Life) Baron Gueterbock 2000. Born 20 September 1939; Son of late Brigadier Ernest Adolphus Leopold Gueterbock and late Hon. Cynthia Ella Gueterbock; Married Diana (Dido) Townsend 1965 (2 sons 1 daughter); married Rosalind Clarke 1999 (divorced 2011); married Marian Bennett 2017.

Education: Eton College; Trinity College, Cambridge (MA mechanical sciences 1961); French, German.

Non-political career: Civil engineer, Sir Alexander Gibb and Partners 1961-67; George Wimpey plc 1967-87; Public affairs manager, Eurotunnel 1987-95; Chair: Piggyback Consortium 1995-98, Rail Freight Group 1997-2018.

Political career: *House of Lords:* Created a life peer as Baron Gueterbock, of Cranford in the London Borough of Hillingdon 2000. First entered House of Lords 1992; Opposition Spokesperson for Transport 1996-97; Opposition Whip 1996-97. Member: European Union 1997-2001, EU Internal Market Sub-committee 2019-20, EU Goods Sub-committee 2020-.

Political interests: Transport, environment; European Union member states.

Other: Honorary President, UK Maritime Pilots' Association 2001-; European Rail Freight Association: Board member 2007-, Chair 2009-10; Trustee, Plymouth Marine Laboratories Ltd 2011-17; Vice-president, ALLRAIL 2017-; Board member, Isles of Scilly Transport Board 2019-; MICE; FRSA; FCILT; Honorary FIMechE; Honorary degree, Brighton University; OBE 1989.

Recreations: Sailing, skiing.

The Lord Berkeley OBE, House of Lords, London SW1A 0PW
Tel: 020 7219 0611 *Email:* berkeleyafg@parliament.uk
Tel: 07710 431542 *Twitter:* @tonyberkeley1

CROSSBENCH

BERKELEY OF KNIGHTON, LORD

BERKELEY of KNIGHTON (Life Baron), Michael Fitzhardinge Berkeley; cr 2013. Born 29 May 1948; Son of Sir Lennox and Freda Berkeley; Married Deborah Coltman-Rogers (died 2012) (1 daughter); Married Elizabeth Jane West 2014.

Education: Westminster Cathedral Choir School; The Oratory School; Royal Academy of Music.

Non-political career: Phlebotomist, St Bartholomew's Hospital 1969-71; Presentation Assistant, LWT 1973; Announcer, BBC Radio 3 1974-79; Associate Composer, Scottish Chamber Orchestra 1979; Joint Artistic Director, Spitalfields Festival 1994-97; Artistic

Director, Cheltenham Festival 1995-2004; Associate Composer, BBC National Orchestra of Wales 2001-08; Radio Presenter.

Political career: *House of Lords:* Raised to the peerage as Baron Berkeley of Knighton, of Knighton in the County of Powys 2013. *Other:* General Advisory Council, BBC 1990-95.

Other: Member: Executive committee, Association of Professional Composers 1982-84, New music sub-committee, Arts Council of Great Britain 1984-86, Central music advisory committee, BBC 1986-90; Music panel adviser, Arts Council 1986-90; Visiting professor, Huddersfield University 1991-94; Governor, National Youth Orchestra 1994-96; Director, Britten-Pears Foundation 1996-2009; Member, Board of Directors, Royal Opera House, Covent Garden 1996-2001; Chair, Royal Ballet 2003-; Fellow: Royal Academy of Music, Royal Northern College of Music, Royal Welsh College of Music and Drama; Hon DMus, University of East Anglia; CBE 2012. Campden Hill Tennis Club; Holland Park Tennis Club.

Publications: The Music Pack (1994).

Recreations: Walking, tennis.

The Lord Berkeley of Knighton CBE, House of Lords, London SW1A 0PW
Tel: 020 7219 5353 *Email:* berkeleym@parliament.uk Website: www.michaelberkeley.co.uk
Twitter: @MichaelBerkele2

CONSERVATIVE

BERRIDGE, BARONESS

Parliamentary Under-Secretary of State for the School System and Government Spokesperson, Department for Education and Minister for Women and Government Spokesperson, Government Equalities Office

BERRIDGE (Life Baroness), Elizabeth Rose Berridge; cr 2011. Born 22 March 1972.

Education: Catmose College, Rutland; Emmanuel College (BA law 1995).

Non-political career: Barrister, Kings Chambers 1996-2005; Project Director, Commonwealth Initiative for Freedom of Religion or Belief 2015-.

Political career: *House of Commons:* Contested (Conservative) Stockport 2005 general election. *House of Lords:* Raised to the peerage as Baroness Berridge, of the Vale of Catmose in the County of Rutland 2011. Government Whip (Baroness in Waiting) 2019-20; Government Spokesperson for Education (Higher Education) 2019-20; Parliamentary Under-Secretary of State for the School System and Government Spokesperson, Department for Education 2020-; Minister for Women and Government Spokesperson, Government Equalities Office 2020-. Member: Joint Committee on Statutory Instruments 2010-12, Joint Committee on Human Rights 2011-15, Social Mobility 2015-16, Ecclesiastical Committee 2015-19, Sentencing (Pre-consolidation Amendments) Bill 2019. *Other:* Director, Conservative Christian Fellowship, CCHQ 2005-11.

Political interests: Religious freedom, policing, human rights, black and minority ethnic affairs; Central African Republic, Commonwealth.

Other: Member: International Panel, Parliamentarians for Freedom of Religion or Belief, Executive Committee, Commonwealth Parliamentary Association United Kingdom 2017-19; Trustee: Kainos Community (prison charity) 2006-14, More than Gold Olympic charity 2011-13, Member: Advisory board, Theos Think Tank 2011-, Advisory council, Federation for Relief and Reconciliation in the Middle East 2011-15; Trustee, Freedom Declared Foundation 2017-.

Recreations: Tennis, Swimming.

The Baroness Berridge, House of Lords, London SW1A 0PW
Tel: 020 7219 8943 *Email:* berridgee@parliament.uk Website: www.baronessberridge.com
Twitter: @BaronessEB

CONSERVATIVE

BERTIN, BARONESS

BERTIN (Life Baroness), Gabrielle Louise Bertin; cr 2016. Born 14 March 1978; Married Chris Glenny 2007 (divorced); married Michael Grist (2 daughters).

Non-political career: Press Officer to Liam Fox; Researcher, Atlantic Bridge; Press Secretary to David Cameron: as Leader of the Opposition 2005-10, as Prime Minister 2010-12; Director of External Relations, Prime Minister's Office 2013-16; Director of Strategic Communications and Campaigns, BT 2017-.

Political career: *House of Lords:* Raised to the peerage as Baroness Bertin, of Battersea in the London Borough of Wandsworth 2016. Member: Communications 2017-19, Joint Committee on the Draft Domestic Abuse Bill 2019.

Other: Trustee, KIDS (disabled children charity) 2013-.

The Baroness Bertin, House of Lords, London SW1A 0PW
Tel: 020 7219 3000

CROSSBENCH

BEST, LORD

BEST (Life Baron), Richard Stuart Best; cr. 2001. Born 22 June 1945; Son of late Walter Best, DL, JP and late Frances Best, née Chignell; Married Belinda Stemp 1978 (2 daughters 2 sons).

Education: Shrewsbury School; Nottingham University (BA social administration 1967).

Non-political career: Chief executive: British Churches Housing Trust 1970-73, National Federation of Housing Associations 1973-88, Joseph Rowntree Foundation 1988-2006, Joseph Rowntree Housing Trust 1988-2006.

Political career: *House of Lords:* Raised to the peerage as Baron Best, of Godmanstone in the County of Dorset 2001. Chair, House of Lords Audit Committee 2004-09; Member: Joint Committee on the Charities Bill 2004, Economic Affairs 2007-12, Economic Affairs Finance Bill Sub Committee 2009-, Information 2013-14, Olympic and Paralympic Legacy 2013-14; Chair, Communications 2014-17; Member, EU Home Affairs Sub-committee 2018-20. *Other:* Commissioner, Rural Development Commission 1989-98; Chair, Hull Partnership Liaison Board 2003-05; Member, Audit Commission's Advisory Board on Housing, Communities and Environment 2003-10; Local Government Association: President 2005-15, Vice-president 2015-; Chair: Westminster Housing Commission 2005-06, Hanover Housing Association 2006-15, Office of Public Management's Public Interest Council 2007-12; Deputy chair, Standards Committee, Westminster City Council 2008-12; Chair: Commission on Housing in Northern Ireland 2009-10, Property Ombudsman 2009-17, Housing for an Ageing Population 2009, CLG/LGA Housing Commission 2010; DL, North Yorkshire 2012-; Church Commissioner 2018-21; Board member, Shadow Sponsor Body for the Houses of Parliament Restoration and Renewal Programme 2020-.

Political interests: Housing, regeneration, social policy.

Other: Chair, International Board, South East European Research Centre; Royal Society of Arts: Trustee 2006-12, Treasurer 2009-12; Patron, Housing Associations Charitable Trust 2007-; Chair, Hanover Housing Group 2006-15; Joint Chair of the Judges, International Property Awards 2013-; Vice-President, Town and Country Planning Association 2015-; Chair: Regulation of Property Agents Working Group 2018-, Centre for Social Justice Housing Commission 2018-, Affordable Housing Commission: Smith Institute and Nationwide Foundation 2018-; Member, Trust for London Housing Advisory Board 2018-; President, Sustainable Energy Association 2018-; Hon. Fellow RIBA 2001; Hon. Life Member, Chartered Institute of Housing 2003; Fellow, Academy of Social Sciences; Honorary degrees: Sheffield University 2006, York University 2008; Parliamentarian of the Year, CAB 2010; UK Social Policy Association Award 2012; OBE 1988. Travellers Club, Farmers Club.

Publications: Contributor to various books and numerous articles for magazines and journals.

The Lord Best OBE, House of Lords, London SW1A 0PW
Tel: 020 7219 6799 *Email:* best@parliament.uk

CONSERVATIVE

BETHELL, LORD

Parliamentary Under-Secretary of State for Innovation and Government Spokesperson, Department of Health and Social Care

BETHELL (5th Baron, UK), James Nicholas Bethell; cr 1922; 5th Bt of Park House (UK) 1911. Born 1 October 1967; Son of 4th Baron; Married Melissa 2004 (2 sons 2 daughters).

Education: Harrow School; Edinburgh University (MA history and politics 1990).

Non-political career: Reporter *Sunday Times* 1991-93; Managing director, Ministry of Sound 1993-2001; Group head of business development, Capital Radio 2001-04; Managing partner, Portland 2005-08; Communications director, Policy Exchange 2009; Westbourne Communications: Managing director 2009-18, Senior Counsel 2018.

Political career: *House of Commons:* Contested Tooting 2005 general election. *House of Lords:* Elected hereditary peer 2018-; Government Whip (Lord in Waiting) 2019-20; Parliamentary Under-Secretary of State for Innovation and Government Spokesperson, Department of Health and Social Care 2020-. Member, Communications 2019. *Other:* Governor, Hall School Charitable Trust 2016-.

Political interests: Taiwan, USA.

Other: Chair, development board, Scar Free Foundation 2017-; Member, development council, Sadler's Wells 2018-.

The Lord Bethell, House of Lords, London SW1A 0PW
Tel: 020 7219 3000 *Email:* bethellj@parliament.uk *Twitter:* @JimBethell

CROSSBENCH

BEW, LORD

BEW (Life Baron), Paul Anthony Elliott; cr 2007. Born 22 January 1950; Son of Dr Kenneth Bew and Dr Mary Bew, née Leahy; Married Dr Greta Jones 1977 (1 son).

Education: Campbell College, Belfast; Pembroke College, Cambridge (BA modern history, MA; PhD 1974).

Non-political career: Humanities Lecturer, Ulster College 1975-79; Queen's University, Belfast 1979-: European and American History Lecturer 1979-84, Politics Lecturer 1984-87, Reader, Politics 1987-91, Professor of Politics 1991-, Emeritus Professor 2014-; Visiting Professor, King's College London 2015-.

Political career: *House of Lords:* Raised to the peerage as Baron Bew, of Donegore in the County of Antrim 2007. Member: Joint Committee on the Draft Defamation Bill 2011, Joint Committee on Parliamentary Privilege 2013, Procedure/Procedure and Privileges 2019-. *Other:* Chair: Committee on Standards in Public Life 2013-18, House of Lords Appointments Commission 2018-.

Political interests: Nationalism, foreign policy, education.

Other: Chairman: British-Irish Association 2007-13, Anglo-Israel Association 2007-; Member, British-Irish Parliamentary Assembly 2013-; Chairman, Key Stage 2 Assessment Review 2010-11; President, Airey Neave Trust 2013-; MRIA; Honorary Fellow, Pembroke College, Cambridge.

Recreations: Five-a-side football.

The Lord Bew, House of Lords, London SW1A 0PW
Tel: 020 7219 5353

NON-AFFILIATED

BHATIA, LORD

BHATIA (Life Baron), Amirali Alibhai Bhatia; cr. 2001. Born 18 March 1932; Married Nurbanu Amersi Kanji 1954 (3 daughters).

Education: Schools in Tanzania and India.

Non-political career: Chair and managing director, Forbes Campbell International Ltd 1980-2001; Director, Casley Finance Ltd 1985-2001.

Political career: *House of Lords:* Raised to the peerage as Baron Bhatia, of Hampton in the London Borough of Richmond upon Thames 2001. Suspended from membership October 2010-June 2011, April-December 2016. Member, Religious Offences 2002-03.

Political interests: Africa, Bangladesh, India, Middle East, Pakistan, Sri Lanka.

Other: Chair, Forbes Trust 1985-; Chair and Co-founder, Ethnic Minority Foundation 1999-2009; British Muslim Research Centre; British Edutrust Foundation; Vice-chair, India800 Foundation; Oxfam, Ethnic Minority Foundation; FRSA; UK Charity Awards Personality of the Year 2001; Beacon Prize 2003; OBE 1997. Commonwealth Club, Institute of Directors.

Recreations: Swimming, walking, reading, music.

The Lord Bhatia OBE, House of Lords, London SW1A 0PW
Tel: 020 7219 5652 *Email:* bhatiaa@parliament.uk
Forbes House, 9 Artillery Lane, London E1 7LP *Tel:* 020 7377 8484
Email: abhatia@casley.co.uk

CROSSBENCH

BICHARD, LORD

BICHARD (Life Baron), Michael George Bichard; cr 2010. Born 31 January 1947; Son of George and Nora Bichard; Married Gillian Guy 2008.

Education: King Edward VI Grammar School, Southampton; Manchester University (LLB, Hon Fellow 1968); Birmingham University (Master's social science 1973).

Non-political career: Solicitor; Chief executive: London Borough of Brent Council 1980-86, Gloucestershire County Council 1986-90, Social Security Benefits Agency 1990-95; Permanent secretary: Department for Employment 1995, Department for Education and Employment 1995-2001; Rector, London Institute/University of the Arts, London 2001-08; Chair, Rathbone Training Ltd 2001-08.

Political career: *House of Lords:* Raised to the peerage as Baron Bichard, of Nailsworth in the County of Gloucestershire 2010. Member, Leader's Group Reforming Working Practices 2010-11; Deputy Chair of Committees 2012-16. Member: Leader's Group on the Working Practices of the House of Lords 2010-11, Secondary Legislation Scrutiny 2012-15, Public Service and Demographic Change 2012-13, Charities 2016-17, Intergenerational Fairness and Provision 2018-19, Public Services 2020-. *Other:* Vice-President, Local Government Association 2011-.

Political interests: Social policy, education, public service reform, child protection.

Other: Member, Economic and Social Research Council 1989-92; Non-executive director, Reed Executive plc 2002-04; Director, River and Rowing Museum Foundation 2002-; Non-executive chair, RSe Consulting 2003-08; Chair: Soham Murders Inquiry 2004, Legal Services Commission 2005-08, Film Club 2007; Henley Business School Strategy Board 2008-13; Chair, Design Council 2008-12; Institute for Government: Director 2008-10, Senior fellow 2010-12; Chair: Social Care Institute for Excellence 2013-17, National Audit Office 2015-21 Shakespeare's Globe 2015-18, Bristol Business School 2016-; Non-executive director, The Key; Honorary Doctorates: Leeds Metropolitan University, Birmingham University, Bradford University, Middlesex University, Southampton Solent University, Cranfield University, Gloucestershire University, University of the West of England; KCB 1999.

Recreations: Food, gardening, Manchester United FC.

The Lord Bichard KCB, House of Lords, London SW1A 0PW
Tel: 020 7219 5353
Email: m.bichard@btinternet.com

CROSSBENCH

BILIMORIA, LORD

BILIMORIA (Life Baron), Karan Faridoon Bilimoria; cr 2006. Born 26 November 1961; Son of late Lt General Faridoon Noshir Bilimoria PVSM ADC and Yasmin Bilimoria; Married Heather Walker 1993 (2 sons 2 daughters).

Education: Hebron School, Lushington Hall, Ooty, India; Indian Institute of Management and Commerce, Osmania University, Hyderabad, India (BComm 1981); School of Business Studies, City of London Polytechnic (Diploma accounting 1982); ACA 1986; Sidney Sussex College, Cambridge (BA law 1988, MA) (Vice-president, Cambridge Union 1988); Cranfield University School of Management 1998; London Business School 2008; Harvard Business School 2011; French, Hindi.

Non-political career: Trainee and qualified chartered accountant, Ernst & Young 1982-86; Consulting accountant, Crevsale Ltd, London 1988; Sales and marketing director, European Accounting Focus magazine 1989; Cobra Beer: Founder 1989, Chief executive 1989-2007, Chair 2007-09; Founder, General Bilimoria Wines 1989-; Founder and publishing director, *Tandoori Magazine* 1994-2003; UK Chair, Indo British Partnership 2003-09; Non-executive director, Brake Brothers Ltd 2004-07; Visiting entrepreneur, Cambridge University 2004-; Member, advisory board, Boston Analytics, Boston, USA 2005-10; Senior independent director and non-executive director, Booker Group plc 2007-16; Visiting Professor, London Metropolitan University 2009; Chairman: Cobra Beer Partnership Limited 2009-, Molson Coors Cobra India Pvt Ltd 2011-; Vice-chair, Asian Business Association 2003-08; Chair: Faridoon Wines 2015-, PictoSo 2015-.

Political career: *House of Lords:* Raised to the peerage as Baron Bilimoria, of Chelsea in the Royal Borough of Kensington and Chelsea 2006. Member, Economic Affairs Finance Bill Sub-committee 2012-13, 2014, 2015-16, 2016-17. *Other:* Member: New Deal Task Force, Department for Education and Employment 1999-2001, National Employment Panel 2001-07; DL, Greater London 2001-; Representative DL, Hounslow 2005-10; Deputy President, London Chamber of Commerce 2008-10.

Political interests: Manufacturing and industry, armed forces, defence, economic affairs, business and finance, banking, higher education and universities, international students, inter faith, capital and financial markets, culture and creativity, SMEs, EU; Commonwealth, EU, India, USA.

Other: Member: UK-India Round Table, 2005–17, Prime Minister of India's Global Advisory Council 2009-14; Founding President, UK India Business Council 2009-12; Chair, advisory board, Loomba Foundation 2001-; President's Committee, London First 2002-06; Vice-chair, Asian Business Association 2003-08; Patron, Rethink Severe Mental Illness 2003-; Ditchley Foundation: Governor 2004-11, Council member 2011-20; Member: UK-India Round Table 2005-, Asia Task Force 2005-10, Advisory board, Birmingham Business School 2005-; Trustee, British Cardiac Research Trust 2006-; Commissioner, Royal Hospital, Chelsea 2006-12; Member, HRH The Duke of York's Business Advisory Council 2006-09; Adab Trust 2007-; UK-India Business Council: Chair 2007-09, President 2009-11; Trustee, British Cardiac Research Trust 2006-; Patron, Child in Need India (CINI) UK 2008-; Roundhouse Trust 2008-; Enterprise Leader, Princes Trust 2008-; Patron, Pratham UK 2008-; Deputy President, London Chamber of Commerce and Industry 2008-10; Advisory board, Judge Business School, Cambridge University: Member 2008-16, Chair 2016-; Member, advisory board, Cranfield School of Management 2009-; Chair, University of Cambridge India Partnership 2009-12; Trustee, St Paul's Cathedral Foundation 2011-; Member, World President's Organization 2012-; Vice Chancellor’s Circle of Advisors for India, Cambridge University 2012-; Seven Hills 2013-; President, UKCISA 2015-; Chair, Manufacturing Commission 2016-; Ambassador: SkillForce 2016-, Tutu Foundation; Confederation of British Industry (CBI): Vice-president 2019-20, President 2020-; FCA 2002; Honorary Life Fellow, Royal Society of Arts 2004-; Fellow, Institute of Directors 2005-; Companion, Chartered Management Institute 2005-; Liveryman: Drapers' Company City of London 2008-, Brewers' Company City of London 2008-, Worshipful Company of Chartered Accountants in England and Wales 2010-; Freedom: City of London, Guild of Entrepreneurs 2015; Chancellor: Thames Valley University (University of West London) 2005-10, Birmingham University 2014-; Hon. Life Fellow, RSA 2004; Hon. Fellow, Sidney Sussex College, Cambridge 2009-; Eleven honorary doctorates; Hon. Fellow, Sidney Sussex College, Cambridge 2007; Bynum Tudor Fellow, Kellogg College, Oxford, for the Academic Year 2017-18; Non-resident Indian Millennium Honour 2001; CBE 2004. Secunderabad Club, University Pitt Club Cambridge,

Kelvin Grove Club Cape Town, Hawks' Club, Carlton Club; Delhi Golf Club; Guards Polo Club, Ascot; Hawks' Club.

Publications: Bottled for Business (Capstone, 2007); Against the Grain (Capstone, 2009).

Recreations: Reading, current affairs, travel, art, music, theatre, tennis, horse riding, golf, scuba diving, sailing.

The Lord Bilimoria CBE DL, House of Lords, London SW1A 0PW
Tel: 020 7219 6040 *Fax:* 020 7219 5979 *Email:* bilimoria@parliament.uk
Cobra Beer Partnership Limited, Welken House, 10-11 Charterhouse Square, London EC1M 6EH *Tel:* 020 7788 2880 *Email:* karan.bilimoria@cobrabeerpartnership.com
Website: www.lordbilimoria.co.uk *Twitter:* @Lord_Bilimoria

LABOUR

BILLINGHAM, BARONESS

BILLINGHAM (Life Baroness), Angela Theodora Billingham; cr. 2000. Born 31 July 1939; Daughter of late Theodore and Eva Case; Married Peter Billingham 1962 (died 1992) (2 daughters).

Education: Aylesbury Grammar School; College of Education (London); Department of Education, Oxford University (MEd).

Non-political career: Teacher 1960-90; Examiner for Education Board 1990-95; Chair, Catalyst Corby urban regeneration company 2001-07. Member: NUT, GMB.

Political career: *House of Commons:* Contested (Labour) Banbury 1992 general election. *House of Lords:* Raised to the peerage as Baroness Billingham, of Banbury in the County of Oxfordshire 2000. Opposition Spokesperson for Culture, Media and Sport 2010-13. Member: European Union 2000-05, EU Sub-committee D (Environment, Agriculture, Public Health and Consumer Protection/Environment and Agriculture) 2000-05, Draft Climate Change Bill Joint Committee 2007, Information 2008-10; Co-opted member, EU Sub-committee F (Home Affairs) 2009-10, Member: Olympic and Paralympic Legacy 2013-14, EU Sub-committee C: External Affairs 2014-16, Joint Committee on the Draft Health Service Safety Investigations Bill 2018. Vice-chair PLP Departmental Committee for Culture, Media and Sport 2005-06. *Other:* European Parliament: MEP for Northamptonshire and Blaby 1994-99: Chief Whip, Socialist Group. Councillor: Banbury Borough Council 1970-74, Cherwell District Council 1974-84: Leader of Labour Group; Mayor of Banbury 1976; JP 1976-; Councillor, Oxfordshire County Council 1993-94.

Political interests: Europe, education, health, sport, urban regeneration, planning; European Union, India, USA.

Other: Patron: Supporters Direct (football and all professional sport), CSCS (Centre for supporting comprehensive education in the UK); Chair: Banbury and District Sport for the Disabled, Early Education; Member, advisory board, Save the Children; Chair: Northampton Osteoporosis, Council for the Advancement of Arts, Recreation and Education (CAARE); One World, Oxfam, Imperial Cancer.

Recreations: Family, tennis, cinema, bridge, gardening.

The Baroness Billingham, House of Lords, London SW1A 0PW
Tel: 020 7219 5481
Email: a.billingham77@btinternet.com

CROSSBENCH

BIRD, LORD

BIRD (Life Baron), John Anthony Bird; cr 2015. Born 30 January 1946; Married 3rd Parveen 2004 (1 son 1 daughter) (1 son 2 daughters from previous marriages).

Education: St Thomas More's Secondary Modern School; Chelsea School of Art, University of the Arts London (Foundation Diploma in Art and Design); Ealing College of Higher Education, University of West London, (BA human anthropology).

Non-political career: Printer: Pictorial Charts Educational Trust 1974-75, Broadoak Press 1978-83; Print and publishing consultant 1983-91; Anti-poverty campaigner; Founder and Editor-in-Chief, *The Big Issue* 1991-; Founder: International Network of Street Papers 1994-, The Big Issue Foundation 2005-; Director, The Big Issue Group 2005-; Social Enterprise Ambassador, Cabinet Office 2010-; Visiting Professor, Lincoln University 2015-; Expert, Rough Sleeping Advisory Panel.

Political career: *House of Lords:* Raised to the peerage as Baron Bird, of Notting Hill in the Royal Borough of Kensington and Chelsea 2015. Member, Lord Speaker's Advisory Panel on Works of Art 2017-.

Political interests: Arts and culture, economic empowerment, poverty prevention, sociable housing, political reform, financial inclusion, social business; Australia, Ireland, Japan, South Africa, USA.

Other: Director: Wedge Card Ltd, The Big Issue Digital Ltd, Burgeon Creative Ideas Ltd; The Big Issue Foundation; Worshipful Company of Stationers and Newspaper Makers; Honorary Fellow: Liverpool John Moores University, Goldsmiths, University of London; Beacon Fellow, UK Community Foundations; Fellow: Workers' Educational Association, Social Enterprise UK; Senior Fellow, Ashoka; Hon Doctorate of Business, Portsmouth University; Hon D.Litt, Oxford Brookes University; Editors' Editor of the Year, British Society of Magazine Editors 1992; Revd. Marcus Morris Award, Professional Publishers Association 2000; London's Living Legend, BBC London 2003; Scroll of Honour, UN-HABITAT 2004; Entrepreneur of the Year, Ernst & Young 2008; Lifetime Recognition Award, Lotus 2018; Hall of Fame, Publishers Association 2018; MBE 1994.

Publications: Dickens the Socially Mobile Cat (1990); Some Luck (autobiography, 2002); How to Change Your Life in Seven Steps (2006); The Ten Keys to Success (2008); The Necessity of Poverty (2012); Why Drawing Naked Women is Good for the Soul (2013).

Recreations: Writing, painting, cycling, poetry.

The Lord Bird MBE, House of Lords, London SW1A 0PW
Tel: 020 7219 3000 *Email:* birdja@parliament.uk
The Big Issue Group, 113-115 Fonthill Road, London N4 3HH *Tel:* 020 7526 3200
Email: john.bird@bigissue.com *Twitter:* @johnbirdswords

NON-AFFILIATED

BIRMINGHAM, LORD BISHOP OF

BIRMINGHAM (9th Bishop of), David Andrew Urquhart. Born 14 April 1952.

Education: Croftinloan School, Perthshire; Rugby School; Ealing Business School (BA 1977); Wycliffe Hall, Oxford (1984).

Non-political career: Volunteer, Uganda 1971; BP plc 1972-82; Ordained Deacon 1984; Priest 1985; Curate, St Nicholas, Kingston-upon-Hull 1984-87; Vicar: Drypool 1987-92, Holy Trinity, Coventry 1992-2000; Hon. Canon, Coventry Cathedral 1999-2000; Bishop Suffragen of Birkenhead 2000-06; Prelate of the Most Distinguished Order of St Michael and St George 2005-; Archbishop of Canterbury's Envoy to China 2005-; Bishop of Birmingham 2006-.

Political career: *House of Lords:* Entered House of Lords 2010; Convenor of the Lords Spiritual 2015-. Member, Financial Exclusion 2016-17. *Other:* Governor, Rugby School 2001-; Chair, Ridley Hall Council, Cambridge 2011-.

Political interests: Local government, economy, foreign affairs; China, DR Congo, Malawi.

Other: Chair: Church Mission Society 1994-2008, Chester Diocese Education Board 2001-06; Trustee, Hippodrome Theatre, Birmingham 2009-; Church Mission Society, Institut Pan-Africain deSanté Communitaire, DR Congo; Hon Freedom, Metropolitan Borough of Wirral 2006; Hon

DD, Birmingham University 2009; Hon DUniv, Birmingham City University 2014; KCMG 2018. Athenæum Club; Jesters.

Recreations: Rugby fives, Scottish hill-walking.

Rt Rev the Lord Bishop of Birmingham KCMG, House of Lords, London SW1A 0PW
Tel: 020 7219 5353
Bishop's Croft, Old Church Road, Harborne, Birmingham B17 0BG *Tel:* 0121-427 1163
Email: bishop@cofebirmingham.com Website: www.cofebirmingham.com
Twitter: @David_Urq

CROSSBENCH

BIRT, LORD

BIRT (Life Baron), John Birt; cr. 2000. Born 10 December 1944; Son of late Leo and Ida Birt; Married Jane Lake 1965 (divorced 2006) (1 son 1 daughter); married Eithne Wallis, CB 2006.

Education: St Mary's College, Liverpool; St Catherine's College, Oxford (BA engineering science 1966, MA).

Non-political career: Granada TV 1968-70: Producer, *Nice Time* 1968-69, Joint editor, *World in Action* 1969-70; London Weekend Television 1971-87: Producer, *The Frost Programme* 1971-72, Executive producer, *Weekend World* 1972-74, Head of current affairs 1974-77, Producer, *The Nixon Interviews* 1977, Controller of features and current affairs 1977-81, Director of programmes 1981-87; BBC 1987-2000: Deputy Director-General 1987-92, Director-General 1992-2000; Visiting Fellow, Nuffield College, Oxford 1991-99; Chair, Lynx Capital Ventures 2000-04; Strategy adviser to Tony Blair as Prime Minister 2000-05; Adviser, McKinsey's Global Media Practice 2000-05; Member: Cabinet Office Strategy Board 2003-05, Civil Service Reform Programme Board 2004-05 PayPal (Europe) Ltd, an eBay subsidiary: Non-executive director 2004-10, Chair 2010-14; Non-executive director, Infinis 2006-13; Eutelsat: Non-executive director 2006-12, Vice-chair 2012-; Adviser: Terra Firma 2006, Capgemini 2006-10; Chair: Waste Recycling Group 2006, Maltby Capital (EMI Holding Company) 2007-10; Non-executive director, Shopcade 2011-17; Chair: Host Europe Group 2013-17, CPA Global 2015-17.

Political career: *House of Lords:* Raised to the peerage as Baron Birt, of Liverpool in the County of Merseyside 2000.

Political interests: Broadcasting, digital Britain, crime, transport, constitution, humanism, energy, public sector management, London; China, France, Japan, South Africa, USA.

Other: Member, Wilton Park Academic Council 1980-83; Royal Television Society: Fellow 1989, Vice-president 1994-2001; Member, Advisory Board, GovernUp 2014; Chair, JLA 2018-; Two honorary university fellowships, three honorary doctorates; Emmy Award, US National Academy of Television, Arts and Sciences 1995; Kt 1998. Groucho Club, Ivy Club.

Publications: The Harder Path (2002).

Recreations: Walking, cinema, football.

The Lord Birt, House of Lords, London SW1A 0PW
Tel: 020 7219 8723 *Email:* gomesd@parliament.uk
Millbank House, 1-2 Milbank, London SW1P 3JU

CONSERVATIVE

BLACK OF BRENTWOOD, LORD

BLACK OF BRENTWOOD (Life Baron), Guy Vaughan Black; cr 2010. Born 6 August 1964; Son of late Thomas and late Monica Black; Married Mark Bolland 2015.

Education: Brentwood School, Essex; Peterhouse, Cambridge (BA history 1985, MA).

Non-political career: Graduate trainee, corporate banking division, BZW 1985-86; Desk officer, Conservative Research Department 1986-89; Special adviser to Rt Hon John Wakeham MP as Secretary of State for Energy 1989-92; Account director, Westminster Strategy 1992-94; Associate director, Lowe Bell Good Relations 1994-96; Director, Press Complaints Commission 1996-2003; Press secretary to Rt Hon Michael Howard MP as Leader of the Opposition 2004-05; Director of Media, Conservative Central Office 2004-05; Telegraph Media Group: Corporate affairs director 2005-09, Executive director 2009-18, Deputy chair 2018-.

Political career: *House of Lords:* Raised to the peerage as Baron Black of Brentwood, of Brentwood in the County of Essex 2010. Member: Information 2011-15, Joint Committee on Privacy and Injunctions 2011-12, Sexual Violence in Conflict 2015-16, Democracy and Digital Technologies 2019-. *Other:* Member, Association of Conservative Peers. Councillor, Brentwood District Council 1988-92.

Political interests: Media and creative industries, health, education, energy, animal welfare; Commonwealth, Italy.

Other: Director, Advertising Standards Board of Finance 2005-; Press Standards Board of Finance: Director 2006-, Chair 2009-; Trustee: Sir Edward Heath's Charitable Foundation 2006-10, Imperial War Museum 2007-; Chair, Commonwealth Press Union Media Trust 2009-; Royal College of Music: Member of Council 2009-17, Chair 2017-; President: London Press Club 2012-, The Printing Charity 2013-; Member, Chartered Institute of Public Relations; Cats Protection, National Osteoporosis Society; Fellow, Royal Society of Arts.

Recreations: Music, history.

The Lord Black of Brentwood, House of Lords, London SW1A 0PW
Tel: 020 7219 5353 *Email:* blackgv@parliament.uk
Tel: 020 7931 3806 Website: www.guyblack.org.uk

NON-AFFILIATED

BLACK OF CROSSHARBOUR, LORD

BLACK OF CROSSHARBOUR (Life Baron), Conrad Moffat Black; cr 2001. Born 25 August 1944; Son of George M Black and Jean Elizabeth Riley; Married Shirley Gail Hishon 1978 (divorced and annulled 1992) (2 sons 1 daughter); married Barbara Amiel 1992.

Education: Carleton University, Canada (BA history and political science 1965); Laval University, Canada (LLL law 1970); McGill University, Canada (MA history 1973); French.

Non-political career: Co-founded, Sterling Newspapers Ltd 1971; Argus Corporation Ltd: President 1978-79, Chair 1979-2004; Chair: Telegraph Group Ltd, London 1985-2003, Hollinger International Inc, USA 1985-2003, Hollinger International Inc, Canada 1986-2004. Honorary Colonel, Governor-General's Foot Guards 1997-.

Political career: *House of Lords:* Raised to the peerage as Baron Black of Crossharbour, of Crossharbour in the London Borough of Tower Hamlets 2001. On leave of absence June 2012-.

Political interests: Canada, EU, Israel, United States.

Other: Advisory Member, Jubilee Appeal for Veterans; Honorary Chair, Black Family Foundation; Honorary Publisher, National Interest (Washington); McMaster L.L.D.; Carlton L. L.D.; St. Francis Xavier, L.L.D.; Windsor Lit. D.; Knight Commander of the Order of St Gregory the Great (Holy See) 2001. Athenæum, Beefsteak, Garrick, Century (New York), Everglades (Palm Beach, Florida), Beach (Palm Beach, Florida), York (Toronto), Mount Royal (Montreal), University Club (Montreal); Granite Club, Toronto Golf Club.

Publications: Duplessis (1976) revised as Render unto Caesar (1998); A Life in Progress (1993); Franklin Delano Roosevelt, Champion of Freedom (2003); The Invincible Quest: The Life of Richard Milhous Nixon (2007); A Matter of Principle (2011); Flight of the Eagle: A Strategic History of the United States (2013); Rise to Greatness: The History of Canada from the Vikings to the Present (2014); Backward Glances (2016); Donald J. Trump: A President Like No Other (2018); The Canadian Manifesto (2019).

Recreations: Reading, Writing, Chess.

The Lord Black of Crossharbour OC, House of Lords, London SW1A 0PW
Tel: 020 7219 5353
Conrad Black Capital Corporation, Suite 296, 2869 Bloor Street West, Toronto Ontario M8X 1B3 *Tel:* +1 647 970 6315 *Email:* dconnors@blackam.net
Website: www.conradmblack.com *Twitter:* @ConradMBlack

NON-AFFILIATED

BLACKBURN, LORD BISHOP OF

BLACKBURN (9th Bishop of), Julian Tudor Henderson. Born 23 July 1954; Married Heather 1984 (1 son 1 daughter).

Education: Radley College; Keble College, Oxford (MA theology); Ridley Hall, Cambridge.

Non-political career: Ordained deacon 1979; Priest 1980; Curate, St Mary's Islington 1979-83; Vicar: Emmanuel and St Mary in the Castle, Hastings 1983-92, Holy Trinity, Claygate 1992-2005; Rural Dean of Emly 1996-2001; Honorary Canon, Guildford Cathedral 2002-13; Archdeacon of Dorking 2005-13; Bishop of Blackburn 2013-.

Political career: *House of Lords:* Entered House of Lords 2019.

Recreations: Gardening, design and DIY, walking, reading, tennis, cycling.

Rt Rev the Lord Bishop of Blackburn, House of Lords, London SW1A 0PW

LABOUR INDEPENDENT

BLACKSTONE, BARONESS

BLACKSTONE (Life Baroness), Tessa Ann Vosper Blackstone; cr. 1987. Born 27 September 1942; Daughter of late Geoffrey Blackstone and late Joanna Blackstone, née Vosper; Married Tom Evans 1963 (divorced 1975) (1 son 1 daughter).

Education: Ware Grammar School; London School of Economics (BScSoc sociology 1964; PhD 1969); Some French and German.

Non-political career: Associate Lecturer, Enfield College 1965-66; Assistant Lecturer then Lecturer, Department of Social Administration, London School of Economics 1966-75; Fellow, Centre for Studies in Social Policy 1972-74; Adviser, Central Policy Review Staff, Cabinet Office 1975-78; Professor of Educational Administration, University of London Institute of Education 1978-83; Deputy Education Officer (Resources), Inner London Education Authority 1983-86; Fellow, Policy Studies Institute 1987; Master, Birkbeck College, London University 1987-97; Vice-chancellor, Greenwich University 2004-11.

Political career: *House of Lords:* Raised to the peerage as Baroness Blackstone, of Stoke Newington in the County of Greater London 1987. Opposition Spokesperson for: Education and Science 1988-96, Treasury Matters 1990-91; Principal Opposition Spokesperson for Education and Science 1990-92; Opposition Spokesperson for Trade and Industry 1992-96; Principal Opposition Spokesperson for Foreign Affairs 1992-97; Minister of State and Government Spokesperson for: Department for Education and Employment (Minister of State for Education and Employment) 1997-2001, Department for Culture, Media and Sport (Minister of State for the Arts) 2001-03. Member: Public Service and Demographic Change 2012-13, Economic Affairs 2013-16, Sub-committee on Economic Affairs Finance Bill 2014-15, Long-Term Sustainability of the NHS 2016-17, Secondary Legislation Scrutiny 2017-18, Intergenerational Fairness and Provision 2018-19, International Relations/International Relations and Defence 2019-. *Other:* Chair, BBC General Advisory Council 1987-91; Chair and founder member, Institute for Public Policy Research 1988-97; Chair: British Library 2010-18, Bar Standards Board 2018-.

Political interests: Education, social policy, foreign affairs, arts; France, India, Palestine, USA.

Other: Royal Opera House: Board member 1987-97, 2009-14, Chair, Ballet Board 1991-97, Chair, Education and Access Committee 2011-; Trustee, Natural History Museum 1992-97; Chair, Royal Institute of British Architects Trust 2003-10; Non-executive director: Thames Television, VT Group 2004-10, Mott MacDonald 2005-08; Chair: Great Ormond Street Hospital Trust 2009-17, Orbit Group 2013-; Chair of trustees, Franco-British Council 2013-; Chair, British Lung Foundation 2017-; Chair of trustees, Royal College of Obstetricians and Gynaecologists 2019-; Chair, Bar Standards Board 2018-; Vice-president VSO, Patron Why Me?; Twelve honorary doctorates; Three honorary fellowships; Lifetime Award for Higher Education, *The Times* Higher Education awards 2011; PC 2001; Legion d'Honneur 2016.

Publications: A Fair Start (1971); Co-author: Students in Conflict (1967), The Academic Labour Market (1974), Educational Policy and Educational Inequality (1982), Disadvantage and Education (1982), Response to Adversity (1983), Inside the Think Tank: Advising the Cabinet 1971-84 (1988); Author, Prison and Penal Reform (1992); Co-edited, Race Relations in Britain (1998).

Recreations: Tennis, walking, ballet, opera, cinema.

Rt Hon the Baroness Blackstone, House of Lords, London SW1A 0PW
Tel: 020 7219 5409 *Email:* blackstonet@parliament.uk
The British Library, 96 Euston Road, London NW1 2DB *Tel:* 020 7412 7262

CONSERVATIVE

BLACKWELL, LORD

BLACKWELL (Life Baron), Norman Roy Blackwell; cr. 1997. Born 29 July 1952; Son of Albert and Frances Blackwell; Married Brenda Clucas 1974 (3 sons 2 daughters).

Education: Latymer Upper School, London; Royal Academy of Music (Junior Exhibitioner); Trinity College, Cambridge (BA natural sciences 1973, MA); Wharton Business School, University of Pennsylvania (AM, MBA 1975; PhD finance and economics 1976).

Non-political career: Plessey Company 1976-78; McKinsey & Co 1978-95: Partner 1984-95; Prime Minister's Policy Unit: Special adviser 1986-87, Head 1995-97; Director: Group Development, NatWest Group 1997-2000, Dixons Group 2000-03; Special adviser, KPMG Corporate Finance 2000-08; Director: Corporate Services Group 2000-06, SEGRO plc (formerly Slough Estates) 2001-10, SmartStream Technologies Ltd 2001-06; Chair, Akers Biosciences Inc 2002-03; Director, Standard Life Assurance 2003-12; Chair, Interserve plc 2006-16; Director: Halma plc 2010-14; Lloyds Banking Group plc: Director 2012-, Chairman 2014-; Chair, Scottish Widows Group Ltd 2012-14.

Political career: *House of Lords:* Raised to the peerage as Baron Blackwell, of Woodcote in the County of Surrey 1997. Member: Joint Committee on Tax Simplification 2001-, EU Sub-committee A (Economic and Financial Affairs) 2003-07, Economic Affairs Sub-committee on the Finance Bill 2004–10, European Union 2005-08, Joint Committee on Tax Law Rewrite Bills 2005-10; EU Sub-committee E (Law and Institutions): Member 2007-08, Co-opted member 2008-10; Member: Delegated Powers and Regulatory Reform 2008-13, EU Sub-committee E (Justice and Institutions) 2010-12, Secondary Legislation Scrutiny 2013-14. *Other:* Board member, Office of Fair Trading 2003-10; Office of Communications (Ofcom): Non-executive board member 2009-14, Member, content board 2012-14.

Political interests: Economic policy and taxation, public services, European Union.

Other: Chair: Centre for Policy Studies 2000-09, Global Vision 2007-09; Governor, Yehudi Menuhin School 2016-. Carlton, Royal Automobile Club.

Publications: Funding the Basic State Pension (CPS, 2001); Towards Smaller Government (CPS, 2001); Better Healthcare for all (CPS, 2002); A defining moment? – the European Constitutional Convention (CPS, 2003); Freedom annd Responsibility: A manifesto for a smaller state, bolder nation! (CPS, 2003); What if Britain says No to the EU Constitution? (CPS, 2004); Better Schools and Hospitals – Why parent and patient choice will work (CPS, 2004); Sleepwalking into an EU Legal System (CPS, 2006); From principle to policy – an outline manifesto (CPS, 2006); Three cheers for selection – How Grammar Schools help the poor (CPS, 2007).

Recreations: Classical music, walking.

The Lord Blackwell, House of Lords, London SW1A 0PW
Tel: 020 7219 8672 *Email:* blackwelln@parliament.uk
Tel: 020 7356 1390

CONSERVATIVE

BLACKWOOD OF NORTH OXFORD, BARONESS

BLACKWOOD OF NORTH OXFORD (Life Baroness), Nicola Claire Blackwood; cr 2019. Born 16 October 1979; Married Paul Bate 2016.

Education: Home schooled; Trinity College of Music; St Anne's College, Oxford (BA music 2003); Emmanuel College, Cambridge (MPhil musicology 2004).

Non-political career: Parliamentary researcher to Andrew Mitchell MP -2006; Policy fellow, Public.io 2017-; Senior adviser, Global Counsel Consulting Ltd 2018-; Honorary Professor, Department of Science, Technology, Engineering and Public Policy, University College London 2018-.

Political career: *House of Commons:* MP for Oxford West and Abingdon 2010-17; PPS to Matthew Hancock as Minister of State: for Skills and Enterprise, Department for Business, Innovation and Skills 2013-14, for Business and Enterprise and Minister for Portsmouth, Department for Business, Innovation and Skills and Minister of State for Energy, Department of Energy and Climate Change 2014-15; Board Member, Parliamentary Office of Science and Technology (POST) 2015-16; Parliamentary Under-Secretary of State for Public Health and Innovation, Department of Health 2016-17. Member: Home Affairs 2010-15, Joint Committee on the Draft Enhanced Terrorism Prevention and Investigation Measures Bill 2012-13, Liaison 2015-16; Chair, Science and Technology 2015-16. *House of Lords:* Raised to the peerage as Baroness Blackwood of North Oxford, of North Oxford in the County of Oxfordshire 2019. Parliamentary Under-Secretary of State and Government Spokesperson, Department of Health and Social Care 2019-20. Member, Science and Technology 2020-. *Other:* Vice-chairman (social action), Conservative Party 2010-13. Chair, Human Tissue Authority 2018-19.

Political interests: Civil liberties and human rights, home affairs, international development, universities, science and environment; Afghanistan, Democratic Republic of Congo, Iran, Rwanda, Sudan.

Other: Trustee, Northern House School 2007-; Member, advisory council: ZANE, Oxford Philharmonic Orchestra 2015-; Ambassador, One HealthTech; Board member: Eagle Genomics 2017-, Campaign for Science and Engineering 2017-, Oxford University Innovations 2018-, Push Doctor 2018-; Chair, Public Policy Projects 2020-; The Ley Community, Archway Foundation, National Osteoporosis Society.

Recreations: Music.

The Baroness Blackwood of North Oxford, House of Lords, London SW1A 0PW
Tel: 020 7219 3000 *Twitter:* @nicolablackwood

CROSSBENCH

BLAIR OF BOUGHTON, LORD

BLAIR OF BOUGHTON (Life Baron), Ian Warwick Blair; cr 2010. Born 19 March 1953; Son of Francis James Blair and Sheila Kathleen Blair; Married Felicity White 1980 (1 son 1 daughter).

Education: Wrekin College, Shropshire; Harvard High School, Los Angeles, USA; Christ Church, Oxford (BA English language and literature 1974, MA).

Non-political career: Metropolitan Police: Police Constable, Sergeant, then Inspector (uniform and CID) 1974-85, Detective Chief Inspector, CID, Kentish Town 1985-88, Manager, Crime Investigation Project 1988-89, Superintendent, Kensington Division 1989-91, Chief Superintendent and Staff Officer to HM Chief Inspector of Constabulary, Home Office 1991-93, Officer in charge of Operation Gallery 1993-96, Deputy Commissioner 2000-05, Commissioner 2005-08; Thames Valley Police: Assistant Chief Constable 1994-97, Deputy Chief Constable 1997-98; Chief Constable, Surrey Police 1998-2000.

Political career: *House of Lords:* Raised to the peerage as Baron Blair of Boughton, of Boughton in the County of Cheshire 2010. Member: EU Sub-committee E (Justice, Institutions and Consumer Protection) 2013-15, European Union 2015-16, EU Justice Sub-committee 2015-16, Licensing Act 2003 2016-17, Joint Committee on the Draft Domestic Abuse Bill 2019. *Other:* Commissioner, Commission on Assisted Dying 2010-.

Political interests: India.

Other: Visiting fellow: International Centre for Advanced Studies, New York University 1998, Nuffield College, Oxford 2001; Visiting Professor, John Jay College, New York 2010; Trustee: Michael Sieff Foundation, Longford Trust 2010-19, Shakespeare's Globe 2010-18; Chairman: Woolf Institute, Cambridge 2015-, Helen and Douglas House Children's Hospice, Oxford 2018-; Freeman, City of London; Hon. LLD, Lincoln University 2013; QPM 1998; Kt 2003. MCC, Athenæum Club.

Publications: Author: Investigating Rape: A New Approach for Police (1985); Policing Controversy (Profile Books, 2009).

Recreations: Theatre, opera, tennis.

The Lord Blair of Boughton QPM, House of Lords, London SW1A 0PW
Tel: 020 7219 3000

LABOUR

BLAKE OF LEEDS, BARONESS

BLAKE OF LEEDS (Life Barones), Judith Vivienne Blake; cr 2021. Born 23 July 1953; 3 daughters (including Olivia Blake (qv), MP for Sheffield, Hallam) 1 son.

Education: Leeds Girls' High School; Kent University (history).

Non-political career: Member, GMB.

Political career: *House of Commons:* Contested Leeds North West 2005 and 2010 general elections. *House of Lords:* Raised to the peerage as Baroness Blake of Leeds, of Gledhow in the City of Leeds 2021. *Other:* Member: Co-operative Party, SERA, National Policy Forum, Labour Party. Leeds City Council: Councillor 1996-, Deputy Leader of the Council 2010-15, Leader of the Council 2015-; Chair, Children and Young People's Board, Local Government Association; Governor: Cockburn John Charles Academy, Westwood Primary School; Board Member, Transport for the North; Member, West Yorkshire Combined Authority.

Other: Member, Middleton Elderly Aid 2004-10, 2018-; Director, Rail North; Trustee: Leeds United Foundation 2017-, Northern Ballet 2018-, Leeds International Piano Competition; Board member, Leeds Culture Trust 2019-; Member, UK 2070 Commission; CBE 2017.

The Baroness Blake of Leeds, House of Lords, London SW1A 0PW *Twitter:* @cllrjudithblake

CONSERVATIVE

BLENCATHRA, LORD

Chair, Select Committee on Delegated Powers and Regulatory Reform

BLENCATHRA (Life Baron), David John Maclean; cr 2011. Born 16 May 1953.

Education: Fortrose Academy; Aberdeen University.

Non-political career: Director, Cayman Islands Government Office, London 2011-14.

Political career: *House of Commons:* MP (Conservative) for Penrith and The Border 1983 by-election to 2010; Assistant Government Whip 1987-89; Government Whip 1988-89; Parliamentary Secretary, Ministry of Agriculture, Fisheries and Food 1989-92; Minister of State: Department of the Environment 1992-93, Home Office 1993-97; Opposition Chief Whip 2001-03, 2003-05; Member House of Commons Commission 2006. Chair, Joint Committee on Statutory Instruments 2006; Member, Liaison 2006. *House of Lords:* Raised to the peerage as Baron Blencathra, of Penrith in the County of Cumbria 2011. Member: EU Sub-committee F: (Home Affairs) 2011-12, (Home Affairs, Health and Education) 2012-15, Procedure 2012-15; Chair: Joint Committee on the Draft Communications Data Bill 2012-13, Delegated Powers and Regulatory Reform 2017-. *Other:* Vice-President, Conservatives for Britain 2015-16. Board Member and Deputy Chair, Natural England 2018-.

Other: PC 1995.

Rt Hon the Lord Blencathra, House of Lords, London SW1A 0PW
Tel: 020 7219 5353

CONSERVATIVE

BLOOMFIELD OF HINTON WALDRIST, BARONESS

Government Spokesperson, Wales Office; Government Whip (Baroness in Waiting)

BLOOMFIELD OF HINTON WALDRIST (Life Baroness), Olivia Caroline Bloomfield; cr 2016. Born 30 June 1960; Married Andrew 1984 (1 son 2 daughters).

Education: Atlantic College; St Hugh's college, Oxford (BA philosophy, politics and economics 1982).

Non-political career: Bank of America 1982-86; Russell Reynolds Associates 1986-93; Chief of Staff to Michael Spencer as Treasurer of CCHQ 2006-10; Partner: Atlantic Superconnection Corporation 2011-16, Disruptive Capital Finance 2011-16.

Political career: *House of Lords:* Raised to the peerage as Baroness Bloomfield of Hinton Waldrist, of Hinton Waldrist in the County of Oxfordshire 2016. Conservative Party Whip 2017-19; Government Whip (Baroness in Waiting) 2019-; Government Spokesperson, Wales Office 2019-20, 2020-. Member: Joint Committee on Statutory Instruments 2017-19, Science and Technology 2019. *Other:* Chairman, Wantage Conservative Group 2002-15. Governor, Cheltenham Ladies College 2003-09.

Other: Chair: Wandage Group 2005-16, Pump House Project 2013-; Member, advisory board, Terrestrial Energy 2018-.

The Baroness Bloomfield of Hinton Waldrist, House of Lords, London SW1A 0PW
Tel: 020 7219 0465 *Email:* bloomfieldo@parliament.uk

LABOUR

BLOWER, BARONESS

BLOWER (Life Baroness), Christine Blower; cr 2019.

Non-political career: Teacher, Holland Park School 1973-80; Head of Modern Languages, St Edmunds Secondary School, Fulham 1980-83; Head of Department, Quintin Kynaston School, Westminster 1983-90; Member, Hammersmith and Fulham's Primary Behaviour Support Team. National Union of Teachers (NUT): President 1997, Deputy General Secretary 2005-08, Acting General Secretary 2008-09, General Secretary 2009-16; International Secretary, NUT section, National Education Union; President, European Trade Union Committee for Education (ETUCE).

Political career: *House of Lords:* Raised to the peerage as Baroness Blower, of Starch Green in the London Borough of Hammersmith and Fulham 2019. Member, National Plan for Sport and Recreation 2020-. *Other:* Contested (London Socialist Alliance) 2000 London Assembly election. Member, Labour Party 2016-.

The Baroness Blower, House of Lords, London SW1A 0PW
Email: blower@parliament.uk

LABOUR

BLUNKETT, LORD

BLUNKETT (Life Baron), David Blunkett; cr 2015. Born 6 June 1947; Son of late Arthur and Doris Blunkett; Married Ruth Gwynneth Mitchell 1970 (divorced 1990) (3 sons); (1 son); married Dr Margaret Williams 2009 (3 stepdaughters).

Education: Royal National Normal College for the Blind; Shrewsbury Technical College; Sheffield Richmond College of Further Education (day release and evening courses); Sheffield University (BA political theory and institutions 1972); Huddersfield College of Education (PGCE 1973); Esperanto.

Non-political career: Office work, East Midlands Gas Board 1967-69; Tutor in industrial relations and politics, Barnsley College of Technology 1973-81; Professor of Politics in Practice, Sheffield University 2015-. Shop steward, GMB EMGB 1967-69; Member: NATFHE 1973-87, Unison 1973-.

Political career: *House of Commons:* Contested (Labour) Sheffield Hallam February 1974 general election. MP for Sheffield Brightside 1987-2010, for Sheffield Brightside and Hillsborough 2010-15; Opposition Spokesperson for Local Government 1988-92; Shadow Secretary of State for: Health 1992-94, Education 1994-95, Education and Employment 1995-97; Secretary of State for: Education and Employment 1997-2001, Home Department (Home Secretary) 2001-04, Work and Pensions 2005. *House of Lords:* Raised to the peerage as Baron Blunkett, of Brightside and Hillsborough in the City of Sheffield 2015. Member: Citizenship and Civic Engagement 2017-18, Joint Committee on the Draft Parliamentary Buildings (Restoration and Renewal) Bill 2018-19. *Other:* Labour Party: Member, National Executive Committee 1983-98, Vice-chair 1992-93, Chair 1993-94. Councillor, Sheffield City Council 1970-88, Chair, Social Services Committee 1976-80, Leader 1980-87; Councillor, South Yorkshire County Council 1973-77; Former chair, Race Relations Forum.

Political interests: Local government, employment and welfare to work, citizenship and civil renewal, education; France, USA.

Other: Former Council Member, Guide Dogs for the Blind Association; Former Trustee, Community Service Volunteers; Fellow, Industry and Parliament Trust 1991; Vice-president, Alzheimer's Society 2009; Patron, Society of Occupational Medicine; Board Member, National Citizens Service -2018; Vice President: Alzheimers Society, Royal National Institute for the Blind; President, Association of Citizenship Teaching; Chair: Heathrow Airport Implementation Steering Group for skills and Employment, Sheffield City Partnership Board 2017-; Trustee, FSI 2019-; Joint Chair, Higher Education Commission 2019-; Fellow, Academy of Social Sciences; Member, Political Studies Association; Guide Dogs for the Blind, RNIB; Fellow, Academy of Social Science; Honorary Doctorate: Haifa University, Israel 2005, Open University 2016, Sheffield University 2016, Huddersfield University 2017, Middlesex University 2018; Fellow, Sheffield Hallam University; PC 1997.

Publications: Building from the Bottom (1983); Democracy in Crisis – the Town Halls Respond (1987); On a Clear Day (autobiography) (1995, 2002); Politics and Progress (2001); The Blunkett Tapes – My Life in the Bear Pit (2006).

Recreations: Walking, sailing, music, poetry.

Rt Hon the Lord Blunkett, House of Lords, London SW1A 0PW
Tel: 020 7219 3000

LABOUR

BOATENG, LORD

BOATENG (Life Baron), Paul Yaw Boateng; cr 2010. Born 14 June 1951; Son of Kwaku Boateng, barrister, and Eleanor Boateng, teacher; Married Janet Alleyne 1980 (2 sons 3 daughters).

Education: Achimota School, Ghana; Accra Academy, Ghana; Apsley Grammar School, Ghana; Bristol University (LLB 1972); College of Law (solicitor 1975); French (colloquial).

Non-political career: Solicitor 1975; Barrister-at-law; High Commissioner, South Africa 2005-09; Advisory Board, Aegis; Chair, advisory board, Aventa Capital Partners; Member: Health policy advisory board, Gilead Sciences Inc, Non-executive director, 4G Africa AG; Director, Akyen Law and Advisory Science Ltd. Member, GMB.

Political career: *House of Commons:* Contested Hertfordshire West 1983 general election. MP (Labour) for Brent South 1987-2005; Opposition Frontbench Spokesperson on: Treasury and Economic Affairs 1989-92, Lord Chancellor's Department 1992-97; Parliamentary Under-Secretary of State, Department of Health 1997-98; Home Office: Minister of State (Minister for Criminal Policy) 1998-99, Minister of State and Deputy Home Secretary 1999-2001; Minister for Young People 2000-01; HM Treasury 2001-05: Financial Secretary 2001-02, Chief Secretary 2002-05. Member, Public Accounts 2001-02. *House of Lords:* Raised to the peerage as Baron Boateng, of Akyem in the Republic of Ghana and of Wembley in the London Borough of Brent 2010. Member, Joint Committee on National Security Strategy 2014-17. *Other:* Member: Labour Party NEC Human Rights sub-committee 1979-83, Labour Party Joint Committee on Crime and Policing 1984-86. Member Greater London Council 1981-86: Chair, Police Committee 1981-86, Vice-chair, Ethnic Minority Committee 1981-86; Governor: Museum of London 2009-, London School of Economics 2011.

Political interests: Home affairs, housing, inner cities, overseas aid and development, environment, children and young people's policy; Africa, Caribbean, Southern Africa, USA.

Other: Chair: Afro-Caribbean Education Resource Project 1978-84, Westminster Community Relations Council 1979-81; Legal adviser, Scrap Sus Campaign 1977-81; Home Office Advisory Council on Race Relations 1981-86; World Council of Churches Commission on programme to combat racism 1984-91; Vice-Moderator 1984-91; Police Training Council 1981-85; Executive NCCL 1980-86; Governor, Police Staff College Bramshill 1981-84; Board of English National Opera 1984-97; Governor, Ditchley Park 2007-11; Board of Governors, English Speaking Union 2009-; Board member, Food for the Hungry 2009-; Trustee, Duke of Edinburgh International Youth Award 2009-; Non-executive director, Ghana International Bank plc London; Member, Gray's Inn; DL, Lincoln College, Philadelphia, USA; LLD, Bristol University; PC 1999.

Publications: Contributor, Reclaiming the Ground; Introduction to Sense and Sensibility: The Complete Jane Austen.

Recreations: Family, swimming, opera.

Rt Hon the Lord Boateng, House of Lords, London SW1A 0PW
Tel: 020 7219 3000 *Email:* boatengp@parliament.uk

LIBERAL DEMOCRAT

BONHAM-CARTER OF YARNBURY, BARONESS

Liberal Democrat Lords Spokesperson for Digital, Culture, Media and Sport

BONHAM-CARTER OF YARNBURY (Life Baroness), Jane Bonham Carter; cr. 2004. Born 20 October 1957; Daughter of Mark Bonham Carter and Leslie Nast; Partner Lord Razzall (qv).

Education: St Paul's Girls' School, London; University College, London (BA philosophy).

Non-political career: Producer, BBC Television's *Panorama* and *Newsnight* 1988-93; Editor, *A Week in Politics*, Channel Four 1993-96; Director of communications, Liberal Democrat Party 1996-98; Independent television producer, Brook Lapping Productions 1998-2004; Associate, Brook Lapping Productions, Ten Alps plc 2004-09.

Political career: *House of Lords:* Raised to the peerage as Baroness Bonham-Carter of Yarnbury, of Yarnbury in the County of Wiltshire 2004. Liberal Democrat Spokesperson for Culture, Media and Sport (Broadcasting and the Arts) 2004-10; Deputy Convener of the Liberal Democrat Peers 2010-15; Trade Envoy to Mexico 2013-; Liberal Democrat: Principal Spokesperson for Culture, Media and Sport 2010-15, Shadow Secretary of State/Spokesperson for: Culture, Media and Sport 2015-17, Digital, Culture, Media and Sport 2017-. Member: EU Sub-committee F (Home Affairs) 2004-07, Review of the BBC Charter 2005-06, Communications 2007-10, 2015-19, Joint Committee on Privacy and Injunctions 2011-12, EU Sub-committee C: (Foreign Affairs, Defence and Development Policy) 2010-12, (External Affairs) 2012-15. Co-Chair, Liberal Democrat Parliamentary Party Committee on Culture, Media and Sport 2010-15. *Other:* Member, Liberal Democrats Campaigns and Communications Committee 1998-2006.

Political interests: Ethiopia, Italy, Mexico, USA, Zimbabwe.

Other: Advisory committee, Centre Forum 1998-2015; Council member, Britain in Europe 1998-2005; Member: RAPt Rehabilitation of Addicted Prisoners Trust/Forward Trust 1999-, Referendum Campaign team 2004-05; Trustee, The Lowry 2011-; Board member, National Campaign for the Arts 2010-12; Patron, The Studio Theatre, Salisbury 2017-, Regional Champion, British Museum 2018-, Patron, Messums, Wiltshire 2018-; Visiting Parliamentary Fellow of St Antony's College, Oxford 2013-14; Gold Medal, NY International Festival 2003. Academicians' Room Royal Academy of Arts, Groucho Club.

The Baroness Bonham-Carter of Yarnbury, House of Lords, London SW1A 0PW
Tel: 020 7219 2717 *Email:* bonhamcarterj@parliament.uk *Twitter:* @jbonham_carter

CROSSBENCH

BOOTHROYD, BARONESS

BOOTHROYD (Life Baroness), Betty Boothroyd; cr. 2001. Born 8 October 1929; Daughter of late Archibald and Mary Boothroyd.

Education: Dewsbury College of Commerce and Art.

Non-political career: Personal/political assistant to: Barbara Castle MP 1956-58, Lord Walston as Minister of State, Foreign and Commonwealth Office 1962-73; Legislative assistant, US congressman Silvio O Conte 1960-62.

Political career: *House of Commons:* Contested Leicester South East 1957 by-election, Peterborough 1959 general election, Nelson and Colne 1968 by-election and Rossendale 1970 general election. MP for West Bromwich 1973-74, for West Bromwich West 1974-2000 (Labour 1973-92, Speaker 1992-2000); Assistant Government Whip 1974-76; Second Deputy Chairman of Ways and Means and Deputy Speaker 1987-92; Speaker 1992-2000; Chairman, House of Commons Commission 1992-2000. *House of Lords:* Raised to the peerage as Baroness Boothroyd, of Sandwell in the County of West Midlands 2001. *Other:* European Parliament: MEP 1975-77. Member, National Executive Committee, Labour Party 1981-87. Councillor, Hammersmith Borough Council 1965-68.

Political interests: Constitutional affairs; Commonwealth.

Other: Patron: London International Orchestra 2000-, National Benevolent Fund for the Aged 2009-, Commonwealth Countries League 2011-14, CHICKS (Country Holidays for Inner City Kids) 2012-, David Nott Foundation 2016-; Memorial to the Women of World War Two, Friends of the Elderly, London Trust, Silver Trust; Worshipful Company of: Feltmakers 1994, Glovers of London 2001 (Special Member), Lightmongers 2001 (Special Member), Grocers 2005 (Honorary Member); Freedom: Metropolitan Borough of Sandwell, Metropolitan Borough of Kirklees, City of London; Chancellor, Open University 1994-2006; Ten honorary degrees, including Oxford, Cambridge and St Andrews; Honorary Master of the Bench, Middle Temple 2011; *The Spectator*: Parliamentarian of the Year Award 1992, Personality of the Year 1993, Communicator of the Year 1994; Lifetime Achievement, *House Magazine* awards 2012; PC 1992; OM 2005. Reform Club, University Women's Club.

Publications: The Autobiography Betty Boothroyd (2001).

Recreations: Gardening.

Rt Hon the Baroness Boothroyd OM, House of Lords, London SW1A 0PW
Tel: 020 7219 3000 *Email:* boothroyd@parliament.uk

CONSERVATIVE

BORWICK, LORD

BORWICK (5th Baron, UK) Geoffrey Robert James (Jamie) Borwick; cr 1922; 5th Bt of Eden Lacy (UK) 1916. Born 7 March 1955; Son of late Hon. Robin Sandbach Borwick; Married Victoria Lorne Peta Borwick 1981, London Assembly Member 2008-15, Deputy Mayor of London 2012-15, MP for Kensington 2015-17 (3 sons 1 daughter).

Education: Eton College.

Non-political career: Sir Robert McAlpine & Sons Ltd 1972-81; Non-executive director, Hansa Trust plc 1984-2012; Manganese Bronze Holdings plc: Chief executive 1987-2001, Chair 2001-03; Chair, Federated Trust Corporation Ltd 1987-; Director: Mayfield Market Towns Ltd 2012-, Penso Ltd 2018-.

Political career: *House of Lords:* Elected hereditary peer 2013-. Member: Secondary Legislation Scrutiny 2014-15, European Union 2015-16, EU Financial Affairs Sub-committee 2015-16, Science and Technology 2016-, Services 2018-. *Other:* Director and trustee, Board, Science Museum 2014-.

Political interests: Business, economy, planning, transport; USA.

Other: Trustee: Federated Foundation 1985-, Ewing Foundation 1985-, British Lung Foundation 2001-08, 2011-16, Royal Brompton and Harefield Charity 2012-; Fellow, Ewing Foundation. Garrick Club.

Recreations: Travel, swimming, walking.

The Lord Borwick, House of Lords, London SW1A 0PW
Email: borwickgr@parliament.uk
15 Great College Street, London SW1P 3RX

NON-AFFILIATED

BOSWELL OF AYNHO, LORD

BOSWELL OF AYNHO (Life Baron), Timothy Eric Boswell; cr 2010. Born 2 December 1942; Son of late Eric Boswell and Joan Boswell; Married Helen Delahay 1969, née Rees (died 2019) (3 daughters, including Victoria Prentis (qv) MP for Banbury).

Education: Marlborough College, Wiltshire; New College, Oxford (BA classics 1965, MA; Diploma agricultural economics 1966); French, German, Italian.

Non-political career: Conservative Research Department 1966-73: Head, economic section 1970-73; Farmer 1974-87; Part-time special adviser to Minister of Agriculture 1984-86. Chair, Leicestershire, Northamptonshire and Rutland NFU County Branch 1983.

Political career: *House of Commons:* Contested Rugby February 1974 general election. MP (Conservative) for Daventry 1987-2010; PPS to Peter Lilley as Financial Secretary to Treasury 1989-90; Assistant Government Whip 1990-92; Government Whip 1992; Parliamentary Under-Secretary of State, Department for Education 1992-95; Parliamentary Secretary, Ministry of Agriculture, Fisheries and Food 1995-97; Opposition Spokesperson for: the Treasury 1997,

Trade and Industry 1997-99, Education 1999-2001, Work and Pensions (People with Disabilities) 2001; Shadow Minister for: Education and Skills (People with Disabilities) 2002-03, Home, Constitutional and Legal Affairs 2003-04, Home Affairs 2004, Work and Pensions 2004-06, Welfare Reform 2004-05; PPS to Francis Maude as Chairman, Conservative Party 2005-07. Member: Innovation, Universities[, Science] and Skills/Science and Technology 2007-10. Member, Executive, 1922 Committee 2007-10. *House of Lords:* Raised to the peerage as Baron Boswell of Aynho, of Aynho in the County of Northamptonshire 2010. Principal Deputy Chairman of Committees 2012-19; Deputy Speaker 2018-19. Chair, European Union 2012-19. *Other:* Chair, Daventry Constituency Conservative Association 1979-83; Acting Chairman, Milton Keynes Conservatives 2009-10. Member, Agriculture and Food Research Council 1988-90; DL, Northamptonshire 2010-17.

Political interests: Agriculture, finance, European Union, education, equalities; Europe.

Other: Perry Foundation: Council member 1967-90, President 1984-90; Governor: University of Wales Institute, Cardiff 2007-12, Northampton University 2010-12; Fellow: City and Guilds Institutes, Society of Antiquaries of London. Farmers Club.

Recreations: Shooting.

The Lord Boswell of Aynho, House of Lords, London SW1A 0PW
Tel: 020 8767 6931 *Email:* boswellte@parliament.uk
Tel: 020 8767 6931

CROSSBENCH

BOTHAM, LORD

BOTHAM (Life Baron), Ian Terence Botham; cr 2020. Born 24 November 1955; Son of Herbert Leslie and Violet Marie Botham; Married Kathryn Waller (1 son 2 daughters).

Education: Buckler's Mead Secondary School, Yeovil.

Non-political career: Professional Cricketer 1974-92: Somerset 1974-87, Worcestershire 1987-91, Durham 1992-93, England Test cricketer 1977-92; Cricket commentator and writer 1994-2020; Partner, Botham Wines 2018-.

Political career: *House of Lords:* Raised to the peerage as Baron Botham, of Ravensworth in the County of North Yorkshire 2020.

Political interests: Countryside, sports and stadiums survival during and after the Covid pandemic; Australia, New Zealand.

Other: Chair, Mission Sports Management 2000-12; President, Leukaemia and Lymphoma Research/Blood Cancer UK 2003-; Beefy's Charity Foundation; Freeman: Yeovil, Epworth; DLitt, Chester University 2006; LLD, Bath University 2008; Doctorate of Sports Science, Leeds Metropolitan University 2008; Honorary Graduate, Exeter University 2010; Doctorate for Science, Lincoln University 2010; BBC Sports Personality of the Year Lifetime Achievement Award 2004; OBE 1992; Kt 2007. Member, MCC, Sunningdale, Portmarnock, Yoevil, Rockliffe Hall, Archerfield, Darlington, Desert Springs Golf Clubs; Chair, Durham County Cricket Club 2017-; President, Scunthorpe United FC 2017-.

Publications: Botham – Don't tell Kath (Harper Collins, 1995); Head On – Ian Botham: The Autobiography (Ebury Press, 2008); Beefy's Cricket Tales: My Favourite Stories from On and Off the Field (Simon & Schuster UK, 2014).

Recreations: Charity walks, fishing, countryside sports, wine, sport.

The Lord Botham OBE, House of Lords, London SW1A 0PW
Tel: 020 7219 3000 *Email:* bothami@parliament.uk Website: ianbotham.com
Twitter: @BeefyBotham

CONSERVATIVE

BOTTOMLEY OF NETTLESTONE, BARONESS

BOTTOMLEY OF NETTLESTONE (Life Baroness), Virginia Hilda Brunette Maxwell Bottomley; cr 2005. Born 12 March 1948; Daughter of late W. John Garnett, CBE; Married Peter Bottomley (qv) 1967 (later Sir Peter, MP for Worthing West) (1 son 2 daughters).

Education: Putney High School; Essex University (BA sociology); London School of Economics (MSc social administration 1975).

Non-political career: Behavioural scientist 1971-84; Executive director, Odgers Berndston (executive search) 2000-; Member, Supervisory Board, Akzo Nobel NV 2000-12; NED; BUPA 2007-13; Non-executive director, Smith & Nephew 2012-.

Political career: *House of Commons:* Contested Isle of Wight 1983 general election. MP (Conservative) for South West Surrey 1984 by-election to 2005; PPS: to Chris Patten as Minister of State: Department of Education and Science 1985-86, Overseas Development Administration 1986-87, to Sir Geoffrey Howe as Foreign Secretary 1987-88; Parliamentary Under-Secretary of State, Department of Environment 1988-89; Department of Health: Minister of State 1989-92, Secretary of State 1992-95; Secretary of State for National Heritage 1995-97. *House of Lords:* Raised to the peerage as Baroness Bottomley of Nettlestone, of St Helens in the County of Isle of Wight 2005. *Other:* Magistrate, Inner London Juvenile Courts 1975-84; Chairman, Lambeth Juvenile Court 1980-84; Governor, London School of Economics 1985-; Chair, Millennium Commission 1995-97; Government Co-chair, Women's National Commission 1991-92; Vice-chair, British Council 1997-2001; Governor, University of the Arts, London 1999-2004; DL, Surrey 2006; Sheriff of Hull 2013-; Member, State Honours Committee -2018.

Political interests: Health, universities, prison reform, diversity, business enterprise, regulatory reform, children and family policy; China, India, Japan, Netherlands.

Other: Fellow, Industry and Parliament Trust 1987; Council member: Ditchley Foundation 1991-, Prince of Wales International Business Leaders Forum 2002-09; Lay Canon, Guildford Cathedral 2002-; President: Farnham Castle (Centre for International Briefing) 2003-, Abbeyfield Society 2004-09; International Chamber of Commerce, UK Advisory Council 2004-; Advisory Council, Cambridge Judge Business School 2004-09; Trustee, *The Economist* 2005-; Freedom, City of London 1988; Pro-chancellor, Surrey University 2005-15; Chancellor, Hull University 2006-; Honorary LLD, Portsmouth University 1993; Honorary doctorate, Aston University; PC 1992. Athenæum Club.

Publications: Various articles on criminal justice, poverty, children and corporate governance.

Recreations: Grandchildren.

Rt Hon the Baroness Bottomley of Nettlestone DL, House of Lords, London SW1A 0PW
Tel: 020 7219 1060 *Email:* bottomleyv@parliament.uk

CONSERVATIVE

BOURNE OF ABERYSTWYTH, LORD

BOURNE OF ABERYSTWYTH (Life Baron), Nicholas Henry Bourne; cr 2013. Born 1 January 1952; Son of late John Morgan Bourne, systems engineer, and late Joan Mary Bourne, housewife.

Education: King Edward VI School, Chelmsford; University College of Wales, Aberystwyth (LLB law 1973; LLM 1976); Trinity College, Cambridge (LLM 1975); Honourable Society of Gray's Inn (Barrister-at-Law 1976); French.

Non-political career: Supervisor in law: Corpus Christi College, Cambridge 1974-82, St Catharine's College, Cambridge 1974-82, London School of Economics 1975-77; Principal, Chart University Tutors Ltd 1979-88; Company secretary, Chart Foulks Lynch plc 1984-88; Director of studies, Holborn Law Tutors Ltd 1988-91; Senior lecturer in law, South Bank University 1991-92; Dean, Swansea Law School 1992-96; Assistant principal, Swansea Institute 1996-98; Visiting lecturer, Hong Kong University 1996-. Former member, NATFHE.

Political career: *House of Commons:* Contested (Conservative) Chesterfield 1983 general election and 1984 by-election and Worcester 1997 general election. *House of Lords:* Raised to the peerage as Baron Bourne of Aberystwyth, of Aberystwyth in the County of Ceredigion and of Wethersfield in the County of Essex 2013. Government Whip (Lord in Waiting) 2014-16; Government Spokesperson for: Culture, Media and Sport (Broadcasting) 2014-15, International

Development 2014-15, Work and Pensions 2014-15, Wales Office 2014-17, Energy and Climate Change 2015-16, Communities and Local Government 2016-19; Parliamentary Under-Secretary of State: Wales Office 2015-17, Department of Energy and Climate Change 2015-16; Department for Communities and Local Government/Ministry of Housing, Communities and Local Government: Parliamentary Under-Secretary of State: for Faith and Integration 2016-17, (Minister for Faith) 2017-19; Parliamentary Under-Secretary of State: Northern Ireland Office 2017, Wales Office 2017-19. Member: Delegated Powers and Regulatory Reform 2014, Public Services 2020-. *Other:* National Assembly for Wales: Contested Brecon and Radnorshire constituency 1999, 2003, 2007 and 2011 elections, AM for Mid and West Wales region 1999-2011, Leader, Conservative Group in the National Assembly 1999-2011, Welsh Conservative Spokesperson for: Finance 1999, 2001-02, 2006-07, Europe and Constituional Affairs 2007-09, Leader of the Official Opposition 2007-11, Shadow Minister for: Finance 2008-11, Heritage 2010, Contested Mid and West Wales region 2011 election. Member: North East Thames Regional Health Authority 1990-92, West Glamorgan Health Authority 1994-97, Doctor and Dentist Review Body 1998-99, Silk Commission 2011-13, Commission on Public Service Governance and Delivery 2013.

Political interests: Foreign affairs, economy, education, health, constitutional issues; France, Greece, India, Italy, Malaysia, Singapore.

Other: Patron: Kidney Wales, Heart of Wales Line Association; Member, Advisory Committee: British Council, Wales Governance Centre; Member, Honourable Society of Gray's Inn; BHF, NSPCC; Fellow, Aberystwyth University 2015; Hon. LLD, University of Trinity St David 2018. Society of Authors, United Oxford and Cambridge University Club.

Publications: Various company law and business law text books; Editor of a series of legal text books; Editorial board, Business Law Review.

Recreations: Badminton, squash, tennis, walking, theatre, cinema.

The Lord Bourne of Aberystwyth, House of Lords, London SW1A 0PW
Tel: 020 7219 8758 *Email:* bournen@parliament.uk *Twitter:* @lordnickbourne

LIBERAL DEMOCRAT

BOWLES OF BERKHAMSTED, BARONESS

BOWLES OF BERKHAMSTED (Life Baroness), Sharon Margaret Bowles; cr 2015. Born 12 June 1953; Daughter of late Percy Bowles and late Florence Bowles; Married Andrew Horton (2 sons).

Education: Our Lady's Convent, Abingdon; Reading University (BSc chemical physics and mathematics 1974); Lady Margaret Hall, Oxford (research 1974-77).

Non-political career: Chartered Patent Attorney, Registered Trademark Agent and European Patent Attorney 1981-; Professional Representative, Office for Harmonisation of the Single Market; Partner, Bowles Horton partnership 1981-2005; Non-executive Director: London Stock Exchange Group 2014-16, London Stock Exchange plc 2014-.

Political career: *House of Lords:* Raised to the peerage as Baroness Bowles of Berkhamsted, of Bourne End in the County of Hertfordshire 2015. Member: Economic Affairs 2016-, Economic Affairs Finance Bill Sub-committee 2016-17, 2020-, Intellectual Property (Unjustified Threats) Bill 2016, SLSC Sub-committee A 2018-19. *Other:* European Parliament: MEP for South East 2005-14: Bureau member, ALDE group 2009-14, Chair, Economic and Monetary Affairs Committee 2009-14. Liberal Democrats: Secretary, Chilterns region 1990-95, Member, federal executive and federal finance committee 2000-03; Co-founder, Association of Liberal Democrat Engineers and Scientists; Vice-president and bureau member, ELDR group 2004-14; Chair, Liberal Democrat International Relations Committee.

Political interests: Financial services, science and technology, intellectual property, company law.

Other: Vice-president, Liberal International; Member, advisory board, Centre for Progressive Capitalism 2016-; Anti-Slavery International. National Liberal Club.

The Baroness Bowles of Berkhamsted, House of Lords, London SW1A 0PW
Tel: 020 7219 3000 *Email:* bowless@parliament.uk *Twitter:* @SharonBowlesUK

NON-AFFILIATED

BOWNESS, LORD

BOWNESS (Life Baron), Peter Spencer Bowness; cr. 1996. Born 19 May 1943; Son of late Hubert Bowness and Doreen Bowness; Married Marianne Hall 1969 (divorced 1983) (1 daughter); married Patricia Cook 1984 (1 stepson).

Education: Whitgift School, Croydon; Law Society School of Law, College of Law.

Non-political career: Admitted Solicitor 1966; Partner, Weightman Sadler, Solicitors, Purley, Surrey 1970-2002; Notary Public 1977; Consultant, Streeter Marshall Solicitors, Warlingham/Purley/Croydon 2002-11. Hon. Colonel 151 (Greater London) RCT Regiment (V) 1988-93.

Political career: *House of Lords:* Raised to the peerage as Baron Bowness, of Warlingham in the County of Surrey and of Croydon in the London Borough of Croydon 1996. Opposition Spokesperson for Local Government 1997-98; House of Lords representative to Convention to Draft an EU Charter of Fundamental Rights 1999-2000. Chair, Draft Local Government (Organisation and Standards) Bill Joint Committee 1999; Member: EU Sub-committee C (Common Foreign and Security Policy) 2000-03, Chinook ZD567 2001-02, Joint Committee on Human Rights 2002-06, 2008-12, European Union 2003-07; Chair, EU Sub-committee C (Foreign Affairs, Defence and Development Policy) 2003-06; EU Sub-committee E (Law and Institutions): Co-opted Member 2006-09, Co-opted Chair 2009-10; Member, European Union 2009-14; Chair, EU Sub-committee E: (Justice and Institutions) 2010-12, (Justice, Institutions and Consumer Protection) 2012-13; Member: EU Sub-committee D (Agriculture, Fisheries, Environment and Energy) 2013-15, Secondary Legislation Scrutiny 2014-17, EU Energy and Environment Sub-Committee 2015-16. *Other:* Left Conservatives November 2020, now sits as Non-affiliated. London Borough of Croydon Council: Councillor 1968-98, Leader 1976-94, Mayor 1979-80; Deputy Chair, Association of Metropolitan Authorities 1978-80; Chair, London Boroughs Association 1978-94; DL, Greater London 1981-; Member: Audit Commission 1983-95, London Residuary Body 1985-93, National Training Task Force 1989-92.

Political interests: European Union, local government, London; Europe, particularly Balkans and Baltics, Caucasus.

Other: Member, UK Delegation to: Congress of Regional and Local Authorities of Europe, Council of Europe 1990-98, EU Committee of the Regions 1994-98; Member, Inter-Parliamentary Union; UK Delegation, Parliamentary Assembly of the Organisation for Security and Co-operation in Europe: Member 2007-, Leader 2014-17, Vice-President 2015-21, President 2021-; Freedom, City of London 1984; Honorary Freedom, London Borough of Croydon 2002; CBE 1981; Kt 1987.

Recreations: Travel, gardening.

The Lord Bowness CBE DL, House of Lords, London SW1A 0PW
Tel: 020 7219 2575 *Email:* bownessp@parliament.uk

CROSSBENCH

BOYCE, LORD

BOYCE (Life Baron), Michael Cecil Boyce; cr. 2003. Born 2 April 1943; Son of late Commander Hugh Boyce DSC RN and late Madeleine Boyce, née Manley; Married Harriette Fletcher 1971 (separated 1994, divorced 2005) (1 son 1 daughter); married Fleur Rutherford, née Smith 2006 (died 2016).

Education: Hurstpierpoint College; Britannia Royal Naval College, Dartmouth (1964); Royal College of Defence Studies (1988).

Non-political career: Non-executive Director: WS Atkins plc 2004-13, VT Group plc 2004-10. Royal Navy 1961-2003: Served HM Submarines Anchorite, Valiant and Conqueror 1965-72; Commanded HM Submarines: Oberon 1973-74, Opossum 1974-75, Superb 1979-81, HMS Brilliant 1983-84; Captain Submarine Sea Training 1984-86; Royal College of Defence Studies 1988; Senior Naval Officer, Middle East 1989; Director, Naval Staff Duties 1989-91; Flag Officer Sea Training 1991-92, Surface Flotilla 1992-95; Commander Anti-Submarine Warfare Striking Force 1992-94; Second Sea Lord and Commander-in-Chief Naval Home Command 1995-97; Commander-in-Chief Fleet and Eastern Atlantic Area and Commander Naval Forces North Western Europe 1977-98; First Sea Lord and Chief of Naval Staff 1988-2001; Chief of the Defence Staff 2001-03; Colonel Commandant Special Boat Service 2003-.

Political career: *House of Lords:* Raised to the peerage as Baron Boyce, of Pimlico in the City of Westminster 2003. European Union Sub-committee C (Foreign Affairs, Defence and Development Policy): Member 2005-06, Co-opted member 2006-08. *Other:* DL, Greater London.

Other: Officers Association: President 2003-11, Senior President 2009-11; President, St John Ambulance (London District) 2003-11; Patron: Sail 4 Cancer 2003-, Submarine Association 2003-, Trafalgar Woods 2004-; Lord Warden and Admiral of the Cinque Ports and Constable of Dover Castle 2004-; UK Defence Forum; Vice-Patron, Tall Ships Youth Trust; Forces in Mind Trust; Historic Dockyard Chatham; President, Royal Navy Submarine Museum 2005-; Vice-President, Forces Pension Society 2006-; Elder Brother, Trinity House 2007-; Chair, Council White Ensign Association 2007-10; Chair and Trustee, RNLI 2008-13; Patron, Forces in Mind Trust 2012-; Chair, HMS Victory Preservation Company 2012-; Honorary Bencher, Middle Temple 2012-; Chair, RBL Centre for Blast Injury Studies Advisory Board; Draper's Company: Master 2013-14; Freedom, City of London; Honorary doctorates: Portsmouth University 2005, Canterbury Christ Church University 2011, Kent University 2013, Imperial College 2016; King of Arms Order of the Bath; OBE 1982; KCB 1995; GCB 1999; KStJ 2002; Commander, Legion of Merit (USA) 2003; King of Arms Order of the Bath 2009-18 KG 2011. Naval and Military, Garrick Club; RNSA; RYA; Jester; West Withering Windsurfing Club; Queen's.

Recreations: Tennis, real tennis, squash, windsurfing, opera.

Admiral of the Fleet the Lord Boyce KG GCB OBE DL, House of Lords, London SW1A 0PW
Tel: 020 7219 8714 *Email:* boycem@parliament.uk

CROSSBENCH

BOYCOTT, BARONESS

BOYCOTT (Life Baroness), Rosel Marie Boycott; cr 2018. Born 13 May 1951; Married David Leitch 1983 (dissolved 1998) (1 daughter); married Charles Howard 1999.

Education: Kent University (pure maths); Cheltenham Ladies' College.

Non-political career: Editor: *Esquire* 1992-96, *Independent on Sunday* 1996-98, *The Independent* 1998, *Daily Express* 1998-2001.

Political career: *House of Lords:* Raised to the peerage as Baroness Boycott, of Whitefield in the County of Somerset 2018. Member, Food, Poverty, Health and the Environment 2019-. *Other:* Chair, London Food Board 2008-18.

Other: Director: Soil Association 2003-04, School Food Matters 2009-11; Trustee, Food Foundation.

Publications: A Nice Girl Like Me (2009).

The Baroness Boycott, House of Lords, London SW1A 0PW
Tel: 020 7219 3000 *Twitter:* @RosieBoycott

NON-AFFILIATED

BOYD OF DUNCANSBY, LORD

BOYD OF DUNCANSBY (Life Baron), Colin David Boyd; cr 2006. Born 7 June 1953; Son of Dr David Boyd and Bette Boyd, née Mutch; Married Fiona McLeod 1979 (2 sons 1 daughter).

Education: Wick High School; George Watson's College, Edinburgh; Manchester University (BA Econ 1974); Edinburgh University (LLB 1976).

Non-political career: Solicitor 1978-82, 2007-12; Advocate, Scotland 1983-2007; Legal associate, Royal Town Planning Institute 1990; Advocate depute 1993-95; QC (Scotland) 1995; Scottish Executive: Solicitor General for Scotland 1997-2000, Lord Advocate for Scotland 2000-06; Commissioner, Northern Lighthouse Board 1997-2006; Consultant and head of public law, Dundas & Wilson CS LLP 2007-12; Honorary Professor of Law, Glasgow University 2007-12; Senator of the College of Justice in Scotland 2012-.

Political career: *House of Lords:* Raised to the peerage as Baron Boyd of Duncansby, of Duncansby in Caithness 2006. As a senior member of the judiciary, disqualified from participation 2012-. Member: Delegated Powers and Regulatory Reform 2007-10, EU

Sub-committee E (Justice and Institutions) 2010-12. *Other:* Member, Commission on Scottish Devolution 2008-09; Vice-president, Investigatory Powers Tribunal 2019-.

Political interests: Constitutional affairs, criminal justice, planning and built environment.

Other: Fellow: Legal Associate Royal Town Planning Institute; Writer to the Signet; PC 2000.
Recreations: Watching rugby, reading, walking.

Rt Hon the Lord Boyd of Duncansby QC, House of Lords, London SW1A 0PW
Tel: 020 7219 5353

CONSERVATIVE

BRABAZON OF TARA, LORD

BRABAZON OF TARA (3rd Baron, UK), Ivon Anthony Moore-Brabazon; cr. 1942. Born 20 December 1946; Son of 2nd Baron, CBE; Married Harriet Frances de Courcy Hamilton 1979 (1 son 1 daughter).

Education: Harrow School.

Non-political career: Member, Stock Exchange 1972-84.

Political career: *House of Lords:* First entered House of Lords 1977; Government Whip 1984-86; Government Spokesperson for: Transport 1984-85, Trade and Industry, Treasury and Energy 1985-86; Parliamentary Under-Secretary of State, Department of Transport 1986-89; Minister of State: Foreign and Commonwealth Office 1989-90, Department of Transport 1990-92; Opposition Spokesperson for Transport 1998-2000; Elected hereditary peer 1999-; Principal Deputy Chairman of Committees 2001-02; Chairman of Committees 2002-12; Deputy Speaker 2002-12. House of Lords' Offices/House: Member 2001-03, 2006-12, Chair 2003-06; Procedure: Member 2001-03, 2010-11, 2015-19, Chair 2003-10, 2011-12; Chair: European Union 2001-02, Hybrid Instruments 2003-12, Liaison 2003-12, Personal Bills 2003-09, Privileges/Privileges and Conduct 2003-12, Selection 2003-12, Standing Orders (Private Bills) 2003-12, 2013, Administration and Works 2003-10, 2011-12, Refreshment 2008-12, Sub-committee on Leave of Absence 2011-12, Joint Committee on Parliamentary Privilege 2013, Hybrid Instruments 2013-14; Member: Affordable Childcare 2014-15, High Speed Rail (London-West Midlands) Bill 2016, Middle Level Bill 2018, Joint Committee on the Draft Parliamentary Buildings (Restoration and Renewal) Bill 2018-19, Joint Committee on Human Rights 2019-, High Speed Rail (West Midlands-Crewe) Bill 2020-. *Other:* DL, Isle of Wight 1993-.

Political interests: Transport; Switzerland.

Other: President, United Kingdom Warehousing Association 1992-2018; Deputy Chair, Foundation for Sport and the Arts 1992-2012; Shipwrecked Mariners' Society: Council member 1993-2011, Vice-President 2011-; President, Natural Gas Vehicles Association 1995-97; Institute of the Motor Industry: Deputy President 1997-98, Fellow 1997-, President 1998-2004, Vice-President 2008-; President, British International Freight Association 1997-98; Shipwrecked Mariners' Society; PC 2013. Royal Yacht Squadron (Cowes) Club.

Recreations: Sailing, golf.

Rt Hon the Lord Brabazon of Tara DL, House of Lords, London SW1A 0PW
Tel: 020 7219 6796 *Email:* brabazoni@parliament.uk

LABOUR

BRADLEY, LORD

BRADLEY (Life Baron), Keith John Charles Bradley; cr 2006. Born 17 May 1950; Son of late John Bradley and late Mrs Beatrice Harris; Married Rhona Graham 1987 (2 sons 1 daughter).

Education: Bishop Vesey's Grammar School, Sutton Coldfield; Manchester Polytechnic (BA social science 1976); York University (MPhil social policy 1978).

Non-political career: Charles Impey and Co, chartered accountants 1969-73; Research Officer, Manchester City Council Housing Department 1978-81; Secretary, Stockport Community Health Council 1981-87; Manchester University: Special Adviser to President and Vice-chancellor 2005-10, 2013-, Associate Vice-president 2010-13. Member, Unite.

Political career: *House of Commons:* MP (Labour) for Manchester Withington 1987-2005; Opposition Spokesperson for: Social Security 1991-96, Transport 1996-97; Parliamentary Under-Secretary of State, Department of Social Security 1997-98; Deputy Chief Whip 1998-2001; Minister of State, Home Office 2001-02. *House of Lords:* Raised to the peerage as Baron Bradley, of Withington in the County of Greater Manchester 2006. Opposition Spokesperson for: Health 2013-15, Work and Pensions 2013-15. Member: House 2007-10, Long-Term Sustainability of the NHS 2016-17, Liaison 2019-. *Other:* Member: Co-operative Party, Labour Party. Manchester City Council: Councillor 1983-88, Chair, Environment and Consumer Services Committee 1984-88; City Council Director: Manchester Ship Canal Co 1984-87, Manchester Airport plc 1984-87; Non-executive Chair, Manchester, Salford and Trafford Lift Company 2007-; Council Member, Medical Protection Society 2007-15; Non-executive Chair: Christie Hospital NHS Foundation Trust 2011-14, Bury Tameside and Glossop Lit Company 2014-; Non-executive Director, Pennine Care NHS Foundation Trust 2015-18.

Political interests: Local and regional government, housing, health, pensions, poverty, sport; China, France, USA.

Other: Trustee: Centre for Mental Health 2011-, Prison Reform Trust 2011-; Pro-Chancellor, Salford University; PC 2001.

Publications: The Bradley Report [a review of people with mental health problems or learning disabilities in the criminal justice system] (Department of Health, 2009).

Recreations: All sports, theatre, cinema.

Rt Hon the Lord Bradley, House of Lords, London SW1A 0PW
Tel: 020 7219 4207 *Email:* bradleykj@parliament.uk
Tel: 0161-275 3963 *Email:* keith.bradley@manchester.ac.uk

LIBERAL DEMOCRAT

BRADSHAW, LORD

BRADSHAW (Life Baron), William Peter Bradshaw; cr. 1999. Born 9 September 1936; Son of late Leonard Bradshaw and Ivy Bradshaw; Married Jill Hayward 1957 (died 2002) (1 son 1 daughter); married Diana Ayris 2003.

Education: Slough Grammar School; Reading University (BA political economy 1957, MA 1960); Little French.

Non-political career: British Railways/Rail 1959-85: Management trainee, Western Region 1959-62, Various appointments, London and West of England Division 1962-73, Divisional manager, Liverpool 1973-75, Chief operating manager, London Midland (LM) Region, Crewe 1976, Deputy general manager, LM Region 1977, Chief operations manager, BR Headquarters 1978-80, Director, Policy Unit 1980-83, General manager, Western Region 1983-85, Professor of transport management, Salford University 1986-92; Chair, Ulsterbus and Citybus Ltd Belfast 1987-93; Special adviser to Transport Select Committee 1992-97. National Service 1957-59. Transport Salaried Staffs Association 1961-77.

Political career: *House of Lords:* Raised to the peerage as Baron Bradshaw, of Wallingford in the County of Oxfordshire 1999. Liberal Democrat Spokesperson for: Transport 2001-15 (and Industry Contact 2015). Co-opted Member, EU Sub-committee B (Internal Market) 2007-10; Member, EU Sub-committee B (Internal Market, Energy and Transport) 2010-12. Chair, Liberal Democrat Parliamentary Party Committee on Transport 2010-15. *Other:* Councillor, Oxfordshire County Council 1993-2008, Thames Valley Police Authority: Member 1993-95, 1997-2008, Vice-chair 1999-2003; Member: Commission for Integrated Transport -2001, British Railways Board (Shadow Strategic Rail Authority) 1999-2001.

Political interests: Transport, environment, planning, police.

Other: President, Friends of the Ridgeway; National Trust, Salvation Army; Honorary Fellow, Wolfson College, Oxford. National Liberal Club.

Publications: Many chapters and articles on transport issues.

Recreations: Growing hardy perennial plants.

Professor the Lord Bradshaw, House of Lords, London SW1A 0PW
Tel: 020 7219 8621 *Email:* bradshaww@parliament.uk
Priory Garden, 14a Wood Street, Wallingford, Oxon OX10 0BD *Tel:* 01491 839142
Email: billbradshaw@btinternet.com

CONSERVATIVE

BRADY, BARONESS

BRADY (Life Baroness), Karren Rita Brady; cr 2014. Born 4 April 1969; Daughter of Terry and Rita Brady; Married Paul Peschisolido 1995 (1 daughter 1 son).

Non-political career: Saatchi & Saatch 1987-88; Sales executive, London Broadcasting Company 1988-89; Sport Newspapers Ltd 1989-1993; Managing director, Birmingham Football Club 1993-2010; Vice-chair, West Ham Football Club 2010-; Management consultant, Syco Entertainment; Appears on BBC The Apprentice TV show; Non-executive chair, Taveta Investments Ltd 2017-19; Director, BKB Media Ltd.

Political career: *House of Lords:* Raised to the peerage as Baroness Brady, of Knightsbridge in the City of Westminster 2014. Member, National Plan for Sport and Recreation 2020-. *Other:* Small business ambassador, Conservative Party. Member, women and sport advisory board, Department for Culture, Media and Sport.

Other: Board member: Mothercare plc, Channel 4 Television, Sport England, Britain Stronger in Europe 2015-16; Stroke Association, Wellchild, Teenage Cancer Trust; Hon. doctorate (business), Birmingham University; Business Woman of the Year; Cosmopolitan Woman of the Year; Spirit of Everywoman Award; Britain's Most Influential Woman Award; CBE 2013.

Publications: Playing to Win: 10 Steps to Achieving Your Goals (2004); Strong Woman: The Truth About Getting To The Top (2013).

Recreations: Football, family.

The Baroness Brady CBE, House of Lords, London SW1A 0PW
Tel: 020 7219 5353
West Ham United Football Club, London Stadium, Queen Elizabeth Olympic Park, London E20 2ST *Email:* pa@karrenbrady.com Website: www.karrenbrady.com *Twitter:* @karren_brady

LABOUR

BRAGG, LORD

BRAGG (Life Baron), Melvyn Bragg; cr. 1998. Born 6 October 1939; Son of Stanley and Mary Bragg; Married Marie-Elisabeth Roche 1961 (died 1971) (1 daughter); married Catherine Haste 1973 (divorced 2018) (1 son 1 daughter); married Gabriel Clare-Hunt 2019.

Education: Nelson-Thomlinson Grammar School, Wigton; Wadham College, Oxford (BA modern history 1961, MA); French.

Non-political career: BBC radio and TV producer 1961-67; Novelist 1964-; Writer and Broadcaster 1967-; Television Presenter and Editor 1973-; Radio Presenter 1988-; London Weekend Television: Controller of Arts 1990-2010, Head of Arts 1982-90; Border Television: Chair 1990-95, Deputy Chair 1985-90; Director, Directors Cut Productions Ltd 2010-.

Political career: *House of Lords:* Raised to the peerage as Baron Bragg, of Wigton in the County of Cumbria 1998. Member, Communications 2010-13. *Other:* Governor, London School of Economics 1997; DL, Cumbria 2003.

Political interests: Broadcasting, universities, the arts, countryside; France, North of England, USA.

Other: Chair, Literature Panel of Arts Council 1977-80; President: Mind 1996-2011, Cumbrians for Peace 1982-86, Northern Arts 1983-87, National Campaign for the Arts 1986-2005; Chair, RNIB Talking Books Appeal 2000-05; BAFTA; MIND, RNIB, St. Mungo's; Chancellor, Leeds University 1999-2017; Fellow: Royal Society of Literature, Royal Television Society, Royal Society, British Academy, BAFTA; Twelve honorary doctorates; Four honorary fellowships; Royal Television Society Gold Medal; John Llewllyn-Rhys Memorial Award for *Without a City Wall*; PEN Awards for Fiction for *The Hired Man*; Outstanding Contribution to Television, Richard Dimbleby award 1987; Best Musical (*The Hired Man*), Ivor Novello award 1985; Numerous prizes for *The South Bank Show* including four Prix Italias; Television and Radio Industries Club (TRIC) award: Radio Programme of the Year for *Start the Week* 1990, Radio Personality of the Year for *Start the Week* 1991; WHS Literary award for *The Soldier's Return*; Viewers and Listeners Broadcaster of the Year 2007-08; Bafta Fellowship 2010; Media Brief Award 2010; Outstanding Achievement South Bank Show Awards 2010;

Sandford St. Martin Personal Award 2014; Parliamentarian Book Award for Now Is The Time 2016; CH 2018. The Garrick Club, Chelsea Arts Club.

Publications: For Want of a Nail (1965); The Second Inheritance (1966); Without a City Wall (1968); The Hired Man (1969); A Place in England (1970); The Nerve (1971); Josh Lawton (1972); The Silken Net (1974); A Christmas Child (1976); Speak for England (1976); Mardi Gras (musical 1976); Orion (TV play 1977); Autumn Manoeuvres (1978); Kingdom Come (1980); Love and Glory (1983); Land of the Lakes (1983); Laurence Olivier (1984); The Hired Man (musical 1984); The Maid of Buttermere (1987); Rich: The Life of Richard Burton (1988); A Time to Dance (1990); Crystal Rooms (1992); King Lear in New York (play 1992); The Seventh Seal: a study of Ingmar Bergman (1993); Credo (1996); On Giants' Shoulders (1998); The Soldier's Return (1999); A Son of War (2001); Crossing the Lines (2003); The Adventure of English (2003); 12 Books that Changed the World (2006); Remember Me (2008); In Our Time (2009); Final Cut: The South Bank Show (2010); The Book of Books: The Radical Impact of the King James Bible 1611-2011 (Hodder & Stoughton, 2011); Grace and Mary (2012); Now Is The Time (2016); William Tyndale: A Very Brief History (2017); In Our Time (2018); Love Without End (2019); Screenplays: Isadora, Jesus Christ Superstar, Clouds of Glory.

Recreations: Walking, books.

The Lord Bragg CH, House of Lords, London SW1A 0PW
Tel: 020 7219 8741
12 Hampstead Hill Gardens, London WW3 2PL *Tel:* 07979 966675
Email: melvyn.bragg@dcptv.co.uk

NON-AFFILIATED

BRENNAN, LORD

BRENNAN (Life Baron), Daniel Joseph Brennan; cr. 2000. Born 19 March 1942; Son of late Daniel and Mary Brennan; Married Pilar Sanchez 1968 (4 sons).

Education: St Bede's Grammar School, Bradford; Manchester University (LLB 1964).

Non-political career: Called to the Bar, Gray's Inn 1967 (Bencher 1993); Crown Court Recorder 1982-; QC 1985; Member, Criminal Injuries Compensation Board 1989-97; Deputy High Court Judge 1994-; Chair, General Council of the Bar 1999; Independent assessor to Home Office on Miscarriages of Justice 2001-.

Political career: *House of Lords:* Raised to the peerage as Baron Brennan, of Bibury in the Country of Gloucestershire 2000. Member: Constitution 2014-17, Joint Committee on the National Security Strategy 2017-. *Other:* Left Labour February 2020, now sits as non-affiliated.

Other: Councillor, International Bar Association; President: Catholic Union of Great Britain 2001-, Consortium for Street Children; FRSA; Two honorary doctorates; QC 1985; Cruz de Honor of the Order of St Raimond de Penafort (Spain) 2000. Garrick Club.

Publications: General editor, Bullen and Leake on Pleadings (2003).

The Lord Brennan QC, House of Lords, London SW1A 0PW
Tel: 020 7219 5353
Matrix Chambers, Griffin Building, Gray's Inn, London WC1R 5LN *Tel:* 020 7404 3447
Email: danbrennan@matrixlaw.co.uk

CONSERVATIVE

BRIDGEMAN, VISCOUNT

BRIDGEMAN (3rd Viscount, UK), Robin John Orlando Bridgeman; cr. 1929. Born 5 December 1930; Son of late Brigadier Hon. Geoffrey Bridgeman, MC, FRCS, second son of 1st Viscount; Married Victoria Turton (CBE 2014) 1966 (3 sons 1 son deceased).

Education: Eton College.

Non-political career: Partner, Henderson Crosthwaite and Co., Stockbrokers 1973-86; Director: The Bridgeman Art Library Limited 1972-, Guinness Mahon and Co. Ltd 1988-90, Nestor-BNA plc 1988-2000. 2nd Lieutenant, The Rifle Brigade 1950-51.

Political career: *House of Lords:* First entered House of Lords 1982; Opposition Whip 1998-2010; Elected hereditary peer 1999-; Opposition Spokesperson for: Home Affairs 2001-10, Northern Ireland 2001-07, 2009-10. Member: Information 2010-11, EU Sub-committees: G (Social Policies and Consumer Protection) 2011-12, F (Home Affairs, Health and Education) 2012-15, Joint Committee on Consolidation, &c, Bills 2015-. *Other:* Reed's School: Chair of Governors 1994-2002, Joint life president 2002-.

Political interests: Health, social services, environment, home affairs, local government.

Other: Member, British-Irish Parliamentary Assembly; Chairman, Friends of Lambeth Palace Library 1992-2008; Special Trustee, Hammersmith and Queen Charlotte's Hospital Authority 1992-2000; Trustee, Music at Winchester 1995-2006; Treasurer: Florence Nightingale Aid in Sickness Trust 1995-2006, New England Company 1996-2006; Chairman: Hospital of St John and St Elizabeth 1999-2007, CORESS 2006-12; Trustee, Parliament Choir 2011-; MCC; Sovereign Military Order of Malta, Knight, 1995. Beefsteak, Pitt Club.

Recreations: Gardening, music, shooting.

The Viscount Bridgeman, House of Lords, London SW1A 0PW
Tel: 020 7219 3000 *Email:* bridgemanr@parliament.uk

CONSERVATIVE

BRIDGES OF HEADLEY, LORD

Chair, Economic Affairs Finance Bill Sub-committee

BRIDGES OF HEADLEY (Life Baron), James George Robert Bridges; cr 2015. Born 15 July 1970; Married Alice Hickman (1 son 2 daughters).

Education: Eton College; Exeter College, Oxford (modern history); University of Pennsylvania (government administration).

Non-political career: Director of Communications, British Digital Broadcasting 1997-98; Lead writer, *The Times* 1998-2000; Quiller Consultants: Consultant 2000-04, 2007-09, Chief Executive 2010-13; Senior Adviser to: UK Chief Executive, Santander 2014-15, Group Executive Chairman, Banco Santander SA 2017-.

Political career: *House of Lords:* Raised to the peerage as Baron Bridges of Headley, of Headley Heath in the County of Surrey 2015. Parliamentary Secretary and Government Spokesperson, Cabinet Office 2015-16; Parliamentary Under-Secretary of State and Government Spokesperson, Department for Exiting the European Union 2016-17. Economic Affairs Finance Bill Sub-committee: Member 2019-20, Chair 2020-. *Other:* Assistant Political Secretary to the Prime Minister 1994-97; Chair, Conservative Research Department 2004-05; Campaign Director, Conservative Party 2006-07.

Other: Freedom, City of London; MBE 1997.

The Lord Bridges of Headley MBE, House of Lords, London SW1A 0PW
Tel: 020 7219 3000 *Email:* bridgesg@parliament.uk

LIBERAL DEMOCRAT

BRINTON, BARONESS

Liberal Democrat Lords Spokesperson for Health

BRINTON (Life Baroness), Sarah (Sal) Virginia Brinton; cr 2011. Born 1 April 1955; Daughter of late Tim Brinton (MP 1979-87) and late Jane-Mari Shearing, née Coningham; Married Tim Whittaker 1983 (2 sons 1 daughter 2 wards – 1 male 1 female).

Education: Benenden, Cranbrook; Central School of Speech and Drama (1973); London College of Secretaries (1974); Churchill College, Cambridge (BA 1984, MA); Conversational French.

Non-political career: Floor manager, BBC radio and television 1974-81; Venture capitalist 1984-90; Bursar: Lucy Cavendish College, Cambridge 1992-97, Selwyn College, Cambridge 1997-2002; Consultant, IDeA 2003-06; Director, Association of Universities in the East of England 2006-11.

Political career: *House of Commons:* Contested (Liberal Democrat) Cambridgeshire South East 1997 and 2001 and Watford 2005 and 2010 general elections. *House of Lords:* Raised to the peerage as Baroness Brinton, of Kenardington in the County of Kent 2011. Liberal Democrat Lords Spokesperson for: Social Care 2017-19, Health 2020-. Member, Equality Act 2010 and Disability 2015-16. *Other:* Liberal Democrat Party: Education and Higher Education Working Group 1993-97, Federal Conference Committee: Member 2004-08, Vice-chair 2010-; Federal Policy Committee: Member 2004-08, 2010-, Vice-chair 2006-08; Schools Working Group 2008-, Member, Manifesto Working Group 2013-15, Chair, Diversity Engagement Group 2011-14, President 2015-19, Joint Interim Leader 2019-20. Cambridgeshire County Council 1993-2004: Councillor 1993-2004, Education portfolio holder 1993-97, Leader, Liberal Democrat group 1997-2004; East of England Development Agency: Board Member 1999-2004, Deputy Chair 2002-04; Chair, Cambridgeshire Learning and Skills Council 2000-06; Vice-President, Local Government Association 2018-.

Political interests: Education, including further and higher education and skills, health and social care, economic development, disability; France, Palestine.

Other: St Johns Innovation Centre, Cambridge 1992-2010; Director and trustee, Christian Blind Mission 2003-13; Director: UFI Charitable Trust 2003-, East of England International 2006-11; Trustee, Unicef UK 2013-; Director, Joseph Rowntree Reform Trust 2013-; Member: Institute of Directors, RSA; Fellow, Birkbeck College 2013; Honorary Doctorate Anglia Ruskin University (for services to education and skills) 2003; East Anglian Entrepreneurial Businesswoman of the Year 1997.

Recreations: Theatre, football, cooking, swimming.

The Baroness Brinton, House of Lords, London SW1A 0PW
Tel: 020 7219 3234 *Email:* brintons@parliament.uk
Liberal Democrats, 8-10 Great George Street, London SW1P 3AE
Email: president@libdems.org.uk *Twitter:* @SalBrinton

NON-AFFILIATED

BRISTOL, LORD BISHOP OF

BRISTOL (56th Bishop of), Vivienne Frances Faull. Born 20 May 1955; Married Michael Duddridge.

Education: The Queen's School, Chester; Saint Hilda's College, Oxford (BA modern history 1974, MA 1979); Saint John's College, Nottingham (1981); Nottingham University (BA theology 1981); Open University (MBA 1983).

Non-political career: Teacher, Church Mission Society, North India 1977-79; Youth work, Shrewsbury House, Everton 1979; Deaconess, Saint Matthew and Saint James, Mossley Hill, Diocese of Liverpool 1982-85; Chaplain, later Fellow, Clare College, Cambridge 1985-90; Deacon, Diocese of Ely 1987; Chaplain, Gloucester Cathedral 1990-94; Ordained priest 1994; Coventry Cathedral: Canon Pastor 1994-2000, Vice Provost 1995-2000; Provost, then Dean of Leicester 2000-12; Dean of York 2012-18; Bishop of Bristol 2018-.

Political career: *House of Lords:* Entered House of Lords 2018.

Political interests: Human trafficking.

Other: Member, General Synod 2003-12, 2018-; Chair, Association of English Cathedrals 2009-15; Member, English Anglican Roman Catholic Committee for Ecumenical Conversations 2007-17; Chair, Deans' Conference 2015-17 House of Bishops 2013-; Honorary Fellow, Clare College Cambridge; DPhil Gloucester University 2014; DLit Chester University 2015; DUniv York University 2015.

Rt Rev the Lord Bishop of Bristol, House of Lords, London SW1A 0PW
Bishop of Bristol's Office, Church Lane, Winterbourne, Bristol BS36 1SG *Tel:* 01454 777728
Email: bishop.bristol@bristoldiocese.org Website: www.bristol.anglican.org
Twitter: @Bishopviv1

CROSSBENCH

BROERS, LORD

BROERS (Life Baron), Alec Nigel Broers; cr. 2004. Born 17 September 1938; Son of late Alec Broers and Constance Broers, née Cox; Married Marie Phelan 1964 (2 sons).

Education: Geelong Church of England Grammar School, Australia; Melbourne University, Australia (BSc physics 1959, electronics 1960); Gonville and Caius College, Cambridge (BA mechanical sciences 1962; PhD electrical engineering 1965; ScD 1991).

Non-political career: IBM 1965-84: Research staff, TJ Watson Research Center 1965-81, Manager: Photon and electron optics 1977-81, Advanced development East Fishkill Laboratory 1982-84, Member, corporate technical committee, corporate headquarters 1984; Cambridge University: Professor of electrical engineering 1984-96, Professor emeritus 1996-, Fellow, Trinity College 1985-90, Churchill College: Fellow 1990-, Master 1990-96, Vice-chancellor 1996-2003.

Political career: *House of Lords:* Raised to the peerage as Baron Broers, of Cambridge in the County of Cambridgeshire 2004. Chair, Science and Technology 2004-07; Member, Science and Technology Sub-committees: II (Energy Efficiency) 2004-08, I (Scientific Aspects of Ageing) 2005-07; Co-opted Member, Science and Technology Sub-committee II (Genomic Medicine) 2008-09; Member, Science and Technology 2009-13; Chair, Science and Technology Sub-committee I (Radioactive Waste Management: a further update) 2010; Member, Science and Technology Sub-committee I 2012-13. *Other:* President, Royal Academy of Engineering 2001-06; Member: Board of Trustees, American University of Shaijah, Singapore, One-North Resource Advisory Board, AIST (Japanese Instutite of Advanced Industrial Science and technology); Chair, Board of Diamond Light Source.

Political interests: Energy, industry, education; Australia, USA.

Other: Trustee: British Museum, Needham Research Institute; Foreign associate, US National Academy of Engineering; Foreign member: Chinese Academy of Engineering, American Philosophical Society; Honorary Fellow, Australian Academy of Technological Sciences and Engineering; FIEE 1984; FREng 1985; FRS 1986; FIME; FInstP; FMedSci 2004; Numerous honorary doctorates and fellowships; American Institute of Physics Prize for Industrial Applications of Physics 1981; IEEE Cledo Brunetti Award 1985; Prince Philip Medal of Royal Academy of Engineering 2001; Kt 1998. Athenæum Club.

Publications: Numerous papers and book chapters on electron microscopy, micro-electronics and nanotechnology; Reith Lectures – Triumph of Technology (Cambridge University Press, 2005).

Recreations: Sailing, skiing, listening to music.

Professor the Lord Broers, House of Lords, London SW1A 0PW
Tel: 020 7219 5353
Email: anb1000@cam.ac.uk

LABOUR

BROOKE OF ALVERTHORPE, LORD

BROOKE OF ALVERTHORPE (Life Baron), Clive Brooke; cr. 1997. Born 21 June 1942; Son of John and Mary Brooke; Married Lorna Roberts 1967.

Education: Thornes House School, Wakefield.

Non-political career: Inland Revenue Staff Federation: Assistant Secretary 1964-82, Deputy General Secretary 1982-88, General Secretary 1988-95; Joint General Secretary, Public Services Tax and Commerce Union 1996-98; Member, TUC: General Council 1989-96, Executive Committee 1993-96; Senior strategic adviser, Accenture plc 1997-2010; Self-employed consultant 1997-2010. Member, Public and Commercial Services Union.

Political career: *House of Lords:* Raised to the peerage as Baron Brooke of Alverthorpe, of Alverthorpe in the County of West Yorkshire 1997. Chair, European Communities Sub-committee B (Energy, Industry and Transport) 1999-2002; Member, Information 2005-09, 2015-16; EU Sub-committee D (Environment and Agriculture): Member 2007, Co-opted member 2008-10; Member: Crossrail Bill 2008, EU Sub-committee B: (Internal Market, Energy and Transport) 2010-12, (Internal Market, Infrastructure and Employment) 2012-15, Licensing Act 2003 2016-17. Vice-chair, PLP Departmental Groups for: Cabinet Office 1998-2010, Home Affairs 2010, Transport 2010-15. *Other:* Member: House of Commons

Speaker's Commission on Citizenship 1988, Council of Churches for Britain and Ireland Enquiry into Unemployment and the Future of Work 1995-97, Pensions Compensation Board 1996-2005; Government Partner Director, NATS Limited 2001-06.

Political interests: Public health and wellbeing, particularly related to alcohol and sugar abuse; Sweden.

Other: Member: Inter-Parliamentary Union, Commonwealth Parliamentary Association; Trustee: Community Service Volunteers 1989-2008, Duke of Edinburgh's Study Conference 1993-2007; Institute for Public Policy Research: Trustee 1997-2010, Policy advisory council 2010-; Member, Fabian Society; Patron, Sparrow Foundation 2002-; Trustee, Action on Addiction 2002-13; Patron: Kenward Trust 2008-, Everyman Project 2010-, British Liver Trust 2013-; Cancer Research UK, Royal Marsden Hospital, Trinity Hospice Clapham, Sparrow Foundation, Woodland Trust; FRSA.

Recreations: Spiritual pursuits, meditation, painting, association football, Chelsea FC.

The Lord Brooke of Alverthorpe, House of Lords, London SW1A 0PW
Tel: 020 7219 0478 *Email:* brookec@parliament.uk

CROSSBENCH

BROOKEBOROUGH, VISCOUNT

BROOKEBOROUGH (3rd Viscount, UK), Alan Henry Brooke; cr. 1952; 7th Bt of Colebrooke (UK) 1822. Born 30 June 1952; Son of 2nd Viscount, PC; Married Janet Cooke 1980.

Education: Harrow School; Millfield School, Somerset; Royal Agricultural College, Cirencester 1978.

Non-political career: Owner, Colebrooke Park 1973-; Non-executive director: Green Park Healthcare Trust 1993-2001, Basel International (Jersey) 1997-2010; Personal Lord in Waiting to HM The Queen 1997-. Commission, 17th/21st Lancers 1971; Ulster Defence Regiment 1977, Royal Irish Regiment 1992; Lieutenant-Colonel 1993; Hon. Colonel, 4th/5th Battalion, Royal Irish Rangers 1997-2008.

Political career: *House of Lords:* First entered House of Lords 1987; Elected hereditary peer 1999-. Member: EU Sub-committee D 1988-92, 1993-97, European Communities 1998-2002, Procedure 2003-05; Co-opted member, EU Sub-committee D (Environment and Agriculture) 2006-10; Member: EU Sub-committee A (Economic and Financial Affairs) 2012-15, Financial Exclusion 2016-17. *Other:* County Fermanagh: DL 1987-2012, High Sheriff 1995, Lord Lieutenant 2012-; Board member, Northern Ireland Policing Board 2000-04.

Political interests: Northern Ireland, agriculture, tourism, defence, health; Europe, UK.

Other: Vice-President, Somme Association 1990-; President, Army Benevolent Fund, Northern Ireland 1995-; Fellow, Industry and Parliament Trust 1999; Member, Duke of Edinburgh Award Advisory Council, Northern Ireland; President, Northern Ireland Outward Bound Association; Trustee, Winston Churchill Memorial Trust 2013-; Military, cancer and disabled charities; KG 2018. Cavalry and Guards, Pratt's, Farmers' Club.

Recreations: Shooting, fishing, gardening, sailing.

The Viscount Brookeborough KG, House of Lords, London SW1A 0PW
Tel: 020 7219 1668
Colebrooke Park, Brookeborough, Enniskillen BT94 4DW *Tel:* 028 8953 1402
Email: ahb@colebrooke.info Website: www.colebrooke.info

CONSERVATIVE

BROUGHAM AND VAUX, LORD

BROUGHAM AND VAUX (5th Baron, UK), Michael John Brougham; cr. 1860. Born 2 August 1938; Son of 4th Baron; Married Olivia Gray 1963 (divorced 1967, died 1986) (1 daughter); married Catherine Gulliver 1969 (divorced 1981) (1 son).

Education: Lycée Jaccard, Lausanne, Switzerland; Millfield School, Somerset; Northampton Institute of Agriculture.

Political career: *House of Lords:* First entered House of Lords 1968; Deputy Chair of Committees 1993-97, 1997-; Deputy Speaker 1995-; Elected hereditary peer 1999-. Member: Statutory Instruments Joint Committee 2001-07, Information 2003-07, Standing Orders (Private Bills) 2003-06, Refreshment 2007-12, Administration and Works 2009-14. *Other:* Vice-chair Association of Conservative Peers 1998-2002, 2003-10.

Political interests: Road safety, transport, motor industry, aviation; France, Spain.

Other: Royal Society for the Prevention of Accidents: President 1986-89, Vice-President 1999-; Chair, Tax Payers' Society 1989-91; Fellow, Industry and Parliament Trust 1990, 1993; Chair, European Secure Vehicle Alliance 1992-2015; President, National Health Safety Groups Council/Safety Groups UK 1994-; Honorary Vice-President, Institute of Occupational Safety and Health 2008-; CBE 1995.

Recreations: Photography, bridge, shooting.

The Lord Brougham and Vaux CBE, House of Lords, London SW1A 0PW
Tel: 020 7219 5353 *Fax:* 020 7219 5979 *Email:* broughamm@parliament.uk

CROSSBENCH

BROWN OF CAMBRIDGE, BARONESS

BROWN OF CAMBRIDGE (Life Baroness), Julia Elizabeth King; cr 2015. Born 11 July 1954; Daughter of Jane King and Derrick King; Married Dr Colin Brown 1984.

Education: Godolphin and Latymer Girls' School, London; New Hall, Cambridge (BA natural sciences (metallurgy) 1975; MA 1978; PhD 1979); French.

Non-political career: Rolls-Royce Research Fellow, Girton College, Cambridge 1978-80; Lecturer, Nottingham University 1980-87; Cambridge University: British Gas/Fellowship of Engineering Senior Research Fellow 1987-92, University Lecturer, Department of Materials Science and Metallurgy 1992-94; Fellow, Churchill College, Cambridge 1987-94; Rolls-Royce plc 1994-2002: Head of Materials, Director of Advanced Engineering, Rolls-Royce Industrial Power Group, Managing Director, Rolls-Royce Fan Systems; Director, Engineering and Technology, Rolls-Royce Marine Business 2002-02; Chief Executive, Institute of Physics 2002-04; Principal, Engineering Faculty, Imperial College London 2004-06; Vice-Chancellor, Aston University 2006-16.

Political career: *House of Lords:* Raised to the peerage as Baroness Brown of Cambridge, of Cambridge in the County of Cambridgeshire 2015. Member: European Union 2016-, EU External Affairs Sub-committee 2016-19, EU Environment Sub-committee 2020-. *Other:* Non-executive director, Department of Business, Innovation and Skills 2009-13; Chair, Defence Scientific Advisory Council 2003-07; Member, National Security Forum 2009-10; Board member, Technology Strategy Board 2004-09; Committee on Climate Change: Member 2008-, Deputy Chair 2015-21, Chair, Adaptation Sub-Committee 2017-; Review Chair, King Review of Decarbonising Road Transport 2006; UK Low Carbon Business Ambassador 2009-19; Member: Browne Review of HE Funding 2009–10, Stern Review of the Research Excellence Framework 2015-16, UK Airports Commission 2012-15, Science and Technology Honours Committee 2012-18, Innovate UK Council 2018-; Non-executive Director, UK Green Investment Bank 2012-17; Offshore Wind Sector Deal Champion 2018-; Member, Defence Innovation Advisory Board 2018-.

Political interests: Science and engineering issues, energy, transport, climate change, science education, higher education, diversity; China, Europe, India, Vietnam.

Other: World Economic Forum Automotive Council 2008-12; World Economic Forum Global Agenda Council on Decarbonizing Energy 2014-17; Trustee: Rolls-Royce Pension Fund 1997-2000, Institute of Physics Pension Fund 2002-04; Non-executive director: Birmingham Technology Limited (Innovation Birmingham) 2007-16, Higher Education Statistics Agency 2007-11; Member, Governing Board, European Institute of Innovation and Technology (EIT)

2008-12; Trustee, Forum for the Future 2011-13; Non-executive director: UniversitiesUK 2011-15, Angel Trains 2012-15, National Centre for Universities and Business 2013-15, Cumberland Lodge 2013-15; Non-executive director, Marketing Birmingham 2015-16; Chair: Henry Royce Institute for Advanced Materials, Manchester University 2015-, STEM Learning Ltd 2016-, Carbon Trust 2018-; Fellow: Institute of Materials, Mining and Metallurgy, Institute of Physics; Member, Women's Engineering Society; Oxfam, Murray Edwards College Cambridge, Aston University, RSPB, WWF; Liveryman, Goldsmiths' Company; Freedom, City of London 1998; Fellow: Royal Academy of Engineering FREng 1997, Royal Society of London FRS 2017; Honorary Fellow: Murray Edwards College, Cambridge, Cardiff University, Churchill College, Cambridge, Society for the Environment, British Science Association, Polymer Processing Academy India, Institute of Engineering and Technology, Institute of Materials, Minerals and Mining; Honorary DSc: Queen Mary, University of London, Manchester University, Exeter University, Brunel University, Aston University, Strathclyde University; Grunfeld Medal 1992; Bengough Medal 1995; Kelvin Medal 2001; John Collier Medal 2009; Lunar Society Medal 2011; President's Prize, Engineering Professors' Council 2012; Constance Tipper Silver Medal (International Congress on Fracture) 2013; Erna Hamburger Prize (WISH Foundation, EPFL, Switzerland) 2013; Leonardo Da Vinci Medal (European Society for Engineering Education) 2014; LowCVP Low Carbon Champion Award 'Outstanding Individual in Promoting Low Carbon Transport' 2014; CBE 1999; DBE 2012.

Publications: Over 160 papers on fatigue and fracture in structural materials and developments in aerospace and marine propulsion technology.

Recreations: Walking, growing orchids, gardening, collecting modern prints and sculpture.

Professor the Baroness Brown of Cambridge DBE, House of Lords, London SW1A 0PW
Tel: 020 7219 5463 *Email:* kingjb@parliament.uk

CROSSBENCH

BROWN OF EATON-UNDER-HEYWOOD, LORD

BROWN OF EATON-UNDER-HEYWOOD (Life Baron), Simon Denis Brown; cr. 2004. Born 9 April 1937; Son of late Denis Baer Brown and Edna Brown, née Abrahams; Married Jennifer Buddicom 1963 (2 sons 1 daughter).

Education: Stowe School, Buckinghamshire; Worcester College, Oxford (BA law 1960).

Non-political career: Barrister 1961; Recorder 1979-84; First Junior Treasury Counsel, Common Law 1979-84; Judge of the High Court of Justice Queen's Bench Division 1984-92; President, Security Service Tribunal 1989-2000; Lord Justice of Appeal 1992-2004; President, Intelligence Services Tribunal 1995-2000; Intelligence Services Commissioner 2000-06; Vice-president, Court of Appeal Civil Division 2001-03; Lord of Appeal in Ordinary 2004-09; Justice of the Supreme Court of the United Kingdom 2009-12. Army national service 1955-57.

Political career: *House of Lords:* Raised to the peerage as Baron Brown of Eaton-under-Heywood, of Eaton-under-Heywood in the County of Shropshire 2004. Lord of Appeal in Ordinary 2004-09; As Justice of the Supreme Court, disqualified from participation 2009-12. Chair, European Union Sub-committee E (Law and Institutions) 2005-07; Member: European Union 2005-07, Privileges and Conduct 2013-; Chair, Sub-committee on Lords' Conduct 2013-18; Member, Extradition Law 2014-15; Alternate member, Procedure 2015-19; Member, Conduct 2019-.

Political interests: The law and constitution.

Other: Butcher's Company; Honorary Fellow, Worcester College, Oxford 1993-; Visitor, Pembroke College, Cambridge 2010; High Steward, Oxford University 2011-12; Visitor, St Hugh's College, Oxford 2011-; Kt 1984; PC 1992. Garrick Club; Denham Golf Club; Church Stretton Golf Club.

Recreations: Golf, reading, theatre.

Rt Hon the Lord Brown of Eaton-under-Heywood, House of Lords, London SW1A 0PW
Tel: 020 7219 1639
Email: sdbrown@blueyonder.co.uk

DEMOCRATIC UNIONIST PARTY

BROWNE OF BELMONT, LORD

BROWNE OF BELMONT (Life Baron), Wallace Hamilton Browne; cr 2006. Born 29 October 1947; Son of Gerald Browne and Phyllis Hamilton Browne; Married.

Education: Campbell College, Belfast; Queen's University, Belfast (BSc zoology 1970).

Non-political career: A-level biology teacher, Rainey Endowed School, Magherafelt 1970-2000. Member, NASUWT (retirement association).

Political career: *House of Lords:* Raised to the peerage as Baron Browne of Belmont, of Belmont in the County of Antrim 2006. *Other:* Northern Ireland Assembly: MLA for East Belfast 2007-11, Chair, Committee on Procedures 2010-11. Belfast City Council: Councillor 1985-2011, Alderman 1993, Lord Mayor 2005-06; High Sheriff of Belfast 2002-.

Political interests: Education, Northern Ireland affairs, Balkan affairs; Brazil, Canada, Croatia, France, Germany, Italy, Montenegro, Serbia.

Other: Trustee, Somme Association, Northern Ireland.

Recreations: Golf, football, cricket, rugby.

The Lord Browne of Belmont, House of Lords, London SW1A 0PW
Tel: 020 7219 5353 *Fax:* 020 7219 2347 *Email:* brownew@parliament.uk

LABOUR

BROWNE OF LADYTON, LORD

BROWNE OF LADYTON (Life Baron), Desmond Henry Browne; cr 2010. Born 22 March 1952; Son of late Peter Browne, process worker, and Maureen Browne, catering manageress; Married Maura Taylor 1983 (2 sons).

Education: Saint Michael's Academy, Kilwinning; Glasgow University (LLB 1973).

Non-political career: Qualified as solicitor 1976; Solicitor, Jas Campbell & Co, WS Ross Haper & Murphy and McCluckey Browne 1976-1993; Called to Scottish Bar 1993; Advocate, Faculty of Advocates 1993-. Member, Unison.

Political career: *House of Commons:* Contested Argyll and Bute 1992 general election. MP (Labour) for Kilmarnock and Loudoun 1997-2005, for Kilmarnock and Loudon (revised boundary) 2005-10; PPS to: Donald Dewar as Secretary of State for Scotland 1998-99, Adam Ingram as Minister of State, Northern Ireland Office 2000; Parliamentary Under-Secretary of State, Northern Ireland Office 2001-03; Minister of State: Department for Work and Pensions (Work) 2003-04, Home Office (Citizenship, Immigration and Nationality) 2004-05; Chief Secretary to the Treasury 2005-06; Secretary of State for: Defence 2006-08, Scotland 2007-08; Prime Minister's Special Envoy to Sri Lanka 2009-10. Member: Northern Ireland Affairs 1997-98, Public Administration 1999-2000, Joint Committee on Human Rights 2001-09, Joint Committee on National Security Strategy 2010. *House of Lords:* Raised to the peerage as Baron Browne of Ladyton, of Ladyton in Ayrshire and Arran 2010. Opposition Spokesperson for Scotland 2011-12; On leave of absence October 2015-April 2017. Member: Partnerships (Prosecution) (Scotland) Bill 2013, Science and Technology 2019-, Risk Assessment and Risk Planning 2020-.

Political interests: Legal affairs, human rights, disability, education, Northern Ireland, constitution, international affairs; Afghanistan, Burundi, Colombia, Rwanda, South Africa.

Other: Member, Scottish Council for Civil Liberties 1976-; Council member, Law Society of Scotland 1988-92; Chair, Scottish Child Law Centre 1988-92; Fellow, Industry and Parliament Trust 2002; PC 2005.

Publications: Report for Lord MacAulay's Working Party on the Prison System (1990).

Recreations: Sports, football, tennis, swimming, reading, computing.

Rt Hon the Lord Browne of Ladyton, House of Lords, London SW1A 0PW
Tel: 020 7219 4501 *Email:* browned@parliament.uk

CROSSBENCH

BROWNE OF MADINGLEY, LORD

BROWNE OF MADINGLEY (Life Baron), Edmund John Phillip Browne; cr 2001. Born 20 February 1948.

Education: King's School, Ely; St John's College, Cambridge (BA physics 1969, MA); Stanford University, USA (MS business 1980).

Non-political career: BP plc 1966-2007: Exploration and production posts in USA, UK and Canada 1969-83, Group treasurer and chief executive, BP Finance International 1984-86, Executive vice-president and chief financial officer, BP America and chief executive officer (CEO), Standard Oil Production Company 1986-89, CEO, BP Exploration, London 1989-91, Managing director, British Petroleum Company plc 1991-95, Group chief executive 1995-2007; Numerous non-executive directorships, including Intel Corporation -2006 and Goldman Sachs -2007; Partner, Riverstone LLC 2007-15; Chair: Advisory Board, Mubadala International Oil and Gas -2014, Accenture Global Energy Board, Cuadrilla Resource Holdings Ltd -2015, Advisory Board, Stanhope Capital; Member, Deutsche Bank: Advisory Board for Climate Change -2014, Bank Europe Advisory Board -2014; Letterone Petroleum Ltd/L1 Energy Advisory Board: Former member, Chair; Advisory Group, Schlumberger Business Consulting; PCCW Group of Advisers -2016; Former adviser, Fidelity International; Chair, Huawei Technologies UK Ltd 2015-; Executive Chair, L1 Energy 2015-; Director: IHS Markit 2018-, Wintershall Dea 2019-, Windward, Pattern Energy; Member, Advisory Board: Edelman, Schillings, Afiniti, Kayrros.

Political career: *House of Lords:* Raised to the peerage as Baron Browne of Madingley, of Cambridge in the County of Cambridgeshire 2001. Lead Non-Executive Director, Cabinet Office Board 2010-15; On leave of absence March 2018-December 2019. EU Sub-committee A (Economic and Financial Affairs and International Trade): Co-opted member 2008-10, Member 2010-11. *Other:* Board of trustees, Tate Galleries: Trustee 2007-17, Chair 2009-17; Non-executive director, Cabinet Office 2010-15.

Political interests: Arts, culture, education, energy, environment.

Other: Trustee: British Museum 1995-2005, Eisenhower Fellowships, Holocaust Educational Trust; Vice-President, Prince of Wales Business Leaders Forum 1997-2007; Council member, Foundation for Science and Technology; President, British Association for Advancement of Science -2008; Chair: International Advisory Board, Blavatnik School of Government, Queen Elizabeth Prize for Enginneering Foundation, Donmar Theatre; Vice-president, Flora and Fauna International; Senior fellow, St Anthony's College, Oxford; Elder Brother, Corporation of Trinity House; President, Royal Academy of Engineering 2006-11; Chair: Independent Review of Higher Education Funding and Student Finance 2009-10, Advisory board, Judge Business School, Cambridge -2010; Emeritus chairman, Graduate School of Business, Stanford University; Fellow, American Academy of Arts and Sciences; Honorary member, School of Economics and Management, Tsinghua University, Beijing; Co-chair, International Advisory Board, Russian Museum; Chair: Queen Elizabeth Prize Foundation, John Browne Charitable Trust, Courtauld Institute 2017-, Francis Crick Institute 2017-; Member: Blavatnik School of Government Foundation, Needham Resarch Institute, Cambridge China Development Trust, Cambridge Foundation -2017, Jewish Museum and Tolerance Centre, Russia, Stanford University Knight-Hennessey Scholarships; FREng; FRS; FIMM; FInstP; FInstPet; 19 honorary doctorates from UK, western European, Russian and US universities; 9 honorary fellowships; Royal Academy of Engineering Prince Philip medal for outstanding contribution to engineering 1999; *Management Today* Most Admired CEO 1999-2002; Institute of Energy Melchett Medal 2001; Institute of Management Gold Medal 2001; Institution of Chemical Engineers Commemorative Medal 2003; British American Business Inc Channing Corporate Citizen Award 2004; World Petroleum Congress Dewhurst Award 2005; Kt 1998.

Publications: Beyond Business (2010); Seven Elements that have Changed the World (2013); The Glass Closet: Why Coming Out is Good Business (2014); Connect: How Companies Succeed by Engaging Radically with Society (2015); Make, Think, Imagine: Engineering the Future of Civilisation (2019).

Recreations: Opera, photography, pre-Columbian art, 17th- and 18th-century printed works.

The Lord Browne of Madingley, House of Lords, London SW1A 0PW
Tel: 020 7219 5353
Email: spaynter@l1energy.co.uk *Twitter:* @lordjohnbrowne

CONSERVATIVE

BROWNING, BARONESS

BROWNING (Life Baroness), Angela Frances Browning; cr 2010. Born 4 December 1946; Daughter of late Thomas Pearson and late Linda Chamberlain; Married David Browning 1968 (2 sons).

Education: Westwood Grammar School; Reading College of Technology; Bournemouth College of Technology.

Non-political career: Teacher, home economics, adult education 1968-74; Auxiliary nurse 1976-77; Self-employed consultant, manufacturing industry 1977-85; Management consultant specialising in training, corporate communications and finance 1985-94; Director, Small Business Bureau 1985-94; Chair, Women Into Business 1988-92; Member, Department of Employment Advisory Committee for Women's Employment 1989-92.

Political career: *House of Commons:* Contested Crewe and Nantwich 1987 general election. MP (Conservative) for Tiverton 1992-97, for Tiverton and Honiton 1997-2010; PPS to Michael Forsyth as Minister of State, Department of Employment 1993-94; Parliamentary Secretary, Ministry of Agriculture, Fisheries and Food 1994-97; Opposition Spokesperson on Education and Employment (Education and Disability) 1997-98; Member, Shadow Cabinet 1999-2001: Shadow Secretary of State for Trade and Industry 1999-2000, Shadow Leader of the House 2000-01. Member: Agriculture 1992-93, Modernisation of the House of Commons 2000-01, Public Accounts 2004-06, 2007-10, Standards and Privileges 2004-06. *House of Lords:* Raised to the peerage as Baroness Browning, of Whimple in the County of Devon 2010. Government Spokesperson, Home Office 2011; Minister of State for Crime Prevention and Anti-Social Behaviour Reduction, Home Office 2011. Member: Liaison 2012-15, Mental Capacity Act 2005 2013-14, The Arctic 2014-15; Procedure/Procedure and Privileges 2015-; Member: Equality Act 2010 and Disability 2015-16, Joint Committee on the Draft Investigatory Powers Bill 2015-16, European Union 2016-18, EU Home Affairs Sub-committee 2016-18, Lord Speaker's Committee on the Size of the House 2016-, Delegated Powers and Regulatory Reform 2019-. *Other:* Conservative Party: Vice-chair 2001-05, Deputy chair (organisation and campaigning) 2005-07. Government co-chair, Women's National Commission 1995-97; Electoral Commissioner 2010-12; Advisory Committee on Business Appointments: Member 2014, Chair 2015-20; Member, House of Lords Appointments Commission 2018-.

Political interests: Small businesses, education (special needs), mental health, learning disabilities.

Other: Vice-president: National Autistic Society, Institute of Sales and Marketing Management 1997-; National vice-president, Alzheimer's Society 1997-; Patron: Research Autism, Action on Elder Abuse; Fellow, Institute of Sales and Marketing Management.

Recreations: Theatre, cooking.

The Baroness Browning, House of Lords, London SW1A 0PW
Tel: 020 7219 5353

CONSERVATIVE

BROWNLOW OF SHURLOCK ROW, LORD

BROWNLOW OF SHURLOCK ROW (Life Baron), David Ellis Brownlow; cr 2019.

Education: Newcastle Polytechnic (BA economics 1986).

Non-political career: Police officer, Thames Valley Police 1+97-88; Recruitment manager: Hays Accounting and Finance 1988-92, Douglas Llambias Associates 1992-96; Co-founder: Huntswood 1996-, Havisham 2013-.

Political career: *House of Lords:* Raised to the peerage as Baron Brownlow of Shurlock Row, of Shurlock Row in the Royal County of Berkshire 2019. *Other:* Vice-chair (Campaigning and Incumbency), Conservative Party 2017-. DL, Berkshire 2018-.

Other: Patron: Royal Osteoporosis Society, Prince of Wales Hospice, Pontefract, Landmark Trust, Royal Drawing School; Founding patron, Royal Albert Hall's President's Circle; Vice-president, Berkshire Community Foundation; Trustee: Dumfries House 2013-17, The Prince's Regeneration Trust 2016-17; Trustee, David Brownlow Charitable Foundation; Emerging Entrepreneur of the Year, Ernst & Young/Sunday Times/Coutts Awards 2005; CVO 2018.

The Lord Brownlow of Shurlock Row CVO DL, House of Lords, London SW1A 0PW
Tel: 020 7219 3000 *Email:* brownlowd@parliament.uk Website: davidbrownlow.com
Twitter: @DavidEBrownlow

LIBERAL DEMOCRAT

BRUCE OF BENNACHIE, LORD

Liberal Democrat Lords Spokesperson for Scotland

BRUCE OF BENNACHIE (Life Baron), Malcolm Gray Bruce; cr 2015. Born 17 November 1944; Son of David Bruce, agricultural merchant and hotelier, and Kathleen Bruce; Married Veronica Wilson 1969 (divorced 1992) (1 son 1 daughter); married Rosemary Vetterlein 1998 (2 daughters 1 son).

Education: Wrekin College, Shropshire; St Andrews University (MA economics and political science 1966); Strathclyde University (MSc marketing 1971); CPE and Inns of Court School of Law, Gray's Inn 1995; French, German (a little).

Non-political career: Trainee journalist, *Liverpool Post* 1966-67; Boots section buyer 1968-69; Research and information officer, NE Scotland Development Authority 1971-75; Director, Noroil Publishing House (UK) Ltd 1975-81; Joint editor/publisher, Aberdeen Petroleum Publishing 1981-84. Member, NUJ.

Political career: *House of Commons:* Contested Angus North and Mearns October 1974 and Aberdeenshire West 1979 general elections. MP (Liberal Democrat) for Gordon 1983-97, for Gordon (revised boundary) 1997-2005, for Gordon (revised boundary) 2005-15; Liberal Spokesperson for Energy 1985-87; Scottish Liberal Spokesperson for Education 1986-87; Alliance Spokesperson for Employment 1987; Liberal Spokesperson for Trade and Industry 1987-88; SLD Spokesperson for Natural Resources (energy and conservation) 1988-89; Liberal Democrat Spokesperson for: the Environment and Natural Resources 1989-90, Scottish Affairs 1990-92, Trade and Industry 1992-94, the Treasury 1994-99; Chair, Liberal Democrat Parliamentary Party 1999-2001; Liberal Democrat Shadow Secretary of State for: Environment, Food and Rural Affairs 2001-02, Trade and Industry 2003-05. Member: Scottish Affairs 1990-92, Trade and Industry 1992-94, Treasury 1997-99, Standards and Privileges 1999-2001; Chair: International Development 2005-15; Member: Liaison 2005-15, Quadripartite (Committees on Strategic Export Controls)/Arms Export Controls 2006-15, Joint Committee on National Security Strategy 2010-15. *House of Lords:* Raised to the peerage as Baron Bruce of Bennachie, of Torphins in the County of Aberdeen 2015. Liberal Democrat Shadow Minister/ Lords Spokesperson for: Scotland 2016-, Northern Ireland 2018-20. Member: EU Financial Affairs Sub-committee 2017-20, EU Services Sub-committee 2020-, Common Frameworks Scrutiny 2020-. *Other:* Leader, Scottish Social and Liberal Democrats 1988-89; Scottish Liberal Democrats: Leader 1989-92, President 2000-15; Deputy Leader, Liberal Democrats 2014-15. Rector, Dundee University 1986-89.

Political interests: Energy, gas industry, oil industry, industrial policy, trade policy, deaf children, Scottish home rule and federalism; Balkans, Baltic States, Canada, Czech Republic, Eastern Europe, Hungary, Russia, Scandinavia, South Africa, USA, Zimbabwe.

Other: Member: UK Delegation, Parliamentary Assembly of the Council of Europe/Western European Union 2000-05, Executive Committee, Inter-Parliamentary Union, British Group 2010-15, Executive Committee, Commonwealth Parliamentary Association (UK Branch) 2014-15, British-Irish Parliamentary Association 2019-; Hon. Vice-President, National Deaf Children's Society; Hon. President, Grampian Branch; Hon. Vice-President: Combined Heat and Power Association, Action on Hearing Loss; Council member, Overseas Development Institute; National Deaf Children's Society; PC 2006; Kt 2012.

Recreations: Golf, cycling, walking, theatre and music.

Rt Hon the Lord Bruce of Bennachie, House of Lords, London SW1A 0PW
Tel: 020 7219 3000 *Twitter:* @malcolmbruce

LABOUR

BRYAN OF PARTICK, BARONESS

BRYAN OF PARTICK (Life Baroness), Pauline Christina Bryan; cr 2018. Married.

Education: Kingsway College, London.

Non-political career: Daily Mirror; Independent Labour Party, Bradford; Fabian Society; Editor, *The Citizen* magazine, Scottish Labour Campaign for Socialism.

Political career: *House of Lords:* Raised to the peerage as Baroness Bryan of Partick, of Partick in the City of Glasgow 2018. Lead for updating policy on federalism and Lords reform 2018-. Member: EU Energy and Environment Sub-committee 2019-20, EU Environment Sub-committee 2020-. *Other:* Former chair, Scottish Labour Campaign for Socialism.

Publications: Editor: Class, Nation and Socialism: The Red Paper on Scotland 2014 (Glasgow Caledonian University, 2013), What would Keir Hardie Say?: Exploring Hardie's vision and relevence to 21st Century politics (Luath Press Ltd, 2015); The Bryan Paper (Red Paper Collective, 2019).

The Baroness Bryan of Partick, House of Lords, London SW1A 0PW
Tel: 020 7219 3000

CROSSBENCH

BULL, BARONESS

BULL (Life Baroness), Deborah Clare Bull; cr 2018. Born 22 March 1963; Daughter of Revd M John Bull and late Doreen A Bull, née Plumb.

Education: Royal Ballet School.

Non-political career: Dancer, The Royal Ballet 1981-2002; Presenter/writer for television and radio 1998-; Royal Opera House: Creative Director, ROH2 2002-08, Creative Director 2008-12; King's College London: Director, Cultural Partnerships 2012-15, Assistant Principal (London) 2015-18, Vice-president and Vice-principal (London) 2018-, Senior Advisory Fellow for Culture 2018-.

Political career: *House of Lords:* Raised to the peerage as Baroness Bull, of Aldwych in the City of Westminster 2018. Member: Communications/Communications and Digital 2019-, Lord Speaker's Advisory Panel on Works of Art 2019-. *Other:* Council member, Arts Council England 1998-2005; Governor, BBC 2003-06; Council member, Arts and Humanities Research Council 2012-19.

Other: Board member, South Bank Centre 1997-2003; Judge, 2010 Booker Prize; Vice-president, cultural development, British Science Association 2015-18; Honorary doctorate: Derby University 1998, Sheffield Hallam University 2001, Open University 2005, Kent University 2010, Lincoln University 2017; CBE 1998.

Publications: The Vitality Plan, (Dorling Kindersley, 1998); Dancing Away (Methuen, 1998); Co-author (with Luke Jennings), The Faber Guide to Classical Ballets (2005); The Everyday Dancer (2011).

The Baroness Bull CBE, House of Lords, London SW1A 0PW
Tel: 020 7219 3000 *Email:* bulld@parliament.uk
1.10 Somerset House East Wing, King's College London, London WC2R 2LS
Website: www.deborahbull.com *Twitter:* @BullDeborah

LIBERAL DEMOCRAT

BURNETT, LORD

BURNETT (Life Baron), John Patrick Aubone Burnett; cr 2006. Born 19 September 1945; Son of late Lt-Col Aubone Burnett OBE and Joan Burnett, née Bolt; Married Elizabeth Sherwood, née de la Mare 1971 (2 sons 2 daughters).

Education: Ampleforth College, Yorkshire; Royal Marines Commando Training Centre; Britannia Royal Naval College, Dartmouth; College of Law, London.

Non-political career: Farmer 1976-98; Solicitor 1975; Partner, senior partner Burd Pearse solicitors, Okehampton, Devon 1976-97. Royal Marines 1964-70: Troop Commander, 42 Commando in Borneo and Singapore, Troop Commander and Company Second-in-Command, 40 Commando in Far East and Middle East. Member, NFU.

Political career: *House of Commons:* Contested Torridge and West Devon 1987 general election. MP (Liberal Democrat) for Torridge and West Devon 1997-2005; Spokesperson for: Home and Legal Affairs 1997-2004, Solicitor General's Department 2004-05. *House of Lords:* Raised to the peerage as Baron Burnett, of Whitchurch in the County of Devon 2006. Liberal Democrat Spokesperson for: Planning 2007-09, Environment, Food and Rural Affairs 2009-10. Co-opted Member, EU Sub-committee E (Law and Institutions) 2006-10.

Political interests: Economic policy, defence, agriculture.

Other: Member: Law Society, Devon and Exeter Law Society, Law Society's Revenue (Tax) Law Committee 1984-96, Council of Devon Cattle Breeders' Association, Royal Marine Association, Royal British Legion.

Recreations: Breeding Devon cattle, walking, sport.

The Lord Burnett, House of Lords, London SW1A 0PW
Tel: 020 7219 8730

NON-AFFILIATED

BURNETT OF MALDON, LORD

BURNETT OF MALDON (Life Baron), Ian Duncan Burnett; cr 2017. Born 28 February 1958; Married Caroline Monks 1991 (1 son 1 daughter).

Education: Pembroke College, Oxford (MA).

Non-political career: Called to the Bar, Middle Temple 1980; Bencher 2001; Temple Garden Chambers: Barrister 1982-2008, Head of Chambers 2003-08; Junior Counsel to the Crown, Common Law 1992-98; QC 1998; Assistant Recorder 1998-2000; Recorder 2000-08; Deputy High Court Judge 2008; Judge of the High Court, Queen's Bench Division 2008-14; Deputy Chamber, Security Vetting Appeals Panel 2009-14; Presiding Judge, Western Circuit 2011-14; Lord Justice of Appeal 2014-17; Lord Chief Justice of England and Wales 2017-.

Political career: *House of Lords:* Raised to the peerage as Baron Burnett of Maldon, of Maldon in the County of Essex 2017. As a senior member of the judiciary, disqualified from participation 2017-. *Other:* Vice-chair, Judicial Appointments Commission 2015-17.

Other: Kt 2008; PC 2014.

Rt Hon the Lord Burnett of Maldon, House of Lords, London SW1A 0PW
Tel: 020 7219 3000

CROSSBENCH

BURNS, LORD

Chair, Lord Speaker's Committee on the Size of the House

BURNS (Life Baron), Terence Burns; cr. 1998. Born 13 March 1944; Son of Patrick and Doris Burns; Married Anne Powell 1969 (1 son 2 daughters).

Education: Houghton-le-Spring Grammar School; Manchester University (BA economics 1965).

Non-political career: London Business School (LBS): Research posts 1965-70, Lecturer in economics 1970-74, Senior lecturer in economics 1974-79, Director, LBS Centre for Economic Forecasting 1976-79, Professor of economics 1979, Fellow 1989; Member, HM Treasury Academic Panel 1976-79; Chief Economic Adviser to HM Treasury and Head of Government Economic Service 1980-91; Visiting Fellow, Nuffield College, Oxford 1989-97; Permanent Secretary, HM Treasury 1991-98; Non-executive director: Legal and General Group plc 1999-2001, Pearson plc 1999-2010; British Land Company plc 2000-05; Chair: Glas Cymru (Welsh Water) 2001-10, Santander UK plc (formerly Abbey National plc) 2002-15; Marks and Spencer plc: Deputy chair 2005-06, Chair 2006-07; Channel 4 Television Corporation: Chairman Designate 2009-10, Chair 2010-16.

Political career: *House of Lords:* Raised to the peerage as Baron Burns, of Pitshanger in the London Borough of Ealing 1998. Chair: Financial Services and Markets Joint Committee 1999, Trade Union and Party Funding 2016; Member, Economic Affairs 2016-; Chair, Lord Speaker's Committee on the Size of the House 2016-. *Other:* Non-executive member, Office for Budget Responsibility 2012-18; Chair: Freedom of Information Commission 2015-16, Office of Communications (Ofcom) 2018-20, South East Wales Transport Commission 2019-.

Other: Society of Business Economists: Vice-President 1985-98, President 1998-; Fellow, London Business School 1989-; Vice-President, Royal Economic Society 1992-; Board Member, Manchester Business School 1992-98; Non-executive director, Queens Park Rangers FC 1996-2001; Royal Academy of Music: Governor 1998-2002, Chair of governing body 2002-14, Vice-President 2014-; Monteverdi Choir and Orchestra: Trustee 1998-2001, Chair of trustees 2001-07; Chair, National Lottery Commission 2000-01; Member, Hansard Society Commission on Scrutiny Role of Parliament 1999-; Chair, Committee of Inquiry into Hunting with Dogs in England and Wales 2000; Governor, National Institute of Economic and Social Research; Chair, Independent Adviser on BBC Charter Review 2003-04; Vice-chair, Hay Festival of Literature and Arts Ltd 2015-; Young Classical Artists Trust 2017-; Four honorary degrees; Kt 1983; GCB 1995. Reform Club.

Recreations: Watching football, music, golf.

The Lord Burns GCB, House of Lords, London SW1A 0PW
Tel: 020 7219 0312 *Email:* burnst@parliament.uk
Santander UK plc, 2 Triton Square, Regent's Place, London NW1 3AN *Tel:* 020 7756 5550
Email: terry.burns@santander.co.uk

LIBERAL DEMOCRAT

BURT OF SOLIHULL, BARONESS

BURT OF SOLIHULL (Life Baroness), Lorely Jane Burt; cr 2015. Born 10 September 1954; Daughter of Hazel Baker, née Abbiss, and Raymond Baker; Married Richard Burt 1992 (1 daughter from previous marriage 1 stepson).

Education: High Arcal Grammar School, Dudley; University College of Wales, Swansea (BSc Econ economics 1975); Open University (MBA 1997); Financial Times Non-executive Director Diploma.

Non-political career: Assistant governor, Pucklechurch Remand Centre and HMP Holloway 1975-78; Personnel and training posts, Beecham, Eurocar, Forte and Mercers 1978-84; Managing director, Kudos Leisure Ltd training company 1984-97; Director: Ace Creative Enterprises Ltd marketing company 1994-99, Mansion House Group 1999-2002; Self-employed estate planning consultant 2002-05; Board adviser: Total Training 2015-, DBS Law 2016-; Non-executive director, DBS Heart CIC 2016-.

Political career: *House of Commons:* Contested Dudley South 2001 general election. MP (Liberal Democrat) for Solihull 2005-10, for Solihull (revised boundary) 2010-15. Contested Solihull 2015 general election; Liberal Democrat: Whip 2005-06, Shadow Minister for: Northern Ireland 2005-06, Small Business, Women and Equality 2006-07, Business, Enterprise and Regulatory Reform 2007-09, Business, Innovation and Skills 2009-10; PPS to Danny Alexander as Chief Secretary to the Treasury 2012-14; Government Ambassador for Women and Enterprise 2014-15; Assistant Government Whip 2014-15. Member: Treasury 2005-06, Regulatory Reform 2006-10, Joint Committee on Voting Eligibilty (Prisoners) Bill 2013. Chair, Liberal Democrat Parliamentary Party Committee on Business, Innovation and Skills 2010-12. *House of Lords:* Raised to the peerage as Baroness Burt of Solihull, of Solihull in the County of West Midlands 2015. Liberal Democrat: Spokesperson for Business, Innovation and Skills 2015-16, Shadow Secretary of State for Equalities 2016-17, Spokesperson for: Women 2017-19, Small Business 2019. Member, Joint Committee on the Draft Domestic Abuse Bill 2019. *Other:* Contested West Midlands region 2004 European Parliament election. Liberal Democrats: Member: Federal Policy Committee 2002-03, West Midlands regional executive 2002-, Chair, Liberal Democrat Parliamentary Party 2007-12, Member, Federal Executive, President, West Midlands Liberal Democrats 2016-. Councillor, Dudley Metropolitan Borough Council 1998-2003.

Political interests: Industry, manufacturing, equalities, planning, women in enterprise, osteoporosis, funerals and bereavement, personal and company debt, management, prisons; Guinea-Bissau, Israel, Japan, Palestine, Papua New Guinea, Tunisia.

Other: Fellow, Institute of Sales and Marketing Management 1998; Small Business Friendly Award, Federation of Small Businesses 2008; International Luminary Award, Women's Business Enterprise National Council 2009; Small Business Friendly Award, Federation of Small Businesses Warwickshire and Coventry region 2009; Community Inspiration Award, Community Foundation 2014. President, Colebridge Table Tennis Club 2013-.

Recreations: Theatre, cinema, socialising, food, keeping fit.

The Baroness Burt of Solihull, House of Lords, London SW1A 0PW
Tel: 020 7219 8269 *Email:* burtl@parliament.uk *Twitter:* @lorelyburt

CONSERVATIVE

BUSCOMBE, BARONESS

BUSCOMBE (Life Baroness), Peta Jane Buscombe; cr. 1998. Born 12 March 1954; Married Philip John Buscombe 1980 (twin sons 1 daughter).

Education: Hinchley Wood School, Surrey; Rosebery Grammar School, Epsom; Inns of Court School of Law; Columbia Law School, New York; French.

Non-political career: Called to the Bar, Inner Temple 1977; Director, R Buxton textile marketing company 1977-79; Legal adviser, Dairy Trade Federation 1979-80; Barclays Bank 1980-84: Legal counsel, New York, Head office lawyer and inspector, London; Legal adviser and assistant secretary, Institute of Practitioners in Advertising 1984-87; Non-executive director, Affinity Water plc 2006-; Chief executive, Advertising Association 2007-; Director: Advertising Standards Board of Finance 2007-, Committee of Advertising Practice 2007-; Non-executive Director, Local World Ltd 2013-.

Political career: *House of Commons:* Contested (Conservative) Slough 1997 general election. *House of Lords:* Raised to the peerage as Baroness Buscombe, of Goring in the County of Oxfordshire 1998. Opposition Spokesperson for: Law Officers and Lord Chancellor's Department/Legal Affairs 1999-2005, Social Security 1999-2001, Trade and Industry 1999-2000, 2001, Cabinet Office 2000-01, Home Office 2001-02, Culture, Media and Sport 2002-05, Education and Skills 2005-07; Government Whip (Baroness in Waiting) 2016-17; Parliamentary Under-Secretary of State and Government Spokesperson, Department for Work and Pensions 2017-19. Member: EU Sub-committee B (Internal Market, Infrastructure and Employment) 2012-13, Inquiries Act 2005 2013-14, Joint Committee on Human Rights 2014-16, Joint Committee on the National Security Strategy 2015-17, Communications and Digital 2020-. *Other:* Vice-chair, Conservative Party 1997-99; President, Slough Conservative Association 1997-2001; Patron, Inns of Court School of Law Conservative Association; President, Henley Constituency Association 2015-. Councillor, South Oxfordshire District Council 1995-99; Chair, Press Complaints Commission 2009-11.

Political interests: Law and order, legal affairs, defence, media.

Other: Member, Inter-Parliamentary Union; Patron, PALS (Partnership for Active Leisure Scheme); Vice-president, Henley Society; Ambassador, Guide Association; Chair, Samaritans Advisory Board; Foundation for International and Commercial Arbitration and Alternative Dispute Resolution.

Recreations: Gardening, riding, tennis, theatre, cinema, shooting.

The Baroness Buscombe, House of Lords, London SW1A 0PW
Tel: 020 7219 5353 *Email:* buscombep@parliament.uk Website: petabuscombe.com

CROSSBENCH

BUTLER OF BROCKWELL, LORD

BUTLER OF BROCKWELL (Life Baron), Frederick Edward Robin Butler; cr. 1998. Born 3 January 1938; Son of late Bernard and Nora Butler; Married Gillian Galley 1962 (1 son 2 daughters).

Education: Harrow School; University College, Oxford (BA literae humaniores 1961, MA).

Non-political career: Civil Service 1961-98: HM Treasury (HMT) 1961-72: Private secretary to Niall MacDermot as Financial Secretary to Treasury 1964-65; Secretary Budget Committee 1965-69; Seconded to Cabinet Office as Member Central Policy Review Staff 1971-72; Private Secretary to Prime Ministers: Edward Heath 1972-74, Harold Wilson 1974-75; HMT 1975-82:

Assistant Secretary-General, Expenditure Intelligence Division 1975-77, Under Secretary, General Expenditure Policy Group 1977-80, Principal Establishment Officer 1980-82; Principal Private Secretary to Rt Hon Margaret Thatcher as Prime Minister 1982-85; Second Permanent Secretary, Public Expenditure, HMT 1985-87; Secretary of the Cabinet and Head of the Home Civil Service 1988-98; Master, University College, Oxford 1998-2008; Non-executive director: ICI plc 1998-2008, HSBC Holdings plc 1998-2008; Member, Marsh and McLennan International Advisory Board 2005-09; Kings Health Partners Academic Health Science Centre: Chair 2009-15, Board Member 2015-.

Political career: *House of Lords:* Raised to the peerage as Baron Butler of Brockwell, of Herne Hill in the London Borough of Lambeth 1998. Member: Intelligence and Security Committee 2010-15, Parliamentary and Political Service Honours Committee 2012-18. Member: Delegated Powers and Regulatory Reform 2009-13, Leader's Group on the Working Practices of the House of Lords 2010-11, Procedure 2012-15, EU Financial Affairs Sub-committee 2015-19, Joint Committee on the Draft Investigatory Powers Bill 2015-16, Social and Economic Impact of the Gambling Industry 2019-, Economic Affairs Finance Bill Sub-committee 2020-. *Other:* Member, Royal Commission on the Reform of the House of Lords 1999; Chair, Review of Intelligence on Weapons of Mass Destruction 2004.

Political interests: Higher education, civil service, constitutional matters.

Other: Chair of Governors: Harrow School 1988-91, Dulwich College 1997-2003; Visitor, Ashmolean Museum 2001-08; Trustee, Rhodes Trust 2002-09; The Salters' Company: Hon. Member, Master 2011-12; Six honorary degrees from UK and US universities; Hon. Fellow, King's College, London; CVO 1986; KCB 1988; GCB 1992; KG 2003; PC 2004. Athenæum, Brooks's, Beefsteak, Anglo-Belgian Club; MCC; Dulwich and Sydenham Golf Club; St Enodoc Golf Club.

Recreations: Competitive games.

Rt Hon the Lord Butler of Brockwell KG GCB CVO, House of Lords, London SW1A 0PW
Tel: 020 7219 5353
Tel: 020 7630 5247 *Email:* lord.butler@univ.ox.ac.uk

CROSSBENCH

BUTLER-SLOSS, BARONESS

Chair, Ecclesiastical Committee

BUTLER-SLOSS (Life Baroness), (Ann) Elizabeth Oldfield Butler-Sloss; cr 2006. Born 10 August 1933; Daughter of Sir Cecil Havers, High Court Judge Queen's Bench Division and Lady Havers, née Enid Snelling; Married Joseph Butler-Sloss 1958 (2 sons 1 daughter).

Education: Wycombe Abbey School; French.

Non-political career: Barrister, Inner Temple 1955; Practising barrister 1955-70; Registrar Principal Registry of Probate/Family Division 1970-79; High Court Judge Family Division 1979-88; Lord Justice of Appeal 1988-99; President Family Division 1999-2005.

Political career: *House of Commons:* Contested (Conservative) Lambeth, Vauxhall 1959 general election. *House of Lords:* Raised to the peerage as Baroness Butler-Sloss, of Marsh Green in the County of Devon 2006. Member: Merits of Statutory Instruments 2007-12, Statutory Instruments 2010; Ecclesiastical Committee: Member 2010-18, 2020, Chair 2018-19, 2020-; Chair, Adoption Legislation 2012-13; Member, Joint Committee on the Draft Modern Slavery Bill 2014. *Other:* Chair: Cleveland Child Abuse Inquiry 1987-88, Security Commission 1995-2005; Commission on Appointment of Archbishop of Canterbury 2002.

Political interests: Education, children, family, intelligence/security, Commonwealth, legal issues, human trafficking, interfaith relations, Forced Marriages Commission 2013; Hong Kong, India, Kenya, Malaysia, Pakistan, Singapore.

Other: Former chair, St Paul's Cathedral Council; Governor, Coram and Merchant Taylors School; Inner Temple: Bencher, Treasurer 1998; Vice-President, Devon Hospice Care; President, Devon Branch National Trust; Patron, Grandparents' Association; Visitor, St Hilda's College, Oxford; Trustee: Muzaffarabad Earthquake Appeal, Human Trafficking Foundation; Chair, Commission on Religion and Belief in British Public Life; Honorary Freeman, Merchant Taylors; Freedom, City of London; Chancellor, University of West of England 1993-2011; Honorary FCP; FCPaed; FCPsych; FSM; 18 honorary degrees; Honorary fellow: King's

College, London, St Hilda's College, Oxford, Peterhouse Cambridge, Corpus Christi College, Cambridge; DBE 1979; PC 1988; GBE 2005. RSM, Landsdowne Club.

Rt Hon the Baroness Butler-Sloss GBE, House of Lords, London SW1A 0PW
Tel: 020 7219 4044 *Email:* butlerslosse@parliament.uk

CONSERVATIVE

CAINE, LORD

CAINE (Life Baron), Jonathan Michael Caine; cr 2016. Born 11 April 1966.

Education: Temple Moor High School; Leicester University (history).

Non-political career: Research Department, Conservative Central Office; Special Adviser to Secretaries of State for Northern Ireland: Tom King 1988-89, Peter Brooke 1989-92, Patrick Mayhew 1992-97, Owen Paterson 2010-12, Theresa Villiers 2012-16, James Brokenshire 2016-18, Karen Bradley 2018-19.

Political career: *House of Lords:* Raised to the peerage as Baron Caine, of Temple Newsam in the City of Leeds 2016. Deputy Chairman of Committees 2020-. Member, Common Frameworks Scrutiny 2020-.

Other: Member, British-Irish Parliamentary Assembly 2020-.

Recreations: Leeds Rhinos RLFC, Yorkshire County Cricket Club.

The Lord Caine, House of Lords, London SW1A 0PW
Tel: 020 7219 3000

CONSERVATIVE

CAITHNESS, EARL OF

CAITHNESS (20th Earl of, S), Malcolm Ian Sinclair; cr. 1455; Lord Berriedale; 15th Bt of Canisbay (NS) 1631. Born 3 November 1948; Son of 19th Earl; Married Diana Caroline Coke 1975 (died 1994) (1 son 1 daughter); married Leila Jenkins 2004 (divorced); married Diana Penelope Wilson 2015.

Education: Marlborough College, Wiltshire; Royal Agricultural College, Cirencester.

Non-political career: Savills 1972-78; Brown and Mumford 1978-80; Director of various companies 1980-84; Consultant, Rickett Tinne Property Consultants, and other companies 1994-.

Political career: *House of Lords:* First entered House of Lords 1969; Government Spokesperson for DHSS 1984-85; Government Whip 1984-85; Government Spokesperson for Scotland 1984-86; Parliamentary Under-Secretary of State, Department of Transport 1985-86; Minister of State: Home Office 1986-88, Department of Environment 1988-89; Paymaster General and Treasury Minister 1989-90; Minister of State: Foreign and Commonwealth Office 1990-92, Department of Transport 1992-94; Elected hereditary peer 1999-. Member: EU Sub-committee G 1979, EU Sub-committee D 1979-82, Consolidation Bills (Joint Committee) 1979-84, Procedure Committee 1997-2004, House of Lords Offices Committee 1997-2000, EU Sub-committee F (Home Affairs) 2003-07, Draft Climate Change Bill Joint Committee 2007; Co-opted member, EU Sub-committee D (Environment and Agriculture) 2008-10; Member: EU Sub-committee D: (Agriculture, Fisheries and Environment) 2010-12, (Agriculture, Fisheries, Environment and Energy) 2012-13, EU Sub-committee A (Economic and Financial Affairs) 2013-15, European Union 2014-16, EU Financial Affairs Sub-committee 2015-16, Communications 2016-17, Natural Environment and Rural Communities Act 2006 2017-18, Rural Economy 2018-19, Food, Poverty, Health and the Environment 2019-. *Other:* Chair, West Oxfordshire Conservative Association 1985-2001.

Other: Trustee: Queen Elizabeth Castle of Mey Trust 1996-2016, Clan Sinclair Trust 1998-; Chair, Caithness Archaeological Trust 2002-2011; FRICS; PC 1990.

Rt Hon the Earl of Caithness, House of Lords, London SW1A 0PW
Tel: 020 7219 5442 *Email:* caithness@parliament.uk

CONSERVATIVE

CALLANAN, LORD

Parliamentary Under-Secretary of State (Minister for Climate Change and Corporate Responsibility) and Government Spokesperson, Department for Business, Energy and Industrial Strategy

CALLANAN (Life Baron), Martin John Callanan; cr 2014. Born 8 August 1961; Married Jayne Burton 1997 (1 son).

Education: Heathfield Senior High School; Newcastle Polytechnic (BSc electrical and electronic engineering 1995).

Non-political career: Project engineer, Scottish and Newcastle Breweries 1986-98.

Political career: *House of Lords:* Raised to the peerage as Baron Callanan, of Low Fell in the County of Tyne and Wear 2014. Parliamentary Under-Secretary of State for Aviation, International and Security and Government Spokesperson, Department for Transport 2017; Minister of State and Government Spokesperson, Department for Exiting the European Union 2017-20; Parliamentary Under-Secretary of State (Minister for Climate Change and Corporate Responsibility) and Government Spokesperson, Department for Business, Energy and Industrial Strategy 2020-. Member: Information 2015-16, Trade Union and Party Funding 2016, EU Financial Affairs Sub-committee 2016-17. *Other:* European Parliament: MEP for North East 1999-2014: PPS to Leader of Conservative MEPs 2003-05, Chief whip, European Conservatives and Reformists group 2009-14, Conservative Spokesperson for Transport 2009-14, Leader, Conservative Delegation 2010-14. Conservative Party: Member, Gateshead East and Washington West constituency party, President, Newcastle University Conservative Future. Member: Tyne and Wear County Council 1981-85, Gateshead Metropolitan Borough Council 1987-96.

Recreations: Squash, restoring vintage cars.

The Lord Callanan, House of Lords, London SW1A 0PW
Tel: 020 7219 5353 *Twitter:* @LordCallanan

CROSSBENCH

CAMERON OF DILLINGTON, LORD

CAMERON OF DILLINGTON (Life Baron), Ewen James Hanning Cameron; cr. 2004. Born 24 November 1949; Son of Major Allan and Elizabeth Cameron; Married Caroline Ripley 1975 (3 sons 1 daughter).

Education: Harrow School; Oxford University (BA modern history 1972, MA).

Non-political career: Manager, Dillington Estate, Somerset 1971-2017; Chair, Orchard Media Ltd 1989-99; President, Somerset Young Farmers 1990-91; Director, Village Retail Services Association 1992-99; National president, Country Land and Business Association 1995-97; Member, Round Table for Sustainable Development 1997-2000; Chair: Let's Go Travel Ltd 1998-2006, Countryside Agency 1999-2004, Government's rural advocate for England 2000-04, Airport Direct Travel Ltd 2006-; Royal Bath and West Society: President 2006-07, Director 2008-15.

Political career: *House of Lords:* Raised to the peerage as Baron Cameron of Dillington, of Dillington in the County of Somerset 2004. Member: EU Sub-committee D (Environment and Agriculture) 2005-09, Administration and Works 2009-14, EU Sub-committee D: (Agriculture, Fisheries and Environment) 2010-12, (Agriculture, Fisheries, Environment and Energy) 2012-15, European Union 2012-15, Science and Technology 2015-17; Chair, Natural Environment and Rural Communities Act 2006 2017-18; Member: EU Energy and Environment Sub-committee 2018-20, EU Environment Sub-committee 2020-. *Other:* High Sheriff of Somerset 1986-87; DL, Somerset 1989.

Political interests: Countryside, agriculture, environment, food and rural affairs, fisheries, housing, international development and aid, Africa, food and agriculture in developing world; (Agriculture in) Sub-Saharan Africa.

Other: Fellow, Royal Agricultural Societies 1995; Chair, Somerset Strategic Partnership 2004-11; Trustee, Lawes Agricultural Trust 2005-; President, British Guild of Agricultural Journalists 2010-15; Chair: Strategic Advisory Board of the Governments' Global Food Security Programme 2012-, Board of Trustees, Centre for Ecology and Hydrology 2015-;

President, Royal Association of British Dairy Farmers 2019-; FRICS 1992-; Hon. LLD Exeter 2004; Hon. degree Royal Agricultural University, Cirencester 2015; Kt 2003.

Recreations: Golf, shooting.

The Lord Cameron of Dillington, House of Lords, London SW1A 0PW
Tel: 020 7219 2530 *Email:* camerone@parliament.uk
Clouds, Golf Hill Road, Rock TA19 9EG

CROSSBENCH

CAMPBELL OF LOUGHBOROUGH, BARONESS

CAMPBELL OF LOUGHBOROUGH (Life Baroness), Susan Catherine Campbell; cr 2008. Born 10 October 1948.

Education: Long Eaton Grammar School, Derbyshire; Bedford College of Further Education; Leicester University (Advanced DipEd, MEd 1975).

Non-political career: Physical Education Teacher, Whalley Range High School, Manchester 1970-72; Director of PE, Leicester University 1972-76; Lecturer, Department of PE and Sports Science, Loughborough University 1976-80; East Midlands Regional Officer, Sports Council 1980-84; National Coaching Foundation 1984-95: Deputy Chief Executive 1984, Chief Executive 1985-95; Youth Sport Trust 1995-2017: Chief Executive 1995-2005, Chair 2005-17; PE Adviser to Departments for Culture, Media and Sport and for Education and Science 2000-04; UK Sport 2003-13: Reform Chair 2003-05, Chair 2005-13; Football Association: Head of Women's Football 2016-17, Director of Women's Football 2018-.

Political career: *House of Lords:* Raised to the peerage as Baroness Campbell of Loughborough, of Loughborough in the County of Leicestershire 2008.

Political interests: Africa, Asia.

Other: Chair, Commonwealth Advisory Board on Sport 2004-08; Trustee, International Development through Sport; Hon. Fellow: Leeds Polytechnic 1990, Sheffield Polytechnic 1991; UK Sport Fellowship 2015; Hon DEd: Leicester University, Council for National Academic Awards 1992, De Montfort University 1996; Hon DSc, Brighton University 1993; Hon DTech, Loughborough University 1997; Hon doctorate: Bedford University, Leeds Metropolitan University 2006, City and Guilds 2010, Exeter University 2010, Endicott College Boston, USA 2011, Queen's University 2013, Nottingham Trent University 2016; MBE 1991; CBE 2003; DBE 2020.

Recreations: Competitive squash and hockey, kayaking, golf, tennis, cycling.

The Baroness Campbell of Loughborough DBE, House of Lords, London SW1A 0PW
Tel: 020 7219 5353

LIBERAL DEMOCRAT

CAMPBELL OF PITTENWEEM, LORD

CAMPBELL OF PITTENWEEM (Life Baron), Walter Menzies Campbell; cr 2015. Born 22 May 1941; Son of late George and Elizabeth Campbell; Married Elspeth Urquhart 1970.

Education: Hillhead High School, Glasgow; Glasgow University (MA arts 1962; LLB law 1965); Stanford University, California (Postgraduate Studies international law 1966-67).

Non-political career: Competed: 1964 (Tokyo) Olympics, 1966 Commonwealth Games (Jamaica); UK Athletics Team Captain 1965-66; UK 100 metres record holder 1967-74; Called to the Bar (Scotland) 1968; QC (Scotland) 1982; Chair, Royal Lyceum Theatre Company, Edinburgh 1984-87.

Political career: *House of Commons:* Contested Greenock and Port Glasgow February and October 1974, East Fife 1979, and North East Fife 1983 general elections. MP for North East Fife 1987-2005, for North East Fife (revised boundary) 2005-15 (Liberal/All 1987-88, Liberal Democrat 1988-2015); Liberal Spokesperson for Arts, Broadcasting and Sport 1987-88; Liberal Democrat Spokesperson for: Scotland (Legal Affairs, Lord Advocate) 1988-99, Defence and Sport 1988-89, Defence and Disarmament and Sport 1989-94, Foreign Affairs and Defence and Sport 1994-97, Foreign Affairs (Defence and Europe) 1997-99, Liberal Democrat Principal Spokesperson for Defence and Foreign Affairs 1999-2001; Contested Speaker election 2000; Liberal Democrat Shadow Secretary of State for Foreign and Commonwealth Affairs 2001-06;

Member, Intelligence and Security Committee 2010-15. Member: Trade and Industry 1990-92, Defence 1992-97, 1997-99, Foreign Affairs 2008-15, Joint Committees on: Intelligence and Security 2008-15, the Draft Detention of Terrorist Suspects (Temporary Extension) Bills 2011, Parliamentary Privilege 2013. *House of Lords:* Raised to the peerage as Baron Campbell of Pittenweem, of Pittenweem in the County of Fife 2015. Liberal Democrat Spokesperson for Defence 2017-19. Member, Joint Committee on the National Security Strategy 2017-. *Other:* Chair, Scottish Liberal Party 1975-77; Liberal Democrats: Deputy Leader 2003-06, Leader 2006-07, Chair, Home Rule Commission 2011-12.

Political interests: Defence, foreign affairs, legal affairs, sport, arts; North America, Middle East.

Other: North Atlantic Assembly (now NATO Parliamentary Assembly): Member 1989-, Leader, UK Delegation 2010-15; Parliamentary Assembly of OSCE: Member, UK Delegation 1992-97, 1999-2001, Vice-President 2017-; Member: Board of the British Council 1998-2002, Council of the Air League 1999-2006, Olympic Board 2010-12; President, European Movement in Scotland 2016-; Member, Faculty of Advocates; Patron, Lymphoma Association 2016-; Chancellor, St Andrews University 2006-; Three honorary doctorates: Glasgow University, Strathclyde University, St Andrews University; Member to Watch, Highland Park/*Spectator* 1996; Opposition Politician of the Year, Channel 4 2004; Opposition Politician of the Year, *House Magazine* 2004; Westminster Politician of the Year, *Herald*/Diageo 2004; Politician of the Year, *Oldie* magazine 2005; Parliamentarian of the Year, Political Studies Association 2005; Lifetime Achievement Award, *Herald* 2016; CBE 1987; PC 1999; Kt 2004; CH 2013. Reform, National Liberal Club.

Publications: Menzies Campbell: My Autobiography (2008).

Recreations: All sports, theatre, music.

Rt Hon the Lord Campbell of Pittenweem CH CBE QC, House of Lords, London SW1A 0PW
Tel: 020 7219 6910 *Email:* campbellm@parliament.uk

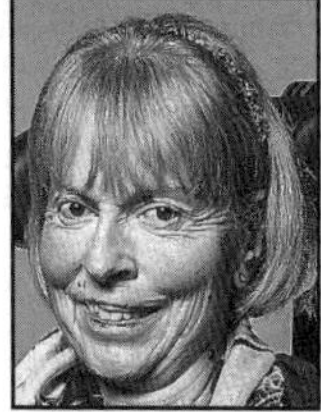

CROSSBENCH

CAMPBELL OF SURBITON, BARONESS

CAMPBELL OF SURBITON (Life Baroness), Jane Susan Campbell; cr 2007. Born 19 April 1959; Daughter of Ronald Campbell, engineer, and Jessie Campbell, nursery nurse; Married Roger Symes 2000.

Education: Hereward College, Coventry; Hatfield Polytechnic (BA history 1979); Sussex University (MA political history 1982).

Non-political career: Equal opportunities liaison officer, Greater London Council 1984-86; Disability training development officer, London Boroughs Joint Disability Committee 1986-87; Principal disability adviser, Hounslow Council 1987-88; Director of training, London Boroughs Disability Resource Team 1988-94; Freelance consultant 1994-96; Co-director, National Centre for Independent Living 1996-2000; Chair: Social Care Institute for Excellence 2001-05, Independent Living Strategy Group 2016-.

Political career: *House of Lords:* Raised to the peerage as Baroness Campbell of Surbiton, of Surbiton in the Royal Borough of Kingston upon Thames 2007. Independent member, House of Lords Appointments Commission 2008-13; Disability adviser, Department for Work and Pensions and Department of Health 2007-12. Member: Joint Committee on Human Rights 2010-12, Equality Act 2010 and Disability 2015-16. *Other:* Chair, British Council of Disabled People 1991-95; Governor, National Institute for Social Work 1995-2001; Commissioner, Disability Rights Commission 2000-06; Chair, Disability Committee and Commissioner, Commission for Equality and Human Rights 2006-09.

Political interests: Health and social care, social policy, medical ethics, independent living, equality and human rights, disability rights, end of life issues; Sweden.

Other: Founder and co-director, Not Dead Yet UK 2006-; President, National Disability Archive (Shape, London) 2013-; Patron: National Disability Arts Collection and Archive 2013-, Just Fair (UK) 2014-; Member, Justice Advisory Group (justice.org.uk) 2015; Disability Rights UK, Power International; Honorary LLD, Bristol University 2002; Honorary Doctorate: Sheffield Hallam University 2003, Birmingham University 2009; Lifetime Achievement Award, Liberty Human Rights Awards (2012); Lifetime Achievement Award, Bevan Prize for Health and Wellbeing (2015); MBE 2000; DBE 2006.

Publications: With Mike Oliver, Disability Politics (Routledge, 1996); Contributor, Disabled People and the Right to Life (Routledge, 2008).

Recreations: Theatre, cinema, reading, gardening.

The Baroness Campbell of Surbiton DBE, House of Lords, London SW1A 0PW
Tel: 020 7219 5124 *Email:* campbelljs@parliament.uk *Twitter:* @BnsJaneCampbell

LABOUR

CAMPBELL-SAVOURS, LORD

CAMPBELL-SAVOURS (Life Baron), Dale Norman Campbell-Savours; cr 2001. Born 23 August 1943; Son of late John Lawrence and Cynthia Lorraine Campbell-Savours; Married Gudrun Kristin Runolfsdottir 1970 (3 sons).

Education: Keswick School; Sorbonne, Paris.

Non-political career: Company director, clock and metal component manufacturing company.

Political career: *House of Commons:* Contested Darwen February and October 1974 general elections and Workington 1976 by-election. MP (Labour) for Workington 1979-2001; Opposition Frontbench Spokesperson for: Development and Co-operation 1991-92, Food, Agriculture and Rural Affairs 1992-94 (resigned from frontbench because of ill health). *House of Lords:* Raised to the peerage as Baron Campbell-Savours, of Allerdale in the County of Cumbria 2001. Member: Administration and Works 2007-12, Liaison 2010-15, Procedure 2010-15, House 2012-16, Services 2016-, Electoral Registration and Administration Act 2013 2019-. *Other:* Councillor, Ramsbottom Urban District Council 1972-74.

Political interests: Investigative political and social work, education and health reform, industrial democracy.

Other: Patron: Cumbria Deaf Association, The Rural Academy Cumbria; President: Allerdale Mind, Cumberland County League.

Publications: The Case for the Supplementary Vote (1990); The Case for a Cattle Traceability Scheme (1993); The Case for The University of the Lakes (1995).

Recreations: Trout fishing, music.

The Lord Campbell-Savours, House of Lords, London SW1A 0PW
Tel: 020 7219 3513 *Email:* campbellsavours@parliament.uk

NON-AFFILIATED

CANTERBURY, LORD ARCHBISHOP OF

CANTERBURY (105th Archbishop of), Justin Portal Welby. Born 6 January 1956; Son of late Gavin Welby and Jane Welby (now Lady Williams of Elvel). Biological son of late Sir Anthony Montague Browne; Married Caroline 1979 (2 sons 3 daughters 1 daughter deceased).

Education: Eton College; Trinity College, Cambridge (BA 1978); St John's College, Durham (BA 1991); French.

Non-political career: Project finance manager, Société Nationale Elf Aquitaine, Paris 1978-83; Treasurer, Elf UK 1983-84; Group Treasurer, Enterprise Oil plc 1984-89; Ordained: Deacon 1992, Priest 1993, Bishop 2011; Curate, All Saints, Chilvers Coton, Nuneaton 1992-95; Rector: St James', Southam 1995-2002, St Michael and All Angels, Ufton 1996-2002; Coventry Cathedral: Co-director, International Ministry and Canon Residentiary 2002-05, Sub-Dean and Canon for Reconciliation Ministry 2005-07; Dean of Liverpool 2007-11; Bishop of Durham 2011-13; Archbishop of Canterbury 2013-.

Political career: *House of Lords:* Entered House of Lords 2011. Member, Parliamentary Commission on Banking Standards 2012-13. *Other:* Southam College: Parent governor 1996-2002, Chair of governors 1998-2002; South Warwickshire General Hospitals NHS Trust: Non-executive director 1998-2000, Chair 2000-02.

Political interests: The 165 countries that have Anglican congregations.

Other: Association Internationale pour l'Enseignement Social Chrétien; Diocesan Trust; Hon. Fellow, Association of Corporate Treasurers; Patron of numerous charities; Skinners; Freedom: City of London City of Coventry; Chancellor, Canterbury Christ Church University; Fellow: Trinity College Cambridge, Liverpool John Moores University; Honorary Degree: Durham

University, Liverpool University, Aberdeen University, Coventry University; Peer of the Year, *Spectator* awards 2012; PC 2013. Athenæum, Liverpool Club.

Publications: Can Companies Sin? (Grove Books, 1992); Dethroning Mammon: Making Money Serve Grace (Bloomsbury Continuum, 2016)' Reimagining Britain: Foundations for Hope (Bloomsbury Continuum, 2018); Various articles in The Treasurer magazine, and numerous other articles on risk management, finance, and on reconciliation; Various chapters in books on reconciliation, conflict management.

Recreations: Sailing, reading, travel.

Most Rev and Rt Hon the Archbishop of Canterbury, House of Lords, London SW1A 0PW
Tel: 020 7219 5353
Lambeth Palace, London SE1 7JU *Tel:* 020 7898 1472
Email: rosemary.nuamahwilliams@lambethpalace.org.uk
Website: www.archbishopofcanterbury.org *Twitter:* @JustinWelby

CROSSBENCH

CAREY OF CLIFTON, LORD

CAREY OF CLIFTON (Life Baron), George Leonard Carey; cr 2002. Born 13 November 1935; Son of late George and Ruby Carey; Married Eileen Harmsworth Hood 1960 (2 sons 2 daughters).

Education: Bifrons School, Barking; King's College, London (PhD); London College of Divinity (ALCD, BD, MTh).

Non-political career: Curate of St Mary's, Islington 1962-66; Lecturer: Oakhill Theological College 1966-70, St John's College, Nottingham; Occasional teacher at Nottingham University 1970-75; Vicar of St Nicholas Church, Durham 1975-82; Principal, Trinity Theological College, Bristol 1982-87; Bishop of Bath and Wells 1987-91; Archbishop of Canterbury 1991-2002. Royal Air Force 1954-56.

Political career: *House of Lords:* Raised to the peerage as Baron Carey of Clifton, of Clifton in the City and Council of Bristol 2002. First entered the House of Lords as Archbishop of Canterbury 1991.

Political interests: Israel, Palestine, Sudan.

Other: President, World Conference for Religion and Peace; Honorary President, International Council for Christians and Jews; Chairman, World Faiths Development Dialogue; International Sports Promotion Society; Vice-President, Tearfund; Fellow: King's College, London, Christchurch University College, Canterbury, Library of Congress; Chair: United Church Schools Trust, Foundation for Reconciliation in the Middle East; Tearfund; Honorary Liveryman, Scriveners' Company; Freedom: City of London, Bath, Wells; 12 honorary doctorates; PC 1991; Royal Victorian Chain 2002. Athenæum, ROSL Club.

Publications: I Believe in Man (1975); God Incarnate (1976); Co-author, The Great Acquittal (1980); The Church in the Market Place (1984); The Meeting of the Waters (1985); The Gate of Glory (1986); The Message of the Bible (1986); The Great God Robbery (1989); I Believe (1991); Sharing a Vision (1993); Spiritual Journey (1994); Co-author, My Journey, Your Journey (1996); Canterbury Letters to the Future (1998); Jesus 2000 (1999); Know The Truth (memoirs, 2004); We Don't Do God (2012).

Recreations: Family life, music, poetry, reading, walking.

Rt Rev and Rt Hon the Lord Carey of Clifton, House of Lords, London SW1A 0PW
Tel: 020 7219 5353
Email: carey.andr@gmail.com

CROSSBENCH

CARLILE OF BERRIEW, LORD

CARLILE OF BERRIEW (Life Baron), Alexander Charles Carlile; cr. 1999. Born 12 February 1948; Married Frances Soley 1968 (divorced) (3 daughters); married Alison Levitt QC 2007 (2 stepdaughters).

Education: Epsom College; King's College, London University (LLB, AKC 1969); Council of Legal Education.

Non-political career: Called to the Bar, Gray's Inn 1970; QC 1984; Crown Court Recorder 1986-2014; Bencher 1992; Honorary Recorder of City of Hereford 1996-2009; Deputy High Court Judge 1998-2014.

Political career: *House of Commons:* Contested (Liberal) Flint East, February 1974 and 1979 general elections. MP for Montgomery 1983-97 (Liberal 1983-88, Liberal Democrat 1988-97); Liberal Spokesperson for Home Affairs, Law 1985-88; Alliance Spokesperson for Legal Affairs 1987; SLD Spokesperson for Foreign Affairs 1988-89; Liberal Democrat Spokesperson for: Legal Affairs 1989-90, Trade and Industry 1990-92, Wales 1992-97, Employment 1992-94, Health 1994-95, Justice, Home Affairs and Immigration 1995-97. *House of Lords:* Raised to the peerage as Baron Carlile of Berriew, of Berriew in the County of Powys 1999. Liberal Democrat Spokesperson for Mental Health and Disability 2007-10; Resigned the Liberal Democrat Whip 2018, now sits as Crossbench. Chair, Mental Health Bill Joint Committee 2005-06; Member, Delegated Powers and Regulatory Reform 2010-12. *Other:* Chair, Welsh Liberal Party 1980-82; Leader, Welsh Liberal Democrat Party 1992-97; President, Liberal Democrats Wales 1997-99; Sat as Non-affiliated in the Lords 2017-January 2018, now sits as a Crossbencher. Lay member, General Medical Council 1989-99; Member, Advisory Council on Public Records 1989-95; Independent Reviewer of Terrorism Legislation 2001-11; Chairman (part-time), Competition Appeals Tribunal 2005-13; Deputy Chief Steward, City of Hereford 2009-; Commissioner, Independent Commission on Freedom of Information 2015-16; Independent Reviewer of Prevent Policy, Home Office 2019.

Political interests: Home affairs, legal affairs, United Nations, arts, Wales, mental health, terrorism; Central and Eastern Europe, Gulf region, Middle East, South Asia.

Other: Patron: National Depression Campaign, Concord Prison Trust, No Panic; White Ensign Association: Council member, Chair; Fellow: Institute of Advanced Legal Studies, Industry and Parliament Trust 1989; President: Howard League for Penal Reform 2006-13, Royal Medical Benevolent Institution (Epsom College); Chair: Lloyd's Enforcement Board, Addaction 2016-; Hope House Children's Hospice, NACRO, Unicef, Rekindle, Howard League for Penal Reform, Addaction, White Ensign Association; Fellow: Royal Society of Arts, King's College London; Hon. LLD: Glamorgan University 2009, Hungarian Institute of Criminology 2010, Manchester Metropolitan University 2011, Swansea University 2019, Chester University 2019; Hon. Professor, Swansea University 2017; QC 1984; CBE 2012. Athenæum Club; President, Berriew FC.

Publications: Too Serious a Thing (National Assembly for Wales review of safety of children in the NHS, 2002); Various articles and reports on Terrorism; If all do their duty they need not fear harm (Report for the Howard League on Children in Custody, 2006).

Recreations: Family, politics, theatre, food, association football.

The Lord Carlile of Berriew CBE QC, House of Lords, London SW1A 0PW
Tel: 020 7219 5353 *Email:* carlilea@parliament.uk
Tel: 020 3432 9891

NON-AFFILIATED

CARLISLE, LORD BISHOP OF

CARLISLE (67th Bishop of), James William Scobie Newcome. Born 24 July 1953; Son of Major John Newcome and Jane Newcome; Married Alison Clarke (2 sons 2 daughters).

Education: Marlborough College; Trinity College, Oxford (BA modern history 1974, MA); Selwyn College, Cambridge (BA theology 1977, MA).

Non-political career: Ordained deacon 1978; Assistant curate, All Saints, Leavesden 1978-82; Priest 1979; Minister, Bar Hill 1982-94; Tutor, Ridley Hall, Cambridge 1983-88; Rural dean 1993-94; Residentiary Canon, Chester Cathedral 1994-2002; Diocesan Director of: Ordinands 1994-2000, Ministry 1996-2002; Bishop Suffragan of Penrith 2002-09; Bishop of Carlisle

2009-; Lead Bishop on Health 2010-; Clerk of the Closet 2014-. Territorial Army Commission 1973.

Political career: *House of Lords:* Entered House of Lords 2013. Member, Long-Term Sustainability of the NHS 2016-17. *Other:* DL, Cumbria 2013-.

Political interests: Healthcare, defence, social care; Africa, Argentina, Norway.

Other: Member, Society for Study for Christian Ethics 1985-; President, St John's College, Durham 2012-; Vice-president, Cumbria Community Foundation; National Chaplain, Royal British Legion 2016-; Chair, Rose Castle Foundation; Christian Aid; Fellow, Royal Society of Arts. Athenæum Club.

Publications: Contributor, Setting the Church of England Free (2003); Great Ideas for Growing Healthy Churches (2012); At the End of the Day (2014); Facing Disappointment (Grove 2016).

Recreations: Film, contemporary novels, sport, furniture restoration.

Rt Rev the Lord Bishop of Carlisle, House of Lords, London SW1A 0PW
Tel: 020 7219 5353
Bishop's House, Ambleside, Keswick CA12 4DD *Tel:* 01768 773430
Email: bishop.carlisle@carlislediocese.org.uk Website: www.carlislediocese.org.uk

CROSSBENCH

CARRINGTON, LORD

CARRINGTON (7th Baron, I), Rupert Francis John Carington; cr. 1796; 7th Baron Carrington (GB) 1797. Born 2 December 1948; Son of 6th Baron, KG, GCMG, CH, MC, PC, DL; Married Daniela 1989 (1 son 2 daughters).

Education: Eton College; Bristol University (BSc politics and sociology 1969).

Non-political career: Director: Morgan Grenfell International 1983-87, Rupert Carington Ltd 1987-, Hartwell plc 1989-2000; Chairman, Schroder Asiapacific Fund plc 1995-2016; Director: Sete Technical Services SA 2002-, Alger Associates Inc 2012-.

Political career: *House of Lords:* Elected hereditary peer 2018-. *Other:* Buckinghamshire: DL 1999-, High Sheriff 2002-03.

Political interests: Foreign affairs, trade and investment, agriculture, culture and heritage; Far East, Middle East, USA.

Other: Trustee, Burks Historic Churches Trust 2000-; Governor, Royal Shakespeare Company 2017-. White's Club, Pratt's Club.

Recreations: Gardening, walking, opera, theatre.

The Lord Carrington DL, House of Lords, London SW1A 0PW
Tel: 020 7219 8892 *Email:* carringtonr@parliament.uk
Carington Estates Ltd, The Courtyard, Manor Farm, Church End, Bledlow HP27 9PD
Tel: 01844 273508 Website: www.carington.co.uk

CONSERVATIVE

CARRINGTON OF FULHAM, LORD

CARRINGTON (Life Baron), Matthew Hadrian Marshall Carrington; cr 2013. Born 19 October 1947; Son of Walter and Dilys Carrington; Married Mary Lou 1975 (1 daughter); married Margaret Millward 2012.

Education: Lycee, London; Imperial College, London; London Business School; French.

Non-political career: Production foreman, GKN Ltd 1969-72; Banker: First National Bank of Chicago 1974-78, Saudi International Bank 1978-87; Chair, Outdoor Advertising Association 1998-2002; Chief executive, Retail Motor Industry Federation 2002-06.

Political career: *House of Commons:* Contested Tottenham 1979 general election and Fulham 1986 by-election. MP (Conservative) for Fulham 1987-97. Contested Hammersmith and Fulham 1997 and 2001 general elections; PPS to: Lord Trefgarne as Minister of State, Department for Trade and Industry 1988-90, John Patten: as Minister of State, Home Office 1990-92, as Secretary of State for Education 1992-94; Assistant Whip 1996-97. Member, Treasury and Civil Service 1994-96; Chair, Treasury 1996. *House of Lords:* Raised to the peerage as Baron Carrington of Fulham, of Fulham in the London Borough of Hammersmith and Fulham 2013.

Member: Economic Affairs 2014-15, Insurance Bill 2014-15. *Other:* Conservative Party: Chair: London Region 2005-08, North West London Area 2002-05, 2008-10.

Political interests: Economy, international affairs, business and industry; Middle East, USA.

Other: Gatehouse Bank plc: Director 2007-17, Deputy chair 2008-17; Director, Arab British Chamber of Commerce 2011-.

Recreations: Political history, cooking.

The Lord Carrington of Fulham, House of Lords, London SW1A 0PW
Tel: 020 7219 5353 *Email:* carringtonm@parliament.uk

NON-AFFILIATED

CARTER OF BARNES, LORD

CARTER OF BARNES (Life Baron), Stephen Andrew Carter; cr 2008. Born 12 February 1964; Married Anna Maria Gorman 1992 (1 son 1 daughter).

Education: Currie High School, Edinburgh; Aberdeen University (LLB 1987); Harvard University (AMP 1997).

Non-political career: Managing director and chief executive, J Walter Thompson Ltd 1992-2000; Chief operating officer and managing director, ntl UK and Ireland 2000-02; Chief executive officer, Office of Communications (Ofcom) 2003-07; Group chief executive, Brunswick Group LLP 2007-08; Chief of strategy and principal adviser to Prime Minister 2008; Chief marketing, strategy and communications officer, EVP solutions division, Alcatel-Lucent, Paris 2010-13; Group chief executive, Informa plc 2013-.

Political career: *House of Lords:* Raised to the peerage as Baron Carter of Barnes, of Barnes in the London Borough of Richmond upon Thames 2008. Parliamentary Under-Secretary of State and Government Spokesperson: Department for Business, Enterprise and Regulatory Reform/ Business, Innovation and Skills (Minister for Communications, Technology and Broadcasting) 2008-09, Department for Culture, Media and Sport 2008-09; On leave of absence July 2011-13. *Other:* Sat with Labour Party in the Lords until February 2017, now sits as Non-Affiliated.

Other: Vice-President, Unicef 2005-; Governor and Chairman, Ashridge Business Management School 2005-; CBE 2007.

The Lord Carter of Barnes CBE, House of Lords, London SW1A 0PW
Tel: 020 7219 5353 *Email:* carterst@parliament.uk
Informa plc, 5 Howick Place, London SW1P 1WG *Tel:* 020 7017 5771
Email: stephen.carter@informa.com

LABOUR

CARTER OF COLES, LORD

CARTER OF COLES (Life Baron), Patrick Robert Carter; cr. 2004. Born 9 February 1946; Married Julia Bourne 1969 (2 daughters).

Education: Brentwood School, Essex; Durham University (BA economics, economic history 1967).

Non-political career: Hambros Bank Ltd 1967-70; Director: Whitecross Equipment Ltd 1970-75, MAI Ltd 1975-85, Westminster Healthcare plc 1975-99; Chair, Sport England 2002-06.

Political career: *House of Lords:* Raised to the peerage as Baron Carter of Coles, of Westmill in the County of Hertfordshire 2004. EU Sub-committee D (Environment and Agriculture): Co-opted member 2009, Chair 2009-10; Member, European Union 2010-13; Chair, EU Sub-committee D: (Agriculture, Fisheries and Environment) 2010-12, (Agriculture, Fisheries, Environment and Energy) 2012-13; Member: EU Sub-committee A (Economic and Financial Affairs) 2013-15, Audit 2013-18, Joint Committee on the Palace of Westminster 2015-16, Rural Economy 2018-19, EU Internal Market Sub-committee 2019-20, EU Environment Sub-committee 2020-. *Other:* Non-executive member: Prisons Board/Strategy Board for Correctional Services 1998-2002, Home Office General Board 2002-06; Chair: National Athletics Review, Review of Payroll Services, Criminal Records Bureau, Review of Offender Services 2006, Review of Pathology 2008, Review of Courts Estate 2009, Competition and

Co-operation Panel -2014, Chair, NHS Procurement and Efficiency Board; Non-executive director, NHS Improvement.

Other: Member, Productivity Panel 2000-; Chair: Commonwealth Games 2002, English National Stadium 2002.

Recreations: Reading, walking, skiing, gardening, opera.

The Lord Carter of Coles, House of Lords, London SW1A 0PW
Tel: 020 7219 3342

CROSSBENCH

CARTER OF HASLEMERE, LORD

CARTER OF HASLEMERE (Life Baron), Harold Mark Carter; cr 2019. Born 21 September 1958; Married Hilary Pharaoh (1 daughter).

Education: Reading University (LLB).

Non-political career: Home Office: Legal Adviser's Branch 1989-2006, Deputy Legal Adviser 2009-16; Legal Adviser's Branch, Foreign and Commonwealth Office 2006-09; Bencher, Gray's Inn 2014; Legal Adviser, No 10, Government Legal Department 2016-.

Political career: *House of Lords:* Raised to the peerage as Baron Carter of Haslemere, of Haslemere in the County of Surrey 2019.

Other: CB 2015.

The Lord Carter of Haslemere CB, House of Lords, London SW1A 0PW

CROSSBENCH

CASEY OF BLACKSTOCK, BARONESS

CASEY OF BLACKSTOCK (Life Baroness), Louise Casey; cr 2020. Born 29 March 1965.

Education: Oaklands RC Comprehensive School, Portsmouth; Goldsmiths' College, London University (BA history).

Non-political career: Co-ordinator, St Mungo Association 1988-90; Director: Homeless Network 1990-92, Shelter 1992-99; Department for Transport, Local Government and the Regions/Office of the Deputy Prime Minister 1999-2003: Director, Rough Sleepers Unit 1999-2002, Director, Homelessness Directorate 2002-03; Home Office 2003-07: Director, Anti-Social Behaviour, Crime Reduction and Community Safety Group 2003-05, Government Co-ordinator, Respect Taskforce, Crime Reduction and Community Safety Group 2005-07; Director, Respect Taskforce, Young People Directorate, Department for Children, Schools and Families 2007-08; Head, Crime and Communities Review, Cabinet Office 2008; Director-General, Neighbourhood Crime and Justice Group, Home Office 2008-10; Commissioner for Victims and Witnesses 2010-11; Director-General, Troubled Families Team, Department for Communities and Local Government 2011-16, Director-General, Casey Review 2015-17; Chair, Institute of Global Homelessness, De Paul University, Chicago 2017-.

Political career: *House of Lords:* Raised to the peerage as Baroness Casey of Blackstock, of Finsbury in the London Borough of Islington 2020.

Other: Woman's Hour Powerlist 2013; CB 2008; DBC 2016.

The Baroness Casey of Blackstock DBE CB, House of Lords, London SW1A 0PW
Tel: 020 7219 3000

NON-AFFILIATED

CASHMAN, LORD

CASHMAN (Life Baron), Michael Maurice Cashman; cr 2014. Born 17 December 1950; Son of John and Mary Cashman; Civil partner Paul Cottingham 2006 (died 2014).

Education: Cardinal Griffin Secondary Modern School; Gladys Dare's Stage School; French.

Non-political career: Actor in theatre, musical theatre, TV films and radio; Associate artist, Birmingham Repertory Theatre 1963-99. Member, Equity.

Political career: *House of Lords:* Raised to the peerage as Baron Cashman, of Limehouse in the London Borough of Tower Hamlets 2014. Member: EU Justice Sub-committee 2017-19, Regenerating Seaside Towns and Communities 2018. *Other:* European Parliament: MEP (Labour) for West Midlands 1999-2014: Vice-chair, Petitions Committee 2004-09, Chair: Lesbian, Gay, Bisexual and Transgender Rights Intergroup 2004-14, South Africa Delegation 2009-14. Labour Party: Member: National Executive Committee 1998-2012, Conference Arrangements Committee 2015-, LGBT global envoy -2016, Patron, LGBT Labour, Resigned May 2019.

Political interests: Human rights, civil liberties, poverty, freedom of information, development, LGBTI; South Africa, Turkey, USA.

Other: Stonewall Group: Founder member, Chair 1988-96; Councillor/honorary treasurer, Equity 1994-98; Sarcoma Unit Royal Marsden Hospital, Peter Tatchell Foundation; Honorary doctorate, Staffordshire University (2007); Special service award, American Association Physicians for Human Rights; Lifetime achievement award, EDA 2012; Lifetime achievement award, *Pink News* 2014; Politican of the Year, Stonewall 2014; CBE 2013.

Recreations: Travel, photography, ceramics.

The Lord Cashman CBE, House of Lords, London SW1A 0PW
Tel: 020 7219 6533 *Email:* cashmanm@parliament.uk Website: www.lordmichaelcashman.com
Twitter: @mcashmanCBE

CONSERVATIVE

CATHCART, EARL

CATHCART (7th Earl, UK), Charles Alan Andrew Cathcart; cr. 1814; 7th Viscount Cathcart and Baron Greenock (UK) 1807; 16th Lord Cathcart (S) c.1442. Born 30 November 1952; Son of Major-General 6th Earl and Rosemary Smyth-Osbourne; Married Vivien Skinner 1981 (1 son 1 daughter).

Education: Eton College.

Non-political career: Chartered accountant: Whinney Murray 1976-79, Ernst and Whinney 1979-83 (ICAEW 1981); Director and Lloyd's underwriter: Gardner Mountain and Capel-cure Agencies 1983-94, Murray Lawrence Members Agencies 1995-96; Director, Reinsurance Group of America (UK) 1996-2011; Chairman, Equator Films plc (now Handmade Films Ltd) 1998-2004; Finance director, Vivien Greenock Ltd 2001-; Director, Spring Gardens Eggs Ltd. Command Scots Guards 1972-75.

Political career: *House of Lords:* First entered House of Lords 1999; Elected hereditary peer 2007-; Opposition Whip 2007-10; Opposition Spokesperson for: Communities and Local Government 2007-10, Environment, Food and Rural Affairs 2007-10, Northern Ireland 2007-09, Scotland 2009-10. Member: Administration and Works 2015-16, Privileges and Conduct 2016-. *Other:* President: Mid Norfolk Conservative Association 2009-11, Mid Norfolk Patrons Club 2010-; Executive Committee of Association of Conservative Peers 2010-13. Councillor, Breckland District Council 1998-2007.

Political interests: Rural affairs, environment, energy, farming, housing; UK.

Other: Member, Queen's Bodyguards for Scotland, Royal Company of Archers; ICAEW.

Recreations: Skiing, sailing, country pursuits.

The Earl Cathcart, House of Lords, London SW1A 0PW
Tel: 020 7219 5422 *Email:* cathcartc@parliament.uk

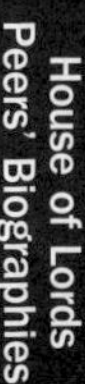

CROSSBENCH

CAVENDISH OF LITTLE VENICE, BARONESS

CAVENDISH OF LITTLE VENICE (Life Baroness), Hilary Camilla Cavendish; cr 2016. Born 20 August 1968; Married 1999 (3 children).

Education: Putney High School; Brasenose College, Oxford (BA philosophy, politics and economics 1989); Harvard School of Government (Kennedy Scholar, MPA 1991).

Non-political career: Business analyst, McKinsey & Co 1991-93; Director of Programmes, London First 1993-95; Chief executive, South Bank Employers Group 1995-99; Adviser to chief executive, Pearsons plc 1999-2002; Columnist and associate editor: *The Times* 2002-13, *Sunday Times* 2013-15; Director of Policy Unit, Prime Minister's Office 2015-16; Senior Fellow, Mossavar-Rahmani Center for Business and Government, Harvard Kennedy School 2018-; Columnist and Contributing Editor, *Financial Times* 2018-.

Political career: *House of Lords:* Raised to the peerage as Baroness Cavendish of Little Venice, of Mells in the County of Somerset 2016. *Other:* Resigned from Conservative Party December 2016, sat as Non-affiliated December 2016-October 2019, now sits as a Crossbencher. Non-executive Director, Care Quality Commission 2013-15.

Other: Trustee: Policy Exchange 2002-, Foundation Years Trust 2013-15; Chair, Frontline 2017-; Senior Fellow, Harvard University; Paul Foot Award for Campaigning Journalism 2008; Wincott Senior Financial Journalist 2011.

Publications: Extra Time: Ten Lessons for an Ageing World (Harper Collins, 2019).

The Baroness Cavendish of Little Venice, House of Lords, London SW1A 0PW
Tel: 020 7219 3000 *Twitter:* @camcavendish

CONSERVATIVE

CHADLINGTON, LORD

CHADLINGTON (Life Baron), Peter Selwyn Gummer; cr. 1996. Born 24 August 1942; Son of late Rev Canon Selwyn Gummer and late Sybille Selwyn Gummer, née Mason; Married Lucy Dudley-Hill 1982 (3 daughters 1 son).

Education: King's School, Rochester; Selwyn College, Cambridge (BA moral sciences tripos 1964, MA).

Non-political career: Portsmouth and Sunderland Newspaper Group Ltd 1964-65; Viyella International 1965-66; Hodgkinson and Partners 1966-67; Industrial and Commercial Finance Corporation 1967-74; Shandwick International plc 1974-2000: Founder and chief executive 1974-94, Chairman 1994-2000; Non-executive director, CIA Group plc 1990-94; Chairman, Marketing Group of GB 1993-95; Halifax Building Society/plc: Non-executive director, London Bonds 1990-94, Non-executive director 1994-2001; Chairman, International Public Relations 1998-2000; Director: Black Box Music Ltd 1999-2001, Walbrook Club 1999-2004; Chairman, Hotcourses Ltd 2000-04; Huntsworth plc: Chief executive 2000-05, Sept 2005-, Executive chairman May-Sept 2005; Director, Hill Hay Saddle Ltd 2002-; Non-executive director, Britax Childcare Holdings Ltd 2005-11.

Political career: *House of Lords:* Raised to the peerage as Baron Chadlington, of Dean in the County of Oxfordshire 1996. Member: European Union Sub-committee B (Energy, Industry and Transport) 2000-03, Information 2005-06, Charities 2016-17. *Other:* Member: NHS Policy Board 1991-95, Arts Council of England 1991-96; Chairman: National Lottery Advisory Board for Arts and Film 1994-96, Royal Opera House 1996-97; Council member, Cheltenham Ladies College 1998-2003; Non-executive director, Oxford Resources 1999-2002; Non-executive chairman, guideforlife.com 2000-02.

Other: Chairman, Understanding Industry Trust 1991-96; Trustee, Atlantic Partnership 1999-; Board of Trustees, American University 1999-2001; Action on Addiction: Trustee 1999-2000, Chairman 2000-07; Governor, Ditchley Foundation 2008; Committee member, British Heart Foundation Mending Broken Hearts Appeal 2010-; Chairman, LAPADA (professional art and antique dealers' trade association) 2011-; Freedom, City of London; FRSA; FIPR; Honorary Fellow, Bournemouth University 1999-; *PR Week* Award for outstanding individual contribution to public relations 1984; Institute of Public Relations Presidents' Medal 1988; Ernst & Young Entrepreneur of the Year, Master Entrepreneur London Region 2008. White's, Garrick, Carlton, Walbrook Club; MCC.

Publications: Various articles and booklets on public relations.

Recreations: Opera, rugby, cricket.

The Lord Chadlington, House of Lords, London SW1A 0PW
Tel: 020 7219 5172 *Email:* chadlingtonp@parliament.uk

LABOUR

CHAKRABARTI, BARONESS

CHAKRABARTI (Life Baroness), Sharmishta Chakrabarti; cr 2016. Born 16 June 1969; Married Martyn Hopper 1995 (divorced 2014) (1 son).

Education: Harrow Weald Sixth Form College; London School of Economics (LLB).

Non-political career: Called to the Bar, Middle Temple 1994; Associate Tenant, 39 Essex Chambers; Legal Adviser's Branch, Home Office 1996-2001; Liberty: Lawyer 2001-03, Director 2003-15; Leveson Inquiry 2011-12.

Political career: *House of Lords:* Raised to the peerage as Baroness Chakrabarti, of Kennington in the London Borough of Lambeth 2016. Shadow Attorney General 2016-20. *Other:* Governor, London School of Economics 2005-11.

Other: Governor, British Film Institute 2006-13; Chancellor: Oxford Brookes University 2008-15, Essex University 2014-17; Channel 4 News Most Inspiring Political Figure 2006; CBE 2007; PC 2018.

Rt Hon the Baroness Chakrabarti CBE, House of Lords, London SW1A 0PW
Tel: 020 7219 3000 *Email:* chakrabartis@parliament.uk

CONSERVATIVE

CHALKER OF WALLASEY, BARONESS

CHALKER OF WALLASEY (Life Baroness), Lynda Chalker; cr. 1992. Born 29 April 1942; Daughter of late Sidney Bates and late Marjorie Randell; Married Eric Chalker 1967 (divorced 1973); married Clive Landa 1981 (divorced 2003).

Education: Roedean School, Sussex; Heidelberg University (technical German 1961); London University; Central London Polytechnic (statistics 1965).

Non-political career: Statistician, Unilever's Research Bureau Ltd 1963-69; Market researcher, Shell Mex and BP 1969-72; Executive director (International), Opinion Research International Ltd 1972-74; Adviser, Barclays Bank International 1976-79; Independent Consultant on Africa and Development 1997-; Africa Matters Limited: Chair 1997-16, President 2016-; Director: Unilever plc 1998-2007, Ashanti Goldfields Ltd 1998-2007, Group Five Construction Pty (SA) 2001-2012. Hon. Colonel, Royal Logistic Corps (156 Transport Regiment NW) 1995-2001.

Political career: *House of Commons:* MP (Conservative) for Wallasey February 1974-92. Contested Wallasey 1992 general election; Parliamentary Under-Secretary of State, Department of Health and Social Security 1979-82, Department of Transport: Parliamentary Under-Secretary of State 1982-83, Minister of State 1983-86; Foreign and Commonwealth Office: Minister of State 1986-97, Deputy to Foreign Secretary 1987-97, Minister for Overseas Development 1989-92. *House of Lords:* Raised to the peerage as Baroness Chalker of Wallasey, of Leigh-on-Sea in the County of Essex 1992. Minister of Overseas Development and Minister for Africa and Commonwealth, Foreign and Commonwealth Office 1992-97. Member: EU External Affairs Sub-committee 2018-20, EU Goods Sub-committee 2020-. *Other:* National vice-chair, Young Conservatives 1970-71; Hon. Life member, Tory Reform Group. Member, BBC Advisory Committee 1974-76.

Political interests: Voluntary sector, European co-operation, Africa, overseas development, trade, transport, construction; Sub-Saharan Africa, Egypt, Jordan.

Other: Adviser, World Bank 1997-2005; Co-ordinator, Presidential International Investment Council for Nigeria 2001-; Member: Kenyan National Economic and Social Council 2004-09, Ugandan Presidential Investment Round Table 2004-, Tanzania National Business Council 2004-; Chair: London School of Hygiene and Tropical Medicine 1998-2006, Medicines for Malaria Venture 2006-11; Trustee: Global Leadership Foundation, Investment Climate Facility for Africa; British Executive Services Overseas, Intermediate Technology Development Group, African Medical Research Foundation, British Red Cross, Red R, Water Aid; Fellow: Royal Geographical Society, London School of Hygiene and Tropical Medicine, Institute of

Highways and Transportation, Royal Statistical Society; Nine honorary degrees; PC 1987. Royal Overseas League, St James Club.

Publications: Police in Retreat (1968); Unhappy Families (1972); We're Richer than We Think (1978); Africa – Turning the Tide (1989).

Recreations: Theatre, cooking, gardening, jazz.

Rt Hon the Baroness Chalker of Wallasey, House of Lords, London SW1A 0PW
Tel: 020 7219 3000 *Email:* chalkerl@parliament.uk
13-15 Carteret Street, London SW1H 9DJ *Tel:* 020 7976 6850 *Email:* pa@africamatters.com
Twitter: @BaronessChalker

LABOUR

CHANDOS, VISCOUNT

CHANDOS (3rd Viscount, UK), Thomas Orlando Lyttelton; cr. 1954; (Life) Baron Lyttelton of Aldershot 2000. Born 12 February 1953; Son of 2nd Viscount; Married Arabella Sarah Bailey 1985 (2 sons 1 daughter).

Education: Eton College; Worcester College, Oxford (BA).

Non-political career: Director: Kleinwort Benson 1985-93, Botts & Company Limited 1993-98, Capital and Regional Properties plc 1993-, Cine-UK Limited 1995-, Video Networks Limited 1996-99, Chair: Lopex plc 1997-99, Mediakey plc 1998-2000, Capital and Regional plc 2000-; Director: Global Natural Energy plc 2000-, Northbridge (UK) Limited 2001-.

Political career: *House of Lords:* Created a life peer as Baron Lyttelton of Aldershot, of Aldershot in the County of Hampshire 2000. First entered House of Lords 1982; Formerly SDP Spokesperson for Finance and Trade; Opposition Spokesperson on Treasury and Economic Affairs 1995-97. Member: Works of Art 2003-07, Information 2015-16, Natural Environment and Rural Communities Act 2006 2017-18, Intergenerational Fairness and Provision 2018-19, Economic Affairs 2019-, Economic Affairs Finance Bill Sub-committee 2020-.

Other: Director, English National Opera 1995-; Trustee: 21st Century Learning Initiative 1995-, Education Low-Priced Sponsored Texts 1996-99; Governor, National Film and Television School 1996-2001; President, National Kidney Research Fund 2001-; Director, Social Market Foundation 2001-.

The Viscount Chandos, House of Lords, London SW1A 0PW
Tel: 020 7219 6307
Northbridge UK Ltd, 9 Park Place, London SW1A 1LP

LABOUR

CHAPMAN OF DARLINGTON, BARONESS

CHAPMAN OF DARLINGTON (Life Baroness), Jennifer Chapman; cr 2021. Born 25 September 1973; Married Nick Smith (qv) 2014 (MP for Blaenau Gwent).

Education: Hummersknott School, Darlington; Brunel University (BSc psychology 1996); Durham University (MA medieval archaeology 2004).

Non-political career: Senior parliamentary researcher to Alan Milburn MP 1997-2005. Member, USDAW.

Political career: *House of Commons:* MP for Darlington 2010-19; Shadow Minister for: Justice 2011-16, Education 2016, Exiting the European Union 2016-19. Member: Procedure 2010-16, 2016-17, Joint Committee on Consolidation, Etc, Bills 2010-15. *House of Lords:* Raised to the peerage as Baroness Chapman of Darlington, of Darlington in the County of Durham 2021. *Other:* Darlington Council: Councillor 2007-10, Cabinet Member for Children and Young People; Governor, Branksome School; Member, Darlington Partnership Board.

Political interests: Justice, children, families, employment, transport, economy, skills.

Other: Member, National Trust; Trustee, Darlington Rape Crisis Centre; Vice-chair, Progress 2012-; Chair of trustees, Newblood Live.

Publications: Contributor, The Purple Book (Progress, 2011).

The Baroness Chapman of Darlington, House of Lords, London SW1A 0PW
Twitter: @JennyChapman

CROSSBENCH

CHARTRES, LORD

CHARTRES (Life Baron), Richard John Carew Chartres; cr 2017. Born 11 July 1947; Son of late Richard Chartres and Charlotte Chartres; Married Caroline Mary McLintock 1982 (2 sons 2 daughters).

Education: Hertford Grammar School; Trinity College, Cambridge (MA history 1968); Cuddesdon Theological College, Oxford; Lincoln Theological College (BD (Lambeth) 1984); French.

Non-political career: Deacon 1973; Assistant Curate, St Andrew's, Bedford 1973-75; Priest 1974; Bishop's Domestic Chaplain, St Albans 1975-80; Archbishop of Canterbury's Chaplain 1980-84; Vicar, St Stephen with St John, Westminster 1984-92; Director of Ordinands for the London Area 1985-92; Gresham Professor of Divinity 1986-92; Area Bishop of Stepney 1992-95; Hon Bencher, Middle Temple; Bishop of London 1995-2017.

Political career: *House of Lords:* Raised to the peerage as Baron Chartres, of Wilton in the County of Wiltshire 2017. First Entered House of Lords as Bishop of London 1996. Member: Secondary Legislation Scrutiny 2018-, SLSC Sub-committee A 2018-19. *Other:* Dean of HM Chapels Royal 1996-; Independent member, House of Lords Appointment Commission 2019-.

Political interests: London, environment, constitutional matters; China, Russia.

Other: Ecclesiastical Patron, Prayer Book Society; Life President, St Ethelburga's Centre for Reconciliation and Peace; Vice-president, Bible Society; Ambassador, World Wildlife Fund; Liveryman: Drapers' Company, Pewterers Company; Hon. Freeman: Merchant Taylors' Company, Weavers' Company, Leathersellers' Company, Woolmen Company, Vintners, Grocers, Water Conservators, Arts Scholars; Freedom, City of London 1997; FSA 1999; Hon. Fellow, Trinity College, Cambridge; Hon DLitt, London Guildhall; Hon DD: Queen Mary London, City University, Brunel University, King's College, London, University of the South, Tennessee, USA; PC 1995; Ehrendomprediger (Germany) 2001; KCVO 2009; GCVO 2019. Garrick Club.

Publications: A Brief History of Gresham College (1997); Tree of Knowledge, Tree of Life (2004).

Recreations: Family.

Rt Rev and Rt Hon the Lord Chartres GCVO, House of Lords, London SW1A 0PW
Tel: 020 7219 3000 *Email:* chartresr@parliament.uk

NON-AFFILIATED

CHICHESTER, LORD BISHOP OF

CHICHESTER (104th Bishop of), Martin Clive Warner. Born 24 December 1958; Single.

Education: King's School; Maidstone Grammar School; St Chad's College, Durham; St Stephen's House, Oxford.

Non-political career: Ordained Deacon 1984, Priest 1985; Curate, St Peter's Plymouth 1984-88; Team Vicar, Parish of the Resurrection, Leicester 1988-93; Priest Administrator, Shrine of Our Lady of Walsingham 1993-2002; Priest-in-charge, Hempton and Pudding Norton 1998-2000; Honorary Canon of Norwich 2000-02; Canon, St Paul's Cathedral, London 2003-10; Suffragan Bishop of Whitby 2010-12; Bishop of Chichester 2012-.

Political career: *House of Lords:* Entered House of Lords 2018.

Other: Chair, Council of St Stephen's House, Oxford 2013-; President and Trustee, Sussex Historic Churches Trust; Patron: Family Support Work 2012-, Sussex Snowdrop Trust 2014-, Streetlight UK 2015-, Trustee, John Booth Foundation 2015-; Trustee and Chair, Bishop Otter Trust.

Publications: Walsingham, an Ever-circling Year (1996); Say Yes to God (1999); The Habit of Holiness (2004); Known to the Senses (2004); Between Heaven and Charing Cross (2009); Contributor, *Church Times*.

Recreations: Cycling, the arts.

Rt Rev Dr the Lord Bishop of Chichester, House of Lords, London SW1A 0PW
Tel: 020 7219 3000
The Palace, Chichester PO19 1PY *Tel:* 01243 782161 *Email:* bishop@chichester.anglican.org
Website: www.chichester.anglican.org

LIBERAL DEMOCRAT

CHIDGEY, LORD

Liberal Democrat Lords Spokesperson for Africa

CHIDGEY (Life Baron), David William George Chidgey; cr 2005. Born 9 July 1942; Son of Major Cyril and Winifred Chidgey; Married April Idris-Jones 1964 (1 son 2 daughters).

Education: Brune Park County High School, Gosport; Portsmouth Polytechnic (Dip CivilEng 1965, CEng); Portsmouth Naval College; Graduate, Institute of Mechanical Engineers; French.

Non-political career: Consulting civil engineer; Senior civil engineer, Hampshire County Council 1964-73; Brian Colquhoun and Partners 1973-93: Associate partner 1988-93, Projects director, West Africa and South East Asia 1978-87, Managing director, Ireland 1981-88; Chief consultant to Dublin Transport Authority 1987-88; Associate director and projects director, Central Southern England Thorburn Colquhoun 1994.

Political career: *House of Commons:* Contested Eastleigh 1992 general election. MP (Liberal Democrat) for Eastleigh 1994 by-election to 2005; Liberal Democrat Spokesperson for: Employment 1994-95, Transport 1995-97, Trade and Industry 1997-99, Foreign Affairs 1999-2005. Member: Accomodation and Works 1998-2001, Standards and Privileges 2001, Foreign Affairs 1999-2005, Chairman's Panel 2001-05, Joint Committee on Human Rights 2003-05. *House of Lords:* Raised to the peerage as Baron Chidgey, of Hamble-le-Rice in the County of Hampshire 2005. Liberal Democrat Spokesperson for: Defence (Royal Navy, Defence Procurement) 2005-06, International Development and Foreign and Commonwealth Office (Africa) -2010, International Development 2015, Africa 2020-. Co-opted Member, EU Sub-committee C (Foreign Affairs, Defence and Development Policy) 2006-10. Chair, Liberal Democrat Parliamentary Party Committee on International Affairs (International Development) 2010-15. *Other:* Contested (SLD) Hampshire Central 1988 by-election and 1989 European Parliament election. Regional chair, Hampshire and Wight Liberal Democrats 1992-94; Joint founder and president, Association of Liberal Democrat Engineers and Applied Scientists. Councillor, Winchester City Council 1987-91.

Political interests: Foreign affairs, international development, transport, built environment; Africa, Pacific Rim and South East Asia, Indian sub-continent, Middle East, Europe.

Other: AWEPA (European Parliamentarians with Africa): UK Parliament Representative 2007-, Director, Governing Council 2010-, Political co-ordinator for aid effectiveness, SADC region 2011-; Member, advisory board, UK Transatlantic Leadership Academy SLLF/Europe 2007-12; Chair, international advisory board, CPSU (Commonwealth Policy Studies Unit) 2008-12; Member, advisory board, TI (UK) 2008-; Delegate, Parliamentary Assembly Council of Europe and Western European Union 2009-11; Member, Chartered Institute of Transport; Companion, Royal Aeronautical Society; Fellow, Industry and Parliament Trust 1999; Save The Children; Liveryman Worshipful Company of Carmen; Freedom: City of London 1997, Borough of Eastleigh 2005; Fellow: Institution of Civil Engineers, Institution of Engineers of Ireland, Institution of Highways and Transportation, Association of Consulting Engineers of Ireland. National Liberal Club.

Recreations: Reading, walking, following cricket.

The Lord Chidgey, House of Lords, London SW1A 0PW
Tel: 020 7219 6944 *Fax:* 020 7219 5436 *Email:* chidgeyd@parliament.uk

CONSERVATIVE

CHISHOLM OF OWLPEN, BARONESS

CHISHOLM OF OWLPEN (Life Baroness), Caroline (Carlyn) Elizabeth Chisholm; cr 2014. Born 23 December 1951; Daughter of Baron Egremont MBE; Married Colin Chisholm 1976 (2 sons 1 daughter).

Non-political career: Nurse.

Political career: *House of Lords:* Raised to the peerage as Baroness Chisholm of Owlpen, of Owlpen in the County of Gloucestershire 2014. Government Whip (Baroness in Waiting) 2015-16, 2017-18, 2019-20; Government Spokesperson for Cabinet Office 2015-16. Member: Joint Committee on the Draft Health Service Safety Investigations Bill 2018, Communications 2018-19, COVID-19 2020-. *Other:* Senior volunteer, Conservative Party; Chair, Conservative Candidates Committee; President, Stroud Conservative Association.

Other: Nelson Trust, National Autistic Society, Trustee, National Osteoporosis Society.

The Baroness Chisholm of Owlpen, House of Lords, London SW1A 0PW
Tel: 020 7219 5353

NON-AFFILIATED

CHOLMONDELEY, MARQUESS OF

CHOLMONDELEY (7th Marquess of, UK), David George Philip Cholmondeley; cr. 1815; 10th Earl of Cholmondeley (E) 1706; 7th Earl of Rocksavage (UK) 1815; 10th Viscount Malpas (E) 1706; 11th Viscount Cholmondeley (I) 1661; 10th Baron Cholmondeley (E) 1689; 10th Baron Newburgh (GB) 1716; 10th Baron Newborough (I) 1715. Born 27 June 1960; Son of 6th Marquess, GCVO, MC, DL; Married Rose Hanbury 2009 (twin sons 1 daughter).

Education: Eton College; Sorbonne.

Non-political career: Page of Honour to HM The Queen 1974-76; Joint Hereditary Lord Great Chamberlain of England (acting for the reign of Queen Elizabeth II) 1990-.

Political career: *House of Lords:* First entered House of Lords 1990; On leave of absence.

Other: KCVO 2007.

Most Hon the Marquess of Cholmondeley KCVO, House of Lords, London SW1A 0PW
Tel: 020 7219 5353
Houghton Hall, King's Lynn PE31 6UA *Tel:* 01829 720202

CONSERVATIVE

CHOUDREY, LORD

CHOUDREY (Life Baron), Zameer Mohammed Choudrey; cr 2019.

Education: Kent University.

Non-political career: Bestway Group: Financial Controller 1984-87, Managing Director 1987-90, Finance Director 1990-95, Chief Executive, Bestway Cement 1995-2004, Chief executive, Bestway Group 2004-.

Political career: *House of Lords:* Raised to the peerage as Baron Choudrey, of Hampstead in the London Borough of Barnet 2019. *Other:* Chair, Conservative Friends of Pakistan. Governor, John Kelly colleges/schools (Crest Academies) 1992-2002.

Other: Chair, Bestway Foundation Pakistan; Trustee: Bestway Foundation UK, Crimestoppers, GroceryAid; Member: HRH Prince of Wales Pakistan Recovery Fund International Leadership Team, UK Advisory Council, British Asian Trust; Governor, Rainbow Foundation; Fellow, Institute of Chartered Accountants in England and Wales; Honorary Doctor of Civil Law, Kent University; CBE 2016.

The Lord Choudrey CBE, House of Lords, London SW1A 0PW
Email: choudreyz@parliament.uk

LABOUR

CHRISTOPHER, LORD

CHRISTOPHER (Life Baron), Anthony (Tony) Martin Grosvenor Christopher; cr. 1998. Born 25 April 1925; Son of late George and Helen Christopher; Married Adela Thompson 1962.

Education: Cheltenham Grammar School; Westminster College of Commerce.

Non-political career: Articled Pupil Agricultural Valuers, Gloucester 1941-44; Inland Revenue 1948-57; Civil Service Building Society: Director 1958-87, Chair 1978-87; General Secretary, Inland Revenue Staff Federation 1976-88; TUC General Council: Member 1976-89, Chair 1988-89; TU Fund Managers Ltd: Director 1981-2013, Chair 1983-2013; Director, Birmingham Midshires Building Society 1987-88; Industrial and Public Affairs Consultant 1988-. RAF 1944-48.

Political career: *House of Lords:* Raised to the peerage as Baron Christopher, of Leckhampton in the County of Gloucestershire 1998. Member: Consolidation, Etc, Bills Joint Committee 2000-16, Audit 2003-06, European Union Sub-committee D (Environment and Agriculture) 2003-06, Tax Law Rewrite Bills Joint Committee 2007-09. *Other:* Member, Inner London Probation and After-care Committee 1966-79; Chair, NACRO 1973-98; Member: Tax Reform Committee 1974-80, Royal Commission on Distribution of Income and Wealth 1978-79, Independent Broadcasting Authority 1978-83; Chair, Tyre Industry Economic Development Council 1983-86; Member: Council of Institute of Manpower Studies 1984-89, Economic and Social Research Council 1985-88; Vice-President, Building Societies Association 1985-90; Member: General Medical Council 1989-94, Audit Commission 1989-95, Broadcasting Complaints Commission 1989-97.

Political interests: Agriculture, financial services, pensions, penal affairs and policy, economics, industry, the elderly; Africa, China, Egypt.

Other: Members' Auditor, International Confederation of Free Trades Unions 1983-2007; Trustee: Trades Union Unit Trust Charitable Trust 1981-, Commonwealth Trades Union Council Charitable Trust 1985-89, Save The Children Fund 1985-90; Institute for Public Policy Research: Trustee 1989-94, Treasurer 1990-94; Trustee, Douglas Houghton Memorial Fund 1998-; Hon. Fellow, Association of Taxation Technicians 2015; FRSA 1989; CBE 1984. Beefsteak, Wig and Pen Club.

Publications: Co-author: Policy for Poverty (1970); The Wealth Report (1979); The Wealth Report 2 (1982).

Recreations: Gardening, dog walking.

The Lord Christopher CBE, House of Lords, London SW1A 0PW
Tel: 020 7219 6162
TU Fund Managers Ltd, Congress House, Great Russell Street, London WC1B 3LQ
Tel: 020 7637 7114

CROSSBENCH

CLANCARTY, EARL OF

CLANCARTY (9th Earl of, I), Nicholas Power Richard Le Poer Trench; cr. 1803; 9th Viscount Dunlo (I), 1800; 8th Viscount Clancarty (UK) 1823; 9th Baron Kilconnel (I) 1797; 8th Baron Trench (UK) 1815; 8th Marquess of Heusden in the Netherlands 1818. Born 1 May 1952; Son of late Hon Power Edward Ford Le Poer (Terry) Trench and late Jocelyn Louise (Joy) Courtney; Married Victoria Frances Lambert 2005 (1 daughter).

Education: Westminster School; Ashford County Grammar School; Plymouth Polytechnic (BA geography and geology 1975); University of Colorado, USA (MA geography 1978); Sheffield Polytechnic (BA fine art 1987); French, German.

Non-political career: Artist and writer; Company secretary, Dysart Press.

Political career: *House of Lords:* First entered House of Lords 1995. Sits as Viscount Clancarty; Elected hereditary peer 2010-. Member, Lord Speaker's Advisory Panel on Works of Art 2019-.

Political interests: Arts and cultural issues, welfare, education; France, Germany, Netherlands.

The Earl of Clancarty, House of Lords, London SW1A 0PW
Tel: 020 7219 8929 *Email:* clancartyn@parliament.uk *Twitter:* @NickClancarty

CROSSBENCH

CLARK OF CALTON, BARONESS

CLARK OF CALTON (Life Baroness), Lynda Margaret Clark; cr 2005. Born 26 February 1949.

Education: Queen's College, St Andrews University (LLB 1970); Edinburgh University (PhD 1975).

Non-political career: Dundee University: Part-time tutor 1971-73, Lecturer in jurisprudence 1973-76; Advocate, Scots Bar 1977-89; QC 1989-99 in practice at Scots Bar; Called to the English Bar 1990; Governing bencher, Inner Temple 2000; Senator of the College of Justice in Scotland 2006-.

Political career: *House of Commons:* Contested North East Fife 1992 general election. MP (Labour) for Edinburgh Pentlands 1997-2005; Advocate General for Scotland 1999-2005. *House of Lords:* Raised to the peerage as Baroness Clark of Calton, of Calton in the City of Edinburgh 2005. Advocate General for Scotland 2005-06; Lord of Appeal 2006-08; As a senior member of the judiciary, disqualified from participation 2006-19; On Leave of absence February-September 2019.

Political interests: Constitutional reform, justice system, health, education, pensions.

Other: Former member: Scottish Legal Aid Board, Edinburgh University Court; QC (Scot) 1989; PC 2013.

Rt Hon the Baroness Clark of Calton QC, House of Lords, London SW1A 0PW
Tel: 020 7219 5353

LABOUR

CLARK OF KILWINNING, BARONESS

CLARK OF KILWINNING (Life Baroness), Kathryn Sloan Clark; cr 2020. Born 3 July 1967; Daughter of Dr Norman Clark and Esther Clark; 1 daughter.

Education: Kyle Academy, Ayr; Aberdeen University (LLB 1990); Edinburgh University (Diploma legal practice 1991).

Non-political career: Qualified solicitor – Scotland, England and Wales; Private practice, Edinburgh and Musselburgh -1998; Head of membership legal services, Unison 1998-2005; Political Secretary to Jeremy Corbyn 2015-19. Member: GMB, CWU.

Political career: *House of Commons:* Contested Galloway and Upper Nithsdale 1997 general election. MP for North Ayrshire and Arran 2005-15. Contested North Ayrshire and Arran 2015 general election. Member: Scottish Affairs 2005-10, Procedure 2005-10, Crossrail Bill 2006-07, European Scrutiny 2006-10, Joint Committee on the Draft Human Tissue and Embryos Bill 2007, Chairmen's Panel/Panel of Chairs 2010-15, Environmental Audit 2010-15, Business, Innovation and Skills 2010-15, Arms Export Controls 2011-15. *House of Lords:* Raised to the peerage as Baroness Clark of Kilwinning, of Kilwinning in the County of Ayrshire 2020. *Other:* Contested London region 2019 European Parliament election. Member: Labour Party 1985-, Co-operative Party; Contested Scottish Labour deputy leadership election 2014.

Political interests: Equality, human rights, economic and social justice, transport, environment.

The Baroness Clark of Kilwinning, House of Lords, London SW1A 0PW
Tel: 020 7219 3000 *Email:* clarkk@parliament.uk *Twitter:* @KatySClark

LABOUR

CLARK OF WINDERMERE, LORD

CLARK OF WINDERMERE (Life Baron), David George Clark; cr. 2001. Born 19 October 1939; Son of George Clark; Married Christine Kirkby 1970 (1 daughter).

Education: Windermere Grammar School; Manchester University (BA economics 1963, MSc 1965) Sheffield University (PhD 1978).

Non-political career: Forester 1956-57; Laboratory worker in textile mill 1957-59; Student teacher, Salford 1959-60; President, Manchester University Union 1963-64; Lecturer in public administration, Salford University 1965-70; Professor of History and Politics, Huddersfield University 2015-. Member, Unison.

Political career: *House of Commons:* Contested Manchester Withington 1966 general election. MP (Labour) for Colne Valley 1970-74, for South Shields 1979-2001; Opposition Spokesperson for: Agriculture, Fisheries and Food 1972-74, Defence 1980-81, Environment 1981-87, Food, Agricultural and Rural Affairs 1987-92, Defence, Disarmament and Arms Control 1992-97; Chancellor of the Duchy of Lancaster 1997-98. *House of Lords:* Raised to the peerage as Baron Clark of Windermere, of Windermere in the County of Cumbria 2001. Member, Joint Committee on National Security Strategy 2013-16. Vice-chair, PLP Departmental Group for Defence 2010-15. *Other:* Chair, Forestry Commission 2001-10; DL, Cumbria 2006; Member, House of Lords Appointments Commission 2017-.

Political interests: Open spaces, forestry, defence, security.

Other: UK Delegation of the North Atlantic Assembly 1980-2005: Member 1980-97, 1998-2005, Leader 2001-05; Executive member, National Trust 1980-94; Patron, Vindolanda Trust 1983-; Trustee, History of Parliament Trust 1986-; Freedom, Borough of South Tyneside 1998-; Hon. Fellow, Cumbria University 2009; PC 1997. Director, Carlisle United AFC 2002-.

Publications: Industrial Manager (1966); Colne Valley: Radicalism to Socialism (1981); Victor Grayson: Labour's Lost Leader (1985); We Do Not Want The Earth (1992); The Labour Movement in Westmorland (2012); Voices from Labour's Past (2015); Victor Grayson: The Man and the Mystery (2016).

Recreations: Gardening, fell-walking, reading, watching football.

Rt Hon the Lord Clark of Windermere DL, House of Lords, London SW1A 0PW
Tel: 020 7219 2558 *Email:* clarkd@parliament.uk

LABOUR

CLARKE OF HAMPSTEAD, LORD

CLARKE OF HAMPSTEAD (Life Baron), Anthony James Clarke; cr. 1998. Born 17 April 1932; Son of Henry Clarke and Elizabeth Clarke; Married Josephine Turner 1954 (1 son 1 daughter).

Education: St Dominic's Roman Catholic School, Kentish Town; Ruskin College, Oxford (Correspondence course trade union studies).

Non-political career: Post Office: Telegraph boy, Postman, Postman higher grade (sorter); Union of Postal Workers (UPW): Full-time trade union officer 1979-93, Editor, UPW journal *The Post* 1979, Deputy General Secretary 1981-93. National Service, Royal Signals 1950-52; TA and Army Emergency Reserve 1952-68. Branch Secretary, UPW 1962-69; Member: London Trades Council 1965-69 (EC Member 1967-68), TUC Disputes Panel 1972-93, TUC South East Regional Council 1974-79, London Council of Post Office Unions 1975-79, Midlands Council of Post Office Unions 1975-79; President, TU Friends of Israel.

Political career: *House of Commons:* Contested (Labour) Camden Hampstead February and October 1974 general elections. *House of Lords:* Raised to the peerage as Baron Clarke of Hampstead, of Hampstead in the London Borough of Camden 1998. *Other:* Member, Executive Committee, Labour Friends of Israel 1972-2001; Labour Party: Member, National Executive Committee 1983-93, St Albans Labour Party 1986-2013, Chair 1992-93. Councillor, London Borough of Camden 1971-78.

Political interests: Overseas aid and development, industrial relations.

Other: Organiser and Lecturer, Postal and Telegraph International, Malaysia and India; Trustee, Post Office Pension Funds 1991-97; Governor, Westminster Foundation for Democracy 1992-98; Founder member, One World Action; RAF Museum; Knight of St Gregory (Papal Order) 1994; CBE 1998.

Recreations: Arsenal FC, *The Archers*, reading.

The Lord Clarke of Hampstead CBE, House of Lords, London SW1A 0PW
Tel: 020 7219 1379 *Email:* clarkeaj@parliament.uk

CONSERVATIVE

CLARKE OF NOTTINGHAM, LORD

CLARKE OF NOTTINGHAM (Life Baron), Kenneth Harry Clarke; cr 2020. Born 2 July 1940; Son of late Kenneth Clarke, watchmaker and jeweller, and Doris Clarke; Married Gillian Edwards 1964 (died 2015) (1 son 1 daughter).

Education: Nottingham High School; Gonville and Caius College, Cambridge (BA law 1962; LLB 1963) (President, Cambridge Union 1963).

Non-political career: Called to the Bar 1963; Member, Midland Circuit, practising from Birmingham; QC 1980; Bencher, Gray's Inn; Deputy Chair, British American Tobacco 1998-2007; Director: Independent News and Media (UK), Independent News and Media plc; Member, Advisory Board, Centaurus Capital.

Political career: *House of Commons:* Contested Mansfield Notts 1964 and 1966 general elections. MP for Rushcliffe 1970-2010, for Rushcliffe (revised boundary) 2010-19; PPS to Sir Geoffrey Howe as Solicitor General 1971-72; Assistant Government Whip 1972-74; Government Whip 1974; Opposition Spokesperson for: Social Services 1974-76, Industry 1976-79; Parliamentary Secretary, Ministry of Transport 1979-80; Parliamentary Under-Secretary of State, Department of Transport 1980-82; Minister for Health 1982-85; Paymaster General and Employment Minister 1985-87; Chancellor, Duchy of Lancaster and Minister of Trade and Industry 1987-88; Secretary of State for: Health 1988-90, Education and Science 1990-92; Home Secretary 1992-93, Chancellor of the Exchequer 1993-97; Shadow Secretary of State for Business, Enterprise and Regulatory Reform/Innovation and Skills 2009-10; Lord Chancellor and Secretary of State for Justice 2010-12; Government Anti-Corruption Champion 2010-12; Minister without Portfolio, Cabinet Office 2012-14; Father of the House 2017-19. Member, Joint Committee on House of Lords Reform 2003-10; Joint Committee on Tax Law Rewrite Bills: Member 2005-09, Chair 2007-09. *House of Lords:* Raised to the peerage as Baron Clarke of Nottingham, of West Bridgford in the County of Nottinghamshire 2020. *Other:* Chair: Cambridge University Conservative Association 1961, Federation Conservative Students 1963-65; Contested Conservative Party leadership 1997, 2001 and 2005; Chair, Democracy Task Force; President, Tory Reform Group; Conservative Party whip suspended September 2019.

Political interests: Economic policy, National Health Service.

Other: Member, Justice and Home Affairs Council, Council of the European Union 2010-12; President, Industry and Parliament Trust 2010-12; Liveryman, The Clockmakers' Company; Three honorary law doctorates; Honorary Fellow, Gonville and Caius College, Cambridge; Double Act of the Year (with Theresa May MP), *Spectator* awards 2011; Oldie of the Year, *Oldie* awards 2012; PC 1984; CH 2014. Garrick Club.

Publications: Kind of Blue: A Political Memoir (Macmillan, 2016).

Recreations: Birdwatching, football, cricket, jazz, Formula 1 motor racing.

Rt Hon the Lord Clarke of Nottingham CH QC, House of Lords, London SW1A 0PW
Tel: 020 7219 3000

LIBERAL DEMOCRAT

CLEMENT-JONES, LORD

Liberal Democrat Lords Spokesperson for Digital

CLEMENT-JONES (Life Baron), Timothy Francis Clement-Jones; cr. 1998. Born 26 October 1949; Son of late Maurice Clement-Jones and late Margaret Clement-Jones, née Hudson; Married Dr Vicky Yip 1973 (died 1987); married Jean Whiteside 1994 (1 son).

Education: Haileybury College, Hertford; Trinity College, Cambridge (MA economics and law 1971); French, German.

Non-political career: Solicitor; Head of legal services, London Weekend Television 1980-83; Legal director, Grand Metropolitan Retailing 1984-86; Group company secretary and legal adviser, Kingfisher plc 1986-95; Chair: Context Group Ltd 1997-2009, Upstream (government and media relation practice of DLA Piper Rudick Gray Cary) 1999-2006; Co-chair, DLA Piper Global Government Relations 1999-2010; DLA Piper: London Managing Partner 2011-16, Partner 2016-18, Consultant 2018-.

Political career: *House of Lords:* Raised to the peerage as Baron Clement-Jones, of Clapham in the London Borough of Lambeth 1998. Liberal Democrat Spokesperson for: Health 1998-2004, Culture, Media and Sport 2004-10; Member, Speakers' Working Group on All-Party Groups 2011-12; Liberal Democrat Spokesperson for: Business, Innovation and Skills 2015, Culture, Media, Sport and Tourism 2015, Digital 2020-. Member: Communications 2010-15, Built Environment 2015-16, Licensing Act 2003 2016; Chair, Artificial Intelligence 2017-18; Member: Services 2020-, Risk Assessment and Risk Planning 2020-. *Other:* Chair, Association of Liberal Lawyers 1981-86; Liberal Democrats: Member, National Executive 1988-98, Chair, Federal Finance Committee 1991-98, Director, Campaign for the European Parliamentary elections 1994, Chair, London mayoral and Assembly campaign 2000, 2004, Federal Treasurer 2005-10; Chair, Liberal Democrats in Communications. Chair, Ombudsman Services 2016-.

Political interests: Cancer, inner cities, autism, crime prevention, creative industries, intellectual property, higher education; Central Asia, China, Iraq, Turkey, UAE.

Other: Trustee, Cancerbackup 1986-2008; Chairman and director, Crime Concern 1988-99; Council member, London Lighthouse 1989-93; Director, Brixton City Challenge 1994-98; Patron, Tymes Trust; Director, British America Business Inc; Member, 48 Group Club (promotion of relations with China); Chair: Treehouse Trust (charity for autistic children) 2001-08, Lambeth Crime Prevention Trust 2004-09, Council, School of Pharmacy, London University 2008-12; President, Ambitious About Autism 2011-; Member, Council, University College London 2012-17; Trustee: Space for Giants, Barbican Centre Trust 2012-; Council Member, Heart of the City 2013-; Chair, Council, Queen Mary University of London 2017-; Fellow, Public Relations Consultants Association; Law Society of England and Wales (City Ambassador); Fellow, Chartered Institute of Public Relations; Ambitious About Autism, Macmillan Cancer Support, Target Ovarian Cancer, Learning Skills Foundation; Freedom, City of London; FIPR; FCPRA; Hon. Fellow, UCL School of Pharmacy; CBE 1988. Arts Club.

Recreations: Travelling, eating, talking, reading, walking, the arts.

The Lord Clement-Jones CBE, House of Lords, London SW1A 0PW
Tel: 020 7219 5353 *Email:* clementjonest@parliament.uk
DLA Piper UK LLP, 3 Noble Street, London EC2V 7EE *Tel:* 020 7796 6169
Email: tim.clement-jones@dlapiper.com *Twitter:* @whiterhino1949

LABOUR

COAKER, LORD

COAKER (Life Baron), Vernon Rodney Coaker; 2021. Born 17 June 1953; Son of Edwin Coaker; Married Jacqueline Heaton 1978 (1 son 1 daughter).

Education: Drayton Manor Grammar School, London; Warwick University (BA politics 1974); Trent Polytechnic (PGCE 1976).

Non-political career: Humanities teacher, Nottinghamshire: Manvers School 1976-82, Arnold Hill School 1982-89, Bramcote Park School 1989-95, Big Wood School 1995-97. Member: NUT, Unite.

Political career: *House of Commons:* Contested Gedling 1987 and 1992 general elections. MP for Gedling 1997-2010, for Gedling (revised boundary) 2010-19; PPS: to Stephen Timms: as Minister of State, Department of Social Security 1999, as Financial Secretary, HM Treasury 1999-2001, as Minister of State for Schools and Learners, Department for Education and Skills 2001-02, as Minister of State, Department of Trade and Industry 2002, to Estelle Morris as Secretary of State for Education and Skills 2002, to Tessa Jowell as Secretary of State for Culture, Media and Sport 2002-03; Assistant Government Whip 2003-05; Government Whip 2005-06; Home Office: Parliamentary Under-Secretary of State (Crime Reduction) 2006-08, Minister of State (Policing, Crime and Security) 2008-09; Minister of State, Department of Children, Schools and Families 2009-10; Shadow Minister for: Education 2010, Policing 2010-11; Shadow Secretary of State for: Northern Ireland 2011-13, 2015-16, Defence 2013-15. Member: Social Security 1998-99, European Standing Committee B 1998, Business, Energy and Industrial Strategy 2017-19. *House of Lords:* Raised to the peerage as Baron Coaker, of Gedling in the County of Nottinghamshire 2021. *Other:* Member, International – Britain's Global Role Policy Commission. Councillor, Rushcliffe Borough Council 1983-97.

Political interests: Environment, education, welfare reform, foreign policy, sport; Angola, France, Kosovo, Macedonia.

Other: Substitute Member, UK Delegation to Parliamentary Assembly of Council of Europe 2017-19; UNICEF; *House Magazine* Opposition Frontbencher of the Year, Dods Parliamentary Awards 2014.

Recreations: Sport, walking.

The Lord Coaker, House of Lords, London SW1A 0PW *Twitter:* @Vernon_Coaker

CONSERVATIVE

COE, LORD

COE (Life Baron), Sebastian Newbold Coe; cr. 2000. Born 29 September 1956; Son of late Peter and Angela Coe; Married Nicola McIrvine 1990 (2 sons 2 daughters); married Carole Annett, née Smith 2011.

Education: Tapton Secondary Modern School, Sheffield; Abbeydale Grange School; Loughborough University (BSc economics and social history 1979).

Non-political career: Athlete; Associate member, Academy of Sport (France) 1982; Sports Council: Member 1983-89, Vice-chair 1986-89; Member, Health Education Authority 1987-92; Administrative Steward, British Boxing Board of Control; International Olympic Committee Member: Athletes and Medical Commission of International Olympic Committee 1997, Tokyo 2020 Coordination Commission 2013-, European Olympic Commission Executive Committee 2014-17; Private Secretary to William Hague MP as Leader of the Opposition 1997-2001; President, Amateur Athletics Association 2000-03; Founding member, Laureus World Sports Academy 2000-18; Global adviser to Nike 2001-15; Athletics commentator, Channel 7, Australia; Consultant, Chelsea Football Club 2011-; London 2012 Olympic Bid: Vice-chair 2003-04, Chair 2004-05; Chair, LOCOG (London Organising Committee of the Olympic Games and Paralympic Games) 2005-13; International Association of Athletics Federations (IAAF): Vice-president 2007-15, President 2015-, Chair: British Olympic Association 2012-16, Working Group on Youth; Strategic Advisor and Ambassador, Vitality Health, Wellness Programme 2013-; Columnist: *Daily Telegraph* 2013-17, *Evening Standard* 2017-; Ambassador, Lexus UK 2017-; Senior Adviser, Morgan Stanley & Co International plc 2017-; Executive Board Member, Association of Summer Olympic International Federations 2017-; Adviser, McLaren Formula One 2018-.

Political career: *House of Commons:* MP (Conservative) for Falmouth and Camborne 1992-97; PPS: to Roger Freeman: as Minister of State for Defence Procurement 1994-95, as Chancellor of the Duchy of Lancaster and Minister of Public Service 1995-96, to Nicholas Soames as Minister of State for the Armed Forces 1994-95, to Michael Heseltine as First Secretary of State and Deputy Prime Minister 1995-96; Assistant Government Whip 1996-97. *House of Lords:* Raised to the peerage as Baron Coe, of Ranmore in the County of Surrey 2000. Olympics legacy ambassador 2012-14; On leave of absence October 2016-June 2017. *Other:* Member, UK Government Honours Main Committee and chair, Sports Honours Committee -2017.

Political interests: Health, foreign affairs, education, environment, economy, voluntary movement.

Other: Director: Complete Leisure Group Ltd 2005-, Sebastian Coe Ltd 2005-; Executive Chair, CSM Sport and Entertainment LLP 2013-; Founder and Director, Seb Coe Charitable Foundation 2014-; Director, Diamond League AG 2015-; Non Executive Director: Vitality Companies 2015-, Fortescue Metals Group 2018-; Progressive Supranuclear Palsy Association, Greenhouse Sports; Chancellor, Loughborough University 2017-; Hon. DSc, Hull University 1988; Hon. LLD, Sheffield University; Honorary Fellow, UWIC; Hon. D Tech, Loughborough University 1985; Hon. DSc, University of East London; Hon. DLetters, Sunderland University 2011; Honorary Fellow, RIBA 2010; Gold 1,500m and silver 800m medals at Moscow Olympic Games 1980 and Los Angeles Olympic Games 1984; European Champion for 800m Stuttgart 1986; Set nine world records; BBC Sports Personality of the Year 1979; Sportswriters' Sportsman of the Year: 1979, 1980, 1981, 1984; Lifetime Achievement Award, BBC Sports Personality of the Year 2012; MBE 1982; OBE 1990; KBE 2006; CH 2013. East India Club, 5 Hertford Street, Marks Club.

Publications: Autobiography, Running My Life (Hodder & Stoughton, 2012).

Recreations: Jazz, theatre, reading.

The Lord Coe CH KBE, House of Lords, London SW1A 0PW
Tel: 020 7219 5353 *Twitter:* @sebcoe

LABOUR

COHEN OF PIMLICO, BARONESS

COHEN OF PIMLICO (Life Baroness), Janet Cohen; cr. 2000. Born 4 July 1940; Daughter of late George Neel and Mary Isabel Neel; Married James Lionel Cohen 1971 (2 sons 1 daughter).

Education: South Hampstead High School, London; Newnham College, Cambridge (BA law 1962) (Associate Fellow 1988-91); Good French, some German.

Non-political career: Articled clerk, Frere Cholmeley 1963-65; Admitted solicitor 1965; Consultant: ABT Associates, USA 1965-67, John Laing Construction 1968-69; Department of Trade and Industry: Principal 1969-78, Assistant secretary 1978-82; Charterhouse Bank Ltd: Assistant director 1982-88, Director 1988-2000; Chair, Café Pelican Ltd 1984-90; Yorkshire Building Society: Director 1991-94, Vice-chair 1994-99; BPP Holdings: Non-executive director 1994-2002, Non-executive chair 2002-06; Non-executive director: Waddington plc 1994-97, London and Manchester Assurance 1997-98, ISI Ltd 1998-2002, United Assurance 1999-2000, Defence Logistics Organisation 1999-2005, London Stock Exchange 2001-13; Vice-chair, Borsa Italiana 2001-14; Non-executive director: Management Consulting Group plc 2003-10, Freshwater UK plc 2007-09, Inviseo Media Holdings 2007-09. Member, First Division Association 1969-82.

Political career: *House of Lords:* Raised to the peerage as Baroness Cohen of Pimlico, in the City of Westminster 2000. Member: Tax Law Rewrite Bills Joint Committee 2001-07, EU Sub-committee B (Internal Market, Energy and Transport) 2002-06, European Union 2006-10; Chair, EU Sub-committee A (Economic and Financial Affairs) 2006-10; Member: Small- and Medium-Sized Enterprises 2012-13, Joint Committee on the Draft Communications Data Bill 2012-13; Audit: Member 2013-15, 2016-18, Chair 2015-16. *Other:* Sheffield Development Corporation 1993-97; Governor, BBC 1994-99; Board Member, Parkside Federation Academies Trust 2016-; Governor, University Technical College Cambridge 2016-.

Political interests: Finance, City affairs, education; France, Germany, Italy, New Zealand.

Other: Chair, Cambridge Arts Theatre 2007-15; BPP University College: President 2008-13, Chancellor 2013-17; Hon President, Cambridge Arts Theatre Trust 2015–; Law Society; Cambridge Arts Theatre Trust, Arthur Rank Hospice Trust; Hon. Fellow: Lucy Cavendish College Cambridge, St Edmund's College Cambridge; Hon. DLitt, Humberside 1995.

Publications: As Janet Neel: Death's Bright Angel (1988); Death on Site (1989); Death of a Partner (1991); Death among the Dons (1993); A Timely Death (1999); To Die For (1998); O Gentle Death (2000); Ticket to Ride (2005); As Janet Cohen: The Highest Bidder (1992); Children of a Harsh Winter (1994).

Recreations: Writing, theatre.

The Baroness Cohen of Pimlico, House of Lords, London SW1A 0PW
Tel: 020 7219 5353
Email: janet@bnsjcohen.com

CONSERVATIVE

COLGRAIN, LORD

COLGRAIN (4th Baron, UK), Alastair Colin Leckie Campbell; cr 1946. Born 16 September 1951; Son of David Colin Campbell, 3rd Baron Colgrain, and Veronica Webster; Married Annabel (Bella) Warrender 1979 (2 sons).

Education: Eton College; Trinity College, Cambridge (MA English 1973); Royal Agricultural College, Cirencester.

Non-political career: J Henry Schroder Wagg & Co; Welbeck Group Ltd; Managing Director, Webster and Partners 2002-; Partner, Campbell Brothers (farming partnership).

Political career: *House of Lords:* Elected hereditary peer 2017-. Member: Finance 2017-, Rural Economy 2018-19, Joint Committee on Statutory Instruments 2019-. *Other:* High Sherriff of Kent 2013-14; Governor, Sevenoaks School; DL, Kent 2017-.

Political interests: Environment, agriculture, armed forces and police, employment.

Other: Special Constable, London; Trustee: Belmont House, Arvon Foundation, Belnor Farms, Rochester Cathedral; Non-executive director, Cripps 2014-; President, Kent County Agricultural Society 2015-. Brooks's Club.

The Lord Colgrain DL, House of Lords, London SW1A 0PW
Tel: 020 7219 3000

LABOUR

COLLINS OF HIGHBURY, LORD

Opposition Spokesperson for Foreign and Commonwealth Office and International Development; Opposition Whip

COLLINS OF HIGHBURY (Life Baron), Raymond Edward Harry Collins; cr 2011. Born 21 December 1954; Son of late Harry and Isobel Collins; Married Rafael Ballesteros 2005.

Education: Matthew Arnold School, Staines; Richmond College; Kent University, Canterbury (BA industrial relations and politics 1980); Conversational Spanish.

Non-political career: Transport and General Workers' Union/Unite: Assistant librarian 1972-74, Specialist assistant, Education 1974-77, Policy adviser and special assistant to General Secretary 1980-84, National administrative officer 1984-99, Assistant General Secretary 1999-2008. Member: TGWU/Unite 1972-, Branch Committee, Staff Negotiating Committee.

Political career: *House of Lords:* Raised to the peerage as Baron Collins of Highbury, of Highbury in the London Borough of Islington 2011. Opposition Whip 2011-; Opposition Spokesperson for: Work and Pensions 2012-13, International Development 2013-, Foreign and Commonwealth Office 2015-, Women and Equalities 2020. Member, Finance 2016-. *Other:* Labour Party: Member 1970-, Member, National Policy Forum 1997-2003, Elected Member, National Constitution Committee 2001-08, General Secretary 2008-11, Patron, LGBT Labour. Governing Body, Ruskin College, Oxford.

Political interests: Equality, international affairs, justice and opportunity; South America, Spain.

Other: Director, Lionel Cook Memorial Fund 2008-; Stonewall, Positive East, Human Dignity Trust.

Recreations: Arsenal FC, cinema, reading, swimming.

The Lord Collins of Highbury, House of Lords, London SW1A 0PW
Tel: 020 7219 1675 *Fax:* 020 7219 0699 *Email:* collinsr@parliament.uk
Twitter: @Lord_Collins

CROSSBENCH

COLLINS OF MAPESBURY, LORD

COLLINS OF MAPESBURY (Life Baron), Lawrence Antony Collins; cr 2009. Born 7 May 1941; Son of Sol and Phoebe Collins; Married Sara Shamni 1982 (divorced 2003) (1 son 1 daughter); married Patti Langton 2012.

Education: City of London School; Downing College, Cambridge (BA 1963; LLB 1964); Columbia University, New York (LLM 1965); Cambridge University (LLD 1994).

Non-political career: Solicitor 1968; Herbert Smith Solicitors: Partner 1971-2000, Head of Litigation and Arbitration Department 1995-98; Visiting Professor, Queen Mary College, London 1982-; QC 1997; Deputy High Court Judge 1997-2000; High Court Judge Chancery Division, High Court of Justice 2000-07; Bencher Inner Temple 2001; Lord Justice of Appeal 2007-09; Justice of the Supreme Court of the United Kingdom 2009-11; Professor of law, Faculty of Laws, University College London 2011-; Non-Permanent Judge, Hong Kong Court of Final Appeal 2011-; Arbitrator member, Essex Court Chambers 2012-; Visiting Professor, New York University Law School 2014-.

Political career: *House of Lords:* Raised to the peerage as Baron Collins of Mapesbury, of Hampstead Town in the London Borough of Camden 2009. Lord of Appeal in Ordinary 2009; As Justice of the Supreme Court, disqualified from participation 2009-11. *Other:* Member, Department for Constitutional Affairs/Ministry of Justice Advisory Committee on Private International Law 2004-.

Other: Member, Institut de Droit International 1989; Hon. Member, Society of Legal Scholars 1993; Fellow, British Academy 1994; Hon. Life Member, Law Society 2000; Vice-President, British Institute of International and Comparative Law 2011-; Takeover Appeal Board: Deputy Chair 2013-14, Chair 2014-; Wolfson College, Cambridge: Fellow 1975-, Hon Fellow 2009-; Hon Fellow, Downing College, Cambridge 2000; Hon LLD, College of Law 2008; Kt 2000; PC 2007. Athenæum, Ronnie Scott's Club.

Publications: General editor, Dicey & Morris/Dicey, Morris & Collins Conflict of Laws 1987-; Essays in International Litigation and the Conflict of Laws (1994); European Community Law in the United Kingdom (1st ed 1975, 4th ed 1990).

Rt Hon the Lord Collins of Mapesbury QC, House of Lords, London SW1A 0PW
Tel: 020 7219 5353
24 Lincoln's Inn Fields, London WC2A 3EG *Tel:* 020 7813 8000 *Email:* lcollins@essexcourt.net

CROSSBENCH

COLVILLE OF CULROSS, VISCOUNT

COLVILLE OF CULROSS (5th Viscount, UK), Charles Mark Townshend Colville; cr. 1902; 14th Lord Colville of Culross (S) 1604; 5th Baron Colville of Culross (UK) 1885. Born 5 September 1959; Son of late 4th Viscount and Mary Colville, née Webb-Bowen.

Education: Rugby School; Durham University (BA history 1981); French, Russian.

Non-political career: Former reporter: *Ludlow Advertiser*, *Worcester Evening News*, *Weekend World*, LWT; BBC: Moscow producer 1989-92, New York producer 1992-94, Newsnight Producer, Day Editor, *Newsnight* 1994-99, Producer: *Money Programme* 1999-2004, *Horizon* 2004-09, Senior producer: BBC Science 2005-10, BBC History 2010-16; Series producer: ITN Productions 2016-17, Arrow Media 2018-. BECTU.

Political career: *House of Lords:* Elected hereditary peer 2011-. Member, Communications/ Communications and Digital 2017-.

Political interests: Media, science, foreign affairs; China, Japan, Russia.

Other: Trustee, Tree Council 2014-.

Recreations: Theatre, trees, learning Russian.

The Viscount Colville of Culross, House of Lords, London SW1A 0PW
Tel: 020 7219 5353 *Email:* colvillec@parliament.uk

CONSERVATIVE

COLWYN, LORD

COLWYN (3rd Baron, UK), Ian Anthony Hamilton-Smith; cr. 1917; 3rd Bt of Colwyn Bay (UK) 1912. Born 1 January 1942; Son of 2nd Baron; Married Sonia Morgan 1964 (divorced 1976) (1 son 1 daughter); married Nicola Tyers 1977 (2 daughters).

Education: Cheltenham College; St Bartholomew's Hospital and Royal Dental Hospital, London University (BDS London University 1966, LDS, RCS (England) 1966).

Non-political career: Dental practice 1965-2005; Non-executive director, Medical Protection Society 1989-2002; Chair, Dental Protection Ltd 1995-2001; Non-executive director, Project Hope 1996-2001; Bandleader, Lord Colwyn Organisation; Chair: RAW FM (Radio) 1998-99, Banbury Local Radio 2003-05, Campbell, Montague International 2005-08, Dental Sedation Practice 2005-08. Member, Musicians' Union 1966-.

Political career: *House of Lords:* First entered House of Lords 1967; Elected hereditary peer 1999-; Deputy Chairman of Committees 2007-16; Deputy Speaker 2008-16; Contested Lord Speaker election 2011. Member: Administration and Works Sub-committee 1997-2003, Finance and Staff Sub-committee 1997-2003; Chair, Refreshment Sub-committee 1997-2003; Co-opted member: Science and Technology Sub-committee I (Complementary and Alternative Medicine) 2000, EU Sub-committee G (Social Policy and Consumer Affairs) 2003-07; Member: Science and Technology 2006-10, Science and Technology Sub-committees: I (Allergy) 2007, II (Genomic Medicine) 2008-09, Refreshment 2012-15. *Other:* Member, Conservative Medical Society; Executive member, Association of Conservative Peers 2004-10.

Political interests: Health, dentistry, complementary medicine, arts, sport, cycling.

Other: FDI Federation Dentaire International; Member, Royal Society of Medicine; President, Natural Medicines Society 1988-2005; Member, Eastman Research Institute Trust 1990-2001; President: Huntington's Disease Association 1991-98, Society for Advancement of Anaesthesia in Dentistry 1993-98, Arterial Health Foundation 1993-2004, Metropolitan Branch, British Dental Association 1994-95; Council member, Medical Protection Society 1994-2001; Fellow, Industry and Parliament Trust 2000; Trustee, Portman Estates 2004-08; Fellow, Institute of Directors 1999-2001; Fellowship, British Dental Association 2005; Macmillan, Fight for Sight, AF Foundation; CBE 1989. Ronnie Scott's, 606 Club; Life member: Cheltenham Rugby Club, Colwyn Bay Rugby Club, Hennerton Golf Club, Leander.

Recreations: Bandleader, music, riparian pursuits, golf, rugby.

The Lord Colwyn CBE, House of Lords, London SW1A 0PW
Tel: 020 7219 3184 *Fax:* 020 7219 0318 *Email:* colwyna@parliament.uk

NON-AFFILIATED

COOPER OF WINDRUSH, LORD

COOPER OF WINDRUSH (Life Baron), Andrew Timothy Cooper; cr 2014. Born 9 June 1963; Married Elizabeth Campbell 2000 (3 daughters).

Education: Reigate Grammar School, Surrey; London School of Economics.

Non-political career: Head of research, Social Market Foundation 1994-96; Conservative Party: Deputy director of research 1996-97, Director of strategy 1997-99, Director, Political Operations 2011-13; Populus: Founder 2003-, Board Director.

Political career: *House of Lords:* Raised to the peerage as Baron Cooper of Windrush, of Chipping Norton in the County of Oxfordshire 2014. Member, Information 2015-16. *Other:* Conservative Party whip suspended May 2019-.

Political interests: Political reform, elections, economy, health, human rights; Australia, Middle East, North and South America.

Other: Member, advisory board, Centre for Progressive Capitalism 2016-.

The Lord Cooper of Windrush, House of Lords, London SW1A 0PW
Tel: 020 7219 5353 *Email:* cooperac@parliament.uk
Populus, 10 Northburgh Street, London EC1V 0AT *Tel:* 020 7253 9900
Twitter: @AndrewCooper__

CROSSBENCH

CORK AND ORRERY, EARL OF

CORK AND ORRERY (15th Earl of, I), John Richard Boyle; cr 1620 and 1660; 15th Viscount Dungarvan (I) 1620; 16th Viscount Boyle of Kinalmeaky and Baron of Bandon Bridge (I) 1627; 15th Baron Boyle of Youghal (I) 1616; 15th Baron Boyle of Broghill (I) 1621; 12th Baron Boyle of Marston (GB) 1711. Born 3 November 1945; Married Hon Rebecca Noble 1973 (1 son 2 daughters).

Education: Harrow School; RNC Dartmouth.

Non-political career: Officer, Royal Navy 1963-79; E D and F Man Sugar Ltd: Employee 1979-94, Director 1994-2014; Chair, Commodity Handling Ltd 1986-2014.

Political career: *House of Lords:* Elected hereditary peer 2016-. Member, Ecclesiastical Committee 2017-.

Political interests: Maritime affairs, Royal Navy, security, AI, drones, ecclesiastical affairs, charity governance.

Other: Chair, Society for the Advancement of the Christian Faith 2003-; Trustee, MapAction 2007-14; Council member, International Dendrology Society 2008-; Trustee, Chichester Cathedral Trusts 2009-; Chair, Chichester Cathedral Restoration and Development Trust 2009-15.

Recreations: Dendrology, sailing, cathedrals.

The Earl of Cork and Orrery, House of Lords, London SW1A 0PW
Tel: 020 7219 3884 *Email:* corkj@parliament.uk

CONSERVATIVE

CORMACK, LORD

CORMACK (Life Baron), Patrick Thomas Cormack; cr 2010. Born 18 May 1939; Son of late Thomas Cormack, local government officer; Married Kathleen McDonald 1967 (2 sons).

Education: St James' Choir School, Grimsby; Havelock School, Grimsby; Hull University (BA English and history 1961); French (basic).

Non-political career: Industrial consultant; Second master, St James' Choir School, Grimsby 1961-66; Training and education officer, Ross Group Ltd 1966-67; Assistant housemaster, Wrekin College, Shropshire 1967-69; Head of history, Brewood Grammar School, Staffordshire 1969-70; Associate editor, *Time and Tide* 1977-79; *The House Magazine*: Chairman editorial board 1976-, Editor 1979-2005, Life president 2005-; Company director, Historic House Hotels 1980-88, Aitken Dott 1984-90; Visiting lecturer, University of Texas 1984; St Antony's College, Oxford: Visiting parliamentary fellowship 1994, Senior member 1995-; Visiting senior lecturer, Hull University 1994-; *First* magazine: International president 1994-, President 2004-.

Political career: *House of Commons:* Contested Bolsover 1964 and Grimsby 1966 general elections. MP (Conservative) for Cannock 1970-74, for South West Staffordshire 1974-83, for South Staffordshire 1983-2010; PPS to Joint Parliamentary Secretaries, Department of Health and Social Security 1970-73; Deputy Shadow Leader of the House of Commons 1997-2000; Contested Speaker election 2000, 2009; Opposition Spokesperson for Constitutional Affairs 1997-2000; Member, House of Commons Commission 2002-05. Member: Ecclesiastical Committee 1970-2010, Lord Chancellor's Advisory Committee on Public Records 1982-87, Accommodation and Works 1987-2001, Modernisation of the House of Commons 1997-98, Joint Committee on Parliamentary Privilege 1997-2000, Foreign Affairs 2001-03, Standing Orders 2001-10, Joint Committee on Human Rights 2001, Joint Committee on Consolidation Etc Bills 2001-09; Chair, Northern Ireland Affairs 2005-10; Member, Liaison 2005-10. Chairman: Conservative Parliamentary Arts and Heritage Committee 1979-83, Conservative Party's Advisory Committee on Arts and Heritage 1987-99; Member, Executive, 1922 Committee 2002-05. *House of Lords:* Raised to the peerage as Baron Cormack, of Enville in the County of Staffordshire 2010. Member: Works of Art 2012-13, 2014-15, Ecclesiastical Committee 2015-, EU Home Affairs Sub-committee 2015-17, Lord Speaker's Advisory Panel on Works of Art 2019-, EU Environment Sub-Committee 2020-. *Other:* Chair, Lincolnshire Young Conservative 1960-66; Executive, 1922 Committee 2000-05; Life Patron, South Staffordshire Conservative Association 2010-. Member, Council of Historical Association 1963-66; Founder and vice-chairman, Heritage in Danger 1974-97; Member, Historic Buildings Council 1979-84; Chairman, Council for Independent Education 1980-95; Royal Commission on Historical Manuscripts/National Archives 1981-2004; Member, General Synod of the Church of England 1995-2005; Governor, English Speaking Union 1999-2006; DL, Staffordshire 2011.

Political interests: Arts, heritage, defence and NATO, Parliamentary history, education, constitutional affairs, industrial relations, human rights; Bosnia, Croatia, Finland, Lithuania, Netherlands, former Soviet Union, USA.

Other: Vice-chairman, De Burght Conference; Commonwealth Parliamentary Association (CPA) UK Branch 1970: Member, executive committee 1997-99, Joint vice-chairman 1999-2000, Treasurer 2000-03; Member, Council for Peace in the Balkans 1992-2000; Historic Churches Preservation Trust/National Churches Trust: Trustee 1973-, Vice-President 2004-; Society of Antiquaries: Fellow 1978-, Vice-President 1994-98; History of Parliament Trust: Member 1979-, Trustee 1983-, Chair 2001-16, Patron 2016-; Member, Institute of Journalists 1979-89; Museum of Garden History 1980-2000; Member, Council of Winston Churchill Memorial Trust 1983-93; Chair, William Morris Craft Fellowships 1986-; President, Staffordshire Historic Buildings Trust 1992-; Vice-President, Lincolnshire Historic Churches Trust 1997-; Director, Parliamentary Broadcasting Unit 1997-2010; President, Staffordshire Historic Churches Trust 1998-2012; Chair, Campaign for an Effective Second Chamber 2001-; President, Staffordshire Parks and Gardens Trust 2006-15; Vice-President, Tennyson Society 2009-; President, Prayer Book Society 2011-; Chair, Historic Lincoln Trust 2012; Deputy High Steward, Lincoln Cathedral 2018-; President, Heritage Lincolnshire 2018-; Save the Children, Historic Churches Preservation Trust, RNLI, Aid to the Church in Need; Member, Worshipful Company of Glaziers; Company of Art Scholars; Freedom, City of London 1980; Fellow, Royal Historical Society 2010-; Hon. Fellow, Historical Association 2010-; Hon Fellow: Historical

Association 2010, Golden Jubilee Parliamentarians, the Political Studies Association 2010; Hon DLitt, Hull University 2011, Hon Doctor of Laws, Catholic University of America 2011; Political Studies Jubilee Award 2011; Hon. Citizen of Texas 1985; Kt 1995; Commander of the Order of the Lion (Finland) 1998. Athenæum.

Publications: Heritage in Danger (1976); Right Turn (1978); Westminster: Palace and Parliament (1981); Castles of Britain (1982); Wilberforce – The Nation's Conscience (1983); English Cathedrals (1984); Responsible Capitalism (2009); Responsible Capitalism II (2017).

Recreations: Walking, talking, fighting Philistines.

The Lord Cormack, House of Lords, London SW1A 0PW
Tel: 020 7219 5353

LABOUR

CORSTON, BARONESS

CORSTON (Life Baroness), Jean Ann Corston; cr 2005. Born 5 May 1942; Daughter of late Laurie Parkin, trade union official, and late Eileen Parkin; Married Christopher Corston 1961 (1 son 1 daughter 1 daughter stillborn); married Professor Peter Townsend 1985 (died 2009).

Education: Yeovil Girls' High School; Open University; London School of Economics (LLB 1989); Inns of Court School of Law 1989-90.

Non-political career: Barrister. Former Member, Unite.

Political career: *House of Commons:* MP (Labour) for Bristol East 1992-2005; PPS to David Blunkett as Secretary of State for Education and Employment 1997-2000. Chair, Joint Committee on Human Rights 2001-05; Member: Agriculture 1992-95, Home Affairs 1995-97. Co-chair, Parliamentary Labour Party Women's Group 1992-97; Chair: PLP Children and Family Group 1995-97, PLP Civil Liberties Group 1997-2001. *House of Lords:* Raised to the peerage as Baroness Corston, of St George in the County and City of Bristol 2005. Member: Liaison 2009-13, Joint Committee on Privacy and Injunctions 2011-12; EU Sub-committee E (Justice, Institutions and Consumer Protection): Member 2012-13, Chair 2013-14; Member, European Union 2013-14; Chair, Social Mobility 2015-16; Member, Constitution 2017-. *Other:* Labour Party: Regional organiser, South West Region 1981-85, Assistant national agent, London 1985-86, Secretary, Annual Conference Arrangements 1985-86, Parliamentary Labour Party: Deputy chair 1997-2001, Chair 2001-05, Vice-chair, Labour Peers 2012-.

Political interests: Equal opportunities, human rights, complementary medicine, women in prison; India, Kenya, USA.

Other: Member, Executive Committee, Commonwealth Parliamentary Association (UK Branch) 1999-2005, 2010-; Chair, Commonwealth Women Parliamentarians 2000; Member, British-Irish Parliamentary Assembly 2015-17; Fellow, Royal Society of Arts; Chair, Fawcett Society Commission on Women in the Criminal Justice System 2007-08; Vice-chair and Trustee, Parliament Choir 2011-17; Patron: Women in Prison, Working Chance, Award Scheme Development Accreditation Network, Battle Against Tranquilizers, Elizabeth Fry Approved Premises, Meningitis Trust; Addiction Recovery Agency, Battle Against Tranquilisers, Organisation for Sickle Cell Anaemia Research, Elizabeth Fry Approved Premises, Bristol Children's Playhouse, Meningitis Trust; Honorary Fellow, Royal College of Chiropractors; Fellow, Royal Society of Arts; PC 2003.

Publications: The Corston Report (Home Office, 2007).

Recreations: Gardening, reading.

Rt Hon the Baroness Corston, House of Lords, London SW1A 0PW
Tel: 020 7219 4575 *Email:* corstonj@parliament.uk

LIBERAL DEMOCRAT

COTTER, LORD

COTTER (Life Baron), Brian Joseph Cotter; cr 2006. Born 24 August 1936; Son of late Michael Cotter and late Mary Cotter; Married Eyleen Wade 1963 (2 sons 1 daughter).

Education: Downside School, Somerset; London Polytechnic (business studies).

Non-political career: Plasticable Ltd 1990-2003: Sales manager, Managing director. National Service 1956-58.

Political career: *House of Commons:* Contested Weston-Super-Mare 1992 general election. MP (Liberal Democrat) for Weston-Super-Mare 1997-2005; Liberal Democrat Spokesperson for Small Businesses 1997-2005. *House of Lords:* Raised to the peerage as Baron Cotter, of Congresbury in the County of Somerset 2006. Liberal Democrat Spokesperson for: Small Business 2006-10, Skills 2007-10. Co-opted Member, EU Sub-committee G (Social Policy and Consumer Affairs) 2008-10; Member EU Sub-committees: G (Social Policies and Consumer Protection) 2010-12, B (Internal Market, Infrastructure and Employment) 2013-15, Internal Market 2015. *Other:* Councillor, Woking Borough Council 1986-90.

Political interests: Business, tourism, foreign affairs, youth affairs, apprenticeships and skills; China, Ireland, Rwanda.

Other: MIND, Oxfam, Cafod, Survivors' Fund (Rwandan Widows Charity).

Publications: Creating an Entrepreneurial Culture (2001).

Recreations: Reading, walking, gardening, films.

The Lord Cotter, House of Lords, London SW1A 0PW
Tel: 020 7219 8271 *Email:* cotterb@parliament.uk

CONSERVATIVE

COURTOWN, EARL OF

Lords Deputy Chief Whip (Captain of the Queen's Bodyguard of the Yeomen of the Guard)

COURTOWN (9th Earl of, I), James Patrick Montagu Burgoyne Winthrop Stopford; cr. 1762; Viscount Stopford; 9th Baron Courtown (I) 1758; 8th Baron Saltersford (GB) 1796. Born 19 March 1954; Son of 8th Earl, OBE, TD; Married Elisabeth Dunnett 1985 (1 son 2 daughters).

Education: Eton College; Berkshire College of Agriculture; Royal Agricultural College, Cirencester.

Non-political career: Land agent: Bruton Knowles, Gloucester 1987-90, John German, Shrewsbury 1990-93; Landscape Contractor 2001-10.

Political career: *House of Lords:* First entered House of Lords 1975. Sits as Baron Saltersford; Government Spokesperson for the Home Office, Scotland and Transport 1995-97; Government Whip 1995-97; Opposition Whip 1997-2000; Elected hereditary peer 1999-; Government Whip (Lord in Waiting) 2015-16; Government Spokesperson for: Business, Innovation and Skills 2015-16, Culture, Media and Sport 2015-16, International Development 2015-16, Foreign and Commonwealth Office 2015-16; Lords Deputy Chief Whip, Captain of the Queen's Bodyguard of the Yeomen of the Guard 2016-; Government Spokesperson for: International Trade 2020, Treasury 2020. Member: Bodmin Moor Commons Bill 1994, EU Sub-committees: G (Social Policies and Consumer Protection) 2011-12, D (Agriculture, Fisheries, Environment and Energy) 2012-13; Member: Inheritance and Trustees' Powers Bill 2013, Digital Skills 2014-15, Finance 2016-.

Political interests: Agriculture, environment, property, landscape industry, West Country; Ireland, Switzerland.

Other: Patron, Stroud Court Community Trust.

Recreations: Skiing, gardening.

The Earl of Courtown, House of Lords, London SW1A 0PW
Tel: 020 7219 3129 *Email:* courtownp@parliament.uk *Twitter:* @LordCourtown

CROSSBENCH

COUSSINS, BARONESS

COUSSINS (Life Baroness), Jean Elizabeth Coussins; cr 2007. Born 26 October 1950; Daughter of Jessica Coussins, née Hughes, and Walter Coussins; Divorced (1 son 2 daughters).

Education: Godolphin and Latymer Girls' School, London; Newnham College, Cambridge (BA modern and medieval languages 1973, MA); French, Spanish, basic Arabic.

Non-political career: Secretary, United Nations Association 1973-75; Women's rights officer, National Council for Civil Liberties 1975-80; Deputy director, Child Poverty Action Group 1980-83; Senior education officer, Inner London Education Authority 1983-88; Commission for Racial Equality 1988-96: Director: Social policy 1988-94, Equality assurance 1994-96; Chief executive officer, Portman Group 1996-2006; Independent consultant on corporate responsibility 2006-.

Political career: *House of Lords:* Raised to the peerage as Baroness Coussins, of Whitehall Park in the London Borough of Islington 2007. Member: Information 2007-12, EU Sub-committee C (External Affairs) 2013-16, International Relations 2016-19. *Other:* Member: DTI Crime Prevention Panel 1999, Scottish Ministerial Advisory Group on Alcohol Problems 2001-06, Advisory council, British Board of Film Classification 2002-05, Advertising Standards Authority 2003-09, Alcohol Education and Research Council 2004-07, Better Regulation Commission 2004-07; Governor, Channing School 2007-12.

Political interests: Modern languages and linguists, corporate social responsibility, regulation, social justice and equal opportunity, international affairs, UN; Latin America, especially Chile, Peru and Colombia, Cuba, EU, France, South Africa, Spain.

Other: President, Money Advice Trust 2010-; Vice-President, Chartered Institute of Linguists 2010-; President: Peru Support Group 2012-, Speak to the Future 2015-; Member, MOD's LEC Assurance Committee 2016-19; President, Speak to the Future 2016-; Newnham College, Cambridge: Associate Fellow 2003-05, Hon Fellow 2015-; Hon Fellow: University College London 2010-, Chartered Institute of Linguists 2010-; Hon. Doctorate, Open University 2019; British Academy President's Medal 2013.

Recreations: Family, travel, food, swimming, football, Fulham FC, crosswords.

The Baroness Coussins, House of Lords, London SW1A 0PW
Tel: 020 7219 5353 *Email:* coussinsj@parliament.uk

CONSERVATIVE

COUTTIE, BARONESS

COUTTIE (Life Baroness), Philippa Marion Roe; cr 2016. Born 25 September 1962; Daughter of Dame Marion Roe (former MP for Broxbourne) and James Roe; Married Stephen Couttie 2002 (twin son and daughter).

Education: Roedean School, Brighton; St Andrews University (BSc psychology 1984); French.

Non-political career: Various PR roles 1984-90; Managing director, Cornerstone Communications and CPP Brussels 1990-92; Chief executive, PR Consultants 1992-99; Associate director, J Henry Schroder 1999-2000; Director, Citigroup 2000-06; Non-executive Senior Adviser, FTI Consulting 2014-17; Mitie plc: Non-executive Director 2017-, Chair, Corporate and Social Responsibility Board Sub-group 2019-.

Political career: *House of Lords:* Raised to the peerage as Baroness Couttie, of Downe in the County of Kent 2016. Member: Political Polling and Digital Media 2017-18, European Union 2019-, EU Financial Affairs Sub-committee 2019-20, EU Services Sub-committee 2020-. *Other:* Conservative Party: Private Finance Panel, Treasury Team, James Committee, Party Whip 2017-; Executive board member, Conservative Group, Local Government Association 2012-; Executive member, Association of Conservative Peers 2018-. Westminster City Council: Councillor 2006-17, Cabinet Member for: Housing 2008-11, Finance 2011-12, Council Leader 2012-17; Board member, Royal Parks 2012-17; President, Local Government Association 2018-; Commissioner, Guernsey Financial Services Commission 2020-.

Political interests: Local government, economy, business, welfare; Europe, Middle East.

Other: Council member, Imperial College London 2006-14; Member, London Crime Reduction Board 2012-14; Board member, Canal and River Trust 2013-14; Chair, West End Partnership 2013-17; Board member, London Local Enterprise Partnership 2014-16; Deputy Leader: London Councils 2013-17, Local Government Association 2014-17; Non-executive

Director, Mitie plc; Member, Worshipful Company of Gardeners; Breast Cancer Haven, Macmillan; Freedom, City of London.

Recreations: Skiing, antiquities, theatre, opera, gardening.

The Baroness Couttie, House of Lords, London SW1A 0PW
Tel: 020 7219 3000

NON-AFFILIATED

COVENTRY, LORD BISHOP OF

COVENTRY (9th Bishop of), Christopher John Cocksworth. Born 12 January 1959; Son of late Stanley Cocksworth and Auriol Cocksworth; Married Charlotte Pytches 1979 (5 sons).

Education: Forest School for Boys, Horsham; Manchester University (BA theology 1980; PhD 1989); Didsbury School of Education, Manchester Polytechnic (PGCE 1981); German.

Non-political career: Teacher, King Edward's School, Witley 1981-84; Doctoral research 1986-88; Ordained deacon 1988; Assistant curate, Christ Church, Epsom 1988-92; Ordained priest 1989; Chaplain, Royal Holloway and Bedford New College 1992-97; Director, Southern Theological Education and Training Scheme 1997-2001; Hon. Canon, Guildford Cathedral 2000-01; Principal, Ridley Hall, Cambridge 2001-08; Bishop of Coventry 2008-.

Political career: *House of Lords:* Entered House of Lords 2012.

Political interests: Education, international affairs, reconciliation, beginning and end of life issues; Egypt, Germany, Israel, Jordan, Nigeria, Palestine, Syria.

Other: Member, House of Bishops' Standing Committee; Co-chair, Joint Implementation Commission for the Anglican Methodist Covenant; Chair, Faith and Order Commission of the Church of England; Chair of Trustees, Coventry 2020 Educational Trust 2008-; President, Dudley Lodge Family Assessment Centre, Coventry 2008-; Trustee, Frauenkirche Foundation, Dresden 2008-; Member, Consultative Council, Shakespeare Birthplace Trust 2008-; Chair, Inter-Religious Platform for Article 18 2015-; Society for the Study of Theology; Society for the Study of Liturgy; Doctor of Divinity, University of London. Farmers Club.

Publications: Numerous theological articles in journals, chapters in books and book reviews; Evangelical Eucharistic Thought in the Church of England (CUP, 1993); Co-author, An Anglican Companion (CHP/SPCK, 1996); Holy, Holy, Holy: Worshipping the Trinitarian God (DLT, 1997); Co-author, Being a Priest Today (Cantebury Press-SCM, 2004); Holding Together: Gospel, Church and Spirit – the Essentials of Christian Identity (Canterbury Press-SCM, 2008); Seeing Jesus and Being Seen by Him (SPCK, 2014).

Recreations: Organic fruit and vegetable growing.

Rt Rev Dr the Lord Bishop of Coventry, House of Lords, London SW1A 0PW
Tel: 020 7219 5353 *Email:* cocksworthc@parliament.uk
Bishop's House, 23 Davenport Road, Coventry CV5 6PW *Tel:* 024 7667 2244
Email: bishop@bishop-coventry.org Websites: www.dioceseofcoventry.org
www.bishop-coventry.org

CROSSBENCH

COX, BARONESS

COX (Life Baroness), Caroline Anne Cox; cr. 1983. Born 6 July 1937; Daughter of late Robert McNeill Love and Dorothy Borland; Married Dr Murray Cox 1959 (died 1997) (2 sons 1 daughter).

Education: Channing School, Highgate, London; London Hospital (SRN 1958); London University external student (BScSoc 1967; MSc(Econ) 1969); French (basic); Italian; Russian (basic).

Non-political career: Staff nurse, Edgware General Hospital 1960; North London Polytechnic: Lecturer, senior lecturer and principal lecturer 1969-74, Head, Department of Sociology 1974-77; Director, Nursing Education Research Unit, Chelsea College, London University 1977-84; Royal College of Nursing: Fellow, Vice-President 1990-; Humanitarian Aid Relief Trust (HART): Chief executive officer 2005-16, 2017- President 2016-17.

Political career: *House of Lords:* Raised to the peerage as Baroness Cox, of Queensbury in Greater London 1983. Government Whip 1985; Deputy Speaker 1986-2005; Deputy Chair of Committees 1986-2004.

Political interests: Human rights, humanitarian aid, education, health, nursing; Armenia, Burma, Nigeria, North Korea, Poland, Sudan, South Sudan, Syria, East Timor, Uganda.

Other: Patron: Medical Aid for Poland Fund 1983-, Physicians for Human Rights, UK 1990-; Standing Conference on Women's Organisations 1990-; Vice-President, Girl Guides Association 1995-; Hon. vice-chair, International Islamic Christian Organisation for Reconciliation and Reconstruction 2002-; Patron, Christian Solidarity Worldwide UK 2006-; Vice-President, Liverpool School of Tropical Medicine 2006-; Honorary Freeman, Worshipful Society of Apothecaries; Chancellor: Bournemouth University 1992-2001, Liverpool Hope University 2006-13; Hon. FRCN; Hon. FRCS 1997; 14 honorary doctorates and fellowships; Wilberforce Award 1995; Fridej of Nansen International Foundation Award 2004; International Mother Teresa Award 2005; Commander Cross of the Order of Merit of the Republic of Poland 1990; Mkhitar Gosh Medal (Armenia) 2005; Polish Solidarity Movement Medal 2005. Royal Over-Seas League Club.

Publications: Author of numerous publications on education and health care, including: Co-editor, A Sociology of Medical Practice (1975); Co-author, The Rape of Reason: The Corruption of the Polytechnic of North London (1975); The Right to Learn (1982); Sociology: A Guide for Nurses, Midwives and Health Visitors (1983); Editor, Trajectories of Despair: Misdiagnosis and Maltreatment of Soviet Orphans (1991); Co-author: Ethnic Cleansing in Progress: War in Nagorno Karabakh (1993), Made to Care: The Case for Residential and Village Communities for People with a Mental Handicap (1995), The 'West', Islam and Islamism: Is Ideological Islam Compatible With Liberal Democracy? (2003, 2006); Cox's Book of Modern Saints and Martyrs (Continuum, 2006); This Immoral Trade: Slavery in the 21st Century (Monarch, 2006, revised edition 2013); The Very Stones Cry Out: The Persecuted Church: Pain, Passion and Praise (Continuum, 2011).

Recreations: Campanology, hill-walking, tennis.

The Baroness Cox, House of Lords, London SW1A 0PW
Tel: 020 7219 8638 *Email:* coxc@parliament.uk
Humanitarian Aid Relief Trust, Unit 1, Jubilee Business Centre, 213 Kingsbury Road, London NW9 8AQ *Tel:* 020 8205 4608 *Email:* caroline.cox@hart-uk.org Websites: www.hart-uk.org www.baronesscox.com

CROSSBENCH

CRAIG OF RADLEY, LORD

CRAIG OF RADLEY (Life Baron), David Brownrigg Craig; cr. 1991. Born 17 September 1929; Son of late Major Francis Brownrigg Craig and Hannah Olivia (Olive) Craig; Married June Derenburg 1955 (died 2016) (1 son 1 daughter).

Education: Radley College; Lincoln College, Oxford (BA pure maths 1951, MA).

Non-political career: Commissioned into RAF 1951; Flying instructor on Meteors and Hunter pilot in Fighter Command 1953-55; CO, No. 35 Squadron 1963-65; Military Assistant to Chief of the Defence Staff 1965-68; Group Captain 1968; Station CO, RAF College, Cranwell 1968-70; ADC to HM The Queen 1969-71; Director, Plans and Operations, HQ Far East Command 1970-71; OC, RAF Akrotiri (Cyprus) 1972-73; Assistant Chief of Air Staff (Operations), Ministry of Defence 1975-78; Air Officer Commanding No 1 Group 1978-80; Vice-Chief of Air Staff 1980-82; Air Officer Commanding-in-Chief Strike Command and Commander-in-Chief UK Air Forces 1982-85; Chief of the Air Staff 1985-88; Air ADC to HM The Queen 1985-88; Marshal of the Royal Air Force 1988; Chief of the Defence Staff 1988-91.

Political career: *House of Lords:* Raised to the peerage as Baron Craig of Radley, of Helhoughton in the County of Norfolk 1991. Convenor of Crossbench Peers 1999-2004. Member: Privileges 2000-04, Liaison 2000-04, 2013-16, Procedure 2000-04, Selection 2000-04, 2016-, House 2002-04, 2007-13, Administration and Works 2002-04, Information 2004-07. *Other:* Chairman of Council, King Edward VII's Hospital 1998-2004.

Political interests: Defence, foreign and Commonwealth affairs.

Other: Vice-chair, RAF Benevolent Fund 1991-2013; President: (RAF) The "Not Forgotten" Association 1993-2014, RAF Club 2002-12; King Edward VII's Hospital for Officers; RAF Benevolent Fund; Freedom, City of London; FRAeS; Hon. Fellow, Lincoln College, Oxford

1984; Hon. DSc, Cranfield Institute of Technology 1988; OBE (Mil) 1967; CB 1978; KCB 1981; GCB (Mil) 1984. RAF Club.

Recreations: Fishing, shooting, woodwork.

Marshal of the Royal Air Force the Lord Craig of Radley GCB OBE, House of Lords, London SW1A 0PW
Tel: 020 7219 2200 *Email:* craigd@parliament.uk

CROSSBENCH

CRAIGAVON, VISCOUNT

CRAIGAVON (3rd Viscount, UK), Janric Fraser Craig; cr. 1927; 3rd Bt of Craigavon (UK) 1918. Born 9 June 1944; Son of 2nd Viscount.

Education: Eton College; London University (BA; BSc).

Non-political career: Chartered accountant.

Political career: *House of Lords:* First entered House of Lords 1974; Elected hereditary peer 1999-. Member, Hybrid Instruments 1993-97, 1999-2005; Alternate member, Procedure 2010-15.

Political interests: Netherlands, Nordic countries.

Other: Commander of the Order of the Lion (Finland) 1998; Commander of the Royal Order of the Polar Star (Sweden) 1999; Knight of the Order of Dannebrog (Denmark) 2006; Commander of the Royal Norwegian Order of Merit 2010; Grand Decoration of Honour in Gold for Services to the Republic of Austria 2019.

The Viscount Craigavon, House of Lords, London SW1A 0PW
Tel: 020 7219 3881 *Email:* craigavonj@parliament.uk
54 Westminster Mansions, 1 Little Smith Street, London SW1P 3DQ *Tel:* 020 7222 1949

CONSERVATIVE

CRATHORNE, LORD

CRATHORNE (2nd Baron, UK), (Charles) James Dugdale; cr. 1959; 2nd Bt of Crathorne (UK) 1945. Born 12 September 1939; Son of 1st Baron, PC, TD; Married Sylvia Montgomery 1970 (died 2009) (1 son 2 daughters).

Education: Eton College; Trinity College, Cambridge (MA fine arts 1963).

Non-political career: Impressionist painting department, Sotheby & Co. 1963-66; Assistant to president, Parke-Bernet Galleries, New York 1966-69; Independent fine art consultancy, James Dugdale & Associates/James Crathorne & Associates 1969-; Lecture tours to the USA 1969-99; Director, Blakeney Hotels Ltd 1979-96; Lecture series *Aspects of England*, in Metropolitan Museum, New York 1981; Australian bicentennial lecture tour 1988; Director: Woodhouse Securities Ltd 1988-99, Cliveden plc 1996-99, Cliveden Ltd 1999-2002, Hand Picked Hotels 2000-01.

Political career: *House of Lords:* First entered House of Lords 1977; Elected hereditary peer 1999-. Lord Speakers Advisory Panel on Works of Art: Member 1983-2004, 2012-13, 2014-15, 2017-, Chair 2003-07. *Other:* Member, Conservative Advisory Group on Arts and Heritage 1988-99. DL, County of Cleveland 1983-96; Member of Court, Leeds University 1985-97; President, Cleveland and North Yorkshire Magistrates' Association 1997-2003; County of North Yorkshire: DL 1996-98, Lord Lieutenant 1999-2014; JP 1999-; Member of Court: York University 1999-, Hull University 1999-2014.

Political interests: Visual and performing arts, country houses; India, USA.

Other: Trustee, Georgian Theatre Royal, Richmond, Yorkshire 1970-; Fellow, Royal Society of Arts 1972; Captain Cook Birthplace Museum Trust: Trustee 1978-, Chair 1993-2017; Editorial Board, *House Magazine* 1983-; Council, RSA 1982-88; Georgian Group: Executive Committee 1985-, Chair 1990-99, President 1999-2016; President: Cleveland Family History Society 1988-, Cleveland Sea Cadets 1988-2014; Hambleton District, Council for the Protection of Rural England 1988-; Trustee, Yorkshire Regional Committee, National Trust 1988-94; Vice-President, Cleveland Wildlife Trust 1989-; Patron: Attingham Trust for Study of British Country House 1990-, Cleveland Community Foundation 1990-2004; Trustee, National Heritage Memorial Fund 1992-95; Joint Committee of National Amenity Societies: Deputy chair 1993-96, Chair 1996-99; Vice-President, Public Monuments and Sculpture Association 1997-; President, Cleveland Search and Rescue Team 1998-2016; Patron, Friends of Public Record Office 1998-2018; President: North Yorkshire County Scout Council 1999-2014, St John Ambulance North Yorkshire and Teesside 1999-; Yorkshire and Humberside Reserve Forces and Cadets' Association (RFCA): Vice-President 1999-2014, President 2006-09; Patron, British Red Cross, North Yorkshire Branch 1999-2014; Vice-President, North of England (RFCA) 2001-14; Patron, Tees Valley Community Foundation 2004-; Fellow, Society of Antiquaries 2009, Chair, Sylvia Crathorne Memorial Trust 2009-; Patron, Middlesbrough Institute of Modern Art (MIMA) 2012; Marie Curie Cancer Care, Georgian Theatre Royal; Freedom: Richmond, North Yorkshire 2014, City of York, City of London; Hon. LLD: Teeside University 2013, York University 2015; KStJ 1999; Queen's Golden Jubilee Medal 2002; Queen's Diamond Jubilee Medal 2012; KCVO 2013. Pratts, Garrick Club.

Publications: Articles in The Connoisseur and Apollo; Edouard Vuillard (1967); Co-author: Tennant's Stalk (1973), A Present from Crathorne (1989); Cliveden, the Place and the People (1995); The Royal Crescent Book of Bath (1998); Co-Photographer, Parliament in Pictures (1999).

Recreations: Photography, jazz, collecting, country pursuits, travel.

The Lord Crathorne KCVO, House of Lords, London SW1A 0PW
Tel: 020 7219 5224 *Email:* crathornej@parliament.uk
Crathorne House, Yarm TS15 0AT *Tel:* 01642 700431 *Email:* james.crathorne@btconnect.com

LABOUR

CRAWLEY, BARONESS

CRAWLEY (Life Baroness), Christine Mary Crawley; cr. 1998. Born 9 January 1950; Daughter of Thomas Louis Quinn and Joan Ryan; Married (1 son 2 daughters, including twins).

Education: Notre Dame Girls School, Plymouth; Digby Stuart Teacher Training College, Roehampton, London.

Non-political career: Former teacher and youth theatre leader, Oxfordshire. Member: MSF, Unison.

Political career: *House of Commons:* Contested (Labour) Staffordshire South East 1983 general election. *House of Lords:* Raised to the peerage as Baroness Crawley, of Edgbaston in the County of West Midlands 1998. Government Whip 2002-08, 2009-10; Government Spokesperson for: Defence 2002-08, Foreign and Commonwealth Office 2002-05, International Development 2002-04, 2008, Transport 2004-05, 2007-08, Education and Skills/ Children, Schools and Families and for Innovation, Universities and Skills 2005-08, Northern Ireland 2007-08; Opposition Spokesperson for: Communities and Local Government 2010, Foreign and Commonwealth Office 2010, Health 2010; Opposition Deputy Chief Whip 2010-12. Member: European Union -2000, European Union Sub-committee A (Economic and Financial Affairs, Trade and External Relations) 2000-01, Refreshment 2011-12, Lord Speaker's Committee on the Size of the House 2016-, Intergenerational Fairness and Provision 2018-19, Common Frameworks Scrutiny 2020-. *Other:* European Parliament: MEP for Birmingham East 1984-99: Chair, Women's Rights Committee 1989-94. Member: Co-operative Party, Labour Movement in Europe. Former Town and District Councillor, South Oxfordshire; Chair: Women's National Commission 1999-2002, West Midlands Regional Cultural Consortium 1999-2002.

Political interests: Women's rights, equal opportunities, European Union.

Other: Member: Amnesty International, Fabian Society; Fellow, Royal Society of Arts; Chartered Trading Standards Institute: President 2009-17, Vice-president 2017-.

Recreations: Latin American literature, amateur dramatics, attending local football matches in Birmingham.

The Baroness Crawley, House of Lords, London SW1A 0PW
Tel: 020 7219 4650 *Fax:* 020 7219 6837 *Email:* crawleyc@parliament.uk
Email: ccrawley@enterprise.net

CROSSBENCH

CRISP, LORD

CRISP (Life Baron), (Edmund) Nigel Ramsay Crisp; cr. 2006. Born 14 January 1952; Married Siân Jenkins 1976 (1 daughter 1 son).

Education: Uppingham School, Rutland; St John's College, Cambridge (BA moral sciences 1973, MA).

Non-political career: Deputy director, Halewood Community Council 1973-77; Production manager, Trebor plc 1977-81; Director, Cambridgeshire Community Council 1981-86; General manager, East Berkshire Health Authority 1986-88; Wexham Park Hospital and Heatherwood Hospital 1988-93: Chief executive 1992-93; Chief executive, Oxford Radcliffe Hospital 1993-97; Regional director: South Thames Regional Office 1997-98, London Regional Office 1999-2000; Permanent Secretary for Health and Chief Executive, NHS, Department of Health 2000-06.

Political career: *House of Lords:* Raised to the peerage as Baron Crisp, of Eaglescliffe in the County of Durham 2006. Member: Merits of Statutory Instruments 2007-09, European Union 2017-18, EU Home Affairs Sub-committee 2017-18.

Political interests: Developing world.

Other: Honorary Professor, London School of Hygiene and Tropical Medicine; Senior Fellow, Institute for Health Care Improvement; KCB 2003.

Recreations: Countryside.

The Lord Crisp KCB, House of Lords, London SW1A 0PW
Tel: 020 7219 3873 *Email:* crisp@parliament.uk Website: www.nigelcrisp.com
Twitter: @LordNigelCrisp

CROSSBENCH

CROMWELL, LORD

CROMWELL (7th Baron, E), Godfrey John Bewicke-Copley; cr 1375. Born 4 March 1960; Son of 6th Baron Cromwell and Vivian de Lisle Penfold; Married Elizabeth Hawksley 1990 (3 sons 1 daughter).

Education: Eton College; Selwyn College, Cambridge (BA 1982).

Non-political career: Director/economist, international development NGOs 1987-2006; Director, British East-West Centre 2000-; Executive director, Russo-British Chamber of Commerce 2003-07; Director, British-Georgian Chamber of Commerce 2007-09; Vice-president, Barclays Wealth and Investment Management 2007-16; Divisional Director, Brewin Dolphin 2017-18; Executive chair, Banking Competition Remedies Ltd 2018-.

Political career: *House of Lords:* Elected hereditary peer 2014-. Member: EU Justice Sub-committee 2015-19, Finance 2016-, European Union 2017-19.

Political interests: Business education; Africa, Russia and CIS Countries.

The Lord Cromwell, House of Lords, London SW1A 0PW
Tel: 020 7219 5678 *Email:* cromwellg@parliament.uk

CONSERVATIVE

CRUDDAS, LORD

CRUDDAS (Life Baron), Peter Andrew Cruddas; cr 2021. Born September 1953; Married (2 children); married Fiona (2 children).

Education: Shoreditch Comprehensive.

Non-political career: Telex operator, Western Union; Trader, Marine Midland and Bank of Iran; Chief dealer, SCF Equity Services 1982-89; Founder and chief executive officer, Currency Management Consultants Ltd/CMC Markets 1989-; Visiting Professor of Enterprise, Loughborough University 2009-.

Political career: *House of Lords:* Raised to the peerage as Baron Cruddas, of Shoreditch in the London Borough of Hackney 2021. *Other:* Treasurer, Conservative and Unionist Party 2011-12.

Other: Ambassador to Team Programme, The Prince's Trust 2007; Founder: Peter Cruddas Foundation, Peter Cruddas Social Innovation Initiative 2008-; Founding Fellow, The Prince's Trust Enterprise Fellowship Oxford University; Founding Chair, Youth United 2009-11; Trustee, Royal Opera House 2012-; Honorary Fellow, Harris Manchester College, Oxford; Honorary Doctorate, Loughborough University 2011; Entrepreneur of the Year, Management Today (2007).

Recreations: Golf.

The Lord Cruddas, House of Lords, London SW1A 0PW *Twitter:* @peteratcmc

CONSERVATIVE

CUMBERLEGE, BARONESS

CUMBERLEGE (Life Baroness), Julia Frances Cumberlege; cr. 1990. Born 27 January 1943; Daughter of Dr LU Camm and MGG Camm; Married Patrick Cumberlege 1961 (3 sons).

Education: Convent of the Sacred Heart, Tunbridge Wells.

Non-political career: Executive director, MJM Healthcare Solutions 1997-2001; Non-executive director, Huntsworth plc 2001-03; Consultant, Quo Health 2001-05; Founded Cumberlege Connections 2001; Founder, Cumberlege Eden and Partners Ltd 2013, Director: Assuring Better Practice (UK) Ltd 2004-07, South East Water plc 2006-08.

Political career: *House of Lords:* Raised to the peerage as Baroness Cumberlege, of Newick in the County of East Sussex 1990. Joint Parliamentary Under-Secretary of State, Department of Health 1992-97; Opposition Spokesperson for Health 1997. Member, Draft Mental Health Bill Joint Committee 2004-05. *Other:* Lewes District Council: Councillor 1966-79, Leader 1977-78; Councillor, East Sussex County Council 1974-85: Chair, Social Services Committee 1979-82; Chair, Brighton Health Authority 1981-88; Member, Press Council 1984-90; Chair, Review of Community Nursing for England (Report: Neighbourhood Nursing) 1985, DL, East Sussex 1986-; Member, DHSS Expert Advisory Group on AIDS 1987-89, Chair, South West Thames Regional Health Authority 1988-92; Vice-President, Royal College of Nursing 1989-; Member, NHS Policy Board for England 1989-97; Council Member, UK Central Council for Nursing, Midwifery and Health Visiting 1989-92; Vice-Lord Lieutenant, East Sussex 1992; Chair: Review of Maternity Services for England (Report: Changing Childbirth) 1993, St George's Medical School Council 2000-06; Council Member, Sussex University 2001-09; Vice-President, Royal College of Midwives; Chair, Review of National Maternity Services 2016.

Political interests: Local government, NHS, media, education.

Other: Patron, National Childbirth Trust; Fellow, Royal Society of Arts 1989; Trustee: Chailey Heritage Foundation School 1990-2014; Leeds Castle Foundation 2005-16; Governor, Lancing College 2013-; Chair, National Association of Health Authorities 1987-88; Fellow: Royal College of Physicians 2006, Royal College of General Practioners 2006, Royal College of Nursing 2010, Royal College of Obstetrics and Gynaecology 2012; Royal Society of Medicine, Rural College of Midwives; Fellow: RCM, RCN; Ten honorary doctorates; CBE 1985.

Recreations: Other people's gardens, bicycling.

The Baroness Cumberlege CBE DL, House of Lords, London SW1A 0PW
Email: cumberlegej@parliament.uk *Twitter:* @JuliaCumberlege

LABOUR

CUNNINGHAM OF FELLING, LORD

CUNNINGHAM OF FELLING (Life Baron), John Anderson (Jack) Cunningham; cr 2005. Born 4 August 1939; Son of late Andrew and Freda Cunningham; Married Maureen Appleby 1964 (1 son 2 daughters).

Education: Jarrow Grammar School; Bede College, Durham University (BSc chemistry 1962; PhD 1966).

Non-political career: Research fellow, Durham University 1966-68; Executive Chairman and Director, Navitas Resources (UK) Ltd -2019. Full-time officer, GMWU 1969-70.

Political career: *House of Commons:* MP (Labour) for Whitehaven 1970-83, for Copeland 1983-2005; PPS to James Callaghan as Foreign Secretary and Prime Minister 1974-76; Parliamentary Under-Secretary for Energy 1976-79; Shadow Environment Secretary 1983-89; Shadow Leader of the House 1989-92; Shadow Secretary of State for: Foreign and Commonwealth Affairs 1992-94, Trade and Industry 1994-95, National Heritage 1995-97; Minister of Agriculture, Fisheries and Food 1997-98; Minister for the Cabinet Office, and Chancellor of the Duchy of Lancaster 1998-99. Chair, Joint Committee on House of Lords Reform 2002-05. *House of Lords:* Raised to the peerage as Baron Cunningham of Felling, of Felling in the County of Tyne and Wear 2005. Chair, Conventions Joint Committee 2006; Member: Science and Technology Sub-committee I: (Nanotechnologies and food) 2008-10, (Radioactive Waste Management: a further update) 2010, Science and Technology 2009-13, Science and Technology Sub-committee I 2012-13, EU Sub-committee D: Agriculture, Fisheries, Environment and Energy 2014-15, EU Energy and Environment Sub-Committee 2015-17, Finance 2016-, Secondary Legislation Scrutiny 2018-; Chair, SLSC Sub-committee B 2018-19; Member, Economic Affairs 2019-. *Other:* General Election Campaign Co-ordinator 1989-92; Labour Whip withdrawn June 2013-January 2014. DL, Cumbria 1991; Commissioner, Millennium Commission 1998-99.

Political interests: Regional policy, environment, foreign affairs, industry, energy; China, Europe, Japan, South Africa, USA.

Other: UK-Japan 21st Century Group: Chairman 2004-11, Member, UK Board; Fellow, Industry and Parliament Trust 1981; PC 1993; Order of the Rising Sun Gold and Silver Star, Japan 2016.

Recreations: Fell-walking, gardening, music, reading, fishing, theatre.

Rt Hon the Lord Cunningham of Felling DL, House of Lords, London SW1A 0PW
Tel: 020 7219 5222

CROSSBENCH

CURRIE OF MARYLEBONE, LORD

CURRIE OF MARYLEBONE (Life Baron), David Anthony Currie; cr. 1996. Born 9 December 1946; Son of late Kennedy Currie and Marjorie Currie; Married Shaziye Gazioglu 1975 (divorced 1992) (2 sons); married Angela Dumas 1995 (1 stepson).

Education: Battersea Grammar School; Manchester University (BSc maths 1968); Birmingham University (MSocSci Econs 1971); London University (PhD economics 1978).

Non-political career: Economist, Hoare Govett 1971-72; Lecturer, reader and professor of economics, Queen Mary College, London University 1972-88; Visiting scholar, International Monetary Fund 1987; London Business School: Professor of economics 1988-2000, Research dean 1989-92, Governor 1989-95, 1999-2000, Deputy principal 1992-95, Deputy dean, External Relations 1999-2000; Director: Joseph Rowntree Reform Trust 1991-2002, International Schools of Business Management 1992-95; Visiting professor, European University Institute 1992-95; Director: Charter 88 1994-98, Gas and Electricity Markets Authority 2000-02; Member, Terra Firma, Advisory Board of Nomura Private Finance Group 2000-02; Dean, City University Business School/Cass Business School, City of London 2001-08; Director, Abbey National plc 2001-02; Member, advisory board, Terra Firma Capital Partners 2002-05; Director: Dubai Financial Services Authority 2005-, London Philharmonic Orchestra 2007-12; Chair, Semperian PPP Investment Partners 2007-12; Director: BDO 2008-12, Royal Mail 2009-12; Chair, International Centre for Financial Regulation 2009-12; Director, IG Group 2010-12.

Political career: *House of Lords:* Raised to the peerage as Baron Currie of Marylebone, of Marylebone in the City of Westminster 1996. Member, Economic Affairs 2008-12. *Other:* Houblon-Norman resident fellow, Bank of England 1985-86; Member: Retail Price Index Advisory Committee 1992-95, Treasury's Panel of Independent Forecasters 1992-95, Management Board, OFGEM 1999-2000; Chairman, Ofcom 2002-09; Panel member, Leveson Inquiry 2011-12; Chair: Competition and Markets Authority 2012-18, Advertising Standards Authority 2017-.

Political interests: Economic policy, media and communications, regulation.

Other: Research Fellow, Centre for Economic Policy Research 1983-98; Governor, Institute for Government 2008-; Council of Essex University: Member 2008-13, 2015-, Chair 2011-13, 2016-; Chair, Alacrity Foundation 2010-13; Honorary fellowship and doctorate: Queen Mary,

University of London 1997, Glasgow University 1998, Birmingham University 2003, City University, London 2012, Essex University 2014.

Publications: Advances in Monetary Economics (1985); Co-author: The Operation and Regulation of Financial Markets (1986), Macroeconomic Interactions Between North and South (1988), Rules, Reputation and Macroeconomic Policy Co-ordination (1993), EMUs Problems in the Transition to a Single European Currency (1995), North-South Linkages and International Macroeconomic Policy (1995); The Pros and Cons of EMU (1997); Will the Euro Work? (1998); Articles in journals.

Recreations: Music, literature, swimming.

Professor the Lord Currie of Marylebone, House of Lords, London SW1A 0PW
Tel: 020 7219 5353

CROSSBENCH

CURRY OF KIRKHARLE, LORD

CURRY OF KIRKHARLE (Life Baron); Donald Thomas Younger Curry cr. 2011. Born 4 April 1944; Married Rhoda Murdie 1966 (2 sons 1 daughter).

Education: Northumberland College of Agriculture.

Non-political career: Farmer, Northumberland 1971-; Founder and chairman: North Country Primestock 1990-2001, At Home in the Community 1992-; NFU Mutual Insurance Society: Non-executive director 1997-2011, Vice-chairman 2000-03, Chairman 2003-11; Chair: Leckford Estate Management Committee, Waitrose Farm 2009-16, Better Regulation Executive, Department for Business, Innovation and Skills 2009-15, Cawood Scientific Group 2014-.

Political career: *House of Lords:* Raised to the peerage as Baron Curry of Kirkharle, of Kirkharle in the County of Northumberland 2011. Member: Refreshment 2014-16, EU Energy and Environment Sub-committee 2015-18, Rural Economy 2018-19. *Other:* Commissioner, Crown Estate 2000-07; Chair, Commission on the Future of Farming and Food 2001-02; Government Strategy for Sustainable Farming and Food 2002-09.

Political interests: Agriculture and food, social care; South Sudan.

Other: Fellow: Royal Agricultural Society 1995, British Veterinary Association 1998, Myerscough College 2000, Scottish Agricultural College 2006; Trustee: NFU Mutual Charitable Trust 2002-, Lawes Agricultural Trust 2009-17, Clinton Devon Estate 2009-, The Prince's Countryside Fund 2010-, Anglican International Development 2010-; Chair: Centre of Excellence for UK Farming 2010-, Royal Veterinary College 2012-19, National Land Based College; Anglican International Development; Hon. BSc, Cranfield University 2004; Hon. doctorate, Gloucester University 2005; Hon. DCL, Newcastle University 2008; CBE 1997; Kt 2001. Farmers Club.

Recreations: Church, Newcastle United FC.

The Lord Curry of Kirkharle CBE, House of Lords, London SW1A 0PW
Tel: 020 7219 8952 *Email:* curryd@parliament.uk

CROSSBENCH

DANNATT, LORD

DANNATT (Life Baron), Francis Richard Dannatt; cr 2011. Born 23 December 1950; Son of Mary Dannatt, née Chilvers, and Anthony Dannatt; Married Philippa Gurney 1977 (3 sons 1 daughter).

Education: St Lawrence College, Ramsgate; Royal Military Academy, Sandhurst; Durham University (BA economic history 1976).

Non-political career: British Army/Ministry of Defence (MoD) 1969-2009: Chief of Staff, 20th Armoured Brigade 1983-84, Military Assistant to Minister of State for Armed Forces 1986-89, Commanding Officer, 1 Green Howards 1989-91, Colonel, Higher Command and Staff Course, Camberley 1992-94, Commander, 4th Armoured Brigade 1994-96, Director, Defence Programmes, MoD 1996-98, General Officer Commanding, 3rd UK Division 1999-2000, Deputy Commander, Operations, HQ Stabilisation Force 2000-01, Assistant Chief of the General Staff 2001-02, Commander, Allied Rapid Reaction Corps 2003-05, Commander in Chief, Land Command 2005-06, Chief of the General Staff 2006-09; Constable, HM Tower of London 2009-16.

Political career: *House of Lords:* Raised to the peerage as Baron Dannatt, of Keswick in the County of Norfolk 2011. Member, Rural Economy 2018-19. *Other:* DL: Greater London 2010, Norfolk 2011; Royal Armouries: Trustee, Chair 2016-18.

Political interests: Defence, security, agriculture, human rights; Africa, South Asia, Middle East.

Other: Patron, Military Mission International 2010-; President, Royal Norfolk Agricultural Association 2008; Trustee: Windsor Leadership Trust, Historic Royal Palaces; Vice-President, Officers Christian Union 1998-, President: Army Rifle Association 2000-08, Army Winter Sports Association 2003-09, Army Rugby Union 2003-09, The Soldiers' and Airmen's Scripture Readers Association 2003-; Chairman, Strategic Advisory Board, Durham Global Security Institute, Durham University; Help for Heroes, Street Child of Sierra Leone, The Soldier's Charity, Combat Stress, Blind Veterans UK, Royal British Legion, Haig Housing Trust; Hon. Freeman, Merchant Taylors; Hon. Liveryman, Security Professionals; Honorary Doctorate of Civil Law: Durham University 2009, Kent University 2009; Honorary Doctorate of Technology, Anglia Ruskin University 2010; Military Cross 1973; CBE 1996; KCB 2004; GCB 2009. Army & Navy; Cavalry and Guards Club; Norfolk County Cricket Club.

Publications: Autobiography, Leading from the Front (Bantam Press, 2010); Boots on the Ground: Britain and her Army since 1945 (Profile Books, 2016).

Recreations: Sport, reading.

General the Lord Dannatt GCB CBE MC, House of Lords, London SW1A 0PW
Tel: 020 7219 8949 *Email:* dannattr@parliament.uk
Tel: 07899 950320 *Email:* richard@richarddannat.com

CROSSBENCH

DARROCH OF KEW, LORD

DARROCH OF KEW (Life Baron), Nigel Kim Darroch; cr 2019. Born 30 April 1954; Married Vanessa Jackson 1978 (1 daughter 1 son).

Education: Abingdon School; Durham University (BSc zoology 1975); Italian.

Non-political career: HM Diplomatic Service 1976-2019: First Secretary, Tokyo Embassy 1980-84, Foreign and Commonwealth Office (FCO), London 1985-89: Private Secretary to Minister of State 1987-89, First Secretary, Rome Embassy 1989-92, FCO 1993-97: Deputy Head, European Integration Department 1993-95, Head, Eastern Adriatic Department 1995-97; Counsellor, External Affairs, UK Permanent Representation to European Union, Brussels 1997-98, FCO 1998-2004: Head, News Department 1998-2000, Director, European Union Department 2000-03, Director-General, European Union Policy 2003-04, Prime Minister's European Policy Adviser and Head of European Secretariat, Cabinet Office 2004-07; Permanent Representative to the EU 2007-11, Prime Minister's National Security Adviser, Prime Minister's Office 2012-15, Ambassador to the United States 2016-19.

Political career: *House of Lords:* Raised to the peerage as Baron Darroch of Kew, of St Mawes in the County of Cornwall 2019.

Other: CMG 1998; KCMG 2008.

Recreations: Skiing, sailing, squash, cinema.

The Lord Darroch of Kew KCMG, House of Lords, London SW1A 0PW
Twitter: @KimDarroch

NON-AFFILIATED

DARZI OF DENHAM, LORD

DARZI OF DENHAM (Life Baron), Ara Warkais Darzi; cr 2007. Born 7 May 1960; Married Wendy Hutchinson 1991 (1 son 1 daughter).

Education: Royal College of Surgeons of Ireland (MB BCh BAO 1984); Trinity College, Dublin (MD 1992).

Non-political career: Consultant surgeon and senior lecturer, Central Middlesex Hospital 1993-94; Consultant, St Mary's Hospital, Paddington 1994-98; Honorary consultant surgeon: Imperial College Healthcare NHS Trust 1994-, Royal Marsden Hospital NHS Foundation Trust 1994-, Great Ormond Street Hospital 1995-, Central Middlesex Hospital 1995-; Imperial College, London: Professor of surgery 1998-, Head of surgery, oncology, reproductive biology and anaesthesia 2002-07, Head of surgery division 2009-12; Adviser on surgery, Department of Health 2001-07; Professor of surgery, Institute of Cancer Research 2005-; Paul Hamlyn chair of surgery 2005-; Director, Institute of Global Health Innovation 2010-; Chair, Imperial College Healthcare Partners 2012-13; Executive Chair, World Innovation Summit for Health 2012-; Vice-Dean, Health Policy and Engagement, Imperial College London 2013-17; Chair, London Health Commission 2013-14; Director: Imperial CRUK Centre 2016-, Imperial NIHR Patient Safety Translational Research Centre 2012-.

Political career: *House of Lords:* Raised to the peerage as Baron Darzi of Denham, of Gerrards Cross in the County of Buckinghamshire 2007. Department of Health: Parliamentary Under-Secretary of State 2007-09, Government Spokesperson 2007-09; UK Business Ambassador, Department of Business, Innovation and Skills 2009-13. *Other:* Resigned Labour Whip July 2019-. Non-executive director, NHS England 2015-; Member, Council, Engineering and Physical Sciences Research Council 2013-18; Chair, Accelerated Access Collaborative 2018-.

Other: Member, advisory board, Helen Hamlyn Centre for Design, Royal College of Arts; Royal Society of Medicine; Surgical Research Society; Irish Society of Gastroenterology; American Society of Colon and Rectal Surgeons; Society of Minimally Invasive Therapy; European Association of Endoscopic Surgery; Association of Endoscopic Surgeons of Great Britain and Ireland; Association of Surgeons of Great Britain and Ireland; Association of Coloproctology of Great Britain and Ireland; Society of American Gastrointestinal Endoscopic Surgeons; Société Internationale de Chirurgie; World Association of Hepato-Pancreato-Biliary Surgery; American College of Surgeons; Association for Surgical Education; International Surgical Group; International Society of Surgery; Society of Laparoscopic Surgery; American Surgical Association; Beating Bowel Cancer, Meningitis Now, Barrett's Oesophagus Campaign, Chordoma UK, National Competitiveness Foundation of Armenia, Lord Leonard and Lady Estelle Wolfson of Marylebone Charitable Trust for Preventative Medicine, Rangoon Hospital Reinvigoration Charitable Trust, Cyberbullying Foundation, N Sethia Foundation, Smile Support and Care, Pathway Charity; Numerous fellowships including: Hon. Fellowship, American Surgical Association, USA, Hon. Fellow, Anatomical Society, Hon. Fellow, National Institute of Clinical Excellence, Visiting Professor, London School of Economics and Political Science, Foreign Associate Member, Institute of Medicine of the National Academies, USA, Hon. Fellowship, American Society for Colon and Rectal Surgeons, Hon. Fellow, Royal College of Radiologists, FRS Fellow, Royal Society, Hon. Membership, Japan Society for Endoscopic Surgery, Hon. Professor, Department of Surgery, University of Hong Kong, Hon. Fellow, American College of Surgeons, Fellow, Royal College of Physicians, Fellow, Royal College of Physicians in Ireland, Fellow, Academy of Medical Sciences, Hon. Fellow, Royal Academy of Engineering; Numerous honorary academic degrees, including: Hon FRCSI, Royal College of Surgeons, Ireland, Hon DH, Bradford University, Hon MEng, Bradford University, Hon. DCard, Cardiff University, Hon. DEbor, York University, Hon LLD, Trinity College Dublin, Hon DSc, De Montfort University, Hon MD, Newcastle University, Hon DEng, Bath University, Hon DSc, Cranfield University; Queen's Anniversary Prize in Higher and Further Education 2001; Hamdan Award for Medical Research Excellence 2004; Scientific Achievement Award, Armenian Medical World Congress, New York 2009; Distinguished Graduates Medal, Royal College of Surgeons, Ireland 2009; Qatari Sash of Independence 2014; Armenia Order of Honour 2017; Order of the Rising Sun, Gold Rays with Neck Ribbon, Japan 2019; KBE 2002; PC 2009; OM 2016.

Publications: Over 1,100 peer reviewed articles in academic journals.

Rt Hon Professor the Lord Darzi of Denham OM KBE, House of Lords, London SW1A 0PW
Tel: 020 7219 5416
Department of Surgery and Cancer, Tenth Floor QEQM Building, St Mary's Hospital Campus,

Imperial College London, Praed Street, London W2 1NY *Tel:* 020 3312 1310
Email: s.mcateer@imperial.ac.uk Website: www.imperial.ac.uk/people/a.darzi

LABOUR

DAVIDSON OF GLEN CLOVA, LORD

Shadow Advocate General for Scotland; Opposition Spokesperson for Law Officers and Scotland

DAVIDSON OF GLEN CLOVA (Life Baron), Neil Forbes Davidson; cr 2006. Born 13 September 1950; Son of John and Flora Davidson; Married Regina Sprissler 1980.

Education: Stirling University (BA economics 1971); Bradford University (MSc international business 1972); Edinburgh University (LLB 1977; LLM 1979).

Non-political career: Faculty of Advocates 1979; Standing Junior Counsel to: Registrar General 1982-88, Departments of Health and Social Security 1988-93; Barrister Inner Temple, London 1990; QC (Scot) 1993; Solicitor General for Scotland 2000-01; Director City Disputes Panel 1993-2000; Advocate, Axiom Advocates.

Political career: *House of Lords:* Raised to the peerage as Baron Davidson of Glen Clova, of Glen Clova in Angus 2006. Advocate General for Scotland 2006-10; Government Spokesperson for Scotland 2008-10; Shadow Advocate General for Scotland and Opposition Spokesperson for Law Officers 2010-; Opposition Spokesperson for: Treasury 2010-20, Scotland 2010-12, 2018-. Member, Insurance Bill 2014-15.

Political interests: China.

Other: Chair, Human Rights Committee, Faculty of Advocates 1997-2000; DUniv, Stirling University 2012.

The Lord Davidson of Glen Clova QC, House of Lords, London SW1A 0PW
Tel: 020 7219 5353
Email: lord.davidson@axiomadvocates.com

CONSERVATIVE

DAVIDSON, RUTH – Peerage pending at time of going to press

Born 10 November 1978; Engaged to Jennifer Wilson (1 son).

Education: Buckhaven High School; Edinburgh University; Glasgow University (international development).

Non-political career: Journalist and presenter, BBC Scotland -2009; Former journalist: Real Radio, Kingdom FM, Johnson Press. Territorial Army.

Political career: *House of Commons:* Contested Glasgow North East 2009 by-election and 2010 general election. *Other:* Contested Glasgow Kelvin constituency 2011 Scottish Parliament election. MSP for Glasgow region 2011-16, for Edinburgh Central constituency since 5 May 2016: Scottish Conservatives Spokesperson for Culture 2011, Leader of the opposition 2016-19, Member, Scottish Parliamentary Corporate Body 2019-20, Leader, Scottish Conservative Group in the Scottish Parliament 2020-. Leader, Scottish Conservative and Unionist Party 2011-19.

Political interests: Sport.

Other: Politician of the Year, Stonewall awards 2012; PC 2016.

Publications: Yes She Can: Why Women Own The Future (Hodder & Stoughton, 2018).

Recreations: Hill-walking, kickboxing, walking the dog.

Rt Hon Ruth Davidson, House of Lords, London SW1A 0PW *Twitter:* @ruthdavidsonmsp

NON-AFFILIATED

DAVIES OF ABERSOCH, LORD

DAVIES OF ABERSOCH (Life Baron), (Evan) Mervyn Davies; cr 2009. Born 21 November 1952; Son of late Richard Davies and Margaret Davies; Married Jeanne Gammie 1979 (1 son 1 daughter).

Education: Rydal School, Colwyn Bay; Harvard Business School (PMD 1989); Welsh.

Non-political career: Senior credit officer, Citibank 1983-93; Standard Chartered plc and predecessors 1993-2009: Director 1997-2009, Director, Hong Kong 1997-2001, Group chief executive 2001-06, Chair 2006-09; Chair and partner, Corsair Capital 2010-; Non-executive chairman, PineBridge Investments Ltd 2010-; Moelis & Co: Chair, advisory board 2010-15, Senior adviser to CEO 2015-16; Non-executive director: Bharti Airtel Ltd 2010-12, Diageo plc 2010-; Chairman, Chime Communications 2012-15; Director, Glyndebourne Productions Ltd 2012-; Chair, Jack Wills 2014-; Deputy Chair, LetterOne Holdings 2015-.

Political career: *House of Lords:* Raised to the peerage as Baron Davies of Abersoch, of Abersoch in the County of Gwynedd 2009. Minister of State and Government Spokesperson, Department for Business, Enterprise and Regulatory Reform/Business, Innovation and Skills and Foreign and Commonwealth Office (Minister for Trade, Investment and Small Business) 2009-10; Trade Envoy to Sri Lanka 2020-; On leave of absence December 2020-. *Other:* Resigned from Labour 2016; now sits as Non-affiliated. Chair, Council, University of Wales, Bangor -2014; JP, Hong Kong.

Political interests: Labour, free trade, equality; Africa, Asia, Middle East.

Other: Former chair: British Chamber of Commerce, Hong Kong, Hong Kong Association of Banks; Chair: Royal Academy of Arts Trustees 2012-18, Garden Bridge Trust 2013-; Member, International Advisory Board, Discovery Insurance; Director: Glyndebourne Productions Ltd, The All England Lawn Tennis Ground plc, LTA Operations Limited, Artfarm Group Limited, Made By Dyslexia; Chair: UK India Business Council, Lawn Tennis Association, Corsair Capital LLP, LetterOne Holdings S.A., Cydar Limited, Andrew Martin Limited, UK Agricultural Finance, Play On Football Ltd, Byhiras, Double Dutch Ltd; Member, World Rugby Executive Committee; Adviser, Teneo Holdings; Fellow, Institute of Bankers; Breakthrough Breast Cancer, Hope House Children's Hospice; CBE 2002. Shek O, Arts/Alfred's Club; Abersoch GC; Morla Nefyn GC.

Recreations: Soccer, skiing, golf, music, Welsh art.

The Lord Davies of Abersoch CBE, House of Lords, London SW1A 0PW
Tel: 020 7219 3000
Tel: 020 7152 6536 *Email:* hilderly@corsair-capital.com

LABOUR

DAVIES OF BRIXTON, LORD

BARON DAVIES OF BRIXTON (Life Baron), Brinley Howard Davies; cr 2020. Born 17 May 1944; Married Prof Dame Til Wykes 2006.

Education: Hull University (BSc (Econ) 1966); London School of Economics (MSc 2006).

Non-political career: Pensions Officer, Trades Union Congress 1974-81; Director, Pensions and Investment Research Consultants 1984; Research Actuary, then Partner, Bacon and Woodrow (Consulting Actuaries) 1985-89; Director, Union Pension Services 1989-; Special Adviser, House of Commons Social Security Committee 1996-97. Member, Unite and its predecessors 1966-.

Political career: *House of Lords:* Raised to the peerage as Baron Davies of Brixton, of Brixton in the London Borough of Lambeth 2020. *Other:* Councillor, Croydon Council 1971-74; Member, Occupational Pensions Board 1976-81; Councillor, Lambeth Council 1978-81; Member, Greater London Council 1980-85; Leader, Inner London Education Authority 1981-83.

Political interests: Pensions, mental health, transport; London.

Other: Chair, Independent Pensions Research Group 1980-; Treasurer, European Network for Research on Supplementary Pensions 1995-; Fellow, Institute of Actuaries (Qualified 1974).

The Lord Davies of Brixton, House of Lords, London SW1A 0PW
Tel: 020 7219 3000 *Email:* daviesofbirxton@parliament.uk *Twitter:* @DaviesofBrixton

CONSERVATIVE

DAVIES OF GOWER, LORD

DAVIES OF GOWER (Life Baron), Henry Byron Davies; cr 2019. Born 4 September 1952; Son of William and Gladys Davies; Married Gillian Davies 1978 (1 son).

Education: Gowerton Boys' Grammer School; Thames Valley University (LLB 1993); Romanian, Welsh.

Non-political career: Police officer 1971-2003: Detective, Metropolitan Police, Senior investigating officer, National Crime Squad of England and Wales, Adviser on combating organised crime, seconded to European Union; Adviser to Romanian National Police; Self-employed consultant 2003-11. Former member, Royal Air Force Volunteer Reserve.

Political career: *House of Commons:* Contested Gower 2010 general election. MP for Gower 2015-17. Member: Welsh Affairs 2015-17, Armed Forces Bill 2015 2015-16, Home Affairs 2016-17. Chairman, Conservative Backbench Policy Committee on Home Affairs 2015-17. *House of Lords:* Raised to the peerage as Baron Davies of Gower, of Gower in the County of Swansea 2019. Member, Public Services 2020-. *Other:* Contested Gower constituency 2007 National Assembly for Wales election. AM for South Wales West region 2011 to 15 May 2015: Welsh Conservatives: Shadow Minister for Transport and Regeneration 2011-15, Whip 2011-15. Founding member, Conservatives for Reform in Europe 2016; Welsh Conservative Party: Chair 2017-20, President 2020-.

Political interests: Home affairs, policing, foreign affairs, EU enlargement, transport; Balkans, Eastern Europe.

Other: Member, Executive Committee, Commonwealth Parliamentary Association United Kingdom 2020-; Fellow, Institute of Professional Investigators; Royal British Legion, Wales Air Ambulance. Royal Air Force, Piccadilly London, Gowerton Conservative and Unionist Club.

Recreations: Aviation (holds pilot's licence), rugby, cycling.

The Lord Davies of Gower, House of Lords, London SW1A 0PW
Tel: 020 7219 3000 *Email:* daviesbh@parliament.uk *Twitter:* @Byron_Davies

LABOUR

DAVIES OF OLDHAM, LORD

DAVIES OF OLDHAM (Life Baron), Bryan Davies; cr. 1997. Born 9 November 1939; Son of late George and Beryl Davies; Married Monica Shearing 1963 (2 sons 1 daughter).

Education: Redditch High School; University College, London (BA history 1961); Institute of Education (PGCE 1962); London School of Economics (BSc economics 1968).

Non-political career: History teacher, Latymer School, London 1962-65; History and social science lecturer, Middlesex Polytechnic, Enfield 1965-74. Divisional executive officer, NATFHE 1967-74; Member, Transport and General Workers' Union/Unite 1979-.

Political career: *House of Commons:* Contested Norfolk Central 1966 general election. MP (Labour) for Enfield North 1974-79. Contested Enfield North 1979 and Newport West 1983 general elections. MP for Oldham Central and Royton 1992-97; Assistant Government Whip 1978-79; Opposition Spokesperson for: Education 1993-95, Education and Employment 1995-97. *House of Lords:* Raised to the peerage as Baron Davies of Oldham, of Broxbourne in the County of Hertfordshire 1997. Government Whip 2000-03; Government Spokesperson for: Home Office 2000-02, Education and Skills 2001-03, Culture, Media and Sport 2001-08, Transport 2002-07, Trade and Industry 2003-04; Deputy Chief Whip (Captain, the Queen's Body Guard of the Yeomen of the Guard) 2003-10; Government Spokesperson for: Cabinet Office 2007-08, Treasury 2007-08, Environment, Food and Rural Affairs 2008, Scotland 2008, Wales 2008-10; Parliamentary Under-Secretary of State and Government Spokesperson, Department for Environment, Food and Rural Affairs 2009-10; Opposition Spokesperson for: Transport 2010-15, Treasury 2010-20, Wales 2010-13. Member: Refreshment 2005-08, 2009-11, Joint Committee on Security 2010, Liaison 2020-. *Other:* Secretary, Parliamentary Labour Party and Shadow Cabinet 1979-92. Member, Medical Research Council 1977-79; Chair, Further Education Funding Council 1998-2000.

Political interests: Economic policy, employment, training, education, arts, transport; Nepal, Sri Lanka.

Other: President, Royal Society for the Prevention of Accidents 1999-2000; Oxfam; Honorary Doctorate, Middlesex University 1996; PC 2007.

Recreations: Sport, literature.

Rt Hon the Lord Davies of Oldham, House of Lords, London SW1A 0PW
Tel: 020 7219 1475 *Email:* daviesb@parliament.uk
Email: bm.davies@ntlworld.com

LABOUR

DAVIES OF STAMFORD, LORD

DAVIES OF STAMFORD (Life Baron), Quentin Davies; cr 2010. Born 29 May 1944; Son of late Dr M I Davies, general practitioner, and Thelma Davies; Married Chantal Tamplin 1983 (2 sons).

Education: Leighton Park School, Reading; Gonville and Caius College, Cambridge (BA history 1966, MA); Harvard University, USA (Frank Knox Fellow); French, German, Italian, Russian.

Non-political career: HM Diplomatic Service 1967-74: Third Secretary, FCO 1967-69, Second Secretary, Moscow 1969-72, First Secretary, FCO 1972-74; Manager then assistant director, Morgan Grenfell & Co Ltd 1974-78; Director-general and President, Morgan Grenfell France 1978-81; Morgan Grenfell Co Ltd and certain group subsidiaries: Director, main board 1981-87, Consultant 1987-93; Consultant, National Westminster Securities plc 1993-99; Dewe Rogerson International 1987-94; Société Genérale d'Entreprises 1999-2000; Consultant, Royal Bank of Scotland 1999-2002; Director: Vinci 2003-08, Vinci UK 2003-08; Lloyd's of London: Director, Member of the Council 2004-07.

Political career: *House of Commons:* Contested Birmingham Ladywood 1977 by-election. MP (Conservative) for Stamford and Spalding 1987-97, for Grantham and Stamford 1997-2010 (Labour June 2007-10); PPS to Angela Rumbold as Minister of State: Department of Education and Science 1988-90, Home Office 1990-91; Shadow Minister for Pensions 1998-99; Shadow Paymaster General 1999-2000; Shadow Minister for Defence 2000-01; Shadow Secretary of State for Northern Ireland 2001-03; Parliamentary Under-Secretary of State (Minister for Defence Equipment and Support), Ministry of Defence 2008-10. Member: Standards and Privileges 1995-97, 1997-98, Treasury 1997-98, European Scrutiny 1998, International Development 2003-07, Joint Committee on Tax Law Rewrite Bills 2007-09, Regulatory Reform 2007-10. Secretary, Conservative Parliamentary Committees on: Finance 1991-97, Trade and Industry 1991-95; Vice-chair, Conservative Party Committee for Trade and Industry 1995-98; Chair, Conservative Group for Europe 2006-07. *House of Lords:* Raised to the peerage as Baron Davies of Stamford, of Stamford in the County of Lincolnshire 2010. Member: Selection 2011, Joint Committee on the Draft Detention of Terrorist Suspects (Temporary Extension) Bills 2011, Consumer Insurance (Disclosure and Representations) Bill 2011-12, Joint Committee on Parliamentary Privilege 2013, EU Sub-committee A (Economic and Financial Affairs) 2013-15, European Union 2015-16, EU Financial Affairs Sub-committee 2015-16, Joint Committee on Statutory Instruments 2016, Licensing Act 2003 2016-17, EU External Affairs Sub-committee 2019-20, EU Services Sub-committee 2020-.

Political interests: Defence, trade and industry, finance, agriculture, health, welfare, pensions, overseas development, Europe; EU, Russia, USA.

Other: Parliamentary adviser, Chartered Institute of Taxation 1993-2008; Fellow, Industry and Parliament Trust 1995; Trustee and member, Executive Committee, Council for Economic Policy Research 1996-2008; Liveryman, Goldsmiths' Company. Beefsteak, Brooks's, Travellers, RAF Club.

Publications: Britain and Europe: A Conservative View (1996); Co-author, Report of Inquiry into National Recognition of our Armed Forces (2008).

Recreations: Reading, walking, skiing, travel.

The Lord Davies of Stamford, House of Lords, London SW1A 0PW
Tel: 020 7219 5353 *Email:* daviesq@parliament.uk

CROSSBENCH

DEAR, LORD

DEAR (Life Baron), Geoffrey James Dear; cr 2006. Born 20 September 1937; Son of late Cecil Dear and Violet Dear, née Mackney; Married Judith Stocker 1958 (died 1996) (1 son 2 daughters); married Alison Martin Jones 1998.

Education: Fletton Grammar School, Huntingdonshire; University College, London (Bramshill Scholarship, LLB 1968).

Non-political career: Mid-Anglia Constabulary 1965; Assistant Chief Constable (operations), Nottinghamshire 1972-80; Seconded as director of command training, Bramshill Police College 1975-77; Metropolitan Police 1980-85: Personnel and training 1981-84, Operations 1984-85; Chief Constable, West Midlands Police 1985-90; HM Inspector of Constabulary 1990-97; Hon Bencher, Gray's Inn 2008; Non-executive chair, Blaythorne Group plc.

Political career: *House of Lords:* Raised to the peerage as Baron Dear, of Willersey in the County of Gloucestershire 2006. Deputy Chairman of Committees 2015-; Deputy Speaker 2015-. EU Sub-committee F (Home Affairs): Co-opted member 2007-09, Member 2009-12; Member: European Union 2009-14, EU Sub-committee A (Economic and Financial Affairs) 2012-15, Joint Committee on the Rookery South (Resource Recovery Facility) Order 2012-13, Works of Art 2015-16, Privileges and Conduct 2015-, Lord Speaker's Advisory Panel on Works of Art 2017-19. *Other:* DL, West Midlands 1985-96; Worcestershire: DL 1996-, Vice-Lord Lieutenant 1998-2001.

Political interests: Egypt, India, Middle East, USA.

Other: Trustee: The Country Trust 1987-2012, Police Rehabilitation Trust 1991-2018; Police Foundation 2008-13; World Horse Welfare 2010-15; Freeman, City of London 2004; Fellow, University College, London; Hon. fellow, Birmingham City University; Hon. Bencher, Gray's Inn; Queen's Commendation for Bravery 1979; QPM 1982; Commander Order of St John 1996; Kt 1997. East India Club, Special Forces Club; Vice-President, Warwickshire County Cricket Club.

Recreations: Country sports, cricket, rugby football, gardening, music, literature.

The Lord Dear QPM DL, House of Lords, London SW1A 0PW
Email: deargj@parliament.uk

CONSERVATIVE

DEBEN, LORD

DEBEN (Life Baron), John Selwyn Gummer; cr 2010. Born 26 November 1939; Son of late Rev Canon Selwyn Gummer and late Sybille Gummer, née Mason; Married Penelope Gardner 1977 (2 sons, including Ben Gummer, MP for Ipswich 2010-17, 2 daughters).

Education: King's School, Rochester; Selwyn College, Cambridge (BA history 1961, MA 1971) (Union President 1962); French (reasonable).

Non-political career: Editor, Business Publications 1962-64; Editor-in-Chief, Max Parrish & Oldbourne Press 1964-66; Director, Shandwick Publishing Co 1966-81; BPC Publishing: Special assistant to chairman 1967, Publisher, special projects 1967-69, Editorial co-ordinator 1969-70; Siemssen Hunter Ltd: Director 1973-80, Chairman 1979-80; Chairman: Selwyn Shandwick International 1976-81, Sancroft International Ltd (corporate responsibility consultants) 1997-, Marine Stewardship Council 1997-2006; Vivendi UK/Veolia Water UK: Director 1997-2013, Chairman 2004-13; Chairman, Valpak Ltd 1998-; International Commission on Consumption 1998-2005; Association of Professional Financial Advisers (formerly Association of Independent Financial Advisers) 2003-17; President, Association of Mortgage Intermediaries; Chairman, Zero C Holdings Ltd 2008-14; Non-executive directorships, including: Catholic Herald, Castle Trust 2011-; Personal Investment Management and Financial Advice Association 2017-.

Political career: *House of Commons:* Contested Greenwich 1964 and 1966 general elections. MP (Conservative) for Lewisham West 1970-February 1974. Contested Lewisham West February 1974 general election. MP for Eye 1979-83, for Suffolk Coastal 1983-2010; PPS: to Jim Prior as Minister of Agriculture, Fisheries and Food 1971-72, to Patrick Jenkin as Secretary of State for Social Services 1979-81; Government Whip 1981-83; Department of Employment: Parliamentary Under-Secretary of State 1983, Minister of State 1983-84; Paymaster General 1984-85; Minister of State, Ministry of Agriculture, Fisheries and Food 1985-88; Minister for Local Government, Department of Environment 1988-89; Minister of Agriculture, Fisheries and

Food 1989-93; Secretary of State for the Environment 1993-97. *House of Lords:* Raised to the peerage as Baron Deben, of Winston in the County of Suffolk 2010. *Other:* Chairman, Cambridge University Conservative Association 1961; Conservative Party: Vice-chairman 1972-74, Chairman 1983-85; Chairman, Conservative Group for Europe 1997-2000. Councillor, Inner London Education Authority 1967-70; Chairman, Committee on Climate Change 2012-.

Political interests: Energy, environment, European affairs, business, industry, consumers.

Other: Member: General Synod, Church of England (for St Edmundsbury and Ipswich Diocese) 1978-92, Panel on Takeovers and Mergers 2018-; Hon. Doctorate, Westminster University 2014; PC 1985.

Publications: When the Coloured People Come (1966); The Permissive Society (1971); Co-author, The Christian Calendar (1974); Faith in Politics (1987).

Recreations: Architecture, walking.

Rt Hon the Lord Deben, House of Lords, London SW1A 0PW
Tel: 020 7219 5353
46 Queen Anne's Gate, London SW1H 9AP *Tel:* 020 7960 7900 *Email:* office@sancroft.com
Twitter: @lorddeben

CROSSBENCH

DEECH, BARONESS

DEECH (Life Baroness), Ruth Lynn Deech; cr 2005. Born 29 April 1943; Daughter of Josef Fraenkel and Dora, née Rosenfeld; Married Dr John Deech 1967 (1 daughter).

Education: Christ's Hospital, Hertford; St Anne's College, Oxford (BA law 1965, MA); Brandeis University, USA (MA Jewish studies 1966).

Non-political career: Called to the Bar Inner Temple 1967 (later Hon. Bencher); St Anne's College, Oxford: Fellow and law tutor 1970-91, Principal 1991-2004; QC 2013.

Political career: *House of Lords:* Raised to the peerage as Baroness Deech, of Cumnor in the County of Oxfordshire 2005. Member: Merits of Statutory Instruments 2007-10, Draft Human Tissue and Embryos Bill Joint Committee 2007, Communications 2010-15; Chair, Equality Act 2010 and Disability 2015-16; Member, EU Justice Sub-committee 2019-20. *Other:* Chair, Human Fertilisation and Embryology Authority 1994-2002; BBC Governor 2002-06; Independent Adjudicator for Higher Education 2004-08; Gresham Professor of Law 2008-12; Chair, Bar Standards Board 2009-14.

Political interests: Higher education, family law, broadcasting, reproductive technology; Israel, Poland, USA.

Other: Fellow: Royal Society of Medicine, International Society of Family Law; Non-executive board member, Law Commission 2019-; Liveryman, Drapers' Company; Pro-vice-chancellor, Oxford University 2001-04; Honorary LLD: Strathclyde University 2003, Richmond American International University 2006, Ben Gurion University, Israel 2012; DBE 2002. Royal Society of Medicine Club.

Publications: Co-editor, Biomedicine, the Family and Human Rights (Kluwer, 2002); From IVF to Immortality (OUP, 2007).

Recreations: Opera, travel, after-dinner speaking.

The Baroness Deech DBE QC, House of Lords, London SW1A 0PW
Tel: 020 7219 5353 *Email:* deechr@parliament.uk
Email: ruth.deech@st-annes.ox.ac.uk
Websites: www.law.ox.ac.uk/people/profile.php?who=deechr
lordsoftheblog.net/category/baroness-deech *Twitter:* @BaronessDeech

CONSERVATIVE

DEIGHTON, LORD

DEIGHTON (Life Baron), Paul Clive Deighton; cr 2012. Born 18 January 1956; Son of late Walter Deighton and late Mabel King; Married Alison Klebanoff 1985 (2 sons).

Education: Wallington County Grammar School for Boys; Trinity College, Cambridge (BA economics 1978).

Non-political career: Bank of America 1978-81; Security Pacific 1981-83; Goldman Sachs 1983-2006; Chief executive officer, LOCOG 2006-12; Non-executive chair, Heathrow Airport Holdings Ltd 2016-.

Political career: *House of Lords:* Raised to the peerage as Baron Deighton, of Carshalton in the County of Surrey 2012. Commercial Secretary and Government Spokesperson, HM Treasury 2013-15. Member, Joint Committee on the Palace of Westminster 2015-16. *Other:* Chair, governing body, King's College School, Wimbledon.

Other: Board member, England Rugby 2015 (organising body for the Rugby World Cup) 2013-15; Chair, Audit and Finance Commission, International Association of Athletics Federations 2016-; Non-executive director, Square 2016-; Non-executive chair: Holdingham Group 2018-, Economist Group 2018-; Honorary fellow, Institution of Civil Engineers; Honorary doctorate, Sheffield Hallam University; KBE 2013.

The Lord Deighton KBE, House of Lords, London SW1A 0PW
Tel: 020 7219 5353

CONSERVATIVE

DE MAULEY, LORD

DE MAULEY (7th Baron, UK), Rupert Charles Ponsonby; cr. 1838. Born 30 June 1957; Son of late Colonel Hon Thomas Maurice Ponsonby, TD, DL, younger son of 5th Baron; Married Hon Lucinda Royle 2002.

Education: Eton College.

Non-political career: Director, Samuel Montagu & Co Ltd 1990-93; Standard Chartered Merchant Bank Asia Ltd 1994-99; Master of the Horse 2019-. Royal Wessex Yeomanry: Lt Col (Commanded) 2003-04, Honorary Colonel 2015-; Colonel Commandant, The Yeomanry 2011-.

Political career: *House of Lords:* Elected hereditary peer 2005-; Opposition Whip 2005-10; Opposition Spokesperson for: Trade and Industry/Business, Enterprise and Regulatory Reform/ Business, Innovation and Skills 2005-10, Cabinet Office 2006-09, Energy and Climate Change 2008-09, Innovation, Universities and Skills 2008-09, Children, Schools and Families 2008-09, Treasury 2009-10; Government Whip 2010-12; Government Spokesperson for: Business, Innovation and Skills 2010-12, Home Office 2010, HM Treasury 2010-12, Environment, Food and Rural Affairs 2010-15, Work and Pensions 2011-12; Department for Environment, Food and Rural Affairs: Parliamentary Under-Secretary of State: (Resource Management, the Local Environment and Environmental Science) 2012-13, (Natural Environment and Science) 2013-15. Member: Joint Committee on Security 2010-12, Consumer Insurance (Disclosure and Representations) Bill 2011-12, Trade Union and Party Funding 2016, EU Financial Affairs Sub-committee 2016-19, Lord Speaker's Advisory Panel on Works of Art 2019-. *Other:* President, Conservative Rural Affairs Group 2016-.

Political interests: South east Asia, China, Europe.

Other: President: UK Council, Reserve Forces and Cadets Associations 2010-, Society for the Protection of Animals Abroad 2010-; Panel member, Youd Andrews 2016-; Trustee, Horse Trust 2016-; Institute of Chartered Accountants in England and Wales; FCA 1990; TD.

Recreations: Country sports, woodland management.

The Lord de Mauley TD, House of Lords, London SW1A 0PW
Tel: 020 7219 3000 *Email:* demauley@parliament.uk

CONSERVATIVE

DENHAM, LORD

DENHAM (2nd Baron, UK), Bertram Stanley Mitford Bowyer; cr. 1937; 10th Bt of Denham (E) 1660; 2nd Bt of Weston Underwood (UK) 1933. Born 3 October 1927; Son of 1st Baron, MC; Married Jean McCorquodale 1956 (3 sons 1 daughter).

Education: Eton College; King's College, Cambridge (BA English literature 1951).

Non-political career: Countryside Commissioner 1993-99.

Political career: *House of Lords:* First entered House of Lords 1948; Government Whip 1961-64, 1970-72; Opposition Whip 1964-70; Deputy Chief Whip 1972-74; Opposition Deputy Chief Whip 1974-78; Opposition Chief Whip 1978-79; Government Chief Whip 1979-91; Extra Lord in Waiting to HM The Queen 1998-; Elected hereditary peer 1999-.

Political interests: Machinery of Government.

Other: PC 1981; KBE 1991. Pratt's, Garrick Club.

Publications: The Man Who Lost His Shadow (1979); Two Thyrdes (1983); Foxhunt (1988); Black Rod (1997); A Thing of Shreds and Patches (a read anthology of own selection of light verse, 2000); Victorian Plums (CD including The Hunting of the Snark, The Rubaiyat of Omar Khayyam and the Ballad of Reading Gaol).

Recreations: Field sports.

Rt Hon the Lord Denham KBE, House of Lords, London SW1A 0PW
Tel: 020 7219 6056 *Fax:* 020 7219 6056
The Laundry Cottage, Weston Underwood, Olney MK46 5JZ *Tel:* 01234 711535

NON-AFFILIATED

DERBY, LORD BISHOP OF

DERBY (8th Bishop of), Elizabeth (Libby) Jane Holden Lane. Born 8 December 1966; Daughter of Dennis and Helen Holden; Married George Lane 1990 (1 son 1 daughter).

Education: Manchester High School for Girls; St Peter's College, Oxford (MA); St John's College, Cranham Hall, Durham (DipMin).

Non-political career: Ordained deacon 1993, Priest 1994; Curate, St James Blackburn, Diocese of Blackburn 1993-96; Permission to Officiate, Diocese of York 1996-99; Chaplain, Diocese of York 1998-2000; Diocese of Chester: Social Responsibility Officer 2000-02, Assistant Director of Ordinands 2005-07, Team Vicar, St George's Stockport 2002-07; Vicar, St Peter's, Hale and St Elizabeth's, Ashley 2007-14; Dean of Women in Ministry 2010-14; Suffragan Bishop of Stockport 2015-19; Bishop of Derby 2019-.

Political career: *House of Lords:* Entered House of Lords 2019.

Other: Vice-chair of the Board, The Children's Society; Chair of the board: Cranmer Hall, St John's College, Durham University, Multi-Faith Centre, Derby University; The Church of England's Children's Society; Hon. Fellow, St Peter's College, Oxford University; Hon. Doc.: University of Wales, Bath University, Chester University.

Rt Rev the Lord Bishop of Derby, House of Lords, London SW1A 0PW
Tel: 020 7219 3000
The Bishop's Office, 6 King Street, Duffield, Belper DE56 4EU *Tel:* 01332 840132
Email: bishop@bishopofderby.org Website: derby.anglican.org

NON-AFFILIATED

DESAI, LORD

DESAI (Life Baron), Meghnad Jagdishchandra Desai; cr. 1991. Born 10 July 1940; Son of late Jagdishchandra and Mandakini Desai; Married Gail Wilson 1970 (1 son 2 daughters) (divorced 2004); married Kishwar Ahluwalia, née Rosha 2004.

Education: Sayaji High School, Baroda; Premier High School, Bombay; University of Bombay (BA economics 1958, MA 1960); University of Pennsylvania (PhD economics 1964); French, Gujarati, Hindi, Marathi, Sanskrit.

Non-political career: Associate specialist, Department of Agricultural Economics, University of California, Berkeley 1963-65; London School of Economics 1965-2003: Lecturer in economics 1965-77, Senior lecturer 1977-80, Reader 1980-83, Professor 1983-2004, Convenor, Economics Department 1987-90, Head, Development Studies Institute 1990-95, Director, Centre for the Study of Global Governance 1992-2003; Chair: Cape Claims Services 2007-, Advisory Board, Official Monetary and Financial Institutions Forum 2010-.

Political career: *House of Lords:* Raised to the peerage as Baron Desai, of St Clement Danes in the City of Westminster 1991. Opposition Whip 1991-94; Opposition Spokesperson for: Health 1991-93, Treasury and Economic Affairs 1992-93; Contested Lord Speaker election 2011. Member: Science and Technology 1991-92, European Community, Sub Committee A (Economic and Financial Affairs, Trade and External Relations) 1995-99, Delegated Powers Scrutiny 2001-05, Speakership of the House 2003, Merits of Statutory Instruments 2003-04, Intergovernmental Organisations 2007-08, EU Financial Affairs Sub-committee 2016-20, Economic Affairs Finance Bill Sub-committee 2019-20. *Other:* Labour Party: Chair, Islington South and Finsbury CLP 1986-92, Resigned from Party November 2020, now sits as Non-affiliated.

Political interests: Economic policy, education, development; Australia, Bangladesh, Brazil, Canada, China, India, Malaysia, Mauritius, Pakistan, Sierra Leone, Singapore, Sri Lanka, USA.

Other: Member: Executive Committee, Inter-Parliamentary Union British Group 1995-2003, Marshall Aid Commission 1998-2002; Member of Senate, London University 1980-88; Chair: City Life (drug rehabilitation charity) 1992-2000, Gandhi Statue Memorial Trust 2014-; FRSA; Five honorary doctorates; Honorary Fellow, London School of Economics 2005; Pravasi Bharatiya Purnskar Award for Overseas Indians of Distinction granted by Indian Government 2004; Padma Bhushan awarded by the Government of India 2008.

Publications: Several on economics.

Recreations: Reading, writing, cricket.

Professor the Lord Desai, House of Lords, London SW1A 0PW
Tel: 020 7219 5066 *Email:* desaim@parliament.uk
Tel: 020 7274 5561 *Email:* lord.mdesai@gmail.com

CROSSBENCH

DEVON, EARL OF

DEVON (19th Earl of, E), Charles Peregrine Courtenay; cr 1553; 15th Bt of Powderham Castle (E) 1644. Born 14 August 1975; Son of 18th Earl; Married Allison Joy Langer 2004 (1 son 1 daughter).

Education: Eton College; St John's College, Cambridge (BA history of art 1997); College of Law, London (CPE 1998); Inns of Court School of Law, London (BVC 1999).

Non-political career: Called to the Bar, Inner Temple 1999; Tenant, Maitland Chambers 2000-05; Admitted to California Bar 2004; Chancery Barrister, Lincoln's Inn, London; Latham & Watkins LLP: Associate, Los Angeles 2005-13, Counsel 2014-18, Head of Intellectual Property Litigation, Europe 2015-18; Partner, Michelmores LLP 2019-.

Political career: *House of Lords:* Elected hereditary peer 2018-.

Other: Member: Property Bar Association, Chancery Bar Association: Patron: Music in the Castle 2015-, Kenn Valley Young Farmers 2015-, Prison Choir Project 2017-. Patron, Starcross Yacht Club.

The Earl of Devon, House of Lords, London SW1A 0PW
Tel: 020 7219 3000

LIBERAL DEMOCRAT

DHOLAKIA, LORD

Deputy Leader, Liberal Democrat Peers

DHOLAKIA (Life Baron), Navnit Dholakia; cr. 1997. Born 4 March 1937; Son of Permananddas Mulji Dholakia and Shantabai Permananddas Dholakia; Married Ann McLuskie 1967 (2 daughters).

Education: Indian public schools in Moshi, Arusha, Tabora and Morogoro in Tanzania; Institute of Science, Bhavnager, Gujarat, India; Brighton Technical College; Gujarari, Hindi, Swahili.

Non-political career: Medical laboratory technician, Southlands Hospital, Shoreham-by-Sea 1960-66; Development officer, National Committee for Commonwealth Immigrants 1966-68; Community Relations Commission: Senior development officer 1968-74, Principal officer and secretary 1974-76; Commission for Racial Equality 1976-94: Head, administration of justice section 1984-94.

Political career: *House of Lords:* Raised to the peerage as Baron Dholakia, of Waltham Brooks in the County of West Sussex 1997. Liberal Democrat: Spokesperson for Home Affairs 1998-2007, Deputy Chief Whip 1998-2002; Member, House of Lords Appointments Commission 2000-10; Deputy Leader, Liberal Democrat Peers 2004-; Liberal Democrat Spokesperson for Communities 2007-10. Co-opted Member, European Communities Sub-committee F (Social Affairs, Education and Home Affairs) 1997-2000; Member: House of Lords Offices 1998-2001, Sub-committee on Lords' Interests 2008-10, Sub-committee on Lords' Conduct 2010-18, Joint Committee on Voting Eligibilty (Prisoners) Bill 2013, EU Justice Sub-committee 2019-20, EU Security and Justice Sub-committee 2020-. *Other:* Chair: Brighton Young Liberals 1959-62, Brighton Liberal Association 1962-64; Secretary, Race and Community Relations Panel, Liberal Party 1969-74; Member: Liberal Democrat Federal Policy Committee 1996-97, Federal Executive Committee; President: Liberal Democrat Party 2000-04, Liberal Democrat Federal Conference Committee 2001-; Chair, Diversity Engagement Group 2014-. Councillor, County Borough of Brighton 1961-64; Member: Lord Hunt's Committee on Immigration and Youth Service 1967-69, Board of Visitors, HM Prison Lewes 1978-95; JP, Mid Sussex 1978; Member: Home Office Inter-departmental Committee on Racial Attacks and Harassment 1987-92, Sussex Police Authority 1991-94, Ethnic Minority Advisory Committee of Judicial Studies Board 1992-96, Police Complaints Authority 1994-98; DL, West Sussex 1999-2014; Member: Lord Carlisle's Committee on Parole Systems Review 1999-, Home Secretary's Race Forum 1999-, Prime Minister's Advisory Committee on Business Appointments 2009-.

Political interests: Home affairs; East Africa, South East Asia, India.

Other: Member, Executive Committee: Inter-Parliamentary Union, British Group, Commonwealth Parliamentary Association; Patron, vice-patron and trustee numerous organisations, particularly those concerned with ethnic minorities; Council member: Save the Children Fund 1986-99, Howard League of Penal Reform 1992-2002; Editorial Board, *Howard Journal of Criminology* 1993-2012; President, National Association of Care and Resettlement of Offenders 1998-; Governor, Commonwealth Institute 1998-2005; Vice-chair, Policy Research Institute on Ageing and Ethnicity 1998-2013; Member, Governing Body, Commonwealth Institute 1999-; Vice-president, Mental Health Foundation 2002-; Trustee, Police Foundation 2010-; Melvin Jones Fellowship, Lions Club; Hon. Doctor of Laws: Hertfordshire University 2009, York University 2010, East London University 2010; Asian of the Year 2000; Pravasi Bharatiya Samman Award (Government of India) 2003; Pride of India Award 2004, 2005; OBE 1994; PC 2010.

Publications: Various articles on criminal justice matters.

Recreations: Photography, travel, gardening, cooking exotic dishes.

Rt Hon The Lord Dholakia OBE DL, House of Lords, London SW1A 0PW
Tel: 020 7219 5203 *Email:* dholakian@parliament.uk

CONSERVATIVE

DIXON-SMITH, LORD

DIXON-SMITH (Life Baron), Robert William Dixon-Smith; cr. 1993. Born 30 September 1934; Son of late Dixon and Alice Smith; Married Georgina Cook 1960 (1 son 1 daughter).

Education: Oundle School, Northamptonshire; Writtle Agricultural College, Essex.

Non-political career: Farmer. Second Lieutenant, King's Dragoon Guards (National Service) 1956-57.

Political career: *House of Lords:* Raised to the peerage as Baron Dixon-Smith, of Bocking in the County of Essex 1993. Opposition Spokesperson for: Environment, Transport and the Regions (Local Government) December 1998-2001, Home Affairs 2001-02, Environment 2003-07, Communities and Local Government 2007-09. Member: Science and Technology 1994-97, 2012-15, European Communities 1994-97, Communications 2010-11. *Other:* Essex County Council: Councillor 1965-93, Chair 1986-89; DL, Essex 1986; Chair, Association of County Councils 1992-93.

Political interests: Agriculture, environment, transport.

Other: Writtle Agricultural College: Governor 1967-94, Chair 1973-85, Fellow; Anglia Polytechnic University (formerly Anglia Polytechnic): Governor 1973-2000, Chair of Governors 1993-94; Fellow, Industry and Parliament Trust 1998; Liveryman, Farmers' Company 1990; Honorary Doctorate, Anglia Polytechnic University.

Recreations: Country sports, golf.

The Lord Dixon-Smith DL, House of Lords, London SW1A 0PW
Tel: 020 7219 5351
Houchins, Coggeshall, Colchester CO6 1RT *Tel:* 01376 561448

CONSERVATIVE

DOBBS, LORD

DOBBS (Life Baron), Michael John Dobbs; cr 2010. Born 14 November 1948; Son of Eric and Eileen Dobbs.

Education: Hertford Grammar School; Christ Church, Oxford (BA); Fletcher School of Law and Diplomacy (MA, MALD, PhD).

Non-political career: Government special adviser 1981-87; Deputy chairman, Saatchi & Saatchi 1983-86, 1988-91; Presenter, *Despatch Box*, BBC 1999-2001.

Political career: *House of Lords:* Raised to the peerage as Baron Dobbs, of Wylye in the County of Wiltshire 2010. Member: Joint Committee on Privacy and Injunctions 2011-12, Communications 2015, Democracy and Digital Technologies 2019. *Other:* Conservative Party: Chief of Staff 1986-87, Joint deputy chairman 1994-95.

Political interests: Constitution, foreign affairs, arts; China, Middle East, USA.

Other: Royal Automobile Club.

Publications: House of Cards (1989); Wall Games (1990); Last Man to Die (1991); To Play the King (1992); The Touch of Innocents (1994); The Final Cut (1995); Goodfellowe MP (1996); The Buddha of Brewer Street (1998); Whispers of Betrayal (2000); Winston's War (2002); Never Surrender (2003); Churchill's Hour (2004); Churchill's Triumph (2005); First Lady (2006); The Lord's Day (2007); The Edge of Madness (2008); The Reluctant Hero (2009); Old Enemies (2010); A Sentimental Traitor (2012); A Ghost at the Door (2013).

The Lord Dobbs, House of Lords, London SW1A 0PW
Tel: 020 7219 5353 *Email:* dobbsm@parliament.uk Website: www.michaeldobbs.com
Twitter: @dobbs_michael

DEMOCRATIC UNIONIST PARTY

DODDS OF DUNCAIRN, LORD

DODDS OF DUNCAIRN (Life Baron), Nigel Alexander Dodds; cr 2020. Born 20 August 1958; Son of late Joseph Dodds, civil servant, and Doreen Dodds, née McMahon; Married Diane Harris 1985, MLA for Belfast West 2003-07 as Diane Dodds, MEP for Northern Ireland 2009-20, now MLA for Upper Bann and Minister for the Economy (2 sons 1 daughter).

Education: Portora Royal School, Enniskillen; St John's College, Cambridge (BA law 1980); Queen's University, Belfast Institute of Professional Legal Studies (Cert PLS 1981); French.

Non-political career: Barrister 1981-83; European Parliament Secretariat (non-attached members) 1984-96; Member of Senate, Queen's University, Belfast 1985-93.

Political career: *House of Commons:* Contested East Antrim 1992 general election. MP for Belfast North 2001-10, for Belfast North (revised boundary) 2010-19. Contested Belfast North 2019 general election; DUP Chief Whip 2001-08; DUP Spokesperson for: Treasury 2005-07, Work and Pensions 2005-07, Business of the House 2005-10, Justice 2007-10, Business, Enterprise and Regulatory Reform 2007-10; DUP Parliamentary Group Leader 2010-19; Spokesperson for: Reform and Constitutional Agenda/Constitutional Issues 2010-19, Foreign Affairs 2010-19, Culture, Olympics, Media and Sport 2012-15, Exiting the European Union 2017-19. Member: Members' Allowances 2009-10, Joint Committee on Statutory Instruments and Commons Committee on Statutory Instruments 2009-10. *House of Lords:* Raised to the peerage as Baron Dodds of Duncairn, of Duncairn in the City of Belfast 2020. *Other:* Member Northern Ireland Forum for Political Dialogue 1996-98; MLA for Belfast North 1998-2010: Minister of: Social Development 1999-2000, 2001-02, Enterprise, Trade and Investment 2007-08, Finance and Personnel 2008-09. DUP: Secretary 1992-2008, Deputy Leader 2008-. Belfast City Council: Councillor 1985-2010, Lord Mayor of Belfast 1988-89, 1991-92, Vice-President, Association of Local Authorities of Northern Ireland 1989-90.

Political interests: Foreign affairs, constitution, senior citizens; The Commonwealth, USA.

Other: Member, UK Delegation to NATO Parliamentary Assembly 2014-19; Board member, Vote Leave 2016; OBE 1997; PC 2010.

Rt Hon the Lord Dodds of Duncairn OBE, House of Lords, London SW1A 0PW
Tel: 020 7219 3000 *Email:* doddsn@parliament.uk *Twitter:* @NigelDoddsDUP

LABOUR

DONAGHY, BARONESS

Chair, EU Services Sub-committee

DONAGHY (Life Baroness), Rita Margaret Donaghy; cr 2010. Born 9 October 1944; Married James Donaghy 1968 (died 1986); married Ted Easen-Thomas 2000.

Education: Leamington College for Girls; Durham University (BA English language and literature 1967).

Non-political career: Technical assistant, National Union of Teachers 1967-68; Institute of Education, London University: Assistant registrar 1968-84, Permanent secretary, Students' Union 1984-2000; Chair, Advisory, Conciliation and Arbitration Service 2000-07. Member: National Executive Committee, NALGO/Unison 1973-2000, General council, Trades Union Congress 1987-2000; President: NALGO 1989-90, Trades Union Congress 2000.

Political career: *House of Lords:* Raised to the peerage as Baroness Donaghy, of Peckham in the London Borough of Southwark 2010. Member, Personal Service Companies 2013-14; Chair, Information 2014-16; EU Internal Market Sub-committee: Member 2015-19, Chair 2019-20; Member: SLSC Sub-committee B 2018-19, Conduct 2019-, European Union 2019-; Chair, EU Services Sub-committee 2020-. *Other:* Member, Low Pay Commission 1997-2000; Committee on Standards in Public Life: Member 2001-07, Interim chair 2007; Chair, Department of Work and Pensions Inquiry into Fatal Construction Accidents 2009.

Other: Non-executive director, King's College Hospital NHS Trust 2005-; Fellow, Chartered Institute of Personnel and Development 2002; OBE 1998; CBE 2005.

The Baroness Donaghy CBE, House of Lords, London SW1A 0PW
Tel: 020 7219 5353 *Email:* donaghyr@parliament.uk

LABOUR

DONOUGHUE, LORD

DONOUGHUE (Life Baron), Bernard Donoughue; cr. 1985. Born 8 September 1934; Son of late Thomas Donoughue; Married Carol Goodman 1959 (divorced 1989) (2 sons 2 daughters); married The Hon. Sarah, Lady Berry 2009.

Education: Campbell Secondary Modern School, Northampton; Northampton Grammar School; Lincoln College, Oxford (BA history 1957); Harvard University, USA (1958-59); Nuffield College, Oxford (DPhil 1963).

Non-political career: Editorial staff, *The Economist* 1959-60; Senior research officer, Political and Economic Planning Institute 1960-63; Senior lecturer, London School of Economics 1963-74; Senior policy adviser to Prime Ministers: Harold Wilson 1974-76, James Callaghan 1976-79; Development director, Economist Intelligence Unit 1979-81; Assistant editor, *The Times* 1981-82; Head of research and investment policy, Grieveson Grant and Co. 1982-86; Head of international research and director, Kleinwort Grieveson Securities Ltd 1986-88; Executive vice-chair, LBI 1988-91; Director, Towcester Racecourse Ltd 1992-97; Visiting Professor of Government, LSE 2000-01. Member, GMBW.

Political career: *House of Lords:* Raised to the peerage as Baron Donoughue, of Ashton in the County of Northamptonshire 1985. Opposition Spokesperson for: Energy 1991-92, Treasury Affairs 1991-92, National Heritage 1992-97; Parliamentary Secretary, Ministry of Agriculture, Fisheries and Food (Minister for Farming and the Food Industry) 1997-99. *Other:* Member: Sports Council 1965-71, LSE Court of Governors 1968-97.

Political interests: Arts, finance, sport; France, Ireland, Italy.

Other: Member, British-Irish Parliamentary Assembly 2020-; Member, Commission of Enquiry into Association Football 1966-68; London Symphony Orchestra: Chair Executive 1979-91, Patron 1989-95, Associate 2000-; Member: London Arts Board 1992-97, Dorneywood Trust 1998-2015, Victoria County History of Northamptonshire; Consultant member, Horse Industry Confederation 1999-2003; British Horseracing Board: Member: Committee on VAT 2000-03, Commission of Enquiry into Stable and Stud Staff 2003-04; Vice-President, Comprehensive Schools Association 2000-08; Chair: Starting Price Regulatory Board 2003-, Future Funding of Racing Group 2005-, Review of Regulation of Greyhound Racing 2007-08; Global Warming Policy Foundation 2018-19; World Horse Welfare, Trustee Global Warming Policy Foundation 2010-; Hon. Fellow, Lincoln College, Oxford; Hon. LLD, Leicester; Hon. Fellow: LSE, Northampton University. Beefsteak, Pratt's, Farmers', 1795 Club.

Publications: Books on history and politics including: Trade Unions in a Changing Society (1963); British Politics and the American Revolution (1964); Herbert Morrison (1973); Prime Minister (1987); The Heat of the Kitchen (2003); Downing Street Diaries, Vol 1, Harold Wilson (2005); Downing Street Diaries, Vol 2, James Callaghan (2008); Westminster Diaries 1995-98 (2010).

Recreations: Music, theatre, sport.

The Lord Donoughue, House of Lords, London SW1A 0PW
Tel: 020 7219 5353

LIBERAL DEMOCRAT

DOOCEY, BARONESS

DOOCEY (Life Baroness), Elizabeth Dee Doocey; cr 2010. Born 2 May 1948; Daughter of Joseph and Sheila O'Keefe; Married James Doocey (1 son).

Non-political career: Liberal Democrat Party: Finance director, Financial adviser; Group managing director, international fashion company; Management consultant.

Political career: *House of Lords:* Raised to the peerage as Baroness Doocey, of Hampton in the London Borough of Richmond upon Thames 2010. Coalition representative, Criminal Justice Board, Home Office; Liberal Democrat Principal Spokesperson for Culture, Media, Sport and Tourism 2015; Member, House of Lords Commission 2016-19; Liberal Democrat Spokesperson without Portfolio 2017-19. Member: Refreshment 2012-15, Joint Committee on the Draft Enhanced Terrorism Prevention and Investigation Measures Bill 2012-13, Joint Committee on the Draft Modern Slavery Bill 2014, Leader's Group on Governance 2015; Chair, Finance 2016-. *Other:* Election Agent to Dr Vincent Cable, Twickenham 1992-2015. Richmond-upon-Thames Borough Council: Councillor 1986-94, Chair, Housing Committee; London Assembly: Member 2004-12, Chair, Economy, Culture and Sport Committee 2004-10,

2011-12, Chair 2010-11, Deputy Chair 2011-12; Metropolitan Police Authority: Member 2005-12, Chair, Finances and Resources Committee 2011-12; Member, Home Office Olympic Security Board 2008-12.

Political interests: Police, economic development, housing, people with disabilities, ending child trafficking, culture, sport, tourism, Olympic legacy; Ireland, USA.

Other: Member, British-Irish Parliamentary Assembly; OBE.

The Baroness Doocey OBE, House of Lords, London SW1A 0PW
Tel: 020 7219 0926 *Email:* dooceyd@parliament.uk

LABOUR

DRAKE, BARONESS

DRAKE (Life Baroness), Jean Lesley Patricia Drake; cr 2010. Born 16 January 1948.

Non-political career: Research officer, NUPE; Assistant general secretary, Civil and Public Services Association 1978-85; Deputy general secretary, National Communications Union 1985-95; Deputy general secretary (telecommunications and financial services), Communication Workers' Union 1996-2008. Trades Union Congress: Member, general council and executive committee 1986-2008, President 2004-05.

Political career: *House of Lords:* Raised to the peerage as Baroness Drake, of Shene in the County of Surrey 2010. Member: Joint Committee on the Draft Financial Services Bill 2011-12, Small-and Medium-Sized Enterprises 2012-13, Delegated Powers and Regulatory Reform 2014-17, Economic Affairs Finance Bill Sub-committee 2014, 2015-16, 2016-17, 2018-19, Trade Union and Party Funding 2016, Constitution 2017-. Vice-chair, PLP Departmental Group for Work and Pensions 2010-15. *Other:* Member, Employment Tribunal 1988-2001; Commissioner, Equal Opportunities Commission 2000-07; Member, Employment Appeals Tribunal 2001-; Board member, Sector Skills Development Agency 2001-08; Member, Pensions Commission 2002-06; Non-executive board member, Pension Protection Fund 2004-; Supervisory board member, Union Moderation Fund (BERR) 2005-; Commissioner, Equal and Human Rights Commission 2006-09; Chair, Railway Pensions Commission 2006-08; Personal Accounts Delivery Authority: Member 2007-08, Acting chair 2008-; Governor, Pensions Policy Institute; Non-executive director, Pensions Advisory Service.

Other: Trustee: Alliance and Leicester Group Pension Fund 1991-, O2 Pension Trustee Company 2003-; Non-executive director, Communication Workers' Friendly Society -2010; OBE; CBE.

The Baroness Drake CBE, House of Lords, London SW1A 0PW
Tel: 020 7219 5353

LABOUR

DRAYSON, LORD

DRAYSON (Life Baron), Paul Rudd Drayson; cr. 2004. Born 5 March 1960; Son of Michael Rudd and Ruth Irene Drayson; Married Elspeth Jane Bellhouse 1994 (2 daughters 3 sons).

Education: St Dunstan's College, London; Aston University (BSc production engineering 1982; PhD robotics 1985).

Non-political career: Undergraduate engineer, BL Cars 1978-82; Development engineer, Trebor Group 1982-86; Managing director, Lambourn Food Co 1986-91; Founder and managing director, Genisys Development Ltd 1991-95; Chief executive, Powerject Pharmaceuticals plc 1993-2003; Chairman, BioIndustry Association 2001-02; Entrepreneur in Residence, Saïd Business School, Oxford University 2003-05; Co-founder, Drayson Racing Technologies 2007-; Chair and chief executive, Drayson Technologies Group 2015-.

Political career: *House of Lords:* Raised to the peerage as Baron Drayson, of Kensington in the Royal Borough of Kensington and Chelsea 2004. Ministry of Defence: Government Spokesperson 2005-07, Parliamentary Under-Secretary of State 2005-07, Minister of State (MoS) (Minister for Defence Equipment and Support) 2007; MoS (Business and Regulatory Reform), Department for Business, Enterprise and Regulatory Reform 2007; MoS (Science and Innovation) and Government Spokesperson, Department for Innovation, Universities and Skills/ Business, Innovation and Skills (attending Cabinet) 2008-10; MoS (Strategic Defence Acquisition Reform) and Government Spokesperson, Ministry of Defence 2009-10. Member:

Science and Technology Committee 2004-05, Information 2005-09, Science and Technology Sub-committee I (Scientific Aspects of Ageing) 2005.

Political interests: Science, business innovation, entrepreneurship; France.

Other: Trustee, Drayson Foundation; Oxford Children's Hospital (Chairman Campaign 2002-05); PC 2008. Salle d'Armes Club.

Recreations: Motor racing, sword fencing.

Rt Hon the Lord Drayson, House of Lords, London SW1A 0PW
Tel: 020 7219 4147 *Email:* draysonp@parliament.uk
Nether Lypiatt Manor, Nether Lypiatt, Nr Stroud GL6 7LS *Twitter:* @lorddrayson

CROSSBENCH

D'SOUZA, BARONESS

D'SOUZA (Life Baroness), Frances Gertrude Claire D'Souza; cr. 2004. Born 18 April 1944; Daughter of Robert Russell and Pauline Russell, née Parmet; Married Stanislaus D'Souza 1959 (divorced 1974) (2 daughters); married Martin Griffiths 1985 (divorced 1994); remarried Stanislaus D'Souza 2003 (died 2011).

Education: University College, London (BSc anthropology 1970); Lady Margaret Hall, Oxford (DPhil evolutionary models 1976).

Non-political career: Ford Foundation research fellow in comparative reproductive physiology, Nuffield Institute of Comparative Medicine 1973-77; Part-time lecturer, London School of Economics 1973-80; Senior lecturer, department of humanities, Oxford Brookes University 1977-80; Founder director and research director, International Relief and Development Institute 1977-85; Editor, 'Disasters' Journal 1977-84; Independent research consultant for UN, Save the Children Fund, Ford Foundation 1985-88; Research fellow, Overseas Development Administration 1988-89; Executive director, Article 19 anti-censorship organisation 1989-98; Redress Trust: Director 2003-04, Consultant 2004-06.

Political career: *House of Lords:* Raised to the peerage as Baroness D'Souza, of Wychwood in the County of Oxfordshire 2004. Convenor of the Crossbench Peers 2007-11; Lord Speaker 2011-16. Member, Procedure 2005-16; Co-opted Member, European Union Sub-committee F (Home Affairs) 2006-07; Member: Selection 2007-11, Liaison 2007-11, Administration and Works 2007-11, Privileges/Privileges and Conduct 2007-11, 2011-12; House: Member 2007-11, Chair 2011-16; Member: Joint Committee on Security 2010-11, Joint Committee on Consolidation & Bills.

Political interests: Human rights and development, House of Lords Reform; Afghanistan, Japan, India, Jordan, Nordic countries, Southern Africa (SADC countries), South Korea, Taiwan, West Balkans.

Other: Executive Committee, Commonwealth Parliamentary Association (UK Branch): President 2011-16, Member 2016-; Inter-Parliamentary Union, British Group: Hon President 2011-16, Executive Committee Member 2016-, Vice-chair 2020-; BIFG 2011-16; Co-founder, Marefat High School, Kabul, Afghanistan 2002-; President: Hansard Society 2011-16, Industry and Parliament Trust 2011-16, Parliament Choir 2011-16, PICTFOR 2011-16; Chair, David Nott Foundation 2016-; Hazara Charitable Trust, David Nott Foundation, NSPCC, Cancer Research, Macmillan Cancer, Marie Curie, Medecins sans Frontiers, LMH Oxford, St John's Hospice, El Shaddai Orphanage (Goa), Forward Assist, Guide Dogs, The Circle; Hon Doctorate, Hull University 2016; CMG 1999; PC 2009.

Recreations: Music (opera, string quartets, jazz and flamenco).

Rt Hon the Baroness D'Souza CMG, House of Lords, London SW1A 0PW
Tel: 020 7219 3670 *Email:* dsouzaf@parliament.uk

LABOUR

DUBS, LORD

DUBS (Life Baron), Alfred Dubs; cr. 1994. Born 5 December 1932; Married (1 son 1 daughter).

Education: London School of Economics (BSc Econ).

Non-political career: Former local government officer; Chief executive, Refugee Council 1988-95; Deputy chair, ITC 2000; Chair: Broadcasting Standards Commission 2001-03, Appeals Panel, Association of Energy Suppliers 2004-. Member, TGWU.

Political career: *House of Commons:* Contested Cities of London and Westminster 1970 and Hertfordshire South February and October 1974 general elections. MP (Labour) for Battersea South 1979-83, for Battersea 1983-87. Contested Battersea 1987 and 1992 general elections; Opposition Spokesperson for Home Affairs 1983-87. *House of Lords:* Raised to the peerage as Baron Dubs, of Battersea in the London Borough of Wandsworth 1994. Opposition Whip 1995-97; Opposition Spokesperson for: The Environment (Health and Safety) 1996-97, Energy 1996-97; Parliamentary Under-Secretary of State, Northern Ireland Office (Minister for Environment and Agriculture) 1997-99; Chair, Labour Party in Lords 2000-05. Member, European Union 2003-06; Procedure: Member 2005-07, Alternate member 2007-10; Co-opted member, European Union Sub-committee F (Home Affairs) 2006-07; Member: Human Rights Joint Committee 2007-12, 2019-, Communications 2012-15, EU External Affairs Sub-Committee 2015-19. Vice-chair: PLP Departmental Committee for Culture, Media and Sport -2005, PLP Departmental Groups for: Justice 2010-15, Northern Ireland 2010-15, DPM/ Constitutional Affairs 2011-15. *Other:* Member, Co-operative Party. Councillor, Westminster City Council 1971-78; Chair, Westminster Community Relations Council 1972-77; Member, Kensington, Chelsea and Westminster Area Health Authority 1975-78; Broadcasting Standards Council: Member 1988-94, Deputy Chairman 1994-97; Non-executive director, Pathfinder NHS Trust 1995-97.

Political interests: Civil liberties, penal reform, race relations, immigration, health service, Ireland, human rights.

Other: Member: Executive Committee, British Group, Inter-Parliamentary Union, UK Delegation, Organisation for Security and Co-operation in Europe Parliamentary Assembly, British-Irish Parliamentary Assembly; Trustee, Action Aid 1989-97; Chair, Liberty 1990-92; Trustee, Immigration Advisory Service 1992-97; Chair, Fabian Society 1993-94; Fellow, Industry and Parliament Trust 2003; Trustee, Open University 2004-09; Patron, Naz Project London.

Publications: Lobbying: An Insider's Guide to the Parliamentary Process (1989).

Recreations: Walking in the Lake District.

The Lord Dubs, House of Lords, London SW1A 0PW
Tel: 020 7219 3590 *Fax:* 020 7219 3981 *Email:* dubsa@parliament.uk *Twitter:* @AlfDubs

CONSERVATIVE

DUNCAN OF SPRINGBANK, LORD

DUNCAN OF SPRINGBANK (Life Baron), Ian James Duncan; cr 2017. Born 13 February 1973; Son of Robert Duncan and Audrey Duncan, née Doig; Married Benjamin Neal Brust 2012.

Education: Alyth High School; St Andrews University (BSc geology 1994); Bristol University (PhD palaeontology 1997); French.

Non-political career: Analyst, BP 1998-99; Deputy Chief Executive/Secretary, Scottish Fishermen's Federation 1999-2003; Director, Policy and Communications, Scottish Refugee Council 2004-05; Head, Scottish Parliament Office, Brussels 2005-11; Clerk, Scottish Parliament 2011-13; EU Adviser, European Committee, Scottish Parliament 2011-13.

Political career: *House of Commons:* Contested (Con) Perth and North Perthshire 2017 general election. *House of Lords:* Raised to the peerage as Baron Duncan of Springbank, of Springbank in the County of Perth 2017. Parliamentary Under-Secretary of State and Government Spokesperson: Scotland Office 2017-19, Wales Office 2017, Northern Ireland Office 2017-20; Parliamentary Under-Secretary of State (Minister for Climate Change) and Government Spokesperson, Department for Business, Energy and Industrial Strategy 2019-20; Deputy Chairman of Committees 2020-. Member, COVID-19 2020-. *Other:* Contested Aberdeen constituency South 2003 Scottish Parliament election. MEP for Scotland 2014-17; Chief Whip,

UK Conservative Delegation, European Parliament 2014-17; Energy and Climate Change Spokesperson, UK Conservative Delegation, European Parliament 2014-17; Fisheries Spokesperson, UK Conservative Delegation, European Parliament 2014-17; Vice-President, South Asia Delegation, European Parliament 2014-17. Member of Court, St Andrews University 2021-.

Political interests: Energy and climate Change policy, fisheries management, constitutional affairs.

Other: Secretary-general, Foundation for European Reform 2014-17; English Speaking Union (Scotland): Chair 2014-, Honorary President 2017-; Board member, Schwarzenegger Institute, University of Southern California 2016-; Chair: National Forest Company 2020-, Confederation of Forest Industries (Confor) 2020-; Member, International Advisory Board, Terrestrial Energy 2020-; Honorary President, Association for Decentralised Energy 2020-; Board member, Westminster Foundation for Democracy 2020-; Consulting partner, Charlotte Street Partners 2021-; Fellow, Geological Society of London. The New Club, Edinburgh.

Recreations: Oil painting, hill walking, carpentry.

The Lord Duncan of Springbank, House of Lords, London SW1A 0PW
Tel: 020 7219 3000 *Email:* duncani@parliament.uk
1 Melville Crescent, Edinburgh EH3 7HW *Tel:* 020 7270 6806 *Twitter:* @IanDuncanHMG

CONSERVATIVE

DUNDEE, EARL OF

DUNDEE (12th Earl of, S), Alexander Henry Scrymgeour; cr. 1660; Viscount Dudhope (S) 1641; Lord Scrymgeour (S) 1641; Lord Inverkeithing (S) 1660; Baron Glassary (UK) 1954. Born 5 June 1949; Son of 11th Earl, PC, DL; Married Siobhan Mary Llewellyn 1979 (died 2019) (1 son 3 daughters).

Education: Eton College; St Andrews University.

Political career: *House of Commons:* Contested (Conservative) Hamilton 1978 by-election. *House of Lords:* First entered House of Lords 1983; Government Whip 1986-89; Government Spokesperson for: Education 1986-88, Scottish Affairs 1986-89, Home Affairs and for Energy 1987-89; Elected hereditary peer 1999-. Member: Joint Committee on Consolidation, Etc, Bills 2000-05, 2006-15, EU Sub-committee G (Social Policy and Consumer Affairs) 2003-07; EU Sub-committee D (Environment and Agriculture): Member 2007-08, Co-opted member 2008-10; Member: EU Sub-committee D (Agriculture, Fisheries and Environment) 2010-12, Public Service and Demographic Change 2012-13. *Other:* DL, Fife.

Other: Member: UK delegation, Organisation for Security and Co-operation in Europe 1992-97, Council of Europe parliament 1992-99, Western European parliament 1992-99, UK delegation, Parliamentary Assembly of the Council of Europe 2015-; Fellow, Industry and Parliament Trust 2002; Hereditary Banner Bearer for Scotland. White's, New (Edinburgh) Club.

The Earl of Dundee, House of Lords, London SW1A 0PW
Tel: 020 7219 6781 *Email:* dundeea@parliament.uk

CONSERVATIVE

DUNLOP, LORD

DUNLOP (Life Baron), Andrew James Dunlop; cr 2015. Born 21 June 1959; Son of the late Shirley and the late Robert Dunlop; Married to Lucia (3 daughters).

Education: Glasgow Academy; Trinity College, Glenalmond; Edinburgh University (MA politics and modern history 1981); King's College, London (Postgraduate Diploma European competition law); French.

Non-political career: Midland Bank International 1981-82; Head of Policy and Research, Scottish Conservative and Unionist Party 1982-84; Conservative Research Department 1984-86; Special Adviser: to Defence Secretary, Ministry of Defence 1986-88, Prime Minister's Policy Unit 1988-90; Founder and Managing Director, Politics International Ltd 1991-2008; Interel Consulting UK: Managing Director 2008-10, Executive Chairman 2010-11; Member, Management Board, Interel Group, Brussels 2008-11; Special Adviser to the Prime Minister 2012-15; Government Communications Service Board 2016-17; Senior Deployable

Adviser, National School of Government International, UK Stabilisation Unit 2017-; Prime Minister's Independent Reviewer of UK Government Union Capability.

Political career: *House of Lords:* Raised to the peerage as Baron Dunlop, of Helensburgh in the County of Dunbarton 2015. Parliamentary Under-Secretary of State and Government Spokesperson, Scotland Office 2015-17; Government Spokesperson for Northern Ireland 2015-17; Parliamentary Under-Secretary of State, Northern Ireland Office 2016-17. Member, Constitution 2017-. *Other:* Chair, Scottish Future Growth Council. Councillor, Horsham District Council 2011-13.

Political interests: Scotland, Northern Ireland, devolution, constitutional issues, economy, business, sport and culture; Central Asia, China, Russia, USA.

Other: Chair, UK Government, Scottish Business Taskforce; Non-executive Director, Scottish Council for Development and Industry 2017-; Board Director, Scottish Swimming; Advisory Board Member, Scottish Policy Foundation; Advisory Council Member, Ionad Hiort 2017; Chair, City of Portsmouth Athletics Club; Glasgow Children's Hospital Charity, The Archie Foundation, The Archie Tayside Appeal, Maggie's Centres; Glasgow Incorporation of Bakers. Reform Club, London; Chair, Atlantis Swimming Club, Horsham 2007-12; Member, Management Committee: Sussex Amateur Swimming Association 2009-11, South East Region Amateur Swimming Association 2011-12.

Recreations: Reading, tennis, skiing, swimming, sailing, horse-riding, gardening, watching football, walking.

The Lord Dunlop, House of Lords, London SW1A 0PW
Tel: 020 7219 0645 *Email:* dunlopa@parliament.uk *Twitter:* @ScotlandDunlop

NON-AFFILIATED

DURHAM, LORD BISHOP OF

DURHAM (76th Bishop of), Paul Roger Butler. Born 18 September 1955; Son of Denys and Jean Butler; Married Rosemary Johnson 1982 (2 sons 2 daughters).

Education: Kingston Grammar School; Nottingham University (BA English and history 1977); Wycliffe Hall, Oxford (BA theology 1982).

Non-political career: Ordained deacon 1983; Curate, Holy Trinity, Wandsworth 1983-87; Priest 1984; Scripture Union: Inner London Evangelist 1987-92, Deputy head of missions 1992-94; St Paul, East Ham 1988-94; Priest-in-charge: St Mary with St Stephen, and St Luke, Walthamstow 1994-97, St Gabriel, Walthamstow 1997; Team rector, Parish of Walthamstow 1997-2004; Area dean, Waltham Forest 2000-04; Honorary Canon, St Paul's Cathedral, Rwanda 2001-; Bishop Suffragan of Southampton 2004-09; Bishop of: Southwell and Nottingham 2009-14, Durham 2014-.

Political career: *House of Lords:* Entered House of Lords 2014.

Political interests: Children and family, welfare, migration – refugees and asylum seekers, overseas aid; Burundi, Iran, Israel, Lesotho, Palestine, Russia, Rwanda, South Africa, Uganda.

Other: Chair, Friends of Byumba Trust 2001-; Advocate for Children on behalf of Bishops 2004-; Chair, Church Mission Society 2007-10; President, Scripture Union 2011-17; Trustee: Safe Families for Children 2017-, Child Theology Movement 2017-; Director, Reset Communities and Refugees 2017-; Christian Aid, Tearfund, Church Mission Society, Safe Families for Children, National Trust, RHS, Scripture Union; Doctor of Divinity, Nottingham University 2016. Farmers Club.

Publications: Reaching Children (1992); Reaching Families (1994); God's Friends (1994); Following Jesus (1994); Want to be in God's Family? (1998); Growing Up in God's Family (1998); Temptation and Testing (2007); Contributor: Through the Eyes of a Child (2009), Offering the Best Children's Ministry (2011); Co-author, Living Your Confirmation (2012); Contributor: On Being a Curate (2014), Clergy in a Complex Age (2016); Co-author with Sandra Millar, We Welcome You (2016).

Rt Rev the Lord Bishop of Durham, House of Lords, London SW1A 0PW
Tel: 020 7219 5353
Auckland Castle, Bishop Auckland DL14 7NR *Tel:* 01388 602576
Email: bishop.of.durham@durham.anglican.org Website: www.durham.anglican.org
Twitter: @BishopPaulB

CROSSBENCH

DYKES, LORD

DYKES (Life Baron), Hugh John Maxwell Dykes; cr. 2004. Born 17 May 1939; Son of Richard and Doreen Dykes; Married Susan Smith 1965 (divorced 2000) (2 sons and 1 son deceased); partner Sarah.

Education: Weston-Super-Mare Grammar School; College de Normandie, France; Pembroke College, Cambridge (MA economics 1963); Speaks many European languages.

Non-political career: Assistant to Edward Heath MP as Leader of the Conservative Party 1965-66; Partner, Simon and Coates stockbrokers 1968-78; Founder shareholder, Dewe Rogerson Ltd 1972-98; Associate member, Quilter Goodison stockbrokers 1978-87; Group director, Far East Division of Dixons plc 1985-90; EU special adviser to Rogers and Wells 1990-97; Member, Securities Institute (MSI) 1993-2003.

Political career: *House of Commons:* Contested Tottenham 1966 and Harrow East 1997 general elections. MP (Conservative) for Harrow East 1970-97; PPS to: Lord Lambton at Ministry of Defence 1971-72, Kenneth Baker as Civil Service Minister in Cabinet Office 1972-74; Chief Sponsor, Heavy Commercial Vehicles Act (Dykes Act) 1973. *House of Lords:* Raised to the peerage as Baron Dykes, of Harrow Weald in the London Borough of Harrow 2004. Liberal Democrat Spokesperson for: Foreign and Commonwealth Affairs (Europe) 2005-10, Environment, Food and Rural Affairs (CAP Reform) 2006-10. Member, Statutory Instruments Joint Committee 2005-09; Co-opted member, EU Sub-committee C (Foreign Affairs, Defence and Development Policy) 2005-06; EU Sub-committee B (Internal Market): Co-opted member 2006-07, Member 2007-10; Member: European Union 2007-12, EU Sub-committee E: (Justice and Institutions) 2010-12, (Justice, Institutions and Consumer Protection) 2012-15, Hybrid Instruments 2017-, Electoral Registration and Administration Act 2013 2019-. *Other:* European Parliament: MEP (Conservative) 1974-76; Contested (Lib Dem) London region 1999 European Parliament election. Joined Liberal Democrat Party after 1997 election; joined Crossbenches July 2015. Governor, North London Collegiate School 1981-97.

Political interests: EU, economics, taxation, transport; China, Europe, South Africa, USA.

Other: Chair, UK-European Movement 1990-96; Official International EU Observer to first South African Elections 1994; Chair, Mid-Atlantic Club 2002-05; European-Atlantic Group: Chair 2005-08, President 2008-10; Vice-president, British German Association; President, League of Friends, Royal National Orthopaedic Hospital 1986-97; Freedom, City of London 1979; Visiting Fellow, European Institution, London School of Economics 1998-2003; Order of Merit (Germany) 1991; Medaille pour l'Europe (Luxembourg) 1993; Légion d'Honneur (France) 2004. Garrick, Beefsteak Club; Harrow Rugby Club.

Publications: Many articles and pamphlets on foreign affairs and Europe; Co-author, Britain on the Edge (2012).

Recreations: Music, theatre, swimming, travel, languages.

The Lord Dykes, House of Lords, London SW1A 0PW
Tel: 020 7219 2729 *Email:* dykesh@parliament.uk

CROSSBENCH

EAMES, LORD

EAMES (Life Baron), Robert (Robin) Henry Alexander Eames; cr. 1995. Born 27 April 1937; Son of Revd. William and Mary Eames; Married Ann Christine Daly OBE 1966 (2 sons).

Education: Belfast Royal Academy; Methodist College, Belfast; Queen's University, Belfast (LLB 1957, PhD ecclesiastical and constitutional law 1963, LLD 1990); Trinity College, Dublin (divinity test 1963).

Non-political career: Research scholar and tutor, Faculty of Laws, Queen's University, Belfast 1960-63; Curate assistant, Bangor Parish Church 1963-66; Rector of St Dorothea's, Belfast 1966-74; Examining Chaplain to Bishop of Down 1973; Rector St Mark's, Dundela 1974-75; Bishop of Derry and Raphoe 1975-80; Bishop of Down and Dromore 1980-86; Archbishop of Armagh and Primate of All Ireland and Metropolitan 1986-2006; Hon. Bencher, Lincoln's Inn 1998; Senior Primate of Anglican Communion 2000-06.

Political career: *House of Lords:* Raised to the peerage as Baron Eames, of Armagh in the County of Armagh 1995. Member: Works of Art 2006-07, Privileges/Privileges and Conduct 2007-19, Consolidation of Private/Public Bills 2007-; Co-opted member, EU Sub-committee G

(Social Policy and Consumer Affairs) 2007-10; Chair, Leader's Group on the Code of Conduct 2009; Member: Joint Committee on Consolidation, Etc, Bills 2009-, EU Sub-committee G (Social Policies and Consumer Protection) 2010-12, Merits of Statutory Instruments/Secondary Legislation Scrutiny 2010-15, Procedure/Procedure and Privileges 2019-. *Other:* Select Preacher, Oxford University 1987; Chair: Commission on Communion and Women in the Episcopate (Eames Commission) 1988-, Commission on Inter-Anglican Relations (Virginia Report) 1988-; Select Preacher, Cambridge University 1990; Chair, Inter-Anglican Theological and Doctrinal Commission 1991; Select Preacher, Edinburgh University 1993; Chair, Inter-Anglican Finance Committee 1997-2005; Select Preacher, St Andrews University 2001-; Chair, Lambeth Commission Communion (Windsor Report) 2003-04; Co-chair: Consultative Commission on Northern Ireland's Past 2007-08, Consultative Group on Legacy of Northern Ireland Conflict 2008-09 (Co-chairman, Report 2009); Member: Independent Police Commission in England and Wales 2012-, Independent Commission on Referendums 2018-19.

Political interests: Northern Ireland, social issues, community care, broadcasting; Middle and Far East, North Korea, South Korea, USA.

Other: Member, Anglican International Consultative Council; Member, Institute of Advanced Motorists 1965-; Life Member, Royal Yachting Association 1973-; Governor, Church Army 1985-88; Chair: Board of Governors, Royal School, Armagh 1986-2006, Armagh Observatory and Planetarium 1986-2006; Council member, St George's House, Windsor 2008-; Christian Aid, Save the Children, RNLI; Member, Livery Company of Carmen; Freedom: City of London 1989, City of Armagh 2007; Eleven honorary doctorates from British, Irish and US universities, including Hon LLD Queen's University, Belfast 1990; Archbishop of Canterbury's award for Outstanding Service to the International Anglican Communion 2006; OM 2007. Kildare Street and University (Dublin), Athenæum Club; Member, Strangford Lough Yacht Club, Co Down; Carrickfergus Marina, Co Antrim.

Publications: A Form of Worship for Teenagers (1965); The Quiet Revolution – Irish Disestablishment (1970); Through Suffering (1973); Thinking through Lent (1978); Through Lent (1984); Chains to be Broken (1992); Biography Nobody's Fool (McCreery, 2004); Contributor to: Irish Legal Quarterly, Criminal Law Review, New Divinity, Cambridge Law Review, Conflict, Freedom and Religion (2008); Unfinished Search (2017).

Recreations: Sailing, rugby union, reading, travel.

Rt Rev the Lord Eames OM, House of Lords, London SW1A 0PW
Tel: 020 7219 5353
Email: robin.eames@yahoo.co.uk

CONSERVATIVE

EATON, BARONESS

EATON (Life Baroness), (Ellen) Margaret Eaton; cr 2010. Born 1 June 1942; Daughter of John and Evelyn Midgley; Married John Eaton 1969 (1 son 1 daughter).

Education: Hanson Grammar School; Balls Park Teacher Training College; German.

Non-political career: Former teacher.

Political career: *House of Lords:* Raised to the peerage as Baroness Eaton, of Cottingley in the County of West Yorkshire 2010. Member: Merits of Statutory Instruments/Secondary Legislation Scrutiny 2011-13, Adoption Legislation 2012-13, Joint Committee on the Draft Care and Support Bill 2013, Refreshment 2015-16, Licencing Act 2003 2016-17, Citizenship and Civic Engagement 2017-18, Joint Committee on the Draft Health Service Safety Investigations Bill 2018, Electoral Registration and Administration Act 2013 2019-, Ecclesiastical Committee 2020-. *Other:* Conservative Party Local Government Committee. Bradford Metropolitan Borough Council: Councillor 1986-2016, Leader, Conservative Group 1995-2006, Council Leader 2000-06; Former chair: Bradford Local Strategic Partnership Board, Bradford Cultural Consortium, Bradford Safer Communities Partnership; Director: Bradford Centre Regeneration Company, Leeds Bradford International Airport; Member, Yorkshire and Humber Assembly; Local Government Association: Vice-chair, Conservative Group, Chair, Conservative Group, Chair 2008-11, Vice-President 2011-; DL, West Yorkshire 2008.

Political interests: Education, children's services; Eastern Europe, Germany.

Other: Member, EU Committee of the Regions 2003-06; Substitute member, UK delegation, Parliamentary Assembly of the Council of Europe 2012-17; FRSA; Hon Lay Canon, Bradford Cathedral; Member, Beckfoot Multi-Academy Trust, Bingley 2016-; Guardian Emeritus, Holy Shrine of our Lady of Walsingham; Near Neighbours, Angelus Foundation, Candlelighters; Fellow, Bradford College; Hon. degree, Bradford University; Lifetime Achievement Award, Variety Club; OBE; DBE 2010. United, Cecil Club.

The Baroness Eaton DBE, House of Lords, London SW1A 0PW
Tel: 020 7219 6380 *Email:* eatonm@parliament.uk

LABOUR

EATWELL, LORD

EATWELL (Life Baron), John Leonard Eatwell; cr. 1992. Born 2 February 1945; Son of late Harold Eatwell and Mary Eatwell; Married Hélène Seppain 1970 (divorced 2002) (2 sons 1 daughter); married Mrs Susan Digby 2006.

Education: Headlands Grammar School, Swindon; Queens' College, Cambridge (BA economics 1967, MA 1971); Harvard University (PhD economics 1975).

Non-political career: Teaching fellow, Graduate School of Arts and Sciences, Harvard University 1968-69; Research fellow, Queens' College, Cambridge 1969-70; Fellow, Trinity College, Cambridge 1970-96; Faculty of Economics and Politics, Cambridge University: Assistant lecturer 1975-77, Lecturer 1977-2002; Visiting professor of economics, New School for Social Research, New York 1982-96; Economic adviser to Neil Kinnock as Leader of the Labour Party 1985-92; Chair, Extemporary Dance Theatre 1990; Non-executive director: Anglia Television Group Ltd 1994-2001, Cambridge Econometrics Ltd 1996-2007; President, Queens' College, Cambridge 1997-2020; Director: Cambridge Endowment for Research in Finance, and Professor of Financial Policy, Cambridge University 2002-12, SAV Credit Ltd (now NewDay Ltd) 2007-16; Professor of Economics, University of Southern California 2012-. Member, Association of University Teachers.

Political career: *House of Lords:* Raised to the peerage as Baron Eatwell, of Stratton St Margaret in the County of Wiltshire 1992. Opposition Spokesperson for: Trade and Industry 1992-96, Treasury and Economic Affairs 1992-93; Principal Opposition Spokesperson for Treasury and Economic Affairs 1993-97; Opposition Spokesperson for Treasury 2010-14. Member: Economic Affairs 2008-10, Consumer Insurance (Disclosure and Representations) Bill 2011-12. *Other:* Director, Securities and Futures Authority 1997-2002; Chair: British Screen 1997-2000, British Library 2001-06; Commissioner, Jersey Financial Services Commission 2010-.

Political interests: Economics, trade and industry, arts.

Other: Institute for Public Policy Research: Trustee 1988-, Secretary 1988-97, Chair 1997-2001, 2016-; Governor, Contemporary Dance Trust 1991-95; Director, Arts Theatre Trust, Cambridge 1991-98; Chair, Crusaid, the national fundraiser for AIDS 1993-98; Director, Royal Opera House 1998-2006; Chair: Commercial Radio Companies Association 2000-04, British Library 2001-06; Director, Cambridge Endowment for Research in Finance 2002-12; Governor, Royal Ballet School 2003-06; Chair, Royal Opera House Pension Fund Trustees 2007-; Jersey Financial Services Commission: Commissioner 2010-, Chair 2014-. Harvard Club of New York City, Bohemian Club, San Francisco; House of Lords and House of Commons RUFC.

Publications: Co-author An Introduction to Modern Economics (1973); Whatever happened to Britain? (1982); Co-author Keynes's Economics and the Theory of Value and Distribution (1983); The New Palgrave: A Dictionary of Economics, 4 vols (1987); The New Palgrave Dictionary of Money and Finance, 3 vols (1992); Editor Global Unemployment: Loss of Jobs in the '90s (1996); Co-author Not Just Another Accession: The Political Economy of EU Enlargement to the East (1997); Understanding Globalisation: The Nation-State, Democracy and Economic Policies in the New Epoch (1998); Global Finance at Risk: The Case for International Regulation (2000); Hard Budgets and Soft States: Social Policy Choices in Central and Eastern Europe (2000); Co-author, The Fall and Rise of Keynesian Economics (2011); Articles in scientific journals and other collected works.

Recreations: Classical and contemporary dance, rugby union football.

The Lord Eatwell, House of Lords, London SW1A 0PW
Tel: 020 7219 6947

CONSERVATIVE

ECCLES, VISCOUNT

ECCLES (2nd Viscount, UK), John Dawson Eccles; cr. 1964; 2nd Baron Eccles (UK) 1962. Born 20 April 1931; Son of 1st Viscount and late Hon. Sybil Dawson, daughter of 1st Viscount Dawson of Penn; Married Diana Sturge 1955, now Baroness Eccles of Moulton (qv) (1 son 3 daughters).

Education: Winchester College; Magdalen College, Oxford (BA philosophy, politics and economics 1954).

Non-political career: Head Wrightson 1954; Director, Nuclear Power Group 1968-74; Head Wrightson & Co Ltd: Managing director 1968-77, Chair 1976-77; Director: Glynwed International plc 1972-96, Investors in Industry plc (3i) 1974-88, Davy International Ltd 1977-81; Commonwealth Development Corporation: Member 1982-85, General manager and subsequently chief executive 1985-94; Chair, Chamberlin & Hill plc 1982-2004; Member, Industrial Development Advisory Board 1989-93; Courtaulds Textiles plc: Director 1992-2000, Chair 1995-2000; Chair, Acker Deboeck corporate psychologists 1994-2004. National service 1st Battalion KRRC (60th Rifles) 2nd Lieutenant.

Political career: *House of Lords:* First entered House of Lords 1999; Elected hereditary peer 2005-. Member: Information 2005-07, Merits of Statutory Instruments 2005-09, Delegated Powers and Regulatory Reform 2007-10, Adoption Legislation 2012-13, EU Sub-committee E (Justice, Institutions and Consumer Protection) 2012-15, Joint Committee on Consolidation, &c, Bills 2015-. *Other:* Monopolies and Mergers Commission: Member 1976-85, Deputy chair 1981-85.

Political interests: Economy, education, Third World development, museums and the arts, secondary legislation, local government; Third World.

Other: Chair: Board of Trustees, Royal Botanical Gardens, Kew 1983-91, Hospital for Tropical Diseases Foundation 2000-, Bowes Museum Trust, Co Durham 2000-08; Council member, Eccles Centre for American Studies, British Library 2003-; Hon. DSc, Cranfield Institute of Technology 1989; CBE 1985. Brooks's Club.

Recreations: Arts, gardening, bridge.

The Viscount Eccles CBE, House of Lords, London SW1A 0PW
Tel: 020 7219 5353 *Email:* ecclesj@parliament.uk
Tel: 020 7222 4040

CONSERVATIVE

ECCLES OF MOULTON, BARONESS

ECCLES OF MOULTON (Life Baroness), Diana Catherine Eccles; cr. 1990. Born 4 October 1933; Daughter of late Raymond and Margaret Sturge; Married Hon John Eccles 1955, now 2nd Viscount Eccles (qv) (1 son 3 daughters).

Education: St James's School, West Malvern; Open University (BA 1978).

Non-political career: Voluntary work, Middlesbrough Community Council 1955-58; Partner in graphic design business 1963-77; Vice-chair, National Council for Voluntary Organisations 1981-87; Director: Tyne Tees Television 1986-94, J. Sainsbury plc 1986-95, Yorkshire Electricity Group plc 1990-97, National and Provincial Building Society 1991-96, Times Newspapers Holdings Ltd 1998-2016, Opera North 1998-2011, London Clinic 2003-08.

Political career: *House of Lords:* Raised to the peerage as Baroness Eccles of Moulton, of Moulton in the County of North Yorkshire 1990. Member: Animals in Scientific Procedures 2001-02, EU Sub-committee B (Internal Market) 2003-07, Pre-legislative Scrutiny on Mental Health Bill 2005, Communications 2007-10, Intergovernmental Organisations 2007-08, EU Sub-committee F (Home Affairs) 2010-12, Joint Committee on Statutory Instruments 2010-12, European Union 2012-15, EU Sub-committees: C (External Affairs) 2012-13, E (Justice, Institutions and Consumer Protection) 2013-15, EU Justice Sub-committee 2015-16, Liaison 2016-17. *Other:* Member, North Eastern Electricity Board 1974-85; Durham University Council: Lay Member 1981-, Vice-chair 1985-2004; Chair, Tyne Tees Television Programme Consultative Council 1982-84; Member: Advisory Council on Energy Conservation (Department of Energy) 1982-84, Widdicombe Inquiry into Local Government 1985-86, Home

Office Advisory Panel on Licences for Experimental Community Radio 1985-86, British Rail Eastern Board 1986-92, Teesside Urban Development Corporation 1987-98; Chair, Ealing District Health Authority 1988-93; Member, Unrelated Live Transplant Regulatory Authority 1990-99; Chair, Ealing, Hammersmith and Hounslow Health Authority 1993-2000; DL, North Yorkshire 1998-2008.

Other: Member, UK delegation, Parliamentary Assembly of the Council of Europe 2010-; Trustee: Charities Aid Foundation 1982-89, York Minster Trust Fund 1989-99, 2006-09; Member, British Heart Foundation 1989-98; Hon. DCL, Durham 1995.

The Viscountess Eccles, Lady Eccles of Moulton DL, House of Lords, London SW1A 0PW
Tel: 020 7219 5353 *Email:* ecclesd@parliament.uk

LABOUR

ELDER, LORD

ELDER (Life Baron), Thomas Murray Elder; cr. 1999. Born 9 May 1950.

Education: Kirkcaldy High School; Edinburgh University (MA economic history).

Non-political career: Bank of England 1972-80; Research assistant to Shadow Secretary of State for Trade and Industry 1980-84; Labour Party Scotland 1984-92, General Secretary 1988-92; Chief of Staff to John Smith MP as Leader of the Labour Party 1992-94; Special adviser, Scottish Office 1997-99.

Political career: *House of Commons:* Contested (Labour) Ross, Cromarty and Skye 1983 general election. *House of Lords:* Raised to the peerage as Baron Elder, of Kirkcaldy in Fife 1999. Member: Monetary Policy of the Bank of England/Economic Affairs 2000-05, Refreshment 2008-13, High Speed Rail (London-West Midlands) Bill 2016, Joint Committee on the Draft Health Service Safety Investigations Bill 2018, Member, COVID-19 2020-.

Recreations: Walking, reading, opera.

The Lord Elder, House of Lords, London SW1A 0PW
Tel: 020 7219 8512

NON-AFFILIATED

ELIS-THOMAS, LORD

ELIS-THOMAS (Life Baron), Dafydd Elis-Thomas; cr. 1992. Born 18 October 1946; Son of Rev William Ellis Thomas and Eirlys Thomas; Married Elen Williams 1970 (divorced) (3 sons); married Mair Parry Jones 1993.

Education: Ysgol Dyffryn Conwy; University College of Wales (PhD); Welsh.

Non-political career: Tutor in Welsh studies, Coleg Harlech 1971-74; Lecturer: University College of North Wales, Bangor, Aberystwyth, Cardiff, Open University; Broadcaster on BBC Wales, HTV, S4C, Radio Wales; Consultant to: S4C, Welsh Development Agency, Rural Initiative Programme, Assembly of European Regions, Government of Catalonia; Chairman, Screen Wales; Director and deputy chair, Cynefin Environmental; Director and chair, New Media Agency; Director: Oriel Mostyn, National Botanical Gardens, MFM Marcher.

Political career: *House of Commons:* Contested Conway 1970 general election. MP (Plaid Cymru) for Meirionnydd February 1974-83, for Meirionnydd Nant Conwy 1983-92. *House of Lords:* Raised to the peerage as Baron Elis-Thomas, of Nant Conwy in the County of Gwynedd 1992. Member: European Communities 1997-98, European Communities Sub-committee C (Environment, Public Health and Consumer Protection) 1997-98. *Other:* National Assembly for Wales: AM for Meirionnydd Nant Conwy constituency 1999-2007, for Dwyfor Meirionnydd constituency 3 May 2007-5 May 2020, MS for Dwyfor Meirionnydd constituency since 6 May 2020: Presiding Officer 1999-2011, Chair, Assembly Committee on Environment and Sustainability 2011-14, Plaid Cymru: Spokesperson for: Environment, Energy and Planning 2011-12, Rural Affairs, Fisheries and Food 2012-13, Transport 2013-14, Society 2013-14, Shadow Minister for Wales Bill, Government Liaison and Constitution 2016; Minister/Deputy Minister for Culture, Sport and Tourism 2017-. Plaid Cymru: President 1984-91, Contested leadership election 2012, Whip withdrawn 18-20 July 2012, Resigned from Party October 2016.

Political interests: Rural affairs, environment, constitutional affairs; Wales.

Other: President, Commonwealth Parliamentary Association (Wales Branch) 1999-2011; President: Hay-on-Wye Literature Festival, Ramblers Association in Wales -1999, Snowdonia National Park Society -1999, Abbeyfield -1999; Member: Welsh Arts Council -1999, Welsh Film Council -1999, Welsh Film Board -1999, Wales Committee of National Trust; BBC General Consultative Council -1999; Chair, Welsh Language Board 1993-96, 1996-99; Trustee: Big Issue Foundation -1999, Theatr Bara Caws -1999; Fellow, International Centre for Intercultural Studies, Institute of Education, London; Patron, Prince of Wales Trust – Bro; Chair, Future Landscapes Wales 2015-17; Surname changed from Thomas to Elis-Thomas by deed poll 1992; Chancellor, Bangor University 2001-17; Welsh Politician of the Year 2008, ITV Wales; PC 2004.

Recreations: Welsh literature and art, music, theatre, films, hill- and mountain-walking, jogging.

Rt Hon the Lord Elis-Thomas, House of Lords, London SW1A 0PW
Tel: 020 7219 8701 *Email:* elisthomasd@parliament.uk
7 Bank Place, Porthmadog LL49 9AA *Tel:* 01766 515028
Email: dafydd.elis-thomas@senedd.wales *Twitter:* @ElisThomasD

NON-AFFILIATED

ELY, LORD BISHOP OF

ELY (69th Bishop of), Stephen David Conway. Born 22 December 1957; Son of late David Conway and Dorothy Lambert.

Education: Archbishop Tenison's Grammar School, London; Keble College, Oxford (BA modern history 1980); Selwyn College, Cambridge (BA theology 1985).

Non-political career: Assistant master, Glenalmond College 1981-83; Ordained deacon 1986; Priest 1987; Curate: Heworth 1986-89, Bishopwearmouth 1989-90, St Margaret, Durham 1990-94; Diocesan director of ordinands, Durham 1989-94; Priest then Vicar, Cockerton 1994-98; Senior chaplain to Bishop of Durham and Diocesan communications officer 1998-2002; Archdeacon of Durham 2002-06; Area Bishop of Ramsbury 2006-10; Bishop of Ely 2010-.

Political career: *House of Lords:* Entered House of Lords 2014. *Other:* Member, General Synod of Church of England 1995-2000, 2011-.

Political interests: Mental health, education, rural affairs, disability; Germany, India, Rwanda.

Other: Chair: National Society Council, Development and Appointments Group, House of Bishops 2013-15, Westcott House Council; Faith and Order Commission, World Council of Churches; L'Arche Community, Arthur Rank Hospice, Romsey Mill, Arts and Minds, National Youth Arts Trust; Honorary Fellow, Harris Manchester College, Oxford 2017-.

Publications: Editor, Living the Eucharist (2001); Contributor: This is Our Calling (2004), The Vicar's Guide (2005), 'Generous Episcopacy' in Generous Ecclesiology (SCM, 2013); 'A Good Easter' in Mark Oakley's "A Good Year" (2016).

Recreations: Reading detective fiction, biographies and history, film, travel.

Rt Rev the Lord Bishop of Ely, House of Lords, London SW1A 0PW
Tel: 020 7219 5353
The Bishop's House, Ely CB7 4DW *Tel:* 01353 662749 *Email:* bishop@elydiocese.org
Website: www.elydiocese.org *Twitter:* @Bishop_S_Conway

ULSTER UNIONIST PARTY

EMPEY, LORD

EMPEY (Life Baron), Reginald Norman Morgan Empey; cr 2011. Born 26 October 1947; Son of late Samuel Empey and late Emily Empey, née Morgan; Married Stella Donnan 1977 (1 son 1 daughter).

Education: Royal School, Armagh; Queen's University, Belfast (BSc (Econ) 1969).

Non-political career: 1970-1986: Industrial rubber products division, Goodyear International Corporation; House of Fraser/Switzer and Company; McMahon Co; Self-employed clothing retailer 1986-.

Political career: *House of Commons:* Contested (UUP) Belfast East 1997 and 2005 and (UCUNF) South Antrim 2010 general elections. *House of Lords:* Raised to the peerage as Baron Empey, of Shandon in the City and County of Belfast 2011. Member: Small- and Medium-Sized Enterprises 2012-13, Personal Service Companies 2013-14, Extradition Law 2014-15, Information 2015-16, Financial Exclusion 2016-17, Bribery Act 2010 2018-19, Food, Poverty, Health and the Environment 2019-. *Other:* Member: Northern Ireland Convention 1975, UUP Talks Team: Brooke/Mayhew Talks 1991, Castle Buildings Talks 1996-98; Northern Ireland Assembly: MLA for Belfast East 1998-2011, Minister for Enterprise, Trade and Investment 1999-2002, Acting First Minister 2001, Minister for Employment and Learning 2007-10. Vice-president, Ulster Unionist Council 1996-2004; Ulster Unionist Party: Leader 2005-10, Chair 2012-. Belfast City Council: Councillor 1985-2010, Mayor 1989, 1993; Member, Police Authority of Northern Ireland 1992-2001.

Political interests: Economic policy, education, UK-US relations, EU, small- and medium-sized enterprises; Canada, India, USA.

Other: Member: EU Committee of the Regions 1994-2002, British-Irish Parliamentary Assembly 2017-; Vice-president, Institute of Export; OBE 1994; Kt 1999. Army and Navy Club.

Recreations: Walking, gardening.

The Lord Empey OBE, House of Lords, London SW1A 0PW
Tel: 020 7219 8482 *Email:* empeyr@parliament.uk
Room 6-06, Millbank House, 1 Millbank, London SW1A 0PW

CROSSBENCH

ERROLL, EARL OF

ERROLL (24th Earl of, S), Merlin Sereld Victor Gilbert Hay; cr. 1452. 25th Lord Hay (S) 1429, 24th Lord Slains (S) 1452; 12th Bt (NS) 1685; 28th Hereditary Lord High Constable of Scotland, 1314; 32nd Chief of The Hays since 1160 (Celtic Title) Mac Garadh Mhor. Born 20 April 1948; Son of Sir Iain Moncreiffe of that Ilk, 11th Bt and Diana Denyse, Countess of Erroll (23rd in line); Married Isabelle Jacqueline Laline Astell 1982 (died 2020) (2 sons 2 daughters).

Education: Eton College; Trinity College, Cambridge.

Non-political career: Hayway Partners (Marketing) 1991-; Computer consultant -1993; Group director, Applications and Development, Girovend Holdings plc 1993-94; Chair: CRC Ltd 1995-, Fonem Ltd 2004-. Lieutenant, Atholl Highlanders 1974; TA 1975-90; Hon. Colonel, RMPTA 1992-97.

Political career: *House of Lords:* First entered House of Lords 1978; Elected hereditary peer 1999-. Board Member, Parliamentary Office of Science and Technology 2000-; Council Member, PITCOM 2000-; Member, Information 2003-05, 2007-08, 2009-12.

Political interests: Defence, ICT, science, Scotland, environment.

Other: Member, Queen's Body Guard for Scotland, Royal Company of Archers; Fishmongers Company Charitable Trust; Billingsgate Christian Mission; Trustee, Mar Estate Trust; Royal Caledonian Ball; Member, Court of Assistants of Fishmongers' Company, Prime Warden 2000-01; Freedom, City of London; Page to the Lord Lyon 1956; OStJ 1977. White's, Pratt's, Puffin's (Edinburgh) Club.

Recreations: Country pursuits.

The Earl of Erroll, House of Lords, London SW1A 0PW
Tel: 020 7219 3885 *Email:* errollm@parliament.uk
Woodbury Hall, Everton, Sandy SG19 2HR *Tel:* 01767 650251

CROSSBENCH

ETHERTON, LORD

ETHERTON (Life Baron), Terence Michael Elkan Barnet Etherton; cr 2020. Married Andrew Stone 2014 (civil partnership 2006).

Non-political career: Called to the Bar, Gray's Inn 1974; In practice, Chancery Bar 1975-2000; QC 1990; High Court Judge, Chancery Division 2001-08; Chairman, Law Commission of England and Wales 2006-09; Lord Justice of Appeal 2008-13; President of the Councils of the Inns of Court 2009-12; Chancellor of the High Court of England and Wales 2013-16; Master of the Rolls and Head of Civil Justice 2016-21.

Political career: *House of Lords:* Raised to the peerage as Baron Etherton, of Marylebone in the City of Westminster 2020.

Other: Chair, Trust Law Committee; President, Property Bar Association; Member, editorial board, Conveyancing and Property Law Journal; Patron, Birkbeck Law Review; Visiting law professor: Birkbeck, London University, Kent University; Honorary fellow: Corpus Christi College, Cambridge, Royal Holloway, London University; Honorary LLD, City University; Kt 2001; PC 2008.

Rt Hon the Lord Etherton QC, House of Lords, London SW1A 0PW
Tel: 020 7219 3000

CONSERVATIVE

EVANS OF BOWES PARK, BARONESS

Leader of the House of Lords and Lord Privy Seal

EVANS OF BOWES PARK (Life Baroness), Natalie Jessica Evans; cr 2014. Born 29 November 1975; Married James Wild 2010 (MP for North West Norfolk).

Education: Henrietta Barnett School; Cambridge University (social and political sciences).

Non-political career: Head of policy, British Chambers of Commerce; Deputy director, Policy Exchange 2008-11; New Schools Network: Chief operating officer 2011-13 Director 2013-15.

Political career: *House of Lords:* Raised to the peerage as Baroness Evans of Bowes Park, of Bowes Park in the London Borough of Haringey 2014. Government Whip (Baroness in Waiting) 2015-16; Government Spokesperson for: Education 2015-16, Justice 2015-16, Work and Pensions 2015-16; Leader of the House of Lords and Lord Privy Seal 2016-; Member, House of Lords Commission 2016-. Member: House 2016, Liaison 2016-19, Privileges and Conduct 2016-19, Procedure/Procedure and Privileges 2016-, Selection 2016-. *Other:* Deputy director, research department, Conservative Party 2000-02.

Political interests: Education, crime and justice, sport.

Other: Chair, board of trustees, Chevening House; PC 2016.

Rt Hon the Baroness Evans of Bowes Park, House of Lords, London SW1A 0PW
Tel: 020 7219 3200
Email: psleaderofthelords@cabinetoffice.gov.uk

LABOUR

EVANS OF WATFORD, LORD

EVANS OF WATFORD (Life Baron), David Charles Evans; cr. 1998. Born 30 November 1942; Son of Arthur Charles Evans and Phyllis Connie Evans; Married June Scaldwell 1966 (divorced) (2 sons 1 daughter).

Education: Hampden Secondary School; Watford College of Technology (Full Tech 1962).

Non-political career: Apprentice Printer, Stone and Cox Ltd 1957; Sales Executive and Sales Director at various printers; Centurion Press: Founder 1971, Chair, and of subsidiary companies in UK, Netherlands and the USA -2002; Former Chair: Personnel Publications Ltd, Redactive Publishing Ltd, Indigo Publishing Ltd, Iconic Images Ltd, Advanced Oncotherapy plc, Newsdesk Media Ltd; Chair: Senate Publishing Ltd, TU Ink Ltd, Evans Mitchell Books, Kennedy Scott Ltd; Stormount Energy Ltd; Non-executive Chair, Institute for Collaborative Working. Unite.

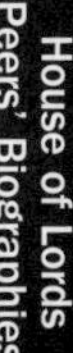

Political career: *House of Lords:* Raised to the peerage as Baron Evans of Watford, of Chipperfield in the County of Hertfordshire 1998. Departmental Liaison Peer for Department of Trade and Industry 1999-2004. Member, Small-and Medium-Sized Enterprises 2012-13.

Political interests: Trade and industry, industrial relations, current affairs, education, travel, voluntary sector; Europe, Far East, Middle East, USA.

Other: Honorary Fellow, Cancer Research UK; Assisted in creation of One World group/One World Action; Voluntary lecturer for Postal Telegraph and Telephone International in trade union studies and media public relations; Non-executive director, Hendon Museum Enterprises Ltd; Patron: Watford Peace Hospice, VITAL, Alma Hospital Trust, Eliminating Domestic Violence; Cancer Research UK, Royal British Legion, British Red Cross, Peace Hospice Care, Prostate Cancer UK; Member, Worshipful Company of Marketors; Fellow: Chartered Institute of Marketing, City and Guilds Institute. George, 5 Hertford Street Club.

Recreations: Theatre, the arts, reading, travel.

The Lord Evans of Watford, House of Lords, London SW1A 0PW
Tel: 020 7219 6184 *Fax:* 020 7219 1733
Senate Publishing, 5 Wythburn Place, London W1H 7BU *Tel:* 020 7723 9825
Email: lordevans@senatepublishing.co.uk Website: www.senatepublishing.co.uk

CROSSBENCH

EVANS OF WEARDALE, LORD

EVANS OF WEARDALE (Life Baron), Jonathan Douglas Evans; cr 2014. Born 17 February 1958.

Education: Sevenoaks School, Kent; Bristol University (Degree classical studies); Institute of Directors (Certificate company direction).

Non-political career: Security Service 1980-2013: Roles including counter-espionage investigations, protective security policy, international and domestic counter-terrorism, Secondment to the Home Office, Director of international counter-terrorism, Security Service's Management Board, Deputy Director-General 2005-07, Director-General 2007-13; Non-executive director: HSBC 2013-, Ark Data Centres Ltd.

Political career: *House of Lords:* Raised to the peerage as Baron Evans of Weardale, of Toys Hill in the County of Kent 2014. *Other:* Governor, Skinners' Kent Academy, Tunbridge Wells; DL, Kent 2015; Member, Parliamentary and Political Service Honours Committee 2017-18; Chair, Committee on Standards in Public Life 2018-.

Other: Non-executive Director: HSBC Holdings plc, Ark Data Centres Ltd; Senior Adviser, Accenture plc -2015; Member, Advisory Board: Darktrace Ltd, Facewatch Ltd; Patron: West Kent YMCA, Sevenoaks School, Member, Council of Reference, Westminster Abbey Institute; Freedom, City of London; Senior associate fellow, Royal United Services Institute; Honorary professor, St Andrews University; Hon LLD, Bristol University; KCB 2013.

Recreations: Classic cars, town and country walks.

The Lord Evans of Weardale KCB DL, House of Lords, London SW1A 0PW
Tel: 020 7219 5353

CONSERVATIVE

FAIRFAX OF CAMERON, LORD

FAIRFAX OF CAMERON (14th Lord, S), Nicholas John Albert Fairfax; cr 1627. Born 4 January 1956; Son of 13th Lord and late Sonia Gunston; Married Annabel Morriss 1982 (3 sons).

Education: Eton College; Downing College, Cambridge (Postgraduate LLB international law subjects 1981); French, German, Italian, Russian.

Non-political career: Called to the Bar, Gray's Inn 1977; Director: Thomas Miller P&I and Thomas Miller Defence 1987-90, Sedgwick Marine and Cargo Ltd 1995-96, Sovcomflot (UK) Ltd 2005-, North of England P&I Association Ltd 2012-; Chair: SCF Overseas Holding Ltd 2012-, SCF Management Services Ltd 2012-, Advisory board, Hawk-i Worldwide Ltd 2015-, Consultant, Burford Capital 2014-.

Political career: *House of Lords:* First entered House of Lords 1977; Elected hereditary peer 2015-.

Political interests: Shipping, marine insurance and law, exiting the European Union, artificial intelligence, security, motorcycling, choice at end of life, mental health, homelessness; Eastern Europe, Russia, former Soviet Union, USA.

Other: Patron, Downside Up; Patron: Wildlife Vets International, Downside Up, Warm House, Friends of Fairfax House; Liveryman, Shipwrights' Company; Freedom, City of London. Royal Yacht Squadron Club.

Recreations: Sailing, motorcycling, astronomy, photography.

The Lord Fairfax of Cameron, House of Lords, London SW1A 0PW
Tel: 020 7219 3000 *Email:* fairfaxn@parliament.uk

CONSERVATIVE

FAIRHEAD, BARONESS

FAIRHEAD (Life Baroness), Rona Alison Fairhead; cr 2017. Born 28 August 1961; Daughter of Douglas and Isabel Haig; Married Thomas Fairhead 1992 (2 sons 1 daughter).

Education: Yarm Grammar School/Conyer's School, Yarm; St Catharine's College, Cambridge (law 1983); Harvard Business School (MBA 1989); French, German, limited Spanish.

Non-political career: Senior Consultant, Bain & Co 1983-87, 1989-90; Summer Associate, Morgan Stanley 1988; Industrial Consultant, British Aerospace 1991; Bombardier/Shorts Aerospace: Vice-president, Corporate Strategy and Public Affairs 1991-94, Vice-president and general manager, UK Aerospace Services 1994-96; ICI plc 1996-2001: Director, Planning and Acquisitions 1996-97, Executive Vice-president, Communications, Strategy and Financial Control 1997-2001; Pearson plc 2001-06: Deputy chief financial director 2001-02, Chief Financial Officer 2002-06; Chairman and Chief Executive, Financial Times Group and Professional Education 2006-13.

Political career: *House of Lords:* Raised to the peerage as Baroness Fairhead, of Yarm in the County of North Yorkshire 2017. Minister of State for Trade and Export Promotion and Government Spokesperson, Department for International Trade 2017-19. *Other:* Non-executive director, Cabinet Office 2011-14; UKTI Business Ambassador, UK Trade & Investment (UKTI) 2014-15; Chairman, BBC Trust 2014-17.

Other: Non-executive director: Laganside Corporation, Belfast 1994-2000, HSBC Holdings plc 2004-16, Economist Group 2006-14, PepsiCo Inc; Chairman of Board, Interactive Data Corporation 2007-10; Non-executive director, Oracle Corporation 2019-; Member, External Advisory Group, McKinsey & Co 2020-; Senior Executive, Chairman Mentors International 2020-; Member, Advisors' Group, Edge Investments 2020-; Non-executive director, survivorNET 2020-; Non-executive chair, Electrocomponents 2020-; Honorary fellow, St Catharine's College, Cambridge; Honorary doctorate: Teesside University, Queen's University Belfast; CBE 2012.

The Baroness Fairhead CBE, House of Lords, London SW1A 0PW
Tel: 020 7219 3000

LABOUR

FALCONER OF THOROTON, LORD

Shadow Attorney General; Opposition Spokesperson for Law Officers and Justice

FALCONER OF THOROTON (Life Baron), Charles Leslie Falconer; cr. 1997. Born 19 November 1951; Son of late John Leslie Falconer and Anne Mansel Falconer; Married Marianna Catherine Thoroton Hildyard (later QC) 1985 (3 sons 1 daughter).

Education: Trinity College, Glenalmond; Queens' College, Cambridge.

Non-political career: Called to the Bar, Inner Temple 1974; QC 1991; Elected Master, Bench of the Inner Temple 1997; Senior Counsel, Gibson Dunn and Crutcher LLP.

Political career: *House of Lords:* Raised to the peerage as Baron Falconer of Thoroton, of Thoroton in the County of Nottinghamshire 1997. Solicitor General 1997-98; Minister of State and Government Spokesperson for: Cabinet Office 1998-2001, Department for Transport, Local Government and the Regions (Minister for Housing, Planning and Regeneration) 2001-02, Home Office (Criminal Justice, Sentencing and Law Reform) 2002-03; Secretary of State and Government Spokesperson for Constitutional Affairs/Justice and Lord Chancellor 2003-07; Opposition Spokesperson for Justice (Constitutional Affairs) 2010-16; Shadow Lord Chancellor and Secretary of State for Justice 2015-16; Shadow Attorney General 2020-; Opposition Spokesperson for Law Officers 2020-, Justice 2020-. Member: Procedure 2003-07, Sentencing (Pre-consolidation Amendments) Bill 2019. *Other:* Adviser on Planning and Transition into Government 2013-. Chair, Commission on Assisted Dying 2010-.

Other: Vice-President, Commonwealth Parliamentary Association (UK Branch); Peer of the Year, *Spectator* awards 2014; PC 2003.

Rt Hon the Lord Falconer of Thoroton QC, House of Lords, London SW1A 0PW
Tel: 020 7219 5159
Email: cfalconer@gibsondunn.com *Twitter:* @LordCFalconer

CROSSBENCH

FALKLAND, VISCOUNT OF

FALKLAND (15th Viscount of, S), Lucius Edward William Plantagenet Cary; cr. 1620; Lord Cary 1620. Born 8 May 1935; Son of 14th Viscount; Married Caroline Butler 1962 (divorced 1990) (1 son 2 daughters and 1 daughter deceased); married Nicole Mackey 1990 (1 son).

Education: Wellington College, Berkshire; French, German.

Non-political career: Journalist, Theatrical agent, Chartered shipbroker; Chief executive, C T Bowring Trading (Holdings) Ltd 1974-80; Marketing consultant 1980-86. 2nd Lieutenant, 8th Hussars.

Political career: *House of Lords:* First entered House of Lords 1984; Liberal Democrat: Deputy Chief Whip 1988-2001, Spokesperson for: National Heritage 1995-97, Culture, Media and Sport 1997-2005; Elected hereditary peer 1999-; Former Deputy Chair of Committees. Member: Overseas Trade 1984-85, Pre-legislative Gambling Joint Committee 2004-05; Works of Art: Member 2005-07, 2014-16, Chair 2007-13; Member, Lord Speaker's Advisory Panel on Works of Art 2017-19. *Other:* Resigned Liberal Democrat Whip March 2011, now sits as Crossbench.

Political interests: Theatre, Europe, film industry, alcohol and drug addiction, transport (particularly motorcycling), racing and bloodstock; France, Sub-Saharan Africa.

Other: Tower Hamlets Mission, U Can Do It. Brooks's Club; Sunningdale Golf.

Recreations: Golf, cinema, motorcycling, reading, racing.

The Viscount of Falkland, House of Lords, London SW1A 0PW
Tel: 020 7219 3230
Email: lordfalkland@aol.com

CROSSBENCH

FALKNER OF MARGRAVINE, BARONESS

FALKNER OF MARGRAVINE (Life Baroness), Kishwer Falkner; cr. 2004. Born 9 March 1955; Daughter of Ahsan Mohammad Khan and Saeeda Ahsan; Married Robert Falkner 1996 (1 daughter).

Education: St Joseph's Convent School, Karachi, Pakistan; London School of Economics (BSc (Econ) international relations 1992); Kent University (MA international relations and European studies 1994).

Non-political career: Deputy manager, Saudi Arabian Airlines, France and USA 1982-86; Senior researcher, Liberal Democrats, House of Commons 1992-93; Liberal Democrats: Director: International Affairs 1993-99, Policy 1997-98; Chief programme officer, Political Affairs Division, Commonwealth Secretariat 1999-2003; Chief executive, Student Partnerships Worldwide 2003-04; Visiting Professor, King's College, London 2015-. Commonwealth Secretariat Staff Association: Member 1999-2003, Vice-chair 2000-03.

Political career: *House of Commons:* Contested (Liberal Democrat) Kensington and Chelsea 2001 general election. *House of Lords:* Raised to the peerage as Baroness Falkner of Margravine, of Barons Court in the London Borough of Hammersmith and Fulham 2004. Liberal Democrat Spokesperson for: Home Affairs 2004-05, 2009-10, Communities and Local Government 2005-06, Children, Schools and Families 2007-08, Justice 2008-09, Foreign and Commonwealth Affairs 2009-10, 2015. Co-opted Member, EU Sub-committee C (Foreign Affairs, Defence and Development Policy) 2005-06; Member: Joint Committee on Human Rights 2005, 2009-10, Draft Legal Services Bill Joint Committee 2006, Intergovernmental Organisations 2007-08, Constitution 2010-11, 2012-15, Joint Committee on National Security Strategy 2014-17, European Union 2015-19; Chair, EU Financial Affairs Sub-committee 2015-19; Member, Procedure 2019. Chair, Liberal Democrat Parliamentary Party Committee on International Affairs (FCO) 2010-15. *Other:* Contested London region 2004 European Parliament election. Liberal Democrats: Member, Federal Policy Committee 1999-2001, Chair, policy, London Liberal Democrats 2000-04, Member, Federal Executive 2010-19, Left Liberal Democrats July 2019, non-affiliated July 2019-August 2020, now sits as Crossbench. Member, advisory board, British Library 2014-; Chair, Equality and Human Rights Commission 2020-.

Political interests: European and foreign affairs, political Islam, diversity and equality, constitution, governance, transitional democracies; Middle East, USA.

Other: Non-executive director, Hyde Group 2006-15; Chancellor, Northampton University 2008-16; Fellow: Kennedy School of Government, Harvard University 2006, St Antony's College, Oxford 2008; Hon. Doc, Northampton University 2008.

Recreations: Travel, reading, cooking, running, cinema.

The Baroness Falkner of Margravine, House of Lords, London SW1A 0PW
Tel: 020 7219 2809 *Email:* falknerk@parliament.uk *Twitter:* @KishwerFalkner

CONSERVATIVE

FALL, BARONESS

FALL (Life Baroness), Catherine Susan Fall; cr 2015. Born 2 October 1967; Daughter of Sir Brian Fall, diplomat, and Delmar Alexandra Roos; Married Ralph Ward-Jackson 1996 (divorced 2010) (1 son 1 daughter).

Education: King's School, Canterbury (music scholar); St Hilda's College, Oxford (philosophy, politics, economics 1986).

Non-political career: Research assistant to Patricia Rawlings MEP; Special adviser to the Deputy Director-general, Confederation of British Industry; Conservative Research Department: Desk officer for Europe and agriculture, Head of Home Affairs Section; Assistant to: Michael Howard MP as Shadow Foreign Secretary, John Maples MP as Shadow Health Secretary; Political adviser, 1999 European Parliament election; Deputy Chief of Staff to David Cameron MP as: Leader of the Opposition 2005-10, Prime Minister 2010-16; Senior Adviser, Brunswick Group LLP 2016-.

Political career: *House of Lords:* Raised to the peerage as Baroness Fall, of Ladbroke Grove in the Royal Borough of Kensington and Chelsea 2015. Member: Political Polling and Digital Media 2017-18, International Relations/International Relations and Defence 2019-.

Other: Trustee, Atlantic Partnership 2017-; Member, advisory board, Onward 2018-.

The Baroness Fall, House of Lords, London SW1A 0PW
Tel: 020 7219 3000

CONSERVATIVE

FARMER, LORD

FARMER (Life Baron), Michael Stahel Farmer; cr 2014. Born 17 December 1944; Married Jenny (3 children).

Non-political career: Head of base metal trading, Phibro Salomon 1987-89; Chief executive, Metal & Commodity Company Ltd 1989-99; Managing Director: Merchanting, MG plc 1999-2000, Base metal trading, Enron Europe Ltd 2000-01; Senior partner, RK Capital Management 2005-.

Political career: *House of Lords:* Raised to the peerage as Baron Farmer, of Bishopsgate in the City of London 2014. Member: Social Mobility 2015-16, Joint Committee on the Draft Domestic Abuse Bill 2019. *Other:* Treasurer, Conservative and Unionist Party 2011-15. Council member, Oakhill Theological College 2001-14; Sponsor governor, Ark All Saints Camberwell 2013-18.

Other: Chair, Great St Helen's Trust 1996-2015; Trustee, Kingham Hill Trust 2001-14; Chair, Farmer Review on Importance of Strengthening Offenders' Family Ties to Prevent Re-offending and Intergenerational Crime 2016-; Deputy chair, Council for Christians and Jews 2016-.

The Lord Farmer, House of Lords, London SW1A 0PW
Tel: 020 7219 3000 *Email:* callans@parliament.uk

LABOUR

FAULKNER OF WORCESTER, LORD

FAULKNER OF WORCESTER (Life Baron), Richard Oliver Faulkner; cr. 1999. Born 22 March 1946; Son of late Harold and Mabel Faulkner; Married Susan Heyes 1968 (2 daughters).

Education: Merchant Taylors' School, Northwood; Worcester College, Oxford (BA philosophy, politics and economics 1967, MA).

Non-political career: Research assistant and journalist, Labour Party 1967-69; Public relations officer, Construction Industry Training Board 1969-70; Editor, *Steel News* 1971; Account director, F J Lyons (Public Relations) Ltd 1971-73; Director, PPR International 1973-76; Government relations adviser to various companies, unions, councils and bodies 1973-99; *The House Magazine*: Co-founder, Member, Editorial Board 2003-; Communications adviser to Leader of the Opposition and Labour Party (unpaid) in general elections 1987, 1992, 1997; Communications adviser to Bishop at Lambeth 1990; Deputy chair, Citigate Westminster 1997-99 (Joint Managing Director, Westminster Communications Group 1989-97); Cardiff Millennium Stadium plc: Director 1997-2004, Deputy chair 2004-08; Strategy adviser, Littlewoods Leisure 1999-2009; Alderney Gambling Control Commission: Adviser 2005-08, Commissioner 2013-, Chairman 2014; Adviser on Railway Heritage, New South Wales Government 2012. Graduate Armed Forces Parliamentary Scheme, attached to Royal Navy 2002-07.

Political career: *House of Commons:* Contested (Labour) Devizes 1970, February 1974, Monmouth October 1974, Huddersfield West 1979 general elections. *House of Lords:* Raised to the peerage as Baron Faulkner of Worcester, of Wimbledon in the London Borough of Merton 1999. Departmental Liaison Peer: Department of the Environment, Transport and the Regions 2000-01, Cabinet Office 2001-05; Deputy Chairman of Committees 2007-09, 2010-; Deputy Speaker 2008-09, 2010-; Government Whip 2009-10; Trade Envoy to Taiwan 2016-. Chair, London Local Authorities Private Bill 2006; Member: Draft Gambling Bill Joint Scrutiny Committee 2003-04, London Local Authorities Private Bill 2006, Delegated Powers and Regulatory Reform 2007-09; Co-opted Member, European Union Sub-committee F (Home Affairs) 2009; Member: Administration and Works 2011-15, Joint Committee on the Rookery South (Resource Recovery Facility) Order 2012-13, Selection 2013-17, Olympic and Paralympic Legacy 2013-14, Sub-committee F: Home Affairs, Health and Education 2013-15; Alternate Member, Procedure 2014-15; Member: Equality Act 2010 and Disability 2015-16, Information 2015-16, EU Home Affairs Sub-committee 2015-16, Ecclesiastical Committee 2015-, Lord Speaker's Advisory Panel on Works of Art 2017-, Secondary Legislation Scrutiny 2017-19, Natural Environment and Rural Communities Act 2006 2017-18, SLSC Sub-committee A 2018-19, Joint Committee on the Draft Registration of Overseas Entities Bill 2019, European Union 2019-, EU External Affairs Sub-committee 2019-20, EU Goods Sub-committee 2020-. *Other:* Member, National Policy Commission 2014. Councillor, Merton Borough Council 1971-78; Member of Court, Bedfordshire University 1999-2009; ROSPA:

President 2001-04, Vice-president 2004-; Science Museum Group: Trustee 2007-09, 2011-18, Deputy Chair 2015-18; President, College of Fellows, Worcester University 2014-18.

Political interests: Transport, sport, human rights, smoking and health, sex equality; Argentina, Australia, Canada, Jamaica, Namibia, New Zealand, Norway, South Africa, Taiwan.

Other: Member: Inter-Parliamentary Union, Executive committee, Commonwealth Parliamentary Association UK 2003-05; Various posts numerous sports, especially football, including directorships of four football clubs; Patron, Roy Castle Lung Cancer Foundation 1999-2003, 2006-; Trustee, Foundation for Sports and the Arts 2000-12; Vice-president, Campaign for Better Transport (formerly Transport 2000 Ltd) 2001-; Director, West Somerset Railway 2004-05; Chair, Railway Heritage Committee 2004-09; Trustee: Gamcare 2005-09, National Football Museum 2007-09, 2012-16; Vice-president, Level Playing Field 2007-09, 2010-; President, Cotswold Line Promotion Group 2007-09, 2010-; First Great Western Trains Advisory Board (now Great Western Railway Advisory Board): Member 2010-, Chair 2014-; President, Heritage Railway Association 2011-; Vice-president, Football Conference 2011-15; President, Old Merchant Taylors' Society 2011-12; Worcester Live: Patron and director 2011, Chairman 2014-18; Patron, Myriad Centre 2012-; Chair, Railway Heritage Designation Advisory Board 2013-; Patron, Guild of Battlefield Guides 2013-; President, Worcester College Oxford Society 2014-; Vice-president, National League 2015-; Chair, advisory board, Museum of Science and Industry 2017-; Associate Member, Retired Railway Officers Association; Hon. Fellow, Worcester College, Oxford 2002; Hon. Doctor of Law, Luton University 2003; Fellow, Worcester University 2008; Diplomatic Medal of Honour, Government of Taiwan 2004; Order of the Brilliant Star with Grand Cordon, Government of Taiwan 2008.

Publications: Co-author, Holding the Line - How Britain's Railways Were Saved (Oxford Publishing Company, 2012); Disconnected! – Broken Links in Britain's Rail Policy (Oxford Publishing Company, 2015).

Recreations: Travelling by railway, collecting Lloyd George memorabilia, tinplate trains, watching Association Football.

The Lord Faulkner of Worcester, House of Lords, London SW1A 0PW
Tel: 020 7219 8503 *Fax:* 020 7219 1460 *Email:* faulknerro@parliament.uk
Website: www.lordfaulkner.net

NON-AFFILIATED

FAULKS, LORD

FAULKS (Life Baron), Edward Peter Lawless Faulks; cr 2010. Born 19 August 1950; Son of His Honour Peter Faulks MC and Pamela Faulks, née Lawless; Married Catherine Turner 1990 (2 sons).

Education: Wellington College, Berkshire; Jesus College, Oxford (MA jurisprudence); French.

Non-political career: Called to the Bar, Middle Temple 1973; Literary agent, Curtis Brown 1980-81; QC 1996; Assistant recorder 1996-2000; Recorder 2000-10; Bencher 2002; Chair, Professional Negligence Bar Association 2002-04; Special adviser to Department for Constitutional Affairs on compensation culture 2005-06; Part-time Judge, Astana International Financial Court 2015-.

Political career: *House of Lords:* Raised to the peerage as Baron Faulks, of Donnington in the Royal County of Berkshire 2010. Ministry of Justice: Government Spokesperson 2013-16, Minister of State for: Civil Justice 2013-16, Legal Policy 2013-15. Member: Selection 2011, Joint Committee on the Draft Detention of Terrorist Suspects (Temporary Extension) Bills 2011, Joint Committee on Human Rights 2012-14, Join Committee on the Draft Communications Data Bill 2012-13; Mental Capacity Act 2005 2013, Joint Committee on the Draft Registration of Overseas Entities Bill 2019, Constitution 2019-, Sentencing (Pre-consolidation Amendments) Bill 2019. *Other:* Left Conservatives July 2019, now sits as non-affiliated.

Political interests: Legal issues, constitution, education, medicine, conservation, human rights; India, Sri Lanka, USA.

Publications: Contributing editor, Local Authority Liability (2012).

Recreations: Sports, the arts.

The Lord Faulks QC, House of Lords, London SW1A 0PW
Tel: 020 7219 5353
1 Chancery Lane, London WC2A 1LF *Tel:* 020 7092 2900 *Email:* efaulks@1chancerylane.com

LIBERAL DEMOCRAT

FEATHERSTONE, BARONESS

FEATHERSTONE (Life Baroness), Lynne Choona Featherstone; cr 2015. Born 20 December 1951; Daughter of late Joseph Woolf and Gladys Ryness; Married Stephen Featherstone 1982 (divorced 2002) (2 children).

Education: South Hampstead High School, London; Oxford Polytechnic (Diploma communications and design 1974); French.

Non-political career: Graphic designer, London and Australia 1974-77; Freelance designer 1977-80; Managing director, Inhouse Outhouse Design 1980-87; Strategic design consultant 1987-97; Director, Ryness Electrical Supplies Ltd 1991-2002.

Political career: *House of Commons:* Contested Hornsey and Wood Green 1997 and 2001 general elections. MP for Hornsey and Wood Green 2005-15. Contested Hornsey and Wood Green 2015 general election; Liberal Democrat: Spokesperson for: Home Affairs 2005-06, London 2006-07, Shadow Secretary of State for International Development 2006-07; Shadow Minister for Youth and Equalities 2008-10; Parliamentary Under-Secretary of State: (Minister for Equalities), Home Office and Government Equalities Office 2010-12, Department for International Development 2012-14; Minister of State for Crime Prevention, Home Office 2014-15. Member, Environmental Audit 2005-06. *House of Lords:* Raised to the peerage as Baroness Featherstone, of Highgate in the London Borough of Haringey 2015. Liberal Democrat Spokesperson for Energy and Climate Change 2015-19. *Other:* Member, Human Rights Committee, Liberal International 2016-17. London Borough of Haringey Council: Councillor 1998-2006, Leader of Opposition 1998-2003; London Assembly: Member 2000-05, Chair, Assembly Committee on Transport 2000-05; Member, Metropolitan Police Authority 2000-05.

Political interests: Energy and climate change, female genital mutilation, gay rights in Africa and Asia, disability in the Developing World, contaminated blood scandal; Africa, Asia.

Other: Member, Human Rights Committee Liberal International 2016-17; Unsung Hero award, *Daily Mail* 2002; Best Campaign Website, Orange Digital award 2010; Politician of the Year, *Attitude Magazine* 2012; Ally of the Year, *PinkNews* 2014; Politician of the Year, Stonewall 2014; PC 2014.

Publications: Marketing and Communications Techniques for Architects (Longman, 1992); Equal Ever After (Biteback, 2016).

Recreations: Writing poetry, film.

Rt Hon the Baroness Featherstone, House of Lords, London SW1A 0PW
Tel: 020 7219 3000 *Email:* featherstonel@parliament.uk *Twitter:* @lfeatherstone

CONSERVATIVE

FELDMAN OF ELSTREE, LORD

FELDMAN OF ELSTREE (Life Baron), Andrew Simon Feldman; cr 2010. Born 25 February 1966; Son of Malcolm and Marcia Feldman; Married Gabrielle Gourgey (2 sons 1 daughter).

Education: Haberdashers' Aske's School, Elstree; Brasenose College, Oxford (BA jurisprudence 1988).

Non-political career: Management Consultant, Bain & Company 1988-90; Barrister, 1 Essex Court 1991-95; Chief Executive, Jayroma 1995-2018; Partner, Macro Advisory Partners 2018-19; Managing Partner, Tulchan Communications 2019–.

Political career: *House of Lords:* Raised to the peerage as Baron Feldman of Elstree, of Elstree in the County of Hertfordshire 2010. On leave of absence June 2020-. *Other:* Conservative Party: Deputy Treasurer 2005-08, Chief Executive 2008-10, Co-chair 2010-16, Chair, party board 2010-16; Trustee, Conservative Party Foundation 2019-. Board member, UK Holocaust Memorial Foundation 2015-.

Other: PC 2015.

Recreations: Tennis, golf.

Rt Hon the Lord Feldman of Elstree, House of Lords, London SW1A 0PW
Tel: 020 7219 5353

CROSSBENCH

FELLOWES, LORD

FELLOWES (Life Baron), Robert Fellowes; cr. 1999. Born 11 December 1941; Son of late Sir William Fellowes, KCVO and Lady Fellowes; Married Lady Jane Spencer, daughter of 8th Earl Spencer, LVO, and Hon. Mrs Shand Kydd 1978 (1 son 2 daughters).

Education: Eton College.

Non-political career: Director, Allen Harvey & Ross Ltd 1968-77; Private Office of HM The Queen: Assistant Private Secretary 1977-86, Deputy Private Secretary 1986-90, Private Secretary 1990-99; Barclays Private Bank: Vice-chair 1999-2000, Chair 2000-09; Non-executive director, SAB Miller 1999-2010; Secretary and registrar, Order of Merit 2003-. Short Service Commission, Scots Guards 1960-63.

Political career: *House of Lords:* Raised to the peerage as Baron Fellowes, of Shotesham in the County of Norfolk 1999. Member: Constitution 2001-04, Liaison 2009-13, Joint Committee on National Security Strategy 2010-14, Financial Exclusion 2016-17, Standing Orders (Private Bills) 2017-. *Other:* Board member, British Library 2007-16.

Political interests: Prison reform, constitution; USA.

Other: Winston Churchill Memorial Trust: Trustee 2001-16, Chair 2009-16; Rhodes Trust 2001-10; Chair, Prison Reform Trust 2001-08; Mandela-Rhodes Foundation 2003-10; Scots Guards 2006-; Vice-chair, Commonwealth Education Trust 2007-16; Goodenough College: President, Advisory Council 2008-13, Governor Emeritus 2014-; Trustee, King Edward VII Hospital, Sister Agnes 2010-13; Liveryman, Goldsmith's Company; LVO 1983; CB 1987; KCVO 1989; PC 1990; KCB 1991; GCVO 1996; GCB 1998; QSO 1999. White's, Pratt's, Royal Overseas League Club; MCC.

Recreations: Golf, watching cricket, reading.

Rt Hon the Lord Fellowes GCB GCVO QSO, House of Lords, London SW1A 0PW
Tel: 020 7219 8754 *Email:* fellowesr@parliament.uk

CONSERVATIVE

FELLOWES OF WEST STAFFORD, LORD

FELLOWES OF WEST STAFFORD (Life Baron), Julian Alexander Kitchener-Fellowes; cr 2011. Born 17 August 1949; Son of late Peregrine Fellowes and Olwen Fellowes, née Stuart-Jones; Married Emma Kitchener LVO 1990 (1 son).

Education: Ampleforth College, Yorkshire; Magdalene College, Cambridge (BA 1970); Webber Douglas Academy (1973); Inadequate French.

Non-political career: Actor: Joking Apart, Queen's Theatre 1978, Present Laughter, Vaudeville Theatre 1981, Futurists, Royal National Theatre 1986, For the Greater Good 1991, Shadowlands 1993, Damage 1993, Our Friends in the North 1996, Tomorrow Never Dies 1997, Place Vendôme 1998, Aristocrats 1999, Monarch of the Glen 1999-2005; Producer, A Married Man 1982; Writer, Little Lord Fauntleroy 1994; Writer and co-producer, The Prince and the Pauper 1997; Writer: Gosford Park 2001, Mary Poppins 2004; Writer and director, Separate Lies 2005; Writer: Vanity Fair 2005, The Young Victoria 2009; Writer and director, From Time to Time 2010; Writer and creator, Downton Abbey 2010-15; Writer: School of Rock 2015, Half a Sixpence 2016, The Wind in the Willows 2017. Member, Equity.

Political career: *House of Lords:* Raised to the peerage as Baron Fellowes of West Stafford, of West Stafford in the County of Dorset 2011. *Other:* DL, Dorset 2008; Member, Arts and Media Honours Committee -2018.

Political interests: The arts (particularly film and television), education; Ireland, USA.

Other: Chairman, Talking Books Appeal, RNIB 2003-; Patron, Rainbow Trust 2005-; Vice-President, Weldmar Hospicecare Trust 2006-; Patron: Help the Aged/Age UK 2007-, Changing Faces 2007-; President, Thomas Hardy Society 2007-; Ambassador: The Haven 2007-, Alzheimer's Society 2008-; Patron: Moviola 2008-, Lewiston School Appeal 2009-; Member, Appeal Council, National Memorial Arboretum 2009-; Vice-President, Catholic Association of Performing Arts 2010-; Patron: AdLib, Association of Friends of Dorset Libraries 2010-, Bay Theatre, Weymouth College 2010-; Member, National Advisory Council,

RicNic Trust 2011-; Vice-Patron, Priory of England and the Islands, of the Order of St. John; Honorary Patron, Sleaford Playhouse 2011-; Vice-President, RNIB 2016-; Hon. DLitt, Bournemouth 2007; Hon. DArts, Southampton Solent 2010; Best Screenplay, New York Film Critics' Award 2001; Best Screenplay, National Film Critics' Award 2001; Screenwriter of the Year, ShoWest 2002; Best Original Screenplay, Writer's Guild Award 2002; Best Original Screenplay, Academy Award 2002; Best Directorial Debut, National Board of Review 2006; Best Writer, British Press Guild Awards 2011; Outstanding Writing for a Mini-series, Emmy Awards 2011; International Emmy Award 2015. 5 Hertford Street, Boodle's, Pratt's Club.

Publications: Author: Snobs (2004), The Curious Adventures of the Abandoned Toys (2007), Past Imperfect (2008), Belgravia (2016).

Recreations: History.

The Lord Fellowes of West Stafford, House of Lords, London SW1A 0PW
Tel: 020 7219 5353

CROSSBENCH

FIELD OF BIRKENHEAD, LORD

FIELD OF BIRKENHEAD (Life Baron), Frank Field; cr 2020. Born 16 July 1942; Son of late Walter Field.

Education: St Clement Danes Grammar School, London; Hull University (BSc economics 1963).

Non-political career: Teacher in further education 1964-69; Director: Child Poverty Action Group 1969-79, Low Pay Unit 1974-80; Non-executive director, Medicash 2003-.

Political career: *House of Commons:* Contested (Lab) Buckinghamshire South 1966 general election. MP for Birkenhead 1979-2010, for Birkenhead (revised boundary) 2010-19. Contested (Birkenhead Social Justice Party) Birkenhead 2019 general election; Opposition Spokesperson for Education 1980-81; Minister of State, Department of Social Security (Welfare Reform) 1997-98; Led Independent Review on Poverty and Life Chances. Chair, Social Security 1990-97; Member: Public Accounts 2002-05, Ecclesiastical Committee 2002-19; Chair: Joint Committee on the Draft Modern Slavery Bill 2014, Work and Pensions 2015-19; Member, Liaison 2015-19. *House of Lords:* Raised to the peerage as Baron Field of Birkenhead, of Birkenhead in the County of Merseyside 2020. *Other:* Resigned Labour Whip August 2018. Councillor, Hounslow Borough Council 1964-68; DL 2011.

Political interests: Poverty and income redistribution, church affairs; Poland.

Other: Chair: Churches Conservation Trust 2001-07, King James Bible Trust 2007-12; Chair, Feeding Britain 2015-; Member, Campaign Committee, Vote Leave 2016; Founding Supporter, Change Britain 2016-; Trustee, Cathedral Fabrics Commission for England; Chair, Birkenhead Education Trust; Three honorary doctorates; Two honorary fellowships; *The House Magazine* Home Affairs Campaigner of the Year, Dods Parliamentary Awards 2014; PC 1997.

Publications: Publications on low pay, poverty and social issues 1971-; Neighbours From Hell (2003); Attlee's Great Contemporaries (2009); Saints and Heroes (2010); Contributor, The Purple Book (Progress, 2011); Fixing Broken Britain? An audit of working-age welfare reform since 2010 (2016).

Rt Hon the Lord Field of Birkenhead, House of Lords, London SW1A 0PW
Tel: 020 7219 3000 *Twitter:* @frankfieldteam

LABOUR

FILKIN, LORD

FILKIN (Life Baron), David Geoffrey Nigel Filkin; cr. 1999. Born 1 July 1944; Son of late Donald and Winifred Filkin; Married Elizabeth Tompkins 1974 (divorced 1994) (3 daughters); married Brigitte Paupy 2005.

Education: King Edward VI School, Birmingham; Clare College, Cambridge (MA history 1966); Manchester University (DipTP 1972); Birmingham University (management in local government); French.

Non-political career: Teacher on VSO, Ghana 1966-67; Town planner, Redditch Development Corporation (New Town) 1969-72; Manager, Brent Housing Aid Centre, London Borough of Brent 1972-75; Deputy chief executive, Merseyside Improved Housing 1975-79; Borough housing officer, Ellesmere Port and Neston Borough Council 1979-82; Director of housing, London Borough of Greenwich 1982-88; Chief executive: Reading Borough Council 1988-91, Association of District Councils 1991-97; Local government adviser, Joseph Rowntree Foundation 1997-2001; Director, New Local Government Network 1997-2001; Policy analyst and writer 1997-2001; Adviser, Capgemini plc 2005-12; Non-executive director, Accord plc 2005-07; Adviser: Serco 2006-, NCP 2006-; Chair: Public Sector Reform Group 2005-08, St Alban's Cathedral Music Trust 2006-10; Founder chair, 2020 Public Services Trust 2008-11; Chair, Centre for Ageing Better 2014-18.

Political career: *House of Lords:* Raised to the peerage as Baron Filkin, of Pimlico in the City of Westminster 1999. Government Spokesperson for: Transport, Local Government and the Regions 2001-02, Health 2001-02; Government Whip 2001-02; Parliamentary Under-Secretary of State and Government Spokesperson for: Home Office 2002-03, Department for Constitutional Affairs 2003-04, Department for Education and Skills and Department for Work and Pensions 2004-05. Chair, Merits of Statutory Instruments 2005-09; Member, Leader's Group on the Working Practices of the House of Lords 2010-11; Procedure: Alternate member 2011-13, Member 2012-13; Chair, Public Service and Demographic Change 2012-13; Member: Social and Economic Impact of the Gambling Industry 2019-, Public Services 2020-. *Other:* Vice-president, Local Government Association 2020-.

Political interests: Policy development, policy implementation, housing; Southern Africa, West Africa.

Other: Parliament Choir: Founder chair 2000-, Trustee; Trustee, Southbank Sinfonia; Former member, Royal Town Planning Institute; Former associate member, Institute of Housing; Honorary Fellow, Chartered Institute of Purchasing and Supplies; CBE 1997.

Publications: Best Value for the Public; Political Leadership of Best Value; Partnerships for Best Value; Modernising Local Government; Starting to Modernise; Achieving Best Value; Towards a New Localism; Winning the e-Revolution; Strategic Partnering for Local Services; Co-author: Public Matters – Renewing the Public Realm (Methuen, 2007), Better Outcomes (2009).

Recreations: Music, walking, swimming, singing, church.

The Lord Filkin CBE, House of Lords, London SW1A 0PW
Tel: 020 7219 0640 *Email:* filking@parliament.uk
Email: gfilkin1@aol.com

CONSERVATIVE

FINK, LORD

FINK (Life Baron), Stanley Fink; cr 2011. Born 15 September 1957; Married Barbara Paskin (2 sons 2 daughters).

Education: Manchester Grammar School; Trinity Hall, Cambridge (LLB 1979).

Non-political career: Chartered accountancy training, Arthur Andersen 1980-82; Financial planning team, Mars Confectionery 1982-83; Vice-President, Citibank 1983-87; Man Group plc: Director, mergers acquisitions and treasury 1987-2000, Chief executive officer 2000-07, Deputy chairman 2008; International Standard Asset Management: Chief executive officer 2008-15, Chair 2015-; Special adviser, eToro 2018-.

Political career: *House of Lords:* Raised to the peerage as Baron Fink, of Northwood in the County of Middlesex 2011. Member: Refreshment 2014, Audit 2014-, EU Financial Affairs Sub-committee 2016. *Other:* Treasurer, Conservative Party 2010-12, 2012-13.

Other: Trustee: ARK (Absolute Return for Kids), Mayor's Fund for London; Chair, board of governors, Oxford Centre for Hebrew and Jewish Studies; Chair Emeritus, board of governors, Burlington Danes Academy; Non-executive director, British Pearl 2016-; Member, Institute of Chartered Accountants 1982; Hon. Fellow, King's College London 2011.

Recreations: Skiing, golf.

The Lord Fink, House of Lords, London SW1A 0PW
Tel: 020 7219 5353

CONSERVATIVE

FINKELSTEIN, LORD

FINKELSTEIN (Life Baron), Daniel William Finkelstein; cr 2013. Born 30 August 1962; Son of late Prof Ludwik Finkelstein OBE and Mirjam Emma Weiner; Married Dr Nicola Ruth 1993 (3 sons).

Education: Hendon Preparatory School; University College School; London School of Economics (BSc economics 1984); City University (MSc 1986).

Non-political career: Political adviser to Dr David Owen MP as Leader of the Social Democrat Party 1986-91; Journalist, *Network* Magazine 1987-89; Editor, Connexion 1989-92; Associate editor, *New Moon* Magazine 1990-97; Director: Social Market Foundation 1992-95, Conservative Party Research Department 1995-98, Policy Unit, Conservative Central Office 1999-2001; *The Times*: Associate editor 2001-10, Comment editor 2004-08, Chief leader writer 2008-, Executive editor 2010-; Columnist, *Jewish Chronicle* 2004-; Editor, Comment Central, *Times* Online 2006-; Chair, Policy Exchange 2012-14.

Political career: *House of Commons:* Contested (SDP/All) Brent East 1987 and (Conservative) Harrow West 2001 general elections. *House of Lords:* Raised to the peerage as Baron Finkelstein, of Pinner in the County of Middlesex 2013. Member: Works of Art 2014-16, Lord Speaker's Advisory Panel on Works of Art 2017-19, Communications 2017. *Other:* Member, national committee, SDP 1986-90.

Other: Enterprise Europe: Chair 1990-95, Board member 1990-; Non-executive director, Equitable Life Assurance Society; OBE 1997.

The Lord Finkelstein OBE, House of Lords, London SW1A 0PW
Tel: 020 7219 5353 *Twitter:* @Dannythefink

CROSSBENCH

FINLAY OF LLANDAFF, BARONESS

FINLAY OF LLANDAFF (Life Baroness), Ilora Gillian Finlay; cr 2001. Born 23 February 1949; Daughter of Charles Beaumont Benoy Downman and Thaïs Helène, née Barakan; Married Andrew Yule Finlay CBE 1972 (1 son 1 daughter).

Education: Wimbledon High School, London; St Mary's Hospital Medical School, London University (MB BS 1972); French.

Non-political career: General practitioner 1981-86; Consultant, Palliative medicine 1987-; Velindre NHS Trust Cancer Centre, Cardiff 1994-; National Cancer Forum 1997-2000; Vice-dean, School of Medicine, University of Wales College of Medicine 2000-05.

Political career: *House of Lords:* Raised to the peerage as Baroness Finlay of Llandaff, of Llandaff in the County of South Glamorgan 2001. Contested Crossbench Convener election 2011; Deputy Chairman of Committees 2017-; Deputy Speaker 2018-. Member: Science and Technology 2003-08, Science and Technology Sub-committees: I (Fighting Infection) 2003, II (Science and the Regional Development Agencies) 2003, I (Science and International Agreements) 2003-04, I (Ageing) 2004-05, Assisted Dying for the Terminally Ill Bill 2004-05, Mental Health Bill 2004-05, Science and Technology Sub-committees: I (Avian Flu) 2005-06, II (Conservation Science) 2005-06; Chair, Science and Technology Sub-committee I (Allergy) 2006-07; Co-opted member: Science and Technology Sub-committee II (Genomic Medicine) 2008-09, Science and Technology (Pandemic Influenza) 2008-09; Member: Public Service and Demographic Change 2012-13, Built Environment 2015-16, Procedure/Procedure and Privileges 2019-. *Other:* Non-executive director, Gwent Health Authority 1995-2001; Member: Cancer Strategy Board, National Assembly for Wales 2006-07, End of Life Care Strategy Board, Department of Health 2007-09, UK Drugs Policy Commission 2008-13; Cardiff

Metropolitan University: Governor 2012-14, Chair of Board of Governors 2018-; Chair, National Mental Capacity Forum 2015-; Bevan Commissioner, Wales 2017-; European Advisory Group, Welsh Government 2018-; Vice-chair, NICE guideline on myalgic encephalitis/chronic fatigue syndrome 2019-.

Political interests: Medical ethics, Welsh affairs, health and medicine; China (Hong Kong), France, Netherlands, Spain.

Other: President, vice-president, patron of several organisations, especially concerned with palliative care, end of life care, multiple sclerosis, music and Foodbanks Cymru; Member, Expert Advisory Group on Cancers 1993-97; Chair, Association for Palliative Medicine 1995-98; President: Medical Women's Federations 2001-02, Chartered Society of Physiotherapy 2002-; Member, Science Committee, Cancer Research UK 2002-04; Vice-president, Marie Curie Cancer Care 2004-; Associate, Girls' Day School Trust 2005-; Vice-President, Full Stop 2005-07; President, Royal Society of Medicine 2006-08; Chair: Palliative Care Strategy (Wales) Implementation Board 2008-14, Palliative Care Implementation Group Wales 2008-18; Member, BMA Medical Ethics Committee 2009-; Director (non-remunerated), Living and Dying Well 2010-; Chair, Royal College of General Practitioners' Inquiry into Generalism 2011; Chair: Welsh Medical and Dental Academic Advisory Board 2012-14, UK Bioethics Programme (UNESCO) 2015-, National Council for Palliative Care 2015-17; Vice-president, Hospice UK 2017-; Founder patron, SKIP (Students for Kids International Project); Royal College of Physicians; Royal College of General Practitioners; Royal Society of Medicine; Association for Palliative Medicine, Great Britain and Ireland; President, British Medical Association 2014-15; Marie Curie Care, Changing Faces, MNDA, MS Society, Trussell Trust, Hospice UK, NSPCC Wales; FRCP, FRCGP, F Med Sci; Fellow, Academy of Medical Sciences 2014; Honorary Fellow: Royal Society of Medicine 2009, Royal College of Surgeons Faculty of Dentistry 2009; Learned Society of Wales 2010; College of Emergency Medicine 2014; Faculty of Public Health 2015; Honorary Doctor of Science: Glamorgan University, University of Wales Trinity St David, Worcester University; Honorary Fellow: Cardiff University, University of Wales Institute, Cardiff; Johanna Bijtel Professor, Gröningen University, Netherlands 2000-02; Honorary Professorial Associate, University of Melbourne 1996-2001; Welsh Woman of the Year 1996-97; Peer of the Year, Women in Public Life Awards 2008; Lifetime Achievement, Livery Company of Wales 2014 Innovator, Grassroots Diplomat 2015; Royal College of Physicians Clinical Care Excellence 2019. Patron, Llandaff Rowing Club.

Publications: Co-author Care of the Dying – a clinical handbook (Churchill Livingstone, 1984); Co-editor: Medical Humanities, (BMJ Press, 2001), The Effective Management of Cancer Pain (Aesculapius Medical Press, 2000, 2001); Oral Care in Advanced Disease (Oxford University Press, 2005); Communication in Cancer (Oxford University Press, 2010); Many chapters in books and papers on palliative medicine, medical education, ethics and service provision.

Recreations: Cycling, family events.

The Baroness Finlay of Llandaff, House of Lords, London SW1A 0PW
Tel: 020 7219 6693 *Email:* finlayi@parliament.uk
Email: finlayig@cardiff.ac.uk

CONSERVATIVE

FINN, BARONESS

FINN (Life Baroness), Simone Jari Finn; cr 2015. Born 10 June 1968; Daughter of Professor Jan Kubes and Morwenna Talfan Davies; Married Alex 1996 (1 son 1 daughter).

Education: Lady Margaret Hall, Oxford (BA history); French.

Non-political career: Manager, Coopers & Lybrand/PricewaterhouseCoopers 1991-98; Senior accountant, Financial Service Authority 1998-2001; Adviser on industrial relations to Cabinet Office 2010-11; Special adviser: to Francis Maude MP as Minister for the Cabinet Office and Paymaster General, Cabinet Office 2012-15, to Lord Maude of Horsham as Minister of State for Trade and Investment, Foreign and Commonwealth Office and Department for Business, Innovation and Skills 2015-16, to Sajid Javid MP as Secretary of State for Business, Innovation and Skills 2016; Partner, Francis Maude Associates.

Political career: *House of Lords:* Raised to the peerage as Baroness Finn, of Swansea in the County of West Glamorgan 2015. Member: Secondary Legislation Scrutiny 2017-19, SLSC Sub-committee A 2018-19, EU External Affairs Sub-committee 2019-20, EU Security and Justice Sub-committee 2020-. *Other:* Member, Conservative Party's Implementation Team

2009-10; Director, Conservative Party Foundation Ltd. Non-executive Board Member, Cabinet Office 2020-.

Political interests: Industrial relations, efficiency, Civil Service reform and diversity; China, Czech Republic, Hong Kong, India, Indonesia, Japan, Singapore, USA.

Other: Member: Advisory Board, Centre for Politics, Philosophy and Law, King's College London; Development Committee, Clean Break; Trustee, Demos; Board Member, Open Europe; Member, Audit Committee, Arbuthnot Latham & Co Ltd; Independent Non-executive Director and Chair of Audit and Risk Committees, Morses Club; ACA; ICAEW.

The Baroness Finn, House of Lords, London SW1A 0PW
Tel: 020 7219 3000 *Email:* finns@parliament.uk

CROSSBENCH

FLATHER, BARONESS

FLATHER (Life Baroness), Shreela Flather; cr. 1990. Born 13 February 1934; Daughter of Aftab and Krishna Rai; Married Gary Flather 1965 (2 sons).

Education: Attended schools in Buenos Aires, Delhi and Rio de Janerio; University College, London (LLB 1956); Hindi, some Spanish.

Non-political career: Called to the Bar, Inner Temple 1962; Infant teacher, ILEA 1965-67; Teacher of English as second language: Altwood Comprehensive School, Maidenhead 1968-74, Broadmoor Hospital 1974-78; Member, Committee of Management, Servite Houses Ltd 1987-94; Director: Meridian Broadcasting (MAI) Ltd 1990-2000, Marie Stopes International 1996-2017, Cable Corporation 1997-2000; Director, Kiss FM and Magic FM 1999-2002; Chair and Director, Club Asia 2002-06; Member, LWT Advisory Board 1993-2000; Chair, Star FM.

Political career: *House of Lords:* Raised to the peerage as Baroness Flather, of Windsor and Maidenhead in the Royal County of Berkshire 1990. Member: European Communities Sub-committee C 1990-95, Medical Ethics 1993-94, Intergovernmental Organisations 2007-08. *Other:* Member: Conservative Women's National Committee 1978-88, Anglo-Asian Conservative Society 1979-83, National Union Executive Committee, Conservative Party 1989-90; Resigned the Conservative Whip December 1998, rejoined November 1999, moved to Crossbenches 2008. JP, Maidenhead 1971-90; Royal Borough of Windsor and Maidenhead: Councillor 1976-91, Mayor 1986-87; Senior posts in numerous organisations involved in refugee, community, carer, race relations and prison work, including: Member: Commission for Racial Equality 1980-86, BBC South and East Regional Advisory Council 1987-89, Social Security Advisory Committee 1987-90; Vice-chair, Refugee Council 1991-94; Governor, Commonwealth Institute 1993-98; President, Ethics Committee Broadmoor Hospital 1993-97; DL, Berkshire 1994-2009; Chair, Alcohol Education and Research Council 1995-2001; Joint President, Family Planning Association 1995-98; Member, Council of University College London 2000-06.

Political interests: Role of four million Indians in two World Wars, empowerment of women in South Asia and Africa, assisting family planning financially and with advocacy, negative impact of sharia law, disability of children from first cousin marriages; Africa, Indian sub-continent, including Burma.

Other: UK Representative, EU Advisory Commission on Racism and Xenophobia 1995-97; UK Member, Economic and Social Committee, European Community 1987-90; Trustee: Hillingdon Hospital 1990-98, Rajiv Gandhi (UK) Foundation 1993-2002; Member, Council, Winston Churchill Memorial Trust 1993-2008; Patron, Cedar Centre (community centre Isle of Dogs) 1994-2007; Member, Council of St George's House, Windsor Castle 1996-2002; Chair, Memorial Gates Trust (memorial on Constitution Hill) 1998-2009; Fellow, Industry and Parliament Trust 1998; Bookpower (providing low priced educational texts in developing countries) 2001-07; Pan African Health Foundation (auto disable syringe factory in Nigeria) 2004-; Member, Advisory Council, American Intercontinental University 2004-06; Patron: Population Matters 2011-, L'orchestre du Monde 2014-, Asian Women's Resource Centre 2014-, Commonwealth Countries League Education Fund, Corona Worldwide; Vice-president, Townswomen's Guilds; Associate Member, National Secular Society; Patron, Women's Council; Chair and Founder, Women Matter 2015-; Memorial Gates, Fistula Hospital Addis Ababa, Trustee Friends of Seva Mandir; Fellow: University College London, Royal Society of Arts; Honorary DUniv, Open University 1994; Honorary LLD, Leeds University 2008; Honorary Doctorate, Northampton University 2010; Asian of the Year, *Asian Who's Who* 1996;

Asian Jewel Award 2003; Lifetime Achievement Award, Global NRI Institute 2011; Lifetime Achievement Award, GG2 2012; Pravasi Diwas Samman by President of India 2009.

Publications: Woman: Acceptable Exploitation for Profit (2010).

Recreations: Reading, cinema, travel.

The Baroness Flather DL, House of Lords, London SW1A 0PW
Tel: 020 7219 5353
Tel: 01628 625408

CONSERVATIVE

FLEET, BARONESS

FLEET (Life Baroness), Veronica Judith Colleton Wadley; cr 2020. Born 28 February 1952; Daughter of Neville John Pierce Wadley and Anne Hawise Colleton Wadley; Married Tom Bower 1985 (1 daughter 1 son 2 stepsons).

Education: Francis Holland School; Benenden School.

Non-political career: Journalist 1971-1986: *Mail on Sunday*, *Telegraph Magazine*, Capital Radio, Freelance writer/editor in Southern and East Africa, Mafeking Mail, UPITN; Deputy Editor/Features Editor, *Daily Telegraph* 1986-96; Deputy Editor/Assistant Editor, *Daily Mail* 1996-2002; Editor, *Evening Standard* 2002-09; Senior adviser to Boris Johnson as Mayor of London 2012-16.

Political career: *House of Lords:* Raised to the peerage as Baroness Fleet, of Hampstead in the London Borough of Camden 2020. *Other:* Governor: Yehudi Menuhin School 2012-, Shoreditch Park Academy 2019-; Chair, Department for Education's Expert Panel for the Model Music Curriculum 2019-.

Political interests: Music, arts, creative industries, education, volunteering.

Other: Chair, Arts Council London and Board member, Arts Council England 2010-18; Independent director, *Times* Newspapers 2011-20; Chair and co-founder, London Music Fund 2011-; Non-executive director, Berkeley Group 2012-21; Board member: City of London Education Board 2016-20, Royal College of Music 2018-; Board trustee, ABRSM 2020-; CBE 2019.

Recreations: Music, theatre, swimming, walking, ski-ing, cooking for family and friends.

The Baroness Fleet CBE, House of Lords, London SW1A 0PW
Tel: 020 7219 3000 *Email:* fleet@parliament.uk

CONSERVATIVE

FLIGHT, LORD

FLIGHT (Life Baron), Howard Emerson Flight; cr 2011. Born 16 June 1948; Son of late Bernard Flight and late Doris Flight; Married Christabel Norbury 1973 (1 son 3 daughters).

Education: Brentwood School, Essex; Magdalene College, Cambridge (MA economics 1969); University of Michigan, USA (Power exchange scholar, MBA 1971); French.

Non-political career: Investment adviser, N M Rothschild 1970-73; Manager: Cayzer Ltd 1973-76, Wardley Ltd (HSBC) Hong Kong 1976-78, Merchant banking division, Hong Kong Bank, Bombay, India 1978-79; Director, investment division, Guinness Mahon 1979-86; Joint managing director, Guinness Flight Global Asset Management Ltd 1986-99; Investec Asset Management Ltd: Director 1987-, Chairman 1999-2003; Director, Panmure Gordon & Co 2002-07; Chairman: EIS Association 2005-, CIM Investment Management Ltd 2006-, Flight and Partners 2007-; Director, Marechale Capital 2007-; Chairman: Downing Structured Opportunities VCT 1 plc 2009-; Director, Metrobank plc 2010-; Chairman, Aurora Investment Trust plc 2011-; Director: Edge Performance VCT plc 2011-, R5FX; Consultant: TISA, Kinetic Partners, Arden Partners plc; Member, advisory board: Financial Services Forum, Guinness Renewable Energy EIS Fund.

Political career: *House of Commons:* Contested Southwark (Bermondsey) February and October 1974 general elections. MP (Conservative) for Arundel and South Downs 1997-2005; Whip withdrawn March 2005; Shadow Economic Secretary, HM Treasury 1999-2001; Shadow Paymaster General 2001-02; Shadow Chief Secretary to the Treasury 2002-04; Special envoy to City of London 2004-05. Member: Environment, Transport and Regional Affairs 1997-98,

Environment, Transport and Regional Affairs (Environment Sub-Committee) 1997-98, Social Security 1998-99. Joint Secretary, Conservative Party Committee for International Development 1997-98; Joint Chairman, Conservative Party Committee for Hong Kong 1997-2005; Secretary, Conservative Party Committees for: Finance 1999-2005, Social Security 1999-2005. *House of Lords:* Raised to the peerage as Baron Flight, of Worcester in the County of Worcestershire 2011. Member, EU Sub-committee A: (Economic and Financial Affairs and International Trade) 2011-12, (Economic and Financial Affairs) 2012-15; Member: Delegated Powers and Regulatory Reform 2015-19, Economic Affairs Finance Bill Sub-committee 2017, High Speed Rail (West Midlands-Crewe) Bill 2019-20. *Other:* Chair, Cambridge University Conservative Association 1968-69; Vice-chair, Federation of Conservative Students 1969; Conservative City Circle: Chairman 2002-05, President 2006-10; Deputy Chairman, Conservative Party 2004-05; Vice-President, Conservatives for Britain 2015-16. Member, HMG Tax Consultative Committee to HM Treasury 1985-92; Commissioner, Guernsey Financial Services Commission 2005-20; Governor and trustee, Brentwood School.

Political interests: Taxation, pensions, economic policy, farming, charities, venture capital, EMU, private finance initiative; China, India, South East Asia, USA.

Other: Trustee, Elgar Foundation 1979-; Fellow, Royal Society of Arts; Advisory Board, Institute for Economic Affairs; Chairman, Enterprise Investment Scheme Association 2005-; Trustee, Africa Research Institute 2006-; Council Member, Centre for Policy Studies 2008-; Chairman: 1900 Club 2008-18, National Trust Croome Court Appeal Committee 2009-; Worcester Porcelein Museum, Wedgewood Collection Trust, Magdalene College Cambridge; Liveryman, Carpenters' Company; Freedom, City of London 1999. Carlton, Pratt's, Boodles Club; Marden (Skiing).

Publications: All You Need to Know About Exchange Rates (1988).

Recreations: Skiing, classical music, antique collecting, gardening.

The Lord Flight, House of Lords, London SW1A 0PW
Tel: 020 7219 5353 *Email:* flighth@parliament.uk
Tel: 020 7222 7559 *Email:* hflight@btinternet.com

CONSERVATIVE

FOOKES, BARONESS

FOOKES (Life Baroness), Janet Evelyn Fookes; cr. 1997. Born 21 February 1936; Daughter of late Lewis Fookes, company director, and late Evelyn Fookes, née Holmes.

Education: Hastings and St Leonards Ladies' College; Hastings High School for Girls; Royal Holloway College, London University (BA history 1957).

Non-political career: History and English teacher in independent schools 1958-70.

Political career: *House of Commons:* MP (Conservative) for Merton and Morden 1970-74, for Plymouth Drake 1974-97; Deputy Speaker and Second Deputy Chairman of Ways and Means 1992-97; Sponsored as Private Member's Bill: Sexual Offences Act 1985, Dangerous Dogs Act 1989. Chair, Education, Arts and Home Affairs sub-committee 1975-79; Member: Panel of Chairs 1976-92, Home Affairs 1984-92. *House of Lords:* Raised to the peerage as Baroness Fookes, of Plymouth in the County of Devon 1997. Deputy Chair of Committees 2002-; Deputy Speaker 2002-; Contested Lord Speaker election 2006. Member: Consolidation, Etc, Bills Joint Committee 2000-10, Hybrid Instruments 2002-10; Chair, Refreshments 2003-07; Member: Crossrail Bill 2008, Communications 2010-15; Delegated Powers and Regulatory Reform: Member 2013-15, Chair 2015-17; Member: Bribery Act 2010 2018-19, Constitution 2019-. *Other:* Member, Association of Conservative Peers. County Borough of Hastings: Councillor 1960-61, 1963-70, Chair, Education Committee 1967-70; DL, East Sussex -2001.

Political interests: Health, defence, animal welfare, equal opportunities; Canada, New Zealand.

Other: Fellow, Industry and Parliament Trust 1978; Member: Commonwealth War Graves Commission 1987-97, Council of Management, College of St Mark and St John 1989-2004; Chair, Ambassadors group, Tomorrow's People 1998-2016; Member, Armed Forces Parliamentary Scheme 2001-; Governor, Kelly College, Tavistock 2002-14; President, War Widows Association of Great Britain 2002-; RSPCA, SSAFA, Fellowship of St Nicholas, NSPCC, National Trust, Royal Horticultural Society; Worshipful Company of Gardeners 2005-; Hon. Freedom, City of Plymouth 2000; Freedom, City of London 2005; Hon. Fellow, Royal Holloway; Honorary DLitt, Plymouth University; Honorary fellow, Royal Holloway College; DBE 1989.

Recreations: Swimming, gardening, theatre, yoga, opera.

The Baroness Fookes DBE, House of Lords, London SW1A 0PW
Tel: 020 7219 5899 *Email:* fookesj@parliament.uk

CROSSBENCH

FORD, BARONESS

FORD (Life Baroness), Margaret Anne Ford; cr 2006. Born 16 December 1957; Daughter of Edward Garland and Susan Garland, née Townsley; Married David Bolger 1990 (1 son 1 daughter from previous marriage 1 stepson).

Education: St Michael's Academy, Kilwinning; Glasgow University (MA arts 1979, MPhil economics 1984).

Non-political career: Local government officer, Cunninghame District Council 1979-82; Scottish organiser, Banking Insurance and Finance Union 1982-87; Management consultant, Price Waterhouse & Co 1987-90; Director, Scottish Homes 1990-93; Founder and managing director, Eglinton Management Centre 1993-99; Founder and chief executive, Good Practice Ltd 2000-07; Managing director, Royal Bank of Canada Capital Markets 2007-09. Branch secretary, NALGO 1979-82; Scottish organiser, BIFU 1982-87.

Political career: *House of Lords:* Raised to the peerage as Baroness Ford, of Cunninghame in North Ayrshire 2006. On leave of absence May 2020-. Member, Political Polling and Digital Media 2017-18. *Other:* Resigned Labour Whip February 2013; Joined Crossbenches October 2016. Non-executive director, Scottish Prison Service 1993-97; Chair, Lothian Health Board 1997-2000; Non-executive director, Gas and Electrical Markets Authority (Ofgem) 2000-04; Chair: English Partnerships 2002-07, Olympic Park Legacy Company 2009-12.

Political interests: Regeneration, housing, planning, energy, public sector reform; Australia, USA.

Other: Member, Scottish Economic Council 1997-2000; Non-executive director: Thus plc 2002-05, Serco plc 2003-10; Chairman, Irvine Bay Urban Regeneration Company 2006-10; Non-executive director, Grainger plc 2008-16; President, British Epilepsy Association 2008-; Chair: May Gurney Integrated Services plc 2011-13, Barchester Healthcare Ltd 2011-15; Non-executive director: Segro plc 2013-, Taylor Wimpey plc 2013-16; Chair: STV plc 2013-, STV Appeal 2013-; Trustee, Tennis Foundation 2013-; Senior independent non-executive director, NewRiver 2017-; Hon. Member, Royal Institute of Chartered Surveyors; Member, Royal Television Society; Epilepsy Action; Fellow, Royal Society of Edinburgh 2015-; D.BA, Napier University; D.Univ, Stirling University.

Publications: Contributor, Anatomy of New Scotland (Mainstream Publishing, 2002); Leadership Development: How Government Works (Audit Scotland, 2005).

Recreations: Family, fine art, music, gardening, sport (all kinds).

The Baroness Ford, House of Lords, London SW1A 0PW
Tel: 020 7219 5439 *Email:* fordm@parliament.uk

CONSERVATIVE

FORSYTH OF DRUMLEAN, LORD

Chair, Select Committee on Economic Affairs

FORSYTH OF DRUMLEAN (Life Baron), Michael Bruce Forsyth; cr. 1999. Born 16 October 1954; Son of John T. Forsyth; Married Susan Clough 1977 (1 son 2 daughters).

Education: Arbroath High School; St Andrews University (MA).

Non-political career: Director, Robert Fleming & Co Ltd 1997-2000; J P Morgan 2000-: Vice-chair, investment banking Europe 2000-02, Deputy chair (UK) 2002-05; Non-executive director: J & J Denholm 2005-, Denholm Industrial Service (Holdings) Ltd 2006-; Evercore Partners: Senior adviser 2006-07, Senior managing director 2007-.

Political career: *House of Commons:* MP (Conservative) for Stirling 1983-97; PPS to Geoffrey Howe as Foreign Secretary 1986-87; Parliamentary Under-Secretary of State, Scottish Office 1987-90; Minister of State: Scottish Office with responsibility for Health, Education, Social Work and Sport 1990-92, Department of Employment 1992-94, Home Office 1994-95;

Secretary of State for Scotland 1995-97. *House of Lords:* Raised to the peerage as Baron Forsyth of Drumlean, of Drumlean in Stirling 1999. Member: Monetary Policy of the Bank of England 2000-01, House of Lords Reform Joint Committee 2002-05, Barnett Formula 2008-09; Economic Affairs: Member 2008-13, 2015-17, Chair 2017-; Member: Soft Power and the UK's Influence 2013-14, Joint Committee on National Security Strategy 2014-15; Economic Affairs Finance Bill Sub-committee: Member 2015-16, 2020-, Chair 2018-20. *Other:* President, St Andrews University Conservative Association 1973-76; Member, Executive Committee, National Union of Conservative and Unionist Associations 1975-77; Chair: Federation of Conservative Students 1976-77, Scottish Conservative Party 1989-90; Vice-President, Conservatives for Britain 2015-16. Councillor, Westminster City Council 1978-83; Member: Commission on Strengthening Parliament 1999-2000, Development Board, National Portrait Gallery 2000-03; Chair, Tax Reform Commission 2005-06.

Political interests: Local government, privatisation, economics, healthcare, education, environment, constitution.

Other: Director, Centre for Policy Studies 2006-; Patron: Craighalbent Centre for Children with motor impairments, Children in Need Institute (UK), working in India 2008-; Vote Leave: Board member 2016, Member, Campaign committee 2016; President, Steam Boat Association of Great Britain; Save the Children, Debra, St Mungus; Highland Park/*The Spectator*: Member to Watch 1993, Parliamentarian of the Year 1996; PC 1995; KB 1997.

Publications: Various pamphlets on privatisation and local government.

Recreations: Mountaineering, photography, gardening, fly-fishing, astronomy.

Rt Hon the Lord Forsyth of Drumlean, House of Lords, London SW1A 0PW
Tel: 020 7219 3000 *Email:* forsythm@parliament.uk

LIBERAL DEMOCRAT

FOSTER OF BATH, LORD

FOSTER OF BATH (Life Baron), Donald Michael Ellison Foster; cr 2015. Born 31 March 1947; Son of late John Foster, vicar, and late Iris Foster, née Ellison; Married Victoria Pettegree 1968 (died 2017) (1 son 1 daughter).

Education: Lancaster Royal Grammar School; Keele University (BSc physics and psychology 1969; CEd 1969); Bath University (MEd 1981); French (enthusiastic).

Non-political career: Science teacher, Sevenoaks School, Kent 1969-75; Science project director, Resources for Learning Development Unit, Avon LEA 1975-80; Education lecturer, Bristol University 1980-89; Management consultant, Pannell Kerr Forster 1989-92; Associate, Global Partners Governance 2016-.

Political career: *House of Commons:* Contested (Liberal/All) Bristol East 1987 general election. MP (Liberal Democrat) for Bath 1992-2010, for Bath (revised boundary) 2010-15; Liberal Democrat: Spokesperson for: Education 1992-95, Education and Employment 1995-97; Principal Spokesperson for: Environment, Transport, the Regions and Social Justice 1999-2001, Transport, Local Government and the Regions 2001-02, Shadow Secretary of State for: Transport 2002-03, Culture, Media and Sport 2003-10; Sponsored Live Music Act 2012; Parliamentary Under-Secretary of State, Department for Communities and Local Government 2012-13; Member, Parliamentary and Political Service Honours Committee 2013-15; Deputy Chief Whip (Comptroller of HM Household) 2013-15. Member: Education and Employment 1996-99, Education and Employment (Education Sub-Committee) 1997-99, Joint Committee on Security 2013-15. Chair, Liberal Democrat Parliamentary Party Committee on Culture, Media and Sport 2010-12. *House of Lords:* Raised to the peerage as Baron Foster of Bath, of Bath in the County of Somerset 2015. Liberal Democrat Shadow Secretary of State for Business and Industrial Strategy 2016-17. Member, Licensing Act 2003 2016-17; Chair, Rural Economy 2018-19; Member: Social and Economic Impact of the Gambling Industry 2019-, EU International Agreements Sub-committee 2020-. *Other:* President, Liberal Democrat Youth and Students 1993-95. Councillor, Avon County Council 1981-89; Executive, Association of County Councils 1985-89; Joint Hon. President, British Youth Council 1992-99.

Political interests: Education, local and regional government, transport, culture, media, sport and tourism, international development; Africa, Iraq.

Other: Vice-chair, British Association for Central and Eastern Europe 1994-97; Trustee, Open School and Education Extra 1993-99; National Campaign for Nursery Education: Vice-chair 1993-99, President 1999-2001; President, British Association for Early Childhood Education

1998-2002; Governor, Westminster Foundation for Democracy 2010-; Member, Olympic Board 2010-12; Water Aid, Patron, Designability; CPhys; MInstP; Honorary Fellow, Bath College of High Education 1995; Honorary Doctor of Letters, Bath University 2016; Sports Parliamentarian of the Year 2011; PC 2010.

Publications: Resource-based Learning in Science (1979); Science With Gas (1981); Co-author: Aspects of Science (1984), Reading About Science (1984), Nuffield Science (1986); Teaching Science 11-13 (1987); From the Three Rs to the Three Cs (2003); Numerous educational and political articles and pamphlets.

Recreations: Classical music, travel, sport, modern ballet.

Rt Hon the Lord Foster of Bath, House of Lords, London SW1A 0PW
Tel: 020 7219 6332 *Email:* fosterdon@parliament.uk *Twitter:* @TheDon_Foster

CONSERVATIVE

FOSTER OF OXTON, BARONESS

FOSTER OF OXTON (Life Baroness), Jacqueline Foster; cr 2021. Born 30 December 1947.

Education: Prescot Girls' Grammar School; French, German.

Non-political career: British Airways 1969-81, 1985-99; Area manager, Horizon tour operator, Austria 1981-85; Consultant and adviser to defence and aviation industries, Brussels 2005-09. Founder member and deputy general secretary, Cabin Crew '89 (trade union for UK airline crew).

Political career: *House of Commons:* Contested Newham South 1992 and Peterborough 1997 general elections. *House of Lords:* Raised to the peerage as Baroness Foster of Oxton, of Oxton in the County of Merseyside 2021. *Other:* MEP for North West 1999-2004, 2009-19: Conservative Spokesperson for Transport and Tourism 1999-2004, 2009-19, Member: Employment and Social Affairs Committee 1999, Women's Rights and Equal Opportunities Committee 1999, ACP-EU Joint Parliamentary Assembly 1999-2004, Regional Policy, Transport and Tourism Committee 2001-04, Improving safety at Sea Committee 2003-04, Transport and Tourism Committee 2009-19, Euro-Mediterranean Parliamentary Assembly Delegation 2009-12, Maghreb and Arab Maghreb Union Delegation 2009-12, Maghreb countries and the Arab Maghreb Union Delegation 2009-12, Australia and New Zealand Delegation 2014-19. President, North-West England Conservative Association.

Political interests: Civil air transport, aerospace and defence, protecting national sovereignty; North West of England.

Other: DBE 2019; Member: Carlton Club, Royal Aeronautical Society (Brussels branch), European Aviation Club, Brussels.

Recreations: Skiing, ice-skating, tennis, walking the dogs.

The Baroness Foster of Oxton DBE, House of Lords, London SW1A 0PW
Twitter: @jfoster2019

LABOUR/
CO-OPERATIVE

FOULKES OF CUMNOCK, LORD

FOULKES OF CUMNOCK (Life Baron), George Foulkes; cr 2005. Born 21 January 1942; Son of late George Horace Foulkes, engineer, and late Jessie Foulkes, principal nursing officer; Married Elizabeth Hope 1970 (2 sons 1 daughter).

Education: Keith Grammar School, Banffshire; Haberdashers' Aske's School; Edinburgh University (BSc psychology 1964) (President, Edinburgh University SRC 1963-64); Conversational Spanish.

Non-political career: President, Scottish Union of Students 1964-66; Director, European League for Economic Co-operation 1966-68; Scottish organiser, European Movement 1968-69; Director: Enterprise Youth 1969-73, Age Concern Scotland 1973-79; Chairman, advisory committee, GovNet 2008-. Territorial Army 1961-64. Member, GMB.

Political career: *House of Commons:* Contested Edinburgh West 1970 and Edinburgh Pentlands October 1974 general elections. MP (Labour) for South Ayrshire 1979-83, for Carrick, Cumnock and Doon Valley 1983-2005; Opposition Frontbench Spokesperson for: Europe 1983-85, Foreign and Commonwealth Affairs 1985-92, Defence, Disarmament and Arms Control

1992-93, Overseas Development 1994-97; Parliamentary Under-Secretary of State, Department of International Development 1997-2001; Minister of State, Scotland Office 2001-02. *House of Lords:* Raised to the peerage as Baron Foulkes of Cumnock, of Cumnock in East Ayrshire 2005. Member, Intelligence and Security Committee 2007-10. Co-opted Member, European Union Sub-committee F (Home Affairs) 2006-07; Member: Joint Committee on National Security Strategy 2010-13, EU Sub-Committee G (Social Policies and Consumer Protection) 2011-12, European Union 2011-15, EU Sub-committee C (External Affairs) 2012-15, Soft Power and the UK's Influence 2013-14, Liaison 2015-19; Procedure/Procedure and Privileges: Alternate Member 2015-18, Member 2018-20; Member: Charities 2016-17, Political Polling and Digital Media 2017-18, Common Frameworks Scrutiny 2020-. *Other:* Scottish Parliament: MSP for Lothians region 2007-11 (as George Foulkes). Chair, Labour Campaign for a Scottish Parliament 1979-97; Member, Co-operative Party; Chair, Scottish Group PLP 2015-17. Councillor: Edinburgh City Council 1970-75, Lothian Regional Council 1974-79; Chair: Lothian Region Education Committee 1974-79, Education Committee, Convention of Scottish Local Authorities 1975-78; JP, Edinburgh 1975.

Political interests: International development, foreign affairs, devolution, energy, human rights, defence, Scotland, financial regulation; Latin America, Caribbean, China, EU, Russia.

Other: Delegate, Parliamentary Assemblies of the Council of Europe and Western European Union 1979-80; Executive Committee, Commonwealth Parliamentary Association (UK Branch): Member 1989-97, 2011-15, Vice-chair 2015-; Executive member: British Section, Inter-Parliamentary Union 1989-97, Socialist International 2004-08; Member, Parliamentary Assembly, Council of Europe 2016-; Rector's assessor, Edinburgh University 1968-71; Director, Co-operative Press 1990-97; Chair, John Wheatley Centre 1990-97; Trustee, Commonwealth Parliamentary Association Funds 1998-2008; Chair, Heart of Midlothian FC 2004-05; President, Caribbean Council 2011-16, Treasurer, Climate Parliament 2015-16; Chair, Age Scotland 2016-; Age Scotland, Ayrshire Hospice, Garvald Edinburgh; Wilberforce Medal 1998; Order of Merit of Duarte, Sanchez & Mejia (Dominican Republic); PC 2000. Royal Scots Club.

Publications: Editor, 80 Years On (History of Edinburgh University SRC); Chapters in: Scotland – A Claim of Right, Football and the Commons People.

Recreations: Boating, Heart of Midlothian FC season ticket holder and shareholder.

Rt Hon the Lord Foulkes of Cumnock, House of Lords, London SW1A 0PW
Tel: 020 7219 3474 *Email:* foulkesg@parliament.uk *Twitter:* @GeorgeFoulkes

LORD SPEAKER

FOWLER, LORD

Lord Speaker

FOWLER (Life Baron), Peter Norman Fowler; cr. 2001. Born 2 February 1938; Son of late N F and Katherine Fowler; Married Fiona Poole, née Donald 1979 (2 daughters).

Education: King Edward VI School, Chelmsford; Trinity Hall, Cambridge (BA economics and law 1961, MA).

Non-political career: *The Times*: Special correspondent 1961-66, Home affairs correspondent 1966-70; Non-executive director, NFC plc 1990-97; Non-executive chair: Midland Independent Newspapers 1991-98, National House Building Council 1992-98, Regional Independent Media 1998-2002, Numark plc 1998-2005, Aggregate Industries plc 2000-06; Non-executive director, Holcim Ltd 2006-09; Member, Advisory Council, Electra QMC Europe Development Capital Fund plc 2006-08; Non-executive director, ABTA 2009-16. Commissioned national service, Essex Regiment 1956-58.

Political career: *House of Commons:* MP (Conservative) for Nottingham South 1970-74, for Sutton Coldfield February 1974-2001; PPS to Minister of State for Northern Ireland 1972-74; Opposition Spokesperson for Home Affairs 1974-75; Chief Opposition Spokesperson for: Social Services 1975-76, Transport 1976-79; Minister of Transport 1979-81; Secretary of State for: Transport 1981, Social Services 1981-87, Employment 1987-90; Shadow Secretary of State for: Environment, Transport and the Regions 1997-98, the Home Department 1998-99. *House of Lords:* Raised to the peerage as Baron Fowler, of Sutton Coldfield in the County of West Midlands 2001. Lord Speaker 2016-; Chair, House of Lords Commission 2016-. Chair: Review of the BBC Charter 2005-06, Communications 2007-10, HIV and AIDS in the UK 2010-11; Member, Procedure/Procedure and Privileges 2016-. *Other:* Chair, Cambridge University Conservative Association 1960; Editorial board, *Crossbow* 1962-70; Vice-chair,

North Kensington Conservative Association 1967-68; Chair: East Midlands Conservative Political Centre 1970-73, Conservative Party 1992-94; Member, Executive Association of Conservative Peers 2001-04; Vice-chairman, Association of Conservative Peers 2005-10.

Political interests: HIV/AIDS, media; Middle East.

Other: President, Commonwealth Parliamentary Association (UK Branch) 2016-; Hon. President, Inter-Parliamentary Union, British Group 2016-; Council member, Bow Group 1967-69; Patron, British HIV Association 2011-; Chairman: Thomson Foundation, Hansard Society 2015-; Honorary Bencher, The Inner Temple 2018; Honorary Fellowship, Trinity Hall, Cambridge; Honorary Doctorate: City of Birmingham University 2011, Hull University 2019; PC 1979; Kt 1990. Garrick, Hurlingham, Seaview Yacht Club.

Publications: After the Riots (1979); Ministers Decide (1991); A Political Suicide (2008); AIDS: Don't Die of Prejudice (2014).

Rt Hon the Lord Fowler, House of Lords, London SW1A 0PW
Tel: 020 7219 6444 *Email:* lordspeaker@parliament.uk *Twitter:* @LordSpeaker

LIBERAL DEMOCRAT

FOX, LORD

Liberal Democrat Lords Spokesperson for Business, Energy and Industrial Strategy

FOX (Life Baron), Christopher Francis Fox; cr 2014. Born 27 September 1957; Son of Andrew and Elizabeth Fox; Married Sarah (1 daughter).

Education: Minster School, Leominster; Imperial College (BSc analytical chemistry and geology 1979) (President, Imperial College Students' Union 1980).

Non-political career: Field Engineer, Schlumberger Oilfield Services 1981-85; Editor, Offshore Engineer magazine 1985-90; Communications manager, Schlumberger Inc 1990-98; Director of corporate relations, Tate & Lyle 1998-2005; Director of communications, Smiths Group 2005-09; Director of group communications, GKN plc 2012-17; Executive chair, Vulpes Advisory Ltd 2017-.

Political career: *House of Lords:* Raised to the peerage as Baron Fox, of Leominster in the County of Herefordshire 2014. Liberal Democrat: Shadow Secretary of State/Lords Spokesperson for: Enterprise/Energy 2017-19, Business and Industrial Strategy 2017-19, Environment and Climate Change 2019, Business, Energy and Industrial Strategy 2020-. Member: Science and Technology 2015-19, Economic Affairs 2019-. *Other:* Chief Executive, Liberal Democrats 2009-11. Councillor, Hounslow Borough Council 1994-98.

Political interests: Engineering, manufacturing, technology, education, business.

Other: Ambassador, Wave Trust 2013-. MCC.

Recreations: Season ticket holder, Arsenal FC.

The Lord Fox, House of Lords, London SW1A 0PW
Tel: 020 7219 3215 *Email:* foxc@parliament.uk

NON-AFFILIATED

FOX OF BUCKLEY, BARONESS

FOX OF BUCKLEY (Life Baroness), Claire Regina Fox; cr 2020. Born 5 June 1960.

Education: St Richard Gwyn High School, Flint; Warwick University (BA English and American literature 1981).

Non-political career: English lecturer, West Herts College 1991-97; Founder and director, Academy of Ideas 2000-; Director, Battle of Ideas 2005-.

Political career: *House of Lords:* Raised to the peerage as Baroness Fox of Buckley, of Buckley in the County of Flintshire 2020. *Other:* MEP (Brexit Party) for North West 2019-20.

Publications: No Strings Attached! Why arts funding should say no to instrumentalism (2007); I STILL Find That Offensive! (2018).

The Baroness Fox of Buckley, House of Lords, London SW1A 0PW
Tel: 020 7219 3000 *Email:* foxcr@parliament.uk
Email: clairefox@academyofideas.org.uk Website: clairefox.org.uk *Twitter:* @Fox_Claire

CONSERVATIVE

FRAMLINGHAM, LORD

FRAMLINGHAM (Life Baron), Michael Nicholson Lord; cr 2011. Born 17 October 1938; Son of late John Lord, headmaster; Married Jennifer Childs 1965 (1 son 1 daughter).

Education: William Hulme's Grammar School, Manchester; Christ's College, Cambridge (MA agriculture 1962) (Cambridge Rugby Blue).

Non-political career: Farmer and agriculture tutor 1962-66; Director, Power Line Maintenance Ltd 1966-68; Founded Lords Tree Services Ltd 1968; Aboricultural Consultant 1983.

Political career: *House of Commons:* Contested Manchester Gorton 1979 general election. MP (Conservative) for Central Suffolk 1983-97, for Central Suffolk and North Ipswich 1997-2010; PPS to John MacGregor: as Minister of Agriculture, Fisheries and Food 1984-85, as Chief Secretary to the Treasury 1985-87; Second Deputy Chairman, Ways and Means and Deputy Speaker 1997-2010; Contested Speaker elections 2000, 2009. Member: Chairmen's Panel 1997-2010, Court of Referees 1997-2010, Standing Orders 1998-2010, Unopposed Bills (Panel) 2000-10. *House of Lords:* Raised to the peerage as Baron Framlingham, of Eye in the County of Suffolk 2011. *Other:* North Bedfordshire Borough Council: Councillor 1974-77, Chair, Policy Committee 1974-77; Bedfordshire County Council: Councillor 1981-83, Chair, Further Education Committee 1981-83.

Political interests: Agriculture, forestry, environment.

Other: Parliamentary delegate, Council of Europe and Western European Union 1987-91; Member, Executive Committee, Inter-Parliamentary Union British Group 1995-97; President, Arboricultural Association 1989-95; Captain, Parliamentary Golfing Society 1999-2002; FArbA; Kt 2001. Hawks Club.

Recreations: Golf, sailing, gardening.

The Lord Framlingham, House of Lords, London SW1A 0PW
Tel: 020 7219 5353

CONSERVATIVE

FRASER OF CRAIGMADDIE, Baroness

FRASER OF CRAIGMADDIE (Life Baroness), Stephanie Mary Fraser; cr 2021. Married Jamie Fraser 1997 (3 daughters 1 son).

Education: Stowe School, Buckingham; Arts Education School, Tring Park; Trinity College, Cambridge (MA history 1990); Benesh Institute of Choreology (Diploma benesh notation 1995).

Non-political career: Account director, J Walter Thompson 1990-95; English National Ballet: Choreologist 1995-97, Development director 1997-2000; Head of development, Scottish Ballet 2005-11; Chief Executive, Cerebral Palsy Scotland 2012-20.

Political career: *House of Commons:* Contested Cumbernauld, Kilsyth and Kirkintilloch East 2010 general election. *House of Lords:* Raised to the peerage as Baroness Fraser of Craigmaddie, of Craigmaddie in the County of Stirlingshire 2021. *Other:* Contested Strathkelvin and Bearsden constituency 2007 and 2011 Scottish Parliament elections. National Advisory Committee for Neurological Conditions, Scottish Government: Deputy Chair 2016-19, Chair 2019-.

Other: Member, Royal Academy of Dance; Director, Dance House Glasgow 2011-16; Executive Board Member, Neurological Alliance of Scotland 2013-; Director, Horsecross Arts 2015-19; Board Member: Office of the Scottish Charity Regulator 2018-, Creative Scotland 2019-.

Recreations: Scuba diving, baking.

The Baroness Fraser of Craigmaddie, House of Lords, London SW1A 0PW
Twitter: @StephanieFraser

CONSERVATIVE

FRASER OF CORRIEGARTH, LORD

FRASER OF CORRIEGARTH (Life Baron), Alexander Andrew Macdonell Fraser; cr 2016. Born 2 December 1946; Son of Lord Fraser of Tullybelton; Married Sarah Joanna Jones 1982 (divorced); Married Rebecca Shaw-Mackenzie 2010.

Education: Eton College; St John's College, Oxford (MA philosophy, politics and economics); French.

Non-political career: Worked in the City, including Vickers da Costa, Sun Hung Kai Securities; Director, Barings Bank; Chief executive, Baring Securities; Director, Asia Frontier Capital Ltd.

Political career: *House of Lords:* Raised to the peerage as Baron Fraser of Corriegarth, of Corriegarth in the County of Inverness 2016. Member: EU Financial Affairs Sub-committee 2017-18, EU External Affairs Sub-committee 2019-20, EU International Agreements Sub-committee 2020. *Other:* Treasurer, Conservative Party 2015-16.

Political interests: Financial affairs, defence, Scotland; China, North Korea, Scotland, Vietnam.

Other: Treasurer, Better Together Campaign 2013-14; New Foundation Fellow, Eton College; Member: Court of Benefactors, Oxford University, Queen's Body Guard for Scotland, Royal Company of Archers 1996-. Pratt's, White's, Brooks's, Leander Club.

The Lord Fraser of Corriegarth, House of Lords, London SW1A 0PW
Tel: 020 7219 3000
Email: andrewfraser.1946@gmail.com

CONSERVATIVE

FREUD, LORD

FREUD (Life Baron), David Anthony Freud; cr 2009. Born 24 June 1950; Son of late Anton Freud and late Annette Freud, née Krarup; Married Priscilla Dickinson 1978 (1 son 2 daughters).

Education: Whitgift School, Croydon; Merton College, Oxford (BA philosophy, politics and economics 1972).

Non-political career: Journalist 1972-83: *Western Mail* 1972-75, *Financial Times* 1976-83; Investment banker, Rowe and Pitman and successors, ultimately UBS AG 1984-2003; Chief executive, Portland Trust 2005-08; Adviser on welfare reform to Secretary of State for Work and Pensions 2008-09. Member, National Union of Journalists 1972-83.

Political career: *House of Lords:* Raised to the peerage as Baron Freud, of Eastry in the County of Kent 2009. Shadow Minister for Welfare Reform and Opposition Spokesperson for Work and Pensions 2009-10; Department for Work and Pensions: Parliamentary Under-Secretary of State (Minister for Welfare Reform) 2010-15, Government Spokesperson 2010-16, Minister of State for Welfare Reform 2015-16.

Political interests: Welfare reform.

Other: Trustee, Jecda Foundation; PC 2015.

Publications: Freud in the City (Bene Factum Publishing, 2006); Reducing Dependency, Increasing Opportunity: Options for the Future of Welfare to Work (Independent Report to DWP).

Recreations: Cycling, swimming, skiing, tennis, history.

Rt Hon the Lord Freud, House of Lords, London SW1A 0PW
Tel: 020 7219 4907 *Email:* freudd@parliament.uk

CROSSBENCH

FREYBERG, LORD

FREYBERG (3rd Baron, UK), Valerian Bernard Freyberg; cr. 1951. Born 15 December 1970; Son of Colonel 2nd Baron, and Ivry Perronelle Katharine Guild; Married Dr Harriet Atkinson 2002 (1 son 2 daughters).

Education: Eton College; Camberwell College of Arts (BA 1994); Slade School of Fine Art (MA 2006).

Non-political career: Artist.

Political career: *House of Lords:* First entered House of Lords 1994; Elected hereditary peer 1999-. Member House of Lords Offices Sub-committees: House of Lords Library and Computers 1995-98, Advisory Panel on Works of Art 1999-2002. *Other:* Member, Design Council 2001-04.

Political interests: Visual arts; New Zealand.

The Lord Freyberg, House of Lords, London SW1A 0PW
Tel: 020 7219 5101 *Email:* freybergv@parliament.uk

CROSSBENCH

FRITCHIE, BARONESS

FRITCHIE (Life Baroness), Irene Tordoff Fritchie; cr 2005. Born 29 April 1942; Daughter of Charles Fennell and Eva, née Tordoff; Married Don Fritchie 1960 (1 son 1 son deceased).

Education: Ribston Hall Grammar School for Girls.

Non-political career: Insurance 1970-76; Training posts Food and Drink Industry Training Board 1976-80; Consultant, Social Ecology Associates 1980-81; Director: Transform Ltd 1981-85, Rennie Fritchie Consultancy 1985-89; Managing director, Working Choices Ltd 1989-91; Consultant, Mainstream Development 1991-; Vice-chair, Stroud and Swindon Building Society 2004-08; Chair, Nominet 2010-; Non-executive, UK SBS 2013.

Political career: *House of Lords:* Raised to the peerage as Baroness Fritchie, of Gloucester in the County of Gloucestershire 2005. Member: Delegated Powers and Regulatory Reform 2007-09, Refreshment 2008-12, Audit 2015-. *Other:* Chair: Gloucester Health Authority 1988-92, South Western Regional Health Authority 1992-94, South and West Regional Health Authority 1994-96; Civil Service Commissioner 1999-2005; Commissioner for Public Appointments 1999-2005; Chair, Independent Appointments Selection Board, Royal Institution of Chartered Surveyors 2007-10; Board member and deputy chair, Scottish Public Services Ombudsman Audit Advisory Board 2007-10; Chair, 2gether NHS Mental Health Foundation Trust 2008-12.

Political interests: China, New Zealand, Turkey, USA.

Other: President and Founder Member, Pennell Initiative, focusing on the health of women in later life 1997-2006; Gloucestershire Ambassador 2000-; Patron: Pied Piper Appeal 2002-, Winston's Wish (grief support for children) 2002-; St Andrew's Ambassador 2004-; Vice-president, British Lung Foundation 2005-10; President, Chronic Pain Policy Coalition 2005-08; Chair, Advisory Board, Web Science Research Initiative 2006-09; Patron, Women in Banking and Finance 2008-12; President, Hospital Caterers Association 2009-10; Chair, Lloyds Bank Foundation England and Wales 2015-; Companion, Institute of Management; Member, Royal Society of Medicine; Pro-chancellor, Southampton University 1998-2007; Chancellor, Gloucestershire University 2012-; Seven honorary doctorates; Two fellowships; DBE 1996.

Publications: Working Choices (Dent, 1988), Co-author: The Business of Assertiveness (BBC Books, 1991), Resolving Conflicts in Organisations (Lemos & Crane, 1998), Career Life Planning – a tutor's guide (Manpower Services Commission), Interpersonal Skills for Managers, a tutor's guide (Manpower Services Commission), Women, Work and Training (Manpower Services Commission); Articles in training and management journals; Member, editorial board, Whitehall & Westminster World.

Recreations: Gardening, writing, reading, babysitting, *The Archers*.

The Baroness Fritchie DBE, House of Lords, London SW1A 0PW
Tel: 020 7219 5353 *Email:* fritchiei@parliament.uk
Tel: 01452 414542/01452 301266 *Email:* renniefritchie@hotmail.com

CONSERVATIVE

FROST, LORD

FROST (Life Baron), David George Hamilton Frost; cr 2020.

Education: Nottingham High School; St John's College, Oxford (MA French and history 1986); French, German, Danish, Greek.

Non-political career: Tax adviser, KPMG 1990-92; Foreign and Commonwealth Office: Various roles in London, including Private Secretary to Permanent Secretary and diplomatic postings to Brussels, New York and Cyprus 1987-2001, Counsellor, British Embassy, Paris 2001-2003, Head, EU-Internal Department, then Director, European Union 2003-06, Ambassador to Denmark 2006-08, Director, Strategy and Policy Planning 2008-10; Director, Europe, Trade and International (on secondment), Department of Business, Innovation and Skills 2010-13; Chief executive, Scotch Whiskey Association 2014-16; Special Adviser to Boris Johnson as Foreign Secretary 2016-18; Chief executive, London Chamber of Commerce and Industry 2019; Sherpa and EU Adviser to Boris Johnson as Prime Minister 2019-21, Prime Minister's Representative on Brexit and International Policy 2021-.

Political career: *House of Lords:* Raised to the peerage as Baron Frost, of Allenton in the County of Derbyshire 2020. On leave of absence September 2020-.

Other: Former member, Scottish Government's Advisory Council on Europe; Advisory council member, Open Europe 2014-16.

The Lord Frost CMG, House of Lords, London SW1A 0PW
Tel: 020 7219 3000 *Twitter:* @DavidGHFrost

CONSERVATIVE

FULLBROOK, BARONESS

FULLBROOK (Life Baroness), Lorraine Fullbrook; cr 2020. Born 1959; Married Mark.

Non-political career: Former press and media adviser; Consultant 2000-.

Political career: *House of Commons:* Contested South Ribble 2005 general election. MP for South Ribble 2010-15. Member, Home Affairs 2010-15. *House of Lords:* Raised to the peerage as Baroness Fullbrook, of Dogmersfield in the County of Hampshire 2020. *Other:* Hart District Council: Councillor 2002-04, Leader 2003-04.

Political interests: Law and order, economy, immigration, EU.

Recreations: Reading, collecting advertising memorabilia, travel.

The Baroness Fullbrook, House of Lords, London SW1A 0PW
Tel: 020 7219 3000

NON-AFFILIATED

GADHIA, LORD

GADHIA (Life Baron), Jitesh Kishorekumar Gadhia; cr 2016. Born 27 May 1971; Married Angeli, née Saujani (1 daughter 1 son).

Education: Cambridge University (BA economics 1991); London Business School (MSc management 2000).

Non-political career: Director, Baring Brothers 1991-98; Managing Director, ABN AMRO 2001-08; Managing Director and Head of Advisory, Barclays Capital 2008-10; Senior Managing Director, Blackstone Group 2010-15.

Political career: *House of Lords:* Raised to the peerage as Baron Gadhia, of Northwood in the County of Middlesex 2016. *Other:* Co-Founder, Conservative Friends of India; Joined House of Lords as Conservative; now sits as Non-affiliated. Non-executive board member: UK Financial Investments Ltd 2014, UK Government Investments Ltd 2016-.

Political interests: Brazil, Russia, India, China, South Africa.

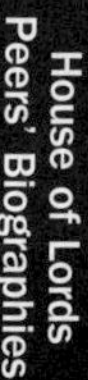

Other: Young Global Leader, World Economic Forum; Trustee: Guy's & St Thomas' Charity 1999-2009, Nesta 2007-13; Advisory Board, City Hindus Network; Vice-Chancellor's Circle of Advisors on India, Cambridge University; Member, UK-India CEO Council 2015-; Board member, BGL Group 2016-.

The Lord Gadhia, House of Lords, London SW1A 0PW
Tel: 020 7219 3000 *Twitter:* @JiteshGadhia

LABOUR

GALE, BARONESS

GALE (Life Baroness), Anita Gale; cr. 1999. Born 28 November 1940; Daughter of late Arthur Gale, coalminer, and late Lillian Gale, housewife; Married Morcom Holmes 1959 (divorced 1983) (2 daughters).

Education: Treherbert Secondary Modern School; Pontypridd Technical College 1970-73; University College of Wales, Cardiff (BSc Econ politics 1976).

Non-political career: Sewing machinist, clothing factory 1956-57; Shop assistant 1957-59; Sewing machinist 1965-69; Wales Labour Party: Women's Officer and Assistant Organiser 1976-84, General Secretary 1984-99. Shop steward, Tailors and Garment Workers' Union 1967-70; GMB Labour Organisers' Branch 1976-: Chair, Wales and South West Section 1986-99, Equal opportunities officer 1991-99.

Political career: *House of Lords:* Raised to the peerage as Baroness Gale, of Blaenrhondda in the County of Mid Glamorgan 1999. Opposition Whip 2010-13; Assistant Opposition Whip 2015-20; Opposition Spokesperson for Women and Equalities 2016-20. Member, Joint Committee on Statutory Instruments 2003-07, 2020-; Co-opted member, EU Sub-Committee G (Social Policy and Consumer Affairs) 2006-09; Member: Works of Art 2009-11, 2013, 2014-16, Refreshment 2012-13, Charities 2016-17, Lord Speaker's Advisory Panel on Works of Art 2017-19. Vice-chair, PLP Departmental Group for Women 2006-10, 2014-. *Other:* Vice-chair, Labour Animal Welfare Society 1995-; Member: Wales Labour Women's Committee 2000-; Labour Women's Network National Committee 2001-09; Joint Vice-chair, Parliamentary Labour Party Women's Committee 2013-. Commissioner for Wales, Women's National Commission 2004-09.

Political interests: Animal welfare, women's equality, children's rights, Wales, devolution, smoking and health, environment; India, Rwanda, Taiwan, USA.

Other: Member: Inter-Parliamentary Union 1999-, Parliamentary Assembly of Council of Europe 2008-10, CPA 2005-; President, Treherbert and District branch, Royal British Legion 2003-; Patron, Kidney Wales Foundation 2008-; President, National Association of Old Age Pensioners in Wales 2010-; Hon. Vice-President, James Whale Fund for Kidney Cancer 2010-; Patron, Bees for Development 2013-; President, Cardiff and District Rhondda Society 2013-; NSPCC, Parkinson's UK, Royal British Legion, AFASIC; Welsh Woman of the Year, Val Feld award 2005.

Recreations: Swimming, walking, travel.

The Baroness Gale, House of Lords, London SW1A 0PW
Tel: 020 7219 8511 *Email:* galea@parliament.uk *Twitter:* @BaronessGale

LIBERAL DEMOCRAT

GARDEN OF FROGNAL, BARONESS

GARDEN OF FROGNAL (Life Baroness), Susan (Sue) Elizabeth Garden; cr 2007. Born 22 February 1944; Daughter of late Henry Button and Peggy, née Heslop; Married Timothy Garden (later Air Marshal Lord Garden KCB, died 2007) 1965 (2 daughters).

Education: Westonbirt School, Gloucestershire; St Hilda's College, Oxford (BA modern and medieval languages 1965, MA); French, Spanish.

Non-political career: Schoolteacher, various posts in England and Germany 1966-84; City & Guilds: Administrator/manager 1988-2000, Consultant 2000-18.

Political career: *House of Commons:* Contested (Liberal Democrat) Finchley and Golders Green 2005 general election. *House of Lords:* Raised to the peerage as Baroness Garden of Frognal, of Hampstead in the London Borough of Camden 2007. Liberal Democrat: Whip

2008-10, Spokesperson for: Children, Schools and Families 2008-09, Innovation, Universities and Skills 2009-10; Government Whip 2010-13, 2014-15; Government Spokesperson for: Business, Innovation and Skills (Higher Education) 2010-13, Culture, Olympics Media and Sport: (Olympics, Sport, Tourism and Lottery) 2010-12, (Women and Equalities) 2014-15, Education 2010-13, 2014-15, Defence 2012-13 Environment, Food and Rural Affairs 2014-15; Liberal Democrat Spokesperson for Higher and Further Education and Skills 2015; Deputy Chairman of Committees 2015-; Deputy Speaker 2018-. EU Sub-committee F (Home Affairs): Co-opted Member 2008-10, Member 2010; Member: Digital Skills 2014, Liaison 2015-19; Member, Highgate Cemetery Bill [HL] 2020-. *Other:* Member, Liberal Democrat Federal Conference Committee 2004-08; President, Camden Liberal Democrats 2007-.

Political interests: Education and skills.

Other: Director, UK-Japan 21st Century Group; St Hilda's College Association 1965-: Chairman 1996-2000; President, Relate central Middlesex 1997-2001; Caseworker, SSAFA Forces Help 2000-05; Vice-chairman: Oxford University Society 2005-07; Council member, Air League 2012-; FRSA 1993; Master World Traders' Livery Company 2008-09; Freedom, City of London; Fellow, City & Guilds 2010; Hon. FCIL 2012; Birkbeck Collge 2018; PC 2015. National Liberal, Royal Air Force Club.

Rt Hon the Baroness Garden of Frognal, House of Lords, London SW1A 0PW
Tel: 020 7219 2747 *Email:* gardens@parliament.uk
14 Alvanley Court, 200 Finchley Road, London NW3 6DL
Email: sue.garden@blueyonder.co.uk

CONSERVATIVE

GARDINER OF KIMBLE, LORD

Parliamentary Under-Secretary of State for Rural Affairs and Biosecurity and Government Spokesperson, Department for Environment, Food and Rural Affairs

GARDINER OF KIMBLE (Life Baron), John Eric Gardiner; cr 2010. Born 17 March 1956; Son of Anthony Gardiner and Heather Gardiner, née Robarts; Married Olivia Musgrave 2004.

Education: Uppingham School, Rutland; Royal Holloway College, London University (BA modern history and politics 1977).

Non-political career: Partner, family farm, Kimble, Buckinghamshire; Private secretary to Chairmen of Conservative Party 1989-95: Kenneth Baker MP 1989-90, Chris Patten MP 1990-92, Sir Norman Fowler MP 1992-94, Jeremy Hanley MP 1994-95, Brian Mawhinney MP 1995; British Field Sports Society/Countryside Alliance: Director of political affairs 1995-2004, Deputy chief executive 2004-10, Executive director and board member 2010-12.

Political career: *House of Lords:* Raised to the peerage as Baron Gardiner of Kimble, of Kimble in the County of Buckinghamshire 2010. Party Whip 2010-12; Government Whip 2012-15; Government Spokesperson for: Cabinet Office 2012-15, Business, Innovation and Skills 2012-13, Energy and Climate Change 2012-15, Culture, Media and Sport 2013-15, Justice (Criminal Justice and Courts Bill) 2014, Environment, Food and Rural Affairs 2015-; Deputy Chief Whip (Captain of the Queen's Bodyguard of the Yeomen of the Guard) 2015-16; Parliamentary Under-Secretary of State Rural Affairs and Biosecurity, Department for Environment, Food and Rural Affairs 2016-. Member: HIV and AIDS in the UK 2010-11, Joint Committee on Security 2013-15, Refreshment 2015-16. *Other:* Member, Quality of Life Commission Rural Affairs Group, Conservative Party 2008-10.

Political interests: Agriculture, rural affairs, housing, conservation, heritage; Australia, Greece, Ireland, Zimbabwe.

Other: Chair, Vale of Aylesbury with Garth and South Berks Hunt 1992-2006; Federation of Associations for Hunting and Conservation of the European Union: Chair (UK) 1998-2012, Treasurer (Europe) 2003-, Treasurer 2012-13; Vice-President: Buckinghamshire Agricultural Association, Suffolk Agricultural Association; President, Buckinghamshire County Show 2007; Vice-president, Peterborough Royal Foxhound Show; Member: British Horse Society, Countryside Alliance, National Farmers' Union, National Trust, Royal Horticultural Society; Honorary Member, Kimblewick Hunt. Pratt's Club.

Recreations: Hunting, gardening.

The Lord Gardiner of Kimble, House of Lords, London SW1A 0PW
Tel: 020 7219 3000 *Email:* gardinerj@parliament.uk

CONSERVATIVE

GARDNER OF PARKES, BARONESS

GARDNER OF PARKES (Life Baroness), Rachel Trixie Anne Gardner; cr. 1981. Born 17 July 1927; Daughter of late Hon. J. J. Gregory McGirr and late Rachel McGirr, OBE, LC; Married Kevin Gardner 1956 (died 2007) (3 daughters).

Education: Monte Sant Angelo College, north Sydney, Australia; East Sydney Technical College; Sydney University (BDS 1954); Cordon Bleu de Paris (Diploma 1956).

Non-political career: Came to UK 1954; Dentist in general practice 1955-90; Director: Gateway Building Society 1987-88, Woolwich Building Society 1988-93; Chair (UK), Plan International 1989-2003.

Political career: *House of Commons:* Contested (Conservative) Blackburn 1970 and North Cornwall February 1974 general elections. *House of Lords:* Raised to the peerage as Baroness Gardner of Parkes, of Southgate in Greater London and of Parkes in the State of New South Wales and Commonwealth of Australia 1981. Deputy Chair of Committees 1999-2002; Deputy Speaker 1999-2002. Member: Information 2003-05, Delegated Powers and Regulatory Reform 2005-09, 2010-13. *Other:* Member: Inner London Executive Council NHS 1966-71, Standing Dental Advisory Committee for England and Wales 1968-76, Industrial Tribunal Panel for London 1974-97; Councillor, Westminster City Council 1968-78: Lady Mayoress of Westminster 1987-88; Councillor, GLC 1970-86; JP, North Westminster 1971-97; Member, Westminster, Kensington and Chelsea Area Health Authority 1974-81; Department of Employment's Advisory Committee on Women's Employment 1980-89; North Thames Gas Consumer Council 1980-82; Member: General Dental Council 1984-86, 1987-91, London Electricity Board 1984-90; Vice-chair, North East Thames Regional Health Authority 1990-94; Trustee, Parliamentary Advisory Council on Transport Safety 1992-98; Vice-President, National House Building Council 1992-99; Chair, Royal Free Hampstead NHS Trust 1994-97.

Political interests: Transport, housing, health, planning, energy; Commonwealth, Latin America, Scandinavia.

Other: British chair, European Union of Women 1978-82; UK representative on the UN Status of Women Commission 1982-88; Member, Executive Committee, Inter-Parliamentary Union, British Group -1997, 2008-11; UK representative to Euro-Mediterranean Women's Forum 2000-02; Governor: Eastman Dental Hospital 1971-80, National Heart Hospital 1974-90; Hon. President, War Widows' Association of Great Britain 1984-87; Sydney University UK Alumni Association: President 1990-2012, Patron 2012; President, British Fluoridation Society 1990-93; Chair, Suzy Lamplugh Trust 1993-96; President, Women's Guild of Friendship 1995-2011; Chair, Cook Society 1996; President, Married Women's Association 1998-2010; Honorary Vice-President, British Legion, Women's Section 2001-06; PLAN International UK, Multiple Sclerosis Trust; Freedom, City of London 1992; DU, Middlesex 1997; Fellow, University of Sydney, Australia 2005; International Achievement Award, Sydney University; Peer Contribution to Central Lobby, *PoliticsHome* awards 2012; Lifetime Achievement Award, Sydney University Alumni Association 2018; AM (Order of Australia) 2003.

Recreations: Family life, gardening, needlework, travel.

The Baroness Gardner of Parkes AM, House of Lords, London SW1A 0PW
Tel: 020 7219 6611 *Email:* gardnert@parliament.uk
25 Caroline Place, London W2 4AN *Tel:* 020 7229 9488

CONSERVATIVE

GARNIER, LORD

GARNIER (Life Baron), Edward Henry Garnier; cr 2018. Born 26 October 1952; Son of late Colonel William d'Arcy Garnier and Hon Mrs Garnier; Married Anna Mellows 1982 (2 sons 1 daughter).

Education: Wellington College, Berkshire; Jesus College, Oxford (BA modern history 1974, MA); College of Law, London; French.

Non-political career: Called to the Bar, Middle Temple 1976; One Brick Court: Barrister 1976-, Head of Chambers 2017-19; QC 1995; Crown Court Recorder 1998-2015; Bencher: Middle Temple 2001, Inn Court of Northern Ireland 2010; QC, 4 Pump Court 2019-.

Political career: *House of Commons:* Contested Hemsworth 1987 general election. MP (Con) for Harborough 1992-2010, for Harborough (revised boundary) 2010-17; PPS to: Alastair Goodlad and David Davis as Ministers of State, Foreign and Commonwealth Office 1994-95, Sir Nicholas Lyell as Attorney-General and Sir Derek Spencer as Solicitor-General 1995-97, Roger Freeman as Chancellor of the Duchy of Lancaster 1996-97; Shadow Minister, Lord Chancellor's Department 1997-99; Shadow Attorney General 1999-2001, 2009-10; Shadow Minister for: Home Affairs 2005-07, Justice 2007-09; Solicitor General 2010-12. Member: Home Affairs 1992-95, Statutory Instruments 1992, Joint Committee on Human Rights 2014-15. Member, Executive, 1922 Committee 2002-05. *House of Lords:* Raised to the peerage as Baron Garnier, of Harborough in the County of Leicestershire 2018. Member: Joint Committee on the Draft Registration of Overseas Entities Bill 2019, Sentencing (Pre-consolidation Amendments) Bill 2019, Common Frameworks Scrutiny 2020-. *Other:* Treasurer, Macleod Group of Conservative MPs 1995-97; Chair, Executive Committee, Society of Conservative Lawyers 2003-05; Founding member, Conservatives for Reform in Europe 2016.

Political interests: Agriculture, defence, foreign affairs, education, constitutional affairs.

Other: Foreign Affairs Forum: Secretary 1988-92, Vice-chair 1992-97; Director, Great Britain-China Centre 1998-2012; Trustee, China-Oxford Scholarship Fund 2005-10, 2013-; Advisory Board, Samaritans 2013-18; Trustee, Prison Reform Trust 2015-; Member, Prosecution Counsel Panel, Serious Fraud Office 2017-; Freedom, City of London 2015; Visiting Parliamentary Fellow, St Antony's College, Oxford 1996-97; Kt 2012; PC 2015. White's Club, Pratt's Club, Beefsteak Club, Vincent's Club Oxford.

Publications: Co-author, Bearing the Standard: Themes for a Fourth Term (1991); Facing the Future (1993); Contributor to: Halsbury's Laws of England (4th edition, 1985), Lissack & Horlick on Bribery (2nd edition, 2014).

Recreations: Shooting, cricket, tennis, skiing, opera, biographical research.

Rt Hon the Lord Garnier QC, House of Lords, London SW1A 0PW
Tel: 020 7219 3000

CONSERVATIVE

GEDDES, LORD

GEDDES (3rd Baron, UK), Euan Michael Ross Geddes; cr. 1942. Born 3 September 1937; Son of 2nd Baron, KBE, DL; Married Gillian Butler 1966 (died 1995) (1 son 1 daughter); married Susan Hunter, née Carter 1996.

Education: Rugby School; Gonville and Caius College, Cambridge (BA history 1961, MA); Harvard Business School 1969.

Non-political career: Trinity College London: Chair 1992-2009, Life President. Royal Navy 1956-58; Lieutenant-Commander, RNR (Rtd).

Political career: *House of Lords:* First entered House of Lords 1975; Elected hereditary peer 1999-; Deputy Chair of Committees 2000-; Deputy Speaker 2002-. Member: European Union 1994-2000, EU Sub-committee A 1985-90, 2000-03; EU Sub-committee B: Member 1990-94, 1995-99, Chair 1996-99; Member: Science and Technology Sub-committee I 1990-92, Refreshment Sub-committee 2000-03, Procedure/Procedure and Privileges 2003-05, 2017-, European Union 2003-07, EU Sub-committee B (Internal Market) 2003-07, Personal Bills 2003-09, Standing Orders (Private Bills) 2003-, Liaison 2003-08, Refreshment 2007-12, Intergovernmental Organisations 2007-08, Joint Committees on: Statutory Instruments 2012, the Rookery South (Resource Recovery Facility) Order 2012-13. *Other:* Executive of Association of Conservative Peers: Member 1999-, Treasurer 2000-.

Political interests: Shipping, Anglo-Chinese relations, immigration, energy, transport, industry, tourism; South East Asia, Hong Kong.

Other: Trustee, Portman; Hon. FTCL. Brooks's, Hong Kong, Noblemen and Gentlemen's Catch Club; Hong Kong Golf.

Recreations: Golf, music, bridge, gardening, shooting.

The Lord Geddes, House of Lords, London SW1A 0PW
Tel: 020 7219 4633 *Fax:* 020 7219 0034 *Email:* geddese@parliament.uk

CROSSBENCH

GEIDT, LORD

GEIDT (Life Baron), Christopher Edward Wollaston MacKenzie Geidt; cr 2017. Born 17 August 1961; Married Emma (2 children).

Education: Dragon School, Oxford; Trinity College, Glenalmond; King's College London (war studies); Trinity Hall, Cambridge (international relations).

Non-political career: Royal United Services Institute 1987-90; Intelligence Corps 1987-94; Foreign and Commonwealth Office (Sarajevo, Geneva and Brussels) 1994-2001; Assistant Private Secretary to The Queen 2002-05; Deputy Private Secretary to The Queen 2005-07; Private Secretary to The Queen and Keeper of The Queen's Archives 2007-17; Permanent Lord-in-Waiting to The Queen 2019-. Honorary Regimental Colonel, London Scottish Regiment 2016-.

Political career: *House of Lords:* Raised to peerage as Baron Geidt, of Crobeg in the County of Ross and Cromarty 2017. *Other:* Board member, Shadow Sponsor Body for the Houses of Parliament Restoration and Renewal Programme 2018-20.

Other: Chair of Council, King's College London 2016-; Chair, The Queen's Commonwealth Trust 2017-; Freedom, City of London 2018; Fellow, King's College London 2011; Honorary Bencher, Middle Temple 2013; Fellow, Kennedy School of Government, Harvard University 2014; Honorary Fellow, Magdalen College, Oxford 2016; OBE 1997; Officier, Légion d'honneur (France) 2004; CVO 2007; PC 2007; KCVO 2011; KCB 2014; Grand-officier, Légion d'honneur (France) 2014; GCVO 2017; QSO 2018; GCB 2018.

Rt Hon the Lord Geidt GCB GCVO OBE QSO, House of Lords, London SW1A 0PW
Tel: 020 7219 3000

LIBERAL DEMOCRAT

GERMAN, LORD

Liberal Democrat Lords Spokesperson for Rehabilitation and Probation

GERMAN (Life Baron), Michael James German; cr 2010. Born 8 May 1945; Son of Arthur Ronald German, retired, and Molly German, retired; Divorced (2 daughters); married Veronica Watkins (later AM as Veronica German 2010-11) 2006 (3 stepchildren).

Education: St Illtyd's College, Cardiff; St Mary's College London; Open University (BA educational studies 1972); Bristol Polytechnic (Postgraduate Diploma education management 1974); French.

Non-political career: Primary school teacher 1966-97; Secondary school teacher, Mostyn High School 1967-70; Head of music: Lady Mary High School, Cardiff 1970-86, Corpus Christi High School, Cardiff 1986-91; Director, European unit, Welsh Joint Education Committee 1991-99.

Political career: *House of Commons:* Contested (Liberal) Cardiff North October 1974 and 1979, Cardiff Central (Liberal/All) 1983 and 1987 general elections. *House of Lords:* Raised to the peerage as Baron German, of Llanfrechfa in the County Borough of Torfaen 2010. Liberal Democrat Spokesperson for: Work and Pensions 2015, Rehabilitation and Probation 2020-. Member: EU Internal Market Sub-committee 2015-19, Democracy and Digital Technologies 2019-, Secondary Legislation Scrutiny 2020-. Chair, Liberal Democrat Parliamentary Party Committee on Work and Pensions 2010-15. *Other:* National Assembly for Wales: Contested

Caerphilly constituency 1999 and Torfaen constituency 2003 elections, AM for South Wales East region 1999-2010: Welsh Liberal Democrat Spokesperson for Economic Development 1999-2001, Deputy First Minister 2000-01, 2002-03, Minister for: Economic Development 2000-01, Rural Development and Wales Abroad 2002-03, Welsh Liberal Democrat Spokesperson for: Local Government 2004-05, Local Government and European Affairs 2005-07, Europe 2007-10, Shadow Minister for Environment 2010. Liberal Party/Welsh Liberal Democrats: Member 1974-, Federal Executive Committee 1989-91; Welsh Liberal Democrats: General election director 1992-97, Leader, Welsh Liberal Democrats in the National Assembly 1998-2008, Leader, Welsh Liberal Democrats 2007-08; Liberal Democrats: Member: Federal Executive Committee 2001-03, Federal Policy Committee 2010-, Treasurer 2016-. Cardiff City Council: Councillor 1983-96, Group Leader 1983-96, Joint Leader 1987-91; Member, Advisory Committee on Business Appointments 2015-.

Political interests: Small businesses, education and skills, governance and constitutional affairs; European Union, Oman, Moldova, Sub-Saharan Africa.

Other: Executive member, Wales branch, Commonwealth Parliamentary Association 2004-10; Member, British-Irish Parliamentary Assembly; President, Dolen Cymru (The Wales-Lesotho Link) 2008-; Parliament Choir: Chair and trustee 2011-13, Vice-chair 2013-; President, Monmouth, Brecon and Abergavenny Canals Trust 2011-; OBE 1996. National Liberal Club.

Recreations: Reading, music, travel.

The Lord German OBE, House of Lords, London SW1A 0PW
Tel: 020 7219 6942 *Email:* germanm@parliament.uk *Twitter:* @mjgerman

LABOUR

GIDDENS, LORD

GIDDENS (Life Baron), Anthony Giddens; cr. 2004. Born 18 January 1938; Son of Thomas George and Nell Maude Giddens; Married Alena Ledeneva 2005 (divorced).

Education: Minchenden Grammar School, London; Hull University (BA sociology and psychology 1959); London School of Economics (MA sociology 1961); Cambridge University (PhD 1976); French, some German.

Non-political career: Lecturer in sociology, Leicester University 1961-70; Cambridge University: Sociology lecturer 1970-84, Reader/professor of sociology 1984-96, Fellow, King's College; Former chair and director, Polity Press Ltd; London School of Economics: Director 1997-2004, Emeritus professor.

Political career: *House of Lords:* Raised to the peerage as Baron Giddens, of Southgate in the London Borough of Enfield 2004. Co-opted Member, EU Sub-committee A (Economic and Financial Affairs) 2006-08; Member EU Sub-committee D: (Agriculture, Fisheries and Environment) 2010-12, (Agriculture, Fisheries, Environment and Energy) 2012-13; Member: Digital Skills 2014-15, Artificial Intelligence 2017-18, EU Financial Affairs Sub-committee 2018-20, EU Environment Sub-committee 2020-.

Political interests: Welfare, social policy, foreign policy, global issues; Latin America, China, EU, Russia.

Other: BBC Reith Lecturer 1998; Member, Academy of Social Sciences; 22 honorary doctorates from Europe, South America and China; Asturias Prize for Social Sciences 2002; Fellow American Academy of Arts and Sciences; Academician of the Russian Academy of Sciences; Order of the Southern Cross (Brazil); Order of the Finnish Lion (Finland). Queen's Club.

Publications: Over 40 books on sociology, politics and psychology.

Recreations: Watching Spurs, tennis, travel.

The Lord Giddens, House of Lords, London SW1A 0PW
Tel: 020 7219 6710 *Email:* giddensa@parliament.uk

CONSERVATIVE

GILBERT OF PANTEG, LORD

Chair, Select Committee on Communications and Digital

GILBERT OF PANTEG (Life Baron), Stephen Gilbert; cr 2015. Born 24 July 1963.

Non-political career: Political Secretary to David Cameron as Prime Minister 2010-15; Director, Stephen Gilbert Consulting; Consultant, Populus 2015-.

Political career: *House of Lords:* Raised to the peerage as Baron Gilbert of Panteg, of Panteg in the County of Monmouthshire 2015. Communications/Communications and Digital: Member 2016-17, Chair 2017-. *Other:* Deputy Chair (Campaigning) and Member, Party Board, Conservative Party 2015-16. Commissioner, Electoral Commission 2018-.

Other: Member, Executive Committee, Inter-Parliamentary Union (British Group) 2016-. Carlton Club.

The Lord Gilbert of Panteg, House of Lords, London SW1A 0PW
Tel: 020 7219 3000 *Email:* gilberts@parliament.uk

LIBERAL DEMOCRAT

GLASGOW, EARL OF

GLASGOW (10th Earl of, S), Patrick Robin Archibald Boyle; cr. 1703; Viscount of Kelburn; 10th Lord Boyle (S) 1699/1703; 4th Baron Fairlie (UK) 1897. Born 30 July 1939; Son of Rear-Admiral 9th Earl, CB, DSC; Married Isabel James 1975 (1 son 1 daughter).

Education: Eton College; Sorbonne, Paris.

Non-political career: Television and film production: Assistant film director 1962-67, Documentary producer/director, Yorkshire TV 1968-70, Freelance television documentary producer 1971-86; Owner/manager, Kelburn Country Centre country park and visitor attraction. Royal Navy national service 1959-60; Sub-Lieutenant, RNR 1960. Former member, ACTT.

Political career: *House of Lords:* First entered House of Lords 1990; Elected hereditary peer 2005-; Liberal Democrat Spokesperson for: Transport 2005-10, Culture, Media and Sport 2008-10. Member: Works of Art 2005-09, 2015-16, Lord Speaker's Advisory Panel on Works of Art 2017-19. *Other:* DL, Ayrshire and Arran 1995.

Political interests: Tourism, television, performing arts, small businesses, assisted dying.

Other: Arthritis Care.

Publications: Occasional articles for the *Spectator* and other magazines.

Recreations: Theatre, cinema, skiing.

The Earl of Glasgow DL, House of Lords, London SW1A 0PW
Tel: 020 7219 5419 *Email:* glasgowp@parliament.uk
Kelburn Country Centre, Fairlie KA29 0BE *Tel:* 01475 568685
Email: admin@kelburncountrycentre.com Websites: www.kelburncastle.com
www.kelburncountrycentre.com

LABOUR

GLASMAN, LORD

GLASMAN (Life Baron), Maurice Mark Glasman; cr 2011. Born 8 March 1961; Married Catherine (3 sons 1 daughter).

Education: JFS Comprehensive School; St Katherine's College, Cambridge (BA modern history); York University (MA political philosophy); European University Institute, Florence (PhD unnecessary suffering 1989).

Non-political career: Senior lecturer in political theory, London Guildhall University; Senior lecturer in political theory and director of faith and citizenship programme, London Metropolitan University.

Political career: *House of Lords:* Raised to the peerage as Baron Glasman, of Stoke Newington and of Stamford Hill in the London Borough of Hackney 2011.

Other: London Citizens; Patron, Change Britain 2016-.

Publications: Unnecessary Suffering: Managing Market Utopia (Verso, 1996).

The Lord Glasman, House of Lords, London SW1A 0PW
Tel: 020 7219 5353

CONSERVATIVE

GLENARTHUR, LORD

GLENARTHUR (4th Baron, UK), Simon Mark Arthur; cr. 1918; 4th Bt of Carlung (UK) 1903. Born 7 October 1944; Son of 3rd Baron, OBE, DL; Married Susan Barry 1969 (1 son 1 daughter).

Education: Eton College.

Non-political career: Captain, British Airways Helicopters Ltd 1976-82; Director: Aberdeen and Texas Corporate Finance Ltd 1977-82, ABTEX Computer Systems Ltd 1979-82; Hanson plc: Senior executive 1989-96, Consultant 1996-99; Deputy chair, Hanson Pacific Ltd 1994-98; Director, Whirly Bird Services Ltd 1995-2004; Consultant, British Aerospace 1989-99; Director, Lewis Group plc 1993-94; Consultant, Chevron UK Ltd 1994-97; Director, Millennium Chemicals Inc 1996-2004; Consultant, Imperial Tobacco Group plc 1996-98; Audax Trading Ltd: Consultant 2001-02, Director 2003-05; Director: Medical Defence Union 2002-06, Audax Global S.à.r.l. 2005-; Non-executive Chair, British European Aviation Group Ltd 2015-. Commissioned 10th Royal Hussars (PWO) 1963; ADC to High Commissioner, Aden 1964-65; Retired 1975 as Major; Major, The Royal Hussars (PWO) TAVR 1976-80; Honorary Colonel, 306 Hospital Support Medical Regiment (Volunteers) 2001-11; Honorary Air Commodore, 612 (County of Aberdeen) Squadron, Royal Auxiliary Air Force 2004-14.

Political career: *House of Lords:* First entered House of Lords 1976; Government Whip 1982-83; Government Spokesperson for: the Treasury 1982-85, Home Office, Employment and Industry 1982-83, Defence 1983-89; Parliamentary Under-Secretary of State: Department of Health and Social Security 1983-85, Home Office 1985-86; Minister of State: Scottish Office 1986-87, Foreign and Commonwealth Office 1987-89; Elected hereditary peer 1999-. Member: Refreshment 2007-10, Ecclesiastical Committee 2010-. *Other:* DL, Aberdeenshire 1988-; Chair, St Mary's Hospital, Paddington, NHS Trust 1991-98; President, National Council for Civil Protection 1991-2003; Member, National Employers Liaison Committee for HM Reserve Forces 1996-2002; Governor, Nuffield Hospitals (now Nuffield Health) 2000-09; Commissioner, Royal Hospital, Chelsea 2001-07; Chair, National Employer Advisory Board for Britain's Reserve Forces 2002-09; King Edward VII's Hospital, Sister Agnes: Governor 2010-13, Chairman of council 2012-13; Governor, Sutton's Hospital, Charterhouse 2011-.

Political interests: Aviation, foreign affairs, defence, penal policy, health, Scotland; South Pacific.

Other: Member, Queen's Bodyguard for Scotland (Royal Company of Archers); Trustee, Hanson Research Trust 1990-; Fellow, Royal Aeronautical Society 1992-2010; British Helicopter Association: Chair 1992-2004, President 2004-; Special Trustee, St Mary's Hospital, Paddington 1991-2000; Scottish Patron, Butler Trust 1994-2014; Council member, Air League 1994-2009; Chair: European Helicopter Association 1996-2003, International Federation of Helicopter Associations 1997-2004; Trustee, Philip Alison Foundation 2000-; Royal College of Organists: Member 2003, Co-opted Council Trustee 2014-; Chartered Institute of Transport (now Chartered Institute of Logistics and Transport): Member 1978-2011, Fellow 1999-2011; Guild of Air Pilots and Air Navigators: Freeman 1992, Liveryman 1996-2011; Freedom, City of London 1996; Grand Cross, Order of Crown of Tonga; Royal Military Order of St George, Tonga. Cavalry and Guards Club.

Recreations: Field sports, gardening, choral singing, organ playing, antique barometers.

The Lord Glenarthur DL, House of Lords, London SW1A 0PW
Tel: 020 7219 5353 *Email:* glenarthurs@parliament.uk
Northbrae Farmhouse, Crathes, Banchory AB31 6JQ *Tel:* 01330 844467
Email: glenarthur@northbrae.co.uk

CONSERVATIVE

GLENDONBROOK, LORD

GLENDONBROOK (Life Baron), Michael David Bishop; cr 2011. Born 10 February 1942; Son of Clive Bishop.

Education: Mill Hill School.

Non-political career: Mercury Airlines, Manchester 1963; Chair: British Midland Airways 1964-2009, Airlines of Britain Holdings/British Midland plc 1978-2009, British Regional Air Lines Group plc 1982-2001, Manx Airlines 1982-2001; Airtours plc: Director 1987-2001, Deputy Chairman 1996-2001; Chairman, D'Oyly Carte Opera Trust Ltd 1989-2008; Channel 4 Television: Deputy Chairman 1991-93, Chairman 1993-97; Director, Williams Holdings plc 1993-2000; Non-executive director, Kidde plc 2000-02.

Political career: *House of Lords:* Raised to the peerage as Baron Glendonbrook, of Bowdon in the County of Cheshire 2011. *Other:* Member, East Midlands Electricity Board 1980-83.

Other: Member, East Midlands Regional Board, Central Television 1981-89; Honorary member, Royal Society of Musicians of Great Britain 1989; Chair of Trustees, Michael Bishop Foundation 1989-; Trustee and director, Friends in the UK, Royal Flying Doctor Service of Australia 2005; Chair, The Glendonbrook Foundation, Sydney 2007-; Liveryman, Guild of Air Pilots and Air Navigators; CBE 1986; Kt 1991. Brooks's Club.

The Lord Glendonbrook CBE, House of Lords, London SW1A 0PW
Tel: 020 7219 5353
Tel: 01530 564388 *Email:* charl.newall@btconnect.com

NON-AFFILIATED

GLOUCESTER, LORD BISHOP OF

GLOUCESTER (41st Bishop of), Rachel Treweek. Born 4 February 1963; Daughter of Robert and Marian Montgomery; Married Guy Treweek 2006.

Education: Broxbourne School; Reading University (BA linguistics and language pathology 1985); Wycliffe Hall, Oxford (BTh theology 1994).

Non-political career: Paediatric speech and language therapist, Hampstead Heath Authority 1985-91; Manager of Paediatric Speech and Language Therapists in Health Centres across three Health Authorities (Bloomsbury, Hampstead and Islington) 1989-91; Ordained deacon 1994; Priest 1995; St George's, Tufnell Park: Assistant Curate 1994-97, Associate Vicar 1997-99; Vicar, St James-the-Less, Bethnal Green 1999-2006; Continuing Ministerial Education Officer 1999-2001; Archdeacon of Northolt 2006-11; Archdeacon of Hackney 2011-15; Bishop of Gloucester 2015-.

Political career: *House of Lords:* Entered House of Lords 2015; First female Bishop to enter the House of Lords. *Other:* Governor: Tufnell Park Primary School 1996-99, Bonner Primary School, Tower Hamlets 1999-2006; Member: Church Commissioners' Pastoral Committee 2007-11, General Synod 2010-; Adviser to the House of Bishop's Working Group on Human Sexuality 2011-13.

Political interests: Conflict resolution, education, gospel transformation in society, justice, gender equality, overseas aid, young people, children and families; India, Mozambique, South Africa, Sweden, Tanzania, USA.

Other: Member, Management Committee, Whittington Community Centre 1995-99; Trustee: RADICLE 1999-2003, Ignite Trust 2007-11; Chair, Board of Reference for Heathrow Multi-faith Chaplaincy 2008-11; Member, Bridge Builders' Council of Reference 2012-; Trustee: Gloucester Magdalen Charity 2015-, Children's Society 2015-, Church of England Foundation for Educational Leadership 2017-; Ambassador, RESTORED; Patron, Gloucestershire Action for Refugees and Asylum Seekers; Honorary Degree of Doctor of Letters, Reading University 2016.

Recreations: Walking, canoeing, reading and writing.

Rt Rev the Lord Bishop of Gloucester, House of Lords, London SW1A 0PW
Tel: 020 7219 3000
2 College Green, Gloucester GL1 2LR *Tel:* 01452 835511 *Email:* bgloucester@glosdioc.org.uk
Website: www.gloucester.anglican.org *Twitter:* @BishGloucester

LIBERAL DEMOCRAT

GODDARD OF STOCKPORT, LORD

GODDARD OF STOCKPORT (Life Baron), David Goddard; cr 2014. Born 2 October 1952; Married Helen (1 son).

Education: Brinnington Secondary Modern; City & Guilds Qualification in gas fitting; IDEA Senior Leadership Academy (Leeds Castle).

Non-political career: Taxi driver; British Gas.

Political career: *House of Lords:* Raised to the peerage as Baron Goddard of Stockport, of Stockport in the County of Greater Manchester 2014. Member: Refreshment 2015-16, Secondary Legislation Scrutiny 2015-19, SLSC Sub-committee B 2018-19, Delegated Powers and Regulatory Reform 2019-, High Speed Rail (West Midlands-Crewe) Bill 2020-. *Other:* Stockport Metropolitan Council: Member 1990-2012, 2014-, Leader of the Council 2007-12; Governor, Stockport School; Member: Greater Manchester Local Enterprise Board, Greater Manchester Fire and Rescue Committee, Greater Manchester Police Authority.

Political interests: Northern powerhouse, housing, planning and development, aviation, transport; China, USA.

Other: Environment Commissioner, Great Manchester Combined Authority; Board Member, Manchester Airport Group; Age Concern, Wellspring Homeless Charity, Schools for Kenya.

The Lord Goddard of Stockport, House of Lords, London SW1A 0PW
Tel: 020 7219 6563 *Email:* goddardd@parliament.uk *Twitter:* @GoddardLord

CONSERVATIVE

GODSON, LORD

GODSON (Life Baron), Dean Aaron Godson; cr 2021.

Education: Sussex House; St Paul's School; Cambridge University.

Non-political career: Feature and Profile Writer, *Sunday Telegraph*; Chief Leader Writer, *Daily Telegraph* 1995-2004; Associate Editor, *The Spectator* 1997-2004; Contributing Editor, *Prospect Magazine*; Policy Exchange: Head, security research 2005-13, Director 2013-.

Political career: *House of Commons:* Contested Great Grimsby 1997 general election. *House of Lords:* Raised to the peerage as Baron Godson, of Thorney Island in the City of Westminster 2021. *Other:* Deputy Chairman, Kensington and Chelsea Conservative Association 1995-98.

Publications: Author, Himself Alone: David Trimble and the Ordeal of Unionism (Harper Collins, 2004).

The Lord Godson, House of Lords, London SW1A 0PW
Tel: 020 7219 3000

CONSERVATIVE

GOLD, LORD

GOLD (Life Baron), David Laurence Gold; cr 2011. Born 1 March 1951; Son of Michael and Betty Gold; Married Sharon Levy 1978 (1 daughter 2 sons).

Education: Westcliff High School for Boys; London School of Economics (LLB 1972).

Non-political career: Admitted solicitor 1975; Herbert Smith: Head of litigation 2003-05, Senior partner 2005-10; Corporate Monitor BAE Systems plc 2010-; Principal, David Gold and Associates 2011-.

Political career: *House of Lords:* Raised to the peerage as Baron Gold, of Westcliffe-on-Sea in the County of Essex 2011. Member: Joint Committee on Privacy and Injunctions 2011-12, EU Justice Sub-committee 2017-18, 2019-20, Bribery Act 2010 2018-19, EU International Agreements Sub-committee 2020-. *Other:* Chairman, Conservative Party Disciplinary Committee 2010-12.

Other: Governor, London School of Economics 2010-; Law Society of England and Wales.

Recreations: Theatre, cinema, travel, family.

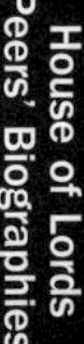

The Lord Gold, House of Lords, London SW1A 0PW
Tel: 020 7219 5353 *Email:* goldd@parliament.uk
3 Fitzhardinge Street, London W1H 6EF *Tel:* 020 3535 8989
Email: david.gold@davidgoldassociates.com Website: www.davidgoldassociates.com

CONSERVATIVE

GOLDIE, BARONESS

Minister of State and Government Spokesperson, Ministry of Defence

GOLDIE (Life Baroness), Annabel MacNicoll Goldie; cr 2013. Born 27 February 1950; Daughter of Alexander and Margaret Goldie.

Education: Greenock Academy, Greenock; Strathclyde University (LLB law 1971).

Non-political career: Admitted Solicitor 1974; Apprentice Solicitor, McClure Naismith Brodie & Co, Glasgow 1971-73; Assitant Solicitor, Haddow & McLay/Dickson, Haddow & Co 1973-77; Partner, Dickson, Haddow & Co/Donaldson, Alexander, Russell & Haddow, Glasgow 1978-2006.

Political career: *House of Commons:* Contested (Conservative) Renfrew West and Inverclyde 1992 general election. *House of Lords:* Raised to the peerage as Baroness Goldie, of Bishopton in the County of Renfrewshire 2013. Government Whip (Baroness in Waiting) 2016-19; Minister of State and Government Spokesperson, Ministry of Defence 2019-. Member, Communications 2016. *Other:* Scottish Parliament: Contested West Renfrewshire constituency 1999, 2003 and 2007 and Renfrewshire North and West constituency 2011 elections, MSP (as Annabel Goldie) for: West of Scotland region 1999-2011, West Scotland region 2011-16, Scottish Conservative Spokesperson for: Economy, Industry and Finance 1999-2001, Enterprise and Lifelong Learning 2001-03, Justice and Home Affairs 2003-05, Home Affairs 2005-06, Leader, Conservatives in the Scottish Parliament 2005-11, Scottish Conservative Spokesperson for: Culture and Communities 2011-13, Constitution 2013-16. Scottish Conservatives: Vice-chair 1992-95, Deputy Chair 1995-97, 1997-98, Chair March-July 1997, Deputy Leader 1998-2005. DL, Renfrewshire 1993-.

Other: Notary Public 1978-2007; Elder, Church of Scotland, Bishopton; Member: Glasgow Charing Cross Rotary Club, RSPB, West Scotland advisory board, Salvation Army; Director, Prince's Scottish Youth Business Trust 1995-2010; Honorary Fellow, Royal Incorporation of Architects in Scotland; Honorary fellow, Strathclyde University.

Recreations: Countryside, walking, bird-watching, wildlife, music.

The Baroness Goldie DL, House of Lords, London SW1A 0PW
Tel: 020 7219 5353

LABOUR

GOLDING, BARONESS

GOLDING (Life Baroness), Llinos Golding; cr. 2001. Born 21 March 1933; Daughter of late Ness Edwards (MP for Caerphilly 1939-68); Married Dr Roland Lewis 1957 (1 son 2 daughters); married John Golding 1980 (MP 1969-86) (died 1999).

Education: Caerphilly Girls Grammar School; Cardiff Royal Infirmary School of Radiography (1952).

Non-political career: Radiographer, NHS 1952-80; Secretary and assistant to John Golding MP 1972-86. Former branch secretary, NUPE; Secretary, Newcastle Staffs and District Trades Council 1976-86.

Political career: *House of Commons:* MP (Labour) for Newcastle-under-Lyme 1986-2001; Opposition Whip 1987-92; Opposition Spokesperson for: Social Security 1992-93, Children and Families 1993-95, Food, Agriculture and Rural Affairs 1995-97. *House of Lords:* Raised to the peerage as Baroness Golding, of Newcastle-under-Lyme in the County of Staffordshire 2001. *Other:* Member: BBC Advisory Committee 1989-92, Commonwealth War Graves Commission 1992-2001.

Political interests: Health service, trade unions, children, racing, gambling, fishing; Spain.

Other: Executive Committee Member, Inter-Parliamentary Union British Group 1996-99; Trustee, NSPCC 1988-2001; Chair: Second Chance 1988-, Citizen Card 2001-; Citizencard; Member, Board of Countryside Alliance 2002-, Vice-President; Administrative Steward, British Boxing Board of Control.

Recreations: Fishing.

The Baroness Golding, House of Lords, London SW1A 0PW
Tel: 020 7219 4209 *Email:* goldingll@parliament.uk

LABOUR

GOLDSMITH, LORD

Chair, EU International Agreements Sub-committee

GOLDSMITH (Life Baron), Peter Henry Goldsmith; cr. 1999. Born 5 January 1950; Son of late Sydney Goldsmith and Myra Nurick; Married Joy Elterman 1974 (3 sons 1 daughter).

Education: Quarry Bank High School, Liverpool; Gonville and Caius College, Cambridge (MA law 1971); University College, London (LLM 1972); French, German.

Non-political career: Called to the Bar, Gray's Inn 1972; In practice 1972-; QC 1987; Assistant Recorder, then Recorder of the Crown Court 1987-; Member, Paris Bar (Avocat a la Cour) 1997; Fellow, American Law Institute; European and Asian chair, Litigation Debevoise & Plimpton LLP 2007-.

Political career: *House of Lords:* Raised to the peerage as Baron Goldsmith, of Allerton in the County of Merseyside 1999. Attorney General and Government Spokesperson for Law Officers' Departments 2001-07. Member: Procedure 2009-12, Constitution 2010-15; Chair, EU International Agreements Sub-committee 2020-; Member, European Union 2020-. *Other:* Chair, Financial Reporting Review Panel 1997-2000.

Other: Prime Minister's Representative on Convention for a Charter of Fundamental Rights of the EU 1999-2000; Executive committee member, Great Britain China Centre 1996-2001; Council member, Public Concern at Work 1996-2001; Bar Pro Bono Unit: Founder 1996, President 2001-; Various offices international law organisations, including American Law Institute 1996-; Chair, Access to Justice Foundation 2008-; Council member: Hong Kong International Arbitration Centre, CEELI (Central and Eastern European Law Initiative); Chair, Commission on Crime and Problem Gambling, Howard League for Penal Reform 2019-; Chair: Bar Council of England and Wales 1995, Bar Council International Relations Committee 1996, IBA Standing Committee on Globalisation 1996-98; Co-chair, IBA Human Pro Rights Institute 1998-2001; Freedom, City of London; Fellow, University College London; PC 2002.

Rt Hon the Lord Goldsmith QC, House of Lords, London SW1A 0PW
Tel: 020 7219 7500 *Email:* goldsmithp@parliament.uk
Debevoise & Plimpton LLP, 65 Gresham Street, London EC2V 7NQ *Tel:* 020 7786 9088
Email: phgoldsmith@debevoise.com Website: www.debevoise.com/lordgoldsmithqc

CONSERVATIVE

GOLDSMITH OF RICHMOND PARK, LORD

Minister of State for the Pacific and Environment and Government Spokesperson, Foreign, Commonwealth and Development Office and Department for Environment, Food and Rural Affairs

GOLDSMITH OF RICHMOND PARK (Life Baron), Frank Zacharias Robin Goldsmith; cr 2020. Born 20 January 1975; Son of Sir James Goldsmith and Lady Annabel Vane-Tempest-Stewart; Married Sheherazade Ventura-Bentley 1999 (divorced 2010) (1 son 2 daughters); married Alice Rothschild 2013 (1 son 2 daughters).

Education: Eton College.

Non-political career: Redefining Progress, San Francisco, USA 1994-95; International Society for Ecology and Culture 1995-97; Editor, *Ecologist* 1997-2007.

Political career: *House of Commons:* Member (Con) for Richmond Park 2010 to 25 October 2016. Contested (Ind) Richmond Park 2016 by-election. Member (Con) for Richmond Park 2017-19; Illegal Wildlife Trade Conference Champion 2018-; Department for Environment,

Food and Rural Affairs and Department for International Development: Parliamentary Under-Secretary of State 2019, Minister of State (also attending Cabinet) 2019. Member, Environmental Audit 2010-16, 2017-19. *House of Lords:* Raised to the peerage as Lord Goldsmith of Richmond Park, of Richmond Park in the London Borough of Richmond upon Thames 2020. Minister of State for the Pacific and Environment and Government Spokesperson: Department for Environment, Food and Rural Affairs 2020-, Foreign and Commonwealth Office and Department for International Development 2020, Foreign, Commonwealth and Development Office 2020-. *Other:* Contested 2016 London mayoral election. Deputy Chair, Quality of Life Policy Group, Conservative Party 2005-07.

Political interests: Climate change, environment, animal welfare, democratic reform.

Other: Beacon Prize for Young Philanthropist of the Year 2003; Mikhail Gorbachev's International Environmental Leadership Award 2004; Richmond Green Champion 2010; Politician of the Year, Business Leaders Award 2011; Sustainable National Politician of the Year, Blue & Green Tomorrow 2013; MP of the year, Patchwork 2014, 2015; The Newcomer (Conservative) MP of the Year 2014; Overall MP for Year 2014-15; Backbencher of the year, Asian Voices 2015; Change Opinions (Political) Award, Westbourne 2015; PC 2019.

Publications: Author, The Constant Economy (Atlantic Books, 2009).

Rt Hon the Lord Goldsmith of Richmond Park, House of Lords, London SW1A 0PW
Tel: 020 7219 3000
Email: zac@zacgoldsmith.com *Twitter:* @ZacGoldsmith

CONSERVATIVE

GOODLAD, LORD

GOODLAD (Life Baron), Alastair Robertson Goodlad; cr 2005. Born 4 July 1943; Son of late Dr. John Goodlad and Isabel Goodlad, née Sinclair; Married Cecilia Hurst 1968 (2 sons).

Education: Marlborough College, Wiltshire; King's College, Cambridge (BA 1966, MA, LLB).

Non-political career: Former director, Bowater Overseas Holdings Ltd; President, Water Companies Association 1989; High Commissioner to Australia 2000-05.

Political career: *House of Commons:* Contested Crewe 1970 general election. MP (Conservative) for Northwich February 1974-83, for Eddisbury 1983-99; Government Whip 1981-84; Parliamentary Under-Secretary of State, Department of Energy 1984-87; Government Whip 1989-92; Minister of State, Foreign and Commonwealth Office 1992-95; Government Chief Whip 1995-97; Member, Shadow Cabinet 1997-98: Shadow Secretary of State for International Development 1997-98. Chairman, Conservative Party Committee for International Development 1997-98. *House of Lords:* Raised to the peerage as Baron Goodlad, of Lincoln in the County of Lincolnshire 2005. Contested Lord Speaker election 2011. Constitution: Member 2007, Chair 2007-10; Chair: Merits of Statutory Instruments/Secondary Legislation Scrutiny 2010-15, Leader's Group on the Working Practices of the House of Lords 2010-11; Member: Standing Orders (Private Bills) 2015-19, Communications 2015-16, 2017-19.

Other: PC 1992; KCMG 1997. Brooks's, Beefsteak, Pratt's Club.

Rt Hon the Lord Goodlad KCMG, House of Lords, London SW1A 0PW
Tel: 020 7219 3427

LABOUR

GORDON OF STRATHBLANE, LORD

GORDON OF STRATHBLANE (Life Baron), James Stuart Gordon; cr. 1997. Born 17 May 1936; Son of late James and Elsie Gordon, née Riach; Married Margaret Anne Stevenson 1971 (1 daughter 2 sons).

Education: St Aloysius' College, Glasgow; Glasgow University (MA classics 1958).

Non-political career: Political editor, Scottish Television 1965-73; Managing director, Radio Clyde 1973-96; Scottish Advisory Board, BP 1990-2002; Scottish Radio Holdings: Chief executive 1991-96, Chair 1996-2005; Vice-chair, Melody Radio 1991-97; Director: Clydeport Holdings 1992-98, Johnston Press plc 1996-2007, AIM Trust plc (now Active Capital Trust) 1996-2009; Chair, RAJAR (Radio Audience Research) 2003-06.

Political career: *House of Commons:* Contested (Labour) East Renfrewshire 1964 general election. *House of Lords:* Raised to the peerage as Baron Gordon of Strathblane, of Deil's Craig in Stirling 1997. Member, Communications/Communications and Digital 2009-13, 2017-. *Other:* Member, Scottish Development Agency 1981-90; Chair, Scottish Exhibition Centre 1983-89; Member of Court, Glasgow University 1984-97; Committee member, Inquiry into Teacher's Pay 1986; Chair, Advisory Group on Listed Events on TV 1997-98; Member, Independent Review Panel on Funding of BBC 1998-99; Board member, British Tourist Authority 1998-2001.

Political interests: Broadcasting, tourism, constitutional affairs, Scotland; China, India, Middle East.

Other: Trustee: John Smith Memorial Trust 1995-2007, National Galleries of Scotland 1998-2001; Scottish Tourist Board: Board member 1997-2001, Chair 1998-2001; Hon. DLitt, Glasgow Caledonian 1994; DUniv, Glasgow University 1998; Sony Award for outstanding services to radio 1984; Fellow, Radio Academy 1994; Lord Provost's Award for Public Service in Glasgow 1994; CBE 1984. New (Edinburgh), Glasgow Art Club; Prestwick Golf.

Recreations: Skiing, walking, genealogy.

The Lord Gordon of Strathblane CBE, House of Lords, London SW1A 0PW

CONSERVATIVE

GOSCHEN, VISCOUNT

GOSCHEN (4th Viscount, UK), Giles John Harry Goschen; cr. 1900. Born 16 November 1965; Son of 3rd Viscount, KBE; Married Sarah Penelope Horsnail 1991 (2 daughters 1 son).

Education: Eton College.

Non-political career: Deutsche Bank 1997-2000; Director: Barchester Advisory 2000-02, Korn/Ferry International 2005-.

Political career: *House of Lords:* First entered House of Lords 1986; Government Whip (Lord-in-Waiting to HM The Queen) 1992-94; Government Spokesperson for Environment, Employment, Social Security, Transport and Trade and Industry 1992-94; Parliamentary Under-Secretary of State, Department of Transport 1994-97; Opposition Spokesperson for Environment, Transport and the Regions (Transport) 1997; Elected hereditary peer 1999-.

Political interests: Sub-Saharan Africa.

Other: Chair, Kasanka Trust. Air Squadron, Pratt's Club.

The Viscount Goschen, House of Lords, London SW1A 0PW
Tel: 020 7219 3198

LABOUR

GOUDIE, BARONESS

GOUDIE (Life Baroness), Mary Teresa Goudie; cr. 1998. Born 2 September 1946; Daughter of Martin and Hannah Brick; Married James Goudie QC 1969 (2 sons).

Education: Our Lady of The Visitation, Greenford; Our Lady of St Anselm, Hayes.

Non-political career: Assistant director, Brent People's Housing Association 1977-81; Director: The Hansard Society for Parliamentary Government 1985-90, *The House Magazine* 1989-90; European director of public affairs, World Wide Fund for Nature (UK) 1990-95; Independent public affairs consultant 1995-98; Strategic and management consultant 1998-; Member, global advisory board, WEConnect International 2012-; Director, Center for Talent Innovations 2012-. Member: APEX, GMB.

Political career: *House of Lords:* Raised to the peerage as Baroness Goudie, of Roundwood in the London Borough of Brent 1998. Co-opted Member, European Union Sub-committee E (Law and Institutions) 1998-2000; Member: Procedure 2001-04, House of Lords' Offices Finance and Staff Sub-committee 2002-03, Information Committee 2003-05, Statutory Instruments Joint Committee 2005-06, Selection 2008-13, Joint Committee on Tax Law Rewrite Bills 2009-10, Soft Power and the UK's Influence 2013-14, Insurance Bill 2014-15, Sexual Violence in Conflict 2015-16, Licensing Act 2003 2016-17, Finance 2016-, EU Justice Sub-committee 2019-20, EU Security and Justice Sub-committee 2020-. Vice-chair, PLP Departmental Group for International Development 2010-15. *Other:* Secretary, Labour Solidarity Campaign 1981-87;

Campaign manager to Roy Hattersley MP, Labour Party Deputy leadership election 1983; Member, Labour Parliamentary general election campaign team 1998-2001; Vice-chair, Labour Peers 2001-03; Member: Society of Labour Lawyers, Labour Movement in Europe. London Borough of Brent: Councillor 1971-78, Chair, Housing and Planning Committees, Deputy Whip.

Political interests: Women and children, regional development, human rights, charity law, human trafficking, sexual violence and conflict, women on boards, European Commission and Parliament; Azerbaijan, Europe, India, Ireland, Middle East, Northern Ireland, Scotland, USA.

Other: Member, Inter-Parliamentary Union, British-Irish Inter-Parliamentary Committee; Chair, Women Leaders' Council to Fight Human Trafficking, UN; Member: Fabian Society, Smith Institute; Trustee: Piggybank Kids, Share Gift; Patron: National Childbirth Trust, Northern Ireland Community Foundation; Ambassador, World Wildlife Federation; Member, executive and board of directors, Vital Voices Global Partnership; Founding member, 30% Club 2010-; Trustee, El-Hibri Charitable Foundation 2012-; Honorary doctorate, Napier University 2000; Global Power award, Centre for Women Policy Studies 2012. SBCC Tennis Club.

Recreations: Family, travelling, gardening, food and wine, art.

The Baroness Goudie, House of Lords, London SW1A 0PW
Tel: 020 7219 5880 *Email:* goudie@parliament.uk Website: www.baronessgoudie.com
Twitter: @BaronessGoudie

CROSSBENCH

GRABINER, LORD

GRABINER (Life Baron), Anthony Stephen Grabiner; cr. 1999. Born 21 March 1945; Son of late Ralph and Freda Grabiner, née Cohen; Married Jane Portnoy 1983 (3 sons 1 daughter).

Education: Central Foundation Boys' Grammar School, London; London School of Economics (LLB 1966; LLM 1967); Lincoln's Inn (Hardwicke Scholar 1966, Droop Scholar 1968).

Non-political career: Called to the Bar, Lincoln's Inn 1968; Standing Junior Counsel to Department of Trade, Export Credits Guarantee Department 1976-81; Junior Counsel to the Crown 1978-81; QC 1981; Bencher 1989; Recorder of the Crown Court 1990-99; Deputy High Court Judge 1994-; Non-executive director, Next plc 2002; Non-executive chair, Arcadia Group Limited 2002-; Bank of England Financial Services Law Committee 2002-05.

Political career: *House of Lords:* Raised to the peerage as Baron Grabiner, of Aldwych in the City of Westminster 1999. Member, Religious Offences 2002-03; Co-opted Member, European Union Sub-committee E (Law and Institutions) 2003-06; Member: Joint Committee on Privacy and Injunctions 2011-12, Bribery Act 2010 2018-19. *Other:* Resigned Labour whip October 2015; now sits on Crossbenches.

Political interests: Law reform, commercial and company law, city, pensions, higher education.

Other: Chair: Court of Governors, LSE 1998-2007, Management and Standards Committee, News Corporation 2011-. Garrick Club; Brocket Hall Golf; Non-executive director Wentworth Golf Club 2005-.

Publications: Co-editor, Sutton and Shannon on Contract (7th edition, 1970); The Informal Economy (Report to Chancellor of the Exchequer, March 2000).

Recreations: Golf, theatre, reading.

The Lord Grabiner QC, House of Lords, London SW1A 0PW
Tel: 020 7219 5353
1 Essex Court, Temple, London EC4Y 9AR *Tel:* 020 7583 2000 *Email:* agrabiner@oeclaw.co.uk

CONSERVATIVE

GRADE OF YARMOUTH, LORD

Chair, Select Committee on Social and Economic Impact of the Gambling Industry

GRADE OF YARMOUTH (Life Baron), Michael Ian Grade; cr 2011. Born 8 March 1943; Son of Leslie Grade; Married Penelope Levinson 1967 (divorced 1981) (1 son 1 daughter); married Hon Sarah Lawson 1982 (divorced 1991); Married Francesca Leahy 1998 (1 son).

Education: St Dunstan's College, London; French.

Non-political career: *Daily Mirror*: Trainee journalist 1960s, Sports columnist 1964-66; Theatrical agent, Grade Organisation 1966; London Management and Representation: Joint managing director -1973, London Weekend Television: Deputy controller of programmes (entertainment) 1973, Director of programmes 1977-81; President, Embassy Television 1981-84; Controller, BBC1 1984-86; Director of programmes, BBC TV 1986-87; Chief executive, Channel Four 1988-97; Director: ITN 1989-93, Delfont Macintosh Theatres Ltd 1994-99, New Millennium Experience Co 1997-2001; Former director, Charlton Athletic Football Club; Pinewood-Shepperton plc: Chair 2000-16, Senior Consultant 2016-18; Camelot Group: Director 2000-04, Chair 2002-04; Director: Reel Enterprises Ltd 2002-04, SMG 2003-04, Television Corporation 2003-04; Chair, Ocado 2006-13; Executive chair and chief executive, ITV 2007-09; Chair, James Grant Group 2010-12; Director, WRG Group 2011-14; Chair, Infinity Creative Media 2014-; Director: Grade Linnit Company, Performing Right Society for Music 2015-18.

Political career: *House of Lords:* Raised to the peerage as Baron Grade of Yarmouth, of Yarmouth in the County of Isle of Wight 2011. Member: Joint Committee on the Draft Defamation Bill 2011, Small- and Medium-Sized Enterprises 2012-13, Regenerating Seaside Towns and Communities 2018-19; Chair, Social and Economic Impact of the Gambling Industry 2019-. *Other:* Chairman, Fear of Crime Working Group 1989; Member, National Committee of Inquiry into Prevention of Child Abuse 1994-96; Chairman: Index on Censorship 2000-04, Board of Governors, BBC 2004-06; Member, Panel on Fair Access to the Professions 2009; Lay member, Press Complaints Commission 2011-14; Trustee, Science Museum 2011-19; Chair: Media Museum, Bradford 2011-19, Charity Fundraising Regulator 2015-18.

Political interests: Media, arts, business; Middle East.

Other: Council member: LAMDA 1981-93, RADA 1996-2004; BAFTA: Council member 1981-82, 1986-88, Fellowship 1994, Vice-President 2004-; Member, British Screen Advisory Council 1986-97; Fellow, Royal Television Society 1991; Council member, Royal Albert Hall 1997-2004; Chair advisory board, National Science and Media Museum 2011-19; The Healing Foundation, Samaritans, Royal National Lifeboat Institute, Tall Ships Trust, Royal National Mission for Deep Sea Fishermen; Honorary Professor, Thames Valley University (1994); Hon. LLD, Nottingham University (1997); CBE 1998. Royal Thames Yacht Club; Royal Solent Yacht Club.

Publications: It Seemed Like a Good Idea at the Time (autobiography, 1999).

Recreations: Sailing, theatre, opera, cricket.

The Lord Grade of Yarmouth CBE, House of Lords, London SW1A 0PW
Tel: 020 7219 3000
GradeLinnit Company Ltd, 17 Old Park Lane, London W1K 1QT *Tel:* 020 3150 2471
Email: ros@michaelgrade.com

LABOUR

GRANTCHESTER, LORD

Opposition Spokesperson for Environment, Food and Rural Affairs and Business, Energy and Industrial Strategy and International Trade (Energy); Opposition Whip

GRANTCHESTER (3rd Baron, UK), Christopher John Suenson-Taylor; cr. 1953. Born 8 April 1951; Son of late 2nd Baron, CBE, QC and late Betty, née Moores; Married Jacqueline Jaffé 1973 (divorced) (2 sons 2 daughters).

Education: Winchester College; London School of Economics (BSc economics 1973).

Non-political career: Dairy farmer and cattle breeder; Director: Littlewoods Organisation various companies 1993-97, Everton Football Club Company 1994-2000, Dairy Farmers of Britain 2003-09, Cheshire and Warrington Economic Alliance 2005-10.

Political career: *House of Lords:* First entered House of Lords 1995; Elected hereditary peer 2003-; Opposition Whip 2010-15, 2020-; Opposition Spokesperson for: Environment, Food and Rural Affairs 2014-, Energy and Climate Change 2015-16, Business, Energy and Industrial Strategy 2016-, International Trade 2020-. Member: EU Sub-Committee D Agriculture, Fisheries and Food 1996-99, Hybrid Instruments 2005-.

Political interests: Rural economy, the environment, sport, Merseyside, Cheshire and the North West; China, Denmark, Taiwan.

Other: Member of the Executive Council, Cheshire Agricultural Society 1986-99; Cheshire Representative to The Royal Agricultural Society of England 1994-97; Trustee, Foundation for Sports and the Arts 1997-; President: Western Holstein Breeders Club 1999-2000, President, Royal Association of British Dairy Farmers 2001-03; Chair: Cheshire County Country Lane and Business Association 2002-04, Local Football Partnership, Liverpool County FA 2001-06; Chairman, Everton Collection Charitable Trust 2005-; Vice-president, Wingate Special Children's Trust 2008. Vice-president, Oulton Park Cricket Club 2006.

Recreations: Sport (football, cricket, tennis), Everton FC, countryside and gardens, the arts.

The Lord Grantchester, House of Lords, London SW1A 0PW
Tel: 020 7219 5421 *Fax:* 020 7219 5979 *Email:* grantchesterj@parliament.uk

LIBERAL DEMOCRAT

GREAVES, LORD

GREAVES (Life Baron), Anthony Robert Greaves; cr. 2000. Born 27 July 1942; Son of late Geoffrey Lawrence and Moyra Louise Greaves; Married Heather Ann Baxter 1968 (2 daughters).

Education: Queen Elizabeth Grammar School, Wakefield; Hertford College, Oxford (BA geography 1963); French.

Non-political career: Teacher 1969-74; Organising secretary, Association of Liberal Councillors 1977-85; Manager, Liberal Party Publications 1985-90; Book dealer.

Political career: *House of Commons:* Contested (Liberal) Nelson and Colne February and October 1974 and (Liberal Democrat) Pendle 1997 general elections. *House of Lords:* Raised to the peerage as Baron Greaves, of Pendle in the County of Lancashire 2000. Liberal Democrat Spokesperson for: Environment, Food and Rural Affairs 2001-03, Deputy Prime Minister, Regional and Local Government 2003, Environment, Food and Rural Affairs 2005-10, Communities and Local Government 2007-10. Member: Standing Orders (Private Bills) 2000-05, Personal Bills 2005-09; Co-opted member, European Union Sub-committee D (Environment and Agriculture) 2006-08; Member, Procedure 2014-17. Chair, Liberal Democrat Parliamentary Party Committee on Energy and Climate Change; Environment, Food and Rural Affairs (Environment, Food and Rural Affairs) 2010-12. *Other:* Chairman: Union of Liberal Students 1965-66, National League of Young Liberals 1970-71; Member, Liberal Democrat Federal Policy Committee. Councillor: Colne Borough Council 1971-74, Pendle Borough Council 1973-92, 1994-98, 2004-, Lancashire County Council 1973-97; Vice-President, Local Government Association 2011-16.

Political interests: Local government and democracy, environment, railways, elections, human rights, asylum seekers and refugees, countryside access; Bosnia-Herzegovina, Croatia, France.

Other: Patron, British Mountaineering Council 2005-; Vice-president, Open Spaces Society 2010-.

Publications: Co-author, Merger: The Inside Story (1989).

Recreations: Climbing, mountaineering, botany, cycling.

The Lord Greaves, House of Lords, London SW1A 0PW
Tel: 020 7219 8620 *Email:* greavesa@parliament.uk
3 Hartington Street, Winewall, Colne BB8 8DB *Tel:* 01282 864346
Email: tonygreaves@cix.co.uk Website: liberallord.com

CROSSBENCH

GREEN OF DEDDINGTON, LORD

GREEN OF DEDDINGTON (Life Baron), Andrew Fleming Green; cr 2014. Born 6 August 1941; Married Jane Churchill (1 son 1 daughter).

Education: Cambridge University (natural sciences and economics); Arabic.

Non-political career: Diplomatic Service 1965-2000: Ambassador to Syria 1991-94, Director for Middle East, Foreign and Commonwealth Office 1994-96, Ambassador to Saudi Arabia 1996-2000; Founder chair, Migration Watch 2001-. Short Service Commission in the Royal Green Jackets 1962-65.

Political career: *House of Lords:* Raised to the peerage as Baron Green of Deddington, of Deddington in the County of Oxfordshire 2014.

Political interests: Immigration, Christian persecution; Middle East.

Other: Former chair, Medical Aid for Palestinians; Former member, advisory board, Concordis; Former board member, Christian Solidarity Worldwide; CMG 1991; KCMG 1998.

Recreations: Tennis, bridge.

The Lord Green of Deddington KCMG, House of Lords, London SW1A 0PW
Tel: 020 7219 3000 *Email:* greena@parliament.uk

NON-AFFILIATED

GREEN OF HURSTPIERPOINT, LORD

GREEN OF HURSTPIERPOINT (Life Baron), Stephen Keith Green; cr 2010. Born 7 November 1948; Son of late Dudley and Rosamund Green; Married Janian Joy (1971) (2 daughters).

Education: Lancing College, West Sussex; Exeter College, Oxford (BA philosophy, politics and economics); Massachusetts Institute of Technology, USA (MSc political science); French, German.

Non-political career: Overseas Development Agency, Foreign and Commonwealth Office 1970-77; McKinsey & Co Inc. 1977-82; HSBC plc 1982-2010: Chief executive officer, Group Chairman 2006-10; Ordained deacon 1987; Priest 1988; Member, board of directors, BASF 2009-10.

Political career: *House of Lords:* Raised to the peerage as Baron Green of Hurstpierpoint, of Hurstpierpoint in the County of West Sussex 2010. Minister of State for Trade and Investment and Government Spokesperson, Department for Business, Innovation and Skills and Foreign and Commonwealth Office 2011-13. Member: European Union 2015-17, EU Internal Market Sub-committee 2015-17. *Other:* Left Conservatives July 2019, now sits as non-affiliated. Chair, Natural History Museum 2014-.

Political interests: Asia, France, Germany.

Other: Member, Steering Group, Centre for Excellence in Finance, Sabanci University; Trustee: Archbishop of Canterbury's Anglican Communion Fund, Wintershall Charitable Trust; Chair, Asia House 2017-; President, Institute of Export 2017-; Freedom, City of London. Athenæum Club.

Publications: Serving God? Serving Mammon? (1996); Good Value: reflections on money, morality and an uncertain world (2009); Reluctant Meister: How Germany's Past is Shaping its European Future (2014); The European Identity: Historical and Cultural Realities we Cannot Deny (2015).

Recreations: Art, European literature, opera.

The Lord Green of Hurstpierpoint, House of Lords, London SW1A 0PW
Tel: 020 7219 3000

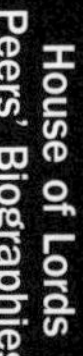

CROSSBENCH

GREENFIELD, BARONESS

GREENFIELD (Life Baroness) Professor Susan Adele Greenfield; cr 2001. Born 1 October 1950; Daughter of Reginald Greenfield and Doris Thorpe; Married Professor Peter Atkins 1991 (divorced 2003).

Education: Godolphin and Latymer Girls' School, London; St Hilda's College, Oxford (BA experimental psychology 1973, MA; DPhil pharmacology 1977); French.

Non-political career: Medical Research Council (MRC) research scholarship, pharmacology department, Oxford 1973-76; MRC-INSERM exchange fellowship, College de France, Paris 1979-80; Junior research fellowship, Green College, Oxford 1981-84; Lecturer in synaptic pharmacology, Oxford 1985-96; Tutorial fellowship in medicine, Lincoln College, Oxford 1985-98; Deputy director, Squibb Projects 1988-95; Gresham Chair of Physics, Gresham College, London 1995-99; Professor of synaptic pharmacology, Oxford University and Director, Institute for the Future of the Mind 1996-2013; Distinguished visiting scholar, Queen's University, Belfast 1996; Senior research fellowship, Lincoln College 1998-2016; Director: Royal Institution of Great Britain 1998-2010, Synaptica Ltd 1998-2003, BrainBoost Ltd 2003-06, Neurodiagnostics Ltd 2004-05; Thinker in Residence, Adelaide, South Australia 2004-05; Director: Enkephala 2005-13, MindWeavers 2006-09; Chair of Innovation, Queen's University, Belfast 2006; Director, Greenfield PPS Ltd 2007-; Founder and chief executive, Neuro-Bio Ltd 2013-; Director, Tekcapital Ltd 2014-16.

Political career: *House of Lords:* Raised to the peerage as Baroness Greenfield, of Ot Moor in the County of Oxfordshire 2001. Member, Information 2005-08. *Other:* Vice-President, Local Government Association 2018-19.

Political interests: Biotech, science, higher education, women's rights; Australia, France, Israel, Middle East.

Other: Various posts in numerous organisations, particularly in fields of neurological illnesses and promotion of science; Science Museum: Trustee 1998-2003, Fellow 2010-; Vice-President, Association of Woman in Science and Engineering 2001-03; Chair, Women in Science Group 2002; Board of Governors, Weizmann Institute of Science 2004-13; President, Classical Association 2004-05; Fellow, James Martin Institute 2004-; Editorial Board, Common Knowledge 2004-; Trustee: Carnegie Mellon University Proposal 2004-, John Porter National Trust 2004, Alexandria Library, Egypt 2006-; Board of Trustees, Cyprus Research Institute 2006-14; Trustee: Institute for Food, Brain and Behaviour (formerly National Justice) 2007-, Science for Humanities 2007-; Science Media Centre Board, Australia 2007-, Royal Institution Australia 2008-16; Governor, Florey Institute for Neuroscience and Mental Health 2012; British Association for the Advancement of Science 2006; Alzheimer's Research UK; Chancellor, Heriot-Watt University 2005-12; Senior Research Fellow, Department of Pharmacology, Lincoln College, Oxford; Honorary Fellow: St Hildas College, Oxford 1999, Royal College of Physicians 2000, Cardiff University 2000, College of Teachers 2001, Royal Society of South Australia 2005; Honorary Senior Fellow, Higher Education Academy 2007; Fellow: Royal Society of Edinburgh 2007-, Australian Davos Connection 2007-; 32 honorary doctorates from UK, US, Israeli and Australian universities; Honorary Fellowship, Royal College of Physicians 2000; Honorary Fellow, Institute of Risk Management 2012; Honorary Professor, Melbourne University Medical School 2014-17; Dame Catherine Fulford Senior Scholarship, St Hugh's College, Oxford 1974; J.H. Burn Trust Scholarship, pharmacology department, Oxford 1977; MRC training fellowship, physiology department, Oxford 1977-81; Royal Society study visit award, College de France, Paris 1978; Woman of Distinction of the Year (Jewish Care) 1998; Royal Society Michael Faraday Award 1998; *Observer* Woman of the Year 2000; Golden Plate Award, American Academy of Achievement 2003; Honorary Australian of the Year 2006; British Inspiration Award – Science and Technology 2010; Australian Society for Medical Research Medal 2010; CBE 2000; Ordre National de la Légion d'Honneur (France) 2003. Hospital Club.

Publications: Co-editor, Mindwaves: Thoughts on Intelligence, Identity and Consciousness (Basil Blackwell, 1987); Co-author, Journey to the Centres of the Brain (BBC Education Publishers, 1994); Editor, The Human Mind Explained (Reader's Digest, USA; Cassell UK, 1994); Author, The Human Brain: A Guided Tour (Weidenfield & Nicolson/Basic Books, 1997, Paperback Phoenix Press, 1998); Editor, Brainpower (Ivy Press, 1999); Author: The Private Life of the Brain (Penguin, 2000), Brain Story (BBC Books, 2000), Set Fair; a report on Women in Science, Engineering and Technology to the Secretary of State for Trade and Industry (2002), Tomorrow's People (Penguin, 2003); 'ID' The Quest for Identity in the 21st Century (Hodder & Stoughton, 2008); You and Me: Neuroscience and Identity (Notting Hill Education,

2011); 2121: A Tale from the Next Century (Head of Zeus, 2013); Mind Change: How digital technologies are leaving their mark on our Brains (Random House, 2014), A Day in the Life of the Brain: The Neuroscience of Consciousness from Dawn 'til Dusk (Penguin, 2016).

Recreations: Squash, dancing.

Professor the Baroness Greenfield CBE, House of Lords, London SW1A 0PW
Tel: 020 7219 6451 *Email:* greenfieldsu@parliament.uk
Building F5, Culham Science Centre, Abingdon OX14 3DB *Tel:* 01865 407158
Email: sagpa@susangreenfield.com Website: www.susangreenfield.com
Twitter: @baroness_susan

CROSSBENCH

GREENGROSS, BARONESS

GREENGROSS (Life Baroness), Sally Ralea Greengross; cr. 2000. Born 29 June 1935; Married Sir Alan Greengross 1959 (1 son 3 daughters).

Education: Brighton and Hove High School; London School of Economics (BA 1972); French, Spanish.

Non-political career: Formerly a linguist, executive in industry, lecturer and researcher; Age Concern England: Assistant director 1977-82, Deputy director 1982-87, Director-General (formerly director) 1987-2000; International Federation on Ageing: Secretary General 1982-87, Vice-President (Europe) 1987-2001; Joint chair, Age Concern Institute of Gerontology, King's College London 1987-2000; Chair, Experience Corps 2001-04; International Longevity Centre UK: Executive chair 2000-04, Chief executive 2004-; Co-president, ILC Global Alliance 2007-17.

Political career: *House of Lords:* Raised to the peerage as Baroness Greengross, of Notting Hill in the Royal Borough of Kensington and Chelsea 2000. Co-opted Member, European Union Sub-committee F (Social Affairs, Education and Home Affairs) 2000-03; Member: European Union Sub-committee G (Social Policy and Consumer Affairs) 2003-07, Joint Committee on the Draft Care and Support Bill 2013, Intergenerational Fairness and Provision 2018-19. *Other:* Commissioner, Equlity and Human Rights Commission 2006-12; Vice-President, Local Government Association 2010-.

Other: Independent member, UN and WHO Networks on Ageing 1983-2000; Member, advisory council, European Movement 1992-; Vice-chair, Britain in Europe 2000-; Past and current member of several advisory bodies concerned with older people; Founder and Patron, Action on Elder Abuse 1994-; Vice-President, EXTEND 1996; Patron, Family Planning Association; President: Pensions Policy Institute, Association of Retirement Housing Managers; Royal Society for Public Health; Royal Society of Medicine; Patron to various charities; FRSH 1994; FRSA 1994; Eight honorary doctorates; UK Woman of Europe 1990; Outstanding achievement awards from the British Society of Gerontology and the British Geriatrics Society Medal; OBE 1993. Hurlingham, Reform Club.

Publications: Consultant, Journal of Educational Gerontology 1987-; Editor, Ageing: an adventure in living (1985); Has edited and contributed to other publications on ageing issues and social policy.

Recreations: Countryside, music.

The Baroness Greengross OBE, House of Lords, London SW1A 0PW
Tel: 020 7219 5494 *Email:* greengrosss@parliament.uk
Website: baronessgreengross.wordpress.com

CONSERVATIVE

GREENHALGH, LORD

Minister of State for Building Safety and Communities and Government Spokesperson, Ministry of Housing, Communities and Local Government and Home Office

GREENHALGH (Life Baron), Stephen John Greenhalgh; cr 2020. Born 4 September 1967; Married (3 children).

Education: St Paul's School; Trinity College, Cambridge (BA history and law 1989).

Non-political career: Brand Manager: Procter and Gamble 1989-94, PwC 1994-99; Biba Medical: Managing Director 1994-2018, Business Development Director 2018-; Deputy Mayor for Policing and Crime, London Mayoral Office 2012-16.

Political career: *House of Lords:* Raised to the peerage as Baron Greenhalgh, of Fulham in the London Borough of Hammersmith and Fulham 2020. Minister of State for Building Safety and Communities and Government Spokesperson: Ministry of Housing, Communities and Local Government 2020-, Home Office 2020-. *Other:* Hammersmith and Fulham Council: Councillor 1996-2003, Opposition Leader 2003-06, Leader 2006-12.

The Lord Greenhalgh, House of Lords, London SW1A 0PW
Tel: 020 7219 3000 *Twitter:* @team_greenhalgh

CROSSBENCH

GREENWAY, LORD

GREENWAY (4th Baron, UK), Ambrose Charles Drexel Greenway; cr. 1927; 4th Bt of Stanbridge Earls (UK) 1919. Born 21 May 1941; Son of 3rd Baron; Married Rosalynne Peta Schenk, née Fradgley 1985.

Education: Winchester College; Working French and German.

Non-political career: Marine photographer; Shipping consultant, Eurolist International Ltd -2017.

Political career: *House of Lords:* First entered House of Lords 1975; Elected hereditary peer 1999-. Member, Statutory Instruments Joint Committee 2000-07.

Political interests: Shipping, marine industry.

Other: Trinity House: Younger Brother 1987, Elder Brother 2007; Chair, Marine Society 1994-2000; Vice-President, Sail Training Association 1995-2004; President, Cruise Europe 1996-2003; Chair, World Ship Trust 2003-13; Hon. Fellow: Institute of Marine Engineering, Science and Technology, Nautical Institute; Mission to Seafarers, RNLI, Tall Ships Youth Trust. House of Lords Yacht Club.

Publications: Soviet Merchant Ships (1976); Comecon Merchant Ships (1978); A Century of Cross-Channel Passenger Ferries (1981); A Century of North Sea Passenger Steamers (1986); Cargo Liners (2009).

Recreations: Sailing, swimming.

The Lord Greenway, House of Lords, London SW1A 0PW
Tel: 020 7219 4943 *Email:* greenwaya@parliament.uk

LIBERAL DEMOCRAT

GRENDER, BARONESS

Liberal Democrat Lords Spokesperson for Housing

GRENDER (Life Baroness), Rosalind (Olly) Grender; cr 2013. Born 19 August 1962; Married (1 child).

Non-political career: Office of Paddy Ashdown MP: Speechwriter and responsible for housing and transport policy, Head of communication as Leader of Liberal Democrats 1990-95; Director of Communications, Shelter; Deputy Director of Communications, Number 10; Political co-ordinator and director for special projects to Lord Ashdown of Norton-sub-Hamdon as Chair of the Liberal Democrat's 2015 general election campaign 2012-15.

Political career: *House of Lords:* Raised to the peerage as Baroness Grender, of Kingston upon Thames, in the London Borough of Kingston upon Thames 2013. Liberal Democrat Lords Spokesperson for Housing 2020-. Member: Licensing Act 2003 2016-17, Artificial Intelligence 2017-18, Communications/Communications and Digital 2019-. *Other:* Member, Liberal Party/ Liberal Democrats 1981-; Deputy Local and General Election Co-ordinator 2015.

Political interests: Housing.

Other: Trustee: Homeless Link, Wandle Housing Association; MBE 1996.

The Baroness Grender MBE, House of Lords, London SW1A 0PW
Tel: 020 7219 3000 *Email:* grenderr@parliament.uk *Twitter:* @OllyGrender

CROSSBENCH

GREY-THOMPSON, BARONESS

GREY-THOMPSON (Life Baroness), Carys Davina (Tanni) Grey-Thompson; cr 2010. Born 26 July 1969; Daughter of Peter Grey and Sulwen Grey, née Jones; Married Dr Ian Thompson 1999 (1 daughter).

Education: St Cyres School, Penarth; Loughborough University (BA politics and administration 1991).

Non-political career: Paralympic Athlete, GB Paralympic Team 1988-2004; Development officer, UK Athletics 1996-2000; Director: TGT International Limited 2002-, Tanni Grey-Thompson Ltd 2006-.

Political career: *House of Lords:* Raised to the peerage as Baroness Grey-Thompson, of Eaglescliffe in the County of Durham 2010. Member, National Plan for Sport and Recreation 2020-. *Other:* Member: Sports Council for Wales 1996-2002, UK Sport 1998-2003, Sport Honours Committee 2006-17; Board member: Transport for London 2008-18, London Legacy Development Corporation 2012-; Vice-president, Local Government Association; Non-executive member, BBC Board 2017-.

Political interests: Sport, women's issues, disability rights; Developing countries.

Other: Council member, Winston Churchill Memorial Trust 2006-; Trustee and vice-chair, Laureus Sport for Good Foundation 2007-; Chair, Commission of the Future of Women's Sport; Non-executive director, UK Athletics 2007-12; Board member, London Marathon 2007-; President, Sports Leaders UK; Ambassador, International Inspiration; Trustee: Jane Tomlinson Trust, Tony Blair Sports Foundation, Snowdon Award Scheme 2012-; President, National Council for Voluntary Organisations; Member, executive committee, British Wheelchair Sports Foundation; Trustee: Spirit of 2012 Trust, Wembley National Stadium Trust 2013-, Sportsaid Foundation 2014-, Duke of Edinburgh Award 2014-; Chair, ukactive 2015-; Trustee, Stadium of Light Foundation 2018-; Adviser, EQUIIDA 2019-; V Charity; Freedom: City of Cardiff, Borough of Redcar and Cleveland; Pro-chancellor, Staffordshire University 2005-13; Chancellor, Northumbria University 2015-; 28 honorary degrees; Bronze 400m medal Seoul Paralympics 1988; Gold 100m, 200m, 400m, 800m medals Barcelona Paralympics 1992; Gold 800m and Silver 100m, 200m, 400m medals Atlanta Paralympics 1996; Gold 100m, 200m, 400m, 800m medals Sydney Paralympics 2000; Gold 100m, 400m medals Athens Paralympics 2004; MBE 1993; OBE 2000; DBE 2005. Cardiff Amateur Athletics Club; New Marske Harriers; Cleveland Wheelers Cycling Club.

Publications: Seize the Day (autobiography, 2001); Aim High (2007).

Recreations: Handcycling, wheelchair sports.

The Baroness Grey-Thompson DBE, House of Lords, London SW1A 0PW
Tel: 020 7219 3143 *Email:* greythompsont@parliament.uk Website: www.tanni.co.uk
Twitter: @Tanni_GT

LABOUR

GRIFFITHS OF BURRY PORT, LORD

GRIFFITHS OF BURRY PORT (Life Baron), Leslie John Griffiths; cr. 2004. Born 15 February 1942; Son of Olwen Griffiths, née Thomas, and Sidney Griffiths; Married Margaret Rhodes 1969 (1 daughter 2 sons).

Education: Llanelli Grammar School; University College of Wales, Cardiff (BA medieval English 1963); Fitzwilliam College, Cambridge (MA theology 1969); School of Oriental and African Studies, London University (PhD 1987); French, Haitian Créole.

Non-political career: Assistant lecturer in English, University of Wales 1964-67; Methodist minister: Port-au-Prince, Haiti 1970-74, Reading, Berkshire 1974-77, Cap Haitien, Haiti 1997-80, Loughton, Essex 1980-86, West London Mission 1986-91, Golders Green 1991-96; President, Methodist Conference 1994-95; Methodist minister, Wesley's Chapel, City of London 1997-2017; Canon, St Paul's Cathedral 2000-17. Member Association of University Teachers 1964-67.

Political career: *House of Lords:* Raised to the peerage as Baron Griffiths of Burry Port, of Pembrey and Burry Port in the County of Dyfed 2004. Opposition Whip 2017-20; Opposition Spokesperson for: Digital, Culture, Media and Sport 2017-20, Wales 2017-20. Member, Ecclesiastical Committee 2010-17.

Political interests: Education, international affairs, urban affairs, ethical issues; Cambodia, Dominican Republic, Fiji, Ghana, Haiti.

Other: Addiction Recovery Foundation 1989-2004, Patron 2004-; Christian Aid 1991-99; Birnbeck Housing Association 1991-96; Trustee, Sir Halley Stewart Trust 1999-; Art and Christianity Enquiry 1999-2008; Wesley House, Cambridge 2001-05; Central Foundation Schools of London 2002-; Abraham Path Initiative; Chairman, Central Foundation Schools of London; Paul Harris fellow, Rotary International 2008; Associate member, Learned Society of Wales; President, Boys' Brigade 2011-; Chair of Trustees, Central Foundation Schools of London 2011-; Patron, Waldensian Society in Britain 2012-; Trustee, Premier Christian Radio 2017-; Christian Aid, Shelter; Freedom, City of London 1997; Fellow: Sarum College, Salisbury 2001, Sion College 2003, Cardiff University 2005, University of Wales, Lampeter 2006; Knight of the Order of St John of Jerusalem 1989; Office of the Order of Christopher Columbus (Dominican Republic) 2011. Graduate Centre Club, Cambridge.

Publications: History of Haitian Methodism (1991); Letters Home (Methodist Publishing House, 1995); The Aristide Factor (1996); Worship in Our Diverse World (1998); Voices from the Desert (Canterbury Press, 2003); World Without End? (Epworth Press, 2007); A View from the Edge (Continuum, 2010).

Recreations: Cricket, rugby union, the post-colonial world, poetry.

The Lord Griffiths of Burry Port, House of Lords, London SW1A 0PW
Tel: 020 7219 8313 *Email:* griffithslj@parliament.uk
26 Stroud Road, Croydon London *Email:* lesliejohngriffiths@gmail.com

CONSERVATIVE

GRIFFITHS OF FFORESTFACH, LORD

GRIFFITHS OF FFORESTFACH (Life Baron), Brian Griffiths; cr. 1991. Born 27 December 1941; Son of Ivor and Phyllis Griffiths; Married Rachel Jones 1965 (1 son 2 daughters).

Education: Dynevor Grammar School; London School of Economics (BScEcon 1963; MScEcon 1965).

Non-political career: Lecturer in economics, London School of Economics 1965-76; Professor of banking and Director of Centre, Banking and International Finance, City University 1977-82; Dean, Business School, City University 1982-85; Director, Bank of England 1983-85; Head, Prime Minister's Policy Unit and special adviser to Margaret Thatcher 1985-90; Director: Thorn EMI 1990-96, Herman Miller Inc. 1991-2011, Times Newspapers Ltd 1991-; International adviser, Goldman Sachs 1991; Director: Servicemaster 1992-2007, HTV 1992-93, Telewest 1995-98, English, Welsh, Scottish Railway 1996-2007; Chair: Trillium 1998-2000, Westminster Health Care 1999-2002, Trillium Land Securities 2000-08; Vice-chair, Goldman Sachs (International) 2007; Adviser, Telereal Trillium 2009-.

Political career: *House of Lords:* Raised to the peerage as Baron Griffiths of Fforestfach, of Fforestfach in the County of West Glamorgan 1991. Member: European Union Sub-committee F (Social Affairs, Education and Home Affairs) 1999-2003, Religious Offences 2002-03, Economic Affairs 2007-10, Economic Affairs Finance Bill Sub-Committee 2011, Public Service and Demographic Change 2012-13, Sub-committee on Economic Affairs Finance Bill 2012-13, Economic Affairs 2013-16, Science and Technology 2017-19. *Other:* Chairman, Centre for Policy Studies 1991-2001; Member, board of directors Conservative Christian Fellowship 2000-02. Chair, Schools Examinations and Assessment Council 1991-93.

Political interests: Economic policy, education, broadcasting, social policy; China, Eastern and Central Europe.

Other: Freedom, City of London; Honorary doctorates: City University, University of Wales; Richmond University; Fellow: Trinity College, Carmarthen 1996, Swansea Institute of Higher Education 2003, Swansea University 2006. Garrick Club.

Publications: Several books on economics including: The Creation of Wealth (1984); Morality and the Market Place (1989).

The Lord Griffiths of Fforestfach, House of Lords, London SW1A 0PW
Tel: 020 7219 5353
Email: brian.griffiths@gs.com

CONSERVATIVE

GRIMSTONE OF BOSCOBEL, LORD

Minister of State for Investment and Government Spokesperson, Department for International Trade and Department for Business, Energy and Industrial Strategy

GRIMSTONE OF BOSCOBEL (Life Baron), Gerald Edgar Grimstone; cr 2020. Born 27 August 1949; Divorced (2 daughters 1 son).

Education: Merton College, Oxford (MSc chemistry).

Non-political career: Department of Health and Social Security 1982-86; Assistant Secretary, HM Treasury 1982-86; Schroders 1986-99: Director, Corporate Finance, Head, International Finance, Deputy chair and Head of Investment in Asia-Pacific, Head, Investment Banking in North America. Board Member, RAF Strike Command/Air Command 1999-2007; Chair, RAF Audit Committee; Member, Defence Audit Committee.

Political career: *House of Lords:* Raised to the peerage as Baron Grimstone of Boscobel, of Belgravia in the City of Westminster 2020. Minister of State for Investment and Government Spokesperson: Department for International Trade 2020-, Department for Business, Energy and Industrial Strategy 2020-. *Other:* Lead Non-executive board member, Ministry of Defence 2012-20.

Other: Standard Life: Board member 2003, Chair -2019; Chair, TheCityUK; Board member, HDFC Life; Independent Non-executive board member, Deloitte LLP 2011-20; Barclays Bank: Deputy chair, Chair -2019; Kt 2014.

The Lord Grimstone of Boscobel, House of Lords, London SW1A 0PW
Tel: 020 7219 3000

LABOUR

GROCOTT, LORD

GROCOTT (Life Baron), Bruce Joseph Grocott; cr. 2001. Born 1 November 1940; Son of late Reginald and Helen Grocott; Married Sally Ridgway 1965 (2 sons).

Education: Hemel Hempstead Grammar School; Leicester University (BA politics 1962); Manchester University (MA economics 1966).

Non-political career: Administrative officer, London County Council 1963-64; Tutor in politics, Manchester University 1964-65; Lecturer then senior lecturer in politics, Birmingham Polytechnic 1965-72; Principal lecturer, North Staffs Polytechnic 1972-74; Presenter then producer, Central Television 1979-87. Member: National Union of Journalists, Unite.

Political career: *House of Commons:* Contested South West Hertfordshire 1970 and Lichfield and Tamworth February 1974 general elections. MP (Labour) for Lichfield and Tamworth October 1974-79. Contested Lichfield and Tamworth 1979 and The Wrekin 1983 general elections. MP for The Wrekin 1987-97, for Telford 1997-2001; PPS to John Silkin: as Minister for Planning and Local Government 1975-76, as Minister of Agriculture 1976-78; Deputy Shadow Leader of the House and Deputy Campaigns Co-ordinator 1987-92; Opposition Frontbench Spokesperson for Foreign and Commonwealth Affairs 1992-93; PPS to Tony Blair: as Leader of the Labour Party 1994-2001, as Prime Minister 1997-2001. *House of Lords:* Raised to the peerage as Baron Grocott, of Telford in the County of Shropshire 2001. Government Spokesperson for: Defence 2001-02, Foreign and Commonwealth Office 2001-02, International Development 2001-02, Work and Pensions 2001-02; Government Whip 2001-02; Chief Whip 2002-08; Deputy Chair of Committees 2002-08; Deputy Speaker 2002-08. Member: Privileges 2002-08, Procedure 2002-08, Selection 2002-08, House of Lords' Offices Administration and Works Sub-committee 2002-08, Refreshment 2003-05, Communications 2008, Leader's Group on the Working Practices of the House of Lords 2010-11, International Relations/International Relations and Defence 2016-, Joint Committee on Fixed-Term Parliaments Act 2020-. *Other:* Councillor, Bromsgrove Urban District Council 1971-74; Governor, Birmingham City University 2010-18.

Political interests: Foreign affairs, media, health service, machinery of government.

Other: Chairman, Hansard Society 2012-15; Chancellor, Leicester University 2013-18; Hon. Doctorates: Birmingham City University 2006, Leicester University 2011; PC 2002. Trench Labour Club.

Recreations: Steam railways, sport.

Rt Hon the Lord Grocott, House of Lords, London SW1A 0PW
Tel: 020 7219 5097 *Email:* grocottb@parliament.uk

CONSERVATIVE

HAGUE OF RICHMOND, LORD

HAGUE OF RICHMOND (Life Baron), William Jefferson Hague; cr 2015. Born 26 March 1961; Son of Nigel and Stella Hague; Married Ffion Jenkins 1997.

Education: Wath-upon-Dearne Comprehensive School, Yorkshire; Magdalen College, Oxford (BA philosophy, politics and economics 1982) (President, Oxford Union 1981); INSEAD Business School, France 1985-86.

Non-political career: Shell UK 1982-83; McKinsey and Company 1983-88; Political adviser to Sir Geoffrey Howe as Chancellor of the Exchequer and Leon Brittan as Chief Secretary to the Treasury 1983; Political and economic adviser, JCB 2001-; Non-executive director, AES Engineering 2001-09; Member, Political Council of Terra Firma Capital Partners 2001-; Columnist, *News of the World* 2003-05; Non-executive director: AMT Sybex 2003-09, Intercontinental Exchange 2015-; Chair, International Advisory Group, Linklaters 2015-; Senior adviser, Teneo Holdings 2015-; Columnist, *Daily Telegraph* 2015-; Consultant, Citigroup 2017-.

Political career: *House of Commons:* Contested Wentworth 1987 general election. MP (Conservative) for Richmond (Yorkshire) 23 February 1989 by-election to 2010, for Richmond (Yorkshire) (revised boundary) 2010-15; PPS to Norman Lamont as Chancellor of the Exchequer 1990-93; Department of Social Security: Joint Parliamentary Under-Secretary of State 1993-94, Minister of State for Social Security and Disabled People 1994-95; Secretary of State for Wales 1995-97; Leader of the Opposition 1997-2001; Shadow Foreign Secretary and Senior Member of the Shadow Cabinet 2005-10; First Secretary of State 2010-15; Secretary of State for Foreign and Commonwealth Affairs (Foreign Secretary) 2010-14; Leader of the House of Commons 2014-15; Member: House of Commons Commission 2014-15, Speaker's Committee for the Independent Parliamentary Standards Authority 2014-15, Public Accounts Commission 2014-15. Member, Joint Committee on House of Lords Reform 2002-05. *House of Lords:* Raised to the peerage as Baron Hague of Richmond, of Richmond in the County of North Yorkshire 2015. On leave of absence January 2021-. *Other:* President Oxford University Conservative Association 1981; Leader Conservative Party June 1997-2001.

Political interests: Agriculture, economic policy.

Other: International Democrat Union, Global Alliance of Conservative, Christian Democrat and like-minded parties: Chair 1999-2002, Deputy Chair 2002-05, Assistant chair 2005-; Vice-President, Commonwealth Parliamentary Association (UK Branch) 2010-14; Member, Foreign Affairs Council, Council of the European Union 2010-14; Chairman: United for Wildlife Transport Taskforce 2014-, Royal United Services Institute 2015-; Fellow, Royal Society of Literature; *The Spectator*/Highland Park Parliamentarian of the Year 1998; National Book Awards History Book of the Year for biography of Pitt the Younger 2005; Threadneedle/ *Spectator* Speech of the Year 2007; Lifetime Achievement Award, *Spectator* awards 2014; PC 1995. Beefsteak, Carlton, Buck's, Pratt's, Budokwai Club.

Publications: Speaking with Conviction (Conservative Policy Forum, 1998); I Will Give you Back your Country (Conservative Policy Forum, 2000); Biography of William Pitt the Younger (2004); Biography of William Wilberforce (2007).

Recreations: Walking, sailing, cross country, skiing, judo.

Rt Hon the Lord Hague of Richmond, House of Lords, London SW1A 0PW
Tel: 020 7219 3000
Email: general@williamjhague.com Website: www.williamhague.com
Twitter: @WilliamJHague

CONSERVATIVE

HAILSHAM, VISCOUNT

HAILSHAM (3rd Viscount, UK), Douglas Martin Hogg; cr 1929; 3rd Baron Hailsham (UK) 1928; (Life) Baron Hailsham of Kettlethorpe 2015. Born 5 February 1945; Son of late Baron Hailsham of St Marylebone, former Lord Chancellor who disclaimed his hereditary honours for life 1963 and was subsequently created a life peer; succeeded his father 2001 as 3rd Viscount Hailsham and 3rd Baron Hailsham; Married Hon Sarah Boyd-Carpenter 1968 (now Baroness Hogg (qv)) (1 son 1 daughter).

Education: Eton College; Christ Church, Oxford (MA history 1968) (President, Oxford Union 1966).

Non-political career: Called to the Bar, Lincoln's Inn 1968 (Kennedy Law Scholar); QC 1990.

Political career: *House of Commons:* MP (Conservative) for Grantham 1979-97, for Sleaford and North Hykeham 1997-2010; PPS to Leon Brittan as Chief Secretary to the Treasury 1982-83; Government Whip 1983-84; Parliamentary Under-Secretary, Home Office 1986-89; Minister of State: Department of Trade and Industry (Minister for Industry and Enterprise) 1989-90, Foreign and Commonwealth Office 1990-95; Minister of Agriculture, Fisheries and Food 1995-97. Member: Home Affairs 1997-98, Justice 2009-10. *House of Lords:* Created a life peer as Baron Hailsham of Kettlethorpe, of Kettlethorpe in the County of Lincolnshire 2015.

Other: PC 1992.

Rt Hon the Viscount Hailsham QC, House of Lords, London SW1A 0PW
Tel: 020 7219 3000

LABOUR

HAIN, LORD

HAIN (Life Baron), Peter Gerald Hain; cr 2015. Born 16 February 1950; Son of Walter and Adelaine Hain; Married Patricia Western 1975 (divorced 2002) (2 sons); married Elizabeth Haywood 2003.

Education: Pretoria Boys High School, South Africa; Emanuel School, Wandsworth, London; Queen Mary College, London University (BSc economics and political science 1973); Sussex University (MPhil political science 2000).

Non-political career: Head of research, Union of Communication Workers 1976-91. Member, GMB.

Political career: *House of Commons:* Contested Putney 1983 and 1987 general elections. MP (Labour) for Neath 4 April 1991 by-election to 2010, for Neath (revised boundary) 2010-15; Opposition Whip 1995-96; Opposition Spokesperson for Employment 1996-97; Parliamentary Under-Secretary of State, Welsh Office 1997-99; Minister of State: Foreign and Commonwealth Office 1999-2001, Department of Trade and Industry (Energy and

Competitiveness) 2001, Foreign and Commonwealth Office (Europe) 2001-02; Government representative European Union Convention 2002-03; Secretary of State for Wales 2002-08; Leader of the House of Commons and Lord Privy Seal 2003-05; Secretary of State for: Northern Ireland 2005-07, Work and Pensions 2007-08, Wales 2009-10; Shadow Secretary of State for Wales 2010-12. Chair, Modernisation of the House of Commons 2003-05. *House of Lords:* Raised to the peerage as Baron Hain, of Neath in the County of West Glamorgan 2015. Member, COVID-19 2020-. *Other:* Leader, Young Liberals 1971-73; Member: Labour Party 1977-, Labour Party NEC 2011-12; Chair, National Policy Forum 2010-12.

Political interests: Social justice, democratic renewal, including Lords reform, electoral reform and devolution, environmental policy, including renewable energy, foreign affairs; Southern Africa, Spain.

Other: Former Member, Anti-Apartheid Movement; Chair, 'Stop the Seventy Tour' (which disrupted the South African rugby tour, and stopped the South African cricket tour to Britain) 1969-70; Founder, *Anti-Nazi League* 1977; Director, *Tribune* Newspaper 1991-97; Founder, Unite Against Fascism 2005; Honorary President, Unite Against Fascism, Wales 2009-; Non-executive Director, Amara Mining PCC 2013-16; Vice-President, Action for Southern Africa 2014-; Visiting Professor, University of South Wales 2014-; Chair, Board of Trustees, Donald Woods Foundation 2014-; Ambassador, Desmond Tutu Foundation 2015-; Trustee, Listen Charity 2015-; Global and Governmental adviser, Gordon Dadds LLP 2016-; Strategic adviser, Cyrus IM LLP 2016-; Visiting Adjunct Professor, University of Witwatersrand 2016-; Adviser, MOTI Group, Johannesburg 2018-; Patron, Canon Collins Trust; Chair: OR Tambo Centenary Committee 2017, Nelson Mandela Centenary Committee 2018; Fellow: Swansea University, Queen Mary University 2017; Hon. doctorate: University of South Wales 2013, University of Wales Trinity St David 2017; Welsh Politician of the Year, *am.pm* 2006; Welsh MP of the Year, BBC 2007; PC 2001; OR Tambo Presidential National Award (South Africa) 2015. Ynysygerwn Cricket Club; Resolven Rugby Club.

Publications: 21 books including: Ayes to the Left: A future for socialism (Lawrence and Wishart, 1995), Mandela (Spruce, 2010), Outside In (autobiography) (Biteback, 2012), Ad & Wal (Biteback, 2014), Back to the Future of Socialism (Policy Press, 2015) The Hain Diaries 1998-2007 (Biteback Publishing, 2015), Mandela: His Essential Life (Rowman & Littlefield, 2018).

Recreations: Rugby, soccer, cricket, motor racing, rock and folk music.

Rt Hon the Lord Hain, House of Lords, London SW1A 0PW
Tel: 020 7219 3000 *Email:* peter.hain@parliament.uk Website: peterhain.uk *Twitter:* @peterhain

HALE OF RICHMOND, BARONESS

NON-AFFILIATED

HALE OF RICHMOND (Life Baroness), Brenda Marjorie Hale; cr. 2004. Born 31 January 1945; Daughter of Cecil Hale and Marjorie Hale, née Godfrey; Married Anthony Hoggett 1968 (divorced 1992) (1 daughter); married Dr Julian Farrand QC 1992 (1 stepson 2 stepdaughters).

Education: Richmond High School for Girls, Yorkshire; Girton College, Cambridge (BA law 1966, MA 1969); Gray's Inn (Barrister 1969).

Non-political career: Manchester University law faculty 1966-89: Assistant lecturer, Lecturer, Senior lecturer, Reader, Professor; Barrister 1969-1972; On leave 1984-89; Commissioner, Law Commission 1984-93; QC 1989; High Court judge 1994-99; Lord Justice of Appeal 1999-2004; Visitor, Girton College, Cambridge 2004-; Supreme Court of the United Kingdom: Justice 2009-13, Deputy President 2013-17, President 2017-20.

Political career: *House of Lords:* Raised to the peerage as Baroness Hale of Richmond, of Easby in the County of North Yorkshire 2004. Lord of Appeal in Ordinary 2004-09; Disqualified from participation as: Justice of the Supreme Court 2009-13, Deputy President of the Supreme Court 2013-17, President of the Supreme Court 2017-20. *Other:* Member, Council on Tribunals 1980-84; Chair then President, National Family Mediation 1989-; Governor, Centre for Policy on Ageing 1990-93; Member: Human Fertilisation and Embryology Authority 1990-93, Judicial Studies Board, Civil and Family Committee 1990-94; Chair, Royal Courts of Justice Advice Bureau 2001-03.

Other: Managing trustee, Nuffield Foundation 1987-2002; Patron: Richmond Open Spaces Appeal 2004-, Hammersmith and Fulham Law Centre 2010-; President: Association of Women Barristers 1997-2005; UK Association of Women Judges 2003-; International Association of

Women Judges: President-elect 2008-10, President 2010-12; Fellmongers Company of Richmond, North Yorkshire; Chancellor, Bristol University 2004-16; Twenty honorary law doctorates; Hon. FBA; Hon. FRC Psych; Honorary degree, Bristol University 2017; DBE 1994; PC 1999. Athenæum Club.

Publications: Women and the Law (Blackwell, 1984); Parents and Children (Sweet and Maxwell, 4th edition 1993); From the Test Tube to the Coffin (Stevens, 1996); The Family, Law and Society (Butterworth, 6th edition 2008); Mental Health Law (Sweet and Maxwell, 5th edition 2010).

Recreations: Domesticity, drama, duplicate bridge.

Rt Hon the Baroness Hale of Richmond DBE, House of Lords, London SW1A 0PW
Tel: 020 7219 5353

CROSSBENCH

HALL OF BIRKENHEAD, LORD

HALL OF BIRKENHEAD (Life Baron), Anthony (Tony) William Hall; cr 2010. Born 3 March 1951; Son of late Donald Hall and Mary Hall; Married Cynthia Davis 1977 (1 son 1 daughter).

Education: King Edward's School, Birmingham; Birkenhead School; Keble College, Oxford (BA philosophy, politics and economics).

Non-political career: BBC 1973-2001: News trainee 1973, Producer, *World Tonight* 1976, Senior producer, *World at One* 1978, Output editor, *Newsnight* 1980, Senior producer, *Six O'Clock News* 1984, Assistant editor, *Nine O'Clock News* 1985, Editor, news and 1987 general election 1987, News and Current Affairs Department: Editor 1988-90, Director 1990-93, Managing director 1993-96, Chief executive, BBC News 1996-2001, Director-General, BBC 2013-20; Chief executive, Royal Opera House 2001-13.

Political career: *House of Lords:* Raised to the peerage as Baron Hall of Birkenhead, of Birkenhead in the County of Cheshire 2010. *Other:* Non-executive director, HM Customs and Excise 2002-05; Chair, Creative and Culture Skills 2004-09; Non-executive director, Channel 4 Television 2005-20; Member, Olympics Cultural Advisory Board, Department for Culture, Media and Sport 2006-08; Board member, London Organising Committee of the Olympic Games 2009-13; Chair, Cultural Olympiad Board 2009-13; Mayor of London's Cultural Forum; Chair, National Gallery 2020-.

Political interests: Arts, culture, broadcasting, skills; China, Italy.

Other: Fellow, Royal Society of Arts 1997; Chair, Theatre Royal, Stratford 2001-09; Non-executive director, University for Industry 2003-06; Trustee, British Council 2008-13; Honorary DLitt, London University 2009; CBE 2006.

Recreations: Ballet, TV and radio, gardening, walking, books, opera.

The Lord Hall of Birkenhead CBE, House of Lords, London SW1A 0PW
Tel: 020 7219 5353 *Email:* halla@parliament.uk
NBH 04A Director-General's Office, BBC Broadcasting House, Portland Place, London W1A 1AA *Tel:* 020 3614 2255 *Email:* tony.hall@bbc.co.uk

CROSSBENCH

HALLETT, BARONESS

HALLETT (Life Baroness), Heather Carol Hallett; cr 2019. Born 16 December 1949; Married Nigel Wilkinson 1974 (2 sons).

Education: St Hugh's College, Oxford (MA).

Non-political career: Called to the Bar, Inner Temple 1972; Bencher 1993; QC 1989; Recorder 1989-99; Deputy High Court Judge 1995-99; Leader, South Eastern Circuit 1995-97; QBD: Judge of the High Court of Justice 1999-2005, Vice-president 2012-14; Presiding Judge, Western Circuit 2001-04; Lord Justice of Appeal 2005-; Vice-president, Court of Appeal (Criminal Division) 2013-19.

Political career: *House of Lords:* Raised to the peerage as Baroness Hallett, of Rye in the County of East Sussex 2019. Chair, Highgate Cemetery Bill [HL] 2020-. *Other:* Judicial Appointments Commission: Member 2006-07, Vice-chair 2007-10; Chair, Security Vetting Appeals Panel 2019-.

Other: Chair, Judicial College 2010-14; General Council of the Bar: Vice-chair 1997, Chair 1998; Hon LLD: Derby University 2000, UCL 2012, Portsmouth University 2012; DBE 1999; PC 2005.

Rt Hon the Baroness Hallett DBE, House of Lords, London SW1A 0PW

CROSSBENCH

HAMEED, LORD

HAMEED (Life Baron), Khalid Hameed; cr 2007. Born 1 July 1941; Son of late Prof Dr M Abdul Hameed and Rashida Abdul Hameed; Married Dr Ghazala Afzal 1989 (3 daughters 3 sons).

Education: Colvin Taluqdars College, Lucknow, India; Lucknow University (BSc, DPA, MBBS 1966); London University (Diploma tropical medicine and hygiene 1972); Hindi, Urdu.

Non-political career: Clinical assistant, University College Hospital, London; Senior house officer, St George's Hospital, London; Registrar, St Mary's Hospital, London; Private and corporate medicine, London 1980-90; Chief executive officer, Cromwell Hospital, London 1990-2005; Chair, Alpha Hospitals 2003-17; Director, London International Hospital 2005-15.

Political career: *House of Lords:* Raised to the peerage as Baron Hameed, of Hampstead in the London Borough of Camden 2007. *Other:* Chair, Commonwealth Youth Exchange Council 1997-; High Sheriff of Greater London 2006-07; DL, Greater London 2007-.

Political interests: Commonwealth.

Other: Parliament of the World Religions, Brussels; Chair, Woolf Institute; President: Little Foundation, Friends of British Library; Trustee, International Students House; Member: Royal Society of Medicine, Medical Defence Union, General Medical Council; Save the Children, MacMillan Cancer Research, Royal Academy School of Art, British Red Cross, MENCAP; Freedom, City of London; Honorary Fellow, Royal College of Physicians; DSc Lucknow University 1999; Honorary Fellow, Royal College of Physicians, London 2006; Honorary doctorates: Middlesex University 2008, Metropolitan University 2009; Several awards from UK and overseas organisations and universities; Padma Shri (India) 1992; Sitare Qaide Azam (Pakistan) 1996; Hilali-Quaid-i-Azam (Pakistan) 1999; PGDB (Nepal) 1999; Order of the Burning Spear (Kenya) 2001; CBE 2004; Padma Bhushan (India) 2009. Athenæum, Marks, Mossiman Dining Club; Member, Guards Polo Club; Life Member: MCC, Lucknow Golf Club.

Publications: Published speeches on Interfaith Harmony.

Recreations: Chess, bridge, cricket, poetry, polo.

The Lord Hameed CBE DL, House of Lords, London SW1A 0PW
Email: hameed@parliament.uk
94 Harley Street, London W1G 7HX *Tel:* 020 7935 5012

CONSERVATIVE

HAMILTON OF EPSOM, LORD

HAMILTON OF EPSOM (Life Baron), Archibald (Archie) Gavin Hamilton; cr 2005. Born 30 December 1941; Son of late 3rd Baron Hamilton of Dalzell, GCVO, MC; Married Anne Napier 1968 (3 daughters).

Education: Eton College.

Non-political career: Director, Tower Assets 1971-73; Managing Director, British Quadruplex 1974; Director, Jupiter Dividend & Growth Trust plc 1998-. Lieutenant, Coldstream Guards 1960-62.

Political career: *House of Commons:* Contested Dagenham February and October 1974 general elections. MP (Conservative) for Epsom and Ewell 1978 by-election to 2001; PPS to David Howell as Secretary of State for: Energy 1979-81, Transport 1981-82; Assistant Government Whip 1982-84; Government Whip 1984-86; Ministry of Defence: Parliamentary Under-Secretary of State for Defence Procurement 1986-87, Minister of State for the Armed Forces 1988-93; PPS to Margaret Thatcher as Prime Minister 1987-88; Member, Committee on Intelligence and Security 1994-97. 1922 Committee: Member, Executive 1995-97, Chair 1997-2001; Member, Conservative Ethics and Integrity Committee 1999. *House of Lords:*

Raised to the peerage as Baron Hamilton of Epsom, of West Anstey in the County of Devon 2005. Co-opted Member, EU Sub-committee C (Foreign Affairs, Defence and Development Policy) 2006-10; Member: EU Sub-committee A: (Economic and Financial Affairs and International Trade) 2010-12, (Economic and Financial Affairs) 2012-15, Joint Committee on the National Security Strategy 2015-19. *Other:* Vice-President, Conservatives for Britain 2015-16. Councillor, Royal Borough of Kensington and Chelsea 1968-71; Trustee, National Army Museum 2012-.

Political interests: Finance, tax, economic policy, trade and industry, defence.

Other: Member, UK Delegation to NATO Parliamentary Assembly 2014-; Governor, Westminster Foundation for Democracy 1993-97; President, Lest We Forget; PC 1991; Knighted 1994. White's Club.

Rt Hon the Lord Hamilton of Epsom, House of Lords, London SW1A 0PW
Tel: 020 7219 3000 *Email:* hamiltona@parliament.uk

CONSERVATIVE

HAMMOND OF RUNNYMEDE, LORD

HAMMOND OF RUNNYMEDE (Life Baron), Philip Hammond; cr 2020. Born 4 December 1955; Son of Bernard Hammond, civil engineer and local government officer; Married Susan Williams-Walker 1991 (2 daughters 1 son).

Education: Shenfield School, Brentwood, Essex; University College, Oxford (MA politics, philosophy and economics 1977).

Non-political career: Assistant to Chair, then marketing manager, Speywood Laboratories Ltd 1977-81; Director, Speywood Medical Ltd 1981-83; Established and ran medical equipment manufacturing and distribution companies 1983-94; Director various medical equipment manufacturing companies 1983-96; Director, Castlemead Ltd 1984-; Partner, CMA Consultants 1993-95; Director, Castlemead Homes Ltd 1994-2004; Consultant to Government of Malawi 1995-97; Director: Consort Resources Ltd 1999-2003, Matrix Partners 2020-.

Political career: *House of Commons:* Contested Newham North East 1994 by-election. MP for Runnymede and Weybridge 1997-2019; Opposition Spokesperson for: Health and Social Services 1998-2001, Trade and Industry 2001-02; Shadow Minister for Local and Devolved Government Affairs 2002-05; Shadow Chief Secretary to the Treasury 2005; Shadow Secretary of State for Work and Pensions 2005-07; Shadow Chief Secretary to the Treasury 2007-10; Secretary of State for: Transport 2010-11, Defence 2011-14, Foreign and Commonwealth Affairs (Foreign Secretary) 2014-16; Chancellor of the Exchequer 2016-19. Member: Unopposed Bills (Panel) 1997-2004, Environment, Transport and Regional Affairs 1998, Environment, Transport and Regional Affairs (Transport Sub-Committee) 1998, Trade and Industry 2002. Secretary, Conservative Party Committee for Health 1997-98. *House of Lords:* Raised to the peerage as Baron Hammond of Runnymede, of Runnymede in the County of Surrey 2020. *Other:* Chair, East Lewisham Conservative Association 1989-96; Member, Executive Council, Greater London Area 1989-96; Conservative Party whip removed September 2019.

Political interests: Economic policy, international trade, European Union, defence, social security, transport, housing and planning, energy, health; Southern and Eastern Africa, Germany, Italy, Latin America.

Other: Joint President, Weybridge Youth Club; Vice-president, Basingstoke Canal Society; Patron, White Lodge, Chertsey; Non-executive director, Ardagh Group 2019-; Senior Adviser, OakNorth Bank 2020-; Partner, Buckthorn Partners 2020-; Chair, Future Economy Surrey Commission 2020-; Member of Panel of Senior Advisers, Chatham House 2020-; PC 2010. Carlton Club.

Recreations: Travel, cinema, walking.

Rt Hon the Lord Hammond of Runnymede, House of Lords, London SW1A 0PW
Tel: 020 7219 3000 *Email:* hammondp@parliament.uk *Twitter:* @PhilipHammondUK

LIBERAL DEMOCRAT

HAMWEE, BARONESS

Liberal Democrat Lords Spokesperson for Immigration

HAMWEE (Life Baroness), Sally Rachel Hamwee; cr. 1991. Born 12 January 1947; Daughter of late Alec and Dorothy Hamwee.

Education: Manchester High School for Girls; Girton College, Cambridge (BA law 1969, MA).

Non-political career: Admitted Solicitor 1972; Clintons Solicitors: Partner 1984-2004, Consultant 2004-10.

Political career: *House of Lords:* Raised to the peerage as Baroness Hamwee, of Richmond upon Thames in the London Borough of Richmond upon Thames 1991. Liberal Democrat Spokesperson for: Local Government 1991-98, Housing and Planning 1993-98, Local Government and Planning 1998-2000, Environment, Transport and the Regions 1999-2000, Local Government and the Regions 2001-04, ODPM/Communities and Local Government 2004-10, Regional and Local Government 2006-09, Home Affairs 2009-10, 2015, Immigration 2017-. Member, Economic Affairs 2008-10; Alternate member, Procedure 2009-14; Member: Leader's Group on Code of Conduct 2009, Merits of Statutory Instruments/ Secondary Legislation Scrutiny 2010-15, Leader's Group on the Working Practices of the House of Lords 2010-11, Adoption Legislation 2012-13, Inquiries Act 2005 2013-14, Inheritance and Trustees' Powers Bill 2013, Extradition Law 2014-15, Joint Committee on Human Rights 2015-19, European Union 2019-, EU Justice Sub-committee 2019-20, EU Security and Justice Sub-committee 2020-. Chair, Liberal Democrat Parliamentary Party Committee on Home Affairs, Justice and Equalities (Home Office) 2010-15. *Other:* Member, National Executive, Liberal Party 1987-88; Liberal Democrats, Member: Federal Executive 1989-91, General election team 1992, 1997, Federal Policy Committee 1996-98. Councillor, London Borough of Richmond upon Thames 1978-98: Chair: Planning Committee 1983-94, London Planning Advisory Committee 1986-94; Joint President, Association of London Government; London Assembly: Member 2000-08, Deputy chair 2000-01, 2002-03, 2004-05, 2006-07, Chair 2001-02, 2003-04, 2005-06, 2007-08; Joint President, London Councils.

Political interests: Local government, planning, London, arts, home affairs, immigration and asylum, penal policy.

Other: Council Member, Parents for Children 1977-86; Legal Adviser, Simon Community 1980-; Council Member, Refuge 1991-2005; Member: Joseph Rowntree Foundation Inquiry, Planning for Housing 1991, Advisory Board, Compact Advocacy Advisory Group, NCVO; Family Policy Studies Centre: Governing Council -2000, Council Member 1994-2001; Town and Country Planning Association: President 1995-2002, Vice-president 2002-; Chair, Xfm Ltd 1996-98; Member, Advisory Board, Centre for Public Scrutiny 2000-; Board Member, Arts Council London 2006-08; Trustee, Rose Theatre Kingston 2009-; Vice-President, Chartered Institute of Environmental Health; Member, Advisory Board, Equality and Diversity Forum, Human Rights Project; Trustee, Safer London 2014-; Member, Missing People, Policy and Research Advisory group 2014-.

The Baroness Hamwee, House of Lords, London SW1A 0PW
Tel: 020 7219 5353 *Email:* hamwees@parliament.uk

CONSERVATIVE

HANNAN OF KINGSCLERE, LORD

HANNAN OF KINGSCLERE (Life Baron), Daniel John Hannan; cr 2021. Born 1 September 1971; Married Sara Maynard 2000 (2 daughters).

Education: Marlborough College; Oriel College, Oxford (MA modern history 1993); French, Spanish.

Non-political career: Director, European Research Group 1994-99; Leader writer, *Daily Telegraph* 1996-; Political adviser to Michael Howard as shadow foreign secretary 1997-98.

Political career: *House of Lords:* Raised to the peerage as Baron Hannan of Kingsclere, of Kingsclere in the County of Hampshire 2021. *Other:* MEP for South East 1999-2020: Member: Citizens' Freedoms and Rights, Justice and Home Affairs Committee 1999-2002, Kazakhstan, Kyrgyzstan, Uzbekistan, Tajikistan, Turkmenistan and Mongolia Delegation 1999-2002, Employment and Social Affairs Committee 2002, Constitutional Affairs Committee 2002-07, 2011-14, 2019-20, Central America and Mexico Delegation 2002-04, Mercosur Delegation

2004-08, Internal Market and Consumer Protection Committee 2007-08, Euro-Latin American Delegation 2007-08, Fisheries Committee 2008-09, Afghanistan Delegation 2008-09, Legal Affairs Committee 2009-11; ACP-EU Delegation: Member 2009-14; Vice-chair 2014-19; Member: Petitions Committee 2014-19, Andean Community Delegation 2019-20, Euro-Latin American Parliamentary Assembly Delegation 2019-20; Vice-chair, European Conservatives and Reformists Group 2019-20. President, Oxford University Conservative Association 1992; Vice-chair, Conservative Students 1993; Chair, National Association of Conservative Graduates 1995.

Political interests: South America, Spain.

Other: Co-founder, Direct Democracy; Member, Freedom Association.

Publications: A Treaty Too Far (1992); Time for a Fresh Start in Europe (1993); Towards 1996: Britain in a Multi-Speed Europe (1994); The Challenge of the East (1996); A Guide to the Amsterdam Treaty (1997); The Euro: Bad for Business (1998); What if Britain Votes No? (2002); The Case for EFTA (2004); Co-author: Direct Democracy: An Agenda for a New Model Party (2005), The Plan: Twelve Months to Renew Britain (2008).

Recreations: Shakespeare.

The Lord Hannan of Kingsclere, House of Lords, London SW1A 0PW
Tel: 020 7219 3000 *Twitter:* @DanielJHannan

CROSSBENCH

HANNAY OF CHISWICK, LORD

HANNAY OF CHISWICK (Life Baron), David Hugh Alexander Hannay; cr 2001. Born 28 September 1935; Son of late Julian Hannay and late Eileen Hannay; Married Gillian Rex 1961 (died 2015) (4 sons).

Education: Craigflower School; Winchester College; New College, Oxford (BA modern history 1959); French.

Non-political career: Foreign Office (FCO) 1959-95: London 1959-60, Language student, Tehran 1960-61, Oriental secretary, Kabul 1961-63, Second secretary, FCO 1963-65, First secretary, Brussels (EC) 1965-70, Brussels negotiating team 1970-72, Chef de Cabinet to Vice-President EC Commission 1973-77, FCO 1977-84: Head of: Energy, science and space department 1977-79, Middle East department 1979, Assistant under-secretary, EC 1979-84; Minister, Washington 1984-85, Ambassador, permanent representative to: EC 1985-90, UN, New York 1990-95; Special Representative for Cyprus 1996-2003; Non-executive director: Chime Communications 1999-2006, Aegis 2000-03; Member, advisory board, GPW 2011-. National Service 1954-56 (2nd Lieutenant 8th King's Royal Irish Hussars). First Division Association 1959-95.

Political career: *House of Lords:* Raised to the peerage as Baron Hannay of Chiswick, of Bedford Park in the London Borough of Ealing 2001. Member: EU Sub-committee A (Economic and Financial Affairs, Trade and External Relations/Economic and Financial Affairs) 2001-05, European Union 2003-06, 2008-14; EU Sub-committee C (Foreign Affairs, Defence and Development Policy): Member 2005-06, Co-opted member 2006-08; Member, Intergovernmental Organisations 2007-08, EU Sub-committee F (Home Affairs) 2008-12: Chair, EU Sub-committee F (Home Affairs, Health and Education) 2012-14; Member: The Arctic 2014-15, Sexual Violence in Conflict 2015-16, International Relations/International Relations and Defence 2016-. *Other:* Council Member: Birmingham University 1997-2006, Kent University 2009-15; Council Chair and Pro-Chancellor, Birmingham University 2001-06.

Political interests: Foreign and development policy, EU, energy policy and climate change, higher education.

Other: Adviser to Executive Committee, World Federation of United Nations Associations 1995-2000; Member, UN Secretary-General High Level Panel on Threats, Challenges and Change 2003-04; Chair, United Nations Association, UK 2006-11; Member: Top Level Group for Nuclear Disarmament and Non-proliferation 2011-, Future of Europe Forum 2013-16; Advisory Board: Prospect 1995-2005, Centre for European Reform 1996-, European Foreign Affairs Review 1996-; Salzburg Seminar 2001-05; Chair, International Advisory Board, EDHEC Business School, France 2002-09; TANGGUH Independent Advisory Panel 2002-09; Judge, School of Management, Cambridge 2004-10; Governor, Ditchley Foundation 2005-20; Children at Risk Foundation (UK); Fellow: New College, Oxford, Regent's University 2019; Honorary Fellow, New College, Oxford; Hon DLitt, Birmingham University; Sir Brian

Urquhart Award for Distinguished Service to the United Nations 2015; CMG 1981; KCMG 1986; GCMG 1995; CH 2003. Travellers Club.

Publications: Editor, Britain's Entry into the European Community, Report on the Negotiations (1970-72); Cyprus: The Search for a Solution (I.B. Tauris, 2004); New World Disorder – The UN after the Cold War, an Insider's View (I.B. Tauris, 2008); Britain's Quest for a Role: A Diplomatic Memoir from Europe to the UN (I.B. Tauris, 2012).

Recreations: Travel, photography, gardening, grandchildren.

The Lord Hannay of Chiswick GCMG CH, House of Lords, London SW1A 0PW
Tel: 020 7219 1358
3 The Orchard, London W4 1JZ *Tel:* 020 8994 7004 *Email:* d.h.a.hannay@gmail.com

NON-AFFILIATED

HANNINGFIELD, LORD

HANNINGFIELD (Life Baron), Paul Edward Winston White; cr. 1998. Born 16 September 1940; Son of late Edward Ernest William White and Irene Joyce Gertrude, née Williamson.

Education: King Edward VI Grammar School, Chelmsford; Nuffield Scholarship for Agriculture (research in USA specialising in marketing in farming).

Non-political career: Farmer.

Political career: *House of Lords:* Raised to the peerage as Baron Hanningfield, of Chelmsford in the County of Essex 1998. Opposition Whip 2003-07; Opposition Spokesperson for: Office of the Deputy Prime Minister/Communities and Local Government 2003-07, Education and Skills 2004-05, Transport 2005-09, Business, Innovation and Skills 2009-10; Suspended from membership: July 2011-May 2012, May 2014-May 2015. *Other:* Chair: Conservative Party National Local Government Advisory Committee, Board of Conservative Party 1997-2001; Conservative Whip suspended February 2010. Essex County Council: Councillor 1970-2010, Council Leader 1998-99, 2001-10, Leader, Conservative Group 2001-10; DL, Essex 1991-; Deputy Chair and Conservative Group Leader, Local Government Association 1997-2001.

Political interests: Local government, education, transport and infrastructure, agriculture, constitutional affairs, foreign policy.

Other: President, Assembly of European Regions Sub-Commission 1990-2005; EU Committee of the Regions: Leader, Conservative Group, UK Delegation -2005, Chair: Enlargement Group 1998-2005, Bulgarian Joint Consultative Committee 2002-05; Vice-President, Commission on Transport and the Information Society 1998-2000; Board member, Commonwealth Local Government Forum 2007-; Association of County Councils: Member 1981-97, Conservative Leader 1995-97; Chair: Council of Local Education Authorities 1990-92; Eastern Region Further Education Funding Council 1992-97; Chair and co-founder, Localis 2001-; Member of Court, Essex University; President, Society of Emergency Planning Officers 2003-; Vice-Patron, Helen Rollason Cancer Centre Appeal; Two honorary doctorates: Essex University, Anglia Ruskin University.

Publications: Several contributions to local government journals.

Recreations: Botany, politics and current affairs, travel, food and wine.

The Lord Hanningfield DL, House of Lords, London SW1A 0PW
Tel: 020 7219 5353

LABOUR

HANWORTH, VISCOUNT

HANWORTH (3rd Viscount, UK), David Stephen Geoffrey Pollock; cr. 1936; 3rd Baron Hanworth (UK) 1926; 3rd Bt of Hanworth (UK) 1922. Born 16 February 1946; Son of 2nd Viscount Hanworth; Married Elizabeth 1968 (2 daughters).

Education: Wellington College, Berkshire; Guildford Technical College; Sussex University (BSc economics 1969); Southampton University (MSc economics and statistics 1970); Amsterdam University (PhD 1988); French.

Non-political career: University of London 1972-2007: Lecturer, Reader; Professor, Leicester University 2007-.

Political career: *House of Lords:* First entered House of Lords 1996; Elected hereditary peer 2011-. Member: Joint Committee on Consolidation, Etc, Bills 2013-, Inheritance and Trustees' Powers Bill 2013, Partnerships (Prosecution) (Scotland) Bill 2013, The Arctic 2014-15, EU Energy and Environment Sub-Committee 2015-19, Intellectual Property (Unjustified Threats) Bill 2016, Economic Affairs Finance Bill Sub-committee 2018-19, Secondary Legislation Scrutiny 2019-.

Political interests: Economic policy, financial regulation, energy, transport, environment, foreign affairs; Austria, France, Germany, Italy, Netherlands.

Publications: The Algebra of Econometrics (1979); Handbook of Time Series Analysis Signal Processing and Dynamics (1999); Co-author, Innovations in Multivariate Statistical Analysis (2000).

The Viscount Hanworth, House of Lords, London SW1A 0PW
Tel: 020 7219 5353 *Email:* pollockd@parliament.uk
Department of Economics, Astley Clarke Building, A108, University of Leicester, Leicester LE1 7RH *Email:* stephen_pollock@sigmspi.u-net.com Website: www.le.ac.uk/users/dsgp1

CROSSBENCH

HARDIE, LORD

HARDIE (Life Baron), Andrew Rutherford Hardie; cr 1997. Born 8 January 1946; Son of late Andrew Rutherford and late Elizabeth Currie Hardie; Married Catherine Storrar Elgin 1971 (2 sons 1 daughter).

Education: St Modan's High School, Stirling; Edinburgh University (MA French and German 1966; LLB 1969).

Non-political career: Solicitor 1971; Member, Faculty of Advocates 1973; Advocate Depute 1979-83; QC (Scot) 1985; Treasurer, Faculty of Advocates 1989-94, Dean 1994-97; Lord Advocate 1997-2000; Senator of the College of Justice in Scotland 2000-13; Honorary Bencher, Lincoln's Inn.

Political career: *House of Lords:* Raised to the peerage as Baron Hardie, of Blackford in the City of Edinburgh 1997. As a senior member of the judiciary, disqualified from participation 2009-13; On leave of absence July 2016-. Chair, Mental Capacity Act 2005 2013-14.

Political interests: Law and the constitution, human rights, issues relating to families and children, care and rehabilitation of prisoners (particularly young offenders), disability issues, asylum and immigration, energy and environment; China, India, Sri Lanka, Taiwan.

Other: Non-practising member, Faculty of Advocates; Capability (Scotland), Children's Charities, Christian Aid; PC 1997.

Recreations: Cricket, travel, grandchildren.

Rt Hon the Lord Hardie, House of Lords, London SW1A 0PW
Tel: 020 7219 5353 *Email:* hardiera@parliament.uk

CONSERVATIVE

HARDING OF WINSCOMBE, BARONESS

HARDING OF WINSCOMBE (Life Baroness), Diana (Dido) Mary Harding; cr 2014. Born 9 November 1967; Daughter of Lord and Lady Harding of Petherton; Married John Penrose (qv) 1995 (MP for Weston-Super-Mare) (2 daughters).

Education: St Antony's Leweston School, Dorset; Oxford University (BA philosophy, politics and economics 1988); Harvard Business School (MBA 1992).

Non-political career: Consultant, McKinsey & Co 1988-90; Marketing Director, Thomas Cook 1995-98; Global Sourcing Director, Kingfisher plc 1998-2000; Commercial Director, Woolworths 1998-99; Commercial Director and International Support Director, Tesco plc 2000-08; Convenience Director, Sainsbury's 2008-10; Chief Executive, TalkTalk Telecom Group plc 2010-17.

Political career: *House of Lords:* Raised to the peerage as Baroness Harding of Winscombe, of Nether Compton in the County of Dorset 2014. Member, Economic Affairs 2017-. *Other:* Non-executive director, Bank of England 2014-; Board member, UK Holocaust Memorial Foundation 2015-; Chair, NHS Improvement 2017-; Member, Health Honours Committee

2018-; Chair, Covid-19 Test and Trace Programme 2020-; Interim Executive Chair, National Institute for Health Protection 2020-.

Political interests: Business, digital economic and social issues; China, India.

Other: Non-executive director: British Land Company plc 2010-14, Cheltenham Racecourse 2011-14; Trustee: Go-On, Digital Skills Alliance 2013-, Doteveryone 2016-; Liveryman, Worshipful Company of Goldsmiths; Honorary Doctor of Business Administration, Anglia Ruskin University. Member, Jockey Club.

Recreations: Horse racing, hunting.

The Baroness Harding of Winscombe, House of Lords, London SW1A 0PW
Tel: 020 7219 5353 *Email:* hardingd@parliament.uk

CROSSBENCH

HARRIES OF PENTREGARTH, LORD

HARRIES OF PENTREGARTH (Life Baron), Richard Douglas Harries; cr 2006. Born 2 June 1936; Son of late Brigadier W. D. J. Harries, CBE; Married Josephine Bottomley, MB, BChir, DCH 1963 (1 son 1 daughter).

Education: Wellington College, Berkshire; RMA, Sandhurst; Selwyn College, Cambridge (MA theology 1965); Cuddesdon College, Oxford.

Non-political career: Curate, Hampstead Parish Church 1963-69; Chaplain, Westfield College 1966-69; Lecturer, Wells Theological College 1969-72; Vicar, All Saints, Fulham 1972-81; Dean, King's College, London 1981-87; Bishop of Oxford 1987-2006; Visiting Professor, Liverpool Hope University College 2002; Nuffield Council on Bioethics 2002-08; Hon. Professor of Theology, Kings College, London 2006-; Gresham College: Professor of Divinity 2008-12, Fellow and Emeritus Professor 2012-. Lieutenant, Royal Corps of Signals 1955-58.

Political career: *House of Lords:* Raised to the peerage as Baron Harries of Pentregarth, of Ceinewydd in the County of Dyfed 2006. First entered House of Lords as Bishop of Oxford 1993; Convener of Bench of Bishops 1998-2006. Member, House of Lords' Offices 1997-2001; Chair, Stem Cell Research 2001-02; Member: Procedure 2007-12, Joint Committee on Privacy and Injunctions 2011-12, Works of Art 2012-13, 2014-15, Charities 2016-17, Citizenship and Civic Engagement 2017-18. *Other:* General Ordination examiner in Christian Ethics 1972-76; Director, Post Ordination Training, Kensington Jurisdiction 1973-79; Member, Home Office Advisory Committee for reform of sexual offences law 1981-85; Chair, Southwark Ordination Course 1982-87; Vice-chair, Council for Arms Control 1982-87; Chair: Council of Christians and Jews 1992-2001, Board of Social Responsibility for Church of England 1996-2001; Member, Royal Commission on Reform of House of Lords 1999-2000; Nuffield Council on Bioethics 2002-07; Human Fertilisation and Embryo Authority 2003-09.

Political interests: Dalits, religion and belief in British public life, ethics in relation to end of life issues, use of armed forces, poverty, human rights; Georgia, India, West Papua.

Other: Member, Anglican Consultative Council 1994-2003; Consultant, Anglican Peace and Justice Network 1984-94; Vice-chair, Council for Christian Action 1979-87; President, Johnson Society 1988-89; Board member, Christian Aid 1994-2000; Five honorary doctorates; Two honorary Oxbridge fellowships; Fellow, King's College, London; Hon. Fellow: Academy of Medical Sciences, Institute of Biology; Fellow: Learned Society of Wales, Royal Society of Literature; President's Medal, British Academy 2012.

Publications: Prayers of Hope (1975); Turning to Prayer (1978); Prayers of Grief and Glory (1979); Being a Christian (1981); Should Christians Support Guerillas? (1982); The Authority of Divine Love (1983); Praying Round the Clock (1983); Prayer and the Pursuit of Happiness (1985); Morning Has Broken (1985); Christianity and War in a Nuclear Age (1986); C. S. Lewis: the man and his God (1987); Christ is Risen (1988); Is There a Gospel for the Rich (1992); Art and the Beauty of God (1993); The Real God: A Response to Anthony Freeman (1994); Questioning Belief (1995); A Gallery of Reflections – The Nativity in Art (1995); Co-editor, Two Cheers For Secularism (1998); In The Gladness of Today (2000); Co-editor, Christianity: Two Thousand Years (2001); God outside the Box: Why spiritual people object to Christianity (2002); After the Evil: Christianity and Judaism in the Shadow of the Holocaust (2003); The Passion in Art (2004); Praying the Eucharist (2004); The Re-enchantment of Morality (2008); Faith in Politics? Rediscovering the Christian Roots of our Political Values (2010, 2014); Issues of Life and Death: Christian Faith and Medical Intervention (2010); Co-editor, Reinhold Niebuhr and Contemporary Politics (2010); Reinhold Niebuhr Considered

(2011); The Image of Christ in Modern Art (2013); The Beauty and the Horror: searching for God in a suffering world (2016); Haunted by Christ: modern writers and the struggle for faith (2018); Seeing God in Art: The Christian faith in 30 images (2020); Has edited and contributed to other Christian publications as well as articles in the press and periodicals.

Recreations: Theatre, literature, the visual arts, sport.

Rt Rev the Lord Harries of Pentregarth, House of Lords, London SW1A 0PW
Email: harriesr@parliament.uk

LABOUR

HARRIS OF HARINGEY, LORD

HARRIS OF HARINGEY (Life Baron), Jonathan Toby Harris; cr. 1998. Born 11 October 1953; Son of late Professor Harry and Muriel Harris; Married Ann Herbert 1979 (2 sons 1 daughter).

Education: Haberdashers' Aske's School, Elstree; Trinity College, Cambridge (BA natural sciences and economics 1975) (Union President 1974).

Non-political career: Economics division, Bank of England 1975-79; Electricity Consumers' Council 1979-86: Deputy director 1983-86; Director, Association of Community Health Councils for England and Wales 1987-98; Senior associate, The King's Fund 1998-2004; Chair, Toby Harris Associates 1998-; Consultant adviser to: Harrogate Management Centre 1998-2004, Infolog Training 1998-2005, Vantage Point 1998-2001, KPMG 1999-2013, DEMSA 2001-03. Member, Unite.

Political career: *House of Lords:* Raised to the peerage as Baron Harris of Haringey, of Hornsey in the London Borough of Haringey 1998. Member: House of Lords Offices Finance and Staff Sub-committee 2000-02, Science and Technology Sub-committee on Personal Internet Security 2006-07, Joint Committee on National Security Strategy 2010-14; Chair, Olympic and Paralympic Legacy 2013-14; Member: Joint Committee on the National Security Strategy 2016-, Democracy and Digital Technologies 2019-, COVID-19 2020-. Member, Labour Peers' Co-ordinating Committee 2004-. *Other:* Chair: Cambridge University Labour Club 1973, Hornsey Labour Party 1978, 1979, 1980, Labour Group of Local Government Association 1995-2004; Member: Labour Party National Policy Forum 1992-2004, Labour Party Local Government Committee 1993-2004, Greater London Labour Party Regional Board 1993-2004, Labour Peers Co-ordinating Committee 2004-; Labour Peers: Vice-chair 2008-12, Chair 2012-. London Borough of Haringey: Councillor 1978-2002, Council Leader 1987-99; Deputy chair, National Fuel Poverty Forum 1981-86; Governor, National Institute for Social Work 1986-94; Member, London Drug Policy Forum 1990-98; Deputy chair, Association of Metropolitan Authorities 1991-97; Member: National Nursery Examination Board 1992-94, Home Office Advisory Council on Race Relations 1992-97; Chair: Association of London Authorities 1993-95, Local Government Anti-Poverty Unit 1994-97, Association of London Government 1995-2000; Member: Court of Middlesex University 1995-, Joint London Advisory Panel 1996-97, London Ambulance Service NHS Trust 1998-2006, London Pension Fund Authority 1998-2000, Metropolitan Police Committee 1998-2000; Local Government Association: Member, Executive 1999-2003, Vice-President 2005-10; Association of Police Authorities: Member, Executive 2000-06, Vice-President 2007-12; Member: Greater London Authority for Brent and Harrow 2000-04; Metropolitan Police Authority: Chair 2000-04, Member (representing the Home Secretary) 2004-12; Special adviser to Board, Transport for London 2004-08; Founding chair, Institute of Commissioning Professionals 2007-08; Member: Police Counter-Terrorism Board 2007-12, Police Counter-Terrorism Ministerial Advisory Group 2008-10; Chair: Independent Advisory Panel on Deaths in Custody 2009-15, Audit Panel, Metropolitan Police and Mayor's Office for Policing and Crime 2012, National Trading Standards Board 2013-; Independent Review into Self-Inflicted Deaths in NOMS Custody of 18-24 year olds 2014-15; Reviewer, Independent Review of London's Preparedness to deal with a Major Terrorist Attack 2016; Chair: Independent Reference Group, National Crime Agency 2017-, Fundraising Regulator 2019-.

Political interests: Local government, health, policing, information technology, homeland security, consumer protection; Australia, Canada, Cyprus, France, Greece, Italy, USA.

Other: EU Committee of the Regions: Member 1994-98, Alternate member 1998-2002; Chair, Young Fabian Group 1976-77; Board member, London First 1993-2002; Executive council member, RNIB 1993-94; Trustee: *Evening Standard* Blitz Memorial Appeal 1995-99, Help for Health Trust 1995-97, Learning Agency 1996-98; Chair, Wembley National Stadium Trust 1996-2018; Vice-patron: Artificial Heart Fund 2004, Vocaleyes 2004; Trustee, Safer London

Foundation 2004-08; London Ambassador, Community Service Volunteers 2005-10; Member, Public Sector Advisory Council, Anite 2005-06; Burned Children's Club 2007; Trustee, Bilimankhwe Arts 2008-15; Chair: Freedom Trust 2010-15, Advisory Council, Cities Security and Resilience Network 2011-; Member, Advisory Board, Resilience First 2019-; Fellow, British Computer Society 2011-; Member, Trading Standards Institute 2013-; President and Fellow, Institute of Strategic Risk Management 2019-; Freedom, City of London 1998; FRSA; Honorary doctorate, Middlesex University 1999.

Publications: Co-author, Why Vote Labour? (1979); Contributor to Economics of Prosperity (1980); Co-editor, Energy and Social Policy (1983).

Recreations: Reading, theatre, classical music, opera.

The Lord Harris of Haringey, House of Lords, London SW1A 0PW
Tel: 020 7219 8513 *Email:* harrist@parliament.uk *Twitter:* @LordTobySays

CONSERVATIVE

HARRIS OF PECKHAM, LORD

HARRIS OF PECKHAM (Life Baron), Philip Charles Harris; cr. 1996. Born 15 September 1942; Son of Charles Harris, MC and Ruth Harris; Married Pauline Chumley (later DBE) 1960 (3 sons 1 daughter).

Education: Streatham Grammar School.

Non-political career: Harris Queensway plc: Chairman 1964-88, Chief executive 1987-88; Non-executive director: Great Universal Stores 1986-2004, Fisons plc 1986-94; Chairman: Harris Ventures Ltd 1988-, C. W. Harris Properties 1988-97; Non-executive director, Molyneux Estates 1990-95; Carpetright plc: Chairman 1993-2014, Non-executive chair 2014-; Non-executive director: Matalan 2004-06, Arsenal FC 2005-; Consultant, Tapi Carpets and Floors Ltd 2015-.

Political career: *House of Lords:* Raised to the peerage as Baron Harris of Peckham, of Peckham in the London Borough of Southwark 1996. Member, Works of Art 2005-09. *Other:* Deputy Chairman, Conservative Party Treasurers 1993. Governor, United Medical and Dental School of Guy's and St Thomas's Hospitals 1983-98; Member, Court of Patrons, Royal College of Gynaecologists 1984-; Chair, Guy's and Lewisham NHS Trust 1991-93; Deputy chair, Lewisham NHS Trust 1993-97; Council member, University of London Court 1994-96; University College London Council 1996-99.

Other: British Showjumping Association 1974-; Chair: Prostate Cancer Charity: Investing in Life Campaign, Generation Trust, Guy's Hospital 1984-2004; Trustee: National Hospital for Neurology and Neurosurgery Development Foundation 1984-92, Westminster Abbey Trust 1987-96; Sponsor, Harris Federation of Schools 1989-; Director and co-sponsor, Bacon's City Technology College 1990-; Trustee, Tavistock Trust for Aphasia 1993-2003; NSPCC National Appeal Board and Executive Committee 1998-2008; Deputy chair, Full-Stop Campaign 1998-2008; President, Friends of Guy's Hospital 1999-; Trustee: Royal Academy of Arts 1999-2005, Outward Bound Trust 2001-03; Sponsor, Harris HospisCare, Orpington 2002-13; Bowel Cancer and Research Trust: Trustee 2005-10, Patron 2010-; Non-executive Director, Arsenal Holdings plc 2005-; Trustee, Westminster Abbey Campaign Development Board 2011-; Great Ormond Street Hospital, Wellbeing of Women, Prostate Cancer Charity; Liveryman: Broderers' Company 1992, Clockmakers Company 2003; Freedom, City of London 1992; Hon. Fellow, Royal College of Radiologists 1992; Three honorary doctorates; Four honorary University Fellowships; Hambro Business Man of the Year 1983; Ernst and Young Entrepreneur of the Year 2007; Beacon Award 2015; Kt 1985. 5 Hertford Street, Mosimanns, Mark's Club; Queens Club.

Publications: Magic Carpet Ride – The Story Of My Life (2017).

Recreations: Football, cricket, show jumping, tennis.

The Lord Harris of Peckham, House of Lords, London SW1A 0PW
Harris Ventures Ltd, Philip Harris House, 1a Spur Road, Orpington BR6 0PH *Tel:* 01689 886886
Email: judy.willett@harrisventures.co.uk

LIBERAL DEMOCRAT

HARRIS OF RICHMOND, BARONESS

Liberal Democrat Lords Whip

HARRIS OF RICHMOND (Life Baroness), Angela Felicity Harris; cr. 1999. Born 4 January 1944; Daughter of late Rev. G H Hamilton Richards and Eva Richards; Married 2nd John Harris 1976 (1 son from previous marriage).

Education: Canon Slade Grammar School, Bolton; Ealing Hotel and Catering College (University of West London).

Political career: *House of Lords:* Raised to the peerage as Baroness Harris of Richmond, of Richmond in the County of North Yorkshire 1999. Liberal Democrat: Whip 2000-08, 2018-, Spokesperson for: Northern Ireland 2003-10, Home Office (Police) 2005-10; Deputy Speaker 2008-17; Deputy Chairman of Committees 2008-17; Contested Lord Speaker election 2011. Chair, European Union Sub-committee F (Social Affairs, Education and Home Affairs/Home Affairs) 2000-04; Member: European Union 2000-04, Refreshment 2003-07, Administration and Works 2007-12, Ecclesiastical Committee 2013-, Procedure/Procedure and Privileges 2019-. *Other:* Contested Yorkshire and the Humber region 1999 European Parliament election. Richmond Town Council (Yorkshire): Councillor 1978-81, 1991-99, Mayor 1993-94; Richmondshire District Council: Councillor 1979-89, Chair 1987-88; North Yorkshire County Council: Councillor 1981-2001, Chair 1991-92, Honorary Alderman 2000; JP, North Yorkshire 1982-99; Non-executive director, Northallerton NHS Trust 1989-97; DL, North Yorkshire 1994-2019; Chair, North Yorkshire Police Authority 1994-2001; Deputy Chair, National Association of Police Authorities 1997-2001; High Steward, Ripon Cathedral 2000-.

Political interests: Police, Northern Ireland; Canada, Ireland, Nepal, Qatar.

Other: Member: British-American Parliamentary Group 1999-, Inter-Parliamentary Union 2003-, British-Irish Parliamentary Assembly 2005-17, Liberal Democrat Friends of India; Patron, Herriot Hospice Homecare, Northallerton 1987-; President, National Association of Chaplains to the Police 1990-16; York University: Member, Court 1995-, Member, Nominations Committee 2012-; Police Rehabilitation Trust (Flint House) 2003-18; Industry and Parliament Trust: Fellow 2003, Trustee 2006-14, Chair of Trustees 2010-14; Patron, Northern Ireland Hospice; Visitor, Harrogate Ladies College 2011-; Trustee, Fellowship of St John Trust 2013-; Chair, advisory panel, Police Federation of England and Wales 2014-16; President, Police Treatment Centres, Harrogate 2018-; Hon. President, RAF Regiment Dinner Club; Master, Fellmongers Company of Richmond 2018-; Herriot Hospice Homecare, Police Treatment Centres, Richmondshire Museum, Richmondshire Building Preservation Trust, Friends of the Friary Hospital Richmond; Freedom, City of London; Honorary Freedom, Richmond, North Yorkshire 2004; Honorary Alderman, North Yorkshire County Council 2000-. RAF Club, Civil Service Club.

Recreations: Music, political biographies.

The Baroness Harris of Richmond DL, House of Lords, London SW1A 0PW
Tel: 020 7219 6709 *Email:* harrisa@parliament.uk

LABOUR

HARRISON, LORD

HARRISON (Life Baron), Lyndon Henry Arthur Harrison; cr. 1999. Born 28 September 1947; Son of late Charles and Edith Harrison; Married Hilary Plank 1980 (1 son 1 daughter).

Education: Oxford School; Warwick University (BA English and American studies 1970); Sussex University (MA American studies 1971); Keele University (MA American studies 1978).

Non-political career: Research officer, UMIST Union, Manchester 1975-78; Manager, North East Wales Institute Student Union, Clwyd 1978-89. Member, GMB.

Political career: *House of Lords:* Raised to the peerage as Baron Harrison, of Chester in the County of Cheshire 1999. Departmental Liaison Peer for Northern Ireland 1999-2001. Member: EU Sub-committee C (Common Foreign and Security Policy) 1999-2003, Delegated Powers and Regulatory Reform 2003-07, EU Sub-committee G (Social Policy and Consumer Affairs) 2003-07, Hybrid Instruments 2003-, European Union 2004-08, 2010-15; EU Sub-committee F (Home Affairs): Member 2006-08, Co-opted member 2008-10; Chair, EU Sub-committee A: (Economic and Financial Affairs and International Trade) 2010-12, (Economic and Financial

Affairs) 2012-15; Member: Equality Act 2010 and Disability 2015-16, Financial Exclusion 2016-17, Natural Environment and Rural Communities Act 2006 2017. *Other:* European Parliament: MEP for: Cheshire West 1989-94: Cheshire West and Wirral 1994-99; Secretary, European Parliamentary Labour Party 1991-94. Councillor, Cheshire County Council 1981-90; Deputy Chair, North West Tourist Board 1986-89; Vice-President, Association of County Councils 1990-97.

Political interests: Small businesses, tourism, monetary union, children, European Union; Commonwealth, EU member and applicant countries, USA.

Other: Member: Inter-Parliamentary Union 1999-, Commonwealth Parliamentary Association 2007-; Vice-President, Cheshire Landscape Trust 1999-; President, Chester and District Parkinson's Disease Society 2005-; Honorary Council Member NSPCC.

Publications: Everything you wanted to know about the Euro...and were afraid to ask; Tourism means Jobs.

Recreations: Chess, the arts, sport, bridge.

The Lord Harrison, House of Lords, London SW1A 0PW
Tel: 020 7219 6424 *Fax:* 020 7219 5979 *Email:* harrisonlh@parliament.uk
Tel: 01244 343428

CONSERVATIVE

HASELHURST, LORD

HASELHURST (Life Baron), Alan Gordon Barraclough Haselhurst; cr 2018. Born 23 June 1937; Son of late John Haselhurst and Alice Haselhurst, née Barraclough; Married Angela Bailey 1977 (2 sons 1 daughter).

Education: King Edward VI School, Birmingham; Cheltenham College; Oriel College, Oxford.

Non-political career: Secretary, treasurer, librarian, Oxford Union Society 1959-60; Industrial executive: ICI 1960-65, Slater Walker 1965-68, British Vita 1968-70; Public affairs consultant 1974-97.

Political career: *House of Commons:* MP (Con) for Middleton and Prestwich 1970-February 1974. Contested Middleton and Prestwich February 1974 general election. MP for Saffron Walden 7 July 1977 by-election to 2010, for Saffron Walden (revised boundary) 2010-17; PPS to Mark Carlisle as Secretary of State, Education and Science 1979-81; Chairman Ways and Means and Deputy Speaker 1997-2010; Contested Speaker elections 2000, 2009. Ex-officio chair, Chairmen's Panel 1997-2010; Ex-officio Member: Court of Referees 1997-2010, Standing Orders 1998-2010, Unopposed Bills (Panel) 2000-10; Member: Finance and Services 2008-15, Ecclesiastical Committee 2010-15, Liaison 2010-15; Chair, Administration 2010-15; Member: Works of Art 2011-15, Finance 2015-17. *House of Lords:* Raised to the peerage as Baron Haselhurst, of Saffron Walden in the County of Essex 2018. Member: EU Home Affairs Sub-committee 2018-19, Delegated Powers and Regulatory Reform 2019-, High Speed Rail (West Midlands-Crewe) Bill 2019-. *Other:* President, Oxford University Conservative Association 1958; National Chair, Young Conservative Movement 1966-68; Deputy Chair, Conservative Group for Europe 1982-85. Governor, Felsted School 1985-2012; Member, Parliamentary and Political Service Honours Committee 2019-.

Political interests: Education, aerospace, aviation, youth affairs, European Union, agriculture, community development; Commonwealth countries, USA.

Other: Chair, Commonwealth Youth Exchange Council 1978-81; Commonwealth Parliamentary Association: Chair: UK branch 2010-15, International Executive Committee 2011-14, Member, Executive Committee 2015-17, 2018-; Fellow, Industry and Parliament Trust 1982; Chair of trustees, Community Projects Foundation 1986-97; Kt 1995; PC 1999. MCC; Member, executive committee, Essex County Cricket Club 1996-2008.

Publications: Occasionally Cricket (Queen Anne Press, 1999); Eventually Cricket (Queen Anne Press, 2001); Incidentally Cricket (Queen Anne Press, 2003); Accidentally Cricket (Professional and Higher Partnership, 2009); Unusually Cricket (Professional and Higher Partnership, 2010); Fatally Cricket (Professional and Higher Partnership, 2014); Politically Cricket (Professional and Higher Partnership, 2016).

Recreations: Hi-fi, watching cricket, gardening, theatre, writing novels.

Rt Hon the Lord Haselhurst, House of Lords, London SW1A 0PW
Tel: 020 7219 3000 *Email:* haselhursta@parliament.uk Website: www.alanhaselhurst.org.uk
Twitter: @Alan_Haselhurst

LABOUR

HASKEL, LORD

HASKEL (Life Baron), Simon Haskel; cr. 1993. Born 8 October 1934; Son of late Isaac and Julia Haskel; Married Carole Lewis 1962 (1 son 1 daughter).

Education: Sedbergh School; Salford College of Advanced Technology (ARTCS textile technology 1955); French, Spanish.

Non-political career: Joined Perrotts Ltd 1961; Chairman, Perrotts Group plc and associated companies 1973-97. National service commission, Royal Artillery 1957.

Political career: *House of Lords:* Raised to the peerage as Baron Haskel, of Higher Broughton in the County of Greater Manchester 1993. Opposition Spokesperson for Trade and Industry 1994-97; Opposition Whip 1994-97; Government Whip (Lord in Waiting) 1997-98; Government Spokesperson for: Social Security 1997-98, Trade and Industry 1997-98, the Treasury 1997-98; Deputy Chair of Committees 2002-; Deputy Speaker 2002-; Board member, Parliamentary Office of Science and Technology (POST). Member: Science and Technology 1994-97, 1999-2002, 2005-10, Procedure 2002-05, Science and Technology Sub-committee I (Fighting Infection) 2002-03, EU Sub-committee B (Internal Market) 2003-07, Information 2003-07, Joint Committee on Tax Law Rewrite Bills 2005-10, Science and Technology Sub-Committee I 2007-10 (Allergy/Waste Reduction 2007-08, Nanotechnologies and food 2008-10), Information 2009-14, Delegated Powers and Regulatory Reform 2009-14, EU Sub-committee B: (Internal Market, Energy and Transport) 2010-12, (Internal Market, Infrastructure and Employment) 2012-15, Small- and Medium-Sized Enterprises 2012-13, Digital Skills 2014-15, Secondary Legislation Scrutiny 2015-19, Built Environment 2015, Financial Exclusion 2016-17, Bribery Act 2010 2018-19, Audit 2018-, SLSC Sub-committee A 2018-19, Joint Committee on Statutory Instruments 2019-, Delegated Powers and Regulatory Reform 2019-. *Other:* Labour Party 1972 Industry Group: Founder Member, Secretary 1976-81; Chair, Labour Finance and Industry Group 1980-92.

Political interests: Trade and industry, science and technology, overseas development; Europe, USA.

Other: Chair, Thames Concerts Society 1982-90; Trustee, Smith Institute 1998-2008; Patron, Chronic Disease Research Foundation 1999-2006; Trustee, Haskel Family Foundation 2000-; President, Environment Industries Commission 2000-; Patron, Society of Operations Engineers 2000-04; President, Institute for Jewish Policy Research 2002-; Trustee, Foundation for Science and Technology 2010-; International President, Textile Institute 2002-05; Hon. President, Materials UK 2006-; Hon. Doctorate, Bolton University 2007. Cyclists' Touring Club; Tandem Club.

Recreations: Music, cycling.

The Lord Haskel, House of Lords, London SW1A 0PW
Tel: 020 7219 4076 *Email:* haskels@parliament.uk
Tel: 020 8948 7711 *Email:* haskel@blueyonder.co.uk

CROSSBENCH

HASTINGS OF SCARISBRICK, LORD

HASTINGS OF SCARISBRICK (Life Baron), Michael John Hastings; cr 2005. Born 29 January 1958; Son of late Petain Hastings and Olive Hastings; Married Jane 1990 (2 daughters 1 son).

Education: Scarisbrick Hall School, Ormskirk; Cornwall College, Montego Bay, Jamaica; London School of Theology (BA theology and sociology 1979); Westminster College, Oxford (PGCE).

Non-political career: BBC 1994-2006: Political and parliamentary affairs department, Head of public affairs 1995-2006, Head of corporate social responsibility 2003-06; Chair, Crime Concern 1995-2008; Board member, Responsible and Sustainable Business Committee, BT

2004-; KPMG: International Director for Corporate Citizenship 2006-, Global Head, Citizenship and Diversity 2007-.

Political career: *House of Lords:* Raised to the peerage as Baron Hastings of Scarisbrick, of Scarisbrick in the County of Lancashire 2005. Member, Communications 2007-09. *Other:* Commissioner, Commission for Racial Equality 1993-2001; Member, Government Social Security Advisory Committee 1993-95; Founding member, Metropolitan Police Advisory Committee 1995-97.

Other: Patron: Zane, Child Brain Injury Trust; Founding chair: Childnet International, Springboard for Children; Trustee, Vodafone Group Foundation 2008-; Vice-President, Unicef; Chairman, Millenium Promise UK; Council member, Overseas Development Institute; Chancellor, Regent's University London 2017-; Unicef award 2005; CBE 2002.

The Lord Hastings of Scarisbrick CBE, House of Lords, London SW1A 0PW
Tel: 020 7219 3781 *Email:* hastingsm@parliament.uk *Twitter:* @LordHastings

LABOUR

HAUGHEY, LORD

HAUGHEY (Life Baron), William Haughey; cr 2013. Born 2 July 1956; Married Susan 1978.

Education: St Francis; Holyrood Secondary; Springburn College.

Non-political career: Engineering supervisor, Turner Refrigeration 1973-83; Head of engineering, UTS Carrier, UAE 1983-85; Founder, City Refrigeration 1985-.

Political career: *House of Lords:* Raised to the peerage as Baron Haughey, of Hutchesontown in the City of Glasgow 2013.

Other: Chair: Scottish Enterprise Glasgow, Asset Skills; Non-executive: Dunedin Enterprise Trust, Glasgow Culture and Leisure; Charter member, Duke of Edinburgh Awards Scheme; Member, Growth Fund Panel, Prince's Trust Youth Business Scotland; Director, Celtic Football Club; Founder, City Charitable Trust; Honorary doctorate, Glasgow Caledonian University; The Loving Cup 2001; St Mungo Prize 2006; OBE 2003; Kt 2012.

The Lord Haughey OBE, House of Lords, London SW1A 0PW
Tel: 020 7219 5353

LABOUR

HAWORTH, LORD

HAWORTH (Life Baron), Alan Robert Haworth; cr. 2004. Born 26 April 1948; Son of late John Haworth, retail grocer, and Hilma Haworth, née Westhead; Married Gill Cole 1973 (divorced); married Maggie Rae 1991.

Education: Blackburn Technical and Grammar School; Barking Regional College of Technology (BSc Soc London University external 1971).

Non-political career: North East London Polytechnic 1972-75: Registrar, Faculty of Art and Design 1972-73, Assistant to director of course development 1973-75; Parliamentary Labour Party: Committee Officer 1975-85, Senior Committee Officer 1985-92, Secretary 1992-2004. Member, Transport and General Workers' Union 1975-2005.

Political career: *House of Lords:* Raised to the peerage as Baron Haworth, of Fisherfield in Ross and Cromarty 2004. Member, Joint Committee on the Draft Registration of Overseas Entities Bill 2019.

Political interests: Energy, environment, transport, health, Royal Navy; Cambodia, Georgia, Iran, Kazakhstan, Kyrgyzstan, Laos, Russia, Tibet, Vietnam.

Other: Member: Munro Society, Mountain Bothies Association, Marine Conservation Society, Scottish Wild Land Group, National Trust for Scotland, RSPB, John Muir Trust, Mountaineering Scotland, Wildfowl and Wetlands Trust, Ramblers.

Publications: Co-editor (with Baroness Hayter of Kentish Town), Men Who Made Labour (Routledge, 2006).

Recreations: Hillwalking, mountaineering, first member of Lords to have climbed all the Munros.

The Lord Haworth, House of Lords, London SW1A 0PW
Tel: 020 7219 6620 *Email:* hawortha@parliament.uk

DEMOCRATIC UNIONIST PARTY

HAY OF BALLYORE, LORD

HAY OF BALLYORE (Life Baron), William Alexander Hay; cr 2014. Born 16 April 1950; Divorced (3 sons 2 daughters); married 2010.

Education: Faughen Valley High School.

Non-political career: Haulage contractor.

Political career: *House of Commons:* Contested (DUP) Foyle 1997, 2001 and 2005 general elections. *House of Lords:* Raised to the peerage as Baron Hay of Ballyore, of Ballyore in the City of Londonderry 2014. *Other:* Northern Ireland Assembly: MLA for: Foyle 1998-2011, Foyle (revised boundary) 2011 to 13 October 2014, Speaker 2007-14, Chair: Assembly Commission 2007-14, Business Committee 2007-14. Londonderry City Council: Councillor 1981-2010, Deputy Mayor 1992, Mayor 1993; Member: Western Education and Library Board 1998, Northern Ireland Housing Council 1998, Northern Ireland Policing Board 2001-07.

Other: President, Commonwealth Parliamentary Association (Northern Ireland Assembly Branch); Member: Loyal Orders, Londonderry Port and Harbour Commission 1998-; Spokesperson, Apprentice Boys.

The Lord Hay of Ballyore, House of Lords, London SW1A 0PW
Tel: 020 7219 5353

CROSSBENCH

HAYMAN, BARONESS

HAYMAN (Life Baroness), Helene Valerie Hayman; cr. 1996. Born 26 March 1949; Daughter of late Maurice and Maude Middleweek; Married Martin Hayman 1974 (4 sons).

Education: Wolverhampton High School for Girls; Newnham College, Cambridge (BA law 1969) (Union President 1969).

Non-political career: Shelter, National Campaign for the Homeless 1969-71; Social Services Department, London Borough of Camden 1971-74; Deputy director, National Council for One Parent Families 1974.

Political career: *House of Commons:* Contested Wolverhampton South West February 1974 general election. MP (Labour) for Welwyn and Hatfield October 1974-79. Contested Welwyn and Hatfield 1979 general election. *House of Lords:* Raised to the peerage as Baroness Hayman, of Dartmouth Park in the London Borough of Camden 1996. Opposition Spokesperson for Health 1996-97; Parliamentary Under-Secretary of State: Department of the Environment, Transport and the Regions (Minister for Roads) 1997-98, Department of Health 1998-99; Minister of State, Ministry of Agriculture, Fisheries and Food 1999-2001; Lord Speaker 2006-11; Member, Parliamentary and Political Service Honours Committee 2012-18. Member: Constitution 2005-06, Liaison 2005-06, Procedure 2006-11; Chair, House 2006-11. *Other:* Member, Royal College of Gynaecologists Ethics Committee 1982-97; Committee on Ethics of Clinical Investigation, University College London/University College Hospital: Member 1987-97, Vice-chair 1990-97; Vice-chair: Bloomsbury Health Authority 1988-90, Bloomsbury and Islington Health Authority 1991-92; Council member, University College, London 1992-97; Chair, Whittington Hospital NHS Trust 1992-97; Member: Review Committee of Privy Counsellors of the Anti-terrorism, Crime and Security Act 2002-04, General Medical Council 2013-.

Political interests: Health, education, overseas development; Sub-Saharan Africa.

Other: Commonwealth Parliamentary Association (UK Branch): President 2006-11, Vice-President 2011-14, Member, Executive Committee 2014-16; Hon. President, Inter-Parliamentary Union, British Group 2006-11; Chair, Cancer Research UK 2001-04; Roadsafe: Board member 2001-05, Patron 2006-; Board of Trustees, Royal Botanical Gardens, Kew 2002-06; Chair: Specialised Health Care Alliance 2004-06, Human Tissue Authority 2005-06; Trustee, Tropical Health and Education Trust 2005-06; Patron, Anne Frank Trust UK 2009-; President: Hansard Society 2010-11, Industry and Parliament Trust -2011, Parliament

Choir -2011; Trustee: Sabin Vaccine Institute 2013-17, Malaria Consortium 2013-16, Disaster Emergency Committee 2014-; Chair: Cambridge University Health Partners 2014-, Ethics and Governance Council UK Biobank 2015-; Fellow, Newnham College, Cambridge; Honorary degree: University of North London, Hertfordshire University, Wolverhampton University, Birmingham University, Brunel University; PC 2001; GBE 2012.

Rt Hon the Baroness Hayman GBE, House of Lords, London SW1A 0PW
Tel: 020 7219 5083 *Email:* haymanh@parliament.uk

LABOUR

HAYMAN OF ULLOCK, BARONESS

Opposition Spokesperson for Environment, Food and Rural Affairs; Opposition Whip

HAYMAN OF ULLOCK (Life Baroness), Susan Mary Hayman; cr 2020. Born 28 July 1962; Married Ross (2 children).

Non-political career: Constituency office manager to: Tess Kingham MP, Michael John Foster MP; Business development director, 3G Communications/Copper Consultancy; Community relations consultant. Former member, Trade and General Workers' Union; Member, GMB.

Political career: *House of Commons:* Contested Preseli Pembrokeshire 2005 and Halesowen and Rowley Regis 2010 general elections. MP for Workington 2015-19. Contested Workington 2019 general election; Opposition Whip 2015-16; Shadow Minister for Flooding and Coastal Communities 2016-17; Shadow Secretary of State for Environment, Food and Rural Affairs 2017-19. Member, Justice 2015. *House of Lords:* Raised to the peerage as Baroness Hayman of Ullock, of Ullock in the County of Cumbria 2020. Opposition Spokesperson for Environment, Food and Rural Affairs 2020-; Opposition Whip 2020-. *Other:* Contested West Midlands region 2004 European Parliament election. Cumbria County Council: Councillor 2013-15, Vice-chair, Children and Young People's Scrutiny Committee; Former chair of school governors.

Political interests: Energy, NHS, human rights, local transport, cost of living, arts funding.

The Baroness Hayman of Ullock, House of Lords, London SW1A 0PW
Tel: 020 7219 3000 *Twitter:* @SueHayman1

LABOUR/
CO-OPERATIVE

HAYTER OF KENTISH TOWN, BARONESS

Shadow Deputy Leader of the House of Lords; Opposition Spokesperson for Business, Energy and Industrial Strategy and International Trade, Cabinet Office, Constitutional and Devolved Issues, Digital, Culture, Media and Sport and Wales

HAYTER OF KENTISH TOWN (Life Baroness); Dianne Hayter; cr 2010. Born 7 September 1949; Daughter of late Alec Hayter and late Nancy Hayter; Married Prof. David Caplin 1994.

Education: Penrhos College, Colwyn Bay; Aylesbury High School; Durham University (BA sociology and social administration 1970); London University (PhD 2004); French (basic).

Non-political career: Research assistant: General and Municipal Workers Union 1970-72, European Trade Union Confederation, Brussels 1973; Research officer, Trade Union Advisory Committee to OECD, Paris 1973-74; Fabian Society: Assistant general secretary 1974-76, General secretary 1976-82, Member, executive committee 1986-95, Chair 1992-93; Journalist, *A Week in Politics*, Channel 4 1982-84; Director, Alcohol Concern 1984-90; Chief executive, European Parliamentary Labour Party 1990-96; Director of corporate affairs, Wellcome Trust 1996-99; Chief executive, Pelican Centre 1999-2001; Member, Board for Actuarial Standards 2006-11; Chair: Consumer panel, Bar Standards Board 2006-09, Property Standards Board 2008-10, Legal Services Consumer Panel 2009-11; Visiting Professor, Westminster University 2012-. GMB.

Political career: *House of Lords:* Raised to the peerage as Baroness Hayter of Kentish Town, of Kentish Town in the London Borough of Camden 2010. Opposition Whip 2011-15; Opposition Spokesperson for: Business, Innovation and Skills/Business, Energy and Industrial Strategy (Consumer Affairs) 2012-, Cabinet Office 2012-17, 2018-20, Women and Equalities 2015-16,

2020, Exiting the European Union 2016-20, Consumer Affairs 2017-19; Shadow Deputy Leader of the House of Lords 2017-; Opposition Spokesperson for: Constitutional Affairs 2018-20, Digital, Culture Media and Sport (Charities) 2020-, Wales 2020-, International Trade 2020-, Cabinet Office, Constitutional and Devolved Issues 2020-. Member: Joint Committee on the Draft Defamation Bill 2011, Liaison 2017-. *Other:* Member: Executive committee, London Labour Party 1977-83, National Constitution Committee, Labour Party 1987-98; National Executive Committee, Labour Party: Member 1998-2010, Vice-chair 2006-07, Chair 2007-08; Chair, Holborn and St Pancras Labour Party 1990-93.

Political interests: Trade unions, consumer affairs, women; France, New Zealand, Sri Lanka.

Other: Member, Royal Commission on Criminal Procedure 1978-80; Vice-chair, Webb Memorial Trust 1997-2018; Member: National board, Patient Safety Agency 2001-04, Dr Foster Ethics Committee 2001-10; Financial Services Consumer Panel: Member 2001-05, Vice-chair 2003-05; Board member, National Consumer Council 2001-08; Member: Determinations Panel, Pensions Regulator 2005-10, Insolvency Practices Council 2006-10; Pelican Cancer Trust, Dartmouth Street Trust; Hon. Doctor of Letters, Westminster University 2015.

Publications: Author, Fightback! Labour's Traditional Right in the 1970s and 1980s (2005); Co-editor (with Lord Haworth), Men Who Made Labour (2006); Contributor, The Prime Ministers Who Never Were (2011).

Recreations: Reading, travel.

The Baroness Hayter of Kentish Town, House of Lords, London SW1A 0PW
Tel: 020 7219 8926 *Email:* hayterd@parliament.uk *Twitter:* @HayteratLords

CONSERVATIVE

HAYWARD, LORD

HAYWARD (Life Baron), Robert Antony Hayward; cr 2015. Born 11 March 1949; Son of late Ralph and Mary Hayward.

Education: Abingdon School; Maidenhead Grammar School; University College of Rhodesia (BSc (Econ) 1970).

Non-political career: Personnel Manager: Esso Petroleum 1971-75, Coca Cola Bottlers 1975-79, GEC Large Machines 1979-82; Director-General, British Soft Drink Association 1993-99; Director, British Beer and Pub Association 1999-2009.

Political career: *House of Commons:* Contested Carmarthen October 1974 general election. MP (Conservative) for Kingswood 1983-92; PPS: to Minister for: Corporate and Consumer Affairs 1985-87, Industry 1986-87, to Secretary of State for Transport 1987-89. *House of Lords:* Raised to the peerage as Baron Hayward, of Cumnor in the County of Oxfordshire 2015. Member: Licensing Act 2003 2016, Political Polling and Digital Media 2017-18, Electoral Registration and Administration Act 2013 2019-, National Plan for Sport and Recreation 2020-. *Other:* National vice-chairman, Young Conservatives 1975. Councillor, Coventry City Council 1976-78.

Political interests: Economics, transport, defence.

Other: Director, Stonewall 1997-2003; Board Member and Treasurer, Dignity in Dying 2012-16; Director, Portcullis Public Affairs 2012-14; Chair, Public Sector Equality Duty Review 2012-13; Deputy Chair, Central YMCA 2014-17; Board Member, YMCA Training 2013-; Business Breakfast Presenter, Colourful Radio 2014-15; OBE 1991. Founder Chairman, Kings Cross Steelers RFC 1996-99.

Recreations: Former RFU rugby referee.

The Lord Hayward OBE, House of Lords, London SW1A 0PW
Tel: 020 7219 7058
Email: robertahayward11@gmail.com

LABOUR

HEALY OF PRIMROSE HILL, BARONESS

HEALY OF PRIMROSE HILL (Life Baroness), Anna Mary Healy; cr 2010. Born 10 May 1955; Daughter of late Martin Healy and Kathleen Healy; Married Jon Cruddas (qv) 1992 (MP for Dagenham and Rainham) (1 son).

Education: St Aloysius Convent; Royal Holloway College, London (BA modern history/economic history/politics 1976); Birkbeck College, London (MSc politics 1982); City University, London (Diploma journalism 1982-83).

Non-political career: Labour Party HQ 1978-88: Personal assistant to the international secretary 1978-81, Personal assistant to director of communications 1981-85; Press officer, later campaigns press officer 1985-88; Press office, Parliamentary Labour Party 1988-96; Press officer to Tony Blair MP as Leader of the Opposition 1996-97; Special adviser to: Mo Mowlam MP as Secretary of State for Northern Ireland 1997-98, Jack Cunningham MP as Minister for the Cabinet Office and Chancellor of the Duchy of Lancaster 1998-99; Communications strategist, Carlton TV 2000; Senior consultant, GPC 2000-01; Special adviser to Lord Macdonald of Tradeston as: Minister for Transport 2001, Minister for the Cabinet Office 2001-03; Head of office of Jon Cruddas MP 2003-07; Special adviser to Harriet Harman MP as Leader of the House of Commons and Lord Privy Seal 2007-10; Chief of staff to Harriet Harman MP as Leader of the Opposition 2010. Former Member: NUJ, Unite.

Political career: *House of Lords:* Raised to the peerage as Baroness Healy of Primrose Hill, of Primrose Hill in the London Borough of Camden 2010. Deputy Chairman of Committees 2020-. Member: HIV and AIDS in the UK 2010-11, Joint Committee on Parliamentary Privilege 2013, Communications 2013-16, Joint Committee on the National Security Strategy 2017-.

Political interests: Labour Party, health and welfare policies, penal reform; China, Ireland, Italy, Middle East, Spain, USA.

Other: Commonwealth Parliamentary Association; Anaphylaxis Campaign.

Recreations: Music, film, literature.

The Baroness Healy of Primrose Hill, House of Lords, London SW1A 0PW
Tel: 020 7219 8912 *Email:* healyab@parliament.uk

CONSERVATIVE

HELIC, BARONESS

BARONESS HELIC (Life Baroness), Arminka Helic; cr 2014. Born 20 April 1968.

Education: High school, Gracanica, Bosnia and Herzegovina; University of Sarajevo; London School of Economics.

Non-political career: Freelance consultant (Eastern Europe and Balkans) BBC and ITV 1993-94; International affairs and defence adviser, House of Commons 1997-98; Defence adviser to Conservative Shadow Secretaries of State for Defence 1999-2005; Risk analyst, MMC Ventures Ltd 2001-02; Senior adviser to William Hague as Shadow Foreign Secretary 2005-10; Special adviser to William Hague as: Foreign Secretary 2010-14, Leader of the House of Commons 2014-15; Preventing Sexual Violence Initiative (PSVI): Co-author 2012-, Member, Advisory Board 2015-; Director, JP D H London Ltd/JDH Office Ltd 2015-.

Political career: *House of Lords:* Raised to the peerage as Baroness Helic, of Millbank in the City of Westminster 2014. Member, International Relations/International Relations and Defence 2016-.

Political interests: Foreign policy, defence and international security, human rights, post-conflict issues.

Other: Board member, Western European and Others Group (WEOG), Trust Fund for Victims, International Criminal Court 2015-; Member, UN Secretary-General's Advisory Board on Disarmament Matters 2018-; Member, advisory board, Centre for Women, Peace and Security, LSE 2015-.

The Baroness Helic, House of Lords, London SW1A 0PW
Tel: 020 7219 5353 *Twitter:* @arminkahelic

LABOUR

HENDY, LORD

HENDY (Life Baron), John Hendy; cr 2019. Born 11 April 1948; Married (3 daughters).

Education: Ealing Technical College (LLB); Queen's University Belfast (DipLL; LLM).

Non-political career: Called to the Bar, Gray's Inn 1972; Director, Newham Rights Centre 1973-76; Lecturer, Middlesex Polytechnic 1976-77; Barrister 1977-; QC 1987; Bencher 1995; Admitted to Bar of New South Wales 1998; Head, Old Square Chambers 1999-2008; Visiting Professor: School of Law, Kings College, London 1999-2005, Faculty of Law, University College, London 2014-; Consultant to International Trade Union Confederation, Brussels 2015.

Political career: *House of Lords:* Raised to the peerage as Baron Hendy, of Hayes and Harlington in the London Borough of Hillingdon 2019.

Other: President, International Centre for Trade Union Rights 2011-; Vice-president, Campaign for Trade Union Freedom 2014-; Chair: Institute of Employment Rights 1989-, Employment Law Bar Association 2003-05; Fellow: Royal Society of Medicine, Society of Advanced Legal Studies.

The Lord Hendy QC, House of Lords, London SW1A 0PW *Twitter:* @JohnHendyQC

LABOUR

HENIG, BARONESS

Deputy Speaker

HENIG (Life Baroness), Ruth Beatrice Henig; cr. 2004. Born 10 November 1943; Daughter of Kurt and Elfrieda Munzer; Married Stanley Henig 1966 (divorced 1993) (2 sons); married Jack Johnstone 1994 (died 2013).

Education: Wyggeston Girls' Grammar School, Leicester; Bedford College, London (BA history 1965); Lancaster University (PhD history 1978); French, German.

Non-political career: Lancaster University 1968-2002: History lecturer 1968-93, Senior history lecturer 1993-2002, Head of department 1995-97, Dean of arts and humanities 1997-2000; Chair, Security Industry Authority 2007-13. Member, AUT 1968-2002.

Political career: *House of Commons:* Contested (Labour) Lancaster 1979 and 1992 general elections. *House of Lords:* Raised to the peerage as Baroness Henig, of Lancaster in the County of Lancashire 2004. Deputy Chairman of Committees 2015-; Deputy Speaker 2018-. Member: EU Sub-committee F (Home Affairs) 2005-09, Draft Legal Services Bill Joint Committee 2006, Refreshment 2009-10, 2011-14; Co-opted member, EU Sub-committee G (Social Policy and Consumer Affairs) 2009-10; Member EU Sub-committees: G (Social Policies and Consumer Protection) 2010-12, C (External Affairs) 2012-15; Member: European Union 2014-15, Licensing Act 2003 2016-17, Joint Committee on the National Security Strategy 2017-. Vice-chair, PLP Departmental: Committee for Home Affairs 2006-10, Group for Home Affairs 2010-15. *Other:* Vice-chair, PLP Departmental Group for Home Affairs 2006-09, 2011-. Lancashire County Council: Councillor 1981-2005, Chair 1999-2000; Magistrate, Lancaster Bench 1984-2005; Chair, Lancashire Police Authority 1995-2005; Member, Lawrence Steering Group (Home Office) 1998-2005; Association of Police Authorities: Chair 1997-2005, President 2005-12; DL, Lancashire 2002; Member: Street Crime Action Group 2002-04, National Criminal Justice Board 2003-05; Chair, Security Industry Authority 2007-13.

Political interests: Policing and private security, criminal justice system, foreign affairs, Europe; China, Japan, Malaysia, Thailand.

Other: Chair, Storey Creative Industries Centre, Lancaster 2006-10; Royal National Lifeboat Institute, Save the Children, International Red Cross, Well-being of Women, Prince's Trust, Be Your Best Foundation; Member, Worshipful Company of Security Professionals; Hon. Fellow, Lancaster University; Outstanding Contribution to Industry, Security Excellence Awards 2012; Imbert Prize for Security Industry Professional of the Year, ASC 2013; CBE 2000.

Publications: The League of Nations (Oliver and Boyd, 1973); Versailles and After (Routledge, 1984, 1995); Origins of the Second World War (Routledge, 1985); The Weimer Republic 1919-33 (Routledge, 1988); Origins of the First World War (Routledge, 1989, 1993, 2002); Co-author: Europe 1870-1945 (Longmans, 1997), Women and Political Power (Routledge, 2000); History of the League of Nations (Haus, 2010) (republished as The Peace that Never Was, 2019).

Recreations: Bridge, fell-walking, gardening, wine.

The Baroness Henig CBE, House of Lords, London SW1A 0PW
Tel: 020 7219 5133 *Email:* henigr@parliament.uk
Email: ruthhenig@gmail.com Website: ruthhenigassociates.co.uk

CONSERVATIVE

HENLEY, LORD

HENLEY (8th Baron, I), Oliver Michael Robert Eden; cr. 1799; 6th Baron Northington (UK) 1885. Born 22 November 1953; Son of 7th Baron; Married Caroline Patricia Sharp 1984 (3 sons 1 daughter).

Education: Dragon School, Oxford; Clifton College, Bristol; Durham University (BA modern history 1975).

Non-political career: Called to the Bar, Middle Temple 1977.

Political career: *House of Lords:* First entered House of Lords 1977. Sits as Baron Northington; Government Whip 1989; Government Spokesperson for Health 1989; Joint Parliamentary Under-Secretary of State: Department of Social Security 1989-93, Department of Employment 1993-94, Ministry of Defence 1994-95; Minister of State, Department of Education and Employment 1995-97; Opposition Spokesperson for: Defence 1997, Education and Employment 1997, Treasury 1997-98, Home Affairs 1997-98, Constitutional Affairs 1998-99; Opposition Chief Whip 1998-2001; Elected hereditary peer 1999-; Deputy Speaker 1999-2001; Deputy Chairman of Committees 1999-2001; Opposition Spokesperson for: Cabinet Office June 1999-2000, Legal Affairs 2003-07, Constitutional Affairs 2005-07, Home Affairs 2006-07, Justice 2007-10; Parliamentary Under-Secretary of State and Government Spokesperson, Department for Environment, Food and Rural Affairs 2010-11; Government Spokesperson for: Business, Innovation and Skills 2011, Home Office 2011-12; Minister of State for Crime Prevention and Anti-Social Behaviour Reduction, Home Office 2011-12; Government Whip (Lord in Waiting) 2016-17; Parliamentary Under-Secretary of State and Government Spokesperson: Department for Work and Pensions 2016-17, Department for Business, Energy and Industrial Strategy 2017-19; Ministerial Champion for Salisbury 2019. Member: House of Lords Offices Administration and Works Sub-committee 1998-2001, Procedure 1998-2001, Privileges 1998-2002, Selection 1999-2001, House of Lords Offices -2001; Co-opted Member, European Union Sub-committee E (Law and Institutions) 2003-06; Member: Inheritance and Trustees' Powers Bill 2013, Extradition Law 2014-15, Joint Committee on Human Rights 2015-16, Joint Committee on the Draft Investigatory Powers Bill 2015-16; Chair, Communications 2017. *Other:* Penrith and the Border Conservative Association: Chair 1987-89, President 1989-94. President, Cumbria Association of Local Councils 1981-89; Councillor, Cumbria County Council 1986-89.

Other: PC 2013. Brooks's Club.

Rt Hon the Lord Henley, House of Lords, London SW1A 0PW
Tel: 020 7219 3108 *Email:* henleyo@parliament.uk

CROSSBENCH

HENNESSY OF NYMPSFIELD, LORD

HENNESSY OF NYMPSFIELD (Life Baron), Peter John Hennessy; cr 2010. Born 28 March 1947; Son of William Gerald and Edith Hennessy; Married Enid Candler 1969 (2 daughters).

Education: Marling School, Stroud; St John's College, Cambridge (BA 1969; PhD 1990); London School of Economics; Harvard University, USA.

Non-political career: Reporter, *Times Higher Education Supplement* 1972-74, *The Times*: Reporter 1974-76, Whitehall Correspondent 1976-82, Home leader writer and columnist 1982-84; Lobby Correspondent, *Financial Times* 1976; Journalist, *The Economist* 1982; Columnist: *New Statesman* 1986-87, *The Independent* 1987-91; Visiting professor of government, Strathclyde University 1989-94; Professor of contemporary history, Queen Mary University, London 1992-2000; Professor of rhetoric, Gresham College 1994-97; Member, Steering group, Sharman Review of Audit and Accountability for Central Government 2001-01; Attlee professor of contemporary British history 2001-; Member, Cabinet Office advisory group on security and intelligence records 2004-10; Mile End Institute of Contemporary British

Government, Intelligence and Society, Queen Mary University, London: Director 2006-11, Patron 2011-.

Political career: *House of Lords:* Raised to the peerage as Baron Hennessy of Nympsfield, of Nympsfield in the County of Gloucestershire 2010. Member: Joint Committee on the Draft House of Lords Reform Bill 2011-12, Science and Technology 2014-17, Constitution 2019-.

Other: Vice-President, Politics Association 1985-90; Trustee, Attlee Foundation 1985-98; Institute of Contemporary British History: Founder and co-director 1986-89, Board member 1989-98; Board member, Institute of Historical Research 1992-97; President, Johnian Society 1995; Chairman, Kennedy Memorial Trust 1995-2000; Vice-President, RHists 1996-2000; Governor, Ditchley Foundation 2001-; Trustee: Geffrye Museum 2002-04, Orwell Memorial Trust 2002-04; Director, The Tablet 2003-; Fellow, British Academy 2003-; Patron, Bletchley Park Trust 2011-; Visiting fellow: Policy Studies Institute 1986-91, Reading University 1988-94, Nottingham University 1989-95; Honorary research fellow, Department of Politics and Sociology, Birkbeck College, London 1990-91; Visiting scholar, Centre for Australian Public Sector Management, Griffith University, Brisbane 1991; Honorary fellow, Institute of Contemporary British History 1995; Fellow, Gresham College 1997; Hon. DLitt, Universities of: West of England 1995, Westminster 1996, Kingston 1998, Strathclyde 2005; Hon. Fellow, St Benet's Hall, Oxford 2008; DUniv, Open University 2009; Hon. DLitt, Reading University 2011; Hon. Master of the Bench, Middle Temple 2012; Duff Cooper Prize 1993; NCR Prize 1994; Orwell Prize for Political Writing 2007.

Publications: What the Papers Never Said (1985); Never Again: Britain 1945-51 (1992); The Hidden Wiring: Unearthing the British Constitution (1995); Muddling Through (1996); The Prime Minister: the office and its holders since 1945 (2000); The Secret State (2002, 2nd edn 2010); Having it So Good: Britain in the Fifties (2006); Editor, The New Protective State: Government, Intelligence and Terrorism (Continuum, 2007); Cabinets and the Bomb (2007); Distilling the Frenzy: Writing the History of One's Own Times (Biteback, 2012).

Professor the Lord Hennessy of Nympsfield, House of Lords, London SW1A 0PW
Tel: 020 7219 5790 *Email:* hennessyp@parliament.uk

CONSERVATIVE

HERBERT OF SOUTH DOWNS, LORD

HERBERT OF SOUTH DOWNS (Life Baron), Nicholas Le Quesne Herbert; cr 2020. Born 7 April 1963; Civil partner Jason Eades 2008.

Education: Haileybury College, Hertford; Magdalene College, Cambridge (BA law and land economy 1985).

Non-political career: British Field Sports Society 1990-96: Director of political affairs 1992-96 (co-founder Countryside Movement); Chief executive, Business for Sterling 1998-2000 (founder of the 'No' Campaign); Director, Reform 2001-05.

Political career: *House of Commons:* Contested Berwick-upon-Tweed 1997 general election. MP for Arundel and South Downs 2005-10, for Arundel and South Downs (revised boundary) 2010-19; Shadow Minister for Police Reform 2005-07; Shadow Secretary of State for: Justice 2007-09, Environment, Food and Rural Affairs 2009-10; Minister of State for Policing and Criminal Justice, Home Office and Ministry of Justice 2010-12. Member, Home Affairs 2005-06. *House of Lords:* Raised to the peerage as Baron Herbert of South Downs, of Arundel in the County of West Sussex 2020. *Other:* Chair, College of Policing 2021-.

Political interests: Rural affairs, public services, the economy, international development.

Other: Co-chair, Global TB Caucus; Chair: Project for Modern Democracy 2013-, Global TB Caucus 2014-, Global Equality Caucus 2019-, Countryside Alliance 2019-; PC 2010; CBE 2016.

Publications: Why Vote Conservative 2015.

Recreations: Watching cricket, racing, country sports, cinema, theatre, opera.

Rt Hon the Lord Herbert of South Downs CBE, House of Lords, London SW1A 0PW
Tel: 020 7219 3000
Email: nick@nickherbert.com Website: www.nickherbert.com *Twitter:* @nickherbertcbe

NON-AFFILIATED

HESELTINE, LORD

HESELTINE (Life Baron), Michael Ray Dibdin Heseltine; cr. 2001. Born 21 March 1933; Son of late Colonel R. D. Heseltine and Mrs Eileen Heseltine; Married Anne Williams 1962 (1 son 2 daughters).

Education: Shrewsbury School; Pembroke College, Oxford (BA philosophy, politics and economics 1954) (Union President).

Non-political career: Chair: Haymarket Press (Magazine Publishers) 1964-70, Haymarket Media Group 1999-2010, Haymarket Group 1997-, Regional Growth Fund 2010-17; Thames Estuary 2050 Commission 2016-17, Regeneration Advisory Panel 2016-17; Commissioner, National Infrastructure Commission 2015-17. Commissioned Welsh Guards 1979.

Political career: *House of Commons:* Contested Gower 1959 and Coventry North 1964 general elections. MP (Conservative) for Tavistock 1966-74, for Henley February 1974-2001; Parliamentary Secretary, Ministry of Transport June-October 1970; Parliamentary Under-Secretary of State, Department of the Environment 1970-72; Minister for Aerospace and Shipping, Department of Trade and Industry 1972-74; Opposition Spokesperson for: Industry 1974-76, Environment 1976-79; Secretary of State for: Environment 1979-83, 1990-92, Defence 1983-86, President of the Board of Trade and Secretary of State for Trade and Industry 1992-95; Deputy Prime Minister and First Secretary of State 1995-97. *House of Lords:* Raised to the peerage as Baron Heseltine, of Thenford in the County of Northamptonshire 2001. Government Adviser on Local Growth 2015-17. *Other:* Chair, Conservative Mainstream Group; President, Conservative Group for Europe; Contested Conservative Party leadership November 1990; Patron, Tory Reform Group; Conservative Whip suspended May 2019-. Commissioner, National Infrastructure Commission 2015-.

Political interests: Industrial strategy, urban renaissance.

Other: Member, Millennium Commission 1994-2001; Chair, Anglo/Chinese Forum 1998-2004; Vice-President, Royal Horticultural Society 2009-; Chair, Tees Valley Inward Investment Initiative 2015-17; Honorary Liveryman of the Worshipful Company of Marketors 2015; Freedom: City of Liverpool 2012, City of London 2012; Royal Institute of British Architects 1991; The 48 Group Club 2003; Hon fellow, Pembroke College 1986; Hon degree, Leeds Metropolitan University 1989; Hon LLD, Liverpool University 1990; Hon degree: Swansea University 2001, Aston University 2013; Hon doctorate, University of South Wales 2013; Hon fellow: Northampton University 2013, Liverpool John Moores University 2013; Birmingham City University 2014; PPA Marcus Morris Award 2003; Publicity Club of London Cup 2005; Lifetime Achievment, National Business Awards 2005; Goldie Oldie of the Year, *The Oldie* awards 2013; PC 1979; CH 1997. Carlton, Pratt's, Brooks's, White's, Beefsteak Club.

Publications: Where There's a Will (1987); The Challenge of Europe: Can Britain Win? (1989); Life in the Jungle (autobiography) (2000); No Stone Unturned (2012); Co-author with Lady Heseltine, Thenford: The Creation of an English Garden (2016); Industrial Strategy (2017).

Recreations: Gardening.

Rt Hon the Lord Heseltine CH, House of Lords, London SW1A 0PW
Tel: 020 7219 5353
Email: privateoffice@haymarket.com

CONSERVATIVE

HILL OF OAREFORD, LORD

HILL OF OAREFORD (Life Baron), Jonathan Hopkin Hill; cr 2010. Born 24 July 1960; Son of Rowland Hill and Paddy Henwood; Married Alexandra Nettelfield 1988 (1 son 2 daughters).

Education: Highgate School, London; Trinity College, Cambridge (BA history 1982).

Non-political career: RIT & Northern 1983; Hamish Hamilton 1984-85; Conservative Research Department 1985-86; Special adviser to Rt Hon Kenneth Clarke MP: as Paymaster General and Employment Minister 1986-87, as Chancellor of the Duchy of Lancaster and Minister of Trade and Industry 1987-88, as Secretary of State for Health 1988-89; Lowe Bell Communications 1989-91; Number 10 Policy Unit 1991-92; Political Secretary to Rt Hon John Major MP as Prime Minister 1992-94; Senior consultant, Bell Pottinger Consultants 1994-98; Founding director, Quiller Consultants 1998-2010; Commissioner for Financial Stability, Financial Services and Capital Markets Union, European Commission 2014-16; Independent

National Director, Times Newspapers 2017-; Senior Adviser, Freshfields Bruckhaus Deringer 2017-.

Political career: *House of Lords:* Raised to the peerage as Baron Hill of Oareford, of Oareford in the County of Somerset 2010. Parliamentary Under-Secretary of State for Schools and Government Spokesperson, Department for Education 2010-13; Leader of the House of Lords 2013-14; Chancellor of the Duchy of Lancaster 2013-14; On leave of absence October 2014-October 2016. Member: House 2013-14, Liaison 2013-14, Privileges and Conduct 2013-14, Procedure 2013-14, Selection 2013-14. *Other:* Governor: Highgate School 1995-2010, Hanford School 2004-10; Lead non-executive board member (with responsibility for the Union), HM Treasury 2019-.

Other: Trustee, National Literacy Trust 1995-2009; Member, advisory board, Reform 2004-10; Trustee, Teach First; Member, Council of Management, Ditchley Foundation; Resignation of the Year, *Spectator* awards 2012; CBE 1995; PC 2013.

Publications: Co-author, Too Close to Call: John Major, Power and Politics in No.10 (1995).

Recreations: Reading, gardening, walking on Exmoor.

Rt Hon the Lord Hill of Oareford CBE, House of Lords, London SW1A 0PW
Tel: 020 7219 5353

LABOUR

HILTON OF EGGARDON, BARONESS

HILTON OF EGGARDON (Life Baroness), Jennifer Hilton; cr. 1991. Born 12 January 1936; Daughter of late John Hilton, CMG and Margaret Hilton.

Education: Bedales School, Hampshire; Manchester University (BA psychology 1970; MA (police scholarship) 1971); London University (Diploma criminology 1973; Diploma history of art 1980); French.

Non-political career: Metropolitan Police 1956-90; Directing staff, National Police Staff College; Metropolitan Police Management Services 1975-76; Superintendent/Chief Superintendent 1977-83; Senior Command Course, National Staff College 1979; New Scotland Yard 1983-87; North West London, responsible for Complaints/Discipline, Personnel, Community Relations 1987-88; Peel Centre, Hendon, responsible for all Metropolitan Police training 1988-90.

Political career: *House of Lords:* Raised to the peerage as Baroness Hilton of Eggardon, of Eggardon in the County of Dorset 1991. Opposition Whip 1991-95; Opposition Spokesperson for: the Environment 1991-97, Home Affairs 1994-97. EU Sub-committee D (Environment): Member 1991-97, Chair 1995-97; Member: Science and Technology 1992-95, 2010-15, 2019-, European Union 1997-99; Chair: EU Sub-committee C (Environment, Public Health and Consumer Protection) 1997-99, Advisory Panel on Works of Art 1998-2003, EU Sub-committee C (Foreign Affairs and Defence): Member 2000-03, Chair 2000-01; Member: House of Lords Offices 2000-03, Science and Technology Sub-committees: I (Science and International Agreements) 2003-04, I (Scientific Aspects of Ageing) 2004-05, Works of Art 2007-09, Science and Technology Sub-committee I 2012-14, Sexual Violence in Conflict 2015-16, International Relations 2016-19. *Other:* Patron, LGBT Labour.

Political interests: Environment, race relations, criminal justice; All countries of the old Russian empire.

Other: Member, UK Delegation, Organisation for Security and Co-operation in Europe Parliamentary Assembly -2019; Member: ACPOs Executive Committee, Equal Opportunities, Extended Interview Panel, Various Home Office Committees; Trustee, Life in Fresh 2005-; QPM 1989.

Publications: The Gentle Arm of the Law (1967); Co-author, Individual Development and Social Experience (1974).

Recreations: Gardening, travel, art.

The Baroness Hilton of Eggardon QPM, House of Lords, London SW1A 0PW
Tel: 020 7219 3182 *Email:* hiltonj@parliament.uk

CONSERVATIVE

HODGSON OF ABINGER, BARONESS

BARONESS HODGSON OF ABINGER (Life Baroness), Fiona Ferelith Hodgson; cr 2013. Daughter of Keith Allom and Jean Allom, née Robertson; Married Robin Granville Hodgson 1982 (MP Walsall North 1976-79, now Lord Hodgson of Astley Abbotts (qv)) (3 sons 1 daughter 1 twin son deceased).

Education: Queen Anne's School Caversham; Guildford High School.

Non-political career: Personal Secretary to Prime Minister's Private Secretary 1973-76; Research executive, Reader's Digest Association Ltd 1980-83; Managing director, Kensington Carnival Co Ltd 1984-87; Director: Johnson Brothers Design 1991-2006, Johnson Bros & Co Ltd 1991-. Armed Forces Parliamentary Scheme 2014-18; Royal College of Defence Studies 2017-18; Hon Col Outreach Group 77th Brigade.

Political career: *House of Lords:* Raised to the peerage as Baroness Hodgson of Abinger, of Abinger in the County of Surrey 2013. Member: Sexual Violence in Conflict 2015-16, Rural Economy 2018-19, Joint Committee on the National Security Strategy 2019-. *Other:* Conservative Women's Organisation: Deputy chair 2002-05, Chair 2005-08, President 2008-11, Honorary vice-president 2011-; Conservative National Convention: Vice-president 2009-11, President 2011-12; Chair, 2011 Conservative Party Conference; Member, Conservative Human Rights Commission 2009-; Vice-chair, Conservative Policy Forum 2010-13; Patron, Conservative Friends of International Development 2012-; Conservative Party Whip 2014-17. Member, Farm Animal Welfare Council 1989-97; Non-executive director, Barnet Health Authority 1992-94; Member, Advisory Committee on Animal Food Stuffs, Food Standards Agency 2001-04.

Political interests: International development, international women's rights, foreign affairs, equality, defence, health; Afghanistan, Middle East, conflict and post-conflict countries, developing countries.

Other: Member, Wellbeing general council and appeals committee, Royal College of Obstetricians and Gynaecologists 1993-2006; Member, International Social Services UK 2003-04; Delegate, Commission on the Status of Women 2008-; Chair, GAPS (Gender Action in Peace and Security) advisory group 2009-; Member, Oxfam Association 2009-15; Trustee, Chalker Foundation 2010-; Women's Justice Task Force 2010-16; Independent Doctors Federation (ISAAC Group) 2010-13; Patron, Afghan Connection 2011-; Chair, governance board, Independent Sector Complaints and Adjudication Service 2012-; Member, steering board, Preventing Sexual Violence Initiative in Conflict and Post Conflict Countries 2012-; Founder member, Afghan Women's Support Forum in the UK 2012-; CBE 2012.

Recreations: Cooking, reading, riding, walking.

The Baroness Hodgson of Abinger CBE, House of Lords, London SW1A 0PW
Tel: 020 7219 8283 *Email:* hodgsonf@parliament.uk *Twitter:* @hodgsonfiona

CONSERVATIVE

HODGSON OF ASTLEY ABBOTTS, LORD

Chair, Select Committee on Secondary Legislation Scrutiny

HODGSON OF ASTLEY ABBOTTS (Life Baron), Robin Granville Hodgson; cr. 2000. Born 25 April 1942; Son of late Henry and Natalie Hodgson; Married Fiona Ferelith Allom 1982, now Baroness Hodgson of Abinger (qv) (3 sons 1 daughter 1 twin son deceased).

Education: Shrewsbury School; Oxford University (BA modern history 1964); Wharton School of Finance, Pennsylvania University (MBA 1969).

Non-political career: Investment banker, New York and Montreal 1964-67; Industry in Birmingham 1969-72; Director, Johnson Brothers & Co Ltd, Walsall 1970-; Granville Baird Group: Director 1972-2003, Group chief executive 1979-95, Chair 1995-2002; Director: Domnick Hunter plc 1989-2002, Staffordshire Building Society 1995-2005, Community Hospitals plc 1995-2001; Chair: Market Touch plc 2001-02, Nova Capital Management 2002-15, Carbo plc 2002-05; Director, Marstons plc (formerly Wolverhampton and Dudley Breweries plc) 2002-14; Chair: RFIB Group Limited 2007-15, Tenet Group Ltd 2007-12, EIS Optics Ltd 2009-11, CMS Ltd/CMSpi Ltd 2014-, Green River Capital Partners Ltd 2019-.

Political career: *House of Commons:* Contested Walsall North February and October 1974 general elections. MP (Conservative) for Walsall North November 1976 by-election to 1979. *House of Lords:* Raised to the peerage as Baron Hodgson of Astley Abbotts, of Nash in the County of Shropshire 2000. Opposition Spokesperson for: Home Office 2002-06, Trade and Industry 2002-06. EU Sub-committee F (Home Affairs): Co-opted member 2007-10, Member 2010-12; Member: Consumer Insurance (Disclosure and Representations) Bill 2011-12, EU Sub-committee E (Justice, Institutions and Consumer Protection) 2012-15, Soft Power and the UK's Influence 2013-14, Joint Committee on Draft Protection of Charities Bill 2014-15; Secondary Legislation Scrutiny: Member 2015-17, Chair 2019-; Chair, Citizenship and Civic Engagement 2017-18; Member: Bribery Act 2010 2018-19, SLSC Sub-committee B 2018-19. *Other:* Chairman: National Union of Conservative Associations 1996-98, National Conservative Convention 1998-2000; Deputy Chairman, Conservative Party 1998-2000. Member: Council for Securities Industry 1980-85, Securities and Investment Board 1985-89, West Midlands Industrial Development Board 1989-97, Securities and Futures Authority 1993-2001; President, National Council for Voluntary Organisation (NCVO) 2007-12; Official Reviewer of: Charities Act 2011-12, Transparency in Lobbying Act 2015-16.

Political interests: Trade and industry, charities and voluntary sector, demography.

Other: Chair, Armed Forces Charity Advisory Committee 2008-18; Trustee, Fair Trials International 2012-19; Salvation Army, Fair Trials International, Freedom from Torture, Howard League, Tree Aid; Liveryman, Goldsmith's Company 1983; Trustee and Honorary Fellow, St Peter's College, Oxford; CBE 1992.

Publications: Britain's Home Defence Gamble (1978); Unshackling Good Neighbours (2011); Britain's Demographic Challenge (2017).

Recreations: Fishing, theatre, books.

The Lord Hodgson of Astley Abbotts CBE, House of Lords, London SW1A 0PW
Tel: 020 7219 8526 *Email:* hodgsonr@parliament.uk
Tel: 07500 706917 *Email:* hadowv@parliament.uk

HOEY, BARONESS

NON-AFFILIATED

HOEY (Life Baroness), Catharine (Kate) Letitia Hoey; cr 2020. Born 21 June 1946; Daughter of Thomas and late Letitia Hoey.

Education: Belfast Royal Academy; Ulster College of Physical Education (Diploma teaching 1964); City of London College, London (BSc economics 1968).

Non-political career: Lecturer, Southwark College 1972-76; Senior Lecturer, Kingsway College 1976-85; Educational Adviser to Arsenal Football Club 1985-89. Member, CWU; Chair, Fire Brigades Union Parliamentary Group.

Political career: *House of Commons:* Contested Dulwich 1983 and 1987 general elections. MP (Lab) for Vauxhall 15 June 1989 by-election to 2010, for Vauxhall (revised boundary) 2010-19; Opposition Spokesperson for Citizen's Charter and Women 1992-93; PPS to Frank Field as Minister of State, Department of Social Security 1997-98; Parliamentary Under-Secretary of State: Home Office (Metropolitan Police, European Union, Judicial Co-operation) 1998-99, Department for Culture, Media and Sport (Minister for Sport) 1999-2001. Member: Broadcasting 1991-97, Social Security 1994-97, Science and Technology 2004-05, Northern Ireland Affairs 2007-10, 2010-19, Public Administration and Constitutional Affairs 2015-17, European Scrutiny 2015-19. *House of Lords:* Raised to the peerage as Baroness Hoey, of Lylehill and Rathlin in the County of Antrim 2020. *Other:* Mayor of London's Commissioner for Sport -2016. Co-Chair, Labour Leave 2016. Councillor: Hackney Borough Council 1978-82, Southwark Borough Council 1988-89.

Political interests: Sport, foreign affairs, housing, countryside, European Union; Angola, Bosnia, Oman, Tibet, Zimbabwe.

Other: Chair, Countryside Alliance 2005-14; Hon Vice-President, British Wheelchair Basketball Association; Former chair, London Sport; Founding member, Grassroots Out 2016; *The Spectator*/Highland Park Debater of the Year Award 1998; University of Ulster Distinguished Graduate 2000; *The House Magazine* International Campaigner of the Year, Dods Parliamentary Awards 2014. Hon Vice-President, Surrey County Cricket Club; Hon President, British Pistol Club.

Publications: Occasional articles on sport in the press.

The Baroness Hoey, House of Lords, London SW1A 0PW
Tel: 020 7219 3000 *Twitter:* @CatharineHoey

CROSSBENCH

HOFFMANN, LORD

HOFFMANN (Life Baron), Leonard Hubert Hoffmann; cr. 1995. Born 8 May 1934; Married Gillian Lorna Sterner 1957 (2 daughters).

Education: South African College School, Cape Town; University of Cape Town (BA); Queen's College, Oxford (Rhodes Scholar, MA, BCL, Vinerian Law Scholar).

Non-political career: Advocate of Supreme Court of South Africa 1958-60; Stowell Civil Law Fellow, University College, Oxford 1961-73; Called to the Bar, Gray's Inn 1964; QC 1977-85; Judge of the Courts of Appeal of Jersey and Guernsey 1980-85; Bencher 1984; Judge of the High Court of Justice, Chancery Division 1985-92; Lord Justice of Appeal 1992-95; Non-Permanent Judge, Hong Kong Court of Final Appeal 1998-; Visiting Professor: of Law, Oxford University 2009-, of Intellectual Property Law, London University 2009-.

Political career: *House of Lords:* Raised to the peerage as Baron Hoffmann, of Chedworth in the County of Gloucestershire 1995. Lord of Appeal in Ordinary 1995-2009; Leave of absence October 2013-November 2016. Chair, European Communities Sub-committee E (Law and Institutions) 1997-2000. *Other:* Member, Royal Commission on Gambling 1976-78; Council of Legal Education: Member 1983-92, Chair 1989-92.

Other: Director, English National Opera 1985-90, 1991-94; President, British-German Jurists Association 1991-2009; Chair, Financial Market Law Committee 2009-; Three honorary doctorates; Hon. fellow: Queen's College, Oxford 1992, University College, Oxford 1995; Gold Bauhinia Star (2014); Kt 1985; PC 1992.

Publications: The South African Law of Evidence (1963).

Recreations: Music, cycling.

Rt Hon the Lord Hoffmann, House of Lords, London SW1A 0PW
Tel: 020 7219 6067
Surrey Lodge, 23 Keats Grove, London NW3 2RS

CROSSBENCH

HOGAN-HOWE, LORD

HOGAN-HOWE (Life Baron), Bernard Hogan-Howe; cr 2017. Born 25 October 1957; Married Marion White.

Education: Hinde House Comprehensive School; Merton College, Oxford (MA law); Cambridge University (Diploma applied criminology); Sheffield University (MBA).

Non-political career: South Yorkshire Police 1979-97: District Commander, Doncaster W Area 1996-97; Merseyside Police: Assistant Chief Constable 1997-99, Head, Area Operations 1999-2001, Chief Constable of Merseyside 2004-09; Metropolitan Police: Assistant Commissioner 2001-04, Commissioner 2011-17; HM Inspector of Constabulary 2009-11.

Political career: *House of Lords:* Raised to the peerage as Baron Hogan-Howe, of Sheffield in the County of South Yorkshire 2017. Member: SLSC Sub-committee A 2018-19, Public Services 2020-. *Other:* Non-executive Board Member, Cabinet Office 2020-.

Other: Member, Cabinet, Association of Chief Police Officers 2001-04; Senior associate fellow, RUSI; Trustee: Lowland Rescue 2017-, Arise Foundation 2018-; Honorary Fellow, Liverpool John Moores University 2010; Honoary LLD: Sheffield Hallam University 2012, Sheffield University 2013; QPM 2003; Kt 2013.

The Lord Hogan-Howe QPM, House of Lords, London SW1A 0PW
Tel: 020 7219 3000

CROSSBENCH

HOGG, BARONESS

HOGG (Life Baroness), Sarah Elizabeth Mary Hogg; cr. 1995. Born 14 May 1946; Daughter of late Rt Hon Baron Boyd-Carpenter; Married Douglas Martin Hogg 1968 (MP for Grantham 1979-97 and for Sleaford and North Hykeham 1997-2001, QC, 3rd Viscount Hailsham (qv)) (1 son 1 daughter).

Education: St Mary's Convent, Ascot; Lady Margaret Hall, Oxford (BA philosophy, politics and economics 1967).

Non-political career: *The Economist* 1967-81: Literary editor 1970-77, Economics editor 1977-81; Economics editor, *The Sunday Times* 1981-82; Presenter, *Channel 4 News* 1982-83; Director, London Broadcasting Company 1982-90; Economics editor and deputy executive editor, finance and industry, *The Times* 1984-86; Assistant editor and business and city editor, *The Independent* 1986-89; Economics editor, *Daily Telegraph* and *Sunday Telegraph* 1989-90; Head, Prime Minister's Policy Unit, with rank of Second Permanent Secretary 1990-95; Director, London School of Economics 1995-97; Chairman: Chair, London Economics 1997-99, Frontier Economics Ltd 1999-2013; Foreign and Colonial Smaller Companies Trust: Non-executive director 1995-2002, Chairman 1997-2002; International advisory board, National Westminster Bank 1995-98; Advisory board, Bankinter 1995-98; NPI 1996-99; Non-executive director, Energy Group 1996-98; GKN: Non-executive director 1996-2006, Deputy Chair 2003-06; 3i: Director 1997-, Deputy Chair 2000-01, Chair 2002-10; Non-executive director: Scottish Eastern Investment Trust 1998-99, Martin Currie Portfolio Trust 1999-2002, P&O 1999-2000, P&O Princess Cruises 2000-03, Carnival Corporation and Carnival plc 2003-08, BG Group plc 2005-; Cadbury plc 2008-10; Chairman, Financial Reporting Council 2010-14, Non-executive director, John Lewis Partnership 2011-18.

Political career: *House of Lords:* Raised to the peerage as Baroness Hogg, of Kettlethorpe in the County of Lincolnshire 1995. Member: Science and Technology Committee 1996-99, Monetary Policy of the Bank of England/Economic Affairs 2000-03. *Other:* Governor, BBC 2000-04; Non-executive director: HM Treasury Board 2010-, Financial Conduct Authority 2016-.

Other: Governor, Centre for Economic Policy Research 1985-92; Director, Royal National Theatre 1988-91; Trustee, St Mary's School, Ascot 1994-; Fellow, Eton College 1996-2008; Council Member: Royal Economic Society 1996-2004, Institute for Fiscal Studies 1996-2005, 2010-, Hansard Society for Parliamentary Government 1996-2000, Lincolnshire Foundation 1996-98, Lincoln University 2002-05; Trustee, Trusthouse Charitable Foundation 2003-; Governor, London Business School 2004-10; Trustee: Cicely Saunders International 2009-10, Historic Lincoln Trust 2013-, Queen Elizabeth Jubilee Memorial Trust 2013-; Governor, NIESR 2014-; Member: Mentoring Foundation, Panel of Takeovers and Mergers; Honorary MA, Open University, 1987; Honorary DLitt, Loughborough, 1992; Honorary Fellow, Lady Margaret Hall, 1994; Honorary LLD, Lincoln, 2001; Honorary DPhil: City University, 2002, Cranfield, 2006; Wincott Foundation Financial Journalist of the Year 1985; CBI First Women Lifetime Award 2005.

Publications: Co-author, Too Close to Call (1995).

Viscountess Hailsham, The Baroness Hogg, House of Lords, London SW1A 0PW
Tel: 020 7219 5353

LABOUR

HOLLICK, LORD

HOLLICK (Life Baron), Clive Richard Hollick; cr. 1991. Born 20 May 1945; Son of late Leslie Hollick and Olive Hollick; Married Susan Woodford 1977 (3 daughters).

Education: Taunton's School, Southampton; Nottingham University (BA sociology 1966).

Non-political career: Hambros Bank: Joined 1967, Director 1973-96; Managing director, MAI plc 1974-96; Director, Mills and Allen Ltd 1975-89; Chair, Shepperton Studios Ltd 1976-84; Member, National Bus Company 1984-91; Director: Logica plc 1987-91, Avenir Havas Media SA (France) 1988-92, National Opinion Polls Ltd 1989-97, Satellite Information Services 1990-94; Chair, Meridian Broadcasting 1991-96; Director, British Aerospace 1992-97; Member, Financial Law Panel 1993-97; Director, Anglia Television 1994-97; Member, Commission on Public Policy and British Business 1995-97; Chair, United Broadcasting and Entertainment Ltd 1995-2000; Chief executive, United Business Media plc 1996-2005; Special adviser to Margaret Beckett MP as President of the Board of Trade 1997-98; Director: Express Newspapers plc 1998-2000, TRW Inc 2000-02, Diageo plc 2001-12; Chair, South Bank Centre 2002-08; Director, Honeywell International Inc 2003-; Kohlberg Kravis Roberts: Partner 2005-09, Senior adviser 2009-10; Partner, GP Bullhound 2010-; Senior adviser, Jefferies Inc 2011-.

Political career: *House of Lords:* Raised to the peerage as Baron Hollick, of Notting Hill in the Royal Borough of Kensington and Chelsea 1991. Trade Envoy to Kenya and Tanzania 2014-18. Economic Affairs: Member 2010-14, Chair 2014-17; Member, Joint Committee on Privacy and Injunctions 2011-12; Economic Affairs Finance Bill Sub-committee: Member 2012-13, 2014, 2015-16, 2018-19, Chair 2016-17; Member: Artificial Intelligence 2017-18, Intergenerational Fairness and Provision 2018-19, Science and Technology 2019-.

Political interests: Business, economic policy, constitutional affairs, transport, media.

Other: Founder, Institute for Public Policy Research 1988-; Governor, London School of Economics and Political Science 1997-2002; Trustee: Dorneywood, Heart of England Forest; Hon. LLD, Nottingham University 1993.

Recreations: Reading, countryside, cinema, theatre, tennis, golf.

The Lord Hollick, House of Lords, London SW1A 0PW
Tel: 020 7219 8942 *Email:* hollickrc@parliament.uk *Twitter:* @clivehollick

HOLLINS, BARONESS

CROSSBENCH

HOLLINS (Life Baroness), Sheila Clare Hollins; cr 2010. Born 22 June 1946; Daughter of late Captain Adrian Kelly and late Monica Kelly, née Edwards; Married Martin Prior Hollins 1969 (1 son 3 daughters).

Education: Notre Dame High School, Sheffield; St Thomas' Hospital Medical School, London (MB BS medicine 1970); French.

Non-political career: Senior registrar in child psychiatry, Earl's Court Child Guidance Unit and Westminster Child's Hospital 1979-81; Senior lecturer in psychiatry of learning disability 1981-90; Honorary Consultant Psychiatrist 1981-2011: Wandsworth Community Health Trust, Richmond, Twickenham and Roehampton Healthcare Trust, South West London and St George's Mental Health Trust; St George's, University of London: Professor of psychiatry of disability 1990-2011, Chair, Academic Division of Mental Health 2002-05; Policy adviser on learning disability, Department of Health (on secondment) 1992-93, 2001-03; Member, Minister's Advisory Group on Learning Disability 1999-2001; Chair, NHS Working Party on Breast and Cervical Screening in Learning Disability 1999-2000; Deputy chair, National Specialist Commissioning Advisory Group 2006-08; Chair, WHO Europe Steering and Drafting Groups on developing a declaration about children with intellectual disabilities for agreement by Ministers of Health across Europe 2008-10; Chair, External Advisory Group, National Confidential Inquiry into Suicides and Homicides 2007-11; Honorary Professor, Department of Theology and Religion, Durham University 2013-; Chair, Scientific Advisory Group, Centre for Çhild Protection, Pontifical Gregorian University, Rome 2014-; Chair, Expert Reference Group on workforce for Transforming Care programme, Health Education England 2015-17. President, BMA 2012-13; Chair, Board of Science 2013-16.

Political career: *House of Lords:* Raised to the peerage as Baroness Hollins, of Wimbledon in the London Borough of Merton and of Grenoside in the County of South Yorkshire 2010. Member, Mental Capacity Act 2005 2013-14.

Political interests: Health and social care (especially mental health and learning disability), welfare reform, special education (long term conditions), human rights abuses of disabled people; Africa, South Asia.

Other: Member, Pontifical Commission for the Protection of Minors Rome 2014-18; Member: Community Care and Disability Sub-committee, Joseph Rowntree Foundation 1989-93, Academy of Medical Royal Colleges 2005-08; Founder and Chair, Books Beyond Word CIC; Patron, Respond 2011-; Honorary fellow and vice-president, Institute of Psychotherapy and Disability; Patron: Wimbledon Bookfest 2010-, Living and Dying Well 2012-, St Teresa's School, Effingham 2014-, Home Renaissance Foundation 2018-, DanceSyndrome 2019-; Royal College of Psychiatrists: Vice-President 2003-04, President 2005-08; British Medical Association: President 2012-13, Chair, Board of Science 2013-; President, Royal College of Occupational Therapists 2015-; Books Beyond Words, Respond, Lay Community of St

Benedict; MRCPsych 1978; FRCPsych 1988; FRCPCH 1990; Honorary FRCP 2007; FHEA; Honorary Fellow, Medical Women's Federation; FIPD 2009; Fellow, City Lit 2015; Honorary Fellow, Academy of Medical Educators 2019; Honorary fellow, Colleges of Medecine, South Africa 2005; DD, University of London 2013; MD, Sheffield University 2014; DL, Bath University 2014; DS, Worcester University 2014; DL, Durham University 2016; Doctor of the University, Australian Catholic University, Melbourne 2016; D Ed, Oxford Brookes University 2019. Farmers Club, RSM, Lansdowne Club.

Publications: Over 200 academic and professional articles on mental health and learning disability; 50 books in the Books Beyond Words series for adults with intellectual disabilities.

Recreations: Walking, music, oil painting.

Professor the Baroness Hollins, House of Lords, London SW1A 0PW
Tel: 020 7219 0520 *Email:* hollinss@parliament.uk *Twitter:* @baronesshollins

CONSERVATIVE

HOLMES OF RICHMOND, LORD

HOLMES OF RICHMOND (Life Baron), Christopher Holmes; cr 2013. Born 15 October 1971; Son of Michael and Margaret Holmes; Engaged.

Education: Harry Cheshire High School, Kidderminster; King's College, Cambridge (BA 1994).

Non-political career: Paralympic swimmer; Public Speaker 1992-; Ashurst 2002-07; Admitted solicitor 2004.

Political career: *House of Lords:* Raised to the peerage as Baron Holmes of Richmond, of Richmond in the London Borough of Richmond upon Thames 2013. Member: Digital Skills 2014-15, Social Mobility 2015-16, Financial Exclusion 2016-17, Artificial Intelligence 2017-18, Intergenerational Fairness and Provision 2018-19, Democracy and Digital Technologies 2019-. *Other:* Left Conservatives July 2019; Non-affiliated July 2019-October 2020; Conservatives October 2020-. Non-executive director: Disability Rights Commission 2002-07, UK Sport 2005-13; Director, Paralympic integration, London Organising Committee of 2012 Olympic and Paralympic Games 2009-13; Non-executive director, Equality and Human Rights Commission (Disability Commissioner) 2013-17; Diversity adviser, Cabinet Office 2015-; Deputy Chair, Channel 4 2018-; Lead, Review for the Government into Disability and Public Appointments; Trustee, Industry and Parliament Trust.

Political interests: Economy, pensions, education, employment, diversity and inclusion, digital, foreign affairs, broadcasting, media, sport, culture; Australia, Canada, Japan, Malawi, Middle East, Singapore, South Korea, USA.

Other: Patron, Help for Heroes 2008-; Chair, Global Disability Innovation Hub; Trustee, Industry and Parliament Trust; Solicitors Regulation Authority; Nick Webber Trust, Queen Elizabeth Diamond Jubilee Trust, Duke of Edinburgh Award; BPP University: Deputy Chancellor 2015-17, Chancellor 2017-; Honorary LLD, Bath University 2012; Six Paralympic gold medals at Barcelona Games 1992; Sports Personality of the Year 1992; Bass Midlander of the Year 1992; Three Paralympic gold medals at Atlanta Games 1996; Saf Paul Zetter Award 1996; Sports Personality of the Year, Variety Club of GB 1997; MBE 1993. Hawks' Club, Cambridge University.

Recreations: Skiing, theatre, reading, music.

The Lord Holmes of Richmond MBE, House of Lords, London SW1A 0PW
Tel: 020 7219 8617 *Email:* holmesc@parliament.uk Website: chrisholmes.co.uk
Twitter: @LordCHolmes

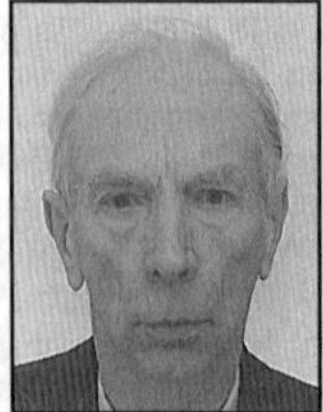

CONSERVATIVE

HOME, EARL OF

HOME (15th Earl of, S), David Alexander Cospatrick Douglas-Home; cr. 1604; Lord Dunglass; 20th Lord Home (S) 1473; 5th Baron Douglas (UK) 1875. Born 20 November 1943; Son of 14th Earl, KT, PC, DL, who disclaimed the earldom 1963 to become Prime Minister as Sir Alec Douglas-Home, and who was subsequently made a life peer as Baron Home of the Hirsel 1974; Married Jane Williams-Wynne 1972 (1 son 2 daughters).

Education: Eton College; Christ Church, Oxford (BA philosophy, politics and economics 1966).

Non-political career: Douglas and Angus Estates: Director 1966-, Chair 1995-; Director: Morgan Grenfell & Co Ltd 1974-99, Arab-British Chamber of Commerce 1975-84; Morgan Grenfell (Asia) Ltd: Director 1978-82, Deputy chair 1979-82; Director: Arab Bank Investment Co 1979-87, Agricultural Mortgage Corporation plc 1979-93; Tandem Group plc (formerly EFG plc): Director 1981-96, Chair 1993-96; Chair: Morgan Grenfell Export Services 1984-98, Morgan Grenfell (Scotland) 1986-98, Committee for Middle East Trade 1986-92, Morgan Grenfell International Ltd 1987-98; Director: Morgan Grenfell Asia (Hong Kong) Ltd/Deutsche Morgan Grenfell Hong Kong Ltd 1989-99, Morgan Grenfell Asia Holdings Pte Ltd/Deutsche Morgan Grenfell Asia Holdings Pte Ltd 1989-99, K & N Kenanga Holdings Bhd 1993-99; Non-executive director, Grosvenor Estate Holdings 1993-2000; Director: Kenanga DMG Futures Sdn Bhd/Kenanga Deutsche Futures Sdn Bhd 1995-99, Deutsche Morgan Grenfell Group plc 1996-99; Board member: Deva Group/Wheatsheaf Investments Ltd 1999-, Deva Holding Ltd/Deva Group 1999-2010; Chair: Coutts and Company 1999-2012, Coutts Switzerland Ltd/RBS Coutts/Coutts & Co Ltd 2000-17, MAN Ltd 2000-09; Board member: Oryx Fund 2004-07, Dubai Financial Services Authority 2005-12; Grosvenor Group Ltd: Board member 2005-10, Chair 2007-10.

Political career: *House of Lords:* First entered House of Lords 1995; Opposition Frontbench Spokesperson for: Trade 1997-98, the Treasury 1997-98; Elected hereditary peer 1999-. *Other:* Member, Export Guarantee Advisory Council, ECGD 1988-93.

Political interests: Foreign affairs, Scottish affairs, industry, agriculture; Middle and Far East.

Other: President, British Malaysian Society 2006-; Trustee: Grosvenor Estate 1993-2010, Royal Agricultural Society of England 1999-2003; Chairman: Coutts Charitable Trust -2017, Coutts Foundation -2017; Fellow, Chartered Institute of Bankers 1999-; Lymphoma Association; CBE 1991; CVO 1997; KT 2014. Turf Club.

Recreations: Outdoor sports.

The Earl of Home KT CVO CBE, House of Lords, London SW1A 0PW
Tel: 020 7219 3168
Email: linda.bracha@coutts.com

CONSERVATIVE

HOOPER, BARONESS

HOOPER (Life Baroness), Gloria Dorothy Hooper; cr. 1985. Born 25 May 1939; Daughter of late Frederick Hooper and late Frances Hooper, née Maloney.

Education: La Sainte Union Convent; Royal Ballet School; Southampton University (BA law 1960); Universidad Central, Ecuador (Rotary Foundation Fellow 1965-66); French, Spanish.

Non-political career: Assistant to chief registrar, John Lewis Partnership 1960-61; Editor, Current Law, Sweet & Maxwell, Law Publishers 1961-62; Information officer, Winchester City Council 1962-67; Assistant solicitor, Taylor and Humbert 1967-72; Legal adviser, Slater Walker France S.A. 1972-73; Partner, Taylor and Humbert (Solicitors), now Taylor Wessing 1974-84.

Political career: *House of Lords:* Raised to the peerage as Baroness Hooper, of Liverpool and St James's in the City of Westminster 1985. Government Whip 1985-87; Parliamentary Under-Secretary of State, Department of: Education and Science 1987-88, Energy 1988-89, Health 1989-92; Deputy Speaker 1993-2018; Deputy Chairman of Committees 1993-2018; PPS to William Hague as Leader of the Opposition 1999-2001; Trade Envoy to Costa Rica, Dominican Republic and Panama 2020-. Member, Intergovernmental Organisations 2008; EU Sub-committee A (Economic and Financial Affairs and International Trade): Co-opted member 2008-10, Member 2010-12; Member EU Sub-committees: A (Economic and Financial Affairs) 2012-13, B (Internal Market, Infrastructure and Employment) 2013-15; Member, European

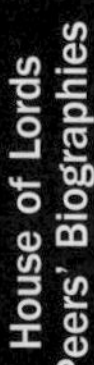

Union 2014-15. *Other:* European Parliament: MEP for Liverpool 1979-84: Deputy chief whip, European Democratic Group. Member, Association of Conservative Peers 1985-; President, Greater London Women's Conservative Association 2006-.

Political interests: European Union, cultural heritage, education, energy, international relations; Mercosur countries, Andean Pact countries, CAFTA countries, Commonwealth countries, NAFTA countries, Council of Europe countries, Overseas Territories.

Other: Member: Parliamentary Delegation to Council of Europe and to Western European Union 1992-97, 2001-09, Executive Committee, Commonwealth Parliamentary Association (UK Branch) 2008-17; Vice-chair, Inter-Parliamentary Union, British Group 2017-20; Member, Law Society; President, British Educational Equipment and Supplies Association; Vice-President, Canning House (Hispanic and Luso Brazilian Council); President: Good Guy's Cancer Appeal, Friends of Colombia for Social Aid, European Foundation For Heritage Skills, Friends of Gibraltar; Chair: Institute of the Americas UCL, Dance Teachers Benevolent Fund; Trustee/Governor, Centre for Global Energy Studies; Industry and Parliament Trust: Fellow 1983, Trustee 1996-2012; Trustee: Tablet Trust 2004-, St George's House, Windsor Castle 2007-13; Fellow: Royal Geographical Society, RSA; Hon. LLD, Southampton University 2009; Order of Francisco de Miranda (Venezuela) 1999; CMG 2003; Order of Boyaca Gran Cruz (Colombia) 2004; Order of Merit (Ecuador) 2004; Order of Bernardo O'Higgins (Chile) 2004; Dame of the Order of St Gregory the Great 2005. In and Out Club.

Recreations: Theatre, travel, gardening.

The Baroness Hooper CMG, House of Lords, London SW1A 0PW
Tel: 020 7219 5489 *Email:* hooperg@parliament.uk

CROSSBENCH

HOPE OF CRAIGHEAD, LORD

Chair, Select Committee on High Speed Rail (West Midlands-Crewe) Bill

HOPE OF CRAIGHEAD (Life Baron), James Arthur David Hope; cr. 1995. Born 27 June 1938; Son of late Arthur Hope, OBE, WS; Married Mary Kerr 1966 (twin sons 1 daughter).

Education: Edinburgh Academy; Rugby School; St John's College, Cambridge (Scholarship 1956, BA classics 1962, MA); Edinburgh University (LLB 1965).

Non-political career: Admitted Faculty of Advocates 1965; Standing Junior Counsel in Scotland to Board of Inland Revenue 1974-78; Advocate-Depute 1978-82; QC (Scotland) 1978; Legal Chairman, Pensions Appeal Tribunal 1985-86; Chairman, Medical Appeal Tribunals 1985-86; Dean, Faculty of Advocates 1986-89; Lord Justice General of Scotland and Lord President of the Court of Session 1989-96; Hon. Bencher: Gray's Inn 1989, Inn of Court of Northern Ireland 1995; Deputy President, Supreme Court of the United Kingdom 2009-13; HM Lord High Commissioner to the General Assembly of the Church of Scotland 2015-16. National service, Seaforth Highlanders 1957-59.

Political career: *House of Lords:* Raised to the peerage as Baron Hope of Craighead, of Bamff in the District of Perth and Kinross 1995. Lord of Appeal in Ordinary 1996-2009: Second Senior Law Lord 2009; As Deputy President of the Supreme Court, disqualified from participation 2009-13; Convenor of the Crossbench Peers 2015-19; Member, House of Lords Commission 2016-19. Member, European Communities 1998-2001; Chair, European Communities Sub-committee E (Law and Institutions) 1998-2001; Member: Personal Service Companies 2013-14, Privileges and Conduct 2014-; Chair, Joint Committee on the Draft Protection of Charities Bill 2014-15; Member: Administration and Works 2015-16, House 2015-16, Liaison 2015-19, Procedure 2015-19, Selection 2015-19, Services 2016-19; Chair, High Speed Rail (West Midlands-Crewe) Bill 2020-; Member, Common Frameworks Scrutiny 2020-.

Political interests: Scotland.

Other: Board of Trustees, National Library of Scotland 1989-96; Trustee, Bute House Trust, Edinburgh 1996-; Member, University of Strathclyde Charitable Foundation 1998-2001; Chair, Advisory Council, Institute of Advanced Legal Studies 1998-2013; President: Stair Society 1993-2013, International Criminal Law Association 2000-13; Fellow: Strathclyde University 2000, Royal Society of Edinburgh 2003; Commonwealth Magistrates' and Judges' Association: President 2003-06, Life Vice-President; Chair, Botanic Cottage Trust, Edinburgh 2009-12;

Chancellor, Strathclyde University 1998-2013; Hon. LLD: Aberdeen 1991, Strathclyde 1993, Edinburgh 1995; Hon. Fellow, St John's College, Cambridge 1995; Hon. DUniv, Strathclyde 2013; Hon. LLD: Glasgow 2013, BPP (London) 2014, Abertay 2014; PC 1989; KT 2010. New Club (Edinburgh).

Publications: Co-editor, Gloag and Henderson's Introduction to the Law of Scotland (6th-9th eds 1956-87); Armour on Valuation for Rating (4th-5th eds, 1971, 1985); Co-author, The Rent (Scotland) Act (1984, 1986); Contributor, Stair Memorial Encyclopaedia of Scots Law; Gloag and Henderson's The Law of Scotland (11th ed, 2002); Court of Session Practice (2005) with regular updates; Lord Hope's Diaries: Senior Counsel 1976-1986 (2017), Dean of Faculty 1996-1998 (2018), Lord President 1998-1996 (2018).

Recreations: Walking, ornithology, music.

Rt Hon the Lord Hope of Craighead KT, House of Lords, London SW1A 0PW
Tel: 020 7219 1414/8054 *Email:* hopejad@parliament.uk

CONSERVATIVE

HORAM, LORD

HORAM (Life Baron), John Rhodes Horam; cr 2013. Born 7 March 1939; Son of Sydney and Catherine Horam; Married Judith Jackson 1987 (2 sons from previous marriage).

Education: Silcoates School, Wakefield; St Catharine's College, Cambridge (MA economics 1960).

Non-political career: Market research officer, Rowntree & Co 1960-62; Leader and feature writer: *Financial Times* 1962-65, *The Economist* 1965-68; Managing director: Commodities Research Unit Ltd 1968-70, 1983-87, CRU Holdings Ltd 1988-92; CRU International Ltd: Deputy chair 1992-95, Non-executive director 1997-.

Political career: *House of Commons:* Contested Folkstone and Hythe 1966 general election. MP for Gateshead West 1970-83 (Labour 1970-81, SDP 1981-83). Contested Newcastle upon Tyne Central (SDP/All) 1983 general election. MP (Conservative) for Orpington 1992-2010; Parliamentary Under-Secretary of State, Department of Transport 1976-79; Labour Spokesperson for Economic Affairs 1979-81; SDP Spokesperson for Economic Affairs 1981-83; Parliamentary Secretary, Office of Public Service 1995; Parliamentary Under-Secretary of State, Department of Health 1995-97. Member: Public Accounts 1992-95, Liaison 1997-2003; Environmental Audit: Chair 1997-2003, Member 2003-05, Member: Foreign Affairs 2005-10. *House of Lords:* Raised to the peerage as Baron Horam, of Grimsargh in the County of Lancashire 2013. Member: Delegated Powers and Regulatory Reform 2013-14, Communications 2014-15, EU External Affairs Sub-Committee 2015-19, High Speed Rail (West Midlands-Crewe) Bill 2020-. *Other:* Member, Executive, 1922 Committee 2004-07. Electoral Commissioner 2012-18.

Political interests: Economic policy, transport, health, foreign affairs; France, Germany, USA.

Other: St Catharine's Society Cambridge: Chair 2006-13, President 2014; Fellow Commoner, St Catherine's College Cambridge, 2010-.

Publications: Making Britain Competitive (1993).

Recreations: Opera, gardening, walking, golf, cooking.

The Lord Horam, House of Lords, London SW1A 0PW
Tel: 020 7219 8759
Tel: 020 7736 8521 *Email:* jrhoram@gmail.com

CROSSBENCH

HOUGHTON OF RICHMOND, LORD

HOUGHTON OF RICHMOND (Life Baron), John Nicholas Reynolds Houghton; cr 2017. Born 18 October 1954; Married Maggie (1 son 1 daughter).

Education: Woodhouse Grove School, Bradford; Royal Military Academy, Sandhurst; St Peter's College, Oxford (modern history); Army Command and Staff Course, Shrivenham and Camberley; Higher Command and Staff Course 1997.

Non-political career: Army 1974-2016: Commissioned into Green Howards, Military Assistant to the Chief of Staff, British Army of the Rhine, Member of Directing Staff, Royal Military College of Science, Shrivenham, Deputy Assistant Chief of Staff, G3 (Operations and Deployment), HQ Land Command 1993-97, Director of Military Operations, Ministry of Defence 1999-2002, Chief of Staff, Allied Rapid Reaction Corps 2002-04, Assistant Chief of Defence Staff (Operations) 2004-05, Deputy Commanding General, Multi-national Force in Iraq 2005-06, Chief of Joint Operations, Permanent Joint Headquarters 2006-09; Ministry of Defence: Vice-Chief of the Defence Staff 2009-13, Chief of the Defence Staff 2013-16; Constable of Her Majesty's Tower of London 2016-.

Political career: *House of Lords:* Raised to the peerage as Baron Houghton of Richmond, of Richmond in the County of North Yorkshire 2017.

Other: President, Combined Services Golf; Vice-patron, Royal Edinburgh Military Tattoo; Fellow, St Peter's College, Oxford; ADC Gen CBE GCB. Army and Navy; Combined Winter Sports; President, Combined Services Golf.

Recreations: Golf, sailing, shooting, cooking, history.

General the Lord Houghton of Richmond GCB CBE ADC Gen, House of Lords, London SW1A 0PW
Tel: 020 7219 3000
HM Tower of London, London EC3N 4AB *Tel:* 020 3166 6220
Email: natalie.gough@hrp.org.uk

CONSERVATIVE

HOWARD OF LYMPNE, LORD

HOWARD OF LYMPNE (Life Baron), Michael Howard; cr 2010. Born 7 July 1941; Son of late Bernard and Hilda Howard; Married Sandra Paul 1975 (1 son 1 daughter 1 stepson).

Education: Llanelli Grammar School; Peterhouse, Cambridge (MA economics and law; LLB 1963).

Non-political career: Called to the Bar, Inner Temple 1964; Junior Counsel to the Crown 1980-82; QC 1982.

Political career: *House of Commons:* Contested Liverpool Edge Hill 1966 and 1970 general elections. MP (Conservative) for Folkestone and Hythe 1983-2010; PPS to Sir Patrick Mayhew as Solicitor-General 1984-85; Parliamentary Under-Secretary of State, Department of Trade and Industry 1985-87; Minister of State, Department of the Environment 1987-90; Secretary of State for: Employment 1990-92, the Environment 1992-93; Home Secretary 1993-97; Member, Shadow Cabinet 1997-99, 2001-05: Shadow Foreign Secretary 1997-99, Shadow Chancellor of the Exchequer 2001-03, Leader of the Opposition 2003-05. Chair, Conservative Policy Committee for Economic Affairs/Enterprise/Pensions/Social Affairs 2001-03. *House of Lords:* Raised to the peerage as Baron Howard of Lympne, of Lympne in the County of Kent 2010. *Other:* Chair, Coningsby Club 1972-73; Member, Conservative Policy Board 2001-03; Contested Conservative Party leadership June 1997; Leader, Conservative Party 2003-05; Patron, Tory Reform Group. Member, House of Lords Appointments Commission 2010-18; Commissioner, Independent Commission on Freedom of Information 2015-.

Political interests: Home affairs, foreign affairs; USA.

Other: Chair, Bow Group 1970; President and founding chair, Atlantic Partnership 2003-; Chair, Hospice UK; *Spectator* Parliamentarian of the Year 2003; PC 1990; CH 2011. Carlton, Pratt's, Buck's Club.

Recreations: Football, baseball.

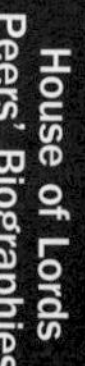

Rt Hon the Lord Howard of Lympne CH QC, House of Lords, London SW1A 0PW
Tel: 020 7219 3964 *Email:* howardm@parliament.uk
Tel: 01883 713249 *Email:* murrellt@parliament.uk Website: www.michaelhoward.org

CONSERVATIVE

HOWARD OF RISING, LORD

HOWARD OF RISING (Life Baron), Greville Patrick Charles Howard; cr. 2004. Born 22 April 1941; Son of Lt Col H R G Howard; Married Mary Cortland Culverwell 1981 (2 sons 1 daughter).

Education: Eton College.

Non-political career: Private secretary to J Enoch Powell MP 1968-70; Director: Keep Trust 1980-87, Fortress Trust 1989-93, Fortress Holdings 1993-2008.

Political career: *House of Lords:* Raised to the peerage as Baron Howard of Rising, of Castle Rising in the County of Norfolk 2004. Opposition Whip 2005-09; Opposition Spokesperson for: Treasury 2005-09, Work and Pensions 2005-06, Constitutional Affairs 2006, Cabinet Office 2006-09, Culture, Media and Sport 2006-10. Member: Joint Committee on Statutory Instruments 2005-07, Refreshment 2012-14. *Other:* Vice-President, Conservatives for Britain 2015-16. Councillor, King's Lynn and West Norfolk 2003-.

Other: Vice-president, National Playing Fields Association. Captain, Lords and Commons tennis team.

Publications: Editor, Enoch at 100 (Biteback, 2012).

The Lord Howard of Rising, House of Lords, London SW1A 0PW
Tel: 020 7219 5353 *Email:* howardgr@parliament.uk

CROSSBENCH

HOWARTH OF BRECKLAND, BARONESS

HOWARTH OF BRECKLAND (Life Baroness), Valerie Georgina Howarth OBE; cr 2001. Born 5 September 1940; Daughter of George Howarth and Edith Steele.

Education: Abbeydale Girls Grammar School, Sheffield; Leicester University (Diploma social studies 1963; Certificate applied social studies); Home Office Certificate childcare.

Non-political career: Caseworker, Family Welfare Association 1963-68; London Borough of Lambeth 1968-82: Senior child care worker and training officer 1968-70, Area co-ordinator 1970-72, Chief co-ordinator of social work 1972-76, Assistant director of personal services 1976-82; Director of social services, London Borough of Brent 1982-86; Chief executive, ChildLine charity 1987-2001.

Political career: *House of Lords:* Raised to the peerage as Baroness Howarth of Breckland, of Parson Cross in the County of South Yorkshire 2001. EU Sub-committee G (Social Policy and Consumer Affairs): Member 2003-07, Chair 2007-10; Member: European Union 2007-12, EU Sub-committee D: (Agriculture, Fisheries and Environment) 2010-12, (Agriculture, Fisheries, Environment and Energy) 2012-15, Adoption Legislation 2012-13, Ecclesiastical Committee 2015-. *Other:* UK Representative, European Forum for Child Welfare 1994-97; Chair, UK Group on Child Exploitation (linked with EFCW); Board member: Food Standards Agency 2000-07, National Care Standards Commission 2001-04, Meat Hygiene Services Board 2004-07; Cafcass (Children and Families Advisory and Support Services): Board member 2004-08, Chair 2008-12; Vice-President, Local Government Association 2010-19, 2020-; Director and committee member, ICSTIS (Independent Committee for the Supervision of Television Information Systems) 1988-2000.

Political interests: Social care, children, consumer affairs, energy, animal welfare, environment; Canada, Europe.

Other: Founder and first chair, King's Cross Homeless Project 1986-87; Founder member, London Homeless Forum 1986-87; Trustee and vice-chair, National Council for Voluntary Child Care Organisations 1990-95, Member NCH Commission considering Children as Abusers 1991-92; Trustee and vice-chair, Lucy Faithfull Foundation 1992-; Chair, 'Stop it Now' Steering Group 2009-11; Trustee, National Children's Bureau 1993-94; Member, NSPCC Professional Advisory Panel 1993-95; Adviser and trustee, Sieff Foundation 1994-2004;

Founder member and first chair, Telephone Helplines Association 1995-96; Resident, John Grooms Association for Disabled People and Chair of Care and Development Committee 2000-07; Patron and trustee, Little Hearts Matter 2002-; Chair, Children's International Helplines Association 2003-07; Patron: Voice 2006-, TRACKS 2011-; Senior Vice-President, Livability 2013-; British Association of Social Workers; Association of Directors of Adult Social Care; President, Child Helpline International; Honorary Doctorate, Open University 2007; Children's Champion, Charity Champion awards 2012; OBE 1999.

Recreations: People, gardening, reading, walking dog, church.

The Baroness Howarth of Breckland OBE, House of Lords, London SW1A 0PW
Tel: 020 7219 8744 *Fax:* 020 7219 0269 *Email:* howarthv@parliament.uk

LABOUR

HOWARTH OF NEWPORT, LORD

HOWARTH OF NEWPORT (Life Baron), Alan Thomas Howarth; cr 2005. Born 11 June 1944; Son of late T. E. B. Howarth MC, TD, and Margaret Howarth, née Teakle; Married Gillian Chance 1967 (divorced 1996) (2 sons 2 daughters); partner Baroness Hollis of Heigham (died 2018).

Education: Rugby School; King's College, Cambridge (BA history 1965); French.

Non-political career: Senior research assistant to Field-Marshal Montgomery on *A History of Warfare* 1965-67; English and history teacher, Westminster School 1968-74; Private secretary to Conservative Party Chairmen William Whitelaw and Lord Thorneycroft 1975-79; Vice-chair and chief executive, Conservative Central Office 1979-81; Co-ordinated campaign planning for 1979 election; Director, Conservative Research Department 1979-81; Investment department, Baring Brothers 1982-87.

Political career: *House of Commons:* MP for Stratford-on-Avon 1983-97, for Newport East 1997-2005 (Conservative 1983-95, Labour 1995-2005); PPS to Sir Rhodes Boyson as Minister of State, Northern Ireland Office and Department of Environment 1985-87; Assistant Government Whip 1987-88; Government Whip 1988-89; Parliamentary Under-Secretary of State, Department for Education and Science 1989-92, Minister for Schools 1989-90, Minister for Higher Education and Science 1990-92; Resigned from Conservative Party and joined Labour Party, October 1995; Parliamentary Under-Secretary of State: Department for Education and Employment, Employment Minister and Minister for Disabled People 1997-98, Department for Culture, Media and Sport (Minister for the Arts) 1998-2001; Member, Intelligence and Security Committee 2001-05. *House of Lords:* Raised to the peerage as Baron Howarth of Newport, of Newport in the County of Gwent 2005. Member: Intergovernmental Organisations 2007-08, Political Polling and Digital Media 2017-18, Constitution 2019-. Vice-chair PLP Departmental Committee for Culture, Media and Sport 2006-15. *Other:* Vice-chair, Conservative Party 1980-81. Vice-President, Local Government Association 2001-.

Political interests: Economic policy, education, disability, charities, voluntary sector, social security, arts, heritage, constituencies; Brazil, South Africa, Uganda, Vietnam.

Other: Leader, UK Parliamentary Trade Delegation to Washington 2003; Governor, Royal Shakespeare Company 1984-97; Founder and chair, Friends of the Huntington's Disease Association 1985-87; Board member: Retirement Security Ltd 1987, Institute of Historical Research 1992-97; Member, Constitution Unit Advisory Committee 1992-97; Vice-president, British Dyslexia Association 1992-97; Patron, Neurological Alliance 1992-97; Trustee, Employment Policy Institute 1992-97; Member, Executive Committee, Fabian Society 1995-96; Chair, Trustees and Governors, Friends of the Royal Pavilion, Brighton 2006-11; Board member, Norwich Heritage and Economic Regeneration Trust 2006-; Trustee: Poetry Archive 2006-13, Foundation for International Cultural Diplomacy 2006-11; Chair, Working Group on UK Literary Heritage 2006-12; Patron, Tourism for All UK 2006-; Vice-President, Victorian Society 2009-; Hon Fellow, Royal Institute of British Architects 2004; Fellow, Society of Antiquaries 2007; CBE 1982; PC 2000.

Publications: Co-author: Changing Charity (1984), Monty at Close Quarters (1985), Save Our Schools (1986), The Arts: The Next Move Forward (1987); Articles in the *Guardian*, *Independent*, *Observer*, *Daily Telegraph*.

Recreations: The arts, heritage, reading, walking.

Rt Hon the Lord Howarth of Newport CBE, House of Lords, London SW1A 0PW
Tel: 020 7219 5077 *Email:* howartha@parliament.uk

CONSERVATIVE

HOWE, EARL

Deputy Leader of the House of Lords

HOWE (7th Earl, UK), Frederick Richard Penn Curzon; cr. 1821; 8th Viscount Curzon (UK) 1802; 9th Baron Howe (GB) 1788; 8th Baron Curzon (GB) 1794. Born 29 January 1951; Son of late Commander Chambré George William Penn Curzon, RN, grandson of 3rd Earl, GCVO, CB, and late Mrs Jane Curzon, née Fergusson; Married Elizabeth Stuart 1983 (1 son 3 daughters).

Education: Rugby School; Christ Church, Oxford (MA literae humaniores 1973).

Non-political career: Arable farmer; Director: Adam & Company plc 1987-90, Provident Life Association Ltd 1988-91; Barclays Bank plc 1973-87, Senior manager 1984-87; Chair, LAPADA 1999-2010; Director, Andry Montgomery Ltd 2000-10; Trustee, Kedleston and Portman Estates 2006-. Member, National Farmers' Union.

Political career: *House of Lords:* First entered House of Lords 1984; Government Whip 1991-92; Parliamentary Secretary, Ministry of Agriculture, Fisheries and Food 1992-95; Parliamentary Under-Secretary of State, Ministry of Defence 1995-97; Elected hereditary peer 1999-; Opposition Spokesperson for: Defence May-October 1997, Health October 1997-2010, the Family 2004-05; Parliamentary Under-Secretary of State (Quality) and Government Spokesperson, Department of Health 2010-15; Minister of State and Government Spokesperson, Ministry of Defence 2015-19; Deputy Leader of the House of Lords 2015-; Government Spokesperson for Cabinet Office 2020. Member, Liaison 2019-. *Other:* President, Beaconsfield Constituency Conservative Association 2005-.

Political interests: Agriculture, health and social care, defence; Republic of Korea.

Other: Governor, King William IV Naval Foundation 1984-; National Society for Epilepsy: Vice-President 1984-86, President 1986-2010; President: South Bucks Association for the Disabled 1984-, Chilterns Branch, RNLI 1985-; Governor, Trident Trust 1985-2008; President: CPRE (Penn Country Branch) 1986-92, Epilepsy Society 1986-2010; Trustee, Milton's Cottage 1986-2012; Member, RNLI Council 1997-2014; Trustee: Sir William Borlase's Grammar School, Marlow 1998-2010, Restoration of Appearance and Function Trust (RAFT) 1999-2010; Patron: Demand 1999-2010, Chiltern Society 2001-; Chairman, Patrons of Buckinghamshire County Museum and Art Gallery 2005-; President, Institute of Clinical Research 2008-10; Associate, Chartered Institute of Bankers 1976-; Hon FRCP 2008-; Lords Minister of the Year, *House Magazine* awards 2012; PC 2013.

Recreations: Old films.

Rt Hon the Earl Howe, House of Lords, London SW1A 0PW
Tel: 020 7219 5353 *Email:* howef@parliament.uk
Tel: 020 7218 7346

CONSERVATIVE

HOWELL OF GUILDFORD, LORD

HOWELL OF GUILDFORD (Life Baron), David Arthur Russell Howell; cr. 1997. Born 18 January 1936; Son of late Arthur Howell, retired army officer and businessman; Married Davina Wallace 1967 (1 son 2 daughters).

Education: Eton College; King's College, Cambridge (BA economics 1959, MA).

Non-political career: Economic section, HM Treasury 1959-60; Leader writer, *Daily Telegraph* 1960-64; Editor, *Crossbow* 1962-64; Chair, UK-Japan 21st Century Group 1990-2000; Director, Trafalgar House 1990-2006; Visiting Fellow, Nuffield College, Oxford 1992-2000; Director: Monks Investment Trust 1993-2004, Jardine Insurance 1994-97; Advisory director, UBS-Warburg 1997-2000; Director, John Laing 2000-03; Financial advisory board, Kuwait Investment Authority 2003-10, 2012-. Second Lieutenant, 2nd Btn Coldstream Guards 1954-56.

Political career: *House of Commons:* Contested Dudley 1964 general election. MP (Conservative) for Guildford 1966-97; Parliamentary Secretary, Civil Service Department 1970-72; Parliamentary Under-Secretary of State: Department of Employment 1971-72, Northern Ireland Office March-November 1972; Minister of State: Northern Ireland Office 1972-74, Department of Energy 1974; Secretary of State for: Energy 1979-81, Transport

1981-83. Chair, Foreign and Commonwealth Affairs 1987-97. Chairman, One Nation Group of Conservative MPs 1988-97. *House of Lords:* Raised to the peerage as Baron Howell of Guildford, of Penton Mewsey in the County of Hampshire 1997. Opposition Spokesperson for Foreign and Commonwealth Affairs 2000-10; Deputy Leader of the Opposition 2005-10; Minister of State and Government Spokesperson, Foreign and Commonwealth Office 2010-12. Member, European Communities Sub-committee B (Energy, Industry and Transport) 1997-99; Chair: European Communities Sub-committee C (Defence and Foreign Policy) 1999-2000, Soft Power and the UK's Influence 2013-14, International Relations 2016-19, Constitution 2019-. *Other:* Director, Conservative Political Centre 1964-66.

Political interests: Economics, international finance, energy, oil, foreign affairs; All Central European countries, China, India, Japan, Middle East.

Other: Chair: Bow Group 1962, Council of Commonwealth Societies; Trustee, 800th Anniversary Magna Carta Trust; Chair, Windsor Energy Group 2000-; President, British Institute of Energy Economics 2005-14; Director, Shakespeare Globe Theatre 2008-10; President: Royal Commonwealth Society 2012-, Energy Industries Council 2013-16; Liveryman, Clothworkers' Company; Grand Cordon of Order of Sacred Treasure (Japan) 2002; PC 1979. Beefsteak Club.

Publications: Co-author, Principles in Practice (1960); The Conservative Opportunity (1965); Freedom and Capital (1981); Blind Victory: a study in income, wealth and power (1986); The Edge of Now (2000); Out of the Energy Labyrinth (2007); Old Links and New Ties (2013); Empires in Collision – the green versus black struggle for our energy future (2016).

Recreations: Writing, travel, do-it-yourself.

Rt Hon the Lord Howell of Guildford, House of Lords, London SW1A 0PW
Tel: 020 7219 5415 *Email:* howelld@parliament.uk *Twitter:* @Lordhowell

LABOUR

HOYLE, LORD

HOYLE (Life Baron), Eric Douglas Harvey Hoyle; cr. 1997. Born 17 February 1930; Son of late William Hoyle; Married Pauline Spencer 1952 (died 1991) (1 son, Lindsay Hoyle (qv) MP for Chorley).

Education: Adlington School; Horwich Technical College (HNC mechanical engineering).

Non-political career: British Rail 1945-51; AEI 1951-53; Sales engineer, C. Weston Ltd, Salford 1953-74; Warrington Rugby League plc: Chair 1999-2009, President 2009-. ASTMS: Vice-President 1972-74, 1981-85, President 1977-81, 1985-88; Merged with TASS 1988; MSF: Joint President 1988-90, President 1990-91; Unite: Member, Chair, Lords Parliamentary Group.

Political career: *House of Commons:* Contested Clitheroe 1964, Nelson and Colne 1970 and February 1974 general elections. MP (Labour) for Nelson and Colne October 1974-79, for Warrington 1981 by-election to 1983, for Warrington North 1983-97; Member Shadow Cabinet 1992-97. Chair: PLP Trade and Industry Committee 1987-92, PLP 1992-97. *House of Lords:* Raised to the peerage as Baron Hoyle, of Warrington in the County of Cheshire 1997. Government Spokesperson for: Defence 1997-99, Home Office 1997-99, Agriculture 1997-99; Government Whip 1997-99. Member, Procedure 2003-05. Member (HoL representative), PLP Parliamentary Committee 2001-05. *Other:* Member, Labour Party National Executive 1978-82, 1983-85. JP 1958; Member, North West Regional Health Authority 1968-74.

Political interests: Trade, employment, industrial relations, health, immigration, arts, sport; Australia, Europe, Gibraltar, New Zealand, South Africa.

Other: Freedom: Gibraltar, Warrington; Hon Doctorate, Chester University. President: Adlington Cricket Club 1974-, Chorley Rugby League Club 1989-96; Warrington Wolves RLFC: Chair 1999-2009, President 2010-.

Recreations: Cricket, rugby league, theatre, cinema, sport.

The Lord Hoyle, House of Lords, London SW1A 0PW
Tel: 020 7219 3000

LABOUR

HUGHES OF STRETFORD, BARONESS

HUGHES OF STRETFORD (Life Baroness), Beverley June Hughes; cr 2010. Born 30 March 1950; Daughter of late Norman Hughes and late Doris Hughes; Married Thomas McDonald 1973 (1 son 2 daughters).

Education: Ellesmere Port Girls' Grammar School; Manchester University (BSc 1971; MSc 1978); Liverpool University (Diploma applied social studies 1974).

Non-political career: Trainee probation officer, Merseyside 1971; Probation officer, Merseyside 1972-76; Manchester University: Research associate 1976-81; Lecturer 1981-93, Senior lecturer and head of department 1993-97, Honorary Professor of Politics 2018-. Member, USDAW.

Political career: *House of Commons:* MP (Labour) for Stretford and Urmston 1997-2010; PPS to Hilary Armstrong as Minister of State, Department of the Environment, Transport and the Regions (DETR) 1998-99; Parliamentary Under-Secretary of State, DETR 1999-2001; Home Office 2001-04: Parliamentary Under-Secretary of State 2001-02, Minister of State 2002-04: (for Citizenship, Immigration and Community Cohesion 2002-03, (Citizenship, Immigration and Counter Terrorism 2003-04); Minister of State, Department for Education and Skills/ Children, Schools and Families 2005-09 (Children, Young People and Families 2005-07, Children and Youth Justice 2007-09) (attending cabinet 2008-09); Minister for the North West 2007-09. Member, Home Affairs 1997-98. Joint Vice-chair, PLP Departmental Committee for Women 1999-2000. *House of Lords:* Raised to the peerage as Baroness Hughes of Stretford, of Ellesmere Port in the County of Cheshire 2010. Opposition Spokesperson for Education 2010-15. Member, EU Justice Sub-committee 2015-17. *Other:* Trafford Metropolitan Borough Council: Councillor 1986-97, Labour Group Leader 1992-97, Council Leader 1995-97; Director: Trafford Park Development Corporation 1992-97, Manchester Airport plc 1995-97; Chair of Governing Council, Salford University 2014-17; Deputy Mayor for Greater Manchester (Police, Crime, Fire and Resilience/Policing, Crime, Criminal Justice and Fire) 2017-.

Political interests: Economic regeneration, investment, local and regional government, health and community care, families, regional development, education, criminal justice, child protection and safety; Commonwealth countries, USA.

Other: Member, Executive Committee, Commonwealth Parliamentary Association (UK Branch) 2014-15; Strategic Policy Adviser, Greater Manchester Chamber of Commerce 2010-17; Trustee: Lowry Theatre 2011-, M20 Learning Trust 2018-; PC 2004.

Publications: Older People and Community Care: Critical Theory and Practice (1995); Numerous academic and professional publications.

Recreations: Jazz, fell-walking.

Rt Hon the Baroness Hughes of Stretford, House of Lords, London SW1A 0PW
Tel: 020 7219 5353 *Email:* hughesb@parliament.uk *Twitter:* @DeputyMayorofGM

LABOUR

HUGHES OF WOODSIDE, LORD

HUGHES OF WOODSIDE (Life Baron), Robert Hughes; cr. 1997. Born 3 January 1932; Son of Mitchell Hughes and Jessie Anderson; Married Ina Miller 1957 (2 sons 3 daughters).

Education: Robert Gordon's College, Aberdeen; Benoni High School, Transvaal, South Africa; Pietermaritzburgh Technical College, Natal, South Africa; Pietermaritzburg Technical College South Africa (Higher National Diploma engineering 1953).

Non-political career: Emigrated to South Africa 1947; Returned UK 1954; CF Wilson and Co (1932) Ltd, Aberdeen: Draughtsman 1954-64, Chief draughtsman 1964-70. Member, Unite.

Political career: *House of Commons:* Contested North Angus and Mearns 1959 general election. MP (Labour) for Aberdeen North 1970-97; Parliamentary Under-Secretary of State, Scottish Office 1974-75; Piloted the Rating (Disabled Persons) Act 1978 as Private Member's Bill. Chair, Scottish Affairs 1991-94. *House of Lords:* Raised to the peerage as Baron Hughes of Woodside, of Woodside in the City of Aberdeen 1997. *Other:* Chairman, Aberdeen City Labour Party 1963-69. Councillor, Aberdeen Town Council 1962-71; Member: North East Scotland Regional Hospital Board 1964-70, General Medical Council 1976-81.

Political interests: Agriculture, fishing industry, transport, health service, overseas aid and development; Countries in Southern Africa.

Other: Founder member, CND; Anti-Apartheid Movement: Vice-chair 1976, Chair 1977-94; Action for Southern Africa: Chair 1994-98, Hon. President 1998-; Hon. President, Mozambique, Angola Committee 2001-; South African Government National Order, Grand Companion of Oliver Tambo 2004.

Recreations: Fishing.

The Lord Hughes of Woodside, House of Lords, London SW1A 0PW
Tel: 020 7219 1451 *Fax:* 020 7219 2772 *Email:* hughesr@parliament.uk

LIBERAL DEMOCRAT

HUMPHREYS, BARONESS

Liberal Democrat Lords Spokesperson for Wales and Deputy Chief Whip

HUMPHREYS (Life Baroness), Christine Mary Humphreys; cr 2013. Born 26 May 1947.

Education: Welsh.

Non-political career: Former teacher and head of vocational education, Welsh Medium School; Part-time tutor, Welsh for adults courses, Bangor University.

Political career: *House of Lords:* Raised to the peerage as Baroness Humphreys, of Llanrwst in the County of Conwy 2013. Liberal Democrat: Deputy Chief Whip 2015-16, 2020-, Shadow Minister/Shadow Secretary of State/Spokesperson for Wales 2016-. Member: Joint Committee on Statutory Instruments 2013-16, Secondary Legislation Scrutiny 2014-17, Procedure 2015-19, Services 2016-18, Rural Economy 2018-19. *Other:* National Assembly for Wales: AM for North Wales region 1999-2001: Liberal Democrats Spokesperson on Economics and Environment. Welsh Liberal Democrats: Member, National Executive Committee, President 2007-. Councillor, Colwyn Bay Borough Council 1984-88, 1990-94.

Other: Chair of trustees, Llanrwst Almshouse Museum; President, Conwy Valley Rotary Club 2011-.

The Baroness Humphreys, House of Lords, London SW1A 0PW
Tel: 020 7219 5353 *Twitter:* @WelshChrisHumph

CROSSBENCH

HUNT OF BETHNAL GREEN, BARONESS

HUNT OF BETHNAL GREEN (Life Baroness), Ruth Elizabeth Hunt; cr 2019.

Education: New College School Cardiff; King Edward VI Camp Hill School for Girls; Oxford University (BA English language and literature 2001) (President Oxford Student Union 2001-02).

Non-political career: Policy officer, Equality Challenge Unit 2004-05; Stonewall: Senior policy officer 2005-07, Head of policy and research 2007-09, Deputy director of public affairs 2009-10, Director of public affairs 2011-13, Deputy chief executive 2014; Chief executive 2014-19.

Political career: *House of Lords:* Raised to the peerage as Baroness Hunt of Bethnal Green, of Bethnal Green in the London Borough of Tower Hamlets 2019.

Other: Trustee and vice-chair, Shelter UK 2015-.

The Baroness Hunt of Bethnal Green, House of Lords, London SW1A 0PW
Tel: 020 7219 3000 *Email:* huntr@parliament.uk *Twitter:* @ruth_hunt

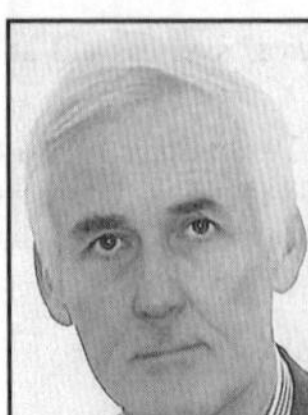

LABOUR

HUNT OF CHESTERTON, LORD

HUNT OF CHESTERTON (Life Baron), Julian Charles Roland Hunt; cr. 2000. Born 5 September 1941; Son of Roland Hunt CMG and Pauline Hunt, née Garnett; Married Marylla Shephard 1965 (1 son, Tristram Hunt, MP for Stoke-on-Trent Central 2010-17, 2 daughters).

Education: Westminster School; Trinity College, Cambridge (BA engineering 1963; PhD engineering 1967); Warwick University (engineering on secondment from Cambridge); French.

Non-political career: Cambridge University: Fellow 1966-, Senior research fellow 1998-99; Post-doctoral research, Cornell University, USA 1967; Research officer, Central Electricity Research Laboratories 1968-70; Trinity College: Lecturer in applied mathematics and in engineering 1970-78, Reader in fluid mechanics 1978-90, Professor 1990-92, Hon. Professor 1992-; Visiting professor: Colorado State University, USA 1975, National Center for Atmospheric Research, Boulder, Colorado, USA 1983; Cambridge Environmental Research Consultants Ltd: Company Director 1985-91, Chair 1997-, Chair 2000-; Chief executive, Meteorological Office 1992-97; Visiting scientist, Cerfacs, Toulouse, France 1997, 1998, 2007, 2008; Visiting professor: Arizona State University, USA 1997-98, 2007-11, Stanford University, USA 1998, Delft University of Technology 1998-; Professor in climate modelling, and director, Lighthill Institute for Mathematical Science, University College, London 1999-2008, Emeritus 2008-; Visiting professor, Cornell University 2003-06; Pierre Fermat Visiting Professor, Toulouse 2007-08; Visiting fellow, Malaysian Commonwealth Studies Centre, Cambridge; Visiting professor, Hong Kong University 2011-; Chair, Advisory Committee Tokamak Solutions Ltd. Electrical Power Engineers Association: Member 1968-70, Branch secretary 1970; Member: AUT 1970-91, 1999-2008, IPCS 1992-97.

Political career: *House of Lords:* Raised to the peerage as Baron Hunt of Chesterton, of Chesterton in the County of Cambridgeshire 2000. Member: Animals in Scientific Procedures 2001-02, Science and Technology Sub-committees: II (Innovations in Microprocessing) 2002-03, I (Science and International Agreements) 2003-04; Member: The Arctic 2014-15, Science and Technology 2015-19. *Other:* Cambridge City Council: Councillor 1971-74, Leader, Labour Group 1972; President, National Society of Clean Air 2006-09.

Political interests: Environment, science, government – civil service issues, informational aspects; France, India, USA.

Other: Member, Management board, European Research Community for Flow Turbulence and Combustion 1988-95; Member, Executive council, World Meteorological Organisation 1992-97; President, Institute of Mathematics and its Applications 1993-95; Council member, Royal Society 1998-99; ACOPS (Advisory Committee on Protection of the Sea): Chair 2001-04, President 2004-; Vice-President, Globe International 2009; Trustee, Royal Institution 2015-; Hon. Fellow: Institution of Civil Engineers, Institute of Mathematics and its applications, Royal Meteorological Society; Oxfam, Unipal; FRS 1989; Eight honorary doctorates from England, Scotland, France and Sweden; European Geophysical Society, LF Richardson Medal 2001; CB 1998. Meteorological Club.

Publications: Editor four volumes including London's Environment (Imperial College Press, 2005); Articles in mathematical and scientific publications, and newspapers.

Recreations: Swimming, history, rough gardening.

Professor the Lord Hunt of Chesterton CB, House of Lords, London SW1A 0PW
Tel: 020 7219 6193
Department of Earth Sciences, University College London, Gower Street, London WC1E 6BT
Email: julian.hunt@ucl.ac.uk

LABOUR/ CO-OPERATIVE

HUNT OF KINGS HEATH, LORD

HUNT OF KINGS HEATH (Life Baron), Philip Alexander Hunt; cr. 1997. Born 19 May 1949; Son of late Rev. Philip Hunt and Muriel Hunt; Married 1974 (divorced) (1 daughter); married Selina Stewart 1988 (3 sons 1 daughter).

Education: City of Oxford High School; Oxford School; Leeds University (BA political studies 1970).

Non-political career: Oxford Regional Hospital Board 1972-74; Nuffield Orthopaedic Centre 1974-75; Secretary, Edgware/Hendon Community Health Council 1975-78; National Association of Health Authorities: Assistant secretary 1978-79, Assistant director 1979-84, Director 1984-90; Director, National Association of Health Authorities and Trusts 1990-96; Chief executive, NHS Confederation 1996-97. Member, Unison.

Political career: *House of Lords:* Raised to the peerage as Baron Hunt of Kings Heath, of Birmingham in the County of West Midlands 1997. Government Spokesperson for Education and Employment 1998-99; Government Whip 1998-99; Parliamentary Under-Secretary of State and Government Spokesperson for: Department of Health 1999-2003, Department for Work and Pensions 2005-06; Minister of State for Quality, Department of Health and Government Spokesperson for Health 2006-07; Parliamentary Under-Secretary of State and Government Spokesperson, Ministry of Justice 2007-08; Minister of State and Government Spokesperson: Department for Environment, Food and Rural Affairs 2008-09, Department of Energy and Climate Change 2008-10; Deputy Leader of the House of Lords 2008-10; Opposition Spokesperson for: Cabinet Office 2010-12, Energy and Climate Change 2010, Home Office 2010-12; Shadow Deputy Leader of the House of Lords 2010-17; Opposition Spokesperson for: Health 2012-18, Constitutional Affairs 2015-17, Further and Higher Education 2017-18, Cabinet Office 2017-18. Member, Consolidation, Etc, Bills Joint Committee 1998; Chair, Merits of Statutory Instruments 2003-05; Member: Leader's Group on Members Leaving the House 2010-15, House 2015-16, Liaison 2015-17, Middle Level Bill 2018, Public Services 2020-. *Other:* Councillor, Oxford City Council 1973-79; Member, Oxfordshire Area Health Authority 1975-77; Councillor, Birmingham City Council 1980-82; Chair, National Patient Safety Agency 2004-05; Chairman, Heart of England NHS Foundation Trust, Birmingham 2011-14.

Political interests: Transport, constitutional affairs, energy and climate change.

Other: Council, International Hospital Federation 1986-91; Association for Public Health: Council 1992, Co-chair 1994-98; President: Family Planning Association 1997-98, Royal Society for Public Health 2010-; Oxfam, Living Streets, St Mary's Hospice Birmingham, Birmingham Contemporary Music Group, City of Birmingham Symphony Orchestra; Honorary Doctorate: Birmingham University, Birmingham City University, Aston University; OBE 1993; PC 2009. Warwickshire CCC.

Recreations: Cycling, swimming, Birmingham City FC, music.

Rt Hon the Lord Hunt of Kings Heath OBE, House of Lords, London SW1A 0PW
Tel: 020 7219 2030 *Email:* huntp@parliament.uk *Twitter:* @LordPhilofBrum

CONSERVATIVE

HUNT OF WIRRAL, LORD

HUNT OF WIRRAL (Life Baron), David James Fletcher Hunt; cr. 1997. Born 21 May 1942; Son of late Alan Hunt, OBE, shipping agent, and late Jessie Ellis Hunt; Married Paddy Orchard 1973 (2 sons 2 daughters).

Education: Liverpool College; Montpellier University, France (1962); Bristol University (LLB 1965); Guildford College of Law (1968).

Non-political career: Solicitor; DAC Beachcroft LLP: Partner 1968-, Senior Partner 1996-2005, Chair, Financial Services Division 2005-; Director, BET Omnibus Services Ltd 1980-81; Chair, Beachcroft Regulatory Consulting 2002-08.

Political career: *House of Commons:* Contested Bristol South 1970 and Kingswood 1974 general elections. MP (Conservative) for Wirral 1976-83, for Wirral West 1983-97; Opposition Spokesperson for Shipping and Shipbuilding 1977-79; PPS to John Nott as Secretary of State for: Trade 1979-81, Defence 1981; Assistant Whip 1981-83; Government Whip 1983-84; Parliamentary Under-Secretary of State, Department of Energy 1984-87; Deputy Chief Whip (Treasurer of HM Household) 1987-89; Minister for Local Government and Inner Cities

1989-90; Secretary of State: for Wales 1990-93, for Employment 1993-94; Chancellor of the Duchy of Lancaster and Minister for Public Service and Science 1994-95. *House of Lords:* Raised to the peerage as Baron Hunt of Wirral, of Wirral in the County of Merseyside 1997. Opposition Spokesperson for Business, Enterprise and Regulatory Reform/Business, Innovation and Skills 2008-10. Member: Offices 1999-2001, European Communities Sub-committee E (Law and Institutions) 1999-2002, House 2003-07; Chair, Draft Legal Services Bill Joint Committee 2006; Alternate member, Procedure 2007-08, 2008-11; Member, EU Sub-committee G (Social Policies and Consumer Protection) 2010-12; Chair, Leader's Group on Members Leaving the House 2010-15; Member, Constitution 2015-19. *Other:* Vice-chair, Bristol Conservative Association 1970; Chair, National Young Conservatives 1972-73; Vice-President, European Conservative and Christian Democratic Youth Community 1974-76; Vice-chair, Conservative Party 1983-84; Tory Reform Group: President 1991-97, Patron 1997-; Chairman, Association of Conservative Peers 2016-. Chair, British Youth Council 1971-74; Member: South West Economic Planning Council 1972-76, Government Advisory Committee on Pop Festivals 1972-75; President, British Youth Council 1978-80; English Speaking Union: Governor 1998-2011, Deputy chair 2000-05, Chair 2005-11, International chair 2008-11; Professional Standards Board, Chartered Insurance Institute: Chair 2004-06, President 2007-08; Chair: McEdCo 2009-15, Lending Standards Board 2011-17, Press Complaints Commission 2011-14, British Insurance Brokers' Association 2014-.

Political interests: Europe, business and economy, skills; Commonwealth, European Union, USA.

Other: Governor, European Youth Foundation at Strasbourg 1972-75; Chair, British Atlantic Group of Young Politicians 1979-81; President, Atlantic Association for Young Political Leaders 1981-83; Vice-President and trustee, Holocaust Educational Trust 1995-; Honorary Fellow: International Institute of Risk and Safety Management 2000, Institute of Actuaries 2003, Chartered Insurance Institute 2004; Member, Law Society of England and Wales 1968-; Honorary Freedom, Worshipful Company of Insurers 2009-; Fellow: Chartered Insurance Institute, Institute of Chartered Secretaries and Administrators, International Risk and Safety Management, Institute of Actuaries; Hon LLD, Bristol University 2008; Doctor of Letters, Chester University 2013; MBE 1973; PC 1990. Hurlingham Club.

Recreations: Cricket, walking.

Rt Hon the Lord Hunt of Wirral MBE, House of Lords, London SW1A 0PW
Tel: 020 7219 6688 *Email:* huntd@parliament.uk
DAC Beachcroft LLP, The Walbrook Building, 25 Walbrook, London EC4N 8AF
Tel: 020 7831 6630 *Email:* lordhunt@dacbeachcroft.com Website: www.dacbeachcroft.com

LIBERAL DEMOCRAT

HUSSAIN, LORD

HUSSAIN (Life Baron), Qurban Hussain; cr 2011. Born 27 March 1956; Married (6 children).

Education: Rochdale College; Bedford College; Luton University.

Non-political career: Secretary, Luton TUC 1994-96.

Political career: *House of Commons:* Contested (Liberal Democrat) Luton South 2005 and 2010 general elections. *House of Lords:* Raised to the peerage as Baron Hussain, of Luton in the County of Bedfordshire 2011. Member, Extradition Law 2014-15. *Other:* Member: Labour Party 1996-2003, Liberal Democrats 2003-. Luton Borough Council: Councillor 2003-11, Deputy leader 2005-07.

Political interests: Luton.

Other: Member: Luton Law Centre, Justice Foundation, Islamic Cultural Society.

Recreations: Badminton, swimming, walking, writing.

The Lord Hussain, House of Lords, London SW1A 0PW
Tel: 020 7219 3159 *Email:* hussainq@parliament.uk

LIBERAL DEMOCRAT

HUSSEIN-ECE, BARONESS

Liberal Democrat Lords Spokesperson for Equality

HUSSEIN-ECE (Life Baroness), Meral Hussein Ece; cr 2010. Born 10 October 1953; Daughter of late Hasan Nihet Hussein and Ayshe Hussein, née Abdullah; 3 children.

Education: Edith Cavell Secondary School, Hackney; Art school (BA); Turkish.

Non-political career: Special adviser to Nick Clegg MP on community cohesion and minority ethnic communities 2006-12; Member, Government BME Women Councillors' Task Force 2008-10.

Political career: *House of Lords:* Raised to the peerage as Baroness Hussein-Ece, of Highbury in the London Borough of Islington 2010. Liberal Democrat Lords Spokesperson for Equality 2015-. Member: HIV and AIDS in the UK 2010-11, Soft Power and the UK's Influence 2013-14, Sexual Violence in Conflict 2015-16, Conduct 2019-. *Other:* Liberal Democrats: Member: Executive, London Liberal Democrats 1998-2003, Federal Policy Committee 2005-06, Federal Executive 2005-10, Chair, Ethnic Minority Liberal Democrats 2006-10. London Borough of Hackney Council: Councillor 1994-2002, Deputy Leader 1995-96; London Borough of Islington Council: Councillor 2002-10, Cabinet Member for Health and Social Care 2002-06; Board member, Islington Primary Care Trust 2002-06; Non-executive director, Camden and Islington Mental Health and Social Care Trust 2004-06; Chair, Islington Health Partnership Board 2004-06; Commissioner, Equality and Human Rights Commission 2009-12.

Political interests: Local government, health, equality and diversity, women, youth, community cohesion, European and foreign affairs; Cyprus, Middle East, Turkey.

Other: Hon DLitt Coventry University 2012; OBE 2009.

The Baroness Hussein-Ece OBE, House of Lords, London SW1A 0PW
Tel: 020 7219 5353 *Email:* ecem@parliament.uk *Twitter:* @meralhece

LABOUR

HUTTON OF FURNESS, LORD

HUTTON OF FURNESS (Life Baron), John Matthew Patrick Hutton; cr 2010. Born 6 May 1955; Son of late George Hutton, salesman and general labourer, and Rosemary Hutton, orthoptist; Married Rosemary Caroline Little 1978 (divorced 1993) (3 sons 1 daughter and 1 son deceased); married Heather Rogers 2004.

Education: Westcliffe High School, Southend; Magdalen College, Oxford (BA law 1976; BCL 1978).

Non-political career: Legal assistant, CBI 1978-80; Research fellow, Templeton College, Oxford 1980-81; Senior law lecturer, Newcastle Polytechnic 1981-92; Adviser, Bechtel 2011-; Special Adviser, PWC LLP 2013-17; Consultant, Lockheed Martin 2014-.

Political career: *House of Commons:* Contested Penrith and the Border 1987 general election. MP (Labour) for Barrow and Furness 1992-2010; PPS to Margaret Beckett: as President of the Board of Trade and Secretary of State for Trade and Industry 1997-98, as President of the Council and Leader of the House of Commons 1998; Department of Health: Parliamentary Under-Secretary of State 1998-99, Minister of State for Health 1999-2005; Chancellor of the Duchy of Lancaster and Minister for the Cabinet Office 2005; Secretary of State for: Work and Pensions 2005-07, Business, Enterprise and Regulatory Reform 2007-08, Defence 2008-09. Member, Home Affairs 1994-97. Chair PLP Departmental Committees for: Defence 1992-94, Home Affairs 1994-97. *House of Lords:* Raised to the peerage as Baron Hutton of Furness, of Aldingham in the County of Cumbria 2010. Member: Public Service and Democratic Change 2012-13, Bribery Act 2010 2018-19, Economic Affairs Finance Bill Sub-committee 2018. *Other:* Contested Cumbria and North Lancashire 1989 European Parliament election. Chair, Independent Public Service Pensions Commission 2010-.

Political interests: Defence, welfare state, home affairs, legal affairs.

Other: Chair: Royal United Services Institute 2010-, Nuclear Industry Association 2011-, Cuba Initiative 2011-; Trustee, RAF Museum 2012-; Non-executive director: Sirius Minerals 2012-, Circle Holdings plc, Total Decom Ltd; Terence Higgins Trust; PC 2001.

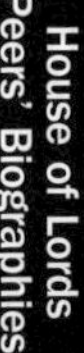

Publications: Kitchener's Men (2008); August 1914 – Surrender at St Quentin (2010); A Doctor on the Western Front (2013).

Recreations: Cricket, football, films, music, history.

Rt Hon the Lord Hutton of Furness, House of Lords, London SW1A 0PW
Tel: 020 7219 5353

CROSSBENCH

HYLTON, LORD

HYLTON (5th Baron, UK), Raymond Hervey Jolliffe; cr. 1866; 5th Bt of Merstham (UK) 1821. Born 13 June 1932; Son of 4th Baron; Married Joanna de Bertodano 1966 (4 sons 1 daughter).

Education: Eton College; Trinity College, Oxford (MA history 1955); French, some Italian.

Non-political career: Assistant Private Secretary to the Governor-General of Canada 1960-62; Farmer (organic), forester and land-owner 1968-. National Service, commissioned Coldstream Guards 1951-52.

Political career: *House of Lords:* First entered House of Lords 1971; Private Member's Bills: Sexual Offences (Amendment) Bill, Overseas Domestic Workers (Protection) Bill; Elected hereditary peer 1999-. Member, Selection 2008-13. *Other:* Councillor, Frome RDC 1968-72; Governor: Kilmersdon Primary School 1967-87, Writhlington Comprehensive School 1969-75; DL, Somerset 1970-90; President, Northern Ireland Association for Care and Resettlement of Offenders 1988-2009.

Political interests: Northern Ireland, housing, British-Irish relations, human rights, prisons, penal affairs and policy, conflict resolution, peace building, inter-faith relations, foreign affairs and policy, asylum issues; Caucasus (North and South), Europe, Iraq, Israel, Middle East, Moldova, Palestine, Russia, South East Europe, former Soviet Union.

Other: Member, Chatham House; Associated in various capacities 1962-: Abbeyfield Society, Catholic Housing Aid Society, London Housing Aid Centre, National Federation of Housing Associations 1970-73, Age Concern, L'Arche Ltd, Royal MENCAP, Foundation for Alternatives, Mendip Wansdyke Local Enterprise Group, Action around Bethlehem Children with Disability (ABCD); Trustee and governor, Ammerdown Centre Ltd, near Bath 1970-; Housing Associations Charitable Trust; Acorn Christian Healing Trust 1976-99; Chair: St Francis and St Sergius Trust Fund (for the churches and youth in Russia) 1993-2001, MICOM – Moldova Initiatives Committee of Management 1994; Soul of Europe (Kosovo, Bosnia and others); Trustee, Forward Thinking (Re Israel and Palestine etc) 2004-19; Chair, Advisory Council, Foundation for Reconciliation and Relief in Middle East (Iraq) 2006-15; Associate, Royal Institute of Chartered Surveyors 1964-; ARICS 1960; Hon. DSocSci, Southampton University 1994. Lansdowne Club.

Publications: Numerous articles.

The Lord Hylton, House of Lords, London SW1A 0PW
Tel: 020 7219 3883 *Fax:* 020 7219 5979 *Email:* hyltonr@parliament.uk
Website: lordsoftheblog.net/category/lord-hylton

NON-AFFILIATED

INGLEWOOD, LORD

INGLEWOOD (2nd Baron, UK), William Richard Fletcher-Vane; cr. 1964. Born 31 July 1951; Son of 1st Baron, TD, DL and Mary, neé Proby; Married Cressida Pemberton-Pigott 1986 (1 son 2 daughters).

Education: Eton College; Trinity College, Cambridge (BA English/land economy 1973, MA); Cumbria College of Agriculture and Forestry (City and Guilds Levels III and IV 1982); French, German.

Non-political career: Called to the Bar, Lincoln's Inn 1975; CN Group: Non-executive director 1997-2018, Chair 2002-16; Chair, Reviewing Committee on Export of Works of Art and Objects of Cultural Interest 2003-14; Carrs Milling Industries plc: Non-executive director 2004-05, Chair 2005-13; Chair, Gen2 2016-18.

Political career: *House of Commons:* Contested (Conservative) Houghton and Washington 1983 general election. *House of Lords:* First entered House of Lords 1989; Government Whip 1994-95; Government Deputy Chief Whip 1995; Parliamentary Under-Secretary of State and Government Spokesperson, Department of National Heritage 1995-97; Opposition Spokesperson for Environment, Transport and the Regions 1997-98; Elected hereditary peer 1999-. Member: EU Sub-committee E 1997-99, EU Sub-committee A 2004-07, Communications 2007-10; Co-opted member, EU Sub-committee G (Social Policy and Consumer Affairs) 2008-10; Member, EU Sub-committee G (Social Policies and Consumer Protection) 2010-11; Chair: Communications 2010-14, Extradition Law 2014-15; Member: Works of Art 2015-16, Built Environment 2015-16, International Relations 2016-17, Lord Speaker's Advisory Panel on Works of Art 2017-19. *Other:* European Parliament: Contested Durham 1984 election, MEP for Cumbria and Lancashire North 1989-94, Contested Cumbria and Lancashire North 1994 election, MEP for North West region 1999-2004, Vice-President, EP-China Delegation 1999-2004. Left Conservatives June 2018, now sits as non-affiliated. Member, Lake District Special Planning Board 1984-90; Chair, Development Control Committee 1985-89; Member, North West Water Authority 1987-89; DL, Cumbria 1993; Chair, Reviewing Committee Export of Works of Art 2003-14; Governor, Skinners' Academy, Hackney 2008-11; Vice Lord-Lieutenant, Cumbria 2013-; Chair of board, Cumbria LEP 2018-.

Political interests: Rural affairs, agriculture, environment, Europe, local and regional government, regional policy, legal affairs, media, arts, constitutional affairs; China, Egypt, EU, Iceland, Turkey.

Other: Adviser and Member of the Advisory Board, Knowledge City Cairo 2015-; President, Cumbria Tourist Board 2004-19; Cumbria Local Nature Partnership: Chair 2013-17, Member 2017-; Visiting Parliamentary Fellow, St Antony's College Oxford 2014-15; President: British Art Market Federation 2014-, Uplands Alliance 2015-, Ancient Monuments Society 2015-; Member, Advisory Board, Reuters' Institute, Oxford University 2015-19; President, National Sheep Association 2017-; Member, Royal Institution of Chartered Surveyors; Barrister, Lincolns Inn; Fellow, Society of Antiquaries of London; Liveryman, Skinners' Company; FSA. Travellers Club, Pratt's Club.

The Lord Inglewood, House of Lords, London SW1A 0PW
Tel: 020 7219 3190 *Email:* inglewoodw@parliament.uk
Hutton-in-the-Forest, Penrith CA11 9TH *Tel:* 01768 484500
Email: inglewood@hutton-in-the-forest.co.uk Website: www.hutton-in-the-forest.co.uk

LABOUR

IRVINE OF LAIRG, LORD

IRVINE OF LAIRG (Life Baron), Alexander Andrew Mackay Irvine; cr. 1987. Born 23 June 1940; Son of Alexander and Margaret Christina Irvine; Married Alison Mary McNair 1974 (2 sons).

Education: Inverness Royal Academy; Hutchesons' Boys' Grammar School, Glasgow; Glasgow University (MA, LLB); Christ's College, Cambridge (Scholar, BA, LLB).

Non-political career: University lecturer, London School of Economics 1965-69; Called to the Bar, Inner Temple 1967; QC 1978; Head, 11 King's Bench Walk Chambers 1981-97; Bencher of the Inner Temple, 1985; Recorder 1985-88; Deputy High Court Judge 1987-97.

Political career: *House of Commons:* Contested (Labour) Hendon North 1970 general election. *House of Lords:* Raised to the peerage as Baron Irvine of Lairg, of Lairg in the District of Sutherland 1987. Opposition Spokesperson for Legal Affairs and Home Affairs 1987-92; Shadow Lord Chancellor 1992-97; Lord Chancellor and Government Spokesperson for Legal Affairs and Lord Chancellor's Department 1997-2003; Lord of Appeal -2008. Member: Privileges/Privileges and Conduct 2008-, Sub-committee on Lords' Interests 2008-10, Constitution 2009-14, Sub-committee on Lords' Conduct 2010-18. *Other:* Church Commissioner.

Political interests: Legal affairs, home affairs, constitutional affairs.

Other: Vice-Patron, World Federation of Mental Health; Joint President: Inter-Parliamentary Union, Commonwealth Parliamentary Association; Vice-President, Commonwealth Parliamentary Association (UK Branch); President, Magistrates Association; Chair, Glasgow 2001 Committee; Member, Committee of the Slade School of Fine Art 1990-; Foundation trustee, Whitechapel Art Gallery 1990-97; Trustee: John Smith Memorial Trust 1992-97, Hunterian Collection 1997-; Joint President, Industry and Parliament Trust 1997-; Hon. Fellow,

Society for Advanced Legal Studies; Fellow, US College of Trial Lawyers 1998-; Hon. Fellow, Christ's College, Cambridge 1996; Hon. LLD, Glasgow 1997; Hon. Bencher, Inn of Court of Northern Ireland 1998; Hon. Doctorate, Siena 2000; Fellowship, LSE 2000; Member, Polish Bar 2000; George and Thomas Hutchison Award 1998; PC 1997; Knight Commander of the Order of Merit of the Republic of Poland, with Star 2004. Garrick Club.

Publications: Articles on constitutional and legal topics in legal journals.

Recreations: Collecting paintings, travel, reading, cinema and theatre.

Rt Hon the Lord Irvine of Lairg, House of Lords, London SW1A 0PW
Tel: 020 7219 1446

CONSERVATIVE

JAMES OF BLACKHEATH, LORD

JAMES OF BLACKHEATH (Life Baron), David Noel James; cr 2006. Born 7 December 1937; Son of Captain Francis James and Alsina James, née Burdett; Married Caroline Webster 2004.

Education: Christ's College, Blackheath.

Non-political career: Lloyds Bank 1959-64; Ford Motor Co (UK) 1964-73; Rank Organisation plc 1974-81; Chairman: Central and Sherwood plc 1984-88, Eagle Trust 1989-97; LFP Group plc 1991-95, Henleys Group plc 1991-96, Robinson Group plc 1997-2001, New Millennium Experience Co 2000-01, Litigation Control Group Ltd 2002-06, Vidapulse Ltd 2003-.

Political career: *House of Lords:* Raised to the peerage as Baron James of Blackheath, of Wildbrooks in the County of West Sussex 2006. Co-opted Member, EU Sub-committee B (Internal Market) 2007-10; Member: Merits of Statutory Instruments 2007-10, Crossrail Bill 2008, EU Sub-committee B (Internal Market, Energy and Transport) 2010-12. *Other:* James Review of Taxpayer Value 2004-05.

Political interests: Horseracing industry, NHS finances, MoD procurement, funding and organisation of 2012 Olympics, renewable energy; Libya.

Other: Fellow, Institute of Directors; Trustee, David James Musical charity, Aphasia Society; Lifetime Achievement, Society of Turnaround Practitioners 2003; CBE 1992. Savile, Jockey Club Rooms; MCC, Lords' Taverners.

Publications: Future Capital Structure of Lloyd's of London (1996); James Report on Public Expenditure (2005).

Recreations: Opera, ballet, cricket, rugby, tennis, horseracing, golf.

The Lord James of Blackheath CBE, House of Lords, London SW1A 0PW
Tel: 020 7219 4954
Tel: 01798 812349 *Email:* dnjcbe@aol.com

LIBERAL DEMOCRAT

JANKE, BARONESS

Liberal Democrat Lords Spokesperson for Work and Pensions and Whip

JANKE (Life Baroness), Barbara Lilian Janke; cr 2014. Born 5 June 1947; Daughter of Esther and Alfred Kearns; Married John (1 son 1 daughter).

Education: Waterloo Park Girls Grammar School; College St Matteas, Bristol (Cert. Ed. 1968); Open University (economic and politics 1981); French.

Non-political career: Languages and economics teacher 1968-95; Caseworker to Don Foster MP 1994.

Political career: *House of Commons:* Contested (Liberal Democrat) Surbiton 1992 general election. *House of Lords:* Raised to the peerage as Baroness Janke, of Clifton in the City and County of Bristol 2014. Liberal Democrat Spokesperson for: Communities and Local Government 2015, Treasury 2015, Work and Pensions 2019-, Whip 2020-. Member: EU Home Affairs Sub-committee 2015-19, Political Polling and Digital Media 2017-18, Food, Poverty, Health and the Environment 2019-. *Other:* Member, Liberal Party 1978; Leader,

Bristol Liberal Democrats 1997-. Councillor, London Borough of Kingston-upon-Thames 1986; Bristol City Council: Councillor 1995-2015, Leader of the Council 2003-04, 2005-07, 2009-12; Vice-President, Local Government Association 2016-.

Political interests: Local government, health, care, treasury, finance, constitutional reform.

The Baroness Janke, House of Lords, London SW1A 0PW
Tel: 020 7219 5353 *Email:* jankeb@parliament.uk

CROSSBENCH

JANVRIN, LORD

JANVRIN (Life Baron), Robin Berry Janvrin; cr 2007. Born 20 September 1946; Married Isabelle de Boissonneaux de Chevigny 1977 (2 sons 2 daughters).

Education: Marlborough College, Wiltshire; Brasenose College, Oxford (BA philosophy, politics and economics 1969).

Non-political career: HM Diplomatic Service 1975-87: First secretary, UK delegation to NATO 1976-78, New Delhi High Commission 1981-84, Counsellor 1985; HM the Queen: Press secretary to 1987-90, Assistant private secretary to 1990-95, Deputy private secretary to 1996-99, Private secretary to and Keeper of the Queen's Archives 1999-2007, Permanent Lord-in-waiting 2007-; Senior adviser, HSBC Private Bank (UK) 2008-. Various positions, Royal Navy 1964-75.

Political career: *House of Lords:* Raised to the peerage as Baron Janvrin, of Chalford Hill in the County of Gloucestershire 2007. Trade Envoy to Turkey; Member, Intelligence and Security Committee 2015-19. Member: Joint Committee on Privacy and Injunctions 2011-12, Soft Power and the UK's Influence 2013-14, Digital Skills 2014-15, Secondary Legislation Scrutiny 2015-19, SLSC Sub-committee B 2018-19, Electoral Registration and Administration Act 2013 2019-. *Other:* Trustee, National Portrait Gallery 2008-16; Board member, British Library 2017-.

Political interests: Constitutional issues, foreign and commonwealth affairs, philanthropy; France, India.

Other: Chair, Royal Foundation 2010-16; Trustee, Gurkha Welfare Trust 2010-16; LVO 1983; CVO 1994; CB 1997; PC 1998; KCVO 1998; KCB 2003; GCB 2007; GCVO 2007; QSO 2008.

Recreations: Family, painting.

Rt Hon the Lord Janvrin GCB GCVO QSO, House of Lords, London SW1A 0PW
Tel: 020 7219 6989 *Email:* janvrinr@parliament.uk

CROSSBENCH

JAY OF EWELME, LORD

JAY OF EWELME (Life Baron), Michael Hastings Jay; cr 2006. Born 19 June 1946; Son of late Alan Jay and Vera Effa Vickery; Married Sylvia Mylroie 1975.

Education: Winchester College; Magdalen College, Oxford (BA philosophy, politics and economics 1968, MA); School of Oriental and African Studies, London University (MSc economic development 1969); French.

Non-political career: Volunteer teacher, Zambia 1965; Assistant principal, Ministry of Overseas Development (ODM) 1969-73; Technical assistant, UK delegation to International Monetary Fund and International Bank for Reconstruction and Development (World Bank), Washington DC 1973-75; Principal, ODM 1976-78; First Secretary (Development), New Delhi High Commission 1978-81; Foreign and Commonwealth Office (FCO), London 1981-85: Deputy Head, FCO Policy Planning Staff 1981-82, Private Secretary to Permanent Under Secretary 1982-85; Counsellor, European Secretariat, Cabinet Office 1985-87; Financial and Commercial Counsellor, British Embassy, Paris 1987-90; FCO 1990-96: Assistant Under-Secretary for European Affairs 1990-94, Deputy Under-Secretary of State for Economic and Economic Affairs 1994-96; Ambassador to France 1996-2001; Permanent Under-Secretary, FCO and Head of the Diplomatic Service 2002-06; Prime Minister's Personal Representative for G8 Presidency and Summits 2005-06; Non-executive director: Associated British Foods 2006-15, Valeo SA 2007-15, Credit Agricole SA 2007-11, Candover Investments plc 2008-14, EDF 2009-14; Trustee, Thomson Reuters Founders Share Company 2014-.

Political career: *House of Lords:* Raised to the peerage as Baron Jay of Ewelme, of Ewelme in the County of Oxfordshire 2006. Co-opted Member, EU Sub-committee E (Law and Institutions) 2006-08; Member: Draft Climate Change Bill Joint Committee 2007, Intergovernmental Organisations 2007-08; EU Sub-committee C (Foreign Affairs, Defence and Development Policy): Co-opted Member 2008-10, Member 2010-12; Member: EU Sub-committee C (External Affairs) 2012-13, Joint Committee on the Draft Enhanced Terrorism Prevention and Investigation Measures Bill 2012-13, EU Sub-committee F (Home Affairs, Health and Education) 2014-15, European Union 2015-20; EU Home Affairs Sub-committee: Member 2015-17, Chair 2017-20; Member, Joint Committee on Fixed-Term Parliaments Act 2020-. *Other:* Chair, House of Lords Appointments Commission 2008-13.

Political interests: Foreign and European policy, energy policy, environment and climate change, development; Africa, EU, India.

Other: Vice-chair, Business for New Europe 2006-; Chair: Merlin (international medical charity) 2007-13, British Library Advisory Council: Member 2011-, Chair 2014-; Francis Crick Institute, Friends of Ewelme Church; Hon. Fellow, Magdalen College, Oxford; Senior associate member, St Antony's College, Oxford 1996; Honorary Fellow, Magdalen College, Oxford 2004; CMG 1992; KCMG 1997; GCMG 2006. Special Forces Club.

The Lord Jay of Ewelme GCMG, House of Lords, London SW1A 0PW
Tel: 020 7219 3941 *Email:* jaymh@parliament.uk *Twitter:* @LordJayEwelme

LABOUR

JAY OF PADDINGTON, BARONESS

JAY OF PADDINGTON (Life Baroness), Margaret Ann Jay; cr. 1992. Born 18 November 1939; Daughter of late James Callaghan, former Prime Minister, and late Audrey Moulton; Married Hon Peter Jay 1961 (divorced 1986) (1 son 2 daughters); married Professor Michael Adler CBE 1994.

Education: Blackheath High School, London; Somerville College, Oxford (BA philosophy, politics and economics 1961).

Non-political career: Various production posts with BBC Television in current affairs and further education 1965-77; Former reporter for: BBC Television's *Panorama*, Thames Television's *This Week*; Founder director, National AIDS Trust 1988-92; Non-executive director: Carlton Television 1996-97, Scottish Power 1996-97, Independent News and Media UK 2001-12, BT 2002-08; Political consultant to Currie and Brown 2004-07; Non-executive director, British Telecom Committee for Responsible and Sustainable Business 2008-17. Member, National Union of Journalists.

Political career: *House of Lords:* Raised to the peerage as Baroness Jay of Paddington, of Paddington in the City of Westminster 1992. Opposition Spokesperson for Health 1992-97, Minister of State, Department of Health 1997-98; Deputy Leader, House of Lords 1997-98; Leader of the House of Lords and Lord Privy Seal; Minister for Women 1998-2001; Opposition Whip 1992-95. Member: House of Lords Offices 1997-2001, Assisted Dying 2004-05, Leader's Group on Code of Conduct 2009; Constitution: Member 2009-10, Chair 2010-14; Member: Extradition Law 2014-15, Communications 2015-16, Privileges and Conduct 2016-, Political Polling and Digital Media 2017-18, Food, Poverty, Health and the Environment 2019, COVID-19 2020-. *Other:* Member, Labour Party Donations Committee 2002-05; President, One Thousand Club 2002-06; Member, Lionel Cooke Memorial Fund Trust 2008-. Member, Kensington and Chelsea and Westminster Health Authority 1993-97; Former Member, Central Research and Development Committee for NHS.

Political interests: Health, overseas aid and development, media, broadcasting, constitution; China, India, South Africa, USA.

Other: Former Member, President World Bank International Advisory Group on Health; Member, International Advisory Board Independent News and Media 2002-; Associate member, InterAction Council; Member of the Board, United Europe Organisation 2016; Trustee, Europaeum 2018; Former Governor, South Bank University; Former Member, Governing Board: Queen Charlotte's Maternity Hospital, Chelsea Hospital for Women; Chair: Overseas Development Institute 2002-10; Bringing Research to Life Development Board, Great Ormond Street Hospital 2010-; Overseas Development Institute: Chair 2002-10, Council member; Trustee, Hansard Society 2012-; Member: Court of Governors, South Bank University 2012-, Oxford University Alumni Board 2016; Two honorary degrees; Senior Honorary Fellow,

Somerville College, Oxford; Honorary Fellow: Sunderland University, South Bank University, Greenwich University; PC 1998.

Publications: How Rich Can We Get? (1972); Co-author, Battered – The Story of Child Abuse (1986).

Rt Hon the Baroness Jay of Paddington, House of Lords, London SW1A 0PW
Tel: 020 7219 4912 *Email:* jaym@parliament.uk

CONSERVATIVE

JENKIN OF KENNINGTON, BARONESS

JENKIN OF KENNINGTON (Life Baroness), Anne Caroline Jenkin; cr 2011. Born 8 December 1955; Daughter of late Hon. Charles Strutt and Hon. Jean Strutt, née Davidson; Married Bernard Jenkin (qv) 1988 (MP for Harwich and North Essex) (2 sons).

Political career: *House of Lords:* Raised to the peerage as Baroness Jenkin of Kennington, of Hatfield Peverel in the County of Essex 2011. Member: Refreshment 2012-15, Equality Act 2010 and Disability 2015-16, Charities 2016-17, Intergenerational Fairness and Provision 2018-19, Hybrid Instruments 2019-. *Other:* Founder and co-chair, Women2Win; Chair, Conservative Friends of International Development.

Other: Patron, Restless Development; Trustee: Unicef UK, Sir Simon Milton Foundation -2015, Cool Earth, WRAP 2016-.

The Baroness Jenkin of Kennington, House of Lords, London SW1A 0PW
Tel: 020 7219 5353 *Twitter:* @BaronessJenkin

CONSERVATIVE

JOHNSON OF MARYLEBONE, LORD

JOHNSON OF MARYLEBONE (Life Baron), Joseph Edmund Johnson; cr 2020. Born 23 December 1971; Son of Stanley Johnson and Charlotte Johnson, née Fawcett; Married Amelia Gentleman (2 children).

Education: European School, Uccle, Brussels; Ashdown House, Sussex; Hall School, Hampstead; Eton College; Balliol College, Oxford (BA modern history 1994); Institut d'Etudes Europennes, Universite Libre de Bruxelles (Licence Speciale 1995); INSEAD (MBA 2000); French.

Non-political career: Corporate Finance, Deutsche Bank; *Financial Times*: Lex column 1997, Paris Correspondent 2001-05, Bureau Chief, South Asia 2005-08, Associate Editor and Head of Lex 2008-10.

Political career: *House of Commons:* MP for Orpington 2010-19; PPS to Mark Prisk as Minister of State for Business and Enterprise 2011-12; Assistant Government Whip 2012-14; Head of Number 10 Policy Unit 2013-15; Cabinet Office: Parliamentary Secretary 2013-14, Minister of State 2014-15; Minister of State for: Universities and Science, Department for Business, Innovation and Skills 2015-16, Universities, Science, Research and Innovation, Department for Business, Energy and Industrial Strategy and Department for Education 2016-18, 2019 (also attending Cabinet 2019); Minister of State, Department for Transport 2018; Minister for London 2018. Member, Public Accounts 2010-12. *House of Lords:* Raised to the peerage as Baron Johnson of Marylebone, of Marylebone in the City of Westminster 2020. *Other:* Chair, Number 10 Policy Board 2013-15.

Political interests: Education and technology policy, business, finance, trade and investment; China, European Union, India.

Other: Member: European Council on Foreign Relations, UK-India Roundtable; Co-founder, Prabodhan: India Conclave; Non-executive chair, TES Global 2019-; President's Professional Fellow, Kings College London 2020-; Senior Fellow, Harvard Kennedy School 2020-; Chair, Applyboard 2020-; Council member and non-executive director, Dyson Institute of Technology Engineering 2020-; Non-executive director, Tech Nation 2020-; PC 2019.

Publications: Co-author, The Man Who Tried To Buy The World (2003); Co-editor, Reconnecting Britain and India: Ideas for an Enhanced Partnership (2011).

Rt Hon the Lord Johnson of Marylebone, House of Lords, London SW1A 0PW
Tel: 020 7219 3000
Email: jo@jo-johnson.com Website: www.jo-johnson.com *Twitter:* @JoJohnsonUK

LIBERAL DEMOCRAT

JOLLY, BARONESS

JOLLY (Life Baroness), Judith Anne Jolly; cr 2010. Born 27 April 1951; Married (2 sons).

Education: The King's High School for Girls, Warwick; Leeds University (BSc engineering); Nottingham University (PGCE).

Non-political career: Maths teacher 1974-97; Chief of staff to Robin Teverson MEP 1997-99; Taught English as a foreign language, British Council, Oman 1990s.

Political career: *House of Lords:* Raised to the peerage as Baroness Jolly, of Congdon's Shop in the County of Cornwall 2010. Government Whip 2013-15; Government Spokesperson for: Culture, Media and Sport (Arts, Tourism and Sport; Women and Equalities) 2013-15, Defence 2013-15, Health 2013-15; Liberal Democrat: Spokesperson/Shadow Secretary of State for Defence 2015-17, Spokesperson for Health 2017-19. Member: Ecclesiastical Committee 2012-13, Joint Committee on the Draft Care and Support Bill 2013, EU Home Affairs Sub-committee 2019-20, EU Environment Sub-committee 2020-. Chair, Liberal Democrat Parliamentary Party Committee on Health and Social Care 2011-15. *Other:* Member, Liberal Party/Liberal Democrats 1984-; Election Agent to Paul Tyler MP 1997; Vice-chair, Parliamentary Candidates' Assocation 1999-2008; Member, Federal Policy Committee 2002-10; Chair, Devon and Cornwall Regional Executive 2007-10. Non-executive director, Mental Health and Learning Disability NHS Trust 1997-2007; Former chair, North and East Cornwall NHS Primary Care Trust; Former lay member, Commission for Health Improvement; President, Society of Chiropodists and Podiatrists 2013-; Chair, Digital Services Cornwall CIC.

Political interests: Defence, international affairs, poverty, rural affairs, global health, music; Middle East, Oman.

Other: Chair, HFT WEF 2016-.

Recreations: Singing, reading modern novels.

The Baroness Jolly, House of Lords, London SW1A 0PW
Tel: 020 7219 1286 *Email:* jollyj@parliament.uk *Twitter:* @jollyjudith

LABOUR

JONES, LORD

JONES (Life Baron), Stephen Barry Jones; cr. 2001. Born 26 June 1937; Son of late Stephen Jones, steelworker, and late Grace Jones; Married Janet Davies (1 son).

Education: Hawarden Grammar School; Teacher training, Normal College, UCNW Bangor.

Non-political career: Head of English department, Deeside Secondary School, Flintshire; Regional officer, National Union of Teachers. Member, Transport and General Workers Union.

Political career: *House of Commons:* Contested Northwich, Cheshire 1966 general election. MP (Labour) for East Flint 1970-83, for Alyn and Deeside 1983-2001; PPS to Denis Healey as Chancellor of the Exchequer 1972-74; Parliamentary Under-Secretary of State for Wales 1974-79; Member, Public Accounts Committee 1979-80; Opposition Frontbench Spokesperson for Employment 1980-83; Member: Shadow Cabinet 1983-92, Prime Minister's Intelligence and Security Committee 1994-97, 1997-2001; Madam Speaker's Chairman Panel 1997-2001; Chairman: Welsh Grand Committee 1997-2001, Advisory Committee on Registration of Political Parties 1999-2001; Deputy Speaker, Westminster Hall 2000-01. *House of Lords:* Raised to the peerage as Baron Jones, of Deeside in the County of Clwyd 2001. Member, EU Sub-committee A (Economic and Financial Affairs, Trade and External Relations/Economic and Financial Affairs) 2003-06; EU Sub-committee C (Foreign Affairs, Defence and Development Policy): Co-opted member 2008-10, Member 2010-12; Member: Joint Committee on the Draft Communications Data Bill 2012-13, Inheritance and Trustees' Powers Bill 2013, Extradition Law 2014-15, Delegated Powers and Regulatory Reform 2015-19, Ecclesiastical Committee 2020-. *Other:* Chair, Flint East Constituency Labour Party 1964-66; Member, Executive of Labour Party, Wales 1966-70. Governor: National Museum of Wales, National Library of Wales.

Political interests: Manufacturing industries, regional policy, NHS, education, aerospace; Austria, Germany.

Other: Member, Delegation of Council of Europe and Western European Union 1971-74; Hon. Life Member, Royal Liverpool Philharmonic Society 1980-; Chair, Diocesan Board of Continuing Education, St Asaph 2004-; Trustee: Friends of Africa Foundation, Winnicot Clinic, Bodelwyddan Castle Trust (NPG Wales); President: Deeside Hospital League of Friends, North East Wales Institute of Higher Education 2007-09, North Wales Exporters Club, Neighbourhood Watch, Flintshire 2008-, Hawarden Singers, Saltney History Society; Vice-President, Federation of Economic Development Authorities; Chair, Diocesan Education Board (St Asaph); Dementia Champion Wales 2012-; President: Army Cadet Forces Association Wales 2013, Royal Buckley Town Band, Wrexham and Bidston Rail Users Association, Chester and East Clwyd Advanced Motorists, Deeside Business Forum, Arthritis Care, Flintshire, Flintshire County Business Week 2014; Sain Clwyd Sound (Talking Newspaper); Patron: Brain Injury Rehabilitation and Development Learning Centre, Chester, Neuro Centre, Chester and North Wales; President: Mersey Dee Alliance, Cornerstone Flintshire (L'Arche UK); Alzheimer's Disease Society, Wales Ambassador and Dementia Friend, Royal Academy, Tate Galleries, Merseyside Museum and Gallery, Patron, Welsh Association of ME and CFS Support (Wales Neurological Alliance); Founding Chancellor, Glyndwr University 2009-12; Hon. Fellow: Bangor University 2012, Gladstone's Library, Hawarden; PC 1999. Patron, GAP Connah's Quay Nomads Football Club.

Recreations: Soccer, cricket, watching tennis.

Rt Hon the Lord Jones, House of Lords, London SW1A 0PW
Tel: 020 7219 3556

LIBERAL DEMOCRAT

JONES OF CHELTENHAM, LORD

JONES OF CHELTENHAM (Life Baron), Nigel David Jones; cr 2005. Born 30 March 1948; Son of late A J and Nora Jones; Married Katy Grinnell 1981 (1 son twin daughters).

Education: Prince Henry's Grammar School, Evesham; Arabic, French, German, Swedish.

Non-political career: Clerk; Computer operator, Westminster Bank 1965-67; Computer programmer, ICL Computers 1967-70; Systems analyst, Vehicle and General Insurance 1970-71; Systems programmer, Atkins Computing 1971; Systems designer; Consultant; Project manager, ICL Computers 1971-92.

Political career: *House of Commons:* Contested Cheltenham 1979 general election. MP (Liberal Democrat) for Cheltenham 1992-2005; Liberal Democrat Spokesperson for: England, Local Government and Housing 1992-93, Science and Technology 1993-2005, Consumer Affairs 1995-97, Sport 1997-99, Science and Technology 1997-99, International Development 1999-2002. *House of Lords:* Raised to the peerage as Baron Jones of Cheltenham, of Cheltenham in the County of Gloucestershire 2005. Member: Information 2007-09, Crossrail Bill 2008, High Speed Rail (London-West Midlands) Bill 2016, High Speed Rail (West Midlands-Crewe) Bill 2019-20. *Other:* Councillor, Gloucestershire County Council 1989-93.

Political interests: Trade and industry, transport, restructuring of defence industries, information technology, sport, international development; Africa, Bahrain, Botswana, Gambia, Ghana, Kenya, Kuwait, Lesotho, Malawi, Middle East, St Helena, Sierra Leone, Swaziland, Tanzania, Turks and Caicos Islands, Uganda, UAE, Zambia, Zimbabwe.

Other: Member, Executive Committee: Governing Body British Association for Central and Eastern Europe 1996-2001, Inter-Parliamentary Union British Group 1997-2005, Commonwealth Parliamentary Association UK Branch 1999-2005; NSPCC, Help the Aged, WWF, Smile Train. National Liberal, Reform Club; Gloucestershire County Cricket Club; Cheltenham Town FC Season Ticket Holder.

Recreations: Watching Swindon Town FC and Cheltenham Town FC, playing cricket, gardening.

The Lord Jones of Cheltenham, House of Lords, London SW1A 0PW
Tel: 020 7219 4415 *Email:* jonesn@parliament.uk

GREEN PARTY

JONES OF MOULSECOOMB, BARONESS

JONES OF MOULSECOOMB (Life Baroness), Jennifer Helen Jones; cr 2013. Born 23 December 1949; 2 daughters.

Education: Westlain Grammar, Brighton; University College, London (BSc environmental archaeology 1994); Arabic (a little), French, German.

Non-political career: Housewife, Secretary, Office Manager with some political activism 1970-90; Archaeologist/Political Activist 1991-99; Financial Controller, Metro Inspection Services (a fire safety company) 1999-2000.

Political career: *House of Commons:* Contested (Green) Dulwich and West Norwood 2001 and 2005 and Camberwell and Peckham 2010 general elections. *House of Lords:* Raised to the peerage as Baroness Jones of Moulsecoomb, of Moulsecoomb in the County of East Sussex 2013. *Other:* Contested London region 1999 European Parliament election. London Assembly: AM for Londonwide region 2000-16, Chair, Standards Committee 2000-03, Mayor of London's Road Safety Ambassador 2002-08, Deputy Mayor of London 2003-04, Chair: Mayor of London's Walking Advisory Panel 2003-08, Mayor of London's Green Transport Adviser 2006-08, Planning and Housing Committee 2009-10, 2011-12, Economy Committee 2014-16; Contested London Mayoral 2012 election. Chair, Green Party 1996-98. Member, Metropolitan Police Authority 2000-12; Chair, London Food 2004-08; Councillor, London Borough of Southwark Council 2006-10; Vice-president, Local Government Association.

Political interests: Sustainability, social justice; Middle East.

Other: WWF, Southwark Day Centre for Asylum Seekers, Green Gathering Charity.

Recreations: Yoga, films, walking.

The Baroness Jones of Moulsecoomb, House of Lords, London SW1A 0PW
Tel: 020 7219 3000 *Email:* jonesjb@parliament.uk
Email: contact@jennyjones.org Website: jennyjones.org *Twitter:* @GreenJennyJones

LABOUR

JONES OF WHITCHURCH, BARONESS

Opposition Spokesperson for Environment, Food and Rural Affairs

JONES OF WHITCHURCH (Life Baroness), Margaret (Maggie) Beryl Jones; cr 2006. Born 22 May 1955; Daughter of Bill and Audrey Jones.

Education: Whitchurch High School, Cardiff; Sussex University (BA sociology 1976).

Non-political career: Inland Revenue Staff Federation 1977-78; National Union of Bank Employees 1978-79; National Union of Public Employees/Unison 1979-2006: Regional official 1979-89, National officer 1989-95, Director, policy and public affairs 1995-2006; Chair, Circle 33 Housing Association 2006-12; Non-executive board member: Circle Housing 2006-16, WRAP (Waste and Resources Action Programme) 2006-15, Ombudsman Services 2013-19; Chair, Rothamsted Enterprises 2019-. Unison.

Political career: *House of Commons:* Contested (Labour) Blaenau Gwent 2005 general election. *House of Lords:* Raised to the peerage as Baroness Jones of Whitchurch, of Whitchurch in the County of South Glamorgan 2006. Opposition Whip 2010-11; Opposition Spokesperson for: Culture, Media and Sport 2010-14, Education 2011-15, Environment, Food and Rural Affairs 2015-, Energy and Climate Change 2016. Co-opted Member, EU Sub-committee D (Environment and Agriculture) 2006-09; Member, Statutory Instruments Joint Committee 2007-10; Co-opted Member, EU Sub-committee G (Social Policy and Consumer Affairs) 2009-10. *Other:* Labour Party: Member, National Executive Committee trade union section 1993-2005, Chair: Local Government Committee 1996-2004, Housing, Transport and the Regions Commission 1999-2004, Labour Party 2000-01, Labour's Joint Policy Committee 2003-05. General Medical Council, Fitness to Practice Panel 2006-13; Chair, Ombudsman Services: Property 2007-13.

Political interests: Housing, public service reform, food and nutrition, education, culture and media; China.

Other: Trustee, Shelter 2003-09; Deputy chair, School Food Trust 2005-09; Farming and Countryside Education Strategy Group 2007-11; Member, Fabian Society; Patron, Empty Homes Agency 2010-; Fundraising Committee, Passage Homeless Centre 2011-15; Chair,

Surveyors Ombudsman Service 2007-13; ClientEarth Development Board 2016–; Q Bot energy saving 2017-; President, South Downs Society 2018; Shelter, Passage Homeless Centre, ClientEarth. Athenæum Club.

Recreations: Walking, sailing, horse riding.

The Baroness Jones of Whitchurch, House of Lords, London SW1A 0PW
Tel: 020 7219 8272 *Email:* jonesmag@parliament.uk *Twitter:* @WhitchurchGirl

CONSERVATIVE

JOPLING, LORD

JOPLING (Life Baron), Thomas Michael Jopling; cr. 1997. Born 10 December 1930; Son of Mark Jopling; Married Gail Dickinson 1958 (2 sons).

Education: Cheltenham College; King's College, Newcastle upon Tyne (BSc agriculture 1952).

Non-political career: Farmer 1955-.

Political career: *House of Commons:* Contested Wakefield 1959 general election. MP (Conservative) for Westmorland 1964-83, for Westmorland and Lonsdale 1983-97; PPS to James Prior as Minister of Agriculture, Fisheries and Food 1970-71; Government: Assistant Whip 1971-73, Whip 1973-74; Opposition Spokesperson for Agriculture 1974-79; Shadow Minister for Agriculture 1975-76; Government Chief Whip 1979-83; Minister of Agriculture, Fisheries and Food 1983-87. Member, Foreign Affairs 1987-97; Chair, Sittings of the House (Jopling Report) 1991-92. *House of Lords:* Raised to the peerage as Baron Jopling, of Ainderby Quernhow in the County of North Yorkshire 1997. Member, European Union 1999-2003, 2007-12; EU Sub-committee C (Common Foreign and Security Policy): Member 1999-2003, Chair 2000-03, Member: Procedure 2003-06, 2010-12, Merits of Statutory Instruments 2003-07; EU Sub-committee F (Home Affairs): Co-opted Member 2006-07, Chair 2007-10; Member: EU Sub-committee C: (Foreign Affairs, Defence and Development Policy) 2010-12, (External Affairs) 2012-15, International Relations 2016-19. *Other:* Committee member, Association of Conservative Peers 1997-2000. Councillor, Thirsk Rural District Council 1958-64; DL: Cumbria 1991-97, North Yorkshire 1998-2005.

Other: UK branch, Commonwealth Parliamentary Association (CPA): Executive Committee 1974-79, 1987-97, Vice-chair 1977-78; President, EU Councils of Agriculture and Fishery Ministers 1986; Executive, CPA HQ 1988-89; North Atlantic Assembly and NATO Parliamentary Assembly: UK delegate 1987-97, 2001-, Vice-President 2014-; OSCE Parliamentary Assembly: Leader, UK Delegation 1991-97, UK delegate 2000-01; Member, Executive Committee, Inter-Parliamentary Union, British Group 1999-; Chair, Committee on Civilian Aspects of Security 2011-14; Member, National Council, NFU 1962-65; Fellow, Industry and Parliament Trust 1979; Auto Cycle Union: President 1990-2004, President Emeritus 2004-; President, Despatch Association 2002-07; Hon. DCL, Newcastle 1992; PC 1979. Honorary Member, Royal Automobile Club, Buck's Club.

Rt Hon the Lord Jopling DL, House of Lords, London SW1A 0PW
Tel: 020 7219 0801

LABOUR

JORDAN, LORD

JORDAN (Life Baron), William Brian Jordan; cr. 2000. Born 28 January 1936; Son of Walter and Alice Jordan; Married Jean Ann Livesey 1958 (3 daughters).

Education: Barford Road Secondary Modern School, Birmingham.

Non-political career: Machine Toolmaker; Convener of shop stewards, Guest, Keen and Nettlefold 1966; Full-time AUEW divisional organiser 1976; President, AEU then AEEU 1986-95; Member, TUC General Council 1986-95; General Secretary, ICFTU (International Confederation of Free Trade Unions) 1995-2002. Royal Air Force 1954-56. Member: AEEU England, Amicus, Unite.

Political career: *House of Lords:* Raised to the peerage as Baron Jordan, of Bournville in the County of West Midlands 2000. Member EU Sub-committee A: (Economic and Financial Affairs) 2005-07, 2008-09, 2012-13, (Economic and Financial Affairs and International Trade) 2010-12. *Other:* Member, National Economic Development Council 1986-92; Governor, Henley College; Member, Council, Industrial Society 1987-; Manchester Business School

1987-92; Governor, BBC 1988-98; Engineering Industry Training Board 1986-91; Governor, LSE 1987-2002; Victim Support Advisory Committee 1990-2007; Council Winston Churchill Trust 1990-; Governor, Ashridge Management College 1992-2015; Board Member, English Partnerships 1993-2002; Chair, Housing and Communities Agency Pension Scheme 2004-; UK National Contact Point (NCP) Steering Board 2007-.

Political interests: Labour Party; Bahrain, India, Jordan.

Other: President: European Metal Workers Federation 1986-95, International Metal Workers Federation 1986-95; UN High Panel on Youth Employment 2001-; UN Global Compact Advisory Council 2001; Fellow, World Economic Forum; President, RoSPA; FRSA 1996; City and Guilds London Institute (Honoris Causa); DUniv, Central England 1993; Hon. DSc, Cranfield 1995; Silver Medal, Institute of Sheet Metal Engineering; CBE 1992.

Recreations: Reading, watching football.

The Lord Jordan CBE, House of Lords, London SW1A 0PW
Tel: 020 7219 5648 *Email:* jordanw@parliament.uk
352 Heath Road South, Northfield, Birmingham B31 2BH *Tel:* 0121-475 7319
Email: lordjordan@btinternet.com

LABOUR

JUDD, LORD

JUDD (Life Baron), Frank Ashcroft Judd; cr. 1991. Born 28 March 1935; Son of late Charles Judd, CBE, and late Helen Judd, JP; Married Christine Willington 1961 (2 daughters).

Education: City of London School; London School of Economics (BSc economics 1956).

Non-political career: General Secretary, International Voluntary Service 1960-66; Associate director, International Defence and Aid Fund for Southern Africa 1979-80; Director: Voluntary Service Overseas 1980-85, Oxfam 1985-91; Chair, International Council of Voluntary Agencies 1986-90; Consultant (professional) to De Montfort University (Faculty of Health and Life Sciences and Scholarship Board) 1993-2012; Adviser to: Forbes Trust 1992-2000, Saferworld 1992-2002; Non-executive director, Portsmouth Harbour Renaissance 1998-2006. Short Service Commission, RAF 1957-59. Member: Unite, GMB.

Political career: *House of Commons:* Contested Sutton and Cheam 1959 and Portsmouth West 1964 general elections. MP (Labour) for Portsmouth West 1966-74, for Portsmouth North 1974-79; PPS to: Anthony Greenwood as Minister of Housing 1967-70, Harold Wilson as Leader of Opposition 1970-72; Shadow Defence Team 1972-74; Parliamentary Under-Secretary of State (Royal Navy), Ministry of Defence 1974-76; Minister of State: Overseas Development 1976-77, Foreign and Commonwealth Office 1977-79. *House of Lords:* Raised to the peerage as Baron Judd, of Portsea in the County of Hampshire 1991. Opposition Spokesperson for Foreign Affairs 1991-92; Principal Opposition Spokesperson for: Development and Co-operation 1992-97, Education 1992-94; Opposition Spokesperson for Defence 1995-97. Member: Procedure 2001-04, Ecclesiastical Committee 2002-, Joint Committee on Human Rights 2003-07, EU Sub-committee F: (Home Affairs) 2010-12, (Home Affairs, Health and Education) 2012-15, EU Justice Sub-committee 2015-19. *Other:* LSE: Member of the Court 1982-2012, Member, advisory board, Centre for Human Rights/Human Rights Strategy Committee 2007-, Emeritus governor 2012-, Member, Commission on Diplomacy 2014-15; Vice-President, Campaign for National Parks 1998-; Lancaster University Court: Member 2002-11, Life member 2011-; Newcastle University Court: Member 2004-13, Life member 2013-; Member, Lancaster University 2018-.

Political interests: Foreign affairs, overseas development, defence, education, refugees, migration, race relations, penal affairs, environment policy, human rights.

Other: Member, Parliamentary Delegation to Council of Europe and WEU 1969-72, 1997-2005: Chair: Sub-committee on Refugees 1998-2001, Rapporteur and Co-chair, Ad Hoc Committee on the conflict in Chechnya, Council of Europe 1999-2003; Chair, Conference on the Future of Southern Africa, World Economic Forum 1990, 1991; Member, Commission on Global Governance 1992-2001; Member Advisory Panel, United Nations Association; Member: WHO Task Force on Health and Development 1994-98, Justice Richard Goldstone's Commission on Human Duties and Responsibilities 1997-99; President, Middle East Committee, Inter-Parliamentary Union 2012-15; President, YMCA (England) 1996-2005; Trustee: Saferworld 2002-15, Ruskin Foundation 2002-11; Member: British Council, Royal Institute for International Affairs; Fellow, Royal Society of Arts; Member and Former Chair,

Fabian Society; Member: Christians on the Left, Advisory board, Institute for Global Challenges, Rutgers University, New Jersey, USA Member, Advisory Panel, UNA-UK; Friends of the Royal Naval Museum: President 2002-12, Honorary Vice-President 2012-; Friends of the Lake District: President 2005-12, Patron 2012-; Hospice at Home, West Cumbria: President 2008-15, Vice-President 2015-; Freedom, City of Portsmouth 1995; Hon. DLitt, Bradford University 1987; Hon. Fellow: Portsmouth University 1995, Selly Oak Colleges, Birmingham 1997; Hon. DLitt, Portsmouth University 1997; Hon. LLD, Greenwich University 1999; Hon. DLitt, De Montfort University 2006; Hon. Fellow, Lancaster University 2015. Royal OverSeas League.

Publications: Co-author: Radical Future (1967); Purpose in Socialism (1973); Imagining Tomorrow (2000).

Recreations: Enjoying the countryside, family holidays, music, theatre.

The Lord Judd, House of Lords, London SW1A 0PW
Tel: 020 7219 5353 *Email:* juddf@parliament.uk

CROSSBENCH

JUDGE, LORD

Convenor of the Crossbench Peers

JUDGE (Life Baron), Igor Judge; cr 2008. Born 19 May 1941; Son of Raymond Judge and Rosa Judge, née Micallef; Married Judith Robinson 1965 (1 son 2 daughters).

Education: St Edward's College, Malta; Oratory School, Woodcote; Magdalene College, Cambridge (BA 1962); Middle Temple, London; Maltese.

Non-political career: Called to the Bar, Middle Temple 1963; Recorder 1976-88; QC 1979; Bencher Middle Temple 1987; Midland and Oxford Circuit: Leader 1988, High Court Judge, Queens Bench Division 1988-96, Presiding Judge 1993-96; Lord Justice of Appeal 1996-2005; Senior Presiding Judge for England and Wales 1998-2003; Deputy Chief Justice of England and Wales 2003-05; President, QBD 2005-08; Lord Chief Justice of England and Wales 2008-13; Treasurer, Middle Temple 2014; Visiting Professor, King's College, London 2014-; Commissary, Cambridge University 2017-.

Political career: *House of Lords:* Raised to the peerage as Baron Judge, of Draycote in the County of Warwickshire 2008. As a senior member of the judiciary, disqualified from participation 2008-13; Convenor of the Crossbench Peers 2019-; Member, House of Lords Commission 2019-. Member, Constitution 2015-19; Chair, Sentencing (Pre-consolidation Amendments) Bill 2019; Member: Services 2019-, Liaison 2019-, Procedure/Procedure and Privileges 2019-, Selection 2019-. *Other:* Surveillance Commissioner 2015; Chief Surveillance Commissioner 2015-17.

Political interests: Malta.

Other: Commissary, Cambridge University; Hon. LLD: Cambridge University, Kings College London, Aberystwyth University, Swansea University, Nottingham Trent University, Northampton University, Kingston University; Buckingham University; Kt 1988; PC 1996. Athenæum Club.

Publications: Co-author, Magna Carter Uncovered (2014); The Safest Shield (2015).

Recreations: History, music, cricket.

Rt Hon the Lord Judge, House of Lords, London SW1A 0PW
Tel: 020 7219 1414

CROSSBENCH

KAKKAR, LORD

KAKKAR (Life Baron), Ajay Kumar Kakkar; cr 2010. Born 28 April 1964; Son of Prof. Vijay Vir Kakkar and Dr Savitri Kakkar; Married Nicola Lear 1993 (2 daughters).

Education: Alleyn's School, Dulwich, London; King's College School of Medicine and Dentistry (BSc 1985; MBBS 1988); Imperial College, London (PhD 1998).

Non-political career: House surgeon and physician, King's College Hospital 1988-89; Junior surgical trainee 1989-92; Hammersmith Hospital/Royal Postgraduate Medical School (Medical Research Council): Clinical training fellow 1993-96, Clinical scientist fellow 1996-99; Senior lecturer in surgery and consultant surgeon, Hammersmith Hospital 1999-2004; Professor of surgical sciences, St Barts and the London School of Medicine and Dentistry, Queen Mary University, London 2004-11; Consultant Surgeon: St Barts and the London NHS Trust 2004-11, University College Hospitals NHS Foundation Trust 2011-; Director, Thrombosis Research Institute 2008-; Professor of surgery, University College, London 2011-; Chair, UCL Partners 2013-.

Political career: *House of Lords:* Raised to the peerage as Baron Kakkar, of Loxbeare in the County of Devon 2010. Member: EU Sub-committee B (Internal Market, Infrastructure and Employment) 2012-15, Science and Technology 2015-16, 2017-, Long-Term Sustainability of the NHS 2016-17. *Other:* Chair, Alleyn's School Governors 2008-15; UK Business Ambassador for Pharmaceutical and Healthcare 2012-19; Chair, House of Lords Appointments Commission 2013-18; Member, UK Government Honours Main Committee and Chair, Health Honours Committee 2013-; Chair, Judicial Appointments Commission 2016-.

Political interests: India, USA.

Other: Fellow, Royal College of Surgeons 1992; Association of Surgeons of Great Britain and Ireland; Royal College of Surgeons; Member, General Medical Council 2012-16; Worshipful Company of Barbers; Hon. Fellow, Harris Manchester College, Oxford; James VI Association of Surgeons Fellow 1992; Hunterian Professor, Royal College of Surgeons of England 1996; David Patey Prize, Surgical Research Society of Great Britain and Ireland 1996; Knoll William Harvey Prize, International Society on Thrombosis and Haemostasis 1997; Wellcome Lecture, Royal Society of Medicine 2009; PC 2014. Athenæum Club.

Publications: Numerous academic publications.

Rt Hon Professor the Lord Kakkar, House of Lords, London SW1A 0PW
Tel: 020 7219 3000 *Email:* kakkara@parliament.uk

NON-AFFILIATED

KALMS, LORD

KALMS (Life Baron), Harold Stanley Kalms; cr. 2004. Born 21 November 1931; Son of Charles and Cissie Kalms; Married Pamela Jimack 1954 (3 sons).

Education: Christ's College, Finchley.

Non-political career: Dixons Group/DSG International plc 1948-: Managing director 1962-72, Chair 1972-2002, President 2002-; Director, British Gas 1987-97; Chair, Volvere 2001-11.

Political career: *House of Lords:* Raised to the peerage as Baron Kalms, of Edgware in the London Borough of Barnet 2004. Member: Review of the BBC Charter 2005-06, Information 2006-09. *Other:* Treasurer, Conservative Party 2001-03. Governor, Dixons Bradford City Technology College 1988-2002; Chair, Kings Healthcare NHS Trust 1993-96; Member, Funding Agency for Schools 1994-97.

Political interests: Islamism, reforming EU, dignity in dying; Europe, Israel.

Other: Director, Centre for Policy Studies 1991-2001; Trustee: Economic Trust 1993-2002, Industry in Education 1993-; Member, Business for Sterling 1998-2001; Five honorary doctorates; Honorary fellow London Business School 1995; Kt 1996. Saville, Portland Club.

Publications: A Time for Change (1996).

Recreations: Opera, ballet, bridge.

The Lord Kalms, House of Lords, London SW1A 0PW
Tel: 020 7219 5353
Email: lordkalmsoffice@btinternet.com

CONSERVATIVE

KAMALL, LORD

KAMALL (Life Baron), Syed Salah Kamall; cr 2021. Born 15 February 1967; Married Sandira Beekoo 1997 (2 sons).

Education: Latymer School, Edmonton, London; Liverpool University (BEng electronic engineering 1988); London School of Economics (MSc economics 1989); City University, London (PhD organisational change 2004); French.

Non-political career: Business systems analyst, NatWest Bank 1989-91; Fellow, Management School, Bath University 1994-96; Research fellow, Leeds University Business School 1996-97; Associate director and consultant, Omega Partners 1997-2001; Consultant and director, SSK Consulting 2001-05; Visiting fellow, Leeds University Business School 2004-.

Political career: *House of Commons:* Contested West Ham 2001 general election. *House of Lords:* Raised to the peerage as Baron Kamall, of Edmonton in the London Borough of Enfield 2021. *Other:* MEP for London 2005-19: Member: Legal Affairs Committee 2005, International Trade Committee 2005-09, Internal Market and Consumer Protection Committee 2008 Constitutional Affairs Committee: Member 2009, Vice-chair 2009-11; Member: Switzerland, Iceland and Norway and EEA Delegation 2009-12, Legal Affairs Committee 2011, Economic and Monetary Affairs Committee 2011-14; European Conservatives and Reformists Group: Bureau Member 2013-14, Chair 2014-19; Member: Environment, Public Health and Food Safety Committee 2014-15, 2016, Conference of Presidents 2014-19, Transport and Tourism Committee 2014, Maghreb Delegation 2014-15, Mediterranean Delegation 2014-15, Foreign Affairs Committee 2014-15, Japan Delegation 2015-17, United States Delegation 2016, Culture and Education Committee 2016-17, Cariforum Delegation 2017-19. Contested London region 2019 European Parliament election. Conservative Party: Former: Honorary secretary, Conservative Political Forum, Bath Conservative Association, Chair, Stockwell ward, Vauxhall, London, Executive member, London Eastern Area Committee, Treasurer, Conservative delegation 2010.

Political interests: International trade, financial services, social justice, fighting global poverty, information and communications technology, media and broadcasting.

Publications: Spicer's European Union Policy Briefings: Telecommunications (Longman, 1996); Numerous articles on international business and foreign investment.

Recreations: Touch rugby, football, cricket.

The Lord Kamall, House of Lords, London SW1A 0PW *Twitter:* @syedkamall

CONSERVATIVE

KEEN OF ELIE, LORD

KEEN OF ELIE (Life Baron), Richard Sanderson Keen; cr 2015. Born 29 March 1954; Married (1 son 1 daughter).

Education: King's School, Rochester; Dollar Academy; Edinburgh University (LLB 1976).

Non-political career: Faculty of Advocates: Admitted 1980, Dean 2007-14; Standing junior counsel to the DTI in Scotland 1986-93; QC 1993; Chairman: Appeal Committee, Institute of Chartered Accountants in Scotland 2000-04, Police Appeals Tribunal 2004-10; Member: Bar of England and Wales, Blackstone Chambers (non-practising); Bencher, Middle Temple 2013.

Political career: *House of Lords:* Raised to the peerage as Baron Keen of Elie, of Elie in Fife 2015. Advocate General for Scotland 2015-20; Government Spokesperson: Law Officers 2015-20, Home Office 2016, Justice 2016-20. Member, Sentencing (Pre-consolidation Amendments) Bill 2019. *Other:* Chairman, Scottish Conservative Party 2014-15.

Other: Member, Scottish Public Law Group; PC 2017. Hon. Company of Edinburgh Golfers, Muirfield; Golf Home Club, Elie; New Club, Edinburgh.

Rt Hon the Lord Keen of Elie QC, House of Lords, London SW1A 0PW
Tel: 020 7219 3000

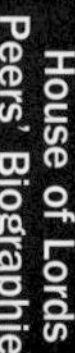

NON-AFFILIATED

KENNEDY OF CRADLEY, BARONESS

KENNEDY OF CRADLEY (Life Baroness), Alicia Pamela Kennedy; cr 2013. Born 22 March 1969; Daughter of Mary and Frank Chater; Married Roy Kennedy 2004, now Lord Kennedy of Southwark (qv).

Education: King Edward VI College; Warwick University (BSc pyschology 1991).

Non-political career: Labour Party: Regional organiser 1995-97, Policy officer, Partnership in Power February 2000, Head of General Secretary's Office 2000-01, Chief of Staff 2001-05, Field of Operation, Task Force Leader 2003-05, 2009-10, Director of Campaigns, Organisation, Membership and Equalities 2005-06, Deputy General Secretary 2006-11; Political adviser to Joan Ruddock MP as Parliamentary Under-Secretary of State for Women 1997-98; Policy analyst, Leader's Office, London Borough of Lambeth 1998-2000; Strategic adviser to Ed Miliband MP as Leader of the Opposition 2011-13. GMB.

Political career: *House of Lords:* Raised to the peerage as Baroness Kennedy of Cradley, of Cradley in the Metropolitan Borough of Dudley 2013. Member: Joint Committee on the Draft Modern Slavery Bill 2014, Affordable Childcare 2014-15. *Other:* Chief of Staff to Tom Watson as Deputy Leader of the Labour Party 2015-19; Left Labour Party June 2020, now sits as Non-affiliated. Councillor, London Borough of Lewisham Council 2014-16.

Political interests: International development, home affairs, community development, consumer protection; South Asia, Sub-Saharan Africa.

Other: Trustee, APT Action on Poverty -2017; Member: Black Country Society, Institute of Marketing, Amnesty International, Child Poverty Action Group.

The Baroness Kennedy of Cradley, House of Lords, London SW1A 0PW
Tel: 020 7219 6495 *Email:* alicia.kennedy@parliament.uk *Twitter:* @aliciakennedy07

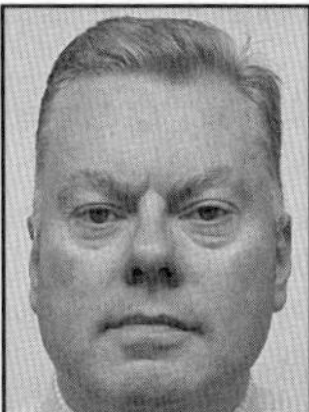

LABOUR/ CO-OPERATIVE

KENNEDY OF SOUTHWARK, LORD

Opposition Spokesperson for Home Office and Communities and Local Government and Housing; Opposition Whip

KENNEDY OF SOUTHWARK (Life Baron), Roy Francis Kennedy; cr 2010. Born 9 November 1962; Son of John and Frances Kennedy; Married Alicia 2004, now Baroness Kennedy of Cradley (qv) (no children).

Education: St Thomas the Apostle School, Peckham.

Non-political career: Director, London Mutual Credit Union. Member, GMB.

Political career: *House of Lords:* Raised to the peerage as Baron Kennedy of Southwark, of Newington in the London Borough of Southwark 2010. Opposition Whip 2011-12, 2014-19, 2020- Opposition Spokesperson for: Communities and Local Government 2015-, Housing 2015-, Home Office 2015-; Opposition Senior Whip 2019-20. Member: Joint Committee on Statutory Instruments 2010-15, Refreshment 2013-16. *Other:* Contested East Midlands region 2009 European Parliament election. Labour Party: Regional director, East Midlands 1997-2005, Director of Finance and Compliance 2005-10; Vice-chair (Lords), Co-operative Parliamentary Group. London Borough of Southwark Council: Councillor 1986-94, Former deputy leader, Former chair, Highways Committee; Commissioner, Electoral Commission 2010-13; Councillor, London Borough of Lewisham Council 2014-18; Vice-President, Local Government Association 2016-.

Political interests: Low pay, credit unions, diabetes, co-operatives, mutuals; EU, Ireland.

Other: Member: Fabian Society, Diabetes UK, Ramblers Association, Amnesty International; Trustee: National Association of Racing Staff, Millwall FC Community Trust; President, College of Podiatry; Trustee and Chair, Credit Union Foundation; Hon. Alderman, London Borough of Southwark. Member, Surrey County Cricket Club; Season ticket holder at Millwall FC.

Recreations: Reading, walking, theatre, football.

The Lord Kennedy of Southwark, House of Lords, London SW1A 0PW
Tel: 020 7219 1772 *Fax:* 020 7219 1506 *Email:* kennedyro@parliament.uk
Email: lordroykennedy@gmail.com *Twitter:* @LordRoyKennedy

LABOUR

KENNEDY OF THE SHAWS, BARONESS

KENNEDY OF THE SHAWS (Life Baroness), Helena Ann Kennedy; cr. 1997. Born 12 May 1950; Daughter of late Joshua Kennedy and Mary Kennedy; Partner Roger Mitchell 1977-84 (1 son); married Dr Iain Hutchison 1986 (1 son 1 daughter).

Education: Holyrood Secondary School, Glasgow; Council of Legal Education.

Non-political career: Called to the Bar, Gray's Inn 1972; Established Chambers at: Garden Court 1974, Tooks Court 1984, Doughty Street 1990; Broadcaster: First female moderator, Hypotheticals (Granada) on surrogate motherhood and artificial insemination; Presenter: *Heart of the Matter*, BBC 1987, *Putting Women in the Picture*, BBC2 1987, *Time Gentlemen Please*, BBC Scotland 1994; QC 1991; Bencher of Gray's Inn 1999; Investigating Commissioner, Inquiry into Human Trafficking in Scotland, Equality and Human Rights Commission 2011.

Political career: *House of Lords:* Raised to the peerage as Baroness Kennedy of The Shaws, of Cathcart in the City of Glasgow 1997. Member: Joint Committee on Human Rights 2012-15, European Union 2015-19; Chair, EU Justice Sub-committee 2015-19.

Other: IBA's International Task Force on Terrorism 2001-02; Haldane Society: Chair 1983-86, Vice-President 1986-; Member, National Board, Women's Legal Defence Fund 1989-91; Council member, Howard League for Penal Reform 1989-; Board Member: *New Statesman* 1990-96, *Counsel Magazine* 1990-; Committee member, Association of Women Barristers 1991-92; Chair: Charter '88 1992-97, Standing Committee for Youth Justice, NACRO 1993-, London International Festival of Theatre 1993-2002, British Council 1998-, Human Genetics Commission 2000-07, Advisory Council, World Bank Institute; Member, Independent Newspaper Board; Chair of council, JUSTICE; Vice-President, Haldane Society; Patron, Liberty; President, National Children's Bureau; Member, Bar Council 1990-93; Chancellor, Oxford Brookes University 1994-2001; Fellow, Royal Society of Arts; Hon. Fellow: Institute of Advanced Legal Studies 1997, City and Guilds London Institute, Institute of Advanced Legal Studies; Hon. Member, Paris-based Academie Universelle des Cultures; Eighteen honorary law doctorates; Honorary degree: City University London 2016, Essex University 2017; Women's Network Award for her work on women and justice 1992; UK Woman of Europe Award 1995; National Federation of Women's Institutes Making a World of Difference Award Institutes for her work on equal rights 1996; *The Times* (Joint) Lifetime Achievement Award 1997.

Publications: Co-author: The Bar on Trial (1978), Child Abuse Within the Family (1984), Balancing Acts (1989); Eve was Framed (1992); Leader of enquiry into health, environmental and safety aspects of Atomic Weapons Establishment Secrecy Versus Safety (1994); Inquiry into Violence in Penal Institutions for Young People (1995); Learning Works Official report for the FEFC on widening participation in Further Education (1997); Lectures; Has contributed articles on law, civil liberties and women.

Recreations: Theatre, spending time with family and friends.

The Baroness Kennedy of The Shaws QC, House of Lords, London SW1A 0PW
Tel: 020 7219 5353
Tel: 01708 379482 *Email:* hilary.hard@btinternet.com Website: www.helenakennedy.co.uk

CROSSBENCH

KERR OF KINLOCHARD, LORD

KERR OF KINLOCHARD (Life Baron), John Olav Kerr; cr. 2004. Born 22 February 1942; Son of Dr and Mrs J D O Kerr; Married Elizabeth Kalaugher 1965 (2 sons 3 daughters).

Education: Glasgow Academy; Pembroke College, Oxford (BA modern history 1963); French, Russian.

Non-political career: HM Diplomatic Service 1966-2002: Foreign Office, Moscow embassy, Rawalpindi, Pakistan High Commission, Foreign and Commonwealth Office (FCO), Private secretary to Permanent Under Secretary FCO 1974-79, Seconded to HM Treasury 1979-84: Principal private secretary to Sir Geoffrey Howe MP and Nigel Lawson MP as Chancellors of Exchequer 1981-84, Head of chancery, Washington DC, USA embassy 1984-87, Assistant Under-Secretary FCO 1987-90, Ambassador and UK Permanent Representative to EC/EU Brussels 1990-95, Ambassador to USA 1995-97, Permanent Under-Secretary and Head of Diplomatic Service, FCO 1997-2002; Secretary-General, European Convention 2002-03;

Director: Scottish American Investment Trust 2002-19, Shell Transport and Trading Co plc 2002-05, Rio Tinto plc 2003-15; Deputy chairman, Royal Dutch Shell plc 2005-12; Member, Advisory Board, BAe Systems 2008-11; Scottish Power: Director 2009-12, Deputy Chairman 2012-; Adviser, Edinburgh Partners 2012-.

Political career: *House of Lords:* Raised to the peerage as Baron Kerr of Kinlochard, of Kinlochard in Perth and Kinross 2004. Member: EU Sub-committee A: (Economic and Financial Affairs) 2006-08, 2012-15, (Economic and Financial Affairs and International Trade) 2011-12, European Union 2007-10, 2014-15, 2019-, EU Sub-committee E: (Law and Institutions) 2008-10, (Justice and Institutions) 2010-11, Economic Affairs 2015-19, Economic Affairs Finance Bill Sub-committee 2015-16, EU Energy and Environment Sub-committee 2019-20, EU International Agreements Sub-committee 2020-. *Other:* Trustee and Deputy Chair, National Gallery 2002-10; Member, Scottish Government's Standing Council on Europe 2016-.

Political interests: International affairs, economic affairs; China, EU, Korea, Russia, USA.

Other: Trustee: Rhodes Trust 1997-2010, National Gallery 2002-10, Fulbright Commission 2004-09; Hon President, Universities Association for Contemporary European Studies 2004-07; Carnegie Trust for the Universities of Scotland: Trustee 2005-18, Deputy Chair 2013-18; Chairman of Court/Council, Imperial College, London 2005-11; Centre for European Reform: Member of Council 2005-, Chair 2008-; Member of Council, European Policy Centre 2007-; President, UK-Korea Forum for the Future 2007-14; St Andrews Clinics for Children: Hon President 2010-, Trustee 2019-; Advisory Board Member, Burrell Collection Glasgow 2011-; Deputy Chair, Scottish Power 2012-; Member of Council, British Influence in Europe 2014-15; Trustee, Refugee Council 2016-; Scottish Centre on European Relations 2017-; Hon. Fellow: Pembroke College, Oxford 1991, Royal Society of Edinburgh 2006, Imperial College, London 2012; Honorary LLD: St Andrews 1996, Glasgow University 1999; Honorary DLitt, Aston University 2010; CMG 1987; KCMG 1991; GCMG 2001. Garrick Club.

Publications: Various articles.

Recreations: Travel, books, film, following Queen's Park Rangers FC.

The Lord Kerr of Kinlochard GCMG, House of Lords, London SW1A 0PW
Tel: 020 7219 5353

CROSSBENCH

KERSLAKE, LORD

KERSLAKE (Life Baron), Robert Walter Kerslake. Born 24 February 1955; Son of Robert James Kerslake and Maura Kerslake; Married Anne (1 son 1 daughter).

Education: Blue School, Somerset; Warwick University (BSc mathematics).

Non-political career: Greater London Council: CIPFA trainee 1979-82, Transport Finance 1982-85, Inner London Education Authority 1985-89, Director, Finance 1989-90; Chief Executive: London Borough of Hounslow 1990-97, Sheffield City Council 1997-2008, Homes and Communities Agency 2008-10; Permanent Secretary, Department for Communities and Local Government 2010-15; Head of the Civil Service 2012-14; Endcliffe Services 2015-.

Political career: *House of Lords:* Raised to the peerage as Baron Kerslake, of Endcliffe in the City of Sheffield 2015. Member: Administration and Works 2015-16, Finance 2016-. *Other:* President, Local Government Association 2015-; Chair, King's College Hospital Foundation Trust 2015-17.

Political interests: Local government, housing, local growth and regeneration, devolution.

Other: Chair: Peabody 2015-, Centre for Public Scrutiny 2015-, IPPR London Housing Commission 2015-; Member, CIPFA; Honorary degree: Sheffield University, Sheffield Hallam University; Kt 2005.

Recreations: Music, walking.

The Lord Kerslake, House of Lords, London SW1A 0PW
Tel: 020 7219 3000 *Email:* kerslakeb@parliament.uk *Twitter:* @sirbobkerslake

LABOUR

KESTENBAUM, LORD

KESTENBAUM (Life Baron) Jonathan Andrew Kestenbaum; cr 2011. Born 5 August 1959; Son of Ralph and Gaby Kestenbaum; Married Deborah Zackon 1984 (3 sons 1 daughter).

Education: London School of Economics (BA 1982); Wolfson College, Cambridge; Hebrew University (MA 1989); Cass Business School (MBA 1994).

Non-political career: Chief executive: Office of Chief Rabbi 1991-96, UJIA 1996-2002, Portland Trust 2002-06; Chief of staff to Sir Ronald Cohen, chairman of Apax Partners 2002-06; Chief executive, National Endowment for Science, Technology and the Arts 2005-10; Chairman, Five Arrows Ltd 2010-; Chief operating officer, RIT Capital Partners plc 2011-.

Political career: *House of Lords:* Raised to the peerage as Baron Kestenbaum, of Foxcote in the county of Somerset 2011.

Other: Governing Board, Royal Shakespeare Company; Rowley Lane Recreational Trust; Chancellor, Plymouth University; Honorary Doctorate of Technology, Plymouth University 2010; Honorary Fellowship, Royal College of Art 2011. MCC Club.

The Lord Kestenbaum, House of Lords, London SW1A 0PW
Tel: 020 7219 5353 *Email:* kestenbaumj@parliament.uk
RIT Capital Partners, 27 St James' Place, London SW1A 1NR *Tel:* 020 7647 8565
Email: jkestenbaum@ritcap.co.uk Website: www.ritcap.com

LABOUR

KHAN OF BURNLEY, LORD

KHAN OF BURNLEY (Life Baron), Wajid Iltaf Khan; cr 2021. Born 15 October 1979; Married Anam (2 children).

Education: Central Lancashire University (law 2002); Masters European law (2004).

Non-political career: Central Lancashire University: Senior lecturer, Course leader, community leadership programme.

Political career: *House of Lords:* Raised to the peerage as Baron Khan of Burnley, of Burnley in the County of Lancashire 2021. *Other:* MEP for North West 2017-19: Member: Economic and Monetary Affairs Committee 2017-18, Arab Peninsula Delegation 2017-19, Foreign Affairs Committee 2018-19, Human Rights Sub-committee 2018-19, S&D Group Special Envoy to Muslim Communities. Contested North West region 2019 European Parliament. Burnley Council: Councillor 2007-19, Mayor of Burnley 2020-21.

Political interests: Workers' rights, youth empowerment, human rights.

Other: Sitara-i-Qaide Azam Award by the President of Pakistan.

The Lord Khan of Burnley, House of Lords, London SW1A 0PW *Twitter:* @WajidKhanMayor

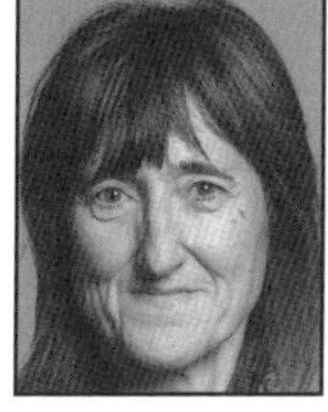

CROSSBENCH

KIDRON, BARONESS

KIDRON (Life Baroness), Beeban Tania Kidron; cr 2012. Born 2 May 1961; Daughter of Nina Kidron and late Michael Kidron; Married Lee Hall (1 son 1 daughter from previous marriage).

Education: Camden School for Girls, London; National Film and Television School (1981-85).

Non-political career: Director: *Carry Greenham Home* 1983, *Oranges Are Not the Only Fruit* 1989, *Antonia and Jane* 1990, *Vroom* 1990, *Itch* 1991, *Used People* 1992, *Great Moments in Aviation* 1993, *Hookers, Hustlers, Pimps and their Johns* 1993, *To Wong Foo Thanks for Everything, Julie Newmar* 1995, *Eve Arnold in Retrospect* 1996, *Swept from the Sea* 1997, *Texarkana* 1998, *Cinderella* 2000, *Murder* 2002, *Bridget Jones: The Edge of Reason* 2004, *Antony Gormley: Making Space* 2007, *Storyville: Sex, Death and the Gods* 2011, *In Real Life* 2013; Producer, Cross Street Films.

Political career: *House of Lords:* Raised to the peerage as Baroness Kidron, of Angel in the London Borough of Islington 2012. Member: Communications 2015-19, Democracy and Digital Technologies 2019-. *Other:* Member, Children's Commissioner for England's Taskforce for Growing Up Digital 2016-17; Commissioner, Arts Council England and Durham University Commission on Creativity and Education 2018-.

Political interests: Justice, arts, education, media, children, young people, internet; China, India, Liberia, Somalia, USA.

Other: Commissioner, UNESCO Broadband Commission for Sustainable Development 2016-; Founder, IntoFilm (previously Film Club) 2007-19; Co-founder and Vice-chair, Film Club Educational Charity; Trustee, UK Film Council 2008-10; Governor, British Film Institute 2010-12; Council member, Institute of Contemporary Art 2011-16; Trustee, Paul Hamlyn Foundation 2012-15; President, Voluntary Arts 2013-19; Patron: Legal Aid Worldwide 2014-, Artangel; Member: Royal Foundation Taskforce for the Prevention of Cyberbullying 2016-, WeProtect Child Dignity Alliance Technical Working Group 2017-, Council for Extended Intelligence 2018-; Directors' Guild of America 1990-; Directors UK; Academy of Motion Picture Sciences 1992-; Fellow, National Film and Television School; Honorary doctorate, Kingston University 2010; OBE 2012.

The Baroness Kidron OBE, House of Lords, London SW1A 0PW
Tel: 020 7219 5353 *Email:* kidronb@parliament.uk
Email: nicola@crosstreefilms.com

CROSSBENCH

KILCLOONEY, LORD

KILCLOONEY (Life Baron), John David Taylor; cr. 2001. Born 24 December 1937; Son of late George David Taylor, architect, and Georgina Taylor, née Baird; Married Mary Todd 1970 (1 son 5 daughters).

Education: Royal School, Armagh; Queen's University, Belfast (BSc applied science and technology 1950); French.

Non-political career: Company director; Chairman: West Ulster Estates Ltd 1965-, Alpha Newspaper Group 1977-, Sovereign Properties (NI) Ltd 1981-, Midland Tribune Ltd 2002-, Alpha Publications (Ireland) Ltd 2002-, Northern Media Group Ltd 2006-14, Northern Newspapers Ltd, Bramley Apples Restaurant Ltd.

Political career: *House of Commons:* MP (UUP) for Strangford 1983-2001; Spokesperson for: Trade and Industry 1992-97, Foreign and Commonwealth Affairs 1997-2001. *House of Lords:* Raised to the peerage as Baron Kilclooney, of Armagh in the County of Armagh 2001. *Other:* MP for South Tyrone, Northern Ireland Parliament 1965-73: Parliamentary Secretary, Ministry of Home Affairs 1969-70, Minister of State, Home Affairs 1970-72, Member for: Fermanagh and South Tyrone, Northern Ireland Assembly 1973-75, North Down, Northern Ireland Constitutional Convention 1976-77, North Down, Northern Ireland Assembly 1982-86; European Parliament: MEP for Northern Ireland 1979-89; Member Northern Ireland Forum for Political Dialogue 1996-98; Northern Ireland Assembly: MLA for Strangford 1998-2007. Chair: Queen's University Conservative and Unionist Association 1959-60, Ulster Young Unionist Council 1961-62; Ulster Unionist Party: Hon. Secretary 1994-96, Deputy Leader 1995-2001. Governor, Royal School, Armagh City 1973-; Castlereagh Borough Council: Councillor 1989-97, Leader, UUP 1989-94; Member, Northern Ireland Policing Board 2001-06.

Political interests: Irish politics, European Union, regional policy, agriculture; Asia, Cyprus, Gibraltar, Ireland, Latin America, Middle East, Taiwan, Turkey.

Other: Member: Council of Europe Assembly 1997-2005, Western European Union 1997-2011; Member: Charles Sheils Charity Homes Board 1973-, Royal Horticultural Society; Elder, Presbyterian Church in Ireland; Member, Loyal Orange Institution of Ireland; Tear Fund; AMICEI; AMInstHE; Eastern Mediterranean University, Famagusta (PhD international relations 1999); PC (Northern Ireland) 1970. Farmers Club, County Club, Armagh; City of Armagh Cricket Club.

Publications: Ulster – The Economic Facts (1974).

Recreations: Antiques, Irish art, travelling, horticulture.

Rt Hon the Lord Kilclooney, House of Lords, London SW1A 0PW
Tel: 020 7219 6443
Tel: 020 7931 7211 *Email:* johnkilclooney@hotmail.co.uk *Twitter:* @KilclooneyJohn

LABOUR

KING OF BOW, BARONESS

KING OF BOW (Life Baroness), Oona Tamsyn King; cr 2011. Born 22 October 1967; Daughter of Preston King, professor of political science, and Hazel King, teacher; Married Tiberio Santomarco 1994 (1 adopted son 2 adopted daughters 1 son).

Education: Haverstock Comprehensive Secondary School, London; York University (BA politics 1990); Berkeley-University of California, USA (Scholarship); French, Italian.

Non-political career: Researcher, Socialist Group, European Parliament 1990; Political assistant to Glyn Ford MEP 1991-93; John Smith's Labour Party leadership campaign team 1992; Freelance speech-writer/ghost writer 1993-94; Political assistant to Glenys Kinnock MEP 1994-95; Trade union organiser, GMB Southern Region 1995-97; Diversity executive, Channel 4 2009-16; Director of diversity, YouTube 2016-. Southern region equality officer, GMB.

Political career: *House of Commons:* MP (Labour) for Bethnal Green and Bow 1997-2005. Contested Bethnal Green and Bow 2005 general election; PPS to: Stephen Timms as Minister of State, Department of Trade and Industry 2002-03, Patricia Hewitt as Secretary of State for Trade and Industry 2003-05; Senior Policy Adviser on equalities to Gordon Brown as Prime Minister 2007-09. Member: International Development 1997-2001, Transport, Local Government and the Regions 2001-02, Transport, Local Government and the Regions (Urban Affairs Sub-Committee) 2001-02. Member, Labour Party Departmental Committees for: Education and Employment 1997-99, Home Affairs 1997-2001. *House of Lords:* Raised to the peerage as Baroness King of Bow, of Bow in the London Borough of Tower Hamlets 2011. Opposition Whip 2014-15; Opposition Spokesperson for: Culture, Media and Sport 2015, Equalities 2015; On leave of absence November 2016-. Member: Adoption Legislation 2012-13, Olympic and Paralympic Legacy 2013-14. *Other:* Joint vice-chair, London Regional Group of Labour MPs 1997-2005; Chair, Labour Campaign for Electoral Reform; Contested Labour Party London Mayor candidacy 2010. Governor, British Film Institute.

Political interests: Race relations, employment, education, health, development, equal opportunities, housing, European affairs, electoral reform, poverty; Bangladesh, France, Great Lakes Region, Italy, Nicaragua, Rwanda, South Africa, USA.

Other: Member: Oxfam, Amnesty International, Jewish Council for Racial Equality, One World Action, Fabian Society, Unicef; Member, 1990 Trust, Toynbee Hall; Vice-chair, British Council 1999-; Patron, Dane Ford Trust; Vice-chair, British Council 2001-; Patron: Positive Care Link, Council for Education in the World, Riverside Gallery; Associate fellow, Chatham House; Chair: Institute for Community Cohesion, Rich Mix Cultural Foundation; Hon. degree, Sussex University 2013.

Publications: Oona King Diaries (Bloomsbury, 2007).

Recreations: Ice skating, cycling, pilates, cinema, history.

The Baroness King of Bow, House of Lords, London SW1A 0PW
Tel: 020 7219 5353 *Email:* miahr@parliament.uk *Twitter:* @oona_king

CONSERVATIVE

KING OF BRIDGWATER, LORD

KING OF BRIDGWATER (Life Baron), Thomas Jeremy King; cr. 2001. Born 13 June 1933; Son of John H King, JP; Married Jane Tilney 1960 (1 son 1 daughter).

Education: Rugby School; Emmanuel College, Cambridge (MA classics, archaeology and anthropology 1956).

Non-political career: E. S. and A. Robinson Ltd, Bristol 1956-69: Divisional General Manager 1964-69; Chair, Sale, Tilney & Co Ltd industrial holding company 1971-79; Non-executive director, Electra Investment Trust 1992-2008; London International Exhibition Centre plc: Chair 1994-2008, Non-executive director 2008-. Army national service 1952-53; Service in East Africa; TA 1953-56.

Political career: *House of Commons:* MP (Conservative) for Bridgwater 3 March 1970 by-election to 2001; PPS to Christopher Chataway: as Minister of Posts and Telecommunications 1970-72, as Minister for Industrial Development 1972-74; Opposition Spokesperson for: Industry 1975-76, Energy 1976-79; Minister for Local Government and Environmental Services 1979-83; Secretary of State for: Environment January-June 1983, Transport June-October 1983, Employment 1983-85, Northern Ireland 1985-89, Defence

1989-92; Chair, Intelligence and Security Committee 1994-2001. *House of Lords:* Raised to the peerage as Baron King of Bridgwater, of Bridgwater in the County of Somerset 2001. Trade Envoy to Saudi Arabia 2014-19. Member: Review of the BBC Charter 2005-06, Communications 2007-10, Joint Committee on the Draft Enhanced Terrorism Prevention and Investigation Measures Bill 2012-13, Inquiries Act 2005 2013-14, Joint Committee on the National Security Strategy 2017-.

Other: PC 1979; CH 1992.

Recreations: Cricket, skiing.

Rt Hon the Lord King of Bridgwater CH, House of Lords, London SW1A 0PW
Tel: 020 7219 4467

CROSSBENCH

KING OF LOTHBURY, LORD

KING OF LOTHBURY (Life Baron), Mervyn Allister; cr. 2013. Born 30 March 1948; Son of Eric King and Kathleen Passingham; Married Barbara Melander.

Education: Wolverhampton Grammar School; King's College, Cambridge (BA 1969); Harvard University (Kennedy Scholar 1971-72); French.

Non-political career: Lecturer, Faculty of Economics, Cambridge 1976-77; Esmée Fairbairn professor of investment, Birmingham University 1977-84; Managing editor, Review of Economic Studies 1978-83; Associate editor, Journal of Public Economics 1982-98; Professor of economics, London School of Economics 1984-95; Associate editor, American Economic Review 1985-88; Bank of England: Non-executive director 1990-91, Chief economist and executive director 1991-98, Deputy Governor 1998-2003, Governor 2003-13.

Political career: *House of Lords:* Raised to the peerage as Baron King of Lothbury, of Lothbury in the City of London 2013. *Other:* Trustee, National Gallery 2005-09, 2014-18.

Other: Member, Meade Committee 1975-78; Council and executive, Royal Economic Society 1981-86, 1992-97; Visiting professor of economics: Harvard University 1982-83, 1990, Massachusetts Institute of Technology 1983-84; Board member, Securities Association 1987-89; London School of Economics: Co-director, Financial Markets Group 1987-91, Visiting professor of economics 1996-2015, School professor of economics 2015-; Member, City Capital Markets Committee 1989-91; Trustee, Kennedy Memorial Trust 1990-2000; President, European Economic Association 1993; Member, Group of Thirty 1997-; Monetary Policy Committee: Founder member 1997, Chair 2003-13; President, Institute for Fiscal Studies 1999-2003; Member, Advisory Council, London Symphony Orchestra 2001-; Chair, Interim Financial Policy Committee 2011-13; Vice-chair, European Systematic Risk Board 2011-13; Visiting professor of economics, New York University 2014-; President, Chance to Shine; Fellow, St John's College, Cambridge 1972-77; Honorary fellow, King's College, Cambridge; Fellow, Econometric Society 1982; FBA; Honorary degree: London Guildhall 2001, Birmingham University 2002, City University, London 2002, London School of Economics 2003, Wolverhampton University 2003, Edinburgh University 2005, Helsinki Univeristy 2006; Honorary LLD, Cambridge Univeristy 2006, Honorary degree: Worcestershire University 2008, Kent University 2012, Abertay University 2013; GBE 2011; KG 2014. Athenæum, Brook's Club, Garrick Club; MCC; AELTC Club; Honorary President, Ekenäs Cricket Club, Finland; President, Worcestershire County Cricket Club 2015-17.

Publications: Public Policy and the Corporation (1977); The British Tax System (1978); The Taxation of Income from Capital (1984); The End of Alchemy (2016); Co-author, Radical Uncertainty (2020).

The Lord King of Lothbury KG GBE, House of Lords, London SW1A 0PW
Tel: 020 7219 5353
Tel: 020 7099 0450 *Email:* office@mervynking.com

LABOUR

KINGSMILL, BARONESS

KINGSMILL (Life Baroness), Denise Patricia Byrne Kingsmill; cr 2006. Born 24 April 1947; Daughter of Patrick Henry and Hester Jean Byrne; Married David Kingsmill 1970 (divorced 2002) (2 children); married Richard Wheatly 2006.

Education: Croesy Ceiliog Grammar School, Wales; Girton College, Cambridge (BA economics and anthropology 1968); Solicitor 1980.

Non-political career: ICI, International Wool Secretariat 1968-75; Robin Thompson & Partners 1979-82; Russell Jones and Walker 1982-85; Denise Kingsmill & Co 1985-90; Partner, D J Freeman 1990-93; Consultant, Denton Hall 1994-2000; Non-executive director, British Airways 2004-10; Chair, advisory forum, Laing O'Rourke 2004-06; Senior adviser, Royal Bank of Scotland 2005-08; Non-executive director: E.ON AG, Betfair plc 2011-12, APR Energy plc; Member, European Advisory Council, Microsoft 2007-12; Non-executive director, Korn/Ferry International 2009-12; Independent non-executive director, International Consolidated Airlines Group SA; Columnist, *Management Today*; Chair, European Advisory Board.

Political career: *House of Lords:* Raised to the peerage as Baroness Kingsmill, of Holland Park in the Royal Borough of Kensington and Chelsea 2006. Co-opted Member, European Union Sub-committee E (Law and Institutions) 2006-09; Member: Merits of Statutory Instruments 2007-09, Economic Affairs 2008-13, 2017-, EU Financial Affairs Sub-committee 2015-16, Economic Affairs Finance Bill Sub-committee 2016-17. *Other:* Deputy chair, Monopolies and Mergers/Competition Commission 1997-2003.

Political interests: International business, women; Australia, China, India, New Zealand, USA.

Other: Member, UK delegation, NATO Parliamentary Assembly 2020-; Member, advisory board, IESE Business School; Theatre Royal Stratford East: Board Member 2018-, Chair, Development Board 2018-; Pro-Chancellor, Brunel University 2002-06; Fellow, University of Wales 2000; Hon. LLD: Brunel University 2001, Stirling University 2003, Cranfield University 2007; CBE 2000.

Recreations: Fly-fishing, walking.

The Baroness Kingsmill CBE, House of Lords, London SW1A 0PW
Tel: 020 7219 4537 *Email:* kingsmilldp@parliament.uk
Tel: 020 7221 1700 *Email:* tess@dkingsmill.com *Twitter:* @denisekingsmill

LABOUR

KINNOCK, LORD

KINNOCK (Life Baron), Neil Gordon Kinnock; cr 2005. Born 28 March 1942; Son of late Gordon H Kinnock, steelworker and coalminer, and Mary, née Howells, district nurse; Married Glenys Elizabeth Parry 1967 (MEP for South East Wales 1994-99 and Wales region 1999-2009, now Baroness Kinnock of Holyhead (qv)) (1 son, Stephen Kinnock (qv) MP for Aberavon, 1 daughter).

Education: Lewis School, Pengam; University College of Wales, Cardiff (BA industrial relations and history 1966).

Non-political career: University College of Wales, Cardiff: President: Socialist Society 1963-65, Students' Union 1965-66; Tutor and organiser, Workers' Educational Association 1966-70; European Commission: Commissioner 1995-2004: Commissioner for Transport 1995-99, Vice-president for Administrative Reform, Internal Audit, Personnel, Language Services and Logistics 1999-2004. Member, Transport and General Workers Union 1966-.

Political career: *House of Commons:* MP (Labour) for Bedwellty 1970-83, for Islwyn 1983-95; PPS to Michael Foot as Secretary of State for Employment 1974-75; Principal Opposition Spokesperson for Education 1979-83; Leader of the Opposition 1983-92. *House of Lords:* Raised to the peerage as Baron Kinnock, of Bedwellty in the County of Gwent 2005. *Other:* Labour Party: NEC: Member 1978-94, Chair 1987-88; Leader 1983-92. Member, BBC Advisory Council 1976-79; Chair, British Council 2004-09.

Other: President of the Council (Chancellor), Cardiff University 1998-2009; PC 1983.

Publications: Making Our Way – Investing in Britain's Future (1986); Thorns and Roses (1992).

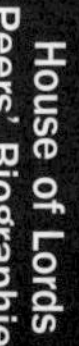

Recreations: Opera, male choral music, theatre, rugby, soccer, cricket, grandchildren.

Rt Hon the Lord Kinnock, House of Lords, London SW1A 0PW
Tel: 020 7219 8304 *Email:* kinnockn@parliament.uk

LABOUR

KINNOCK OF HOLYHEAD, BARONESS

KINNOCK OF HOLYHEAD (Life Baroness); Glenys Elizabeth Kinnock; cr 2009. Born 7 July 1944; Daughter of Cyril Parry, railway signalman, and Elizabeth Parry; Married Neil Kinnock 1967 (MP for Bedwellty 1970-83 and Islwyn 1983-95, Labour Party Leader 1983-92, European Commissioner 1995-2004, now Lord Kinnock (qv)) (1 son, Stephen Kinnock (qv) MP for Aberavon, 1 daughter).

Education: Holyhead Comprehensive School, Anglesey; University College of Wales, Cardiff (Degree history and education 1964; DipEd 1965); Welsh.

Non-political career: Primary and secondary school teacher 1965-93. Member: GMB, National Union of Teachers.

Political career: *House of Lords:* Raised to the peerage as Baroness Kinnock of Holyhead, of Holyhead in the County of Ynys Môn 2009. Minister of State and Government Spokesperson, Foreign and Commonwealth Office 2009-10: Minister for Europe 2009, Minister for Africa and UN 2009-10; Opposition Spokesperson for: Foreign and Commonwealth Office 2011, International Development 2011-12. Member, Sexual Violence in Conflict 2015-16. *Other:* European Parliament: MEP for: South East Wales 1994-99, Wales 1999-2009, Labour Spokesperson for International Development, Co-President, ACP-EU Joint Parliamentary Assembly. Co-president, Labour Campaign for International Development.

Political interests: International development, regions, gender issues, children's rights, education; African countries, Burma, Sudan, South Sudan.

Other: Board member, Burma Campaign UK -2017; Council member, Overseas Development Institute -2017; Patron: Saferworld, Womankind, Waging Peace; Various charities supported; Honorary Fellow: University of Wales, Newport, University of Wales, Bangor; Honorary Doctorate: Thames Valley University, Brunel University, Kingston University.

Publications: Voices for One World (Fontana, 1988); Eritrea – Images of War and Peace (Chatto and Windus, 1988); Namibia: Birth of a Nation (Quartet, 1990); By Faith and Daring (Virago, 1993); Changing States (Heinemann, 1996); Could do Better (1996); Zimbabwe on the Brink (Centurion, 2003).

Recreations: Grandchildren, cooking, theatre, cinema, reading.

The Baroness Kinnock of Holyhead, House of Lords, London SW1A 0PW
Tel: 020 7219 1297 *Email:* kinnockg@parliament.uk *Twitter:* @GlenysKinnock

NON-AFFILIATED

KINNOULL, EARL OF

Principal Deputy Chairman of Committees; Chair, Select Committee on European Union

KINNOULL (16th Earl of, S), Charles William Harley Hay; cr. 1633; Viscount Dupplin and Lord Hay of Kinfauns, 1627, 1633, 1697; Baron Hay (GB), 1711. Born 20 December 1962; Son of 15th Earl; Married Clare (1 son 3 daughters).

Education: Eton College; Christ Church, Oxford; City University (Diploma law); Inns of Court School of Law; French, German.

Non-political career: Associate, Credit Suisse First Boston 1985-88; Called to the Bar, Middle Temple 1990; Underwriter, Roberts & Hiscox/Hiscox Syndicates Ltd 1990-95; Hiscox Insurance Company: Managing director, Europe 1995-2000, Chief executive officer 2009-12; Director of mergers and acquisitions, Hiscox Ltd 2000-14; Company secretary, Hiscox Group 2009-12.

Political career: *House of Lords:* Elected hereditary peer 2015-; Principal Deputy Chairman of Committees 2019-. Member: Social Mobility 2015-16, Trade Union and Party Funding 2016, European Union 2016-19, EU Justice Sub-committee 2016-19; Chair, European Union 2019-.

Other: Left Crossbench September 2019, now sits as non-affiliated. DL, Perth and Kinross 2018-.

Political interests: Science and technology, insurance and financial services, art and the art market, red squirrels, rural issues, Scotland, constitutional issues, Post Office; Austria, Bermuda.

Other: Member: Association of Bermuda Insurers and Reinsurers 2009-12, Reinsurance Association of America 2009-12; President, Royal Caledonian Charities Trust 2013-; Chair, Red Squirrel Survival Trust 2013-; Director, Horsecross Arts Ltd 2014-; Chair, Culture Perth & Kinross; Freedom, City of London 2008. Whites, Turf Club, Pratt's, Royal Perth, Jockey Club (Vienna); MCC.

Recreations: Real tennis, lawn tennis, philately, skiing.

The Earl of Kinnoull, House of Lords, London SW1A 0PW
Tel: 020 7219 3000 *Email:* kinnoull@parliament.uk

CONSERVATIVE

KIRKHAM, LORD

KIRKHAM (Life Baron), Graham Kirkham; cr. 1999. Born 14 December 1944; Son of Tom and Elsie Kirkham; Married Pauline Fisher 1965 (1 son 1 daughter).

Education: Maltby Grammar School.

Non-political career: Founder, DFS Furniture Company Ltd 1969-2010: Director, Iceland Frozen Foods 2012-14.

Political career: *House of Lords:* Raised to the peerage as Baron Kirkham, of Old Cantley in the County of South Yorkshire 1999. Member: Administration and Works 2003-05, Leader's Group on Governance 2015. *Other:* Chairman, Conservative Party Treasurers 1997.

Political interests: Business, children.

Other: Chair of trustees, Duke of Edinburgh's Award Scheme; Deputy patron, Outward Bound Trust; Deputy president, Animal Health Trust; Honorary Liveryman Worshipful Company of Furniture Makers 2007; Hon. Member, Emmanuel College, Cambridge 1995; Hon. Doctorate, Bradford University 1997; Kt 1995; CVO 2001.

The Lord Kirkham CVO, House of Lords, London SW1A 0PW
Tel: 020 7219 5353
Black Diamond Investments LP, Redhouse Interchange, Adwick-le-Street, Doncaster DN6 7FE
Tel: 01302 337215 *Email:* lord.kirkham@bdinvestments.co.uk

CONSERVATIVE

KIRKHOPE OF HARROGATE, LORD

KIRKHOPE OF HARROGATE (Life Baron), Timothy John Robert Kirkhope; cr 2016. Born 29 April 1945; Son of late John Kirkhope and late Dorothy Kirkhope; Married Caroline Maling 1969 (4 sons).

Education: Royal Grammar School, Newcastle; College of Law, Guildford (1965, 1970).

Non-political career: Solicitor 1973-: Principal, Timothy J R Kirkhope Solicitors 1973-77, 1997-, Partner, Wilkinson Maughan Solicitors 1977-87; Director, Newcastle International Airport 1983-86; Business consultant on central and eastern Europe 1997-99; Timothy Kirkhope Consultancy 1997-; Director, Bournemouth and West Hampshire Water Company plc 1999-2011.

Political career: *House of Commons:* MP for Leeds North East 1987-97; Assistant Government Whip 1990-92; Government Whip: Lord Commissioner of HM Treasury 1992-95, Vice-Chamberlain of HM Household 1995; Parliamentary Under-Secretary of State, Home Office 1995-97. *House of Lords:* Raised to the peerage as Baron Kirkhope of Harrogate, of Harrogate in the County of North Yorkshire 2016. Member: EU Home Affairs Sub-committee 2017-20, Sentencing (Pre-consolidation Amendments) Bill 2019, EU Security and Justice Sub-committee 2020-. *Other:* MEP for Yorkshire and the Humber 1999-2016: Conservative Spokesperson on Citizens' Freedoms and Rights, Justice and Home Affairs 1999-2009, Chief Whip 1999-2001, Member, Convention on the Future of Europe 2002-04, Leader, UK Conservative Party delegation in European Parliament 2004-07, 2008-10; Vice-President, EPP-ED Group 2007-08; ECR Group: Deputy Chair 2009-11, Interim First Chair 2009; ECR

Spokesperson on Justice and Home Affairs 2009-14, 2014-16. Officer, Young Conservatives at Local and Northern Regional level 1965-73; Treasurer, Hexham Association 1982-85; Member, Conservative Party Board 2005-07, 2008-10. Member: Northumberland County Council 1981-85, Northern Regional Health Authority 1982-86; Founder member, Mental Health Act commission 1983-86; Governor, Newcastle Royal Grammar School 1989-99.

Political interests: Defence, home affairs, environment, broadcasting, health, aviation, Trans-atlantic relations, immigration; Germany, United States.

Other: Vice-chair, Governing Bodies Association for Independent Schools 1990-98; Member: Fountain Society (for restoration of water features), Bentley Drivers Club, Porsche Owners Club; Trustee: Biwater Retirement and Security Scheme Pension Trust 2011-, Yorkshire Conservative Trust; Member: Institute of Directors, The Law Society; Dunstanburgh Castle Golf Club Charitable Events. Northern Counties Club, Newcastle-upon-Tyne; Dunstanburgh Castle Golf Club Northumberland, Collingham Lawn Tennis Club.

Recreations: Tennis, swimming, flying, golf, holds a private pilot's licence.

The Lord Kirkhope of Harrogate, House of Lords, London SW1A 0PW
Tel: 020 7219 3107
Biwater House, Dorking RH4 1TZ *Email:* timothy@kirkhope.org.uk
Website: www.kirkhope.org.uk *Twitter:* @LordKirkhope

LABOUR/ CO-OPERATIVE

KNIGHT OF WEYMOUTH, LORD

KNIGHT OF WEYMOUTH (Life Baron), James Philip Knight; cr 2010. Born 6 March 1965; Son of Philip John Knight, accountant, and Hilary Jean Howlett, neé Harper, craftswoman; Married Anna Wheatley 1989 (separated) (1 daughter 1 son).

Education: Eltham College, London; Fitzwilliam College, Cambridge (BA geography, social and political sciences 1987); French.

Non-political career: Works Theatre Co-operative 1986-88; Manager, Central Studio Basingstoke 1988-90; Director, West Wiltshire Arts Centre Ltd 1990-91; Dentons Directories Ltd 1991-2001: Sales Executive 1991-96, General Manager 1997-98, Director 1998-2000, Production Manager 2000-01; Board Member, Arsenal Fanshare Society Ltd 2010-13; Chief Education and External Officer, TES Global 2015-; Founder and Chair, XRapid 2015-. Member: Unite 1995-2010, GMB 2001-.

Political career: *House of Commons:* Contested South Dorset 1997 general election. MP (Lab/ Co-op) for South Dorset 2001-10. Contested South Dorset 2010 general election; PPS at Department of Health 2003-05: to Rosie Winterton as Minister of State 2003-04, Team PPS 2004-05; Parliamentary Under-Secretary of State, Department for Environment, Food and Rural Affairs 2005-06; Minister of State: Department for Education and Skills/Children, Schools and Families (Schools and Learners) 2006-09, Department for Work and Pensions 2009-10; Minister for the South West 2009-10. Member, Defence 2001-03. *House of Lords:* Raised to the peerage as Baron Knight of Weymouth, of Weymouth in the County of Dorset 2010. Opposition Spokesperson for: Work and Pensions 2010-11, Environment, Food and Rural Affairs 2011-14. Member: Regenerating Seaside Towns and Communities 2018-19, Democracy and Digital Technologies 2019-, National Plan for Sport and Recreation 2020-. *Other:* Contested South West region 1999 European Parliament election. Various posts local constituency party 1990-. Frome Town Council: Councillor 1993-2001, Mayor 1998-2001; Mendip District Council: Councillor 1997-2001, Deputy leader 1999-2001, Labour group leader 1999-2001; Vice-President, Local Government Association 2010-13.

Political interests: Rural and coastal affairs, digital policy, education.

Other: Nominet Trust: Deputy Chair, Chair -2015; Chair and trustee, Tinder Foundation -2017; Director: Whole Education Ltd, Centre of Acceleration of Social Technology Ltd; Hon. Fellow, Institute of Employability Professionals; Visiting Professor, Institute of Education, University of London; Campaigner of the Year, *House Magazine* 2006; PC 2008.

Recreations: Football, tennis, cooking.

Rt Hon the Lord Knight of Weymouth, House of Lords, London SW1A 0PW
Tel: 020 7219 3000 *Email:* knightja@parliament.uk
51 Manwood Road, London SE4 1AB *Twitter:* @LordJimKnight

LIBERAL DEMOCRAT

KRAMER, BARONESS

Liberal Democrat Lords Spokesperson for Treasury

KRAMER (Life Baroness), Susan Veronica Kramer; cr 2010. Born 21 July 1950; Daughter of Harry Victor (Bill) Richards and Elisabeth Richards; Married John Kramer 1972 (died 2006) (1 daughter 1 son).

Education: St Paul's Girls' School, London; St Hilda's College, Oxford (BA philosophy, politics and economics 1972, MA); Illinois University, USA (MBA business/finance 1982).

Non-political career: Staff associate, National Academy of Engineering 1972-73; Second vice-president, Continental Bank, USA 1982-88; Vice-president, corporate finance, Citibank/ Citicorp, USA 1988-92; Chief operating officer, Future Water International 1992-95; Partner, Kramer and Associates 1995-99; Board member, CAIB Infrastructure Project Advisers 1997-99; Director, Infrastructure Capital Partners Ltd 1999-2006; Board member, Transport for London 2000-05; Director, Speciality Scanners plc 2001-11.

Political career: *House of Commons:* Contested Dulwich and West Norwood 1997 general election. MP (Liberal Democrat) for Richmond Park 2005-10. Contested Richmond Park 2010 general election; Liberal Democrat: Spokesperson for the Treasury 2005-06, Shadow Secretary of State for: International Development 2006, Trade and Industry 2006-07, Transport 2007, Shadow Minister for the Cabinet Office and Shadow Chancellor of the Duchy of Lancaster 2007-09. Member, Treasury 2005-06. *House of Lords:* Raised to the peerage as Baroness Kramer, of Richmond Park in the London Borough of Richmond upon Thames 2010. Minister of State and Government Spokesperson, Department for Transport 2013-15; Liberal Democrat: Lords Spokesperson for Economy/Treasury 2015-19, Shadow Chancellor of the Exchequer 2015-17, Spokesperson for Treasury 2017-. Member: Economic Affairs Finance Bill Sub-Committee 2011, 2012-13, 2018-, Consumer Insurance (Disclosure and Representations) Bill 2011-12, Small- and Medium-Sized Enterprises 2012-13, Parliamentary Commission on Banking Standards 2012-13, EU Internal Market Sub-committee 2020, EU Goods Sub-committee 2020-. Chair, Liberal Democrat Parliamentary Party Committee on Treasury 2012-15. *Other:* Contested London region 1999 European Parliament election and London mayoral 2000 election. Liberal Democrats: Member: Women executive 1997-2000, London Region executive 1997-2003, Federal executive 2001-04, Chair, Twickenham and Richmond Liberal Democrats 2001-02.

Political interests: Environment, finance, transport; Eastern Europe, USA.

Other: President, Oxford Union Trinity term 1971; Advisory board member, Centre for Reform 2001-04; Board member, Institute for Government; Holly Lodge, Richmond Park Charitable Trust, Orange Tree Theatre; PC 2014. National Liberal Club.

Publications: Orange Book chapter 'Harnessing the Markets to Achieve Environmental Goals' (Profile Books, 2004).

Recreations: Theatre, reading, walking.

Rt Hon the Baroness Kramer, House of Lords, London SW1A 0PW
Tel: 020 7219 1492 *Email:* kramers@parliament.uk *Twitter:* @BaronessKramer

CROSSBENCH

KREBS, LORD

Chair, Select Committee on Food, Poverty, Health and the Environment

KREBS (Life Baron), John Richard Krebs; cr 2007. Born 11 April 1945; Son of Sir Hans Adolf Krebs FRCP FRS, Nobel Prize winning scientist, and Margaret Cicely Krebs; Married Katharine Fullerton 1968 (divorced 2012) (2 daughters); married Sarah Margaret Phibbs 2013.

Education: City of Oxford High School; Pembroke College, Oxford (BA zoology 1966, MA; DPhil 1970); German.

Non-political career: Oxford University: Departmental demonstrator in ornithology, Edward Grey Institute 1969-70, Research officer, Animal Behaviour Research Group 1975-76, Zoology lecturer, Edward Grey Institute 1976-88, Fellow, Wolfson College 1976-81, Pembroke College: EP Abraham Fellow 1981-88, Official Fellow 1988-2005; Royal Society Research Professor 1988-2005: Seconded as Chief executive, National Environment Research Council 1994-99; Principal, Jesus College 2005-15, Emeritus Professor of Zoology 2015-; Assistant professor of animal resource ecology, University of British Columbia, Canada 1970-73; Zoology lecturer, University College of North Wales, Bangor 1973-75; Chair, Food Standards Agency 2000-05.

Political career: *House of Lords:* Raised to the peerage as Baron Krebs, of Wytham in the County of Oxfordshire 2007. Board member, Parliamentary Office of Science and Technology (POST) -2014. Science and Technology: Member 2007, 2008-10, Chair 2010-14, Co-opted member 2015-16; Chair, Science and Technology Sub-committee I (Nanotechnologies and food) 2008-10; Member, Science and Technology Sub-committees: II (Genomic Medicine) 2008-09, I 2012-13; Member, EU Energy and Environment Sub-Committee 2015-19; Chair, Food, Poverty, Health and the Environment 2019-; Member, National Plan for Sport and Recreation 2020-. *Other:* Chair, Adaptation Sub-Committee 2009-17; Member, Committee on Climate Change 2010-17.

Political interests: Science, environment, food, education.

Other: Trustee and Deputy Chair, Nuffield Foundation 2013-; President, Campden BRI 2010-14; Chair, Wellcome Trust Advisory Group on Sustaining Health 2014-19; Scientific Adviser to: Marks and Spencer plc 2015-, Ajinomoto Co Inc 2015-. Tesco plc 2017-19; FRS 1984; FMedSci 2004; Foreign member: US National Academy of Science, American Philosophical Society, American Academy of Arts and Science; German National Academy of Sciences, Leopoldina; 14 honorary fellowships; 17 honorary doctorates; Numerous awards, including: Linnean Society Bicentenary Medal 1983, Frink medal, Zoological Society 1997, Harben Gold Medal, Royal Institute of Public Health 2006; Kt 1999.

Publications: 250-plus books and articles on ecology and animal behaviour.

Recreations: Running, tennis, walking, food including cooking, music, gardening, family.

Professor the Lord Krebs, House of Lords, London SW1A 0PW
Tel: 020 7219 5353 *Email:* krebsj@parliament.uk
Zoology Research and Administration Building, 11a Mansfield Rd, Oxford OX1 3SZ
Email: john.krebs@zoo.ox.ac.uk

CROSSBENCH

LAMING, LORD

Chair, Select Committee on Services

LAMING (Life Baron), (William) Herbert Laming; cr. 1998. Born 19 July 1936; Son of William and Lillian Laming; Married Aileen Pollard 1962 (died 2010).

Education: Durham University (Diploma applied social sciences 1960); Rainer House (probation training 1960-61); London School of Economics (mental health course 1964-65).

Non-political career: Nottingham Probation Service: Probation officer 1961-66, Senior probation officer 1966-68; Assistant chief probation Officer, Nottingham City and County Probation Service 1968-71; Hertfordshire County Council Social Services: Deputy Director 1971-75, Director 1975-91; Chair, Independent Inquiry for Somerset Health Authority 1989; Chief Inspector, Social Services Inspectorate, Department of Health 1991-98; Chair: Review of Management of the Prison Service 1999-2000, Independent Statutory Inquiry following the murder of Victoria Climbié 2001-03, Review of Protection of Children in England 2010, In Care, Out of Trouble 2016. Royal Navy 1954-56.

Political career: *House of Lords:* Raised to the peerage as Baron Laming, of Tewin in the County of Hertfordshire 1998. Convener of the Crossbench Peers 2011-15; Chairman of Committees 2015-16; Member, House of Lords Commission 2016-. Member: Ecclesiastical Committee 2003-15, House 2011-16, Joint Committee on Security 2011-15; Administration and Works: Member 2011-15, Chair 2015-16; Liaison: Member 2011-15, Chair 2015-16; Procedure: Member 2011-15, Chair 2015-16; Selection: Member 2011-15, Chair 2015-16; Member: Privileges and Conduct 2011-16, Sub-committee on Leave of Absence 2011; Member, Joint Committee on the Palace of Westminster 2015-16; Chair: Refreshment 2015-16, Standing Orders (Private Bills) 2015-16, Hybrid Instruments 2015-16, Privileges and Conduct 2015-16; Chair, Services 2016-. *Other:* DL, Hertfordshire 1999-; Vice-President, Local Government Association 2012-15.

Political interests: Public services; China, Europe.

Other: President, Association of Directors of Social Services 1982-83; President and Patron of social care charities; Freedom, City of London 1996; Five honorary doctorates; CBE 1985; Kt 1996; PC 2014.

Publications: Lessons from America: the balance of services in social care (1985).

Rt Hon the Lord Laming CBE DL, House of Lords, London SW1A 0PW
Tel: 020 7219 8907 *Email:* lamingh@parliament.uk

CONSERVATIVE

LAMONT OF LERWICK, LORD

LAMONT OF LERWICK (Life Baron), Norman Stewart Hughson Lamont; cr. 1998. Born 8 May 1942; Son of late Daniel Lamont and Helen Irene Lamont; Married Rosemary White 1971 (divorced) (1 son 1 daughter).

Education: Loretto School, Musselburgh (Scholar); Fitzwilliam College, Cambridge (BA economics 1965) (Union President 1964).

Non-political career: NM Rothschild and Sons Ltd 1968-79, 1993-95; Director: Rothschild Asset Management 1978-79, NM Rothschild and Sons 1993-95; Consultant to Monsanto Corporation 1994-99; Director, Balli Group plc 1995-2012; Adviser to Romanian Government 1995-97; Chair, East European Food Fund 1995-2006; Director: Cie International de Participations Bancaires et Financieres 1999-, Banca Commerciala Robank 2000-05; President, British Romanian Chamber of Commerce 2002-16; Director, Scottish Re 2002-07; Chair, British Iranian Chamber of Commerce 2004-; Director: RAB Capital 2004-11, Jupiter Second Split 2005-; Chair, Jupiter Adria 2006-; Consultant to Western Union Company 2006-08; Chair: Advisory board, Uniastrum Bank 2006-08, Smaller Companies Dividend Trust 2008-; Director, Phorm plc.

Political career: *House of Commons:* Contested Kingston-upon-Hull East 1970 general election. MP (Conservative) for Kingston-upon-Thames 1972 by-election to 1997. Contested Harrogate and Knaresborough 1997 general election; PPS to Norman St John Stevas as Minister for the Arts 1974; Parliamentary Under-Secretary of State, Department of Energy 1979-81; Minister of State, Department of Trade and Industry 1981-85; Minister for Defence Procurement, Ministry of Defence 1985-86; HM Treasury 1986-93: Financial Secretary 1986-89, Chief Secretary 1989-90, Chancellor of the Exchequer 1990-93. *House of Lords:* Raised to the peerage as Baron Lamont of Lerwick, of Lerwick in the Shetland Islands 1998. Trade Envoy to Iran 2016-. Member: Economic Affairs 2005-08, 2015-19, Economic Affairs Taxation Sub-committee 2005-08, EU Sub-committee C: (Foreign Affairs, Defence and Development Policy) 2010-12, (External Affairs) 2012-15, European Union 2019-, EU Internal Market Sub-committee 2019-20, EU Goods Sub-committee 2020-. *Other:* Bruges Group: Vice-President 1994-2003, Co-chair 2003-07; Vice-President, Conservatives for Britain 2015-16.

Political interests: Economics, European Union, foreign affairs; Chile, Iran, Middle East, Romania.

Other: Chair, Bow Group 1971-72; Trustee, Romanian Orthodox Church in London 2005-08; Chair: Clan Lamont Society 2006-08, Le Cercle 2007-08; Member, advisory board, Iran Heritage Foundation 2008-; President, Economic Research Council 2009-; Honorary Fellow, Fitzwilliam College, Cambridge; PC 1986; Order of Faithful Service (Romania) 2010. Garrick, Beefsteak, White's Club.

Publications: Sovereign Britain (1995); In Office (1999).

Recreations: Theatre, history, ornithology.

Rt Hon the Lord Lamont of Lerwick, House of Lords, London SW1A 0PW
Tel: 020 7219 5353
Seventh Floor, 33 Cavendish Square, London W1G OPW *Tel:* 020 7306 2138
Email: beverley.gaynor@lhcap.co.uk

CONSERVATIVE

LANCASTER OF KIMBOLTON, LORD

LANCASTER OF KIMBOLTON (Life Baron), John Mark Lancaster; cr 2020. Born 12 May 1970; Son of Revd Ron Lancaster MBE and Kath Lancaster; Married Katherine Reader 1995 (divorced) (1 daughter); married Caroline Dinenage (qv) 2014 (MP for Gosport).

Education: Kimbolton School, Huntingdon; Buckingham University (BSc business studies 1991); Exeter University (MBA 1994); French, Nepali.

Non-political career: Director, Kimbolton Fireworks Ltd 1990-2005. Royal Engineers: Officer 1988-90; Lt Colonel, Colonel, Brigadier, Army Reserve 1990-.

Political career: *House of Commons:* Contested Nuneaton 2001 general election. MP for Milton Keynes North East 2005-10, for Milton Keynes North 2010-19; Opposition Whip 2006-07; Shadow Minister for International Development 2007-10; PPS to Andrew Mitchell as Secretary of State for International Development 2010-12; Government Whip 2012-15; Ministry of Defence: Parliamentary Under-Secretary of State: Defence Personnel and Veterans 2015-16, Defence Veterans, Reserves and Personnel 2016-17, Minister of State for the Armed Forces 2017-19. Member: Office of the Deputy Prime Minister 2005-06, Defence 2006, Communities and Local Government 2008-09, International Development 2009-10, Armed Forces Bill 2011. *House of Lords:* Raised to the peerage as Baron Lancaster of Kimbolton, of Kimbolton in the County of Cambridgeshire 2020. *Other:* Huntingdon District Council: Councillor 1995-99, Chair, Leisure Committee 1996-99.

Political interests: Defence, international development, commerce, international relations; East Africa, China, India, Nepal, Overseas Territories, USA.

Other: Vice-chair: British Fireworks Association 1999-2006, MK SNAP 2004-; Patron, Willen Hospice 2006-; Member, Global Advisory Board, GFG Alliance 2020-; Fellow, Institute of Royal Engineers; Member, Worshipful Company of Fanmakers; Freeman, City of London; Hon DSc, Buckingham University 2007; TD 2002; VRSM 2012; PC 2017. United and Cecil Club; House of Commons and House of Lords Cricket Club; Associate member, MCC; Non-executive director, Hampshire Cricket Club 2020-.

Publications: Contributor, Fireworks Principles and Practice (Chemical Publishing, 1999).

Recreations: Cricket, football, collecting classic British motorcycles.

Rt Hon the Lord Lancaster of Kimbolton TD, House of Lords, London SW1A 0PW
Tel: 020 7219 3000 *Twitter:* @MarkLancasterMK

CROSSBENCH

LANE-FOX OF SOHO, BARONESS

LANE-FOX OF SOHO (Life Baroness), Martha Lane Fox; cr 2013. Born 10 February 1973; Partner Chris Gorell Barnes (twin sons).

Education: Oxford High School; Westminster School; Oxford University (BA ancient and modern history).

Non-political career: Co-founder: lastminute.com 1998-2003, Lucky Voice 2005-; Founder and chair: Antigone Foundation 2007-15, Go On UK 2012-16, Doteveryone 2015-; Chair, MakieLab 2012-17.

Political career: *House of Lords:* Raised to the peerage as Baroness Lane-Fox of Soho, of Soho in the City of Westminster 2013. Member, Joint Committee on National Security Strategy 2017-; Chair, COVID-19 2020-. *Other:* Board member, Channel 4 2007-11; Government Digital Champion 2009-13; Non-executive director, Efficiency and Reform Board, Cabinet Office 2010-12; Member, advisory board, Government Digital Service 2016-.

Political interests: Entrepreneurship, government policy, open data, women, security, cyber.

Other: Non-executive director, Marks and Spencer 2007-15; Patron: AbilityNet, Reprieve, Just for Kids Law 2009-, Camfed; Non-executive director: Women's Prize for Fiction 2011-, Twitter Inc 2016-; Convenor, MoreUnited.uk 2016-; Non-executive director: Queen's Commonwealth Trust 2018-, Donmar Warehouse 2018-, Chanel 2018-; Chancellor, Open University 2014-; CBE 2013.

The Baroness Lane-Fox of Soho CBE, House of Lords, London SW1A 0PW
Tel: 020 7219 5353
Email: martha@marthalanefox.com Website: marthalanefoxblog.wordpress.com
Twitter: @Marthalanefox

CONSERVATIVE

LANG OF MONKTON, LORD

LANG OF MONKTON (Life Baron), Ian Bruce Lang; cr. 1997. Born 27 June 1940; Son of late James Lang, DSC; Married Sandra Montgomerie 1971 (2 daughters).

Education: Lathallan School, Montrose; Rugby School; Sidney Sussex College, Cambridge (BA history 1962).

Non-political career: Marsh and McLennan Companies Inc: Director 1997-2016, Chair 2011-16; Executive Adviser, Aquiline Capital LLC 2016-; Chair, Lovat Parks Ltd 2018-.

Political career: *House of Commons:* Contested Ayrshire Central 1970 and Glasgow Pollok February 1974 general elections. MP (Conservative) for Galloway 1979-83, for Galloway and Upper Nithsdale 1983-97; Assistant Government Whip 1981-83; Government Whip 1983-86; Parliamentary Under-Secretary of State, Department of Employment 1986; Scottish Office: Parliamentary Under-Secretary of State 1986-87, Minister of State 1987-90, Secretary of State for Scotland 1990-95; President of the Board of Trade and Secretary of State for Trade and Industry 1995-97. *House of Lords:* Raised to the peerage as Baron Lang of Monkton, of Merrick and the Rhinns of Kells in Dumfries and Galloway 1997. Constitution: Member 2001-05, 2012-14, Chair 2014-17; Member, Barnett Formula 2008-09; Member, Liaison 2017-. *Other:* Governor, Rugby School 1997-2007; DL, Ayrshire and Arran 1998-; Prime Minister's Advisory Committee on Business Appointments: Member 2009-14, Chairman 2009-14.

Political interests: Constitutional, economic.

Other: Member, Queen's Bodyguard for Scotland, Royal Company of Archers 1974-; President, Association for the Protection of Rural Scotland 1998-2001; Chair, Patrons of the National Galleries of Scotland 1999-2007; Officer of the Order of St John 1974; PC 1990. Pratt's Club; Prestwick Golf Club.

Publications: Blue Remembered Years (2002).

Rt Hon the Lord Lang of Monkton DL, House of Lords, London SW1A 0PW
Tel: 020 7219 5792

CONSERVATIVE

LANSLEY, LORD

LANSLEY (Life Baron), Andrew David Lansley; cr 2015. Born 11 December 1956; Son of Thomas Lansley, OBE, and Irene Lansley; Married Marilyn Biggs 1985 (divorced 2001) (3 daughters); married Sally Low 2001 (1 daughter 1 son).

Education: Brentwood School, Essex; Exeter University (BA politics 1979) (President, Guild of Students 1977-78).

Non-political career: Department of [Trade and] Industry 1979-87: Private Secretary to Norman Tebbit as Secretary of State for Trade and Industry 1984-85; Principal Private Secretary to Norman Tebbit as Chancellor of the Duchy of Lancaster 1985-87; British Chambers of Commerce 1987-90: Policy Director 1987-89, Deputy Director-General 1989-90; Director: Conservative Research Department 1990-95, Public Policy Unit 1995-97; Speaker, Dods Training 2015-; Consultant, Bain & Company 2015-17; Adviser, UK Active 2015-; Director, Low Associates 2015-.

Political career: *House of Commons:* MP (Conservative) for South Cambridgeshire 1997-2010, for South Cambridgeshire (revised boundary) 2010-15; Member Shadow Cabinet 1999-2001: Shadow Minister for the Cabinet Office and Policy Renewal 1999-2001; Shadow Chancellor of the Duchy of Lancaster 1999-2001; Member Shadow Cabinet 2003-10: Shadow Secretary of State for Health 2003-10; Secretary of State for Health 2010-12; Leader of the House of Commons, Lord Privy Seal 2012-14; Member: House of Commons Commission 2012-14, Speaker's Committee for the Independent Parliamentary Standards Authority 2012-14, Public Accounts Commission 2012-14. Member: Health 1997-98, Trade and Industry 2001-04. *House of Lords:* Raised to the peerage as Baron Lansley, of Orwell in the County of Cambridgeshire

2015. Member: EU Internal Market Sub-committee 2016-20, EU International Agreements Sub-committee 2020-. *Other:* Vice-chair, Conservative Party (with responsibility for policy renewal) 1998-99. DL, Cambridgeshire.

Political interests: Health, local and regional government, economic policy, trade and industry; Egypt, France, Germany, Israel, Japan, South Africa, USA.

Other: Patron: ASPIRE (Spinal injury), Headway (Acquired Brain injury); Member, National Union Executive Committee 1990-95; Chair, UK-Japan 21st Century Group 2015-; Trustee, Radix (think tank) 2016-; CBE 1996; PC 2010.

Publications: A Private Route (1988); Co-author Conservatives and the Constitution (1997); Do the right thing – Why Conservatives must achieve greater fairness and diversity in candidate selection (2002); Extending the Reach (2003).

Recreations: Spending time with my children, films, biography, history, cricket.

Rt Hon the Lord Lansley CBE, House of Lords, London SW1A 0PW
Tel: 020 7219 3000 *Email:* lansleya@parliament.uk *Twitter:* @andrewdlansley

LABOUR

LAWRENCE OF CLARENDON, BARONESS

LAWRENCE OF CLARENDON (Life Baroness), Doreen Delceita Lawrence; cr 2013. Born 24 October 1952.

Education: Greenwich University (BA humanities 1995; Postgraduate counselling skills 1997).

Non-political career: Campaigner for justice, race equality and better policing; Stephen Lawrence Charitable Trust: Founder 1998, Director 2002-15; Founder, Stephen Lawrence Day 2019-.

Political career: *House of Lords:* Raised to the peerage as Baroness Lawrence of Clarendon, of Clarendon in the Commonwealth Realm of Jamaica 2013. Member: Joint Committee on Human Rights 2015-19, Joint Committee on Fixed-Term Parliaments Act 2020-. *Other:* Race Relations Adviser, Labour Party 2020-.

Other: Trustee, Liberty -2017; Stop Hate UK; Freedom: Royal Borough of Greenwich, London Borough of Lewisham, City of London 2019; Chancellor, De Montfort University, Leicester; Honorary Fellow: Royal Institute of British Architects 2010, Goldsmith's University of London 2012; Hon. doctorate (Civil Law), University of East Anglia 1999; Hon. LLD, Bradford University 2000; Hon. doctorate: Staffordshire University 2001, Greenwich University 2006; Bishop Grosseteste University College Lincoln 2008, University of East London 2012, York University 2013, Sheffield Hallam University 2013, Oxford Brookes University 2014, Exeter University 2014, University of West London 2017; Hon. Doctor of Law 2019; Special award for the Legal Aid Lawyer of the Year 2012; Lifetime Achievement at Pride of Britain Awards 2012; Londoner of the Year at London Press Club Awards 2013; OBE 2003.

Publications: And Still I Rise (2006).

The Baroness Lawrence of Clarendon OBE, House of Lords, London SW1A 0PW
Tel: 020 7219 5353 *Twitter:* @DLawrenceOBE

CONSERVATIVE

LAWSON OF BLABY, LORD

LAWSON OF BLABY (Life Baron), Nigel Lawson; cr. 1992. Born 11 March 1932; Son of late Ralph Lawson and late Joan Lawson, née Davis; Married Vanessa Salmon 1955 (divorced 1980, died 1985) (1 son 2 daughters 1 daughter deceased); married Thérèse Maclear 1980 (divorced 2012) (1 son 1 daughter).

Education: Westminster School; Christ Church, Oxford (Scholar, BA philosophy, politics and economics 1954).

Non-political career: Member editorial staff, *Financial Times* 1956-60; City editor, *Sunday Telegraph* 1961-63; Special assistant to Sir Alec Douglas-Home as Prime Minister 1963-64; *Financial Times* columnist and BBC broadcaster 1965; Editor, *The Spectator* 1966-70; Director, Barclays Bank plc 1990-98; Chair: Central Europe Trust Co Ltd 1990-2012; Oxford Investment Partners 2006-13; Founding Chair: Global Warming Policy Foundation 2009-,

Global Warming Policy Forum 2014-; Mousquetaire d'Armagnac 2010-. Royal Navy national service 1954-56; Sub-Lt RNVR, CO HMMTB Gay Charger.

Political career: *House of Commons:* Contested Eton and Slough 1970 general election. MP (Conservative) for Blaby February 1974-92; Opposition Whip 1976-77; Opposition Spokesperson on Treasury and Economic Affairs 1977-79; Financial Secretary to the Treasury 1979-81; Secretary of State for Energy 1981-83; Chancellor of the Exchequer 1983-89. *House of Lords:* Raised to the peerage as Baron Lawson of Blaby, of Newnham in the County of Northamptonshire 1992. Member: Economic Affairs 2004-08, 2010-15, Barnett Formula 2008-09, Parliamentary Commission on Banking Standards 2012-13, EU Financial Affairs Sub-committee 2015-16. *Other:* President, Conservatives for Britain 2015-16.

Political interests: Climate change, economics, finance, banking, Europe.

Other: President, British Institute of Energy Economics 1995-2004; Member, Governing Body, Westminster School 1999-2005; Vote Leave: Interim chair 2016, Member, Campaign Committee 2016; Founding supporter, Change Britain 2016-; Fellow, Nuffield College, Oxford 1972-73; Hon. Student, Christ Church, Oxford 1996; Fellow, Westminster School 2005; Hon. DSc, Buckingham University 2011; IEA National Free Enterprise Award 2008; *The House Magazine* Lifetime Achievement Award, Dods Parliamentary Awards 2014; PC 1981. Beefsteak, Garrick, Pratt's Club.

Publications: Co-author, The Power Game (1976); The View from Number 11: (Memoirs 1992) [abridged and updated as Memoirs of a Tory Radical, 2010]; Co-author, The Nigel Lawson Diet Book (1996); An Appeal to Reason: A Cool Look at Global Warming (2008).

Rt Hon the Lord Lawson of Blaby, House of Lords, London SW1A 0PW
Tel: 020 7219 4464 *Email:* lawsonn@parliament.uk

LABOUR

LAYARD, LORD

LAYARD (Life Baron) (Peter) Richard Grenville Layard; cr. 2000. Born 15 March 1934; Son of Dr John Layard and Doris Layard; Married Molly Meacher 1991, née Reid, now Baroness Meacher (qv).

Education: Eton College; King's College, Cambridge (BA history 1957); London School of Economics (MSc economics 1967).

Non-political career: History master, London comprehensive secondary schools 1959-61; Senior research officer, Robbins Committee on Higher Education 1961-63; London School of Economics 1964-: Deputy director, Higher Education Research Unit 1964-74, Lecturer in economics 1968-75, Reader in economics of labour 1975-80, Head, Centre for Labour Economics 1974-90, Professor of Economics 1980-99, Emeritus Professor of Economics 1999-; Director, Centre for Economic Performance 1990-2003; Economic Consultant to the Russian Government 1991-97; Consultant: Department for Education and Employment 1997-2001, Cabinet Office 2001; Programme director, Well-Being Programme, LSE Centre for Economic Performance 2003-; Adviser, Improved Access to Psychological Therapy Programme, Department of Health 2006-. Member, Association of University Teachers.

Political career: *House of Lords:* Raised to the peerage as Baron Layard, of Highgate in the London Borough of Haringey 2000. Member: European Union Sub-Committee A (Economic and Financial Affairs, Trade and External Relations) 2001-02, Economic Affairs 2005-08, 2015-19, Social and Economic Impact of the Gambling Industry 2019-.

Political interests: Economic policy, employment, inequality, well-being, mental health; Bhutan.

Other: Member, UGC 1985-89; Chair, Employment Institute 1987-92; Member, Good Childhood Inquiry Panel 2007-09; Fellow: Econometric Society 1986, British Academy 2003, European Economics Association 2004, Society of Labour Economists 2007; Honorary Fellow, London School of Economics 2000; WW Leontief Medal of the Russian Academy of Natural Sciences 2005; 12A Prize (Joint) in Labour Economics 2008; Royal College of Psychiatrists Medal 2010.

Publications: Co-author: The Causes of Graduate Unemployment in India (1969), The Impact of Robbins: Expansion in Higher Education (1969), Qualified Manpower and Economic Performance (1971); Editor, Cost-Benefit Analysis (1973, 1994); Co-author: Microeconomic Theory (1978), The Causes of Poverty (1978); Author: More Jobs, Less Inflation (1982), How to Beat Unemployment (1986); Co-author: Handbook of Labour Economics (1986), The Performance of the British Economy (1988), Unemployment: Macroeconomic Performance and the Labour Market (1991), Reform in Eastern Europe (1991), East-West Migration: the alternatives (1992), Post-Communist Russia: pain and progress (1993), Macroeconomics: a text for Russia (1994), The Coming Russian Boom (1996); Author, What Labour Can Do (1997); Co-author, Emerging from Communism: Lessons from Russia, China and Eastern Europe (1998); Author: Tackling Unemployment (1999), Tackling Inequality (1999); Co-author, What the Future Holds (2001); Author, Happiness (2005, 2011); Co-author: A Good Childhood: Searching for Values in a Competitive Age (2009), Combatting Unemployment (2011); Thrive: The Power of Evidence-based Psychological Therapies (2014).

Recreations: Tennis, sailing.

Professor the Lord Layard, House of Lords, London SW1A 0PW
Tel: 020 7219 5353
Centre for Economic Performance, London School of Economics, Houghton Street, London WC2A 2AE *Tel:* 020 7955 7048 *Email:* r.layard@lse.ac.uk Website: cep.lse.ac.uk/layard

NON-AFFILIATED

LEA OF CRONDALL, LORD

LEA OF CRONDALL (Life Baron), David Edward Lea; cr. 1999. Born 2 November 1937; Son of late Edward and Lilian Lea.

Education: Farnham Grammar School, Surrey; Christ's College, Cambridge (MA economics 1961) (Inaugural chair Cambridge University Students Representative Council 1961); French.

Non-political career: Economist Intelligence Unit 1961-63; Trades Union Congress: Research/Economic Department 1964-67, Assistant secretary, Economic and Social Affairs 1968-70, Head, Economic and Social Affairs 1970-77, Assistant general secretary 1978-99. National Service, Royal Horse Artillery 1955-57. Member, TGWU 1962-; TUC: Member, Mission to Study Employment and Technology in the USA 1980, Secretary: Nuclear Energy Review Body 1986-88, Task Force on Representation at Work 1994-99; European TUC: Chair, Economic Committee 1980-90, Member, Executive Committee and Steering Group 1991-99, Vice-President 1997-99.

Political career: *House of Lords:* Raised to the peerage as Baron Lea of Crondall, of Crondall in the County of Hampshire 1999. Member: European Communities Sub-committees: A (Economic and Financial Affairs, Trade and External Relations) 2000-03, C (Foreign Affairs, Defence and Development Policy) 2003-07, G (Social Policy and Consumer Affairs) 2007-09, Insurance Bill 2014-15. *Other:* President, Cambridge University Liberal Club 1960-61; Secretary, TUC-Labour Party: Liaison Committee 1972-86, Contact Group 1987-96; Suspended from Labour Party January 2020-. Member: DTI Investment Mission in Japan 1974, Channel Tunnel Advisory Committee 1974-75, Bullock Committee on Industrial Democracy 1975-77, Royal Commission on the Distribution of Income and Wealth 1975-79, Delors Committee on Economic and Social Concepts in the Community 1977-79, Energy Commission 1977-79, NEDC Committee on Finance for Industry 1978-82, Franco-British Council 1982-99; Retail Prices Index Advisory Committee 1985-99, Kreisky Commission on Employment Issues in Europe 1987-89, Round Table on Sustainable Development 1995-99, Advisory Committee on Vehicle Emissions 1998-99, Treasury Advisory Committee on EMU 1998-99, Central Arbitration Committee 2000-10.

Political interests: European Union, employment, energy, economy, constitution; Africa, Bolivia, Madagascar, Nepal.

Other: Member: UN Commission on Transnational Corporations 1977-82, Tripartite Mission EU, Japan 1990, European Social Dialogue Joint Steering Committee 1992, UK Delegation Earth Summit, Rio 1992, EU High Level Group on Benchmarking 1998-99; Editorial board member, New Economy (IPPR) 1991-99; Governor, National Institute of Economic and Social Research; Council member, Britain in Europe 2000-05; Election monitor: Congo (DRC) 2007, Nepal 2008; Chair, Hammarskjold Inquiry Trust 2012-13; OBE 1978. Bourne Club, Farnham, Lords/Commons Tennis and Ski Clubs.

Publications: Trade Unionism (1966); Co-author, Europe and Your Rights at Work (2006).

Recreations: Tennis, music, theatre, skiing.

The Lord Lea of Crondall OBE, House of Lords, London SW1A 0PW
Tel: 020 7219 8518 *Email:* lead@parliament.uk

CROSSBENCH

LEBEDEV, LORD

LEBEDEV (Life Baron), Evgeny Alexandrovich Lebedev; cr 2020. Born May 1980.

Non-political career: Director: Lebedev Holdings 2008-, Evening Standard 2008-13, 2017-, Independent Print 2010-13, Independent Digital News and Media 2010-.

Political career: *House of Lords:* Raised to the peerage as Baron Lebedev, of Hampton in the London Borough of Richmond upon Thames and of Siberia in the Russian Federation 2020.

Other: Director: Pies Pub 2011-, Elton John Aids Foundation 2016-.

Recreations: Theatre, art, literature.

The Lord Lebedev, House of Lords, London SW1A 0PW
Tel: 020 7219 3000 Website: evgenylebedev.com *Twitter:* @mrevgenylebedev

LIBERAL DEMOCRAT

LEE OF TRAFFORD, LORD

LEE OF TRAFFORD (Life Baron), John Robert Louis Lee; cr 2006. Born 21 June 1942; Son of Basil Lee, doctor; Married Anne Bakirgian 1975 (2 daughters).

Education: William Hulme's Grammar School, Manchester; Chartered accountant 1964.

Non-political career: Founding director, Chancery Consolidated Ltd (investment bankers), Manchester; Various non-executive directorships.

Political career: *House of Commons:* Contested Manchester Moss-side October 1974. MP (Conservative) for Nelson and Colne 1979-83, for Pendle 1983-92. Contested Pendle 1992 general election; PPS to: Kenneth Baker as Minister of State for Industry 1981-83, Cecil Parkinson as Secretary of State for Industry 1983; Parliamentary Under-Secretary of State: Ministry of Defence 1983-86, Department of Employment 1986-89; Minister for Tourism 1987-89. *House of Lords:* Raised to the peerage as Baron Lee of Trafford, of Bowdon in the County of Cheshire 2006. Liberal Democrat: Spokesperson for: Trade and Industry 2006-07, Culture, Media and Sport (Tourism) 2006-10, Defence 2007-10, Whip 2007-10. Co-opted Member, EU Sub-committee B (Internal Market) 2006-07; Member: Refreshment 2007-12, 2015-16, Joint Committee on National Security Strategy 2010-14, Economic Affairs Finance Bill Sub-committee 2018-19. Chair, Liberal Democrat Parliamentary Party Committee on International Affairs (Defence) 2010-12. *Other:* Joined Liberal Democrats 2001; Chairman, Liberal Democrat Friends of Armed Forces 2010-12. Chair, Association of Leading Visitor Attractions 1990-; Member, English Tourist Board 1992-99; Chair: Museum of Science and Industry, Manchester 1992-99, Christie Hospital NHS Trust 1992-98; DL, Greater Manchester 1995; High Sheriff, Greater Manchester 1998-99.

Political interests: Defence, tourism, trade and industry, investment; UK.

Other: Chairman, Association of Leading Visitor Attractions; Trustee and Deputy Chair, Museum of Richmond.

Publications: Portfolio Man (Willow Publishing, 2005); How to Make a Million - Slowly (2014); Yummi Yoghurt – A First Taste of Stock Market Investment! (2019).

Recreations: Stock market, salmon fishing, antiques.

The Lord Lee of Trafford, House of Lords, London SW1A 0PW
Tel: 020 7219 3949 *Email:* leej@parliament.uk

NON-AFFILIATED

LEEDS, LORD BISHOP OF

LEEDS (1st Bishop of), Nicholas Baines. Born 13 November 1957; Son of Frank and Beryl Baines; Married Linda Higgins 1980 (2 sons 1 daughter).

Education: Holt Comprehensive School, Liverpool; Bradford University (BA modern languages); Trinity College, Bristol (BA theological studies); German, French, Russian.

Non-political career: Linguist specialist, GCHQ, Cheltenham 1980-84; Ordained deacon 1987; Assistant curate, St Thomas, Kendal 1987-91; Priest 1988; Assistant Priest, Holy Trinity with St John, Leicester 1991-92; Vicar, St Mary and St John, Leicester 1992-2000; Archdeacon of Lambeth 2000-03; Bishop of: Croydon 2003-11, Bradford 2011-14, Leeds 2014-.

Political career: *House of Lords:* Entered House of Lords as the Bishop of Leeds 2014. *Other:* Member, General Synod 1995-2005.

Political interests: Foreign affairs; Germany, Kazakhstan, Russia, Sri Lanka, Sudan, Tanzania.

Other: Anglican co-chair, Meissen Commission 2007-17; Chair, Sandford St Martin Trust 2008-17; Honorary doctorate: Bradford University, Friedrich-Schiller-University Jena, Germany; Honorary fellow, Bradford College.

Publications: Hungry for Hope (1991, 2007); Speedbumps and Potholes (2003); Jesus and People Like Us (2004); Marking Time: 47 Reflections on Mark's Gospel for Lent, Holy Week and Easter (2005); Finding Faith: Stories of Music and Life (2008); Scandal of Grace: The Danger of Following Jesus (2008); Why Wish You a Merry Christmas?: What Matters (and What Doesn't) in the Festive Season (2009); Freedom is Coming (SPCK, 2019).

Recreations: Sport, literature, music, theatre.

Rt Rev the Lord Bishop of Leeds, House of Lords, London SW1A 0PW
Tel: 020 7219 5353 *Email:* bainesn@parliament.uk
Hollin House, Weetwood Avenue, Leeds LS16 5NG *Tel:* 0113-284 4301
Email: bishop.nick@leeds.anglican.org Websites: www.leeds.anglican.org
nickbaines.wordpress.com *Twitter:* @nickbaines

CONSERVATIVE

LEIGH OF HURLEY, LORD

LEIGH OF HURLEY (Life Baron), Howard Darryl Leigh; cr 2013. Born 3 April 1959; Married Jennifer Peach 1998 (2 daughters).

Education: Clifton College, Bristol; Southampton Univeristy (BSc Soc Sci Economics 1980); Chartered Accountant 1983.

Non-political career: Deloitte Haskins & Sells 1981-88: Chartered Accountant, Corporate Tax Department, Mergers and Acquisitions Group; Cavendish Corporate Finance: Founder 1988, Senior Partner 2010-.

Political career: *House of Lords:* Raised to the peerage as Baron Leigh of Hurley, of Hurley in the Royal County of Berkshire 2013. Member: Economic Affairs Finance Bill Sub-committee 2014, 2016-17, 2018-19, Administration and Works 2014-15, Finance 2016-17. *Other:* Conservative Party: Treasurer 2000-05, Chair, Leader's Group 2010-, Senior treasurer 2005-; Member, executive board, Conservative Friends of Israel; Westminster North Conservative Association: President 2010-17, Patron 2017-.

Other: Member: Chartered Institute of Taxation 1985, Deregulation Taskforce, DTI 1994-97; ICAEW: Council Member 1998-2004, Chair, Corporate Finance Faculty 1998-2004, Member: Takeover Panel Appeal Committee 1998-, Jewish Care Business Group 2000-; Vice-President, Jewish Leadership Council 2010-; President, Westminster Synagogue 2010-; Member, Deliver Life Board Wateraid 2015-16; President, Institute for Jewish Policy Research 2016-; Member Advisory Board, Metro Bank plc 2017-; ICAEW; Chartered Institute of Taxation; Jewish Care, Wateraid; Member of Court, Worshipful Company of Chartered Accountants 2003-15; Freedom, City of London; Lifetime Achievement Award, Corporate Finance Faculty ICAEW. Carlton Club.

Publications: Lecturer, author and broadcaster on mergers and acquisitions; Good Practice Guideline: Selling a Business (Institute of Chartered Accountants).

Recreations: Running.

The Lord Leigh of Hurley, House of Lords, London SW1A 0PW
Tel: 020 7219 5353
Cavendish Corporate Finance LLP, 40 Portland Place, London W1B 1NB *Tel:* 020 7908 6000
Twitter: @HowardDLeigh

LABOUR

LEITCH, LORD

LEITCH (Life Baron), Alexander Park Leitch; cr. 2004. Born 20 October 1947; Son of Donald Leitch and Agnes Smith, née Park; Married (3 daughters); married Noelle Kristin Dowd 2003 (1 daughter 1 son).

Education: Dunfermline High School.

Non-political career: Chief systems designer, National Mutual Life/Hambro Life 1969-75; Allied Dunbar plc: Chief executive 1993-96, Chair 1996-2001; Chair: Dunbar Bank 1994-2001, Eagle Star 1996-2004, Threadneedle Asset Management 1996-2004; Director, BAT Industries 1997-98; Chief executive, Zurich Financial Services (UKISA Asia Pacific) 1998-2004; Chair: Association of British Insurers 1998-2000, National Employment Panel 2000-07; Intrinsic FS 2005-17; Director: Lloyds TSB plc 2005, UBM plc 2005-09, Paternoster 2006-10; Chair, BUPA 2006-18; Scottish Widows plc: Director 2007-13, Chair 2008-13; Deputy chair, Lloyds Banking Group plc 2011-13; Chair, FNZ 2013; Adviser, Guggenheim Investments 2014; Director, Old Mutual Wealth 2014-17.

Political career: *House of Lords:* Raised to the peerage as Baron Leitch, of Oakley in Fife 2004.

Political interests: Skills and education, pensions, financial services, charity, Scotland, health, Fintech; Africa, Australia, Chile, China, France, India, Italy, Latin America, Poland, Saudi Arabia, Spain, Switzerland, Turkey, USA.

Other: Chair, Stoner School 1990-2003; Deputy chair, BITC 1996-2004; Chair, Sane 1999-2000; Trustee, National Galleries of Scotland 1999-2003; Deputy chair, Commonwealth Education Fund 2001-06; Vice-President, UK Cares 2004; Chair: Balance Foundation 2004-05, Leitch Review of UK Skills 2005-07, Medical Aid Films 2010-14; Trustee, Lloyds TSB Foundation 2011-13; Founder, W.I.M Foundation (What Is More?) 2017-; Member, Worshipful Company of Insurers 2002; Freedom, City of London 2002; Chancellor, Carnegie College, Dunfermline 2010; Fellow, Carnegie College; Hon. Doctorate, Sunderland University; City and Guilds; Prince of Wales Ambassador's Award for Charitable Work 2001. Caledonia Club, Athenæum Club.

Recreations: Antiquarian books, antiques, poetry, malt whisky, art, painting, exploring religion/spirituality.

The Lord Leitch, House of Lords, London SW1A 0PW
Tel: 020 7219 3000

LABOUR

LENNIE, LORD

Opposition Whip

LENNIE (Life Baron), Christopher (Chris) John Lennie; cr 2014. Born 22 February 1953; Son of Magnus and Elizabeth Lennie; Partner Anne (2 children).

Education: West Kent College; Newcastle University (history and English literature 1976).

Non-political career: National campaigns manager and Northern political officer, Unison; Labour Party: Regional director (Northern England) 1999-2001, Deputy Secretary-general, Acting Secretary-general 2008-09, External relations adviser. Member, Unison.

Political career: *House of Lords:* Raised to the peerage as Baron Lennie, of Longsands Tynemouth in the County of Tyne and Wear 2014. Opposition Whip 2016-.

Political interests: Social mobility, economic security, North East region of England; Europe, USA.

Other: Tynemouth CIU Club.

Recreations: Newcastle United FC.

The Lord Lennie, House of Lords, London SW1A 0PW
Tel: 020 7219 5353 *Email:* lenniec@parliament.uk

CROSSBENCH

LEVENE OF PORTSOKEN, LORD

LEVENE OF PORTSOKEN (Life Baron), Peter Keith Levene; cr. 1997. Born 8 December 1941; Son of late Maurice and Rose Levene; Married Wendy Fraiman 1966 (2 sons 1 daughter).

Education: City of London School; Manchester University (BA economics 1963); French, German, Italian.

Non-political career: United Scientific Holdings 1963-85: Managing director 1968-85, Chair 1982-85; Member, South East Asia Trade Advisory Group 1979-83; Defence Manufacturers' Association: Council member 1982-85, Chair 1984-85, President 2005-09; Personal adviser to Michael Heseltine as Secretary of State for Defence 1984; Chief of Defence Procurement, Ministry of Defence 1985-91; UK National Armaments Director 1988-91; Chair, European National Armaments Directors 1989-90; Personal adviser to Michael Heseltine as Secretary of State for the Environment 1991-92; Chair, Docklands Light Railway Ltd 1991-94; Deputy chair, Wasserstein Perella & Co Ltd 1991-94; Personal adviser on competition and purchasing to Norman Lamont as Chancellor of the Exchequer 1992; Member, Citizen's Charter Advisory Panel 1992-93; Personal adviser to the President of the Board of Trade 1992-95; Adviser on efficiency and effectiveness to John Major as Prime Minister 1992-97; Chair and chief executive, Canary Wharf Ltd 1993-96; Senior adviser, Morgan Stanley & Co Ltd 1996-98; Director, Haymarket Group Ltd 1997-; Chair: Bankers Trust International plc 1998-99, Investment Banking Europe Deutsche Bank 1999-2001; Vice-chair, Deutsche Bank AG London 2001-02; Director, J Sainsbury plc 2001-04; Chair: General Dynamics UK Ltd 2001-, World Trade Centre Disaster Fund (UK) 2001-03, Lloyd's 2002-11; Member, supervisory board, Deutsche Boerse ag 2004-05; Board member, TOTAL SA 2005-11; Director, China Construction Bank 2006-12; Chair: Ministry of Defence Reform Group 2010-16, NBNK Investments plc 2011-12; Vice-chair, Starr International Company Inc 2012-; Chair, Starr Underwriting Agents Ltd 2012-; Director: Getlink (formerly Eurotunnel SA) 2012-, China Construction Bank (Asia) 2013-; Chair, Tikehau Investments Ltd 2013-. Hon. Col. Comdt, Royal Logistic Corps 1993-2006.

Political career: *House of Lords:* Raised to the peerage as Baron Levene of Portsoken, of Portsoken in the City of London 1997. Member: Economic Affairs 2008-13, Joint Committee on National Security Strategy 2013-16, Personal Service Companies 2013-14, Artificial Intelligence 2017-18. *Other:* Court of Common Council, City of London: Member 1983-84, Alderman 1984-2012; JP, City of London 1984-2002; Governor, City of London School 1986-; Sheriff, City of London 1995-96; Lord Mayor of London 1998-99.

Other: Chair: Board of management, London Homes for the Elderly 1990-93, Bevis Marks Trust; LEUKA 2000; Carmen's Company: Liveryman 1984-, Master 1992-93; Liveryman: Information Technologists 1992-, Management Consultant (Honorary) 2004-; Chancellor, City University 1998-99; CIMgt; FCIPS; Fellow, Queen Mary and Westfield College 1995; Two honorary doctorates; KBE 1989; KStJ 1998; Commandeur, Ordre National du Merite (France) 1996; Knight Commander Order of Merit (Germany) 1998; Middle Cross Order of Merit (Hungary) 1999. Guildhall, Royal Automobile Club, Walbrook Club.

Recreations: Skiing, watching football, travel.

The Lord Levene of Portsoken KBE, House of Lords, London SW1A 0PW
Tel: 020 7219 5353
Fourth Floor, 30 Fenchurch Avenue, London EC3M 5AD *Tel:* 020 7398 5087
Email: peter.levene@starrcompanies.com

LABOUR

LEVY, LORD

LEVY (Life Baron), Michael Abraham Levy; cr. 1997. Born 11 July 1944; Son of Samuel and Annie Levy; Married Gilda Altbach 1967 (1 son 1 daughter).

Education: Hackney Downs Grammar School, London; FCA 1966.

Non-political career: Lubbock Fine (Chartered Accountants) 1961-66; Principal, M Levy & Co 1966-69; Partner, Wagner Prager Levy & Partners 1969-73; Chair, Magnet Group of Companies 1973-88; Vice-chair: Phonographic Performance Ltd 1979-84, British Phonographic Industry Ltd 1984-87; Chair: D & J Securities Ltd 1988-92, M & G Records Ltd 1992-97, Chase Music Ltd (formerly M & G Music Ltd) 1992-2008, Wireart Ltd 1992-2008; Principal, Global Consultancy Services 2005-; Chair, International Standard Asset Management 2008-11; Director, Chase Mill Hill Ltd 2013-.

Political career: *House of Lords:* Raised to the peerage as Baron Levy, of Mill Hill in the London Borough of Barnet 1997. Personal Envoy to the Prime Minister and Special Adviser on the Middle East 1998-2007. *Other:* Member, Labour Party Donations Committee 2002-07. JFS (Jews Free School): Governor 1990-95, Hon. President 1995-2001, President 2001; President, Barnet and Southgate College 2017-.

Political interests: Voluntary sector, social welfare, education, Middle East; European countries, North Africa, Latin and Central America, Middle East.

Other: International Peace Institute; United Joint Israel Appeal: National Campaign Chair 1982-85, Honorary Vice-President 1994-2000, Honorary President 2000-; Member, World Board of Governors: Jewish Agency 1990-95, Keren Hayesod 1991-95; World Chair, Youth Aliyah Committee, Jewish Agency Board of Governors 1991-95; Chair: British Music Industry Trust Awards Committee 1992-95, Jewish Care 1992-97, Chief Rabbinate Awards for Excellence 1992-2007, Foundation for Education 1993-2006; Vice-chair, Central Council for Jewish Social Services 1994-2006; Patron, British Music Industry Trust Awards 1995; Chair, Jewish Care Community Foundation 1995-2010; Member: World Commission on Israel-Diaspora Relations 1995-, International Board of Governors, Peres Centre for Peace 1997-2009, Advisory Council, Foreign Policy Centre 1997-2006; Patron, Prostate Cancer Charitable Trust 1997-2011; President: Jewish Care 1997-, Volunteering Matters 1998-; Patron, Friends of Israel Educational Trust 1998-2001; Member: National Council for Voluntary Organisations Advisory Committee 1998-2011, Community Legal Service Champions Panel 1999-2010; Patron, Save A Child's Heart Foundation 2000-04; Member, Honorary Committee, Israel Britain and the Commonwealth Association 2000-04; Chair, Board of Trustees, New Policy Network Foundation 2000-07; Hon. Patron, Cambridge University Jewish Society 2000-; Executive Committee Member, Chai-Lifeline 2001-02; Patron, Simon Marks Jewish Primary School Trust 2002-; Former Trustee and Co-chair, Academy Sponsors Trust; President, Specialist Schools and Academics Trust 2005-08; Trustee and Member, executive committee, Jewish Leadership Council (JLC) 2006-11; President, Jewish Lads' and Girls' Brigade (JLGB) 2006-; Member, Development Board, British Library 2008-11; Patron: Mathilda Marks-Kennedy Jewish Primary School 2011-, Etz Chaim Jewish Primary School 2011; Member: Advisory Council, "Step Up to Serve Campaign" under the patronage of HRH The Princes of Wales 2014-, Board, International Peace Institute 2015-19; President: Barnet and Southgate College 2017-, Sense 2019-, Sense International 2019-; Fellow, Institute of Chartered Accountants; FCA 1966; Honorary Doctorate, Middlesex University 1999; B'nai B'rith First Lodge Award 1994; Friends of the Hebrew University of Jerusalem Scopus Award 1998; Israel Policy Forum (USA) Special Recognition Award 2003; *Jewish Chronicle* Award for an outstanding, unique and long term contribution to British communal life 2016; Who's Who Marquis Lifetime Achievement Award 2018.

Publications: A Question of Honour (2008).

Recreations: Tennis, swimming.

The Lord Levy, House of Lords, London SW1A 0PW
Tel: 020 7219 5353
3 Marylebone Mews, London W1G 8PU *Tel:* 020 7487 5174 *Email:* ml@lordlevy.com

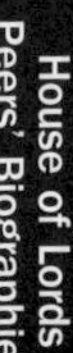

CONSERVATIVE

LEXDEN, LORD

LEXDEN (Life Baron), Alistair Basil Cooke; cr 2010. Born 20 April 1945; Son of Dr Basil and Nancy Cooke.

Education: Framlingham College, Suffolk; Peterhouse, Cambridge (BA, MA 1970); Queen's University, Belfast (PhD 1979).

Non-political career: Lecturer and tutor in modern history, Queen's University, Belfast 1971-77; Political adviser to Shadow Minister for Northern Ireland 1977-79; Conservative Research Department: Desk officer 1977-83, Assistant director 1983-85, Deputy director 1985-97; Director, Conservative Political Centre 1988-97; Official historian of the Conservative Party 2009-.

Political career: *House of Lords:* Raised to the peerage as Baron Lexden, of Lexden in the County of Essex and of Strangford in the County of Down 2010. Deputy Chairman of Committees 2017-; Deputy Speaker 2018-. Member: EU Sub-committee G (Social Policies and Consumer Protection) 2012, Constitution 2012-15, Joint Committee on Statutory Instruments 2015-19, Ecclesiastical Committee 2017-, Electoral Registration and Administration Act 2013 2019-, EU Home Affairs Sub-committee 2019-20, EU Security and Justice Sub-committee 2020-. *Other:* Co-chair, Conservative History Group 2012-. General Secretary, Independent Schools Council 1997-2004.

Political interests: Northern Ireland, education, constitutional and electoral affairs; All countries of the United Kingdom.

Other: Member, British-Irish Parliamentary Assembly 2017-20; President, Northern Ireland Schools Debating Competition 2001-18; Co-Chairman, London Friends of the Belfast Buildings Preservation Trust 2006-18; Vice-President, Council of British International Schools 2011-; President: Independent Schools Association 2013-, Council for Independent Education 2013-; Trustee, Hansard Society 2014-; OBE 1988. Carlton Club.

Publications: Joint-editor, Lord Carlingford's Journal (1971); Co-author, The Governing Passion: Cabinet Government and Party Politics in Britain 1885-86 (1974); Editor: The Ashbourne Papers 1869-1913 (1974), The Conservative Party's Campaign Guides, Seven Volumes (1987-2005), The Conservative Party: Seven Historical Studies (1997), The Conservative Research Department 1929-2004 (2004); Co-author, The Carlton Club 1832-2007 (2007); Tory Heroine: Dorothy Brant and the Rise of Conservative Women (2008); A Party of Change: A Brief History of the Conservatives (2008); Contributor, Between the Thin Blue Lines (2008); Editor and co-author, Tory Policy Making: The Conservative Research Department 1929-2009 (2009); A Gift from the Churchills: The Primrose League 1883-2004 (2010); Contributor, Enoch at 100: A Re-evaluation of Enoch Powell (2012); Neville Chamberlain: Redressing the Balance (2018); Editor and co-author, Stanley Baldwin: A Statesman in Bronze (2018).

Recreations: Writing letters to the press (and getting them published), collecting royal and political memorabilia, book reviewing.

The Lord Lexden OBE, House of Lords, London SW1A 0PW
Tel: 020 7219 8216 *Email:* lexdena@parliament.uk Website: www.alistairlexden.org.uk

LABOUR

LIDDELL OF COATDYKE, BARONESS

LIDDELL OF COATDYKE (Life Baroness), Helen Lawrie Liddell; cr 2010. Born 6 December 1950; Daughter of Hugh and Bridget Reilly; Married Dr Alistair Liddell 1972 (1 son 1 daughter).

Education: St Patrick's High School, Coatbridge; Strathclyde University (BA economics 1972); French.

Non-political career: Head, Economic Department, Scottish TUC 1971-76; Economics correspondent, BBC Scotland 1976-77; General secretary, Labour Party in Scotland 1977-88; Director, personnel and public affairs, Scottish Daily Record and Sunday Mail (1986) Ltd 1988-92; Chief executive, Business Venture Programme 1993-94; High Commissioner to Australia 2005-09. GMB; NUJ.

Political career: *House of Commons:* Contested Fife East October 1974 general election. MP (Labour) for Monklands East 30 June 1994 by-election to 1997, and for Airdrie and Shotts 1997-2005; Opposition Spokesperson on Scotland 1995-97; Economic Secretary, HM Treasury 1997-98; Minister of State: Scottish Office (Minister for Education) 1998-99, Department of the Environment, Transport and the Regions (Minister for Transport) 1999, Department of Trade and Industry (Minister for Energy and Competitiveness in Europe) 1999-2001; Secretary of State for Scotland 2001-03. Member, Labour Party Departmental Committee for the Treasury 1997-2001. *House of Lords:* Raised to the peerage as Baroness Liddell of Coatdyke, of Airdrie in Lanarkshire 2010. Member: Selection 2011, Joint Committee on the Draft Detention of Terrorist Suspects (Temporary Extension) Bills 2011, EU Sub-committee E: Justice, Institutions and Consumer Protection 2013-15, Partnerships (Prosecution) (Scotland) Bill 2013, EU Financial Affairs Sub-committee 2016-20, EU International Agreements Sub-committee 2020-. *Other:* Commissioner, BBC Privacy Commission 2011; Member: Inquiry into the Mull of Kintyre Helicopter Accident 2010-11, Advisory Committee on Business Appointments.

Political interests: Media, foreign affairs, economic policy, trade and industry, small businesses, energy and climate change, defence and security; Australia, China, Europe, USA.

Other: Vice-chair, Rehab Scotland 1990-92; Chair, Independent Review into the future of the Scottish Symphony Orchestra and Orchestra of Scottish Opera 1993-94; Chair, UN5O: Scotland 1994; Associate member, BUPA 2010; Director, British-Australia Society 2011-; Cook Society 2011-; Trustee: Northcote Educational Trust, Arthur Philip Trust; Non Executive director: Visit Britain 2010-14, Offshore Renewable Energy Catapult 2013-16; St Andrew's Hospice Airdrie, Maggie's Centres; Honorary Doctor of Laws, Strathclyde University 2005; PC 1998.

Publications: Elite (1990).

Recreations: Cooking, hill-walking, music, writing.

Rt Hon the Baroness Liddell of Coatdyke, House of Lords, London SW1A 0PW
Tel: 020 7219 6960 *Email:* liddellh@parliament.uk

LABOUR

LIDDLE, LORD

LIDDLE (Life Baron), Roger John Liddle; cr 2010. Born 14 June 1947; Son of late John Thwaites Liddle, railway clerk, and late Elizabeth Liddle, née Temple; Married Caroline Thomson 1983 (1 son).

Education: Carlisle Grammar School; Queen's College, Oxford (BA modern history 1968, MA; MPhil management studies 1970).

Non-political career: Oxford School of Social and Administrative Studies 1970-74; Industrial relations officer, Electricity Council 1974-76; Special adviser to William Rodgers MP 1976-81: as Secretary of State for Transport 1976-79; Director, Public Policy Centre 1982-87; Managing director, Prima Europe Ltd 1987-97; Special adviser to Tony Blair MP as Prime Minister 1997-2004; European Commission: Member of cabinet of Peter Mandelson as Trade Commissioner 2004-06, Principal adviser to the President of the European Commission 2006-07; Chair, advisory board, New Industry New Jobs Panel, Department for Business, Innovation and Skills 2008-10. Member, GMB.

Political career: *House of Lords:* Raised to the peerage as Baron Liddle, of Carlisle in the County of Cumbria 2010. Opposition Whip 2011-13; Opposition Spokesperson for: Foreign and Commonwealth Office (Europe) 2012-14, Business, Innovation and Skills 2013-14. Member: European Union 2010, 2015-19, EU Sub-committee G (Social Policies and Consumer Protection) 2011, EU Internal Market Sub-committee 2015-19, High Speed Rail (West Midlands-Crewe) Bill 2019-, Secondary Legislation Scrutiny 2020-. *Other:* Member: National committee, Social Democratic Party 1981-86, Advisory Board, Progress. Oxford City Council: Councillor 1971-76, Deputy Leader 1973-76; Councillor, Lambeth Borough Council 1982-86, 1994-95; Chair, Cumbria Vision 2007-10; Councillor, Cumbria County Council 2013-.

Political interests: Future of European Union, European social democracy, industrial economic questions, regional policy, future of welfare state, universities; France, Germany, Italy, Sweden, USA.

Other: Member: Fabian Society, Progress; Policy Network: Vice-chair 2007-09, Chair 2009-15, Co-Chair 2015-; Pro-Chancellor, Lancaster University 2013-. Reform Club.

Publications: Co-author (with Peter Mandelson), The Blair Revolution (1996); Author, The New Case for Europe (2005); Co-author: Global Europe, Social Europe (2006), Beyond New Labour (2009); The Europe Dilemma (2014); The Risk of Brexit (2015).

Recreations: Tennis, opera, reading history and politics, walking.

The Lord Liddle, House of Lords, London SW1A 0PW
Tel: 020 7219 2132 *Email:* liddler@parliament.uk

CONSERVATIVE

LILLEY, LORD

LILLEY (Life Baron), Peter Bruce Lilley; cr 2018. Born 23 August 1943; Son of Arnold Lilley and Lilian Lilley, née Elliott; Married Gail Ansell 1979.

Education: Dulwich College, London; Clare College, Cambridge (BA natural sciences and economic sciences 1965); French.

Non-political career: Economic adviser in developing countries 1966-72; Investment adviser on North Sea oil and other energy industries 1972-84; Partner, W Greenwell & Co 1979-86; Director: Great Western Resources Ltd 1985-87, Greenwell Montague Stockbrokers (head, oil investment department) 1986-87, JP Morgan Claverhouse Investment Trust 1997-2008, Idox plc 2002-18, Melchior Japan Investment Trust 2006-10; Non-executive director and vice-chairman, Tethys Petroleum Ltd 2006-14.

Political career: *House of Commons:* Contested Haringey, Tottenham October 1974 general election. MP (Con) for St Albans 1983-97, for Hitchin and Harpenden 1997-2010, for Hitchin and Harpenden (revised boundary) 2010-17; PPS: to Lord Bellwin as Minister of State and William Waldegrave as Parliamentary Under-Secretary of State, Department of Environment 1984, to Nigel Lawson as Chancellor of the Exchequer 1984-87; HM Treasury: Economic Secretary 1987-89, Financial Secretary 1989-90; Secretary of State for: Trade and Industry 1990-92, Social Security 1992-97; Member, Shadow Cabinet and Shadow Chancellor of the Exchequer 1997-98; Deputy Leader of the Opposition (with overall responsibility for development of party policy) 1998-99. Chair, Joint Committee on the Draft Financial Services Bill 2011-12; Member: Energy and Climate Change 2012-15, Environmental Audit 2015-17, Exiting the European Union 2016-17. Chairman, Conservative Party Committee for Finance 1997-98. *House of Lords:* Raised to the peerage as Baron Lilley, of Offa in the County of Hertfordshire 2018. Member: SLSC Sub-committee A 2018-19, EU Internal Market Sub-committee 2019-20, EU Goods Sub-committee 2020-. *Other:* Consultant director, Conservative Research Department 1979-83; Contested Conservative Party leadership election 1997; Chair, Globalisation and Global Poverty Policy Group 2006-07; Member, Number 10 Policy Advisory Board (Foreign Affairs) 2011-15. Member, School of Management Advisory Board, Southampton University 2002-12.

Political interests: Economic policy, European Union, education, race relations; Central Asia, France.

Other: Trustee, Parliamentary Contributory Pension Fund; Chair: House of Commons Members Fund, Bow Group 1973-75; Stairways (Mencap) Harpenden; Hon. LLD, Hertfordshire University; PC 1990. Carlton Club, Beefsteak Club.

Publications: Do You Sincerely Want to Win? – Defeating Terrorism in Ulster (Bow Group, 1972); Lessons for Power (1974); Co-author, Delusions of Income Policy (Bow Group, 1977); Contributor, End of the Keynesian Era (1980); Thatcherism, the Next Generation (CPS, 1989); The Mais Lecture Benefits and Costs: Securing the Future of the Social Security (1993); Patient Power (Demos, 2000); Common Sense on Cannabis (Social Market Foundation, 2001); Taking Liberties (Adam Smith Institute, 2002); Save Our Pensions (Social Market Foundation, 2003); Identity Crisis (Bow Group, 2004); Too Much of a Good Thing (Centre for Policy Studies, 2005); Tony Duke of York (Bow Group, 2006); In It Together – Report of Commission on Global Poverty (Conservative Party, 2007); Paying for Success (Policy Exchange, 2008); What is Wrong with Stern? – The failings of the Stern Review of the Economics of Climate Change (GWPF, 2012); £300 billion – the Cost of the Climate Change Act (GWPF, 2017); Helm Review and the Climate Industrial Complex (GWPF, 2018); Fact Not Friction – exploding the myths of leaving the Customs Union (Global Britain/ERG, 2018); 30 Truths about Leaving on WTO Terms – Why WTO offers a safer haven than the Backstop (Global Britain/Labour Leave, 2019).

Recreations: Mending ancient walls.

Rt Hon the Lord Lilley, House of Lords, London SW1A 0PW
Tel: 020 7219 3000 *Email:* lilleyp@parliament.uk

NON-AFFILIATED

LINCOLN, LORD BISHOP OF

LINCOLN (72nd Bishop of), Christopher Lowson. Born 3 February 1953; Married Susan Osborne 1976 (1 son 1 daughter).

Education: Newcastle Cathedral School; Consett Grammar School; King's College London (Associateship of King's College in Theology 1975); Pacific School of Religion, Berkeley (Master of Sacred Theology 1976); Heythrop College London (Master of Theology in pastoral theology 1996); Cardiff Law School (Master of Laws in canon law 2003).

Non-political career: Ordained 1978; Assistant Curate, Richmond, Surrey 1977-82; Holy Trinity, Eltham: Priest-in-charge 1982-83, Vicar 1983-91; Chaplain: Avery Hill College 1982-85, Thames Polytechnic 1985-91; Vicar of Petersfield and Rector of Buriton 1991-99; Rural Dean of Petersfield 1995-99; Archdeacon of Portsmouth/Archdeacon of Portsdown 1999-2006; Bishop's Liaison Officer for Prisons, Portsmouth 2000-03; Bishop's Adviser to Hospital Chaplaincy, Portsmouth 2003-06; Director, Ministry Division, Archbishops' Council and Priest Vicar, Westminster Abbey 2006-11; Bishop of Lincoln 2011- (suspended May 2019-).

Political career: *House of Lords:* Entered House of Lords 2017. Member, Regenerating Seaside Towns and Communities 2018-19.

Other: Garrick Club.

Rt Rev the Lord Bishop of Lincoln, House of Lords, London SW1A 0PW
Tel: 020 7219 3000
Edward King House, Minster Yard, Lincoln LN2 1PU *Tel:* 01522 504090
Email: bishop.lincoln@lincoln.anglican.org Website: www.lincoln.anglican.org
Twitter: @BishopofLincoln

CONSERVATIVE

LINDSAY, EARL OF

LINDSAY (16th Earl of, S), James Randolph Lindesay-Bethune; cr. 1633; Viscount Garnock (S) 1703; Lord Lindsay of the Byres (S) 1445; Lord Parbroath (S) 1633; Lord Kilbirnie, Kingsburn and Drumry (S) 1703. Born 19 November 1955; Son of 15th Earl and Hon. Mary-Clare Douglas Scott Montagu, daughter of 2nd Baron Montagu of Beaulieu, KCIE, CSI, DL; Married Diana Mary Chamberlayne-Macdonald 1982 (2 sons 3 daughters inc. twins).

Education: Eton College; Edinburgh University (MA economic history 1978); University of California, Davis (land use).

Non-political career: Chair, Assured British Meat Ltd 1997-2001; Non-executive director, UA Group plc 1998-2005; Chair: Scottish Quality Salmon 1999-2006, UA Properties Ltd 1999-2000, UA Forestry Ltd 1999-2000, Genesis Quality Assurance Ltd 2001-02, Elmwood College Board of Management 2001-09; Managing director, Marine Stewardship Council International 2001-04; Non-executive director, Mining (Scotland) Ltd/Scottish Resources Group Ltd 2001-13; British Polythene Industries plc: Non-executive director 2006-15, Adviser; Associate director, National Non-Food Crops Centre 2007-12; Chair: Scottish Agricultural College Ltd/SRUC-Scotland's Rural College 2007-15, British Polythene Pension Scheme 2009-; Non-executive director, Hargreaves Energy Projects 2015-17; Adviser: Hargreaves (UK) Services 2015-17, 3R Energy Ltd; Non-executive Director, Brockwell Energy Ltd 2017-.

Political career: *House of Lords:* First entered House of Lords 1989; Government Whip 1995; Parliamentary Under-Secretary of State, Scottish Office 1995-97; Opposition Spokesperson for Green Issues June-October 1997; Elected hereditary peer 1999-. Member: European Communities Sub-committee C (Environment and Social Affairs) 1993-95, 1997-98, Sustainable Development 1994-95, Science and Technology Sub-committee II (Energy Efficiency) 2004-05, Partnerships (Prosecution) (Scotland) Bill 2013, EU Financial Affairs Sub-committee 2015-19, European Union 2019, Secondary Legislation Scrutiny 2019-. *Other:* Board member, Cairngorms Partnership 1998-2003; Member: Secretary of State's Advisory Group on Sustainable Development 1998-99, UK Round Table on Sustainable Development 1998-99; Chair: United Kingdom Accreditation Service 2002-; Better Regulation Commission:

Member 2006-08, Deputy chair 2007-08; DL, Fife 2007-; Member: Advisory board, Business and a Sustainable Environment 2007-15, Commission on Scottish Devolution 2008-09, Risk and Regulation Advisory Council 2008-10, Better Regulation Strategy Group 2013-15.

Political interests: Environment, agriculture, rural affairs, energy, food industry, Scotland, risk regulation, accreditation, standards.

Other: Inter-Parliamentary Union Committee on Environment: Member 1993-95, Vice-chair 1994-95; Chair, Landscape Foundation 1992-95; International Tree Foundation: President 1995-2005, Vice-President 2005-; Vice-President, Royal Smithfield Club 1998-; Director, West Highland Rail Heritage Trust Ltd 1998-2006; RSPB: Chair, Scotland 1998-2003, UK vice-president 2004-; Royal Scottish Geographical Society: President 2005-12, Vice-President 2012-; President, Royal Highland Agriculture Society of Scotland 2005-06; Chair, Moorland Forum 2007-18; Director and Trustee, Leven Valley Development Trust 2009-18; President, National Trust (Scotland) 2012-17; Trustee, Prince's Countryside Fund 2018-; Chair, Business Banking Grant Implementation Steering Committee, ClearBank and Tide 2019-; Freedom, City of London 2015; Hon. Fellow, Institute of Wastes Management 1998-; Fellow, Royal Agricultural Societies 2003; Honorary doctorate, Glasgow University 2012; Green Ribbon Political Award 1995. New Club (Edinburgh).

The Earl of Lindsay, House of Lords, London SW1A 0PW
Tel: 020 7219 5353 *Email:* lindsayj@parliament.uk
Lahill, Upper Largo KY8 6JE

CONSERVATIVE

LINGFIELD, LORD

LINGFIELD (Life Baron), Robert George Alexander Balchin; cr 2010. Born 31 July 1942; Son of late Leonard George and Elizabeth Balchin; Married Jennifer Kinlay 1970 (twin sons, 1 deceased).

Education: Bec School; London University; Hull University.

Non-political career: Teacher 1964-69; Researcher, Institute of Education, Hull University 1969-71; Chairman, HSW Ltd 1972-2000; St John Ambulance: Assistant director-general 1982-84, Director-general 1984-90, Member, Chapter-General, Order of St John 1984-99; Joint founder and treasurer, Catch 'em Young Project Trust 1984-98; Chairman: Grant-Maintained Schools Foundation 1989-99, Pardoe-Blacker (Publishing) Ltd 1989-99, CEFM Ltd 1994-; Imperial Society of Knights Bachelor: Council Member 1995-, Knight Registrar 1998-2006, Knight Principal and Chairman of Knight Bachelors' Council 2006-12, Knight President 2012-; President: English Schools Orchestra 1998-, League of Mercy 1999-; Chair: Blacker-Publishing Ltd 2003-09, Education Commission 2003-10, Government Review, Professionalism in Further Education (Lingfield Report) 2012; Chartered Institution for Further Education 2014-; Chair, Association of Super Recognisers 2018-. Honorary Colonel: Humberside & South Yorkshire ACF 2004-12, Reserve Forces and Cadets Music 2018-.

Political career: *House of Lords:* Raised to the peerage as Baron Lingfield, of Lingfield in the County of Surrey 2010. Member: EU Sub-committee F (Home Affairs, Health and Education) 2012-13, Lord Speaker's Advisory Panel on Works of Art 2019-. *Other:* Councillor, Surrey County Council 1981-85; Member, Funding Agency for Schools 1994-97; DL, Greater London 2001-.

Political interests: Education, stroke rehabilitation, arts, conservation, restoration; UK.

Other: Chairman, Balchin Family Society 1993-; Member of Court, Leeds University 1995-2000; Goldsmith' College, London: Council member 1997-2005, Deputy chair of council 1999-2005; Patron, Gateway Training Centre for Homeless 1999-2010; Chairman: ARNI Institute 2008-, Maritime Heritage Foundation 2011-; CVQO 2012-; Goldsmiths' Company 1980; Broderers' Company 2004-12; Apothecaries' Society 2014; Freedom, City of London 1980; Pro-chancellor, Brunel University 2008-13; FCP 1971; Honorary FHS 1987; Honorary FCP 1987; Honorary FCGI 1998; DLitt, Hull University; EdD, Brunel University; KStJ 1984; SMOM 1987; Kt 1993; GCFO 2014; GCEO 2014; Grand Officer of Merit SMOM 2017. Athenæum Club.

Publications: Emergency Aid in Schools (1984); Choosing a State School (1989); Many articles on politics and education.

Recreations: Restoration of ancient house.

The Lord Lingfield DL, House of Lords, London SW1A 0PW
Tel: 020 7219 5353

LABOUR

LIPSEY, LORD

LIPSEY (Life Baron), David Lawrence Lipsey; cr. 1999. Born 21 April 1948; Son of late Lawrence Lipsey and Penelope Lipsey; Married Margaret Robson 1982 (1 daughter 2 stepsons).

Education: Bryanston School, Dorset; Magdalen College, Oxford (BA philosophy, politics and economics 1970).

Non-political career: Research assistant, GMWU 1970-72; Political adviser to Anthony Crosland (in Opposition, DoE and FCO) 1972-77; Adviser to 10 Downing Street 1977-79; *New Society*: Journalist 1979-80, Editor 1986-88; Journalist, then economics editor, *Sunday Times* 1980-86; Founder/deputy editor, *Sunday Correspondent* 1988-90; Associate (acting deputy) editor, *The Times* 1990-92; Journalist, political editor, public policy editor, *The Economist* 1992-99; Visiting professor, Ulster University 1993-98; Public interest director, Personal Investment Authority 1994-2000; Chairman: Impower 2001-03, Shadow Racing Trust 2002-07, British Greyhound Racing Board 2004-08; Non-executive director, LWT/ITV London 2004-06; Visiting professor, Salford University 2008-12; Visiting fellow, Centre for European Studies, Harvard University, USA 2011.

Political career: *House of Lords:* Raised to the peerage as Baron Lipsey, of Tooting Bec in the London Borough of Wandsworth 1999. Member, Speakers' Working Group on All-Party Groups 2011-12. Member: Economic Affairs 2009-14, Sub-committee on Economic Affairs Finance Bill 2012-13, Information 2013-15, Long-Term Sustainability of the NHS 2016-17; Chair, Political Polling and Digital Media 2017-18; Member, Democracy and Digital Technologies 2019-. *Other:* Secretary, Streatham Labour Party 1970-72; Sat as non-affiliated December 2017-September 2019. Member: Jenkins Commission on Electoral Reform 1998, Royal Commission on Long-term Care of the Elderly 1998-99, Davies Panel on BBC Licence Fee 1999; Council member, Advertising Standards Authority 1999-2005; Chair, Financial Services' Consumers Panel 2008.

Political interests: Elderly people, electoral reform, psephology, machinery of government, greyhound welfare, racing, music.

Other: Chair: Fabian Society 1982-83, Make Votes Count 1999-2006, Social Market Foundation 2000-10; Member, advisory council, Constitution Unit; President, British Harness Racing Club 2015; Patron, Glasbury Arts Festival; Trustee, Mid Wales Music Trust; Chair, Straight Statistics 2008-11; President, Society of Later Life Advisers 2009-; Chair, Trinity Laban Conservatoire of Music and Dance 2012-17; Sidney Nolan Trust: Chair, President 2017-.

Publications: Labour and Land (1972); Editor, The Socialist Agenda (1981); The Name of the Rose (1992); The Secret Treasury (2000); In the Corridors of Power (autobiography) (Biteback, 2012); Counter Coup (2014).

Recreations: Music, golf, harness, point-to-point and greyhound racing, National Trust, opera, walking, cooking.

The Lord Lipsey, House of Lords, London SW1A 0PW
Tel: 020 7219 5353 *Email:* lipseyd@parliament.uk

LABOUR

LISTER OF BURTERSETT, BARONESS

LISTER OF BURTERSETT (Life Baroness), Margot Ruth Aline Lister; cr 2011. Born 3 May 1949; Daughter of Dr Werner Bernard and Daphne Lister.

Education: Moreton Hall, Shropshire; Essex University (BA sociology 1970); Sussex University (MA multi-racial studies 1971); Rusty French and German.

Non-political career: Child Poverty Action Group: Legal research officer 1971-75, Assistant director 1975-77, Deputy director 1977-79, Director 1979-87; Professor of Applied Social Studies, Bradford University 1987-93; Loughborough University: Professor of Social Policy 1994-2010, Emeritus Professor of Social Policy 2010-; Donald Dewar Visiting Professor of Social Justice, Glasgow University 2005-06. University and College Union (when employed).

Political career: *House of Lords:* Raised to the peerage as Baroness Lister of Burtersett, of Nottingham in the County of Nottinghamshire 2011. Member: Joint Committee on Human Rights 2012-15, Citizenship and Civic Engagement 2017-18. Vice-chair, PLP Departmental Group for Women 2015-.

Political interests: Poverty, social security, welfare reform, gender, children, refugees and asylum seekers; Australia, Japan, Nordic countries, USA.

Other: Vice-chair, NVCO 1991-93; Founding Academician, Academy of Social Sciences 1999; Member: Opsahl Commission 1992-93, Commission for Social Justice 1992-94, Commission on Poverty, Participation and Power 1999-2000; Trustee, Community Development Foundation (Government appointment) 2000-10; Member: Fabian Commission on Life Chances and Child Poverty 2004-06, National Equality Panel (Government appointment) 2009-10; Fellow, British Academy 2009; Honorary President, Child Poverty Action Group 2010-; Board Member, Smith Institute; Compass: Chair, Management Committee 2011-, Board 2019-; Patron, Just Fair 2012-; Honorary President, Social Policy Association 2016-; Patron, Project for the Registration of Children as British Citizens 2019-; Member, Forde Inquiry Panel 2020-; Hon LLD, Manchester University 1987; Hon DLitt, Glasgow Caledonian University 2011; Hon LLD, Brighton University 2012; DUniv, Essex University 2012; Hon DSc, Lincoln University; Hon LLD, Bath University 2014; Hon D.Litt, Loughborough University 2015; Lifetime Achievement Award, Social Policy Association; CBE 1999.

Publications: Supplementary Benefit Rights (1974); Welfare Benefits (1981); The Exclusive Society (1990); Women's Economic Dependency and Social Security (1992); Citizenship: feminist perspectives (1997, 2003); Poverty (2004); Co-author, Gendering Citizenship in Western Europe (2007); Co-editor, Why Money Matters (2008); Understanding Theories and Concepts in Social Policy (2010).

Recreations: Walking, watching tennis, tai chi, music, films, theatre, mindfulness.

The Baroness Lister of Burtersett CBE, House of Lords, London SW1A 0PW
Tel: 020 7219 8984 *Email:* listerr@parliament.uk
Website: www.lboro.ac.uk/departments/socialsciences/staff/academicandresearch/lister-ruth.html

CROSSBENCH

LISTOWEL, EARL OF

LISTOWEL (6th Earl of, I), Francis Michael Hare; cr. 1822; 6th Viscount Ennismore and Listowel (I) 1816; 6th Baron Ennismore (I) 1800; 4th Baron Hare (UK) 1869. Born 28 June 1964; Son of 5th Earl.

Education: Westminster School; Queen Mary and Westfield College, London (BA English literature 1992).

Political career: *House of Lords:* First entered House of Lords 1997. Sits as Baron Hare; Elected hereditary peer 1999-; On leave of absence January 2020-. Member: House of Lords Offices Library and Computers Sub-committee 2000-02, European Union Sub-committee F (Home Affairs) 2003-07. *Other:* Vice-President, Local Government Association 2018-.

Political interests: Young under-privileged; Angola.

Other: Trustee, Michael Sieff Foundation; Patron: Voice, Who Cares? Trust, Caspari Foundation; Anna Freud Centre, Beanstalk; Hon. doctorate, University of East London. Reform Club.

Recreations: Singing, music, art.

The Earl of Listowel, House of Lords, London SW1A 0PW
Tel: 020 7219 2247 *Email:* listowelf@parliament.uk
Email: francis.listowel@googlemail.com

CROSSBENCH

LISVANE, LORD

LISVANE (Life Baron), Robert James Rogers; cr 2014. Born 5 February 1950; Son of late Francis Barry Day Rogers and late Jeanne Turner Prichard Rogers; Married Revd Constance Jane Perkins 1981 (2 daughters).

Education: Tonbridge School (Scholar); Lincoln College, Oxford (Scholar and Judd exhibitioner, BA Anglo-Saxon, Norse and Celtic languages 1971, MA 1977; Rhodes Research Scholar 1971); French.

Non-political career: Ministry of Defence 1971; House of Commons 1972-2014: Assistant Clerk 1972, Various Procedural and Select Committee posts, Clerk of Select Committee on Defence 1983-89, Clerk of Private Members' Bills 1989-92, Clerk of the European Legislation Committee 1993-97, Principal Clerk 1997, Principal Clerk of Select Committees 1999-2001, Secretary to the House of Commons Commission 2001-03, Clerk of the Journals 2003-04, Principal Clerk of the Table Office 2004-06, Clerk of Legislation 2006-09, Clerk Assistant 2009-11, Clerk of the House and Chief Executive 2011-14.

Political career: *House of Lords:* Raised to the peerage as Baron Lisvane, of Blakemere in the County of Herefordshire and of Lisvane in the City and County of Cardiff 2014. Member: Delegated Powers and Regulatory Reform 2015-19, Ecclesiastical Committee 2015-, Secondary Legislation Scrutiny 2019-. *Other:* Independent Chair, Standards Committee: Herefordshire Council 2002-09, Herefordshire and Worcestershire Fire and Rescue Authority 2002-09; West Mercia Police Authority: Member, Standards Committee 2002-09, Independent Chair, Selection Committee 2004-09; Member, Parliamentary and Political Service Honours Committee 2014-; DL, Herefordshire 2016-; Independent Vice-President, Local Government Association 2016-17; Chief Steward, City of Hereford 2016-.

Political interests: Constitution, Parliament and the judiciary, rural issues, heritage, the arts (especially music); Australia, France, Italy, Greece, Oman, New Zealand.

Other: Chair: Hereford Cathedral Perpetual Trust 2007-09, Hereford Cathedral Fabric Committee 2018; Patron, Herefordshire Headway; Trustee: History of Parliament, Voces8 Foundation; Governor, Hereford Cathedral Perpetual Trust; Skinners' Company: Liveryman, Extra Member of the Court 2004-06; Renter Warden 2016; First Warden 2017, Master 2018; Freedom, City of London; Honorary Fellow, Lincoln College, Oxford; Honorary Bencher, Middle Temple; *Spectator* Parliamentarian of the Year 2014; KCB 2013. Travellers, Reform Club.

Publications: How Parliament Works (with Dr Rhodri Walters) (seventh edition 2015); Parliamentary Miscellanies: Order! Order! (2011); Who Goes Home? (2013) eighth edition (Besly and Goldsmith 2018).

Recreations: Music (church organist), cricket, sailing, shooting, natural history.

The Lord Lisvane KCB DL, House of Lords, London SW1A 0PW
Tel: 020 7219 5353 *Email:* lisvane@parliament.uk

LABOUR

LIVERMORE, LORD

LIVERMORE (Life Baron), Spencer Elliot Livermore; cr 2015. Born 12 June 1975; Married Seb Dance 2016 (Former MEP for London region).

Education: Beauchamps Comprehensive School, Wickford; London School of Economics (BSc economics 1996).

Non-political career: Labour Party: Economic Secretariat 1996-98, Senior adviser 1997, 2001 and 2005 general election campaigns, General election campaign director 2014-15; HM Treasury: Special adviser 1998-2003, Chief strategy adviser to Gordon Brown MP as Chancellor of the Exchequer 2003-07; Director of political strategy, Prime Minister's Office 2007-08; Senior strategist, Saatchi & Saatchi 2008-09; Head of strategy, Blue Rubicon 2009-14; Founder, Thirty Six Strategy 2012-14; Partner, BritainThinks 2016-18.

Political career: *House of Lords:* Raised to the peerage as Baron Livermore, of Rotherhithe in the London Borough of Southwark 2015. Opposition Whip 2020; Opposition Spokesperson for Treasury 2020; On leave of absence July 2020-. Member, Economic Affairs 2016-19. *Other:* Patron, LGBT Labour.

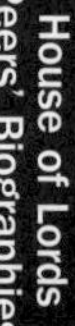

Political interests: Economy and finance, business, industry and consumers, social mobility, education, employment and training, parliament, government and politics, election campaigns; Australia, China, European Union, India, Israel, United Kingdom, USA.

Other: Chair, Lowick Associates Group 2019-.

The Lord Livermore, House of Lords, London SW1A 0PW
Tel: 020 7219 3000 *Twitter:* @SpenceLivermore

CONSERVATIVE

LIVERPOOL, EARL OF

LIVERPOOL (5th Earl of, UK), Edward Peter Bertram Savile Foljambe; cr. 1905; Viscount Hawkesbury; 5th Baron Hawkesbury (UK) 1893. Born 14 November 1944; Son of Captain Peter George William Savile Foljambe; Married Lady Juliana Noel 1970 (divorced 1994) (2 sons); married Comtesse Marie-Ange de Pierredon 1995 (divorced 2001); married Georgina Lederman 2002.

Education: Shrewsbury School; Perugia University, Italy (Italian and Italian art 1963).

Non-political career: Melbourns Brewery Ltd, Stamford, Lincolnshire: Managing director 1971-76, Joint chair and managing director 1977-87; Director: Hilstone Developments Ltd 1986-91, Hart Hambleton plc 1986-92, Rutland Properties Ltd 1987-, J W Cameron & Co Ltd 1987-91; Chair and managing director, Maxador Ltd 1987-97; Chair, Rutland Management Ltd 1997-.

Political career: *House of Lords:* First entered House of Lords 1969; Elected hereditary peer 1999-. Member, EU Sub-committee B (Internal Market, Infrastructure and Employment) 2012-15.

Political interests: Environment, renewables, green energy, transport, IT, aviation.

Other: Turf, Pratt's, Air Squadron Club.

Recreations: Flying, golf, shooting.

The Earl of Liverpool, House of Lords, London SW1A 0PW
Tel: 020 7219 5406 *Fax:* 020 7219 0318 *Email:* liverpoole@parliament.uk

CONSERVATIVE

LIVINGSTON OF PARKHEAD, LORD

LIVINGSTON OF PARKHEAD (Life Baron), Ian Paul Livingston; cr 2013. Born 28 July 1964; Married Debbie (1 son 1 daughter).

Education: Manchester University (BA economics).

Non-political career: Arthur Andersen 1984-87; Bank of America International 1987-88; 3i Group plc 1988-91; Senior management roles 1991-96; Chief finance officer, Dixons Group plc 1996-2002; BT Group plc: Chief finance director 2002-05, Chief executive officer, BT Retail 2005-08, Chief executive officer 2008-13; Dixons Carphone plc: Deputy Chair 2015-17, Chair 2017-; Chair, Man Group plc 2016-.

Political career: *House of Lords:* Raised to the peerage as Baron Livingston of Parkhead, of Parkhead in the City of Glasgow 2013. Minister of State for Trade and Investment and Government Spokesperson, Department for Business, Innovation and Skills and Foreign and Commonwealth Office 2013-15. Member, Economic Affairs 2019-.

Other: Associate, Institute of Chartered Accountants; Non-executive director: Freeserve plc 1999-2001, Hilton Group plc 2003-06, Celtic Football Club 2007-17, Belmond Ltd 2015-19, Jewish Care 2015-; Advisory board member, Livingbridge 2016-; Member, ICAEW (Institute of Chartered Accountants in England and Wales).

Recreations: Football, theatre.

The Lord Livingston of Parkhead, House of Lords, London SW1A 0PW
Email: livingstoni@parliament.uk *Twitter:* @Lord_Livingston

CONSERVATIVE

LLEWELLYN OF STEEP, LORD

LLEWELLYN OF STEEP (Life Baron), Edward David Gerard Llewellyn; cr 2016. Born 23 September 1965; Married Anne (3 children).

Education: Eton College; New College, Oxford (BA modern languages).

Non-political career: Conservative Research Department 1988-92: Private Secretary to Margaret Thatcher (on secondment) 1990-91; Personal Adviser to Chris Patten as Governor of Hong Kong 1992-97; Office of UN High Representative, Sarajevo 1997-99; Cabinet of Chris Patten as EU Commissioner for External Relations 1999-2002; Chief of Staff to Lord Ashdown of Norton-sub-Hamdon as UN High Representative, Sarajevo 2002-05; Chief of Staff to David Cameron: as Leader of the Opposition 2005-10, as Prime Minister 2010-16; Ambassador to France 2016-.

Political career: *House of Lords:* Raised to the peerage as Baron Llewellyn of Steep, of Steep in the County of Hampshire 2016. Leave of absence November 2016-.

Other: MBE 1997; OBE 2006; PC 2015.

Rt Hon the Lord Llewellyn of Steep OBE, House of Lords, London SW1A 0PW
Tel: 020 7219 3000 *Twitter:* @EdLlewellynFCO

NON-AFFILIATED

LONDON, LORD BISHOP OF

LONDON (133rd Bishop of), Sarah Elisabeth Mullally. Born 26 March 1962; Married Eamonn James Mullally 1987 (1 daughter 1 son).

Education: Polytechnic of the Southbank (BSc nursing 1984; MSc health and welfare studies 1992); Kent University (Diploma theology 2001); Heythrop College, London (MA pastoral theology 2006).

Non-political career: St Thomas' Hospital, London 1984-87: Staff Nurse 1984-87, Clinical Teacher 1987; Staff Nurse, Royal Marsden Hospital, London 1987-88; Ward Sister, Westminster Hospital, London 1988-90; Senior Nurse, Riverside Health Authority, London 1990-92; Assistant Chief Nurse, Riverside Hospital 1992-94; Director of Nursing and Deputy Chief Executive, Chelsea and Westminster Healthcare Trust, London 1994-99; Chief Nursing Officer, Department of Health 1999-2004; Ordained deacon 2001; Non-stipendiary minister, Battersea Fields 2001-04; Team rector, Sutton 2006-12; Canon Resident and Treasurer, Salisbury Cathedral 2012-15; Bishop Suffragan of Crediton, Diocese of Exeter 2015-17; Bishop of London 2018-.

Political career: *House of Lords:* Entered House of Lords 2018. *Other:* Governor, South Bank University 2005-15; Non-executive director: Royal Marsden NHS Foundation Trust 2005-13, Salisbury NHS Foundation Trust 2013-16; Governor, King's College London 2016-.

Other: Honorary Fellow, South Bank University 2000; Honorary degree: Bournemouth University 2004, Wolverhampton University 2004, Hertfordshire University 2005; DBE 2005; PC 2018.

Recreations: Pottery.

Rt Rev and Rt Hon the Bishop of London DBE, House of Lords, London SW1A 0PW
Tel: 020 7219 3000
St Michael Paternoster Royal, College Hill, London EC4R 2RL *Tel:* 020 3837 5200
Email: bishop.london@london.anglican.org Website: bishopoflondon.org
Twitter: @bishopSarahM

CROSSBENCH

LOOMBA, LORD

LOOMBA (Life Baron), Rajinder Paul Loomba; cr 2011. Born 13 November 1943; Son of late Shri Jagiri Lal Loomba and late Shrimati Pushpa Wati Loomba; Married Veena (2 daughters 1 son).

Education: D.A.V. College, Jalandhar, India; State University of Iowa, USA (1962); Hindi, Punjabi.

Non-political career: Founder and chairman: Rinku Group 1980-, The Loomba Group of Companies 1980-, The Loomba Foundation 1997-, India First Ltd 1999-.

Political career: *House of Lords:* Raised to the peerage as Baron Loomba, of Moor Park in the County of Hertfordshire 2011. *Other:* Left Liberal Democrats December 2016; now sits as a Crossbencher. Member, board of governors, University of East London 2008-12.

Political interests: Humanitarian causes, raise awareness of the plight of widows around the world, international development aid projects for empowermment; South Asia, Bangladesh, Chile, Gabon, India, Kenya, Malawi, Nepal, Rwanda, South Africa, Sri Lanka, Uganda, UK, USA.

Other: Vice-patron, Gates 1998-2005; London First: Board member 2000-04, Member, President's Council 2004-06; Member, Royal Institute of International Affairs 2002-09; Patron, Children in Need, India 2002-12; Founding patron, World Punjabi Organisation 2002-; Trustee, Maharajah Ranjit Singh Trust, India 2004-16; Vice-president: Barnardo's 2005-, Safer London Foundation 2006-12; Chairman, Friends of the Three Faiths Forum 2007-12; Member, Board of development, Oxfam 2008-11; Ambassador, Global Partnership Forum 2011-15; Oxfam, Barnardo's, YBI, Virgin Unite; Freedom, City of London 2000; Fellow, Royal Society of Arts 2004-; Honorary Fellowship, Northampton University 2014; International Excellence Award 1991; Hind Rattan Award 1991; Asian of the Year Award 1997; Pride of India Gold Medal 1998; Highly Commended New Initiative, Beacon Prize 2004; Priyadarshni Academy Global Award 2006; Charity of the Year, The Asian Who's Who awards 2006; Forbes India NRI Philanthropy Award 2012; First Founding Champion of the Widows Rights, UN Women 2013; Pravasi Saman Patra Award 2015; Life Time Achievement Award, UN Association 2016; CBE 2008. Rotary Club of London 2001-; Moor Park Golf Club.

Publications: Invisible Forgotten Sufferers: The Plight of Widows Around the World; Hidden Calamaties; One Man Walking; World Widows Report.

Recreations: Walking, reading, cooking.

The Lord Loomba CBE, House of Lords, London SW1A 0PW
Tel: 020 7219 3000 *Email:* loombar@parliament.uk
Loomba House, 622 Western Avenue, London W3 0TF *Tel:* 020 8102 0351
Email: raj@loomba.com Website: www.theloombafoundation.org

CONSERVATIVE

LOTHIAN, MARQUESS OF

LOTHIAN (13th Marquess of, S), Michael Andrew Foster Jude Kerr; cr 1701; 14th Earl of Lothian (S) 1606; 15th Earl of Ancram (S) 1633; Viscount of Briene (S) 1701; Lord Newbottle (S) 1591; Lord Jedburgh (S) 1622; Lord Kerr (S) 1633; 8th Baron Ker (UK) 1821; (Life) Baron Kerr of Monteviot 2010. Born 7 July 1945; Son of late 12th Marquess of Lothian, KCVO, DL; Married Lady Jane Fitzalan-Howard 1975, daughter of 16th Duke of Norfolk (2 daughters).

Education: Ampleforth College, Yorkshire; Christ Church, Oxford (BA history 1966, MA); Edinburgh University (LLB 1968); French.

Non-political career: Advocate, Scottish Bar 1970-79; QC (Scot) 1996.

Political career: *House of Commons:* Contested West Lothian 1970 general election. MP (Conservative) for Berwickshire and East Lothian February-October 1974. Contested Berwickshire and East Lothian October 1974 general election. MP for Edinburgh South 1979-87. Contested Edinburgh South 1987 general election. MP for Devizes 1992-2010; Parliamentary Under-Secretary of State, Scottish Office 1983-87; Northern Ireland Office: Parliamentary Under-Secretary of State 1993-94, Minister of State 1994-97; Member Shadow Cabinet 1997-2005: Frontbench Spokesperson for Constitutional Affairs, with overall responsibility for Scottish and Welsh issues 1997-98, Deputy Leader of the Opposition 2001-05; Shadow Secretary of State for: Foreign and Commonwealth Affairs 2001-05, International

Affairs 2003-05, Defence 2005; Member, Intelligence and Security Committee 2006-10. Member: Energy 1980-83, Public Accounts 1992-93. Chair: Conservative Parliamentary Constitutional Committee 1992-93, Conservative Party Committee for Constitutional Affairs, Scotland and Wales 1997-98, Conservative Defence/Foreign Affairs Policy Committee 2001-05. *House of Lords:* Created a life peer as Baron Kerr of Monteviot, of Monteviot in Roxburghshire 2010. Member, Intelligence and Security Committee 2010-19. *Other:* Chair, Conservative Party in Scotland 1980-83; Conservative Party: Deputy Chair June-October 1998, Chair 1998-2001, Contested leadership election 2001, Member, Policy Board 2001-05; Vice-President, Conservatives for Britain 2015-16. DL, Roxburgh, Ettrick and Lauderdale 1990-.

Political interests: Housing, defence, agriculture; Middle East.

Other: Member, Board of Scottish Homes 1988-90; Chairman, Global Strategy Forum 2006-; Freedom: City of Gibraltar 2010-, Devizes Town 2011-; PC 1996; Grand Prior, Order of Saint Lazarus of Jerusalem 2013-. New (Edinburgh), Whites, Beefsteak, Pratt's Club.

Publications: Numerous pamphlets published by Global Strategy Forum.

Recreations: Skiing, photography, folksinging.

Most Hon the Marquess of Lothian PC QC DL, House of Lords, London SW1A 0PW
Tel: 020 7219 5353 *Email:* lothianm@parliament.uk

CROSSBENCH

LOW OF DALSTON, LORD

LOW OF DALSTON (Life Baron), Colin MacKenzie Low; cr 2006. Born 23 September 1942; Son of Arthur Eric Low and Catherine Cameron Low, née Anderson; Married Jill Irene Coton 1969 (1 son 1 daughter).

Education: Worcester College for the Blind; Queen's College, Oxford (BA jursiprudence 1965, MA); Churchill College, Cambridge (Diploma criminology 1966).

Non-political career: Law lecturer, Leeds University 1968-84; Director, Disability Resource Team (initially within GLC) 1984-94; City University, London: Senior research fellow 1994-2000, Visiting professor 2001-. Member: Association of University Teachers 1968-84, 1994-2000, NALGO/Unison 1984-94.

Political career: *House of Lords:* Raised to the peerage as Baron Low of Dalston, of Dalston in the London Borough of Hackney 2006. Member: Procedure 2007-12, Liaison 2016-. *Other:* Member: Special Educational Needs Tribunal 1994-, National Disability Council 1996-2000, Disability Rights Commission 2000-02; Independent member, House of Lords Appointment Commission 2014-19; Equality and Human Rights Commission, Disability Advisory Committee 2018-.

Political interests: Disability, higher education, arts, music, broadcasting, crime and delinquency, assisted dying; Australia, South Africa, USA.

Other: Life member and holder of various offices, National Federation of the Blind 1969-92; Member and various positions, Association of Blind and Partially Sighted Teachers and Students 1970-; SKILL (National Bureau for Students with Disabilities): Member 1974-2011, Vice-president 2003-11; Disability Alliance: Chair 1991-97, President 1997-2010; Royal National Institute of the Blind: Chair 2000-09, Vice-President 2009-; President: European Blind Union 2003-11, International Council for the Education of all Visually Impaired People 2010-16; Hon. Fellow, The Queen's College Oxford 2006; Hon. Doctorate: Open University 2011, Worcester University 2014; Hon. Doctor of Laws, Leeds University 2017; Liberty Campaigner of the Year 2014; CBE 2000.

Publications: Co-author: An Equal Say in Our Own Affairs (National Federation of the Blind of the United Kingdom [NFBUK] 1971), Educational Provision for the Visually Handicapped (NFBUK and Association of Blind and Partially Sighted Teachers and Students, 1973); Plus numerous articles on provision for the disabled, particularly education.

Recreations: Music, wine.

The Lord Low of Dalston CBE, House of Lords, London SW1A 0PW
Tel: 020 7219 4119 *Email:* lowc@parliament.uk

CONSERVATIVE

LUCAS OF CRUDWELL AND DINGWALL, LORD

LUCAS OF CRUDWELL (11th Baron, E) cr. 1663, and DINGWALL (de facto 8th Lord, 14th but for the attainder) (S) cr. 1609; Ralph Matthew Palmer. Born 7 June 1951; Son of late Major Hon. Robert Jocelyn Palmer, MC, and Anne Rosemary, Baroness Lucas of Crudwell (10th in line); Married Clarissa Lockett 1978 (divorced 1995) (1 son 1 daughter); married Amanda Atha 1995 (died 2000); married Antonia Rubinstein 2001 (1 daughter).

Education: Eton College; Balliol College, Oxford (BA physics 1972).

Non-political career: Articles with various firms once part of Arthur Andersen 1972-76; With S G Warburg & Co Ltd 1976-88; Director of various companies, principally those associated with the Good Schools Guide.

Political career: *House of Lords:* First entered House of Lords 1991; Government Whip 1994-97; Government Spokesperson for: Education 1994-95, Social Security and the Welsh Office 1994-97, Agriculture, Fisheries and Food and Environment 1995-97; Opposition Spokesperson for: Agriculture, Fisheries and Food 1997, Constitutional Affairs, Scotland and Wales (Wales) 1997, Environment, Transport and the Regions (Environment) 1997, International Development 1997-98; Elected hereditary peer 1999-. Member: Animals in Scientific Procedures 2001-02, Sub-committee on House of Lords' Offices Library and Computers, Information -2003; Co-opted Member, European Union Sub-committee E (Law and Institutions) 2006-07; Member: Merits of Statutory Instruments 2007-11, Science and Technology Sub-committee I 2012-13, Digital Skills 2014-15, Intellectual Property (Unjustified Threats) Bill 2016, Regenerating Seaside Towns and Communities 2018-19, Democracy and Digital Technologies 2019-.

Political interests: Education, liberty, planning, finance, electronic government, copyright.

Other: Safe Ground; Fellow, Institute of Chartered Accountants in England and Wales; Liveryman, Mercers' Company; FCA.

The Lord Lucas of Crudwell and Dingwall, House of Lords, London SW1A 0PW
Tel: 020 7219 4177 *Email:* lucasr@parliament.uk *Twitter:* @LordLucasCD

LIBERAL DEMOCRAT

LUDFORD, BARONESS

Liberal Democrat Lords Spokesperson for Existing European Union

LUDFORD (Life Baroness), Sarah Ann Ludford; cr. 1997. Born 14 March 1951; Daughter of Joseph Campbell Ludford and Valerie Kathleen, née Skinner; Married Stephen Hitchins 1982 (died 2019).

Education: Portsmouth High School for Girls; London School of Economics (BSc Econ international history 1972; MSc Econ European studies 1977); Inns of Court School of Law; French, German.

Non-political career: Civil servant, Department of the Environment 1972-73; Independent Broadcasting Authority 1973-75; Called to the Bar, Gray's Inn 1979; Official, European Commission, Brussels 1979-85; European adviser, Lloyd's of London 1985-87; American Express Europe 1987-90; European affairs consultant 1990-99.

Political career: *House of Commons:* Contested (Liberal Democrat) Islington North 1992 and Islington South and Finsbury 1997 general elections. *House of Lords:* Raised to the peerage as Baroness Ludford, of Clerkenwell in the London Borough of Islington 1997. As an MEP, disqualified from participation 2009-14; Liberal Democrat Lords Spokesperson for: Europe 2015-16, Exiting the European Union 2016-19, Existing European Union 2020-. Member: EU Justice Sub-committee 2015-19, Joint Committee on Human Rights 2019-. *Other:* European Parliament: Contested Hampshire East and Wight 1984 and London Central 1989 and 1994 elections, MEP for London region 1999-2014 (as Sarah Ludford): ALDE spokesperson on justice and home affairs, Rapporteur on anti-racism 2000-09, Vice-chair, Anti-racism and Diversity Intergroup, Co-ordinator, Kurdish Network, Contested London region 2014 election. Liberal Democrat Party: Vice-chair, Federal Policy Committee, Vice-president, Liberal Democrat LGBT Group; Council member, European Liberal Democrat and Reform Party; Vice-president, Liberal Democrat Friends of Israel. Councillor, London Borough of Islington 1991-99.

Political interests: Europe, justice and home affairs, foreign affairs; Balkans, Cyprus, Middle East, Turkey, USA.

Other: Council member, Justice; Federal Trust; Member: Royal Institute of International Affairs (Chatham House), European Movement; Parliamentary Fellow, Institute of Public Affairs, London School of Economics.

Recreations: Theatre, ballet.

The Baroness Ludford, House of Lords, London SW1A 0PW
Tel: 020 7219 5353 *Email:* ludfords@parliament.uk *Twitter:* @SarahLudford

NON-AFFILIATED

LUPTON, LORD

LUPTON (Life Baron), James Roger Crompton Lupton; cr 2015. Born 15 June 1955; Married Beatrice 1983 (3 daughters 1 son).

Education: Sedbergh School; Lincoln College, Oxford (BA law 1976); French.

Non-political career: Lovell White & King 1977-79; Qualified Solicitor 1979; S G Warburg & Co 1979-80; Deputy Chair, Barings Bank 1980-95; Managing director, Greenhill & Co 1998-; Chair, Greenhill Europe 2011-17; Non-executive director, Lloyds Banking Group plc 2017-.

Political career: *House of Lords:* Raised to the peerage as Baron Lupton, of Lovington in the County of Hampshire 2015. Member, Charities 2016-17. *Other:* Co-treasurer, Conservative Party 2013-16; Left Conservatives July 2019, now sits as non-affiliated. Governor, Downe House School 1998-2006; Trustee, British Museum 2012-17; Chairman, Dulwich Picture Gallery 2006-11.

Political interests: Child welfare, business, the City, the arts, responsible capitalism; France, Spain, UK.

Other: Advisory Board, Grange Park Opera 1997-2011; Member, international advisory board, Global Leadership Foundation 2008-; Chair, Lovington Foundation 2014-; Member, Law Society; Lovington Foundation, Kids Company, Emmaus Hampshire, Dulwich Picture Gallery, British Museum; CBE 2012. Brooks' Club, 5 Hertford Street, City Capital Club.

Recreations: Opera, skiing, shooting, collecting art, music and family.

The Lord Lupton CBE, House of Lords, London SW1A 0PW
Tel: 020 7219 3000 *Email:* luptonj@parliament.uk
Tel: 020 7198 7424 *Email:* jlupton@greenhill.com

CROSSBENCH

LYTTON, EARL OF

LYTTON (5th Earl, UK), John Peter Michael Scawen Lytton; cr. 1880; Viscount Knebworth; 17th Baron Wentworth (E) 1529; 6th Baron Lytton (UK) 1866; 6th Bt of Knebworth (UK) 1838. Born 7 June 1950; Son of 4th Earl of Lytton; Married Ursula Alexandra (2 sons 1 daughter).

Education: Downside School, Somerset; College of Estate Management; Reading University (BSc estate management 1972).

Non-political career: Valuation officer, Inland Revenue 1975-81; Associate partner, Permutt Brown & Co 1982-86; Cubitt and West 1986-87; Founder, John Lytton & Co Chartered Surveyors 1988- (John Lytton & Co Ltd 2009-).

Political career: *House of Lords:* First entered House of Lords 1985; Sponsor Party Wall etc. Bill 1996; Elected hereditary peer 2011-. Member: Information 2012-15, Built Environment 2015-16. *Other:* Vice-president: National Association of Local Councils, Local Government Association.

Political interests: Communities and local government finance, countryside conservation, agriculture, rural economy, town and country planning, property taxation.

Other: Council member, Country Landowners' Association 1993-; Horsham Chamber of Commerce: Chair 1993-95, President 1995-; Chairman: Leasehold Enfranchisement Advisory Service 1994-97, Leasehold Advisory Service 1997-; President: Newsted Abbey Byron Society, Institute of Heraldic and Genealogical Studies, 1st Shipley Scout Group, West Sussex, Sussex Association of Local Councils 1997-; Member, Countryside Alliance; Trustee, Shipley

Windmill Trust; Hon. Fellow, Association of Building Engineers; Member, Chartered Institute of Arbitrators; FRICS; Elected member, Institute of Revenues, Rating and Valuation 1990.

The Earl of Lytton, House of Lords, London SW1A 0PW
Tel: 020 7219 5353 *Email:* lyttonj@parliament.uk

LABOUR/
CO-OPERATIVE

MCAVOY, LORD

Shadow Chief Whip in the House of Lords

McAVOY (Life Baron), Thomas McLaughlin McAvoy; cr 2010. Born 14 December 1943; Son of late Edward McAvoy, steelworker, and late Frances McLaughlin McAvoy; Married Eleanor Kerr 1968 (4 sons).

Education: St Columbkilles Secondary School.

Non-political career: Hoover plc, Cambuslang 1974-87. AEU shop steward, USDAW 1974-87; Member, Unite 1974-.

Political career: *House of Commons:* MP (Lab/Co-op) for Glasgow Rutherglen 1987-2005, for Rutherglen and Hamilton West 2005-10; Opposition Whip 1991-93, 1996-97; Government Whip 1997-2010; Deputy Chief Whip 2008-10. Member: Northern Ireland Affairs 1994-96, Finance and Services 1997-2009, Selection 2008-10, Administration 2009, Members' Allowances 2009-10. PLP Departmental Committee on Northern Ireland: Member 1996-2010, Co-vice-chair 1996-97. *House of Lords:* Raised to the peerage as Baron McAvoy, of Rutherglen in the County of Lanarkshire 2010. Opposition Whip 2011-15; Opposition Spokesperson for: Northern Ireland 2012-18, Scotland 2012-18; Opposition Deputy Chief Whip 2015-18; Shadow Chief Whip in the House of Lords 2018-; Deputy Chairman of Committees 2018-; Deputy Speaker 2018-. Member: Administration and Works 2012-15, Partnerships (Prosecution) (Scotland) Bill 2013, Privileges and Conduct 2018-19, Procedure/Procedure and Privileges 2018-, Selection 2018-, Services 2018. *Other:* Member, Co-operative Party. Chair, Rutherglen Community Council 1980-82; Councillor, Strathclyde Regional Council 1982-87.

Political interests: Social services; Ireland, USA.

Other: PC 2003. South Lanarkshire Council, Eastfield Lifestyles.

Rt Hon the Lord McAvoy, House of Lords, London SW1A 0PW
Tel: 020 7219 5009 *Email:* mcavoyto@parliament.uk

CONSERVATIVE

MCCOLL OF DULWICH, LORD

McCOLL OF DULWICH (Life Baron), Ian McColl; cr. 1989. Born 6 January 1933; Son of late Frederick and Winifred McColl; Married Dr Jean Lennox, née McNair 1960 (1 son 2 daughters) (died 2012); married Dr Evy Lise Kaarvang 2015.

Education: Hutchesons' Grammar School, Glasgow; St Paul's School, London (Foundation Scholarship classics); London University (Master of Surgery 1965; MB BS 1957).

Non-political career: Consultant surgeon and Sub Dean, St Bartholomew's Hospital 1967-71; Research fellow, Harvard Medical School 1967; Professor and Director of Surgery, Guy's Hospital 1971-98; Professor of Surgery, London University 1971-98; Consultant Surgeon to the Army 1980-98; Chair, Government Working Party on Artificial Limbs and Wheelchair Service (The McColl Report) 1984-86; Vice-chair, Disablement Services Authority 1987-91; Chair, Department of Surgery of the United Medical Schools of Guy's and St Thomas' Hospital 1988-92. Honorary Consultant Surgeon 1980-90; Honorary Group Captain, RAF, Armed Forces Parliamentary Scheme. BMA 1957-.

Political career: *House of Lords:* Raised to the peerage as Baron McColl of Dulwich, of Bermondsey in the London Borough of Southwark 1989. PPS to John Major as Prime Minister 1994-97; Deputy Speaker 1994-97, 1998-2002; Deputy Chairman of Committees 1994-97, 1998-2002; Opposition Spokesperson for Health 1997-2010. Member: European Communities Sub-committee F (Environment) 1991-94, Medical Ethics 1993-94, Science and Technology 2000-03, Science and Technology Sub-committees: IIA (Human Genetic Databases) 2000-01, II (Aircraft Cabin Environment) 2001, I (Systematic Biology and Biodiversity/Fighting Infection) 2002-03, I (Science and International Agreements) 2003-10, Patient-Assisted Dying for the terminally ill 2004, HIV and AIDS in the UK 2010-11, Joint Committee on the Draft Modern Slavery Bill 2014, Equality Act 2010 and Disability 2015-16, Long-Term Sustainability of the NHS 2016-17, Standing Orders (Private Bills) 2019-. *Other:* Member, governing council, Conservative Christian Fellowship.

Political interests: Anti-slavery legislation, anti-obesity epidemic campaign, disability, higher education, health service, forestry, medicine; Benin, Gambia, Ghana, Liberia, Madagascar, Malawi, Norway, Romania, Sierra Leone, Tanzania, Togo, Uganda.

Other: Commonwealth Parliamentary Association UK Branch: Member, executive committee 1999-2005, 2006-11, 2015-19, Vice-chair 2011-15; Vice-chair, Inter-Parliamentary Union, British Group 2014-15; Chair, UK Board of Mercy Ships; Governor-at-large for England, Board of Governors, American College of Surgeons 1982-86; Mildmay Mission Hospital: President 1985-2000, Vice-President 2000-; Council member, Royal College of Surgeons 1986-94; President: Society of Minimally Invasive Surgery 1991-94, National Association of Limbless Disabled 1992-; Vice-President, John Groom's Association for Disabled People 1992-; President: Hospital Saving Association 1994-2001, Association of Endoscopic Surgery of Great Britain and Ireland 1994-96, Leprosy Mission 1996-; Royal College of Surgeons; Shaftesbury Society, Mercyships, Livability, Bridge2Aid, Burrswood, British Home; Master, Worshipful Company of Barbers; FRCS 1962; FACS; FKC; MS; Fellow, King's College, London 2001; Hon. FDS RCS 2007; George and Thomas Hutchesons Award 2000; Great Scot Award for medical charity work 2002; National Maritime Historical Society Distinguished service award 2002; CBE 1997; Order of Mercy 2007. Palace of Westminster; Jags of Dulwich.

Publications: Intestinal Absorption in Man (1976); NHS Data Book (1984); Government Report on Artificial Limb and Appliance Centre Service (1986); As well as articles in medical journals.

Recreations: Forestry, ornithology.

Professor the Lord McColl of Dulwich CBE, House of Lords, London SW1A 0PW
Tel: 020 7219 5141 *Email:* mccolli@parliament.uk

LABOUR

MCCONNELL OF GLENSCORRODALE, LORD

McCONNELL OF GLENSCORRODALE (Life Baron), Jack Wilson McConnell; cr 2010. Born 30 June 1960; Son of William Wilson McConnell, tenant farmer, and Elizabeth McConnell; Married Bridget McLuckie 1990 (1 son 1 daughter).

Education: Arran High School, Isle of Arran; Stirling University (BSc mathematics; Dip Ed 1983).

Non-political career: Maths teacher, Lornshill Academy 1983-92; General secretary, Scottish Labour Party 1992-98; Education adviser, Clinton Hunter Development Initiative 2007-11; Prime Minister's Special Representative for Peace-Building 2008-10; Member, advisory board, PricewaterhouseCoopers. Member, Community.

Political career: *House of Commons:* Contested (Labour) Perth and Kinross 1987 general election. *House of Lords:* Raised to the peerage as Baron McConnell of Glenscorrodale, of the Isle of Arran in Ayrshire and Arran 2010. *Other:* Scottish Parliament: MSP for Motherwell and Wishaw constituency 1999-2011: Scottish Labour: Minister for: Finance 1999-2000, Education, Europe and External Affairs 2000-01, First Minister 2001-07. Member, Labour Scottish Executive 1989-92; Scottish Labour Party: General Secretary 1992-98, Leader 2001-07. Stirling District Council: Councillor 1984-93, Treasurer 1988-92, Council leader 1990-92; Member: Scottish Constitutional Convention 1989-98, Convention of Scottish Local Authorities 1990-92.

Political interests: Education, economic policy, international development, conflict and peacebuilding; China, EU, Japan, Malawi, Rwanda, USA.

Other: Member: Congress of Local and Regional Authorities in Europe 1999-2001, EU Committee of the Regions 2000-07; President, European Regions with Legislative Power 2004; Board Member, UK-Japan 21st Century Group 2010-; Ambassador: Action for Children, SSE's Scotland Sustainable Fund Panel; Pump Aid; Patron: Positive Women, Diana Awards; Advisory board, Institute for Cultural Diplomacy; Chair: Radio Clyde Cash for Kids, McConnell International Foundation, SSE Community Funding Panel 2013-; Patron, European Movement in Scotland 2016-; Various charities supporting international development and vulnerable children; Fellow, 48 Group Club; Honorary Doctorate, Stirling University 2008;

Scottish Politician of the Year 2001; UK Public Health Champion 2005; Scottish Politics Lifetime Achievement Award 2010; PC 2001. Lamlash Golf Club.

Recreations: Golf, music, sports, gardening.

Rt Hon the Lord McConnell of Glenscorrodale, House of Lords, London SW1A 0PW
Tel: 020 7219 8913 *Email:* mcconnellj@parliament.uk *Twitter:* @LordMcConnell

DEMOCRATIC UNIONIST PARTY

MCCREA OF MAGHERAFELT AND COOKSTOWN, LORD

McCREA OF MAGHERAFELT AND COOKSTOWN (Life Baron), Robert Thomas William McCrea; cr 2018. Born 6 August 1948; Son of late Robert Thomas McCrea, farmer, and late Sarah McCrea; Married Anne McKnight 1971 (2 sons 3 daughters).

Education: Cookstown Grammar School; Marietta Bible College, Ohio, USA (doctorate of divinity 1989); Theological College of Free Presbyterian Church of Ulster.

Non-political career: Civil servant, Northern Ireland Department of Health and Social Services 1966-82; Director, Daybreak Recording Company 1981-; Gospel recording artist.

Political career: *House of Commons:* MP for Mid Ulster 1983 to 17 December 1985 (resigned seat in protest against Anglo-Irish Agreement), 23 January 1986 by-election to 1997. Contested Mid Ulster 1997 general election. MP for South Antrim 21 September 2000 by-election to 2001. Contested South Antrim 2001 general election. MP for South Antrim 2005-10, for South Antrim (revised boundary) 2010-15. Contested South Antrim 2015 general election; Member, Public Accounts Commission -2011; DUP: Spokesperson for: Environment, Food and Rural Affairs 2005-10, Local Government 2009-10; Shadow Leader of the House/House Issues 2009-15; Spokesperson for Justice and Home Affairs 2010-15; Shadow Deputy Prime Minister 2012-15. Member: Chairmen's Panel/Panel of Chairs 2006-15, Joint Committee on the Draft House of Lords Reform Bill 2011-12. *House of Lords:* Raised to the peerage as Baron McCrea of Magherafelt and Cookstown, of Magherafelt in the County of Londonderry and Cookstown in the County of Tyrone 2018. *Other:* Northern Ireland Assembly: Member 1982-86; Member, Northern Ireland Forum for Political Dialogue 1996-98; MLA for Mid Ulster 1998-2007, for South Antrim 2007-10: DUP Spokesperson for Environment 1998, Chair, Committee on Environment 1999-2002, Deputy Whip, DUP Assembly Group, Member, Preparation for Government Committee 2006-07, Chair, Committee on Agriculture and Rural Development 2007-09. Board of Governors, Magherafelt High School; Magherafelt District Council: Councillor 1973-2010, Chair 1977-81, 2002-03.

Political interests: Agriculture, health, elderly issues, environment, special needs education, planning; USA.

Other: Member: Woodland Trust, The Loyal Orange Order, Royal Black Institution and Apprentice Boys of Derry; Autism Northern Ireland (PAPA); RSPB Northern Ireland.

Publications: In His Pathway – The Story of the Reverend William McCrea (1980).

Recreations: Gospel music, horse riding.

Dr the Lord McCrea of Magherafelt and Cookstown, House of Lords, London SW1A 0PW
Tel: 020 7219 3000

LABOUR

MCDONAGH, BARONESS

McDONAGH (Life Baroness), Margaret Josephine McDonagh; cr. 2004. Born 26 June 1961; Daughter of Breda, née Doogue, psychiatric nurse, and Cumin McDonagh, building labourer.

Education: Holy Cross Secondary Modern, New Malden; Kingston College of Further Education, Surrey; Brunel University (BSc politics and modern history with statistics 1984); Kingston Business School (MA advanced marketing 1994); Harvard Business School, USA (advanced management programme 2002).

Non-political career: Labour Party 1987-2001: General election co-ordinator 1997, Secretary General 1998-2001; General manager, *Express* Newspapers 2001; Non-executive director: TBI plc 2004, Standard Life plc 2007. Amicus.

Political career: *House of Lords:* Raised to the peerage as Baroness McDonagh, of Mitcham and of Morden in the London Borough of Merton 2004. Member, House 2013-16.

The Baroness McDonagh, House of Lords, London SW1A 0PW
Tel: 020 7219 3000 *Email:* mcdonaghm@parliament.uk
Tel: 020 7636 9002

CROSSBENCH

MACDONALD OF RIVER GLAVEN, LORD

MACDONALD OF RIVER GLAVEN (Life Baron), Kenneth Donald John Macdonald; cr 2010. Born 4 January 1953; Married Linda Zuck 1980 (2 sons 1 daughter).

Education: St Edmund Hall, Oxford (BA philosophy, politics and economics 1974).

Non-political career: Called to the Bar, Inner Temple 1978; Practising criminal lawyer 1978-; QC 1997; Recorder 2001-; Director of public prosecutions 2003-08; Bencher 2004; Member, Matrix Chambers 2008-; Visiting Professor of Law, London School of Economics 2009-; Warden, Wadham College, Oxford; Deputy High Court Judge 2010-.

Political career: *House of Lords:* Raised to the peerage as Baron Macdonald of River Glaven, of Cley-next-the-Sea in the County of Norfolk 2010. Member, Constitution 2012-13. *Other:* Left Liberal Democrat group March 2018; Sat as Non-affiliated March 2018-March 2019; now sits as Crossbencher. Member: Treasury Counsel Selection Committee, Central Criminal Court 2001-03, Sentencing Guidelines Council 2003-08, Criminal Procedure Rules Committee 2003-08, Independent Commission on Youth Crime 2008-; Trustee, Index on Censorship 2009-; Advisory board, Centre for Criminology, Oxford University.

Political interests: Security, criminal justice, civil liberties.

Other: Member, Bar Council 2000; Bar Public Affairs Group: Member 2001-03, Vice-chair 2001-02; Criminal Bar Association: Vice-chair 2002-03, Chair 2003-; Kt 2007.

The Lord Macdonald of River Glaven QC, House of Lords, London SW1A 0PW
Tel: 020 7219 5353

CROSSBENCH

MCDONALD OF SALFORD, LORD

McDONALD OF SALFORD (Life Baron), Simon Gerard McDonald; cr 2021. Married Olivia Wright, daughter of Lord Wright of Richmond (4 children).

Education: Pembroke College, Cambridge.

Non-political career: Foreign and Commonwealth Office (FCO) 1982-2007: Benelux desk officer, WED 1982-83, Arabic language training, SOAS and UKAS 1983-85, Third Secretary, later second secretary, British Embassy, Jeddah, later Riyadh 1985-88, Second secretary (economic), British Embassy, Bonn 1988-90, Speech writer to the Foreign Secretary 1990-93, Private Secretary to PUS 1993-95, First Secretary, British Embassy, Washington DC 1995-98, Deputy Head of Mission, Counsellor and Consul-General, British Embassy, Riyadh 1998-2001, Principal Private Secretary to the Foreign Secretary 2001-03, Ambassador to Israel 2003-06; Prime Minister's Foreign Policy Adviser and Head of Foreign and Defence Policy, Cabinet Office 2007-10; FCO: Ambassador to Germany 2010-15, Permanent Under Secretary and Head of the Diplomatic Service 2015-20.

Political career: *House of Lords:* Raised to the peerage as Baron McDonald of Salford, of Pendleton in the City of Salford 2021.

Other: CMG 2004; KCMG 2014; KCVO 2015.

The Lord McDonald of Salford KCMG KCVO, House of Lords, London SW1A 0PW
Twitter: @SimonMcDonaldUK

NON-AFFILIATED

MCFALL OF ALCLUITH, LORD

Senior Deputy Speaker

McFALL OF ALCLUITH (Life Baron), John Francis McFall; cr 2010. Born 4 October 1944.

Political career: *House of Commons:* MP (Labour) for Dumbarton 1987-2005, for West Dunbartonshire 2005-10; Member Public Accounts Commission -2010; Opposition Whip 1989-91; Opposition Spokesperson for Scottish Affairs 1992-97; Government Whip 1997-98; Parliamentary Under-Secretary of State, Northern Ireland Office 1998-99 (Minister for Education, Training and Employment, Health and Community Relations 1998-99, for Economy and Education 1999). Chair, Treasury 2001-10; Member: Public Administration 2000-01, Treasury Sub-committee 2001-10, Liaison 2001-10, Liaison Sub-committee 2007-10. *House of Lords:* Raised to the peerage as Baron McFall of Alcluith, of Dumbarton in the County of Dunbartonshire 2010. Senior Deputy Speaker 2016-; Member, House of Lords Commission 2016-. Member: Economic Affairs Finance Bill Sub-Committee 2011, Joint Committee on the Draft Financial Services Bill 2011-12, Economic Affairs 2012-15, Parliamentary Commission on Banking Standards 2012-13, EU Financial Affairs Sub-committee 2015-16, European Union 2016; Chair: Privileges and Conduct 2016, Procedure/Procedure and Privileges 2016-, Liaison 2016-, Selection 2016-, Hybrid Instruments 2016-, Standing Orders (Private Bills) 2016-; Member, Parliamentary Works Estimates Commission 2020-. *Other:* Member, Co-operative Party.

Political interests: Defence, education, economic policy, co-operative development, Third World; Latin America, Middle East, Romania.

Other: Fellow, Industry and Parliament Trust 1989, 2003; DUniv: Strathclyde University 2010, Glasgow University 2011, Stirling University 2011; Hon. doctorate of business administration, BPP Business School, London 2011; DUniv, West of Scotland University 2012; PC 2004.

Recreations: Jogging, golf, reading.

Rt Hon the Lord McFall of Alcluith, House of Lords, London SW1A 0PW
Tel: 020 7219 6000 *Email:* hlseniordeputyspeaker@parliament.uk

CONSERVATIVE

MCGREGOR-SMITH, BARONESS

MCGREGOR-SMITH (Life Baroness), Ruby McGregor-Smith; cr 2015. Born 22 February 1963; Married Graham (2 children).

Education: Lowlands Sixth Form College; Kingston Polytechnic (BA economics 1985).

Non-political career: BDO Stoy Hayward; Serco Group plc; Mitie Group: Group Finance Director 2002-05, Group Chief Operating Officer 2005-07, Chief Executive 2007-16.

Political career: *House of Lords:* Raised to the peerage as Baroness McGregor-Smith, of Sunninghill in the Royal County of Berkshire 2015. Member: EU Internal Market Sub-committee 2017-19, Democracy and Digital Technologies 2019-, Risk Assessment and Risk Planning 2020-. *Other:* UK Business Ambassador for Professional and Business Services 2014-19; Non-executive board member: Department for Culture, Media and Sport -2015, Department for Education 2015-; Chair, Office for Tackling Injustices 2019-.

Other: Non-executive director, PageGroup 2007-17; Chair: Public Services Strategy Board, Confederation of British Industry, Women's Business Council; Corporate board member, Great Ormond Street Hospital; Chair, Airport Operators Association 2019-; Trustee, Cumberland Lodge 2019-; President, British Chambers of Commerce 2020-; Hon DLitt, Kingston University 2011; First Woman of Business Services, CBI 2007; Business Woman of the Year, Asian Woman of Achievement Awards 2008.

The Baroness McGregor-Smith CBE, House of Lords, London SW1A 0PW
Tel: 020 7219 3000

CONSERVATIVE

MCINNES OF KILWINNING, LORD

McINNES OF KILWINNING (Life Baron), Mark McInnes; cr 2016. Born 4 November 1976.

Education: Kilwinning Academy; Edinburgh University (MA 1998).

Non-political career: Director, Scottish Conservative and Unionist Party 2003-.

Political career: *House of Lords:* Raised to the peerage as Baron McInnes of Kilwinning, of Kilwinning in the County of Ayrshire 2016. Member: Communications/Communications and Digital 2019-, Common Frameworks Scrutiny 2020-. *Other:* Councillor, Edinburgh City Council 2003-17; Governor, George Watson's College 2007-16.

Other: Curator of Patronage, Edinburgh University 2007-17; Director: Changeworks Resources for Life -2010, Eric Liddell Centre -2011, Better Together 2013-15, Trustee, Merchant Company Endowment Trust; CBE 2016.

The Lord McInnes of Kilwinning CBE, House of Lords, London SW1A 0PW
Tel: 020 7219 3000 *Email:* mcinnesm@parliament.uk *Twitter:* @Morningsidemark

LABOUR

MCINTOSH OF HUDNALL, BARONESS

McINTOSH OF HUDNALL (Life Baroness), Genista Mary McIntosh; cr. 1999. Born 23 September 1946; Daughter of late Geoffrey and Maire Tandy; Married Neil McIntosh 1971 (divorced 1990) (1 son 1 daughter).

Education: Hemel Hempstead Grammar School; York University (BA philosophy and sociology 1968).

Non-political career: Press Secretary, York Festival of Arts 1968-69; Royal Shakespeare Company: Casting director 1972-77, Planning controller 1977-84, Senior administrator 1986-90, Associate producer 1990; Executive director, Royal National Theatre 1990-January 1997, October 1997-2002; Chief executive, Royal Opera House, Covent Garden 1997; Principal, Guildhall School of Music and Drama 2002-03.

Political career: *House of Lords:* Raised to the peerage as Baroness McIntosh of Hudnall, of Hampstead in the London Borough of Camden 1999. Deputy Chairman of Committees 2007-; Deputy Speaker 2008-; Member: Consultative Panel on Parliamentary Security, House of Lords Commission 2016-. Member: Joint Scrutiny Committees on: Draft Mental Incapacity Bill 2003, Draft Charities Bill 2004, Draft Mental Health Bill 2004-05, Liaison 2005-09; Chair, London Local Authorities Bill 2006; Member: Communications/Communications and Digital 2007-10, 2016-, Administration and Works 2007-11, 2012-15, House 2010-12, HIV and AIDS in the UK 2010-11, Mental Capacity Act 2005 2013-14, Procedure 2013-16, Ecclesiastical Committee 2014-, Leader's Group on Governance 2015, Lord Speaker's Advisory Panel on Works of Art 2019-.

Political interests: Arts, public health, education, sustainable transport.

Other: Trustee: Roundhouse Trust 2000-17, Southbank Sinfonia 2000-, National Opera Studio 2006-16, Artis Foundation 2018-; Board member, Royal Shakespeare Company 2010-; Patron: Helena Kennedy Bursary Scheme, Cantate; Fellow, Royal Society of Arts; Childline, National Trust, Cancer Research; Three honorary degrees; Honorary fellowship, Goldsmith's College 2003.

Recreations: Gardening, music.

The Baroness McIntosh of Hudnall, House of Lords, London SW1A 0PW
Tel: 020 7219 8732 *Email:* mcintoshg@parliament.uk

CONSERVATIVE

MCINTOSH OF PICKERING, BARONESS

McINTOSH OF PICKERING (Life Baroness), Anne Caroline Ballingall McIntosh; cr 2015. Born 20 September 1954; Daughter of late Dr Alastair McIntosh, medical practitioner, and late Grethe-Lise McIntosh; Married John Harvey 1992.

Education: Harrogate Ladies' College; Edinburgh University (LLB 1977); Åarhus University, Denmark (European law 1978); French, Danish, Spanish, German, Italian.

Non-political career: Trainee, EEC Competition Directorate, Brussels 1978; Legal adviser, Didier & Associates, Brussels 1979-80; Apprentice, Scottish Bar, Edinburgh 1980-82; Advocate, practising with European Community Law Office, Brussels 1982-83; Adviser, European Democratic Group, principally on Transport, Youth Education, Culture, Tourism, Relations with Scandinavia, Austria and Yugoslavia 1983-89; Strategic Adviser, Anne McIntosh Consulting Ltd 2015-.

Political career: *House of Commons:* Contested Workington 1987 general election. MP (Conservative) for Vale of York 1997-2010, for Thirsk and Malton 2010-15; Opposition Spokesperson for Culture, Media and Sport 2001-02; Shadow Minister for: Transport 2002-03, Environment and Transport 2003-05, Foreign Affairs 2005, Work and Pensions 2005-06, Children, Young People and Families 2006-07, Environment, Food and Rural Affairs 2007-10. Member: Environment, Transport and Regional Affairs 1999-2001, Environment, Transport and Regional Affairs (Transport Sub-Committee) 1999-2001, European Standing Committee C 1999-2001, European Scrutiny 2000-03, Transport, Local Government and the Regions (Transport Sub-Committee) 2001-02, Transport, Local Government and the Regions (Urban Affairs Sub-Committee) 2001-02, Transport, Local Government and the Regions 2001-02, Transport 2003-05; Environment, Food and Rural Affairs: Member 2007-10, Chair 2010-15; Member: Chairmen's Panel/Panel of Chairs 2010-15, Liaison 2010-15, Liaison (National Policy Statements Sub-committee) 2010-15. Joint Vice-chair, Conservative Party Committee for Social Security. *House of Lords:* Raised to the peerage as Baroness McIntosh of Pickering, of the Vale of York in the County of North Yorkshire 2015. Chair, Licensing Act 2003 2016-17; Member: EU Energy and Environment Sub-committee 2019-20, EU Environment Sub-committee 2020-. *Other:* European Parliament: MEP for: Essex North East 1989-94, Essex North and Suffolk South 1994-99: Bureau Member, European People's Party 1994-97. Executive Member, 1922 Committee 2000-01. Vice-President, Local Government Association 2018-19.

Political interests: Transport, tourism, legal affairs, environment, farming and animal husbandry; Central and Eastern Europe, Scandinavia.

Other: President, Anglia Enterprise in Europe 1989-99; Co-chair, European Transport Safety Council 1994-99; Member, Executive Committee, Commonwealth Parliamentary Association (UK Branch) 2014-15; President, Yorkshire First – Enterprise in Yorkshire; Member: Yorkshire Agricultural Society, Anglo-Danish Society; Vice-President, National Eye Research (Yorkshire) Advisory Board; Patron, Thirsk Museum Society; Fellow, Industry and Parliament Trust 1995; Graduate, Armed Forces Parliamentary Scheme, Royal Navy 2000; Vice-president, Association of Drainage Authorities 2014-; President, North Yorkshire Moore Railway 2016-; Vice-president: National Encephalitis Society 2016-, National Association of Child Contact Centres 2017-; Chair, PASS 2018-; Member, Faculty of Advocates 1982-; Honorary Doctorate of Laws, Anglia Polytechnic University 1997. Yorkshire Agricultural Society, Royal Over-seas League, Royal Automobile Club.

Recreations: Swimming, reading, cinema.

The Baroness McIntosh of Pickering, House of Lords, London SW1A 0PW
Tel: 020 7219 3000 *Email:* mcintoshac@parliament.uk *Twitter:* @AnneCMcIntosh

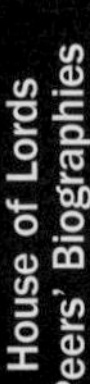

CONSERVATIVE

MACKAY OF CLASHFERN, LORD

MACKAY OF CLASHFERN (Life Baron), James Peter Hymers Mackay; cr. 1979. Born 2 July 1927; Son of late James Mackay, railwayman; Married Elizabeth Gunn Hymers 1958 (1 son 2 daughters).

Education: George Heriot's School, Edinburgh; Edinburgh University (MA mathematics and natural philosophy 1948; LLB 1955); Trinity College, Cambridge (BA maths 1952).

Non-political career: Lecturer in mathematics, St Andrews University 1948-50; Advocate 1955; QC (Scotland) 1965; Sheriff Principal, Renfrew and Argyll 1972-74; Dean, Faculty of Advocates 1976-79; Director, Stenhouse Holdings Ltd 1976-78; Judge of Supreme Court of Scotland 1984-85; Lord of Appeal in Ordinary 1985-87; Lord Clerk, Register of Scotland 2007-.

Political career: *House of Lords:* Raised to the peerage as Baron Mackay of Clashfern, of Eddrachillis in the District of Sutherland 1979. Lord Advocate 1979-84; Government Spokesperson for Legal Affairs in Scotland 1983-84; Lord of Appeal in Ordinary 1985-87; Lord High Chancellor 1987-97. Member, Privileges/Privileges and Conduct 1999-2019; Chair, Assisted Dying Bill 2004-05; Member: Draft Human Tissue and Embryos Bill Joint Committee 2007, Joint Committee on the Draft Care and Support Bill 2012-13. *Other:* Chair, Conservative Party Constitutional Commission 1998-99.

Other: Vice-President, Commonwealth Parliamentary Association (UK Branch); Elder Brother, Trinity House; Part-time Member, Scottish Law Commission 1976-79; Member, Insurance Brokers' Registration Council 1978-79; Senator, College of Justice in Scotland 1984-85; Chair: Legal Reform Commission, Mauritius 1997-98, Legal Commission, Trinidad and Tobago 2000; Commissioner, Cambridge University 2003-16; Lord High Commission to General Assembly of Church of Scotland 2005, 2006; Cancer UK, Barnardo's, Army Benevolent Fund, Mission Aviation Fellowship, Mercy Ships; Hon. Freeman, Woolman's Company; Chancellor, Heriot-Watt University 1991-2005; Royal College of Surgeons of Edinburgh 1989; Royal Society of Edinburgh; RICE; Royal College of Physicians Edinburgh 1990; Royal College of Obstetrics and Gynaecology; Chartered Institute of Taxation; Hon. Fellow: Trinity College, Cambridge, Girton College, Cambridge; Several Honorary Degrees; PC 1979; KT 1997. New (Edinburgh), Caledonian, Athenæum Club.

Publications: Senior Editor, Armour: Valuation for Rating (third edition, 1961); General Editor-in-chief, Halsbury's Laws of England 1999-2015.

Recreations: Walking, travel.

Rt Hon the Lord Mackay of Clashfern KT, House of Lords, London SW1A 0PW
Tel: 020 7219 6041 *Email:* mackayjp@parliament.uk

LABOUR

MACKENZIE OF CULKEIN, LORD

MACKENZIE OF CULKEIN (Life Baron), Hector Uisdean MacKenzie; cr. 1999. Born 25 February 1940; Son of late George MacKenzie, lighthouse keeper, and late Williamina Budge, née Sutherland; Married Anna Morrison 1961 (divorced 1991) (1 son 3 daughters).

Education: Isle of Erraid Public School, Argyll; Aird Public School, Isle of Lewis; Nicolson Institute, Stornoway, Isle of Lewis; Portree High School, Skye; Leverndale School of Nursing, Glasgow (RMN 1961); West Cumberland School of Nursing, Whitehaven (SRN 1966).

Non-political career: Student nurse, Leverndale Hospital 1958-61; Assistant lighthouse keeper, Clyde Lighthouses Trust 1961-64; West Cumberland Hospital: Student nurse 1964-66, Staff nurse 1966-69; Confederation of Health Service Employees: Assistant regional secretary 1969, Regional secretary, Yorkshire and East Midlands 1970-74, National officer 1974-83, Assistant General Secretary 1983-87, General Secretary 1987-93; Member, executive board, Public Services International 1987-2000; Associate General Secretary, Unison 1993-2000; Company secretary, UIA Insurance Ltd 1996-2000; TUC: President 1998-99, Senior Vice-President 1999-2000. Member, Unison.

Political career: *House of Lords:* Raised to the peerage as Baron MacKenzie of Culkein, of Assynt in Highland 1999. *Other:* Member, Labour Party Policy: Forum 1997-2000, Commission on Health 1998-2000.

Political interests: Health, nursing, defence, aviation, maritime affairs, land reform; Australia, Falkland Islands, USA.

Other: First Substitute Member, World Executive of Public Services International 1987-2000; Inter-Parliamentary Union (British Group); Trustee, COHSE 1974 Pension and Assurance Scheme; Governor member, RNLI; RGN; RMN; Lindsay Robertson Gold Medal for Nurse of the Year 1966. St Elpheges, Wallington, Ruskin Club, Croydon.

Recreations: Reading, Celtic music, shinty, aviation, travel.

The Lord MacKenzie of Culkein, House of Lords, London SW1A 0PW
Tel: 020 7219 8515 *Fax:* 020 7219 8712 *Email:* mackenzieh@parliament.uk

NON-AFFILIATED

MACKENZIE OF FRAMWELLGATE, LORD

MACKENZIE OF FRAMWELLGATE (Life Baron), Brian Mackenzie; cr. 1998. Born 21 March 1943; Son of Frederick Mackenzie and Lucy Mackenzie, née Ward; Married Jean Seed 1965 (2 sons); married Deborah Glaister 2009 (divorced 2012).

Education: Eastbourne Boys' School, Darlington; London University (LLB 1974); FBI National Academy, Quantico, USA (Graduate 1985).

Non-political career: Durham Constabulary 1963-98: Chief Superintendent 1989-98. Member, Police Federation of England and Wales 1963-80; National President, Police Superintendents' Association 1995-98; Member, National Association of Retired Police Officers 1998-; Vice-President, BALPA 2003-.

Political career: *House of Lords:* Raised to the peerage as Baron Mackenzie of Framwellgate, of Durham in the County of Durham 1998. Suspended from membership December 2013-June 2014. EU Sub-committee F (Home Affairs): Co-opted member 2009-10, Member 2010-12; Member EU Sub-committee F (Home Affairs, Health and Education) 2012-13. *Other:* Labour Whip withdrawn June 2013.

Political interests: Police, home affairs, legal affairs; India, Poland, Russia, USA.

Other: Member: FBI National Academy Associates, International Association of Chiefs of Police; President/patron, various police, security, defence and hospice organisations; Honorary Billetmaster, City of Durham 1989-2004; Patron: Loomba Trust, Finchale Training College for Disabled, Durham; Managing Director, Mack Diligence Ltd; St Oswald's Hospice, Newcastle; OBE 1998. Dunelm Club, Durham City.

Publications: Two Lives of Brian – From Policing to Politics (autobiography, Memoir Club, 2004).

Recreations: Herpetology, after-dinner speaking, swimming, fitness, singing.

The Lord Mackenzie of Framwellgate OBE, House of Lords, London SW1A 0PW
Tel: 020 7219 8632 *Email:* mackenzieb@parliament.uk

LABOUR

MCKENZIE OF LUTON, LORD

McKENZIE OF LUTON (Life Baron), William David McKenzie; cr. 2004. Born 24 July 1946; Son of Elsie May Doust and George McKenzie; Married Diane Joyce Angliss 1972.

Education: Reading School; Bristol University (BA economics and accounting 1967).

Non-political career: Articled clerk to salaried partner Martin Rata and Partners 1968-73; Price Waterhouse, London 1973-86: Senior to senior manager 1973-80, Partner 1980-86; Sundry consultancy projects 1986-92; Price Waterhouse, Hong Kong 1992-98: Consultant 1992-93, Partner 1993-98, Partner in charge, Vietnam 1996-98. Member, GMB 1980s-.

Political career: *House of Commons:* Contested (Labour) Luton South 1987 and 1992 general elections. *House of Lords:* Raised to the peerage as Baron McKenzie of Luton, of Luton in the County of Bedfordshire 2004. Government Spokesperson for: Trade and Industry 2005-07, Treasury 2005-07; Government Whip 2005-07; Parliamentary Under-Secretary of State and Government Spokesperson: Department for Work and Pensions 2007-10, Department for Communities and Local Government 2009-10; Opposition Spokesperson for: Communities and Local Government 2010-15, Work and Pensions 2010-13, 2015-20. Member: Merits of

Statutory Instruments 2005, Financial Exclusion 2016-17. *Other:* Various constituency party posts. Luton Borough Council: Councillor 1976-92, 1999-2005, Leader 1999-2003.

Political interests: Local government, local government finance, taxation systems, education, airports.

Other: FCA 1979.

Recreations: Swimming, reading.

The Lord McKenzie of Luton, House of Lords, London SW1A 0PW
Tel: 020 7219 6339 *Email:* mckenziew@parliament.uk

CONSERVATIVE

MCLOUGHLIN, LORD

Chair, Joint Committee on Fixed-Term Parliaments Act

McLOUGHLIN (Life Baron), Patrick Alan McLoughlin; cr 2020. Born 30 November 1957; Son of Patrick Alphonsos McLoughlin; Married Lynne Newman 1984 (1 son 1 daughter).

Education: Cardinal Griffin Comprehensive School, Cannock; Staffordshire College of Agriculture.

Non-political career: Agricultural worker 1974-79; Various positions with National Coal Board (including underground) 1979-86.

Political career: *House of Commons:* Contested Wolverhampton South East 1983 general election. MP for West Derbyshire 8 May 1986 by-election to 2010, for Derbyshire Dales 2010-19; PPS to: Angela Rumbold as Minister of State, Department of Education 1987-88, Lord Young of Graffham as Secretary of State for Trade and Industry 1988-89; Parliamentary Under-Secretary of State, Department of Transport (Minister for Aviation and Shipping) 1989-92; Joint Parliamentary Under-Secretary of State, Department of Employment 1992-93; Parliamentary Under-Secretary of State, Department of Trade and Industry (Trade and Technology) 1993-94; Assistant Government Whip 1995-96; Government Whip 1996-97; Opposition Pairing Whip 1997-98; Opposition Deputy Chief Whip 1998-2005; Opposition Chief Whip 2005-10; Parliamentary Secretary to the Treasury 2010-12; Chief Whip 2010-12; Member, Parliamentary and Political Service Honours Committee 2012; Secretary of State for Transport 2012-16; Chancellor of the Duchy of Lancaster (also attending Cabinet) 2016-18. Member: Broadcasting 1994-95, Selection 1997-2001, Finance and Services 1998-2005, Accommodation and Works 2001-05, Modernisation of the House of Commons 2004-05, Selection 2005, Administration 2005, Business, Energy and Industrial Strategy 2018-19, Liaison 2018-19; Chair, European Statutory Instruments 2018-19. *House of Lords:* Raised to the peerage as Baron McLoughlin, of Cannock Chase in the County of Staffordshire 2020. Chair, Joint Committee on Fixed-Term Parliaments Act 2020-. *Other:* National Vice-chair, Young Conservatives 1982-84; Chairman, Conservative Party 2016-18. Councillor: Cannock Chase District Council 1980-87, Staffordshire County Council 1981-87; Chair, VisitBritain 2020-.

Political interests: Agriculture, education.

Other: Vice-president, Youth Hostel Association; Chair, board of trustees, Chequers and Dorneywood 2016-18; PC 2005; Kt 2016; CH 2019.

Rt Hon the Lord McLoughlin CH, House of Lords, London SW1A 0PW
Tel: 020 7219 3000 *Twitter:* @Patrick4Dales

LIBERAL DEMOCRAT

MCNALLY, LORD

McNALLY (Life Baron), Tom McNally; cr. 1995. Born 20 February 1943; Son of late John and Elizabeth McNally; Married Eileen Powell 1970 (divorced 1990); married Juliet Lamy Hutchinson 1990 (2 sons 1 daughter).

Education: College of St Joseph, Blackpool; University College, London (BSc economics 1966) (President, Students Union 1965-66).

Non-political career: Political adviser to James Callaghan: as Secretary of State for Foreign and Commonwealth Affairs 1974-76, as Prime Minister 1976-79; Public affairs adviser, GEC 1983-84; Director and chief executive, British Retail Consortium 1985-87; Head of public affairs: Hill & Knowlton 1987-93, Shandwick 1993-96; Vice-chair, Weber Shandwick 1993-2004. Vice-President, National Union of Students 1966-67.

Political career: *House of Commons:* MP for Stockport South (Labour 1979-81, SDP 1981-83). Contested (SDP) Stockport 1983 general election; SDP Spokesperson for Education and Sport 1981-83. Member, Industry and Trade 1979-83. *House of Lords:* Raised to the peerage as Baron McNally, of Blackpool in the County of Lancashire 1995. Liberal Democrat Spokesperson for: Broadcasting and Trade and Industry 1996-97, Home Affairs 1998-2002, Broadcasting 2002-04, Home Office 2004; Liberal Democrat peers: Deputy Leader 2001-04, Leader 2004-13; Liberal Democrat Spokesperson for Constitutional Affairs 2006-10; Deputy Leader of the House of Lords 2010-13; Minister of State and Government Spokesperson, Ministry of Justice 2010-13. Member: Public Service 1996-97, Freedom of Information 1999, Draft Communications Bill Joint Committee 2002, Liaison 2005-13, Privileges/Privileges and Conduct 2005-13, Procedure 2005-13, Selection 2005-13, 2014, House 2005-13, Conventions Joint Committee 2006, Inheritance and Trustees' Powers Bill 2013, Insurance Bill 2014-15, Regenerating Seaside Towns and Communities 2018-19, EU Home Affairs Sub-committee 2019-20, EU Services Sub-committee 2020-. *Other:* Labour Party Researcher 1967-68; International Secretary, Labour Party 1969-74. Chairman, Youth Justice Board for England and Wales 2014-17.

Political interests: Penal reform, future of the BBC, media plurality; China, EU, India, Tunisia.

Other: Assistant General Secretary, Fabian Society 1966-67; Fellow, Industry and Parliament Trust 1981; Fellow, Chartered Institute of Public Relations (FCIPR) 2000; Fellow, University College, London 1995; Doctor of Law, Hertfordshire University 2011; PC 2004. National Liberal Club.

Recreations: Watching sport, reading history.

Rt Hon the Lord McNally, House of Lords, London SW1A 0PW
Tel: 020 7219 5443 *Email:* mcnallyt@parliament.uk

LABOUR

MCNICOL OF WEST KILBRIDE, LORD

McNICOL OF WEST KILBRIDE (Life Baron), Iain Mackenzie McNicol; cr 2018. Born 17 August 1969; Son of Iain McNicol and Zoe McNicol, née Coles; Married Shelley 1995 (1 son 1 daughter).

Education: Ardrossan Academy; Dundee Institute of Technology (HND building management 1991) (Students' Union President 1991-93).

Non-political career: Labour Party: Campaigns officer, Labour Students 1993-94, Organiser and agent 1994-97, General secretary 2011-18; GMB Union: Industrial organiser 1997-2004, National political officer 2004-11. GMB.

Political career: *House of Lords:* Raised to the peerage as Baron McNicol of West Kilbride, of West Kilbride in the County of Ayrshire 2018. Opposition Whip 2018-April 2020; Deputy Chairman of Committees 2020-.

Political interests: Housing, homelessness, farming, social mobility, education, building industry, trade unions; Canada.

Other: Trustee, Polka Theatre 2014-; Trustee and board member, National Citizen Service Trust 2018-. Karate Union of Great Britain (KUGB).

Recreations: Cooking, walking, skiing, golf, karate (black belt).

The McNicol of West Kilbride, House of Lords, London SW1A 0PW
Tel: 020 7219 3000 *Email:* mcnicoli@parliament.uk *Twitter:* @IainMcNicol

CROSSBENCH

MACPHERSON OF EARL'S COURT, LORD

MACPHERSON OF EARL'S COURT (Life Baron), Nicholas Ian Macpherson; cr 2016. Born 14 July 1959; Son of Ewen A. Macpherson and Nicolette (née Van der Bijl); Married Suky Jane Appleby 1983 (2 sons).

Education: Eton College; Balliol College, Oxford (BA philosophy, politics and economics 1981); University College, London (MSc economics of public policy 1982).

Non-political career: Economist, Confederation of British Industry 1982-83; Senior Analyst, Peat, Marwick and Mitchell Management Consultancy 1983-85; HM Treasury 1985-2016: Principal Private Secretary to Kenneth Clarke as Chancellor of the Exchequer 1993-97, Head, Work Incentives Policy 1997-98, Director, Budget and Public Finances 1998-2001, Managing Director: Public Services 2001-04, Budget and Public Finances Directorate 2004-05, Permanent Secretary 2005-16.

Political career: *House of Lords:* Raised to the peerage as Baron Macpherson of Earl's Court, of Earl's Court in the Royal Borough of Kensington and Chelsea 2016. Member: Audit 2018-, Parliamentary Works Estimates Commission 2020-.

Political interests: Economy, public spending, European Union.

Other: Non-executive director, HM Revenue and Customs 2005-07; Chairman, C Hoare & Co 2016-; Non-executive director: Scottish American Investment Trust 2016-, British Land plc 2016-; Trustee, Royal Mint Museum 2015-; Board member (Private Banking), UK Finance 2017-20; Visiting Professor, King's College London University 2014-; KCB 2009; GCB 2015.

The Lord Macpherson of Earl's Court GCB, House of Lords, London SW1A 0PW
Tel: 020 7219 3000 *Email:* macphersonn@parliament.uk *Twitter:* @nickmacpherson2

CONSERVATIVE

MAGAN OF CASTLETOWN, LORD

MAGAN OF CASTLETOWN (Life Baron), George Morgan Magan; cr 2011. Born 14 November 1945; Son of Brigadier William Magan CBE and Maxine Mitchell; Married Wendy Chilton 1972 (2 sons 1 daughter).

Education: Winchester College.

Non-political career: Peat Marwick Mitchell 1964-70; Kleinwort Benson Ltd 1971-74; Director, Morgan Grenfell and Co Ltd 1974-88; Co-founder and chair, JO Hambro Magan 1988-96; Chair: Hawkpoint Partners 1997-2001, eMuse 2001-, Lion Capital Partners 2001-08, Mallett plc 2001-08, Morgan Shipley Ltd (Dubai) 2001-; Director: Edmiston and Co. 2001-, Allied Investment Partners (Abu Dhabi) 2007-12.

Political career: *House of Lords:* Raised to the peerage as Baron Magan of Castletown, of Kensington in the Royal Borough of Kensington and Chelsea 2011. On leave of absence September 2020-. Member: Works of Art 2015-16, Lord Speaker's Advisory Panel on Works of Art 2017-18. *Other:* Conservative Party: Deputy treasurer 2002-03, Treasurer 2003, Board member 2003; Conservative Party Foundation: Director 2003-13, Deputy chairman 2009-13. Royal Opera House, Covent Garden 1995-2001.

Other: Trustee: London Philharmonic Orchestra 1992-2006, British Museum Development Trust 1999-2003. Royal Yacht Squadron Club.

The Lord Magan of Castletown, House of Lords, London SW1A 0PW
Tel: 020 7219 5353

INDEPENDENT ULSTER UNIONIST

MAGINNIS OF DRUMGLASS, LORD

MAGINNIS OF DRUMGLASS (Life Baron), Kenneth Wiggins Maginnis; cr 2001. Born 21 January 1938; Son of late Gilbert and Margaret Maginnis, née Wiggins; Married Joy Stewart 1961 (2 sons 2 daughters).

Education: Royal School, Dungannon; Stranmillis Teacher Training College, Belfast 1958.

Non-political career: Teacher: Cookstown Secondary School 1959-60, Drumglass Primary School, Dungannon 1960-66; Principal, Pomeroy Primary School 1966-82. Major (Rtd), 8 Battalion, Ulster Defence Regiment 1970-81.

Political career: *House of Commons:* Contested Fermanagh and South Tyrone August 1981 by-election. MP (UUP) for Fermanagh and South Tyrone 1983-2001 (Resigned December 1985 in protest against the Anglo-Irish Agreement; Re-elected 23 January 1986 by-election); UUP Spokesperson for: Defence and Home Office 1997-2000, Defence, Trade and Industry 2000-01. *House of Lords:* Raised to the peerage as Baron Maginnis of Drumglass, of Carnteel in the County of Tyrone 2001. Suspended from membership December 2020-. *Other:* Member: Northern Ireland Assembly 1982, Northern Ireland Forum 1996-98. Treasurer, Ulster Unionist Council -2008; UUP Whip withdrawn June 2012; Resigned from UUP August 2012. Councillor, Dungannon and South Tyrone Borough Council 1981-93, 2001-05; Member, Southern Health and Social Services Council 1989-93.

Political interests: Terrorism and internal security, defence, autism; Turkish Republic of Northern Cyprus.

Other: Chair: Moygashel Regeneration Group, Independent Review of Autism Services for DHSSPS(NI) 2008, Northern Ireland Regional ASD Reference Group 2009-11; Martin Residential Trust Belfast. Ulster Reform Club; President, Dungannon Rugby Club 2001-02.

Recreations: Rugby.

The Lord Maginnis of Drumglass, House of Lords, London SW1A 0PW

CROSSBENCH

MAIR, LORD

MAIR (Life Baron), Robert James Mair; cr 2015. Born 20 April 1950; Married Margaret O'Connor 1981 (1 son 1 daughter).

Education: Clare College, Cambridge (engineering 1971; PhD tunnelling in soft ground 1979).

Non-political career: Engineer, London and Hong Kong 1971-76; Cambridge University: Research assistant, Department of Engineering 1976-79, Professor of geotechnical engineering and Head of civil and environmental engineering 1998-; Senior engineer, London 1980-83; Founding director, Geotechnical Consulting Group 1983-; Department of Civil Engineering, Nottingham University 1994-97; Master, Jesus College, Cambridge 2001-11; Chief engineering adviser to Laing O'Rourke Group 2011-; Principal investigator, Cambridge Centre for Smart Infrastructure and Construction 2011-; Recent international projects: Railway tunnels in Amsterdam, Barcelona, Bologna, Florence, Rome, Singapore and Warsaw, Motorway tunnels in Turkey; Closely involved with the design and construction of: Jubilee Line Extension for London Underground, Channel Tunnel Rail Link (now HS1), Crossrail projects.

Political career: *House of Lords:* Raised to the peerage as Baron Mair, of Cambridge in the County of Cambridgeshire 2015. Member: Science and Technology 2016-, Risk Assessment and Risk Planning 2020-.

Other: Chair, international advisory board, Singapore Land Transport Authority; International Society of Soil Mechanics and Foundation Engineering: Board member, Chair, Technical Committee on Underground Construction in Soft Ground; Member, Crossrail's Engineering Expert Panel; Chair, Royal Society/Royal Academy of Engineering Review of Shale Gas Extraction in the UK (report published 2012); Fellow: Institution of Civil Engineers, Royal Society; Royal Academy of Engineering: Fellow, Senior vice-president 2008-11; Fellow, John's College, Cambridge 1998-2001; British Geotechnical Society Prize 1980; Institution of Civil Engineers: Geotechnical Research Medal 1994, Gold Medal 2004; CBE 2010.

Publications: Has published many papers, mainly on the geotechnical aspects of soft ground tunnelling and excavations.

Professor the Lord Mair CBE, House of Lords, London SW1A 0PW
Tel: 020 7219 3000

LABOUR

MALLALIEU, BARONESS

MALLALIEU (Life Baroness), Ann Mallalieu; cr. 1991. Born 27 November 1945; Daughter of late Sir William Mallalieu and Lady Mallalieu; Married Timothy Cassel 1979 (later Sir Timothy Bt) (divorced 2007) (2 daughters).

Education: Holton Park Girls' Grammar School, Wheatley; Newnham College, Cambridge (MA, LLM law 1968).

Non-political career: Called to the Bar, Inner Temple 1970; Elected Member, General Council of the Bar 1973-75; Recorder 1985-94; Bencher 1992; QC.

Political career: *House of Lords:* Raised to the peerage as Baroness Mallalieu, of Studdridge in the County of Buckinghamshire 1991. Opposition Spokesperson for: Home Affairs 1992-97, Legal Affairs 1992-97. Member Joint Committees on: Consolidation, Etc, Bills 1998-2005, 2006-, Statutory Instruments 2013-16; Member: Rural Economy 2018-19, Electoral Registration and Administration Act 2013 2019-. *Other:* Exmoor National Park Consultative Forum.

Political interests: Law, home affairs, agriculture, environment, animal welfare.

Other: Chair: Council, Ombudsman for Corporate Estate Agents 1993-2000, Suzy Lamplugh Trust 1996-2000; President: Countryside Alliance 1998-, British Hawking Association 1999-; Member, British Horseracing Board 2004-07; President, Horse Trust 2009-; Trustee: Racing Welfare 2009-19, National Association of Stable Staff 2009-18; Hon. Fellow, Newnham College, Cambridge 1992; Peer of the Year: *House Magazine* 2005, *Spectator* 2005.

Recreations: Hunting, poetry, sheep, fishing, racing.

The Baroness Mallalieu QC, House of Lords, London SW1A 0PW
Tel: 020 7219 2000
Tel: 01643 831468

CROSSBENCH

MALLOCH-BROWN, LORD

MALLOCH-BROWN (Life Baron), George Mark Malloch-Brown; cr 2007. Born 16 September 1953; Son of late Robert Malloch-Brown and Ursula Malloch-Brown, née Pelly; Married Patricia Cronan 1989 (1 son 3 daughters).

Education: Marlborough College, Wiltshire; Magdalene College, Cambridge (BA history 1975); University of Michigan, USA (MA political science 1977).

Non-political career: Political correspondent, *Economist* 1977-79; Field operations for Cambodian refugees, Thailand 1979-81; Deputy chief emergency unit, UN High Commission for Refugees, Geneva 1981-83; Founder and editor, Economist Development Report 1983-86; Lead international partner, Sawyer-Miller Group 1986-94; World Bank 1994-99: Director, external affairs 1994-96, Vice-President, external affairs and UN affairs 1996-99; Administrator, UN Development Programme 1999-2005; UN 2005-06: Chef de Cabinet to Secretary-General Kofi Annan 2005-06, Deputy Secretary-General 2006; Vice-chair: Soros Fund Management 2007, Open Society Institute 2007, World Economic Forum 2009; Chair, EMEA operations, FTI Consulting 2010-16; Adviser, SouthWest Energy 2010-; Chair, SGO 2016-.

Political career: *House of Lords:* Raised to the peerage as Baron Malloch-Brown, of St Leonard's Forest in the County of West Sussex 2007. Minister of State for Africa, Asia and UN and Government Spokesperson, Foreign and Commonwealth Office (also attending Cabinet) 2007-09; On leave of absence June-December 2012, September 2015-October 2016, June 2020-.

Political interests: Development, foreign policy; Africa and Asia.

Other: Chair, Royal Africa Society; Board member: Open Society Institute, Save the Children International, Children's Investment Fund Foundation; Founder and board member, International Crisis Group 1995-; Board member: Centre for Global Development, Shell

Foundation; Governor, Marlborough College; Honorary doctorates from three US and one Peruvian University; Honorary Fellow, Magdalene College, Cambridge; KCMG 2007; PC 2007.

Recreations: Reading, jogging, family.

Rt Hon the Lord Malloch-Brown KCMG, House of Lords, London SW1A 0PW
Tel: 020 7219 5353
Tel: 020 7290 4891 *Email:* mary.tait@smartmatic.com

CROSSBENCH

MANCE, LORD

MANCE (Life Baron), Jonathan Hugh Mance; cr 2005. Born 6 June 1943; Son of Sir Henry and Lady Mance, née Joan Erica Robertson Baker; Married Mary Arden, later Rt Hon Dame Mary Arden, Lady Justice Arden 1973 (1 son 2 daughters).

Education: Charterhouse, Surrey; University College, Oxford (BA jurisprudence 1964, MA); French, German, mainly reading Spanish.

Non-political career: Called to the Bar, Middle Temple 1965; QC 1982; Bencher 1989; Recorder 1990-93; Judge commercial list High Court Queen's Bench Division 1993-99; Lord Justice of Appeal 1999-2005; Supreme Court of the United Kingdom: Justice 2009-17, Deputy President 2017-18.

Political career: *House of Lords:* Raised to the peerage as Baron Mance, of Frognal in the London Borough of Camden 2005. Lord of Appeal in Ordinary 2005-09; As Justice of the Supreme Court, disqualified from participation 2009-18. European Union Sub-committee E (Law and Institutions): Co-opted Member 2006-07, Chair 2007-09; Member, European Union 2007-09; Chair, Conduct 2019-. *Other:* Chair, various Banking Appeals Tribunals 1992-93.

Political interests: Europe, Democratic Republic of the Congo.

Other: Council of Europe's Consultative Council of Judges: UK Representative Judge -2011, Chair 2000-03; Member, seven-person panel on the functioning of the European Union (established by the Lisbon Treaty, under Article 255 TFEU) 2010-14, 2014-; Member, Judicial Integrity Group; Chair, Lord Chancellor's Advisory Committee on Private International Law; Trustee, European Law Academy -2011; High Steward, Oxford University 2012-; Chair, International Law Association 2009-; President, British-German Jurists Association 2009-; Hampstead Counselling Service; Hon Fellow, American College of Trial Lawyers; Hon. Fellow: University College, Oxford, Wolfson College, Oxford, Liverpool John Moores University, John F Kennedy University, Buenos Aires, Argentina; Hon. Doc: Canterbury Church University, Oxford University; Kt 1993; PC 1999. Cumberland Lawn Tennis Club.

Publications: Editor and author various legal works and articles.

Recreations: Languages, music, tennis, skiing.

Rt Hon the Lord Mance, House of Lords, London SW1A 0PW
Tel: 020 7219 5353 *Email:* mancej@parliament.uk

NON-AFFILIATED

MANCHESTER, LORD BISHOP OF

MANCHESTER (12th Bishop of), David Stuart Walker. Married Sue (2 children).

Education: Queen's College, Birmingham (theology).

Non-political career: Curate, St Mary Handsworth, Sheffield 1983-86; Team Vicar and Industrial Chaplain, Maltby Team Ministry, Sheffield 1986-91; Vicar of Bramley and Ravenfield, Sheffield, later Team Rector of Bramley and Ravenfield with Hooton Roberts and Braithwell 1991-95; Honorary Canon of Sheffield Cathedral 2000; Suffragan Bishop of Dudley 2000-13; Bishop of Manchester 2014-.

Political career: *House of Lords:* Entered House of Lords 2020.

Political interests: Social housing, equalities, monasticism.

Other: Member, Equality and Diversity Panels: Homes and Communities Agency, National Policing Improvement Agency; Vice-chair, Church of England Pensions Board; Deputy Chair, Church Commissioners.

Recreations: Cricket, rambling, mathematical puzzles, reading.

Rt Rev the Lord Bishop of Manchester, House of Lords, London SW1A 0PW
Tel: 020 7219 3000
Bishopscourt, Bury New Road, Manchester M7 4LE *Tel:* 0161-792 2096
Email: bishop@bishopscourt.manchester.anglican.org Website: www.manchester.anglican.org
Twitter: @BishManchester

CONSERVATIVE

MANCROFT, LORD

MANCROFT (3rd Baron, UK), Benjamin Lloyd Stormont Mancroft; cr. 1937; 3rd Bt of Mancroft (UK) 1932. Born 16 May 1957; Son of 2nd Baron KBE TD and late Diana, née Lloyd; Married Emma Peart 1990 (2 sons 1 daughter).

Education: Eton College.

Non-political career: Chair: Inter Lotto (UK) Ltd 1995-, Scratch-n-Win Lotteries Ltd 1995-98; Non-executive director: St Martin's Magazines plc, Rok Corporation (and deputy chair) 2003-; Chair, New Media Lottery Services plc.

Political career: *House of Lords:* First entered House of Lords 1987; Elected hereditary peer 1999-. Member: Statutory Instruments Joint Committee 2002-07, Pre-legislative Scrutiny Committee on Draft Gambling Bill 2003-04, Administration and Works 2009-14, Licensing Act 2003 2016-17, Procedure/Procedure and Privileges 2019-, Social and Economic Impact of the Gambling Industry 2019-, Joint Committee on Fixed-Term Parliaments Act 2020-. *Other:* Member, Executive: National Union of Conservative Associations 1989-94, Association of Conservative Peers 1989-94, 1999-.

Political interests: Drug addiction, alcoholism, rural affairs.

Other: Joint Master, Vale of White Horse Fox Hounds 1987-89; Chair, Addiction Recovery Foundation 1989-; Phoenix House Housing Association: Director 1991-96, Vice-chairman 1992-96; Deputy chair, British Field Sports Society 1992-97; Chair, Drug and Alcohol Foundation 1994-; President, Alliance of Independent Retailers 1996-2000; Patron, Osteopathic Centre for Children 1996-; Lotteries Council: Executive Committee 1999-, President; Chair, Mentor (UK) 2001-; Vice-chair, Countryside Alliance 2005-; President, European Association for the Treatment of Addiction; Chair, Master of Foxhounds Association. Pratt's Club.

Recreations: Hunting, stalking, shooting, fishing.

The Lord Mancroft, House of Lords, London SW1A 0PW
Tel: 020 7219 5353

LABOUR

MANDELSON, LORD

MANDELSON (Life Baron); Peter Benjamin Mandelson; cr 2008. Born 21 October 1953; Son of late George Mandelson and Hon Mary Joyce Morrison, daughter of late Baron Morrison of Lambeth.

Education: Hendon Grammar School; St Catherine's College, Oxford (BA philosophy, politics and economics 1976); French.

Non-political career: Producer, London Weekend Television 1982-85; Director, campaigns and communications, Labour Party 1985-90; Industrial consultant, SRU Group 1990-92; Economic department, Trade Union Congress (TUC) 1977-78; Commissioner for Trade, European Commission 2004-08; Chairman, Global Counsel LLP; Senior Adviser, Lazard Ltd. Member, GMB.

Political career: *House of Commons:* MP (Labour) for Hartlepool 1992-2004; Opposition Whip 1994-95; Opposition spokesperson: Civil service 1995-96, Election planning 1996-97; Minister without Portfolio 1997-98; Secretary of State for: Trade and Industry 1998, Northern Ireland 1999-2001. *House of Lords:* Raised to the peerage as Baron Mandelson, of Foy in the County of Herefordshire and Hartlepool in the County of Durham 2008. Secretary of State and Government Spokesperson for Business, Enterprise and Regulatory Reform/Business, Innovation and Skills 2008-10; First Secretary of State 2009-10; Lord President of the Council

2009-10. *Other:* Chair, PLP General Election Campaign (Planning) 1999-2001; Patron, LGBT Labour. Councillor, London Borough of Lambeth 1979-82; High Steward, Hull 2013-.

Other: Chair, British Youth Council 1978-80; President, Central School of Speech and Drama 2001-; Chair, Policy Network 2001-; UK Chair, UK-Japan 21st century Group; President, Hartlepool United FC -2016; Board Member, Britain Stronger in Europe 2015-16; President: Great Britain-China Centre 2015-, Supervisory board, German British Forum; Chair, Design Museum 2017-; Chancellor, Manchester Metropolitan University 2016-; Hon Fellow, St Catherine's College, Oxford; Politicians' Politician, Channel 4 Political awards 2009; PC 1998; Grand Officer, Order of the Star of Italy 2016; Order of Légion d'Honneur (France) 2017.

Publications: Several books including: Broadcasting and Youth (1980), Labour's Next Steps: Tackling Social Exclusion (Fabian Society, 1997); Co-author: The Blair Revolution – Can New Labour Deliver? (Faber and Faber, 1996), The Blair Revolution Revisited (Politico's, 2004); Author, The Third Man (Harper Press, 2010); Contributor, The Purple Book (Progress, 2011).

Recreations: Cinema, theatre.

Rt Hon the Lord Mandelson, House of Lords, London SW1A 0PW
Tel: 020 7219 5353

NON-AFFILIATED

MANN, LORD

MANN (Life Baron), John Mann; cr 2019. Born 10 January 1960; Son of James Mann and Brenda Cleavin; Married Joanna White 1986 (2 daughters 1 son).

Education: Bradford Grammar School; Manchester University (BA Econ 1982); ITD Diploma 1992; French, German.

Non-political career: Head research and education, AEU 1988-90; National training officer, TUC 1990-95; Liaison officer, National Trade Union and Labour Party 1995-2000; Director, Abraxas Communications Ltd 1998-2002. Member, AEEU 1985-.

Political career: *House of Commons:* Member (Lab) for Bassetlaw 2001-10, for Bassetlaw (revised boundary) 2010 to 28 October 2019; PPS: to Richard Caborn as Minister for Sport 2005-07, to Tessa Jowell as Minister for: the Olympics and London 2007-08, the Olympics 2008, the Olympics and Paymaster General 2009; Independent adviser on anti-Semitism to Ministry for Housing, Communities and Local Government 2019. Member, Information 2001-05; Treasury: Member 2003-05, 2009-19, Acting Chair, September 2019; Treasury Sub-committee: Member 2003-10, Chair 2017-19; Member, Unopposed Bills (Panel) 2004-15. *House of Lords:* Raised to the peerage as Baron Mann, of Holbeck Moor in the City of Leeds 2019. Independent adviser to The Government on anti-Semitism 2019-. *Other:* Contested East Midlands 1999 European Parliament election. Councillor, London Borough of Lambeth 1986-90.

Political interests: Small businesses, training, economic regeneration, sport, drugs.

Other: Fellow, Industry and Parliament Trust 2003; Founding supporter, Change Britain 2016-; MIPD. Manton Miners Club.

Publications: Labour and Youth: The Missing Generation (Fabian Society, 1985); Heroin in Bassetlaw (2002); The Real Deal (Fabian Society, 2006); The Bassetlaw Anti-Social Behaviour Handbook (2007); Co-Writer, Antisemitism in European Football: A scar on the beautiful game (2008); Miner Compensation – The Legal Complaints Service and the Coal Health Compensation Scheme (2009); What Every Parent and Grandparent Needs to Know about Drugs and Alcohol (2009).

Recreations: Football, cricket, fell-walking, mountaineering.

The Lord Mann, House of Lords, London SW1A 0PW
Tel: 020 7219 8130 *Email:* mannjl@parliament.uk *Twitter:* @LordJohnMann

CROSSBENCH

MANNINGHAM-BULLER, BARONESS

MANNINGHAM-BULLER (Life Baroness), Eliza(beth) Lydia Manningham-Buller; cr 2008. Born 14 July 1948; Daughter of 1st Viscount Dilhorne; Married.

Education: Northampton High School; Benenden School, Kent; Lady Margaret Hall, Oxford (BA English 1970).

Non-political career: Security Service 1974-2007: Deputy director-general 1997-2002, Director-general 2002-07.

Political career: *House of Lords:* Raised to the peerage as Baroness Manningham-Buller, of Northampton in the County of Northamptonshire 2008. Member, Privileges/Privileges and Conduct 2008-13; Sub-committee on Lords' Interests: Member 2008-09: Chair 2009-13; Member: Joint Committee on National Security Strategy 2010-13, Science and Technology 2013-16, 2019-.

Political interests: National security, foreign policy, defence, health, higher education.

Other: Chair: Council, Imperial College London 2011-15, Wellcome Trust 2015-; Co-President, Chatham House 2016-; Honorary fellow: Lady Margaret Hall, Oxford, Northampton University, Cardiff University, City & Guilds; Six honorary doctorates: St Andrews University, Cranfield University, Open University, Oxford University, Leeds University 2012, Dundee University 2017; Women in Public Life Awards: Outstanding Achievement award 2007, Public Servant of the Year 2007; DCB 2005; LG 2014.

Publications: Securing Freedom (Based on 2011 Reith lectures) (Profile Books, 2012).

The Baroness Manningham-Buller LG DCB, House of Lords, London SW1A 0PW
Tel: 020 7219 5353

CONSERVATIVE

MANZOOR, BARONESS

MANZOOR (Life Baroness), Zahida Parveen Manzoor; cr 2013. Born 25 May 1958; Married Dr Madassar Manzoor 1984 (2 daughters).

Education: Leeds University (1982); New College, Durham University (Further Education Teaching Certificate 1984); Queen Elizabeth Hospital, Birmingham (State Certified Midwife 1984); Bradford University (MA applied social studies 1989).

Non-political career: West Suffolk Area Health Authority 1977-80: Student nurse, Staff nurse; Health visitor, Durham Area Health Authority 1983-84; Lecturer, Thomas Danby College 1984-86, 1987-88; North east regional programme director, Common Purpose Charitable Trust 1990-92; Intellisys Ltd: Director 1996-2003, Managing director, Property Development and Private Equity 2011-.

Political career: *House of Lords:* Raised to the peerage as Baroness Manzoor, of Knightsbridge in the Royal Borough of Kensington and Chelsea 2013. Liberal Democrat Spokesperson for: International Development 2015, Welfare, Work and Pensions 2015-16; Government Whip (Baroness in Waiting) 2018-19. Member: House 2015-16, EU External Affairs Sub-committee 2017-18. *Other:* Member: Liberal Democrats -2016, Conservatives October 2016-. Non-executive director, Bradford Hospitals NHS Trust 1991-92; Chair, Service Equity Committee 1991-92; Governor: Sheffield Hallam University 1991-93, Bradford and Airedale College of Health 1992-93; Chair, Bradford Health Authority 1992-97; Member of Court, Bradford University 1992-98; Deputy chair, Commission for Racial Equality 1993-98; Chair: CRE Complaints Committee 1994-98, CRE Audit Committee 1995-98; Governor, Keighley College 1994-95; Trustee, West Yorkshire Police Community Trust 1996-98; Policy board member, NHS England and Wales 1997-2001; Regional chair, Northern and Yorkshire Regions for the NHS Executive of England and Wales 1997-2001; Member, Race Equality Advisory Panel, Home Office 2003-; Legal Services Ombudsman for England and Wales 2003-11; Legal Services Complaints Commissioner 2004-10; Chair, Financial Ombudsman Service 2019-.

Other: Governor: Sheffield Hallam University 1991-93, Airedale College of Health 1992-93; Member, Bradford Congress 1992-96; Court Member, Bradford University 1992-98; Director, Bradford City Challenge 1993-96; Trustee: Uniting Britain Trust 1996-2000, West Yorkshire Police Charitable Trust 1996-98, NSPCC 1997-2003; Vice Patron, Regional Crime Stoppers 1998-2007; Patron, Ethnic Minority Disability Association 1999-; Independent Assessor, Foreign Office 1999-2013; Board Member: Diversity Focus Group for the Cabinet Office

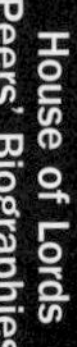

1999-2000; Middle East Association 2013-; Chair, Middle East Technical Advisory Council for The Phoenix Partnership 2016-; Vice-patron, Regional Crime Stoppers 1998; Honorary Fellowship, Bolton Institute 1999 Honorary Doctorate: Bradford University 1999, Leeds Metropolitan University 2003, Bolton University 2010, Sheffield Hallam University 2016; Yorkshire Asian Business Personality of the Year 1992; National Asian Woman of the Year 1999; G22 National Leadership Award for ' Best Contribution to Public Services 2003; Lloyds Asian Jewel Award 2004; Top 100 most influential people in the UK in the Public Sector 2006; Top Three Most Successful Asian Women, Success Magazine 2007; One of the most influential Muslim women in the country, *The Times* and The Human Rights Commission 2009; CBE 1998.

The Baroness Manzoor CBE, House of Lords, London SW1A 0PW
Tel: 020 7219 3599 *Email:* manzoorz@parliament.uk

LIBERAL DEMOCRAT

MARKS OF HENLEY-ON-THAMES, LORD

Liberal Democrat Lords Spokesperson for Justice

MARKS OF HENLEY-ON-THAMES (Life Baron), Jonathan Clive Marks; cr 2011. Born 19 October 1952; Son of late Geoffrey Marks and Patricia Marks, née Bowman; Married Sarah Russell 1982 (divorced 1991) (1 son 1 daughter); married Clementine Cafopoulous 1993 (3 sons 2 daughters).

Education: Harrow School; University College, Oxford (BA jurisprudence 1974); Inns of Court School of Law (1975); French, Greek.

Non-political career: Called to the Bar, Inner Temple 1975; Visiting lecturer in advocacy: Malaya University 1985, 1989-91, Mauritius University 1988, Sri Lanka University Law College 1992; QC 1995; Barrister, 4 Pump Court Chambers; Arbitrator and Family Law Arbitration.

Political career: *House of Commons:* Contested (SDP/All) Weston-Super-Mare 1983 and Falmouth and Camborne 1987 general elections. *House of Lords:* Raised to the peerage as Baron Marks of Henley-on-Thames, of Henley-on-Thames in the County of Oxfordshire 2011. Liberal Democrat: Spokesperson for Justice 2012-16, 2017-, Shadow Lord Chancellor and Secretary of State for Justice 2016-17. Member: Joint Committee on the Draft Defamation Bill 2011, Delegated Powers and Regulatory Reform 2012-15. Chair, Liberal Democrat Parliamentary Party Committee on Home Affairs, Justice and Equalities (Justice) 2012-15. *Other:* Contested Cornwall and Plymouth 1984 European Parliament election. Member, Liberal Democrat Committee for England 1988-89; Chair, Liberal Democrat Lawyers Association 2001-07; Member, Federal Policy Committee, Liberal Democrat 2004-10, 2012-.

Political interests: Justice issues, constitutional reform, human rights, education, health; Greece.

Other: Vice-patron, Jubilee; Sailing Trust; Fellow, Chartered Institute of Arbitrators 2012-; Worshipful Company of Pattenmakers. Royal Automobile Club.

Recreations: Tennis, skiing, theatre, opera, travel.

The Lord Marks of Henley-on-Thames QC, House of Lords, London SW1A 0PW
Tel: 020 7219 6270 *Email:* marksj@parliament.uk
4 Pump Court, London EC4Y 7AN *Tel:* 020 7842 5555 *Email:* jmarks@4pumpcourt.com
Website: www.4pumpcourt.com

CONSERVATIVE

MARLAND, LORD

MARLAND (Life Baron), Jonathan Peter Marland; cr 2006. Born 14 August 1956; Son of Peter Greaves Marland and Audrey Joan Marland; Married Penelope Mary Lamb 1983 (2 sons 2 daughters).

Education: Shrewsbury School.

Non-political career: Director, Lloyd Thompson 1982-99; Partner, JLT Risk Solutions 1999-2006; Chair: Herriot Ltd 2000-10, Janspeed Performance Exhaust Systems Ltd 2002-10; Non-executive director, Clareville Capital LLP 2006-10; Director: Insurance Capital Partners LLP, Hunter Boot Ltd 2007-10; Chair, Jubilee/Appleclaim; Non-executive director: Essex Court Management, WH Ireland Ltd, Test Match Extra -2017.

Political career: *House of Commons:* Contested (Conservative) Somerset and Frome 2001 general election. *House of Lords:* Raised to the peerage as Baron Marland, of Odstock in the County of Wiltshire 2006. Opposition Whip 2009-10; Opposition Spokesperson for: Cabinet Office 2009-10, Energy and Climate Change 2009-10; Parliamentary Under-Secretary of State and Government Spokesperson, Department for: Energy and Climate Change 2010-12, Business, Innovation and Skills 2012-13. *Other:* Conservative Party: Treasurer 2003-07, Board member 2005-07; Director, C&UCO Properties (Party property company) 2006-05; Treasurer, Boris Johnson's London Mayoral Campaign 2007-08. Royal Academy of Arts Development Committee 2008-10.

Political interests: Sport, arts, environment, business, finance.

Other: Advisory committee member, Airey Neave Trust 1992-; J P Marland Charitable Trust 1995-; Harnham Water Meadows Trust 2001-10; Trustee: Atlantic Partnership 2001-, Guggenheim (Museum) UK 2002-, Invercauld Estate 2002-15, Sports Nexus 2003-10; President, Salisbury FC 2008-10; International Churchill Society: Trustee 2009-, Chairman 2012-; Chairman: Tickets for Troops 2009-, Tricouni Brand Ltd 2014-, Commonwealth Enterprise and Investment Council 2014-; President, Commonwealth Youth Orchestra and Choir 2014; Chairman, Eco World Management and Advisory Services UK Ltd 2015-; FRSA 2008-. RSA, MCC, Brooks's, Garrick Club.

Recreations: Sport, British art.

The Lord Marland, House of Lords, London SW1A 0PW
Tel: 020 7219 8738 *Email:* marland@parliament.uk
78 Belgrave Road, London SW1V 2BJ *Tel:* 020 7752 0177 *Email:* marland@odstock.net

CONSERVATIVE

MARLESFORD, LORD

MARLESFORD (Life Baron), Mark Shuldham Schreiber; cr. 1991. Born 11 September 1931; Son of late John Shuldham Schreiber, AE, DL and Maureen Schreiber, née Dent; Married Gabriella Federica 1969, daughter of Count Teodoro Veglio di Castelletto d'Uzzone (2 daughters).

Education: Eton College; Trinity College, Cambridge (BA economics 1956, MA); French.

Non-political career: Fisons Ltd 1957-63; Conservative Research Department 1963-70; Special adviser: to HM Government 1970-74, to Leader of the Opposition 1974-75; *The Economist*: Editorial consultant 1974-91, Lobby correspondent 1976-91; Director, Eastern Group plc 1990-96; Adviser to Mitsubishi Corporation International NV 1990-2003; Independent national director, Times Newspaper Holdings 1991-2014; Adviser to Board, John Swire and Sons Ltd 1992-2009; Non-executive director, Baring New Russia Fund 1996-2007; Adviser, Sit Investment Associates, Minneapolis, USA 2001-; Non-executive director, Gave-Kal Research (Hong Kong) 2004-. National Service, Coldstream Guards, 2nd Lieutenant 1950-51.

Political career: *House of Lords:* Raised to the peerage as Baron Marlesford, of Marlesford in the County of Suffolk 1991. Member, EU Sub-committee A: (Economic and Financial Affairs, Trade and External Relations/Economic and Financial Affairs) 2000-05, (Economic and Financial Affairs and International Trade) 2010-12, (Economic and Financial Affairs) 2012-14; Member, European Union 2003-07, 2012-14; EU Sub-committee F (Home Affairs): Member 2005-07, Co-opted member 2007-09. *Other:* Councillor, East Suffolk County Council 1968-70; Chair, Marlesford Parish Council 1978-; Member: Countryside Commission 1980-92, Rural Development Commission 1985-93; DL, Suffolk 1991-.

Political interests: Conservation, defence, EU economy; China, Egypt, Hong Kong, Iran.

Other: Chair, Council for the Protection of Rural England 1993-98; President: Suffolk ACRE 1995-2004, Suffolk Preservation Society 1997-. Pratt's Club.

Recreations: Planting trees and hedges, collecting minerals.

The Lord Marlesford DL, House of Lords, London SW1A 0PW
Tel: 020 7219 5480 *Fax:* 020 7219 5979 *Email:* marlesford@parliament.uk
Marlesford Hall, Woodbridge IP13 0AU

CROSSBENCH

MASHAM OF ILTON, BARONESS

MASHAM OF ILTON (Life Baroness), Susan Lilian Primrose Cunliffe-Lister; cr. 1970. Born 14 April 1935; Daughter of late Major Sir Ronald Sinclair, 8th Bt, TD, DL and Rebecca Sinclair; Married Lord Masham, later 2nd Earl of Swinton 1959 (died 2006) (1 son 1 daughter both adopted).

Education: Heathfield School, Ascot; London Polytechnic.

Non-political career: Voluntary social work/health matters. Member, NFU.

Political career: *House of Lords:* Raised to the peerage as Baroness Masham of Ilton, of Masham in the North Riding of the County of Yorkshire 1970. Chair, Home Office Crime Prevention Working Group on Young People and Alcohol 1987. Member: Science and Technology Sub-committee I (Resistance to Anti-Microbial Agents) 1997-98, Administration and Works 2005-09, HIV and AIDS in the UK 2010-11. *Other:* Member: Peterlee and Newton Aycliffe Corporation 1973-85, Yorkshire Regional Health Authority 1982-90; DL, North Yorkshire 1991-; Member: North Yorkshire Family Health Service Authority 1990-96, Board of Visitors, Wetherby Young Offenders Institute.

Political interests: Health, disability, penal affairs and policy, drug abuse, farming, horticulture; Europe.

Other: North Yorkshire Red Cross: President 1963-88, Patron 1989-; Council member, Winston Churchill Trust 1980-2005; Hon. President, Ripon St Cecilia Orchestra 2008; Chair, Howard League Inquiry into Girls in Prison; Patron: International Spinal Research Trust, Northern Counties Trust for People Living with HIV/AIDS; Animal Health Trust; John Mordaunt Trust; Yorkshire Wildlife Trust; Highland Pony Society; Vice-President, Ponies UK; Former and current president, patron, chair, member of numerous charities, especially in areas of health and disability; Freedom: Ripon 1960, Harrogate 1989; Hon. Fellowship: RCGP 1981, Chartered Society of Physiotherapy 1996; Six honorary degrees; Four honorary fellowships; Rome Paralympics 1960: Gold 25m breaststroke swimming medal, Silver 25m backstroke swimming medal, Bronze women's doubles table tennis medal; Tokyo Paralympics 1964: Gold women's doubles table tennis medal, Silver 25m breaststroke swimming, 25m freestyle prone swimming, 25m freestyle supine swimming and women's singles table tennis medals; Tel Aviv Paralympics 1968: Silver women's doubles table tennis medal, Bronze women's singles table tennis medal.

Publications: The World Walks By (1986).

Recreations: Breeding Highland ponies, long haired dachshunds, gardening, swimming.

The Countess of Swinton, Baroness Masham of Ilton DL, House of Lords, London SW1A 0PW
Tel: 020 7219 3000 *Email:* mashams@parliament.uk
Dykes Hill House, Masham, Nr Ripon HG4 4NS *Tel:* 01765 689241
Email: masham.swinton@gmail.com Website: mashamridingcentre.com

LABOUR

MASSEY OF DARWEN, BARONESS

MASSEY OF DARWEN (Life Baroness), Doreen Elizabeth Massey; cr. 1999. Born 5 September 1938; Daughter of late Jack and Mary Ann Hall, née Sharrock; Married Dr Leslie Massey 1966 (2 sons 1 daughter).

Education: Darwen Grammar School, Lancashire; Birmingham University (BA French 1961; DipEd 1962); London University (MA health education 1985); French, some Russian.

Non-political career: Graduate service overseas, Gabon 1962-63; French teacher, South Hackney School 1964-67; French and English teacher, Springside School, Philadelphia 1967-69; Running community playgroup 1970-77; Teacher/Head of year/Senior teacher in charge of health education, Walsingham School, London 1979-83; Director of training, Family Planning Association (FPA) 1981-89; Adviser in personal, social and health education, Inner London Education Authority 1983-85; Director of Young People's Programme, Health Education Authority 1985-87; Director, FPA 1989-94; Independent consultant in health education 1994-2001; Chair, National Treatment Agency for Substance Misuse 2002-13. Former member: NUT, MSF.

Political career: *House of Lords:* Raised to the peerage as Baroness Massey of Darwen, of Darwen in the County of Lancashire 1999. Member: Selection 2005-08, Ecclesiastical Committee 2005-10, Works of Art 2007-11, Information 2010-15, Affordable Childcare 2014-15, EU Home Affairs Sub-committee 2015-19, Joint Committee on Human Rights 2019-, Lord Speaker's Advisory Panel on Works of Art 2019-. Vice-chair, PLP Departmental Group for Education 2010-15.

Political interests: Education, health, children and young people, sport, substance misuse; Central Asia, France, Russia, USA.

Other: Member, UK delegation, Parliamentary Assembly of the Council of Europe 2017-; President, Brook Advisory Centres; Patron: The Maya Centre, Association for Young People's Health, Bedfordshire University Child Trafficking Unit; ENO, Opera North, Terrence Higgins Trust, Stonewall, Brook Advisory, Women and Children First, Association for Young People's Health, The Maya Centre; FRSA; Fellow, University of Central Lancashire 2005; Honorary Doctorate, Birmingham University 2014; Honorary Professor of Social Studies, Nottingham Trent University. Farmers Club, Lady Taverners Club.

Publications: Teaching About HIV/AIDS (1988); Co-author, Sex Education Factpack (1988); Sex Education: Why, What and How (1988); Editor, The Sex Education Source Book (1995); Lovers' Guide Encyclopaedia (1996); Love and Death in Shanghai – a novel (2018); Articles on health education in a variety of journals.

Recreations: Theatre, opera, reading, walking, pilates, travel, sports.

The Baroness Massey of Darwen, House of Lords, London SW1A 0PW
Tel: 020 7219 8653 *Email:* masseyd@parliament.uk Website: elizabethjhall.com

CONSERVATIVE

MAUDE OF HORSHAM, LORD

MAUDE OF HORSHAM (Life Baron), Francis Anthony Aylmer Maude; cr 2015. Born 4 July 1953; Son of late Angus Maude (MP for Ealing South 1950-58 and Stratford-on-Avon 1963-83, later Lord Maude of Stratford-upon-Avon) and late Lady Maude; Married Christina Hadfield 1984 (2 sons 3 daughters).

Education: Abingdon School; Corpus Christi, Cambridge (MA history 1976) (Hulse Prize and Avory Studentship); College of Law (Forster Boulton Prize and Inner Temple Law Scholarship 1977).

Non-political career: Called to Bar, Inner Temple 1977; Practising barrister 1977-85; Head of global privatisation, Salomon Bros International 1992-93; Managing director, global privatisation, Morgan Stanley & Co Ltd 1993-97; Chair, Deregulation Task Force 1993-97; Benfield Group plc: Non-executive director 1999-, Deputy chair 2003-08; Non-executive director, Businesses for Sale Company plc 2000-02; Chair: Prestbury Holdings plc 2002-08, Jubilee Investment Trust plc 2003-07, Mission Marketing Group 2006-09; Senior adviser: Covington & Burling LLP 2016-, Stephens Europe Ltd 2017-; Partner, FMA Partners LLP.

Political career: *House of Commons:* MP (Conservative) for North Warwickshire 1983-92. Contested North Warwickshire 1992 general election. MP for Horsham 1997-2010, for Horsham (revised boundary) 2010-15; PPS to Peter Morrison as Minister of State for Employment 1984; Government Whip 1985-87; Parliamentary Under-Secretary of State, Department of Trade and Industry 1987-89; Minister of State, Foreign and Commonwealth Office 1989-90; Financial Secretary to the Treasury 1990-92; Member, Shadow Cabinet 1997-2001: Shadow Secretary of State for: National Heritage 1997, Culture, Media and Sport 1997-98; Shadow Chancellor of the Exchequer 1998-2000; Shadow Secretary of State for Foreign and Commonwealth Affairs 2000-01; Shadow Minister for the Cabinet Office and Shadow Chancellor of the Duchy of Lancaster 2007-10; Minister for the Cabinet Office; Paymaster General 2010-15. Member, Public Accounts 1990-92. Member, Executive 1922 Committee 1997; Chair, Conservative Party Committees for: Culture, Media and Sport 1997-98, Finance 1998-2000, European Affairs 2000-01, Foreign and Commonwealth Affairs 2000-01. *House of Lords:* Raised to the peerage as Baron Maude of Horsham, of Shipley in the County of West Sussex 2015. Minister of State for Trade and Investment and Government Spokesperson, Department for Business, Innovation and Skills and Foreign and Commonwealth Office 2015-16. *Other:* Chair, Conservative Party 2005-07. Councillor, Westminster City Council 1978-84; Chair of governors, Abingdon School 1994-2003.

Other: Advisory board member, Anvest Partners 2016-; Chair, Cogent Elliott Group Ltd 2016-; Advisory board member: OakNorth Bank 2016-, GPW 2017-; Chair, board, Brighton College International Schools 2017-; Advisory board member, Fine Instrument Fund 2017-; Member, International Consultative Council, Astana International Financial Centre 2017-; PC 1992.

Recreations: Skiing, reading, opera.

Rt Hon the Lord Maude of Horsham, House of Lords, London SW1A 0PW
Tel: 020 7219 3000

CROSSBENCH

MAWSON, LORD

MAWSON (Life Baron), Andrew Mawson; cr 2007. Born 8 November 1954; Son of Jack and Mary Mawson; Married Susan Barnes 1975 (1 daughter 2 sons).

Education: Hanson Boys' School, Bradford; Manchester University (BA theology 1979; MPhil urban spirituality 1990).

Non-political career: Ordained minister, United Reformed Church 1979; Founder and director, Church Action on Central America 1980-92; Founder, chief executive, chair, president, Bromley by Bow Centre (community and primary care facilities) 1984-; Co-founder, executive director, president, Community Action Network 1998-; Director: Andrew Mawson Partnerships 2007-, St Paul's Way CIC, Water City CIC 2011-, St Paul's Way Transformation Project; Founder: Poplar Harca, Leaside Regeneration.

Political career: *House of Lords:* Raised to the peerage as Baron Mawson, of Bromley-by-Bow in the London Borough of Tower Hamlets 2007. EU Sub-committee F (Home Affairs): Co-opted Member 2007-10, Member 2010-12; Member: Small- and Medium-Sized Enterprises 2012-13, Refreshment 2012-15, Joint Committee on the Draft Deregulation Bill 2013, Information 2014-16, European Union 2015-16, EU Internal Market Sub-committee 2015-18, Regenerating Seaside Towns and Communities 2018-19.

Political interests: Public services, international affairs, health, education, enterprise; Europe, UK.

Other: Non-executive director, Olympic Park Legacy Company 2009-18; Trustee, Legacy List 2015-16; Chair, SS Robin Trust 2015-17; Executive chair, Well North 2015-; Member, University Schools Trust, East London 2017-; Executive chair, Well North Enterprises CIC Ltd 2018-; Honorary doctorate; OBE 2000.

Publications: The Social Entrepreneur: Making Communities Work (2007).

Recreations: Music, walking, travel.

The Lord Mawson OBE, House of Lords, London SW1A 0PW
Tel: 020 7219 6197
c/o HLM Architects, Ground Floor, 46 Loman Street, London SE1 0EH *Tel:* 020 7620 6000
Email: andrew@amawsonpartnerships.com Website: www.amawsonpartnerships.com

LABOUR

MAXTON, LORD

MAXTON (Life Baron), John Alston Maxton; cr. 2004. Born 5 May 1936; Son of late John Maxton, agricultural economist, and late Jenny Maxton; Married Christine Waine 1970 (3 sons).

Education: Lord William's Grammar School, Thame; University College, Oxford (BA modern history 1960; DipEd 1961).

Non-political career: Teacher, Glasgow Academy 1961-70; Lecturer in social studies, Hamilton College 1970-79. Member: MSF, Educational Institute of Scotland.

Political career: *House of Commons:* MP (Labour) for Glasgow Cathcart 1979-2001; Opposition Scottish and Treasury Whip 1985; Opposition Frontbench Spokesperson for Scotland 1985-92. Chair PLP National Heritage/Culture, Media and Sport Committee, Member 1992-97. *House of Lords:* Raised to the peerage as Baron Maxton, of Blackwaterfoot in Ayrshire and Arran 2004. Member: Review of the BBC Charter 2005-06, Communications 2007-10, Information 2011-15, Science and Technology 2015-19, EU Energy and Environment Sub-committee 2019-20.

Political interests: Broadcasting, internet; France, Spain.

Other: Member: Association of Lecturers in Colleges of Education, Socialist Educational Association. Shiskine Golf and Tennis Club; Virgin Active; Hamilton Rugby Club.

Recreations: Listening to Jazz, fitness, holiday golf on the Isle of Arran, technology.

The Lord Maxton, House of Lords, London SW1A 0PW
Tel: 020 7219 6475 *Email:* maxtonj@parliament.uk
Email: maxtonj@yahoo.co.uk

CROSSBENCH

MEACHER, BARONESS

MEACHER (Life Baroness), Molly Christine Meacher; cr 2006. Born 15 May 1940; Daughter of William Frederick and Lucy Marie Reid; Married Michael Meacher 1962 (MP for Oldham West 1970-97 and Oldham West and Royton 1997-2015) (divorced 1987, died 2015) (2 sons 2 daughters); married Professor Richard Layard 1991, now Lord Layard (qv).

Education: Berkhamsted School for Girls; York University (BA economics 1970); London University (CQSW 1980); Russian and French.

Non-political career: Manager, National Association of Citizens Advice Bureaux 1982-84; Parliamentary officer, British Association of Social Workers 1984-86; Director, Campaign for Work 1986-91; Chief adviser to Russian Government on employment 1991-94; Member and deputy chair, Police Complaints Authority 1994-2002; Chair, Security Industry Authority 2002-04.

Political career: *House of Lords:* Raised to the peerage as Baroness Meacher, of Spitalfields in the London Borough of Tower Hamlets 2006. Alternate member, Procedure 2015-19; Member: Joint Committee on Statutory Instruments 2015-19, Delegated Powers and Regulatory Reform 2019-. *Other:* Commissioner, Mental Health Act 1987-92; Non-executive director, Tower Hamlets Healthcare Trust 1994-98; Chair: Home Office Forum for Forensic Physicians 2002-04, Clinical Ethics Committee, Central and North West London Mental Health Trust 2004-08, East London NHS Foundation Trust 2004-13.

Political interests: Mental health, criminal justice, welfare benefits, social care; Russia.

Other: Chair, European Initiative on Drug Policy 2014-16; President, Haemophilia Society 2012-; Chair, Dignity in Dying 2016-; Russian European Trust, Taxaid; *Spectator* Peer of the Year 2015; Oldie Campaigner of the Year 2015. Hampstead Golf Club 2004-.

Publications: Scrounging on the Welfare (Hutchinson, 1972); To Him Who Hath (Penguin, 1977); New Methods of Mental Health Care (Penguin, 1979); Contributor: The Mentally Disordered Offender (Butterworth-Heinemann, 1991), Mental Health Services Today and Tomorrow (Radcliffe Publishing Oxford, 2008).

Recreations: Music, golf.

The Baroness Meacher, House of Lords, London SW1A 0PW
Tel: 020 7219 4081 *Email:* meachermc@parliament.uk

LABOUR

MENDELSOHN, LORD

MENDELSOHN (Life Baron), Jonathan Neil Mendelsohn; cr 2013. Born 30 December 1966.

Non-political career: Policy and communications adviser to Leader of the Opposition 1995-97; Business adviser and co-founder, LLM Communications 1997-2007; Financial Dynamics: Managing director 2005-07, Chair, Global Issues Division 2005-07; Partner, Oakvale Capital LLP.

Political career: *House of Lords:* Raised to the peerage as Baron Mendelsohn, of Finchley in the London Borough of Barnet 2013. Opposition Whip 2014-15; Opposition Spokesperson for: Business, Innovation and Skills 2015-16, Business, Energy and Industrial Strategy 2016-18, International Trade 2016-18. Member, International Relations/International Relations and Defence 2019-. *Other:* Labour Party: Director of general election resources 2007-10, Assistant treasurer 2009-11.

The Lord Mendelsohn, House of Lords, London SW1A 0PW
Tel: 020 7219 3199

CONSERVATIVE

MENDOZA, LORD

MENDOZA (Life Baron), Neil Francis Jeremy Mendoza; cr 2020. Born 2 November 1959; Married.

Education: Haberdashers' Aske's Boys School; Oxford University (MA geography 1981); Stanford University (Professional Qualification genetics and genomics 2016).

Non-political career: Banker, JP Morgan 1981-83; Director, Albion Films 1983-87; Chief executive and co-founder, Forward 1987-2001; Megalomedia plc 1995-2000; Chief executive, Hammer Films 2000-07; Director, Cross Asset Management 2000-05; Provost, Oriel College, Oxford 2018-.

Political career: *House of Lords:* Raised to the peerage as Baron Mendoza, of King's Reach in the City of London 2020. *Other:* Department for Culture, Media and Sport/Digital, Culture, Media and Sport: Non-executive Board Member 2016-20, Government Lead Reviewer Museums in England 2016-18; Commissioner for Cultural Recovery and Renewal 2020-; Chair, Culture Heritage Capital Board 2020-; Member: Cultural Recovery Board 2020-, Cultural Renewal Taskforce 2020-.

Other: Trustee: Forward Arts Foundation 1994-2013, Almeida Theatre 1998-2002; Vice-chair, Soho Theatre 2007-18; Trustee, Shakespeare Schools Festival 2010-15; Chair: Victoria Private Investment Office 2010-18, Landmark Trust 2010-, Prince's Foundation for Children and the Arts 2013-17; Non-executive director, Meira GTx 2015-; Commissioner, Historic England 2016-19; Chair, Illuminated River Foundation 2017-; Trustee, Mail Force CIO 2020-; Honorary Fellow, Trinity College Dublin. Army & Navy, Portland Club.

The Lord Mendoza, House of Lords, London SW1A 0PW
Tel: 020 7219 3000 *Email:* mendozan@parliament.uk *Twitter:* @neilfmendoza

LABOUR

MERRON, BARONESS

MERRON (Life Baroness), Gillian Joanna Merron; cr 2021. Born 12 April 1959; Daughter of late Harry Merron, factory store keeper, and of late Bessie Merron, shop assistant.

Education: Wanstead High School; Lancaster University (BSc management sciences 1981).

Non-political career: Business development adviser Derbyshire Co-operative Development Agency 1982-85; Local government officer Derbyshire County Council 1985-87; Full-time official East Midlands National Union of Public Employees (now UNISON) 1987-95; Senior regional officer for Lincolnshire, UNISON 1995-97; Divisional director, Cool Milk Group 2010-14; Chief executive, Board of Deputies of British Jews 2014-. Member, Armed Forces Parliamentary Scheme (RAF) 1997-98.

Political career: *House of Commons:* MP for Lincoln 1997-2010. Contested Lincoln 2010 general election; Sponsored, Football Sponsorship Levy Bill 1997; PPS: to Ministers of State, Ministry of Defence: Doug Henderson 1998-99, Baroness Symons of Vernham Dean 1999-2001, to Dr John Reid as Secretary of State for Northern Ireland 2001-02; Assistant Government Whip 2002-04; Government Whip 2004-06; Parliamentary Under-Secretary of State, Department for Transport 2006-07; Minister, Cabinet Office 2007-08; Minister for the East Midlands 2007-08; Parliamentary Under-Secretary of State: Department for International Development 2008, Foreign and Commonwealth Office 2008-09, Minister of State, Department of Health 2009-10. Member: Trade and Industry 1997-98, Selection 2005-06. *House of Lords:* Raised to the peerage as Baroness Merron, of Lincoln in the County of Lincolnshire 2021. *Other:* Co-ordinated Shadow Cabinet Central Region campaign in 1992 general election and 1994 European Parliament election; Vice-chair: Regional Labour Party Executive, Central Region Group of Labour MPs 1997-99; Chair, East Midlands Regional Group of Labour MPs 1999-2002; Member, Co-operative Party.

Political interests: Health, exercise and sport, vocational training, transport.

Other: Associate member, British-Irish Parliamentary Body 2001-02; Member, Holocaust Educational Trust; Board member, Westminster Foundation for Democracy 1998-2001; Fellow, Industry and Parliament Trust 2002; Non-executive director, National Grid Electricity System Operator 2019-.

Recreations: Football, running, films, gym, Lincoln City FC.

The Baroness Merron, House of Lords, London SW1A 0PW

CONSERVATIVE

MEYER, BARONESS

MEYER (Life Baroness), Catherine Irene Jacqueline Meyer; cr 2018. Born 26 January 1953; Daughter of the late Maurice and Olga Laÿlle (born Olga Iosivna Ilyina); Married Sir Christopher Meyer (British Ambassador to the United States 1997-2003) 1997 (2 sons, 2 step-sons).

Education: French Lycée, London (Baccalauréat); School of Slavonic and East European Studies (SSEES) (BA economics and Russian regional studies 1976); French (bi-lingual), Russian and Italian (fluent), German (conversational).

Non-political career: Account Executive: Merrill Lynch, Pierce, Fenner and Smith 1976-79, Dean Witter Reynolds 1979-80, EF Hutton 1980-85; Interdealer Broker, Tradition Bond Brokers 1992-93; Account Executive, Deutsche Bank 1993-94; Senior Account Executive, San Paolo Bank 1994-96; Founder and Chief Executive, Parents and Abducted Children Together/ Action Against Abduction 1997-2017; Senior Adviser, Pagefield Communications 2017-18.

Political career: *House of Lords:* Raised to the peerage as Baroness Meyer, of Nine Elms in the London Borough of Wandsworth 2018. Trade Envoy to Ukraine 2020-. Member: Social and Economic Impact of the Gambling Industry 2019, Communications/Communications and Digital 2019-20. *Other:* National treasurer, Conservative Party 2010-15.

Political interests: International relations, Brexit, children's issues; European Union, France, Russia, USA.

Other: Co-founder and trustee, International Center for Missing and Exploited Children 1998-2002; Non-executive director, London International Financial Futures and Options Exchange 2003-08; Trustee, London Institute for Mathematical Sciences 2013-14; Founder and President, Action Against Abduction 2017-; Ambassador, Missing People 2019-; Missing People; Honorary Texan (USA) 1998; Fellow, Royal Society of Arts; Rainbow Award for outstanding contributions to children's causes; CBE 2012. The Walkbrook, Ivy Club.

Publications: Handbook on the Mechanism of the London Metal Exchange Option Market (1982); These are My Children, Too (PublicAffairs, 1989); Two Children Behind a Wall (Random House, 1997); Documentary film "Sarah Cecilie" (2015); Various articles and reports on missing and abducted children.

Recreations: Family and friends, browsing antique markets, skiing and walking in the mountains.

The Baroness Meyer CBE, House of Lords, London SW1A 0PW
Tel: 020 7219 3000 *Email:* meyerc@parliament.uk *Twitter:* @ladylilo2

LIBERAL DEMOCRAT

MILLER OF CHILTHORNE DOMER, BARONESS

MILLER OF CHILTHORNE DOMER (Life Baroness), Susan Elisabeth Miller; cr. 1998. Born 1 January 1954; Daughter of Frederick Taylor and Norah Langham; Married John Miller 1980 (divorced 1998) (2 daughters 1 deceased); married Humphrey Temperley 1999.

Education: Sidcot School, Winscombe, Somerset; Oxford Polytechnic (book publishing 1975); French.

Non-political career: In publishing: David & Charles, Weidenfeld & Nicolson, Penguin Books 1975-79; Bookshop owner 1979-89; Vineyard owner 2009-.

Political career: *House of Lords:* Raised to the peerage as Baroness Miller of Chilthorne Domer, of Chilthorne Domer in the County of Somerset 1998. Liberal Democrat Spokesperson for: Agriculture and Rural Affairs 1999-2001, Environment, Food and Rural Affairs 2001-07, Home Affairs 2007-09; On leave of absence April-September 2020. Member: European Union

Sub-committee D (Environment and Agriculture) 2005-07, Draft Climate Change Bill Joint Committee 2007, Draft Marine Bill Joint Committee 2008. *Other:* Member, Liberal Democrat Federal Policy Committee. South Somerset District Council: Councillor 1991-98, Leader 1996-98; Councillor, Somerset County Council 1997-2005.

Political interests: Environment, street children, human rights, nutrition and food, sovereignty, nuclear non proliferation and disarmament; Central and South America, France.

Other: Member: Inter-Parliamentary Union, Parliamentarians for Nuclear Non-proliferation and Disarmament (PNND); Vice-president: British Trust for Conservation Volunteers, Wildlife Link; Patron, ECOS Homes; TCF; President, Josephine Butler Society; Charlotte Miller Art Project, International Children's Trust (Juconi), Save the Children, Marine Conservation Society, Baby Milk Action, Wildlife Trusts, Oxfam, War on Want; Fellow, Joint University (Exeter and Bournemouth).

Publications: Stuck or Spiked – What Happened to eco-labelling in the UK (2002); Hungry for Change – A UK Food Policy (2004).

Recreations: Horse riding, reading, friends, gardening vegetables, wine.

The Baroness Miller of Chilthorne Domer, House of Lords, London SW1A 0PW
Tel: 020 7219 6042 *Email:* millers@parliament.uk

LABOUR

MITCHELL, LORD

MITCHELL (Life Baron), Parry Andrew Mitchell; cr. 2000. Born 6 May 1943; Son of late Leon Mitchell and Rose Mitchell; Married Doreen Hargreaves 1972 (divorced) (1 daughter); married Hannah Lowy 1988 (twin sons).

Education: Christ's College Grammar School, London; London University (BSc economics 1964); Graduate School of Business, Columbia University, New York (MBA 1966).

Non-political career: Information technology entrepreneur; Chair and founder: United Leasing plc 1976-87, Syscap plc 1992-2006, Zuse Inc New York 2012-, Instant Impact Ltd 2014-17.

Political career: *House of Lords:* Raised to the peerage as Baron Mitchell, of Hampstead in the London Borough of Camden 2000. Opposition Spokesperson for Business, Innovation and Skills 2012-13. Member: House of Lords Offices Library and Computers Sub-committee 2001-03, Science and Technology Sub-committee II (Innovations in Computer Processors/ Microprocessors/Science and the Regional Development Agencies) 2002-03, Science and Technology Committee 2003-06; Chair, Science and Technology Sub-committee I (Science and International Agreements) 2003-04; Member, Science and Technology Sub-committee I (Scientific Aspects of Ageing) 2004-05; Co-opted Member: EU Sub-committee B (Internal Market) 2006-10, Science and Technology Sub-committee I (Nanotechnologies and food) 2009-10; Member: Small- and Medium-Sized Enterprises 2012, Joint Committee on National Security Strategy 2014-17, Democracy and Digital Technologies 2019-. *Other:* Labour's Business Ambassador 2013-16; Adviser to Shadow Ministerial Business, Innovation and Skills team 2013-16; Left the Labour Party September 2016, Crossbencher September 2016-April 2020, returned to Labour April 2020.

Political interests: Information technology, small businesses, foreign affairs, education, alcohol abuse; Israel, USA.

Other: Trustee, Lowy Mitchell Foundation; Honorary fellow, College of Teachers 2011. Players Club, New York Club.

Recreations: Scuba diving, theatre, jazz, opera.

The Lord Mitchell, House of Lords, London SW1A 0PW
Tel: 020 7219 8657 *Email:* mitchellp@parliament.uk
Tel: 020 7433 3238 *Email:* parrym@mac.com *Twitter:* @lordparry

CONSERVATIVE

MOBARIK, BARONESS

MOBARIK (Life Baroness), Nosheena Shaheen Mobarik; cr 2014. Born 16 October 1957; Daughter of Tufail Shaheen; Married Iqbal (2 children).

Education: Glasgow Caledonian University (business); Open University; Strathclyde University (English literature and history).

Non-political career: Small business owner; Lecturer, Social policy in healthcare, Anniesland College; Co-founder, M Computer Technologies 1997-.

Political career: *House of Lords:* Raised to the peerage as Baroness Mobarik, of Mearns in the County of Renfrewshire 2014. Government Whip (Baroness in Waiting) 2016-17; As an MEP, disqualified from participation September 2017-January 2020. Member: Refreshment 2015, EU Financial Affairs Sub-committee 2016, Intellectual Property (Unjustified Threats) Bill 2016. *Other:* Contested Scotland region 2014 European Parliament election. MEP (replacement) for Scotland 8 September 2017 to 31 January 2020: Spokesperson for Women's Rights and Gender Equality Issues, Conservative delegation, European Parliament 2018-20. Governor, Craigholme School for Girls.

Other: Chair, CBI Scotland; Founder and trustee, Save the Bosnian People Campaign; Founder and convener, Scotland Pakistan Network; Member, Edinburgh Direct Aid; Chair, Pakistan Britain Trade and Investment Forum 2012-; Board member, Glasgow Film Theatre; OBE 2004; CBE 2014.

The Baroness Mobarik CBE, House of Lords, London SW1A 0PW
Suite 26-27, Spiersbridge House, Spiersbridge Business Park, Spiersbridge Way, Thornliebank, Glasgow G46 8NG *Tel:* 0141-212 6270 Website: www.nosheenamobarik.com
Twitter: @NosheenaMobarik

CONSERVATIVE

MONE, BARONESS

MONE (Life Baroness), Michelle Georgina Mone; cr 2015. Born 8 October 1971; Daughter of Duncan and Isobel Allan; Married Michael Mone (divorced 2013) (3 children); Engaged to Douglas Barrowman.

Non-political career: Head of sales and marketing for Scotland, Labatt Brewers -1996; Founder: Ultimo 1996-2014, UTan 2012-.

Political career: *House of Lords:* Raised to the peerage as Baroness Mone, of Mayfair in the City of Westminster 2015. Leads a government review on supporting business start-ups in disadvantaged communities.

Political interests: Enterprise.

Other: Board of directors, Prince's Scottish Youth Business Trust; Princes Trust; Hon. Doctorate: Paisley University 2002, Hertfordshire University 2010; World Young Business Achiever Award 2000, USA; Business Woman of the Year, Corporate Elite Awards; Best Newcomer, British Apparel Export Awards; OBE 2010.

Publications: My Fight to the Top (autobiography, 2015).

The Baroness Mone OBE, House of Lords, London SW1A 0PW
Tel: 020 7219 3000 *Email:* monem@parliament.uk
MGM Media Limited, 86-90 Paul Street, London EC2A 4NE *Tel:* 020 3823 6900
Email: enquiries@michellemone.com Website: michellemone.com *Twitter:* @MichelleMone

MONKS, LORD

LABOUR

MONKS (Life Baron), John Stephen Monks; cr 2010. Born 5 August 1945; Son of Charles Monks, parks superintendent, and Bessie Monks, teacher; Married Francine Schenk 1970 (2 sons 1 daughter).

Education: Ducie Technical High School, Manchester; Nottingham University (BA economic history 1967); French.

Non-political career: Trades Union Congress 1969-2003: Head of organisation and industrial relations department 1977-87, Deputy General Secretary 1987-93, General Secretary 1993-2003; General Secretary, European Trades Union Confederation 2003-11; Non-executive director, Thompsons' Solicitors 2010-19; Special adviser to José Manuel Barroso as President, European Commission 2011-14; Trustee director, NOW: Pensions 2011-17. President, British Airline Pilots' Association 2011-18.

Political career: *House of Lords:* Raised to the peerage as Baron Monks, of Blackley in the County of Greater Manchester 2010. Member: Economic Affairs 2014-16, 2020-, Economic Affairs Finance Bill Sub-committee 2015-16, 2020-. *Other:* Council member, ACAS 1979-95; Vice-chair, Learning and Skills Council 2001-04; Chairman, Co-operative Commission 2000-01.

Political interests: Europe, the economy and employment, trade unions; Europe, North America.

Other: Council member, Economic and Social Research Council 1988-91; People's History Museum: Trustee 1988-2016, Chair of Trustees 2004-16; President, British Airline Pilots Association 2011-18; Member, Panel on Takeovers and Mergers 2018-; MS Society, People's History Museum; Honorary doctorates: Nottingham University, Salford University, Manchester University, Cranfield University, Cardiff University, Kingston University, Southampton University, Open University; Fellow, City & Guilds of London; Chevalier, Legion D'Honneur.

Recreations: Music, film, football, cricket, rugby (especially league).

The Lord Monks, House of Lords, London SW1A 0PW
Tel: 020 7219 6943 *Email:* monksj@parliament.uk

MONTROSE, DUKE OF

CONSERVATIVE

MONTROSE (8th Duke of, S), James Graham; cr. 1707; Marquis of Montrose (S) 1644; Marquess of Graham and Buchanan (S) 1707; Earl of Montrose (S) 1505; Earl of Kincardine (S) 1707; Earl Graham (GB) 1722; Viscount Dundaff (S) 1707; Lord Graham (S) 1445; Lord Aberuthven, Mugdock and Fintrie (S) 1707; Baron Graham (GB) 1722; 12th Bt of Braco (NA) 1625. Born 6 April 1935; Son of 7th Duke and late Isobel Sellar; Married Catherine MacDonnell, née Young 1970 (died 2014) (2 sons 1 daughter).

Education: Loretto School, Musselburgh; French.

Non-political career: Farmer, landowner; Director, Montrose Estates Ltd 1992-.

Political career: *House of Lords:* First entered House of Lords 1996; Elected hereditary peer 1999-; Opposition Spokesperson for: Scotland 2001-10, Environment 2001-06, 2008-10, Food and Rural Affairs 2001-10; Opposition Whip 2001-10; Opposition Spokesperson for: Northern Ireland 2007, Wales 2007-08, 2009-10. Member: Partnerships (Prosecution) (Scotland) Bill 2013, Science and Technology 2015-16, EU Energy and Environment Sub-Committee 2016-19, EU Environment Sub-committee 2020-. *Other:* Chair, Buchanan Community Council 1982-93; Vice-chair, Secretary of State's Working Party for Loch Lomond and the Trossachs.

Political interests: Europe, agriculture, rural affairs; Ethiopia, Sudan.

Other: Member: Inter-Parliamentary Union 1997-, Commonwealth Parliamentary Association 1997-; Queen's Bodyguard for Scotland (Royal Company of Archers): Member 1965-, Captain 2006-14; Hereditary Sheriff, Dunbartonshire; Member: Council, Scottish National Farmers Union 1981-90, Royal Scottish Pipers Society; President, Royal Highland and Agricultural Society 1997-98; Scottish Landowners Federation; President, National Sheep Association 2013-17; Royal Agricultural Benevolent Society; OStJ 1978. Farmers Club.

Recreations: Walking, shooting, golf.

His Grace the Duke of Montrose, House of Lords, London SW1A 0PW
Tel: 020 7219 4487 *Fax:* 020 7219 5979 *Email:* montrosej@parliament.uk
Montrose Estates Ltd, Buchanan Castle, Drymen G63 0HY *Tel:* 01360 870382
Email: jeanetta@buchanancastlegolfclub.co.uk

NON-AFFILIATED

MOONIE, LORD

MOONIE (Life Baron), Lewis George Moonie; cr 2005. Born 25 February 1947; Son of late George Moonie, accountant, and Eva Moonie; Married Sheila Burt 1971 (2 sons).

Education: Grove Academy, Dundee; St Andrews University (MB, ChB 1970); Edinburgh University (DPM 1975; MRCPsych 1979; MSc community medicine 1981; MFCM 1984); French, Dutch.

Non-political career: Registrar training in psychiatry 1973-75; Full-time research clinical pharmacologist and medical adviser in pharmaceutical industry in Netherlands, Switzerland and Edinburgh 1975-80; Fife Health Board: Trainee community medicine 1980-84, Community medicine specialist 1984-87. Member: TGWU, MSF.

Political career: *House of Commons:* MP (Labour) for Kirkcaldy 1987-2005; Opposition Frontbench Spokesperson for: Technology, Trade and Industry 1989-92, Science and Technology 1992-94, Trade and Industry 1994-95, Broadcasting and Telecommunications 1995-97; Member House of Commons Commission 1997-2000; Parliamentary Under-Secretary of State (Minister for Veterans), Ministry of Defence 2000-03. *House of Lords:* Raised to the peerage as Baron Moonie, of Bennochy in Fife 2005. Member: Economic Affairs 2007-12, Finance Bill Sub-committee 2008-10, Economic Affairs Finance Bill Sub-Committee 2011. *Other:* Member, Co-operative Party; Left Labour Party May 2019. Councillor, Fife Regional Council 1982-86.

Political interests: Industry, technology, economic policy, defence.

Other: RSPB, Oxfam.

Recreations: Fishing, walking, golf, bridge.

The Lord Moonie, House of Lords, London SW1A 0PW
Tel: 020 7219 4097 *Email:* mooniel@parliament.uk *Twitter:* @Moonie_1

NON-AFFILIATED

MOORE OF ETCHINGHAM, LORD

MOORE OF ETCHINGHAM (Life Baron), Charles Hilary Moore; cr 2020. Married Caroline Baxter (twin son and daughter).

Education: Eton College; Trinity College, Cambridge (MA history).

Non-political career: *Daily Telegraph*: Political correspondent 1979-1982, Deputy Editor 1992-95, Editor 1995-2003, Group Consulting Editor 2003-; *The Spectator*: Political Columnist 1982-84, Editor 1984-90; Editor, *Sunday Telegraph* 1992-95.

Political career: *House of Lords:* Raised to the peerage as Baron Moore of Etchingham, of Etchingham in the County of East Sussex 2020.

Other: Trustee, Global Warming Policy Foundation; Chair of trustees, Rectory Society; DLitt, Buckingham University 2007.

Publications: Margaret Thatcher: The Authorized Biography, Volume One: Not For Turning (2013); Margaret Thatcher: The Authorized Biography, Volume Two: Everything She Wants (2016); Margaret Thatcher: The Authorized Biography, Volume Three: Herself Alone (2019).

The Lord Moore of Etchingham, House of Lords, London SW1A 0PW
Tel: 020 7219 3000

LABOUR

MORGAN, LORD

MORGAN (Life Baron), Kenneth Owen Morgan; cr. 2000. Born 16 May 1934; Son of late David Morgan and Margaret Morgan, née Owen; Married Jane Keeler 1973 (died 1992) (1 son 1 daughter); married Dr Elizabeth Gibson 2009.

Education: University College School, Hampstead; Oriel College, Oxford (BA modern history 1955, MA; DPhil 1958; DLitt 1985).

Non-political career: Lecturer, later senior lecturer in history, University College of Wales, Swansea 1958-66; Columbia University: Visiting Fellow 1962-63, Visiting Professor 1965; Fellow and praelector, modern history and politics, Queen's College, Oxford 1966-89; Visiting Professor, University of South Carolina 1972; O'Donnell lecturer, University of Wales 1981-82; Neale lecturer, University College, London 1986; Principal, then Vice-Chancellor, University College of Wales, Aberystwyth; University of Wales: Professor 1989-95, Senior Vice-Chancellor 1993-95, Emeritus Professor 1999; AH Dodd lecturer, University of Wales, Bangor 1992, 2004; Lloyd George Memorial lecturer 1993; Visiting lecturer, University of Texas (Austin) 1994, 1999, 2007, 2010, 2014; Faculty lecturer, Oxford University 1995-2000; BBC (Wales) annual lecturer 1995; Prothero lecturer, Royal Historical Society 1996; Callaghan lecturer, University College of Wales, Swansea 1996; Visiting Professor, Witwatersrand University, South Africa 1997, 1998, 2000; British Academy lecturer 1998; Benjamin Meaker Visiting Professor, Bristol University 2000; Merlyn-Rees lecturer, Glamorgan University 2002; Presidential lecturer, Rouen University 2003; Ford special lecturer, Oxford University 2005; London Guildhall lecturer 2006, 2007; Gresham College Lecturer 2007; Speaker's House lecture 2011; Visiting Professor, King's College, London 2012-; King's College London annual lecture 2012; SAES lecture, Limoges 2012; Visiting Lecturer: Texas University 2014, Riga University 2014. Member, AUT -1995.

Political career: *House of Lords:* Raised to the peerage as Baron Morgan, of Aberdyfi in the County of Gwynedd 2000. Member, Constitution 2001-04, 2015-19; Joint Committee on Draft Constitutional Bill 2008.

Political interests: Education, Europe, foreign affairs, constitutional reform, civil liberties, children; France, India, South Africa, Wales, USA.

Other: Chair, Curatorium, Celtic Studies Centre, Tubingen University 1998-2005; President, Committee for Advanced Studies, Rouen University 2002-; Vice-President, Hon Society Cymmrodorion, Llafur, International Eisteddfod of Llangollen; Yr Academi Gymreig; Board member, Celtic Studies 1972-2003; Council member, Royal Historical Society 1983-86; Trustee, St Deiniol's, Hawarden 1989-96; Council member, National Library of Wales 1991-95; Academic assessor, Leverhulme Devolution project 1999-2002; Chair, Fabian Society Commission on the Monarchy 2002-03; Trustee, History of Parliament Trust 2002-; Chair, University Committee on Student Radicalisation 2015; Fellow: Royal Historical Society 1964, British Academy 1983; Founding Fellow, Learned Society of Wales 2009; Imperial Cancer Research, Royal Institute for the Deaf; Hon. Fellow: Queen's College, Oxford 1992, Oriel College, Oxford 2003; Honorary doctorate: Wales University, Glamorgan University, Greenwich University; ACLS Fellowship, Columbia University 1962-63; Honorary Druid, Welsh National Eisteddfod 2008; Gold Medal for Lifetime Achievement, Honourable Society of Cymmrodorion 2009; Awards for Lifetime Achievement: Parliamentary Archives and History Group 2014, Welsh Parliamentarian of the Year 2014. Reform Club; Member, Middlesex County Cricket Club.

Publications: Editor, Welsh History Review 1961-2003; Wales in British Politics 1868-1922 (1963, 1992); David Lloyd George: Welsh radical as world statesman (1963); Freedom or Sacrilege? (1967); Keir Hardie (1967); The Age of Lloyd George (1971); Editor, Lloyd George Family Letters (1973); Lloyd George (1974); Keir Hardie, Radical and Socialist (1975) (Arts Council prize); Consensus and Disunity (1979); Co-author, Portrait of a Progressive (1980); Rebirth of a Nation: Wales 1880-1980 (1981) (Arts Council prize); David Lloyd George (1981); Labour in Power, 1945-1951 (1984); Editor, The Oxford Illustrated History of Britain (1984, new updated edn, 2009); Labour People (1987); Editor, The Oxford History of Britain (1988, 2001, updated 2010); The Red Dragon and the Red Flag (1989); The People's Peace (1990, 2001); Co-editor, Twentieth Century British History (1994-99); Modern Wales: politics, places and people (1995); Britain and Europe (1995); Editor, The Young Oxford History of Britain and Ireland (1996, 2006); Callaghan: a life (1997); Co-editor, Crime, Protest and Police in Modern British Society (1999); The Twentieth Century (2000); The Great Reform Act (2001); 25 contributions to Oxford Dictionary of National Biography (2004) and supplements (2009) and (2014); Michael Foot: a Life (2007); Ages of Reform (2011); Editor, David Lloyd George

(2013); Author and editor of many other works, as well as articles and reviews; Frequent broadcaster on history, politics and Welsh affairs; Revolution to Devolution (2014); My Histories (2015).

Recreations: Music, travel, sport (cricket), architectural history.

Professor the Lord Morgan, House of Lords, London SW1A 0PW
Tel: 020 7219 8616
Email: kenneth.morgan@hotmail.co.uk

CONSERVATIVE

MORGAN OF COTES, BARONESS

MORGAN OF COTES (Life Baroness), Nicola Ann Morgan; cr 2020. Born 10 October 1972; Daughter of Peter and Jennifer Griffith; Married Jonathan Morgan 2000 (1 son).

Education: Surbiton High School, Kingston-upon-Thames; St Hugh's College, Oxford (BA law 1993, MA); Legal Practice Course 1994.

Non-political career: Trainee/assistant solicitor, Theodore Goddard 1994-97; Assistant solicitor, Allen & Overy 1998-2002; Corporate professional support lawyer, Travers Smith 2002-10; Consultant, Travers Smith LLP 2020-; Political adviser, StepChange Debt Charity 2020-.

Political career: *House of Commons:* Contested Islington South and Finsbury 2001 and Loughborough 2005 general elections. Member for Loughborough 2010-19; PPS to David Willetts as Minister of State for Universities and Science 2010-12; Assistant Government Whip 2012-13; HM Treasury: Economic Secretary 2013-14, Financial Secretary 2014; Minister for Women, Department for Culture, Media and Sport (attending Cabinet) 2014; Secretary of State for: Education and Minister for Women and Equalities 2014-16, Digital, Culture, Media and Sport 2019. Member, Business, Innovation and Skills 2010; Ex-officio Member, Public Accounts 2013-14; Chair, Treasury 2017-19; Member: Liaison 2017-19, Treasury Sub-committee 2017-19. *House of Lords:* Raised to the peerage as Baroness Morgan of Cotes, of Cotes in the County of Leicestershire 2020. Secretary of State for Digital, Culture, Media and Sport 2020. Member, COVID-19 2020-. *Other:* Chair, Wessex Young Conservatives 1995-97; Vice-chair, Battersea Conservatives 1997-99.

Political interests: DCMS matters, business, financial services, economy, higher education, mental health; Bangladesh.

Other: Founder, Bluelist Organisation 2002-04; Member, advisory board: Finito Education Ltd 2016-19, Carnegie Centre of Excellence for Mental Health in Schools 2017-19; Non-executive director: Great Central Railway 2020-, Careers & Enterprise Company 2020-, Financial Services Compensation Scheme 2020-; Member, Law Society; RNIB, Mind, Rethink, Rainbows Hospice, Carpenters Arms, World Vision; Industry and Parliament Trust; PC 2014.

Publications: Ombudsmen – Time for Reform? (Bretwalda Books); The Civil War in Loughborough; Taught Not Caught: Educating for 21st Century Character (John Catt Educational Ltd, 2017).

Recreations: Choral singing, cookery, reading, theatre, cinema, running.

Rt Hon the Baroness Morgan of Cotes, House of Lords, London SW1A 0PW
Tel: 020 7219 3000 *Email:* morganna@parliament.uk *Twitter:* @nickymorgan01

CROSSBENCH

MORGAN OF DREFELIN, BARONESS

MORGAN OF DREFELIN (Life Baroness), Delyth Jane Morgan; cr. 2004. Born 30 August 1961; Daughter of David Elias Julian Morgan and Ann George, née Stedman; Married Jim Shepherd 1991 (1 daughter).

Education: Elliott Comprehensive, London; Putney College of Further Education; University College, London (BSc physiology 1986).

Non-political career: President, London University Union 1985-86; Campaigns organiser, Shelter 1986-88; Director, Workplace Nurseries Campaign 1988-92; Director of communications, National Asthma Campaign 1992-96; Chief executive: Breakthrough Breast Cancer 1996-2005, Breast Cancer Campaign 2011-15, Breast Cancer Now 2015-.

Political career: *House of Lords:* Raised to the peerage as Baroness Morgan of Drefelin, of Drefelin in the County of Dyfed 2004. Government Whip 2007-08; Government Spokesperson for: Communities and Local Government 2007-08, Work and Pensions 2007-08, Scotland 2007-08, Wales 2007-08; Parliamentary Under-Secretary of State (Intellectual Property and Quality) and Government Spokesperson, Department for Innovation, Universities and Skills 2008; Government Spokesperson for Cabinet Office 2008; Parliamentary Under-Secretary of State and Government Spokesperson, Department for Children, Schools and Families 2008-10; Opposition Spokesperson for Education 2010-11. Member: Merits of Statutory Instruments 2005-07, Draft Children (Contact and Adoption) Bill Joint Committee 2005. *Other:* Labour until July 2011 (on taking up position of chief executive of Breast Cancer Campaign); now sits as Crossbencher July 2011-.

Political interests: Science, health, women, children, voluntary sector; Wales.

Other: Chair, Childcare Umbrella 1989-92; Long Term Conditions Alliance: Trustee 1994-2000, Chair of trustees 1996-98; Member, Cancer Task Force 2000-05; Association of Medical Research Charities Trustee 2001-04; Member, NHS Modernisation Board 2002-05; Chair, Choice in Primary Care 2003-04; Patron, Sheila McKechnie Foundation 2004-; Chair of trustees, Foundations UK 2004-07; Trustee, Children with Leukaemia 2005-07; Chair, Patient Voices 2005-07; Member, Ethics Committee, Royal College of Obstetricians and Gynaecologists 2006-07; Patron, Breast Cancer Campaign 2007; Chair, National Cancer Research Institute 2015-; Fellow: University College London, Cardiff University, Institute of Cancer Research, London University.

Recreations: Photography, singing, reading, watching rugby.

The Baroness Morgan of Drefelin, House of Lords, London SW1A 0PW
Tel: 020 7219 8727 *Email:* morgand@parliament.uk *Twitter:* @delythjmorgan

LABOUR

MORGAN OF ELY, BARONESS

MORGAN OF ELY (Life Baroness), Mair Eluned Morgan; cr 2011. Born 16 February 1967; Daughter of Rev Bob Morgan and Elaine Morgan; Married Rev Dr Rhys Jenkins 1996 (1 son 1 daughter).

Education: Atlantic College; Glantaf Welsh Language Comprehensive; Hull University (BA European studies); French, Spanish, Welsh.

Non-political career: Programme sales 1991; TV reporter 1992-93; Documentaries researcher, BBC 1993-94; Director of national business development, Wales, Scottish and Southern Energy plc 2009-13. Member, Unite.

Political career: *House of Lords:* Raised to the peerage as Baroness Morgan of Ely, of Ely in the City of Cardiff 2011. Opposition Whip 2013-16; Opposition Spokesperson for: Wales 2013-16, 2016-17, Foreign and Commonwealth Office 2014-16. *Other:* European Parliament: MEP for: Mid and West Wales 1994-99, Wales 1999-2009: Labour spokesperson on: Budgetary control, Energy, Industry; National Assembly for Wales: AM for Mid and West Wales region 5 May 2016-5 May 2020, MS for Mid and West Wales region since 6 May 2020: Minister for: Lifelong Learning and Welsh Language 2017-20, Mental Health, Wellbeing and Welsh Language 2020-.

Political interests: European Union reform and economic development, devolution, tourism, minority languages, business, energy.

Other: Live Music Now Charity: Chair (Wales) 2012-16, Trustee (UK) 2012-16; Fellow, Trinity College Carmarthen; Cardiff University: Honorary Professor 2010-, Fellow.

Recreations: Walking, reading, having fun with family.

The Baroness Morgan of Ely, House of Lords, London SW1A 0PW
Tel: 020 7219 5353 *Email:* morganeluned@parliament.uk
Welsh Parliament, Cardiff Bay, Cardiff CF99 1SN *Tel:* 0300 200 7264
Email: eluned.morgan@senedd.wales Website: www.elunedmorgan.wales
Twitter: @Eluned_Morgan

LABOUR

MORGAN OF HUYTON, BARONESS

MORGAN OF HUYTON (Life Baroness), Sally Morgan; cr. 2001. Born 28 June 1959; Daughter of Albert Morgan and Margaret Morgan; Married John Lyons 1984 (2 sons).

Education: Belvedere School for Girls, Liverpool; Van Mildert College, Durham University (BA geography 1980); King's College, London (PGCE 1981); Institute of Education, London (MA education 1988).

Non-political career: Secondary school geography teacher 1981-85; Labour Party: Student organiser 1985-88, Key seats organiser 1989-92, Director of campaigns and elections 1993-95, Head of party liaison to Tony Blair as Leader of the Opposition 1995-97; Prime Minister's Office 1997-2005: Political secretary to Tony Blair as Prime Minister 1997-2001, Director, government relations 2001-05; Adviser to ARK (Absolute Return for Kids) 2005-. Member, GMB.

Political career: *House of Lords:* Raised to the peerage as Baroness Morgan of Huyton, of Huyton in the County of Merseyside 2001. Cabinet Office: Minister of State 2001, Government Spokesperson for Women's Issues 2001. Co-opted Member, EU Sub-committee G (Social Policy and Consumer Affairs) 2006-09; Member: Public Service and Demographic Change 2012-13, Personal Service Companies 2013-14; Chair, Digital Skills 2014-15; Member, Science and Technology 2015-19. *Other:* Councillor, Wandsworth Borough Council 1986-90; Trustee, Olympic Delivery Authority 2006-12; Chair: Office for Standards in Education (OFSTED) 2011-14, Royal Brompton and Harefield NHS Foundation Trust 2017-.

Political interests: Equality issues, education, health.

Other: Non-executive director, Carphone Warehouse plc/Dixons Carphone 2005-17; Member, advisory board, Virgin Holdings; Trustee, Mayor's Fund 2009-; Member, advisory board, Institute of Education, University of London; Vice-chair, King's College London 2013-19; Chair, Ambition School Leadership 2019-; Master-elect, Fitzwilliam College Cambridge 2019-; Children's charities.

Recreations: Gardening, family, cooking, theatre.

The Baroness Morgan of Huyton, House of Lords, London SW1A 0PW
Tel: 020 7219 5500 *Email:* morgan@parliament.uk

LABOUR

MORRIS OF ABERAVON, LORD

MORRIS OF ABERAVON (Life Baron), John Morris; cr. 2001. Born 5 November 1931; Son of late D W Morris and late M O A Lewis, formerly Morris; Married Margaret Lewis 1959 (3 daughters).

Education: Ardwyn School, Aberystwyth; University College of Wales, Aberystwyth (LLB 1952); Gonville and Caius College, Cambridge (LLM 1953); Gray's Inn (Holker Senior Exhibitioner); Welsh.

Non-political career: Called to the Bar, Gray's Inn 1954; QC 1973; Recorder of Crown Court 1982-97; Bencher, Gray's Inn 1984. Commissioned Welch Regiment and served Royal Welch Fusiliers. Member, GMB.

Political career: *House of Commons:* MP (Labour) for Aberavon 1959-2001; Parliamentary Secretary, Ministry of Power 1964-1966; Joint Parliamentary Secretary, Ministry of Transport 1966-1968; Minister of Defence for Equipment 1968-70; Secretary of State for Wales 1974-79; Shadow Attorney General and Principal Opposition Frontbench Spokesperson for Legal Affairs 1979-81, 1983-97; Attorney General 1997-99. *House of Lords:* Raised to the peerage as Baron Morris of Aberavon, of Aberavon in the County of West Glamorgan and of Ceredigion in the County of Dyfed 2001. Member: European Union Sub-committee C (Common Foreign and Security Policy/Foreign Affairs, Defence and Development Policy) 2002-05, Constitution 2006-09, Joint Committee on the Draft Defamation Bill 2011, EU Sub-committee E (Justice and Institutions) 2011-12, Inquiries Act 2005 2013-14, Procedure/Procedure and Privileges 2016-, Electoral Registration and Administration Act 2013 2019, European Union 2019-20; Chair, EU Justice Sub-committee 2019-20; Member, EU International Agreements Sub-committee 2020-. *Other:* Chair: Joint Review of British Railways 1966-67, National Road Safety Advisory Council 1967-68; Committee member, Implementation of Nolan Report 1997; Member, Prime Minister's Advisory Committee on Business Appointments 2002-09; Lord Lieutenant, Dyfed 2002-06.

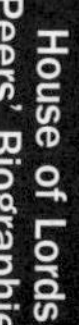

Political interests: Legal matters, armed forces, steel industry, agriculture; Spain.

Other: Member: UK Delegation, Consultative Assemblies Council of Europe and Western European Union 1963-64, 1982-83, UK Delegates to North Atlantic Assembly 1970, Executive Committee, Inter-Parliamentary Union, British Group, UK Delegation to US Senate (British-American Parliamentary Group) 2011; President, London Welsh Association 2001-08; Member, Prince's Trust Council (Cymru) 2002-08; Patron: London Welsh Lawyers Association 2010-, Edmund-Davies Charitable Trust; Freedom, Borough of Port Talbot 1992; Chancellor: Glamorgan University 2001-13, University of South Wales 2013-14; Hon. LLD: University of Wales, University of South Wales; Hon. Fellow: University College, Aberystwyth, Trinity College, Carmarthen, University College, Swansea, Gonville and Caius College, Cambridge, University College, Lampeter; Lifetime Achievement, *Wales Yearbook* awards 2011; PC 1970; Kt 1999; KG 2003.

Publications: Endowed Lecture, David Lloyd George Memorial (Hon. Society of Cymrodorion, London, 2005); Autobiography, Fifty Years in Politics and the Law (University of Wales Press, Cardiff, 2011); Youard Lecture, The Development by Attorney Generals of the Doctrine of Armed Intervention by States, without Security Council Authorisation, to Avert an Overwhelming Human Catastrophe (Swansea University, 2011); The Welsh and the United Kingdom (National Library of Wales Website, November 2013).

Recreations: Fishing, shooting.

Rt Hon the Lord Morris of Aberavon KG QC, House of Lords, London SW1A 0PW
Tel: 020 7219 3156 *Email:* maggiestevenson@parliament.uk

CONSERVATIVE

MORRIS OF BOLTON, BARONESS

MORRIS OF BOLTON (Life Baroness), Patricia Morris; cr. 2004. Born 16 January 1953; Daughter of late James Sydney and Alice Whittaker; Married William Patrick Morris 1978 (1 daughter 1 son).

Education: Bolton School; Clifton and Didsbury Colleges of Education.

Non-political career: PA to: Northern Regional Director, Slater Walker Ltd 1974-75, Chevalier Dr Harry D. Schultz 1975; Fund manager, PPS 1975-77; Technical analyst: Foster & Braithwaite 1977-78, Charlton, Seal, Dimmock & Co 1979-83; Adviser to Abbot of Ampleforth 1998-2004; Policy and political adviser to Conservative MEP 1999-2001.

Political career: *House of Commons:* Contested (Conservative) Oldham Central and Royton 1992 general election. *House of Lords:* Raised to the peerage as Baroness Morris of Bolton, of Bolton in the County of Greater Manchester 2004. Opposition Whip 2004-10; Opposition Spokesperson for: Health 2004-06, 2009-10, Education and Skills 2004-07, Women 2005-10, Children, Schools and Families 2007-09, Work and Pensions 2009-10; Deputy Chairman of Committees 2010-; Deputy Speaker 2011-; Trade Envoy to Jordan, Kuwait and Palestinian Territories 2012-. Member: Joint Committee on Human Rights 2010-11, Adoption Legislation 2012-13, Soft Power and the UK's Influence 2013-14, Affordable Childcare 2014-15, European Union 2016; Chair, EU External Affairs Sub-committee 2016; Member, Services 2017-. *Other:* Conservative Party: Member, National Union Executive Committee 1991-96, Chair, North West Area Women's Committee 1993-96, Member: Conferences Committee 1998-2001, Field Operations Panel 1998-2001, Agents' Remuneration Panel 1998-2001, Vice-chair (Candidates) 2001-05. Deputy chair, Salford Royal Hospitals NHS Trust 1993-97; DL, Greater Manchester 2008-.

Other: Chair, Bolton Cancer Research Campaign 1992-95; Trustee, Bolton Lads and Girls Club 1994-2002; Member, advisory board, Women 2 Win 2005-; President, National Benevolent Institution 2006-; Patron, Oxford Parent Infant Project (OXPIP) 2006-; Trustee: Agbis 2006-, Disability Partnership 2007-, Unicef UK 2007-; Co-chair, Women in Public Policy 2007-; Vice-president, Catholic Union of Great Britain 2008-; President, World Travel Market Advisory Council; Chair: Governance Group, Register of Providers of Cosmetic Injectable Treatments, Centre for Islamic Finance; OBE. Special Forces Club.

Recreations: Music, reading, football (Bolton Wanderers FC).

The Baroness Morris of Bolton OBE DL, House of Lords, London SW1A 0PW
Tel: 020 7219 5353 *Email:* whitbycollinsa@parliament.uk *Twitter:* @MorrisofBolton

LABOUR

MORRIS OF YARDLEY, BARONESS

MORRIS OF YARDLEY (Life Baroness), Estelle Morris; cr 2005. Born 17 June 1952; Daughter of late Charles Morris (MP 1963-83) and late Pauline Morris, née Dunn.

Education: Whalley Range High School, Manchester; Coventry College of Education, Warwick University (BEd 1974).

Non-political career: Teacher, Sidney Stringer School and Community College 1974-92. Member, CWU.

Political career: *House of Commons:* MP (Labour) for Birmingham Yardley 1992-2005; Opposition Whip 1994-95; Opposition Spokesperson for Education and Employment 1995-97; Department for Education and Employment/Skills 1997-2002: Parliamentary Under-Secretary of State 1997-98, Minister of State 1998-2001, Secretary of State for Education and Skills 2001-02; Minister of State (Minister for the Arts), Department for Culture, Media and Sport 2003-05. *House of Lords:* Raised to the peerage as Baroness Morris of Yardley, of Yardley in the County of West Midlands 2005. Member: Merits of Statutory Instruments/Secondary Legislation Scrutiny 2009-14, Social Mobility 2015-16, Citizenship and Civic Engagement 2017-18, Democracy and Digital Technologies 2019-, National Plan for Sport and Recreation 2020-. *Other:* Warwick District Council: Councillor 1979-91, Leader, Labour Group 1982-89.

Political interests: Education and training, political engagement, arts.

Other: Fellow, Industry and Parliament Trust 1994; Trustee: Hamlyn Foundation 2005-15, The Roundhouse 2008-15; Chair, Goldsmiths College, University of London 2012-18; Trustee, National Poetry Archive 2013-; Seven honorary degrees; PC 1999.

Rt Hon the Baroness Morris of Yardley, House of Lords, London SW1A 0PW
Tel: 020 7219 3000 *Email:* morrise@parliament.uk

CONSERVATIVE

MORRISSEY, BARONESS

MORRISSEY (Life Baroness), Helena Louise Morrissey; cr 2020. Born 22 March 1966; Married Richard Morrissey (3 sons 6 daughters).

Education: Cambridge University (MA philosophy 1987).

Non-political career: Schroders: Global Bond Analyst, New York 1988-90, Global Bond Fund Manager 1987-94; Newton Investment Management: Global Bond Fund Manager 1994-2004, Head of Fixed Income 1999-2001, Chief executive 2001-16; Head of Personal Investing, Legal & General Investment Management 2017-19.

Political career: *House of Lords:* Raised to the peerage as Baroness Morrissey, of Chapel Green in the Royal County of Berkshire 2020. *Other:* Diversity Adviser, UK Civil Service 2015-; Lead Non-Executive Director, Foreign, Commonwealth and Development Office 2020-.

Other: Panel member, FSA Practitioner Panel 2007-13; Founder and chair, 30% Club 2010-15; Chair: Royal Academy of Arts 2012-15 Eve Appeal 2013-15, Investment Association 2013-17; Board member: Financial Trade and Investment Services Board 2015-, Endowment Investment, Cambridge University 2013-15; Member, IPPR Commission on Economic Justice 2016-; Non-executive director, St James's Place 2019-; Chartered Institute of Management Accountants; Fellow, London Business School; Honorary doctorate: Cranfield University, Essex University, Queen's University Belfast, Cambridge University.

Publications: A Good Time To Be A Girl (William Collins, 2018).

The Baroness Morrissey DBE, House of Lords, London SW1A 0PW
Tel: 020 7219 3000 *Twitter:* @MorrisseyHelena

DEMOCRATIC UNIONIST PARTY

MORROW, LORD

MORROW (Life Baron), Maurice George Morrow; cr 2006. Born 27 September 1948; Son of Ernest and Eliza Jane Morrow; Married Jennifer Reid 1976 (2 daughters).

Education: Drumglass High School; East Tyrone College of Further and Higher Education.

Non-political career: Self-employed auctioneer, estate agent and valuer.

Political career: *House of Lords:* Raised to the peerage as Baron Morrow, of Clogher Valley in the County of Tyrone 2006. *Other:* Member, Northern Ireland Forum for Political Dialogue 1996-98; Northern Ireland Assembly: MLA for Fermanagh and South Tyrone 1998-2017 (as Maurice Morrow), Minister for Social Development 2000-01, 2016, DUP Chief Whip -2002, Member, Preparation for Government Committee 2006-07, Chair, Assembly Committees on: Procedures 2007-10, Justice 2010-11. Contested 2017 Fermanagh and South Tyrone Northern Ireland Assembly election. Chair, Democratic Unionist Party. Councillor, Dungannon and South Tyrone Borough Council 1973-2017.

Political interests: Israel, USA.

Other: Alternate member, EU Committee of the Regions 2006-10; Member, Apprentice Boys of Derry; Director: Moygashel Development Association, Dungannon Enterprise Centre -2013.

Recreations: Field sports.

The Lord Morrow, House of Lords, London SW1A 0PW
Tel: 020 7219 5353
19 Church Street, Dungannon BT71 6AB *Tel:* 028 8775 2799
Email: mauricemorrow@hotmail.com

CROSSBENCH

MOUNTEVANS, LORD

MOUNTEVANS (4th Baron, UK), Jeffrey Richard de Corban Evans; cr 1945. Born 13 May 1948; Son of 2nd Baron Mountevans; Married Hon Juliet Wilson 1972 (2 sons).

Education: Nautical College, Pangbourne; Pembroke College, Cambridge; Norwegian, French.

Non-political career: Clarksons Platou: Shipbroker 1972-, Tanker broker 1972-79, Head, Gas and Specialised Tankers 2000-01, Managing director, Gas 2001-, Director 2014-17. Honorary Commander, RNR 2015.

Political career: *House of Lords:* Elected hereditary peer 2015-. Member, EU Internal Market Sub-committee 2019-20. *Other:* City of London Corporation: Alderman 2007-, Sheriff 2012-13, Lord Mayor of London 2015-16.

Political interests: Maritime, international business, education.

Other: Director and trustee, White Ensign Association; President, City of London Sea Cadets 2007-; Almoner and director, Christ's Hospital 2010-; Trustee: Seafarers UK 2011-, Mansion House Scholarship Scheme 2011-, St Paul's Chorister Trust 2013-; Chair: Maritime London 2013-, Maritime UK 2014-15, Maritime Growth Study: Keeping the UK Competitive; Younger Brother, Trinity House; Member, Institute of Chartered Shipbrokers; Lord Mayor's Appeal 2015-16, JDRF, Sea Cadets; Liveryman: Worshipful Company of Shipwrights 1979-, Worshipful Company of World Traders 2010-, Worshipful Company of Goldsmiths 2012-, Worshipful Company of Wheelwrights 2013-, Worshipful Company of Security Professionals 2013-; Freedom, City of London; Knight, Order of St John.

Recreations: Walking, skiing.

The Lord Mountevans, House of Lords, London SW1A 0PW
Tel: 020 7219 3000

CONSERVATIVE

MOYLAN, LORD

MOYLAN (Life Baron), Daniel Michael Gerald Moylan; cr 2020. Born 1 March 1956; Son of the late James and Susan Moylan.

Education: Oxford University (BA philosophy and modern languages 1978) (President, Oxford Union 1978).

Non-political career: Financial training consultant, Egan Associates 1987-2016; Adviser to Boris Johnson as Mayor of London 2008-16.

Political career: *House of Lords:* Raised to the peerage as Baron Moylan, of Kensington in the Royal London Borough of Kensington and Chelsea 2020. *Other:* Trustee, Kensington, Chelsea and Fulham Conservative Association 1996-. Councillor, Kensington and Chelsea Council 1990-2018.

Political interests: European and other international relations, transport, infrastructure, planning and construction; Southern Africa, South-East Asia, China, European Union, Russia.

Other: Honorary Fellow, Royal Institute of British Architects.

The Lord Moylan, House of Lords, London SW1A 0PW
Tel: 020 7219 3000 *Email:* moyland@parliament.uk Website: www.danielmoylan.com
Twitter: @danielmgmoylan

CONSERVATIVE

MOYNIHAN, LORD

MOYNIHAN (4th Baron, UK), Colin Berkeley Moynihan; cr. 1929; 4th Bt of Carr Manor (UK) 1922. Born 13 September 1955; Son of 2nd Baron; Married Gaynor-Louise Metcalf 1992 (2 sons 1 daughter).

Education: Monmouth School (Music Scholar); University College, Oxford (BA philosophy, politics and economics 1977, MA 1982) (President of the Oxford Union); Brasenose College, Oxford (J A Fiddian Research Scholarship 1977); French.

Non-political career: Personal assistant to chair, Tate and Lyle Ltd 1978-80; Manager, Tate and Lyle Agribusiness 1980-82; Ridgways Tea and Coffee Merchants: Chief executive 1982-83, Chair 1983-87; Chair, CMA Consultants 1993-; Managing director, Independent Power Corporation plc 1996-2001; Director, Rowan Group of Companies 1996-2016; Chair and chief executive, Consort Resources Group of Companies 2000-03; Director, Clipper Windpower UK Ltd 2001-07, Executive chair, Clipper UK Ltd 2004-07, Chair, Clipper EU Ltd 2004-07; Non-executive chair, Pelamis Wave Energy Ltd 2005-11; Chair, British Olympic Association 2005-12; Director, London Organising Committee for Olympic Games (LOCOG) 2006-12; Member: International Olympic Committee (IOC) International Relations Commission 2008-12, IOC Candidature Acceptance Working Group for the 2016 Olympic Games 2008-16; Non-executive Chair, Hydrodec 2012-; Chair, Buckthorn Partners.

Political career: *House of Commons:* MP (Conservative) for Lewisham East 1983-92. Contested Lewisham East 1992 general election; PPS to Kenneth Clarke MP: as Minister of Health 1985, as Paymaster-General 1985-87; Parliamentary Under-Secretary of State: Department of Environment (Minister for Sport) 1987-90, Department of Energy 1990-92. *House of Lords:* First entered House of Lords 1997; Senior Opposition Spokesperson for Foreign and Commonwealth Affairs 1997-2000; Elected hereditary peer 1999-; Shadow Minister for Sport 2003-05. Co-opted Member, European Union Sub-committee D (Environment and Agriculture) 2006-07; Member: Olympic and Paralympic Legacy 2013-14, The Arctic 2014-15, Delegated Powers and Regulatory Reform 2015-19, National Plan for Sport and Recreation 2020-. *Other:* Governor, Sports Aid Foundation (London and South East) 1980-82.

Political interests: Foreign affairs, trade and industry, sport, inner cities, refugees, overseas aid and development.

Other: Member, Bow Group 1978-: Chair, Trade and Industry Standing Committee 1983-87; Director, Canterbury Festival 1999-2001; Executive council member, Association of National Olympic Committees (ANOC) 2006-12; Ex-officio member, Olympic Board; Spinal Injuries Association; Liveryman, Worshipful Company of Haberdashers 1981; Court of Assistants 2003-; Freedom, City of London 1978; Hon. doctorate, London Metropolitan University 2007; Oxford Double Blue, Rowing and Boxing 1976 and 1977; World Gold Medal for Lightweight

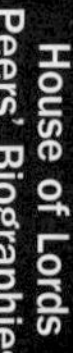

Rowing, International Rowing Federation 1978; Silver Medal for Rowing at Moscow Olympic Games 1980; World Silver Medal for Rowing 1981. Club at The Ivy, Le Beaujolais Club, Vincent's Club; London Rowing, Leander.

Recreations: Reading, sport, music.

The Lord Moynihan, House of Lords, London SW1A 0PW
Tel: 020 7219 5879
Westburn Business Centre, Westburn House, McNee Road, Prestwick KA9 2PB
Email: c.moynihan@cmagroup.org.uk

CROSSBENCH

MURPHY, BARONESS

MURPHY (Life Baroness), Elaine Murphy; cr. 2004. Born 16 January 1947; Daughter of Roger Lawson, engineer, and Nell Lawson, née Allitt; Married John Murphy 1969 (divorced 2001); married Michael Robb 2001.

Education: West Bridgford Grammar School, Nottingham; Manchester University (MB ChB 1971, MD 1979); University College, London (PhD history of medicine 2000).

Non-political career: Professor of old age psychiatry, Guy's Hospital, United Medical Schools, University of London 1983-96; Chair: City and Hackney Community Services NHS Trust 1995-98, East London and City Health Authority 1998-2001, North East London Strategic Health Authority 2001-06, St George's Hospital Medical School, University of London 2006-10.

Political career: *House of Lords:* Raised to the peerage as Baroness Murphy, of Aldgate in the City of London 2004. Member: Science and Technology Sub-committee I (Scientific Aspects of Ageing) 2005, Leader's Group on Members Leaving the House 2010-11. *Other:* Commissioner, Commission on Assisted Dying 2010-11.

Political interests: Mental health, NHS, mental capacity, ageing, higher education; Italy.

Other: Vice-President, Alzheimer's Society; Fellow, Royal College of Psychiatrists; Alzheimer's Society; MRCPsych 1976; FRCPsych 1983; Three honorary doctorates.

Publications: 100-plus publications and books; After the Asylums (Faber, 1991); Co-author, The Falling Shadow (Duckworth, 1995); The Moated Grange (Book Guild, 2015); Monks Hall, the History of a Waveney Valley Manor (Poppyland Publishing, 2018).

Recreations: Italy, Norfolk, entertaining friends.

The Baroness Murphy, House of Lords, London SW1A 0PW
Email: murphyel@parliament.uk

LABOUR

MURPHY OF TORFAEN, LORD

MURPHY OF TORFAEN (Life Baron), Paul Peter Murphy; cr 2015. Born 25 November 1948; Son of late Ronald Murphy and late Marjorie Murphy.

Education: St Francis School, Abersychan; West Monmouth School, Pontypool; Oriel College, Oxford (MA modern history 1970); French (basic).

Non-political career: Management trainee, CWS 1970-71; Lecturer in government, Ebbw Vale College of Further Education 1971-87; Visiting Parliamentary Fellow, St Anthony's College, Oxford 2006-07. Member, TGWU-Unite.

Political career: *House of Commons:* Contested Wells 1979 general election. MP (Labour) for Torfaen 1987-2015; Opposition Spokesperson on: Welsh Affairs 1988-94, Northern Ireland 1994-95, Foreign Affairs 1995, Defence, Disarmament and Arms Control 1995-97; Minister of State, Northern Ireland Office (Minister for Political Development) 1997-99; Secretary of State for: Wales 1999-2002, 2008-09, Northern Ireland 2002-05; Chairman, Intelligence and Security Committee 2005-08. Member, Joint Committee on National Security Strategy 2010-15. Chair, PLP Departmental Committee for Northern Ireland 2010-15. *House of Lords:* Raised to the peerage as Baron Murphy of Torfaen, of Abersychan in the County of Gwent 2015. Chair, Joint Committee on the Draft Investigatory Powers Bill 2015-16; Member, Common Frameworks Scrutiny 2020-. *Other:* Secretary, Torfaen CLP 1971-87; Chair, Welsh Group,

Labour MPs 1996-97. Torfaen Borough Council: Councillor 1973-87, Chair, Finance Committee 1976-86; National Assembly for Wales Ambassador for Oxbridge 2013-14.

Political interests: Local and regional government, Wales, education, housing, foreign affairs; France, Ireland, Northern Ireland.

Other: Vice-chair, British-American Parliamentary Group 2004-05, 2007-09; British-Irish Parliamentary Assembly: Co-chair 2006-07, 2009-10, Vice-chair 2010-15, Member 2017-; Vice-chair, Franco-British Friendship Group; Hon. Fellow, Oriel College, Oxford 2001; Parliamentary Visiting Fellow, St Antony's College, Oxford 2006-07; Hon. Fellow, Glyndwr University, Wrexham 2009-; Hon. Doc. University of South Wales 2014; Hon. D.Litt University of Wales Trinity Saint David; Knight of St Gregory (Papal Order); PC 1999; KCMCO. Oxford and Cambridge Club.

Recreations: Classical music, cooking.

Rt Hon the Lord Murphy of Torfaen, House of Lords, London SW1A 0PW
Tel: 020 7219 6193 *Email:* murphypp@parliament.uk

CROSSBENCH

MYNERS, LORD

MYNERS (Life Baron), Paul Myners; cr 2008. Born 1 April 1948; Married 2nd Alison Macleod 1995 (1 son 1 daughter 3 daughters from previous marriage).

Education: Truro School, Cornwall; London University Institute of Education (BEd); Stanford Executive Program, Stanford School of Business, USA.

Non-political career: *Daily Telegraph* 1970-74; N M Rothschild & Sons Ltd 1974-85; Gartmore plc 1985-2001: Chief executive 1985-93, 1999-2000, Chair 1987-2001; Deputy chair, Powergen plc 1999-2001; Director, National Westminster Bank 1997-2000; Chair, Guardian Media Group 2000-08; Personal accounts delivery authority, Department for Work and Pensions 2007-09; Chair and managing partner, Cevian Capital 2011-; Chair, Edelman 2015-.

Political career: *House of Lords:* Raised to the peerage as Baron Myners, of Truro in the County of Cornwall 2008. Financial Services Secretary and Government Spokesperson, HM Treasury 2008-10. Member: Joint Committee on Privacy and Injunctions 2011-12, Works of Art 2012-13, Personal Service Companies 2013-14. Vice-chair, PLP Departmental Group for Treasury 2010-15. *Other:* Sat as Labour until January 2014, now sits as a Crossbencher. Member: Financial Reporting Council 1995-2004, Company Law Review Consultative Committee 1998-2000; Court of Directors, Bank of England 2005-; Chair, Low Pay Commission 2006-.

Other: Trustee, Royal Academy Trust 2000-03; Tate Gallery: Trustee 2003-, Chair 2004-; Trustee: Glyndbourne 2003-, Smith Institute 2003-, National Gallery 2007-; Senior independent director, Co-operative Group Board 2014; Chancellor, Exeter University 2016-; CBE 2003.

The Lord Myners CBE, House of Lords, London SW1A 0PW
Tel: 020 7219 6760

CONSERVATIVE

NASEBY, LORD

NASEBY (Life Baron), Michael Wolfgang Laurence Morris; cr. 1997. Born 25 November 1936; Son of late Cyril Morris and Margaret Morris; Married Dr Ann Appleby 1960 (2 sons 1 daughter).

Education: Bedford School; St Catharine's College, Cambridge (BA economics 1960, MA); French.

Non-political career: Marketing manager, Reckitt and Colman Group 1960-64; Director: Service Advertising 1964-71, Benton & Bowles Ltd 1971-81; Chairman: Children's Mutual 1997-2005, Invesco Recovery Trust 2011 1995-2011; Non-executive director: Mansell Ltd 1998-2003, City Disputes Panel Ltd 2015-17. National service pilot (RAF and NATO) 1955-57.

Political career: *House of Commons:* Contested Islington North 1966 general election. MP (Conservative) for Northampton South 1974-97; PPS to Hugh Rossi and Michael Alison as Ministers of State, Northern Ireland 1979-81; Deputy Speaker and Chairman of Ways and Means 1992-97. *House of Lords:* Raised to the peerage as Baron Naseby, of Sandy in the County of Bedfordshire 1997. Member: Standing Orders (Private Bills) 2003-, Administration and Works 2005-09; EU Sub-committee F (Home Affairs): Co-opted member 2009-10, Member 2010-11; Member, Joint Committee on the Draft Deregulation Bill 2013. *Other:* London Borough of Islington: Councillor 1968-74, Leader 1969-71, Alderman 1971-74.

Political interests: Energy, health service, exports, marketing, parliamentary procedure, financial services, questioning government of the day; Caribbean, Cayman Islands, Chile, France, India, Maldives, Singapore, Sri Lanka.

Other: Member, Council of Europe and Western European Union 1983-91; Trustee: Victoria County History Society Northamptonshire 1992-, Parliamentary Contributory Pension Fund 2007-; Patron, Naseby Battlefield Project Trust 2008-14; President, Lords and Commons Golf Society 2010-; Patron, Cromwell Museum 2016-; Bedford School Foundation, Northamptonshire VCH Trust, Northamptonshire County Cricket Club Youth Trust, Royal Opera House; Hon. Fellow in History, Northampton University; Honorary fellow in history, Northampton University 2007; PC 1994; Sri Lanka Ratna 2005; Bernardo O'Higgins medal (Chile) 2013. Carlton Club, Chamberlain, Ordre des Cofeaux de Champagne, Confrérie des Chevalier du Tasterin, Chevalier, Commanderie de Bordeaux à Londres, Chairman, Cofradia del Vino Chileno; President, Northamptonshire County Cricket 2012-; MCC; John O'Gaunt Golf Club; Port Stanley Golf; All England Lawn Tennis; Lords Taverners; Northampton Saints Rugby.

Publications: Helping The Exporter (1967); Co-author, Marketing Below The Line (1970); The Disaster of Direct Labour (1978).

Recreations: Golf, tennis, forestry, wine, cricket.

Rt Hon the Lord Naseby, House of Lords, London SW1A 0PW
Tel: 020 7219 5353
Email: amnaseby@btinternet.com

CONSERVATIVE

NASH, LORD

NASH (Life Baron), John Alfred Stoddard; cr 2013. Born 22 March 1949; Son of John and Josephine Nash; Married Caroline 1983 (1 son 1 daughter).

Education: Milton Abbey School, Dorset; Corpus Christi College, Oxford (MA law 1971).

Non-political career: Barrister, Inner Temple 1972-74; William Brandts Sons & Co Ltd 1974-75; Lazard Brothers & Co Ltd 1975-83: Assistant director 1981-83; Advent Ltd 1983-88: Managing director 1987-88; Nash, Sells & Partners/Sovereign Capital Partners: Founder 1988, Chairman 1988-2010, Non-executive partner 2010-13.

Political career: *House of Lords:* Raised to the peerage as Baron Nash, of Ewelme in the County of Oxfordshire 2013. Department for Education: Government Spokesperson 2013-17, Parliamentary Under-Secretary of State for: Schools 2013-16, School System 2016-17. *Other:* Non-executive Director, Department for Education 2010-13; Lead Non-executive Director, Cabinet Office 2020-.

Political interests: Education.

Other: Chair, British Venture Capital Association 1988-89; Corpus Christi College, Oxford: Foundation Fellow, Member, Investment Committee 2005-, Deputy Chair, Development Committee 2005-; Chair: Future (charity) 2005-, Pimlico Academy 2008-, Future Academies Trust 2008-; Board Member, Centre for Policy Studies 2003-13; Trustee, Education Policy Institute 2018-; Foundation fellow, Corpus Christi College, Oxford. Athenæum Club, Turf Club; Sunningdale Golf Club; Pine Valley Golf Club, USA.

Recreations: Golf, tennis, skiing.

The Lord Nash, House of Lords, London SW1A 0PW
Tel: 020 7219 5353

CROSSBENCH

NEUBERGER, BARONESS

NEUBERGER (Life Baroness), Julia Babette Sarah Neuberger; cr. 2004. Born 27 February 1950; Daughter of late Walter Schwab, civil servant, and Alice Schwab, née Rosenthal, art collector; Married Anthony Neuberger 1973 (1 daughter 1 son).

Education: South Hampstead High School, London; Newnham College, Cambridge (BA Hebrew/Assyriology 1973, MA); Leo Baeck College, London (rabbinic ordination 1977).

Non-political career: Rabbi, author, broadcaster; Rabbi, South London Liberal Synagogue 1977-89; Visiting fellow: King's Fund Institute 1989-91, Harvard Medical School (Harkness fellowship) 1991-92; Chief executive, King's Fund 1997-2004; Consultant, Clore Duffield Foundation 2004-; Adviser to Trustees, Sainsbury Centre for Mental Health 2006-11; Bloomberg Professor, Harvard Divinity School, spring semester 2006; Senior Rabbi, West London Synagogue 2011-.

Political career: *House of Commons:* Contested (Liberal Democrat) Tooting 1983 general election. *House of Lords:* Raised to the peerage as Baroness Neuberger, of Primrose Hill in the London Borough of Camden 2004. Liberal Democrat Spokesperson for Health 2004-07; Prime Minister's Champion for Volunteering 2007-10. Member: EU Sub-committee G (Social Policy and Consumer Affairs) 2005-08, Draft Human Tissue and Embryos Bill Joint Committee 2007, Science and Technology Sub-committee I (Nanotechnologies and food) 2008-10, Science and Technology 2009-12; Chair, Science and Technology Sub-committee I (Behaviour Change) 2010-11; Member: Science and Technology Sub-committee I 2012-13, EU Justice Sub-committee 2015-19. *Other:* Trustee, Liberal Democrats 2004-08; Left Liberal Democrats September 2011 (on taking up position of Senior Rabbi of West London Synagogue), now sits as Crossbencher. Chair, Camden and Islington Community Health Services NHS Trust 1993-97; Trustee, Imperial War Museum 1999-2006; Civil Service Commissioner 2001-02; Member, Committee on Standards in Public Life 2001-04; Trustee, British Council 2004-07; Member: One Housing Group 2008-12, Responsible Gambling Strategy Board 2008-11; Advisory Panel, Judicial Diversity 2009-10; Chair, University College London Hospitals, NHS Foundation Trust 2019-.

Political interests: Health, citizens' rights, asylum and refugees; Ireland.

Other: Patron, North London Hospice; Trustee: Booker Prize Foundation 2002-11, New Philanthropy Capital 2008-11, Van Leer Group Foundation 2012-; Board member and trustee, Social Market Foundation 2012-13; Chair, Review of How the Liverpool Care Pathway for Dying Patients is Used in Practice 2013-15; Trustee, Rayne Foundation 2015-; Vice-chair, Independent Review of the Mental Health Act 2018-; Chancellor, Ulster University 1994-2000; Thirteen honorary doctorates; 5 honorary fellowships; Hon. Doctorate of Divinity, Cambridge University 2015; DBE 2004.

Publications: Caring for Dying Patients of Different Faiths (1986, 1994, 2004); The Story of Judaism (for children) (Dinosaur/Collins, 1987); Whatever's Happening to Women? (Kyle Cathie, 1991); Ethics and Healthcare: Research Ethics Committees in the UK (Kings Fund Institute, 1992); The Things That Matter; An Anthology of Women's Spiritual Poetry (Kyle Cathie, 1993); On Being Jewish (Heinemann, 1996); Dying Well: a guide to enabling a good death (1999, 2004); The Moral State We're In (HarperCollins, 2006); Not Dead Yet: A Manifesto for Old Age (HarperCollins, 2008); Is That All There Is? (Rider, 2011); Frequent broadcaster and press contributor.

Recreations: Opera, gardening, Irish life, novels, food, sailing.

The Baroness Neuberger DBE, House of Lords, London SW1A 0PW
Tel: 020 7219 2716 *Email:* neubergerj@parliament.uk
West London Synagogue, 33 Seymour Place, London W1H 5AU *Tel:* 020 7535 0255
Email: julia.neuberger@wls.org.uk Website: www.wls.org.uk

CROSSBENCH

NEUBERGER OF ABBOTSBURY, LORD

NEUBERGER OF ABBOTSBURY (Life Baron), David Edmond Neuberger; cr. 2006. Born 10 January 1948; Son of Prof Albert Neuberger CBE FRS and Lilian Dreyfus; Married Angela Holdsworth 1976 (2 sons 1 daughter).

Education: Westminster School; Christ Church, Oxford (BA chemistry 1970, MA); French.

Non-political career: NM Rothschild & Sons 1970-73; Called to the Bar, Lincoln's Inn 1974; QC 1987; Recorder 1990-96; Bencher 1993; High Court Judge, Chancery Division 1996-2004; Supervisory Chancery Judge, Midland, Wales and Chester, and Western Circuits 2001-04; Lord Justice of Appeal 2004-07; Judge in charge of Modernisation 2004-06; Lord of Appeal in Ordinary 2007-09; Master of the Rolls 2009-12; President of the Supreme Court 2012-17; Arbitrator and Legal Expert 2018-.

Political career: *House of Lords:* Raised to the peerage as Baron Neuberger of Abbotsbury, of Abbotsbury in the County of Dorset 2006. Lord of Appeal in Ordinary 2007-09; As a senior member of the judiciary, disqualified from participation 2009-17. *Other:* Chair, Advisory Committee on Spoliation of Art during the Holocaust 1997-; Governor, University of the Arts, London 2000-10.

Other: Chair, Schizophrenia Trust 2003-14; Patron, MHRUK 2014-; Prisoners Aboard, GRIT, BIICL, Westminster School Bursaries; Freeman: Company of Drapers 2011, Skinners Company 2018; Freedom, City of London; Chancellor, University of Law 2018-; Hon. Student, Christ Church College, Oxford; Hon. Fellow, Royal Society; Honorary Doctorate of Law: UCL, Queen Mary University of London, Exeter University, York University, Oxford University; Kt 1996; PC 2004. Garrick Club.

Rt Hon the Lord Neuberger of Abbotsbury, House of Lords, London SW1A 0PW
Tel: 020 7219 5353
One Essex Court Temple, London EC4Y 9AR

CONSERVATIVE

NEVILLE-JONES, BARONESS

NEVILLE-JONES (Life Baroness), (Lilian) Pauline Neville-Jones; cr 2007. Born 2 November 1939; Daughter of Roland Neville-Jones and Cecilia Winn.

Education: Leeds Girls' High School; Lady Margaret Hall, Oxford (BA modern history 1961); French, German, some Spanish.

Non-political career: HM Diplomatic Service 1963-96: Third secretary, Salisbury, Rhodesia High Commission 1964-65, Third, second secretary, Singapore High Commission 1965-68, Foreign and Commonwealth Office, London (FCO) 1968-71, First secretary, Washington DC embassy 1971-75, FCO 1975-77, Member/chef de cabinet to European Commissioner Christopher Tugendhat, Brussels 1977-82, Head of planning staff, FCO 1983-87, Bonn embassy 1987-91: Minister (economics) 1987-88, Minister 1988-91, Seconded as Deputy Secretary to the Cabinet and Head of Defence and Overseas Secretariat, Cabinet Office 1991-94; Chair, Joint Intelligence Committee 1993-94; Political director, FCO 1994-96; Seconded as senior adviser to High Representative for Bosnia 1996; BBC International Governor 1998-2004; Chair: Information Assurance Advisory Council 2004-07, Qinetiq Group plc 2002-05; Senior Adviser, Ridge Global 2015-.

Political career: *House of Lords:* Raised to the peerage as Baroness Neville-Jones, of Hutton Roof in the County of Cumbria 2007. Shadow Minister for Security and National Security Adviser to the Leader of the Opposition 2007-10; Minister of State for Security and Government Spokesperson, Home Office 2010-11; Special Representative to Business on Cyber Security 2011-14. Member: Joint Committee on the National Security Strategy 2012-15, 2019-, Joint Committee on the Draft Enhanced Terrorism Prevention and Investigation Measures Bill 2012-13, The Arctic 2014-15, Science and Technology 2015-19. *Other:* BBC Governor 1997-2005; Member: City University Council 1997-2001, Oxford University Council 2001-04, Engineering and Physical Sciences Research Council 2013-19, Lancaster University Council 2014-.

Political interests: National security issues, foreign affairs, science and technology; Asia, Europe, Middle East.

Other: Chair, Advisory Panel of Cyber Security, Bank of England 2014-16; Patron and Chair, Advisory Board, Cyber Security Challenge 2014-; Cyclotion Trust, Unique; Freedom, City of London; Hon. doctorates: University of London, Open University, City University; Hon. fellow, Lady Margaret Hall, Oxford; CMG 1987; DCMG 1996; Légion d'Honneur (France) 2009; PC 2010.

Rt Hon the Baroness Neville-Jones DCMG, House of Lords, London SW1A 0PW
Tel: 020 7219 3208 *Email:* nevillejonesp@parliament.uk

CONSERVATIVE

NEVILLE-ROLFE, BARONESS

NEVILLE-ROLFE (Life Baroness), Lucy Jeanne Neville-Rolfe; cr 2013. Born 2 January 1953; Daughter of late Edmund and late Margaret Neville-Rolfe; Married Sir Richard Packer (4 sons).

Education: St Mary's Convent, Shaftesbury and Cambridge; Somerville College, Oxford (MA philosophy, politics and economics); Some French and German.

Non-political career: Ministry of Agriculture, Fisheries and Food 1973-92: Private Secretary to John Silkin as Minister of Agriculture, Fisheries and Food 1977-79, EC Sheepmeat and Milk 1979-86, Land Use 1986-88, Food Safety Act 1988-90, Head of Personnel 1990-92; Member, Prime Minister's Policy Unit 1992-94; Under Secretary 1994; Director, Deregulation Unit, Department of Trade and Industry/Better Regulation Unit, Cabinet Office 1995-97; Tesco plc: Group director of corporate affairs 1997-2006, Company Secretary 2003-06, Executive director, corporate and legal affairs 2006-12.

Political career: *House of Lords:* Raised to the peerage as Baroness Neville-Rolfe, of Chilmark in the County of Wiltshire 2013. Parliamentary Under-Secretary of State for Intellectual Property and Government Spokesperson: Department for Business, Innovation and Skills 2014-16, Department for Culture, Media and Sport 2015-16; Minister of State for Energy and Intellectual Property and Government Spokesperson, Department for Business, Energy and Industrial Strategy 2016; Commercial Secretary and Government Spokesperson, HM Treasury 2016-17. Member: Affordable Childcare 2014, Intellectual Property (Unjustified Threats) Bill 2016, European Union 2017-, EU Financial Affairs Sub-committee 2017-20, EU Services Sub-committee 2020-. *Other:* Member, Deputy Prime Minister's Local Government Funding Committee 2003-04; Efficiency Board, Cabinet Office 2010-13; Governor, London Business School 2011-; Strategic Advisory Group, UK Trade & Investment 2011-13.

Political interests: Agriculture, animals, food, rural affairs, business, industry and consumers, culture, media and sport, European Union including Brexit, international affairs, roll out of broadband, vocational education, digital, economic and financial affairs, productivity; China, Eastern Europe, Germany, India, Ireland, Italy, South Asia, USA.

Other: Non-executive director, John Laing Construction 1991-92; British Retail Consortium: Member, management board 1998-2012, Member, Economics and European Committee 1998-2013, Deputy chair 2003-12; EuroCommerce: Vice-president 1998-2008, President 2012-14; Board of Management, Foreign and Commonwealth Office 2000-05; Corporate Leaders Group on Climate Change 2005-13; Foresight Obesity Project 2005-07; China-Britain Business Council 2005-13; Chair, Dobbies Garden Centres plc 2007-10; Non-executive director, Carbon Trust 2008-13; UK-India Business Council 2008-13; Non-executive director, ITV plc 2010-14; Member: Advisory board, PWC 2013-14, Supervisory board, Metro AG 2013-14; Non-executive director: Boparan Ltd (2 Sisters Food Group) 2013-14, Hermes Equity Ownership Services 2013-14, Capita plc 2017-; Chair, Assured Food Standards 2017-; Adviser, Bridge Farm Group 2018-; Non-executive director: Health Data Research UK 2018-, Secure Trust Bank 2018-, Thomson Reuters Founders Share Company 2019-; Chair, UK ASEAN Business Council 2019-; Fellow, Institute of Chartered Secretaries; FCIS 2010; Hon. Fellow, Somerville College, Oxford; Women of Achievement Award 2007; PR Week Lifetime Achievement Award 2013; CMG 2005; DBE 2012.

Recreations: Gardening, art and architecture, racing, cricket, theatre.

The Baroness Neville-Rolfe DBE CMG, House of Lords, London SW1A 0PW
Tel: 020 7219 5353 *Email:* nevillerolfel@parliament.uk *Twitter:* @LNevilleRolfe

LIBERAL DEMOCRAT

NEWBY, LORD

Leader, Liberal Democrat Peers

NEWBY (Life Baron), Richard Mark Newby; cr 1997. Born 14 February 1953; Son of Frank and Kathleen Newby; Married Ailsa Ballantyne Thomson 1978 (2 sons).

Education: Rothwell Grammar School; St Catherine's College, Oxford (BA philosophy, politics and economics 1974, MA).

Non-political career: HM Customs and Excise: Administration trainee 1974, Private secretary to Permanent Secretary 1977-79, Principal, Planning Unit 1979-81; Secretary, SDP Parliamentary Committee 1981; SDP headquarters 1981-88: National Secretary 1983-88; Corporate affairs director, Rosehaugh plc 1988-92; Director: Matrix Communications Consultancy Ltd 1992-99, Flagship Group Ltd 1999-2001; Chair: Live Consulting 2001-12, Live Sport CIC 2009-12.

Political career: *House of Lords:* Raised to the peerage as Baron Newby, of Rothwell in the County of West Yorkshire 1997. Liberal Democrat Spokesperson for: Trade and Industry 1998-2000, Treasury 1998-2010; Sponsored Public Services (Social Value) Act 2012; Deputy Chief Whip (Captain of the Queen's Bodyguard of the Yeomen of the Guard) 2012-15; Government Spokesperson for Treasury 2012-15; Liberal Democrat: Chief Whip 2012-16, Leader, Liberal Democrat Peers 2016-; Member, House of Lords Commission 2016-. Member: Monetary Policy of the Bank of England/Economic Affairs 1998-2003, Ecclesiastical Committee 2002-12, Economic Affairs Sub-committee on Financial Bill 2004, Joint Committee on the Draft Financial Services Bill 2011-12, Administration and Works 2012-16, Privileges and Conduct 2012-19, Procedure/Procedure and Privileges 2012-, Sub-committee on Leave of Absence 2012-13, Selection 2012-, Refreshment 2012-15, Joint Committee on Security 2012-15, Insurance Bill 2014-15, Finance 2016, Liaison 2016-19. Chair, Liberal Democrat Parliamentary Party Committee on Treasury 2010-12. *Other:* Deputy Chair, Liberal Democrat General Election Team 1995-97; Liberal Democrat Campaigns and Communications Committee 1995-2006; Chief of Staff to Charles Kennedy as Leader of the Liberal Democrats 1999-2006.

Political interests: Europe, regional development; Eastern Caribbean, Pakistan, South Africa.

Other: Sport Legacy Foundation, Transformation Trust; OBE 1990; PC 2014. MCC.

Recreations: Football, cricket, tennis.

Rt Hon the Lord Newby OBE, House of Lords, London SW1A 0PW
Tel: 020 7219 8501 *Email:* newbyr@parliament.uk *Twitter:* @RichardNewby3

NON-AFFILIATED

NEWCASTLE, LORD BISHOP OF

NEWCASTLE (12th Bishop of), Christine Elizabeth Hardman. Born 27 August 1951; Married Roger (2 daughters).

Education: Queen Elizabeth's Girls' Grammar School, Barnet; University of London (BSc (Econ) 1973); Oxford University (MTh applied theology 1994).

Non-political career: Articled clerk; Estate agency; Deaconess 1984; Curate, St John the Baptist, Markyate Street 1984-88; Ordained Deacon 1987; St Albans Ministerial Training Scheme/Oxford Ministry Course 1988-96: Tutor and course director, Director of Mission Studies; Ordained Priest 1994; Vicar, Holy Trinity and Christ the King, Stevenage 1996-2001; Rural Dean of Stevenage 1999-2001; Archdeacon of Lewisham and Greenwich 2001-12; Honorary Assistant Priest, Cathedral and Collegiate Church of St Saviour and St Mary Overie Southwark 2012-15; Bishop of Newcastle 2015-.

Political career: *House of Lords:* Entered House of Lords 2015. *Other:* Member: General Synod 1998-, Archbishops' Council 2010-15; Church Commissioner 2017-.

Political interests: Rural and urban issues; North East region, economic and business affairs; Botswana, Norway.

Other: Committee Member, Ecclesiastical Law Society; Doctor of Business Administration, Greenwich University.

Recreations: Theatre, being in the mountains, cycling.

Rt Rev the Lord Bishop of Newcastle, House of Lords, London SW1A 0PW
Tel: 020 7219 3000
Bishop's House, 29 Moor Road South, Gosforth, Newcastle upon Tyne NE3 1PA
Tel: 0191-285 2220 *Email:* bishop@newcastle.anglican.org
Website: www.newcastle.anglican.org *Twitter:* @BishopNewcastle

CONSERVATIVE

NEWLOVE, BARONESS

NEWLOVE (Life Baroness), Helen Margaret Newlove; cr 2010. Born 28 December 1961; Married Garry Newlove 1986 (died 2007) (3 daughters).

Non-political career: Campaigner against anti-social behaviour; Founder, Newlove Warrington 2009.

Political career: *House of Lords:* Raised to the peerage as Baroness Newlove, of Warrington in the County of Cheshire 2010. Government Champion for Active, Safer Communities: Home Office 2010-11, Department for Communities and Local Government 2011-12; Deputy Chairman of Committees 2017-; Deputy Speaker 2018-. Member: EU Justice Sub-committee 2015-17, Citizenship and Civic Engagement 2017-18, EU Home Affairs Sub-committee 2019, Joint Committee on Statutory Instruments 2019-. *Other:* Victims' Commissioner for England and Wales, Ministry of Justice 2013-19.

Political interests: Community, policing, volunteering, anti-social behaviour, alcohol, victims, justice, national citizen service; Caribbean, Dubai, New Zealand, USA.

Other: Warrington Wolves Foundation, SAFE Place Merseyside, Fybromyalgia UK; Doctor of Laws, Bolton University 2017; Best Magazine Bravery Award 2008; Cheshire Woman of the Year 2009; Local Heroes Community Project of the Year 2009; Business Woman of the Year Achievement Award 2015.

The Baroness Newlove, House of Lords, London SW1A 0PW
Tel: 020 7219 6464 *Email:* newloveh@parliament.uk Website: victimscommissioner.org.uk
Twitter: @baronessnewlove/@VictimsComm

CONSERVATIVE

NICHOLSON OF WINTERBOURNE, BARONESS

NICHOLSON OF WINTERBOURNE (Life Baroness), Emma Harriet Nicholson; cr. 1997. Born 16 October 1941; Daughter of late Sir Godfrey Nicholson, 1st and last Bt and late Lady Katharine Lindsay, daughter of 27th Earl of Crawford, KT, PC; Married Sir Michael Harris Caine 1987 (died 1999) (2 stepchildren 1 deceased).

Education: Portsdown Lodge School, Bexhill; St Mary's School, Wantage; Royal Academy of Music (LRAM 1962, ARCM 1962); French.

Non-political career: ICL 1961-64; Computer consultant, John Tyzack and Partners 1964-69; Computer management consultant: McLintock Mann and Whinney Murray 1969-73, John Tyzack and Partners 1973-74; Save the Children Fund 1974-85: Director of Fundraising 1977-85; Consultant inter alia Dr Barnardos, Westminster Children's Hospital, The Duke of Edinburgh's Award Scheme, Foster Parents Plan, Association of Girl Guides and Scouts et al 1985-87; St Antony's College, Oxford: Visiting fellow 1995-96, Senior associate member 1997-98, 1998-99.

Political career: *House of Commons:* Contested (Conservative) Blyth 1979 general election. MP for Devon West and Torridge 1987-97 (Conservative 1987-95, Liberal Democrat 1995-97); PPS to Michael Jack as Minister of State: Home Office 1992-93, Ministry of Agriculture, Fisheries and Food 1993-95, Treasury 1995; Liberal Democrat Spokesperson for Overseas Development and Human Rights 1996-97. *House of Lords:* Raised to the peerage as Baroness Nicholson of Winterbourne, of Winterbourne in the Royal County of Berkshire 1997. Member, Liberal Democrat Foreign Affairs Team 1997-2016; Frontbench Spokesperson for Data Protection 1998-99; Trade Envoy to: Iraq 2014-, Azerbaijan and Turkmenistan 2016-, Kazakhstan 2017-. Member, Soft Power and the UK's Influence 2013-14; Chair, Sexual Violence in Conflict 2015-16; Member, Joint Committee on Human Rights 2018-19. *Other:* European Parliament: MEP for South East region 1999-2009: First Vice-President, Foreign Affairs, Human Rights, Common Defence and Security Policy/Foreign Affairs Committee 1999-2007; Rapporteur for: Romania 1999-2007, Iraq 2000-02, Kashmir 2007-09; Chair, interparliamentary Committee for Iraq; Deputy Chair, Euromed committee for Women; Member inter alia committee for Finance, subcommittee for women's Affairs, Agriculture Committee etc; Member, Council for Lome Convention; Official observer including leader for 32 Parliamentary and Presidential elections in Africa, Europe and the Middle East; Member, Monitoring Committee. Former treasurer, Positive European Group (Conservative); Vice-chair, Conservative Party 1983-87; Member, Federal Executive Committee, Liberal Democrats 1999-2003; Sat as Liberal Democrat in the Lords until September 2016; now sits as Conservative.

Political interests: Foreign affairs, fundamental freedoms, democracy and the rule of law.

Other: Parliamentary Assembly of the Council of Europe: Member, UK Delegation 2011-15, Honorary Life Member; Chair, AMAR International Charitable Foundation 1991-; Founder President, Iraq-Britain Business Council; Vice President, Man Booker Prize for English Fiction; Chair, Booker Prize for Russian fiction; President, Caine Prize for African Writing; Board member, GWPF; Patron, Blind in Business; Freeman, Worshipful Company of Information Technologists; Freedom, City of London; LRAM; ARCM; FRSA; Honorary D; Honorary doctorate: Oklahoma City University, USA, Birmingham University, London Metropolitan University, Victor Babes University of Medicine and Pharmacy, Romania, Dimitrie Cantemir Christian University, Bucharest, Romania, Brigham Young University, USA 2017, Kingston University 2014, University of Craiova 2015, Academy of Economic Studies, Bucharest 2001. Royal Over-seas League, Reform Club.

Publications: Why Does the West Forget? (1993); Secret Society – Inside and Outside the Conservative Party (1996); Co-editor, The Iraqi Marshlands (2002); Co-author, Religious Persecution – The Driver for Forced Migration (2018).

The Baroness Nicholson of Winterbourne, House of Lords, London SW1A 0PW
Tel: 020 7219 0059 *Twitter:* @Baroness_Nichol

CONSERVATIVE

NOAKES, BARONESS

NOAKES (Life Baroness), Sheila Valerie Noakes; cr. 2000. Born 23 June 1949; Daughter of Albert and Iris Masters; Married (Colin) Barry Noakes 1985.

Education: Eltham Hill Grammar School; Bristol University (LLB 1970).

Non-political career: Peat Marwick Mitchell & Co/KPMG/KPMG Peat Marwick 1970-2000: Partner 1983-2000; Seconded to: HM Treasury 1979-81, Department of Health, as Director of Finance, NHS Management Executive 1988-91; Bank of England: Director 1994-2001, Senior non-executive director 1998-2001; Non-executive director: Carpetright plc 2001-14, SThree plc 2001-07, Hanson plc 2001-07, English National Opera 2001-08, John Laing plc 2002-04, Imperial Chemical Industries plc 2004-08, Severn Trent plc 2008-14, Royal Bank of Scotland Group plc 2011-.

Political career: *House of Lords:* Raised to the peerage as Baroness Noakes, of Goudhurst in the County of Kent 2000. Opposition Spokesperson for: Health 2001-03, Work and Pensions 2001-06, Treasury 2003-10. Member: Audit 2011-14, Economic Affairs Finance Bill Sub-Committee 2012-13, 2016, 2018-19, Joint Committee on Voting Eligibilty (Prisoners) Bill 2013; Chair, Personal Service Companies 2013-14; Member: Economic Affairs 2013-14, Affordable Childcare 2014-15, Insurance Bill 2014-15, EU Internal Market Sub-committee 2015-19, European Union 2018-19, Finance 2020-. *Other:* Member: Inland Revenue Management Board 1992-99, NHS Policy Board 1992-95, Chancellor of the Exchequer's Private Finance Panel 1993-97; Commissioner, Public Works Loan Board 1995-2001; Member, Public Services Productivity Panel 1998-2000; Governor: London Business School 1998-2001, Eastbourne College 2000-04; Deputy Chairman, Ofcom 2014-18.

Political interests: Health, public finance, trade and industry, public service management, horse racing, rural issues.

Other: Trustee, Thomson Reuters Founder Share Company 1998-2013; Board member, Social Market Foundation 2002-05; Institute of Chartered Accountants of England and Wales: Fellow, Council member 1987-2002, President 1999-2000; Board member, Companions, Institute of Management 1996-2002; Childrens Society, Dogs Trust, Cats Protection Society; Freedom, City of London; FCA; Three honorary doctorates; DBE 1996. Farmers Club.

Recreations: Skiing, horse racing, opera, early classical music.

The Baroness Noakes DBE, House of Lords, London SW1A 0PW
Tel: 020 7219 5230 *Fax:* 020 7219 4215 *Email:* noakess@parliament.uk *Twitter:* @1SVN

NON-AFFILIATED

NORFOLK, DUKE OF

NORFOLK (18th Duke of, E), Edward William Fitzalan-Howard; cr. 1483; 29th Earl of Arundel (E) 1139/1289; Earl of Surrey (E) 1483; 16th Earl of Norfolk (E) 1644; 13th Baron Beaumont (E) 1309; 20th Baron Maltravers (E) 1330; 16th Baron FitzAlan, Clun, and Oswaldestre (E) 1627; 5th Baron Howard of Glossop (UK) 1869. Born 2 December 1956; Son of Major-General 17th Duke, KG, GCVO, CB, MC, DL; Married Georgina Susan Temple Gore 1987 (3 sons 2 daughters).

Education: Ampleforth College, Yorkshire; Lincoln College, Oxford (BA philosophy, politics and economics 1978, MA).

Non-political career: Chair: Sigas Ltd 1979-88, Parkwood Group Ltd 1989-2002.

Political career: *House of Lords:* Entered House of Lords 2002; On leave of absence June 2012-September 2016, April 2017-June 2017, January 2021-. *Other:* DL, West Sussex 2002-.

Other: Trustee: Tablet Trust, College of Arms Trust; Arundel and Littlehampton District Scouts; Arundel Branch, Royal British Legion; Friends of Arundel Cathedral; Oxford and Cambridge Catholic Education Board; Premier Duke and Earl of England; Earl Marshal and Hereditary Marshal and Chief Butler of England. British Racing Drivers Club (Silverstone).

Recreations: Skiing, motor-racing, shooting.

His Grace the Duke of Norfolk DL, House of Lords, London SW1A 0PW
Tel: 020 7219 5353
Arundel Castle, Arundel BN18 9AB *Tel:* 01903 883400

CONSERVATIVE

NORTHBROOK, LORD

NORTHBROOK (6th Baron, UK), Francis Thomas Baring; cr. 1866; 8th Bt of The City of London (GB) 1793. Born 21 February 1954; Son of 5th Baron; Married Amelia Taylor 1987 (divorced 2006) (3 daughters); married Charlotte Pike 2013.

Education: Winchester College; Bristol University (BA 1976).

Non-political career: Trainee accountant, Dixon Wilson & Co 1976-80; Credit and investment analyst/private client investment manager, Baring Bros & Co Ltd 1981-89; Senior investment manager, Taylor Young Investment Management Ltd 1990-93; Investment fund manager, Smith and Williamson 1993-95; Managing director, Northbrook Farms Ltd 1995-; Director, Mars Asset Management 1996-2006.

Political career: *House of Lords:* First entered House of Lords 1990; Elected hereditary peer 1999-; Opposition Whip 1999-2000. Member: Equality Act 2010 and Disability 2015-16, Financial Exclusion 2016-17.

Political interests: Finance and industry, agriculture, constitution.

Other: Trustee, Fortune Forum 2006-; Member, advisory board, Iman Foundation 2016-; Freedom, City of London; Royal Geographical Society. White's, Pratt's, Beefsteak, Gunmakers Club.

Recreations: Cricket, skiing, shooting.

The Lord Northbrook, House of Lords, London SW1A 0PW
Tel: 020 7219 4090 *Email:* northbrookf@parliament.uk

LIBERAL DEMOCRAT

NORTHOVER, BARONESS

Liberal Democrat Lords Spokesperson for Foreign and Commonwealth Affairs

NORTHOVER (Life Baroness), Lindsay Patricia Northover; cr. 2000. Born 21 August 1954; Daughter of Charles and Patricia Granshaw; Married John Northover 1988 (separated) (2 sons 1 daughter).

Education: Brighton and Hove High School; St Anne's College, Oxford (BA modern history 1976, MA); Bryn Mawr College, Pennsylvania University, USA (MA history and philosophy of science 1978; PhD 1981).

Non-political career: Research Fellow: University College London and St Mark's Hospital 1980-83, St Thomas's Hospital Medical School, London 1983-84; Lecturer, University College London 1984-91; Historian of twentieth century medicine, Wellcome Institute, London 1984-91. Member, AUT 1984-91.

Political career: *House of Commons:* Contested (as Lindsay Granshaw) (SDP/All) Welwyn Hatfield 1983 and 1987 and (Liberal Democrat) Basildon 1997 general elections. *House of Lords:* Raised to the peerage as Baroness Northover, of Cissbury in the County of West Sussex 2000. Liberal Democrat Spokesperson for: Health 2001-02, International Development 2002-10, Equality Bill 2009-10; Government Whip 2010-14; Government Spokesperson for: Advocate General for Scotland 2010, Law Officers 2010, Wales 2010, Justice 2010-12, Health 2010-13, Women and Equalities 2010-14; Department for International Development: Government Spokesperson 2010-15, Parliamentary Under-Secretary of State 2014-15; Government Spokesperson for: Environment, Food and Rural Affairs 2012-14, Culture, Media and Sport 2013-14, Education 2013-14; Liberal Democrat: Spokesperson for International Development 2015-16, Shadow Minister/Lords Spokesperson for Foreign and Commonwealth Affairs 2016-; Trade Envoy to: Angola 2016-20, Zambia 2017-20. Member: Stem Cell Research 2001-02, EU Sub-committee C (Foreign Affairs, Defence and Development Policy) 2003-04, Procedure 2005-09, EU Sub-committee A (Economic and Financial Affairs and International Trade) 2008-10. *Other:* Chair: SDP Health and Social Welfare Association 1987-88, Liberal Democrats' Parliamentary Candidates Association 1988-91, Women Liberal Democrats 1992-95; Trustee, Liberal Democrats 2009-11; President, Liberal Democrat Women 2014-.

Other: Vice-chair, Commonwealth Parliamentary Association 2008-10; Trustee, Bryn Mawr College Association, Great Britain; Council member, Overseas Development Institute 2005-10; Trustee: Tropical Health and Education Trust 2007-10, Unicef UK 2009-10; Honorary Associate Professor, Institute of Global Health Innovation, Imperial College, London 2016-; Member of Advisory Council, Wilton Park 2016-; Trustee, Malaria Consortium 2016-; Fellow, Royal Society of Arts 2013; English-Speaking Union award to study in USA 1972; St Anne's College Exhibition 1973; Herbert Plumer Bursary for postgraduate study overseas 1976; English-speaking Union Fellowship 1976-79; Mrs Giles Whiting Fellowship in the Humanities 1979-80; PC 2015.

Publications: Various academic publications.

Rt Hon the Baroness Northover, House of Lords, London SW1A 0PW
Tel: 020 7219 8623 *Email:* northoverl@parliament.uk *Twitter:* @LPNorthover

CONSERVATIVE

NORTON OF LOUTH, LORD

NORTON OF LOUTH (Life Baron), Philip Norton; cr. 1998. Born 5 March 1951; Son of late George and Ena Norton.

Education: King Edward VI Grammar School, Louth; Sheffield University (BA political theory and institutions 1972; PhD 1977) (Nalgo Prize); University of Pennsylvania (Thouron Scholar, MA political science 1975).

Non-political career: Hull University: Politics lecturer 1977-82, Senior lecturer 1982-84, Reader 1984-86, Professor of Government 1986-, Director, Centre of Legislative Studies 1992-, Head of Department of Politics and International Studies 2002-07; Associate editor, *Political Studies* 1987-93; Editor, *Journal of Legislative Studies* 1995-.

Political career: *House of Lords:* Raised to the peerage as Baron Norton of Louth, of Louth in the County of Lincolnshire 1998. Constitution: Chair 2001-04, Member 2007-12, 2015-19; Co-opted member, EU Sub-committee E (Law and Institutions) 1999-2001, 2006-09; Member: Regulators 2006-07, Joint Committee on Draft Constitutional Bill 2008, Merits of Statutory Instruments/Secondary Legislation Scrutiny 2009-14, Joint Committee on Draft House of Lords Reform Bill 2011-12, Joint Committee on Voting Eligibilty (Prisoners) Bill 2013, Information 2014-15. *Other:* Chair, Conservative Academic Group 2000-; Executive Committee: Association of Conservative Peers 2001-14, Conservative History Group 2003-. Chair, Standards Committee, Kingston-upon-Hull City Council 1999-2003.

Political interests: Constitutional affairs, parliamentary reform, legislatures, British politics, American politics, education.

Other: Executive committee member: Study of Parliament Group 1981-93, 2012-, Political Studies Association 1983-89; Member, Society and Politics Research Development Group, Economic and Social Research Council 1987-90; President, British Politics Group (USA) 1988-90; Warden, King Edward VI Grammar School, Louth 1990-93; President, Politics Association 1993-2008; Co-chair, Research Committee of Legislative Specialists, International Political Science Association 1994-2003; Hansard Society: Council member 1997-, Director of Studies 2002-; Chair, Commission to Strengthen Parliament 1999-2001; Vice-President, Political Studies Association 1999-; Trustee, History of Parliament Trust 1999-; Co-founder, Campaign for an Effective Second Chamber 2001; Trustee, Jo Carby-Hall Poland and Cyprus Scholarships/Fellowships 2009-; Member, advisory board, Opposition Studies Forum 2009-; Co-chair, Higher Education Commission 2012-; President, Study of Parliament Group 2019-; Honorary Freeman, City of Kingston-Upon-Hull 2016; FRSA 1995; ACSS 2001; FRHistS 2018; Hon. LLD, Lincoln University 2011; Honorary Senior Fellow, Regent's University, London 2019. Royal Overseas League Club.

Publications: Author or editor: Dissension in the House of Commons 1945-74 (1975); Conservative Dissidents (1978); Dissension in the House of Commons 1974-79 (1980); The Commons in Perspective (1981); Co-author, Conservatives and Conservatism (1981); The Constitution in Flux (1982); Law and Order and British Politics (1984); The British Polity (1984, 5th edition 2010); Parliament in the 1980s (1985); Co-editor, The Political Science of British Politics (1986); Legislatures (1990); Parliaments in Western Europe (1990); New Directions in British Politics? (1991); Co-editor, Parliamentary Questions (1993); Co-author, Back from Westminster (1993); Does Parliament Matter? (1993); National Parliaments and the European Union (1996); Co-editor, The New Parliaments of Central and Eastern Europe (1996); The Conservative Party (1996); Legislatures and Legislators (1998); Parliaments and Governments in Western Europe (1998); Parliaments and Pressure Groups in Western Europe (1998); Co-editor, Parliaments in Asia (1999); Parliaments and Citizens in Western Europe (2002); Co-editor: Post-Communist and Post-Soviet Legislatures: The Initial Decade (2007), The Internet and Parliamentary Democracy in Europe (2008); A Century of Constitutional Reform (2011); Eminent Parliamentarians (2012); Parliament in British Politics (2nd edition 2013); The Voice of the Backbenchers (2013); Reform of the House of Lords (2017); Co-author: Politics UK (9th edition, 2018).

Recreations: Table tennis, walking, writing.

Professor the Lord Norton of Louth, House of Lords, London SW1A 0PW
Tel: 020 7219 0669 *Email:* nortonp@parliament.uk
Faculty of Business, Law and Politics, School of Law and Politics, Hull University, Hull HU6 7RX *Email:* andersoni@parliament.uk
Websites: www.hull.ac.uk/faculties/contact-list/philip-norton-lord-norton-of-louth
nortonview.wordpress.com *Twitter:* @LordNortonLouth

LABOUR

NYE, BARONESS

NYE (Life Baroness), Susan Jane Nye; cr 2010. Born 17 May 1955; Married Gavyn Davies (2 sons 1 daughter).

Non-political career: Civil servant: Department of Employment 1974-76, Downing Street 1976-79; Office of the Leader of the Opposition 1979-92; Office manager to Gordon Brown MP as Shadow Chancellor of the Exchequer 1992-97; Political secretary to Gordon Brown MP as Chancellor of the Exchequer 1997-2007; Director of government relations, Downing Street 2007-10.

Political career: *House of Lords:* Raised to the peerage as Baroness Nye, of Lambeth in the London Borough of Lambeth 2010.

Other: Partner: Barnsham Barns (Norfolk) LLP, Machrie Golf LLP; General Partner, SPKRBM LP; Director: Actev II Ltd Trading Group, Machrie Golf Links and Hotel Ltd, Another Place Ltd; Board member, Burma Campaign UK; Trustee, Young Women's Trust.

The Baroness Nye, House of Lords, London SW1A 0PW
Tel: 020 7219 5353

NON-AFFILIATED

OAKESHOTT OF SEAGROVE BAY, LORD

OAKESHOTT OF SEAGROVE BAY (Life Baron), Matthew Alan Oakeshott; cr. 2000. Born 10 January 1947; Son of late Keith Oakeshott CMG, diplomat, and late Jill Oakeshott; Married Dr Philippa Poulton 1976 (2 sons 1 daughter).

Education: Charterhouse, Surrey (Senior Foundation Scholar); University and Nuffield Colleges, Oxford (BA philosophy, politics and economics 1968, MA); French, German, Spanish.

Non-political career: ODI/Nuffield Fellow, Kenya Ministry of Finance and Economic Planning 1968-70; Special adviser to Roy Jenkins MP 1972-76; Director, Warburg Investment Management 1976-81; Manager, Courtaulds Pension Fund 1981-85; Founder director, OLIM Ltd and Investment director, Value and Income Trust plc 1986-; Chairman, OLIM Property Ltd 2012-.

Political career: *House of Commons:* Contested (Labour) Horsham and Crawley October 1974 and (SDP/All) Cambridge 1983 general elections. *House of Lords:* Raised to the peerage as Baron Oakeshott of Seagrove Bay, of Seagrove Bay in the County of the Isle of Wight 2000. Liberal Democrat Spokesperson for: Treasury 2001-11, Work and Pensions 2002-10; Chair, Business Advisory Group to Vince Cable as Secretary of State for Business, Innovation and Skills 2010; On leave of absence May 2014-October 2015, February 2020-. Member: Economic Affairs 2001-04, House of Lords' Offices Finance and Staff Sub-committee 2001-02, Reform of House of Lords Joint Committee 2002-03, Economic Affairs 2007-08. *Other:* Member, SDP: National Committee 1981-82, National Economic Policy Committee 1981-85; Member, Liberal Democrat Taxation Group 2007-10; Resigned from Liberal Democrats May 2014; now sits as Non-affiliated. Oxford City Councillor 1972-76.

Political interests: Economic policy, housing, overseas development, elections; France, Germany, Kenya, Norway.

Other: Governor, National Institute of Economic and Social Research; Chair, Coltstaple Trust; Coltstaple Trust.

Publications: Chapter in By-Elections in British Politics (1973).

Recreations: Music, elections, Arsenal FC.

The Lord Oakeshott of Seagrove Bay, House of Lords, London SW1A 0PW
Email: oakeshottm@parliament.uk
Tel: 020 7647 6701 *Twitter:* @oakeshottm

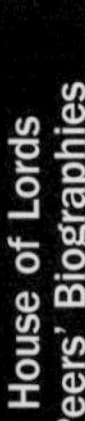

LIBERAL DEMOCRAT

OATES, LORD

Liberal Democrat Lords Spokesperson for Energy and Climate Change

OATES (Life Baron), Jonathan Oates; cr 2015. Born 28 December 1969; Son of Revd Canon John Oates and Sylvia Mary West; Civil partner David Hill 2006.

Education: Marlborough College; Exeter University (BA politics).

Non-political career: Teaching in Zimbabwe 1988; Account manager, Westminster Strategy 1992-99; Political and media adviser, South African Parliament 1999-2001; Communications adviser, Youth Justice Board 2001; Associate, Mark Bolland Associates 2002-04; Bell Pottinger: Director 2004-07, Strategic media director 2008-09; Liberal Democrats: Director of policy and communications 2007-08, Director, general election communications 2009-10; Deputy communications director, Number 10 2010; Chief of Staff to Nick Clegg as the Deputy Prime Minister 2010-15; Director, H&O Communications Ltd.

Political career: *House of Lords:* Raised to the peerage as Baron Oates, of Denby Grange in the County of West Yorkshire 2015. On leave of absence September 2017-July 2018; Liberal Democrat Lords Spokesperson for Energy and Climate Change 2020-. Member: EU Justice Sub-committee 2016-17, EU External Affairs Sub-committee 2019-20, European Union 2019-, EU International Agreements Sub-committee 2020-. *Other:* Election agent to: Ed Davey 1997, Jenny Tonge 2001; Campaign manager to Jeremy Browne 2005. Kingston upon Thames Council: Councillor 1994-98, Deputy Leader 1997-98.

Political interests: International development, mental health, youth justice; Ethiopia, South Africa, Zimbabwe.

Other: Non-executive director, NHS Blood and Transplant 2017-; Member, governing council, Association of European Parliamentarians with Africa; External adviser, International Planned Parenthood Federation. National Liberal Club.

Publications: Author, I Never Promised You A Rose Garden (2020).

Recreations: Poetry, football (Tottenham Hotspur FC), running.

The Lord Oates, House of Lords, London SW1A 0PW
Tel: 020 7219 3000

CONSERVATIVE

O'CATHAIN, BARONESS

O'CATHAIN (Life Baroness), Detta O'Cathain; cr. 1991. Born 3 February 1938; Daughter of late Caoimhghin and Margaret O'Cathain; Married William Bishop 1968 (died 2001).

Education: Laurel Hill, Limerick; University College, Dublin (BA economics, English and French 1961); French.

Non-political career: Assistant economist, Aer Lingus 1959-66; Group economist, Tarmac 1966-69; Economic adviser to Chair, Rootes Motors/Chrysler 1969-72; Senior economist, Carrington Viyella 1972; British Leyland: Economic adviser 1973-74, Director, Market Planning 1974-76; Corporate planning executive, Unigate plc 1976-81; Milk Marketing Board 1981-88: Managing director 1985-88; Managing director, Barbican Centre 1990-95; Numerous non-executive directorships.

Political career: *House of Lords:* Raised to the peerage as Baroness O'Cathain, of The Barbican in the City of London 1991. Member: Monetary Policy of the Bank of England/Economic Affairs 1998-2005, European Communities Sub-committee B (Energy, Industry and Transport) 1998-2002, European Union 1999-2001, 2010-15, Joint Committee on House of Lords Reform 2002-05, Constitution 2005-08; Co-opted Member, EU Sub-committee E (Law and Institutions) 2007-10; Chair EU Sub-committee B: (Internal Market, Energy and Transport) 2010-12, (Internal Market, Infrastructure and Employment) 2012-15; Member: Leader's Group on the Working Practices of the House of Lords 2010-11, Consumer Insurance (Disclosure and Representations) Bill 2011-12, Digital Skills 2014-15; Chair, Built Environment 2015-16; Member: High Speed Rail (London-West Midlands) Bill 2016, Joint Committee on Human Rights 2017-18, Rural Economy 2018. *Other:* Chair, Conservative Friends of Azerbaijan. Past President, Agricultural Section British Association for the Advancement of Science; Member: Design Council 1978-80, Engineering Council 1980-83; Council member, Industrial Society 1986-92; Patron, Women in Banking and Finance 2000-07.

Political interests: Arts, agriculture, industry, commerce, finance, retail industry, disabled, economic policy, family, energy; Azerbaijan, EU, Ireland, Israel, USA.

Other: Member, British-Irish Parliamentary Assembly 2017-20; Fellow: Royal Society of Arts 1986, Chartered Institute of Marketing 1987; Chair, Chichester Cathedral Council 2010-; President, Chartered Institute of Marketing 1998-2001; Freedom, City of London; Fellow, Harris Manchester College, Oxford; Honorary Fellow, Harris Manchester College, Oxford 2009; OBE 1983; Commander: Royal Norwegian Order 1993, Order of the Lion of Finland 1994, Order of Friends of Azerbaijan 2011. Athenæum Club.

Recreations: Music, reading, swimming, walking, gardening.

The Baroness O'Cathain OBE, House of Lords, London SW1A 0PW
Tel: 020 7219 0662 *Email:* ocathaind@parliament.uk

O'DONNELL, LORD

CROSSBENCH

O'DONNELL (Life Baron), Augustine (Gus) Thomas O'Donnell; cr 2012. Born 1 October 1952; Son of late James O'Donnell and late Helen McLean; Married Melanie Timmis 1979 (1 daughter).

Education: Salesian College, Battersea; Warwick University (BA economics 1973); Nuffield College, Oxford (MPhil economics 1975).

Non-political career: Lecturer in Political Economy, Glasgow University 1975-79; HM Treasury 1979-2005: Economist 1979-85, First Secretary (Economic), Washington DC embassy 1985-88, Senior Economic Adviser 1988-89, Press Secretary to John Major: as Chancellor of Exchequer 1989-90, as Prime Minister 1990-94, Under Secretary, Monetary Group 1994-95, Deputy Director, Macroeconomic Policy and Prospects Directorate 1995-96, UK's Executive Director to IMF and World Bank 1997-98, Economic Minister, Washington DC embassy 1997-98, Director, Macroeconomic Policy and Prospects 1998-99, Head of Government Economic Service 1998-2003, Managing Director, Macroeconomic Policy and International Finance Directorate 1999-2002, Permanent Secretary and Chair HMT Management Board 2002-05; Secretary of the Cabinet and Head of the Home Civil Service, Cabinet Office 2005-11, Secretary of the Cabinet and Head of the Civil Service 2011; Chair, Main Honours Advisory Committee -2012; Senior fellow, Civil Service College, Singapore; Chair, Commission on Wellbeing Policy, Legatum Institute 2012; Strategic Adviser to the chief executive, Toronto Dominion Bank 2012-; Chair, Frontier Economics 2013-; Non-executive Director and Strategic Adviser, Brookfield Asset Management 2013-; Chair, Public Interest Board, PwC 2016-; President of the Council, Institute for Fiscal Studies 2016-; Chair of Trustees, Pro Bono Economics 2016-.

Political career: *House of Lords:* Raised to the peerage as Baron O'Donnell, of Clapham in the London Borough of Wandsworth 2012.

Political interests: Public sector, especially the civil service, economic and financial issues, wellbeing, behavioural science; Australia, Brazil, Canada, New Zealand, USA.

Other: Trustee, *The Tablet*; Member: Economist Trust, Tech UK Brexit Advisory Panel; Society of Business Economists; Pro Bono Economics, Anchor House, Paul's Charity, Shine; Freedom, City of London; Fellow, Institute for Government 2012; Hon. Fellow, British Academy 2014; Honorary degrees from Glasgow and Warwick universities; Honorary fellow, Nuffield College, Oxford; CB 1994; KCB 2005; GCB 2011. Committee member, All England Lawn Tennis and Croquet Club.

Publications: Numerous articles on policy.

Recreations: Tennis, opera, golf.

The Lord O'Donnell GCB, House of Lords, London SW1A 0PW
Tel: 020 7219 5353 *Email:* odonnellg@parliament.uk
Frontier Economics, 71 High Holborn, London WC1V 6DA *Tel:* 020 7031 7000
Website: www.frontier-economics.com *Twitter:* @Gus_ODonnell

CROSSBENCH

O'LOAN, BARONESS

O'LOAN (Life Baroness), Nuala Patricia O'Loan; cr 2009. Born 20 December 1951; Daughter of Gerard Herbert and Sara Herbert; Née St Clair-Herbert; Married Declan O'Loan (MLA 2007-11) 1975 (5 sons).

Education: Holy Child School, Harrogate; King's College, London (LLB 1973); College of Law, London (Law 1976).

Non-political career: Articled clerk, Stephenson Harwood solicitors, London 1974-76; Law lecturer, Ulster Polytechnic 1976-80; Raised family in Kenya where her husband was teaching 1980-83: Teacher, St Patrick's School, Iten, Kenya 1982-83; Ulster University 1984-2000: Law lecturer, then senior lecturer 1984-92, Jean Monnet chair, European law 1992-2000; External examiner, Aberystwyth University, Trinity College Dublin and IPSERA 1996-2000; Visiting professor, School of Law, Ulster University; Member, Independent Group for Dialogue and Peace, Basque Country 2007-10; Ireland's roving ambassador for conflict resolution and special envoy to Timor Leste 2008-11; UN special envoy, women and peace-keeping 2009-11; Roving ambassador and special envoy of Ireland, women, peace and security 2009-11; Member, International Contact Group, Basque Country 2011-.

Political career: *House of Lords:* Raised to the peerage as Baroness O'Loan, of Kirkinriola in the County of Antrim 2009. Member: Delegated Powers and Regulatory Reform 2010-15, EU Sub-committee E: (Justice and Institutions) 2011-12, (Justice, Institutions and Consumer Protection) 2012-15, Joint Committee on Human Rights 2012-15, Secondary Legislation Scrutiny 2015-19, SLSC Sub-committee B 2018-19. *Other:* Member: General Consumer Council, Northern Ireland 1991-96, UK Domestic Coal Consumers Council 1992-95, Ministerial Working Group on Green Economy 1993-95, Northern Health and Social Services Board 1993-97, Northern Ireland Police Authority 1997-2000; Chair, Northern Ireland Consumer Committee for Electricity 1997-2000; Strategy group 2010, Department for Economic Development 1998-99; Police Ombudsman for Northern Ireland 1999-2007; Special Commissioner, Commission for Racial Equality 2004-05; Chair, human rights inquiry, Equality and Human Rights Commission 2008-09; Independent Review for Home Office 2009-10; Chair: Governing Authority Maynooth University 2010, Daniel Morgan Independent Panel 2014; Member, BMA Ethics Committee 2014.

Political interests: Justice, security, human rights, life issues; Africa, South East Asia, Spain.

Other: Member, Consumers Consultative Council, European Commission 1994-95; Associate member, British-Irish Parliamentary Assembly; Member, Commonwealth Parliamentary Association; NetPLUSS, Club of Madrid; Member: Society of Public Teachers of Law 1992-2000, Irish Association of Law Teachers 1992-2000, International Purchasing and Supply Educational Research Association 1992-2000; Patron: Living and Dying Well, Drumalis Retreat Centre, British Irish Association; Member, Royal Irish Academy 2013-; Chair, Catholic Council for Independent Inquiry into Child Sexual Abuse; Former Member: Law Society of England and Wales, Solicitor of Supreme Court England and Wales, Association of Women Solicitors; Trustee, CONCERN Worldwide 2008-12; Hon. Doctor of Laws: Ulster University 2008, National University of Ireland, Maynooth 2008, Higher Education and Technical Awards Council, Ireland, Queen's University, Belfast 2010, Open University; Outstanding Achievement Award, American Association for the Civilian Oversight of Law Enforcement 2007; Northern Ireland Woman of the Year, Irish Tatler Awards 2007; Person of the Year, RTE Awards 2008; DBE 2008. Royal Irish Academy; Royal Dublin Society.

Publications: Many (100+) in reviewed journals, books and papers; Review editor and member of editorial board, Public Procurement Law Review (Sweet and Maxwell) 1991-96.

Recreations: Reading.

The Baroness O'Loan DBE, House of Lords, London SW1A 0PW
Tel: 020 7219 8724 *Email:* oloann@parliament.uk
Email: nualaoloan@googlemail.com

CROSSBENCH

O'NEILL OF BENGARVE, BARONESS

O'NEILL OF BENGARVE (Life Baroness), Onora Sylvia O'Neill; cr. 1999. Born 23 August 1941; Daughter of late Hon. Sir Con O'Neill, GCMG and late Lady Garvey, née Pritchard; Married Edward Nell 1963 (divorced 1976) (2 sons).

Education: St Paul's Girls' School, London; Somerville College, Oxford (BA philosophy, psychology and physiology 1962, MA); Harvard University (PhD philosophy 1969); French, German.

Non-political career: Philosophy assistant, then associate professor, Barnard College, Columbia University 1970-77; Essex University: Philosophy lecturer 1977-78, Senior lecturer 1978-83, Reader 1983-87, Professor of philosophy 1987-92; Principal, Newnham College, Cambridge 1992-2006.

Political career: *House of Lords:* Raised to the peerage as Baroness O'Neill of Bengarve, of The Braid in the County of Antrim 1999. Member: Stem Cell Research 2002, BBC Charter Review 2005-06; Co-opted member: Science and Technology Sub-committee II (Genomic Medicine) 2008-09, Science and Technology Sub-committee I (Nanotechnologies and Food) 2009-10; Science and Technology Sub-committee I (Behavioural Change) 2010-11; Member: Sub-committee on Lords' Interests 2009-10, Sub-committee on Lords' Conduct 2010-18, Political Polling and Digital Media 2017-18. *Other:* Chair, Equalities and Human Rights Commission 2012-16.

Political interests: Constitutional reform, education especially higher education, medical ethics, languages, communication, copyright and publishing; Germany, Northern Ireland, Republic of Ireland.

Other: President, Aristotelian Society 1988-89; Fellow, Wissenschaftskolleg, Berlin 1989-90; Member, Animal Procedures Committee 1990-94; Nuffield Council on Bioethics: Member 1991-98, Chair 1996-98; Foreign Hon member, American Academy of Arts and Sciences 1993-; Human Genetics Advisory Commission: Member 1996-99, Chair 1998-99; Chair, Nuffield Foundation 1998-2010; Ditchley Foundation: Governor 2001-11, Council member 2003-11; Foreign Hon member, Austrian Academy of Sciences 2002-; Foreign member, American Philosophical Society 2003-; Hon member, Royal Irish Academy 2003-; President, Mind Association 2003-04; Trustee, Sense about Science 2004-14; Foreign member, Leopoldina 2004-; President, British Academy 2005-09; Trustee, American University of Sharjah 2005-15; Foundation for Science and Technology 2006-20; Foreign member, Norwegian Academy of Sciences 2006-; Board member, Medical Research Council 2012-18; Trustee and Council Member, Foundation for Science and Technology; American University of Sharjah; British Philosophical Association; FBA 1993, PBA 2005-09; F Med Sci 2002; Honorary FRS 2007; Over 20 honorary degrees; Kant Prize 2015; Holberg Prize 2017; Berggruen Prize 2017; CBE 1995; CH 2014. Athenæum Club.

Publications: Faces of Hunger (1986); Constructions of Reason (1989), Towards Justice and Virtue (1996); Bounds of Justice (2000); Autonomy and Trust in Bioethics (2002); A Question of Trust (2002); Acting on Principle (2nd edition 2013); Co-author, Rethinking Informed Consent in Bioethics; Constructing Authorities: Reason, Politics and Interpretation in Kant's Philosophy (2016); Justice Across Boundaries: Whose Obligations? (2016); From Principles to Practice: Normativity in Ethics and Politics (2018).

Recreations: Walking and talking.

The Baroness O'Neill of Bengarve CH CBE, House of Lords, London SW1A 0PW
Tel: 020 7219 4120

CROSSBENCH

O'NEILL OF GATLEY, LORD

O'NEILL OF GATLEY (Life Baron), Terence James (Jim) O'Neill; cr 2015. Born 17 March 1957.

Education: Sheffield University (BA economics 1978; MA); Surrey University (PhD 1982).

Non-political career: Economist: Bank of America 1982-83, Marine Midland Bank 1983-88; Swiss Bank Corporation 1988-95: Head of research 1991-95; Goldman Sachs 1995-2013: Head of Global Economics Research and chief currency economist 1995-2001, Chief economist 2001-10, Head of Global Economics, Commodities and Strategy Research 2008-10, Chair, Goldman Sachs Asset Management 2010-13.

Political career: *House of Lords:* Raised to the peerage as Baron O'Neill of Gatley, of Gatley in the County of Greater Manchester 2015. Commercial Secretary and Government Spokesperson, HM Treasury 2015-16. *Other:* Non-executive director, Department of Education -2015; Vice-president, Local Government Association 2017-.

Other: Honorary chair of economics, Manchester University; Visiting research fellow, Bruegel; Member, economic advisory board, IFC; Board member, Teach for All; Non-executive director, Manchester United FC; Chair, Cities Growth Commission 2013-14; Board member, Northern Powerhouse Partnership 2016-; Trustee, SHINE 2017-; Member, Steering Group: Royal Society 2017-, British Academy 2017-; Advisory board member, Project for Modern Democracy 2017-; Commissioner, Independent Commission on Social Housing, Shelter 2018-; Chair of Council, Chatham House 2018-; Distinguished Fellow, Chatham House 2018-; Honorary degrees: Institute of Education, University of London, City University, Sheffield University.

The Lord O'Neill of Gatley, House of Lords, London SW1A 0PW
Tel: 020 7219 3000

LABOUR

OSAMOR, BARONESS

OSAMOR (Life Baroness), Martha Otito Osamor; cr 2018. Born 24 September 1940; Widowed (4 children, including Kate Osamor (qv), MP for Edmonton).

Non-political career: Teacher; Community activist; Legal adviser, Tottenham Law Centre.

Political career: *House of Lords:* Raised to the peerage as Baroness Osamor, of Tottenham in the London Borough of Haringey and of Asaba in the Republic of Nigeria 2018. Member, Food, Poverty, Health and the Environment 2019-. *Other:* Former member, Socialist Workers' Party; Member, Labour Party 1979/1980-. Haringey Council: Councillor 1986-90, Former Deputy Council Leader.

Political interests: Community empowerment, access to justice.

Other: Founding member, United Black Women's Action Group; Trustee, African Women's Welfare Association.

The Baroness Osamor, House of Lords, London SW1A 0PW
Tel: 020 7219 3000 *Email:* osamorm@parliament.uk

CONSERVATIVE

O'SHAUGHNESSY, LORD

O'SHAUGHNESSY (Life Baron), James Richard O'Shaughnessy; cr 2015. Born 26 March 1976; Married Lucy Sheppard 2005 (1 son 2 daughters).

Education: Wellington College; St Hugh's College, Oxford (BA philosophy, politics and economics 1998).

Non-political career: Conservative Party: Special adviser, Education and Skills 2001-03, Director of policy and research 2007-10; Head of research, LLM Communications 2003-04; Deputy director, Policy Exchange 2004-07; Director of policy to David Cameron as Prime Minister 2010-11; Head of group strategy, Wellington College 2012-14; Visiting fellow, Policy Exchange 2012-; Chief policy adviser, Portland Communications 2012-15; Director, Mayforth Consulting 2012-17; Honorary senior research fellow, Birmingham University 2012-17;

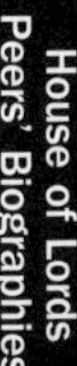

Managing director, Floreat Education 2013-16; Founder and non-executive director, Edspace 2014-; Senior fellow, Legatum Institute 2016-17.

Political career: *House of Lords:* Raised to the peerage as Baron O'Shaughnessy, of Maidenhead in the Royal County of Berkshire 2015. Government Whip (Lord in Waiting) 2016-17; Parliamentary Under-Secretary of State for Health and Government Spokesperson, Department of Health/Department of Health and Social Care 2016-18. Member, Risk Assessment and Risk Planning 2020-. *Other:* Governor, Lena Gardens School 2013-; Chair of governors: Floreat Wandsworth Primary School -2016, Floreat Brentford Primary School -2017; Member, Department for Education Counter-Extremism Reference Group -2017.

Other: Visiting Professor, Imperial College London 2019-; Director, Mayforth Consulting 2019-; Advisory member and patron, Tessa Jowell Brain Cancer Mission 2019-; Member: Project Steering Committee, Price Waterhouse Coopers 2019-, Advisory Council, Portland Communications 2019-; Advisory Board, Onward Thinktank 2019-; Member, advisory council, Centre for Science and Policy, Cambridge University 2019-; Non-executive director: Albion Development VCT 2019-, Board, Health Data Research UK 2019-; External Adviser, Bain & Co 2020-.

The Lord O'Shaughnessy, House of Lords, London SW1A 0PW
Tel: 020 7219 3000 *Email:* oshaughnessyj@parliament.uk *Twitter:* @jamesosh

INDEPENDENT SOCIAL DEMOCRAT

OWEN, LORD

OWEN (Life Baron), David Anthony Llewellyn Owen; cr. 1992. Born 2 July 1938; Son of late Dr John Owen, general practitioner, and Molly Owen, alderman; Married Deborah Schabert 1968 (2 sons 1 daughter).

Education: Bradfield College; Sidney Sussex College, Cambridge (BA natural sciences 1959; MB BChir 1962); St Thomas's Hospital, London 1956-61.

Non-political career: Various house appointments, St Thomas's Hospital 1962-64; Neurological and psychiatric registrar 1964-66; Research Fellow, Medical Unit 1966-68; Director, Deborah Owen Ltd 1972-2015; Non-executive director: New Crane Publishing 1992-2005, Coats Viyella 1994-2001; Executive chair, Global Natural Energy plc 1995-2006; Director, Abbott Laboratories plc 1995-2011; Chair, NEU Ltd 1999-2005; Non-executive chair, Europe-Steel Company 2000-15; Chair, Yukos International UK BV 2002-05; Member, Supervisory Council of Mazeikiu Nafta Oil Refinery, Lithuania 2002-05; Director: Intelligent Energy 2003-05, Hyperdynamics Corporation 2009-14.

Political career: *House of Commons:* Contested Torrington 1964 general election. MP for Plymouth Sutton 1966-74, for Plymouth Devonport 1974-92 (Labour 1966-81, SDP 1981-92); PPS to Gerry Reynolds as Minister of Defence 1966-68; Parliamentary Under-Secretary of State for Defence (Royal Navy) 1968-70; Opposition Spokesperson for Defence 1970-72; Parliamentary Under-Secretary of State, Department of Health and Social Security 1974, Minister of State 1974-76; Minister of State, Foreign Office 1976-77; Secretary of State for Foreign and Commonwealth Affairs 1977-79; Principal Opposition Spokesperson for Energy 1979-80. *House of Lords:* Raised to the peerage as Baron Owen, of the City of Plymouth 1992. *Other:* Social Democratic Party: Co-founder March 1981, Chairman, Parliamentary Committee 1981-82, Deputy Leader of the Party 1982-83, Leader 1983-87, Resigned over merger with Liberal Party 1987; Re-elected SDP Leader 1988-90.

Political interests: International affairs (foreign and defence).

Other: Member: Palme Commission on Disarmament and Security Issues 1980-89, Independent Commission on International Humanitarian Issues 1983-88; EU Co-chair, International Conference on former Yugoslavia 1992-95; Carnegie Commission on Preventing Deadly Conflict 1994-99; Director, Center for International Humanitarian Co-operation 1996-; Eminent Persons Group on curbing illicit traffic in small arms and light weapons 1999-2001; Vice-President, Commonwealth Parliamentary Association (UK Branch); Patron: Social Market Foundation 1989-, James Callaghan Centre for Conflict Studies, University of Wales 2002-, Greenham Common Community Trust 2004-16; President, River Thames Society 2009-; Chairman of Trustees, Daedalus Trust 2010-17; Member, Campaign Committee, Vote Leave 2016; Founding Supporter, Change Britain 2016-; Fellow, Royal College of Physicians 2005; Freedom, City of Plymouth 2000; Chancellor, Liverpool University 1996-2009; Three honorary degrees; PC 1976; CH 1994.

Publications: A Unified Health Service (1968); The Politics of Defence (1972); In Sickness and in Health (1976); Human Rights (1978); Face the Future (1981); A Future that will Work (1984); A United Kingdom (1986); Personally Speaking (to Kenneth Harris) (1987); Our NHS (1988); Time to Declare (autobiography 1991); Seven Ages (poetry anthology 1992); Balkan Odyssey (1995); The Hubris Syndrome (2007); In Sickness and in Power: Illness in Heads of Government during the last 100 years (2008, revised editions 2011, 2016); Time to Declare: Second Innings (updated and abridged autobiography, 2009); Nuclear Papers (2009); Europe Restructured (2012, revised edition 2016); Bosnia and Herzegovina: The Vance Owen Peace Plan (2013); The Hidden Perspective: The Military Conversations of 1906-1914 (Haus, 2014); The Health of the Nation: NHS in Peril (Meuthen, 2014); Cabinet's Finest Hour: The Hidden Agenda of May 1940 (2016); British Foreign Policy After Brexit (2017); Hubris: The Road to Donald Trump. Power, populism, narcissism (Methuen, 2018).

Recreations: Sailing.

Rt Hon the Lord Owen CH, House of Lords, London SW1A 0PW
Tel: 01442 872617 *Email:* davidowen@lorddavidowen.co.uk
Website: www.lorddavidowen.co.uk

CROSSBENCH

OXBURGH, LORD

OXBURGH (Life Baron), Ernest Ronald Oxburgh; cr. 1999. Born 2 November 1934; Son of Ernest Oxburgh and Violet, née Bugden; Married Ursula Mary Brown 1958 (1 son 2 daughters).

Education: Liverpool Institute; Oxford University (BA natural sciences (geology) 1957, MA); Princeton University, USA (PhD geology 1960).

Non-political career: Oxford University: Departmental demonstrator 1960-61, Lecturer in geology 1961-78, Fellow, St Edmund Hall 1964-78, Emeritus Fellow 1978; California Institute of Technology: Visiting Professor 1967-68, Fairchild Fellow 1995-96; Visiting Professor, Stanford and Cornell Universities 1973-74; Cambridge University: Professor of mineralogy and petrology 1978-91, Head of Department of Earth Sciences 1980-88, Fellow of Trinity Hall 1978-82, President, Queens' College 1982-89, Professorial Fellow 1989-91; Chief scientific adviser, Ministry of Defence 1988-93; Rector, Imperial College of Science, Technology and Medicine, London 1993-2001; Chair: SETNET 2002-05, Shell Transport and Trading plc 2004-05, D1 Oils plc 2007-08, 20C 2007-17, Falck Renewables 2007-10; Adviser: Climate Change Capital 2005-10, Deutsche Bank 2008-12, McKinsey 2010-13; Non-executve director, Green Energy Options 2011-; Carbon-12 2017-.

Political career: *House of Lords:* Raised to the peerage as Baron Oxburgh, of Liverpool in the County of Merseyside 1999. Board member, Parliamentary Office of Science and Technology (POST) 2000-. Science and Technology: Member 1999-2005, 2016-19, Chair 2001-05, Co-opted Member 2009-12; Member: Science and Technology Sub-committees: II (Science and Society) 1999-2000, II (Aircraft Cabin Environment) 2000-01; Chair, Science and Technology Sub-committee IIA (Human Genetic Databases) 2000-01; Member, Science and Technology Sub-committees: I (Fighting Infection) 2002-03, II (Innovations in Computer Processors/Microprocessing/Science and the Regional Development Agencies) 2002-03, I (Science and International Agreements) 2003-04; Chair, Science and Technology Sub-committee II (Renewable Energy) 2003-04; Member: Science and Technology Sub-committees: I (Scientific Aspects of Ageing) 2004-05, II (Energy Efficiency) 2004-05, Opposed Private Bills Committee (Broads) 2009; Co-opted Member, Science and Technology Sub-committee I (Radioactive Waste Management: a further update) 2010; Member: The Arctic 2014-15, Information 2015-16. *Other:* Member, National Committee of Inquiry into Higher Education (Dearing Committee) 1996-97; Council member, Foundation for Science and Technology; Chair, Scientific Programme Review Committee British Antarctic Survey.

Political interests: Higher education, health, energy, research and development, climate change; China, Singapore, USA.

Other: Member: ASTAR Singapore, SERC Singapore; President, European Union of Geosciences 1985-87; Member, geological and scientific academies and societies in USA, Germany, Austria, Australia and Venezuela; Natural History Museum: Trustee 1995-2002, Chairman 1999-2002; Vice-President, Globe UK; Council member, Winston Churchill Memorial Trust 1995-2008; President, Geological Society 1999-2001; Chair, Friends of Natural History Museum 2004-07; President, Carbon Capture and Storage Association 2006-16; Geological Society of London; Geological Society of America; Geologists' Association;

American Geophysical Union; FRS 1978, Hon. FIMechE 1993, Hon. FCGI 1996, Hon. FREng 2000, Foreign Associate, US Academy of Sciences 2001, American Philosophical Society 2005; Hon. Fellow: Trinity Hall, Cambridge 1982, University College, Oxford 1983, St Edmund Hall, Oxford 1986; Queens' College, Cambridge 1992; Ten honorary doctorates; Bigsby Medal, Geological Society 1979; KBE 1992; Officier, Ordre des Palmes Académiques (France) 1995; Public Service Medal (Singapore) 2009; Honorary Citizen (Singapore) 2012. Athenæum Club; Climbers, West Anglia Orienteering.

Publications: Contributor to geological, defence and scientific journals.

Recreations: Mountaineering, theatre, orienteering.

The Lord Oxburgh KBE, House of Lords, London SW1A 0PW
Tel: 020 7219 4341 *Fax:* 020 7219 5979 *Email:* oxburghe@parliament.uk

NON-AFFILIATED

OXFORD, LORD BISHOP OF

OXFORD (43rd Bishop of), Steven John Lindsey Croft. Born 29 May 1957; Son of James and Marian Croft; Married Ann Baker 1978 (2 sons 2 daughters).

Education: Heath School, Halifax; Worcester College, Oxford (BA 1980, MA); St John's College, Durham (PhD 1984).

Non-political career: Ordained deacon 1983; Priest 1984; Curate, St Andrew's, Enfield 1983-87; Vicar, St George's, Ovenden 1987-96; Mission consultant, Diocese of Wakefield 1993-96; Priest-in-charge, St Augustine, Halifax 1994-96; Warden, Cranmer Hall, St John's College, Durham 1996-2004; Archbishop's Missioner and Team Leader, Fresh Expressions 2004-09; Bishop of: Sheffield 2009-16, Oxford 2016-.

Political career: *House of Lords:* First entered House of Lords as Bishop of Sheffield 2013-16; Entered House of Lords as Bishop of Oxford 2016. Member, Artificial Intelligence 2017-18. *Other:* Board Member, Centre for Data Ethics and Innovation 2018–.

Other: Member, Archbishop's Council 2010-17; Hon. Fellow, Worcester College, Oxford 2018.

Publications: The Identity of the Individual in the Psalms (1987); Growing New Christians (1993); Making New Disciples (1994); Co-author, Emmaus, The Way of Faith volumes one to six (1996), volumes seven to eight (1998); Man to Man: friendship and faith (1999); Co-author, Travelling Well (2000); The Lord is Risen (2001); Missionary Journeys, Missionary Church (2001); Transforming Communities: re-imagining the Church for the 21st-century (2002); Co-author, Learning for Ministry: making the most of study and training (2005); Moving On in a Mission-Shaped Church (2005); The Advent Calendar (2006); Editor: The Future of the Parish System (2006), Mission-shaped Questions (2008); Jesus' People: what the church should do next (2009); Editor, Fresh Expressions in the Sacramental Tradition (2010); Exploring God's Mercy (2011); Exploring God's Love (2011); Pilgrim (2014); The Gift of Leadership, According to the Scriptures (2016).

Recreations: Walking, cooking, films.

Rt Rev the Lord Bishop of Oxford, House of Lords, London SW1A 0PW
Tel: 020 7219 3000
Church House Oxford, Langford Locks, Kidlington, Oxford OX5 1GF *Tel:* 01865 208222
Email: bishopoxon@oxford.anglican.org Websites: www.oxford.anglican.org
blogs.oxford.anglican.org *Twitter:* @Steven_Croft

OXFORD AND ASQUITH, EARL OF

NON-AFFILIATED

OXFORD AND ASQUITH (3rd Earl of, UK), Raymond Benedict Bartholomew Michael Asquith; cr. 1925; Viscount Asquith. Born 24 August 1952; Son of 2nd Earl, KCMG; Married Clare 1978 (1 son 4 daughters).

Education: Ampleforth College; Balliol College, Oxford (MA); Russian, Ukrainian, French.

Non-political career: HM Diplomatic Service 1980-97: Moscow 1983-85, Cabinet Office 1985-92, British Embassy, Kiev 1992-97; Chair, Zander Corporation 2006-.

Political career: *House of Lords:* Elected hereditary peer 2014-. Member, EU External Affairs Sub-Committee 2015-19. *Other:* Left Liberal Democrats September 2019, now sits as non-affiliated.

Political interests: Energy, environment, foreign affairs; Eastern Europe, Iran, Middle East, Russia, Ukraine.

Other: Non-executive director: JKX Oil and Gas, Zander Corporation, Meteor; Director: Hansa Trust, British Ukrainian Society; Trustee, Ukrainian Catholic Foundation; OBE 1992.

The Earl of Oxford and Asquith OBE, House of Lords, London SW1A 0PW
Tel: 020 7219 5353 *Email:* oxfordr@parliament.uk
Email: dessna.company@tuta.io

PADDICK, LORD

LIBERAL DEMOCRAT

Liberal Democrat Lords Spokesperson for Home Affairs

PADDICK (Life Baron), Brian Leonard Paddick; cr 2013. Born 24 April 1958; Married Mary 1983 (divorced); married Petter Belsvik 2009.

Education: Bec Grammar School, Tooting Bec, London; Sutton Manor High School, London; Queen's College, Oxford (BA philosophy, politics and economics 1986); Warwick Business School (MBA 1990); Fitzwilliam College, Cambridge (Diploma applied criminology and policing).

Non-political career: Metropolitan Police 1976-2007: Constable 1977-80, Sergeant 1980-83, Inspector 1983-89, Chief Inspector 1989-96, Superintendent 1996-97, Chief Superintendent 1997-2000, Commander 2001-03, Deputy Assistant Commissioner 2003-07; Senior consultant, Policing and Public Sector, Public Partners.

Political career: *House of Lords:* Raised to the peerage as Baron Paddick, of Brixton in the London Borough of Lambeth 2013. Liberal Democrat: Lords Spokesperson for Home Affairs 2015-19, 2020-, Shadow Home Secretary 2016-17. *Other:* Contested Liberal Democrat London mayoral candidacy 2008 and 2012.

Political interests: Crime, civil law, justice and rights, housing and planning, social security and pensions; Norway, South Africa, USA.

Publications: Line of Fire (Simon & Schuster UK, 2008).

The Lord Paddick, House of Lords, London SW1A 0PW
Tel: 020 7219 5353 *Email:* paddickb@parliament.uk Website: www.brianpaddick.com
Twitter: @brianpaddick

CROSSBENCH

PALMER, LORD

PALMER (4th Baron, UK), Adrian Bailie Nottage Palmer; cr. 1933; 4th Bt of Grosvenor Crescent (UK) 1916. Born 8 October 1951; Son of Colonel Hon Sir Gordon Palmer, KCVO and Hon Lady Palmer, DL; Married Cornelia Wadham 1977 (divorced 2004) (2 sons 1 daughter); married Loraine McMurrey 2006 (divorced 2013).

Education: Eton College; Edinburgh University (Certificate farming practice 1979); French.

Non-political career: Apprentice, Huntley and Palmers Ltd 1970-73; Sales manager, southern Belgium and Luxembourg 1974-77; Scottish representative to European Landowning Organisation 1986-91; Farmer. Member, National Farmers Union of Scotland.

Political career: *House of Lords:* First entered House of Lords 1990; Elected hereditary peer 1999-. Member: Advisory Panel on Works of Art 1995-98, 2000-02, 2005-09, Refreshment 1997-2000, 2003-05, Standing Orders (Private Bills) 2005-17; Co-opted Member, EU Sub-committee D (Environment and Agriculture) 2000-03, 2007-10; Procedure: Member 2007, Alternate Member 2007-10. *Other:* Member: Executive Council, Historic Houses Association 1981-99, Council, Scottish Landowners' Federation 1986-92; Secretary, Royal Caledonian Hunt 1989-2005; President, Palm Tree Silk Co (St Lucia) 1992-; Historic Houses Association for Scotland: Vice-chair 1993-94, Chair 1994-99; President: British Association of Biofuels and Oils 1999-, Renewable Energy Authority (transport division) 2006-.

Political interests: Agriculture, environment, heritage, media, tourism; St Lucia, Scotland, Zimbabwe.

Other: Member, Queen's Bodyguard for Scotland (Royal Company of Archers) 1990-96; Chair, Country Sports Defence Trust 1994-; Secretary, Scottish Peers Association 2007-. New (Edinburgh), Pratt's, Chair, Lords and Commons Cigar Club; Patron, Manderston Cricket Club 1978-.

Recreations: Gardening.

The Lord Palmer, House of Lords, London SW1A 0PW
Tel: 020 7219 6452 *Fax:* 020 7219 5979 *Email:* palmerad@parliament.uk
Manderston, Duns TD11 3PP *Tel:* 01361 883450/01361 882636
Email: palmer@manderston.co.uk

LIBERAL DEMOCRAT

PALMER OF CHILDS HILL, LORD

PALMER OF CHILDS HILL (Life Baron), Monroe Edward Palmer; cr 2011. Born 30 November 1938; Son of William and Sybil Polikoff; Married Susette Cardash 1962 (2 sons 1 daughter).

Education: Orange Hill Grammar School; Open University (BA 2005).

Non-political career: Chartered accountant 1963; Treasurer, Disablement Association, London Borough of Barnet 1971-88; Chair, Hendon Citizens Advice Bureau 1981-83; Barnet Citizens Advice Bureau: Vice-chair 1986-88, Chair 1988-90; Director, Barnet Homes 1994-2010.

Political career: *House of Commons:* Contested (Liberal) Hendon South 1979, (Liberal/All) 1983 and 1987 and (Liberal Democrat) Hastings and Rye 1992 and 1997 general elections. *House of Lords:* Raised to the peerage as Baron Palmer of Childs Hill, of Childs Hill in the London Borough of Barnet 2011. Liberal Democrat Spokesperson for: Defence 2011-15, Business, Innovation and Skills 2015-16; Party Lead Spokesperson on Small and Medium-sized Enterprises; Deputy Chairman of Committees 2017-; Deputy Speaker 2018-. Member: Refreshment 2012-15, Personal Service Companies 2013-14. Chair, Liberal Democrat Parliamentary Party Committee on International Affairs (Defence) 2012-15. *Other:* Joint Treasurer, Liberal Parliamentary Party 1977-83; Liberal Democrat Friends of Israel: Chair 1987-2010, Vice-President 2010-16, President 2016-; Treasurer, London Region, Liberal Democrats 2008-09. London Borough of Barnet Council: Councillor 1986-94, 1998-2014, Chair, Audit Committee 2010-14.

Political interests: Business (including small businesses), taxation, local government, foreign affairs; Israel, Middle East, Palestine.

Other: Fellow, Institute of Chartered Accountants; OBE 1982. National Liberal Club.

Recreations: Horse riding, reading, music.

The Lord Palmer of Childs Hill OBE, House of Lords, London SW1A 0PW
Tel: 020 7219 2561 *Email:* palmerm@parliament.uk
Tel: 020 8455 5140 *Twitter:* @palmermonroe

LIBERAL DEMOCRAT

PALUMBO OF SOUTHWARK, LORD

PALUMBO OF SOUTHWARK (Life Baron), James Rudolph Palumbo; cr 2013. Born 6 June 1963; Son of Peter Garth Palumbo (now Lord Palumbo) and Denia Wigram; 1 son.

Education: Eton College; Worcester College, Oxford.

Non-political career: Property developer; Merchant banker: Merrill Lynch, Morgan Grenfell; Founder and chair, Ministry of Sound Group.

Political career: *House of Lords:* Raised to the peerage as Baron Palumbo of Southwark, of Southwark in the London Borough of Southwark 2013.

Publications: Tomas (2009); Tancredi (2011).

The Lord Palumbo of Southwark, House of Lords, London SW1A 0PW
Tel: 020 7219 5353

CROSSBENCH

PANNICK, LORD

PANNICK (Life Baron), David Philip Pannick; cr 2008. Born 7 March 1956; Son of late Maurice Pannick and late Rita Pannick; Married Denise Sloam 1978 (died 1999) (2 sons 1 daughter); married Nathalie Trager-Lewis 2003 (1 son 2 daughters).

Education: Bancroft's School, Essex; Hertford College, Oxford (MA 1977; BCL 1978); Gray's Inn, London.

Non-political career: Called to the Bar 1979; Barrister, Blackstone Chambers, Temple 1980-; Junior counsel to Crown (Common Law) 1988-92; QC 1992; Bencher, Gray's Inn 1998; Deputy High Court Judge 1998-2005.

Political career: *House of Lords:* Raised to the peerage as Baron Pannick, of Radlett in the County of Hertfordshire 2008. Member, Constitution 2008-13, 2016-.

Political interests: Legal matters; Israel, USA.

Other: Chair, British Legal Friends of the Hebrew University 2009-; Fellow, All Souls College, Oxford 1978-; Hon. fellow: Hertford College, Oxford, Hebrew University of Jerusalem; Hon. doctorate, Hertfordshire University.

Recreations: Cinema, theatre, Arsenal FC.

The Lord Pannick QC, House of Lords, London SW1A 0PW
Tel: 020 7219 5353
Blackstone Chambers, Temple, London EC4Y 9BW *Tel:* 020 7583 1770
Email: davidpannick@blackstonechambers.com

LABOUR

PAREKH, LORD

PAREKH (Life Baron), Bhikhu Chhotalal Parekh; cr. 2000. Born 4 January 1935; Son of Chhotalal and Gajaraben Parekh; Married Pramila Dalal 1959 (3 sons).

Education: HDS High School, Amalsad, India; Bombay University (BA economics 1954; MA political science 1956); London University (PhD the idea of equality in English political thought 1966); Gujarati, Hindi.

Non-political career: London School of Economics: Politics tutor 1962-63, Centennial Professor 2001-03; Assistant lecturer in politics, Glasgow University 1963-64; Hull University: Politics lecturer, senior lecturer and reader 1964-82, Professor of political theory 1982-2001, Emeritus Professor 2000-; Visiting Professor: University of British Columbia, Canada 1967-68, Concordia University 1974-75, McGill University 1976-77, Harvard University 1996, Institute for Advanced Study, Vienna 1997, University of Pompeu Fabra, Barcelona 1997, University of

Pennsylvania 1998, École des Hautes Études en Sciences Sociales 2000; Westminster University: Professor of political philosophy 2001-09, Emeritus Professor of Political Philosophy 2009-.

Political career: *House of Lords:* Raised to the peerage as Baron Parekh, of Kingston upon Hull in the East Riding of Yorkshire 2000. Member, Human Rights Joint Committee 2001-03. *Other:* Member, Rampton/Swann Committee of Inquiry into Educational Problems of Ethnic Minority Children 1978-82; Deputy chair, Commission for Racial Equality 1985-90; Vice-President, UK Council for Overseas Students Affairs 1989-99; Chair, Commission on Future of Multi-Ethnic Britain 1998-2001; President, British Association of South Asia Scholars 2004-07.

Political interests: Race relations, higher education, ethnic conflicts, global justice, international politics, multiculturalism; Canada, India, USA.

Other: Founding Member and Past President, Research Committee on Political Philosophy of International Political Science Association; Council Member, Policy Studies Institute 1985-90; Runnymede Trust: Trustee 1986-2003, Patron 2003; Gandhi Foundation: Trustee 1988, Patron 2002-, President 2012-; Council member, Institute for Public Policy Research 1990-96; Trustee: Anne Frank Educational Trust 1992-, Nirman Foundation 2000-; Fellow, Asiatic Society India 2003; Trustee: Rathbone Society 2003-, Black Umbrella 2005-; Patron: Institute of Advanced Study, Durham University 2008-10, Whistling Woods International, Mumbai 2008-; Cancer Research Society, Royal Society for the Blind, Barnardo's; Vice-chancellor, University of Baroda, India 1981-84; FRSA 1988; Fellow, British Academy 2003; President, Academy of Learned Societies for the Social Sciences 2004-08; Fellow, European Academy 2009; Sixteen honorary doctorates; Honorary Professor, University of Wales; Distinguished Professorial Fellow, Centre for the Study of Developing Societies, Delhi; Distinguished Visiting Professor, Cardozo Law School, New York; Distinguished Visiting Fellow, University of Maine, USA; British Asian of the Year 1991; Gujarati of the Year 1994; BBC's Special Lifetime Achievement Award for Asians 1999; Sir Isaiah Berlin Prize for Lifetime Contribution to Political Studies 2003; Pravasi Bharatiya Samman, by President of India 2005; Interdependence Prize, Campaign for Democracy, New York 2006; Pride of India 2006; Distinguished Global Thinker, India International Centre, Delhi 2006; Padma Bhushan, President of India 2007.

Publications: Politics and Experience (1968); Dissent and Disorder (1971); The Morality of Politics (1972); Knowledge and Belief in Politics (1973); Bentham's Political Thought (1973); Colour, Culture and Consciousness (1974); Jeremy Bentham: ten critical essays (1974); The Concept of Socialism (1975); Hannah Arendt and the Search for a new Political Philosophy (1981); Karl's Marx's Theory of Ideology (1982); Contemporary Political Thinkers (1982); Political Discourse (1986); Gandhi's Political Philosophy (1989); Colonialism, Tradition and Reform (1989); Jeremy Bentham: critical assessments (1993); The Decolonisation of Imagination (1995); Crisis and Change in Contemporary India (1995); Gandhi (1997); Race Relations in Britain (1998); Rethinking Multiculturalism (2000); The Future of Multi Ethnic Britain: The Parekh Report (2000); Culture and Economy in the Indian Diaspora (2003); A New Politics of Identity (2008); Conversations with Bhikhu Parekh (2012); Numerous articles in various learned journals.

Recreations: Reading, music, walking.

Professor the Lord Parekh, House of Lords, London SW1A 0PW
Tel: 020 7219 5353 *Fax:* 020 7219 5979
211 Victoria Avenue, Hull HU5 3EF *Tel:* 01482 345530 *Email:* profparekh@gmail.com

CROSSBENCH

PARKER OF MINSMERE, LORD

Lord Chamberlain

PARKER OF MINSMERE (Life Baron), Andrew David Parker; cr 2021. Born 1962; Married (2 children).

Education: Cambridge University (natural sciences).

Non-political career: Security Service (MI5) 1983-2020: Postings in the fields of international terrorism, counter-espionage, Northern Ireland terrorism, serious and organised crime, protective security and policy, Liaison posting with FBI and CIA, USA 1991, On secondment as Director Intelligence, HM Customs & Excise 1999-2002, Director for Northern Ireland terrorism, Protective Security and Serious Crime 2002-05, Director, International Terrorism 2005-07,

Deputy Director General 2007-13, Director-General 2013-20; Lord Chamberlain of the Queen's Household 2021-.

Political career: *House of Lords:* Raised to the peerage as Baron Parker of Minsmere, of Minsmere in the County of Suffolk 2021.

Other: KCB 2019.

The Lord Parker of Minsmere KCB, House of Lords, London SW1A 0PW

Lord Chamberlain, Buckingham Palace, London SW1A 1AA

CONSERVATIVE

PARKINSON OF WHITLEY BAY, LORD

Government Whip, Lord in Waiting

PARKINSON OF WHITLEY BAY (Life Baron), Stephen Graeme Parkinson; cr 2019. Born 1983.

Education: Emmanuel College, Cambridge (history) (Union President).

Non-political career: Conservative Research Department 2004-06; Director of Research, Centre for Policy Studies 2006-07; Conservative Central Office 2007-10; Consultant, Quiller Consultants 2010-12; Special Adviser to Theresa May as Home Secretary 2012-15; National Organiser, Vote Leave campaign 2015-16; Political Secretary to Theresa May as Prime Minister 2016-19.

Political career: *House of Commons:* Contested Newcastle upon Tyne North 2010 general election. *House of Lords:* Raised to the peerage as Baron Parkinson of Whitley Bay, of Beyton in the County of Suffolk 2019. Government Whip, Lord in Waiting 2020-. Member, Social and Economic Impact of the Gambling Industry 2019-20.

Other: Member, advisory council, Centre for Policy Studies 2019-.

Publications: Arena of Ambition: A History of the Cambridge Union (Icon Books Ltd, 2009).

The Lord Parkinson of Whitley Bay, House of Lords, London SW1A 0PW

LIBERAL DEMOCRAT

PARMINTER, BARONESS

PARMINTER (Life Baroness), Kathryn Jane Parminter; cr 2010. Born 24 June 1964; Daughter of James and June Parminter; Married Neil Sherlock 1994 (2 daughters).

Education: Millais School, West Sussex; Collyers Sixth Form College, Horsham; Lady Margaret Hall, Oxford (BA theology 1986, MA).

Non-political career: Graduate trainee, Nestle 1986-88; Parliamentary researcher to Simon Hughes MP 1988-89; Account executive, Juliette Hellman Public Relations 1989-90; Royal Society for the Prevention of Cruelty to Animals: Public relations officer 1990-92, Head of campaigns and events 1992-95, Head of public affairs 1995-96, Head of press and public affairs 1996-98; Chief executive, Campaign to Protect Rural England 1998-2004; Freelance consultant advising corporations and charities on CSR and charitable issues 2004-10.

Political career: *House of Lords:* Raised to the peerage as Baroness Parminter, of Godalming in the County of Surrey 2010. Deputy Leader, Liberal Democrat Peers 2015-17; Shadow Secretary of State for Environment, Food and Rural Affairs 2015-17. Member, EU Sub-committee D: (Agriculture, Fisheries and Environment) 2010-12, (Agriculture, Fisheries, Environment and Energy) 2012-15; Member: European Union 2013-15, Built Environment 2015-16, Natural Environment and Rural Communities Act 2006 2017-18, Food, Poverty, Health and the Environment 2019-. Chair, Liberal Democrat Policy Committees on: Energy and Climate Change; Environment, Food and Rural Affairs (Environment, Food and Rural Affairs) 2012, Environment, Food and Rural Affairs 2012-15. *Other:* Liberal Democrat: Policy Review Group 2005-07, Reform Commission 2008, Federal Executive 2008-10; Trustee, Liberal Democrat Party 2011-. Councillor, Horsham District Council 1987-95; Member, House of Lords Appointments Commission 2020-.

Political interests: Environment, food policy, mental health.

Other: Chair, Campaign for Protection of Hunted Animals 1997-98; Trustee, Institute for Public Policy Research 2007-18; Advisory group, Every Child A Reader 2007-10; Vice-president, RSPCA 2011-15; Meath Trust; Honorary Fellow, CIWEM. National Liberal Club.

Recreations: Walking.

The Baroness Parminter, House of Lords, London SW1A 0PW
Tel: 020 7219 4195 *Email:* parminterk@parliament.uk *Twitter:* @kateparminter

CROSSBENCH

PATEL, LORD

Chair, Select Committee on Science and Technology

PATEL (Life Baron), Naren Babubhai Patel; cr. 1999. Born 11 May 1938; Son of Babubhai and Lalita Patel; Married Dr Helen Dally 1970 (twin sons 1 daughter).

Education: Government Secondary School, Dar Es Salaam, Tanzania; Harrow High School; St Andrews University (MB ChB 1964).

Non-political career: Consultant obstetrician, Ninewells Hospital, Dundee 1974-2003; Professor, Dundee University.

Political career: *House of Lords:* Raised to the peerage as Baron Patel, of Dunkeld in Perth and Kinross 1999. Board Member, Parliamentary Office of Science and Technology 2017-. Science and Technology: Member 1999-2003, 2005-09, 2010-15, Co-opted member 2015-16; Member: Science and Technology Sub-committees: II (Aircraft Cabin Environment) 2000-02, IIA (Human Genetic Databases) 2000-01, I (Fighting Infection) 2002-10, II (Innovations in Computer Processors/Microprocessing) 2002; Chair, Science and Technology Sub-committee II (Science and the Regional Development Agencies) 2003; Member, Science and Technology Sub-committee II: (Renewable Energy/Energy Efficiency) 2003-04, (Water Management) 2006, (Pandemic Influenza) 2006; Chair, Science and Technology Sub-committee II (Genomic Medicine) 2008-09; Member: Procedure 2012-15, Science and Technology Sub-committee I 2012-13, Affordable Childcare 2014-15, Social Mobility 2015-16; Chair: Long-Term Sustainability of the NHS 2016-17, Science and Technology 2017-. *Other:* President, Royal College of Obstetricians 1995-98; Chair, Academy of Medical Royal Colleges 1996-98; Council, General Medical Council 1998-2003; Chair: Specialist Training Authority of Medicine 1998-2001, NHS Quality Improvement, Scotland 1999-2006, Clinical Standards Board of Scotland 1999-2002; Member, Armed Forces Pay Review Body 2000-06; Chair: UK Stem Cell Oversight Committee 2005-10, National Patient Safety Agency 2006-10, Armed Forces Diversity and Equality Committee 2006-09, UK National Stem Cell Network 2007-09; Council member, Medical Research Council 2008-12.

Political interests: Women's health, higher education, regulation of medicine, ethnic minority issues, standards in medicine, care of obstetric fistulas worldwide, NHS, medical research; France, India, South Africa, Sweden, Tanzania, USA.

Other: European Board of Obstetrics and Gynaecology 2000-03; Vice-President, International Federation of Obstetrics and Gynaecology 2000-03; President, European Association of Obstetricians and Gynaecologists 2005-07; Fistula Fund, WellBeing, Safe Hands, South Asia Health Foundation; Chancellor, Dundee University 2006-17; FMedSci; FRCOG; FRSE; Numerous honorary degrees and fellowships from universities in the UK and worldwide; Kt 1997; KT 2010.

Publications: Several books, chapters, articles on maternal/foetal medicine, epidemiology, obstetrics, gynaecology, quality healthcare.

Recreations: Walking, travel.

The Lord Patel KT, House of Lords, London SW1A 0PW
Tel: 020 7219 8702
Tel: 01350 727366 *Email:* patel_naren@hotmail.com

NON-AFFILIATED

PATEL OF BRADFORD, LORD

PATEL OF BRADFORD (Life Baron), Kamlesh Kumar Patel; cr 2006. Born 28 September 1960; Son of Sudhindra Kumar and Savita Devi Patel; Married Yasmin Saloojee 1998 (2 sons 2 stepdaughters).

Education: Belle Vue Boys Grammar School, Bradford; Huddersfield Polytechnic (CQSW 1987).

Non-political career: West Yorkshire Police Service 1981-91; Ambulanceman West Yorkshire Ambulance Service 1981-83; Bradford Social Services: Social worker 1983-87, Specialist caseworker (alcohol and drugs team) 1987-89; Manager, Bridge Project (drugs and mental health care organisation) 1989-95; University of Central Lancashire 1995-2010: Senior lecturer in social work 1995-97, Senior researcher in health 1997-98, Principal lecturer/research in health 1998-99, Professor and Head of Centre for Ethnicity and Health and of Institute for Philosophy, Diversity and Mental Health 1999-2008; Seconded as national strategic director, National Institute for Mental Health England 2003-04; Seconded as national director, Department of Health national delivering race equality mental health programme 2004-07; UK member, Unicef's Global Task Force on Water, Sanitation and Hygiene 2006-10; Ministerial adviser to Hazel Blears as Secretary of State for Communities and Local Government 2008-09; Professor and Head of International School for Communities, Rights and Inclusion 2008-10; Professor, senior management team, De Montfort University March-October 2010; Director of strategic partnerships and senior adviser to the Vice-Chancellor, University of East London 2010-.

Political career: *House of Lords:* Raised to the peerage as Baron Patel of Bradford, of Bradford in the County of West Yorkshire 2006. Sat as Crossbench Peer 2006-08; Government Whip 2008-09; Opposition Spokesperson for Communities and Local Government 2010-11. Member, Mental Capacity Act 2005 2013-14. *Other:* Left Labour group March 2018; now sits as Non-affiliated. Home Office Advisory Council for the Misuse of Drugs: Member, Criminal Justice Advisory Working Group 1990-96, Council member 1993-96; Mental Health Act Commission 1995-2008: Non-executive board member 1995-2001, Member 1995-2001, Vice-chair 2001-02, Chair 2002-08; Non-executive board member, Central Council for Education and Training and Social Work 1997-98; National Treatment Agency for Substance Misuse: Non-executive board member 2001-08, Chair, Audit and Risk Committee 2001-08; Non-executive board member, Healthcare Commission 2003-05; Commissioner and trustee, UK Drug Policy Commission 2007-09; Chair, National Prison Drug Treatment Review Group 2008-10; Leicestershire Partnership NHS Trust: Associate non-executive director 2008-, Adviser to Communities, Rights and Inclusion Programme 2008-, Chair, Communities, Rights and Inclusion Governance Committee 2010-; Chair, Integrated Equality and Human Rights Committee, Leicestershire County and Rutland NHS Trust 2010-; Chair: Bradford Teaching Hospitals NHS Foundation Trust 2014-16, Bradford City Producer Board 2014-16, Social Work England 2020-.

Political interests: Africa, India, Middle East.

Other: UK Member, Unicef's Global Task Force on Water, Sanitation and Hygiene 2006-10; Patron: National Men's Health Forum 2003-, Sharing Voices 2007-12, Bridge Project 2008-; President, Bradford Magistrates Chaplaincy Service 2008-; Patron: Westminster Health Forum 2009-, British Muslim Heritage Centre 2009-, Equity Partnership 2009-, Bradford Cryrenians 2010-, Safe Inside – Safe Outside 2010-; President, Royal Society of Public Health London 2010-18; Chair: International Deaf 2010-, International Forum for Community Innovations 2011-, Community Innovations Enterprise 2011-; Patron: Mental Health First Aid 2011-, Awaaz 2011-, Engage Communities 2012-, Lily Project 2012-, Intercultural Communication and Leadership School 2012-; Vice-president, Institute of Healthcare Management 2014-; President, National Appropriate Adult Network (NAAN) 2014-; Trustee, Milestone Group 2014-; Patron, Kala Sangam 2015-; Chair, EDV 2015-16; Ambassador, Tutu Foundation 2015-; Patron, Yorkshire Enterprise Network 2015-; President, Asian Sports Foundation 2015-; Vice-President, Yorkshire Society 2015-; Director, England and Wales Cricket Board (ECB) 2015-; Trustee, Noon Memorial Legacy Trust 2016-; Paton: Maya Centre 2016-, Revolving Doors 2016-; Member, General Medical Council 2019-; Professorial fellow: Mental Health (Institute of Mental Health), Public Health (Royal Society of Public Health) 2012-; Two honorary doctorates; Long Service Medal, West Yorkshire Police 1991; Plaque of Recognition for Contributions to the Enhancement of Human Welfare and International Understanding, India High Commission, London 1999; Glory of India Award and Certificate of Excellence, India International Friendship Society 2009; Achievement Award for Services to Education, India

International Foundation 2009; GG2 Man of the Year: Award for consistent lifetime achievement and contribution to public sector services, AMG Awards London 2015; Yorkshire Man of the Year: Award for lifetime contribution to the County of Yorkshire, Yorkshire Society 2016; OBE 1999. Northowram Fields Community Cricket Club.

Recreations: Member of several cricket clubs.

The Lord Patel of Bradford OBE, House of Lords, London SW1A 0PW
Tel: 020 7219 4557 *Email:* patelkk@parliament.uk *Twitter:* @LordKPatel

CONSERVATIVE

PATTEN, LORD

PATTEN (Life Baron), John Haggitt Charles Patten; cr. 1997. Born 17 July 1945; Son of late Jack Patten; Married Louise Alexandra Virginia Charlotte Rowe 1978 (1 daughter).

Education: Wimbledon College, London; Sidney Sussex College, Cambridge (MA; PhD).

Non-political career: Oxford University: University lecturer 1969-79, Fellow and tutor, Hertford College 1972-81, Supernumary Fellow, Hertford College 1981-94; Business adviser and company director 1995-.

Political career: *House of Commons:* MP (Conservative) for Oxford 1979-83, for Oxford West and Abingdon 1983-97; PPS to the Ministers of State at the Home Office 1980-81; Parliamentary Under-Secretary of State for: Northern Ireland 1981-83, Health 1983-85; Minister of State: Department of Environment 1985-87, Home Office 1987-92; Secretary of State for Education 1992-94. *House of Lords:* Raised to the peerage as Baron Patten, of Wincanton in the County of Somerset 1997. *Other:* Oxford City Councillor 1973-76.

Other: Liveryman, Drapers' Company; Hon. Fellow, Harris Manchester College, Oxford; PC 1990.

Publications: Co-editor, The Conservative Opportunity (1976); Things to Come: The Tories in the 21st Century (1995) and other volumes.

Recreations: Talking with my wife and daughter.

Rt Hon the Lord Patten, House of Lords, London SW1A 0PW
Tel: 020 7219 1282

CONSERVATIVE

PATTEN OF BARNES, LORD

PATTEN OF BARNES (Life Baron), Christopher Francis Patten; cr 2005. Born 12 May 1944; Son of late Francis Patten, music publisher, and Joan McCarthy; Married Mary St Leger, née Thornton 1971 (3 daughters).

Education: St Benedict's School, West London; Balliol College, Oxford (BA modern history 1965, MA).

Non-political career: Conservative Research Department: Research officer 1966-70, Director 1974-79; Research officer: Cabinet Office 1970-72, Home Office 1972; Governor and Commander-in-Chief, Hong Kong 1992-97; Chair, Independent Commission on Policing in Northern Ireland 1998-99; Commissioner for External Relations, European Commission 1999-2004.

Political career: *House of Commons:* MP (Conservative) for Bath 1979-92. Contested Bath 1992 general election; PPS: to Norman St John Stevas as Leader of the House of Commons and Chancellor of the Duchy of Lancaster 1979-81, to Patrick Jenkin as Secretary of State for Social Services 1981; Parliamentary Secretary, Northern Ireland Office 1983-85; Minister of State: Department of Education and Science 1985-86, for Overseas Development, Foreign and Commonwealth Office 1986-89; Secretary of State for the Environment 1989-90; Chancellor of the Duchy of Lancaster 1990-92. *House of Lords:* Raised to the peerage as Baron Patten of Barnes, of Barnes in the London Borough of Richmond 2005. *Other:* Personal assistant to Chairman Conservative Party 1972-74; Chair, Conservative Party 1990-92; Patron, Tory Reform Group. Chairman, BBC Trust 2011-14.

Other: Chancellor: Newcastle University 1999-2009, Oxford University 2003-; Honorary Fellow: Balliol College, Oxford, St Antony's College, Oxford; Nine honorary doctorates; PC 1989; CH 1998.

Publications: The Tory Case (1983); East and West (1998); Not Quite the Diplomat (2005); What Next? Surviving the 21st Century (2008); First Confession – A Sort of Memoir (2017).

Rt Hon the Lord Patten of Barnes CH, House of Lords, London SW1A 0PW
Tel: 020 7219 8736 *Email:* pattenc@parliament.uk

NON-AFFILIATED

PAUL, LORD

PAUL (Life Baron), Swraj Paul; cr. 1996. Born 18 February 1931; Son of late Payare Lal and Mongwati Lal; Married Aruna Vij 1956 (2 sons 1 daughter 1 son and 1 daughter deceased).

Education: Foreman Christian College, Lahore, Pakistan; Punjab University (BSc physics, chemistry and maths 1949); Massachusetts Institute of Technology (BSc, MSc 1952, mechanical engineering); Hindi.

Non-political career: Partner in family firm in India, Apeejay Surrendra Group 1953; Came to the UK in 1966, establishing first business Natural Gas Tubes Ltd; Chair and Founder Caparo Group Ltd 1978-; Chair, Caparo BullMoose USA.

Political career: *House of Lords:* Raised to the peerage as Baron Paul, of Marylebone in the City of Westminster 1996. Ambassador for British Business 1998-2010; Deputy Speaker 2008-10; Deputy Chairman of Committees 2008-10; Suspended from membership October 2010-February 2011. Member: European Communities Sub-committee B (Energy, Industry and Transport) 1997-2001, Monetary Policy of the Bank of England/Economic Affairs 2000, 2001-03, 2005-09, Science and Technology 2003-07, Science and Technology Sub-committee II (Energy Efficiency) 2004-05; EU Sub-committee B (Internal Market): Co-opted member 2007-08, Member 2008-10; Member: Finance Bill Sub-committee 2008-10, European Union 2008-10, EU Sub-committee B (Internal Market, Energy and Transport) 2010. *Other:* Resigned Labour Whip October 2010. Board Member: London Development Agency 2000-08, London 2012 2003-05; Chairman, Olympic Delivery Committee 2005-11.

Political interests: Foreign affairs, economic affairs, education, manufacturing; Austria, Bangladesh, China, Dubai, Germany, India, Pakistan, Poland, Spain, Sri Lanka, Switzerland, Turkey, USA.

Other: Member, Foreign Policy Advisory Council 1998-; Co-Chair, Indo-British Round Table 2000-05; Founder and Chair, Ambika Paul Foundation 1978-; President, UK Steel Producers Association 1994-95; Director, Royal Albert Hall 2001-06; Chair: Piggy Bank Kids 2002-15, Piggy Bank Kids Projects Ltd 2002-13, Theirworld 2013-15; Magic Bus, Chance to Shine, Hospices, ZSL; Freedom, City of London 1998; Thames Valley University: Pro-chancellor 1998-2000, Chancellor 2000-01; Chancellor: Wolverhampton University 1998-, Westminster University 2006-14; Member, Royal Society of Arts 1984-2017; Fifteen honorary doctorates from England, Switzerland, Russia, USA and India; Corporate Leadership Award, MIT 1987; First Asian of the Year Award, Asian Who's Who 1987; Corporate Leadership Award, MIT 1989; Donald C. Burnham Manufacturing Management Award, Society of Manufacturing Engineers USA 1995; Lifetime Achievement Award, Asian Business Awards 2008; Lifetime Achievement Award, Global Skill Tree Consortium 2014; International Icon of the Decade Award, World Consulting Research Corporation 2014; Golden Peacock Award for Lifetime Achievement in Business Leadership, Institute of Directors 2018; International Iconic Leader Award for Lifetime Achievement, WCRC 2018; Padma Bhushan (Government of India) 1983; PC 2009. Royal Calcutta Golf Club; Cricket Club of India (Bombay); Marylebone Cricket Club.

Publications: Indira Gandhi (1984); Beyond Boundaries (autobiography, 1998).

Recreations: Grandchildren.

Rt Hon the Lord Paul, House of Lords, London SW1A 0PW
Tel: 020 7219 5353
Caparo Group Ltd, Caparo House, 103 Baker Street, London W1U 6LN *Tel:* 020 7486 1417
Email: lp@caparogrp.com Website: www.caparo.com *Twitter:* @RtHonLordPaulPC

NON-AFFILIATED

PEARSON OF RANNOCH, LORD

PEARSON OF RANNOCH (Life Baron), Malcolm Everard MacLaren Pearson; cr. 1990. Born 20 July 1942; Son of late Colonel John MacLaren Pearson; Married Francesca Frua de Angeli 1965 (divorced 1970) (1 daughter); married Hon. Mary Charteris 1977 (divorced 1995) (2 daughters); married Caroline St Vincent Rose 1997.

Education: Eton College.

Non-political career: Founded PWS Group of reinsurance brokers 1964.

Political career: *House of Lords:* Raised to the peerage as Baron Pearson of Rannoch, of Bridge of Gaur in the District of Perth and Kinross 1990. Member, European Communities and Sub-committee on Social Affairs and the Environment 1992-96. *Other:* UK Independence Party: Leader 2009-10, Left Party October 2019, now sits as Non-affiliated. Council for National Academic Awards: Member 1983-93, Hon. Treasurer 1986-93.

Political interests: European Union, intellectual impairment, Islamism, education.

Other: Co-founder, Global Britain; Patron, Register of Chinese Herbal Medicine; Founded Rannoch Charitable Trust 1984; Patron, RESCARE (Society for Children and Adults with Learning Disabilities and their Families) 1994-; Hon. LLD, CNAA 1992. White's Club; Swinley Forest Golf.

Recreations: Stalking, fishing, shooting, golf.

The Lord Pearson of Rannoch, House of Lords, London SW1A 0PW
Tel: 020 7219 5353
Email: lordpearsonofrannoch@gmail.com

CROSSBENCH

PEEL, EARL

PEEL (3rd Earl, UK), William James Robert Peel; cr. 1929. 4th Viscount Peel (UK) 1895; Viscount Clanfield (UK) 1929; 8th Bt of Drayton Manor (GB) 1800. Born 3 October 1947; Son of 2nd Earl; Married Veronica Timpson 1973 (divorced 1987) (1 son 1 daughter); married Hon Charlotte Hambro 1989, née Soames (1 daughter).

Education: Ampleforth College, Yorkshire; Tours University, France; Royal Agricultural College, Cirencester.

Non-political career: Lord Chamberlain of the Queen's Household and Chancellor of the Royal Victorian Order 2006-21.

Political career: *House of Lords:* First entered House of Lords 1979; Elected hereditary peer 1999-. Co-opted Member, European Union Sub-committee D (Environment and Agriculture Policy) 2003-06. *Other:* DL, North Yorkshire 1998-.

Other: Chair, North of England Grouse Research Project 1979-96; Member: Yorkshire Dales National Parks Committee 1981-87, Moorland Association Executive Committee 1988-2006; President, Yorkshire Wildlife Trust 1989-96; Council member, Nature Conservancy Council for England, then English Nature 1991-96; President, Gun Trade Association 1993-99; Duchy of Cornwall: Member, Prince's Council 1993-96, Lord Warden of the Stannaries 1994-2006; Game and Wildlife Conservation Trust: Chair 1994-2000, President 2000-08, Vice-president 2008-; Chair, Standing Conference on Country Sports 2001-06; GCVO 2006; PC 2006. White's Club.

Recreations: Shooting, cricket, photography, ornithology.

Rt Hon the Earl Peel GCVO DL, House of Lords, London SW1A 0PW
Tel: 020 7219 5353

House of Lords
Peers' Biographies

LABOUR

PENDRY, LORD

PENDRY (Life Baron), Thomas Pendry; cr 2001. Born 10 June 1934; Son of late Leonard Pendry; Married Moira Smith 1966 (separated 1983) (1 son 1 daughter).

Education: St Augustine's School, Ramsgate; Plater Hall, Oxford University.

Non-political career: Official, National Union of Public Employees 1960-70. RAF national service 1955-57. Member, AEEU.

Political career: *House of Commons:* MP (Labour) for Stalybridge and Hyde 1970-2001; Opposition Whip 1971-74; Government Whip 1974-77 (resigned); Parliamentary Under-Secretary of State, Northern Ireland Office 1978-79; Opposition Frontbench Spokesperson for: Northern Ireland 1979-82, Overseas Development 1981-82, Regional Affairs and Devolution 1982-92, National Heritage (Sport and Tourism) 1992-97. *House of Lords:* Raised to the peerage as Baron Pendry, of Stalybridge in the County of Greater Manchester 2001. Member: Refreshment 2014-16, Regenerating Seaside Towns and Communities 2018. *Other:* Chair, Derby Labour Party 1966. Councillor, Paddington Borough Council 1962-65.

Political interests: Industrial relations, housing, sport, recreation, finance, social security, environment; Hong Kong, Japan, Malta, USA.

Other: Member, Council of Europe and Western European Union 1973-75; President, Stalybridge Public Band; Patron, Football Supporter's Federation; Fellow, Industry and Parliament Trust 1979, 1988; President: Ramsgate FC, Stalybridge Labour Club; Football Foundation: Chair 2001-03, President 2003-; Patron, Teenage Cancer Trust; Freedom: Borough of Tameside, Lord Mottram of Longendale; Lordship of Mottram in Longendale 1995; PC 2001; Knight of Malta; Freeman, Tameside Borough Council. Royal Air Force, Garrick Club; Stalybridge Labour Club; Boxed for Oxford University 1957-59; Middleweight Colonial boxing champion, Hong Kong 1957; Lord's Taverners; MCC; Vincent's, Oxford University.

Publications: Taking It on the Chin (autobiography) (Biteback Publishing, 2016).

Recreations: Watching all sport, meeting sportspersons, jazz.

Rt Hon the Lord Pendry, House of Lords, London SW1A 0PW
Tel: 020 7219 4590 *Fax:* 020 7219 4419 *Email:* pendryt@parliament.uk

CONSERVATIVE

PENN, BARONESS

Government Whip (Baroness in Waiting)

PENN (Life Baroness), Joanna Carolyn Penn; cr 2019. Born 1985.

Education: Oxford University (BA history and politics 2006); Harvard University (Masters public policy 2015).

Non-political career: Special adviser, Conservative Party 2007-10; Home Office: Policy adviser 2010-11, Senior policy adviser 2015-16; Tony Blair Africa Governance Initiative: Governance adviser, Sierra Leone 2011-12, Deputy Country Head, Malawi 2012-13; Deputy Chief of Staff to Theresa May as Prime Minister 2016-19.

Political career: *House of Lords:* Raised to the peerage as Baroness Penn, of Teddington in the London Borough of Richmond 2019. Government Whip (Baroness in Waiting) 2020-. Member, Science and Technology 2019-20.

The Baroness Penn, House of Lords, London SW1A 0PW

NON-AFFILIATED

PETERBOROUGH, LORD BISHOP OF

PETERBOROUGH (38th Bishop of), Donald Spargo Allister. Born 27 August 1952; Son of Charles and Barbara Allister; Married Janice 1976 (3 children).

Education: Birkenhead School; Peterhouse, Cambridge (BA theology 1974); Trinity College, Bristol 1974.

Non-political career: Ordained deacon 1976; Curate: St George's, Hyde 1976-79, St Nicholas, Sevenoaks 1979-83; Part-time consultant editor, *Church of England Newspaper* 1976-83; Vicar, Christ Church, Birkenhead 1983-89; Rector, St Mary's, Cheadle 1989-2002; Rural Dean of Cheadle 1999-2002; Archdeacon of Chester 2002-10; Bishop of Peterborough 2010-; Assistant Bishop in the Diocese of Ely 2011-.

Political career: *House of Lords:* Entered House of Lords 2014. *Other:* Member: General Synod 2005-, Women Bishops Legislative Drafting Group 2006-08; Council for Christian Unity: Member 2006-13; Chair 2013-18.

Political interests: Farming and rural affairs, prisons and criminal justice, mental health; Korea (North and South).

Other: Vice-President, The Leprosy Mission; Honorary Doctorate in Theology, Chester University (2011). Farmers Club.

Rt Rev the Lord Bishop of Peterborough, House of Lords, London SW1A 0PW
Tel: 020 7219 5353 *Email:* allisterd@parliament.uk
Bishop's Lodging, The Palace, Peterborough PE1 1YA *Tel:* 01733 562492
Email: bishop@peterborough-diocese.org.uk Website: www.peterborough-diocese.org.uk

CROSSBENCH

PHILLIPS OF WORTH MATRAVERS, LORD

PHILLIPS OF WORTH MATRAVERS (Life Baron), Nicholas Addison Phillips; cr. 1999. Born 21 January 1938; Son of Michael Pennington Phillips and Dora Phillips, née Hassid; Married Christylle Marie-Thérèse Rouffiac, née Doreau 1972 (2 daughters 1 stepson 1 stepdaughter).

Education: Bryanston School; King's College, Cambridge (BA law 1961, MA).

Non-political career: Called to the Bar, Middle Temple (Harmsworth Scholar) 1962; In practice at the Bar 1962-87; Junior Counsel to Ministry of Defence and to Treasury in Admiralty matters 1973-78; QC 1978; Recorder 1982-87; Judge of the High Court of Justice (Queen's Bench Division) 1987-95; Lord Justice of Appeal 1995-98; Chairman of the BSE Inquiry 1998-2000; Master of the Rolls 2000-05; Head of Civil Justice 2000-05; Lord Chief Justice 2005-08; President of the Supreme Court of the United Kingdom 2009-12; Visiting Professor: King's College London 2010-, Oxford University 2013-16. Royal Navy national service commissioned RNVR 1956-58.

Political career: *House of Lords:* Raised to the peerage as Baron Phillips of Worth Matravers, of Belsize Park in the London Borough of Camden 1999. Lord of Appeal in Ordinary 1999-2000; Senior Lord of Appeal in Ordinary 2008-09; As President of the Supreme Court, disqualified from participation 2009-12. Member: Joint Committee on Voting Eligibilty (Prisoners) Bill 2013, Selection 2015-16. *Other:* Member, Panel of Wreck Commissioners 1979; Chair: Law Advisory Committee, British Council 1991-97, Council of Legal Education 1992-97; Advisory Council of Institute of European and Comparative Law 1999-; Council of Management, British Institute of International and Comparative Law 1999-; Chair, Lord Chancellor's Advisory Committee on Public Records 2000-05; President, British Maritime Law Association 2005-; Chair: Sentencing Guidelines Council 2005-08, Criminal Procedure Rules Committee 2005-08.

Other: The Draper's Company; Worshipful Company of Shipwrights; Freedom, City of London; Chancellor, Bournemouth University 2009-18; Honorary LLD, Exeter University 1998; Honorary Fellow, Society for Advanced Legal Studies 1999; Visitor: Nuffield College, Oxford 2000-05, University College, London 2000-05; Hon. Fellow, King's College, Cambridge 2003; Doctor of Civil Law, City University, London; Honorary LLD: London University, Birmingham University; Visitor, Darwin College, Cambridge 2005; International Maritime Law Institute 2007; Kt 1987; PC 1995; KG 2011; Officier of the Legion d'Honneur 2017. Brooks's; Garrick Club.

Recreations: Sea, mountains.

Rt Hon the Lord Phillips of Worth Matravers KG, House of Lords, London SW1A 0PW
Tel: 020 7219 5353
Email: phillipsofworth@gmail.com

CONSERVATIVE

PICKLES, LORD

PICKLES (Life Baron), Eric Jack Pickles; cr 2018. Born 20 April 1952; Son of late Jack Pickles and Constance Pickles; Married Irene 1976.

Education: Greenhead Grammar School, Keighley, Yorkshire; Leeds Polytechnic.

Non-political career: Industrial trainer.

Political career: *House of Commons:* MP (Con) for Brentwood and Ongar 1992-2010, for Brentwood and Ongar (revised boundary) 2010-17; Opposition Spokesperson for Social Security 1998-2001; Shadow Minister for Transport 2001-02; Shadow Secretary of State for: Local Government and the Regions 2002-03, Local Government 2003-05; Shadow Minister for Local Government 2005-07; Shadow Secretary of State for Communities and Local Government 2007-09; Secretary of State for Communities and Local Government 2010-15; Minister for Faith 2014-15; UK Government Anti-Corruption Champion 2015-17; Chair Inter-Ministerial Group on Anti-Corruption 2015-17. Member: Environment, Transport and Regional Affairs 1997-98, Environment, Transport and Regional Affairs (Transport Sub-Committee) 1997-98. *House of Lords:* Raised to the peerage as Baron Pickles, of Brentwood and Ongar in the County of Essex 2018. Member, COVID-19 2020-. *Other:* Member, Conservative Party National Union Executive Committee 1975-97; National chair, Young Conservatives 1980-81; Member: Conservative Party National Local Government Advisory Committee 1985-, One Nation Forum 1987-91; Deputy leader, Conservative Group on Association of Metropolitan Authorities 1989-91; Local government editor, *Newsline* 1990-92; Conservative Party: Vice-chair 1993-97, Deputy chair (local government) 2005-07, Chair 2009-10; Chair, Conservative Friends of Israel 2015-; Patron, Conservatives for Reform in Europe 2016. Bradford Metropolitan District Council: Councillor 1979-91, Leader, Conservative Group 1987-91; Member, Yorkshire Regional Health Authority 1982-90; Chair: Joint Committee Against Racism 1982-87, National Local Government Advisory Committee 1992-95; Vice-President, Local Government Association 1997-2010; UK Holocaust Memorial Foundation: Board member 2015-, Co-chair 2018-; UK Special Envoy for Post-Holocaust Issues 2015-; Chair, Advisory Committee on Business Appointments 2020-.

Political interests: Housing, health, social services, local government; Eastern Europe, India, Poland, USA.

Other: Non-executive board member, Leo Group Ltd 2016-; Member, advisory board, Community Security Trust 2016-; *The House Magazine* Social Media Moment of the Year, Dods Parliamentary Awards 2014; PC 2010; Kt 2015. Carlton Club.

Recreations: Films, opera, bird watching, golf.

Rt Hon the Lord Pickles, House of Lords, London SW1A 0PW
Tel: 020 7219 3000 *Twitter:* @EricPickles

CONSERVATIVE

PIDDING, BARONESS

PIDDING (Life Baroness), Emma Samantha Pidding; cr 2015. Born 13 January 1966; Partner Tim Butcher.

Education: Dr Challoner's High School, Little Chalfont.

Non-political career: Lloyds Bank; Marketing and events manager, IT consultancy, Buckinghamshire; Owner, consultancy specialising in organising seminar and conferences.

Political career: *House of Lords:* Raised to the peerage as Baroness Pidding, of Amersham in the County of Buckinghamshire 2015. Member, Electoral Registration and Administration Act 2013 2019-. *Other:* Chair, Chesham and Amersham Young Conservatives 1991-94; Chesham and Amersham Conservative Association: Deputy chair 1997-2000, Chair 2000-03; Oxfordshire and Buckinghamshire Area Team: Deputy Chair (membership and fundraising) 2002-04, Area Chair 2004-06; National Convention: Vice-President 2006-09, President 2009-10, Chair 2012-15; President, Northern Ireland Conservatives 2007-; National volunteer by-election co-ordinator 2010-12; Deputy Chair, Conservative Party Board 2012-15; Executive Member, Association of Conservative Peers 2017-. Councillor, Chiltern District Council 1991-99.

Other: CBE 2014.

The Baroness Pidding CBE, House of Lords, London SW1A 0PW
Tel: 020 7219 3000 *Email:* piddinge@parliament.uk *Twitter:* @EmmaPidding

LIBERAL DEMOCRAT

PINNOCK, BARONESS

Liberal Democrat Lords Spokesperson for Communities and Local Government and Whip

PINNOCK (Life Baroness), Kathryn (Kath) Mary Pinnock; cr 2014. Born 25 September 1946.

Education: Keele University (Degree history and chemistry; Diploma teaching).

Non-political career: Secondary school teacher, various schools in Birmingham and West Yorkshire; Deputy Chief Examiner for GCE history.

Political career: *House of Commons:* Contested (Liberal Democrat) Batley and Spen 1997 and 2001 general elections. *House of Lords:* Raised to the peerage as Baroness Pinnock, of Cleckheaton in the County of West Yorkshire 2014. Liberal Democrat: Spokesperson for Children 2015, Shadow Secretary of State/Lords Spokesperson for Communities and Local Government 2016-, Lords Spokesperson for Housing 2019, Whip 2020-. Member: EU Home Affairs Sub-committee 2015-19, Public Services 2020-. *Other:* Leader, Kirklees Liberal Democrats 1991-2014; President, Association of Liberal Democrat Councillors. Kirklees Council: Councillor 1987-, Leader of the Council 2000-06; Governor, Whitcliffe Mount School, Cleckheaton; Board member, Yorkshire Forward 2001-11; Non-executive director, Yorkshire Water 2008-; Vice-President, Local Government Association 2015-.

Other: Association of West Yorkshire Authorities; Mayor of Borough of Kirklees Appeal Fund; CO2 Sense Limited; Council member, Huddersfield University.

The Baroness Pinnock, House of Lords, London SW1A 0PW
Tel: 020 7219 5353 *Twitter:* @KathPinnock

LABOUR

PITKEATHLEY, BARONESS

PITKEATHLEY (Life Baroness), Jill Elizabeth Pitkeathley; cr. 1997. Born 4 January 1940; Daughter of Roland and May Bisson; Married W. Pitkeathley 1961 (divorced 1978) (1 son 1 daughter); married David Emerson 2008.

Education: Ladies' College, Guernsey; Bristol University (BA economics 1960).

Non-political career: Social Worker 1961-68; Voluntary Service Co-ordinator, West Berkshire Health Authority 1970-83; National Consumer Council 1983-86; Director, National Council for Carers 1986 until merger with Association of Carers 1988; Carers National Association: Chief Executive 1988-98, Vice-President 2001-; Chair: Children and Families Court Advisory and Support Service 2003-08, Council for Health Care Regulatory Excellence/Professional Standards Authority 2009-15.

Political career: *House of Lords:* Raised to the peerage as Baroness Pitkeathley, of Caversham in the Royal County of Berkshire 1997. Deputy Speaker 2002-; Deputy Chair of Committees 2002-. Member: House of Lords' Offices Refreshment Sub-committee 2001-09, Information 2010-13, Joint Committee on the Draft Care and Support Bill 2013, Equality Act 2010 and Disability 2015-16; Chair, Charities 2016-17; Member: Citizenship and Civic Engagement 2017-18, Rural Economy 2018-19, Public Services 2020-. *Other:* Adviser to Griffith's Review of Community Care 1986-88; Community Council for Berkshire: Vice-President 1990-98, President 1998-2013; Chair: New Opportunities Fund 1998-2004, Future Builders Advisory Panel 2005-08, Advisory Board, Office of Third Sector 2008-10; Interim Chair, General Social Care Council 2008.

Political interests: Health, social care, voluntary sector, charities; Channel Islands.

Other: Vice-President, Carers UK 1998-; Big Society Trust: Trustee 2011-14, Chair 2015-; Cumberland Lodge: Trustee 2014-, Vice-chair 2019-; President, National Council for Voluntary Organisations (NCVO) 2018-; Carers UK; Hon. RCGP; Hon. City and Guilds 2009; DL: Bristol 2002, London Metropolitan 2002; OBE 1993.

Publications: When I Went Home (1978); Mobilising Voluntary Resources (1984); Supporting Volunteers (1985); It's my duty, isn't it? (1989); Co-author: Age Gap Relationships (1996), Only Child (1994); Fiction: Cassandra and Jane (2004), Dearest Cousin Jane (2009).

Recreations: Gardening, grandchildren, writing.

The Baroness Pitkeathley OBE, House of Lords, London SW1A 0PW
Tel: 020 7219 0358 *Email:* pitkeathleyj@parliament.uk

LABOUR

PLANT OF HIGHFIELD, LORD

PLANT OF HIGHFIELD (Life Baron), Raymond Plant; cr. 1992. Born 19 March 1945; Son of late Stanley Plant and Marjorie Plant; Married Katherine Dixon 1967 (3 sons).

Education: Havelock School, Grimsby; King's College, London (BA philosophy 1966); Hull University (PhD political philosophy 1971); French, German.

Non-political career: Lecturer, then senior lecturer in philosophy, Manchester University 1967-79; Philosophy lecturer in several universities 1981-91; Professor of politics, Southampton University 1979-94; Master, St Catherine's College, Oxford 1994-2000; Professor of: European politics, Southampton University 2000-02, Law and philosophy, King's College, London 2002-: Head of Law School 2006-08; Visiting professor of law and philosophy, Institut d'Etudes Politiques, Paris 2008; Hon. professor of humanities, Winchester University; Part-time professor of law, Tallinn University, Estonia.

Political career: *House of Lords:* Raised to the peerage as Baron Plant of Highfield, of Weelsby in the County of Humberside 1992. Opposition Spokesperson for Home Affairs 1992-96. Member: Relations between Central and Local Government 1995-96, European Communities Sub-committee E 2000-03, Joint Committee on Human Rights 2003-07, Merits of Statutory Instruments/Secondary Legislation Scrutiny 2010-15, Joint Committee on the Draft Enhanced Terrorism Prevention and Investigation Measures Bill 2012-13, Inheritace and Trustees' Powers Bill 2013, Joint Committee on Able Marine Energy Park Development Consent Order 2014 2014-15, Ecclesiastical Committee 2014-, High Speed Rail (London-West Midlands) Bill 2016, Joint Committee on Consolidation, &c, Bills 2016-, Intellectual Property (Unjustified Threats) Bill 2016, Selection 2017-, Bribery Act 2010 2018-19. *Other:* Chair, Labour Party Commission on Electoral Systems 1991-93.

Political interests: France, Germany, Portugal, Russia.

Other: President, National Council for Voluntary Organisations (NCVO) 1998-2002; Fellow, Industry and Parliament Trust 1998; Chair: Hope Medical Trust, Southampton 2000-06, Centrepoint 2001-04, Southampton University Development Trust 2007-08; Pro-Chancellor, Southampton University 1996-2000; FRSA 1992; ACSS (Academy of Learned Societies in the Social Sciences); Six honorary doctorates; Fellow: King's College, London, Catherine's College, Oxford, Cardiff University, Harris Manchester College, Oxford; Isiah Berlin prize 2010. Athenæum Club.

Publications: Hegel (1974); Community and Ideology (1974); Political Philosophy and Social Welfare (1981); Philosophy, Politics and Citizenship (1984); Contributor to *The Times* (1988-91); Conservative Capitalism in Britain and the United States: a critical appraisal (1988); Modern Political Thought (1991); Politics, Theology and History (2001); The Neo-liberal State (OUP, 2009).

Recreations: Music, opera, reading.

Professor the Lord Plant of Highfield, House of Lords, London SW1A 0PW
Tel: 020 7219 5424
School of Law, King's College, Strand, London WC2R 2LS *Tel:* 020 7836 5454
Email: raymond.plant@kcl.ac.uk

CONSERVATIVE

POLAK, LORD

POLAK (Life Baron), Stuart Polak; cr 2015. Born 28 March 1961.

Non-political career: Youth Officer, United Synagogue; Conservative Friends of Israel: Director 1989-2015, Honorary President 2015-; Director, Markham Services Ltd; Senior consultant, Jardine Lloyd Thompson Group plc.

Political career: *House of Lords:* Raised to the peerage as Baron Polak, of Hertsmere in the County of Hertfordshire 2015. Member: EU Justice Sub-committee 2016-20, European Union 2018-19, EU Security and Justice Sub-committee 2020-.

Other: Chair, TWC Associates; Senior consultant, Jardine Lloyd Thompson; Chair, European Friends of Israel; Trustee, Langdon Foundation; Director, Yavneh Foundation Trust; Board member, Europe Near East Forum; CBE 2015.

The Lord Polak CBE, House of Lords, London SW1A 0PW
Tel: 020 7219 3000

LABOUR

PONSONBY OF SHULBREDE, LORD

Opposition Spokesperson for Justice

PONSONBY OF SHULBREDE (4th Baron, UK), Frederick Matthew Thomas Ponsonby; cr. 1930; (Life) Baron Ponsonby of Roehampton 2000. Born 27 October 1958; Son of 3rd Baron; Married Sarah Jackson 1995 (1 daughter 1 son).

Education: Holland Park Comprehensive School; University College, Cardiff (BSc physics 1980); Imperial College, London (MSc DIC petroleum engineering 1983).

Non-political career: Member, Unite.

Political career: *House of Lords:* Created a life peer as Baron Ponsonby of Roehampton, of Shulbrede in the County of West Sussex 2000. First entered House of Lords 1990; Opposition Spokesperson for: Education 1992-97, Justice 2020-. Member: Science and Technology 1998-99, Science and Technology Sub-committee II (Science and Society) 1999, Constitution 2001, Joint Committee on the Draft Domestic Abuse Bill 2019. *Other:* Councillor, London Borough of Wandsworth 1990-94; JP: Westminster Bench 2005-11, Inner London Youth Panel 2008-11, Central London Bench 2012-, Central London Youth Panel 2012-, Greater London Family Panel 2012-.

Political interests: Foreign affairs.

Other: Delegate to: Council of Europe 1997-2001, Western European Union 1997-2001; Organisation for Security and Co-operation in Europe 2001-10; FIMM.

The Lord Ponsonby of Shulbrede, House of Lords, London SW1A 0PW
Tel: 020 7219 0071 *Email:* ponsonbyf@parliament.uk

CONSERVATIVE

POPAT, LORD

POPAT (Life Baron), Dolar Amarshi Popat; cr 2010. Born 14 June 1953; Son of Amarshibhai Haridas Popat and Parvatiben Amarshibhai Popat; Married Sandhya Popat 1980 (3 sons).

Education: Manjasi High School, Torono, Uganda; Kilburn Polytechnic; City of London Polytechnic, Moorgate; Chartered Institute of Management Accounting (management accounting 1977); Gujarati, Hindi, Swahili.

Non-political career: Practicing accountant 1980-82; Harrow Chamber of Commerce 1982-1987; Chief executive, Fast Finance plc 1982-91; Founding Patron, Harrow Grange Hospice St Luke's Hospice 1984-; Founder and chief executive, TLC Group 1991-2010.

Political career: *House of Lords:* Raised to the peerage as Baron Popat, of Harrow in the London Borough of Harrow 2010. Government Whip 2013-15; Government Spokesperson: Business, Innovation and Skills 2013-15, Transport 2013-15, Communities and Local Government (Faith and Communities) 2014-15; Conservative Party Whip 2015-; Trade Envoy to: Uganda and Rwanda 2016-, Democratic Republic of Congo. Member, Small- and

Medium-Sized Enterprises 2012-13. *Other:* Secretary, Anglo-Asian Conservative Association; Chair, One Nation Forum, Barnet; President, Harrow East Conservative Association; Member, Conservative Ethnic Diversity Council; Co-chair, Conservative Friends of India 2012-13.

Political interests: International affairs, international development, small- and medium-sized businesses, banking and finance, community, exports; Africa, India, Kenya, Malawi, Tanzania, Uganda.

Other: Affiliate member, Institute of Chartered Management Accountants; Charities supported through the Lord Dolar Popat Foundation, St Luke's Hospice.

Recreations: Reading, tennis, walking, community work, travelling, Tottenham Hotspur FC.

The Lord Popat, House of Lords, London SW1A 0PW
Tel: 020 7219 0295 *Email:* popatd@parliament.uk Website: www.lordpopat.com

CONSERVATIVE

PORTER OF SPALDING, LORD

PORTER OF SPALDING (Life Baron), Gary Andrew Porter; cr 2015. Born 8 September 1960; Married Karen (2 children).

Education: Collenswood School, Stevenage; De Montfort University (BA history and politics 2000); Canterbury Christ Church University (Postgraduate Certificate shared services 2011).

Non-political career: Industrial bakery; Labourer, warehouse building site; Contracts manager for a construction firm; Owner of small building firm.

Political career: *House of Lords:* Raised to the peerage as Baron Porter of Spalding, of Spalding in the County of Lincolnshire 2015. Member, High Speed Rail (West Midlands-Crewe) Bill 2019-20. *Other:* Chair, Conservative Councillors Association 2013-16; Member, Conservative Party Board. South Holland District Council: Councillor 2001-, Leader 2003-; Local Government Association: Chair, environment, housing and planning board 2009-11, Leader, Conservative Group and Vice-chair 2011-15, Chair 2015-19.

Other: Director: South Holland Homes, Local Government Information House Ltd, Improvement and Development Agency for Local Government; Chair, District Council Network 2009-11.

The Lord Porter of Spalding CBE, House of Lords, London SW1A 0PW
Tel: 020 7219 3000
c/o Council Offices, Priory Road, Spalding PE11 2XE *Twitter:* @garyporterlga

NON-AFFILIATED

PORTSMOUTH, LORD BISHOP OF

PORTSMOUTH (9th Bishop of), Christopher Richard James Foster. Born 7 November 1953; Son of late Joseph James Frederick and late Elizabeth Foster, née Gibbs; Married Julia 1982 (died 2001) (1 son 1 daughter); married Sally 2006.

Education: Royal Grammar School, Guildford; Durham University (BA economics and politics 1975); Manchester University (MA (Econ) econometrics 1977); Trinity Hall, Cambridge (MA theology 1979); Westcott House, Cambridge.

Non-political career: Economics lecturer; Ordained deacon 1980; Assistant curate, Tettenhall Regis, Wolverhampton 1980-82; Chaplain, Wadham College, Oxford 1982-86; Assistant Priest, University Church of St Mary the Virgin 1982-86; Vicar, Christ Church, Southgate, London 1986-94; Director, CME, Edmonton Episcopal Area 1988-94; Sub-Dean and residentiary canon, St Albans Cathedral 1994-2001; Bishop of: Hertford 2001-10, Portsmouth 2010-.

Political career: *House of Lords:* Entered House of Lords 2014. *Other:* Hertfordshire University: Governor 2002-10, Chair, finance committee 2007-10; Council Member, Westcott House, Cambridge 2004-12; Member: Church Commissioners Pastoral Committee 2013-14, Dioceses Commission 2014-, Ministry Council 2017-; Chair of Governors, Ripon College, Cuddesdon 2014-; Governor, Portsmouth University 2014-; Chair: Remuneration and Conditions of Service Committee, Archbishops' Council 2017-, Churches Funerals Group 2017-; Co-Chair, Anglican Roman Catholic Committee 2018-.

Political interests: Ghana.

Other: Director, Churches Together in England 2012-17; DLitt, Hertfordshire University 2011. Athenæum, Royal Yacht Squadron Club.

Rt Rev the Lord Bishop of Portsmouth, House of Lords, London SW1A 0PW
Tel: 020 7219 5353 *Email:* fostercrj@parliament.uk
Bishopsgrove, 26 Osborn Road, Fareham PO16 7DQ *Tel:* 01329 280247
Email: bishop@portsmouth.anglican.org Website: www.portsmouth.anglican.org

CROSSBENCH

POWELL OF BAYSWATER, LORD

POWELL OF BAYSWATER (Life Baron), Charles David Powell; cr. 2000. Born 6 June 1941; Son of late Air Vice Marshal John Powell, OBE; Married Carla Bonardi 1964 (2 sons).

Education: Canterbury Cathedral Choir School; King's School, Canterbury; New College, Oxford (BA modern history 1963); Finnish, French, German, Italian.

Non-political career: Diplomatic Service 1963-83; Private Secretary to Prime Ministers: Margaret Thatcher 1983-90, John Major 1990-91; Director: Matheson & Co 1991-, Mandarin Oriental Hotel Group 1991-2018, Hong Kong Land Holdings 1991-2001, 2018-, Jardine Matheson Holdings 1991-2001, Jardine Strategic Holdings 1991-2000, 2018-, National Westminster Bank (Chairman, International Advisory Board) 1991-2000, J Rothschild Name Company 1992-2003, Said Holdings 1993-2000, Arjo Wiggins Appleton 1993-2000, Louis Vuitton Moët Hennessy 1995-, British Mediterranean Airways 1997-2007; Member, international advisory board: GEMS Private Equity 1999-2013, Phillips de Pury Luxembourg 2000-02; Director: Sagitta Asset Management 2001-05, Caterpillar Inc 2001-13, Textron Corporation 2001-17, Yell Group 2002-09, Schindler Holding 2003-14, Northern Trust Global Services 2004-14; Member, international advisory board: Thales UK 2004-, Alfa Capital 2005-10, Chubb Insurance 2006-, Barrick Gold 2006-; Chairman: International advisory board, Rolls Royce 2006-17, Capital Generation Partners 2006-13, Magna Holdings International 2006-12, Bowmark 2008-; Geopolitical adviser, BAe Systems 2009-; Director, Northern Trust Corporation 2015-; Adviser, Technologies 2016-; Geopolitical adviser: Brunswick Group 2017-, Rolls Royce 2017-.

Political career: *House of Lords:* Raised to the peerage as Baron Powell of Bayswater, of Canterbury in the County of Kent 2000. Co-opted Member, EU Sub-committee C (Common Foreign and Security Policy/Foreign Affairs, Defence and Development Policy) 2000-04; Member: Economic Affairs 2005-07, European Union 2006-10, EU Sub-committee B (Internal Market) 2006-10, Finance Bill Sub-committee 2006-11, Constitution 2010-15, Procedure 2015-19, Joint Committee on the National Security Strategy 2016-. *Other:* Chair, Singapore British Business Council 1993-2001; President, China-Britain Business Council 1997-2007; Co-chair, Asia Task Force 2007-14; UK Business Ambassador 2012-19; Vice-president: Great Britain-China Centre, Asia House.

Political interests: Foreign affairs, defence, intelligence, trade; Asia, Europe, North America.

Other: Trustee, Aspen Institute, USA 1995-; Asia House International Advisory Board 1996-; Chair of Trustees, Oxford University Business School Foundation 1997-; Trustee, British Museum 2000-10; Chair, Atlantic Partnership 2000-; Trustee: Saïd Foundation 2008-, International Institute of Strategic Studies 2010-17; Chair, British Museum Trust 2011-; Member, International Advisory Board, New York Council on Foreign Relations 2011-17; Deputy chair, Fudan University School of Management Advisory Board 2012-; Aspen Institute; Honorary Fellow, Ashmolean Museum, Oxford; Foundation Fellow, Somerville College, Oxford; Honorary Fellow, King's College, London; DSc (Hons), Shiv Nadar University, India; KCMG 1990; Public Service Star (Singapore) 2001. Turf Club.

Recreations: Walking.

The Lord Powell of Bayswater KCMG, House of Lords, London SW1A 0PW
LVMH House, 15 St George Street, London W1S 1FH *Tel:* 020 7199 3916
Email: pa@charlespowell.com

CROSSBENCH

PRASHAR, BARONESS

PRASHAR (Life Baroness), Usha Kumari Prashar; cr. 1999. Born 29 June 1948; Daughter of late Naurhia Lal and Durga Devi Prashar; Married Vijay Kumar Sharma 1973.

Education: Duchess of Gloucester School, Nairobi, Kenya; Wakefield Girls' High School, Yorkshire; Leeds University (BA political science 1970); Glasgow University (Dip Soc Admin 1971); Hindi.

Non-political career: Conciliation officer, Race Relations Board 1971-75; Director, Runnymede Trust 1976-84; Research fellow, Policy Studies Institute 1984-86; Director, National Council of Voluntary Organisations 1986-91; National Literacy Trust: Deputy chair 1992-2000, Chair 2000-05; First Civil Service Commissioner 2000-05; Non-executive director: Unite plc 2000-04, Nationwide Building Society 2017-.

Political career: *House of Lords:* Raised to the peerage as Baroness Prashar, of Runnymede in the County of Surrey 1999. Member: Joint Committee on Human Rights 2000-04, 2008-10, Privileges 2008-09; Chair, Sub-committee on Lords' Interests 2008-09; EU Sub-committee F (Home Affairs, Health and Education): Member 2012-14, Chair 2014-15; Member, European Union 2014-17; Chair, EU Home Affairs Sub-committee 2015-17; Member: Joint Committee on the Draft Parliamentary Buildings (Restoration and Renewal) Bill 2018-19, EU Internal Market Sub-committee 2019-20, EU Services Sub-committee 2020-. *Other:* Member: Arts Council of Great Britain 1979-81, 1994-97, Study Commission on the Family 1980-83, Social Security Advisory Committee 1980-83, London Food Commission 1984-90, BBC Educational Broadcasting Council 1987-89, Solicitor's Complaints Bureau 1989-90, Royal Commission on Criminal Justice 1991-93; Part-time Civil Service Commissioner 1991-96; Member, Lord Chancellor's Advisory Committee on Legal Education and Conduct 1991-97; Non-executive director: Channel 4 1992-98, Ealing, Hammersmith and Hounslow Health Authority 1993-96; Executive chairman, Parole Board of England and Wales 1997-2000; Chair: Royal Commonwealth Society 2002-08, ITV Board 2005-10, Judicial Appointments Commission 2005-10; Member, Iraq Inquiry 2009-16; British Council: Deputy chair 2012-, Acting chair 2016.

Political interests: Education, criminal justice, human rights, race relations, international affairs; Africa, Europe, India, Mauritius.

Other: Board member, Salzburg Seminar 2000-04; Member, executive committee, Child Poverty Action Group 1984-85; Trustee, Camelot Foundation 1995-2000; Management board, King's Fund 1997-2002; Trustee, Ethnic Minority Foundation 1997-2002; Tara Arts 1999-; President, Community Foundation Network 2000-; Chair, National Literacy Trust 2000-05; Trustee, BBC World Service Trust 2002-05; Wise Thoughts 2002-; Ditchley Foundation: Governor and member, Management Committee 2003, Trustee 2004-; President, UKCIS (UK Council for International Student Affairs) 2006-16; Trustee, Miriam Rothschild and John Foster Trust 2007-10; Cumberland Lodge: Trustee 2007-, Chair of trustees 2019-; Senior Fellow, Salzberg Global Seminar; Companion, Chartered Management Institute; Chancellor and Governor, De Montfort University 1998-2008; Fellow, Royal Society of Arts; Hon. Fellow, Goldsmith's College, London University; Ten honorary doctorates; Elected Master of the Bench of Inner Temple 2011; CBE 1994; PC 2009. Royal Commonwealth Society Club; Foxhills Golf Club.

Publications: Contributor to several publications on health and race relations.

Recreations: Golf, music, art, reading.

Rt Hon the Baroness Prashar CBE, House of Lords, London SW1A 0PW
Tel: 020 7219 6792 *Email:* prasharu@parliament.uk

LABOUR

PRESCOTT, LORD

PRESCOTT (Life Baron), John Leslie Prescott; cr 2010. Born 31 May 1938; Son of late John Herbert Prescott, railway controller, and late Phyllis Prescott; Married Pauline Tilston 1961 (2 sons).

Education: Ellesmere Port Secondary Modern School; Ruskin College, Oxford (DipEcon/Pol 1965); Hull University (BSc (Econ) 1968).

Non-political career: Steward, Merchant Navy 1955-63; Union official, National Union of Seamen 1968-70. TU Official, National Union of Seamen, RMT (resigned 2002).

Political career: *House of Commons:* Contested Southport 1966 general election. MP (Labour) for Kingston-upon-Hull East 1970-83, for Hull East 1983-2010; PPS to Peter Shore as Secretary of State for Trade 1974-76; Opposition Spokesperson for: Transport 1979-81, Regional Affairs and Devolution 1981-83; Member Shadow Cabinet 1983-97: Shadow Secretary of State for: Transport 1983-84, 1988-93, Employment 1984-87, 1993-94, Energy 1987-89; Deputy Prime Minister 1997-2007; Secretary of State for the Environment, Transport and the Regions 1997-2001; First Secretary of State 2001-07. *House of Lords:* Raised to the peerage as Baron Prescott, of Kingston upon Hull in the County of East Yorkshire 2010. Adviser on climate change (unpaid) to Ed Miliband as Leader of the Opposition 2015. *Other:* Deputy Leader: Labour Party 1994-2007, Labour Party National Executive Committee 1997-2007; Contested Labour Party treasurer 2010.

Political interests: Climate change; China.

Other: Member, Council of Europe 1972-75; Delegate, EEC Parliamentary 1975; Leader, Labour Party Delegation to European Parliament 1976-79; UK Delegation Parliamentary Assembly, Council of Europe: Leader 2007-19, Member 2020-, Rapporteur for the Committee on Social Affairs, Health and Sustainable Development; Hon. professor on Climate Change, Xiamen University; Hon. degree: Ningbo University, Nottingham University, Universiapolis, University in Agadir, Morocco; North of England Zoological Society Gold Medal 1999; Priyadarshni Award 2002; Political Tweeter of the Year, *PoliticsHome* awards 2012; PC 1994 (resigned July 2013).

Publications: Prezza: Pulling No Punches (2008).

Recreations: Jazz, theatre, music, aqua diving.

The Lord Prescott, House of Lords, London SW1A 0PW
Tel: 020 7219 5353 *Twitter:* @johnprescott

CONSERVATIVE

PRICE, LORD

PRICE (Life Baron), Mark Ian Price; cr 2016. Born 2 March 1961; Married Judith Bolt 1991 (2 daughters).

Education: Crewe County Grammar School for Boys; Lancaster University (BA archaeology and ancient history).

Non-political career: John Lewis 1982-1998: Graduate trainee, Store manager: High Wycombe 1992-95, Cheadle 1995-98; Waitrose: Director of retail and marketing 1998-05, Managing director 2007-16, John Lewis Partnership: Director of Development 2005-07, Deputy chairman 2013-16.

Political career: *House of Lords:* Raised to the peerage as Baron Price, of Sturminster Newton in the County of Dorset 2016. Minister of State for Trade and Investment and Government Spokesperson, Department for Business, Innovation and Skills and Foreign and Commonwealth Office 2016; Minister of State for Trade Policy and Government Spokesperson, Department for International Trade 2016-17. Member, Intergenerational Fairness and Provision 2018-19. *Other:* Channel 4: Non-executive director 2010-13, Deputy Chairman 2013-16; Non-executive member, Cabinet Office Board 2015-16; Lay member, Lancaster University Council 2018-.

Other: Chair: Prince's Countryside Fund 2010-16, Business in the Community 2011-15; Patron, Grocery Aid; Chair, Board of Trustees, Fairtrade Foundation 2018-; Member, Trade and Agriculture Commission 2020-; President, Chartered Management Institute 2020-; Honorary degree: Lancaster University, Roehampton University; Fellowship: Aberystwyth University, Marketing Society; CVO 2014.

Publications: The Great British Picnic Guide (Ebury Press, 2008); The Food Lover's Handbook (Ebury Press, 2016); The Foolish King (David Fickling Books, 2016); Fairness for All: Unlocking the Power of Employee Engagement (David Fickling Books, 2017); Workplace Fables: 145 True Life Stories (Stour Publishing, 2017).

Recreations: Writing, golf, ancient history.

The Lord Price CVO, House of Lords, London SW1A 0PW
Tel: 020 7219 4930 *Email:* dewdneyherbertl@parliament.uk Website: lordmarkprice.com
Twitter: @LORDMARKPRICE

LABOUR

PRIMAROLO, BARONESS

PRIMAROLO (Life Baroness), Dawn Primarolo; cr 2015. Born 2 May 1954; Née Gasson; Married Michael Primarolo 1972 (divorced) (1 son); married Thomas Ducat 1990.

Education: Thomas Bennett Comprehensive School, Crawley; Bristol Polytechnic (BA social science 1984).

Non-political career: Secretary 1972-73; Secretary and advice worker, Law Centre, East London; Secretary, Avon County Council 1975-78; Voluntary work 1978-81; Mature student 1981-87. Member, Unison.

Political career: *House of Commons:* MP (Labour) for Bristol South 1987-2010, for Bristol South (revised boundary) 2010-15; Opposition Spokesperson for: Health 1992-94, Treasury and Economic Affairs 1994-97; HM Treasury: Financial Secretary 1997-99, Paymaster General 1999-2007; Minister of State: for Public Health, Department of Health 2007-09, for Children, Young People and Families, Department for Children, Schools and Families 2009-10; Shadow Minister for Children 2010; Second Deputy Chairman, Ways and Means and Deputy Speaker 2010-15. Member: Public Accounts 1997-98, Panel of Chairs 2010-15. *House of Lords:* Raised to the peerage as Baroness Primarolo, of Windmill Hill in the City of Bristol 2015. Member: Financial Exclusion 2016-17, Bribery Act 2010 2018-19, European Union 2019-, EU Home Affairs Sub-committee 2019-20, Economic Affairs Finance Bill Sub-Committee 2019-20, EU Security and Justice Sub-committee 2020-. *Other:* Councillor, Avon County Council 1985-87; Chair, Remuneration Board, National Assembly for Wales 2015-.

Political interests: Education, housing, social security, health, economic policy, equal opportunities.

Other: Non-executive Director and Chair, Supervisory Board, Thompson's Solicitors London 2016-; Honorary Doctorate in Philosophy, Bristol University 2016; PC 2002; DBE 2014.

Rt Hon the Baroness Primarolo DBE, House of Lords, London SW1A 0PW
Tel: 020 7219 3000 *Email:* dawn.primarolo@parliament.uk

NON-AFFILIATED

PRIOR OF BRAMPTON, LORD

PRIOR OF BRAMPTON (Life Baron), David Gifford Leathes Prior; cr 2015. Born 3 December 1954; Son of late James Prior (MP for Lowestoft 1959-83 and Waveney 1983-87, later Lord Prior) and Lady Prior; Married Caroline Holmes 1987 (1 son 1 daughter).

Education: Charterhouse School; Pembroke College, Cambridge (MA law 1976).

Non-political career: Called to the Bar, Gray's Inn 1977; Lehman Brothers and Lazard Freres, investment banks 1977-80; Senior executive, British Steel 1980-87; Investor and manager of various industrial businesses; Adviser to the health authority of Abu Dhabi.

Political career: *House of Commons:* MP (Conservative) for North Norfolk 1997-2001. Contested North Norfolk 2001 general election. *House of Lords:* Raised to the peerage as Baron Prior of Brampton, of Swannington in the County of Norfolk 2015. Parliamentary Under-Secretary of State and Government Spokesperson, Department of Health: (NHS Productivity) 2015-16, (Health) 2016, Parliamentary Under-Secretary of State and Government Spokesperson, Department for Business, Energy and Industrial Strategy 2016-17. *Other:* Chair, Mid Norfolk Conservative Association 1995-96; Conservative Party: Vice-chairman 1998-99, Deputy chairman and chief executive 1999-2001, Resigned Party Whip October 2018, now sits as Non-affiliated. Chair: NHS Workforce Race Equality Standard Strategic Advisory Group

-2015, Norfolk and Norwich University Hospital 2002-13, Care Quality Commission 2013-15, Two free schools and an academy, University College of London Hospital Foundation Trust 2017-, NHS England 2018-.

Other: Trustee, Inspiration Trust; Senior Adviser: Lazard 2018-, Carnall Farrar 2018-.

The Lord Prior of Brampton, House of Lords, London SW1A 0PW
Tel: 020 7219 3000

LABOUR

PROSSER, BARONESS

PROSSER (Life Baroness), Margaret Theresa Prosser; cr. 2004. Born 22 August 1937; Daughter of Frederick James and Lilian James, née Barry; Divorced (1 son 2 daughters).

Education: St Philomena's Convent, Carshalton, Surrey; North East London Polytechnic (Postgraduate Diploma housing, law and social security 1977).

Non-political career: Advice centre organiser, Southwark Community Development Project 1974-77; Legal adviser, Southwark Law Project 1977-83; Transport and General Workers' Union 1983-2002: District organiser 1983-84, National women's secretary 1984-92, National organiser 1992-98, Deputy secretary-general 1998-2002; President, Trades Union Congress 1995-96; Chair: Women's National Commission 2002-07, Women and Work Commission 2004-06. Member, Unite (T&G) 1977-.

Political career: *House of Lords:* Raised to the peerage as Baroness Prosser, of Battersea in the London Borough of Wandsworth 2004. Member, Information 2005-09; Co-opted member, EU Sub-committee G (Social Policy and Consumer Affairs) 2009-10; Member EU Sub-committees: G (Social Policies and Consumer Protection) 2010-12, A (Economic and Financial Affairs) 2012-13; Member: Soft Power and the UK's Influence 2013-14, Joint Committee on Human Rights 2015-19. *Other:* National treasurer, Labour Party 1996-2001. Member: Equal Opportunities Commission 1985-92, Employment Appeal Tribunal 1994-2006, Low Pay Commission 2000-05; Deputy Chair, Equality and Human Rights Commission 2006-12.

Political interests: World of work, equalities, equal pay; Middle East, USA.

Other: Fellow, Royal Society of Arts 1996-; Director, Trade Union Fund Managers 1998-; Non-executive director, Royal Mail Holdings 2004-10; Industry and Parliament Trust: Trustee 2012-16, Deputy Chair, board of trustees 2016-17, Chair, board of trustees 2017-20, Vice-president 2020-; Director, Involvement and Participation Association 2013-19; Two honorary doctorates; Honorary degree, Open University; OBE 1997. Athenæum Club.

Recreations: Walking, cooking.

The Baroness Prosser OBE, House of Lords, London SW1A 0PW
Tel: 020 7219 3000 *Email:* prosserm@parliament.uk *Twitter:* @BaronessProsser

LIBERAL DEMOCRAT

PURVIS OF TWEED, LORD

Liberal Democrat Lords Spokesperson for International Trade

PURVIS OF TWEED (Life Baron), Jeremy Purvis; cr 2013. Born 15 January 1974; Son of George Purvis, ambulance technician, and Eileen Purvis.

Education: Berwick-upon-Tweed High School; Brunel University (BSc politics and modern history 1996).

Non-political career: Research assistant to Sir David Steel MP, House of Commons 1993; Parliamentary assistant: Liberal International 1994, ELDR Group, European Parliament 1995; Personal assistant to Sir David Steel MP (later Lord Steel of Aikwood) 1996-98; Director: GJW Scotland 1998-2001, McEwan Purvis 2001-03; Policy and strategy adviser to Willie Rennie as Leader, Scottish Liberal Democrat; Leader, Devo Plus Group 2011-13; Director, Keep Scotland Beautiful 2012.

Political career: *House of Lords:* Raised to the peerage as Baron Purvis of Tweed, of East March in the Scottish Borders 2013. Liberal Democrat: Principal Spokesperson for Energy and Climate Change 2015, Shadow Minister/Lords Spokesperson for International Trade 2016-. Member, International Relations/International Relations and Defence 2016-. *Other:* Scottish

Parliament: MSP for Tweeddale, Ettrick and Lauderdale constituency 2003-11: Scottish Liberal Democrat Spokesperson for: Finance 2003-05, Justice 2005-07; Member, Scottish Parliament Arts Advisory Group 2007-11; Scottish Liberal Democrat: Shadow Cabinet Secretary for Education and Lifelong Learning 2007-08, Shadow Minister for Children and Early Years 2007-08, Spokesperson on Economy and Finance 2008-11, Contested Midlothian South, Tweeddale and Lauderdale constituency 2011 election.

Political interests: Economy and enterprise, Europe and foreign affairs, youth policies, rural development, design and architecture, Scottish affairs, democratic governance, constitutional reform.

Other: Member, Executive Committees: Commonwealth Parliamentary Association United Kingdom 2015-17, Inter-Parliamentary Union 2016-; Member, Amnesty International; Selkirk Merchant Company; Member, Scottish Parliament Commission on Parliamentary Reform 2016-17.

Recreations: Classic cars, reading, painting.

The Lord Purvis of Tweed, House of Lords, London SW1A 0PW
Tel: 020 7219 5353 Website: www.jeremypurvis.org

LABOUR

PUTTNAM, LORD

Chair, Select Committee on Democracy and Digital Technologies

PUTTNAM (Life Baron), David Terence Puttnam; cr. 1997. Born 25 February 1941; Son of late Leonard and Marie Puttnam; Married Patricia Jones 1961 (1 son 1 daughter).

Education: Minchenden Grammar School, London; City and Guilds 1958-62.

Non-political career: Advertising 1958-68; Film production 1968-98, 2017-; Producer of films including: *Stardust*, 1974, *Bugsy Malone*, 1976 (four BAFTA Awards), *Midnight Express*, 1978 (two Academy Awards, three BAFTA Awards, Golden Globe for Best Film), *Chariots of Fire*, 1981 (four Academy Awards, three BAFTA Awards including awards for best film, Golden Globe for Best Film), *Local Hero*, 1982 (two BAFTA Awards); *The Killing Fields*, 1984 (three Academy Awards, seven nominations: eight BAFTA Awards including Best Film); *The Mission*, 1986 (Palme D'Or, Cannes, one Academy Award, seven nominations; three BAFTA Awards); *Memphis Belle*, 1990, as well as many others; Chair, Enigma Productions Ltd 1978-; Director: National Film Finance Corporation 1980-85, Anglia Television Group 1982-98; Visiting Professor, Bristol University 1984-96; Chair and chief executive officer, Columbia Pictures 1986-88; Director, Village Roadshow plc 1988-98; Adviser, Department for Children, Schools and Families 1997-2005; Visiting lecturer, London School of Economics 1997-2002; Non-executive chair, Spectrum Strategy Consultants 1999-2006; Deputy chair, Channel 4 2006-12; Chair, Futurelab 2006-11; Non-executive director, Huntsworth plc 2007-12; Deputy chair, Profero 2010-14; Senior non-executive director, Promethean World 2006-15; Hon. Fellow of the Institute of Education, University of London 2007; Chairman, Atticus Education 2012-; Director, EMPGI Ireland. Hon. Member, BECTU.

Political career: *House of Lords:* Raised to the peerage as Baron Puttnam, of Queensgate in the Royal Borough of Kensington and Chelsea 1997. Trade envoy to: Vietnam, Laos and Cambodia 2012-17, Burma 2012-16. Chair: Draft Communications Bill Joint Committee 2002, Hansard Society's Commission on the Communication of Parliamentary Democracy 2004-05; Member, Information 2005-09; Chair, Draft Climate Change Bill Joint Committee 2007; Member, Artificial Intelligence 2017-18; Chair, Democracy and Digital Technologies 2019-. *Other:* Digital Champion, Republic of Ireland 2012-17. Chair, Film, Television and Video Advisory Committee, British Council 1992-2001; Member: British Screen Advisory Council 1988-98, Arts Council Lottery Panel 1995-98; Member, Education Standards Task Force 1997-2001; Chair: British Council Arts Advisory Committee 2001-03, Hansard Commission "Parliament in the Public Eye" 2004-05.

Political interests: Education, culture, environment; Ireland, USA.

Other: Fellow, World Economic Forum, Davos, Switzerland 1997; President, Unicef UK 2002-09; National Film and Television School: Governor 1974-87, Chair 1987-96, Life President 2017; Council for the Protection of Rural England: President 1986-92, Vice-President 1997-2007; Trustee: Sundance Institute 1985-90, Tate Gallery 1985-93; Governor, American Film Institute 1986-88; Member, Tate Gallery Liverpool Advisory

Committee 1988-94; Trustee: National Aids Trust 1988-, Landscape Institute; Chair, National Memorial Arboretum Trustees 1993-2003, Vice-President, BAFTA 1993-2002; Chair, National Museum of Photography, Film and Television 1994-2003; Trustee, Science Museum 1996-2004; Governor and Visiting Professor, London School of Economics 1997-2002; Governor, London Institute 1997-2002; Vice-President, Royal Geographical Society 1997-99; Trustee and fellow, World Economic Forum 1997-2008; Member: Academic Board, Bristol University, Arts and Humanities Research Board, UK-China Forum 1998-2002; Chair: Teaching Awards Trust 1998-2008, National Endowment for Science, Technology and Arts 1998-2003, General Teaching Council 1998-2001, BAFTA Trustees 2002-04; Honorary Life Member, BECTU 1999; Trustee: Institute for Public Policy Reform, Thomson Foundation 2003-14; Chair, Sage Gateshead (North Music Trust) 2007-12; President, Film Distributors Association 2007-; Trustee: Eden Project 2009-13, Transformation Trust 2009-11, Baker Dearing Educational Trust 2010-13; Non-executive adviser, TSL Advisory Board 2010-18; Chair, A Future for Public Service Television Inquiry 2015-16; Patron, Dublin Bid World Summit on Media for Children 2020/2023; Unicef; Freedom, City of Sunderland 2007; Chancellor: Sunderland University 1998-2007, Open University 2006-14; FRGS; FRSA; FRPS; FCGI; BAFTA; National Film & Television School; Sam Spiegal Film School; Fellow: The British Film Institute, Royal Television Society; Over 50 honorary degrees, diplomas and fellowships in UK and overseas; Ten Academy awards, 25 BAFTA awards and Ten Golden Globes, and numerous other awards, including: BAFTA Michael Balcon Award for outstanding contribution to British Film Industry 1982, RSA Benjamin Franklin Award 1996, World Economic Forum Crystal Award 1997, Honorary BECTU 1998, President's Medal, Royal Photographic Society 2003, BAFTA Fellowship 2006, RSA Bicentenary Medal 2007, New Media Consortium Fellows Award (USA) 2012; CBE 1983; Chevalier de l'Ordre des Arts et des Lettres (France) 1985; Officier de l'Ordre des Arts et des Lettres (France) 1992; Kt 1995; Commander de l'Ordre des Arts et des Lettres (France) 2006. Chelsea Arts, Athenæum Club; Trustee, Sunderland AFC Foundation; MCC.

Publications: Contributor, The Third Age of Broadcasting (1982); Co-author, Rural England (1988); A Submission to the EC Think Tank on Audio-Visual Policy (1994); The Creative Imagination in 'What Needs to Change' (1996); The Undeclared War (1997); Movies and Money (1998); Members Only? Parliament in the Public Eye: Report of the Hansard Society Commission on the Communication of Parliamentary Democracy (Hansard Society, 2005); Parliament in the Public Eye 2006: Coming into Focus? (Hansard Society, 2006).

Recreations: Reading, cinema, landscape gardening.

The Lord Puttnam CBE, House of Lords, London SW1A 0PW
Tel: 020 7219 6822 *Fax:* 020 7219 5794 *Email:* puttnamd@parliament.uk
Website: www.davidputtnam.com *Twitter:* @Dputtnam

LABOUR

QUIN, BARONESS

QUIN (Life Baroness), Joyce Gwendolen Quin; cr. 2006. Born 26 November 1944; Daughter of late Basil Godfrey Quin, schoolmaster, and late Ida Quin, neé Ritson, teacher; Married (Francis) Guy MacMullen 2010.

Education: Whitley Bay Grammar School; Newcastle University (BA French 1967); London School of Economics (MSc international relations 1969); French, some Italian, German and Spanish.

Non-political career: Research officer, International Department, Labour Party HQ 1969-72; Lecturer in French, Bath University 1972-76; Tutor and lecturer in French and politics, Durham University 1976-79. Member, TGWU/Unite.

Political career: *House of Commons:* MP (Labour) for Gateshead East 1987-97, for Gateshead East and Washington West 1997-2005; Opposition Spokesperson for: Trade and Industry 1989-92, Employment 1992-93, Foreign and Commonwealth Affairs 1993-97; Minister of State: Home Office 1997-98, Foreign and Commonwealth Office 1998-99; Minister of State and Deputy Minister, Ministry of Agriculture, Fisheries and Food 1999-2001. Member, Joint Committee on House of Lords Reform 2003-05. Chair, PLP Regional Government Group 2001-05. *House of Lords:* Raised to the peerage as Baroness Quin, of Gateshead in the County of Tyne and Wear 2006. Opposition Spokesperson for Environment, Food and Rural Affairs 2010-11. Member: Constitution 2007-10, EU Sub-committee C (External Affairs) 2013-14, European Union 2013-15; EU Justice, Institutions and Consumer Protection Sub-committee:

Member 2014, Chair 2014-15; Member, Communications/Communications and Digital 2016-. *Other:* European Parliament: MEP for Tyne and Wear 1979-89. Member, Review Committee of Privy Counsellors of Anti-terrorism, Crime and Security Act 2002-05.

Political interests: European affairs, industrial policy, regional policy; Europe (including Eastern Europe).

Other: President, Northumberland Pipers Society 2009-; Chair, strategic board, Tyne and Wear Museums 2017-; Hon. Freedom, Borough of Gateshead 2006; Hon. Fellow: Sunderland Polytechnic 1986, St Mary's College, Durham University 1996; PC 1998; Officier de la Légion d'Honneur (France) 2010.

Publications: Author, The British Constitution – Continuity and Change (Northern Writers, 2010); Author (with Moira Kilkenny) Angels of the North – Notable Women of the North-East (Tyne Bridge Publishers, 2018).

Recreations: North East local history, walking, music, reading, cycling, playing Northumbrian pipes.

Rt Hon the Baroness Quin, House of Lords, London SW1A 0PW
Tel: 020 7219 4009 *Email:* quinjg@parliament.uk

LABOUR

RADICE, LORD

RADICE (Life Baron), Giles Heneage Radice; cr. 2001. Born 4 October 1936; Married Lisanne Koch 1971.

Education: Winchester College; Magdalen College, Oxford (BA history 1960); French.

Non-political career: Head of research department, General and Municipal Workers Union 1966-73. Member, GMB.

Political career: *House of Commons:* Contested Chippenham 1964 and 1966 general elections. MP (Labour) for Chester-le-Street 1 March 1973 by-election to 1983, for Durham North 1983-2001; PPS to Shirley Williams as Secretary of State for Education and Science 1978-79; Opposition Frontbench Spokesperson for: Foreign Affairs 1981, Employment 1982-83, Education 1983-87; Member, Shadow Cabinet 1983-87. Chair: Public Service 1996-97, Treasury 1997-2001. *House of Lords:* Raised to the peerage as Baron Radice, of Chester-le-Street in the County of Durham 2001. Member, European Union 2003-06; Chair, EU Sub-committee A (Economic and Financial Affairs, Trade and External Relations/Economic and Financial Affairs) 2003-06; Member EU Sub-committee C: (Foreign Affairs, Defence and Development Policy) 2010-12, (External Affairs) 2012-15.

Political interests: Economic and European affairs, Labour Party policy revision, foreign policy; France, Germany, India, Italy, Poland, Sweden.

Other: Chair: European Movement 1995-2001, Franco British Council 2002-07; Chair: British Association for Central and Eastern Europe 1997-2008, Policy Network 2007-09; Parliamentary Fellow, St Anthony's College Oxford 1994-95; Order of Merit (Germany) 1995, Légion d'Honneur (France) 2005; PC 1999.

Publications: Democratic Socialism (1965); Co-editor, More Power to People (1968); Co-author, Will Thorne (1974); The Industrial Democrats (1978); Co-author, Socialists in the Recession: a Survey of European Socialism (1986); Labour's Path to Power: the New Revisionism (1989); Offshore – Britain and the European Idea (1992); The New Germans (1995); Editor, What Needs to Change (1996); Friends and Rivals (2002); Diaries 1980-2001 (2004); The Tortoise and the Hares (2008); Trio: Blair, Brown and Mandelson (2010); Odd Couples (2015).

Recreations: Reading, tennis, gardening.

Rt Hon the Lord Radice, House of Lords, London SW1A 0PW
Tel: 020 7219 4194
Email: gh@radice.plus.com

LABOUR

RAMSAY OF CARTVALE, BARONESS

RAMSAY OF CARTVALE (Life Baroness), Meta Ramsay; cr. 1996. Born 12 July 1936; Daughter of Alexander Ramsay and Sheila, née Jackson.

Education: Hutchesons' Girls' Grammar School, Glasgow; Glasgow University (MA 1958; MEd 1961); Graduate Institute for International Affairs, Geneva 1967-68.

Non-political career: HM Diplomatic Service 1969-91: Stockholm embassy 1970-73, Helsinki embassy 1981-85, Counsellor, FCO London 1986-91; Foreign policy adviser to John Smith as Leader of the Labour Party 1992-94; Special adviser to John Cunningham as Shadow Secretary of State for Trade and Industry 1994-95. Member, GMB.

Political career: *House of Lords:* Raised to the peerage as Baroness Ramsay of Cartvale, of Langside in the City of Glasgow 1996. Government Spokesperson for: Culture, Media and Sport 1997-98, Health 1997-98, Scotland 1997-2001; Government Whip December 1997-2001; Member, Intelligence and Security Committee 1997, 2001-06; Government Spokesperson for Foreign Affairs and Europe 1998-2001; Deputy Speaker 2002-08. Member, Joint Committee on National Security Strategy 2010-14. *Other:* Member: Co-operative Party, Labour Finance and Industry Group, Labour Movement in Europe; Labour Friends of Israel. Member, Lewisham Community Health Council 1992-94.

Political interests: Foreign affairs, defence, intelligence, women's affairs, Scotland; Finland, Israel, Sweden.

Other: Member, UK delegation to: Parliamentary Assembly of Organisation for Security and Co-operation in Europe 1997, NATO Parliamentary Assembly 2003-19; Trustee, Smith Institute 1996-2008; Chair, Atlantic Council of the United Kingdom 1997, 2001-10; Member: Fabian Society, RIIA, Institute for Jewish Policy Research, 300 Group; Chair: Wyndham Deedes Trust, Kenneth Lindsay Trust; Blind Veterans UK; FRSA; Three honorary doctorates: Bradford University 1997, Glasgow University 2004, Stirling University 2009; Commander of the Order of the White Rose of Finland 2002. University Women's Club, Reform Club.

Recreations: Theatre, opera, ballet.

The Baroness Ramsay of Cartvale, House of Lords, London SW1A 0PW
Tel: 020 7219 3145 *Fax:* 020 7219 5979 *Email:* ramsaym@parliament.uk

CROSSBENCH

RAMSBOTHAM, LORD

RAMSBOTHAM (Life Baron), David John Ramsbotham; cr 2005. Born 6 November 1934; Son of late Rev John Alexander Ramsbotham, Bishop of Wakefield, and Eirian Morgan-Owen; Married Susan Dickinson 1958 (2 sons).

Education: Haileybury College, Hertford; Corpus Christi College, Cambridge (BA history 1957, MA 1971).

Non-political career: Director of International Affairs, DSL Ltd 1994-97. Army national service 1952-54; Rifle Brigade, UK and Germany 1957-62; Seconded to King's African Rifles 1962-63; Staff College 1964; Service in Far East 1965; 7 Armoured Brigade 1966-68; Royal Green Jackets, Germany 1968-71; Military assistant to Chief of the General Staff 1971-73; Commanding officer 2 Royal Green Jackets 1974-76; Commander, 39 Infantry Brigade 1978-80; Royal College of Defence Studies 1981; Director of Public Relations (Army) 1982-84; 4 Armoured Division, Germany 1976-78; Commander: 3 Armoured Division 1984-87, UK Field Army and Inspector General Territorial Army 1987-90; Adjutant General 1990-93; ADC General to HM the Queen 1990-93.

Political career: *House of Lords:* Raised to the peerage as Baron Ramsbotham, of Kensington in the Royal Borough of Kensington and Chelsea 2005. Member: Regulators 2006-07, Soft Power and the UK's Influence 2013-14, Joint Committee on National Security Strategy 2014-17. *Other:* Chair, Hillingdon Hospital NHS Trust 1994-95; Chief Inspector of Prisons for England and Wales 1995-2001.

Political interests: Penal reform, youth justice, education and employment, UN peace keeping and reform, mental health particularly in prisons, post-conflict reconstruction, including demining.

Other: Council member, International Institute of Strategic Affairs 1997-2003; Advisory board, Youth at Risk 1999-; Vice-chair, Prisoners Education Trust 2001-; Chair, Keostler Arts Trust 2001-06; President, UNLOCK (National Association of Ex-Prisoners) 2004-; Vice-chair, NAOPV (National Association of Official Prison Visitors) 2005-; Chair, Criminal Justice and Acquired Brain Injury Interest Group 2010-; Vice-president, Centre for Mental Health 2010-; President, Institute of Food, Brain and Behaviour 2015-; Honorary Liveryman: Worshipful Company of Weavers 2008-, The Skinners' Company 2008-; Fellow: City and Guilds Institute 2001, Royal Society of Arts 2001, Royal College of Speech and Language Therapists 2013; Seven honorary doctorates; Honorary bencher, Grey's Inn 2001; Honorary fellow, Corpus Christi Cambridge 2001; OBE 1971; CBE 1980; KCB 1987; GCB 1993. MCC, Beefsteak Club.

Publications: Prisongate (2003).

Recreations: Sailing, walking, arts, art history.

General the Lord Ramsbotham GCB CBE, House of Lords, London SW1A 0PW
Tel: 020 7219 8752 *Email:* ramsbothamd@parliament.uk

CONSERVATIVE

RANA, LORD

RANA (Life Baron), Diljit Singh Rana; cr. 2004. Born 20 September 1938; Son of Paras Ram Rana; Married Uma Kumari Passi 1966 (died 2002) (2 sons); married Shruti 2009 (divorced).

Education: AS High School, Khanna, Punjab, India; Punjab University (BA economics 1958); Hindi, Punjabi, Urdu.

Non-political career: Café and restaurant owner; Property developer, hotel owner, Belfast; Founder, Andras House Ltd office, hotel and retail property management company 1981; Founder and chair, Indian Business Forum 1985; President: Belfast Chamber of Trade 1991-92, Northern Ireland Chamber of Commerce 2004-06; Founder: Cordia Technologies Software Development, Europe India Chamber of Commerce; Indian Community Centre.

Political career: *House of Lords:* Raised to the peerage as Baron Rana, of Malone in the County of Antrim 2004.

Political interests: International development, global living wage, education, poverty alleviation, rural development, healthcare, human rights, non-violence, peaceful resolution of problems; India, Ireland, Mauritius, Namibia, Taiwan.

Other: Member, Confederation of British Industry; Northern Ireland Chamber of Commerce; Founder, Rana Charitable Trust 1996; Chair, Thanksgiving Square 2002-; JD Memorial Trust, India 2005-; President, Global Organisation for People of Indian Origin 2009-; Shardhanjali Trust, India; Honorary Consul: of India in Northern Ireland 2004-, of Namibia in Northern Ireland 2012-; Member, Institute of Directors; Three honorary doctorates: Ulster University 1999, Queen's University, Belfast 2003, Bengal Engineering and Science University 2009; MBE 1996; Non-resident Indian of the Year Award 2005; Samman Bharat Divas Award 2007.

Recreations: Community activities, charitable work, travel.

The Lord Rana MBE, House of Lords, London SW1A 0PW
Tel: 020 7219 3295 *Email:* ranad@parliament.uk
Andras House, 60 Great Victoria Street, Belfast BT2 7BB *Tel:* 028 9087 8787
Email: mail@andrashouse.co.uk Website: www.diljitrana.com *Twitter:* @LordRana1

CONSERVATIVE

RANDALL OF UXBRIDGE, LORD

RANDALL OF UXBRIDGE (Life Baron), Alexander John Randall; cr 2018. Born 5 August 1955; Son of late Alec Randall, company director, and late Joyce Randall, née Gore; Married Katherine Gray 1986 (2 sons 1 daughter).

Education: Merchant Taylors' School, Northwood; School of Slavonic and East European Studies, London University (BA Serbo-Croat 1979); French, Russian, Serbo-Croat.

Non-political career: Randall's of Uxbridge: Sales assistant 1973-79, Buyer 1979, Director 1980-2012, Managing director 1988-97; Tour leader, Birdquest Holidays and Limosa Holidays as specialist ornithologist 1986-97; Special adviser on environment to Theresa May as Prime Minister 2017-.

Political career: *House of Commons:* MP (Con) for Uxbridge 31 July 1997 by-election to 2010, for Uxbridge and South Ruislip 2010-15; Opposition Whip 2000-03, 2003-05; Opposition Assistant Chief Whip 2005-10; Deputy Chief Whip (Treasurer of HM Household) 2010-13. Member: Deregulation 1997-2001, Environment, Transport and Regional Affairs 1998-2000, Environment, Transport and Regional Affairs (Environment Sub-Committee) 1998-2000, Transport 2003-05, Finance and Services 2005-06, Selection 2005-07, Administration 2007-09, Members' Allowances 2009-10; Chair, Joint Committee on Security 2010-13; Member: Selection 2012-13, Joint Committee on the Draft Modern Slavery Bill 2014, Privileges 2014-15, Standards 2014-15. *House of Lords:* Raised to the peerage as Baron Randall of Uxbridge, of Uxbridge in the London Borough of Hillingdon 2018. *Other:* Uxbridge Conservative Association: Hon. Treasurer 1994, Chair 1994-97. Independent Lead, Department for Transport inquiry into Port Connectivity 2017.

Political interests: Environment, particularly biodiversity and conservation, foreign affairs; Balkans, Caucasus, Russia.

Other: Chair, Uxbridge Retailers' Association -1997; Vice-chair of Trustees, Human Trafficking Foundation 2013-; Trustee, Saracens Sports Foundation 2016-; Director, Colne Valley Park Community Interest Company 2015-17; PC 2010; Kt 2013. Oriental Club; Member: Saracens Rugby Football Club, Middlesex County Cricket Club.

Recreations: Local history, ornithology, theatre, opera, travel, music (plays piano), cricket, football, rugby.

Rt Hon the Lord Randall of Uxbridge, House of Lords, London SW1A 0PW
Tel: 020 7219 3000 *Email:* randallj@parliament.uk

LIBERAL DEMOCRAT

RANDERSON, BARONESS

Liberal Democrat Lords Spokesperson for Transport

RANDERSON (Life Baroness), Jennifer Elizabeth Randerson; cr 2011. Born 26 May 1948; Married Dr Peter Randerson 1970 (1 son 1 daughter).

Education: Wimbledon High School, London; Bedford College, London University (BA history 1969); London University Institute of Education (PGCE 1970); French, Welsh learner.

Non-political career: History, economics and politics teacher: Sydenham High School 1970-72, Spalding High School 1972-74, Llanishen High School, Cardiff 1974-76; Coleg Glan Hafren, Cardiff: Business studies lecturer 1976-, Manager 1994-99. Former branch chair and member, Association for College Management.

Political career: *House of Commons:* Contested (Liberal/All) Cardiff South and Penarth 1987 and (Liberal Democrat) Cardiff Central 1992 and 1997 general elections. *House of Lords:* Raised to the peerage as Baroness Randerson, of Roath Park in the City of Cardiff 2011. Parliamentary Under-Secretary of State and Government Spokesperson, Wales Office 2012-15; Government Spokesperson for Northern Ireland 2012-15; Liberal Democrat: Principal Spokesperson for Wales 2015, Shadow Secretary of State/Spokesperson for Transport 2015-. Member: EU Internal Market Sub-Committee 2015-19, Common Frameworks Scrutiny 2020-. Chair, Liberal Democrat Parliamentary Party Committee on Wales 2011-12. *Other:* National Assembly for Wales: AM for Cardiff Central constituency 1999-2011: Welsh Liberal Democrat: Whip 1999-2000, Spokesperson for Education (under-16) 1999-2000, Minister for Culture, Sports and Welsh Language 2000-03, Acting Deputy First Minister 2001-02, Welsh Liberal Democrat: Spokesperson for: Economic Development, Finance and Transport 2003-05, Health and

Finance/Health, Finance and Equal Opportunities 2005-07, Finance, Health and Well-being 2007-08, Shadow Minister for: Enterprise, Transport and Education 2008-09, Economy, Transport and Education 2009-10, Economy and Education 2010-11, Shadow Minister for Transport 2011. Former member: Welsh Campaigns and Candidates Committee, Federal Executive, Federal Policy Committee, Welsh Policy Committee; Contested Welsh Liberal Democrats leadership election 2008; Welsh Liberal Democrats Spokesperson for a Democratic Wales 2018-. Cardiff City Council: Councillor 1983-2000, Opposition Leader 1995-99; JP (Supplemental list).

Political interests: Transport, higher education, health, culture, devolution; Australia, Canada, Europe, France.

Other: Member: Friends of Nant Fawr, Institute of Welsh Affairs; Patron: Cardiff and Vale of Glamorgan Youth Wind Band 2010-, African Mothers' Foundation 2011-, Wales Council for Deaf People 2011-, Cardiff Centre for the Deaf 2018-; RNID, British Deaf Association, Alzheimers Society, Mencap, Kidney Wales Foundation, The Living Room; Pro-Chancellor, Cardiff University 2017-; Honorary Fellowship, Cardiff University 2011. National Liberal Club.

Recreations: Travel, concert and theatre going, walking, gardening.

The Baroness Randerson, House of Lords, London SW1A 0PW
Tel: 020 7219 2538 *Email:* randersonj@parliament.uk *Twitter:* @jennyranderson

CONSERVATIVE

RANGER, LORD

RANGER (Life Baron), Raminder Singh Ranger; cr 2019. Born 1947; Married Renu (3 daughters).

Education: Government College, Chandigarh (BA).

Non-political career: Founder and chair: Sea, Air and Land Forwarding Ltd 1987-, Sun Mark Ltd 1995-.

Political career: *House of Lords:* Raised to the peerage as Baron Ranger, of Mayfair in the City of Westminster 2019.

Other: Chair, British-Sikh Association; Trustee, Gandhi Memorial Trust; Fellow, Prince's Trust; Hon DLitt, West London University 2016; MBE 2005; CBE 2016.

Publications: From Nothing to Everything (autobiography) (Harriman House, 2014).

The Lord Ranger CBE, House of Lords, London SW1A 0PW

CROSSBENCH

RAVENSDALE, LORD

RAVENSDALE (4th Baron), Daniel Nicholas Mosley; cr 1911. Born 10 October 1982; Married Rachel 2010 (3 sons).

Education: Sheffield University (MEng aerospace engineering 2006).

Non-political career: Atkins: Graduate engineer 2006-07, CBRN Segment lead 2007-10, Lead Systems engineer 2010-11, Project director/Technical lead 2011-.

Political career: *House of Lords:* Elected hereditary peer 2019-.

The Lord Ravensdale, House of Lords, London SW1A 0PW
Tel: 020 7219 3000

CONSERVATIVE

RAWLINGS, BARONESS

RAWLINGS (Life Baroness), Patricia Elizabeth Rawlings; cr. 1994. Born 27 January 1939; Daughter of late Louis Rawlings and Mary Rawlings, née Boas de Winter; Married Sir David Wolfson 1962, now Lord Wolfson of Sunningdale (divorced 1967).

Education: Le Manoir, Lausanne, Switzerland; Oak Hall, Haslemere, Surrey; Florence University; University College, London (BA English 1979); London School of Economics (Postgraduate Diploma international relations 1983).

Non-political career: LEC Childrens Care Committee 1959-1961; Nurse, Westminster Hospital; Director: California Dress Company 1969-82, Rheims and Laurent, French Fine Art Auctioneers 1969-71, Nigel Greenwood Inc 1969-86; Member: Peace through NATO Council 1985-88, British Video Classification Council 1986-89; Special adviser to Sir David Trippier as Minister for Inner Cities, Department of the Environment 1987-88; Board member, British Association for Central and Eastern Europe 1994-2008.

Political career: *House of Commons:* Contested (Conservative) Sheffield Central 1983 and Doncaster Central 1987 general elections. *House of Lords:* Raised to the peerage as Baroness Rawlings, of Burnham Westgate in the County of Norfolk 1994. Opposition Whip 1997-98; Opposition Spokesperson for: Culture, Media and Sport 1997-98, Foreign and Commonwealth Affairs December 1998-2010, International Development December 1998-2010; Government Whip (Baroness in Waiting) 2010-12; Government Spokesperson for: Scotland 2010-12, Culture, Olympics, Media and Sport (Arts, Culture, and Media) 2010-12, Attorney General's Office 2010-12, Advocate General for Scotland 2010-12. Member: House of Lords Offices Sub-committee (Advisory Panel on Works of Art) 2000-02, Information 2013-14, Works of Art 2014-16, Built Environment 2015-16, Lord Speaker's Advisory Panel on Works of Art 2017-19, International Relations/International Relations and Defence 2019-. *Other:* European Parliament: MEP for Essex South West 1989-94, Contested Essex West and Hertfordshire East 1994 election. Extra Baroness in Waiting, Lord Chamberlain's Office 2012-.

Political interests: International affairs, culture, heritage, media; Brazil, Bulgaria, Oman, Russia.

Other: British Red Cross Society: Member 1964-, Chair, London Branch, Hon. Vice-President 1988-; Director, English Chamber Orchestra and Music Society 1980-2001; Governor, American University in Bulgaria 1991-; Member, British Council 1997-; Council member, NACF; Member: European Academy of Sciences and Arts, Advisory Council, The Prince's Youth Business Trust; Chair of Council, King's College, London 1998-2007; Trustee, Chevening Estate 2002-; Patron, Afghan Mother and Child Health Care 2002; President: British Freight Forwarders Association, NCVO 2002-07, British Antique Dealers Association 2005-12; Chairman of Governors, English College in Prague 2008-16; President, Friends of BADA 2008-; Hon. DLitt, Buckingham University; Fellow: King's College, London, University College, London; National Badge of Honour, British Red Cross 1987; Order of the Rose (Silver) (Bulgaria) 1991; Grand Official, Order of the Southern Cross (Brazil) 1997; Hon Plaquette National Assembly of Republic of Bulgaria 2007. Royal West Norfolk Golf.

Recreations: Music, art, architecture, gardening, travel, golf.

The Baroness Rawlings, House of Lords, London SW1A 0PW
Tel: 020 7219 0664 *Email:* rawlingspe@parliament.uk

LIBERAL DEMOCRAT

RAZZALL, LORD

RAZZALL (Life Baron), Edward Timothy (Tim) Razzall; cr. 1997. Born 12 June 1943; Son of Leonard Razzall and Muriel Razzall; Married Deirdre Bourke 1982 (divorced 2003) (1 son 1 daughter from previous marriage); partner Baroness Bonham-Carter of Yarnbury (qv).

Education: St Paul's School, London; Open Scholar Worcester College, Oxford (BA jurisprudence 1965); French.

Non-political career: Teaching associate, North Western University, Chicago, USA 1965-66; Frere Cholmeley Bischoff, solicitors 1966-96: Partner 1973-96, Managing Partner 1990-93; Director, Cala plc 1973-99; Chair, Abaco Investments plc 1974-90; Partner, Argonaut Associates 1995-; Director, Erinaceous Group plc 2002-09; Chair, Boxhill Technologies plc 2010-19; Director: Just Loans plc 2013-19, ZeUCrypto Network 2018-, Lawthority Ltd 2019-.

Political career: *House of Lords:* Raised to the peerage as Baron Razzall, of Mortlake in the London Borough of Richmond 1997. Liberal Democrat Spokesperson for: Trade and Industry/ Business, Enterprise and Regulatory Reform 1998-2010, Civil Service and Public Sector Reform 2015-16, Manufacturing 2016-. Member: Joint Committee on Consolidation, Etc, Bills 1998-2005, 2006-, Delegated Powers and Regulatory Reform 2007-10, Communications 2010-15, Lord Speaker's Advisory Panel on Works of Art 2019-. Chair, Liberal Democrat Parliamentary Party Committee on: Business, Innovation and Skills 2010-14, Treasury 2014-15. *Other:* Treasurer, Liberal Party 1986-87; Liberal Democrats: Treasurer 1987-2000, Member, Federal Executive Committee 1987-2010, Chair: General Election Campaign 1999-2006, Campaigns and Communications Committee 2000-06, Member, Campaigns and Communications Committee 2006-; President, Association of Liberal Democrat Councillors 1990-95. London Borough of Richmond: Councillor 1974-98, Deputy Leader 1983-96.

Political interests: Manufacturing, business, civil service; Greenland, Iceland, Sub-Saharan Africa.

Other: Member, board of director, ZeU Crypto Networks 2018-; European Lawyer of the Year 1992; CBE 1993. National Liberal, MCC, Soho House Club.

Publications: Chance Encounters: Tales from a Varied Life (autobiography) (Biteback Publishing, 2014).

Recreations: All sports.

The Lord Razzall CBE, House of Lords, London SW1A 0PW
Tel: 020 7219 5888

CONSERVATIVE

REAY, LORD

REAY (15h Lord, S), Aeneas Simon Mackay; cr. 1628; 15h Bt of Far (NS) 1627; 8th Baron Mackay van Ophemert (Netherlands) 1822. Born 20 March 1965; Son of 14th Lord and Hon Annabel Fraser; Married Mia 2010 (2 sons 1 daughter).

Education: Westminster School; Brown University, USA (BA economics 1987).

Non-political career: Associate, Salomon Brothers 1987-97; Robert Fleming, later JP Morgan 1992-2003; Principal and co-founder, Montrose Partners LLP 2003-11; Founder, Montrose Advisers LLP 2011-; Director/Corporate Finance, London Court Limited 2016-.

Political career: *House of Lords:* Elected hereditary peer 2019-.

Other: Advisory board member, ScreenHits Limited 2012-; Non-executive director, Public-i Group Ltd 2014-; Advisory board member, Orbitt 2018-; Chief of the Clan Mackay.

The Lord Reay, House of Lords, London SW1A 0PW
Tel: 020 7219 3000

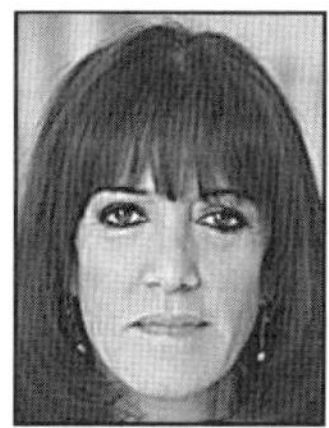

LABOUR

REBUCK, BARONESS

REBUCK (Life Baroness), Gail Ruth Rebuck; cr 2014. Born 10 February 1952; Daughter of Gordon and Mavis Rebuck; Married Philip Gould 1985 (later Lord Gould of Brookwood) (died 2011) (2 daughters).

Education: Sussex University (BA); Wharton Business School (Diploma); French, Spanish.

Non-political career: Production assistant, Grisewood & Dempsey 1975-76; Robert Nicholson Publications 1976-78: Editor, Publisher; Publisher, Hamlyn Paperbacks 1978-82; Publishing director, Century Publishing 1982-85; Publisher, Century Hutchinson 1985-89; Chair, Random Century 1989-91; Chair and Chief executive, Random House UK/Random House Group Ltd 1991-2013; Director, Penguin Random House 2013-.

Political career: *House of Lords:* Raised to the peerage as Baroness Rebuck, of Bloomsbury in the London Borough of Camden 2014. Member, Communications and Digital 2020-.

Other: Member, Creative Industries Taskforce 1997-2000; Co-founder, World Book Day 1998; Royal College of Art: Trustee 1999-2014, Chair 2015-; Non-executive director: Work Foundation 2001-08, BskyB 2002-12; Chair, Quick Reads Charity 2006-18; National Literacy Trust: Trustee 2007-14, Patron 2014-; Chair, Cheltenham Literature Festival 2013-17;

Non-executive Director: Koovs plc 2014-, Belmond Ltd 2015-19, The Guardian Media Group 2016-; Hon. Fellow, London Business School; Hon. doctorate: Sussex University, Essex University, Oxford Brookes University, Kingston University, The Open University; CBE 2000; DBE 2009.

The Baroness Rebuck DBE, House of Lords, London SW1A 0PW
Tel: 020 7219 5353 *Email:* rebuckg@parliament.uk
Penguin Random House, 20 Vauxhall Bridge Road, London SW1V 2SA *Tel:* 020 7840 8877
Email: grebuck@penguinrandomhouse.co.uk *Twitter:* @gailrebuck

LIBERAL DEMOCRAT

REDESDALE, LORD

REDESDALE (6th Baron, UK), Rupert Bertram Mitford; cr. 1902; (Life) Baron Mitford 2000. Born 18 July 1967; Son of 5th Baron; Married Helen Shipsey 1998 (2 sons 2 daughters).

Education: Highgate School, London; Newcastle University (BA archaeology 1989).

Non-political career: Chairman: Anaerobic Digestion and Biogas Association 2009-, Carbon Management Association 2012-, Energy Managers Association 2012-.

Political career: *House of Lords:* Created a life peer as Baron Mitford, of Redesdale in the County of Northumberland 2000. First entered House of Lords 1991; Liberal Democrat Spokesperson for: Overseas Development 1994-99, Northern Ireland 1999, Tourism 2000, International Development 2000-01, Defence 2001-05, Energy 2005-09, Agriculture 2006-09; Contested Lord Speaker elections 2006, 2011.

Political interests: Environment, archaeology; Qatar.

Other: York Archaelogical Trust; Council member, Institute of Advanced Motorists 1994-2010; Kids Kabin, Rainbow Trust; Fellow, Society of Antiquaries.

Recreations: Caving, climbing, skiing.

The Lord Redesdale, House of Lords, London SW1A 0PW
Tel: 020 7219 4342 *Email:* redesdaler@parliament.uk *Twitter:* @RupertRedesdale

CONSERVATIVE

REDFERN, BARONESS

REDFERN (Life Baroness), Elizabeth Marie Redfern; cr 2015. Born 25 September 1947; Married Gordon 1974 (died 2009) (2 daughters).

Education: French.

Non-political career: Former director, chemical and machinery company; Owner of a seed merchant business.

Political career: *House of Lords:* Raised to the peerage as Baroness Redfern, of the Isle of Axholme in the County of Lincolnshire 2015. Member: Long-Term Sustainability of the NHS 2016-17, Citizenship and Civic Engagement 2017-18, SLSC Sub-committee B 2018-19, Food, Poverty, Health and the Environment 2019-20, Common Frameworks Scrutiny 2020-. *Other:* Chair, Brigg and Goole Conservative Association 1997-2002. Member, Belton Parish Council 1987-2016; Councillor, Boothferry Borough Council 1992-96; North Lincolnshire Council: Councillor 1995-2019, Conservative group: Deputy Leader 1995-2006, Leader 2006-17, Deputy Council Leader 2003-06, Cabinet Member for: Adult Social Care 2003-07, Regeneration 2011-15, Devolution 2015-17; Council Leader 2006-07, 2011-17; Member, Epworth Town Council 2007-16.

Other: Director: Humberside International Airport Board 2011-17, Greater Lincolnshire Local Enterprise Partnership 2011-17; Board member, Humber University Technology College 2011-17; Chair, Humber Bridge Board 2012-14; Director, Rail North Limited 2013-17; Committee member, Epworth and District Agricultural Society; Chancellor, North Lincolnshire Children's University 2016-.

Recreations: Walking dogs, keen gardener, travel, theatre.

The Baroness Redfern, House of Lords, London SW1A 0PW
Tel: 020 7219 3000
Tel: 01427 872008 *Email:* eredfern008@btinternet.com

NON-AFFILIATED

REED OF ALLERMUIR, LORD

REED OF ALLERMUIR (Life Baron), Robert John Reed; cr 2020. Born 7 September 1956; Married Jane Mylne 1988 (2 daughters).

Education: George Watson's College; Edinburgh University (LLB); Balliol College, Oxford (DPhil).

Non-political career: Admitted Faculty of Advocates 1983; Standing Junior Counsel: Scottish Education Department 1988-89, Scottish Office Home and Health Department 1989-95; Called to the Bar, Inner Temple 1991, Bencher 2012; QC (Scot) 1995; Advocate Depute 1996-98; Senator, College of Justice in Scotland 1998-2012; Judge, Outer House of the Court of Session 1998-2008; Judge, European Court of Human Rights 1999-; Expert adviser, EU/Council of Europe Joint Initiative with Turkey 2002-04; Principal Commercial Judge 2006-08; Member, Inner House 2008-12; Supreme Court of the United Kingdom: Justice 2012-18, Deputy President 2018-20, President 2020-; Non-permanent judge, Hong Kong Court of Financial Appeal 2017-.

Political career: *House of Lords:* Raised to the peerage as Baron Reed of Allermuir, of Sundridge Park in the London Borough of Bromley 2020. Disqualified from participation as President of the Supreme Court 2020-.

Other: Chair, Franco-British Judicial Co-operation Committee 2005-12; President, EU Forum of Judges for the Environment 2006-08; Hon LLD, Glasgow University 2013; PC 2008.

Rt Hon the Lord Reed of Allermuir, House of Lords, London SW1A 0PW
Tel: 020 7219 3000

CROSSBENCH

REES OF LUDLOW, LORD

REES OF LUDLOW (Life Baron), Martin John Rees; cr 2005. Born 23 June 1942; Son of late Reginald Jackson Rees and Joan Rees, née Bett; Married Professor Caroline Humphrey (later Dame) 1986.

Education: Shrewsbury School; Trinity College, Cambridge (BA mathematics 1963; PhD 1967).

Non-political career: Research associate, California Institute of Technology, USA 1967-68, 1971; Member, Institute for Advanced Study Princeton University, USA 1969-70; Professor, Sussex University 1972-73; Cambridge University: Professor of astronomy and experimental philosophy 1973-91, Professor of cosmology and astrophysics 2002-09, Master, Trinity College 2004-12; Royal Society: Research professor 1992-2003, President 2005-10; Astronomer Royal 1995-; Visiting professor, Leicester University and Imperial College, London 2000-.

Political career: *House of Lords:* Raised to the peerage as Baron Rees of Ludlow, of Ludlow in the County of Shropshire 2005. Member: Science and Technology 2010-15, Science and Technology Sub-committee I 2012-13, EU Internal Market Sub-committee 2015-19, Risk Assessment and Risk Planning 2020-.

Political interests: Science and technology, education, developing world, energy.

Other: Trustee: British Museum 1994-2000, Institute for Advanced Studies 1996-; Kennedy Memorial Trust 1999-2004; IPPR 2000-09; National Museum of Science and Industry 2002-; Gates Cambridge Trust 2005-14; Royal Institution 2008-09; Chair of Longitude Prize Committee, Nesta; Former President: Royal Astronomical Society, British Science Association; Royal Society of Arts; City and Guild; FRS, Hon FBA Hon FAcad Med Sci; Hon FREng; Hon Fellow: Learned Society of Wales, City and Guilds, Five Cambridge University Colleges; Numerous fellowships and honorary doctorates; Hon. Member: US National Academy of Science, Russian Academy of Science, American Philosophical Society, Pontifical Academy of Science, Japan Academy and other foreign academies; Numerous UK and international awards; Templeton Prize 2011; FRS 1979; Officer Order des Artes et lettres (France) 1991; Kt 1992; OM 2007; Order of the Rising Sun – Gold and Silver Star 2015 (Japan). Athenæum Club; Oxford and Cambridge Club Hon, Walbrook Club.

Publications: Scientific and general articles, plus nine books.

Recreations: Writing, music, rural pursuits.

Professor the Lord Rees of Ludlow OM, House of Lords, London SW1A 0PW
Tel: 020 7219 5353
Trinity College, Cambridge CB2 1TQ *Tel:* 01223 338412/01223 369043
Email: mjr36@cam.ac.uk

LABOUR

REID OF CARDOWAN, LORD

REID OF CARDOWAN (Life Baron), John Reid; cr 2010. Born 8 May 1947; Son of late Thomas Reid, postman, and late Mary Reid, factory worker; Married Cathie McGowan 1969 (died 1998) (2 sons); married Carine Adler 2002.

Education: St Patrick's Senior Secondary School, Coatbridge; Stirling University (MA history 1978; PhD economic history 1987); French.

Non-political career: Insurance clerk late 1960s; Scottish research officer, Labour Party 1979-83; Adviser to Neil Kinnock MP as Leader of Labour Party 1983-85; Scottish organiser, Trade Unionists for Labour 1985-87; Hon Professor, University College London; Director, John Reid Advisory Ltd. Fellow, Armed Forces Parliamentary Scheme 1990-. Member, TGWU.

Political career: *House of Commons:* MP (Labour) for Motherwell North 1987-97, for Hamilton North and Bellshill 1997-2005, for Airdrie and Shotts 2005-10; Deputy Opposition Spokesperson for: Children 1989-90, Defence, Disarmament and Arms Control 1990-97; Shadow Deputy Secretary of State for Defence 1995-97; Minister of State (Minister for the Armed Forces), Ministry of Defence 1997-98; Minister of State (Minister for Transport), Department of the Environment, Transport and the Regions 1998-99; Secretary of State for: Scotland 1999-2001, Northern Ireland 2001-02; Minister without Portfolio and Party Chair 2002-03; Leader of the House of Commons and President of the Council 2003; Secretary of State for: Health 2003-05, Defence 2005-06, the Home Department (Home Secretary) 2006-07. Chair, Modernisation of the House of Commons 2003. *House of Lords:* Raised to the peerage as Baron Reid of Cardowan, of Stepps in Lanarkshire 2010. Member, International Relations/International Relations and Defence 2016-. *Other:* Member, Labour Party National Executive Committee 2002-03.

Political interests: Security, foreign affairs, defence, cyber.

Other: Chair, Institute for Security and Resilience Studies/Institute for Strategy, Resilience and Security, University College, London; Chair, advisory board, Shearwater Group plc; Hon doctorate, Stirling University 2009; Best Scot at Westminster 2001; Peace Person of the Year (Northern Ireland) 2002; Minister to Watch, *Spectator* 2005; Politician of the Year, *Spectator* 2006; PC 1998.

Publications: Co-author, Cyber Doctrine: Towards a framework for learning resilience (2011).

Recreations: Football, crosswords.

Rt Hon the Lord Reid of Cardowan, House of Lords, London SW1A 0PW
Tel: 020 7219 8537 *Email:* reidja@parliament.uk

CONSERVATIVE

RENFREW OF KAIMSTHORN, LORD

RENFREW OF KAIMSTHORN (Life Baron), Andrew Colin Renfrew; cr. 1991. Born 25 July 1937; Son of late Archibald and Helena Renfrew; Married Jane Margaret Ewbank 1965 (2 sons 1 daughter).

Education: St Albans School; St John's College, Cambridge (Exhibitioner, BA archaeology and anthropology 1962, MA; PhD 1965, ScD 1976); British School of Archaeology, Athens; French, Greek.

Non-political career: Sheffield University 1965-72: Lecturer in prehistory and archaeology 1965-70, Senior lecturer 1970-72, Reader 1972; Visiting lecturer, University of California 1967; Professor of archaeology, Southampton University 1972-81; Cambridge University: Disney Professor of Archaeology 1981-2004, Research director, McDonald Institute for Archaeological Research 2013; St John's College, Cambridge: Professional fellow 1981-86, Hon. fellow 2004-; Jesus College, Cambridge: Master 1986-97, Fellow 1986-2004, Honorary fellow 2004-, Emeritus fellow 2004-; Has lectured on archaeology in numerous British and American universities; Has excavated in Greece and the United Kingdom. RAF national service 1956-58 .

Political career: *House of Commons:* Contested (Conservative) Sheffield Brightside 1968 by-election. *House of Lords:* Raised to the peerage as Baron Renfrew of Kaimsthorn, of Hurlet in the District of Renfrew 1991. Chair, Library and Computing Sub-committee 1995-2003; Member: House 2003-07, Science and Technology 2017-19. *Other:* Chair, Hampshire Archaeological Committee 1974-81; Member: Ancient Monuments Board for England 1974-84, Royal Commission for Historical Monuments (England) 1977-87; Vice-president, Royal Archaeological Institute 1982-85; Member: Historical Buildings and Monuments Commission for England 1984-86, Ancient Monuments Advisory Committee 1984-2001, UK National Commission for UNESCO 1984-86; Trustee, British Museum 1991-2000; Board member, Parliamentary Office of Science and Technology (POST) 1997-98; Member, executive committee, National Art Collections Fund Committee 2001-10.

Political interests: National heritage, arts, museums and galleries, education, foreign affairs; France, Greece, USA.

Other: Foreign associate, US National Academy of Sciences 1997; Corresponding Member: Austrian Academy of Sciences 2000, German Archaeological Institute 2004; Foreign member, Russian Academy of Sciences 2006; Trustee: Society of Antiquaries of London -2017, Antiquity Trust -2017; Freedom, City of London; FSA; Hon FSA (Scotland); FBA 1980; Hon FRSE 2001; Seven honorary doctorates; Huxley Memorial Medal 1991; Fyssen Prize 1996; European Science Foundation Latsis Prize 2003; Balzan Foundation Prize 2004. Athenæum, United Oxford and Cambridge University Club.

Publications: The Emergence of Civilisation (1972); Editor The Explanation of Culture Change (1973); Before Civilisation (1973); Editor British Prehistory, a New Outline (1974); Investigations in Orkney (1979); Problems in European Prehistory (1979); An Island Polity (1982); Approaches to Social Archaeology (1984); The Prehistory of Orkney (1985); The Archaeology of Cult (1985); Archaeology and Language (1987); The Cycladic Spirit (1991); Loot, Legitimacy and Ownership: the Ethical Crisis in Archaeology (2000); Figuring It Out (2003); Prehistory, the Making of the Human Mind (2008); Collaboration with other authors on archaeological subjects, as well as contributions to archaeological journals.

Recreations: Contemporary art.

Professor the Lord Renfrew of Kaimsthorn, House of Lords, London SW1A 0PW
Tel: 020 7219 5353
McDonald Institute for Archaeological Research, Downing Street, Cambridge CB2 3ER
Tel: 01223 333521 *Email:* acr10@cam.ac.uk

LIBERAL DEMOCRAT

RENNARD, LORD

RENNARD (Life Baron), Christopher John Rennard; cr. 1999. Born 8 July 1960; Son of late Cecil and Jean Rennard; Married Ann McTegart 1989.

Education: Liverpool Blue Coat School; Liverpool University (BA politics and economics 1982).

Non-political career: Director, Rennard & McTegart Ltd 2009-; Director of Communications, British Healthcare Trades Association 2011-. Former member, GMB.

Political career: Member, Liberal Democrat Parliamentary Teams: Political and Constitutional Reform 2010-, Health 2014-, Peers Finance Committee 2016-. *House of Lords:* Raised to the peerage as Baron Rennard, of Wavertree in the County of Merseyside 1999. Liberal Democrat Spokesperson for: Communities and Local Government 2009-10, Constitutional Affairs 2009-10. Member: Information 2009-14, Constitution 2011-12, Political Polling and Digital Media 2017-18, Secondary Legislation Scrutiny 2020. *Other:* Treasurer, Liverpool Church Ward Liberals 1974–76; Secretary, Liverpool Wavertree Liberals 1976-78; Chair: Liverpool Young Liberals, Liverpool University Liberals, Liverpool University Liberal and Social Democratic Society; Deputy Chair, Liverpool Liberal Party 1978–82; Agent, Liberal Party Liverpool 1982–84; Constituency Agent, Liverpool Mossley Hill 1983; Area Agent, Liberal Party HQ East Midlands 1984-88; Election Co-ordinator, Social and Liberal Democrats 1988-89; Liberal Democrats: Director of Campaigns and Elections 1989-2003, Chief

Executive 2003-09, Overall responsibility for all party election campaigns 1989-2009, Party membership suspended 2013-14.

Political interests: Health, disability, public health, diabetes, constitutional and political reform, international democracy building, human rights.

Other: Member: Inter-Parliamentary Union, Commonwealth Parliamentary Association; Former Vice-President, Liberal International; Former Council Member, European Liberal Democrat and Reform Group; Chair: Commission on the Big Society (Association of Chief Executives of Voluntary Organisations) 2010-11, Primary Care Diabetes Society Commission on 'Keeping patients with diabetes out of hospital' 2011; Director and Trustee, Action on Smoking and Health 2011-14; Vice-president, Local Government Association 2011-13; Member and former Council Member, Electoral Reform Society; MBE 1989.

Publications: Winning Here: My Campaigning Life: Memoirs Volume 1 (Biteback Publishing, 2018).

Recreations: Cooking, wine, France.

The Lord Rennard MBE, House of Lords, London SW1A 0PW
Tel: 020 7219 6717 *Fax:* 020 7219 2458 *Email:* rennardc@parliament.uk
Website: chrisrennard.uk *Twitter:* @LordRennard

CONSERVATIVE

RIBEIRO, LORD

RIBEIRO (Life Baron), Bernard Francisco Ribeiro; cr 2010. Born 20 January 1944; Son of late Miguel and Matilda Ribeiro; Married Elisabeth Orr 1968 (1 son 3 daughters including twins).

Education: Dean Close School, Cheltenham; Middlesex Hospital Medical School, London University (MBBS, LRCP 1967).

Non-political career: Registrar, then Senior Registrar, Middlesex Hospital 1972-78; Lecturer in Urology, Ghana Medical School, Accra 1974; Consultant General Surgeon, Basildon University Hospital 1979-2008; Surgical Adviser to Expert Advisory Group on Aids (EAGA) and UK Advisory Panel for health care workers infected with blood-borne viruses (UKAP), Department of Health 1994-2003; President, Royal College of Surgeons of England 2005-08; Visiting Professor, University of North Carolina at Chapel Hill, USA 2006-07. Drum Major, Combined Cadet Force 1958-62.

Political career: *House of Lords:* Raised to the peerage as Baron Ribeiro, of Achimota in the Republic of Ghana and of Ovington in the County of Hampshire 2010. Member: Refreshment 2015-16, EU Home Affairs Sub-committee 2015-19, Long-Term Sustainability of the NHS 2016-17. *Other:* Member, Executive Committee, Association of Conservative Peers. Member, Board of Visitors, HM Prison Chelmsford 1982-92; Council Member, Dean Close School, Cheltenham 2006-; Chair, Independent Reconfiguration Panel 2012-; President, Dean Close School Council 2016-.

Political interests: Health, education, prison reform; Africa (Ghana), USA.

Other: Royal College of Surgeons: Member 1967-, Fellow 1972-, Council member 1998-2008, Member, court of examiners 1998-2004, Chairman, Quality Assurance and Inspection 2000-05, Senior vice-president 2004-05, Chair, Honours Committee 2005-13, President 2005-08; Court of Patrons 2011-; Association of Surgeons of Great Britain and Ireland: Honorary secretary 1991-96, President 1999-2000, Chair, Distinction Awards Committee 2000-04; Consultant to advisory board, Health Policy Research Institute, American College of Surgeons 2000-10; Medical vice-chair, East of England Advisory Committee on Clinical Excellence Awards 2002-05; Member, Test and Itchen Association; Chair: Research Review Panel, Pelican Foundation 2009-, CORESS (Confidential Reporting System in Surgery) 2012-, Independent Reconfiguration Panel 2012-; Member: Royal Society of Medicine, British Medical Association; Achimota Trust in London 2010-, Operation Hernia 2011-, Partnership in Health Information, Old Deacanians Society 2014-; Hon. Liveryman, Worshipful Company of Cutlers 2008-; Worshipful Company of Barbers: Middle Warden 2011-12, Upper Warden 2012-13, Master 2013-14, Deputy Master 2014-15; Freedom, City of London 1991; Honorary Fellow, American Association of Surgeons 2013-; Fellow ad hominem, Royal College of Surgeons, Edinburgh 2000; Hon. Fellow, Ghana College of Physicians and Surgeons 2006; Fellow: Royal College of Physicians 2006, Academy of Medicine of Malaysia 2006; Hon. Fellow, Caribbean College of Surgeons 2007; Hon. Member, Académie Chirurgie de Paris 2008; Hon. Fellow: Royal College of Surgeons in Ireland 2008, Royal College of Physicians and Surgeons of Glasgow 2008, American College of Surgeons 2008; Fellow, College of Anaesthetists 2008; Hon. DSc, Anglia Ruskin University 2008; Hon. DEng, Bath University 2012; Charles Saint Medal, South Africa 2007; Arthur Li Oration, Hong Kong 2007; CBE 2004; Officer, Order of the Volta 2008; Kt 2009. Surgical Sixty Club; Flyfishers' Club.

Publications: Chapters in surgical textbooks; Papers on rectal cancer and biliary manometry; Contributions to Royal College of Surgeons bulletins.

Recreations: Fishing, shooting, history of warfare.

The Lord Ribeiro CBE, House of Lords, London SW1A 0PW
Tel: 020 7219 4819 *Email:* ribeirob@parliament.uk

CROSSBENCH

RICHARDS OF HERSTMONCEUX, LORD

RICHARDS OF HERSTMONCEUX (Life Baron), David Julian Richards; cr 2014. Born 4 March 1952; Son of Colonel Jim and Pamela Richards; Married Caroline 1978 (2 daughters).

Education: Eastbourne College; University College, Cardiff (international relations 1974).

Non-political career: Commissioned into Royal Artillery 1971; Parachute and Commando trained; Chief of Staff, Berlin Infantry Brigade; Commanding Officer 3rd Regiment RHA; Instructor, Staff College, Camberley; Colonel, Army Plans, Ministry of Defence 1994-96; Commanding Officer 3rd Regiment RHA; Chief Joint Force Operations, Permanent Joint Headquarters 1998-2001; Chief of Staff, Allied Rapid Reaction Corps 2001-02; Assistant Chief of the General Staff 2002-05; Commander: Allied Rapid Reaction Corps 2005-06, International Stabilisation and Assistance Force Afghanistan 2006-07; Commander-in-Chief of UK Land Forces 2008-09; Chief of the General Staff 2009-10; Member, Defence Council 2009-13; Chief of the Defence Staff 2010-13; Senior adviser, International Institute for Strategic Studies 2013-18; Executive Chairman, Equilibrium Global 2013-; Chairman, Palliser Associates Ltd 2013-; Visiting professor, Exeter University 2013-; Director, CQS 2015-19.

Political career: *House of Lords:* Raised to the peerage as Baron Richards of Herstmonceux, of Emsworth in the County of Hampshire 2014. *Other:* DL, Hampshire 2014-.

Political interests: Defence, foreign policy; Middle East and Gulf, SW Asia, SE Asia, Africa.

Other: Deputy Grand President, Royal Commonwealth Ex-Services League; Member, European Leadership Foundation; Chair, Gurkha Welfare Trust 2007-11; Deputy grand president, Royal Commonwealth Ex-Services League 2013-; President, Military Historical Society 2014-; Vice-president, Blind Veterans UK 2014-; Governor, Ditchley Park 2014-; Member, European Leaders Network (ELN) 2014-; President, League of Remembrance 2015-; Member, Advisory Panel, Homes for Heroes 2016-; Armed Forces Muslim Association, Lt Dougie Dalzell Memorial Trust, Afghan Appeal Fund, Sierra Leone Blind Schools Association, Combined Operations Pilotage Parties Trust, Garrison Military Re-enactment Group, Military Historical Society, Plant For Peace, Care After Combat, James Myatt Trust, Combined Services Polo Association, Speakers For Schools, Tickets 4 Troops, Forces Trust, Row2Recovery, L'Orchestre du Monde, Toe In The Water, London Taxi Benevolent Association for War Disabled; Freedom, City of London 2012; Fellow: Cardiff University 2013, Kings College London 2015; Annual Churchillian Award for Leadership, Churchillian Society of the UK 2011; Tufts University Boston Global Citizenship Award 2016; CBE 2000; DSO 2001; KCB 2007; GCB 2011. Army and Navy, Cavalry and Guards Club; Royal Cruising Club; Royal Artillery Yacht Club; British Kiel Yacht Club; Royal Yacht Squadron.

Publications: Contributor: Oxford Handbook of Modern War (2012), Blair's Wars (2013); Taking Command (autobiography, 2014); Victory Among People (2011).

Recreations: Sailing, riding, military history.

General the Lord Richards of Herstmonceux GCB CBE DSO, House of Lords, London SW1A 0PW
Tel: 020 7219 5353 *Email:* richardsd@parliament.uk

CROSSBENCH

RICKETTS, LORD

Chair, EU Security and Justice Sub-committee

RICKETTS (Life Baron), Peter Forbes Ricketts; cr 2016. Born 30 September 1952; Married Suzanne Julia Horlington 1980 (1 daughter 1 son).

Education: Bishop Vesey's Grammar School, Sutton Coldfield; Pembroke College, Oxford (MA); French.

Non-political career: HM Diplomatic Service 1974-2016: UK Mission to United Nations, New York 1974, Foreign and Commonwealth Office, London (FCO) 1975-76, Third Secretary, Singapore High Commission 1976-78, UK Delegation to North Atlantic Treaty Organisation (NATO) 1978-81, FCO 1981-85: Second Secretary, Near East and North African Department 1981-83, Assistant Private Secretary to Geoffrey Howe as Foreign Secretary 1983-85; First Secretary, Washington DC embassy 1986-89, FCO 1989-94: Deputy Head, Security Policy Department 1989-91, Head, Hong Kong Department 1991-94, Counsellor, Finance and Economic, Paris embassy 1994-97, FCO 1997-2003: Deputy Political Director 1997-99, Director, International Security 1999-2000, Chair, Joint Intelligence Committee, Cabinet Office (seconded to) 2000-01, Director-General, Political 2001-03, UK Permanent Representative to NATO 2003-06, Permanent Secretary and Head of the Diplomatic Service, FCO 2006-10, Prime Minister's National Security Adviser 2010-12, Ambassador to France 2012-16; Non-executive director, Engie Paris 2016-; Strategic adviser, Lockheed Martin 2016-.

Political career: *House of Lords:* Raised to the peerage as Baron Ricketts, of Shortlands in the County of Kent 2016. Member: EU Home Affairs Sub-committee 2017-20, European Union 2018-; Chair, EU Security and Justice Sub-committee 2020-.

Political interests: Europe, France, USA.

Other: Visiting Professor, King's College London 2016-; Trustee: Royal Academy Development Trust 2016-, Leighton House Museum 2016-; Chair, Normandy Memorial Trust 2017-; Secretary for Foreign Correspondence, Royal Academy 2018-; Honorary Doctorate: Bath University, Kent University, London University; CMG 1999; KCMG 2003; GCMG 2011; GCVO 2014.

Recreations: Victorian art and literature, restoring Normandy farmhouse.

The Lord Ricketts GCMG GCVO, House of Lords, London SW1A 0PW
Tel: 020 7219 3000 *Twitter:* @LordRickettsP

CONSERVATIVE

RIDLEY, VISCOUNT

RIDLEY, (5th Viscount, UK) Matthew White Ridley; cr 1900; Baron Wensleydale; 9th Bt of Blagdon (GB) 1756. Born 7 February 1958; Son of 4th Viscount and Lady Anne Lumley; Married Anya Hurlbert 1989 (1 son 1 daughter).

Education: Eton College; Magdalen College, Oxford (BA zoology 1979; DPhil zoology 1983).

Non-political career: *The Economist* 1983-92: Science editor 1983-87, Washington correspondent 1987-90, American editor 1990-92; Columnist, *Daily Telegraph* and *Sunday Telegraph* 1993-2000; Northern Rock: Director 1994-2007, Non-executive chairman 2004-07; Director, Northern Investors 1994-2007; Founding chairman, International Centre for Life 1996-2003; Chairman, Northern 2 VCT 1999-2008; PA Holdings Ltd 1999-2008; Columnist: *Wall Street Journal*, *The Times*.

Political career: *House of Lords:* Elected hereditary peer 2013-. Member: Science and Technology 2014-17, 2019-, Artificial Intelligence 2017-18. *Other:* Vice-President, Conservatives for Britain 2015-16. DL, Northumberland.

Other: Fellow: Royal Society of Literature, Academy of Medical Sciences; Foreign honorary member, American Academy of Arts and Sciences; Hon. DCL: Buckingham University 2003, Newcastle University 2007; Hon. DSc, Cold Spring Harbor Laboratory 2006.

Publications: Warts and All: The Men Who Would be Bush (Viking, 1989); The Red Queen: The Sex and the Evolution of Human Nature (Prentice Hall & IBD, 1994); The Origins of Virtue (Viking, 1996); Genome: The Auto-biography of a Species in 23 Chapters (Fourth Estate, 1999); Nature via Nurture: Genes, Experience and What Makes us Human (Fourth Estate, 2003); Francis Crick: Discoverer of the Genetic Code (Harper Press, 2006); The Rational

Optimist: How Prosperity Evolves (Fourth Estate, 2010); The Evolution of Everything (Fourth Estate, 2015).

The Viscount Ridley, House of Lords, London SW1A 0PW
Tel: 020 7219 7763 *Email:* ridleywm@parliament.uk
Blagdon Estate Office, Seaton Burn, Newcastle NE13 6DD *Tel:* 01670 789325
Email: mwridley@gmail.com Website: www.mattridley.co.uk *Twitter:* @mattwridley

CONSERVATIVE

RISBY, LORD

RISBY (Life Baron), Richard John Grenville Spring; cr 2010. Born 24 September 1946; Son of late H J A Spring and late Marjorie Watson-Morris; Married Hon Jane Henniker-Major 1979 (divorced 1993) (1 son 1 daughter).

Education: Rondebosch, Cape Town, South Africa; University of Cape Town; Magdalene College, Cambridge (BA economics, MA); French.

Non-political career: Merrill Lynch Ltd 1971-86: Vice-President 1976-86; Deputy managing director, Hutton International Associates 1986-88; Executive director, Shearson Lehman Hutton 1988-90; Managing director, Xerox Furman Selz 1990-92.

Political career: *House of Commons:* Contested Ashton-Under-Lyne 1983 general election. MP (Conservative) for Bury St Edmunds 1992-97, for West Suffolk 1997-2010; PPS to: Sir Patrick Mayhew as Secretary of State for Northern Ireland 1994-95, Tim Eggar as Minister for Trade and Industry 1995-96, Nicholas Soames and James Arbuthnot as Ministers of State, Ministry of Defence 1996-97; Opposition Spokesperson for: Culture, Media and Sport November 1997-2000, Foreign Affairs 2000-04; Shadow Minister for the Treasury 2004-05. Member: Northern Ireland Affairs 1995-97, Health 1995-96, Deregulation 1997, Home Affairs 2006-07. *House of Lords:* Raised to the peerage as Baron Risby, of Haverhill in the County of Suffolk 2010. Trade Envoy to: Algeria 2012-, Lebanon 2019-. Member: EU External Affairs Sub-Committee 2015-19, European Union 2018-19, EU International Agreements Sub-committee 2020-. *Other:* Various offices in Westminster Conservative Association 1976-87, including CPC Chair 1990; Vice-chair: Conservative Industrial Fund 1993-96, Conservative Party (Business) 2005-10. Member, Horserace Betting Levy Board 2016-.

Political interests: Treasury, small business, foreign affairs; China, Europe, Middle East, Pacific Rim, South Africa, USA.

Other: Deputy chair, Small Business Bureau 1992-; Fellow, Industry and Parliament Trust 1994; Governor, Westminster Foundation for Democracy 2001-10; Director, British Syria Society 2005-11; Chair, British-Ukrainian Society 2007-; President, Association for Decentralised Energy 2012; Patron: *London Magazine* 2013, Open Road 2013. Boodle's Club.

Recreations: Country pursuits, tennis, swimming.

The Lord Risby, House of Lords, London SW1A 0PW
Tel: 020 7219 8996 *Email:* risbyr@parliament.uk

NON-AFFILIATED

RITCHIE OF DOWNPATRICK, BARONESS

RITCHIE OF DOWNPATRICK (Life Baroness), Margaret Mary Ritchie; cr 2019. Born 25 March 1958; Daughter of late John Ritchie and late Rose Ritchie, née Drumm; Single.

Education: St Mary's High School; Queen's University Belfast (BA geography and political science 1979); Postgraduate Qualification administrative management.

Non-political career: Assistant to Eddie McGrady MP 1987-2003.

Political career: *House of Commons:* MP (SDLP) for South Down 2010-17. Contested South Down 2017 general election; SDLP: Spokesperson for: Political Affairs 2010-15, Energy and Climate Change 2010-15, Environment, Food and Rural Affairs 2010-15, Chief Whip 2015-17. Member: Environment, Food and Rural Affairs 2012-17, Environment, Food and Rural Affairs Sub-committee 2015-16. *House of Lords:* Raised to the peerage as Baroness Ritchie of Downpatrick, of Downpatrick in the County of Down 2019. Member: Food, Poverty, Health and the Environment 2020-, Common Frameworks Scrutiny 2020-. *Other:* Member, Northern Ireland Forum 1996; MLA for South Down 2003-11, and for South Down (revised boundary)

2011-12: SDLP Spokesperson for Regional Development 2003-07, Minister for Social Development 2007-10. Social Democratic and Labour Party: Member 1980-2019, Member General Council, International Secretary -2007, Leader 2010-11. Down District Council: Councillor 1985-2009, Chair 1993-94.

Political interests: Health, environment, Europe, provision facilities for the young, economy, regional development; Belgium, France.

Other: Alternate member, EU Committee of the Regions 2005-09; President, St Patrick's Choral Society; Honorary associate member, Northern Ireland Veterinary Association 2016-.

Recreations: Walking, reading.

The Baroness Ritchie of Downpatrick, House of Lords, London SW1A 0PW
Twitter: @MRitchieSD

CONSERVATIVE

ROBATHAN, LORD

ROBATHAN (Life Baron), Andrew Robert George Robathan; cr 2015. Born 17 July 1951; Son of late Douglas Robathan and Sheena Robathan, née Gimson; Married Rachael Maunder 1991 (1 son 1 daughter).

Education: Merchant Taylors' School, Northwood; Oriel College, Oxford (BA modern history 1973, MA); RMA, Sandhurst; Army Staff College (psc 1984); French, German (colloquial).

Non-political career: BP 1991-92. Regular Army officer, Coldstream Guards and SAS 1974-89; Rejoined Army for Gulf War January-April 1991.

Political career: *House of Commons:* MP (Conservative) for Blaby 1992-2010, for South Leicestershire 2010-15; PPS to Iain Sproat as Minister of State, Department of National Heritage 1995-97; Shadow Minister for: Trade and Industry 2002-03, International Development 2003, Defence 2004-05; Opposition Deputy Chief Whip 2005-10; Ministry of Defence: Parliamentary Under-Secretary of State (Defence Personnel, Welfare and Veterans) 2010-12, Minister of State for the: Armed Forces 2012-13, Northern Ireland Office 2013-14. Member: International Development 1997-2002, 2003-04, Administration 2005-07, Selection 2006-10, Armed Forces Bill 2011, Joint Committee on Statutory Instruments 2014-15. Chair, Conservative Parliamentary Committee on Defence 1994-95; Vice-chair: Conservative Parliamentary Committee on Northern Ireland 1994-2002, Conservative Defence/Foreign Affairs Policy Committee 2001-02; Member, Executive, 1922 Committee 2001-02, 2003-04. *House of Lords:* Raised to the peerage as Baron Robathan, of Poultney in the County of Leicestershire 2015. Member: Trade Union and Party Funding 2016, EU Internal Market Sub-committee 2018-20, EU International Agreements Sub-committee 2020-. *Other:* Councillor, London Borough of Hammersmith and Fulham 1990-92.

Political interests: International development, environment, transport, defence, Northern Ireland; Africa, Indian Sub-Continent, Middle East.

Other: Chairman, Halo Trust 2003-06; Freeman, Merchant Taylors' Company; Freedom, City of London; PC 2010. Special Forces Club, Pratts Club.

Recreations: Mountain walking, skiing, wildlife, shooting.

Rt Hon the Lord Robathan, House of Lords, London SW1A 0PW
Tel: 020 7219 3550 *Email:* robathana@parliament.uk

LIBERAL DEMOCRAT

ROBERTS OF LLANDUDNO, LORD

ROBERTS OF LLANDUDNO (Life Baron), John Roger Roberts; cr. 2004. Born 23 October 1935; Son of Thomas Charles and Alice Ellen Roberts; Married Eirlys Ann 1962 (died 1995) (2 daughters 1 son).

Education: John Bright Grammar School, Llandudno; University College of North Wales (BA history, biblical history 1957); Handsworth Methodist College; Welsh.

Non-political career: Methodist Church 1959-: Superintendent minister: Llangollen 1965-70, Llandudno 1983-2002; Minister, Toronto Welsh Church 2003-04; Part-time lecturer, Llandrillo College.

Political career: *House of Commons:* Contested Conwy (Liberal) 1979, (Liberal/All) 1983, 1987, (Liberal Democrat) 1992 and 1997 general elections. *House of Lords:* Raised to the peerage as Baron Roberts of Llandudno, of Llandudno in the County of Gwynedd 2004. Liberal Democrat: Spokesperson for: International Development 2004-10, Wales 2004-10, Whip 2005-10. Member, Works of Art 2010-11, 2012-13, 2014-15. *Other:* Contested Wales 1999 European Parliament election. Chair, Union of University Liberal Societies 1956-57; Former President: Welsh Liberal Party, Welsh Liberal Democrats; Deputy President, Liberal Democrats. Group leader, Aberconwy Borough Council 1976-87; Former Vice-President, Local Government Association.

Political interests: Human rights, international affairs, Welsh affairs, child welfare, asylum seekers, migrant workers; Canada, Israel, Poland, Uganda.

Other: President, Wales International Eisteddford 2008-14; Trustee, Fund for Human Need; Patron, Bite the Ballot; Chair, Grassroutes; Director, Commonwealth Carnival of Music; Vice-President, Llangollen International Music Eisteddford.

Publications: Author, Hel Tai (Gwasg y Bwthyn, 2010).

Recreations: Music, travel, walking.

The Lord Roberts of Llandudno, House of Lords, London SW1A 0PW
Tel: 020 7219 8739 *Email:* robertsr@parliament.uk

LABOUR

ROBERTSON OF PORT ELLEN, LORD

ROBERTSON OF PORT ELLEN (Life Baron), George Islay MacNeill Robertson; cr. 1999. Born 12 April 1946; Son of late George Robertson, police inspector, and late Marion Robertson; Married Sandra Wallace 1970 (2 sons 1 daughter).

Education: Dunoon Grammar School, Argyll; Dundee University (MA economics 1968).

Non-political career: Research Assistant, Tayside Study, Economics Group 1968-69; Scottish Organiser, GMWU 1969-78; Secretary-General, North Atlantic Treaty Organisation 1999-2003; Executive Deputy Chair, Cable and Wireless plc 2004-06; Chair, Cable and Wireless International 2006-08; Senior Counsellor, Cohen Group 2004-; Non-executive Director: Weir Group plc 2004-15, The Smiths Group 2004-06; Special Adviser, BP plc 2006-; Non-executive Director, Western Ferries (Clyde) Ltd 2006-13; Deputy Chair, TNK-BP 2006-13; Senior International Adviser, Cable and Wireless Communications plc 2008-15; Senior Adviser, Chatham House 2014-. Hon. Regimental Colonel, London Scottish Regiment 2001-. Member, GMB 1965-.

Political career: *House of Commons:* MP (Labour) for Hamilton May 1978 by-election to 1997, for Hamilton South 1997 to 24 August 1999; PPS to David Ennals as Secretary of State for Social Services February-May 1979; Opposition Frontbench Spokesperson for: Scotland 1979-80, Defence 1980-81, Foreign and Commonwealth Affairs 1981-93, European and Community Affairs 1985-93; Shadow Secretary of State for Scotland 1993-97; Secretary of State for Defence 1997-99. *House of Lords:* Raised to the peerage as Baron Robertson of Port Ellen, of Islay in Argyll and Bute 1999. Secretary of State for Defence August-October 1999. Member, Risk Assessment and Risk Planning 2020-. *Other:* Chair, Scottish Labour Party 1977-78. Vice-chair, British Council 1985-94; Chair: Commission on Global Road Safety 2006-15, Commission on National Security (IPPR) 2007-09.

Political interests: Foreign affairs, defence, road safety.

Other: Fellow, Industry and Parliament Trust 1983; Joint President, Royal Institute of International Affairs 2001-11; Elder Brother, Corporation of Trinity House 2002-; Chair: John Smith Memorial Trust 2004-08, Maggies (Cancer Care) Centre, Lanarkshire Appeal 2004-; Trustee, British Forces Foundation 2004-; Patron: Glasgow Islay Association 2004-, Alzheimer's Research UK 2004-; Member, advisory board: Centre for European Reform 2004-, European Council for Foreign Affairs 2007-; Museum of Islay Life 2008-; Patron, Islay Book Festival 2008-; Governor, Ditchley Foundation 2009-20; Patron: Dunblane Centre 2010-, Disabilities Trust 2010-; Member, advisory board, International Institute for Strategic Studies 2013-; Chair, FIA Foundation 2016-; Freedom: City of Glasgow 2012, City of London 2016; Chancellor, Order of St Michael and St George 2011-; FRSA 1999; Hon FRSE 2003; Fourteen honorary doctorates from UK, Azerbaijan, Kyrgyzstan, Romania and Armenia; Hon. Professor, politics department, Stirling University 2009-; International Academy of Achievement, Golden Plate Award 2000; English Speaking Union Winston Churchill Medal of Honour 2003; Atlantic

Council of USA Distinguished International Leadership Award 2003; Parliamentarian of the Year (Jt) 2003; Licentiate, Royal Photographic Society 2010; PC 1997; Honours from Italy, Germany, Poland, Hungary, Luxembourg, Netherlands, Spain, Belgium, Portugal, Lithuania, Romania, Bulgaria, Croatia, Estonia, Ukraine, Slovakia, Latvia, Slovenia; Presidential Medal of Freedom (USA) 2003; Distinguished Service Medal, US Department of Defence 2003; Golden Medal of Freedom, Kosovo 2016; KT 2004; GCMG 2004. Army and Navy; Hamilton Rugby; Islay Golf; Dunblane New Golf.

Publications: Author, Islay and Jura: Photographs (Birlinn, 2006).

Recreations: Photography, golf, reading.

Rt Hon the Lord Robertson of Port Ellen KT GCMG, House of Lords, London SW1A 0PW
Tel: 020 7219 6235 *Email:* robertsong@parliament.uk

NON-AFFILIATED

ROCHESTER, LORD BISHOP OF

ROCHESTER (107th Bishop of), James Henry Langstaff. Born 27 June 1956; Son of Henry and Jillian Langstaff; Married Bridget Streatfeild 1977 (1 son 1 daughter).

Education: St Catherine's College, Oxford (BA philosophy, politics and economics 1977); Nottingham University (BA theology 1980); St John's College, Nottingham (Diploma pastoral studies).

Non-political career: Ordained deacon 1981; Assistant curate, St Peter, Farnborough 1981-86; Priest 1982; Vicar, St Matthew, Duddeston and St Clement, Nechells 1986-96; Rural dean, Birmingham City 1995-96; Chaplain to Bishop of Birmingham 1996-2000; Rector, Holy Trinity Sutton Coldfield 2000-04; Area Dean, Sutton Coldfield 2002-04; Bishop Suffragan of Lynn 2004-10; Bishop of Rochester 2010-; Bishop to Prisons 2013-.

Political career: *House of Lords:* Entered House of Lords 2014. *Other:* Non-executive director, Good Hope Hospital NHS Trust 2003-04; Member, East of England Regional Assembly 2006-10.

Other: Tutor, Aston Training Scheme 1987-97; Board member, FCH Housing and Care 1988-2002; Chair: Flagship Housing Group 2006-10, Housing Justice 2008-.

Rt Rev the Lord Bishop of Rochester, House of Lords, London SW1A 0PW
Tel: 020 7219 5353 *Email:* langstaffj@parliament.uk
Bishopscourt, 24 St Margaret's Street, Rochester ME1 1TS *Tel:* 01634 842721
Email: bishop.rochester@rochester.anglican.org Website: www.rochester.anglican.org
Twitter: @Jameslangstaff

CONSERVATIVE

ROCK, BARONESS

ROCK (Life Baroness), Kate Harriet Alexandra Rock; cr 2015. Born 9 October 1968; Married Caspar Rock 1999 (1 son 1 daughter).

Education: Sherborne School for Girls; Oxford Polytechnic (BA).

Non-political career: Retail and luxury brands team, College Hill 1996-2008; Conservative Party: Head of business development 2008-10, Director of business engagement 2010-15; Senior adviser, Instinctif Partners 2017-; Speaker, Speakers for Schools.

Political career: *House of Lords:* Raised to the peerage as Baroness Rock, of Stratton in the County of Dorset 2015. Member: Artificial Intelligence 2017-18, Rural Economy 2018-19, Science and Technology 2019-. *Other:* Vice-chair (business), Conservative Party 2015-16. Governor, Burlington Danes Academy 2012-.

Political interests: Business, technology, skills and education.

Other: Non-executive director and Chair, Remuneration Committee, Imagination Technologies 2014-17; Non-executive director: First News (UK) Ltd 2014-17, Wrackleford Farms Ltd 2017-, Real World Technologies 2018-, Keller Group plc 2018-; Advisory Board, Onward; Board member, Centre for Data Ethics and Innovation 2018-; Visiting Parliamentary Fellow, St Antony's College, Oxford 2017.

The Baroness Rock, House of Lords, London SW1A 0PW
Tel: 020 7219 3000

LIBERAL DEMOCRAT

RODGERS OF QUARRY BANK, LORD

RODGERS OF QUARRY BANK (Life Baron), William Thomas Rodgers; cr. 1992. Born 28 October 1928; Son of William and Gertrude Rodgers; Married Silvia Szulman 1955 (died 2006) (3 daughters).

Education: Sudley Road Council School; Quarry Bank High School, Liverpool; Magdalen College, Oxford (Open Exhibitioner, BA modern history 1951).

Non-political career: General Secretary: Fabian Society 1953-60, Publishing 1960-64, 1970-72; Director-General, Royal Institute of British Architects 1987-94; Chair, Advertising Standards Authority 1995-2000. National Service 1947-49.

Political career: *House of Commons:* Contested Bristol West 1957 by-election. MP for Stockton-on-Tees 1962-74, for Teesside, Stockton 1974-83 (Labour 1962-81, SDP 1981-83). Contested (SDP) Stockton North 1983 and (SDP/All) Milton Keynes 1987 general elections; Parliamentary Under-Secretary of State: Department of Economic Affairs 1964-67, Foreign Office 1967-68; Minister of State: Board of Trade 1968-69, HM Treasury 1969-70, Ministry of Defence 1974-76; Secretary of State for Transport 1976-79; Shadow Secretary of State for Defence 1979-80. *House of Lords:* Raised to the peerage as Baron Rodgers of Quarry Bank, of Kentish Town in the London Borough of Camden 1992. Liberal Democrat Spokesperson for Home Office Affairs 1994-97. Member: House of Lords' Offices 1998-2001, Liaison 1998-2001, Privileges 1998-2001, Procedure 1998-2001, Selection 1998-2001, House 2003-05, Constitution 2007-12, Standing Orders (Private Bills) 2013-. *Other:* Social Democratic Party: Joint founder 1981, Vice-president 1982-87; Leader, Liberal Democrat Peers 1998-2001. Borough Councillor, St Marylebone 1958-62.

Other: Leader, UK Delegation to the Council of Europe and WEU 1967-68; Hon. FRIBA; Hon. FIStructE; Honorary LLD, Liverpool University; Honorary Fellow, Liverpool John Moore University; PC 1975.

Publications: Editor, Hugh Gaitskell 1906-1963 (1964); Co-author, The People into Parliament (1966); The Politics of Change (1982); Editor, Government and Industry (1986); Fourth Among Equals (2000).

Rt Hon the Lord Rodgers of Quarry Bank, House of Lords, London SW1A 0PW
Tel: 020 7219 3607

ULSTER UNIONIST PARTY

ROGAN, LORD

ROGAN (Life Baron), Dennis Robert David Rogan; cr. 1999. Born 30 June 1942; Son of late Robert Henderson Rogan; Married Lorna Colgan 1968 (2 sons).

Education: The Wallace High School; Belfast Institute of Technology; Open University (BA economics, politics 1976).

Non-political career: Moygashel Ltd 1960-69; William Ewart & Sons Ltd 1969-72; Lamont Holdings plc 1972-78; Managing director, Dennis Rogan and Associates 1978-; Chair: Associated Processors Ltd 1985-, Events Management 2002-, Stakeholder Group 2005-; Council member, TLFCA-NI; Member, International Advisory Board, Parker Green International 2008-. Hon. Colonel, 40 (Ulster) Signal Regiment (Volunteers) 2008-.

Political career: *House of Lords:* Raised to the peerage as Baron Rogan, of Lower Iveagh in the County of Down 1999. Leader in the Lords, Ulster Unionist Party 2001-; Deputy Chairman of Committees 2017-; Deputy Speaker 2018-. *Other:* Chair: Ulster Young Unionist Council 1968-69, South Belfast Constituency Association 1992-96; Ulster Unionist Party: Chair 1996-2001, Honorary secretary 2001-04, President 2004-06, Party officer 2012-. Chair, Lisburn Unit of Management Health Board 1984-85; Member, Northern Ireland Police Fund 2001-05.

Political interests: Northern Ireland, trade and industry, defence.

Other: Member: CPA (UK) 2000-, IPU (UK) 2001-, British-Irish Parliamentary Assembly; Patron, Somme Association 1999-; Friend of the Salvation Army, Army Benevolent Fund. Ulster Reform, Belfast, Army and Navy Club.

Recreations: Rugby football, oriental carpets, gardening, shooting.

The Lord Rogan, House of Lords, London SW1A 0PW
Tel: 020 7219 8625 *Email:* rogand@parliament.uk
31 Notting Hill, Malone Road, Belfast BT9 5NS *Tel:* 028 9066 2468

LABOUR

ROGERS OF RIVERSIDE, LORD

ROGERS OF RIVERSIDE (Life Baron), Richard George Rogers; cr. 1996. Born 23 July 1933; Son of Dada Geiringer and Nino Rogers; Married Su Brumwell 1961 (3 sons); married Ruth Elias 1973 (1 son 1 son deceased).

Education: Kingswood House School, Epsom, Surrey; Downs Lodge, Sutton; St John's School, Leatherhead; Architectural Association (AA Dip 1959); Yale University (MArch, Fulbright, Edward D. Stone and Yale Scholar 1961-62); RIBA; French, Italian.

Non-political career: Team 4 1963-67; Richard & Su Rogers 1968-70; Piano + Rogers 1970-78; Visiting professor, Yale University and University College, London 1978; Chair, Richard Rogers Architects Ltd 1978- (Rogers Stirk Harbour + Partners 2006-); Gave the BBC Reith Lectures entitled 'Cities for a Small Planet' 1995; Masterplans for many city centres.

Political career: *House of Lords:* Raised to the peerage as Baron Rogers of Riverside, of Chelsea in the Royal Borough of Kensington and Chelsea 1996. *Other:* Vice-chair, Arts Council of England 1994-96; Adviser to the Mayor, Barcelona Urban Strategies Council; Greater London Authority: Mayor's Chief Adviser on Architecture and Urbanism 2000-08; Member, Mayor of London's Advisory Cabinet 2008-09; UK Business Ambassador 2008-.

Political interests: Sustainable built environment, arts, New York City; Brazil, Italy, Mexico, UK.

Other: Director, River Cafe; Member, United Nations Architects' Committee; Patron, Society of Black Architects; Membre de l'Acadamie d'Architecture 1983; Member, RIBA Council and Policy Committees 1984-87; Chair, Board of Trustees, Tate Gallery 1984-88; Honorary member, Bund Deutscher Architekten 1989; President, National Communities Resource Centre 1991-; Chair, Architecture Foundation 1991-2001; Honorary Trustee, MOMA 2001-; Chair, Urban Task Force 1997-2005; Trustee, Doctors of the world 1997-2017; United Nations World Commissions on 21st Century Urbanisations; Royal Designer for Industry, RSA 2014; Member, Barcelona Urban Strategy Council; Member, Royal Institute of British Architects; Maggie's Centres, Reprieve, Doctors of the World, Trees for Cities; Freeman of the City 2014; Hon. Fellow: Royal Academy of Art, The Hague, American Institute of Architects 1983; Royal Academician, Royal Academy of London 1984; Hon. Fellow, Tokyo Society of Architects and Building Engineers 1996; Fellow, Royal Society for the Arts 1996; Academician, International Academy of Architecture; Fellow: Royal Academy of Engineering 2005, University of Wales Institute, Wales 2007; Doctor Honoris Causa, Universidad Alfonso X El Sabio, Madrid 2008; Honorary degrees from British, Chinese, Czech and Spanish universities; International Union of Architects August Perret Prize for most outstanding international work (Centre Pompidon) 1975-78; Royal Gold Medal for Architecture 1985; American Academy and Institute of Arts and Letters, Arnold W Brunner Memorial Prize 1989; Friend of Barcelona 1997; Thomas Jefferson Memorial Foundation Medal in Architecture 1999; Japan Art Association Praemium Imperiale Award for Architecture 2000; Golden Lion for Lifetime Achievement 2006; Pritzker Architecture Prize Laureate 2007; Mario Pani Prize Mexico 2014; Senior Loeb, Harvard Graduate School of Design 2016; Honorary Fellow, The Architectural Institute of Taiwan 2017; Kt 1991; Chevalier l'Ordre National de la Légion d'Honneur (France) 1986; Officier de l'Ordre des Arts et des Lettres (France) 1995; CH 2008.

Publications: Richard Rogers + Architects (1985); A + U: Richard Rogers 1978-88 (1988); Architecture: A Modern View (1990); (jointly) A New London (1992); Richard Rogers (1995); Cities for a Small Planet (1997); Towards an Urban Renaissance (Urban Task Force, 1999); Richard Rogers, Complete Works, Vol 1 (1999); Paying for an Urban Renaissance (2000); Co-author Cities for a Small Country (2000); Richard Rogers, Complete Works, Vol 2 (2001); Delivering an Urban Renaissance (2002); Towards a Strong Urban Renaissance (2005); Richard Rogers, Architecture of the Future (2005); Richard Rogers, Complete Works, Vol 3

(2006); Richard Rogers + Architects, From the House to the City (2010); British Museum Word Conservation and Exhibitions Centre (2014); A Place For All People (2017).

Recreations: Friends, food, art, architecture, travel.

The Lord Rogers of Riverside CH, House of Lords, London SW1A 0PW
Rogers Stirk Harbour and Partners, The Leadenhall Building, 122 Leadenhall Street, London EC3V 4AB *Tel:* 020 7385 1235 *Email:* enquiries@rsh-p.com Website: www.rsh-p.com

LABOUR

ROOKER, LORD

ROOKER (Life Baron), Jeffrey William Rooker; cr. 2001. Born 5 June 1941; Son of late William Rooker and Mary Rooker; Married Angela Edwards 1972 (died 2003); married Helen Hughes 2010.

Education: Aldridge Road Secondary Modern; Handsworth Technical School; Handsworth Technical College 1957-60; Aston University (BSc production engineering 1964); Warwick University (MA industrial relations 1972).

Non-political career: Apprentice toolmaker, Kings Heath Engineering Company 1957-63; Manager, Geo Salter & Co 1964-67; Production manager, Rola Celestion Ltd 1967-70; Lecturer, Lanchester Polytechnic, Coventry 1972-74. Member: Community 2010, GMB 2016-.

Political career: *House of Commons:* MP (Labour) for Birmingham Perry Barr February 1974-2001; PPS to Peter Archer as Solicitor General 1974-77; Opposition Frontbench Spokesperson for: Social Services 1979-80, Social Security 1980-83, Treasury and Economic Affairs 1983-84, Environment 1984-88, Community Care and Social Services 1990-92, Education 1992-93; Shadow Deputy Leader of the House of Commons 1994-97; Minister of State and Deputy Minister, Ministry of Agriculture, Fisheries and Food (Minister for Food Safety) 1997-99; Minister of State, Department of Social Security 1999-2001. *House of Lords:* Raised to the peerage as Baron Rooker, of Perry Barr in the County of West Midlands 2001. Minister of State and Government Spokesperson for: Home Office 2001-02, Office of the Deputy Prime Minister 2002-05; Minister of State, Northern Ireland Office 2005-06; Government Spokesperson for Northern Ireland 2005-08; Deputy Leader of the Lords 2005-08; Minister of State and Government Spokesperson, Department for Environment, Food and Rural Affairs 2006-08. Member: Procedure 2005-07, Barnett Formula 2008-09, Joint Committee on the Draft House of Lords Reform Bill 2011-12; Chair, Joint Committee on the Draft Deregulation Bill 2013; Member: EU Energy and Environment Sub-Committee 2015-19, Charities 2016-17, SLSC Sub-committee B 2018-19, Food, Poverty, Health and the Environment 2019-20. *Other:* Birmingham Education Committee 1972-74; Council member, Institution of Production Engineers 1975-80; Lay Member of Council, Aston University 2008-10; Chair, Food Standards Agency 2009-13.

Political interests: Food, agriculture, planning, constitutional affairs, science and technology, housing, energy, fairness; New Zealand, Sweden.

Other: Chair, British Motorsport Training Trust 2011-; Fellow, Institution Engineering and Technology; Member, Institute of Management; DSc, Aston University 2001; DUniv, University of Central England 2002; Minister of the Year, *House Magazine* awards 2004; Peer of Year, Channel 4 2007; Lords Minister of the Year, *House Magazine* awards 2008; PC 1999.

Recreations: Walking, reading, motorsport (spectator).

Rt Hon the Lord Rooker, House of Lords, London SW1A 0PW
Tel: 020 7219 6469 *Email:* rookerj@parliament.uk *Twitter:* @JeffRooker

CONSERVATIVE

ROSE OF MONEWDEN, LORD

ROSE OF MONEWDEN (Life Baron), Stuart Alan Ransom Rose; cr 2014. Born 17 March 1949; Son of Harry and Margaret Rose; Married Jennifer Cook 1973 (divorced 2010) (1 daughter 1 son); Married Anna Hartropp 2019.

Education: Bootham School, York.

Non-political career: Marks & Spencer plc: Trainee 1971, Commercial director for Europe 1988-89, Chief Executive 2004-09, Chair 2009-10; Chief Executive: Burton Group 1989-97, Argos Plc 1998, Booker Plc 1998-2000, Iceland Group 2000, Arcadia Plc 2000-02; Ocado: Chair 2013-, Non-executive Director 2013-; Chair, Fat Face 2013-; Government Adviser on NHS leadership 2014.

Political career: *House of Lords:* Raised to the peerage as Baron Rose of Monewden, of Monewden in the County of Suffolk 2014.

Political interests: Business and sustainability.

Other: Non-executive Director: NSB Retail Systems plc 2000-04, Land Securities 2000-13; Chair: British Fashion Council 2003-08, Business in the Community 2004-08; Member, Advisory Committee, Bridgepoint 2010-; Non-executive Director: Woolworths Holdings 2011-18, Oasis Dental Care 2013-18 Chair, Britain Stronger in Europe 2015-16; Director, Soak & Sleep Holdings Ltd 2015-; Scar Free Foundation, Mvumi Secondary School; Hon. Degree: Leeds University, Aston University, Heriot Watt University, Suffolk University, York University; Kt 2008. Groucho Club.

The Lord Rose of Monewden, House of Lords, London SW1A 0PW
Tel: 020 7219 5353

LABOUR

ROSSER, LORD

Opposition Spokesperson for Home Office and Transport

ROSSER (Life Baron), Richard Andrew Rosser; cr. 2004. Born 5 October 1944; Son of Gordon Rosser and Kathleen Rosser, née Moon; Married Sheena Denoon 1973 (2 sons 1 daughter).

Education: St Nicholas Grammar School for Boys, Northwood; University of London (BSc (Econ) economics 1970).

Non-political career: London Transport: Clerk 1962-65, PA to operating manager (railways) 1965-66; Transport Salaried Staffs' Association: Research officer 1966-76, Finance and organising officer 1976-77, London Midland regional division secretary 1977-82, Assistant general secretary 1982-89, General secretary 1989-2004; Non-executive director, Correctional Services Board/National Offender Management Service Board 2000-09; Chair, Prison Service/ National Offender Management Service Audit Committee 2003-09. Transport Salaried Staffs' Association (TSSA) 1963-; GMB 1966-; Member, TUC general council 2000-04.

Political career: *House of Commons:* Contested (Labour) Croydon Central 1974 general election. *House of Lords:* Raised to the peerage as Baron Rosser, of Ickenham in the London Borough of Hillingdon 2004. Opposition Whip 2010-11; Opposition Spokesperson for: Home Office 2011-, Defence 2011-15, Transport 2011-. Member, Procedure 2005-09; Co-opted Member, EU Sub-committee E (Law and Institutions) 2007-10; Merits of Statutory Instruments: Member 2008-10, Chair 2009-10. Vice-chair, PLP Departmental Committee for Work and Pensions 2006-10. *Other:* Labour Party: Member, National Executive Committee 1988-98, Chair 1997-98. London Borough of Hillingdon: Councillor 1971-78, Chair, Labour Group 1975-78; JP 1978.

Political interests: Transport, employment, criminal justice system, treatment of offenders; Taiwan.

Other: Honorary Vice-president, Ryman Isthmian Football League 2008-; Vice-president, Level Playing Field 2009-; Trustee, White Rose Children's Charity -2017; Chartered member, Institute of Logistics and Transport (formerly Institute of Transport) 1967.

Recreations: Walking, reading, going to non-league football matches.

The Lord Rosser, House of Lords, London SW1A 0PW
Tel: 020 7219 4589 *Email:* rosserr@parliament.uk

CROSSBENCH

ROSSLYN, EARL OF

ROSSLYN (7th Earl of, UK), Peter St Clair-Erskine; cr. 1801; 7th Baron Loughborough (GB) 1795; 11th Bt of Alva (NS) 1666. Born 31 March 1958; Son of 6th Earl; Married Helen Watters 1982 (2 sons 2 daughters).

Education: Eton College; Bristol University (BA Hispanic and Latin American studies 1980); Cambridge University (MSt applied criminology 2002).

Non-political career: Metropolitan Police 1980-94; Thames Valley Police 1994-2000; Commander, Metropolitan Police 2000-14: Royalty and diplomatic protection department 2003-14; Master of the Household to The Prince of Wales and The Duchess of Cornwall 2014-.

Political career: *House of Lords:* First entered House of Lords 1979; Elected hereditary peer 1999-.

Other: Member, Queen's Body Guard for Scotland, Royal Company of Archers; Trustee, Dunimarle Museum; Chair of Governors, Ludgrove School; QPM 2009; CVO 2014. White's Club.

The Earl of Rosslyn CVO QPM, House of Lords, London SW1A 0PW
Tel: 020 7219 5353

CONSERVATIVE

ROTHERWICK, LORD

ROTHERWICK (3rd Baron, UK), Herbert Robin Cayzer; cr. 1939; 6th Bt of Gartmore (UK) 1904; 3rd Bt of Tylney (UK) 1924. Born 12 March 1954; Son of 2nd Baron; Married Sara Jane McAlpine 1982 (divorced 1994) (2 sons 1 daughter); married Tania Fox 2000 (1 son 1 daughter).

Education: Harrow School; RMA, Sandhurst; Royal Agricultural College, Cirencester (Diploma agriculture 1982).

Non-political career: Barings Bank 1976-78; Bristol Helicopters 1978-80; Farming and estate management 1982-. Acting Captain, The Life Guards 1973-76; Household Cavalry, Territorial 1977-83; Member, Armed Forces Parliamentary Scheme 2010-12.

Political career: *House of Lords:* First entered House of Lords 1996; Elected hereditary peer 1999-; Opposition Whip 2001-05; Opposition Spokesperson for: Education and Skills, Work and Pensions 2001-03, Environment, Food and Rural Affairs 2003-05, Transport 2004-05.

Political interests: Defence, aviation, agriculture.

Other: Member: Council of Europe 2000-01, Western European Union 2000-01; Vice-chair, Popular Flying Association 1999-2001; President, General Aviation Awareness Council; Board director, Cayzer Continuation PCC Ltd 2004-; Fellow, Industry and Parliamentary Trust 2005; Non-executive chair, Air Touring Ltd 2006-11; Director: Light Aviation Association, Cornbury Estates Company Limited, Cornbury Maintenance Company Limited; Succeeded his kinsman as 6th Bt of Gartmore 2012. White's Club.

Recreations: Flying, Conservation.

The Lord Rotherwick, House of Lords, London SW1A 0PW
Tel: 020 7219 0660
Cornbury Park, Charlbury OX7 3EH *Tel:* 01608 811276 *Email:* r@cpark.co.uk

CROSSBENCH

ROWE-BEDDOE, LORD

ROWE-BEDDOE (Life Baron), David Sydney Rowe-Beddoe; cr 2006. Born 19 December 1937; Son of late Sydney and Dolan Rowe-Beddoe, née Evans; Married Malinda Collison 1962 (divorced 1982) (3 daughters); married Madeleine Harrison 1984 (1 stepson 1 stepdaughter).

Education: Cathedral School, Llandaff; Stowe School, Buckinghamshire; St John's College, Cambridge (BA economics/law 1961, MA); Graduate School of Business Administration, Harvard University (PMD 1974); French, Spanish.

Non-political career: Thomas De la Rue & Co 1961-76: Chief executive 1971-76, Executive director, De la Rue Co plc 1974-76; Revlon Inc 1976-81: President, Latin America and Caribbean 1976-77, President, Europe, Middle East and Africa 1977-81; President: GFTA Trendanalysen 1981-87, Morgan Stanley-GFTA Ltd 1983-91; Chair: Cavendish Services Ltd 1987-93, EHC International Ltd 2001-13; Deputy chair, Toye & Company plc 2002-14; Director: Mitel (Canada) 2002-06, Newport Networks Group plc 2004-09; Chair: GFTA – Euro/Dollar Technology Co Ltd 2005-14, Cardiff Wales Airport 2013-16. Sub-lieutenant, Royal Navy national service 1956-58; Lieutenant, Royal Naval Reserve 1958-66.

Political career: *House of Lords:* Raised to the peerage as Baron Rowe-Beddoe, of Kilgetty in the County of Dyfed 2006. Co-opted member, EU Sub-committee B (Internal Market) 2007-10; Member: Barnett Formula 2008-09, Administration and Works 2009-14, EU Sub-committee B (Internal Market, Energy and Transport) 2010-12, Economic Affairs 2012-15, Economic Affairs Finance Bill Sub-committee 2012-15, 2019-, Procedure 2015-19, Joint Committee on Statutory Instruments 2016-, Citizenship and Civic Engagement 2017-18. *Other:* Chairman: Welsh Development Agency 1993-2001, Development Board for Rural Wales 1994-98; Wales Millennium Centre: Chairman 2001-10, Life President 2010-; Chairman, Representative Body of the Church in Wales 2002-13; Member, Governing Body, Church in Wales 2002-13; DL, Gwent 2003-; President, Royal Welsh College of Music and Drama 2004-; Deputy Chairman, UK Statistics Authority 2008-12; Chair, Office of National Statistics 2008-12.

Political interests: Arts and heritage, management, university, armed forces, faith and society; Argentina, Brazil, Central America, China, Mexico, North Korea, South America, UAE.

Other: Commonwealth Parliamentary Association; Inter-Parliamentary Union; President, British-Australia Society (Wales Branch); FRSA; Fellow, Institute of Welsh Affairs; Prince of Wales Trust, Church in Wales; Freedom, City of London; Pro-chancellor, University of South Wales 2007-; Honorary doctorates: University of Wales, University of Glamorgan/University of South Wales; Fellow: Cardiff University, Aberystwyth University, Newport University, Cardiff Metropolitan University; Beacon Prize 2004; Lifetime Achievement Award, *Western Mail* 2005; Achievement Award, Worshipful Livery Company of Wales 2009; Kt 2000; Order of the Rising Sun, Gold Rays with Neck Ribbon (Japan) 2008. Garrick, Cardiff and County, Brook Club (New York).

Recreations: Music, theatre, country pursuits.

The Lord Rowe-Beddoe DL, House of Lords, London SW1A 0PW
Tel: 020 7219 6255
Royal Welsh College of Music and Drama, Castle Grounds, Cathays Park, Cardiff CF10 3ER
Tel: 029 2039 1344 *Email:* david@rbinternet.com

LABOUR

ROWLANDS, LORD

ROWLANDS (Life Baron), Edward (Ted) Rowlands; cr. 2004. Born 23 January 1940; Son of William Samuel Rowlands, Clerk of Works; Married Janice Williams 1968 (died 2004) (2 sons 1 daughter).

Education: Rhondda Grammar School; Wirral Grammar, Cheshire; King's College, London (BA history 1962).

Non-political career: Research student 1962; Research assistant, History of Parliament Trust 1963-65; Lecturer: Modern history and government, Welsh College of Advanced Technology 1965-66, Law Department, London School of Economics 1972-74. Member: Association of University Teachers 1965-72, ASTMS 1972-2001.

Political career: *House of Commons:* MP (Labour) for Cardiff North 1966-70, for Merthyr Tydfil 13 April 1972 by-election to 1983, for Merthyr Tydfil and Rhymney 1983-2001; Parliamentary Under-Secretary of State (PUS), Welsh Office 1969-70, 1974-75; Foreign and

Commonwealth Office 1975-79: PUS 1975-76, Minister of State 1976-79; Opposition Frontbench Spokesperson for: Foreign and Commonwealth Affairs 1979-80, Energy 1981-87. Member, Foreign Affairs 1987-2001; Former chair, Quadripartite Committee. *House of Lords:* Raised to the peerage as Baron Rowlands, of Merthyr Tydfil and Rhymney in the county of Mid Glamorgan 2004. Member: Constitution 2005-09, EU Sub-committee E: (Justice and Institutions) 2010-12, (Justice, Institutions and Consumer Protection) 2012-14, Extradition Law 2014-15, Joint Committee on Statutory Instruments 2015-19, Secondary Legislation Scrutiny 2016-17, Delegated Powers and Regulatory Reform 2017-, EU Justice Sub-committee 2019-20, EU Security and Justice Sub-committee 2020-. *Other:* Member, Richard Commission 2003-04.

Political interests: International energy, constitution; Botswana, South Africa, former Soviet Eastern Europe.

Other: Fellow, Industry and Parliament Trust 1982; Judge, Booker McConnel Novel of the Year Competition 1984; Council member, Winston Churchill Memorial Trust 1989-2010; History of Parliamentary Trust: Chair 1993-2001, Trustee; President, National Training Federation for Wales; WaterAid; Freedom, Merthyr County Borough; Honorary degree, Glamorgan University; CBE 2003.

Publications: 'Something Must be Done' South Wales v Whitehall 1921-1951; Robert Harley and the Battle for Power in Radnorshire 1690-1693 (Welsh History Review, 1990); A Golden Age – Peer Power in the Early Eighteenth Century (2008); Revolution and Reform (2019).

Recreations: Gardening, golf.

The Lord Rowlands CBE, House of Lords, London SW1A 0PW
Tel: 020 7219 3842

ROYALL OF BLAISDON, BARONESS

LABOUR/ CO-OPERATIVE

ROYALL OF BLAISDON (Life Baroness), Janet Anne Royall; cr. 2004. Born 20 August 1955; Daughter of Basil and Myra Royall; Married Stuart Hercock 1980 (died 2010) (1 daughter 2 sons).

Education: Royal Forest of Dean Grammar School; Westfield College, London University (BA Spanish and French 1977); French, Spanish, some Italian.

Non-political career: Continental Farms (Europe) Ltd 1978; Secretary-General, British Labour Group, European Parliament 1979-85; Policy adviser/PA to Neil Kinnock MP as Leader of the Opposition 1986-92; Researcher/Press officer to Neil Kinnock MP 1992-95; Member, Cabinet of Neil Kinnock as: European Commissioner for Transport 1995-99, Vice-president of the Commission 1999-2001; Parliamentary co-ordinator, Press and communications directorate-general, European Commission 2001-03; Head of European Commission Office in Wales 2003-04; Visiting Professor, Institute of Global Health Innovation, Imperial College, London 2016-; Principal, Somerville College, Oxford 2017-. Member, USDAW.

Political career: *House of Lords:* Raised to the peerage as Baroness Royall of Blaisdon, of Blaisdon in the County of Gloucestershire 2004. Government Spokesperson for: Health 2005-08, International Development 2005-08, Foreign and Commonwealth Office 2005-08; Government Whip 2005-08; Chief Whip 2008; Leader of the House of Lords 2008-10; Lord President of the Council 2008-09; Government Spokesperson for: Equality 2008-10, Northern Ireland 2008-10, Cabinet Office 2009-10; Chancellor of the Duchy of Lancaster 2009-10; Shadow Leader of the House of Lords 2010-15; Opposition Spokesperson for: Cabinet Office 2010-12, Education 2010, Northern Ireland 2010-11, Work and Pensions 2010, Equalities Office 2010-12, International Development 2012-13. Member: Merits of Statutory Instruments 2005, Administration and Works 2008, Privileges/Privileges and Conduct 2008-15, Procedure 2008-15, Liaison 2008-15, House 2008-15, Selection 2008-15. *Other:* Member, Politics – Better Politics Policy Commission.

Political interests: Foreign policy, development, carers, democratic engagement, penal affairs, youth policies; Central and Latin America, Australia, Balkans, European Union, India, New Zealand, South Africa, USA.

Other: Vice-president, Party of European Socialists 2012-; Former Patron, Kidney Wales Foundation; Former President, Autism Cymru; Former Trustee: IPPR, National Botanic Garden of Wales, Generation Europe, Forest of Dean Crossroads, Better Learning Together – Our Co-operative Trust; Patron, ASHA Centre; Trustee: Paladin 2014-18, City Year UK

2015-18; Chair: DRIVE, People's History Museum 2016-; Member Advisory Council, Step up to Serve; Chair: Centre for Opposition Studies 2018-, Oxford Strategic Partnership 2018-; Pro-chancellor, Bath University 2014-17; *The House Magazine* Peer of the Year, Dods Parliamentary Awards 2014; PC 2008.

Recreations: Reading, travel, gardening, swimming.

Rt Hon the Baroness Royall of Blaisdon, House of Lords, London SW1A 0PW
Tel: 020 7219 1435 *Email:* royallj@parliament.uk
Somerville College, Woodstock Road, Oxford OX2 6HD *Twitter:* @LabourRoyall

CROSSBENCH

RUSSELL OF LIVERPOOL, LORD

RUSSELL OF LIVERPOOL (3rd Baron, UK), Simon Gordon Jared Russell; cr 1919. Born 30 August 1952; Son of late Captain Hon Langley Gordon Haslingden Russell; Married Dr Gilda Albano 1984 (2 sons 1 daughter).

Education: Charterhouse; Trinity College, Cambridge (BA history 1982); INSEAD, Fontainebleau, France (MBA 1982); Italian, French.

Non-political career: Spencer Stuart Management Consultants NV: Senior Adviser 2017-19, Senior Director 1994-2017; Consultant, Corporate Consulting Group 1986-94.

Political career: *House of Lords:* First entered House of Lords 1982; Left House of Lords 1999; Elected hereditary peer 2014-; Deputy Chairman of Committees 2020-. Member: EU Internal Market Sub-committee 2018-20, EU Goods Sub-committee 2020-.

Political interests: Asylum, immigration and nationality, children and young people, education, human rights; European Union.

Other: Substitute Member, UK Delegation to Parliamentary Assembly of Council of Europe 2017-; Coram: Trustee 2009-17, Governor 2017-; Chair: Coram Life Education 2009-17, Life Education Centres UK 1994-2009; Trustee: Perseverance Trust 2011-17, Baldwin Bewdley Trust 2000-, Robin Howard Foundation 1992-2011; Liveryman, Fishmongers' Company; Freedom, City of London. Brooks's Club.

The Lord Russell of Liverpool, House of Lords, London SW1A 0PW
Tel: 020 7219 5353

CONSERVATIVE

RYDER OF WENSUM, LORD

RYDER OF WENSUM (Life Baron), Richard Ryder; cr. 1997. Born 4 February 1949; Son of Stephen Ryder, JP, DL, farmer; Married Caroline Stephens (later CVO MBE) 1981 (1 daughter 1 son deceased).

Education: Radley College; Magdalene College, Cambridge (BA history 1971).

Non-political career: Former journalist; Director of family businesses in Suffolk; Political Secretary to Margaret Thatcher as Leader of the Opposition and Prime Minister 1975-81; Founding chair, Eastern Counties Radio 1997-2001; Chair: Institute of Cancer Research 2005-13, UCanDoIt 2011-14, Child Bereavement UK 2013-.

Political career: *House of Commons:* Contested Gateshead East February and October 1974 general elections. MP (Conservative) for Norfolk Mid 1983-97; PPS to: John Moore as Financial Secretary to the Treasury 1984, Geoffrey Howe as Foreign Secretary 1984-86; Government Whip 1986-88; Parliamentary Secretary, Ministry of Agriculture, Fisheries and Food 1988-89; HM Treasury: Economic Secretary 1989-90, Paymaster General July-November 1990; Government Chief Whip 1990-95. *House of Lords:* Raised to the peerage as Baron Ryder of Wensum, of Wensum in the County of Norfolk 1997. Co-opted Member, EU Sub-committee B (Internal Market) 2008-10; Member, EU Sub-committee B (Internal Market, Energy and Transport) 2010-12. *Other:* Chairman, Conservative Foreign and Commonwealth Council 1984-89. BBC Governors: Vice-chair 2002-04, Acting chair 2004-05.

Other: OBE 1981; PC 1990.

Rt Hon the Lord Ryder of Wensum OBE, House of Lords, London SW1A 0PW
Tel: 020 7219 5353

CONSERVATIVE

SAATCHI, LORD

SAATCHI (Life Baron), Maurice Saatchi; cr. 1996. Born 21 June 1946; Son of Nathan and Daisy Saatchi; Married Josephine Hart 1984 (died 2011) (1 son 1 stepson).

Education: Tollington Grammar School, Muswell Hill, London; London School of Economics (BSc economics 1967); French.

Non-political career: Co-founder, Saatchi & Saatchi 1970; Partner, M & C Saatchi 1995-.

Political career: *House of Lords:* Raised to the peerage as Baron Saatchi, of Staplefield in the County of West Sussex 1996. Opposition Spokesperson for: Treasury 1999-2003, Cabinet Office 2001-03. *Other:* Co-chair, Conservative Party 2003-05. Governor, London School of Economics 1985-.

Political interests: UK.

Other: Director, Museum of Garden History; Centre for Policy Studies: Director 1999-, Chair 2009-.

Publications: The War of Independence (1999); Happiness Can't Buy Money (1999); The Bad Samaritan (2000); The Science of Politics (2001); Poor People! Stop Paying Tax! (2001); If this is Conservatism, I am a Conservative (2005); In Praise of Ideology (2007); Enemy of the People (2008); The Myth of Inflation Targeting (2009).

The Lord Saatchi, House of Lords, London SW1A 0PW
Tel: 020 7219 5353
M & C Saatchi plc, 36 Golden Square, London W1F 9EE *Tel:* 020 7543 4510
Email: maurices@mcsaatchi.com

CONSERVATIVE

SAINSBURY OF PRESTON CANDOVER, LORD

SAINSBURY OF PRESTON CANDOVER (Life Baron), John Davan Sainsbury; cr. 1989. Born 2 November 1927; Son of late Lord Sainsbury (Life Peer); Married Anya Eltenton 1963 (2 sons 1 daughter).

Education: Stowe School, Buckinghamshire; Worcester College, Oxford (BA history).

Non-political career: Joined J. Sainsbury in buying departments 1950: Director 1958-92, Vice-chair 1967-69, Chair and chief executive 1969-92, President 1992-; Director, *The Economist* 1972-80. Served Life Guards 1945-48.

Political career: *House of Lords:* Raised to the peerage as Baron Sainsbury of Preston Candover, of Preston Candover in the County of Hampshire 1989. On leave of absence 2010-. Member, Joint Parliamentary Scrutiny Committee on Draft Charities Bill 2004-05. *Other:* Member, National Committee for Electoral Reform 1976-85.

Political interests: Commerce, arts.

Other: Governor, Royal Ballet School 1965-76, 1987-91; Contemporary Arts Society: Honorary secretary 1965-71, Vice-chair 1971-74, Vice-President 1984-96, Vice-Patron 1998-2006; Royal Opera House, Covent Garden: Director 1969-85, Chair 1987-91, Hon. Vice-President 2009-; Chair, Council of Friends of Covent Garden 1969-81; Joint Hon. Treasurer, European Movement 1972-75; Director, Royal Opera House Trust 1974-84, 1987-97; Trustee: National Gallery 1976-83, Westminster Abbey Trust 1977-83; President's Committee, CBI 1982-84; Trustee: Tate Gallery 1982-83, Rhodes Trust 1984-98; Honorary Bencher, Inner Temple 1985; Chair, Benesh Institute of Choreology 1986-87; Royal Ballet: Governor 1987-2003, Chair of governors 1995-2003; President, Sparsholt College, Hampshire 1993-2000; Dulwich Picture Gallery: Chair of trustees 1994-2000, Patron 2004-; Director, Friends of the Nelson Mandela Children's Fund 1996-2000; Chair of trustees, Royal Opera House Endowment Fund 2001-05; Rambert School, chairman: Development committee 2002-03, Steering committee 2005-09; Visitor, Ashmolean Museum 2003-; Trustee, Saïd Business School Foundation 2003; Director, Rambert School of Ballet and Contemporary Dance 2003-05; Patron, Sir Harold Hillier Gardens and Arboretum 2005-; Chairman, Rambert School Trust 2005-10; Director, Centre for Policy Studies 2009-12; British Retail Consortium: Council member 1975-79, President 1993-97; Fellow, Institute of Grocery Distribution 1973-;

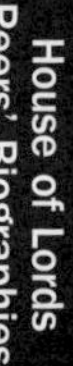

Hon. FRIBA 1993; Hon. Fellow, Worcester College, Oxford 1982; Hon. DSc, Economics (London) 1985; Hon. DLitt, South Bank University 1992; Hon. LLD, Bristol University 1993; Hon. D.EconSc, Cape Town 2000; Hon. Fellow, British School at Rome 2002; Albert Medal, Royal Society of Arts 1989; Hadrian Award 2000; Prince of Wales Medal for Arts Philanthropy 2008; Sheldon Medal, Oxford University 2010; The Gjergi Kastrioti-Skenderbeg Presidential Award 2014; Kt 1980; KG 1992. Garrick, Beefsteak Club.

The Lord Sainsbury of Preston Candover KG, House of Lords, London SW1A 0PW
Tel: 020 7219 5353
Tel: 020 7695 6663 *Email:* ginny.key@sainsburys.co.uk

LABOUR

SAINSBURY OF TURVILLE, LORD

SAINSBURY OF TURVILLE (Life Baron), David John Sainsbury; cr 1997. Born 24 October 1940; Son of late Sir Robert and Lady Lisa Sainsbury; Married Susan Reid 1973 (3 daughters).

Education: Eton College; King's College, Cambridge (BA history and psychology 1963); Columbia University, New York (MBA 1971).

Non-political career: Joined J. Sainsbury plc 1963: Finance director 1973-90, Deputy chair 1988-92, Chief executive 1992-97, Chair 1992-98; Visiting Fellow, Nuffield College, Oxford 1987-95.

Political career: *House of Lords:* Raised to the peerage as Baron Sainsbury of Turville, of Turville in the County of Buckinghamshire 1997. Parliamentary Under-Secretary of State and Government Spokesperson, Department of Trade and Industry (Minister for Science and Innovation) 1998-2006; On leave of absence July 2013-. *Other:* Trustee, Social Democratic Party 1982-90. Member, Committee of Review of Post Office (Carter Committee) 1975-77; London Business School: Member, governing body 1985-, Chair 1991-98.

Political interests: Science and innovation, policy, industry and education; Africa, China, India, USA.

Other: Settlor Gatsby Charitable Foundation; Chair, Institute for Government 2009-; Chancellor, Cambridge University 2011-; Honorary doctorate from Universities of Cambridge, Oxford and Manchester, and Imperial College; Hon. Fellowship, London Business School 1990; Hon. FREng 1994; Hon. FRS 2008; Hon. Fellow, Academy of Medical Sciences 2008; Andrew Carnegie Medal of Philanthropy (on behalf of Sainsbury Family) 2003.

Publications: Government and Industry: a new partnership (1981); Co-author, Wealth Creation and Jobs (1987); The Race to the Top – report for the Government on its science and innovation policies (2007); Progressive Capitalism: How to Achieve Economic Growth, Liberty and Social Justice (2013).

The Lord Sainsbury of Turville, House of Lords, London SW1A 0PW
Tel: 020 7219 5353

NON-AFFILIATED

ST ALBANS, LORD BISHOP OF

ST ALBANS (10th Bishop of), Alan Gregory Clayton Smith. Born 14 February 1957; Son of Frank Smith and Rosemary Smith.

Education: Trowbridge Grammar School for Boys; John of Gaunt School; Birmingham University (BA 1978; MA 1979); University of Wales, Bangor (PhD 2002).

Non-political career: Curate, Pudsey St Lawrence 1981-84; Chaplain, Lee Abbey Community 1984-90; Team vicar, St Matthew's, Walsall 1990-97; Diocesan Missioner 1990-97; Archdeacon, Stoke-on-Trent 1997-2001; Honorary canon, Lichfield Cathedral 1997-2001; Area Bishop, Shrewsbury 2001-09; Bishop of St Albans 2009-.

Political career: *House of Lords:* Entered House of Lords 2013. Member, Social and Economic Impact of the Gambling Industry 2019-. *Other:* Member, General Synod 1999-2001, 2009-; Vice-President, Local Government Association 2018-.

Political interests: Caribbean, West and East Malaysia.

Other: Member: Amnesty International, Rural Bishops' Panel 2006-; Chair, Local Strategic Partnership, Shropshire; Hon DD, Birmingham University 2010.

Publications: Contributor: Changing Rural Life (2004), Celebrating Community: God's Gift for Today's World (2006); Growing up in Multifaith Britain: Explorations in Youth, Ethnicity and Religion (2007); God-Shaped Mission: A Perspective from the Rural Church (2007); The Reflective Leader (2011); Joint editor, Faith in the Future of the Countryside (2012); Saints and Pilgrims in the Diocese of St Albans (2013).

Recreations: Skiing, travelling, gardening, playing and listening to music.

Rt Rev Dr the Lord Bishop of St Albans, House of Lords, London SW1A 0PW
Tel: 020 7219 5353 *Email:* smithab@parliament.uk
Abbey Gate House, Abbey Mill Lane, St Albans AL3 4HD *Tel:* 01727 853305
Email: bishop@stalbans.anglican.org Website: www.stalbans.anglican.org
Twitter: @BishopStAlbans

CROSSBENCH

ST JOHN OF BLETSO, LORD

ST JOHN OF BLETSO (21st Baron, E), Anthony Tudor St John; cr. 1558; 18th Bt of Bletso (E) 1660. Born 16 May 1957; Son of 20th Baron, TD; Married Dr Helen Jane Westlake 1994 (divorced 2012) (2 sons 2 daughters); married Sabina McTaggart 2015.

Education: Diocesan College, Cape Town, South Africa; University of Cape Town (BSocSc 1977; BA law 1979; BProc law 1982); London University (LLM 1983); Afrikaans, German, Xhosa.

Non-political career: Solicitor; Financial Consultant; Attorney in South Africa 1983-85; Oil Analyst/Stockbroker, County Natwest 1985-88; Consultant to Merrill Lynch 1988-2008; Director, Albion VCT 2012-; Chair: GRIT Plc 2014-, Strand Hanson 2014-, IDH Plc 2015-; Advisory Board Member: Silicon Valley Bank 2015-, Betway 2015-.

Political career: *House of Lords:* First entered House of Lords 1978; Extra Lord in Waiting to HM The Queen 1998-; Elected hereditary peer 1999-. Member: European Communities/Union Sub-committee A (Economic and Financial Affairs, Trade and External Relations) 1997-2003, Library and Computers Sub-committee 1998-2000, European Union Sub-committee B (Internal Market) 2003-07, Information 2008-13, 2015-16, Communications 2009-14, Artificial Intelligence 2017-18, Joint Committee on the Draft Registration of Overseas Entities Bill 2019.

Political interests: Foreign affairs, finance, legal affairs, sport, information technology, environment; China, Egypt, Kenya, Mozambique, Sierra Leone, South Africa, Zimbabwe.

Other: Chair: Governing Board of Certification International, Sierra Leone Business Forum; Trustee: TUSK 1997-2012, Citizens-on-Line 2000-08, TVE (Television for the Environment) 2002-12, Life Neurological Trust 2004, M'Afrika Tikkun 2006-, Alexandra Rose Charities: Member 2008-14, Deputy Chair 2014-; Christel House, Co-existence Trust, Helen Feather Memorial Trust; Trustee, Emeritas TVE 2012-; Unicef. Alfreds Club; Sunningdale Golf; Hurlingham; Royal Cape Golf.

Recreations: Skiing, golf, tennis, bridge.

The Lord St John of Bletso, House of Lords, London SW1A 0PW
Tel: 020 7219 3886 *Email:* stjohna@parliament.uk
Email: stjohn1957@gmail.com

NON-AFFILIATED

SALISBURY, LORD BISHOP OF

SALISBURY (78th Bishop of), Nicholas Roderick Holtam. Born 8 August 1954; Son of late Sydney Holtam and Kathleen Holtam; Married Helen Harris 1981 (3 sons 1 daughter).

Education: Latymer Grammar School; Collingwood College, Durham University (BA geography 1975); King's College London (BA divinity 1978); Durham University (MA theology 1989).

Non-political career: Ordained deacon 1979; Priest 1980; Assistant curate, St Dunstan and All Saints Stepney 1979-83; Tutor, Lincoln Theology College 1983-87; Vicar: Christ Church and St John with St Luke's, Isle of Dogs 1988-95, St Martin-in-the-Fields 1995-2011; Bishop of Salisbury 2011-.

Political career: *House of Lords:* Entered House of Lords 2014.

Political interests: Environment, disability, homelessness; Latvia, Scandinavia, South Africa, South Sudan, Sudan.

Other: Trustee, National Churches Trust 2008-; Vice-President, Royal School of Church Music 2012-; Honorary Fellow, Guild of Church Musicians 2013; Hon. DCL, Durham University 2005; FKC King's College London 2005. Farmers Club.

Publications: A Room With a View: Ministry with the World at your Door (2008); The Art of Worship (2011).

Recreations: Theatre, museums, walking, cycling, reading, writing.

Rt Rev the Lord Bishop of Salisbury, House of Lords, London SW1A 0PW
Tel: 020 7219 5353 *Email:* holtamn@parliament.uk
South Canonry, 71 The Close, Salisbury SP1 2ER *Tel:* 01722 334031
Email: bishop.salisbury@salisbury.anglican.org Website: www.salisbury.anglican.org

CONSERVATIVE

SANDERSON OF WELTON, BARONESS

SANDERSON OF WELTON (Life Baroness), Elizabeth Jenny Rosemary Sanderson; cr 2019.

Non-political career: Journalist, *Mail on Sunday*; Special Adviser to Theresa May as Home Secretary 2014-16; Head of Features, Prime Minister's Office 2016-17.

Political career: *House of Lords:* Member, Food, Poverty, Health and the Environment 2020-. *Other:* Raised to the peerage as Baroness Sanderson of Welton, of Welton in the East Riding of Yorkshire 2019.

The Baroness Sanderson of Welton, House of Lords, London SW1A 0PW

CROSSBENCH

SANDWICH, EARL OF

SANDWICH (11th Earl of, E), John Edward Hollister Montagu; cr. 1660; Viscount Hinchingbrooke and Baron Montagu. Born 11 April 1943; Son of Rosemary Maud Peto and Victor Montagu (10th Earl, formerly Viscount Hinchingbrooke MP, who disclaimed the earldom and other honours for life in 1964); Married (Susan) Caroline Hayman 1968 (2 sons 1 daughter).

Education: Eton College; Trinity College, Cambridge (BA history and modern language Tripos 1965, MA); Open University (Certificate European studies 1973); French, German.

Non-political career: Assistant editor, Bodley Head 1966-68; Editor, India Tourism Development Corporation 1968-69; Christian Aid: Information officer 1974-85, Research officer 1985-86, Board 1999-2004; Joint owner/administrator, Mapperton Estate, Dorset 1982-; Consultant, CARE Britain 1987-93; Editor, Save the Children 1990-92. Former member, National Union of Journalists.

Political career: *House of Lords:* First entered House of Lords 1995; Elected hereditary peer 1999-. Member: Standing Orders (Private Bills) 2000-01, Library and Computers Sub-committee 2001-04, Constitution 2005-07; Co-opted Member, EU Sub-committee E (Law and Institutions) 2009-10; Member: European Union 2010-15, EU Sub-committee E: (Justice and Institutions) 2010-12, (Justice, Institutions and Consumer Protection) 2012-13, EU Sub-committee C (External Affairs) 2013-15, EU External Affairs Sub-committee 2019-20, EU International Agreements Sub-committee 2020-.

Political interests: Aid and development, international affairs, national heritage; Afghanistan, India, Mozambique, Nepal, South Africa, South Sudan, Sudan, Uganda, Zimbabwe.

Other: President, Samuel Pepys Club 1985-; Associate, Care International 1993-98; Trustee, Britain-Afghanistan Trust 1994-2001; Council, Anti-Slavery International 1997-2006; Vice-President, Worldaware 1997-2001; International Development Affairs Committee, Church House 1997-2001; Patron: Trust for Africa's Orphans 2000-, Haslar Visitors 2002-15; Independent Asylum Commission 2007-09; Dorset Expeditionary Society 2011-13; Member, British College Advisory Panel, Kathmandu 2013-.

Publications: The Book of the World (1971); Prospects for Africa (1988); Prospects for Africa's Children (1990); Children at Crisis Point (1992); Co-editor, Hinch: A Celebration (1997); Sandwich Man (2016).

Recreations: Walking, tennis, sailing, skiing.

The Earl of Sandwich, House of Lords, London SW1A 0PW
Tel: 020 7219 3882 *Email:* sandwichj@parliament.uk
Tel: 01308 862645

CONSERVATIVE

SARFRAZ, LORD

SARFRAZ (Life Baron), Aamer Ahmad Sarfraz; cr 2020. Born 25 September 1981; Son of Naeem and Salma Sarfraz; Married Maryam Sayeed Sarfraz.

Education: Boston University (BS business administration and management 2002); London School of Economics (MSc information systems 2005); Urdu.

Non-political career: Analyst, Technology Venture Capital, 3i Group plc 2005-06; Managing director, Electrum Group (UK) 2006-15; Director, Indus Basin Holding 2010-; Founder, Better Grain Ltd 2011-; Venture Partner, Draper Associates 2019-.

Political career: *House of Lords:* Raised to the peerage as Baron Sarfraz, of Kensington in the Royal London Borough of Kensington and Chelsea 2020. *Other:* Conservative Party: Adviser on Outreach to the Party Leadership 2018-20, Treasurer 2018-20.

Other: Member: International advisory board, Texas A&M University, Dean's advisory board, Pardee School of Global Studies, Boston University, Board of directors, WWF, Pakistan, Conservation Council, Panthera.

The Lord Sarfraz, House of Lords, London SW1A 0PW
Tel: 020 7219 4421 *Email:* lordsarfrazoffice@parliament.uk Website: www.lordsarfraz.com

CONSERVATIVE

SASSOON, LORD

SASSOON (Life Baron), James Meyer Sassoon; cr 2010. Born 11 September 1955; Son of Hugh Sassoon and Marion Sassoon, née Schiff; Married Sarah Barnes 1981 (1 son 2 daughters).

Education: Eton College; Christ Church, Oxford (BA philosophy, politics and economics 1977, MA).

Non-political career: Thomson McLintock & Co (KPMG) 1977-86; S G Warburg & Co 1987-95: Director 1991-95; Warburg Dillon Read/UBS Warburg: Managing director 1995-2002, Vice-chair, Corporate Finance 2000-02; HM Treasury (HMT) 2002-08: Managing Director, Finance Regulation and Industry Directorate 2002-06, HMT Representative for Promotion of the City 2006-08; Member: Financial Stability Forum 2002-06, EU Financial Services Committee 2003-06; President, Financial Action Task Force 2007-08; Adviser to George Osborne MP as Shadow Chancellor of the Exchequer 2008-10; Member, Economic Recovery Committee, Shadow Cabinet 2009-10; Executive director, Jardine Matheson 2013-; Director, Jardine Lloyd Thompson 2013-19.

Political career: *House of Lords:* Raised to the peerage as Baron Sassoon, of Ashley Park in the County of Surrey 2010. Commercial Secretary and Government Spokesperson, HM Treasury 2010-13. Member, Consumer Insurance (Disclosure and Representations) Bill 2011-12. *Other:* Trustee, British Museum 2009-10, 2013-.

Political interests: Trade and investment, financial services; China, UK's major trading partners and inward/outward investors.

Other: Director, Partnerships UK 2002-06; Trustee, National Gallery Trust 2002-09; Merchants Trust plc: Director 2006-10, Chair 2010; Director, Nuclear Liabilities Fund 2008-10; Chair: ifs School of Finance 2009-10, China-Britain Business Council 2013-; Committee member, Hong Kong Association 2013-; Member, Global Advisory Board, Mitsubishi UFJ Financial Group 2013-; FCA; Kt 2008.

Publications: Author, The Tripartite Review (2009).

Recreations: Travel, the arts, gardening.

The Lord Sassoon, House of Lords, London SW1A 0PW
Tel: 020 7219 5353 *Email:* sassoonjm@parliament.uk

CONSERVATIVE

SATER, BARONESS

SATER (Life Baroness), Amanda Jacqueline Sater; cr 2018. Born 21 June 1963; Married Roisen Mark Sater 1988 (1 daughter 1 son).

Non-political career: Director, Institute of Sales Promotion 1996-97; Managing director, Control Promotions Ltd 1989-97.

Political career: *House of Commons:* Contested Luton North 2001 general election. *House of Lords:* Raised to the peerage as Baroness Sater, of Kensington in the Royal Borough of Kensington and Chelsea 2018. Member: Food, Poverty, Health and the Environment 2019-, National Plan for Sport and Recreation 2020-. *Other:* Conservative and Unionist Party: Vice-chair (responsible for Women) 2014-15, Co-chair, Candidates Committee 2015-, Deputy chairman 2016-18, Board member 2015-18, 2018-. Magistrate, Central London Youth Panel 1995-2018; Board member: Metropolitan Police Authority 2010-12, Youth Justice Board 2013-17; Magistrate, Central London LJA 2016-18; Supplemental list, Central London Youth Panel 2019-.

Political interests: Justice, sport.

Other: Chair and trustee, North Kensington Opportunity Centre 1999-2003; Trustee: Addaction 2002-05, British Lung Foundation 2005-11; Vice-chair and trustee, Queen's Club 2009-15; Chair, Queen's Club Foundation 2015-; StreetGames: Chair and trustee 2015-18, Patron 2018-; Freedom, City of London; FRSA.

The Baroness Sater, House of Lords, London SW1A 0PW
Tel: 020 7219 3000 *Email:* satera@parliament.uk

CROSSBENCH

SAVILLE OF NEWDIGATE, LORD

SAVILLE OF NEWDIGATE (Life Baron), Mark Oliver Saville; cr. 1997. Born 20 March 1936; Son of Kenneth and Olivia Saville; Married Jill Gray 1961 (2 sons).

Education: Rye Grammar School; Brasenose College, Oxford (Vinerian Scholar, BA law 1959; BCL 1960).

Non-political career: Called to the Bar, Middle Temple 1962; QC 1975; Bencher 1983; Judge of the High Court, Queen's Bench Division 1985-93; Lord Justice of Appeal 1994-97; Justice of the Supreme Court of the United Kingdom 2009-10. Second Lieutenant, Royal Sussex Regiment 1954-56.

Political career: *House of Lords:* Raised to the peerage as Baron Saville of Newdigate, of Newdigate in the County of Surrey 1997. Lord of Appeal in Ordinary 1997-2009; As Justice of the Supreme Court, disqualified from participation 2009-10. Chair: Intellectual Property (Unjustified Threats) Bill 2016, Bribery Act 2010 2018-19.

Other: Two honorary law doctorates; Kt 1985; PC 1994. Garrick Club.

Recreations: Sailing, flying, gardening, computers.

Rt Hon the Lord Saville of Newdigate, House of Lords, London SW1A 0PW
Tel: 020 7219 5353

LABOUR

SAWYER, LORD

SAWYER (Life Baron), Lawrence Sawyer; cr. 1998. Born 12 May 1943.

Education: Dodmire School; Eastbourne School; Darlington Technical School and College.

Non-political career: Engineering apprentice, Robert Stephenson and Hawthorne 1958-63; Engineering inspector, Lockhead Brakes, Leamington Spa 1963-65; Engineering inspection and work study officer, Cummins Engines, Darlington 1965-71; NUPE: Officer 1971-75, Northern Regional Officer 1975-81, Deputy General Secretary, NUPE/Unison 1981-94; Director: Investors in People UK 1998-2005, Reed Executive plc 1998-2001, Britannia Building Society 1999-2009; Visiting Professor, Cranfield Business School 1999-2013; Chair, Notting Hill Housing Association 1999-2004; Union Income Benefit Advisory Board 2000-; Royal Mail

Partnership Board 2001-08; Reed Healthcare plc 2001-04; Thompsons Solicitors Supervisory Board 2001-10; Chair, Norlife 2004-. Member, Unison: Deputy General Secretary 1982-94.

Political career: *House of Lords:* Raised to the peerage as Baron Sawyer, of Darlington in the County of Durham 1998. Member: Affordable Childcare 2014-15, Refreshment 2015-16. *Other:* Labour Party: Member, National Executive 1982-94, 1998-2001, Chair, Labour Home Policy Committee 1989-94, Party Chair 1992, General Secretary 1994-98.

Political interests: Housing, employment, education, Royal Mail; Americas, Europe, South Africa.

Other: Member: Post Office Northern Advisory Board 1997-99, Nurses' and Midwives' Whitley Council 1997-99, NJIC for Manual Workers 1997-99; President, William Morris Society 2017-; Cystic Fibrosis; Chancellor, Teesside University 2005-17.

Recreations: Antiquarian book dealer and collector.

The Lord Sawyer, House of Lords, London SW1A 0PW
Tel: 020 7219 8668

LABOUR

SCOTLAND OF ASTHAL, BARONESS

SCOTLAND OF ASTHAL (Life Baroness), Patricia Janet Scotland; cr. 1997. Born 19 August 1955; Daughter of Arthur and Dellie Marie Scotland; Married Richard Mawhinney 1985 (2 sons).

Education: Walthamstow School for Girls; London University (LLB 1976).

Non-political career: Called to the Bar, Middle Temple 1977; Founding member, later head of chambers, 1 Gray's Inn Square 1979-; QC 1991; Assistant recorder 1992; Bencher 1997; Barrister specialising in family and administrative law 1997-91; Recorder 2000; Member, Bar of Antigua and Bar of the Commonwealth of Dominica; Secretary-General of the Commonwealth of Nations 2016-.

Political career: *House of Lords:* Raised to the peerage as Baroness Scotland of Asthal, of Asthal in the County of Oxfordshire 1997. Parliamentary Under-Secretary of State and Government Spokesperson for Foreign and Commonwealth Office 1999-2001; Parliamentary Secretary, Lord Chancellor's Department and Government Spokesperson for Law Officers' Department 2001-03; Minister of State and Government Spokesperson for Home Office 2003-07; Government Spokesperson for: Trade and Industry 2004-05, Women's Issues/Equal Agenda; Attorney General and Government Spokesperson for the Law Officers (attending cabinet) 2007-10; Shadow Attorney General 2010-11; Opposition Spokesperson for the Law Officers 2010-11; Trade envoy to South Africa 2012-16; On leave of absence March 2016-. Member: Privileges and Conduct 2012-16, Communications 2013-16. *Other:* Former member, Commission for Racial Equality; Alderman, Corporation of London 2014-.

Other: Alternate UK Government Representative, European Convention 2002-03; Member: Millennium Commission 1994-99, Thomas More Society, Lawyers' Christian Fellowship; Patron: Margaret Beaufort Institute, GAP; Vice-patron: CFAB, Almshouses Association; Chancellor, Greenwich University 2014-19; Five honorary doctorates, Universities of Westminster, Buckingham, Leicester, East London and West Indies; Honorary Fellow: Wolfson College, Cambridge, Cardiff University; Peer of the Year, *House Magazine* awards 2004; Peer of the Year, Channel 4 2004; Parliamentarian of the Year, Political Studies Association 2004; Parliamentarian of the Year, *Spectator* 2005; Kathleen Carlin Justice Seekers award 2008; Lifetime Achievement award, Black Solicitors Network 2009; Female Personality of the Year award, GV Media Group 2009; Anti-corruption award, Doha 2009; European Women in Business Law Lifetime Achievement award, Euromoney Legal Media Group 2011; PC 2001.

Rt Hon the Baroness Scotland of Asthal QC, House of Lords, London SW1A 0PW
Tel: 020 7219 3000 *Twitter:* @PScotlandCSG

CONSERVATIVE

SCOTT OF BYBROOK, BARONESS

Government Whip, Baroness in Waiting

SCOTT OF BYBROOK (Life Baroness), Jane Antoinette Scott; cr 2015. Born 13 June 1947; Widowed (3 children).

Education: Lancashire College of Agriculture.

Non-political career: Dairy industry; Public relations; Marketing; Lecturer.

Political career: *House of Lords:* Raised to the peerage as Baroness Scott of Bybrook, of Upper Wraxall in the County of Wiltshire 2015. Government Whip, Baroness in Waiting 2020-; Government Spokesperson for: Justice 2020, Law Officers 2020. Member: Natural Environment and Rural Communities Act 2006 2017, EU Home Affairs Sub-committee 2019-20, Communications/Communications and Digital 2019-20. *Other:* Wiltshire County Council: Councillor 1997-2009, Leader 2003-09; Wiltshire Council: Councillor 2009-20, Leader 2009-19; Member: Court, Bath University, Independent taskforce, Royal Borough of Kensington recovery plan (following Grenfell Tower fire) 2017-; Vice-president, Local Government Association -2020.

Other: Chair, Wiltshire Strategic Board; Wiltshire and Swindon Local Enterprise Partnership; OBE 2010.

The Baroness Scott of Bybrook OBE, House of Lords, London SW1A 0PW
Tel: 020 7219 3000

LIBERAL DEMOCRAT

SCOTT OF NEEDHAM MARKET, BARONESS

SCOTT OF NEEDHAM MARKET (Life Baroness), Rosalind Carol Scott; cr. 2000. Born 10 August 1957; Daughter of Kenneth Vincent and Carol Leadbeater; Married Mark Valladares 2008 (1 son 1 daughter from previous marriage).

Education: Whitby Grammar School; Kent School; University of East Anglia (BA European studies 1999).

Political career: *House of Lords:* Raised to the peerage as Baroness Scott of Needham Market, of Needham Market in the County of Suffolk 2000. Liberal Democrat: Whip 2001-02, Deputy Chief Whip 2002, Spokesperson for: Transport, Local Government and the Regions 2001-02, Transport 2002-04, Office of the Deputy Prime Minister/Communities and Local Government 2004-09. Member: Liaison 2003-07, Delegated Powers and Regulatory Reform 2005-07, Communications 2007-10, Leader's Group on Members Leaving the House 2010-15, EU Sub-Committee G (Social Policies and Consumer Protection) 2011-12, Joint Committee on the Draft House of Lords Reform Bill 2011-12, European Union 2012-16, EU Sub-committee B (Internal Market, Infrastructure and Employment) 2012-13; Chair: EU Sub-committee D (Agriculture, Fisheries, Environment and Energy) 2013-15, EU Energy and Environment Sub-committee 2015-16; Member: Joint Committee on Statutory Instruments 2016-, Charities 2016-17, Natural Environment and Rural Communities Act 2006 2017-18. *Other:* President, Liberal Democrat Party 2008-10; Vice-President, Alliance Liberal Democrats in Europe 2016-17. Councillor, Mid Suffolk District Council 1991-94; Suffolk County Council: Councillor 1993-2005, Vice-chair 1996-97, Chair, Transport Committee, Local Government Association 2002-04; Member, House of Lords Appointments Commission 2010-20; Vice-president, Local Government Association; Board member: National Archives 2018-, Shadow Sponsor Body for the Houses of Parliament Restoration and Renewal Programme 2018-.

Political interests: Transport, Europe; Commonwealth, India, USA.

Other: Member: North Sea Commission 1997-2005, Council of European Municipalities and Regions 1997-2003, Congress of Local and Regional Authorities in Europe 1997-2003, EU Committee of the Regions 1998-2002, Inter-Parliamentary Union 2000-; Commonwealth Parliamentary Association 2000-; Patron, ACE Anglia; Member, Shadow Sponsor Board, Restoration and Renewal Programme; Board member: Audit Commission 2002-05, Lloyds Register 2003-09, Harwich Haven Authority 2012-; Trustee: Industry and Parliament Trust 2015-, Community Action Suffolk 2018-; Hon. Member, Chartered Institute Highways and Transportation; Suffolk Foundation. Royal Commonwealth Society Club.

Recreations: Walking, political biography, genealogy.

The Baroness Scott of Needham Market, House of Lords, London SW1A 0PW
Tel: 020 7219 8660 *Email:* scottrc@parliament.uk *Twitter:* @BaronessRos

LIBERAL DEMOCRAT

SCRIVEN, LORD

SCRIVEN (Life Baron), Paul James Scriven; cr 2014. Born 7 February 1966; Partner.

Education: Rawthorpe High School, Huddersfield; Huddersfield Technical College; Manchester Polytechnic (BA); Sheffield University (Postgraduate Course health economics).

Non-political career: Senior manager, NHS; Director, Apps2Connect; Managing partner, Scriven Consulting 2010-.

Political career: *House of Commons:* Contested (Liberal Democrat) Sheffield Central 2010 general election. *House of Lords:* Raised to the peerage as Baron Scriven, of Hunters Bar in the City of Sheffield 2014. Member: EU Justice Sub-committee 2015-16, Long-Term Sustainability of the NHS 2016-17, Procedure/Procedure and Privileges 2017-, Democracy and Digital Technologies 2019-. *Other:* Sheffield City Council: Councillor 2000-12, 2016-19, Leader of the Council 2008-11; Member, South Yorkshire Fire Authority 2001-12; Sheffield Executive Board 2006-11; Sheffield Local Enterprise Partnership 2010-11; Vice-president, Local Government Association 2017-.

Political interests: Local government, health, international LGBTI issues, civil liberties; Malaysia, Philippines, Singapore, Thailand.

Other: Patron, Gay Professional Network 2018-.

Recreations: Walking, travel.

The Lord Scriven, House of Lords, London SW1A 0PW
Tel: 020 7219 5353 *Twitter:* @Paulscriven

CONSERVATIVE

SECCOMBE, BARONESS

SECCOMBE (Life Baroness), Joan Anna Dalziel Seccombe; cr. 1991. Born 3 May 1930; Daughter of late Robert Owen and Olive Barlow Owen; Married Henry Seccombe 1950 (died 2008) (2 sons).

Education: St Martin's, Solihull.

Political career: *House of Lords:* Raised to the peerage as Baroness Seccombe, of Kineton in the County of Warwickshire 1991. Opposition Whip 1997-2001; Opposition Deputy Chief Whip 2001-10; Opposition Spokesperson for: Education and Skills 2003-04, Legal Affairs 2003-06, Home Affairs 2004-07; Extra Baroness in Waiting to HM The Queen 2004-; Opposition Spokesperson for: Constitutional Affairs 2005-06, Constitutional and Legal Affairs/Justice 2006-10; Party Whip 2010-. Member: Information 2012-15, Consolidation, Etc, Bills Joint Committee 2014-, Liaison 2015-17. *Other:* Chairman: West Midlands Conservative Women's Committee 1975-78, Conservative Women's National Committee 1981-84; National Union of Conservative and Unionist Associations: Chairman 1987-88, Vice-chairman 1984-87, Member of Executive 1975-97; Chairman, Conservative Party Annual Conference, Blackpool 1987; Vice-chairman, Conservative Party with special responsibility for Women 1987-97. JP, Solihull 1968-2000, Chairman of Bench 1981-84; Chairman, Lord Chancellor's Advisory Committee, Solihull 1975-93; Councillor, West Midlands County Council 1977-81, Chairman, Trading Standards Committee 1979-81; Member, Women's National Commission 1984-90; Governor, Nuffield Hospitals 1988-2001; Vice-President, Institute of Trading Standards Administration/Chartered Trading Standards Institute 1992-.

Political interests: Women's issues, family, criminal justice.

Other: Chair, Trustees of Nuffield Hospitals Pension Scheme 1992-2001; Trustee, Industry and Parliament Trust; DBE 1984. President, St Enedoc Golf Club 1992-.

Recreations: Golf, needlework.

The Baroness Seccombe DBE, House of Lords, London SW1A 0PW
Tel: 020 7219 4558 *Email:* seccombej@parliament.uk

CROSSBENCH

SEDWILL, LORD

SEDWILL (Life Baron), Mark Philip Sedwill; cr 2020. Born 21 October 1964; Married Sarah-Jane Lakeman (1 daughter).

Education: St Andrews University (BSc); St Edmunds Hall, Oxford (MPhil).

Non-political career: Foreign and Commonwealth Office (FCO): Second Secretary: Security Co-ordination Department 1989-91, Cairo 1991-94, First Secretary: Resource Management Department 1994-96, Attached to UN Special Commission 1996-98, First Secretary for Political-Military Affairs and Counter-Terrorism, Nicosia 1998-2000, Private Secretary to the Secretary of State for Foreign and Commonwealth Affairs (Robin Cook, then Jack Straw) 2000-02, Deputy High Commissioner to Pakistan 2003-05, Deputy Director, Middle East and North Africa 2005; Director: UK Visas 2006-08, International Group, UK Border Agency 2008-09; FCO: Ambassador to Afghanistan 2009-10, Senior Civilian Representative to Afghanistan, NATO 2010-11, UK Special Representative for Afghanistan and Pakistan 2011-13, Director-General, Political 2012-13; Permanent Secretary, Home Office 2013-17; Prime Minister's Adviser, National Security 2017-20; Cabinet Secretary and Head of the Civil Service 2018-20.

Political career: *House of Lords:* Raised to the peerage as Baron Sedwill, of Sherborne in the County of Dorset 2020.

Other: Senior adviser, Rothschild & Co 2020-; CMG 2008; KCMG 2018.

Recreations: Golf, squash, scuba diving, windsurfing, hill-walking.

Lord Sedwill KCMG, House of Lords, London SW1A 0PW
Tel: 020 7219 3000 *Twitter:* @marksedwill

CONSERVATIVE

SELKIRK OF DOUGLAS, LORD

SELKIRK OF DOUGLAS (Life Baron), James Alexander Douglas-Hamilton; cr. 1997. Born 31 July 1942; Son of late 14th Duke of Hamilton and Brandon, KT, PC, GCVO, AFC, DL, and late Lady Elizabeth Percy, OBE, DL, daughter of 8th Duke of Northumberland, KG, CBE, MVO; Married Hon Susan Buchan 1974 (4 sons including twins).

Education: Eton College; Balliol College, Oxford (BA modern history 1964) (Oxford Boxing Blue 1961-62); President, Oxford Union Society Summer 1964); Edinburgh University (LLB Scots law 1967).

Non-political career: Scots Advocate 1968-76; Depute Procurator Fiscal: Dumfries 1969, Edinburgh 1972; QC 1996. Officer 6/7th Btn, Cameronians TA 1961-66; 2nd Btn Lowland Volunteers, TAVR 1971-74; Captain Cameronians TA 1973; Hon. Air Commodore No 2 (City of Edinburgh), Maritime Headquarters Unit 1995-99; Hon. Air Commodore No 603 (City of Edinburgh) Squadron 2000-15.

Political career: *House of Commons:* MP (Conservative) for Edinburgh West 1974-97. Contested Edinburgh West 1997 general election; Opposition Whip 1976-79; Government Whip 1979-81; PPS to Malcolm Rifkind: as Minister of State, Foreign Office 1983-85, as Secretary of State for Scotland 1986-87; Scottish Office 1987-95: Parliamentary Under-Secretary of State 1987-95, Minister of State 1995-97. *House of Lords:* Raised to the peerage as Baron Selkirk of Douglas, of Cramond in the City of Edinburgh 1997. EU Sub-committee C (Foreign Affairs, Defence and Development Policy): Co-opted member 2008-10, Member 2011-12; Member Joint Committees on: Statutory Instruments 2012-15, Draft Deregulation Bill 2013; Member: EU Energy and Environment Sub-Committee 2015-19, European Union 2016-18. *Other:* Scottish Parliament: Contested Edinburgh West constituency 1999 and 2003 elections, MSP for Lothians region 1999-2007 (as Lord James Douglas-Hamilton): Member, Parliamentary Bureau 1999-2001, Business Manager/Chief Whip, Conservative Group 1999-2001, Conservative Spokesperson for: Justice 2001-03, Education 2003-07. President, Oxford University Conservative Association Winter 1963. Councillor, Edinburgh Corporation 1972-74; President: Royal Commonwealth Society in Scotland 1979-87, Scottish National Council, UN Association 1981-87; Member, Commission on Scottish Devolution (Calman Commission) 2008-09.

Political interests: Foreign affairs, defence, Scottish affairs, law reform, conservation, arts, housing, health, education, local government, environment, heritage; Africa, Asia, Australasia, Europe, Middle East, North America.

Other: Hon. President, Scottish Boxing Association 1975-98; President, International Rescue Corps 1995-; Edinburgh Support Group of Hope and Homes for Children: Chairman 2002-07, Patron 2007-; President: Scottish Veterans' Garden City Association 2007-, Chair, Scottish Advisory Committee, SkillForce; Member, Royal Company of Archers, Queen's Bodyguard for Scotland; Trustee, Selkirk Charitable Trust; Lord High Commissioner, General Assembly, Church of Scotland 2012-13; Chair, Scottish Peers' Association 2016-; Disclaimed the Earldom of Selkirk, November 1994; PC 1996. Honorary Member, Royal Scots Club, Sloane Club; Member, Muirfield (Honorable Company of Edinburgh Golfers).

Publications: Motive for a Mission: The Story Behind Hess's Flight to Britain (1971); The Air Battle for Malta: The Diaries of a Fighter Pilot (1981); Roof of the World: Man's First Flight over Everest (1983); The Truth About Rudolf Hess (1993, new edition 2016); After You, Prime Minister (Stacey International, 2010).

Recreations: Golf, boxing, forestry, debating, history.

Rt Hon the Lord Selkirk of Douglas QC, House of Lords, London SW1A 0PW
Tel: 020 7219 2131 *Email:* selkirkj@parliament.uk

CONSERVATIVE

SELSDON, LORD

SELSDON (3rd Baron, UK), Malcolm McEacharn Mitchell-Thomson; cr. 1932; 4th Bt of Polmood (UK) 1900. Born 27 October 1937; Son of 2nd Baron, DSC.

Education: Winchester College; French, German.

Non-political career: Plastics products manager, Universal Asbestos (UAM) 1959-63; Director, market analysis and research services, London Press Exchange Group 1964-72; European mergers and acquisitions, Singer & Friedlander (CT Bowring Group) 1972-76; Midland Bank Group 1976-90; International board member, Merloni Group, Italy 1978-98; Peasant farmer, Provence, France (vineyard and olive groves) 1987-; Deputy chairman, Comcap plc 1988-93; UK board member, Raab Karcher, Germany 1994-98; Director, MJ Gleeson Group plc 1996-2006; Director international banking, Samuel Montagu & Co; EU and public finance adviser. Sub-Lieutenant RNVR, Royal Navy 1956-58.

Political career: *House of Lords:* First entered House of Lords 1963; Elected hereditary peer 1999-. Member: EC Sub-committee B (Internal Market, Energy and Transport) 1974-76, EC Sub-committee A (Economic and Financial Affairs and International Trade) 1974-84, Draft Human Tissue and Embryos Bill Joint Committee 2007, Information 2008-13. *Other:* Treasurer, Conservative Group on Europe. Chair: Greater London and South East Council for Sport and Recreation 1977-83, Committee for Middle East Trade 1979-86; Member: British Overseas Trade Board 1983-86, East European Trade Council 1983-86.

Political interests: Trade and industry, foreign affairs, defence, economic and finance, health and technology, construction and planning; Africa, China, Commonwealth and overseas territories, EU, Middle East, Russia and former Soviet Union.

Other: British Delegate, Council of Europe and Western European Union 1972-78; President: British Exporters' Association 1992-98, Anglo Swiss Society 2001-. Secretary and treasurer, House of Lords Yacht Club; Member, MCC 1958-.

Recreations: Skiing, sailing, tennis, lawn tennis, golf.

The Lord Selsdon, House of Lords, London SW1A 0PW
Tel: 020 7219 6668 *Email:* selsdonm@parliament.uk

CROSSBENCH

SENTAMU, JOHN – Peerage pending at time of going to press

John Tucker Mugabi Sentamu. Born 10 June 1949; Son of late John and Ruth Walakira; Married Margaret Wanambwa 1973.

Education: Kitante and Old Kampala Secondary Schools, Uganda; Makerere University, Uganda (LLB 1971); Diploma in legal practice, Uganda 1972; Selwyn College, Cambridge (BA 1976; PhD 1984); Ridley Hall, Cambridge.

Non-political career: Advocate, High Court of Uganda 1971-; Ordained 1979; Assistant chaplain, Selwyn College, Cambridge 1979; Chaplain, HM Remand Centre, Latchmere House 1979-82; Assistant curate: St Andrew, Ham 1979-82, St Paul, Herne Hill, London 1982-83; Holy Trinity and St Mathias, Tulse Hill London: Respectively priest and vicar 1983-84; Vicar 1985-96; Priest, St Saviour, Brixton Hill, London 1987-89; Honorary Canon, Southwark Cathedral 1993-96; Stepney Area Bishop, London 1996-2002; Bishop of Birmingham 2002-05; Archbishop of York 2005-20; Hon. Master Bencher, Gray's Inn 2007-.

Political career: *House of Lords:* First entered House of Lords as Archbishop of York 2005. *Other:* Member, General Synod 1985-96, 2002-20.

Political interests: Legal, community, young people, faith; Africa.

Other: Chair, Sickle Cell and Thalassaemia Screening Programme 2001-13; President: Youth for Christ 2004-, YMCA England 2005-; Sponsor, York Fairness Commission 2011-12; Fellow, Royal Society of Arts; Chair, Living Wage Commission 2013-14; Freedom: City of London 2000, Montego Bay, Jamaica 2007; Chancellor: York St John University 2006-20, Cumbria University 2007-; Fellow: University College Christ Church, Canterbury 2001, Queen Mary College, University of London 2001; Honorary fellow, Selwyn College, Cambridge 2005; Harold Turner Visiting fellow, University of Otago, New Zealand 2014; Honorary fellow, St Margaret's College, Dunedin, New Zealand 2014; Twenty honorary doctorates from UK, Canada, Caribbean and US universities; Midlander of the Year 2003; Yorkshire Man of the Year 2007; Speaker of the Year 2007; York Ambassador, York Tourism Awards 2010; PC 2005.

Recreations: Cooking, music, rugby, football, athletics.

Most Rev and Rt Hon John Sentamu, House of Lords, London SW1A 0PW
Twitter: @JohnSentamu

CONSERVATIVE

SHACKLETON OF BELGRAVIA, BARONESS

SHACKLETON OF BELGRAVIA (Life Baroness), Fiona Sara Shackleton; cr 2010. Born 26 May 1956; Daughter of late Jonathan Charkham CBE; Married Ian Shackleton (2 daughters).

Education: Francis Holland School; Benenden School; Exeter University (LLB 1977).

Non-political career: Articled clerk, Herbert Smith 1978-80; Admitted solicitor 1980; Partner: Brecher and Co. 1981-84, Farrer and Co. 1987-2000; Personal solicitor to: The Prince of Wales 1996-2005, Prince William of Wales 1996-, Prince Harry of Wales 1996-; Partner, Payne Hicks Beach Solicitors.

Political career: *House of Lords:* Raised to the peerage as Baroness Shackleton of Belgravia, of Belgravia in the City of Westminster 2010. Member, EU Justice Sub-committee 2015-19. *Other:* Governor, Benenden School 1986-2007.

Other: Inaugural member, International Academy of Matrimonial Lawyers 1986-; Trustee: Broad Cairn Foundation, Glen Beg Foundation, Sir Frank Lowe's Football Trust -2017, Royal Opera House Endowment Fund; Director, Diana, Princess of Wales Memorial Fund Trustee Company -2017; Member, advisory council, London Philharmonic Orchestra; Hon. LLD, Exeter University 2010; Elected Master of the Bench, Inner Temple 2011; LVO 2005.

Publications: Co-author, The Divorce Handbook (1992).

The Baroness Shackleton of Belgravia LVO, House of Lords, London SW1A 0PW
Tel: 020 7219 5353
Email: fshackleton@phb.co.uk

CROSSBENCH

SHAFIK, BARONESS

SHAFIK (Life Baroness), Nemat (Minouche) Talaat Shafik; cr 2020. Born 13 August 1962; Married Raffael Jovine (2 children 3 step children).

Education: Massachusetts-Amherst University (BA economics and politics 1983); London School of Economics (MSc economics 1986); St Antony's College, Oxford (DPhil economics 1989); Arabic, French.

Non-political career: Researcher and tutor, Oxford University 1987-89; World Bank: Economist, Research Department 1990-92, Economist, World Development Report on Environment and Development 1992, Senior Economist, Central and Eastern Europe 1992-94, Director, Private Sector and Finance, Middle East and North Africa Region 1996-99, Vice-President, Private Sector Development and Infrastructure 1999-2003; Adjunct Professor, Georgetown University 1989-94; Visiting Associate Professor, Wharton Business School, University of Pennsylvania 1996; Department for International Development: Director-General, Country/Regional Programmes Division 2004-08, Permanent Secretary 2008-11; Deputy Managing Director, International Monetary Fund 2011-14; Deputy Governor of Bank of England 2014-17; Director, London School of Economics and Political Science 2017-.

Political career: *House of Lords:* Raised to the peerage as Baroness Shafik, of Camden in the London Borough of Camden and of Alexandria in the Arab Republic of Egypt 2020. *Other:* Trustee, British Museum 2016-.

Political interests: International economics, development, central banking, environment, education.

Other: Member: Supervisory Board, Siemens, Council, Institute for Fiscal Studies; Governor, National Institute for Economic and Social Research, Board member, Russell Group; International board, Bangladesh Rural Advancement Committee (BRAC); Honorary Fellow, St Antony's College, Oxford; Honorary doctorate: Warwick University, Glasgow University, Reading University; Woman of the Year, GG2 Global Leadership and Global Diversity Awards 2009; DBE 2015.

Publications: Reviving Private Investment in Developing Countries (1992); Editor: Prospects for the Middle East and North African Economies: from Boom to Bust and Back? (1998), Economic Challenges Facing Middle Eastern and North African Countries (1998); Numerous articles in academic journals and books.

Recreations: Family, theatre, reading, swimming, walking, cooking.

The Baroness Shafik DBE, House of Lords, London SW1A 0PW
Tel: 020 7219 3000 *Email:* shafikn@parliament.uk

LIBERAL DEMOCRAT

SHARKEY, LORD

SHARKEY (Life Baron), John Kevin Sharkey; cr 2010. Born 24 September 1947; Married (3 daughters).

Education: Manchester University (BSc Mathematics 1968).

Non-political career: Benton & Bowles, KMP; Saatchi & Saatchi: Joined 1984, Deputy Chair 1986, Managing Director 1987; Chair, Broad Street Group, BDDP; Founder, Joint Chair and Chief Executive, Bainsfair Sharkey Trott/BST-BDDP 1990-97; Joint Chair, BDDP GGT 1997-98; Managing Director, Europe Manpower plc 1998; Chair, Sharkey Associates Ltd; Chief Operating Officer, Blue Arrow plc; Communications Adviser to Nick Clegg 2006-10.

Political career: *House of Lords:* Raised to the peerage as Baron Sharkey, of Niton Undercliff in the County of Isle of Wight 2010. Liberal Democrat Spokesperson for Personal Finances 2015-. Member: EU Sub-committee F (Home Affairs, Health and Education) 2012-15, Joint Committee on the Draft Deregulation Bill 2013, Information 2014-16, Economic Affairs 2015-19, SLSC Sub-committee A 2018-19, European Union 2019-; Chair, EU Financial Affairs Sub-committee 2019-20; Member, EU Services Sub-committee 2020-. *Other:* Liberal Democrats: Chair, general election campaign 2010, Campaign director, YES to Fairer Votes for the 2011 Referendum.

Political interests: Finance, health, education, NW England, Isle of Wight; Cyprus, Middle East, Turkey.

Other: Non-executive Chair, Highland Partners Europe -2006; Hansard Society: Member 2004-, Hon Treasurer 2007-, Chair 2016-; Governor, Institute for Government 2013-; Chair, Association of Medical Research Charities 2015-; Director: New City Agenda 2014-, Full Fact Ltd 2015-; Chair: Specialised Healthcare Alliance 2017-, Member of Council, UCL 2017.

The Lord Sharkey, House of Lords, London SW1A 0PW
Tel: 020 7219 5353 *Email:* sharkeyjk@parliament.uk

CONSERVATIVE

SHARPE OF EPSOM, LORD

SHARPE OF EPSOM (Life Baron), Andrew Michael Gordon Sharpe; cr 2020. Born 15 June 1962; Son of Michael and Gillian Sharpe; Married Fiona Sharpe.

Education: Dorking Grammar School/The Ashcombe School; Westminster University (MA 2003); Buckingham University (Master's military history 2013); Spoken Cantonese.

Non-political career: Inspector, Royal Hong Kong Police 1987-91; Salesman, Smith New Court/HSBC/UBS, Hong Kong/Tokyo/New York 1991-2000; Morgan Stanley, London 2000-03, UBS Investment Bank, London 2003-06; Partner, Redburn Partners 2006-12; Founding Partner, Sharpe Lankester & Associates 2012-14; Vice-president, Green Street Advisors 2014-18; Director, Battenhall 2013-; Founding Partner, Primary Access & Research 2019-.

Political career: *House of Lords:* Raised to the peerage as Baron Sharpe of Epsom, of Epsom in the County of Surrey 2020. *Other:* Conservative Party: National Conservative Convention: Regional Chairman, South East 2012-15, Vice-President 2015-17; Deputy Chairman, Party Board 2018-, Chairman, Finance and Audit Committee 2018-, Vice-chairman, Candidates Committee 2019-.

Political interests: Financial markets regulation, policing, defence, international trade; China, Hong Kong, Japan, Switzerland, United Kingdom, USA.

Other: Patron, National Army Museum; National Brain Appeal, Gurkha Welfare Trust; OBE 2018. Royal Automobile Club, In & Out (Naval & Military) Club; Royal Hong Kong Yacht Club.

Publications: The Indianisation of the Indian Army, History Today (March 1984); The Battle of Neuve Chapelle and The Indian Corps, History Today (August 2015).

Recreations: Reading history, golf, cycling.

The Lord Sharpe of Epsom OBE, House of Lords, London SW1A 0PW
Tel: 020 7219 3000 *Email:* sharpea@parliament.uk *Twitter:* @amgsharpe

LIBERAL DEMOCRAT

SHEEHAN, BARONESS

Liberal Democrat Lords Spokesperson for International Development

SHEEHAN (Life Baroness), Shaista (Shas) Ahmad Sheehan; cr 2015. Born 29 July 1959; Married Patrick (3 children).

Education: Rosa Bassett Grammar School; University College London (BSc chemistry 1978); Imperial College (MSc environmental technology 1990).

Non-political career: Chemistry teacher; Nursing auxiliary, New Cross Hospital; Senior planner and buyer in advertising 1981-2005; Head of office to Susan Kramer MP 2005-08; Charity worker, Wimbledon Guild Daycentre and Faith in Action project for homeless people 2010-15.

Political career: *House of Commons:* Contested (Liberal Democrat) Wimbledon 2010 and 2015 general elections. *House of Lords:* Raised to the peerage as Baroness Sheehan, of Wimbledon in the London Borough of Merton and of Tooting in the London Borough of Wandsworth 2015. Liberal Democrat Shadow Secretary of State/Spokesperson for International Development 2016-. Member: EU Energy and Environment Sub-committee 2015-19, Science and Technology 2019-. *Other:* Contested Londonwide region 2012 London Assembly election. Member, Green Lib Dems. London Borough of Richmond upon Thames: Councillor 2006-10,

Assistant Cabinet Member for Energy and Climate Change; Governor, Queen's CoE Primary School.

Other: Chair, Wimbledon Cancer Friendship Group; Trustee, Merton and Lambeth Citizen's Advice Bureau; Founding Member, 20's Plenty for Merton Steering Group; RSPB, Amnesty International, London Wildlife Trust.

Recreations: Spending time with family, walking, reading, cooking.

The Baroness Sheehan, House of Lords, London SW1A 0PW
Tel: 020 7219 3000 *Twitter:* @sheehanshas

CONSERVATIVE

SHEIKH, LORD

SHEIKH (Life Baron), Mohamed Iltaf Sheikh; cr 2006. Born 13 June 1941; Son of Mohamed Abdullah Sheikh and Kalsum Ara, née Bux; Married Shaida Begum Thantrey 1986 (1 daughter from previous marriage).

Education: Government Secondary School, Mbale, Uganda; City of London College (associateship Chartered Insurance Institute 1966); Holborn College (FCII 1968).

Non-political career: Section manager, Sun Alliance Insurance Co 1962-66; Accident underwriter, Household and General Insurance Company 1966-68; Principal officer, Guardian Royal Exchange 1968-78; Chair and chief executive, Camberford Law plc 1978-2008.

Political career: *House of Lords:* Raised to the peerage as Baron Sheikh, of Cornhill in the City of London 2006. Member, Communications 2016-17. *Other:* Conservative Muslim Forum: Chair 2004-14, President 2014-; Chair, Conservative Ethnic Diversity Council 2005-.

Political interests: Ethnic issues, environment, financial services, economy, home and international affairs, pensions.

Other: President, chair, council member several financial, especially insurance, bodies; British Insurance Brokers Association (BIBA): Regional chair 1991-92, 1996-97, Director; Director, South London Training and Enterprise Council 1998-99, 1999-2003; Freedom, City of London 1995.

Recreations: Keep-fit, walking, countryside, travel.

The Lord Sheikh, House of Lords, London SW1A 0PW
Tel: 020 7219 4542 *Email:* sheikhm@parliament.uk Website: lordsheikh.com

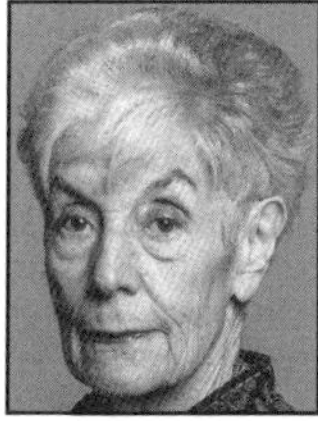

CONSERVATIVE

SHEPHARD OF NORTHWOLD, BARONESS

SHEPHARD OF NORTHWOLD (Life Baroness), Gillian Patricia Shephard; cr 2005. Born 22 January 1940; Daughter of late Reginald and Bertha Watts; Married Thomas Shephard 1975 (2 stepsons).

Education: North Walsham Girls' High School; St Hilda's College, Oxford (BA modern languages 1961, MA); French, rusty German.

Non-political career: Education officer and schools inspector, Norfolk County Council 1963-75; Part-time lecturer, Workers' Educational Association and Cambridge Extra Mural Board 1965-87; Anglia TV 1975-77.

Political career: *House of Commons:* MP (Conservative) for South West Norfolk 1987-2005; PPS to Peter Lilley as Economic Secretary to the Treasury 1988-89; Parliamentary Under-Secretary of State, Department of Social Security 1989-90; Minister of State, HM Treasury 1990-92; Secretary of State for Employment and for Women's Issues 1992-93; Minister of Agriculture, Fisheries and Food 1993-94; Secretary of State for Education (and Employment) 1995-97; Shadow Leader of the House of Commons 1997-98; Member House of Commons Commission 1997-99; Shadow Chancellor of the Duchy of Lancaster 1997-98; Shadow Secretary of State for the Environment, Transport and the Regions 1998-99. *House of Lords:* Raised to the peerage as Baroness Shephard of Northwold, of Northwold in the County of Norfolk 2005. Member, Speakers' Working Group on All-Party Groups 2011-12. Member: Selection 2007-10, Procedure 2007-10, Joint Committee on the Draft House of Lords Reform Bill 2011-12, Public Service and Demographic Change 2012-13, Mental Capacity Act 2005 2013-14, Affordable Childcare 2014-15; Chair, Leader's Group on Governance 2015. *Other:*

Conservative Party: Joint deputy chair 1991-92, Head, Candidates Development Unit 2001-03, Deputy chair 2002-03, Chair, Association of Conservative Peers 2007-12, Board member Board 2007-12. JP 1973-; Norfolk County Council: Councillor 1977-89, Deputy Leader 1982-87; Government co-chair, Women's National Commission 1990; DL, Norfolk 2003-; Member, Committee on Standards in Public Life 2003-07; President, Norfolk Association of Local Councils 2009-; Deputy chair, Social Mobility Commission 2013-17.

Political interests: Constitution, education, agriculture and rural affairs; Latin America, France.

Other: Member, Franco-British Council 2000-07; Oxford University: Council member 2002-06, Member, Continuing Education Board 2004-; Chair, Franco-British Society 2005-11; Member, Fawcett Commission 2005-; Patron, WEA 2006-; Royal Veterinary College: Chair of council 2006-, Fellow 2012-; Chair, Oxford University Society 2009-; Chair of council, Institute of Education 2010-15; Council member, Royal Norfolk Agricultural Association; Trustee, Norwich Cathedral; Vice-chair, Social Mobility Commission 2013-17; EDP We Care Appeal; Fellow, Royal Veterinary College; Hon. fellow: St Hilda's College, Oxford, Queen Mary, University of London, UCL, University of London 2015; Hon. Doctorate, University of East Anglia 2018; PC 1992; Légion d'Honneur (France) 2009. Norfolk Club.

Publications: Reforming Local Government (1999); Shephard's Watch (2000); Knapton Remembered (2007); Twentieth Century Village Voices (2011); The Real Iron Lady – Working with Margaret Thatcher (2013).

Recreations: Music, gardening, France.

Rt Hon the Baroness Shephard of Northwold, House of Lords, London SW1A 0PW
Tel: 020 7219 6241

CONSERVATIVE

SHERBOURNE OF DIDSBURY, LORD

SHERBOURNE OF DIDSBURY (Life Baron), Stephen Ashley Sherbourne; cr 2013. Born 15 October 1945; Son of late Jack and Blanche Sherbourne.

Education: Burnage Grammar School, Manchester; St Edmund Hall, Oxford (MA philosophy, politics and economics); French, Italian.

Non-political career: Conservative Research Department: Head of economic section 1973-74, Assistant director 1974-75; Head of office for Edward Heath MP 1975-76; Special adviser to Patrick Jenkin as Secretary of State for Industry 1982-83; Political secretary to Margaret Thatcher as Prime Minister 1983-88; Senior corporate communications consultant, Lowe Bell Communications 1988-92; Managing director, Lowe Bell Consultants/Bell Pottinger Consultants 1992-99; Chair, Lowe Bell Political/Bell Pottinger Public Affairs 1994-2001; Director, Chime Communications plc 2001-03; Chief of Staff to Michael Howard as Leader of the Opposition 2003-05; Director: Smithfield Consultants 2006-, Newscounter 2007-10, Trufflenet 2010-; Chair, Interel Consulting UK 2012-13.

Political career: *House of Lords:* Raised to the peerage as Baron Sherbourne of Didsbury, of Didsbury in the City of Manchester 2013. Member: Communications 2014-17, Joint Committee on Statutory Instruments 2015-17, Trade Union and Party Funding 2016, Secondary Legislation Scrutiny 2017-, SLSC Sub-committee B 2018-19, Constitution 2020-. *Other:* Chair, Parliamentary and Political Service Honours Committee 2018-.

Political interests: Economy, education, business; France, Germany, Italy, USA.

Other: Trustee, China Oxford Scholarship Fund 2006-11; Member, policy advisory board, Social Market Foundation 2007-; CBE 1988; Kt 2006.

Recreations: Cinema, music, theatre, tennis.

The Lord Sherbourne of Didsbury CBE, House of Lords, London SW1A 0PW
Tel: 020 7219 5353 *Email:* sherbournes@parliament.uk

LABOUR

SHERLOCK, BARONESS

Opposition Spokesperson for Work and Pensions

SHERLOCK (Life Baroness), Maeve Christina Mary Sherlock; cr 2010. Born 10 November 1960; Daughter of Roisin and William Sherlock.

Education: Our Lady's Senior School, Abingdon; Liverpool University (BA sociology 1984); Open University (MBA 1997); Durham University (MA theology 2007).

Non-political career: Treasurer, Liverpool University Guild 1984-85; National Union of Students: Executive officer 1985-86, Treasurer 1986-88, President 1988-90; Director, Endsleigh Insurance 1986-90; UKCOSA: Deputy director 1990-91, Director 1991-97; Director, National Council for One Parent Families 1997-2000; Special adviser to Gordon Brown MP as Chancellor of the Exchequer 2000-03; Chief executive, British Refugee Council 2003-06.

Political career: *House of Lords:* Raised to the peerage as Baroness Sherlock, of Durham in the County of Durham 2010. Opposition Whip 2013-15; Opposition Spokesperson for Work and Pensions 2013-; Opposition Senior Whip 2015-20. *Other:* Member, Equality and Human Rights Commission 2007-10; Board member, Financial Ombudsman Service 2008-; Non-executive director, Child Maintenance and Enforcement Commission 2008-10; Member, Riot Communities and Victims Panel 2011-.

Political interests: Families with children, poverty, welfare state, health, communities, faith and politics.

Other: Court member, Warwick University 1993-95, Executive board member, European Association for International Education 1994-97, Assembly member, Greenwich University 1995-97; Governor, Sheffield Hallam University 1997-2000; Trustee: National Family and Parenting Institute 1999-2000, Demos 2004-07; Member: Advisory board, Naturalisation and Integration 2004-, National Refugee Integration Forum 2006-; Chair, National Students Forum 2008-10; Council member, St John's College, Durham University 2009-; NEPACS, Chapel Street; DUniv, Sheffield Hallam University; Hon. fellow, St Chad's College, Durham University; OBE 2000.

Recreations: Cookery, music, books.

The Baroness Sherlock OBE, House of Lords, London SW1A 0PW
Tel: 020 7219 8905 *Email:* sherlockm@parliament.uk *Twitter:* @maevesherlock

CONSERVATIVE

SHIELDS, BARONESS

SHIELDS (Life Baroness), Joanna Shields; cr 2014. Born 12 July 1962; Daughter of Kaye and Thomas Shields; Married Andy Stevenson (1 son).

Education: Pennsylvania State University (BSc 1984); George Washington University (MBA 1987); Hebrew.

Non-political career: Product manager, National Digital 1986-89; Vice-president, Electronics for Imaging, USA 1989-97: Chief executive officer, Veon, USA 1997-2000; Vice-president, International: Real Networks, USA 2000-02, Decru, USA 2002-03; Managing director, Syndication, Business Development, Google EMEA 2004-07; Chief executive officer, Bebo 2007-09; President, People Networks AOL 2010; Vice-president and managing director, Facebook EMEA 2010-13; Chair, TechCity UK 2013-15; Chief executive, Benevolent AI 2018-.

Political career: *House of Lords:* Raised to the peerage as Baroness Shields, of Maida Vale in the City of Westminster 2014. Adviser to the Prime Minister on Digital Economy 2014-15; Parliamentary Under-Secretary of State for Internet Safety and Security and Government Spokesperson: Department for Culture, Media and Sport and Home Office 2015-16, Home Office 2016-17; Prime Minister's Special Representative on: Internet Crime and Harms 2016-17, Internet Safety 2017-18; On leave of absence May 2018-December 2019. *Other:* UK Business Ambassador for Digital Industries 2013-15; Founder and Member, WeProtect Global Alliance – End Child Sexual Exploitation Online (formerly US/UK Taskforce to combat child online abuse and exploitation) 2014-; Co-Chair, UK Council for Child Internet Safety; Member: Child Protection Implementation Taskforce, Tackling Extremism in Communities

Implementation Taskforce, Inter-Ministerial Group on Violence Against Women and Girls, Inter-Ministerial Group on Child Sexual Abuse.

Political interests: Digital agenda, child online protection, cyber-security, counter-terrorism and extremism, conflict zones; USA.

Other: Trustee: NSPCC's There4Me 2005-09, Save the Children UK 2008-12, Prince's Trust Internet and Media Leadership Group, Women's Business Council, American School in London 2011-15; Member, EU Web Entrepreneurs Leaders' Club 2013-14; Non-executive director, London Stock Exchange Group 2014-15; Member, Advisory board, Elbi; Commissioner, Transatlantic Commission on Election Integrity 2018-; Non-executive chair, CognitionX 2018-; Honorary doctorate, Public Service and for the WeProtect Initiative, George Washington University; Most Influential Woman in the UK IT industry, *Computer Weekly* 2013; Lifetime Achievement Award, British Interactive Media Association 2013; OBE 2014.

The Baroness Shields OBE, House of Lords, London SW1A 0PW
Tel: 020 7219 5353 *Email:* shieldsj@parliament.uk Website: www.joannashields.com
Twitter: @joannashields

CONSERVATIVE

SHINKWIN, LORD

SHINKWIN (Life Baron) Kevin Joseph Maximilian Shinkwin; cr 2015. Born 7 June 1971.

Education: Hull University (BA British politics and legislative studies).

Non-political career: Parliamentary affairs manager: Macmillan Cancer Relief 2001-05, Cancer Research UK 2005-08; Head of public affairs, Royal British Legion 2008-13; Parliamentary affairs and campaigns director, Wine and Spirits Trade Association 2013-15.

Political career: *House of Lords:* Raised to the peerage as Baron Shinkwin, of Balham in the London Borough of Wandsworth 2015. Member, Financial Exclusion 2016-17. *Other:* Commissioner, Equality and Human Rights Commission 2017-18.

Other: Trustee, National Council for Palliative Care 2016-17.

The Lord Shinkwin, House of Lords, London SW1A 0PW
Tel: 020 7219 3000

LIBERAL DEMOCRAT

SHIPLEY, LORD

Liberal Democrat Lords Whip

SHIPLEY (Life Baron), John Warren Shipley; cr 2010. Born 5 July 1946; Son of Edward Shipley and Grace Shipley, née Horton; Married Margaret Pattison 1969 (1 son 1 daughter).

Education: Whitby Grammar School; University College London (history 1969) (Union President 1968-69).

Non-political career: Brand management, Procter and Gamble 1969-71; Administrator, various roles then retired as regional director for the north of England and EU, Open University 1971-2005.

Political career: *House of Commons:* Contested (Liberal) Blyth February and October 1974, Hexham 1979, (Liberal/All) Newcastle upon Tyne North 1983 and 1987 general elections. *House of Lords:* Raised to the peerage as Baron Shipley, of Gosforth in the County of Tyne and Wear 2010. Liberal Democrat: Spokesperson for Decentralisation and the Northern Powerhouse 2015, Shadow Minister/Spokesperson for Housing 2016-19, Whip 2020-. Member: Economic Affairs 2010-15, Economic Affairs Finance Bill Sub-Committee 2011, EU Internal Market Sub-committee 2019-20, EU Goods Sub-committee 2020-. *Other:* Member, Liberal Democrat Manifesto Working Group 2013-. Newcastle City Council: Councillor 1975-2012, Opposition Leader 1988-98, Council Leader 2006-10; Member: Northumbria Police Authority 1980s, Tyne and Wear Passenger Transport Authority 1990s, 2004-06; Former board member, Newcastle International Airport Local Authority Holding Company 2004-06; Board member, One North East 2005-12; Vice-President, Local Government Association 2010-.

Political interests: Local government, regeneration; Central and eastern Europe.

Other: Former director: Northern Development Company 1990s, Tyne and Wear Development Company 1990s, 2004-08; Executive member, Universities for the North East; Former board member: NewcastleGateshead City Development Company (1NG), Newcastle Science City Company, Newcastle Local Strategic Partnership, Northern Way Transport Compact, Newcastle Theatre Royal Trust; Chair, Prince's Trust (North East); Doctor of Civil Law, Northumbria University 2011; OBE 1995.

Recreations: Classical music, theatre, First World War, Sunderland AFC.

The Lord Shipley OBE, House of Lords, London SW1A 0PW
Tel: 020 7219 5353 *Email:* shipleyj@parliament.uk

CONSERVATIVE

SHREWSBURY AND WATERFORD, EARL OF

SHREWSBURY (22nd Earl of, E), cr. 1442, AND WATERFORD (22nd Earl of, I), cr. 1446; Charles Henry John Benedict Crofton Chetwynd Chetwynd-Talbot; Earl Talbot and Viscount Ingestre (GB) 1784; Baron Talbot (GB) 1733. Born 18 December 1952; Son of 21st Earl; Married Deborah Hutchinson 1974 (2 sons 1 daughter).

Education: Harrow School.

Non-political career: Joint Deputy Chairman, Britannia Building Society 1987-92; Director, Richmount Enterprise Zone Trust 1988-94; Director: PMI Limited 1996-98, Banafix Limited 1996-98, Minibusplus 1997-2001, Talbot Consulting Limited. Hon. Colonel, 'A' Squadron RMLY 2003-06.

Political career: *House of Lords:* First entered House of Lords 1980; Elected hereditary peer 1999-; Assistant Party Whip 2013-. Member: Works of Art 2009-10, 2012-13, Services 2016-18, Intellectual Property (Unjustified Threats) Bill 2016. *Other:* Member, Association of Conservative Peers. DL, Staffordshire 1994-; Chair, Firearms Consultative Committee 1994-99.

Political interests: Agriculture, environment, construction industry, property, West Midlands, mineral extraction, firearms and shooting sports, fishing; Scotland.

Other: President and National Executive Director, British Institute of Innkeeping 1996-98; Hon. President, Gun Trade Association 2002-; British Shooting Sports Council: Chair 2002-08, President 2008-14; Deputy Chair, Standing Conference on Country Sports 2011-; President, Staffordshire Historic Churches Trust 2012-; High Steward, Sheffield Cathedral 2014-; President, Building Societies Association 1993-97; St Giles' Hospice, Lichfield; Member: Worshipful Company of Weavers, Worshipful Company of Gunmakers; Chancellor, Wolverhampton University 1993-99; Hon. LLD, Wolverhampton University 1994; Premier Earl on Rolls of both England and Ireland; Hereditary Lord High Steward of Ireland. Army and Navy, Pratt's Club.

Recreations: Shooting, fishing.

The Earl of Shrewsbury and Waterford DL, House of Lords, London SW1A 0PW
Tel: 020 7219 3158 *Email:* shrewsburyc@parliament.uk *Twitter:* @lordshrewsbury

LABOUR

SIKKA, LORD

SIKKA (Life Baron), Prem Nath Sikka; cr 2020.

Education: Upton House Secondary School.

Non-political career: Professor, Essex University 1996-2016; Professor of Accounting, Sheffield University 2017-.

Political career: *House of Lords:* Raised to the peerage as Baron Sikka, of Kingswood in Basildon in the County of Essex 2020.

Professor the Lord Sikka, House of Lords, London SW1A 0PW *Twitter:* @premnsikka

LABOUR

SIMON, VISCOUNT

SIMON (3rd Viscount, UK), Jan David Simon; cr. 1940. Born 20 July 1940; Son of 2nd Viscount, CMG; Married Mary Elizabeth Burns 1969 (died 2020) (1 daughter).

Education: Westminster School; School of Navigation, Southampton University; Sydney Technical College.

Political career: *House of Lords:* First entered House of Lords 1993; Deputy Chairman of Committees 1998-; Deputy Speaker 1999-; Elected hereditary peer 1999-. Member: Dangerous Dogs (Amendment) Bill 1995-96, London Local Authorities Bill 1998, Procedure 1999-2002, Personal Bills 2004-09, Standing Orders (Private Bills) 2004-; Co-opted Member, Science and Technology Sub-committee I (Allergy) 2006-07.

Political interests: Disability, motor industry, police, road safety, science and technology, aviation; Australia, Qatar.

Other: Trustee, Guild of Experienced Motorists, Road Safety Charity 1999-2019; President: Driving Instructors Association 2000-13, GEM Motoring Assist 2004-19; Younger Brother, Trinity House 2007-; Patron, Road Victims Trust 2010-; Graduate and Postgraduate, Police Service Parliamentary Scheme with Essex Police 2010-13; Trustee: Safety House 2015-16, Road Safety Trust 2015-16; Honorary Vice-President, GEM Motoring Assist 2019-; Fellow, Hertfordshire University 2013; Award, Police Federation of England and Wales 2013 and 2015.

Recreations: Photography, baroque music.

The Viscount Simon, House of Lords, London SW1A 0PW
Tel: 020 7219 5353 *Email:* simonj@parliament.uk

CROSSBENCH

SINGH OF WIMBLEDON, LORD

SINGH OF WIMBLEDON (Life Baron); Indarjit Singh cr. 2011. Born 17 September 1932; Son of Dr Diwan Singh and Kundan Kaur; Married Dr Kanwaljit Kaur 1962 (2 daughters).

Education: Bishop Vesey's Grammar School, Sutton Coldfield; Birmingham University (MCom; MBA); MiminE CEng 1967; French, Hindi, Punjabi.

Non-political career: National Coal Board 1955-59, 1965-67; Mines manager, India 1959-65; Costain 1967-75; Management consultant, London 1975-2002; Editor, *Sikh Messenger* 1984-; Director, Network of Sikh Organisations UK 1995-; Founder Member, Interfaith Network UK. Head of Sikh Armed Services Chaplaincy.

Political career: *House of Lords:* Raised to the peerage as Baron Singh of Wimbledon, of Wimbledon in the London Borough of Merton 2011. Adviser to: Ministry of Justice on Sikhs in Prisons, Ministry of Defence on Sikhs in the Armed Services. Member, Joint Committee on Human Rights 2019-. *Other:* JP, Wimbledon 1984; Member, Interfaith Network UK.

Political interests: Resolution of conflict, liaising with all political parties to ensure greater weightage of ethical considerations in decision-making; Canada, France, India, USA.

Other: Member, World Parliament of Religions and the Global Sikh Organisation; Contributor, Thought for the Day, BBC Radio 4 1984-; Prison Chaplaincy and Director, Sikh Chaplaincy Service UK 2004-; Member, Institution of Mining Engineers 1967; Amnesty International, Save the Children Fund, Unicef; Hon. DLitt, Coventry University 2002; Hon. DLaws, Leicester University 2004; Hon. DArts, Leeds Metropolitan University 2007; Hon. DLitt, York St Johns University 2014; Promotion of Inter-faith Understanding, UK Templeton Prize 1989; Inter-faith Medallion for Services to Religious Broadcasting 1991; Jewel of Punjab Award, World Punjabi Organisation; OBE 1996; CBE 2009.

The Lord Singh of Wimbledon CBE, House of Lords, London SW1A 0PW
Tel: 020 7219 8951
Tel: 020 8540 4148 *Email:* sikhmessenger@aol.com

CROSSBENCH

SKIDELSKY, LORD

SKIDELSKY (Life Baron), Robert Jacob Alexander Skidelsky; cr. 1991. Born 25 April 1939; Son of late Boris Skidelsky and Galia Skidelsky, née Sapelkin; Married Augusta Hope 1970 (2 sons 1 daughter).

Education: Brighton College; Jesus College, Oxford (BA modern history 1961); Nuffield College, Oxford (DPhil 1968).

Non-political career: Research fellow, Nuffield College, Oxford 1965-68; Associate professor, School of Advanced International Studies, Johns Hopkins University, Washington DC 1970-76; Head of department of history, philosophy and European studies, Polytechnic of North London 1976-78; Warwick University: Professor of: International studies 1978-90, Political economy 1990-2006; Director, Janus Capital 2001-11; Founder and chair, Centre for Global Studies 2002-; Director: Greater Europe Fund 2005-09, Sistema JSC 2008-10, Rusnano Capital 2010-. Member, AUT.

Political career: *House of Lords:* Raised to the peerage as Baron Skidelsky, of Tilton in the County of East Sussex 1991. Opposition Spokesperson for: Culture, Media and Sport 1997-98, the Treasury 1998-99. Member: Economic Affairs 2003-08, 2012-15, 2019-, Refreshment 2009-14, EU Sub-committee G (Social Policies and Consumer Protection) 2010-12, Joint Committee on the Draft Financial Services Bill 2011-12, EU Financial Affairs Sub-committee 2015-18. *Other:* Member: Lord Chancellor's Advisory Council on Public Records 1987-92, School Examinations and Assessment Council 1992-93; Governor, Portsmouth University 1994-97; Brighton College: Governor 1998-, Chair 2004-; Governor, Moscow School of Political Studies 1999-; Founder member, World Political Forum 2002-; Member, Academic Council, Wilton Park 2002-09.

Political interests: Education, economic policy, Europe, transition economies, arts; China, Russia.

Other: Member, Inter-Parliamentary Union; Fellow: Royal Historical Society 1973, Royal Society of Literature 1978, Chair: Charleston Trust 1987-92, Social Market Foundation 1991-2001; Fellow, British Academy 1994; Trustee, Daedatus Trust 2011-; Freedom, Knoxville, Tennessee, USA 1998; Hon DLitt, Buckingham University; Hon Fellow, Jesus College, Oxford 1997; Hon doctorate, University of Rome 2010; Hon DLitt, Warwick University 2011; Wolfson Prize for History 1992; Duff Cooper Prize for *Fighting for Britain, 1937-1946*, 2000; Lionel Gelber Prize for International Relations 2001; Council on Foreign Relations Prize 2002; James Tait Black Memorial Prize for *Fighting for Britain, 1937-1946*, 2002; Cavaliere di gran Croce (Italy) 2010. Grillion's Club.

Publications: Includes: Politicians and the Slump (1967); English Progressive Schools (1969); Oswald Mosley (1975); Biographies of John Maynard Keynes: Hopes Betrayed, 1883-1920 (1983), The Economist as Saviour, 1920-1937 (1992), Fighting for Britain, 1937-1946 (2000), (abridged, single volume edition 2003); The World After Communism (1995); Keynes – The Return of the Master (2009); Co-author, How Much Is Enough? (Allen Lane, 2012); Britain Since 1900 – A Success Story? (Vintage, 2014).

Recreations: Opera, listening to music, tennis, table tennis, good conversation.

Professor the Lord Skidelsky, House of Lords, London SW1A 0PW
Tel: 020 7219 8721 *Email:* skidelskyr@parliament.uk
Room 207, Fielden House, 13 Little College Street, London SW1P 3SH

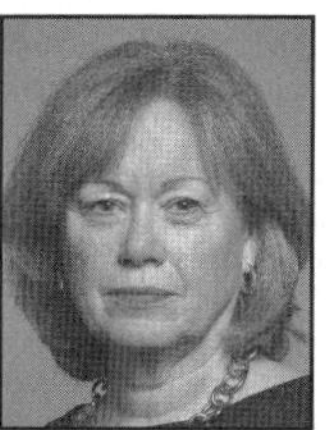

LABOUR/
CO-OPERATIVE

SMITH OF BASILDON, BARONESS

Shadow Leader of the House of Lords; Opposition Spokesperson for Cabinet Office, Constitutional and Devolved Issues and Northern Ireland

SMITH OF BASILDON (Life Baroness), Angela Evans Smith; cr 2010. Born 7 January 1959; Daughter of Patrick Evans, retired factory worker, and Emily Evans, neé Russell, supervisor of church pre-school; Married Nigel Smith 1978.

Education: Chalvedon Comprehensive, Basildon; Leicester Polytechnic (BA public administration 1981).

Non-political career: Trainee accountant, London Borough of Newham 1981-83; League Against Cruel Sports, finally head of political and public relations 1983-95; Research assistant to Alun Michael MP 1995-97. Member, USDAW.

Political career: *House of Commons:* Contested Southend West 1987 general election. MP (Lab/Co-op) for Basildon 1997-2010. Contested South Basildon and East Thurrock 2010 general election; PPS to Paul Boateng as Minister of State, Home Office 1999-2001; Assistant Government Whip 2001-02; Parliamentary Under-Secretary of State: Northern Ireland Office 2002-06, Department for Communities and Local Government 2006-07; PPS to Gordon Brown as Prime Minister 2007-09; Minister of State, Cabinet Office 2009-10. Joint Vice-chair, PLP Departmental Committee for International Development 1999-2000. *House of Lords:* Raised to the peerage as Baroness Smith of Basildon, of Basildon in the County of Essex 2010. Opposition Spokesperson for: Energy and Climate Change 2010-13, Northern Ireland 2011-12, 2018-, Home Office 2012-15; Opposition Deputy Chief Whip 2012-15; Shadow Leader of the House of Lords 2015-; Opposition Spokesperson for Constitutional Affairs 2015-20; Member, House of Lords Commission 2016-; Opposition Spokesperson for: Cabinet Office 2018-20, Cabinet Office, Constitutional and Devolved Issues 2020-. Member: Selection 2015-, House 2015, Liaison 2015, Privileges and Conduct 2015-19, Procedure/Procedure and Privileges 2015-, Joint Committee on the Palace of Westminster 2015-16. *Other:* Essex County Council: Councillor 1989-97, Chief Whip 1993-96; Vice-president, Local Government Association 2011-.

Political interests: Home affairs, animal welfare, international development, employment, third sector, fire service; Cuba, Germany, Ireland, USA.

Other: Patron, Basildon Women's Aid; Vice-chair, Cuba Solidarity Campaign; President, Basildon Ladies Football Club -2015; Vice-president, League Against Cruel Sports; Patron, Captive Animals Protection Society; Honorary President, St Clere's Co-op Academy Trust 2012-; Chair, Resolving Chaos 2012-14; Patron, Stanford and Corringham Schools Trust 2013-14; Chair, Production Exchange 2014-; Political Studies Association, Parliamentarian of the Year 2016; PC 2009.

Recreations: Swimming, reading, theatre, watching *Coronation Street.*

Rt Hon the Baroness Smith of Basildon, House of Lords, London SW1A 0PW
Tel: 020 7219 3237 *Email:* smithangela@parliament.uk *Twitter:* @LadyBasildon

NON-AFFILIATED

SMITH OF FINSBURY, LORD

SMITH OF FINSBURY (Life Baron), Christopher Robert Smith; cr 2005. Born 24 July 1951; Son of Colin Smith, civil servant, and Gladys Smith, teacher.

Education: George Watson's College, Edinburgh; Pembroke College, Cambridge (BA English 1972; PhD 1979) (President, Cambridge Union 1972); Harvard University (Kennedy Scholar 1975-76); French, German (rusty).

Non-political career: Housing Corporation 1976-77; Shaftesbury Society Housing Association 1977-80; Society for Co-operative Dwellings 1980-83; Senior Adviser, Walt Disney Company 2001-07; Visiting Professor, University of the Arts London 2002-10; Chair: Environment Agency 2008-14, Immidtown Business Improvement District 2014; Master, Pembroke College, Cambridge 2015-; Chair, Intellectual Property Regulatory Board (IPReg) 2018-. ASTMS: Branch secretary 1977-80, Branch chair 1980-83.

Political career: *House of Commons:* Contested Epsom and Ewell 1979 general election. MP (Labour) for Islington South and Finsbury 1983-2005; Opposition London Whip 1986-87; Shadow Treasury Minister 1987-92; Shadow Secretary of State for: Environmental Protection 1992-94, National Heritage 1994-95, Social Security 1995-96, Health 1996-97; Sponsored Environment and Safety Information Act 1988 (Private Member's Bill); Secretary of State for: National Heritage May-July 1997, Culture, Media and Sport July 1997-2001; Chair, Millennium Commission 1997-2001. *House of Lords:* Raised to the peerage as Baron Smith of Finsbury, of Finsbury in the London Borough of Islington 2005. *Other:* Chair, Labour Campaign for Criminal Justice 1985-88; Vice-President, Christian Socialist Movement 1987-; President, SERA 1992-2007; Patron, LGBT Labour. Islington Borough Council: Councillor 1978-83, Chief Whip 1978-79, Chair of Housing 1981-83; Co-opted member, Council for National Parks 1980-89; Member: Committee on Standards in Public Life 2001-05, Review Committee of Privy Counsellors of the Anti-terrorism, Crime and Security Act 2002-03; Founding director,

Clore Leadership Programme 2003-08; Chair: London Cultural Consortium 2004-08, Advertising Standards Authority 2007-17.

Political interests: Culture, media, sport, housing, local and regional government, foreign affairs, environment, civil liberties, criminal justice, economic policy, social security, health, higher education; Argentina, Australia, Brazil, China, Cyprus, Europe, Hong Kong, New Zealand, South Africa, USA.

Other: Tribune Group: Secretary 1984-88, Chair 1988-89, Chair of board, *Tribune* newspaper 1990-93; Member: Shelter Board 1986-92, Executive, National Council for Civil Liberties 1986-88; Sadlers Wells Theatre: Board member 1986-92, Governor 1992-97; Vice-President, Wildlife Link 1986-90; Fabian Society: Member, Executive 1990-98, Vice-chair 1995-96, Chair 1997-98; Trustee, John Muir Trust 1992-97; Chair of board, *New Century* Magazine 1993-96; Executive Committee, National Trust 1994-96; Senior associate, Judge Institute, Cambridge University 2001-06; Wordsworth Trust: Trustee 2001-17, Chair 2003-17, Honorary President 2018-; Board member, Royal National Theatre 2001-09; Chair, Classic FM Consumer Panel 2001-07; Donmar Warehouse: Board member 2001-15, Chair 2003-15; Board member: Terrence Higgins Trust 2001-05, Poetry Archive 2002-07; Chair of Judges, Man Booker Prize 2004; Governor, University of Arts, London 2005-08; Windsor Leadership Trust 2006-08; Board member, Phonographic Performance Ltd 2007-; International Advisory Committee, Russian State Museum, St Petersburg 2008-14; Chair of Judges, Museum of the Year Prize 2012; Trustee, The Sixteen 2013-; Chair, Art Fund 2014-; Non-executive director, Spencer Ogden 2014-17; Independent Non-executive Director, South Staffs and Cambridge Water Companies 2018-; Chair, Intellectual Property Regulation Board 2018-; Honorary Liveryman, Company of Arts Scholars 2017-; Freedom, London Borough of Islington 2011; Honorary fellow, Royal Institute of British Architects 2000; Honorary Doctor of Arts, City University 2003; Honorary fellow, Pembroke College, Cambridge 2004-; Senior Fellow, Royal College of Art 2007; Visiting fellow, Ashridge Business School 2007-10; Honorary fellow: King's College London 2008, Cumbria University 2010; Honorary doctorate, Lancaster University 2011; Honorary fellow, Royal Incorporation of Architects in Scotland 2012; Honorary doctorate: Westminster University 2015, London Metropolitan University 2016; PC 1997.

Publications: National Parks (Fabian Society, 1977); New Questions for Socialism (Fabian Society, 1996); Creative Britain (Faber, 1998); Co-author, Suicide of the West (Continuum, 2006).

Recreations: Mountaineering, literature, theatre, music, art.

Rt Hon the Lord Smith of Finsbury, House of Lords, London SW1A 0PW
Pembroke College, Cambridge CB2 1RF *Tel:* 01223 338129 *Email:* master@pem.cam.ac.uk

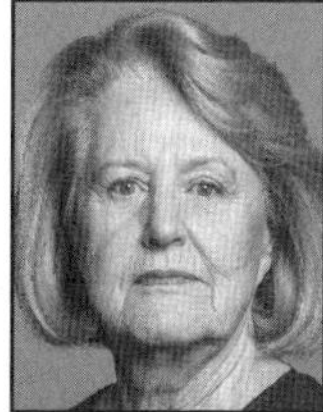

LABOUR

SMITH OF GILMOREHILL, BARONESS

SMITH OF GILMOREHILL (Life Baroness), Elizabeth Margaret Smith; cr. 1995. Born 4 June 1940; Daughter of late Frederick William Moncrieff Bennett and late Elizabeth Waters Irvine Shanks; Married John Smith 1967 (MP 1970-94, Leader of the Labour Party 1992-94) (died 1994) (3 daughters).

Education: Hutchesons' Girls' Grammar School, Glasgow; Glasgow University (MA French and Russian 1962).

Non-political career: Chair, Lamda Development Board -2001; Non-executive director: Deutsche Bank, Scotland -2004, City Inn Ltd -2011; BP Advisory Board for Scotland -2004.

Political career: *House of Lords:* Raised to the peerage as Baroness Smith of Gilmorehill, of Gilmorehill in the District of the City of Glasgow 1995. Opposition Spokeswoman on National Heritage (Tourism) 1996-97. *Other:* Member, Press Complaints Commission 1995-2001; DL, City of Edinburgh 1996.

Political interests: Arts; Russia, Former Soviet Union.

Other: Executive Committee Member, Inter-Parliamentary Union British Group -2002; Board member, Edinburgh International Festival -1999; Council member, Britain in Europe Campaign; Member: British Heart Foundation -2000, Future of Europe Trust -2000, John Smith Memorial Trust, Know How Fund Advisory Board -2000; Trustee, Hakluyt Foundation -2001; Member: English Speaking Union, Russo-British Chamber of Commerce, Centre for European Reform -2004; 21st Century Trust -2008; President, Scottish Opera -2012; Chair, Edinburgh Festival

Fringe -2012; Member: RIIA – Chatham House Mariinsky Theatre Trust; John Smith Memorial Trust, Dash Arts; Chancellor, Birkbeck College, London 1998-2003; Hon. LLD, University of Glasgow.

The Baroness Smith of Gilmorehill DL, House of Lords, London SW1A 0PW
Tel: 020 7219 5353 *Email:* smithlady@parliament.uk

CONSERVATIVE

SMITH OF HINDHEAD, LORD

SMITH OF HINDHEAD (Life Baron), Philip Roland Smith; cr 2015. Born 16 February 1966; Son of late John Smith and Ann Smith; Married Emma Clarke 1989 (1 son 1 daughter).

Education: Woolmer Hill School, Haslemere.

Non-political career: Association of Conservative Clubs: Joined 1987, Chief Executive 1999-.

Political career: *House of Lords:* Raised to the peerage as Baron Smith of Hindhead, of Hindhead in the County of Surrey 2015. Party Whip 2016-. Member: Licensing Act 2003 2016-17, Liaison 2017-, Political Polling and Digital Media 2017-18, Regenerating Seaside Towns and Communities 2018-19, Social and Economic Impact of the Gambling Industry 2019-. *Other:* Treasurer, Conservative Party 2001-; Chairman, National Conservative Draws Society 2001-; Financial Trustee of the Conservative Agents' Benevolent Association (registered charity) 2014-; Trustee, Conservative Party Agents' Pension Fund 2014-; Member, Conservative Party's Finance and Audit Committee 2016-; Trustee, Conservative Party Archive 2017.

Political interests: Licensing, gambling, clubs, not-for-profit organisations; Estonia, Latvia, Lithuania.

Other: Chairman: Committee of Registered Clubs Associations, Best Bar None 2017-; Freedom, City of London 2007; CBE 2013. Farnham Conservative, Carlton Club.

Publications: Club Law and Management (2008); Questions & Answers on Club Law and Management (2017).

The Lord Smith of Hindhead CBE, House of Lords, London SW1A 0PW
Tel: 020 7219 3000

CROSSBENCH

SMITH OF KELVIN, LORD

SMITH OF KELVIN (Life Baron), Robert Haldane Smith; cr 2008. Born 8 August 1944; Married Alison Bell 1969 (2 daughters).

Education: Allan Glen's School, Glasgow; Articles, Robb Ferguson & Co 1963-68; Qualified chartered accountant 1968.

Non-political career: Industrial and Commercial Finance Corporation 1968-82; Managing Director, National Commercial & Glyns Ltd 1983-85; General Manager, Corporate Finance Division, Royal Bank of Scotland plc; Managing Director, Charterhouse Development Capital Ltd 1985-89; Morgan Grenfell Development Capital Ltd 1989-2001: Chair 1989-2001, Chief Executive 1989-96; Chief Executive, Morgan Grenfell Asset Management Ltd 1996-2000; Member, Management Committee, Deutsche Bank AG 1996-2000; Deutsche Asset Management: Chief Executive 1999-2000, Vice-chair 2000-02; Chair, Weir Group plc 2002-13; Director, Standard Bank Group 2003-15; Chair: Scottish and Southern Energy plc 2005-16, Smith Group 2005-12; Member, Council of Economic Advisers to First Minister of Scotland 2007-11; Chair: IMI plc 2015-, Forth Ports Limited 2015-, Clyde Gateway 2015-, Alliance Trust plc 2016-.

Political career: *House of Lords:* Raised to the peerage as Baron Smith of Kelvin, of Kelvin in the City of Glasgow 2008. Chair, Smith Commission 2014. *Other:* Member, Museums Advisory Board 1983-85; National Museums of Scotland: Trustee 1985-2002, Chair, Board of Trustees 1993-2002; Museums and Galleries Commission: Commissioner 1988-98, Vice-chair 1997-98; Member, Financial Services Authority 1997-2000; BBC Governor and Chair, Broadcasting Council for Scotland 1999-2004; Financial Reporting Council: Member 2001-04, Chair, FRC Group on Audit Committees Combined Code of Guidance – The Smith Report 2003; Member, Judicial Appointments Board for Scotland 2002-07; Chair: Glasgow 2014

Commonwealth Games Organising Committee 2008-14, Code of Governance for Higher Education in Scotland 2012-13, UK Green Investment Bank 2012-17.

Political interests: South Africa.

Other: Director and Treasurer, Sussex Heritage Trust 1975-82; Non-executive Director: Tip Europe plc 1987-89, MFI Furniture Group 1987-2000, Bank of Scotland plc 1998-2000; Deputy Chair, Bristow Helicopter Group 1991-95; President: British Association of Friends and Museums 1995-2005, Institute of Chartered Accountants of Scotland 1996-97; Statkis plc: Director 1997-99, Chair 1998-99; Non-executive Director: Network Rail 2002-03, Aegon UK plc 2002-09; Member, Board of Trustees, British Council 2002-05; Chair, BBC Children in Need 2003-04; Vice-chair: China Britain Business Council 2003-08, Kelvingrove Museum Appeal 2003-07; Non-executive Director, 3i Group plc 2004-09; Prince's Ambassador for CSR, Scottish Business in the Community 2006-07; Chair, Riverside Museum Appeal 2007-11; Patron, Foundation Scotland 2008-15; President, Royal Highland and Agricultural Society of Scotland 2010-11; Patron, Capital Appeal for Prince and Princess of Wales Hospice 2013-; Chair, International Public Policy Unit 2014-; Non-executive chair, British Business Bank 2017-; President, Institute of Chartered Accountants of Scotland 1996-97; Chancellor: University of the West of Scotland 2003-13, Strathclyde University 2013-; Honorary degree: Edinburgh University 1999, Glasgow University 2001, Paisley University 2003; Hon. Fellowship: Institute of Internal Auditors 2010, Royal College of Physicians and Surgeons of Glasgow 2014; British Venture Capital Association Hall of Fame 2006; Business Leader of the Year, Elite Insider 2008; Lifetime Achievement Award, Scottish Accounts Association 2010; Board Member of the Year, Scotland plc Award 2012; Outstanding Achievement, NED Awards 2012; Wallace Award, American Scottish Foundation 2012; Chairman's Award, Insitute of Directors 2014; Lifetime Achievement Award, Inspiring City: Glasgow 2014; Outstanding Achievement, Great London Scot Award 2014; Shackleton Medal, Royal Scottish Geographical Society 2015; Adam Smith Medal, Royal Society of Edinburgh 2015; Knighted 1999; KT 2014; CH 2016.

Publications: Co-author, Managing Your Company's Finances.

Recreations: Chanteclair Estate, guest house and vineyard in South Africa, highland cattle breeding.

The Lord Smith of Kelvin KT CH, House of Lords, London SW1A 0PW
Tel: 020 7219 5353

LABOUR

SMITH OF LEIGH, LORD

SMITH OF LEIGH (Life Baron), Peter Richard Charles Smith; cr. 1999. Born 24 July 1945; Son of Ronald and Kathleen Smith; Married Joy Booth 1968 (1 daughter).

Education: Bolton School; London School of Economics (BSc economics 1967); Garnett College, London University (CertEd(FE) 1969); Salford University (MSc urban studies 1983).

Non-political career: Lecturer: Walbrook College, London 1969-74, Manchester College of Art and Technology 1974-2000 (part-time 1991-2000); Manchester Airport plc: Board director 1986-2001, Chair 1989-90; Board director, Manchester Airport Group 2001-09. Member, NATFHE -2001.

Political career: *House of Lords:* Raised to the peerage as Baron Smith of Leigh, of Wigan in the County of Greater Manchester 1999. Vice-chair: PLP Departmental Committee for Office of the Deputy Prime Minister 2006-07, PLP Departmental Group for Communities and Local Government 2010-15. *Other:* Wigan Metropolitan Borough Council: Councillor 1978-, Chair, Finance Committee 1982-91, Council Leader 1991-2018; Member: Association of Metropolitan Authorities Policy Committee 1991-97, Local Government Association Policy and Strategy Committee 1997-2000; Vice-chair, Special Interest Group for Municipal Authorities 1997-; Member, Improvement and Development Agency 1999-2003; North West Regional Assembly: Chair 1999-2000, Executive Board 2005-09; Chair, Association of Greater Manchester Authorities 2000-17; Vice-President, Local Government Association 2010-; Chairman, Greater Manchester Combined Authority 2011-15.

Political interests: Local government, regionalism, airports, health; Australia, France, New Zealand, USA.

Other: Oxfam, Wigan and Leigh Hospice; Freedom, Wigan Metropolitan Borough 2011; Doctor of Laws, Manchester Metropolitan University.

Recreations: Gardening, sport, jazz.

The Lord Smith of Leigh, House of Lords, London SW1A 0PW
Tel: 020 7219 8631 *Email:* smithprc@parliament.uk
Town Hall, Library Street, Wigan WN1 1YN *Tel:* 01942 827001 *Twitter:* @Lord_PeterSmith

LIBERAL DEMOCRAT

SMITH OF NEWNHAM, BARONESS

Liberal Democrat Lords Spokesperson for Defence

SMITH OF NEWNHAM (Life Baroness), Julie Elizabeth Smith; cr 2014. Born 1 June 1969; Daughter of Hugh Francis Smith and Eileen Elizabeth Smith, née Murphy.

Education: Merchant Taylor's School for Girls, Crosby; Brasenose College, Oxford (MA philosophy, politics and economics 1991); St Antony's College, Oxford (MPhil; DPhil politics 1995); French, German.

Non-political career: Fellow, Robinson College, Oxford 1997-; Lecturer/Teaching Fellow, Centre for International Studies, Cambridge 1997-2004; Head of European programme, Chatham House 1999-2003; Deputy director, Centre of International Studies, Cambridge University 2004-08; Department of Politics and International Studies (POLIS), Cambridge University: Senior lecturer of international relations 2009-18, Reader in European politics 2018-.

Political career: *House of Lords:* Raised to the peerage as Baroness Smith of Newnham, of Crosby in the County of Merseyside 2014. Liberal Democrat Lords Spokesperson for Defence 2015, 2019-. Member, International Relations/International Relations and Defence 2016-. *Other:* Vice-chair, Liberal Democrat Federal Policy Committee. Cambridge City Council: Councillor 2003-15, Executive Councillor for: Arts and Recreation 2006-10, Customer Services and Resources 2012-14, Honorary Councillor 2015-.

Political interests: Europe, defence, higher education; France, Germany.

Other: Trustee: Cambridge University Catholic Association 2008-, Gladstone's Library, Hawarden 2014-; Gladstone's Library Hawarden, Cambridge University Catholic Association.

Publications: Voice of the people: European Parliament in the 1990s (1995); Eminent Europeans: Personalities who shaped contemporary Europe (1996); A Sense of Liberty: A Short History of the Liberal International 1947-97 (1997); Democracy in the New Europe (1999); Europe's Elected Parliament (1999); The New Bilateralism: The UK's Bilateral Relations within the EU (2002); Co-editor, Through the Paper Curtain: Insiders and Outsiders in the New Europe (2003); Reinvigorating European Elections: the Implications of Electing the European Commission (2005); New Horizons in European Politics Series (2011-); Co-editor and contributor, Palgrave Handbook on National Parliaments and the European Union (2015).

Recreations: Yoga, ballet, travelling.

The Baroness Smith of Newnham, House of Lords, London SW1A 0PW
Tel: 020 7219 3214 *Email:* jes42@parliament.uk
Department of Politics and International Studies, Alison Richard Building, 7 West Road, Cambridge CB3 9DT *Tel:* 01223 766259

LABOUR

SNAPE, LORD

SNAPE (Life Baron), Peter Charles Snape; cr. 2004. Born 12 February 1942; Son of late Thomas Snape, Railway Chargeman; Married Winifred Grimshaw 1963 (divorced 1980) (2 daughters); married Janet Brenda Manley 2004.

Education: Dial Stone Secondary Modern School, Cheshire.

Non-political career: British Railways/Rail: Railway signalman 1957-60, Goods guard 1967-70, Clerical officer 1970-74; Travel West Midlands: Non-executive director 1992-95, Chair 1995-2000; Transport consultant 2000-. Regular Army service 1961-67: Royal Engineers 1961-64, Royal Corps of Transport 1964-67. National Union of Railwaymen: Member 1957-61, 1969-94, Branch chair 1970-74; Member, Rail Maritime and Transport Union 1994-.

Political career: *House of Commons:* MP (Labour) for West Bromwich East 1974-2001; Assistant Government Whip 1975-77; Government Whip 1977-79; Opposition Frontbench Spokesperson on: Defence 1979-82, Home Affairs 1982-84, Transport 1984-92. *House of Lords:* Raised to the peerage as Baron Snape, of Wednesbury in the County of West Midlands 2004. Member: Procedure 2005-07, Crossrail Bill 2008, High Speed Rail (West Midlands-Crewe) Bill 2019-, National Plan for Sport and Recreation 2020-. *Other:* Bredbury and Romiley Urban District Council: Leader 1971-74, Chair, Finance Committee 1972-74.

Political interests: Transport.

Recreations: Golf, football.

The Lord Snape, House of Lords, London SW1A 0PW
Tel: 020 7219 5877

LABOUR

SOLEY, LORD

SOLEY (Life Baron), Clive Stafford Soley; cr 2005. Born 7 May 1939; Son of Joseph Soley and Doris Despard; Married Rosslyn Brown (separated) (1 son 1 daughter).

Education: Downshall Secondary Modern, Ilford; Newbattle Abbey Adult Education College (1963); Strathclyde University (BA politics and psychology 1968); Southampton University (Diploma applied social studies 1970).

Non-political career: British Council, London and Madrid 1968-69; Probation Officer and Senior Probation Officer, Inner London Probation Service 1970-79; Chairman and Director, Good Governance Foundation 2011-15. RAF national service 1959-61; RCDS International Security and Strategic Leadership Course 2017; Member, Armed Forces Parliamentary Trust. Member, GMB.

Political career: *House of Commons:* MP (Labour) for Hammersmith North 1979-83, for Hammersmith 1983-97, for Ealing, Acton and Shepherds Bush 1997-2005; Opposition Spokesperson for: Northern Ireland 1982-85, Home Affairs 1985-87, Housing and Local Government 1987-89, Housing and Planning 1989-92. Chair, Northern Ireland Affairs 1995-97; Member: Joint Committee on House of Lords Reform 2002-05, Constitutional Affairs 2003-05. *House of Lords:* Raised to the peerage as Baron Soley, of Hammersmith in the London Borough of Hammersmith and Fulham 2005. Leader, Parliamentary Delegation to Bahrain 2014. Chair: Draft Children (contact) and Adoption Bill Joint Committee 2005, Intergovernmental Organisations 2007-08; Member: Delegated Powers and Regulatory Reform 2009-13, Inquiries Act 2005 2013-14, The Arctic 2014-15, EU Home Affairs Sub-committee 2015-20, European Union 2018-19. *Other:* Chair: Labour Campaign for Criminal Justice 1983-97, Parliamentary Labour Party 1997-2001; Member, Labour Party National Executive Committee 1998-2001; Chair, London Selection Board for Labour candidate for Mayor 1999. Councillor, Hammersmith and Fulham Council 1974-78.

Political interests: Environment, civil liberties, foreign policy, aviation policy, good governance; China, South East Asia.

Other: International Observer at: First national elections in Mongolia 1990, Peruvian general election 1995; Leader, Westminster Foundation Group to Kosovo 1999; Chair, Alcohol Education Centre, Maudsley Hospital 1974-84; Fellow, Industry and Parliament Trust 1984; Chair: Mary Seacole Memorial Statue Appeal 2004-16, Arab-Jewish Forum 2005-14; Campaign Director, Future Heathrow 2005-10; Member, International Institute for Strategic Studies 2005-; Life Patron, Mary Seacole Trust 2016-; Member, Chatham House 2018-; Vice-chair, Scottish Peers Association 2019-. Commonwealth Club.

Publications: 'The Politics of the Family' in Rewriting the Sexual Contract (Institute of Community Studies, 1997); Co-author: Regulating the Press (Pluto Press, 2000), A Statue for Mary: the Seacole Legacy, ed. Jean Gray (Mary Seacole Memorial Statue Appeal, 2016).

Recreations: Walking, photography, scuba diving.

The Lord Soley, House of Lords, London SW1A 0PW
Tel: 020 7219 5118 *Email:* soleyc@parliament.uk *Twitter:* @CliveSoley

SOMERSET, DUKE OF

CROSSBENCH

SOMERSET (19th Duke of, E), John Michael Edward Seymour; cr 1547; Baron Seymour; 17th bt of Berry Pomeroy (E) 1611. Born 30 December 1952; Son of 18th Duke; Married Judith-Rose 1984 (2 sons 2 daughters).

Education: Eton College; University of Neuchâtel; Royal Agricultural University.

Non-political career: Director, Duchy of Somerset Estates; Member, Witham Water LLP.

Political career: *House of Lords:* First entered House of Lords 1985; Elected hereditary peer 2014-. Member: Sub-committee D 1987-91, 1993-96, European Communities 1990-97, Sub-committee F 1992. *Other:* DL: Wiltshire 1993, Devon 1999-; Chair, advisory committee, Royal Agricultural University.

Political interests: Foreign affairs, accountability of the EU, rural society and economy, including conservation and heritage; Eastern Europe, India.

Other: Trustee: Motorsport Endeavour, Mount Edgcumbe Estate; Fellow, Royal Institute of Chartered Surveyors.

His Grace the Duke of Somerset DL, House of Lords, London SW1A 0PW
Tel: 020 7219 5353

SOUTHWARK, LORD BISHOP OF

NON-AFFILIATED

SOUTHWARK (10th Bishop of), Christopher Thomas James Chessun. Born 5 August 1956; Son of late Thomas Chessun and Joyce Chessun.

Education: Hampton Grammar School; University College, Oxford (BA modern history 1978); Trinity Hall, Cambridge (BA theology 1982); Westcott House Theology College, Cambridge.

Non-political career: Ordained Deacon 1983; Priest 1984; Assistant Curate, St Michael and All Angels Sandhurst 1983-87; Senior Curate, St Mary Portsea 1987-89; Chaplain and Minor Canon, St Paul's Cathedral 1989-93; Vocations Adviser, Diocese of London 1991-93; Rector, St Dunstan and All Saint's Stepney 1993-2001; Area Dean, Tower Hamlets 1997-2001; Archdeacon of Northolt 2001-05; Area Bishop of Woolwich 2005-11; Bishop of Southwark 2011-.

Political career: *House of Lords:* Entered House of Lords 2014. *Other:* Bishops Spokesperson on Immigration 2015-.

Political interests: Immigration, foreign affairs, international development; Israel, Palestine, Zimbabwe.

Other: Bishop for Urban Life and Faith 2010-14; Patron: Embrace the Middle East 2013-, Friends of the Holy Land 2013-; Chaplain to the Needlemakers' Company; Freedom, City of London 1993. Athenæum.

Rt Rev the Lord Bishop of Southwark, House of Lords, London SW1A 0PW
Tel: 020 7219 5353
Trinity House, 4 Chapel Court, Borough High Street, London SE1 1HW *Tel:* 020 7939 9420
Email: bishop.christopher@southwark.anglican.org Website: www.southwark.anglican.org
Twitter: @BishopSouthwark

SPENCER OF ALRESFORD, LORD

CONSERVATIVE

SPENCER OF ALRESFORD (Life Baron), Michael Alan Spencer; cr 2020.

Education: Worth Abbey Benedictine School; Oxford University (physics 1976).

Non-political career: Chief executive, ICAP 1986-2016; Chair, Numis 2003-09; Owner, Exotix 2007-; Chair: BI Wines & Spirits 2011-, IPGL (Holdings) 2014-; Chief executive, NEX Group 2016-.

Political career: *House of Lords:* Raised to the peerage as Baron Spencer of Alresford, of Alresford in the County of Hampshire 2020. *Other:* Treasurer, Conservative Party 2006-10.

Other: Board of directors, CME Group 2018-; Honorary Fellow, Corpus Christi College, Oxford 2008; Honorary doctorate, Loughborough University 2012.

The Lord Spencer of Alresford, House of Lords, London SW1A 0PW
Tel: 020 7219 3000

CROSSBENCH

STAIR, EARL OF

STAIR (14th Earl of, S), John David James Dalrymple; cr. 1703; Viscount Dalrymple and Lord Newliston, Glenluce and Stranraer; 15th Viscount Stair and Lord Glenluce and Stranraer (S) 1690; 7th Baron Oxenfoord (UK) 1841; 15th Bt of Stair (S) 1664; 11th Bt of Killock (S) 1698. Born 4 September 1961; Son of 13th Earl; Married Hon Emily Stonor 2006 (1 son 1 daughter).

Education: Harrow School; Royal Military Academy, Sandhurst.

Non-political career: Land management. Commissioned Scots Guards 1982.

Political career: *House of Lords:* First entered House of Lords 1996; Elected hereditary peer 2008-. Member: EU Sub-committee F (Home Affairs, Health and Education) 2012-15, Refreshment 2015-16, EU Energy and Environment Sub-committee 2017-19, EU Environment Sub-committee 2020-. *Other:* Board member: Scottish Enterprise Dumfries and Galloway 1999-2008, Scottish Environment Protection Agency 2002-09; Vice Lord-Lieutenant, Wigtown 2017-.

Political interests: Scottish affairs, agriculture, tourism, defence.

The Earl of Stair, House of Lords, London SW1A 0PW
Tel: 020 7219 5353 *Email:* dalrymplej@parliament.uk

CONSERVATIVE

STEDMAN-SCOTT, BARONESS

Parliamentary Under-Secretary of State and Government Spokesperson, Department for Work and Pensions

STEDMAN-SCOTT (Life Baroness), Deborah Stedman-Scott; cr 2010. Born 23 November 1955; Daughter of Jack Scott and Doreen-Margaret Scott; Civil partner Gabrielle Joy Stedman-Scott 2006.

Education: Ensham Secondary School for Girls; Southwark Technical College (1972).

Non-political career: Salvation Army 1978-83; Co-ordinator youth training scheme, Royal Tunbridge Wells Chamber of Commerce 1983-84; Tomorrow's People: Development manager 1984-86, Manager, Kent and Sussex 1986-88, South east regional manager 1988-93, Operations director 1993-95, Trust director 1995-2005, Chief executive 2005-15.

Political career: *House of Lords:* Raised to the peerage as Baroness Stedman-Scott, of Rolvenden in the County of Kent 2010. Deputy Chair of Committees 2014-17; Government Whip (Baroness in Waiting) 2017-19; Parliamentary Under-Secretary of State and Government Spokesperson, Department for Work and Pensions 2019-. Member: Information 2011-15, Joint Committee on Parliamentary Privilege 2013, Social Mobility 2015-16, Charities 2016-17, Citizenship and Civic Engagement 2017. *Other:* DL, East Sussex 2007-; Governor, Bexhill Academy 2015-.

Political interests: Unemployment, young people, education; New Zealand.

Other: Member, Advisory Board, International Centre for Drugs Policy 2004-07; Member, CBI: Employment Advisory Group 2004-09, Public Service Industry Forum; Employment Related Services Association: Founding Member, Chair 2007-09; Deputy Chair, Social Justice Policy Group; Trustee, New Philanthropy Capital 2011-17; Fellow, Centre for Social Justice, Trustee: Stefanou Foundation 2015-, Allia 2017; Charity Principal of the Year 2005; Regional Entrepreneur of the Year, Ernst and Young 2010; Outstanding Leadership Award, Private Equity Foundation 2011; Women of The Year, Outstanding Achievement, Vitalise Woman of The Year Awards 2015; OBE 2008.

Recreations: Reading, travelling, art, particularly Lowry.

The Baroness Stedman-Scott OBE, House of Lords, London SW1A 0PW
Tel: 020 7219 8919 *Email:* stedmanscottd@parliament.uk

LIBERAL DEMOCRAT

STEPHEN, LORD

STEPHEN (Life Baron), Nicol Ross Stephen; cr 2011. Born 23 March 1960; Son of Nicol Stephen, teacher, and Sheila Stephen, teacher; Married Caris Doig 1996 (2 sons 2 daughters).

Education: Robert Gordon's College, Aberdeen; Aberdeen University (LLB 1980); Edinburgh University (Diploma legal practice 1981); French.

Non-political career: Trainee solicitor, C & P H Chalmers 1981-83; Solicitor, Milne & Mackinnon 1983-88; Senior manager, Touche Ross Corporate Finance 1988-91; Director, Glassbox Ltd 1992-99.

Political career: *House of Commons:* Contested Kincardine and Deeside 1987 general election. MP (Liberal Democrat) for Kincardine and Deeside November 1991 by-election to 1992. Contested Kincardine and Deeside 1992 and Aberdeen South 1997 general elections. *House of Lords:* Raised to the peerage as Baron Stephen, of Lower Deeside in the City of Aberdeen 2011. Liberal Democrat Spokesperson for Scotland 2015-16. Member, Partnerships (Prosecution) (Scotland) Bill 2013. Chair, Liberal Democrat Parliamentary Party Committee on Scotland 2012-15. *Other:* Scottish Parliament: MSP for Aberdeen South constituency 1999-2011: Deputy Minister for Enterprise and Lifelong Learning 1999-2000, Minister for Higher Education 1999-2000, Deputy Minister for: Education, Europe and External Affairs 2000-01, Education and Young People 2001-03, Minister for Transport 2003-05, Deputy First Minister 2005-07, Minister for Enterprise and Lifelong Learning 2005-07. General election agent, Kincardine and Deeside 1983; Scottish Liberal Democrat Spokesperson for Health 1995-97; Party Spokesperson for Education and Heritage, Team Leader; Leader, Scottish Liberal Democrats 2005-08. Councillor, Grampian Regional Council 1982-92.

Political interests: Economic development, education, health; China, India, Japan, USA.

Other: EU Committee of the Regions: Member 2002-05, Alternate member 2010-11; Former chair: CREATE (Campaign for Rail Electrification Aberdeen to Edinburgh), STAR Campaign (Save Tor-na-Dee Hospital and Roxburghe House); Founding director, Grampian Enterprise; Director, Grampion Youth Orchestra. Deeside Golf.

Recreations: Golf.

The Lord Stephen, House of Lords, London SW1A 0PW
Tel: 020 7219 2964 *Email:* stephenn@parliament.uk

CONSERVATIVE

STERLING OF PLAISTOW, LORD

STERLING OF PLAISTOW (Life Baron), Jeffrey Maurice Sterling; cr. 1991. Born 27 December 1934; Son of late Harry and Alice Sterling; Married Dorothy Smith 1985 (1 daughter).

Education: Reigate Grammar School; Preston Manor County School, Brent; Guildhall School of Music, London.

Non-political career: Paul Schweder and Co. (Stock Exchange) 1955-57; G Eberstadt & Co 1957-62; Financial director, General Guarantee Corporation 1962-64; Managing director, Gula Investments Ltd 1964-69; Chair, Sterling Guarantee Trust plc 1969, merging with P&O 1985; Board member, British Airways 1979-82; Executive chair, Peninsular and Oriental Steam Navigation Company 1983-2005; Special adviser: to Patrick Jenkin MP as Secretary of State for Industry 1982-83, to Secretaries of State for Trade and Industry 1983-90; P&O Princess Cruises plc: Chair 2000-03, Life President 2003-; Chair: Swan Hellenic 2007-, Hebridean Island Cruises 2009-. RAF National Service; Royal Naval Reserve: Honorary Captain 1991, Honorary Rear Admiral 2010, Honorary Vice Admiral 2015-.

Political career: *House of Lords:* Raised to the peerage as Baron Sterling of Plaistow, of Pall Mall in the City of Westminster 1991. Member: Joint Committee on National Security Strategy 2010-14, Sexual Violence in Conflict 2015-16.

Political interests: Shipping, economics, disability, arts, music, international affairs.

Other: Organisation for Rehabilitation through Training (ORT): Vice-President, British ORT 1978-; Deputy chair and Hon. treasurer, London Celebrations Committee, Queen's Silver Jubilee 1975-83; Chair, Young Vic Company 1975-83; Motability: Joint founder 1977, Chair 1994-; Chair of Governors, Royal Ballet School 1983-99; Governor, Royal Ballet 1986-99; Elder Brother, Trinity House 1991-; Chair: Board of Trustees, National Maritime Museum (which incorporates The Royal Observatory Greenwich and Royal Museums Greenwich) 2005-13, Cutty Sark Trust 2011-15; President, Ajex (Association of Jewish Ex-Servicemen and Women) 2012-; President: General Council, British Shipping 1990-91, European Community Shipowners' Associations 1992-94; Motability; Worshipful Company of Coopers; Freedom, City of London; Hon. Fellow: Institute of Marine Engineers 1991, Institute of Chartered Shipbrokers 1992; Hon. Member, Royal Institute of Chartered Surveyors 1993; Fellow, Incorporated Society of Valuers and Auctioneers 1995; Hon. Fellow, Royal Institute of Naval Architects 1997; Three honorary doctorates; Interfaith Medallion 2003; CBE 1977; Kt 1985; KStJ 1998; GCVO 2002; Grand Officer Order of May (Argentina) 2002; Officer's Cross Order of Merit (Germany) 2004; Officier de l'Ordre National de Légion d'Honneur (France) 2005. Garrick, Hurlingham Club.

Recreations: Music, swimming, arts.

The Lord Sterling of Plaistow GCVO CBE, House of Lords, London SW1A 0PW
15 St James's Place, London SW1A 1NP *Tel:* 020 7647 8522 *Email:* pa@lordsterling.co.uk

CROSSBENCH

STERN, BARONESS

STERN (Life Baroness) Vivien Helen Stern; cr. 1999. Born 25 September 1941; Daughter of Frederick Stern and Renate Mills; Married Professor Andrew Coyle CMG.

Education: Kent College, Pembury, Kent; Bristol University (BA English literature 1963; MLitt 1964; CertEd 1965).

Non-political career: Lecturer in education 1970; Principal officer, Community Relations Commission 1970-77; Director, NACRO 1977-96; Visiting fellow, Nuffield College, Oxford 1984-91; Senior research fellow, International Centre for Prison Studies, King's College London 1997-2010; Visiting professor, Essex University 2011-14.

Political career: *House of Lords:* Raised to the peerage as Baroness Stern, of Vauxhall in the London Borough of Lambeth 1999. Member: European Union 2000-03, Joint Committee on Human Rights 2004-08, Joint Committee on Statutory Instruments 2010-15, Inquiries Act 2005 2013-14, Secondary Legislation Scrutiny 2014-17. *Other:* Committee Member, Prison Disciplinary System 1984-85.

Political interests: Criminal justice, foreign affairs, human rights, international development, penal reform, prisons, rape and sexual violence, death penalty, violence against children; Afghanistan, Algeria, Argentina, Chile, Dominican Republic, Kazakhstan, Kenya, Kyrgyzstan, Tajikistan, Uzbekistan.

Other: Member: Special Programmes Board, Manpower Services Commission 1980-82, Youth Training Board 1982-88, General Advisory Council, IBA 1982-87; Penal Reform International: Honorary secretary-general 1989-2006, Honorary president 2006-; Member, Advisory Council, PSI 1993-96; Board member, Association for Prevention of Torture, Geneva 1993-2000; Trustee, Milton S Eisenhower Foundation, Washington 1993-2007; British Council: Member: Law Advisory Committee 1995-2000, Governance Advisory Committee 2002-06; Patron: Clean Break 1998-, Prisoners' Education Trust 1998-2019; President, New Bridge 2001-06; Vice-president, Comité de Soutien, Français Incarcérés au Loin (FIL) 2001-07; Convener, Scottish Consortium on Crime and Criminal Justice 2003-09; President, Association of Members of Independent Monitoring Boards 2005-; Patron, Amicus 2007-; Member, advisory council, Legal Policy Research Centre, Kazakhstan 2008-19; International Legal Foundation, New York: Advisory Committee member 2009-14, Board member 2009-; Patron: Alternatives to Violence Project 2010-, Venture Trust 2010-, UK Network of Sex Work Projects 2011-, London Havens (Sexual Assault Referral Centres) 2012-; Survivors' Network, Brighton 2013; Co-chair, KNOW Violence Global Learning Initiative 2014-18; Trustee: Institute for Criminal Policy Research 2014-18, Redress 2015-; Six honorary doctorates; Hon. Fellow, LSE 1996; Peer of the Year, Women in Public Life Awards 2010; CBE 1992.

Publications: Bricks of Shame (1987); Imprisoned by Our Prisons (1989); Deprived of their Liberty, a report for Caribbean Rights (1990); A Sin Against the Future: imprisonment in the world (1998); Alternatives to Prison in Developing Countries (1999); Editor, Sentenced to Die:

The Problems of TB in Prisons in Eastern Europe and Central Asia (2000); Creating Criminals: People and Prisons in a Market Society (2006); Report of an Independent Review into how rape complaints are handled by public authorities in England and Wales (The Stern Review, 2010).

The Baroness Stern CBE, House of Lords, London SW1A 0PW
Tel: 020 7219 5353 *Email:* sternvh@parliament.uk
Tel: 020 3926 1693 *Email:* fairh@parliament.uk

CROSSBENCH

STERN OF BRENTFORD, LORD

STERN OF BRENTFORD (Life Baron), Nicholas Herbert Stern; cr 2007. Born 22 April 1946; Son of late Adalbert and Marion Stern, née Swann; Married Susan Ruth Chesterton 1968 (1 daughter 2 sons).

Education: Peterhouse, Cambridge (BA mathematics 1967); Nuffield College, Oxford (DPhil economics 1972); French.

Non-political career: Lecturer in industrial mathematics, Oxford, and Fellow in economics, St Catherine's College, Oxford 1970-77; Professor of economics, Warwick University 1978-85; London School of Economics and Political Science: Sir John Hicks Professor of Economics 1986-94, Professor of economics 1999-2003, IG Patel Chair 2007-; Chief Economist and Special Counsellor to the President, European Bank for Reconstruction and Development 1994-99; Chief Economist and Senior Vice-President, World Bank, Washington DC 2000-03; HM Treasury 2003-07: Managing director, Budget and Public Finance 2003-05, Second Permanent Secretary 2003-05, Head of Government Economic Service 2003-07, Adviser on Economics of Climate Change and Development (Stern Review) 2005-06.

Political career: *House of Lords:* Raised to the peerage as Baron Stern of Brentford, of Elsted in the County of West Sussex and of Wimbledon in the London Borough of Merton 2007. Member, Economic Affairs 2019-. *Other:* Trustee, British Museum.

Other: Member, United Nations High Level Group on Development Strategy and Management of the Market Economy 1997; Fellow: British Academy, Econometric Society 1978; Eleven honorary doctorates; Foreign Honorary Member, American Academy of Arts and Sciences; Great Briton of the Year (Environment) 2006; Royal Geographical Society Patron's Royal Medal 2009; Asahi Glass Foundation Blue Planet Prize 2009; Kt 2004; CH 2017.

Publications: Crime, the Police and Criminal Statistics (1979); Editor, Journal of Public Economics 1981-97; Palanpur: The Economy of an Indian Village (1982); The Theory of Taxation for Developing Countries (World Bank, 1987); The Role of the State in Economic Development (1991); The Theory and Practice of Tax Reform in Developing Countries (1991); Economic Development in Palanpur over Five Decades (1998); A Case for Aid (World Bank, 2002); A Strategy for Development (World Bank, 2002); Co-author, Growth and Empowerment (2005); A Blueprint for a Safer Planet (2009).

Recreations: Walking, reading, football.

Professor the Lord Stern of Brentford CH, House of Lords, London SW1A 0PW
Tel: 020 7219 1300 *Twitter:* @lordstern1

CROSSBENCH

STEVENS OF KIRKWHELPINGTON, LORD

STEVENS OF KIRKWHELPINGTON (Life Baron), John Arthur Stevens; cr 2005. Born 21 October 1942; Married (2 sons 1 daughter).

Education: St Lawrence College, Ramsgate; Leicester University (LLB, LLD 2000); Southampton University.

Non-political career: Metropolitan Police 1963-83; Directing staff, Police Staff College 1983-84; Assistant Chief Constable, Hampshire Constabulary 1986-89; Deputy Chief Constable, Cambridgeshire Constabulary 1989-91; Chief Constable, Northumbria 1991-96; HM Inspector of Constabulary 1996-98; Metropolitan Police 1998-2005: Deputy Commissioner 1998-99, Commissioner 2000-05; Senior international security adviser to Prime Minister 2007-10; Chair: Border Policing Committee 2007, Independent Police Commission 2011. Honorary Colonel, Northumbria Army Cadets 2006-; Honorary Air Commodore, No 3 (Royal Auxiliary) Air Force Police Squadron 2007-.

Political career: *House of Lords:* Raised to the peerage as Baron Stevens of Kirkwhelpington, of Kirkwhelpington in the County of Northumberland 2005. *Other:* Chair, Independent Review into the Future of Policing in England and Wales 2011-. Chair: Stevens Enquiries (into NI security forces and paramilitary collusion) 1989-92, 1999-2003, Joint Committee on Offender Profiling 1991, Inquiry into death of Princess Diana 2003-06, Strategic Advisory Panel, Interpol 2005-.

Other: Northumbria Youth Action, Newcastle Cathedral Restoration; Freedom, City of London 2002; Chancellor, Northumbria University 2005-15; Fellow, Wolfson College, Cambridge; QPM 1992; Kt 2000; Knight of St John 2002; Star of Romania; Emeritus Lay Cannon, Newcastle Cathedral. RAF Club.

Publications: Not for the Faint Hearted (2005).

The Lord Stevens of Kirkwhelpington QPM, House of Lords, London SW1A 0PW
Tel: 020 7219 5488

CONSERVATIVE INDEPENDENT

STEVENS OF LUDGATE, LORD

STEVENS OF LUDGATE (Life Baron), David Robert Stevens; cr. 1987. Born 26 May 1936; Son of late A Edwin Stevens, CBE and Kathleen James; Married Patricia Rose 1961 (divorced 1971) (1 son 1 daughter); married Melissa Sadoff, née Milicevic 1977 (died 1989); married Meriza Giori, née Dzienciolsky 1990.

Education: Stowe School, Buckinghamshire; Sidney Sussex College, Cambridge (BA economics 1959, MA); French.

Non-political career: Management trainee, Elliot Automation 1959; Hill Samuel Securities 1959-68; Drayton Group 1968-74; United News and Media plc (formerly United Newspapers): Director 1974-, Chair 1981-99; Chair: City and Foreign/Alexander Proudfoot 1976-95, Drayton Far East 1976-93, English and International 1976-89, Consolidated Venture 1979-93, Drayton Consolidated 1980-92, Drayton Japan 1980-88; MIM Britannia Ltd (formerly Montagu Investment Management Ltd): Chair and chief executive 1980-89, Chair 1989-93; Chair, Express Newspapers plc 1985-99; Deputy chair, Britannia Arrow Holdings plc 1987-89; Chair: Invesco MIM plc (formerly Britannia Arrow Holdings) 1989-92, Oak Industries 1989-1995, Premier Asset Management 1997-2001, Personal Number Company 1998-2003; Express National Newspapers Ltd: Chair 1998-99, Deputy Chair 2014-18. Second Lieutenant, Royal Artillery, National Service, Hong Kong 1954-56.

Political career: *House of Lords:* Raised to the peerage as Baron Stevens of Ludgate, of Ludgate in the City of London 1987. *Other:* Member: Conservative Party 1987-2004, UK Independence Party 2013-December 2018; Conservative Independent 2004-13, December 2018-. Chair, EDC for Civil Engineering 1984-86.

Political interests: European Union, tax and financial affairs; France, Italy, USA.

Other: Director, English National Opera 1980-87; Founder and Chair, Helicopter Emergency Rescue Services 1988-90; National Association of Almshouses, Action Against Cancer, St George's Hospital (Cancer)Charity, Cancer Research, Prostate Cancer, UCH Cancer; Patron, Royal College of Surgeons; Hon. Fellow, Sidney Sussex College, Cambridge 1991; Grand Official, Order of the Southern Cross (Brazil) 1993. White's Club; Sunningdale Golf, Swinley Forest Golf.

Recreations: Gardening, golf.

The Lord Stevens of Ludgate, House of Lords, London SW1A 0PW
Tel: 020 7219 5353 *Email:* stevensdavid@parliament.uk

LABOUR

STEVENSON OF BALMACARA, LORD

STEVENSON OF BALMACARA (Life Baron), Robert Wilfrid (Wilf) Stevenson; cr 2010. Born 19 April 1947; Son of late James Stevenson and late Elizabeth Macrae; Married Jennifer Antonio 1972 (divorced 1979); married Ann Minogue 1991 (1 son 2 daughters).

Education: Edinburgh Academy; University College, Oxford (BA natural sciences, chemistry, MA 1970); Napier Polytechnic (FCCA 1986).

Non-political career: Research officer, Edinburgh University Students' Association 1970-74; Secretary, Napier College, Edinburgh 1974-87; British Film Institute: Deputy Director 1987-88, Director 1988-97; Director, Smith Institute 1997-2008; Senior Policy Adviser, Prime Minister's Office 2008-10. Member, Unite 1974-.

Political career: *House of Lords:* Raised to the peerage as Baron Stevenson of Balmacara, of Little Missenden in the County of Buckinghamshire 2010. Opposition Whip 2011-21; Opposition Spokesperson for: Business, Innovation and Skills 2011-16, Culture, Media and Sport 2011-17, Business, Energy and Industrial Strategy 2016-17, 2020-21, Higher Education 2016-17, Scotland 2018, International Trade 2019, 2020-21, Digital, Culture Media and Sport (Charities) 2020-21. Member: Communications 2011, Intellectual Property (Unjustified Threats) Bill 2016.

Political interests: Intellectual property, the Arts, Scotland; Burma, Eire, Iran, Laos, Spain, Turkey.

Other: Member, ACCA (retired); Hypospadias UK, Catalyst Trust; Hon DArts, Napier University 2008.

Publications: Editor: Gordon Brown Speeches (2006), Moving Britain Forward (2006), The Change We Choose: Speeches 2007-2009 (2010).

Recreations: Cinema, gardening, beekeeping.

The Lord Stevenson of Balmacara, House of Lords, London SW1A 0PW
Tel: 020 7219 8914 *Email:* stevensonw@parliament.uk
Email: wilf@wilfstevenson.co.uk *Twitter:* @WilfStevenson

CROSSBENCH

STEVENSON OF CODDENHAM, LORD

STEVENSON OF CODDENHAM (Life Baron), Henry Dennistoun (Dennis) Stevenson; cr. 1999. Born 19 July 1945; Son of late Alexander and Sylvia Stevenson, née Ingleby; Married Charlotte Susan Vanneck 1972 (4 sons).

Education: Trinity College, Glenalmond; King's College, Cambridge (MA classics 1970).

Non-political career: Saxton Bampfylde International plc 1986-98; J Rothschild Assurance plc 1991-97; English Partnerships 1993-99; British Sky Broadcasting Group plc 1994-2000; Governor, London School of Economics 1995-99; Lazard Brothers & Co Ltd 1997-2000; The Economist Newspapers Ltd 1998-2011; Waterstones Holdings plc 2011-16; Chair, SRU Group of Companies 1972-96; Non-executive director, Manpower Inc 1988-2006; Chair: Sinfonia 21 1989-99, AerFi Group plc 1993-2000, Pearson plc 1996-05, Halifax plc 1999-2008, HBOS plc 2001-08, Non-executive director: Western Union Company 2006-12, Culture and Sport Glasgow 2007-09, Loudwater Investment Partners Ltd 2007-12.

Political career: *House of Lords:* Raised to the peerage as Baron Stevenson of Coddenham, of Coddenham in the County of Suffolk 1999. Member, Works of Art 2009-14. *Other:* Chair, House of Lords Appointments Commission 2000-08; Westminster City Council Standards Committee 2008-12.

Political interests: Holland, Japan, Sierra Leone, USA.

Other: Chair: Government Working Party on role of voluntary movements and youth in the environment 1971, Newton Aycliffe and Peterlee New Town Development Corporation 1971-80, Independent Advisory Committee on Pop Festivals 1972-76, National Association of Youth Clubs 1973-81; Director, National Building Agency 1977-81; Adviser on agricultural marketing to Minister of Agriculture 1979-83; Director, London Docklands Development Corporation 1981-88; Chair: Intermediate Technology Development Group 1983-90, Trustees, Tate Gallery 1988-98; Member, Panel on Takeovers and Mergers 1992-2000; Board member, British Council 1996-2003; Governor: London School of Economics 1996-2002, London

Business School 1996-2002; Director, Glyndebourne Productions 1998-2016; Hon. Member, Royal Society of Musicians of Great Britain 1998-; Trustee, Tate Gallery Foundation 1998-; Chair, Aldeburgh Music Ltd 2000-12; Chancellor, University of the Arts London 2000-10; Trustee, Horse's Mouth 2006-15; Board of Governors, Institute for Government 2008-13; Arts & Media Honours Committee 2008-12; MQ: Transforming Mental Health 2010-15; Director, London Music Masters 2011-; Chair of Trustees, Inter Mediate 2015-; Director, Think Ahead 2016-; Chancellor, University of the Arts, London 2000-10; CBE 1981; Kt 1998. Garrick, Brooks's, MCC Club.

Publications: Stevenson Commission Information and Communications Technology in UK Schools Report (1997).

The Lord Stevenson of Coddenham CBE, House of Lords, London SW1A 0PW
Tel: 020 7219 5353
Email: dennis@hdstevenson.co.uk

CONSERVATIVE

STEWART OF DIRLETON, LORD

Advocate General for Scotland and Government Spokesperson, Law Officers

STEWART OF DIRLETON (Life Baron), Keith Douglas Stewart; cr 2020. Married (2 children).

Education: George Heriot's School, Edinburgh; Keble College, Oxford (MA English language and literature 1986); Edinburgh University (LLB 1989); Strathclyde University (Diploma legal practice 1990).

Non-political career: Trainee solicitor, Shepherd & Wedderburn WS 1990-92; Faculty of Advocates 1993-: Advocate-depute 2003-05, Senior Advocate-depute 2005-09, Advocate-depute ad hoc 2002, 2009-; QC 2011.

Political career: *House of Lords:* Raised to the peerage as Baron Stewart of Dirleton, of Dirleton in the County of East Lothian 2020. Advocate General for Scotland 2020-; Government Spokesperson for Law Officers 2020-.

Other: Curator, Advocates' Library; Member, Scottish Criminal Bar Association.

The Lord Stewart of Dirleton QC, House of Lords, London SW1A 0PW
Tel: 020 7219 3000

CROSSBENCH

STIRRUP, LORD

STIRRUP (Life Baron), Graham Eric (Jock) Stirrup; cr 2011. Born 4 December 1949; Son of William Stirrup and Jacqueline Stirrup, née Coulson; Married Mary Elliott 1976 (1 son).

Education: Merchant Taylors' School, Northwood; Royal Air Force College.

Non-political career: Qualified as flying instructor 1971; Service in the Sultan of Oman's Air Force 1973-75; Fighter reconnaissance pilot 1976-78; US Air Force 1978-81; Flight Commander 1982-84; Officer Commanding (OC) No II (Army Co-operation) Squadron 1985-87; Personal Staff Officer to Chief of the Air Staff 1987-90; OC RAF Marham 1990-92; Royal College of Defence Studies 1993; Director, Air Force Plans and Programmes, MoD 1994-97; Air OC No I 1997-98; Assistant Chief of Air Staff 1998-2000; Deputy Commander-in-Chief, Strike Command; Commander NATO Combined Air Operations Centre 9 and Director, European Air Group 2000-02; Deputy Chief of Defence Staff (Equipment Capability) 2002-03; Chief of the Air Staff 2003-06; Chief of the Defence Staff 2006-10.

Political career: *House of Lords:* Raised to the peerage as Baron Stirrup, of Marylebone in the City of Westminster 2011. Member: House 2013-16, EU External Affairs Sub-Committee 2015-19, Joint Committee on Statutory Instruments 2020-.

Political interests: Australia, Middle East, USA.

Other: FRAeS; FIMgt; Hon. DSc, Cranfield University 2005; AFC 1982; CB 2000; KCB 2002; GCB 2005; KG 2013. Royal Air Force, Beefsteak Club.

Recreations: History, music, theatre, golf.

Marshal of the Royal Air Force the Lord Stirrup KG GCB AFC ADC, House of Lords, London SW1A 0PW
Tel: 020 7219 5979 *Email:* stirrupg@parliament.uk

NON-AFFILIATED

STONE OF BLACKHEATH, LORD

STONE OF BLACKHEATH (Life Baron), Andrew Zelig Stone; cr. 1997. Born 7 September 1942; Son of Sydney and Louise Stone; Married Vivienne Lee 1973 (1 son 2 daughters).

Education: Cardiff High School.

Non-political career: Marks and Spencer plc 1966-99: Personal assistant to chair 1978-80, Joint managing director 1994-99; Director: N Brown 2002-13, Ted Baker plc 2002-04, McDonalds Advisory Board 2005-07, Deal Group Media plc 2005-07; Deputy chair, Sindicatum Carbon Capital Holdings Ltd 2005-09; Director, Falcon Power Holdings 2012-.

Political career: *House of Lords:* Raised to the peerage as Baron Stone of Blackheath, of Blackheath in the London Borough of Greenwich 1997. Departmental Liaison Peer to Baroness Jay as Leader of the House of Lords 1999-2001. Member, House of Lords Offices Refreshment Sub-committee 2000-02. *Other:* Suspended from Labour Peers Group October 2019, now sits as non-affiliated.

Political interests: Conflict resolution, art and science, health, ecology; China, Middle East.

Other: British Overseas Trade Board for Israel: Chair 1991-99, President 1995-2000; Governor, Weizmann Institute Foundation 1993-; Council member, Arts and Business 1994-2001; Member, national advisory committee, Creative and Cultural Education 1998-2000; Director, Science Media Centre 2001-05; Governor, Tel Aviv University 2001-04; Hon Vice-President, Movement for Reform Judaism; Chair, Dipex (Direct Patient Experiences) 2005-17; Trustee, Olive Tree Trust 2005-09; Governor, British University of Egypt 2006-; Member, Risk Commission (RSA); Chair, Sindicatum Climate Change Foundation 2009-11; Trustee, Prism the Gift Fund 2009-; Orphaids, Gauchers Association, DIPEX; Two honorary degrees.

Recreations: Reading, walking, thinking, meditating.

The Lord Stone of Blackheath, House of Lords, London SW1A 0PW
Tel: 020 7219 4556 *Fax:* 020 7219 5979 *Email:* stonea@parliament.uk

LIBERAL DEMOCRAT

STONEHAM OF DROXFORD, LORD

Liberal Democrat Chief Whip in the Lords

STONEHAM OF DROXFORD (Life Baron), Benjamin Russell Mackintosh Stoneham; cr 2011. Born 24 August 1948; Son of Major B J R Stoneham and Beryl Stoneham; Married Anne 1975 (2 sons 1 daughter).

Education: Harrow School; Christ's College, Cambridge (BA economics 1970); Warwick University (MA industrial relations 1971).

Non-political career: Research officer, Social and Administrative Studies Department, Oxford University 1971-74; NCB 1974-78; National officer, National Union of Railwaymen 1979-82; Portsmouth and Sunderland Newspapers 1982-89; Managing director, Portsmouth Publishing and Printing Ltd 1989-99; Group production and personnel director, News International 2000-03; Operations director, Liberal Democrat HQ 2003-10; Chair and director, First Wessex Housing Group Ltd 2007-12; Chair, Housing and Care 21 2011-.

Political career: *House of Commons:* Contested (Labour) Saffron Walden 1977 and 1979 and (SDP/All) Stevenage 1983 and 1987 general elections. *House of Lords:* Raised to the peerage as Baron Stoneham of Droxford, of the Meon Valley in the County of Hampshire 2011. Liberal Democrat: Whip 2011-15, Spokesperson for Business, Innovation and Skills 2015, Chief Whip in the Lords 2016-; Deputy Speaker 2018-. Member: EU Sub-committee E (Justice, Institutions and Consumer Protection) 2012-15, Olympic and Paralympic Legacy 2013-14, Finance 2016-, Privileges and Conduct 2016-19, Procedure/Procedure and Privileges 2016-, Selection 2016-, Services 2018-. *Other:* Councillor, Hertfordshire County Council 1985-89.

Political interests: Pensions, housing and regeneration, media; France, South Africa, USA.

Other: Director, Make Votes Count; Trustee, Coltstaple Trust.

The Lord Stoneham of Droxford, House of Lords, London SW1A 0PW
Tel: 020 7219 8629 *Twitter:* @lordstoneham

LIBERAL DEMOCRAT

STOREY, LORD

Liberal Democrat Lords Spokesperson for Education and Whip

STOREY (Life Baron), Michael John Storey; cr 2011. Born 25 May 1949; Married (1 daughter).

Education: Liverpool University (BEd).

Non-political career: Teacher: Prescot CoE Primary School 1972-77, New Hutte Primary School, Halewood 1977-82; Deputy headteacher, Halsnead Primary School, Whiston 1982-85; Headteacher: St Gabriel's CoE Primary School, Huyton 1985-90, Plantation County Primary School, Halewood 1990-2012.

Political career: *House of Lords:* Raised to the peerage as Baron Storey, of Childwall in the City of Liverpool 2011. Liberal Democrat: Whip 2011-14, 2020-, Shadow Minister/Lords Spokesperson for Education 2015-, Spokesperson on Young People 2017-19. Member: Small- and Medium-Sized Enterprises 2012-13, Communications/Communications and Digital 2019-. Chair, Liberal Democrat Parliamentary Committee for Education, Families and Young People 2013-15. *Other:* Liverpool City Council: Councillor 1973-2011, Leader, Liberal Democrat opposition 1991-98, Council Leader 1998-2005, Lord Mayor of Liverpool 2009-10; Vice-president, Local Government Association 2017-; Foundation Governor, Liverpool College 2019-.

Political interests: Education, regeneration, the arts, local authorities, Merseyside; France, Germany, Switzerland, USA.

Other: Patron: Strawberry Fields 2017-, Royal Life Saving Institution 2018-, Careers Connect 2018-; OBE 1994; CBE 2002.

Recreations: Reading, theatre, cinema, gardening.

The Lord Storey CBE, House of Lords, London SW1A 0PW
Tel: 020 7219 1972 *Email:* storeym@parliament.uk *Twitter:* @LordStorey

NON-AFFILIATED

STOWELL OF BEESTON, BARONESS

STOWELL OF BEESTON (Life Baroness), Tina Wendy Stowell; cr 2011.

Education: Chilwell Comprehensive School; Broxtowe College of Further Education (1985).

Non-political career: Civil servant 1986-96: Ministry of Defence 1986-88, British Embassy, Washington DC 1988-91, Downing Street Press Office 1991-96; Private Sector (various, including Paradine Productions, Granada Media) 1996-98; Deputy Chief of Staff to William Hague MP as Leader of the Conservative Party 1998-2001; BBC: Deputy Secretary 2001-03, Head of communications to the Chairman and Board of Governors/BBC Trust 2003-08, Head of corporate affairs 2008-10; Consultant, Tina Stowell Associates 2010-11; Chair, Charity Commission 2018-.

Political career: *House of Lords:* Raised to the peerage as Baroness Stowell of Beeston, of Beeston in the County of Nottinghamshire 2011. Party Whip 2011; Government Whip 2011-13; Government Spokesperson for: Energy and Climate Change 2011-12, International Development 2011-12, Home Office 2011-13, Culture, Media and Sport 2012-13, Northern Ireland September-October 2012, Women and Equalities 2012-13, Work and Pensions 2012-13; Parliamentary Under-Secretary of State and Government Spokesperson, Department for Communities and Local Government 2013-14; Leader of the House of Lords and Lord Privy Seal 2014-16. Member Joint Committees on: Human Rights 2011, Security 2012-13; Member: House 2014-16, Liaison 2014-16, Privileges and Conduct 2014-16, Procedure 2014-16, Selection 2014-16; Chair, Joint Committee on the Palace of Westminster 2015-16; Member, Communications 2017-18. *Other:* Resigned from Conservative Party and Whip following appointment as Charity Commission Chair February 2018; now sits as Non-affiliated.

Political interests: Social mobility, political reform.

Other: Non-executive director: ABTA Ltd 2017-, Impellam Group plc 2017-; Honorary Doctorate, Nottingham University 2016; MBE 1996; PC 2014.

Rt Hon the Baroness Stowell of Beeston MBE, House of Lords, London SW1A 0PW
Tel: 020 7219 5353 *Email:* stowellt@parliament.uk Website: www.tinastowell.co.uk
Twitter: @tinastowell

LIBERAL DEMOCRAT

STRASBURGER, LORD

STRASBURGER (Life Baron), Paul Cline Strasburger; cr 2011. Born 31 July 1946; Married.

Non-political career: IT and security industries; Property management.

Political career: *House of Lords:* Raised to the peerage as Baron Strasburger, of Langridge in the County of Somerset 2011. Member: Joint Committee on the Draft Communications Data Bill 2012-13, Information 2014-16, Joint Committee on the Draft Investigatory Powers Bill 2015-16.

Political interests: Civil liberties, the environment, unleashing potential, protecting citizens from the State and corporations.

Other: The Prince's Trust. MCC.

Recreations: All music (almost), sport, theatre, adventure.

The Lord Strasburger, House of Lords, London SW1A 0PW
Tel: 020 7219 5353 *Email:* strasburgerp@parliament.uk *Twitter:* @LordStras

CONSERVATIVE

STRATHCLYDE, LORD

STRATHCLYDE (2nd Baron, UK), Thomas Galloway Dunlop du Roy de Blicquy Galbraith; cr. 1955. Born 22 February 1960; Son of late Hon Sir Thomas Galbraith KBE (former MP, eldest son of 1st Baron, PC); Married Jane Skinner 1992 (3 daughters).

Education: Wellington College, Berkshire; University of East Anglia 1978-82; University of Aix-en-Provence 1981.

Non-political career: Lloyd's insurance broker; Bain Clarkson Ltd 1982-88; Chair, Trafalgar Capital Management Ltd 2001-10; Director: Scottish Mortgage Investment Trust plc 2004-10, Galena Asset Management Ltd 2004-10, Marketform Group Ltd 2004-10, Hampden Agencies Ltd 2008-10; Director, Trafigura Beheer BV Supervisory Board 2013-.

Political career: *House of Lords:* First entered House of Lords 1985; Government Whip 1988-89; Government Spokesperson for Trade and Industry, Treasury and Scotland 1988-89; Parliamentary Under-Secretary of State: Department of Employment (Tourism) 1989-90, Department of Environment 1990, 1992-93; Scottish Office (Agriculture and Fisheries) 1990-92; Department of Trade and Industry: Parliamentary Under-Secretary of State 1993-94, Minister of State 1994; Government Chief Whip 1994-97; Member, Shadow Cabinet 1997-2010; Opposition Chief Whip 1997-98; Deputy Speaker 1997-98; Deputy Chairman of Committees 1997-98; Leader of the Opposition 1998-2010; Opposition Spokesperson for Constitutional Affairs December 1998-2005; Elected hereditary peer 1999-; Leader of the House of Lords and Chancellor of the Duchy of Lancaster 2010-13. Member: House -2013, Liaison -2013, Privileges/Privileges and Conduct -2013, Procedure -2013, Selection -2013. *Other:* Contested Merseyside East 1984 European Parliament election. Chair: Commission on the Future Structure of the Scottish Conservative and Unionist Party 1997-98, Commission on the Future Governance of Scotland. Governor, Wellington College 2010-.

Other: President, Quoted Companies Alliance 2003-09; Board Member, Centre for Policy Studies; Chair: Battersea Power Station Foundation 2015-, B & C (Bank) plc 2016-; Peer of 2000 Channel 4 and *The House Magazine*; Peer of the Year, *Spectator* 2004; PC 1995; CH 2013.

Publications: New Frontiers for Reform (CPS, 2001); Working in Harness: parliamentary government and the role of the Lords (Politeia, 2005).

Rt Hon the Lord Strathclyde CH, House of Lords, London SW1A 0PW
Tel: 020 7219 5353

CONSERVATIVE

STROUD, BARONESS

STROUD (Life Baroness), Philippa Claire Stroud; cr 2015. Born 2 April 1965; Married David Stroud 1989 (1 son twin daughters).

Education: St Catherine's School, Bramley; Birmingham University (BA French 1987); French, some knowledge of spoken Chinese.

Non-political career: Voluntary worker, drug rehabilitation centre, Hong Kong and Macau 1987-89; Founder, King's Arms Project, Bedford 1989-96; Director: Care Confidential -2004, Bridge Project Birmingham 2001-03; Executive Director, Centre for Social Justice 2004-10, 2015-16; Special Adviser to Iain Duncan Smith MP as Secretary of State for Work and Pensions 2010-15; Chief Executive, Legatum Institute 2016-.

Political career: *House of Commons:* Contested (Conservative) Birmingham Ladywood 2005 and Sutton and Cheam 2010 general elections. *House of Lords:* Raised to the peerage as Baroness Stroud, of Fulham in the London Borough of Hammersmith and Fulham 2015. *Other:* Former Governor, Blue Coat School.

Political interests: Social justice, education, health, crime, voluntary sector, family, social policy.

Other: Board member, SCOLA 2008-; Patron, Elevate 2008-. United and Cecil Club.

Recreations: Travelling, eating out, movies, sport – especially skiing and sailing.

The Baroness Stroud, House of Lords, London SW1A 0PW
Tel: 020 7219 3000 *Email:* stroudp@parliament.uk
c/o Legatum Institute, 11 Charles Street, London W1J 5DW *Tel:* 020 7148 5400

NON-AFFILIATED

STUART OF EDGBASTON, BARONESS

STUART OF EDGBASTON (Life Baroness), Gisela Stuart; 2020. Born 26 November 1955; Daughter of late Martin Gschaider and Liane Krompholz; Married Robert Scott Stuart 1980 (divorced 2000) (2 sons); married Derek Scott 2010 (died 2012).

Education: Staatliche Realschule, Vilsbiburg, Bavaria; Manchester Polytechnic (business studies 1979); London University (LLB 1992); German.

Non-political career: Deputy director, London Book Fair 1983; Translator; Lawyer and lecturer, Worcester College of Technology and Birmingham University 1992-97. Member, Amicus.

Political career: *House of Commons:* MP (Lab) for Birmingham Edgbaston 1997-2010, for Birmingham, Edgbaston (revised boundary) 2010-17; PPS to Paul Boateng as Minister of State, Home Office 1998-99; Parliamentary Under-Secretary of State, Department of Health 1999-2001; Parliamentary representative Convention on Future of Europe 2002-04; Member, Intelligence and Security Committee 2015-17. Member: Social Security 1997-98, Foreign Affairs 2001-10, Joint Committee on Conventions 2006, Defence 2010-15, Arms Export Controls 2010-11, Joint Committee on Privacy and Injunctions 2011-12, Administration 2015-17, Speaker's Advisory Committee on Works of Art 2015-17. Chair, PLP Departmental Group for Defence 2011-15. *House of Lords:* Raised to the peerage as Baroness Stuart of Edgbaston, of Edgbaston in the City of Birmingham 2020. *Other:* Chair, Wilton Park 2018-; Lead Non-executive Board Member (with responsibility for the Union), Cabinet Office 2020-.

Political interests: Pension law, constitutional reform, European Union.

Other: Member, advisory board, Birmingham University Business School; Board member, External System, London University; Trustee, Henry Jackson Society; Fellow, Industry and Parliament Trust 2002; Skills for Birmingham; Vote Leave: Chair 2016, Co-convenor, Campaign Committee 2016; Chair, Change Britain 2016-19; Trustee, Reading Force; Hon Doctorate, Aston University; Bundesverdienstkreuz, Germany; PC 2015.

Publications: The Making of Europe's Constitution (Fabian Society, 2003); Editor, *The House Magazine* 2005-17.

Rt Hon the Baroness Stuart of Edgbaston, House of Lords, London SW1A 0PW
Tel: 020 7219 3000 *Twitter:* @GiselaStuart

LIBERAL DEMOCRAT

STUNELL, LORD

STUNELL (Life Baron), Robert Andrew Stunell; cr 2015. Born 24 November 1942; Son of late Robert Stunell and Trixie Stunell; Married Gillian Chorley 1967 (3 sons 2 daughters).

Education: Surbiton Grammar School; Manchester University (architecture RIBA Pt. II exemption 1963); Liverpool Polytechnic; (Some) German, French.

Non-political career: Architectural assistant: CWS Manchester 1965-67, Runcorn New Town 1967-81; Freelance architectural assistant 1981-85; Association of Liberal Democrat Councillors: Various posts including political secretary 1985-97, Head of Service 1989-96. Member, NALGO: New Towns Whitley Council 1977-81.

Political career: *House of Commons:* Contested City of Chester 1979, 1983, 1987, Hazel Grove 1992 general elections. MP (Liberal Democrat) for Hazel Grove 1997-2010, for Hazel Grove (revised boundary) 2010-15; Liberal Democrat: Spokesperson for Energy 1997-2005, Deputy Chief Whip 1997-2001, Chief Whip 2001-06, Shadow Secretary of State for Office of the Deputy Prime Minister/Communities and Local Government 2006-07; Parliamentary Under-Secretary of State, Department for Communities and Local Government 2010-12. Member: Broadcasting 1997-2000, Modernisation of the House of Commons 1997-2006, Procedure 1997-2001, Unopposed Bills (Panel) 1997-2001, Standing Orders 1998-2001, Finance and Services 2001-06, Selection 2001-06, International Development 2009-10, Arms Export Controls 2009-10, Joint Committee on the Draft Modern Slavery Bill 2014. *House of Lords:* Raised to the peerage as Baron Stunell, of Hazel Grove in the County of Greater Manchester 2015. Liberal Democrat Lords Spokesperson on the Construction Industry 2016-. Member: Bribery Act 2010 2018-19, Joint Committee on the Draft Parliamentary Buildings (Restoration and Renewal) Bill 2018-19. *Other:* Member, Liberal Democrat Federal Party: Executive Committee 2001-06, Conference Committee 2001-06; Chair, Local Election Campaign 2007-12; President, NW Liberal Democrats Regional Party 2015-18. Councillor: Chester City Council 1979-90, Cheshire County Council 1981-91; Vice-chair, Association of County Councils 1985-90; Councillor, Stockport Metropolitan Borough Council 1994-2002; Vice-president, Local Government Association 1997-2010; Member, Committee on Standards in Public Life 2016-.

Political interests: Local democracy and regional devolution, sustainable construction, energy and climate change, social cohesion; North and Sub-Saharan Africa, European Union.

Other: President, Goyt Valley Rail Users Association; Vice-president, Macclesfield Canal Society 1998-2015; Member, North West Constitutional Convention 1999-2001; Fellow, Industry and Parliament Trust 2000; Patron, Marple Civic Society 2012-; Governor, Westminster Foundation for Democracy 2013-15; Trustee, Mellor Archaeological Trust; Fellow, Institute of Civil Engineers 2018; OBE 1995; PC 2012; Kt 2013.

Publications: Budgeting For Real (1984, 1994, 1999); Life In The Balance (1986); Thriving In The Balance (1995); Open Active & Effective (1995); Local Democracy Guaranteed (1996); Energy – Clean and Green to 2050 (1999); Nuclear Waste – Cleaning up the Mess (2001).

Recreations: Theoretical astronomy, camping, table tennis.

Rt Hon the Lord Stunell OBE, House of Lords, London SW1A 0PW
Tel: 020 7219 3000 *Email:* andrew.stunell.hg@parliament.uk

CROSSBENCH

SUGAR, LORD

SUGAR (Life Baron), Alan Michael Sugar; cr 2009. Born 24 March 1947; Married Ann Simons 1968 (2 sons 1 daughter).

Non-political career: Amstrad and post-1997 successors Betacom and Viglen: Founder chair 1968-97, Chair 1991-2001, Chief executive 1998-2000; Presenter, *The Apprentice* BBC TV 2005-.

Political career: *House of Lords:* Raised to the peerage as Baron Sugar, of Clapton in the London Borough of Hackney 2009. Government Enterprise Champion 2009-10, 2016-.

Other: Jewish Care, Great Ormond Street; Doctorate of Science: Brunel University, City University; Kt 2000.

Publications: What You See Is What You Get: My Autobiography (2011); The Way I See It: Rants, Revelations And Rules For Life (2011); Unscripted: My Ten Years in Telly (2015).

Recreations: Cycling, flying.

The Lord Sugar, House of Lords, London SW1A 0PW
Tel: 020 7219 5353
Amshold House, Goldings Hill, Loughton IG10 2RW *Twitter:* @Lord_Sugar

CONSERVATIVE

SUGG, BARONESS

SUGG (Life Baroness) Elizabeth Grace Sugg; cr 2016. Born 2 May 1977.

Education: Newcastle University (politics).

Non-political career: Sky News; Media, Conservative MEP Team; Aide to Ken Clarke MP; Prime Minister's Office 2005-16: Head of Operations, Director of Operations and Campaigns.

Political career: *House of Lords:* Raised to the peerage as Baroness Sugg, of Coldharbour in the London Borough of Lambeth 2016. Government Whip (Baroness in Waiting) 2017; Government Spokesperson, Department for International Trade September 2017; Parliamentary Under-Secretary of State and Government Spokesperson: Department for Transport 2017-19, Department for International Development 2019-20; Parliamentary Under-Secretary of State (Minister for Overseas Territories and Sustainable Development) and Government Spokesperson: Department for International Development and Foreign and Commonwealth Office 2020, Foreign, Commonwealth and Development Office 2020; Prime Minister's Special Envoy for Girls' Education 2020.

Other: Board member, Cricket World Cup England and Wales 2019.

The Baroness Sugg CBE, House of Lords, London SW1A 0PW
Tel: 020 7219 3000

CONSERVATIVE

SURI, LORD

SURI (Life Baron), Ranbir Singh Suri; cr 2014. Born 10 February 1935.

Non-political career: Chair and Founder, Oceanic Jewellers 1976-.

Political career: *House of Lords:* Raised to the peerage as Baron Suri, of Ealing in the London Borough of Ealing 2014. *Other:* Chair, Anglo-Asian Conservative Association 1978-; British Asian Conservative Links: Founder, Chair 1997-2011; President, Conservative Ethnic Diversity Council. Voluntary Associate: HM Prison Wormwood Scrubs 1982-85, Middlesex Probation Committee 1983-85; Member: Board of Visitors, HM Prison Pentonville 1985-2000, Advisory Council on Race Relations, Home Office 1988-92, Middlesex Probation Committee 1990-91, Local Review Committee, HM Prison Pentonville 1990-93; JP, Ealing 1991-2005; Member, Lord Chancellor's Advisory Committee on General Commissioners of Income Tax 2003-05.

Other: Honorary Correspndent to the British High Commissioner, Kenya 1973-74; Member, London Chamber of Commerce; Mentor, Prince's Youth Business Trust 1997-2003; Executive Committee Member, British Heart Foundation, Ealing 1995-96; Member, Institute of Directors 1991-2012; Friends of Shakespeare Globe; General Secretary, Board of British Sikhs 1991-92;

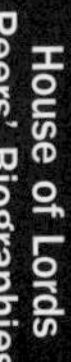

Executive Committee Member, Bharatiya Vidya Bhavan; Adviser, Khalsa College 1988-89; Vice-President, Shepherd's Bush Gurdwara 1980-81; Shiromani Award 1979; Scroll of Honour 1985.

The Lord Suri, House of Lords, London SW1A 0PW
Tel: 020 7219 5353

LIBERAL DEMOCRAT

SUTTIE, BARONESS

Liberal Democrat Lords Spokesperson for Northern Ireland

BARONESS SUTTIE (Life Baroness), Alison Mary Suttie; cr 2013. Born 27 August 1968; Daughter of late Dr Alastair M Suttie and Dr Gillian Suttie.

Education: Hawick High School; Heriot-Watt University (BA French and Russian 1990); French, Russian.

Non-political career: English Teacher, St Petersburg 1990-91; Liberal Democrat Adviser, House of Commons 1991-96; Adviser, ELDR group, European Parliament; Press Attaché and Adviser 1999-2001; Office of Pat Cox as President of the European Parliament; Press Secretary 2002-04; Head of Office to leaders of the Liberal Democrats Sir Menzies Campbell and Nick Clegg 2006-10; Deputy Chief of Staff, Office of Nick Clegg as the Deputy Prime Minister 2010-11; Consultant on democracy building projects specializing in the North Africa, Middle East and the countries of the former Soviet Union 2012; Training courses for UK civil servants, NGOs and charities 2012-; Associate, Global Partners Governance 2015-.

Political career: *House of Lords:* Raised to the peerage as Baroness Suttie, of Hawick in the Scottish Borders 2013. Liberal Democrat: Shadow Secretary of State/Lords Spokesperson for Northern Ireland 2016-18, Spokesperson for Northern Ireland 2020-. Member: European Union 2015-19, EU External Affairs Sub-Committee 2015-19, Electoral Registration and Administration Act 2013 2019-. *Other:* Liberal Democrats: Campaign Manager,2010 general election campaign, Co-ordinator, negotiation team leading to the establishment of the Coalition Government 2010, Party Whip 2013-, Member, Foreign Affairs Team 2013-.

Political interests: European affairs, international development (in particular global health and TB), political and constitutional reform, international relations, human rights; Middle East, North Africa, Russia and the countries of the former Soviet Union.

Other: Member, British-Irish Parliamentary Association 2017-19; Trustee of Board, IPPR.

The Baroness Suttie, House of Lords, London SW1A 0PW
Tel: 020 7219 5353 *Email:* suttiea@parliament.uk

CONSERVATIVE

SWINFEN, LORD

SWINFEN (3rd Baron, UK), Roger Mynors Swinfen Eady; cr. 1919. Born 14 December 1938; Son of 2nd Baron; Married Patricia Blackmore 1962 (1 son 3 daughters).

Education: Westminster School; RMA, Sandhurst.

Non-political career: Director, Swinfen Charitable Trust 1998-. Lieutenant, The Royal Scots (The Royal Regiment).

Political career: *House of Lords:* First entered House of Lords 1977; Elected hereditary peer 1999-. Member: Greater Manchester Bill 1979, European Communities House of Lords: Sub-committees: C 1990-94, B 2004-05; Co-opted member: EU Sub-committees: B (Internal Market) 2005-06, C (Foreign Affairs, Defence and Development Policy) 2007-10; Member: Hybrid Instruments 2010-, Joint Committee on Consolidation, Etc, Bills 2010-15, Mental Capacity Act 2005 2013-14, Artificial Intelligence 2017-18. *Other:* JP, Kent 1983-85.

Political interests: Disability, telemedicine.

Other: President, South East Region, British Sports Association for the Disabled; Member, Direct Mail Services Standards Board 1983-97; Fellow, Industry and Parliament Trust 1983; Patron: Disablement Income Group 1988-, Labrador Rescue South East 1996-, World Orthopaedic Concern, MOET Iraq (Management of Obstetric Emergency Trauma), KunDe Foundation; Director, American Telemedicine Association 2009-13; Liveryman, Worshipful

Company of Drapers; Honorary Research Fellow, Centre for Online Health, University of Queensland 2001-10; MBE 2015.

Publications: Co-author: An Evaluation of the First Year's Experience with a Low-cost Telemedicine Link in Bangladesh (2001), Store-and-Forward Teleneurology in Developing Countries (2001), Experience with a Low-cost Telemedicine System in Three Developing Countries (2001); Low Cost Telemedicine in the Developing World (2002); Telemedicine: The Way Ahead for Medicine in the Developing World (2003); Prospective Case Review of a Global E-health System for Doctors in Developing Countries (2004); Telemedicine Support for Iraq (2005); Low-cost Telemedicine in Iraq: analysis of referrals in the first 15 months (2005); Supporting Hospital Doctors in the Middle East by Email Telemedicine: Something the industrial world can do (2007).

Recreations: Gardening, painting, reading history.

The Lord Swinfen MBE, House of Lords, London SW1A 0PW
Tel: 020 7219 3500 *Email:* swinfenr@parliament.uk

LABOUR

SYMONS OF VERNHAM DEAN, BARONESS

SYMONS OF VERNHAM DEAN (Life Baroness), Elizabeth Conway Symons; cr. 1996. Born 14 April 1951; Daughter of Ernest Vize Symons and Elizabeth Megan, née Jenkins; Married Philip Bassett 2001 (1 son).

Education: Putney High School for Girls; Girton College, Cambridge (MA history 1974).

Non-political career: Research, Girton College, Cambridge 1972-74; Administration trainee, Department of the Environment 1974-77; Inland Revenue Staff Federation: Assistant secretary 1977-78, Deputy general secretary 1978-89; General secretary, Association of First Division Civil Servants 1989-97. Member, General Council, TUC 1989-96.

Political career: *House of Lords:* Raised to the peerage as Baroness Symons of Vernham Dean, of Vernham Dean in the County of Hampshire 1996. Parliamentary Under-Secretary of State, Foreign and Commonwealth Office 1997-99; Minister of State for: Defence Procurement, Ministry of Defence 1999-2001, International Trade and Investment, Foreign and Commonwealth Office and Department of Trade and Industry 2001-03; Government Spokesperson for: Foreign and Commonwealth Office 2001-05, Trade and Industry 2001-05; Deputy Leader of the Lords 2001-05; Minister of State for Middle East, Foreign and Commonwealth Office 2003-05; Opposition Spokesperson for Foreign and Commonwealth Office 2010-11. Member: EU Sub-committee C (Foreign Affairs, Defence and Development Policy): Co-opted member 2005-06, Member 2006-09; Member: Conventions Joint Committee 2006, European Union 2006-10; Co-opted Member, EU Sub-committee D (Environment and Agriculture) 2009-10; Member: National Security Strategy Joint Committee 2010, Joint Committee on the Draft House of Lords Reform Bill 2011-12, The Arctic 2014-15, EU External Affairs Sub-committee 2016-20, Risk Assessment and Risk Planning 2020-. *Other:* Member, Parliamentary Labour Party Parliamentary Committee 2001-10. Governor: Polytechnic of North London 1989-94, London Business School 1993-97; Member, Employment Appeal Tribunal 1995-97; Board Member, Manchester Airports Group 2013-16.

Other: Council member, RIPA 1989-97; Hon. Associate, National Council of Women 1989; Member: Executive Council, Campaign for Freedom of Information 1989-97, Hansard Society Council 1992-97, Advisory Council, Civil Service College 1992-97; Council member: Industrial Society 1994-97, Open University 1994-97; FRSA; Lords Select Committee Member of the Year, *House Magazine* awards 2012; PC 2001.

Recreations: Reading, gardening.

Rt Hon the Baroness Symons of Vernham Dean, House of Lords, London SW1A 0PW
Tel: 020 7219 5837

LIBERAL DEMOCRAT

TAVERNE, LORD

TAVERNE (Life Baron), Dick Taverne; cr. 1996. Born 18 October 1928; Son of late Dr N J M Taverne and Mrs L V Taverne; Married Janice Hennessey 1955 (2 daughters).

Education: Charterhouse School, Surrey; Balliol College, Oxford (MA literae humaniores 1951); Dutch.

Non-political career: Called to the Bar, Middle Temple 1954; QC 1965; Director, Equity & Law 1972-87; Institute for Fiscal Studies: Director 1970-79, Director-General 1979-81, Chair 1981-83; Director, BOC Group 1975-95; Director, Axa Equity & Law 1987-2001; PRIMA Europe Ltd: Director 1987-98, Chair 1991-93, President 1993-98; Chair, OLIM Investment Trust 1989-99; Deputy Chair, Central European Growth Fund 1994-2000; Chair, Axa Equity & Law Monitoring Board 2001-08; Founder and Chair, Sense about Science 2002-12; President, Research Defence Society 2003-08; Chair, IFG 2004-07.

Political career: *House of Commons:* Contested Wandsworth, Putney 1959 general election. MP (Labour) for Lincoln 1962-72 (resigned), (Democratic Labour) for Lincoln March 1973 by-election to September 1974. Contested (SDP) Southwark, Peckham 1982 by-election and Dulwich 1983 general election; Parliamentary Under-Secretary of State, Home Office 1966-68; HM Treasury: Minister of State 1968-69, Financial Secretary 1969-70. *House of Lords:* Raised to the peerage as Baron Taverne, of Pimlico in the City of Westminster 1996. Liberal Democrat Spokesperson for Treasury 1998-2005 (Euro 2001-05). Member: Monetary Policy of the Bank of England 2000-03, Animals in Scientific Procedures 2001-02, European Union Sub-committee A (Economic and Financial Affairs, Trade and External Relations/Economic and Financial Affairs) 2003-05; Science and Technology: Member 2004-09, Co-opted Member 2009; Member, Science and Technology Sub-committee II (Genomic Medicine) 2008-09. *Other:* Member: National Committee, Social Democratic Party 1981-87; Federal Policy Committee, Liberal Democrats 1989-90. Chair: Public Policy Centre 1983-87, Alcohol and Drug Abuse Prevention and Treatment Ltd 1996-2008.

Political interests: Science and technology, European Union, crime and drugs, tax, economic policy.

Other: Member, International Independent Review Body to review workings of European Commission 1979; Refugee Council; Honorary Fellow Mansfield College, Oxford; Association of British Science Writers Parliamentary Science Communicator of the Year 2006.

Publications: The Future of the Left: Lincoln and after (1974); The March of Unreason – Science, Democracy and the New Fundamentalism (2005); Against the Tide (autobiography) (Biteback Publishing, 2014).

The Lord Taverne QC, House of Lords, London SW1A 0PW
Tel: 020 7219 3000
25 Tufton Court, Tufton Street, London SW1P 3QH *Tel:* 020 7233 2409
Email: dick.taverne@gmail.com

LABOUR

TAYLOR OF BOLTON, BARONESS

Chair, Select Committee on Constitution

TAYLOR OF BOLTON (Life Baroness), Ann Taylor; cr 2005. Born 2 July 1947; Daughter of late John Walker and late Doreen Bowling; Married David Taylor 1966 (1 son 1 daughter).

Education: Bolton School; Bradford University (BSc politics and economic history 1969); Sheffield University (MA economic history 1970).

Non-political career: Part-time tutor, Open University 1971-74; Monitoring officer, Housing Corporation 1985-87; Member, Intelligence Review Committee 2004; Parliamentary Fellowship, St Anthony's College, Oxford; Member, advisory board, Thales UK 2010-. Member: Association of University Teachers, GMB.

Political career: *House of Commons:* Contested Bolton West February 1974 general election. MP (Labour) for Bolton West October 1974-83. Contested Bolton North East 1983 general election. MP for Dewsbury 1987-2005; PPS to Fred Mulley as Secretary of State for: Education and Science 1975-76, Defence 1976-77; Government Whip 1977-79; Opposition Frontbench Spokesperson for: Education 1979-81, Housing 1981-83, Home Office 1987-88, Environment 1988-92; Shadow Secretary of State for Education 1992-94; Shadow Chancellor of the Duchy of Lancaster 1994-95; Shadow Leader of the House 1994-97: Member House of Commons Commission 1994-98, President of the Council and Leader of the House of Commons 1997-98; Member Public Accounts Commission 1997-98; Government Chief Whip 1998-2001; Chair, Intelligence and Security Committee 2001-05. *House of Lords:* Raised to the peerage as Baroness Taylor of Bolton, of Bolton in the County of Greater Manchester 2005. Parliamentary Under-Secretary of State and Government Spokesperson: Ministry of Defence 2007-10 (Defence Equipment and Support 2007-08, International Defence and Security 2008-10), Foreign and Commonwealth Office 2009-10. Member: Joint Committee on National Security Strategy 2010-14, Constitution 2014-17, Leader's Group on Governance 2015, Lord Speaker's Committee on the Size of the House 2016-; Chair, Constitution 2017-. *Other:* Holmfirth UDC 1972-74.

Political interests: Education, Home Office, intelligence and security, defence.

Other: Member, UK Delegation to NATO Parliamentary Assembly 2014-15; Hon. Fellow, Birkbeck College, London University; Hon. Doctorate, Bradford University; PC 1997.

Publications: Choosing Our Future – Practical Politics of the Environment (1992).

Recreations: Bolton Wanderers FC.

Rt Hon the Baroness Taylor of Bolton, House of Lords, London SW1A 0PW
Tel: 020 7219 5183 *Email:* taylora@parliament.uk *Twitter:* @AnnTaylor_HoL

LIBERAL DEMOCRAT

TAYLOR OF GOSS MOOR, LORD

TAYLOR OF GOSS MOOR (Life Baron), Matthew Owen John Taylor; cr 2010. Born 3 January 1963; Son of late Ken Taylor, screenwriter, and Jill Taylor, née Black; Married Victoria Garner 2009 divorced 2017 (3 sons).

Education: Treliske School, Truro; University College School, London; Lady Margaret Hall, Oxford (BA philosophy, politics and economics 1986, MA).

Non-political career: Sabbatical President, Oxford University Student Union 1985-86; Economic Policy Researcher, Parliamentary Liberal Party, attached to David Penhaligon MP 1986-87; Director, Taylor & Garner Ltd (own planning consultancy) 2009-; Chair: National Housing Federation 2009-15, St Austell Ecotown Strategic Partnership Board 2010-, Kensa Heat Pumps Ltd 2012-, Bridgehall Real Estate 2013-19; Non-executive Director, Mayfield Towns Ltd 2013-.

Political career: *House of Commons:* MP for Truro 12 March 1987 by-election to 1997, for Truro and St Austell 1997-2010 (Liberal/All 1987-88, Liberal Democrat 1988-2010); Liberal Spokesperson for Energy 1987-88; Liberal Democrat Spokesperson for: England (Local Government, Housing and Transport) 1988-89, Trade and Industry 1989-90, Education 1990-92, Citizen's Charter 1992-94; Principal Spokesperson for: Environment 1994-97, the Environment and Transport 1997-99, Economy 1999-2003, Cabinet Office and Social Exclusion 2006-07. Member: Broadcasting 1992-94, Environment 1996-97. *House of Lords:* Raised to the peerage as Baron Taylor of Goss Moor, of Truro in the County of Cornwall 2010. *Other:* Chair, Liberal Democrat Campaigns and Communications 1989-95; Author, Liberal Democrat General Election manifesto 2001, 2005; Chair, Liberal Democrat Parliamentary Party 2003-05. Non-executive director, South West Water 2010-; Chair, National Housing Federation 2009-15; President, National Association of Local Councils 2015-18.

Political interests: Environment, economy, education, international development, rural communities, housing, sustainable development, planning.

Other: Chair, Carclaze Garden Village Strategic Board 2010-; Visiting Professor of Planning, Plymouth University 2015-; Honorary Member, Royal Town Planning Institute 2016-; Visiting Senior Fellow, Cambridge University Planning School 2016-; Fellow, Academy of Social Sciences 2017-.

Publications: Living Working Countryside (DCLG Review of Rural Housing and Rural Economy, 2008); The Rural Coalition (2010); Planning Practice Guidance Review (DCLG, 2013); Garden Villages (Policy Exchange, 2015).

The Lord Taylor of Goss Moor, House of Lords, London SW1A 0PW
Tel: 020 7219 5353 *Email:* taylormoj@parliament.uk

CONSERVATIVE

TAYLOR OF HOLBEACH, LORD

TAYLOR OF HOLBEACH (Life Baron), John Derek Taylor; cr 2006. Born 12 November 1943; Son of late Percy Taylor and Ethel Taylor, née Brocklehurst; Married Julia Cunnington 1968 (2 sons).

Education: Bedford School; Conversational French and Dutch.

Non-political career: Director, Taylors Bulbs of Spalding 1968-2010. Member, NFU Bulb sub-committee 1982-87.

Political career: *House of Commons:* Contested (Conservative) Chesterfield February and October 1974 general elections. *House of Lords:* Raised to the peerage as Baron Taylor of Holbeach, of South Holland in the County of Lincolnshire 2006. Opposition Whip 2006-10; Opposition Spokesperson for: Environment 2006-07, Wales 2006-07, Work and Pensions 2006-10, Environment, Food and Rural Affairs 2007-10; Government Whip 2010-11; Government Spokesperson for: Cabinet Office 2010-11, Energy and Climate Change 2010-11, Work and Pensions 2010-11; Parliamentary Under-Secretary of State, Department for Environment, Food and Rural Affairs 2011-12; Parliamentary Under-Secretary of State (Criminal Information) and Government Spokesperson, Home Office 2012-14; Chief Whip (Captain of the Honourable Corps of the Gentlemen-at-Arms) 2014-19; Deputy Chairman of Committees 2014-19; Deputy Speaker 2018-19. Member: Procedure 2014-19, Privileges and Conduct 2014-, Selection 2014-19, Administration and Works 2014-16, Services 2016-19. *Other:* Contested Nottingham 1979 European Parliament election. Member, Executive Committee, East Midlands Conservative Council 1966-98; Chair, Candidates Committee 1997-98, 2002-05; Member, Conservative Board of: Finance 1985-89, Management 1996-98, 2000-03; President and Conservative Conference Chair 1997-98; Deputy chair, Conservative Party 2000-03; Chair: National Conservative Convention 2000-03, Conservatives Abroad 2001-09, Conservative Agents Superannuation Fund 2006-10. Member, Horticulture Development Council 1986-91; Minister of Agriculture's Regional Panel: Eastern Region 1990-92, East Midlands Region 1992-96, Lincoln Diocesan Assets Committee 1995-2001, 2004-.

Political interests: Agriculture and horticulture, environment, energy, waste, freight, democracy and political parties; France, Netherlands, Slovenia.

Other: Chair, EC Working Party on European Bulb Industry 1982; Fellow, Royal Society of Arts 1994; Trustee, International Bomber Command Memorial Trust; Associate, Royal Agricultural Society 2012; Chartered Member, Institute of Horticulture 2015; Holbeach and East Elloe Hospital Trust; Liveryman: Worshipful Company of Farmers, Worshipful Company of Gardeners; Freedom, City of London; Fellow, Chartered Institute of Horticulture 2014; Peer of the Year, *House Magazine* awards 2011; Personality of the Year, *Farm Business Magazine* 2012; CBE 1992; PC 2014. Farmers Club, Carlton Club.

Publications: Taylors Bulb Book.

Recreations: Travel, arts, literature, music.

Rt Hon the Lord Taylor of Holbeach CBE, House of Lords, London SW1A 0PW
Tel: 020 7219 5353 *Email:* taylorjl@parliament.uk

NON-AFFILIATED

TAYLOR OF WARWICK, LORD

TAYLOR OF WARWICK (Life Baron), John David Beckett Taylor; cr. 1996. Born 21 September 1952; Son of late Derief Taylor, Warwickshire professional cricketer, and Mrs Enid Taylor, nurse; Married 1981 (divorced 2005) (1 son 2 daughters); married Laura Colleen Taylor 2015 (1 son 4 daughters).

Education: Moseley Church of England School, Birmingham; Moseley Grammar School; Keele University (BA law 1977); Gray's Inn, Inns of Court School of Law.

Non-political career: Barrister-at-Law, called Gray's Inn 1978; Television and radio presenter; Author and Journalist; International Keynote Speaker; Special Adviser to the Home Secretary and Home Office Ministers 1990-91; Non-executive director: Currencies Direct Ltd -2010, Asia Now Resources Inc, Canada, International Small Business Congress; Bank Consultant; Judge 2001-06. Member, NUJ.

Political career: *House of Commons:* Contested (Conservative) Cheltenham 1992 general election. *House of Lords:* Raised to the peerage as Baron Taylor of Warwick, of Warwick in the County of Warwickshire 1996. Introduced the Criminal Evidence (Amendment) Bill which came into force March 1997 as the Criminal Evidence (Amendment) Act 1997; Suspended from membership May 2011-June 2012. Member, Information 2007-11. *Other:* Member, Association of Conservative Peers -2010; Resigned Conservative Whip July 2010. Councillor, Solihull Borough Council 1986-91; Member: North West Thames Regional Health Authority 1992-93, Greater London Further Education Funding Council 1992-95; Vice-President, British Board of Film Classification 1998-; Member, Independent Football Commission 2002-03.

Political interests: International peace-making, diversity, immigration, media, business, trade, security and defence; Africa, China, Europe, Israel, Italy, Jamaica, Japan, USA.

Other: Member: International Trade Commission, Inter-Parliamentary Union, Commonwealth Parliamentary Association; Founder, Warwick Leadership Academy 1997-; Director, Warwick Leadership Foundation 1999-; Life Patron, West Indian Senior Citizens Association (WISCA); Patron: Parents Need Children Adoption Charity, Kidscape Charity; Executive Committee Member, Sickle Cell Anaemia Relief Charity; Member: Royal Television Society, Radio Academy; Vice-President, National Small Business Bureau; President, African Caribbean Westminster Business Initiative; Barker, Variety Club of Great Britain; Member, Industry and Parliament Trust; Member: Bar Council, Institute of Directors; Freedom: City of London 1998, City of Lexington, Kentucky, USA 2004, City of Las Vegas, USA 2007; Chancellor, Bournemouth University 2002-07; Honorary LLD: Warwick University 2001, Asbury College, Kentucky, USA 2004; Gray's Inn Advocacy Prize 1978. Hon. President, Ilford Town FC.

Publications: The System on Trial (BBC Publications, 1996); No Blacks, No Irish, No Dogs.

Recreations: Music, wife and family, sport, travel.

The Lord Taylor of Warwick, House of Lords, London SW1A 0PW
Tel: 020 7219 5604 *Email:* taylorjdb@parliament.uk Website: www.lordtaylor.org
Twitter: @Lord_ofWarwick

CONSERVATIVE

TEBBIT, LORD

TEBBIT (Life Baron), Norman Beresford Tebbit; cr. 1992. Born 29 March 1931; Son of late Leonard Albert Tebbit; Married Margaret Daines 1956 (died 2020) (2 sons 1 daughter).

Education: Edmonton County Grammar School.

Non-political career: Journalist 1947-49; Publicist and publisher 1951-53; Airline pilot 1953-70; Assistant director of information, National Federation of Building Trades Employers 1975-79; Company director: Sears Holdings plc 1987-99, British Telecom 1987-96, BET 1987-96, Spectator (1828) Ltd 1989-2004; Political commentator on Sky Television's Target programme 1989-98; Company director, Onix Ltd 1990-92; Columnist: *The Sun* 1995-97, *Mail on Sunday* 1997-2001; Former director and adviser to JCB Excavators Ltd; Blogger, *Daily Telegraph* 2010-. RAF pilot 1949-51, Commissioned; Served 604 Squadron RAuxAF 1952-55. Member and office holder, BALPA.

Political career: *House of Commons:* MP (Conservative) for Epping 1970-74, for Chingford 1974-92; PPS to Robin Chichester-Clarke as Minister of State, Department of Employment 1972-73; Parliamentary Under-Secretary of State, Department of Trade 1979-81; Minister of State for Industry 1981; Secretary of State for: Employment 1981-83, Trade and Industry and President of the Board of Trade 1983-85; Chancellor of the Duchy of Lancaster 1985-87. *House of Lords:* Raised to the peerage as Baron Tebbit, of Chingford in the London Borough of Waltham Forest 1992. *Other:* Chair, Conservative Party 1985-87; Vice-President, Conservatives for Britain 2015-16.

Political interests: Europe, industrial relations, aviation; UK.

Other: President, Air League 1994-98; Chair, Battle of Britain London Monument Appeal 2003-06; President: Nuffield Ortholics Appeal 2005-, Nuffield Orthopaedic Appeal 2005-; Member, Royal Aeronautical Society 2005-; Liveryman, Guild of Air Pilots and Air Navigators; Freedom, City of London; PC 1981; CH 1987. Royal Air Force, Beefsteak, The Other Club.

Publications: Upwardly Mobile (1988); Unfinished Business (1991); The Game Cook (2009) (new edition 2017); Ben's Story (2014).

Recreations: Shooting.

Rt Hon the Lord Tebbit CH, House of Lords, London SW1A 0PW
Tel: 020 7219 5353 *Email:* tebbitn@parliament.uk

LIBERAL DEMOCRAT

TEVERSON, LORD

Chair, EU Environment Sub-committee

TEVERSON (Life Baron), Robin Teverson; cr 2006. Born 31 March 1952; Son of Dr Crofton and Joan Teverson; Married Rosemary Young 1975 (2 daughters); married Terrye Lynn Jones 2006 (3 stepdaughters).

Education: Chigwell School, Essex; Waltham Forest Technical College; Exeter University (BA economics 1973).

Non-political career: Director, Exel Logistics 1986-89; Managing director: SPD Ltd 1986-89, Rationale Ltd supply chain consultancy 1989-2002; Chair, Finance South West Ltd 1999-2002; Chief executive, Finance Cornwall 2002-06; Director: Finance South West Ltd 2004-06, Devon and Cornwall Business Council 2006-16, KCS Print Ltd 2006-, UK-Japan 21st Century Group Ltd 2007-, Thornparks Ltd 2008-09; Chair, Wessex Investors Ltd 2008-.

Political career: *House of Commons:* Contested (Liberal Democrat) South East Cornwall 1992 general election. *House of Lords:* Raised to the peerage as Baron Teverson, of Tregony in the County of Cornwall 2006. Liberal Democrat: Whip 2006-09, Spokesperson for: Environment, Food and Rural Affairs 2006-08, Energy and Climate Change 2008-10, Principal Spokesperson for Transport 2015. Co-opted Member, EU Sub-committee F (Home Affairs) 2006-08; Member: Draft Climate Change Bill Joint Committee 2007, European Union 2008-13; Chair EU Sub-committee C: (Foreign Affairs, Defence and Development Policy) 2008-12, (External Affairs) 2012-13; Chair, The Arctic 2014-15; Member: Economic Affairs 2015-16, Economic Affairs Finance Bill Sub-committee 2015-16, European Union 2016-; Chair: EU Energy and Environment Sub-Committee 2016-20, EU Environment Sub-committee 2020-. Chair, Liberal Democrat Parliamentary Party Committees on: Environment, Food and Rural Affairs (Energy and Climate Change) 2010-12, Energy and Climate Change 2012-15. *Other:* European Parliament: MEP for Cornwall and West Plymouth 1994-99, Contested South West region 1999 election. Liberal Democrats: Chair, Federal Finance and Administration Committee 1999-2002, Member, Federal Executive 1999-2002, 2005-. Member, Cornwall Council 2009-14.

Political interests: Business, transport, Europe, financial markets, international affairs; Australia, Chile, Denmark, India, Ireland.

Other: Member, Securities and Investment Institute (MSI).

Recreations: Running, history, science.

The Lord Teverson, House of Lords, London SW1A 0PW
Tel: 020 7219 3566 *Email:* teversonr@parliament.uk *Twitter:* @lordtev

CROSSBENCH

THOMAS OF CWMGIEDD, LORD

Chair, Joint Committee on Consolidation, &c, Bills

THOMAS OF CWMGIEDD (Life Baron), Roger John Laugharne Thomas; cr 2013. Born 22 October 1947; Son of Roger and Dinah Thomas; Married Elizabeth Ann.

Education: Rugby School; Trinity Hall, Cambridge (1969); University of Chicago Law School (JD 1970).

Non-political career: Assistant teacher 1965-66; Called to Bar, Gray's Inn 1969 (Bencher 1992); Barrister, Essex Court Chambers 1972-96; QC 1984; Recorder 1987-96; Judge: High Court of Justice 1996-2003, Commercial Court 1996-2003; Presiding Judge, Wales and Chester Circuit 1998-2001; Senior Presiding Judge, England and Wales 2003-06; Lord Justice of Appeal 2003-11; Queen's Bench Division: Vice-President 2008-11, President 2011-13; Deputy Head, Criminal Justice 2008-13; Lord Chief Justice of England and Wales 2013-17.

Political career: *House of Lords:* Raised to the peerage as Baron Thomas of Cwmgiedd, of Cwmgiedd in the County of Powys 2013. As a senior member of the judiciary, disqualified from participation 2013-17. Member, EU Financial Affairs Sub-committee 2018-20; Chair, Middle

Level Bill 2018; Member: EU Services Sub-committee 2020-, European Union 2020-; Chair, Joint Committee on Consolidation, &c, Bills 2020-; Member, Common Frameworks Scrutiny 2020-. *Other:* President, Sentencing Council 2013-17 Chair: Criminal Procedure Rule Committee 2013-17, Financial Markets Law Committee, Commission on Justice in Wales (established by Welsh Government).

Political interests: Administration of justice, devolution.

Other: DTI Inspector, Mirror Group Newspapers plc 1992; Vice-President, British Maritime Law Association 1996-; AIDA Reinsurance and Insurance Arbitration Society: Deputy President 1996-2014, President 2014-; European Law Institute: Fellow, Executive Committee Member; President: British Insurance Law Association 2004-06, European Network of the Councils of the Judiciary 2008-10; International Law Book Fund; Drapers; Chancellor, Aberystwyth University 2018-; Faculty fellow, Law School, Southampton University 1990; Lord Morris of Borth-y-Gest Lecturer, University of Wales 2000; Honorary fellow: Cardiff University, Aberystwyth University, Bangor University, Swansea University, Trinity Hall, Cambridge; Honorary LLD: University of South Wales, University of the West of England, Cardiff Metropolitan University; Fellow, Learned Society of Wales; Kt 1996; PC 2003.

Recreations: Gardens, walking.

Rt Hon the Lord Thomas of Cwmgiedd, House of Lords, London SW1A 0PW
Tel: 020 7219 5353 *Email:* thomasjl@parliament.uk

LIBERAL DEMOCRAT

THOMAS OF GRESFORD, LORD

Liberal Democrat Shadow Attorney General

THOMAS OF GRESFORD (Life Baron), Donald Martin Thomas; cr. 1996. Born 13 March 1937; Son of late Hywel Thomas and Olwen Thomas; Married Nan Thomas 1961, née Kerr (died 2000) (3 sons 1 daughter); married Baroness Walmsley (qv) 2005.

Education: Grove Park Grammar School, Wrexham; Peterhouse, Cambridge (MA classics; LLB).

Non-political career: Solicitor, Wrexham 1961-66; Lecturer in law 1966-68; Called to the Bar, Gray's Inn 1967, Bencher 1989; Barrister, Wales and Chester Circuit 1968-; Deputy Circuit Judge 1974-76; Recorder of the Crown Court 1976-2002; QC 1979; Deputy High Court Judge 1985-2009.

Political career: *House of Commons:* Contested (Liberal) West Flintshire 1964, 1966, 1970, and Wrexham February and October 1974, 1979, 1983, 1987 general elections. *House of Lords:* Raised to the peerage as Baron Thomas of Gresford, of Gresford in the County Borough of Wrexham 1996. Liberal Democrat: Spokesperson for: Welsh Affairs -2004, Home Office -2004; Shadow Attorney General 2004-06, 2007-10, 2015-, Shadow Lord Chancellor 2006-07, Spokesperson for: Justice 2007-10, Law Officers 2015-19, Wales 2015-16. Member: Joint Committee on Privacy and Injunctions 2011-12, Delegated Powers and Regulatory Reform 2015-19, Bribery Act 2010 2018-19, Sentencing (Pre-consolidation Amendments) Bill 2019. Chair, Liberal Democrat Parliamentary Party Committees on Home Affairs, Justice and Equalities (Justice) 2010-12, Wales 2012-15. *Other:* Welsh Liberal Party: Vice-chair 1967-69, Chair 1969-74; President: Wrexham Liberal Association 1975-, Welsh Liberal Party 1977, 1978, 1979; Welsh Liberal Democrats: Vice-President 1991-93, President 1993. Member, Criminal Injury Compensation Board 1985-93.

Political interests: Criminal justice; China, Hong Kong, Wales.

Other: Marcher Sound: Chair 1991-2000, Vice-chair 1983-91; President: Gresford Memorial Trust 1993-, London Welsh Chorale 2000-; OBE 1982. Reform, Western (Glasgow) Club.

Recreations: Rugby football, rowing, golf, fishing, cooking, harp, piano, bagpipes, singing.

The Lord Thomas of Gresford OBE QC, House of Lords, London SW1A 0PW
Tel: 020 7219 5453 *Email:* thomasm@parliament.uk

LIBERAL DEMOCRAT

THOMAS OF WINCHESTER, BARONESS

THOMAS OF WINCHESTER (Life Baroness), Celia Marjorie Thomas; cr 2006. Born 14 October 1945; Daughter of David Thomas and Marjorie Thomas, née Best.

Education: St Swithun's School, Winchester.

Non-political career: Winchester Diocesan Board of Finance 1963-65; Winchester Cathedral Appeal 1965-66; The Pilgrims' School, Winchester 1967-72; Christ Church Cathedral School, Oxford 1972-74; Liberal/Liberal Democrat Lords Whips Office 1977-2006: Head of Office.

Political career: *House of Lords:* Raised to the peerage as Baroness Thomas of Winchester, of Winchester in the County of Hampshire 2006. Liberal Democrat Spokesperson for: Work and Pensions 2007-10, Disability 2015-. Member: Liaison 2007-10, Merits of Statutory Instruments 2007-10, Refreshment 2007-12; Procedure/Procedure and Privileges: Member 2007, 2009-13, 2017-, Alternate Member 2008-09; Chair, Delegated Powers and Regulatory Reform 2010-15; Member: Equality Act 2010 and Disability 2015-16, Joint Committee on Consolidation, &c, Bills 2015-. *Other:* Liberal/Liberal Democrat election agent: Winchester October 1974, Brecon and Radnor 1987 and 1992; President, Winchester Liberal Democrats.

Political interests: Disability, prisons, bee health, voting reform and machinery of government.

Other: Vice-president and trustee, Muscular Dystrophy; Patron: Winchester Churches Nightshelter, Avonbrook Projects Abroad, Thrive, Driving Mobility, Pinotage Youth Development Academy, SA; Chair, Liberal Summer School, now Keynes Forum 2001-09; Vice-President, Lloyd George Society 2005-; Management Board, Centre Forum 2006-09; Member, MCC Disability Access Group; Target Ovarian Cancer, Butterfly Conservation, Plantlife, Salvation Army, Muscular Dystrophy UK; Health Champion, Charity Champion awards 2012; MBE 1985.

Recreations: Music, theatre, gardening, butterfly conservation, watching cricket.

The Baroness Thomas of Winchester MBE, House of Lords, London SW1A 0PW
Tel: 020 7219 5353

LIBERAL DEMOCRAT

THORNHILL, BARONESS

Liberal Democrat Deputy Chief Whip

THORNHILL (Life Baroness), Dorothy Thornhill; cr 2015. Born 26 May 1955; Married Dr Iain Sharpe (1 daughter 1 son).

Education: Park School, Preston; BEd English; MEd education of children with learning and behavioural difficulties.

Non-political career: Teacher for 25 years, including: Assistant head teacher, Queens School, Bushey 1995-2002.

Political career: *House of Commons:* Contested (Liberal Democrat) Watford 2015 general election. *House of Lords:* Raised to the peerage as Baroness Thornhill, of Watford in the County of Hertfordshire 2015. Liberal Democrat: Spokesperson for Communities and Local Government 2015-16, Whip 2020, Deputy Chief Whip 2020-. Member: Intergenerational Fairness and Provision 2018-19, Social and Economic Impact of the Gambling Industry 2019-. *Other:* Watford Borough Council: Councillor 1992-2002, Directly Elected Mayor 2002-18; Vice-president, Local Government Association 2017-.

Political interests: Housing, planning, education.

Other: Trustee, Work Place Matters; MBE 2011.

Recreations: Watching rugby, cycling, walking, reading, theatre, architecture.

The Baroness Thornhill MBE, House of Lords, London SW1A 0PW
Tel: 020 7219 3000 *Email:* thornhilld@parliament.uk Website: www.dorothythornhill.com

LABOUR/ CO-OPERATIVE

THORNTON, BARONESS

Opposition Spokesperson for Health

THORNTON (Life Baroness), Dorothea Glenys Thornton; cr. 1998. Born 16 October 1952; Daughter of Peter and Jean Thornton; Married John Carr 1977 (1 son 1 daughter).

Education: Thornton Secondary School, Bradford; London School of Economics (BSc economics 1976).

Non-political career: National co-ordinator, Gingerbread 1977-79; Area officer, Citizens Advice Bureau 1979-81; Public affairs adviser, Co-operative Wholesale Society 1981-93; Director of development and general secretary, Fabian Society 1993-96; Chair, Pall Mall Consult 2001-08; Senior associate, Social Business International 2010-; Chief executive, Young Foundation 2015-17. Member, GMB.

Political career: *House of Lords:* Raised to the peerage as Baroness Thornton, of Manningham in the County of West Yorkshire 1998. Government Whip 2008-10; Government Spokesperson for: Work and Pensions 2008, Equality 2008, Health 2008, 2009-10; Parliamentary Under-Secretary of State, Department of Health 2010; Opposition Spokesperson for: Health 2010-12, 2017-, Work and Pensions 2010, Equalities Office 2010-15, Culture, Media and Sport 2014-15. Member, EU Sub-committee C (Environment, Public Health and Consumer Protection) 1999-2000. *Other:* Member, Co-operative Party 1974-; Chair, Greater London Labour Party 1986-91; Labour Party Policy Forum 2005-08. London School of Economics: Member, Court of Governors 1999-, Emeritus governor 2016-.

Political interests: Children, media, social enterprise, Yorkshire.

Other: NCH, Circusspace, One World Action, Theodora Childrens Trust, Patron Social Enterprise UK; RSA; Hon Doctorate, Bradford University 2015.

Recreations: Canoeing, hill-walking in Yorkshire.

The Baroness Thornton, House of Lords, London SW1A 0PW
Tel: 020 7219 8502 *Email:* thorntong@parliament.uk *Twitter:* @GlenysThornton

CROSSBENCH

THURLOW, LORD

THURLOW (9th Baron), Roualeyn Robert Hovell-Thurlow-Cumming-Bruce; cr 1792. Born 13 April 1952; Son of Lord Francis Thurlow, diplomat, and late Yvonne Wilson, artist; Married Bridget 1980 (2 sons 2 daughters).

Education: Milton Abbey School.

Non-political career: Chartered Surveyor, RICS 1979-2016; Jones Lang Wootton/Jones Lang LaSalle: Partner 1985-99, Managing director 1999-2007; Principal, RCB Advisors 2007-.

Political career: *House of Lords:* Elected hereditary peer 2015-. Member, Delegated Powers and Regulatory Reform 2016-. *Other:* Councillor, Mapledurham Parish Council 2000-.

Political interests: Europe, rural affairs, built environment, mental health; Commonwealth.

Other: Chair, Investors' Committee, UK Property Fund -2016; Senior Consultant and member, Investment Committee, Castleforge Partners; MRICS 1979; MIND, Charlie Waller Foundation. White's, Pratt's Club; Friends of Hardwick Tennis Court.

Recreations: Country sports, golf.

The Lord Thurlow, House of Lords, London SW1A 0PW
Tel: 020 7219 3000 *Email:* thurlowr@parliament.uk

LIBERAL DEMOCRAT

THURSO, VISCOUNT

THURSO (3rd Viscount, UK) John Archibald Sinclair; cr 1952; 6th Bt of Ulbster (GB) 1786. Born 10 September 1953; Son of late Robin, 2nd Viscount Thurso, and late Margaret, née Robertson; Married Marion Ticknor, née Sage 1976 (2 sons 1 daughter).

Education: Eton College; Westminster Technical College (FIH Membership Exam 1974); French.

Non-political career: Managing Director: Lancaster Hotel 1981-85, Cliveden House Ltd 1985-93; Non-executive Director, Savoy Hotel plc 1993-98; Managing director, Fitness and Leisure Holdings Ltd 1995-2001; Chair: Thurso Fisheries Ltd 1995-, Scrabster Harbour Trust 1996-2001; Director: Profile Recruitment and Management Ltd 1996-2002, Walker Greenbank plc 1997-2002, Anton Mosiman Ltd 1997-2002; Chair, International Wine and Spirit Competition 1999-; Deputy Chair, Millennium and Copthorn's Hotels plc 2002-09.

Political career: *House of Commons:* MP (Liberal Democrat) for Caithness, Sutherland and Easter Ross 2001-05, for Caithness, Sutherland and Easter Ross (revised boundary) 2005-15. Contested Caithness, Sutherland and Easter Ross 2015 general election (First former hereditary member of House of Lords to become an MP); Liberal Democrat: Whip 2001-02, Spokesperson for: Tourism 2001-05, Scotland 2001-03, Shadow Secretary of State for: Transport 2003-05, Scotland 2003-06, Business, Enterprise and Regulatory Reform 2008-09, Business, Innovation and Skills 2009-10; Member, House of Commons Commission 2010-15. Member: Culture, Media and Sport 2001-05, Administration 2005-10, Treasury 2006-15, Liaison 2010-15; Chair, Finance and Services 2010-15; Member: Joint Committee on the Draft House of Lords Reform Bill 2011-12, Parliamentary Commission on Banking Standards 2012-13. Chair, Liberal Democrat Parliamentary Party Committees on: Scotland 2010-15, Constitutional and Political Reform 2012-15. *House of Lords:* First entered House of Lords 1995: Liberal Democrat Spokesperson for: Tourism 1996-99, Food 1998-99; Elected hereditary peer 2016-. Member, Risk Assessment and Risk Planning 2020-. *Other:* Member, Liberal Democrat Party Federal Policy Committee 1999-2001. Board member, Independent Parliamentary Standards Authority 2016; Chair, VisitScotland Board 2016-; Lord Lieutenant, Caithness 2017-.

Political interests: Tourism, House of Lords reform, treasury, financial services, banking reform, energy.

Other: Chair: Bucks Game Conservancy 1990-92, BHA Clubs Panel 1992-96, Master Innholders Association 1995-97; President, Licensed Victuallers Schools 1996-97; President and Fellow, Tourism Society 1999-; Patron: Hotel Catering and International Management Association 1997-2003, Institute of Management Services 1998-; President, Academy of Food and Wine Service 1998-; Chair, UK Springboard Festival Year 2000; Trustee: Castle of Mey Trust, La Foundation pour la Formation Hoteliere (Zurich); Chancellor, Wine Guild UK 2017-; Liveryman, Innholders' Company 1997; Freedom, City of London 1991; FHCIMA 1991; FInstD 1997; Hon. DBA, Oxford Brookes University 2004; PC 2014. Brook's, New Edinburgh Club.

Publications: Tourism Tomorrow (1998).

Rt Hon the Viscount Thurso, House of Lords, London SW1A 0PW
Tel: 020 7219 3000

LABOUR/ CO-OPERATIVE

TOMLINSON, LORD

TOMLINSON (Life Baron), John Edward Tomlinson; cr. 1998. Born 1 August 1939; Son of Frederick and Doris Tomlinson; Married 2nd Paulette Fuller 1998.

Education: Westminster City School; Co-operative College, Loughborough (Diploma political, economic and social studies 1961); Brunel University (health services management 1974-76); Warwick University (MA industrial relations 1982).

Non-political career: Head of research, AUEW 1968-70; Senior lecturer in industrial relations and management, Solihull College of Technology 1979-84. Member, TGWU.

Political career: *House of Commons:* MP (Labour) for Meriden 1974-79; PPS to Harold Wilson as Prime Minister 1975-76; Parliamentary Under-Secretary of State, Foreign and Commonwealth Office 1976-79; Parliamentary Secretary, Ministry of Overseas Development 1977-79. *House of Lords:* Raised to the peerage as Baron Tomlinson, of Walsall in the County of

West Midlands 1998. Member, European Union 1998-2002, 2005-08, 2010-15; EU Sub-committee A (Economic and Financial Affairs, Trade and External Relations): Member 1998-2002, Chair 2000-01; Member: House of Lords' Offices 2001-02, EU Sub-committee C (Foreign Affairs, Defence and Development Policy) 2003-07, Joint Committee on Conventions 2006; EU Sub-committee E (Law and Institutions): Member 2007-08, Co-opted member 2008-10; Member: EU Sub-committee F (Home Affairs) 2010-12, Audit 2011-13, EU Sub-committee F (Home Affairs, Health and Education) 2012-13, 2014-15, Insurance Bill 2014-15. *Other:* European Parliament: MEP for Birmingham West 1984-99. Councillor, Sheffield City Council 1963-67; Dartford Borough Council: Councillor 1970-74, Deputy Leader.

Political interests: Finance, Europe, international development, foreign policy.

Other: House of Lords Representative on Convention on Future of Europe 2002-03; Member Parliamentary Assembly: Council of Europe, Western European Union; Vice-chair, Election of Judges Committee to the European Court of Human Rights; Industry and Parliament Trust: Trustee 1987, Chair of Trustees -2007; Vice-President, Hansard Society -2006; Chair, advisory board, London School of Commerce 2004-; President: British Fluoridation Society 2004-11, Association of Independent Higher Education Providers 2005-13; Anglia Ruskin University: Board of Governors 2008-, Chair 2010-; Chair of council, Association of Business Executives; Honorary doctorate, Birmingham University; Honorary Fellowship, University of Wales Institute, Cardiff 2007. West Bromwich Labour Club.

Publications: Left, Right: The March of Political Extremism in Britain (Calders, 1981).

Recreations: Walking, reading, sport.

The Lord Tomlinson, House of Lords, London SW1A 0PW
Tel: 020 7219 3770 *Email:* tomlinsonj@parliament.uk

LIBERAL DEMOCRAT

TOPE, LORD

TOPE (Life Baron), Graham Norman Tope; cr. 1994. Born 30 November 1943; Son of late Leslie Tope; Married Margaret East 1972 (2 sons).

Education: Whitgift School, Croydon.

Non-political career: Company secretary and insurance manager 1965-72; Deputy general secretary, Voluntary Action Camden 1975-90; Chair, Community Investors Ltd 1995-98. London Scottish TA 1962-64.

Political career: *House of Commons:* MP (Liberal) Sutton and Cheam 7 December 1972 by-election to February 1974. Contested Sutton and Cheam February and October 1974 general elections; Liberal Spokesperson for Environment 1972-74. *House of Lords:* Raised to the peerage as Baron Tope, of Sutton in the London Borough of Sutton 1994. Liberal Democrat: Spokesperson for Education 1994-2000, Assistant Whip 1998-2000, Spokesperson for Communities and Local Government 2008-15, Spokesperson for London 2015-. Member: Relations between Central and Local Government 1995-96, EU Sub-committee F (Home Affairs) 2011-12, Public Service and Demographic Change 2012-13, Delegated Powers and Regulatory Reform 2019-. Chair, Liberal Democrat Parliamentary Party Committee on Communities and Local Government 2010-15. *Other:* Member, Liberal Party National Council 1970-76; National League of Young Liberals: Vice-chair 1971-73, President 1973-75; President: London Liberal Democrats 1991-2000, Sutton Liberal Democrats 2014-. London Borough of Sutton: Councillor 1974-2014, Leader, Liberal (later Liberal Democrat) Group 1974-99, Opposition Leader 1984-86, Council Leader 1986-99, Executive Councillor for Community Safety Leisure and Libraries 1999-2012; Member, London Fire and Civil Defence Authority 1995-97; Vice-president, Local Government Association 1997-2005, 2013-; Vice-chair, Association of London Government 1997-2000; London Assembly: Member 2000-08, Leader, Liberal Democrat Group 2000-06, Member, Metropolitan Police Authority 2000-08, Chair, Finance 2000-08, Mayor of London Cabinet 2000-04; Member: Croydon Strategic Partnership Board 2002-08, Sutton Strategic Partnership Board 2003-12, Safer Croydon Partnership Board 2004-08, Safer Sutton Partnership Board: Member 2004-12, Chair 2009-12; Chair, Local Government Group for Europe 2005-.

Political interests: Local government, Europe, London; Bermuda, EU, Western Balkans.

Other: EU Committee of the Regions: Member 1994-2014, Vice-chair, UK Delegation 1996-2014, Bureau member 1996-2014, President: European Liberal Democrat and Reform Group 1998-2002, Constitutional Affairs and European Governance Commission 2002-04, Political co-ordinator, ALDE Group 2007-14, Member, Political Monitoring Group 2008-10, Western Balkans Working Group 2008-14; Member, Congress of Local and Regional Authorities in Europe, Council of Europe 1996-2000; Rapporteur, Smarter Regulation 2010-11; Member, High Level Group of Independent Stakeholders on Administrative Burdens, European Commission; Member, Needle Makers Company; Freedom: City of London 1998, London Borough of Sutton 2014; CBE 1991.

Publications: Co-author: Liberals and the Community (1974), A Political Life (2011).

Recreations: Garden, history, walking, stamps.

The Lord Tope CBE, House of Lords, London SW1A 0PW
Tel: 020 7219 3098 *Fax:* 020 7219 0967 *Email:* topeg@parliament.uk
Tel: 020 8642 5292

LABOUR/ CO-OPERATIVE

TOUHIG, LORD

TOUHIG (Life Baron), James Donnelly (Don) Touhig; cr 2010. Born 5 December 1947; Son of late Michael and Catherine Touhig; Married Jennifer Hughes 1968 (died 2014) (2 sons 2 daughters).

Education: St Francis School, Abersychan; East Monmouth College.

Non-political career: Apprentice radio and tv engineer; Journalist 1968-76; Editor, Free Press of Monmouthshire 1976-90; General manager and editor-in-chief, Free Press Group of Newspapers 1988-92; General manager (business development): Bailey Group 1992-93, Bailey Print 1993-95. Member, TGWU.

Political career: *House of Commons:* Contested Richmond and Barnes 1992 general election. MP (Lab/Co-op) for Islwyn 16 February 1995 by-election to 2010; Public Interest Disclosure (Private Member's Bill) 1995; PPS to Gordon Brown as Chancellor of the Exchequer 1997-99; Assistant Government Whip 1999-2001; Parliamentary Under-Secretary of State, Wales Office 2001-05; Parliamentary Under-Secretary of State and Minister for Veterans, Ministry of Defence 2005-06; Member, Speaker's Committee for the Independent Parliamentary Standards Authority 2009-10. Member: European Standing Committee B 1995-96, Welsh Affairs 1996-97, Public Accounts 2006-10, Liaison 2009-10; Chair: Members' Allowances 2009-10. Hon. Secretary, PLP Welsh Regional Group 1995-99, 2007-08. *House of Lords:* Raised to the peerage as Baron Touhig, of Islwyn and Glansychan in the County of Gwent 2010. Opposition Whip 2015-16; Opposition Spokesperson for Defence 2015-17, 2020-21. Member: Public Service and Demographic Change 2012, Liaison 2013-16, Services 2018-. *Other:* Member, Labour Leadership Campaign Team (responsible for Devolution in Wales) 1996-97; Co-operative Party: Member, Chair, Parliamentary Group 1999, 2010. Gwent County Council: Councillor 1973-95, Chair, Finance Committee 1992-94.

Political interests: Treasury, employment, health, education, local and regional government; France.

Other: Substitute Member, UK Delegation to Parliamentary Assembly of Council of Europe 2017-; Past President, South Wales Newspaper Society; Member: Mensa, Mencap, Amnesty International; President: Caerphilly County Borough Access Group, Caerphilly Citizens Advice Bureau, Newbridge and District Ladies Choir; Vice-president, National Autistic Society; Fellow, Industry and Parliament Trust 2003; Patron, Everyone's Child Romania; Freedom, City of London 2013; Papal Knight of the Order of St Sylvester 1991; PC 2006.

Recreations: Reading, cooking for family and friends, music, walking.

Rt Hon the Lord Touhig, House of Lords, London SW1A 0PW
Tel: 020 7219 7248 *Email:* touhigjd@parliament.uk

CROSSBENCH

TREES, LORD

TREES (Life Baron), Alexander John Trees; cr 2012. Born 12 June 1946; Son of John Trees, chemical engineer, and Margaret Trees, née Bell; Married Frances McAnally 1970 (1 daughter).

Education: Brigg Grammar School, Lincolnshire; Edinburgh University (BVMS 1969; PhD 1976); French, Italian.

Non-political career: Assistant in general veterinary practice, Derby 1970-71; Research assistant, Edinburgh University 1971-76; Elanco Products Ltd, Rome, Italy: Veterinary adviser 1977-80, Head of animal science 1980; Liverpool School of Tropical Medicine, Liverpool University: Lecturer, Department of Veterinary Parasitology 1980-91, Senior lecturer 1991-94, Head of: Veterinary Parasitology 1992-2001, Parasite and Vector Biology Division 1994-97, Professor of Veterinary Parasitology 1994-2011; Liverpool University: Dean, Faculty of Veterinary Science 2001-08, Emeritus professor 2011-; Glasgow University: Visiting professor, School of Veterinary Medicine, Professor James McCall Memorial Lecture 2010; Editor-in-chief, *Veterinary Record* 2011-; Chair, Moredun Research Institute 2011-.

Political career: *House of Lords:* Raised to the peerage as Baron Trees, of The Ross in Perth and Kinross 2012. Member: EU Sub-committee D (Agriculture, Fisheries, Environment and Energy) 2014-15, European Union 2015-17, EU Energy and Environment Sub-committee 2015-17, Middle Level Bill 2018.

Political interests: Veterinary matters, animal health and welfare, aspects of public health, tropical medicine and overseas development, higher education, professional regulation, the environment; Africa, Middle East.

Other: European Veterinary Parasitology College: Founding diplomate 2003, Vice-president 2006-09; Executive council, World Association of Veterinary Parasitology 2007-; British Society of Parasitology 1980-; Royal Society of Tropical Medicine and Hygiene: Fellow 1986-, Council 1997-2000; Hon. fellow, Myerscough College; Royal College of Veterinary Surgeons: Member 1969-, Council member 2000, Junior vice-president 2008-09, President 2009-10, Senior vice-president; President, Association of Veterinary Teachers and Research Workers 1996-97; British Veterinary Association: Member 1980-, Veterinary Policy Group 1997-2001, Chair, Education Group; Hon. FRSE; FMedSci; DVM, Royal Veterinary College, London University; DVMS, Glasgow University; Peter Bridge Award, BCVA; Selborne medal, Association of Veterinary Teachers and Research Workers 2005; Wooldridge lecture and medal, British Veterinary Association 2009; Amoroso award, British Small Animal Veterinary Association 2011. Farmers Club.

Publications: 170+ papers in peer-reviewed academic journals.

Recreations: Natural history, outdoors, mountaineering, DIY.

Professor the Lord Trees, House of Lords, London SW1A 0PW
Tel: 020 7219 7278 *Fax:* 020 7219 1991 *Email:* treesa@parliament.uk

CONSERVATIVE

TREFGARNE, LORD

TREFGARNE (2nd Baron, UK), David Garro Trefgarne; cr. 1947. Born 31 March 1941; Son of 1st Baron; Married Rosalie Lane 1968 (2 sons 1 daughter).

Education: Haileybury College, Hertford; Princeton University, USA; French.

Non-political career: Non-executive director, Siebe plc 1991-98; Chairman: Engineering and Marine Training Authority (now SEMTA) 1994-2006, Scotty Group plc 2006-11.

Political career: *House of Lords:* First entered House of Lords 1962; Opposition Whip 1977-79; Government Whip 1979-80; Parliamentary Under-Secretary of State: Department of Trade 1980-81, Foreign and Commonwealth Office 1981-82, Department of Health and Social Security 1982-83, for the Armed Forces June 1983-85; Minister of State: for Defence Support 1985-86, for Defence Procurement 1986-89, Department of Trade and Industry (Minister for Trade) 1989-90; Elected hereditary peer 1999-. Member: Procedure 2000-03, Privileges 2002-05, Speakership of the House 2003-05; Co-opted Member, EU Sub-committee G (Social Policy and Consumer Affairs) 2006-08; Member: EU Sub-committee A (Economic and Financial Affairs and International Trade) 2010-11, Joint Committee on the Draft House of Lords Reform Bill 2011-12, Inquiries Act 2005 2013-14; Chair, Secondary Legislation Scrutiny

2015-19; Member, Highgate Cemetery Bill [HL] 2020-. *Other:* Association of Conservative Peers: Treasurer 1997-2000, Chair 2000-04.

Political interests: Aviation, defence, constitutional reform; North Africa.

Other: President, Mechanical and Metal Trades Confederation 1990-2000; Governor, Guildford School of Acting 1992-2001; Member, Mary Rose Trust 1992-2001; Hon. President, Popular Flying Association 1992-2003; Life Governor and council member, Haileybury 1993-2001; Hon. President, British Association of Aviation Consultants 1993-; Vice-chair, Army Cadet Force 1993-2001; Patron, Catering Equipment Suppliers Association 2000-; Director, Arab-British Chamber of Commerce 2000-; Chair, Brooklands Museum Trust 2001-14; Director, UK Skills 2001-05; Libyan British Business Council: Chair 2003-13, President 2013-; President, TWI 2006; Honorary fellowship, IET; Hon. doctorate: Staffordshire University, University of Central Lancashire; Royal Aero Club Bronze Medal 1963; PC 1989. RAF Club.

Recreations: Photography.

Rt Hon the Lord Trefgarne, House of Lords, London SW1A 0PW
Tel: 020 7219 5450 *Email:* trefgarned@parliament.uk
Email: dgt@trefgarne.co.uk

CONSERVATIVE

TRENCHARD, VISCOUNT

TRENCHARD (3rd Viscount, UK), Hugh Trenchard; cr. 1936; 3rd Baron Trenchard (UK) 1930; 3rd Bt of Wolfeton (UK) 1919. Born 12 March 1951; Son of 2nd Viscount, MC and Patricia Bailey; Married Fiona 1975 (daughter of 2nd Baron Margadale) (2 sons 2 daughters).

Education: Eton College; Trinity College, Cambridge (BA archaeology and anthropology 1973); German, Japanese.

Non-political career: Kleinwort Benson Ltd 1973-96: Chief Representative in Japan 1980-85, Director 1986-96; Director, Dover Japan Inc 1985-87; Kleinwort Benson International Inc: General manager (Tokyo branch) 1985-88, President 1988-95, Deputy chair 1995-96; Director, ACP Holdings Ltd 1990-94; Securities Committee, European Business Community in Japan: Chair 1993-95, Vice-chair of Council 1995; Director: Japan Securities Dealers Association 1994-95, Bond Underwriters Association of Japan 1994-95, Robert Fleming and Co Ltd 1996-98, Robert Fleming International Ltd 1998-2000; Non-executive director, Berkeley Technology Limited 1999-2011; Director, Westhall Capital Limited (formerly AC European Finance Limited) 2001-03; Non-executive chair, Dejima Fund Ltd 2001-09; Senior adviser, Prudential Financial Inc 2002-08; Non-executive director, Dryden Wealth Management Limited 2004-05; Stratton Street PCC Limited: Non-executive director 2005-, Chair 2009-, Director-general, European Fund and Asset Management Association 2006; Director, Standon Lordship Ltd 2006-; Managing director, Mizuho International plc 2007-12; Director: Bache Global Series 2008-15, UK Koyu Corporation Ltd 2009-, Lotte Chemical UK Ltd 2010-; Consultant and senior adviser, Mizuho Bank Ltd 2013-14; Consultant: Simon Robertson Associates LLP 2013-, Rolls-Royce Power Engineering plc 2014-15 Optum Health Solutions UK Ltd 2014-; Director, Adamas Finance Asia Ltd 2017-; Consultant, Japan Bank for International Co-operation 2017-. Captain, 4th Battalion, The Royal Green Jackets, TA 1972-80; Honorary Air Commodore, 600 (City of London) Squadron, Royal Auxiliary Air Force 2006-.

Political career: *House of Lords:* First entered House of Lords 1987; Elected hereditary peer 2004-. Member: Joint Committee on Financial Services and Markets 1999, EU Financial Affairs Sub-committee 2019-20, EU Services Sub-committee 2020-. *Other:* Chair, Conservatives Abroad in Japan 1986-88; President, North East Hertfordshire Conservative Association 2001-. DL, Hertfordshire 2008-; Lieutenant, City of London 2014-.

Political interests: Financial services, defence, foreign affairs; China, Japan, Korea, USA.

Other: Member, Japan Association of Corporate Executives 1987-95; Chair, Japan Society 2000-04; RAF Benevolent Fund: Council and board of trustees 2006-13, Deputy chair of council 2014-. Brooks's, Pratt's, Royal Air Force, Cavalry and Guards, Tokyo Club.

Recreations: Shooting, fishing, skiing.

The Viscount Trenchard DL, House of Lords, London SW1A 0PW
Tel: 020 7219 5353 *Email:* trenchardh@parliament.uk
Simon Robertson Associates LLP, 2 St James's Place, London SW1A 1NP *Tel:* 020 7318 8882
Email: hugh.trenchard@simonrobertsonassociates.com

CROSSBENCH

TREVETHIN AND OAKSEY, LORD

TREVETHIN (5th Baron, UK), cr 1921 AND OAKSEY (3rd Baron, UK), cr 1947; Patrick John Tristram Lawrence (known as Lord Oaksey). Born 29 June 1960; Son of 4th Baron, OBE JP; Married Lucinda 1987 (1 son 2 daughters).

Education: Christ Church, Oxford (philosophy, politics and economics).

Non-political career: Called to the Bar 1985; QC 2002; Barrister, 4 New Square.

Political career: *House of Lords:* Elected hereditary peer 2015-. Member, Social and Economic Impact of the Gambling Industry 2019-.

Other: Trustee, Associated Studios (charity).

The Lord Trevethin and Oaksey QC, House of Lords, London SW1A 0PW
Tel: 020 7219 3000

LABOUR

TRIESMAN, LORD

TRIESMAN (Life Baron), David Maxim Triesman; cr. 2004. Born 30 October 1943; Son of Michael Triesman and Rita Triesman, née Lubran; Married Lucy Hooberman 2004 (1 daughter).

Education: Stationers' Company's School, London; Essex University (BA social sciences 1968; MA philosophy of science 1969); King's College, Cambridge (postgraduate research 1970-73); French.

Non-political career: Senior researcher, addiction research unit, London University 1970-74; Senior lecturer and co-ordinator of postgraduate research, South Bank Polytechnic 1975-84; Non-executive chair, MCC (UBS) 1975-97; Visiting professor of economics, S Lawrence University, USA 1977; National negotiating secretary and deputy general secretary, NATFHE 1984-93; Chair, Victoria Management Ltd 1989-2001; General secretary and chief executive officer, Association of University Teachers 1993-2001; Visiting scholar in economics, Cambridge University 2000; Visiting fellow in economics, Wolfson College, Cambridge 2000-; Senior associate fellow, Manufacturing Group, Warwick University 2003-; Senior visiting fellow in politics, London School of Economics 2005-; Chairman, Football Association 2008-10; Director, Wembley National Stadium Ltd 2008-10; Chair, Board of Advisers, Templewood Merchant Bank 2010-13; Board member, Augur Buchler 2010-13; Chairman: Triesman Associates 2011-, International Board, Joule Africa 2011-, International Board, Hibernia College 2012-; Director: Havin Bank 2013-, Funding Affordable Homes Ltd 2013-18, Salamanca Group Merchant Bank 2015-, Gravity Ltd. 2017-. AUT/University and College Union 1970-.

Political career: *House of Lords:* Raised to the peerage as Baron Triesman, of Tottenham in the London Borough of Haringey 2004. Government Spokesperson for: Education and Skills 2004-05, Trade and Industry 2004-05, Transport 2004, International Development 2004-05; Government Whip 2004-05; Foreign and Commonwealth Office: Government Spokesperson 2004-07, Parliamentary Under-Secretary of State 2005-07; Parliamentary Under-Secretary of State (Intellectual Property and Quality) and Government Spokesperson, Department for Innovation, Universities and Skills 2007-08; Opposition Spokesperson for: Business, Innovation and Skills 2010-11, Foreign and Commonwealth Office 2011-14. Member: EU External Affairs Sub-committee 2015-19, Risk Assessment and Risk Planning 2020-. *Other:* Labour Party: General secretary 2001-03, Resigned Whip July 2019-June 2020. Member: Home Office Committee on Prison Education 1980-83, Greater London Manpower Board 1981-86; Chair, Burnham FHE Committee Teachers' Side 1985-86; Member: Bett Inquiry into Higher Education 1998-99, Ruskin College Governors 1999-2002, Better Regulations Task Force 2000-01; HM Treasury Public Services Productivity Panel 2000-02; Chair, National Inquiry into Housing Benefit (Cabinet Office) 2001; Member, England 2018/2022 FIFA World Cup bid -2010; Chair, The Design Commission 2016-18.

Political interests: Economics, industry, banking, foreign affairs, intelligence, broadcasting, higher education, public diplomacy, sports, arts, governance and ethics; Africa, the Americas, Caribbean, Cuba, China, Commonwealth, Europe, India, Middle East, UK Overseas Territories.

Other: British North American Committee; Board member, The European Leadership Group 2016-; Chair, Usecolour Foundation 2000-02; Trustee: Public Management Foundation 2000-02; Football Foundation 2008-10; Patron, Tottenham Hotspurs Foundation 2008-; Chair, SHTIB Banking 2017-; Non-Executive Board Member: Salamanca Topaz Ltd 2017-, City Centre Colleges Group 2018-; Royal Statistical Society; One World Action, Amber Rocks, UNICEF; Liveryman, Worshipful Company of Stationers and Newspaper Makers; Freeman, Worshipful Company of Stationers and City of London 2016-; Fellow: Royal Statistical Society 1984, Royal Society of Arts 1992; Fellow, Northampton University 1996; Honorary Doctor of Laws, London Southbank University 2009; Honorary Doctorate, Essex University 2010. Reform Club; Tottenham Hotspur Supporters Club; Middlesex County Cricket Club.

Publications: Co-author, Football Mania (Ocean Books, 1972); Reconstructing Social Psychology (Penguin Books, 1974); Five Ring Circus: The Olympics (Pluto Press, 1984); College Administration (Longmans, 1988); c.50 academic papers in economics and epidemology.

Recreations: Family, football, blues and rock guitar, mountain walking, reading.

The Lord Triesman, House of Lords, London SW1A 0PW
Tel: 020 7219 6224 *Email:* triesmand@parliament.uk *Twitter:* @DavidTriesman

CONSERVATIVE

TRIMBLE, LORD

TRIMBLE (Life Baron), William David Trimble; cr 2006. Born 15 October 1944; Son of late William and Ivy Trimble; Married Daphne Orr 1978 (2 sons 2 daughters).

Education: Bangor Grammar School; Queen's University, Belfast (LLB 1968).

Non-political career: Queen's University, Belfast: Lecturer in Law 1968-77, Senior Lecturer 1977-90.

Political career: *House of Commons:* MP (UUP) for Upper Bann 1990 by-election to 2005; UUP Spokesperson for: Constitutional Affairs, Treasury 2002-05, Trade and Industry 2004-05, Work and Pensions 2004-05. *House of Lords:* Raised to the peerage as Baron Trimble, of Lisnagarvey in the County of Antrim 2006. EU Sub-committee A (Economic and Financial Affairs and International Trade): Co-opted member 2007-08, Member 2008-10; Member: European Union 2008-13, Barnett Formula 2008-09, EU Sub-committee C (Foreign Affairs, Defence and Development Policy) 2010-12, Joint Committee on the Draft House of Lords Reform Bill 2011-12, EU Sub-committee C (External Affairs) 2012-15, Inquiries Act 2005 2013-14, Delegated Powers and Regulatory Reform 2014-15, Joint Committee on the National Security Strategy 2015-19, Joint Committee on Human Rights 2016-. *Other:* Member: Northern Ireland Constitutional Convention for South Belfast 1975-76, Northern Ireland Forum for Political Dialogue 1996-98; Northern Ireland Assembly: MLA for Upper Bann 1998-2007, First Minister 1998-July 2001, November 2001-03. Chair, Lagan Valley Unionist Association 1985-90; Leader, Ulster Unionist Party 1995-2005; Patron, Tory Reform Group; Sat in the Lords as Ulster Unionist 2006-07, now sits as Conservative 2007-.

Political interests: Legal affairs, arts and culture, foreign policy.

Other: Chair, Ulster Society 1985-90; Several honorary degrees; Nobel Peace Prize (jointly) 1998; Major Political Achievement House Award, Channel 4 and *The House* Magazine 1999; Parliamentarian of the Year, *Spectator* 2001; St Angela's Peace and Justice Group Award 2002; PC 1998; Légion d'Honneur (France) 2002.

Recreations: Music, reading.

Rt Hon the Lord Trimble, House of Lords, London SW1A 0PW
Tel: 020 7219 2421 *Fax:* 020 7219 5979

CONSERVATIVE

TRUE, LORD

Minister of State and Government Spokesperson, Cabinet Office

TRUE (Life Baron), Nicholas Edward True; cr 2010. Born 31 July 1951; Son of Edward and Kathleen True; Married Anne-Marie Hood 1979 (2 sons 1 daughter).

Education: Nottingham High School; Peterhouse, Cambridge (BA classics and history 1973); Italian.

Non-political career: Member, Conservative Research Department 1975-82; Assistant to Conservative Party Deputy Leader 1978-82; Special adviser to Secretary of State for Health and Social Security 1982-86; Director, Public Policy Unit 1986-90; Deputy head, Prime Minister's Policy Unit 1991-95; Special adviser, Prime Minister's Office 1997; House of Lords: Private Secretary to Leader of the Opposition 1997-2010, Director, Opposition Whips' Office 1997-2010.

Political career: *House of Lords:* Raised to the peerage as Baron True, of East Sheen in the County of Surrey 2010. Minister of State and Government Spokesperson, Cabinet Office 2020-. Procedure: Member 2011-12, 2015-19, Alternate member 2012-15; Member, House 2012-15; Chair, Intergenerational Fairness and Provision 2018-19; Member, Constitution 2019-20. *Other:* Conservative Councillors' Association. Royal Borough of Richmond-upon-Thames Council: Councillor 1986-90, 1998-2017, Deputy Leader 2002-06, Opposition Leader 2006-10, Council Leader 2010-17; Board member, Royal Parks -2017; Vice-President, Local Government Association 2016-.

Political interests: Local government, education, constitution, arts; Guatemala, Italy.

Other: Olga Havel Foundation 1990-94; Sir Harold Hood's Charitable Trust 1996-; Richmond Civic Trust 2006-10; Venice in Peril Foundation, British School at Rome; CBE 1993. Beefsteak, Brook's, Traveller's Club.

Recreations: Books, history, art, gardens, Byzantium.

The Lord True CBE, House of Lords, London SW1A 0PW
Email: truen@parliament.uk

INDEPENDENT LABOUR

TRUSCOTT, LORD

TRUSCOTT (Life Baron), Peter Derek Truscott; cr. 2004. Born 20 March 1959; Son of late Derek and Dorothy Truscott; Married Svetlana Chernikova 1991.

Education: Newton Abbot Grammar School; Knowles Hill Comprehensive School, Newton Abbot; Exeter College, Oxford (BA modern history 1981, MA; DPhil 1985).

Non-political career: Political organiser, Labour Party 1986-89; National Association for the Care and Resettlement of Offenders (NACRO) 1989-94; Author 1997-; Senior expert, European Commission 1999; Institute for Public Policy Research (IPPR): Visiting research fellow 1999-2000, Associate research fellow 2001-06; Associate fellow, Royal United Services Institute for Defence and Security Studies 2005-06, 2008-; Director: Energy Enterprises Ltd 2008-, Gulf Keystone Petroleum Ltd 2008-12, Eastern Petroleum Corporation 2008-11, African Minerals Ltd 2008-09; Associate Partner, Special Adviser and Chairman, advisory board, Opus Executive Partners 2008-11. Formerly TGWU, various posts in TU movement.

Political career: *House of Commons:* Contested (Labour) Torbay 1992 general election. *House of Lords:* Raised to the peerage as Baron Truscott, of St James's in the City of Westminster 2004. Parliamentary Under-Secretary of State for Energy and Government Spokesperson, Department of Trade and Industry 2006-07; Ministry of Defence Liaison Peer 2005-06; Suspended from membership May-November 2009. Member, EU Sub-committee C (Foreign Affairs, Defence and Development) 2007-09. *Other:* European Parliament: MEP for Hertfordshire 1994-99: Vice-president, Security Committee 1996-99, Contested Eastern region 1999 election. Labour Party: Member, NEC Domestic and International Policy Sub-committee 1997-99, Former National Membership Champion; Former member, Co-operative Party; Resigned Labour Party Whip 2009; now sits as Independent Labour. Councillor, Colchester Borough Council 1988-92.

Political interests: Foreign affairs, defence, energy, international trade; Russia and former Soviet Union, EU.

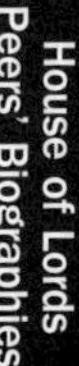

Other: Election expert, Organisation for Security and Co-operation in Europe 1995, 1996, 1999, 2003; Parliamentary Ambassador for Russian Federation and Former Soviet Union, British Council; Fellow, Industry and Parliament Trust 2006; Children's Fire and Burn Trust.

Publications: Russia First (1997); European Defence (IPPR, 2000); Kursk: Russia's Lost Pride (Simon and Schuster, 2002); Putin's Progress (Simon and Schuster, 2004); The Ascendancy of Political Risk Management (RUSI, 2006); European Energy Security (RUSI, 2009); Numerous articles.

Recreations: Walking, swimming, theatre, travel.

The Lord Truscott, House of Lords, London SW1A 0PW
Tel: 020 7219 3241

CONSERVATIVE

TUGENDHAT, LORD

TUGENDHAT (Life Baron), Christopher Samuel Tugendhat; cr. 1993. Born 23 February 1937; Son of late Dr Georg and Mairé Tugendhat; Married Julia Dobson 1967 (2 sons).

Education: Ampleforth College, Yorkshire; Gonville and Caius College, Cambridge (BA history 1960, MA).

Non-political career: Journalist, *Financial Times* 1960-70; Director: Sunningdale Oils 1971-76, Phillips Petroleum International (UK) Ltd 1972-76, EEC Commission: Commissioner for Budget and Financial Control, Financial Institutions Personnel and Administration 1977-85: Vice-President 1981-85; Director: National Westminster Bank 1985-91, The BOC Group 1985-96; Chair, Civil Aviation Authority 1986-91; Director, Commercial Union Assurance 1988-91; Deputy chair, National Westminster Bank 1990-91; Director, LWT (Holdings) plc 1991-94, Chairman: Abbey National plc 1991-2002, Blue Circle Industries plc 1996-2001; Board member, Eurotunnel plc 1991-2003; Director, Rio Tinto plc 1997-2004; Chairman: Lehman Brothers, Europe 2002-06, Lehman Brothers European Advisory Board 2006-07. Army national service Essex Regiment 1955-57.

Political career: *House of Commons:* MP (Conservative) for Cities of London and Westminster 1970-74, for City of London and Westminster South 1974-76. *House of Lords:* Raised to the peerage as Baron Tugendhat, of Widdington in the County of Essex 1993. Member: Economic Affairs 2008-13, 2016-, Economic Affairs Finance Bill Sub-committee 2012-13, 2016-17, European Union 2013-16; Chair, EU Sub-committee C (External Affairs) 2013-16; Member, The Arctic 2014-15. *Other:* Chair, Imperial College Healthcare NHS Trust 2007-11.

Political interests: Economy, foreign affairs, European Union.

Other: Chair, Royal Institute for International Affairs, Chatham House 1986-95; Governor, Council, Ditchley Foundation 1986-2010; Chair, European Policy Forum 1997-; Member, advisory board, OMFIF 2012-; Freedom, City of London; Chancellor, Bath University 1998-2013; Hon. LLD, Bath University 1998; Hon. DLitt, UMIST 2002; Kt 1990. Athenæum Club.

Publications: Oil: the biggest business (1968); The Multinationals (1971); Making Sense of Europe (1986); Co-author Options for British Foreign Policy in the 1990s (1988); A History of Britain Through Books 1900-1964 (2019).

Recreations: Family, reading, conversation.

The Lord Tugendhat, House of Lords, London SW1A 0PW
Tel: 020 7219 5353 *Email:* tugendhatc@parliament.uk

LABOUR

TUNNICLIFFE, LORD

Opposition Deputy Chief Whip; Opposition Spokesperson for Treasury, Defence and Transport

TUNNICLIFFE (Life Baron), Denis Tunnicliffe; cr 2004. Born 17 January 1943; Son of Harold and Nellie Tunnicliffe; Married Susan Dale 1968 (2 sons 1 deceased).

Education: Henry Cavendish School, Derby; University College, London (BSc mathematics 1965); College of Air Training, Hamble.

Non-political career: BOAC/British Airways 1966-86: Co-pilot 1966-72, Chief executive, International Leisure Group, Aviation Division 1986-88; London Underground Ltd: Managing director 1988-98, Chair 1998-2000; Chief executive, London Transport 1998-2000; Chair: United Kingdom Atomic Energy Authority 2002-04, Rail Safety and Standards Board 2003-08. Member, British Airline Pilots Association 1966-72.

Political career: *House of Lords:* Raised to the peerage as Baron Tunnicliffe, of Bracknell in the Royal County of Berkshire 2004. Government Whip 2008-10; Government Spokesperson for: International Development 2008-09, Work and Pensions 2008; Opposition Deputy Chief Whip 2010-; Opposition Spokesperson for: Defence 2010-11, 2016-, Business, Innovation and Skills 2012, Treasury 2014-, Transport 2018-. Member: Merits of Statutory Instruments 2005-08, Joint Committee on Security 2010-15, Refreshment 2013-14. *Other:* Councillor: Royal Borough of New Windsor 1972-75, Royal County of Berkshire 1974-78; Bracknell District Council: Councillor 1983-87, Leader 1985-87.

Political interests: Finance, justice, defence, climate change; Antigua.

Other: Trustee, Homerton College Cambridge 1998-2008; Council member, Royal Holloway College, University of London 2004-08; Board member, ACT (a property company that gives its profits to charity) 2004-08; Non-executive director, Defence Equipment and Support 2007-08; CBE 1993. RAC, RAF Club.

Recreations: Theatre, boating, flying.

The Lord Tunnicliffe CBE, House of Lords, London SW1A 0PW
Tel: 020 7219 4326 *Email:* tunnicliffed@parliament.uk

LABOUR

TURNBERG, LORD

TURNBERG (Life Baron), Leslie Arnold Turnberg; cr. 2000. Born 22 March 1934; Son of Hyman and Dora Turnberg; Married Edna Barme 1968 (1 daughter 1 son deceased).

Education: Stand Grammar School, Whitefield; Manchester University (MB, ChB 1957; MD 1966).

Non-political career: Junior medical posts 1957-61, 1964-66: Manchester Jewish Hospital, Northern Hospital, Ancoats Hospital, Manchester Royal Infirmary; Registrar, University College Hospital, London 1961-64; Lecturer, Royal Free Hospital, London 1967; Research fellow, University of Texas South-Western Medical School, Dallas, Texas 1968; Manchester University: Lecturer, then senior lecturer 1968-73, Professor of medicine 1973-97, Dean, Faculty of medicine 1986-89; Scientific adviser, Association of Medical Research Charities 1997-.

Political career: *House of Lords:* Raised to the peerage as Baron Turnberg, of Cheadle in the County of Cheshire 2000. Science and Technology: Member 2001-06, Co-opted member 2013; Member: Science and Technology Sub-committees: I (Systematic Biology and Biodiversity/Fighting Infection) 2002-03, II (Renewable Energy) 2003-04, I (Scientific Aspects of Ageing) 2004-05, Draft Human Tissue and Embryos Bill Joint Committee 2007, Mental Capacity Act 2005 2013-14, Works of Art 2014-16, Long-Term Sustainability of the NHS 2016-17. *Other:* Member, Labour Friends of Israel 2001-; Resigned Labour Whip July 2019-April 2020. Member: Salford Health Authority 1974-81, 1990-92, North West Regional Health Authority 1986-89; Chair: Conference of Medical Royal Colleges 1994-96, Specialist Training Authority 1996-98, Public Health Laboratory Service Board 1997-2002; President: Medical Council on Alcoholism 1997-2002, Medical Protection Society 1997-2007; Chair, Medical Advisory Board, Nations Healthcare 2004-07.

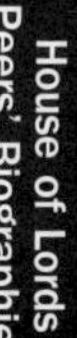

Political interests: NHS, social care, integrated care, medical research, medical education, medical ethics; Middle East, Israel.

Other: Trustee: Haddasah UK 1996-2015, Wolfson Foundation 1997-; Vice-president, Academy of Medical Sciences 1998-2004; Chair, Health Quality Service 1999-2004; President: British Society of Gastroenterology 1999-2000, Association of Physicians 2000; Trustee: Foulkes Foundation 2000-17, Dipex 2004-10; Chairman, National Centre for Replacement, Reduction and Refinement of use of Animals in Research 2004-07; Board member, Renovo 2006-11; Trustee: Ovarian Cancer Action 2007-18, Weizmann UK 2010-; President, Royal College of Physicians 1992-97; MRCP 1961; FRCP 1973; FRCPE 1993; FRCP(I) 1993; Hon. Fellow: Academy of Medicine, Singapore 1994, College of Medicine, South Africa 1994; FRCPSGlas 1994; FCPPak 1994; Hong Kong College of Physicians 1995; FRAustCP 1995; FRCS 1996; FRCOphth 1996; FRCOG 1996; FRCPsych 1997; Malaysia College of Medicine 1997; FMedSci 1998; Physiological Society 2005; Four honorary doctorates; Kt 1994.

Publications: Author of publications on intestinal research and clinical gastroenterology; Beyond the Balfour Declaration. The Hundred Year Quest for Israeli Palestinian Peace (Biteback, 2017).

Recreations: Reading, antiquarian books, painting, Chinese ceramics, walking, writing.

The Lord Turnberg, House of Lords, London SW1A 0PW
Email: turnbergl@parliament.uk
Tel: 020 7435 8223

CROSSBENCH

TURNBULL, LORD

TURNBULL (Life Baron), Andrew Turnbull; cr 2005. Born 21 January 1945; Son of Anthony and Mary Turnbull; Married Diane Clarke 1967 (2 sons).

Education: Enfield Grammar School; Christ's College, Cambridge (BA economics 1967).

Non-political career: Economist, Government Republic of Zambia 1968-70; HM Treasury (HMT) 1970-94, 1998-2002: Seconded to International Monetary Fund 1976-78, Private Secretary (Economics) to Margaret Thatcher as Prime Minister 1983-85, Head, General Expenditure Policy Group 1985-88, Principal Private Secretary to Margaret Thatcher as Prime Minister 1988-92, Deputy Secretary, Public Finance and Monetary Policy 1992-93, Second Permanent Secretary, Public Expenditure 1993-94, Permanent Secretary 1998-2002; Permanent Secretary: Department of the Environment 1994-97, Department of Environment, Transport and the Regions 1997-98; Secretary of the Cabinet and Head of the Home Civil Service, Cabinet Office 2002-05; Non-executive director: Prudential plc 2006-15, British Land Company plc 2006-17, Frontier Economics 2006-17, BH Global Ltd (Chair) 2008-12.

Political career: *House of Lords:* Raised to the peerage as Baron Turnbull, of Enfield in the London Borough of Enfield 2005. Member: Audit 2011-13, Parliamentary Commission on Banking Standards 2012-13; Chair, Audit 2013-15; Member: Leader's Group on Governance 2015, Economic Affairs 2015-19, Economic Affairs Finance Bill Sub-committee 2015-16, 2016-17, 2018-19, EU Financial Affairs Sub-committee 2019-20, Procedure/Procedure and Privileges 2019-, EU Goods Sub-committee 2020-. *Other:* Chair of Governors, Dulwich College 2009-15.

Political interests: Public services, the economy, financial services, energy, climate change; Zambia.

Other: Trustee, Global Warming Policy Foundation; Zambia Orphan Aid UK; Honorary doctorates: Middlesex University, Cranfield University; Honorary fellow, Christ's College, Cambridge; CB 1990; CVO 1992; KCB 1998.

Recreations: Golf, opera, sailing, walking, Tottenham Hotspur FC.

The Lord Turnbull KCB CVO, House of Lords, London SW1A 0PW
Tel: 020 7219 5353 *Email:* turnbulla@parliament.uk

CROSSBENCH

TURNER OF ECCHINSWELL, LORD

TURNER OF ECCHINSWELL (Life Baron), (Jonathan) Adair Turner; cr 2005. Born 5 October 1955; Son of Geoffrey Turner and Kathleen Turner, née Broadhurst; Married Orna Ni Chionna 1985 (2 daughters).

Education: Glenalmond School, Perthshire; Gonville and Caius College, Cambridge (BA history and economics 1978, MA) (Union President).

Non-political career: Economics Supervisor (part-time), Gonville and Caius College, Cambridge 1979-82; BP 1979; Chase Manhattan Bank 1979-82; McKinsey & Co 1982-95: Director 1994-95; Director-General, Confederation of British Industry 1995-99; Vice-chair, Merrill Lynch Europe 2000-06; Director: United Business Media 2000-08, Siemens UK plc 2006-08, Standard Chartered Bank 2006-08, Paternoster 2006-08; Chair: ESRC 2007-08, ODI 2007-10, Financial Services Authority 2008-13, Institute of New Economic Thinking (INET) 2013-, Centre for Financial Studies (Frankfurt) 2014-; Senior Independent Director, Oak North 2014-17; Non-executive director, Prudential plc 2015-; Chair, Energy Transitions Commission 2016-.

Political career: *House of Lords:* Raised to the peerage as Baron Turner of Ecchinswell, of Ecchinswell in the County of Hampshire 2005. Member, Economic Affairs 2007-08. *Other:* Chair: Low Pay Commission 2002-06, Pension Commission 2003-06, Committee on Climate Change 2008-12; Trustee, British Museum 2014-.

Political interests: China.

Other: Fellow, World Wide Fund for Nature (WWF) UK; Honorary Fellow, Royal Society of Edinburgh; Member, Advisory Council, People's Bank of China School of Finance, Tsighua University, Beijing 2014-; Save the Children, WWF UK; Fellow, Royal Society 2016-; Visiting professor: London School of Economics, Cass Business School; Honorary fellow, London Business School; Doctor of Law, Cambridge University 2017.

Publications: Author, Just Capital (MacMillan, 2001); Declining Populations in Philosophical Transactions of the Royal Society (2009); Economics After the Crisis (Lionel Robbins Memorial Lectures, MIT, 2012); Between Debt and the Devil: Money, Credit and Fixing Global Finance (Princeton University Press, 2015).

The Lord Turner of Ecchinswell, House of Lords, London SW1A 0PW
Tel: 020 7219 3000
Tel: 020 7499 4288 *Email:* adair.turner@ineteconomics.org Website: adairturner.com
Twitter: @AdairTurnerUK

LIBERAL DEMOCRAT

TYLER, LORD

TYLER (Life Baron), Paul Archer Tyler; cr 2005. Born 29 October 1941; Son of Oliver and Grace Tyler; Married Nicola Ingram 1970 (1 daughter 1 son).

Education: Sherborne School, Dorset; Exeter College, Oxford (BA modern history 1963, MA).

Non-political career: Director, public affairs, Royal Institute of British Architects 1972-73; Board member, Shelter: National Campaign for the Homeless 1975-76; Managing director, Cornwall Courier Newspaper Group 1976-81; Public affairs division, Good Relations plc: Chief executive 1984-86, Chair 1986-87, Senior consultant, Public Affairs 1987-92; Director, Western Approaches Public Relations Ltd 1987-92. National Union of Journalists 1973-82.

Political career: *House of Commons:* Contested Totnes 1966 and Bodmin 1970 general elections. MP (Liberal) for Bodmin February-October 1974. Contested Bodmin 1979 general election and Beaconsfield 1982 by-election. MP (Liberal Democrat) for North Cornwall 1992-2005; Liberal Democrat: Spokesperson for: Agriculture and Rural Affairs 1992-97, Agriculture, Tourism, Transport and Rural Affairs 1994-96, Food 1997-99, Chief Whip 1997-2001, Shadow Leader of the House 1997-2005, Spokesperson for Constitutional Reform 2001-05. *House of Lords:* Raised to the peerage as Baron Tyler, of Linkinhorne in the County of Cornwall 2005. Liberal Democrat: Spokesperson for: Constitutional Affairs 2006-10, Environment, Food and Rural Affairs 2008-09, Constitutional and Political Reform 2015-16, Shadow Minister/Spokesperson for Political and Constitutional Reform 2016-17, Constitutional and Political Reform 2017-19. Member: Conventions Joint Committee 2006, Draft Constitutional Renewal Bill Joint Committee 2008, Procedure 2008-13, Joint Committee on the Draft House of Lords Reform Bill 2011-12, Delegated Powers and Regulatory Reform 2015-19,

Trade Union and Party Funding 2016, Liaison 2019-. Chair, Liberal Democrat Parliamentary Party Committee on Constitutional and Political Reform 2010-15. *Other:* Contested (SLD) Cornwall and Plymouth 1989 European Parliament election. Chair: Devon and Cornwall Region Liberal Party 1981-82, Liberal Party National Executive Committee 1983-86; Campaign adviser to David Steel MP in 1983 and 1987 general elections. Councillor, Devon County Council 1964-70; Member, Devon and Cornwall Police Authority 1965-70; Vice-chair, Dartmoor National Park Committee 1965-70; DL, Cornwall 2005-10.

Political interests: Tourism, rural affairs, constitutional reform; Australia, Canada, Finland, Germany, Sweden.

Other: Chair, Council for the Protection of Rural England Working Party on the future of the village 1974-81; Vice-President: British Resorts and Destinations Association 1995-, Youth Hostels Association 1996-2014; Director, Make Votes Count 2005-10; Chair, Faiths and Civil Society Unit, Goldsmiths College, London 2008-; Vice-chair, Hansard Society 2009-18; Chair, advisory board, Interclimate Network 2010-; Patron, Joe Homan Charity 2011-18; Ambassador, Concern Universal/United Purpose 2012-; Shelter; Parliamentarian of the Year, *Country Life* 1997; CBE 1985; PC 2014.

Publications: Co-author, Power to the Provinces (1968); A New Deal for Rural Britain (1978); Country Lives, Country Landscapes (1996); Britain's Democratic Deficit (2003); Co-author, Reforming the House of Lords – Breaking the Deadlock (2005); Co-author, Beating the Retreat – The Government's Flight from Constitutional Reform (2008); Constitutional Renewal Bill (2009); Lords Reform: A Guide for MPs (2012); Funding a Democracy: Breaking the Deadlock (2013); Who Decides? (2014).

Recreations: Sailing, gardening, walking.

Rt Hon the Lord Tyler CBE, House of Lords, London SW1A 0PW
Tel: 020 7219 6355 *Email:* tylerp@parliament.uk Website: www.paultylerlibdems.org
Twitter: @ptylerlords

LIBERAL DEMOCRAT

TYLER OF ENFIELD, BARONESS

Liberal Democrat Lords Spokesperson for Mental Health

TYLER OF ENFIELD (Life Baroness) Claire Tyler; cr 2011. Born 4 June 1957.

Education: Latymer Grammar School, Edmonton; Southampton University (BA law and politics); Diploma (management studies).

Non-political career: Greater London Council/Inner London Education Authority 1978-88; Department of Employment 1988-2000: Assistant Regional Director, Government Office for London, Head, 16-19 Policy Unit; Deputy Chief Executive, Connexions Service 2000-02; Director, Social Exclusion Unit, Office of the Deputy Prime Minister/Department for Communities and Local Government 2002-06; Director, Vulnerable Children's Group, Department for Education and Skills 2006-07; Relate: Chief Executive 2007-12, Vice-president 2012-; President, National Children's Bureau 2012-19; Chair, Making Every Adult Matter Coalition 2013-.

Political career: *House of Lords:* Raised to the peerage as Baroness Tyler of Enfield, of Enfield in the London Borough of Enfield 2011. Chair, Growing Giving Parliamentary Inquiry; Liberal Democrat Spokesperson for Mental Health 2015, 2017-. Member: Public Service and Demographic Change 2012-13, Affordable Childcare 2014-15, Social Mobility 2015-16; Chair, Financial Exclusion 2016-17; Member: Intergenerational Fairness and Provision 2018-19, Public Services 2020-. *Other:* Chair, Liberal Democrat Policy Working Group on Balanced Working. Chair, CAFCASS (Children and Family Court Advisory and Support Service) 2012-18.

Political interests: Health and social care, welfare reform, financial exclusion, social mobility, wellbeing, children and family policy, machinery of government, voluntary sector.

Other: Member, Joseph Rowntree Foundation Poverty and Disadvantage Committee 2002-06; Chair, Values-Based Child and Adolescent Mental Health System Commission -2016; Fellow: Chartered Institute for Personnel and Development, Academy of Social Sciences.

The Baroness Tyler of Enfield, House of Lords, London SW1A 0PW
Tel: 020 7219 3606 *Email:* tylerc@parliament.uk Website: baronessclairetyler.com
Twitter: @ClaireT_UKLords

NON-AFFILIATED

TYRIE, LORD

TYRIE (Life Baron), Andrew Guy Tyrie; cr 2018. Born 15 January 1957; Son of the late Derek and Patricia Tyrie.

Education: Felsted School, Essex; Trinity College, Oxford (BA philosophy, politics and economics 1979, MA); College of Europe, Bruges (Diploma economics 1980); Wolfson College, Cambridge (MPhil international relations 1981); French.

Non-political career: Group head office, British Petroleum 1981-83; Adviser to Chancellors of the Exchequer: Nigel Lawson 1986-89, John Major 1989-90; Fellow, Nuffield College, Oxford 1990-91; Senior economist, European Bank for Reconstruction and Development 1992-97.

Political career: *House of Commons:* Contested Houghton and Washington 1992 general election. MP (Con) for Chichester 1997-2017; Public Accounts Commission: Member 1997-2017, Chair 2010-11; Shadow Financial Secretary 2003-04; Shadow Paymaster General 2004-05. Member: Joint Committee on Consolidation of Bills Etc 1997-2001, Public Administration 1997-2001; Treasury: Member 2001-03, 2009-10, Chair 2010-17; Member: Treasury (Treasury Sub-Committee) 2001-04, Constitutional Affairs/Justice 2005-10, Joint Committee on Conventions 2006, Joint Committee on Draft Constitution Renewal Bill 2008, Reform of the House of Commons 2009-10; Joint Committee on Tax Law Rewrite Bills: Member 2009-10, Chair 2010; Liaison: Member 2010-15, Chair 2015-17; Chair, Parliamentary Commission on Banking Standards 2012-13. Member, Executive, 1922 Committee 2005-06. *House of Lords:* Raised to the peerage as Baron Tyrie, of Chichester in the County of West Sussex 2018. Member, Economic Affairs Finance Bill Sub-committee 2020. *Other:* Chair, Competition and Markets Authority 2018-20.

Political interests: Economic policy, European constitutional reform, international affairs.

Other: Member, Inter-Parliamentary Union 1999-2017; Trustee, Pallant House Gallery 2017-; Hon. Fellow, Trinity College, Oxford; *Spectator* awards: Backbencher of the Year 2000, 2009, Select Committee Chairman of the Year 2011; PC 2015. Royal Automobile Club, Garrick Club; MCC; Chichester Yacht Club; Goodwood Golf and Country Clubs.

Publications: Various works on economic and monetary union in Europe and other European issues; The Prospects for Public Spending (1996); Reforming the Lords: a Conservative Approach (Conservative Policy Forum, 1998); Sense on EMU (1998); Co-author, Leviathan at Large: The New Regulator for the Financial Markets (Centre for Policy Studies, 2000); Mr Blair's Poodle: An Agenda for Reviving the House of Commons (2000); Back from the Brink (2001); Co-author, Statism by Stealth: New Labour, New Collectivism (Centre for Policy Studies, 2002); Axis of Anarchy: America, Britain and the New World Order after Iraq (2003); Mr Blair's Poodle goes to War: The House of Commons, Congress and Iraq (Centre for Policy Studies, 2004); Pruning the Politicians: The Case for a smaller House of Commons (2004); The Conservative Party's proposals for the funding of political parties (2006); One Nation Again (One Nation Group, 2006); An Elected Second Chamber: A Conservative View (Constitution Unit, 2009); Extraordinary Rendition: Closing the Gap (2009); After the Age of Abundance (Centre for Policy Studies, 2011); The IMF and the Eurozone (Centre for Policy Studies, 2012); Neither Just nor Secure: The Justice and Security Bill (Centre for Policy Studies, 2013).

Recreations: Golf.

Rt Hon the Lord Tyrie, House of Lords, London SW1A 0PW
Tel: 020 7219 3000 *Email:* tyriea@parliament.uk

UDDIN, BARONESS

NON-AFFILIATED

UDDIN (Life Baroness), Pola Manzila Uddin; cr. 1998. Born 17 July 1959; Daughter of Mr and Mrs Khan; Married Komar Uddin 1976 (4 sons 1 daughter).

Education: Plashet School for Girls, Newham; Polytechnic of North London (Diploma social work 1990).

Non-political career: Youth and community worker, YWCA 1980-82; Liaison officer, Tower Hamlets Social Services 1982-84; Manager, Women's Health Project 1984-88; Asian Family Counselling Service 1989-90; Social worker, subsequently management consultant, Social Services Department, London Borough of Newham Council 1993-98; Non-executive director, Carlton Media Group 1999-2001; Project Leader, Addaction.

Political career: *House of Lords:* Raised to the peerage as Baroness Uddin, of Bethnal Green in the London Borough of Tower Hamlets 1998. Suspended from membership October 2010-May 2012. Co-opted Member, European Union Sub-committee G (Social Policy and Consumer Affairs) 2006-08. *Other:* Labour Whip suspended October 2010; now sits as Non-affiliated. London Borough of Tower Hamlets: Councillor 1990-98, Deputy Leader 1994-96.

Political interests: Women, international affairs, human rights and equality; Bangladesh, Morocco, Qatar, Saudi Arabia, Tunisia, UAE.

Other: Patron: Bethnal Green and Victoria Park Housing Association, Social Action for Health, Women's Aid, Black Women's Health Project, Disability Trust, Student Partnership Worldwide, ORBIS International; NSPCC, East London Asian Family Counselling; Honorary degrees, universities of East London and Exeter.

The Baroness Uddin, House of Lords, London SW1A 0PW
Tel: 020 7219 8506 *Email:* uddinm@parliament.uk *Twitter:* @baroness_uddin

CONSERVATIVE

UDNY-LISTER, LORD

UDNY-LISTER (Life Baron), Edward Julian Udny-Lister; cr 2020.

Non-political career: Director of Government Relations, Tyco Fire & Security 2008-11; Director of Government Relations EMEA, ADT Fire & Security 2008-11; Chief of Staff to Boris Johnson as Mayor of London and Deputy Mayor for Planning, Greater London Authority 2011-16; Senior Strategic Adviser to Boris Johnson as Prime Minister 2019-.

Political career: *House of Lords:* Raised to the peerage as Baron Udny-Lister, of Wandsworth in the London Borough of Wandsworth 2020.

The Lord Udny-Lister, House of Lords, London SW1A 0PW
Tel: 020 7219 3000

CONSERVATIVE

ULLSWATER, VISCOUNT

ULLSWATER (2nd Viscount, UK), Nicholas James Christopher Lowther; cr. 1921. Born 9 January 1942; Son of late Lieutenant John Lowther, MVO, RNVR, grandson of 1st Viscount, PC, GCB; Married Susan Weatherby 1967 (2 sons 2 daughters).

Education: Eton College; Trinity College, Cambridge (BA agriculture 1963, MA).

Non-political career: Chair, Wincanton Races Co Ltd 1986-93; Private Secretary and Comptroller to Princess Margaret, Countess of Snowdon 1998-2002. Captain, Royal Wessex Yeomanry, Retired.

Political career: *House of Lords:* First entered House of Lords 1963; Government Whip 1989-90; Parliamentary Under-Secretary of State, Department of Employment 1990-93; Government Chief Whip 1993-94; Minister of State, Department of the Environment (Construction and Planning) 1994-95; Elected hereditary peer 2003-; Deputy Speaker 2004-20; Deputy Chair of Committees 2004-; Contested Lord Speaker election 2006. Co-opted Member, EU Sub-Committee F (Home Affairs) 2003-07; Member: Merits of Statutory Instruments 2003-05, Administration and Works 2005-09; Co-opted Member, EU Sub-committee D (Environment and Agriculture) 2006-10; Member: Procedure/Procedure and Privileges 2009-14, 2019-, Liaison 2010-15, Privileges and Conduct 2013-19, Delegated Powers and

Regulatory Reform 2014-15; Chair, Joint Committee on Able Marine Energy Park Development Consent Order 2014 2014-15; Member: Selection 2015-, EU Energy and Environment Sub-Committee 2015-19. *Other:* JP 1971-88; Councillor, King's Lynn and West Norfolk Borough Council 2003-11.

Other: Wiltshire Association of Boys Clubs: Chair 1966-74, Vice-President 1975-; PC 1994; LVO 2002. Jockey (Newmarket), Pratt's Club.

Recreations: Racing, golf.

Rt Hon the Viscount Ullswater LVO, House of Lords, London SW1A 0PW
Tel: 020 7219 5219 *Email:* ullswatern@parliament.uk
Whiteacres, Cross Lane, Brancaster, King's Lynn PE31 8AE *Tel:* 01485 210488

NON-AFFILIATED

VADERA, BARONESS

VADERA (Life Baroness), Shriti Vadera; cr 2007. Born 23 June 1962.

Non-political career: Executive director, UBS Warburg 1984-99; Adviser to the Chancellor of the Exchequer and member, Council of Economic Advisers, HM Treasury 1999-2007; Adviser on the Eurozone crisis, banking sector, debt restructuring and markets 2010-14; Chair, Santander UK plc 2015-.

Political career: *House of Lords:* Raised to the peerage as Baroness Vadera, of Holland Park in the London Borough of Kensington and Chelsea 2007. Parliamentary Under-Secretary of State: Department for International Development 2007-08, Department for Business, Enterprise and Regulatory Reform/Business, Innovation and Skills (Minister for Economic Competitiveness, Small Business and Enterprise) 2008-09, Cabinet Office 2008-09; On leave of absence December 2011-. *Other:* Joined the House of Lords as Labour; now sits as Non-affiliated. Adviser at Republic of Korea as Chair G20 2009-10.

Other: BHP Billiton: Non-executive director 2011-, Senior independent director 2015-; Pro-chancellor, St Mary's University 2017-; PC 2009.

Rt Hon the Baroness Vadera, House of Lords, London SW1A 0PW
Santander UK plc, Santander House, 2 Triton Square, Regent's Place, London NW1 3AN

CONSERVATIVE

VAIZEY OF DIDCOT, LORD

VAIZEY OF DIDCOT (Life Baron), Edward Henry Butler Vaizey; cr 2020. Born 5 June 1968; Son of late Lord Vaizey of Greenwich and Marina Vaizey CBE; Married Alexandra Holland 2005 (1 son 1 daughter).

Education: St Paul's School, London; Merton College, Oxford (BA modern history 1989, MA); City University (Diploma law 1992); Inns of Court School of Law (Diploma law 1993).

Non-political career: Desk officer, Conservative Research Department 1989-91; Called to the Bar, Middle Temple 1993; Barrister specialising in family law and child care 1994-96; Director: Public Policy Unit 1996-97, Politics International 1997-98; Director and partner, Consolidated Communications 1998-2003; Freelance journalist 2001-; Speechwriter to Michael Howard MP as Leader of the Opposition 2003-05.

Political career: *House of Commons:* Contested Bristol East 1997 general election. MP for Wantage 2005-10, for Wantage (revised boundary) 2010-19; Shadow Minister for the Arts 2006-10; Parliamentary Under-Secretary of State (Minister for Culture, Communications and Creative Industries), Departments for: Business, Innovation and Skills 2010-11, Culture, Media and Sport 2010-14; Minister of State for Culture and the Digital Economy, Departments for Business, Innovation and Skills and Culture, Media and Sport 2014-16; Trade Envoy to Vietnam, Cambodia and Laos 2017-19. Member: Modernisation of the House of Commons 2005-07, Environmental Audit 2006-07, Works of Art 2016-19. *House of Lords:* Raised to the peerage as Baron Vaizey of Didcot, of Wantage in the County of Oxfordshire 2020. Member, Communications and Digital 2020-. *Other:* Election aide to Iain Duncan Smith MP 2001 general election; Deputy chair, Conservative Globalisation and Global Poverty Policy Group 2006; Conservative Party whip removed September-October 2019.

Political interests: Arts, architecture, digital technology, media, telecommunications, energy, science and technology, environment; India, Israel, Middle East, Vietnam, USA.

Other: Hon. Fellow, Royal Institute of British Architects 2011; Consultant, LionTree Europe 2016-; Trustee: BRITDOC Charitable Trust 2016-, National Youth Theatre of Great Britain 2016-; Chair, advisory board: Creative Fuse North East 2016-; Member, advisory board, *The Sunday Times* Short Story Award 2017-18; President, advisory board, British Esports Association Ltd 2017-; Adviser, esports, International Group Management 2017-18; Judge, Indigo Index Prize 2017-; Adviser, Digital Theatre+ 2017-; Hon Fellow, Radio Centre 2018; Member, advisory board: NEC Europe Ltd 2018-19, Salary Finance 2019-, NewsGuard Technologies 2019-, Acess Partnership 2019-; Trustee, London Music Masters 2019-; Adviser: FTI Consulting 2019-, Digitalis 2020-, Common Sense Media 2020-; Member, advisory board: Edge Investments 2020-, Perlego 2020-, Interactive Savings Association 2020-; Culture Editor, *Country & Townhouse* Magazine; SUDEP, Didcot Train; PC 2016. Deputy President, Old Pauline Club 2020-.

Publications: Editor: A Blue Tomorrow (Politicos, 2001), The Blue Book on Health (Politicos, 2002), The Blue Book on Transport (Politicos, 2002).

Recreations: Watching football, running, the arts.

The Lord Vaizey of Didcot, House of Lords, London SW1A 0PW
Tel: 020 7219 3000 *Email:* vaizeye@parliament.uk Website: www.vaizey.com
Twitter: @edvaizey

VALENTINE, BARONESS

CROSSBENCH

VALENTINE (Life Baroness), Josephine (Jo) Clare Valentine; cr 2005. Born 8 December 1958; Daughter of Michael and Shirley Valentine; Married Simon Acland 1990 (2 daughters).

Education: St Paul's Girls' School, London; St Hugh's College, Oxford (BA maths and philosophy 1981); Casual French.

Non-political career: Manager, Barings 1981-88; Chief executive officer, Blackburn Partnership 1988-90; Senior manager, BOC Group 1990-95; Chief executive officer, Central London Partnership 1995-97; London First 1997-2016: Chief operating officer 2000-03, Chief executive officer 2003-16; Director of Place, Business in the Community 2019-.

Political career: *House of Lords:* Raised to the peerage as Baroness Valentine, of Putney in the London Borough of Wandsworth 2005. Member: Works of Art 2009-10, 2012-13, EU Sub-committee B: (Internal Market, Energy and Transport) 2010-12, (Internal Market, Infrastructure and Employment) 2012-15, Regenerating Seaside Towns and Communities 2018-19. *Other:* Commissioner, National Lottery Commission 2000-05; Non-executive Director, Crossrail 2019-.

Political interests: Higher education, devolution, housing, transport and infrastructure, London, Europe, Blackpool, the Fylde Coast, Lancashire.

Other: Board member, Skills Festival Company 2005-16; Non-executive director, Peabody 2012-17; Board member: University College London 2014-, HS2 2014-18; Chair, Heathrow Southern Railway 2017-; Director, Business in the Community, Blackpool 2017-; Orchid Project, Aspired Futures; Honorary fellow: St Hugh's College, Oxford, Birkbeck College; Honorary doctorate, Roehampton University; Honorary degree, University of London.

Recreations: Piano, bridge, travel.

The Baroness Valentine, House of Lords, London SW1A 0PW
Tel: 020 7219 5353

CROSSBENCH

VAUX OF HARROWDEN, LORD

VAUX OF HARROWDEN (12th Baron, UK), Richard Hubert Gordon Gilbey; cr 1523. Born 16 March 1965; Son of 11th Baron; Married (2 children).

Education: Ampleforth College; Aberdeen University (MA economic science with accountancy 1987).

Non-political career: Chartered accountant, Price Waterhouse 1987-97; Investment manager, Indochina Asset Management 1997-2000; Chief financial officer, Reech Capital plc 2000-03; Managing director, corporate development, SunGard Data Systems Inc 2003-16; Self-employed consultant 2016-.

Political career: *House of Lords:* Elected hereditary peer 2017-. Member: EU Financial Affairs Sub-committee 2018-20, EU Services Sub-committee 2020-.

Political interests: Renewable energy, farming, technology, finance; Scotland, South East Asia.

Other: Chairman, Fleet District Salmon Fishery Board; Trustee, Harrowden Chapel Trust; Member, Institute of Chartered Accountants in England and Wales; Freedom, City of London. Kandahar Ski Club.

The Lord Vaux of Harrowden, House of Lords, London SW1A 0PW
Tel: 020 7219 3000 *Email:* vaux@parliament.uk

CONSERVATIVE

VERE OF NORBITON, BARONESS

Parliamentary Under-Secretary of State and Government Spokesperson, Department for Transport

VERE OF NORBITON (Life Baroness), Charlotte Sarah Emily Vere; cr 2016. Born 9 March 1969; Daughter of Colonel Roger Vere MBE RA and Mrs Karin Terry; Married (2 children from previous marriage).

Education: Stover School, Newton Abbot; University College London (BSc biochemical engineering 1989); Kellogg Graduate School of Management, Northwestern University, USA (MBA 1997).

Non-political career: Various positions, financial services 1989-99; Finance director, Recruit Media Ltd 2005-07; Chief executive, Big White Wall 2007-09; Founder and director, Women On... 2011-14; Executive director, Girls' Schools Association 2012-16; Independent Schools Council: Director 2012-16, Acting General-secretary 2014-15.

Political career: *House of Commons:* Contested Brighton Pavilion 2010 general election. *House of Lords:* Raised to the peerage as Baroness Vere of Norbiton, of Norbiton in the Royal London Borough of Kingston upon Thames 2016. Government Whip (Baroness in Waiting) 2016-19; Parliamentary Under-Secretary of State and Government Spokesperson, Department for Transport 2019-. *Other:* Finance director, NO to AV 2010-11; Executive director, Conservatives In 2016. Governor, Lovelace Primary School 2012-19.

Political interests: Education, business, economy, mental health; Europe, South East Asia.

Other: Chair, Young Ambassadors with Samaritans 2003-07; Founder, Women On 2011-14; Trustee: Fatherhood Institute 2012-15, National Youth Arts Trust 2013-16, Shrewsbury House School Trust Ltd 2015-19.

Recreations: Singing, running.

The Baroness Vere of Norbiton, House of Lords, London SW1A 0PW
Tel: 020 7219 3000 *Email:* verec@parliament.uk *Twitter:* @CharlotteV

LIBERAL DEMOCRAT

VERJEE, LORD

VERJEE (Life Baron), Rumi Verjee; cr 2013. Born 26 June 1957.

Education: Haileybury School; Downing College, Cambridge (law).

Non-political career: Lawyer, Middle Temple; Entrepreneur and philanthropist; Founder, Domino's Pizza UK; Chair, Thomas Goode & Co; Founder, Rumi Foundation 2006-.

Political career: *House of Lords:* Raised to the peerage as Baron Verjee, of Portobello in the Royal Borough of Kensington and Chelsea 2013. Member, Citizenship and Civic Engagement 2017-18.

Other: Chair: Brompton Capital Ltd, Ipanema Properties, WE UK (formerly Free The Children UK); Member: World Presidents' Organization, Global Leadership Foundation, British Olympic Association advisory board for the 2012 Olympic Games; Convenor, MoreUnited.uk 2016-; Fellow, Downing College, Cambridge; CBE 2009.

The Lord Verjee CBE, House of Lords, London SW1A 0PW
Tel: 020 7219 5353 Website: rumifoundation.com

CONSERVATIVE

VERMA, BARONESS

Chair, EU Goods Sub-committee

VERMA (Life Baroness), Sandip Verma; cr 2006. Born 30 June 1959; Daughter of Shivcharan Singh Rana and Ravinder Rana; Married Ashok Kumar Verma 1977 (1 daughter 1 son).

Education: De Montfort University, Leicester (Deferred Degree business management); Hindi, Punjabi.

Non-political career: Managing Director, Domiciliary Care Services UK Ltd 2000-12, 2016-; Director, DCS Foods; Global Chair, WWG; International Advisor to Amity University (India); Special Adviser to Sir John Cass Foundation; Director, Applebright Cleaning Services.

Political career: *House of Commons:* Contested (Conservative) Hull East 2001 and Wolverhampton South West 2005 general elections. *House of Lords:* Raised to the peerage as Baroness Verma, of Leicester in the County of Leicestershire 2006. Opposition Whip 2006-10; Opposition Spokesperson for: Health 2006-07, Education and Skills 2006-07, Innovation, Universities and Skills 2007-09, Children, Schools and Families 2007-08, 2009-10, Universities and Skills 2009-10; Government Whip 2010-12; Government Spokesperson for: Cabinet Office 2010-12, International Development 2010-11, Women and Equalities 2010-12, Business, Innovation and Skills 2011-12; Parliamentary Under-Secretary of State and Government Spokesperson: Department of Energy and Climate Change 2012-15, Department for International Development 2015-16. Member, European Union 2016-; Chair: EU External Affairs Sub-committee 2016-20, EU Goods Sub-committee 2020-. *Other:* Area chair, Conservative Women 2001-02; Area officer 2001-03; Executive National Conservative (Women) 2001-03; Chair, Leicester South Conservative Association 2006-08; President, City of Leicester Conservative Association 2008-09, 2010-11; Patron: Tory Reform Group, British Asian Conservative Link, Friends of Conservative Society of Indians; Vice-chair, Syston branch, Rutland Conservative Association.

Political interests: Health, education, overseas development, home affairs; Africa, Europe, South Asia.

Other: Patron: CST – Protecting the Jewish Community, India Association, British Sikh Association, Bucks Punjabi Society, Pakistan-India and UK-Friendship Forum, Punjab Link Council; Extraordinary Champion, Roko Cancer (Breast Cancer); Board member, Football Foundation; NRI Institute, India; Punjab House Trust; Patron, Dil Trust UK; Chair, UN Women National Committee; Director and Chair of Advisers, Nexus Green; Non-executive director, Renewal Energy Association; Freedom, City of London; FRSA; Distinguished Fellowship, Institute of Directors, India; Hon. Doctorate: Wolverhampton University, Amity University; Pravasi Bharatiya Saman, President of India 2011; Ellis Island Medal of Honour (USA).

Recreations: Socialising, walking, travel.

The Baroness Verma, House of Lords, London SW1A 0PW
Tel: 020 7219 5216 *Email:* vermas@parliament.uk *Twitter:* @Baroness_Verma

CONSERVATIVE

VINSON, LORD

VINSON (Life Baron), Nigel Vinson; cr. 1985. Born 27 January 1931; Son of late Ronald Vinson, farmer; Married Yvonne Collin 1972 (3 daughters).

Education: Nautical College, Pangbourne.

Non-political career: Founder, Plastic Coatings Ltd 1952 (floated on London Stock Exchange 1970); Director, British Airports Authority 1973-80; Co-founder and director, Centre for Policy Studies 1974-80; Director, Barclays Bank UK 1982-87; Deputy chair, Electra Investment Trust 1990-98; Chair: St Cuthbert's Newcastle Estates 1990-2000, Fleming Income and Growth Trust 1995-2000. Lieutenant, Queen's Royal Regiment 1948-50.

Political career: *House of Lords:* Raised to the peerage as Baron Vinson, of Roddam Dene in the County of Northumberland 1985. Member: Pollution 1997-98, Monetary Policy of the Bank of England/Economic Affairs 1998-2004, Draft Climate Change Bill Joint Committee 2007. *Other:* President, Berwick upon Tweed Conservative Association 2000-05. Member: Crafts Advisory Committee 1971-77, Design Council 1973-80; President, Industrial Participation Association 1979-90; Chair, Rural Development Commission 1980-90; DL, Northumberland 1990.

Political interests: Small businesses, deregulation, tax, pensions; UK.

Other: CBI: Member, Grand Council 1975-, Deputy Chair, Smaller Firms Council 1979-84; Hon Director, Queen's Silver Jubilee Appeal 1974-78; Member, Regional Committee, National Trust 1977-84; Northumbrian National Parks: Member, Countryside Committee 1977-87, Chair, Rural Development Committee 1980-90; Member, Industry Year Steering Committee, Royal Society of Arts 1985; Institute of Economic Affairs: Chair of trustees 1988-95, Vice-President 1995-; Trustee, St George's House, Windsor 1990-96; Member, Foundation of Science and Technology 1991-; Chair: North East Civic Trust 1996-2001, Prince's Trust (NE) 1997-99; Trustee: Civitas 2003-, Chillingham Wild Cattle Association 2008; Council member, Freedom Association; Foundation Donor, Vinson Centre for Liberal Economics and Enterprise, Buckingham University 2017; Nigel Vinson Charitable Trust; CBIM; FRSA; Hon. Degree in Science, Buckingham University 2017; Queen's Award to Industry 1971; LVO 1979. Boodle's, Pratt's Club.

Publications: Personal Pensions for All (1984); Take Upon Retiring (Late Extra) (2005).

Recreations: Objets d'art, farming, horses.

The Lord Vinson LVO DL, House of Lords, London SW1A 0PW
Tel: 020 7219 5353
34 Kynance Mews, London SW7 4QR *Tel:* 020 7937 4183/01668 217230
Email: roddamdene@btinternet.com

CONSERVATIVE

WAKEHAM, LORD

WAKEHAM (Life Baron), John Wakeham; cr. 1992. Born 22 June 1932; Son of late Major Walter John Wakeham; Married Anne Bailey 1965 (died 1984) (2 sons); married Alison Ward 1985 (1 son).

Education: Charterhouse School.

Non-political career: Chair: Genner Holdings 1994-, Genner Securities, Press Complaints Commission 1995-2002, British Horseracing Board 1996-98. Army national service 1955-57, commissioned Royal Artillery.

Political career: *House of Commons:* Contested Coventry East 1966 and Putney 1970 general elections. MP (Conservative) for Maldon 1974-83, for South Colchester and Maldon 1983-92; Assistant Government Whip 1979-81; Government Whip 1981; Parliamentary Under-Secretary of State, Department of Industry 1981-82; Minister of State, HM Treasury 1982-83; Government Chief Whip 1983-87; Lord Privy Seal and Leader of the House of Commons 1987-88; Lord President of the Council and Leader of the House of Commons 1988-89; Secretary of State for Energy 1989-92; Given additional responsibility for co-ordinating the development and presentation of Government policies 1990-92. *House of Lords:* Raised to the peerage as Baron Wakeham, of Maldon in the County of Essex 1992. Lord Privy Seal and

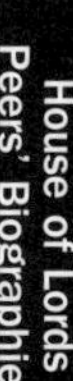

Leader of the House of Lords 1992-94; Member, House of Lords Commission 2016-. Economic Affairs: Member 2003-06, Chair 2006-09; Member: Procedure 2003-07, 2010-15, Liaison 2007-10, House 2007-13, 2015-16, Finance Bill Sub-committee 2008-10, Selection 2010-15, Joint Committee on Security 2010-15, Economic Affairs Finance Bill Sub-Committee 2012-13, 2014, 2016-17, Lord Speaker's Committee on the Size of the House 2016-. *Other:* JP, Inner London 1972; DL, Hampshire 1997; Chair, Royal Commission on the Reform of the House of Lords 1999.

Political interests: Economic affairs, energy, reform of the constitution.

Other: Member, Governing Body, Charterhouse 1986-2004; Governor, Sutton's Hospital, Charterhouse 1992-; Trustee, RNLI: Management 1995-2003, Council 2003-05; Trustee: HMS Warrior 1860 1997-2017; President: GamCare 1997-2003, Brendoncare Foundation 1998-2011, Printers' Charitable Corporation 1998; Chair: Alexandra Rose Day 1998-2010, Cothill Education Trust 1998-2011; Chartered Accountant; Chancellor, Brunel University 1997-2012; FCA; Hon. PhD, Anglia Ruskin University 1992; Hon. DUniv, Brunel University 1998; PC 1983. Buck's, St Stephen's Constitutional, Garrick, Royal Yacht Squadron (Cowes), Chair, Carlton Club 1992-98; Royal Yacht Squadron, Royal Southern Yacht Club, RAF Yacht Club.

Recreations: Sailing, racing, reading.

Rt Hon the Lord Wakeham DL, House of Lords, London SW1A 0PW
Tel: 020 7219 3162 *Fax:* 020 7219 6807 *Email:* wakehamj@parliament.uk

CONSERVATIVE

WALDEGRAVE OF NORTH HILL, LORD

WALDEGRAVE OF NORTH HILL (Life Baron), William Arthur Waldegrave; cr. 1999. Born 15 August 1946; Son of 12th Earl Waldegrave, KG, GCVO, TD, DL and Mary Hermione Grenfell; Married Caroline Burrows OBE 1977 (1 son 3 daughters).

Education: Eton College; Corpus Christi College, Oxford (Open Scholar, BA literae humaniores 1969) (Union President 1968); Harvard University (Kennedy Scholar) 1969-70.

Non-political career: Fellow, All Souls, Oxford 1971-86, 1999-; Member: Central Policy Review Staff, Cabinet Office 1971-73, Political Staff at 10 Downing Street 1973-74; Leader of Opposition's Office 1974-75; With GEC Ltd 1975-81; Non-executive Director: Waldegrave Farms Ltd 1975-, Bristol and West plc (formerly Bristol and West Building Society) 1997-2006, Biotech Growth Trust plc (formerly Finsbury Life Sciences Investment Trust plc) 1997-2016, Henry Sotheran Ltd 1998-2015; Dresdner Kleinwort Wasserstein 1998-2003: Managing Director, Investment Banking, UBS; Vice-chairman and Managing Director, Investment Banking 2003-08; Non-executive Director, Bank of Ireland UK Holdings plc 2002-06; Member: International Advisory Board, Teijin Ltd 2006-08, Remuneration and Nomination Committee, Bergeson Worldwide Gas ASA 2006-08; Provost, Eton College 2009-; Chair: Biotech Growth Trust plc 2012-16, Coutts and Co 2014-, Coutts Foundation 2016-; Director, GW Pharmaceuticals plc 2017-.

Political career: *House of Commons:* MP (Conservative) for Bristol West 1979-97; Parliamentary Under-Secretary of State: Department of Education and Science 1981-83, Department of Environment (DoE) 1983-85; Minister of State: DoE 1985-88, Foreign and Commonwealth Office 1988-90; Secretary of State for Health 1990-92; Chancellor of the Duchy of Lancaster and Minister for Public Service and Science 1992-94; Minister of Agriculture, Fisheries and Food 1994-95; Chief Secretary to HM Treasury 1995-97. *House of Lords:* Raised to the peerage as Baron Waldegrave of North Hill, of Chewton Mendip in the County of Somerset 1999. President Parliamentary and Scientific Committee 2000-03. Member, Joint Committee on National Security Strategy 2010-14. *Other:* Hon. Life member, Tory Reform Group. JP, Inner London Juvenile Court 1975-79.

Other: Rhodes Trust: Trustee 1992-2011, Chair 2002-11; Trustee: Beit Memorial Fellowships 1998-2006, Strawberry Hill Trust 2002-14; Chair, National Museum of Science and Industry 2002-10; Trustee, Mandela Rhodes Foundation, South Africa 2003-11; President, Royal Bath and West Society 2006; Trustee, Cumberland Lodge, Windsor 2008-; Liveryman, Merchant Taylors' Company; Freedom: City of London, City of Bristol; Chancellor, Reading University 2016-; Hon. Fellow, Corpus Christi College, Oxford; Hon. DLitt, Reading University; Royal Society of Chemistry Parliamentary Award 2001; PC 1990. Whites, Beefsteak, Pratt's, Clifton (Bristol), Leander Club; Eton Vikings.

Publications: The Binding of Leviathan (1978); A Different Kind of Weather (2015); Various pamphlets.

Rt Hon the Lord Waldegrave of North Hill, House of Lords, London SW1A 0PW
Tel: 020 7219 5353
Eton College, Windsor SL4 6DH *Tel:* 01753 671234
Email: provostsecretary@etoncollege.org.uk

CROSSBENCH

WALKER OF ALDRINGHAM, LORD

WALKER OF ALDRINGHAM (Life Baron), Michael John Dawson Walker; cr. 2006. Born 7 July 1944; Son of William Walker and Dorothy Walker; Married Victoria Holme 1973 (2 sons 1 daughter).

Education: Milton School, Bulawayo, Zimbabwe; Woodhouse Grove School, Yorkshire; RMA Sandhurst (commissioned 1966).

Non-political career: Regimental and staff duties, Royal Anglian Regiment 1966-82; Military Assistant to Chief of the General Staff 1982-85; Commanding Officer, 1 Royal Anglian Regiment 1985-87; Commander, 20th Armoured Brigade 1987-89; Chief of Staff 1 (Br) Corps 1989-91; Colonel Commandant, Queen's Division 1991-2000; General Officer Commanding: North East District and Commander 2nd Infantry Division 1991-92, Eastern District 1992; Assistant Chief of the General Staff, Ministry of Defence 1992-94; Commander, Allied Command Europe Rapid Reaction Corps 1994-97; Colonel Commandant, Army Air Corps 1994-2004; Commander, Land Component Peace Implementation Force, Bosnia 1995-96; Commander-in-Chief, Land Command 1997-2000; Colonel, Royal Anglian Regiment 1997-2002; Aide de Camp General to the Queen 1997-2006; Chief of the General Staff 2000-03; Chief of the Defence Staff 2003-06; Governor, Royal Hospital Chelsea 2006-11.

Political career: *House of Lords:* Raised to the peerage as Baron Walker of Aldringham, of Aldringham in the County of Suffolk 2006. *Other:* DL, Greater London 2007-; Member, Prime Minister's Advisory Committee on Business Appointments.

Political interests: Defence, foreign affairs, international relations, country sports, sports; Africa, eastern Europe.

Other: Former chair, Army Benevolent Fund; Chair, Tutu Foundation UK; President, Museum of Army Flying 2002-; Patron, British South Africa Police Trust 2003-; President, Stoll (Sir Oswald Stoll Foundation) 2010-; Trustee, Veteran's Aid 2010-; Hon. Doctor of Civil Law, University of East Anglia 2002; Hon. Doctor of Science in Social Science, Cranfield University 2003; OBE 1982; CBE 1990; KCB 1995; CMG 1997; Legion of Merit (USA) 1997; GCB 2000; Cross of Merit (Czechoslovakia) 2001.

Recreations: Golf, shooting, tennis, sailing, motorcycling, skiing.

The Lord Walker of Aldringham GCB CMG CBE DL, House of Lords, London SW1A 0PW
Tel: 020 7219 8956 *Email:* walkermjd@parliament.uk

CROSSBENCH

WALKER OF GESTINGTHORPE, LORD

WALKER OF GESTINGTHORPE (Life Baron), Robert Walker; cr. 2002. Born 17 March 1938; Son of late Ronald Robert Antony Walker and late Mary Helen Walker, née Welsh; Married Suzanne Diana Leggi 1962 (3 daughters 1 son).

Education: Downside School, Somerset; Trinity College, Cambridge (BA classics and law 1959); French, Italian.

Non-political career: Barrister, Lincoln's Inn 1960; QC 1982; High Court Judge, Chancery Division 1994-97; Lord Justice of Appeal 1997-2002; Justice of the Supreme Court of the United Kingdom 2009-13; Non-permanent Judge, Court of Final Appeal, Hong Kong 2009-. 2nd Lieutenant R.A (National Service) 1959-61.

Political career: *House of Lords:* Raised to the peerage as Baron Walker of Gestingthorpe, of Gestingthorpe in the County of Essex 2002. Lord of Appeal in Ordinary 2002-09; As Justice of the Supreme Court, disqualified from participation 2009-13. Chair, High Speed Rail

(London-West Midlands) Bill 2016; Member, SLSC Sub-committee A 2018-19; Chair, High Speed Rail (West Midlands-Crewe) Bill 2019-20.

Other: Patron, International Advocacy Training Council; Honorary fellow, Trinity College, Cambridge 2006; Honorary doctorate, London Metropolitan University 2008; Kt 1994; PC 1997.

Publications: Articles in legal periodicals.

Recreations: Walking, gardening.

Rt Hon the Lord Walker of Gestingthorpe QC, House of Lords, London SW1A 0PW
Tel: 020 7219 5353

LIBERAL DEMOCRAT

WALLACE OF SALTAIRE, LORD

Liberal Democrat Lords Spokesperson for the Cabinet Office

WALLACE OF SALTAIRE (Life Baron), William John Lawrence Wallace; cr. 1995. Born 12 March 1941; Son of late William Edward Wallace and late Mary Agnes Tricks; Married Helen Rushworth 1968 (1 son 1 daughter).

Education: Westminster Abbey Choir School; St Edward's School, Oxford; King's College, Cambridge (BA history 1962); Cornell University, USA (PhD government 1968); Nuffield College, Oxford (MA 1965).

Non-political career: Lecturer in government, Manchester University 1967-77; Director of studies, Royal Institute of International Affairs 1978-90; Walter F. Hallstein Fellow, St Antony's College, Oxford 1990-95; London School of Economics 1995-: International relations reader 1995-99, Professor 1999-2005, Emeritus Professor 2005-.

Political career: *House of Lords:* Raised to the peerage as Baron Wallace of Saltaire, of Shipley in the County of West Yorkshire 1995. Liberal Democrat: Spokesperson for: Defence 1997-2001, Foreign and Commonwealth Affairs 1998-2010, Deputy Leader Liberal Democrat peers 2004-10, Spokesperson for Justice 2007-08; Government Whip 2010-15; Government Spokesperson for: Education (Higher Education) 2010, Foreign and Commonwealth Office 2010-15, Defence 2010-12, Business, Innovation and Skills 2010, Home Office (Security) 2010-11, Cabinet Office 2011-15; Liberal Democrat: Spokesperson for Foreign and Commonwealth Affairs 2015-16, Shadow Minister/Lords Spokesperson for the Cabinet Office 2016-. Member: Ecclesiastical Committee 1997-2010, European Union 1997-2000, 2001-02; Chair, European Union Sub-committee F (Social Affairs, Education and Home Affairs) 1997-2000; Member, European Union Sub-committee C (Common Foreign and Security Policy) 2001-02. *Other:* vice-chair, Liberal Party Standing Committee (later Policy Committee) 1974-84; Chair, Manifesto Drafting Committee 1979, 1997.

Political interests: Foreign affairs, defence, Europe, constitutional affairs; Armenia, EU member states, Georgia, Russia, Ukraine, USA.

Other: Voces Cantabiles Music/Gresham Centre 2004-; National Children's Choir of Great Britain -2017; Honorary doctorate, Université Libre de Bruxelles 1992; Chevalier, Ordre pour le Mérite (France) 1995; Légion d'Honneur (France) 2005; PC 2012. Saltaire Tennis Club.

Publications: The Foreign Policy Process in Britain (1977); The Transformation of Europe (1990); The Dynamics of European Integration (1990); Regional Integration – The West European Experience (1994); Policy-making in the European Union, with Helen Wallace (1996, 2000, 2005); Why Vote Liberal Democrat? (1997).

Recreations: Singing, swimming, walking, gardening.

Rt Hon the Lord Wallace of Saltaire, House of Lords, London SW1A 0PW
Tel: 020 7219 3125 *Email:* wallacew@parliament.uk

NON-AFFILIATED

WALLACE OF TANKERNESS, LORD

WALLACE OF TANKERNESS (Life Baron), James Robert Wallace; cr 2007. Born 25 August 1954; Son of John Fergus Thomson Wallace and Grace Wallace, née Maxwell; Married Rosemary Fraser 1983 (2 daughters).

Education: Annan Academy, Dumfriesshire; Downing College, Cambridge (BA economics and law 1975, MA); Edinburgh University (LLB law 1977).

Non-political career: Called to the Scottish Bar 1979; QC (Scot) 1997; Jim Wallace Consultancy Ltd 2007-10; Hon. Professor, Institute of Petroleum Engineering, Heriot-Watt University 2007-10; Advocate, Terra Firma Chambers, Edinburgh 2010; Hon. Bencher, Lincoln's Inn 2012; Moderator, General Assembly of the Church of Scotland 2021-.

Political career: *House of Commons:* Contested Dumfries 1979 general election. MP for Orkney and Shetland 1983-2001 (Liberal 1983-88, Liberal Democrat 1988-2001). *House of Lords:* Raised to the peerage as Baron Wallace of Tankerness, of Tankerness in Orkney 2007. Liberal Democrat Spokesperson for: Justice 2009-10, Scotland 2009-10, Equality Bill 2009-10; Advocate General for Scotland 2010-15; Government Spokesperson for: Scotland 2010-15, Wales 2010-12, Attorney General's Office/Law Officers 2010-15; Leader, Liberal Democrat Peers 2013-16; Deputy Leader of the House of Lords 2013-15; Member, House of Lords Commission 2016. Co-opted Member, EU Sub-committee D (Environment and Agriculture) 2008; Member: Constitution 2008-10, Partnerships (Prosecution) (Scotland) Bill 2013; House 2013-16, Liaison 2013-16, Privileges and Conduct 2013-16, Procedure 2013-16, Selection 2013-16, Joint Committee on the Palace of Westminster 2015-16, Constitution 2018-. *Other:* Contested South Scotland 1979 European Parliament election; Scottish Parliament: MSP for Orkney 1999-2007: Deputy First Minister 1999-2005, Minister for: Justice 1999-2003, Enterprise and Lifelong Learning 2003-05. Scottish Liberal Party: Member, Executive 1976-85, Vice-chair (policy) 1982-85; Hon. President, Scottish Young Liberals 1984-85; Leader, Scottish Liberal Democrats 1992-2005; As Moderator of the General Assembly of the Church of Scotland does not take the Liberal Democrat whip, now sits as non-affiliated January 2021-. Member: Scottish Office Consultative Steering Group on Scottish Parliament 1998, Calman Commission on Scottish Devolution 2008-09.

Political interests: Constitutional reform, Scottish home rule and federalism, Scottish law, rural development, energy conservation, shipping, Amnesty International, renewable energy; China, New Zealand, Norway, USA.

Other: Board member, St Magnus International Festival 2007-14; Chair, Relationships Scotland 2008-10; Co-convener, Scottish Poverty Truth Commission 2009-10; Patron, European Movement in Scotland; Non-executive director, Water Retail Company 2017-; Member and chair of Regulation Board, Institute of Chartered Accountants of Scotland 2017-; Chair, board of trustees, Reprieve 2017-; Member, Faculty of Advocates 1979-; RNLI, Christian Aid, Amnesty International, British Red Cross, Reprieve; Fellow, Royal Society of Edinburgh 2018; DLitt, Heriot-Watt University 2007; DUniv, Open University 2009; Doctor honoris causa, Edinburgh University 2009; Joint recipient Saltire Society's Andrew Fletcher Award for Services to Scotland 1998; Scottish Politician of the Year, *The Herald* 2000; Devolved Politician of the Year, Channel Four 2002; Lifetime Achievement Award, *The Herald* 2008; PC 2000. Caledonian, Scottish Liberal Club; Orkney Golf Club.

Recreations: Golf, travel, music.

Rt Hon the Lord Wallace of Tankerness QC, House of Lords, London SW1A 0PW
Tel: 020 7219 3526 *Email:* wallacej@parliament.uk *Twitter:* @jrwallace54

LIBERAL DEMOCRAT

WALMSLEY, BARONESS

Deputy Leader, Liberal Democrat Peers

WALMSLEY (Life Baroness), Joan Margaret Walmsley; cr. 2000. Born 12 April 1943; Daughter of Leo and Monica Watson; Married John Richardson 1966 (divorced 1980) (1 son 1 daughter); married Christopher Walmsley 1986 (died 1995) (1 stepson 2 stepdaughters); married Lord Thomas of Gresford (qv) 2005 (3 stepsons 1 stepdaughter).

Education: Notre Dame High School, Liverpool; Liverpool University (BSc biology 1966); Manchester Polytechnic (PGCE 1979).

Non-political career: Cytologist, Christie Hospital, Manchester 1965-67; Teacher, Buxton College, Derbyshire 1979-86; Public relations consultant 1987-2003.

Political career: *House of Commons:* Contested (Liberal Democrat) Leeds South and Morley 1992 and Congleton 1997 general elections. *House of Lords:* Raised to the peerage as Baroness Walmsley, of West Derby in the County of Merseyside 2000. Liberal Democrat Spokesperson for: Early Years Education, Education and Skills 2001-03, Home Office 2003-04, Education and Children/Children, Schools and Families 2004-10, Education, Families and Young People 2010-13; Convener of the Liberal Democrat Peers 2014-15; Liberal Democrat Shadow Minister/Lords Spokesperson for Health 2015-17; Deputy Leader, Liberal Democrat Peers 2017-. Member, Science and Technology 2000-05, 2019-; Chair, Science and Technology Sub-committee I (Systematic Biology and Biodiversity) 2002; Member, Science and Technology Sub-committees: I (Fighting Infection) 2002-03, I (Science and International Agreements) 2003-04, I (Scientific Aspects of Ageing) 2004-05; Co-opted Member, Science and Technology 2008; Member: Adoption Legislation 2012-13, House 2014-15, Liaison 2014-15, 2019-, Affordable Childcare 2014-15. Chair, Liberal Democrat Parliamentary Party Committee on Education, Families and Young People 2010-12. *Other:* Member, Liberal Democrat Conference Committee 2000-03; President, Women Liberal Democrats 2002-04; Member, Liberal Democrats Federal Executive 2003-04.

Political interests: Child protection, young offenders, prisoner education, environment, early years education.

Other: Patron: Family Planning Association, Helena Kennedy Trust; Infant Trust; WAVE Trust; Ambassador: NSPCC, 4Children; Honorary fellow, Unicef; Member, Parliament Choir; Amnesty International. Reform Club, Pall Mall; Rex Boat Club.

Publications: Chaired report What on Earth? The threats to the Science Underpinning Conservation (2002).

Recreations: Music, theatre, gardening, rowing, good company, bee-keeping.

The Baroness Walmsley, House of Lords, London SW1A 0PW
Tel: 020 7219 6047 *Email:* walmsleyj@parliament.uk Website: www.joanwalmsley.org.uk
Twitter: @joan_walmsley

NON-AFFILIATED

WALNEY, LORD

WALNEY (Life Baron), John Zak Woodcock; cr 2020. Born 14 October 1978; Married Mandy Telford (2 daughters) (divorced); partner Isabel Hardman (1 son).

Education: Tapton Secondary School, Sheffield; Edinburgh University (MA English literature and history 2002); King's College London (MA international security and strategy 2019).

Non-political career: Journalist, *Scotsman* 1999-2002; Researcher, Labour Party 2003-05; Special adviser: to John Hutton MP: as Chancellor of the Duchy of Lancaster and Minister for the Cabinet Office 2005, as Secretary of State for Work and Pensions 2005-07, as Secretary of State for Business, Enterprise and Regulatory Reform 2007-08, to Gordon Brown MP as Prime Minister (on political press issues) 2009; Consultant on counter extremism, Tony Blair Institute for Global Change 2020-.

Political career: *House of Commons:* MP (Lab) for Barrow and Furness 2010-19; Shadow Minister for: Transport 2010-13, Education 2015. Member: Defence 2010, 2013-15, Arms Export Controls 2010, Home Affairs 2018-19. PLP Departmental Group for Defence: Vice-chair 2010-11, Chair 2015-17; Chair, PLP Departmental Group for Foreign Affairs 2017-18. *House of Lords:* Raised to the peerage as Baron Walney, of the Isle of Walney in the

County of Cumbria 2020. *Other:* Former chair, Labour Friends of Israel; Labour Party: Whip suspended April 2018, Resigned July 2018. Governor, Walney School.

Political interests: Civil nuclear power, manufacturing industry.

Other: Member, UK Delegation, Organisation for Security and Co-operation in Europe Parliamentary Assembly 2014-17; Former chair, Progress; Special Envoy for countering violent extremism, Home Office 2020-; Sports Parliamentarian of the Year, Sport and Recreation Alliance 2011.

Publications: Columnist, *PR Week*; Contributor, The Purple Book (Progress, 2011).

Recreations: Barrow Athletic FC, Barrow Raiders RLFC, Sheffield Wednesday FC.

The Lord Walney, House of Lords, London SW1A 0PW
Tel: 020 7219 3000
PO Box 208, Walney Island LA14 9EB *Email:* enquiries@lordwalney.uk
Website: lordwalney.uk *Twitter:* @LordWalney

CROSSBENCH

WARNER, LORD

WARNER (Life Baron), Norman Reginald Warner; cr. 1998. Born 8 September 1940; Son of Albert and Laura Warner; Married Anne Lawrence 1961 (divorced 1981) (1 son 1 daughter); married Suzanne Reeve 1990 (1 son).

Education: Dulwich College, London; University of California, Berkeley (MPH) (Harkness Fellowship 1971-73).

Non-political career: Ministry of Health/DHSS 1959-85: Assistant private secretary: to Minister of Health 1967-68, to Secretary of State for Social Services 1968-69, Executive Councils Division 1969-71, NHS Reorganisation 1973-74, Principal private secretary to Secretary of State for Social Services 1974-76, Supplementary Benefits Division 1976-78, Management services 1979-81, Controller, Wales and South Western Region 1981-83, Under-Secretary, Supplementary Benefits Division 1984-85; Director of social services, Kent County Council 1985-91; Managing director, Warner Consultancy and Training Services Ltd 1991-97; Senior policy adviser to Home Secretary 1997-99; Chair: Youth Justice Board for England and Wales 1998-2003, London Sports Board 2003.

Political career: *House of Lords:* Raised to the peerage as Baron Warner, of Brockley in the London Borough of Lewisham 1998. Department of Health: Government Spokesperson 2003-06, Parliamentary Under-Secretary of State 2003-05, Minister of State: (NHS Delivery) 2005-06, (NHS Reform) 2006. Member: Science and Technology 2008-12, Science and Technology Sub-committee II (Genomic Medicine) 2008-09, Science and Technology Sub-committee I (Radioactive Waste Management: a further update) 2010, Adoption Legislation 2012-13; Member, Joint Committees on: the Draft Care and Support Bill 2013, the Draft Modern Slavery Bill 2014; Member, Long-Term Sustainability of the NHS 2016-17. *Other:* Resigned Labour Party and Whip October 2015; now sits as Crossbencher. Chair: City and East London FHSA 1991-94, National Inquiry into Selection, Development and Management of Staff in Children's Homes 1991-92; Member, Local Government Commission 1995-96; Chair, NHS London Provider Agency 2007-09; Member, Commission on Funding of Care and Support (Dilnot Commission) 2010-11; Children's Commissioner, Birmingham City Council 2014-.

Political interests: Law and order, children, social and health care, end of life, Palestine; Commonwealth countries, North Africa/Middle East, USA.

Other: Member, Carers National Association 1991-94; Royal Philanthropic Society: Member 1991-, Chair 1993-98; Trustee: Leonard Cheshire Foundation 1994-96, MacIntyre Care 1994-97; Chair: Expert Panel for UK Harkness Fellowships 1994-97, Residential Forum, in Association with National Institute for Social Work 1994-97; National Council for Voluntary Organisations 2001-03; Oxfam, Amnesty International, Samaritans; Harkness Fellowship 1971-73; Gwilym Gibbon Fellow, Nuffield College, Oxford 1984; PC 2006.

Publications: Editor, Commissioning Community Alternatives in European Social and Health Care (1993); Articles in specialised journals and national newspapers; A Suitable Case for Treatment: The NHS and Reform (2011); Solving the NHS Care and Cash Crisis (2014).

Recreations: Reading, cinema, theatre, exercise, travel.

Rt Hon the Lord Warner, House of Lords, London SW1A 0PW
Tel: 020 7219 4540 *Email:* warnern@parliament.uk

CONSERVATIVE

WARSI, BARONESS

WARSI (Life Baroness), Sayeeda Hussain Warsi; cr 2007. Born 28 March 1971; Married (divorced) (1 daughter); Married Iftikhar (4 stepchildren).

Education: Dewsbury College; Leeds University (LLB 1992).

Non-political career: Trainee solicitor, Crown Prosecution Service 1994-96; Solicitor, Whitfield Hallam Goodall Solicitors 1996-97; Managing partner, George Warsi Solicitors 1997-2002; Legal draftsman, Ministry of Law, Pakistan 2002-03; Director, Shire Bed Company 2015-.

Political career: *House of Commons:* Contested (Conservative) Dewsbury 2005 general election. *House of Lords:* Raised to the peerage as Baroness Warsi, of Dewsbury in the County of West Yorkshire 2007. Shadow Minister for: Community Cohesion 2007-10, Social Action 2007-10; Minister without Portfolio 2010-12; Government Spokesperson for Cabinet Office 2011-12; Senior Minister of State (Faith and Communities) and Government Spokesperson, Department for Communities and Local Government and Foreign and Commonwealth Office 2012-14. Member, Sexual Violence in Conflict 2015-16. *Other:* Conservative Party: Vice-chairman (with responsibility for cities) 2005-07, Chairman 2010-12.

Political interests: Foreign affairs, faith, integration, freedom of religion, social action; Afghanistan, Central Asia, Bangladesh, Pakistan.

Other: Founder and chair, Savayra Foundation, UK 2003-; Pro Vice-Chancellor, Bolton University 2016-; Honorary Doctorate, University of Law; PC 2010.

Publications: The Enemy Within, A Tale of Muslim Britain (Allen Lane, 2017).

Recreations: Writing, family life.

Rt Hon the Baroness Warsi, House of Lords, London SW1A 0PW
Tel: 020 7219 0262 *Email:* warsis@parliament.uk Website: sayeedawarsi.com
Twitter: @SayeedaWarsi

LABOUR

WARWICK OF UNDERCLIFFE, BARONESS

WARWICK OF UNDERCLIFFE (Life Baroness), Diana Warwick; cr. 1999. Born 16 July 1945; Daughter of Jack and Olive Warwick; Married Sean Bowes Young 1969.

Education: St Joseph's College, Bradford; Bedford College, London University (BA 1967).

Non-political career: Technical assistant to general secretary, NUT 1969-72; Assistant secretary, Civil and Public Services Association 1972-83; General secretary, Association of University Teachers 1983-92; Chief executive: Westminster Foundation for Democracy 1992-95, Universities UK (previously Committee of Vice-Chancellors and Principals/ Universities UK) 1995-2009; Non-executive director: Lattice plc 2000-02, Universities Superannuation Scheme Ltd 2001-09; Chair: Human Tissue Authority 2010-, National Housing Federation 2015-. Member, TUC General Council 1989-92.

Political career: *House of Lords:* Raised to the peerage as Baroness Warwick of Undercliffe, of Undercliffe in the County of West Yorkshire 1999. Member: Science and Technology 1999-2005, Science and Technology Sub-committees: II (Aircraft Cabin Environment) 2000-01, (Stem Cell Research) 2001-02, II (Innovations in Computer Processors) 2001-02, I (Fighting Infection) 2002-03, (Science and International Agreements) 2003-04, Advisory Panel on Works of Art 2003-05, Joint Committee on the Draft Protection of Charities Bill 2014-15, Procedure/Procedure and Privileges 2016-, Joint Committee on the Draft Parliamentary Buildings (Restoration and Renewal) Bill 2018-19. *Other:* Board member, British Council 1985-95; Member: Employment Appeal Tribunal 1987-99, Executive and Council, Industrial Society 1987-97, Commonwealth Institute 1988-95, Nolan/Neill Committee on Standards in Public Life 1994-99, OST Technology Foresight Steering Group 1997-2000.

Political interests: Higher education, science and technology, health, heritage, international development, pensions, corporate social responsibility.

Other: Member: Inter-Parliamentary Union 1999-, Commonwealth Parliamentary Association 1999-, British American Parliamentary Group 1999-; Trustee, Royal Anniversary Trust 1991-93; Council member, Duke of Edinburgh's Seventh Commonwealth Study Conference 1991; Voluntary Service Overseas: Chair 1994-2003, Life Vice-president 2003-; Member, RIIA 1995-; Trustee, St Catherine's Foundation, Windsor 1996-2008; Chair of trustee, International Students House 2000-; Chair, Modern Records Centre, Warwick University 2009-; Council member, University College London 2010-; Board member, Pensions Protection Fund 2011-; VSO, Womankind Worldwide; FRSA 1984; Five honorary doctorates.

Recreations: Theatre, opera, looking at pictures.

The Baroness Warwick of Undercliffe, House of Lords, London SW1A 0PW
Tel: 020 7219 5086 *Email:* warwickd@parliament.uk

CONSERVATIVE

WASSERMAN, LORD

WASSERMAN (Life Baron), Gordon Joshua Wasserman; cr 2011. Born 26 July 1938; Son of late John Wasserman QC and Prof Rachel Wasserman; Married Cressida Frances 1964.

Education: Westmount High School, Montreal, Canada; New College, Oxford (BA); McGill University, Canada (Rhodes Scholar 1959).

Non-political career: Senior research scholar, St Antony's College, Oxford 1961-64; Lecturer in economics, Merton College, Oxford 1963-64; Research Fellow, New College Oxford 1964-67; Home Office: Economic adviser 1967, Senior economic adviser 1972, Assistant secretary 1977-81; Head, Urban Deprivation Unit 1973-77; Civil service travelling fellowship, USA 1977-78; Under Secretary, Central Policy Review Staff, Cabinet Office 1981-83; Assistant Under Secretary of State, Home Office 1983-95; Special adviser (science and technology) to Police Commissioner, New York 1996-98; Chief of staff to Police Commissioner, New York 1998-2002; Special adviser to Police Commissioner, Philadelphia 1998-2003; Chair, ION Track Inc 2000-02; Chair and chief executive officer, Gordon Wasserman Group LLC 2003-.

Political career: *House of Lords:* Raised to the peerage as Baron Wasserman, of Pimlico in the City of Westminster 2011. Government Adviser on Policing and Criminal Justice 2011-. Member: EU Sub-committee F (Home Affairs, Health and Education) 2013-15, EU Home Affairs Sub-committee 2015-16, EU Justice Sub-committee 2018-19.

Other: Vice-President, English Basketball Association 1983-86; Executive member, ELITE Group 1993-96; Board member, SEARCH Group Inc 1994-2000; Member, US Justice Department Advisory Panel on Science and Technology 1996-2003.

The Lord Wasserman, House of Lords, London SW1A 0PW
Tel: 020 7219 5353

CROSSBENCH

WATKINS OF TAVISTOCK, BARONESS

WATKINS OF TAVISTOCK (Life Baroness), Mary Jane Watkins; cr 2015. Born 5 March 1955; Married Roger Watkins 1981 (1 son 1 daughter).

Education: St Helen and St Katharine School, Abingdon; Wolfson School of Nursing, Westminster Hospital (qualified general nurse 1976); South London and Maudsley Nursing School (qualified mental health nurse 1979); Nightingale Scholar 1985; University of Wales (Masters nursing); King's College, University of London (PhD 1985).

Non-political career: Tutor, Nightingale School 1979-81; Nurse, Westminster Hospital London 1980; Tutor, Maudsley School of Nursing 1981-83; Academic director and senior tutor, Tor and South West College of Health; Plymouth University: Dean, Faculty of Health and Social Work, Emeritus Professor of Nursing 2012-17, Pro Vice-Chancellor, Health, Deputy Vice-Chancellor 2009-12; Nurse adviser to BUPA Medical Advisory Panel 2006-.

Political career: *House of Lords:* Raised to the peerage as Baroness Watkins of Tavistock, of Buckland Monachorum in the County of Devon 2015. Deputy Chairman of Committees 2020-. Member: Licensing Act 2003 2016-17, Secondary Legislation Scrutiny 2017-18, Joint Committee on the Draft Health Service Safety Investigations Bill 2018, SLSC Sub-committee B 2018-19, Secondary Legislation Scrutiny 2019-. *Other:* Non-executive Director: South West

Ambulance NHS Foundation Trust 2008-16, Aster Housing Association 2010-; Chair: National Institute for Health Research (NIHR), South West Peninsula 2014-, Acorn Academy Schools, Cornwall 2014-16.

Political interests: Health, housing, higher education, secondary education.

Other: Member: UK Central Council for Nursing and Midwifery and Health Visiting 1996-2001, Council for Professions Supplementary to Medicine 1997-2001; Former nurse member, appraisal committee, National Institute for Health and Clinical Excellence 2001-07; Member, BUPA Global Quality Clinical Committee 2014-18; Trustee, Florence Nightingale Museum Trust 2014-; Member, Brightwell Academy Trustee Board 2016-; Trustee, Plymouth Marine Laboratory 2017-; Member, Royal College of Nursing; Nightingale Fellowship 1980; Honorary doctorate, Plymouth University 2012.

Publications: Published in the field of nursing education and leadership; Inaugural editor, Journal of Clinical Nursing.

Professor the Baroness Watkins of Tavistock, House of Lords, London SW1A 0PW
Tel: 020 7219 5459 *Email:* watkinsm@parliament.uk
King's College London *Tel:* 020 7848 3325 *Email:* sadaf.qureshi@kcl.ac.uk

LABOUR

WATSON OF INVERGOWRIE, LORD

Opposition Spokesperson for Education

WATSON OF INVERGOWRIE (Life Baron), Michael (Mike) Goodall Watson; cr. 1997. Born 1 May 1949; Son of late Clarke and late Senga Watson, née Goodall; Married Lorraine McManus 1986 (divorced); married Clare Thomas 2004 (1 son).

Education: Dundee High School; Heriot-Watt University, Edinburgh (BA economics and industrial relations 1974); French.

Non-political career: Development officer, Workers Educational Association East Midlands District 1974-77; MSF: Full-time official 1977-89, Industrial officer 1977-79, Regional officer based in Glasgow 1979-89; Director, PS Communication Consultants Ltd, Edinburgh 1997-99; Associate director, Caledonia Consulting, Edinburgh 2007-12. Member, Unite 1975-.

Political career: *House of Commons:* MP (Labour) for Glasgow Central 1989-97. Chairman, Parliamentary Labour Party Committee on Overseas Development Aid 1991-97. *House of Lords:* Raised to the peerage as Baron Watson of Invergowrie, of Invergowrie in Perth and Kinross 1997. Opposition Spokesperson for Education 2015-. Member, Joint Committee on the Draft Protection of Charities Bill 2014-15. *Other:* Scottish Parliament: MSP for Glasgow Cathcart constituency 1999-2005 (as Mike Watson): Minister for Tourism, Culture and Sport 2001-03. Labour Party: Member, Scottish Executive Committee 1987-90, Party Whip suspended 2004, Re-admitted November 2012.

Political interests: Economy, social inclusion policy, overseas aid and development, extension of devolution throughout the UK; France.

Other: Fellow, Industry and Parliament Trust 1999; Oxfam, Epilepsy Action Scotland, Shelter; Visiting Research Fellow, Department of Government, Strathclyde University 1993-96, 1999-2002; Hon LLD, Abertay Dundee University 1998. Director, Dundee United Football Company Ltd 2003-05.

Publications: Rags to Riches: The Official History of Dundee United FC (1985); The Tannadice Encyclopedia (1997); Year Zero: An Inside View of the Scottish Parliament (2001).

Recreations: Dundee United FC, cycling, running.

The Lord Watson of Invergowrie, House of Lords, London SW1A 0PW
Tel: 020 7219 8731 *Email:* watsonm@parliament.uk

LIBERAL DEMOCRAT

WATSON OF RICHMOND, LORD

WATSON OF RICHMOND (Life Baron), Alan John Watson; cr. 1999. Born 3 February 1941; Son of Rev. John William Watson and Edna Mary, née Peters; Married Karen Lederer 1965 (2 sons).

Education: Diocesan College, Cape Town, South Africa; Kingswood School, Bath; Jesus College, Cambridge (Open Scholar history 1959; State Scholar 1959, MA 1963) (Vice-president, Cambridge Union); German.

Non-political career: Research assistant, Cambridge University 1962-64; BBC 1965-68: General trainee 1965-66, Reporter, *The Money Programme*, BBC TV 1966-68; Chief public affairs commentator, London Weekend Television 1969-70; Presenter: *Panorama*, BBC TV 1971-74, *The Money Programme* 1974-75; Head of TV, radio, audio-visual division, EEC, and Editor, European Community Newsreel service to Lomé Convention Countries 1975-79; Charles Barker City Ltd: Director 1980-85, Chief executive 1980-83; Deputy chair, Sterling Public Relations 1985-86; Chair: City and Corporate Counsel Ltd 1987-94, Threadneedle Publishing Group 1987-94, Corporate Vision Ltd 1989-98; Presenter: BBC 1 1990 *You and 92*, Documentary Series *The Germans*, Channel 4 1992; Chair, Corporate Television Networks 1992-; Member, Y&R Partnership Board; Chair: Burson-Marsteller UK 1994-2004, Burson-Marsteller Europe 1996-2007, The Cola Cola Company European Advisory Board 2002-06, Raisin Social Ltd (Wine Importers) 2005-, Nexus Publishing 2007-, Havas Media/ Havas Media Group 2008-.

Political career: *House of Commons:* Contested (Liberal) Richmond, Surrey 1974 and 1979 and (Liberal/All) Richmond and Barnes 1983 and 1987 general elections. *House of Lords:* Raised to the peerage as Baron Watson of Richmond, of Richmond in the London Borough of Richmond upon Thames 1999. Liberal Democrat Spokesperson for: Foreign and Commonwealth Affairs (Europe) 2000-01, 2002-05, Universities 2007-09. Member, EU Sub-committee C (Common Foreign and Security Policy) 2000-03; Co-opted Member, EU Sub-committee A (Economic and Financial Affairs) 2006-10. *Other:* President, Cambridge University Liberal Club 1961-; Chair, Liberal Party Parliamentary Association 1982-84; Member, Liberal Party National Executive 1982-86; President, Liberal Party 1984-85. Chair of Governors, Westminster College, Oxford 1988-94.

Political interests: Worldwide use of English, EU enlargement, transatlantic relationship; Germany, Romania, Russia, USA.

Other: Member: Executive board, Unicef 1985-92, High Level EU-Romania Group 2000-02; Chair, Royal Television Society 1990-91; Visiting Fellow, Louvanium International Business Centre, Brussels 1990-95; Visiting Erasmus Professor in European studies, Louvain University 1990; President, Heathrow Association for Control of Aircraft Noise 1992-95; British-German Association: Chair 1992-2000; President 2000-; Vice-chair, European Movement 1995-2001; Prince of Wales Business Leaders Forum 1996-; Hon. Professor, German Studies, Birmingham University 1997-; Council member, British Studies Centre, Humboldt University, Berlin 1998-; Chair, Father Thames Trust 1999-; English Speaking Union: Chair 1999-2005, Chair, British Jamestown Committee 2005-07, International chair Emeritus 2006-, Vice-President 2012-; Trustee and Patron, Richmond Museum 2002-; Patron, Richmond Society 2002-; Visiting Fellow, Oriel College, Oxford 2003-; Chair: UK Steering Committee of Koenigswinter Conference 2003-10, Chemistry Advisory Board, Cambridge 2004-13; Hon. Fellow, Jesus College, Cambridge 2004-; Chair: Cambridge Foundation 2005-, Council of Commonwealth Societies 2005-12; Marsh Memorial Homes, Cape Town, South Africa; High Steward (Deputy Chancellor), Cambridge University 2010-; FRSA; FIPR; FIVCA; FRTS; Ten honorary doctorates from Russian, Romania, Moldovan, US and UK universities; Jean Monnet Prize for European TV coverage 1974; The Churchill Medal 2005; CBE 1985; Order of Merit (Germany) 1995; Grand Cross Order of Merit (Germany) 2001; Grand Cross Order of Merit (Romania) 2004; Knights Grand Cross (Germany) 2007; Order of the Red Eagle (Albania) 2014. Brooks's, Royal Automobile Club, Kennel Club, Beefsteak Club; House of Lords Yacht Club.

Publications: Europe at risk (1972); The Germans: who are they now? (1992); Thatcher and Kohl: old rivalries revisited (1996); Jamestown: The Voyage of English (2007); The Queen and the USA (2012).

Recreations: Boating, wines, foreign travel, art.

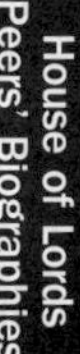

The Lord Watson of Richmond CBE, House of Lords, London SW1A 0PW
Tel: 020 7219 8661
CTN Communications, 114 St Martin's Lane, London WC2N 4BE *Tel:* 020 7395 4485
Email: alan.watson@ctn.co.uk

LABOUR

WATTS, LORD

WATTS (Life Baron), David Leonard Watts; cr 2015. Born 26 August 1951; Son of Leonard and Sarah Watts; Married Avril Davies 1972 (2 sons).

Education: Seel Road Secondary Modern School.

Non-political career: Labour Party organiser; Research assistant to: Angela Eagle MP 1992-93, John Evans MP 1993-97. Shop steward, United Biscuits AEU.

Political career: *House of Commons:* MP (Labour) for St Helens North 1997-2010, for St Helens North (revised boundary) 2010-15; PPS: to John Spellar: as Minister of State, Ministry of Defence 1999-2001, as Minister of Transport, Department for Transport, Local Government and the Regions 2001-02, as Minister of State, Department for Transport 2002-03, to John Prescott as Deputy Prime Minister 2003-05; Government Whip 2005-10; Opposition Whip 2010. Member: Finance and Services 1997-2001, 2005-06, Foreign Affairs 2010-12, Administration 2010-15, Arms Export Controls 2011-12, House of Commons Governance 2014-15. Chair: PLP North West Regional Group 2000-01, Parliamentary Labour Party 2012-15. *House of Lords:* Raised to the peerage as Baron Watts, of Ravenhead in the County of Merseyside 2015. Member: EU Home Affairs Sub-committee 2016-20, Social and Economic Impact of the Gambling Industry 2019-, EU International Agreements Sub-committee 2020-. *Other:* St Helens Metropolitan Borough Council: Councillor 1979-97, Leader 1993-97; Vice-chair, Association of Metropolitan Authorities.

Political interests: Regional policy, education, training.

Other: UK President, Euro Group of Industrial Regions 1989-93.

Recreations: Watching football and rugby, reading.

The Lord Watts, House of Lords, London SW1A 0PW
Tel: 020 7219 3000

CROSSBENCH

WAVERLEY, VISCOUNT

WAVERLEY (3rd Viscount, UK), John Desmond Forbes Anderson; cr. 1952. Born 31 October 1949; Son of 2nd Viscount.

Non-political career: Adviser to Chairman, CCC Group 1993-; Founder and Chairman, supplyfinder.com 2015-.

Political career: *House of Lords:* First entered House of Lords 1993; Elected hereditary peer 1999-; On leave of absence November 2013-March 2016.

Political interests: International affairs.

Other: Order of San Carlos (Grand Cross) (Colombia) 1998; Jubilee Medal (Kazakhstan) 2002; Chieftaincy (Yoruba) 2010; Anniversary Medal (Kyrgyzstan) 2010.

The Viscount Waverley, House of Lords, London SW1A 0PW
Tel: 020 7219 3174
Email: jd@lordwaverley.com Website: lordwaverley.com *Twitter:* @LordWaverley

CONSERVATIVE

WEI, LORD

WEI (Life Baron), Nathanael Ming-Yan Wei; cr 2010. Born 19 January 1977; Son of Rev Edward Wei and Mrs Meggy Wei; Married Cynthia Wei 2003 (2 sons).

Education: Sir Frank Markham School, Milton Keynes; Jesus College, Oxford (BA modern languages 1999); Chinese (basic Mandarin and Cantonese), French, German.

Non-political career: Consultant, McKinsey 1999-2001; Co-founder: Teach First 2001-05, Future Leaders 2005-07, The Challenge Network; Co-founder and partner, Shaftesbury Partnership 2006-10; Head of new ventures and strategic adviser, Absolute Return for Kids 2007-10; Community Foundation Network 2011-.

Political career: *House of Lords:* Raised to the peerage as Baron Wei, of Shoreditch in the London Borough of Hackney 2010. Government adviser, Big Society (unpaid), Cabinet Office 2010-11. Member, EU Internal Market Sub-committee 2015-18. *Other:* Founding co-chair, Conservative Friends of the Chinese.

Political interests: East Asia (including China, Japan, Mongolia, South Korea) and South East Asia.

Other: Young Global Leader, World Economic Forum; Fellow, Young Foundation 2005-10; Board member, Asia House 2012-.

The Lord Wei, House of Lords, London SW1A 0PW
Tel: 020 7219 5353 *Email:* wein@parliament.uk *Twitter:* @natwei

CROSSBENCH

WELLINGTON, DUKE OF

WELLINGTON (9th Duke of, UK), Arthur Charles Valerian Wellesley; cr 1814; Marquess of Wellington (UK) 1812; Marquess of Douro (UK) 1814; Earl of Mornington (I) 1760; Earl of Wellington (UK) 1812; Viscount Wellesley (I) 1760; Viscount Wellington (UK) 1809; Baron Mornington (I) 1746; Baron Douro (UK) 1809. Born 19 August 1945; Son of 8th Duke; Married Antonia Elizabeth Bridgid Luise OBE 1977 (daughter of HRH the late Prince Friedrich Georg Wilhelm Christoph of Prussia) (2 sons 3 daughters).

Education: Eton College; Christ Church, Oxford (MA PPE).

Non-political career: Deputy chair, Thames Valley Broadcasting 1975-84; Director: Antofagasta and Bolivia Railway 1977-80, Eucalyptus Pulp Mills 1979-88, Transatlantic Holdings 1983-95, Global Asset Management Worldwide 1984-2013; Deputy chair, Deltec Panamerica 1985-89; Chair, Deltec Securities 1985-89; Director, Continental and Industrial Trust 1987-90; Deputy chair, Guinness Mahon Holdings 1988-91; Chair: Dunhill Holdings 1991-93, Richemont Holdings 1993-, Framlington Group 1994-2005, Sun Life and Provincial Holdings 1995-2000; Director: Compagnie Financière Richemont 1999-2017, Sanofi 2002-14, Pernod Richard 2003-11, RIT Capital Partners 2010-.

Political career: *House of Commons:* Contested (Conservative) Islington North October 1974 general election. *House of Lords:* Succeeded his father to the dukedom of Ciudad Rodrigo 2010 and to the dukedom of Wellington and other honours 2014. Prince of Waterloo (Netherlands) 1815; Duke of Victoria and Marquess of Torres Vedras (Portugal); Count of Vimiero (Portugal) 1811; Duke of Ciudad Rodrigo and a Grandee of Spain (1st Class) (Spain) 1812. Elected hereditary peer 2015-. Member, EU Financial Affairs Sub-committee 2016-17. *Other:* European Parliament: MEP for: Surrey 1979-84, Surrey West 1984-89. Left Conservatives September 2019, non-affiliated September 2019-September 2020, now sits as Crossbench. Councillor, Basingstoke Borough Council 1978-79; Member of council, Royal College of Art 1991-97; DL, Hampshire 1999.

Other: Commissioner, English Heritage 2003-07; Chair of council, King's College London 2007-16; Trustee, Royal United Services Institute 2017-; Freeman, City of London 2016; Hon D. Litt King's College London 2016; Order of Isabel the Catholic (Spain): Knight 1986, Grand Cross 2000; Grand Officer, Order of Merit (Portugal) 1987; OBE 1999. Honorary Member: Cavalry and Guards Club, Army and Navy Club.

His Grace the Duke of Wellington OBE, House of Lords, London SW1A 0PW
Tel: 020 7219 3000 *Email:* wellington@parliament.uk
Tel: 020 7514 2717

LABOUR

WEST OF SPITHEAD, LORD

WEST OF SPITHEAD (Life Baron), Alan William John West; cr 2007. Born 21 April 1948; Son of Walter West, Admiralty civil servant, and Jacqueline West, née Bliss; Married Rosemary Linington Childs 1973 (2 sons 1 daughter).

Education: Windsor Grammar School; Clydebank High School; Dartmouth (Britannia Royal Naval College); RN staff course 1978; Royal College of Defence Studies 1992; Higher Command and Staff course 1993; French (basic).

Non-political career: Royal Navy 1965-: Seagoing posts 1966-73; Commanding officer (CO) HMS Yarnton 1973; HMSs Juno 1976, Ambuscade 1977, Norfolk 1979; CO HMS Ardent 1980; Naval Staff, Ministry of Defence (MoD) 1982; CO HMS Bristol 1987; Defence Intelligence Staff, MoD 1989; MoD 1993-96: Director Naval Staff Duties 1993, Naval Secretary 1994-96; Commander UK Task Group and of Anti-submarine Warfare Striking Force 1996-97; Chief of Defence Intelligence, MoD 1997-2001; Commander-in-Chief Fleet and East Atlantic and Commander Allied Naval Forces North 2001-02; Chief of Naval Staff and First Sea Lord, MoD 2002-06; Chairman, defence advisory board, QinetiQ 2006-07; Member, foreign advisory board, HSBC 2010-11; Strategic adviser, Primetake plc 2011-12; Chairman: Magic Industries Ltd 2012-13, Spearfish 2012-, MCM Solutions 2013-. Active List, Royal Navy.

Political career: *House of Lords:* Raised to the peerage as Baron West of Spithead, of Seaview in the County of Isle of Wight 2007. Parliamentary Under-Secretary of State (Security and Counter-terrorism) and Government Spokesperson, Home Office 2007-10; Minister for Cyber Security 2009-10; Member, Intelligence and Security Committee of Parliament 2020-. Member, Joint Committee on National Security Strategy 2014-17. *Other:* Trustee, Imperial War Museum 2007-.

Political interests: Security, defence, foreign affairs, shipping/maritime; South West Asia, Horn of Africa, Gulf, Japan, Pakistan, Scandinavian countries, Ukraine.

Other: ELN; Younger Brother, Trinity House 1986-; President, Merchant Navy Medal Fund 2006-; Chairman, National Security Forum 2008-10; Member, RUSI; Master Mariner; President: Transport on Water, Great River Race, Merchant Navy Association; Member: Naval Review, Top Level Group, Global Strategy Fourm, Woodland Trust, UK National Defence Association, UK Defence Forum, Friends of the City Churches; St Anne's Lime House, Bollington Sea Cadet Unit, Dockland Sinfonia, Medway Queen, Albert McKenzie Memorial Fund, Ardent Association; Liveryman, Honourable Company of Master Mariners; Company of Watermen and Lightermen of the River Thames; Chancellor, Southampton Solent University 2006-18; Honorary doctorate 2006; Trench Gascoigne prize winner; DSC 1982; KCB 2000; ADC 2002; GCB 2004; PC 2010. Navy Club of 1765 & 85, Royal Naval Club, Royal Yacht Squadron, St Barbara Association, British American Forces Dining Club, Anchorites, Britannia Association, Pepys Club, Destroyer Club, Pilgrims, Merchant Trading with the Continent, RNSA, Woodroffes, The Cachalots, The Old Gang Club.

Publications: Seaford House Paper (2002); Contributor, The Oxford Handbook of War.

Recreations: Boating, military history, OMRS.

Rt Hon Admiral the Lord West of Spithead GCB DSC, House of Lords, London SW1A 0PW
Tel: 020 7219 5953 *Email:* westaa@parliament.uk
Email: westbuzz1@btinternet.com

CONSERVATIVE

WHARTON OF YARM, LORD

WHARTON OF YARM (Life Baron), James Stephen Wharton; cr 2020. Born 16 February 1984.

Education: Yarm School; Durham University (LLB 2005); College of Law, York (LPC 2006).

Non-political career: Solicitor, BHP Law 2006-10; Hume Brophy: Senior Advisor 2017-18, Chair, UK Corporate and Public Affairs 2018-.

Political career: *House of Commons:* MP for Stockton South 2010-17. Contested Stockton South 2017 general election; Parliamentary Under-Secretary of State: (Minister for Local Growth and the Northern Powerhouse), Department for Communities and Local Government 2015-16, Department for International Development 2016-17. Member, Public Accounts

2010-12. *House of Lords:* Raised to the peerage as Baron Wharton of Yarm, of Yarm in the County of North Yorkshire 2020. *Other:* Constituency chair 2002-06; *Other:* Chair, Office for Students 2021-; Campaign manager, Boris Johnson leadership campaign 2019.

Political interests: Education, young people, law and order; Sri Lanka.

Other: Senior adviser, Squire Patton Boggs 2017-; Adviser to the Board, AQUIND 2017-; Senior fellow, Policy Exchange 2018-; Law society; *The House Magazine* Rising Star, Dods Parliamentary Awards 2014. United and Cecil Club.

Recreations: Countryside, walking, eating out, friends and family.

The Lord Wharton of Yarm, House of Lords, London SW1A 0PW
Tel: 020 7219 3000

CROSSBENCH

WHEATCROFT, BARONESS

WHEATCROFT (Life Baroness), Patience Jane Wheatcroft; cr 2010. Born 28 September 1951; Daughter of Anthony and Ruth Wheatcroft; Married Anthony Salter 1976 (2 sons 1 daughter).

Education: Wolverhampton High School for Girls; Queen Elizabeth's Grammar School, Tamworth; Birmingham University (LLB 1972).

Non-political career: Deputy city editor, *The Times* 1984-86; Assistant city editor, *Daily Mail* 1986-88; Editor, *Retail Week* 1988-93; Deputy city editor, *Mail on Sunday* 1994-97; Business and city editor, *The Times* 1997-2006; Editor, *Sunday Telegraph* 2006-07; Non-executive director: Barclays plc 2008-09, Shaftesbury plc 2008-09; Editor-in-chief, *Wall Street Journal Europe* 2009-10; Non-executive director: St James's Place plc, Fiat Chrysler Automobiles.

Political career: *House of Lords:* Raised to the peerage as Baroness Wheatcroft, of Blackheath in the London Borough of Greenwich 2010. Member: EU Sub-committee G (Social Policies and Consumer Protection) 2011-12, Joint Committee on the Draft Financial Services Bill 2011-12, Constitution 2012-14, Economic Affairs Finance Bill Sub-committee 2012-13, 2014, 2015-16, Olympic and Paralympic Legacy 2013-14, Economic Affairs 2014-17. *Other:* Left Conservatives November 2019 Non-affiliated November 2019-January 2021; Crossbench January 2021-.

Political interests: Business, finance, economics, arts; China, India.

Other: Director, Association of Leading Visitor Attractions; Chair, *Financial Times* Complaints Commission; Action Aid, St James's Place Foundation; Hon. Doctorate, City University, London.

Recreations: Opera, skiing, theatre.

The Baroness Wheatcroft, House of Lords, London SW1A 0PW
Tel: 020 7219 5353
Email: patiencewheatcroft@googlemail.com

LABOUR

WHEELER, BARONESS

Opposition Deputy Chief Whip; Opposition Spokesperson for Health and Social Care

WHEELER (Life Baroness), Margaret Eileen Joyce Wheeler; cr 2010. Born 25 March 1949; Partner.

Education: St Ursula's Convent School, Greenwich; Nottingham University (BA politics and psychology 1971).

Non-political career: Publishing/editorial trainee, Routledge and Kegan Paul 1971-73; Confederation of Health Service Employees 1973-93: Head of editorial department, Press officer, Campaigns strategies, Parliamentary and international officer 1973-88, Director of specialist and support services 1988-93; Unison: Director of organisation development 1993-97, Director of organisation and staff development 1997-2010; Natural carers strategy implementation team, Department of Health 2009-10. Member: National Union of Journalists 1972-2010, Unison 1997-2010.

Political career: *House of Lords:* Raised to the peerage as Baroness Wheeler, of Blackfriars in the City of London 2010. Opposition Whip 2010-13; Opposition Senior Whip 2013-18; Opposition Spokesperson for Health/Health and Social Care 2015-; Opposition Deputy Chief Whip 2018-. Member: Consumer Insurance (Disclosure and Representations) Bill 2011-12, Services 2018-. *Other:* Former member: Commission on Social Justice, Enquiry panel into productivity and high performance, Department of Trade and Industry/Work Foundation; Investors in People Advisory Board, UK Commission for Employment and Skills.

Political interests: Health and social care; disabilities; China, India.

Other: Trustee and board member: One World Action, Carer Support, Elmbridge -2017; Chair and board member, Blackfriars Settlement; Christian Aid; MBE 2005.

Recreations: Walking, theatre, arts, music.

The Baroness Wheeler MBE, House of Lords, London SW1A 0PW
Tel: 020 7219 8909 *Email:* wheelerm@parliament.uk

WHITAKER, BARONESS

LABOUR

WHITAKER (Life Baroness), Janet Alison Whitaker; cr. 1999. Born 20 February 1936; Daughter of Alan Stewart and Ella Stewart, née Saunders; Married Ben Whitaker CBE 1964 (died 2014) (2 sons 1 daughter).

Education: Nottingham High School for Girls; Girton College, Cambridge (BA English 1957); Bryn Mawr College, USA (MA English 1959); Harvard University, USA (Radcliffe Fellow 1960); French.

Non-political career: Editor, André Deutsch (Publishers) 1961-66; Various posts, Health and Safety Executive 1974-88; Department of Education and Employment 1988-96: Head of sex equality branch 1992-96; Consultant: Commission for Racial Equality 1995-96, Commonwealth Secretariat 1996; Assessor, Citizens' Charter Chartermark 1996; Consultant, Committee of Reference, Friends Provident Group 2000-08. Member, FDA.

Political career: *House of Lords:* Raised to the peerage as Baroness Whitaker, of Beeston in the County of Nottinghamshire 1999. International Development Liaison Peer 1999-2007. Member: European Union Select Committee Sub-committee F (Social Affairs, Education and Home Affairs) 1999-2003, Joint Committee on Human Rights 2000-03, Joint Committee on Draft Corruption Bill 2003, Intergovernmental Organisations 2007-08, Joint Committee on Draft Bribery Bill 2009, Built Environment 2015-16, Natural Environment and Rural Communities Act 2006 2017-18, Regenerating Seaside Towns and Communities 2018-19, Sentencing (Pre-consolidation Amendments) Bill 2019, Highgate Cemetery Bill [HL] 2020-. *Other:* Magistrate 1985-2006; Member, Employment Tribunal 1995-2000; Deputy chair and chair, Camden Racial Equality Council 1996-99; Non-executive director, Tavistock and Portman NHS Trust 1997-2001; Member, Immigration Complaints Audit Committee 1998-99; Chair, Department for Education Stakeholder Group for Gypsy, Roma and Traveller Education 2014-.

Political interests: Architecture and design, international development, race relations; Africa, Asia, Europe.

Other: Member: Inter-Parliamentary Union, Commonwealth Parliamentary Association, UK advisory panel, United Nations Association 2006-; Member/associate, Fabian Society 1962; Council member, SOS Sahel 1997-2011; Chair, Working Men's College for Men and Women 1998-2001; Advisory council, Transparency International (UK) 2001-09; Deputy chair, Independent Television Commission (ITC) 2001-03; Patron, Runnymede Trust 2001-; Overseas Development Institute: Council member 2003-11, Trustee 2006-09; Trustee, Unicef UK 2003-09; Patron, British Stammering Association 2003-; Practical Action (formerly Intermediate Technology Development Group) 2004-10; British Humanist Association: Vice-President 2004-, Patron 2014-; Patron, One World Trust 2004-; Member, Advisory Board, British Institute of Human Rights 2005-; Patron, Student Partnerships Worldwide 2005-10; President: South Downs Society 2012-16, Friends, Families and Travellers 2013-, Advisory Council for the Education of Romany and Other Travellers 2014-, Newhaven Historical Society 2015-; Patron, Hillcrest Community Centre 2017; Newhaven Coastal Communities Team: Chair 2017-19, President 2019-; FRIBA; Fellow, Working Men's College; Hon. Doctorate, Buckinghamshire New University 2019.

Recreations: Travel, walking, art, music, reading.

The Baroness Whitaker, House of Lords, London SW1A 0PW
Tel: 020 7219 5353

CONSERVATIVE

WHITBY, LORD

WHITBY (Life Baron), Michael John Whitby; cr 2013. Born 6 February 1948; Married Gaynor.

Education: James Watt Technical Grammar School, Birmingham; German.

Non-political career: Worked in the cultural sector in Liverpool; Lecturer in business and management studies; Chair and managing director, Skeldings Ltd.

Political career: *House of Commons:* Contested (Conservative) Delyn 1992 general election. *House of Lords:* Raised to the peerage as Baron Whitby, of Harborne in the City of Birmingham 2013. *Other:* Contested Midlands West 1987 European Parliament by-election. Member, Conservative Party 1979-; Board member, Conservative Councillors' Association. Birmingham City Council: Councillor 1997-2014, Leader, Conservative Group 2003-14, Council Leader 2004-12; Member, West Midlands Police and Crime Panel; Governor, Baskerville School, Harborne, Birmingham; Vice-president, Local Government Association.

Other: Fellow, Institute of Directors; Director: Birmingham Science Park Aston Ltd, Marketing Birmingham Ltd; Member, Greater Birmingham and Solihull Local Enterprise Partnership; Board member: Advantage West Midlands, National Exhibition Centre; Committee member, THSH Trust.

The Lord Whitby, House of Lords, London SW1A 0PW
Tel: 020 7219 5353

LABOUR

WHITTY, LORD

WHITTY (Life Baron), John Lawrence (Larry) Whitty; cr. 1996. Born 15 June 1943; Son of late Frederick James and Kathleen May Whitty; Married Tanya Gibson 1969 (divorced 1986) (2 sons); married Angela Forrester 1993.

Education: Latymer Upper School, London; St John's College, Cambridge (BA economics 1965); French, German.

Non-political career: Hawker Siddeley Aviation 1960-62; Civil servant, Ministry of Aviation and Ministry of Technology 1965-70; Assistant secretary, Trades Union Congress 1970-73; Research officer, General, Municipal, Boilermakers and Allied Trade Union 1973-85; Chair, Cofeely East London Energy 2005-10. Member, GMB.

Political career: *House of Lords:* Raised to the peerage as Baron Whitty, of Camberwell in the London Borough of Southwark 1996. Government Whip 1997-98; Government Spokesperson for European Affairs, International Development, Foreign and Commonwealth Affairs, Education and Employment 1997-98; Parliamentary Under-Secretary of State and Government Spokesperson: Department of the Environment, Transport and the Regions (Minister for Roads and Road Safety) 1998-2001, Department for Environment, Food and Rural Affairs 2001-05. Member, Draft Climate Change Bill Joint Committee 2007; Co-opted member, EU Sub-committee B (Internal Market) 2007-10; Member: EU Sub-committees: G (Social Policies and Consumer Protection) 2010-12, D (Agriculture, Fisheries, Environment and Energy) 2012-15, European Union 2015-19; Chair, EU Internal Market Sub-committee 2015-19; Member: Trade Union and Party Funding 2016, Food, Poverty, Health and the Environment 2019-, Procedure and Privileges 2020-. Vice-chair, PLP Departmental Group for Energy and Climate Change 2010-15. *Other:* Labour Party: General Secretary 1985-94, European Co-ordinator 1994-97. Chair, National Consumer Council 2006-08; Member, National Water Regulation Authority (Ofwat) 2006; Non-executive director, Environment Agency 2006-12; Chair, Consumer Focus 2008-10; Vice-president, Local Government Association; Member, Advisory Committee on Business Appointments 2019-.

Political interests: Employment, energy, environment, food, Europe, consumers, education; China, France, Germany, Ireland, Italy, Japan.

Other: Member: Friends of the Earth, Fabian Society; President, Combined Heat and Power Association 2005-11; Chair: Housing Voice 2009-10, Cheshire Lehman Fund 2009-16, Road Safety Foundation 2014-; President, Environmental Protection UK 2016-; Member, Forde Inquiry Panel 2020-; Alzheimer's Society; PC 2005.

Recreations: Theatre, cinema, swimming.

Rt Hon the Lord Whitty, House of Lords, London SW1A 0PW
Tel: 020 7219 3118 *Email:* whittyl@parliament.uk

PLAID CYMRU

WIGLEY, LORD

WIGLEY (Life Baron), Dafydd Wigley; cr 2011. Born 1 April 1943; Son of Elfyn and Myfanwy Wigley; Married Elinor Bennett 1967 (1 son 1 daughter 2 sons deceased).

Education: Caernarfon Grammar School; Rydal School, Colwyn Bay; Manchester University (BSc physics 1964); Welsh (fluent), French (modest).

Non-political career: Finance staff, Ford Motor Co 1964-67; Chief cost accountant and financial planning manager, Mars Ltd 1967-71; Financial controller, Hoover Ltd, Merthyr Plant 1971-74; Chair, Alpha-Dyffryn Ltd (Electronics) 1987-91; Board member, S4C 2003-06. Former member, Association of Scientific, Technical and Managerial Staffs (ASTMS).

Political career: *House of Commons:* Contested Merioneth 1970 general election. MP (Plaid Cymru) for Caernarfon February 1974-2001; Sponsor Disabled Persons Act 1981; Plaid Cymru: Whip 1987-91, Spokesperson for Constitutional Affairs 1997-2000. *House of Lords:* Raised to the peerage as Baron Wigley, of Caernarfon in the County of Gwynedd 2011. Member: Olympic and Paralympic Legacy 2013-14, EU Internal Market Sub-committee 2017-20, EU Goods Sub-committee 2020-. *Other:* Contested North Wales region 1994 European Parliament election; National Assembly for Wales: AM for Caernarfon constituency 1999-2003: Shadow First Minister 1999-2000, Shadow Secretary for Finance 1999-2000, Contested North Wales region 2007 election. Leader and president, Plaid Cymru 1981-84, 1991-2000. Councillor, Merthy Tydfil County Borough Council 1972-74; Vice-president, Local Government Association 2017-.

Political interests: Industry, employment, disability, Europe, minority languages; Argentina, Ireland, New Zealand, Slovenia, USA.

Other: Vice-President, Wales Council for the Disabled; President, Spastic Society for Wales 1985-90; Member, Mencap Profound Mental Handicap Study Committee 1987-97; Vice-President: Mencap in Wales 1990-, Federation of Economic Development Authorities (FEDA); Patron, Autism Wales 2003-; President: Gwynedd Family History Society 2005-, National Library of Wales 2008-12; Hon. member, Welsh Gorsedd of Bards; NSPCC, Mencap Wales, Contact a Family; Freedom: Borough of Arfon 1996, Town of Caernarfon 2001; Pro-chancellor, University of Wales 2003-06; Honorary fellowship, Bangor University; Hon. LLB University of Wales; National Federation of the Blind Grimshaw Memorial Award 1981; PC 1997. Clwb y Castell Club, Caernarfon.

Publications: Co-author: An Economic Plan for Wales (1970), O Ddifri (1992), A Democratic Wales in an United Europe (1994), A Fair Choice for Wales (1996); Columnist, *Daily Post* 2009-.

Recreations: Chess, walking, soccer, Caernarfon Town FC, rugby, gardening.

Rt Hon the Lord Wigley, House of Lords, London SW1A 0PW
Tel: 020 7219 0780 *Email:* wigleyd@parliament.uk *Twitter:* @Dafydd_Wigley

LABOUR

WILCOX OF NEWPORT, BARONESS

Opposition Spokesperson for Women and Equalities; Opposition Whip

WILCOX OF NEWPORT (Life Baroness), Deborah Ann Wilcox; cr 2019.

Education: Central School of Speech and Drama (BEd drama, education 1979); University of Wales, Cardiff (MA media studies 1997).

Non-political career: Head of Performing Arts Faculty, Hawthorn High School 1994-2014.

Political career: *House of Lords:* Raised to the peerage as Baroness Wilcox of Newport, of Newport in the City of Newport 2019. Opposition Whip 2020-; Opposition Spokesperson for Women and Equalities 2020-. *Other:* Contested South Wales East region 2011 and 2016 National Assembly for Wales elections. Newport City Council: Councillor 2004-19, Cabinet Member for Education and Young People 2004-16, Leader of the Council 2016-19; Leader, Welsh Local Government Association 2017-; Vice-president, Local Government Association 2020-.

Other: Member, Forde Inquiry Panel 2020-; Fellow, Royal Society of Arts 2018-.

The Baroness Wilcox of Newport, House of Lords, London SW1A 0PW
Twitter: @TheLadyWilcox

CONSERVATIVE

WILLETTS, LORD

WILLETTS (Life Baron), David Lindsay Willetts; cr 2015. Born 9 March 1956; Son of John and Hilary Willetts; Married Hon Sarah Butterfield 1986 (1 son 1 daughter).

Education: King Edward's School, Birmingham; Christ Church, Oxford (BA philosophy, politics and economics 1978); German (fluent).

Non-political career: HM Treasury 1978-84: Private secretary to Nicholas Ridley MP as Financial Secretary 1981-82, Principal, Monetary Policy Division 1982-84; Prime Minister's Downing Street Policy Unit 1984-86; Director of Studies, Centre for Policy Studies 1987-92; Consultant director, Conservative Research Department 1987-92; Director: Retirement Security Ltd 1988-94, Electra Corporate Ventures Ltd 1988-94; Governor, Ditchley Foundation 1998-; Visiting Fellow, Nuffield College, Oxford 1999-2006; Member, Global Commission on Ageing 2000-10; Visiting Fellow, Cass Business School 2004-07; Non-executive board member, National Council for Universities and Business 2015-; Executive chair, Resolution Foundation 2015-; Senior non-executive director, Surrey Satellite Technologies Ltd 2015-; Visiting Professor, King's College London; Honorary Fellow, Nuffield College, Oxford 2016-.

Political career: *House of Commons:* MP (Conservative) for Havant 1992-2010, for Havant (revised boundary) 2010-15; PPS to Sir Norman Fowler as Chairman of Conservative Party 1993-94; Assistant Government Whip 1994-95; Government Whip July-November 1995; Office of Public Service: Parliamentary Secretary 1995-96, Paymaster General July-December 1996; Opposition Spokesperson for Employment 1997-98; Shadow Secretary of State for: Education and Employment 1998-99, Social Security 1999-2001, Work and Pensions 2001-05, Welfare Reform 2004-05, Trade and Industry 2005, Education and Skills/Innovation, Universities and Skills 2005-09; Shadow Minister for Universities and Skills 2009-10; Minister of State for Universities and Science, Department for Business, Innovation and Skills 2010-14. Member, Social Security 1992-93. Member, Conservative Economic Affairs/Enterprise/ Pensions/Social Affairs Policy Committee. *House of Lords:* Raised to the peerage as Baron Willetts, of Havant in the County of Hampshire 2015. Member, Risk Assessment and Risk Planning 2020-. *Other:* Conservative Party: Chair, Conservative Research Department 1997, Member, Policy Board, Head of policy co-ordination 2003-04. Member: Lambeth and Lewisham Family Practitioners' Committee 1987-90, Parkside Health Authority 1988-90, Social Security Advisory Committee 1989-92; Trustee, Science Museum Group.

Political interests: Economic policy, health, social security, education, science; China, Germany, USA.

Other: Member, Competitiveness Council, Council of the European Union 2010-15; Board member, Biotech Industry Association 2015-; Non-executive director, Biotech Growth Trust 2015-; Chair, British Science Association 2015-; Trustee director, Francis Crick Institute 2015-; Honorary President, International Student Foundation 2016-; Chancellor, Leicester University 2018-; Honorary degree, Bath University 2017; PC 2010. Hurlingham, Garrick Club.

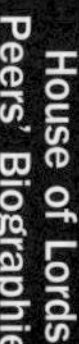

Publications: Modern Conservatism (1992); Civic Conservatism (1994); Blair's Gurus (1996); Why Vote Conservative (1997); Welfare to Work (1998); After the Landslide (1999); Browned-off: What's Wrong with Gordon Brown's Social Policy (2000); Co-author, Tax Credits: Do They Add Up? (2002); Left Out, Left Behind (2003); Old Europe? Demographic Change and Pension Reform (2003); Conservatives in Birmingham (2008); The Pinch – How the baby boomers took their children's future – and why they should give it back (Atlantic Books, 2010); A University Education (OUP Oxford, 2019).

Recreations: Swimming, reading, cycling.

Rt Hon the Lord Willetts, House of Lords, London SW1A 0PW
Tel: 020 7219 3000
Resolution Foundation, 2 Queen Anne's Gate, London SW1H 9AA
Email: david.willetts@resolutionfoundation.org

CONSERVATIVE

WILLIAMS OF TRAFFORD, BARONESS

Minister of State and Government Spokesperson, Home Office

WILLIAMS OF TRAFFORD (Life Baroness), Susan Frances Maria Williams; cr 2013. Born 16 May 1967; Daughter of John McElroy and Mary McElroy; Married Alex Williams 2005 (1 son 2 daughters).

Education: La Sagesse High School, Jesmond; Huddersfield Polytechnic (BSc applied nutrition 1989).

Non-political career: Nutritionist, Action and Research into Multiple Sclerosis (ARMS) 1992-2002; Leadership consultant, Local Government Improvement and Development 2006-12; Director, North West Rail Campaign 2011-14; Executive director, Atlantic Gateway 2012-14.

Political career: *House of Commons:* Contested (as Susan Fildes) (Conservative) Wythenshawe and Sale East 2001 and (as Susan Williams) Bolton West 2010 general elections. *House of Lords:* Raised to the peerage as Baroness Williams of Trafford, of Hale in the County of Greater Manchester 2013. Government Whip 2014-15; Government Spokesperson for: Communities and Local Government 2014-15, Home Office 2014-15, 2016-, Law Officers 2014-15, Northern Ireland 2014-15, Scotland 2014-15, Wales 2014, Education (Women and Equalities) 2015-16; Parliamentary Under-Secretary of State, Department for Communities and Local Government 2015-16; Government Spokesperson for Women and Equalities 2016-20; Home Office: Minister of State 2016-17, 2020-, Minister of State for Countering Extremism 2017-20; Minister for Equalities, Government Equalities Office 2018-20. *Other:* Trafford Metropolitan Borough Council: Councillor 1998-2011, Leader, Conservative group 2002-09, Council Leader 2004-09; Non-executive director, North West Development Agency 2007-11; Authority member, Greater Manchester Police Authority 2008-09; Vice-President, Local Government Association 2018-19.

Political interests: Local government, transport, foreign affairs.

Other: Board member, Central Salford Urban Regeneration Company 2008-10; Chair (North West), Heritage Lottery Fund.

Recreations: Walking, cycling, gardening.

The Baroness Williams of Trafford, House of Lords, London SW1A 0PW
Tel: 020 7219 8110 *Email:* williamssb@parliament.uk *Twitter:* @SusanBaroness

LIBERAL DEMOCRAT

WILLIS OF KNARESBOROUGH, LORD

Chair, Select Committee on National Plan for Sport and Recreation

WILLIS OF KNARESBOROUGH (Life Baron), Philip George Willis; cr 2010. Born 30 November 1941; Son of late George Willis, postman, and late Norah Willis, nurse; Married Heather Sellars 1974 (1 son 1 daughter).

Education: Burnley Grammar School; City of Leeds and Carnegie College (Cert Ed 1963); Birmingham University (BPhil education 1978); French.

Non-political career: Head teacher: Ormesby School, Cleveland 1978-82, John Smeaton Community High School, Leeds 1983-97. Member, Secondary Heads Association.

Political career: *House of Commons:* MP (Liberal Democrat) for Harrogate and Knaresborough 1997-2010; Liberal Democrat: Whip 1997-99, Spokesperson for Further, Higher and Adult Education 1997-99, Principal Spokesperson for Education and Employment 1999-2000, Shadow Secretary of State for Education and Skills 2000-05. Member: Education and Employment (Education Sub-Committee) 1999-2000, Education and Employment 1999-2000, Liaison 2005-10; Chair: Science and Technology 2005-07, Joint Committee on the Draft Human Tissue and Embryos Bill 2007, Innovation, Universities[, Science] and Skills/Science and Technology 2007-10, National Plan for Sport and Recreation 2020-. *House of Lords:* Raised to the peerage as Baron Willis of Knaresborough, of Harrogate in the County of North Yorkshire 2010. Science and Technology: Co-opted member 2010-11, Member 2011-15; Member: Science and Technology Sub-committee I 2012-13, Long-Term Sustainability of the NHS 2016-17. *Other:* Member, Association of Liberal Democrat Councillors. Harrogate Borough Council: Councillor 1988-99, First Liberal Democrat Leader 1990-97; North Yorkshire County Council: Councillor 1993-97, Deputy Group Leader 1993-97; Vice-President, Local Government Association 2010-11.

Political interests: Inclusive education, health, local and regional government, science policy, higher education reform; Ireland.

Other: Council member, Foundation for Science and Technology; Chair, Association of Medical Research Charities 2010-15; Council member, National Environment Research Council 2011-; Chair: NIHR Collaboration for Leadership in Applied Health Research and Care, Yorkshire and the Humber 2014-19, Applied Research Collaboration (Yorks and Humber) 2019-; National Children's Homes, St Michael's Hospice, Harrogate, Horticap, Bluecoat Wood Nursery, Harrogate Homeless Project; Royal Society of Arts; Royal College of Nursing; Doctor of Science: Salford University, London City University; Man of the Year, *Times Educational Supplement* 2002.

Publications: Quality and Compassion: the future of nursing (2012); Shape of Caring - Raising the Bar (2017).

Recreations: Theatre, music, dance (especially ballet), football (Leeds United FC).

The Lord Willis of Knaresborough, House of Lords, London SW1A 0PW
Tel: 020 7219 5709 *Email:* willisg@parliament.uk *Twitter:* @LordWillisg

NON-AFFILIATED

WILLOUGHBY DE BROKE, LORD

WILLOUGHBY DE BROKE (21st Baron, E), Leopold David Verney; cr. 1491. Born 14 September 1938; Son of 20th Baron, MC, AFC; Married Petra Aird 1965 (divorced 1989) (3 sons); married Mrs Alexandra du Luart 2003.

Education: Le Rosey, Switzerland; New College, Oxford (BA modern languages 1961).

Non-political career: Chair: St Martin's Magazines 1992-2008, SM Theatre Ltd 1992-; President, Heart of England Tourist Board 1999-2004.

Political career: *House of Lords:* First entered House of Lords 1986; Elected hereditary peer 1999-. Member: European Union 1997-2000, European Union Sub-committee D (Environment, Agriculture, Public Health and Consumer Protection) 1997-2001. *Other:* Vice-President, Conservatives Against a Federal Europe (CAFE) 1997-2007. DL, Warwickshire 1999-2016.

Political interests: Rural affairs, EU; Europe, Hong Kong, Tibet.

Other: Patron, Warwickshire Association of Boys' Clubs 1990-04; Honorary governor, Royal Shakespeare Theatre 1992-; President, CPRE Warwickshire 2002-16; Chair, Warwickshire Hunt Ltd 2005-12. All England Lawn Tennis.

The Lord Willoughby de Broke DL, House of Lords, London SW1A 0PW
Tel: 020 7219 4941 *Email:* willoughbyl@parliament.uk
Ditchford Farm, Moreton in Marsh GL56 9RD *Tel:* 01608 661990

LABOUR

WILLS, LORD

WILLS (Life Baron), Michael David Wills; cr 2010. Born 20 May 1952; Son of late Stephen Wills and Elizabeth Wills; Married Jill Freeman 1984 (3 sons 2 daughters).

Education: Haberdashers' Aske's, Elstree; Clare College, Cambridge (BA history 1973).

Non-political career: Third secretary, later second secretary, HM Diplomatic Service 1976-80; Researcher, later producer, London Weekend Television 1980-84; Director, Juniper Productions TV production company 1984-97. Member, TGWU.

Political career: *House of Commons:* MP (Labour) for North Swindon 1997-2010; Parliamentary Under-Secretary of State: Department of Trade and Industry (Minister for Small Firms, Trade and Industry) 1999, Department for Education and Employment 1999-2001; Parliamentary Secretary, Lord Chancellor's Department 2001-02; Parliamentary Under-Secretary of State, Home Office 2002-03: (for Criminal Justice System IT 2002, Information Technology in the Criminal Justice System 2003); Minister of State, Ministry of Justice 2007-10. *House of Lords:* Raised to the peerage as Baron Wills, of North Swindon in the County of Wiltshire and Woodside Park in the London Borough of Barnet 2010. Member, Electoral Registration and Administration Act 2013 2019-.

Other: Board member), Institute of Germanic and Romance Studies, University of London; President, Wiltshire Association of Local Councils; Member, advisory council, Transparency International UK; PC 2008.

Rt Hon the Lord Wills, House of Lords, London SW1A 0PW
Tel: 020 7219 5353

CROSSBENCH

WILSON OF DINTON, LORD

WILSON OF DINTON (Life Baron), Richard Thomas James Wilson; cr. 2002. Born 11 October 1942; Son of late Richard Ridley and Frieda Bell Wilson, née Finlay; Married Caroline Margaret Lee 1972 (1 son 1 daughter).

Education: Radley College; Clare College, Cambridge (BA law 1964; LLM 1965).

Non-political career: Called to Bar, Middle Temple 1965; Assistant principal, Board of Trade 1966-71; Principal, Cabinet Office 1971-73; Department of Energy 1974-86: Principal establishment and finance officer 1983-86; Seconded to Cabinet Office 1986-90: Head, economic secretariat 1987-90; Deputy secretary, industry, HM Treasury 1990-92; Permanent Secretary, Department of the Environment 1992-94; Permanent Under-Secretary, Home Office 1994-97; Cabinet Secretary and Head, Home Civil Service 1998-2002; Master of Emmanuel College, Cambridge 2002-12.

Political career: *House of Lords:* Raised to the peerage as Baron Wilson of Dinton, of Dinton in the County of Buckinghamshire 2002.

Other: Trustee, Ewing Foundation 1995-; Non-executive director, BSkyB 2003-12; Trustee, Cicely Saunders Foundation 2004-; President, Chartered Institute of Personnel and Development 2004-06; Chairman, Radley College 2004-10; Trustee, Syndic Fitzwilliam Museum 2005-11; Chairman: C Hoare & Co 2006-16, Prince's Teaching Institute 2006-09; Trustee, Cambridge Arts Theatre 2008-12; CB 1991; KCB 1997; GCB 2001.

Recreations: Home, garden.

The Lord Wilson of Dinton GCB, House of Lords, London SW1A 0PW
Tel: 020 7219 5353
Email: rw272@cam.ac.uk

CROSSBENCH

WILSON OF TILLYORN, LORD

WILSON OF TILLYORN (Life Baron), David Clive Wilson; cr. 1992. Born 14 February 1935; Son of late Rev. William Skinner Wilson and late Enid Wilson; Married Natasha Alexander 1967 (2 sons).

Education: Trinity College, Glenalmond; Keble College, Oxford (Scholar, BA history 1958, MA); London University (PhD modern Chinese history 1973); Chinese (Mandarin), French.

Non-political career: Foreign Service 1958-68: Served Vientiane, Laos 1959-60, Language student, Hong Kong 1960-62, First Secretary, Peking Embassy 1963-65, FCO 1965-68; Editor, *China Quarterly* 1968-74; Visiting Scholar, Columbia University, New York 1972; Rejoined Diplomatic Service 1974-92: Seconded to Cabinet Office 1974-77, Political adviser, Hong Kong 1977-81, FCO 1981-87: Head of Southern European Department 1981-84, Assistant Under-Secretary of State 1984-87, Governor and Commander-in-Chief, Hong Kong 1987-92; Chair, Scottish Hydro Electric plc (now Scottish and Southern Energy plc) 1993-2000); Master, Peterhouse, Cambridge 2002-08; Deputy vice-chancellor, Cambridge University 2005-08. Army national service (Black Watch) 1953-55.

Political career: *House of Lords:* Raised to the peerage as Baron Wilson of Tillyorn, of Finzean in the District of Kincardine and Deeside and of Fanling in Hong Kong 1992. Chair, Revised Red Deer Act (Scotland) 1996; Co-opted member, EU Sub-committee B (Energy, Industry and Transport) 2000-02; Member: EU Sub-committee B (Internal Market, Infrastructure and Employment) 2012-15, European Union 2013-15. *Other:* Board member, British Council 1993-2002; Chair, Scottish Committee of the British Council 1993-2002; Prime Minister's Advisory Committee on Public Appointments: Member 2000-09, Chair 2008-09.

Political interests: Scottish affairs, education; China (including Hong Kong SAR), East and South East Asia.

Other: Substitute Member, UK Delegation to Parliamentary Assembly of Council of Europe 2016-17; Member: Oxford University Expedition to Somaliland 1957, British Mount Kongur Expedition (North West China) 1981; Council member, CBI Scotland 1993-2000; Member, Hopetoun House Preservation Trust 1993-98; President: Bhutan Society of the UK 1993-2008, Hong Kong Society 1994-2012, Hong Kong Association 1994-; Glenalmond College: Council member 1994-2005, Chair 2000-05; Vice-President, Royal Scottish Geographical Society 1996-; Scottish Peers Association: Vice-chair 1998-2000, Chair 2000-02; Trustee, Scotland's Churches Scheme (later Scotland's Churches Trust) 1999-2002, 2009-; Museums of Scotland: Trustee 1999-2006, Chair 2002-06; Member, Royal Society for Asian Affairs; Royal Society of Edinburgh: Council member 2000-04, President 2008-11; Carnegie Trust for the Universities of Scotland 2000-; Registrar, Order of Saint Michael and Saint George 2001-10; Chair, Advisory Council, St Paul's Cathedral 2009-; Chancellor, Aberdeen University 1997-2013; FRSE; Six honorary doctorates; Honorary Fellow: Keble College, Oxford 1987, Peterhouse, Cambridge 2008; CMG 1985; KCMG 1987; KStJ 1987; GCMG 1991; KT 2000. Alpine, New (Edinburgh), Royal Northern and University (Aberdeen) Club.

Recreations: Mountaineering, reading, theatre.

The Lord Wilson of Tillyorn KT GCMG, House of Lords, London SW1A 0PW
Tel: 020 7219 5353 *Email:* wilsondc@parliament.uk

NON-AFFILIATED

WINCHESTER, LORD BISHOP OF

WINCHESTER (97th Bishop of), Tim Dakin. Born 6 February 1958; Married Sally (1 son 1 daughter).

Education: University College of Saint Mark and St John, Plymouth; King's College, London; Christ Church, Oxford.

Non-political career: Principal, Carlile College, Kenya 1993-2000; Curate, Nairobi Cathedral 1993-2000; General secretary, Church Mission Society 2000-12; Honorary Canon Theologian, Coventry Cathedral 2001-; Bishop of Winchester 2012-.

Political career: *House of Lords:* Entered House of Lords 2012.

Political interests: Burundi, Democratic Republic of Congo, Kenya, Rwanda, Uganda.

Recreations: Reading, walking, films.

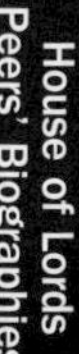

Rt Revd Bishop of Winchester, House of Lords, London SW1A 0PW
Tel: 020 7219 5353 *Email:* dakint@parliament.uk
Wolvesey, Winchester SO23 9ND *Tel:* 01962 854050
Email: bishop.tim@winchester.anglican.org Website: www.winchester.anglican.org
Twitter: @bishoptimdakin

LABOUR

WINSTON, LORD

WINSTON (Life Baron), Robert Maurice Lipson Winston; cr. 1995. Born 15 July 1940; Son of late Laurence Winston and Ruth Winston-Fox, MBE; Married Lira Helen Feigenbaum 1973 (2 sons 1 daughter).

Education: St Paul's School, London; London Hospital Medical College, London University (MB, BS 1964).

Non-political career: Wellcome research senior lecturer, Institute of Obstetrics and Gynaecology 1974-78; Other posts in UK, Belgium and USA; Consultant obstetrician and gynaecologist, Hammersmith Hospital 1978-2005; Former Dean, Institute of Obstetrics and Gynaecology, Royal Postgraduate Medical School (RPMS), London; Former Chair, British Fertility Society; Institute of Obstetrics and Gynaecology, RPMS, London University: Professor of Fertility Studies 1987-2005, Professor Emeritus 2005-; President, British Association of Advancement of Science 2005; Professor of Science and Society, Imperial College, London 2008; Chair, Advisory Board, DeVOS Cohort Project, Singapore 2012-; Presenter: *Your Life in Their Hands*, BBC TV 1978-84; *An Eye for the Job*, ITV 1990; *Making Babies*, BBC TV 1995, *The Human Body*, BBC TV 1998, *Secret Life of Twins*, BBC TV 1999; *Millennium Babies*, BBC TV 1999; *Superhuman*, BBC TV 2000; *Child of our Time*, BBC TV 2000-16, *Human Instinct*, BBC TV 2002, *Threads of Life*, BBC TV 2002, *Human Mind*, BBC TV 2003, *Walking with Cavemen*, BBC TV 2003, *The Story of God*, BBC TV 2005; *Superdoctors*, BBC TV 2010; *How Science Changed Our World*, BBC TV 2011; *My Favourite Things*, BBC/Sky Arts 2016; Various music programmes, BBC Radio 4, Radio 3. British Medical Association.

Political career: *House of Lords:* Raised to the peerage as Baron Winston, of Hammersmith in the London Borough of Hammersmith and Fulham 1995. Parliamentary Office of Science and Technology (POST): Member 1998-2006, Vice-chair 2006-. Science and Technology: Member 1996-2006, 2010-15, Chair 1998-2001; Member: Innovation Exploitation Barrier 1997, Science and Technology Sub-committees: II (Cannabis) 1998, II (Antibiotic Resistance) 1999-2000, I (Non-food Crops) 1999, II (Science and Society) 1999-2000, II (Aircraft Cabin Environment) 2000-01, IIA (Human Genetic Databases) 2000-01; Chair, Science and Technology Sub-committee I (Science in Schools) 2000-01; Member, Science and Technology Sub-committees: II (Renewable Energy) 2003-04, II Science and Treaties 2003-04, II (Science and RDAs) 2003, II (Energy Efficiency) 2004-08; Member: Pandemic Influenza 2005-06, Draft Human Tissue and Embryos Bill Joint Committee 2007; Co-opted Member, Science and Technology Sub-committee II (Genomic Medicine) 2008-09; Member: Nuclear Research and Developmental Capabilities 2010-12, Science and Technology Sub-committee I 2012-13, Sport and Exercise Science and Medicine, Higher Education in Science, Technology, Engineering and Mathematics Subjects.

Political interests: Health, science and technology, education, arts; New Zealand, Israel, Switzerland.

Other: Chair, Council, Royal College of Music 2007-17; Commissioner, UK Pavilion Expo 2001; Council member: Cancer Research UK -2007, Surrey University -2014, Engineering and Physical Sciences Research Council 2006-14; Chair, Genesis Research Trust; Board Member, Twig, Educational Films; Trustee: Royal Institution, British Science Association, UK Stem Cell Foundation; Member, Cancer Research UK; DreamLearners Ltd; Patron, Euphonia; Vice-President, Royal College of Music; Academy of Medical Sciences; Royal Academy of Engineering; Natural History Museum, Cheltenham Festival, Royal College of Music, Glyndebourne Opera, Royal Opera House, Reach Out Lab Imperial College, Genesis Research Trust, Winston's Wish, Listening Books, Garsington Opera, Lyric Theatre, UJIA, Jewish Care, New Israel Fund, Traverse Theatre Edinburgh; Chancellor, Sheffield Hallam University 2001-18; Hon FREng; FRSB, FRCOG; FRCP; FRSA; FMedSci; FRCM; FRCSE; FRCPS; FCGI; Hon. Fellow: Queen Mary Westfield College, Institute of Education, Endocrine Society; Twenty four honorary doctorates; Cedric Carter Medal, Clinical Genetics Society 1993; Victor Bonney Triennial Prize, Royal College of Surgeons of England 1993;

Chief Rabbi's Award for Contribution to Community 1994; Gold Medal, Royal Society for Promotion of Health 1998; Michael Faraday Gold Medal, Royal Society 1999; Robert Menzies Medal 2001; BMA Gold Medal Book Prize, Human 2001 Edwin Stevens Medal, Royal Society of Medicine 2003; Gold Medal, North of England Zoological Society 2004; Peer of the Year, *House Magazine* 2008; Medallist, Olumuc Film Festival 2014; Science Book Prize, Royal Society 2005, 2013, 2016, 2017. Athenæum, MCC, Garrick Club.

Publications: Reversibility of Sterilization (1978); Co-author Tubal Infertility (1981); Infertility, a Sympathetic Approach (1987); The IVF Revolution (1999); Superhuman (2000); Human Instinct (2002); Predictions (2002); The Human Mind (2003); The Story of God (2005); A Child Against All Odds (2006); Bad Ideas (2010); Science Year by Year (2013); Growing Up (2017); 16 illustrated books about science for children; Over 330 papers in scientific journals on human and experimental reproduction.

Recreations: Theatre, broadcasting, music, wine.

Professor the Lord Winston, House of Lords, London SW1A 0PW
Tel: 020 7219 6020 *Email:* winstonr@parliament.uk
11 Denman Drive, London NW11 6RE *Tel:* 020 8455 7475 *Email:* r.winston@imperial.ac.uk
Website: www.robertwinston.org.uk *Twitter:* @ProfRWinston

NON-AFFILIATED

WOLF OF DULWICH, BARONESS

WOLF OF DULWICH (Life Baroness), Alison Margaret Wolf; cr 2014. Born 31 October 1949; Married Martin Wolf 1970 (2 sons 1 daughter).

Education: Oxford High School; Oxford University (MA; MPhil); French (good), Italian (moderate to poor).

Non-political career: Research associate, National Institute of Education, Washington 1975-82; Institute of Education, University of London: Research officer 1983-85, Senior research officer 1985-95, Professor 1995-2004; King's College London: Sir Roy Griffiths Professor of Public Sector Management 2006-, Director, International Centre for University Policy Research 2012-.

Political career: *House of Lords:* Raised to the peerage as Baroness Wolf of Dulwich, of Dulwich in the London Borough of Southwark 2014. *Other:* Left Crossbench January 2020, now sits as Non-affiliated. Governor, King's College London Mathematics School; Member, King's College London Council; Vice-President, Local Government Association 2018-19.

Political interests: Training and skills policy, universities, medical workforce; Canada, France, Italy, Sweden, USA.

Other: Trustee: Abbeyfield Society, Newbury 2000-, Social Market Foundation 2013-16, King's College London Mathematics School; Academic Member, Council of King's College London; Abbeyfield (Newbury), Friends of King's College London Mathematics School; Sam Aaronovitch memorial prize 2008; CBE 2012.

Publications: Does Education Matter? (2002); The XX Factor: How Working Women are Creating a New Society (2013).

Professor the Baroness Wolf of Dulwich CBE, House of Lords, London SW1A 0PW
Tel: 020 7219 8619 *Email:* wolfa@parliament.uk
Department of Management, King's College London, 150 Stamford Street, London SE1 9NH
Website: www.kcl.ac.uk/aboutkings/governance/council/members/alisonwolf.aspx
Twitter: @XXFactorFacts

CONSERVATIVE

WOLFSON OF ASPLEY GUISE, LORD

WOLFSON OF ASPLEY GUISE (Life Baron), Simon Adam Wolfson; cr 2010. Born 27 October 1967; Son of David Wolfson, now Lord Wolfson of Sunningdale, and Susan Davis; Married Eleanor Shawcross 2012 (2 sons).

Education: Radley College; Trinity College, Cambridge (LLB 1989).

Non-political career: Next plc: Director 1997-, Managing director 1999-2001, Chief executive 2001-.

Political career: *House of Lords:* Raised to the peerage as Baron Wolfson of Aspley Guise, of Aspley Guise in the County of Bedfordshire 2010.

Political interests: Industry, economy.

Other: Trustee, Charles Wolfson Charitable Trust.

The Lord Wolfson of Aspley Guise, House of Lords, London SW1A 0PW
Tel: 020 7219 5353

CONSERVATIVE

WOLFSON OF TREDEGAR, LORD

Parliamentary Under-Secretary of State and Government Spokesperson, Ministry of Justice

WOLFSON OF TREDEGAR (Life Baron), David Wolfson; cr 2020. Born 1968.

Education: King David High School, Liverpool; Yeshiva HaKotel, Jerusalem; Selwyn College, Cambridge (oriental studies and law 1991); Inns of Court School of Law.

Non-political career: Call to the Bar at Inner Temple 1992; QC 2009; Barrister in commercial law, One Essex Court, Temple.

Political career: *House of Lords:* Raised to the peerage as Baron Wolfson of Tredegar, of Tredegar in the County of Gwent 2020. Parliamentary Under-Secretary of State and Government Spokesperson, Ministry of Justice 2020-.

Other: Commercial Litigation Silk of the Year 2020, The Legal 500; Commercial Litigation Silk of the Year, Chambers UK Bar Awards 2020.

The Lord Wolfson of Tredegar QC, House of Lords, London SW1A 0PW
Tel: 020 7219 3000 *Email:* wolfsond@parliament.uk

LABOUR

WOOD OF ANFIELD, LORD

WOOD OF ANFIELD (Life Baron), Stewart Martin Wood; cr 2011. Born 25 March 1968; Son of Brian and Gisela Wood; Married Camilla Bustani 1998 (2 sons).

Education: Judd School, Tonbridge; University College, Oxford (BA philosophy, politics and economics); Harvard University (Fulbright Scholar, government department, PhD 1997); French, German.

Non-political career: Script consultant, BBC Documentaries 1995-2000; Junior research fellow, St John's College, Oxford 1996; Fellow in politics and lecturer, Magdalen College, Oxford 1996-2011; Special adviser to Gordon Brown: as Chancellor of the Exchequer 2001-07, as Prime Minister 2007-10; Adviser to Ed Miliband as Leader of the Opposition 2010-15. Member, Community.

Political career: *House of Lords:* Raised to the peerage as Baron Wood of Anfield, of Tonbridge in the County of Kent 2011. Opposition Spokesperson for Cabinet Office 2011-12, 2014-15; Shadow Minister without Portfolio, Cabinet Office 2011-15. Member: International Relations 2016-19, SLSC Sub-committee A 2018-19, European Union 2019-, EU External Affairs Sub-committee 2019-20, EU Goods Sub-committee 2020-. *Other:* Ed Miliband Labour leadership campaign 2010; Member, Co-operative Party 2010-.

Political interests: Foreign policy, economic policy, sport, media and creative industries, Northern Ireland; China, EU, Germany, Russia, USA.

Other: Chair, United Nations Associations (UK) 2016-; Co-Founder and co-director, Nexus 1996-99; Member, British Film Institute; Board member, English Stage Company, Royal Court Theatre, London 2008-; Patron, Camden Psychotherapy Unit; Board member, YouGov/ Cambridge; Fellow-In-Practice, Blavatnik School of Government, Oxford University 2016-.

Publications: Numerous articles and chapters on political economy, West European politics, education policy.

Recreations: Guitar, alt-country music, film and movie history, cricket, football (Liverpool FC).

The Lord Wood of Anfield, House of Lords, London SW1A 0PW
Tel: 020 7219 5854 *Email:* stewart.wood@parliament.uk *Twitter:* @StewartWood

LABOUR

WOODLEY, LORD

WOODLEY (Life Baron), Anthony Jonathan Woodley; cr 2020. Born 2 January 1948.

Non-political career: Ellesmere Port factory, Vauxhall Motors 1967-89; Transport and General Workers' Union (TGWU): District official 1989-91, National official 1991-92, Deputy General secretary 2002-03, General Secretary 2003-07 (merger with Amicus); Unite the Union: Joint General Secretary 2007-11, Executive officer 2011-13, Adviser 2013-.

Political career: *House of Lords:* Raised to the peerage as Baron Woodley, of Wallasey in the Metropolitan Borough of Wirral 2020.

Other: Chair, Vauxhall Motors Football Club.

The Lord Woodley, House of Lords, London SW1A 0PW
Tel: 020 7219 3000

CROSSBENCH

WOOLF, LORD

WOOLF (Life Baron), Harry Kenneth Woolf; cr. 1992. Born 2 May 1933; Son of late Alexander and Leah Woolf; Married Marguerite Sassoon 1961 (3 sons).

Education: Fettes College, Edinburgh; University College, London (LLB 1954).

Non-political career: Called to Bar, Inner Temple 1954; Started practice at Bar 1956; Recorder of the Crown Court 1972-79; Junior Counsel, Inland Revenue 1973-74; First Treasury Junior Counsel (Common Law) 1974-79; Bencher 1976; Judge of the High Court of Justice, Queen's Bench Division 1979-86; Presiding Judge, South Eastern Circuit 1981-84; Member: Senate, Inns of Court and Bar 1981-85, Board of Management, Institute of Advanced Legal Studies 1985-93; Chair, Lord Chancellor's Advisory Committee on Legal Education 1986-90; Lord Justice of Appeal 1986-92; Chair, Board of Management, Institute of Advanced Legal Studies 1986-93; Held inquiry into: Prison disturbances 1990, part II with Judge Tumim, report 1991, Access to Justice 1994-96 (interim report 1995, final report and rules 1996); Master of the Rolls 1996-2000; Chair, Advisory Committee on Public Records 1996; Visitor: University College, London 1996-2000, Nuffield College, Oxford 1996-2000; Lord Chief Justice of England and Wales 2000-05; Visitor, Downing College, Cambridge 2005-; Judge of final appeal, Hong Kong; President, Qatar Financial Services Court; Chair of Council, University College London 2005-07; Chair, Woolf Committee 2007-08; President of the Civil and Commercial Court of Qatar. Commissioned (National Service) 15/19th Royal Hussars 1954; Seconded to Army Legal Services 1954; Captain 1955.

Political career: *House of Lords:* Raised to the peerage as Baron Woolf, of Barnes in the London Borough of Richmond 1992. Lord of Appeal in Ordinary 1992-2006. Chair, Sub-committee on Lords' Interests 2006-08; Member: Constitution 2006-10, Privileges 2007-08, Inquiries Act 2005 2013-14; Chair, Insurance Bill 2014-15; Member, Joint Committee on Human Rights 2015-19.

Other: President: Association of Law Teachers 1985-89, South West London Magistrates Association 1987-92, Central Council of Jewish Social Services 1989-99; Governor, Oxford Centre of Hebrew Studies (Emeritus) 1990-93; Butler Trust: Chair 1992-96, President 1996-; Trustee, St Mary's Hospital Special Trustees 1993-97; Mogen Dovid Adom 1995-; Honorary Liveryman, Drapers' Company; Pro-Chancellor, London University 1994-2002; Chancellor, Open University of Israel 2005-; FBA; Fellow: University College, London 1981, British

Academy 2000; Twelve honorary doctorates; Hon. Fellow: Leeds Municipal University, Academy of Medical Sciences 2002-; Kt 1979; PC 1986; CH 2015. Garrick, Royal Automobile Club.

Publications: Protection of the public: A New Challenge (Hamlyn lecture, 1990); Co-author: Zamir and Woolf: The Declaratory Judgement (2nd edition, 1993), De Smith, Woolf and Jowell (5th edition, 1995), Principles of Judicial Review; De Smith Administrative Law (6th edition, 2008); The Pursuit of Justice (Oxford University Press); Ethical Conduct in BAE Systems plc – The Way Forward.

Recreations: Theatre, music.

Rt Hon the Lord Woolf CH, House of Lords, London SW1A 0PW
Tel: 020 7219 1788 *Email:* maggiestevenson@parliament.uk

CROSSBENCH

WOOLLEY OF WOODFORD, LORD

WOOLLEY OF WOODFORD (Life Baron), Simon Andrew Woolley; cr 2019. Born 24 December 1961; Partner Begona Juarros (1 son).

Education: Middlesex University (BA English literature and Spanish 1993); Queen Mary University of London (MA Hispanic studies 1994).

Non-political career: Founder/Chief executive, Operation Black Vote 1996-.

Political career: *House of Lords:* Raised to the peerage as Baron Woolley of Woodford, of Woodford in the London Borough of Redbridge 2019. *Other:* Member, Equality and Human Rights Commission 2009-12; Chair, Race Disparity Unit Advisory Group 2018-.

Other: Board member, Youth Futures Foundation 2019-.

The Lord Woolley of Woodford, House of Lords, London SW1A 0PW

NON-AFFILIATED

WORCESTER, LORD BISHOP OF

WORCESTER (113th Bishop of), John Geoffrey Inge. Born 26 February 1955.

Education: Kent College, Canterbury; St Chads College, Durham (BSc chemistry); Keble College, Oxford (PGCE); College of the Resurrection, Mirfield, Yorkshire.

Non-political career: Chemistry teacher, Lancing College; Diocese of Chichester: Ordained deacon 1983, Ordained priest 1984; Chaplain: Lancing College, Harrow School; Vicar, St Luke's Church, Wallsend; Ely Cathedral: Residentiary Canon, Vice Dean 1999-2003; Bishop of Huntingdon 2003-08; Bishop of Worcester 2008-.

Political career: *House of Lords:* Entered House of Lords 2012. Member, Communications/ Communications and Digital 2019-. *Other:* Lord High Almoner to HM The Queen 2013-.

Other: Member: World Development Movement, Amnesty International; Trustee, Common Purpose.

Publications: A Christian Theology of Place (Ashgate, 2003); Living Love: In Conversation with the No. 1 Ladies' Detective Agency (Inspire, 2007).

Rt Rev the Lord Bishop of Worcester, House of Lords, London SW1A 0PW
Tel: 020 7219 5353
The Old Palace, Deansway, Worcester WR1 2JE *Tel:* 01905 20537
Email: generalinfo@cofe-worcester.org.uk Website: www.cofe-worcester.org.uk
Twitter: @BishopWorcester

CROSSBENCH

WORTHINGTON, BARONESS

WORTHINGTON (Life Baroness) Bryony Katherine Worthington; cr 2011. Born 19 September 1971; Married Dr Srivas Chennu 2010 (1 son).

Education: Queens' College, Cambridge (BA English literature 1993).

Non-political career: Fundraiser, Operation Raleigh; Wildlife and Countryside Link; Campaigner, Friends of the Earth; Department of Energy and Climate Change (on secondment); Policy adviser, Scottish and Southern Electricity; Founder and director, Sandbag 2008-.

Political career: *House of Lords:* Raised to the peerage as Baroness Worthington, of Cambridge in the County of Cambridgeshire 2011. Opposition Whip 2012-15; Opposition Spokesperson for Energy and Climate Change 2013-15. *Other:* Left the Labour group in the Lords April 2017; Non-Affiliated April 2017-December 2018; now sits as a Crossbencher.

Political interests: Environment, climate change.

The Baroness Worthington, House of Lords, London SW1A 0PW
Tel: 020 7219 8987 *Email:* worthingtonb@parliament.uk *Twitter:* @bryworthington

LIBERAL DEMOCRAT

WRIGGLESWORTH, LORD

WRIGGLESWORTH (Life Baron), Ian William Wrigglesworth; cr 2013. Born 8 December 1939; Son of late Edward Wrigglesworth; Married Patricia Truscott 1967 (2 sons 1 daughter).

Education: Stockton Grammar School; Stockton-Billingham Technical College; College of St Mark and St John, Chelsea (Music and English Teaching Qualification 1966).

Non-political career: Personal assistant to Sir Ronald Gould as General Secretary of National Union of Teachers; Press and public affairs manager, National Giro; Divisional director, Smith's Industries 1976-2000; Deputy chair, John Livingston and Sons Ltd 1987-95; Director: CIT Holdings Ltd 1987-2003, Northern Development Co 1997-99, Tyne Tees TV 2002-06; Port of Tyne: Director 2003-05, Chair 2005-12; Chair, Bluehall Properties (now Durham Group) 2008-. Former Member: NUT; USDAW; NUJ.

Political career: *House of Commons:* MP for Teesside, Thornaby February 1974-83, for Stockton South 1983-87 (Labour/Co-op 1974-81, SDP/All 1981-87). Contested Stockton South 1987 general election; PPS to: Alex Lyon as Minister of State, Home Office March-November 1974, Roy Jenkins as Home Secretary 1974-76; Opposition Spokesperson on the Civil Service 1979-80; SDP Spokesperson on Economic Affairs and Taxation, Trade and Industry, Energy, Small Businesses and Consumer Affairs. *House of Lords:* Raised to the peerage as Baron Wrigglesworth, of Norton on Tees in the County of Durham 2013. Member: Economic Affairs Finance Bill Sub-committee 2014, 2017, Trade Union and Party Funding 2016. *Other:* Research officer, Co-operative Party; Member, Labour Party 1962-81; Founder member, Social Democrats 1981; Liberal Democrats: President 1988-90, Chair: Business Forum, National Trustees 2002-12, National Treasurer 2012-15. Governor and Deputy Chair, Teesside University 1993-2002; DL, Tyne and Wear 2005-13; Deputy Chair, Regional Growth Fund Advisory Panel 2010-12.

Political interests: Economic, industrial and regional policy; India, USA.

Other: Chair: Northern region, CBI 1992-94, Northern Business Forum 1996-98, UK Land Estates 1995-2009, Government Policy Consultants Ltd 1998-2000, Newcastle-Gateshead Initiative 1999-2004, Baltic Centre for Contemporary Art 2004-09; Liveryman, Worshipful Company of Founders; Freedom, City of London 1995; Honorary Doctorate of: Music, Northumbria University 2011, Business Administration, Teesside University 2012; Kt 1991. Groucho, Reform Club.

Recreations: Skiing, music, walking, cycling.

The Lord Wrigglesworth, House of Lords, London SW1A 0PW
Tel: 020 7219 8743 *Email:* wrigglesworthi@parliament.uk

CONSERVATIVE

WYLD, BARONESS

WYLD (Life Baroness), Laura Lee Wyld; cr 2017. Born 13 January 1978.

Education: Cambridge University (BA history).

Non-political career: Campaigns officer, Conservative Central Office; Research consultant, Quiller Consultants; Consultant, Lexington Communications 2003-07; Fishburn Hedges: Consultant 2007-09, Associate Director 2009-13; Head, Prime Minister's Appointments Unit 2013-16; Senior adviser, Strategic Communications Alliance.

Political career: *House of Lords:* Raised to the peerage as Baroness Wyld, of Gosforth in the City of Newcastle upon Tyne 2017. Member: Regenerating Seaside Towns and Communities 2018-19, Social and Economic Impact of the Gambling Industry 2019, Public Services 2020-. *Other:* Non-executive board member, Department for Digital, Culture, Media and Sport 2020-.

Other: Council member, Institute of Directors; Board member, Urology Foundation 2017-.

The Baroness Wyld, House of Lords, London SW1A 0PW
Tel: 020 7219 3000

NON-AFFILIATED

YORK, LORD ARCHBISHOP OF

YORK (98th Archbishop of), Stephen Geoffrey Cottrell. Born 31 August 1958; Son of John and Eileen Cottrell; Married Rebecca Stirling 1984 (3 sons).

Education: Belfairs High School for Boys; Polytechnic of Central London (BA media studies 1979); St Stephen's House, Oxford.

Non-political career: Ordained deacon 1984; Curate, Christ Church, Forest Hill 1984-88; Priest 1985; Priest-in-charge, St Wilfrid's Chichester 1988-93; Assistant director, Pastoral Studies, Chichester Theological College 1988-93; Diocesan missioner, Wakefield 1993-98; Springboard missioner 1998-2001; Canon Pastor, Peterborough Cathedral 2001-04; Area Bishop of Reading 2004-10; Bishop of Chelmsford 2010-20; Archbishop of York 2020-.

Political career: *House of Lords:* Entered House of Lords 2014. Member, Communications 2015-19.

Other: Visitor, Society of the Precious Blood; Chair, Church Army; PC 2020.

Publications: Many publications including: I Thirst (2003), The Adventures of Naughty Nora (2008), Hit the Ground Kneeling: seeing leadership differently (2008), The Things He Said: the story of the first Easter Day (2009), How to Pray (2011), The Nail: being part of the Passion (2011), Christ in the Wilderness: reflecting on the paintings by Stanley Spencer (2012).

Recreations: Writing, reading, cooking, music, football.

Most Rev and Rt Hon the Archbishop of York, House of Lords, London SW1A 0PW
Tel: 020 7219 5353 *Email:* cottrells@parliament.uk
The Office of the Archbishop of York, Bishopthorpe Palace, Bishopthorpe, York YO23 2GE
Tel: 01904 707021 *Email:* office@archbishopofyork.org Websites: dioceseofyork.org.uk
www.archbishopofyork.org *Twitter:* @cottrellstephen

CONSERVATIVE

YOUNG OF COOKHAM, LORD

YOUNG OF COOKHAM (Life Baron), George Samuel Knatchbull Young; cr 2015. Born 16 July 1941; Son of late Sir George Young, 5th Bt, CMG, and Elizabeth Young, née Knatchbull-Hugessen; Married Aurelia Nemon-Stuart 1964 (2 sons 2 daughters).

Education: Eton College; Christ Church, Oxford (BA philosophy, politics and economics 1963, MA); Surrey University (MPhil economics 1971).

Non-political career: Economic adviser, Post Office 1969-74.

Political career: *House of Commons:* MP (Conservative) for Ealing Acton February 1974-97, for North West Hampshire 1997-2010, for North West Hampshire (revised boundary) 2010-15; Opposition Whip 1976-79; Parliamentary Under-Secretary of State: Department of Health and Social Services 1979-81, Department of Environment 1981-86; Government Whip 1990; Department of Environment: Minister for Housing and Planning 1990-93, Minister for

Housing, Inner Cities and Construction 1993-94; Financial Secretary, HM Treasury 1994-95; Secretary of State for Transport 1995-97; Shadow Secretary of State for Defence 1997-98; Shadow Leader of the House of Commons 1998-99, 2009-10; Member, House of Commons Commission 1998-99, 2009-12; Shadow Chancellor of the Duchy of Lancaster 1998-99; Shadow Leader of the House of Commons and Constitutional Affairs 1999-2000; Contested Speaker election 2000, 2009; Member, Speaker's Committee for the Independent Parliamentary Standards Authority 2009-12; Leader of the House of Commons, Lord Privy Seal 2010-12; Member, Public Accounts Commission 2010-12; Parliamentary Secretary to the Treasury; Chief Whip 2012-14; Member, Parliamentary and Political Service Honours Committee 2012-14. Member: Public Accounts 1994-95, Modernisation of the House of Commons 1998-2000, Selection 2001-09; Chair, Standards and Privileges 2001-09; Member: Liaison 2001-09, Liaison (Liaison Sub-Committee) 2002-09, Reform of the House of Commons 2009. Chair, Conservative Party: Committee for Defence 1997-98, Constitution Committee 1998-2000. *House of Lords:* Raised to the peerage as Baron Young of Cookham, of Cookham in the Royal County of Berkshire 2015. Government Whip (Lord in Waiting) 2016-19; Government Spokesperson for: HM Treasury 2016, 2019, Cabinet Office 2016-19. Member: Privileges and Conduct 2015-16, Public Services 2020-. *Other:* Patron, Tory Reform Group; Former Vice-chair, Association of Conservative Peers. Councillor: London Borough of Lambeth 1968-71, GLC 1970-73.

Political interests: Housing, disability, health education, constitutional reform.

Other: Trustee: Guinness Trust 1986-90, Foundations Independent Living Trust 2002-10; Backbencher of the Year, *Spectator* awards 1988; Resurrection of the Year, *Spectator* awards 2012; 6th Baronet, created 1813, succeeded his father 1960; PC 1993; CH 2012.

Publications: Tourism – Blessing or Blight (1970); I'm Keeping Young (2015).

Recreations: Bicycling, opera.

Rt Hon the Lord Young of Cookham CH, House of Lords, London SW1A 0PW
Tel: 020 7219 6665 *Email:* youngg@parliament.uk

CONSERVATIVE

YOUNG OF GRAFFHAM, LORD

YOUNG OF GRAFFHAM (Life Baron), David Ivor Young; cr. 1984. Born 27 February 1932; Son of late Joseph Young; Married Lita Marianne Shaw 1956 (2 daughters).

Education: Christ's College, Finchley; University College, London (LLB 1954).

Non-political career: Solicitor 1956; Executive, Great Universal Stores 1956-61; Chair: Eldonwall Ltd 1961-75, Manufacturers Hanover Property Services Ltd 1974-84; Industrial adviser/special adviser, Department of Industry 1979-82; Chair, Manpower Services Commission 1982-84; Fellow, University College London 1988; Executive Chair, Cable and Wireless plc 1990-95; Director, Salomon Inc 1990-94; Chair of several companies, including: Young Associates Ltd 1996-, Pixology Ltd 1997-, Newhaven Management Services 1997-, Spectrum Interactive plc, TSSI Ltd, Camcon Ltd; Director: Deeptek Ltd, Kashflow Software Ltd.

Political career: *House of Lords:* Raised to the peerage as Baron Young of Graffham, of Graffham in the County of West Sussex 1984. Cabinet Minister without Portfolio 1984-85; Secretary of State for: Employment 1985-87, Trade and Industry 1987-89; Adviser to the Prime Minister on: Health and Safety Law and Practice 2010, Enterprise 2010, 2011-17. Member: Science and Technology 2003-06, Science and Technology Sub-committees: II (Science and the Regional Development Agencies) 2003, II (Renewable Energy) 2003-04, II (Energy Efficiency) 2004-. *Other:* Deputy chair, Conservative Party 1989-90. DL, West Sussex 1999-.

Other: Chair, West Sussex Economic Forum 1993-2001; President, Institute of Directors 1993-2004; Chair of Council, University College, London 1995-2005; Chair, Chichester Festival Theatre Ltd 1997-; Prince's Trust: Chair, Development Board 2003-07, Trustees council member 2004-07; Chair and trustee, Peter Cruddas Foundation 2006-; Trustee, MBI AL Jaber Foundation 2007-; President and trustee, Chai Cancer Care 2007-; Honorary Doctorate of Science, Cranfield University 1986; Doctor of Laws, Honoris Causa, University College London 2006; PC 1984; CH 2015.

Publications: The Enterprise Years (1990).

Recreations: Photography, music, book collecting, fishing.

Rt Hon the Lord Young of Graffham CH DL, House of Lords, London SW1A 0PW
Tel: 020 7219 5353 *Twitter:* @TheLordYoung

CROSSBENCH

YOUNG OF HORNSEY, BARONESS

YOUNG OF HORNSEY (Life Baroness), Margaret Omolola (Lola) Young; cr. 2004. Born 1 June 1951; Daughter of Maxwell Fela Young and Yele Santos; Married Barrie Birch 1984 (1 son).

Education: Parliament Hill School for Girls, London; New College of Speech and Drama (Diploma dramatic art 1975; Teaching Certificate 1976); Middlesex Polytechnic/University (BA contemporary cultural studies 1988; PhD British film 1995).

Non-political career: Residential social worker, London Borough of Islington 1971-73; Professional actor 1976-84; Co-director and training and development manager, Haringey Arts Council 1985-89; Freelance lecturer and arts consultant 1989-1991; Lecturer in media studies, Polytechnic of West London/Thames Valley University 1990-92; Middlesex University 1992-2001: Lecturer, Senior lecturer, Principal lecturer, Professor of cultural studies, Emeritus professor; Project director, Archives and Museum of Black Heritage 1997-2001; Head of culture, Greater London Authority 2002-04; Visiting professor, Birkbeck College, London; Founder, Cultural Brokers Arts and Heritage Consultancy 2004-.

Political career: *House of Lords:* Raised to the peerage as Baroness Young of Hornsey, of Hornsey in the London Borough of Haringey 2004. Co-opted Member, EU Sub-committee G (Social Policy and Consumer Affairs) 2007-10; Chair, EU Sub-committee G (Social Policies and Consumer Protection) 2010-12; Member: European Union 2010-13, Joint Committee on the Draft House of Lords Reform Bill 2011-12, EU Sub-committee C (External Affairs) 2012-15, Sexual Violence in Conflict 2015-16.

Political interests: Arts and culture, children and young people in care, mental health, equalities, London, North and South West England; Commonwealth, Sub-saharan Africa, USA.

Other: Commissioner, Royal Commission on Historical Manuscripts 2000-01; Board member: National Theatre 2000-03, South Bank Centre 2002-08; Chair: Arts Advisory Committee, British Council 2004-08, Nitro Theatre Company 2004-09; Patron, Post-adoption Centre 2004-; Council member, RSA 2005-08; Patron, Josephine Wolf Trust 2007-; Chair, Commonwealth group on Culture and Development 2008-12; Commissioner, English Heritage 2011-; Freeman, Tallow Chandlers Company; Chancellor, Nottingham University 2020-; FRSA 2000; OBE 2001. RSA, Hospital Club.

Publications: Numerous newspaper articles and radio and television broadcasts; Fear of the Dark: 'Race', Gender and Sexuality in Cinema (Routledge, 1996).

Recreations: Walking, cinema, theatre, visual arts, gardening, reading.

Professor the Baroness Young of Hornsey OBE, House of Lords, London SW1A 0PW
Tel: 020 7219 5991 *Email:* younglo@parliament.uk
Email: lola.young@culturalbrokers.co.uk *Twitter:* @LolaHornsey

LABOUR

YOUNG OF NORWOOD GREEN, LORD

YOUNG OF NORWOOD GREEN (Life Baron), Anthony Ian Young; cr. 2004. Born 16 April 1942; Son of late Henry and Sheila Young; Married Doreen Goodman (divorced 1984) (1 son 2 daughters); married Margaret Newnham 1985 (1 son 1 daughter).

Education: Harrow County Grammar School.

Non-political career: GPO (General Post Office) telecommunications apprentice 1958; Post Office Engineering Union: Union branch officer 1967, Member, National Executive Committee 1989-95; General secretary, National Communications Union 1989-95; Communication Workers' Union: Joint General secretary 1995-98, Senior deputy general secretary 1998-2002; Trades Union Council: Member, General Council 1989-2002, President 2001-02. Member, Communication Workers Union (CWU).

Political career: *House of Lords:* Raised to the peerage as Baron Young of Norwood Green, of Norwood Green in the London Borough of Ealing 2004. Parliamentary Under-Secretary of State (Skills and Apprenticeships 2008-09, Postal Affairs and Employment Relations 2009-10) and Government Spokesperson, Department for Innovation, Universities and Skills/Business, Innovation and Skills 2008-10; Government Whip 2008-10; Opposition Spokesperson for Business, Innovation and Skills 2010-15. Co-opted Member, European Union Sub-committee F (Home Affairs) 2007-08; Member: Crossrail Bill 2008, High Speed Rail (London-West Midlands) Bill 2016, EU Energy and Environment Sub-committee 2017-19, EU Environment Sub-committee 2020-. *Other:* Member: Wilton Park Academic Council 1996-2005, Employment Tribunal Steering Board 1997-2003; Governor, BBC 1998-2002; Vice-chair, Ethical Trading Initiative; Chair, One World Broadcasting Trust 2002-09; Member, Armed Forces Pay Review Board -2008; Governor, Three Bridges Primary School.

Political interests: China, Italy, USA.

Other: Member, board of trustees, Industry and Parliament Trust 2020-; Kt 2002.

Recreations: Cycling, tennis, table tennis, reading, gardening.

The Lord Young of Norwood Green, House of Lords, London SW1A 0PW
Tel: 020 7219 3176 *Email:* younga@parliament.uk

LABOUR

YOUNG OF OLD SCONE, BARONESS

YOUNG OF OLD SCONE (Life Baroness), Barbara Scott Young; cr. 1997. Born 8 April 1948; Daughter of late George Young and late Mary Young.

Education: Perth Academy; Edinburgh University (MA classics 1970); Strathclyde University (DipSocSci 1971); DipHSM 1974; Chartered Environmentalist 2005.

Non-political career: Sector administrator, Glasgow Health Board 1973-78; Director of planning and development, St Thomas' Health District, London 1978-79; District general administrator, Kensington and Chelsea and Westminster Area Health Authority 1979-82; District administrator, Haringey Health Authority (HA), London 1982-85; District general manager: Paddington and North Kensington HA 1985-88, Parkside HA 1988-91; Chief executive, Royal Society for the Protection of Birds 1991-98; Chair, English Nature 1998-2000; Non-executive director, Anglian Water 1998-2000; Chief executive: Environment Agency 2000-08, Diabetes UK 2010-15.

Political career: *House of Lords:* Raised to the peerage as Baroness Young of Old Scone, of Old Scone in Perth and Kinross 1997. Member: Built Environment 2015-16, Science and Technology 2016-, Rural Economy 2018-19. *Other:* BBC: Member, General Advisory Council 1985-88, Vice-chair 1998-2000; Committee member, Secretary of State for the Environment's Going for Green Initiative 1994-96; Member: UK Round Table on Sustainability 1995-2000, Commission on the Future of the Voluntary Sector 1995-97, Committee on the Public Understanding of Science 1996-97; Chair, Care Quality Commission 2008-09; Commissioner, Commission on Assisted Dying 2010-.

Political interests: Environment, broadcasting, health and social care, equality and rights, higher education.

Other: President, Institute of Health Services Management 1987-88; Patron, Institute of Ecological and Environment Management 1993-; Trustee, National Council for Voluntary Organisations 1994-98; Vice-President: Flora and Fauna International 1998-, World Council, Birdlife International 1999-, Plantlife 2000-15, RSPB 2000-; Trustee, Institute for Public Policy Research 2000-09; President: Beds, Cambs, Northants and Peterborough Wildlife Trust 2001-, British Trust of Ornithology 2004-13, South Georgia Heritage Trust 2008-; Bedfordshire Symphony Orchestra; Patron, Lantra; Chair: Environmentalists for Europe 2015-19, Woodland Trust 2016-, Royal Veterinary College 2019-; Woodland Trust, RSPB, Action Aid, Plantlife, Dignity in Dying, Diabetes UK, Birdlife International, South Georgia Heritage Trust, Bedfordhsire, Cambridgeshire and Northamptonshire Wildlife Trust; Chancellor, Cranfield University 2010-; Honorary member, RICS; Honorary fellow: Geologists Association, Linnean Society, Royal Society of Edinburgh; Eminent fellow, IAgrE; CIWEM Chartered Environmentalist; CIWM; Fifteen honorary doctorates; Honorary Fellow, Sydney Sussex College.

Recreations: Cinema, gardening, dressage.

The Baroness Young of Old Scone, House of Lords, London SW1A 0PW
Tel: 020 7219 1000 *Email:* youngb@parliament.uk *Twitter:* @youngb48

YOUNGER OF LECKIE, VISCOUNT

CONSERVATIVE

Government Spokesperson, Scotland Office and Northern Ireland Office; Government Whip (Lord in Waiting)

YOUNGER OF LECKIE (5th Viscount, UK), James Edward George Younger; cr. 1923; 5th Bt of Leckie (UK) 1911. Born 11 November 1955; Son of 4th Viscount and Diana Tuck; Married Jennie Wootton 1988 (1 son 2 daughters).

Education: Cargilfield School, Edinburgh; Winchester College; St Andrews University (MA Hons medieval history 1979); Henley Management College (MBA 1993).

Non-political career: Personnel manager, Coats Patons 1979-84; Recruitment consultant, Angela Mortimer Ltd 1984-86; Executive search consultant, Stephens Consultancies 1986-92; Director, McInnes Younger 1992-94; Human Resources director, UBS Wealth Management 1994-2004; Director, Culliford Edmunds Associates 2004-07; Consultant, Eban Ltd 2007-10.

Political career: *House of Lords:* Elected Hereditary peer 2010-; Party Whip 2010-12; Government Whip (Lord in Waiting) 2012-13, 2015-19; 2020-; Government Spokesperson for: Culture, Olympics, Media and Sport/Culture, Media and Sport 2012-13, Scotland 2012-13, 2015-16, 2019-20, 2020-, Attorney General's Office 2012, Advocate General for Scotland 2012, Law Officers 2012-13, 2015-16, Transport 2012-13, 2015-16, Communities and Local Government 2015-16, Energy and Climate Change 2015-16, Northern Ireland 2015-16, 2020-, Wales 2015-16, Higher Education 2016-19; Parliamentary Under-Secretary of State and Government Spokesperson, Department for Business, Innovation and Skills 2013-14; Parliamentary Under-Secretary of State (Minister for Faith and Communities) and Government Spokesperson, Ministry of Housing, Communities and Local Government 2019-20. Member: Public Service and Demographic Change 2012, Joint Committee on the Draft Protection of Charities Bill 2014-15. *Other:* Head of Fundraising, Wandsworth Tooting Conservative Association 1994-96; Chair, Buckingham Conservative Constituency Association 2006-10; Member, Association of Conservative Peers 2006-; Elected member, area board, Oxfordshire and Buckinghamshire Conservatives 2009-13; Chair, Milton Keynes Conservative Association 2010-13.

Political interests: Big Society, tourism, War Widows Association, localism, sports in schools, diversity and corporate responsibility, human resources, employment law, intergenerational; Scotland.

Other: Member, Queen's Bodyguard for Scotland, Royal Company of Archers; Highland Society of London: Director 2005-12, President 2012-; Member, Parliamentary Choir; President of Life Members, Kate Kennedy Club; Vice-president, War Widows Association; Trustee, Mrs W Wootton Trust; Patron: Almshouses Association, Garsington Opera, Brands Museum, Buckinghamshire County Museum; Trustee, Globe Run; London Committee Member, National Trust for Scotland; Member: Chartered Institute of Marketing, Association of MBAs; Pace Aylesbury, Aylesbury Museum. White Hunter Cricket Club.

Recreations: Sailing, cricket, skiing, running, tennis, DIY, highland dancing, country pursuits.

The Viscount Younger of Leckie, House of Lords, London SW1A 0PW
Tel: 020 7219 3527 *Email:* youngerj@parliament.uk
The Old Vicarage, Dorton, Aylesbury HP18 9NH *Tel:* 01844 238396

ANALYSIS OF PEERS 1086

Peers' Political Interests

For precise details of individuals' stated interests, see relevant biography. The interests listed are supplied by Peers themselves.

Animals

See also:
Animal health
Animal rights and welfare

Benefits

See also:
Benefits payment systems

Business and industry

See also:
Business
Economics and finance
Economy
Enterprise
Finance
Financial services
Personal finance
Tax
Trade

Children and Families

See also:
Childcare
Children
Family

Communities, planning and local government

See also:
Communities
Construction industry
Housing
Local government
Planning
Urban renewal

Culture, media and sport

See also:
Alcohol licensing
Architecture
Arts
Broadcasting
Creative industries
Culture
Culture, Media and Sport
Gambling and lotteries
Heritage
Media
Music
Tourism

Defence and security

See also:
Armed Forces
Defence
Security

Disability

See also:
Disability equality
Disability rights
Disabled children
Learning disabilities

Education and skills

See also:
Education
Further and higher education
Schools
Skills
Student finance

Employment and welfare

See also:
Employment
Employment Law
Employment rights
Equal opportunities and diversity
Unemployment and jobseeking
Welfare

Energy and Utilities

See also:
Electricity
Energy
Energy Industry
Energy Security
Energy sources
Telecommunications

Environment, agriculture and rural affairs

See also:
Agriculture
Countryside
Environment
Farming
Fisheries
Recycling
Rural affairs
Rural communities
Sustainable development
Waste management

European affairs

See also:
European Union
Internal Market
Justice and Home Affairs
Regional policy

Government, politics and public administration

See also:
- Civil Service
- Constitutional Affairs
- Democracy and elections
- Ireland
- Public administration
- Scotland

Health, wellbeing and care

See also:
- Addiction
- Care
- Cosmetic surgery
- Food and drink
- Health
- Mental health
- National Health Service

Home affairs

See also:
- Animal health
- Charities and volunteers
- Consumer affairs
- Counter-terrorism
- Crime
- Human rights
- Immigration and nationality
- Justice system
- Law
- Police
- Prisons
- Security
- Sentencing
- Social affairs
- Social inclusion
- Social justice
- Youth justice

Information and communication

See also:
- Communications
- Information and communication technology
- Intellectual property

International affairs

See also:
- Foreign policy
- International development and aid
- Terrorism
- Third World

Religion

See also:
- Church Affairs

Science, technology and research

See also:
- Biotechnology
- Engineering
- Research and development
- Science
- Technology

Transport

See also:
- Aviation
- Infrastructure
- Road safety
- Road transport

Age discrimination

Baroness Barker	*Lib Dem*	p609

Agriculture

Baroness Bakewell of Hardington Mandeville	*Lib Dem*	p607
Lord Bellingham	*Con*	p615
Lord Boswell of Aynho	*NA*	p634
Viscount Brookeborough	*CB*	p647
Lord Burnett	*Lib Dem*	p654
Lord Carrington	*CB*	p666
Lord Christopher	*Lab*	p676
Lord Colgrain	*Con*	p682
Earl of Courtown	*Con*	p688
Lord Curry of Kirkharle	*CB*	p697
Lord Dannatt	*CB*	p697
Lord Davies of Stamford	*Lab*	p703
Lord Dixon-Smith	*Con*	p710
Lord Framlingham	*Con*	p746
Lord Gardiner of Kimble	*Con*	p751
Lord Garnier	*Con*	p753
Lord Hague of Richmond	*Con*	p774
Lord Hanningfield	*NA*	p782
Lord Haselhurst	*Con*	p788
Earl of Home	*Con*	p806
Earl Howe	*Con*	p812
Lord Hughes of Woodside	*Lab*	p814
Lord Inglewood	*NA*	p820
Lord Kilclooney	*CB*	p838
Earl of Lindsay	*Con*	p861
Marquess of Lothian	*Con*	p868
Earl of Lytton	*CB*	p871
Lord McCrea of Magherafelt and Cookstown	*DUP*	p874
Lord McLoughlin	*Con*	p881
Baroness Mallalieu	*Lab*	p885
Duke of Montrose	*Con*	p900
Lord Morris of Aberavon	*Lab*	p905

Baroness Neville-Rolfe	*Con*	p915
Lord Northbrook	*Con*	p919
Baroness O'Cathain	*Con*	p923
Lord Palmer	*CB*	p932
Lord Rooker	*Lab*	p975
Lord Rotherwick	*Con*	p977
Baroness Shephard of Northwold	*Con*	p995
Earl of Shrewsbury and Waterford	*Con*	p999
Lord Taylor of Holbeach	*Con*	p1026

Air transport

Lord Kirkhope of Harrogate	*Con*	p843

Airports

Lord McKenzie of Luton	*Lab*	p880
Lord Smith of Leigh	*Lab*	p1005

Alcoholism

Lord Brooke of Alverthorpe	*Lab*	p646
Lord Mancroft	*Con*	p887
Lord Mitchell	*Lab*	p898
Baroness Newlove	*Con*	p917

Animal rights and welfare

Lord Black of Brentwood	*Con*	p625
Baroness Fookes	*Con*	p740
Baroness Gale	*Lab*	p750
Lord Goldsmith of Richmond Park	*Con*	p761
Baroness Howarth of Breckland	*CB*	p810
Baroness Mallalieu	*Lab*	p885
Lord Trees	*CB*	p1035

Animals

Baroness Neville-Rolfe	*Con*	p915

Anti-social behaviour

Baroness Newlove	*Con*	p917

Apprenticeships

Lord Cotter	*Lib Dem*	p688

Architecture

Lord Beith	*Lib Dem*	p614
Lord Purvis of Tweed	*Lib Dem*	p952
Lord Vaizey of Didcot	*Con*	p1047
Baroness Whitaker	*Lab*	p1066

Armed Forces

Lord Bilimoria	*CB*	p622
Lord Colgrain	*Con*	p682
Lord Harries of Pentregarth	*CB*	p784
Lord Morris of Aberavon	*Lab*	p905
Lord Rowe-Beddoe	*CB*	p978

Arts

Lord Aberdare	*CB*	p586
Lord Adebowale	*CB*	p587
	NA	p600
Lord Archer of Weston-super-Mare		
Baroness Bakewell	*Lab*	p606
Baroness Benjamin	*Lib Dem*	p615
Lord Bird	*CB*	p624
Baroness Blackstone	*Lab Ind*	p627
Lord Bragg	*Lab*	p642
Lord Browne of Madingley	*CB*	p651
Lord Campbell of Pittenweem	*Lib Dem*	p661
Lord Carlile of Berriew	*CB*	p665
Earl of Clancarty	*CB*	p676
Lord Colwyn	*Con*	p684
Lord Cormack	*Con*	p686
Lord Davies of Oldham	*Lab*	p702
Lord Dobbs	*Con*	p710
Lord Donoughue	*Lab*	p712
Lord Eatwell	*Lab*	p720
Viscount Eccles	*Con*	p721
Lord Fellowes of West Stafford	*Con*	p733
Baroness Fleet	*Con*	p739
Lord Grade of Yarmouth	*Con*	p765
Lord Hall of Birkenhead	*CB*	p777
Baroness Hamwee	*Lib Dem*	p780
Baroness Hayman of Ullock	*Lab*	p792
Lord Howarth of Newport	*Lab*	p811
Lord Hoyle	*Lab*	p813
Lord Inglewood	*NA*	p820
Baroness Kidron	*CB*	p837
Earl of Kinnoull	*NA*	p842
Lord Lisvane	*CB*	p865
Lord Low of Dalston	*CB*	p869
Lord Lupton	*NA*	p871
Baroness McIntosh of Hudnall	*Lab*	p877
Lord Marland	*Con*	p890
Baroness Morris of Yardley	*Lab*	p907
Baroness O'Cathain	*Con*	p923
Lord Renfrew of Kaimsthorn	*Con*	p964
Lord Rowe-Beddoe	*CB*	p978
Lord Selkirk of Douglas	*Con*	p990
Lord Skidelsky	*CB*	p1001
Lord Sterling of Plaistow	*Con*	p1010
Lord Stevenson of Balmacara	*Lab*	p1014
Lord Storey	*Lib Dem*	p1017
Lord Triesman	*Lab*	p1037
Lord Trimble	*Con*	p1038
Lord True	*Con*	p1039
Lord Vaizey of Didcot	*Con*	p1047
Baroness Wheatcroft	*CB*	p1065
Lord Winston	*Lab*	p1074

Asylum

Baroness Barran	*Con*	p610
Baroness Hamwee	*Lib Dem*	p780
Lord Hardie	*CB*	p783
Lord Hylton	*CB*	p820

Lord Russell of Liverpool	*CB*	p980
Autism		
Lord Clement-Jones	*Lib Dem*	p679
Lord Maginnis of Drumglass	*Ind UU*	p884
Aviation		
Lord Brougham and Vaux	*Con*	p648
Lord Glenarthur	*Con*	p757
Lord Goddard of Stockport	*Lib Dem*	p759
Lord Haselhurst	*Con*	p788
Earl of Liverpool	*Con*	p866
Lord MacKenzie of Culkein	*Lab*	p879
Lord Rotherwick	*Con*	p977
Viscount Simon	*Lab*	p1000
Lord Soley	*Lab*	p1007
Lord Tebbit	*Con*	p1027
Lord Trefgarne	*Con*	p1035
Banking and finance		
Lord Lawson of Blaby	*Con*	p850
Lord Popat	*Con*	p946
Banking services		
Lord Triesman	*Lab*	p1037
Big Society		
Viscount Younger of Leckie	*Con*	p1084
Biodiversity		
Lord Randall of Uxbridge	*Con*	p958
Biotechnology		
Baroness Greenfield	*CB*	p768
Broadband		
Baroness Neville-Rolfe	*Con*	p915
Broadcasting		
Lord Birt	*CB*	p625
Lord Bragg	*Lab*	p642
Baroness Deech	*CB*	p705
Lord Eames	*CB*	p718
Lord Gordon of Strathblane	*Lab*	p762
Lord Griffiths of Fforestfach	*Con*	p772
Lord Hall of Birkenhead	*CB*	p777
Lord Holmes of Richmond	*Con*	p805
Baroness Jay of Paddington	*Lab*	p824
Lord Lipsey	*Lab*	p863
Lord Low of Dalston	*CB*	p869
Lord Maxton	*Lab*	p894
Lord Triesman	*Lab*	p1037
Baroness Young of Old Scone	*Lab*	p1083
Built environment		
Lord Chidgey	*Lib Dem*	p674
Business		
Lord Allen of Kensington	*Lab*	p592
Lord Bilimoria	*CB*	p622
Lord Borwick	*Con*	p634
Baroness Bottomley of Nettlestone	*Con*	p636
Baroness Brady	*Con*	p642
Lord Cotter	*Lib Dem*	p688
Baroness Couttie	*Con*	p689
Lord Cromwell	*CB*	p694
Lord Drayson	*Lab*	p713
Lord Fox	*Lib Dem*	p745
Lord Grade of Yarmouth	*Con*	p765
Baroness Harding of Winscombe	*Con*	p783
Lord Hollick	*Lab*	p803
Lord Hunt of Wirral	*Con*	p817
Lord Johnson of Marylebone	*Con*	p825
Lord Jones of Cheltenham	*Lib Dem*	p827
Lord Kirkham	*Con*	p843
Lord Lupton	*NA*	p871
Lord Marland	*Con*	p890
Baroness Morgan of Cotes	*Con*	p903
Baroness Morgan of Ely	*Lab*	p904
Bishop of Newcastle	*NA*	p916
Baroness O'Cathain	*Con*	p923
Lord Palmer of Childs Hill	*Lib Dem*	p932
Lord Razzall	*Lib Dem*	p960
Baroness Rock	*Con*	p972
Lord Rose of Monewden	*Con*	p976
Lord Taylor of Warwick	*NA*	p1026
Lord Teverson	*Lib Dem*	p1028
Baroness Vere of Norbiton	*Con*	p1049
Baroness Wheatcroft	*CB*	p1065
Business and industry		
Lord Broers	*CB*	p646
Lord Christopher	*Lab*	p676
Lord Davies of Stamford	*Lab*	p703
Lord Deben	*Con*	p704
Lord Evans of Watford	*Lab*	p725
Lord Geddes	*Con*	p753
Lord Heseltine	*NA*	p798
Lord Hodgson of Astley Abbotts	*Con*	p800
Earl of Home	*Con*	p806
Lord Jones of Cheltenham	*Lib Dem*	p827
Lord Lee of Trafford	*Lib Dem*	p853
Lord Livermore	*Lab*	p865
Lord Moonie	*NA*	p901
Lord Moynihan	*Con*	p909
Baroness Neville-Rolfe	*Con*	p915
Baroness Noakes	*Con*	p918
Baroness O'Cathain	*Con*	p923
Baroness Quin	*Lab*	p954
Lord Rogan	*UUP*	p973
Lord Sainsbury of Turville	*Lab*	p982
Lord Selsdon	*Con*	p991
Lord Triesman	*Lab*	p1037
Lord Wigley	*PlC*	p1068
Lord Wolfson of Aspley Guise	*Con*	p1076

Cancer

Lord Clement-Jones	*Lib Dem*	p679

Capital and financial markets

Lord Bilimoria	*CB*	p622

Care

Baroness Barker	*Lib Dem*	p609
Baroness Barran	*Con*	p610
Earl Howe	*Con*	p812
Baroness Janke	*Lib Dem*	p822
Lord McAvoy	*Lab/Co-op*	p872
Baroness Royall of Blaisdon	*Lab/Co-op*	p979
Lord Turnberg	*Lab*	p1041
Baroness Tyler of Enfield	*Lib Dem*	p1044

Care for the elderly

Baroness Bakewell	*Lab*	p606
Lord Christopher	*Lab*	p676
Lord Lipsey	*Lab*	p863

Charities and volunteers

Lord Allen of Kensington	*Lab*	p592
Earl of Arran	*Con*	p601
Baroness Chalker of Wallasey	*Con*	p671
Earl of Cork and Orrery	*CB*	p685
Lord Evans of Watford	*Lab*	p725
Lord Flight	*Con*	p739
Baroness Goudie	*Lab*	p763
Lord Hodgson of Astley Abbotts	*Con*	p800
Lord Howarth of Newport	*Lab*	p811
Lord Levy	*Lab*	p857
Baroness Morgan of Drefelin	*CB*	p903
Baroness Newlove	*Con*	p917
Baroness Pitkeathley	*Lab*	p944
Baroness Tyler of Enfield	*Lib Dem*	p1044

Child poverty

Earl of Listowel	*CB*	p864

Child protection

Baroness Barran	*Con*	p610
Lord Bichard	*CB*	p621
Baroness Hughes of Stretford	*Lab*	p814
Baroness Shields	*Con*	p997
Baroness Walmsley	*Lib Dem*	p1056

Children

Baroness Bakewell of Hardington Mandeville	*Lib Dem*	p607
Baroness Benjamin	*Lib Dem*	p615
Lord Boateng	*Lab*	p632
Baroness Bottomley of Nettlestone	*Con*	p636
Baroness Butler-Sloss	*CB*	p658
Bishop of Durham	*NA*	p717
Baroness Eaton	*Con*	p719
Baroness Gale	*Lab*	p750
Baroness Golding	*Lab*	p760
Baroness Goudie	*Lab*	p763
Lord Hardie	*CB*	p783
Lord Harrison	*Lab*	p787
Baroness Howarth of Breckland	*CB*	p810
Baroness Kidron	*CB*	p837
Baroness Kinnock of Holyhead	*Lab*	p842
Lord Kirkham	*Con*	p843
Baroness Lister of Burtersett	*Lab*	p863
Baroness Massey of Darwen	*Lab*	p892
Baroness Meyer	*Con*	p897
Baroness Miller of Chilthorne Domer	*Lib Dem*	p897
Lord Morgan	*Lab*	p902
Baroness Morgan of Drefelin	*CB*	p903
Lord Russell of Liverpool	*CB*	p980
Baroness Stern	*CB*	p1011
Baroness Thornton	*Lab/Co-op*	p1031
Baroness Tyler of Enfield	*Lib Dem*	p1044
Lord Warner	*CB*	p1057

Children and Families

Bishop of Gloucester	*NA*	p758
Lord Hardie	*CB*	p783

Church Affairs

Lord Field of Birkenhead	*CB*	p734

Citizenship

Lord Alton of Liverpool	*CB*	p595
Lord Blunkett	*Lab*	p631

Civil Service

Lord Butler of Brockwell	*CB*	p657
Baroness Finn	*Con*	p737
Lord Hunt of Chesterton	*Lab*	p816
Lord O'Donnell	*CB*	p924
Lord Razzall	*Lib Dem*	p960

Climate change

Baroness Altmann	*Con*	p594
Baroness Brown of Cambridge	*CB*	p648
Lord Duncan of Springbank	*Con*	p715
Baroness Featherstone	*Lib Dem*	p732
Lord Goldsmith of Richmond Park	*Con*	p761
Lord Hannay of Chiswick	*CB*	p781
Lord Hunt of Kings Heath	*Lab/Co-op*	p817
Lord Jay of Ewelme	*CB*	p823
Lord Lawson of Blaby	*Con*	p850
Baroness Liddell of Coatdyke	*Lab*	p858
Lord Oxburgh	*CB*	p929
Lord Prescott	*Lab*	p950
Lord Stunell	*Lib Dem*	p1020
Lord Turnbull	*CB*	p1042

Coasts

Lord Knight of Weymouth	*Lab/Co-op*	p844

Commonwealth

Lord Craig of Radley	*CB*	p691

Communications

Lord Currie of Marylebone	*CB*	p696
Baroness O'Neill of Bengarve	*CB*	p926

Communities

Baroness Barran	*Con*	p610
Earl of Lytton	*CB*	p871
Baroness Newlove	*Con*	p917
Lord Popat	*Con*	p946

Community Cohesion

Baroness Hussein-Ece	*Lib Dem*	p819

Community Development

Lord Haselhurst	*Con*	p788
Baroness Kennedy of Cradley	*NA*	p834

Company law

Baroness Bowles of Berkhamsted	*Lib Dem*	p637

Conservation areas

Lord Marlesford	*Con*	p891
Lord Randall of Uxbridge	*Con*	p958

Constituencies

Lord Howarth of Newport	*Lab*	p811

Constitutional Affairs

Lord Beith	*Lib Dem*	p614
Lord Birt	*CB*	p625
Lord Bourne of Aberystwyth	*Con*	p636
Lord Brown of Eaton-under-Heywood	*CB*	p649
Lord Browne of Ladyton	*Lab*	p650
Lord Butler of Brockwell	*CB*	p657
Lord Chartres	*CB*	p673
Lord Cormack	*Con*	p686
Lord Dobbs	*Con*	p710
Lord Dodds of Duncairn	*DUP*	p711
Lord Duncan of Springbank	*Con*	p715
Lord Dunlop	*Con*	p716
Lord Elis-Thomas	*NA*	p722
Baroness Falkner of Margravine	*CB*	p728
Lord Faulks	*NA*	p731
Lord Fellowes	*CB*	p733
Lord Forsyth of Drumlean	*Con*	p741
Lord German	*Lib Dem*	p754
Lord Gordon of Strathblane	*Lab*	p762
Lord Hanningfield	*NA*	p782
Lord Hollick	*Lab*	p803
Lord Hunt of Kings Heath	*Lab/Co-op*	p817
Lord Inglewood	*NA*	p820
Lord Irvine of Lairg	*Lab*	p821
Baroness Jay of Paddington	*Lab*	p824
Earl of Kinnoull	*NA*	p842
Lord Lang of Monkton	*Con*	p849
Lord Lea of Crondall	*NA*	p852
Lord Lisvane	*CB*	p865
Lord Northbrook	*Con*	p919
Lord Norton of Louth	*Con*	p920
Lord Rooker	*Lab*	p975
Baroness Shephard of Northwold	*Con*	p995
Lord True	*Con*	p1039
Lord Wallace of Saltaire	*Lib Dem*	p1054

Constitutional reform

Lord Bird	*CB*	p624
Baroness Clark of Calton	*CB*	p677
Baroness Janke	*Lib Dem*	p822
Lord Lexden	*Con*	p858
Lord Marks of Henley-on-Thames	*Lib Dem*	p890
Lord Morgan	*Lab*	p902
Lord Norton of Louth	*Con*	p920
Baroness O'Neill of Bengarve	*CB*	p926
Lord Purvis of Tweed	*Lib Dem*	p952
Lord Rennard	*Lib Dem*	p965
Baroness Stuart of Edgbaston	*NA*	p1019
Baroness Suttie	*Lib Dem*	p1022
Lord Trefgarne	*Con*	p1035
Lord Tyler	*Lib Dem*	p1043
Lord Tyrie	*NA*	p1045
Lord Wakeham	*Con*	p1051
Lord Wallace of Tankerness	*NA*	p1055
Lord Young of Cookham	*Con*	p1080

Construction industry

Baroness Chalker of Wallasey	*Con*	p671
Lord Selsdon	*Con*	p991
Earl of Shrewsbury and Waterford	*Con*	p999
Lord Stunell	*Lib Dem*	p1020

Consumer affairs

Baroness Hayter of Kentish Town	*Lab/Co-op*	p792
Baroness Howarth of Breckland	*CB*	p810
Baroness Kennedy of Cradley	*NA*	p834
Baroness Neville-Rolfe	*Con*	p915
Lord Whitty	*Lab*	p1067

Consumer rights

Baroness Altmann	*Con*	p594
Lord Deben	*Con*	p704
Lord Harris of Haringey	*Lab*	p785

Copyright

Lord Lucas of Crudwell and Dingwall	*Con*	p870
Baroness O'Neill of Bengarve	*CB*	p926

Corporate Social Responsibility

Baroness Coussins	*CB*	p689
	Lab	p1058

Baroness Warwick of Undercliffe		

Countryside

Lord Botham	*CB*	p635
Lord Bragg	*Lab*	p642
Lord Cameron of Dillington	*CB*	p660
Lord Greaves	*Lib Dem*	p766
Baroness Hoey	*NA*	p801

Countryside conservation

Earl of Lytton	*CB*	p871

Creative industries

Lord Black of Brentwood	*Con*	p625
Lord Clement-Jones	*Lib Dem*	p679
Baroness Fleet	*Con*	p739
Lord Wood of Anfield	*Lab*	p1076

Crime

Lord Bach	*Lab*	p605
Baroness Barran	*Con*	p610
Lord Birt	*CB*	p625
Baroness Evans of Bowes Park	*Con*	p725
Lord Low of Dalston	*CB*	p869
Lord Paddick	*Lib Dem*	p931
Baroness Stroud	*Con*	p1019
Lord Taverne	*Lib Dem*	p1024

Crime prevention

Lord Clement-Jones	*Lib Dem*	p679

Culture

Lord Aberdare	*CB*	p586
Lord Allen of Kensington	*Lab*	p592
Baroness Andrews	*Lab*	p598
Lord Bassam of Brighton	*Lab/Co-op*	p612
Baroness Benjamin	*Lib Dem*	p615
Lord Bilimoria	*CB*	p622
Lord Browne of Madingley	*CB*	p651
Lord Carrington	*CB*	p666
Earl of Clancarty	*CB*	p676
Baroness Doocey	*Lib Dem*	p712
Lord Dunlop	*Con*	p716
Lord Foster of Bath	*Lib Dem*	p742
Lord Hall of Birkenhead	*CB*	p777
Lord Holmes of Richmond	*Con*	p805
Baroness Hooper	*Con*	p806
Baroness Jones of Whitchurch	*Lab*	p828
Baroness Neville-Rolfe	*Con*	p915
Lord Puttnam	*Lab*	p953
Baroness Randerson	*Lib Dem*	p958
Baroness Rawlings	*Con*	p960
Lord Smith of Finsbury	*NA*	p1002
Lord Trimble	*Con*	p1038

Culture, media and sport

Lord Allen of Kensington	*Lab*	p592
Lord Holmes of Richmond	*Con*	p805
Baroness Morgan of Cotes	*Con*	p903

Cycling

Lord Colwyn	*Con*	p684

Deaf children

Lord Bruce of Bennachie	*Lib Dem*	p653

Defence

Lord Arbuthnot of Edrom	*Con*	p599
Lord Astor of Hever	*Con*	p603
Earl Attlee	*Con*	p604
Lord Bach	*Lab*	p605
Lord Balfe	*Con*	p608
Lord Bellingham	*Con*	p615
Lord Bilimoria	*CB*	p622
Viscount Brookeborough	*CB*	p647
Lord Burnett	*Lib Dem*	p654
Baroness Buscombe	*Con*	p657
Lord Campbell of Pittenweem	*Lib Dem*	p661
Lord Clark of Windermere	*Lab*	p677
Lord Cormack	*Con*	p686
Lord Craig of Radley	*CB*	p691
Lord Dannatt	*CB*	p697
Lord Davies of Stamford	*Lab*	p703
Earl of Erroll	*CB*	p724
Baroness Fookes	*Con*	p740
Lord Foulkes of Cumnock	*Lab/Co-op*	p743
Lord Fraser of Corriegarth	*Con*	p747
Lord Garnier	*Con*	p753
Lord Glenarthur	*Con*	p757
Lord Hamilton of Epsom	*Con*	p778
Lord Hammond of Runnymede	*Con*	p779
Lord Hayward	*Con*	p793
Baroness Helic	*Con*	p794
Baroness Hodgson of Abinger	*Con*	p800
Earl Howe	*Con*	p812
Lord Hutton of Furness	*Lab*	p819
Baroness Jolly	*Lib Dem*	p826
Lord Jones of Cheltenham	*Lib Dem*	p827
Lord Judd	*Lab*	p830
Lord Kirkhope of Harrogate	*Con*	p843
Lord Lancaster of Kimbolton	*Con*	p848
Lord Lee of Trafford	*Lib Dem*	p853
Baroness Liddell of Coatdyke	*Lab*	p858
Marquess of Lothian	*Con*	p868
Lord McFall of Alcluith	*NA*	p876
Lord MacKenzie of Culkein	*Lab*	p879
Lord Maginnis of Drumglass	*Ind UU*	p884
Baroness Manningham-Buller	*CB*	p889
Lord Marlesford	*Con*	p891
Lord Moonie	*NA*	p901
Baroness Nicholson of Winterbourne	*Con*	p917
Lord Powell of Bayswater	*CB*	p948
Baroness Ramsay of Cartvale	*Lab*	p956
Lord Reid of Cardowan	*Lab*	p964

Lord Richards of Herstmonceux	*CB*	p967
Lord Robathan	*Con*	p970
Lord Robertson of Port Ellen	*Lab*	p971
Lord Rogan	*UUP*	p973
Lord Rotherwick	*Con*	p977
Lord Selkirk of Douglas	*Con*	p990
Lord Selsdon	*Con*	p991
Lord Sharpe of Epsom	*Con*	p994
Baroness Smith of Newnham	*Lib Dem*	p1006
Baroness Taylor of Bolton	*Lab*	p1024
Lord Taylor of Warwick	*NA*	p1026
Lord Trefgarne	*Con*	p1035
Viscount Trenchard	*Con*	p1036
Lord Walker of Aldringham	*CB*	p1053
Lord Wallace of Saltaire	*Lib Dem*	p1054
Lord West of Spithead	*Lab*	p1064

Defence and security

Lord Bach	*Lab*	p605

Defence equipment and weapon systems

Lord James of Blackheath	*Con*	p822

Democracy and elections

Lord Campbell-Savours	*Lab*	p663
Lord Goldsmith of Richmond Park	*Con*	p761
Lord Greaves	*Lib Dem*	p766
Baroness Morris of Yardley	*Lab*	p907
Lord Purvis of Tweed	*Lib Dem*	p952
Baroness Royall of Blaisdon	*Lab/Co-op*	p979
Lord Taylor of Holbeach	*Con*	p1026

Dentists

Lord Colwyn	*Con*	p684

Development and education

Baroness D'Souza	*CB*	p714

Devolved administrations

Baroness Gale	*Lab*	p750
Lord Thomas of Cwmgiedd	*CB*	p1028

Devolved government

Baroness Morgan of Ely	*Lab*	p904
Baroness Randerson	*Lib Dem*	p958
Lord Watson of Invergowrie	*Lab*	p1060

Diabetes

Lord Kennedy of Southwark	*Lab/Co-op*	p834
Lord Rennard	*Lib Dem*	p965

Disability

Lord Addington	*Lib Dem*	p587
Baroness Brinton	*Lib Dem*	p644
Lord Browne of Ladyton	*Lab*	p650
Baroness Corston	*Lab*	p687
Baroness Doocey	*Lib Dem*	p712
Bishop of Ely	*NA*	p723
Lord Hardie	*CB*	p783
Lord Howarth of Newport	*Lab*	p811
Lord Low of Dalston	*CB*	p869
Lord McColl of Dulwich	*Con*	p872
Baroness Masham of Ilton	*CB*	p892
Baroness O'Cathain	*Con*	p923
Lord Rennard	*Lib Dem*	p965
Bishop of Salisbury	*NA*	p983
Viscount Simon	*Lab*	p1000
Lord Sterling of Plaistow	*Con*	p1010
Baroness Thomas of Winchester	*Lib Dem*	p1030
Lord Wigley	*PlC*	p1068
Lord Young of Cookham	*Con*	p1080

Disability rights

Baroness Campbell of Surbiton	*CB*	p662
Baroness Grey-Thompson	*CB*	p771

Disabled children

Baroness Flather	*CB*	p738

Domestic violence

Baroness Barran	*Con*	p610

Drug-related crime

Lord Taverne	*Lib Dem*	p1024

Drugs use and abuse

Lord Brooke of Alverthorpe	*Lab*	p646
Lord Mancroft	*Con*	p887
Baroness Masham of Ilton	*CB*	p892
Baroness Massey of Darwen	*Lab*	p892

Economic development

Baroness Brinton	*Lib Dem*	p644
Baroness Doocey	*Lib Dem*	p712
Lord Mann	*NA*	p888

Economics and finance

Lord Christopher	*Lab*	p676
Lord Dykes	*CB*	p718
Lord Eatwell	*Lab*	p720
Lord Forsyth of Drumlean	*Con*	p741
Lord Hague of Richmond	*Con*	p774
Lord Hayward	*Con*	p793
Lord Howell of Guildford	*Con*	p812
Lord Lamont of Lerwick	*Con*	p847
Lord Lawson of Blaby	*Con*	p850
Baroness Liddell of Coatdyke	*Lab*	p858
Lord Lilley	*Con*	p860
Lord McConnell of Glenscorrodale	*Lab*	p873
Lord McFall of Alcluith	*NA*	p876
Baroness McIntosh of Pickering	*Con*	p878
Lord Moonie	*NA*	p901
Baroness Neville-Rolfe	*Con*	p915
Lord Oakeshott of Seagrove Bay	*NA*	p922
Baroness O'Cathain	*Con*	p923

Economy

Education

Bishop of Ely	*NA*	p723
Lord Empey	*UUP*	p723
Baroness Evans of Bowes Park	*Con*	p725
Lord Evans of Watford	*Lab*	p725
Lord Faulks	*NA*	p731
Lord Fellowes of West Stafford	*Con*	p733
Baroness Finn	*Con*	p737
Baroness Fleet	*Con*	p739
Lord Forsyth of Drumlean	*Con*	p741
Lord Foster of Bath	*Lib Dem*	p742
Lord Fox	*Lib Dem*	p745
Baroness Garden of Frognal	*Lib Dem*	p750
Lord Garnier	*Con*	p753
Lord German	*Lib Dem*	p754
Bishop of Gloucester	*NA*	p758
Lord Griffiths of Burry Port	*Lab*	p772
Lord Griffiths of Fforestfach	*Con*	p772
Lord Hanningfield	*NA*	p782
Lord Haselhurst	*Con*	p788
Baroness Hayman	*CB*	p791
Lord Holmes of Richmond	*Con*	p805
Baroness Hooper	*Con*	p806
Lord Howarth of Newport	*Lab*	p811
Baroness Hughes of Stretford	*Lab*	p814
Lord Johnson of Marylebone	*Con*	p825
Lord Jones	*Lab*	p826
Baroness Jones of Whitchurch	*Lab*	p828
Lord Judd	*Lab*	p830
Baroness Kidron	*CB*	p837
Baroness King of Bow	*Lab*	p839
Baroness Kinnock of Holyhead	*Lab*	p842
Lord Knight of Weymouth	*Lab/Co-op*	p844
Lord Krebs	*CB*	p845
Lord Levy	*Lab*	p857
Lord Lexden	*Con*	p858
Lord Lilley	*Con*	p860
Lord Lingfield	*Con*	p862
Lord Livermore	*Lab*	p865
Lord Lucas of Crudwell and Dingwall	*Con*	p870
Lord McConnell of Glenscorrodale	*Lab*	p873
Lord McFall of Alcluith	*NA*	p876
Baroness McIntosh of Hudnall	*Lab*	p877
Lord McKenzie of Luton	*Lab*	p880
Lord McLoughlin	*Con*	p881
Lord McNicol of West Kilbride	*Lab*	p882
Lord Marks of Henley-on-Thames	*Lib Dem*	p890
Baroness Massey of Darwen	*Lab*	p892
Lord Mawson	*CB*	p894
Lord Mitchell	*Lab*	p898
Lord Morgan	*Lab*	p902
Baroness Morgan of Huyton	*Lab*	p905
Baroness Morris of Yardley	*Lab*	p907
Lord Mountevans	*CB*	p908
Lord Murphy of Torfaen	*Lab*	p910
Lord Nash	*Con*	p912
Baroness Neville-Rolfe	*Con*	p915
Lord Norton of Louth	*Con*	p920
Baroness O'Neill of Bengarve	*CB*	p926
Lord Paul	*NA*	p939
Lord Pearson of Rannoch	*NA*	p940
Baroness Prashar	*CB*	p949
Baroness Primarolo	*Lab*	p951
Lord Puttnam	*Lab*	p953
Lord Ramsbotham	*CB*	p956
Lord Rana	*Con*	p957
Lord Rees of Ludlow	*CB*	p963
Lord Renfrew of Kaimsthorn	*Con*	p964
Baroness Rock	*Con*	p972
Lord Russell of Liverpool	*CB*	p980
Lord Sainsbury of Turville	*Lab*	p982
Lord Sawyer	*Lab*	p986
Lord Selkirk of Douglas	*Con*	p990
Baroness Shafik	*CB*	p993
Lord Sharkey	*Lib Dem*	p993
Baroness Shephard of Northwold	*Con*	p995
Lord Skidelsky	*CB*	p1001
Baroness Stedman-Scott	*Con*	p1009
Lord Stephen	*Lib Dem*	p1010
Lord Storey	*Lib Dem*	p1017
Baroness Stroud	*Con*	p1019
Baroness Taylor of Bolton	*Lab*	p1024
Lord Taylor of Goss Moor	*Lib Dem*	p1025
Lord Touhig	*Lab/Co-op*	p1034
Lord True	*Con*	p1039
Baroness Vere of Norbiton	*Con*	p1049
Baroness Verma	*Con*	p1050
Lord Watts	*Lab*	p1062
Lord Wharton of Yarm	*Con*	p1064
Lord Whitty	*Lab*	p1067
Lord Willetts	*Con*	p1069
Lord Willis of Knaresborough	*Lib Dem*	p1071
Lord Wilson of Tillyorn	*CB*	p1073
Lord Winston	*Lab*	p1074

Education and skills

Lord Aberdare	*CB*	p586
Baroness Garden of Frognal	*Lib Dem*	p750
Lord German	*Lib Dem*	p754
Lord Kirkhope of Harrogate	*Con*	p843
Lord Leitch	*Lab*	p855
Baroness Thornhill	*Lib Dem*	p1030
Baroness Watkins of Tavistock	*CB*	p1059

Electoral reform

Lord Hain	*Lab*	p775

Baroness King of Bow	*Lab*	p839
Lord Lipsey	*Lab*	p863
Baroness Thomas of Winchester	*Lib Dem*	p1030

Electoral services

Lord Lexden	*Con*	p858

Employment

Lord Davies of Oldham	*Lab*	p702
Lord Holmes of Richmond	*Con*	p805
Lord Hoyle	*Lab*	p813
Baroness King of Bow	*Lab*	p839
Lord Layard	*Lab*	p851
Lord Lea of Crondall	*NA*	p852
Lord Livermore	*Lab*	p865
Lord Monks	*Lab*	p900
Lord Ramsbotham	*CB*	p956
Lord Rosser	*Lab*	p976
Lord Sawyer	*Lab*	p986
Lord Touhig	*Lab/Co-op*	p1034
Lord Whitty	*Lab*	p1067
Lord Wigley	*PlC*	p1068

Employment and welfare

Lord Blunkett	*Lab*	p631

Employment Law

Viscount Younger of Leckie	*Con*	p1084

Energy

Lord Birt	*CB*	p625
Lord Black of Brentwood	*Con*	p625
Lord Broers	*CB*	p646
Baroness Brown of Cambridge	*CB*	p648
Lord Browne of Madingley	*CB*	p651
Lord Bruce of Bennachie	*Lib Dem*	p653
Earl Cathcart	*Con*	p669
Lord Cunningham of Felling	*Lab*	p695
Lord Deben	*Con*	p704
Lord Duncan of Springbank	*Con*	p715
Baroness Featherstone	*Lib Dem*	p732
Baroness Ford	*CB*	p741
Lord Foulkes of Cumnock	*Lab/Co-op*	p743
Baroness Gardner of Parkes	*Con*	p752
Lord Geddes	*Con*	p753
Lord Hammond of Runnymede	*Con*	p779
Lord Hannay of Chiswick	*CB*	p781
Viscount Hanworth	*Lab*	p782
Lord Hardie	*CB*	p783
Lord Haworth	*Lab*	p790
Baroness Hayman of Ullock	*Lab*	p792
Baroness Hooper	*Con*	p806
Baroness Howarth of Breckland	*CB*	p810
Lord Howell of Guildford	*Con*	p812
Lord Hunt of Kings Heath	*Lab/Co-op*	p817
Lord Jay of Ewelme	*CB*	p823
Lord Lea of Crondall	*NA*	p852
Baroness Liddell of Coatdyke	*Lab*	p858
Earl of Lindsay	*Con*	p861
Baroness Morgan of Ely	*Lab*	p904
Lord Naseby	*Con*	p911
Baroness O'Cathain	*Con*	p923
Lord Oxburgh	*CB*	p929
Earl of Oxford and Asquith	*NA*	p931
Lord Rees of Ludlow	*CB*	p963
Lord Rooker	*Lab*	p975
Lord Stunell	*Lib Dem*	p1020
Lord Taylor of Holbeach	*Con*	p1026
Viscount Thurso	*Lib Dem*	p1032
Lord Turnbull	*CB*	p1042
Lord Vaizey of Didcot	*Con*	p1047
Lord Wakeham	*Con*	p1051
Lord Whitty	*Lab*	p1067

Energy Conservation

Lord Wallace of Tankerness	*NA*	p1055

Engineering

Earl Attlee	*Con*	p604
Baroness Brown of Cambridge	*CB*	p648
Lord Fox	*Lib Dem*	p745
Lord Pendry	*Lab*	p941

Enterprise

Lord Mawson	*CB*	p894
Baroness Mone	*Con*	p899
Lord Purvis of Tweed	*Lib Dem*	p952

Environment

Lord Alton of Liverpool	*CB*	p595
Baroness Armstrong of Hill Top	*Lab*	p600
Lord Barker of Battle	*Con*	p610
Lord Bassam of Brighton	*Lab/Co-op*	p612
Lord Beecham	*Lab*	p613
Lord Berkeley	*Lab*	p617
Baroness Blackwood of North Oxford	*Con*	p628
Lord Boateng	*Lab*	p632
Lord Bradshaw	*Lib Dem*	p641
Viscount Bridgeman	*Con*	p643
Lord Browne of Madingley	*CB*	p651
Lord Cameron of Dillington	*CB*	p660
Earl Cathcart	*Con*	p669
Lord Chartres	*CB*	p673
Baroness Clark of Kilwinning	*Lab*	p677
Lord Coe	*Con*	p681
Lord Colgrain	*Con*	p682
Earl of Courtown	*Con*	p688
Lord Cunningham of Felling	*Lab*	p695
Lord Deben	*Con*	p704
Lord Dixon-Smith	*Con*	p710
Lord Elis-Thomas	*NA*	p722

Earl of Erroll	*CB*	p724
Lord Forsyth of Drumlean	*Con*	p741
Lord Framlingham	*Con*	p746
Baroness Gale	*Lab*	p750
Lord Goldsmith of Richmond Park	*Con*	p761
Lord Grantchester	*Lab*	p765
Lord Greaves	*Lib Dem*	p766
Viscount Hanworth	*Lab*	p782
Lord Hardie	*CB*	p783
Lord Haworth	*Lab*	p790
Baroness Hilton of Eggardon	*Lab*	p799
Baroness Howarth of Breckland	*CB*	p810
Lord Hunt of Chesterton	*Lab*	p816
Lord Inglewood	*NA*	p820
Lord Jay of Ewelme	*CB*	p823
Lord Judd	*Lab*	p830
Baroness Kramer	*Lib Dem*	p845
Lord Krebs	*CB*	p845
Earl of Lindsay	*Con*	p861
Earl of Liverpool	*Con*	p866
Lord McCrea of Magherafelt and Cookstown	*DUP*	p874
Baroness McIntosh of Pickering	*Con*	p878
Baroness Mallalieu	*Lab*	p885
Lord Marland	*Con*	p890
Baroness Miller of Chilthorne Domer	*Lib Dem*	p897
Earl of Oxford and Asquith	*NA*	p931
Lord Palmer	*CB*	p932
Baroness Parminter	*Lib Dem*	p935
Lord Pendry	*Lab*	p941
Lord Puttnam	*Lab*	p953
Lord Randall of Uxbridge	*Con*	p958
Lord Redesdale	*Lib Dem*	p962
Baroness Ritchie of Downpatrick	*NA*	p969
Lord Robathan	*Con*	p970
Lord St John of Bletso	*CB*	p983
Bishop of Salisbury	*NA*	p983
Lord Selkirk of Douglas	*Con*	p990
Baroness Shafik	*CB*	p993
Lord Sheikh	*Con*	p995
Earl of Shrewsbury and Waterford	*Con*	p999
Lord Smith of Finsbury	*NA*	p1002
Lord Soley	*Lab*	p1007
Lord Strasburger	*Lib Dem*	p1018
Lord Taylor of Goss Moor	*Lib Dem*	p1025
Lord Taylor of Holbeach	*Con*	p1026
Lord Trees	*CB*	p1035
Lord Vaizey of Didcot	*Con*	p1047
Baroness Walmsley	*Lib Dem*	p1056
Lord Whitty	*Lab*	p1067
Baroness Young of Old Scone	*Lab*	p1083

Environment, agriculture and rural affairs

Lord Hannan of Kingsclere	*Con*	p780
Lord Kirkhope of Harrogate	*Con*	p843

Equal opportunities and diversity

Baroness Afshar	*CB*	p588
Baroness Bakewell	*Lab*	p606
Baroness Barker	*Lib Dem*	p609
Baroness Benjamin	*Lib Dem*	p615
Baroness Berridge	*Con*	p618
Lord Boswell of Aynho	*NA*	p634
Baroness Bottomley of Nettlestone	*Con*	p636
Baroness Brady	*Con*	p642
Baroness Burt of Solihull	*Lib Dem*	p656
Baroness Campbell of Surbiton	*CB*	p662
Lord Cashman	*NA*	p669
Lord Collins of Highbury	*Lab*	p683
Baroness Corston	*Lab*	p687
Baroness Coussins	*CB*	p689
Baroness Crawley	*Lab*	p693
Lord Davies of Abersoch	*NA*	p701
Baroness Falkner of Margravine	*CB*	p728
Lord Faulkner of Worcester	*Lab*	p730
Baroness Finn	*Con*	p737
Baroness Fookes	*Con*	p740
Baroness Gale	*Lab*	p750
Bishop of Gloucester	*NA*	p758
Baroness Goudie	*Lab*	p763
Baroness Greenfield	*CB*	p768
Baroness Grey-Thompson	*CB*	p771
Baroness Hayter of Kentish Town	*Lab/Co-op*	p792
Baroness Hodgson of Abinger	*Con*	p800
Lord Holmes of Richmond	*Con*	p805
Baroness Hussein-Ece	*Lib Dem*	p819
Baroness King of Bow	*Lab*	p839
Baroness Kinnock of Holyhead	*Lab*	p842
Lord Layard	*Lab*	p851
Baroness Morgan of Huyton	*Lab*	p905
Baroness Primarolo	*Lab*	p951
Baroness Prosser	*Lab*	p952
Baroness Ramsay of Cartvale	*Lab*	p956
Baroness Seccombe	*Con*	p989
Lord Taylor of Warwick	*NA*	p1026

Equal pay

Baroness Altmann	*Con*	p594
Baroness Prosser	*Lab*	p952

EU economy

Lord Marlesford	*Con*	p891

EU enlargement

Lord Davies of Gower	*Con*	p702

European affairs

Lord Davies of Stamford	*Lab*	p703
Lord Deben	*Con*	p704
Viscount of Falkland	*CB*	p728
Baroness Falkner of Margravine	*CB*	p728
Baroness Henig	*Lab*	p795
Lord Hunt of Wirral	*Con*	p817
Baroness Hussein-Ece	*Lib Dem*	p819
Baroness King of Bow	*Lab*	p839
Lord Lawson of Blaby	*Con*	p850
Lord Monks	*Lab*	p900
Duke of Montrose	*Con*	p900
Lord Morgan	*Lab*	p902
Lord Moylan	*Con*	p909
Lord Newby	*Lib Dem*	p916
Lord Purvis of Tweed	*Lib Dem*	p952
Baroness Quin	*Lab*	p954
Lord Radice	*Lab*	p955
Baroness Scott of Needham Market	*Lib Dem*	p988
Lord Skidelsky	*CB*	p1001
Baroness Smith of Newnham	*Lib Dem*	p1006
Baroness Suttie	*Lib Dem*	p1022
Lord Tebbit	*Con*	p1027
Lord Thurlow	*CB*	p1031
Lord Tomlinson	*Lab/Co-op*	p1032
Lord Tope	*Lib Dem*	p1033
Baroness Valentine	*CB*	p1048
Lord Wallace of Saltaire	*Lib Dem*	p1054
Lord Whitty	*Lab*	p1067
Lord Wigley	*PlC*	p1068

European Commission

Baroness Goudie	*Lab*	p763

European Union

Lord Ahmad of Wimbledon	*Con*	p590
Baroness Altmann	*Con*	p594
Lord Bilimoria	*CB*	p622
Lord Blackwell	*Con*	p628
Lord Boswell of Aynho	*NA*	p634
Lord Bowness	*NA*	p638
Lord Chartres	*CB*	p673
Baroness Crawley	*Lab*	p693
Lord Dykes	*CB*	p718
Lord Empey	*UUP*	p723
Baroness Fullbrook	*Con*	p749
Baroness Goudie	*Lab*	p763
Lord Hammond of Runnymede	*Con*	p779
Lord Hannay of Chiswick	*CB*	p781
Lord Harrison	*Lab*	p787
Lord Haselhurst	*Con*	p788
Baroness Hoey	*NA*	p801
Baroness Hooper	*Con*	p806
Lord Inglewood	*NA*	p820
Lord Kalms	*NA*	p832
Lord Kilclooney	*CB*	p838
Lord Lamont of Lerwick	*Con*	p847
Lord Lea of Crondall	*NA*	p852
Lord Liddle	*Lab*	p859
Lord Lilley	*Con*	p860
Lord Macpherson of Earl's Court	*CB*	p883
Baroness Morgan of Ely	*Lab*	p904
Baroness Neville-Rolfe	*Con*	p915
Lord Pearson of Rannoch	*NA*	p940
Baroness Stuart of Edgbaston	*NA*	p1019
Lord Taverne	*Lib Dem*	p1024
Lord Teverson	*Lib Dem*	p1028
Lord Tugendhat	*Con*	p1040
Lord Tyrie	*NA*	p1045
Lord Watson of Richmond	*Lib Dem*	p1061
Lord Willoughby de Broke	*NA*	p1071

Exports

Lord Naseby	*Con*	p911
Lord Popat	*Con*	p946

Faith schools

Baroness Warsi	*Con*	p1058

Family

Baroness Barran	*Con*	p610
Baroness Bottomley of Nettlestone	*Con*	p636
Baroness Butler-Sloss	*CB*	p658
Bishop of Durham	*NA*	p717
Lord Hardie	*CB*	p783
Baroness Hughes of Stretford	*Lab*	p814
Baroness Miller of Chilthorne Domer	*Lib Dem*	p897
Baroness O'Cathain	*Con*	p923
Baroness Seccombe	*Con*	p989
Baroness Stroud	*Con*	p1019
Baroness Tyler of Enfield	*Lib Dem*	p1044

Farming

Earl Cathcart	*Con*	p669
Lord Flight	*Con*	p739
Baroness McIntosh of Pickering	*Con*	p878
Lord McNicol of West Kilbride	*Lab*	p882
Baroness Masham of Ilton	*CB*	p892
Bishop of Peterborough	*NA*	p942
Lord Vaux of Harrowden	*CB*	p1049

Film Industry

Viscount of Falkland	*CB*	p728
Lord Fellowes of West Stafford	*Con*	p733

Finance

Lord Ahmad of Wimbledon	*Con*	p590
Lord Bilimoria	*CB*	p622

Lord Boswell of Aynho	*NA*	p634
Baroness Cohen of Pimlico	*Lab*	p682
Lord Davies of Stamford	*Lab*	p703
Lord Donoughue	*Lab*	p712
Lord Fraser of Corriegarth	*Con*	p747
Lord Hamilton of Epsom	*Con*	p778
Baroness Janke	*Lib Dem*	p822
Lord Johnson of Marylebone	*Con*	p825
Baroness Kramer	*Lib Dem*	p845
Lord Lawson of Blaby	*Con*	p850
Lord Lucas of Crudwell and Dingwall	*Con*	p870
Earl of Lytton	*CB*	p871
Lord Marland	*Con*	p890
Lord Northbrook	*Con*	p919
Baroness O'Cathain	*Con*	p923
Lord O'Donnell	*CB*	p924
Lord Pendry	*Lab*	p941
Lord St John of Bletso	*CB*	p983
Lord Selsdon	*Con*	p991
Lord Sharkey	*Lib Dem*	p993
Lord Teverson	*Lib Dem*	p1028
Lord Tomlinson	*Lab/Co-op*	p1032
Lord Vaux of Harrowden	*CB*	p1049
Baroness Wheatcroft	*CB*	p1065

Financial services

Baroness Altmann	*Con*	p594
Baroness Bowles of Berkhamsted	*Lib Dem*	p637
Lord Christopher	*Lab*	p676
Earl of Cork and Orrery	*CB*	p685
Earl of Kinnoull	*NA*	p842
Lord Leitch	*Lab*	p855
Baroness Morgan of Cotes	*Con*	p903
Lord Naseby	*Con*	p911
Lord Sassoon	*Con*	p985
Lord Sheikh	*Con*	p995
Viscount Thurso	*Lib Dem*	p1032
Viscount Trenchard	*Con*	p1036
Lord Turnbull	*CB*	p1042

Financial services regulation

Lord Foulkes of Cumnock	*Lab/Co-op*	p743
Lord Sharpe of Epsom	*Con*	p994

Fisheries

Lord Cameron of Dillington	*CB*	p660
Lord Duncan of Springbank	*Con*	p715
Baroness Golding	*Lab*	p760
Lord Hughes of Woodside	*Lab*	p814
Earl of Shrewsbury and Waterford	*Con*	p999

Food and drink

Lord Cameron of Dillington	*CB*	p660
Lord Curry of Kirkharle	*CB*	p697
Baroness Jones of Whitchurch	*Lab*	p828
Lord Krebs	*CB*	p845
Baroness Miller of Chilthorne Domer	*Lib Dem*	p897
Baroness Parminter	*Lib Dem*	p935
Lord Rooker	*Lab*	p975

Food industry

Earl of Lindsay	*Con*	p861
Baroness Neville-Rolfe	*Con*	p915
Lord Whitty	*Lab*	p1067

Foreign policy

Lord Austin of Dudley	*NA*	p604
Lord Balfe	*Con*	p608
Lord Bates	*Con*	p612
Lord Bellingham	*Con*	p615
Lord Bew	*CB*	p620
Lord Craig of Radley	*CB*	p691
Lord Davies of Gower	*Con*	p702
Lord Garnier	*Con*	p753
Lord Giddens	*Lab*	p755
Lord Hanningfield	*NA*	p782
Baroness Helic	*Con*	p794
Baroness Hodgson of Abinger	*Con*	p800
Baroness Hoey	*NA*	p801
Lord Holmes of Richmond	*Con*	p805
Lord Hylton	*CB*	p820
Lord Jay of Ewelme	*CB*	p823
Lord Kirkhope of Harrogate	*Con*	p843
Baroness Manningham-Buller	*CB*	p889
Lord Palmer of Childs Hill	*Lib Dem*	p932
Lord Radice	*Lab*	p955
Lord Richards of Herstmonceux	*CB*	p967
Baroness Royall of Blaisdon	*Lab/Co-op*	p979
Lord Soley	*Lab*	p1007
Baroness Stern	*CB*	p1011
Lord Tomlinson	*Lab/Co-op*	p1032
Lord Trimble	*Con*	p1038
Lord Tugendhat	*Con*	p1040
Baroness Williams of Trafford	*Con*	p1070
Lord Wood of Anfield	*Lab*	p1076

Forestry

Lord Clark of Windermere	*Lab*	p677
Lord Framlingham	*Con*	p746
Lord McColl of Dulwich	*Con*	p872

Freedom of information

Lord Cashman	*NA*	p669

Freight transport

Lord Taylor of Holbeach	*Con*	p1026

Further and higher education

Lord Bilimoria	*CB*	p622
Baroness Blackwood of North Oxford	*Con*	p628
Baroness Bottomley of Nettlestone	*Con*	p636
Lord Bragg	*Lab*	p642

Lord Oxburgh	*CB*	p929
Lord Pickles	*Con*	p943
Baroness Pitkeathley	*Lab*	p944
Baroness Primarolo	*Lab*	p951
Lord Rana	*Con*	p957
Baroness Randerson	*Lib Dem*	p958
Lord Rennard	*Lib Dem*	p965
Baroness Ritchie of Downpatrick	*NA*	p969
Lord Scriven	*Lib Dem*	p989
Lord Selkirk of Douglas	*Con*	p990
Lord Selsdon	*Con*	p991
Lord Sharkey	*Lib Dem*	p993
Lord Smith of Finsbury	*NA*	p1002
Lord Smith of Leigh	*Lab*	p1005
Lord Stephen	*Lib Dem*	p1010
Baroness Stroud	*Con*	p1019
Baroness Suttie	*Lib Dem*	p1022
Lord Touhig	*Lab/Co-op*	p1034
Lord Trees	*CB*	p1035
Baroness Tyler of Enfield	*Lib Dem*	p1044
Baroness Verma	*Con*	p1050
Baroness Warwick of Undercliffe	*Lab*	p1058
Lord Willetts	*Con*	p1069
Lord Willis of Knaresborough	*Lib Dem*	p1071
Lord Winston	*Lab*	p1074

Health and social care professionals

Lord Warner	*CB*	p1057
Baroness Young of Old Scone	*Lab*	p1083

Health, wellbeing and care

Baroness Watkins of Tavistock	*CB*	p1059

Heritage

Lord Aberdare	*CB*	p586
Lord Allan of Hallam	*Lib Dem*	p592
Baroness Andrews	*Lab*	p598
Lord Carrington	*CB*	p666
Lord Cormack	*Con*	p686
Lord Gardiner of Kimble	*Con*	p751
Baroness Hooper	*Con*	p806
Lord Howarth of Newport	*Lab*	p811
Lord Lisvane	*CB*	p865
Lord Palmer	*CB*	p932
Baroness Rawlings	*Con*	p960
Lord Renfrew of Kaimsthorn	*Con*	p964
Lord Rowe-Beddoe	*CB*	p978
Lord Selkirk of Douglas	*Con*	p990
Duke of Somerset	*CB*	p1008
Baroness Warwick of Undercliffe	*Lab*	p1058

HIV and AIDS

Lord Fowler	*Lord Speaker*	p744

Home affairs

Lord Allan of Hallam	*Lib Dem*	p592
Lord Allen of Kensington	*Lab*	p592
Lord Bassam of Brighton	*Lab/Co-op*	p612
Baroness Blackwood of North Oxford	*Con*	p628
Lord Boateng	*Lab*	p632
Viscount Bridgeman	*Con*	p643
Lord Carlile of Berriew	*CB*	p665
Lord Davies of Gower	*Con*	p702
Lord Dholakia	*Lib Dem*	p709
Baroness Hamwee	*Lib Dem*	p780
Lord Howard of Lympne	*Con*	p809
Lord Hutton of Furness	*Lab*	p819
Lord Irvine of Lairg	*Lab*	p821
Baroness Kennedy of Cradley	*NA*	p834
Lord Mackenzie of Framwellgate	*NA*	p880
Baroness Mallalieu	*Lab*	p885
Lord Sheikh	*Con*	p995
Baroness Verma	*Con*	p1050

Homelessness

Lord Fairfax of Cameron	*Con*	p726
Lord McNicol of West Kilbride	*Lab*	p882
Bishop of Salisbury	*NA*	p983

Horse racing

Viscount of Falkland	*CB*	p728
Baroness Golding	*Lab*	p760
Lord James of Blackheath	*Con*	p822
Lord Lipsey	*Lab*	p863
Baroness Noakes	*Con*	p918

House of Lords

Baroness D'Souza	*CB*	p714

Housing

Lord Alton of Liverpool	*CB*	p595
Baroness Andrews	*Lab*	p598
Lord Austin of Dudley	*NA*	p604
Baroness Bakewell of Hardington Mandeville	*Lib Dem*	p607
Lord Barwell	*Con*	p611
Lord Bassam of Brighton	*Lab/Co-op*	p612
Lord Best	*CB*	p619
Lord Bird	*CB*	p624
Lord Boateng	*Lab*	p632
Lord Bradley	*Lab*	p640
Lord Cameron of Dillington	*CB*	p660
Earl Cathcart	*Con*	p669
Earl of Courtown	*Con*	p688
Baroness Doocey	*Lib Dem*	p712
Lord Filkin	*Lab*	p735
Baroness Ford	*CB*	p741
Lord Gardiner of Kimble	*Con*	p751
Baroness Gardner of Parkes	*Con*	p752

Lord Goddard of Stockport	*Lib Dem*	p759
Baroness Grender	*Lib Dem*	p770
Lord Hammond of Runnymede	*Con*	p779
Baroness Hoey	*NA*	p801
Lord Hylton	*CB*	p820
Baroness Jones of Whitchurch	*Lab*	p828
Lord Kerslake	*CB*	p836
Baroness King of Bow	*Lab*	p839
Marquess of Lothian	*Con*	p868
Lord McNicol of West Kilbride	*Lab*	p882
Lord Murphy of Torfaen	*Lab*	p910
Lord Oakeshott of Seagrove Bay	*NA*	p922
Lord Paddick	*Lib Dem*	p931
Lord Pendry	*Lab*	p941
Lord Pickles	*Con*	p943
Baroness Primarolo	*Lab*	p951
Lord Rooker	*Lab*	p975
Lord Sawyer	*Lab*	p986
Lord Selkirk of Douglas	*Con*	p990
Earl of Shrewsbury and Waterford	*Con*	p999
Lord Smith of Finsbury	*NA*	p1002
Lord Taylor of Goss Moor	*Lib Dem*	p1025
Baroness Thornhill	*Lib Dem*	p1030
Baroness Valentine	*CB*	p1048
Baroness Watkins of Tavistock	*CB*	p1059
Lord Young of Cookham	*Con*	p1080

Human rights

Lord Alton of Liverpool	*CB*	p595
Baroness Anelay of St Johns	*Con*	p598
Baroness Barker	*Lib Dem*	p609
Baroness Berridge	*Con*	p618
Baroness Blackwood of North Oxford	*Con*	p628
Lord Browne of Ladyton	*Lab*	p650
Baroness Campbell of Surbiton	*CB*	p662
Lord Cashman	*NA*	p669
Lord Cooper of Windrush	*NA*	p685
Lord Cormack	*Con*	p686
Baroness Corston	*Lab*	p687
Baroness Cox	*CB*	p690
Lord Dannatt	*CB*	p697
Baroness D'Souza	*CB*	p714
Lord Dubs	*Lab*	p715
Lord Faulkner of Worcester	*Lab*	p730
Lord Faulks	*NA*	p731
Lord Foulkes of Cumnock	*Lab/Co-op*	p743
Baroness Goudie	*Lab*	p763
Lord Greaves	*Lib Dem*	p766
Lord Hardie	*CB*	p783
Lord Harries of Pentregarth	*CB*	p784
Baroness Hayman of Ullock	*Lab*	p792
Baroness Helic	*Con*	p794
Lord Hylton	*CB*	p820
Lord Judd	*Lab*	p830
Lord Macdonald of River Glaven	*CB*	p875
Lord Marks of Henley-on-Thames	*Lib Dem*	p890
Baroness Miller of Chilthorne Domer	*Lib Dem*	p897
Lord Morgan	*Lab*	p902
Baroness Neuberger	*CB*	p913
Baroness Nicholson of Winterbourne	*Con*	p917
Baroness O'Loan	*CB*	p925
Lord Paddick	*Lib Dem*	p931
Baroness Prashar	*CB*	p949
Lord Rana	*Con*	p957
Lord Rennard	*Lib Dem*	p965
Lord Russell of Liverpool	*CB*	p980
Lord Scriven	*Lib Dem*	p989
Lord Smith of Finsbury	*NA*	p1002
Lord Soley	*Lab*	p1007
Baroness Stern	*CB*	p1011
Lord Strasburger	*Lib Dem*	p1018
Baroness Suttie	*Lib Dem*	p1022

Humanitarian aid

Lord Allen of Kensington	*Lab*	p592
Baroness Cox	*CB*	p690

Hunting

Earl of Shrewsbury and Waterford	*Con*	p999

Immigration and nationality

Baroness Barran	*Con*	p610
Lord Barwell	*Con*	p611
Lord Dubs	*Lab*	p715
Bishop of Durham	*NA*	p717
Lord Geddes	*Con*	p753
Lord Green of Deddington	*CB*	p767
Baroness Hamwee	*Lib Dem*	p780
Lord Hardie	*CB*	p783
Lord Hoyle	*Lab*	p813
Lord Russell of Liverpool	*CB*	p980
Bishop of Southwark	*NA*	p1008
Lord Taylor of Warwick	*NA*	p1026

Infrastructure

Lord Hanningfield	*NA*	p782
Lord Moylan	*Con*	p909
Lord Thurlow	*CB*	p1031
Baroness Valentine	*CB*	p1048

Insurance

Lord Fairfax of Cameron	*Con*	p726
Earl of Kinnoull	*NA*	p842

Intellectual property

Baroness Bowles of Berkhamsted	*Lib Dem*	p637
Lord Clement-Jones	*Lib Dem*	p679
Lord Stevenson of Balmacara	*Lab*	p1014

Intelligence Services

Lord Powell of Bayswater	*CB*	p948
Baroness Ramsay of Cartvale	*Lab*	p956
Baroness Taylor of Bolton	*Lab*	p1024
Lord Triesman	*Lab*	p1037

International affairs

Lord Ahmad of Wimbledon	*Con*	p590
Baroness Anelay of St Johns	*Con*	p598
Lord Arbuthnot of Edrom	*Con*	p599
Bishop of Birmingham	*NA*	p624
Baroness Blackstone	*Lab Ind*	p627
Lord Bourne of Aberystwyth	*Con*	p636
Lord Browne of Ladyton	*Lab*	p650
Lord Campbell of Pittenweem	*Lib Dem*	p661
Lord Chidgey	*Lib Dem*	p674
Lord Coe	*Con*	p681
Lord Collins of Highbury	*Lab*	p683
Viscount Colville of Culross	*CB*	p684
Lord Cotter	*Lib Dem*	p688
Baroness Coussins	*CB*	p689
Bishop of Coventry	*NA*	p690
Lord Dobbs	*Con*	p710
Lord Dodds of Duncairn	*DUP*	p711
Lord Foulkes of Cumnock	*Lab/Co-op*	p743
Lord Glenarthur	*Con*	p757
Lord Griffiths of Burry Port	*Lab*	p772
Lord Hain	*Lab*	p775
Viscount Hanworth	*Lab*	p782
Baroness Henig	*Lab*	p795
Earl of Home	*Con*	p806
Lord Horam	*Con*	p808
Lord Howard of Lympne	*Con*	p809
Lord Howell of Guildford	*Con*	p812
Baroness Jolly	*Lib Dem*	p826
Lord Judd	*Lab*	p830
Lord Kerr of Kinlochard	*CB*	p835
Lord Lamont of Lerwick	*Con*	p847
Lord Lancaster of Kimbolton	*Con*	p848
Bishop of Leeds	*NA*	p854
Baroness Liddell of Coatdyke	*Lab*	p858
Lord Mawson	*CB*	p894
Baroness Meyer	*Con*	p897
Lord Mitchell	*Lab*	p898
Lord Morgan	*Lab*	p902
Lord Moylan	*Con*	p909
Lord Moynihan	*Con*	p909
Lord Murphy of Torfaen	*Lab*	p910
Baroness Neville-Jones	*Con*	p914
Baroness Neville-Rolfe	*Con*	p915
Baroness Nicholson of Winterbourne	*Con*	p917
Lord Owen	*Ind Soc Dem*	p928
Earl of Oxford and Asquith	*NA*	p931
Lord Parekh	*Lab*	p933
Lord Paul	*NA*	p939
Lord Ponsonby of Shulbrede	*Lab*	p946
Lord Popat	*Con*	p946
Lord Powell of Bayswater	*CB*	p948
Baroness Prashar	*CB*	p949
Lord Purvis of Tweed	*Lib Dem*	p952
Baroness Ramsay of Cartvale	*Lab*	p956
Lord Randall of Uxbridge	*Con*	p958
Baroness Rawlings	*Con*	p960
Lord Reid of Cardowan	*Lab*	p964
Lord Renfrew of Kaimsthorn	*Con*	p964
Lord Risby	*Con*	p969
Lord Robertson of Port Ellen	*Lab*	p971
Lord St John of Bletso	*CB*	p983
Lord Selkirk of Douglas	*Con*	p990
Lord Selsdon	*Con*	p991
Lord Sheikh	*Con*	p995
Duke of Somerset	*CB*	p1008
Bishop of Southwark	*NA*	p1008
Lord Sterling of Plaistow	*Con*	p1010
Baroness Suttie	*Lib Dem*	p1022
Lord Teverson	*Lib Dem*	p1028
Viscount Trenchard	*Con*	p1036
Lord Triesman	*Lab*	p1037
Lord Tyrie	*NA*	p1045
Lord Wallace of Saltaire	*Lib Dem*	p1054
Baroness Warsi	*Con*	p1058
Lord West of Spithead	*Lab*	p1064

International development and aid

Lord Ahmad of Wimbledon	*Con*	p590
Baroness Andrews	*Lab*	p598
Baroness Armstrong of Hill Top	*Lab*	p600
Earl Attlee	*Con*	p604
Lord Barker of Battle	*Con*	p610
Baroness Blackwood of North Oxford	*Con*	p628
Lord Boateng	*Lab*	p632
Lord Cameron of Dillington	*CB*	p660
Baroness Chalker of Wallasey	*Con*	p671
Lord Chidgey	*Lib Dem*	p674
Lord Christopher	*Lab*	p676
Lord Clarke of Hampstead	*Lab*	p678
Lord Davies of Stamford	*Lab*	p703
Bishop of Durham	*NA*	p717
Lord Foster of Bath	*Lib Dem*	p742
Lord Foulkes of Cumnock	*Lab/Co-op*	p743
Bishop of Gloucester	*NA*	p758
Lord Hannay of Chiswick	*CB*	p781
Lord Haskel	*Lab*	p789

Lord Herbert of South Downs	*Con*	p797
Baroness Hodgson of Abinger	*Con*	p800
Lord Hughes of Woodside	*Lab*	p814
Baroness Jay of Paddington	*Lab*	p824
Baroness Kennedy of Cradley	*NA*	p834
Baroness Kinnock of Holyhead	*Lab*	p842
Lord Lancaster of Kimbolton	*Con*	p848
Lord McConnell of Glenscorrodale	*Lab*	p873
Lord Moynihan	*Con*	p909
Lord Oakeshott of Seagrove Bay	*NA*	p922
Lord Oates	*Lib Dem*	p923
Lord Popat	*Con*	p946
Lord Rana	*Con*	p957
Lord Robathan	*Con*	p970
Bishop of Southwark	*NA*	p1008
Baroness Stern	*CB*	p1011
Baroness Suttie	*Lib Dem*	p1022
Lord Taylor of Goss Moor	*Lib Dem*	p1025
Lord Tomlinson	*Lab/Co-op*	p1032
Lord Trees	*CB*	p1035
Baroness Verma	*Con*	p1050
Baroness Warwick of Undercliffe	*Lab*	p1058
Lord Watson of Invergowrie	*Lab*	p1060
Baroness Whitaker	*Lab*	p1066

Internet

Baroness Kidron	*CB*	p837
Lord Maxton	*Lab*	p894

Investment

Lord Carrington	*CB*	p666
Baroness Hughes of Stretford	*Lab*	p814
Lord Johnson of Marylebone	*Con*	p825
Lord Lee of Trafford	*Lib Dem*	p853
Lord Sassoon	*Con*	p985

Ireland

Lord Dubs	*Lab*	p715
Lord Kilclooney	*CB*	p838

Islam

Baroness Afshar	*CB*	p588
Lord Kalms	*NA*	p832
Lord Pearson of Rannoch	*NA*	p940

Justice system

Lord Bach	*Lab*	p605
Lord Beecham	*Lab*	p613
Lord Beith	*Lib Dem*	p614
Baroness Clark of Calton	*CB*	p677
Bishop of Gloucester	*NA*	p758
Baroness Henig	*Lab*	p795
Baroness Hilton of Eggardon	*Lab*	p799
Baroness Kidron	*CB*	p837
Lord Kirkhope of Harrogate	*Con*	p843
Lord Macdonald of River Glaven	*CB*	p875
Lord McNally	*Lib Dem*	p882
Lord Marks of Henley-on-Thames	*Lib Dem*	p890
Baroness Meacher	*CB*	p895
Baroness Newlove	*Con*	p917
Baroness O'Loan	*CB*	p925
Lord Paddick	*Lib Dem*	p931
Baroness Prashar	*CB*	p949
Lord Rosser	*Lab*	p976
Baroness Sater	*Con*	p986
Baroness Seccombe	*Con*	p989
Lord Smith of Finsbury	*NA*	p1002
Baroness Stern	*CB*	p1011
Lord Thomas of Cwmgiedd	*CB*	p1028
Lord Thomas of Gresford	*Lib Dem*	p1029

Labour Party

Lord Davies of Abersoch	*NA*	p701
Baroness Healy of Primrose Hill	*Lab*	p794
Lord Jordan	*Lab*	p829
Lord Radice	*Lab*	p955

Law

Lord Arbuthnot of Edrom	*Con*	p599
Lord Brown of Eaton-under-Heywood	*CB*	p649
Lord Hardie	*CB*	p783
Baroness Mallalieu	*Lab*	p885
Lord Selkirk of Douglas	*Con*	p990

Law and order

Baroness Buscombe	*Con*	p657
Lord Warner	*CB*	p1057
Lord Wharton of Yarm	*Con*	p1064

Learning disabilities

Baroness Browning	*Con*	p652

Legal affairs

Lord Bellingham	*Con*	p615
Lord Browne of Ladyton	*Lab*	p650
Baroness Buscombe	*Con*	p657
Baroness Butler-Sloss	*CB*	p658
Lord Campbell of Pittenweem	*Lib Dem*	p661
Lord Carlile of Berriew	*CB*	p665
Lord Hutton of Furness	*Lab*	p819
Lord Inglewood	*NA*	p820
Lord Irvine of Lairg	*Lab*	p821
Baroness McIntosh of Pickering	*Con*	p878
Lord Mackenzie of Framwellgate	*NA*	p880
Lord Morris of Aberavon	*Lab*	p905
Lord Pannick	*CB*	p933
Lord St John of Bletso	*CB*	p983
Lord Trimble	*Con*	p1038

Legal aid

Lord Beecham	*Lab*	p613

Local government

Lord Bach	*Lab*	p605
Baroness Bakewell of Hardington Mandeville	*Lib Dem*	p607
Lord Bassam of Brighton	*Lab/Co-op*	p612
Lord Beecham	*Lab*	p613
Bishop of Birmingham	*NA*	p624
Lord Blunkett	*Lab*	p631
Lord Bowness	*NA*	p638
Lord Bradley	*Lab*	p640
Viscount Bridgeman	*Con*	p643
Baroness Couttie	*Con*	p689
Baroness Cumberlege	*Con*	p695
Viscount Eccles	*Con*	p721
Lord Forsyth of Drumlean	*Con*	p741
Lord Greaves	*Lib Dem*	p766
Baroness Hamwee	*Lib Dem*	p780
Lord Hanningfield	*NA*	p782
Lord Harris of Haringey	*Lab*	p785
Baroness Hughes of Stretford	*Lab*	p814
Baroness Hussein-Ece	*Lib Dem*	p819
Lord Inglewood	*NA*	p820
Baroness Janke	*Lib Dem*	p822
Lord Kerslake	*CB*	p836
Lord Lansley	*Con*	p849
Earl of Lytton	*CB*	p871
Lord McKenzie of Luton	*Lab*	p880
Lord Murphy of Torfaen	*Lab*	p910
Lord Palmer of Childs Hill	*Lib Dem*	p932
Lord Pickles	*Con*	p943
Lord Scriven	*Lib Dem*	p989
Lord Selkirk of Douglas	*Con*	p990
Lord Shipley	*Lib Dem*	p998
Lord Smith of Finsbury	*NA*	p1002
Lord Smith of Leigh	*Lab*	p1005
Lord Storey	*Lib Dem*	p1017
Lord Stunell	*Lib Dem*	p1020
Lord Tope	*Lib Dem*	p1033
Lord Touhig	*Lab/Co-op*	p1034
Lord True	*Con*	p1039
Baroness Williams of Trafford	*Con*	p1070
Lord Willis of Knaresborough	*Lib Dem*	p1071

London economy

Baroness Valentine	*CB*	p1048

Manufacturing

Lord Austin of Dudley	*NA*	p604
Lord Bilimoria	*CB*	p622
Baroness Burt of Solihull	*Lib Dem*	p656
Lord Fox	*Lib Dem*	p745
Lord Jones	*Lab*	p826
Lord Paul	*NA*	p939
Lord Razzall	*Lib Dem*	p960
Lord Renfrew of Kaimsthorn	*Con*	p964
Lord Taylor of Goss Moor	*Lib Dem*	p1025

Media

Lord Allen of Kensington	*Lab*	p592
Earl of Arran	*Con*	p601
Baroness Benjamin	*Lib Dem*	p615
Lord Black of Brentwood	*Con*	p625
Baroness Buscombe	*Con*	p657
Viscount Colville of Culross	*CB*	p684
Baroness Cumberlege	*Con*	p695
Lord Currie of Marylebone	*CB*	p696
Lord Fowler	*Lord Speaker*	p744
Lord Grade of Yarmouth	*Con*	p765
Lord Grocott	*Lab*	p773
Lord Hollick	*Lab*	p803
Lord Holmes of Richmond	*Con*	p805
Lord Inglewood	*NA*	p820
Baroness Jay of Paddington	*Lab*	p824
Baroness Jones of Whitchurch	*Lab*	p828
Baroness Kidron	*CB*	p837
Baroness Liddell of Coatdyke	*Lab*	p858
Lord McNally	*Lib Dem*	p882
Baroness Neville-Rolfe	*Con*	p915
Lord Palmer	*CB*	p932
Baroness Rawlings	*Con*	p960
Lord Smith of Finsbury	*NA*	p1002
Lord Taylor of Warwick	*NA*	p1026
Baroness Thornton	*Lab/Co-op*	p1031
Lord Vaizey of Didcot	*Con*	p1047
Lord Wood of Anfield	*Lab*	p1076

Medical ethics

Baroness Campbell of Surbiton	*CB*	p662
Baroness Finlay of Llandaff	*CB*	p736
Baroness O'Neill of Bengarve	*CB*	p926

Medical schools

Lord Turnberg	*Lab*	p1041

Medicines

Lord Faulks	*NA*	p731
Baroness Finlay of Llandaff	*CB*	p736
Lord McColl of Dulwich	*Con*	p872
Lord Patel	*CB*	p936

Medicines in the Third World

Lord Trees	*CB*	p1035

Mental health

Lord Alderdice	*Lib Dem*	p591
Baroness Browning	*Con*	p652
Lord Davies of Brixton	*Lab*	p701
Bishop of Ely	*NA*	p723
Lord Fairfax of Cameron	*Con*	p726
Lord Layard	*Lab*	p851
Baroness Meacher	*CB*	p895
Baroness Morgan of Cotes	*Con*	p903
Baroness Murphy	*CB*	p910

Lord Oates	*Lib Dem*	p923
Baroness Parminter	*Lib Dem*	p935
Bishop of Peterborough	*NA*	p942
Lord Ramsbotham	*CB*	p956
Lord Thurlow	*CB*	p1031
Baroness Vere of Norbiton	*Con*	p1049

Mineral extraction

Earl of Shrewsbury and Waterford	*Con*	p999

Motor industry

Lord Brougham and Vaux	*Con*	p648
Viscount Simon	*Lab*	p1000

Museums and galleries

Viscount Eccles	*Con*	p721
Lord Renfrew of Kaimsthorn	*Con*	p964

Music

Baroness Fleet	*Con*	p739
Baroness Jolly	*Lib Dem*	p826
Lord Lipsey	*Lab*	p863
Lord Low of Dalston	*CB*	p869
Lord Sterling of Plaistow	*Con*	p1010

National Health Service

Lord Clarke of Nottingham	*Con*	p679
Baroness Cumberlege	*Con*	p695
Lord Dubs	*Lab*	p715
Lord Grocott	*Lab*	p773
Baroness Hayman of Ullock	*Lab*	p792
Lord James of Blackheath	*Con*	p822
Lord Jones	*Lab*	p826
Lord McColl of Dulwich	*Con*	p872
Baroness Murphy	*CB*	p910
Lord Naseby	*Con*	p911
Lord Patel	*CB*	p936
Lord Turnberg	*Lab*	p1041

National security

Baroness Manningham-Buller	*CB*	p889
Baroness Neville-Jones	*Con*	p914

National Service

Baroness Newlove	*Con*	p917

NATO

Lord Cormack	*Con*	p686

Northern Ireland

Lord Alderdice	*Lib Dem*	p591
Lord Alton of Liverpool	*CB*	p595
Lord Bellingham	*Con*	p615
Viscount Brookeborough	*CB*	p647
Lord Browne of Ladyton	*Lab*	p650
Lord Dunlop	*Con*	p716
Lord Eames	*CB*	p718
Baroness Harris of Richmond	*Lib Dem*	p787
Lord Hylton	*CB*	p820
Lord Lexden	*Con*	p858
Lord Robathan	*Con*	p970
Lord Rogan	*UUP*	p973
Lord Wood of Anfield	*Lab*	p1076

Nuclear weapons

Baroness Miller of Chilthorne Domer	*Lib Dem*	p897

Nursing

Baroness Cox	*CB*	p690
Lord MacKenzie of Culkein	*Lab*	p879

Obesity

Lord McColl of Dulwich	*Con*	p872

Osteoporosis

Baroness Burt of Solihull	*Lib Dem*	p656

Parliamentary administration

Lord Lisvane	*CB*	p865
Lord Livermore	*Lab*	p865
Lord Naseby	*Con*	p911

Peacekeeping operations

Lord Taylor of Warwick	*NA*	p1026

Pensions

Baroness Altmann	*Con*	p594
Baroness Bakewell	*Lab*	p606
Lord Bradley	*Lab*	p640
Lord Christopher	*Lab*	p676
Baroness Clark of Calton	*CB*	p677
Lord Davies of Brixton	*Lab*	p701
Lord Davies of Stamford	*Lab*	p703
Lord Flight	*Con*	p739
Lord Grabiner	*CB*	p764
Lord Holmes of Richmond	*Con*	p805
Lord Leitch	*Lab*	p855
Lord Lipsey	*Lab*	p863
Lord Paddick	*Lib Dem*	p931
Lord Sheikh	*Con*	p995
Baroness Stuart of Edgbaston	*NA*	p1019
Lord Vinson	*Con*	p1051
Baroness Warwick of Undercliffe	*Lab*	p1058

Performing arts

Earl of Glasgow	*Lib Dem*	p756

Personal finance

Baroness Altmann	*Con*	p594
Baroness Hayman of Ullock	*Lab*	p792

Planning

Baroness Andrews	*Lab*	p598
Baroness Billingham	*Lab*	p623
Lord Borwick	*Con*	p634
Lord Bradshaw	*Lib Dem*	p641
Baroness Burt of Solihull	*Lib Dem*	p656
Baroness Ford	*CB*	p741
Baroness Gardner of Parkes	*Con*	p752
Lord Goddard of Stockport	*Lib Dem*	p759
	Con	p779

Lord Hammond of Runnymede		
Baroness Hamwee	*Lib Dem*	p780
Lord Lucas of Crudwell and Dingwall	*Con*	p870
Earl of Lytton	*CB*	p871
Lord McCrea of Magherafelt and Cookstown	*DUP*	p874
Lord Moylan	*Con*	p909
Lord Paddick	*Lib Dem*	p931
Lord Rooker	*Lab*	p975
Lord Selsdon	*Con*	p991
Lord Taylor of Goss Moor	*Lib Dem*	p1025
Baroness Thornhill	*Lib Dem*	p1030

Police

Baroness Berridge	*Con*	p618
Lord Bradshaw	*Lib Dem*	p641
Lord Colgrain	*Con*	p682
Lord Davies of Gower	*Con*	p702
Baroness Doocey	*Lib Dem*	p712
Lord Harris of Haringey	*Lab*	p785
Baroness Harris of Richmond	*Lib Dem*	p787
Baroness Henig	*Lab*	p795
Lord Mackenzie of Framwellgate	*NA*	p880
Baroness Newlove	*Con*	p917
Lord Sharpe of Epsom	*Con*	p994
Viscount Simon	*Lab*	p1000

Policy making

Lord Sainsbury of Turville	*Lab*	p982

Political parties

Lord Taylor of Holbeach	*Con*	p1026

Politics

Lord Norton of Louth	*Con*	p920

Postal Services

Earl of Kinnoull	*NA*	p842
Lord Sawyer	*Lab*	p986

Poverty

Lord Adebowale	*CB*	p587
Lord Bird	*CB*	p624
Lord Bradley	*Lab*	p640
Lord Cashman	*NA*	p669
Lord Field of Birkenhead	*CB*	p734
Lord Harries of Pentregarth	*CB*	p784
Baroness Jolly	*Lib Dem*	p826
Baroness King of Bow	*Lab*	p839
Baroness Lister of Burtersett	*Lab*	p863
Lord Rana	*Con*	p957

Prison reform

Lord Addington	*Lib Dem*	p587
Baroness Bottomley of Nettlestone	*Con*	p636
Lord Dubs	*Lab*	p715
Lord Fellowes	*CB*	p733
Lord Ramsbotham	*CB*	p956
Baroness Stern	*CB*	p1011

Prisoners

Lord Hardie	*CB*	p783

Prisons

Baroness Burt of Solihull	*Lib Dem*	p656
Lord Christopher	*Lab*	p676
Lord Glenarthur	*Con*	p757
Baroness Hamwee	*Lib Dem*	p780
Lord Hardie	*CB*	p783
Baroness Healy of Primrose Hill	*Lab*	p794
Lord Hylton	*CB*	p820
Lord Judd	*Lab*	p830
Baroness Masham of Ilton	*CB*	p892
Bishop of Peterborough	*NA*	p942
Baroness Royall of Blaisdon	*Lab/Co-op*	p979
Baroness Stern	*CB*	p1011
Baroness Thomas of Winchester	*Lib Dem*	p1030

Private security services

Baroness Henig	*Lab*	p795

Public finance

Baroness Noakes	*Con*	p918

Public sector pay and conditions

Lord O'Donnell	*CB*	p924

Public service reform

Lord Bichard	*CB*	p621
Baroness Jones of Whitchurch	*Lab*	p828

Public services

Lord Blackwell	*Con*	p628
Lord Herbert of South Downs	*Con*	p797
Lord Laming	*CB*	p846
Lord Mawson	*CB*	p894
Baroness Noakes	*Con*	p918
Lord Turnbull	*CB*	p1042

Rail transport

Lord Greaves	*Lib Dem*	p766

Rape

Baroness Stern	*CB*	p1011

Recreation

Lord Pendry	*Lab*	p941

Refugees and asylum seekers

Lord Alton of Liverpool	*CB*	p595
Bishop of Durham	*NA*	p717
Lord Greaves	*Lib Dem*	p766
Lord Judd	*Lab*	p830
Baroness Lister of Burtersett	*Lab*	p863
Lord Moynihan	*Con*	p909
Baroness Neuberger	*CB*	p913

Regeneration

Lord Adebowale	*CB*	p587
Lord Best	*CB*	p619
Baroness Ford	*CB*	p741
Lord Shipley	*Lib Dem*	p998
Lord Storey	*Lib Dem*	p1017

Regional assemblies

Lord Dunlop	*Con*	p716
Lord Touhig	*Lab/Co-op*	p1034

Regional policy

Baroness Armstrong of Hill Top	*Lab*	p600
Lord Beecham	*Lab*	p613
Baroness Hughes of Stretford	*Lab*	p814
Lord Inglewood	*NA*	p820
Lord Jones	*Lab*	p826
Lord Kilclooney	*CB*	p838
Lord Liddle	*Lab*	p859
Lord Newby	*Lib Dem*	p916
Baroness Quin	*Lab*	p954
Lord Smith of Leigh	*Lab*	p1005
Lord Wrigglesworth	*Lib Dem*	p1079

Regulatory Reform

Baroness Bottomley of Nettlestone	*Con*	p636

Religion

Baroness Berridge	*Con*	p618
Lord Harries of Pentregarth	*CB*	p784
Lord Hylton	*CB*	p820

Renewables

Baroness Finn	*Con*	p737
Lord Hain	*Lab*	p775
Lord James of Blackheath	*Con*	p822
Earl of Liverpool	*Con*	p866
Lord Vaux of Harrowden	*CB*	p1049
Lord Wallace of Tankerness	*NA*	p1055

Research and development

Baroness Bowles of Berkhamsted	*Lib Dem*	p637
Lord Cashman	*NA*	p669
Lord Haskel	*Lab*	p789
Lord Oxburgh	*CB*	p929
Lord Patel	*CB*	p936
Lord Rooker	*Lab*	p975
Lord Turnberg	*Lab*	p1041
Lord Vaizey of Didcot	*Con*	p1047
Baroness Warwick of Undercliffe	*Lab*	p1058
Lord Winston	*Lab*	p1074

Retail industry

Baroness O'Cathain	*Con*	p923

Road safety

Lord Brougham and Vaux	*Con*	p648
Lord Robertson of Port Ellen	*Lab*	p971
Viscount Simon	*Lab*	p1000

Royal Navy

Lord Haworth	*Lab*	p790

Rural affairs

Baroness Bakewell of Hardington Mandeville	*Lib Dem*	p607
Lord Cameron of Dillington	*CB*	p660
Earl Cathcart	*Con*	p669
Lord Elis-Thomas	*NA*	p722
Bishop of Ely	*NA*	p723
Lord Gardiner of Kimble	*Con*	p751
Lord Herbert of South Downs	*Con*	p797
Lord Inglewood	*NA*	p820
Baroness Jolly	*Lib Dem*	p826
Earl of Kinnoull	*NA*	p842
Lord Knight of Weymouth	*Lab/Co-op*	p844
Earl of Lindsay	*Con*	p861
Lord Lisvane	*CB*	p865
Lord Mancroft	*Con*	p887
Duke of Montrose	*Con*	p900
Baroness Neville-Rolfe	*Con*	p915
Bishop of Newcastle	*NA*	p916
Baroness Noakes	*Con*	p918
Bishop of Peterborough	*NA*	p942
Lord Purvis of Tweed	*Lib Dem*	p952
Lord Rana	*Con*	p957
Baroness Shephard of Northwold	*Con*	p995
Lord Thurlow	*CB*	p1031
Lord Tyler	*Lib Dem*	p1043
Lord Wallace of Tankerness	*NA*	p1055
Lord Willoughby de Broke	*NA*	p1071

Rural communities

Lord Taylor of Goss Moor	*Lib Dem*	p1025

Rural economy

Earl of Lytton	*CB*	p871

Science

Baroness Andrews	*Lab*	p598
Baroness Blackwood of North Oxford	*Con*	p628
Baroness Bowles of Berkhamsted	*Lib Dem*	p637
Baroness Brown of Cambridge	*CB*	p648
Viscount Colville of Culross	*CB*	p684
Lord Drayson	*Lab*	p713
Earl of Erroll	*CB*	p724
Baroness Greenfield	*CB*	p768
Lord Haskel	*Lab*	p789
Lord Hunt of Chesterton	*Lab*	p816
Lord Krebs	*CB*	p845
Baroness Morgan of Drefelin	*CB*	p903
Baroness Neville-Jones	*Con*	p914

Lord O'Donnell	*CB*	p924
Lord Rees of Ludlow	*CB*	p963
Lord Rooker	*Lab*	p975
Lord Sainsbury of Turville	*Lab*	p982
Viscount Simon	*Lab*	p1000
Lord Taverne	*Lib Dem*	p1024
Lord Vaizey of Didcot	*Con*	p1047
Baroness Warwick of Undercliffe	*Lab*	p1058
Lord Willetts	*Con*	p1069
Lord Willis of Knaresborough	*Lib Dem*	p1071
Lord Winston	*Lab*	p1074

Science, technology and research

Baroness Bowles of Berkhamsted	*Lib Dem*	p637
Lord Haskel	*Lab*	p789
Earl of Kinnoull	*NA*	p842

Scotland

Lord Dunlop	*Con*	p716
Earl of Erroll	*CB*	p724
Lord Foulkes of Cumnock	*Lab/Co-op*	p743
Lord Fraser of Corriegarth	*Con*	p747
Lord Glenarthur	*Con*	p757
Lord Gordon of Strathblane	*Lab*	p762
Earl of Home	*Con*	p806
Earl of Kinnoull	*NA*	p842
Lord Leitch	*Lab*	p855
Earl of Lindsay	*Con*	p861
Lord Purvis of Tweed	*Lib Dem*	p952
Baroness Ramsay of Cartvale	*Lab*	p956
Lord Selkirk of Douglas	*Con*	p990
Lord Stevenson of Balmacara	*Lab*	p1014
Lord Wilson of Tillyorn	*CB*	p1073

Scottish Government

Lord Wallace of Tankerness	*NA*	p1055

Scottish home rule

Lord Wallace of Tankerness	*NA*	p1055

Security

Lord Bach	*Lab*	p605
Baroness Butler-Sloss	*CB*	p658
Lord Clark of Windermere	*Lab*	p677
Earl of Cork and Orrery	*CB*	p685
Lord Dannatt	*CB*	p697
Lord Fairfax of Cameron	*Con*	p726
Lord Harris of Haringey	*Lab*	p785
Baroness Liddell of Coatdyke	*Lab*	p858
Lord Macdonald of River Glaven	*CB*	p875
Baroness O'Loan	*CB*	p925
Lord Reid of Cardowan	*Lab*	p964
Baroness Taylor of Bolton	*Lab*	p1024
Lord Taylor of Warwick	*NA*	p1026
Lord West of Spithead	*Lab*	p1064

Sexual abuse

Baroness Stern	*CB*	p1011

Sexually Transmitted Diseases

Baroness Barker	*Lib Dem*	p609

Skills

Lord Aberdare	*CB*	p586
Baroness Brinton	*Lib Dem*	p644
Lord Cotter	*Lib Dem*	p688
Baroness Garden of Frognal	*Lib Dem*	p750
Lord German	*Lib Dem*	p754
Lord Hall of Birkenhead	*CB*	p777
Lord Hunt of Wirral	*Con*	p817
Baroness Rock	*Con*	p972
Baroness Wolf of Dulwich	*NA*	p1075

Small businesses

Lord Aberdare	*CB*	p586
Lord Bellingham	*Con*	p615
Baroness Browning	*Con*	p652
Lord Empey	*UUP*	p723
Lord German	*Lib Dem*	p754
Earl of Glasgow	*Lib Dem*	p756
Lord Harrison	*Lab*	p787
Baroness Liddell of Coatdyke	*Lab*	p858
Baroness McIntosh of Pickering	*Con*	p878
Lord Mann	*NA*	p888
Lord Mitchell	*Lab*	p898
Lord Palmer of Childs Hill	*Lib Dem*	p932
Lord Popat	*Con*	p946
Lord Risby	*Con*	p969
Lord Vinson	*Con*	p1051

Smoking

Lord Faulkner of Worcester	*Lab*	p730
Baroness Gale	*Lab*	p750

Social affairs

Baroness Andrews	*Lab*	p598
Lord Beecham	*Lab*	p613
Lord Best	*CB*	p619
Lord Bichard	*CB*	p621
Baroness Blackstone	*Lab Ind*	p627
Baroness Campbell of Surbiton	*CB*	p662
Lord Eames	*CB*	p718
Lord Griffiths of Fforestfach	*Con*	p772

Social inclusion

Baroness Armstrong of Hill Top	*Lab*	p600
Lord Stunell	*Lib Dem*	p1020
Lord Watson of Invergowrie	*Lab*	p1060

Social justice

Lord Hain	*Lab*	p775
Baroness Stroud	*Con*	p1019

Tourism

Viscount Brookeborough	*CB*	p647
Lord Cotter	*Lib Dem*	p688
Baroness Doocey	*Lib Dem*	p712
Lord Foster of Bath	*Lib Dem*	p742
Lord Geddes	*Con*	p753
Earl of Glasgow	*Lib Dem*	p756
Lord Gordon of Strathblane	*Lab*	p762
Lord Harrison	*Lab*	p787
Lord Lee of Trafford	*Lib Dem*	p853
Baroness McIntosh of Pickering	*Con*	p878
Baroness Morgan of Ely	*Lab*	p904
Lord Palmer	*CB*	p932
Viscount Thurso	*Lib Dem*	p1032
Lord Tyler	*Lib Dem*	p1043
Viscount Younger of Leckie	*Con*	p1084

Trade

Lord Aberdare	*CB*	p586
Lord Bruce of Bennachie	*Lib Dem*	p653
Lord Carrington	*CB*	p666
Baroness Chalker of Wallasey	*Con*	p671
Lord Davies of Abersoch	*NA*	p701
Lord Davies of Stamford	*Lab*	p703
Lord Evans of Watford	*Lab*	p725
Lord Hammond of Runnymede	*Con*	p779
Lord Haskel	*Lab*	p789
Lord Hodgson of Astley Abbotts	*Con*	p800
Lord Hoyle	*Lab*	p813
Lord Johnson of Marylebone	*Con*	p825
Lord Jones of Cheltenham	*Lib Dem*	p827
Lord Lansley	*Con*	p849
Lord Lee of Trafford	*Lib Dem*	p853
Lord Moynihan	*Con*	p909
Baroness Noakes	*Con*	p918
Lord Rogan	*UUP*	p973
Lord Selsdon	*Con*	p991
Lord Sharpe of Epsom	*Con*	p994
Lord Taylor of Warwick	*NA*	p1026

Trade Unions

Lord Balfe	*Con*	p608
Baroness Golding	*Lab*	p760
Baroness Hayter of Kentish Town	*Lab/Co-op*	p792
Lord McNicol of West Kilbride	*Lab*	p882
Lord Monks	*Lab*	p900

Transatlantic relations

Lord Watson of Richmond	*Lib Dem*	p1061

Transport

Earl Attlee	*Con*	p604
Lord Berkeley	*Lab*	p617
Lord Birt	*CB*	p625
Lord Borwick	*Con*	p634
Lord Brabazon of Tara	*Con*	p640
Lord Bradshaw	*Lib Dem*	p641
Lord Brougham and Vaux	*Con*	p648
Baroness Brown of Cambridge	*CB*	p648
Baroness Chalker of Wallasey	*Con*	p671
Lord Chidgey	*Lib Dem*	p674
Baroness Clark of Kilwinning	*Lab*	p677
Lord Davies of Brixton	*Lab*	p701
Lord Davies of Gower	*Con*	p702
Lord Davies of Oldham	*Lab*	p702
Lord Dixon-Smith	*Con*	p710
Lord Dykes	*CB*	p718
Viscount of Falkland	*CB*	p728
Lord Faulkner of Worcester	*Lab*	p730
Lord Foster of Bath	*Lib Dem*	p742
Baroness Gardner of Parkes	*Con*	p752
Lord Geddes	*Con*	p753
Lord Goddard of Stockport	*Lib Dem*	p759
Lord Hammond of Runnymede	*Con*	p779
Lord Hanningfield	*NA*	p782
Viscount Hanworth	*Lab*	p782
Lord Haworth	*Lab*	p790
Baroness Hayman of Ullock	*Lab*	p792
Lord Hayward	*Con*	p793
Lord Hollick	*Lab*	p803
Lord Horam	*Con*	p808
Lord Hughes of Woodside	*Lab*	p814
Lord Hunt of Kings Heath	*Lab/Co-op*	p817
Lord Jones of Cheltenham	*Lib Dem*	p827
Baroness Kramer	*Lib Dem*	p845
Earl of Liverpool	*Con*	p866
Baroness McIntosh of Hudnall	*Lab*	p877
Baroness McIntosh of Pickering	*Con*	p878
Lord Moylan	*Con*	p909
Baroness Randerson	*Lib Dem*	p958
Lord Robathan	*Con*	p970
Lord Rosser	*Lab*	p976
Lord Teverson	*Lib Dem*	p1028
Baroness Valentine	*CB*	p1048
Baroness Williams of Trafford	*Con*	p1070

Tuberculosis

Baroness Suttie	*Lib Dem*	p1022

Unemployment and jobseeking

Lord Colgrain	*Con*	p682
Baroness Stedman-Scott	*Con*	p1009

United Nations

Lord Carlile of Berriew	*CB*	p665
Baroness Coussins	*CB*	p689
Lord Ramsbotham	*CB*	p956

Urban communities

Lord Griffiths of Burry Port	*Lab*	p772

Urban renewal

Lord Heseltine	*NA*	p798

Venture capital

Lord Flight	*Con*	p739

Veterinary services

Lord Trees	*CB*	p1035

Victims of crime

Baroness Newlove	*Con*	p917

Visual arts

Lord Freyberg	*CB*	p748

Waste policies and regulation

Lord Taylor of Holbeach	*Con*	p1026

Welfare

Lord Bach	*Lab*	p605
Earl of Clancarty	*CB*	p676
Baroness Couttie	*Con*	p689
Lord Davies of Stamford	*Lab*	p703
Bishop of Durham	*NA*	p717
Lord Giddens	*Lab*	p755
Baroness Healy of Primrose Hill	*Lab*	p794
Lord Hutton of Furness	*Lab*	p819
Lord Levy	*Lab*	p857
Lord Liddle	*Lab*	p859
Baroness Lister of Burtersett	*Lab*	p863
Baroness Meacher	*CB*	p895
Lord Paddick	*Lib Dem*	p931
Lord Smith of Finsbury	*NA*	p1002
Lord Turnberg	*Lab*	p1041
Baroness Tyler of Enfield	*Lib Dem*	p1044

Welsh Government

Lord Carlile of Berriew	*CB*	p665

Young offenders

Lord Hardie	*CB*	p783
Baroness Walmsley	*Lib Dem*	p1056

Youth justice

Lord Oates	*Lib Dem*	p923
Lord Ramsbotham	*CB*	p956

Youth services

Lord Purvis of Tweed	*Lib Dem*	p952

Peers' Countries of Interest

For precise details of individuals' stated interests, see relevant biography. The interests listed are supplied by Peers themselves.

Afghanistan

Lord Arbuthnot of Edrom	*Con*	p599
Baroness Blackwood of North Oxford	*Con*	p628
Lord Browne of Ladyton	*Lab*	p650
Baroness D'Souza	*CB*	p714
Baroness Featherstone	*Lib Dem*	p732
Baroness Hodgson of Abinger	*Con*	p800
Earl of Sandwich	*CB*	p984
Baroness Stern	*CB*	p1011
Baroness Warsi	*Con*	p1058

Albania

Lord Bates	*Con*	p612

Algeria

Baroness Stern	*CB*	p1011

Angola

Baroness Hoey	*NA*	p801
Earl of Listowel	*CB*	p864

Antigua And Barbuda

Lord Tunnicliffe	*Lab*	p1041

Argentina

Bishop of Carlisle	*NA*	p665
Lord Faulkner of Worcester	*Lab*	p730
Lord Rowe-Beddoe	*CB*	p978
Lord Smith of Finsbury	*NA*	p1002
Baroness Stern	*CB*	p1011
Lord Wigley	*PlC*	p1068

Armenia

Baroness Cox	*CB*	p690
Baroness Nicholson of Winterbourne	*Con*	p917
Lord Wallace of Saltaire	*Lib Dem*	p1054

Australia

Lord Arbuthnot of Edrom	*Con*	p599
Lord Archer of Weston-super-Mare	*NA*	p600
Lord Barker of Battle	*Con*	p610
Lord Bassam of Brighton	*Lab/Co-op*	p612
Lord Bird	*CB*	p624
Lord Botham	*CB*	p635
Lord Broers	*CB*	p646
Lord Cooper of Windrush	*NA*	p685
Lord Desai	*NA*	p708
Lord Faulkner of Worcester	*Lab*	p730
Baroness Ford	*CB*	p741
Lord Gardiner of Kimble	*Con*	p751
Baroness Greenfield	*CB*	p768
Lord Harris of Haringey	*Lab*	p785
Lord Holmes of Richmond	*Con*	p805
Earl of Home	*Con*	p806
Lord Hoyle	*Lab*	p813
Baroness Kingsmill	*Lab*	p841
Lord Kirkhope of Harrogate	*Con*	p843
Lord Leitch	*Lab*	p855
Baroness Liddell of Coatdyke	*Lab*	p858
Baroness Lister of Burtersett	*Lab*	p863
Lord Lisvane	*CB*	p865
Lord Livermore	*Lab*	p865
Lord Low of Dalston	*CB*	p869
Lord MacKenzie of Culkein	*Lab*	p879
Lord O'Donnell	*CB*	p924
Baroness Randerson	*Lib Dem*	p958
Baroness Royall of Blaisdon	*Lab/Co-op*	p979
Viscount Simon	*Lab*	p1000
Lord Smith of Finsbury	*NA*	p1002
Lord Smith of Leigh	*Lab*	p1005
Lord Stirrup	*CB*	p1015
Lord Teverson	*Lib Dem*	p1028
Lord Tyler	*Lib Dem*	p1043

Austria

Viscount Hanworth	*Lab*	p782
Lord Jones	*Lab*	p826
Earl of Kinnoull	*NA*	p842
Lord Paul	*NA*	p939

Azerbaijan

Baroness Goudie	*Lab*	p763
Lord Haworth	*Lab*	p790
Baroness Nicholson of Winterbourne	*Con*	p917
Baroness O'Cathain	*Con*	p923

Bahrain

Lord Jones of Cheltenham	*Lib Dem*	p827
Lord Jordan	*Lab*	p829

Bangladesh

Lord Ahmad of Wimbledon	*Con*	p590
Lord Bhatia	*NA*	p621
Lord Desai	*NA*	p708
Baroness King of Bow	*Lab*	p839
Lord Loomba	*CB*	p868
Baroness Morgan of Cotes	*Con*	p903
Lord Paul	*NA*	p939
Baroness Uddin	*NA*	p1046
Baroness Warsi	*Con*	p1058

Belgium

Lord Astor of Hever	*Con*	p603
Baroness Ritchie of Downpatrick	*NA*	p969

Benin

Lord McColl of Dulwich	*Con*	p872

Bermuda

Earl of Kinnoull	*NA*	p842
Lord Tope	*Lib Dem*	p1033

Bhutan

Lord Layard	*Lab*	p851
Lord O'Donnell	*CB*	p924

Bolivia

Lord Lea of Crondall	*NA*	p852

Bosnia/Herzegovina

Lord Cormack	*Con*	p686
Lord Greaves	*Lib Dem*	p766
Baroness Hoey	*NA*	p801

Botswana

Lord Jones of Cheltenham	*Lib Dem*	p827
Bishop of Newcastle	*NA*	p916
Lord Rowlands	*Lab*	p978

Brazil

Baroness Bakewell	*Lab*	p606
Lord Bates	*Con*	p612
Lord Browne of Belmont	*DUP*	p650
Lord Desai	*NA*	p708
Lord Gadhia	*NA*	p749
Lord Howarth of Newport	*Lab*	p811
Lord Oakeshott of Seagrove Bay	*NA*	p922
Lord O'Donnell	*CB*	p924
Baroness Rawlings	*Con*	p960
Lord Rogers of Riverside	*Lab*	p974
Lord Rowe-Beddoe	*CB*	p978
Lord Smith of Finsbury	*NA*	p1002

Bulgaria

Baroness Nicholson of Winterbourne	*Con*	p917
Baroness Rawlings	*Con*	p960

Burma (Myanmar)

Lord Alton of Liverpool	*CB*	p595
Baroness Cox	*CB*	p690
Baroness Flather	*CB*	p738
Baroness Jones of Whitchurch	*Lab*	p828
Baroness Kinnock of Holyhead	*Lab*	p842
Lord Stevenson of Balmacara	*Lab*	p1014

Burundi

Lord Browne of Ladyton	*Lab*	p650
Archbishop of Canterbury	*NA*	p663
Bishop of Durham	*NA*	p717
Bishop of Winchester	*NA*	p1073

Cambodia

Lord Griffiths of Burry Port	*Lab*	p772
Lord Haworth	*Lab*	p790

Canada

Lord Beith	*Lib Dem*	p614
Lord Black of Crossharbour	*NA*	p626
Lord Browne of Belmont	*DUP*	p650
Lord Bruce of Bennachie	*Lib Dem*	p653
Lord Desai	*NA*	p708
Lord Empey	*UUP*	p723
Lord Faulkner of Worcester	*Lab*	p730
Baroness Fookes	*Con*	p740
Lord Harris of Haringey	*Lab*	p785
Baroness Harris of Richmond	*Lib Dem*	p787
Lord Holmes of Richmond	*Con*	p805
Baroness Howarth of Breckland	*CB*	p810
Lord O'Donnell	*CB*	p924
Lord Parekh	*Lab*	p933
Baroness Randerson	*Lib Dem*	p958
Lord Roberts of Llandudno	*Lib Dem*	p970
Lord Singh of Wimbledon	*CB*	p1000
Lord Tyler	*Lib Dem*	p1043
Baroness Wolf of Dulwich	*NA*	p1075

Cayman Islands

Lord Naseby	*Con*	p911

Chile

Lord Bach	*Lab*	p605
Baroness Coussins	*CB*	p689
Lord Lamont of Lerwick	*Con*	p847
Lord Leitch	*Lab*	p855
Lord Loomba	*CB*	p868
Lord Naseby	*Con*	p911
Baroness Stern	*CB*	p1011
Lord Teverson	*Lib Dem*	p1028

China

Lord Aberdare	*CB*	p586
Lord Ahmad of Wimbledon	*Con*	p590
Lord Alton of Liverpool	*CB*	p595
Baroness Amos	*Lab*	p596
Lord Bates	*Con*	p612
Bishop of Birmingham	*NA*	p624
Lord Birt	*CB*	p625
Baroness Bottomley of Nettlestone	*Con*	p636
Lord Bradley	*Lab*	p640
Baroness Brown of Cambridge	*CB*	p648
Lord Chartres	*CB*	p673
Lord Christopher	*Lab*	p676
Lord Clement-Jones	*Lib Dem*	p679
Viscount Colville of Culross	*CB*	p684
Lord Cotter	*Lib Dem*	p688
Lord Cunningham of Felling	*Lab*	p695
Lord Davidson of Glen Clova	*Lab*	p700
Lord de Mauley	*Con*	p706
Lord Desai	*NA*	p708
Lord Dobbs	*Con*	p710
Lord Dunlop	*Con*	p716
Lord Dykes	*CB*	p718

Baroness Finlay of Llandaff	*CB*	p736
Baroness Finn	*Con*	p737
Lord Flight	*Con*	p739
Lord Foulkes of Cumnock	*Lab/Co-op*	p743
Lord Fraser of Corriegarth	*Con*	p747
Baroness Fritchie	*CB*	p748
Lord Gadhia	*NA*	p749
Lord Giddens	*Lab*	p755
Lord Goddard of Stockport	*Lib Dem*	p759
Lord Gordon of Strathblane	*Lab*	p762
Lord Grantchester	*Lab*	p765
Lord Griffiths of Fforestfach	*Con*	p772
Lord Hall of Birkenhead	*CB*	p777
Lord Hardie	*CB*	p783
Baroness Harding of Winscombe	*Con*	p783
Baroness Healy of Primrose Hill	*Lab*	p794
Baroness Henig	*Lab*	p795
Lord Howell of Guildford	*Con*	p812
Lord Inglewood	*NA*	p820
Baroness Jay of Paddington	*Lab*	p824
Lord Johnson of Marylebone	*Con*	p825
Baroness Jones of Whitchurch	*Lab*	p828
Lord Kerr of Kinlochard	*CB*	p835
Baroness Kidron	*CB*	p837
Baroness Kingsmill	*Lab*	p841
Lord Laming	*CB*	p846
Lord Lancaster of Kimbolton	*Con*	p848
Lord Leitch	*Lab*	p855
Baroness Liddell of Coatdyke	*Lab*	p858
Lord Livermore	*Lab*	p865
Lord McConnell of Glenscorrodale	*Lab*	p873
Lord McNally	*Lib Dem*	p882
Lord Marlesford	*Con*	p891
Lord Moylan	*Con*	p909
Baroness Neville-Rolfe	*Con*	p915
Lord Oxburgh	*CB*	p929
Lord Paul	*NA*	p939
Lord Prescott	*Lab*	p950
Lord Risby	*Con*	p969
Lord Rowe-Beddoe	*CB*	p978
Lord Sainsbury of Turville	*Lab*	p982
Lord St John of Bletso	*CB*	p983
Lord Sassoon	*Con*	p985
Lord Selsdon	*Con*	p991
Lord Sharpe of Epsom	*Con*	p994
Lord Skidelsky	*CB*	p1001
Lord Smith of Finsbury	*NA*	p1002
Lord Soley	*Lab*	p1007
Lord Stephen	*Lib Dem*	p1010
Lord Stone of Blackheath	*NA*	p1016
Lord Taylor of Warwick	*NA*	p1026
Lord Thomas of Gresford	*Lib Dem*	p1029
Viscount Trenchard	*Con*	p1036
Lord Triesman	*Lab*	p1037
Lord Turner of Ecchinswell	*CB*	p1043
Lord Wallace of Tankerness	*NA*	p1055
Lord Wei	*Con*	p1063
Baroness Wheatcroft	*CB*	p1065
Baroness Wheeler	*Lab*	p1065
Lord Whitty	*Lab*	p1067
Lord Willetts	*Con*	p1069
Lord Wood of Anfield	*Lab*	p1076
Lord Young of Norwood Green	*Lab*	p1082

Colombia

Lord Alderdice	*Lib Dem*	p591
Lord Allan of Hallam	*Lib Dem*	p592
Lord Browne of Ladyton	*Lab*	p650
Baroness Coussins	*CB*	p689

Croatia

Lord Bates	*Con*	p612
Lord Browne of Belmont	*DUP*	p650
Lord Cormack	*Con*	p686
Lord Greaves	*Lib Dem*	p766

Cuba

Baroness Coussins	*CB*	p689
Baroness Smith of Basildon	*Lab/Co-op*	p1001
Lord Triesman	*Lab*	p1037

Cyprus

Lord Harris of Haringey	*Lab*	p785
Baroness Hussein-Ece	*Lib Dem*	p819
Lord Kilclooney	*CB*	p838
Baroness Ludford	*Lib Dem*	p870
Lord Maginnis of Drumglass	*Ind UU*	p884
Lord Sharkey	*Lib Dem*	p993
Lord Smith of Finsbury	*NA*	p1002

Czech Republic

Lord Bruce of Bennachie	*Lib Dem*	p653
Baroness Finn	*Con*	p737

Democratic Republic of Congo

Lord Alton of Liverpool	*CB*	p595
Bishop of Birmingham	*NA*	p624
Baroness Blackwood of North Oxford	*Con*	p628
Archbishop of Canterbury	*NA*	p663
Lord Mance	*CB*	p886
Bishop of Winchester	*NA*	p1073

Denmark

Lord Grantchester	*Lab*	p765
Lord Teverson	*Lib Dem*	p1028

Dominican Republic

Lord Griffiths of Burry Port	*Lab*	p772
Baroness Stern	*CB*	p1011

East Timor

Baroness Cox	*CB*	p690

Ecuador

Lord Allan of Hallam	*Lib Dem*	p592

Egypt

Lord Alton of Liverpool	*CB*	p595
Baroness Berridge	*Con*	p618
Baroness Chalker of Wallasey	*Con*	p671
Lord Christopher	*Lab*	p676
Bishop of Coventry	*NA*	p690
Lord Dear	*CB*	p704
Lord Lansley	*Con*	p849
Lord Marlesford	*Con*	p891
Lord St John of Bletso	*CB*	p983

Estonia

Lord Smith of Hindhead	*Con*	p1004

Ethiopia

Lord Bates	*Con*	p612
Baroness Bonham-Carter of Yarnbury	*Lib Dem*	p633
Duke of Montrose	*Con*	p900
Lord Oates	*Lib Dem*	p923

Falkland Islands

Lord MacKenzie of Culkein	*Lab*	p879

Fiji

Lord Griffiths of Burry Port	*Lab*	p772

Finland

Lord Cormack	*Con*	p686
Baroness Ramsay of Cartvale	*Lab*	p956
Lord Tyler	*Lib Dem*	p1043

France

Baroness Afshar	*CB*	p588
Lord Anderson of Swansea	*Lab*	p597
Lord Arbuthnot of Edrom	*Con*	p599
Lord Astor of Hever	*Con*	p603
Baroness Benjamin	*Lib Dem*	p615
Lord Birt	*CB*	p625
Baroness Blackstone	*Lab Ind*	p627
Lord Blunkett	*Lab*	p631
Lord Bourne of Aberystwyth	*Con*	p636
Lord Bradley	*Lab*	p640
Lord Bragg	*Lab*	p642
Baroness Brinton	*Lib Dem*	p644
Lord Brougham and Vaux	*Con*	p648
Lord Browne of Belmont	*DUP*	p650
Archbishop of Canterbury	*NA*	p663
Earl of Clancarty	*CB*	p676
Baroness Cohen of Pimlico	*Lab*	p682
Baroness Coussins	*CB*	p689
Lord Donoughue	*Lab*	p712
Lord Drayson	*Lab*	p713
Viscount of Falkland	*CB*	p728
Baroness Finlay of Llandaff	*CB*	p736
Lord Greaves	*Lib Dem*	p766
Lord Green of Hurstpierpoint	*NA*	p767
Baroness Greenfield	*CB*	p768
Viscount Hanworth	*Lab*	p782
Lord Harris of Haringey	*Lab*	p785
Baroness Hayter of Kentish Town	*Lab/Co-op*	p792
Lord Horam	*Con*	p808
Lord Hunt of Chesterton	*Lab*	p816
Lord Janvrin	*CB*	p823
Baroness King of Bow	*Lab*	p839
Lord Lansley	*Con*	p849
Lord Leitch	*Lab*	p855
Lord Liddle	*Lab*	p859
Lord Lilley	*Con*	p860
Lord Lisvane	*CB*	p865
Lord Lupton	*NA*	p871
Baroness Massey of Darwen	*Lab*	p892
Lord Maxton	*Lab*	p894
Baroness Meyer	*Con*	p897
Baroness Miller of Chilthorne Domer	*Lib Dem*	p897
Lord Morgan	*Lab*	p902
Lord Murphy of Torfaen	*Lab*	p910
Lord Naseby	*Con*	p911
Baroness Nicholson of Winterbourne	*Con*	p917
Lord Oakeshott of Seagrove Bay	*NA*	p922
Lord Patel	*CB*	p936
Lord Plant of Highfield	*Lab*	p945
Lord Radice	*Lab*	p955
Baroness Randerson	*Lib Dem*	p958
Lord Renfrew of Kaimsthorn	*Con*	p964
Lord Ricketts	*CB*	p968
Baroness Ritchie of Downpatrick	*NA*	p969
Baroness Shephard of Northwold	*Con*	p995
Lord Sherbourne of Didsbury	*Con*	p996
Lord Singh of Wimbledon	*CB*	p1000
Lord Smith of Leigh	*Lab*	p1005
Baroness Smith of Newnham	*Lib Dem*	p1006
Lord Stevens of Ludgate	*Con Ind*	p1013
Lord Stoneham of Droxford	*Lib Dem*	p1016
Lord Storey	*Lib Dem*	p1017
Lord Taylor of Holbeach	*Con*	p1026
Lord Touhig	*Lab/Co-op*	p1034
Lord Watson of Invergowrie	*Lab*	p1060
Lord Whitty	*Lab*	p1067
Baroness Wolf of Dulwich	*NA*	p1075

Gabon

Lord Loomba	*CB*	p868

Gambia

Lord Jones of Cheltenham	*Lib Dem*	p827
Lord McColl of Dulwich	*Con*	p872

Georgia

Lord Harries of Pentregarth	*CB*	p784
Lord Haworth	*Lab*	p790
Baroness Nicholson of Winterbourne	*Con*	p917
Lord Wallace of Saltaire	*Lib Dem*	p1054

Germany

Lord Anderson of Swansea	*Lab*	p597
Lord Arbuthnot of Edrom	*Con*	p599
Lord Barker of Battle	*Con*	p610
Lord Browne of Belmont	*DUP*	p650
Earl of Clancarty	*CB*	p676
Baroness Cohen of Pimlico	*Lab*	p682
Bishop of Coventry	*NA*	p690
Baroness Eaton	*Con*	p719
Bishop of Ely	*NA*	p723
Lord Green of Hurstpierpoint	*NA*	p767
Lord Hammond of Runnymede	*Con*	p779
Viscount Hanworth	*Lab*	p782
Lord Horam	*Con*	p808
Lord Jones	*Lab*	p826
Lord Lansley	*Con*	p849
Bishop of Leeds	*NA*	p854
Lord Liddle	*Lab*	p859
Baroness Neville-Rolfe	*Con*	p915
Baroness Nicholson of Winterbourne	*Con*	p917
Lord Oakeshott of Seagrove Bay	*NA*	p922
Baroness O'Neill of Bengarve	*CB*	p926
Lord Paul	*NA*	p939
Lord Plant of Highfield	*Lab*	p945
Lord Radice	*Lab*	p955
Lord Sherbourne of Didsbury	*Con*	p996
Baroness Smith of Basildon	*Lab/Co-op*	p1001
Baroness Smith of Newnham	*Lib Dem*	p1006
Lord Storey	*Lib Dem*	p1017
Lord Tyler	*Lib Dem*	p1043
Lord Watson of Richmond	*Lib Dem*	p1061
Lord Whitty	*Lab*	p1067
Lord Willetts	*Con*	p1069
Lord Wood of Anfield	*Lab*	p1076

Ghana

Baroness Benjamin	*Lib Dem*	p615
Lord Griffiths of Burry Port	*Lab*	p772
Lord Jones of Cheltenham	*Lib Dem*	p827
Lord McColl of Dulwich	*Con*	p872
Bishop of Portsmouth	*NA*	p947
Lord Ribeiro	*Con*	p966

Gibraltar

Lord Hoyle	*Lab*	p813
Lord Kilclooney	*CB*	p838

Greece

Lord Bates	*Con*	p612
Lord Bourne of Aberystwyth	*Con*	p636
Lord Gardiner of Kimble	*Con*	p751
Lord Harris of Haringey	*Lab*	p785
Lord Lisvane	*CB*	p865
Lord Marks of Henley-on-Thames	*Lib Dem*	p890
Lord Renfrew of Kaimsthorn	*Con*	p964

Greenland

Lord Razzall	*Lib Dem*	p960

Guatemala

Lord True	*Con*	p1039

Guinea-Bissau

Baroness Burt of Solihull	*Lib Dem*	p656

Haiti

Lord Griffiths of Burry Port	*Lab*	p772

Hong Kong

Baroness Butler-Sloss	*CB*	p658
Baroness Finlay of Llandaff	*CB*	p736
Baroness Finn	*Con*	p737
Lord Geddes	*Con*	p753
Lord Marlesford	*Con*	p891
Lord Pendry	*Lab*	p941
Lord Sharpe of Epsom	*Con*	p994
Lord Smith of Finsbury	*NA*	p1002
Lord Thomas of Gresford	*Lib Dem*	p1029
Lord Willoughby de Broke	*NA*	p1071
Lord Wilson of Tillyorn	*CB*	p1073

Hungary

Lord Bruce of Bennachie	*Lib Dem*	p653

Iceland

Lord Inglewood	*NA*	p820
Lord Razzall	*Lib Dem*	p960

India

Baroness Afshar	*CB*	p588
Lord Ahmad of Wimbledon	*Con*	p590
Baroness Amos	*Lab*	p596
Lord Arbuthnot of Edrom	*Con*	p599
Lord Archer of Weston-super-Mare	*NA*	p600
Lord Bach	*Lab*	p605
Baroness Bakewell	*Lab*	p606
Baroness Barker	*Lib Dem*	p609
Lord Barwell	*Con*	p611
Lord Bassam of Brighton	*Lab/Co-op*	p612
Lord Bhatia	*NA*	p621
Lord Bilimoria	*CB*	p622
Baroness Billingham	*Lab*	p623
Baroness Blackstone	*Lab Ind*	p627
Lord Blair of Boughton	*CB*	p629
Baroness Bottomley of Nettlestone	*Con*	p636

Lord Bourne of Aberystwyth	*Con*	p636
Baroness Brown of Cambridge	*CB*	p648
Baroness Butler-Sloss	*CB*	p658
Bishop of Carlisle	*NA*	p665
Lord Clement-Jones	*Lib Dem*	p679
Baroness Corston	*Lab*	p687
Lord Crathorne	*Con*	p692
Lord Dear	*CB*	p704
Lord Desai	*NA*	p708
Lord Dholakia	*Lib Dem*	p709
Baroness D'Souza	*CB*	p714
Bishop of Ely	*NA*	p723
Lord Empey	*UUP*	p723
Lord Faulks	*NA*	p731
Baroness Featherstone	*Lib Dem*	p732
Baroness Finn	*Con*	p737
Lord Flight	*Con*	p739
Lord Gadhia	*NA*	p749
Baroness Gale	*Lab*	p750
Bishop of Gloucester	*NA*	p758
Lord Gordon of Strathblane	*Lab*	p762
Baroness Goudie	*Lab*	p763
Lord Hardie	*CB*	p783
Baroness Harding of Winscombe	*Con*	p783
Lord Harries of Pentregarth	*CB*	p784
Lord Howell of Guildford	*Con*	p812
Lord Hunt of Chesterton	*Lab*	p816
Lord Janvrin	*CB*	p823
Lord Jay of Ewelme	*CB*	p823
Baroness Jay of Paddington	*Lab*	p824
Lord Johnson of Marylebone	*Con*	p825
Lord Jordan	*Lab*	p829
Lord Kakkar	*CB*	p832
Baroness Kidron	*CB*	p837
Baroness Kingsmill	*Lab*	p841
Lord Lancaster of Kimbolton	*Con*	p848
Lord Leitch	*Lab*	p855
Lord Livermore	*Lab*	p865
Lord Loomba	*CB*	p868
Lord Mackenzie of Framwellgate	*NA*	p880
Lord McNally	*Lib Dem*	p882
Lord Morgan	*Lab*	p902
Lord Naseby	*Con*	p911
Baroness Neville-Rolfe	*Con*	p915
Lord Parekh	*Lab*	p933
Lord Patel	*CB*	p936
Lord Patel of Bradford	*NA*	p937
Lord Paul	*NA*	p939
Lord Pickles	*Con*	p943
Lord Popat	*Con*	p946
Baroness Prashar	*CB*	p949
Lord Radice	*Lab*	p955
Lord Rana	*Con*	p957
Baroness Royall of Blaisdon	*Lab/Co-op*	p979
Lord Sainsbury of Turville	*Lab*	p982
Earl of Sandwich	*CB*	p984
Baroness Scott of Needham Market	*Lib Dem*	p988
Lord Singh of Wimbledon	*CB*	p1000
Duke of Somerset	*CB*	p1008
Lord Stephen	*Lib Dem*	p1010
Lord Teverson	*Lib Dem*	p1028
Lord Triesman	*Lab*	p1037
Lord Vaizey of Didcot	*Con*	p1047
Baroness Wheatcroft	*CB*	p1065
Baroness Wheeler	*Lab*	p1065
Lord Wrigglesworth	*Lib Dem*	p1079

Indonesia

Lord Ahmad of Wimbledon	*Con*	p590
Baroness Finn	*Con*	p737

Iran

Baroness Afshar	*CB*	p588
Baroness Blackwood of North Oxford	*Con*	p628
Baroness D'Souza	*CB*	p714
Bishop of Durham	*NA*	p717
Lord Haworth	*Lab*	p790
Lord Lamont of Lerwick	*Con*	p847
Lord Marlesford	*Con*	p891
Baroness Nicholson of Winterbourne	*Con*	p917
Earl of Oxford and Asquith	*NA*	p931
Lord Stevenson of Balmacara	*Lab*	p1014

Iraq

Lord Alton of Liverpool	*CB*	p595
Baroness Berridge	*Con*	p618
Lord Clement-Jones	*Lib Dem*	p679
Lord Foster of Bath	*Lib Dem*	p742
Lord Hylton	*CB*	p820
Baroness Nicholson of Winterbourne	*Con*	p917

Ireland

Lord Bird	*CB*	p624
Lord Cotter	*Lib Dem*	p688
Earl of Courtown	*Con*	p688
Lord Donoughue	*Lab*	p712
Baroness Doocey	*Lib Dem*	p712
Lord Fellowes of West Stafford	*Con*	p733
Lord Gardiner of Kimble	*Con*	p751
Baroness Goudie	*Lab*	p763
Baroness Harris of Richmond	*Lib Dem*	p787
Baroness Healy of Primrose Hill	*Lab*	p794
Lord Kennedy of Southwark	*Lab/Co-op*	p834
Lord Kilclooney	*CB*	p838
Lord McAvoy	*Lab/Co-op*	p872
Lord Murphy of Torfaen	*Lab*	p910
Baroness Neuberger	*CB*	p913

Baroness O'Cathain	*Con*	p923
Baroness O'Neill of Bengarve	*CB*	p926
Lord Puttnam	*Lab*	p953
Lord Rana	*Con*	p957
Baroness Smith of Basildon	*Lab/Co-op*	p1001
Lord Stevenson of Balmacara	*Lab*	p1014
Lord Teverson	*Lib Dem*	p1028
Lord Whitty	*Lab*	p1067
Lord Wigley	*PlC*	p1068
Lord Willis of Knaresborough	*Lib Dem*	p1071

Israel

Lord Ahmad of Wimbledon	*Con*	p590
Lord Arbuthnot of Edrom	*Con*	p599
Lord Beecham	*Lab*	p613
Baroness Burt of Solihull	*Lib Dem*	p656
Archbishop of Canterbury	*NA*	p663
Lord Carey of Clifton	*CB*	p664
Bishop of Coventry	*NA*	p690
Baroness Deech	*CB*	p705
Bishop of Durham	*NA*	p717
Baroness Greenfield	*CB*	p768
Lord Hylton	*CB*	p820
Lord Kalms	*NA*	p832
Lord Lansley	*Con*	p849
Lord Livermore	*Lab*	p865
Lord Mitchell	*Lab*	p898
Lord Morrow	*DUP*	p908
Baroness O'Cathain	*Con*	p923
Lord Palmer of Childs Hill	*Lib Dem*	p932
Lord Pannick	*CB*	p933
Baroness Ramsay of Cartvale	*Lab*	p956
Lord Roberts of Llandudno	*Lib Dem*	p970
Bishop of Southwark	*NA*	p1008
Lord Taylor of Warwick	*NA*	p1026
Lord Turnberg	*Lab*	p1041
Lord Vaizey of Didcot	*Con*	p1047

Italy

Lord Adebowale	*CB*	p587
Lord Arbuthnot of Edrom	*Con*	p599
Lord Bach	*Lab*	p605
Lord Black of Brentwood	*Con*	p625
Baroness Bonham-Carter of Yarnbury	*Lib Dem*	p633
Lord Bourne of Aberystwyth	*Con*	p636
Lord Browne of Belmont	*DUP*	p650
Baroness Cohen of Pimlico	*Lab*	p682
Lord Donoughue	*Lab*	p712
Lord Hall of Birkenhead	*CB*	p777
Lord Hammond of Runnymede	*Con*	p779
Viscount Hanworth	*Lab*	p782
Lord Harris of Haringey	*Lab*	p785
Baroness Healy of Primrose Hill	*Lab*	p794
Baroness King of Bow	*Lab*	p839
Lord Leitch	*Lab*	p855
Lord Liddle	*Lab*	p859
Lord Lisvane	*CB*	p865
Baroness Murphy	*CB*	p910
Lord Radice	*Lab*	p955
Lord Rogers of Riverside	*Lab*	p974
Lord Sherbourne of Didsbury	*Con*	p996
Lord Stevens of Ludgate	*Con Ind*	p1013
Lord Taylor of Warwick	*NA*	p1026
Lord Whitty	*Lab*	p1067
Baroness Wolf of Dulwich	*NA*	p1075
Lord Young of Norwood Green	*Lab*	p1082

Jamaica

Lord Faulkner of Worcester	*Lab*	p730
Lord Taylor of Warwick	*NA*	p1026

Japan

Lord Bates	*Con*	p612
Lord Bird	*CB*	p624
Lord Birt	*CB*	p625
Baroness Bottomley of Nettlestone	*Con*	p636
Baroness Burt of Solihull	*Lib Dem*	p656
Viscount Colville of Culross	*CB*	p684
Lord Cunningham of Felling	*Lab*	p695
Baroness D'Souza	*CB*	p714
Baroness Finn	*Con*	p737
Baroness Henig	*Lab*	p795
Lord Holmes of Richmond	*Con*	p805
Lord Howell of Guildford	*Con*	p812
Lord Lansley	*Con*	p849
Baroness Lister of Burtersett	*Lab*	p863
Lord McConnell of Glenscorrodale	*Lab*	p873
Lord Pendry	*Lab*	p941
Lord Sharpe of Epsom	*Con*	p994
Lord Stephen	*Lib Dem*	p1010
Lord Stevenson of Coddenham	*CB*	p1014
Lord Taylor of Warwick	*NA*	p1026
Viscount Trenchard	*Con*	p1036
Lord Wei	*Con*	p1063
Lord West of Spithead	*Lab*	p1064
Lord Whitty	*Lab*	p1067

Jordan

Baroness Chalker of Wallasey	*Con*	p671
Bishop of Coventry	*NA*	p690
Baroness D'Souza	*CB*	p714
Lord Jordan	*Lab*	p829

Kazakhstan

Lord Haworth	*Lab*	p790
Bishop of Leeds	*NA*	p854
Lord Levy	*Lab*	p857
Baroness Nicholson of Winterbourne	*Con*	p917
Baroness Stern	*CB*	p1011

Kenya

Lord Aberdare	*CB*	p586
Lord Allan of Hallam	*Lib Dem*	p592
Lord Alton of Liverpool	*CB*	p595
Baroness Armstrong of Hill Top	*Lab*	p600
Baroness Barker	*Lib Dem*	p609
Baroness Butler-Sloss	*CB*	p658
Archbishop of Canterbury	*NA*	p663
Baroness Corston	*Lab*	p687
Lord Jones of Cheltenham	*Lib Dem*	p827
Lord Loomba	*CB*	p868
Lord Oakeshott of Seagrove Bay	*NA*	p922
Bishop of Peterborough	*NA*	p942
Lord Popat	*Con*	p946
Lord St John of Bletso	*CB*	p983
Baroness Stern	*CB*	p1011
Bishop of Winchester	*NA*	p1073

Korea, North

Lord Alton of Liverpool	*CB*	p595
Lord Bates	*Con*	p612
Baroness Cox	*CB*	p690
Lord Eames	*CB*	p718
Lord Fraser of Corriegarth	*Con*	p747
Earl Howe	*Con*	p812
Lord Kerr of Kinlochard	*CB*	p835
Bishop of Peterborough	*NA*	p942
Lord Rowe-Beddoe	*CB*	p978
Viscount Trenchard	*Con*	p1036

Korea, South

Lord Bates	*Con*	p612
Baroness Benjamin	*Lib Dem*	p615
Baroness D'Souza	*CB*	p714
Lord Eames	*CB*	p718
Lord Holmes of Richmond	*Con*	p805
Lord Kerr of Kinlochard	*CB*	p835
Bishop of Peterborough	*NA*	p942
Viscount Trenchard	*Con*	p1036
Lord Wei	*Con*	p1063

Kuwait

Lord Jones of Cheltenham	*Lib Dem*	p827
Baroness Nicholson of Winterbourne	*Con*	p917

Kyrgzstan

Lord Haworth	*Lab*	p790
Baroness Stern	*CB*	p1011

Latvia

Bishop of Salisbury	*NA*	p983
Lord Smith of Hindhead	*Con*	p1004

Lebanon

Baroness Nicholson of Winterbourne	*Con*	p917

Lesotho

Bishop of Durham	*NA*	p717
Lord Jones of Cheltenham	*Lib Dem*	p827

Liberia

Baroness Kidron	*CB*	p837
Lord McColl of Dulwich	*Con*	p872

Libya

Lord James of Blackheath	*Con*	p822

Liechtenstein

Baroness Smith of Basildon	*Lab/Co-op*	p1001

Lithuania

Lord Cormack	*Con*	p686
Lord Smith of Hindhead	*Con*	p1004

Madagascar

Lord Lea of Crondall	*NA*	p852
Lord McColl of Dulwich	*Con*	p872

Malawi

Bishop of Birmingham	*NA*	p624
Lord Holmes of Richmond	*Con*	p805
Lord Jones of Cheltenham	*Lib Dem*	p827
Lord Loomba	*CB*	p868
Lord McColl of Dulwich	*Con*	p872
Lord McConnell of Glenscorrodale	*Lab*	p873
Lord Popat	*Con*	p946

Malaysia

Lord Bourne of Aberystwyth	*Con*	p636
Baroness Butler-Sloss	*CB*	p658
Lord Desai	*NA*	p708
Baroness Henig	*Lab*	p795
Lord Scriven	*Lib Dem*	p989

Maldives

Lord Naseby	*Con*	p911

Malta

Lord Judge	*CB*	p831
Lord Pendry	*Lab*	p941

Mauritius

Lord Desai	*NA*	p708
Baroness Prashar	*CB*	p949
Lord Rana	*Con*	p957

Mexico

Baroness Bonham-Carter of Yarnbury	*Lib Dem*	p633
Lord Rogers of Riverside	*Lab*	p974
Lord Rowe-Beddoe	*CB*	p978

Moldova

Lord German	*Lib Dem*	p754
Lord Hylton	*CB*	p820
Baroness Nicholson of Winterbourne	*Con*	p917

Mongolia

Lord Wei	*Con*	p1063

Montenegro

Lord Browne of Belmont	*DUP*	p650

Morocco

Baroness Barker	*Lib Dem*	p609
Baroness Uddin	*NA*	p1046

Mozambique

Bishop of Gloucester	*NA*	p758
Lord St John of Bletso	*CB*	p983
Earl of Sandwich	*CB*	p984

Namibia

Lord Faulkner of Worcester	*Lab*	p730
Lord Rana	*Con*	p957

Nepal

Lord Davies of Oldham	*Lab*	p702
Baroness Featherstone	*Lib Dem*	p732
Baroness Harris of Richmond	*Lib Dem*	p787
Lord Lancaster of Kimbolton	*Con*	p848
Lord Lea of Crondall	*NA*	p852
Lord Loomba	*CB*	p868
Earl of Sandwich	*CB*	p984

Netherlands

Baroness Bottomley of Nettlestone	*Con*	p636
Earl of Clancarty	*CB*	p676
Lord Cormack	*Con*	p686
Viscount Craigavon	*CB*	p692
Baroness Finlay of Llandaff	*CB*	p736
Viscount Hanworth	*Lab*	p782
Lord Stevenson of Coddenham	*CB*	p1014
Lord Taylor of Holbeach	*Con*	p1026

New Zealand

Lord Botham	*CB*	p635
Baroness Cohen of Pimlico	*Lab*	p682
Lord Faulkner of Worcester	*Lab*	p730
Baroness Fookes	*Con*	p740
Lord Freyberg	*CB*	p748
Baroness Fritchie	*CB*	p748
Baroness Hayter of Kentish Town	*Lab/Co-op*	p792
Lord Hoyle	*Lab*	p813
Baroness Kingsmill	*Lab*	p841
Lord Lisvane	*CB*	p865
Baroness Newlove	*Con*	p917
Lord O'Donnell	*CB*	p924
Lord Rooker	*Lab*	p975
Baroness Royall of Blaisdon	*Lab/Co-op*	p979
Lord Smith of Finsbury	*NA*	p1002
Lord Smith of Leigh	*Lab*	p1005
Baroness Stedman-Scott	*Con*	p1009
Lord Wallace of Tankerness	*NA*	p1055
Lord Wigley	*PIC*	p1068

Nicaragua

Baroness King of Bow	*Lab*	p839

Nigeria

Lord Adebowale	*CB*	p587
Baroness Barker	*Lib Dem*	p609
Archbishop of Canterbury	*NA*	p663
Bishop of Coventry	*NA*	p690
Baroness Cox	*CB*	p690

Norway

Lord Anderson of Swansea	*Lab*	p597
Bishop of Carlisle	*NA*	p665
Lord Faulkner of Worcester	*Lab*	p730
Lord McColl of Dulwich	*Con*	p872
Bishop of Newcastle	*NA*	p916
Lord Oakeshott of Seagrove Bay	*NA*	p922
Lord Paddick	*Lib Dem*	p931
Lord Wallace of Tankerness	*NA*	p1055

Oman

Lord German	*Lib Dem*	p754
Baroness Hoey	*NA*	p801
Baroness Jolly	*Lib Dem*	p826
Lord Lisvane	*CB*	p865
Baroness Rawlings	*Con*	p960

Pakistan

Lord Ahmad of Wimbledon	*Con*	p590
Lord Arbuthnot of Edrom	*Con*	p599
Lord Bhatia	*NA*	p621
Baroness Butler-Sloss	*CB*	p658
Lord Desai	*NA*	p708
Baroness Featherstone	*Lib Dem*	p732
Lord Newby	*Lib Dem*	p916
Lord Paul	*NA*	p939
Baroness Warsi	*Con*	p1058
Lord West of Spithead	*Lab*	p1064

Papua New Guinea

Baroness Burt of Solihull	*Lib Dem*	p656

Peru

Baroness Coussins	*CB*	p689

Philippines

Lord Scriven	*Lib Dem*	p989

Poland

Baroness Cox	*CB*	p690
Baroness Deech	*CB*	p705
Lord Field of Birkenhead	*CB*	p734
Lord Leitch	*Lab*	p855
Lord Mackenzie of Framwellgate	*NA*	p880
Lord Paul	*NA*	p939
Lord Pickles	*Con*	p943
Lord Radice	*Lab*	p955
Lord Roberts of Llandudno	*Lib Dem*	p970

Portugal

Lord Bach	*Lab*	p605
Lord Plant of Highfield	*Lab*	p945

Qatar

Baroness Harris of Richmond	*Lib Dem*	p787
Lord Redesdale	*Lib Dem*	p962
Viscount Simon	*Lab*	p1000
Baroness Uddin	*NA*	p1046

Romania

Lord Lamont of Lerwick	*Con*	p847
Lord McColl of Dulwich	*Con*	p872
Lord McFall of Alcluith	*NA*	p876
Baroness Nicholson of Winterbourne	*Con*	p917
Lord Watson of Richmond	*Lib Dem*	p1061

Russia

Lord Aberdare	*CB*	p586
Lord Ahmad of Wimbledon	*Con*	p590
Lord Arbuthnot of Edrom	*Con*	p599
Lord Barker of Battle	*Con*	p610
Lord Bruce of Bennachie	*Lib Dem*	p653
Lord Chartres	*CB*	p673
Viscount Colville of Culross	*CB*	p684
Lord Cromwell	*CB*	p694
Lord Davies of Stamford	*Lab*	p703
Lord Dunlop	*Con*	p716
Bishop of Durham	*NA*	p717
Lord Fairfax of Cameron	*Con*	p726
Lord Foulkes of Cumnock	*Lab/Co-op*	p743
Lord Gadhia	*NA*	p749
Lord Giddens	*Lab*	p755
Lord Haworth	*Lab*	p790
Lord Hylton	*CB*	p820
Lord Kerr of Kinlochard	*CB*	p835
Bishop of Leeds	*NA*	p854
Lord Mackenzie of Framwellgate	*NA*	p880
Baroness Massey of Darwen	*Lab*	p892
Baroness Meacher	*CB*	p895
Baroness Meyer	*Con*	p897
Lord Moylan	*Con*	p909
Earl of Oxford and Asquith	*NA*	p931
Lord Plant of Highfield	*Lab*	p945
Lord Randall of Uxbridge	*Con*	p958
Baroness Rawlings	*Con*	p960
Lord Selsdon	*Con*	p991
Lord Skidelsky	*CB*	p1001
Baroness Smith of Gilmorehill	*Lab*	p1003
Baroness Suttie	*Lib Dem*	p1022
Lord Truscott	*Ind Lab*	p1039
Lord Wallace of Saltaire	*Lib Dem*	p1054
Lord Watson of Richmond	*Lib Dem*	p1061
Lord Wood of Anfield	*Lab*	p1076

Rwanda

Baroness Blackwood of North Oxford	*Con*	p628
Lord Browne of Ladyton	*Lab*	p650
Lord Cotter	*Lib Dem*	p688
Bishop of Durham	*NA*	p717
Bishop of Ely	*NA*	p723
Baroness Gale	*Lab*	p750
Baroness King of Bow	*Lab*	p839
Lord Loomba	*CB*	p868
Lord McConnell of Glenscorrodale	*Lab*	p873
Bishop of Winchester	*NA*	p1073

Saint Lucia

Lord Palmer	*CB*	p932

Saudi Arabia

Lord Leitch	*Lab*	p855
Baroness Nicholson of Winterbourne	*Con*	p917
Baroness Uddin	*NA*	p1046

Scotland

Lord Fraser of Corriegarth	*Con*	p747
Baroness Goudie	*Lab*	p763
Lord Hope of Craighead	*CB*	p807
Lord Palmer	*CB*	p932
Earl of Shrewsbury and Waterford	*Con*	p999
Lord Vaux of Harrowden	*CB*	p1049
Viscount Younger of Leckie	*Con*	p1084

Serbia

Lord Browne of Belmont	*DUP*	p650

Sierra Leone

Lord Desai	*NA*	p708
Lord Jones of Cheltenham	*Lib Dem*	p827
Lord McColl of Dulwich	*Con*	p872
Lord St John of Bletso	*CB*	p983
Lord Stevenson of Coddenham	*CB*	p1014

Singapore

Lord Bourne of Aberystwyth	*Con*	p636
Baroness Butler-Sloss	*CB*	p658
Lord Desai	*NA*	p708
Baroness Finn	*Con*	p737
Lord Holmes of Richmond	*Con*	p805
Lord Naseby	*Con*	p911
Lord Oxburgh	*CB*	p929
Lord Scriven	*Lib Dem*	p989

Slovenia

Lord Taylor of Holbeach	*Con*	p1026
Lord Wigley	*PlC*	p1068

Somalia

Baroness Kidron	*CB*	p837

South Africa

Lord Anderson of Swansea	*Lab*	p597
Baroness Armstrong of Hill Top	*Lab*	p600
Baroness Benjamin	*Lib Dem*	p615
Lord Bilimoria	*CB*	p622
Lord Bird	*CB*	p624
Lord Birt	*CB*	p625
Lord Browne of Ladyton	*Lab*	p650
Lord Bruce of Bennachie	*Lib Dem*	p653
Lord Cashman	*NA*	p669
Baroness Coussins	*CB*	p689
Lord Cunningham of Felling	*Lab*	p695
Bishop of Durham	*NA*	p717
Lord Dykes	*CB*	p718
Lord Faulkner of Worcester	*Lab*	p730
Lord Gadhia	*NA*	p749
Bishop of Gloucester	*NA*	p758
Lord Howarth of Newport	*Lab*	p811
Lord Hoyle	*Lab*	p813
Lord Hughes of Woodside	*Lab*	p814
Baroness Jay of Paddington	*Lab*	p824
Baroness King of Bow	*Lab*	p839
Lord Lansley	*Con*	p849
Lord Loomba	*CB*	p868
Lord Low of Dalston	*CB*	p869
Lord Morgan	*Lab*	p902
Lord Newby	*Lib Dem*	p916
Lord Oates	*Lib Dem*	p923
Lord Paddick	*Lib Dem*	p931
Lord Patel	*CB*	p936
Lord Risby	*Con*	p969
Lord Rowlands	*Lab*	p978
Baroness Royall of Blaisdon	*Lab/Co-op*	p979
Lord St John of Bletso	*CB*	p983
Bishop of Salisbury	*NA*	p983
Earl of Sandwich	*CB*	p984
Lord Sawyer	*Lab*	p986
Lord Smith of Finsbury	*NA*	p1002
Lord Smith of Kelvin	*CB*	p1004
Lord Stoneham of Droxford	*Lib Dem*	p1016

Spain

Lord Arbuthnot of Edrom	*Con*	p599
Lord Bach	*Lab*	p605
Lord Bassam of Brighton	*Lab/Co-op*	p612
Lord Brougham and Vaux	*Con*	p648
Lord Collins of Highbury	*Lab*	p683
Baroness Coussins	*CB*	p689
Baroness Finlay of Llandaff	*CB*	p736
Baroness Golding	*Lab*	p760
Lord Hain	*Lab*	p775
Baroness Healy of Primrose Hill	*Lab*	p794
Lord Leitch	*Lab*	p855
Lord Lupton	*NA*	p871
Lord Maxton	*Lab*	p894
Lord Morris of Aberavon	*Lab*	p905
Baroness O'Loan	*CB*	p925
Lord Paul	*NA*	p939

Sri Lanka

Lord Bhatia	*NA*	p621
Baroness Cox	*CB*	p690
Lord Davies of Oldham	*Lab*	p702
Lord Desai	*NA*	p708
Lord Faulks	*NA*	p731
Lord Hardie	*CB*	p783
Baroness Hayter of Kentish Town	*Lab/Co-op*	p792
Bishop of Leeds	*NA*	p854
Lord Loomba	*CB*	p868
Lord Naseby	*Con*	p911
Lord Paul	*NA*	p939

Sudan

Lord Alton of Liverpool	*CB*	p595
Baroness Blackwood of North Oxford	*Con*	p628
Lord Carey of Clifton	*CB*	p664
Baroness Cox	*CB*	p690
Lord Curry of Kirkharle	*CB*	p697
Baroness Kinnock of Holyhead	*Lab*	p842
Bishop of Leeds	*NA*	p854
Duke of Montrose	*Con*	p900
Bishop of Salisbury	*NA*	p983
Earl of Sandwich	*CB*	p984

Swaziland

Lord Jones of Cheltenham	*Lib Dem*	p827

Sweden

Lord Brooke of Alverthorpe	*Lab*	p646
Baroness Campbell of Surbiton	*CB*	p662
Bishop of Gloucester	*NA*	p758
Lord Liddle	*Lab*	p859
Lord Patel	*CB*	p936
Lord Radice	*Lab*	p955
Baroness Ramsay of Cartvale	*Lab*	p956
Lord Rooker	*Lab*	p975
Lord Tyler	*Lib Dem*	p1043
Baroness Wolf of Dulwich	*NA*	p1075

Switzerland

Lord Brabazon of Tara	*Con*	p640
Earl of Courtown	*Con*	p688
Lord Leitch	*Lab*	p855
Lord Paul	*NA*	p939
Lord Sharpe of Epsom	*Con*	p994
Baroness Smith of Basildon	*Lab/Co-op*	p1001
Lord Storey	*Lib Dem*	p1017

Syria

Lord Alton of Liverpool	*CB*	p595
Bishop of Coventry	*NA*	p690

Baroness Cox	*CB*	p690
Baroness Nicholson of Winterbourne	*Con*	p917
Lord Wharton of Yarm	*Con*	p1064

Taiwan

Lord Arbuthnot of Edrom	*Con*	p599
Lord Bethell	*Con*	p620
Baroness D'Souza	*CB*	p714
Lord Faulkner of Worcester	*Lab*	p730
Baroness Gale	*Lab*	p750
Lord Grantchester	*Lab*	p765
Lord Hardie	*CB*	p783
Lord Kilclooney	*CB*	p838
Lord Rana	*Con*	p957
Lord Rosser	*Lab*	p976

Tajikistan

Baroness Stern	*CB*	p1011

Tanzania

Baroness Armstrong of Hill Top	*Lab*	p600
Bishop of Gloucester	*NA*	p758
Lord Jones of Cheltenham	*Lib Dem*	p827
Bishop of Leeds	*NA*	p854
Lord McColl of Dulwich	*Con*	p872
Lord Patel	*CB*	p936
Lord Popat	*Con*	p946

Thailand

Baroness Henig	*Lab*	p795
Lord Scriven	*Lib Dem*	p989

Togo

Lord McColl of Dulwich	*Con*	p872

Tunisia

Baroness Burt of Solihull	*Lib Dem*	p656
Lord McNally	*Lib Dem*	p882
Baroness Uddin	*NA*	p1046

Turkey

Baroness Bakewell	*Lab*	p606
Lord Balfe	*Con*	p608
Lord Cashman	*NA*	p669
Lord Clement-Jones	*Lib Dem*	p679
Baroness Fritchie	*CB*	p748
Baroness Hussein-Ece	*Lib Dem*	p819
Lord Inglewood	*NA*	p820
Lord Kilclooney	*CB*	p838
Lord Leitch	*Lab*	p855
Baroness Ludford	*Lib Dem*	p870
Baroness Nicholson of Winterbourne	*Con*	p917
Lord Paul	*NA*	p939
Lord Sharkey	*Lib Dem*	p993
Lord Stevenson of Balmacara	*Lab*	p1014

Turkmenistan

Baroness Nicholson of Winterbourne	*Con*	p917

Turks & Caicos Islands

Lord Jones of Cheltenham	*Lib Dem*	p827

Uganda

Lord Alton of Liverpool	*CB*	p595
Baroness Armstrong of Hill Top	*Lab*	p600
Baroness Cox	*CB*	p690
Bishop of Durham	*NA*	p717
Lord Howarth of Newport	*Lab*	p811
Lord Jones of Cheltenham	*Lib Dem*	p827
Lord Loomba	*CB*	p868
Lord McColl of Dulwich	*Con*	p872
Lord Popat	*Con*	p946
Lord Roberts of Llandudno	*Lib Dem*	p970
Earl of Sandwich	*CB*	p984
Bishop of Winchester	*NA*	p1073

Ukraine

Earl of Oxford and Asquith	*NA*	p931
Lord Wallace of Saltaire	*Lib Dem*	p1054
Lord West of Spithead	*Lab*	p1064

United Arab Emirates

Lord Clement-Jones	*Lib Dem*	p679
Lord Jones of Cheltenham	*Lib Dem*	p827
Baroness Newlove	*Con*	p917
Lord Rowe-Beddoe	*CB*	p978
Baroness Uddin	*NA*	p1046

United Kingdom

Lord Baker of Dorking	*Con*	p606
Viscount Brookeborough	*CB*	p647
Earl Cathcart	*Con*	p669
Lord Lee of Trafford	*Lib Dem*	p853
Lord Lexden	*Con*	p858
Lord Lingfield	*Con*	p862
Lord Livermore	*Lab*	p865
Lord Loomba	*CB*	p868
Lord Lupton	*NA*	p871
Lord Mawson	*CB*	p894
Lord Rogers of Riverside	*Lab*	p974
Lord Saatchi	*Con*	p981
Lord Tebbit	*Con*	p1027
Lord Vinson	*Con*	p1051

USA

Lord Aberdare	*CB*	p586
Lord Adebowale	*CB*	p587
Lord Ahmad of Wimbledon	*Con*	p590
Lord Allan of Hallam	*Lib Dem*	p592
Lord Allen of Kensington	*Lab*	p592
Lord Arbuthnot of Edrom	*Con*	p599
Lord Astor of Hever	*Con*	p603
Lord Bach	*Lab*	p605

Lord Balfe	*Con*	p608
Lord Barker of Battle	*Con*	p610
Lord Barwell	*Con*	p611
Lord Bassam of Brighton	*Lab/Co-op*	p612
Lord Bates	*Con*	p612
Baroness Benjamin	*Lib Dem*	p615
Lord Bethell	*Con*	p620
Lord Bilimoria	*CB*	p622
Baroness Billingham	*Lab*	p623
Lord Bird	*CB*	p624
Lord Birt	*CB*	p625
Baroness Blackstone	*Lab Ind*	p627
Lord Blunkett	*Lab*	p631
Lord Boateng	*Lab*	p632
Baroness Bonham-Carter of Yarnbury	*Lib Dem*	p633
Lord Borwick	*Con*	p634
Lord Bradley	*Lab*	p640
Lord Bragg	*Lab*	p642
Lord Broers	*CB*	p646
Lord Bruce of Bennachie	*Lib Dem*	p653
Lord Carrington of Fulham	*Con*	p666
Lord Cashman	*NA*	p669
Lord Cormack	*Con*	p686
Baroness Corston	*Lab*	p687
Lord Crathorne	*Con*	p692
Lord Cunningham of Felling	*Lab*	p695
Lord Davies of Stamford	*Lab*	p703
Lord Dear	*CB*	p704
Baroness Deech	*CB*	p705
Lord Desai	*NA*	p708
Lord Dobbs	*Con*	p710
Lord Dodds of Duncairn	*DUP*	p711
Baroness Doocey	*Lib Dem*	p712
Lord Dunlop	*Con*	p716
Lord Dykes	*CB*	p718
Lord Eames	*CB*	p718
Lord Empey	*UUP*	p723
Lord Evans of Watford	*Lab*	p725
Lord Fairfax of Cameron	*Con*	p726
Baroness Falkner of Margravine	*CB*	p728
Lord Faulks	*NA*	p731
Baroness Featherstone	*Lib Dem*	p732
Lord Fellowes	*CB*	p733
Lord Fellowes of West Stafford	*Con*	p733
Baroness Finn	*Con*	p737
Lord Flight	*Con*	p739
Baroness Ford	*CB*	p741
Baroness Fritchie	*CB*	p748
Baroness Gale	*Lab*	p750
Bishop of Gloucester	*NA*	p758
Lord Goddard of Stockport	*Lib Dem*	p759
Baroness Goudie	*Lab*	p763
Lord Harris of Haringey	*Lab*	p785
Lord Harrison	*Lab*	p787
Lord Haselhurst	*Con*	p788
Lord Haskel	*Lab*	p789
Baroness Healy of Primrose Hill	*Lab*	p794
Lord Holmes of Richmond	*Con*	p805
Lord Horam	*Con*	p808
Lord Howard of Lympne	*Con*	p809
Baroness Hughes of Stretford	*Lab*	p814
Lord Hunt of Chesterton	*Lab*	p816
Lord Hunt of Wirral	*Con*	p817
Baroness Jay of Paddington	*Lab*	p824
Lord Kakkar	*CB*	p832
Lord Kerr of Kinlochard	*CB*	p835
Baroness Kidron	*CB*	p837
Baroness King of Bow	*Lab*	p839
Baroness Kingsmill	*Lab*	p841
Lord Kirkhope of Harrogate	*Con*	p843
Baroness Kramer	*Lib Dem*	p845
Lord Lancaster of Kimbolton	*Con*	p848
Lord Lansley	*Con*	p849
Lord Leitch	*Lab*	p855
Lord Lennie	*Lab*	p855
Baroness Liddell of Coatdyke	*Lab*	p858
Lord Liddle	*Lab*	p859
Baroness Lister of Burtersett	*Lab*	p863
Lord Livermore	*Lab*	p865
Lord Loomba	*CB*	p868
Lord Low of Dalston	*CB*	p869
Baroness Ludford	*Lib Dem*	p870
Lord McAvoy	*Lab/Co-op*	p872
Lord McConnell of Glenscorrodale	*Lab*	p873
Lord McCrea of Magherafelt and Cookstown	*DUP*	p874
Lord MacKenzie of Culkein	*Lab*	p879
Lord Mackenzie of Framwellgate	*NA*	p880
Baroness Massey of Darwen	*Lab*	p892
Baroness Meyer	*Con*	p897
Lord Mitchell	*Lab*	p898
Lord Morgan	*Lab*	p902
Lord Morrow	*DUP*	p908
Baroness Newlove	*Con*	p917
Baroness Nicholson of Winterbourne	*Con*	p917
Baroness O'Cathain	*Con*	p923
Lord O'Donnell	*CB*	p924
Lord Oxburgh	*CB*	p929
Lord Paddick	*Lib Dem*	p931
Lord Pannick	*CB*	p933
Lord Parekh	*Lab*	p933
Lord Patel	*CB*	p936
Lord Paul	*NA*	p939
Lord Pendry	*Lab*	p941
Lord Pickles	*Con*	p943
Baroness Prosser	*Lab*	p952
Lord Puttnam	*Lab*	p953

Lord Renfrew of Kaimsthorn	*Con*	p964
Lord Ribeiro	*Con*	p966
Lord Ricketts	*CB*	p968
Lord Risby	*Con*	p969
Baroness Royall of Blaisdon	*Lab/Co-op*	p979
Lord Sainsbury of Turville	*Lab*	p982
Baroness Scott of Needham Market	*Lib Dem*	p988
Lord Sharpe of Epsom	*Con*	p994
Lord Sherbourne of Didsbury	*Con*	p996
Baroness Shields	*Con*	p997
Lord Singh of Wimbledon	*CB*	p1000
Baroness Smith of Basildon	*Lab/Co-op*	p1001
Lord Smith of Finsbury	*NA*	p1002
Lord Smith of Leigh	*Lab*	p1005
Lord Stephen	*Lib Dem*	p1010
Lord Stevens of Ludgate	*Con Ind*	p1013
Lord Stevenson of Coddenham	*CB*	p1014
Lord Stirrup	*CB*	p1015
Lord Stoneham of Droxford	*Lib Dem*	p1016
Lord Storey	*Lib Dem*	p1017
Lord Taylor of Warwick	*NA*	p1026
Viscount Trenchard	*Con*	p1036
Lord Vaizey of Didcot	*Con*	p1047
Lord Wallace of Saltaire	*Lib Dem*	p1054
Lord Wallace of Tankerness	*NA*	p1055
Lord Warner	*CB*	p1057
Lord Watson of Richmond	*Lib Dem*	p1061
Lord Wigley	*PlC*	p1068
Lord Willetts	*Con*	p1069
Baroness Wolf of Dulwich	*NA*	p1075
Lord Wood of Anfield	*Lab*	p1076
Lord Wrigglesworth	*Lib Dem*	p1079
Baroness Young of Hornsey	*CB*	p1082
Lord Young of Norwood Green	*Lab*	p1082

Uzbekistan

Baroness Stern	*CB*	p1011

Vietnam

Baroness Brown of Cambridge	*CB*	p648
Lord Fraser of Corriegarth	*Con*	p747
Lord Haworth	*Lab*	p790
Lord Howarth of Newport	*Lab*	p811
Lord Vaizey of Didcot	*Con*	p1047

Wales

Lord Aberdare	*CB*	p586
Lord Elis-Thomas	*NA*	p722
Lord Morgan	*Lab*	p902
Baroness Morgan of Drefelin	*CB*	p903
Lord Thomas of Gresford	*Lib Dem*	p1029

Yemen

Baroness Nicholson of Winterbourne	*Con*	p917

Zambia

Lord Jones of Cheltenham	*Lib Dem*	p827
Lord Turnbull	*CB*	p1042

Zimbabwe

Lord Beith	*Lib Dem*	p614
Baroness Bonham-Carter of Yarnbury	*Lib Dem*	p633
Lord Bruce of Bennachie	*Lib Dem*	p653
Lord Gardiner of Kimble	*Con*	p751
Baroness Hoey	*NA*	p801
Lord Jones of Cheltenham	*Lib Dem*	p827
Lord Oates	*Lib Dem*	p923
Lord Palmer	*CB*	p932
Lord St John of Bletso	*CB*	p983
Earl of Sandwich	*CB*	p984
Bishop of Southwark	*NA*	p1008

MPs who are now Peers

Irene Adams
Baroness Adams of Craigielea
Richard Allan
Lord Allan of Hallam
David Alton
Lord Alton of Liverpool
Donald Anderson
Lord Anderson of Swansea
James Arbuthnot
Lord Arbuthnot of Edrom
Jeffrey Archer
Lord Archer of Weston-super-Mare
Hilary Armstrong
Baroness Armstrong of Hill Top
Ian Austin
Lord Austin of Dudley
Kenneth Baker
Lord Baker of Dorking
Gregory Barker
Lord Barker of Battle
Gavin Barwell
Lord Barwell
Michael Bates
Lord Bates
Alan Beith
Lord Beith
Henry Bellingham
Lord Bellingham
Richard Benyon
Lord Benyon
David Maclean
Lord Blencathra
David Blunkett
Lord Blunkett
Paul Boateng
Lord Boateng
Betty Boothroyd
Baroness Boothroyd
Timothy Boswell
Lord Boswell of Aynho
Virginia Bottomley
Baroness Bottomley of Nettlestone
Keith Bradley
Lord Bradley
Des Browne
Lord Browne of Ladyton
Angela Browning
Baroness Browning
Malcolm Bruce
Lord Bruce of Bennachie
John Burnett
Lord Burnett
Lorely Burt
Baroness Burt of Solihull
Menzies Campbell
Lord Campbell of Pittenweem
Dale Campbell-Savours
Lord Campbell-Savours
Alexander Carlile
Lord Carlile of Berriew
Matthew Carrington
Lord Carrington of Fulham
Lynda Chalker
Baroness Chalker of Wallasey
Jenny Chapman
Baroness Chapman of Darlington
David Chidgey
Lord Chidgey
Lynda Clark
Baroness Clark of Calton
Katy Clark
Baroness Clark of Kilwinning
David Clark
Lord Clark of Windermere
Kenneth Clarke
Lord Clarke of Nottingham
Vernon Coaker
Lord Coaker
Sebastian Coe
Lord Coe
Patrick Cormack
Lord Cormack
Jean Corston
Baroness Corston
Brian Cotter
Lord Cotter
Jack Cunningham
Lord Cunningham of Felling

Byron Davies
Lord Davies of Gower
Bryan Davies
Lord Davies of Oldham
Quentin Davies
Lord Davies of Stamford
John Gummer
Lord Deben
Nigel Dodds
Lord Dodds of Duncairn
Alf Dubs
Lord Dubs
Hugh Dykes
Lord Dykes
Dafydd Elis-Thomas
Lord Elis-Thomas
Lynne Featherstone
Baroness Featherstone
Frank Field
Lord Field of Birkenhead
Howard Flight
Lord Flight
Janet Fookes
Baroness Fookes
Michael Forsyth
Lord Forsyth of Drumlean
Donald Foster
Lord Foster of Bath
George Foulkes
Lord Foulkes of Cumnock
Norman Fowler
Lord Fowler
Michael Lord
Lord Framlingham
Lorraine Fullbrook
Baroness Fullbrook
Edward Garnier
Lord Garnier
Llin Golding
Baroness Golding
Zac Goldsmith
Lord Goldsmith of Richmond Park
Alastair Goodlad
Lord Goodlad
Bruce Grocott
Lord Grocott

William Hague
Lord Hague of Richmond
Douglas Hogg
Viscount Hailsham
Peter Hain
Lord Hain
Archie Hamilton
Lord Hamilton of Epsom
Philip Hammond
Lord Hammond of Runnymede
Alan Haselhurst
Lord Haselhurst
Helene Hayman
Baroness Hayman
Sue Hayman
Baroness Hayman of Ullock
Robert Hayward
Lord Hayward
Nick Herbert
Lord Herbert of South Downs
Michael Heseltine
Lord Heseltine
Robin Hodgson
Lord Hodgson of Astley Abbotts
Kate Hoey
Baroness Hoey
John Horam
Lord Horam
Michael Howard
Lord Howard of Lympne
Alan Howarth
Lord Howarth of Newport
David Howell
Lord Howell of Guildford
Douglas Hoyle
Lord Hoyle
Beverley Hughes
Baroness Hughes of Stretford
Robert Hughes
Lord Hughes of Woodside
David Hunt
Lord Hunt of Wirral
John Hutton
Lord Hutton of Furness
Jo Johnson
Lord Johnson of Marylebone

Barry Jones
Lord Jones
Nigel Jones
Lord Jones of Cheltenham
Michael Jopling
Lord Jopling
Frank Judd
Lord Judd
John Taylor
Lord Kilclooney
Oona King
Baroness King of Bow
Tom King
Lord King of Bridgwater
Neil Kinnock
Lord Kinnock
Timothy Kirkhope
Lord Kirkhope of Harrogate
Jim Knight
Lord Knight of Weymouth
Susan Kramer
Baroness Kramer
Norman Lamont
Lord Lamont of Lerwick
Mark Lancaster
Lord Lancaster of Kimbolton
Ian Lang
Lord Lang of Monkton
Andrew Lansley
Lord Lansley
Nigel Lawson
Lord Lawson of Blaby
John Lee
Lord Lee of Trafford
Helen Liddell
Baroness Liddell of Coatdyke
Peter Lilley
Lord Lilley
Michael Ancram
Marquess of Lothian
Thomas McAvoy
Lord McAvoy
William McCrea
Lord McCrea of Magherafelt and Cookstown
John McFall
Lord McFall of Alcluith
Anne McIntosh
Baroness McIntosh of Pickering
Patrick McLoughlin
Lord McLoughlin
Tom McNally
Lord McNally
Ken Maginnis
Lord Maginnis of Drumglass
Peter Mandelson
Lord Mandelson
John Mann
Lord Mann
Francis Maude
Lord Maude of Horsham
John Maxton
Lord Maxton
Gillian Merron
Baroness Merron
Lewis Moonie
Lord Moonie
Nicky Morgan
Baroness Morgan of Cotes
John Morris
Lord Morris of Aberavon
Estelle Morris
Baroness Morris of Yardley
Colin Moynihan
Lord Moynihan
Paul Murphy
Lord Murphy of Torfaen
Michael Morris
Lord Naseby
Emma Nicholson
Baroness Nicholson of Winterbourne
David Owen
Lord Owen
John Patten
Lord Patten
Christopher Patten
Lord Patten of Barnes
Tom Pendry
Lord Pendry
Eric Pickles
Lord Pickles
John Prescott
Lord Prescott

Dawn Primarolo
Baroness Primarolo
David Prior
Lord Prior of Brampton
Joyce Quin
Baroness Quin
Giles Radice
Lord Radice
John Randall
Lord Randall of Uxbridge
John Reid
Lord Reid of Cardowan
Richard Spring
Lord Risby
Margaret Ritchie
Baroness Ritchie of Downpatrick
Andrew Robathan
Lord Robathan
George Robertson
Lord Robertson of Port Ellen
William Rodgers
Lord Rodgers of Quarry Bank
Jeffrey Rooker
Lord Rooker
Ted Rowlands
Lord Rowlands
Richard Ryder
Lord Ryder of Wensum
James Douglas-Hamilton
Lord Selkirk of Douglas
Gillian Shephard
Baroness Shephard of Northwold
Angela Smith
Baroness Smith of Basildon
Chris Smith
Lord Smith of Finsbury
Peter Snape
Lord Snape
Clive Soley
Lord Soley
Nicol Stephen
Lord Stephen
Gisela Stuart
Baroness Stuart of Edgbaston
Andrew Stunell
Lord Stunell
Dick Taverne
Lord Taverne
Ann Taylor
Baroness Taylor of Bolton
Matthew Taylor
Lord Taylor of Goss Moor
Norman Tebbit
Lord Tebbit
John Thurso
Viscount Thurso
John Tomlinson
Lord Tomlinson
Graham Tope
Lord Tope
Don Touhig
Lord Touhig
David Trimble
Lord Trimble
Christopher Tugendhat
Lord Tugendhat
Paul Tyler
Lord Tyler
Andrew Tyrie
Lord Tyrie
Ed Vaizey
Lord Vaizey of Didcot
John Wakeham
Lord Wakeham
William Waldegrave
Lord Waldegrave of North Hill
Jim Wallace
Lord Wallace of Tankerness
John Woodcock
Lord Walney
Mike Watson
Lord Watson of Invergowrie
David Watts
Lord Watts
James Wharton
Lord Wharton of Yarm
Dafydd Wigley
Lord Wigley
David Willetts
Lord Willetts
Phil Willis
Lord Willis of Knaresborough
Michael Wills
Lord Wills
Ian Wrigglesworth
Lord Wrigglesworth

George Young
Lord Young of Cookham

Hereditary Peer Members

Under the 1999 House of Lords Act, which abolished the right of most hereditary peers to sit in the Upper Chamber, 92 hereditary peers retained their seats. These include two hereditary office holders, the Duke of Norfolk (Earl Marshal), and the Marquess of Cholmondeley (Lord Great Chamberlain).

Peers of Ireland are marked *, with their British honours in parenthesis.

A number of other peers sit under their hereditary titles, although they are members by virtue of life peerages, the titles of which appear in bold.

Lord Aberdare cr. 1873
Lord Addington cr. 1887
Earl of Arran cr. 1762* (Baron Sudley)
Lord Ashton of Hyde cr. 1911
Viscount Astor cr. 1917
Lord Astor of Hever cr. 1956
Earl Attlee cr. 1955
Lord Berkeley cr. 1421 (LP **Baron Gueterbock** 2000)
Lord Bethell cr. 1922
Lord Borwick cr. 1922
Lord Brabazon of Tara cr. 1942
Viscount Bridgeman cr. 1929
Viscount Brookeborough cr. 1952
Lord Brougham and Vaux cr. 1860
Earl of Caithness cr. 1455
Lord Carrington cr. 1796
Earl Cathcart cr. 1814
Viscount Chandos cr. 1954 (LP **Baron Lyttelton of Aldershot** 2000)
Marquess of Cholmondeley cr. 1815
Earl of Clancarty cr. 1803* (Baron Trench)
Lord Colgrain cr. 1946
Viscount Colville of Culross cr. 1902
Lord Colwyn cr. 1917
Earl of Cork and Orrery cr. 1620/1660* (Baron Boyle of Marston)
Earl of Courtown cr. 1762* (Baron Saltersford)
Viscount Craigavon cr. 1927
Lord Crathorne cr. 1959
Lord Cromwell cr. 1375
Lord de Mauley cr. 1838
Lord Denham cr. 1937
Earl of Devon cr. 1553
Earl of Dundee cr. 1660
Viscount Eccles cr. 1964
Earl of Erroll cr. 1452
Lord Fairfax of Cameron cr. 1627
Viscount of Falkland cr. 1620
Lord Freyberg cr. 1951
Lord Geddes cr. 1942
Earl of Glasgow cr. 1703
Lord Glenarthur cr. 1918
Viscount Goschen cr. 1900
Lord Grantchester cr. 1953
Lord Greenway cr. 1927
Viscount Hailsham cr. 1929 (LP **Baron Hailsham of Kettlethorpe** 2015)
Viscount Hanworth cr. 1936
Lord Henley cr. 1799* (Baron Northington)
Earl of Home cr. 1604
Earl Howe cr. 1821
Lord Hylton cr. 1866
Lord Inglewood cr. 1964
Earl of Kinnoull cr. 1633
Earl of Lindsay cr. 1633
Earl of Listowel cr. 1822* (Baron Hare)
Earl of Liverpool cr. 1905
Marquess of Lothian cr. 1701 (LP **Baron Kerr of Monteviot** 2010)
Lord Lucas of Crudwell and Dingwall cr. 1663/1609
Earl of Lytton cr. 1880
Lord Mancroft cr. 1937
Duke of Montrose cr. 1707
Lord Mountevans cr. 1945
Lord Moynihan cr. 1929
Duke of Norfolk cr. 1483
Lord Northbrook cr. 1866
Earl of Oxford and Asquith cr. 1925
Lord Palmer cr. 1933
Earl Peel cr. 1929
Lord Ponsonby of Shulbrede cr. 1930 (LP **Baron Ponsonby of Roehampton** 2000)
Lord Ravensdale cr. 1911
Lord Reay cr. 1628
Lord Redesdale cr. 1902 (LP **Baron Mitford** 2000)
Viscount Ridley cr. 1900
Earl of Rosslyn cr. 1801
Lord Rotherwick cr. 1939
Lord Russell of Liverpool cr. 1919
Earl of Sandwich cr. 1660
Lord Selsdon cr. 1932
Earl of Shrewsbury and Waterford cr. 1442/1446
Viscount Simon cr. 1940
Duke of Somerset cr. 1547
Lord St John of Bletso cr. 1558
Earl of Stair cr. 1703
Lord Strathclyde cr. 1955
Lord Swinfen cr. 1919
Lord Thurlow cr. 1792
Viscount Thurso cr. 1952
Lord Trefgarne cr. 1947
Viscount Trenchard cr. 1936
Lord Trevethin and Oaksey cr. 1921/1947
Viscount Ullswater cr. 1921
Lord Vaux of Harrowden cr. 1523
Viscount Waverley cr. 1952
Duke of Wellington cr. 1814
Lord Willoughby de Broke cr. 1491
Viscount Younger of Leckie cr. 1923

Bishops

Since the mid-nineteenth century the number of bishops in the House (known as Lords Spiritual as opposed to Lords Temporal) has been limited by statute to 26. By ancient usage the two Anglican Archbishops and the Bishops of London, Durham and Winchester automatically have seats in the House of Lords. The remaining 21 diocesan bishops usually qualify for membership according to seniority. However until 2025, where there is a woman amongst those bishops awaiting a place in the Lords, she will be given priority in filling the vacancy under the terms of the Lords Spiritual (Women) Act 2015.

Email: parliamentary@churchofengland.org Website: churchinparliament.org Twitter: @churchstate

ARCHBISHOPS (2) AND DIOCESAN BISHOPS (3) EX-OFFICIO

		Entered Lords
Most Rev and Rt Hon Justin Welby	Canterbury	2011
Most Rev and Rt Hon Stephen Cottrell	York	2014
Rt Rev Paul Butler	Durham	2014
Rt Rev Tim Dakin	Winchester	2012
Rt Rev and Rt Hon Sarah Mullally	London	2018

BISHOPS IN ORDER OF SENIORITY (21)

		Entered Lords
Rt Rev David Urquhart	Birmingham	2010
Rt Rev John Inge	Worcester	2012
Rt Rev Dr Christopher Cocksworth	Coventry	2012
Rt Rev Steven Croft	Oxford	2016
Rt Rev Dr Alan Smith	St Albans	2013
Rt Rev James Newcome	Carlisle	2013
Rt Rev Donald Allister	Peterborough	2014
Rt Rev Christopher Foster	Portsmouth	2014
Rt Rev James Langstaff	Rochester	2014
Rt Rev Stephen Conway	Ely	2014
Rt Rev Christopher Chessun	Southwark	2014
Rt Rev Nicholas Baines	Leeds	2014
Rt Rev Nicholas Holtam	Salisbury	2014
Rt Rev Rachel Treweek	Gloucester	2015
Rt Rev Christine Hardman	Newcastle	2015
Rt Rev Christopher Lowson	Lincoln	2017
Rt Rev Dr Martin Warner	Chichester	2018
Rt Rev Vivienne Faull	Bristol	2018
Rt Rev Libby Lane	Derby	2019
Rt Rev Julian Henderson	Blackburn	2019
Rt Rev David Walker	Manchester	2020

Law Lords

Senior members of the judiciary are unable to sit or vote in the House of Lords until they retire.

Supreme Court Justice: Lord Reed of Allermuir
Lord Chief Justice of England and Wales: Lord Burnett of Maldon
Senator of the College of Justice in Scotland: Lord Boyd of Duncansby

Peers on leave of absence (22)

Baroness Ashton of Upholland	NA	Earl of Listowel	CB
Lord Barker of Battle	Con	Lord Livermore	Lab
Lord Black of Crossharbour	NA	Lord Llewellyn of Steep	Con
Marquess of Cholmondeley	NA	Lord Magan of Castletown	Con
Lord Davies of Abersoch	NA	Lord Malloch-Brown	CB
Lord Feldman of Elstree	Con	Duke of Norfolk	NA
Baroness Ford	CB	Lord Oakeshott of Seagrove Bay	NA
Lord Frost	Con	Lord Sainsbury of Preston Candover	Con
Lord Hague of Richmond	Con	Lord Sainsbury of Turville	Lab
Lord Hardie	CB	Baroness Scotland of Asthal	Lab
Baroness King of Bow	Lab	Baroness Vadera	NA

Women Members (230)

Women were first admitted into the House of Lords by the Life Peerage Act, 1958. Women peers by succession were not admitted into the Upper House until 1963. There are currently no Women peers by succession sitting in the House of Lords. Women Bishops were first admitted into the House of Lords by the Lords Spiritual (Women) Act, 2015.

Baroness Adams of Craigielea	Lab	Baroness Campbell of Surbiton	CB
Baroness Afshar	CB	Baroness Casey of Blackstock	CB
Baroness Altmann	Con	Baroness Cavendish of Little Venice	CB
Baroness Amos	Lab	Baroness Chakrabarti	Lab
Baroness Andrews	Lab	Baroness Chalker of Wallasey	Con
Baroness Anelay of St Johns	Con	Baroness Chapman of Darlington	Lab
Baroness Armstrong of Hill Top	Lab	Baroness Chisholm of Owlpen	Con
Baroness Ashton of Upholland	NA	Baroness Clark of Calton	CB
Baroness Bakewell	Lab	Baroness Clark of Kilwinning	Lab
Baroness Bakewell of Hardington Mandeville	Lib Dem	Baroness Cohen of Pimlico	Lab
Baroness Barker	Lib Dem	Baroness Corston	Lab
Baroness Barran	Con	Baroness Coussins	CB
Baroness Benjamin	Lib Dem	Baroness Couttie	Con
Baroness Bennett of Manor Castle	Green	Baroness Cox	CB
Baroness Berridge	Con	Baroness Crawley	Lab
Baroness Bertin	Con	Baroness Cumberlege	Con
Baroness Billingham	Lab	Baroness D'Souza	CB
Baroness Blackstone	Lab Ind	Baroness Deech	CB
Baroness Blackwood of North Oxford	Con	Bishop of Derby	NA
Baroness Blake of Leeds	Lab	Baroness Donaghy	Lab
Baroness Bloomfield of Hinton Waldrist	Con	Baroness Doocey	Lib Dem
Baroness Blower	Lab	Baroness Drake	Lab
Baroness Bonham-Carter of Yarnbury	Lib Dem	Baroness Eaton	Con
Baroness Boothroyd	CB	Baroness Eccles of Moulton	Con
Baroness Bottomley of Nettlestone	Con	Baroness Evans of Bowes Park	Con
Baroness Bowles of Berkhamsted	Lib Dem	Baroness Fairhead	Con
Baroness Boycott	CB	Baroness Falkner of Margravine	CB
Baroness Brady	Con	Baroness Fall	Con
Baroness Brinton	Lib Dem	Baroness Featherstone	Lib Dem
Bishop of Bristol	NA	Baroness Finlay of Llandaff	CB
Baroness Brown of Cambridge	CB	Baroness Finn	Con
Baroness Browning	Con	Baroness Flather	CB
Baroness Bryan of Partick	Lab	Baroness Fleet	Con
Baroness Bull	CB	Baroness Fookes	Con
Baroness Burt of Solihull	Lib Dem	Baroness Ford	CB
Baroness Buscombe	Con	Baroness Foster of Oxton	Con
Baroness Butler-Sloss	CB	Baroness Fox of Buckley	NA
Baroness Campbell of Loughborough	CB	Baroness Fraser of Craigmaddie	Con
		Baroness Fritchie	CB

Baroness Fullbrook	Con
Baroness Gale	Lab
Baroness Garden of Frognal	Lib Dem
Baroness Gardner of Parkes	Con
Bishop of Gloucester	NA
Baroness Goldie	Con
Baroness Golding	Lab
Baroness Goudie	Lab
Baroness Greenfield	CB
Baroness Greengross	CB
Baroness Grender	Lib Dem
Baroness Grey-Thompson	CB
Baroness Hale of Richmond	NA
Baroness Hallett	CB
Baroness Hamwee	Lib Dem
Baroness Harding of Winscombe	Con
Baroness Harris of Richmond	Lib Dem
Baroness Hayman	CB
Baroness Hayman of Ullock	Lab
Baroness Hayter of Kentish Town	Lab/Co-op
Baroness Healy of Primrose Hill	Lab
Baroness Helic	Con
Baroness Henig	Lab
Baroness Hilton of Eggardon	Lab
Baroness Hodgson of Abinger	Con
Baroness Hoey	NA
Baroness Hogg	CB
Baroness Hollins	CB
Baroness Hooper	Con
Baroness Howarth of Breckland	CB
Baroness Hughes of Stretford	Lab
Baroness Humphreys	Lib Dem
Baroness Hunt of Bethnal Green	CB
Baroness Hussein-Ece	Lib Dem
Baroness Janke	Lib Dem
Baroness Jay of Paddington	Lab
Baroness Jenkin of Kennington	Con
Baroness Jolly	Lib Dem
Baroness Jones of Moulsecoomb	Green
Baroness Jones of Whitchurch	Lab
Baroness Kennedy of Cradley	NA
Baroness Kennedy of The Shaws	Lab
Baroness Kidron	CB
Baroness King of Bow	Lab
Baroness Kingsmill	Lab
Baroness Kinnock of Holyhead	Lab
Baroness Kramer	Lib Dem
Baroness Lane-Fox of Soho	CB
Baroness Lawrence of Clarendon	Lab
Baroness Liddell of Coatdyke	Lab
Baroness Lister of Burtersett	Lab
Bishop of London	NA
Baroness Ludford	Lib Dem
Baroness Mallalieu	Lab
Baroness Manningham-Buller	CB
Baroness Manzoor	Con
Baroness Masham of Ilton	CB
Baroness Massey of Darwen	Lab
Baroness McDonagh	Lab
Baroness McGregor-Smith	Con
Baroness McIntosh of Hudnall	Lab
Baroness McIntosh of Pickering	Con
Baroness Meacher	CB
Baroness Merron	Lab
Baroness Meyer	Con
Baroness Miller of Chilthorne Domer	Lib Dem
Baroness Mobarik	Con
Baroness Mone	Con
Baroness Morgan of Cotes	Con
Baroness Morgan of Drefelin	CB
Baroness Morgan of Ely	Lab
Baroness Morgan of Huyton	Lab
Baroness Morris of Bolton	Con
Baroness Morris of Yardley	Lab
Baroness Morrissey	Con
Baroness Murphy	CB
Baroness Neuberger	CB
Baroness Neville-Jones	Con
Baroness Neville-Rolfe	Con
Bishop of Newcastle	NA
Baroness Newlove	Con
Baroness Nicholson of Winterbourne	Con
Baroness Noakes	Con
Baroness Northover	Lib Dem
Baroness Nye	Lab
Baroness O'Cathain	Con
Baroness O'Loan	CB
Baroness O'Neill of Bengarve	CB
Baroness Osamor	Lab
Baroness Parminter	Lib Dem
Baroness Penn	Con
Baroness Pidding	Con
Baroness Pinnock	Lib Dem
Baroness Pitkeathley	Lab
Baroness Prashar	CB
Baroness Primarolo	Lab
Baroness Prosser	Lab
Baroness Quin	Lab
Baroness Ramsay of Cartvale	Lab
Baroness Randerson	Lib Dem
Baroness Rawlings	Con
Baroness Rebuck	Lab
Baroness Redfern	Con
Baroness Ritchie of Downpatrick	NA
Baroness Rock	Con
Baroness Royall of Blaisdon	Lab/Co-op
Baroness Sanderson of Welton	Con
Baroness Sater	Con
Baroness Scotland of Asthal	Lab
Baroness Scott of Bybrook	Con
Baroness Scott of Needham Market	Lib Dem
Baroness Seccombe	Con
Baroness Shackleton of Belgravia	Con
Baroness Shafik	CB

Baroness Sheehan	Lib Dem
Baroness Shephard of Northwold	Con
Baroness Sherlock	Lab
Baroness Shields	Con
Baroness Smith of Basildon	Lab/Co-op
Baroness Smith of Gilmorehill	Lab
Baroness Smith of Newnham	Lib Dem
Baroness Stedman-Scott	Con
Baroness Stern	CB
Baroness Stowell of Beeston	NA
Baroness Stroud	Con
Baroness Stuart of Edgbaston	NA
Baroness Sugg	Con
Baroness Suttie	Lib Dem
Baroness Symons of Vernham Dean	Lab
Baroness Taylor of Bolton	Lab
Baroness Thomas of Winchester	Lib Dem
Baroness Thornhill	Lib Dem
Baroness Thornton	Lab/Co-op
Baroness Tyler of Enfield	Lib Dem
Baroness Uddin	NA
Baroness Vadera	NA
Baroness Valentine	CB
Baroness Vere of Norbiton	Con
Baroness Verma	Con
Baroness Walmsley	Lib Dem
Baroness Warsi	Con
Baroness Warwick of Undercliffe	Lab
Baroness Watkins of Tavistock	CB
Baroness Wheatcroft	CB
Baroness Wheeler	Lab
Baroness Whitaker	Lab
Baroness Wilcox of Newport	Lab
Baroness Williams of Trafford	Con
Baroness Wolf of Dulwich	NA
Baroness Worthington	CB
Baroness Wyld	Con
Baroness Young of Hornsey	CB
Baroness Young of Old Scone	Lab

Peers by Age

(Ages as at 1 February 2021)

	Conservative	%	Labour	%	Lib Dem	%	CB	%	Other	%	Total
40–49	19	7.4	1	0.6	1	1.1	4	0.5	2	2.1	23
50–59	43	16.8	14	7.9	11	12.6	18	6.0	10	10.3	78
60–69	72	28.1	34	19.1	27	31.0	43	14.8	46	47.4	179
70–79	70	27.3	78	43.8	37	42.5	81	20.2	26	26.8	211
80–89	40	15.6	49	27.5	9	10.3	34	4.9	13	13.4	111
Over 90	8	3.1	2	1.1	2	2.3	2	1.1	0	0.0	12
	256		178		87		183		97		801*
Average age	**68.1**		**73.6**		**70.3**		**71.7**		**68.4**		

*The average age has been calculated on supplied dates of birth only.

Peers who have not supplied date of birth

Baroness Blower (Lab)
Lord Brownlow of Shurlock Row (Con)
Baroness Bryan of Partick (Lab)
Lord Choudrey (Con)
Lord Etherton (CB)
Lord Frost (Con)
Lord Godson (Con)
Baroness Hodgson of Abinger (Con)
Baroness Hunt of Bethnal Green (CB)
Bishop of Manchester (Non-Affiliated)
Lord Moore of Etchingham (Non-Affiliated)
Baroness Sanderson of Welton (Con)
Lord Sikka (Lab)
Lord Spencer of Alresford (Con)
Lord Stewart of Dirleton (Con)
Baroness Stowell of Beeston (Non-Affiliated)
Lord Udny-Lister (Con)
Baroness Wilcox of Newport (Lab)

Baroness Penn	35/36
Lord Wharton of Yarm	36
Lord Parkinson of Whitley Bay	37/38
Lord Ravensdale	38
Lord Sarfraz	39
Lord Lebedev	40
Baroness Blackwood of North Oxford	41
Baroness Bertin	42
Lord Walney	42
Baroness Sugg	43
Baroness Wyld	43
Lord McInnes of Kilwinning	44
Lord O'Shaughnessy	44
Lord Wei	44
Earl of Devon	45
Baroness Evans of Bowes Park	45
Lord Livermore	45
Lord Goldsmith of Richmond Park	46
Lord Duncan of Springbank	47
Baroness Lane-Fox of Soho	47
Lord Purvis of Tweed	47
Baroness Berridge	48
Baroness Morgan of Cotes	48
Lord Barwell	49
Lord Gadhia	49
Lord Hannan of Kingsclere	49
Lord Holmes of Richmond	49
Lord Johnson of Marylebone	49
Baroness Mone	49
Lord Shinkwin	49
Baroness Warsi	49
Baroness Worthington	49
Lord Bridges of Headley	50
Lord Freyberg	50
Lord Lancaster of Kimbolton	50
Baroness Brady	51
Baroness Chakrabarti	51
Baroness Grey-Thompson	51
Baroness Kennedy of Cradley	51
Lord McNicol of West Kilbride	51
Lord Oates	51
Baroness Smith of Newnham	51
Baroness Vere of Norbiton	51
Lord Ahmad of Wimbledon	52
Baroness Cavendish of Little Venice	52
Baroness Finn	52
Baroness Helic	52
Baroness Rock	52
Baroness Suttie	52
Lord Vaizey of Didcot	52
Lord Wolfson of Tredegar	52/53
Lord Wood of Anfield	52
Lord Bethell	53
Baroness Clark of Kilwinning	53
Baroness Fall	53
Lord Greenhalgh	53
Baroness Harding of Winscombe	53
Baroness King of Bow	53
Baroness Morgan of Ely	53
Lord Redesdale	53
Baroness Williams of Trafford	53
Lord Wolfson of Aspley Guise	53

Lord Allan of Hallam	54
Lord Barker of Battle	54
Baroness Bennett of Manor Castle	54
Lord Caine	54
Bishop of Derby	54
Lord Feldman of Elstree	54
Lord Mendelsohn	54
Baroness Morrissey	54
Lord Scriven	54
Lord Smith of Hindhead	54
Lord Austin of Dudley	55
Baroness Casey of Blackstock	55
Viscount Goschen	55
Lord Knight of Weymouth	55
Lord Llewellyn of Steep	55
Baroness Pidding	55
Lord Reay	55
Baroness Stroud	55
Lord Vaux of Harrowden	55
Lord Alli	56
Lord Black of Brentwood	56
Lord Carter of Barnes	56
Lord Kakkar	56
Earl of Listowel	56
Lord Livingston of Parkhead	56
Baroness Parminter	56
Lord Sedwill	56
Lord Addington	57
Lord Adonis	57
Baroness Bull	57
Lord Cooper of Windrush	57
Lord Gilbert of Panteg	57
Bishop of Gloucester	57
Lord Herbert of South Downs	57
Baroness McGregor-Smith	57
Lord Palumbo of Southwark	57
Baroness Sater	57
Lord Adebowale	58
Baroness Couttie	58
Lord Finkelstein	58
Baroness Grender	58
Baroness Hayman of Ullock	58
Lord Kennedy of Southwark	58
Earl of Kinnoull	58
Bishop of London	58
Baroness Shafik	58
Lord Sharpe of Epsom	58
Baroness Shields	58
Lord Taylor of Goss Moor	58
Baroness Vadera	58
Lord Anderson of Ipswich	59
Lord Bates	59
Lord Bilimoria	59
Lord Callanan	59
Baroness Fairhead	59
Lord Geidt	59
Lord Glasman	59
Lord Hague of Richmond	59
Baroness Kidron	59
Baroness McDonagh	59
Baroness Morgan of Drefelin	59
Baroness Newlove	59
Lord Polak	59
Lord Price	59
Earl of Stair	59
Lord Woolley of Woodford	59
Lord Agnew of Oulton	60
Baroness Barker	60
Baroness Bloomfield of Hinton Waldrist	60
Marquess of Cholmondeley	60
Lord Cromwell	60
Lord Darzi of Denham	60
Lord Drayson	60
Baroness Fox of Buckley	60
Lord Hill of Oareford	60
Lord McConnell of Glenscorrodale	60
Lord Patel of Bradford	60
Lord Porter of Spalding	60
Lord Rennard	60
Baroness Sherlock	60
Lord Stephen	60
Lord Strathclyde	60
Lord Trevethin and Oaksey	60
Baroness Barran	61
Baroness Campbell of Surbiton	61
Viscount Colville of Culross	61
Lord Dunlop	61
Baroness Fullbrook	61/62
Lord Kestenbaum	61
Lord Leigh of Hurley	61
Lord Macpherson of Earl's Court	61
Lord Mann	61
Lord Mendoza	61
Baroness Morgan of Huyton	61
Baroness Sheehan	61
Lord Truscott	61
Baroness Uddin	61
Baroness Verma	61
Lord Ashton of Hyde	62
Lord Burnett of Maldon	62
Lord Carter of Haslemere	62
Bishop of Chichester	62
Bishop of Coventry	62
Lord Dodds of Duncairn	62
Lord Evans of Weardale	62
Baroness Manzoor	62
Lord Paddick	62
Lord Ponsonby of Shulbrede	62
Viscount Ridley	62
Baroness Ritchie of Downpatrick	62
Earl of Rosslyn	62
Baroness Smith of Basildon	62
Baroness Valentine	62
Bishop of Winchester	62

Archbishop of York	62
Baroness Bonham-Carter of Yarnbury	63
Lord de Mauley	63
Bishop of Ely	63
Lord Fink	63
Baroness Ford	63
Lord Fox	63
Lord Hastings of Scarisbrick	63
Lord Hogan-Howe	63
Bishop of Leeds	63
Lord Mancroft	63
Lord McLoughlin	63
Baroness Mobarik	63
Lord O'Neill of Gatley	63
Bishop of Oxford	63
Baroness Scott of Needham Market	63
Bishop of St Albans	63
Lord St John of Bletso	63
Baroness Tyler of Enfield	63
Lord Verjee	63
Lord Allen of Kensington	64
Baroness Altmann	64
Baroness Ashton of Upholland	64
Earl Attlee	64
Lord Coe	64
Lord Gardiner of Kimble	64
Lord Haughey	64
Lord Hussain	64
Lord Lansley	64
Lord Marland	64
Lord Moylan	64
Duke of Norfolk	64
Lord Pannick	64
Lord Reed of Allermuir	64
Bishop of Rochester	64
Baroness Shackleton of Belgravia	64
Bishop of Southwark	64
Lord Tyrie	64
Lord Willetts	64
Lord Alderdice	65
Lord Bellingham	65
Lord Borwick	65
Lord Botham	65
Baroness Brinton	65
Bishop of Bristol	65
Archbishop of Canterbury	65
Lord Deighton	65
Bishop of Durham	65
Lord Fairfax of Cameron	65
Baroness Falkner of Margravine	65
Lord Hammond of Runnymede	65
Baroness Healy of Primrose Hill	65
Lord Hutton of Furness	65
Baroness Jenkin of Kennington	65
Baroness Jones of Whitchurch	65
Lord Kerslake	65
Earl of Lindsay	65
Lord Lupton	65
Lord Moynihan	65
Baroness Nye	65
Lord Randall of Uxbridge	65
Baroness Royall of Blaisdon	65
Lord Sassoon	65
Baroness Scotland of Asthal	65
Baroness Stedman-Scott	65
Baroness Stuart of Edgbaston	65
Baroness Thornhill	65
Lord Turner of Ecchinswell	65
Baroness Watkins of Tavistock	65
Bishop of Worcester	65
Viscount Younger of Leckie	65
Baroness Amos	66
Bishop of Blackburn	66
Baroness Brown of Cambridge	66
Baroness Burt of Solihull	66
Baroness Buscombe	66
Lord Collins of Highbury	66
Earl of Courtown	66
Lord Darroch of Kew	66
Lord Forsyth of Drumlean	66
Lord Houghton of Richmond	66
Lord Keen of Elie	66
Lord Mawson	66
Baroness McIntosh of Pickering	66
Lord Northbrook	66
Baroness Northover	66
Baroness Primarolo	66
Lord Prior of Brampton	66
Lord Rotherwick	66
Bishop of Salisbury	66
Lord Wallace of Tankerness	66
Lord Bassam of Brighton	67
Lord Blair of Boughton	67
Lord Blencathra	67
Baroness Bowles of Berkhamsted	67
Lord Boyd of Duncansby	67
Bishop of Carlisle	67
Viscount Chandos	67
Lord Harris of Haringey	67
Lord Henley	67
Baroness Hussein-Ece	67
Lord Lennie	67
Bishop of Lincoln	67
Lord Malloch-Brown	67
Lord Mandelson	67
Lord Maude of Horsham	67
Baroness Miller of Chilthorne Domer	67
Lord Newby	67
Lord Popat	67
Bishop of Portsmouth	67
Viscount Thurso	67
Lord Arbuthnot of Edrom	68
Bishop of Birmingham	68
Lord Blackwell	68

Viscount Brookeborough	68
Lord Browne of Ladyton	68
Earl Cathcart	68
Earl of Clancarty	68
Lord Davies of Abersoch	68
Lord Davies of Gower	68
Baroness Fleet	68
Lord Garnier	68
Lord Goddard of Stockport	68
Baroness Lawrence of Clarendon	68
Lord Macdonald of River Glaven	68
Lord Marks of Henley-on-Thames	68
Baroness Meyer	68
Baroness Morris of Bolton	68
Baroness Morris of Yardley	68
Baroness Neville-Rolfe	68
Lord O'Donnell	68
Earl of Oxford and Asquith	68
Bishop of Peterborough	68
Lord Pickles	68
Baroness Rebuck	68
Lord Richards of Herstmonceux	68
Lord Ricketts	68
Lord Russell of Liverpool	68
Earl of Shrewsbury and Waterford	68
Duke of Somerset	68
Lord Taylor of Warwick	68
Lord Teverson	68
Baroness Thornton	68
Lord Thurlow	68
Lord Wills	68
Lord Alton of Liverpool	69
Viscount Astor	69
Lord Boateng	69
Lord Bourne of Aberystwyth	69
Baroness Boycott	69
Baroness Chisholm of Owlpen	69
Lord Colgrain	69
Lord Crisp	69
Lord Falconer of Thoroton	69
Baroness Featherstone	69
Lord Gold	69
Lord Grantchester	69
Lord Hall of Birkenhead	69
Lord Inglewood	69
Baroness Jolly	69
Lord Lucas of Crudwell and Dingwall	69
Baroness Ludford	69
Bishop of Newcastle	69
Lord Norton of Louth	69
Baroness O'Loan	69
Lord Palmer	69
Lord Robathan	69
Lord Smith of Finsbury	69
Baroness Symons of Vernham Dean	69
Viscount Trenchard	69
Lord True	69
Lord Watts	69
Baroness Wheatcroft	69
Baroness Young of Hornsey	69
Lord Bradley	70
Lord Cashman	70
Baroness Coussins	70
Lord Dannatt	70
Lord Davidson of Glen Clova	70
Lord Elder	70
Lord Faulks	70
Lord Freud	70
Baroness Goldie	70
Baroness Greenfield	70
Lord Hain	70
Lord Hay of Ballyore	70
Earl Howe	70
Baroness Hughes of Stretford	70
Baroness Kennedy of The Shaws	70
Baroness Kramer	70
Baroness Liddell of Coatdyke	70
Lord Lisvane	70
Earl of Lytton	70
Lord Mair	70
Baroness Neuberger	70
Baroness Bakewell of Hardington Mandeville	71
Baroness Benjamin	71
Lord Bew	71
Lord Cameron of Dillington	71
Baroness Clark of Calton	71
Lord Clement-Jones	71
Baroness Crawley	71
Earl of Dundee	71
Lord Fellowes of West Stafford	71
Baroness Finlay of Llandaff	71
Lord Goldsmith	71
Lord Grimstone of Boscobel	71
Baroness Hallett	71
Baroness Hayman	71
Baroness Hayter of Kentish Town	71
Lord Hayward	71
Lord Hunt of Kings Heath	71
Baroness Jones of Moulsecoomb	71
Baroness Lister of Burtersett	71
Lord Nash	71
Baroness Noakes	71
Lord Rose of Monewden	71
Lord Ryder of Wensum	71
Lord Stirrup	71
Lord Storey	71
Lord Watson of Invergowrie	71
Viscount Waverley	71
Baroness Wheeler	71
Baroness Wolf of Dulwich	71
Lord Berkeley of Knighton	72
Baroness Bottomley of Nettlestone	72
Lord Browne of Madingley	72

Earl of Caithness	72
Baroness Campbell of Loughborough	72
Lord Carlile of Berriew	72
Lord Carrington	72
Lord Dobbs	72
Baroness Doocey	72
Earl of Erroll	72
Lord Flight	72
Lord Green of Hurstpierpoint	72
Lord Haworth	72
Lord Hendy	72
Lord Jones of Cheltenham	72
Lord King of Lothbury	72
Lord Lipsey	72
Baroness Manningham-Buller	72
Lord McCrea of Magherafelt and Cookstown	72
Lord Morrow	72
Lord Mountevans	72
Lord Murphy of Torfaen	72
Lord Myners	72
Baroness Prashar	72
Baroness Randerson	72
Lord Stoneham of Droxford	72
Lord West of Spithead	72
Lord Whitby	72
Baroness Young of Old Scone	72
Lord Aberdare	73
Baroness Adams of Craigielea	73
Baroness Anelay of St Johns	73
Lord Blunkett	73
Lord Browne of Belmont	73
Lord Carrington of Fulham	73
Lord Chartres	73
Baroness Drake	73
Lord Empey	73
Lord Foster of Bath	73
Lord Harrison	73
Lord Hennessy of Nympsfield	73
Baroness Humphreys	73
Baroness Janke	73
Baroness Kingsmill	73
Lord Leitch	73
Lord Liddle	73
Lord Moonie	73
Lord Neuberger of Abbotsbury	73
Earl Peel	73
Lord Ranger	73/74
Baroness Redfern	73
Lord Reid of Cardowan	73
Baroness Scott of Bybrook	73
Lord Sharkey	73
Lord Stevenson of Balmacara	73
Lord Sugar	73
Baroness Taylor of Bolton	73
Lord Thomas of Cwmgiedd	73
Lord Touhig	73
Lord Woodley	73
Lord Astor of Hever	74
Lord Bach	74
Lord Bichard	74
Lord Brabazon of Tara	74
Baroness Browning	74
Lord Carter of Coles	74
Lord Currie of Marylebone	74
Lord Elis-Thomas	74
Lord Faulkner of Worcester	74
Lord Fraser of Corriegarth	74
Baroness Goudie	74
Baroness Hamwee	74
Viscount Hanworth	74
Baroness Hoey	74
Baroness Hogg	74
Baroness Hollins	74
Lord Janvrin	74
Lord Jay of Ewelme	74
Baroness McIntosh of Hudnall	74
Lord McKenzie of Luton	74
Baroness Murphy	74
Lord Oakeshott of Seagrove Bay	74
Baroness Pinnock	74
Lord Risby	74
Lord Robertson of Port Ellen	74
Lord Saatchi	74
Lord Shipley	74
Lord Stern of Brentford	74
Lord Strasburger	74
Lord Trees	74
Lord Waldegrave of North Hill	74
Baroness Armstrong of Hill Top	75
Lord Bamford	75
Lord Best	75
Lord Bird	75
Lord Burnett	75
Earl of Cork and Orrery	75
Lord Eatwell	75
Lord German	75
Lord Grabiner	75
Viscount Hailsham	75
Lord Hardie	75
Lord Hollick	75
Lord Kirkhope of Harrogate	75
Lord Krebs	75
Lord Lexden	75
Marquess of Lothian	75
Lord Magan of Castletown	75
Baroness Mallalieu	75
Lord Monks	75
Lord Patten	75
Lord Plant of Highfield	75
Lord Sherbourne of Didsbury	75
Lord Smith of Leigh	75
Lord Stevenson of Coddenham	75
Baroness Thomas of Winchester	75
Baroness Warwick of Undercliffe	75

Duke of Wellington	75
Baroness Afshar	76
Lord Balfe	76
Lord Beecham	76
Lord Birt	76
Lord Black of Crossharbour	76
Lord Bruce of Bennachie	76
Lord Burns	76
Viscount Craigavon	76
Lord Curry of Kirkharle	76
Lord Davies of Brixton	76
Lord Davies of Stamford	76
Baroness Donaghy	76
Baroness D'Souza	76
Lord Farmer	76
Lord Filkin	76
Baroness Garden of Frognal	76
Lord Glenarthur	76
Baroness Hale of Richmond	76
Lord Howarth of Newport	76
Baroness Kinnock of Holyhead	76
Lord Kirkham	76
Lord Levy	76
Earl of Liverpool	76
Lord McFall of Alcluith	76
Lord Patten of Barnes	76
Baroness Quin	76
Lord Rosser	76
Lord Smith of Kelvin	76
Lord Trimble	76
Lord Turnbull	76
Lord Walker of Aldringham	76
Baroness Andrews	77
Lord Beith	77
Lord Bowness	77
Lord Boyce	77
Lord Campbell-Savours	77
Baroness Deech	77
Lord Goodlad	77
Lord Grade of Yarmouth	77
Baroness Harris of Richmond	77
Baroness Henig	77
Earl of Home	77
Lord Lilley	77
Lord Loomba	77
Lord Mackenzie of Framwellgate	77
Lord Mance	77
Lord McAvoy	77
Lord McNally	77
Lord Mitchell	77
Lord Razzall	77
Lord Ribeiro	77
Earl of Sandwich	77
Lord Sawyer	77
Lord Taylor of Holbeach	77
Lord Tope	77
Lord Triesman	77
Baroness Walmsley	77
Lord Whitty	77
Lord Wigley	77
Baroness Blackstone	78
Lord Boswell of Aynho	78
Lord Brennan	78
Lord Brooke of Alverthorpe	78
Lord Chadlington	78
Baroness Chalker of Wallasey	78
Lord Chidgey	78
Baroness Corston	78
Baroness Cumberlege	78
Baroness Eaton	78
Lord Evans of Watford	78
Lord Field of Birkenhead	78
Baroness Fritchie	78
Lord Glendonbrook	78
Lord Greaves	78
Lord Griffiths of Burry Port	78
Lord Harris of Peckham	78
Lord Hodgson of Astley Abbotts	78
Lord Hunt of Wirral	78
Lord Kerr of Kinlochard	78
Lord Kinnock	78
Lord Lamont of Lerwick	78
Lord Lee of Trafford	78
Lord Lingfield	78
Lord Low of Dalston	78
Lord Pearson of Rannoch	78
Lord Rees of Ludlow	78
Lord Rogan	78
Lord Selkirk of Douglas	78
Lord Snape	78
Lord Stevens of Kirkwhelpington	78
Lord Stone of Blackheath	78
Lord Stunell	78
Lord Tunnicliffe	78
Lord Wilson of Dinton	78
Lord Young of Norwood Green	78
Lord Campbell of Pittenweem	79
Lord Collins of Mapesbury	79
Lord Colwyn	79
Lord Fellowes	79
Lord Foulkes of Cumnock	79
Lord Green of Deddington	79
Lord Greenway	79
Lord Griffiths of Fforestfach	79
Lord Hameed	79
Lord Hamilton of Epsom	79
Lord Howard of Lympne	79
Lord Howard of Rising	79
Lord Hunt of Chesterton	79
Lord Judge	79
Lord Levene of Portsoken	79
Baroness Nicholson of Winterbourne	79
Baroness O'Neill of Bengarve	79
Lord Powell of Bayswater	79

Name	Age
Lord Puttnam	79
Lord Rooker	79
Lord Sheikh	79
Baroness Stern	79
Lord Trefgarne	79
Lord Tyler	79
Viscount Ullswater	79
Lord Wallace of Saltaire	79
Lord Watson of Richmond	79
Lord Willis of Knaresborough	79
Lord Young of Cookham	79
Lord Archer of Weston-super-Mare	80
Lord Clarke of Nottingham	80
Baroness Cohen of Pimlico	80
Lord Desai	80
Baroness Gale	80
Lord Grocott	80
Lord Hanningfield	80
Baroness Howarth of Breckland	80
Lord Irvine of Lairg	80
Lord Lang of Monkton	80
Lord MacKenzie of Culkein	80
Baroness Meacher	80
Baroness Osamor	80
Lord Sainsbury of Turville	80
Viscount Simon	80
Baroness Smith of Gilmorehill	80
Lord Warner	80
Lord Winston	80
Lord Anderson of Swansea	81
Lord Berkeley	81
Baroness Billingham	81
Lord Bragg	81
Lord Clark of Windermere	81
Lord Cormack	81
Lord Crathorne	81
Lord Cunningham of Felling	81
Lord Davies of Oldham	81
Lord Deben	81
Lord Dykes	81
Earl of Glasgow	81
Baroness Hooper	81
Lord Horam	81
Baroness Jay of Paddington	81
Baroness Neville-Jones	81
Baroness Pitkeathley	81
Lord Rowlands	81
Baroness Shephard of Northwold	81
Lord Skidelsky	81
Lord Soley	81
Lord Tomlinson	81
Lord Wrigglesworth	81
Earl of Arran	82
Lord Broers	82
Lord Brougham and Vaux	82
Lord Fowler	82
Lord Framlingham	82
Lord Hope of Craighead	82
Baroness Massey of Darwen	82
Baroness O'Cathain	82
Lord Owen	82
Lord Palmer of Childs Hill	82
Lord Patel	82
Lord Prescott	82
Lord Rana	82
Baroness Rawlings	82
Lord Swinfen	82
Lord Walker of Gestingthorpe	82
Lord Wasserman	82
Lord Willoughby de Broke	82
Lord Brown of Eaton-under-Heywood	83
Lord Butler of Brockwell	83
Baroness Cox	83
Lord Dear	83
Lord Dholakia	83
Lord Eames	83
Lord Geddes	83
Lord Giddens	83
Lord Haselhurst	83
Lord James of Blackheath	83
Lord Jones	83
Lord Kilclooney	83
Lord Lea of Crondall	83
Lord Maginnis of Drumglass	83
Lord Phillips of Worth Matravers	83
Baroness Prosser	83
Lord Renfrew of Kaimsthorn	83
Lord Rowe-Beddoe	83
Lord Selsdon	83
Lord Thomas of Gresford	83
Lord Tugendhat	83
Lord Bradshaw	84
Lord Cotter	84
Baroness Fookes	84
Lord Gordon of Strathblane	84
Lord Harries of Pentregarth	84
Lord Laming	84
Lord Maxton	84
Lord Naseby	84
Lord Radice	84
Baroness Ramsay of Cartvale	84
Lord Saville of Newdigate	84
Lord Stevens of Ludgate	84
Baroness Whitaker	84
Lord Carey of Clifton	85
Viscount of Falkland	85
Baroness Greengross	85
Lord Hannay of Chiswick	85
Baroness Hilton of Eggardon	85
Lord Howell of Guildford	85
Lord Jordan	85
Lord Judd	85
Baroness Masham of Ilton	85
Duke of Montrose	85

Lord Roberts of Llandudno 85
Lord Suri 85
Lord Wilson of Tillyorn 85
Lord Baker of Dorking 86
Lord Dixon-Smith 86
Lord Donoughue 86
Baroness Flather 86
Lord Haskel 86
Lord Hoffmann 86
Lord Layard 86
Lord Morgan 86
Lord Oxburgh 86
Lord Parekh 86
Lord Pendry 86
Lord Ramsbotham 86
Lord Sterling of Plaistow 86
Lord Turnberg 86
Baroness Bakewell 87
Baroness Butler-Sloss 87
Baroness Eccles of Moulton 87
Baroness Golding 87
Lord Heseltine 87
Lord King of Bridgwater 87
Lord Rogers of Riverside 87
Lord Woolf 87
Lord Alliance 88
Lord Bhatia 88
Lord Clarke of Hampstead 88
Lord Dubs 88
Lord Hylton 88
Lord Lawson of Blaby 88
Lord McColl of Dulwich 88
Lord Singh of Wimbledon 88
Lord Wakeham 88
Lord Young of Graffham 88
Viscount Eccles 89
Lord Hughes of Woodside 89
Lord Kalms 89
Lord Marlesford 89
Lord Morris of Aberavon 89
Lord Paul 89
Lord Tebbit 89
Viscount Bridgeman 90
Lord Hoyle 90
Lord Jopling 90
Baroness Seccombe 90
Lord Vinson 90
Baroness Boothroyd 91
Lord Craig of Radley 91
Lord Rodgers of Quarry Bank 92
Lord Taverne 92
Lord Denham 93
Baroness Gardner of Parkes 93
Lord Mackay of Clashfern 93
Lord Sainsbury of Preston Candover 93
Lord Christopher 95

Peers by Party

Conservative

AGNEW OF OULTON Lord
AHMAD OF WIMBLEDON Lord
ALTMANN Baroness
ANELAY OF ST JOHNS Baroness
ARBUTHNOT OF EDROM Lord
ARRAN Earl of
ASHTON OF HYDE Lord
ASTOR Viscount
ASTOR OF HEVER Lord
ATTLEE Earl
BAKER OF DORKING Lord
BALFE Lord
BAMFORD Lord
BARKER OF BATTLE Lord
BARRAN Baroness
BARWELL Lord
BATES Lord
BELLINGHAM Lord
BENYON Lord
BERRIDGE Baroness
BERTIN Baroness
BETHELL Lord
BLACK OF BRENTWOOD Lord
BLACKWELL Lord
BLACKWOOD OF NORTH OXFORD Baroness
BLENCATHRA Lord
BLOOMFIELD OF HINTON WALDRIST Baroness
BORWICK Lord
BOTTOMLEY OF NETTLESTONE Baroness
BOURNE OF ABERYSTWYTH Lord
BRABAZON OF TARA Lord
BRADY Baroness
BRIDGEMAN Viscount
BRIDGES OF HEADLEY Lord
BROUGHAM AND VAUX Lord
BROWNING Baroness
BROWNLOW OF SHURLOCK ROW Lord
BUSCOMBE Baroness
CAINE Lord
CAITHNESS Earl of
CALLANAN Lord
CARRINGTON OF FULHAM Lord
CATHCART Earl
CHADLINGTON Lord
CHALKER OF WALLASEY Baroness
CHISHOLM OF OWLPEN Baroness
CHOUDREY Lord
CLARKE OF NOTTINGHAM Lord
COE Lord
COLGRAIN Lord
COLWYN Lord
CORMACK Lord
COURTOWN Earl of
COUTTIE Baroness
CRATHORNE Lord
CRUDDAS Lord
CUMBERLEGE Baroness
DAVIES OF GOWER Lord
DE MAULEY Lord
DEBEN Lord
DEIGHTON Lord
DENHAM Lord
DIXON-SMITH Lord
DOBBS Lord
DUNCAN OF SPRINGBANK Lord
DUNDEE Earl of
DUNLOP Lord
EATON Baroness
ECCLES Viscount
ECCLES OF MOULTON Baroness
EVANS OF BOWES PARK Baroness
FAIRFAX OF CAMERON Lord
FAIRHEAD Baroness
FALL Baroness
FARMER Lord
FELDMAN OF ELSTREE Lord
FELLOWES OF WEST STAFFORD Lord
FINK Lord
FINKELSTEIN Lord
FINN Baroness
FLEET Baroness
FLIGHT Lord
FOOKES Baroness
FORSYTH OF DRUMLEAN Lord
FOSTER OF OXTON Baroness
FRAMLINGHAM Lord
FRASER OF CORRIEGARTH Lord
FRASER OF CRAIGMADDIE Baroness
FREUD Lord
FROST Lord
FULLBROOK Baroness
GARDINER OF KIMBLE Lord
GARDNER OF PARKES Baroness
GARNIER Lord
GEDDES Lord
GILBERT OF PANTEG Lord
GLENARTHUR Lord
GLENDONBROOK Lord
GODSON Lord
GOLD Lord
GOLDIE Baroness
GOLDSMITH OF RICHMOND PARK Lord
GOODLAD Lord
GOSCHEN Viscount

GRADE OF YARMOUTH Lord
GREENHALGH Lord
GRIFFITHS OF FFORESTFACH Lord
GRIMSTONE OF BOSCOBEL Lord
HAGUE OF RICHMOND Lord
HAILSHAM Viscount
HAMILTON OF EPSOM Lord
HAMMOND OF RUNNYMEDE Lord
HANNAN OF KINGSCLERE Lord
HARDING OF WINSCOMBE Baroness
HARRIS OF PECKHAM Lord
HASELHURST Lord
HAYWARD Lord
HELIC Baroness
HENLEY Lord
HERBERT OF SOUTH DOWNS Lord
HILL OF OAREFORD Lord
HODGSON OF ABINGER Baroness
HODGSON OF ASTLEY ABBOTTS Lord
HOLMES OF RICHMOND Lord
HOME Earl of
HOOPER Baroness
HORAM Lord
HOWARD OF LYMPNE Lord
HOWARD OF RISING Lord
HOWE Earl
HOWELL OF GUILDFORD Lord
HUNT OF WIRRAL Lord
JAMES OF BLACKHEATH Lord
JENKIN OF KENNINGTON Baroness
JOHNSON OF MARYLEBONE Lord
JOPLING Lord
KAMALL Lord
KEEN OF ELIE Lord
KING OF BRIDGWATER Lord
KIRKHAM Lord
KIRKHOPE OF HARROGATE Lord
LAMONT OF LERWICK Lord
LANCASTER OF KIMBOLTON Lord
LANG OF MONKTON Lord
LANSLEY Lord
LAWSON OF BLABY Lord
LEIGH OF HURLEY Lord
LEXDEN Lord
LILLEY Lord
LINDSAY Earl of
LINGFIELD Lord
LIVERPOOL Earl of
LIVINGSTON OF PARKHEAD Lord
LLEWELLYN OF STEEP Lord
LOTHIAN Marquess of
LUCAS OF CRUDWELL AND DINGWALL Lord
MACKAY OF CLASHFERN Lord
MAGAN OF CASTLETOWN Lord
MANCROFT Lord
MANZOOR Baroness
MARLAND Lord
MARLESFORD Lord
MAUDE OF HORSHAM Lord
MCCOLL OF DULWICH Lord
MCGREGOR-SMITH Baroness
MCINNES OF KILWINNING Lord
MCINTOSH OF PICKERING Baroness
MCLOUGHLIN Lord
MENDOZA Lord
MEYER Baroness
MOBARIK Baroness
MONE Baroness
MONTROSE Duke of
MORGAN OF COTES Baroness
MORRIS OF BOLTON Baroness
MORRISSEY Baroness
MOYLAN Lord
MOYNIHAN Lord
NASEBY Lord
NASH Lord
NEVILLE-JONES Baroness
NEVILLE-ROLFE Baroness
NEWLOVE Baroness
NICHOLSON OF WINTERBOURNE Baroness
NOAKES Baroness
NORTHBROOK Lord
NORTON OF LOUTH Lord
O'CATHAIN Baroness
O'SHAUGHNESSY Lord
PARKINSON OF WHITLEY BAY Lord
PATTEN Lord
PATTEN OF BARNES Lord
PENN Baroness
PICKLES Lord
PIDDING Baroness
POLAK Lord
POPAT Lord
PORTER OF SPALDING Lord
PRICE Lord
RANA Lord
RANDALL OF UXBRIDGE Lord
RANGER Lord
RAWLINGS Baroness
REAY Lord
REDFERN Baroness
RENFREW OF KAIMSTHORN Lord
RIBEIRO Lord
RIDLEY Viscount
RISBY Lord
ROBATHAN Lord
ROCK Baroness
ROSE OF MONEWDEN Lord
ROTHERWICK Lord
RYDER OF WENSUM Lord
SAATCHI Lord
SAINSBURY OF PRESTON CANDOVER Lord

SANDERSON OF WELTON Baroness
SARFRAZ Lord
SASSOON Lord
SATER Baroness
SCOTT OF BYBROOK Baroness
SECCOMBE Baroness
SELKIRK OF DOUGLAS Lord
SELSDON Lord
SHACKLETON OF BELGRAVIA Baroness
SHARPE OF EPSOM Lord
SHEIKH Lord
SHEPHARD OF NORTHWOLD Baroness
SHERBOURNE OF DIDSBURY Lord
SHIELDS Baroness
SHINKWIN Lord
SHREWSBURY AND WATERFORD Earl of
SMITH OF HINDHEAD Lord
SPENCER OF ALRESFORD Lord
STEDMAN-SCOTT Baroness
STERLING OF PLAISTOW Lord
STEWART OF DIRLETON Lord
STRATHCLYDE Lord
STROUD Baroness
SUGG Baroness
SURI Lord
SWINFEN Lord
TAYLOR OF HOLBEACH Lord
TEBBIT Lord
TREFGARNE Lord
TRENCHARD Viscount
TRIMBLE Lord
TRUE Lord
TUGENDHAT Lord
UDNY-LISTER Lord
ULLSWATER Viscount
VAIZEY OF DIDCOT Lord
VERE OF NORBITON Baroness
VERMA Baroness
VINSON Lord
WAKEHAM Lord
WALDEGRAVE OF NORTH HILL Lord
WARSI Baroness
WASSERMAN Lord
WEI Lord
WHARTON OF YARM Lord
WHITBY Lord
WILLETTS Lord
WILLIAMS OF TRAFFORD Baroness
WOLFSON OF ASPLEY GUISE Lord
WOLFSON OF TREDEGAR Lord
WYLD Baroness
YOUNG OF COOKHAM Lord
YOUNG OF GRAFFHAM Lord
YOUNGER OF LECKIE Viscount

Labour

ADAMS OF CRAIGIELEA Baroness
ADONIS Lord
ALLEN OF KENSINGTON Lord
ALLI Lord
AMOS Baroness
ANDERSON OF SWANSEA Lord
ANDREWS Baroness
ARMSTRONG OF HILL TOP Baroness
BACH Lord
BAKEWELL Baroness
BEECHAM Lord
BERKELEY Lord
BILLINGHAM Baroness
BLAKE OF LEEDS Baroness
BLOWER Baroness
BLUNKETT Lord
BOATENG Lord
BRADLEY Lord
BRAGG Lord
BROOKE OF ALVERTHORPE Lord
BROWNE OF LADYTON Lord
BRYAN OF PARTICK Baroness
CAMPBELL-SAVOURS Lord
CARTER OF COLES Lord
CHAKRABARTI Baroness
CHANDOS Viscount
CHAPMAN OF DARLINGTON Baroness
CHRISTOPHER Lord
CLARK OF KILWINNING Baroness
CLARK OF WINDERMERE Lord
CLARKE OF HAMPSTEAD Lord
COAKER Lord
COHEN OF PIMLICO Baroness
COLLINS OF HIGHBURY Lord
CORSTON Baroness
CRAWLEY Baroness
CUNNINGHAM OF FELLING Lord
DAVIDSON OF GLEN CLOVA Lord
DAVIES OF BRIXTON Lord
DAVIES OF OLDHAM Lord
DAVIES OF STAMFORD Lord
DONAGHY Baroness
DONOUGHUE Lord
DRAKE Baroness
DRAYSON Lord
DUBS Lord
EATWELL Lord
ELDER Lord
EVANS OF WATFORD Lord
FALCONER OF THOROTON Lord
FAULKNER OF WORCESTER Lord
FILKIN Lord
GALE Baroness
GIDDENS Lord
GLASMAN Lord
GOLDING Baroness

GOLDSMITH Lord
GORDON OF STRATHBLANE Lord
GOUDIE Baroness
GRANTCHESTER Lord
GRIFFITHS OF BURRY PORT Lord
GROCOTT Lord
HAIN Lord
HANWORTH Viscount
HARRIS OF HARINGEY Lord
HARRISON Lord
HASKEL Lord
HAUGHEY Lord
HAWORTH Lord
HAYMAN OF ULLOCK Baroness
HEALY OF PRIMROSE HILL Baroness
HENDY Lord
HENIG Baroness
HILTON OF EGGARDON Baroness
HOLLICK Lord
HOWARTH OF NEWPORT Lord
HOYLE Lord
HUGHES OF STRETFORD Baroness
HUGHES OF WOODSIDE Lord
HUNT OF CHESTERTON Lord
HUTTON OF FURNESS Lord
IRVINE OF LAIRG Lord
JAY OF PADDINGTON Baroness
JONES Lord
JONES OF WHITCHURCH Baroness
JORDAN Lord
JUDD Lord
KENNEDY OF THE SHAWS Baroness
KESTENBAUM Lord
KHAN OF BURNLEY Lord
KING OF BOW Baroness
KINGSMILL Baroness
KINNOCK Lord
KINNOCK OF HOLYHEAD Baroness
LAWRENCE OF CLARENDON Baroness
LAYARD Lord
LEITCH Lord
LENNIE Lord
LEVY Lord
LIDDELL OF COATDYKE Baroness
LIDDLE Lord
LIPSEY Lord
LISTER OF BURTERSETT Baroness
LIVERMORE Lord
MACKENZIE OF CULKEIN Lord
MALLALIEU Baroness
MANDELSON Lord
MASSEY OF DARWEN Baroness
MAXTON Lord
MCCONNELL OF GLENSCORRODALE Lord
MCDONAGH Baroness
MCINTOSH OF HUDNALL Baroness
MCKENZIE OF LUTON Lord
MCNICOL OF WEST KILBRIDE Lord
MENDELSOHN Lord
MERRON Baroness
MITCHELL Lord
MONKS Lord
MORGAN Lord
MORGAN OF ELY Baroness
MORGAN OF HUYTON Baroness
MORRIS OF ABERAVON Lord
MORRIS OF YARDLEY Baroness
MURPHY OF TORFAEN Lord
NYE Baroness
OSAMOR Baroness
PAREKH Lord
PENDRY Lord
PITKEATHLEY Baroness
PLANT OF HIGHFIELD Lord
PONSONBY OF SHULBREDE Lord
PRESCOTT Lord
PRIMAROLO Baroness
PROSSER Baroness
PUTTNAM Lord
QUIN Baroness
RADICE Lord
RAMSAY OF CARTVALE Baroness
REBUCK Baroness
REID OF CARDOWAN Lord
ROBERTSON OF PORT ELLEN Lord
ROGERS OF RIVERSIDE Lord
ROOKER Lord
ROSSER Lord
ROWLANDS Lord
SAINSBURY OF TURVILLE Lord
SAWYER Lord
SCOTLAND OF ASTHAL Baroness
SHERLOCK Baroness
SIKKA Lord
SIMON Viscount
SMITH OF GILMOREHILL Baroness
SMITH OF LEIGH Lord
SNAPE Lord
SOLEY Lord
STEVENSON OF BALMACARA Lord
SYMONS OF VERNHAM DEAN Baroness
TAYLOR OF BOLTON Baroness
TRIESMAN Lord
TUNNICLIFFE Lord
TURNBERG Lord
WARWICK OF UNDERCLIFFE Baroness
WATSON OF INVERGOWRIE Lord
WATTS Lord
WEST OF SPITHEAD Lord
WHEELER Baroness
WHITAKER Baroness
WHITTY Lord
WILCOX OF NEWPORT Baroness

WILLS Lord
WINSTON Lord
WOOD OF ANFIELD Lord
WOODLEY Lord
YOUNG OF NORWOOD GREEN Lord
YOUNG OF OLD SCONE Baroness

Labour/Co-operative

BASSAM OF BRIGHTON Lord
FOULKES OF CUMNOCK Lord
HAYTER OF KENTISH TOWN Baroness
HUNT OF KINGS HEATH Lord
KENNEDY OF SOUTHWARK Lord
KNIGHT OF WEYMOUTH Lord
MCAVOY Lord
ROYALL OF BLAISDON Baroness
SMITH OF BASILDON Baroness
THORNTON Baroness
TOMLINSON Lord
TOUHIG Lord

Crossbench

ABERDARE Lord
ADEBOWALE Lord
AFSHAR Baroness
ALTON OF LIVERPOOL Lord
ANDERSON OF IPSWICH Lord
BERKELEY OF KNIGHTON Lord
BEST Lord
BEW Lord
BICHARD Lord
BILIMORIA Lord
BIRD Lord
BIRT Lord
BLAIR OF BOUGHTON Lord
BOOTHROYD Baroness
BOTHAM Lord
BOYCE Lord
BOYCOTT Baroness
BROERS Lord
BROOKEBOROUGH Viscount
BROWN OF CAMBRIDGE Baroness
BROWN OF EATON-UNDER-HEYWOOD Lord
BROWNE OF MADINGLEY Lord
BULL Baroness
BURNS Lord
BUTLER OF BROCKWELL Lord
BUTLER-SLOSS Baroness
CAMERON OF DILLINGTON Lord
CAMPBELL OF LOUGHBOROUGH Baroness
CAMPBELL OF SURBITON Baroness
CAREY OF CLIFTON Lord
CARLILE OF BERRIEW Lord
CARRINGTON Lord
CARTER OF HASLEMERE Lord
CASEY OF BLACKSTOCK Baroness
CAVENDISH OF LITTLE VENICE Baroness
CHARTRES Lord
CLANCARTY Earl of
CLARK OF CALTON Baroness
COLLINS OF MAPESBURY Lord
COLVILLE OF CULROSS Viscount
CORK AND ORRERY Earl of
COUSSINS Baroness
COX Baroness
CRAIG OF RADLEY Lord
CRAIGAVON Viscount
CRISP Lord
CROMWELL Lord
CURRIE OF MARYLEBONE Lord
CURRY OF KIRKHARLE Lord
DANNATT Lord
DARROCH OF KEW Lord
DEAR Lord
DEECH Baroness
DEVON Earl of
D'SOUZA Baroness
DYKES Lord
EAMES Lord
ERROLL Earl of
ETHERTON Lord
EVANS OF WEARDALE Lord
FALKLAND Viscount of
FALKNER OF MARGRAVINE Baroness
FELLOWES Lord
FIELD OF BIRKENHEAD Lord
FINLAY OF LLANDAFF Baroness
FLATHER Baroness
FORD Baroness
FREYBERG Lord
FRITCHIE Baroness
GEIDT Lord
GRABINER Lord
GREEN OF DEDDINGTON Lord
GREENFIELD Baroness
GREENGROSS Baroness
GREENWAY Lord
GREY-THOMPSON Baroness
HALL OF BIRKENHEAD Lord
HALLETT Baroness
HAMEED Lord
HANNAY OF CHISWICK Lord
HARDIE Lord
HARRIES OF PENTREGARTH Lord
HASTINGS OF SCARISBRICK Lord
HAYMAN Baroness
HENNESSY OF NYMPSFIELD Lord
HOFFMANN Lord

HOGAN-HOWE Lord
HOGG Baroness
HOLLINS Baroness
HOPE OF CRAIGHEAD Lord
HOUGHTON OF RICHMOND Lord
HOWARTH OF BRECKLAND Baroness
HUNT OF BETHNAL GREEN Baroness
HYLTON Lord
JANVRIN Lord
JAY OF EWELME Lord
JUDGE Lord
KAKKAR Lord
KERR OF KINLOCHARD Lord
KERSLAKE Lord
KIDRON Baroness
KILCLOONEY Lord
KING OF LOTHBURY Lord
KREBS Lord
LAMING Lord
LANE-FOX OF SOHO Baroness
LEBEDEV Lord
LEVENE OF PORTSOKEN Lord
LISTOWEL Earl of
LISVANE Lord
LOOMBA Lord
LOW OF DALSTON Lord
LYTTON Earl of
MACDONALD OF RIVER GLAVEN Lord
MCDONALD OF SALFORD Lord
MACPHERSON OF EARL'S COURT Lord
MAIR Lord
MALLOCH-BROWN Lord
MANCE Lord
MANNINGHAM-BULLER Baroness
MASHAM OF ILTON Baroness
MAWSON Lord
MEACHER Baroness
MORGAN OF DREFELIN Baroness
MOUNTEVANS Lord
MURPHY Baroness
MYNERS Lord
NEUBERGER Baroness
NEUBERGER OF ABBOTSBURY Lord
O'DONNELL Lord
O'LOAN Baroness
O'NEILL OF BENGARVE Baroness
O'NEILL OF GATLEY Lord
OXBURGH Lord
PALMER Lord
PANNICK Lord
PARKER OF MINSMERE Lord
PATEL Lord
PEEL Earl
PHILLIPS OF WORTH MATRAVERS Lord
POWELL OF BAYSWATER Lord
PRASHAR Baroness
RAMSBOTHAM Lord
RAVENSDALE Lord
REES OF LUDLOW Lord
RICHARDS OF HERSTMONCEUX Lord
RICKETTS Lord
ROSSLYN Earl of
ROWE-BEDDOE Lord
RUSSELL OF LIVERPOOL Lord
SANDWICH Earl of
SAVILLE OF NEWDIGATE Lord
SEDWILL Lord
SHAFIK Baroness
SINGH OF WIMBLEDON Lord
SKIDELSKY Lord
SMITH OF KELVIN Lord
SOMERSET Duke of
ST JOHN OF BLETSO Lord
STAIR Earl of
STERN Baroness
STERN OF BRENTFORD Lord
STEVENS OF KIRKWHELPINGTON Lord
STEVENSON OF CODDENHAM Lord
STIRRUP Lord
SUGAR Lord
THOMAS OF CWMGIEDD Lord
THURLOW Lord
TREES Lord
TREVETHIN AND OAKSEY Lord
TURNBULL Lord
TURNER OF ECCHINSWELL Lord
VALENTINE Baroness
VAUX OF HARROWDEN Lord
WALKER OF ALDRINGHAM Lord
WALKER OF GESTINGTHORPE Lord
WARNER Lord
WATKINS OF TAVISTOCK Baroness
WAVERLEY Viscount
WELLINGTON Duke of
WHEATCROFT Baroness
WILSON OF DINTON Lord
WILSON OF TILLYORN Lord
WOOLF Lord
WOOLLEY OF WOODFORD Lord
WORTHINGTON Baroness
YOUNG OF HORNSEY Baroness

Liberal Democrat

ADDINGTON Lord
ALDERDICE Lord
ALLAN OF HALLAM Lord
ALLIANCE Lord
BAKEWELL OF HARDINGTON MANDEVILLE Baroness
BARKER Baroness
BEITH Lord

BENJAMIN Baroness
BONHAM-CARTER OF YARNBURY Baroness
BOWLES OF BERKHAMSTED Baroness
BRADSHAW Lord
BRINTON Baroness
BRUCE OF BENNACHIE Lord
BURNETT Lord
BURT OF SOLIHULL Baroness
CAMPBELL OF PITTENWEEM Lord
CHIDGEY Lord
CLEMENT-JONES Lord
COTTER Lord
DHOLAKIA Lord
DOOCEY Baroness
FEATHERSTONE Baroness
FOSTER OF BATH Lord
FOX Lord
GARDEN OF FROGNAL Baroness
GERMAN Lord
GLASGOW Earl of
GODDARD OF STOCKPORT Lord
GREAVES Lord
GRENDER Baroness
HAMWEE Baroness
HARRIS OF RICHMOND Baroness
HUMPHREYS Baroness
HUSSAIN Lord
HUSSEIN-ECE Baroness
JANKE Baroness
JOLLY Baroness
JONES OF CHELTENHAM Lord
KRAMER Baroness
LEE OF TRAFFORD Lord
LUDFORD Baroness
MARKS OF HENLEY-ON-THAMES Lord
MCNALLY Lord
MILLER OF CHILTHORNE DOMER Baroness
NEWBY Lord
NORTHOVER Baroness
OATES Lord
PADDICK Lord
PALMER OF CHILDS HILL Lord
PALUMBO OF SOUTHWARK Lord
PARMINTER Baroness
PINNOCK Baroness
PURVIS OF TWEED Lord
RANDERSON Baroness
RAZZALL Lord
REDESDALE Lord
RENNARD Lord
ROBERTS OF LLANDUDNO Lord
RODGERS OF QUARRY BANK Lord
SCOTT OF NEEDHAM MARKET Baroness
SCRIVEN Lord
SHARKEY Lord
SHEEHAN Baroness
SHIPLEY Lord
SMITH OF NEWNHAM Baroness
STEPHEN Lord
STONEHAM OF DROXFORD Lord
STOREY Lord
STRASBURGER Lord
STUNELL Lord
SUTTIE Baroness
TAVERNE Lord
TAYLOR OF GOSS MOOR Lord
TEVERSON Lord
THOMAS OF GRESFORD Lord
THOMAS OF WINCHESTER Baroness
THORNHILL Baroness
THURSO Viscount
TOPE Lord
TYLER Lord
TYLER OF ENFIELD Baroness
VERJEE Lord
WALLACE OF SALTAIRE Lord
WALMSLEY Baroness
WATSON OF RICHMOND Lord
WILLIS OF KNARESBOROUGH Lord
WRIGGLESWORTH Lord

Non-Affiliated

ARCHER OF WESTON-SUPER-MARE Lord
ASHTON OF UPHOLLAND Baroness
AUSTIN OF DUDLEY Lord
BHATIA Lord
BIRMINGHAM Lord Bishop of
BLACK OF CROSSHARBOUR Lord
BLACKBURN Lord Bishop of
BOSWELL OF AYNHO Lord
BOWNESS Lord
BOYD OF DUNCANSBY Lord
BRENNAN Lord
BRISTOL Lord Bishop of
BURNETT OF MALDON Lord
CANTERBURY Lord Archbishop of
CARLISLE Lord Bishop of
CARTER OF BARNES Lord
CASHMAN Lord
CHICHESTER Lord Bishop of
CHOLMONDELEY Marquess of
COOPER OF WINDRUSH Lord
COVENTRY Lord Bishop of
DARZI OF DENHAM Lord
DAVIES OF ABERSOCH Lord
DERBY Lord Bishop of
DESAI Lord
DURHAM Lord Bishop of
ELIS-THOMAS Lord
ELY Lord Bishop of

FAULKS Lord
FOX OF BUCKLEY Baroness
GADHIA Lord
GLOUCESTER Lord Bishop of
GREEN OF HURSTPIERPOINT Lord
HALE OF RICHMOND Baroness
HANNINGFIELD Lord
HESELTINE Lord
HOEY Baroness
INGLEWOOD Lord
KALMS Lord
KENNEDY OF CRADLEY Baroness
KINNOULL Earl of
LEA OF CRONDALL Lord
LEEDS Lord Bishop of
LINCOLN Lord Bishop of
LONDON Lord Bishop of
LUPTON Lord
MACKENZIE OF FRAMWELLGATE Lord
MANCHESTER Lord Bishop of
MANN Lord
MCFALL OF ALCLUITH Lord
MOONIE Lord
MOORE OF ETCHINGHAM Lord
NEWCASTLE Lord Bishop of
NORFOLK Duke of
OAKESHOTT OF SEAGROVE BAY Lord
OXFORD Lord Bishop of
OXFORD AND ASQUITH Earl of
PATEL OF BRADFORD Lord
PAUL Lord
PEARSON OF RANNOCH Lord
PETERBOROUGH Lord Bishop of
PORTSMOUTH Lord Bishop of
PRIOR OF BRAMPTON Lord
REED OF ALLERMUIR Lord
RITCHIE OF DOWNPATRICK Baroness
ROCHESTER Lord Bishop of
SALISBURY Lord Bishop of
SMITH OF FINSBURY Lord
SOUTHWARK Lord Bishop of
ST ALBANS Lord Bishop of
STONE OF BLACKHEATH Lord
STOWELL OF BEESTON Baroness
STUART OF EDGBASTON Baroness
TAYLOR OF WARWICK Lord
TYRIE Lord
UDDIN Baroness
VADERA Baroness
WALLACE OF TANKERNESS Lord
WALNEY Lord
WILLOUGHBY DE BROKE Lord
WINCHESTER Lord Bishop of
WOLF OF DULWICH Baroness
WORCESTER Lord Bishop of
YORK Lord Archbishop of

Democratic Unionist Party

BROWNE OF BELMONT Lord
DODDS OF DUNCAIRN Lord
HAY OF BALLYORE Lord
MCCREA OF MAGHERAFELT AND COOKSTOWN Lord
MORROW Lord

Independent Labour

TRUSCOTT Lord

Ulster Unionist Party

EMPEY Lord
ROGAN Lord

Green Party

BENNETT OF MANOR CASTLE Baroness
JONES OF MOULSECOOMB Baroness

Independent Social Democrat

OWEN Lord

Independent Ulster Unionist

MAGINNIS OF DRUMGLASS Lord

Lord Speaker

FOWLER Lord

Plaid Cymru

WIGLEY Lord

Conservative Independent

BLACKSTONE Baroness
STEVENS OF LUDGATE Lord

Select Committees

Legislative Committees

Common Frameworks Scrutiny

Tel: 020 7219 8664
Email: hlcommonframeworks@parliament.uk
committees.parliament.uk/committee/474/common-frameworks-scrutiny-committee
Twitter: @HLFrameworksCom

Baroness Andrews (Chair)	*Lab*
Lord Bruce of Bennachie	*Lib Dem*
Lord Caine	*Con*
Baroness Crawley	*Lab*
Lord Foulkes of Cumnock	*Lab/Co-op*
Lord Garnier	*Con*
Lord Hope of Craighead	*CB*
Lord McInnes of Kilwinning	*Con*
Lord Murphy of Torfaen	*Lab*
Baroness Randerson	*Lib Dem*
Baroness Redfern	*Con*
Baroness Ritchie of Downpatrick	*NA*
Lord Thomas of Cwmgiedd	*CB*

Staff: Erik Tate (Clerk)

Constitution

Examines constitutional implications of all public bills; reviews operation of the constitution.

Tel: 020 7219 5960
Email: constitution@parliament.uk
committees.parliament.uk/committee/172/constitution-committee
Twitter: @HLConstitution

Baroness Taylor of Bolton (Chair)	*Lab*
Lord Beith	*Lib Dem*
Baroness Corston	*Lab*
Baroness Drake	*Lab*
Lord Dunlop	*Con*
Lord Faulks	*NA*
Baroness Fookes	*Con*
Lord Hennessy of Nympsfield	*CB*
Lord Howarth of Newport	*Lab*
Lord Howell of Guildford	*Con*
Lord Pannick	*CB*
Lord Sherbourne of Didsbury	*Con*
Lord Wallace of Tankerness	*NA*

Staff: Matt Korris (Clerk), Matt Byatt (Policy Analyst), Katy Durrans (Press Officer), Alasdair Johnston (Committee Assistant)

Delegated Powers and Regulatory Reform

Reports whether the provisions of any bill inappropriately delegate legislative powers or whether they subject the exercise of legislative power to an inappropriate degree of parliamentary scrutiny.

Tel: 020 7219 3103
Email: hldelegatedpowers@parliament.uk
committees.parliament.uk/committee/173/delegated-powers-and-regulatory-reform-committee

Lord Blencathra (Chair)	*Con*
Baroness Andrews	*Lab*
Baroness Browning	*Con*
Lord Goddard of Stockport	*Lib Dem*
Lord Haselhurst	*Con*
Lord Haskel	*Lab*
Baroness Meacher	*CB*
Lord Rowlands	*Lab*
Lord Thurlow	*CB*
Lord Tope	*Lib Dem*

Staff: Christine Salmon Percival (Clerk)

Hybrid Instruments

Tel: 020 7219 3231
committees.parliament.uk/committee/186/hybrid-instruments-committee-lords

Lord McFall of Alcluith (Chair)	*NA*
Lord Addington	*Lib Dem*
Lord Dykes	*CB*
Lord Grantchester	*Lab*
Lord Harrison	*Lab*
Baroness Jenkin of Kennington	*Con*
Lord Swinfen	*Con*

Staff: Christine Salmon Percival (Clerk)

Secondary Legislation Scrutiny

Tel: 020 7219 8821
Email: hlseclegscrutiny@parliament.uk
committees.parliament.uk/committee/255/secondary-legislation-scrutiny-committee

Lord Hodgson of Astley Abbotts (Chair)	*Con*
Baroness Bakewell of Hardington Mandeville	*Lib Dem*
Lord Chartres	*CB*
Lord Cunningham of Felling	*Lab*
Lord German	*Lib Dem*
Viscount Hanworth	*Lab*
Lord Liddle	*Lab*
Earl of Lindsay	*Con*
Lord Lisvane	*CB*
Lord Sherbourne of Didsbury	*Con*
Baroness Watkins of Tavistock	*CB*

Staff: Christine Salmon Percival (Clerk)

Standing Orders (Private Bills)

Reviews compliance with standing orders.

Tel: 020 7219 3103
Email: prbohol@parliament.uk

committees.parliament.uk/committee/198/standing-orders-private-bills-committee-lords

Lord McFall of Alcluith (Chair) *NA*
Lord Fellowes *CB*
Lord Geddes *Con*
Lord McColl of Dulwich *Con*
Lord Naseby *Con*
Lord Rodgers of Quarry Bank *Lib Dem*
Viscount Simon *Lab*

Staff: John Turner (Clerk)

Ad Hoc Committees

Covid-19

Tel: 020 7219 6772
Email: hlcovid19cmttee@parliament.uk
committees.parliament.uk/committee/460/covid19-committee
Twitter: @HLCOVID19Com

Baroness Lane-Fox of Soho (Chair) *CB*
Lord Alderdice *Lib Dem*
Baroness Benjamin *Lib Dem*
Baroness Chisholm of Owlpen *Con*
Lord Duncan of Springbank *Con*
Lord Elder *Lab*
Lord Hain *Lab*
Lord Harris of Haringey *Lab*
Baroness Jay of Paddington *Lab*
Baroness Morgan of Cotes *Con*
Lord Pickles *Con*
Baroness Young of Hornsey *CB*

Staff: Alexandra McMillan (Clerk)

Democracy and Digital Technologies

Tel: 020 7219 6075
Email: hldemocracydigital@parliament.uk
committees.parliament.uk/committee/407/democracy-and-digital-technologies-committee
Twitter: @HLDemoDigital

Lord Puttnam (Chair) *Lab*
Lord Black of Brentwood *Con*
Lord German *Lib Dem*
Lord Harris of Haringey *Lab*
Lord Holmes of Richmond *Con*
Baroness Kidron *CB*
Lord Knight of Weymouth *Lab/Co-op*
Lord Lipsey *Lab*
Lord Lucas of Crudwell and Dingwall *Con*
Baroness McGregor-Smith *Con*
Lord Mitchell *Lab*
Baroness Morris of Yardley *Lab*
Lord Scriven *Lib Dem*

Staff: Olivia Crabtree (Clerk)

Electoral Registration and Administration Act 2013

Tel: 020 7219 2466
Email: hlelecregact@parliament.uk
committees.parliament.uk/committee/405/electoral-registration-and-administration-act-2013-committee

To be appointed (Chair)
Baroness Adams of Craigielea *Lab*
Lord Campbell-Savours *Lab*
Lord Dykes *CB*
Baroness Eaton *Con*
Lord Hayward *Con*
Lord Janvrin *CB*
Lord Lexden *Con*
Baroness Mallalieu *Lab*
Baroness Pidding *Con*
Baroness Suttie *Lib Dem*
Lord Wills *Lab*

Food, Poverty, Health and the Environment

Tel: 020 7219 4878
Email: hlfoodpoverty@parliament.uk
committees.parliament.uk/committee/408/food-poverty-health-and-environment-committee

Lord Krebs (Chair) *CB*
Baroness Boycott *CB*
Earl of Caithness *Con*
Lord Empey *UUP*
Baroness Janke *Lib Dem*
Baroness Osamor *Lab*
Baroness Parminter *Lib Dem*
Baroness Ritchie of Downpatrick *NA*
Baroness Sanderson of Welton *Con*
Baroness Sater *Con*
Lord Whitty *Lab*

Highgate Cemetery Bill [HL]

Email: hlprivatebills@parliament.uk

Baroness Hallett (Chair) *CB*
Lord Aberdare *CB*
Baroness Garden of Frognal *Lib Dem*
Lord Trefgarne *Con*
Baroness Whitaker *Lab*

National Plan for Sport and Recreation

Tel: 020 7219 4384
Email: hlsportandrec@parliament.uk
committees.parliament.uk/committee/482/national-plan-for-sport-and-recreation-committee Twitter: @HLSportandRec

Lord Willis of Knaresborough (Chair) *Lib Dem*
Lord Addington *Lib Dem*
Baroness Blower *Lab*
Baroness Brady *Con*
Baroness Grey-Thompson *CB*
Lord Hayward *Con*
Lord Knight of Weymouth *Lab/Co-op*

Lord Krebs	*CB*
Baroness Morris of Yardley	*Lab*
Lord Moynihan	*Con*
Baroness Sater	*Con*
Lord Snape	*Lab*
Lord Triesman	*Lab*
Lord Willetts	*Con*

Risk Assessment and Risk Planning

Tel: 020 7219 4878
Email: hlriskcmttee@parliament.uk
committees.parliament.uk/committee/483/risk-assessment-and-risk-planning-committee

Lord Arbuthnot of Edrom (Chair)	*Con*
Lord Browne of Ladyton	*Lab*
Lord Clement-Jones	*Lib Dem*
Lord Mair	*CB*
Baroness McGregor-Smith	*Con*
Lord O'Shaughnessy	*Con*
Lord Rees of Ludlow	*CB*
Lord Robertson of Port Ellen	*Lab*
Baroness Symons of Vernham Dean	*Lab*
Viscount Thurso	*Lib Dem*

Social and Economic Impact of the Gambling Industry

Tel: 020 7219 4384
Email: hlgamblingindustry@parliament.uk
committees.parliament.uk/committee/406/gambling-industry-committee
Twitter: @HLGamblingCom

Lord Grade of Yarmouth (Chair)	*Con*
Baroness Armstrong of Hill Top	*Lab*
Lord Butler of Brockwell	*CB*
Lord Filkin	*Lab*
Lord Foster of Bath	*Lib Dem*
Lord Layard	*Lab*
Lord Mancroft	*Con*
Lord Smith of Hindhead	*Con*
Bishop of St Albans	*NA*
Baroness Thornhill	*Lib Dem*
Lord Trevethin and Oaksey	*CB*
Lord Watts	*Lab*

Joint Committees

See Lords and Commons Joint Select Committees on p1164

Domestic Committees

Audit

To support the House of Lords Commission by examining and monitoring audit and accountability arrangements in the House of Lords.

Tel: 020 7219 5961
Email: hlauditcommittee@parliament.uk
committees.parliament.uk/committee/169/audit-committee-lords

Lord Fink	*Con*
Baroness Fritchie	*CB*
Lord Haskel	*Lab*
Lord Macpherson of Earl's Court	*CB*

External Members:
Mathew Duncan
Caroline Gardner

Staff: Joseph Topping (Clerk)

Finance

To support the House of Lords Commission by considering expenditure on services provided from the Estimate for the House of Lords.

Tel: 020 7219 3736
Email: hlfinancecommittee@parliament.uk
committees.parliament.uk/committee/364/finance-committee-lords

Baroness Doocey (Chair)	*Lib Dem*
Lord Colgrain	*Con*
Lord Collins of Highbury	*Lab*
Earl of Courtown	*Con*
Lord Cromwell	*CB*
Lord Cunningham of Felling	*Lab*
Baroness Goudie	*Lab*
Lord Kerslake	*CB*
Baroness Noakes	*Con*
Lord Stoneham of Droxford	*Lib Dem*

Staff: Gabby Longdin (Clerk)

Services

To support the House of Lords Commission by agreeing day-to-day policy on member-facing services, providing advice on strategic policy decisions and overseeing the delivery and implementation of both.

Tel: 020 7219 3736
Email: hlservicescommittee@parliament.uk
committees.parliament.uk/committee/363/services-committee

Lord Laming (Chair)	*CB*
Lord Ashton of Hyde	*Con*
Lord Borwick	*Con*
Lord Campbell-Savours	*Lab*
Lord Clement-Jones	*Lib Dem*
Lord Judge	*CB*
Baroness Morris of Bolton	*Con*
Lord Stoneham of Droxford	*Lib Dem*
Lord Touhig	*Lab/Co-op*
Baroness Wheeler	*Lab*

Staff: Gabby Longdin (Clerk)

Lord Speaker's Advisory Panel on Works of Art

To support the House of Lords Commission by reporting and making recommendations to the Lord Speaker on the House of Lords Works of Art collection.

Tel: 020 7219 7517
Email: hlworksofartcmttee@parliament.uk
committees.parliament.uk/committee/371/lord-speakers-advisory-panel-on-works-of-art

Lord Bird	*CB*
Baroness Bull	*CB*
Earl of Clancarty	*CB*
Lord Cormack	*Con*
Lord Crathorne	*Con*
Lord de Mauley	*Con*
Lord Faulkner of Worcester	*Lab*
Lord Lingfield	*Con*
Baroness Massey of Darwen	*Lab*
Baroness McIntosh of Hudnall	*Lab*
Lord Razzall	*Lib Dem*

Staff: Edward McCarthy (Clerk), Owen Williams (Head)

Procedural Committees

Conduct

Tel: 020 7219 8796
Email: mawsonc@parliament.uk
committees.parliament.uk/committee/402/conduct-committee

Lord Mance (Chair)	*CB*
Baroness Anelay of St Johns	*Con*
Lord Brown of Eaton-under-Heywood	*CB*
Baroness Donaghy	*Lab*
Baroness Hussein-Ece	*Lib Dem*

Lay Members:
Cindy Butts
Mark Castle
Andrea Coomber
Vanessa Davies

Staff: Chloe Mawson (Clerk)

Liaison

Co-ordinates and allocates resources for committee work.

Tel: 020 7219 6678
Email: hlliaisoncmttee@parliament.uk
committees.parliament.uk/committee/187/liaison-committee-lords

Lord McFall of Alcluith (Chair)	*NA*
Lord Bradley	*Lab*
Lord Davies of Oldham	*Lab*
Baroness Hayter of Kentish Town	*Lab/Co-op*
Earl Howe	*Con*
Lord Judge	*CB*
Lord Lang of Monkton	*Con*
Lord Low of Dalston	*CB*
Lord Smith of Hindhead	*Con*
Lord Tyler	*Lib Dem*
Baroness Walmsley	*Lib Dem*

Staff: Philippa Tudor (Clerk), Owen Williams (Press Officer), Lucy Molloy (Research Assistant), Heather Fuller (Committee Assistant)

Procedure and Privileges

Considers the operation of procedures for parliamentary business in the Lords.

Tel: 020 7219 8796
Email: mawsonc@parliament.uk
committees.parliament.uk/committee/191/procedure-committee-lords

Lord McFall of Alcluith (Chair)	*NA*
Lord Ashton of Hyde	*Con*
Lord Bew	*CB*
Baroness Browning	*Con*
Lord Eames	*CB*
Baroness Evans of Bowes Park	*Con*
Baroness Finlay of Llandaff	*CB*
Lord Fowler	*Lord Speaker*
Lord Geddes	*Con*
Baroness Harris of Richmond	*Lib Dem*
Lord Judge	*CB*
Lord Mancroft	*Con*
Lord McAvoy	*Lab/Co-op*
Lord Morris of Aberavon	*Lab*
Lord Newby	*Lib Dem*
Lord Scriven	*Lib Dem*
Baroness Smith of Basildon	*Lab/Co-op*
Lord Stoneham of Droxford	*Lib Dem*
Baroness Thomas of Winchester	*Lib Dem*
Lord Turnbull	*CB*
Viscount Ullswater	*Con*
Baroness Warwick of Undercliffe	*Lab*
Lord Whitty	*Lab*

Staff: Chloe Mawson (Clerk)

Selection

Proposes members for select committees and other bodies.

Tel: 020 7219 3736
committees.parliament.uk/committee/197/committee-of-selection-lords

Lord McFall of Alcluith (Chair)	*NA*
Lord Ashton of Hyde	*Con*
Lord Craig of Radley	*CB*
Baroness Evans of Bowes Park	*Con*
Lord Judge	*CB*
Lord McAvoy	*Lab/Co-op*
Lord Newby	*Lib Dem*

Lord Plant of Highfield	*Lab*
Baroness Smith of Basildon	*Lab/Co-op*
Lord Stoneham of Droxford	*Lib Dem*
Viscount Ullswater	*Con*

Staff: Matthew Smith (Clerk)

Investigative Committees

Communications and Digital

Tel: 020 7219 8662
Email: holcommunications@parliament.uk
committees.parliament.uk/committee/170/communications-and-digital-committee
Twitter: @LordsCommsCom

Lord Gilbert of Panteg (Chair)	*Con*
Lord Allen of Kensington	*Lab*
Baroness Bull	*CB*
Baroness Buscombe	*Con*
Viscount Colville of Culross	*CB*
Baroness Grender	*Lib Dem*
Lord McInnes of Kilwinning	*Con*
Baroness McIntosh of Hudnall	*Lab*
Baroness Quin	*Lab*
Baroness Rebuck	*Lab*
Lord Storey	*Lib Dem*
Lord Vaizey of Didcot	*Con*
Bishop of Worcester	*NA*

Staff: Alasdair Love (Clerk), Theo Demolder (Policy Analyst), Kiran Dhaliwal (Press Officer), Rita Cohen (Committee Assistant)

Economic Affairs

Tel: 020 7219 5358
Email: economicaffairs@parliament.uk
committees.parliament.uk/committee/175/economic-affairs-committee
Twitter: @LordsEconCom

Lord Forsyth of Drumlean (Chair)	*Con*
Baroness Bowles of Berkhamsted	*Lib Dem*
Lord Burns	*CB*
Viscount Chandos	*Lab*
Lord Cunningham of Felling	*Lab*
Lord Fox	*Lib Dem*
Baroness Harding of Winscombe	*Con*
Baroness Kingsmill	*Lab*
Lord Livingston of Parkhead	*Con*
Lord Monks	*Lab*
Lord Skidelsky	*CB*
Lord Stern of Brentford	*CB*
Lord Tugendhat	*Con*

Staff: Adrian Hitchins (Clerk), William Harvey (Policy Analyst), Dervish Mertcan (Press Officer), Mithula Parayoganathan (Committee Assistant)

Economic Affairs Finance Bill Sub-committee

Tel: 020 7219 2228
Email: financebill@parliament.uk
www.parliament.uk/hlfinancebill

Lord Bridges of Headley (Chair)	*Con*
Baroness Bowles of Berkhamsted	*Lib Dem*
Lord Butler of Brockwell	*CB*
Viscount Chandos	*Lab*
Lord Forsyth of Drumlean	*Con*
Baroness Kramer	*Lib Dem*
Lord Monks	*Lab*
Lord Rowe-Beddoe	*CB*

Staff: Tristan Stubbs (Clerk), Dervish Mertcan (Press), Claire Coast-Smith (Committee Assistant)

European Union

Tel: 020 7219 6083
Email: euclords@parliament.uk
committees.parliament.uk/committee/176/european-union-committee
Twitter: @LordsEUCom

Earl of Kinnoull (Chair)	*NA*
Baroness Brown of Cambridge	*CB*
Baroness Couttie	*Con*
Baroness Donaghy	*Lab*
Lord Faulkner of Worcester	*Lab*
Lord Goldsmith	*Lab*
Baroness Hamwee	*Lib Dem*
Lord Kerr of Kinlochard	*CB*
Lord Lamont of Lerwick	*Con*
Baroness Neville-Rolfe	*Con*
Lord Oates	*Lib Dem*
Baroness Primarolo	*Lab*
Lord Ricketts	*CB*
Lord Sharkey	*Lib Dem*
Lord Teverson	*Lib Dem*
Lord Thomas of Cwmgiedd	*CB*
Baroness Verma	*Con*
Lord Wood of Anfield	*Lab*

Staff: Christopher Johnson (Principal Clerk), Stuart Stoner (Clerk), Roberto Robles (Policy Analyst), Alex Horne (Legal Advisers), Tim Mitchell (Legal Advisers), Owen Williams (Press Officer), Sam Lomas (Committee Assistant)

EU Environment Sub-committee

Tel: 020 7219 6798
Email: ayresl@parliament.uk
committees.parliament.uk/committee/444/eu-environment-subcommittee

Lord Teverson (Chair)	*Lib Dem*
Baroness Brown of Cambridge	*CB*
Baroness Bryan of Partick	*Lab*
Lord Cameron of Dillington	*CB*
Lord Carter of Coles	*Lab*

Lord Cormack	*Con*
Lord Giddens	*Lab*
Baroness Jolly	*Lib Dem*
Baroness McIntosh of Pickering	*Con*
Duke of Montrose	*Con*
Earl of Stair	*CB*
Lord Young of Norwood Green	*Lab*

Staff: Jennifer Mills (Clerk)

EU Goods Sub-committee
Tel: 020 7219 6099
Email: euclords@parliament.uk
committees.parliament.uk/committee/445/eu-goods-subcommittee

Baroness Verma (Chair)	*Con*
Lord Berkeley	*Lab*
Baroness Chalker of Wallasey	*Con*
Lord Faulkner of Worcester	*Lab*
Lord Inglewood	*NA*
Baroness Kramer	*Lib Dem*
Lord Lamont of Lerwick	*Con*
Lord Lilley	*Con*
Lord Russell of Liverpool	*CB*
Lord Shipley	*Lib Dem*
Lord Turnbull	*CB*
Lord Wigley	*PlC*
Lord Wood of Anfield	*Lab*

Staff: Jennifer Martin-Kohlmorgen (Clerk)

EU Services Sub-committee
Tel: 020 7219 3140
Email: garwellh@parliament.uk
committees.parliament.uk/committee/447/eu-services-subcommittee

Baroness Donaghy (Chair)	*Lab*
Lord Bruce of Bennachie	*Lib Dem*
Baroness Couttie	*Con*
Lord Davies of Stamford	*Lab*
Lord McNally	*Lib Dem*
Baroness Neville-Rolfe	*Con*
Baroness Prashar	*CB*
Lord Sharkey	*Lib Dem*
Lord Thomas of Cwmgiedd	*CB*
Viscount Trenchard	*Con*
Lord Vaux of Harrowden	*CB*

Staff: Dee Goddard (Clerk)

EU Security and Justice Sub-committee
Tel: 020 7219 5945
Email: euclords@parliament.uk
committees.parliament.uk/committee/446/eu-security-and-justice-subcommittee

Lord Ricketts (Chair)	*CB*
Lord Anderson of Ipswich	*CB*
Lord Anderson of Swansea	*Lab*
Lord Arbuthnot of Edrom	*Con*
Lord Dholakia	*Lib Dem*
Baroness Finn	*Con*
Baroness Goudie	*Lab*
Baroness Hamwee	*Lib Dem*
Lord Kirkhope of Harrogate	*Con*
Lord Lexden	*Con*
Lord Polak	*Con*
Baroness Primarolo	*Lab*
Lord Rowlands	*Lab*

Staff: Simon Pook (Clerk)

EU International Agreements Sub-committee
Tel: 020 7219 4840
Email: hlintlagreements@parliament.uk
committees.parliament.uk/committee/448/eu-international-agreements-subcommittee

Lord Goldsmith (Chair)	*Lab*
Lord Foster of Bath	*Lib Dem*
Lord Gold	*Con*
Lord Kerr of Kinlochard	*CB*
Lord Lansley	*Con*
Baroness Liddell of Coatdyke	*Lab*
Lord Morris of Aberavon	*Lab*
Lord Oates	*Lib Dem*
Lord Risby	*Con*
Lord Robathan	*Con*
Earl of Sandwich	*CB*
Lord Watts	*Lab*

Staff: Dominique Gracia (Clerk)

International Relations and Defence

Tel: 020 7219 7412
Email: hlintlrelations@parliament.uk
committees.parliament.uk/committee/360/international-relations-and-defence-committee
Twitter: @LordsIRCom

Baroness Anelay of St Johns (Chair)	*Con*
Lord Alton of Liverpool	*CB*
Baroness Blackstone	*Lab Ind*
Baroness Fall	*Con*
Lord Grocott	*Lab*
Lord Hannay of Chiswick	*CB*
Baroness Helic	*Con*
Lord Mendelsohn	*Lab*
Lord Purvis of Tweed	*Lib Dem*
Baroness Rawlings	*Con*
Lord Reid of Cardowan	*Lab*
Baroness Smith of Newnham	*Lib Dem*

Staff: Eva George (Clerk), Joseph Dobbs (Policy Analyst), Owen Williams (Press and Media Officer), Thomas Cullen (Committee Assistant)

Public Services

Tel: 020 7219 8654
Email: hlpublicservices@parliament.uk
committees.parliament.uk/committee/430/

public-services-committee
Twitter: @LordsPublicSCom

Baroness Armstrong of Hill Top (Chair)	*Lab*
Lord Bichard	*CB*
Lord Bourne of Aberystwyth	*Con*
Lord Davies of Gower	*Con*
Lord Filkin	*Lab*
Lord Hogan-Howe	*CB*
Lord Hunt of Kings Heath	*Lab/Co-op*
Baroness Pinnock	*Lib Dem*
Baroness Pitkeathley	*Lab*
Baroness Tyler of Enfield	*Lib Dem*
Baroness Wyld	*Con*
Lord Young of Cookham	*Con*

Staff: Tristan Stubbs (Clerk)

Science and Technology
Tel: 020 7219 5750
Email: hlscience@parliament.uk
committees.parliament.uk/committee/193/science-and-technology-committee-lords
Twitter: @LordsSTCom

Lord Patel (Chair)	*CB*
Baroness Blackwood of North Oxford	*Con*
Lord Borwick	*Con*
Lord Browne of Ladyton	*Lab*
Baroness Hilton of Eggardon	*Lab*
Lord Hollick	*Lab*
Lord Kakkar	*CB*
Lord Mair	*CB*
Baroness Manningham-Buller	*CB*
Viscount Ridley	*Con*
Baroness Rock	*Con*
Baroness Sheehan	*Lib Dem*
Baroness Walmsley	*Lib Dem*
Baroness Young of Old Scone	*Lab*

Staff: Simon Cran-McGreehin (Clerk), Amy Creese (Policy Analyst), Kiran Dhaliwal (Press Officer), Cerise Burnett-Stuart (Committee Assistant)

Principal Office Holders and Staff

Lord Speaker: Rt Hon Lord Fowler 020 7219 6444 Email: lordspeaker@parliament.uk
Senior Deputy Speaker: Rt Hon Lord McFall of Alcluith 020 7219 6000
Email: hlseniordeputyspeaker@parliament.uk
Principal Deputy Chairman of Committees: Earl of Kinnoull 020 7219 3000
Email: kinnoull@parliament.uk
Clerk of the Parliaments: Edward Ollard 020 7219 3171 Email: ollardec@parliament.uk
Clerk Assistant: Simon Burton 020 7219 3187 Email: burtons@parliament.uk
Reading Clerk and Clerk of the Overseas Office: Jake Vaughan 020 7219 3152
Email: vaughanj@parliament.uk
Lady Usher of the Black Rod: Sarah Clarke OBE 020 7219 3100 Email: clarkes@parliament.uk
Commissioner for Standards: Lucy Scott-Moncrieff CBE 020 7219 7152
Email: lordsstandards@parliament.uk
Registrar of Lords' Interests: Tom Wilson 020 7219 3112/020 7219 3120
Email: wilsont@parliament.uk
Clerk of Committees: Dr Philippa Tudor 020 7219 3130 Email: tudorfp@parliament.uk
Director of Facilities: Carl Woodall 020 7219 5501 Email: woodallc@parliament.uk
Finance Director: Fehintola Akinlose 020 7219 5524 Email: akinlosef@parliament.uk
Acting Director of Human Resources: James Taylor
Director of Parliamentary Digital Service: Tracey Jessup 020 7219 0745
Email: jessupt@parliament.uk
Clerk of Legislation: Andrew Makower 020 7219 3152 Email: makowera@parliament.uk
Examiners of Petitions for Private Bills: James Cooper 020 7219 3211
Email: cooperjj@parliament.uk, Daniel Greenberg 020 7219 5552
Email: greenbergd@parliament.uk, Colin Lee 020 7219 3255 Email: leecg@parliament.uk,
Christine Salmon Percival 020 7219 3233 Email: salmonc@parliament.uk
Organisational Culture Lead: Duncan Sagar 020 7219 3828 Email: sagard@parliament.uk
Clerk of the Journals: Chloe Mawson 020 7219 8796 Email: mawsonc@parliament.uk
Director of Library Services: Patrick Vollmer 020 7219 5805 Email: vollmerp@parliament.uk
Director of the Parliamentary Archives: Adrian Brown 020 7219 3071
Email: brownad@parliament.uk
Director of Communications: Michael Winders 020 7219 0671 Email: windersm@parliament.uk
Editor of the Official Report: John Vice 020 7219 3397 Email: vicej@parliament.uk
Counsel to the Chairman of Committees: James Cooper 020 7219 3211
Email: cooperjj@parliament.uk
Deputy Counsel to the Chairman of Committees: Nicholas Beach 020 7219 3243
Email: beachn@parliament.uk
Assistant Counsel to the Chairman of Committees: Che Diamond 020 7219 5332
Email: diamondc@parliament.uk
Counsel to the Joint Committee on Human Rights, Chamber and Committees: Ellie Hourigan
020 7219 3033 Email: hourigane@parlimament.uk
Director of Parliamentary Procurement and Commercial Service: Richard Blake 020 7219 8122
Email: blaker@parliament.uk
Head of Catering and Retail Services: Stephen Perkins 020 7219 4222
Email: perkinss@parliament.uk
Head of Property and Office Services: Justin Hills 020 7219 3213 Email: hillsj@parliament.uk
Head of Internal Audit: Paul Thompson 020 7219 3353 Email: thompsonp@parliament.uk
Internal Communications Manager: Sarah Kears-Burke 020 7219 4155
Email: kears-burkes@parliament.uk
Head of Information Compliance: Frances Grey 020 7219 0100 Email: greyf@parliament.uk
Private Secretary to the Lord Speaker: Patrick Milner 020 7219 6644 Email: milnerp@parliament.uk
Private Secretary to the Senior Deputy Speaker: Matthew Smith 020 7219 7539
Email: hlseniordeputyspeaker@parliament.uk
Head of Secretariat: Sarah Jones 020 7219 2997 Email: jonessa@parliament.uk
Principal Private Secretary to the Leader of the House: Victoria Warren 020 7219 1113
Email: victoria.warren@cabinetoffice.gov.uk

Private Secretary to the Leader of the House: Philip Lloyd 020 7219 6782
Email: philip.lloyd@cabinetoffice.gov.uk
Principal Clerk of Select Committees: Christopher Johnson DPhil 020 7219 5458
Email: johnsonc@parliament.uk
Clerk of Select Committees: Nicolas Besly 020 7219 6072 Email: beslyn@parliament.uk
Deputy Head of Legislation Office: Christine Salmon Percival 020 7219 3233
Email: salmonc@parliament.uk

House of Lords Communications

Westminster, London SW1A 0PW
Website: www.parliament.uk/lords

Director of Communications: Michael Winders 020 7219 0671 Email: windersm@parliament.uk
Head of Enquiry Service: Mark Simpson 020 7219 3107/Freephone: 0800 223 0855
Email: hlinfo@parliament.uk
Head of External Affairs and Engagement: Ciarán Norris 020 7219 4366
Email: norrisc@parliament.uk
Head of Internal Communications: Sarah Kears-Burke 020 7219 4155
Email: kears-burkes@parliament.uk
Head of Marketing and Digital Communications: Alexander Fleming 020 7219 4420
Email: fleminga@parliament.uk
Head of Press and Media: Owen Williams 020 7219 8659 Email: williamso@parliament.uk

Political Offices

Government

Tel: 020 7219 3131
Email: holgovernmentwhips@parliament.uk Website: www.lordswhips.org.uk

Leader of the House of Lords' Office 020 7219 3200
Government Whips' Office 020 7219 3131

Official Opposition

Leader's Office 020 7219 3237
Opposition Chief Whip's Office 020 7219 3237 Email: holoppositionwhips@parliament.uk

Liberal Democrats

Leader's Office 020 7219 3178
Chief Whip's Office 020 7219 3114

Crossbenchers

Convenor: Rt Hon Lord Judge
Private Secretary: Kate Long 020 7219 1414 Email: lordscrossbenchconvenor@parliament.uk

PARLIAMENT

Joint Committees

Joint Committee on Consolidation, &c, Bills

These Bills fall into five categories:
Consolidation Bills, whether public or private, which are limited to re-enacting existing law;
Statute Law Revision Bills, which are limited to repeal of obsolete, spent, unnecessary or superseded enactments;
Bills presented under the Consolidation of Enactments (Procedure) Act 1949, which include corrections and minor improvements to the existing law;
Bills to consolidate any enactments with amendments to give effect recommendations made by the Law Commissions;
Bills prepared by the Law Commissions to promote the reform of the Statute Law by the repeal of enactments which are no longer of practical utility.

Tel: 020 7219 5438
committees.parliament.uk/committee/171/consolidation-bills-joint-committee

Lord Thomas of Cwmgiedd (Chair)	*CB*
Baroness Andrews	*Lab*
Duncan Baker	*Con*
Simon Baynes	*Con*
Viscount Bridgeman	*Con*
Richard Burgon	*Lab*
Elliot Colburn	*Con*
Baroness D'Souza	*CB*
Maria Eagle	*Lab*
Lord Eames	*CB*
Viscount Eccles	*Con*
Viscount Hanworth	*Lab*
Simon Jupp	*Con*
Baroness Mallalieu	*Lab*
Lord Plant of Highfield	*Lab*
Lord Razzall	*Lib Dem*
Christina Rees	*Lab/Co-op*
Baroness Seccombe	*Con*
Andy Slaughter	*Lab*
Jane Stevenson	*Con*
Julian Sturdy	*Con*
Baroness Thomas of Winchester	*Lib Dem*
Owen Thompson	*SNP*
Suzanne Webb	*Con*

Staff: John Turner (Clerk)

Joint Committee on Fixed-Term Parliaments Act

Tel: 020 7219 3315
Email: jcftpa@parliament.uk
committees.parliament.uk/committee/491/joint-committee-on-the-fixedterm-parliaments-act

Lord McLoughlin (Chair)	*Con*
Lord Beith	*Lib Dem*
Aaron Bell	*Con*
Chris Bryant	*Lab*
Jackie Doyle-Price	*Con*
Angela Eagle	*Lab*
Maria Eagle	*Lab*
Peter Gibson	*Con*
Robert Goodwill	*Con*
Lord Grocott	*Lab*
Lord Jay of Ewelme	*CB*
Baroness Lawrence of Clarendon	*Lab*
David Linden	*SNP*
Alan Mak	*Con*
Lord Mancroft	*Con*
Maria Miller	*Con*
John Spellar	*Lab*
Alexander Stafford	*Con*
Shailesh Vara	*Con*
Craig Whittaker	*Con*

Staff: Eve Samson (Clerk), Ian Hook (Senior Executive Officer)

Joint Committee on Human Rights

Tel: 020 7219 2467
Email: jchr@parliament.uk
committees.parliament.uk/committee/93/human-rights-joint-committee Twitter: @HumanRightsCtte

Harriet Harman (Chair)	*Lab*
Lord Brabazon of Tara	*Con*
Fiona Bruce	*Con*
Karen Buck	*Lab*
Joanna Cherry	*SNP*
Lord Dubs	*Lab*
Pauline Latham	*Con*
Baroness Ludford	*Lib Dem*
Baroness Massey of Darwen	*Lab*
Dean Russell	*Con*
Lord Singh of Wimbledon	*CB*
Lord Trimble	*Con*

Staff: Robin James, George Webber (Clerks)

Joint Committee on the National Security Strategy

Tel: 020 7219 8092 (Commons enquiries)
Email: jcnss@parliament.uk
committees.parliament.uk/committee/111/national-security-strategy-joint-committee
Twitter: @JointCtteNSS

Margaret Beckett (Chair)	*Lab*
Lord Brennan	*NA*
Lord Campbell of Pittenweem	*Lib Dem*
Sarah Champion	*Lab*

Yvette Cooper	*Lab*
Tobias Ellwood	*Con*
Richard Graham	*Con*
Lord Harris of Haringey	*Lab*
Baroness Healy of Primrose Hill	*Lab*
Baroness Henig	*Lab*
Baroness Hodgson of Abinger	*Con*
Darren Jones	*Lab*
Alicia Kearns	*Con*
Lord King of Bridgwater	*Con*
Baroness Lane-Fox of Soho	*CB*
Edward Leigh	*Con*
Angus MacNeil	*SNP*
Robert Neill	*Con*
Baroness Neville-Jones	*Con*
Lord Powell of Bayswater	*CB*
Bob Stewart	*Con*
Tom Tugendhat	*Con*

Staff: Simon Fiander (Commons Clerk), Eva George (Lords Clerk), Ashlee Godwin (Commons Senior Committee Specialist), Estelle Currie (Press Officer), Carolyn Bowes (Commons Committee Assistant), Breda Twomey (Lords Committee Assistant)

Joint Committee on Statutory Instruments

Commons members of the Joint Committee also meet separately as the Select Committee on Statutory Instruments.

Tel: 020 7219 7599/2026 (Commons)
Email: jcsi@parliament.uk
committees.parliament.uk/committee/148/statutory-instruments-joint-committee

Jessica Morden (Chair)	*Lab*
Lord Colgrain	*Con*
James Davies	*Con*
Baroness Gale	*Lab*
Lord Haskel	*Lab*
Paul Holmes	*Con*
John Lamont	*Con*
Baroness Newlove	*Con*
Lord Rowe-Beddoe	*CB*
Baroness Scott of Needham Market	*Lib Dem*
Lord Stirrup	*CB*
Robert Syms	*Con*
Owen Thompson	*SNP*
Liz Twist	*Lab*

Staff: Christine Salmon Percival (Clerk), Liz Booth (Committee Assistant)

Statutory Committees

These committees are not select committees or committees of Parliament, but statutory committees of parliamentarians, which are required by law to be made up of Members of the two Houses. Generally, however, they model their procedure closely on that of select committees, and, with the exception of the Intelligence and Security Committee and Parliamentary and Political Service Honours Committee, draw their secretariats from parliamentary staff.

Ecclesiastical Committee

This Committee examines draft Measures presented to it by the Legislative Committee of the General Synod of the Church of England. It reports to Parliament on whether or not it considers the measures to be expedient. The members of the Committee are appointed by the Speaker and Lord Speaker for the duration of each Parliament.

Tel: 020 7219 3233 (Lords)
Email: eccctee@parliament.uk
committees.parliament.uk/committee/174/ecclesiastical-committee-joint-committee

Baroness Butler-Sloss (Chair)	*CB*
Fleur Anderson	*Lab*
Peter Bottomley	*Con*
Ben Bradshaw	*Lab*
Fiona Bruce	*Con*
Lisa Cameron	*SNP*
Miriam Cates	*Con*
Earl of Cork and Orrery	*CB*
Lord Cormack	*Con*
Baroness Eaton	*Con*
Lord Faulkner of Worcester	*Lab*
Roger Gale	*Con*
Lord Glenarthur	*Con*
Baroness Harris of Richmond	*Lib Dem*
Baroness Howarth of Breckland	*CB*
Lord Jones	*Lab*
Lord Judd	*Lab*
David Lammy	*Lab*
Lord Lexden	*Con*
Lord Lisvane	*CB*
Rachael Maskell	*Lab/Co-op*
Baroness McIntosh of Hudnall	*Lab*
Lord Plant of Highfield	*Lab*
Gary Sambrook	*Con*
Andrew Selous	*Con*
Jim Shannon	*DUP*
Desmond Swayne	*Con*
Stephen Timms	*Lab*
Martin Vickers	*Con*

Speaker's Committee on the Electoral Commission

The Speaker's Committee is a statutory body established under the Political Parties, Elections

and Referendums Act 2000.
Of the appointed members, one is a Member of the House of Commons who is a Minister with responsibilities in relation to local government. This appointment is made by the Prime Minister. The other appointed members are Members of the House of Commons who are not Ministers and are appointed by the Speaker. Appointed members serve for the full length of the Parliament, unless they cease to be Members of the House, resign from the Committee, or another member is appointed in their place. They may be reappointed.

Tel: 020 7219 3351
Email: speakerscommittee@parliament.uk
committees.parliament.uk/committee/144/speakers-committee-on-the-electoral-commission

Lindsay Hoyle (Chair)	*Speaker*
Michael Gove	*Con*
Luke Hall	*Con*
Karl McCartney	*Con*
Craig Mackinlay	*Con*
Chris Matheson	*Lab*
Cat Smith	*Lab*
Owen Thompson	*SNP*
William Wragg	*Con*

Staff: Robin James (Clerk), Kevin Maddison (Secretary), Jackie Storer (Media Officer), Jim Lawford (Committee Assistant)

Speaker's Committee for the Independent Parliamentary Standards Authority

The Committee considers the candidates proposed by the Speaker, following fair and open competition, for the posts of Chair and members of the Independent Parliamentary Standards Authority (IPSA). The candidates for these posts must then be considered by the House of Commons before their appointment by the Queen.
The Committee also reviews the IPSA's annual estimate of the resources it needs.
The Speaker, the Leader of the House and the Chair of the Committees on Standards and Privileges are *ex-officio* members.

Tel: 020 7219 3351 Fax: 020 7219 2269
Email: scipsa@parliament.uk
committees.parliament.uk/committee/143/speakers-committee-for-the-independent-parliamentary-standards-authority

Lindsay Hoyle (Chair)	*Speaker*
Chris Bryant	*Lab*
Marion Fellows	*SNP*
Cheryl Gillan	*Con*
Jacob Rees-Mogg	*Con*
Desmond Swayne	*Con*
Valerie Vaz	*Lab*
Charles Walker	*Con*

Lay Members: Peter Blausten, Cindy Butts, Shrinvas Honap
Staff: Robin James, Kevin Maddison (Clerks), Jackie Storer (Media Officer), Jim Lawford (Committee Assistant)

Intelligence and Security Committee of Parliament

Tel: 020 7276 1215
isc.independent.gov.uk

Julian Lewis (Chair)	*Con*
John Hayes	*Con*
Stewart Hosie	*SNP*
Diana Johnson	*Lab*
Kevan Jones	*Lab*
Mark Pritchard	*Con*
Bob Stewart	*Con*
Theresa Villiers	*Con*
Lord West of Spithead	*Lab*

Parliamentary and Political Service Honours Committee

Tel: 020 7276 2777
Email: honours@cabinetoffice.gov.uk

Lord Sherbourne of Didsbury (Chair)	*Con*
Nick Brown	*Lab*
Lord Haselhurst	*Con*
Lord Lisvane	*CB*
Mark Spencer	*Con*

Non-parliamentary Members: Susan Griffiths, Denise Platt, Paul Silk

Staff: Alison Bennett (Head of Honours and Appointments Secretariat)

Parliamentary Works Estimates Commission

Lilian Greenwood	*Lab*
Eleanor Laing	*Con*
Lord Macpherson of Earl's Court	*CB*
Lord McFall of Alcluith	*NA*

Public Accounts Commission

The Commission's principal duties are to examine the National Audit Office Estimates, and (if satisfied) present them to the House of Commons, agree the National Audit Office (NAO)'s corporate strategy, appoint non-executive members of the NAO board (other than the chair) and consider value for money reports from the appointed auditor for the National Audit Office. The Leader of the House and Chair of the Public Accounts Committee are *ex-officio* members.

Tel: 020 7219 3261

www.parliament.uk/business/committees/committees-a-z/other-committees/public-accounts-commission

Edward Leigh (Chair)	*Con*
Richard Bacon	*Con*
Jack Brereton	*Con*
Nick Brown	*Lab*
Clive Efford	*Lab*
Peter Grant	*SNP*
Meg Hillier	*Lab/Co-op*
Alan Mak	*Con*
Jacob Rees-Mogg	*Con*

Staff: Kevin Maddison (Secretary), Christine McGrane (Assistant)

Party Committees

CONSERVATIVE PARTY 1922 COMMITTEE

The 1922 Committee exists to give Conservative Backbench MPs a voice and as a mechanism for consultation between the backbenches and the Government.

The 1922 conducts the early stages of leadership elections in the Party and the Chairman has the role of the Returning Officer throughout the process, which includes a vote by the entire countrywide membership of the Conservative Party.

In Opposition, the membership extends to all members of the Parliamentary Party whether front or back benchers. Conservative Peers are invited to all 1922 meetings. When in Government, the 1922 is comprised of all the backbenchers of the Party; the Whips come to the weekly meetings by invitation, as do other Government Ministers.

Chairman: Sir Graham Brady
Vice-chairmen: Dame Cheryl Gillan, Sir Charles Walker
Treasurer: Sir Geoffrey Clifton-Brown
Secretaries: Bob Blackman, Pauline Latham
Members, Executive: Steve Baker, Dr James Davies, Robert Halfon, Sir Bernard Jenkin, Jason McCartney, Karl McCartney, David Morris, Sheryll Murray, Mark Pawsey, Nicola Richards, Gary Sambrook, William Wragg

PARLIAMENTARY LABOUR PARTY DEPARTMENTAL GROUPS

Business, Energy and Industrial Strategy
Chair: Andrew Gwynne

Cabinet Office
Chair: Yvonne Fovargue

Communities and Local Government
Chair: Fleur Anderson

Defence
Chair: Derek Twigg

Digital, Culture, Media and Sport
Chair: Darren Jones

Education
Chair: Ian Mearns

Employment Rights and Protection
Chair: Tonia Antoniazzi

Environment, Food and Rural Affairs
Chair: Barry Sheerman

Foreign Affairs
Chair: Catherine McKinnell

Future Relationship with the European Union
Chair: Judith Cummins

Health
Chair: Sarah Owen

Home Affairs
Chair: Dame Diana Johnson

Housing
Chair: Karen Buck

International Development
Chair: Julie Elliott

International Trade
Chair: Mick Whitley

Justice
Chair: Maria Eagle

Northern Ireland
Chair: Kevin Brennan

Transport
Chair: Lilian Greenwood

Treasury
Chair: Dame Angela Eagle

Women
Chair: Rosie Duffield
Vice-chairs: Jess Phillips *(Commons)*, Yasmin Qureshi *(Commons)*, Baroness Gale *(Lords)*, Baroness Lister of Burtersett *(Lords)*

Work and Pensions
Chair: Neil Coyle

Golf
Chair: Craig Tracey *Con*
Vice-chairs:
Steve Brine *Con*
Wendy Chamberlain *Lib Dem*
Sir Jeffrey Donaldson *DUP*
Dame Cheryl Gillan *Con*
Lord Goddard of Stockport *Lib Dem*
Julian Knight *Con*
Lord Lennie *Lab*
Karl McCartney *Con*
Lord Moynihan *Con*
Gavin Newlands *SNP*
Baroness Nye *Lab*
Laurence Robertson *Con*
Lord Robertson of Port Ellen *Lab*
Michael Tomlinson *Con*

Contact: Craig Tracey, House of Commons, London SW1A 0AA Tel: 020 7219 5646
Email: craig.tracey.mp@parliament.uk
Website: www.parliamentary.golf
Twitter: @ParliamentGolf

Governance and Inclusive Leadership
Chair: Dawn Butler *Lab*
Vice-chairs:
Sir Peter Bottomley *Con*
Anne McLaughlin *SNP*
Officers:
Clive Lewis *Lab*
Lord Woolley of Woodford *CB*

Contact: Dawn Butler, House of Commons, London SW1A 0AA Tel: 020 7219 8591
Email: dawn.butler.mp@parliament.uk

Green Deal Misselling
Chairs:
Anne McLaughlin *SNP*
Gavin Newlands *SNP*
Vice-chairs:
Andrew Bowie *Con*
Alan Brown *SNP*
Bambos Charalambous *Lab*
Margaret Ferrier *Ind*
Patricia Gibson *SNP*

Contact: Gavin Newlands, 6 Porterfield Road, Renfrew PA4 8HG Tel: 01413 780600

Green New Deal
Chairs:
Clive Lewis *Lab*
Dr Caroline Lucas *Green*
Vice-chairs:
Debbie Abrahams *Lab*
Claire Hanna *SDLP*
Lord Randall of Uxbridge *Con*
Liz Saville Roberts *PlC*
Treasurer: Dr Stephen Farry *APNI*

Contact: Dr Caroline Lucas, House of Commons, London SW1A 0AA
Tel: 020 7219 7025
Email: caroline.lucas.mp@parliament.uk

Greyhound
President: Lord Lipsey *Lab*
Chairs:
Ian Lavery *Lab*
Andrew Rosindell *Con*
Vice-chairs:
Baroness Golding *Lab*
Stephen Hammond *Con*
Conor McGinn *Lab*
Ian Mearns *Lab*
Grahame Morris *Lab*
Kate Osborne *Lab*

Contact: Andrew Rosindell, House of Commons, London SW1A 0AA
Tel: 020 7219 8475
Email: andrew.rosindell.mp@parliament.uk

Gypsies, Travellers and Roma
Honorary President: Lord Bourne of Aberystwyth *Con*
Chairs:
Martin Docherty-Hughes *SNP*
Baroness Whitaker *Lab*
Vice-chairs:
Baroness Bakewell of Hardington Mandeville *Lib Dem*
Sir Peter Bottomley *Con*
Andy Slaughter *Lab*
Officers:
Baroness Brinton *Lib Dem*
Deidre Brock *SNP*
Gill Furniss *Lab*
Alex Sobel *Lab/Co-op*

Contact: Martin Docherty-Hughes, House of Commons, London SW1A 0AA
Tel: 020 7219 4609
Email: martin.docherty.mp@parliament.uk
Website: www.gypsy-traveller.org/appg

Hadrian's Wall
Chair: Mary Glindon *Lab*
Vice-chairs:
Catherine McKinnell *Lab*
Ian Mearns *Lab*
Secretary: Trudy Harrison *Con*

Contact: Mary Glindon, House of Commons, London SW1A 0AA Tel: 020 7219 3000
Email: mary.glindon.mp@parliament.uk

Haemophilia and Contaminated Blood

Chairs:
Sir Peter Bottomley *Con*
Dame Diana Johnson *Lab*
Vice-chairs:
Barbara Keeley *Lab*
Jason McCartney *Con*
Jessica Morden *Lab*
Chris Stephens *SNP*
Jo Stevens *Lab*
Catherine West *Lab*
Dr Philippa Whitford *SNP*
Officer: Baroness Ritchie of Downpatrick *NA*

Contact: Dame Diana Johnson, House of Commons, London SW1A 0AA
Tel: 020 7219 5647
Email: johnsond@parliament.uk
Website: www.haemophilia.org.uk/get-involved/campaigning/access-to-care/appg

Hairdressing, Barbering and Cosmetology

Chairs:
John McNally *SNP*
Christina Rees *Lab/Co-op*
Officers:
Sir David Amess *Con*
Catherine West *Lab*

Contact: John McNally, House of Commons, London SW1A 0AA Tel: 020 7219 6525
Email: john.mcnally.mp@parliament.uk

Hajj and Umrah

Chairs:
Yasmin Qureshi *Lab*
Baroness Uddin *NA*
Vice-chairs:
Tahir Ali *Lab*
Robert Goodwill *Con*
Lord Hussain *Lib Dem*
Imran Hussain *Lab*
Afzal Khan *Lab*
Alex Norris *Lab/Co-op*
Steve Reed *Lab/Co-op*
Naz Shah *Lab*
Baroness Warsi *Con*
Mohammad Yasin *Lab*

Contact: Yasmin Qureshi, House of Commons, London SW1A 0AA Tel: 020 7219 7019
Email: yasmin.qureshi.mp@parliament.uk
Website: www.appghajjumrah.org
Twitter: @appghajjumrah

Health

Chairs:
Dr Lisa Cameron *SNP*
Peter Dowd *Lab*
Baroness Finlay of Llandaff *CB*
Baroness Masham of Ilton *CB*
Baroness Walmsley *Lib Dem*
Treasurer: Lord Hunt of Kings Heath *Lab/Co-op*
Officers:
Sir Paul Beresford *Con*
Sir Peter Bottomley *Con*
Dr Luke Evans *Con*
Sarah Jones *Lab*
Lord Rennard *Lib Dem*
Karin Smyth *Lab*
Munira Wilson *Lib Dem*

Contact: Dr Lisa Cameron, House of Commons, London SW1A 0AA Tel: 020 7219 6855
Email: lisa.cameron.mp@parliament.uk
Website: www.healthinparliament.org.uk
Twitter: @HealthAPPG

Health in all Policies

Chair: Debbie Abrahams *Lab*
Vice-chairs:
Jackie Doyle-Price *Con*
Jim Shannon *DUP*
Dr Philippa Whitford *SNP*

Contact: Debbie Abrahams, House of Commons, London SW1A 0AA
Tel: 020 7219 1041
Email: abrahamsd@parliament.uk

Healthy Homes and Buildings

Chairs:
Mary Glindon *Lab*
Jim Shannon *DUP*
Vice-chairs:
Eddie Hughes *Con*
Marco Longhi *Con*
Earl of Lytton *CB*
Secretary: Derek Thomas *Con*
Treasurer: Paul Girvan *DUP*

Contact: Jim Shannon, House of Commons, London SW1A 0AA Tel: 020 7219 7160
Email: jim.shannon.mp@parliament.uk
Website: healthyhomesbuildings.org.uk
Twitter: @APPGHHB

Heart Valve Disease

Chair: Steve McCabe *Lab*
Vice-chairs:
Chris Evans *Lab/Co-op*
Chris Green *Con*
Baroness Masham of Ilton *CB*
Jim Shannon *DUP*
Virendra Sharma *Lab*
Henry Smith *Con*
Dr Philippa Whitford *SNP*

Contact: Steve McCabe, House of Commons, London SW1A 0AA Tel: 020 7219 3509
Email: mccabes@parliament.uk
Twitter: @APPG_HVD

Heathrow Expansion and Regional Connectivity

Chairs:
Ruth Cadbury *Lab*
David Simmonds *Con*
Vice-chairs:
Adam Afriyie *Con*
Fleur Anderson *Lab*
Bob Blackman *Con*
Baroness Hamwee *Lib Dem*
Baroness Jones of Moulsecoomb *Green*
Andy Slaughter *Lab*
Munira Wilson *Lib Dem*

Contact: David Simmonds, House of Commons, London SW1A 0AA Tel: 0207 219 3000
Email: david.simmonds.mp@parliament.uk
Website: www.appgheathrowexpansion.com

Heritage Rail

Chair: Liz Saville Roberts *PlC*
Vice-chairs:
Lord Faulkner of Worcester *Lab*
Mark Garnier *Con*
Lord Grocott *Lab*
Kevin Hollinrake *Con*
Baroness Morgan of Cotes *Con*
Lord Snape *Lab*
Treasurer: Martin Vickers *Con*

Contact: Liz Saville Roberts, Angorfa, Heol Meurig, Dolgellau LL40 1LN
Tel: 01341 422661
Email: liz.savilleroberts.mp@parliament.uk

British Hindus

Chair: Bob Blackman *Con*
Vice-chairs:
Maria Miller *Con*
Virendra Sharma *Lab*
Alison Thewliss *SNP*
Theresa Villiers *Con*

Contact: Bob Blackman, House of Commons, London SW1A 0AA Tel: 020 7219 7082
Email: bob.blackman.mp@parliament.uk
Twitter: @BritishHindus

Historic Counties

Chairs:
Andrew Rosindell *Con*
Henry Smith *Con*
Vice-chairs:
Andrew Gwynne *Lab*
Lord Randall of Uxbridge *Con*

Contact: Andrew Rosindell, House of Commons, London SW1A 0AA
Tel: 020 7219 8475
Email: andrew.rosindell.mp@parliament.uk

Historic Vehicles

Chair: Sir Greg Knight *Con*
Vice-chair: Mark Tami *Lab*
Secretary: Sir Christopher Chope *Con*
Treasurer: John Cryer *Lab*

Contact: Sir Greg Knight, House of Commons, London SW1A 0AA Tel: 020 7219 4077
Email: sothcottt@parliament.uk
Website: www.historicvehicles.org.uk

HIV and AIDS

Chair: Stephen Doughty *Lab/Co-op*
Vice-chairs:
Baroness Barker *Lib Dem*
Lord Black of Brentwood *Con*
Sarah Champion *Lab*
Lord Collins of Highbury *Lab*
Dr Peter Kyle *Lab*
Baroness Masham of Ilton *CB*
Mark Menzies *Con*
Dr Ben Spencer *Con*
Treasurer: Lloyd Russell-Moyle *Lab/Co-op*

Contact: Stephen Doughty, House of Commons, London SW1A 0AA Tel: 020 7219 5348
Email: stephen.doughty.mp@parliament.uk
Website: www.appghivaids.org.uk
Twitter: @appg_hiv_aids

Hockey

Chairs:
Ben Bradley *Con*
Luke Pollard *Lab/Co-op*
Vice-chairs:
Stephen Hammond *Con*
Abena Oppong-Asare *Lab*
Rob Roberts *Con*
Treasurer: Tim Loughton *Con*

Contact: Luke Pollard, House of Commons, London SW1A 0AA Tel: 020 7219 2749
Email: luke.pollard.mp@parliament.uk

Holiday Parks and Campsites

Chair: Peter Aldous *Con*
Vice-chairs:
Lord Carter of Coles *Lab*
Lord Redesdale *Lib Dem*
Liz Saville Roberts *PlC*

Contact: Peter Aldous, House of Commons, London SW1A 0AA Tel: 020 7219 7182
Email: peter.aldous.mp@parliament.uk
Website: www.appgholidayparkcampsite.org

Holocaust Memorial
President: Lord Pickles *Con*
Chair: Bob Blackman *Con*
Vice-chairs:
Sir Peter Bottomley *Con*
Dr Lisa Cameron *SNP*
Stephen Crabb *Con*
Rosie Duffield *Lab*
Secretary: Nicola Richards *Con*
Treasurer: Lord Polak *Con*
Officers:
Dame Margaret Hodge *Lab*
Dr John Howell *Con*
Lord Shinkwin *Con*
Alex Sobel *Lab/Co-op*

Contact: Bob Blackman, House of Commons, London SW1A 0AA Tel: 020 7219 7082
Email: bob.blackman.mp@parliament.uk

Holy See
Chairs:
Baroness Hollins *CB*
Mike Kane *Lab*
Sir Edward Leigh *Con*
Vice-chair: Patrick Grady *SNP*
Secretaries:
Baroness Hooper *Con*
Mark Menzies *Con*
Treasurers:
Lord Balfe *Con*
Angus MacNeil *SNP*

Contact: Sir Edward Leigh, House of Commons, London SW1A 0AA
Tel: 020 7219 6480
Email: edward.leigh.mp@parliament.uk

Homelessness
Chairs:
Bob Blackman *Con*
Neil Coyle *Lab*
Vice-chairs:
Nickie Aiken *Con*
Tonia Antoniazzi *Lab*
Lord Bird *CB*
Alex Chalk *Con*
Jason McCartney *Con*
Justin Madders *Lab*
Rachael Maskell *Lab/Co-op*
Stephen Timms *Lab*
Mike Wood *Con*
Officers:
Mike Amesbury *Lab*
Rosie Duffield *Lab*
Colleen Fletcher *Lab*
Emma Hardy *Lab*
Chris Matheson *Lab*
Angela Richardson *Con*
Lord Shipley *Lib Dem*
Chris Stephens *SNP*
Daniel Zeichner *Lab*

Contact: Neil Coyle, House of Commons, London SW1A 0AA Tel: 020 7232 4640
Email: neil.coyle.mp@parliament.uk
Website: www.crisis.org.uk/ending-homelessness/appg-for-ending-homelessness
Twitter: @HomelessAPPG

"Honour" Based Abuse
Chair: Virendra Sharma *Lab*
Vice-chair: Philip Davies *Con*
Secretary: Baroness Cox *CB*
Treasurer: Lord Dholakia *Lib Dem*

Contact: Virendra Sharma, House of Commons, London SW1A 0AA Tel: 020 7219 6080
Email: sharmav@parliament.uk

Hormone Pregnancy Tests
Chair: Yasmin Qureshi *Lab*
Vice-chairs:
Lord Alton of Liverpool *CB*
Sir Ed Davey *Lib Dem*
Yvonne Fovargue *Lab*
Robert Goodwill *Con*
Sir Mike Penning *Con*

Contact: Yasmin Qureshi, House of Commons, London SW1A 0AA Tel: 020 7219 7019
Email: yasmin.qureshi.mp@parliament.uk
Twitter: @APPGHPTs

Horse
Chair: Saqib Bhatti *Con*
Officers:
Dr Neil Hudson *Con*
Baroness Mallalieu *Lab*
Caroline Nokes *Con*
Laurence Robertson *Con*

Contact: Saqib Bhatti, House of Commons, London SW1A 0AA Tel: 020 7219 3423
Email: saqib.bhatti@parliament.uk

Hospice and End of Life Care
Chairs:
Jack Dromey *Lab*
Baroness Finlay of Llandaff *CB*
Officers:
Peter Gibson *Con*
Catherine McKinnell *Lab*
Baroness Walmsley *Lib Dem*
Dr Philippa Whitford *SNP*

Contact: Jack Dromey, House of Commons, London SW1A 0AA Tel: 020 7219 0903
Email: jack.dromey.mp@parliament.uk

Hospitality and Tourism
Chair: Steve Double *Con*
Vice-chairs:
Scott Mann *Con*
Alison Thewliss *SNP*
Secretary: Lord Pendry *Lab*
Treasurer: Michael Tomlinson *Con*

Contact: Steve Double, House of Commons, London SW1A 0AA Tel: 020 7219 4408
Email: steve.double.mp@parliament.uk
Website: www.ukhospitality.org.uk/page/appg

Housing and Care for Older People
Chairs:
Peter Aldous *Con*
Lord Best *CB*
Vice-chairs:
Baroness Andrews *Lab*
Baroness Barker *Lib Dem*
Ruth Cadbury *Lab*
Baroness Greengross *CB*
Baroness Jolly *Lib Dem*
Lord Stoneham of Droxford *Lib Dem*

Contact: Peter Aldous, House of Commons, London SW1A 0AA Tel: 020 7219 7182
Email: peter.aldous.mp@parliament.uk
Website: www.housingandcare21.co.uk/about-us/appg-housing-and-care-for-older-people

Housing and Planning
Chair: David Simmonds *Con*
Vice-chairs:
Fleur Anderson *Lab*
Lord Best *CB*
Ben Everitt *Con*
Jane Hunt *Con*
Andrew Lewer *Con*
Tony Lloyd *Lab*
Jerome Mayhew *Con*
Gagan Mohindra *Con*
Mark Pawsey *Con*
Officers:
Karen Buck *Lab*
Helen Hayes *Lab*
Paul Howell *Con*

Contact: David Simmonds, House of Commons, London SW1A 0AA Tel: 0207 219 3000
Email: david.simmonds.mp@parliament.uk

Housing and Social Mobility
Chairs:
Peter Aldous *Con*
Liz Twist *Lab*
Vice-chairs:
Richard Bacon *Con*
Bob Blackman *Con*
Sally-Ann Hart *Con*

Contact: Peter Aldous, House of Commons, London SW1A 0AA Tel: 020 7219 7182
Email: peter.aldous.mp@parliament.uk
Website: www.communitiesthatwork.co.uk/appg

Housing in the North
Chair: Ian Mearns *Lab*
Vice-chairs:
Mary Foy *Lab*
Lord Goddard of Stockport *Lib Dem*
Richard Holden *Con*
Kevin Hollinrake *Con*
Grahame Morris *Lab*
Kate Osborne *Lab*

Contact: Ian Mearns, House of Commons, London SW1A 0AA Tel: 020 7219 7074
Email: ian.mearns.mp@parliament.uk
Website: www.northern-consortium.org.uk/services/policy/parliament/appg-for-housing-in-the-north

Housing Market and Housing Delivery
Chair: Ben Everitt *Con*
Vice-chairs:
Peter Gibson *Con*
Paul Holmes *Con*
Lloyd Russell-Moyle *Lab/Co-op*

Contact: Ben Everitt, House of Commons, London SW1A 0AA Tel: 020 7219 5898
Email: ben.everitt.mp@parliament.uk
Website: appghousing.org.uk
Twitter: @HousingAPPG

Human Microbiome
Chair: Julie Elliott *Lab*
Vice-chairs:
Baroness Bennett of Manor Castle *Green*
Jessica Morden *Lab*
Secretary: Robert Goodwill *Con*
Treasurer: Siobhain McDonagh *Lab*

Contact: Julie Elliott, House of Commons, London SW1A 0AA Tel: 020 7219 7165
Email: julie.elliott.mp@parliament.uk

Human-Relevant Science
Chair: Grahame Morris *Lab*
Vice-chairs:
Sir David Amess *Con*
Baroness Hayman of Ullock *Lab*
Officer: Chris Stephens *SNP*

Contact: Grahame Morris, House of Commons, London SW1A 0AA Tel: 020 7219 1283
Email: grahame.morris.mp@parliament.uk
Website: www.humanrelevantscience.org/all-party-parliamentary-group

Human Rights
Chairs:
Margaret Ferrier *Ind*
Dame Diana Johnson *Lab*
Baroness Stern *CB*
Vice-chairs:
Marsha De Cordova *Lab*
Lord Garnier *Con*
Tony Lloyd *Lab*
Baroness Whitaker *Lab*
Treasurer: Stephen Timms *Lab*

Contact: Dame Diana Johnson, House of Commons, London SW1A 0AA
Tel: 020 7219 5647
Email: johnsond@parliament.uk
Website: appg-humanrights.org.uk
Twitter: @HumanRightsAPPG

Human Trafficking and Modern Slavery
Chairs:
Karen Bradley *Con*
Baroness Butler-Sloss *CB*
Vice-chairs:
Sarah Champion *Lab*
Darren Jones *Lab*
Lord Randall of Uxbridge *Con*
Andrew Selous *Con*
Secretaries:
Lord McColl of Dulwich *Con*
Alex Norris *Lab/Co-op*

Contact: Karen Bradley, House of Commons, London SW1A 0AA Tel: 020 7219 7215
Email: karen.bradley.mp@parliament.uk

Humanist
Chairs:
Baroness Bakewell *Lab*
Crispin Blunt *Con*
Vice-chairs:
Baroness Burt of Solihull *Lib Dem*
Clive Lewis *Lab*
Viscount Ridley *Con*
Tommy Sheppard *SNP*
Jeff Smith *Lab*
Lord Taverne *Lib Dem*
Secretary: Baroness Massey of Darwen *Lab*
Treasurer: Lord Dubs *Lab*

Contact: Crispin Blunt, House of Commons, London SW1A 0AA Tel: 020 7219 2254
Email: crispinbluntmp@parliament.uk
Website: www.humanism.org.uk/about/humanists-in-parliament

Hydrogen
Chair: Jacob Young *Con*
Vice-chairs:
Sir Roger Gale *Con*
Andrew Griffith *Con*
Mark Jenkinson *Con*
Lord Moynihan *Con*
Lia Nici *Con*
Alex Sobel *Lab/Co-op*
Alexander Stafford *Con*
Lord Wigley *PlC*
Lord Young of Norwood Green *Lab*
Officers:
Peter Aldous *Con*
Paula Barker *Lab*
Sir Paul Beresford *Con*
Lord Colwyn *Con*
Sir Ed Davey *Lib Dem*
Steve Double *Con*
Bill Esterson *Lab*
Baroness Goudie *Lab*
Lord Grantchester *Lab*
Damian Hinds *Con*
Baroness Hooper *Con*
Lord Lucas of Crudwell and Dingwall *Con*
Lord Mackay of Clashfern *Con*
Lord Mackenzie of Framwellgate *NA*
Angus MacNeil *SNP*
Baroness Meacher *CB*
Lord Moonie *NA*
Charlotte Nichols *Lab*
Lord Oates *Lib Dem*
Ian Paisley *DUP*
Richard Thomson *SNP*
Dr Alan Whitehead *Lab*

Contact: Jacob Young, House of Commons, London SW1A 0AA Tel: 0207 219 3936
Email: jacob.young.mp@parliament.uk
Website: www.connectpa.co.uk/appg-hydrogen
Twitter: @HydrogenAPPG

Illicit Trade
Chair: Dr Matthew Offord *Con*
Vice-chair: Kenny MacAskill *SNP*
Officers:
Baroness Bakewell *Lab*
Mary Glindon *Lab*
Craig Mackinlay *Con*
John McNally *SNP*

Contact: Dr Matthew Offord, House of Commons, London SW1A 0AA
Tel: 020 7219 7083
Email: matthew.offord.mp@parliament.uk
Website: www.connectpa.co.uk/illicit-trade-party-parliamentary-group
Twitter: @IAppg

Immigration Detention
Chair: Alison Thewliss *SNP*
Vice-chairs:
Christine Jardine *Lib Dem*

Bell Ribeiro-Addy *Lab*
Officers:
Baroness Bennett of Manor Castle *Green*
Sir Peter Bottomley *Con*
Stephen Doughty *Lab/Co-op*
Richard Fuller *Con*
Baroness Hamwee *Lib Dem*
Harriet Harman *Lab*
Helen Hayes *Lab*
Baroness Lister of Burtersett *Lab*
Stuart C McDonald *SNP*
Kate Osamor *Lab/Co-op*
Earl of Sandwich *CB*
Hywel Williams *PlC*

Contact: Alison Thewliss, House of Commons, London SW1A 0AA Tel: 020 7219 6447
Email: alison.thewliss.mp@parliament.uk
Website: www.appgdetention.org.uk
Twitter: @APPGDetention

Immigration Law and Policy

Chair: Stephen Timms *Lab*
Vice-chairs:
Adam Afriyie *Con*
Dr Stephen Farry *APNI*
Jonathan Lord *Con*
Stuart C McDonald *SNP*
Christina Rees *Lab/Co-op*

Contact: Stephen Timms, House of Commons, London SW1A 0AA Tel: 020 7219 4000
Email: timmss@parliament.uk

Inclusive Entrepreneurship

Chair: Dr Lisa Cameron *SNP*
Vice-Chairs:
Earl of Erroll *CB*
Baroness Grey-Thompson *CB*
Yasmin Qureshi *Lab*
Craig Tracey *Con*
Vice-Chairand Treasurer: Baroness Uddin *NA*

Contact: Dr Lisa Cameron, House of Commons, London SW1A 0AA Tel: 020 7219 6855
Email: lisa.cameron.mp@parliament.uk
Twitter: @APPG_IE

Independent Education

Chair: Andrew Lewer *Con*
Vice-chairs:
Brendan Clarke-Smith *Con*
Baroness Garden of Frognal *Lib Dem*
Ranil Jayawardena *Con*
Lord Knight of Weymouth *Lab/Co-op*
Michael Tomlinson *Con*
William Wragg *Con*

Contact: Andrew Lewer, House of Commons, London SW1A 0AA Tel: 020 7219 3870
Email: andrew.lewer.mp@parliament.uk

Indian Traditional Sciences

Chairs:
Bob Blackman *Con*
Virendra Sharma *Lab*
Vice-chairs:
Tanmanjeet Singh Dhesi *Lab*
Lord Hussain *Lib Dem*
Lord Ranger *Con*
Lord Sheikh *Con*
Baroness Uddin *NA*
Baroness Verma *Con*

Contact: Virendra Sharma, House of Commons, London SW1A 0AA Tel: 020 7219 6080
Email: sharmav@parliament.uk

Industrial Heritage

Chair: Stephanie Peacock *Lab*
Vice-chairs:
Wayne David *Lab*
Paul Howell *Con*
Andrew Lewer *Con*
Conor McGinn *Lab*
Jim McMahon *Lab/Co-op*
Secretary: Christina Rees *Lab/Co-op*

Contact: Stephanie Peacock, House of Commons, London SW1A 0AA
Tel: 020 7219 4129
Email: stephanie.peacock.mp@parliament.uk

Infant Feeding and Inequalities

Chair: Alison Thewliss *SNP*
Vice-chairs:
Fleur Anderson *Lab*
Kirsty Blackman *SNP*
Alex Davies-Jones *Lab*
Anneliese Dodds *Lab/Co-op*
Julie Elliott *Lab*
Sir Oliver Heald *Con*
Sharon Hodgson *Lab*
Julian Knight *Con*
Ben Lake *PlC*
Gavin Newlands *SNP*
Jonathan Reynolds *Lab/Co-op*
Gareth Thomas *Lab/Co-op*
Stephen Timms *Lab*

Contact: Alison Thewliss, 33 London Road, Glasgow G1 5NW Tel: 01415 527117
Email: alison.thewliss.mp@parliament.uk
Website: www.infantfeedingappg.uk
Twitter: @APPGIFI

Infrastructure

Chairs:
Alan Brown *SNP*
Andrew Jones *Con*
Officers:
Lord Berkeley *Lab*
Lord Chidgey *Lib Dem*
Stephen Hammond *Con*
Baroness Neville-Rolfe *Con*
Chi Onwurah *Lab*
Lord Stunell *Lib Dem*

Contact: Andrew Jones, House of Commons, London SW1A 0AA Tel: 020 7219 3000
Email: andrew.jones.mp@parliament.uk

Inheritance and Intergenerational Fairness

Chair: John Stevenson *Con*
Officers:
Sir George Howarth *Lab*
Holly Lynch *Lab*
Dr Matthew Offord *Con*

Contact: John Stevenson, House of Commons, London SW1A 0AA Tel: 020 7219 3000
Email: john.stevenson.mp@parliament.uk
Website: www.step.org/appg

Innovation Corridor

Chairs:
Julie Marson *Con*
Daniel Zeichner *Lab*
Vice-chair: Feryal Clark *Lab*
Secretaries:
Lord Harris of Haringey *Lab*
Lord Haselhurst *Con*

Contact: Daniel Zeichner, House of Commons, London SW1A 0AA Tel: 020 7219 8462
Email: daniel@danielzeichner.co.uk

Insurance and Financial Services

Chairs:
Lord Hunt of Wirral *Con*
Craig Tracey *Con*
Officers:
Sir Peter Bottomley *Con*
Barry Gardiner *Lab*
Rob Roberts *Con*
Christian Wakeford *Con*

Contact: Craig Tracey, House of Commons, London SW1A 0AA Tel: 020 7219 5646
Email: craig.tracey.mp@parliament.uk

Intellectual Property

Chair: Pete Wishart *SNP*
Vice-chairs:
Baroness Neville-Rolfe *Con*
John Whittingdale *Con*
Secretary: Dr Rupa Huq *Lab*
Treasurer: Lord Clement-Jones *Lib Dem*

Contact: Pete Wishart, House of Commons, London SW1A 0AA Tel: 020 7219 8303
Email: pete.wishart.mp@parliament.uk
Website: www.allpartyipgroup.org.uk

Intelligent Energy

Chair: Peter Aldous *Con*
Vice-chair: Lord Redesdale *Lib Dem*
Secretary: Alan Brown *SNP*
Treasurer: Dr Alan Whitehead *Lab*

Contact: Peter Aldous, House of Commons, London SW1A 0AA Tel: 020 7219 7182
Email: peter.aldous.mp@parliament.uk
Twitter: @appgie

International Conservation

Chairs:
Theo Clarke *Con*
Barry Gardiner *Lab*
Vice-chairs:
Bim Afolami *Con*
Ian Byrne *Lab*
Feryal Clark *Lab*
Rosie Duffield *Lab*
Chris Grayling *Con*
Kerry McCarthy *Lab*
Anna McMorrin *Lab*
Lord Randall of Uxbridge *Con*
Andrew Rosindell *Con*
Alex Sobel *Lab/Co-op*

Contact: Barry Gardiner, House of Commons, London SW1A 0AA Tel: 020 7219 4046
Email: gardinerb@parliament.uk

International Freedom of Religion or Belief

Chairs:
Baroness Cox *CB*
Preet Kaur Gill *Lab/Co-op*
Jim Shannon *DUP*
Vice-chairs:
Lord Alton of Liverpool *CB*
Baroness Anelay of St Johns *Con*
Fiona Bruce *Con*
Sir Jeffrey Donaldson *DUP*
Tommy Sheppard *SNP*
Lord Singh of Wimbledon *CB*
Alexander Stafford *Con*
Lord Suri *Con*
Secretaries:
Sir George Howarth *Lab*
Chris Matheson *Lab*
Brendan O'Hara *SNP*
Treasurer: Dr Lisa Cameron *SNP*

Contact: Jim Shannon, House of Commons, London SW1A 0AA Tel: 020 7219 7160
Email: jim.shannon.mp@parliament.uk
Website: appgfreedomofreligionorbelief.org
Twitter: @APPGFoRB

International Relations

Chair: Khalid Mahmood — *Lab*
Vice-chairs:
Afzal Khan — *Lab*
Bob Stewart — *Con*
Lord Taylor of Warwick — *NA*
Mohammad Yasin — *Lab*

Contact: Khalid Mahmood, House of Commons, London SW1A 0AA
Tel: 020 7219 8141
Email: mahmoodk@parliament.uk

International Students

Chairs:
Lord Bilimoria — *CB*
Paul Blomfield — *Lab*
Vice-chairs:
Alison Thewliss — *SNP*
Baroness Warwick of Undercliffe — *Lab*
Lord Willetts — *Con*
Secretary: Mark Logan — *Con*
Treasurer: Baroness Uddin — *NA*

Contact: Paul Blomfield, House of Commons, London SW1A 0AA Tel: 020 7219 7142
Email: paul.blomfield.mp@parliament.uk
Website: www.exeduk.com/appg-for-international-students
Twitter: @APPGIS

International Trade and Investment

Chair: Craig Williams — *Con*
Vice-chairs:
Gareth Bacon — *Con*
Chris Evans — *Lab/Co-op*
Lord Gold — *Con*
Mark Menzies — *Con*
Gagan Mohindra — *Con*
Baroness Northover — *Lib Dem*
Gary Sambrook — *Con*
Treasurer: Lord Davies of Gower — *Con*

Contact: Craig Williams, House of Commons, London SW1A 0AA Tel: 020 7219 3000
Email: craig.williams.mp@parliament.uk

Internet, Communications and Technology

Chairs:
Darren Jones — *Lab*
Baroness Neville-Rolfe — *Con*
Vice-chairs:
Lord Arbuthnot of Edrom — *Con*
Bob Blackman — *Con*
Sir Peter Bottomley — *Con*
Kevin Brennan — *Lab*
Lord Clement-Jones — *Lib Dem*
Lord Cotter — *Lib Dem*
Lord Cromwell — *CB*
Martyn Day — *SNP*
Tanmanjeet Singh Dhesi — *Lab*
Flick Drummond — *Con*
Chris Elmore — *Lab*
Bill Esterson — *Lab*
Lord Goddard of Stockport — *Lib Dem*
Lord Harris of Haringey — *Lab*
Kevin Hollinrake — *Con*
Jane Hunt — *Con*
John Lamont — *Con*
Lord Mackenzie of Framwellgate — *NA*
Anna McMorrin — *Lab*
Scott Mann — *Con*
Carol Monaghan — *SNP*
Chi Onwurah — *Lab*
Lord Patel — *CB*
Tulip Siddiq — *Lab*
Alex Sobel — *Lab/Co-op*
Lord Teverson — *Lib Dem*
Owen Thompson — *SNP*
Stephen Timms — *Lab*
Daniel Zeichner — *Lab*
Treasurer: Lord McNally — *Lib Dem*

Contact: Darren Jones, House of Commons, London SW1A 0AA Tel: 0117-959 6545
Email: darren.jones.mp@parliament.uk
Website: www.pictfor.org.uk
Twitter: @Pictfor

Islamic Finance

Chairs:
Naz Shah — *Lab*
Lord Sheikh — *Con*
Vice-chairs:
Lord Alderdice — *Lib Dem*
Baroness Bowles of Berkhamsted — *Lib Dem*
Lord Hussain — *Lib Dem*
Earl of Lindsay — *Con*
Wes Streeting — *Lab*
Stephen Timms — *Lab*
Secretary: Baroness Uddin — *NA*

Contact: Naz Shah, House of Commons, London SW1A 0AA Tel: 020 7219 8603
Email: naz.shah.mp@parliament.uk
Website: www.appgif.org.uk

ITV

Chairs:
Jason McCartney — *Con*
Ian Murray — *Lab*
Vice-chairs:
Lord Black of Brentwood — *Con*

Baroness Bonham-Carter of Yarnbury *Lib Dem*
Lord Dubs *Lab*
Emma Hardy *Lab*
Mark Menzies *Con*

Contact: Jason McCartney, House of Commons, London SW1A 0AA Tel: 020 7219 3000
Email: jason.mccartney.mp@parliament.uk

Key Cities

Chairs:
Julie Elliott *Lab*
John Stevenson *Con*
Vice-chairs:
Imran Ahmad Khan *Con*
Tracy Brabin *Lab/Co-op*
Stephen Morgan *Lab*
Jane Stevenson *Con*

Contact: John Stevenson, House of Commons, London SW1A 0AA Tel: 020 7219 3000
Email: john.stevenson.mp@parliament.uk

Knife Crime and Violence Reduction

Chairs:
Florence Eshalomi *Lab/Co-op*
Taiwo Owatemi *Lab*
Vice-chairs:
Felicity Buchan *Con*
Vicky Foxcroft *Lab*
Huw Merriman *Con*
Kate Osamor *Lab/Co-op*
Lord Paddick *Lib Dem*
Officers:
Imran Ahmad Khan *Con*
Fleur Anderson *Lab*
Crispin Blunt *Con*
Ian Byrne *Lab*
Ruth Cadbury *Lab*
Tanmanjeet Singh Dhesi *Lab*
Marcus Fysh *Con*
Jo Gideon *Con*
Helen Hayes *Lab*
Meg Hillier *Lab/Co-op*
Jason McCartney *Con*
Bell Ribeiro-Addy *Lab*
Claudia Webbe *Ind*

Contact: Florence Eshalomi, House of Commons, London SW1A 0AA
Tel: 020 7219 6552
Email: florence.eshalomi.mp@parliament.uk
Website: www.preventknifecrime.co.uk

Land Value Capture

Chairs:
Lord Greaves *Lib Dem*
Helen Hayes *Lab*
Kevin Hollinrake *Con*
Dr Caroline Lucas *Green*

Contact: Helen Hayes, House of Commons, London SW1A 0AA Tel: 020 7219 6971
Email: helen.hayes.mp@parliament.uk
Website: www.c4ej.com/appg

Learning Disability

Chair: Mark Harper *Con*
Vice-chairs:
Kate Green *Lab*
Baroness Hollins *CB*
Officers:
Lord Adebowale *CB*
Sir David Amess *Con*
Tonia Antoniazzi *Lab*
Dr Lisa Cameron *SNP*
Neil Coyle *Lab*
Bishop of Ely *NA*
Barbara Keeley *Lab*
Andy McDonald *Lab*
Stephen McPartland *Con*
Rachael Maskell *Lab/Co-op*
Maria Miller *Con*
Grahame Morris *Lab*
Barry Sheerman *Lab/Co-op*
Henry Smith *Con*
Baroness Thomas of Winchester *Lib Dem*
Lord Wigley *PlC*
Mike Wood *Con*
William Wragg *Con*

Contact: Mark Harper, House of Commons, London SW1A 0AA Tel: 020 7219 5056
Email: mark.harper.mp@parliament.uk
Website: www.mencap.org.uk/get-involved/campaign-mencap/our-work-parliament/all-party-parliamentary-group-learning-disability

Leasehold and Commonhold Reform

Chairs:
Sir Peter Bottomley *Con*
Sir Ed Davey *Lib Dem*
Justin Madders *Lab*
Vice-chairs:
Marie Rimmer *Lab*
Andrew Selous *Con*

Contact: Sir Peter Bottomley, House of Commons, London SW1A 0AA
Tel: 020 7219 5060
Email: bottomleyp@parliament.uk
Website: www.leaseholdknowledge.com/category/news/parliament/mps-appg-on-leasehold

"Left Behind" Neighbourhoods

Chairs:
Gill Furniss *Lab*
Paul Howell *Con*

Vice-Chairs:
Dame Diana Johnson *Lab*
Nicola Richards *Con*
Officers:
Jack Brereton *Con*
Sharon Hodgson *Lab*
Ian Levy *Con*

Contact: Paul Howell, House of Commons, London SW1A 0AA Tel: 020 7219 3000
Email: paul.howell.mp@parliament.uk
Website: www.appg-leftbehindneighbourhoods.org.uk
Twitter: @appgleftbehind

Legal Aid

Chair: Karen Buck *Lab*
Vice-chairs:
Lord Bach *Lab*
Gareth Bacon *Con*
Baroness Bennett of Manor Castle *Green*
Daisy Cooper *Lib Dem*
James Daly *Con*
Yvonne Fovargue *Lab*
Baroness Kennedy of The Shaws *Lab*
Lord Low of Dalston *CB*
Andy Slaughter *Lab*

Contact: Karen Buck, House of Commons, London SW1A 0AA Tel: 020 7219 3000
Email: buckk@parliament.uk
Website: www.apg-legalaid.org

Legal and Constitutional Affairs

Chairs:
Laura Farris *Con*
Lord Hunt of Wirral *Con*
Officers:
Joanna Cherry *SNP*
James Daly *Con*
Maria Eagle *Lab*
Kenny MacAskill *SNP*

Contact: Laura Farris, House of Commons, London SW1A 0AA Tel: 020 7219 3000
Email: laura.farris.mp@parliament.uk

Life Sciences

Chair: Daniel Zeichner *Lab*
Vice-chairs:
Anthony Browne *Con*
Chris Green *Con*
Officers:
Jerome Mayhew *Con*
Lord Patel *CB*

Contact: Daniel Zeichner, House of Commons, London SW1A 0AA Tel: 020 7219 8462
Email: daniel@danielzeichner.co.uk
Twitter: @LifeScienceAPPG

Light Rail

Chair: Andy Carter *Con*
Vice-chair: Stephen Metcalfe *Con*
Secretaries:
Stephen Hammond *Con*
Baroness Randerson *Lib Dem*
Treasurer: Clive Betts *Lab*
Officers:
Mike Amesbury *Lab*
Lord Faulkner of Worcester *Lab*
Drew Hendry *SNP*
Wera Hobhouse *Lib Dem*
Gavin Newlands *SNP*

Contact: Andy Carter, House of Commons, London SW1A 0AA Tel: 020 7219 3000
Email: andy.carter.mp@parliament.uk
Website: www.applrguk.co.uk

Limits to Growth

Chair: Dr Caroline Lucas *Green*
Vice-chair: Clive Lewis *Lab*
Officers:
Sir Peter Bottomley *Con*
Alison Thewliss *SNP*
Baroness Tyler of Enfield *Lib Dem*

Contact: Dr Caroline Lucas, House of Commons, London SW1A 0AA
Tel: 020 7219 7025
Email: caroline.lucas.mp@parliament.uk
Website: www.limits2growth.org.uk
Twitter: @appg_L2G

Listed Properties

Chair: Craig Mackinlay *Con*
Vice-chairs:
Lord Dear *CB*
Rosie Duffield *Lab*
Kevin Hollinrake *Con*
Chris Law *SNP*
Bill Wiggin *Con*
Hywel Williams *PlC*

Contact: Craig Mackinlay, House of Commons, London SW1A 0AA Tel: 020 7219 4442
Email: craig.mackinlay.mp@parliament.uk

Liver Health

Chairs:
Sir David Amess *Con*
Baroness Masham of Ilton *CB*
Baroness Randerson *Lib Dem*
Vice-chairs:
Sir Peter Bottomley *Con*
Lord Brooke of Alverthorpe *Lab*
Virendra Sharma *Lab*
Jeff Smith *Lab*

Contact: Sir David Amess, House of Commons, London SW1A 0AA Tel: 020 7219 3452
Email: amessd@parliament.uk
Website: www.appghep.org.uk
Twitter: @APPGLiverHealth

Liverpool City Region

Chair: Alison McGovern *Lab*
Vice-chairs:
Lord Alton of Liverpool *CB*
Mike Amesbury *Lab*
Paula Barker *Lab*
Ian Byrne *Lab*
Margaret Greenwood *Lab*
Lord Heseltine *NA*
Sir George Howarth *Lab*
Marie Rimmer *Lab*
Derek Twigg *Lab*
Mick Whitley *Lab*
Secretary: Conor McGinn *Lab*
Treasurer: Lord Hunt of Wirral *Con*

Contact: Alison McGovern, House of Commons, London SW1A 0AA
Tel: 020 7219 7190
Email: alison.mcgovern.mp@parliament.uk
Website: www.appglcr.org.uk
Twitter: @LCRAPPG

Loan Charge

Chairs:
Ruth Cadbury *Lab*
Sir Ed Davey *Lib Dem*
Sir Mike Penning *Con*
Vice-chairs:
Andrea Jenkyns *Con*
Baroness Kramer *Lib Dem*
Sammy Wilson *DUP*

Contact: Sir Ed Davey, House of Commons, London SW1A 0AA Tel: 020 7219 4530
Email: edward.davey.mp@parliament.uk
Website: www.loanchargeappg.co.uk
Twitter: @loanchargeAPPG

Local Authority Pension Funds

Chair: Clive Betts *Lab*
Vice-chairs:
Baroness Altmann *Con*
Lord Goddard of Stockport *Lib Dem*
Lord Kerslake *CB*
Secretary: David Simmonds *Con*

Contact: Clive Betts, House of Commons, London SW1A 0AA Tel: 020 7219 5114
Email: officeofclivebettsmp@parliament.uk
Website: www.appglocalpensionfunds.org

Local Democracy

Chairs:
Richard Holden *Con*
Cherilyn Mackrory *Con*
Vice-chair: Lord Greaves *Lib Dem*
Secretary: Earl of Lytton *CB*
Treasurer: Karen Buck *Lab*

Contact: Richard Holden, House of Commons, London SW1A 0AA Tel: 0207 219 3059
Email: richard.holden.mp@parliament.uk
Website: www.nalc.gov.uk/our-work/parliament-and-political-engagement

Local Government

Chair: Chris Clarkson *Con*
Vice-chairs:
Jack Brereton *Con*
Rachel Hopkins *Lab*
Secretary: Baroness Eaton *Con*
Treasurer: Lord Shipley *Lib Dem*

Contact: Chris Clarkson, House of Commons, London SW1A 0AA Tel: 020 7219 3000
Email: chris.clarkson.mp@parliament.uk
Website: www.lgiu.org/workstream/local-gov-appg

London

Chairs:
Sir Robert Neill *Con*
Steve Reed *Lab/Co-op*
Vice-chairs:
Florence Eshalomi *Lab/Co-op*
David Simmonds *Con*
Lord Tope *Lib Dem*
Secretary: Catherine West *Lab*

Contact: Sir Robert Neill, House of Commons, London SW1A 0AA Tel: 020 7219 8169
Email: bob.neill.mp@parliament.uk
Website: www.londoncouncils.gov.uk/appg
Twitter: @APPGforLondon

London's Planning and Built Environment

Chairs:
Dr Rupa Huq *Lab*
David Simmonds *Con*
Deputy Chairs:
Fleur Anderson *Lab*
Jon Cruddas *Lab*
Baroness Kramer *Lib Dem*
James Murray *Lab/Co-op*

Contact: Dr Rupa Huq, House of Commons, London SW1A 0AA Tel: 020 7219 6865
Email: rupa.huq.mp@parliament.uk

Loneliness
Chair: Neil O'Brien *Con*
Vice-chairs:
Dean Russell *Con*
Alison Thewliss *SNP*
Officers:
Lord Barwell *Con*
Karen Bradley *Con*
Jack Brereton *Con*
Baroness Greengross *CB*
Anne McLaughlin *SNP*
Alan Mak *Con*
Seema Malhotra *Lab/Co-op*
Jerome Mayhew *Con*
Kirsten Oswald *SNP*
Ellie Reeves *Lab*
Barry Sheerman *Lab/Co-op*
Liz Twist *Lab*
Matt Vickers *Con*
Giles Watling *Con*

Contact: Neil O'Brien, House of Commons, London SW1A 0AA Tel: 020 7219 1802
Email: neil.obrien.mp@parliament.uk

Longevity
Chair: Damian Green *Con*
Vice-chairs:
Sir Peter Bottomley *Con*
Baroness Cavendish of Little Venice *CB*
Lord Kerslake *CB*
Jonathan Lord *Con*
Lord O'Shaughnessy *Con*
Lord Willetts *Con*
Secretary: Lord Filkin *Lab*
Treasurer: Baroness Greengross *CB*

Contact: Damian Green, c/o Hardy House, The Street, Bethersden, Ashford TN26 3AG
Tel: 01233 820454
Website: www.appg-longevity.org
Twitter: @APPGLongevity

Looked After Children and Care Leavers
Chair: Steve McCabe *Lab*
Vice-chairs:
Tim Loughton *Con*
Baroness Young of Old Scone *Lab*
Officers:
Lucy Allan *Con*
Bill Esterson *Lab*
Marie Rimmer *Lab*
David Simmonds *Con*

Contact: Steve McCabe, House of Commons, London SW1A 0AA Tel: 020 7219 3509
Email: mccabes@parliament.uk
Website: www.becomecharity.org.uk/improving-the-care-system/appg

Malaria and Neglected Tropical Diseases
Chair: Catherine West *Lab*
Vice-chairs:
Tanmanjeet Singh Dhesi *Lab*
Baroness Hayman *CB*
Pauline Latham *Con*
Lord Trees *CB*

Contact: Catherine West, House of Commons, London SW1A 0AA Tel: 020 7219 6141
Email: catherine.west.mp@parliament.uk
Website: www.appg-malariantds.org.uk
Twitter: @MalariaNTDAPPG

Management
Chair: Barry Sheerman *Lab/Co-op*
Vice-chairs:
Lord Bilimoria *CB*
Kevin Hollinrake *Con*
Kirsten Oswald *SNP*
Richard Thomson *SNP*
Lord Young of Norwood Green *Lab*

Contact: Barry Sheerman, House of Commons, London SW1A 0AA Tel: 020 7219 5037
Email: sheermanb@parliament.uk

Greater Manchester
Chair: Lucy Powell *Lab/Co-op*
Vice-chairs:
Yvonne Fovargue *Lab*
Lord Goddard of Stockport *Lib Dem*
Afzal Khan *Lab*
Jim McMahon *Lab/Co-op*
Navendu Mishra *Lab*
Baroness Newlove *Con*
Secretary: Jonathan Reynolds *Lab/Co-op*
Treasurer: Yasmin Qureshi *Lab*

Contact: Lucy Powell, House of Commons, London SW1A 0AA Tel: 020 7219 4402
Email: contact@lucypowell.org.uk
Website: gmappg.org.uk
Twitter: @GMAPPG

Manufacturing
Chairs:
Jack Dromey *Lab*
Mark Pawsey *Con*
Vice-chairs:
Lord Bilimoria *CB*
Baroness Burt of Solihull *Lib Dem*
Vicky Ford *Con*
Drew Hendry *SNP*
Jonathan Reynolds *Lab/Co-op*
Barry Sheerman *Lab/Co-op*

Contact: Jack Dromey, House of Commons, London SW1A 0AA Tel: 020 7219 0903
Email: jack.dromey.mp@parliament.uk

Website: www.policyconnect.org.uk/apmg
Twitter: @TheAPMG

Marine Energy

Chair: Richard Graham *Con*
Vice-chairs:
Andrew Bowie *Con*
Deidre Brock *SNP*
Alan Brown *SNP*
Alistair Carmichael *Lib Dem*
Stephen Crabb *Con*
Virginia Crosbie *Con*
Simon Fell *Con*
Nusrat Ghani *Con*
Mark Jenkinson *Con*
Darren Jones *Lab*
Ben Lake *PlC*
Sheryll Murray *Con*
Bob Seely *Con*
Jim Shannon *DUP*
Secretary: Christine Jardine *Lib Dem*
Treasurer: Liz Saville Roberts *PlC*

Contact: Richard Graham, House of Commons, London SW1A 0AA Tel: 020 7219 7077
Email: richard.graham.mp@parliament.uk

Maritime and Ports

Chairs:
Jackie Doyle-Price *Con*
Lord Greenway *CB*
Deputy Chairs:
Natalie Elphicke *Con*
Stephen Hammond *Con*
Stephen Metcalfe *Con*
Stephen Morgan *Lab*
Lord Mountevans *CB*
Dr Alan Whitehead *Lab*
Secretary: Lord Berkeley *Lab*

Contact: Jackie Doyle-Price, House of Commons, London SW1A 0AA
Tel: 020 7219 7171
Email: jackie.doyleprice.mp@parliament.uk

Maternity

Chair: Sir David Amess *Con*
Vice-chair: Baroness Cumberlege *Con*
Officers:
Tulip Siddiq *Lab*
Alison Thewliss *SNP*

Contact: Sir David Amess, House of Commons, London SW1A 0AA Tel: 020 7219 3452
Email: amessd@parliament.uk

Mayflower 400

Chairs:
Anthony Mangnall *Con*
Luke Pollard *Lab/Co-op*
Vice-chairs:
Brendan Clarke-Smith *Con*
Simon Jupp *Con*
Sheryll Murray *Con*
Martin Vickers *Con*
Secretary: Lord Taylor of Holbeach *Con*
Officers:
Sir Peter Bottomley *Con*
Sir Gary Streeter *Con*
Treasurer: Lord Mann *NA*

Contact: Luke Pollard, House of Commons, London SW1A 0AA Tel: 020 7219 2749
Email: luke.pollard.mp@parliament.uk

Media

Chair: Andy Carter *Con*
Vice-chairs:
Lord Birt *CB*
Baroness Bottomley of Nettlestone *Con*
Sir Peter Bottomley *Con*
Alun Cairns *Con*
Dr Lisa Cameron *SNP*
Rosie Cooper *Lab*
Alex Davies-Jones *Lab*
Lord Foster of Bath *Lib Dem*
Sir Roger Gale *Con*
Andrew Griffith *Con*
Christine Jardine *Lib Dem*
Mark Logan *Con*
Mark Pritchard *Con*
Jamie Stone *Lib Dem*
Lord Taylor of Holbeach *Con*
Owen Thompson *SNP*

Contact: Andy Carter, House of Commons, London SW1A 0AA Tel: 020 7219 3000
Email: andy.carter.mp@parliament.uk
Website: www.appgmedia.org

Media Freedom

Chair: Damian Collins *Con*
Vice-chairs:
Lord Black of Brentwood *Con*
Theo Clarke *Con*
Lord Foulkes of Cumnock *Lab/Co-op*
Sir Roger Gale *Con*
Chris Matheson *Lab*

Contact: Damian Collins, House of Commons, London SW1A 0AA Tel: 020 7219 7072
Email: damian.collins.mp@parliament.uk

Media Literacy

Chairs:
Damian Collins *Con*
Lord Hastings of Scarisbrick *CB*
Vice-chairs:
Damian Hinds *Con*
Lord Knight of Weymouth *Lab/Co-op*

Siobhain McDonagh *Lab*
John Nicolson *SNP*

Contact: Damian Collins, House of Commons, London SW1A 0AA Tel: 020 7219 7072
Email: damian.collins.mp@parliament.uk

Medical Cannabis under Prescription

Chairs:
Tonia Antoniazzi *Lab*
Sir Mike Penning *Con*
Vice-chairs:
Ronnie Cowan *SNP*
Emma Hardy *Lab*
Baroness Meacher *CB*
Stephanie Peacock *Lab*

Contact: Sir Mike Penning, House of Commons, London SW1A 0AA
Tel: 020 7219 3000
Email: mike.penning.mp@parliament.uk
Twitter: @MedCannAPPG

Medical Research

Chair: Chris Green *Con*
Vice-chair: Daniel Zeichner *Lab*
Secretaries:
Anne Marie Morris *Con*
Lord Turnberg *Lab*
Treasurer: Lord Willis of Knaresborough *Lib Dem*

Contact: Chris Green, House of Commons, London SW1A 0AA Tel: 020 7219 8685
Email: chris.green.mp@parliament.uk
Website: www.amrc.org.uk/our-work/appg-medical-research

Medicines and Medical Devices

Chair: Anne Marie Morris *Con*
Officers:
Martyn Day *SNP*
Steve McCabe *Lab*
Baroness Masham of Ilton *CB*
Dr Dan Poulter *Con*
Lord Rennard *Lib Dem*
Andrew Selous *Con*
Jim Shannon *DUP*
Martin Vickers *Con*

Contact: Anne Marie Morris, House of Commons, London SW1A 0AA
Tel: 020 7219 3000
Email: annemarie.morris.mp@parliament.uk

Medomsley Detention Centre

Chair: Richard Holden *Con*
Vice-Chair: Baroness Armstrong of Hill Top *Lab*
Secretary: Rachael Maskell *Lab/Co-op*
Treasurer: Kevin Hollinrake *Con*

Contact: Richard Holden, House of Commons, London SW1A 0AA Tel: 020 7219 3059
Email: richard.holden.mp@parliament.uk

Mental Health

Chair: Jeff Smith *Lab*
Vice-chairs:
Virginia Crosbie *Con*
Baroness Hollins *CB*
Earl of Listowel *CB*
Marco Longhi *Con*
Rachael Maskell *Lab/Co-op*
Baroness Meacher *CB*
Dean Russell *Con*
Dr Ben Spencer *Con*
Baroness Tyler of Enfield *Lib Dem*
Officers:
Neil Coyle *Lab*
Helen Hayes *Lab*
Lord Moynihan *Con*
Matt Western *Lab*
Munira Wilson *Lib Dem*

Contact: Jeff Smith, House of Commons, London SW1A 0AA Tel: 020 7219 5878
Email: jeff.smith.mp@parliament.uk

Mentoring

Chairs:
Dr Lisa Cameron *SNP*
Lord Hastings of Scarisbrick *CB*
Vice-chairs:
Fleur Anderson *Lab*
Ian Paisley *DUP*
Lord Rennard *Lib Dem*
Officers:
Jim Shannon *DUP*
Alexander Stafford *Con*

Contact: Dr Lisa Cameron, House of Commons, London SW1A 0AA Tel: 020 7219 6855
Email: lisa.cameron.mp@parliament.uk
Twitter: @AppgMentoring

Mersey Dee North Wales

Chair: Dr James Davies *Con*
Vice-chairs:
Lord Jones *Lab*
David Jones *Con*
Justin Madders *Lab*
Rob Roberts *Con*

Contact: Dr James Davies, House of Commons, London SW1A 0AA Tel: 020 7219 3000
Email: james.davies.mp@parliament.uk

Metal, Stone and Heritage Crime

Chairs:
Lord Faulkner of Worcester *Lab*
Andrew Selous *Con*

Vice-chairs:
Lord Birt *CB*
Baroness Browning *Con*
Officer: Ruth Jones *Lab*

Contact: Andrew Selous, House of Commons, London SW1A 0AA Tel: 020 7219 8134
Email: andrew.selous.mp@parliament.uk
Website: www.recyclemetals.org/appgmshc.html

Micromobility
Chair: Elliot Colburn *Con*
Vice-Chairs:
Lord Berkeley *Lab*
Ben Everitt *Con*
Tom Hunt *Con*
Gary Sambrook *Con*
Virendra Sharma *Lab*

Contact: Elliot Colburn, House of Commons, London SW1A 0AA Tel: 020 7219 3000
Email: elliot.colburn.mp@parliament.uk
Twitter: @APPGmicromob

Microplastics
Chair: Alberto Costa *Con*
Vice-chairs:
Lord Brennan *NA*
Ruth Jones *Lab*
Liz Twist *Lab*
Secretary: Anne-Marie Trevelyan *Con*
Treasurer: Mark Pawsey *Con*

Contact: Alberto Costa, House of Commons, London SW1A 0AA Tel: 020 7219 4936
Email: alberto.costa.mp@parliament.uk
Website: www.thewi.org.uk/campaigns/key-and-current-campaigns/end-plastic-soup/all-party-parliamentary-group-on-microplastics
Twitter: @APPGPlastics

Midlands Engine
Chairs:
Darren Henry *Con*
Lord Ravensdale *CB*
Vice-Chairs:
Lilian Greenwood *Lab*
Kate Griffiths *Con*
Nicola Richards *Con*
Baroness Verma *Con*
Secretary: Karl McCartney *Con*

Contact: Darren Henry, House of Commons, London SW1A 0AA Tel: 020 7219 3000
Email: darren.henry.mp@parliament.uk

Migration
Chair: David Simmonds *Con*
Vice-chairs:
Steve Double *Con*
Bishop of Durham *NA*
Tim Farron *Lib Dem*
Baroness Hamwee *Lib Dem*
Lord Teverson *Lib Dem*
Secretary: Neil Coyle *Lab*

Contact: David Simmonds, House of Commons, London SW1A 0AA Tel: 020 7219 3000
Email: david.simmonds.mp@parliament.uk
Website: appgmigration.org.uk
Twitter: @APPGMigration

Mindfulness
Chairs:
Tim Loughton *Con*
Jessica Morden *Lab*
Vice-chairs:
Baroness Burt of Solihull *Lib Dem*
Tracey Crouch *Con*
Margaret Ferrier *Ind*
Baroness Harris of Richmond *Lib Dem*
Baroness Healy of Primrose Hill *Lab*
Lord Howarth of Newport *Lab*
Baroness Lawrence of Clarendon *Lab*
Baroness Lister of Burtersett *Lab*
Dr Caroline Lucas *Green*
Sir Desmond Swayne *Con*

Contact: Tim Loughton, House of Commons, London SW1A 0AA Tel: 020 7219 4471
Email: loughtont@parliament.uk
Website: www.themindfulnessinitiative.org/mindfulness-all-party-parliamentary-group

Miscarriages of Justice
Chair: Barry Sheerman *Lab/Co-op*
Vice-chair: Crispin Blunt *Con*
Officers:
Sir Robert Neill *Con*
Lucy Powell *Lab/Co-op*
Ellie Reeves *Lab*
Baroness Stern *CB*

Contact: Barry Sheerman, House of Commons, London SW1A 0AA Tel: 020 7219 5037
Email: sheermanb@parliament.uk
Website: www.appgmiscarriagesofjustice.wordpress.com
Twitter: @APPGMJ

Modern Languages
Chairs:
Nia Griffith *Lab*
Baroness Coussins *CB*
Vice-chairs:
Tonia Antoniazzi *Lab*
Lord Dykes *CB*
Baroness Garden of Frognal *Lib Dem*
Lord Sherbourne of Didsbury *Con*

Contact: Nia Griffith, House of Commons, London SW1A 0AA Tel: 020 7219 4903
Email: nia.griffith.mp@parliament.uk
Website: www.britishcouncil.org/education/schools/support-for-languages/thought-leadership/appg
Twitter: @APPGMFL

Mortgage Prisoners

Chairs:
Seema Malhotra *Lab/Co-op*
Lord Sharkey *Lib Dem*
Vice-chairs:
Feryal Clark *Lab*
Kevin Hollinrake *Con*

Contact: Seema Malhotra, House of Commons, London SW1A 0AA Tel: 020 7219 8957
Email: seema.malhotra.mp@parliament.uk
Website: www.appgmortgageprisoners.com
Twitter: @APPGMortgage

Motor

(Motor and motorsport industries)

Chair: Matt Western *Lab*
Vice-chairs:
Greg Clark *Con*
Jack Dromey *Lab*
Andrew Griffith *Con*
Julian Knight *Con*
Justin Madders *Lab*
Officers:
Lord Fox *Lib Dem*
Lord Hain *Lab*
Sharon Hodgson *Lab*
Baroness McIntosh of Pickering *Con*

Contact: Matt Western, House of Commons, London SW1A 0AA Tel: 020 7219 2051
Email: matt.western.mp@parliament.uk

Motor Neurone Disease

Chair: Andrew Lewer *Con*
Vice-chairs:
Brendan Clarke-Smith *Con*
Chris Evans *Lab/Co-op*
Christine Jardine *Lib Dem*
Mark Tami *Lab*
Secretary: Rosie Duffield *Lab*

Contact: Andrew Lewer, House of Commons, London SW1A 0AA Tel: 0207 219 3870
Email: andrew.lewer.mp@parliament.uk
Website: www.mndassociation.org/get-involved/campaigning-influencing/all-party-parliamentary-group-appg-on-mnd

Motorcycle Speedway

Chair: Nick Brown *Lab*
Vice-chairs:
Lord Snape *Lab*
James Wild *Con*
Secretary: Mark Pawsey *Con*

Contact: Nick Brown, House of Commons, London SW1A 0AA Tel: 020 7219 6814
Email: nickbrownmp@parliament.uk

Motorcycling

Chair: Chris Law *SNP*
Vice-chairs:
Fabian Hamilton *Lab*
Stewart Hosie *SNP*
Sammy Wilson *DUP*
Treasurer: Robert Goodwill *Con*

Contact: Chris Law, House of Commons, London SW1A 0AA
Email: chris.law.mp@parliament.uk

Motorsport

Chairs:
Lord Hain *Lab*
Karl McCartney *Con*
Greg Smith *Con*
James Sunderland *Con*
Vice-chairs:
Tracey Crouch *Con*
John Spellar *Lab*
Stephen Timms *Lab*
James Wild *Con*

Contact: Karl McCartney, House of Commons, London SW1A 0AA Tel: 020 7219 3000
Email: karl.mccartney.mp@parliament.uk
Website: www.parliamentary.racing

Mountaineering

Chair: Derek Twigg *Lab*
Vice-chair: Bob Stewart *Con*
Secretary: Lord Haworth *Lab*
Treasurer: Lilian Greenwood *Lab*

Contact: Derek Twigg, House of Commons, London SW1A 0AA Tel: 020 7219 1039
Email: derek.twigg.mp@parliament.uk

Multiple Sclerosis (MS)

Chair: Simon Hoare *Con*
Vice-chairs:
Lord Dubs *Lab*
Chris Law *SNP*
Lord Monks *Lab*
Christina Rees *Lab/Co-op*
Officers:
Alistair Carmichael *Lib Dem*
Helen Hayes *Lab*
Catherine McKinnell *Lab*

Angus MacNeil *SNP*
Ian Mearns *Lab*
Gavin Robinson *DUP*
Andrew Selous *Con*

Contact: Simon Hoare, House of Commons, London SW1A 0AA Tel: 020 7219 5697
Email: simon.hoare.mp@parliament.uk

Muscular Dystrophy
Chair: Mary Glindon *Lab*
Vice-chairs:
Dame Cheryl Gillan *Con*
Jim Shannon *DUP*
Baroness Thomas of Winchester *Lib Dem*
Liz Twist *Lab*

Contact: Mary Glindon, House of Commons, London SW1A 0AA Tel: 020 7219 3000
Email: mary.glindon.mp@parliament.uk

Museums
Chair: Chris Skidmore *Con*
Vice-chairs:
Felicity Buchan *Con*
Theo Clarke *Con*
Lord Faulkner of Worcester *Lab*
Alison McGovern *Lab*
Alison Thewliss *SNP*
Secretary: Chris Bryant *Lab*
Treasurer: Kim Johnson *Lab*

Contact: Chris Skidmore, House of Commons, London SW1A 0AA Tel: 020 7219 7094
Email: chris.skidmore.mp@parliament.uk
Website: www.nationalmuseums.org.uk/what-we-do/museums-appg
Twitter: @AppgMuseums

Music
Chairs:
Kevin Brennan *Lab*
Sharon Hodgson *Lab*
David Warburton *Con*
Pete Wishart *SNP*
Vice-chairs:
Sir Peter Bottomley *Con*
Dawn Butler *Lab*
Lord Clement-Jones *Lib Dem*
Dehenna Davison *Con*
Dr Rupa Huq *Lab*
Jack Lopresti *Con*
Kerry McCarthy *Lab*
David Morris *Con*
Jeff Smith *Lab*
Alex Sobel *Lab/Co-op*
Lord Tyrie *NA*
Valerie Vaz *Lab*
Lord Watts *Lab*
Secretary: Conor McGinn *Lab*
Treasurer: Andrea Jenkyns *Con*

Contact: David Warburton, House of Commons, London SW1A 0AA Tel: 020 7219 5229
Email: david.warburton.mp@parliament.uk
Website: allpartymusicgroup.org.uk

Music Education
Chairs:
Lord Black of Brentwood *Con*
Dame Diana Johnson *Lab*
Vice-chairs:
Lord Aberdare *CB*
Baroness Bonham-Carter of Yarnbury *Lib Dem*
Earl of Clancarty *CB*
Alex Davies-Jones *Lab*
Baroness Finlay of Llandaff *CB*
Sharon Hodgson *Lab*
Baroness Nicholson of Winterbourne *Con*
David Warburton *Con*

Contact: Dame Diana Johnson, House of Commons, London SW1A 0AA
Tel: 020 7219 5647
Email: johnsond@parliament.uk

Muslim Women
Chairs:
Caroline Nokes *Con*
Naz Shah *Lab*
Vice-chairs:
Nusrat Ghani *Con*
Jess Phillips *Lab*
Officers:
Apsana Begum *Lab*
Baroness Hussein-Ece *Lib Dem*
Afzal Khan *Lab*

Contact: Naz Shah, House of Commons, London SW1A 0AA Tel: 020 7219 8603
Email: naz.shah.mp@parliament.uk
Website: www.mwnuk.co.uk/appg.php

British Muslims
Chairs:
Mark Eastwood *Con*
Wes Streeting *Lab*
Vice-chairs:
Steve Baker *Con*
Tanmanjeet Singh Dhesi *Lab*
Colleen Fletcher *Lab*
Afzal Khan *Lab*
Mark Logan *Con*
Kirsten Oswald *SNP*
Naz Shah *Lab*
Treasurer: Baroness Warsi *Con*

Contact: Wes Streeting, House of Commons, London SW1A 0AA Tel: 020 7219 6132

Email: wes.streeting.mp@parliament.uk
Website: appgbritishmuslims.org
Twitter: @APPGBritMuslims

Myalgic Encephalomyelitis (ME)

Chairs:
Sharon Hodgson *Lab*
Stephen Metcalfe *Con*
Carol Monaghan *SNP*
Vice-chair: Ben Lake *PlC*
Secretary: Hywel Williams *PlC*
Treasurer: Olivia Blake *Lab*

Contact: Carol Monaghan, House of Commons, London SW1A 0AA Tel: 020 7219 6396
Email: carol.monaghan.mp@parliament.uk

National Food Strategy

Chair: Jo Gideon *Con*
Vice-chairs:
Ian Byrne *Lab*
Earl of Caithness *Con*
Sharon Hodgson *Lab*
Kerry McCarthy *Lab*
Lord McColl of Dulwich *Con*
Dean Russell *Con*
Selaine Saxby *Con*

Contact: Jo Gideon, House of Commons, London SW1A 0AA Tel: 020 7219 8131
Email: jo.gideon.mp@parliament.uk

Nature

Chair: Barry Gardiner *Lab*
Officers:
Steve Double *Con*
Dr Caroline Lucas *Green*
Kerry McCarthy *Lab*
Baroness Young of Old Scone *Lab*

Contact: Barry Gardiner, House of Commons, London SW1A 0AA Tel: 020 7219 4046
Email: gardinerb@parliament.uk
Website: www.cieem.net/i-am/influencing-policy/appg-for-nature

Net Zero

Chair: Alex Sobel *Lab/Co-op*
Vice-chairs:
Duncan Baker *Con*
Sara Britcliffe *Con*
Rosie Duffield *Lab*
Vicky Ford *Con*
Sir Bernard Jenkin *Con*
Kerry McCarthy *Lab*
Anna McMorrin *Lab*
Lord Teverson *Lib Dem*
Liz Twist *Lab*
Secretary: Angus MacNeil *SNP*
Treasurer: Helen Hayes *Lab*

Contact: Alex Sobel, House of Commons, London SW1A 0AA Tel: 020 7219 8295
Email: alex.sobel.mp@parliament.uk
Website: www.netzeroappg.org.uk

Netball

Chair: Gareth Johnson *Con*
Vice-chairs:
Tonia Antoniazzi *Lab*
Peter Bone *Con*
Chris Bryant *Lab*

Contact: Gareth Johnson, House of Commons, London SW1A 0AA Tel: 020 7219 7047
Email: gareth.johnson.mp@parliament.uk
Website: appgnetball.org.uk
Twitter: @AppgNetball

Northern Powerhouse

Chairs:
Julie Elliott *Lab*
Kevin Hollinrake *Con*
Catherine McKinnell *Lab*
John Stevenson *Con*
Vice-chairs:
Mike Amesbury *Lab*
Baroness Armstrong of Hill Top *Lab*
Lord Goddard of Stockport *Lib Dem*
Jason McCartney *Con*
Lord O'Neill of Gatley *CB*
Treasurer: Mark Jenkinson *Con*

Contact: Julie Elliott, House of Commons, London SW1A 0AA Tel: 020 7219 7165
Email: julie.elliott.mp@parliament.uk
Website: www.northernpowerhouseappg.org.uk
Twitter: @NPAPPG

Nuclear Energy

Chair: Ian Liddell-Grainger *Con*
Vice-chairs:
Peter Aldous *Con*
Lord Broers *CB*
Neil Coyle *Lab*
Simon Fell *Con*
Viscount Hanworth *Lab*
Trudy Harrison *Con*
Mike Hill *Lab*
Mark Jenkinson *Con*
Mark Menzies *Con*
Layla Moran *Lib Dem*
Baroness Neville-Rolfe *Con*
Charlotte Nichols *Lab*
Lord Ravensdale *CB*
Liz Saville Roberts *PlC*
John Stevenson *Con*
Jamie Stone *Lib Dem*
John Whittingdale *Con*

Contact: Ian Liddell-Grainger, House of Commons, London SW1A 0AA
Tel: 020 7219 8149 Email: ianlg@parliament.uk

Nursery Schools, Nursery and Reception Classes
Chair: Lucy Powell *Lab/Co-op*
Vice-chair: William Wragg *Con*
Secretary: Jack Dromey *Lab*
Treasurer: Steve Brine *Con*

Contact: Lucy Powell, House of Commons, London SW1A 0AA Tel: 020 7219 4402
Email: contact@lucypowell.org.uk
Website: www.early-education.org.uk/all-party-parliamentary-group-nursery-schools-nursery-and-reception-classes
Twitter: @APPG_Nursery

Nutrition for Growth
Chairs:
Lord Collins of Highbury *Lab*
David Linden *SNP*
Baroness Manzoor *Con*
Vice-chairs:
Lord Cameron of Dillington *CB*
Greg Hands *Con*
Jessica Morden *Lab*
David Mundell *Con*

Contact: David Linden, House of Commons, London SW1A 0AA Tel: 020 7219 1801
Email: david.linden.mp@parliament.uk
Website: appg-n4g.org.uk
Twitter: @APPGNutrition

Obesity
Chair: Mary Glindon *Lab*
Vice-chairs:
Lord Brooke of Alverthorpe *Lab*
Dr James Davies *Con*
Baroness Jenkin of Kennington *Con*
Jim Shannon *DUP*
Baroness Walmsley *Lib Dem*

Contact: Mary Glindon, Swans Centre for Innovation, Station Road, Wallsend NE28 6HJ
Tel: 01912 342493
Website: www.obesityappg.com
Twitter: @ObesityAPPG

Occupational Safety and Health
President: Lord Hunt of Wirral *Con*
Chair: Jo Stevens *Lab*
Vice-chair: Lord McKenzie of Luton *Lab*
Honorary Secretary: Martin Docherty-Hughes *SNP*

Contact: Jo Stevens, House of Commons, London SW1A 0AA Tel: 020 7219 8290
Email: jo.stevens.mp@parliament.uk

Ocean Conservation
Chair: Steve Double *Con*
Vice-chairs:
Geraint Davies *Lab/Co-op*
Dr Caroline Lucas *Green*
Kerry McCarthy *Lab*
Cherilyn Mackrory *Con*
Secretary: Derek Thomas *Con*
Treasurer: Scott Mann *Con*

Contact: Steve Double, House of Commons, London SW1A 0AA Tel: 020 7219 4408
Email: steve.double.mp@parliament.uk

Olympic and Paralympic Games
Chairs:
Sir David Amess *Con*
Lord Moynihan *Con*
Vice-chairs:
Lord Addington *Lib Dem*
Lord Bates *Con*
Sir Peter Bottomley *Con*
Dr Lisa Cameron *SNP*
Lord Campbell of Pittenweem *Lib Dem*
Feryal Clark *Lab*
Lord Coe *Con*
Baroness Doocey *Lib Dem*
Baroness Grey-Thompson *CB*
Lord Hunt of Kings Heath *Lab/Co-op*
Christina Rees *Lab/Co-op*
Lord Stone of Blackheath *NA*
Vice-Chairand Chair of Working Group on Tokyo Olympic and Paralympic Games: Lord McConnell of Glenscorrodale *Lab*

Contact: Sir David Amess, House of Commons, London SW1A 0AA Tel: 020 7219 3452
Email: amessd@parliament.uk

Online and Home Electrical Safety
Chair: Carolyn Harris *Lab*
Vice-chair: Yvonne Fovargue *Lab*
Vice-chairand Secretary: Derek Thomas *Con*
Treasurer: Gerald Jones *Lab*
Officers:
Margaret Ferrier *Ind*
Lord Tope *Lib Dem*

Contact: Carolyn Harris, House of Commons, London SW1A 0AA Tel: 020 7219 4316
Email: carolyn.harris.mp@parliament.uk
Twitter: @APPGElecSafety

Open Banking and Payments
Chair: Ian Liddell-Grainger *Con*
Vice-Chairs:
Lord Cromwell *CB*
Simon Fell *Con*
Earl of Lindsay *Con*

Chi Onwurah *Lab*
Treasurer: Lord Sharkey *Lib Dem*

Contact: Ian Liddell-Grainger, House of Commons, London SW1A 0AA
Tel: 020 7219 8149 Email: ianlg@parliament.uk

Opera
Chair: Sir Robert Neill *Con*
Vice-chairs:
Lord Aberdare *CB*
Lord Trimble *Con*
Baroness Whitaker *Lab*
Secretaries:
Nick Brown *Lab*
Mark Pritchard *Con*

Contact: Sir Robert Neill, House of Commons, London SW1A 0AA Tel: 020 7219 8169
Email: bob.neill.mp@parliament.uk

Oracy
Chair: Emma Hardy *Lab*
Officers:
Tanmanjeet Singh Dhesi *Lab*
Ian Mearns *Lab*
Stephanie Peacock *Lab*
William Wragg *Con*

Contact: Emma Hardy, House of Commons, London SW1A 0AA
Email: emma.hardy.mp@parliament.uk
Website: www.oracyappg.org.uk
Twitter: @AppgOracy

Outdoor Learning
Chairs:
Tim Farron *Lib Dem*
Robin Millar *Con*
Vice-chairs:
Simon Baynes *Con*
Virginia Crosbie *Con*
Richard Drax *Con*
Dr Neil Hudson *Con*
Jessica Morden *Lab*
Liz Saville Roberts *PlC*
Hywel Williams *PlC*

Contact: Robin Millar, House of Commons, London SW1A 0AA Tel: 020 7219 3000
Email: robin.millar.mp@parliament.uk

Ovarian Cancer
Chair: Sharon Hodgson *Lab*
Vice-chairs:
Paul Bristow *Con*
Lord Clement-Jones *Lib Dem*
Alex Davies-Jones *Lab*
Christina Rees *Lab/Co-op*
Lee Rowley *Con*
Henry Smith *Con*
Alison Thewliss *SNP*

Contact: Sharon Hodgson, House of Commons, London SW1A 0AA Tel: 020 7219 5160
Email: sharon.hodgson.mp@parliament.uk
Website: targetovariancancer.org.uk/appg

Packaging Manufacturing Industry
Chair: Mark Pawsey *Con*
Vice-chairs:
Peter Aldous *Con*
Anna McMorrin *Lab*
Secretary: Tom Tugendhat *Con*
Treasurer: Gerald Jones *Lab*

Contact: Mark Pawsey, House of Commons, London SW1A 0AA Tel: 020 7219 7136
Email: mark.pawsey.mp@parliament.uk

Pakistani Minorities
Chairs:
Lord Alton of Liverpool *CB*
Jim Shannon *DUP*
Vice-chairs:
Steve Reed *Lab/Co-op*
Lord Singh of Wimbledon *CB*
Secretary: Martyn Day *SNP*
Treasurer: Fiona Bruce *Con*

Contact: Jim Shannon, House of Commons, London SW1A 0AA Tel: 020 7219 7160
Email: jim.shannon.mp@parliament.uk

Pancreatic Cancer
Chair: Jim Shannon *DUP*
Vice-chairs:
Lord Aberdare *CB*
Colleen Fletcher *Lab*
Sir George Howarth *Lab*
Lord Patel *CB*
Lord Porter of Spalding *Con*
Officer: Henry Smith *Con*

Contact: Jim Shannon, House of Commons, London SW1A 0AA Tel: 020 7219 7160
Email: jim.shannon.mp@parliament.uk
Website: www.pancanappg.org.uk

PANS and PANDAS
Chair: Ruth Cadbury *Lab*
Vice-Chairs:
Robin Millar *Con*
Munira Wilson *Lib Dem*
Officers:
Baroness Boycott *CB*
Lord Dubs *Lab*

Contact: Ruth Cadbury, House of Commons, London SW1A 0AA Tel: 020 7219 8590

Email: ruthcadburymp@parliament.uk
Website: www.panspandasuk.org/appg

Parental Participation in Education
Chair: Ian Mearns *Lab*
Vice-chairs:
Baroness Blower *Lab*
John McDonnell *Lab*
Tom Tugendhat *Con*

Contact: Ian Mearns, House of Commons, London SW1A 0AA Tel: 020 7219 7074
Email: ian.mearns.mp@parliament.uk

Park Homes
Chair: Sir Christopher Chope *Con*
Vice-chairs:
Peter Aldous *Con*
Sir Peter Bottomley *Con*
Lord Carter of Coles *Lab*
Alex Sobel *Lab/Co-op*

Contact: Sir Christopher Chope, House of Commons, London SW1A 0AA
Tel: 020 7219 5808
Email: chopec@parliament.uk
Website: www.parkhome.org.uk/appg

Parkinson's
Chairs:
Mary Glindon *Lab*
Baroness Gale *Lab*
Vice-chairs:
Seema Malhotra *Lab/Co-op*
Baroness Masham of Ilton *CB*
Sheryll Murray *Con*
Nick Thomas-Symonds *Lab*
Secretary: Sir David Amess *Con*
Treasurer: Baroness Finlay of Llandaff *CB*

Contact: Mary Glindon, Swans Centre for Innovation, Station Road, Wallsend NE28 6HJ
Tel: 01912 342493
Website: www.parkinsons.org.uk

Parkrun
Chair: Nick Smith *Lab*
Vice-chair: Alun Cairns *Con*
Officers:
Tonia Antoniazzi *Lab*
Janet Daby *Lab*
Wayne David *Lab*
Thangam Debbonaire *Lab*
Gerald Jones *Lab*
David Linden *SNP*
Chris Matheson *Lab*
Alex Norris *Lab/Co-op*
Nicola Richards *Con*

Contact: Nick Smith, House of Commons, London SW1A 0AA Tel: 020 7219 7018
Email: nick.smith.mp@parliament.uk

Parks and Green Spaces
Chair: Lilian Greenwood *Lab*
Vice-chairs:
Fleur Anderson *Lab*
Bob Blackman *Con*
Ian Byrne *Lab*
Rosie Duffield *Lab*
Helen Hayes *Lab*
Sir John Hayes *Con*
Liz Twist *Lab*
Matt Western *Lab*

Contact: Lilian Greenwood, House of Commons, London SW1A 0AA
Tel: 020 7219 7122
Email: lilian.greenwood.mp@parliament.uk

Peak District
Chair: Robert Largan *Con*
Vice-chairs:
Karen Bradley *Con*
Chris Clarkson *Con*
Nigel Mills *Con*
Jonathan Reynolds *Lab/Co-op*

Contact: Robert Largan, House of Commons, London SW1A 0AA Tel: 020 7219 3000
Email: robert.largan.mp@parliament.uk

Penal Affairs
Chairs:
Paul Maynard *Con*
Lord Ramsbotham *CB*
Vice-chairs:
Lord Beecham *Lab*
Marie Rimmer *Lab*
Andrew Selous *Con*
Secretary: Lord Hodgson of Astley Abbotts *Con*

Contact: Paul Maynard, House of Commons, London SW1A 0AA Tel: 020 7219 7017
Email: paul.maynard.mp@parliament.uk
Website: www.prisonreformtrust.org.uk/presspolicy/parliament/allpartyparliamentarypenalaffairsgroup

Pension Scams
Chair: Bob Blackman *Con*
Vice-chairs:
Lord Kirkhope of Harrogate *Con*
Rob Roberts *Con*
Nick Smith *Lab*

Contact: Bob Blackman, House of Commons, London SW1A 0AA Tel: 020 7219 7082

Email: bob.blackman.mp@parliament.uk
Twitter: @APPGpensionscam

Pensions
Chair: Nigel Mills *Con*
Vice-chairs:
Baroness Altmann *Con*
Baroness Drake *Lab*
Chris Elmore *Lab*
Neale Hanvey *SNP*
David Simmonds *Con*
Richard Thomson *SNP*

Contact: Nigel Mills, House of Commons, London SW1A 0AA Tel: 020 7219 7233
Email: nigel.mills.mp@parliament.uk

Performers' Alliance
Chair: Alison McGovern *Lab*
Officers:
Deidre Brock *SNP*
Earl of Clancarty *CB*
Lord Clement-Jones *Lib Dem*
Damian Collins *Con*
Thangam Debbonaire *Lab*
Kerry McCarthy *Lab*
Baroness McIntosh of Hudnall *Lab*
Ian Murray *Lab*
David Warburton *Con*
Giles Watling *Con*
Pete Wishart *SNP*

Contact: Alison McGovern, House of Commons, London SW1A 0AA
Tel: 020 7219 7190
Email: alison.mcgovern.mp@parliament.uk

Period Equality
Chair: Ruth Cadbury *Lab*
Vice-chair: Sir Peter Bottomley *Con*
Officers:
Debbie Abrahams *Lab*
Rachel Hopkins *Lab*

Contact: Ruth Cadbury, House of Commons, London SW1A 0AA Tel: 020 7219 8590
Email: ruthcadburymp@parliament.uk

Personal Banking and Fairer Financial Services
Chair: Peter Gibson *Con*
Vice-chairs:
Tonia Antoniazzi *Lab*
Aaron Bell *Con*
Kevin Hollinrake *Con*
Robert Largan *Con*

Contact: Peter Gibson, House of Commons, London SW1A 0AA Tel: 020 7219 3000
Email: peter.gibson.mp@parliament.uk

Personalised Medicine
Chairs:
Sir David Amess *Con*
Lord Warner *CB*
Vice-chairs:
Lord Hunt of Kings Heath *Lab/Co-op*
Chi Onwurah *Lab*
Lord Patel *CB*
Treasurer: Lord Willis of Knaresborough *Lib Dem*

Contact: Sir David Amess, House of Commons, London SW1A 0AA Tel: 020 7219 3452
Email: amessd@parliament.uk
Website: www.personalisedmedicineappg.org
Twitter: @personmedAPPG

Pharmacy
Chair: Jackie Doyle-Price *Con*
Officers:
Sir David Amess *Con*
Paul Bristow *Con*
Feryal Clark *Lab*
Lord Clement-Jones *Lib Dem*
Baroness Cumberlege *Con*
Jason McCartney *Con*
Taiwo Owatemi *Lab*
Julian Sturdy *Con*

Contact: Jackie Doyle-Price, House of Commons, London SW1A 0AA
Tel: 020 7219 7171
Email: jackie.doyleprice.mp@parliament.uk
Website: www.pharmacyappg.co.uk
Twitter: @APPGPharmacy

Philanthropy and Social Investment
Chair: Rushanara Ali *Lab*
Vice-chairs:
Tom Hunt *Con*
Lord Janvrin *CB*
Baroness Kennedy of The Shaws *Lab*
Baroness Pitkeathley *Lab*
Baroness Prashar *CB*
Baroness Royall of Blaisdon *Lab/Co-op*
Lord Triesman *Lab*
Lord Wasserman *Con*
Lord Wei *Con*

Contact: Rushanara Ali, House of Commons, London SW1A 0AA Tel: 020 7219 7200
Email: rushanara.ali.mp@parliament.uk

Philately
Chair: Andrew Rosindell *Con*
Vice-chairs:
Sir David Amess *Con*
Sir Jeffrey Donaldson *DUP*
Alexander Stafford *Con*

Lord West of Spithead *Lab*
Secretary: Lord Jones of Cheltenham *Lib Dem*

Contact: Andrew Rosindell, House of Commons, London SW1A 0AA
Tel: 020 7219 8475
Email: andrew.rosindell.mp@parliament.uk

Photography
Chairs:
Sir David Amess *Con*
Lord Robertson of Port Ellen *Lab*
Vice-chair: Tim Loughton *Con*
Secretary: Lord Crathorne *Con*
Treasurer: Viscount Simon *Lab*
Officer: Sir Peter Bottomley *Con*

Contact: Sir David Amess, House of Commons, London SW1A 0AA Tel: 020 7219 3452
Email: amessd@parliament.uk

Photonics and Quantum
Chair: Carol Monaghan *SNP*
Vice-chairs:
Douglas Chapman *SNP*
Kevan Jones *Lab*
Secretary: Marcus Fysh *Con*
Treasurer: Chris Green *Con*

Contact: Carol Monaghan, House of Commons, London SW1A 0AA Tel: 020 7219 6396
Email: carol.monaghan.mp@parliament.uk

Pigeon Racing
Chair: Craig Williams *Con*
Vice-chairs:
Chris Evans *Lab/Co-op*
Jim Shannon *DUP*
Officers:
Alex Chalk *Con*
Conor McGinn *Lab*
Lord Moynihan *Con*
Lord Naseby *Con*

Contact: Craig Williams, House of Commons, London SW1A 0AA Tel: 020 7219 3000
Email: craig.williams.mp@parliament.uk

Policing and Security
Chairs:
Sir Paul Beresford *Con*
Lord Harris of Haringey *Lab*
Vice-chairs:
Judith Cummins *Lab*
Dr John Howell *Con*
Secretary: Baroness Harris of Richmond *Lib Dem*

Contact: Sir Paul Beresford, House of Commons, London SW1A 0AA
Tel: 020 7219 5018
Email: annie.winsbury@parliament.uk

Polo
Chair: Mark Garnier *Con*
Vice-chairs:
Lord Astor of Hever *Con*
Nusrat Ghani *Con*
James Gray *Con*
Chris Matheson *Lab*
Caroline Nokes *Con*

Contact: Mark Garnier, House of Commons, London SW1A 0AA Tel: 020 7219 7198
Email: mark.garnier.mp@parliament.uk

Population, Development and Reproductive Health
Chair: Pauline Latham *Con*
Vice-chairs:
Baroness Hussein-Ece *Lib Dem*
Holly Lynch *Lab*
Baroness Northover *Lib Dem*
Lord Patel *CB*
Secretaries:
Tommy Sheppard *SNP*
Baroness Uddin *NA*
Treasurers:
Baroness Jenkin of Kennington *Con*
Virendra Sharma *Lab*
Officers:
Baroness Barker *Lib Dem*
Baroness Blackstone *Lab Ind*
Lord Cameron of Dillington *CB*
Baroness Flather *CB*
Lord Hussain *Lib Dem*
Lord Mann *NA*
Baroness Massey of Darwen *Lab*
Baroness Sheehan *Lib Dem*

Contact: Pauline Latham, House of Commons, London SW1A 0AA Tel: 020 7219 7110
Email: pauline.latham.mp@parliament.uk
Website: www.appg-popdevrh.org.uk
Twitter: @APPGPopDevRep

Post Offices
Chair: Marion Fellows *SNP*
Vice-chairs:
Dame Diana Johnson *Lab*
Kevan Jones *Lab*
Derek Thomas *Con*
Secretary: Lord Arbuthnot of Edrom *Con*
Treasurer: Lord Hain *Lab*

Contact: Marion Fellows, House of Commons, London SW1A 0AA Tel: 020 7219 5784
Email: marion.fellows.mp@parliament.uk

Post-Brexit Funding for Nations, Regions and Local Areas

Chair: Stephen Kinnock *Lab*
Vice-chairs:
Anna McMorrin *Lab*
Scott Mann *Con*
Christina Rees *Lab/Co-op*
Nick Smith *Lab*
Chris Stephens *SNP*

Contact: Stephen Kinnock, House of Commons, London SW1A 0AA Tel: 020 7219 8801
Email: stephen.kinnock.mp@parliament.uk
Website: www.postbrexitappg.org

Poverty

Chairs:
Neil Gray *SNP*
Kevin Hollinrake *Con*
Vice-chairs:
Lord Bird *CB*
Lyn Brown *Lab*
Afzal Khan *Lab*
Baroness Lister of Burtersett *Lab*
Tony Lloyd *Lab*

Contact: Kevin Hollinrake, House of Commons, London SW1A 0AA Tel: 020 7219 4746
Email: kevin.hollinrake.mp@parliament.uk
Twitter: @APPGPoverty

Premature and Sick Babies

Chair: David Linden *SNP*
Vice-chairs:
Alex Davies-Jones *Lab*
Darren Henry *Con*
Sharon Hodgson *Lab*
Ranil Jayawardena *Con*
Lord Moynihan *Con*

Contact: David Linden, House of Commons, London SW1A 0AA Tel: 020 7219 1801
Email: david.linden.mp@parliament.uk
Website: neonatalappg.org.uk
Twitter: @NeonatalAPPG

Prescribed Drug Dependence

Chairs:
Lord Crisp *CB*
Danny Kruger *Con*
Officers:
Debbie Abrahams *Lab*
Steve Brine *Con*
Baroness Hollins *CB*
Baroness Masham of Ilton *CB*
Lucy Powell *Lab/Co-op*
Earl of Sandwich *CB*
Baroness Stroud *Con*

Contact: Danny Kruger, House of Commons, London SW1A 0AA Tel: 020 7219 7050
Email: danny.kruger.mp@parliament.uk
Website: prescribeddrug.org

Preventing Sexual Violence in Conflict Initiative

Chair: Anthony Mangnall *Con*
Vice-chairs:
Nickie Aiken *Con*
Fleur Anderson *Lab*
Baroness Hodgson of Abinger *Con*
Baroness Uddin *NA*
Treasurer: Chris Clarkson *Con*

Contact: Anthony Mangnall, House of Commons, London SW1A 0AA
Tel: 020 7219 5579
Email: anthony.mangnall.mp@parliament.uk

Private Rented Sector

Chair: Andrew Lewer *Con*
Vice-chairs:
Karen Buck *Lab*
Baroness Grender *Lib Dem*
Kevin Hollinrake *Con*

Contact: Andrew Lewer, House of Commons, London SW1A 0AA Tel: 020 7219 3870
Email: andrew.lewer.mp@parliament.uk

Professional Sales

Chair: Mark Pawsey *Con*
Vice-Chairs:
Robert Courts *Con*
Martyn Day *SNP*
Dr Peter Kyle *Lab*
Jack Lopresti *Con*
Jim Shannon *DUP*

Contact: Mark Pawsey, Albert Buildings, 2 Castle Mews, Rugby CV21 2XL
Tel: 01788 579499
Website: www.the-aps.com/appg

Pro-Life

(In relation to abortion, euthanasia and research on the human embryo)

Chair: Fiona Bruce *Con*
Vice-chairs:
Dr Lisa Cameron *SNP*
Sir Jeffrey Donaldson *DUP*
Mary Glindon *Lab*
Baroness Masham of Ilton *CB*
Jim Shannon *DUP*
Martin Vickers *Con*
Treasurer: Sir Edward Leigh *Con*

Contact: Fiona Bruce, House of Commons, London SW1A 0AA Tel: 020 7219 7042
Email: fiona.bruce.mp@parliament.uk

Psychology

Chair: Dr Lisa Cameron *SNP*
Vice-chair: Baroness Hamwee *Lib Dem*
Officers:
Lord Alderdice *Lib Dem*
Lord Balfe *Con*
Sarah Champion *Lab*

Contact: Dr Lisa Cameron, House of Commons, London SW1A 0AA Tel: 020 7219 6855
Email: lisa.cameron.mp@parliament.uk

Publishing

Chair: Andrew Lewer *Con*
Vice-chairs:
Baroness Bonham-Carter of Yarnbury *Lib Dem*
Lord Foster of Bath *Lib Dem*
Baroness Rebuck *Lab*
John Whittingdale *Con*
Officer: Lord Clement-Jones *Lib Dem*

Contact: Andrew Lewer, House of Commons, London SW1A 0AA Tel: 020 7219 3870
Email: andrew.lewer.mp@parliament.uk
Website: www.allpartypublishinggroup.org.uk

Pubs

Chair: Charlotte Nichols *Lab*
Vice-chairs:
Dr Lisa Cameron *SNP*
Rachel Hopkins *Lab*
Laurence Robertson *Con*
Matt Western *Lab*

Contact: Charlotte Nichols, House of Commons, London SW1A 0AA
Tel: 020 7219 3000
Email: charlotte.nichols.mp@parliament.uk

Race and Community

Chair: Clive Lewis *Lab*
Vice-chairs:
Debbie Abrahams *Lab*
Sir Peter Bottomley *Con*
Dawn Butler *Lab*
Imran Hussain *Lab*
Afzal Khan *Lab*
Naz Shah *Lab*
Lord Sheikh *Con*
Baroness Whitaker *Lab*
Officers:
Apsana Begum *Lab*
Helen Grant *Con*

Contact: Clive Lewis, House of Commons, London SW1A 0AA Tel: 020 7219 5593
Email: clive.lewis.mp@parliament.uk
Website: www.runnymedetrust.org/projects-and-publications/parliament/appg-2.html

Racing and Bloodstock Industries

Chairs:
Conor McGinn *Lab*
Laurence Robertson *Con*
Vice-chairs:
Dan Carden *Lab*
Philip Davies *Con*
Viscount of Falkland *CB*
Victoria Prentis *Con*
Secretary: Lord Donoughue *Lab*
Treasurer: Grahame Morris *Lab*

Contact: Laurence Robertson, House of Commons, London SW1A 0AA
Tel: 020 7219 4196
Email: robertsonl@parliament.uk

Radiotherapy

Chair: Tim Farron *Lib Dem*
Vice-chairs:
Grahame Morris *Lab*
Henry Smith *Con*
Derek Thomas *Con*

Contact: Tim Farron, House of Commons, London SW1A 0AA Tel: 020 7219 8498
Email: farront@parliament.uk
Website: www.actionradiotherapy.org/appg
Twitter: @APPGRT

Rail

Chair: Martin Vickers *Con*
Vice-chairs:
Lord Bradshaw *Lib Dem*
Jack Brereton *Con*
Alan Brown *SNP*
Lilian Greenwood *Lab*
Jonathan Gullis *Con*
Kim Johnson *Lab*
Chris Loder *Con*
Lord Snape *Lab*
Secretary: Lord Berkeley *Lab*
Treasurer: Lord Faulkner of Worcester *Lab*

Contact: Martin Vickers, House of Commons, London SW1A 0AA Tel: 020 7219 7212
Email: martin.vickers.mp@parliament.uk
Twitter: @allpartyrail

Rail in the North

Chair: Ian Mearns *Lab*
Vice-chairs:
Andrew Jones *Con*
Liz Twist *Lab*
Martin Vickers *Con*

Contact: Ian Mearns, 12 Regent Terrace, Gateshead NE8 1LU Tel: 0191-477 0651
Email: ian.mearns.mp@parliament.uk

Rail in Wales
Chair: Chris Elmore *Lab*
Vice-chairs:
Stephen Crabb *Con*
Jessica Morden *Lab*
Christina Rees *Lab/Co-op*
Secretary: Jonathan Edwards *Ind*

Contact: Chris Elmore, House of Commons, London SW1A 0AA Tel: 020 7219 3000
Email: chris.elmore.mp@parliament.uk
Twitter: @APPGRailWales

Rare, Genetic and Undiagnosed Conditions
Chair: Liz Twist *Lab*
Vice-chairs:
Dame Cheryl Gillan *Con*
Baroness Neville-Jones *Con*
Lord Patel *CB*
Lord Turnberg *Lab*
Catherine West *Lab*
Officer: Alex Sobel *Lab/Co-op*

Contact: Liz Twist, House of Commons, London SW1A 0AA Tel: 020 7219 2221
Email: liz.twist.mp@parliament.uk
Website: geneticalliance.org.uk/appg

Recovery from Addictions
Chairs:
Fiona Bruce *Con*
Carolyn Harris *Lab*
Secretary: Sir David Amess *Con*
Treasurer: Baroness Finlay of Llandaff *CB*

Contact: Fiona Bruce, House of Commons, London SW1A 0AA Tel: 020 7219 7042
Email: fiona.bruce.mp@parliament.uk

Refugees
Chairs:
Anne McLaughlin *SNP*
David Simmonds *Con*
Vice-chairs:
Bishop of Durham *NA*
Baroness Lister of Burtersett *Lab*
Tim Loughton *Con*
Dr Caroline Lucas *Green*

Contact: Anne McLaughlin, House of Commons, London SW1A 0AA
Tel: 020 7219 3000
Email: anne.mclaughlin.mp@parliament.uk
Website: appgrefugees.wordpress.com
Twitter: @APPGRefugees

Religion in the Media
Chairs:
Sir Peter Bottomley *Con*
Baroness Butler-Sloss *CB*
Tim Farron *Lib Dem*
Yasmin Qureshi *Lab*
Vice-chairs:
Dr Lisa Cameron *SNP*
Tanmanjeet Singh Dhesi *Lab*
Lord Harries of Pentregarth *CB*
Baroness Hussein-Ece *Lib Dem*
Afzal Khan *Lab*
Charlotte Nichols *Lab*
Lord Parekh *Lab*
Naz Shah *Lab*
Lord Singh of Wimbledon *CB*
Alex Sobel *Lab/Co-op*
Sir Gary Streeter *Con*
Stephen Timms *Lab*
Baroness Uddin *NA*
Martin Vickers *Con*

Contact: Yasmin Qureshi, House of Commons, London SW1A 0AA Tel: 020 7219 7019
Email: yasmin.qureshi.mp@parliament.uk
Website: www.appgreligioninmedia.uk
Twitter: @APPGreligion

Religious Education
Chair: Fiona Bruce *Con*
Vice-chairs:
Sir Peter Bottomley *Con*
Mary Glindon *Lab*
Luke Pollard *Lab/Co-op*
Lord Singh of Wimbledon *CB*

Contact: Fiona Bruce, House of Commons, London SW1A 0AA Tel: 020 7219 7042
Email: fiona.bruce.mp@parliament.uk

Renewable and Sustainable Energy
Chair: Bim Afolami *Con*
Vice-chairs:
Peter Aldous *Con*
Alan Brown *SNP*
Darren Jones *Lab*
Dr Caroline Lucas *Green*

Contact: Bim Afolami, House of Commons, London SW1A 0AA
Email: bim.afolami.mp@parliament.uk
Website: www.praseg.org.uk
Twitter: @PRASEG

Respiratory Health
Chairs:
Yvonne Fovargue *Lab*
Ian Liddell-Grainger *Con*
Jim Shannon *DUP*
Baroness Thornton *Lab/Co-op*
Vice-chairs:
Baroness Blackstone *Lab Ind*
Earl of Dundee *Con*
Baroness Masham of Ilton *CB*

Viscount Simon *Lab*
Liz Twist *Lab*

Contact: Jim Shannon, House of Commons, London SW1A 0AA Tel: 020 7219 7160
Email: jim.shannon.mp@parliament.uk
Twitter: @AppgHealth

Retail Crime
Chair: Steve McCabe *Lab*
Vice-chairs:
Sir Jeffrey Donaldson *DUP*
Baroness Eaton *Con*
Baroness Golding *Lab*
Ian Liddell-Grainger *Con*
Damien Moore *Con*

Contact: Steve McCabe, House of Commons, London SW1A 0AA Tel: 020 7219 3509
Email: mccabes@parliament.uk

Reuniting Britain Post-Brexit
Chair: Stephen Kinnock *Lab*
Vice-chairs:
Sir Peter Bottomley *Con*
Ben Lake *PlC*
Dr Caroline Lucas *Green*
Lucy Powell *Lab/Co-op*
Andrew Rosindell *Con*
Lord Triesman *Lab*

Contact: Stephen Kinnock, House of Commons, London SW1A 0AA Tel: 020 7219 8801
Email: stephen.kinnock.mp@parliament.uk
Twitter: @appg_brexit

River Thames
Chair: Dr John Howell *Con*
Officers:
Alberto Costa *Con*
Mark Menzies *Con*
Sir Robert Neill *Con*
Christina Rees *Lab/Co-op*
Henry Smith *Con*
John Spellar *Lab*
Bob Stewart *Con*

Contact: Dr John Howell, House of Commons, London SW1A 0AA Tel: 020 7219 6676
Email: howelljm@parliament.uk

Road Freight and Logistics
Chair: Sir Mike Penning *Con*
Officers:
Tonia Antoniazzi *Lab*
Sir Peter Bottomley *Con*
Darren Henry *Con*
Gavin Newlands *SNP*
Charlotte Nichols *Lab*

Contact: Sir Mike Penning, The Bury, Queensway, Hemel Hempstead HP1 1HR
Tel: 01442 251126
Email: mike.penning.mp@parliament.uk
Twitter: @roadfreightappg

Roadside Rescue and Recovery
Chair: Sir Mike Penning *Con*
Vice-chair: Tonia Antoniazzi *Lab*
Officers:
Tracey Crouch *Con*
Gareth Johnson *Con*

Contact: Sir Mike Penning, House of Commons, London SW1A 0AA
Tel: 020 7219 3000
Email: mike.penning.mp@parliament.uk

Rohingya
Chairs:
Rushanara Ali *Lab*
Jeremy Hunt *Con*
Vice-chairs:
Lord Alton of Liverpool *CB*
Geraint Davies *Lab/Co-op*
Dr Rupa Huq *Lab*
Imran Hussain *Lab*
Lord McConnell of Glenscorrodale *Lab*
Sir Robert Neill *Con*
Baroness Nye *Lab*
Baroness Sheehan *Lib Dem*
Sam Tarry *Lab*
Viscount Waverley *CB*

Contact: Rushanara Ali, House of Commons, London SW1A 0AA Tel: 020 7219 7200
Email: rushanara.ali.mp@parliament.uk

Rowing
Chairs:
Karl McCartney *Con*
Lord Thomas of Gresford *Lib Dem*
Vice-chairs:
Tonia Antoniazzi *Lab*
Sir Peter Bottomley *Con*
Sir Edward Leigh *Con*
Angus MacNeil *SNP*
Rebecca Pow *Con*

Contact: Karl McCartney, House of Commons, London SW1A 0AA Tel: 020 7219 3000
Email: karl.mccartney.mp@parliament.uk
Website: parliamentaryrowing.org
Twitter: @ParliamentRow

Rugby League
Presidents:
Lord Hoyle *Lab*
Sir Lindsay Hoyle *Speaker*
Chair: Judith Cummins *Lab*

Vice-chairs:
Tracy Brabin *Lab/Co-op*
Lord Caine *Con*
Andy Carter *Con*
Yvonne Fovargue *Lab*
Jason McCartney *Con*
Lord Mann *NA*
Lord Thomas of Gresford *Lib Dem*
Secretary: Marie Rimmer *Lab*
Treasurer: Lord Smith of Leigh *Lab*

Contact: Judith Cummins, House of Commons, London SW1A 0AA Tel: 020 7219 8607
Email: judith.cummins.mp@parliament.uk
Website: www.apprlg.org.uk
Twitter: @UKParliamentRL

Rugby Union Football Club
Chair: Mark Pawsey *Con*
Vice-chairs:
Stephen Crabb *Con*
Sir Mike Penning *Con*
Sam Tarry *Lab*
Lord Thomas of Gresford *Lib Dem*
Secretary: Lord Addington *Lib Dem*
Treasurer: Craig Williams *Con*

Contact: Mark Pawsey, House of Commons, London SW1A 0AA Tel: 020 7219 7136
Email: mark.pawsey.mp@parliament.uk

Rural Business
Chair: Julian Sturdy *Con*
Vice-chairs:
Duncan Baker *Con*
Rosie Cooper *Lab*
Chris Elmore *Lab*
Robert Goodwill *Con*
Simon Hoare *Con*
Richard Holden *Con*
Scott Mann *Con*
Liz Saville Roberts *PlC*

Contact: Julian Sturdy, House of Commons, London SW1A 0AA Tel: 020 7219 7199
Email: julian.sturdy.mp@parliament.uk

Rural Health and Social Care
Chair: Anne Marie Morris *Con*
Vice-chair: and Rt Hon Bishop of London *NA*
Officers:
Brendan Clarke-Smith *Con*
Ruth Edwards *Con*
Lord Hunt of Kings Heath *Lab/Co-op*
Dr Caroline Johnson *Con*
Alicia Kearns *Con*
Scott Mann *Con*
Rob Roberts *Con*

Contact: Anne Marie Morris, House of Commons, London SW1A 0AA
Tel: 020 7219 3000
Email: annemarie.morris.mp@parliament.uk

Rural Services
Chair: Philip Dunne *Con*
Vice-chairs:
Rosie Duffield *Lab*
Chris Loder *Con*
Scott Mann *Con*
Julie Marson *Con*
Selaine Saxby *Con*
Secretary: Lord Cameron of Dillington *CB*
Treasurer: Lord Crathorne *Con*

Contact: Philip Dunne, House of Commons, London SW1A 0AA Tel: 020 7219 2388
Email: philip.dunne.mp@parliament.uk
Website: www.rsnonline.org.uk

Safeguarding in Faith Settings
Chair: Preet Kaur Gill *Lab/Co-op*
Vice-chairs:
Baroness Hollins *CB*
Michael Tomlinson *Con*
Secretary: Tim Farron *Lib Dem*
Officers:
Sir George Howarth *Lab*
Pauline Latham *Con*
Lord Selkirk of Douglas *Con*

Contact: Preet Kaur Gill, House of Commons, London SW1A 0AA Tel: 020 7219 2879
Email: preet.gill.mp@parliament.uk
Website: www.thirtyoneeight.org
Twitter: @APPG_SafeFaith

St George's Day
President: Lord Tebbit *Con*
Chair: Andrew Rosindell *Con*
Vice-chairs:
Scott Benton *Con*
Philip Davies *Con*
Jack Lopresti *Con*
Lord Mann *NA*
Chris Matheson *Lab*
Chris Skidmore *Con*
Henry Smith *Con*
Alexander Stafford *Con*
Lord West of Spithead *Lab*
Secretary: Sir Peter Bottomley *Con*

Contact: Andrew Rosindell, House of Commons, London SW1A 0AA
Tel: 020 7219 8475
Email: andrew.rosindell.mp@parliament.uk

School Exclusions and Alternative Provision

Chairs:
Andy Carter *Con*
Lord Storey *Lib Dem*
Vice-chairs:
Jonathan Gullis *Con*
Sally-Ann Hart *Con*
Lord Knight of Weymouth *Lab/Co-op*
Officers:
Miriam Cates *Con*
Sarah Jones *Lab*

Contact: Andy Carter, House of Commons, London SW1A 0AA Tel: 020 7219 3000
Email: andy.carter.mp@parliament.uk

School Food

Chair: Sharon Hodgson *Lab*
Vice-chairs:
Lord Curry of Kirkharle *CB*
Jonathan Gullis *Con*
Dame Diana Johnson *Lab*
Emma Lewell-Buck *Lab*
Kerry McCarthy *Lab*
Layla Moran *Lib Dem*
Karl Turner *Lab*
Christian Wakeford *Con*
Matt Western *Lab*
Nadia Whittome *Lab*

Contact: Sharon Hodgson, House of Commons, London SW1A 0AA Tel: 020 7219 5160
Email: sharon.hodgson.mp@parliament.uk

Science and Technology in Agriculture

Chair: Julian Sturdy *Con*
Vice-chairs:
Lord Cameron of Dillington *CB*
Robert Goodwill *Con*
Baroness Jones of Whitchurch *Lab*
Earl of Lindsay *Con*

Contact: Julian Sturdy, House of Commons, London SW1A 0AA Tel: 020 7219 7199
Email: julian.sturdy.mp@parliament.uk
Website: www.appg-agscience.org.uk

Scientific

President: Lord Broers *CB*
Vice Presidents:
Sir Peter Bottomley *Con*
Chris Green *Con*
Chair: Stephen Metcalfe *Con*
Vice-chair: Chi Onwurah *Lab*
Honorary Secretary: Carol Monaghan *SNP*
Honorary Treasurer: Lord Willis of Knaresborough *Lib Dem*

Contact: Stephen Metcalfe, House of Commons, London SW1A 0AA Tel: 020 7219 7009
Email: stephen.metcalfe.mp@parliament.uk
Website: www.scienceinparliament.org.uk
Twitter: @ParlSciCom

Scotch Whisky

Chair: Brendan O'Hara *SNP*
Vice-chairs:
Sir Peter Bottomley *Con*
Alistair Carmichael *Lib Dem*
Wendy Chamberlain *Lib Dem*
Drew Hendry *SNP*
John Lamont *Con*
Chris Law *SNP*
Ian Murray *Lab*
John Stevenson *Con*
Secretary: Hannah Bardell *SNP*
Treasurer: Martin Docherty-Hughes *SNP*

Contact: Brendan O'Hara, House of Commons, London SW1A 0AA Tel: 020 7219 8783
Email: brendan.ohara.mp@parliament.uk

Scottish Sport

Chair: Gavin Newlands *SNP*
Vice-chairs:
Allan Dorans *SNP*
Margaret Ferrier *Ind*
Grahame Morris *Lab*
David Mundell *Con*
Jamie Stone *Lib Dem*

Contact: Gavin Newlands, 6 Porterfield Road, Renfrew PA4 8HG Tel: 0141-378 0600
Twitter: @APPGScotSport

Sepsis

Chairs:
Dame Cheryl Gillan *Con*
Christina Rees *Lab/Co-op*
Vice-chairs:
Baroness Masham of Ilton *CB*
Chris Stephens *SNP*
Mike Wood *Con*

Contact: Christina Rees, House of Commons, London SW1A 0AA Tel: 020 7219 5783
Email: christina.rees.mp@parliament.uk
Website: sepsisappg.com
Twitter: @APPGSEPSIS

Sexual and Reproductive Health in the UK

Chairs:
Baroness Barker *Lib Dem*
Dame Diana Johnson *Lab*
Vice-chairs:
Sir Peter Bottomley *Con*
Baroness Flather *CB*
Emily Thornberry *Lab*

Contact: Dame Diana Johnson, House of Commons, London SW1A 0AA
Tel: 020 7219 5647
Email: johnsond@parliament.uk
Website: www.fsrh.org/policy-and-media/all-party-parliamentary-group-on-sexual-and-reproductive-health
Twitter: @APPGSRH

Shipbuilding and Ship Repair
Chair: Kevan Jones *Lab*
Vice-chairs:
Robert Courts *Con*
Carol Monaghan *SNP*
Stephen Morgan *Lab*
Luke Pollard *Lab/Co-op*
Gavin Robinson *DUP*
Chris Stephens *SNP*

Contact: Kevan Jones, House of Commons, London SW1A 0AA Tel: 020 7219 8219
Email: kevanjonesmp@parliament.uk
Twitter: @APPGShipbuild

Shooting and Conservation
Chair: Sir Geoffrey Clifton-Brown *Con*
Vice-chairs:
Lord Cunningham of Felling *Lab*
Mark Tami *Lab*
Secretary: Lord Dear *CB*
Treasurer: Jim Shannon *DUP*

Contact: Sir Geoffrey Clifton-Brown, House of Commons, London SW1A 0AA
Tel: 020 7219 5147
Email: cliftonbrowng@parliament.uk

Short Lets Sector
Chairs:
Nickie Aiken *Con*
Karen Buck *Lab*
Baroness Grender *Lib Dem*
Tommy Sheppard *SNP*
Daniel Zeichner *Lab*

Contact: Karen Buck, House of Commons, London SW1A 0AA Tel: 020 7219 3000
Email: buckk@parliament.uk

Showing Racism the Red Card
Chair: Jo Stevens *Lab*
Vice-chairs:
Baroness Blower *Lab*
James Cleverly *Con*
Damian Collins *Con*
Colum Eastwood *SDLP*
Rachel Hopkins *Lab*
Secretary: Chris Stephens *SNP*

Contact: Jo Stevens, House of Commons, London SW1A 0AA Tel: 020 7219 8290
Email: jo.stevens.mp@parliament.uk

Sickle Cell and Thalassaemia
Chair: Pat McFadden *Lab*
Vice-chair: Janet Daby *Lab*
Officers:
Sir David Amess *Con*
Baroness Benjamin *Lib Dem*
Dawn Butler *Lab*
Florence Eshalomi *Lab/Co-op*
Helen Grant *Con*
Kate Osamor *Lab/Co-op*
Jess Phillips *Lab*
Bell Ribeiro-Addy *Lab*

Contact: Pat McFadden, House of Commons, London SW1A 0AA Tel: 020 7219 4036
Email: mcfaddenp@parliament.uk
Website: www.sicklecellsociety.org

Single Parent Families
Chair: Dr Rupa Huq *Lab*
Vice-chairs:
Tonia Antoniazzi *Lab*
Caroline Nokes *Con*
Officers:
Andrew Bowie *Con*
Rosie Duffield *Lab*
Gavin Newlands *SNP*
Jamie Stone *Lib Dem*

Contact: Dr Rupa Huq, House of Commons, London SW1A 0AA Tel: 020 7219 6865
Email: rupa.huq.mp@parliament.uk

Sixth Form Education
Chairs:
Dame Diana Johnson *Lab*
Jason McCartney *Con*
Vice-chairs:
Peter Aldous *Con*
Rachel Hopkins *Lab*
Dr Caroline Lucas *Green*
Caroline Nokes *Con*
Lloyd Russell-Moyle *Lab/Co-op*
William Wragg *Con*
Officer: Emma Hardy *Lab*

Contact: Dame Diana Johnson, The Avenues Centre, Rooms 0-031 - 0-035, Park Avenue, Hull HU5 4DA Tel: 01482 319135
Email: johnsond@parliament.uk

Skills and Employment
Chair: Sir John Hayes *Con*
Vice-chairs:
Baroness Garden of Frognal *Lib Dem*
Lord Norton of Louth *Con*

Barry Sheerman *Lab/Co-op*
Officers:
Nick Fletcher *Con*
Robert Halfon *Con*
Emma Hardy *Lab*
Lord Lucas of Crudwell and Dingwall *Con*
Nicola Richards *Con*
Rob Roberts *Con*

Contact: Sir John Hayes, House of Commons, London SW1A 0AA Tel: 020 7219 1389
Email: hayesj@parliament.uk
Website: www.policyconnect.org.uk

Skin

(As health issue)
Chair: Sir Edward Leigh *Con*
Vice-chairs:
Baroness Finlay of Llandaff *CB*
Dame Cheryl Gillan *Con*
Baroness Masham of Ilton *CB*
Secretary: Mary Glindon *Lab*

Contact: Sir Edward Leigh, House of Commons, London SW1A 0AA
Tel: 020 7219 6480
Email: edward.leigh.mp@parliament.uk
Website: www.appgs.co.uk

Small and Micro Business

Chair: Robert Courts *Con*
Vice-chair: Matt Western *Lab*
Officers:
Baroness Bennett of Manor Castle *Green*
Saqib Bhatti *Con*
Baroness Burt of Solihull *Lib Dem*
Miriam Cates *Con*
Baroness Nicholson of Winterbourne *Con*

Contact: Robert Courts, House of Commons, London SW1A 0AA Tel: 020 7219 5638
Email: robert.courts.mp@parliament.uk

SME (Small and Medium-sized Enterprises) House Builders

Chair: Andrew Lewer *Con*
Vice-chairs:
Eddie Hughes *Con*
Damien Moore *Con*
Lord Naseby *Con*
Baroness Neville-Rolfe *Con*
Matt Western *Lab*

Contact: Andrew Lewer, House of Commons, London SW1A 0AA Tel: 020 7219 3870
Email: andrew.lewer.mp@parliament.uk

Smoking and Health

Chair: Bob Blackman *Con*
Vice-chairs:
Alex Cunningham *Lab*
Lord Faulkner of Worcester *Lab*
Baroness Finlay of Llandaff *CB*
Lord Rennard *Lib Dem*
Treasurer: Ian Mearns *Lab*

Contact: Bob Blackman, House of Commons, London SW1A 0AA Tel: 020 7219 7082
Email: bob.blackman.mp@parliament.uk
Website: ash.org.uk/category/about-ash/all-party-parliamentary-group-on-smoking-health

Snooker

Chairs:
Karl McCartney *Con*
Nick Smith *Lab*
Vice-chairs:
Hannah Bardell *SNP*
Neil Gray *SNP*
Julian Knight *Con*
Kerry McCarthy *Lab*
Conor McGinn *Lab*
Gavin Newlands *SNP*
Greg Smith *Con*

Contact: Karl McCartney, House of Commons, London SW1A 0AA Tel: 020 7219 3000
Email: karl.mccartney.mp@parliament.uk
Website: www.parliamentarysnooker.org
Twitter: @APPGSnooker

Social Enterprise

Chair: Alex Sobel *Lab/Co-op*
Vice-chairs:
Lord Adebowale *CB*
Harriett Baldwin *Con*
Baroness Barker *Lib Dem*
Lord Bird *CB*
Sir Peter Bottomley *Con*
Alex Davies-Jones *Lab*
Dr John Howell *Con*
Honorary Secretary: Baroness Thornton *Lab/Co-op*

Contact: Alex Sobel, House of Commons, London SW1A 0AA Tel: 020 7219 8295
Email: alex.sobel.mp@parliament.uk
Website: www.socialenterprise.org.uk/appg-on-social-enterprise

Social Integration

Chair: Peter Gibson *Con*
Vice-chairs:
Fleur Anderson *Lab*
Sir Peter Bottomley *Con*
Dr Rupa Huq *Lab*
Jim McMahon *Lab/Co-op*
Virendra Sharma *Lab*
Officers:
Stuart C McDonald *SNP*

All-Party Groups

Subject Groups

All-party groups are unofficial, and have a membership from both Houses. The groups tend to change frequently according to the Members' interests and with the topicality of the various subjects.

22q11 Syndrome

(Condition caused when a tiny part of the long arm of chromosome 22 is missing (at position 11))

Chair: David Duguid *Con*
Vice-chair: Jack Lopresti *Con*
Officers:
Dr Lisa Cameron *SNP*
Baroness Eaton *Con*
Lord Farmer *Con*
Robert Goodwill *Con*
Alex Sobel *Lab/Co-op*
Craig Tracey *Con*
Suzanne Webb *Con*

Contact: David Duguid, House of Commons, London SW1A 0AA Tel: 020 7219 2819
Email: david.duguid.mp@parliament.uk
Twitter: @22qAPPG

Acquired Brain Injury

Chair: Chris Bryant *Lab*
Vice-chairs:
Carolyn Harris *Lab*
Sir John Hayes *Con*
Dr Peter Kyle *Lab*
Dr Caroline Lucas *Green*
Andy McDonald *Lab*
Christina Rees *Lab/Co-op*
Liz Twist *Lab*
Secretary: Scott Mann *Con*
Treasurer: Lord Ramsbotham *CB*

Contact: Chris Bryant, House of Commons, London SW1A 0AA Tel: 020 7219 8315
Email: bryantc@parliament.uk

Adoption and Permanence

Chair: Rachael Maskell *Lab/Co-op*
Officers:
Peter Gibson *Con*
Lord Russell of Liverpool *CB*
Christian Wakeford *Con*

Contact: Rachael Maskell, House of Commons, London SW1A 0AA Tel: 020 7219 4525
Email: rachael.maskell.mp@parliament.uk
Website: appgap.info

Adult Social Care

Chairs:
Damian Green *Con*
Baroness Greengross *CB*
Helen Hayes *Lab*
Vice-chairs:
Baroness Brinton *Lib Dem*
Baroness Healy of Primrose Hill *Lab*
Lord Hunt of Kings Heath *Lab/Co-op*
Lord Low of Dalston *CB*
Sarah Owen *Lab*
Jim Shannon *DUP*
David Warburton *Con*
Mohammad Yasin *Lab*
Officers:
Lord Best *CB*
James Cartlidge *Con*
Marsha De Cordova *Lab*
Paul Girvan *DUP*
Baroness Grey-Thompson *CB*
Kevin Hollinrake *Con*
Baroness Hollins *CB*
Afzal Khan *Lab*
Andrew Lewer *Con*
Jamie Stone *Lib Dem*
Sir Gary Streeter *Con*
Derek Thomas *Con*

Contact: Damian Green, House of Commons, London SW1A 0AA Tel: 020 7219 3911
Email: damian.green.mp@parliament.uk
Website: adultsocialcareappg.com
Twitter: @ASCAPPG

Adverse Childhood Experiences

Chairs:
Wera Hobhouse *Lib Dem*
Julie Marson *Con*
Rachael Maskell *Lab/Co-op*
Treasurer: Rob Butler *Con*

Contact: Wera Hobhouse, House of Commons, London SW1A 0AA Tel: 020 7219 2093
Email: wera.hobhouse.mp@parliament.uk

Aerospace

Chair: Chris Matheson *Lab*
Vice-chairs:
Robert Courts *Con*
Jack Dromey *Lab*
Lord Empey *UUP*
Jack Lopresti *Con*
Carol Monaghan *SNP*
Laurence Robertson *Con*
Gavin Robinson *DUP*
Jamie Stone *Lib Dem*
Dr Philippa Whitford *SNP*

Contact: Chris Matheson, House of Commons, London SW1A 0AA Tel: 020 7219 8078
Email: chris.matheson.mp@parliament.uk

Ageing and Older People

Chairs:
Harriett Baldwin *Con*
Lord Foulkes of Cumnock *Lab/Co-op*
Baroness Greengross *CB*
Baroness Jolly *Lib Dem*
Barbara Keeley *Lab*
Rachael Maskell *Lab/Co-op*
Dr Beth Winter *Lab*
Officers:
Sir Peter Bottomley *Con*
Tim Loughton *Con*

Contact: Rachael Maskell, House of Commons, London SW1A 0AA Tel: 020 7219 4525
Email: rachael.maskell.mp@parliament.uk
Website: www.ageuk.org.uk/our-impact/politics-and-government/all-party-parliamentary-group

Agro-Ecology for Sustainable Food and Farming

Chairs:
Kerry McCarthy *Lab*
Lord Teverson *Lib Dem*
Vice-chairs:
Baroness Bennett of Manor Castle *Green*
Ben Lake *PlC*
Chris Loder *Con*
Robbie Moore *Con*
Officers:
Earl of Caithness *Con*
Lord Cameron of Dillington *CB*
Dr Caroline Lucas *Green*
Baroness Miller of Chilthorne Domer *Lib Dem*
Christina Rees *Lab/Co-op*
Derek Thomas *Con*
Baroness Young of Old Scone *Lab*

Contact: Kerry McCarthy, House of Commons, London SW1A 0AA Tel: 020 7219 4510
Email: kerry.mccarthy.mp@parliament.uk
Website: agroecology-appg.org
Twitter: @APG_Agroecology

Ahmadiyya Muslim Community

Chair: Siobhain McDonagh *Lab*
Vice-chairs:
Fleur Anderson *Lab*
Elliot Colburn *Con*
Sir Ed Davey *Lib Dem*
Tanmanjeet Singh Dhesi *Lab*
Damian Hinds *Con*
Sarah Jones *Lab*
Jason McCartney *Con*
Christina Rees *Lab/Co-op*
Alison Thewliss *SNP*
Lord Tope *Lib Dem*
Matt Western *Lab*
Secretary: Stephen Hammond *Con*
Treasurer: Virendra Sharma *Lab*

Contact: Siobhain McDonagh, House of Commons, London SW1A 0AA
Tel: 020 7219 4678
Email: mcdonaghs@parliament.uk
Website: appg-ahmadiyyamuslim.org.uk
Twitter: @APPG_Muslim

Air Passenger Duty Reform

Chair: Henry Smith *Con*
Vice-chair: Steve Double *Con*
Officers:
Tonia Antoniazzi *Lab*
Jim Shannon *DUP*
Sammy Wilson *DUP*

Contact: Henry Smith, House of Commons, London SW1A 0AA Tel: 020 7219 7043
Email: henry.smith.mp@parliament.uk

Air Pollution

Chair: Geraint Davies *Lab/Co-op*
Vice-chairs:
Karen Buck *Lab*
Helen Hayes *Lab*
Baroness Jones of Moulsecoomb *Green*
John McNally *SNP*
Dr Dan Poulter *Con*
Baroness Sheehan *Lib Dem*
Claudia Webbe *Ind*

Contact: Geraint Davies, House of Commons, London SW1A 0AA Tel: 020 7219 7166
Email: geraint.davies.mp@parliament.uk
Website: appgairpollution.org
Twitter: @APPGairpoll

Alevis

Promoting awareness, recognition and engagement with the Alevi community in Britain and internationally.

Chair: Bambos Charalambous *Lab*
Vice-chairs:
Bob Blackman *Con*
Peter Bone *Con*
Feryal Clark *Lab*
Meg Hillier *Lab/Co-op*
David Lammy *Lab*
Kate Osamor *Lab/Co-op*
Jim Shannon *DUP*
Catherine West *Lab*
Dame Rosie Winterton *Lab*

Contact: Bambos Charalambous, House of Commons, London SW1A 0AA

Tel: 020 7219 3460
Email: bambos.charalambous.mp@parliament.uk

Allergy

Chairs:
Jon Cruddas *Lab*
Baroness Finlay of Llandaff *CB*
Officers:
Sir David Amess *Con*
Baroness Healy of Primrose Hill *Lab*

Contact: Jon Cruddas, House of Commons, London SW1A 0AA Tel: 020 7219 8161
Email: cruddasj@parliament.uk

Alternative Dispute Resolution

Chair: Dr John Howell *Con*
Vice-chairs:
Sir Robert Neill *Con*
Christina Rees *Lab/Co-op*
John Spellar *Lab*
Secretary: Alberto Costa *Con*
Officers:
Alex Chalk *Con*
Bambos Charalambous *Lab*
Lord Low of Dalston *CB*

Contact: Dr John Howell, House of Commons, London SW1A 0AA Tel: 020 7219 6676
Email: howelljm@parliament.uk
Website: www.ciarb.org/policy/uk-appg-on-adr

Alternative Investment Management

Chair: Taiwo Owatemi *Lab*
Vice-chairs:
Geraint Davies *Lab/Co-op*
Lord Fink *Con*
Mark Harper *Con*

Contact: Taiwo Owatemi, House of Commons, London SW1A 0AA Tel: 020 7219 5842
Email: taiwo.owatemi.mp@parliament.uk
Website: www.aima.org/educate/appg.html

Alternative Lending

Chair: Julian Knight *Con*
Vice-chairs:
Chris Evans *Lab/Co-op*
Marion Fellows *SNP*
Lord Flight *Con*
Lord Sharkey *Lib Dem*

Contact: Julian Knight, House of Commons, London SW1A 0AA Tel: 020 7219 3577
Email: julian.knight.mp@parliament.uk
Website: www.appgalternativelending.com

American Football

President: Richard Fuller *Con*
Chair: Peter Bone *Con*
Vice-chairs:
Jon Cruddas *Lab*
Gavin Newlands *SNP*
Alex Norris *Lab/Co-op*
Andrew Percy *Con*
Chris Stephens *SNP*
Lord Taylor of Warwick *NA*

Contact: Peter Bone, House of Commons, London SW1A 0AA Tel: 020 7219 8496
Email: bonep@parliament.uk
Website: www.parliamentary.football

Angling

Chair: Sir Charles Walker *Con*
Vice-chairs:
Jon Cruddas *Lab*
Sir Mike Penning *Con*
Secretary: Baroness Golding *Lab*
Treasurers:
Tracey Crouch *Con*
Scott Mann *Con*

Contact: Sir Charles Walker, House of Commons, London SW1A 0AA
Tel: 020 7219 0338
Email: charles.walker.mp@parliament.uk

Animal Welfare

Chairs:
Tracey Crouch *Con*
Lord Trees *CB*
Vice-chairs:
Baroness Mallalieu *Lab*
Jessica Morden *Lab*
Henry Smith *Con*
Secretaries:
Kirsten Oswald *SNP*
Liz Saville Roberts *PlC*
Lord Taylor of Holbeach *Con*
Treasurers:
Dame Cheryl Gillan *Con*
Giles Watling *Con*

Contact: Tracey Crouch, House of Commons, London SW1A 0AA Tel: 020 7219 7203
Email: tracey.crouch.mp@parliament.uk
Website: www.apgaw.org
Twitter: @apgaw

Antibiotics

Chairs:
Sir Paul Beresford *Con*
Wendy Chamberlain *Lib Dem*
Rosie Cooper *Lab*
Martyn Day *SNP*
Dame Cheryl Gillan *Con*
Kevin Hollinrake *Con*
Baroness Masham of Ilton *CB*
Julian Sturdy *Con*

Secretary: Baroness Bennett of Manor Castle *Green*
Treasurer: Lord Trees *CB*

Contact: Julian Sturdy, House of Commons, London SW1A 0AA Tel: 020 7219 7199
Email: julian.sturdy.mp@parliament.uk
Website: appg-on-antibiotics.com
Twitter: @APPGantibiotics

Anti-Corruption and Responsible Tax

Chairs:
Dame Margaret Hodge *Lab*
Dr Rupa Huq *Lab*
Nigel Mills *Con*
Andrew Mitchell *Con*
Vice-chairs:
Kevin Hollinrake *Con*
Lord Kirkhope of Harrogate *Con*
Baroness Kramer *Lib Dem*
Catherine McKinnell *Lab*
Marie Rimmer *Lab*
Rob Roberts *Con*
Baroness Stern *CB*
Alison Thewliss *SNP*
Lord Wood of Anfield *Lab*

Contact: Dame Margaret Hodge, House of Commons, London SW1A 0AA
Tel: 020 7219 6666
Email: hodgem@parliament.uk
Twitter: @APPGAntiCorrupt

Anti-Semitism

President: Lord Mann *NA*
Vice-Presidents:
Lord Alderdice *Lib Dem*
Lord Boswell of Aynho *NA*
Lord Dholakia *Lib Dem*
Lord Dubs *Lab*
Lord Haskel *Lab*
Lord Stunell *Lib Dem*
Chairs:
Catherine McKinnell *Lab*
Andrew Percy *Con*
Vice-chairs:
Tonia Antoniazzi *Lab*
Bob Blackman *Con*
Sir Graham Brady *Con*
Dr Lisa Cameron *SNP*
Rosie Duffield *Lab*
Lilian Greenwood *Lab*
Louise Haigh *Lab*
Dame Margaret Hodge *Lab*
Anna McMorrin *Lab*
Holly Mumby-Croft *Con*
Dr Matthew Offord *Con*
Kirsten Oswald *SNP*
Nicola Richards *Con*
Liz Saville Roberts *PlC*
Tulip Siddiq *Lab*
Alex Sobel *Lab/Co-op*
Wes Streeting *Lab*
Christian Wakeford *Con*

Contact: Andrew Percy, House of Commons, London SW1A 0AA Tel: 020 7219 7208
Email: andrew.percy.mp@parliament.uk
Twitter: @APPGAA

Apprenticeships

Chairs:
Jack Lopresti *Con*
Karin Smyth *Lab*
Vice-chair: Jonathan Gullis *Con*
Officers:
Lord Aberdare *CB*
Lord Fox *Lib Dem*
Baroness Garden of Frognal *Lib Dem*
Andrew Jones *Con*
Catherine McKinnell *Lab*
Jim McMahon *Lab/Co-op*
Lord Young of Norwood Green *Lab*

Contact: Karin Smyth, House of Commons, London SW1A 0AA
Email: karin.smyth.mp@parliament.uk
Twitter: @ApprenticeAPPG

Archaeology

Chairs:
Tim Loughton *Con*
Lord Renfrew of Kaimsthorn *Con*
Vice-chairs:
Lord Redesdale *Lib Dem*
Lord Stunell *Lib Dem*
Treasurer: Valerie Vaz *Lab*

Contact: Tim Loughton, House of Commons, London SW1A 0AA Tel: 020 7219 4471
Email: loughtont@parliament.uk
Website: www.appag.org.uk
Twitter: @APPGArchaeology

Archives and History

Chairs:
Lord Clark of Windermere *Lab*
Chris Evans *Lab/Co-op*
Vice-chairs:
Lord Boateng *Lab*
Lord Boswell of Aynho *NA*
Richard Graham *Con*
Lord Murphy of Torfaen *Lab*
Christina Rees *Lab/Co-op*
Alexander Stafford *Con*
Secretary: Lord Bew *CB*
Treasurer: Lord Aberdare *CB*

Contact: Chris Evans, House of Commons, London SW1A 0AA Tel: 020 7219 5025
Email: chris.evans.mp@parliament.uk

Armed Forces

Chair: James Gray *Con*
Deputy Chair(Royal Air Force): Robert Courts *Con*
Deputy Chair(Royal Navy and Royal Marines): Luke Pollard *Lab/Co-op*
Deputy Chair(Army): Bob Stewart *Con*
Vice-chair(Army): Stephen Doughty *Lab/Co-op*
Vice-chair(Royal Air Force): Jamie Stone *Lib Dem*
Vice-chair(Royal Navy and Royal Marines): Derek Thomas *Con*
Secretaries:
Dr Lisa Cameron *SNP*
Gavin Robinson *DUP*
Baroness Smith of Newnham *Lib Dem*
Treasurers:
Sheryll Murray *Con*
Lord Rogan *UUP*

Contact: James Gray, House of Commons, London SW1A 0AA Tel: 020 7219 6237
Email: jamesgraymp@parliament.uk

Art, Craft and Design in Education

Chair: Sharon Hodgson *Lab*
Vice-chairs:
Tracy Brabin *Lab/Co-op*
Earl of Clancarty *CB*
Lord Cormack *Con*
Baroness Jones of Whitchurch *Lab*
Baroness Nye *Lab*
David Warburton *Con*

Contact: Sharon Hodgson, House of Commons, London SW1A 0AA Tel: 020 7219 5160
Email: sharon.hodgson.mp@parliament.uk
Website: www.nsead.org/community-activism/all-party-parliamentary-group

Artificial Intelligence

Chairs:
Lord Clement-Jones *Lib Dem*
Stephen Metcalfe *Con*
Vice-chairs:
Lord Broers *CB*
Sir Mark Hendrick *Lab/Co-op*
Lord Holmes of Richmond *Con*
Lord Janvrin *CB*
Darren Jones *Lab*
Baroness Kramer *Lib Dem*
Justin Madders *Lab*
Baroness McGregor-Smith *Con*
Carol Monaghan *SNP*
Lord Willetts *Con*
Secretary: Chris Green *Con*
Treasurer: Bishop of Oxford *NA*

Contact: Stephen Metcalfe, House of Commons, London SW1A 0AA Tel: 020 7219 7009
Email: stephen.metcalfe.mp@parliament.uk
Website: www.appg-ai.org
Twitter: @APPG_AI

Arts and Heritage

President: Lord Cormack *Con*
Vice-Presidents:
Baroness Boothroyd *CB*
Viscount of Falkland *CB*
Lord Howarth of Newport *Lab*
Lord Lea of Crondall *NA*
Daniel Zeichner *Lab*
Chair: Sir Peter Bottomley *Con*
Vice-chairs:
Baroness Hilton of Eggardon *Lab*
Ian Liddell-Grainger *Con*
Honorary Secretary: Lord Crathorne *Con*

Contact: Sir Peter Bottomley, House of Commons, London SW1A 0AA
Tel: 020 7219 5060
Email: bottomleyp@parliament.uk

Arts, Health and Wellbeing

Chairs:
Lord Howarth of Newport *Lab*
Dr Ben Spencer *Con*
Vice-chairs:
Tracy Brabin *Lab/Co-op*
Baroness Morgan of Cotes *Con*
Treasurer: Baroness Andrews *Lab*

Contact: Dr Ben Spencer, House of Commons, London SW1A 0AA Tel: 020 7219 6783
Email: ben.spencer.mp@parliament.uk
Website: www.culturehealthandwellbeing.org.uk/who-we-are/appg

Assistive Technology

Chairs:
Lilian Greenwood *Lab*
Lord Low of Dalston *CB*
Lord Shinkwin *Con*
Officers:
Lord Addington *Lib Dem*
Dr Alex Burghart *Con*
Neil Coyle *Lab*
John Cryer *Lab*
Bill Esterson *Lab*
Sharon Hodgson *Lab*
Lord Holmes of Richmond *Con*
Seema Malhotra *Lab/Co-op*
Lord Rennard *Lib Dem*
Barry Sheerman *Lab/Co-op*
Baroness Uddin *NA*

Contact: Lilian Greenwood, House of Commons, London SW1A 0AA
Tel: 020 7219 7122
Email: lilian.greenwood.mp@parliament.uk
Website: www.policyconnect.org.uk/appgat
Twitter: @AT_APPG

Attention Deficit Hyperactive Disorder

Chair: Bambos Charalambous *Lab*
Vice-chairs:
Tonia Antoniazzi *Lab*
Jackie Doyle-Price *Con*
Alex Sobel *Lab/Co-op*

Contact: Bambos Charalambous, House of Commons, London SW1A 0AA
Tel: 0207 219 3460
Email: bambos.charalambous.mp@parliament.uk

Autism

Chair: Dame Cheryl Gillan *Con*
Vice-chairs:
Jonathan Reynolds *Lab/Co-op*
Lord Touhig *Lab/Co-op*
Officers:
Paul Bristow *Con*
Dr Lisa Cameron *SNP*
James Cartlidge *Con*
Thangam Debbonaire *Lab*
Marion Fellows *SNP*
Baroness Hollins *CB*
Dr John Howell *Con*
Huw Merriman *Con*
Christina Rees *Lab/Co-op*
Cat Smith *Lab*
Lord Sterling of Plaistow *Con*
Lord Warner *CB*

Contact: Dame Cheryl Gillan, House of Commons, London SW1A 0AA
Tel: 020 7219 4061
Email: cheryl.gillan.mp@parliament.uk
Website: www.autism.org.uk/appga

Axial Spondyloarthritis

Chairs:
Lord Campbell-Savours *Lab*
Derek Thomas *Con*
Vice-chair: Tom Randall *Con*
Officers:
Dr Rupa Huq *Lab*
Kerry McCarthy *Lab*
Baroness Masham of Ilton *CB*
Lord Shinkwin *Con*
Andy Slaughter *Lab*
Munira Wilson *Lib Dem*

Contact: Derek Thomas, House of Commons, London SW1A 0AA Tel: 020 7219 4435
Email: derek.thomas.mp@parliament.uk

Baby Loss

Chairs:
Jeremy Hunt *Con*
Cherilyn Mackrory *Con*
Vice-chairs:
Patricia Gibson *SNP*
Sharon Hodgson *Lab*

Contact: Cherilyn Mackrory, House of Commons, London SW1A 0AA
Tel: 020 7219 3000
Email: cherilyn.mackrory.mp@parliament.uk
Website: www.lullabytrust.org.uk/about-us/who-we-are/appg

Bahá'í Faith

Chair: Alistair Carmichael *Lib Dem*
Vice-chairs:
Dame Cheryl Gillan *Con*
Lloyd Russell-Moyle *Lab/Co-op*
Alison Thewliss *SNP*
Secretary: Mary Glindon *Lab*
Treasurer: Jim Shannon *DUP*

Contact: Alistair Carmichael, House of Commons, London SW1A 0AA
Tel: 020 7219 8181
Email: carmichaela@parliament.uk

Baseball and Softball

Chairs:
Jason McCartney *Con*
Alex Norris *Lab/Co-op*
Vice-chairs:
Aaron Bell *Con*
Peter Bone *Con*
Dehenna Davison *Con*
Alex Sobel *Lab/Co-op*
John Spellar *Lab*
Lord Taylor of Warwick *NA*

Contact: Alex Norris, House of Commons, London SW1A 0AA Tel: 020 7219 3899
Email: alex.norris.mp@parliament.uk
Website: www.appgbaseball.org.uk

Basketball

Chairs:
Sir Mike Penning *Con*
Lord Wasserman *Con*
Vice-chairs:
Lord Addington *Lib Dem*
Bambos Charalambous *Lab*
Baroness Grey-Thompson *CB*
Sharon Hodgson *Lab*

Alex Sobel *Lab/Co-op*
Secretary: Jane Hunt *Con*

Contact: Sir Mike Penning, House of Commons, London SW1A 0AA
Tel: 020 7219 3000
Email: mike.penning.mp@parliament.uk
Website: www.appgbasketball.org.uk

BBC
Chair: Huw Merriman *Con*
Vice-chairs:
Sir Peter Bottomley *Con*
Andrew Bowie *Con*
Deidre Brock *SNP*
Theo Clarke *Con*
Ranil Jayawardena *Con*
Jason McCartney *Con*
Alison McGovern *Lab*
Chris Matheson *Lab*
Mark Menzies *Con*
Treasurer: Baroness Bonham-Carter of Yarnbury *Lib Dem*

Contact: Huw Merriman, House of Commons, London SW1A 0AA Tel: 020 7219 8712
Email: huw.merriman.mp@parliament.uk

Beauty, Aesthetics and Wellbeing
Chairs:
Judith Cummins *Lab*
Carolyn Harris *Lab*
Vice-chairs:
Alberto Costa *Con*
Jackie Doyle-Price *Con*
Jessica Morden *Lab*
Secretary: Nick Smith *Lab*
Treasurer: Peter Dowd *Lab*

Contact: Carolyn Harris, House of Commons, London SW1A 0AA Tel: 020 7219 4316
Email: carolyn.harris.mp@parliament.uk
Website: www.baw-appg.com

Beer
President: Nigel Evans *Con*
Chair: Mike Wood *Con*
Deputy Chairs:
Toby Perkins *Lab*
Pete Wishart *SNP*
Vice-chairs:
Tonia Antoniazzi *Lab*
Paula Barker *Lab*
Lord Bilimoria *CB*
Bob Blackman *Con*
Alan Brown *SNP*
Daisy Cooper *Lib Dem*
Lord Davies of Gower *Con*
Lord Dholakia *Lib Dem*
Steve Double *Con*
Lord Jones of Cheltenham *Lib Dem*
Lord Kennedy of Southwark *Lab/Co-op*
Ben Lake *PlC*
Sheryll Murray *Con*
Nicola Richards *Con*
Jim Shannon *DUP*
Lord Smith of Hindhead *Con*
Jo Stevens *Lab*
Craig Williams *Con*

Contact: Mike Wood, House of Commons, London SW1A 0AA Tel: 020 7219 6982
Email: mike.wood.mp@parliament.uk

Betting and Gaming
Chairs:
Laurence Robertson *Con*
Baroness Golding *Lab*
Vice-chairs:
Aaron Bell *Con*
Scott Benton *Con*
Lord Lipsey *Lab*
Conor McGinn *Lab*
Lord Mancroft *Con*
Lord Moynihan *Con*
Mark Pritchard *Con*
Lord Smith of Hindhead *Con*
John Spellar *Lab*
Secretary: Lord Donoughue *Lab*

Contact: Laurence Robertson, House of Commons, London SW1A 0AA
Tel: 020 7219 4196
Email: robertsonl@parliament.uk
Website: www.apbgg.org

Black, Asian and Minority Ethnic Business Owners
Chairs:
Baroness Burt of Solihull *Lib Dem*
Gagan Mohindra *Con*
Vice-chair: Theresa Villiers *Con*
Officers:
Sir Peter Bottomley *Con*
Tanmanjeet Singh Dhesi *Lab*
Dr Rupa Huq *Lab*
Navendu Mishra *Lab*

Contact: Gagan Mohindra, House of Commons, London SW1A 0AA Tel: 020 7219 3000
Email: gagan.mohindra.mp@parliament.uk

Black Country
Chair: Mike Wood *Con*
Vice-chairs:
Stuart Anderson *Con*
Shaun Bailey *Con*
Marco Longhi *Con*
Deputy Chair: Pat McFadden *Lab*

Contact: Mike Wood, House of Commons, London SW1A 0AA Tel: 020 7219 6982
Email: mike.wood.mp@parliament.uk
Website: www.blackcountrychamber.co.uk
Twitter: @APPGBlckCountry

Bladder and Bowel Continence Care
Chairs:
Rosie Cooper *Lab*
Baroness Greengross *CB*
Vice-chairs:
Baroness Finlay of Llandaff *CB*
Baroness Masham of Ilton *CB*
Officers:
Ruth Jones *Lab*
Andrew Selous *Con*

Contact: Rosie Cooper, Suite 108, Malthouse Business Centre, 48 Southport Road, Ormskirk L39 1QR Tel: 01695 570094
Email: rosie@rosiecooper.net
Website: www.appgcontinence.org.uk

Blockchain
Chair: Martin Docherty-Hughes *SNP*
Vice-chairs:
Lord Bridges of Headley *Con*
Lord Holmes of Richmond *Con*
Eddie Hughes *Con*
Darren Jones *Lab*
Viscount Waverley *CB*
Secretary: Earl of Lindsay *Con*
Treasurer: Lord Vaux of Harrowden *CB*

Contact: Martin Docherty-Hughes, House of Commons, London SW1A 0AA
Tel: 020 7219 4609
Email: martin.docherty.mp@parliament.uk
Website: www.appg-blockchain.org
Twitter: @appg_blockchain

Blood Cancer
Chair: Henry Smith *Con*
Vice-chair: Colleen Fletcher *Lab*
Officers:
Jess Phillips *Lab*
Jim Shannon *DUP*
Nick Thomas-Symonds *Lab*

Contact: Henry Smith, House of Commons, London SW1A 0AA Tel: 020 7219 7043
Email: henry.smith.mp@parliament.uk
Website: bloodwise.org.uk/actions/campaign/partnerships/appg
Twitter: @APPGBloodCancer

Boxing
Chair: Chris Evans *Lab/Co-op*
Vice-chairs:
Paula Barker *Lab*
Dr Alex Burghart *Con*
Dr Lisa Cameron *SNP*
Jonathan Djanogly *Con*
Jonathan Gullis *Con*
Imran Hussain *Lab*
Lord Moynihan *Con*
Sir Mike Penning *Con*
Secretary: John Spellar *Lab*
Treasurer: Baroness Golding *Lab*

Contact: Chris Evans, House of Commons, London SW1A 0AA Tel: 020 7219 5025
Email: chris.evans.mp@parliament.uk
Twitter: @APPGBoxing

Brain Tumours
Chair: Derek Thomas *Con*
Vice-chairs:
Lord Carlile of Berriew *CB*
Alistair Carmichael *Lib Dem*
Helen Hayes *Lab*
Baroness Masham of Ilton *CB*
Lee Rowley *Con*
Dean Russell *Con*

Contact: Derek Thomas, House of Commons, London SW1A 0AA Tel: 020 7219 4435
Email: derek.thomas.mp@parliament.uk
Website: www.braintumourresearch.org/appgbt

Breast Cancer
Chairs:
Bambos Charalambous *Lab*
Craig Tracey *Con*
Vice-chairs:
Thangam Debbonaire *Lab*
Sharon Hodgson *Lab*
Baroness Massey of Darwen *Lab*
Dr Philippa Whitford *SNP*

Contact: Craig Tracey, House of Commons, London SW1A 0AA Tel: 020 7219 5646
Email: craig.tracey.mp@parliament.uk
Twitter: @appgbc

Bridge
Chair: Bob Blackman *Con*
Secretary: Lord Hamilton of Epsom *Con*
Officers:
Richard Graham *Con*
Baroness Henig *Lab*
Gavin Newlands *SNP*

Contact: Bob Blackman, House of Commons, London SW1A 0AA Tel: 020 7219 7082
Email: bob.blackman.mp@parliament.uk

Britain-Pakistan Trade and Tourism
Chairs:
Afzal Khan *Lab*
Baroness Warsi *Con*

Vice-chairs:
Tahir Ali *Lab*
Tracy Brabin *Lab/Co-op*
Yasmin Qureshi *Lab*
Baroness Sheehan *Lib Dem*
Lord Sheikh *Con*
Sam Tarry *Lab*
Stephen Timms *Lab*
Secretary: Lord Hussain *Lib Dem*

Contact: Afzal Khan, House of Commons, London SW1A 0AA Tel: 020 7219 3570
Email: afzal.khan.mp@parliament.uk

Britiish Offshore Oil and Gas Industry
Chair: Peter Aldous *Con*
Vice-chairs:
Kirsty Blackman *SNP*
Mary Glindon *Lab*
Lord Goddard of Stockport *Lib Dem*
Secretary: Alistair Carmichael *Lib Dem*

Contact: Peter Aldous, House of Commons, London SW1A 0AA Tel: 020 7219 7182
Email: peter.aldous.mp@parliament.uk
Website: www.oilandgasuk.co.uk/appg

British Bioethanol
Chairs:
Dehenna Davison *Con*
Matt Vickers *Con*
Vice-chairs:
Sir Oliver Heald *Con*
Martin Vickers *Con*
Secretary: Jacob Young *Con*
Officers:
Alan Brown *SNP*
Alex Cunningham *Lab*
Paul Howell *Con*

Contact: Matt Vickers, House of Commons, London SW1A 0AA Tel: 0207 219 3723
Email: matt.vickers.mp@parliament.uk
Website: www.britishbioethanol.co.uk
Twitter: @APPGBioethanol

British Council
Chair: John Baron *Con*
Vice-chairs:
Lord Alton of Liverpool *CB*
Karen Bradley *Con*
Baroness Coussins *CB*
Chris Matheson *Lab*
Baroness Northover *Lib Dem*
Lord Purvis of Tweed *Lib Dem*
Baroness Suttie *Lib Dem*
Baroness Thornton *Lab/Co-op*
Lord Watson of Invergowrie *Lab*
Secretary: Baroness Grey-Thompson *CB*
Treasurer: Stephen Kinnock *Lab*

Contact: John Baron, House of Commons, London SW1A 0AA Tel: 020 7219 8138
Email: baronj@parliament.uk
Website: appg.britishcouncil.org

British Jews
Chairs:
Sir Graham Brady *Con*
Wes Streeting *Lab*
Vice-chairs:
Karen Buck *Lab*
Dr Lisa Cameron *SNP*
Sharon Hodgson *Lab*
Baroness Ludford *Lib Dem*
Ian Mearns *Lab*
Dr Matthew Offord *Con*
Lord Palmer of Childs Hill *Lib Dem*
Secretary: Bob Blackman *Con*
Treasurer: David Lammy *Lab*

Contact: Wes Streeting, House of Commons, London SW1A 0AA Tel: 020 7219 6132
Email: wes.streeting.mp@parliament.uk
Twitter: @APPGBritishJews

British Museum
Chair: Tim Loughton *Con*
Vice-chairs:
Harriett Baldwin *Con*
Baroness Bonham-Carter of Yarnbury *Lib Dem*
Karen Bradley *Con*
Sir Graham Brady *Con*
Theo Clarke *Con*
Baroness Hooper *Con*
Mark Logan *Con*
Holly Lynch *Lab*
Lord Renfrew of Kaimsthorn *Con*
Secretary: Angus MacNeil *SNP*
Treasurer: Chris Bryant *Lab*

Contact: Tim Loughton, House of Commons, London SW1A 0AA Tel: 020 7219 4471
Email: loughtont@parliament.uk

British Sikhs
Chair: Preet Kaur Gill *Lab/Co-op*
Vice-chairs:
Stuart Anderson *Con*
Tanmanjeet Singh Dhesi *Lab*
Martin Docherty-Hughes *SNP*
Kate Green *Lab*
Pat McFadden *Lab*
Joy Morrissey *Con*
Kirsten Oswald *SNP*
Nicola Richards *Con*
John Spellar *Lab*
Wes Streeting *Lab*
Lord Suri *Con*
Alison Thewliss *SNP*

Treasurers:
Lord Ranger *Con*
Lord Singh of Wimbledon *CB*

Contact: Preet Kaur Gill, House of Commons, London SW1A 0AA Tel: 020 7219 2879
Email: preet.gill.mp@parliament.uk
Twitter: @AppgBritSikhs

Broadband and Digital Communication

Chair: Selaine Saxby *Con*
Officers:
Alun Cairns *Con*
Alistair Carmichael *Lib Dem*
Flick Drummond *Con*
Julie Elliott *Lab*
Andrew Griffith *Con*
Jane Hunt *Con*
Julian Knight *Con*
Ian Liddell-Grainger *Con*
Cherilyn Mackrory *Con*
Jerome Mayhew *Con*
Liz Saville Roberts *PlC*
Greg Smith *Con*
Stephen Timms *Lab*

Contact: Selaine Saxby, House of Commons, London SW1A 0AA Tel: 020 7219 5952
Email: selaine.saxby.mp@parliament.uk

Building Communities

Chair: Bob Blackman *Con*
Vice-chairs:
Andrew Lewer *Con*
Alison Thewliss *SNP*
Stephen Timms *Lab*
Liz Twist *Lab*
Secretary: Julie Marson *Con*

Contact: Bob Blackman, House of Commons, London SW1A 0AA Tel: 020 7219 7082
Email: bob.blackman.mp@parliament.uk

Bus and Coach Industry

Chair: Robert Goodwill *Con*
Vice-chairs:
Tony Lloyd *Lab*
John McNally *SNP*
Ian Paisley *DUP*
Treasurer: Lord Bradshaw *Lib Dem*

Contact: Robert Goodwill, House of Commons, London SW1A 0AA Tel: 020 7219 8268
Email: robert.goodwill.mp@parliament.uk

Business in a Pandemic (Covid) World

Chair: Paul Holmes *Con*
Vice-chairs:
Debbie Abrahams *Lab*
Ben Everitt *Con*
Jo Gideon *Con*
Stephen Hammond *Con*
Jane Hunt *Con*
Stephen Morgan *Lab*
Lord Taylor of Warwick *NA*

Contact: Paul Holmes, House of Commons, London SW1A 0AA Tel: 020 7219 3000
Email: paul.holmes.mp@parliament.uk

Business Travel

Chair: Stephen Hammond *Con*
Vice-chairs:
Paul Bristow *Con*
Ian Mearns *Lab*
Andrew Rosindell *Con*
Henry Smith *Con*
Officer: Kim Johnson *Lab*

Contact: Stephen Hammond, House of Commons, London SW1A 0AA
Tel: 020 7219 3401
Email: stephen.hammond.mp@parliament.uk

CAFOD

(Catholic Agency for Overseas Development)
Chair: Catherine McKinnell *Lab*
Vice-chairs:
Patrick Grady *SNP*
Chris Green *Con*
Conor McGinn *Lab*
Alexander Stafford *Con*
James Sunderland *Con*

Contact: Catherine McKinnell, The Lemington Centre, Tyne View, Newcastle NE15 8RZ
Tel: 0191-229 0352
Email: catherine.mckinnell.mp@parliament.uk

Cancer

Chair: Tonia Antoniazzi *Lab*
Vice-chairs:
John Baron *Con*
Amy Callaghan *SNP*
Baroness Finlay of Llandaff *CB*
Colleen Fletcher *Lab*
Dr Rupa Huq *Lab*
Baroness Masham of Ilton *CB*
Baroness Morgan of Drefelin *CB*
Grahame Morris *Lab*
Mark Pritchard *Con*
Christina Rees *Lab/Co-op*
Nicola Richards *Con*
Henry Smith *Con*
Baroness Walmsley *Lib Dem*
Treasurer: Lord Rennard *Lib Dem*

Contact: Tonia Antoniazzi, House of Commons, London SW1A 0AA Tel: 0207 219 1199
Email: tonia.antoniazzi.mp@parliament.uk

Website: www.macmillan.org.uk/appgc
Twitter: @APPGC

Cannabis: Harmful Effects on Developing Brains
Chair: Craig Mackinlay *Con*
Vice-chairs:
Sir David Amess *Con*
Dame Cheryl Gillan *Con*
Mike Hill *Lab*
Lord Mackenzie of Framwellgate *NA*

Contact: Craig Mackinlay, House of Commons, London SW1A 0AA Tel: 020 7219 4442
Email: craig.mackinlay.mp@parliament.uk

Carbon Monoxide
Chairs:
Baroness Finlay of Llandaff *CB*
Barry Sheerman *Lab/Co-op*
Officers:
Sir Peter Bottomley *Con*
Chris Bryant *Lab*
Alex Cunningham *Lab*
Eddie Hughes *Con*
John McNally *SNP*
Maria Miller *Con*
Luke Pollard *Lab/Co-op*
Andrew Selous *Con*
Jim Shannon *DUP*
Liz Twist *Lab*

Contact: Barry Sheerman, House of Commons, London SW1A 0AA Tel: 020 7219 5037
Email: sheermanb@parliament.uk
Website: www.policyconnect.org.uk/appcog
Twitter: @APPCOG_UK

Cats
Chairs:
Andrew Gwynne *Lab*
Sheryll Murray *Con*
Vice-chairs:
Lord Black of Brentwood *Con*
Patricia Gibson *SNP*
Lord Goddard of Stockport *Lib Dem*
Treasurer: Layla Moran *Lib Dem*

Contact: Sheryll Murray, House of Commons, London SW1A 0AA Tel: 020 7219 3000
Email: sheryll.murray.mp@parliament.uk
Website: www.apgocats.co.uk

Celtic Nations
Chair: Dave Doogan *SNP*
Vice-chairs:
Virginia Crosbie *Con*
Colum Eastwood *SDLP*
Conor McGinn *Lab*
Scott Mann *Con*
Andrew Rosindell *Con*
Liz Saville Roberts *PlC*

Contact: Dave Doogan, House of Commons, London SW1A 0AA Tel: 020 7219 3000
Email: dave.doogan.mp@parliament.uk

Celtic Sea
Chair: Selaine Saxby *Con*
Officers:
Geraint Davies *Lab/Co-op*
Steve Double *Con*
Flick Drummond *Con*
Ben Lake *PlC*
Ian Liddell-Grainger *Con*
Cherilyn Mackrory *Con*
Scott Mann *Con*
Sheryll Murray *Con*
Sir Gary Streeter *Con*
Derek Thomas *Con*

Contact: Selaine Saxby, House of Commons, London SW1A 0AA Tel: 020 7219 5952
Email: selaine.saxby.mp@parliament.uk

Ceramics
Chair: Jonathan Gullis *Con*
Vice-chairs:
Jack Dromey *Lab*
Stephanie Peacock *Lab*
Secretary: Aaron Bell *Con*
Treasurer: Jack Brereton *Con*

Contact: Jonathan Gullis, House of Commons, London SW1A 0AA Tel: 0207 219 3000
Email: jonathan.gullis.mp@parliament.uk
Website: www.ceramfed.co.uk/key-topics/all-party-parliamentary-group-for-ceramics

Cerebral Palsy
Chairs:
Mary Foy *Lab*
Paul Maynard *Con*
Vice-chairs:
Dr Lisa Cameron *SNP*
Greg Smith *Con*
Officers:
Baroness Grey-Thompson *CB*
Ruth Jones *Lab*
Jim Shannon *DUP*

Contact: Paul Maynard, House of Commons, London SW1A 0AA Tel: 020 7219 7017
Email: paul.maynard.mp@parliament.uk
Twitter: @CPAPPG

Chalk Streams
Chair: Sir Charles Walker *Con*
Vice-chairs:
Anthony Browne *Con*
Lord Chidgey *Lib Dem*

Daisy Cooper *Lib Dem*
Laura Farris *Con*
Dame Cheryl Gillan *Con*
Sir Oliver Heald *Con*
Rachel Hopkins *Lab*
Maria Miller *Con*
Gagan Mohindra *Con*
Lord Ribeiro *Con*
Matt Western *Lab*
James Wild *Con*
Daniel Zeichner *Lab*
Secretary: Flick Drummond *Con*

Contact: Sir Charles Walker, House of Commons, London SW1A 0AA
Tel: 020 7219 0338
Email: charles.walker.mp@parliament.uk

Challenger Banks and Building Societies
Chair: Karen Bradley *Con*
Vice-chairs:
Baroness Drake *Lab*
Peter Gibson *Con*
Baroness Kramer *Lib Dem*
Jim McMahon *Lab/Co-op*
Mary Robinson *Con*
Baroness Wheatcroft *CB*

Contact: Karen Bradley, House of Commons, London SW1A 0AA Tel: 020 7219 7215
Email: karen.bradley.mp@parliament.uk
Website: www.cbbsappg.org.uk

Channel 4
Chair: Helen Grant *Con*
Vice-chairs:
Baroness Bonham-Carter of Yarnbury *Lib Dem*
Dr Lisa Cameron *SNP*
Andy Carter *Con*
Julie Elliott *Lab*
Jason McCartney *Con*

Contact: Helen Grant, House of Commons, London SW1A 0AA Tel: 020 7219 7107
Email: helen.grant.mp@parliament.uk

Charities and Volunteering
Chairs:
Fleur Anderson *Lab*
Simon Fell *Con*
Lord Hodgson of Astley Abbotts *Con*
Baroness Pitkeathley *Lab*
Vice-chairs:
Baroness Barker *Lib Dem*
Ian Byrne *Lab*
Martin Docherty-Hughes *SNP*
Jo Gideon *Con*
Danny Kruger *Con*

Contact: Fleur Anderson, House of Commons, London SW1A 0AA Tel: 020 7219 3000
Email: fleur.anderson.mp@parliament.uk
Website: www.ncvo.org.uk/about-us/media-centre/all-party-parliamentary-group

Chemical Industry
Chair: Jacob Young *Con*
Vice-chairs:
Mike Amesbury *Lab*
Greg Clark *Con*
Secretary: Martyn Day *SNP*
Treasurer: Lord Monks *Lab*

Contact: Jacob Young, House of Commons, London SW1A 0AA Tel: 020 7219 3936
Email: jacob.young.mp@parliament.uk

Child and Youth Crime
Chair: Sir Mike Penning *Con*
Vice-chairs:
Dawn Butler *Lab*
Nigel Evans *Con*
Tim Farron *Lib Dem*
Jonathan Gullis *Con*
Victoria Prentis *Con*
Secretary: Stephen McPartland *Con*

Contact: Sir Mike Penning, House of Commons, London SW1A 0AA
Tel: 020 7219 3000
Email: mike.penning.mp@parliament.uk

Child Contact Centres and Services
Chairs:
Baroness McIntosh of Pickering *Con*
Alex Norris *Lab/Co-op*
Vice-chairs:
Baroness Finlay of Llandaff *CB*
Jess Phillips *Lab*
Lee Rowley *Con*

Contact: Alex Norris, House of Commons, London SW1A 0AA Tel: 020 7219 3899
Email: alex.norris.mp@parliament.uk

Childcare and Early Education
Chair: Steve Brine *Con*
Vice-chair: Conor McGinn *Lab*
Officers:
Apsana Begum *Lab*
James Daly *Con*
Neil Gray *SNP*
Yasmin Qureshi *Lab*
Christian Wakeford *Con*

Contact: Steve Brine, House of Commons, London SW1A 0AA Tel: 020 7219 7189
Email: steve.brine.mp@parliament.uk
Twitter: @APPGearlyyears

Children

Chairs:
Tim Loughton — *Con*
Baroness Tyler of Enfield — *Lib Dem*
Vice-chairs:
Baroness Howarth of Breckland — *CB*
Baroness Massey of Darwen — *Lab*
Lord Ramsbotham — *CB*
Baroness Walmsley — *Lib Dem*
Secretary: David Simmonds — *Con*

Contact: Tim Loughton, House of Commons, London SW1A 0AA Tel: 020 7219 4471
Email: loughtont@parliament.uk
Website: www.ncb.org.uk/all-party-parliamentary-group-children-0

Children, Teenagers and Young Adults with Cancer

Chair: Thangam Debbonaire — *Lab*
Vice-chairs:
Amy Callaghan — *SNP*
Jack Lopresti — *Con*
Officers:
Lord Moynihan — *Con*
Andrew Selous — *Con*

Contact: Thangam Debbonaire, House of Commons, London SW1A 0AA
Tel: 020 7219 0974
Email: thangam.debbonaire.mp@parliament.uk
Website: www.clicsargent.org.uk/content/all-party-parliamentary-group-children-teenagers-and-young-adults-cancer
Twitter: @APPGyoungcancer

Children's Media and the Arts

Chairs:
Baroness Benjamin — *Lib Dem*
Julie Elliott — *Lab*
Officers:
Baroness McIntosh of Hudnall — *Lab*
Andrew Rosindell — *Con*

Contact: Julie Elliott, House of Commons, London SW1A 0AA Tel: 020 7219 7165
Email: julie.elliott.mp@parliament.uk

Choice at the End of Life

Chair: Karin Smyth — *Lab*
Vice-chairs:
Lucy Allan — *Con*
Paul Blomfield — *Lab*
Christine Jardine — *Lib Dem*
Ben Lake — *PlC*
Dr Caroline Lucas — *Green*
Stuart C McDonald — *SNP*
Baroness Meacher — *CB*

Contact: Karin Smyth, House of Commons, London SW1A 0AA
Email: karin.smyth.mp@parliament.uk

Christianity in the Holy Land

Chair: Steve Double — *Con*
Vice-chairs:
Janet Daby — *Lab*
Brendan O'Hara — *SNP*
Andrew Selous — *Con*
Jim Shannon — *DUP*
Bishop of Southwark — *NA*

Contact: Steve Double, House of Commons, London SW1A 0AA Tel: 020 7219 4408
Email: steve.double.mp@parliament.uk

Christians in Parliament

Chair: Sir Gary Streeter — *Con*
Vice-chairs:
Ian Blackford — *SNP*
Baroness Brinton — *Lib Dem*
Lord Curry of Kirkharle — *CB*
Marsha De Cordova — *Lab*
Sir Jeffrey Donaldson — *DUP*
Lord Farmer — *Con*
Tim Farron — *Lib Dem*
Baroness Sherlock — *Lab*

Contact: Sir Gary Streeter, House of Commons, London SW1A 0AA Tel: 020 7219 5033
Email: deans@parliament.uk
Website: www.christiansinparliament.org.uk
Twitter: @CiPAPPG

Cider

Chair: Ian Liddell-Grainger — *Con*
Vice-chairs:
Sir Mark Hendrick — *Lab/Co-op*
Lord Kilclooney — *CB*
Neil Parish — *Con*
Deputy Chair: Bill Wiggin — *Con*

Contact: Ian Liddell-Grainger, House of Commons, London SW1A 0AA
Tel: 020 7219 8149 Email: ianlg@parliament.uk

City Regions Transport

Chair: Graham Stringer — *Lab*
Vice-chairs:
Lord Shipley — *Lib Dem*
Mike Wood — *Con*
Secretary: Clive Betts — *Lab*

Contact: Graham Stringer, North Manchester Sixth Form College, Rochdale Road, Manchester M9 4AF Tel: 0161-202 6600
Email: graham.stringer.mp@parliament.uk

Classical Music
Chairs:
Lord Berkeley of Knighton *CB*
Barbara Keeley *Lab*
Vice-chairs:
Lord German *Lib Dem*
Sir Bernard Jenkin *Con*
Secretary: William Wragg *Con*
Treasurer: Baroness McIntosh of Hudnall *Lab*

Contact: Barbara Keeley, House of Commons, London SW1A 0AA Tel: 020 7219 8025

Climate Change
Chair: Dr Caroline Lucas *Green*
Vice-chairs:
Daisy Cooper *Lib Dem*
Stephen Doughty *Lab/Co-op*
Wera Hobhouse *Lib Dem*
Clive Lewis *Lab*
Kerry McCarthy *Lab*
Anna McMorrin *Lab*
Lord Oxburgh *CB*
Andrew Selous *Con*
Alex Sobel *Lab/Co-op*
Matt Western *Lab*
Daniel Zeichner *Lab*

Contact: Dr Caroline Lucas, House of Commons, London SW1A 0AA
Tel: 020 7219 7025
Email: caroline.lucas.mp@parliament.uk
Website: www.policyconnect.org.uk/appccg
Twitter: @APPCCG

Coalfield Communities
Chair: Conor McGinn *Lab*
Vice-chairs:
Aaron Bell *Con*
Chris Elmore *Lab*
Yvonne Fovargue *Lab*
Mary Foy *Lab*
Paul Howell *Con*
Christina Rees *Lab/Co-op*
Marie Rimmer *Lab*
Alexander Stafford *Con*
Deputy Chairs:
Alex Davies-Jones *Lab*
Jonathan Gullis *Con*
Secretary: Brendan Clarke-Smith *Con*

Contact: Conor McGinn, House of Commons, London SW1A 0AA Tel: 020 7219 4367
Email: conor.mcginn.mp@parliament.uk

Coastal Communities
Chair: Mike Hill *Lab*
Vice-chairs:
Tim Loughton *Con*
Kate Osborne *Lab*
Jim Shannon *DUP*

Contact: Mike Hill, 23 South Road, Hartlepool TS26 9HD Tel: 01429 290168

Commercial Radio
Chair: Andy Carter *Con*
Vice-chairs:
Baroness Grender *Lib Dem*
Simon Jupp *Con*
Lord Kilclooney *CB*
Steve McCabe *Lab*
Andrew Percy *Con*
Henry Smith *Con*
Iain Stewart *Con*
Secretary and Treasurer: Lord Gordon of Strathblane *Lab*

Contact: Andy Carter, House of Commons, London SW1A 0AA Tel: 020 7219 3000
Email: andy.carter.mp@parliament.uk
Twitter: @RadioAPPG

Commercial Sexual Exploitation
Chair: Dame Diana Johnson *Lab*
Vice-chairs:
Diane Abbott *Lab*
Fiona Bruce *Con*
Carolyn Harris *Lab*
Lord McColl of Dulwich *Con*
Lord Ponsonby of Shulbrede *Lab*
Secretary: Jess Phillips *Lab*
Treasurer: Ronnie Cowan *SNP*

Contact: Dame Diana Johnson, House of Commons, London SW1A 0AA
Tel: 020 7219 5647
Email: johnsond@parliament.uk
Twitter: @APPG_CSE

Commonwealth Games
Chair: Mike Wood *Con*
Vice-chairs:
Lord Addington *Lib Dem*
Lord Bilimoria *CB*
Preet Kaur Gill *Lab/Co-op*
Julian Knight *Con*
Rachel Maclean *Con*
Shabana Mahmood *Lab*
John Spellar *Lab*
Craig Tracey *Con*
Lord Whitby *Con*

Contact: Mike Wood, 111a High Street, Wordsley DY8 5QR Tel: 01384 913123
Website: www.appgcommonwealthgames.org
Twitter: @APPGCGames

Community Development in Europe
Chairs:
Earl of Dundee *Con*
Sir Edward Leigh *Con*
Vice-chairs:
Lord Anderson of Swansea *Lab*
Sir Mark Hendrick *Lab/Co-op*
Secretary: Earl of Dundee *Con*

Contact: Sir Edward Leigh, House of Commons, London SW1A 0AA
Tel: 020 7219 6480
Email: edward.leigh.mp@parliament.uk

Compassionate Politics
Chairs:
Debbie Abrahams *Lab*
Baroness Warsi *Con*
Vice-chairs:
Tracey Crouch *Con*
Martyn Day *SNP*
Bishop of Durham *NA*
Stephen Kinnock *Lab*
Ben Lake *PlC*
Baroness Lister of Burtersett *Lab*
Dr Caroline Lucas *Green*

Contact: Debbie Abrahams, House of Commons, London SW1A 0AA
Tel: 020 7219 1041
Email: abrahamsd@parliament.uk

Complex Needs
Chairs:
Lord Adebowale *CB*
Jane Stevenson *Con*
Officers:
Debbie Abrahams *Lab*
Baroness Armstrong of Hill Top *Lab*
Baroness Finlay of Llandaff *CB*
Damian Hinds *Con*
Steve Reed *Lab/Co-op*
Jeff Smith *Lab*

Contact: Jane Stevenson, House of Commons, London SW1A 0AA Tel: 020 7219 3846
Email: jane.stevenson.mp@parliament.uk
Website: www.turning-point.co.uk/appg.html
Twitter: @APPGComplexNeed

Conception to Age Two – The First 1001 Days
Chair: Tim Loughton *Con*
Vice-chairs:
Caroline Ansell *Con*
Siobhan Baillie *Con*
Sally-Ann Hart *Con*
Sharon Hodgson *Lab*
Baroness Hollins *CB*
Lucy Powell *Lab/Co-op*
Lord Russell of Liverpool *CB*
Treasurer: Fiona Bruce *Con*
Officers:
Miriam Cates *Con*
Wera Hobhouse *Lib Dem*

Contact: Tim Loughton, House of Commons, London SW1A 0AA Tel: 020 7219 4471
Email: loughtont@parliament.uk

Conservation, Places and People
Chair: Layla Moran *Lib Dem*
Vice-chairs:
Paul Howell *Con*
Lord Kerslake *CB*
Alex Sobel *Lab/Co-op*

Contact: Layla Moran, House of Commons, London SW1A 0AA Tel: 020 7219 3905
Email: layla.moran.mp@parliament.uk

Consumer Protection
Chair: Yvonne Fovargue *Lab*
Vice-chairs:
Baroness Altmann *Con*
Patricia Gibson *SNP*
Darren Jones *Lab*

Contact: Yvonne Fovargue, House of Commons, London SW1A 0AA
Tel: 020 7219 3000
Email: yvonne.fovargue.mp@parliament.uk

Coronavirus
Chair: Layla Moran *Lib Dem*
Vice-chairs:
Debbie Abrahams *Lab*
Baroness Jones of Moulsecoomb *Green*
Barbara Keeley *Lab*
Clive Lewis *Lab*
Dr Caroline Lucas *Green*
Dr Dan Poulter *Con*
Liz Saville Roberts *PlC*
Dr Philippa Whitford *SNP*
Munira Wilson *Lib Dem*

Contact: Layla Moran, House of Commons, London SW1A 0AA Tel: 020 7219 3905
Email: layla.moran.mp@parliament.uk
Website: www.marchforchange.uk/appg_coronavirus
Twitter: @AppgCoronavirus

Corporate Governance
Chair: Mark Garnier *Con*
Officers:
Kirsty Blackman *SNP*
Baroness Bowles of Berkhamsted *Lib Dem*
Stephen Timms *Lab*

Contact: Mark Garnier, House of Commons, London SW1A 0AA Tel: 020 7219 7198
Email: mark.garnier.mp@parliament.uk
Website: www.appcgg.co.uk

Corporate Responsibility

Chairs:
Jonathan Djanogly *Con*
Baroness Greengross *CB*
Vice-chairs:
Lord Aberdare *CB*
Baroness Andrews *Lab*
Baroness Burt of Solihull *Lib Dem*
Stephen Hammond *Con*

Contact: Jonathan Djanogly, House of Commons, London SW1A 0AA
Tel: 020 7219 2367
Email: jonathan.djanogly.mp@parliament.uk
Website: www.apcrg.org.uk
Twitter: @CRParliament

Council Housing

Chair: Matt Western *Lab*
Vice-chairs:
Jack Dromey *Lab*
Rachel Hopkins *Lab*
Andrew Lewer *Con*
James Murray *Lab/Co-op*
Officers:
Mike Amesbury *Lab*
Marsha De Cordova *Lab*
Ben Everitt *Con*
Helen Hayes *Lab*
Paul Howell *Con*
Kim Johnson *Lab*
Marco Longhi *Con*
Lloyd Russell-Moyle *Lab/Co-op*
Stephen Timms *Lab*
Mick Whitley *Lab*

Contact: Matt Western, House of Commons, London SW1A 0AA Tel: 0207 219 2051
Email: matt.western.mp@parliament.uk

Council of Sri Lankan Muslim Organisations UK

Chair: Bob Blackman *Con*
Vice-chair: Lord Naseby *Con*
Officers:
Tanmanjeet Singh Dhesi *Lab*
Siobhain McDonagh *Lab*
Gareth Thomas *Lab/Co-op*

Contact: Bob Blackman, House of Commons, London SW1A 0AA Tel: 020 7219 7082
Email: bob.blackman.mp@parliament.uk

County

Chair: Peter Aldous *Con*
Vice-chair: Darren Henry *Con*
Officers:
Baroness Bakewell of Hardington Mandeville *Lib Dem*
Matt Western *Lab*

Contact: Peter Aldous, House of Commons, London SW1A 0AA Tel: 020 7219 7182
Email: peter.aldous.mp@parliament.uk
Website: www.countycouncilsnetwork.org.uk/advocacy/ccn-in-parliament/county-appg
Twitter: @CountyAPPG

Craft

Chair: Sir John Hayes *Con*
Vice-chairs:
Earl of Clancarty *CB*
Lord Cormack *Con*
Baroness Garden of Frognal *Lib Dem*
Sharon Hodgson *Lab*

Contact: Sir John Hayes, House of Commons, London SW1A 0AA Tel: 020 7219 1389
Email: hayesj@parliament.uk
Website: heritagecrafts.org.uk/appg
Twitter: @APPGCraft

Creative Diversity

Chairs:
Baroness Bull *CB*
Chi Onwurah *Lab*
Vice-chairs:
Baroness Benjamin *Lib Dem*
Baroness Bonham-Carter of Yarnbury *Lib Dem*
Tracy Brabin *Lab/Co-op*
Helen Grant *Con*
Dr Rupa Huq *Lab*
Lord Vaizey of Didcot *Con*
Officer: Giles Watling *Con*

Contact: Chi Onwurah, House of Commons, London SW1A 0AA Tel: 020 7219 7114
Email: chi.onwurah.mp@parliament.uk
Twitter: @DiversityAPPG

Credit Unions

Chair: Bim Afolami *Con*
Vice-chairs:
Lord Hunt of Wirral *Con*
Kim Johnson *Lab*
Lord Kennedy of Southwark *Lab/Co-op*
Secretary: Yvonne Fovargue *Lab*
Treasurer: Chris Evans *Lab/Co-op*

Contact: Bim Afolami, House of Commons, London SW1A 0AA
Email: bim.afolami.mp@parliament.uk
Website: www.abcul.coop/news-and-comment/

credit-unions-in-parliament/credit-unions-in-parliament-appg

Cricket

President: Lord Haselhurst *Con*
Chair: Michael Tomlinson *Con*
Vice-chairs:
Vicky Ford *Con*
Baroness Massey of Darwen *Lab*
Baroness Pinnock *Lib Dem*
James Wild *Con*
Secretary: Nigel Mills *Con*
Treasurer: Julian Knight *Con*

Contact: Michael Tomlinson, House of Commons, London SW1A 0AA
Tel: 020 7219 5844
Email: michael.tomlinson.mp@parliament.uk

Critical Minerals

Chair: Steve Double *Con*
Vice-chairs:
Pauline Latham *Con*
Christina Rees *Lab/Co-op*
Alex Sobel *Lab/Co-op*
Alexander Stafford *Con*
Secretary: Scott Mann *Con*

Contact: Steve Double, House of Commons, London SW1A 0AA Tel: 020 7219 4408
Email: steve.double.mp@parliament.uk
Website: www.criticalmineral.org/all-parliamentary-group-appg

Crossrail

Chair: Stephen Timms *Lab*
Vice-chairs:
Lord Bradshaw *Lib Dem*
Lord Brougham and Vaux *Con*
Lord Faulkner of Worcester *Lab*
Dr Rupa Huq *Lab*
Andrew Rosindell *Con*
Virendra Sharma *Lab*
Sam Tarry *Lab*
Lord Tope *Lib Dem*
Treasurer: Abena Oppong-Asare *Lab*

Contact: Stephen Timms, House of Commons, London SW1A 0AA Tel: 020 7219 4000
Email: timmss@parliament.uk

Customer Service

Chairs:
Philip Davies *Con*
Chris Evans *Lab/Co-op*
Officers:
Carolyn Harris *Lab*
Andrew Lewer *Con*

Contact: Philip Davies, House of Commons, London SW1A 0AA Tel: 020 7219 8264
Email: daviesp@parliament.uk
Website: www.instituteofcustomerservice.com/public-affairs/all-party-parliamentary-group

Cyber Security

Chair: Simon Fell *Con*
Vice-chairs:
Lord Arbuthnot of Edrom *Con*
Angela Crawley *SNP*
Sir George Howarth *Lab*
Tony Lloyd *Lab*
Lord Mackenzie of Framwellgate *NA*
Baroness Neville-Jones *Con*
Baroness Neville-Rolfe *Con*
Viscount Waverley *CB*
Lord West of Spithead *Lab*

Contact: Simon Fell, House of Commons, London SW1A 0AA Tel: 020 7219 3000
Email: simon.fell.mp@parliament.uk
Website: www.appgcybersecurity.org

Cycling and Walking

Patrons:
Lord Berkeley *Lab*
Ben Bradshaw *Lab*
Lord Young of Cookham *Con*
Chairs:
Ruth Cadbury *Lab*
Selaine Saxby *Con*
Vice-chairs:
Feryal Clark *Lab*
Virginia Crosbie *Con*
Layla Moran *Lib Dem*
Lord Young of Norwood Green *Lab*
Secretary: Matt Western *Lab*
Treasurer: Fabian Hamilton *Lab*
Officer: Baroness Barker *Lib Dem*
Officers:
Anneliese Dodds *Lab/Co-op*
Lilian Greenwood *Lab*
Meg Hillier *Lab/Co-op*
Rachael Maskell *Lab/Co-op*
Lord Russell of Liverpool *CB*
Daniel Zeichner *Lab*

Contact: Ruth Cadbury, House of Commons, London SW1A 0AA Tel: 020 7219 8590
Email: ruthcadburymp@parliament.uk
Website: allpartycycling.org
Twitter: @allpartycycling

Dairy

Chair: Scott Mann *Con*
Vice-chairs:
Steve Double *Con*
Sir George Howarth *Lab*
Jim Shannon *DUP*
Heather Wheeler *Con*

Contact: Scott Mann, House of Commons, London SW1A 0AA Tel: 020 7219 5744
Email: scott.mann.mp@parliament.uk

Dalits
(Discrimination against Dalits, the former 'untouchables' caste in India)
Chairs:
Lord Harries of Pentregarth *CB*
Yasmin Qureshi *Lab*
Vice-chairs:
Lord Cormack *Con*
Baroness Thornton *Lab/Co-op*
Secretary: Kate Green *Lab*
Treasurer: Lord Cashman *NA*

Contact: Yasmin Qureshi, House of Commons, London SW1A 0AA Tel: 020 7219 7019
Email: yasmin.qureshi.mp@parliament.uk

Dance
Chairs:
Baroness Hooper *Con*
Luke Pollard *Lab/Co-op*
Vice-chairs:
Baroness Bonham-Carter of Yarnbury *Lib Dem*
Sharon Hodgson *Lab*
Secretary: Abena Oppong-Asare *Lab*
Officers:
Baroness McIntosh of Pickering *Con*
Lord Taylor of Warwick *NA*

Contact: Luke Pollard, House of Commons, London SW1A 0AA Tel: 020 7219 2749
Email: luke.pollard.mp@parliament.uk

Dark Skies
Chairs:
Andrew Griffith *Con*
Lord Rees of Ludlow *CB*
Vice-chairs:
Tonia Antoniazzi *Lab*
Baroness Bakewell of Hardington Mandeville *Lib Dem*
Sir Peter Bottomley *Con*
Sir Graham Brady *Con*
Lord Carrington *CB*
Philip Dunne *Con*
Lord Grantchester *Lab*
Fay Jones *Con*
Lord Judd *Lab*
Baroness Neville-Rolfe *Con*
Selaine Saxby *Con*
Greg Smith *Con*
Lord Stunell *Lib Dem*
Lord Taylor of Holbeach *Con*
Anne-Marie Trevelyan *Con*
Lord Vaux of Harrowden *CB*
John Whittingdale *Con*
James Wild *Con*

Contact: Andrew Griffith, House of Commons, London SW1A 0AA Tel: 020 7219 4557
Email: andrew@griffithmp.com
Twitter: @AppgDarkSkies

Darts
Chairs:
Karl McCartney *Con*
Conor McGinn *Lab*
Vice-chairs:
Lord Goddard of Stockport *Lib Dem*
Rachel Hopkins *Lab*
Scott Mann *Con*
John Spellar *Lab*
Jo Stevens *Lab*
Secretaries:
Dr Lisa Cameron *SNP*
Nigel Mills *Con*
Alex Norris *Lab/Co-op*
Treasurers:
Lord Porter of Spalding *Con*
Lord Watts *Lab*

Contact: Conor McGinn, House of Commons, London SW1A 0AA Tel: 020 7219 4367
Email: conor.mcginn.mp@parliament.uk
Website: www.appgdarts.org.uk

Data Analytics
Chair: Daniel Zeichner *Lab*
Vice-chairs:
Earl of Erroll *CB*
Darren Jones *Lab*
Lord Knight of Weymouth *Lab/Co-op*
Rachel Maclean *Con*
Lord Oates *Lib Dem*
Lee Rowley *Con*
Stephen Timms *Lab*
Lord Wallace of Saltaire *Lib Dem*

Contact: Daniel Zeichner, House of Commons, London SW1A 0AA Tel: 020 7219 8462
Email: daniel@danielzeichner.co.uk
Website: www.policyconnect.org.uk/appgda
Twitter: @DataAPG

Deafness
Chair: Lilian Greenwood *Lab*
Vice-chairs:
Rosie Cooper *Lab*
Ian Mearns *Lab*
Sir Mike Penning *Con*
Tommy Sheppard *SNP*
Lord Shipley *Lib Dem*

Contact: Lilian Greenwood, House of Commons, London SW1A 0AA

Tel: 020 7219 7122
Email: lilian.greenwood.mp@parliament.uk
Website: www.deafcouncil.org.uk/about-us/party-parliamentary-group-deafness

Death Penalty

Chairs:
Mark Pritchard *Con*
Baroness Stern *CB*
Vice-chairs:
Baroness Anelay of St Johns *Con*
Alistair Carmichael *Lib Dem*
Lord Dholakia *Lib Dem*
Lord Dubs *Lab*
Lord Faulkner of Worcester *Lab*
Baroness Hooper *Con*
Lord Purvis of Tweed *Lib Dem*
Baroness Whitaker *Lab*

Contact: Mark Pritchard, House of Commons, London SW1A 0AA Tel: 020 7219 8494
Email: pritchardm@parliament.uk
Website: appgdeathpenaltyabolition.uk

Deaths Abroad and Consular Services and Assistance

Chair: Hannah Bardell *SNP*
Vice-chairs:
Anne McLaughlin *SNP*
Justin Madders *Lab*
Lloyd Russell-Moyle *Lab/Co-op*
Naz Shah *Lab*
Secretary: Craig Tracey *Con*
Treasurer: Martin Docherty-Hughes *SNP*

Contact: Hannah Bardell, House of Commons, London SW1A 0AA Tel: 020 7219 5907
Email: hannah.bardell.mp@parliament.uk
Twitter: @APPGDeathAbroad

Debt and Personal Finance

Chair: Yvonne Fovargue *Lab*
Vice-chairs:
Paul Blomfield *Lab*
Jonathan Edwards *Ind*
Andrew Percy *Con*
Treasurer: Nick Smith *Lab*

Contact: Yvonne Fovargue, House of Commons, London SW1A 0AA
Tel: 020 7219 3000
Email: yvonne.fovargue.mp@parliament.uk
Website: www.appgdebt.org

Deliberative Democracy

Chair: Alex Norris *Lab/Co-op*
Vice-chairs:
Alistair Carmichael *Lib Dem*
Wendy Chamberlain *Lib Dem*
Dr Stella Creasy *Lab/Co-op*
Jon Cruddas *Lab*
David Davis *Con*
Dr Caroline Lucas *Green*
David Morris *Con*
Lisa Nandy *Lab*
Bob Stewart *Con*
Lord Tyler *Lib Dem*

Contact: Alex Norris, House of Commons, London SW1A 0AA Tel: 020 7219 3899
Email: alex.norris.mp@parliament.uk

Dementia

Chairs:
Debbie Abrahams *Lab*
Baroness Greengross *CB*
Officers:
Robert Courts *Con*
Sir Mike Penning *Con*

Contact: Debbie Abrahams, House of Commons, London SW1A 0AA
Tel: 020 7219 1041
Email: abrahamsd@parliament.uk
Website: www.alzheimers.org.uk/about-us/policy-and-influencing/all-party-parliamentary-group-dementia

Democracy and Human Rights in the Gulf

Chair: Brendan O'Hara *SNP*
Vice-chairs:
Sir Peter Bottomley *Con*
Alistair Carmichael *Lib Dem*
Chris Law *SNP*
Dr Caroline Lucas *Green*
Alex Norris *Lab/Co-op*
Lord Scriven *Lib Dem*
Andy Slaughter *Lab*
Baroness Stern *CB*

Contact: Brendan O'Hara, House of Commons, London SW1A 0AA Tel: 020 7219 8783
Email: brendan.ohara.mp@parliament.uk

Dentistry and Oral Health

Chair: Sir Paul Beresford *Con*
Vice-chairs:
Lord Colwyn *Con*
Judith Cummins *Lab*
Yasmin Qureshi *Lab*
Baroness Thornton *Lab/Co-op*
Baroness Walmsley *Lib Dem*

Contact: Sir Paul Beresford, House of Commons, London SW1A 0AA
Tel: 020 7219 5018
Email: annie.winsbury@parliament.uk
Website: www.appgdentistry.org

Design and Innovation
Chairs:
Dr John Howell *Con*
Barry Sheerman *Lab/Co-op*
Officers:
Lord Bilimoria *CB*
Jack Brereton *Con*
Lord Freyberg *CB*
Sharon Hodgson *Lab*
Daniel Zeichner *Lab*

Contact: Barry Sheerman, House of Commons, London SW1A 0AA Tel: 020 7219 5037
Email: sheermanb@parliament.uk
Website: www.policyconnect.org.uk/apdig

Devolution
Chair: Andrew Lewer *Con*
Vice-chairs:
Wayne David *Lab*
Baroness Eaton *Con*
Lord Foulkes of Cumnock *Lab/Co-op*
Lord Kerslake *CB*
Lord Purvis of Tweed *Lib Dem*
Henry Smith *Con*
Lord Soley *Lab*
Lord Tyler *Lib Dem*
Dr Jamie Wallis *Con*
Catherine West *Lab*
Craig Williams *Con*

Contact: Andrew Lewer, House of Commons, London SW1A 0AA Tel: 020 7219 3870
Email: andrew.lewer.mp@parliament.uk

Diabetes
Chair: Derek Thomas *Con*
Vice-chairs:
Dr Lisa Cameron *SNP*
Sir George Howarth *Lab*
Secretaries:
Philip Dunne *Con*
Jim Shannon *DUP*
Treasurer: Lord Rennard *Lib Dem*
Officers:
Fabian Hamilton *Lab*
Dr Rupa Huq *Lab*

Contact: Derek Thomas, House of Commons, London SW1A 0AA Tel: 020 7219 4435
Email: derek.thomas.mp@parliament.uk
Twitter: @APPG_Diabetes

Digital Health
Chair: Dean Russell *Con*
Officers:
Saqib Bhatti *Con*
Paul Bristow *Con*
Lord Hunt of Kings Heath *Lab/Co-op*
Anne Marie Morris *Con*

Contact: Dean Russell, House of Commons, London SW1A 0AA Tel: 020 7219 3000
Email: dean.russell.mp@parliament.uk
Website: digitalhealthappg.org

Digital Identity
Chair: Dean Russell *Con*
Vice-chairs:
Lord Arbuthnot of Edrom *Con*
Sir George Howarth *Lab*
Lord Mackenzie of Framwellgate *NA*
Baroness Neville-Rolfe *Con*

Contact: Dean Russell, House of Commons, London SW1A 0AA Tel: 020 7219 3000
Email: dean.russell.mp@parliament.uk
Website: www.appgdigitalid.com

Digital Regulation and Responsibility
Chair: Jeremy Wright *Con*
Deputy Chair: Baroness Kidron *CB*
Vice-chairs:
Hannah Bardell *SNP*
Sarah Champion *Lab*
Lord Clement-Jones *Lib Dem*
Carla Lockhart *DUP*
Maria Miller *Con*
Baroness Morgan of Cotes *Con*
Lord Puttnam *Lab*

Contact: Jeremy Wright, House of Commons, London SW1A 0AA Tel: 020 7219 2008
Email: jeremy.wright.mp@parliament.uk

Digital Skills
Chair: Julie Elliott *Lab*
Vice-chair: Chris Green *Con*
Officers:
Miriam Cates *Con*
Damian Collins *Con*
Lord Knight of Weymouth *Lab/Co-op*
Lord Lucas of Crudwell and Dingwall *Con*

Contact: Julie Elliott, House of Commons, London SW1A 0AA Tel: 020 7219 7165
Email: julie.elliott.mp@parliament.uk
Website: connectpa.co.uk/digital-skills-appg
Twitter: @DigiSkillsAPPG

Disability
Chair: Dr Lisa Cameron *SNP*
Vice-chairs:
Thangam Debbonaire *Lab*
Marsha De Cordova *Lab*
Lord Shinkwin *Con*
Secretary(Lords): Lord Dubs *Lab*
Secretary(Commons): Julia Lopez *Con*
Treasurer: Baroness Uddin *NA*
Officers:
Debbie Abrahams *Lab*

Mary Glindon	*Lab*
Lord Low of Dalston	*CB*
Jim Shannon	*DUP*
Lord Sterling of Plaistow	*Con*

Contact: Dr Lisa Cameron, House of Commons, London SW1A 0AA Tel: 020 7219 6855
Email: lisa.cameron.mp@parliament.uk
Website: disabilityrightsuk.org/policy-campaigns/all-party-parliamentary-disability-group-appdg
Twitter: @DisabilityAPPG

District Councils

Chair: Mark Pawsey *Con*
Vice-chair: Alberto Costa *Con*
Officers:
Baroness Bakewell of Hardington Mandeville *Lib Dem*
Jane Hunt *Con*
Lord Kennedy of Southwark *Lab/Co-op*

Contact: Mark Pawsey, House of Commons, London SW1A 0AA Tel: 020 7219 7136
Email: mark.pawsey.mp@parliament.uk
Website: districtcouncils.info/influencing/appg-micro-site

Diversity and Inclusion in Science, Technology, Engineering and Maths

Chair: Chi Onwurah *Lab*
Officers:
Baroness Benjamin *Lib Dem*
Baroness Brown of Cambridge *CB*
Baroness Grey-Thompson *CB*
Lord Lucas of Crudwell and Dingwall *Con*
Stephen Metcalfe *Con*
Carol Monaghan *SNP*
Alex Norris *Lab/Co-op*
Lord Sheikh *Con*

Contact: Chi Onwurah, House of Commons, London SW1A 0AA Tel: 020 7219 7114
Email: chi.onwurah.mp@parliament.uk
Website: www.britishscienceassociation.org/appg

Domestic Abuse

Chair: Thangam Debbonaire *Lab*
Vice-chairs:
Huw Merriman *Con*
Liz Saville Roberts *PlC*
Secretary: Baroness Bertin *Con*
Treasurer: Gavin Newlands *SNP*

Contact: Thangam Debbonaire, House of Commons, London SW1A 0AA
Tel: 020 7219 0974
Email: thangam.debbonaire.mp@parliament.uk
Website: respect.uk.net/what-we-do/appg-on-perpetrators-of-domestic-abuse

---

Domestic Violence and Abuse

Chair: Apsana Begum *Lab*
Vice-chair: Baroness Bertin *Con*
Officers:
Fleur Anderson *Lab*
Paula Barker *Lab*
Sir Peter Bottomley *Con*
Baroness Burt of Solihull *Lib Dem*
Mark Fletcher *Con*
Vicky Foxcroft *Lab*
Kate Griffiths *Con*
Baroness Hamwee *Lib Dem*
Emma Hardy *Lab*
Kim Johnson *Lab*
Baroness Lister of Burtersett *Lab*
Dr Caroline Lucas *Green*
Maria Miller *Con*
Gavin Newlands *SNP*
Alex Norris *Lab/Co-op*
Jess Phillips *Lab*
Bell Ribeiro-Addy *Lab*
Naz Shah *Lab*
Alison Thewliss *SNP*
Baroness Thornton *Lab/Co-op*
Baroness Verma *Con*

Contact: Apsana Begum, House of Commons, London SW1A 0AA Tel: 020 7219 6826
Email: apsana.begum.mp@parliament.uk
Website: www.womensaid.org.uk/appg

Drones

Chairs:
Gill Furniss *Lab*
Baroness Stern *CB*
Vice-chairs:
Lord Hodgson of Astley Abbotts *Con*
Dr Caroline Lucas *Green*
Alex Sobel *Lab/Co-op*
Lord Wallace of Tankerness *NA*

Contact: Gill Furniss, House of Commons, London SW1A 0AA Tel: 0207 219 0364
Email: gill.furniss.mp@parliament.uk
Website: appgdrones.org.uk
Twitter: @APPGDrones

Drug Policy Reform

Chairs:
Crispin Blunt *Con*
Baroness Meacher *CB*
Jeff Smith *Lab*
Vice-chairs:
Ronnie Cowan *SNP*
Dr Caroline Lucas *Green*

Lord Norton of Louth *Con*
Officer: Alison Thewliss *SNP*

Contact: Crispin Blunt, House of Commons, London SW1A 0AA Tel: 020 7219 2254
Email: crispinbluntmp@parliament.uk
Website: www.drugpolicyreform.net

Dyslexia and other Specific Learning Difficulties
Chair: Sharon Hodgson *Lab*
Vice-chairs:
Lord Addington *Lib Dem*
Janet Daby *Lab*
Dr Peter Kyle *Lab*
Ian Liddell-Grainger *Con*
Yasmin Qureshi *Lab*
Henry Smith *Con*

Contact: Sharon Hodgson, House of Commons, London SW1A 0AA Tel: 020 7219 5160
Email: sharon.hodgson.mp@parliament.uk
Website: www.bdadyslexia.org.uk/about/all-party-parliamentary-group-dyslexia-and-spld-appg

Dyspraxia
Chairs:
Tom Hunt *Con*
Emma Lewell-Buck *Lab*
Vice-chair: Sir David Amess *Con*
Secretary: Lord Addington *Lib Dem*

Contact: Emma Lewell-Buck, House of Commons, London SW1A 0AA
Tel: 020 7219 4468
Email: emma.lewell-buck.mp@parliament.uk

East Coast Main Line
Chair: Catherine McKinnell *Lab*
Vice-chairs:
Lord Beith *Lib Dem*
Jason McCartney *Con*
Stephen McPartland *Con*
Ian Murray *Lab*
Alex Sobel *Lab/Co-op*
Martin Vickers *Con*

Contact: Catherine McKinnell, House of Commons, London SW1A 0AA
Tel: 020 7219 7115
Email: catherine.mckinnell.mp@parliament.uk

East of England
Chairs:
Peter Aldous *Con*
Daniel Zeichner *Lab*
Vice-chairs:
Baroness Cohen of Pimlico *Lab*
Jonathan Djanogly *Con*
Rachel Hopkins *Lab*
Julie Marson *Con*
Giles Watling *Con*
Secretary: Clive Lewis *Lab*
Treasurer: Dr Dan Poulter *Con*

Contact: Daniel Zeichner, House of Commons, London SW1A 0AA Tel: 020 7219 8462
Email: daniel@danielzeichner.co.uk
Website: eastofenglandappg.org.uk
Twitter: @EastEnglandAPPG

East Midlands
Chairs:
Nigel Mills *Con*
Alex Norris *Lab/Co-op*
Vice-chairs:
Dr Luke Evans *Con*
Mark Fletcher *Con*
Lilian Greenwood *Lab*
Darren Henry *Con*
Alicia Kearns *Con*
Tom Randall *Con*
Claudia Webbe *Ind*

Contact: Alex Norris, House of Commons, London SW1A 0AA Tel: 020 7219 3899
Email: alex.norris.mp@parliament.uk

Eating Disorders
Chairs:
Scott Benton *Con*
Wera Hobhouse *Lib Dem*
Vice-chairs:
Dr Lisa Cameron *SNP*
Julie Elliott *Lab*
Tim Farron *Lib Dem*
Sir George Howarth *Lab*
Officers:
Chris Evans *Lab/Co-op*
Baroness Parminter *Lib Dem*

Contact: Wera Hobhouse, House of Commons, London SW1A 0AA Tel: 020 7219 2093
Email: wera.hobhouse.mp@parliament.uk
Website: www.beateatingdisorders.org.uk/appg

Education
Chair: Marcus Fysh *Con*
Vice-chairs:
Jonathan Gullis *Con*
Lord Knight of Weymouth *Lab/Co-op*
Lord Storey *Lib Dem*
James Sunderland *Con*

Contact: Marcus Fysh, House of Commons, London SW1A 0AA Tel: 020 7219 4527
Email: marcus.fysh.mp@parliament.uk
Website: www.educationappg.org.uk
Twitter: @APPGEducation

Education Technology
Chair: Damian Hinds *Con*
Vice-chairs:
Kevin Brennan *Lab*
Conor Burns *Con*
Baroness Hooper *Con*
Lord Knight of Weymouth *Lab/Co-op*
Lord Lucas of Crudwell and Dingwall *Con*
Baroness Morris of Yardley *Lab*
Chris Skidmore *Con*
Christian Wakeford *Con*
Lord Willetts *Con*

Contact: Damian Hinds, House of Commons, London SW1A 0AA Tel: 020 7219 7057
Email: damian.hinds.mp@parliament.uk
Twitter: @edtechappg

Eggs, Pigs and Poultry
Chair: Jim Shannon *DUP*
Vice-chair: Nick Smith *Lab*
Secretary: Craig Williams *Con*
Treasurer: Simon Hoare *Con*
Officers:
Tonia Antoniazzi *Lab*
David Jones *Con*
Carla Lockhart *DUP*

Contact: Jim Shannon, House of Commons, London SW1A 0AA Tel: 020 7219 7160
Email: jim.shannon.mp@parliament.uk

Electoral Campaigning Transparency
Chair: Stephen Kinnock *Lab*
Vice-chairs:
Deidre Brock *SNP*
Dr Caroline Lucas *Green*
John Penrose *Con*
Lord Rennard *Lib Dem*

Contact: Stephen Kinnock, House of Commons, London SW1A 0AA Tel: 020 7219 8801
Email: stephen.kinnock.mp@parliament.uk
Website: www.fairvote.uk/electoral-campaigning-transparency
Twitter: @CampaigningAPPG

Electric Aviation
Chair: Sir Paul Beresford *Con*
Vice-chairs:
Hilary Benn *Lab*
Sir Roger Gale *Con*
Sir Oliver Heald *Con*
Viscount Trenchard *Con*
Officers:
Sir Christopher Chope *Con*
Lord Desai *NA*
Lord Fox *Lib Dem*
Lord Glenarthur *Con*
Lord Jones of Cheltenham *Lib Dem*
Kerry McCarthy *Lab*

Contact: Sir Paul Beresford, House of Commons, London SW1A 0AA
Tel: 020 7219 5018
Email: annie.winsbury@parliament.uk

Electric Vehicles
Chair: Matt Western *Lab*
Officers:
Dame Cheryl Gillan *Con*
Sharon Hodgson *Lab*
Sir Bernard Jenkin *Con*
Anna McMorrin *Lab*
Andrew Selous *Con*
Alex Sobel *Lab/Co-op*
Lord Teverson *Lib Dem*

Contact: Matt Western, House of Commons, London SW1A 0AA Tel: 020 7219 2051
Email: matt.western.mp@parliament.uk
Website: www.r-e-a.net/appgs/appg-on-electric-vehicles

Endometriosis
Chair: Sir David Amess *Con*
Vice-chairs:
Jackie Doyle-Price *Con*
Emma Hardy *Lab*
Dame Diana Johnson *Lab*
Secretary: Gill Furniss *Lab*

Contact: Sir David Amess, House of Commons, London SW1A 0AA Tel: 020 7219 3452
Email: amessd@parliament.uk
Twitter: @Eappg

Energy Costs
Chairs:
Alan Brown *SNP*
Lord Whitty *Lab*
Vice-chairs:
Peter Aldous *Con*
Lord Deben *Con*
Julie Elliott *Lab*
Lord Haworth *Lab*
Lord Palmer *CB*

Contact: Alan Brown, House of Commons, London SW1A 0AA Tel: 020 7219 6093
Email: alan.brown.mp@parliament.uk

Energy Security
Chair: Alun Cairns *Con*
Vice-chairs:
Ben Lake *PlC*
Jessica Morden *Lab*
Craig Williams *Con*

Contact: Alun Cairns, House of Commons, London SW1A 0AA Tel: 020 7219 7175
Email: alun.cairns.mp@parliament.uk

Energy Studies

Chair: Ian Liddell-Grainger *Con*
Officers:
Alan Brown *SNP*
Julie Elliott *Lab*
Vicky Ford *Con*
Lord Hunt of Kings Heath *Lab/Co-op*
Lord Oxburgh *CB*
Lord Ravensdale *CB*
Lord Redesdale *Lib Dem*
Jim Shannon *DUP*
Alexander Stafford *Con*

Contact: Ian Liddell-Grainger, House of Commons, London SW1A 0AA
Tel: 020 7219 8149 Email: ianlg@parliament.uk
Website: pges.org.uk

Engineering

Chairs:
Laurence Robertson *Con*
Lord Broers *CB*
Officers:
Chris Green *Con*
Lord Mair *CB*
Stephen Metcalfe *Con*
Chi Onwurah *Lab*
Lord Willis of Knaresborough *Lib Dem*

Contact: Laurence Robertson, House of Commons, London SW1A 0AA
Tel: 020 7219 4196
Email: robertsonl@parliament.uk
Website: appeg.co.uk

Entrepreneurship

Chair: Seema Malhotra *Lab/Co-op*
Vice-chairs:
Lord Bilimoria *CB*
Dr Lisa Cameron *SNP*
Lord Leigh of Hurley *Con*
Rachel Maclean *Con*
Officers:
Bim Afolami *Con*
Lord Cromwell *CB*
Baroness Kramer *Lib Dem*
Baroness Neville-Jones *Con*

Contact: Seema Malhotra, House of Commons, London SW1A 0AA Tel: 020 7219 8957
Email: seema.malhotra.mp@parliament.uk
Website: appgentrepreneurship.org
Twitter: @appg_e

Environment

Chair: Anthony Browne *Con*
Vice-chairs:
Lord Cameron of Dillington *CB*
Virginia Crosbie *Con*
Sarah Dines *Con*
Jack Dromey *Lab*
Laura Farris *Con*
Dame Cheryl Gillan *Con*
Fay Jones *Con*
Dr Matthew Offord *Con*
Christina Rees *Lab/Co-op*
Dr Alan Whitehead *Lab*

Contact: Anthony Browne, House of Commons, London SW1A 0AA Tel: 020 7219 8089
Email: anthony.browne.mp@parliament.uk

Epilepsy

Chair: Valerie Vaz *Lab*
Vice-chairs:
Sir David Amess *Con*
Dame Cheryl Gillan *Con*
Baroness Hussein-Ece *Lib Dem*
Andy McDonald *Lab*

Contact: Valerie Vaz, House of Commons, London SW1A 0AA Tel: 020 7219 7176
Email: valerie.vaz.mp@parliament.uk
Website: www.epilepsy.org.uk/appg

Equipment for Disabled Children

Chair: Bambos Charalambous *Lab*
Vice-chairs:
Neil Gray *SNP*
Lord Rennard *Lib Dem*
Julian Sturdy *Con*

Contact: Bambos Charalambous, House of Commons, London SW1A 0AA
Tel: 020 7219 3460
Email: bambos.charalambous.mp@parliament.uk
Website: newlifecharity.co.uk/docs/general/The-All-Party-Parliamentary-Group-o.shtml

Equitable Life Policy Holders

Chairs:
Bob Blackman *Con*
Fabian Hamilton *Lab*
Vice-chairs:
Tonia Antoniazzi *Lab*
Mhairi Black *SNP*
Sir Peter Bottomley *Con*
Baroness Kramer *Lib Dem*
Jim Shannon *DUP*
Bob Stewart *Con*
Hywel Williams *PlC*
Secretary: Layla Moran *Lib Dem*

Contact: Bob Blackman, House of Commons, London SW1A 0AA Tel: 020 7219 7082
Email: bob.blackman.mp@parliament.uk
Website: www.emag.org.uk/justice_group.php

Erasmus

Chair: Taiwo Owatemi *Lab*
Officers:
Tonia Antoniazzi *Lab*
Stephen Crabb *Con*
Florence Eshalomi *Lab/Co-op*
Owen Thompson *SNP*

Contact: Taiwo Owatemi, House of Commons, London SW1A 0AA Tel: 020 7219 5842
Email: taiwo.owatemi.mp@parliament.uk

Esports

Chair: Karl McCartney *Con*
Vice-chairs:
Peter Bone *Con*
Lord Moynihan *Con*
Gavin Newlands *SNP*
Tom Pursglove *Con*
Greg Smith *Con*
Alex Sobel *Lab/Co-op*
Chris Stephens *SNP*

Contact: Karl McCartney, House of Commons, London SW1A 0AA Tel: 020 7219 3000
Email: karl.mccartney.mp@parliament.uk
Website: www.appgesports.org
Twitter: @APPGEsports

Ethics and Sustainability in Fashion

Chairs:
Catherine West *Lab*
Baroness Young of Hornsey *CB*
Vice-chairs:
Dr Lisa Cameron *SNP*
Laura Farris *Con*
John McNally *SNP*
Secretary: Lord Young of Norwood Green *Lab*
Treasurer: Baroness Jenkin of Kennington *Con*

Contact: Catherine West, House of Commons, London SW1A 0AA Tel: 020 7219 6141
Email: catherine.west.mp@parliament.uk
Website: www.appg.fashion

Explosive Threats

Chairs:
Lord Dear *CB*
Dr Matthew Offord *Con*
Vice-chairs:
Dan Carden *Lab*
Chris Law *SNP*
Henry Smith *Con*

Contact: Dr Matthew Offord, House of Commons, London SW1A 0AA
Tel: 020 7219 7083
Email: matthew.offord.mp@parliament.uk

Extraordinary Rendition

Chairs:
Stephen Timms *Lab*
Lord Tyrie *NA*
Vice-chairs:
Baroness Ludford *Lib Dem*
Andy Slaughter *Lab*
Lord Tyler *Lib Dem*
Treasurer: Lord Hodgson of Astley Abbotts *Con*

Contact: Stephen Timms, House of Commons, London SW1A 0AA Tel: 020 7219 4000
Email: timmss@parliament.uk
Website: www.extraordinaryrendition.org

Eye Health and Visual Impairment

Chairs:
Marsha De Cordova *Lab*
Lord Low of Dalston *CB*
Vice-chairs:
Lord Blunkett *Lab*
Florence Eshalomi *Lab/Co-op*
Dame Cheryl Gillan *Con*
Lord Holmes of Richmond *Con*
Jim Shannon *DUP*

Contact: Marsha De Cordova, House of Commons, London SW1A 0AA
Tel: 020 7924 1973
Email: marsha.decordova.mp@parliament.uk
Twitter: @EyeHealthAPPG

Fair Business Banking

Chairs:
Kevin Hollinrake *Con*
William Wragg *Con*
Vice-chairs:
Tonia Antoniazzi *Lab*
Harriett Baldwin *Con*
Kirsty Blackman *SNP*
Dr Lisa Cameron *SNP*
James Cartlidge *Con*
Lord Cromwell *CB*
Peter Gibson *Con*
Andrew Griffith *Con*
Julian Knight *Con*
Ben Lake *PlC*
Chris Law *SNP*
Earl of Lindsay *Con*
Chris Matheson *Lab*
Chris Stephens *SNP*
Alison Thewliss *SNP*
Tom Tugendhat *Con*
Sammy Wilson *DUP*

Contact: Kevin Hollinrake, House of Commons, London SW1A 0AA Tel: 020 7219 4746
Email: kevin.hollinrake.mp@parliament.uk
Website: www.appgbanking.org.uk
Twitter: @APPGbanking

Fair Fuel for UK Motorists and UK Hauliers
Chair: Craig Mackinlay *Con*
Vice-chairs:
Rosie Cooper *Lab*
Robert Halfon *Con*
Sammy Wilson *DUP*
Officers:
Peter Aldous *Con*
Mary Glindon *Lab*
Sir Greg Knight *Con*
Julian Knight *Con*
Martin Vickers *Con*

Contact: Craig Mackinlay, House of Commons, London SW1A 0AA Tel: 020 7219 4442
Email: craig.mackinlay.mp@parliament.uk

Fairs and Showgrounds
Chairs:
Sir David Amess *Con*
Lord Mackenzie of Framwellgate *NA*
Vice-chair: Alison Thewliss *SNP*
Secretary and Treasurer: David Linden *SNP*
Officer: Rosie Cooper *Lab*

Contact: Sir David Amess, House of Commons, London SW1A 0AA Tel: 020 7219 3452
Email: amessd@parliament.uk

Fairtrade
Chairs:
Holly Lynch *Lab*
Jason McCartney *Con*
Vice-chairs:
Fleur Anderson *Lab*
Dr Lisa Cameron *SNP*
Stephen Doughty *Lab/Co-op*
Kim Johnson *Lab*
Catherine McKinnell *Lab*
Huw Merriman *Con*
Officers:
Dr Caroline Lucas *Green*
Seema Malhotra *Lab/Co-op*

Contact: Holly Lynch, House of Commons, London SW1A 0AA Tel: 020 7219 6277
Email: holly.lynch.mp@parliament.uk
Website: www.fairtrade.org.uk/get-involved/in-your-community/fairtrade-all-party-parliamentary-group
Twitter: @FairtradeAPPG

Faith and Society
Chair: Stephen Timms *Lab*
Vice-chairs:
Fiona Bruce *Con*
Jon Cruddas *Lab*
David Linden *SNP*
Baroness Neuberger *CB*
Lord Singh of Wimbledon *CB*
Sir Gary Streeter *Con*
Secretary: David Lammy *Lab*
Treasurer: Steve Double *Con*

Contact: Stephen Timms, House of Commons, London SW1A 0AA Tel: 020 7219 4000
Email: timmss@parliament.uk
Website: www.faithandsociety.org

Family Business
Chair: John Stevenson *Con*
Vice-chairs:
Lord Cotter *Lib Dem*
Michelle Donelan *Con*
Julian Sturdy *Con*
Secretary: Mary Glindon *Lab*

Contact: John Stevenson, House of Commons, London SW1A 0AA Tel: 020 7219 3000
Email: john.stevenson.mp@parliament.uk
Website: www.appgfamilybusiness.com

Fatherhood
Chairs:
Steve Double *Con*
David Lammy *Lab*
Vice-chairs:
Tim Loughton *Con*
Matt Western *Lab*
Secretary: Sir Peter Bottomley *Con*

Contact: David Lammy, House of Commons, London SW1A 0AA Tel: 020 7219 0767
Email: lammyd@parliament.uk

Film and Broader Screen
Chair: Nick Smith *Lab*
Vice-chairs:
Richard Bacon *Con*
Baroness Bonham-Carter of Yarnbury *Lib Dem*
Dame Diana Johnson *Lab*
Barbara Keeley *Lab*
Lord McNally *Lib Dem*
Barry Sheerman *Lab/Co-op*
Jeff Smith *Lab*

Contact: Nick Smith, House of Commons, London SW1A 0AA Tel: 020 7219 7018
Email: nick.smith.mp@parliament.uk

Film and Production Industry
Chairs:
Kevin Brennan *Lab*

Mark Pritchard	*Con*
Dean Russell	*Con*
Officers:	
Dehenna Davison	*Con*
Jonathan Gullis	*Con*

Contact: Dean Russell, House of Commons, London SW1A 0AA Tel: 020 7219 3000
Email: dean.russell.mp@parliament.uk

Financial Education for Young People

Chair: Julian Knight	*Con*
Vice-chairs:	
Marion Fellows	*SNP*
Drew Hendry	*SNP*
Jerome Mayhew	*Con*
Jonathan Reynolds	*Lab/Co-op*

Contact: Julian Knight, House of Commons, London SW1A 0AA Tel: 020 7219 3577
Email: julian.knight.mp@parliament.uk
Website: www.young-enterprise.org.uk/home/impact-policy/policy-hub/appg-on-financial-education

Financial Markets and Services

Chair: Bim Afolami	*Con*
Vice-chairs:	
Kirsty Blackman	*SNP*
Alun Cairns	*Con*
Gareth Davies	*Con*
Lord Dykes	*CB*
Ben Everitt	*Con*
Lord Teverson	*Lib Dem*
Alison Thewliss	*SNP*
Stephen Timms	*Lab*
Lord Tyrie	*NA*
Viscount Waverley	*CB*
Secretary: Sir Robert Neill	*Con*

Contact: Bim Afolami, House of Commons, London SW1A 0AA
Email: bim.afolami.mp@parliament.uk
Website: apgfms.org.uk

Financial Technology

Chair: Adam Afriyie	*Con*
Vice-chairs:	
Aaron Bell	*Con*
Lord Holmes of Richmond	*Con*
Stephen Timms	*Lab*
Officers:	
Harriett Baldwin	*Con*
Alan Mak	*Con*
Lord Vaux of Harrowden	*CB*

Contact: Adam Afriyie, House of Commons, London SW1A 0AA Tel: 020 7219 8023
Email: adam.afriyie.mp@parliament.uk
Website: appgfintech.org.uk
Twitter: @APPGFinTech

Fire Safety and Rescue

Chair: Sir David Amess	*Con*
Vice-chairs:	
Baroness Brinton	*Lib Dem*
Felicity Buchan	*Con*
Margaret Ferrier	*Ind*
Mary Glindon	*Lab*
Sir George Howarth	*Lab*
Robbie Moore	*Con*
Lord Porter of Spalding	*Con*
Andy Slaughter	*Lab*
Secretary: Sir Mike Penning	*Con*
Treasurer: Peter Aldous	*Con*

Contact: Sir David Amess, House of Commons, London SW1A 0AA Tel: 020 7219 3452
Email: amessd@parliament.uk

First Do No Harm

Chairs:	
Baroness Cumberlege	*Con*
Jeremy Hunt	*Con*
Vice-chairs:	
Emma Hardy	*Lab*
Sharon Hodgson	*Lab*
Lord Hunt of Kings Heath	*Lab/Co-op*
Lord O'Shaughnessy	*Con*
Lord Patel	*CB*
Yasmin Qureshi	*Lab*
Cat Smith	*Lab*

Contact: Jeremy Hunt, House of Commons, London SW1A 0AA Tel: 020 7219 6813
Email: huntj@parliament.uk

Fisheries

Chair: Peter Aldous	*Con*
Vice-chairs:	
Caroline Ansell	*Con*
Alistair Carmichael	*Lib Dem*
David Duguid	*Con*
Lord Greenway	*CB*
Angus MacNeil	*SNP*
Lord McColl of Dulwich	*Con*
Stephen Morgan	*Lab*
Lia Nici	*Con*
Lord Russell of Liverpool	*CB*
Liz Saville Roberts	*PlC*
Martin Vickers	*Con*
Dr Philippa Whitford	*SNP*

Contact: Peter Aldous, House of Commons, London SW1A 0AA Tel: 020 7219 7182
Email: peter.aldous.mp@parliament.uk
Website: www.fishingappg.org.uk

Fit and Healthy Childhood

Chairs:
Baroness Benjamin *Lib Dem*
Steve McCabe *Lab*
Vice-chairs:
Julie Elliott *Lab*
Adam Holloway *Con*
Dame Diana Johnson *Lab*
Lord McColl of Dulwich *Con*

Contact: Steve McCabe, House of Commons, London SW1A 0AA Tel: 020 7219 3509
Email: mccabes@parliament.uk
Website: royalpa.co.uk/the-aqppg-on-a-fit-and-healthy-childhood
Twitter: @fhcappg

Flags and Heraldry

Chairs:
Andrew Rosindell *Con*
Lord West of Spithead *Lab*
Vice-chairs:
Sir Peter Bottomley *Con*
Philip Hollobone *Con*
Lord Kilclooney *CB*
Angus MacNeil *SNP*
Ian Paisley *DUP*
Tom Randall *Con*
Alexander Stafford *Con*
Secretary: Henry Smith *Con*

Contact: Andrew Rosindell, House of Commons, London SW1A 0AA
Tel: 020 7219 8475
Email: andrew.rosindell.mp@parliament.uk

Flood Prevention

Chair: Rachael Maskell *Lab/Co-op*
Vice-chairs:
Peter Aldous *Con*
Christina Rees *Lab/Co-op*
Laurence Robertson *Con*
Officer: Cat Smith *Lab*

Contact: Rachael Maskell, House of Commons, London SW1A 0AA Tel: 020 7219 4525
Email: rachael.maskell.mp@parliament.uk

Food and Drink

Chair: John Stevenson *Con*
Vice-chairs:
Deidre Brock *SNP*
Sharon Hodgson *Lab*
David Linden *SNP*
Treasurer: Nigel Mills *Con*

Contact: John Stevenson, House of Commons, London SW1A 0AA Tel: 020 7219 3000
Email: john.stevenson.mp@parliament.uk
Website: www.appgfooddrink.org.uk

Food and Health

Chair: Sir David Amess *Con*
Vice-chairs:
Lord Balfe *Con*
Martyn Day *SNP*
Sharon Hodgson *Lab*
Baroness Jenkin of Kennington *Con*
Lord Rooker *Lab*
Baroness Walmsley *Lib Dem*

Contact: Sir David Amess, House of Commons, London SW1A 0AA Tel: 020 7219 3452
Email: amessd@parliament.uk
Website: www.fhf.org.uk

Football

Chair: Clive Betts *Lab*
Vice-chairs:
Lord Addington *Lib Dem*
Karen Bradley *Con*
Ian Byrne *Lab*
Brendan Clarke-Smith *Con*
Dehenna Davison *Con*
Marsha De Cordova *Lab*
Mark Eastwood *Con*
Lord Faulkner of Worcester *Lab*
Alison McGovern *Lab*
Martin Vickers *Con*
Mike Wood *Con*
Treasurer: Ian Murray *Lab*

Contact: Clive Betts, House of Commons, London SW1A 0AA Tel: 020 7219 5114
Email: officeofclivebettsmp@parliament.uk

Football Club

Chairs:
Karl McCartney *Con*
Justin Madders *Lab*
Vice-chairs:
Clive Betts *Lab*
Ben Bradley *Con*
Karen Bradley *Con*
Brendan Clarke-Smith *Con*
Tracey Crouch *Con*
Dehenna Davison *Con*
Mark Eastwood *Con*
Katherine Fletcher *Con*
Lord Hain *Lab*
David Johnston *Con*
Stephen Kinnock *Lab*
Scott Mann *Con*
Chris Matheson *Lab*
Robin Millar *Con*
Ian Murray *Lab*
James Sunderland *Con*
Owen Thompson *SNP*
Edward Timpson *Con*
Martin Vickers *Con*

Contact: Karl McCartney, House of Commons, London SW1A 0AA Tel: 020 7219 3000
Email: karl.mccartney.mp@parliament.uk
Website: www.parliamentary.soccer

Football Supporters

Chair: Ian Mearns *Lab*
Vice-chairs:
Damian Collins *Con*
Tracey Crouch *Con*
Damian Green *Con*
Rachel Hopkins *Lab*
Jason McCartney *Con*
Alex Norris *Lab/Co-op*
Jo Stevens *Lab*
Matt Western *Lab*

Contact: Ian Mearns, House of Commons, London SW1A 0AA Tel: 020 7219 7074
Email: ian.mearns.mp@parliament.uk
Website: thefsa.org.uk/our-work/appg-for-football-supporters

Foreign Affairs

Chair: Imran Ahmad Khan *Con*
Vice-chairs:
Dr Lisa Cameron *SNP*
Sarah Champion *Lab*
Officers:
Bob Blackman *Con*
Andrew Bowie *Con*
Adam Holloway *Con*
David Johnston *Con*
Bob Seely *Con*

Contact: Imran Ahmad Khan, House of Commons, London SW1A 0AA
Tel: 020 7219 3000
Email: imran.mp@parliament.uk
Website: www.appgforeignaffairs.org

Forestry and Tree Planting

Chair: Ben Lake *PlC*
Vice-chairs:
Earl of Caithness *Con*
Lord Carrington *CB*
Lord Clark of Windermere *Lab*
Lord Colgrain *Con*
Drew Hendry *SNP*

Contact: Ben Lake, House of Commons, London SW1A 0AA
Email: ben.lake.mp@parliament.uk

Formula One

Chair: Sir Jeffrey Donaldson *DUP*
Vice-chairs:
Philip Davies *Con*
Lord Hain *Lab*
Conor McGinn *Lab*
Alec Shelbrooke *Con*
James Sunderland *Con*
Secretary: Greg Smith *Con*
Treasurer: Karen Bradley *Con*

Contact: Sir Jeffrey Donaldson, House of Commons, London SW1A 0AA
Tel: 020 7219 3407
Email: jeffrey.donaldson.mp@parliament.uk

Foster Care Work

Chair: Ian Mearns *Lab*
Vice-chairs:
Sir Peter Bottomley *Con*
Bill Esterson *Lab*
Rachel Hopkins *Lab*
Chris Law *SNP*
Kate Osborne *Lab*

Contact: Ian Mearns, House of Commons, London SW1A 0AA Tel: 020 7219 7074
Email: ian.mearns.mp@parliament.uk

Fourth Industrial Revolution

Chair: Alan Mak *Con*
Vice-chairs:
Dr Peter Kyle *Lab*
Wes Streeting *Lab*
Officers:
Anthony Browne *Con*
James Cartlidge *Con*
Andrew Griffith *Con*
Kevin Hollinrake *Con*
Lord Holmes of Richmond *Con*
Stephen Kinnock *Lab*
Pat McFadden *Lab*
Michael Tomlinson *Con*
Lord Willetts *Con*

Contact: Alan Mak, House of Commons, London SW1A 0AA Tel: 020 7219 6266
Email: alan.mak.mp@parliament.uk
Twitter: @4IR_APPG

Fracking

Chair: Lee Rowley *Con*
Vice-chairs:
Ben Bradley *Con*
Mark Fletcher *Con*
Louise Haigh *Lab*
Alexander Stafford *Con*

Contact: Lee Rowley, House of Commons, London SW1A 0AA Tel: 020 7219 4197
Email: lee.rowley.mp@parliament.uk

Freedom of Speech

Chair: Adam Afriyie *Con*
Vice-chairs:
Baroness Cox *CB*
Philip Davies *Con*

Viscount Ridley *Con*
Graham Stringer *Lab*

Contact: Adam Afriyie, House of Commons, London SW1A 0AA Tel: 020 7219 8023
Email: adam.afriyie.mp@parliament.uk

Freeports

Chair: Martin Vickers *Con*
Vice-chairs:
Alun Cairns *Con*
Douglas Chapman *SNP*
Virginia Crosbie *Con*
Dame Diana Johnson *Lab*
Kim Johnson *Lab*
Jack Lopresti *Con*
Mick Whitley *Lab*
Secretary: Lord Berkeley *Lab*
Treasurer: Julia Lopez *Con*

Contact: Martin Vickers, House of Commons, London SW1A 0AA Tel: 020 7219 7212
Email: martin.vickers.mp@parliament.uk
Website: taiwanappg.org.uk

Frozen British Pensions

Chair: Sir Roger Gale *Con*
Vice-chair: Tonia Antoniazzi *Lab*
Officers:
Sir Peter Bottomley *Con*
Lord German *Lib Dem*
Sir George Howarth *Lab*

Contact: Sir Roger Gale, House of Commons, London SW1A 0AA Tel: 020 7219 4087
Email: galerj@parliament.uk
Website: www.frozenbritishpensions.org

Funerals and Bereavement

Chair: Sir John Hayes *Con*
Vice-chairs:
Sir David Amess *Con*
Rosie Cooper *Lab*
Robert Goodwill *Con*
Dame Diana Johnson *Lab*
Mark Pawsey *Con*
Gavin Robinson *DUP*

Contact: Sir John Hayes, House of Commons, London SW1A 0AA Tel: 020 7219 1389
Email: hayesj@parliament.uk

Furniture Industry

Chair: Mike Wood *Con*
Vice-chairs:
Rosie Cooper *Lab*
Mark Eastwood *Con*
Baroness Warsi *Con*

Contact: Mike Wood, House of Commons, London SW1A 0AA Tel: 020 7219 6982
Email: mikej.wood.mp@parliament.uk

Further Education and Lifelong Learning

Chair: Peter Aldous *Con*
Vice-chairs:
Dr Stephen Farry *APNI*
Baroness Garden of Frognal *Lib Dem*
Officer: Emma Hardy *Lab*

Contact: Peter Aldous, House of Commons, London SW1A 0AA Tel: 020 7219 7182
Email: peter.aldous.mp@parliament.uk
Website: www.aoc.co.uk/media-and-parliament/our-work-mps/all-party-parliamentary-group-further-education-and-lifelong

Fusion Energy

Chair: Dr John Howell *Con*
Vice-chair: Mark Menzies *Con*
Officers:
Alberto Costa *Con*
Mark Garnier *Con*
Sir Robert Neill *Con*
Christina Rees *Lab/Co-op*
Henry Smith *Con*
John Spellar *Lab*
Bob Stewart *Con*

Contact: Dr John Howell, House of Commons, London SW1A 0AA Tel: 020 7219 6676
Email: howelljm@parliament.uk

Future Generations

Chairs:
Lord Bird *CB*
Bambos Charalambous *Lab*
Officers:
Lord Balfe *Con*
Simon Fell *Con*
Dame Cheryl Gillan *Con*
Lord Harris of Haringey *Lab*
Lord Hastings of Scarisbrick *CB*
Dr Caroline Lucas *Green*
Anna McMorrin *Lab*
Baroness Prashar *CB*
Lord Rees of Ludlow *CB*
Liz Saville Roberts *PlC*
Baroness Watkins of Tavistock *CB*
Daniel Zeichner *Lab*

Contact: Bambos Charalambous, House of Commons, London SW1A 0AA
Tel: 020 7219 3460
Email: bambos.charalambous.mp@parliament.uk Website: www.appgfuturegenerations.com
Twitter: @FuturesAPPG

Future of Aviation
Chair: Henry Smith *Con*
Vice-chairs:
Alun Cairns *Con*
Rosie Cooper *Lab*
Lord Davies of Gower *Con*
Andrew Griffith *Con*
Seema Malhotra *Lab/Co-op*
Paul Maynard *Con*

Contact: Henry Smith, House of Commons, London SW1A 0AA Tel: 020 7219 7043
Email: henry.smith.mp@parliament.uk

Future of Retail
Chairs:
Liz Twist *Lab*
Matt Vickers *Con*
Vice-chairs:
Dr Lisa Cameron *SNP*
Martyn Day *SNP*
Charlotte Nichols *Lab*
Officers:
Lilian Greenwood *Lab*
Wera Hobhouse *Lib Dem*

Contact: Matt Vickers, House of Commons, London SW1A 0AA Tel: 020 7219 3723
Email: matt.vickers.mp@parliament.uk

Future of Work
Chairs:
David Davis *Con*
Clive Lewis *Lab*
Vice-chairs:
Lord Clement-Jones *Lib Dem*
Jon Cruddas *Lab*
Lord Knight of Weymouth *Lab/Co-op*
Stephen Metcalfe *Con*
Kirsten Oswald *SNP*
Baroness Prosser *Lab*

Contact: Clive Lewis, House of Commons, London SW1A 0AA Tel: 020 7219 5593
Email: clive.lewis.mp@parliament.uk

Gambling Related Harm
Chair: Carolyn Harris *Lab*
Vice-chairs:
Ronnie Cowan *SNP*
Sir Iain Duncan Smith *Con*
Lord Foster of Bath *Lib Dem*
Sir Mark Hendrick *Lab/Co-op*
Stuart C McDonald *SNP*
Sir Mike Penning *Con*
Sammy Wilson *DUP*
Secretary: Gerald Jones *Lab*
Treasurer: Stephen Timms *Lab*

Contact: Carolyn Harris, House of Commons, London SW1A 0AA Tel: 020 7219 4316
Email: carolyn.harris.mp@parliament.uk
Website: www.grh-appg.com
Twitter: @GRHAPPG

Gaps in Support
Chairs:
Tracy Brabin *Lab/Co-op*
Sir Jeffrey Donaldson *DUP*
Dr Caroline Lucas *Green*
Esther McVey *Con*
Jamie Stone *Lib Dem*
Alison Thewliss *SNP*
William Wragg *Con*
Secretary: Dr Stephen Farry *APNI*
Treasurer: Virendra Sharma *Lab*

Contact: Jamie Stone, House of Commons, London SW1A 0AA Tel: 020 7219 1654
Email: jamie.stone.mp@parliament.uk
Website: www.gapsinsupportappg.org
Twitter: @APPGGapsSupport

Gardening and Horticulture
Chairs:
Baroness Fookes *Con*
Ian Liddell-Grainger *Con*
Vice-chairs:
Baroness Bennett of Manor Castle *Green*
Lord Carrington of Fulham *Con*
Dame Cheryl Gillan *Con*
Robert Goodwill *Con*
Lord Taylor of Holbeach *Con*
Secretary: John Spellar *Lab*

Contact: Ian Liddell-Grainger, House of Commons, London SW1A 0AA
Tel: 020 7219 8149 Email: ianlg@parliament.uk

General Aviation
President: Sir Roger Gale *Con*
Vice-President: Lord Kirkhope of Harrogate *Con*
Chairs:
Lord Davies of Gower *Con*
Steve Double *Con*
Vice-chairs:
Robert Courts *Con*
Dr Rupa Huq *Lab*
Stephen Metcalfe *Con*
Ian Paisley *DUP*
Lord Rotherwick *Con*
Lord Stevens of Kirkwhelpington *CB*

Contact: Steve Double, House of Commons, London SW1A 0AA Tel: 020 7219 4408
Email: steve.double.mp@parliament.uk
Website: www.generalaviationappg.uk
Twitter: @GA_APPG

Genetic Haemochromatosis
Chair: Sir John Hayes *Con*
Vice-chair: Ben Lake *PlC*
Officers:
Dr Rupa Huq *Lab*
Angus MacNeil *SNP*

Contact: Sir John Hayes, House of Commons, London SW1A 0AA Tel: 020 7219 1389
Email: hayesj@parliament.uk

Genocide and Crimes Against Humanity
Chairs:
Fleur Anderson *Lab*
Lord Sheikh *Con*
Vice-chairs:
Lord Alderdice *Lib Dem*
Lyn Brown *Lab*
Feryal Clark *Lab*

Contact: Fleur Anderson, House of Commons, London SW1A 0AA Tel: 020 7219 3000
Email: fleur.anderson.mp@parliament.uk
Website: www.aegistrust.org/what-we-do/activities/appg
Twitter: @GenocideAPPG

Geographically Protected Foods
Chairs:
Ruth Edwards *Con*
Alicia Kearns *Con*
Vice-chairs:
Deidre Brock *SNP*
Fay Jones *Con*
Ben Lake *PlC*
Lord McNicol of West Kilbride *Lab*
Lord Tyler *Lib Dem*

Contact: Alicia Kearns, House of Commons, London SW1A 0AA Tel: 020 7219 3000
Email: alicia.kearns.mp@parliament.uk

Global Education
Chair: Harriett Baldwin *Con*
Vice-chairs:
Lord German *Lib Dem*
Lord Low of Dalston *CB*
Chris Matheson *Lab*
Mike Wood *Con*

Contact: Harriett Baldwin, House of Commons, London SW1A 0AA Tel: 020 7219 3000
Email: harriett.baldwin.mp@parliament.uk
Twitter: @appgglobaled

Global Health
Chairs:
Lord Crisp *CB*
Dr Dan Poulter *Con*
Vice-chairs:
Lord Darzi of Denham *NA*
Meg Hillier *Lab/Co-op*
Baroness Northover *Lib Dem*
Lord Ribeiro *Con*
Baroness Watkins of Tavistock *CB*
Treasurer: Lord Kakkar *CB*

Contact: Dr Dan Poulter, House of Commons, London SW1A 0AA Tel: 020 7219 7038
Email: daniel.poulter.mp@parliament.uk
Website: www.appg-globalhealth.org.uk
Twitter: @APPGGlobHealth

Global Lesbian, Gay, Bisexual and Transgender (LGBT+) Rights
Chair: Crispin Blunt *Con*
Vice-chairs:
Baroness Barker *Lib Dem*
Lord Cashman *NA*
Dr Peter Kyle *Lab*
Stewart Malcolm McDonald *SNP*
Treasurer: Lord Collins of Highbury *Lab*

Contact: Crispin Blunt, House of Commons, London SW1A 0AA Tel: 020 7219 2254
Email: crispinbluntmp@parliament.uk
Website: www.appglgbt.org
Twitter: @APPGLGBT

Global Security and Non-Proliferation
Chairs:
Sir Peter Bottomley *Con*
Lord Hannay of Chiswick *CB*
Vice-chairs:
Hilary Benn *Lab*
Lord Browne of Ladyton *Lab*
Baroness Falkner of Margravine *CB*
Baroness Miller of Chilthorne Domer *Lib Dem*
Lord Wood of Anfield *Lab*

Contact: Sir Peter Bottomley, House of Commons, London SW1A 0AA
Tel: 020 7219 5060
Email: bottomleyp@parliament.uk
Website: www.basicint.org/portfolio/appg

Global Tuberculosis
Chairs:
Lord Herbert of South Downs *Con*
Virendra Sharma *Lab*
Vice-chairs:
Pauline Latham *Con*
Baroness Masham of Ilton *CB*
Baroness Sheehan *Lib Dem*
Baroness Suttie *Lib Dem*

Contact: Virendra Sharma, House of Commons, London SW1A 0AA Tel: 020 7219 6080
Email: sharmav@parliament.uk
Website: www.appg-tb.org.uk
Twitter: @APPGTB

Anne McLaughlin *SNP*
Robbie Moore *Con*

Contact: Peter Gibson, House of Commons, London SW1A 0AA Tel: 020 7219 3000
Email: peter.gibson.mp@parliament.uk
Website: www.socialintegrationappg.org.uk
Twitter: @IntegrationAPPG

Social Media
Chair: Chris Elmore *Lab*
Vice-chairs:
Dr Lisa Cameron *SNP*
Bambos Charalambous *Lab*
Damian Hinds *Con*
David Linden *SNP*
Luke Pollard *Lab/Co-op*
Victoria Prentis *Con*
Viscount Waverley *CB*
Secretary: Aaron Bell *Con*

Contact: Chris Elmore, House of Commons, London SW1A 0AA Tel: 020 7219 3000
Email: chris.elmore.mp@parliament.uk
Website: www.rsph.org.uk/socialmediaappg
Twitter: @socialmediaAPPG

Social Mobility
Chairs:
David Johnston *Con*
Justin Madders *Lab*
Baroness Tyler of Enfield *Lib Dem*
Vice-chairs:
Lord Bird *CB*
Judith Cummins *Lab*
Jane Hunt *Con*
Andrea Jenkyns *Con*
Jack Lopresti *Con*
Siobhain McDonagh *Lab*
Baroness Morris of Yardley *Lab*
Lucy Powell *Lab/Co-op*
Stephen Timms *Lab*

Contact: Justin Madders, House of Commons, London SW1A 0AA Tel: 020 7219 6584
Email: justin.madders.mp@parliament.uk
Website: www.suttontrust.com/policy/all-party-parliamentary-group-on-social-mobility
Twitter: @socmobappg

Social Science and Policy
Chair: Sir Peter Bottomley *Con*
Vice-chair: Daniel Zeichner *Lab*
Secretary: Baroness Bottomley of Nettlestone *Con*
Treasurer: Lord Whitty *Lab*

Contact: Sir Peter Bottomley, House of Commons, London SW1A 0AA
Tel: 020 7219 5060
Email: bottomleyp@parliament.uk

South West
Chairs:
Ben Bradshaw *Lab*
Sir Gary Streeter *Con*
Vice-chairs:
Lord Berkeley *Lab*
Sheryll Murray *Con*
Luke Pollard *Lab/Co-op*
Selaine Saxby *Con*
Michael Tomlinson *Con*
David Warburton *Con*

Contact: Sir Gary Streeter, House of Commons, London SW1A 0AA Tel: 020 7219 5033
Email: deans@parliament.uk

South Western Railway
Chair: Chris Loder *Con*
Vice-chairs:
Fleur Anderson *Lab*
Steve Brine *Con*
Sir Ed Davey *Lib Dem*
Flick Drummond *Con*
Stephen Hammond *Con*
Damian Hinds *Con*
Paul Holmes *Con*
Ranil Jayawardena *Con*
Simon Jupp *Con*
Alan Mak *Con*
Maria Miller *Con*
Angela Richardson *Con*
Dr Ben Spencer *Con*
Munira Wilson *Lib Dem*

Contact: Chris Loder, House of Commons, London SW1A 0AA Tel: 01305 818446
Email: chris.loder.mp@parliament.uk
Website: www.rssb.co.uk
Twitter: @appgonswr

Sovereign Defence Capability
Chair: Jack Lopresti *Con*
Vice-chair: Wayne David *Lab*
Secretary: Jamie Stone *Lib Dem*
Treasurer: Mark Menzies *Con*

Contact: Jack Lopresti, House of Commons, London SW1A 0AA Tel: 020 7219 7070
Email: jack.lopresti.mp@parliament.uk

Space
Patron: Adam Afriyie *Con*
Chair: David Morris *Con*
Vice-chairs:
Steve Double *Con*
Mark Garnier *Con*
Dame Cheryl Gillan *Con*

Lord Hunt of Chesterton *Lab*
Angus MacNeil *SNP*
Stephen Metcalfe *Con*
Carol Monaghan *SNP*
Chi Onwurah *Lab*
Ian Paisley *DUP*
Mark Pritchard *Con*
John Spellar *Lab*
Jamie Stone *Lib Dem*
Dr Philippa Whitford *SNP*
Treasurer: Liz Saville Roberts *PlC*

Contact: David Morris, House of Commons, London SW1A 0AA Tel: 020 7219 7234
Email: david.morris.mp@parliament.uk

Special Educational Needs and Disabilities

Chair: Olivia Blake *Lab*
Vice-Chair: Sally-Ann Hart *Con*
Officers:
Rob Butler *Con*
James Daly *Con*
Marsha De Cordova *Lab*
Jack Dromey *Lab*
Tim Farron *Lib Dem*
Emma Hardy *Lab*
Julian Sturdy *Con*
James Sunderland *Con*

Contact: Olivia Blake, House of Commons, London SW1A 0AA Tel: 020 7219 3552
Email: olivia.blake.mp@parliament.uk
Website: www.naht.org.uk/appgsend
Twitter: @APPG_SEND

Speech and Language Difficulties

Chairs:
Geraint Davies *Lab/Co-op*
Lord Ramsbotham *CB*
Vice-chairs:
Peter Aldous *Con*
Steve McCabe *Lab*
Baroness Whitaker *Lab*

Contact: Geraint Davies, House of Commons, London SW1A 0AA Tel: 020 7219 7166
Email: geraint.davies.mp@parliament.uk
Website: www.rcslt.org/policy/england#section-4

Spinal Cord Injury

Chair: Owen Paterson *Con*
Vice-chairs:
Sir Graham Brady *Con*
Baroness Masham of Ilton *CB*
Mark Tami *Lab*
Lord Tebbit *Con*

Contact: Owen Paterson, House of Commons, London SW1A 0AA Tel: 020 7219 5185
Email: patersono@parliament.uk
Website: www.spinal.co.uk/campaigning/all-party-parliamentary-group-on-spinal-cord-injury

Sport

Chair: Ben Bradley *Con*
Vice-chairs:
Lord Addington *Lib Dem*
Lord Archer of Weston-super-Mare *NA*
Lord Campbell of Pittenweem *Lib Dem*
Dehenna Davison *Con*
Baroness Grey-Thompson *CB*
Sharon Hodgson *Lab*
Jane Hunt *Con*
Lord Moynihan *Con*
Christina Rees *Lab/Co-op*
Baroness Sater *Con*

Contact: Ben Bradley, House of Commons, London SW1A 0AA Tel: 020 7219 3594
Email: ben.bradley.mp@parliament.uk
Twitter: @appgsport

Sport, Modern Slavery and Human Rights

Chairs:
Alex Norris *Lab/Co-op*
Baroness Young of Hornsey *CB*
Vice-chairs:
Darren Jones *Lab*
Lord Moynihan *Con*

Contact: Alex Norris, House of Commons, London SW1A 0AA Tel: 020 7219 3899
Email: alex.norris.mp@parliament.uk
Website: www.appgshr.org.uk
Twitter: @APPG_SportandHR

Srebrenica

(To raise awareness of the Srebrenica Genocide)
Chairs:
Lord Bourne of Aberystwyth *Con*
Yasmin Qureshi *Lab*
Vice-chairs:
Kate Green *Lab*
Lord Hussain *Lib Dem*
Imran Hussain *Lab*
Andrew Mitchell *Con*

Contact: Yasmin Qureshi, House of Commons, London SW1A 0AA Tel: 020 7219 7019
Email: yasmin.qureshi.mp@parliament.uk

State Pension Inequality for Women

Chairs:
Carolyn Harris *Lab*
Tim Loughton *Con*
Officers:
Peter Aldous *Con*
Caroline Ansell *Con*
Paula Barker *Lab*

Olivia Blake *Lab*
Douglas Chapman *SNP*
Judith Cummins *Lab*
Alex Davies-Jones *Lab*
Jack Dromey *Lab*
Flick Drummond *Con*
Stephen Flynn *SNP*
Yvonne Fovargue *Lab*
Nia Griffith *Lab*
Sally-Ann Hart *Con*
Rachel Hopkins *Lab*
Christine Jardine *Lib Dem*
Kim Johnson *Lab*
Tony Lloyd *Lab*
Dr Caroline Lucas *Green*
Stuart C McDonald *SNP*
Navendu Mishra *Lab*
Jessica Morden *Lab*
Dr Kieran Mullan *Con*
Kate Osborne *Lab*
Christina Rees *Lab/Co-op*
Liz Saville Roberts *PlC*
Tommy Sheppard *SNP*
Karin Smyth *Lab*
Chris Stephens *SNP*
Richard Thomson *SNP*
Derek Twigg *Lab*
Liz Twist *Lab*
Mick Whitley *Lab*
Dr Beth Winter *Lab*
Dame Rosie Winterton *Lab*

Contact: Carolyn Harris, House of Commons, London SW1A 0AA Tel: 020 7219 4316
Email: carolyn.harris.mp@parliament.uk

Steel and Metal Related Industries

Chairs:
Jessica Morden *Lab*
Holly Mumby-Croft *Con*
Vice-chairs:
Olivia Blake *Lab*
Miriam Cates *Con*
Sarah Champion *Lab*
Marion Fellows *SNP*
Margaret Ferrier *Ind*
Nia Griffith *Lab*
Andrew Percy *Con*
Jacob Young *Con*
Secretary: Stephen Kinnock *Lab*
Treasurer: Stephen Doughty *Lab/Co-op*

Contact: Holly Mumby-Croft, House of Commons, London SW1A 0AA
Tel: 0161-818 9390
Email: holly.mumbycroft.mp@parliament.uk

Stem Cell Transplantation

Chair: Mark Tami *Lab*
Officers:
Colleen Fletcher *Lab*
Henry Smith *Con*
Alison Thewliss *SNP*

Contact: Mark Tami, House of Commons, London SW1A 0AA Tel: 020 7219 8174
Email: tamim@parliament.uk
Website: www.appg-stemcell.org.uk
Twitter: @APPGStemCell

Students

Chair: Paul Blomfield *Lab*
Vice-chairs:
Jane Hunt *Con*
Dr Caroline Lucas *Green*
Jo Stevens *Lab*
Alison Thewliss *SNP*
Lord Willetts *Con*

Contact: Paul Blomfield, House of Commons, London SW1A 0AA Tel: 020 7219 7142
Email: paul.blomfield.mp@parliament.uk
Website: www.appg-students.org.uk
Twitter: @APPGStudents

Suicide and Self Harm Prevention

Chair: Liz Twist *Lab*
Vice-chairs:
Jason McCartney *Con*
Jim Shannon *DUP*
Matt Western *Lab*
Treasurer: Karin Smyth *Lab*

Contact: Liz Twist, House of Commons, London SW1A 0AA Tel: 020 7219 2221
Email: liz.twist.mp@parliament.uk

Surgical Mesh

Chairs:
Emma Hardy *Lab*
Alec Shelbrooke *Con*
Vice-chairs:
Sharon Hodgson *Lab*
Dr Julian Lewis *Con*
Alex Norris *Lab/Co-op*

Contact: Emma Hardy, The Octagon, Walker Street, Hull HU3 2RA Tel: 01482 219211
Email: emma.hardy.mp@parliament.uk

Surrogacy

Chair: Andrew Percy *Con*
Vice-chairs:
Dame Diana Johnson *Lab*
Holly Mumby-Croft *Con*
Catherine West *Lab*

Contact: Andrew Percy, House of Commons, London SW1A 0AA Tel: 020 7219 7208
Email: andrew.percy.mp@parliament.uk
Twitter: @APPGsurrogacy

Sustainable Aviation

Chairs:
Sir Graham Brady *Con*
Catherine McKinnell *Lab*
Vice-chairs:
Mark Garnier *Con*
Henry Smith *Con*

Contact: Sir Graham Brady, House of Commons, London SW1A 0AA
Tel: 020 7219 1260
Email: altsale@parliament.uk

Sustainable Finance

Chair: Sir Ed Davey *Lib Dem*
Vice-Chairs:
Claire Coutinho *Con*
Ed Miliband *Lab*
Alex Sobel *Lab/Co-op*
Officer: Baroness Worthington *CB*

Contact: Sir Ed Davey, House of Commons, London SW1A 0AA Tel: 020 7219 4530
Email: edward.davey.mp@parliament.uk
Website: uk100.org/appg
Twitter: @APPGSustFin

Sustainable Resource

Chairs:
Barry Sheerman *Lab/Co-op*
Dr Alan Whitehead *Lab*
Officers:
Fleur Anderson *Lab*
Sir David Evennett *Con*
Robert Goodwill *Con*
Baroness Jones of Whitchurch *Lab*
Kerry McCarthy *Lab*
Alex Sobel *Lab/Co-op*
Lord Teverson *Lib Dem*

Contact: Barry Sheerman, House of Commons, London SW1A 0AA Tel: 020 7219 5037
Email: sheermanb@parliament.uk
Website: www.policyconnect.org.uk/apsrg
Twitter: @APSRG

Swimming

Chair: Catherine West *Lab*
Vice-chairs:
Tanmanjeet Singh Dhesi *Lab*
Jane Hunt *Con*
Sheryll Murray *Con*
Alison Thewliss *SNP*

Contact: Catherine West, House of Commons, London SW1A 0AA Tel: 020 7219 6141
Email: catherine.west.mp@parliament.uk
Twitter: @APPG_Swimming

Tamils

Chair: Elliot Colburn *Con*
Vice-chairs:
Bob Blackman *Con*
Sarah Champion *Lab*
Bambos Charalambous *Lab*
Feryal Clark *Lab*
Sir Ed Davey *Lib Dem*
Jackie Doyle-Price *Con*
Robert Halfon *Con*
Stephen Hammond *Con*
Siobhain McDonagh *Lab*
Kate Osamor *Lab/Co-op*
Dean Russell *Con*
Wes Streeting *Lab*
Sam Tarry *Lab*
Gareth Thomas *Lab/Co-op*
Theresa Villiers *Con*

Contact: Elliot Colburn, House of Commons, London SW1A 0AA Tel: 020 7219 3000
Email: elliot.colburn.mp@parliament.uk

Taxation

Chair: Ian Liddell-Grainger *Con*
Vice-chairs:
Karen Bradley *Con*
Nigel Mills *Con*
Joy Morrissey *Con*
John Stevenson *Con*
Stephen Timms *Lab*
Secretary: Baroness Kramer *Lib Dem*
Treasurer: Lord McKenzie of Luton *Lab*

Contact: Ian Liddell-Grainger, House of Commons, London SW1A 0AA
Tel: 020 7219 8149 Email: ianlg@parliament.uk

Taxis

Chair: Wes Streeting *Lab*
Vice-chairs:
Sarah Champion *Lab*
Jon Cruddas *Lab*
Andrew Rosindell *Con*
Sir Charles Walker *Con*
Daniel Zeichner *Lab*
Secretary: Yasmin Qureshi *Lab*
Treasurer: Neil Coyle *Lab*

Contact: Wes Streeting, House of Commons, London SW1A 0AA Tel: 020 7219 6132
Email: wes.streeting.mp@parliament.uk
Website: appgtaxis.org

Teaching Profession

Chair: Ian Mearns *Lab*
Vice-chairs:
Baroness Morris of Yardley *Lab*
Lord Storey *Lib Dem*
Officers:
Emma Hardy *Lab*
David Simmonds *Con*

Contact: Ian Mearns, House of Commons, London SW1A 0AA Tel: 020 7219 7074
Email: ian.mearns.mp@parliament.uk
Website: appgteaching.com

Technology and National Security

Chair: Darren Jones *Lab*
Vice-chairs:
Andrew Bowie *Con*
Andrew Griffith *Con*
Lord Houghton of Richmond *CB*
Kevan Jones *Lab*
Tony Lloyd *Lab*
Carol Monaghan *SNP*

Contact: Darren Jones, House of Commons, London SW1A 0AA Tel: 0117-959 6545
Email: darren.jones.mp@parliament.uk
Website: www.appgtechnatsec.com

Tennis

Chairs:
Baroness Billingham *Lab*
Toby Perkins *Lab*
Vice-chairs:
Chris Evans *Lab/Co-op*
Mark Pritchard *Con*
Secretary: Tim Loughton *Con*
Treasurer: Lord Naseby *Con*

Contact: Toby Perkins, House of Commons, London SW1A 0AA Tel: 020 7219 2320
Email: toby.perkins.mp@parliament.uk

Terminal Illness

Chair: Drew Hendry *SNP*
Vice-chairs:
Lord Dykes *CB*
Liz Saville Roberts *PlC*
Jim Shannon *DUP*
Owen Thompson *SNP*
Valerie Vaz *Lab*
Dr Philippa Whitford *SNP*
Officers:
Greg Clark *Con*
Nia Griffith *Lab*
Sir Robert Neill *Con*
Tom Tugendhat *Con*

Contact: Drew Hendry, House of Commons, London SW1A 0AA Tel: 020 7219 6118
Email: drew.hendry.mp@parliament.uk
Website: www.mariecurie.org.uk
Twitter: @scrap6months

Terrorism

Chair: Khalid Mahmood *Lab*
Vice-chairs:
Afzal Khan *Lab*
Bob Stewart *Con*
Lord Taylor of Warwick *NA*
Mohammad Yasin *Lab*

Contact: Khalid Mahmood, House of Commons, London SW1A 0AA
Tel: 020 7219 8141
Email: mahmoodk@parliament.uk

Textiles and Fashion

Chair: Dr Lisa Cameron *SNP*
Vice-chairs:
Martin Docherty-Hughes *SNP*
Sharon Hodgson *Lab*
John McNally *SNP*
Craig Tracey *Con*
Secretary: Nadia Whittome *Lab*
Treasurer: Fleur Anderson *Lab*
Officers:
Baroness Uddin *NA*
Catherine West *Lab*

Contact: Dr Lisa Cameron, House of Commons, London SW1A 0AA Tel: 020 7219 6855
Email: lisa.cameron.mp@parliament.uk
Twitter: @ForAppg

Thalassaemia

Chair: Bambos Charalambous *Lab*
Vice-chairs:
Bob Blackman *Con*
Feryal Clark *Lab*
Alberto Costa *Con*
Judith Cummins *Lab*
Barry Gardiner *Lab*
Fabian Hamilton *Lab*
Kate Osamor *Lab/Co-op*
Taiwo Owatemi *Lab*
Catherine West *Lab*

Contact: Bambos Charalambous, House of Commons, London SW1A 0AA
Tel: 020 7219 3460
Email: bambos.charalambous.mp@parliament.uk

Theatre

Chair: Giles Watling *Con*
Vice-chairs:
Nickie Aiken *Con*
Tracy Brabin *Lab/Co-op*
Baroness Hamwee *Lib Dem*

Lord Kerslake *CB*
Andrew Lewer *Con*
Stephen Metcalfe *Con*
Matt Western *Lab*
Baroness Whitaker *Lab*

Contact: Giles Watling, House of Commons, London SW1A 0AA Tel: 020 7219 0795
Email: giles.watling.mp@parliament.uk
Website: uktheatre.org/theatreappg

Ticket Abuse
Chairs:
Sharon Hodgson *Lab*
Lord Moynihan *Con*
Vice-chairs:
Kevin Brennan *Lab*
Lord Clement-Jones *Lib Dem*
Kerry McCarthy *Lab*
Nick Smith *Lab*
Lord Strasburger *Lib Dem*
Alison Thewliss *SNP*
Pete Wishart *SNP*

Contact: Sharon Hodgson, House of Commons, London SW1A 0AA Tel: 020 7219 5160
Email: sharon.hodgson.mp@parliament.uk
Website: appgticketabuse.wordpress.com

Tidy Britain
Chair: Kevin Hollinrake *Con*
Vice-chairs:
Simon Fell *Con*
Sharon Hodgson *Lab*
Lord Judd *Lab*
Dr Peter Kyle *Lab*
Mark Logan *Con*
Mark Pawsey *Con*
Baroness Pinnock *Lib Dem*
Mark Pritchard *Con*
Steve Reed *Lab/Co-op*

Contact: Kevin Hollinrake, House of Commons, London SW1A 0AA Tel: 020 7219 4746
Email: kevin.hollinrake.mp@parliament.uk
Website: www.keepbritaintidy.org/about/all-party-parliamentary-group

Town Centres
Chair: Stephen Hammond *Con*
Vice-chairs:
Douglas Chapman *SNP*
Peter Gibson *Con*
Officers:
Peter Aldous *Con*
Matt Western *Lab*

Contact: Stephen Hammond, House of Commons, London SW1A 0AA
Tel: 020 7219 3401
Email: stephen.hammond.mp@parliament.uk
Website: www.atcm.org/APPG-for-Town-Centres

Trade and Export Promotion
Chairs:
Gary Sambrook *Con*
Viscount Waverley *CB*
Vice-chairs:
Sir Jeffrey Donaldson *DUP*
Jack Dromey *Lab*
Chris Elmore *Lab*
Lord Lansley *Con*
Lord Mann *NA*
Baroness Baroness Mobarik *Con*
Lord Purvis of Tweed *Lib Dem*
Lord Risby *Con*
Baroness Ritchie of Downpatrick *NA*

Contact: Gary Sambrook, House of Commons, London SW1A 0AA Tel: 020 7219 3000
Email: gary.sambrook.mp@parliament.uk
Website: www.appgtrade.uk

Trade Justice
Chair: Fleur Anderson *Lab*
Vice-chairs:
Earl of Caithness *Con*
Geraint Davies *Lab/Co-op*
Lord Haskel *Lab*
Dr Caroline Lucas *Green*
Kenny MacAskill *SNP*
Lord Purvis of Tweed *Lib Dem*
Hywel Williams *PlC*

Contact: Fleur Anderson, House of Commons, London SW1A 0AA Tel: 020 7219 3000
Email: fleur.anderson.mp@parliament.uk

Trade out of Poverty
Chairs:
Theo Clarke *Con*
Lord Purvis of Tweed *Lib Dem*
Vice-chairs:
Fleur Anderson *Lab*
Lord Boateng *Lab*
Lord Green of Hurstpierpoint *NA*
Lord Lilley *Con*
Stephen Timms *Lab*

Contact: Theo Clarke, House of Commons, London SW1A 0AA Tel: 020 7219 3000
Email: theo.clarke.mp@parliament.uk
Website: tradeoutofpoverty.org
Twitter: @APPG_TOP

Trailer and Towing Safety
Chair: Karin Smyth *Lab*
Officers:
Sir David Amess *Con*

Lord Bassam of Brighton *Lab/Co-op*
Richard Fuller *Con*
Sharon Hodgson *Lab*
Nigel Mills *Con*

Contact: Karin Smyth, House of Commons, London SW1A 0AA
Email: karin.smyth.mp@parliament.uk
Website: www.trailerappg.org.uk
Twitter: @TrailerAPPG

Transatlantic Trade

Chair: John Spellar *Lab*
Vice-chairs:
Lord Anderson of Swansea *Lab*
Alun Cairns *Con*
Jonathan Edwards *Ind*
Lord Empey *UUP*
John Healey *Lab*
Kevan Jones *Lab*
Baroness Kramer *Lib Dem*
Conor McGinn *Lab*
Secretary: Andrew Percy *Con*

Contact: John Spellar, House of Commons, London SW1A 0AA Tel: 020 7219 0674
Email: john.spellar.mp@parliament.uk

Transport Across the North

Chairs:
Andrew Jones *Con*
Grahame Morris *Lab*
Vice-chairs:
Miriam Cates *Con*
Judith Cummins *Lab*
Peter Dowd *Lab*
Nick Fletcher *Con*
Jason McCartney *Con*
Catherine McKinnell *Lab*
Lord Newby *Lib Dem*
Cat Smith *Lab*

Contact: Andrew Jones, House of Commons, London SW1A 0AA Tel: 020 7219 3000
Email: andrew.jones.mp@parliament.uk
Website: transportforthenorth.com/appg

Transport Safety

Chairs:
Sir Peter Bottomley *Con*
Lilian Greenwood *Lab*
Vice-chairs:
Lord Bradshaw *Lib Dem*
Mike Hill *Lab*
Tony Lloyd *Lab*
Baroness Randerson *Lib Dem*
Barry Sheerman *Lab/Co-op*
Viscount Simon *Lab*

Contact: Lilian Greenwood, House of Commons, London SW1A 0AA
Tel: 020 7219 7122
Email: lilian.greenwood.mp@parliament.uk
Website: www.transportsafetyappg.org.uk

Twelve Steps Recovery Programme for Addiction

Chairs:
Lord Brooke of Alverthorpe *Lab*
Dr Lisa Cameron *SNP*
Vice-chair: Fiona Bruce *Con*
Treasurer: Lord Mancroft *Con*

Contact: Dr Lisa Cameron, House of Commons, London SW1A 0AA Tel: 020 7219 6855
Email: lisa.cameron.mp@parliament.uk

UK Islands

Chair: Bob Seely *Con*
Vice-chairs:
Paul Bristow *Con*
Alistair Carmichael *Lib Dem*
Virginia Crosbie *Con*
Angus MacNeil *SNP*
Alan Mak *Con*
Stephen Morgan *Lab*
Derek Thomas *Con*

Contact: Bob Seely, House of Commons, London SW1A 0AA Tel: 020 7219 1840
Email: bob.seely.mp@parliament.uk

Unconscious Bias

Chairs:
Dawn Butler *Lab*
Anne McLaughlin *SNP*
Vice-chairs:
Debbie Abrahams *Lab*
Mhairi Black *SNP*
Angela Crawley *SNP*
Marion Fellows *SNP*
Neale Hanvey *SNP*
Afzal Khan *Lab*
Vice-chairand Treasurer: Stephen Metcalfe *Con*

Contact: Anne McLaughlin, House of Commons, London SW1A 0AA
Tel: 020 7219 3000
Email: anne.mclaughlin.mp@parliament.uk

Union

Chairs:
Dr James Davies *Con*
Sir Jeffrey Donaldson *DUP*
David Mundell *Con*
Laurence Robertson *Con*
Vice-chairs:
Karen Bradley *Con*
Lord Caine *Con*

Mark Logan *Con*
Karin Smyth *Lab*
Secretary: Conor McGinn *Lab*
Treasurer: Ian Paisley *DUP*

Contact: Laurence Robertson, House of Commons, London SW1A 0AA
Tel: 020 7219 4196
Email: robertsonl@parliament.uk

United Nations
Chairs:
Sir Peter Bottomley *Con*
Lord Hannay of Chiswick *CB*
Vice-chairs:
Baroness Anelay of St Johns *Con*
Harriett Baldwin *Con*
Dr Lisa Cameron *SNP*
Baroness Coussins *CB*
Patrick Grady *SNP*
Catherine West *Lab*
Lord Wood of Anfield *Lab*

Contact: Sir Peter Bottomley, House of Commons, London SW1A 0AA
Tel: 020 7219 5060
Email: bottomleyp@parliament.uk

United Nations Global Goals for Sustainable Development
Chairs:
Theo Clarke *Con*
Lord McConnell of Glenscorrodale *Lab*
Vice-chairs:
Harriett Baldwin *Con*
Lord Bird *CB*
Dr Lisa Cameron *SNP*
Lord Chidgey *Lib Dem*
Pauline Latham *Con*
Lord Loomba *CB*
Anna McMorrin *Lab*
Baroness Northover *Lib Dem*

Contact: Theo Clarke, House of Commons, London SW1A 0AA Tel: 020 7219 3000
Email: theo.clarke.mp@parliament.uk
Twitter: @APPG_SDGs

United Nations Women
Chairs:
Maria Miller *Con*
Baroness Verma *Con*
Vice-chairs:
Julie Elliott *Lab*
Laura Farris *Con*
Liz Saville Roberts *PlC*

Contact: Maria Miller, House of Commons, London SW1A 0AA Tel: 020 7219 5749
Email: maria.miller.mp@parliament.uk

Universal Credit
Chair: Debbie Abrahams *Lab*
Vice-chairs:
Peter Aldous *Con*
Anne McLaughlin *SNP*
Secretary: Jonathan Gullis *Con*
Treasurer: Chris Bryant *Lab*

Contact: Debbie Abrahams, House of Commons, London SW1A 0AA
Tel: 020 7219 1041
Email: abrahamsd@parliament.uk
Website: appguniversalcredit.org.uk

University
Chairs:
Baroness Garden of Frognal *Lib Dem*
Daniel Zeichner *Lab*
Vice-chairs:
Ben Lake *PlC*
Jason McCartney *Con*
Alison Thewliss *SNP*
Secretary: Paul Blomfield *Lab*
Treasurer: Lloyd Russell-Moyle *Lab/Co-op*

Contact: Daniel Zeichner, House of Commons, London SW1A 0AA Tel: 020 7219 8462
Email: daniel@danielzeichner.co.uk
Website: appg-universities.org.uk
Twitter: @universityappg

Vaccinations for All
Chair: Dr Philippa Whitford *SNP*
Vice-chairs:
Baroness Greengross *CB*
Lord Oates *Lib Dem*
Lloyd Russell-Moyle *Lab/Co-op*
Lord Selkirk of Douglas *Con*

Contact: Dr Philippa Whitford, House of Commons, London SW1A 0AA
Tel: 020 7219 8158
Email: philippa.whitford.mp@parliament.uk
Website: appg-vfa.org.uk
Twitter: @APPGVaccination

Valproate and other Anti-Epileptic Drugs in Pregnancy
Chair: Cat Smith *Lab*
Vice-chairs:
Fiona Bruce *Con*
Kate Green *Lab*
Lord O'Shaughnessy *Con*
Officers:
Sharon Hodgson *Lab*
Liz Twist *Lab*

Contact: Cat Smith, House of Commons, London SW1A 0AA Tel: 020 7219 6001
Email: cat.smith.mp@parliament.uk

Vaping
Chair: Mark Pawsey *Con*
Vice-chairs:
Mary Glindon *Lab*
Gareth Johnson *Con*
Viscount Ridley *Con*
Secretary: Stephen Metcalfe *Con*
Treasurer: Scott Mann *Con*

Contact: Mark Pawsey, House of Commons, London SW1A 0AA Tel: 020 7219 7136
Email: mark.pawsey.mp@parliament.uk

Vascular and Venous Disease
Chair: Emma Hardy *Lab*
Officers:
Sir Peter Bottomley *Con*
Dame Diana Johnson *Lab*
Baroness Masham of Ilton *CB*

Contact: Emma Hardy, House of Commons, London SW1A 0AA
Email: emma.hardy.mp@parliament.uk
Website: www.vvappg.com
Twitter: @VAPPG

Vegetarianism and Veganism
Chair: Christina Rees *Lab/Co-op*
Vice-chairs:
Thangam Debbonaire *Lab*
Baroness Hussein-Ece *Lib Dem*
Kerry McCarthy *Lab*
Henry Smith *Con*
Alex Sobel *Lab/Co-op*

Contact: Christina Rees, House of Commons, London SW1A 0AA Tel: 020 7219 5783
Email: christina.rees.mp@parliament.uk
Website: vegappg.org.uk

Veterans
Chairs:
Kevan Jones *Lab*
Jim Shannon *DUP*
James Sunderland *Con*
Vice-chairs:
Stuart Anderson *Con*
Sarah Atherton *Con*
Wendy Chamberlain *Lib Dem*
Theo Clarke *Con*
Gareth Davies *Con*
Sir Jeffrey Donaldson *DUP*
Dame Diana Johnson *Lab*
Lord Mendelsohn *Lab*
Carol Monaghan *SNP*
Damien Moore *Con*
Lord Selkirk of Douglas *Con*
Lord Snape *Lab*
Derek Twigg *Lab*

Contact: James Sunderland, House of Commons, London SW1A 0AA
Tel: 0207 219 5032
Email: james.sunderland.mp@parliament.uk

Video Games and Esports
Chair: Alex Sobel *Lab/Co-op*
Vice-chairs:
Fleur Anderson *Lab*
Ben Bradley *Con*
Lord Brooke of Alverthorpe *Lab*
Lord Clement-Jones *Lib Dem*
Dehenna Davison *Con*
Sharon Hodgson *Lab*
Scott Mann *Con*
Lord Taylor of Warwick *NA*
Christian Wakeford *Con*
Matt Western *Lab*
Daniel Zeichner *Lab*

Contact: Alex Sobel, House of Commons, London SW1A 0AA Tel: +020 7219 8295
Email: alex.sobel.mp@parliament.uk

Votes at 16
Chairs:
Sir Peter Bottomley *Con*
Wendy Chamberlain *Lib Dem*
Vicky Foxcroft *Lab*
Dr Caroline Lucas *Green*
Liz Saville Roberts *PlC*
Alison Thewliss *SNP*

Contact: Sir Peter Bottomley, House of Commons, London SW1A 0AA
Tel: 020 7219 6001
Email: cat.smith.mp@parliament.uk

Vulnerable Groups to Pandemics
Chair: Virendra Sharma *Lab*
Vice-chairs:
Bob Blackman *Con*
Lord Lansley *Con*
Jim Shannon *DUP*
Officers:
Dr Lisa Cameron *SNP*
Rachael Maskell *Lab/Co-op*
Lord Mendelsohn *Lab*
Lord Patel *CB*

Contact: Virendra Sharma, House of Commons, London SW1A 0AA Tel: 020 7219 6080
Email: sharmav@parliament.uk
Twitter: @APPG_VGP

Wales in the World
Chair: Craig Williams *Con*
Vice-chairs:
Chris Elmore *Lab*
Lord German *Lib Dem*

Ben Lake *PlC*
Treasurer: Simon Baynes *Con*
Officers:
Tonia Antoniazzi *Lab*
Virginia Crosbie *Con*
Fay Jones *Con*
Gerald Jones *Lab*
Ruth Jones *Lab*
Christina Rees *Lab/Co-op*

Contact: Craig Williams, House of Commons, London SW1A 0AA Tel: 020 7219 3000
Email: craig.williams.mp@parliament.uk

War Heritage
Chairs:
Sir Jeffrey Donaldson *DUP*
Lord Faulkner of Worcester *Lab*
Vice-chairs:
Lord Astor of Hever *Con*
Karen Bradley *Con*
Lord Clark of Windermere *Lab*
Tanmanjeet Singh Dhesi *Lab*
Kevan Jones *Lab*
Lord Selkirk of Douglas *Con*
Treasurer: Gavin Robinson *DUP*

Contact: Sir Jeffrey Donaldson, House of Commons, London SW1A 0AA
Tel: +020 7219 3407
Email: jeffrey.donaldson.mp@parliament.uk
Website: www.wargravesheritage.org.uk

Water
Chairs:
Alex Davies-Jones *Lab*
Baroness McIntosh of Pickering *Con*
Vice-chairs:
Lord Cameron of Dillington *CB*
Baroness Golding *Lab*
Baroness Hooper *Con*
Baroness Pinnock *Lib Dem*
Lord Wigley *PlC*
Treasurer: Lord Moynihan *Con*
Officers:
Philip Dunne *Con*
Darren Jones *Lab*

Contact: Alex Davies-Jones, House of Commons, London SW1A 0AA
Tel: 020 7219 4981
Email: alex.daviesjones.mp@parliament.uk
Website: connectpa.co.uk/water
Twitter: @APPGwater

Water, Sanitation and Hygiene
Chairs:
Fleur Anderson *Lab*
Lord Bates *Con*
Vice-chair: Lord Sheikh *Con*
Officers:
Lord Dubs *Lab*
Patrick Grady *SNP*
Rachel Hopkins *Lab*
Brendan O'Hara *SNP*

Contact: Fleur Anderson, House of Commons, London SW1A 0AA Tel: 020 7219 3000
Email: fleur.anderson.mp@parliament.uk

Waterways
Chair: Michael Fabricant *Con*
Vice-chairs:
Imran Ahmad Khan *Con*
Simon Baynes *Con*
John Cryer *Lab*
Bill Esterson *Lab*
Mark Garnier *Con*
Lord German *Lib Dem*
Jason McCartney *Con*

Contact: Michael Fabricant, House of Commons, London SW1A 0AA
Tel: 020 7219 5022
Website: www.waterways.org.uk

Wellbeing Economics
Chairs:
Jon Cruddas *Lab*
Tim Loughton *Con*
Vice-chairs:
Tracey Crouch *Con*
Lord Layard *Lab*
Lord O'Donnell *CB*
Baroness Tyler of Enfield *Lib Dem*

Contact: Jon Cruddas, House of Commons, London SW1A 0AA Tel: 020 7219 8161
Email: cruddasj@parliament.uk
Twitter: @APPGWellbeing

West Coast Main Line
Chair: John Stevenson *Con*
Vice-chairs:
Rosie Cooper *Lab*
Marie Rimmer *Lab*
Secretary: Lord Foulkes of Cumnock *Lab/Co-op*

Contact: John Stevenson, House of Commons, London SW1A 0AA Tel: 020 7219 3000
Email: john.stevenson.mp@parliament.uk
Website: www.westcoastrail250.co.uk/appg

West Midlands
Chairs:
Preet Kaur Gill *Lab/Co-op*
Jonathan Gullis *Con*
Vice-chairs:
Theo Clarke *Con*
Taiwo Owatemi *Lab*

Mike Wood Con
Secretary: Jack Dromey Lab

Contact: Jonathan Gullis, House of Commons, London SW1A 0AA Tel: 020 7219 3000
Email: jonathan.gullis.mp@parliament.uk
Website: connectpa.co.uk/west-midlands-appg
Twitter: @westmidlandappg

Western Gateway

Chairs:
Mark Harper Con
Jessica Morden Lab
Vice-chairs:
Geraint Davies Lab/Co-op
Anna McMorrin Lab
Laurence Robertson Con
Baroness Wilcox of Newport Lab
Secretary: Chris Skidmore Con

Contact: Jessica Morden, House of Commons, London SW1A 0AA Tel: 020 7219 6213
Email: mordenj@parliament.uk
Twitter: @APPG_WG

Western Rail Link to Heathrow

Chairs:
Tanmanjeet Singh Dhesi Lab
Laura Farris Con
Vice-chairs:
Lord Adonis Lab
Sir Peter Bottomley Con
Secretary: Christina Rees Lab/Co-op
Treasurer: Seema Malhotra Lab/Co-op

Contact: Tanmanjeet Singh Dhesi, House of Commons, London SW1A 0AA
Tel: 020 7219 1946
Email: tan.dhesi.mp@parliament.uk

Whistleblowing

Chairs:
Lord Berkeley Lab
Baroness Kramer Lib Dem
Mary Robinson Con
Vice-chairs:
Mike Amesbury Lab
Philip Davies Con
Kevin Hollinrake Con
Scott Mann Con

Contact: Mary Robinson, House of Commons, London SW1A 0AA Tel: 020 7219 8091
Email: mary.robinson.mp@parliament.uk
Website: www.appgwhistleblowing.co.uk
Twitter: @Awhistleblowing

Wine and Spirits

Honorary President: Nigel Evans Con
Chairs:
Neil Coyle Lab
Helen Grant Con
Vice-chairs:
Lord Blencathra Con
Sir Peter Bottomley Con
Sir Graham Brady Con
Stephen Hammond Con
Sharon Hodgson Lab
Darren Jones Lab
Andy Slaughter Lab

Contact: Neil Coyle, House of Commons, London SW1A 0AA Tel: 020 7232 4640
Email: neil.coyle.mp@parliament.uk

Wine of Great Britain

Chair: Andrew Griffith Con
Vice-Chairs:
Sir Peter Bottomley Con
Feryal Clark Lab
Nusrat Ghani Con
Damian Hinds Con
Alicia Kearns Con
Craig Williams Con
Hywel Williams PlC

Contact: Andrew Griffith, House of Commons, London SW1A 0AA Tel: 020 7219 4557
Email: andrew@griffithmp.com

Women and Enterprise

Chair: Craig Tracey Con
Vice-chairs:
Harriett Baldwin Con
Felicity Buchan Con
Theo Clarke Con
Virginia Crosbie Con
Katherine Fletcher Con
Jo Gideon Con
Carolyn Harris Lab
Selaine Saxby Con

Contact: Craig Tracey, House of Commons, London SW1A 0AA Tel: 020 7219 5646
Email: craig.tracey.mp@parliament.uk
Twitter: @WEAPPG

Women in Parliament

Chair: Maria Miller Con
Vice-chairs:
Baroness Burt of Solihull Lib Dem
Virginia Crosbie Con
Dame Cheryl Gillan Con
Harriet Harman Lab
Baroness Jenkin of Kennington Con
Baroness Northover Lib Dem
Officers:
Nickie Aiken Con
Fleur Anderson Lab
Angela Crawley SNP
Rosie Duffield Lab

Julie Elliott *Lab*
Christine Jardine *Lib Dem*
Dr Caroline Lucas *Green*
Abena Oppong-Asare *Lab*
Rachel Reeves *Lab*
Mary Robinson *Con*

Contact: Maria Miller, House of Commons, London SW1A 0AA Tel: 020 7219 5749
Email: maria.miller.mp@parliament.uk

Women, Peace and Security

Chairs:
Flick Drummond *Con*
Baroness Hodgson of Abinger *Con*
Vice-chairs:
Lord McConnell of Glenscorrodale *Lab*
Maria Miller *Con*
Baroness Prosser *Lab*
Baroness Stern *CB*

Contact: Flick Drummond, House of Commons, London SW1A 0AA Tel: 020 7219 3000
Email: flick.drummond.mp@parliament.uk
Website: gaps-uk.org/about/appg

Women in the Penal System

Chairs:
Debbie Abrahams *Lab*
Baroness Corston *Lab*
Jackie Doyle-Price *Con*
Officers:
Bishop of Gloucester *NA*
Baroness Hamwee *Lib Dem*

Contact: Jackie Doyle-Price, House of Commons, London SW1A 0AA
Tel: 020 7219 7171
Email: jackie.doyleprice.mp@parliament.uk

Women in Transport

Chair: Ruth Cadbury *Lab*
Vice-chair: Baroness Randerson *Lib Dem*
Officers:
Sir Peter Bottomley *Con*
Lilian Greenwood *Lab*
Baroness Prosser *Lab*

Contact: Ruth Cadbury, House of Commons, London SW1A 0AA Tel: 020 7219 8590
Email: ruthcadburymp@parliament.uk
Website: www.panspandasuk.org/appg

Women and Work

Chairs:
Laura Farris *Con*
Jess Phillips *Lab*
Vice-chairs:
Tracy Brabin *Lab/Co-op*
Kirsten Oswald *SNP*
Officers:
Harriett Baldwin *Con*
Sara Britcliffe *Con*
Deidre Brock *SNP*
Baroness Burt of Solihull *Lib Dem*
Wendy Chamberlain *Lib Dem*
Theo Clarke *Con*
Alex Davies-Jones *Lab*
Baroness Garden of Frognal *Lib Dem*
Baroness Goudie *Lab*
Helen Hayes *Lab*
Rachael Maskell *Lab/Co-op*
Baroness Prosser *Lab*
Liz Saville Roberts *PlC*
Baroness Uddin *NA*

Contact: Laura Farris, House of Commons, London SW1A 0AA Tel: 020 7219 3000
Email: laura.farris.mp@parliament.uk
Website: connectpa.co.uk/the-women-and-work-all-party-parliamentary-group
Twitter: @womenworkappg

Women's Football

Chairs:
Tracey Crouch *Con*
Alison McGovern *Lab*
Secretary: Hannah Bardell *SNP*
Treasurer: Dr Rosena Allin-Khan *Lab*

Contact: Tracey Crouch, House of Commons, London SW1A 0AA Tel: 020 7219 7203
Email: tracey.crouch.mp@parliament.uk
Website: apgaw.org

Women's Health

Chairs:
Jackie Doyle-Price *Con*
Carolyn Harris *Lab*
Vice-chairs:
Rachel Maclean *Con*
Kate Osborne *Lab*
Paul Scully *Con*
Alison Thewliss *SNP*

Contact: Jackie Doyle-Price, House of Commons, London SW1A 0AA
Tel: 020 7219 7171
Email: jackie.doyleprice.mp@parliament.uk
Website: www.appgwomenshealth.org
Twitter: @APPG_WH

Wood Panel Industry

Chair: Selaine Saxby *Con*
Vice-chairs:
Alan Brown *SNP*
Mark Jenkinson *Con*
Fay Jones *Con*
Ben Lake *PlC*
Ian Murray *Lab*

Neil Parish *Con*
Jim Shannon *DUP*
Lord Wallace of Tankerness *NA*

Contact: Selaine Saxby, House of Commons, London SW1A 0AA Tel: 020 7219 5952
Email: selaine.saxby.mp@parliament.uk
Website: www.appgwoodpanelindustry.org

Woods and Trees

Chair: Jason McCartney *Con*
Vice-chairs:
Simon Baynes *Con*
Lord Carrington *CB*
Michael Fabricant *Con*
Dame Cheryl Gillan *Con*
Mike Hill *Lab*
Navendu Mishra *Lab*
Theresa Villiers *Con*

Contact: Jason McCartney, House of Commons, London SW1A 0AA Tel: 020 7219 3000
Email: jason.mccartney.mp@parliament.uk

Working at Height

Chair: Alison Thewliss *SNP*
Vice-chairs:
Robert Largan *Con*
Nigel Mills *Con*
Chris Stephens *SNP*
Officers:
Baroness Bennett of Manor Castle *Green*
Chris Bryant *Lab*
Jason McCartney *Con*

Contact: Alison Thewliss, House of Commons, London SW1A 0AA Tel: 020 7219 6447
Email: alison.thewliss.mp@parliament.uk
Website: workingatheight.info
Twitter: @WorkHeight_appg

Wrestling

Chairs:
Alex Davies-Jones *Lab*
Mark Fletcher *Con*
Vice-chairs:
Tonia Antoniazzi *Lab*
Paul Bristow *Con*
Officers:
Ruth Jones *Lab*
Conor McGinn *Lab*

Contact: Alex Davies-Jones, House of Commons, London SW1A 0AA
Tel: 020 7219 4981
Email: alex.daviesjones.mp@parliament.uk
Twitter: @appgwrestling

Writers

Chair: Giles Watling *Con*
Vice-chairs:
Baroness Benjamin *Lib Dem*
Lord Clement-Jones *Lib Dem*
Lord Dubs *Lab*
Julie Elliott *Lab*
Andrew Lewer *Con*
Pete Wishart *SNP*

Contact: Giles Watling, House of Commons, London SW1A 0AA Tel: 020 7219 0795
Email: giles.watling.mp@parliament.uk
Website: allpartywritersgroup.co.uk

Yorkshire and Northern Lincolnshire

Chairs:
Kevin Hollinrake *Con*
Barry Sheerman *Lab/Co-op*
Vice-chairs:
Miriam Cates *Con*
Sarah Champion *Lab*
Lord Kirkhope of Harrogate *Con*
Jason McCartney *Con*
Holly Mumby-Croft *Con*
Lia Nici *Con*
Alexander Stafford *Con*
Jacob Young *Con*
Treasurer: Emma Hardy *Lab*

Contact: Kevin Hollinrake, House of Commons, London SW1A 0AA Tel: 020 7219 4746
Email: kevin.hollinrake.mp@parliament.uk

Young People's Health

Chairs:
Rosie Duffield *Lab*
Baroness Massey of Darwen *Lab*
Officers:
Kerry McCarthy *Lab*
Baroness Newlove *Con*
Lord Ramsbotham *CB*
Baroness Stroud *Con*

Contact: Rosie Duffield, House of Commons, London SW1A 0AA Tel: 020 7219 1183
Email: rosie.duffield.mp@parliament.uk
Website: www.youngpeopleshealth.org.uk/our-work/policy-strategy/appg

Youth Action against Climate Change

Chairs:
Sara Britcliffe *Con*
Alex Chalk *Con*
Geraint Davies *Lab/Co-op*
John McNally *SNP*

Contact: John McNally, House of Commons, London SW1A 0AA Tel: 020 7219 6525
Email: john.mcnally.mp@parliament.uk

Youth Affairs

Chairs:
Lloyd Russell-Moyle *Lab/Co-op*
Amanda Solloway *Con*
Vice-chairs:
Ben Bradley *Con*
John McNally *SNP*
Treasurer: Mary Glindon *Lab*
Officers:
Olivia Blake *Lab*
Sir Peter Bottomley *Con*
Rachel Hopkins *Lab*
Sir George Howarth *Lab*
James Murray *Lab/Co-op*
Claudia Webbe *Ind*

Contact: Lloyd Russell-Moyle, House of Commons, London SW1A 0AA
Tel: 020 7219 2280
Email: lloyd.russellmoyle.mp@parliament.uk
Website: appgyouthaffairs.wordpress.com
Twitter: @YouthAPPG

Youth Employment

Chair: James Daly *Con*
Officers:
Baroness Bennett of Manor Castle *Green*
Sara Britcliffe *Con*
Chris Green *Con*
Andrew Gwynne *Lab*
Ben Lake *PlC*

Contact: James Daly, House of Commons, London SW1A 0AA Tel: 020 7219 3000
Email: james.daly.mp@parliament.uk
Website: appgyouthemployment.org

Zoos and Aquariums

President: Lord Paul *NA*
Chair: Andrew Rosindell *Con*
Vice-chairs:
Sir David Amess *Con*
Virginia Crosbie *Con*
Baroness Hooper *Con*
Daniel Kawczynski *Con*
Angus MacNeil *SNP*
Gavin Robinson *DUP*
Greg Smith *Con*
Sir Charles Walker *Con*
Catherine West *Lab*
Bill Wiggin *Con*
Secretary: Chris Matheson *Lab*

Contact: Andrew Rosindell, House of Commons, London SW1A 0AA
Tel: 020 7219 8475
Email: andrew.rosindell.mp@parliament.uk

Country Groups

Most all-party country groups are formed under the auspices of the Commonwealth Parliamentary Association or the Inter-Parliamentary Union. These organisations have a UK branch, CPA and IPU, which contains affiliated groups of members interested in a particular country.

Afghanistan

Chair: Imran Ahmad Khan *Con*
Vice-chairs:
Khalid Mahmood *Lab*
Baroness Warsi *Con*
Officers:
Flick Drummond *Con*
Tom Tugendhat *Con*

Contact: Imran Ahmad Khan, House of Commons, London SW1A 0AA
Tel: 020 7219 3000
Email: imran.mp@parliament.uk
Twitter: @AfghanistanAPPG

Africa

Chairs:
Lord Chidgey *Lib Dem*
Chi Onwurah *Lab*
Vice-chair(Eastern Africa): Lord Chidgey *Lib Dem*
Vice-chair(Southern Africa): Kim Johnson *Lab*
Vice-chair(Eastern Africa): Pauline Latham *Con*
Vice-chair(Central and West Africa): Lord McConnell of Glenscorrodale *Lab*
Vice-chairs(Southern Africa):
Baroness Northover *Lib Dem*
Lord Oates *Lib Dem*
Vice-chair(Northern Africa): Lord Purvis of Tweed *Lib Dem*
Secretary: Patrick Grady *SNP*
Treasurer: Baroness Uddin *NA*

Contact: Chi Onwurah, House of Commons, London SW1A 0AA Tel: 020 7219 7114
Email: chi.onwurah.mp@parliament.uk
Website: www.royalafricansociety.org/appg-africa
Twitter: @AfricaAPPG

Albania

Chairs:
Lia Nici *Con*
Martin Vickers *Con*
Vice-chairs:
Baroness Barker *Lib Dem*
Lord Bowness *NA*
Lyn Brown *Lab*
Dr Matthew Offord *Con*
Ian Paisley *DUP*

Mark Pritchard *Con*
Viscount Waverley *CB*
John Whittingdale *Con*

Contact: Lia Nici, Tel: 020 7219 6196
Email: lia.nici.mp@parliament.uk

Angola

Chair: Chi Onwurah *Lab*
Vice-chairs:
Lord Boateng *Lab*
Baroness Hooper *Con*
Lord Kilclooney *CB*
Baroness Northover *Lib Dem*
Laurence Robertson *Con*

Contact: Chi Onwurah, House of Commons, London SW1A 0AA Tel: 020 7219 7114
Email: chi.onwurah.mp@parliament.uk

Argentina

Honorary President: Baroness Hooper *Con*
Chair: Mark Menzies *Con*
Vice-chairs:
Lord Addington *Lib Dem*
Chris Bryant *Lab*
Lord Faulkner of Worcester *Lab*
Lord Kilclooney *CB*
Angus MacNeil *SNP*
Chris Matheson *Lab*
David Mundell *Con*
Viscount Waverley *CB*
Treasurer: Lord Wigley *PlC*

Contact: Mark Menzies, House of Commons, London SW1A 0AA Tel: 020 7219 7073
Email: mark.menzies.mp@parliament.uk

Armenia

Chair: Tim Loughton *Con*
Vice-chairs:
Feryal Clark *Lab*
Baroness Cox *CB*
James Gray *Con*
Andrew Rosindell *Con*
Secretary: Mark Pritchard *Con*
Treasurer: James Murray *Lab/Co-op*

Contact: Tim Loughton, House of Commons, London SW1A 0AA Tel: 020 7219 4471
Email: loughtont@parliament.uk

Australia and New Zealand

Chairs:
Andrew Rosindell *Con*
John Spellar *Lab*
Vice-chairs:
Lord Balfe *Con*
Sir Paul Beresford *Con*
Deidre Brock *SNP*
Dr Lisa Cameron *SNP*
Lord Chidgey *Lib Dem*
Lord Goddard of Stockport *Lib Dem*
Gareth Johnson *Con*
Baroness Nicholson of Winterbourne *Con*
Ian Paisley *DUP*
Lord Purvis of Tweed *Lib Dem*
Angela Richardson *Con*
Mary Robinson *Con*
Tommy Sheppard *SNP*
Lord Shinkwin *Con*
Viscount Simon *Lab*
Lord Snape *Lab*
Viscount Waverley *CB*
Catherine West *Lab*
Secretary: Martin Vickers *Con*
Treasurer: Lord Faulkner of Worcester *Lab*

Contact: Andrew Rosindell, House of Commons, London SW1A 0AA
Tel: 020 7219 8475
Email: andrew.rosindell.mp@parliament.uk

Austria

Chairs:
Lord Anderson of Swansea *Lab*
Sir Peter Bottomley *Con*
Vice-chairs:
Lord Dubs *Lab*
Lord Tyler *Lib Dem*
Viscount Waverley *CB*
Secretary: Tim Loughton *Con*

Contact: Sir Peter Bottomley, House of Commons, London SW1A 0AA
Tel: 020 7219 5060
Email: bottomleyp@parliament.uk

Azerbaijan

Chair: Bob Blackman *Con*
Vice-chair: Lord Kilclooney *CB*
Officers:
Lord Evans of Watford *Lab*
Martin Vickers *Con*

Contact: Bob Blackman, House of Commons, London SW1A 0AA Tel: 020 7219 7082
Email: bob.blackman.mp@parliament.uk

Bahrain

Honorary President: Nigel Evans *Con*
Chair: Bob Stewart *Con*
Vice-chairs:
Sir Graham Brady *Con*
Sir Jeffrey Donaldson *DUP*
Dave Doogan *SNP*
Philip Dunne *Con*
David Jones *Con*
Lord Jordan *Lab*
Gagan Mohindra *Con*
Lord Moynihan *Con*

Baroness Northover *Lib Dem*
Lord Richards of Herstmonceux *CB*
Lord Rogan *UUP*
John Spellar *Lab*
Jamie Stone *Lib Dem*
Viscount Waverley *CB*
Secretary: David Morris *Con*
Treasurers:
Lord Kilclooney *CB*
Chris Matheson *Lab*

Contact: Bob Stewart, House of Commons, London SW1A 0AA Tel: 020 7219 7011
Email: bob.stewart.mp@parliament.uk

Bangladesh
Chair: Rushanara Ali *Lab*
Vice-chairs:
Tahir Ali *Lab*
Lord Bilimoria *CB*
Bob Blackman *Con*
Lord Dholakia *Lib Dem*
Tom Hunt *Con*
Shabana Mahmood *Lab*
Naz Shah *Lab*
Virendra Sharma *Lab*
Lord Sheikh *Con*
Mohammad Yasin *Lab*

Contact: Rushanara Ali, House of Commons, London SW1A 0AA Tel: 020 7219 7200
Email: rushanara.ali.mp@parliament.uk

Belarus
Chair: Tony Lloyd *Lab*
Vice-chairs:
Lord Bowness *NA*
Wayne David *Lab*
Lord German *Lib Dem*
Lord Kilclooney *CB*
Lord Moynihan *Con*
Secretary: Daniel Kawczynski *Con*

Contact: Tony Lloyd, House of Commons, London SW1A 0AA Tel: 020 7219 1267
Email: tony.lloyd.mp@parliament.uk

Belgium
Chair: Damien Moore *Con*
Vice-chairs:
Lord Balfe *Con*
Dr Lisa Cameron *SNP*
Rosie Cooper *Lab*
Darren Jones *Lab*
David Linden *SNP*
Ian Paisley *DUP*
Stephanie Peacock *Lab*
Gary Sambrook *Con*

Contact: Damien Moore, House of Commons, London SW1A 0AA Tel: 01704 500577
Email: damien.moore.mp@parliament.uk

Belize
President: Lord Foulkes of Cumnock *Lab/Co-op*
Chair: Bob Stewart *Con*
Vice-chairs:
Sir Graham Brady *Con*
Wayne David *Lab*
Lord Kilclooney *CB*
Kerry McCarthy *Lab*
Chris Matheson *Lab*
Lord Robathan *Con*
Lord Rogan *UUP*
Lord Watts *Lab*
Viscount Waverley *CB*
Secretary: Adam Holloway *Con*

Contact: Bob Stewart, House of Commons, London SW1A 0AA Tel: 020 7219 7011
Email: bob.stewart.mp@parliament.uk

Bermuda
Chair: Sir David Amess *Con*
Vice-chairs:
Rosie Cooper *Lab*
Baroness Hooper *Con*
Lord Moynihan *Con*
Lord Randall of Uxbridge *Con*
Bob Stewart *Con*
Lord Tope *Lib Dem*
Secretary: Andrew Rosindell *Con*
Officer: Viscount Waverley *CB*

Contact: Sir David Amess, House of Commons, London SW1A 0AA Tel: 020 7219 3452
Email: amessd@parliament.uk

Bosnia and Herzegovina
Chairs:
Lord Bourne of Aberystwyth *Con*
Alicia Kearns *Con*
Vice-chairs:
Fleur Anderson *Lab*
Lord Randall of Uxbridge *Con*
James Sunderland *Con*

Contact: Alicia Kearns, House of Commons, London SW1A 0AA Tel: 020 7219 3000
Email: alicia.kearns.mp@parliament.uk

Brazil
Chair: Marco Longhi *Con*
Vice-chairs:
Lee Anderson *Con*
Saqib Bhatti *Con*
Andrew Bowie *Con*
Andy Carter *Con*

Brendan Clarke-Smith	*Con*
Ben Everitt	*Con*
Peter Gibson	*Con*
Robert Halfon	*Con*
Baroness Hooper	*Con*
Chris Matheson	*Lab*
Robin Millar	*Con*
John Spellar	*Lab*
Lord Watts	*Lab*
Secretary: Catherine West	*Lab*
Treasurer: Andrew Lewer	*Con*

Contact: Marco Longhi, House of Commons, London SW1A 0AA Tel: 020 7219 8598
Email: marco.longhi.mp@parliament.uk

Burma

Chair: Rushanara Ali	*Lab*
Vice-chairs:	
Lord Alton of Liverpool	*CB*
Baroness Goudie	*Lab*
Jeremy Hunt	*Con*
Baroness Nye	*Lab*
Sam Tarry	*Lab*
Viscount Waverley	*CB*

Contact: Rushanara Ali, House of Commons, London SW1A 0AA Tel: 020 7219 7200
Email: rushanara.ali.mp@parliament.uk

Canada

Chair: Andrew Rosindell	*Con*
Vice-chairs:	
Lord Balfe	*Con*
Paul Bristow	*Con*
Anthony Browne	*Con*
Lord Chidgey	*Lib Dem*
Tanmanjeet Singh Dhesi	*Lab*
Martin Docherty-Hughes	*SNP*
Lord Foulkes of Cumnock	*Lab/Co-op*
Chris Law	*SNP*
Baroness Northover	*Lib Dem*
Ian Paisley	*DUP*
Lord Purvis of Tweed	*Lib Dem*
Tommy Sheppard	*SNP*
John Spellar	*Lab*
Viscount Waverley	*CB*
Deputy Chair: Andrew Percy	*Con*
Treasurer: Lord Faulkner of Worcester	*Lab*

Contact: Andrew Rosindell, House of Commons, London SW1A 0AA
Tel: 020 7219 8475
Email: andrew.rosindell.mp@parliament.uk

Canada, Australia, New Zealand and the UK (CANZUK)

Chair: Paul Bristow	*Con*
Vice-chairs:	
Imran Ahmad Khan	*Con*
Alex Davies-Jones	*Lab*
Dehenna Davison	*Con*
Antony Higginbotham	*Con*
Alicia Kearns	*Con*
Ian Paisley	*DUP*
Andrew Rosindell	*Con*
Bob Seely	*Con*
Virendra Sharma	*Lab*
Officer: Baroness Stroud	*Con*

Contact: Paul Bristow, House of Commons, London SW1A 0AA Tel: 020 7219 3690
Email: paul.bristow.mp@parliament.uk
Twitter: @Canzuk_APPG

Caribbean

President: Lord Foulkes of Cumnock	*Lab/Co-op*
Chairs:	
Dame Diana Johnson	*Lab*
Andrew Rosindell	*Con*
Deputy Chair: David Lammy	*Lab*
Vice-chairs:	
Sir David Amess	*Con*
Baroness Benjamin	*Lib Dem*
Dawn Butler	*Lab*
Lord Kilclooney	*CB*
Angus MacNeil	*SNP*
David Morris	*Con*
Ian Paisley	*DUP*
Mark Pritchard	*Con*
Lord Randall of Uxbridge	*Con*
Treasurer: Mark Menzies	*Con*

Contact: Andrew Rosindell, House of Commons, London SW1A 0AA
Tel: 020 7219 8475
Email: andrew.rosindell.mp@parliament.uk

Catalonia

Chair: Hywel Williams	*PlC*
Vice-chairs:	
Sarah Champion	*Lab*
Douglas Chapman	*SNP*
Ronnie Cowan	*SNP*
Baroness Garden of Frognal	*Lib Dem*
Baroness Hooper	*Con*
Gareth Johnson	*Con*
Lord Rennard	*Lib Dem*
Andrew Rosindell	*Con*

Contact: Hywel Williams, House of Commons, London SW1A 0AA Tel: 020 7219 8150
Email: hywel.williams.mp@parliament.uk
Website: www.appgcatalonia.org.uk
Twitter: @APPGCatalonia

Cayman Islands

Chair: Sir Graham Brady *Con*
Vice-chairs:
Mark Menzies *Con*
Lord Naseby *Con*
Dr Matthew Offord *Con*
Andrew Rosindell *Con*
John Spellar *Lab*
Viscount Waverley *CB*
Bill Wiggin *Con*

Contact: Sir Graham Brady, House of Commons, London SW1A 0AA
Tel: 020 7219 1260
Email: altsale@parliament.uk

Central America

President: Lord Foulkes of Cumnock *Lab/Co-op*
Chair: Andrew Rosindell *Con*
Vice-chairs:
Baroness Hooper *Con*
Lord Jones of Cheltenham *Lib Dem*
Lord Kilclooney *CB*
Tony Lloyd *Lab*
Ian Paisley *DUP*
Bob Stewart *Con*
Martin Vickers *Con*
Secretary: Mark Menzies *Con*

Contact: Andrew Rosindell, House of Commons, London SW1A 0AA
Tel: 020 7219 8475
Email: andrew.rosindell.mp@parliament.uk

Chagos Islands
(British Indian Overseas Territory)

President: Jeremy Corbyn *Ind*
Chair: Andrew Rosindell *Con*
Vice-chairs:
Patrick Grady *SNP*
Ian Paisley *DUP*
Lord Ramsbotham *CB*
Henry Smith *Con*
Catherine West *Lab*
Baroness Whitaker *Lab*
Secretary: Alan Brown *SNP*

Contact: Andrew Rosindell, House of Commons, London SW1A 0AA
Tel: 020 7219 8475
Email: andrew.rosindell.mp@parliament.uk

Channel Islands

President: Baroness Pitkeathley *Lab*
Chairs:
Andrew Rosindell *Con*
Dr Alan Whitehead *Lab*
Vice-chairs:
Lord Faulkner of Worcester *Lab*
Simon Jupp *Con*
Lord Kilclooney *CB*
Angus MacNeil *SNP*
Lord McNally *Lib Dem*
David Morris *Con*
Sheryll Murray *Con*
Sir Robert Neill *Con*
Dr Matthew Offord *Con*
Lord Pickles *Con*
Greg Smith *Con*
Bob Stewart *Con*

Contact: Andrew Rosindell, House of Commons, London SW1A 0AA
Tel: 020 7219 8475
Email: andrew.rosindell.mp@parliament.uk

Chile

Chair: Dr Lisa Cameron *SNP*
Vice-chairs:
Baroness Hooper *Con*
Lord Kilclooney *CB*
Seema Malhotra *Lab/Co-op*
Lord Mountevans *CB*
Lord Naseby *Con*
Lord Rennard *Lib Dem*
Secretary: Angus MacNeil *SNP*
Treasurer: Kenny MacAskill *SNP*

Contact: Dr Lisa Cameron, House of Commons, London SW1A 0AA Tel: 020 7219 6855
Email: lisa.cameron.mp@parliament.uk

China

Chair: Richard Graham *Con*
Chair(Hong Kong Sub-committee): Lord Wei *Con*
Deputy Chairs:
Alun Cairns *Con*
Lord Clement-Jones *Lib Dem*
Sir Geoffrey Clifton-Brown *Con*
Jonathan Reynolds *Lab/Co-op*
Catherine West *Lab*
Vice-chair(Human Rights): Alistair Carmichael *Lib Dem*
Vice-chair(Environment and Climate Change): Geraint Davies *Lab/Co-op*
Vice-chair: Baroness D'Souza *CB*
Vice-chair(Globalisation and BRI): Baroness Falkner of Margravine *CB*
Vice-chair(Consumer Economy): Yvonne Fovargue *Lab*
Vice-chair(Investment and Industry): Mark Garnier *Con*
Vice-chair: Lord Goddard of Stockport *Lib Dem*
Vice-chair(Trade): Stephen Hammond *Con*
Vice-chair(Scotland): Christine Jardine *Lib Dem*

Vice-chair(Northern Ireland): Lord Kilclooney *CB*
Vice-chair(Media and the North of England): Mark Logan *Con*
Vice-chair: Baroness Northover *Lib Dem*
Vice-chair(Agriculture): Julian Sturdy *Con*
Vice-chair(Cyber): Viscount Waverley *CB*
Vice-chair(Wales): Craig Williams *Con*
Secretary: Lord Cotter *Lib Dem*
Treasurer: Lord Wood of Anfield *Lab*

Contact: Richard Graham, House of Commons, London SW1A 0AA Tel: 020 7219 7077
Email: richard.graham.mp@parliament.uk
Website: www.appcg.org.uk
Twitter: @APPCG

Colombia

Chair: Sir Jeffrey Donaldson *DUP*
Vice-chairs:
Lord Alderdice *Lib Dem*
Greg Clark *Con*
Patrick Grady *SNP*
Mark Menzies *Con*
Lord Mountevans *CB*
Jo Stevens *Lab*
Viscount Waverley *CB*
Secretary: Chris Matheson *Lab*

Contact: Sir Jeffrey Donaldson, House of Commons, London SW1A 0AA
Tel: 020 7219 3407
Email: jeffrey.donaldson.mp@parliament.uk

Commonwealth

Honorary President: Lord Howell of Guildford *Con*
Chairs:
Lord Chidgey *Lib Dem*
Andrew Rosindell *Con*
Vice-chairs:
Lord Addington *Lib Dem*
Paul Bristow *Con*
Deidre Brock *SNP*
Dr Lisa Cameron *SNP*
Baroness Hooper *Con*
Sir Edward Leigh *Con*
Conor McGinn *Lab*
Chi Onwurah *Lab*
Baroness Prashar *CB*
Mary Robinson *Con*
Tommy Sheppard *SNP*
Sammy Wilson *DUP*
Vice-chairand Secretary: Baroness Uddin *NA*

Contact: Andrew Rosindell, House of Commons, London SW1A 0AA
Tel: 020 7219 8475
Email: andrew.rosindell.mp@parliament.uk

Croatia

Chairs:
Earl of Dundee *Con*
Sir Edward Leigh *Con*
Vice-chairs:
Lord Anderson of Swansea *Lab*
Sir Mark Hendrick *Lab/Co-op*
Secretary: Earl of Dundee *Con*

Contact: Sir Edward Leigh, House of Commons, London SW1A 0AA
Tel: 020 7219 6480
Email: edward.leigh.mp@parliament.uk

Cuba

Chair: Grahame Morris *Lab*
Vice-chairs:
Paula Barker *Lab*
Dan Carden *Lab*
Drew Hendry *SNP*
Baroness Hooper *Con*
Kim Johnson *Lab*
Lord Kilclooney *CB*
Angus MacNeil *SNP*
Mark Menzies *Con*
Kate Osborne *Lab*

Contact: Grahame Morris, House of Commons, London SW1A 0AA Tel: 020 7219 1283
Email: grahame.morris.mp@parliament.uk

Cyprus

Chair: Sir Roger Gale *Con*
Vice-chairs:
Bambos Charalambous *Lab*
Christine Jardine *Lib Dem*
Caroline Nokes *Con*
Secretary: Jack Dromey *Lab*
Treasurer: Sheryll Murray *Con*

Contact: Sir Roger Gale, House of Commons, London SW1A 0AA Tel: 020 7219 4087
Email: galerj@parliament.uk
Website: cypriotfederation.org.uk/appgforcyprus

Turkish Republic of Northern Cyprus

Chairs:
Lord Northbrook *Con*
Yasmin Qureshi *Lab*
Vice-chairs:
Lord Harrison *Lab*
Baroness Hussein-Ece *Lib Dem*
Lord Sharkey *Lib Dem*
Graham Stringer *Lab*

Contact: Yasmin Qureshi, House of Commons, London SW1A 0AA Tel: 020 7219 7019
Email: yasmin.qureshi.mp@parliament.uk

Czech Republic and Slovakia

Chairs:
Lord Anderson of Swansea *Lab*
Ian Liddell-Grainger *Con*
Vice-chairs:
Lord Bowness *NA*
Lord Dubs *Lab*
Dr Julian Lewis *Con*

Contact: Ian Liddell-Grainger, House of Commons, London SW1A 0AA
Tel: 020 7219 8149 Email: ianlg@parliament.uk

Denmark

Chairs:
Stephen Kinnock *Lab*
Baroness McIntosh of Pickering *Con*
Vice-chairs:
Angus MacNeil *SNP*
Lord Mountevans *CB*
Andrew Rosindell *Con*
Lord Teverson *Lib Dem*
Secretary: Viscount Craigavon *CB*

Contact: Stephen Kinnock, House of Commons, London SW1A 0AA Tel: 020 7219 8801
Email: stephen.kinnock.mp@parliament.uk

Egypt

Chairs:
Jonathan Lord *Con*
Lord Marlesford *Con*
Vice-chairs:
Sir Jeffrey Donaldson *DUP*
Baroness Hooper *Con*
Lord Houghton of Richmond *CB*
Lord Risby *Con*
Secretary: John Spellar *Lab*
Treasurer: Lord Stone of Blackheath *NA*

Contact: Jonathan Lord, House of Commons, London SW1A 0AA Tel: 020 7219 6913
Email: jonathan.lord.mp@parliament.uk

Eritrea

Chairs:
Thangam Debbonaire *Lab*
Baroness Goudie *Lab*
Kate Osamor *Lab/Co-op*
Vice-chairs:
Lord Alton of Liverpool *CB*
Fleur Anderson *Lab*
Baroness Anelay of St Johns *Con*
Harriett Baldwin *Con*
Lord Chidgey *Lib Dem*
Theo Clarke *Con*
Stephen Doughty *Lab/Co-op*
Flick Drummond *Con*
Philip Hollobone *Con*
Mark Pritchard *Con*
Bishop of Salisbury *NA*

Contact: Kate Osamor, House of Commons, London SW1A 0AA Tel: 020 7219 6602
Email: kate.osamor.mp@parliament.uk

Estonia

Chairs:
Martin Docherty-Hughes *SNP*
Mark Pritchard *Con*
Vice-chairs:
Lord Balfe *Con*
Lord Davies of Stamford *Lab*
Lord Kilclooney *CB*
Alex Sobel *Lab/Co-op*
Viscount Waverley *CB*
Secretary: Greg Hands *Con*
Treasurer: John Whittingdale *Con*

Contact: Mark Pritchard, House of Commons, London SW1A 0AA Tel: 020 7219 8494
Email: pritchardm@parliament.uk

Ethiopia and Djibouti

Chair: Laurence Robertson *Con*
Vice-chairs:
Baroness Anelay of St Johns *Con*
Harriett Baldwin *Con*
Lord Chidgey *Lib Dem*
Sir Jeffrey Donaldson *DUP*
Tim Loughton *Con*
Lord Rogan *UUP*
Lord Sheikh *Con*
Viscount Waverley *CB*
Treasurer: Lord Cameron of Dillington *CB*

Contact: Laurence Robertson, House of Commons, London SW1A 0AA
Tel: 020 7219 4196
Email: robertsonl@parliament.uk

Falkland Islands

Chair: Derek Twigg *Lab*
Vice-chairs:
Baroness Hooper *Con*
Lord Kilclooney *CB*
Brendan O'Hara *SNP*
Alexander Stafford *Con*
James Sunderland *Con*
Secretary: Andrew Rosindell *Con*
Treasurer: Baroness Smith of Newnham *Lib Dem*

Contact: Derek Twigg, House of Commons, London SW1A 0AA Tel: 020 7219 1039
Email: derek.twigg.mp@parliament.uk

Faroe Islands

Chair: Angus MacNeil *SNP*
Vice-chairs:
Fabian Hamilton *Lab*
Anne McLaughlin *SNP*
Lia Nici *Con*
Brendan O'Hara *SNP*
Andrew Rosindell *Con*
Martin Vickers *Con*

Contact: Angus MacNeil, House of Commons, London SW1A 0AA Tel: 020 7219 8476
Email: macneila@parliament.uk

Finland

Chairs:
Baroness Ramsay of Cartvale *Lab*
Dr Ben Spencer *Con*
Vice-chairs:
Lord Balfe *Con*
Lord Beith *Lib Dem*
Kerry McCarthy *Lab*
Angus MacNeil *SNP*
Lord Mountevans *CB*
Lord Reay *Con*
John Spellar *Lab*
Secretary: Viscount Craigavon *CB*

Contact: Dr Ben Spencer, House of Commons, London SW1A 0AA Tel: 020 7219 6783
Email: ben.spencer.mp@parliament.uk

France

Presidents:
Sir Edward Leigh *Con*
Sir Robert Neill *Con*
Chair: Stephen Crabb *Con*
Vice-chairs:
Douglas Chapman *SNP*
Lord Davies of Stamford *Lab*
Baroness Janke *Lib Dem*
Ben Lake *PlC*
Anna McMorrin *Lab*
Secretary: Lord Touhig *Lab/Co-op*
Treasurer: Greg Hands *Con*

Contact: Stephen Crabb, House of Commons, London SW1A 0AA Tel: 020 7219 0907
Email: stephen.crabb.mp@parliament.uk

Friends of Syria

Chairs:
Alison McGovern *Lab*
Andrew Mitchell *Con*
Vice-chairs:
Theo Clarke *Con*
Thangam Debbonaire *Lab*
Alicia Kearns *Con*
Jeff Smith *Lab*

Contact: Alison McGovern, House of Commons, London SW1A 0AA
Tel: 020 7219 7190
Email: alison.mcgovern.mp@parliament.uk
Website: www.appgfriendsofsyria.org
Twitter: @appgsyria

Georgia

Chair: Jonathan Djanogly *Con*
Vice-chairs:
Lord Haworth *Lab*
Mark Pritchard *Con*
Secretary: Jessica Morden *Lab*
Treasurer: Lord Harries of Pentregarth *CB*

Contact: Jonathan Djanogly, House of Commons, London SW1A 0AA
Tel: 020 7219 2367
Email: jonathan.djanogly.mp@parliament.uk

Germany

Chairs:
Greg Hands *Con*
Dr Philippa Whitford *SNP*
Vice-chairs:
Lord Balfe *Con*
Lord Davies of Stamford *Lab*
Lord Goddard of Stockport *Lib Dem*
Drew Hendry *SNP*
Mark Pritchard *Con*
John Spellar *Lab*
Stephen Timms *Lab*
Secretary: Lord Kirkhope of Harrogate *Con*
Treasurer: Sir Mark Hendrick *Lab/Co-op*

Contact: Dr Philippa Whitford, House of Commons, London SW1A 0AA
Tel: 020 7219 8158
Email: philippa.whitford.mp@parliament.uk

Gibraltar

Chair: Sir Robert Neill *Con*
Deputy Chair: Chris Matheson *Lab*
Vice-chairs:
Baroness Butler-Sloss *CB*
Lord Chidgey *Lib Dem*
Sir Jeffrey Donaldson *DUP*
Drew Hendry *SNP*
Jack Lopresti *Con*
Lord Rogan *UUP*
Andrew Rosindell *Con*
Secretary: Bob Stewart *Con*
Treasurers:
Lord Hoyle *Lab*
Angus MacNeil *SNP*

Contact: Sir Robert Neill, House of Commons, London SW1A 0AA Tel: 020 7219 8169
Email: bob.neill.mp@parliament.uk

Greece

Chair: Alberto Costa *Con*

Vice-chairs:

Lord Boswell of Aynho *NA*

Sir Graham Brady *Con*

Lord Dubs *Lab*

Baroness Harris of Richmond *Lib Dem*

Craig Mackinlay *Con*

Secretary: Chris Elmore *Lab*

Treasurer: Sarah Champion *Lab*

Contact: Alberto Costa, House of Commons, London SW1A 0AA Tel: 020 7219 4936
Email: alberto.costa.mp@parliament.uk

Greenland

Chair: Brendan O'Hara *SNP*

Vice-chairs:

Drew Hendry *SNP*

David Linden *SNP*

Carol Monaghan *SNP*

Andrew Rosindell *Con*

Cat Smith *Lab*

Secretary: Alex Sobel *Lab/Co-op*

Treasurer: Gavin Newlands *SNP*

Contact: Brendan O'Hara, House of Commons, London SW1A 0AA Tel: 020 7219 8783
Email: brendan.ohara.mp@parliament.uk

Hong Kong

Chairs:

Baroness Bennett of Manor Castle *Green*

Alistair Carmichael *Lib Dem*

Vice-chairs:

Lord Alton of Liverpool *CB*

Andrew Bowie *Con*

Sarah Champion *Lab*

Geraint Davies *Lab/Co-op*

Steve Double *Con*

Lord Falconer of Thoroton *Lab*

Dame Cheryl Gillan *Con*

Andrew Gwynne *Lab*

Lord Hunt of Kings Heath *Lab/Co-op*

Lord Pendry *Lab*

Mark Pritchard *Con*

Andrew Rosindell *Con*

Bob Seely *Con*

Jim Shannon *DUP*

Lord Shinkwin *Con*

Contact: Alistair Carmichael, House of Commons, London SW1A 0AA
Tel: 020 7219 8181
Email: carmichaela@parliament.uk

Hungary

Chair: Sir Robert Neill *Con*

Vice-chairs:

Lord Anderson of Swansea *Lab*

Craig Mackinlay *Con*

Viscount Waverley *CB*

John Whittingdale *Con*

Contact: Sir Robert Neill, House of Commons, London SW1A 0AA Tel: 020 7219 8169
Email: bob.neill.mp@parliament.uk

Iceland

Chair: Angus MacNeil *SNP*

Vice-chairs:

Viscount Craigavon *CB*

Fabian Hamilton *Lab*

Dame Diana Johnson *Lab*

Martin Vickers *Con*

Secretary: Lia Nici *Con*

Treasurer: Andrew Rosindell *Con*

Contact: Angus MacNeil, House of Commons, London SW1A 0AA Tel: 020 7219 8476
Email: macneila@parliament.uk

India

Chairs:

Bob Blackman *Con*

Virendra Sharma *Lab*

Vice-chairs:

Lord Anderson of Swansea *Lab*

Lord Balfe *Con*

Lord Bilimoria *CB*

Lord Dholakia *Lib Dem*

Baroness Flather *CB*

Lord Kilclooney *CB*

Seema Malhotra *Lab/Co-op*

Lord Naseby *Con*

Lord Sheikh *Con*

Sam Tarry *Lab*

Alison Thewliss *SNP*

Shailesh Vara *Con*

Viscount Waverley *CB*

Secretary: Navendu Mishra *Lab*

Treasurer: Baroness Verma *Con*

Contact: Virendra Sharma, House of Commons, London SW1A 0AA Tel: 020 7219 6080
Email: sharmav@parliament.uk

Indonesia

Chair: Richard Graham *Con*

Vice-chairs:

Lord Astor of Hever *Con*

Lord Clement-Jones *Lib Dem*

Judith Cummins *Lab*

Lord Robathan *Con*

Lord Rogan *UUP*

Lord Sassoon *Con*

John Spellar *Lab*

Secretary: Rosie Cooper *Lab*

Contact: Richard Graham, House of Commons, London SW1A 0AA Tel: 020 7219 7077
Email: richard.graham.mp@parliament.uk

Iran

Chair: Richard Bacon *Con*
Vice-chairs:
Lord Anderson of Swansea *Lab*
Lord Balfe *Con*
John Baron *Con*
Lord Lamont of Lerwick *Con*
Andrew Mitchell *Con*
Viscount Waverley *CB*

Contact: Richard Bacon, House of Commons, London SW1A 0AA Tel: 020 7219 8301
Email: richardbaconmp@parliament.uk

Ireland and the Irish in Britain

Chair: Conor McGinn *Lab*
Vice-chairs:
Martin Docherty-Hughes *SNP*
Baroness Doocey *Lib Dem*
Mark Logan *Con*
Karin Smyth *Lab*
Honorary Secretaries:
Sir Peter Bottomley *Con*
Lord Dubs *Lab*
Officers:
Lord Brennan *NA*
Neil Coyle *Lab*
Jon Cruddas *Lab*
Lord Davies of Stamford *Lab*
Tanmanjeet Singh Dhesi *Lab*
Dave Doogan *SNP*
Stephen Doughty *Lab/Co-op*
Jack Dromey *Lab*
Lord Empey *UUP*
Dr Stephen Farry *APNI*
Claire Hanna *SDLP*
Baroness Harris of Richmond *Lib Dem*
Baroness Healy of Primrose Hill *Lab*
Lord Hendy *Lab*
Simon Hoare *Con*
Mike Kane *Lab*
Lord Kennedy of Southwark *Lab/Co-op*
Pat McFadden *Lab*
Angus MacNeil *SNP*
Huw Merriman *Con*
Carol Monaghan *SNP*
Lord Murphy of Torfaen *Lab*
Baroness Northover *Lib Dem*
Baroness Ritchie of Downpatrick *NA*
Lord Stevenson of Balmacara *Lab*
Catherine West *Lab*

Contact: Conor McGinn, House of Commons, London SW1A 0AA Tel: 020 7219 4367
Email: conor.mcginn.mp@parliament.uk

Isle of Man

Chair: Andrew Rosindell *Con*
Deputy Chair: Gavin Robinson *DUP*
Vice-chairs:
Fleur Anderson *Lab*
Lord Bach *Lab*
Lord Dubs *Lab*
Baroness Harris of Richmond *Lib Dem*
Lord Kilclooney *CB*
Jonathan Lord *Con*
Angus MacNeil *SNP*
David Morris *Con*
Sheryll Murray *Con*
Baroness Nicholson of Winterbourne *Con*
Lia Nici *Con*
Ian Paisley *DUP*
Lord Polak *Con*
Bob Stewart *Con*
Martin Vickers *Con*

Contact: Andrew Rosindell, House of Commons, London SW1A 0AA
Tel: 020 7219 8475
Email: andrew.rosindell.mp@parliament.uk

Israel

Chairs:
Bob Blackman *Con*
Lord Turnberg *Lab*
Vice-chairs:
Steve McCabe *Lab*
Dr Matthew Offord *Con*
Lord Palmer of Childs Hill *Lib Dem*
Baroness Ramsay of Cartvale *Lab*
Mary Robinson *Con*
John Spellar *Lab*
Christian Wakeford *Con*

Contact: Bob Blackman, House of Commons, London SW1A 0AA Tel: 020 7219 7082
Email: bob.blackman.mp@parliament.uk

Italy

Chairs:
Alberto Costa *Con*
Ellie Reeves *Lab*
Vice-chairs:
Baroness Bonham-Carter of Yarnbury *Lib Dem*
Greg Clark *Con*
Robert Courts *Con*
Andrea Jenkyns *Con*
Jack Lopresti *Con*
Lia Nici *Con*
Secretary: Lord Russell of Liverpool *CB*
Treasurer: Lord Anderson of Swansea *Lab*

Contact: Alberto Costa, House of Commons, London SW1A 0AA Tel: 020 7219 4936
Email: alberto.costa.mp@parliament.uk

Jamaica
Chair: Dawn Butler *Lab*
Vice-chairs:
Marsha De Cordova *Lab*
Lord Sheikh *Con*
Secretary: Sarah Champion *Lab*
Treasurer: Laurence Robertson *Con*

Contact: Dawn Butler, House of Commons, London SW1A 0AA Tel: 020 7219 8591
Email: dawn.butler.mp@parliament.uk

Japan
Chair: Jeremy Hunt *Con*
Vice-chairs:
Sir David Amess *Con*
Lord Bates *Con*
Sir Graham Brady *Con*
Deidre Brock *SNP*
Dr Lisa Cameron *SNP*
Judith Cummins *Lab*
Chris Elmore *Lab*
Baroness Finlay of Llandaff *CB*
Lord Holmes of Richmond *Con*
Baroness Hooper *Con*
David Morris *Con*
Lord Moynihan *Con*
Ian Paisley *DUP*
Lord Pendry *Lab*
Gary Sambrook *Con*
John Spellar *Lab*
Dr Ben Spencer *Con*
Viscount Trenchard *Con*
Viscount Waverley *CB*
Heather Wheeler *Con*
Craig Williams *Con*
Secretary: Sir Mark Hendrick *Lab/Co-op*

Contact: Jeremy Hunt, House of Commons, London SW1A 0AA Tel: 020 7219 6813
Email: huntj@parliament.uk
Website: www.bjpg.co.uk

Jordan
Chair: David Jones *Con*
Vice-chairs:
Lord Dubs *Lab*
Alicia Kearns *Con*
Lord Kilclooney *CB*
Mark Logan *Con*
Kerry McCarthy *Lab*
Lord Sheikh *Con*
Bob Stewart *Con*
Viscount Waverley *CB*

Contact: David Jones, House of Commons, London SW1A 0AA Tel: 020 7219 8070
Email: katharine.huggins@parliament.uk

Kashmir
Chair: Debbie Abrahams *Lab*
Senior Vice-chairs:
Jack Brereton *Con*
Imran Hussain *Lab*
Vice-chairs:
Paul Blomfield *Lab*
Paul Bristow *Con*
Sarah Champion *Lab*
Tanmanjeet Singh Dhesi *Lab*
Jonathan Gullis *Con*
Rachel Hopkins *Lab*
Afzal Khan *Lab*
Marco Longhi *Con*
Jason McCartney *Con*
Jim McMahon *Lab/Co-op*
Alex Norris *Lab/Co-op*
Sir Mike Penning *Con*
Viscount Waverley *CB*
Secretary: Lord Hussain *Lib Dem*
Treasurer: James Daly *Con*

Contact: Debbie Abrahams, House of Commons, London SW1A 0AA
Tel: 020 7219 1041
Email: abrahamsd@parliament.uk

Kazakhstan
Chairs:
Lord Astor of Hever *Con*
Bob Stewart *Con*
Vice-chairs:
Sir Graham Brady *Con*
Adam Holloway *Con*
Lord Kilclooney *CB*
Lord Mann *NA*
Chris Matheson *Lab*
Lord Moynihan *Con*
Lord Rogan *UUP*
Lord Sheikh *Con*
Baroness Stern *CB*
Baroness Suttie *Lib Dem*
Martin Vickers *Con*
Lord Wasserman *Con*
Viscount Waverley *CB*
Secretary: Paul Scully *Con*
Treasurer: Craig Mackinlay *Con*

Contact: Bob Stewart, House of Commons, London SW1A 0AA Tel: 020 7219 7011
Email: bob.stewart.mp@parliament.uk

Kosovo
Chair: Martin Vickers *Con*
Vice-chairs:
Sir Peter Bottomley *Con*
Lord Bowness *NA*
Dr Matthew Offord *Con*
Ian Paisley *DUP*

Mark Pritchard *Con*
Alex Sobel *Lab/Co-op*
Viscount Waverley *CB*

Contact: Martin Vickers, House of Commons, London SW1A 0AA Tel: 020 7219 7212
Email: martin.vickers.mp@parliament.uk

Kurdistan in Turkey and Syria

Chair: Lloyd Russell-Moyle *Lab/Co-op*
Vice-chairs:
Crispin Blunt *Con*
Feryal Clark *Lab*
Adam Holloway *Con*
Kate Osamor *Lab/Co-op*
Alexander Stafford *Con*

Contact: Lloyd Russell-Moyle, House of Commons, London SW1A 0AA
Tel: 020 7219 2280
Email: lloyd.russellmoyle.mp@parliament.uk

Kurdistan Region in Iraq

Chairs:
Robert Halfon *Con*
Steve Reed *Lab/Co-op*
Vice-chairs:
Mary Glindon *Lab*
Philip Hollobone *Con*
Sarah Jones *Lab*
Jack Lopresti *Con*
Jason McCartney *Con*
Lord McConnell of Glenscorrodale *Lab*
Lord McNicol of West Kilbride *Lab*
Stephen Metcalfe *Con*
Toby Perkins *Lab*
Baroness Ramsay of Cartvale *Lab*
Henry Smith *Con*
Chris Stephens *SNP*
Michael Tomlinson *Con*
Secretary: Alicia Kearns *Con*
Treasurer: Lord Clement-Jones *Lib Dem*

Contact: Robert Halfon, House of Commons, London SW1A 0AA Tel: 020 7219 7223
Website: www.appgkurdistan.org.uk

Kyrgyzstan

Chair: Bob Stewart *Con*
Vice-chairs:
Sir Graham Brady *Con*
Wayne David *Lab*
Adam Holloway *Con*
Lord Kilclooney *CB*
Khalid Mahmood *Lab*
Lord Mann *NA*
Chris Matheson *Lab*
Lord Moynihan *Con*
Lord Rogan *UUP*
Paul Scully *Con*
Lord Sheikh *Con*
Baroness Stern *CB*
Viscount Waverley *CB*
Secretary: Craig Mackinlay *Con*

Contact: Bob Stewart, House of Commons, London SW1A 0AA Tel: 020 7219 7011
Email: bob.stewart.mp@parliament.uk

Latin America

Honorary President: Baroness Hooper *Con*
Chair: Mark Menzies *Con*
Vice-chairs:
Lord Alderdice *Lib Dem*
Angus MacNeil *SNP*
Chris Matheson *Lab*
Viscount Waverley *CB*

Contact: Mark Menzies, House of Commons, London SW1A 0AA Tel: 020 7219 7073
Email: mark.menzies.mp@parliament.uk

Lebanon

Chair: Sir John Hayes *Con*
Vice-chairs:
Lord Kilclooney *CB*
Viscount Waverley *CB*
Matt Western *Lab*
Secretary: Bob Stewart *Con*

Contact: Sir John Hayes, House of Commons, London SW1A 0AA Tel: 020 7219 1389
Email: hayesj@parliament.uk

Liechtenstein

Chair: Andrew Rosindell *Con*
Vice-chairs:
Sir David Amess *Con*
Dr Lisa Cameron *SNP*
Fabian Hamilton *Lab*
Daniel Kawczynski *Con*
Lord Kilclooney *CB*
Gagan Mohindra *Con*
Lord Northbrook *Con*
Henry Smith *Con*
Viscount Waverley *CB*
Secretary: Mark Menzies *Con*
Treasurer: Angus MacNeil *SNP*

Contact: Andrew Rosindell, House of Commons, London SW1A 0AA
Tel: 020 7219 8475
Email: andrew.rosindell.mp@parliament.uk

Lithuania

Chair: Mark Pritchard *Con*
Vice-chairs:
Lord Bowness *NA*
Stephen Timms *Lab*
Secretary: Daniel Kawczynski *Con*
Treasurer: Tony Lloyd *Lab*

Contact: Mark Pritchard, House of Commons, London SW1A 0AA Tel: 020 7219 8494
Email: pritchardm@parliament.uk

Luxembourg
Chair: Damien Moore *Con*
Vice-chairs:
Lord Balfe *Con*
Dr Lisa Cameron *SNP*
Rosie Cooper *Lab*
Darren Jones *Lab*
David Linden *SNP*
Ian Paisley *DUP*
Stephanie Peacock *Lab*
Gary Sambrook *Con*

Contact: Damien Moore, House of Commons, London SW1A 0AA Tel: 01704 500577
Email: damien.moore.mp@parliament.uk

Malawi
Honorary President: Lord McConnell of Glenscorrodale *Lab*
Chair: Patrick Grady *SNP*
Vice-chairs:
Margaret Ferrier *Ind*
David Mundell *Con*
Kate Osamor *Lab/Co-op*
Jim Shannon *DUP*
Treasurer: Marion Fellows *SNP*

Contact: Patrick Grady, House of Commons, London SW1A 0AA Tel: 020 7219 6398
Email: patrick.grady.mp@parliament.uk
Website: www.scotland-malawipartnership.org/appg

Maldives
Chair: Sir David Amess *Con*
Vice-chairs:
Rosie Cooper *Lab*
Lord German *Lib Dem*
Lord Moynihan *Con*
Viscount Waverley *CB*
Secretary: Mark Pritchard *Con*
Officer: Lord Truscott *Ind Lab*

Contact: Sir David Amess, House of Commons, London SW1A 0AA Tel: 020 7219 3452
Email: amessd@parliament.uk

Malta
Chair: Douglas Chapman *SNP*
Vice-chairs:
Lord Bilimoria *CB*
Yvonne Fovargue *Lab*
Mark Pritchard *Con*
Secretary: Bob Stewart *Con*
Treasurer: Martyn Day *SNP*

Contact: Douglas Chapman, 16 Cromarty Campus, Rosyth Europarc, Rosyth KY11 2WX
Tel: 013 8332 4775

Mexico
Chair: Dan Carden *Lab*
Vice-chairs:
Baroness Bonham-Carter of Yarnbury *Lib Dem*
Lord Brennan *NA*
Baroness Hooper *Con*
Chris Matheson *Lab*
Ian Mearns *Lab*
Bob Seely *Con*
Viscount Waverley *CB*
Secretary: Grahame Morris *Lab*

Contact: Dan Carden, House of Commons, London SW1A 0AA Tel: 020 7219 2673
Email: dan.carden.mp@parliament.uk

Montenegro
Chair: Alex Sobel *Lab/Co-op*
Vice-chairs:
Lord Bowness *NA*
Ian Paisley *DUP*
Lord Randall of Uxbridge *Con*
Martin Vickers *Con*
Viscount Waverley *CB*

Contact: Alex Sobel, House of Commons, London SW1A 0AA Tel: 020 7219 8295
Email: alex.sobel.mp@parliament.uk

Montserrat
Chair: Andrew Rosindell *Con*
Vice-chairs:
Lord Balfe *Con*
Baroness Benjamin *Lib Dem*
Andrew Bowie *Con*
Sir Graham Brady *Con*
Tanmanjeet Singh Dhesi *Lab*
Sir Jeffrey Donaldson *DUP*
Baroness Hooper *Con*
Lord Jones of Cheltenham *Lib Dem*
Angus MacNeil *SNP*
Lord Northbrook *Con*
Secretary: Sheryll Murray *Con*

Contact: Andrew Rosindell, House of Commons, London SW1A 0AA
Tel: 020 7219 8475
Email: andrew.rosindell.mp@parliament.uk

Morocco
Chair: Ian Liddell-Grainger *Con*
Deputy Chair: Fabian Hamilton *Lab*
Vice-chairs:
Lord Harrison *Lab*
Daniel Kawczynski *Con*
Lord Kilclooney *CB*

Dr Andrew Murrison *Con*
Baroness Suttie *Lib Dem*
Secretary: Nigel Evans *Con*
Treasurer: Lord Anderson of Swansea *Lab*

Contact: Ian Liddell-Grainger, House of Commons, London SW1A 0AA
Tel: 020 7219 8149 Email: ianlg@parliament.uk

Nepal

Chair: Virendra Sharma *Lab*
Vice-chairs:
Lord Anderson of Swansea *Lab*
Lord Balfe *Con*
Lord Bilimoria *CB*
Bob Blackman *Con*
Lord Dholakia *Lib Dem*
Baroness Flather *CB*
Lord Kilclooney *CB*
Seema Malhotra *Lab/Co-op*
Lord Naseby *Con*
Baroness Northover *Lib Dem*
Earl of Sandwich *CB*
Lord Sheikh *Con*
Sam Tarry *Lab*
Viscount Waverley *CB*
Secretary: Navendu Mishra *Lab*
Treasurer: Baroness Verma *Con*

Contact: Virendra Sharma, House of Commons, London SW1A 0AA Tel: 020 7219 6080
Email: sharmav@parliament.uk

Netherlands

Chair: Clive Betts *Lab*
Vice-chairs:
Lord Anderson of Swansea *Lab*
Lord Balfe *Con*
Viscount Waverley *CB*
Treasurer: Ben Lake *PlC*

Contact: Clive Betts, House of Commons, London SW1A 0AA Tel: 020 7219 5114
Email: officeofclivebettsmp@parliament.uk

Nigeria

Chair: Kate Osamor *Lab/Co-op*
Vice-chairs:
Lord Chidgey *Lib Dem*
Florence Eshalomi *Lab/Co-op*
Preet Kaur Gill *Lab/Co-op*
Afzal Khan *Lab*
Baroness Northover *Lib Dem*
Taiwo Owatemi *Lab*
Laurence Robertson *Con*

Contact: Kate Osamor, House of Commons, London SW1A 0AA Tel: 020 7219 6602
Email: kate.osamor.mp@parliament.uk
Twitter: @NigeriaAPPG

Norfolk Island

President: Lord Howarth of Newport *Lab*
Chair: Andrew Rosindell *Con*
Deputy Chairs:
Deidre Brock *SNP*
Catherine West *Lab*
Vice-chairs:
Sarah Dines *Con*
Baroness Hooper *Con*
Daniel Kawczynski *Con*
Lord Kilclooney *CB*
Angus MacNeil *SNP*
Sheryll Murray *Con*
Sir Robert Neill *Con*
Ian Paisley *DUP*
Bob Stewart *Con*
Lord West of Spithead *Lab*

Contact: Andrew Rosindell, House of Commons, London SW1A 0AA
Tel: 020 7219 8475
Email: andrew.rosindell.mp@parliament.uk

North Korea

(Democratic People's Republic of Korea)
Chairs:
Lord Alton of Liverpool *CB*
Fiona Bruce *Con*
Sir Geoffrey Clifton-Brown *Con*
Vice-chairs:
Lord German *Lib Dem*
Viscount Waverley *CB*
Catherine West *Lab*

Contact: Fiona Bruce, House of Commons, London SW1A 0AA Tel: 020 7219 7042
Email: fiona.bruce.mp@parliament.uk
Twitter: @APPGNorthKorea

North Macedonia

Chairs:
Alex Sobel *Lab/Co-op*
Martin Vickers *Con*
Vice-chairs:
Baroness Barker *Lib Dem*
Lord Bowness *NA*
Michael Fabricant *Con*
Ian Paisley *DUP*
Lord Randall of Uxbridge *Con*
Viscount Waverley *CB*

Contact: Martin Vickers, House of Commons, London SW1A 0AA Tel: 020 7219 7212
Email: martin.vickers.mp@parliament.uk

Norway

Chair: Sir Mark Hendrick *Lab/Co-op*
Vice-chairs:
Lord Anderson of Swansea *Lab*

Lord Balfe *Con*
Lord Beith *Lib Dem*
Viscount Craigavon *CB*
Lord Faulkner of Worcester *Lab*
Lord Mountevans *CB*
Andrew Rosindell *Con*
Lord Teverson *Lib Dem*
Secretary: Angus MacNeil *SNP*

Contact: Sir Mark Hendrick, House of Commons, London SW1A 0AA
Tel: 020 7219 4791
Email: mark.hendrick.mp@parliament.uk

Oman

Chair: Mark Menzies *Con*
Vice-chairs:
Lord Astor of Hever *Con*
Lord Balfe *Con*
Lord German *Lib Dem*
Dr John Howell *Con*
Afzal Khan *Lab*
Lord Kilclooney *CB*
Jack Lopresti *Con*
Lord Robathan *Con*
Viscount Waverley *CB*
Secretary: Bob Stewart *Con*

Contact: Mark Menzies, House of Commons, London SW1A 0AA Tel: 020 7219 7073
Email: mark.menzies.mp@parliament.uk

UK Overseas Territories

Chair: Andrew Rosindell *Con*
Vice-chairs:
Sir David Amess *Con*
Lord Balfe *Con*
Sir Peter Bottomley *Con*
Sir Graham Brady *Con*
Paul Bristow *Con*
Andrew Griffith *Con*
Baroness Hooper *Con*
Lord Jones of Cheltenham *Lib Dem*
Robin Millar *Con*
John Penrose *Con*
Baroness Smith of Basildon *Lab/Co-op*
John Spellar *Lab*
Derek Twigg *Lab*
Catherine West *Lab*
Secretary: Lord Kilclooney *CB*
Treasurer: Bob Stewart *Con*

Contact: Andrew Rosindell, House of Commons, London SW1A 0AA
Tel: 020 7219 8475
Email: andrew.rosindell.mp@parliament.uk

Pacific Islands

Chair: Andrew Rosindell *Con*
Vice-chairs:
Lord Balfe *Con*
Lord Chidgey *Lib Dem*
Sarah Dines *Con*
Baroness Hooper *Con*
Lord Jones of Cheltenham *Lib Dem*
Angus MacNeil *SNP*
Ian Paisley *DUP*
Catherine West *Lab*

Contact: Andrew Rosindell, House of Commons, London SW1A 0AA
Tel: 020 7219 8475
Email: andrew.rosindell.mp@parliament.uk

Pakistan

Chair: Yasmin Qureshi *Lab*
Vice-chairs:
Imran Ahmad Khan *Con*
Lord Alton of Liverpool *CB*
Lord Hussain *Lib Dem*
Imran Hussain *Lab*
Afzal Khan *Lab*
Dr Matthew Offord *Con*
Viscount Waverley *CB*

Contact: Yasmin Qureshi, House of Commons, London SW1A 0AA Tel: 020 7219 7019
Email: yasmin.qureshi.mp@parliament.uk

Palestine

Chairs:
Julie Elliott *Lab*
Baroness Warsi *Con*
Vice-chairs:
Tahir Ali *Lab*
Imran Hussain *Lab*
Kim Johnson *Lab*
Tommy Sheppard *SNP*
Viscount Waverley *CB*
Matt Western *Lab*
Secretary: Andy Slaughter *Lab*

Contact: Julie Elliott, House of Commons, London SW1A 0AA Tel: 020 7219 7165
Email: julie.elliott.mp@parliament.uk
Twitter: @PalestineAPPG

Philippines

Chair: Sir David Amess *Con*
Vice-chairs:
Rosie Cooper *Lab*
Angus MacNeil *SNP*
Mark Menzies *Con*
Lord Moynihan *Con*
Lord Rogan *UUP*
Viscount Waverley *CB*

Contact: Sir David Amess, House of Commons, London SW1A 0AA Tel: 020 7219 3452
Email: amessd@parliament.uk

Pitcairn Islands

Chair: Andrew Rosindell *Con*
Vice-chairs:
Lord Balfe *Con*
Andrew Bowie *Con*
Fabian Hamilton *Lab*
Baroness Hooper *Con*
Lord Jones of Cheltenham *Lib Dem*
Lord Kilclooney *CB*
Angus MacNeil *SNP*
Sheryll Murray *Con*
Gavin Robinson *DUP*

Contact: Andrew Rosindell, House of Commons, London SW1A 0AA
Tel: 020 7219 8475
Email: andrew.rosindell.mp@parliament.uk

Poland

Chair: Daniel Kawczynski *Con*
Vice-chairs:
Sir Jeffrey Donaldson *DUP*
Robert Halfon *Con*
Dr Rupa Huq *Lab*
Martin Vickers *Con*
Viscount Waverley *CB*

Contact: Daniel Kawczynski, House of Commons, London SW1A 0AA
Tel: 020 7219 6249
Email: daniel.kawczynski.mp@parliament.uk
Website: appgpoland.uk
Twitter: @appgpoland

Polar Regions

Chair: James Gray *Con*
Deputy Chair: Lord Hunt of Chesterton *Lab*
Vice-chairs:
Lord Cromwell *CB*
Lord Haworth *Lab*
Baroness Jay of Paddington *Lab*
Chris Matheson *Lab*
Baroness Neville-Jones *Con*
Brendan O'Hara *SNP*
Baroness Smith of Newnham *Lib Dem*
Matt Western *Lab*
Treasurer: Mark Garnier *Con*

Contact: James Gray, House of Commons, London SW1A 0AA Tel: 020 7219 6237
Email: jamesgraymp@parliament.uk
Twitter: @APPGPolar

Portugal

Chair: Stephen Hammond *Con*
Deputy Chair: Mark Tami *Lab*
Vice-chairs:
Baroness Doocey *Lib Dem*
Lord Dubs *Lab*
Lord Gilbert of Panteg *Con*
Lord McNicol of West Kilbride *Lab*
Valerie Vaz *Lab*
Viscount Waverley *CB*
Secretary: Huw Merriman *Con*
Treasurer: Lord Rogan *UUP*

Contact: Stephen Hammond, House of Commons, London SW1A 0AA
Tel: 020 7219 3401
Email: stephen.hammond.mp@parliament.uk

Qatar

Chairs:
Alistair Carmichael *Lib Dem*
Baroness Morris of Bolton *Con*
Vice-chairs:
Sir David Amess *Con*
Imran Hussain *Lab*
Baroness Northover *Lib Dem*
Lord Redesdale *Lib Dem*
Mark Tami *Lab*

Contact: Alistair Carmichael, House of Commons, London SW1A 0AA
Tel: 020 7219 8181
Email: carmichaela@parliament.uk

Romania

Chairs:
Bob Blackman *Con*
Lord Davies of Stamford *Lab*
Vice-chairs:
Lord Bowness *NA*
Brendan Clarke-Smith *Con*
Lord Dykes *CB*
Greg Hands *Con*
Drew Hendry *SNP*
Stephen Timms *Lab*
Viscount Waverley *CB*
Secretary: Carol Monaghan *SNP*

Contact: Bob Blackman, House of Commons, London SW1A 0AA Tel: 020 7219 7082
Email: bob.blackman.mp@parliament.uk

Russia

Chair: Chris Bryant *Lab*
Vice-chairs:
Richard Bacon *Con*
Lord Balfe *Con*
Dr Lisa Cameron *SNP*
Douglas Chapman *SNP*
Martin Docherty-Hughes *SNP*
Lord Dykes *CB*
Lord Goddard of Stockport *Lib Dem*
Stephen Kinnock *Lab*

Baroness Meyer *Con*
Bob Seely *Con*
Viscount Waverley *CB*
Secretary: Kerry McCarthy *Lab*
Treasurer: Lord Kilclooney *CB*

Contact: Chris Bryant, House of Commons, London SW1A 0AA Tel: 020 7219 8315
Email: bryantc@parliament.uk

Rwanda
Chairs:
Andrew Mitchell *Con*
Lord Popat *Con*
Vice-chairs:
Baroness D'Souza *CB*
Chris Elmore *Lab*
Lord McConnell of Glenscorrodale *Lab*
Lord Sheikh *Con*
Viscount Waverley *CB*
Secretary: Lord Whitby *Con*
Treasurer: Mark Pawsey *Con*

Contact: Andrew Mitchell, House of Commons, London SW1A 0AA Tel: 020 7219 8516
Email: andrew.mitchell.mp@parliament.uk

St Helena
Chair: Andrew Mitchell *Con*
Vice-chairs:
Lord Foulkes of Cumnock *Lab/Co-op*
Baroness Hooper *Con*
Secretary: Andrew Rosindell *Con*
Treasurer: Sir Desmond Swayne *Con*

Contact: Andrew Mitchell, House of Commons, London SW1A 0AA Tel: 020 7219 8516
Email: andrew.mitchell.mp@parliament.uk

San Marino
President: Sir George Howarth *Lab*
Chair: Andrew Rosindell *Con*
Vice-chairs:
Sir David Amess *Con*
Dr Lisa Cameron *SNP*
Lord Dykes *CB*
Baroness Hooper *Con*
Daniel Kawczynski *Con*
Lord Kirkhope of Harrogate *Con*
Angus MacNeil *SNP*
Lord McColl of Dulwich *Con*
Mark Menzies *Con*
Sheryll Murray *Con*
Ian Paisley *DUP*
Secretary: Henry Smith *Con*

Contact: Andrew Rosindell, House of Commons, London SW1A 0AA
Tel: 020 7219 8475
Email: andrew.rosindell.mp@parliament.uk

Saudi Arabia
Chair: Mark Menzies *Con*
Vice-chairs:
Crispin Blunt *Con*
Daniel Kawczynski *Con*
Afzal Khan *Lab*
John Spellar *Lab*
Viscount Waverley *CB*
Secretary: Kevan Jones *Lab*
Treasurer: Lord Robathan *Con*

Contact: Mark Menzies, House of Commons, London SW1A 0AA Tel: 020 7219 7073
Email: mark.menzies.mp@parliament.uk

Singapore
Chair: John Spellar *Lab*
Vice-chairs:
Alun Cairns *Con*
Douglas Chapman *SNP*
Yvonne Fovargue *Lab*
Lord Haselhurst *Con*
Sir Mark Hendrick *Lab/Co-op*
Chris Matheson *Lab*
Mark Menzies *Con*
Lord Naseby *Con*
Lord Rogan *UUP*
Stephen Timms *Lab*
Michael Tomlinson *Con*
Viscount Waverley *CB*
Secretary: Sir Graham Brady *Con*
Treasurer: Sharon Hodgson *Lab*

Contact: John Spellar, House of Commons, London SW1A 0AA Tel: 020 7219 0674
Email: john.spellar.mp@parliament.uk

Slovenia
Chairs:
Lord German *Lib Dem*
Karl McCartney *Con*
Vice-chairs:
Lord Aberdare *CB*
Lord Balfe *Con*
Lord Dubs *Lab*
Craig Mackinlay *Con*
Angus MacNeil *SNP*
Secretary: Baroness Hayman of Ullock *Lab*

Contact: Karl McCartney, House of Commons, London SW1A 0AA Tel: 020 7219 3000
Email: karl.mccartney.mp@parliament.uk

Somaliland
Chair: Clive Betts *Lab*
Vice-chairs:
Baroness Hodgson of Abinger *Con*
Kerry McCarthy *Lab*
Dr Matthew Offord *Con*
Secretary: Stephen Doughty *Lab/Co-op*

Contact: Clive Betts, House of Commons, London SW1A 0AA Tel: 020 7219 5114
Email: officeofclivebettsmp@parliament.uk
Twitter: @AppgSomaliland

South East Asian Nations (ASEAN)

Chair: Mark Garnier *Con*
Officers:
Sir David Amess *Con*
Lord Astor of Hever *Con*
Sir Bill Cash *Con*
Wayne David *Lab*
Baroness Neville-Rolfe *Con*
Paul Scully *Con*
John Spellar *Lab*
Viscount Waverley *CB*

Contact: Mark Garnier, House of Commons, London SW1A 0AA Tel: 020 7219 7198
Email: mark.garnier.mp@parliament.uk

Spain

Chairs:
Lord Brennan *NA*
Chris Bryant *Lab*
Vice-chairs:
Chris Elmore *Lab*
Chris Evans *Lab/Co-op*
Viscount Waverley *CB*
Secretary: Sir Greg Knight *Con*
Treasurer: Kevin Brennan *Lab*

Contact: Chris Bryant, House of Commons, London SW1A 0AA Tel: 020 7219 8315
Email: bryantc@parliament.uk

Sri Lanka

Honorary President: Lord Naseby *Con*
Chair: Dr Matthew Offord *Con*
Vice-chairs:
Bob Blackman *Con*
Elliot Colburn *Con*
Chris Matheson *Lab*
Viscount Waverley *CB*
Officers:
Lord Birt *CB*
Baroness Uddin *NA*

Contact: Dr Matthew Offord, House of Commons, London SW1A 0AA
Tel: 020 7219 7083
Email: matthew.offord.mp@parliament.uk

Sudan and South Sudan

Chair: Harriett Baldwin *Con*
Vice-chairs:
Fleur Anderson *Lab*
Baroness Anelay of St Johns *Con*
Lord Chidgey *Lib Dem*
Theo Clarke *Con*
Baroness Cox *CB*
Stephen Doughty *Lab/Co-op*
Flick Drummond *Con*
Baroness Goudie *Lab*
Philip Hollobone *Con*
Bishop of Leeds *NA*
Kate Osamor *Lab/Co-op*
Mark Pritchard *Con*
Bishop of Salisbury *NA*
Secretary: Lord Alton of Liverpool *CB*
Treasurer: Earl of Sandwich *CB*

Contact: Harriett Baldwin, House of Commons, London SW1A 0AA Tel: 020 7219 3000
Email: harriett.baldwin.mp@parliament.uk
Twitter: @APPGSudans

Sweden

Chair: Andrew Bowie *Con*
Vice-chairs:
Lord Balfe *Con*
Brendan Clarke-Smith *Con*
Kerry McCarthy *Lab*
Angus MacNeil *SNP*
Lord Mountevans *CB*
Dr Ben Spencer *Con*
Secretary: Viscount Craigavon *CB*

Contact: Andrew Bowie, House of Commons, London SW1A 0AA Tel: 020 7219 2791
Email: andrew.bowie.mp@parliament.uk
Twitter: @APPGSweden

Switzerland

Chair: Andrew Rosindell *Con*
Vice-chairs:
Dr Lisa Cameron *SNP*
Lord Davies of Stamford *Lab*
Baroness Hooper *Con*
Lord Kilclooney *CB*
Angus MacNeil *SNP*
Ian Paisley *DUP*
Bob Stewart *Con*
Viscount Waverley *CB*
Jacob Young *Con*
Secretary: Mark Menzies *Con*
Treasurer: Tim Loughton *Con*
Ski Captain: Henry Smith *Con*

Contact: Andrew Rosindell, House of Commons, London SW1A 0AA
Tel: 020 7219 8475
Email: andrew.rosindell.mp@parliament.uk

Taiwan

President: Nigel Evans *Con*
Chairs:
Lord Rogan *UUP*
Martin Vickers *Con*

Vice-chairs:
Wayne David *Lab*
Lord Dholakia *Lib Dem*
Lord Kilclooney *CB*
David Morris *Con*
Baroness Redfern *Con*
Lord Rennard *Lib Dem*
Andrew Rosindell *Con*
Sir Desmond Swayne *Con*
Lord Trimble *Con*
Heather Wheeler *Con*
Secretary: Sheryll Murray *Con*

Contact: Martin Vickers, House of Commons, London SW1A 0AA Tel: 020 7219 7212
Email: martin.vickers.mp@parliament.uk
Website: taiwanappg.org.uk

Thailand
Chair: Sir Graham Brady *Con*
Vice-chairs:
Lord Astor of Hever *Con*
John Spellar *Lab*
Viscount Waverley *CB*

Contact: Sir Graham Brady, House of Commons, London SW1A 0AA
Tel: 020 7219 1260
Email: altsale@parliament.uk

Tibet
Chairs:
Chris Law *SNP*
Tim Loughton *Con*
Officers:
Sir Peter Bottomley *Con*
Marion Fellows *SNP*
Kerry McCarthy *Lab*
Catherine West *Lab*

Contact: Tim Loughton, House of Commons, London SW1A 0AA Tel: 020 7219 4471
Email: loughtont@parliament.uk

Tunisia
Chair: Damien Moore *Con*
Vice-chairs:
Yvonne Fovargue *Lab*
David Linden *SNP*
Andrew Rosindell *Con*
John Spellar *Lab*
Baroness Uddin *NA*
Secretary: Philip Hollobone *Con*

Contact: Damien Moore, House of Commons, London SW1A 0AA Tel: 01704 500577
Email: damien.moore.mp@parliament.uk

Turkey
Chairs:
Sir Jeffrey Donaldson *DUP*
Lord McInnes of Kilwinning *Con*
Lord Sheikh *Con*
Vice-chairs:
Lord Anderson of Swansea *Lab*
Tanmanjeet Singh Dhesi *Lab*
Lord Dykes *CB*
Greg Hands *Con*
Baroness Hussein-Ece *Lib Dem*
Lord Kilclooney *CB*
Viscount Waverley *CB*
Secretary: Lord Balfe *Con*

Contact: Sir Jeffrey Donaldson, House of Commons, London SW1A 0AA
Tel: 020 7219 3407
Email: jeffrey.donaldson.mp@parliament.uk

Turks and Caicos Islands
Chairs:
Alicia Kearns *Con*
John Spellar *Lab*
Vice-chairs:
Baroness Benjamin *Lib Dem*
Rob Butler *Con*
Lord Randall of Uxbridge *Con*
Henry Smith *Con*
James Sunderland *Con*

Contact: Alicia Kearns, House of Commons, London SW1A 0AA Tel: 020 7219 3000
Email: alicia.kearns.mp@parliament.uk

Ukraine
Chair: Mark Pritchard *Con*
Vice-chairs:
Jonathan Djanogly *Con*
Pauline Latham *Con*
Tony Lloyd *Lab*
Stewart Malcolm McDonald *SNP*
Earl of Oxford and Asquith *NA*
Lord Risby *Con*
Secretary: Jason McCartney *Con*
Treasurer: Anthony Mangnall *Con*

Contact: Mark Pritchard, House of Commons, London SW1A 0AA Tel: 020 7219 8494
Email: pritchardm@parliament.uk

United Arab Emirates
Chair: David Jones *Con*
Vice-chairs:
Karen Bradley *Con*
Nick Fletcher *Con*
Yvonne Fovargue *Lab*
John Spellar *Lab*
Viscount Waverley *CB*

Contact: David Jones, House of Commons, London SW1A 0AA Tel: 020 7219 8070
Email: katharine.huggins@parliament.uk

Uzbekistan

Chairs:
Andrew Bridgen *Con*
Baroness Warsi *Con*
Vice-chairs:
Lord Bowness *NA*
Lord Kilclooney *CB*
Baroness Kingsmill *Lab*
Lord Moynihan *Con*
Baroness Stern *CB*
Baroness Suttie *Lib Dem*
Baroness Uddin *NA*
Viscount Waverley *CB*
Hywel Williams *PlC*

Contact: Andrew Bridgen, House of Commons, London SW1A 0AA Tel: 020 7219 7238
Email: andrew.bridgen.mp@parliament.uk

Venezuela

Chair: Andrew Lewer *Con*
Vice-chairs:
Mark Menzies *Con*
John Spellar *Lab*
Viscount Waverley *CB*
Secretary: Chris Matheson *Lab*

Contact: Andrew Lewer, House of Commons, London SW1A 0AA Tel: 020 7219 3870
Email: andrew.lewer.mp@parliament.uk

Vietnam

Chair: Wayne David *Lab*
Vice-chairs:
Lord Balfe *Con*
Lord Dholakia *Lib Dem*
Lord Kilclooney *CB*
Mark Pritchard *Con*
Secretary: Sir Graham Brady *Con*
Treasurer: Sarah Champion *Lab*

Contact: Wayne David, House of Commons, London SW1A 0AA Tel: 020 7219 8152
Email: davidw@parliament.uk

Western Sahara

Chair: Ben Lake *PlC*
Vice-chairs:
Sir Peter Bottomley *Con*
Kim Johnson *Lab*
Secretary: Grahame Morris *Lab*
Treasurer: Navendu Mishra *Lab*

Contact: Ben Lake, House of Commons, London SW1A 0AA
Email: ben.lake.mp@parliament.uk

Yemen

Chair: Tim Loughton *Con*
Vice-chairs:
Baroness Anelay of St Johns *Con*
Harriett Baldwin *Con*
James Cartlidge *Con*
Stephen Doughty *Lab/Co-op*
Sharon Hodgson *Lab*
Philip Hollobone *Con*
Kevan Jones *Lab*
Afzal Khan *Lab*
Lord Kilclooney *CB*
Brendan O'Hara *SNP*
Kirsten Oswald *SNP*
John Spellar *Lab*
Secretary: Alison Thewliss *SNP*

Contact: Tim Loughton, House of Commons, London SW1A 0AA Tel: 020 7219 4471
Email: loughtont@parliament.uk
Twitter: @APPGforYemen

Zimbabwe

Chairs:
Navendu Mishra *Lab*
Lord Oates *Lib Dem*
Vice-chairs:
Lord Chidgey *Lib Dem*
Tanmanjeet Singh Dhesi *Lab*
Lord Hayward *Con*
Kim Johnson *Lab*
Baroness Northover *Lib Dem*
Lord St John of Bletso *CB*
Treasurer: Sir Peter Bottomley *Con*

Contact: Navendu Mishra, House of Commons, London SW1A 0AA Tel: 020 7219 3000
Email: navendu.mishra.mp@parliament.uk

Privy Counsellors

Privy Counsellors historically advised the monarch. The title is now largely honorary; it is given automatically to all cabinet members and the Speaker, the Archbishops of Canterbury and York and the Bishop of London and to holders of certain judicial appointments. Leaders of the main political parties are conventionally nominated. The appointment is for life, unless withdrawn, and holders are addressed as 'Right Honourable' (Rt Hon).

The following lists members of the UK Parliaments and Assemblies who are Privy Counsellors.

Diane Abbott	2017
Lord Adonis	2009
Baroness Amos	2003
Lord Anderson of Swansea	2000
Baroness Anelay of St Johns	2009
Lord Arbuthnot of Edrom	1998
Baroness Armstrong of Hill Top	1999
Lord Ashton of Hyde	2019
Baroness Ashton of Upholland	2006
Lord Astor of Hever	2015
Lord Baker of Dorking	1984
Stephen Barclay	2018
Lord Barker of Battle	2012
Lord Barwell	2017
Lord Bassam of Brighton	2009
Lord Bates	2015
Dame Margaret Beckett	1993
Lord Beith	1992
Hilary Benn	2003
Lord Benyon	2017
Jake Berry	2019
Ian Blackford	2017
Baroness Blackstone	2001
Lord Blencathra	2001
Lord Blunkett	1997
Lord Boateng	1999
Baroness Boothroyd	1992
Baroness Bottomley of Nettlestone	1992
Lord Boyd of Duncansby	2000
Lord Brabazon of Tara	2013
Lord Bradley	2001
Karen Bradley	2016
Ben Bradshaw	2009
Suella Braverman	2020
James Brokenshire	2015
Nick Brown	1997
Lord Brown of Eaton-under-Heywood	1992
Lord Browne of Ladyton	2005
Lord Bruce of Bennachie	2006
Robert Buckland	2019
Lord Burnett of Maldon	2014
Conor Burns	2019
Lord Butler of Brockwell	2004
Baroness Butler-Sloss	1988
Liam Byrne	2008
Alun Cairns	2016
Earl of Caithness	1990
Sir Alan Campbell	2014
Lord Campbell of Pittenweem	1999
Archbishop of Canterbury	2013
Lord Carey of Clifton	1991
Alistair Carmichael	2010
Baroness Chakrabarti	2018
Baroness Chalker of Wallasey	1987
Lord Chartres	1995
Greg Clark	2010
Baroness Clark of Calton	2013
Lord Clark of Windermere	1997
Lord Clarke of Nottingham	1984
James Cleverly	2019
Dr Therese Coffey	2019
Lord Collins of Mapesbury	2007
Yvette Cooper	2007
Jeremy Corbyn	2015
Baroness Corston	2003
Sir Geoffrey Cox	2018
Stephen Crabb	2014
Lord Cunningham of Felling	1993
Lord Darzi of Denham	2009
Ruth Davidson	2016
Lord Davies of Oldham	2006
David Davis	1997
Lord Deben	1985
Lord Denham	1981
Lord Dholakia	2010
Lord Dodds of Duncairn	2010
Sir Jeffrey Donaldson	2007
Oliver Dowden	2019
Mark Drakeford	2019
Lord Drayson	2008
Baroness D'Souza	2009
Sir Iain Duncan Smith	2001
Philip Dunne	2019
Lord Elis-Thomas	2004
Michael Ellis	2019
Tobias Ellwood	2017
Lord Etherton	2008
George Eustice	2020
Baroness Evans of Bowes Park	2016
Sir David Evennett	2015
Lord Falconer of Thoroton	2003
Baroness Featherstone	2014
Lord Feldman of Elstree	2015
Lord Fellowes	1990
Lord Field of Birkenhead	1997
Lord Forsyth of Drumlean	1995

Arlene Foster	2016
Lord Foster of Bath	2010
Lord Foulkes of Cumnock	2002
Lord Fowler	1979
Dr Liam Fox	2010
Mark Francois	2010
Lord Freud	2015
Sir Roger Gale	2019
Baroness Garden of Frognal	2015
Lord Garnier	2015
Lord Geidt	2007
Nick Gibb	2016
Dame Cheryl Gillan	2010
Lord Goldsmith	2002
Lord Goldsmith of Richmond Park	2019
Lord Goodlad	1992
Robert Goodwill	2018
Michael Gove	2010
Chris Grayling	2010
Damian Green	2012
Lord Grocott	2002
Lord Hague of Richmond	1995
Viscount Hailsham	1992
Lord Hain	2001
Baroness Hale of Richmond	1999
Robert Halfon	2015
Baroness Hallett	2005
Lord Hamilton of Epsom	1991
Lord Hammond of Runnymede	2010
Matt Hancock	2014
Greg Hands	2014
Lord Hardie	1997
Harriet Harman	1997
Mark Harper	2015
Simon Hart	2019
Lord Haselhurst	1999
Sir John Hayes	2013
Baroness Hayman	2000
Sir Oliver Heald	2016
John Healey	2008
Lord Henley	2013
Lord Herbert of South Downs	2010
Lord Heseltine	1979
Lord Hill of Oareford	2013
Damian Hinds	2018
Dame Margaret Hodge	2003
Lord Hoffmann	1992
Lord Hope of Craighead	1989
Lord Howard of Lympne	1990
Sir George Howarth	2005
Lord Howarth of Newport	2000
Earl Howe	2013
Lord Howell of Guildford	1979
Sir Lindsay Hoyle	2013
Baroness Hughes of Stretford	2004
Jeremy Hunt	2010
Lord Hunt of Kings Heath	2009
Lord Hunt of Wirral	1980
Lord Hutton of Furness	2001
Lord Irvine of Lairg	1997
Alister Jack	2019
Lord Janvrin	1998
Sajid Javid	2014
Baroness Jay of Paddington	1998
Robert Jenrick	2019
Boris Johnson	2016
Lord Johnson of Marylebone	2019
Lord Jones	1999
Carwyn Jones	2010
David Jones	2012
Kevan Jones	2018
Lord Jopling	1979
Lord Judge	1996
Lord Kakkar	2014
Lord Keen of Elie	2017
Sadiq Khan	2009
Lord King of Bridgwater	1979
Lord Kinnock	1983
Sir Greg Knight	1995
Lord Knight of Weymouth	2008
Baroness Kramer	2014
Kwasi Kwarteng	2019
Dame Eleanor Laing	2017
Lord Laming	2014
David Lammy	2008
Lord Lamont of Lerwick	1986
Lord Lancaster of Kimbolton	2017
Lord Lang of Monkton	1990
Lord Lansley	2010
Lord Lawson of Blaby	1981
Andrea Leadsom	2016
Sir Edward Leigh	2019
Brandon Lewis	2016
Dr Julian Lewis	2015
Baroness Liddell of Coatdyke	1998
Lord Lilley	1990
Lord Llewellyn of Steep	2015
Bishop of London	2018
Marquess of Lothian	1996
Lord McAvoy	2003
Lord McConnell of Glenscorrodale	2001
John McDonnell	2016
Pat McFadden	2008
Lord McFall of Alcluith	2004
Ken Macintosh	2016
Lord Mackay of Clashfern	1979
Lord McLoughlin	2005
Lord McNally	2005
Lord Malloch-Brown	2007
Lord Mance	1999
Lord Mandelson	1998
Lord Maude of Horsham	1992
Theresa May	2003
Ed Miliband	2007

Maria Miller	2012
Amanda Milling	2020
Anne Milton	2015
Andrew Mitchell	2010
Penny Mordaunt	2017
Baroness Morgan of Cotes	2014
Lord Morris of Aberavon	1970
Baroness Morris of Yardley	1999
David Mundell	2010
Lord Murphy of Torfaen	1999
Dr Andrew Murrison	2019
Lord Naseby	1994
Lord Neuberger of Abbotsbury	2004
Baroness Neville-Jones	2010
Lord Newby	2014
Caroline Nokes	2018
Jesse Norman	2019
Baroness Northover	2015
Lord Owen	1976
Priti Patel	2015
Owen Paterson	2010
Lord Patten	1990
Lord Patten of Barnes	1989
Lord Paul	2009
Earl Peel	2006
Lord Pendry	2000
Sir Mike Penning	2014
Lord Phillips of Worth Matravers	1995
Lord Pickles	2010
Christopher Pincher	2018
Baroness Prashar	2009
Baroness Primarolo	2002
Baroness Quin	1998
Dominic Raab	2018
Lord Radice	1999
Lord Randall of Uxbridge	2010
Sir John Redwood	1993
Lord Reed of Allermuir	2008
Jacob Rees-Mogg	2019
Lord Reid of Cardowan	1998
Lord Robathan	2010
Lord Robertson of Port Ellen	1997
Lord Rodgers of Quarry Bank	1975
Lord Rooker	1999
Baroness Royall of Blaisdon	2008
Lord Ryder of Wensum	1990
Lord Saville of Newdigate	1994
Liz Saville Roberts	2019
Baroness Scotland of Asthal	2001
Lord Selkirk of Douglas	1996
John Sentamu [peerage pending]	2005
Grant Shapps	2010
Alok Sharma	2019
Alec Shelbrooke	2019
Baroness Shephard of Northwold	1992
Chris Skidmore	2019
Julian Smith	2017
Baroness Smith of Basildon	2009
Lord Smith of Finsbury	1997
Anna Soubry	2015
John Spellar	2001
Mark Spencer	2019
Sir Keir Starmer	2017
Baroness Stowell of Beeston	2014
Lord Strathclyde	1995
Mel Stride	2017
Baroness Stuart of Edgbaston	2015
Lord Stunell	2012
Nicola Sturgeon	2014
Rishi Sunak	2019
Sir Desmond Swayne	2011
Baroness Symons of Vernham Dean	2001
Mark Tami	2018
Baroness Taylor of Bolton	1997
Lord Taylor of Holbeach	2014
Lord Tebbit	1981
Lord Thomas of Cwmgiedd	2003
Emily Thornberry	2017
Viscount Thurso	2014
Stephen Timms	2006
Lord Touhig	2006
Lord Trefgarne	1989
Anne-Marie Trevelyan	2020
Lord Trimble	1997
Elizabeth Truss	2014
Lord Tyler	2014
Lord Tyrie	2015
Viscount Ullswater	1994
Baroness Vadera	2009
Lord Vaizey of Didcot	2016
Valerie Vaz	2019
Theresa Villiers	2010
Lord Wakeham	1983
Lord Waldegrave of North Hill	1990
Lord Walker of Gestingthorpe	1997
Ben Wallace	2017
Lord Wallace of Saltaire	2012
Lord Wallace of Tankerness	2000
Lord Warner	2006
Baroness Warsi	2010
Lord West of Spithead	2010
John Whittingdale	2015
Lord Whitty	2005
Lord Wigley	1997
Lord Willetts	2010
Gavin Williamson	2015
Lord Wills	2008
Sammy Wilson	2017
Dame Rosie Winterton	2006
Lord Woolf	1986
Jeremy Wright	2014
Archbishop of York	2020
Lord Young of Cookham	1993
Lord Young of Graffham	1984

Political Parties

Conservative and Unionist Party

4 Matthew Parker Street, London SW1H 9HQ
Tel: 020 7222 9000 Fax: 020 7222 1135
Email: chairman@conservatives.com Website: www.conservatives.com Twitter: @Conservatives

Leader: Rt Hon Boris Johnson MP
Chairman and Chairman of the Board: Ben Elliot
Chairman: Rt Hon Amanda Milling MP
Deputy Chairman: Ranil Jayawardena MP
Deputy Chairman of the Board and Chairman of National Conservative Convention: Lord Sharpe of Epsom OBE
Treasurer: Sir Ehud Sheleg
Chief Financial Officer: Simon Day
Chairmen:
Conservative Councillors' Association: Mark Hawthorne MBE
Scottish Conservative Party: Robert Forman MBE
Welsh Conservative Party: Glyn Davies
Association of Conservative Peers: Rt Hon Lord Hunt of Wirral MBE
1922 Committee: Sir Graham Brady MP
Secretary to the Board: Stephen Phillips OBE
Vice-chairmen: Andrew Bowie MP, Rt Hon Sir David Evennett MP, Helen Grant MP, Dr Caroline Johnson MP, Neil O'Brien OBE MP, Rt Hon Alec Shelbrooke MP

Labour Party

Southside, 105 Victoria Street, London SW1E 6QT
Tel: 0345 092 2299/020 7783 1299 Fax: 020 7783 1234
Email: leader@labour.org.uk Website: www.labour.org.uk Twitter: @UKLabour

Leader: Rt Hon Sir Keir Starmer KCB QC MP
Deputy Leader and Party Chair: Angela Rayner MP
General Secretary: David Evans
Treasurer: Diana Holland OBE

National Executive Committee

Chair: Rt Hon Dame Margaret Beckett DBE MP
Vice-chair: Alice Perry
Leader: Rt Hon Sir Keir Starmer KCB QC MP
Deputy Leader and Party Chair: Angela Rayner MP
Treasurer: Diana Holland OBE
Chair of Equalities: James Asser
Members:
Shadow Frontbench: Jim McMahon OBE MP, Jonathan Reynolds MP, Jo Stevens MP
Shadow Scottish Frontbench: To be appointed
Welsh Labour Representative: Rt Hon Carwyn Jones MS
Youth Members Representative: Lara McNeill
Disabled Members Representative: Ellen Morrison
BAME Labour: Carol Sewell

Division I – Trade Unions

Members:
ASLEF: Mike Whelan
BFAWU: Pauline McCarthy
CWU: Andy Kerr
FBU: Ian Murray
GMB: Kathy Abu-Bakir, Tom Warnett

TSSA: Andi Fox
Unison: Mark Ferguson, Wendy Nichols
Unite: Howard Beckett, Jayne Taylor
Usdaw: Joanne Cairns, Michael Wheeler

Division II – Socialist Societies and BAME Labour

Member (Socialist Societies): James Asser
Member (BAME Labour): Carol Sewell

Division III – Constituency Labour Parties

Members: Luke Akehurst, Johanna Baxter, Ann Black, Gemma Bolton, Yasmine Dar, Nadia Jama, Gurinder Singh Josan CBE, Laura Pidcock, Mish Rahman

Division IV – Local Government

Members: Nick Forbes, Alice Perry

Division V – Parliamentary Labour Party

Members: Rt Hon Dame Margaret Beckett DBE MP, Rt Hon Sir George Howarth MP, Shabana Mahmood MP

Parliamentary Labour Party

Chair: John Cryer MP
PLP Secretary: Ben Folley Email: plp@labour.org.uk

Co-operative Party

Unit 13, 83 Crampton Street, London SE17 3BQ
Tel: 020 7367 4150
Email: mail@party.coop Website: www.party.coop Twitter: @CoopParty

Chair: Jim McMahon OBE MP
Vice-chair: Ruth Hall
General Secretary: Joe Fortune
Deputy General Secretary: Karen Wilkie
Chair of Parliamentary Group: Preet Kaur Gill MP

Scottish National Party

Gordon Lamb House, 3 Jackson's Entry, Edinburgh EH8 8PJ
Tel: 0800 633 5432
Email: info@snp.org Website: www.snp.org Twitter: @theSNP

Leader: Rt Hon Nicola Sturgeon MSP
Depute Leader: Keith Brown MSP
President: Ian Hudghton
Chief Executive: Peter Murrell 0131-525 8900 Email: peter.murrell@snp.org

Liberal Democrats

8-10 Great George Street, London SW1P 3AE
Tel: 020 7222 7999
Email: help@libdems.org.uk Website: www.libdems.org.uk Twitter: @LibDems

Leader: Rt Hon Sir Ed Davey MP
Deputy Leader: Daisy Cooper MP
President: Mark Pack
Vice-President (England): Steve Jarvis
Vice-President (Scotland): Sheila Thomson
Vice-President (Wales): Rodney Berman
Vice-President (BAME): Isabelle Parasram
Treasurer: Lord German OBE
Chief Executive: Mike Dixon

Directors:
Communications: Sam Barratt
Elections and Campaigns: Shaun Roberts
Fundraising: Emma Cherniavsky
People: Rachel Palma-Randle
Operations: Lucy Hope
Strategy, Messaging and Research: Mimi Turner
Deputy Director of Elections and Campaigns: David McCobb
Leader's Chief of Staff: Alex Davies
Heads:
Compliance: David Allworthy
Conference: Michael Smith
Finance: Tope Famaks
Content and Creative: Simone Van Beek
International: Isabelle Pucher
Media: Rosy Cobb
Membership: To be appointed
Policy: Christian Moon
Training and Engagement: Dan Purchese
Commons Whip's Office: Jack Fletcher
Lords Whips' Office: Humphrey Amos

Democratic Unionist Party

91 Dundela Avenue, Belfast BT4 3BU
Tel: 028 9047 1155
Email: info@mydup.com Website: www.mydup.com Twitter: @duponline

Assembly Office, Room 207 Parliament Buildings, Stormont, Belfast BT4 3XX
Tel: 028 9052 1323 Twitter: @duponline

Leader: Rt Hon Arlene Foster MLA
Deputy Leader: Rt Hon Lord Dodds of Duncairn OBE
Chair: Lord Morrow
Chief Executive: Timothy Johnston
Secretary: Michelle McIlveen MLA
Treasurer: Gregory Campbell MP
Press Officer: Clive McFarland 028 9065 4479 Email: clivemcfarland@dup.org.uk

Sinn Féin

53 Falls Road, Belfast BT12 4PD
Tel: 028 9034 7350 Fax: 028 9022 3001
Email: theresa.mcardle@sinnfein.ie Website: www.sinnfein.ie Twitter: @sinnfeinireland

44 Parnell Square, Dublin 1
Tel: +353 1 8726932 Fax: +353 1 8733441 Twitter: @sinnfeinireland

Assembly Office:
Tel: 028 9052 1471/028 9052 1470 Fax: 028 9052 1476
Email: sfassembly@outlook.com Twitter: @sinnfeinireland

President: Mary Lou McDonald
Vice-President: Michelle O'Neill MLA
Chair: Declan Kearney MLA
General Secretary: Ken O'Connell
Treasurers: Pearse Doherty, Conor Murphy MLA

Plaid Cymru (The Party of Wales)

Ty Gwynfor, Marine Chambers, Anson Court, Atlantic Wharf, Cardiff CF10 4AL
Tel: 029 2047 2272
Email: post@plaid.cymru Website: www.plaid.cymru Twitter: @plaid_cymru
Assembly Office:
Tel: 0300 200 7351 Twitter: @plaid_cymru

Leader: Adam Price MS
Chair: Alun Ffred Jones
Chief Executive: Gareth Clubb
Treasurer: Marc Phillips

Social Democratic and Labour Party

121 Ormeau Road, Belfast BT7 1SH
Tel: 028 9024 7700 Fax: 028 9023 6699
Email: info@sdlp.ie Website: www.sdlp.ie Twitter: @sdlplive
Press Office:
Tel: 028 9052 1837 Twitter: @sdlplive

Leader: Colum Eastwood MP
Deputy Leader: Nichola Mallon MLA
Chair: Ronan McCay
Vice-chair: Gerard McDonald
General Secretary: Gerry Cosgrove Email: gerry.cosgrove@sdlphq.ie
International Secretary: Dr Naomh Gallagher

Alliance

88 University Street, Belfast BT7 1HE
Tel: 028 9032 4274
Email: alliance@alliancepartyni.org Website: www.allianceparty.org Twitter: @allianceparty
Assembly Office, Room 220 Parliament Buildings, Stormont, Belfast BT4 3XX
Tel: 028 9052 1314
Email: stormont@alliancepartyni.org Twitter: @allianceparty

Leader: Naomi Long MLA
Deputy Leader: Dr Stephen Farry MP
Chair: Helena Young
President: David Ford
General Secretary: Sharon Lowry Email: sharon.lowry@alliancepartyni.org
Joint Hon Treasurers: Stewart Dickson MLA, Billy Webb Email: billy.webb@alliancepartyni.org
Press Officer: Scott Jamison Email: scott.jamison@alliancepartyni.org

Green Party

The Biscuit Factory, Unit 201, A Block, 100 Clements Road, London SE16 4DG
Tel: 020 3691 9400
Email: office@greenparty.org.uk Website: www.greenparty.org.uk Twitter: @TheGreenParty

Co-leaders: Jonathan Bartley, Sian Berry
Deputy Leader: Amelia Womack

Parliamentary Press Gallery

The Parliamentary Lobby Journalists are those journalists authorised to work in Parliament.
Members of the Lobby are marked with an asterisk.
Tel 020 7219 4700; for individual desk numbers prefix 020 7219 in most cases.

Attendants 020 7219 5371
Press Bar 020 7219 4284
Website: www.pressgallery.org.uk Twitter: @PressGalleryUK

Press Gallery

Chairman	Pippa Crerar (Daily Mirror)	
Honorary Secretary	Tony Grew (Sunday Times)	
Honorary Treasurer	Robert Hutton	
Administrator	Elizabeth Johnson admin@pressgallery.org.uk	4395

Lobby

Chairman	Jason Groves (Daily Mail)
Honorary Secretary	Jon Craig (Sky News)
Honorary Treasurer	Nigel Morris (The I)

National Daily Newspapers

Daily Express
Political Editor: *Macer Hall
Deputy Political Editor: *Sam Lister @sam_lister_
*Martyn Brown @MartynInMyanmar

Daily Mail
Political Editor: *Jason Groves @JasonGroves1
Deputy Political Editor: *John Stevens @johnestevens
Policy Editor: *Daniel Martin @Daniel_J_Martin
Sketch Writer: Henry Deeds @HenryDeedes
Larisa Brown @larisamlbrown
*Claire Ellicott @ClaireEllicott1
Administrator (Press Gallery): Nicole Worth

Daily Mirror
Political Editor: *Pippa Crerar @PippaCrerar
Deputy Political Editor: *Ben Glaze @benglaze
*Lizzy Buchan @LizzyBuchan
*Kevin Maguire @Kevin_Maguire
Oliver Milne @OliverMilne

Daily Record
*Torcuil Crichton @Torcuil

Daily Star
To be appointed

Evening Standard
Political Editor: *Joe Murphy @JoeMurphyLondon
Deputy Political Editor: *Nic Cecil @nicholascecil
*Sophia Sleigh @SophiaSleigh
Administrator: Caroline Robertson

Financial Times
Political Editor: *George Parker @GeorgeWParker
*Sebastian Payne @SebastianEPayne
*Jim Pickard @PickardJE

Guardian
Political Editor: *Heather Stewart @GuardianHeather
Deputy Political Editor: Jessica Elgot @jessicaelgot
Rafael Behr @rafaelbehr
*Simon Murphy @murphy_simon
*Rajeev Syal @syalrajeev
*Peter Walker @peterwalker99
Sketch Writer: John Crace @JohnJCrace
Administrator: Maria Remle

Guardian Unlimited
Senior Political Correspondent: Andrew Sparrow @AndrewSparrow

Herald
Political Editor: *Mike Settle @settle_michael
Hannah Rodger

The I
Political Editor: *Nigel Morris @NigelpMorris
Deputy Political Editor: Hugo Gye @HugoGye
*Jane Merrick @janemerrick23
*Richard Vaughan @RichardVaughan1

Independent
Political Editor: *Andrew Woodcock @AndyWoodcock
Deputy Political Editor: *Rob Merrick @Rob_Merrick
Whitehall Editor: *Kate Devlin @_katedevlin

Political Commentators: *Andrew Grice
*John Rentoul @JohnRentoul
*Ashley Cowburn @ashcowburn
Sketch Writer: Tom Peck @tompeck

Scotsman
Alexander Brown @AlexofBrown

Sun
Political Editor: *Harry Cole @MrHarryCole
Deputy Political Editor: *Kate Ferguson @kateferguson4
Jonathan Reilly @thejonnyreilly

Telegraph Media Group
Political Editor: *Gordon Rayner @gordonrayner
Deputy Political Editor: To be appointed
Assistant Editor and Chief Political Correspondent: *Christopher Hope @christopherhope
Whitehall Editor: *Edward Malnick @edwardmalnick
*Amy Jones @amylouisejones
*Harry Yorke @HarryYorke1
Sketch Writer: Michael Deacon @MichaelPDeacon

The Times
Political Editor: *Francis Elliott @elliotttimes
Deputy Political Editor: *Steven Swinford @Steven_Swinford
Editor, Red Box: *Patrick Maguire @patrickkmaguire
Esther Webber, Red Box @estwebber
Policy Editor: *Oliver Wright @oliver_wright
Political and Defence Correspondent: Lucy Fisher @LOS_Fisher
George Grylls @georgegrylls
Administrator: Sian Norris Copson

National Sunday Newspapers

Mail on Sunday
Political Editor: *Glen Owen
Deputy Political Editor: *Anna Mikhailova @AVMikhailova
*Brendan Carlin
Dan Hodges @DPJHodges

Observer
Political Editor: *Toby Helm @tobyhelm
Political Commentator: *Andrew Rawnsley @andrewrawnsley
Policy Editor: Michael Savage @michaelsavage

Sun on Sunday
Political Editor: *David Wooding @DavidWooding
*Ryan Sabey @ryansabey

Sunday Express
Political Editor: *David Maddox @DavidPBMaddox
Deputy Political Editor: *David Williamson @dp_williamson

Sunday People
Political Editor: *Nigel Nelson @NigelNelson

Sunday Times
Political Editor: *Tim Shipman @ShippersUnbound
Deputy Political Editor: *Caroline Wheeler @cazjwheeler
*Tony Grew @ayestotheright

Regional Press

Birmingham Evening Mail/Birmingham Post
*Jon Walker @jonwalker121

Local World
To be appointed

Press and Journal
Dan O'Donoghue @MrDanDonoghue

Western Mail
Ruth Mosalski @ruthmosalski

Yorkshire Post
Geraldine Scott @Geri_E_L_Scott

Magazines

Civil Service World
Editors (job share): Jess Bowie @CSWeditor
Susannah Bracknell @SuzannahCSW

Economist
Matthew Holehouse @mattholehouse

House Magazine
Managing Editor: Daniel Bond @DanBond1
Political Editor: Kate Proctor @Kate_M_Proctor
Policy Editor: Georgina Bailey @georginaebailey

New Statesman
Political Editor: *Stephen Bush @stephenkb
*Harry Lambert @harrytlambert
Assistant Editor: *Isabel Hardman @IsabelHardman

Spectator
Political Editor: *James Forsyth @JGForsyth
Deputy Political Editor: *Katy Balls @katyballs

Tribune
Editor: *Chris McLaughlin
*David Hencke @davidhencke

News Agencies

Agence France Press (AFP)
*Alice Ritchie @alicejritchie

Associated Press
*Jill Lawless @JillLawless

Bloomberg News
Emily Ashton @elashton
Kitty Donaldson @kitty_donaldson
Joe Mayes @Joe_Mayes
Alex Morales @AlexJFMorales
*Thomas Penny @ThomasWPenny
*Tim Ross @TimRoss_1

PA Media
Political Editor, Lobby Office: *David Hughes @DavidHughesPA
Deputy Political Editor: *Harriet Line @HarriLine
Political Reporter: *Sam Blewett @BlewettSam
*Shaun Connolly @shaunconnolly01
*Gavin Cordon @GavinCordon
*Patrick Daly @thepatrickdaly
Parliamentary Editor, Gallery Office: Richard Wheeler @richard_kaputt
Parliamentary Reporters: Elizabeth Arnold @ebrep
Sophie Morris @itssophiemorris
Stefan Rousseau @StefanRousseau
George Ryan @GeorgeMRyan
Josh Thomas @JoshThomas_PA

Parliament Today
*Mike Peters
*Rupert Clark @PTRupertClark
*Julian Robinson

Reuters
Chief Political Correspondent: *Elizabeth Piper @piperliza
*William James @WJames_Reuters
*Kylie MacLellan @kyliemaclellan

Broadcasting

BBC (British Broadcasting Corporation)

BBC Political Programmes
Executive News Editor, BBC Westminster: Katy Searle @KatySearle
News Editor: Alison Macdonald @allimacdonald
Political Editor: *Laura Kuensberg @bbclaurak
Deputy Political Editor: *Victoria Young @BBCVickiYoung
Chief Political Correspondent, BBC News Channel: To be appointed
Political Editor, BBC News Online: *Alex Hunt @iAlexhunt
Diplomatic Correspondent: James Landale @BBCJLandale
*Brian Wheeler (BBC News Online) @BrianWheeler01

Political Correspondents
*Alex Forsyth @AlexForsythBBC
*Eleanor Garnier @BBCEleanorG
*Ross Hawkins @rosschawkins
*Chris Mason @ChrisMasonBBC
*Iain Watson @iainjwatson
*Ben Wright @BBCBenWright

English Regions
Regional Political Editor: *Bob Ledwidge
*Paul Rowley @PaulRowleyBBC

Regional Political Programmes
Kevin Fitzpatrick (North West) @kevfitz21
*Patrick Burns (West Midlands) @PatrickBurnsBBC
*Paul Baltrop (West) @paulbarltrop
*Tim Donovan (London) @BBCTimDonovan
*Peter Henley (South) @BBCPeterH
*Tony Roe (East Midlands) @tonyroe
*Tim Iredale (North/Hull) @iredalepolitics
*Richard Moss (North East) @BBCRichardMoss
*Deborah McGurran (East) @GurranMc
*Martyn Oates (South West) @bbcmartynoates
Paul Siegert (South East)
Len Tingle (North) @Tinglepolitics
*Stephen Walker (NI) @StepWalkTV

National Regional Correspondents
David Cornock (Wales) @davidcornock
*Stephen Walker (NI) @StepWalkTV
David Porter (Scotland)

Parliamentary Correspondents
*Sean Curran @cripeswatson
Mark D'Arcy @DArcyTiP
Susan Hulme @Susanh12
Rachel Byrne @rachelcbyrne

Channel 4 Television

Channel 4 News
Political Editor: *Gary Gibbon @GaryGibbonBlog
*Robert Hamilton
*Rob Thomson

Five News

Political Editor: Andy Bell @andybell5news

Independent Television News

ITV News
Political Editor: *Robert Peston @Peston
News Editor: *Amber de Botton @amberdebotton
*Carl Dinnen @carldinnen
*Libby Wiener @LibbyWienerITV
Producer: Claire Bidmead

Israel Radio

*Jerry Lewis

ITV

Good Morning Britain
*Anne Alexander @Annemariealex
Kieron Clarke @kieronishere

ITV Anglia
*Emma Hutchinson @ITVEmmaH

ITV Central
Westminster News Editor of ITV Regions:
*Simon Mares @SimonMaresITV
*Alison MacKenzie @Alison1mackITV

ITV Granada
*Hannah Miller @hannahITV

ITV Meridian
*Phil Hornby @philhornbyitv

ITV Tyne Tees/ITV Border
*Martin Stew @MartinStewITV

ITV Cymru Wales
Political Editor: *Adrian Masters @adrianmasters84
Head of News: Philip Henfrey
Head of Politics: Nick Powell
Public Affairs Manager: Huw Rossiter

ITV West
*David Wood @davidbevanwood

ITV Westcountry
*Michael Carney

London News Network

*Simon Harris @simonharrisitv

Scottish Television

Westminster Correspondent: *Kathryn Samson @STVKathryn

Sky News

Political Editor: *Beth Rigby @BethRigby
Deputy Political Editor: *Sam Coates @SamCoatesSky
Editor-at-Large: *Adam Boulton @adamboultonSKY
Chief Political Correspondent: *Jon Craig @joncraig
*Tamara Cohen @tamcohen
Lewis Goodall @lewis_goodall
*Kate McCann @KateEMcCann
Nick Martin @NickMartinSKY
Joe Pike @joepike
Rob Powell @robpowellnews
Tom Rayner @RaynerSkyNews
Online Political Reporters: Aubrey Allegretti @breeallegretti
Greg Heffer @GregHeffer
Alan McGuinness @Alan_McGuinness
Head of Politics: Dan Williams @danskywilliams
Senior News Editor: Lucy Plint @lucyplint
News Editors: Louis Degenhardt @LouisDegenhardt
Tom Larkin @TomLarkinSky
Clare Parry @clareparry
Political Producers: George Coote @RealCoote
Liz Lane @LizLaneSky
Editorial Assistant: Kate Wilsea @katewilsea

Times Radio

Tom Newton Dunn @tnewtondunn
Matthew Chorley @MattChorley

UTV

*Ken Reid @KenReid_utv

Websites

Business Insider

Adam Bienkov @AdamBienkov
Adam Payne @adampayne26

Conservative Home

Editor: Paul Goodman @PaulGoodmanCH
Contributing Editor: *Andrew Gimson @AndrewGimson

Huffington Post
Executive Editor, Politics: *Paul Waugh @paulwaugh
Deputy Political Editor: Arj Singh @singharj
*Ned Simons @nedsimons
Rachel Wearmouth @REWearmouth

Mail Online
Political Editor: *James Tapsfield @JamesTapsfield
Deputy Political Editor: *Jack Maidment @jrmaidment
Whitehall Correspondent: *David Wilcock

Mirror Online
Political Editor: *Daniel Bloom @danbloom1
*Mikey Smith @mikeysmith

Politico
Chief UK Political Correspondent: *Charlie Cooper @CharlieCooper8
Editor, London Playbook: *Jack Blanchard @Jack_Blanchard_
Emilio Casalicchio @e_casalicchio
*Annabelle Dickson @NewsAnnabelle
*Cristina Gallardo @gallardo_ortega

Politics.co.uk
Editor: *Ian Dunt @IanDunt

PoliticsHome
Editor-in-Chief: Alan White @aljwhite
Political Editor: Kate Proctor @Kate_M_Proctor
Chief Reporter: Alain Tolhurst @Alain_Tolhurst
Senior Reporter: Kate Forrester @kateforrester
Reporter: Eleanor Langford @eleanormia

Sun Online
Natasha Clark @NatashaC

International

Irish Times
*Denis Staunton @denisstaunton

La Repubblica
Antonello Guerrera @antoguerrera

Le Monde
UK Correspondent: *Cécile Ducourtieux @c_ducourtieux

Middle East News
Adel Darwish @AdelDarwish

New York Times
*Stephen Castle @_StephenCastle

RTE – Irish Broadcasting
London Correspondent: *Fiona Mitchell @mitchefi

Wall Street Journal
Max Colchester @MaximColch
Jason Douglas @wsj_douglasj

Parliamentary Agents

Parliamentary Agents provide general information on Parliament to both individuals and firms, fully reporting on progress of Bills. There are two types of Agent, those registered to propose and oppose bills on behalf of their clients and those who only oppose Bills.

BDB Pitmans LLP
One Bartholomew Close, London EC1A 7BL
Tel: 020 7783 3437
Email: enquiries@bdbpitmans.com Website: www.bdbpitmans.com Twitter: @bdbpitmans
Parliamentary Agents: Ian McCulloch, Nicholas Brown, David Mundy, Nicholas Evans
Partners: Mark Challis, Sarah Clark, Tom Henderson, Richard Marsh, Matthew Smith, Angus Walker
Special Counsel: Jonathan Bracken 020 7783 3408 Email: jonathanbracken@bdbpitmans.com
Head of Public Affairs: Stuart Thomson 020 7783 3439 Email: stuartthomson@bdbpitmans.com
Principal Parliamentary Clerk: Pam Thompson 020 7783 3437
Email: pamthompson@bdbpitmans.com

Bryan Cave Leighton Paisner LLP
Governor's House, 5 Laurence Pountney Hill, London EC4R 0BR
Tel: 020 3400 1000
Email: helen.kemp@bclplaw.com/tim.smith@bclplaw.com Website: www.bclplaw.com Twitter: @BCLPlaw
Parliamentary Agent: Helen Kemp Email: helen.kemp@bclplaw.com
Partner: Tim Smith Email: tim.smith@bclplaw.com

City Remembrancer
City Remembrancer's Office, PO Box 270, London EC2P 2EJ
Tel: 020 7332 1200
Email: rem.parliamentary@cityoflondon.gov.uk/cityremembrancer@theguildhall.org.uk
City Remembrancer: Paul Double LVO

Eversheds Sutherland
1 Wood Street, London EC2V 7WS
Tel: 020 7497 9797 Fax: 020 7919 4919
Website: www.eversheds-sutherland.com Twitter: @ESgloballaw
Parliamentary Agents: Stephen Collings 020 7919 4787
Email: stephencollings@eversheds-sutherland.com, Monica Peto 020 7919 4717
Email: monicapeto@eversheds-sutherland.com, Joe Durkin 07501 057187
Partner: James O'Connor 020 7919 4877 Email: jamesoconnor@eversheds-sutherland.com

Pinsent Masons LLP
30 Crown Place, Earl Street, London EC2A 4ES
Tel: 020 7418 7000
Email: robbie.owen@pinsentmasons.com Website: www.pinsentmasons.com Twitter: @PinsentMasons
Parliamentary Agent (Partner): Robbie Owen 020 7490 6420
Email: robbie.owen@pinsentmasons.com
Parliamentary Agent (Legal Director): Richard Bull 020 7490 9284
Email: richard.bull@pinsentmasons.com
Partner: Francis Tyrrell 020 7490 6994 Email: francis.tyrrell@pinsentmasons.com
Government Affairs and Legislation Clerk: Frances Ellis 020 7667 0164
Email: frances.ellis@pinsentmasons.com

Sharpe Pritchard LLP
Elm Yard, 10-16 Elm Street, London WC1X 0BJ
Tel: 020 7405 4600
Email: alewis@sharpepritchard.co.uk Website: www.sharpepritchard.co.uk Twitter: @SharpePritchard

Partners and Parliamentary Agents: Alastair Lewis Email: alewis@sharpepritchard.co.uk, Emyr Thomas Email: ethomas@sharpepritchard.co.uk

VWV
24 King William Street, London EC4R 9AT
Tel: 020 7405 1234 Fax: 020 7405 4171
Website: www.vwv.co.uk Twitter: @VWVLawFirm

Parliamentary Agent: Ronald Perry Email: rperry@vwv.co.uk

Winckworth Sherwood LLP
Minerva House, 5 Montague Close, London SE1 9BB
Tel: 020 7593 5000 Fax: 020 7593 5099
Email: agorlov@wslaw.co.uk/pirving@wslaw.co.uk Website: www.wslaw.co.uk Twitter: @ws_law

Parliamentary Agent (Partner): Paul Irving
Parliamentary Agents (Consultant): Alison Gorlov, Chris Vine, Stephen Wiggs

DEVOLVED PARLIAMENTS AND ASSEMBLIES

Salaries

Scottish Parliament	Annual salary (£) From 1 April 2020
MSP	64,470
MSP (dual mandate)	21,490

Members who hold any of the following offices are entitled to receive an additional annual salary:

First Minister	93,391
Cabinet Secretary	48,449
Minister	30,351
Presiding Officer	48,449
Deputy Presiding Officer	30,351
Lord Advocate	63,295
Solicitor General for Scotland	45,771

Welsh Parliament	Annual salary (£) From 1 April 2020
MS	67,649

MSs who are also a Member of Parliament have their Welsh Parliamentary salary reduced by an amount equal to two thirds of the basic salary.

Members who hold any of the following offices are entitled to receive an additional annual salary:

First Minister	80,334
Minister	38,052
Deputy Minister	22,197
Presiding Officer	43,338
Deputy Presiding Officer	22,197
Assembly Commissioners	13,741

Northern Ireland Assembly	Annual salary (£) From 1 April 2020
MLA	51,000

Members who hold any of the following offices are entitled to receive an additional annual salary:

First Minister	72,000
Deputy First Minister	72,000
Minister	38,000
Junior Minister	6,000
Speaker	38,000
Principal Deputy Speaker	6,000
Deputy Speaker	6,000

Scottish Government

St Andrew's House, Regent Road, Edinburgh EH1 3DG
Switchboard: 0300 244 4000 Email: scottish.ministers@gov.scot
Website: www.gov.scot Twitter: @scotgov

Cabinet

First Minister	**Nicola Sturgeon**
Deputy First Minister and Cabinet Secretary for Education and Skills	**John Swinney**
Cabinet Secretary for Justice	**Humza Yousaf**
Cabinet Secretary for Health and Sport	**Jeane Freeman**
Cabinet Secretary for Finance	**Kate Forbes**
Cabinet Secretary for the Environment, Climate Change and Land Reform	**Roseanna Cunningham**
Cabinet Secretary for Rural Economy and Tourism	**Fergus Ewing**
Cabinet Secretary for the Constitution, Europe and External Affairs	**Michael Russell**
Cabinet Secretary for Communities and Local Government	**Aileen Campbell**
Cabinet Secretary for Economy, Fair Work and Culture	**Fiona Hyslop**
Cabinet Secretary for Transport, Infrastructure and Connectivity	**Michael Matheson**
Cabinet Secretary for Social Security and Older People	**Shirley-Anne Somerville**
Also attending Cabinet	
Minister for Parliamentary Business and Veterans	**Graeme Dey**
Lord Advocate	**James Wolffe** QC
Solicitor General	**Alison di Rollo** QC

Ministerial Responsibilities and Staff

Office of the First Minister

St Andrew's House, Regent Road, Edinburgh EH1 3DG
Tel: 0300 244 4000
Email: firstminister@gov.scot Website: firstminister.gov.scot Twitter: @ScotGovFM

First Minister Rt Hon **Nicola Sturgeon** MSP

Head of the Scottish Government; responsible for development, implementation and presentation of Government policy; constitutional affairs; promoting and representing Scotland.

Chief of Staff	Liz Lloyd Email: spads_admin@gov.scot	0131-244 5647
Special Advisers		
Head of Communications and Senior Political Spokesperson	Stuart Nicolson Email: spads_admin@gov.scot	0131-244 4779
Head of Policy	Colin McAllister Email: spads_admin@gov.scot	0131-244 3248
Senior Special Adviser		
Government Strategy, Europe and Constitution	Ewan Crawford Email: spads_admin@gov.scot	0131-244 7399

Special Advisers

Deputy Political Spokesperson	Ross Ingebrigtsen	0131-244 4094
	Email: spads_admin@gov.scot	
	John MacInnes	0131-244 2066
	Email: spads_admin@gov.scot	
Principal Private Secretary	John Somers	0131-244 3757
	Email: firstminister@gov.scot	

Education and Skills

St Andrew's House, Regent Road, Edinburgh EH1 3DG
Tel: 0131-556 8400
Email: dfmcse@gov.scot Twitter: @ScotGovEdu

Deputy First Minister and Cabinet Secretary for Education and Skills **John Swinney** MSP

School standards, quality and improvement; school infrastructure and staffing; educational attainment, qualifications and closing the attainment gap; National Improvement Framework; teaching profession; behaviour and measures to combat bullying; modern languages and Gaelic and Scots languages; Named Person; Skills Development Scotland; non-advanced vocational skills; historical abuse enquiry.

Senior Special Adviser	Colin McAllister	0131-244 3248
	Email: colin.mcallister@gov.scot	
Private Secretary	Amy Harron	0131-244 5227
	Email: dfmcse@gov.scot	

Minister for Children and Young People **Maree Todd** MSP

Early learning and childcare; early years; child protection; looked after children including adoption and fostering; youth justice and children's hearings; children's rights; children's services; protection of vulnerable groups; social service workforce; British Sign Language (BSL).

Private Secretary	Chris Inverarity	0131-244 0953
	Email: ministercyp@gov.scot	

Minister for Further Education, Higher Education and Science **Richard Lochhead** MSP

Further education and colleges; higher education and universities; science and STEM (science, technology, engineering and mathematics); student funding; youth work; widening access.

Private Secretary	Grant Moncur	0131-244 1469
	Email: ministerfehes@gov.scot	

Minister for Business, Fair Work and Skills **Jamie Hepburn** MSP

(Also reports to Cabinet Secretary for Finance, Economy and Fair Work) Business, industry and manufacturing; employment policy; labour market strategy, living wage and fair work; employability programmes; youth employment, including implementation of the Wood Commission recommendations; women's employment; bankruptcy and Accountant in Bankruptcy (Scottish government agency); regional economic forums; PACE; non-advanced vocational skills; Skills Development Scotland (Scotland's national skills agency); consumer protection.

Private Secretary	Paul Cavanagh	0131-244 8413
	Email: ministerbfws@gov.scot	

Justice

St Andrew's House, Regent Road, Edinburgh EH1 3DG
Tel: 0131-556 8400
Email: cabsecjustice@gov.scot Twitter: @ScotGovJustice

Cabinet Secretary for Justice **Humza Yousaf** MSP

Police; courts, sentencing; justice system and criminal law procedure; violence reduction; criminal justice social work, victims, witnesses, female offenders; human rights; prisons and prisoners; reducing reoffending; anti-sectarianism; security; youth justice.

Special Adviser	John McFarlane Email: john.mcfarlane@gov.scot	0131-244 1811
Private Secretary	Susan Young Email: cabsecjustice@gov.scot	0131-244 4091

Minister for Community Safety **Ash Denham** MSP

Community safety; access to justice; anti-social behaviour; civil law; fire and rescue services; liquor licensing; legal profession.

Private Secretary	Erin Connell Email: ministercs@gov.scot	0131-244 4579

Health and Sport

St Andrew's House, Regent Road, Edinburgh EH1 3DG
Tel: 0131-244 2125
Email: cabsechs@gov.scot Twitter: @scotgovhealth

Cabinet Secretary for Health and Sport **Jeane Freeman** MSP

NHS and its performance, staff and pay; health care and social integration; patient services and patient safety; primary care; acute services; elective centres; Implementing the 2020 Vision; national clinical strategy; quality strategy and national service planning; allied healthcare services; carers, adult care and support; child and maternal health; dentistry; medical records, health improvement and protection.

Special Adviser	Davie Hutchison Email: david.hutchison@gov.scot	0131-244 4892
Private Secretary	Andrew Corr Email: cabsechs@gov.scot	0131-244 2125

Minister for Public Health, Sport and Wellbeing **Mairi Gougeon** MSP

Covid-19 testing programme; health improvement; public health and healthy working lives; physical activity, sport, sporting events and events legacy; problem alcohol use and recovery; Care Inspectorate; carers; child and maternal health (excluding mental health); health protection; person-centred care; self-directed support; sexual health.

Private Secretary	To be appointed Email: ministerphsw@gov.scot	0131-244 6955

Minister for Mental Health **Clare Haughey** MSP

Mental health; child and adolescent mental health; adult support and protection; autism, sensory impairment and learning difficulties; dementia; Mental Welfare Commission for Scotland (safeguards the rights of people with mental health problems, learning disabilities, dementia and related conditions); survivors of childhood abuse; The State Hospital (Carstairs).

Private Secretary	Craig Hancock Email: ministermh@gov.scot	0131-244 2186

Minister for Drugs Policy **Angela Constance** MSP

Private Secretary	To be appointed Email: ministerdp@gov.scot	

Finance

St Andrew's House, Regent Road, Edinburgh EH1 3DG
Tel: 0131-244 7716
Email: cabsecfinance@gov.scot

Cabinet Secretary for Finance **Kate Forbes** MSP

Budget bill; managing the public finances; fiscal policy and taxation (including income and ADT, fiscal framework); Scottish budget, budgetary monitoring and reporting; government procurement, National Performance Framework, public bodies policy; Scottish futures trust; public sector pay; Digital Economy.

Private Secretary	Christy McCurdy Email: cabsecfinance@gov.scot	0131-244 7716

Environment, Climate Change and Land Reform
St Andrew's House, Regent Road, Edinburgh EH1 3DG
Tel: 0131-244 1556
Email: cabsececclr@gov.scot Twitter: @GreenerScotland

Cabinet Secretary for the Environment, Climate Change and Land Reform **Roseanna Cunningham** MSP

Climate change and environmental protection; biodiversity; Crown Estate; environmental and climate justice; flood prevention and coastal erosion; land use and land reform; animal welfare; wildlife crime; water quality and Scottish Water.

Special Adviser	Máiri McAllan Email: mairi.mcallan@gov.scot	0131-244 7799
Private Secretary	Emma Dilger Email: cabsececclr@gov.scot	0131-244 1556

Minister for Rural Affairs and the Natural Environment **Ben Macpherson** MSP

(Also reports to Cabinet Secretary for Rural Economy) Animal health and welfare; marine planning; National Parks and natural heritage; physical and marine environment; sustainable development.

Private Secretary	Mariella Matheson Email: ministerrane@gov.scot	0131-244 4426

Rural Economy and Tourism
St Andrew's House, Regent Road, Edinburgh EH1 3DG
Tel: 0131-244 2189
Email: cabsecret@gov.scot Twitter: @GreenerScotland

Cabinet Secretary for Rural Economy and Tourism **Fergus Ewing** MSP

Agriculture and crofting; fisheries and aquaculture; food and drink; Highlands and Islands Enterprise; South of Scotland Enterprise Agency; rural Scotland; animal health; forestry; tourism.

Special Adviser	Kate Higgins Email: kate.higgins@gov.scot	0131-244 3460
Private Secretary	Kevin Veitch Email: cabsecret@gov.scot	0131-244 2492

Minister for Rural Affairs and the Natural Environment **Ben Macpherson** MSP

(Also reports to Cabinet Secretary for Environment, Climate Change and Land Reform) Animal health and welfare; marine planning; National Parks and natural heritage; physical and marine environment; sustainable development; plant health (including forestry disease issues); GM; climate change implications related to Agriculture.

Private Secretary	Mariella Matheson Email: ministerrane@gov.scot	0131-244 4426

Constitution, Europe and External Affairs
Scottish Parliament, The Royal Mile, Edinburgh EH99 1SP
Tel: 0131-556 8400
Email: cabsecceaea@gov.scot Twitter: @ScotGovInter

Cabinet Secretary for the Constitution, Europe and External Affairs **Michael Russell** MSP

The UK's exit from the European Union; international relations; Government and parliamentary business; constitutional relations and intra-governmental affairs.

Senior Special Adviser	Ewan Crawford Email: spads_admin@gov.scot	0131-244 7399
Private Secretary	Kirsty Hamilton Email: cabsecceaea@gov.scot	0131-244 2140

Minister for Parliamentary Business and Veterans **Graeme Dey** MSP

Government and parliamentary business; local government elections; Scottish Parliamentary elections; UK frameworks; Freedom of Information (FOI) and open government; veterans.

Private Secretary	Kathryn Stewart	0131-244 7733
	Email: ministerpbv@gov.scot	

Minister for Europe and International Development **Jenny Gilruth** MSP

International development; migration; post-Brexit relations; cross government co-ordination on the European Union; fair trade; Scottish diaspora,

Private Secretary	Barbara Templeton	0131-244 3953
	Email: ministereid@gov.scot	

Communities and Local Government

St Andrew's House, Regent Road, Edinburgh EH1 3DG
Tel: 0131-244 4000
Email: cabsecclg@gov.scot

Cabinet Secretary for Communities and Local Government **Aileen Campbell** MSP

Social justice; tackling inequalities; measures against poverty (with CSSS); place and place-making; community empowerment, community planning, devolution to communities, local governance review and democratic renewal; regeneration including business improvement districts; third sector and social economy; refugees and asylum; religious and faith organisations; medium and long term housing strategy.

Special Advisers	Jeanette Campbell	0131-244 5190
	Email: jeanette.campbell@gov.scot	
	Callum McCaig	0131-244 4534
	Email: callum.mccaig@gov.scot	
Private Secretary	Gillian Cross	0131-244 2784
	Email: cabsecclg@gov.scot	

Minister for Local Government, Housing and Planning **Kevin Stewart** MSP

Housing; local government; planning; building standards; Business Improvement Districts; community planning; homelessness; regeneration; fuel poverty.

Private Secretary	Marissa Gallagher	0131-244 4425
	Email: ministerlghp@gov.scot	

Economy, Fair Work and Culture

St Andrew's House, Regent Road, Edinburgh EH1 3DG
Tel: 0131-556 8400
Email: cabsecefwc@gov.scot Twitter: @scotgoveconomy

Cabinet Secretary for Economy, Fair Work and Culture **Fiona Hyslop** MSP

Scottish national investment bank; Scottish economy; inclusive growth and fair work; trade unions; Scottish Enterprise - national enterprise agency; trade and inward investment; creative industries; culture; architecture and built heritage; broadcasting; co-ordination on bringing major events to Scotland; national records.

Special Advisers	Leanne Dobson	0131-244 3361
	Email: spads_admin@gov.scot	
	Callum McCaig	0131-244 4534
	Email: spads_admin@gov.scot	
Private Secretary	Alistair Paddison	0131-244 4456
	Email: cabsecefwc@gov.scot	

Minister for Trade, Innovation and Public Finance **Ivan McKee** MSP

Trade and inward investment; innovation and increasing productivity; internationalisation and European Structural Funds; life sciences; Low Carbon Economy; fintech; financial services; financial services; Government procurement; Government Statistics; fiscal policy and taxation; public sector pensions; efficient government; Registers of Scotland; Revenue Scotland; digital participation; digital strategy.

Private Secretary	Steven Day Email: ministertipf@gov.scot	0131-244 9554

Minister for Business, Fair Work and Skills **Jamie Hepburn** MSP

(Also reports to Deputy First Minister) Consumer protection bill; business, industry and manufacturing; employment policy; labour market strategy, the living wage and fair work; employability programmes; youth employment (including implementation of the Wood Commission recommendations); women's employment; bankruptcy and Accountant in Bankruptcy (Scottish government agency); regional economic forums; PACE; non-advanced vocational skills; skills development Scotland (Scotland's national skills agency); consumer protection.

Private Secretary	Paul Cavanagh Email: ministerbfws@gov.scot	0131-244 8413

Transport, Infrastructure and Connectivity

St Andrew's House, Regent Road, Edinburgh EH1 3DG
Tel: 0131-244 0585
Email: cabsectic@gov.scot Twitter: @ScotGovEnergy

Cabinet Secretary for Transport, Infrastructure and Connectivity **Michael Matheson** MSP

Transport and public transport; infrastructure investment policy; cities and City Deals; town centres.

Special Advisers		
(Transport)	John McFarlane Email: john.mcfarlane@gov.scot	0131-244 1811
(Connectivity and The Islands)	Kate Higgins Email: kate.higgins@gov.scot	0131-244 3460
(Energy)	Callum McCaig Email: callum.mccaig@gov.scot	0131-244 4534
Private Secretary	Anisah Ijaz Email: cabsectic@gov.scot	0131-244 0585

Minister for Energy, Connectivity and the Islands **Paul Wheelhouse** MSP

Energy and energy consents; renewable energy industries; connectivity including 100 per cent broadband; cross government co-ordination on islands.

Private Secretary	Duncan Stalker Email: ministereci@gov.scot	0131-244 7650

Social Security and Older People

St Andrew's House, Regent Road, Edinburgh EH1 3DG
Tel: 0131-244 2513
Email: cabsecssop@gov.scot

Cabinet Secretary for Social Security and Older People **Shirley-Anne Somerville** MSP

Welfare policy, social security; measures against poverty; Best Start Grant (replacing the UK Government's Sure Start Maternity Grant); Funeral Expense Assistance (replacing the UK Government's Funeral Payment); Carers Allowance; Young Carers Grant; Personal Independence Payments; Disability Living Allowance; Industrial Injuries Disablement Benefit; Attendance Allowance; Severe Disablement Allowance; Cold Weather Payments; Winter Fuel Payments; Gender Recognition and Civil Partnership.

Special Adviser	Jeanette Campbell Email: jeanette.campbell@gov.scot	0131-244 5190
Private Secretary	Stuart McLean Email: cabsecssop@gov.scot	0131-244 2513

Minister for Older People and Equalities **Christina McKelvie** MSP

Equalities; including race, and LGBTI and mainstreaming equalities; protection and development of social and human rights; older people; disabilities; cross government co-ordination of policies in support of women and gender equality; social isolation and loneliness.

Private Secretary	Ciara McCafferty Email: ministerope@gov.scot	0131-244 7460

Whips

Chief Whip	**George Adam**
Depute Whips	**Tom Arthur** **Gordon MacDonald** **Rona Mackay**

Opposition

Scottish Conservatives

Shadow Cabinet

Leader, Scottish Conservative Group in the Scottish Parliament	Rt Hon **Ruth Davidson**
Shadow Cabinet Secretary for Justice	**Liam Kerr**
Chief Whip	**Miles Briggs**
Shadow Cabinet Secretary for Finance	**Murdo Fraser**
Shadow Cabinet Secretary for Health and Sport	**Donald Cameron**
Shadow Cabinet Secretary for Education and Skills	**Jamie Greene**
Shadow Cabinet Secretary for Economy, Fair Work and Culture	**Maurice Golden**
Shadow Cabinet Secretary for Rural Economy and Tourism	**Jamie Halcro Johnston**
Shadow Cabinet Secretary for Social Security and Older People	**Rachael Hamilton**
Shadow Cabinet Secretary for Constitution, Europe and External Affairs	**Dean Lockhart**
Shadow Cabinet Secretary for Communities and Local Government	**Annie Wells**
Shadow Cabinet Secretary for Transport, Infrastructure and Connectivity	**Graham Simpson**
Shadow Cabinet Secretary for Environment, Climate Change and Land Reform	**Liz Smith**

Shadow Ministers

Shadow Minister for Business, Fair Work and Skills	**Gordon Lindhurst**
Shadow Minister for Energy, Connectivity and the Islands	**Alexander Burnett**
Shadow Minister for Public Finance and Migration	**Bill Bowman**
Shadow Minister for Rural Affairs and the Natural Environment	**Finlay Carson**
Shadow Minister for Public Health, Mental Health, Sport and Wellbeing	**Brian Whittle**
Shadow Minister for Europe and International Development	**Peter Chapman**
Shadow Minister for Veterans	**Maurice Corry**
Shadow Minister for Community Safety	**Margaret Mitchell**
Shadow Minister for Older People and Equalities	**Jeremy Balfour**

Shadow Minister for Local Government, Housing and Planning	**Alexander Stewart** MBE
Shadow Minister for Children and Young People	**Alison Harris**

Scottish Labour

Shadow Cabinet

Leader	**Jackie Baillie**
Parliamentary Business Manager and Shadow Cabinet Secretary for the Eradication of Poverty and Social Inequality	**Elaine Smith**
Shadow Cabinet Secretary for Economy, Jobs and Fair Work	**Alex Rowley**
Shadow Cabinet Secretary for Brexit and the Constitution	**Anas Sarwar**
Shadow Cabinet Secretary for Education, Skills and Science	**Iain Gray**
Shadow Cabinet Secretary for Health and Social Care	**Monica Lennon**
Shadow Cabinet Secretary for Environment, Climate Change and Land Reform	**Claudia Beamish**
Shadow Cabinet Secretary for Communities and Equalities	**Pauline McNeill**
Shadow Cabinet Secretary for Justice	**Rhoda Grant**
Shadow Cabinet Secretary for Culture, Tourism and External Affairs	Dr **Claire Baker**
Shadow Cabinet Secretary for Local Government	**Sarah Boyack**
Shadow Cabinet Secretary for Rural Economy, Transport and Connectivity	**Colin Smyth**

Scottish Green Party

Co-convener and Spokesperson for Finance, Economy, Fair Work and Equalities	**Patrick Harvie**
Co-convener and Spokesperson for Health and Sport, Social Security and Children and Young People	**Alison Johnstone**
Spokesperson for Justice, Transport, Tourism and Rural and Island Communities	**John Finnie**
Spokesperson for Climate, Energy, Environment, Food and Farming	**Mark Ruskell**
Spokesperson for Europe and External Affairs, Education and Skills and Culture and Media	**Ross Greer**

Scottish Liberal Democrats

Leader; Spokesperson for Finance, Constitution, Europe and External Affairs	**Willie Rennie**
Spokesperson for Education and Skills	**Beatrice Wishart**
Spokesperson for Justice	**Liam McArthur**
Spokesperson for Health and Sport	**Alexander Cole-Hamilton**

Scottish Parliament

Scottish Parliament, Edinburgh EH99 1SP
Tel: 0131-348 5000/0800 092 7500
Email: info@parliament.scot Website: www.parliament.scot Twitter: @scotparl

Members (MSPs)

State of the Parties (February 2021)

	Constituency	*Regional*	*Total*
Scottish National Party	57*	4	61
Conservative and Unionist Party	7	23	30
Labour (includes Labour/Co-operative Party)	3	20†	23
Green Party	0	5	5
Liberal Democrat	4	1	5
Independent	2	1	3
Presiding Officer	0	1	1
Reform UK	0	1	1
	73	**56**	**129 seats**

* Includes two Deputy Presiding Officers who can participate and vote fully in the Parliament when not in the chair.
† Excludes the Presiding Officer who has no allegiance while in the post.

Changes since 2016 Scottish Parliament election

RESIGNATIONS

Rachael Hamilton	South Scotland - *Con*	2 May 2017
John Lamont	Ettrick, Roxburgh and Berwickshire - *Con*	4 May 2017
Douglas Ross	Highlands and Islands - *Con*	11 June 2017
Ross Thomson	North East Scotland - *Con*	12 June 2017
Tavish Scott	Shetland Islands - *Lib Dem*	15 July 2019
Kezia Dugdale	Lothian - *Lab/Co-op*	15 July 2019

DEATHS

Alex Johnstone	North East Scotland - *Con*	7 December 2016

CHANGE OF PARTY

Mark McDonald	Aberdeen Donside	SNP Whip suspended November 2017, now Independent
Derek Mackay	Renfrewshire North and West	SNP Whip suspended February 2020, now Independent
Michelle Ballantyne	South Scotland	Left Conservative November 2020, now Reform UK
Andy Wightman	Lothian	Left Green Party December 2020, now Independent

REPLACEMENTS

Bill Bowman	North East Scotland - *Con*	Returned 7 December 2016 following the death of Alex Johnstone
Michelle Ballantyne	South Scotland - *Con*	Returned 2 May 2017 following the resignation of Rachael Hamilton
Jamie Halcro Johnston	Highlands and Islands - *Con*	Returned 11 June 2017 following the resignation of Douglas Ross
Tom Mason	North East Scotland - *Con*	Returned 12 June 2017 following the resignation of Ross Thomson
Sarah Boyack	Lothian - *Lab/Co-op*	Returned 15 July 2019 following the resignation of Kezia Dugdale

BY-ELECTIONS

Ettrick, Roxburgh and Berwickshire

8 June 2017 due to the resignation of the Conservative MSP John Lamont

Con	Rachael Hamilton	20,658
SNP	Gail Hendry	11,320
Lab	Sally Prentice	3,406

Lib Dem Catriona Bhatia 3,196

Con majority 9,338 - Con hold (0.42% from SNP to Con)
Electorate 55,395 - Total vote 38,580 - Turnout 69.78%

Shetland Islands

29 August 2019

Lib Dem	Beatrice Wishart	5,659
SNP	Tom Wills	3,822
Ind	Ryan Thomson	1,286

Con Brydon Goodlad 425, *Green* Debra Nicolson 189, *Lab/Co-op* Johan Adamson 152, *Ind* Michael Stout 134, *Ind* Ian Scott 66, *UKIP* Stuart Martin 60, *Ind* Peter Tait 31

Lib Dem majority 1,837 - Lib Dem hold (14.32% from Lib Dem to SNP)
Electorate 17,810 - Total vote 11,824 - Turnout 66.45%

MSPs' Directory

Con	Conservative
Green	Green Party
Ind	Independent
Lab	Labour
Lab/Co-op	Labour/Co-operative
Lib Dem	Liberal Democrat
Pres Off	Presiding Officer
RefUK	Reform UK
SNP	Scottish National Party

ADAM, Mr George *SNP* **Paisley**
SNP Chief Whip
Tel: 0131-348 5869 Email: george.adam.msp@parliament.scot
Constituency office: 4 Johnston Street, Paisley PA1 1XG
Tel: 0141-887 8075
Website: www.paisleysmsp.org Twitter: @georgeadam

ADAMSON, Ms Clare *SNP* **Motherwell and Wishaw**
Convener, Parliamentary Committee on Education and Skills
Tel: 0131-348 6377 Email: clare.adamson.msp@parliament.scot
Constituency office: Suite G2, Dalziel Building, 7 Scott Street, Motherwell ML1 1PN
Tel: 01698 337540
Website: www.clareadamsonmsp.scot Twitter: @ClareAdamsonSNP

ALLAN, Dr Alasdair *SNP* **Na h-Eileanan an Iar**
Tel: 01851 700357 Email: alasdair.allan.msp@parliament.scot
Constituency office: 20 Kenneth Street, Stornoway HS1 2DR
Tel: 01851 700357
Website: alasdairallan.scot Twitter: @alasdairallan

ARTHUR, Mr Tom *SNP* **Renfrewshire South**
SNP Depute Whip
Tel: 0131-348 5863 Email: tom.arthur.msp@parliament.scot
Constituency office: 49 High Street, Johnstone PA5 8AJ
Tel: 01505 331990
Website: www.tomarthursnp.scot Twitter: @ThomasCArthur

BAILLIE, Ms Jackie *Lab* **Dumbarton**
Acting Leader, Scottish Labour Party
Tel: 0131-348 5905 Email: jackie.baillie.msp@parliament.scot
Constituency office: 6 Church Street, Dumbarton G82 1QL
Tel: 01389 734214
Website: www.jackiebaillie.laboursites.org Twitter: @jackiebmsp

---

BAKER, Dr Claire *Lab* **Mid Scotland and Fife**
Scottish Labour Shadow Cabinet Secretary for Culture, Tourism and External Affairs
Tel: 0131-348 6769 Fax: 0131-348 6761 Email: claire.baker.msp@parliament.scot
Regional office: Ore Valley Business Centre, 93 Main Street, Lochgelly, Fife KY5 9AF
Tel: 01592 786726 Email: claire-baker@live.co.uk
Website: www.clairebaker.org Twitter: @clairebakermsp

BALFOUR, Mr Jeremy *Con* **Lothian**
Scottish Conservatives Shadow Minister for Older People and Equalities
Tel: 0131-348 5961 Email: jeremy.balfour.msp@parliament.scot
Regional office: 29 Roseburn Terrace, Edinburgh EH12 5NQ
Tel: 0131-337 9764
Website: www.jeremybalfour.org.uk Twitter: @JBalfourMSP

BALLANTYNE, Mrs Michelle *RefUK* **South Scotland**
Leader, Reform UK Scotland
Tel: 0131-348 5661 Email: michelle.ballantyne.msp@parliament.scot
Regional office: Lower Langbrae, Main Street, St Boswells TD6 0AP
Website: www.michelleballantyne.org.uk Twitter: @MBallantyneMSP

BEAMISH, Ms Claudia *Lab/Co-op* **South Scotland**
Scottish Labour Shadow Cabinet Secretary for Environment, Climate Change and Land Reform
Tel: 0131-348 6889 Email: claudia.beamish.msp@parliament.scot
Regional office: 12 St Vincent Place, Lanark ML11 7LA
Tel: 01555 664065
Website: www.claudiabeamish.com Twitter: @claudiabeamish

BEATTIE, Mr Colin *SNP* **Midlothian North and Musselburgh**
Convener, Scottish Commission for Public Audit
Tel: 0131-348 6373 Email: colin.beattie.msp@parliament.scot
Constituency office: 164 High Street, Dalkeith EH22 1AY
Tel: 0131-454 0204
Website: colinbeattiemsp.org Twitter: @uartlach

BIBBY, Mr Neil *Lab/Co-op* **West Scotland**
Tel: 0131-348 6385 Email: neil.bibby.msp@parliament.scot
Regional office: 3a Mirren Chambers, 41 Gauze Street, Paisley PA1 1EX
Tel: 0141-889 0457
Website: www.neilbibby.com Twitter: @neilbibby

Devolved Parliament and Assemblies

BOWMAN, Mr Bill *Con* **North East Scotland**
Scottish Conservatives Shadow Minister for Public Finance and Migration; Convener, Parliamentary Committee on Delegated Powers and Law Reform
Tel: 0131-348 5649 Email: bill.bowman.msp@parliament.scot
Regional office: 190 East High Street, Forfar, Angus DD8 2HG
Tel: 01307 477784 Twitter: @billabowman

BOYACK, Ms Sarah *Lab* **Lothian**
Scottish Labour Cabinet Secretary for Local Government
Tel: 0131-348 6994 Email: sarah.boyack.msp@parliament.scot
Regional office: 22a Rutland Square, Edinburgh EH1 2BB
Tel: 0131-476 2539
Website: www.sarahboyack.com Twitter: @SarahBoyackMSP

BRIGGS, Mr Miles *Con* **Lothian**
Scottish Conservatives Chief Whip
Tel: 0131-348 5945 Email: miles.briggs.msp@parliament.scot
Regional office: 29 Roseburn Terrace, Edinburgh EH12 5NQ
Tel: 0131-337 9764
Website: www.milesbriggs.scot Twitter: @MilesBriggsMSP

BROWN, Mr Keith *SNP* **Clackmannanshire and Dunblane**
Depute Leader, Scottish National Party
Email: keith.brown.msp@parliament.scot
Constituency office: Unit 4, Townhead Institute, 39 Drysdale Street, Alloa FK10 1JA
Tel: 01259 219333
Website: www.keithbrownmsp.org Twitter: @KeithBrownSNP

BURNETT, Mr Alexander *Con* **Aberdeenshire West**
Scottish Conservatives Shadow Minister for Energy, Connectivity and the Islands
Tel: 0131-348 5642 Email: alexander.burnett.msp@parliament.scot
Constituency office: No constituency office publicised
Website: www.alexanderburnett.com Twitter: @AJABurnett

CAMERON, Mr Donald *Con* **Highlands and Islands**
Scottish Conservatives Shadow Cabinet Secretary for Health and Sport; Convener, Parliamentary Committee on Covid-19
Tel: 0131-348 6989 Email: donald.cameron.msp@parliament.scot
Regional office: 108 George Street, Oban, Argyll PA34 5NT
Tel: 01631 563474
Website: www.donaldcameron.org.uk Twitter: @dajcameron

CAMPBELL, Ms Aileen *SNP* **Clydesdale**
Cabinet Secretary for Communities and Local Government
Tel: 0131-348 6707 Email: aileen.campbell.msp@parliament.scot
Ministerial office: St Andrew's House, Regent Road, Edinburgh EH1 3DG
Tel: 0300 244 4000
Constituency office: Room 1, Kirkton Chambers, 12 Kirkton Street, Carluke ML8 4AB
Tel: 01555 750249
Website: www.aileencampbell.com Twitter: @clydesdaileen

CARLAW, Mr Jackson, CBE *Con* **Eastwood**
Tel: 0131-348 6800 Email: jackson.carlaw.msp@parliament.scot
Constituency office: Spiersbridge House, 1 Spiersbridge Way, Thornliebank, Glasgow G46 8NG
Tel: 0141-465 6611
Website: www.jacksoncarlaw.org.uk Twitter: @Jackson_Carlaw

CARSON, Mr Finlay *Con* **Galloway and West Dumfries**
Scottish Conservatives Shadow Minister for Rural Affairs and the Natural Environment
Tel: 0131-348 5890 Email: kyle.macintyre@parliament.scot/finlay.carson.msp@parliament.scot
Constituency office: 107 King Street, Castle Douglas DG7 1LZ
Tel: 01556 504991 Email: gillian.dykes@parliament.scot
Website: www.finlaycarson.co.uk Twitter: @fincarson

CHAPMAN, Mr Peter *Con* **North East Scotland**
Scottish Conservatives Shadow Minister for Europe and International Development
Tel: 0131-348 6150 Email: peter.chapman.msp@parliament.scot
Regional office: 80 Rosemount Place, Aberdeen AB25 2XN
Tel: 01224 644432 Email: peter.chapman@scottishconservatives.com
Website: www.peter-chapman.org.uk Twitter: @PeterChapmanMSP

COFFEY, Mr Willie *SNP* **Kilmarnock and Irvine Valley**
Tel: 0131-348 6515 Fax: 0131-348 6517 Email: willie.coffey.msp@parliament.scot
Constituency office: 62 John Finnie Street, Kilmarnock KA1 1BS
Tel: 01563 537300 Fax: 01563 537300 Email: willie.coffey@msp-office.co.uk

---

COLE-HAMILTON, Mr Alexander *Lib Dem* **Edinburgh Western**
Scottish Liberal Democrats Spokesperson for Health and Sport
Tel: 0131-348 5821 Email: alex.cole-hamilton.msp@parliament.scot
Constituency office: 151 St John's Road, Edinburgh EH12 7SD
Tel: 0131-334 1814
Website: www.alexcolehamilton.org.uk Twitter: @agcolehamilton

---

CONSTANCE, Ms Angela *SNP* **Almond Valley**
Minister for Drugs Policy
Email: angela.constance.msp@parliament.scot
Ministerial office: St Andrew's House, Regent Road, Edinburgh EH1 3DG
Tel: 0300 244 4000
Constituency office: Unit 4, Ochil House, Beveridge Square, Livingston EH54 6QF
Tel: 01506 460403 Twitter: @AConstanceSNP

CORRY, Mr Maurice *Con* **West Scotland**
Scottish Conservatives Shadow Minister for Veterans
Tel: 0131-348 6155 Email: maurice.corry.msp@parliament.scot
Regional office: Suite 4, Kirk House, Kirk Road, Bearsden G61 3RG
Tel: 0141-942 4942

CRAWFORD, Mr Bruce *SNP* **Stirling**
Convener, Parliamentary Committee on Finance and Constitution
Tel: 0131-348 5687 Email: bruce.crawford.msp@parliament.scot
Constituency office: Office 16, John Player Building, Stirling Enterprise Park, Stirling FK7 7RP
Tel: 01786 471899
Website: www.brucecrawford.scot Twitter: @rhbrucecrawford

CUNNINGHAM, Ms Roseanna *SNP* **Perthshire South and Kinross-shire**
Cabinet Secretary for the Environment, Climate Change and Land Reform
Tel: 0131-348 5697 Fax: 0131-348 5563 Email: roseanna.cunningham.msp@parliament.scot
Ministerial office: St Andrew's House, Regent Road, Edinburgh EH1 3DG
Tel: 0300 244 4000
Constituency office: 63 Glasgow Road, Perth PH2 0PE
Tel: 01738 620540
Website: www.roseannacunningham.com Twitter: @strathearnrose

DAVIDSON, Rt Hon Ruth *Con* **Edinburgh Central**
Leader, Scottish Conservative Group in the Scottish Parliament
Tel: 0131-348 6370 Email: ruth.davidson.msp@parliament.scot
Constituency office: 29 Roseburn Terrace, Edinburgh EH12 5NQ Twitter: @ruthdavidsonmsp

DENHAM, Ms Ash *SNP* **Edinburgh Eastern**
Minister for Community Safety
Tel: 0131-348 5923 Email: ash.denham.msp@parliament.scot
Ministerial office: St Andrew's House, Regent Road, Edinburgh EH1 3DG
Tel: 0300 244 4000
Constituency office: 18 Niddrie Mains Road, Edinburgh EH16 4BG
Tel: 0131-659 4707
Website: www.ashdenham.scot Twitter: @ashtenRD

DEY, Mr Graeme *SNP* **Angus South**
Minister for Parliamentary Business and Veterans
Tel: 0131-348 6292 Email: graeme.dey.msp@parliament.scot
Ministerial office: St Andrew's House, Regent Road, Edinburgh EH1 3DG
Tel: 0300 244 4000
Constituency office: 282-284 High Street, Arbroath, Angus DD11 1JF
Tel: 01241 873058
Website: www.graemedey.info

DORIS, Mr Bob *SNP* **Glasgow Maryhill and Springburn**
Convener, Parliamentary Committee on Social Security
Tel: 0131-348 6547 Fax: 0131-348 6549 Email: bob.doris.msp@parliament.scot
Constituency office: Maryhill Burgh Halls, 10-24 Gairbraid Avenue, Glasgow G20 8YE
Tel: 0141-946 7700
Website: bob-doris.scot Twitter: @BobDorisSNP

DORNAN, Mr James *SNP* **Glasgow Cathcart**
Convener, Parliamentary Committee on Local Government and Communities
Tel: 0131-348 5683 Email: james.dornan.msp@parliament.scot
Constituency office: 2 Clarkston Road, Glasgow G44 4EQ
Tel: 0141-632 5238
Website: www.jamesdornanmsp.org Twitter: @glasgowcathcart

EWING, Ms Annabelle *SNP* **Cowdenbeath**
Tel: 0131-348 6290 Email: annabelle.ewing.msp@parliament.scot
Constituency office: 253-257 High Street, Cowdenbeath KY4 9QF
Tel: 01383 611067 Twitter: @aewingmsp

EWING, Mr Fergus *SNP* **Inverness and Nairn**
Cabinet Secretary for Rural Economy and Tourism
Tel: 0131-348 5732 Email: fergus.ewing.msp@parliament.scot
Ministerial office: St Andrew's House, Regent Road, Edinburgh EH1 3DG
Tel: 0300 244 4000
Constituency office: 112 Church Street, Inverness IV1 1EP
Tel: 01463 713004 Email: fergus@fergusewing.com
Website: www.fergusewing.com Twitter: @fergusewingmsp

FABIANI, Ms Linda *SNP* **East Kilbride**
Deputy Presiding Officer
Tel: 0131-348 5698 Fax: 0131-348 6473 Email: linda.fabiani.msp@parliament.scot
Constituency office: 1/3 Strathmore House, East Kilbride G74 1LF
Tel: 01355 232800 Fax: 01355 232770
Website: www.lindafabiani.scot Twitter: @lindafabianisnp

FEE, Ms Mary *Lab* **West Scotland**
Tel: 0131-348 6391 Email: mary.fee.msp@parliament.scot
Regional office: 3a Mirren Chambers, 41 Gauze Street, Paisley PA1 1EX
Tel: 0141-889 4828
Website: maryfeemsp.com Twitter: @MaryFeeMSP

FINDLAY, Mr Neil *Lab* **Lothian**
Tel: 0131-348 6896 Email: neil.findlay.msp@parliament.scot
Regional office: 4 Northfield Court, West Calder EH55 8DS
Tel: 01506 873242
Website: www.neilfindlaymsp.com Twitter: @NeilFindlay_MSP

FINNIE, Mr John *Green* **Highlands and Islands**
Convener, Justice Sub-committee on Policing; Scottish Green Party Spokesperson for Justice, Transport, Tourism and Rural and Island Communities
Tel: 0131-348 6898 Email: john.finnie.msp@parliament.scot
Regional office: Room 12, 3rd Floor, 2 Baron Taylor's Street, Inverness IV1 1QL
Tel: 01463 710194
Website: johnfinnie.scot Twitter: @JohnFinnieHI

FITZPATRICK, Mr Joe *SNP* **Dundee City West**
Email: joe.fitzpatrick.msp@parliament.scot
Constituency office: 37 Dock Street, Dundee DD1 3DR
Tel: 01382 843244
Website: www.joe.fitzpatrick.scot Twitter: @joefitzsnp

FORBES, Ms Kate *SNP* **Skye, Lochaber and Badenoch**
Cabinet Secretary for Finance
Tel: 01349 863 888 Email: kate.forbes.msp@parliament.scot
Ministerial office: St Andrew's House, Regent Road, Edinburgh EH1 3DG
Tel: 0300 244 4000
Constituency office: 12 High Street, Dingwall IV15 9RU
Tel: 01349 863888
Website: www.kateforbes.scot Twitter: @kateforbesmsp

FRASER, Mr Murdo *Con* **Mid Scotland and Fife**
Scottish Conservatives Shadow Cabinet Secretary for Finance
Tel: 0131-348 5293 Email: murdo.fraser.msp@parliament.scot
Regional office: Control Tower, Perth Airport, Scone, Perth PH2 6PL
Tel: 01738 553990 Email: pkconservatives@gmail.com
Website: www.murdofraser.com Twitter: @murdo_fraser

FREEMAN, Ms Jeane *SNP* **Carrick, Cumnock and Doon Valley**
Cabinet Secretary for Health and Sport
Tel: 0131-348 6745 Email: jeane.freeman.msp@parliament.scot
Ministerial office: St Andrew's House, Regent Road, Edinburgh EH1 3DG
Tel: 0300 244 4000
Constituency office: 46-48 Glaisnock Street, Cumnock KA18 1BY
Tel: 01290 425876
Website: www.jeanefreeman.scot Twitter: @JeaneF1MSP

GIBSON, Mr Kenneth *SNP* **Cunninghame North**
Tel: 0131-348 6536 Fax: 0131-348 6539 Email: kenneth.gibson.msp@parliament.scot
Constituency office: 15 Main Street, Dalry KA24 5DL
Tel: 01294 833687
Website: www.kennethgibson.org

GILRUTH, Ms Jenny *SNP* **Mid Fife and Glenrothes**
Minister for Europe and International Development
Tel: 0131-348 5793 Email: jenny.gilruth.msp@parliament.scot
Ministerial office: St Andrew's House, Regent Road, Edinburgh EH1 3DG
Tel: 0300 244 4000
Constituency office: 12 Commercial Street, Markinch KY7 6DE
Tel: 01592 764815
Website: www.jennygilruthmsp.scot Twitter: @JennyGilruth

GOLDEN, Mr Maurice *Con* **West Scotland**
Scottish Conservatives Shadow Cabinet Secretary for Economy, Fair Work and Culture
Tel: 0131-348 6146 Email: maurice.golden.msp@parliament.scot
Regional office: 4 Kirk House, Kirk Road, Bearsden, Glasgow G61 3RG
Tel: 0141-942 4942
Website: www.mauricegolden.com Twitter: @mgoldenmsp

GOUGEON, Ms Mairi *SNP* **Angus North and Mearns**
Minister for Public Health, Sport and Wellbeing
Email: mairi.gougeon.msp@parliament.scot
Ministerial office: St Andrew's House, Regent Road, Edinburgh EH1 3DG
Tel: 0300 244 4000
Constituency office: 14-18 Swan Street, Brechin DD9 6EF
Tel: 01356 626942 Twitter: @MairiGougeon

GRAHAME, Ms Christine *SNP* **Midlothian South, Tweeddale and Lauderdale**
Deputy Presiding Officer
Tel: 0131-348 5729 Email: christine.grahame.msp@parliament.scot
Constituency office: 46 High Street, Galashiels TD1 1SE
Tel: 01896 759575
Website: www.christinegrahame.com Twitter: @CGrahameMSP

GRANT, Mrs Rhoda *Lab/Co-op* **Highlands and Islands**
Scottish Labour Shadow Cabinet Secretary for Justice
Tel: 0131-348 5766 Email: rhoda.grant.msp@parliament.scot
Regional offices: 3 Gordon Terrace, Inverness IV2 3HD
Tel: 01463 716299
34 Cromwell Street, Stornoway HS1 2DD
Tel: 01851 709 822
Website: www.rhodagrant.org.uk Twitter: @rhodagrant

GRAY, Mr Iain *Lab* **East Lothian**
Scottish Labour Shadow Cabinet Secretary for Education, Skills and Science
Email: iain.gray.msp@parliament.scot
Constituency office: 5a Mitchell's Close, Haddington, East Lothian EH41 3NB
Tel: 01620 822711
Website: www.iaingraymsp.co.uk Twitter: @IainGrayMSP

GREENE, Mr Jamie *Con* **West Scotland**
Scottish Conservatives Shadow Cabinet Secretary for Education
Tel: 0131-348 6137 Email: jamie.greene.msp@parliament.scot
Regional office: 24 Bath Street, Largs KA30 8BL
Tel: 01475 673007
Website: jamiegreene.uk Twitter: @jamiegreeneuk

GREER, Mr Ross *Green* **West Scotland**
Scottish Green Party Spokesperson for Europe and External Affairs, Education and Skills and Culture and Media
Tel: 0131-348 6347 Email: ross.greer.msp@parliament.scot
Regional office: Unit 4, 38 Stewart Street, Milngavie, East Dunbartonshire G62 6BY
Tel: 0141-956 2778
Website: www.rossgreer.greens.scot Twitter: @ross_greer

GRIFFIN, Mr Mark *Lab* **Central Scotland**
Tel: 0131-348 6397 Email: mark.griffin.msp@parliament.scot
Regional office: Unit 32, Coatbridge Business Centre, 204 Main Street, Coatbridge ML5 3RB
Tel: 01236 423555
Website: www.markgriffinmsp.org.uk Twitter: @MarkGriff1n

HALCRO JOHNSTON, Mr Jamie *Con* **Highlands and Islands**
Scottish Conservatives Shadow Cabinet Secretary for Rural Economy and Tourism
Tel: 0131-348 6140 Email: jamie.halcrojohnston.msp@parliament.scot
Regional office: 10 Drummond Street, Inverness IV1 1QD
Tel: 01463 232333
Website: www.jamiehalcrojohnston.org.uk Twitter: @jhalcrojohnston

---

HAMILTON, Ms Rachael *Con* **Ettrick, Roxburgh and Berwickshire**
Scottish Conservatives Shadow Cabinet Secretary for Social Security and Older People
Tel: 0131-348 6971 Email: rachael.hamilton.msp@parliament.scot
Constituency office: 7 Abbey Court, Kelso TD5 7JA
Tel: 01573 224862
Website: www.rachaelhamilton.co.uk Twitter: @Rachael2Win

HARPER, Ms Emma *SNP* **South Scotland**
Tel: 0131-348 6965 Email: emma.harper.msp@parliament.scot
Regional office: Unit 7, Loreburne Centre, High Street, Dumfries DG1 2BD
Tel: 01387 255334 Twitter: @EmmaHarperMSP

HARRIS, Ms Alison *Con* **Central Scotland**
Scottish Conservatives Shadow Minister for Children and Young People
Tel: 0131-348 6152 Email: alison.harris.msp@parliament.scot
Regional office: Suite 4B, 91 Bothwell Road, Hamilton ML3 0DW
Tel: 01698 517011 Twitter: @AlisonHarrisMSP

HARVIE, Mr Patrick *Green* **Glasgow**
Co-leader, Scottish Green Party and Spokesperson for Finance, Economy, Fair Work and Equalities
Tel: 0131-348 6363 Fax: 0131-348 5972 Email: patrick.harvie.msp@parliament.scot
Regional office: 19 Argyle Court, 1103 Argyle Street, Glasgow G3 8ND
Tel: 0141-221 6999
Website: www.patrickharviemsp.com Twitter: @patrickharvie

HAUGHEY, Ms Clare *SNP* **Rutherglen**
Minister for Mental Health
Tel: 0131-348 5756 Email: clare.haughey.msp@parliament.scot
Ministerial office: St Andrew's House, Regent Road, Edinburgh EH1 3DG
Tel: 0300 244 4000
Constituency office: 85 Main Street, Rutherglen, Glasgow G73 2JQ
Tel: 0141-561 5131
Website: clarehaughey.scot Twitter: @haughey_clare

HEPBURN, Mr Jamie *SNP* **Cumbernauld and Kilsyth**
Minister for Business, Fair Work and Skills
Tel: 0131-348 6574 Fax: 0131-348 6575 Email: jamie.hepburn.msp@parliament.scot
Ministerial office: St Andrew's House, Regent Road, Edinburgh EH1 3DG
Tel: 0300 244 4000
Constituency office: Suite 1, Lennox House, Lennox Road, Cumbernauld G67 1LL
Tel: 01236 453969
Website: jamiehepburn.net Twitter: @jamiehepburn

HYSLOP, Ms Fiona *SNP* **Linlithgow**
Cabinet Secretary for Economy, Fair Work and Culture
Tel: 0131-348 5921 Email: fiona.hyslop.msp@parliament.scot
Ministerial office: St Andrew's House, Regent Road, Edinburgh EH1 3DG
Tel: 0300 244 4000
Constituency office: 59 West Main Street, Whitburn, West Lothian EH47 0QD
Tel: 01501 749941 Email: allistair.tatton@parliament.scot
Website: www.fionahyslop.com Twitter: @fionahyslop

JOHNSON, Mr Daniel *Lab* **Edinburgh Southern**
Tel: 0131-348 6462 Email: daniel.johnson.msp@parliament.scot
Constituency office: 134 Comiston Road, Edinburgh EH10 5QN
Tel: 0131-541 2145
Website: www.danieljohnson.org.uk Twitter: @DJohnsonMSP

JOHNSTONE, Ms Alison *Green* **Lothian**
Co-leader, Scottish Green Party Parliamentary Group, Spokesperson for Health and Sport, Social Security and Children and Young People
Tel: 0131-348 6364 Email: alison.johnstone.msp@parliament.scot
Regional office: No regional office
Website: alisonjohnstonemsp.com Twitter: @alisonjohnstone

KELLY, Mr James *Lab/Co-op* **Glasgow**
Tel: 0131-348 6510 Email: james.kelly.msp@parliament.scot
Regional office: Bellahouston Business Centre, 423 Paisley Road West, Glasgow G51 1PZ
Tel: 0141-465 9936 Twitter: @JamesKellyLab

KERR, Mr Liam *Con* **North East Scotland**
Scottish Conservatives Shadow Cabinet Secretary for Justice
Tel: 0131-348 6973 Email: liam.kerr.msp@parliament.scot
Regional office: 80 Rosemount Place, Aberdeen AB25 2XN
Tel: 01224 644432
Website: www.liamkerr.org.uk Twitter: @liamkerrmsp

KIDD, Mr Bill *SNP* **Glasgow Anniesland**
Convener, Parliamentary Committee on Standards, Procedures and Public Appointments
Tel: 0131-348 5691/0131-348 6593 Email: bill.kidd.msp@parliament.scot
Constituency office: 476 Crow Road, Glasgow G11 7DR
Tel: 0141-339 3277
Website: www.billkiddmsp.org Twitter: @BillKiddSNP

LAMONT, Ms Johann *Lab/Co-op* **Glasgow**
Convener, Parliamentary Committee on Public Petitions
Tel: 0131-348 5847 Email: johann.lamont.msp@parliament.scot
Regional office: Bellahouston Business Centre, 423 Paisley Road West, Glasgow G51 1PZ
Tel: 0141-465 9937 Twitter: @johannlamont

LENNON, Ms Monica *Lab* **Central Scotland**
Scottish Labour Shadow Cabinet Secretary for Health and Social Care
Tel: 0131-348 6484 Email: monica.lennon.msp@parliament.scot
Regional office: Unit 32, Coatbridge Business Centre, 204 Main Street, Coatbridge ML5 3RB
Twitter: @monicalennon7

LEONARD, Mr Richard *Lab* **Central Scotland**
Tel: 0131-348 6465 Email: richard.leonard.msp@parliament.scot
Regional office: Coatbridge Business Centre, 204 Main Street, Coatbridge ML5 3RB
Tel: 01236 423555
Website: www.richardleonard.org.uk Twitter: @LabourRichard

LINDHURST, Mr Gordon *Con* **Lothian**
Scottish Conservatives Shadow Minister for Business, Fair Work and Skills; Convener, Parliamentary Committee on Economy, Energy and Fair Work
Tel: 0131-348 5948 Email: gordon.lindhurst.msp@parliament.scot
Regional office: 29 Roseburn Terrace, Edinburgh EH12 5NQ
Tel: 0131-337 9764
Website: www.gordonlindhurst.com Twitter: @GLindhurstMSP

LOCHHEAD, Mr Richard *SNP* **Moray**
Minister for Further Education, Higher Education and Science
Tel: 0131-348 5712 Fax: 0131-348 5737 Email: richard.lochhead.msp@parliament.scot
Ministerial office: St Andrew's House, Regent Road, Edinburgh EH1 3DG
Tel: 0300 244 4000
Constituency office: 80 South Street, Elgin IV30 1JG
Tel: 01343 545077
Website: www.richardlochhead.org Twitter: @richardlochhead

LOCKHART, Mr Dean *Con* **Mid Scotland and Fife**
Scottish Conservatives Shadow Cabinet Secretary for Constitution, Europe and External Affairs
Tel: 0131-348 5993 Email: dean.lockhart.msp@parliament.scot
Regional office: Canmore House, 31 Canmore Street, Dunfermline KY12 7NU
Tel: 01383 720530
Website: www.deanlockhart.org.uk Twitter: @DeanLockhartMSP

LYLE, Mr Richard *SNP* **Uddingston and Bellshill**
Tel: 0131-348 6394 Fax: 0131-348 6798 Email: richard.lyle.msp@parliament.scot
Constituency office: 188 Main Street, Bellshill, North Lanarkshire ML4 1AE
Tel: 01698 479900
Website: www.richardlylemsp.org Twitter: @richardlylesnp

MCALPINE, Ms Joan *SNP* **South Scotland**
Convener, Culture, Tourism, Europe and External Affairs Committee
Tel: 0131-348 6885 Email: joan.mcalpine.msp@parliament.scot
Regional office: Unit 7, Loreburne Shopping Centre, High Street, Dumfries DG1 2BD
Tel: 01387 255334
Website: www.joanmcalpine.com Twitter: @joanmcalpine

MCARTHUR, Mr Liam *Lib Dem* **Orkney Islands**
Scottish Liberal Democrats Spokesperson for Justice
Tel: 0131-348 5815 Fax: 0131-348 5807 Email: liam.mcarthur.msp@parliament.scot
Constituency office: 14 Palace Road, Kirkwall, Orkney KW15 1PA
Tel: 01856 876541 Fax: 01856 876162 Email: msp@msporkney.com
Website: www.liammcarthur.org.uk Twitter: @Liam4Orkney

MACDONALD, Mr Angus *SNP* **Falkirk East**
Tel: 0131-348 5489 Email: angus.macdonald.msp@parliament.scot
Constituency office: 2 York Arcade, Grangemouth FK3 8BA
Tel: 01324 482100
Website: www.angusmacdonald.info Twitter: @Angus4FalkirkE

MACDONALD, Mr Gordon *SNP* **Edinburgh Pentlands**
SNP Depute Whip
Tel: 0131-348 5741 Email: gordon.macdonald.msp@parliament.scot
Constituency office: 9 Kingsknowe Park, Edinburgh EH14 2JQ
Tel: 0131-443 0595 Twitter: @GMacdonaldMSP

MACDONALD, Mr Lewis *Lab* **North East Scotland**
Convener, Parliamentary Committee on Health and Sport; Scottish Labour Shadow Minister for Energy
Tel: 0131-348 5915 Fax: 0131-348 5958 Email: lewis.macdonald.msp@parliament.scot
Regional office: 70 Rosemount Place, Aberdeen AB25 2XJ
Tel: 01224 646333 Fax: 01224 645450
Website: www.lewismacdonald.co.uk Twitter: @LewisMacdMSP

MCDONALD, Mr Mark *Ind* **Aberdeen Donside**
Tel: 0131-348 6522 Email: mark.mcdonald.msp@parliament.scot
Constituency office: Unit 12a, Mastrick Shopping Centre, Greenfern Place, Aberdeen AB16 6JR
Tel: 01224 789457

MACGREGOR, Mr Fulton *SNP* **Coatbridge and Chryston**
Tel: 0131-348 5797 Email: fulton.macgregor.msp@parliament.scot
Constituency office: Coatbridge Business Centre, 204 Main Street, Coatbridge ML5 3RB
Tel: 01236 897540 Twitter: @fultonsnp

MACINTOSH, Rt Hon Ken *Pres Off* **West Scotland**
Presiding Officer
Tel: 0131-348 5324/0131-348 5896 Email: ken.macintosh.msp@parliament.scot
Regional office: 1 Spiersbridge Way, Thornliebank, East Renfrewshire G46 8NG
Tel: 0141-620 6310
Website: www.kenmacintosh.scot Twitter: @KenMacintoshMSP

MACKAY, Mr Derek *Ind* **Renfrewshire North and West**
Email: derek.mackay.msp@parliament.scot
Ministerial office: St Andrew's House, Regent Road, Edinburgh EH1 3DG
Tel: 0300 244 4000
Constituency office: 37 Hairst Street, Renfrew PA4 8QU
Tel: 0141-885 2076
Website: www.derekmackaymsp.org

MACKAY, Ms Rona *SNP* **Strathkelvin and Bearsden**
SNP Depute Whip
Tel: 0131-348 5789 Email: rona.mackay.msp@parliament.scot
Constituency office: 18a Townhead, Kirkintilloch G66 1NL
Tel: 0141-776 1561
Website: ronamackay.scot Twitter: @ronamackaymsp

MCKEE, Mr Ivan *SNP* **Glasgow Provan**
Minister for Trade, Innovation and Public Finance
Tel: 0131-348 6950 Email: ivan.mckee.msp@parliament.scot
Ministerial office: St Andrew's House, Regent Road, Edinburgh EH1 3DG
Tel: 0300 244 4000
Constituency office: 12 Hillfoot Street, Glasgow G31 2LF
Tel: 0141-556 4441
Website: www.ivanmckee.scot Twitter: @ivan_mckee

MCKELVIE, Ms Christina *SNP* **Hamilton, Larkhall and Stonehouse**
Minister for Older People and Equalities
Tel: 0131-348 6680 Fax: 0131-348 6683 Email: christina.mckelvie.msp@parliament.scot
Ministerial office: St Andrew's House, Regent Road, Edinburgh EH1 3DG
Tel: 0300 244 4000
Constituency office: Barncluith Business Centre, Townhead Street, Hamilton ML3 7DP
Tel: 01698 403311 Fax: 01698 403313
Website: www.christina-mckelvie.org Twitter: @christinasnp

MCMILLAN, Mr Stuart *SNP* **Greenock and Inverclyde**
Tel: 0131-348 6810 Email: stuart.mcmillan.msp@parliament.scot
Constituency office: 26 Grey Place, Greenock, Inverclyde PA15 1YF
Tel: 01475 720930
Website: www.stuart-mcmillan.net Twitter: @stumcmillansnp

MCNEILL, Ms Pauline *Lab* **Glasgow**
Scottish Labour Shadow Cabinet Secretary for Communities and Equalities
Tel: 0131-348 6475 Email: pauline.mcneill.msp@parliament.scot
Regional office: Suite 1-11, Bellahouston Business Park, 423 Paisley Road West, Glasgow G51 1PZ
Tel: 0141-465 9932
Website: www.paulinemcneill.org.uk Twitter: @pauline4glasgow

MACPHERSON, Mr Ben *SNP* **Edinburgh Northern and Leith**
Minister for Rural Affairs and the Natural Environment
Tel: 0131-348 5786 Email: ben.macpherson.msp@parliament.scot
Ministerial office: St Andrew's House, Regent Road, Edinburgh EH1 3DG
Tel: 0300 244 4000
Constituency office: 34 Constitution Street, Edinburgh EH6 6RS
Tel: 0131-600 0134
Website: www.benmacpherson.scot Twitter: @benmacpherson

MAGUIRE, Ms Ruth *SNP* **Cunninghame South**
Tel: 0131-348 6953 Email: ruth.maguire.msp@parliament.scot
Constituency office: 14 Eglinton Street, Irvine KA12 8AS
Tel: 01294 276730
Website: ruthmaguire.scot Twitter: @rbfmaguire

MARRA, Ms Jenny *Lab* **North East Scotland**
Convener, Parliamentary Committee on Public Audit and Post-Legislative Scrutiny
Tel: 0131-348 6427 Email: jenny.marra.msp@parliament.scot
Regional office: Office 5/2, Whitehall House, 33 Yeaman Shore, Dundee DD1 4BJ
Tel: 01382 202584 Email: jenny@jennymarra.com
Website: www.jennymarra.com Twitter: @jennymarra

MARTIN, Ms Gillian *SNP* **Aberdeenshire East**
Convener, Parliamentary Committee on Environment, Climate Change and Land Reform
Tel: 0131-348 6956 Email: gillian.martin.msp@parliament.scot
Constituency office: Unit 6, Colpy Business Park, Oldmeldrum, Aberdeenshire AB51 0FU
Tel: 01651 871750 Twitter: @GillianMSP

MASON, Mr John *SNP* **Glasgow Shettleston**
Tel: 0141-550 4327 Email: john.mason.msp@parliament.scot
Constituency office: 1335 Gallowgate, Parkhead Cross, Glasgow G31 4DN
Tel: 0141-550 4327
Website: www.john-mason.org Twitter: @johnmasonmsp

MASON, Mr Tom *Con* **North East Scotland**
Tel: 0131-348 6981 Email: tom.mason.msp@parliament.scot
Regional office: 80 Rosemount Place, Aberdeen AB25 2XN
Tel: 01224 646888
Website: www.tommasonmsp.co.uk Twitter: @TomMasonMSP

MATHESON, Mr Michael *SNP* **Falkirk West**
Cabinet Secretary for Transport, Infrastructure and Connectivity
Email: michael.matheson.msp@parliament.scot
Ministerial office: St Andrew's House, Regent Road, Edinburgh EH1 3DG
Tel: 0300 244 4000
Constituency office: 15a East Bridge Street, Falkirk FK1 1YB
Tel: 01324 629271 Fax: 01324 635576 Email: andrew.maclachlan@parliament.scot
Website: michaelmatheson.org Twitter: @mathesonmichael

MITCHELL, Ms Margaret *Con* **Central Scotland**
Scottish Conservatives Shadow Minister for Community Safety
Tel: 0131-348 5639 Email: margaret.mitchell.msp@parliament.scot
Regional office: Suite 4B, 91 Bothwell Road, Hamilton ML3 0DW
Tel: 01698 282815 Email: liz.mclean@parliament.scot
Website: www.margaretmitchellmsp.scot

MOUNTAIN, Mr Edward *Con* **Highlands and Islands**
Convener, Parliamentary Committee on Rural Economy and Connectivity
Tel: 0131-348 6953 Email: edward.mountain.msp@parliament.scot
Regional office: No regional office publicised Twitter: @1edmountain

MUNDELL, Mr Oliver *Con* **Dumfriesshire**
Tel: 0131-348 5631 Email: oliver.mundell.msp@parliament.scot
Constituency office: 78 High Street, Lockerbie DG11 2EU
Tel: 01576 203910
Website: www.olivermundell.com Twitter: @olivermundell

NEIL, Mr Alex *SNP* **Airdrie and Shotts**
Tel: 0131-348 5703 Fax: 0131-348 5895 Email: alex.neil.msp@parliament.scot
Constituency office: Office 15, Airdrie Business Centre, 1 Chapel Lane, Airdrie ML6 6GX
Tel: 01236 439610 Twitter: @alexneilsnp

PATERSON, Mr Gil *SNP* **Clydebank and Milngavie**
Tel: 0131-348 6812 Fax: 0131-348 6814 Email: gil.paterson.msp@parliament.scot
Constituency office: Suite 1-6, Titan Enterprise Centre, 1 Aurora Avenue, Queens Quay, Clydebank G81 1BF
Tel: 0141-952 9677 Fax: 0141-952 9677
Website: www.gilmsp.com Twitter: @GilMPaterson

RENNIE, Mr Willie *Lib Dem* **North East Fife**
Leader, Scottish Liberal Democrats and Spokesperson for Finance, Constitution, Europe and External Affairs
Tel: 0131-348 5803 Email: willie.rennie.msp@parliament.scot
Constituency office: G3, Granary Business Centre, Cupar, Fife KY15 5YQ
Tel: 01334 656361 Email: willie.c.rennie@gmail.com Twitter: @willie_rennie

ROBISON, Ms Shona *SNP* **Dundee City East**
Tel: 0131-348 6948 Fax: 0131-348 4017 Email: shona.robison.msp@parliament.scot
Constituency office: The Factory Skate Park, 15 Balunie Drive, Dundee DD4 8PS
Tel: 01382 903219 Email: dundee@shona.robison.scot
Website: www.robison.scot Twitter: @shonarobison

ROSS, Ms Gail *SNP* **Caithness, Sutherland and Ross**
Tel: 0131-348 5927 Email: gail.ross.msp@parliament.scot
Constituency office: 106 High Street, Invergordon, Ross-shire IV18 0DR
Tel: 01349 888255
Website: www.gailrosssnp.org Twitter: @gailrosssnp

ROWLEY, Mr Alex *Lab* **Mid Scotland and Fife**
Scottish Labour Shadow Cabinet Secretary for Economy, Jobs and Fair Work
Tel: 0131-348 6827 Email: alex.rowley.msp@parliament.scot
Regional office: Ore Valley Business Centre, 93 Main Street, Lochgelly KY5 9AF
Tel: 01592 786725
Website: www.alexrowley.org Twitter: @Alex_RowleyMSP

RUMBLES, Mr Mike *Lib Dem* **North East Scotland**
Tel: 0131-348 5816 Email: mike.rumbles.msp@parliament.scot
Regional office: No regional office

RUSKELL, Mr Mark *Green* **Mid Scotland and Fife**
Scottish Green Party Spokesperson for Climate, Energy, Environment, Food and Farming
Tel: 0131-348 6468 Email: mark.ruskell.msp@parliament.scot
Regional office: 67a King Street, Stirling FK8 1BN
Tel: 01786 448203 Twitter: @markruskell

RUSSELL, Mr Michael *SNP* **Argyll and Bute**
Cabinet Secretary for the Constitution, Europe and External Affairs
Tel: 0131-348 5738 Email: michael.russell.msp@parliament.scot
Ministerial office: St Andrew's House, Regent Road, Edinburgh EH1 3DG
Tel: 0300 244 4000
Constituency office: 81 Argyll Street, Dunoon, Argyll PA23 7DH
Tel: 01369 702011
Website: michaelrussellmsp.scot Twitter: @feorlean

SARWAR, Mr Anas *Lab* **Glasgow**
Shadow Cabinet Secretary for Brexit and the Constitution
Tel: 0131-348 5830 Email: anas.sarwar.msp@parliament.scot
Regional office: Suite 1-11, Bellahouston Business Park, 423 Paisley Road West, Glasgow G5 1PZ
Tel: 0141-465 9933
Website: www.anassarwar.org Twitter: @AnasSarwar

SCOTT, Mr John *Con* **Ayr**
Tel: 0131-348 5638 Fax: 0131-348 5617 Email: john.scott.msp@parliament.scot
Constituency office: 17 Wellington Square, Ayr KA7 1EZ
Tel: 01292 286251 Fax: 01292 280480

SIMPSON, Mr Graham *Con* **Central Scotland**
Scottish Conservatives Shadow Cabinet Secretary for Transport, Infrastructure and Connectivity
Tel: 0131-348 6983 Email: graham.simpson.msp@parliament.scot
Regional office: No regional office publicised
Website: grahamsimpson.org.uk Twitter: @GrahamSMSP

SMITH, Ms Elaine *Lab* **Central Scotland**
Scottish Labour Parliamentary Business Manager and Shadow Cabinet Secretary for the Eradication of Poverty and Social Inequality
Tel: 0131-348 5824 Email: elaine.smith.msp@parliament.scot
Regional office: Unit 32, Coatbridge Business Centre, 204 Main Street, Coatbridge ML5 3RB
Tel: 01236 423555 Twitter: @elainesmithmsp

SMITH, Miss Liz *Con* **Mid Scotland and Fife**
Scottish Conservatives Shadow Cabinet Secretary for Environment, Climate Change and Land Reform
Tel: 0131-348 6762 Fax: 0131-348 6764 Email: elizabeth.smith.msp@parliament.scot
Regional office: Control Tower, Perth Airport, Scone, Perth PH2 6PL
Tel: 01738 553990 Fax: 01738 553967 Email: pkconservatives@gmail.com
Website: www.ospconservatives.com Twitter: @MSPliz

SMYTH, Mr Colin *Lab* **South Scotland**
Scottish Labour Shadow Cabinet Secretary for Rural Economy, Transport and Connectivity
Tel: 0131-348 6986 Email: colin.smyth.msp@parliament.scot
Regional office: 17 Buccleuch Street, Dumfries DG1 2AT
Tel: 01387 279205 Twitter: @ColinSmythMSP

SOMERVILLE, Ms Shirley-Anne *SNP* **Dunfermline**
Cabinet Secretary for Social Security and Older People
Tel: 0131-348 5778 Email: shirley-anne.somerville.msp@parliament.scot
Ministerial office: St Andrew's House, Regent Road, Edinburgh EH1 3DG
Tel: 0300 244 4000
Constituency office: 34 Chalmers Street, Dunfermline KY12 8DF
Tel: 01383 249200 Twitter: @s_a_somerville

STEVENSON, Mr Stewart *SNP* **Banffshire and Buchan Coast**
Email: stewart.stevenson.msp@parliament.scot
Constituency office: No constituency office publicised
Tel: 01779 470444
Website: www.stewartstevenson.scot Twitter: @zsstevens

STEWART, Mr Alexander, MBE *Con* **Mid Scotland and Fife**
Scottish Conservatives Shadow Minister for Local Government, Housing and Planning
Tel: 0131-348 6134 Email: alexander.stewart.msp@parliament.scot
Regional office: 31 Canmore Street, Dunfermline KY12 5NU
Tel: 01383 720530

STEWART, Mr David *Lab/Co-op* **Highlands and Islands**
Tel: 0131-348 5766 Email: david.stewart.msp@parliament.scot
Regional office: 3 Gordon Terrace, Inverness IV2 3HD
Tel: 01463 716299 Twitter: @Davidstewartmsp

STEWART, Mr Kevin *SNP* **Aberdeen Central**
Minister for Local Government, Housing and Planning
Tel: 0131-348 6382 Email: kevin.stewart.msp@parliament.scot
Ministerial office: St Andrew's House, Regent Road, Edinburgh EH1 3DG
Tel: 0300 244 4000
Constituency office: Third Floor, 27 John Street, Aberdeen AB25 1BT
Tel: 01224 624719 Twitter: @KevinStewartSNP

STURGEON, Rt Hon Nicola *SNP* **Glasgow Southside**
First Minister of Scotland; Leader, Scottish National Party
Tel: 0131-348 5695 Email: nicola.sturgeon.msp@parliament.scot
Ministerial office: St Andrew's House, Regent Road, Edinburgh EH1 3DG
Tel: 0300 244 4000
Constituency office: Unit 3, Govanhill Workspace, 69 Dixon Road, Glasgow G42 8AT
Tel: 0141-424 1174 Twitter: @nicolasturgeon

SWINNEY, Mr John *SNP* **Perthshire North**
Deputy First Minister and Cabinet Secretary for Education and Skills
Tel: 0131-348 5717 Email: john.swinney.msp@parliament.scot
Ministerial office: St Andrew's House, Regent Road, Edinburgh EH1 3DG
Tel: 0300 244 4000
Constituency office: 17-19 Leslie Street, Blairgowrie PH10 6AH
Tel: 01250 876576
Website: www.johnswinney.scot Twitter: @johnswinney

TODD, Ms Maree *SNP* **Highlands and Islands**
Minister for Children and Young People
Email: maree.todd.msp@parliament.scot
Ministerial office: St Andrew's House, Regent Road, Edinburgh EH1 3DG
Tel: 0300 244 4000
Regional office: 12 High Street, Dingwall, Ross-Shire IV15 9RU
Tel: 01349 863888
Website: www.mareetodd.scot Twitter: @MareeToddMSP

TOMKINS, Prof Adam *Con* **Glasgow**
Convener, Parliamentary Committee on Justice
Tel: 0131-348 5963 Email: adam.tomkins.msp@parliament.scot
Regional office: 1018 Maryhill Road, Glasgow G20 9TE
Tel: 0141-946 3335 Twitter: @ProfTomkins

TORRANCE, Mr David *SNP* **Kirkcaldy**
Tel: 0131-348 6892 Email: david.torrance.msp@parliament.scot
Constituency office: 53 Kirk Wynd, Kirkcaldy, Fife KY1 1EH
Tel: 01592 200349
Website: davidtorrancemsp.scot Twitter: @DavidHTorrance

WATT, Ms Maureen *SNP* **Aberdeen South and North Kincardine**
Tel: 0131-348 6675 Email: maureen.watt.msp@parliament.scot
Constituency office: 51 Victoria Road, Torry, Aberdeen AB11 9LS
Tel: 01224 876743 Twitter: @maureenSNP

WELLS, Ms Annie *Con* **Glasgow**
Scottish Conservatives Shadow Cabinet Secretary for Communities and Local Government
Tel: 0131-348 5990 Email: annie.wells.msp@parliament.scot
Regional office: 1018 Maryhill Road, Glasgow G20 9TE
Tel: 0141-945 6465
Website: anniewellsmsp.co.uk Twitter: @AnnieWellsMSP

WHEELHOUSE, Mr Paul *SNP* **South Scotland**
Minister for Energy, Connectivity and the Islands
Tel: 0131-348 6891 Email: paul.wheelhouse.msp@parliament.scot
Ministerial office: St Andrew's House, Regent Road, Edinburgh EH1 3DG
Tel: 0300 244 4000
Regional office: 8 Sandbed, Hawick, Roxburghshire TD9 0HE
Tel: 01450 379572
Website: www.paul-wheelhouse.scot Twitter: @paulwheelhouse

WHITE, Ms Sandra *SNP* **Glasgow Kelvin**
Tel: 0131-348 5688 Fax: 0131-348 5945 Email: sandra.white.msp@parliament.scot
Constituency office: 1274 Argyle Street, Glasgow G3 8AA
Tel: 0141-339 7693
Website: sandrawhitemsp.scot Twitter: @sandrawhitesnp

WHITTLE, Mr Brian *Con* **South Scotland**
Scottish Conservatives Shadow Minister for Public Health, Mental Health, Sport and Wellbeing
Tel: 0131-348 5623 Email: brian.whittle.msp@parliament.scot
Regional office: 25 Portland Road, Kilmarnock KA1 2BT
Tel: 01563 544399
Website: www.brianwhittle.org.uk Twitter: @brianwhittle

WIGHTMAN, Mr Andy *Ind* **Lothian**
Tel: 07984 014368 Email: andy.wightman.msp@parliament.scot
Website: www.andywightman.scot Twitter: @andywightman

WISHART, Ms Beatrice *Lib Dem* **Shetland Islands**
Scottish Liberal Democrats Spokesperson for Education and Skills
Tel: 0131-348 6296 Email: beatrice.wishart.msp@parliament.scot
Constituency office: 171 Commercial Street, Lerwick ZE1 0HX Twitter: @BeatriceWishart

---

YOUSAF, Mr Humza *SNP* **Glasgow Pollok**
Cabinet Secretary for Justice
Tel: 0131-348 6209 Email: humza.yousaf.msp@parliament.scot
Ministerial office: St Andrew's House, Regent Road, Edinburgh EH1 3DG
Tel: 0300 244 4000
Constituency office: 1612-1614 Paisley Road West, Cardonald, Glasgow G52 3QN
Tel: 0141-882 4647
Website: www.humzayousaf.org Twitter: @humzayousaf

Women MSPs (47)

ADAMSON Clare	SNP
BAILLIE Jackie	Lab
BAKER Claire	Lab
BALLANTYNE Michelle	RefUK
BEAMISH Claudia	Lab/Co-op
BOYACK Sarah	Lab
CAMPBELL Aileen	SNP
CONSTANCE Angela	SNP
CUNNINGHAM Roseanna	SNP
DAVIDSON Ruth	Con
DENHAM Ash	SNP
EWING Annabelle	SNP
FABIANI Linda	SNP
FEE Mary	Lab
FORBES Kate	SNP
FREEMAN Jeane	SNP
GILRUTH Jenny	SNP
GOUGEON Mairi	SNP
GRAHAME Christine	SNP
GRANT Rhoda	Lab/Co-op
HAMILTON Rachael	Con
HARPER Emma	SNP
HARRIS Alison	Con
HAUGHEY Clare	SNP
HYSLOP Fiona	SNP
JOHNSTONE Alison	Green
LAMONT Johann	Lab/Co-op
LENNON Monica	Lab
MCALPINE Joan	SNP
MACKAY Rona	SNP
MCKELVIE Christina	SNP
MCNEILL Pauline	Lab
MAGUIRE Ruth	SNP
MARRA Jenny	Lab
MARTIN Gillian	SNP
MITCHELL Margaret	Con
ROBISON Shona	SNP
ROSS Gail	SNP

SMITH Elaine	Lab
SMITH Liz	Con
SOMERVILLE Shirley-Anne	SNP
STURGEON Nicola	SNP
TODD Maree	SNP
WATT Maureen	SNP
WELLS Annie	Con
WHITE Sandra	SNP
WISHART Beatrice	Lib Dem

Constituencies

			Majority	%
Aberdeen Central	Kevin Stewart	SNP	4,349	16.20
Aberdeen Donside	Mark McDonald	Ind*	11,630	37.40
Aberdeen South and North Kincardine	Maureen Watt	SNP	2,755	8.48
Aberdeenshire East	Gillian Martin	SNP	5,837	16.74
Aberdeenshire West	Alexander Burnett	Con	900	2.55
Airdrie and Shotts	Alex Neil	SNP	6,192	23.21
Almond Valley	Angela Constance	SNP	8,393	23.98
Angus North and Mearns	Mairi Gougeon	SNP	2,472	8.38
Angus South	Graeme Dey	SNP	4,304	13.43
Argyll and Bute	Michael Russell	SNP	5,978	20.20
Ayr	John Scott	Con	750	1.99
Banffshire and Buchan Coast	Stewart Stevenson	SNP	6,583	22.84
Caithness, Sutherland and Ross	Gail Ross	SNP	3,913	12.10
Carrick, Cumnock and Doon Valley	Jeane Freeman	SNP	6,006	18.89
Clackmannanshire and Dunblane	Keith Brown	SNP	6,721	22.51
Clydebank and Milngavie	Gil Paterson	SNP	8,432	25.58
Clydesdale	Aileen Campbell	SNP	5,979	17.69
Coatbridge and Chryston	Fulton MacGregor	SNP	3,779	13.30
Cowdenbeath	Annabelle Ewing	SNP	3,041	10.21
Cumbernauld and Kilsyth	Jamie Hepburn	SNP	9,478	33.37
Cunninghame North	Kenneth Gibson	SNP	8,724	27.16
Cunninghame South	Ruth Maguire	SNP	5,693	22.07
Dumbarton	Jackie Baillie	Lab	109	0.32
Dumfriesshire	Oliver Mundell	Con	1,230	3.38
Dundee City East	Shona Robison	SNP	10,898	38.18
Dundee City West	Joe FitzPatrick	SNP	8,828	31.64
Dunfermline	Shirley-Anne Somerville	SNP	4,558	13.84
East Kilbride	Linda Fabiani	SNP	10,979	31.58
Eastwood	Jackson Carlaw	Con	1,610	4.43
Edinburgh Central	Ruth Davidson	Con	610	1.78
Edinburgh Eastern	Ash Denham	SNP	5,087	14.28
Edinburgh Northern and Leith	Ben Macpherson	SNP	6,746	18.06
Edinburgh Pentlands	Gordon MacDonald	SNP	2,456	7.33
Edinburgh Southern	Daniel Johnson	Lab	1,123	2.92
Edinburgh Western	Alexander Cole-Hamilton	Lib Dem	2,960	7.42
Ettrick, Roxburgh and Berwickshire	Rachael Hamilton	Con	9,338	24.16
Falkirk East	Angus MacDonald	SNP	8,312	25.47
Falkirk West	Michael Matheson	SNP	11,280	35.03
Mid Fife and Glenrothes	Jenny Gilruth	SNP	8,276	28.92
North East Fife	Willie Rennie	Lib Dem	3,465	10.14
Galloway and West Dumfries	Finlay Carson	Con	1,514	4.53
Glasgow Anniesland	Bill Kidd	SNP	6,153	21.07
Glasgow Cathcart	James Dornan	SNP	9,390	30.47
Glasgow Kelvin	Sandra White	SNP	4,048	14.18
Glasgow Maryhill and Springburn	Bob Doris	SNP	5,602	23.59

*Elected as Scottish National Party

			Majority	*%*
Glasgow Pollok	Humza Yousaf	SNP	6,482	23.08
Glasgow Provan	Ivan McKee	SNP	4,783	19.73
Glasgow Shettleston	John Mason	SNP	7,323	28.71
Glasgow Southside	Nicola Sturgeon	SNP	9,593	38.09
Greenock and Inverclyde	Stuart McMillan	SNP	8,230	25.85
Hamilton, Larkhall and Stonehouse	Christina McKelvie	SNP	5,437	18.75
Inverness and Nairn	Fergus Ewing	SNP	10,857	28.17
Kilmarnock and Irvine Valley	Willie Coffey	SNP	11,194	32.45
Kirkcaldy	David Torrance	SNP	7,395	23.65
Linlithgow	Fiona Hyslop	SNP	9,335	24.22
East Lothian	Iain Gray	Lab	1,127	2.96
Midlothian North and Musselburgh	Colin Beattie	SNP	7,035	20.20
Midlothian South, Tweeddale and Lauderdale	Christine Grahame	SNP	5,868	16.42
Moray	Richard Lochhead	SNP	2,875	8.57
Motherwell and Wishaw	Clare Adamson	SNP	6,223	21.28
Na h-Eileanan an Iar	Alasdair Allan	SNP	3,496	26.36
Orkney Islands	Liam McArthur	Lib Dem	4,534	42.93
Paisley	George Adam	SNP	5,199	17.57
Perthshire North	John Swinney	SNP	3,336	9.77
Perthshire South and Kinross-shire	Roseanna Cunningham	SNP	1,422	3.92
Renfrewshire North and West	Derek Mackay	Ind*	7,373	23.88
Renfrewshire South	Tom Arthur	SNP	4,408	14.79
Rutherglen	Clare Haughey	SNP	3,743	11.31
Shetland Islands	Beatrice Wishart	Lib Dem	1,837	15.52
Skye, Lochaber and Badenoch	Kate Forbes	SNP	9,043	24.68
Stirling	Bruce Crawford	SNP	6,718	19.58
Strathkelvin and Bearsden	Rona Mackay	SNP	8,100	20.58
Uddingston and Bellshill	Richard Lyle	SNP	4,809	16.18

Regions

			Count elected on
Central Scotland	Mark Griffin	Lab	4
Central Scotland	Alison Harris	Con	7
Central Scotland	Monica Lennon	Lab	3
Central Scotland	Richard Leonard	Lab	1
Central Scotland	Margaret Mitchell	Con	2
Central Scotland	Graham Simpson	Con	5
Central Scotland	Elaine Smith	Lab	6
Glasgow	Patrick Harvie	Green	4
Glasgow	James Kelly	Lab/Co-op	5
Glasgow	Johann Lamont	Lab/Co-op	2
Glasgow	Pauline McNeill	Lab	6
Glasgow	Anas Sarwar	Lab	1
Glasgow	Adam Tomkins	Con	3
Glasgow	Annie Wells	Con	7
Highlands and Islands	Donald Cameron	Con	4
Highlands and Islands	John Finnie	Green	5
Highlands and Islands	Rhoda Grant	Lab/Co-op	2
Highlands and Islands	Jamie Halcro Johnston	Con	–
Highlands and Islands	Edward Mountain	Con	3
Highlands and Islands	David Stewart	Lab/Co-op	7
Highlands and Islands	Maree Todd	SNP	6

*Elected as Scottish National Party

Devolved Parliament and Assemblies

			Count elected on
Lothian	Jeremy Balfour	Con	6
Lothian	Sarah Boyack	Lab	–
Lothian	Miles Briggs	Con	1
Lothian	Neil Findlay	Lab	5
Lothian	Alison Johnstone	Green	2
Lothian	Gordon Lindhurst	Con	4
Lothian	Andy Wightman	Ind*	7
Mid Scotland and Fife	Claire Baker	Lab	4
Mid Scotland and Fife	Murdo Fraser	Con	1
Mid Scotland and Fife	Dean Lockhart	Con	5
Mid Scotland and Fife	Alex Rowley	Lab	2
Mid Scotland and Fife	Mark Ruskell	Green	7
Mid Scotland and Fife	Liz Smith	Con	3
Mid Scotland and Fife	Alexander Stewart	Con	6
North East Scotland	Bill Bowman	Con	–
North East Scotland	Peter Chapman	Con	4
North East Scotland	Liam Kerr	Con	7
North East Scotland	Lewis Macdonald	Lab	5
North East Scotland	Jenny Marra	Lab	2
North East Scotland	Tom Mason	Con	–
North East Scotland	Mike Rumbles	Lib Dem	6
South Scotland	Michelle Ballantyne	RefUK†	–
South Scotland	Claudia Beamish	Lab/Co-op	1
South Scotland	Emma Harper	SNP	4
South Scotland	Joan McAlpine	SNP	2
South Scotland	Colin Smyth	Lab	5
South Scotland	Paul Wheelhouse	SNP	6
South Scotland	Brian Whittle	Con	7
West Scotland	Neil Bibby	Lab/Co-op	1
West Scotland	Maurice Corry	Con	6
West Scotland	Mary Fee	Lab	3
West Scotland	Maurice Golden	Con	4
West Scotland	Jamie Greene	Con	2
West Scotland	Ross Greer	Green	7
West Scotland	Ken Macintosh	Pres Off	5

*Elected as Green Party
†Elected as Conservative

Parliamentary Committees

Conveners Group

The Conveners Group comprises the conveners of the mandatory and subject committees of the Parliament but is not itself a Parliamentary committee.

Tel: 0131-348 5202
Email: vikki.little@parliament.scot
www.scottish.parliament.uk/parliamentarybusiness/21516.aspx

Ken Macintosh (Convener) *Pres Off*
Clare Adamson *SNP*
Bill Bowman *Con*
Donald Cameron *Con*
Bruce Crawford *SNP*
Bob Doris *SNP*
James Dornan *SNP*
Bill Kidd *SNP*
Johann Lamont *Lab/Co-op*
Joan McAlpine *SNP*
Lewis Macdonald *Lab*
Ruth Maguire *SNP*
Jenny Marra *Lab*
Gillian Martin *SNP*
Edward Mountain *Con*
Anas Sarwar *Lab*
Adam Tomkins *Con*

Staff: Susan Duffy (Clerk)

Mandatory Committees

Culture, Tourism, Europe and External Affairs

Tel: 0131-348 5234
Email: europe@parliament.scot
www.parliament.scot/parliamentarybusiness/currentcommittees/european-committee.aspx
Twitter: @SP_European

Joan McAlpine (Convener) *SNP*
Claire Baker (Deputy Convener) *Lab*
Kenneth Gibson *SNP*
Christine Grahame *SNP*
Ross Greer *Green*
Jamie Halcro Johnston *Con*
Dean Lockhart *Con*
Stewart Stevenson *SNP*
Beatrice Wishart *Lib Dem*

Staff: Stephen Herbert (Clerk)

Delegated Powers and Law Reform

Tel: 0131-348 5212
Email: dplr.committee@parliament.scot
www.parliament.scot/parliamentarybusiness/currentcommittees/delegated-powers-committee.aspx Twitter: @SP_subleg

Bill Bowman (Convener) *Con*
Gil Paterson (Deputy Convener) *SNP*
Michelle Ballantyne *RefUK*
Neil Bibby *Lab/Co-op*
Mary Fee *Lab*
Joe FitzPatrick *SNP*
Alex Neil *SNP*

Staff: Andrew Proudfoot (Clerk)

Equalities and Human Rights

Tel: 0131-348 6040
Email: equalities.humanrights@parliament.scot
www.parliament.scot/parliamentarybusiness/currentcommittees/equalities-human-rights-committee.aspx Twitter: @SP_EHRiC

Ruth Maguire (Convener) *SNP*
Alexander Cole-Hamilton (Deputy Convener) *Lib Dem*
Mary Fee *Lab*
Joe FitzPatrick *SNP*
Alison Harris *Con*
Gillian Martin *SNP*
Alexander Stewart *Con*

Staff: Claire Menzies (Clerk)

Finance and Constitution

Tel: 0131-348 5215
Email: finance.constitution@parliament.scot
www.parliament.scot/parliamentarybusiness/currentcommittees/finance-constitution-committee.aspx Twitter: @SP_FinCon

Bruce Crawford (Convener) *SNP*
Murdo Fraser (Deputy Convener) *Con*
Alasdair Allan *SNP*
Tom Arthur *SNP*
Jackie Baillie *Lab*
Alexander Burnett *Con*
Patrick Harvie *Green*
Dean Lockhart *Con*
Fulton MacGregor *SNP*
John Mason *SNP*
Anas Sarwar *Lab*

Staff: Jim Johnston (Clerk)

Public Audit and Post-Legislative Scrutiny

Tel: 0131-348 5390
Email: papls.committee@parliament.scot
www.parliament.scot/parliamentarybusiness/currentcommittees/public-audit-committee.aspx
Twitter: @SP_PAPLS

Jenny Marra (Convener) *Lab*
Graham Simpson (Deputy Convener) *Con*
Colin Beattie *SNP*
Neil Bibby *Lab/Co-op*

Bill Bowman *Con*
Alex Neil *SNP*
Gail Ross *SNP*
Staff: Lucy Scharbert (Clerk)

Public Petitions
Tel: 0131-348 5254
Email: petitions@parliament.scot
www.parliament.scot/parliamentarybusiness/currentcommittees/petitions-committee.aspx
Twitter: @sp_petitions

Johann Lamont (Convener) *Lab/Co-op*
Gail Ross (Deputy Convener) *SNP*
Maurice Corry *Con*
Tom Mason *Con*
David Torrance *SNP*

Staff: Lynn Rusell (Clerk)

Standards, Procedures and Public Appointments
Tel: 0131-348 6924
Email: sppa.committee@parliament.scot
www.parliament.scot/parliamentarybusiness/currentcommittees/standards-committee.aspx

Bill Kidd (Convener) *SNP*
Patrick Harvie (Deputy Convener) *Green*
Neil Findlay *Lab*
Oliver Mundell *Con*
Gil Paterson *SNP*
John Scott *Con*
Maureen Watt *SNP*
Staff: Katy Orr (Clerk)

Subject Committees

Economy, Energy and Fair Work
Tel: 0131-348 5403
Email: economyjobsandfairwork@parliament.scot
www.parliament.scot/parliamentarybusiness/currentcommittees/economy-committee.aspx
Twitter: @SP_Economy

Gordon Lindhurst (Convener) *Con*
Willie Coffey (Deputy Convener) *SNP*
Colin Beattie *SNP*
Maurice Golden *Con*
Richard Lyle *SNP*
Gordon MacDonald *SNP*
Alex Rowley *Lab*
Graham Simpson *Con*
Andy Wightman *Ind*
Staff: Alison Walker (Clerk)

Education and Skills
Tel: 0131-348 5204
Email: es.committee@parliament.scot
www.parliament.scot/parliamentarybusiness/currentcommittees/education-committee.aspx
Twitter: @SP_EduSkills

Clare Adamson (Convener) *SNP*
Daniel Johnson (Deputy Convener) *Lab*
George Adam *SNP*
Kenneth Gibson *SNP*
Iain Gray *Lab*
Jamie Greene *Con*
Ross Greer *Green*
Rona Mackay *SNP*
Oliver Mundell *Con*
Alex Neil *SNP*
Beatrice Wishart *Lib Dem*
Staff: Gary Cocker (Clerk)

Environment, Climate Change and Land Reform
Tel: 0131-348 5242
Email: ecclr.committee@parliament.scot
www.parliament.scot/parliamentarybusiness/currentcommittees/environment-committee.aspx
Twitter: @SP_ECCLR

Gillian Martin (Convener) *SNP*
Finlay Carson (Deputy Convener) *Con*
Claudia Beamish *Lab/Co-op*
Angus MacDonald *SNP*
Mark Ruskell *Green*
Liz Smith *Con*
Stewart Stevenson *SNP*
Staff: Lynn Tullis (Clerk)

Health and Sport
Tel: 0131-348 5224
Email: healthandsport@parliament.scot
www.parliament.scot/parliamentarybusiness/currentcommittees/health-committee.aspx
Twitter: @sp_healthsport

Lewis Macdonald (Convener) *Lab*
Emma Harper (Deputy Convener) *SNP*
George Adam *SNP*
Donald Cameron *Con*
Alexander Cole-Hamilton *Lib Dem*
David Stewart *Lab/Co-op*
David Torrance *SNP*
Sandra White *SNP*
Brian Whittle *Con*
Staff: David Cullum (Clerk)

Justice
Tel: 0131-348 5047
Email: justicecommittee@parliament.scot
www.parliament.scot/parliamentarybusiness/currentcommittees/justice-committee.aspx

Twitter: @SP_Justice

Adam Tomkins (Convener) *Con*
Rona Mackay (Deputy Convener) *SNP*
Annabelle Ewing *SNP*
John Finnie *Green*
Rhoda Grant *Lab/Co-op*
Liam Kerr *Con*
Liam McArthur *Lib Dem*
Fulton MacGregor *SNP*
Shona Robison *SNP*

Staff: Stephen Imrie (Clerk)

Justice Sub-committee on Policing

Tel: 0131-348 5220
Email: justice.committee@scottish.parliament.uk
www.parliament.scot/parliamentarybusiness/currentcommittees/policing-sub-committee.aspx

John Finnie (Convener) *Green*
Margaret Mitchell (Deputy Convener) *Con*
Rhoda Grant *Lab/Co-op*
James Kelly *Lab/Co-op*
Liam McArthur *Lib Dem*
Fulton MacGregor *SNP*
Rona Mackay *SNP*
Shona Robison *SNP*

Staff: Diane Barr (Clerk)

Local Government and Communities

Tel: 0131-348 5206
Email: localgovernmentandcommunities@parliament.scot
www.parliament.scot/parliamentarybusiness/currentcommittees/local-govt-committee.aspx
Twitter: @SP_LocalGovt

James Dornan (Convener) *SNP*
Sarah Boyack (Deputy Convener) *Lab*
Keith Brown *SNP*
Gordon MacDonald *SNP*
Alexander Stewart *Con*
Annie Wells *Con*
Andy Wightman *Ind*

Staff: Peter McGrath (Clerk)

Rural Economy and Connectivity

Tel: 0131-348 5211
Email: rec.committee@parliament.scot
www.parliament.scot/parliamentarybusiness/currentcommittees/rural-economy-committee.aspx Twitter: @SP_RECcttee

Edward Mountain (Convener) *Con*
Maureen Watt (Deputy Convener) *SNP*
Peter Chapman *Con*
John Finnie *Green*
Jamie Halcro Johnston *Con*
Rachael Hamilton *Con*
Emma Harper *SNP*
Richard Lyle *SNP*
Angus MacDonald *SNP*
Mike Rumbles *Lib Dem*
Colin Smyth *Lab*
Stewart Stevenson *SNP*

Staff: Steve Farrell (Clerk)

Social Security

Tel: 0131-348 5320
Email: socialsecuritycommittee@parliament.scot
www.parliament.scot/parliamentarybusiness/currentcommittees/social-security-committee.aspx Twitter: @SP_SocialSecur

Bob Doris (Convener) *SNP*
Pauline McNeill (Deputy Convener) *Lab*
Tom Arthur *SNP*
Jeremy Balfour *Con*
Keith Brown *SNP*
Mark Griffin *Lab*
Rachael Hamilton *Con*
Alison Johnstone *Green*
Shona Robison *SNP*

Staff: Anne Peat (Clerk)

Scottish Commission for Public Audit

The Scottish Commission for Public Audit is not formally a parliamentary committee. The Commission was established under section 12 of the Public Finance and Accountability (Scotland) Act 2000 and is made up of five MSPs.

Tel: 0131-348 5205
Email: scpa@parliament.scot
www.parliament.scot/parliamentarybusiness/101154.aspx

Colin Beattie (Convener) *SNP*
Bill Bowman *Con*
Alison Johnstone *Green*
Rona Mackay *SNP*
Jenny Marra *Lab*
Anas Sarwar *Lab*

Staff: Jane Williams (Secretary)

Principal Officers and Officials

Office of the Presiding Officer
Presiding Officer Rt Hon **Ken Macintosh**

Principal Private Secretary	Joanne McNaughton 0131-348 5302 Email: joanne.mcnaughton@parliament.scot

Deputy Presiding Officers **Linda Fabiani** MSP (SNP), **Christine Grahame** MSP (SNP), **Lewis Macdonald** MSP (Lab)

Scottish Parliamentary Corporate Body
(responsible for administration)

Chair	Rt Hon Ken Macintosh (Pres Off)
Members	Jackson Carlaw CBE (Con) Liam McArthur (Lib Dem) David Stewart (Lab/Co-op) Sandra White (SNP) Andy Wightman (Ind)

Secretariat

Officer	Judith Proudfoot 0131-348 5307 Email: judith.proudfoot@parliament.scot

Parliamentary Bureau
(responsible for all-party business programme and forward planning)

Chair	Rt Hon Ken Macintosh (Pres Off)
Members	Miles Briggs (Con) Graeme Dey (SNP) Patrick Harvie (Green) Willie Rennie (Lib Dem) Elaine Smith (Lab)

Leadership Group

Clerk/Chief Executive	David McGill
Heads	
Legal Services and Audit	Judith Morrison 0131-348 6649 Email: judith.morrison@parliament.scot
Procurement, Business Continuity and Security	Lynsey Hamill 0131-348 6790 Email: lynsey.hamill@parliament.scot
Assistant Clerk/Chief Executive	Michelle Hegarty 0131-348 6070 Email: michelle.hegarty@parliament.scot
Heads	
Human Resources and Digital Services	Alan Balharrie 0131-348 6535 Email: alan.balharrie@parliament.scot
Facilities Management, Visitor Services, Events and Exhibitions	Colin Chisholm 0131-348 6630 Email: colin.chisholm@parliament.scot
Financial Resources	To be appointed
Research, Communications and Public Engagement	Callum Thomson 0131-348 5253 Email: callum.thomson@parliament.scot
Committees and Outreach	Susan Duffy 0131-348 5201 Email: susan.duffy@parliament.scot
Chamber, Reporting and Broadcasting	Tracey White 0131-348 5173 Email: tracey.white@parliament.scot

Scottish Government Civil Service

Permanent Secretary's Office
St Andrew's House, Regent Road, Edinburgh EH1 3DG
Tel: 0131-556 8400/0845 774 1741 Email: permanentsecretary@gov.scot Website: www.gov.scot
Twitter: @PermSecScot

Permanent Secretary: Leslie Evans 0131-244 4176 Email: permanentsecretary@gov.scot

Constitution and External Affairs
St Andrew's House, Regent Road, Edinburgh EH1 3DG
Tel: 0131-244 4000 Email: dgcea@gov.scot Twitter: @ScotGovInter

Director-General: Ken Thomson 0131-244 6923 Email: dgcea@gov.scot

Economy
St Andrew's House, Regent Road, Edinburgh EH1 3DG
Tel: 0131-244 5598 Email: dgeconomy@gov.scot Twitter: @scotgoveconomy/@scotgovocea

Director-General: Liz Ditchburn 0131-244 5598 Email: dgeconomy@gov.scot

Education, Communities and Justice
St Andrew's House, Regent Road, Edinburgh EH1 3DG
Tel: 0131-244 2814 Email: dgecj@gov.scot

Director-General: Paul Johnston 0131-244 2814 Email: dgecj@gov.scot

Health and Social Care
St Andrew's House, Regent Road, Edinburgh EH1 3DG
Tel: 0131-244 2790 Email: dghsc@gov.scot Twitter: @scotgovhealth

Chief Executive of NHS Scotland: John Connaghan CBE 0131 244 2480
Email: john.connaghan@gov.scot
Director-General: Elinor Mitchell 0131-244 7978 Email: elinor.mitchell@gov.scot

Organisational Development and Operations
St Andrews House, Regent Road, Edinburgh EH1 3DG
Tel: 0131-244 6021 Email: dgodo@gov.scot

Director-General: Lesley Fraser 0131-244 6021 Email: dgodo@gov.scot

Scottish Exchequer
Victoria Quay, Edinburgh EH6 6QQ
Tel: 0131-244 4000 Email: dgscottishexchequer@gov.scot

Director-General: Alyson Stafford CBE 0131-244 5692 Email: dgscottishexchequer@gov.scot

Crown Office and Procurator Fiscal Service
25 Chambers Street, Edinburgh EH1 1LA
Tel: 0300 020 3000 Email: enquirypoint@copfs.gov.uk Website: www.copfs.gov.uk
Twitter: @COPFS

Crown Agent and Chief Executive: David Harvie Email: psceca@copfs.gov.uk

Executive Agencies

Accountant in Bankruptcy
1 Pennyburn Road, Kilwinning KA13 6SA
Tel: 0300 200 2600 Fax: 0300 200 2601 Email: aib@aib.gov.uk Website: www.aib.gov.uk
Twitter: @AiB_updates

Chief Executive: Dr Richard Dennis 0300 200 2900 Email: ce@aib.gov.uk
Sponsored by: Economy, Scottish Government

Disclosure Scotland

1 Pacific Quay, Glasgow G51 1DZ
Tel: 0300 020 0040 Email: info@disclosurescotland.gov.scot
Website: www.mygov.scot/organisations/disclosure-scotland Twitter: @disclosurescot
PO Box 250, Glasgow G51 1YU
Chief Executive: Gerard Hart Email: dsadmin@disclosurescotland.gov.scot
Sponsored by: Education, Communities and Justice, Scottish Government

Education Scotland

Denholm House, Almondvale Business Park, Almondvale Way, Livingston EH54 6GA
Tel: 0131-244 4330 Email: enquiries@educationscotland.gov.scot Website: education.gov.scot
Twitter: @EducationScot
Chief Executive: Gayle Gorman 0131-244 4131 Email: gayle.gorman@educationscotland.gov.scot
Sponsored by: Education, Communities and Justice, Scottish Government

Scottish Prison Service

Calton House, 5 Redheughs Rigg, Edinburgh EH12 9HW
Tel: 0131-330 3500 Email: gaolinfo@sps.pnn.gov.uk Website: www.sps.gov.uk
Twitter: @scottishprisons
Chief Executive: Teresa Medhurst 0131-330 3601 Email: sharon.lawson@sps.pnn.gov.uk
Sponsored by: Education, Communities and Justice, Scottish Government

Scottish Public Pensions Agency

7 Tweedside Park, Tweedbank, Galashiels TD1 3TE
Tel: 01896 893000 Fax: 01896 893214 Email: sppacontactus@gov.scot Website: www.sppa.gov.uk
Chief Executive: Penelope Cooper 01896 893202 Email: sppachiefexecutive@gov.scot
Sponsored by: Organisational Development and Operations, Scottish Government

Student Awards Agency Scotland

Saughton House, Broomhouse Drive, Edinburgh EH11 3UT
Tel: 0300 555 0505 Email: saasce@gov.scot Website: www.saas.gov.uk Twitter: @saastweet
Chief Executive: David Robb 0131-244 5867 Email: saasce@gov.scot
Sponsored by: Education, Communities and Justice, Scottish Government

Transport Scotland

Buchanan House, 58 Port Dundas Road, Glasgow G4 0HF
Tel: 0141-272 7100 Email: info@transport.gov.scot Website: www.transport.gov.scot
Twitter: @transcotland
Chief Executive: Roy Brannen 0141-272 7110 Email: chiefexecutive@transport.gov.scot
Sponsored by: Economy, Scottish Government

Non-Ministerial Departments

Food Standards Scotland

Fourth Floor, Pilgrim House, Aberdeen AB11 5RL
Tel: 01224 285100 Email: enquiries@fss.scot Website: foodstandards.gov.scot Twitter: @fsscot
Chair: Ross Finnie
Chief Executive: Geoff Ogle

National Records of Scotland

HM General Register House, 2 Princes Street, Edinburgh EH1 3YY
Tel: 0131-535 1314 Email: rg-keeper@nrscotland.gov.uk Website: www.nrscotland.gov.uk
Twitter: @NatRecordsScot

Ladywell House, Ladywell Road, Edinburgh EH12 7TF
Tel: 0131-334 0380

Keeper of the Records of Scotland: Paul Lowe Email: rg-keeper@nrscotland.gov.uk

Registers of Scotland

Meadowbank House, 153 London Road, Edinburgh EH8 7AU
Tel: 0800 169 9391 Email: customer.services@ros.gov.uk Website: www.ros.gov.uk
Twitter: @registersofscot

Chief Executive and Keeper: Jennifer Henderson 0131-357 8199 Email: rossecretariat@ros.gov.uk

Revenue Scotland

PO Box 24068, Victoria Quay, Edinburgh EH6 9BR
Tel: 0300 020 0310 Email: info@revenue.scot Website: www.revenue.scot
Twitter: @revenuescotland

Chair: Dr Keith Nicholson
Chief Executive: Elaine Lorimer 0300 020 0310 Email: info@revenue.scot

Office of the Scottish Charity Regulator

Second Floor, Quadrant House, 9 Riverside Drive, Dundee DD1 4NY
Tel: 01382 220446 Fax: 01382 220314 Email: info@oscr.org.uk Website: www.oscr.org.uk
Twitter: @ScotCharityReg

Chair: Lindsay Montgomery CBE
Chief Executive: Maureen Mallon Email: maureen.mallon@oscr.org.uk

Scottish Courts and Tribunal Service

Saughton House, Broomhouse Drive, Edinburgh EH11 3XD
Tel: 0131-444 3352 Fax: 0131-443 2610 Email: enquiries@scotcourts.gov.uk
Website: www.scotcourts.gov.uk Twitter: @SCTScourtstribs

Chair: Rt Hon Lord Colin Carloway 0131-240 6701 Email: lppo@scotcourts.gov.uk
Chief Executive: Eric McQueen 0131-244 3306 Email: emcqueen@scotcourts.gov.uk

Scottish Fiscal Commission

Governor's House, Regent Road, Edinburgh EH1 3DE
Tel: 0131-244 0738 Email: info@fiscalcommission.scot Website: www.fiscalcommission.scot
Twitter: @scotfisccomm

Chair: Dame Susan Rice DBE Email: susan.rice@fiscalcommission.scot
Chief Executive: John Ireland Email: john.ireland@fiscalcommission.scot

Scottish Housing Regulator

Buchanan House, 58 Port Dundas Road, Glasgow G4 0HF
Tel: 0141-242 5642 Email: shr@shr.gov.scot Website: www.housingregulator.gov.scot
Twitter: @SHR_news

Chief Executive: Michael Cameron Email: sharon.campbell@shr.gov.scot
Chair: George Walker Email: shr@shr.gov.scot

Political Parties

Scottish National Party

Gordon Lamb House, 3 Jackson's Entry, Edinburgh EH8 8PJ
Tel: 0800 633 5432 Email: info@snp.org Website: www.snp.org Twitter: @theSNP

Leader: Rt Hon Nicola Sturgeon MSP
Depute Leader: Keith Brown MSP
President: Ian Hudghton
Chief Executive: Peter Murrell 0131-525 8900 Email: peter.murrell@snp.org

Scottish Conservative and Unionist Party

67 Northumberland Street, Edinburgh EH3 6JG
Tel: 0131-524 0030 Website: www.scottishconservatives.com Twitter: @scottories

Leader: Douglas Ross MP
Chairman: Robert Forman MBE
Conference Convener: Richard Wilkinson
Director: Lord McInnes of Kilwinning CBE
Treasurer: Bryan Johnston
Director of Strategy and Communications: Eddie Barnes

Scottish Labour

290 Bath Street, Glasgow G2 4RE
Tel: 0141-572 6900 Email: scotland@labour.org.uk Website: www.scottishlabour.org.uk
Twitter: @scottishlabour

Leader: Jackie Baillie MSP
Chair: Cara Hilton
General Secretary: Drew Smith

Scottish Green Party

19b Graham Street, Edinburgh EH6 5QN
Tel: 0870 077 2207 Email: office@scottishgreens.org.uk Website: greens.scot Twitter: @scotgp

Co-leaders: Patrick Harvie MSP, Lorna Slater
Head of Media: Harry Huyten 0131 348 6360 Email: press@scottish.parliament.uk
Senior Party Administrator: Scott Lamb Email: scott@scottishgreens.org.uk
IT Officer: Stuart Leckie Email: stuart.leckie@scottishgreens.org.uk
Operations Manager: Pete Morrison Email: pete.morrison@scottishgreens.org.uk
Finance Officer: Louise Jaundrell Email: finance@scottishgreens.org.uk

Scottish Liberal Democrats

4 Clifton Terrace, Edinburgh EH12 5DR
Tel: 0131-337 2314 Email: hq@scotlibdems.org.uk Website: www.scotlibdems.org.uk
Twitter: @scotlibdems

Leader: Willie Rennie MSP
Deputy Leader: Rt Hon Alistair Carmichael MP
Convener: Sheila Ritchie
President: Willie Wilson
Party Manager: Jenny Wilson 0131-337 2314 Email: jenny.wilson@scotlibdems.org.uk
Chief of Staff, Scottish Parliament: Matthew Clark 0131-348 5818
Email: matthew.clark@parliament.scot
Press Officers: Katie Armour 0131-348 5812 Email: katie.armour@parliament.scot, Max Sefton
0131-348 5812 Email: max.sefton@parliament.scot

Welsh Government

Llywodraeth Cymru

Fifth Floor, Tŷ Hywel, Cardif Bay CF99 1NA
Switchboard: 0300 060 3300 Email: customerhelp@gov.wales
Website: www.gov.wales Twitter: @WelshGovernment

Cabinet

First Minister	**Mark Drakeford** (Lab)
Minister for Finance and Trefnydd	**Rebecca Evans** (Lab/Co-op)
Minister for Health and Social Services	**Vaughan Gething** (Lab/Co-op)
Minister for Environment, Energy and Rural Affairs	**Lesley Griffiths** (Lab)
Minister for Housing and Local Government	**Julie James** (Lab)
Counsel General and Minister for European Transition	**Jeremy Miles** (Lab/Co-op)
Minister for Mental Health, Wellbeing and Welsh Language	**Eluned Morgan** (Lab)
Minister for Economy, Transport and North Wales	**Ken Skates** (Lab)
Minister for Education	**Kirsty Williams** CBE (Lib Dem)

Ministerial Responsibilities and Staff

Office of the First Minister

First Minister Rt Hon **Mark Drakeford** MS (Lab)

Head of the Welsh Government; constitutional affairs, inter-governmental relations; international relations; Wales in Europe; Wales and Africa Programme; Welsh Government international offices; developing links with the Welsh Diaspora; legislative programme; Ministerial code; civil contingencies and resilience; openness in government; public appointments; justice.

Senior Special Adviser	Jane Runeckles Email: jane.runeckles@gov.wales	0300 025 8611
Principal Private Secretary	Carys Evans Email: carys.evans@gov.wales	0300 025 0952
Senior Private Secretary	Rebecca Lewis Email: ps.firstminister@gov.wales	0300 025 8764

Deputy Minister and Chief Whip **Jane Hutt** MS (Lab)

Well-being of Future Generations Act; equality and human rights; domestic abuse, gender-based violence and sexual violence; youth justice and community safety; the voluntary sector and volunteering; advice and advocacy services; relations with the police and other criminal justice agencies; relations with the UK government in respect of prisons and probation.

Private Secretary	Mandy Roberts Email: psdmcw@gov.wales	0300 025 8774

Finance and Trefnydd

Minister for Finance and Trefnydd **Rebecca Evans** MS (Lab/Co-op)

The Welsh Treasury; the Welsh Revenue Authority; provision of strategic direction and management of the resources of the Welsh Government; taxation policy; local taxation policy, Council Tax, non-domestic rates, council tax reduction and the sponsorship of the Valuation Office Agency and Valuation Tribunal Service; budget monitoring and management; strategic investment; Invest to Save; financial accounting and audit; in year budget monitoring and management; value for money and effectiveness; operation and development of the devolved funding settlement and the Statement of Funding Policy; National Procurement Service and Value Wales; acquisition, maintenance and disposal of property and other assets; co-ordination of National Statistics and the Census; management of Government business in the Senedd in line with standing orders; delivery of the weekly Business Statement; represent the government in Business Committee; liaison with other parties on the Government's Legislative Programme (not individual bills which remain the responsibility of the lead minister).

Special Adviser Alex Bevan 0300 025 9282
Email: alex.bevan@gov.wales

Senior Private Secretary Liz Matthews 0300 025 8467
Email: psmft@gov.wales

Health and Social Services

Minister for Health and Social Services **Vaughan Gething** MS (Lab/Co-op)

Public health: Covid-19 response, screening and vaccination; oversight of NHS delivery, performance, new outcome measures; scrutiny of NHS performance against 3-year plans; oversight of escalation procedures; receipt of, response to and direction of reports from Health Inspectorate Wales; oversight of Wales Audit Office (NHS); medical workforce training, exception of years 1-5 of university education for doctors; health innovation and digital; children's and young people's rights and entitlements, including UN Convention on Rights of the Child, the Children's Commissioner for Wales; childcare; Flying Start Initiative children 0-3; Families First, play policies; adoption, fostering services; children, young people's advocacy, including complaints, representations and advocacy under the Social Services and Well-being (Wales) Act 2014; information sharing under Children Act 2004; Cafcass Cymru; policy and oversight of the provision of social services activities of local authorities, including statutory guidance; oversight of Social Care Wales; regulation of residential, domiciliary, adult placements, foster care, under 8s' care provision, private healthcare in Wales; inspection of the provision of social services by local authorities (via Care Inspectorate Wales), including joint reviews and reports of social services; relationships with the Older Peoples' Commissioner for Wales.

Special Adviser Clare Jenkins
Email: clare.jenkins010@gov.wales

Senior Private Secretary Rory Powell 0300 025 8386
Email: psmhss@gov.wales

Deputy Minister for Health and Social Services **Julie Morgan** MS (Lab)

Supports the work of the Minister for Health and Social Services.

Private Secretary Ruth Parness 0300 025 9631
Email: psdmhss@gov.wales

Environment, Energy and Rural Affairs

Minister for Environment, Energy and Rural Affairs **Lesley Griffiths** MS (Lab)

Rural Development Programme; common agricultural policy direct payments, responsibility for cross-compliance; agriculture sector development, including wages and skills; developing agri-food sector, associated supply chains, promotion and marketing of food and drink from Wales; animal health and welfare; bovine TB eradication plan; policy on livestock, artificial insemination, poultry, companion animals, equines, bees; livestock identification, movement policy; holding registration policy (CPH); inland, coastal and sea fisheries: policy regulation and enforcement, including Common Fisheries Policy and management of fishery harbours; marine and fresh water planning, biodiversity, conservation and licensing; power to require provision of information about crop prices; best and most versatile land policy, mineral site restoration advice and Agricultural Land Classification and implementation of the EIA (Agriculture) Regulations; energy policy including small-medium scale energy production, domestic energy, energy efficiency and the reduction of fuel poverty; climate change, emission reduction targets, carbon budgets; national strategy and policy for Natural Resources Management, oversight and implementation of the Environment (Wales) Act and Natural Resources Wales; cross-cutting measures of mitigation and adaptation in relation to climate change, water; land drainage; flood and coastal risk; control of marine and air pollution; national strategy and policy for water; forestry policy and legislation, re-stocking, tree health and forest reproductive material; biodiversity policy, implementation of the Nature Recovery Plan; protection and management of wildlife in Wales, control of pests, injurious weeds, vermin and the regulation of plant health, seeds and pesticides; genetically modified crops; sustainable resource and waste management; allotments and urban green infrastructure; local Environment Quality, including litter, fly-tipping, noise policy and regulation; access to the countryside, coast and rights of way and Areas of Outstanding Natural Beauty and National Parks.

Private Secretary	To be appointed Email: psmeera@gov.wales

Housing and Local Government

Minister for Housing and Local Government **Julie James** MS (Lab)

Housing of local authorities, associations, management, allocation, including supply and quality of market, social and affordable housing; homelessness and housing advice, housing provided by private rented sector, regulation of registered social landlords; aids, adaptations, Disabled Facilities Grants, Physical Adaptation Grants; provision of housing support (not payment of housing benefit); regulation of commercial tenancies let by local authorities; strategic areas, legacy, provision of sites, premises, derelict land and environmental improvements relating to regeneration; structural, democratic, financial constitutional reform of local authorities, co-ordination of regional delivery models, coherence with reform; Local Government Partnership Council; constitutional matters, scrutiny arrangements, cabinets, elected mayors, role of councillors, their diversity, conduct and remuneration; Boundary Commission for Wales, timing of local authority elections; finance policy, un-hypothecated funding of local authorities, police and crime commissioners, through revenue and capital settlements; workforce matters; social partnership; Workforce Partnership Council; mitigation of child poverty; oversight of audit, inspection and regulation of public services, organisational arrangements for Health Inspectorate Wales, Care and Social Services Inspectorate Wales; Fire and Rescue Services, community fire safety; lead policy of armed forces and veterans in Wales; National Infrastructure Commission; implementation of planning acts, planning applications and appeals; Planning gain – Section 106 agreements contained in the Town and Country Planning Act 1990; building regulations; Wales Spatial Plan, National Development Framework; financial inclusion.

Special Advisers	Paul Griffiths Email: paul.griffiths003@gov.wales	0300 025 4979
	Sara Faye Email: sara.faye@gov.wales	0300 025 3645/07896 071038
Senior Private Secretary	Matthew Hall Email: psmhlg@gov.wales	0300 025 8107

Deputy Minister for Housing and Local Government **Hannah Blythyn** MS (Lab)

Supports the work of the Minister for Housing and Local Government.

Private Secretary	Kate Bacon Email: psdmhlg@gov.wales	0300 025 8769

Counsel General and European Transition

Counsel General and Minister for European Transition **Jeremy Miles** MS (Lab/Co-op)

Provision of legal advice to the Government; oversight of the work of the Legal Services Department and Office of the Legislative Counsel; oversight of prosecutions on behalf of the Welsh Government; oversight of representation of the Welsh Government in the courts; consideration of whether Bills passed by the Senedd need to be referred to the Supreme Court for determination as to whether they are within the Senedd's competence (exercised independently of Government); performance of other functions in the public interest including, where the Counsel General considers it appropriate, institute, defend or appear in any legal proceedings relating to functions of the Welsh Government (exercised independently of government); liaison with the legal sector; accessibility of Welsh law; EU exit; JMC(EN); oversight of legislation related to exiting the EU; EU structural funds excluding CAP; shared prosperity fund; chairing the cabinet sub-committee on European Transition; international trade; responsibility for shadowing the UK's international trade negotiations.

Special Advisers	Gareth Williams Email: ps.special.advisers@gov.wales	0300 025 8577

	Jane Runeckles Email: ps.special.advisers@gov.wales	0300 025 8611
Senior Private Secretary	Lauren Stamp Email: ps.counselgeneral@gov.wales	0300 025 8767

Mental Health, Wellbeing and Welsh Language

Minister for Mental Health, Wellbeing and Welsh Language **Eluned Morgan** MS (Lab)

Mental health services; dementia; autism; health impact of problem gambling; substance misuse; Armed Forces and Veterans' Health; health improvement and wellbeing services; Food Standards Agency in Wales, including food safety; genetically-modified food (but not the cultivation of genetically-modified crops); obesity strategy; patient experience, involvement and the citizen's voice; research and development in health and social care; Welsh Language – policy oversight and co-ordination, Ministerial functions emanating from the Welsh Language Measure 2011 and the Welsh Language Commissioner; major events; culture, creativity and the arts, including Creative Wales; sponsorship and remit of the Arts Council of Wales; broadcasting policy; tourism in and to Wales, including the marketing and promotion of Wales as a tourist destination through Visit Wales and regulation of the tourism industry; hospitality; historic environment in Wales; Cadw; National Botanic Garden of Wales; National Museums and Galleries of Wales; National Library of Wales; development of a National Archive for Wales; non-devolved cultural property legislation and tax relief schemes; oversight of the distribution of Lottery funding within Wales; elite sports; community sport, physical activity and active recreation in Wales, including sponsorship of the Sports Council for Wales.

Private Secretary	Peter Kellam Email: psmmhwwl@gov.wales	0300 025 0352

Deputy Minister for Culture, Sport and Tourism Rt Hon **Dafydd Elis-Thomas** MS (Ind)

Supports the work of the Minister for Mental Health, Wellbeing and Welsh Language.

Private Secretary	Kelly Lovell Email: psdmcst@gov.wales	030 0025 8165

Economy, Transport and North Wales

Minister for Economy, Transport and North Wales **Ken Skates** MS (Lab)

Minister for North Wales and Chair of the Standing Committee for Cabinet on North Wales; support and advice to assist the establishment, growth or development of business; support for Inward Investment, foundational economy; promotion of Wales as a location for business and investment; entrepreneurship, enterprise and business information; development Bank of Wales; Community Bank, economic advisory panels; city deals; Council for Economic Development and Social Partnership Strategy Group, simplification and integration of business skills and business development service; social enterprise and the social economy; co-ordination of cross-cutting measures to promote prosperity and tackle poverty; management of Welsh Government-owned property assets relating to economic development; transport for Wales; transport policy; active travel; road safety, safer routes to schools, transport for children and young people, regulation of pedestrian crossings and on-street parking; roads, including construction, improvement and maintenance of motorways and trunk roads; rail services through the Wales and Borders franchise; ports policy; Better Jobs Closer to Home; Living Wage; co-operative economy; Cross Government Digital Policy and Strategy; Business Exploitation of Digital Infrastructure and AI; apprenticeship policy and delivery; youth and adult employability policy and delivery, including Jobs Growth Wales, Essential Skills for Working Adults and the Skills Gateway; work-based learning providers; sector skills including strategies, and development funds Wales Employment and Skills Board; workforce skills development, including the Wales Union Learning Fund core funding for Wales, TUC education and learning services; Careers Policy and the sponsorship of Careers Choices Dewis Gyrfa (CCDG); European programmes relating to skills and employment, except the EU structural funds; regional Skills Partnership; national Occupational Standards; the Valleys Taskforce and programme; The Tech Valleys project; digital connectivity infrastructure, including Public Sector broadband aggregation, fast broadband and mobile; maintaining a modern regulatory framework that supports responsible business practices, growth and competitiveness; strategic communications.

Special Adviser	Andrew Johnson Email: andrew.johnson@gov.wales	0300 025 8673
Senior Private Secretary	Imelda Francombe Email: psmet@gov.wales	0300 025 8768

Deputy Minister for Economy and Transport **Lee Waters** MS (Lab/Co-op)

Supports the work of the Minister for Economy and Transport.

Private Secretary	Euros Evans Email: psdmet@gov.wales	0300 025 8531

Education

Minister for Education **Kirsty Williams** CBE MS (Lib Dem)

School governance, organisation, and admissions; school standards, improvement and pupil attainment, including National Categorisation; Estyn work programme remit; funding of schools; curriculum and assessment up to and including A levels; Welsh medium and bilingual education; foundation Phase; additional learning needs, including needs of pupils with severe, complex and/or specific learning difficulties, disabled pupils, able and talented pupils; support for people with dyslexia; safeguarding and inclusion in schools, including internet safety; complaints against local education authorities and school governing bodies; delivery and management of 21st Century Schools and education programme; sponsorship of Qualifications Wales; education workforce training and development, initial teacher training; teacher's pay and conditions; further education; FE student support: Education Maintenance Allowance (EMA) and Welsh Government Learning Grant (WGLG FE); youth work policy; adult community learning; credit and Qualifications Framework including vocational, key and essential skills qualifications; prisoner learning; higher education policy, strategy and funding; medical education (except for postgraduate training); science: development of science policy, including day to day liaison with the Chief Scientific Adviser for Wales and the National Science Academy; life sciences; research and innovation, including research and development, knowledge transfer and commercialisation; maximising research and innovation incomes; and research centres of excellence; development, retention and attraction of higher level research students for Wales; maximisation of economic benefits of higher education research and development.

Special Adviser	Tom Woodward Email: tom.woodward@gov.wales	0300 025 8141
Senior Private Secretary	Helen Childs Email: psme@gov.wales	0300 025 8783

Opposition

Plaid Cymru

Leader	**Adam Price**
Deputy Leader, Assembly Group; Chief Whip; Shadow Minister for Education, Culture and the Welsh Language	**Siân Gwenllian**
Shadow Minister for Health and Finance	**Rhun ap Iorwerth**
Shadow Minister for Justice and Equalities	**Leanne Wood**
Shadow Minister for Constitutional Affairs, International Relations and Exiting the European Union	Dr **Dai Lloyd**
Shadow Minister for Environment and Rural Affairs	**Llyr Gruffydd**
Shadow Minister for Economy, Tackling Poverty and Transport	**Helen Mary Jones**
Shadow Minister for Post-16 Education, Skills and Innovation	**Bethan Sayed**
Shadow Minister for Public Service Transformation and the Future	**Delyth Jewell**
Shadow Counsel General	Rt Hon **Elfyn Llwyd**

Welsh Conservatives

Leader, Welsh Conservatives in the Senedd	**Andrew R T Davies** CBE

Shadow Minister for Health and Social Services	**Angela Burns**
Shadow Minister for Finance and North Wales; Chief Whip	**Mark Isherwood**
Shadow Minister for Economy, Transport and Mid Wales	**Russell George**
Shadow Minister for Environment, Energy and Rural Affairs	**Janet Finch-Saunders**
Shadow Minister for Mental Health, Wellbeing, Culture and Sport	**David Melding** CBE
Shadow Minister for Education, Skills and the Welsh Language	**Suzy Davies**
Shadow Minister for Housing and Local Government, Equalities, Children and Young People	**Laura Anne Jones**

Welsh Parliament

(SENEDD CYMRU)

Cardiff Bay, Cardiff CF99 1SN
Tel: 0300 200 6565
Email: contact@senedd.wales Website: www.senedd.wales Twitter: @SeneddWales

Members (MSs)

State of the Parties (February 2021)

	Constituency	*Regional*	*Total*
Labour (includes Labour/Co-operative Party)	26*	2	28
Conservative	6	5	11
Plaid Cymru	4†	5	9
Independent	2	2	4
Independent Alliance for Reform	0	3	3
Abolish the Welsh Assembly	0	2	2
Liberal Democrat	1	0	1
Presiding Officer	1	0	1
UK Independence Party	0	1	1
	40	**20**	**60 seats**

* Includes a Deputy Presiding Officer who can participate and vote fully in the Parliament when not in the chair.
† Excludes the Presiding Officer who has no allegiance while in the post.

Changes since 2016 Welsh Parliament election

RESIGNATIONS

Nathan Gill	North Wales - *Brexit Party*	27 December 2017
Simon Thomas	Mid and West Wales - *Plaid Cymru*	25 July 2018

DEATHS

Carl Sargeant	Alyn and Deeside - *Ind*	7 November 2017
Steffan Lewis	South Wales East - *PlC*	11 January 2019
Mohammad Asghar	South Wales East - *Con*	16 June 2020

Devolved Parliament and Assemblies

CHANGE OF PARTY

Dafydd Elis-Thomas	Dwyfor Meirionnydd	Left Plaid Cymru October 2016, now Independent
Mark Reckless	South Wales East	Left UK Independence Party April 2017, now Abolish the Welsh Assembly
Neil McEvoy	South Wales Central	Left Plaid Cymru September 2017, now Independent
Mandy Jones	North Wales	Suspended by UK Independence Party June 2018, now Independent Alliance for Reform
Caroline Jones	South Wales West	Left UK Independence Party September 2018, now Independent Alliance for Reform
Michelle Brown	North Wales	Left UK Independence Party March 2019, now Independent
David Rowlands	South Wales East	Left UK Independence Party May 2019, now Independent Alliance for Reform
Gareth Bennett	South Wales Central	Left UK Independence Party June 2020, now Abolish the Welsh Assembly
Alun Davies	Blaenau Gwent	Suspended by Labour January 2021, now Independent

REPLACEMENTS

Mandy Jones	North Wales - *BP*	Returned 27 December 2017 following the resignation of Nathan Gill
Helen Mary Jones	Mid and West Wales - *PlC*	2 August 2018 following the resignation of Simon Thomas
Delyth Jewell	South Wales East - *PlC*	8 February 2019 following the resignation of Steffan Lewis
Laura Anne Jones	South Wales East - *Con*	6 July 2020 following the death of Mohammad Asghar

BY-ELECTION

Alyn and Deeside

6 February 2018 due to the death of Labour AM Carl Sargeant

Lab	Jack Sargeant	11,267
Con	Sarah Atherton	4,722
Lib Dem	Donna Lalek	1,176

PlC Carrie Harper 1,059, *Green* Duncan Rees 353

Lab majority 6,545 - Lab hold (5.34% from Con to Lab)

Electorate 64,029 - Total vote 18,577 - Turnout 29.07%

MSs' Directory

AWA	Abolish the Welsh Assembly
Con	Conservative
Ind	Independent
IAR	Independent Alliance for Reform
Lab	Labour
Lab/Co-op	Labour/Co-operative
Lib Dem	Liberal Democrat
PlC	Plaid Cymru
Pres Off	Presiding Officer
UKIP	UK Independence Party

ANTONIW, Mr Mick *Lab/Co-op* **Pontypridd**
Chair, Parliamentary Committee on Legislation, Justice and Constitution
Tel: 0300 200 7309 Email: mick.antoniw@senedd.wales
Constituency office: 10 Market Street, Pontypridd CF37 2ST
Tel: 01443 406400
Website: www.mickantoniw.wales Twitter: @MickAntoniw1

AP IORWERTH, Mr Rhun *PlC* **Ynys Môn**
Plaid Cymru Shadow Minister for Health and Finance
Tel: 0300 200 7181 Email: rhun.apiorwerth@senedd.wales/rhun.apiorwerth@cynulliad.cymru
Constituency office: 1B Church Street, Llangefni, Ynys Môn LL77 7DU
Tel: 01248 723599
Website: www.rhunapiorwerth.wales Twitter: @Rhunapiorwerth

BENNETT, Mr Gareth *AWA* **South Wales Central**
Tel: 0300 200 7263 Email: gareth.bennett@senedd.wales
Regional office: No regional office publicised Twitter: @GarethBennettAM

BLYTHYN, Ms Hannah *Lab* **Delyn**
Deputy Minister for Housing and Local Government
Tel: 0300 200 7132 Email: hannah.blythyn@senedd.wales
Ministerial office: Welsh Government, Fifth Floor, Tŷ Hywel, Cardif Bay CF99 1NA
Tel: 0300 060 4400
Constituency office: 38 Church Street, Flint, Flintshire CH6 5AE
Website: www.hannahblythyn.wales Twitter: @hannahblythyn

BOWDEN, Ms Dawn *Lab/Co-op* **Merthyr Tydfil and Rhymney**
Tel: 0300 200 7170 Email: dawn.bowden@senedd.wales
Constituency office: 110 High Street, Merthyr Tydfil CF47 8AP
Tel: 01685 386672
Website: www.dawnbowdenam.co.uk Twitter: @Dawn_Bowden

BROWN, Ms Michelle *Ind* **North Wales**
Tel: 0300 200 7267 Email: michelle.brown@senedd.wales
Regional office: No regional office publicised Twitter: @MishBrownAM

BRYANT, Ms Jayne *Lab* **Newport West**
Chair, Assembly Committee on Standards of Conduct
Email: jayne.bryant@senedd.wales
Constituency office: No constituency office publicised
Tel: 01633 376627
Website: www.jaynebryant.wales Twitter: @JBryantWales

BURNS, Mrs Angela *Con* **Carmarthen West and South Pembrokeshire**
Welsh Conservatives Shadow Minister for Health and Social Services
Tel: 0300 200 7243 Email: angela.burns@senedd.wales
Constituency office: County Chambers, Warren Street, Tenby, Pembrokeshire SA70 7JS
Tel: 01834 843052
Website: www.angelaburns.org.uk Twitter: @AngelaJBurns

DAVID, Dr Hefin *Lab* **Caerphilly**
Tel: 0300 200 7154 Email: hefin.david@senedd.wales
Constituency office: Bargoed YMCA, Aeron Place, Gilfach, Bargoed CF81 8JA
Tel: 01443 838542 Twitter: @hef4caerphilly

DAVIES, Mr Alun *Ind* **Blaenau Gwent**
Tel: 0300 200 7145 Fax: 029 2089 8302 Email: alun.davies@senedd.wales
Constituency office: 23 Beaufort Street, Brynmawr, Blaenau Gwent NP23 4AQ
Tel: 01495 311160
Website: alundaviesam.wordpress.com Twitter: @AlunDaviesMS

DAVIES, Mr Andrew R T, CBE *Con* **South Wales Central**
Leader, Welsh Conservatives in the Senedd
Tel: 0300 200 7228 Email: andrewrt.davies@senedd.wales
Regional office: No regional office publicised
Website: www.andrewrtdavies.co.uk Twitter: @andrewrtdavies

DAVIES, Mr Paul *Con* **Preseli Pembrokeshire**
Tel: 0300 200 7216 Email: paul.davies@senedd.wales
Constituency office: 20 Upper Market Street, Haverfordwest SA61 1QA
Tel: 01437 766425 Fax: 01437 766425
Website: www.paul-davies.org.uk Twitter: @PaulDaviesPembs

DAVIES, Mrs Suzy *Con* **South Wales West**
Welsh Conservatives Shadow Minister for Education, Skills and the Welsh Language
Tel: 0300 200 7208 Email: suzy.davies@senedd.wales
Regional offices: Cornhill Chambers, 8 Christina Street, Swansea SA1 4EW
1a Station Hill, Bridgend CF31 1EA
Website: suzydavies.wales Twitter: @suzydaviesMS

DRAKEFORD, Rt Hon Mark *Lab* **Cardiff West**
First Minister of Wales; Leader, Welsh Labour
Tel: 0300 200 7158 Email: mark.drakeford@senedd.wales
Ministerial office: Welsh Government, Fifth Floor, Tŷ Hywel, Cardif Bay CF99 1NA
Tel: 0300 060 4400
Constituency office: 395 Cowbridge Road East, Canton, Cardiff CF5 1JG
Tel: 029 2022 3207
Website: www.markdrakeford.com Twitter: @MarkDrakeford

ELIS-THOMAS, Rt Hon Dafydd *Ind* **Dwyfor Meirionnydd**
Deputy Minister for Culture, Sport and Tourism
Tel: 0300 200 7175 Email: dafydd.elis-thomas@senedd.wales
Ministerial office: Welsh Government, Fifth Floor, Tŷ Hywel, Cardif Bay CF99 1NA
Tel: 0300 060 4400
Constituency office: 7 Bank Place, Porthmadog, Gwynedd LL49 9AA
Tel: 01766 515028 Twitter: @ElisThomasD

EVANS, Mrs Rebecca *Lab/Co-op* **Gower**
Minister for Finance and Trefnydd
Tel: 0300 200 7160 Email: rebecca.evans@senedd.wales
Ministerial office: Welsh Government, Fifth Floor, Tŷ Hywel, Cardif Bay CF99 1NA
Tel: 0300 060 4400
Constituency office: 9 Pontardulais Road, Gorseinon SA4 4FE
Tel: 01792 899081
Website: www.rebeccaevansms.com Twitter: @RebeccaEvansMS

FINCH-SAUNDERS, Mrs Janet *Con* **Aberconwy**
Chair, Parliamentary Committee on Petitions; Welsh Conservatives Shadow Minister for Environment, Energy and Rural Affairs
Tel: 0300 200 7247 Email: janet.finchsaunders@senedd.wales
Constituency office: 29 Madoc Street, Llandudno LL30 2TL
Tel: 01492 871198
Website: www.janetfinchsaunders.org.uk Twitter: @jfinchsaunders

---

GEORGE, Mr Russell *Con* **Montgomeryshire**
Chair, Parliamentary Committee on Economy, Infrastructure and Skills; Welsh Conservatives Shadow Minister for Economy, Transport and Mid Wales
Tel: 0300 200 7206 Email: russell.george@senedd.wales
Constituency office: 13 Parker's Lane, Newtown, Powys SY16 2LT
Tel: 01686 610887
Website: www.russellgeorge.com Twitter: @russ_george

GETHING, Mr Vaughan *Lab/Co-op* **Cardiff South and Penarth**
Minister for Health and Social Services
Tel: 0300 200 7150 Email: vaughan.gething@senedd.wales
Ministerial office: Welsh Government, Fifth Floor, Tŷ Hywel, Cardif Bay CF99 1NA
Tel: 0300 060 4400
Constituency office: 106 Clare Road, Grangetown CF11 6RU
Website: www.vaughangething.wales Twitter: @vaughangething

GRIFFITHS, Mr John *Lab/Co-op* **Newport East**
Chair, Parliamentary Committee on Equality, Local Government and Communities
Tel: 0300 200 7122 Email: john.griffiths@senedd.wales
Constituency office: Seventh Floor, Clarence House, Clarence Place, Newport NP19 7AA
Tel: 01633 222302
Website: www.johngriffiths.wales Twitter: @JGriffithsLab

GRIFFITHS, Mrs Lesley *Lab* **Wrexham**
Minister for Environment, Energy and Rural Affairs
Email: lesley.griffiths@senedd.wales
Ministerial office: Welsh Government, Fifth Floor, Tŷ Hywel, Cardif Bay CF99 1NA
Tel: 0300 060 4400
Constituency office: Vernon House, 41 Rhosddu Road, Wrexham LL11 2NS
Tel: 01978 355743
Website: www.lesleygriffiths.co.uk Twitter: @lesley4wrexham

GRUFFYDD, Mr Llyr *PlC* **North Wales**
Chair, Parliamentary Committee on Finance; Plaid Cymru Shadow Minister for Environment and Rural Affairs
Email: llyr.gruffydd@senedd.wales
Regional office: Office 3, Ground Floor, Birch House Business Centre, Hen Lon Parcwr, Rhuthun, Denbighshire LL15 1HA
Tel: 01824 703593
Website: www.llyrgruffydd.cymru Twitter: @llyrgruffydd

GWENLLIAN, Ms Siân *PlC* **Arfon**
Deputy Leader and Chief Whip and Shadow Minister for Education, Culture and the Welsh Language, Plaid Cymru Assembly Group
Tel: 0300 200 7192 Email: sian.gwenllian@senedd.wales
Constituency office: 8 Castle Street, Caernarfon LL55 1SE Twitter: @siangwenfelin

---

HAMILTON, Mr Neil *UKIP* **Mid and West Wales**
Leader, UKIP in Wales
Tel: 0300 200 7422 Email: neil.hamilton@senedd.wales
Regional office: No regional office publicised Twitter: @NeilUKIP

HEDGES, Mr Mike *Lab* **Swansea East**
Chair, Parliamentary Committee on Climate Change, Environment and Rural Affairs
Tel: 0300 200 7140 Email: mike.hedges@senedd.wales
Constituency office: 97 Pleasant Street, Morriston, Swansea SA6 6HJ
Tel: 01792 790621 Fax: 01792 794802
Website: www.mikehedges.org.uk Twitter: @mikehedgesam

HOWELLS, Ms Vikki *Lab* **Cynon Valley**
Tel: 0300 200 7163 Email: vikki.howells@senedd.wales
Constituency office: 27 High Street, Aberdare CF44 7AA
Tel: 01685 881388
Website: www.vikkihowells.com

HUTT, Ms Jane *Lab* **Vale of Glamorgan**
Deputy Minister and Chief Whip
Tel: 0300 200 7110 Fax: 029 2089 8129 Email: jane.hutt@senedd.wales
Ministerial office: Welsh Government, Fifth Floor, Tŷ Hywel, Cardif Bay CF99 1NA
Tel: 0300 060 4400
Constituency office: 115 High Street, Barry CF62 7DT
Tel: 01446 740981 Fax: 01446 747106
Website: janehutt.wales Twitter: @janehutt

IRRANCA-DAVIES, Mr Huw *Lab/Co-op* **Ogmore**
Tel: 0300 200 7105 Email: huw.irranca-davies@senedd.wales
Constituency office: Unit 2, 112-113 Commercial Street, Maesteg CF34 9DL
Tel: 01656 737777
Website: www.huwirranca-davies.wales Twitter: @huw4ogmore

ISHERWOOD, Mr Mark *Con* **North Wales**
Welsh Conservatives Shadow Minister for Finance and North Wales and Chief Whip
Tel: 0300 200 7217 Email: mark.isherwood@senedd.wales
Regional office: 8 Chester Street, Mold CH7 1EG
Tel: 01352 710232
Website: www.markisherwood.co.uk Twitter: @MarkIsherwoodMS

JAMES, Ms Julie *Lab* **Swansea West**
Minister for Housing and Local Government
Tel: 0300 200 7137 Email: julie.james@senedd.wales
Ministerial office: Welsh Government, Fifth Floor, Tŷ Hywel, Cardif Bay CF99 1NA
Tel: 0300 060 4400
Constituency office: First Floor, 11 Wind Street, Swansea SA1 1DP
Tel: 01792 460836
Website: www.juliejamesms.co.uk Twitter: @JulieJamesMS

JEWELL, Ms Delyth *PlC* **South Wales East**
Plaid Cymru Shadow Minister for Public Service Transformation and the Future
Tel: 0300 200 6565 Email: delyth.jewell@senedd.wales
Constituency office: Griffiths Building, Victoria Terrace, Newbridge, Caerphilly NP11 4ET
Tel: 0300 200 7138 Twitter: @DelythJewellAM

JONES, Ms Ann *Lab/Co-op* **Vale of Clwyd**
Deputy Presiding Officer
Tel: 0300 200 7173 Email: ann.jones@senedd.wales
Constituency office: The Hub, 69-75 Wellington Road, Rhyl, Denbighshire LL18 1BE
Tel: 01745 332813
Website: www.annjones.org.uk Twitter: @ann_jonesam

JONES, Ms Caroline *IAR* **South Wales West**
Leader, Independent Alliance for Reform Group
Tel: 0300 200 7529 Email: caroline.jones@senedd.wales
Regional office: 88b John Street, Porthcawl CF36 3BD
Tel: 01659 773680
Website: www.carolinejones.wales Twitter: @CarolineJonesMS

JONES, Rt Hon Carwyn *Lab* **Bridgend**
Tel: 0300 200 7095 Email: carwyn.jones@senedd.wales
Constituency office: First and Second Floor Suites, 3 Cross Street, Bridgend CF31 1EX
Tel: 01656 664320 Email: christopher.mainwaring@senedd.wales
Website: www.carwynjonesms.co.uk Twitter: @AMCarwyn

JONES, Ms Elin *Pres Off* **Ceredigion**
Presiding Officer
Email: elin.jones@senedd.wales
Constituency office: Ty Goronwy, 32 Heol y Wig, Aberystwyth, Ceredigion SY23 2LN
Tel: 01970 624516 Fax: 01970 624473 Twitter: @elinceredigion

JONES, Ms Helen Mary *PlC* **Mid and West Wales**
Plaid Cymru Shadow Minister for Economy, Tackling Poverty and Transport; Chair, Parliamentary Committee on Culture, Welsh Language and Communications
Tel: 0300 200 6565 Email: helenmary.jones@senedd.wales
Regional office: No regional office publicised Twitter: @HelenMaryCymru

---

JONES, Ms Laura Anne *Con* **South Wales East**
Welsh Conservatives Shadow Minister for Housing and Local Government, Equalities, Children and Young People
Tel: 0300 200 7238 Email: laura.jones@senedd.wales
Regional office: No regional office publicised
Website: www.lauraannejones.wales Twitter: @LauraJ4SWEast

JONES, Mrs Mandy *IAR* **North Wales**
Tel: 0300 200 7387 Email: mandy.jones@senedd.wales
Regional office: 10 Bridge Street, Menai Bridge LL59 5DW
Tel: 01248 717052 Twitter: @MandyJonesMS

LLOYD, Dr Dai *PlC* **South Wales West**
Chair, Parliamentary Committee on Health, Social Care and Sport; Plaid Cymru Shadow Minister for Constitutional Affairs, International Relations and Exiting the European Union
Tel: 0300 200 7255 Email: dai.lloyd@senedd.wales
Regional office: Uned 2, Ffordd Brunel, Parc Ynni Baglan, Baglan SA11 2FP
Tel: 01639 820530
Website: dailloydam.wixsite.com/dailloyd Twitter: @DaiLloydAS

MCEVOY, Mr Neil *Ind* **South Wales Central**
Tel: 0300 200 7434 Email: neil.mcevoy@senedd.wales
Regional office: 321 Cowbridge Road East, Cardiff CF5 1JD
Website: www.neilmcevoy.wales Twitter: @neiljmcevoy

MELDING, Mr David, CBE *Con* **South Wales Central**
Welsh Conservatives Shadow Minister for Mental Health, Wellbeing, Culture and Sport
Tel: 0300 200 7220 Email: david.melding@senedd.wales
Regional office: Office 2, 20 Pantbach Road, Birchgrove, Cardiff CF14 1UA
Tel: 029 2062 3088 Email: sarah.sharpe@senedd.wales
Website: www.davidmelding.wales Twitter: @DavidMeldingMS

MILES, Mr Jeremy *Lab/Co-op* **Neath**
Counsel General and Minister for European Transition
Tel: 0300 200 7107 Email: jeremy.miles@senedd.wales
Ministerial office: Welsh Government, Fifth Floor, Tŷ Hywel, Cardif Bay CF99 1NA
Tel: 0300 060 4400
Constituency office: 7 High Street, Pontardawe, Swansea SA8 4HU
Tel: 01792 869993 Twitter: @Jeremy_Miles

MILLAR, Mr Darren *Con* **Clwyd West**
Tel: 0300 200 7214 Email: darren.millar@senedd.wales
Constituency office: North Wales Business Park, Abergele LL22 8LJ
Tel: 01745 839117
Website: www.darrenmillar.wales Twitter: @darrenmillarMS

MORGAN, Mrs Julie *Lab* **Cardiff North**
Deputy Minister for Health and Social Services
Tel: 0300 200 7362 Email: julie.morgan@senedd.wales
Ministerial office: Welsh Government, Fifth Floor, Tŷ Hywel, Cardif Bay CF99 1NA
Tel: 0300 060 4400
Constituency office: 17 Plasnewydd, Whitchurch, Cardiff CF14 1NR
Tel: 029 2061 4577
Website: www.juliemorgan.org.uk Twitter: @juliemorganlab

MORGAN, Eluned *Lab* **Mid and West Wales**
Minister for Mental Health, Wellbeing and Welsh Language
Tel: 0300 200 7310 Email: eluned.morgan@senedd.wales
Ministerial office: Welsh Government, Fifth Floor, Tŷ Hywel, Cardif Bay CF99 1NA
Tel: 0300 060 4400
Regional office: 19 Cartlett, Haverfordwest, Pembrokeshire SA61 2LH
Website: www.elunedmorgan.wales Twitter: @Eluned_Morgan

NEAGLE, Ms Lynne *Lab/Co-op* **Torfaen**
Chair, Parliamentary Committee on Children, Young People and Education
Tel: 0300 200 7508 Email: lynne.neagle@senedd.wales
Constituency office: 73 Upper Trosnant Street, Pontypool, Torfaen NP4 8AU
Tel: 01495 740022 Twitter: @lynne_neagle

PASSMORE, Ms Rhianon *Lab/Co-op* **Islwyn**
Tel: 0300 200 7097 Email: rhianon.passmore@senedd.wales
Constituency office: 208 High Street, Blackwood NP12 1AJ
Tel: 01495 225162 Twitter: @rhi4islwyn

PRICE, Mr Adam *PlC* **Carmarthen East and Dinefwr**
Leader, Plaid Cymru
Tel: 0300 200 7177 Email: adam.price@senedd.wales
Constituency office: 37 Wind Street, Ammanford SA18 3DN
Tel: 01269 597677
Website: adam-plaidcarmarthenshire.nationbuilder.com Twitter: @Adamprice

---

RAMSAY, Mr Nick *Con* **Monmouth**
Chair, Parliamentary Committee on Public Accounts
Tel: 0300 200 7211 Email: nicholas.ramsay@senedd.wales
Constituency office: The Grange, 16 Maryport Street, Usk, Monmouthshire NP15 1AB
Tel: 01291 674898 Email: katherine.jordan@senedd.wales
Website: www.nickramsay.org.uk Twitter: @nickramsayam

RATHBONE, Ms Jenny *Lab* **Cardiff Central**
Tel: 0300 200 7134 Email: jenny.rathbone@senedd.wales
Constituency office: 165 Albany Road, Cardiff CF24 3NT
Tel: 029 2025 6255
Website: jennyrathbone.com Twitter: @jennyrathbone

RECKLESS, Mr Mark *AWA* **South Wales East**
Tel: 0300 200 7371 Email: mark.reckless@senedd.wales
Regional office: 20 Commercial Street, Pontypool NP4 6JS Twitter: @MarkReckless

---

REES, Mr David *Lab* **Aberavon**
Chair, Parliamentary Committee on External Affairs and Additional Legislation
Tel: 0300 200 7128 Email: david.rees@senedd.wales
Constituency office: Unit 6, Water Street Business Centre, Port Talbot SA12 6LG
Tel: 01639 870779
Website: www.davidrees.wales Twitter: @DavidReesMS

ROWLANDS, Mr David *IAR* **South Wales East**
Tel: 0300 200 7235 Email: davidj.rowlands@senedd.wales
Regional office: 20 Commercial Street, Pontypool, Torfaen NP4 6JS Twitter: @DavidRowlandsMS

SARGEANT, Mr Jack *Lab* **Alyn and Deeside**
Tel: 0300 200 6565 Email: jack.sargeant@senedd.wales
Constituency office: 70 High Street, Connah's Quay, Flintshire CH5 4DD
Tel: 01244 823547
Website: jacksargeant.wales Twitter: @JackSargeantAM

SAYED, Mrs Bethan *PlC* **South Wales West**
Chair, Assembly Committee on Culture, Welsh Language and Communications; Plaid Cymru Shadow Minister for Post-16 Education, Skills and Innovation
Tel: 0300 200 7185 Email: bethan.sayed@senedd.wales
Regional office: Unit 2, Brunel Way, Baglan Energy Park, Port Talbot SA11 2FP
Tel: 01639 820530 Twitter: @bethanjenkins

SKATES, Mr Ken *Lab* **Clwyd South**
Minister for Economy, Transport and North Wales
Tel: 0300 200 7114 Email: ken.skates@senedd.wales
Ministerial office: Welsh Government, Fifth Floor, Tŷ Hywel, Cardif Bay CF99 1NA
Tel: 0300 060 4400
Constituency office: Unit 22, The Malthouse Business Centre, Regent Street, Llangollen LL20 8HS
Tel: 01978 869058
Website: www.kenskates.co.uk Twitter: @KenSkatesMS

WATERS, Mr Lee *Lab/Co-op* **Llanelli**
Deputy Minister for Economy and Transport
Tel: 0300 200 7100 Email: lee.waters@senedd.wales
Ministerial office: Welsh Government, Fifth Floor, Tŷ Hywel, Cardif Bay CF99 1NA
Tel: 0300 060 4400
Constituency office: 43 Pottery Street, Llanelli, Carmarthenshire SA15 1SU
Tel: 01554 774902
Website: leeforllanelli.wales Twitter: @Amanwy

WATSON, Mrs Joyce *Lab* **Mid and West Wales**
Tel: 0300 200 7093 Email: joyce.watson@senedd.wales
Regional office: 3 Red Street, Carmarthen SA31 1QL
Tel: 01267 233448
Website: www.joycewatson.co.uk Twitter: @JoyceWatsonmsas

WILLIAMS, Ms Kirsty, CBE *Lib Dem* **Brecon and Radnorshire**
Minister for Education
Tel: 0300 200 7277 Email: kirsty.williams@senedd.wales
Ministerial office: Welsh Government, Fifth Floor, Tŷ Hywel, Cardif Bay CF99 1NA
Tel: 0300 060 4400
Constituency office: 4 Water Gate, Brecon, Powys LD3 9AN
Tel: 01874 625739
Website: www.kirstywilliams.org.uk Twitter: @Kirsty_Williams

WOOD, Ms Leanne *PlC* **Rhondda**
Plaid Cymru Shadow Minister for Justice and Equalities
Tel: 0300 200 7202 Email: leanne.wood@senedd.wales
Constituency office: 68 Heol Pontypridd, Porth CF39 9PL
Tel: 01443 681420
Website: www.leannerhondda.wales Twitter: @leannewood

Women MSs (29)

BLYTHYN Hannah	Lab	JONES Caroline	IAR
BOWDEN Dawn	Lab/Co-op	JONES Elin	Pres Off
BROWN Michelle	Ind	JONES Helen Mary	PlC
BRYANT Jayne	Lab	JONES Laura Anne	Con
BURNS Angela	Con	JONES Mandy	IAR
DAVIES Suzy	Con	MORGAN Julie	Lab
EVANS Rebecca	Lab/Co-op	MORGAN Eluned	Lab
FINCH-SAUNDERS Janet	Con	NEAGLE Lynne	Lab/Co-op
GRIFFITHS Lesley	Lab	PASSMORE Rhianon	Lab/Co-op
GWENLLIAN Siân	PlC	RATHBONE Jenny	Lab
HOWELLS Vikki	Lab	SAYED Bethan	PlC
HUTT Jane	Lab	WATSON Joyce	Lab
JAMES Julie	Lab	WILLIAMS Kirsty	Lib Dem
JEWELL Delyth	PlC	WOOD Leanne	PlC
JONES Ann	Lab/Co-op		

Constituencies

			Majority	*%*
Aberavon	David Rees	Lab	6,402	30.51
Aberconwy	Janet Finch-Saunders	Con	754	3.39
Alyn and Deeside	Jack Sargeant	Lab	6,545	35.16
Arfon	Siân Gwenllian	PlC	4,162	20.63
Blaenau Gwent	Alun Davies	Ind*	650	3.04
Brecon and Radnorshire	Kirsty Williams	Lib Dem	8,170	26.78
Bridgend	Carwyn Jones	Lab	5,623	20.85
Caerphilly	Hefin David	Lab	1,575	5.79
Cardiff Central	Jenny Rathbone	Lab	817	3.12
Cardiff North	Julie Morgan	Lab	3,667	9.76
Cardiff South and Penarth	Vaughan Gething	Lab/Co-op	6,921	22.71
Cardiff West	Mark Drakeford	Lab	1,176	3.66
Carmarthen East and Dinefwr	Adam Price	PlC	8,700	29.11
Carmarthen West and South Pembrokeshire	Angela Burns	Con	3,373	11.49
Ceredigion	Elin Jones	Pres Off	2,408	8.14
Clwyd South	Ken Skates	Lab	3,016	13.54
Clwyd West	Darren Millar	Con	5,063	19.23
Vale of Clwyd	Ann Jones	Lab/Co-op	768	3.17
Cynon Valley	Vikki Howells	Lab	5,994	31.01
Delyn	Hannah Blythyn	Lab	3,582	15.36
Dwyfor Meirionnydd	Dafydd Elis-Thomas	Ind†	6,406	31.41
Vale of Glamorgan	Jane Hutt	Lab	777	2.05
Gower	Rebecca Evans	Lab/Co-op	1,829	6.02
Islwyn	Rhianon Passmore	Lab/Co-op	5,106	22.75
Llanelli	Lee Waters	Lab/Co-op	382	1.35
Merthyr Tydfil and Rhymney	Dawn Bowden	Lab/Co-op	5,486	26.34
Monmouth	Nick Ramsay	Con	5,147	16.32

*Elected as Labour
†Elected as Plaid Cymru

			Majority	*%*
Montgomeryshire	Russell George	Con	3,339	14.06
Neath	Jeremy Miles	Lab/Co-op	2,923	11.47
Newport East	John Griffiths	Lab/Co-op	4,896	23.51
Newport West	Jayne Bryant	Lab	4,115	14.75
Ogmore	Huw Irranca-Davies	Lab/Co-op	9,468	40.30
Pontypridd	Mick Antoniw	Lab/Co-op	5,327	20.90
Preseli Pembrokeshire	Paul Davies	Con	3,930	13.78
Rhondda	Leanne Wood	PlC	3,459	14.66
Swansea East	Mike Hedges	Lab	7,452	35.98
Swansea West	Julie James	Lab	5,080	22.73
Torfaen	Lynne Neagle	Lab/Co-op	4,498	19.46
Wrexham	Lesley Griffiths	Lab	1,325	6.48
Ynys Môn	Rhun ap Iorwerth	PlC	9,510	37.63

Regions

			Count elected on
Mid and West Wales	Neil Hamilton	UKIP	1
Mid and West Wales	Helen Mary Jones	PlC	–
Mid and West Wales	Eluned Morgan	Lab	4
Mid and West Wales	Joyce Watson	Lab	2
North Wales	Michelle Brown	Ind*	4
North Wales	Llyr Gruffydd	PlC	2
North Wales	Mark Isherwood	Con	3
North Wales	Mandy Jones	IAR*	–
South Wales Central	Gareth Bennett	AWA†	3
South Wales Central	Andrew R T Davies	Con	1
South Wales Central	Neil McEvoy	Ind†	2
South Wales Central	David Melding	Con	4
South Wales East	Delyth Jewell	PlC	–
South Wales East	Laura Anne Jones	Con	–
South Wales East	Mark Reckless	AWA*	1
South Wales East	David Rowlands	IAR*	3
South Wales West	Suzy Davies	Con	2
South Wales West	Caroline Jones	IAR*	3
South Wales West	Dai Lloyd	PlC	4
South Wales West	Bethan Sayed	PlC	1

Parliament Committees

Chairs' Forum

Tel: 0300 200 6565
Email: coordinationunit@senedd.wales
www.senedd.wales/en/bus-home/committees/pages/committee-profile.aspx?cid=462

Elin Jones (Chair)	*Pres Off*
Mick Antoniw	*Lab/Co-op*
Jayne Bryant	*Lab*
Janet Finch-Saunders	*Con*
Russell George	*Con*
John Griffiths	*Lab/Co-op*
Llyr Gruffydd	*PlC*
Mike Hedges	*Lab*
Ann Jones	*Lab/Co-op*
Dai Lloyd	*PlC*
Lynne Neagle	*Lab/Co-op*
Nick Ramsay	*Con*
David Rees	*Lab*
Bethan Sayed	*PlC*

Staff: Chris Warner, Alun Davidson (Clerks)

Business

Tel: 0300 200 6565
Email: seneddbusiness@senedd.wales
www.senedd.wales/en/bus-home/committees/pages/committee-profile.aspx?cid=425

*Elected as UK Independence Party
†Elected as Plaid Cymru

Elin Jones (Chair) *Pres Off*
Rebecca Evans *Lab/Co-op*
Siân Gwenllian *PlC*
Ann Jones *Lab/Co-op*
Caroline Jones *IAR*
Darren Millar *Con*
Staff: Aled Elwyn Jones (Clerk)

Children, Young People and Education
Tel: 0300 200 6565
Email: seneddcype@senedd.wales
www.senedd.wales/seneddcype
Twitter: @SeneddCYPE

Lynne Neagle (Chair) *Lab/Co-op*
Dawn Bowden *Lab/Co-op*
Hefin David *Lab*
Suzy Davies *Con*
Siân Gwenllian *PlC*
Laura Anne Jones *Con*
Staff: Llinos Madeley (Clerk)

Climate Change, Environment and Rural Affairs
Tel: 0300 200 6565
Email: seneddccera@senedd.wales
www.senedd.wales/seneddccera
Twitter: @SeneddCCERA

Mike Hedges (Chair) *Lab*
Janet Finch-Saunders *Con*
Llyr Gruffydd *PlC*
Neil Hamilton *UKIP*
Jenny Rathbone *Lab*
Joyce Watson *Lab*
Staff: Marc Wyn Jones (Clerk)

Culture, Welsh Language and Communications
Tel: 0300 200 6565
Email: seneddcwlc@senedd.wales
www.senedd.wales/seneddcwlc
Twitter: @SeneddCWLC

Helen Mary Jones (Chair) *PlC*
Mick Antoniw *Lab/Co-op*
John Griffiths *Lab/Co-op*
Carwyn Jones *Lab*
David Melding *Con*
Staff: Rhys Morgan (Clerk)

Economy, Infrastructure and Skills
Tel: 0300 200 6565
Email: senedeis@senedd.wales
www.senedd.wales/seneddeis
Twitter: @SeneddEIS

Russell George (Chair) *Con*
Hefin David *Lab*
Suzy Davies *Con*
Vikki Howells *Lab*
Helen Mary Jones *PlC*
Joyce Watson *Lab*
Staff: Robert Donovan (Clerk)

Equality, Local Government and Communities
Tel: 0300 200 6565
Email: seneddcommunities@senedd.wales
www.senedd.wales/seneddcommunities
Twitter: @SeneddELGC

John Griffiths (Chair) *Lab/Co-op*
Dawn Bowden *Lab/Co-op*
Huw Irranca-Davies *Lab/Co-op*
Mark Isherwood *Con*
Delyth Jewell *PlC*
Mandy Jones *IAR*
Staff: Naomi Stocks (Clerk)

External Affairs and Additional Legislation
Tel: 0300 200 6565
Email: seneddeaal@senedd.wales
www.senedd.wales/seneddeaal
Twitter: @SeneddEAAL

David Rees (Chair) *Lab*
Alun Davies *Ind*
Huw Irranca-Davies *Lab/Co-op*
Laura Anne Jones *Con*
Dai Lloyd *PlC*
David Rowlands *IAR*
Staff: Alun Davidson (Clerk)

Finance
Tel: 0300 200 6372
Email: seneddfinance@senedd.wales
www.senedd.wales/seneddfinance
Twitter: @SeneddFinance

Llyr Gruffydd (Chair) *PlC*
Alun Davies *Ind*
Siân Gwenllian *PlC*
Mike Hedges *Lab*
Rhianon Passmore *Lab/Co-op*
Nick Ramsay *Con*
Mark Reckless *AWA*
Staff: Bethan Davies (Clerk)

Health, Social Care and Sport
Tel: 0300 200 6565
Email: seneddhealth@senedd.wales
www.senedd.wales/seneddhealth
Twitter: @seneddhealth

Dai Lloyd (Chair) *PlC*
Rhun ap Iorwerth *PlC*
Jayne Bryant *Lab*
Andrew R T Davies *Con*
Lynne Neagle *Lab/Co-op*

David Rees *Lab*
Staff: Sarah Beasley (Clerk)

Legislation, Justice and Constitution
Tel: 0300 200 6565
Email: seneddljc@senedd.wales
www.senedd.wales/seneddljc
Twitter: @SeneddLJC

Mick Antoniw (Chair)	*Lab/Co-op*
Carwyn Jones	*Lab*
Dai Lloyd	*PlC*
David Melding	*Con*

Staff: Gareth Williams (Clerk)

Llywydd
Tel: 0300 200 6565
Email: seneddllc@senedd.wales
senedd.wales/en/bus-home/committees/pages/committee-profile.aspx?cid=555

Ann Jones (Chair)	*Lab/Co-op*
Suzy Davies	*Con*
Llyr Gruffydd	*PlC*
Dai Lloyd	*PlC*
Rhianon Passmore	*Lab/Co-op*
David Rowlands	*IAR*

Staff: Huw Gapper (Clerk)

Petitions
Tel: 0300 200 6565
Email: petitions@senedd.wales
www.senedd.wales/seneddpetitions
Twitter: @SeneddPetitions

Janet Finch-Saunders (Chair)	*Con*
Michelle Brown	*Ind*
Neil McEvoy	*Ind*
Jack Sargeant	*Lab*
Leanne Wood	*PlC*

Staff: Graeme Francis (Clerk)

Public Accounts
Tel: 0300 200 6565
Email: seneddpac@senedd.wales
www.senedd.wales/seneddpac
Twitter: @SeneddPAC

Nick Ramsay (Chair)	*Con*
Gareth Bennett	*AWA*
Angela Burns	*Con*
Vikki Howells	*Lab*
Delyth Jewell	*PlC*
Rhianon Passmore	*Lab/Co-op*
Jenny Rathbone	*Lab*

Staff: Fay Bowen (Clerk)

Scrutiny of the First Minister
Tel: 0300 200 6565
Email: scrutinyfm@senedd.wales
www.senedd.wales/scrutinyfm

Ann Jones (Chair)	*Lab/Co-op*
Mick Antoniw	*Lab/Co-op*
Jayne Bryant	*Lab*
Janet Finch-Saunders	*Con*
Russell George	*Con*
John Griffiths	*Lab/Co-op*
Llyr Gruffydd	*PlC*
Mike Hedges	*Lab*
Dai Lloyd	*PlC*
Lynne Neagle	*Lab/Co-op*
Nick Ramsay	*Con*
David Rees	*Lab*
Bethan Sayed	*PlC*

Staff: Graeme Francis (Clerk)

Standards of Conduct
Tel: 0300 200 6565
Email: seneddstandards@senedd.wales
www.senedd.wales/seneddstandards

Jayne Bryant (Chair)	*Lab*
Rhun ap Iorwerth	*PlC*
Andrew R T Davies	*Con*

Staff: Meriel Singleton (Clerk)

Devolved Parliament and Assemblies

Principal Officers and Officials

Office of the Presiding Officer
Presiding Officer **Elin Jones** MS

Head of Private Office — Gwion Evans 0300 200 7403
Email: gwion.evans@senedd.wales

Deputy Presiding Officer **Ann Jones** MS (Lab/Co-op)

Senedd Commission
(responsible for providing property, staff and services to support Senedd Members)

Chair — Elin Jones (Pres Off)

Members	Rhun ap Iorwerth (PlC) Suzy Davies (Con) David Rowlands (IAR) Joyce Watson (Lab)

Senior Management Team

Chief Executive and Clerk of the Parliament	Manon Antoniazzi 0300 200 6230 Email: manon.antoniazzi@senedd.wales
Directors	
Business	Siwan Davies 0300 200 6534 Email: siwan.davies@senedd.wales
Engagement	Arwyn Jones 0300 200 6491 Email: arwyn.jones@senedd.wales
Director of Finance	Nia Morgan 0300 200 6530 Email: nia.morgan@senedd.wales
Director of Resources	Dave Tosh 0300 200 6497 Email: david.tosh@senedd.wales
Chief Legal Adviser (Interim)	Huw Williams 0300 200 6432 Email: huw.williams@senedd.wales
Heads	
Strategic Transformation Service	Anna Daniel 0300 200 6329 Email: anna.daniel@senedd.wales
Policy and Legislation Committee Service	Julian Luke 0300 200 6411 Email: julian.luke@senedd.wales
ICT	Mark Neilson 0300 200 7399 Email: mark.neilson@senedd.wales
Translation and Reporting Service	Mair Parry-Jones 0300 200 6391 Email: mair.parry-jones@senedd.wales
Research Service	Kathryn Potter 0300 200 6587 Email: kathryn.potter@senedd.wales
Communications	Gareth Price 0300 200 6330 Email: gareth.price@senedd.wales
Legal Services	Matthew Richards 0300 200 6435 Email: matthew.richards@senedd.wales
Commission and Member Support Service	Sulafa Thomas 0300 200 6227 Email: sulafa.thomas@senedd.wales
Governance and Assurance	Gareth Watts 0300 200 6537 Email: gareth.watts@senedd.wales
Chamber and Committee Services	Siân Wilkins 0300 200 6380 Email: sian.wilkins@senedd.wales
Human Resources	Lowri Williams 0300 200 6461 Email: lowri.wiliams@senedd.wales
Parliamentary Venues and Visitor Services	Natalie Drury-Styles 0300 200 6234 Email: natalie.drury-styles@senedd.wales
Estates and Facilities Management	Nerys Evans 0300 200 6458 Email: nerys.evans2@senedd.wales
Security	Kevin Tumelty 0300 200 6288 Email: kevin.tumelty@senedd.wales

Welsh Government Civil Service

Welsh Government, Cathays Park, Cardiff, South Glamourgan CF10 3NQ
Tel: 0300 060 3300
Email: [firstname.surname]@wales.gsi.gov.uk Website: gov.wales
Llywodraeth Cymru, Parc Cathays, Caerdydd, South Glamourgan CF10 3NQ
Tel: 0300 060 4400

Permanent Secretary's Group

Permanent Secretary: Dame Shan Morgan DCMG 0300 025 6935
Email: ps.permanentsecretary@gov.wales

Office of the First Minister

Director-General, Office of the First Minister and Brexit: Desmond Clifford 0300 025 7765
Email: desmond.clifford@gov.wales

Education and Public Services Group

Directors-General: Tracey Burke Email: epscomms@gov.wales, Reg Kilpatrick
Email: reg.kilpatrick@gov.wales

Health and Social Services Group

Director-General, Health and Social Services and NHS Wales Chief Executive: Dr Andrew Goodall 029 2080 1182 Email: andrew.goodall@gov.wales

Economy, Skills and Natural Resources Group

Director-General: Andrew Slade 0300 025 6162 Email: andrew.slade@gov.wales

Non-Ministerial Department

Estyn – HM Inspectorate for Education and Training in Wales

Anchor Court, Keen Road, Cardiff CF24 5JW
Tel: 029 2044 6446
Email: enquiries@estyn.gov.wales Website: www.estyn.gov.wales
Twitter: @EstynHMI; @EstynAEM
Llys Angor, Heol Keen, Caerdydd CF24 5JW
Tel: 029 2044 6446
Email: ymholiadau@estyn.llyw.cymru Website: www.estyn.llyw.cymru
HM Chief Inspector of Education and Training in Wales: Meilyr Rowlands 029 2044 6523
Email: chief-inspector@estyn.gov.wales

Political Parties

Welsh Labour (Llafur Cymru)

Unite the Union Building, 1 Cathedral Road, Cardiff CF11 9HA
Tel: 029 2087 7700 Fax: 029 2022 1153
Email: wales@labour.org.uk Website: www.welshlabour.org.uk Twitter: @welshlabour
First Minister of Wales and Welsh Labour Leader: Rt Hon Mark Drakeford MS
Deputy Leader: Carolyn Harris MP
General Secretary: Louise Magee

Welsh Conservatives (Ceidwadwyr Cymreig)
Welsh Conservative Campaign Headquarters, Unit 5, Pro-copy Business Centre, Parc Ty Glas, Cardiff CF14 5DU
Tel: 0333 678 8888
Email: info@welshconservatives.com Website: www.welshconservatives.com
Twitter: @welshconserv

Chair: Glyn Davies
President: Lord Davies of Gower
Campaign Director: Alex Finney 029 2073 6562 Email: alex.finney@conservatives.com
Chief of Staff (Senedd): Paul Smith 07703 056088 Email: paul.smith@senedd.wales
Media Officer (CCHQ Wales): Denise Howard 07795 494059
Email: denise.howard@conservatives.com

Plaid Cymru (The Party of Wales)
Ty Gwynfor, Marine Chambers, Anson Court, Atlantic Wharf, Cardiff CF10 4AL
Tel: 029 2047 2272
Email: post@plaid.cymru Website: www.plaid.cymru Twitter: @plaid_cymru

Assembly Office:
Tel: 0300 200 7351

Leader: Adam Price MS
Chair: Alun Ffred Jones
Chief Executive: Gareth Clubb
Treasurer: Marc Phillips

Welsh Liberal Democrats (Democratiaid Rhyddfrydol Cymru)
Brunel House, 15th Floor, Fitzalan Road, Cardiff CF24 0EB
Tel: 029 2032 9024
Email: enquiries@welshlibdems.wales Website: www.welshlibdems.wales Twitter: @welshlibdems

Leader: Jane Dodds
Media and Policy Officer: Seb Bench
Campaigns and Local Parties Co-ordinator: Matthew Palmer
Email: matt.palmer@welshlibdems.org.uk
Operations Manager: Steffan John Email: steffan.john@welshlibdems.org.uk

Independent Alliance for Reform Group
Twitter: @SeneddIndyGroup

Leader: Caroline Jones MS

UK Independence Party Wales
Tel: 0300 200 7422
Website: ukipwales.com Twitter: @UKIPWales

Leader: Neil Hamilton MS

Northern Ireland Assembly

Parliament Buildings, Stormont, Belfast BT4 3XX
Tel: 028 9052 1137/Textphone: 028 9052 1209 Fax: 028 9052 1961 Email: info@niassembly.gov.uk
Website: www.niassembly.gov.uk Twitter: @niassembly

Executive Committee of Ministers

First Minister	**Arlene Foster** (DUP)
Deputy First Minister	**Michelle O'Neill** (Sinn Féin)
Minister for Agriculture, Environment and Rural Affairs	**Edwin Poots** (DUP)
Minister for Communities	**Deirdre Hargey** (Sinn Féin)
Minister for the Economy	**Diane Dodds** (DUP)
Minister for Education	**Peter Weir** (DUP)
Minister of Finance	**Conor Murphy** (Sinn Féin)
Minister of Health	**Robin Swann** (UUP)
Minister for Infrastructure	**Nichola Mallon** (SDLP)
Minister of Justice	**Naomi Long** (APNI)

Ministerial Responsibilities and Staff

Executive Office

SD03 Stormont Castle, Stormont Estate, Belfast BT4 3TT
Tel: 028 9037 8158/028 9052 8400
Email: ps.ministers@executiveoffice-ni.gov.uk Website: www.executiveoffice-ni.gov.uk
Twitter: @niexecutive

Delivering social change through a framework co-ordinating key actions across government; strategic investment and regeneration through the Social Investment Fund and the Maze Long Kesh site; making Government work through the Programme for Government and support for the Executive; co-operation through the British/Irish, Joint Ministerial Committee, North/South Ministerial Council, European Policy and Co-ordination; promoting international relations through the NI Bureaus in Washington, China and the Office of the Northern Ireland Executive in Brussels; policy responsibility for equality, victims and survivors, human rights, social change, good relations and building a united community; racial equality; actions associated with the implementation of the New Decade, New Approach Deal; Governmental response to the coronavirus Covid-19 pandemic.

First Minister Rt Hon **Arlene Foster** MLA (DUP)

Special Advisers	Dr Philip Weir
	Emma Little Pengelly
Principal Private Secretary	Dr Deirdre Griffith

Deputy First Minister **Michelle O'Neill** MLA (Sinn Féin)

Special Adviser	Stephen McGlade
Principal Private Secretary	Donal Moran

Junior Minister **Gordon Lyons** MLA (DUP)

Private Secretary	Kevin Kerr

Junior Minister **Declan Kearney** MLA (Sinn Féin)

Private Secretary	Marie Muldoon

Department of Agriculture, Environment and Rural Affairs

Dundonald House, Upper Newtownards Road, Ballymiscaw BT4 3SB
Tel: 0300 200 7852
Email: info@daera-ni.gov.uk Website: www.daera-ni.gov.uk Twitter: @daera_ni

Minister of Agriculture, Environment and Rural Affairs **Edwin Poots** MLA (DUP)

Food; farming; environmental; fisheries; forestry and sustainability policy and the development of the rural sector in Northern Ireland; assists the sustainable development of the agri-food, environmental, fishing and forestry sectors of the Northern Ireland economy; having regard for the needs of the consumers; the protection of human, animal and plant health; welfare of animals; conservation and enhancement of the environment.

Special Adviser	Mark Beattie	
	Email: mark.beattie@daera-ni.gov.uk	
Private Secretary	Jonathan McFerran	028 9052 0808
	Email: jonathan.mcferran@daera-ni.gov.uk	

Department for Communities

Causeway Exchange, 1-7 Bedford Street, Belfast BT2 7EG
Tel: 028 9082 3320
Email: private.office@communities-ni.gov.uk Website: www.communities-ni.gov.uk
Twitter: @CommunitiesNI

Minister for Communities **Deirdre Hargey** MLA (Sinn Féin)

Housing; regeneration; sport; benefits and pensions policy and legislation; finding employment; arts and culture; museums and libraries; historic environment; voluntary and community; languages; statistics and research; social inclusion; The Appeals Service; local government; Public Record Office.

Special Adviser	Ronan McGinley	028 9082 3320
	Email: private.office@communities-ni.gov.uk	
Private Secretary	Rosheen Thompson	028 9082 3320
	Email: rosheen.thompson@communities-ni.gov.uk	

Department for the Economy

Adelaide House, 39-49 Adelaide Street, Belfast BT2 8FD
Tel: 028 9052 9900
Email: private.office@economy-ni.gov.uk Website: www.economy-ni.gov.uk
Twitter: @Economy_NI

Minister for the Economy **Diane Dodds** MLA (DUP)

Economic development policy, including business development; energy; telecoms; tourism; assured skills, apprenticeships and youth training, higher education policy; careers; promoting good employment practice; consumer affairs; health and safety at work; Insolvency Service; labour market and economic statistics services; Invest NI; InterTrade Ireland and Tourism Ireland; Health and Safety Executive for NI; the Consumer Council for NI.

Department of Education

Rathgael House, Balloo Road, Rathgill, Bangor BT19 7PR
Tel: 028 9127 9279
Email: private.office@education-ni.gov.uk Website: www.education-ni.gov.uk
Twitter: @Education_NI

Minister of Education **Peter Weir** MLA (DUP)

Curriculum and learning; pupils and parents; teaching staff; non-teaching staff; schools and infrastructure; support and development; children and young people issues; statistics and research; equality and good relations.

Special Adviser	Peter Martin	028 9127 9719
	Email: spad@education-ni.gov.uk	
Private Secretary	Michele Matchett	028 9127 9731
	Email: michele.matchett@education-ni.gov.uk	

Department of Finance
Clare House, 303 Airport Road, Belfast BT3 9ED
Tel: 028 9185 8111
Email: private.office@finance-ni.gov.uk Website: www.finance-ni.gov.uk Twitter: @dptfinance

Minister of Finance **Conor Murphy** MLA (Sinn Féin)

Department of Finance comprising Construction and Procurement Delivery; public spending; programme and project management and assurance; building regulations and energy efficiency of buildings; NICS HR; IT and digital services; public sector policy and reform; statistics and research; Departmental Solicitor's Office; Land & Property Services responsible for property rating, property valuation, land registration and providing geographic mapping data.

Special Adviser — Eoin Rooney
Email: private.office@finance-ni.gov.uk
Private Secretary — Paula Dawson 028 9081 6116
Email: private.office@finance-ni.gov.uk

Department of Health
C5.20, Castle Buildings, Stormont, Belfast BT4 3SQ
Tel: 028 9052 2556
Email: private.office@health-ni.gov.uk Website: www.health-ni.gov.uk Twitter: @Healthdpt

Minister of Health **Robin Swann** MLA (UUP)

Dentistry; finance, procurement and support services; good management, good records; health workforce policy and management; nursing and allied health professionals; governance in health and social care; mental health and learning disabilities; safety and quality standards; public health policy and advice; professional medical and environmental health advice; pharmacy; social services; health policy; DoH statistics and research.

Special Adviser — Mark Ovens 028 9052 2556
Email: spad@health-ni.gov.uk
Private Secretary — Kim Burns 028 9037 8774
Email: kim.burns@health-ni.gov.uk

Department for Infrastructure
Clarence Court, 10-18 Adelaide Street, Belfast BT2 8GB
Tel: 028 9054 0540
Email: private.office@infrastructure-ni.gov.uk Website: www.infrastructure-ni.gov.uk
Twitter: @deptinfra

Minister for Infrastructure **Nichola Mallon** MLA (SDLP)

Road improvement schemes; transport initiatives; roads; public transport; active travel; waterways; DfI Roads procurement; road users; water and sewerage services; ports; statistics and research; Rathlin Island Policy; Crumlin Road Gaol and St Lucia Site; planning; rivers and flooding.

Special Adviser — Tanya McCamphill
Email: spad@infrastructure-ni.gov.uk
Private Secretary — Dr Kathryn McFerran 028 9054 0105
Email: kathryn.mcferran@infrastucture-ni.gov.uk

Department of Justice
Block B, Castle Buildings, Stormont Estate, Belfast BT4 3SG
Tel: 028 9076 3000
Email: private.office@justice-ni.x.gsi.gov.uk Website: www.justice-ni.gov.uk Twitter: @Justice_NI

Minister of Justice **Naomi Long** MLA (APNI)

Justice and the law; legal aid; prisons; youth justice; forensic science; policing and community safety; statistics and research.

Opposition

Ulster Unionist Party

Leader; Spokesperson for Finance	Dr **Stephen Aiken** OBE
Chief Whip; Spokesperson for Education	**Robbie Butler**
Spokesperson for Agriculture, Environment and Rural Affairs	**Rosemary Barton**
Spokesperson for Communities	**Andy Allen** MBE
Spokesperson for Economy	**John Stewart**
Spokesperson for Executive Office	**Mike Nesbitt**
Spokesperson for Health	**Alan Chambers**
Spokesperson for Infrastructure	**Roy Beggs**
Spokesperson for Justice	**Doug Beattie** MC

Social Democratic and Labour Party

Spokesperson for Healthcare	**Colin McGrath**
Spokesperson for Education	**Daniel McCrossan**
Spokesperson for Addressing the Legacy of the Past	**Dolores Kelly**
Spokesperson for Social Justice	**Mark H Durkan**
Spokesperson for Tackling Crime	**Sinéad Bradley**
Spokesperson for Economy	**Sinead McLaughlin**

Alliance

Spokesperson for Agriculture and Environment	**John Blair**
Spokesperson for Communities	**Kellie Armstrong**
Spokesperson for Economy	**Stewart Dickson**
Spokesperson for Education	**Chris Lyttle**
Spokesperson for Justice	**Naomi Long**
Spokesperson for Health	**Paula Bradshaw**
Spokesperson for Infrastructure and Finance	**Andrew Muir**

Members (MLAs)

State of the Parties (February 2021)

	Total
Democratic Unionist Party	28*
Sinn Féin	26†
Social Democratic and Labour Party	12*
Ulster Unionist Party	10*
Alliance Party of Northern Ireland	7
Green Party	2
Independent	2
People Before Profit Alliance	1
The Speaker	1
Traditional Unionist Voice	1
	90 seats

* Includes three Deputy Speakers who can participate and vote fully in the Parliament when not in the chair.
† Excludes the Speaker who has no allegiance while in the post.

Changes since 2017 Northern Ireland Assembly election

RESIGNATIONS

Michelle Gildernew	Fermanagh and South Tyrone - *Sinn Féin*	8 June 2017
Elisha McCallion	Foyle - *Sinn Féin*	8 June 2017
Paul Girvan	South Antrim - *DUP*	8 June 2017
Barry McElduff	West Tyrone - *Sinn Féin*	8 June 2017
Chris Hazzard	South Down - *Sinn Féin*	20 June 2017
David Ford	South Antrim - *Alliance*	30 June 2018
Ian Milne	Mid Ulster - *Sinn Féin*	4 November 2018
Michaela Boyle	West Tyrone - *Sinn Féin*	13 May 2019
Naomi Long	Belfast East - *APNI*	1 July 2019
Simon Hamilton	Strangford - *DUP*	6 September 2019
Steven Agnew	North Down - *Green*	7 October 2019
Stephen Farry	North Down - *APNI*	19 December 2019
Colum Eastwood	Foyle - *SDLP*	7 January 2020
Carla Lockhart	Upper Bann - *DUP*	7 January 2020
Máire Hendron	Belfast East - *APNI*	8 January 2020
Megan Fearon	Newry and Armagh - *Sinn Féin*	9 January 2020
Máirtín Ó Muilleoir	Belfast South - *Sinn Féin*	9 January 2020
Claire Hanna	Belfast South - *SDLP*	10 January 2020
Raymond McCartney	Foyle - *Sinn Féin*	4 February 2020
Catherine Kelly	West Tyrone - *Sinn Féin*	3 November 2020

DEATHS

John Dallat	East Londonderry - *SDLP*	5 May 2020

CHANGE OF PARTY

Trevor Lunn	Lagan Valley	Left Alliance Party March 2020, now Independent

REPLACEMENTS

Name	Constituency - Party	Details
Colm Gildernew	Fermanagh and South Tyrone - *Sinn Féin*	Returned 8 June 2017 following the resignation of Michelle Gildernew
Karen Mullan	Foyle - *Sinn Féin*	Returned 8 June 2017 following the resignation of Elisha McCallion
Trevor Clarke	South Antrim - *DUP*	Returned 8 June 2017 following the resignation of Paul Girvan
Catherine Kelly	West Tyrone - *Sinn Féin*	Returned 8 June 2017 following the resignation of Barry McElduff
Emma Rogan	South Down - *Sinn Féin*	Returned 20 June 2017 following the resignation of Chris Hazzard
John Blair	South Antrim - *APNI*	Returned 30 June 2018 following the resignation of David Ford
Emma Sheerin	Mid Ulster - *Sinn Féin*	Returned 4 November 2018 following the resignation of Ian Milne
Maolíosa McHugh	West Tyrone - *Sinn Féin*	Returned 13 May 2019 following the resignation of Michaela Boyle
Máire Hendron	Belfast East - *APNI*	Returned 1 July 2019 following the resignation of Naomi Long
Harry Harvey	Strangford - *DUP*	Returned 6 September 2019 following the resignation of Simon Hamilton
Rachel Woods	North Down - *Green*	Returned 7 October 2019 following the resignation of Steven Agnew
Andrew Muir	North Down - *APNI*	Returned 19 December 2019 following the resignation of Stephen Farry
Sinead McLaughlin	Foyle - *SDLP*	Returned 7 January 2020 following the resignation of Colum Eastwood
Diane Dodds	Upper Bann - *DUP*	Returned 7 January 2020 following the resignation of Carla Lockhart
Naomi Long	Belfast East - *APNI*	Returned 8 January 2020 following the resignation of Máire Hendron
Liz Kimmins	Newry and Armagh - *Sinn Féin*	Returned 9 January 2020 following the resignation of Megan Fearon
Deirdre Hargey	Belfast South - *Sinn Féin*	Returned 9 January 2020 following the resignation of Máirtín Ó Muilleoir
Matthew O'Toole	Belfast South - *SDLP*	Returned 10 January 2020 following the resignation of Claire Hanna
Martina Anderson	Foyle - *Sinn Féin*	Returned 4 February 2020 following the resignation of Raymond McCartney
Cara Hunter	East Londonderry - *SDLP*	Returned 5 May 2020 following the death of John Dallat
Nicola Brogan	West Tyrone - *Sinn Féin*	Returned 3 November 2020 following the resignation of Catherine Kelly

MLAs' Directory

APNI	Alliance Party of Northern Ireland
DUP	Democratic Unionist Party
Green	Green Party
Ind	Independent
PBPA	People Before Profit Alliance
SDLP	Social Democratic and Labour Party
Speaker	The Speaker
TUV	Traditional Unionist Voice
UUP	Ulster Unionist Party

AIKEN, Dr Stephen, OBE *UUP* **South Antrim**
Leader, Ulster Unionist Party; Spokesperson for Finance; Chair, Assembly Committee on Finance
Tel: 028 9041 8367 Email: steve.aiken@mla.niassembly.gov.uk
Constituency office: 3 The Square, Ballyclare BT39 9BB
Tel: 028 9334 4966 Twitter: @SteveAikenUUP

ALLEN, Mr Andy, MBE *UUP* **Belfast East**
UUP Spokesperson for Communities
Email: andy.allen@mla.niassembly.gov.uk
Constituency office: 174 Albertbridge Road, Belfast BT5 4GS
Tel: 028 9046 3900 Twitter: @AndyAllen88

ALLISTER, Mr Jim *TUV* **North Antrim**
Leader, Traditional Unionist Voice
Tel: 028 9052 1175 Email: jim.allister@mla.niassembly.gov.uk
Constituency offices: 38 Henry Street, Ballykeel, Ballymena, Co Antrim BT42 3AH
Tel: 028 2564 0250 Email: info@jimallister.org
1 Charles Street, Ballymoney, Co Antrim BT53 6DX
Tel: 028 2723 8393
Website: www.jimallister.org Twitter: @jimallister

ANDERSON, Ms Martina *Sinn Féin* **Foyle**
Email: martina.anderson@mla.niassembly.gov.uk
Constituency office: Unit 3, Ráth Mór Business Park, Eastway Road, Derry BT48 0LZ
Tel: 028 7137 7551 Twitter: @M_AndersonSF

ARCHIBALD, Dr Caoimhe *Sinn Féin* **East Londonderry**
Chair, Assembly Committee on Economy
Email: caoimhe.archibald@mla.niassembly.gov.uk
Constituency office: 81 Main Street, Dungiven BT47 4LE
Tel: 028 7774 2488 Twitter: @carchibald_sf

ARMSTRONG, Mrs Kellie *APNI* **Strangford**
Alliance Spokesperson for Communities
Tel: 028 9052 0308 Email: kellie.armstrong@mla.niassembly.gov.uk
Constituency office: 14 South Street, Newtownards BT23 4JT
Tel: 028 9181 1414 Email: kellie.armstrong@alliancepartyni.org
Website: www.kelliearmstrongmla.co.uk Twitter: @Kelmba

BAILEY, Ms Clare *Green* **Belfast South**
Leader, Green Party in Northern Ireland
Tel: 028 9052 1504 Email: clare.bailey@mla.niassembly.gov.uk
Constituency office: 132 University Street, Belfast BT7 1HH
Tel: 028 9031 4455 Twitter: @ClareBaileyGPNI

BARTON, Ms Rosemary *UUP* **Fermanagh and South Tyrone**
UUP Spokesperson for Agriculture, Environment and Rural Affairs
Email: rosemary.barton@mla.niassembly.gov.uk
Constituency offices: 1 Regal Pass, Enniskillen BT74 7NT
Tel: 028 6632 2028
13 Scotch Street, Dungannon BT70 1AR
Tel: 028 8772 3265 Twitter: @RosemaryBarton1

BEATTIE, Mr Doug, MC *UUP* **Upper Bann**
UUP Spokesperson for Justice
Email: doug.beattie@mla.niassembly.gov.uk
Constituency office: 103 Bridge Street, Portadown BT63 5WU Twitter: @beattiedoug

BEGGS, Mr Roy *UUP* **East Antrim**
Deputy Speaker; UUP Spokesperson for Infrastructure
Tel: 028 9052 1546 Email: roy.beggs@mla.niassembly.gov.uk
Constituency offices: 3 St Brides Street, Carrickfergus, Co Antrim BT38 8AF
Tel: 028 9336 2995 Email: roybeggs.office@btopenworld.com
41 Station Road, Inver, Larne, Co Antrim BT40 3AA
Tel: 028 2827 3258 Fax: 028 2827 3258 Email: roybeggs.office3@btopenworld.com
Website: www.roybeggs.co.uk Twitter: @roybeggs

BLAIR, Mr John *APNI* **South Antrim**
Alliance Spokesperson for Agriculture and Environment
Email: john.blair@mla.niassembly.gov.uk
Constituency office: Unit 2, 21 Carnmoney Road, Newtownabbey BT36 6HL
Tel: 028 9084 0930 Email: john.blair@alliancepartyni.org Twitter: @JohnBlairMLA

BOYLAN, Mr Cathal *Sinn Féin* **Newry and Armagh**
Tel: 028 9041 8351 Email: cathal.boylan@mla.niassembly.gov.uk
Constituency office: 59 Thomas Street, Armagh, Co Armagh BT61 7QB
Tel: 028 3751 1797 Email: armaghsinnfein@gmail.com
Website: www.newryarmaghsf.com Twitter: @cathalboylansf

BRADLEY, Mr Maurice *DUP* **East Londonderry**
Email: maurice.bradley@mla.niassembly.gov.uk
Constituency office: 2 Park Street, Coleraine BT52 1BD

BRADLEY, Ms Paula *DUP* **Belfast North**
Chair, Assembly Committee on Communities
Tel: 028 9052 1335 Email: paula.bradley@mla.niassembly.gov.uk
Constituency office: 19-21 Ballyclare Road, Glengormley BT36 5EU
Tel: 028 9083 0066 Twitter: @PaulaBradleyMLA

BRADLEY, Ms Sinéad *SDLP* **South Down**
SDLP Spokesperson for Tackling Crime
Email: sinead.bradley@mla.niassembly.gov.uk
Constituency office: 11-14 Newry Street, Ringmackilroy, Warrenpoint BT34 3JZ
Twitter: @sineadbradleysd

BRADSHAW, Ms Paula *APNI* **Belfast South**
Alliance Spokesperson for Health
Tel: 028 9052 1560 Email: paula.bradshaw@mla.niassembly.gov.uk
Constituency office: 100 University Street, Belfast BT7 1HE
Tel: 028 9032 8162 Email: paula.bradshaw@alliancepartyni.org Twitter: @PaulaJaneB

BROGAN, Ms Nicola *Sinn Féin* **West Tyrone**
Constituency office: Details still to be confirmed Twitter: @nbrogan087

BUCHANAN, Mr Keith *DUP* **Mid Ulster**
Email: keith.buchanan@mla.niassembly.gov.uk
Constituency office: 2 Queens Avenue, Magherafelt BT45 6BU
Tel: 028 7930 0295/028 7930 0296 Twitter: @buchanan_dup

BUCHANAN, Mr Thomas *DUP* **West Tyrone**
Tel: 028 9052 1128 Email: thomas.buchanan@mla.niassembly.gov.uk
Constituency office: 52 Market Street, Omagh, Co Tyrone BT78 1EH
Tel: 028 8224 7702 Email: tombuchananmla@hotmail.co.uk Twitter: @tombbuchanan

BUCKLEY, Mr Jonathan *DUP* **Upper Bann**
Email: jonathan.buckley@mla.niassembly.gov.uk
Constituency office: No constituency office publicised Twitter: @JBuckleyMLA

BUNTING, Ms Joanne *DUP* **Belfast East**
Tel: 028 9079 7100 Email: joanne.bunting@co.niassembly.gov.uk
Constituency office: 220 Knock Road, Belfast BT5 6QD
Tel: 028 9079 7100
Website: joannebunting.co.uk Twitter: @joanne_bunting

BUTLER, Mr Robbie *UUP* **Lagan Valley**
UUP Assembly Chief Whip; Spokesperson for Education
Tel: 028 9244 9898 Email: robbie.butler@mla.niassembly.gov.uk
Constituency office: 59 Bridge Street, Lisburn BT28 1XZ
Website: robbiebutlermla.com Twitter: @RobbieButlerMLA

CAMERON, Mrs Pam *DUP* **South Antrim**
Tel: 028 9052 1816 Email: pam.cameron@mla.niassembly.gov.uk
Constituency office: 12a Beverley Road, Newtownabbey BT36 6QD Twitter: @PamCameronMLA

CARROLL, Mr Gerry *PBPA* **Belfast West**
Email: gerry.carroll@mla.niassembly.gov.uk
Constituency office: 208 Falls Road, Belfast BT12 6AH Twitter: @GerryCarrollPBP

CATNEY, Mr Pat *SDLP* **Lagan Valley**
Email: pat.catney@mla.niassembly.gov.uk
Constituency office: No constituency office publicised Twitter: @PatCatney

CHAMBERS, Mr Alan *UUP* **North Down**
UUP Spokesperson for Health
Email: alan.chambers@mla.niassembly.gov.uk
Constituency office: No constituency office publicised Twitter: @alcham49

CLARKE, Mr Trevor *DUP* **South Antrim**
Email: trevor.clarke@mla.niassembly.gov.uk
Constituency office: 1 Railway Street, Antrim BT41 4AE
Tel: 028 9446 3273 Twitter: @trevorclarkemla

DICKSON, Mr Stewart *APNI* **East Antrim**
Alliance Spokesperson for Economy
Tel: 028 9052 1315 Email: stewart.dickson@mla.niassembly.gov.uk
Constituency office: 8 West Street, Carrickfergus, Co Antrim BT38 7AR
Tel: 028 9335 0286 Email: stewart.dickson@alliancepartyni.org
Website: stewartdicksonmla.com Twitter: @stewartcdickson

DILLON, Ms Linda *Sinn Féin* **Mid Ulster**
Email: linda.dillon@mla.niassembly.gov.uk
Constituency office: 7 The Square, Coalisland BT71 4LN
Tel: 028 8774 8689 Twitter: @LindaDillon81

DODDS, Ms Diane *DUP* **Upper Bann**
Minister for the Economy
Ministerial office: St Andrew's House, Regent Road, Edinburgh EH1 3DG Tel: 0300 244 4000
Constituency office: No constituency office publicised Twitter: @dianedoddsmep

DOLAN, Ms Jemma *Sinn Féin* **Fermanagh and South Tyrone**
Email: jemma.dolan@mla.niassembly.gov.uk
Constituency office: 7 Market Street, Ennskillen BT74 7DS
Tel: 028 6632 8214 Twitter: @jemma_dolan

DUNNE, Mr Gordon, MBE *DUP* **North Down**
Tel: 028 9042 3322 Email: gordon.dunne@mla.niassembly.gov.uk
Constituency office: 8 Church Road, Holywood, Co Down BT18 9BU
Tel: 028 9042 3322 Email: info@gordondunne.org
Website: www.gordondunne.org Twitter: @gordondunnemla

DURKAN, Mr Mark H *SDLP* **Foyle**
SDLP Spokesperson for Social Justice
Tel: 028 9041 8354 Email: markh.durkan@mla.niassembly.gov.uk
Constituency office: 141h Strand Road, Derry, Co Derry BT48 7PB
Tel: 028 7136 5516 Email: mhdurkan@sdlp.ie
Website: www.markhdurkan.com Twitter: @markhdurkan

EASTON, Mr Alex *DUP* **North Down**
Tel: 028 9058 8379 Email: alex.easton@mla.niassembly.gov.uk
Constituency office: 7 High Street, Donaghadee, Co Down BT21 0AA
Tel: 028 9188 9620
Websites: www.nddup.org.uk alexeastonmla.org

ENNIS, Ms Sinéad *Sinn Féin* **South Down**
Chair, Assembly Committee on Standards and Privileges
Email: sinead.ennis@mla.niassembly.gov.uk
Constituency office: No constituency office publicised Twitter: @EnnisSinead

---

FLYNN, Ms Órlaithí *Sinn Féin* **Belfast West**
Email: orlaithi.flynn@mla.niassembly.gov.uk
Constituency office: No constituency office publicised Twitter: @orlaithiflynnsf

---

FOSTER, Rt Hon Arlene *DUP* **Fermanagh and South Tyrone**
First Minister; Leader, Democratic Unionist Party
Tel: 028 9041 8366 Email: arlene.foster@mla.niassembly.gov.uk
Ministerial office: St Andrew's House, Regent Road, Edinburgh EH1 3DG Tel: 0300 244 4000
Constituency office: 1 Quay Lane, Tonystick, Enniskillen, Co Fermanagh BT74 6AG
Tel: 028 6632 0722 Email: office@arlenefoster.org.uk Twitter: @DUPleader

---

FREW, Mr Paul *DUP* **North Antrim**
Tel: 028 9052 1543 Email: paul.frew@mla.niassembly.gov.uk
Constituency office: 9-11 Church Street, Ballymena, Co Antrim BT43 6DD
Tel: 028 2564 1421 Fax: 028 2565 7296 Twitter: @paulfrewDUP

GILDERNEW, Mr Colm *Sinn Féin* **Fermanagh and South Tyrone**
Chair, Assembly Committee on Health
Email: colm.gildernew@mla.niassembly.gov.uk
Constituency office: No constituency office publicised Twitter: @GildernewColm

---

GIVAN, Mr Paul *DUP* **Lagan Valley**
Chair, Assembly Committee on Justice
Tel: 028 9041 8389 Email: paul.givan@mla.niassembly.gov.uk
Constituency office: The Old Town Hall, 29 Castle Street, Lisburn, Co Antrim BT27 4DH
Tel: 028 9266 1100 Email: paul@laganvalley.net Twitter: @paulgivan

---

HARGEY, Ms Deirdre *Sinn Féin* **Belfast South**
Minister for Communities
Email: deirdre.hargey@mla.niassembly.gov.uk
Ministerial office: St Andrew's House, Regent Road, Edinburgh EH1 3DG Tel: 0300 244 4000
Constituency office: 178 Ormeau Road, Malone Lower, Belfast BT7 2ED
Tel: 028 9024 3194

HARVEY, Mr Harry *DUP* **Strangford**
Email: harry.harvey@mla.niassembly.gov.uk
Constituency office: 10a The Square, Ballynahinch BT24 8AE

HILDITCH, Mr David *DUP* **East Antrim**
Tel: 028 9052 1322 Email: david.hilditch@mla.niassembly.gov.uk
Constituency office: Unit 2, Joymount, Carrickfergus BT38 7DN
Tel: 028 9332 9980 Email: davyhilditch.mla@gmail.com Twitter: @davyh_crfc

---

HUMPHREY, Mr William, MBE *DUP* **Belfast North**
Chair, Assembly Committee on Public Accounts
Tel: 028 9052 1322 Email: william.humphrey@mla.niassembly.gov.uk
Constituency office: Park Gate House, 35 Woodvale Road, Belfast BT13 3BN
Tel: 028 9074 4008 Email: williamhy@dup-belfast.co.uk Twitter: @WmHumphreyDUP

HUNTER, Ms Cara *SDLP* **East Londonderry**
Email: cara.hunter@mla.niassembly.gov.uk
Constituency office: No constituency office publicised
Tel: 07903 451135

IRWIN, Mr William *DUP* **Newry and Armagh**
Tel: 028 9052 0313 Email: william.irwin@mla.niassembly.gov.uk
Constituency office: 18 Main Street, Richhill, Co Antrim BT61 9PW
Tel: 028 3887 0500 Fax: 028 3887 0054

KEARNEY, Mr Declan *Sinn Féin* **South Antrim**
Junior Minister, Executive Office
Email: declan.kearney@mla.niassembly.gov.uk
Constituency office: Unit 1, 2 Main Street, Randalstown, Co Antrim BT41 3AB
Tel: 028 9447 3972 Twitter: @declankearneysf

KELLY, Mrs Dolores *SDLP* **Upper Bann**
SDLP Spokesperson for Addressing the Legacy of the Past
Email: dolores.kelly@mla.niassembly.gov.uk
Constituency office: 74 William Street, Lurgan BT66 6JB
Tel: 028 3832 2140 Twitter: @doloreskelly

KELLY, Mr Gerry *Sinn Féin* **Belfast North**
Tel: 028 9052 1471 Email: gerry.kelly@mla.niassembly.gov.uk
Constituency office: 545 Antrim Road, Belfast BT15 3BU
Tel: 028 9521 5649 Email: gerry.kelly@sinn-fein.ie Twitter: @gerrykellymla

---

KIMMINS, Ms Liz *Sinn Féin* **Newry and Armagh**
Email: liz.kimmins@mla.niassembly.gov.uk
Constituency office: 1 Kilmorey Terrace, Patrick Street, Newry BT35 8DW
Tel: 028 3026 1693 Email: lizkimminssf@gmail.com

LONG, Ms Naomi *APNI* **Belfast East**
Minister for Justice
Tel: 028 9052 1314 Email: naomi.long@mla.niassembly.gov.uk
Ministerial office: St Andrew's House, Regent Road, Edinburgh EH1 3DG Tel: 0300 244 4000
Constituency office: 56 Upper Newtownards Road, Belfast BT4 3EL
Tel: 028 9047 2004 Email: naomi.long@alliancepartyni.org Twitter: @naomi_long

---

LUNN, Mr Trevor *Ind* **Lagan Valley**
Tel: 028 9052 1139 Email: trevor.lunn@mla.niassembly.gov.uk
Constituency office: 17 Graham Gardens, Lisburn, Co Antrim BT28 1XE
Tel: 028 9267 1177 Fax: 028 9267 1157 Email: trevor.lunn@allianceparty.org
Twitter: @TrevorLunnLV

LYNCH, Mr Seán *Sinn Féin* **Fermanagh and South Tyrone**
Tel: 028 9052 0350 Email: sean.lynch@mla.niassembly.gov.uk
Constituency office: 115 Main Street, Lisnaskea, Co Fermanagh BT92 0JE
Tel: 028 6772 1642 Email: sean.lynch@sinn-fein.ie Twitter: @seanlynch122

LYONS, Mr Gordon *DUP* **East Antrim**
Junior Minister, Executive Office
Tel: 028 2826 7722 Email: gordon.lyons@mla.niassembly.gov.uk
Constituency office: 116 Main Street, Larne BT40 1RG
Tel: 028 2826 7722 Twitter: @gordonlyons1

LYTTLE, Mr Chris *APNI* **Belfast East**
Chair, Assembly Committee on Education; Alliance Spokesperson for Education
Tel: 028 9052 1314 Email: chris.lyttle@mla.niassembly.gov.uk
Constituency office: 56 Upper Newtownards Road, Belfast, Co Down BT4 3EL
Tel: 028 9047 2004 Email: chris.lyttle.co@alliancepartyni.org Twitter: @chris_lyttle

---

MCALEER, Mr Declan *Sinn Féin* **West Tyrone**
Chair, Assembly Committee on Agriculture, Environment and Rural Affairs
Tel: 028 9052 1470 Email: declan.mcaleer@mla.niassembly.gov.uk
Constituency office: 4-5 James Street, Omagh BT78 1DH
Tel: 028 8225 3040 Fax: 028 8225 3041 Email: declanmcaleer@ymail.com Twitter: @mc_mla

---

MCCANN, Mr Fra *Sinn Féin* **Belfast West**
Tel: 028 9052 1471 Email: fra.mccann@mla.niassembly.gov.uk
Constituency office: 51-55 Falls Road, Belfast, Co Antrim BT12 4PD
Tel: 028 9050 8989 Fax: 028 9050 8988 Email: framccann@hotmail.com Twitter: @framccannmla

---

MCCROSSAN, Mr Daniel *SDLP* **West Tyrone**
Chair, Assembly Committee on Audit; SDLP Spokesperson for Education
Email: daniel.mccrossan@mla.niassembly.gov.uk
Constituency offices: 1 John Street, Omagh BT78 1DW
Tel: 028 8225 0060
Wray House, 1 Church Street, Strabane BT82 8BS
Tel: 028 7188 2828 Twitter: @McCrossanMLA

MCGLONE, Mr Patsy *SDLP* **Mid Ulster**
Deputy Speaker
Tel: 028 9052 0347
Constituency office: 54a William Street, Cookstown, Co Tyrone BT80 8NB
Tel: 028 8675 8175 Email: patsymcglonemla@yahoo.ie
Website: www.patsymcglone.com Twitter: @patsymcglone

MCGRATH, Mr Colin *SDLP* **South Down**
Chair, Assembly Committee on the Executive Office; SDLP Spokesperson for Healthcare
Email: colin.mcgrath@mla.niassembly.gov.uk
Constituency office: 97a Main Street, Ballaghbeg, Co Down BT33 0AE
Tel: 028 4379 8350 Twitter: @colinsdlp

MCGUIGAN, Mr Philip *Sinn Féin* **North Antrim**
Email: philip.mcguigan@mla.niassembly.gov.uk
Constituency office: 12 Main Street, Dunloy BT44 9AA
Tel: 028 2765 7198 Twitter: @mcguigan_philip

MCHUGH, Mr Maolíosa *Sinn Féin* **West Tyrone**
Email: maoliosa.mchugh@mla.niassembly.gov.uk
Constituency office: 1a Melvin Road, Ballycolman, Strabane BT82 9PP Twitter: @MaoliosaMcH

MCILVEEN, Miss Michelle *DUP* **Strangford**
Chair, Assembly Committee on Infrastructure
Tel: 028 9052 1557 Email: michelle.mcilveen@mla.niassembly.gov.uk
Constituency office: 24 Castle Street, Comber, Newtownards BT23 5DZ
Tel: 028 9187 1441 Email: michelle.mcilveen@co.niassembly.gov.uk
Website: www.michellemcilveen.org.uk Twitter: @MMcIlveenDUP

MCLAUGHLIN, Ms Sinead *SDLP* **Foyle**
SDLP Spokesperson for Economy
Email: sinead.mclaughlin@mla.niassembly.gov.uk
Constituency office: Unit 4, Spencer House, 14-22 Spencer Road, Derry BT47 6QA
Tel: 028 7116 2900

MCNULTY, Mr Justin *SDLP* **Newry and Armagh**
Email: justin.mcnulty@mla.niassembly.gov.uk
Constituency office: 15 Trevor Hill, Carneyhough, Newry BT34 1DN
Tel: 028 3026 7933 Twitter: @JustinMcNu1ty

MALLON, Ms Nichola *SDLP* **Belfast North**
Minister for Infrastructure; Deputy Leader, Social Democratic and Labour Party
Tel: 028 9515 0100 Email: nichola.mallon@mla.niassembly.gov.uk
Ministerial office: St Andrew's House, Regent Road, Edinburgh EH1 3DG Tel: 0300 244 4000
Constituency office: 168 Antrim Road, Belfast BT15 2AH
Tel: 028 9515 0100 Twitter: @nicholamallon

MASKEY, Mr Alex *Speaker* **Belfast West**
Speaker; Chair, Assembly Committee on Business
Tel: 028 9052 1224 Email: alex.maskey@mla.niassembly.gov.uk
Constituency office: 147 Andersonstown Road, Ballydownfine, Belfast, Co Antrim BT11 9BW
Tel: 028 9080 8404 Twitter: @AlexMaskeySF

MIDDLETON, Mr Gary *DUP* **Foyle**
Email: gary.middleton@mla.niassembly.gov.uk
Constituency office: First Floor, Waterside Centre, 23 Glendermott Road, Waterside, Co Londonderry BT47 6BG
Tel: 028 7134 6271 Twitter: @Gary_Middleton

MUIR, Mr Andrew *APNI* **North Down**
Alliance Spokesperson for Infrastructure and Finance
Constituency office: No constituency office publicised
Email: andrew.muir@alliancepartyni.org
Website: andrewmuir.net

MULLAN, Ms Karen *Sinn Féin* **Foyle**
Email: karen.mullan@mla.niassembly.gov.uk
Constituency office: Sinn Fein Centre, Ráth Mór Business Park, Eastway Road, Derry BT48 0LZ
Tel: 028 7137 7551 Email: karenmullan@hotmail.com Twitter: @k_mullan

---

MURPHY, Mr Conor *Sinn Féin* **Newry and Armagh**
Minister for Finance
Email: conor.murphy@mla.niassembly.gov.uk
Ministerial office: St Andrew's House, Regent Road, Edinburgh EH1 3DG Tel: 0300 244 4000
Constituency office: 10 Newry Street, Crossmaglen BT35 9JH
Tel: 028 3086 1948 Twitter: @conormurphysf

NESBITT, Mr Mike *UUP* **Strangford**
UUP Spokesperson for Executive Office
Tel: 028 9052 1861 Email: mike.nesbitt@mla.niassembly.gov.uk
Constituency office: 16 South Street, Newtownards, Co Down BT23 4JT
Tel: 028 9182 1587 Twitter: @mikenesbittni

NEWTON, Mr Robin, MBE *DUP* **Belfast East**
Tel: 028 9052 1322 Email: robin.newton@mla.niassembly.gov.uk
Constituency office: 59 Castlereagh Road, Belfast BT5 5FB
Tel: 028 9045 9500 Email: mail@robinnewton.co.uk
Website: www.robinnewton.co.uk Twitter: @RobinNewton4MLA

NÍ CHUILÍN, Ms Carál *Sinn Féin* **Belfast North**
Chair, Assembly Committee on Procedures
Tel: 028 9052 1471 Email: caral.nichuilin@mla.niassembly.gov.uk
Constituency office: 545 Antrim Road, Belfast, Co Antrim BT15 3BU
Tel: 028 9521 5649 Email: caral.nichuilin@sinn-fein.ie Twitter: @CaralNiChuilin

---

O'DOWD, Mr John *Sinn Féin* **Upper Bann**
Tel: 028 9052 1471 Email: john.odowd@mla.niassembly.gov.uk
Constituency office: 77 North Street, Lurgan, Co Armagh BT67 9AH
Tel: 028 3834 9675 Fax: 028 3832 2610 Email: johnodowd@hotmail.com
Website: www.upperbannsf.com Twitter: @johnodowdsf

O'NEILL, Ms Michelle *Sinn Féin* **Mid Ulster**
Deputy First Minister; Leader, Northern Ireland Sinn Féin
Tel: 028 9052 0463 Email: michelle.oneill@mla.niassembly.gov.uk
Ministerial office: St Andrew's House, Regent Road, Edinburgh EH1 3DG Tel: 0300 244 4000
Constituency office: 30F Fairhill Road, Cookstown BT80 8AG
Tel: 028 8627 7680 Twitter: @moneillsf

O'TOOLE, Mr Matthew *SDLP* **Belfast South**
Email: matthew.otoole@mla.niassembly.gov.uk
Constituency office: No constituency office publicised

POOTS, Mr Edwin *DUP* **Lagan Valley**
Minister for Agriculture, Environmental and Rural Affairs
Tel: 028 9052 1114 Email: edwin.poots@mla.niassembly.gov.uk
Ministerial office: St Andrew's House, Regent Road, Edinburgh EH1 3DG Tel: 0300 244 4000
Constituency offices: The Old Town Hall, 29 Castle Street, Lisburn, Co Antrim BT27 4DH
Tel: 028 9260 3003 Email: edwinpoots@outlook.com
3 Church Street, Dromore, Co Down BT25 1AA
Tel: 028 9269 8866 Twitter: @poots2edwin

ROBINSON, Mr George, MBE *DUP* **East Londonderry**
Tel: 028 9052 1322 Email: george.robinson@mla.niassembly.gov.uk
Constituency office: 6-8 Catherine Street, Limavady, Co Londonderry BT49 9DB
Tel: 028 7776 9191 Fax: 028 7776 9111 Email: limavadyhq@dup.org.uk

---

ROGAN, Ms Emma *Sinn Féin* **South Down**
Email: emma.rogan@mla.niassembly.gov.uk
Constituency office: No constituency office publicised
Tel: 028 4461 4405 Email: emmaroganmla@gmail.com Twitter: @emmarogansf

---

SHEEHAN, Mr Pat *Sinn Féin* **Belfast West**
Tel: 028 9052 1471 Email: pat.sheehan@mla.niassembly.gov.uk
Constituency office: 589 Springfield Road, Belfast BT12 7FP
Tel: 028 9062 6670 Email: patsheehansf@gmail.com Twitter: @PatSheehanMLA

SHEERIN, Ms Emma *Sinn Féin* **Mid Ulster**
Email: emma.sheerin@mla.niassembly.gov.uk
Constituency office: 79 Quarry Road, Gulladuff, Knockcloghrim BT45 8NS
Twitter: @SheerinOfficial

STALFORD, Mr Christopher *DUP* **Belfast South**
Principal Deputy Speaker
Email: christopher.stalford@mla.niassembly.gov.uk
Constituency office: 127/145 Sandy Row, Belfast BT12 5ET
Tel: 028 9031 5329 Twitter: @CStalfordMLA

STEWART, Mr John *UUP* **East Antrim**
UUP Spokesperson for Economy
Email: john.stewart@mla.niassembly.gov.uk
Constituency office: 95 Main Street, Larne BT40 1HJ
Tel: 028 2827 2644
Website: johnstewartuup.blogspot.co.uk Twitter: @JohnStewart1983

STOREY, Mr Mervyn *DUP* **North Antrim**
Chair, Assembly Committee on Assembly and Executive Review
Tel: 028 9052 1322 Email: mervyn.storey@mla.niassembly.gov.uk
Constituency office: 3 Market Street, Ballymoney BT53 6EA
Tel: 028 2766 9753 Fax: 028 2766 6143 Email: mervynstoreymla@gmail.com

SUGDEN, Ms Claire *Ind* **East Londonderry**
Tel: 028 9052 0310 Email: claire.sugden@mla.niassembly.gov.uk
Constituency office: 1 Upper Abbey Street, Coleraine BT52 1BF
Tel: 028 7032 7294 Twitter: @ClaireSugden

SWANN, Mr Robin *UUP* **North Antrim**
Minister for Health
Tel: 028 9052 1766 Email: robin.swann@mla.niassembly.gov.uk
Ministerial office: St Andrew's House, Regent Road, Edinburgh EH1 3DG Tel: 0300 244 4000
Constituency office: 13-15 Queen Street, Harryville, Ballymena, Co Antrim BT42 2BB
Tel: 028 2565 9595 Email: robin.swannmla@gmail.com
Website: www.robinswannmla.com Twitter: @RobinSwannUUP

WEIR, Mr Peter *DUP* **Strangford**
Minister for Education
Tel: 028 9052 1296 Fax: 028 9052 1287 Email: peter.weir@mla.niassembly.gov.uk
Ministerial office: St Andrew's House, Regent Road, Edinburgh EH1 3DG Tel: 0300 244 4000
Constituency office: 6a North Street, Newtownards BT23 4DE
Tel: 028 9181 0858 Email: peterweirmla@gmail.com Twitter: @peterweirmla

WELLS, Mr Jim *DUP* **South Down**
Tel: 028 9052 1110 Email: jim.wells@mla.niassembly.gov.uk
Constituency office: 12 Bridge Street, Kilkeel, Co Down BT34 4AD
Tel: 028 4176 9900 Fax: 028 3832 1837 Email: jimwells6@gmail.com Twitter: @jim_wells_mla

WOODS, Ms Rachel *Green* **North Down**
Email: rachel.woods@mla.niassembly.gov.uk
Constituency office: 12 Hamilton Road, Bangor BT20 4LE
Tel: 028 9127 3327 Twitter: @rachelwoods52

Women MLAs (32)

ANDERSON Martina	Sinn Féin	FOSTER Arlene	DUP
ARCHIBALD Caoimhe	Sinn Féin	HARGEY Deirdre	Sinn Féin
ARMSTRONG Kellie	APNI	HUNTER Cara	SDLP
BAILEY Clare	Green	KELLY Dolores	SDLP
BARTON Rosemary	UUP	KIMMINS Liz	Sinn Féin
BRADLEY Paula	DUP	LONG Naomi	APNI
BRADLEY Sinéad	SDLP	MCILVEEN Michelle	DUP
BRADSHAW Paula	APNI	MCLAUGHLIN Sinead	SDLP
BROGAN Nicola	Sinn Féin	MALLON Nichola	SDLP
BUNTING Joanne	DUP	MULLAN Karen	Sinn Féin
CAMERON Pam	DUP	NÍ CHUILÍN Carál	Sinn Féin
DILLON Linda	Sinn Féin	O'NEILL Michelle	Sinn Féin
DODDS Diane	DUP	ROGAN Emma	Sinn Féin
DOLAN Jemma	Sinn Féin	SHEERIN Emma	Sinn Féin
ENNIS Sinéad	Sinn Féin	SUGDEN Claire	Ind
FLYNN Órlaithí	Sinn Féin	WOODS Rachel	Green

Constituencies

			Count elected on
East Antrim	Roy Beggs	UUP	6th
East Antrim	Stewart Dickson	APNI	6th
East Antrim	David Hilditch	DUP	3rd
East Antrim	Gordon Lyons	DUP	8th
East Antrim	John Stewart	UUP	9th
North Antrim	Jim Allister	TUV	7th
North Antrim	Paul Frew	DUP	7th
North Antrim	Philip McGuigan	Sinn Féin	6th
North Antrim	Mervyn Storey	DUP	7th
North Antrim	Robin Swann	UUP	6th
South Antrim	Stephen Aiken	UUP	5th
South Antrim	John Blair	APNI	-
South Antrim	Pam Cameron	DUP	8th
South Antrim	Trevor Clarke	DUP	-
South Antrim	Declan Kearney	Sinn Féin	4th
Belfast East	Andy Allen	UUP	9th
Belfast East	Joanne Bunting	DUP	9th
Belfast East	Naomi Long	APNI	1st
Belfast East	Chris Lyttle	APNI	8th
Belfast East	Robin Newton	DUP	11th
Belfast North	Paula Bradley	DUP	6th
Belfast North	William Humphrey	DUP	6th
Belfast North	Gerry Kelly	Sinn Féin	7th
Belfast North	Nichola Mallon	SDLP	7th
Belfast North	Carál Ní Chuilín	Sinn Féin	7th
Belfast South	Clare Bailey	Green	9th
Belfast South	Paula Bradshaw	APNI	6th
Belfast South	Deirdre Hargey	Sinn Féin	-
Belfast South	Matthew O'Toole	SDLP	-
Belfast South	Christopher Stalford	DUP	9th
Belfast West	Gerry Carroll	PBPA	3rd
Belfast West	Órlaithí Flynn	Sinn Féin	1st
Belfast West	Fra McCann	Sinn Féin	4th
Belfast West	Alex Maskey	Speaker	3rd
Belfast West	Pat Sheehan	Sinn Féin	4th
North Down	Alan Chambers	UUP	1st
North Down	Gordon Dunne	DUP	2nd
North Down	Alex Easton	DUP	1st
North Down	Andrew Muir	APNI	-
North Down	Rachel Woods	Green	-
South Down	Sinéad Bradley	SDLP	3rd
South Down	Sinéad Ennis	Sinn Féin	1st
South Down	Colin McGrath	SDLP	7th
South Down	Emma Rogan	Sinn Féin	-
South Down	Jim Wells	DUP	5th
Fermanagh and South Tyrone	Rosemary Barton	UUP	4th
Fermanagh and South Tyrone	Jemma Dolan	Sinn Féin	3rd
Fermanagh and South Tyrone	Arlene Foster	DUP	2nd
Fermanagh and South Tyrone	Colm Gildernew	Sinn Féin	-
Fermanagh and South Tyrone	Seán Lynch	Sinn Féin	4th
Foyle	Martina Anderson	Sinn Féin	-
Foyle	Mark H Durkan	SDLP	5th
Foyle	Sinead McLaughlin	SDLP	-

			Count elected on
Foyle	Gary Middleton	DUP	6th
Foyle	Karen Mullan	Sinn Féin	-
Lagan Valley	Robbie Butler	UUP	7th
Lagan Valley	Pat Catney	SDLP	8th
Lagan Valley	Paul Givan	DUP	1st
Lagan Valley	Trevor Lunn	Ind*	7th
Lagan Valley	Edwin Poots	DUP	8th
East Londonderry	Caoimhe Archibald	Sinn Féin	12th
East Londonderry	Maurice Bradley	DUP	9th
East Londonderry	Cara Hunter	SDLP	-
East Londonderry	George Robinson	DUP	9th
East Londonderry	Claire Sugden	Ind	8th
Newry and Armagh	Cathal Boylan	Sinn Féin	1st
Newry and Armagh	William Irwin	DUP	1st
Newry and Armagh	Liz Kimmins	Sinn Féin	-
Newry and Armagh	Justin McNulty	SDLP	2nd
Newry and Armagh	Conor Murphy	Sinn Féin	3rd
Strangford	Kellie Armstrong	APNI	4th
Strangford	Harry Harvey	DUP	-
Strangford	Michelle McIlveen	DUP	9th
Strangford	Mike Nesbitt	UUP	9th
Strangford	Peter Weir	DUP	11th
West Tyrone	Nicola Brogan	Sinn Féin	-
West Tyrone	Thomas Buchanan	DUP	1st
West Tyrone	Declan McAleer	Sinn Féin	5th
West Tyrone	Daniel McCrossan	SDLP	5th
West Tyrone	Maolíosa McHugh	Sinn Féin	-
Mid Ulster	Keith Buchanan	DUP	1st
Mid Ulster	Linda Dillon	Sinn Féin	2nd
Mid Ulster	Patsy McGlone	SDLP	5th
Mid Ulster	Michelle O'Neill	Sinn Féin	1st
Mid Ulster	Emma Sheerin	Sinn Féin	-
Upper Bann	Doug Beattie	UUP	5th
Upper Bann	Jonathan Buckley	DUP	4th
Upper Bann	Diane Dodds	DUP	-
Upper Bann	Dolores Kelly	SDLP	6th
Upper Bann	John O'Dowd	Sinn Féin	5th

*Elected as Alliance Party

Assembly Committees

Chairpersons' Liaison Group

Tel: 028 9052 1787
Email: keith.mcbride@niassembly.gov.uk
www.niassembly.gov.uk/assembly-business/committees/chairperson-liaison-group

Stephen Aiken *UUP*
Caoimhe Archibald *Sinn Féin*
Paula Bradley *DUP*
Sinéad Ennis *Sinn Féin*
Colm Gildernew *Sinn Féin*
Paul Givan *DUP*
William Humphrey *DUP*
Chris Lyttle *APNI*
Declan McAleer *Sinn Féin*
Daniel McCrossan *SDLP*
Colin McGrath *SDLP*
Michelle McIlveen *DUP*
Carál Ní Chuilín *Sinn Féin*
Mervyn Storey *DUP*

Staff: Keith McBride (Clerk)

Agriculture, Environment and Rural Affairs

Tel: 028 9052 1475
Email: committee.agrienvrural@niassembly.gov.uk
www.niassembly.gov.uk/assembly-business/committees/2017-2022/agriculture-environment-and-rural-affairs
Twitter: @NIAAgriEnvRA

Declan McAleer (Chair) *Sinn Féin*
Philip McGuigan (Deputy Chair) *Sinn Féin*
Clare Bailey *Green*
Rosemary Barton *UUP*
John Blair *APNI*
Maurice Bradley *DUP*
Harry Harvey *DUP*
William Irwin *DUP*
Patsy McGlone *SDLP*

Staff: Stella McArdle (Clerk)

Assembly and Executive Review

Tel: 028 9052 1843
Email: committee.assemblyexecutivereview@niassembly.gov.uk
www.niassembly.gov.uk/assembly-business/committees/2017-2022/assembly-and-executive-review-committee

Mervyn Storey (Chair) *DUP*
Maolíosa McHugh (Deputy Chair) *Sinn Féin*
Jim Allister *TUV*
Kellie Armstrong *APNI*
Jonathan Buckley *DUP*
Robbie Butler *UUP*
Alex Easton *DUP*
Gerry Kelly *Sinn Féin*
Colin McGrath *SDLP*

Staff: Shane McAteer (Clerk)

Audit

Tel: 028 9052 1843
Email: committee.audit@niasssembly.gov.uk
www.niassembly.gov.uk/assembly-business/committees/2017-2022/audit-committee

Daniel McCrossan (Chair) *SDLP*
Joanne Bunting (Deputy Chair) *DUP*
Jim Allister *TUV*
Alan Chambers *UUP*
Emma Rogan *Sinn Féin*

Staff: Shane McAteer (Clerk)

Ad Hoc Committee on Bill of Rights

Tel: 028 9052 1379
Email: billofrightscommittee@niassembly.gov.uk
www.niassembly.gov.uk/assembly-business/committees/2017-2022/ad-hoc-committee-on-a-bill-of-rights

Emma Sheerin (Chair) *Sinn Féin*
Mike Nesbitt (Deputy Chair) *UUP*
Paula Bradshaw *APNI*
Mark H Durkan *SDLP*
Michelle McIlveen *DUP*
Carál Ní Chuilín *Sinn Féin*
Christopher Stalford *DUP*

Business

Tel: 028 9052 1534
Email: business.office@niassembly.gov.uk
www.niassembly.gov.uk/assembly-business/committees/2017-2022/business-committee

Alex Maskey (Chair) *Speaker*
Kellie Armstrong *APNI*
Clare Bailey *Green*
Keith Buchanan *DUP*
Robbie Butler *UUP*
Sinéad Ennis *Sinn Féin*
Dolores Kelly *SDLP*
Colin McGrath *SDLP*
Gary Middleton *DUP*
Andrew Muir *APNI*
John O'Dowd *Sinn Féin*
John Stewart *UUP*

Staff: Alex McGarel (Clerk)

Communities

Tel: 028 9052 1864
Email: committee.communities@niassembly.gov.uk

www.niassembly.gov.uk/assembly-business/committees/2017-2022/communities
Twitter: @NIA_Communities

Paula Bradley (Chair)	*DUP*
Kellie Armstrong (Deputy Chair)	*APNI*
Andy Allen	*UUP*
Mark H Durkan	*SDLP*
Alex Easton	*DUP*
Sinéad Ennis	*Sinn Féin*
Fra McCann	*Sinn Féin*
Robin Newton	*DUP*

Staff: Janice Thompson (Clerk)

Economy

Tel: 028 9052 1799
Email: committee.economy@niassembly.gov.uk
www.niassembly.gov.uk/assembly-business/committees/2017-2022/economy
Twitter: @NIAEconomy

Caoimhe Archibald (Chair)	*Sinn Féin*
Sinead McLaughlin (Deputy Chair)	*SDLP*
Stewart Dickson	*APNI*
Gordon Dunne	*DUP*
Gary Middleton	*DUP*
John O'Dowd	*Sinn Féin*
Christopher Stalford	*DUP*
John Stewart	*UUP*
Claire Sugden	*Ind*

Staff: Peter Hall (Clerk)

Education

Tel: 028 9052 1628
Email: committee.education@niassembly.gov.uk
www.niassembly.gov.uk/assembly-business/committees/2017-2022/education
Twitter: @NIACfEd

Chris Lyttle (Chair)	*APNI*
Karen Mullan (Deputy Chair)	*Sinn Féin*
Maurice Bradley	*DUP*
Robbie Butler	*UUP*
William Humphrey	*DUP*
Daniel McCrossan	*SDLP*
Justin McNulty	*SDLP*
Robin Newton	*DUP*

Staff: Aoibhinn Treanor (Clerk)

Executive Office

Tel: 028 9052 1019
Email: committee.executive@niassembly.gov.uk
www.niassembly.gov.uk/assembly-business/committees/2017-2022/the-executive-office
Twitter: @NIAEOCttee

Colin McGrath (Chair)	*SDLP*
Doug Beattie (Deputy Chair)	*UUP*
Martina Anderson	*Sinn Féin*
Trevor Clarke	*DUP*
Trevor Lunn	*Ind*
George Robinson	*DUP*
Pat Sheehan	*Sinn Féin*
Emma Sheerin	*Sinn Féin*
Christopher Stalford	*DUP*

Staff: Michael Potter (Clerk)

Finance

Tel: 028 9052 1821
Email: committee.finance@niassembly.gov.uk
www.niassembly.gov.uk/assembly-business/committees/2017-2022/finance
Twitter: @NIAFinance

Stephen Aiken (Chair)	*UUP*
Paul Frew (Deputy Chair)	*DUP*
Jim Allister	*TUV*
Pat Catney	*SDLP*
Jemma Dolan	*Sinn Féin*
Philip McGuigan	*Sinn Féin*
Maolíosa McHugh	*Sinn Féin*
Matthew O'Toole	*SDLP*
Jim Wells	*DUP*

Staff: Peter McCallion (Clerk)

Health

Tel: 028 9052 0348
Email: committee.health@niassembly.gov.uk
www.niassembly.gov.uk/assembly-business/committees/2017-2022/health
Twitter: @niahealth

Colm Gildernew (Chair)	*Sinn Féin*
Pam Cameron (Deputy Chair)	*DUP*
Paula Bradshaw	*APNI*
Gerry Carroll	*PBPA*
Alan Chambers	*UUP*
Alex Easton	*DUP*
Órlaithí Flynn	*Sinn Féin*
Cara Hunter	*SDLP*
Pat Sheehan	*Sinn Féin*

Staff: Éilis Haughey (Clerk)

Infrastructure

Tel: 028 9052 1448
Email: committee.infrastructure@niassembly.gov.uk
www.niassembly.gov.uk/assembly-business/committees/2017-2022/infrastructure
Twitter: @NIAInfra

Michelle McIlveen (Chair)	*DUP*
David Hilditch (Deputy Chair)	*DUP*
Martina Anderson	*Sinn Féin*
Roy Beggs	*UUP*
Cathal Boylan	*Sinn Féin*
Keith Buchanan	*DUP*

Dolores Kelly	*SDLP*
Liz Kimmins	*Sinn Féin*
Andrew Muir	*APNI*

Staff: Cathie White (Clerk)

Justice

Tel: 028 9052 1629
Email: committee.justice@niassembly.gov.uk
www.niassembly.gov.uk/assembly-business/committees/2017-2022/justice
Twitter: @NIAJusticeComm

Paul Givan (Chair)	*DUP*
Linda Dillon (Deputy Chair)	*Sinn Féin*
Doug Beattie	*UUP*
Sinéad Bradley	*SDLP*
Jemma Dolan	*Sinn Féin*
Gordon Dunne	*DUP*
Paul Frew	*DUP*
Emma Rogan	*Sinn Féin*
Rachel Woods	*Green*

Staff: Christine Darrah (Clerk)

Procedures

Tel: 028 9052 1205
Email: committee.procedures@niassembly.gov.uk
www.niassembly.gov.uk/assembly-business/committees/2017-2022/procedures

Carál Ní Chuilín (Chair)	*Sinn Féin*
Thomas Buchanan (Deputy Chair)	*DUP*
Rosemary Barton	*UUP*
Maurice Bradley	*DUP*
Sinéad Bradley	*SDLP*
Nicola Brogan	*Sinn Féin*
Gerry Carroll	*PBPA*
Gary Middleton	*DUP*

Staff: Nick Mitford (Clerk)

Public Accounts

Tel: 028 9052 1208
Email: committee.publicaccounts@niassembly.gov.uk
www.niassembly.gov.uk/assembly-business/committees/2017-2022/public-accounts-committee Twitter: @NIA_PAC

William Humphrey (Chair)	*DUP*
Roy Beggs (Deputy Chair)	*UUP*
Cathal Boylan	*Sinn Féin*
Órlaithí Flynn	*Sinn Féin*
Harry Harvey	*DUP*
David Hilditch	*DUP*
Maolíosa McHugh	*Sinn Féin*
Andrew Muir	*APNI*
Matthew O'Toole	*SDLP*

Staff: Lucia Wilson (Clerk)

Standards and Privileges

Tel: 028 9052 1843
Email: committee.standardsprivileges@niassembly.gov.uk
www.niassembly.gov.uk/assembly-business/committees/2017-2022/standards-and-privileges

Sinéad Ennis (Chair)	*Sinn Féin*
William Irwin (Deputy Chair)	*DUP*
Stephen Aiken	*UUP*
Pam Cameron	*DUP*
Stewart Dickson	*APNI*
Seán Lynch	*Sinn Féin*
Declan McAleer	*Sinn Féin*
Patsy McGlone	*SDLP*
George Robinson	*DUP*

Staff: Shane McAteer (Clerk)

Principal Officers and Officials

Office of the Speaker

Speaker **Alex Maskey**

Principal Deputy Speaker **Christopher Stalford**

Deputy Speakers **Roy Beggs**, **Patsy McGlone**

Principal Officers

Clerk/Chief Executive	Lesley Hogg
Directors	
Legal, Governance and Research Services	Tara Caul
Parliamentary Services	Dr Gareth McGrath
Corporate Services	Richard Stewart
Examiner of Statutory Rules	Angela Kelly
Clerk Assistants	Paul Gill
	Dr Frank Geddis
	Dr Kevin Pelan

Editor of Debates and Head of Public Engagement	Simon Burrowes
Adviser to the Speaker/Head of Corporate Support Unit	Robin Ramsey
Comptroller and Auditor General	Kieran Donnelly CB 028 9025 1000 Email: info@niauditoffice.gov.uk
Northern Ireland Public Services Ombudsman	Margaret Kelly 028 9023 3821 Email: nipso@nipso.org.uk

Northern Ireland Civil Service

Executive Office
GD36 Stormont Castle, Stormont Estate, Belfast BT4 3TT
Tel: 028 9052 8400
Email: info.imcab@executiveoffice-ni.gov.uk Website: www.northernireland.gov.uk
Twitter: @niexecutive

Head of Northern Ireland Civil Service and Secretary to the Executive: Jenny Pyper 028 9037 8131 Email: hocs@executiveoffice-ni.gov.uk

Department of Agriculture, Environment and Rural Affairs
Dundonald House, Upper Newtownards Road, Ballymiscaw BT4 3SB
Tel: 0300 200 7852
Email: daera.helpline@daera-ni.gov.uk Website: www.daera-ni.gov.uk Twitter: @daera_ni

Permanent Secretary: Dr Denis McMahon 028 9052 4608 Email: perm.sec@daera-ni.gov.uk

Department for Communities
Causeway Exchange, 1-7 Bedford Street, Belfast BT2 7EG
Tel: 028 9082 9000
Email: permsecsupport@communities-ni.gov.uk Website: www.communities-ni.gov.uk
Twitter: @CommunitiesNI

Permanent Secretary: Tracy Meharg 028 9082 3301 Email: tracy.meharg@communities-ni.gov.uk

Department for the Economy
Netherleigh, Massey Avenue, Belfast BT4 2JP
Tel: 028 9052 9900
Email: dfemail@economy-ni.gov.uk Website: www.economy-ni.gov.uk Twitter: @Economy_NI

Permanent Secretary: Mike Brennan 028 9052 9441 Email: mike.brennan@economy-ni.gov.uk

Department of Education
Rathgael House, Balloo Road, Rathgill, Bangor BT19 7PR
Tel: 028 9127 9279
Email: de.dewebmail@education-ni.gov.uk Website: www.education-ni.gov.uk
Twitter: @Education_NI

Permanent Secretary: Lianne Patterson

Department of Finance
Clare House, 303 Airport Road West, Belfast BT3 9ED
Tel: 028 9185 8111
Email: dof.enquiries@finance-ni.gov.uk Website: www.finance-ni.gov.uk Twitter: @dptfinance

Permanent Secretary: Sue Gray 028 9081 6590 Email: sue.gray@finance-ni.gov.uk

Department of Health
C5.20, Castle Buildings, Stormont Estate, Belfast BT4 3SQ
Tel: 028 9052 0500
Email: webmaster@health-ni.gov.uk Website: www.health-ni.gov.uk Twitter: @HealthServiceNI

Permanent Secretary: Richard Pengelly 028 9052 0662 Email: richard.pengelly@health-ni.gov.uk

Department for Infrastructure
Clarence Court, 10-18 Adelaide Street, Belfast BT2 8GB
Tel: 028 9054 0540
Email: dcu@infrastructure-ni.gov.uk Website: www.infrastructure-ni.gov.uk Twitter: @deptinfra
Permanent Secretary: Katrina Godfrey 028 9054 1175
Email: katrina.godfrey@infrastructure-ni.gov.uk

Department of Justice
Block B, Castle Buildings, Stormont Estate, Belfast BT4 3SG
Tel: 028 9076 3000/028 9052 7668 (text phone)
Website: www.justice-ni.gov.uk Twitter: @Justice_NI
Permanent Secretary: Peter May

Office of the Attorney General for Northern Ireland
PO Box 1272, Belfast BT1 9LU
Tel: 028 9072 5333
Email: contact@attorneygeneralni.gov.uk Website: www.attorneygeneralni.gov.uk
Attorney General for Northern Ireland: Brenda King

Executive Agencies

Northern Ireland Courts and Tribunals Service
Laganside House, 23-27 Oxford Street, Belfast BT1 3LA
Tel: 0300 200 7812
Website: www.justice-ni.gov.uk/topics/courts-and-tribunals
Chief Executive: Peter Luney Email: peter.luney@courtsni.gov.uk
Sponsored by: Department of Justice

Driver and Vehicle Agency
148-158 Corporation Street, Belfast BT1 3DH
Tel: 0300 200 7861
Email: dva@infrastructure-ni.gov.uk
Website: www.infrastructure-ni.gov.uk/driver-and-vehicle-agency

66 Balmoral Road, Belfast BT12 6QL

County Hall, Castlerock Road, Coleraine BT51 3HS

Chief Executive: Jeremy Logan 028 9025 4125 Email: jeremy.logan@infrastructure-ni.gov.uk
Sponsored by: Department for Infrastructure

Northern Ireland Environment Agency
Klondyke Building, Gasworks Business Park, Lower Ormeau Road, Belfast BT7 2JA
Tel: 028 9056 9210
Email: nieainfo@daera-ni.gov.uk
Website: www.daera-ni.gov.uk/northern-ireland-environment-agency
Chief Executive: Tracey Teague 028 9056 9210 Email: tracey.teague@daera-ni.gov.uk
Sponsored by: Department of Agriculture, Environment and Rural Affairs

Forensic Science Northern Ireland
151 Belfast Road, Carrickfergus BT38 8PL
Tel: 028 9036 1888 Fax: 028 9036 1900
Email: forensic.science@fsni.x.gsi.gov.uk Website: www.justice-ni.gov.uk/fsni
Chief Executive: Gillian Morton 028 9036 1801 Email: generalenquiries@fsni.x.gsi.gov.uk
Sponsored by: Department of Justice

Forest Service
Inishkeen House, Killyhevlin Ind Estate, Enniskillen BT74 4EJ
Tel: 028 6634 3165
Email: forestservicecorporate@daera-ni.gov.uk Website: www.daera-ni.gov.uk/forest-service
Chief Executive: John Joe O'Boyle 028 6634 3086 Email: johnjoe.o'boyle@daera-ni.gov.uk
Sponsored by: Department of Agriculture, Environment and Rural Affairs

Invest Northern Ireland
Bedford Square, Bedford Street, Belfast BT2 7ES
Tel: 0800 181 4422 Fax: 028 9043 6536
Email: enquiry@investni.com Website: www.investni.com Twitter: @InvestNI
Chief Executive: Kevin Holland 028 9069 8260 Email: kevin.holland@investni.com
Chair: Rose Mary Stalker 028 9069 8255 Email: rosemary.stalker@investni.com
Sponsored by: Department for the Economy

Legal Services Agency Northern Ireland
Second Floor, Waterfront Plaza, 8 Langanbank Road, Belfast BT1 3BN
Tel: 028 9040 8888
Email: enquiries@lsani.gov.uk
Website: www.justice-ni.gov.uk/topics/legal-aid/legal-services-agency-northern-ireland
Chief Executive: Paul Andrews Email: paul.andrews@justice-ni.gov.uk
Sponsored by: Department of Justice

Northern Ireland Prison Service
Dundonald House, Upper Newtownards Road, Belfast BT4 3SU
Tel: 028 9052 0929
Email: info@niprisonservice.gov.uk Website: www.justice-ni.gov.uk/topics/prisons
Twitter: @NIPSofficial
Director-General: Ronnie Armour 028 9052 5147 Email: ronnie.armour@justice-ni.x.gsi.gov.uk
Sponsored by: Department of Justice

Northern Ireland Statistics and Research Agency
Colby House, Stranmillis Court, Belfast BT9 5RR
Tel: 028 9038 8400
Email: info@nisra.gov.uk Website: www.nisra.gov.uk Twitter: @NISRA
Registrar General and Chief Executive: Siobhan Carey 028 9034 8102
Email: siobhan.carey@finance-ni.gov.uk
Sponsored by: Department of Finance

Youth Justice Agency
41 Waring Street, Belfast BT1 2DY
Tel: 028 9031 6400
Email: info@yjani.gov.uk Website: www.justice-ni.gov.uk/topics/youth-justice/youth-justice-agency
Twitter: @Y_J_Agency
Chief Executive: Declan McGeown 028 9031 6452 Email: declan.mcgeown@justice-ni.x.gsi.gov.uk
Sponsored by: Department of Justice

Non-Ministerial Department

Public Prosecution Service for Northern Ireland
Belfast Chambers, 93 Chichester Street, Belfast BT1 3JR
Tel: 028 9089 7100
Email: info@ppsni.gsi.gov.uk Website: www.ppsni.gov.uk
Director of Public Prosecutions for Northern Ireland: Stephen Herron
Deputy Director of Public Prosecutions for Northern Ireland: Michael Agnew

Political Parties

Democratic Unionist Party

91 Dundela Avenue, Belfast BT4 3BU
Tel: 028 9047 1155
Email: info@mydup.com Website: www.mydup.com Twitter: @duponline

Assembly Office, Room 207 Parliament Buildings, Stormont, Belfast BT4 3XX
Tel: 028 9052 1323

Leader: Rt Hon Arlene Foster MLA
Deputy Leader: Rt Hon Lord Dodds of Duncairn OBE
Chair: Lord Morrow
Chief Executive: Timothy Johnston
Secretary: Michelle McIlveen MLA
Treasurer: Gregory Campbell MP
Press Officer: Clive McFarland 028 9065 4479 Email: clivemcfarland@dup.org.uk

Sinn Féin

53 Falls Road, Belfast BT12 4PD
Tel: 028 9034 7350 Fax: 028 9022 3001
Email: theresa.mcardle@sinnfein.ie Website: www.sinnfein.ie Twitter: @sinnfeinireland

44 Parnell Square, Dublin 1
Tel: +353 1 8726932 Fax: +353 1 8733441

Assembly Office:
Tel: 028 9052 1471/028 9052 1470 Fax: 028 9052 1476
Email: sfassembly@outlook.com

President: Mary Lou McDonald
Vice-President: Michelle O'Neill MLA
Chair: Declan Kearney MLA
General Secretary: Ken O'Connell
Treasurers: Pearse Doherty, Conor Murphy MLA

Social Democratic and Labour Party

121 Ormeau Road, Belfast BT7 1SH
Tel: 028 9024 7700 Fax: 028 9023 6699
Email: info@sdlp.ie Website: www.sdlp.ie Twitter: @sdlplive

Press Office:
Tel: 028 9052 1837

Leader: Colum Eastwood MP
Deputy Leader: Nichola Mallon MLA
Chair: Ronan McCay
Vice-chair: Gerard McDonald
General Secretary: Gerry Cosgrove Email: gerry.cosgrove@sdlphq.ie
International Secretary: Dr Naomh Gallagher

Ulster Unionist Party

Strandtown Hall, 2-4 Belmont Road, Belfast BT4 2AN
Tel: 028 9047 4630 Fax: 028 9065 2149
Email: uup@uup.org Website: www.uup.org Twitter: @uuponline

Assembly Office, Room 214 Parliament Buildings, Stormont, Belfast BT4 3XX
Tel: 028 9052 1423 Fax: 028 9052 1883

Policy Unit:
Tel: 028 9052 1892

Leader: Dr Stephen Aiken OBE MLA
Chair: Lord Empey OBE
Vice-chair: Roy McCune
Treasurer: Mark Cosgrove
Party Officers: Tom Elliott, James Nicholson, Jenny Palmer, Alexander Redpath, Lord Rogan, George White, Trevor Wilson
Communications and Policy Co-ordinator: John Moore 028 9052 1328 Email: john.moore@uup.org
Press Officer: Stephen Barr 028 9052 1890 Email: stephen.barr@party.niassembly.gov.uk

Alliance

88 University Street, Belfast BT7 1HE
Tel: 028 9032 4274
Email: alliance@alliancepartyni.org Website: www.allianceparty.org Twitter: @allianceparty

Assembly Office, Room 220 Parliament Buildings, Stormont, Belfast BT4 3XX
Tel: 028 9052 1314
Email: stormont@alliancepartyni.org

Leader: Naomi Long MLA
Deputy Leader: Dr Stephen Farry MP
Chair: Helena Young
President: David Ford
General Secretary: Sharon Lowry Email: sharon.lowry@alliancepartyni.org
Joint Hon Treasurers: Stewart Dickson MLA, Billy Webb Email: billy.webb@alliancepartyni.org
Press Officer: Scott Jamison Email: scott.jamison@alliancepartyni.org

Green Party

PO Box 369, Bangor BT20 9FJ
Tel: 028 9145 9110
Email: info@greenpartyni.org Website: www.greenpartyni.org Website: www.greenparty.ie
Twitter: @greenpartyni

Assembly Office:
Tel: 028 9052 1790

Leader, Green Party in Northern Ireland: Clare Bailey MLA 028 9031 4455
Email: clare.bailey@co.niassembly.gov.uk
Chair: Kate Barry
Press Officer: Sinead McIvor 028 9052 1141 Email: greenpartynipress@gmail.com

People Before Profit

13 Westland Avenue, Derry BT48 9JE
Twitter: @pb4p

Leader: Eamonn McCann

Traditional Unionist Voice
38 Henry Street, Ballymena BT42 3AH
Tel: 028 2564 0250
Website: www.tuv.org.uk
Assembly Office:
Tel: 028 9052 1461

Leader: Jim Allister MLA
President: William Ross
Chair: Ivor McConnell
Party Secretary: Joel Johnston
Treasurer: Kenny Loughrin
Press Officer: Samuel Morrison

Greater London Authority

City Hall, The Queens Walk, London SE1 2AA
Tel: 020 7983 4000 Fax: 020 7983 4057 Email: assembly@london.gov.uk
Website: www.london.gov.uk Twitter: @MayorofLondon/@LondonAssembly

Mayoral Team

Mayor of London: Rt Hon Sadiq Khan (Lab)
Tel: 020 7983 5646 Email: mayor@london.gov.uk

Statutory Deputy Mayor; Deputy Mayor for Education and Childcare: Joanne McCartney (Lab/Co-op)
Tel: 020 7983 5504 Email: joanne.mccartney@london.gov.uk

Deputy Mayor for Planning, Regeneration and Skills: Jules Pipe CBE
Tel: 020 7983 4190 Email: jules.pipe@london.gov.uk

Deputy Mayor for Culture and Creative Industries: Justine Simons OBE
Tel: 020 7983 5853 Email: justine.simons@london.gov.uk

Deputy Mayor for Social Integration, Social Mobility and Community Engagement: Dr Debbie Weekes-Bernard
Tel: 020 7983 4015 Email: debbie.weekes-bernard@london.gov.uk

Deputy Mayor for Business: Rajesh Agrawal
Tel: 020 7983 4516 Email: rajesh.agrawal@london.gov.uk

Deputy Mayor for Environment and Energy: Shirley Rodrigues
Tel: 020 7983 4384 Email: shirley.rodrigues@london.gov.uk

Deputy Mayor for Policing and Crime: Sophie Linden
Tel: 020 7983 5696 Email: sophie.linden@mopac.london.gov.uk

Deputy Mayor for Fire and Resilience: Fiona Twycross
Tel: 020 7983 5545 Email: fiona.twycross@london.gov.uk

Deputy Mayor for Transport: Heidi Alexander
Tel: 020 7983 4099 Email: heidi.alexander@london.gov.uk

Deputy Mayor for Housing and Residential Development: Tom Copley
Email: tom.copley@london.gov.uk

Chief of Staff: David Bellamy
Tel: 020 7983 4538 Email: david.bellamy@london.gov.uk

Mayoral Director of Policy: Dr Nick Bowes
Tel: 020 7983 4030 Email: nick.bowes@london.gov.uk

Mayoral Director of Communications: Patrick Hennessy
Tel: 020 7983 4069 Email: patrick.hennessy@london.gov.uk

Mayoral Director for External and International Affairs: Leah Kreitzman
Tel: 020 7983 4030 Email: leah.kreitzman@london.gov.uk

Mayoral Director for Political and Public Affairs: Jack Stenner
Tel: 020 7983 4069 Email: jack.stenner@london.gov.uk

Night Czar: Amy Lamé
Tel: 020 7983 4538 Email: amy.lame@london.gov.uk

Commissioner for Transport: Andy Byford

Commissioner for Walking and Cycling: Dr Will Norman
Tel: 020 3054 1155 Email: willnorman@tfl.gov.uk

Mayoral Health Adviser: Dr Tom Coffey OBE
Email: tom.coffey@london.gov.uk

Victims Commissioner: Claire Waxman
Tel: 020 7983 4646 Email: claire.waxman@mopac.london.gov.uk

Chief Digital Officer: Theo Blackwell MBE
Tel: 020 7983 5505 Email: theo.blackwell@london.gov.uk

Director of Violence Reduction Unit: Lib Peck
Email: lib.peck@london.gov.uk

Spokespeople

Labour Group

Email: cityhalllabour@gmail.com Twitter: @CityHallLabour
Leader, Labour Group on the London Assembly; Spokesperson on Budget and Performance: Len Duvall OBE
Spokesperson on Police and Crime: Unmesh Desai
Spokesperson for Fire and Resilience: Andrew Dismore
Spokesperson on Health: Dr Onkar Sahota
Spokesperson on Education: Jennette Arnold OBE
Spokesperson on Environment and Economy: Leonie Cooper
Spokesperson on Planning: Nicky Gavron

Conservative Group

Email: assembly.tories@gmail.com Website: glaconservatives.co.uk Twitter: @assembly_tories
Leader, Conservative Group on the London Assembly; Spokesperson on Budget, Education, Fire, Resilience and Emergency Planning and Police and Crime: Susan Hall
Deputy Leader, Conservative Group on the London Assembly; Spokesperson on Brexit, Devolution, Health, Housing and Planning and Regeneration: Andrew Boff
Spokesperson on Economy: Shaun Bailey
Spokesperson on Environment: Tony Arbour JP
Spokesperson on Transport: Keith Prince

London Assembly Members' Directory

ARBOUR, Mr Tony, JP *Con* — **South West**
Deputy Chair, London Assembly; Conservative Spokesperson on Environment
Tel: 020 7983 4116 Email: tony.arbour@london.gov.uk

ARNOLD, Ms Jennette, OBE *Lab/Co-op* — **North East**
Labour Spokesperson on Education
Website: jennettearnold.com Twitter: @JennetteArnold

BACON, Mr Gareth *Con* — **Bexley and Bromley**
Tel: 020 7983 5784 Email: gareth.bacon@london.gov.uk
Website: www.garethbacon.com Twitter: @GarethBaconMP

BAILEY, Mr Shaun *Con* — **Londonwide**
Conservative Spokesperson on Economy
Tel: 020 7983 4354 Email: shaun.bailey@london.gov.uk

BERRY, Ms Sian *Green* — **Londonwide**
Tel: 020 7983 4391 Fax: 020 7983 4398 Email: sian.berry@london.gov.uk Twitter: @sianberry

BOFF, Mr Andrew *Con* — **Londonwide**
Deputy Leader, Conservative Group on the London Assembly; Spokesperson on Brexit, Devolution, Health, Housing and Planning and Regeneration
Tel: 020 7983 4366 Email: andrew.boff@london.gov.uk Twitter: @AndrewBoff

COOPER, Ms Leonie *Lab* — **Merton and Wandsworth**
Labour Spokesperson on Environment and Economy
Email: leonie.cooper@london.gov.uk Twitter: @LeonieC

DESAI, Mr Unmesh *Lab* — **City and East**
Labour Spokesperson on Police and Crime
Tel: 020 7983 4430 Email: unmesh.desai@london.gov.uk Twitter: @unmeshdesai

DEVENISH, Mr Tony *Con* — **West Central**
Email: tony.devenish@london.gov.uk Twitter: @Tony_Devenish

DISMORE, Mr Andrew *Lab* — **Barnet and Camden**
Tel: 020 7983 5529 Email: andrew.dismore@london.gov.uk
Website: www.andrewdismore.org.uk Twitter: @Andrew_Dismore

DUVALL, Mr Len, OBE *Lab/Co-op* **Greenwich and Lewisham**
Leader, Labour Group on the London Assembly; Labour Spokesperson on Budget and Performance
Tel: 020 7983 4517 Email: len.duvall@london.gov.uk Twitter: @Len_Duvall

---

ESHALOMI, Ms Florence *Lab/Co-op* **Lambeth and Southwark**
Tel: 020 7983 4427 Email: florence.eshalomi@london.gov.uk
Website: www.florence4vauxhall.org.uk Twitter: @FloEshalomi

GAVRON, Ms Nicky *Lab/Co-op* **Londonwide**
Labour Spokesperson on Planning
Tel: 020 7983 4509 Email: nicky.gavron@london.gov.uk
Website: www.nickygavron.co.uk Twitter: @nickygavron

HALL, Ms Susan *Con* **Londonwide**
Leader, Conservative Group on the London Assembly; Spokesperson on Budget, Education, Fire, Resilience and Emergency Planning and Police and Crime
Email: susan.hall@london.gov.uk Twitter: @Councillorsuzie

KURTEN, Mr David *UKIP* **Londonwide**
Email: david.kurten@london.gov.uk
Website: www.davidkurten.net Twitter: @davidkurten

MCCARTNEY, Ms Joanne *Lab/Co-op* **Enfield and Haringey**
Statutory Deputy Mayor; Deputy Mayor for Education and Childcare
Tel: 020 7983 5524 Email: joanne.mccartney@london.gov.uk
Website: joannemccartney.co.uk Twitter: @JoanneMcCartney

MOORE, Dr Alison *Lab* **Londonwide**
Email: alison.moore@london.gov.uk

O'CONNELL, Mr Steve *Con* **Croydon and Sutton**
Tel: 020 7983 4405 Email: steve.o'connell@london.gov.uk
Website: www.steveoconnell.org Twitter: @SteveO_Connell

PIDGEON, Ms Caroline, MBE *Lib Dem* **Londonwide**
Leader, Liberal Democrat Group on the London Assembly
Tel: 020 7983 4362 Email: caroline.pidgeon@london.gov.uk
Website: www.carolinepidgeon.org Twitter: @CarolinePidgeon

PRINCE, Mr Keith *Con* **Havering and Redbridge**
Conservative Spokesperson on Transport
Tel: 020 7983 4955 Email: keith.prince@london.gov.uk
Website: www.keithprince.london Twitter: @KeithPrinceAM

QURESHI, Mr Murad *Lab/Co-op* **Londonwide**
Email: murad.qureshi@london.gov.uk
Website: muradqureshi.com

RUSSELL, Ms Caroline *Green* **Londonwide**
Leader, City Hall Greens on the Assembly
Email: caroline.russell@london.gov.uk Twitter: @CarolineRussell

---

SAHOTA, Dr Onkar *Lab* **Ealing and Hillingdon**
Labour Spokesperson on Health
Tel: 020 7983 6558 Email: onkar.sahota@london.gov.uk
Website: www.dronkarsahota.com Twitter: @DrOnkarSahota

SHAH, Mr Navin *Lab* **Brent and Harrow**
Chair, London Assembly
Tel: 020 7983 4876 Email: navin.shah@london.gov.uk
Website: www.navinshah.com Twitter: @NavinShah2016

WHITTLE, Mr Peter *Ind* **Londonwide**
Email: peter.whittle@london.gov.uk Twitter: @prwhittle

Constituencies

Barnet and Camden	Andrew Dismore	Lab
Bexley and Bromley	Gareth Bacon	Con
Brent and Harrow	Navin Shah	Lab
City and East	Unmesh Desai	Lab
Croydon and Sutton	Steve O'Connell	Con
Ealing and Hillingdon	Onkar Sahota	Lab
Enfield and Haringey	Joanne McCartney	Lab/Co-op
Greenwich and Lewisham	Len Duvall	Lab/Co-op
Havering and Redbridge	Keith Prince	Con
Lambeth and Southwark	Florence Eshalomi	Lab/Co-op
Merton and Wandsworth	Leonie Cooper	Lab
North East	Jennette Arnold	Lab/Co-op
South West	Tony Arbour	Con
West Central	Tony Devenish	Con

Londonwide list

Shaun Bailey	Con
Sian Berry	Green
Andrew Boff	Con
Nicky Gavron	Lab/Co-op
Susan Hall	Con
David Kurten	UKIP
Alison Moore	Lab
Caroline Pidgeon	Lib Dem
Murad Qureshi	Lab/Co-op
Caroline Russell	Green
Peter Whittle	Ind

Assembly Committees

Budget and Performance

Tel: 020 7983 5526
Email: laura.pelling@london.gov.uk
www.london.gov.uk/about-us/london-assembly/london-assembly-committees/budget-and-performance-committee

Susan Hall (Chair)	*Con*
Len Duvall (Deputy Chair)	*Lab/Co-op*
Sian Berry	*Green*
Unmesh Desai	*Lab*
Tony Devenish	*Con*
Susan Hall	*Con*
Alison Moore	*Lab*
Caroline Pidgeon	*Lib Dem*
Onkar Sahota	*Lab*

Staff: Fiona Bywaters (Principal Committee Manager)

Budget Monitoring Sub-committee

Tel: 020 7983 4000
www.london.gov.uk/about-us/london-assembly/london-assembly-committees/budget-monitoring-sub-committee

Staff:

Confirmation Hearings

Tel: 020 7983 4383
Email: lauren.harvey@london.gov.uk
www.london.gov.uk/about-us/london-assembly/london-assembly-committees/confirmation-hearings-committee

Andrew Boff (Chair)	*Con*
Leonie Cooper	*Lab*
Len Duvall	*Lab/Co-op*
Susan Hall	*Con*
Alison Moore	*Lab*
Keith Prince	*Con*
Caroline Russell	*Green*
Onkar Sahota	*Lab*
Navin Shah	*Lab*
Peter Whittle	*Ind*

Staff: Lauren Harvey (Senior Committee Officer)

Economy

Tel: 020 7983 4383
www.london.gov.uk/about-us/london-assembly/london-assembly-committees/economy-committee

Leonie Cooper (Chair)	*Lab*

Shaun Bailey (Deputy Chair)	*Con*
Unmesh Desai	*Lab*
Susan Hall	*Con*
Murad Qureshi	*Lab/Co-op*
Caroline Russell	*Green*

Staff: Lauren Harvey (Committee Officer)

Environment

Tel: 020 7983 4383
Email: lauren.harvey@london.gov.uk
www.london.gov.uk/about-us/london-assembly/london-assembly-committees/environment-committee

Caroline Russell (Chair)	*Green*
Leonie Cooper (Deputy Chair)	*Lab*
Tony Arbour	*Con*
Jennette Arnold	*Lab/Co-op*
Shaun Bailey	*Con*
Nicky Gavron	*Lab/Co-op*
David Kurten	*UKIP*

Staff: Lauren Harvey (Committee Officer)

Fire, Resilience and Emergency Planning

Tel: 020 7983 5526
Email: laura.pelling@london.gov.uk
www.london.gov.uk/about-us/london-assembly/london-assembly-committees/fire-resilience-and-emergency-planning-committee

Andrew Dismore (Chair)	*Lab*
Susan Hall (Chair)	*Con*
Tony Arbour	*Con*
Leonie Cooper	*Lab*
David Kurten	*UKIP*
Alison Moore	*Lab*

Staff: Diane Richards (Committee Officer)

GLA Oversight

Tel: 020 7983 4425
Email: fiona.bywaters@london.gov.uk
www.london.gov.uk/about-us/london-assembly/london-assembly-committees/gla-oversight-committee

Len Duvall (Chair)	*Lab/Co-op*
Susan Hall (Deputy Chair)	*Con*
Sian Berry	*Green*
Andrew Boff	*Con*
Unmesh Desai	*Lab*
Joanne McCartney	*Lab/Co-op*
Caroline Pidgeon	*Lib Dem*
Keith Prince	*Con*
Onkar Sahota	*Lab*
Navin Shah	*Lab*
Peter Whittle	*Ind*

Staff: Davena Toyinbo (Principal Committee Manager)

Health

Tel: 020 7983 4383
Email: lauren.harvey@london.gov.uk
www.london.gov.uk/about-us/london-assembly/london-assembly-committees/health-committee

Onkar Sahota (Chair)	*Lab*
Andrew Boff (Deputy Chair)	*Con*
Unmesh Desai	*Lab*
Susan Hall	*Con*
Joanne McCartney	*Lab/Co-op*

Staff: Lauren Harvey (Committee Officer)

Housing

Tel: 020 7983 4616
Email: diane.richards@london.gov.uk
www.london.gov.uk/about-us/london-assembly/london-assembly-committees/housing-committee

Murad Qureshi (Chair)	*Lab/Co-op*
Andrew Boff (Deputy Chair)	*Con*
Sian Berry	*Green*
Leonie Cooper	*Lab*
Tony Devenish	*Con*
Nicky Gavron	*Lab/Co-op*
David Kurten	*UKIP*

Staff: Diane Richards (Committee Officer)

Planning and Regeneration

Tel: 020 7983 6559
Email: teresa.young@london.gov.uk
www.london.gov.uk/about-us/london-assembly/london-assembly-committees/planning-and-regeneration-committee

Andrew Boff (Chair)	*Con*
Nicky Gavron (Deputy Chair)	*Lab/Co-op*
Tony Devenish	*Con*
Murad Qureshi	*Lab/Co-op*
Navin Shah	*Lab*

Staff: Diane Richards (Senior Committee Officer)

Police and Crime

Tel: 020 7983 4383
Email: lauren.harvey@london.gov.uk
www.london.gov.uk/about-us/london-assembly/london-assembly-committees/police-and-crime-committee

Unmesh Desai (Chair)	*Lab*
Steve O'Connell (Deputy Chair)	*Con*
Tony Arbour	*Con*
Jennette Arnold	*Lab/Co-op*
Sian Berry	*Green*
Andrew Dismore	*Lab*
Len Duvall	*Lab/Co-op*
Susan Hall	*Con*
Caroline Pidgeon	*Lib Dem*

Peter Whittle *Ind*

Staff: Lauren Harvey (Senior Committee Officer)

Transport

Tel: 020 7983 5526
Email: laura.pelling@london.gov.uk
www.london.gov.uk/about-us/london-assembly/london-assembly-committees/transport-committee

Alison Moore (Chair) *Lab*
Caroline Pidgeon (Deputy Chair) *Lib Dem*
Shaun Bailey *Con*
Tony Devenish *Con*
Florence Eshalomi *Lab/Co-op*
David Kurten *UKIP*
Joanne McCartney *Lab/Co-op*
Keith Prince *Con*
Caroline Russell *Green*
Navin Shah *Lab*

Staff: Fiona Bywaters (Principal Committee Manager)

Audit Panel

Tel: 020 7983 4000
Email: mahvesh.ibrar@london.gov.uk
www.london.gov.uk/about-us/london-assembly/london-assembly-committees/audit-panel

Susan Hall (Chair) *Con*
Len Duvall (Deputy Chair) *Lab/Co-op*
Alison Moore *Lab*
Keith Prince *Con*

Staff: Davena Toyinbo (Senior Committee Officer)

Education Panel

Tel: 020 7983 4000
www.london.gov.uk/about-us/london-assembly/education-panel

Jennette Arnold (Chair) *Lab/Co-op*
Tony Arbour *Con*
Susan Hall *Con*
David Kurten *UKIP*
Alison Moore *Lab*

Staff: Lamide Odanye (Committee Officer)

EU Exit Working Group

Tel: 020 7983 4425
Email: scrutiny@london.gov.uk
www.london.gov.uk/about-us/london-assembly/london-assembly-committees/eu-exit-working-group

Len Duvall (Chair) *Lab/Co-op*
Andrew Boff (Deputy Chair) *Con*
Caroline Pidgeon *Lib Dem*
Caroline Russell *Green*
Peter Whittle *Ind*

Staff: Vishal Seegoolam (Principal Committee Manager), Lauren Harvey (Committee Officer)

Garden Bridge Working Group

Email: lauren.harvey@london.gov.uk
www.london.gov.uk/about-us/london-assembly/london-assembly-committees/garden-bridge-working-group

Sian Berry *Green*
Len Duvall *Lab/Co-op*
Caroline Pidgeon *Lib Dem*
Peter Whittle *Ind*

Staff: Lauren Harvey (Committee Officer)

Police and Crime Commissioners

Avon and Somerset
OPCC, Avon and Somerset Police Headquarters, Valley Road, Portishead BS20 8JJ
Tel: 01278 646188
Email: pcc@avonandsomerset.pnn.police.uk Website: www.avonandsomerset-pcc.gov.uk
Twitter: @AandSPCC
Police and Crime Commissioner: Sue Mountstevens (Ind)

Bedfordshire
OPCC, Bedfordshire Police Headquarters, Woburn Road, Kempston, Bedford MK43 9AX
Tel: 01234 842064
Email: pcc@bedfordshire.pnn.police.uk Website: www.bedfordshire.pcc.police.uk
Twitter: @BedsPCC
Police and Crime Commissioner: Kathryn Holloway (Con)

Cambridgeshire and Peterborough
OPCC, PO Box 688, Huntingdon PE29 9LA
Tel: 0300 333 3456
Email: cambs-pcc@cambs.pnn.police.uk Website: www.cambridgeshire-pcc.gov.uk
Twitter: @PCCCambs
Interim Police and Crime Commissioner: Ray Bisby (Con)

Cheshire
OPCC, Stockton Heath Police Station, Grappenhall Road, Warrington WA4 2AF
Tel: 01606 364000
Email: police.crime.commissioner@cheshire.pnn.police.uk Website: www.cheshire-pcc.gov.uk
Twitter: @CheshirePCC
Police and Crime Commissioner: David Keane (Lab)

Cleveland
OPCC, c/o St Marks House, St Marks Court, Thornaby, Stockton-on-Tees TS17 6QW
Tel: 01642 301861
Email: pcc@cleveland.pnn.police.uk Website: www.cleveland.pcc.police.uk
Twitter: @Cleveland_PCC
Interim Police and Crime Commissioner: Lisa Oldroyd

Cumbria
OPCC, 1-2 Carleton Hall, Penrith CA10 2AU
Tel: 01768 217734
Email: commissioner@cumbria-pcc.gov.uk Website: cumbria-pcc.gov.uk Twitter: @cumbriapcc
Police and Crime Commissioner: Peter McCall (Con)

Derbyshire
OPCC, Butterley Hall, Ripley DE5 3RS
Tel: 0300 122 6000
Email: pccoffice@derbyshire.pnn.police.uk Website: www.derbyshire-pcc.gov.uk
Twitter: @DerbysPCC
Police and Crime Commissioner: Hardyal Dhindsa (Lab)

Devon and Cornwall
OPCC, Andy Hocking House, Alderson Drive, Exeter EX2 7RP
Tel: 01392 225555
Email: opcc@devonandcornwall.pnn.police.uk Website: www.devonandcornwall-pcc.gov.uk
Twitter: @DC_PCC
Police and Crime Commissioner: Alison Hernandez (Con)

Dorset
OPCC, Force Headquarters, Winfrith, Dorchester DT2 8DZ
Tel: 01305 229084/01202 229084
Email: pcc@dorset.pnn.police.uk Website: www.dorset.pcc.police.uk Twitter: @PCCDorset
Police and Crime Commissioner: Martyn Underhill (Ind)

Durham
OPCVC, Durham Police Headquarters, Aykley Heads, Durham DH1 5TT
Tel: 0191-375 2001
Email: general.enquiries@durham.pcc.pnn.gov.uk Website: www.durham-pcc.gov.uk
Twitter: @DurhamPCC
Acting Police, Crime and Victims' Commissioner: Steve White

Dyfed-Powys
OPCC, PO Box 99, Llangunnor, Carmarthen SA31 2PF
Tel: 01267 226440
Email: opcc@dyfed-powys.pnn.police.uk Website: www.dyfedpowys-pcc.org.uk
Twitter: @DPOPCC
Police and Crime Commissioner: Dafydd Llywelyn (PlC)

Essex
OPFCC, Kelvedon Park, London Road, Rivenhall, Witham CM8 3HB
Tel: 01245 291600
Email: pfcc@essex.pnn.police.uk Website: www.essex.pfcc.police.uk Twitter: @EssexPFCC
Police, Fire and Crime Commissioner: Roger Hirst (Con)

Gloucestershire
OPCC, 1 Waterwells, Waterwells Drive, Quedgeley, Gloucester GL2 2AN
Tel: 01452 754348
Email: pcc@gloucestershire.pnn.police.uk Website: www.gloucestershire-pcc.gov.uk
Twitter: @GlosPCC
Police and Crime Commissioner: Martin Surl (Ind)

Gwent
OPCC, Police Headquarters, Croesyceiliog, Cwmbran NP44 2XJ
Tel: 01633 642200
Email: commissioner@gwent.pnn.police.uk Website: www.gwent.pcc.police.uk
Twitter: @GwentPCC
Police and Crime Commissioner: Jeff Cuthbert (Lab)

Hampshire
OPCC, St George's Chambers, St George's Street, Winchester SO23 8AJ
Tel: 01962 871595
Email: opcc@hampshire.pnn.police.uk Website: www.hampshire-pcc.gov.uk Twitter: @HantsPCC
Police and Crime Commissioner: Michael Lane (Con)

Hertfordshire
OPCC, Harpenden Police Station, 15 Vaughan Road, Harpenden AL5 4GZ
Tel: 01707 806100
Email: commissioner@herts.pcc.pnn.gov.uk Website: www.hertscommissioner.org
Twitter: @HertsPCC
Police and Crime Commissioner: David Lloyd (Con)

Humberside
OPCC, The Lawns, Harland Way, Cottingham HU16 5SN
Tel: 01482 220787
Email: pcc@humberside.pnn.police.uk Website: www.humberside-pcc.gov.uk
Twitter: @HumbersidePCC
Police and Crime Commissioner: Keith Hunter (Lab)

Kent
OPCC, Kent Police, Sutton Road, Maidstone ME15 9BZ
Tel: 01622 677055
Email: contactyourpcc@kent.police.uk Website: www.kent-pcc.gov.uk Twitter: @PCCKent
Police and Crime Commissioner: Matthew Scott (Con)

Lancashire
OPCC, County Hall, Preston PR1 0LD
Tel: 01772 533587
Email: commissioner@lancashire-pcc.gov.uk Website: www.lancashire-pcc.gov.uk
Twitter: @LancsPCC
Police and Crime Commissioner: Clive Grunshaw (Lab)

Leicestershire
OPCC, Police Headquarters, St Johns, Enderby, Leicester LE19 2BX
Tel: 0116-229 8980
Email: police.commissioner@leics.pcc.pnn.gov.uk Website: www.leics.pcc.police.uk
Twitter: @LeicsPCC
Police and Crime Commissioner: Lord Bach (Lab)

Lincolnshire
OPCC, Lincolnshire Police Headquarters, Deepdale Lane, Nettleham, Lincoln LN2 2LT
Tel: 01522 947192
Email: lincolnshire-pcc@lincs.pnn.police.uk Website: www.lincolnshire-pcc.gov.uk
Twitter: @MarcJonesLincs
Police, Crime and Victims' Commissioner: Marc Jones (Con)

Merseyside
OPCC, Wavertree Road Police Station, Liverpool L7 1RJ
Tel: 0151-777 5155
Email: info@merseysidepcc.info Website: www.merseysidepcc.info Twitter: @MerseysidePCC
Police and Crime Commissioner: Rt Hon Jane Kennedy (Ind)

Norfolk
OPCC, Building 8, Jubilee House, Falconers Chase, Wymondam NR18 0WW
Tel: 01953 424455
Email: opccn@norfolk.pnn.police.uk Website: www.norfolk-pcc.gov.uk Twitter: @NorfolkPCC
Police and Crime Commissioner: Lorne Green (Con)

Northamptonshire
OPFCC, East House, Force Headquarters, Wootton Hall, Northampton NN4 0JQ
Tel: 01604 888113
Email: commissioner@northantspfcc.pnn.gov.uk Website: www.northantspcc.org.uk
Twitter: @NorthantsOPFCC
Police, Fire and Crime Commissioner: Stephen Mold (Con)

Northumbria
OPCC, Second Floor, Victory House, Balliol Business Park, Benton Lane, Newcastle upon Tyne NE12 8EW
Tel: 0191-221 9800
Email: enquiries@northumbria-pcc.gov.uk Website: www.northumbria-pcc.gov.uk
Twitter: @NorthumbriaPCC
Police and Crime Commissioner: Kim McGuinness (Lab)

Nottinghamshire
OPCC, Arnot Hill House, Arnot Hill Park, Arnold, Nottingham NG5 6LU
Tel: 0115-844 5998
Email: nopcc@nottinghamshire.pnn.police.uk Website: www.nottinghamshire.pcc.police.uk
Twitter: @NottsPCC
Police and Crime Commissioner: Paddy Tipping (Lab)

Staffordshire
Commissioners Office, Block 9, Weston Road, Stafford ST18 0YY
Tel: 01785 232385
Email: pfcc@staffordshire-pfcc.pnn.gov.uk Website: staffordshire-pfcc.gov.uk Twitter: @StaffsPFCC
Police, Fire and Crime Commissioner: Matthew Ellis (Con)

Suffolk
OPCC, Police Headquarters, Portal Avenue, Martlesham Heath, Ipswich IP5 3QS
Tel: 01473 782773
Email: spcc@suffolk.pnn.police.uk Website: www.suffolk-pcc.gov.uk Twitter: @TimSPCC
Police and Crime Commissioner: Tim Passmore (Con)

Surrey
OPCC, PO Box 412, Guildford GU3 1YJ
Tel: 01483 630200
Email: surreypcc@surrey.pnn.police.uk Website: www.surrey-pcc.gov.uk Twitter: @SurreyPCC
Police and Crime Commissioner: David Munro (Ind)

Sussex
OPCC, Sackville House, Brooks Close, Lewes BN7 2FZ
Tel: 01273 481561
Email: pcc@sussex-pcc.gov.uk Website: www.sussex-pcc.gov.uk Twitter: @Sussexpcc
Police and Crime Commissioner: Katy Bourne OBE (Con)

Thames Valley
OPCC, The Farmhouse, Thames Valley Police Headquarters, Oxford Road, Kidlington, Oxon OX5 2NX
Tel: 01865 541957
Email: pcc@thamesvalley.pnn.police.uk Website: www.thamesvalley-pcc.gov.uk Twitter: @TV_PCC
Police and Crime Commissioner: Anthony Stansfeld (Con)

North Wales
OPCC, Police Headquarters, Glan y Don, Colwyn Bay LL29 8AW
Tel: 01492 805486
Email: opcc@nthwales.pnn.police.uk Website: www.northwales-pcc.gov.uk
Twitter: @NorthWalesPCC
Police and Crime Commissioner: Arfon Jones (PlC)

South Wales
OPCC, Ty Morgannwg, Police Headquarters, Bridgend CF31 3SU
Tel: 01656 869366
Email: commissioner@south-wales.pnn.police.uk Website: commissioner.south-wales.police.uk
Twitter: @commissionersw
Police and Crime Commissioner: Rt Hon Alun Michael (Lab/Co-op)

Warwickshire
OPCC, 3 Northgate Street, Warwick CV34 4SP
Tel: 01926 412322
Email: opcc@warwickshire.pnn.police.uk Website: www.warwickshire-pcc.gov.uk
Twitter: @WarwickshirePCC
Police and Crime Commissioner: Philip Seccombe (Con)

West Mercia
OPFCC, West Mercia Police, Hindlip Hall, Worcester WR3 8SP
Tel: 01905 331656
Email: opcc@westmercia.pnn.police.uk Website: www.westmercia-pcc.gov.uk
Twitter: @westmerciapcc
Police, Fire and Crime Commissioner: John Campion (Con)

West Midlands
OPCC, Lloyd House, Colmore Circus Queensway, Birmingham B4 6NQ
Tel: 0121-626 6060
Email: wmpcc@west-midlands.pnn.police.uk Website: www.westmidlands-pcc.gov.uk
Twitter: @WestMidsPCC

Police and Crime Commissioner: David Jamieson (Lab)

Wiltshire
OPCC, London Road, Devizes SN10 2DN
Tel: 01380 734022
Email: pcc@wiltshire.pnn.police.uk Website: www.wiltshire-pcc.gov.uk
Twitter: @PCCWiltsSwindon

Police and Crime Commissioner: Angus Macpherson (Con)

North Yorkshire
OPFCC, 12 Granby Road, Harrogate HG1 4ST
Tel: 01423 569562
Email: info@northyorkshire-pfcc.gov.uk Website: www.northyorkshire-pfcc.gov.uk
Twitter: @northyorkspfcc

Police, Fire and Crime Commissioner: Julia Mulligan (Con)

South Yorkshire
OPCC, South Yorkshire Police HQ, Ground Floor, Carbrook House, Carbrook Hall Road, Sheffield S9 2EH
Tel: 0114-296 4150
Email: info@southyorkshire-pcc.gov.uk Website: www.southyorkshire-pcc.gov.uk Twitter: @SYPCC

Police and Crime Commissioner: Dr Alan Billings (Lab)

West Yorkshire
OPCC, Ploughland House, 62 George Street, Wakefield WF1 1DL
Tel: 01924 294000
Email: contact@westyorkshire.pcc.pnn.gov.uk Website: www.westyorkshire-pcc.gov.uk
Twitter: @WestYorksOPCC

Police and Crime Commissioner: Mark Burns-Williamson (Lab)

Combined Authorities

Cambridgeshire and Peterborough Combined Authority
The Incubator 2, First Floor, Alconbury Weald Enterprise Campus, Alconbury Weald, Huntingdon PE28 4WX
Tel: 01480 277180
Email: contactus@cambridgeshirepeterborough-ca.gov.uk
Website: www.cambridgeshirepeterborough-ca.gov.uk Twitter: @CambsPboroCA
Mayor: James Palmer (Con)

Greater Manchester Combined Authority
Broadhurst House, 56 Oxford Street, Manchester M1 6EU
Tel: 0161-778 7000
Email: enquiries@greatermanchester-ca.gov.uk Website: www.greatermanchester-ca.gov.uk
Twitter: @greatermcr
Mayor: Rt Hon Andy Burnham (Lab)

Liverpool City Region Combined Authority
No 1 Mann Island, Liverpool L3 1BP
Email: info@liverpoolcityregion-ca.gov.uk Website: www.liverpoolcityregion-ca.gov.uk
Twitter: @LpoolCityRegion
Mayor: Steve Rotheram (Lab)

North of Tyne Combined Authority
Quadrant West, 2 Quicksilver Way, Cobalt Business Park, Newcastle upon Tyne NE27 0QQ
Tel: 0191-211 6604/0191-277 4721
Email: enquiries@northoftyne-ca.gov.uk Website: www.northoftyne-ca.gov.uk
Twitter: @NorthTyneCA
Mayor: Jamie Driscoll (Lab/Co-op)

Sheffield City Region Combined Authority
11 Broad Street West, Sheffield S1 2BQ
Tel: 0114-220 3400
Email: enquiries@sheffieldcityregion.org.uk Website: sheffieldcityregion.org.uk
Twitter: @SheffCityRegion
Mayor: Dan Jarvis MBE (Lab)

Tees Valley Combined Authority
Cavendish House, Teesdale Business Park, Stockton-on-Tees, Tees Valley TS17 6QY
Tel: 01642 524400
Email: info@teesvalley-ca.gov.uk Website: teesvalley-ca.gov.uk Twitter: @TeesValleyCA
Mayor: Ben Houchen (Con)

West of England Combined Authority
3 Rivergate, Temple Quay, Bristol BS1 6ER
Tel: 0117-428 6210
Email: info@westofengland-ca.org.uk Website: www.westofengland-ca.org.uk
Twitter: @WestYorkshireCA
Mayor: Tim Bowles (Con)

West Midlands Combined Authority
16 Summer Lane, Birmingham B19 3SD
Tel: 0121-200 2787
Email: andy.street@wmca.org.uk Website: www.wmca.org.uk Twitter: @WestMids_CA
Mayor: Andy Street (Con)

GOVERNMENT AND PUBILC OFFICES

Permanent Secretaries

Departments of State

Business, Energy and Industrial Strategy
Permanent Secretary
Sarah Munby

Cabinet Office
Cabinet Secretary
Dr Simon Case CVO
Chief Operating Officer
Alex Chisholm

Defence
Permanent Secretary
To be appointed

Digital, Culture, Media and Sport
Permanent Secretary
Sarah Healey CB

Education
Permanent Secretary
Susan Acland-Hood

Environment, Food and Rural Affairs
Permanent Secretary
Tamara Finkelstein CB

Foreign, Commonwealth and Development Office
Permanent Under-Secretary
Sir Philip Barton KCMG OBE

Health and Social Care
Permanent Secretary
Sir Chris Wormald KCB
Second Permanent Secretary
David Williams CB

Home Office
Permanent Secretary
Matthew Rycroft CBE
Second Permanent Secretary
Shona Dunn

Housing, Communities and Local Government
Permanent Secretary
Jeremy Pocklington CB

International Trade
Permanent Secretary
John Alty CB
Second Permanent Secretary
Crawford Falconer

Justice
Permanent Secretary
Antonia Romeo

Northern Ireland Office
Permanent Secretary
Madeleine Alessandri CBE

Transport
Permanent Secretary
Bernadette Kelly CB

Treasury
Permanent Secretary
Sir Tom Scholar KCB
Second Permanent Secretary
Charles Roxburgh

Work and Pensions
Permanent Secretary
Peter Schofield CB

Devolved Parliament and Assemblies

Northern Ireland Executive
Head of Northern Ireland Civil Service and Secretary to the Executive
Jenny Pyper

Scottish Government
Permanent Secretary
Leslie Evans

Welsh Government
Permanent Secretary
Dame Shan Morgan DCMG

Departments of State

Prime Minister's Office

10 Downing Street, London SW1A 2AA
Tel: 020 7930 4433
Website: www.gov.uk/number10 Twitter: @10DowningStreet
Prime Minister, First Lord of the Treasury and Minister for the Civil Service, and Minister for the Union: Rt Hon **Boris Johnson** MP
For staff see p13

Attorney General's Office

102 Petty France, London SW1H 9EA
Tel: 020 7271 2440 Fax: 020 7271 2432
Email: correspondence@attorneygeneral.gov.uk Website: www.gov.uk/ago

MINISTERS

Attorney General: Rt Hon Suella Braverman QC MP
Solicitor General: Rt Hon Michael Ellis QC MP

House of Lords Spokesperson: **Lord Stewart of Dirleton** QC

CIVIL SERVANTS

Acting Director-General: Shehzad Charania MBE 020 7271 2412
Email: freya.claydon@attorneygeneral.gov.uk

Department for Business, Energy and Industrial Strategy

1 Victoria Street, London SW1H 0ET
Tel: 020 7215 5000
Email: enquiries@beis.gov.uk Website: www.gov.uk/beis Twitter: @beisgovuk

MINISTERS

Secretary of State: Rt Hon Kwasi Kwarteng MP
Minister of State for Business, Energy and Clean Growth: Rt Hon Anne-Marie Trevelyan MP
Minister of State for Investment: Lord Grimstone of Boscobel
Parliamentary Under-Secretary of State (Minister for Business and Industry): Nadhim Zahawi MP
Parliamentary Under-Secretary of State (Minister for Science, Research and Innovation): Amanda Solloway MP
Parliamentary Under-Secretary of State (Minister for Small Business, Consumers and Labour Markets); Minister for London: Paul Scully MP
Parliamentary Under-Secretary of State (Minister for Climate Change and Corporate Responsibility): Lord Callanan

Head of Parliamentary Unit: Helen Chapman 020 7215 6630

House of Lords Spokespeople: **Lord Callanan**, **Lord Grimstone of Boscobel**

CIVIL SERVANTS

Permanent Secretary: Sarah Munby 020 7215 5914 Email: permanentsecretary@beis.gov.uk
Director-General, Market Frameworks: Jaee Samant 020 7215 5628
Email: jaee.samant@beis.gov.uk
Acting Director-General, Business Sectors: Mike Keoghan 020 7215 1495
Email: michael.keoghan@beis.gov.uk
Director-General, Industrial Strategy, Science and Innovation: Jo Shanmugalingam 020 7215 6374
Email: jo.shanmugalingam@beis.gov.uk
Acting Director-General, Corporate Services: Doug Watkins FCIPD 020 7215 5450
Email: doug.watkins@beis.gov.uk
Director-General, Energy and Security: Joanna Whittington 020 7215 8549
Email: joanna.whittington@beis.gov.uk
Acting Director-General, Trade, Europe and Analysis: Dr Ashley Ibbett 0300 068 6562
Email: ashley.ibbett@beis.gov.uk
Director-General, Energy Transformation and Clean Growth: Julian Critchlow 0300 068 8181
Email: julian.critchlow@beis.gov.uk

Executive Agencies: Companies House, Insolvency Service, Intellectual Property Office, Met Office, UK Space Agency

Cabinet Office

70 Whitehall, London SW1A 2AS
Tel: 020 7276 1234
Email: publiccorrespondence@cabinetoffice.gov.uk Website: www.gov.uk/cabinet-office
Twitter: @cabinetofficeuk

MINISTERS

Chancellor of the Duchy of Lancaster and Minister for the Cabinet Office: Rt Hon Michael Gove MP
Paymaster General: Rt Hon Penny Mordaunt MP
Minister of State for the Constitution and Devolution: Chloe Smith MP
Minister of State for Efficiency and Transformation: Lord Agnew of Oulton DL
Minister of State: Lord True CBE
Minister without portfolio (Conservative Party Chair): Rt Hon Amanda Milling MP
Parliamentary Secretary: Julia Lopez MP
Parliamentary Secretary (Minister for Defence People and Veterans): Johnny Mercer MP
President of the UN COP26 Climate Conference: Rt Hon Alok Sharma MP
Parliamentary Clerk: Ellie Markham 020 7276 7561

House of Lords Spokespeople: **Lord Agnew of Oulton** DL, **Lord True** CBE

CIVIL SERVANTS

Cabinet Secretary and Head of the Civil Service: Dr Simon Case CVO
Email: cabinet.secretary@cabinetoffice.gov.uk
Chief Operating Officer for the Civil Service and Permanent Secretary: Alex Chisholm 020 7271 8822 Email: psalexchisholm@cabinetoffice.gov.uk
Second Permanent Secretary: James Bowler CB
First Parliamentary Counsel: Elizabeth Gardiner CB 020 7276 6541
Email: 1pc@cabinetoffice.gov.uk
Deputy Cabinet Secretary and Head of the Cabinet Secretariat: Helen MacNamara 020 7276 2470
Email: helen.macnamara@cabinetoffice.gov.uk
Acting Director-General, Government Digital Service: Fiona Deans
Director-General, UK Governance: Lucy Smith 07768 646220
Email: ukgg-private-office@cabinetoffice.gov.uk
Director-General, Covid-19: To be appointed
Director-General, Government Property and Chief Operating Officer: Mike Parsons 020 7276 3573
Email: mike.parsons@cabinetoffice.gov.uk
Sherpa, G7/G20: Jonathan Black Email: jonathan.black@cabinetoffice.gov.uk
Chair, Joint Intelligence Committee and Professional Head of Intelligence Analysis: Sir Simon Gass CMG CVO 020 7276 1413 Email: jicchairman@cabinetoffice.gov.uk
Chief Executive, Government Property Agency: Steven Boyd 07851 382960
Email: steven.boyd@gpa.gov.uk
Executive Director, Government Communications: Alex Aiken 020 7276 5134
Email: alex.aiken@cabinetoffice.gov.uk
Executive Director, Implementation Group: Jonathan Nancekivell-Smith 07753 317139
Email: nancekivell.smith@cabinetoffice.gov.uk
Chief Finance Officer: Richard Hornby 07771 900172 Email: richard.hornby@cabinetoffice.gov.uk
Director-General, International Government Service: Kevin Cunnington
Director-General, Economic and Domestic Affairs Secretariat: Mark Sweeney
Email: mark.sweeney@cabinetoffice.gov.uk
Director-General, Civil Service Group: To be appointed
Chief Commercial Officer: Gareth Rhys Williams 07801 405377
Email: gareth.rhyswilliams@cabinetoffice.gov.uk
Government Chief Security Officer: Dominic Fortescue 020 7276 1576
Email: tracey.waltho@cabinetoffice.gov.uk
Chief People Officer: Rupert McNeil 020 7271 6858 Email: rupert.mcneil@cabinetoffice.gov.uk
Chief Negotiator, Taskforce Europe: Lord Frost CMG

Executive Agencies: Crown Commercial Service, Government Property Agency

Ministry of Defence

Main Building, Whitehall, London SW1A 2HB
Tel: 020 7218 9000
Website: www.gov.uk/mod Twitter: @DefenceHQ

MINISTERS
Secretary of State: Rt Hon Ben Wallace MP
Minister of State (Minister for Defence Procurement): Jeremy Quin MP
Minister of State: Baroness Goldie DL
Parliamentary Under-Secretary of State (Minister for the Armed Forces): James Heappey MP
Parliamentary Under-Secretary of State (Minister for Defence People and Veterans): Johnny Mercer MP

House of Lords Spokesperson: **Baroness Goldie** DL

CIVIL SERVANTS
Permanent Secretary: To be appointed 020 7218 2839 Email: pus-privateoffice@mod.gov.uk
Chief of the Defence Staff: General Sir Nicholas Carter GCB CBE DSO ADC Gen 020 7218 6190 Email: cds-privateoffice@mod.gov.uk
Vice Chief of Defence Staff: Adm Tim Fraser CB 020 7218 4402
Email: vcds-groupmailbox@mod.gov.uk
First Sea Lord and Chief of the Naval Staff: Adm Tony Radakin 020 7218 6193
Email: navy-1slcnsgroup@mod.gov.uk
Chief of the General Staff: General Sir Mark Carleton-Smith KCB CBE 020 7218 6153
Email: armycgs-privateoffice-shared@mod.gov.uk
Chief of the Air Staff: Air Chief Marshal Michael Wigston CBE 020 7218 6314
Email: cas-outeroffice@mod.gov.uk
Commander, Joint Forces Command: Gen Patrick Sanders CBE 01923 958529
Email: jfc-comd-outeroffice@mod.gov.uk
Chief of Defence People: Lt Gen James Swift 020 7218 6057 Email: louise.green144@mod.gov.uk
Director-General, Finance: Charlie Pate 020 7218 1519 Email: charlie.pate100@mod.gov.uk
Director-General, Nuclear: Vanessa Nicholls 020 7218 7456
Email: DNO-DGNucPrivateOffice@mod.gov.uk
Director-General, Security Policy: Dominic Wilson 020 7218 6280
Email: dominic.wilson535@mod.gov.uk
Director-General, Strategy and International: Angus Lapsley 020 7218 3830
Email: dgsecpol-privateoffice@mod.gov.uk
Chief Executive, Defence Equipment and Support: Sir Simon Bollom KBE CB 0141-224 2179
Email: desceo-outeroffice@mod.gov.uk
Chief Executive, Defence Infrastructure Organisation: Graham Dalton 07970 896464
Email: diosec-groupmailbox@mod.gov.uk
Deputy Chief of Defence Staff (Military Strategy and Operations): Lt Gen Doug Chalmers 020 7218 8938 Email: dcmc-dcdsdo-office@mod.gov.uk
Deputy Chief of Defence Staff (Financial and Military Capability):
Air Marshal Richard Knighton CB 020 7217 0506 Email: fmc-dcdsmilcap-outeroffice@mod.gov.uk
Chief Operating Officer: Mike Baker 020 7218 1741 Email: coo-privateofficegp@mod.gov.uk
Chief Information Officer: Charles Forte 020 7218 2451 Email: CIO-DG-PrivateOffice@mod.gov.uk

Executive Agencies: Defence Electronics and Components Agency, Defence Equipment and Support, Defence Science and Technology Laboratory, Submarine Delivery Agency, UK Hydrographic Office

---

Department for Digital, Culture, Media and Sport

Department for Digital, Culture, Media and Sport, 100 Parliament Street, London SW1A 2BQ
Tel: 020 7211 6000
Email: enquiries@dcms.gov.uk Website: www.gov.uk/dcms Twitter: @DCMS

MINISTERS
Secretary of State: Rt Hon Oliver Dowden CBE MP
Minister of State for Digital and Culture: Caroline Dinenage MP
Minister of State for Media and Data: Rt Hon John Whittingdale OBE MP
Parliamentary Under-Secretary of State for Digital Infrastructure: Matt Warman MP
Parliamentary Under-Secretary of State for Sport, Tourism and Heritage: Nigel Huddleston MP
Parliamentary Under-Secretary of State for Civil Society and Lords Minister: Baroness Barran MBE

Parliamentary Clerk: To be appointed

House of Lords Spokesperson: **Baroness Barran** MBE

CIVIL SERVANTS
Permanent Secretary: Sarah Healey CB Email: permanent.secretary@culture.gov.uk
Director-General, Digital and Media: Susannah Storey CB Email: dmg.dg@culture.gov.uk

Director-General, Strategy and Operations: Sam Lister Email: psg.dg@culture.gov.uk
Director-General, Culture, Sport and Civil Society: Helen Judge Email: helen.judge@culture.gov.uk
Acting Director, Finance and Commercial: Jacinda Humphry
Email: jacinda.humphry@culture.gov.uk
Commissioner for Cultural Recovery and Renewal: Lord Mendoza

Department for Education

Sanctuary Buildings, Great Smith Street, London SW1P 3BT
Tel: 0370 000 2288
Email: [firstname.surname]@education.gov.uk Website: www.gov.uk/dfe Twitter: @educationgovuk

MINISTERS

Secretary of State: Rt Hon Gavin Williamson CBE MP
Minister of State for Universities: Michelle Donelan MP
Minister of State for School Standards: Rt Hon Nick Gibb MP
Parliamentary Under-Secretary of State for Apprenticeships and Skills: Gillian Keegan MP
Parliamentary Under-Secretary of State for Children and Families: Vicky Ford MP
Parliamentary Under-Secretary of State for the School System; Minister for Women: Baroness Berridge

Parliamentary Clerk: Amy Ross

House of Lords Spokesperson: **Baroness Berridge**

CIVIL SERVANTS

Permanent Secretary: Susan Acland-Hood Email: permanent.secretary@education.gov.uk
Director-General, Social Care, Mobility and Disadvantage: Indra Morris CB 020 7340 8017
Email: indra.morris@education.gov.uk
Director-General, Covid-19 Response and Schools Recovery: Julia Kinniburgh
Director-General, Early Years and Schools: Andrew McCully CB 020 7340 8075
Email: andrew.mccully@education.gov.uk
Director-General, Higher and Further Education: Paul Kett 020 7340 7726
Email: paul.kett@education.gov.uk
Chief Operating Officer and Director-General, Operations: Mike Green CB 020 7340 8208
Email: mike.green@education.gov.uk
Chief Executive, Education and Skills Funding Agency: Eileen Milner 020 7340 8315
Email: eileen.milner@education.gov.uk

Executive Agencies: Education and Skills Funding Agency, Standards and Testing Agency, Teaching Regulation Agency

Department for Environment, Food and Rural Affairs

Seacole Building, 2 Marsham Street, London SW1P 4DF
Tel: 020 7238 6000 Fax: 0345 933 5577
Email: defra.helpline@defra.gov.uk Website: www.gov.uk/defra Twitter: @DefraGovUK

MINISTERS

Secretary of State: Rt Hon George Eustice MP
Minister of State for the Pacific and Environment: Rt Hon Lord Goldsmith of Richmond Park
Parliamentary Under-Secretary of State: Rebecca Pow MP
Parliamentary Under-Secretary of State for Rural Affairs and Biosecurity: Lord Gardiner of Kimble
Parliamentary Under-Secretary of State: Victoria Prentis MP

Parliamentary Clerk: Deirdre Kennedy MBE 020 8026 3042

House of Lords Spokespeople: **Lord Gardiner of Kimble**, Rt Hon **Lord Goldsmith of Richmond Park**

CIVIL SERVANTS

Permanent Secretary: Tamara Finkelstein CB 020 7895 5717 Email: tamara.finkelstein@defra.gov.uk
Chief Operating Officer: Sarah Homer 020 8565 4513 Email: sarah.homer@defra.gov.uk
Acting Director-General, Strategy and Change: Amy Holmes CB 020 8026 2713
Email: amy.holmes@defra.gov.uk
Director-General, Food, Farming and Biosecurity: David Kennedy 020 8225 8709
Email: david.kennedy@defra.gov.uk
Acting Director-General, Europe, International and Constitution: James Quinault CBE
020 8026 3545 Email: james quinault@defra.gov.uk

Director-General, Environment, Rural and Marine: David Hill

Executive Agencies: Animal and Plant Health Agency, Centre for Environment, Fisheries and Aquaculture Science, Rural Payments Agency, Veterinary Medicines Directorate

Foreign, Commonwealth and Development Office

King Charles Street, London SW1A 2AH
Tel: 020 7008 5000
Email: fcdo.correspondence@fcdo.gov.uk
Website: www.gov.uk/government/organisations/foreign-commonwealth-development-office
Twitter: @FCDOGovUK

MINISTERS

First Secretary of State, Secretary of State for Foreign, Commonwealth and Development Affairs (Foreign Secretary): Rt Hon Dominic Raab MP
Minister of State for Middle East and North Africa: Rt Hon James Cleverly MP
Minister of State for the Pacific and Environment: Rt Hon Lord Goldsmith of Richmond Park
Minister of State for Asia: Nigel Adams MP
Minister of State for South Asia and the Commonwealth: Lord Ahmad of Wimbledon
Parliamentary Under-Secretary of State (Minister for Africa): James Duddridge MP
Parliamentary Under-Secretary of State (Minister for the European Neighbourhood and Americas): Wendy Morton MP

Parliamentary Clerk: Nat Dawbarn 020 7008 4005

House of Lords Spokespeople: **Lord Ahmad of Wimbledon**, Rt Hon **Lord Goldsmith of Richmond Park**

CIVIL SERVANTS

Permanent Under-Secretary: Sir Philip Barton KCMG OBE Email: philip.barton@fcdo.gov.uk
Political Director: Sir Tim Barrow GCMG LVO MBE Email: tim.barrow@fcdo.gov.uk
Director-General, Finance and Corporate: Juliet Chua Email: juliet.chua@fcdo.gov.uk
Director-General, Africa: Moazzam Malik CMG Email: moazzam.malik@fcdo.gov.uk
Director-General, Middle East and North Africa, Afghanistan and Pakistan: Thomas Drew CMG Email: tom.drew@fcdo.gov.uk
Director-General, Americas and Overseas Territories: Vijay Rangarajan CMG Email: vijay.rangarajan@fcdo.gov.uk
Director-General, Indo-Pacific: Jenny Bates Email: jenny.bates@fcdo.gov.uk
Director-General, Delivery: Kumar Iyer Email: kumar.iyer@fcdo.gov.uk
Director-General, Transformation: Nic Hailey CMG Email: nic.hailey@fcdo.gov.uk
Legal Director: Sir Iain Macleod KCMG 020 7008 3051 Email: iain.macleod@fcdo.gov.uk

Executive Agency: Wilton Park

Department of Health and Social Care

39 Victoria Street, London SW1H 0EU
Tel: 020 7210 4850
Websites: www.gov.uk/dhsc contactus.dh.gov.uk/?openform Twitter: @DHSCgovuk

MINISTERS

Secretary of State: Rt Hon Matt Hancock MP
Minister of State for Health: Edward Argar MP
Minister of State for Care: Helen Whately MP
Minister of State for Patient Safety, Suicide Prevention and Mental Health: Nadine Dorries MP
Parliamentary Under-Secretary of State for Prevention, Public Health and Primary Care: Jo Churchill MP
Parliamentary Under-Secretary of State for Innovation: Lord Bethell
Parliamentary Under-Secretary of State for COVID Vaccine Deployment: Nadhim Zahawi MP

Parliamentary Clerk: Claire Reading 020 7210 5808

House of Lords Spokesperson: **Lord Bethell**

CIVIL SERVANTS

Permanent Secretary: Sir Chris Wormald KCB 020 7972 4979 Email: permanent.secretary@dhsc.gov.uk
Second Permanent Secretary: David Williams CB 020 7210 5407 Email: david.williams@dhsc.gov.uk
Chief Medical Officer and Chief Scientific Adviser: Prof Chris Whitty 020 7210 5489

Email: chris.whitty@dhsc.gov.uk
Director-General, Global and Public Health: Clara Swinson CB 0207 210 5691
Email: clara.swinson@dhsc.gov.uk
Director-General, Acute Care and Workforce: Lee McDonough 020 7210 6236
Email: lee.mcdonough@dhsc.gov.uk
Director-General, PPE and Public Health: Jonathan Marron 020 7210 4383
Email: jonathan.marron@dhsc.gov.uk
Chief Executive, NHSX: Matthew Gould CMG MBE Email: ceo@nhsx.nhs.uk
Director-General, Commercial: Steve Oldfield 07808 270379 Email: steve.oldfield@dhsc.gov.uk
Director-General, Adult Social Care: Michelle Dyson 07519 615988
Email: michelle.dyson@dhsc.gov.uk
Executive Agencies: Medicines and Healthcare Products Regulatory Agency, Public Health England

Home Office

2 Marsham Street, London SW1P 4DF
Tel: 020 7035 4848 Fax: 020 7035 4745
Email: public.enquiries@homeoffice.gov.uk Website: www.gov.uk/home-office
Twitter: @ukhomeoffice

MINISTERS

Secretary of State: Rt Hon Priti Patel MP
Minister of State for Security: Rt Hon James Brokenshire MP
Minister of State for Crime and Policing: Kit Malthouse MP
Minister of State (Lords): Baroness Williams of Trafford
Minister of State for Building Safety and Communities: Lord Greenhalgh
Parliamentary Under-Secretary of State for Safeguarding: Victoria Atkins MP
Parliamentary Under-Secretary of State for Future Borders and Immigration: Kevin Foster MP
Parliamentary Under-Secretary of State for Immigration Compliance and the Courts: Chris Philp MP
Parliamentary Clerk: Mirsada Dema 07384 455301
House of Lords Spokespeople: **Baroness Williams of Trafford**, **Lord Greenhalgh**

CIVIL SERVANTS

Permanent Secretary: Matthew Rycroft CBE
Email: permanentsecretary.submissions@homeoffice.gov.uk
Second Permanent Secretary: Shona Dunn Email: secondpermanentsecretary@homeoffice.gov.uk
Director-General, Immigration Enforcement: Tyson Hepple CBE 020 8196 4760
Email: tyson.hepple@homeoffice.gov.uk
Director-General, Office for Security and Counter-Terrorism: Tom Hurd OBE 020 7035 8882
Email: dg.osct@homeoffice.x.gov.uk
Director-General, Legal: To be appointed
Director-General, Border Force: Paul Lincoln 07740 928047
Director-General, Borders, Immigration and Citizenship Systems Policy and Strategy:
Glyn Williams CB 020 7035 0395 Email: glyn.williams@homeoffice.gov.uk
Director-General, Serious and Organised Crime: To be appointed
Director-General, Crime, Policing and Fire: Tricia Hayes CB
Director-General, Capabilities and Resources: Charu Gorasia 020 7035 1602
Email: charu.gorasia@homeoffice.gov.uk
Director-General, UK Visas and Immigration: Abigail Tierney
Director-General, HM Passport Office: Abigail Tierney
Director-General, Asylum and Protection: Emma Haddad
Acting Chief People Officer: Jill Hatcher
Director, Visas and Citizenship: Marc Owen OBE Email: vcdirectorsoffice@homeoffice.gov.uk
Director, Communications: Simon Baugh
Chief Digital, Data and Technology Officer: Joanna Davinson 020 7035 5515
Email: cddato@homeoffice.gov.uk

Ministry of Housing, Communities and Local Government

2 Marsham Street, London SW1P 4DF
Tel: 0303 444 0000
Email: contactus@communities.gov.uk Website: www.gov.uk/mhclg Twitter: @mhclg

MINISTERS
Secretary of State: Rt Hon Robert Jenrick MP
Minister of State for Housing: Rt Hon Christopher Pincher MP
Minister of State for Regional Growth and Local Government: Luke Hall MP
Minister of State for Building Safety and Communities: Lord Greenhalgh
Parliamentary Under-Secretary of State for Rough Sleeping and Housing: Eddie Hughes MP
Parliamentary Clerk: Paul B Smith 030 3444 0000
House of Lords Spokesperson: **Lord Greenhalgh**
CIVIL SERVANTS
Permanent Secretary: Jeremy Pocklington CB Email: psperm.sec@communities.gov.uk
Director-General, Local Government, Strategy and Analysis: Catherine Frances 0303 444 3021
Email: catherine.frances@communities.gov.uk
Director-General, Housing and Planning: Tracey Waltho Email: tracey.waltho@communities.gov.uk
Director-General, Stronger Places: Emran Mian 0303 444 1101
Email: emran.mian@communities.gov.uk
Director-General, Building Safety, Grenfell Response and Net Zero: Richard Goodman
Email: richard.goodman@communities.gov.uk
Director-General, Chief Financial Officer: Matt Thurstan
Director, Strategy, Communications and Private Office: Lise-Anne Boissiere 0303 444 8368
Email: lise-anne.boissiere@communities.gov.uk
Director, People, Capability and Change: Ruth Bailey 0303 444 9042
Email: ruth.bailey@communities.gov.uk
Chief Executive, Shielding Programme: Chris Townsend
Executive Agencies: Planning Inspectorate, Queen Elizabeth II Centre

Government and Public Offices

Department for International Trade

55 Whitehall, London SW1A 2AH
Tel: 020 7215 5000
Email: enquiries@trade.gov.uk Website: www.gov.uk/dit Twitter: @tradegovuk
MINISTERS
Secretary of State: Rt Hon Elizabeth Truss MP
Minister of State for Trade Policy: Rt Hon Greg Hands MP
Minister of State for Investment: Lord Grimstone of Boscobel
Parliamentary Under-Secretary of State (Minister for Exports): Graham Stuart MP
Parliamentary Under-Secretary of State (Minister for International Trade): Ranil Jayawardena MP
Parliamentary Clerk: Rachel Williams
House of Lords Spokesperson: **Lord Grimstone of Boscobel**
CIVIL SERVANTS
Acting Permanent Secretary: John Alty CB Email: perm.sec@trade.gov.uk
Second Permanent Secretary and Chief Trade Negotiation Adviser: Crawford Falconer
Chief Operating Officer: Catherine Vaughan
Acting Director-General, Policy and Programmes: Darren Tierney
Email: darren.tiernery@trade.gov.uk
Acting Director-General, Markets and Supply Chains: Andrew Mitchell CMG
Director-General, Trade Policy: To be appointed
Director-General, Trade Relations and Implementation: Jo Crellin
Email: joanna.crellin@trade.gov.uk
Director-General, Chief Executive, UK Export Finance: Louis Taylor
Director-General, Investment: To be appointed
Chief Scientific Adviser: Dr Mike Short CBE

Ministry of Justice

102 Petty France, London SW1H 9AJ
Tel: 020 3334 3555
Email: general.queries@justice.gov.uk Website: www.gov.uk/moj Twitter: @MoJGovUK
MINISTERS
Lord Chancellor and Secretary of State for Justice: Rt Hon Robert Buckland QC MP
Minister of State for Prisons and Probation: Lucy Frazer QC MP
Minister of State for Crime and Policing: Kit Malthouse MP

Parliamentary Under-Secretary of State: Alex Chalk MP
Parliamentary Under-Secretary of State for Immigration Compliance and the Courts: Chris Philp MP
Parliamentary Under-Secretary of State: Lord Wolfson of Tredegar QC
House of Lords Spokesperson: **Lord Wolfson of Tredegar** QC
CIVIL SERVANTS
Permanent Secretary: Antonia Romeo
Acting Chief Financial Officer: James McEwen
Acting Director-General, Policy, Communications and Analysis Group: Melissa Case
Email: melissa.case@justice.gov.uk
Director-General, Probation and Wales, HMPPS: Amy Rees
Director-General, Prisons HMPPS: Phil Copple
Director, Legal: Naomi Mallick Email: naomi.mallick@governmentlegal.gov.uk
Chief People Officer: Dr Neil Wooding
Chief Executive, HM Prison and Probation Service: Dr Jo Farrar CB OBE
Email: ceohmpps@justice.gov.uk
Acting Chief Executive, HM Courts and Tribunals Service: Kevin Sadler CBE 020 3334 3400
Email: kevin.sadler@justice.gov.uk

Executive Agencies: HM Courts and Tribunals Service, Criminal Injuries Compensation Authority, Legal Aid Agency, HM Prison and Probation Service, Office of the Public Guardian

Northern Ireland Office

1 Horseguards Road, Whitehall, London SW1A 2HQ
Tel: 020 7210 0820
Email: enquiries@nio.gov.uk Website: www.gov.uk/nio Twitter: @NIOgov
MINISTERS
Secretary of State: Rt Hon Brandon Lewis CBE MP
Minister of State: Robin Walker MP

Parliamentary Clerk: Louise Newby 020 7210 6575

***House of Lords Spokesperson:* Viscount Younger of Leckie**
CIVIL SERVANTS
Permanent Secretary: Madeleine Alessandri CBE 020 7210 6456 Email: pusmail@nio.gov.uk
Director-General: To be appointed

Government and Public Offices

Privy Council Office

Room G/04, 1 Horse Guards Road, London SW1A 2HQ
Tel: 020 7271 3292
Email: enquiries@pco.gov.uk Website: privycouncil.independent.gov.uk
CIVIL SERVANTS
Clerk of the Council: Richard Tilbrook 020 7271 3292 Email: enquiries@pco.gov.uk
Head of Secretariat and Deputy Clerk of the Council: Ceri King 020 7271 3294
Email: ceri.king@pco.gov.uk
Deputy Clerk: Christopher Berry 020 7271 1406 Email: christopher.berry@pco.gov.uk

Office of the Secretary of State for Scotland

Dover House, Whitehall, London SW1A 2AU
Tel: 020 7270 6754
Email: [firstname.surname]@scotlandoffice.gov.uk Website: www.gov.uk/scotland-office
Twitter: @UKGovScotland
MINISTERS
Secretary of State: Rt Hon Alister Jack MP
Parliamentary Under-Secretary of State (Minister for Scotland): Iain Stewart MP
Parliamentary Under-Secretary of State: David Duguid MP
Parliamentary Clerk: Louise Newby 020 7210 6575
***House of Lords Spokesperson:* Viscount Younger of Leckie**
CIVIL SERVANTS
Director: Laurence Rockey

Office of the Advocate General for Scotland

Victoria Quay, Edinburgh EH6 6QQ
Tel: 020 7270 6770
Email: enquiries@advocategeneral.gov.uk
Website: www.gov.uk/government/organisations/office-of-the-advocate-general-for-scotland

MINISTERS

Advocate General for Scotland: Lord Stewart of Dirleton QC

CIVIL SERVANTS

Director: Neil Taylor Email: neil.taylor@advocategeneral.gov.uk

Department for Transport

Great Minster House, 33 Horseferry Road, London SW1P 4DR
Tel: 0300 330 3000
Email: [firstname.surname]@dft.gov.uk Website: www.gov.uk/dft Twitter: @transportgovuk

MINISTERS

Secretary of State: Rt Hon Grant Shapps MP
Minister of State: Andrew Stephenson MP
Minister of State: Chris Heaton-Harris MP
Parliamentary Under-Secretary of State: Rachel Maclean MP
Parliamentary Under-Secretary of State: Robert Courts MP
Parliamentary Under-Secretary of State: Baroness Vere of Norbiton

Parliamentary Clerk: James Langston 020 7944 4472

House of Lords Spokesperson: **Baroness Vere of Norbiton**

CIVIL SERVANTS

Permanent Secretary: Bernadette Kelly CB 020 7944 3017 Email: bernadette.kelly@dft.gov.uk
Director-General, High Speed Rail and Major Projects Group: Clive Maxwell 020 7944 2112 Email: clive.maxwell@dft.gov.uk
Director-General, Aviation, Maritime, International and Security: Gareth Davies 020 7944 4300 Email: psdavies@dft.gov.uk
Director-General, Rail Group (job share): Polly Payne 020 7944 3368 Email: hannant-payne@dft.gov.uk
Director-General, Rail Group (job share): Ruth Hannant 020 7944 3368 Email: hannant-payne@dft.gov.uk
Director-General, Corporate Delivery Group: Nick Joyce 020 7944 4190 Email: nick.joyce@dft.gov.uk
Director-General, Roads, Places and Environment Group: Emma Ward CBE 020 7944 2400 Email: emma.ward@dft.gov.uk
Director-General, Rail Infrastructure Group: David Hughes
Chief Scientific Adviser: Phil Blythe 07920 581420 Email: philip.blythe@dft.gov.uk
Legal Director: Brett Welch 020 7944 2854 Email: brett.welch@governmentlegal.gov.uk

Executive Agencies: Driver and Vehicle Licensing Agency, Driver and Vehicle Standards Agency, Maritime and Coastguard Agency, Vehicle Certification Agency

HM Treasury

1 Horse Guards Road, London SW1A 2HQ
Tel: 020 7270 5000 Fax: 020 7270 5148
Email: public.enquiries@hmtreasury.gov.uk Website: www.gov.uk/treasury Twitter: @hmtreasury

MINISTERS

Chancellor of the Exchequer: Rt Hon Rishi Sunak MP
Chief Secretary to the Treasury: Rt Hon Stephen Barclay MP
Financial Secretary: Rt Hon Jesse Norman MP
Minister of State for Efficiency and Transformation: Lord Agnew of Oulton DL
Economic Secretary (Minister for the City of London): John Glen MP
Exchequer Secretary; Minister for Equalities: Kemi Badenoch MP

Parliamentary Clerk: Simon Turrell

House of Lords Spokesperson: **Lord Agnew of Oulton** DL

CIVIL SERVANTS
Permanent Secretary: Sir Tom Scholar KCB 020 7270 5743
Email: action.permsec@hmtreasury.gov.uk
Second Permanent Secretary: Charles Roxburgh Email: charles.roxburgh@hmtreasury.gov.uk
Director-General, Tax and Welfare: Beth Russell 020 7270 6259
Email: beth.russell@hmtreasury.gov.uk
Director-General, International and EU: Mark Bowman CB 020 7270 6637
Email: mark.bowman@hmtreasury.gov.uk
Director-General, Public Spending: Cat Little
Director-General, Financial Services: Katharine Braddick CB 020 7270 4448
Email: katharine.braddick@hmtreasury.gov.uk
Director-General, Growth and Productivity: Philip Duffy
Acting Chief Financial Officer and Head of Government Finance Function: James McEwen
Director-General, Economics and Chief Economic Adviser: Clare Lombardelli 020 7270 5004
Email: clare.lombardelli@hmtreasury.gov.uk

Executive Agencies: Government Internal Audit Agency, National Infrastructure Commission, UK Debt Management Office

Office of the Secretary of State for Wales

Gwydyr House, Whitehall, London SW1A 2NP
Tel: 020 7270 0534
Email: correspondence@ukgovwales.gov.uk
Website: www.gov.uk/government/organisations/office-of-the-secretary-of-state-for-wales
Twitter: @UKGovWales

MINISTERS
Secretary of State: Rt Hon Simon Hart MP
Parliamentary Under-Secretary of State: David Davies MP
Parliamentary Clerk: Louise Newby 07554 115063

House of Lords Spokesperson: **Baroness Bloomfield of Hinton Waldrist**

CIVIL SERVANTS
Director: Glynne Jones CBE 020 7270 0559 Email: glynne.jones@ukgovwales.gov.uk

Government and Public Offices

Department for Work and Pensions

Caxton House, Tothill Street, London SW1H 9NA
Tel: 020 3267 5013
Email: correspondence@dwp.gov.uk Website: www.gov.uk/dwp Twitter: @DWP

MINISTERS
Secretary of State: Rt Hon Dr Therese Coffey MP
Minister of State for Disabled People, Health and Work: Justin Tomlinson MP
Parliamentary Under-Secretary of State for Employment: Mims Davies MP
Parliamentary Under-Secretary of State for Pensions and Financial Inclusion: Guy Opperman MP

Parliamentary Under-Secretary of State for Welfare Delivery: Will Quince MP
Parliamentary Under-Secretary of State (Lords): Baroness Stedman-Scott OBE
Parliamentary Clerk: Howard Sargent 020 3267 5159

House of Lords Spokesperson: **Baroness Stedman-Scott** OBE

CIVIL SERVANTS
Permanent Secretary: Peter Schofield CB 020 3267 5013 Email: peter.schofield1@dwp.gov.uk
Director-General, People and Capability: Debbie Alder CB 020 7340 4193
Email: debbie.alder@dwp.gov.uk
Director-General, Change and Senior Responsible Owner Universal Credit: Neil Couling CBE 020 7245 3844 Email: neil.couling@dwp.gov.uk
Director-General, Chief Digital and Information Officer: Simon McKinnon CBE 020 7449 7892
Email: simon.mckinnon@dwp.gov.uk
Director-General, Service Excellence: Amanda Reynolds
Director-General, Work and Health Services: John-Paul Marks 020 7449 5530
Email: john-paul.marks@dwp.gov.uk
Director-General, Policy: Jonathan Mills 020 7449 5516 Email: jonathan.mills@dwp.gov.uk
Director-General, Finance: Nick Joicey CB 020 7449 5780 Email: nick.joicey@dwp.gov.uk

Executive Agencies

ANIMAL AND PLANT HEALTH AGENCY
Corporate Headquarters, Woodham Lane, Addlestone KT15 3NB
Tel: 020 8225 7611
Email: apha.corporatecorrespondence@apha.gov.uk Website: www.gov.uk/apha
Twitter: @APHAgovuk

Chief Executive: Chris Hadkiss

Sponsored by: Department for Environment, Food and Rural Affairs, Scottish Government, Welsh Government

---

CENTRE FOR ENVIRONMENT, FISHERIES AND AQUACULTURE SCIENCE
Lowestoft Laboratory, Pakefield Road, Lowestoft NR33 0HT
Tel: 01502 562244
Email: cmboffice@cefas.co.uk Website: www.cefas.co.uk Twitter: @CefasGovUK

Chief Executive: Neil Hornby

Sponsored by: Department for Environment, Food and Rural Affairs

---

COMPANIES HOUSE
Crown Way, Cardiff CF14 3UZ
Tel: 0303 1234 500
Email: enquiries@companieshouse.gov.uk Website: www.gov.uk/companies-house
Twitter: @CompaniesHouse

Non-Executive Chair: Lesley Cowley OBE Email: lcowley@companieshouse.gov.uk
Chief Executive and Registrar of Companies for England and Wales: Louise Smyth
Email: lsmyth@companieshouse.gov.uk

Sponsored by: Department for Business, Energy and Industrial Strategy

Government and Public Offices

HM COURTS AND TRIBUNALS SERVICE
102 Petty France, London SW1H 9AJ
Tel: 020 3334 3555
Website: www.gov.uk/hmcts Twitter: @HMCTSgovuk

Acting Chief Executive: Kevin Sadler CBE 020 3334 3400 Email: kevin.sadler@justice.gov.uk
Chief Digital and Information Officer: Dave Perry 020 3334 4721 Email: dave.perry@justice.gov.uk

Sponsored by: Ministry of Justice

CRIMINAL INJURIES COMPENSATION AUTHORITY
Alexander Bain House, Atlantic Quay, 15 York Street, Glasgow G2 8JQ
Tel: 0300 003 3601
Email: info@cica.gov.uk Website: www.gov.uk/cica Twitter: @CICAgov

Chief Executive: Linda Brown 07885 242263 Email: linda.brown@cica.gov.uk

Sponsored by: Ministry of Justice

CROWN COMMERCIAL SERVICE
151 Buckingham Palace Road, London SW1W 9SZ
Tel: 0345 410 2222
Email: info@crowncommercial.gov.uk Website: www.crowncommercial.gov.uk
Twitter: @gov_procurement

Chair: Tony van Kralingen
Acting Chief Executive and Accounting Officer: Simon Tse
Email: simon.tse@crowncommercial.gov.uk

Sponsored by: Cabinet Office

DEFENCE ELECTRONICS AND COMPONENTS AGENCY
Welsh Road, Sealand, Deeside CH5 2LS
Tel: 01244 847694
Email: decainfo@deca.mod.uk Website: www.gov.uk/deca
Chair: Alec Don
Chief Executive: Geraint Spearing 01244 847701 Email: jane.twomey@deca.mod.uk
Sponsored by: Ministry of Defence

DEFENCE SCIENCE AND TECHNOLOGY LABORATORY
Porton Down, Salisbury SP4 0JQ
Tel: 01980 950000
Email: centralenquiries@dstl.gov.uk Website: www.gov.uk/dstl Twitter: @dstlmod
Chief Executive: Gary Aitkenhead
Chair: Adrian Belton
Sponsored by: Ministry of Defence

DRIVER AND VEHICLE LICENSING AGENCY
Longview Road, Morriston, Swansea SA6 7JL
Tel: 0300 790 6801 (Drivers)/0300 790 6802 (Vehicles)
Website: www.gov.uk/dvla Twitter: @dvlagovuk
Chief Executive: Julie Lennard 01792 384538 Email: chief.executive@dvla.gov.uk
Sponsored by: Department for Transport

DRIVER AND VEHICLE STANDARDS AGENCY
Berkeley House, Croydon Street, Bristol BS5 0DA
Tel: 0117-954 3200
Email: corporatereputation@dvsa.gov.uk Website: www.gov.uk/dvsa Twitter: @DVSAgovuk
Non-Executive Chair: Shrin Honap Email: shrinivas.honap@dvsa.gov.uk
Chief Executives: Loveday Ryder, Gareth Llewellyn 0117-954 3211
Email: gareth.llewellyn@dvsa.gov.uk
Sponsored by: Department for Transport

EDUCATION AND SKILLS FUNDING AGENCY
Ministerial and Public Communications Division, Department for Education, Piccadilly Gate, Store Street, Manchester M1 2WD
Tel: 0370 000 2288
Website: www.gov.uk/esfa Twitter: @esfagov
Chief Executive: Eileen Milner 020 7340 8315 Email: eileen.milner@education.gov.uk
Sponsored by: Department for Education

FOREST RESEARCH
Alice Holt Lodge Research Station, Farnham GU10 4LH
Tel: 0300 067 5600/01420 22255
Website: www.forestresearch.gov.uk Twitter: @Forest_Research
Chief Executive: Professor James Pendlebury 0300 067 5971
Email: james.pendlebury@forestresearch.gov.uk
Sponsored by: Forestry Commission

FORESTRY ENGLAND
620 Bristol Business Park, Coldharbour Lane, Bristol BS16 1EJ
Tel: 0300 067 4000
Email: info@forestryengland.uk Website: www.forestryengland.uk Twitter: @ForestryEngland
Chief Executive: Mike Seddon 0300 067 4130 Email: michael.seddon@forestryengland.uk
Sponsored by: Forestry Commission

GOVERNMENT INTERNAL AUDIT AGENCY
10 Victoria Street, London SW1H 0NB
Email: correspondence@giaa.gov.uk Website: www.gov.uk/giaa

Chief Executive Officer: Elizabeth Honer

Sponsored by: HM Treasury

GOVERNMENT PROPERTY AGENCY
Email: enquiries@gpa.gov.uk
Website: www.gov.uk/government/organisations/government-property-agency
Twitter: @UKGovPropAgency

Chief Executive: Steven Boyd 07851 382960 Email: steven.boyd@gpa.gov.uk
Chair: Pat Ritchie OBE

Sponsored by: Cabinet Office

THE INSOLVENCY SERVICE
Sixteenth Floor, 1 Westfield Avenue, London E20 1HZ
Tel: 0300 678 0015/020 7637 1110
Email: insolvency.enquiryline@insolvency.gov.uk Website: www.gov.uk/insolvency-service
Twitter: @insolvencygovuk

Chair: Stephen Allinson Email: board.secretariat@insolvency.gov.uk
Chief Executive and Inspector General: Dean Beale Email: dean.beale@insolvency.gov.uk

Sponsored by: Department for Business, Energy and Industrial Strategy

INTELLECTUAL PROPERTY OFFICE
Concept House, Cardiff Road, Newport NP10 8QQ
Tel: 0300 300 2000 Fax: 01633 817777
Email: information@ipo.gov.uk Website: www.gov.uk/ipo Twitter: @The_IPO

Chief Executive and Comptroller General: Tim Moss CBE 01633 814500
Email: tim.moss@ipo.gov.uk
Chair: Tim Suter 01633 814500 Email: tim.suter@ipo.gov.uk

Sponsored by: Department for Business, Energy and Industrial Strategy

LEGAL AID AGENCY
Legal Aid Agency, 102 Petty France, London SW1H 9AL
Tel: 0300 200 2020
Email: contactcivil@justice.gov.uk Website: www.gov.uk/government/organisations/legal-aid-agency
Twitter: @LegalAidAgency

Chief Executive: Jane Harbottle 07713 328383 Email: jane.harbottle@justice.gov.uk

Sponsored by: Ministry of Justice

MARITIME AND COASTGUARD AGENCY
Spring Place, 105 Commercial Road, Southampton SO15 1EG
Tel: 020 3817 2000
Email: infoline@mcga.gov.uk Website: www.gov.uk/mca Twitter: @MCA_media

Chief Executive: Brian Johnson 020 3817 2385 Email: brian.johnson@mcga.gov.uk
Non-Executive Chair: Michael Parker 020 3817 2167 Email: michael.parker@mcga.gov.uk

Sponsored by: Department for Transport

MEDICINES AND HEALTHCARE PRODUCTS REGULATORY AGENCY
10 South Colonnade, London E14 4PU
Tel: 020 3080 6000
Email: info@mhra.gov.uk Website: www.gov.uk/mhra Twitter: @MHRAgovuk

Chair: Stephen Lightfoot
Acting Chief Executive: Dr June Raine OBE 020 3080 7204 Email: june.raine@mhra.gov.uk

Sponsored by: Department of Health and Social Care

MET OFFICE
FitzRoy Road, Exeter EX1 3PB
Tel: 0370 900 0100/01392 885680 Fax: 0370 900 5050/01392 885681
Email: enquiries@metoffice.gov.uk Website: www.metoffice.gov.uk Twitter: @metoffice
Chair: Rob Woodward 0330 135 0113
Chief Executive: Prof Penelope Endersby 0330 135 2819 Email: penny.endersby@metoffice.gov.uk
Sponsored by: Department for Business, Energy and Industrial Strategy

NATIONAL INFRASTRUCTURE COMMISSION
Fourth Floor, Finlaison House, 15-17 Furnival Street, London EC4A 1AB
Email: enquiries@nic.gov.uk Website: www.nic.org.uk Twitter: @NatInfraCom
Chair: Sir John Armitt CBE Email: nicole.kelly@nic.org.uk
Chief Executive: James Heath Email: nicole.kelly@nic.org.uk
Sponsored by: HM Treasury

PLANNING INSPECTORATE
Temple Quay House, 2 The Square, Temple Quay, Bristol BS1 6PN
Tel: 030 3444 5000
Email: enquiries@planninginspectorate.gov.uk Website: www.gov.uk/pins Twitter: @PINSgov
Chair, Planning Inspectorate Board: Trudi Elliott CBE
Chief Executive: Sarah Richards Email: sarah.richards@planninginspectorate.gov.uk
Sponsored by: Ministry of Housing, Communities and Local Government, Welsh Government

HM PRISON AND PROBATION SERVICE
Fifth Floor, 102 Petty France, London SW1H 9AJ
Tel: 020 3193 5921
Email: hmppspublicenquiries@justice.gov.uk Website: www.gov.uk/hmpps Twitter: @hmpps
Chief Executive: Dr Jo Farrar CB OBE Email: ceohmpps@justice.gov.uk
Sponsored by: Ministry of Justice

OFFICE OF THE PUBLIC GUARDIAN
PO Box 16185, Birmingham B2 2WH
Tel: 0300 456 0300
Email: customerservices@publicguardian.gov.uk Website: www.gov.uk/opg Twitter: @OPGGovUK
Chief Executive and Public Guardian: Nick Goodwin 0121-631-6845
Email: nick.goodwin@publicguardian.gov.uk
Sponsored by: Ministry of Justice

PUBLIC HEALTH ENGLAND
Wellington House, 133-155 Waterloo Road, London SE1 8UG
Tel: 020 7654 8000
Email: enquiries@phe.gov.uk Website: www.gov.uk/phe Twitter: @PHE_uk
Acting Chief Executive: Michael Brodie Email: michael.brodie@phe.gov.uk
Sponsored by: Department of Health and Social Care

QUEEN ELIZABETH II CENTRE
Broad Sanctuary, Westminster, London SW1P 3EE
Tel: 020 7798 4000
Email: info@qeiicentre.london Website: www.qeiicentre.london Twitter: @QEIICentre
Chief Executive: Mark Taylor 020 7798 4010 Email: mark.taylor@qeiicentre.london
Sponsored by: Ministry of Housing, Communities and Local Government

RURAL PAYMENTS AGENCY
Northgate House, 21-23 Valpy Street, PO Box 69, Reading RG1 1AF
Tel: 0300 020 0301
Email: ruralpayments@defra.gov.uk Website: www.gov.uk/rpa Twitter: @Ruralpay
Chief Executive: Paul Caldwell 01228 640314 Email: paul.caldwell@rpa.gsi.gov.uk
Sponsored by: Department for Environment, Food and Rural Affairs

STANDARDS AND TESTING AGENCY
Cheylesmore House, Ground Floor South Building, 5 Quinton Road, Coventry CV1 2WT
Tel: 0370 000 2288
Email: assessments@education.gov.uk Website: www.gov.uk/sta
Chief Executive: Una Bennett Email: ceooffice.sta@education.gov.uk
Sponsored by: Department for Education

SUBMARINE DELIVERY AGENCY
Abbey Wood South, Rowan Building 1a #8102, Bristol BS34 8JH
Chief Executive: Ian Booth
Sponsored by: Ministry of Defence

TEACHING REGULATION AGENCY
Ground Floor, South Cheylesmore House, 5 Quinton Road, Coventry CV1 2WT
Website: www.gov.uk/tra
Chief Executive and Accounting Officer: Alan Meyrick
Sponsored by: Department for Education

UK DEBT MANAGEMENT OFFICE
Eastcheap Court, 11 Philpot Lane, London EC3M 8UD
Tel: 020 7862 6500
Email: [firstname.surname]@dmo.gov.uk Website: www.dmo.gov.uk
Chief Executive: Sir Robert Stheeman Email: robert.stheeman@dmo.gsi.gov.uk
Sponsored by: HM Treasury

UK HYDROGRAPHIC OFFICE
Admiralty Way, Taunton TA1 2DN
Tel: 01823 484444
Email: ukho-secretariat@ukho.gov.uk Website: www.gov.uk/ukho Twitter: @UKHO_Online
Non-Executive Chair: Adam Singer Email: adam.singer@ukho.gov.uk
Sponsored by: Ministry of Defence

UK SPACE AGENCY
Polaris House, North Star Avenue, Swindon SN2 1SZ
Tel: 020 7215 5000
Email: info@ukspaceagency.bis.gsi.gov.uk Website: www.gov.uk/uksa Twitter: @spacegovuk
Chair: Sally Howes
Chief Executive: Dr Graham Turnock
Sponsored by: Department for Business, Energy and Industrial Strategy

VALUATION OFFICE AGENCY
Eighth Floor, 10 South Colonnade, Poplar, London W1D 5DA
Tel: 0300 050 1501/0300 050 5505 (Wales)
Website: www.voa.gov.uk Twitter: @VOAgovuk
Acting Chief Executive: Jonathan Russell 0300 050 0031 Email: jonathan.russell@voa.gsi.gov.uk
Sponsored by: HM Revenue & Customs

VEHICLE CERTIFICATION AGENCY
1 The Eastgate Office Centre, Eastgate Road, Bristol BS5 6XX
Tel: 0300 330 5797
Email: enquiries@vca.gov.uk Website: www.vehicle-certification-agency.gov.uk
Chief Executive: Pia Wilkes Email: pia.wilkes@vca.gov.uk
Sponsored by: Department for Transport

VETERINARY MEDICINES DIRECTORATE
Woodham Lane, New Haw, Addlestone KT15 3LS
Tel: 01932 336911
Email: postmaster@vmd.gov.uk Website: www.gov.uk/vmd Twitter: @vmdgovuk
Chief Executive: Prof Peter Borriello 01932 338302 Email: p.borriello@vmd.gov.uk
Sponsored by: Department for Environment, Food and Rural Affairs

WILTON PARK
Wiston House, Steyning BN44 3DZ
Tel: 01903 815020 Fax: 01903 816373
Email: admin@wiltonpark.org.uk Website: www.wiltonpark.org.uk Twitter: @wiltonpark
Chair: Rt Hon Baroness Stuart of Edgbaston 01903 817766
Chief Executive: Tom Cargill
Sponsored by: Foreign, Commonwealth and Development Office

DEFENCE EQUIPMENT AND SUPPORT
DE&S, Abbey Wood, Bristol BS34 8JH
Tel: 0117-913 0000 Fax: 0117-913 0900
Email: DESCDM-CDMCoSouteroffice@mod.gov.uk Website: www.gov.uk/des
Chief Executive: Sir Simon Bollom KBE CB 0141-224 2179 Email: desceo-outeroffice@mod.gov.uk
Chair: Mark Russell
Sponsored by: Ministry of Defence

Non-Ministerial Departments

Non-Ministerial Departments are headed by office-holders, boards or Commissioners with specific statutory responsibilities

CHARITY COMMISSION

102 Petty France, London SW1H 9AJ
Tel: 0300 066 9197
Website: www.charitycommission.gov.uk Twitter: @ChtyCommission

Chair: Rt Hon Baroness Stowell of Beeston MBE 0300 065 2110
Email: tina.stowell@charitycommission.gov.uk
Chief Executive: Helen Stephenson CBE 0300 065 2145
Email: helen.stephenson@charitycommission.gov.uk

COMPETITION AND MARKETS AUTHORITY

The Cabot, 25 Cabot Square, London E14 4QZ
Tel: 020 3738 6000
Email: general.enquiries@cma.gov.uk Website: www.gov.uk/cma Twitter: @CMAgovUK

Acting Chair: Jonathan Scott
Chief Executive: Dr Andrea Coscelli CBE 020 3738 6286 Email: andrea.coscelli@cma.gov.uk

CROWN PROSECUTION SERVICE

102 Petty France, London SW1H 9EA
Tel: 020 3357 0000
Email: enquiries@cps.gov.uk Website: www.cps.gov.uk Twitter: @cpsuk

Director of Public Prosecutions: Max Hill QC
Chief Executive: Rebecca Lawrence

FOOD STANDARDS AGENCY

Floors 6 and 7, Clive House, 70 Petty France, London SW1H 9EX
Tel: 0330 332 7149
Email: helpline@food.gov.uk Website: www.food.gov.uk Twitter: @foodgov

Chair: Heather Hancock 020 7276 8120 Email: toby.garner@food.gov.uk
Chief Executive: Emily Miles 020 7276 8616 Email: chloe.skyrme@food.gov.uk

FORESTRY COMMISSION

Forestry Commission Head Office, Silvan House, 231 Corstorphine Road, Edinburgh EH12 7AT
Tel: 0300 067 5000
Email: enquiries@forestry.gsi.gov.uk Website: www.forestry.gov.uk Twitter: @ForestryCommEng

Chief Executive: Dr David Signorini
Chair: Sir William Worsley

OFFICE OF GAS AND ELECTRICITY MARKETS

10 South Colonnade, London E14 4PU
Tel: 020 7901 7000 Fax: 020 7901 7066
Website: www.ofgem.gov.uk Twitter: @ofgem

Chief Executive: Jonathan Brearley Email: jonathan.brearley@ofgem.gov.uk
Chair: Prof Martin Cave Email: chair@ofgem.gov.uk

GOVERNMENT ACTUARY'S DEPARTMENT

Finlaison House, 15-17 Furnival Street, London EC4A 1AB
Tel: 020 7211 2601 Fax: 020 7211 2650
Email: enquiries@gad.gov.uk Website: www.gov.uk/gad

Government Actuary: Martin Clarke CB 020 7211 2620

GOVERNMENT LEGAL DEPARTMENT
102 Petty France, London SW1H 9GL
Tel: 020 7210 3000
Email: thetreasurysolicitor@governmentlegal.gov.uk Website: www.gov.uk/gld
Acting HM Procurator-General and Treasury Solicitor and Head of the Government Legal Service: Peter Fish

HM REVENUE & CUSTOMS
Her Majesty's Revenue and Customs, 100 Parliament Street, London SW1A 2BQ
Tel: 0300 058 9668
Email: correspondence-team.mincom@hmrc.gov.uk Website: www.gov.uk/hmrc
Twitter: @HMRCgovuk
Chief Executive and Permanent Secretary: Jim Harra Email: perm.secs@hmrc.gov.uk

HM LAND REGISTRY
Head Office, Trafalgar House, 1 Bedford Park, Croydon, London CR0 2AQ
Tel: 0300 006 0004
Email: customersupport@landregistry.gov.uk Website: www.gov.uk/land-registry
Twitter: @HMLandRegistry
Non-Executive Chair: Michael Mire Email: michael.mire@landregistry.gov.uk
Chief Executive and Chief Land Registrar: Simon Hayes Email: simon.hayes@landregistry.gov.uk

THE NATIONAL ARCHIVES
Kew, Richmond TW9 4DU
Tel: 020 8876 3444 Fax: 020 8878 8905
Website: www.nationalarchives.gov.uk Twitter: @UkNatArchives
Chief Executive and Keeper: Jeff James 020 8392 5220 Email: jeff.james@nationalarchives.gov.uk

NATIONAL CRIME AGENCY
1-6 Citadel Place, Tinworth Street, London SE11 5EF
Tel: 0370 496 7622
Email: communication@nca.x.gsi.gov.uk Website: www.nationalcrimeagency.gov.uk
Twitter: @NCA_UK
Director-General: Dame Lynne Owens DCB CBE QPM

NATIONAL SAVINGS AND INVESTMENTS
1 Drummond Gate, Pimlico, London SW1V 2QX
Tel: 020 7932 6600
Website: www.nsandi.com Twitter: @nsandi
Non-Executive Director and Chairman of the Board: Ed Anderson 020 7932 6859
Email: victoria.burnett@nsandi.com
Chief Executive: Ian Ackerley 020 7932 6602 Email: ian.ackerley@nsandi.com

OFFICE OF QUALIFICATIONS AND EXAMINATIONS REGULATION
Earlsdon Park, 53-55 Butts Road, Coventry CV1 3BH
Tel: 0300 303 3344 Fax: 0300 303 3348
Email: public.enquiries@ofqual.gov.uk Website: www.gov.uk/ofqual Twitter: @ofqual
Chair: Ian Bauckham
Acting Chief Regulator: Simon Lebus

OFFICE OF RAIL AND ROAD
25 Cabot Square, London E14 4QZ
Tel: 020 7282 2000
Email: contact.cct@orr.gov.uk Website: www.orr.gov.uk Twitter: @railandroad
Chair: Declan Collier 020 7282 2178 Email: declan.collier@orr.gov.uk
Chief Executive: John Larkinson 020 7282 2193 Email: john.larkinson@orr.gov.uk

SERIOUS FRAUD OFFICE
2-4 Cockspur Street, London SW1Y 5BS
Tel: 020 7239 7272
Email: public.enquiries@sfo.gov.uk Website: www.sfo.gov.uk Twitter: @UKSFO

Director: Lisa Osofsky 020 7239 7045 Email: lisa.osofsky@sfo.gov.uk

OFFICE FOR STANDARDS IN EDUCATION, CHILDREN'S SERVICES AND SKILLS
Piccadilly Gate, Store Street, Manchester M1 2WD
Tel: 0300 123 1231
Email: enquiries@ofsted.gov.uk Website: www.gov.uk/ofsted Twitter: @Ofstednews

Chair: Christine Ryan
HM Chief Inspector of Education, Children's Services and Skills: Amanda Spielman 0300 013 1993
Email: amanda.spielman@ofsted.gov.uk

UK STATISTICS AUTHORITY/OFFICE FOR NATIONAL STATISTICS
1 Drummond Gate, London SW1V 2QQ
Tel: 0845 604 1857 (Authority)/0845 601 3034 (ONS)
Email: authority.enquiries@statistics.gov.uk Email: info@ons.gov.uk
Website: www.statisticsauthority.gov.uk Website: www.ons.gov.uk Twitter: @UKStatsAuth/@ONS

Chair: Sir David Norgrove 01329 447249 Email: david.norgrove@statistics.gov.uk
National Statistician, Chief Executive, UK Statistics Authority, Permanent Secretary, ONS, Head, Government Statistical Service: Prof Sir Ian Diamond 020 7592 8613
Email: national.statistician@statistics.gov.uk

UK SUPREME COURT
Parliament Square, London SW1P 3BD
Tel: 020 7960 1900/020 7960 1500 Fax: 020 7960 1901
Email: enquiries@supremecourt.uk Website: www.supremecourt.uk Twitter: @UKSupremeCourt

Chief Executive: Vicky Fox 020 7960 1906 Email: vicky.fox@supremecourt.uk

WATER SERVICES REGULATION AUTHORITY
Ofwat Birmingham Office, Centre City Tower, 7 Hill Street, Birmingham B5 4UA
Tel: 0121-644 7500
Email: mailbox@ofwat.gsi.gov.uk Website: www.ofwat.gov.uk Twitter: @Ofwat

Chair: Jonson Cox CBE 0121-644 7500 Email: jonson.cox@ofwat.gov.uk
Chief Executive: Rachel Fletcher 0121-644 7818 Email: rachel.fletcher@ofwat.gov.uk

Ombudsmen and Complaint-handling Bodies

ADJUDICATOR'S OFFICE
Adjudicator's Office, PO Box 10280, Nottingham NG2 9PF
Tel: 0300 057 1111 Fax: 0300 059 4513
Website: www.adjudicatorsoffice.gov.uk
Adjudicator: Helen Megarry
Head of Office: Margaret Allcock 0300 057 1781

ADVERTISING STANDARDS AUTHORITY
Castle House, 37-45 Paul Street, London EC2A 4LS
Tel: 020 7492 2222 Fax: 020 7242 3696
Website: www.asa.org.uk Twitter: @ASA_UK
Chair: Professor Lord Currie of Marylebone
Chief Executive: Guy Parker

CHILDREN AND YOUNG PEOPLE'S COMMISSIONER SCOTLAND
Bridgeside House, 99 McDonald Road, Edinburgh EH7 4NS
Tel: 0131-346 5350
Email: info@cypcs.org.uk Website: www.cypcs.org.uk Twitter: @cypcs
Commissioner: Bruce Adamson Email: bruce.adamson@cypcs.org.uk

COMMISSIONER FOR PUBLIC APPOINTMENTS NORTHERN IRELAND
Annex B, Dundonald House, Stormont Estate, Upper Newtownards Road, Belfast BT4 3SB
Tel: 028 9052 4820
Email: info@publicappointmentsni.org Website: www.publicappointmentsni.org
Commissioner: Judena Leslie
Principal Business and Policy Adviser: Pat Neeson

COMMISSIONER FOR ETHICAL STANDARDS IN PUBLIC LIFE IN SCOTLAND
Thistle House, 91 Haymarket Terrace, Edinburgh EH12 5HE
Tel: 0300 011 0550
Email: info@ethicalstandards.org.uk Website: www.ethicalstandards.org.uk
Commissioner for Ethical Standards in Public Life in Scotland: Caroline Anderson 0131-347 3890

FINANCIAL OMBUDSMAN SERVICE
Exchange Tower, London E14 9SR
Tel: 020 7964 1000/0800 023 4567 (consumer) Fax: 020 7964 1001
Email: complaint.info@financial-ombudsman.org.uk Website: www.financial-ombudsman.org.uk
Twitter: @Financialombuds
Chair: Baroness Manzoor CBE
Chief Executive and Chief Ombudsman: Caroline Wayman
Email: caroline.wayman@financial-ombudsman.org.uk

FINANCIAL SERVICES OMBUDSMAN SCHEME FOR THE ISLE OF MAN
Thie Slieau Whallian, Foxdale Road, St John's IM4 3AS
Tel: 01624 686500 Fax: 01624 686504
Email: ombudsman@iomoft.gov.im Website: www.gov.im/oft/ombudsman
Senior Adjudicator: John Wright

GIBRALTAR PUBLIC SERVICES OMBUDSMAN
Office of the Ombudsman, 10 Governor's Lane
Tel: +350 200 46001 Fax: +350 200 46002
Email: info@ombudsman.gi Website: www.ombudsman.org.gi Twitter: @GibraltarOmbuds
Ombudsman: Dilip Dayaram Tirathdas MBE +350 200 46001
Email: dilip.dayaram.tirathdas@ombudsman.gi

GROCERIES CODE ADJUDICATOR

Seventh Floor, The Cabot, London E14 4QZ
Tel: 020 7215 6537
Email: enquiries@groceriescode.gov.uk Website: www.gov.uk/gca Twitter: @UKGCA
Adjudicator: Mark White

INDEPENDENT CASE EXAMINER

PO Box 209, Bootle L20 7WA
Tel: 0800 414 8529 Fax: 0151-221 6601
Email: ice@dwp.gov.uk Website: www.gov.uk/ice
Independent Case Examiner: Joanna Wallace

INDEPENDENT COMPLAINTS REVIEWER

1 Victoria Street, London SW1H 0ET
Tel: 020 7930 0749
Email: enquiries@icrev.org.uk Website: www.icrev.org.uk
Independent Complaints Reviewer for HM Land Registry: Andrea Cook

JUDICIAL APPOINTMENTS AND CONDUCT OMBUDSMAN

1.55, First Floor, The Tower, 102 Petty France, London SW1H 9AJ
Tel: 020 3334 2900
Email: headofoffice@judicialombudsman.gov.uk Website: www.gov.uk/jaco
Judicial Appointments and Conduct Ombudsman: Paul Kernaghan CBE QPM 020 3334 2900
Email: headofoffice@judicialombudsman.gov.uk

LEGAL OMBUDSMAN

For Legal Complaints, PO Box 6806, Wolverhampton WV1 9WJ
Tel: 0300 555 0333
Email: enquiries@legalombudsman.org.uk Website: www.legalombudsman.org.uk
Twitter: @Legal_Ombudsman
Chief Ombudsman: To be appointed

LOCAL GOVERNMENT AND SOCIAL CARE OMBUDSMAN

PO Box 4771, Coventry CV4 0EH
Tel: 0300 061 0614
Email: policyandcomms@lgo.org.uk Website: www.lgo.org.uk Twitter: @LGOmbudsman
Chair and Ombudsman: Michael King 0330 403 4089 Email: s.elford@lgo.org.uk
Chief Executive: Nigel Ellis 0330 403 4089 Email: s.elford@lgo.org.uk

NORTHERN IRELAND PUBLIC SERVICES OMBUDSMAN

Progressive House, 33 Wellington Place, Belfast BT1 6HN
Tel: 028 9023 3821/0800 343 424 Fax: 028 9023 4912
Email: nipso@nipso.org.uk Website: nipso.org.uk/nipso Twitter: @NIPSO_Comms
Ombudsman: Margaret Kelly

OFFICE OF THE INDEPENDENT ADJUDICATOR FOR HIGHER EDUCATION

Second Floor, Abbey Wharf, 57-75 Kings Road, Reading RG1 3AB
Tel: 0118-959 9813
Email: enquiries@oiahe.org.uk Website: www.oiahe.org.uk Twitter: @oiahe
Independent Adjudicator: Felicity Mitchell Email: felicity.mitchell@oiahe.org.uk
Chief Executive: Ben Elger Email: ben.elger@oiahe.org.uk

OFFICE OF THE SCHOOLS ADJUDICATOR

Bishopsgate House, Feethams, Darlington DL1 5QE
Tel: 01325 340402
Email: osa.team@schoolsadjudicator.gov.uk
Website: www.gov.uk/government/organisations/office-of-the-schools-adjudicator

Chief Schools Adjudicator: Shan Scott

OMBUDSMAN ASSOCIATION

Leonard House, 5-7 Newman Road, Bromley BR1 1RJ
Tel: 020 8642 6143
Email: donal.galligan@ombudsmanassociation.org Website: www.ombudsmanassociation.org
Twitter: @OmbudAssoc

Chief Executive: Donal Galligan 020 8642 6143 Email: donal.galligan@ombudsmanassociation.org

OMBUDSMAN SERVICES

The Brew House, Wilderspool Park, Greenall's Avenue, Warrington WA4 6HL
Tel: 0330 440 1624/01925 530263
Email: enquiries@os-communications.org Website: www.ombudsman-services.org
Twitter: @ombudservices

Chair: Lord Clement-Jones CBE
Chief Ombudsman: Matthew Vickers

PARLIAMENTARY AND HEALTH SERVICE OMBUDSMAN

Citygate, Mosley Street, Manchester M2 3HQ
Tel: 0345 015 4033 Fax: 0300 061 4000
Email: phso.enquiries@ombudsman.org.uk Website: www.ombudsman.org.uk
Twitter: @PHSOmbudsman

Chief Executive: Amanda Amroliwala CBE
Ombudsman: Rob Behrens CBE

THE PENSIONS OMBUDSMAN

10 South Colonnade, London E14 4PU
Tel: 020 7630 2200 Fax: 020 7821 0065
Email: enquiries@pensions-ombudsman.org.uk Website: www.pensions-ombudsman.org.uk
Twitter: @PensionsOmbuds

Ombudsman: Anthony Arter
Deputy Ombudsman: Karen Johnston

POLICE OMBUDSMAN FOR NORTHERN IRELAND

New Cathedral Buildings, 11 Church Street, Belfast BT1 1PG
Tel: 028 9082 8600 Fax: 028 9082 8659
Email: info@policeombudsman.org Website: www.policeombudsman.org Twitter: @ponipressoffice

Police Ombudsman for Northern Ireland: Marie Anderson
Chief Executive: Olwen Laird

PRISONS AND PROBATION OMBUDSMAN FOR ENGLAND AND WALES

10 South Colonnade, London E14 4PU
Tel: 020 7633 4100 Fax: 020 7633 4141
Email: mail@ppo.gov.uk Website: www.ppo.gov.uk Twitter: @PPOmbudsman

Ombudsman: Sue McAllister 020 7633 4012 Email: nikki.robinson@ppo.gov.uk

THE PROPERTY OMBUDSMAN

Milford House, 43-55 Milford Street, Salisbury SP1 2BP
Tel: 01722 333306
Email: admin@tpos.co.uk Website: www.tpos.co.uk Twitter: @TPOmb

Ombudsman: Rebecca Marsh

PUBLIC SERVICES OMBUDSMAN FOR WALES

1 Ffordd yr Hen Gae, Pencoed, Bridgend CF35 5LJ
Tel: 0300 790 0203 Fax: 01656 641199
Email: ask@ombudsman.wales Website: www.ombudsman.wales Twitter: @OmbudsmanWales

Public Services Ombudsman for Wales: Nick Bennett

SCOTTISH INFORMATION COMMISSIONER

Kinburn Castle, Doubledykes Road, St Andrews KY16 9DS
Tel: 01334 464610 Fax: 01334 464611
Email: enquiries@itspublicknowledge.info Website: www.itspublicknowledge.info
Twitter: @FOIScotland

Commissioner: Daren Fitzhenry 01334 464610 Email: sic@itspublicknowledge.info

THE SCOTTISH LEGAL COMPLAINTS COMMISSION

The Stamp Office, 10-14 Waterloo Place, Edinburgh EH1 3EG
Tel: 0131-201 2130 Fax: 0131-201 2131
Email: enquiries@scottishlegalcomplaints.org.uk Website: www.scottishlegalcomplaints.org.uk
Twitter: @slcccomplaints

Chair: Jim Martin
Chief Executive: Neil Stevenson

SCOTTISH PUBLIC SERVICES OMBUDSMAN

Bridgeside House, 99 McDonald Road, Edinburgh EH7 4NS
Tel: 0800 377 7330 Fax: 0800 377 7331
Email: ask@spso.gov.scot Website: www.spso.org.uk Twitter: @SPSO_Ombudsman

Ombudsman: Rosemary Agnew

SERVICE COMPLAINTS OMBUDSMAN FOR THE ARMED FORCES

PO Box 72252, London SW1P 9ZZ
Tel: 020 7877 3450
Email: contact@scoaf.org.uk Website: www.scoaf.org.uk Twitter: @SCOAF_UK

Service Complaints Ombudsmen for the Armed Forces: Mariette Hughes 020 7877 3444
Email: ea@scoaf.org.uk

Political and Parliamentary Organisations

AUDIT SCOTLAND

Fourth Floor, 102 West Port, Edinburgh EH3 9DN
Tel: 0131-625 1500
Email: info@audit-scotland.gov.uk Website: www.audit-scotland.gov.uk Twitter: @auditscotland

Auditor General for Scotland: Stephen Boyle
Chair: Prof Alan Alexander OBE

BOUNDARY COMMISSION FOR ENGLAND

35 Great Smith Street, London SW1P 3BU
Tel: 020 7276 1102
Email: information@boundarycommissionengland.gov.uk
Website: boundarycommissionforengland.independent.gov.uk Twitter: @BCEReviews

Chairman: Rt Hon Sir Lindsay Hoyle MP
Deputy Chair: Mr Justice Peter Lane
Secretary: Tim Bowden

BOUNDARY COMMISSION FOR NORTHERN IRELAND

The Bungalow, Stormont House, Stormont Estate, Belfast BT4 3SH
Tel: 028 9052 7821
Email: contact@boundarycommission.org.uk Website: www.boundarycommission.org.uk
Twitter: @BCommNI

Chairman: Rt Hon Sir Lindsay Hoyle MP
Deputy Chairman: Hon Madam Justice Denise McBride DBE QC
Secretary: Eamonn McConville 028 9052 7821
Email: eamonn.mcconville@boundarycommission.org.uk

BOUNDARY COMMISSION FOR SCOTLAND

Thistle House, 91 Haymarket Terrace, Edinburgh EH12 5HD
Tel: 0131-244 2001
Email: bcs@scottishboundaries.gov.uk Website: www.bcomm-scotland.independent.gov.uk
Twitter: @BCommScot

Chairman: Rt Hon Sir Lindsay Hoyle MP
Deputy Chairman: Hon Lord Hugh Matthews
Secretary: Isabel Drummond-Murray

BOUNDARY COMMISSION FOR WALES

Hastings House, Fitzalan Court, Cardiff CF24 0BL
Tel: 029 2046 4819/029 2105 5521
Email: bcw@boundaries.wales Website: bcomm-wales.gov.uk Twitter: @BCommWales

Chairman: Rt Hon Sir Lindsay Hoyle MP
Deputy Chairman: Justice Jefford QC
Secretary: Shereen Williams MBE OStJ

COMMONWEALTH PARLIAMENTARY ASSOCIATION UNITED KINGDOM

Westminster Hall, Houses of Parliament, London SW1A 0AA
Tel: 020 7219 5373
Email: cpauk@parliament.uk Website: www.uk-cpa.org Twitter: @CPA_UK

Joint Presidents: Rt Hon Lord Fowler, Rt Hon Sir Lindsay Hoyle MP
Chair of the Executive Committee: Ian Liddell-Grainger MP
Vice-chairs: Rt Hon Lord Foulkes of Cumnock, Rt Hon Maria Miller MP, Ian Murray MP
Treasurer: Julie Elliott MP
Members, Executive Committee: Sir David Amess MP, Harriett Baldwin MP, Bob Blackman MP, Steve Brine MP, Dr Lisa Cameron MP, Sarah Champion MP, Rt Hon Baroness Corston, Lord Davies of Gower, Rt Hon Lord Dholakia OBE DL, Rt Hon Baroness D'Souza CMG, Chris Elmore MP, Rt Hon Lord Haselhurst, Layla Moran MP, Rt Hon David Mundell MP, Andrew Rosindell MP
Chief Executive: Jon Davies
Deputy Chief Executive: Helen Haywood
Head of Multilateral Projects: Ruth Pope
Acting Head of International Partnerships: Victoria Bower

CONFEDERATION OF BRITISH INDUSTRY

CBI, Cannon Place, 78 Cannon Street, London EC4N 6HN
Tel: 020 7379 7400
Email: enquiries@cbi.org.uk Website: www.cbi.org.uk Twitter: @CBItweets

President: Lord Bilimoria CBE DL
Vice-President: John Allan CBE
Director-General: Tony Danker
Head of Campaigns: Peter McManus 07469 155294 Email: peter.mcmanus@cbi.org.uk

ELECTORAL COMMISSION

3 Bunhill Row, London EC1Y 8YZ
Tel: 0333 103 1928
Email: info@electoralcommission.org.uk Website: www.electoralcommission.org.uk
Twitter: @ElectoralCommUK

Chair of Commission Board: To be appointed
Commissioners: Alex Attwood, Dame Susan Bruce DBE, Sarah Chambers, Lord Gilbert of Panteg, Alasdair Morgan, Professor Dame Elan Closs Stephens DBE, Robert Vincent CBE, Joan Walley
Chief Executive: Bob Posner 020 7271 0605 Email: governance@electoralcommission.org.uk
Secretary to the Commission Board: Zena Khan 020 7271 0506
Email: governance@electoralcommission.org.uk

ELECTORAL OFFICE FOR NORTHERN IRELAND

St Anne's House, 15 Church Street, Belfast BT1 1ER
Tel: 028 9044 6680
Email: [firstname.surname]@eoni.org.uk Website: www.eoni.org.uk Twitter: @eoni_official

Chief Electoral Officer: Virginia McVea Email: virginia.mcvea@eoni.org.uk

ELECTORAL REFORM SOCIETY

15 Blue Lion Place, London SE1 4PU
Tel: 020 3967 1884
Email: ers@electoral-reform.org.uk Website: www.electoral-reform.org.uk Twitter: @electoralreform

Chair: Ruth Kelly
Vice-chair (Management): Justina Cruickshank
Deputy Chair (Campaigns): Lisa French
Chief Executive: Darren Hughes Email: darren.hughes@electoral-reform.org.uk
Treasurer: Andrew Copson

ELECTORAL REFORM SOCIETY CYMRU

Baltic House, Mount Stuart Square, Cardiff CF10 5FH
Tel: 029 2049 6613
Email: wales@electoral-reform.org.uk Website: www.electoral-reform.org.uk/ers-cymru
Twitter: @ERScymru
Director: Jess Blair

ELECTORAL REFORM SOCIETY SCOTLAND

12 South Charlotte Street, Edinburgh EH2 4AX
Tel: 0131-624 9853
Email: scotland@electoral-reform.org.uk Website: www.electoral-reform.org.uk/ers-scotland
Twitter: @ERSScotland
Director: Willie Sullivan

HANSARD SOCIETY

Room 1.17, First Floor, Millbank Tower, 21-24 Millbank, London SW1P 4QP
Tel: 020 3925 3979
Email: contact@hansardsociety.org.uk Website: www.hansardsociety.org.uk
Twitter: @HansardSociety

Chairman: Lord Sharkey
Honorary Treasurer: Shirley Cameron
Director and Head of Research: Dr Ruth Fox 020 7710 6070 Email: ruth.fox@hansardsociety.org.uk

INDEPENDENT PARLIAMENTARY STANDARDS AUTHORITY

Second Floor, 85 Strand, London WC2R 0DW
Tel: 020 7811 6400
Email: info@theipsa.org.uk Website: www.theipsa.org.uk Twitter: @ipsaUK

Interim Chair: Richard Lloyd
Chief Executive: Ian Todd Email: board.office@theipsa.org.uk
Board Members: Helen Jones, William Lifford, Sir Robert Owen
Director of MP Support and Improvement: Georgia Wilson Email: board.office@theipsa.org.uk
Director of Regulation and Insight: Lee Bridges Email: board.office@theipsa.org.uk
Director of Strategy and Change: Karen Walker Email: board.office@theipsa.org.uk
Director of Finance and Corporate Services: Alastair Bridges Email: board.office@theipsa.org.uk

INDUSTRY AND PARLIAMENT TRUST

Suite 101, 3 Whitehall Court, London SW1A 2EL
Tel: 020 7839 9400 Fax: 020 7839 9401
Email: enquiries@ipt.org.uk Website: www.ipt.org.uk Twitter: @indparltrust

Presidents: Rt Hon Lord Fowler, Rt Hon Sir Lindsay Hoyle MP
Vice-President: Baroness Prosser OBE
Chairman, Board of Trustees: Dr John Howell OBE MP
Chairman, Executive Committee: Tony Bellis
Chief Executive: Nick Maher

BRITISH GROUP INTER-PARLIAMENTARY UNION

Palace of Westminster, London SW1A 0AA
Tel: 020 7219 3011 Fax: 020 7219 8780
Email: bgipu@parliament.uk Website: www.bgipu.org Twitter: @BGIPU

Honorary Presidents: Rt Hon Lord Fowler, Rt Hon Sir Lindsay Hoyle MP
Chair: Harriett Baldwin MP
Vice-chairs: Rt Hon Baroness D'Souza CMG, Dame Diana Johnson DBE MP, Ian Liddell-Grainger MP
Treasurer: Alex Sobel MP
Director: Rick Nimmo

NATIONAL AUDIT OFFICE

157-197 Buckingham Palace Road, Victoria, London SW1W 9SP
Tel: 020 7798 7000/020 7798 7400 (Press Office) Fax: 020 7828 7070
Email: enquiries@nao.org.uk Website: www.nao.org.uk Twitter: @NAOorguk

Chair: Dame Fiona Reynolds CBE
Comptroller and Auditor General: Gareth Davies Email: servicedesk.c&ag@nao.org.uk
Executive Directors: Adbool Kara, Daniel Lambauer, Elaine Lewis, Kate Mathers, Rebecca Sheeran, Max Tse
Director, Parliamentary Relations: Adrian Jenner 020 7798 7461 Email: adrian.jenner@nao.org.uk

POLICE AND FIRE SERVICE PARLIAMENTARY SCHEME

13 Cowley Street, London SW1P 3LZ
Tel: 020 7222 0480 Fax: 020 7222 7783
Email: lesley.snape1@btinternet.com Website: www.af-ps.info

Chair: Sir Neil Thorne OBE TD DL

COMMITTEE ON STANDARDS IN PUBLIC LIFE

Room GC.07, 1 Horse Guards Road, London SW1A 2HQ
Tel: 020 7271 2685
Email: public@public-standards.gov.uk Website: www.gov.uk/public-standards
Twitter: @PublicStandards

Chair: Lord Evans of Weardale KCB DL
Members: Rt Hon Dame Margaret Beckett DBE MP, Dr Jane Martin CBE, Dame Shirley Pearce DBE, Monisha Shah, Rt Hon Lord Stunell OBE, Rt Hon Jeremy Wright QC MP
Secretary: Lesley Bainsfair

TRADES UNION CONGRESS

Congress House, Great Russell Street, London WC1B 3LS
Tel: 020 7636 4030
Email: info@tuc.org.uk Website: www.tuc.org.uk Twitter: @tucnews

President: Gail Cartmail
General Secretary: Frances O'Grady
Deputy General Secretary: Paul Nowak
Head of Campaigns, Communications and Digital: Antonia Bance Email: abance@tuc.org.uk
Head of Equality and Strategy: Kudsia Batool Email: kbatool@tuc.org.uk
Head of Management Services and Administration: Matilda Quiney Email: mquiney@tuc.org.uk
Head of Organisation, Services and Skills and Director of unionlearn: Kevin Rowan Email: krowan@tuc.org.uk
Head of Rights, International, Social and Economic: Kate Bell Email: kbell@tuc.org.uk

WALES AUDIT OFFICE

24 Cathedral Road, Cardiff CF11 9LJ
Tel: 029 2032 0500
Email: info@audit.wales Website: www.audit.wales Twitter: @WalesAudit

Auditor-General for Wales: Adrian Crompton

THE WHITEHALL & INDUSTRY GROUP

80 Petty France, London SW1H 9EX
Tel: 020 7222 1166 Fax: 020 7222 1167
Email: info@wig.co.uk Website: www.wig.co.uk Twitter: @wiguk

Chief Executive: Simon Ancona CBE

Diplomatic Representation

British Embassies and High Commissions

Afghanistan

British Embassy, 15th Street, Roundabout Wazir Akbar Khan, PO Box 334, Kabul
Tel: +93 700 102 000 Fax: +93 700 102 250
Email: britishembassy.kabul@fcdo.gov.uk
Website: www.gov.uk/government/world/organisations/british-embassy-kabul
Twitter: @UKinAfghanistan

Ambassador: HE Alison Blake CMG

Albania

British Embassy, Rruga Skenderbeg 12, Tirana
Tel: +355 4 223 4973 Fax: +355 4 224 7697
Email: british.embassytirana@fcdo.gov.uk
Website: www.gov.uk/government/world/organisations/british-embassy-tirana
Twitter: @UKinAlbania

Ambassador (until September 2021): HE Duncan Norman MBE

Ambassador (from September 2021): HE Alastair King-Smith

Algeria

British Embassy, 3 Chemin Capitaine Hocine Slimane (ex Chemin des Glycines), Algiers
Tel: +213 770 085 000 Fax: +213 216 81058
Email: britishembassy.algiers@fcdo.gov.uk
Website: www.gov.uk/government/world/organisations/british-embassy-algiers Twitter: @ukinalgeria

Ambassador: HE Sharon Wardle

Andorra – see Spain

Angola

Non-resident: São Tomé and Príncipe

British Embassy, Rua 17 de Setembro, No 4, Caixa Postal 1244, Ingombotas, Luanda 1244
Tel: +244 222 334 583
Email: britishembassy.luandageral@fcdo.gov.uk
Website: www.gov.uk/government/world/organisations/british-embassy-luanda Twitter: @ukinangola

Ambassador: HE Jessica Hand

Antigua and Barbuda – see Barbados

British High Commission being set up
Website: www.gov.uk/world/organisations/british-high-commission-st-johns

Argentina

British Embassy, Dr Luis Agote 2412, 1425 Buenos Aires
Tel: +54 11 4808 2200 Fax: +54 11 4808 2274
Email: askinformation.baires@fcdo.gov.uk
Website: www.gov.uk/government/world/organisations/british-embassy-buenos-aires
Twitter: @UKinArgentina

Ambassador (until September 2021): HE Mark Kent CMG

Ambassador (from September 2021): HE Kirsty Hayes

Armenia
British Embassy, Eigth Floor, Kamar Business Centre, 0010 Yerevan
Tel: +374 10 264 301
Email: enquiries.yerevan@fcdo.gov.uk
Website: www.gov.uk/government/world/organisations/british-embassy-armenia
Twitter: @UKinArmenia
Ambassador: HE John Gallagher

Australia
British High Commission, Commonwealth Avenue, Yarralumla, Canberra ACT 2600
Tel: +61 2 6270 6666 Fax: +61 2 6273 3236
Email: australia.enquiries@fcdo.gov.uk
Website: www.gov.uk/government/world/organisations/british-high-commission-canberra
Twitter: @ukinaustralia
High Commissioner: HE Victoria Treadell CMG MVO

Austria
British Embassy, Jaurèsgasse 12, 1030 Vienna
Tel: +43 1 716130 Fax: +43 1 71613 2900
Email: press@britishembassy.at
Website: www.gov.uk/government/world/organisations/british-embassy-vienna
Twitter: @UKinAustria
Ambassador (until September 2021): HE Leigh Turner CMG
Ambassador (from September 2021): HE Lindsay Skoll CMG

Azerbaijan
British Embassy, 45 Khagani Street, Baku AZ1010
Tel: +994 12 4377878 Fax: +994 12 4977434
Email: generalenquiries.baku@fcdo.gov.uk
Website: www.gov.uk/government/world/organisations/british-embassy-baku
Twitter: @ukinazerbaijan
Ambassador: HE James Sharp

Bahamas
British High Commission, Balmoral Corporate Centre, Third floor, Sandford Drive, Nassau
Website: www.gov.uk/world/organisations/british-high-commission-nassau
High Commissioner: HE Sarah Dickson

Bahrain
British Embassy, 21 Government Avenue, PO Box 114, Manama 306
Tel: +973 17574100 Fax: +973 17574161
Website: www.gov.uk/government/world/organisations/british-embassy-manama
Twitter: @ukinbahrain
Ambassador: HE Roderick Drummond

Bangladesh
British High Commission, United Nations Road, Baridhara, PO Box 6079, Dhaka 1212
Tel: +880 2 55668700
Email: dhaka.press@fcdo.gov.uk
Website: www.gov.uk/government/world/organisations/british-high-commission-dhaka
Twitter: @ukinbangladesh
High Commissioner: HE Robert Chatterton Dickson

Barbados

Non-resident: Antigua and Barbuda, Dominica, St Kitts and Nevis, St Lucia, St Vincent and the Grenadines

British High Commission, Lower Collymore Rock, PO Box 676, Bridgetown
Tel: +1 246 430 7800
Website: www.gov.uk/government/world/organisations/british-high-commission-barbados

High Commissioner: HE Janet Douglas CMG

Belarus

British Embassy, 37 Karl Marx Street, Minsk 220030
Tel: +375 17 229 8200 Fax: +375 17 229 8206
Email: britishembassy.minsk@fcdo.gov.uk
Website: www.gov.uk/government/world/organisations/british-embassy-minsk
Twitter: @UKinBelarus

Ambassador: HE Jacqueline Perkins

Belgium

British Embassy, Avenue d'Auderghem 10, 1040 Brussels
Tel: +32 2 287 62 11 Fax: +32 2 287 62 50
Email: public.brussels@fcdo.gov.uk
Website: www.gov.uk/government/world/organisations/british-embassy-brussels
Twitter: @ukinbelgium

Ambassador: HE Martin Shearman CVO

Belize

British High Commission, North Ring Road/Melhado Parade, PO Box 91, Belmopan
Tel: +501 822 2146
Email: bhcbelmopan@fcdo.gov.uk
Website: www.gov.uk/government/world/organisations/british-high-commission-belmopan

High Commissioner: HE Claire Evans OBE

Benin – see Ghana

Bolivia

British Embassy, Avenida Arce 2732, La Paz
Tel: +591 2 243 3424 Fax: +591 2 243 1073
Email: belapaz@fcdo.gov.uk
Website: www.gov.uk/government/world/organisations/british-embassy-bolivia
Twitter: @ukinbolivia

Ambassador: HE Jeff Glekin

Bosnia and Herzegovina

British Embassy, 39a Hamdije Cemerlica Street, 71000 Sarajevo
Tel: +387 33 282 200 Fax: +387 33 282 203
Email: britemb@bih.net.ba
Website: www.gov.uk/government/world/organisations/british-embassy-sarajevo

Ambassador: HE Matthew Field

Botswana

British High Commission, Plot 1079-1084 Main Mall, off Queens Road, Gaborone
Tel: +267 395 2841 Fax: +267 395 6105
Email: gaborone.enquiries@fcdo.gov.uk
Website: www.gov.uk/government/world/organisations/british-high-commission-gaborone
Twitter: @UKinBotswana

High Commissioner: HE Sian Price

Brazil
British Embassy, Quadra 801 – Conjunto K – Lote 8, Av. das Nações – Asa Sul, CEP 70408-900, Brasilia
Tel: +55 61 3329 2300 Fax: +55 61 3329 2369
Email: press.brasilia@fcdo.gov.uk
Website: www.gov.uk/government/world/organisations/british-embassy-brazil Twitter: @ukinbrazil
Ambassador: HE Peter Wilson CMG

Brunei
British High Commission, 2.01, Second Floor, Block D, Kompleks Bangunan Yayasan Sultan Haji Hassanal Bokiah, Jalan Pretty, Bandar Seri Begawan PO Box 2197
Tel: +673 2 222231 Fax: +673 2 234315
Email: ukinbrunei@fcdo.gov.uk
Website: www.gov.uk/government/world/organisations/british-high-commission-bandar-seri-begawan Twitter: @ukinbrunei
High Commissioner: HE John Virgoe

Bulgaria
British Embassy, 9 Moskovska Street, 1000 Sofia
Tel: +359 2 933 9222 Fax: +359 2 933 9250
Email: britishembassysofia@fcdo.gov.uk
Website: www.gov.uk/government/world/organisations/british-embassy-sofia Twitter: @ukinbulgaria
Ambassador: HE Dr Rob Dixon

Burkina Faso – see Ghana

Burma – see Myanmar

Burundi – see Rwanda

Cabo Verde – see Senegal

Cambodia
British Embassy, 27-29 Street 75, Sangkat Srah Chak, Khan Daun Penh, Phnom Penh 12201
Tel: +855 61 300 011 Fax: +855 23 427 125
Email: ukincambodia@fcdo.gov.uk
Website: www.gov.uk/government/world/organisations/british-embassy-phnom-penh
Twitter: @ukincambodia
Ambassador: HE Tina Redshaw

Cameroon
Non-resident: Chad, Equatorial Guinea, Gabon
British High Commission, Avenue Winston Churchill, BP 547, Yaoundé
Tel: +237 222 220 796 Fax: +237 222 220 148
Email: bhc.yaounde@fcdo.gov.uk
Website: www.gov.uk/government/world/organisations/british-high-commission-yaounde
Twitter: @ukincameroon
High Commissioner: HE Rowan Laxton

Canada
British High Commission, 80 Elgin Street, Ottawa K1P 5K7
Tel: +1 613 237 1530
Website: www.gov.uk/government/world/organisations/british-high-commission-ottawa
Twitter: @ukincanada
High Commissioner (until August 2021): HE Susan le Jeune d'Allegeershecque CMG
High Commissioner (from August 2021): HE Susannah Goshko

Chad – see Cameroon

Chile

British Embassy, Avda El Bosque Norte 0125, Las Condes, Santiago
Tel: +56 2 370 4100 Fax: +56 2 370 4160
Email: embsan@britemb.cl
Website: www.gov.uk/government/world/organisations/british-embassy-chile Twitter: @ukinchile
Ambassador: HE Louise De Sousa

China

British Embassy, 11 Guang Hua Lu, Jian Guo Men Wai, 100 600 Beijing
Tel: +86 10 5192 4000 Fax: +86 10 5192 4239
Website: www.gov.uk/government/world/organisations/british-embassy-beijing Twitter: @ukinchina
Ambassador: HE Dame Caroline Wilson DCMG

Colombia

British Embassy, Carrera 9 No 76-49, Piso 8, Edificio ING Barings, Bogotá
Tel: +57 1 326 8300
Email: embajadabritanica.bogota@fcdo.gov.uk
Website: www.gov.uk/government/world/organisations/british-embassy-colombia
Twitter: @ukincolombia
Ambassador: HE Colin Martin-Reynolds CMG

Comoros – see Madagascar

Democratic Republic of Congo

Non-resident: Republic of Congo
British Embassy, 83 Avenue Roi Baudouin, Gombe, Kinshasa
Tel: +243 81 556 6200 Fax: +243 81 346 4291
Email: ambassade.britannique@fcdo.gov.uk
Website: www.gov.uk/government/world/organisations/british-embassy-kinshasa
Twitter: @UKinDRC
Ambassador: HE Emily Maltman

Republic of Congo – see Democratic Republic of Congo

Costa Rica

Non-resident: Nicaragua
British Embassy, Edificio Centro Colón, Paseo Colón and Streets 38 and 40, San José
Tel: +506 2258 2025 Fax: +506 2233 9938
Email: ukin.costarica@fcdo.gov.uk
Website: www.gov.uk/government/world/organisations/british-embassy-in-costa-rica
Twitter: @UKinCostaRica
Ambassador: HE Ben Lyster-Binns

Côte d'Ivoire

British Embassy, Cocody Quartier Ambassades, Impasse du Belier, Rue A58, 01 BP, 2581 Abidjan 01
Tel: +225 22 44 26 69 Fax: +225 22 48 95 48
Email: british.embassy.abidjan@fcdo.gov.uk
Website: www.gov.uk/government/world/organisations/british-embassy-abidjan
Ambassador: HE Josephine Gauld

Croatia
British Embassy, Ivana Lučića 4, 10000 Zagreb
Tel: +385 1 6009 100 Fax: +385 1 6009 111
Email: british.embassyzagreb@fcdo.gov.uk
Website: www.gov.uk/government/world/organisations/british-embassy-zagreb Twitter: @ukincroatia
Ambassador (until July 2021): HE Andrew Dalgleish
Ambassador (from July 2021): HE Simon Thomas OBE

Cuba
British Embassy, Calle 34 no. 702e/7ma, Miramar, Playa, La Habana 11300
Tel: +537 214 2200
Email: ukincuba@fcdo.gov.uk
Website: www.gov.uk/government/world/organisations/british-embassy-havana Twitter: @UKinCuba
Ambassador: HE Dr Antony Stokes LVO

Cyprus
British High Commission, Alexander Pallis Street, PO Box 21978, Nicosia 1587
Tel: +357 2 861100 Fax: +357 2 861125
Website: www.gov.uk/government/world/organisations/british-high-commission-nicosia
Twitter: @ukincyprus
High Commissioner: HE Stephen Lillie CMG

Czech Republic
British Embassy, Thunovská 14, 118 00 Prague 1
Tel: +420 257 402 111 Fax: +420 257 402 296
Email: ukinczechrepublic@fcdo.gov.uk
Website: www.gov.uk/government/world/organisations/british-embassy-prague Twitter: @UKinCR
Ambassador: HE Nick Archer MVO

Denmark
British Embassy, Kastelsvej 36-40, 2100 Copenhagen Ø
Tel: +45 35 44 52 00
Email: enquiry.copenhagen@fcdo.gov.uk
Website: www.gov.uk/government/world/organisations/british-embassy-copenhagen
Twitter: @UKinDenmark
Ambassador: HE Emma Hopkins OBE

Djibouti
British Embassy being set up
Website: www.gov.uk/world/djibouti
Ambassador: HE Jo McPhail

Dominica – see Barbados

Dominican Republic
British Embassy, Winston Churchill 1099 Torre Citigroup, Acropolis, Floor 18, Santo Domingo
Tel: +1 809 472 7111
Email: uk.indominicanrepublic@fcdo.gov.uk
Website: www.gov.uk/government/world/organisations/british-embassy-santo-domingo
Twitter: @ukindomrep
Ambassador: HE Mockbul Ali OBE

Ecuador
British Embassy, 14th Floor, Citiplaza Building, Naciones Unidas Avenue and República de El Salvador, PO Box 17-17-830, Quito
Tel: +593 2 3972 200
Email: britishembassy.quito@fcdo.gov.uk
Website: www.gov.uk/government/world/organisations/british-embassy-in-ecuador
Twitter: @ukinecuador
Ambassador: HE Christopher Campbell

Egypt
British Embassy, 7 Ahmed Ragheb Street, Garden City, Cairo
Tel: +20 2 2791 6000 Fax: +20 2 2791 6131
Email: cairo.contact@fcdo.gov.uk
Website: www.gov.uk/government/world/organisations/british-embassy-cairo Twitter: @ukinegypt
Ambassador: HE Sir Geoffrey Adams KCMG

El Salvador
British Embassy, Torre Futura, 14th Floor, Colonia Escalón, San Salvador
Tel: +503 2511 5757
Email: britishembassy.elsalvador@fcdo.gov.uk
Website: www.gov.uk/government/world/organisations/british-embassy-san-salvador
Twitter: @ukinelsalvador
Ambassador: HE David Lelliott OBE

Equatorial Guinea – see Cameroon

Eritrea
British Embassy, 66-68 Mariam Ghimbi Street, Zip Code 174, PO Box 5584, Asmara
Tel: 020 7008 1500 Fax: +291 112 01 04
Website: www.gov.uk/government/world/organisations/british-embassy-asmara
Ambassador: HE Alisdair Walker

Estonia
British Embassy, Wismari 6, Tallinn 15098
Tel: +372 667 4700 Fax: +372 667 4755
Email: infotallinn@fcdo.gov.uk
Website: www.gov.uk/government/world/organisations/british-embassy-tallin Twitter: @ukinestonia
Ambassador (until May 2021): HE Theresa Bubbear
Ambassador (from May 2021): HE Ross Allen

Eswatini
British High Commission being set up
Website: www.gov.uk/world/organisations/british-high-commission-mbabane
High Commissioner: HE John Lindfield MBE

Ethiopia
British Embassy, Comoros Street, Addis Ababa, 858
Tel: +251 11 6170100 Fax: +251 11 6175558
Email: britishembassy.addisababa@fcdo.gov.uk
Website: www.gov.uk/government/world/organisations/british-embassy-addis-ababa
Twitter: @UKinEthiopia
Ambassador: HE Dr Alastair McPhail CMG OBE

Fiji

Non-resident: Kiribati, Marshall Islands, Micronesia and Tuvalu

British High Commission, 47 Gladstone Road, Suva
Tel: +679 322 9100 Fax: +679 322 9132
Email: publicdiplomacysuva@fcdo.gov.uk
Website: www.gov.uk/government/world/organisations/british-high-commission-suva
Twitter: @ukinfiji

High Commissioner: HE George Edgar OBE

Finland

British Embassy, Itäinen Puistotie 17, 00140 Helsinki
Tel: +358 9 2286 5100 Fax: +358 9 2286 5284
Email: info.helsinki@fcdo.gov.uk
Website: www.gov.uk/government/world/organisations/british-embassy-helsinki
Twitter: @ukinfinland

Ambassador (until July 2021): HE Tom Dodd

Ambassador (from July 2021): HE Theresa Bubbear

France

Non-resident: Monaco

British Embassy, 35 rue du Faubourg St Honoré, 75363 Paris Cedex 08
Tel: +33 1 44 51 31 00
Email: france.enquiries@fcdo.gov.uk
Website: www.gov.uk/government/world/organisations/british-embassy-paris Twitter: @ukinfrance

Ambassador: HE Rt Hon Lord Llewellyn of Steep OBE

Gabon – see Cameroon

Gambia

British High Commission, 48 Atlantic Road, Fajara, PO Box 507, Banjul
Tel: +220 4495133
Email: ukinthegambia@fcdo.gov.uk
Website: www.gov.uk/government/world/organisations/british-high-commission-banjul
Twitter: @UKinGambia

High Commissioner: HE David Belgrove OBE

Georgia

British Embassy, 51 Krtsanisi Street, Tbilisi 0114
Tel: +995 32 2274747 Fax: +995 32 2274792
Email: british.embassy.tbilisi@fcdo.gov.uk
Website: www.gov.uk/government/world/organisations/british-embassy-tbilisi
Twitter: @UKinGeorgia

Ambassador: HE Mark Clayton

Germany

British Embassy, Wilhelmstrasse 70, 10117 Berlin
Tel: +49 30 204570
Email: ukingermany@fcdo.gov.uk
Website: www.gov.uk/government/world/organisations/british-embassy-berlin
Twitter: @ukingermany

Ambassador: HE Jill Gallard CMG

Ghana

Non-resident: Benin, Burkina Faso, Togo

British High Commission, Julius Nyerere Link, off Gamel Abdul Nasser Avenue, PO Box 296, Accra
Tel: +233 302 213 200 Fax: +233 302 213 274
Email: high.commission.accra@fcdo.gov.uk
Website: www.gov.uk/government/world/organisations/british-high-commission-accra
Twitter: @ukinghana

High Commissioner: HE Iain Walker

Greece

British Embassy, 1 Ploutarchou Street, 106 75 Athens
Tel: +30 210 7272 600
Email: information.athens@fcdo.gov.uk
Website: www.gov.uk/government/world/organisations/british-embassy-athens Twitter: @ukingreece

Ambassador (until summer 2021): HE Kate Smith CMG

Ambassador (from summer 2021): HE Matthew Lodge

Grenada – see Barbados

British High Commission being set up
Website: www.gov.uk/world/organisations/british-high-commission-st-georges

Guatemala

Non-resident: Honduras

British Embassy, Edificio Torre Internacional, Nivel 11, 16 Calle 0-55, Zona 10, Guatemala City
Tel: +502 2380 7300
Email: embajadabritanicagt@gmail.com
Website: www.gov.uk/government/world/organisations/british-embassy-guatemala
Twitter: @ukinguatemala

Ambassador: HE Nick Whittingham

Guinea

British Embassy, Villa 1, Residence 2000, Corniche Sud, Conakry
Tel: +224 626 26 4040
Email: britishembassy.conakry@fcdo.gov.uk
Website: www.gov.uk/government/world/organisations/british-embassy-conakry
Twitter: @UKinGuinea

Ambassador: HE David McIlroy

Guinea-Bissau – see Senegal

Guyana

Non-resident: Suriname

British High Commission, 44 Main Street, Georgetown
Tel: +592 226 5881 Fax: +592 225 3555
Website: www.gov.uk/government/world/organisations/british-high-commission-georgetown

High Commissioner: To be appointed

Haiti

British Embassy in Port au Prince is currently closed.

Ambassador resident in Dominican Republic.

British Embassy, Entre 73 et 75 Delmas, Port-au-Prince
Email: ukinhaiti@fcdo.gov.uk
Website: www.gov.uk/government/world/organisations/british-embassy-port-au-prince
Twitter: @UKInHaiti

Non-resident Ambassador: HE Mockbul Ali OBE

Holy See
British Embassy, Via XX Settembre 80a, 00187 Rome
Tel: +39 06 4220 4000 Fax: +39 06 4220 4205
Email: holysee@fcdo.gov.uk
Website: www.gov.uk/government/world/organisations/british-embassy-holy-see
Twitter: @ukinholysee

Ambassador (until summer 2021): HE Sally Axworthy MBE

Ambassador (from summer 2021): HE Chris Trott

Honduras – see Guatemala

Hungary
British Embassy, Füge utca 5-7, Budapest 1022
Tel: +36 1 266 2888 Fax: +36 1 266 0907
Website: www.gov.uk/government/world/organisations/british-embassy-budapest
Twitter: @ukinhungary

Ambassador: HE Paul Fox

Iceland
British Embassy, Laufásvegur 31, 101 Reykjavík
Tel: +354 550 5100 Fax: +354 550 5105
Email: info@britishembassy.is
Website: www.gov.uk/government/world/organisations/british-embassy-reykjavik
Twitter: @UKinIceland

Ambassador (until August 2021): HE Michael Nevin

Ambassador (from August 2021): HE Dr Bryony Mathew

India
British High Commission, Shantipath, Chanakyapuri, New Delhi 110021
Tel: +91 11 2419 2100 Fax: +91 11 2419 2400
Email: web.newdelhi@fcdo.gov.uk
Website: www.gov.uk/government/world/organisations/british-high-commission-new-delhi
Twitter: @ukinindia

High Commissioner: HE Alex Ellis

Indonesia
Non-resident: Timor-Leste

British Embassy, Jl Patra Kuningan Raya Blok L5-6, Jakarta 12950
Tel: +62 21 2356 5200 Fax: +62 21 2356 5351
Email: jakarta.mcs@fcdo.gov.uk
Website: www.gov.uk/government/world/organisations/british-embassy-jakarta
Twitter: @ukinindonesia

Ambassador: HE Owen Jenkins

Iran
British Embassy, 172 Ferdowsi Avenue, Tehran 11316-99813
Tel: +98 21 6405 2000
Website: www.gov.uk/government/world/organisations/uk-for-iranians Twitter: @UKinIran

Ambassador: HE Robert Macaire CMG

Iraq
British Embassy, International Zone, Baghdad
Tel: +964 790 192 6280
Website: www.gov.uk/government/world/organisations/british-embassy-baghdad Twitter: @ukiniraq

Ambassador: HE Stephen Hickey

Ireland
British Embassy, 29 Merrion Road, Ballsbridge, Dublin 4
Tel: +353 1 205 3700
Website: www.gov.uk/government/world/organisations/british-embassy-dublin
Twitter: @britembdublin

Ambassador: HE Paul Johnston

Israel
British Embassy, 192 Hayarkon Street, 6340502 Tel Aviv
Tel: +972 3 725 1222
Email: webmaster.telaviv@fcdo.gov.uk
Website: www.gov.uk/government/world/organisations/british-embassy-tel-aviv Twitter: @ukinisrael

Ambassador: HE Neil Wigan OBE

Italy
Non-resident: San Marino

British Embassy, Via XX Settembre 80/a, 00187 Rome
Tel: +39 06 4220 0001 Fax: +39 06 4220 2334
Website: www.gov.uk/government/world/organisations/british-embassy-rome Twitter: @ukinitaly

Ambassador: HE Jill Morris CMG

Ivory Coast – see Côte d'Ivoire

Jamaica
British High Commission, PO Box 575, 28 Trafalgar Road, Kingston 10
Tel: +1 876 936 0700
Email: ppa.kingston@fcdo.gov.uk
Website: www.gov.uk/government/world/organisations/british-high-commission-jamaica

High Commissioner: HE Asif Ahmad CMG

Japan
British Embassy, No 1 Ichiban-cho, Chiyoda-ku, Tokyo 102-8381
Tel: +81 3 5211 1100 Fax: +81 3 5275 3164
Email: public-enquiries.tokyo@fcdo.gov.uk
Website: www.gov.uk/government/world/organisations/british-embassy-tokyo Twitter: @ukinjapan

Ambassador: HE Julia Longbottom CMG

Jordan
British Embassy, (PO Box 87) Abdoun, Amman 11118
Tel: +962 6 590 9200
Email: amman.enquiries@fcdo.gov.uk
Website: www.gov.uk/government/world/organisations/british-embassy-amman
Twitter: @ukinjordan

Ambassador: HE Bridget Brind OBE

Kazakhstan
British Embassy, 62 Kosmonavtov Street, Nur-Sultan 010000
Tel: +7 7172 556200 Fax: +7 7272 556211
Email: ukinkz@fcdo.gov.uk
Website: www.gov.uk/government/world/organisations/british-embassy-astana Twitter: @ukinkz

Ambassador (until summer 2021): HE Michael Gifford
Ambassador (from summer 2021): HE Kathy Leach

Kenya
British High Commission, Upper Hill Road, PO Box 30465-00100, Nairobi
Tel: +254 20 287 3000
Email: nairobi.enquiries@fcdo.gov.uk
Website: www.gov.uk/government/world/organisations/british-high-commission-nairobi
Twitter: @ukinkenya
High Commissioner: HE Jane Marriott OBE

Kiribati – see Fiji

Democratic People's Republic of Korea (North)
British Embassy, Munsu-dong Diplomatic Compound, Pyongyang
Email: pyongyang.enquiries@fcdo.gov.uk
Website: www.gov.uk/government/world/organisations/british-embassy-pyonyang
Ambassador: HE Colin Crooks LVO

Republic of Korea (South)
British Embassy, Sejong-daero 19-gil 24, Seoul Jung-gu 04519
Tel: +82 2 3210 5500 Fax: +82 2 725 1738
Email: enquiry.seoul@fcdo.gov.uk
Website: www.gov.uk/government/world/organisations/british-embassy-seoul Twitter: @ukinkorea
Ambassador: HE Simon Smith CMG

Kosovo
British Embassy, Lidhja e Pejes 177, Pristina 10000
Tel: +383 38 254 700 Fax: +383 38 606 662
Email: britishembassy.pristina@fcdo.gov.uk
Website: www.gov.uk/government/world/organisations/british-embassy-pristina
Twitter: @UKinKosovo
Ambassador: HE Nicholas Abbott

Kuwait
British Embassy, Arabian Gulf Street, Dasman, Kuwait City
Tel: +965 2259 4320 Fax: +965 2259 4339
Website: www.gov.uk/government/world/organisations/british-embassy-kuwait
Twitter: @ukinkuwait
Ambassador (until April 2021): HE Michael Davenport MBE
Ambassador (from April 2021): HE Belinda Lewis

Kyrgyzstan
British Embassy, 21 Erkindik Boulevard, Office 404, Bishkek 720040
Tel: +996 312 303637
Email: ukin.kyrgyzrepublic@fcdo.gov.uk
Website: www.gov.uk/government/world/organisations/british-embassy-bishkek
Twitter: @ukinkyrgyzstan
Ambassador: HE Charles Garrett OBE

Laos
British Embassy, Rue Yokkabat, Phonexay, Saysettha District, Vientaine
Tel: +856 30 770 0000
Email: britishembassy.vientiane@fcdo.gov.uk
Website: www.gov.uk/government/world/organisations/british-embassy-vientiane Twitter: @ukinlaos
Ambassador: HE John Pearson

Latvia

British Embassy, 5 J Alunana Street, Riga LV-1010
Tel: +371 6774 4700 Fax: +371 6777 4707
Email: britishembassy.riga@fcdo.gov.uk
Website: www.gov.uk/government/world/organisations/british-embassy-riga Twitter: @ukinlatvia
Ambassador (until summer 2021): HE Keith Shannon
Ambassador (from summer 2021): HE Paul Brummell CMG

Lebanon

British Embassy, Serail Hill, Embassy Complex, Beirut Central District, PO Box 11-471 Beirut
Tel: +961 1 960800 Fax: +961 1 960855
Website: www.gov.uk/government/world/organisations/british-embassy-beirut
Twitter: @ukinlebanon
Ambassador: HE Chris Rampling MBE

Lesotho

British High Commission being set up
Website: www.gov.uk/world/organisations/british-high-commission-maseru
High Commissioner: HE Anne Macro

Liberia

Leone Compound, 12th Street Beach-side, Sinkor, Monrovia
Tel: +231 77530320
Email: monrovia.generalenquiries@fcdo.gov.uk
Website: www.gov.uk/government/world/organisations/british-embassy-monrovia
Ambassador: HE Neil Bradley

Libya

(Operations suspended since 4 August 2014)
c/o British Embassy in Tunisia, Rue du Lac Windermere, Les Berges du Lac, Tunis 1053
Tel: +216 71 108 700
Website: www.gov.uk/government/world/organisations/british-embassy-tripoli Twitter: @ukinlibya
Ambassador: HE Nicholas Hopton

Liechtenstein – see Switzerland

Lithuania

British Embassy, Antakalnio str. 2, Vilnius LT-10308
Tel: +370 5 246 2900 Fax: +370 5 246 2901
Email: be-vilnius@britain.lt
Website: www.gov.uk/government/world/organisations/british-embassy-vilnius
Twitter: @ukinlithuania
Ambassador: HE Brian Olley

Luxembourg

British Embassy, Boulevard Joseph II 5, 1840 Luxembourg
Tel: +352 22 98 64 Fax: +352 22 98 67
Email: enquirieslux@fcdo.gov.uk
Website: www.gov.uk/government/world/organisations/british-embassy-in-luxembourg
Ambassador (until April 2021): HE John Marshall
Ambassador (from April 2021): HE Fleur Thomas

Madagascar

Non-resident: Comoros

British Embassy, Ninth Floor Tour Zital, Ravoninahitriniarivo Street, Ankorondrano, Antananarivo 101
Tel: +261 2022 33053
Email: british.embassyantananarivo@fcdo.gov.uk
Website: www.gov.uk/government/world/organisations/british-embassy-antananarivo
Twitter: @UKinMadagascar

Ambassador: HE David Ashley

Malawi

British High Commission, PO Box 30042, Lilongwe 3
Tel: +265 177 2122
Email: bhclilongwe@fcdo.gov.uk
Website: www.gov.uk/government/world/organisations/british-high-commission-lilongwe
Twitter: @UKinMalawi

High Commissioner: HE David Beer

Malaysia

British High Commission, Level 27 Menara Binjai, 2 Jalan Binjai, 50450 Kuala Lumpur
Tel: +60 3 2170 2200 Fax: +60 3 2170 2370
Website: www.gov.uk/government/world/organisations/british-high-commission-kuala-lumpur
Twitter: @ukinmalaysia

High Commissioner: HE Charles Hay MVO

Maldives

British High Commission being set up
Tel: +94 11 5390639
Email: bhc.malegeneral@fcdo.gov.uk
Website: www.gov.uk/world/organisations/british-embassy-maldives

High Commissioner: HE Caron Röhsler

Mali

British Embassy, Cité du Niger II, Bamako
Tel: +223 44 97 69 13
Email: bebamako@fcdo.gov.uk
Website: www.gov.uk/government/world/organisations/british-embassy-bamako

Ambassador: HE Barry Lowen

Malta

British High Commission, Whitehall Mansions, Ta'Xbiex Seafront, Ta'Xbiex XBX 1026
Tel: +356 2323 0000 Fax: +356 2323 2216
Website: www.gov.uk/government/world/organisations/british-high-commission-malta
Twitter: @UKinMalta

High Commissioner: HE Katherine Ward LVO OBE

Marshall Islands – see Fiji

Mauritania

British Embassy, Rue 42-163, B.P. 213, Tevragh Zeina, Nouakchott
Tel: +222 45256986
Website: www.gov.uk/world/organisations/british-embassy-nouakchott Twitter: @UkinMauritania

Ambassador: HE Simon Boyden

Mauritius
British High Commission, Seventh Floor, Les Cascades Building, Edith Cavell Street, Port Louis
Tel: +230 202 9400 Fax: +230 202 9408
Website: www.gov.uk/government/world/organisations/british-high-commission-port-louis
High Commissioner: HE Keith Allan

Mexico
British Embassy, Río Lerma 71, Col Cuauhtémoc, 06500 Mexico City
Tel: +52 55 1670 3200
Email: ukinmexico@fcdo.gov.uk
Website: www.gov.uk/government/world/organisations/british-embassy-mexico-city
Twitter: @ukinmexico
Ambassador (until August 2021): HE Corin Robertson
Ambassador (from August 2021): HE Jon Benjamin

Micronesia – see Fiji

Moldova
British Embassy, 18 Nicolae Iorga Str., Chisinau MD-2012
Tel: +373 22 22 59 02 Fax: +373 22 25 18 59
Email: enquiries.chisinau@fcdo.gov.uk
Website: www.gov.uk/government/world/organisations/british-embassy-chisinau
Twitter: @ukinmoldova
Ambassador: HE Steven Fisher

Monaco – see France

Mongolia
British Embassy, Unit 1-3A, Level 19, Shangri-La Offices, Olympic Street 19A, Sukhbaatar District-1, Ulaanbaatar ZIP 14241
Tel: +976 11 458133 Fax: +976 11 458036
Email: enquiries.mongolia@fcdo.gov.uk
Website: www.gov.uk/government/world/organisations/british-embassy-ulaanbaatar
Ambassador: HE Philip Malone LVO

Montenegro
British Embassy, Ulcinjska 8, Gorica C, 81000 Podgorica
Tel: +382 20 420 100 Fax: +382 20 420 140
Email: podgorica@fcdo.gov.uk
Website: www.gov.uk/government/world/organisations/british-embassy-podgorica
Twitter: @ukinmontenegro
Ambassador: HE Karen Maddocks

Morocco
British Embassy, 28 Avenue S.A.R. Sidi Mohammed, Souissi, 10105 (BP 45) Rabat
Tel: +212 537 63 33 33 Fax: +212 537 75 87 09
Email: ukinmorocco.enquiries@fcdo.gov.uk
Website: www.gov.uk/government/world/organisations/british-embassy-rabat
Twitter: @UKinMorocco
Ambassador: HE Simon Martin CMG

Mozambique
British High Commission, Avenida Vladimir Lenine 310, PO Box 55, Maputo
Tel: +258 21 35 60 00 Fax: +258 21 35 60 60
Website: www.gov.uk/government/world/organisations/british-high-commission-maputo
Twitter: @UKinMozambique
High Commissioner: HE NneNne Iwuji-Eme

Myanmar (Burma)
British Embassy, 80 Strand Road, PO Box No 638, Yangon
Tel: +95 1 370865 Fax: +95 1 370866
Website: www.gov.uk/government/world/organisations/british-embassy-rangoon
Twitter: @ukinburma
Ambassador: HE Dan Chugg

Namibia
British High Commission, 116 Robert Mugabe Avenue, PO Box 22202, Windhoek, Khomas
Tel: +264 61 274800 Fax: +264 61 228895
Email: general.windhoek@fcdo.gov.uk
Website: www.gov.uk/government/world/organisations/british-high-commission-windhoek
High Commissioner: HE Charles Moore

Nauru – see Solomon Islands

Nepal
British Embassy, PO Box 106, Lainchaur, Kathmandu
Tel: +977 1 4237100 Fax: +977 1 4411789
Email: bekathmandu@fcdo.gov.uk
Website: www.gov.uk/government/world/organisations/british-embassy-kathmandu
Twitter: @ukinnepal
Ambassador: HE Nicola Pollitt

Netherlands
British Embassy, Lange Voorhout 10, 2514 ED The Hague
Tel: +31 70 4270 427
Email: ukinnl@fcdo.gov.uk
Website: www.gov.uk/government/world/organisations/british-embassy-the-hague Twitter: @ukinnl
Ambassador: HE Joanna Roper CMG

New Zealand
Governor: Pitcairn, Henderson, Ducie and Oeno Islands
British High Commission, 44 Hill Street, Wellington 6011
Tel: +64 4 924 2888 Fax: +64 4 473 4982
Website: www.gov.uk/government/world/organisations/british-high-commission-wellington
Twitter: @ukinnz
High Commissioner: HE Laura Clarke OBE

Nicaragua – see Costa Rica

Niger
British Embassy being set up
Website: www.gov.uk/world/niger
Ambassador: HE Catherine Inglehearn MBE

Nigeria
British High Commission, Plot 1137, Diplomatic Drive, Central Business District, Abuja
Tel: +234 462 3100
Email: ppainformation.abuja@fcdo.gov.uk
Website: www.gov.uk/government/world/organisations/british-high-commission-abuja
Twitter: @ukinnigeria
High Commissioner: HE Catriona Laing CB

North Macedonia
British Embassy, Todor Aleksandrov No. 165, Skopje 1000
Tel: +389 2 3299 299 Fax: +389 2 3179 726
Email: britishembassyskopje@fcdo.gov.uk
Website: www.gov.uk/government/world/organisations/british-embassy-skopje
Twitter: @ukinmacedonia
Ambassador: HE Rachel Galloway

Norway
British Embassy, Thomas Heftyesgate 8, 0264 Oslo
Tel: +47 23 13 27 00 Fax: +47 23 13 27 41
Email: ukinnorway@fcdo.gov.uk
Website: www.gov.uk/government/world/organisations/british-embassy-oslo Twitter: @ukinnorway
Ambassador: HE Richard Wood

Oman
British Embassy, PO Box 185, Mina Al Fahal, 116 Muscat
Tel: +968 2460 9000 Fax: +968 2460 9010
Email: muscat.enquirieswebsite@fcdo.gov.uk
Website: www.gov.uk/government/world/organisations/british-embassy-muscat Twitter: @ukinoman
Ambassador: HE Hamish Cowell CMG

Pakistan
British High Commission, Diplomatic Enclave, Ramna-5, PO Box 1122, Islamabad
Tel: +92 51 201 2000
Email: islamabad-general.enquiries@fcdo.gov.uk
Website: www.gov.uk/government/world/organisations/british-high-commission-islamabad
Twitter: @ukinpakistan
High Commissioner: HE Dr Christian Turner CMG

Palau – see Philippines

Panama
British Embassy, Fourth Floor, Humboldt Tower, Calle 53, Marbella, Panama City
Tel: +507 297 6550 Fax: +507 297 6588
Website: www.gov.uk/government/world/organisations/british-embassy-panama-city
Twitter: @ukinpanama
Ambassador (until July 2021): HE Damion Potter
Ambassador (from July 2021): HE Tim Stew MBE

Papua New Guinea
British High Commission, Sec 411, Lot 1 and 2, Kiroki Street, Waigani, National Capital District, Port Moresby
Tel: +675 303 7600 Fax: +675 325 3547
Email: uk.inpng@fcdo.gov.uk
Website: www.gov.uk/government/world/organisations/british-high-commission-port-moresby
High Commissioner: HE Keith Scott

Paraguay
British Embassy, Edificio Citicenter, Piso 5, Av. Mariscal López y Cruz del Chaco, Asuncion 1892
Tel: +595 21 614 588
Email: ukinparaguay@fcdo.gov.uk
Website: www.gov.uk/government/world/organisations/british-embassy-asuncion
Twitter: @UKinParaguay
Ambassador: HE Ramin Navai

Peru
British Embassy, Torre Parque Mar (Piso 22), Avenida José Larco, 1301 Miraflores, Lima
Tel: +51 1 617 3000 Fax: +51 1 617 3100
Email: belima@fcdo.gov.uk
Website: www.gov.uk/government/world/organisations/british-embassy-peru Twitter: @ukinperu
Ambassador: HE Kate Harrisson

Philippines
Non-resident: Palau
British Embassy, 120 Upper McKinley Road, McKinley Hill, Taguig City, 1634 Manila
Tel: +63 2 8 858 2200 Fax: +63 2 8 858 2216
Email: ukinthephilippines@fcdo.gov.uk
Website: www.gov.uk/government/world/organisations/british-embassy-manila
Twitter: @ukinphilippines
Ambassador: HE Daniel Pruce

Poland
British Embassy, ul. Kawalerii 12, 00-468 Warsaw
Tel: +48 22 311 00 00 Fax: +48 22 311 03 13
Email: info@britishembassy.pl
Website: www.gov.uk/government/world/organisations/british-embassy-warsaw
Twitter: @ukinpoland
Ambassador: HE Anna Clunes CMG OBE

Portugal
British Embassy, Rua de São Bernardo 33, 1249-082 Lisbon
Tel: +351 21 392 40 00
Email: ppa.lisbon@fcdo.gov.uk
Website: www.gov.uk/government/world/organisations/british-embassy-lisbon
Twitter: @ukinportugal
Ambassador: HE Chris Sainty

Qatar
British Embassy, West Bay, Dafna Area, Onaiza Zone 66, Al Shabab Street, PO Box 3 Doha
Tel: +974 496 2000 Fax: +974 496 2086
Email: embassy.doha@fcdo.gov.uk
Website: www.gov.uk/government/world/organisations/british-embassy-doha Twitter: @ukinqatar
Ambassador: HE Jon Wilks CMG

Romania
British Embassy, 24 Strada Jules Michelet, 010463 Bucharest
Tel: +40 21 201 7200
Email: britishembassy.bucharest@fcdo.gov.uk
Website: www.gov.uk/government/world/organisations/british-embassy-bucharest
Twitter: @ukinromania
Ambassador: HE Andrew Noble LVO

Russia
British Embassy, Smolenskaya Naberezhnaya 10, 121099 Moscow
Tel: +7 495 956 7200 Fax: +7 495 956 7481
Email: ukinrussia@fcdo.gov.uk
Website: www.gov.uk/government/world/organisations/british-embassy-moscow
Twitter: @ukinrussia
Ambassador: HE Deborah Bronnert CMG

Rwanda

Non-resident Ambassador: Burundi

British High Commission, KG 7 Ave, Kacyiru-Sud, Kigali PO BOX 576
Tel: +250 252 556 000 Fax: +250 252 582 044
Email: bhc.kigali@fcdo.gov.uk
Website: www.gov.uk/government/world/organisations/british-high-commission-kigali
Twitter: @ukinrwanda

High Commissioner (until July 2021): HE Jo Lomas

High Commissioner (from July 2021): HE Omar Daair

St Kitts and Nevis – see Barbados

St Lucia – see Barbados

St Vincent and the Grenadines – see Barbados

British High Commission being set up
Website: www.gov.uk/world/organisations/british-high-commission-kingstown
Twitter: @UKinCaribbean

Samoa

Cross Island Road (100 metres off Beach Road), Apia
Tel: +64 4 924 2888
Website: www.gov.uk/world/organisations/british-high-commission-apia

High Commissioner: HE David Ward

San Marino – see Italy

São Tomé and Príncipe – see Angola

Saudi Arabia

British Embassy, PO Box 94351, 11693 Riyadh
Tel: +966 1 4819 100 Fax: +966 1 481 9350
Website: www.gov.uk/government/world/organisations/british-embassy-riyadh
Twitter: @ukinsaudiarabia

Ambassador: HE Neil Crompton

Senegal

Non-resident: Cabo Verde, Guinea-Bissau

British Embassy, 20 Rue du Docteur Guillet, BP 6025, Dakar
Tel: +221 33 823 73 92
Email: ukinsenegal@fcdo.gov.uk
Website: www.gov.uk/government/world/organisations/british-embassy-dakar
Twitter: @UKinSenegal

Ambassador: HE Victoria Billing OBE

Serbia

British Embassy, Resavska 46, 11000 Belgrade
Tel: +381 11 3060 900 Fax: +381 11 3061 070
Email: belgrade.ppd@fcdo.gov.uk
Website: www.gov.uk/government/world/organisations/british-embassy-belgrade
Twitter: @ukinserbia

Ambassador: HE Sian MacLeod OBE

Seychelles

British High Commission, Third Floor, Oliaji Trade Centre, Francis Rachel Street, Victoria, Mahé
Tel: +248 283 666 Fax: +248 283 657
Website: www.gov.uk/government/world/organisations/high-commission-victoria
Twitter: @UKinSeychelles

High Commissioner: HE Patrick Lynch

Sierra Leone
British High Commission, 6 Spur Road, Freetown
Tel: +232 77677677
Email: freetown.general.enquiries@fcdo.gov.uk
Website: www.gov.uk/government/world/organisations/british-high-commission-freetown
Twitter: @UKinSierraLeone

High Commissioner: HE Simon Mustard

Singapore
British High Commission, 100 Tanglin Road, Singapore 247919
Tel: +65 6424 4200
Email: enquiries.singapore@fcdo.gov.uk
Website: www.gov.uk/government/world/organisations/british-high-commission-singapore
Twitter: @ukinsingapore

High Commissioner: HE Kara Owen CMG CVO

Slovakia
British Embassy, Panská 16, 811 01 Bratislava
Tel: +421 2 5998 2000 Fax: +421 2 5998 2237
Email: britishembassybratislava@fcdo.gov.uk
Website: www.gov.uk/government/world/organisations/british-embassy-bratislava
Twitter: @UKinSlovakia

Ambassador: HE Nigel Baker OBE MVO

Slovenia
British Embassy, Fourth Floor, Trg Republike 3, 1000 Ljubljana
Tel: +386 1 200 3910 Fax: +386 1 425 0174
Email: info@british-embassy.si
Website: www.gov.uk/government/world/organisations/british-embassy-ljubljana
Twitter: @ukinslovenia

Ambassador: HE Tiffany Sadler

Solomon Islands
Non-resident: Nauru

British High Commission, Tandai Highway, Town Ground, Honiara PO 676
Tel: +677 21705 Fax: +677 21549
Email: bhc@solomon.com.sb
Website: www.gov.uk/government/world/organisations/british-high-commission-honiara
Twitter: @BHCHoniara

High Commissioner: HE Dr Brian Jones

Somalia
British Embassy Mogadishu, Mogadishu
Email: somalia.enquiries@fcdo.gov.uk
Website: www.gov.uk/government/world/organisations/british-embassy-mogadishu
Twitter: @ukinsomalia

Ambassador: HE Kate Foster OBE

South Africa
British High Commission, 255 Hill Street, Arcadia, Pretoria, Gauteng 0002
Tel: +27 12 421 7500
Website: www.gov.uk/government/world/organisations/british-high-commission-pretoria
Twitter: @ukinsouthafrica

High Commissioner: HE Nigel Casey CMG MVO

South Sudan
British Embassy, European Compound, Kololo Road, Juba Na Bair/Tongping, Juba
Email: ukin.southsudan@fcdo.gov.uk
Website: www.gov.uk/government/world/organisations/british-embassy-juba
Twitter: @ukinsouthsudan
Ambassador: HE Jonny Baxter

Spain
Non-resident: Andorra
British Embassy, Torre Espacio, Paseo de la Castellana 259D, 28046 Madrid
Tel: +34 917 146 300 Fax: +34 917 146 301
Website: www.gov.uk/government/world/organisations/british-embassy-madrid Twitter: @ukinspain
Ambassador: HE Hugh Elliott

Sri Lanka
British High Commission, 389 Bauddhaloka Mawatha, Colombo 7
Tel: +94 11 5390639 Fax: +94 11 5390692
Email: colombo.general@fcdo.gov.uk
Website: www.gov.uk/government/world/organisations/british-high-commission-colombo
Twitter: @ukinsrilanka
High Commissioner: HE Sarah Hulton OBE

Sudan
British Embassy, off Sharia Al Baladia, Khartoum East, PO Box No 801
Tel: +249 156 775500 Fax: +249 183 776457
Website: www.gov.uk/government/world/organisations/british-embassy-khartoum
Twitter: @UKinSudan
Ambassador: HE Irfan Siddiq OBE

Suriname – see Guyana

Sweden
British Embassy, Skarpögatan 6-8, Box 27819, 115 93 Stockholm
Tel: +46 8 671 3000 Fax: +46 8 662 9989
Email: stockholm@fcdo.gov.uk
Website: www.gov.uk/government/world/organisations/british-embassy-stockholm
Twitter: @ukinsweden
Ambassador: HE Judith Gough CMG

Switzerland
Non-resident: Liechtenstein
British Embassy, Thunstrasse 50, 3005 Berne
Tel: +41 31 359 77 00 Fax: +41 31 359 77 01
Email: info.berne@fco.gov.uk
Website: www.gov.uk/government/world/organisations/british-embassy-berne
Twitter: @UKEmbassyBerne
Ambassador: HE Jane Owen

Tajikistan
British Embassy, 65 Mirzo Tursunzade Street, Dushanbe 734002
Tel: +992 372 24 2221 Fax: +992 372 27 1726
Website: www.gov.uk/government/world/organisations/british-embassy-dushanbe
Twitter: @ukintajikistan
Ambassador: HE Matthew Lawson

Tanzania
British High Commission, Umoja House, Hamburg Avenue, PO Box 9200, Dar es Salaam
Tel: +255 22 229 0000
Email: bhc.dar@fcdo.gov.uk
Website: www.gov.uk/government/world/organisations/british-high-commission-dar-es-salaam
Twitter: @ukintanzania

High Commissioner: HE David Concar

Thailand
British Embassy, AIA Sathorn Tower, Floor 12a, 11/1 South Sathorn Road, Sathorn, Bangkok 10120
Tel: +66 2 305 8333 Fax: +66 2 255 9278
Email: info.bangkok@fcdo.gov.uk
Website: www.gov.uk/government/world/organisations/british-embassy-bangkok
Twitter: @ukinthailand

Ambassador (until summer 2021): HE Brian Davidson CMG

Ambassador (from summer 2021): HE Mark Gooding OBE

Timor-Leste – see Indonesia

Togo – see Ghana

Tonga
British High Commission being set up
Website: www.gov.uk/world/tonga

High Commissioner: HE Lucy Joyce OBE

Trinidad and Tobago
British High Commission, 19 St Clair Avenue, St Clair, Port of Spain
Tel: +1 868 350 0444
Email: generalenquiries.ptofs@fcdo.gov.uk
Website: www.gov.uk/government/world/organisations/british-high-commission-trinidad-and-tobago
Twitter: @ukintt

High Commissioner: HE Harriet Cross

Tunisia
British Embassy, Rue du Lac Windermere, Les Berges du Lac, Tunis 1053
Tel: +216 71 108 700
Email: britishembassytunis@fcdo.gov.uk
Website: www.gov.uk/government/world/organisations/british-embassy-tunis Twitter: @ukintunisia

Ambassador: HE Edward Oakden CMG

Turkey
British Embassy, Şehit Ersan Caddesi 46/A, Çankaya, Ankara
Tel: +90 312 455 3344 Fax: +90 312 455 3352
Email: info.officer@fco.gov.uk
Website: www.gov.uk/government/world/organisations/british-embassy-ankara Twitter: @ukinturkey

Ambassador: HE Sir Dominick Chilcott KCMG

Turkmenistan
British Embassy, Third Floor Office Building, Four Points Ak Altin Hotel, 744001 Ashgabat
Tel: +993 12 363462 Fax: +993 12 363465
Email: ukembassy.ashgabat@fcdo.gov.uk
Website: www.gov.uk/government/world/organisations/british-embassy-ashgabat

Ambassador: HE Hugh Philpott OBE

Tuvalu – see Fiji

Uganda
British High Commission, 4 Windsor Loop, PO Box 7070, Kampala
Tel: +256 31 2312000 Fax: +256 41 4257304
Email: kampala.bhcinfo@fcdo.gov.uk
Website: www.gov.uk/government/world/organisations/british-high-commission-kampala
Twitter: @ukinuganda

High Commissioner: HE Kate Airey OBE

Ukraine
British Embassy, 9 Desyatynna Street, Kyiv 01025
Tel: +380 44 490 3660 Fax: +380 44 490 3662
Email: ukinukraine@fcdo.gov.uk
Website: www.gov.uk/government/world/organisations/british-embassy-kyiv
Twitter: @UKinUkraine

Ambassador: HE Melinda Simmons

United Arab Emirates
British Embassy, Al Hisn Street, Al Markaziyah West, PO Box 248, Abu Dhabi
Tel: +971 2 610 1100 Fax: +971 2 610 1586
Website: www.gov.uk/government/world/organisations/british-embassy-abu-dhabi Twitter: @ukinuae

Ambassador: HE Patrick Moody

United States of America
British Embassy, 3100 Massachusetts Avenue NW, Washington DC 20008
Tel: +1 202 588 6500
Email: public.affairsdc@fcdo.gov.uk
Website: www.gov.uk/government/world/organisations/british-embassy-washington
Twitter: @ukinusa

Ambassador: HE Dame Karen Pierce DCMG

Uruguay
British Embassy, Calle Marco Bruto 1073, 11300 Montevideo
Tel: +598 2622 3630 Fax: +598 2622 7815
Email: ukinuruguay@adinet.com.uy
Website: www.gov.uk/government/world/organisations/british-embassy-montevideo
Twitter: @ukinuruguay

Ambassador: HE Faye O'Connor OBE

Uzbekistan
British Embassy, 67 Gulyamov Street, Tashkent 100000
Tel: +998 78 120 1500 Fax: +998 78 120 1520
Email: ukin.uzbekistan@fcdo.gov.uk
Website: www.gov.uk/government/world/organisations/british-embassy-tashkent
Twitter: @ukinuzbekistan

Ambassador: HE Mr Tim Torlot

Vanuatu
British High Commission, La Casa D'Andrea E Luciano, Rue Pierre Lamy, Port Vila, Shefa Province
Website: www.gov.uk/world/organisations/british-high-commission-vanuatu

High Commissioner: HE Karen Bell

Venezuela
British Embassy, Torre La Castellana, Piso 11, Avenida La Principal de la Castellana, (Av Eugenio Mendoza) La Castellana, 1061 Caracas
Tel: +58 212 319 5800 Fax: +58 212 267 1275
Email: ukinvenezuela@fcdo.gov.uk
Website: www.gov.uk/government/world/organisations/british-embassy-venezuela
Twitter: @ukinvenezuela

Ambassador: HE Andrew Soper OBE

Vietnam
British Embassy, Fourth Floor, 31 Hai Ba Trung, Hanoi
Tel: +84 4 936 0500 Fax: +84 4 936 0561
Email: generalenquiries.vietnam@fcdo.gov.uk
Website: www.gov.uk/government/world/organisations/british-embassy-hanoi
Twitter: @UKinVietnam

Ambassador: HE Gareth Ward

Yemen
(Operations suspended since 11 February 2015)

British Embassy, 938 Thahr Himyar Street, East Ring Road, near Mövenpick Hotel, Sana'a
Website: www.gov.uk/government/world/organisations/british-embassy-sana-a Twitter: @ukinyemen

Ambassador (until July 2021): HE Michael Aron

Ambassador (from July 2021): HE Richard Oppenheim

Zambia
British High Commission, 5210 Independence Avenue, PO Box 50050, 15101 Ridgeway, Lusaka 10101
Tel: +260 211 423 200
Email: lusakageneralenquiries@fcdo.gov.uk
Website: www.gov.uk/government/world/organisations/british-high-commission-lusaka
Twitter: @ukinzambia

High Commissioner: HE Nicholas Woolley

Zimbabwe
British Embassy, 3 Norfolk Road, Mount Pleasant, Harare
Tel: +263 242 338 809
Email: ukinfo.harare@fcdo.gov.uk
Website: www.gov.uk/government/world/organisations/british-embassy-harare
Twitter: @ukinzimbabwe

Ambassador: HE Melanie Robinson

UK Permanent Representations

UK Mission to ASEAN
Jalan Patra Kuningan Raya Blok L5-6, Jakarta 12950
Tel: +62 21 2356 5334
Website: www.gov.uk/world/organisations/uk-mission-to-asean

Ambassador: HE Jon Lambe

UK Delegation to the Council of Europe
Rue Gottfried 18, 67000 Strasbourg
Tel: +33 3 88 24 71 65
Email: ukdelstrasbourg@fcdo.gov.uk
Website: www.gov.uk/government/world/organisations/uk-delegation-to-the-council-of-europe
Twitter: @UKDelCoE

UK Permanent Representative: HE Neil Holland

UK Joint Delegation to NATO

NATO, Boulevard Leopold III, 1110 Brussels
Tel: +32 2 707 75 01 Fax: +32 2 707 75 96
Email: ukdel.natogeneralenquiries@fcdo.gov.uk
Website: www.gov.uk/government/world/organisations/uk-joint-delegation-to-nato Twitter: @uknato

UK Permanent Representative to the North Atlantic Council: HE Dame Sarah MacIntosh DCMG

UK Permanent Delegation to the OECD

Rue du Faubourg Saint-Honoré 35, 75363 Paris CEDEX
Tel: +33 1 44 51 31 00
Email: ukoecd.admin@fcdo.gov.uk
Website: www.gov.uk/government/world/organisations/uk-permanent-delegation-to-the-oecd
Twitter: @ukoecd

Ambassador: HE Christopher Sharrock

UK Delegation to the OSCE

Jaurèsgasse 12, 1030 Vienna
Tel: +43 1 716 130
Email: ukdel.vienna@fcdo.gov.uk
Website: www.gov.uk/government/world/organisations/organisation-for-security-and-co-opertation-in-europe Twitter: @ukosce

Head of UK Delegation: HE Neil Bush

UK Mission to the EU

Avenue d'Auderghem 10, Brussels 1040
Tel: +32 2 287 82 11 Fax: +32 2 287 82 76
Email: ukmisbrussels@fcdo.gov.uk Website: www.gov.uk/world/organisations/uk-mission-to-the-eu
Twitter: @UKMisBrussels

Head of UK Mission: HE Lindsay Croisdale-Appleby

UK Mission to the UN (New York)

One Dag Hammarskjöld Plaza, 885 Second Avenue, New York 10017
Tel: +1 212 745 9200 Fax: +1 212 745 9316
Website: www.gov.uk/government/world/organisations/uk-mission-to-un-in-new-york
Twitter: @ukun_newyork

UK Permanent Representative to the UN and UK Representative on the Security Council: HE Dame Barbara Woodward DCMG OBE

UK Mission to the UN and other International Organisations (Vienna)

Jaurèsgasse 12, 1030 Vienna
Tel: +43 1 716 130 Fax: +43 1 716 134 900
Email: ukmis.vienna@fcdo.gov.uk
Website: www.gov.uk/government/world/organisations/united-kingdom-mission-to-the-united-nations Twitter: @ukmissionvienna

UK Permanent Representative (until September 2021): HE Leigh Turner CMG
UK Permanent Representative (from September 2021): HE Lindsay Skoll CMG
UK Permanent Representative to the International Atomic Energy Agency and Comprehensive Nuclear-Test-Ban Treaty Organization: HE Corinne Kitsell

UK Mission to the WTO, UN and other International Organisations (Geneva)
Avenue Louis Casaï 58, Case Postale 6, 1216 Cointrin, Geneva
Tel: +41 22 918 23 00 Fax: +41 22 918 23 33
Website: www.gov.uk/government/world/organisations/uk-mission-to-the-united-nations-geneva
Twitter: @ukmissiongeneva

UK Permanent Representative (until spring 2021): HE Julian Braithwaite CMG
UK Permanent Representative (from spring 2021): HE Simon Manley CMG

Conference on Disarmament
UK Permanent Representative: HE Aidan Liddle

London Embassies and High Commissions

Afghanistan
Embassy of the Islamic Republic of Afghanistan, 31 Prince's Gate, Exhibition Road, London SW7 1QQ
Tel: 020 7584 4443
Email: ea@afghanistanembassy.org.uk Website: www.afghanistanembassy.org.uk
Twitter: @Afghan_Emb_LON

Ambassador: To be appointed

Albania
Embassy of the Republic of Albania, 33 St George's Drive, London SW1V 4DG
Tel: 020 7828 8897 Fax: 020 7828 8869
Email: embassy.london@mfa.gov.al Website: www.ambasadat.gov.al/united-kingdom/en
Twitter: @AlEmbassyUK

Ambassador: HE Qirjako Qirko

Algeria
Embassy of the People's Democratic Republic of Algeria, 1-3 Riding House Street, London W1W 7DR
Tel: 020 7299 7077 Fax: 020 7299 7076
Email: info@algerianembassy.org.uk Website: www.algerianembassy.org.uk

Ambassador: HE Abderrahmane Benguerrah

Angola
Embassy of the Republic of Angola, 22 Dorset Street, London W1U 6QY
Tel: 020 7299 9850 Fax: 020 7486 9397
Email: embassy@angola.org.uk Website: www.angola.org.uk

Ambassador: HE Geraldo Nunda

Antigua and Barbuda
High Commission for Antigua and Barbuda, Second Floor, 45 Crawford Place, London W1H 4LP
Tel: 020 7258 0070 Fax: 020 7258 7486
Email: highcommission@antigua-barbuda.com Website: www.antigua-barbuda.com
Twitter: @ABHCUK

High Commissioner: HE Karen-Mae Hill

Argentina
Embassy of the Argentine Republic, 65 Brook Street, London W1K 4AH
Tel: 020 7318 1300 Fax: 020 7318 1301
Email: info@argentine-embassy-uk.org Website: www.argentine-embassy-uk.org
Twitter: @ARGen_UK

Ambassador: HE Javier Esteban Figueroa

Armenia
Embassy of the Republic of Armenia, 25a Cheniston Gardens, London W8 6TG
Tel: 020 7938 5435 Fax: 020 7938 2595
Email: armembassyuk@mfa.am Website: www.uk.mfa.am/en
Ambassador: To be appointed
Chargé d'Affaires: Hrachya Stepanyan

Australia
Australian High Commission, Australia House, Strand, London WC2B 4LA
Tel: 020 7379 4334 Fax: 020 7240 5333
Email: generalenquiries.lhlh@dfat.gov.au Website: www.uk.embassy.gov.au
Twitter: @aushouselondon
High Commissioner: HE Hon George Brandis QC

Austria
Embassy of Austria, 18 Belgrave Mews West, London SW1X 8HU
Tel: 020 7344 3250 Fax: 020 7344 0292
Email: london-ob@bmeia.gv.at Website: www.bmeia.gv.at/en/austrian-embassy-london
Twitter: @austriainuk
Ambassador: HE Dr Michael Zimmermann

Azerbaijan
Embassy of the Republic of Azerbaijan, 4 Kensington Court, London W8 5DL
Tel: 020 7938 3412 Fax: 020 7937 1783
Email: london@mission.mfa.gov.az Website: www.london.mfa.gov.az Twitter: @AzEmbUK
Ambassador: HE Tahir Taghizadeh

Bahamas
High Commission of the Commonwealth of the Bahamas, 10 Chesterfield Street, London W1J 5JL
Tel: 020 7408 4488 Fax: 020 7499 9937
Email: information@bahamashclondon.net Website: www.bahamashclondon.net
Twitter: @BahamasHCLondon
High Commissioner: HE Ellison Greenslade

Bahrain
Embassy of the Kingdom of Bahrain, 30 Belgrave Square, London SW1X 8QB
Tel: 020 7201 9170 Fax: 020 7201 9183
Email: information@bahrainembassy.co.uk Website: www.bahrainembassy.co.uk
Twitter: @BahrainEmbUK
Ambassador: HE Shaikh Fawaz bin Mohammed Al Khalifa

Bangladesh
High Commission for the People's Republic of Bangladesh, 28 Queen's Gate, London SW7 5JA
Tel: 020 7584 0081 Fax: 020 7581 7477
Email: bhclondon@btconnect.com Website: www.bhclondon.org.uk
High Commissioner: HE Saida Muna Tasneem

Barbados
Barbados High Commission, 1 Great Russell Street, London WC1B 3ND
Tel: 020 7631 4975 Fax: 020 7323 6872
Email: london@foreign.gov.bb
High Commissioner: HE Milton Inniss

Belarus
Embassy of the Republic of Belarus, 6 Kensington Court, London W8 5DL
Tel: 020 7937 3288 Fax: 020 7361 0005
Email: uk.london@mfa.gov.by Website: uk.mfa.gov.by/en Twitter: @belarus_emb_UK
Ambassador: HE Maxim Yermalovich

Belgium
Embassy of Belgium, 17 Grosvenor Crescent, London SW1X 7EE
Tel: 020 7470 3700 Fax: 020 7470 3795
Email: london@diplobel.fed.be Website: countries.diplomatie.belgium.be/en/united_kingdom
Twitter: @BelgiuminUK
Ambassador: HE Bruno van der Pluijm

Belize
Belize High Commission, Third Floor, 45 Crawford Place, London W1H 4LP
Tel: 020 7723 3603 Fax: 020 7723 9637
Email: info@belizehighcommission.co.uk Website: www.belizehighcommission.co.uk
Twitter: @BelizeHighComm
Acting High Commissioner: Karen Simplis

Benin
No London Embassy
Embassy of the Republic of Benin, 87 Avenue Victor Hugo, 75116 Paris
Tel: +33 1 45 00 98 82 Fax: +33 1 45 01 82 02
Email: contact@ambassade-benin.fr
Ambassador: To be appointed
UK Consulate
Millennium House, Humber Road, London NW2 6DW
Tel: 020 8830 8612 Fax: 020 7435 0665
Email: beninconsulate@hotmail.co.uk Website: beninconsulate.co.uk/index.html
Honorary Consul: To be appointed

Bhutan
No London Embassy
UK Consulate
2 Windacres Warren Road, Guildford GU1 2HG
Tel: 01483 538189
Email: mrutland@aol.com
Honorary Consul: Michael Rutland

Bolivia
Embassy of Bolivia, 106 Eaton Square, London SW1W 9AD
Tel: 020 7235 4248 Fax: 020 7235 1286
Email: embol@bolivianembassy.co.uk Website: www.bolivianembassy.co.uk Twitter: @boliviaenuk
Ambassador: To be appointed
Chargé d'Affaires: María José Oomen Liebers

Bosnia and Herzegovina
Embassy of Bosnia and Herzegovina, 5-7 Lexham Gardens, London W8 5JJ
Tel: 020 7373 0915 Fax: 020 7373 0871
Email: embassy@bhembassy.co.uk Website: www.bhembassy.co.uk
Ambassador: HE Vanja Filipović

Botswana

Botswana High Commission, 6 Stratford Place, London W1C 1AY
Tel: 020 7499 0031 Fax: 020 7495 8595
Email: bohico@govbw.com

High Commissioner: HE Dr John Seakgosing

Brazil

Embassy of Brazil, 14-16 Cockspur Street, London SW1Y 5BL
Tel: 020 7747 4500
Email: info.london@itamaraty.gov.br Website: londres.itamaraty.gov.br/en-us
Twitter: @BrazilEmbassyUK

Ambassador: HE Fred Arruda

Brunei

Brunei Darussalam High Commission, 19-20 Belgrave Square, London SW1X 8PG
Tel: 020 7581 0521 Fax: 020 7235 9717
Email: info@bruneihighcomm.org.uk

High Commissioner: HE First Admiral Pengiran Dato Seri Pahlawan Norazmi bin Pengiran Haji Muhammad

Bulgaria

Embassy of the Republic of Bulgaria, 186-188 Queen's Gate, London SW7 5HL
Tel: 020 7581 3144 Fax: 020 7584 4948
Email: info@bulgarianembassy.org.uk Website: www.bulgarianembassy-london.org

Ambassador: HE Marin Raykov

Burkina Faso

No London Embassy

Embassy of the Republic of Burkina Faso, Place Guy d'Arezzo 16, 1180 Brussels
Tel: +32 2 345 99 12 Fax: +32 2 345 06 12
Email: ambassade.burkina@skynet.be Website: www.ambassadeduburkina.be

Ambassador: HE Ms Jacqueline Zaba Nikiema

UK Consulate
The Lilacs, Stane Street, Ockley RH5 5LU
Tel: 01306 627225
Email: consul@colinseelig.co.uk Website: www.burkinafasovisa.co.uk
Honorary Consul: To be appointed

Burma – see Myanmar

Burundi

Embassy of the Republic of Burundi, Second Floor, Uganda House, 58-59 Trafalgar Square, London WC2N 5DX
Tel: 020 7930 4958 Fax: 020 7930 4957
Website: www.burundiembassy.org.uk

Ambassador: To be appointed
Chargé d'Affaires: Clothilde Nthahitangira

Cabo Verde
No London Embassy
Embassy of the Republic of Cabo Verde, Avenue Jeane 29, 1050 Brussels
Tel: +32 2 643 62 70 Fax: +32 2 646 33 85
Email: emb.caboverde@skynet.be
Ambassador: To be appointed
Chargé d'Affaires: Octavio Bento Gomes
UK Consulate
33 Buckthorne Road, London SE4 2DG
Email: a.diasborges@googlemail.com
Honorary Consul: Anne-Marie Dias Borges

Cambodia
Royal Embassy of Cambodia, 64 Brondesbury Park, Willesden Green, London NW6 7AT
Tel: 020 8451 7850 Fax: 020 8451 7594
Email: cambodianembassy@btconnect.com
Ambassador: HE Pharidh Kan

Cameroon
High Commission for the Republic of Cameroon, 84 Holland Park, London W11 3SB
Tel: 020 7727 0771 Fax: 020 7792 9353
Email: info@cameroonhighcommission.co.uk Website: www.cameroonhighcommission.co.uk
High Commissioner: HE Albert Njoteh Fotabong

Canada
Canadian High Commission, Canada House, Trafalgar Square, London SW1Y 5BJ
Tel: 0207 004 6000 Fax: 0207 004 6050
Email: ldn@international.gc.ca Website: www.unitedkingdom.gc.ca Twitter: @CanadianUK
High Commissioner: HE Janice Charette

Central African Republic
No London Embassy
Embassy of the Central African Republic, 30 rue des Perchamps, 75016 Paris
Ambassador: To be appointed

Chad
No London Embassy
Embassy of the Republic of Chad, Boulevard Lambermont 52, 1030 Brussels
Tel: +32 2 215 19 75 Fax: +32 2 216 35 26
Email: ambassade.tchad@chello.be
Ambassador: HE Ms Ammo Aziza Baroud

Chile
Embassy of Chile, 37-41 Old Queen Street, London SW1H 9JA
Tel: 020 7222 2361 Fax: 020 7222 0861
Email: embachile@embachile.co.uk Website: chileabroad.gov.cl/reino-unido/en
Twitter: @Chile_in_the_UK
Ambassador: HE David Gallagher

China
Embassy of the People's Republic of China, 49-51 Portland Place, London W1B 1JL
Tel: 020 7299 4049
Website: www.chinese-embassy.org.uk
Ambassador: HE Liu Xiaoming

Colombia
Embassy of Colombia, 3 Hans Crescent, London SW1X 0LN
Tel: 020 7589 9177
Email: elondres@cancilleria.gov.co Website: reinounido.embajada.gov.co
Twitter: @colombianembuk
Ambassador: HE Antonio José Ardila

Comoros
No London Embassy
UK Consulate
11 Park Place, London SW1A 1LP
Tel: 07768 821888
Email: kchehabi@gmail.com
Honorary Consul: Khaled Chehabi

Democratic Republic of Congo
Embassy of the Democratic Republic of Congo, 45-49 Great Portland Street, London W1W 7LD
Tel: 020 7580 3931 Fax: 020 7580 8713
Email: info@ambardc-londres.gouv.cd Website: www.ambardc.london Twitter: @AmbaRDCLondres
Ambassador: HE Marie Ndjeka Opombo

Republic of Congo
No London Embassy
Embassy of the Republic of Congo, 37 bis Rue Paul Valéry, 75116 Paris
Tel: +33 1 45 00 60 57 Fax: +33 1 40 67 17 33
Ambassador: To be appointed
UK Consulate
Third Floor, Holborn Gate, 26 Southampton Buildings, London WC2A 1PN
Tel: 020 7922 0695 Fax: 020 7401 2566
Website: consulateofthecongobrazzaville.webs.com
Honorary Consul: Louis Muzzu

Costa Rica
Embassy of Costa Rica, 23 Woodstock Street, London W1C 2AS
Tel: 020 7629 3111
Email: info@costaricanembassy.co.uk Website: www.costaricanembassy.co.uk
Ambassador: HE Rafael Ortiz Fábrega

Côte d'Ivoire
Embassy of the Republic of Côte d'Ivoire, 2 Upper Belgrave Street, London SW1X 8BJ
Tel: 020 7235 6991 Fax: 020 7259 5320
Ambassador: To be appointed

Croatia
Embassy of the Republic of Croatia, 21 Conway Street, London W1T 6BN
Tel: 020 7387 2022 Fax: 020 7387 0310
Email: vrhlon@mvep.hr Website: uk.mfa.hr Twitter: @CROinUK
Ambassador: HE Igor Pokaz

Cuba
Embassy of the Republic of Cuba, 167 High Holborn, London WC1V 6PA
Tel: 020 7240 2488 Fax: 020 7836 2602
Email: secembajador@uk.embacuba.cu
Website: misiones.minrex.gob.cu/en/united-kingdom/embassy-cuba-united-kingdom
Twitter: @EmbaCuba_UK
Ambassador: HE Bárbara Montalvo Álvarez

Cyprus
High Commission of the Republic of Cyprus, 13 St James's Square, London SW1Y 4LB
Tel: 020 7321 4100 Fax: 020 7321 4164
Email: cyprusinuk@mfa.gov.cy Website: cyprusinuk.com Twitter: @CyprusInUK

High Commissioner: HE Andreas Kakouris

Czech Republic
Embassy of the Czech Republic, 26 Kensington Palace Gardens, London W8 4QY
Tel: 020 7243 1115 Fax: 020 7243 7926
Email: london@embassy.mzv.cz Website: www.mzv.cz/london/en/index.html

Ambassador: HE Libor Sečka

Denmark
Royal Danish Embassy, 55 Sloane Street, London SW1X 9SR
Tel: 020 7333 0200 Fax: 020 7333 0270
Email: lonamb@um.dk Website: storbritannien.um.dk Twitter: @denmarkinuk

Ambassador: HE Lars Thuesen

Djibouti
No London Embassy

Embassy of the Republic of Djibouti, 26 Rue Emilie Ménier, 75116 Paris
Tel: +33 1 47 27 49 22 Fax: +33 1 45 53 50 53
Email: webmaster@amb-djibouti.org

Ambassador: HE Ayeid Mousseid Yahya

Dominica
High Commission for the Commonwealth of Dominica, 1 Collingham Gardens, London SW5 0HW
Tel: 020 7370 5194 Fax: 020 7373 8743
Email: info@dominicahighcommission.co.uk Website: www.dominicahighcommission.co.uk
Twitter: @DHC_London

Acting High Commissioner: Janet Charles

Dominican Republic
Embassy of the Dominican Republic, Second Floor, 81 Cromwell Road, London SW7 5BW
Tel: 020 7262 6856
Email: pa@dominicanembassy.org.uk Website: www.dominicanembassy.org.uk

Ambassador: HE Hugo Guiliani Cury

Ecuador
Embassy of Ecuador, Flat 3b, 3 Hans Crescent, London SW1X 0LS
Tel: 020 7584 1367 Fax: 020 7590 2509
Email: eecugranbretania@mmrree.gov.ec Website: reinounido.embajada.gob.ec
Twitter: @EmbajadaEcuUK

Ambassador: HE Jaime Marchán Romero

Egypt
Embassy of the Arab Republic of Egypt, 26 South Street, London W1K 1DW
Tel: 020 7499 3304 Fax: 020 7491 1542
Email: eg.emb_london@mfa.gov.eg

Ambassador: HE Tarek Adel

El Salvador
Embassy of El Salvador, 8 Dorset Square, London NW1 6PU
Tel: 020 7224 9800 Fax: 020 7224 9878
Email: embajadalondres@rree.gob.sv Twitter: @elsembassy

Ambassador: HE Vanessa Interiano Elfarnawany

Equatorial Guinea
Embassy of the Republic of Equatorial Guinea, 13 Park Place, London SW1A 1LP
Tel: 020 7499 6867 Fax: 020 7499 6782
Email: embarege-londres@embarege-londres.org
Ambassador: To be appointed
Chargé d'Affaires: Maria Jesús Diallo Besari

Eritrea
Embassy of the State of Eritrea, 96 White Lion Street, London N1 9PF
Tel: 020 7713 0096 Fax: 020 7713 0161
Email: pa.ambassador@eritreanembassyuk.org
Ambassador: HE Estifanos Habtemariam Ghebreyesus

Estonia
Embassy of the Republic of Estonia, 44 Queen's Gate Terrace, London SW7 5PJ
Tel: 020 7589 3428 Fax: 020 7589 3430
Email: london@mfa.ee Website: london.mfa.ee Twitter: @estembassyuk
Ambassador: HE Tiina Intelmann

Eswatini
Kingdom of Eswatini High Commission, 20 Buckingham Gate, London SW1E 6LB
Tel: 020 7630 6611 Fax: 020 7630 6564
Email: enquiries@eswatini.org.uk
High Commissioner: HE Christian Muzie Nkambule

Ethiopia
Embassy of the Federal Democratic Republic of Ethiopia, 17 Prince's Gate, London SW7 1PZ
Tel: 020 7589 7212 Fax: 020 7584 7054
Email: info@ethioembassy.org.uk Website: www.ethioembassy.org.uk Twitter: @EthioEmbassyUK
Ambassador: HE Teferi Melesse

Fiji
High Commission of the Republic of the Fiji Islands, 34 Hyde Park Gate, London SW7 5DN
Tel: 020 7584 3661 Fax: 020 7584 2838
Email: mail@fijihighcommission.org.uk Website: www.fijihighcommission.org.uk
Twitter: @FijiHC_London
High Commissioner: HE Jitoko Tikolevu

Finland
Embassy of Finland, 38 Chesham Place, London SW1X 8HW
Tel: 020 7838 6200 Fax: 020 7235 3680
Email: sanomat.lon@formin.fi Website: www.finemb.org.uk Twitter: @finlandinuk
Ambassador: HE Markku Tapio Keinänen

France
Embassy of France, 58 Knightsbridge, London SW1X 7JT
Tel: 020 7073 1000 Fax: 020 7073 1004
Website: www.ambafrance-uk.org Twitter: @FranceintheUK
Ambassador: HE Catherine Colonna

Gabon
Embassy of the Gabonese Republic, 27 Elvaston Place, London SW7 5NL
Tel: 020 7823 9986 Fax: 020 7584 0047
Email: gabonembassyuk@gmail.com
Ambassador: HE Aichatou Sanni Aoudou

Gambia

The Gambia High Commission, 57 Kensington Court, London W8 5DG
Tel: 020 3928 9770
Email: gambiahighcomuk@btconnect.com

High Commissioner: HE Francis Blain

Georgia

Embassy of Georgia, 20 St George's Square, London SW1V 2HP
Tel: 020 7348 1941 Fax: 020 7603 6682
Email: london.emb@mfa.gov.ge Website: www.uk.mfa.gov.ge Twitter: @GeoEmbLondon

Ambassador: HE Sophie Katsarava MBE

Germany

Embassy of the Federal Republic of Germany, 23 Belgrave Square, London SW1X 8PZ
Tel: 020 7824 1300 Fax: 020 7824 1449
Email: info@london.diplo.de Website: www.london.diplo.de Twitter: @germanembassy

Ambassador: HE Andreas Michaelis

Ghana

High Commission for Ghana, 13 Belgrave Square, London SW1X 8PN
Tel: 020 7201 5921 Fax: 020 7245 9552
Email: gh.donlon@gmail.com Website: www.ghanahighcommissionuk.com Twitter: @GhanainUK

Acting High Commissioner: Matilda Osei-Agyeman

Greece

Embassy of Greece, 1a Holland Park, London W11 3TP
Tel: 020 7229 3850 Fax: 020 7229 7221
Email: gremb.lon@mfa.gr Website: www.mfa.gr/uk/en Twitter: @GreeceinUK

Ambassador: HE Ioannis Raptakis

Grenada

High Commission for Grenada, The Chapel, Archel Road, London W14 9QH
Tel: 020 7385 4415 Fax: 020 7381 4807
Email: office@grenada-highcommission.co.uk Website: www.grenada-highcommission.co.uk
Twitter: @grenadahcuk

High Commissioner: HE Lakisha Grant

Guatemala

Embassy of Guatemala, First floor, Suite 1, 105a Westbourne Grove, London W2 4UW
Tel: 020 7221 1525
Email: info@embaguate.com Twitter: @Guatemala_in_UK

Ambassador: To be appointed
Chargé d'Affaires: Olga Perez Tuna

Guinea

Embassy of the Republic of Guinea, 239 Old Marylebone Road, London NW1 5QT
Tel: 020 7258 9640
Email: embassyofguinea@gmail.com

Ambassador: HE Alexandre Cécé Loua

Guinea-Bissau

No London Embassy

Embassy of the Republic of Guinea-Bissau, Rue St Lazare 94, 75009 Paris
Tel: +33 1 48 74 36 39

Ambassador: To be appointed

Guyana
High Commission for Guyana, 3 Palace Court, Bayswater Road, London W2 4LP
Tel: 020 7229 7684 Fax: 020 7727 9809
Email: guyanahc1@btconnect.com Website: www.guyanahclondon.co.uk
High Commissioner: To be appointed

Haiti
Embassy of the Republic of Haiti, 21 Bloomsbury Way, London WC1A 2TH
Tel: 020 3771 1427 Fax: 020 7637 8980
Email: amb.royaumeuni@diplomatie.ht
Ambassador: HE Euvrard Saint Amand

Holy See
Apostolic Nunciature, 54 Parkside, London SW19 5NE
Tel: 020 8944 7189 Fax: 020 8947 2494
Email: nuntius@globalnet.co.uk
Apostolic Nuncio: HE Archbishop Claudio Gugerotti

Honduras
Embassy of Honduras, Fourth Floor, 136 Baker Street, London W1U 6UD
Tel: 020 7486 4880 Fax: 020 7486 4550
Email: hondurasuk@lineone.net Website: www.hondurasembassyuk.co.uk
Twitter: @hondurasembuk
Ambassador: HE Ivan Romero-Martinez

Hungary
Embassy of Hungary, 35 Eaton Place, London SW1X 8BY
Tel: 020 7204 3440 Fax: 020 7823 1348
Email: mission.lon@mfa.gov.hu Website: www.mfa.gov.hu/emb/london
Ambassador: HE Ferenc Kumin

Iceland
Embassy of Iceland, 2a Hans Street, London SW1X 0JE
Tel: 020 7259 3999
Email: icemb.london@utn.stjr.is
Website: www.government.is/diplomatic-missions/embassy-of-iceland-in-london
Twitter: @icelandinuk
Ambassador: HE Sturla Sigurjónsson

India
High Commission of India, India House, Aldwych, London WC2B 4NA
Tel: 020 7836 8484
Email: hc.office@hcilondon.in Website: www.hcilondon.gov.in Twitter: @HCI_London
High Commissioner: HE Gaitri Issar Kumar

Indonesia
Embassy of the Republic of Indonesia, 30 Great Peter Street, London SW1P 2BU
Tel: 020 7499 7661 Fax: 020 7491 4993
Email: kbri@btconnect.com Website: www.indonesianembassy.org.uk Twitter: @KbriLondon
Ambassador: HE Desra Percaya

Iran
Embassy of the Islamic Republic of Iran, 16 Prince's Gate, London SW7 1PT
Tel: 020 7225 4208
Email: iranemb.lon@mfa.gov.ir
Ambassador: HE Hamid Baeidinejad

Iraq
Embassy of the Republic of Iraq, 21 Queen Gate, London SW7 5JE
Tel: 020 7590 7650 Fax: 020 7590 7679
Email: lonemb@mofa.gov.iq Twitter: @iqembassy_uk
Ambassador: HE Mohammed Jaafar M Bakr Haidar Al-Sadr

Ireland
Embassy of Ireland, 17 Grosvenor Place, London SW1X 7HR
Tel: 020 7235 2171 Fax: 020 7589 8450
Email: londonembassymail@dfa.ie Website: www.embassyofireland.co.uk Twitter: @irelandembgb
Ambassador: HE Adrian O'Neill

Israel
Embassy of Israel, 2 Palace Green, London W8 4QB
Tel: 020 7957 9500 Fax: 020 7957 9555
Email: info@london.mfa.gov.il Website: embassies.gov.il/london Twitter: @israelinuk
Ambassador: HE Tsipi Hotovely

Italy
Embassy of Italy, 14 Three Kings Yard, Davies Street, London W1K 4EH
Tel: 020 7312 2200 Fax: 020 7312 2230
Email: ambasciata.londra@esteri.it Website: www.amblondra.esteri.it Twitter: @ItalyinUK
Ambassador: HE Raffaele Trombetta

Ivory Coast - see Côte d'Ivoire

Jamaica
Jamaican High Commission, 1-2 Prince Consort Road, London SW7 2BZ
Tel: 020 7823 9911 Fax: 020 7589 5154
Email: jamhigh@jhcuk.com Website: www.jhcuk.org
High Commissioner: HE Seth Ramocan

Japan
Embassy of Japan, 101-104 Piccadilly, London W1J 7JT
Tel: 020 7465 6500 Fax: 020 7491 9348
Email: info@ld.mofa.go.jp Website: www.uk.emb-japan.go.jp Twitter: @japaninuk
Ambassador: To be appointed

Jordan
Embassy of the Hashemite Kingdom of Jordan, 6 Upper Phillimore Gardens, London W8 7HA
Tel: 020 7937 3685 Fax: 020 7937 8795
Email: london@fm.gov.jo
Ambassador: HE Omar B Nahar

Kazakhstan
Embassy of the Republic of Kazakhstan, 33 Thurloe Square, London SW7 2DS
Tel: 020 7925 1757 Fax: 020 7930 8990
Email: london@kazembassy.org.uk Website: www.mfa.gov.kz/en/london Twitter: @KazEmbassyUK
Ambassador: HE Erlan Idrissov

Kenya
Kenya High Commission, 45 Portland Place, London W1B 1AS
Tel: 020 7636 2371 Fax: 020 7323 6717
Email: mission@kenyahighcom.org.uk Website: www.kenyahighcom.org.uk
Twitter: @KenyaMissionUK
High Commissioner: HE Manoah Esipisu

Kiribati
No London High Commission
Kiribati High Commissioner, c/o Office of the President, PO Box 68, Bairiki, Tarawa
High Commissioner: To be appointed
UK Consulate
The Great House, Llandewi Rydderch NP7 9UY
Tel: 01873 840375 Fax: 01873 840375
Email: mravellwalsh@btopenworld.com
Honorary Consul: Michael Ravell Walsh

Democratic People's Republic of Korea (North)
Embassy of the Democratic People's Republic of Korea, 73 Gunnersbury Avenue, London W5 4LP
Tel: 020 8992 4965 Fax: 020 8992 2053
Email: dprkrepmission@yahoo.co.uk
Ambassador: HE Il Choe

Republic of Korea (South)
Embassy of the Republic of Korea, 60 Buckingham Gate, London SW1E 6AJ
Tel: 020 7227 5500 Fax: 020 7227 5503
Email: koreanembinuk@mofa.go.kr Website: overseas.mofa.go.kr/gb-en/index.do
Twitter: @KoreanEmbassyUK
Ambassador: HE Enna Park

Kosovo
Embassy of the Republic of Kosovo, 8 John Street, London WC1N 2ES
Tel: 020 7405 1010
Email: embassy.uk@ks-gov.net Website: www.kosovoembassy.org.uk Twitter: @KosovoinUK
Ambassador: To be appointed
Chargé d'Affaires: Arrita Gjakova

Kuwait
Embassy of the State of Kuwait, 2 Albert Gate, London SW1X 7JU
Tel: 020 7590 3400 Fax: 020 7823 1712
Ambassador: HE Khaled Al Duwaisan GCVO

Kyrgyzstan
Embassy of the Kyrgyz Republic, Ascot House, 119 Crawford Street, London W1U 6BJ
Tel: 020 7935 1462 Fax: 020 7935 7449
Email: mail@kyrgyz-embassy.org.uk Website: mfa.gov.kg/en/dm/vb Twitter: @kyrgyzembassy
Ambassador: HE Edil Baisalov

Laos
Embassy of the Lao People's Democratic Republic, 49 Porchester Terrace, London W2 3TS
Tel: 020 7402 3770 Fax: 020 7262 1994
Email: laosemblondon@gmail.com
Ambassador: HE Phongsavanh Sisoulath

Latvia
Embassy of the Republic of Latvia, 45 Nottingham Place, London W1U 5LY
Tel: 020 7563 1619 Fax: 020 7312 0042
Email: embassy.uk@mfa.gov.lv Website: www.london.mfa.gov.lv Twitter: @LVembassyUK
Ambassador: HE Ivita Burmistre

Lebanon
Embassy of Lebanon, 21 Palace Gardens Mews, London W8 4QN
Tel: 020 7229 7265 Fax: 020 7243 1699
Email: emb.leb@btinternet.com Website: london.mfa.gov.lb/britain Twitter: @EmbassyLebanon
Ambassador: HE Rami Mortada

Lesotho
High Commission of the Kingdom of Lesotho, 7 Chesham Place, London SW1X 8HN
Tel: 020 7235 5686 Fax: 020 7235 5023
Email: lhc@lesotholondon.org.uk Website: www.lesotholondon.org.uk
High Commissioner: HE Rethabile Mahlompho Mokaeane

Liberia
Embassy of the Republic of Liberia, 23 Fitzroy Square, London W1 6EW
Tel: 020 7388 5489 Fax: 020 7388 2899
Email: info@embassyofliberia.org.uk
Ambassador: HE Gurly Gibson

Libya
Embassy of Libya, 15 Knightsbridge, London SW1X 7LY
Tel: 020 7201 8280 Fax: 020 7245 0588
Ambassador: To be appointed
Chargé d'Affaires: Mohamed Elkoni

Lithuania
Embassy of the Republic of Lithuania, Lithuania House, 2 Bessborough Gardens, London SW1V 2JE
Tel: 020 7592 2840 Fax: 020 7592 2864
Email: amb.uk@urm.lt Website: uk.mfa.lt Twitter: @LTEMBASSYUK
Ambassador: HE Renatas Norkus

Luxembourg
Embassy of Luxembourg, 27 Wilton Crescent, London SW1X 8SD
Tel: 020 7235 6961 Fax: 020 7235 9734
Email: londres.amb@mae.etat.lu Website: londres.mae.lu/en
Ambassador: HE Jean Olinger

Madagascar
Embassy of the Republic of Madagascar, Fifth Floor, One Knightsbridge Green, London SW1X 7NE
Tel: 020 7052 8277
Email: ambamad.contact@madagascarembassy.org.uk
Ambassador: To be appointed
Chargé d'Affaires: Anjaniaina Olivia Rakotonirina

Malawi
High Commission for the Republic of Malawi, 36 John Street, London WC1N 2AT
Tel: 020 7421 6010 Fax: 020 7831 9273
Email: london@malawihighcommission.co.uk Website: www.malawihighcommission.co.uk
Twitter: @MalawiinUK
High Commissioner: HE Kena Mphonda

Malaysia
Malaysian High Commission, 45-46 Belgrave Square, London SW1X 8QT
Tel: 020 3931 6196
Email: mwlondon@kln.gov.my Website: www.kln.gov.my/web/gbr_london/home
Twitter: @MYHicomLondon
High Commissioner: To be appointed

Maldives
High Commission of the Republic of Maldives, 22 Nottingham Place, London W1U 5NJ
Tel: 020 7224 2135
Email: info@maldiveshighcommission.uk Website: maldiveshighcommission.uk
Twitter: @maldivesembuk

High Commissioner: HE Dr Farahanaz Faizal

Mali
No London Embassy
Embassy of the Republic of Mali, Avenue Molière 487, 1050 Brussels
Tel: +32 2 345 74 32 Fax: +32 2 344 57 00
Email: info@amba-mali.be Website: www.amba-mali.be

Ambassador: To be appointed
Chargé d'Affaires: Coulibaly Sira Cisse

Malta
Malta High Commission, Malta House, 36-38 Piccadilly, London W1J 0LE
Tel: 020 7292 4800 Fax: 020 7292 4803
Email: maltahighcommission.london@gov.mt
Website: foreignaffairs.gov.mt/en/embassies/hc_london/pages/hc-london.aspx

High Commissioner: HE Joseph Cole

Mauritania
Embassy of the Islamic Republic of Mauritania, Carlyle House, 235-237 Vauxhall Bridge Road, London SW1V 1EJ
Tel: 020 7233 6158

Ambassador: HE Sidya Ould Elhadj

Mauritius
Mauritius High Commission, 32-33 Elvaston Place, London SW7 5NW
Tel: 020 7581 0294 Fax: 020 7823 8437
Email: londonhc@govmu.org

High Commissioner: HE Girish Nunkoo

Mexico
Embassy of Mexico, 16 St George Street, London W1S 1FD
Tel: 020 7499 8586 Fax: 020 7495 4035
Email: embgbretana@sre.gob.mx Website: embamex.sre.gob.mx/reinounido/index.php/en
Twitter: @embamexru

Ambassador: To be appointed
Chargé d'Affaires: Ana Aureny Aguirre O Sunza

Moldova
Embassy of the Republic of Moldova, 5 Dolphin Square, Edensor Road, London W4 2ST
Tel: 020 8995 6818 Fax: 020 8995 6927
Email: embassy.london@mfa.gov.md Website: regatulunit.mfa.gov.md/en

Ambassador: HE Angela Ponomariov

Monaco
Embassy of the Principality of Monaco, 7 Upper Grosvenor Street, London W1K 2LX
Tel: 020 7318 1081 Fax: 020 7493 4563
Email: embassy.uk@gouv.mc
Website: embassy-to-uk.gouv.mc/en/monaco-embassy-to-united-kingdom

Ambassador: HE Evelyne Genta

Mongolia

Embassy of Mongolia, 7 Kensington Court, London W8 5DL
Tel: 020 7937 0150 Fax: 020 7937 1117
Email: chancery@embassyofmongolia.co.uk Website: www.embassyofmongolia.co.uk
Twitter: @MnEmbassyInUK

Ambassador: HE Tulga Narkhuu

Montenegro

Embassy of Montenegro, 47 De Vere Gardens, London W8 5AW
Tel: 020 3302 7227 Fax: 020 7243 9358
Email: unitedkingdom@mfa.gov.me

Ambassador: HE Vladimir Beratović

Morocco

Embassy of the Kingdom of Morocco, 49 Queen's Gate Gardens, London SW7 5NE
Tel: 020 7581 5001 Fax: 020 7225 3862
Email: ambalondres@maec.gov.ma Website: www.moroccanembassylondon.org.uk
Twitter: @MOROCCOinUK

Ambassador: To be appointed

Mozambique

High Commission for the Republic of Mozambique, 21 Fitzroy Square, London W1T 6EL
Tel: 020 7383 3800 Fax: 020 7383 3801
Website: www.mozambiquehighcommission.org.uk

Acting High Commissioner: Omar Remane

Myanmar (Burma)

Embassy of the Republic of the Union of Myanmar, 19a Charles Street, London W1J 5DX
Tel: 020 7148 0740 Fax: 020 7409 7043
Email: general@myanmarembassylondon.com Website: www.londonmyanmarembassy.com

Ambassador: HE Kyaw Zwar Minn

Namibia

High Commission for the Republic of Namibia, 6 Chandos Street, London W1G 9LU
Tel: 020 7636 6244 Fax: 020 7637 5694
Email: info@namibiahc.org.uk Website: www.namibiahc.org.uk Twitter: @NamibiaUK

High Commissioner: HE Linda Scott

Nauru

No London High Commission

High Commissioner: To be appointed

UK Consulate
Romshed Courtyard, Underriver, nr Sevenoaks TN15 0SD
Tel: 01732 746061 Fax: 01732 746062
Email: nauru@weald.co.uk
Honorary Consul: Martin Weston

Nepal

Embassy of Nepal, 12a Kensington Palace Gardens, London W8 4QU
Tel: 020 7243 7859 Fax: 020 7792 9861
Email: eon@nepembassy.org.uk Website: nepalembassy.gov.np

Ambassador: HE Dr Durga Bahadur Subedi

Netherlands
Embassy of the Kingdom of the Netherlands, 38 Hyde Park Gate, London SW7 5DP
Tel: 020 7590 3200
Email: lon@minbuza.nl Website: www.netherlandsworldwide.nl/countries/united-kingdom
Twitter: @NLinUK
Ambassador: HE Karel van Oosterom

New Zealand
New Zealand High Commission, New Zealand House, 80 Haymarket, London SW1Y 4TQ
Tel: 020 7930 8422 Fax: 020 7839 4580
Email: enquiries@nzhc.uk Website: www.mfat.govt.nz/uk Twitter: @NZinUK
High Commissioner: HE Bede Corry

Nicaragua
Embassy of Nicaragua, Suite 2, Vicarage House, 58-60 Kensington Church Street, London W8 4DB
Tel: 020 7938 2373 Fax: 020 7937 0952
Email: embaniclondon@btconnect.com Twitter: @embaniclondon
Ambassador: HE Guisell Morales-Echaverry

Niger
No London Embassy
Embassy of the Republic of Niger, 154 Rue de Longchamp, 75116 Paris
Tel: +33 1 45 04 80 60 Fax: +33 1 45 04 79 73
Website: ambassadeniger-fr.org
Ambassador: HE Ado Elhadji Abou
UK Consulate
MPC House, 15 Maple Mews, London NW6 5UZ
Tel: 020 7328 8180 Fax: 020 7328 8120
Email: consulate@nigerconsulateuk.org Website: www.nigerconsulateuk.org
Honorary Consul: To be appointed

Nigeria
High Commission for the Federal Republic of Nigeria, Nigeria House, 9 Northumberland Avenue, London WC2N 5BX
Tel: 020 7839 1244 Fax: 020 7839 8746
Email: information@nigeriahc.org.uk Website: www.nigeriahc.org.uk
Acting High Commissioner: Ahmed Sule

North Macedonia
Embassy of the Republic of North Macedonia, Suites 2.1-2.2, Buckingham Court, 75-83 Buckingham Gate, London SW1E 6PE
Tel: 020 7066 0535
Email: sek.london@mfa.gov.mk
Ambassador: HE Aleksandra Miovska

Norway
Royal Norwegian Embassy, 25 Belgrave Square, London SW1X 8QD
Tel: 020 7591 5500 Fax: 020 7591 5501
Email: emb.london@mfa.no Website: www.norway.org.uk Twitter: @norwayinuk
Ambassador: HE Wegger Strømmen

Oman
Embassy of the Sultanate of Oman, 167 Queen's Gate, London SW7 5HE
Tel: 020 7225 0001 Fax: 020 7589 2505
Email: theembassy@omanembassy.org.uk Twitter: @EmbassyOmanUk
Ambassador: HE Abdul Aziz Al Hinai

Pakistan
High Commission for the Islamic Republic of Pakistan, 35-36 Lowndes Square, London SW1X 9JN
Tel: 020 7664 9200 Fax: 020 7664 9224
Email: protocol@phclondon.org Website: www.phclondon.org Twitter: @PakistaninUK
High Commissioner: HE Moazzam Ahmad Khan

Palau
No London Embassy
UK Consulate
Bankfoot Square, Bankfoot Street, Batley WF17 5LH
Tel: 01924 470786 Fax: 01924 474747
Website: palauconsulate.org.uk
Honorary Consul: Q Mohammed

Panama
Embassy of Panama, 40 Hertford Street, London W1J 7SH
Tel: 020 7493 4646 Fax: 020 7493 4333
Email: panama1@btconnect.com Website: www.panamaconsul.co.uk Twitter: @PanamaEmbUK
Ambassador: HE Natalia Royo Ruiz de Hagerman

Papua New Guinea
Papua New Guinea High Commission, Ground Floor, 14 Waterloo Place, London SW1Y 4AR
Tel: 020 7930 0922 Fax: 020 7930 0828
Email: info@png.org.uk Website: www.pnghighcomm.org.uk
High Commissioner: HE Winnie Kiap

Paraguay
Embassy of the Republic of Paraguay, Ground and Lower Ground, Floor 81-83, Cromwell Road, London SW7 5BW
Tel: 020 7610 4180 Fax: 020 7371 4297
Email: embaparuk@paraguayembassy.co.uk Website: www.paraguayembassy.co.uk
Ambassador: HE Genaro Vicente Pappalardo Ayala

Peru
Embassy of Peru, 52 Sloane Street, London SW1X 9SP
Tel: 020 7235 1917
Email: postmaster@peruembassy-uk.com Website: www.peruembassy-uk.com Twitter: @PeruInUK
Ambassador: HE Juan Carlos Gamarra

Philippines
Embassy of the Republic of the Philippines, 6-8 Suffolk Street, London SW1Y 4HG
Tel: 020 7451 1780 Fax: 020 7930 9787
Email: embassy@philemb.co.uk Website: londonpe.dfa.gov.ph Twitter: @philippinesinuk
Ambassador: HE Antonio Lagdameo

Poland
Embassy of the Republic of Poland, 47 Portland Place, London W1B 1JH
Tel: 020 7291 3520
Email: londyn@msz.gov.pl Website: www.gov.pl/web/unitedkingdom Twitter: @polishembassyuk
Ambassador: HE Arkady Rzegocki

Portugal
Embassy of Portugal, 11 Belgrave Square, London SW1X 8PP
Tel: 020 7235 5331 Fax: 020 7245 1287
Email: londres@me.pt Website: www.londres.embaixadaportugal.mne.pt/en
Ambassador: HE Manuel Lobo Antunes

Qatar
Embassy of the State of Qatar, 1 South Audley Street, London W1K 1NB
Tel: 020 7493 2200 Fax: 020 7493 2819
Email: london@mofa.gov.qa Twitter: @QatarEmb_London
Ambassador: HE Yousef Ali Al-Khater

Romania
Embassy of Romania, Arundel House, 4 Palace Green, London W8 4QD
Tel: 020 7937 9666 Fax: 020 7937 8069
Email: roemb@roemb.co.uk Website: londra.mae.ro
Ambassador: To be appointed
Chargé d'Affaires: Daniela-Laura Popescu

Russia
Embassy of the Russian Federation, 6-7 Kensington Palace Gardens, London W8 4QP
Tel: 020 7229 6412 Fax: 020 7727 8625
Email: info@rusemb.org.uk Website: www.rusemb.org.uk Twitter: @russianembassy
Ambassador: HE Andrei Kelin

Rwanda
High Commission for the Republic of Rwanda, 120-122 Seymour Place, London W1H 1NR
Tel: 020 7224 9832 Fax: 020 7724 8642
Email: uk@ambarwanda.org.uk Website: www.rwandahc.org Twitter: @RwandaInUK
High Commissioner: HE Yamina Karitanyi

St Kitts and Nevis
High Commission for Saint Christopher and Nevis, 10 Kensington Court, London W8 5DL
Tel: 020 7937 9718 Fax: 020 7937 7484
Email: mission@sknhc.co.uk Website: www.stkittsnevishcuk.gov.kn Twitter: @sknhcuk
High Commissioner: HE Kevin Isaac

St Lucia
High Commission for Saint Lucia, 1 Collingham Gardens, London SW5 0HW
Tel: 020 7370 7123 Fax: 020 7370 1905
Email: enquiries@stluciahcuk.org
High Commissioner: HE Guy Mayers

St Vincent and the Grenadines
High Commission for Saint Vincent and the Grenadines, 10 Kensington Court, London W8 5DL
Tel: 020 7460 1256 Fax: 020 7937 6040
Email: office@svghighcom.co.uk Website: www.svghighcom.co.uk Twitter: @svghighcom
High Commissioner: HE Cenio Lewis

Samoa
No London High Commission
Embassy of Samoa, Avenue Commandant Lothaire 1, 1040 Brussels
Tel: +32 2 660 84 54 Fax: +32 2 675 03 36
Email: samoaembassy@skynet.be
High Commissioner: HE Fatumanava Dr Pa'olelei Luteru
UK Consulate
Church Cottage, Pedlinge, nr Hythe CT21 5JL
Tel: 01303 260541 Fax: 01303 238058
Honorary Consul: Prunella Scarlett LVO

San Marino

No London Embassy

Embassy of the Republic of San Marino, Department of Foreign Affairs, Palazzo Begni – Contrada Omerelli, 47890 San Marino
Tel: +378 0549 882422
Email: dipartimentoaffariesteri@pa.sm

Ambassador: HE Silvia Marchetti

UK Consulate
Flat 51, 162 Sloane Street, London SW1X 9BS
Tel: 020 7259 9754 Fax: 01268 292629
Email: consolato.londra.sm@gmail.com
Honorary Consul: Eduardo Teodorani-Fabbri

São Tomé and Príncipe

No London Embassy

Embassy of São Tomé and Principé, Avenue de Tervuren 175, 1150 Brussels
Tel: +32 2 734 89 66 Fax: +32 2 734 88 15
Email: ambassade@saotomeeprincipe.be

Ambassador: To be appointed

UK Consulate
11 Briary Court, Turner Street, London E16 1AN
Tel: 07977 260564
Email: chris.buckwell@btopenworld.com
Honorary Consul: Chris Buckwell

Saudi Arabia

Royal Embassy of Saudi Arabia, 30 Charles Street, London W1J 5DZ
Tel: 020 7917 3000
Email: ukemb@mofa.gov.sa Website: www.saudiembassy.org.uk Twitter: @SaudiEmbassyUK

Ambassador: HE HRH Prince Khalid bin Bandar bin Sultan Al Saud

Senegal

Embassy of the Republic of Senegal, 39 Marloes Road, London W8 6LA
Tel: 020 7938 4048 Fax: 020 7938 2546
Email: senegalembassy@hotmail.co.uk

Ambassador: HE Dr Fatimata Dia

Serbia

Embassy of the Republic of Serbia, 28 Belgrave Square, London SW1X 8QB
Tel: 020 7235 9049 Fax: 020 7235 7092
Email: london@serbianembassy.org.uk Website: www.serbianembassy.org.uk

Ambassador: HE Aleksandra Joksimović

Seychelles

High Commission of the Republic of Seychelles, Fourth Floor, 130-132 Buckingham Palace Road, London SW1W 9SA
Tel: 020 7245 0680 Fax: 020 7730 0087
Email: office@seychelleshcl.co.uk

Acting High Commissioner: Terry Romain

Sierra Leone

Sierra Leone High Commission, 41 Eagle Street, London WC1R 4AT
Tel: 020 7404 0140
Email: info@slhc-uk.org.uk Website: www.slhc-uk.org

High Commissioner: HE Dr Morie Komba Manyeh

Singapore
High Commission for the Republic of Singapore, 9 Wilton Crescent, London SW1X 8SP
Tel: 020 7235 8315 Fax: 020 7245 6583
Email: singhc_lon@sgmfa.gov.sg Website: www.mfa.gov.sg/london Twitter: @shclon
High Commissioner: HE Lim Thuan Kuan

Slovakia
Embassy of Slovakia, 25 Kensington Palace Gardens, London W8 4QY
Tel: 020 7313 6470 Fax: 020 7313 6481
Email: emb.london@mzv.sk Website: www.mzv.sk/web/londyn-en Twitter: @SLOVAKIAinUK
Ambassador: HE Róbert Ondrejcsák

Slovenia
Embassy of the Republic of Slovenia, 17 Dartmouth Street, London SW1H 9BL
Tel: 020 7222 5700
Email: sloembassy.london@gov.si Website: www.london.embassy.si Twitter: @SLOinUK
Ambassador: HE Simona Leskovar

Solomon Islands
High Commission for the Solomon Islands, Room 1819, Portland House, Bressenden Place, London SW1E 5RS
High Commissioner: HE Eliam Tangirongo

South Africa
High Commission of the Republic of South Africa, South Africa House, Trafalgar Square, London WC2N 5DP
Tel: 020 7451 7299 Fax: 020 7839 5670
Email: london.sahc@dirco.gov.za Website: www.southafricahouseuk.com
High Commissioner: HE Nomatemba Tambo

South Sudan
Embassy of the Republic of South Sudan, 22-25 Portman Close, London W1H 6BS
Tel: 020 3687 2366
Email: info@embrss.org.uk Website: embrss.org.uk
Ambassador: To be appointed
Chargé d'Affaires: Ashwil Haruun Ruun

Spain
Embassy of Spain, 39 Chesham Place, London SW1X 8SB
Tel: 020 7235 5555 Fax: 020 7259 5392
Email: emb.londres@maec.es Website: www.exteriores.gob.es/embajadas/londres/en
Twitter: @EmbSpainUK
Ambassador: HE Carlos Bastarreche Sagües

Sri Lanka
High Commission for the Democratic Socialist Republic of Sri Lanka, 13 Hyde Park Gardens, London W2 2LU
Tel: 020 7262 1841 Fax: 020 7262 7970
Email: mail@slhc-london.co.uk Website: srilankahc.uk Twitter: @SLHCinLondon
High Commissioner: HE Saroja Sirisena

Sudan
Embassy of the Republic of the Sudan, 3 Cleveland Row, London SW1A 1DD
Tel: 020 7839 8080 Fax: 020 7839 7560
Email: admin@sudanembassy.co.uk
Ambassador: HE Mohamed Abdalla Idris Mohamed

Suriname
No London Embassy

Embassy of the Republic of Suriname, rue du Ranelagh 91, 75016 Paris
Tel: +33 01 45 25 93 00
Email: amb.frankrijk@gov.sr

Ambassador: HE Reggy Martiales Nelson

UK Consulate
127 Pier House, 31 Cheyne Walk, London SW3 5HN
Tel: 020 3084 7143
Email: ajethu@honoraryconsul.info
Honorary Consul: Dr Amwedhkar Jethu

Sweden
Embassy of Sweden, 11 Montagu Place, London W1H 2AL
Tel: 020 7917 6400 Fax: 020 7724 4174
Email: ambassaden.london@gov.se
Website: www.swedenabroad.se/en/embassies/united-kingdom-london Twitter: @swedeninuk

Ambassador: HE Torbjörn Sohlström

Switzerland
Embassy of Switzerland, 16-18 Montagu Place, London W1H 2BQ
Tel: 020 7616 6000 Fax: 020 7724 7001
Email: london@eda.admin.ch Website: www.eda.admin.ch/london Twitter: @swissembassyuk

Ambassador: HE Alexandre Fasel

Tajikistan
Embassy of the Republic of Tajikistan, Suite 309, 3 Shortlands, Hammersmith, London W6 8DA
Tel: 020 8834 1003 Fax: 020 8834 1100
Email: tajemblondon@mfa.tj Website: www.tajembassy.org.uk

Ambassador: HE Masud Khalifazoda

Tanzania
High Commission for the United Republic of Tanzania, 3 Stratford Place, London W1C 1AS
Tel: 020 7569 1470 Fax: 020 7491 3710
Email: balozi@tanzaniahighcomm.co.uk Website: tanzaniahighcomm.co.uk

High Commissioner: HE Dr Asha-Rose Migiro

Thailand
Royal Thai Embassy, 29-30 Queen's Gate, London SW7 5JB
Tel: 020 7589 2944 Fax: 020 7823 7492
Email: thaiduto@btinternet.com Website: www.thaiembassyuk.org.uk Twitter: @ThaiEmbLondon

Ambassador: HE Pisanu Suvanajata

Timor-Leste
Embassy of the Democratic Republic of Timor-Leste, 83 Victoria Street, London SW1H 0HW
Tel: 020 3585 4062
Email: info@tlembassy.co.uk

Ambassador: HE Gil Da Costa

Togo
Embassy of the Republic of Togo, Unit 3, 7 and 8 Lysander Mews, Lysander Grove, London N19 3QP
Tel: 020 3198 9579

Ambassador: To be appointed
Chargé d'Affaires: Komlanvi Dedji

Tonga

Tonga High Commission, 36 Molyneux Street, London W1H 5BQ
Tel: 020 7724 5828 Fax: 020 7723 9074

High Commissioner: HE Titilupe Fanetupouvavau Tuivakano

Trinidad and Tobago

High Commission of the Republic of Trinidad and Tobago, 42 Belgrave Square, London SW1X 8NT
Tel: 020 7245 9351 Fax: 020 7823 1065
Email: hclondon@foreign.gov.tt Twitter: @tnt_london

High Commissioner: HE Orville London

Tunisia

Embassy of Tunisia, 29 Prince's Gate, London SW7 1QG
Tel: 020 7584 8117 Fax: 020 7584 3205
Email: london@tunisianembassy.co.uk

Ambassador: HE Nabil Ben Khedher

Turkey

Embassy of the Republic of Turkey, 43 Belgrave Square, London SW1X 8PA
Tel: 020 7393 0202 Fax: 020 7393 0066
Email: embassy.london@mfa.gov.tr Website: london.emb.mfa.gov.tr Twitter: @TurkEmbLondon

Ambassador: HE Ümit Yalçın

Turkmenistan

Embassy of Turkmenistan, 131 Holland Park Avenue, London W11 4UT
Tel: 020 7610 5239 Fax: 020 7751 1903
Email: tkm-embassy-uk@btconnect.org.uk Website: uk.tmembassy.gov.tm/en

Ambassador: HE Yazmurad Seryaev

Tuvalu

No London High Commission

High Commissioner: HE Mr Aunese Makoi Simati

UK Consulate

Tuvalu House, 230 Worple Road, London SW20 8RH
Tel: 020 8879 0985 Fax: 020 8879 0985
Email: tuvaluconsulate@netscape.net
Honorary Consul: Sir Iftikhar Ayaz KBE

Uganda

Uganda High Commission, Uganda House, 58-59 Trafalgar Square, London WC2N 5DX
Tel: 020 7839 5783 Fax: 020 7839 8925
Email: admin@ugandahighcommission.co.uk Website: london.mofa.go.ug
Twitter: @UGHighCommLDN

High Commissioner: HE Julius Peter Moto

Ukraine

Embassy of Ukraine, 60 Holland Park, London W11 3SJ
Tel: 020 7727 6312 Fax: 020 7792 1708
Email: emb_gb@mfa.gov.ua Website: uk.mfa.gov.ua/en Twitter: @UkrEmbLondon

Ambassador: HE Vadym Prystaiko

United Arab Emirates
Embassy of the United Arab Emirates, 1-2 Grosvenor Crescent, London SW1X 7EE
Tel: 020 7581 1281 Fax: 020 7581 9616
Email: informationuk@mofa.gov.ae
Website: sp.mofaic.gov.ae/en/diplomaticmissions/embassies/london/pages/home.aspx
Twitter: @UAEEmbassyUK
Ambassador: HE Mansoor Abulhoul

United States of America
American Embassy, 33 Nine Elms Lane, London SW11 7US
Tel: 020 7499 9000
Website: uk.usembassy.gov Twitter: @usainuk
Ambassador: To be appointed
Chargé d'Affaires: Yael Lempert

Uruguay
Embassy of Uruguay, Fourth Floor, 150 Brompton Road, Knightsbridge, London SW3 1HX
Tel: 020 7584 4200 Fax: 020 7584 2947
Email: urureinounido@mrree.gub.uy
Ambassador: HE Dr César Rodríguez-Zavalla

Uzbekistan
Embassy of the Republic of Uzbekistan, 41 Holland Park, London W11 3RP
Tel: 020 7229 7679 Fax: 020 7229 7029
Email: info@uzembassy.uk Twitter: @uzbekembassy
Ambassador: HE Said Rustamov

Vanuatu
No London High Commission
High Commission of Vanuatu, Avenue de Tervueren 380, Chemin de Ronde, 1150 Brussels
Tel: +32 2 771 74 94 Fax: +32 2 771 74 94
Email: info@vanuatuembassy.net
High Commissioner: To be appointed

Venezuela
Embassy of the Bolivarian Republic of Venezuela, 1 Cromwell Road, London SW7 2HW
Tel: 020 7584 4206 Fax: 020 7589 8887
Twitter: @VenezEmbassyUK
Ambassador: HE Rocío Maneiro

Vietnam
Embassy of the Socialist Republic of Vietnam, 12-14 Victoria Road, London W8 5RD
Tel: 020 7937 1912 Fax: 020 7937 6108
Website: www.vietnamembassy.org.uk
Ambassador: HE Tran Ngoc An

Yemen
Embassy of the Republic of Yemen, 57 Cromwell Road, London SW7 2ED
Tel: 020 7584 6607
Email: admin@yemenembassy.co.uk
Ambassador: HE Dr Yassin Saeed Ahmed Noman

Zambia
High Commission for the Republic of Zambia, Zambia House, 2 Palace Gate, London W8 5NG
Tel: 020 7581 2142 Fax: 020 7581 1353
Email: info@zambiahc.org.uk Website: www.zambiahc.org.uk Twitter: @zhclondon
High Commissioner: HE Lt Gen Paul Mihova

Zimbabwe
Embassy for the Republic of Zimbabwe, Zimbabwe House, 429 Strand, London WC2R 0JR
Tel: 020 7836 7755
Email: zimebassy@zimlondon.gov.zw
Ambassador: HE Col Christian Katsande

Royal Households

HER MAJESTY'S HOUSEHOLD
Buckingham Palace, London SW1A 1AA Tel: 020 7930 4832
Website: www.royal.uk Twitter: @RoyalFamily

Private Secretary to HM The Queen: Rt Hon Sir Edward Young KCVO

HRH THE PRINCE PHILIP, DUKE OF EDINBURGH
Buckingham Palace, London SW1A 1AA Tel: 020 7930 4832

Private Secretary and Treasurer: Brig. Archie Miller-Bakewell

TRH THE PRINCE OF WALES AND THE DUCHESS OF CORNWALL
Clarence House, London SW1A 1BA Tel: 020 7930 4832
Website: www.princeofwales.gov.uk Twitter: @ClarenceHouse

Principal Private Secretary: Clive Alderton CVO
Private Secretary to The Duchess of Cornwall: Amanda MacManus LVO

TRH THE DUKE AND DUCHESS OF CAMBRIDGE
Kensington Palace, London W8 4PU Tel: 020 7930 4832
Website: www.royal.uk/the-duke-of-cambridge Website: www.royal.uk/the-duchess-of-cambridge
Twitter: @KensingtonRoyal

Private Secretary to The Duke of Cambridge: Christian Jones
Private Secretary to The Duchess of Cambridge: Hannah Cockburn-Logie OBE MVO

TRH THE DUKE AND DUCHESS OF SUSSEX
Buckingham Palace, London SW1A 1AA Tel: 020 7930 4832
Website: sussexroyal.com

HRH THE DUKE OF YORK
Buckingham Palace, London SW1A 1AA Tel: 020 7930 4832
Website: thedukeofyork.org

Assistant Private Secretary: Morag Love

TRH THE EARL AND COUNTESS OF WESSEX
Bagshot Park, Bagshot GU19 5PL Tel: 020 7930 4832

Private Secretary: Captain Andy Aspden RN

HRH THE PRINCESS ROYAL
Buckingham Palace, London SW1A 1AA Tel: 020 7930 4832

Private Secretary: Charles Davies MVO

TRH THE DUKE AND DUCHESS OF GLOUCESTER
Kensington Palace, London W8 4PU Tel: 020 7930 4832

Private Secretary and Comptroller: Lt Col Alastair Todd LVO

TRH THE DUKE AND DUCHESS OF KENT
St James's Palace, London SW1A 1BQ Tel: 020 7930 4872

Private Secretary: Nicholas Turnbull MBE QGM

TRH PRINCE AND PRINCESS MICHAEL OF KENT
Kensington Palace, London W8 4PU
Website: www.princemichael.org.uk

Private Secretary: Camilla Rogers

HRH PRINCESS ALEXANDRA, THE HONOURABLE LADY OGILVY
Buckingham Palace, London SW1A 1AA Tel: 020 7930 4832

Private Secretary and Comptroller: Diane Duke LVO

HM Lord Lieutenants

ENGLAND

Bedfordshire Helen Nellis
Berkshire James Puxley
City and County of Bristol Peaches Golding OBE
Buckinghamshire Countess Howe
Cambridgeshire Julie Spence OBE QPM
Cheshire David Briggs CVO MBE
Cornwall Col Edward Bolitho OBE
Cumbria Claire Hensman
Derbyshire Elizabeth Fothergill CBE
Devon David Fursdon
Dorset Angus Campbell
County Durham Susan Snowdon
Essex Jennifer Tolhurst
Gloucestershire Edward Gillespie OBE
Hampshire Nigel Atkinson
Herefordshire Edward Harley OBE
Hertfordshire Robert Voss CBE CStJ
Isle of Wight Susan Sheldon
Kent Lady Colgrain
Lancashire Lord Shuttleworth KG KCVO
Leicestershire Michael Kapur OBE
Lincolnshire Toby Dennis
Greater London Kenneth Olisa OBE
Greater Manchester Sir Warren Smith KCVO JP
Merseyside Mark Blundell
Norfolk Lady Dannatt MBE
Northamptonshire James Saunders Watson
Northumberland Duchess of Northumberland
Nottinghamshire Sir John Peace
Oxfordshire Tim Stevenson OBE
Rutland Dr Sarah Furness
Shropshire Anna Turner
Somerset Annie Maw
Staffordshire Ian Dudson CBE
Suffolk Countess of Euston
Surrey Michael More-Molyneux
East Sussex Sir Peter Field KCVO JP
West Sussex Susan Pyper
Tyne and Wear Susan Winfield OBE
Warwickshire Timothy Cox
West Midlands John Crabtree OBE
Wiltshire Sarah Troughton
Worcestershire Lt Col Patrick Holcroft LVO OBE

East Riding of Yorkshire	James Dick OBE
North Yorkshire	Johanna Ropner
South Yorkshire	Andrew Coombe
West Yorkshire	Ed Anderson

SCOTLAND

City of Aberdeen*	Lord Provost Barney Crockett
Aberdeenshire	Sandy Manson
Angus	Patricia Sawers
Argyll and Bute	Jane MacLeod
Ayrshire and Arran	Iona McDonald
Banffshire	Christopher Simpson
Berwickshire	Jeanna Swan
Caithness	Rt Hon Viscount Thurso
Clackmannanshire	Lt Col Johnny Stewart
Dumfries	Fiona Armstrong
Dunbartonshire	Real Admiral Michael Gregory OBE
City of Dundee*	Lord Provost Ian Borthwick
City of Edinburgh*	Lord Provost Frank Ross
Fife	Robert Balfour
City of Glasgow*	Lord Provost Philip Braat
Inverness	Donald Cameron of Lochiel CVO
Kincardineshire	Alastair Macphie
Lanarkshire	Lady Susan Haughey CBE
East Lothian	Roderick Urquhart
Midlothian	Lt Col Richard Callander LVO OBE TD
West Lothian	Moira Niven MBE
Moray	Major General Seymour Monro CBE LVO
Nairnshire	George Asher
Orkney	Elaine Grieve
Perth and Kinross	Stephen Leckie
Renfrewshire	Col Peter McCarthy
Ross and Cromarty	Joanie Whiteford
Roxburgh, Ettrick and Lauderdale	Duke of Buccleuch and Queensberry KT KBE CVO
Shetland	Robert Hunter
Stewartry of Kirkcudbright	Elizabeth Gilroy
Stirling and Falkirk	Alan Simpson OBE
Sutherland	Dr Monica Main
Tweeddale	Professor Sir Hew Strachan
Western Isles	Donald Martin
Wigtown	Aileen Brewis

**The Lord Provosts of the four City Districts (Aberdeen, Dundee, Edinburgh and Glasgow) are ex-officio Lord Lieutenants.*

WALES

Clwyd	Henry Fetherstonhaugh OBE
Dyfed	Sara Edwards

Mid Glamorgan	Prof Peter Vaughan QPM
South Glamorgan	Morfudd Meredith
West Glamorgan	Louise Fleet JP
Gwent	Brig Robert Aitken CBE
Gwynedd	Edmund Bailey
Powys	Tia Jones
NORTHERN IRELAND	
County Antrim	David McCorkell
County Armagh	Earl of Caledon KCVO
County Borough of Belfast	Fionnuala Jay-O'Boyle CBE
County Down	David Lindsay CVO
County Fermanagh	Viscount Brookeborough KG
County Londonderry	Alison Millar
County Borough of Londonderry	Dr Angela Garvey
County Tyrone	Robert Scott OBE JP

Association of Lord Lieutenants
Chairman: Col Edward Bolitho OBE
Secretary: Tom Wilson Email: office@lord-lieutenants.uk

British Overseas Territories Governors and Commanders-in-Chief

Anguilla	HE Dileeni Daniel-Selvaratnam *(Governor)*
Bermuda	HE Rena Lalgie *(Governor)*
British Antarctic Territory	Ben Merrick *(Commissioner)* (Non-resident)
British Indian Ocean Territory	Ben Merrick *(Commissioner)* (Non-resident)
British Virgin Islands	HE John Rankin CMG *(Governor)*
Cayman Islands	Martyn Roper OBE *(Governor)*
Falkland Islands	HE Nigel Phillips CBE *(Governor)*
Gibraltar	HE Vice Admiral Sir David Steel KBE *(Governor)*
Montserrat	HE Andrew Pearce OBE *(Governor)*
Pitcairn, Henderson, Ducie and Oeno Islands	HE Laura Clarke OBE *(Governor)* (Non-resident) see New Zealand – British Embassies and High Commissions section
St Helena and Dependencies	HE Dr Philip Rushbrook *(Governor)*
South Georgia and South Sandwich Islands	HE Nigel Phillips CBE *(Commissioner)* (Non-resident)
Turks and Caicos Islands	HE Nigel Dakin CMG *(Governor)*

The Commonwealth

Of the 54 member countries of the Commonwealth, Queen Elizabeth II is Head of State of 16 (including the United Kingdom), 33 are republics, and 5 are monarchies with other sovereigns. The Queen remains symbolically Head of the Commonwealth.

Governors-General

In the overseas realms of which she is Queen, Her Majesty is represented by a Governor-General.

Antigua and Barbuda	HE Sir Rodney Williams GCMG *Prime Minister*: Hon Gaston Browne

Australia	HE David Hurley AC DSC *Prime Minister*: Hon Scott Morrison
Bahamas	HE Sir Cornelius Smith GCMG *Prime Minister*: Hon Dr Hubert Minnis
Barbados	HE Dame Sandra Mason GCMG QC *Prime Minister*: Rt Hon Mia Mottley QC
Belize	HE Sir Colville Young GCMG MBE *Prime Minister*: Hon Johnny Briceño
Canada	HE Rt Hon Julie Payette *Prime Minister*: Rt Hon Justin Trudeau
Grenada	HE Dame Cecile La Grenade GCMG OBE *Prime Minister*: Rt Hon Dr Keith Mitchell
Jamaica	HE Most Hon Sir Patrick Allen ON GCMG *Prime Minister*: Most Hon Andrew Holness ON
New Zealand	HE Rt Hon Dame Patsy Reddy GNZM QSO *Prime Minister*: Rt Hon Jacinda Ardern
Papua New Guinea	HE Sir Bob Dadae GCMG *Prime Minister*: Hon James Marape
St Christopher and Nevis*	HE Sir Tapley Seaton GCMG CVO QC *Prime Minister*: Hon Dr Timothy Harris
St Lucia*	HE Sir Emmanuel Neville Cenac GCMG *Prime Minister*: Hon Allen M Chastanet
St Vincent and The Grenadines*	HE Dame Susan Dougan *Prime Minister*: Hon Dr Ralph Gonsalves
Solomon Islands	HE Sir David Vunagi GCMG *Prime Minister*: Hon Manasseh Sogavare
Tuvalu	HE Teniku Talesi *Prime Minister*: Hon Kausea Natano

*Eastern Caribbean States.

Republics and other Commonwealth Monarchies Heads of State and Heads of Government

Bangladesh	*President and Head of State*: HE Abdul Hamid *Prime Minister*: Hon Sheikh Hasina
Botswana	*President and Head of State*: HE Mokgweetsi Masisi
Brunei Darussalam	*Sultan and Head of Government*: His Majesty Sultan Hassanal Bolkiah of Brunei
Cameroon	*President and Head of State*: HE Paul Biya *Prime Minister and Head of Government*: Joseph Dion Ngute
Cyprus	*President and Head of State*: Nicos Anastasiades
Dominica	*President and Head of State*: HE Charles Savarin *Prime Minister and Head of Government*: Hon Roosevelt Skerrit
Eswatini	*Head of State*: His Majesty King Mswati III *Acting Prime Minister and Head of Government*: Themba Masuku
Fiji Islands	*President and Head of State*: HE Major General Jioji Konrote *Prime Minister and Head of Government*: Rear Admiral Josaia Voreqe Bainimarama
Gambia	*President and Head of State*: HE Adama Barrow

Ghana	*President and Head of State*: HE Nana Akufo-Addo
Guyana	*President and Head of State*: HE Irfaan Ali
	Prime Minister and Head of Government: Mark Phillips
India	*President and Head of State*: HE Shri Ram Nath Kovind
	Prime Minister and Head of Government: Hon Narendra Modi
Kenya	*President and Head of State*: HE Uhuru Kenyatta
Kiribati	*President and Head of State*: HE Taneti Maamau
Lesotho	*Head of State*: His Majesty King Letsie III
	Prime Minister and Head of Government: Thomas Thabane
Malawi	*President and Head of State*: HE Lazarus Chakwera
Malaysia	*Head of State (King of Malaysia)*: His Majesty Al-Sultan Abdullah Al-Haj
	Prime Minister and Head of Government: Muhyiddin Yassin
Maldives	*President and Head of State*: HE Ibrahim Mohamed Solih
Malta	*President and Head of State*: Dr George Vella
	Prime Minister and Head of Government: Robert Abela
Mauritius	*President and Head of State*: HE Prithvirajsing Roopun
	Prime Minister and Head of Government: Hon Pravind Jugnauth
Mozambique	*President and Head of State*: HE Filipe Nyusi
Namibia	*President and Head of State*: HE Dr Hage Geingob
Nauru	*President and Head of Government*: HE Lionel Aingimea
Nigeria	*President and Head of State*: HE Muhammadu Buhari
Pakistan	*President and Head of State*: HE Arif Alvi
	Prime Minister and Head of Government: Imran Khan
Rwanda	*President and Head of State*: HE Paul Kagame
	Prime Minister and Head of Government: Rt Hon Edouard Ngirente
Samoa	*Head of State*: HE Tuimalealiifano Vaaletoa Sualauvi II
	Prime Minister Head of Government: Tuilaepa Aiono Sailele Malielegaoi
Seychelles	*President and Head of State*: HE Wavel Ramkalawan
Sierra Leone	*President and Head of Government*: HE Julius Maada Bio
Singapore	*President and Head of State*: HE Halimah Yacob
	Prime Minister and Head of Government: Lee Hsien Loong
South Africa	*President and Head of State*: HE Cyril Ramaphosa
Sri Lanka	*President and Head of State*: HE Lt Col Gotabaya Rajapaksa
	Prime Minister and Head of Government: Mahinda Rajapaksa
Tanzania	*President and Head of State*: HE Dr John Magufuli
	Prime Minister and Head of Government: Kassim Majaliwa
Tonga	*Head of State*: His Majesty King George Tupou VI
	Prime Minister and Head of Government: Hon Pohiva Tu'i'onetoa
Trinidad and Tobago	*President and Head of State*: HE Paula-Mae Weekes
	Prime Minister and Head of Government: Hon Dr Keith Rowley
Uganda	*President and Head of State*: HE Yoweri Museveni
	Prime Minister and Head of Government: Rt Hon Dr Ruhakana Rugunda

Vanuatu *President and Head of State*: HE Tallis Obed Moses
Prime Minister and Head of Government: Bob Loughman

Zambia *President and Head of State*: HE Edgar Lungu

Forms of Address

Formal modes of address become less formal every year but there are occasions when a person may want to address someone with strict formality. The first form of address given is that which should always be used on the envelope, the second is the formal salutation and conclusion and the third is the less formal salutation and conclusion, respectively (1), (2) and(3).

The honorific prefix 'The Right Honourable' is not now generally used for Peers other than Privy Counsellors.

The courtesy titles Honourable, Lady and Lord to which sons and daughters of Peers (depending on the rank of their father) are not prefixed by the definite article. These are the practices adopted by the Earl Marshal's Office and that of the Lord Chamberlain of the Household and consequently have been followed here.

In the formal mode of address the conclusion '. . . Obedient Servant' has been used. This is a matter of choice as it can be 'humble and obedient servant' or simply 'I am, Sir (my Lord et al) Yours faithfully'.

AMBASSADOR—(1) His Excellency Mr., Dr., etc. as appropriate, (Esquire is never used), Ambassador of the Italian Republic, (the name of the country in full i.e. not The Italian Ambassador). (2) Your Excellency, conclude I am Your Excellency's Obedient Servant. (3) Dear Mr Ambassador, conclude Yours sincerely. In conversation an Ambassador is addressed as 'Your Excellency', but once is sufficient, thereafter 'Sir' is normal.

AMBASSADOR'S PARTNER—(1) As the married partner of the Ambassador they are not 'Your Excellency' nor in the case of a wife 'Ambassadress'.

ARCHBISHOP—(1) The Most Rev The Lord Archbishop of York. Or, The Most Rev John Smith, Lord Archbishop of York. (2) Your Grace or My Lord Archbishop, conclude I am Your Grace's Obedient Servant. (3) Dear Archbishop, conclude Yours sincerely. The Archbishops of Canterbury and York are Privy Counsellors and are therefore addressed as The Most Reverend and Right Honourable.

BARON—(1) The Lord Barton. (2) My Lord, conclude I am, My Lord, Your Obedient Servant. (3) Dear Lord Barton, conclude Yours sincerely.

BARONESS IN HER OWN RIGHT OR BARON'S WIFE—(1) The Lady Barton or, in the case of Baronesses in their own right, most prefer to be styled The Baroness Barton. (2) Dear Madam, conclude Yours faithfully. (3) Dear Lady Barton or Dear Baroness Barton, conclude Yours sincerely.

BARONETS—(1) Sir John Smith, Bt. (the abbreviation Bart. is not much used today but is not incorrect). (2) Dear Sir, conclude Yours faithfully. (3) Dear Sir John, conclude Yours sincerely.

BISHOP WITH A SEAT IN THE HOUSE OF LORDS—(1) The Right Reverend The Lord Bishop of Buxton. Or, The Right Reverend John Smith, Lord Bishop of Buxton. (2) My Lord Bishop, conclude I am, My Lord, Your Obedient Servant. (3) Dear Lord Bishop, Dear Bishop or Dear Bishop of Buxton, conclude Yours sincerely. The Lord is not used for Bishops not sitting in the Lords. Bishops suffragan are addressed by courtesy in the same way as diocesan bishops.

COUNTESS—(1) The Countess of Poole. (2) Dear Madam, conclude Yours faithfully. (3) Dear Lady Poole, conclude Yours sincerely.

DAME—(1) Dame Mary Smith, followed by appropriate post-nominal letters (e.g. DBE). (2) Dear Madam, conclude Yours faithfully. (3) Dear Dame Mary, conclude Yours sincerely.

DUCHESS—(1) Her Grace The Duchess of Avon. (2) Your Grace, conclude I am, Your Grace's Obedient Servant. (3) Dear Duchess of Avon, conclude Yours sincerely.

DUKE—(1) His Grace The Duke of Avon. (2) Your Grace, or My Lord Duke, conclude I am, Your Grace's Obedient Servant. (3) Dear Duke of Avon, conclude Yours sincerely.

EARL—(1) The Earl of Hethe. (2) My Lord, conclude I am my Lord Your Obedient Servant. (3) Dear Lord Hethe, conclude Yours sincerely.

GOVERNORS GENERAL, GOVERNORS AND LIEUTENANT GOVERNORS—As for Ambassadors but followed by description of office, such as Governor General and Commander-in-Chief of New Zealand. (3) Dear Governor General, Governor or Lieutenant-Governor, conclude Yours sincerely. The Lieutenant-Governors of Guernsey, Jersey and the Isle of Man enjoy this style. The Governor General of Canada has the style 'The Right Honourable' for life and a Lieutenant-Governor of a Canadian Province is 'His Honour' for life.

JUDGE (LORD JUSTICE OF APPEAL) —(1) The Right Honourable Sir John Smith, as he is invariably a

Privy Counsellor and a Knight, or the Right Honourable Lord Justice Smith. (2) My Lord, conclude I am My Lord, Your Obedient Servant. (3) Dear Sir John, conclude Yours sincerely.

JUDGE (JUSTICE OF THE HIGH COURT) —(1) The Honourable Sir John Smith, as he is invariably a Knight, or The Honourable Mr Justice Smith. (2) and (3) as for a Lord Justice of Appeal.

JUDGE (CIRCUIT JUDGE) —(1) His Honour Judge Smith. (2) Your Honour, conclude I have the honour to be Your Honour's Obedient Servant. (3) Dear Sir (or Judge Smith), conclude Yours sincerely.

JUDGE (WOMEN JUDGES) —(1) The Right Honourable Dame Ann Smith, DBE (if a Lord of Appeal), The Honourable Dame Anne Smith, DBE (if a High Court Judge). (2) and (3) as for a male Judge with suitable gender changes.

KNIGHT—(1) Sir John Smith, if a Knight Bachelor there is no post-nominal addition in this respect but if a Knight or Knight Grand Cross or Grand Commander of an Order of Chivalry the appropriate post-nominal letters should be added. A Knight may be so addressed when his knighthood is announced, there is now no need to wait for the accolade to have been conferred. (2) Dear Sir, conclude Yours faithfully. (3) Dear Sir John, conclude Yours sincerely.

LORD LIEUTENANT—(1) The normal form of address, followed by, for courtesy, H.M.'s Lord Lieutenant for the County of Newshire. (2) My Lord Lieutenant, conclude I have the honour to be my Lord Lieutenant, Your Obedient Servant. (3) Dear Lord (Sir John or Mr. as appropriate), conclude Yours sincerely.

LORD OF SESSION IN SCOTLAND—(1) The Honourable (or Right Honourable if a Privy Counsellor), Lord Glentie. (2) My Lord, conclude I have the honour to be My Lord, Your Obedient Servant. (3) Dear Lord Glentie, conclude Yours sincerely. Note: The wife of a Lord of Session is styled as the wife of a Baron but her children have no courtesy titles. The Lord Justice General or Lord Justice Clerk is usually so addressed in correspondence, rather than by his juridical title.

MEMBER OF WELSH PARLIAMENT—Address according to rank with the addition of the letters MS after the name.

MEMBER OF NORTHERN IRELAND ASSEMBLY—Address according to rank with the addition of the letters MLA after the name.

MEMBER OF PARLIAMENT—(1) Address according to rank with the addition of the letters MP after the name. Privy Counsellors have the prefix 'The Right Honourable'. Letters to Ministers may start Dear Minister.

MEMBER OF SCOTTISH PARLIAMENT—Address according to rank with the addition of the letters MSP after the name.

PRIME MINISTER—The Prime Minister has the prefix 'The Right Honourable', as a Member of the Privy Council and the letters MP after the name, as a Member of Parliament. Letters to the Prime Minister may start Dear Prime Minister.

PRINCE—(1) HRH The Prince Henry of Wales or, if a Duke, HRH The Duke of Kent; the children of the Sovereign use the definite article before Prince (e.g. The Prince Edward). (2) Your Royal Highness or Sir, conclude I have the honour to be Your Royal Highness's Obedient Servant. In conversation address as Your Royal Highness but once is sufficient, thereafter Sir is normal.

PRINCESS—(1) HRH Princess Beatrice of York, or, if the wife of a Royal Duke, HRH The Duchess of Kent; a daughter of the Sovereign uses the definite article before Princess (e.g. The Princess Anne). (2) Your Royal Highness or Madam, conclude I have the honour to be Your Royal Highness's Obedient Servant. In conversation address as Your Royal Highness but once is sufficient, thereafter Ma'am (pronounced so as to rhyme with lamb) is normal.

PRIVY COUNSELLOR—(1) The Right Honourable prefixes the name and style except in respect of Marquesses and Dukes when the letters PC are placed after the name. The letters follow those indicating membership of Orders of Chivalry. (2) Address according to rank. (See also Member of Parliament).

QUEEN—(1) Her Majesty the Queen, although letters are usually addressed to The Private Secretary to Her Majesty the Queen. (2) Your Majesty or 'May it please your Majesty', conclude I have the honour to be Your Majesty's Obedient Subject. (3) Madam, conclude With my humble duty to Your Majesty. In conversation address as Your Majesty at first thereafter as Ma'am (see Princess).

Parliamentary Terms and Proceedings

For further details see Dod's *Handbook of House of Commons Procedure* by Paul Evans (8th edition, 2012) and Dod's *Handbook of House of Lords Procedure* by Mary Robertson and Thomas Elias (2nd edition, 2006).

References in ***bold italics*** have entries of their own.

accounting officer: the person (usually the permanent secretary of a government department or chief executive of an agency) responsible for accounting to Parliament, in respect of each of the ***Estimates*** (or part of such Estimate), for the resources voted by Parliament for the public service.

address: a motion for an address usually involves either House asking for some matter or request to be communicated to the sovereign.

adjournment motion: although technically a motion moved for the purpose of bringing to a conclusion a sitting, when it is rarely debated, such a motion is often used as a procedural device in the Commons for enabling a debate to take place without having to come to a conclusion in terms (see also ***general debate***).

adjournment debate: a debate on an ***adjournment motion*** (see also ***daily adjournment*** and ***general debate***).

affirmation: see ***oath***.

allocation of time motion: see ***guillotine***.

allotted days: in the Commons, the days allotted to debate a bill under a programme order or a guillotine, also the 20 days allotted each session as opposition days and the 35 days allotted in each session to **backbench business**.

ambit: the description of the scope of expenditure covered by an ***Estimate*** for moneys voted by Parliament for the public services (see also ***appropriation*** and ***Estimates***).

amendment: a proposal to change the terms of a motion or to alter a ***bill***.

annunciator: the television screens situated around Parliament and its precincts on which details of the current proceedings and future business of either House are shown.

appropriation: the allocation of money by Parliament to specified purposes. The Resource Accounts are the ***Comptroller & Auditor General***'s audited accounts showing that money has been spent in accordance with Parliament's instructions embodied in the ***Supply and Appropriation Acts*** (see also ***Consolidated Fund*** and ***Estimates***).

backbench: the backbenches are the places where Members who are not government Ministers or official opposition ***shadows*** sit in each Chamber, hence *backbencher*, the term used to describe a Member who holds no official position in government or in his or her party and who is therefore not bound by the convention of collective responsibility: such a Member may more formally be referred to as a private Member though, strictly speaking, this term applies to any Member not in receipt of a ministerial salary.

backbench business: in the Commons there are 35 days in each session allotted to business which is chosen by the ***Backbench Business Committee*** (27 in the main Chamber and 8 – in the form of 16 Thursday afternoon sessions – in Westminster Hall) which is not government business, ***opposition days*** or private Members' business.

Backbench Business Committee: the committee of the Commons of seven ***backbench*** Members elected by secret ballot of the whole House which is charged with choosing the business to be taken on the days allotted to ***backbench business***.

ballot: the term is used in the House of Commons to refer to the draw for private Members' bills. There is also provision for secret ballots in the House's proceedings relating to the election of its ***Speaker***, the ***Deputy Speakers***, the ***Backbench Business Committee*** and the Chairs of the principal ***select committees***.

Bar of the House: in the Commons, the line across the floor of the Chamber which marks its formal threshold: the Bar is also marked by a rail (now invariably retracted) to which, in former times, ***strangers*** might be summoned to address the House or to be arranged before it: in the Lords, this bar (about waist height) is where Members of the Commons stand to hear the **Queen's Speech** at the State Opening and on **prorogation**.

bill: a proposal for legislation formally presented to either House of Parliament; a bill may be a ***private bill*** or a ***public bill***.

Black Rod: the Gentleman Usher of the Black Rod, a member of the royal household, the broad equivalent in the Lords of the ***Serjeant at Arms***, responsible for the security of the House and sent to summon the Commons to the Lords at the opening and closing of ***sessions***.

book entry: in the Commons, an entry in the ***Votes and Proceedings*** which records as a procedural event something which occurred without any actual proceedings taking place on the floor of the House.

breach of privilege: an abuse of one of the privileges of either House or an attempt to impede or frustrate either House or one of their Members in the exercise of one of their privileges.

budget resolutions: the series of financial resolutions, passed by the House of Commons at the conclusion of the debate on the ***budget statement***, on which the ***Finance Bill*** is founded.

budget statement: the annual statement made by the Chancellor of the Exchequer (usually in October) setting out the government's tax and spending plans and proposals for their reconciliation for the forthcoming financial year: at the end of the debate on the budget, the ***budget resolutions*** are passed and the ***Finance Bill*** is introduced.

business motion: a motion proposing to regulate the time available to the Commons for consideration of a specified item of business at a specified sitting; in the Lords, a business of the House motion is moved by the Leader of the House to allow its standing orders to be suspended or varied or to make other arrangements for organising debates.

business question: in the Commons, the question addressed each Thursday to the ***Leader of the House*** under the urgent question procedure in reply to which the main items of business to be taken on each sitting day for the next week or so are announced.

by-election: an election in a single constituency to fill a vacancy caused by the death or ***disqualification***, etc. of a Member of Parliament (or in the Lords, to fill a vacancy amongst the elected hereditary peers).

C&AG: see ***Comptroller & Auditor General***.

Cabinet: the inner circle of the government to which the Minister in charge of each government department belongs (and certain other Ministers), presided over by the ***Prime Minister***.

casting vote: in the Commons, where any ***division*** (either in the House or in a ***general committee***) results in a tie, it is decided on the vote of the occupant of the Chair, which is given in accordance with precedent.

Central Lobby: the main public area of the Palace of Westminster, equidistant from the two Houses of Parliament, where members of the public are received by Members.

Chairman of Committees: in the Lords, the first Deputy Speaker and chairman of the panel of deputy speakers; also chairs the Committee of Selection, the Liaison Committee and the Procedure Committee, and has special responsibilities for ***private business*** and committees of the whole House. Now also known as the Senior Deputy Speaker.

Chairman of Ways and Means: in the Commons, the first Deputy Speaker, with particular responsibilities for ***private business*** and ***committees of the whole House*** and ***sittings in Westminster Hall***.

Chief Whip: the senior ***Whip*** in each party in each House: the government chief whips attend meetings of the Cabinet.

Chiltern Hundreds: the steward or bailiff of the three Chiltern Hundreds is the mythical 'office of profit under the Crown' to which Members of the Commons are appointed when wishing to resign their seats by disqualifying themselves from membership of the House (see ***disqualification***): the Stewardship of the Manor of Northstead is also used for this purpose.

Clandestine Outlawries Bill: the bill presented *proforma* in the Commons on the first day of each session; in the Lords the Select Vestries Bill; they each signify the right of Parliament to legislate on matters not included in the Queen's Speech.

Clerk Assistant: in each House, the second ***Clerk at the Table***, and first deputy to the ***Clerk of the House*** and the ***Clerk of the Parliaments***.

Clerks at the Table: the senior clerks in each Clerk of the House's Department who sit at the ***Table*** of the House.

Clerk of the House: the principal permanent officer of the House of Commons and principal adviser to the Speaker on the law, procedure and practice of the Commons; also the ***accounting officer*** for the House of Commons Vote.

Clerk of the Parliaments: the principal permanent officer of the House of Lords, and principal adviser to the Lord Speaker on the law, procedure and practice of the Lords. Also the House's ***accounting officer***.

closure: a procedural device for bringing a debate to a conclusion.

code of conduct: the codes adopted by each House to guide Members on questions relating to the interpretation of its resolutions in respect of the declarations in the ***Register of Members' Interests*** (***Register of Members' Financial Interests*** in the Commons), relating to financial and other relationships with outside persons and bodies.

command paper: a government publication (more often than not a ***White Paper***) presented to Parliament by 'command of Her Majesty'.

Commissioner for Standards: the officer of each House appointed to supervise the ***Register of Members' Financial Interests***, to advise Members on the interpretation of the ***code of conduct*** and to assist the ***Committee on Standards and Privileges*** in its work.

committal: the act of sending a ***bill*** to a committee of one kind or another after it has received a ***second reading***; in the Lords also called 'commitment'.

committee: see committee of the whole House, general committee, grand committee, joint committee, public bill committee, select committee.

Committee for Privileges and Conduct: in the Lords, the Committee which investigates allegations of breaches of privilege or contempts and peerage claims; it has a sub-committee on Lords' Conduct.

Committee of Selection: in the Commons, the committee which appoints Members to ***general committees*** and proposes Members to ***select committees***; in the Lords the committee which proposes Members to most select committees.

Committee on Standards: in the Commons, the select committee which investigates allegations of ***breaches of privilege***, ***contempts*** and, with the assistance of the ***Commissioner for Standards***, matters relating to the ***code of conduct***, in particular complaints about Members in relation to outside financial interests and related matters.

committee of the whole House: either House forms itself into a committee of all its Members when it decides to take the committee stage of a ***bill*** on the floor of the House.

committee stage: the next stage of a bill's progress after it has been given a ***second reading*** and committed; it is the stage at which a bill receives the most detailed examination. In the Commons, this generally takes place in a ***public bill committee***, sometimes in ***committee of the whole House***, and very occasionally in another type of committee. In the Lords, this may take place in committee of the whole House or in a Grand Committee, or very occasionally some other type of committee. After a bill has completed its committee stage it is reported back to the House for its ***report stage***.

Commons Amendments: amendments proposed by the Commons to a ***bill*** which has been sent to it by the Lords.

Comptroller & Auditor General: the officer of the House of Commons responsible for the running of the ***National Audit Office*** and for assisting the ***Public Accounts Committee*** in its scrutiny of public expenditure.

consideration: the more formal title for the ***report stage*** of a bill.

Consolidated Fund: the general fund into which almost all government receipts (in the form of taxes, duties, etc.) are paid (under section 10 of the Exchequer and Audit Act 1866) and out of which almost all government expenditure is met: Parliament passes the regular *Supply & Appropriation Bills* which appropriate to the government service out of the Fund the total sums voted for particular purposes by way of the ***Estimates***.

consolidation bill: a ***bill*** which consolidates much of the existing law on a particular subject into one convenient statute: because such bills do not (except within strict and very narrow limits) change the law, they are subject to special procedures distinct from the general procedures applying to public bills.

constituency: each Member of Parliament is elected by the voters in a single geographical division of the UK which is known as a constituency: each has a unique name given by the Boundary Commission, which also recommends the boundaries of each constituency and periodically reviews these. At present each has generally between 60,000 and 80,000 electors (though at the extremes there are wide variations for historical and geographical reasons). At present the UK is divided into 650 constituencies.

contempt: disobedience to, or defiance of, an order of either House, or some other insult to either House or its dignity or a ***breach of privilege***.

Crossbenches: Peers who do not take the Whip of any party in the House of Lords, otherwise 'independents', sit on the crossbenches which face the throne, and are known as 'Crossbench Peers'; however, not all independent peers join the group, which works as an administrative but not political collective. In the Commons those sitting on the few crossbenches are not recognised to speak by the Chair.

crown prerogative: essentially, prerogative actions are those which the executive may take without the sanction of Parliament: they include ***prorogation*** and ***dissolution*** of Parliament (though the latter is a statutory matter under the provisions in the 2011 Fixed-term Parliaments Act), the grant of honours, the declaration of war and, in some circumstances, the making of treaties with foreign governments.

CWH: see ***committee of the whole House***.

daily adjournment: the half-hour debate at the end of each day's sitting in the House of Commons at which a ***backbench*** Member has the opportunity to raise a matter with a Minister.

delegated legislation: legislation made by Ministers under powers granted to them in Acts of Parliament, usually by means of a ***statutory instrument***.

delegated legislation committees: in the Commons, the ***general committees*** which consider items of ***delegated legislation*** referred to them by the House.

departmental select committees: the select committees of the House of Commons established under standing orders to oversee the work of individual government departments.

Deputy Chairmen: the First and Second Deputy Chairmen of Ways and Means in the Commons, who with the ***Chairman of Ways and Means*** share with the ***Speaker*** the duties of presiding over the House. In the Lords, there is a panel of Deputy Chairmen who assist the ***Chairman of Committees***. There is a First Deputy Chairman (also known as the Principal Deputy Chairman of Committees), who chairs the European Union Committee.

Deputy Speakers: see **Chairman of Ways** and Means and **Deputy Chairmen**.

despatch box: two despatch boxes are situated at either side of the ***Table*** in each House and serve as lecterns for those leading debate (or answering questions) from the government and official opposition frontbenches.

dilatory motion: in the Commons a motion for the adjournment of debate or for the adjournment of the House or a committee moved for the purpose of superseding the business in hand.

Director General of the House of Commons: the officer responsible for the delivery of services to Members and the public.

Director of Parliamentary Broadcasting: the officer of both Houses responsible for day to day oversight of the broadcasting of their proceedings.

disqualification: there are a large number of offices the holding of which disqualify a person from sitting as a Member of the House of Commons. Broadly speaking these fall within the general disqualifying category of 'offices of profit under the Crown', though the holders of ministerial office (up to a maximum of 95) are exempt (see also ***Chiltern Hundreds***). There are also general disqualifications for civil servants, police officers, members of the armed forces, some judges and members of non-Commonwealth overseas legislatures. Also disqualified, in general terms, are persons ineligible to vote in a general election, for example Peers entitled to sit in the House of Lords, aliens, persons under the age of 18, sentenced prisoners and persons detained under the Mental Health Act. So too are bankrupts, under the Insolvency Act 1986. Members may also be disqualified after an election for breach of electoral law. In the Lords, peers under the age of 21, aliens, bankrupts and those convicted of treason are disqualified from membership.

dissolution: under the terms of the fixed-term Parliaments Act of 2011 dissolution normally takes place 17 days before the date fixed by statute for the next general election (the first Thursday in May in the fifth year following the last general election) unless an earlier dissolution is triggered by either a vote of two-thirds of the Members of the House of Commons or a vote of no confidence in the government followed by a failure to express confidence in a new government within a fortnight.

division: a vote, that is the means by which either House or one of their committees ascertains the number of Members for and against a proposition before it when the Chair's opinion as to which side is in the majority on a ***Question*** is challenged. A division in the House of Commons on a question which might otherwise take place after the moment of interruption may, in certain circumstances, be automatically deferred; deferred divisions are then taken by collecting voting papers from members on the following Wednesday afternoon.

division bell area: the area from within which it is deemed to be possible to reach the ***division lobbies*** within the period from the ringing of the ***division bells*** to the closing of the lobby doors during a ***division***.

division bells: the bells, situated in the House and its precincts and outbuildings which are rung to summon Members to vote in a ***division***. Their function has been largely superseded off the premises by electronic devices, activated by the ***Whips*** offices.

division lobbies: the lobbies running down either side of each Chamber through which Members must pass to register their votes in a ***division***.

draft bill: a bill presented to Parliament, and published more generally, in draft form (usually as a ***command paper***), to enable consultation on its form and contents to take place before a **bill** is formally introduced into one or other House; the number published has increased in recent years though not steadily; they are now regularly referred to a joint committee or taken up by a select committee for consideration and report.

early day motions: expressions of opinion by Members of the Commons on almost any subject which are published in the form of motions printed in the Notice Paper part of the ***Vote Bundle***, to which other Members may add their names to indicate support. They are not debated.

Ecclesiastical Committee: the statutory committee of Members of both Houses which considers Church of England ***Measures***.

Editor: the officer of the House of Commons in charge of the publication of the ***Official Report*** of debates in the Chamber and in ***general committees*** (aka ***Hansard***). The Lords has its own Hansard, overseen by the Editor of Debates.

EDM: see ***early day motions***.

Electoral Commission: the statutory body established under the Political Parties, Elections and Referendums Act 2000 which has wide-ranging responsibilities in respect of the conduct of elections and referendums and the registration of political parties and related matters. Its funding and work are overseen by a statutory committee of elected parliamentarians called the Speaker's Committee on the Electoral Commission.

English Votes for English Laws (EVEL): To account for the discrepancies caused by devolution and the so-called West Lothian question, a law was passed allowing a committee of MPs from English (or English and Welsh) constituencies to consent to or veto any Bills which would only affect England (or England and Wales).

Erskine May: Erskine May's *Treatise on the Law, Privileges, Proceedings and Usage of Parliament*, first published by the-then Assistant Librarian and subsequently ***Clerk of the House***, Thomas Erskine May in 1844, and revised by his successors as Clerk ever since: it is acknowledged as the authoritative text book on the law and practice of both Houses of Parliament.

Estimates: the form in which the government presents, for approval by the Commons, its requests for the resources needed to cover recurring public expenditure.

Estimates days: the three days in each session set aside in the Commons for consideration of the Estimates, in practice used for debate on one or more select committee reports chosen by the ***Liaison Committee***.

European Committees: in the Commons, the group of ***general committees*** which consider documents referred to them by the European Scrutiny Committee relating to the EU.

Examiner of Petitions: the officer of each House with responsibility for examining certain matters relating to private bills and hybrid bills for compliance with the standing orders relating to ***private business***.

exempted business: business which, under standing orders or under a specific order of the House of Commons, may be carried on after the ***moment of interruption***.

Father of the House: see ***Senior Member***.

Finance Bill: the annual bill, founded on the ***budget resolutions***, which embodies the government's statutory power to levy most taxes and duties, and which may include other provisions relating to taxes management.

financial privilege: the right to approve proposals for taxation or for government expenditure which the Commons asserts as its exclusive privilege, not shared with the Lords.

financial resolutions: the collective term for ***money resolutions***, ***ways and means resolutions***, and supply resolutions.

first reading: the formal first stage of a ***bill***'s progress, which occurs without debate or vote after it has been introduced to either House.

frontbench: the frontbenches are where Ministers and their official opposition ***shadows*** sit in each Chamber, hence *frontbencher* or *frontbench spokesman* (in the Commons the government frontbench is also known as the *Treasury Bench*).

general committees: the family of committees in the Commons (known until recently as "standing committees") which proceed principally by debate rather than inquiry; it includes ***delegated legislation committees***, ***European Committees***, ***grand committees*** and ***public bill committees***.

general debate: debates of a general nature which take place on the motion "that this House has considered [a specified matter]"; the motion is not amendable.

general election: an event initiated by the ***dissolution*** of Parliament under the provisions within the Fixed-term Parliaments Act 2011, when all seats are automatically vacated and elections must be held in each ***constituency*** to elect a Member of Parliament.

grand committees: in the Commons there are three grand committees for Scotland, Wales and Northern Ireland; they are general committees on which all Members having their constituency in the relevant country have an automatic place; in the case of Wales and Northern Ireland additional members from outside those countries may be added; the grand committees generally debate matters (including legislative proposals) relevant to the specific country; they may also conduct other types of proceedings including oral questions and statements. They sometimes meet away from Westminster. The term has a different meaning in the House of Lords, where it is applied to any proceedings of a ***committee of the whole House*** held in parallel with sittings in the main chamber.

guillotine: an order of the House of Commons which limits the time available to debate any stage or stages of a bill, now largely superseded by ***programme*** orders.

Hansard: the colloquial name for the ***Official Report***, the publication containing the accurate and full (though not strictly verbatim as often claimed) reports of what is said and done in the debates of each House and their committees (other than select committees).

health service commissioner: the officer of the House of Commons who acts as the ombudsman for the NHS in England who also holds the office of ***PCA*** and who reports to the Public Administration Select Committee: there are separate commissioners for Wales and Scotland reporting to the devolved legislatures.

House of Commons Commission: the executive body of Members responsible for the running of the House.

House of Lords Commission: Senior Committee to provide high-level strategic and political direction for the House.

Individual Voter Registration: Since 2014 the 'household registration' system has been replaced so each person is responsible for registering themselves, and have to provide identifying information such as national insurance number for verification during the process.

insistence: when one House insists on its own version of the text of a bill or amendment during the exchange of messages ('ping pong') without offering an alternative or compromise.

instruction: after ***committal*** of a bill, either House may give an instruction to any committee to which it is committed to do certain things that the committee might not otherwise be empowered to do.

Joint Committee on Human Rights: a joint select committee of both Houses charged with examining bills, ***remedial orders*** and other matters relating to human rights in the UK.

joint committees: select committees which include Members of both Houses.

Journals: the ***Votes and Proceedings*** of the House of Commons and the ***Minute*** of the House of Lords are each consolidated into the Journals on a sessional basis and these form the authoritative record of the decisions of each House.

law commissions: the law commissions for England and Wales and for Scotland prepare proposals for reform of the law and also for its rationalisation by means of ***consolidation bills*** and statute law repeal bills.

Leader of the House: the Cabinet Minister charged with special responsibility for the management of the House of Commons and its business, part of the ***usual channels***. He or she is a member, *ex officio*, of the ***House of Commons Commission***. He or she also has responsibility for the cabinet committees dealing with the management of the Government's legislative programme. His or her name will frequently appear on motions relating to the business of the House, and he or she will initiate government proposals for the reform of its procedures. His or her most public role is the period of questioning which, each Thursday, follows the ***business question***. The Leader of the House of Lords is also a minister in the Cabinet and has similar responsibilities to those of the Leader of the Commons except that he or she also has a responsibility to the House as well as a responsibility to the Government.

leader of the opposition: the person elected leader of the second largest party in the House of Commons is the leader of the official opposition. He or she receives official recognition in this role in the receipt of a ministerial salary and appointment to the Privy Council. The leader of the opposition has certain well-entrenched conventional rights to initiate certain kinds of business, in particular to demand, and to expect in most circumstances to receive, an opportunity to move a motion of no confidence in the Government. He or she also has certain rights under standing orders (see ***official opposition***). In the Lords, the Leader of the Opposition is the leader of the second largest party in the Commons. He or she receives a salary.

leave: there are a number of types of proceeding which may only be done by leave of the House (or a committee). These include to speak more than once to a Question other than in committee, to withdraw a motion before the House or a committee and to move certain types of motion. Generally leave must be unanimous, that is, any single objection from any Member in the House or in a committee means that leave is thereby denied.

Liaison Committee: in the Commons the select committee consisting mainly of the Chairs of other select committees, which under standing orders has certain powers and duties in relation to the proceedings of the House, as well as a more informal role exercising oversight of the work, and as an advocate of the interests, of select committees in general. It also has a power to examine the Prime Minister on matters of public policy, and certain duties relating to National Policy Statements proposed to be made under the Planning Act 2008. The Lords also has a Liaison Committee, chaired by the Chairman of Committees, which oversees the work of its committees.

lobby correspondents: certain representatives of the various news media who have the authority of the ***Serjeant at Arms*** to enter the ***Members' Lobby*** when the House of Commons is sitting and who enjoy certain other privileges of access to areas of the Palace otherwise closed to persons apart from Members and permanent staff. They also subscribe to a code of conduct relating to the disclosure of the sources of their information (hence the expression 'on lobby terms').

Lord Speaker: Speaker of the House of Lords, having taken the role over from the Lord Chancellor in 2006. Elected by the House from amongst its Members.

Lords Amendments: the amendments proposed by the Lords to a ***bill*** which has been passed by the Commons.

Lords Commissioners: the Peers appointed by the Queen to deliver her ***proclamation*** proroguing Parliament and her ***royal assent*** to Acts agreed just before ***prorogation*** and any other Commission she chooses to send.

Loyal Address: the motion moved in reply to the ***Queen's Speech*** on which the debate on the Queen's Speech takes place.

Mace: the symbol of the Crown's authority in Parliament, which is displayed in each House whenever the House is in session.

maiden speech: the first speech delivered by a Member after he or she first enters the House. By convention, in the Commons, it includes a tribute to his or her predecessor, an encomium to his or her ***constituency***, and avoids controversy (though this latter tradition shows signs of dying out). Also, by tradition, it is heard without interruption from other Members. The latter two points apply also to maiden speeches in the House of Lords.

manuscript amendment: an amendment of which no ***notice*** has been given, which (in the Commons) is presented to the Chair during debate or (in the Lords) is circulated to Members in manuscript or typescript form.

marshalled list: a list of ***amendments*** proposed to a ***bill*** which has been arranged in the order in which the amendments will be considered at ***committee stage***, ***report stage*** or, in the Lords, third reading, rather than in the order in which they were received.

Measure: legislation made by the General Synod of the Church of England.

Member in charge: the Member in charge of a bill is the one who introduces it to the House, and he or she has certain prerogatives in relation to that bill. In the case of a government bill, any Minister (including a ***Whip***) may exercise the rights of the Member in charge.

Members' lobby: the area immediately outside the Commons Chamber generally reserved to Members and ***lobby correspondents*** and staff of the House when the House is sitting. The equivalent in the Lords is the 'Peers Lobby'.

Minister: a member of the government, usually entitled to receive a ministerial salary and bound by the convention of collective responsibility for decisions of government. For procedural purposes, the members of the government (including ***Whips***) are each regarded as being able to act on behalf of any other Minister.

Minute: the document produced after each sitting of the House of Lords recording decisions taken at that sitting and also setting out future business, questions for written answers and other information on the progress of procedural business.

moment of interruption: the time set by standing orders in the House of Commons at which the main business of a day's sitting normally ends after which business may only be taken if it is ***exempted business*** or unopposed business. Currently the moment of interruption is 10 pm on Mondays and Tuesdays, 7 pm on Wednesdays, 6 pm on Thursdays and 2.30 pm on Fridays.

money bill: a bill which is concerned exclusively with raising or spending public money and which, under the terms of the ***Parliament Acts***, cannot be amended by the Lords.

money resolution: a ***resolution*** of the House of Commons, agreed on a motion which may only be moved by a ***Minister***, authorising the provisions of a ***bill*** which entail novel forms of public expenditure.

naming: a Member who persistently defies the authority of the Chair in the House of Commons may be *named* by the Chair, which immediately causes a motion to be moved to suspend the Member from the service of the House.

National Audit Office: the office under the direction of the ***Comptroller & Auditor General*** which audits the expenditure of government departments.

National Policy Statement Committee: a select committee designated by the Commons ***Liaison Committee*** to consider a proposal for a National Policy Statement which a Minister has laid before the House under 5.9 of the Planning Act 2008. It has between 7 and 14 members drawn from the Housing, Communities and Local Government; Health and Social Care; Environmental Audit; Environment, Food and Rural Affairs; Transport and Welsh Affairs Committees.

Northstead, Manor of: see ***Chiltern Hundreds***.

notice: where it is a requirement of standing orders or the rules of the House that a motion requires notice, it means that such a motion cannot be moved unless it appears on the ***Order Paper***. In most circumstances, the latest time for giving notice of a motion to appear on a Paper for the next sitting day is the rising of the House on the previous day. While there is no formal requirement for notice of amendments to bills in committee or on report, the Chair will generally not select ***manuscript amendments*** or ***starred amendments*** for debate. This does not apply in the Lords where manuscript amendments may be moved on Committee and at Report stage without notice. Written notice is required of oral and written ***PQ***s except ***urgent questions*** (Private Notice Questions in the Lords) and ***topical questions*** in the Commons. In the Commons, but not in the Lords, notice is required of presentation of bills.

Notice Paper: the blue pages of the **Vote Bundle** include the Notice Papers for notices of questions, notices of motions for future days, notices of early day motions and notices of amendments to bills.

oath: on their election at a general election or a ***by-election***, each Member of the Commons is required to take the parliamentary oath or to make the required affirmation before taking his or her seat. Witnesses before a committee of the House may also be required to take an oath before giving evidence, though this requirement is generally only imposed on witnesses before a private bill committee. In the Lords, Members take the oath on their first introduction and at the start of each ***session***.

official opposition: the Party with the second largest number of Members in the House of Commons is the official opposition, a status which gains it certain privileges by long-standing convention (such as the right of its official spokespeople to sit on the ***frontbench*** and to address the House from the ***despatch box***) as well as certain rights under the standing orders (to initiate debate on the majority of ***opposition days***) and by statute (such as for certain of its officers to receive ministerial salaries). To an extent, the privileges are shared by members of that same party in the House of Lords.

Official Report: see ***Hansard***.

ombudsman: see ***Parliamentary Commissioner for Administration***.

opposition days: the 20 days each session set aside under standing orders of the House of Commons on which the opposition parties have the right to choose the business for debate.

oral question: see ***PQ***.

order: when either House agrees a motion that something should happen (such as a bill being set down for a second reading or for consideration) it becomes an order of the House (see also ***resolution***). The word is also commonly used in the House of Commons to connote procedural regularity (as in the expression 'in order') or to correct parliamentary behaviour (as in the Chair's call of 'Order, order', which is also used as a form of oral procedural 'punctuation'). In the Lords the word "undesirable" has the same meaning as "out of Order" in the Commons.

Order Paper: the paper, published each sitting day (except the first day of a ***session***), which lists the business of each House and for any sitting in Westminster Hall (or in a Grand Committee of the Lords) for that day, as well as ***parliamentary questions*** (PQs) for oral answer to be asked that day,

PQs for written answer that day, and certain other items such as notices of ***written statements,*** committee notices, ***remaining orders*** (in the Commons) and lists of future business.

Outlawries Bill: see ***Clandestine Outlawries Bill***.

PAC: see ***Public Accounts Committee***.

Parliament Acts: the Parliament Act 1911 as amended and supplemented by the Parliament Act 1949 restrict the powers of the Lords to amend ***money bills*** or reject or delay other ***bills*** agreed by the Commons.

Panel of Chairs: in the Commons, the body of Members appointed by the ***Speaker*** from among whom he chooses the Chair of each ***general committee***. They receive an additional payment for this work. In the Lords, there is a panel of Deputy Chairmen who assist the ***Chairman of Committees***.

Parliamentary Commissioner for Administration: the officer of the House of Commons appointed under statute to investigate complaints of maladministration leading to injustice in the public service, commonly known as the ombudsman. His or her work is overseen by the Public Administration Select Committee (see also ***health service commissioner***).

Parliamentary Commissioner for Standards: see ***Commissioner for Standards***.

Parliamentary Counsel: the civil servants (all lawyers) who draft ***bills*** on the instruction of the government, not to be confused with the ***Speaker's Counsel*** or Counsel of the Chairman of Committees or other lawyers working directly to either House.

parliamentary question: a question addressed (generally) to a Minister for answer orally on the floor of the House at question time, or in writing in ***Hansard***.

PCA: see ***Parliamentary Commissioner for Administration.***

PNQ: see ***urgent question***.

PQ: see ***parliamentary question***.

point of order: properly, a request by a Member of the Commons to the Chair for elucidation of, or a ruling on, a question of procedure, but not infrequently misused by Members who do not have the floor of the House or of a committee to interrupt proceedings for other purposes.

prayers: each sitting of each House begins with prayers, conducted by the Speaker's Chaplain in the Commons or a Bishop in the Lords. The term is also used colloquially to describe a motion to annul a ***statutory instrument*** subject to negative resolution procedure; and to designate the final paragraph of a ***public petition***.

prerogative: see ***Crown prerogative***.

press gallery: the gallery of the Chamber of the Commons above and behind the Speaker's Chair reserved to accredited representatives of the various news media, also used more generally to describe the large area outside and behind this gallery given over to the use of journalists etc. and also to describe collectively the accredited members of the press gallery (see also ***lobby correspondents***). In the Lords there is a much smaller Press Gallery, at the far end from the Throne.

Prime Minister: the First Lord of the Treasury and the head of the government; the person who is elected the leader of the party which can sustain a majority (either alone or in coalition) in the Commons.

Prince of Wales's consent: see ***Queen's consent***.

private bill: a bill to confer on individuals, or more commonly corporate bodies of one kind or another, powers in excess of or in contradiction to the general law.

private business: the business of each House for the most part relating directly or indirectly to ***private bills***.

private Member's bill: a ***public bill*** introduced to either House by a Member who is not a ***Minister***.

private notice question: the former name for what is now called an ***urgent question*** in the Commons. The term is still used in the House of Lords.

privilege: a privilege enjoyed by either House collectively or its Members individually in excess of the general law, which enables it or them to fulfil the functions and duties of the House.

Privy Counsellor: a Member of the Queen's Privy Council, the body of senior royal advisers which in former times was something equivalent to the ***Cabinet***, membership of which is now conferred automatically on Cabinet Ministers and also on certain senior judges; it is also by convention granted to the leaders of parties of any size in the Commons and is occasionally conferred as a mark of honour on senior backbenchers and occasionally others outside these circles. The Council retains certain judicial functions and residual executive functions. Membership once conferred is for life, unless withdrawn. It entitles the holder to the courtesy of the title 'Right Honourable' as in 'the Right Honourable Member for Witney'. In written form this is usually abbreviated to 'Rt Hon'.

Procedure Committee: ***select committees*** of each House appointed to consider proposals for the reform of their procedures.

proclamation: the Queen issues proclamations for the **prorogation** and summoning Parliament.

programme: an order made by the House of Commons after a ***bill***'s ***second reading*** to timetable the subsequent proceedings on that bill.

prorogation: the end of a ***session***.

Public Accounts Commission: the statutory committee of elected parliamentarians which has oversight of the ***National Audit Office***.

Public Accounts Committee: the ***select committee*** of the House of Commons, which works closely with the ***Comptroller & Auditor General*** and the ***National Audit Office***, with particular responsibility for ensuring propriety, efficiency, economy and effectiveness in the spending of public money.

public bill: a proposal for legislation to change the general law; most bills introduced into either House by the government or by private Members are public bills; a minority are ***private bills***.

public bill committee: in the Commons the ***committee stage*** of proceedings on a public bill is usually taken in a public bill committee (until recently a 'standing committee'). Each committee is appointed *ad hoc* to consider each bill and ceases to exist once that bill is reported back to the House. Public bill committees are ***general committees***, but exceptionally in this category, they have power to take written and oral evidence from witnesses, in the manner of ***select committees***, at some of their sittings.

Public Bill Office: the office in each House with particular responsibility for the management of legislation and (in the Commons) for clerking the ***public bill committees*** and other ***general committees*** of the House.

public gallery: the gallery of each Chamber in which members of the public may sit to observe its proceedings; there is also an area designated for the same purpose in each committee room and at ***sittings in Westminster Hall***.

public petition: a petition to either House (but generally to the Commons) for redress of a grievance or other relief.

Queen's consent: where the legislation proposed in a ***bill*** touches on the prerogatives or private interests of the Crown, her consent is required for the bill to proceed: this may be required to be given either before the ***second reading*** or ***third reading*** (or, conceivably, before ***first reading***), depending on the nature of the interest and the extent to which it is fundamental to the bill's purposes. Consent must be obtained from the Queen by a Minister and must be signified at the appropriate time by a ***Privy Counsellor***. The Prince of Wales's consent may also be required, as the heir to the throne, before certain bills may be debated at certain stages.

Queen's recommendation: only the government can propose increases in public expenditure and the recommendation of the 'Crown' is therefore required for a motion in the Commons which proposes to increase or widen the scope of public expenditure: such a motion can therefore be moved only by a Minister.

Queen's Speech: the speech read by the Queen from her throne in the Lords Chamber on the first day of each ***session*** setting out, among other matters, details of the government's proposed legislative programme.

question: see ***parliamentary question***.

Question: in procedural jargon, the matter before either House or a committee awaiting decision at any time.

Questions Book: a daily publication of the House of Commons divided into two parts: Part 1 lists all questions for written answer on that day, Part 2 lists all outstanding PQs for oral or written answer on future days.

question time: the period set aside for ***PQ***s to be asked and answered orally on the floor of either House.

quorum: The minimum number of members needed to be present at a sitting to make proceedings valid. The quorum of the House of Commons is 40 but only for divisions; the quorum for a ***sitting in Westminster Hall*** is three; the quorum of a ***general committee*** (except a ***European Committee***) is one-third of its members, with fractions rounded up; the quorum of a European Committee is three of its appointed members, not including the Chair; the quorum of a ***select committee*** is one-third of its membership or three, whichever is the greater, unless otherwise set out in the standing orders or its order of appointment. The quorum of the Lords is 30 for legislative business or otherwise three.

reasoned amendment: an amendment proposed to the motion to give a ***bill*** a ***second reading*** or ***third reading***.

recess: strictly speaking, the period when Parliament is prorogued; now used to refer to either House's regular holiday adjournments at Christmas, in February, at Easter, at Whitsun and in the summer.

Register of Members' Financial Interests: (in the Lords, Register of Members' Interests) the registers, in which Members of either House record their outside financial interests and the receipt of gifts, free travel, etc.

Registrar of Members' Financial Interests: (in the Lords, Registrar of Members' Interests) the officers of each House responsible for the maintenance of the ***Register of Members' Financial Interests***.

remaining orders: the list of forthcoming government business published with the ***Order Paper*** of the House of Commons each day.

remedial order: a form of ***delegated legislation*** which remedies an incompatibility between UK law and the European Convention on Human Rights.

report stage: the stage of a ***bill***'s progress in each House between its ***committee stage*** and its ***third reading***, at which further detailed amendments may be made.

resolution: when a motion is agreed by either House, it becomes a resolution (unless it is an ***order***).

resource accounts: the audited accounts of ***voted expenditure*** authorised by the ***Estimates***.

return: an answer or response to an address from either House for the deposit of same document.

royal assent: the Queen's assent to a ***bill*** agreed to by both Houses of Parliament is the final act which makes that bill an Act of Parliament.

royal recommendation: see ***Queen's recommendation***.

seconder: no seconder is required for a motion to be proposed to either House, but by tradition the motion for the ***Loyal Address*** is seconded.

second reading: the first stage at which a ***bill*** is debated (and possibly voted on) in each House.

select committees: committees established by either House to inquire into particular matters or subject areas and to report back their findings and recommendations. In the Commons most are appointed permanently, and have members who remain on them for a Parliament unless replaced (and for most of them their Chairs are separately elected by secret ballot of the whole House); some are appointed ad hoc and cease to exist once they have reported on the matter which the House has referred to them. In the Lords most committees are appointed each session. Members remain on them for several ***sessions*** but are subject to a rotation rule.

Select Vestries Bill – see ***Clandestine Outlawries Bill***.

Senior Member: the Member of the House of Commons who has the longest *continuous* period of service in the House, also known as the ***Father of the House***.

Serjeant at Arms: the officer of the House of Commons responsible for security and ceremonial.

session: the period between the state opening of Parliament and its prorogation or dissolution, in the past this has generally been a year running from November to November, but was often altered by the timing of general elections; the present government has indicated its intention to run sessions normally from May to April.

shadow: broadly speaking, the official opposition appoints or elects Members of its party to 'shadow' each government Minister, that is, to take particular responsibility for presenting in and out of Parliament the policies of the opposition for the areas which are that ***Minister***'s responsibility, hence 'Shadow Home Secretary' etc (also called *frontbench spokesperson, spokesmen or spokeswomen*).

shuffle: the process by which the ***PQ***s for oral answer in the Commons are randomly sorted to determine which Members' questions will be printed on the ***Order Paper*** on any given day, and in what order.

sitting: a single meeting of either House or one of their committees.

sittings in Westminster Hall: the 'parallel chamber' of the House of Commons which meets in the Grand Committee Room off Westminster Hall on Tuesdays, Wednesdays and Thursdays. On Tuesdays and Wednesdays it debates subjects chosen by ***backbench*** Members in timed slots of either an hour-and-a-half or half-an-hour; on Thursdays it debates reports from ***select committees*** chosen by the ***Liaison Committee***, or subjects selected by the ***Backbench Business Committee***, for three hours. No decisions are taken at sittings in Westminster Hall, and all its proceedings take place as ***adjournment debates***.

Speaker: the impartial presiding officer of the House of Commons: in the Lords the Lord Speaker and their deputies have far fewer formal powers than their Commons equivalents.

Speaker's Counsel: officers of the House who head its **legal services office**, including those lawyers providing legal advice to the **Speaker** and to certain of the committees of the House.

standing committee: see ***general committees***.

standing orders: the rules formulated by each House to regulate their own proceedings.

starred amendment: an amendment to a bill which has not appeared on a notice paper sufficiently before the sitting at which it is to be considered; as a rule, the Chair in the Commons will not select such an amendment for debate (see also ***notice***). No such problem arises in the Lords.

state opening: the occasion on the first day of each ***session*** on which the Queen usually attends in the House of Lords to deliver the ***Queen's Speech***.

statutory instruments: the form in which most ***delegated legislation*** is made.

strangers: the traditional and now obsolete appellation for anyone who is not a Member, officer or official of the House.

Supply and Appropriation Bills/Acts: the twice yearly Acts of Parliament which give statutory authority to the appropriations made by the House of Commons in agreeing the ***Estimates***.

supply resolution: one of the ***resolutions*** on which the ***Supply and Appropriation bills*** are founded.

Table: the Table of the House, situated between the government and opposition ***frontbenches***, in each House; in former times this was the place where motions, questions, reports etc. were delivered into the possession of the House *via* the Clerks, hence 'tabled' or 'laid upon the Table'.

Table Office: in the Commons the office, situated outside the Chamber of the Commons behind the Speaker's Chair, in which ***PQ***s and ***EDM***s are tabled; it also deals with all matters relating to the business on the floor of the House other than legislation. In the Lords, the office situated near the Prince's Chamber where all business is tabled (including questions) and where the ***Minute*** is compiled.

ten-minute-rule bill: a ***bill*** introduced into the Commons where the Member seeking the ***leave*** of the House to introduce the bill, and a Member who opposes granting it, may each make a short speech before the House comes to a decision on whether to allow the bill to proceed.

Test Roll: the Test Roll must be signed by each new Member after he or she has taken the ***oath*** or affirmed after being elected or appointed to either House.

third reading: the final stage of a whole ***bill***'s passage through either House, though Lords Amendments or Commons Amendments to the bill may subsequently be considered.

topical debate: a debate on a motion "That this House has considered [a specified matter]", on a topic chosen by the ***Backbench Business Committee***. It may last no more than 90 minutes and both frontbench and backbench speeches are time-limited.

topical questions: a procedure whereby the last few minutes of oral question time to particular Ministers are devoted to questions of which no notice needs to be given of the terms of the question; the choice of Members who have the opportunity to ask a topical question is determined by an electronic ballot (see ***shuffle***) of those who have entered their names for a particular question time in advance.

urgent question: an oral parliamentary question in the Commons asked with the consent of the Speaker without published ***notice*** relating to an urgent and important matter. In the Lords, called a ***Private Notice Question***, or PNQ.

usual channels: the colloquial name for the discussions about the business of each House which take place between the ***Whips*** and the Leaders of each House, and in the Lords sometimes (but not always) including the Convenor of the Crossbench Peers.

voted expenditure: the Commons' agreement to an ***Estimate*** followed by a ***Supply and Appropriation Act*** represents the detailed ***appropriation*** of public money to the public service by Parliament.

Votes and Proceedings: the daily minute of the Commons' proceedings.

Vote Bundle: the papers published each day on which the House of Commons sits, including among other things the ***Order Paper***, the ***remaining orders***, the ***Votes and Proceedings***, and the ***notice*** papers (in the Lords the ***Minute*** serves the same general purpose).

ways and means resolution: a ***resolution*** authorising a charge on the people, that is, for the most part, taxes and duties: the ***Finance Bill*** is founded on ways and means resolutions.

Westminster Hall: the oldest remaining part of the Palace of Westminster, now used solely as a public area and for occasional ceremonial purposes (see also ***sittings in Westminster Hall***.)

Whips: the officers of each party in each House with particular responsibilities for party management and organisation of the business of the House and its committees.

White Paper: a ***command paper*** embodying some statement of government policy, often including proposals for legislation.

writ: the issue of a writ is the formal process for initiating a **by-election** (or indeed a general election) in the Commons. In the Lords, new Members are summoned by writ, and all Members receive a writ of summons at the beginning of a new Parliament.

written statement: a vehicle which may be used by a ***minister*** to inform either House on various types of matter relating to his or her responsibilities; they are published in ***Hansard***.

Abbreviations

ABRO	Army Base Repair Organisation
ACA	Associate, Institute of Chartered Accountants
ACAS	Advisory, Conciliation and Arbitration Service
ACPO	Association of Chief Police Officers
ACRE	Action with Communities in Rural England
AcSS	Academy of Learned Societies for the Social Statistics
ADC	Aide-de-camp
AEEU	Amalgamated Engineering and Electrical Union
AEF	Amalgamated Union of Engineering and Foundry Workers
AEU	Amalgamated Engineering Union
AFC	Air Force Cross
AIB	Associate, Institute of Bankers
AIESC	Association Internationale des Étudiants en Sciences Économiques et Commerciales
ALDE	Alliance of Liberals and Democrats for Europe
All	Alliance Party of Northern Ireland
AM	Assembly Member (London Assembly)
AMP	Advanced Management Program; Air Member for Personnel
AO	Officer, Order of Australia
APEX	Association of Professional, Executive, Clerical and Computer Staff
ARA	Associate, Royal Academy
ARCM	Associate, Royal College of Music
ARCS	Associate, Royal College of Science
ARICS	Professional Associate, Royal Institution of Chartered Surveyors
ASBAH	Association for Spina Bifida and Hydrocephalus
ASLEF	Associated Society of Locomotive Engineers and Firemen
ATII	Associate Member, Incorporated Institute of Taxation
AUEW	Amalgamated Union of Engineering Workers
AWA	Abolish the Welsh Assembly Group
BA	Bachelor of Arts
BAFTA	British Academy of Film and Television Arts
BALPA	British Air Line Pilots' Association
BAOR	British Army on the Rhine
BChir	Bachelor of Surgery
BCL	Bachelor of Civil Law
BCom	Bachelor of Commerce
BD	Bachelor of Divinity
BDS	Business Development Service
BE	Bachelor of Engineering
BEc	Bachelor of Economics
BECTU	Broadcasting, Entertainment, Cinematograph and Theatre Union
BEd	Bachelor of Education
BEM	British Empire Medal
BFI	British Film Institute
BIC	British-Irish Council
BIGC	British-Irish Governmental Conference
BIS	Department for Business, Innovation and Skills
BLitt	Bachelor of Literature
BMA	British Medical Association
BMus	Bachelor of Music
BOAC	British Overseas Airways Corporation
BP	The Brexit Party; British Petroleum
Brexit All	Brexit Alliance
BS	Bachelor of Surgery
BSocSci	Bachelor of Social Science

Bt	Baronet
BT	British Telecom
BVC	Bar Vocational Course
CAFCASS	Children and Family Court Advisory and Support Service
CAFOD	Catholic Aid Fund for Overseas Development
CAMRA	Campaign for Real Ale
CAP	Common Agricultural Policy
CB	Companion of the Order of the Bath; Crossbench
CBC	County Borough Council
CBE	Commander of the Order of the British Empire
CBI	Confederation of British Industry
CBIM	Companion, British Institute of Management
CBRN	Chemical, Biological, Radiological and Nuclear
CCHQ	Conservative Party Campagn Headquarters
CCIM	Certified Commercial Investment Member
CCS	Carbon Capture and Storage
CDipAF	Certified Diploma in Accounting and Finance
CEFAS	Centre for Environment, Fisheries and Aquaculture Science
CEng	Chartered Engineer
CEOP	Child Exploitation and Online Protection
CERT	Carbon Emissions Reduction Target
Cert Ed	Certificate of Education
CESP	Community Energy Saving Programme
CFP	Common Fisheries Policy
CH	Companion of Honour
ChB	Bachelor of Surgery
ChM	Master of Surgery
CIE	Companion of the Order of the Indian Empire
CIMA	Chartered Institute of Management Accountants
CIMgt	Companion, Institute of Management
CIPFA	Chartered Institute of Public Finance and Accountancy
CIS	Institute of Chartered Secretaries and Administrators
CLP	Constituency Labour Party
CMEC	Child Maintenance and Enforcement Commission
CMG	Companion of the Order of St Michael and St George
CND	Campaign for Nuclear Disarmament
CoE	Church of England
COI	Central Office of Information
Con	Conservative Party
Con Ind	Conservative Independent
COPD	Chronic Obstructive Pulmonary Disease
CPA	Commonwealth Parliamentary Association; Christian Peoples Alliance
CPE	Common Professional Examination
CPhys	Chartered Physicist
CPRE	Campaign to Protect Rural England
CPS	Crown Prosecution Service
CPsychol	Chartered Psychologist
CQSW	Certificate of Qualification in Social Work
cr	Created
CSA	Child Support Agency; Chief Scentific Adviser
CSCE	Conference on Security and Co-operation in Europe
CSI	Committee on the Intelligence Services; Companion of the Order of the Star of India
CSL	Central Science Laboratory
CStJ	Commander, Most Venerable Order of the Hospital of St. John of Jerusalem
CVO	Commander of the Royal Victorian Order
CWU	Communication Workers Union

DARA	Defence Aviation Repair Agency
DASA	Defence Analytical Services Agency
DBA	Doctor of Business Administration
DBE	Dame Commander of the Order of the British Empire
DCB	Dame Commander of the Order of the Bath
DCL	Doctor of Civil Law
DCLG	Department for Communities and Local Government
DCM	Distinguished Conduct Medal
DCMG	Dame Commander of the Order of St Michael and St George
DCMS	Department for Digital, Culture, Media and Sport
DCSA	Defence Communication Services Agency
DCSF	Department for Children, Schools and Families
DCVO	Dame Commander of the Royal Victorian Order
DD	Doctor of Divinity
DECC	Department of Energy and Climate Change
DEFRA	Department of the Environment, Food and Rural Affairs
DFC	Distinguished Flying Cross
DFID	Department for International Development
DFM	Distinguished Flying Medal
DfT	Department for Transport
DH	Department of Health
DHSS	Department of Health and Social Security
DipAgriSci	Diploma in Agricultural Science
DipEd	Diploma in Education
DipObst	Diploma in Obstetrics
DIUS	Department for Innovation, Universities and Skills
DL	Deputy Lieutenant
Dlitt	Doctor of Letters; Doctor of Literature
DMS	Diploma in Management Studies
DoE	Department of Environment
DoJ	Department of Justice (Northern Ireland)
DPH	Diploma in Public Health
DPhil	Doctor of Philosophy
DPM	Diploma, Personnel Management; Diploma, Psychological Medicine
DSC	Distinguished Service Cross
DSc	Doctor of Science
DSDA	Defence Storage and Distribution Agency
DSO	Distinguished Service Order
DSocSci	Doctor of Social Science
DST	Defence Science and Technology
DStJ	Dame of Grace/or Dame of Justice, Order of the Hospital of St John of Jerusalem
Dstl	Defence Science and Technology Laboratory
DTI	Department of Trade and Industry
DTMA	Defence Transport and Movements Agency
DU	Doctor of the University
DUniv	Doctor of the University
DUP	Democratic Unionist Party
DVA	Defence Vetting Agency
DVP	Democrats and Veterans Party
DWP	Department for Work and Pensions
EC	European Community
ECGD	Export Credits Guarantee Department
ECHR	European Convention on Human Rights
ECO	Energy Company Obligation
Econ	Economics
ECR	European Conservatives and Reformists Group
EdD	Doctor of Education

EFCW	European Forum for Child Welfare
EFD	Europe of Freedom and Democracy Group
EIA	Environmental Investigation Agency
EMR	Electricity Market Reform
EMU	Economic and Monetary Union
EPLP	European Parliament Labour Party
ERD	Emergency Reserve Decoration (Army)
ESRC	Economic and Social Research Council
ETS	Emissions Trading System; Employment Tribunals Service
ETUC	European Trade Union Confederation
EU	European Union
EUL-NGL	European United Left-Nordic Green Left Confederal Group
FACS	Fellow, American College of Surgeons
FArbA	Fellow, Arboricultural Association
FBA	Fellow, British Academy
FBIM	Fellow, British Institute of Management
FC	Football Club
FCA	Fellow, Chartered Accountant
FCCA	Fellow, Chartered Association of Certified Accountants
FCGI	Fellow, City and Guilds
FCILT	Fellow, Chartered Institute of Logistics and Transport
FCIM	Fellow, Chartered Institute of Marketing
FCIPS	Fellow, Chartered Institute of Purchasing and Supply
FCIT	Fellow, Chartered Institute of Transport
FCMA	Fellow, Chartered Institute of Management Accountants
FCO	Foreign and Commonwealth Office
FCP	Fellow, College of Physicians
FCPA	Fellow, Australian Society of Certified Practising Accountants
FCPaed	Fellow, College of Paediatrics
FCPsych	Fellow, College of Psychiatrists
FDA	Association of First Division Civil Servants
FE	Further Education
FHCIMA	Fellow, Hotel, Catering and Institutional Management Association
FICE	Fellow, Institution of Civil Engineers
FICPD	Fellow, Institute of Continuing Professional Development
FIEE	Fellow, Institution of Electrical Engineers
FILA	Fellow, Institute of Landscape Architects
FIMechE	Fellow, Institution of Mechanical Engineers
FIMgt	Fellow, Institute of Management
FIMI	Fellow, Institute of the Motor Industry
FIMM	Fellow, Institute of Mining and Metallurgy
FIMT	Fellow, Institute of the Motor Trade
FInstD	Fellow, Institute of Directors
FInstM	Fellow, Institute of Marketing
FInstP	Fellow, Institute of Physics
FInstPet	Fellow, Institute of Petroleum
FInstPS	Fellow, Institute of Purchasing and Supply
FIPA	Fellow, Institute of Practitioners in Advertising
FIPR	Fellow, Institute of Public Relations
FIQA	Fellow, Institute of Quality Assurance
FIRTE	Fellow, Institute of Road Transport Engineers
FITs	Feed-in Tariffs
FKC	Fellow, King's College, London
FLA	Fellow, Library Association
FMA	Fellow, Museums Association
FMedSci	Fellow, Academy of Medical Sciences
FMI	Foundation for Manufacturing and Industry

FO	Foreign Office
FRAeS	Fellow, Royal Aeronautical Society
FRAM	Fellow, Royal Academy of Music
FRAME	Fund for the Replacement of Animals in Medical Experiments
FRCA	Fellow, Royal College of Anaesthetists; Fellow, Royal College of Art
FRCN	Fellow, Royal College of Nursing
FRCOG	Fellow, Royal College of Obstetricians and Gynaecologists
FRCOphth	Fellow, Royal College of Ophthalmologists
FRCP	Fellow, Royal College of Physicians
FRCPath	Fellow, Royal College of Pathologists
FRCPCH	Fellow, Royal College of Paediatrics and Child Health
FRCPSGlas	Fellow, Royal College of Physicians and Surgeons, Glasgow
FRCPsych	Fellow, Royal College of Psychiatrists
FRCS	Fellow, Royal College of Surgeons of England
FRCVS	Fellow, Royal College of Veterinary Surgeons
FREng	Fellow, Royal Academy of Engineering
FRGS	Fellow, Royal Geographical Society
FRHistS	Fellow, Royal Historical Society
FRIBA	Fellow, Royal Institute of British Architects
FRPS	Fellow, Royal Photographic Society
FRRME	Foundation for Relief and Reconciliation in the Middle East
FRS	Fellow, The Royal Society
FRSA	Fellow, Royal Society of Arts
FRSE	Fellow, Royal Society of Edinburgh
FRSH	Fellow, Royal Society for the Promotion of Health
FRSS	Fellow, Royal Statistical Society
FSA	Fellow, Society of Antiquaries; Financial Services Authority
FSAA	Fellow, Society of Incorporated Accountants and Auditors
FSB	Fellow, Society of Biology
GBE	Knight or Dame Grand Cross of the Order of the British Empire
GC	George Cross
GCB	Knight or Dame Grand Cross of the Order of the Bath
GCFO	Group Chief Financial Officer
GCHQ	Government Communication Headquarters
GCIE	Knight Grand Commander, Order of the Indian Empire
GCMG	Knight or Dame Grand Cross of the Order of St Michael and St George
GCSI	Knight Grand Commander, Order of the Star of India
GCVO	Knight or Dame Grand Cross of the Royal Victorian Order
GLC	Greater London Council
GMB	General Municipal Boilermakers Union
GMBATU	General, Municipal, Boilermakers and Allied Trades Union (see GMB)
GMES	Global Monitoring of Environmental Security
GMOs	Genetically Modified Organisms
GMW	General Municipal Boilermakers and Allied Trades Union
GMWU	General Municipal Workers' Union
GNN	Government News Network
GPMU	Graphical, Paper, Media Union
GPO	General Post Office
Green	Green Party
Greens-EFA	Greens-European Free Alliance
GSM	General Service Medal
HCIMA	Hotel and Catering International Management Association
HE	His/Her Excellency; Higher Education
HEFCE	Higher Education Funding Council for England
HMCI	Her Majesty's Chief Inspector
HMMTB	Her Majesty's Motor Torpedo Boat
HMT	Her Majesty's Treasury

Hon	Honorary; Honourable
HP	Hereditary Peer
IAG	Information, Advice and Guidance
IAR	Independent Alliance for Reform
IB	Incapacity Benefit
ICAEW	Institute of Chartered Accountants in England and Wales
ICFTU	International Confederation of Free Trade Unions
ICI	Imperial Chemical Industries
ICT	Information Communications Technology
IDeA	Improvement and Development Agency for Local Government
IFAW	International Fund for Animal Welfare
IISS	International Institute of Strategic Studies
ILEA	Inner London Education Authority
IMEDE	Institut pour l'Etude des Methodes de Direction de l'Entreprise
IMF	International Monetary Fund
Ind	Independent
Ind Con	Independent Conservative
Ind Lab	Independent Labour
Ind Lib Dem	Independent Liberal Democrat
Ind Soc Dem	Independent Social Democrat
Ind UU	Independent Ulster Unionist
INSEAD	Institut Européen d'Administration des Affaires
IPP	Immigrants Political Party
IPSA	Independent Parliamentary Standards Authority
IPU	Inter-Parliamentary Union
ITU	International Telecommunication Union (UN)
JCR	Junior Common Room
JIC	Joint Intelligence Committee
JMC	Joint Ministerial Committee
JNCC	Joint Nature Conservation Committee
JP	Justice of the Peace
JSD	Doctor of Juristic Science
KBE	Knight Commander of the Order of the British Empire
KCB	Knight Commander of the Order of the Bath
KCIE	Knight Commander of the Order of the Indian Empire
KCMG	Knight Commander of the Order of St Michael and St George
KCSI	Knight Commander of the Order of the Star of India
KCVO	Knight Commander of the Royal Victorian Order
KG	Knight of the Order of the Garter
KM	Knight of Malta
KP	Knight, Order of St Patrick
KRRC	King's Royal Rifle Corps
KStJ	Knight of the Most Venerable Order of the Hospital of St John of Jerusalem
KT	Knight of the Order of the Thistle
Kt	Knight Bachelor; knighted
Lab	Labour Party
Lab/Co-op	Labour Co-operative
LAMDA	London Academy of Music and Dramatic Art
LAPADA	Association for Professional Art and Antiques Dealers
LCC	London County Council
LCO	Legislative Competence Order
LDS	Licentiate in Dental Surgery
LEA	Local Education Authority
LEAF	Linking Environment And Farming
LG	Lady Companion, Order of the Garter
LGIU	Local Government Information Unit
LGSM&D	Licentiate, Guildhall School of Music and Drama

Lib Dem	Liberal Democrat
Libertarian	Libertarian Party
LIBiol	Licentiate, Institute of Biology
LLB	Bachelor of Laws
LLD	Doctor of Laws
LLM	Master of Laws
LLP	Limited Liability Partnership
LOL	Loyal Orange Lodge
Loony	Official Monster Raving Loony Party
LP	Life Peer
LRAM	Licentiate, Royal Academy of Music
LRCP	Licentiate, Royal College of Physicians, London
LSE	London School of Economics
Lt	Lieutenant
LVO	Lieutenant of the Royal Victorian Order
MA	Master of Arts
MAFF	Ministry of Agriculture, Fisheries and Food
MALD	Master of Arts in Law and Diplomacy
MB	Bachelor of Medicine
MBA	Master of Business Administration
MBC	Metropolitan Borough Council
MBE	Member of the Order of the British Empire
MBL	Master in Business Leadership
MC	Military Cross
MCC	Marylebone Cricket Club
MD	Doctor of Medicine
MDC	Metropolitan District Council
ME	Myalgic Encephalomyelitis
MEd	Master of Education
MENA	Middle East North Africa
MENCAP	Royal Society for Mentally Handicapped Children and Adults
MEP	Member of the European Parliament
MFCM	Member, Faculty of Community Medicine
MHCLG	Ministry of Housing, Communities and Local Government
MIBiol	Member, Institute of Biology
MICE	Member, Institution of Civil Engineers
MIMechE	Member, Institution of Mechanical Engineers
MIMinE	Member, Institution of Mining Engineers
MInstP	Member, Institute of Physics
MIPD	Member, Institute of Personnel and Development
MLA	Member of Legislative Assembly (Northern Ireland Assembly)
Mlitt	Master of Letters
MM	Military Medal
MoD	Ministry of Defence
MoJ	Ministry of Justice
MP	Member of Parliament
MPH	Master of Public Health
MPhil	Master of Philosophy
MRCGP	Member, Royal College of General Practitioners
MRCP	Member, Royal College of Physicians
MRCPsych	Member, Royal College of Psychiatrists
MRCS	Member, Royal College of Surgeons
MS	Member of the Senedd (Welsh Parliament); Master of Surgery
MSF	Manufacturing Science Finance Union
MSP	Member of Scottish Parliament
MTh	Master of Theology
MVO	Member of the Royal Victorian Order

NA	Non-Affiliated; Non-attached Group; National Academician (USA)
NACF	National Art Collections Fund
NAO	National Audit Office
NATO	North Atlantic Treaty Organisation
NATS	National Air Traffic Services
NCB	National Coal Board
NCVO	National Council for Voluntary Organisations
NCVQ	National Council for Vocational Qualifications
NDA	Nuclear Decommissioning Agency
NDPB	Non-Departmental Public Body
NEC	National Executive Committee
NEDC	National Economic Development Council
NEET	Not in Education, Employment or Training
NESTA	National Endowment for Science, Technology and the Arts
NF	National Front
NFU	National Farmers' Union
NGO	Non-governmental Organisation
NHS LIFT	NHS Local Improvement Finance Trust
NHSPASA	NHS Purchasing and Supply Agency
NI	Northern Ireland
NICE	National Institute for Health and Clinical Excellence
NICS	Northern Ireland Civil Service
NINOs	National Insurance Numbers
NIO	Northern Ireland Office
NIPS	Northern Ireland Prison Service
NOMS	Naitional Offender Management Service
nr	near
NSPCC	National Society for Prevention of Cruelty to Children
NUJ	National Union of Journalists
NUM	National Union of Mineworkers
NUR	National Union of Railwaymen
NUT	National Union of Teachers
NVQ	National Vocational Qualification
OBE	Officer of the Order of the British Empire
OC	Officer, Order of Canada
OCSC	Office of the Civil Service Commissioners
ODI	Overseas Development Institute
OECD	Organisation for Economic Co-Operation and Development
OFCOM	Office of Communications
Ofgem	Office of Gas and Electricity Markets
OfMDFM	Office of the First Minister and Deputy First Minister
Ofqual	Office of Qualifications and Examinations Regulator
OFSTED	Office for Standards in Education
OFT	Office of Fair Trading
OFWAT	Office of Water Services
OGC	Office of Government Commerce
OJ	Order of Jamaica
OM	Order of Merit
OSCE	Organisation on Security and Co-operation in Europe
OStJ	Officer of the Most Venerable Order of the Hospital of St John of Jerusalem
OUP	Oxford University Press
PC	Privy Counsellor
PCC	Press Complaints Commission
PFI	Private Finance Initiative
PGCE	Post Graduate Certificate of Education
PhD	Doctor of Philosophy
PlC	Plaid Cymru

PLP	Parliamentary Labour Party
PMOS	Prime Minister's Official Spokesman
POST	Parliamentary Office of Science and Technology
PPP	Public Private Partnerships
PPS	Parliamentary Private Secretary; Principal Private Secretary
PR	Proportional Representation; public relations
PSA	Public Services Agreement
PUS	Permanent Under-Secretary
PUSS	Parliamentary Under-Secretary of State
QC	Queen's Counsel
QCDA	Qualifications and Curriculum Development Agency
QIPP	Quality, Innovation, Productivity and Prevention
QPM	Queen's Police Medal
QSO	Queen's Service Order (New Zealand)
RA	Royal Academician; Royal Regiment of Artillery
RAC	Royal Automobile Club; Royal Agricultural College; Royal Armoured Corps
RADA	Royal Academy of Dramatic Art
Radical	Radical Party
RAFVR	Royal Air Force Volunteer Reserve
RAMC	Royal Army Medical Corps
RC	Roman Catholic
RCAC	Royal Canadian Armoured Corps
RCDS	Royal College of Defence Studies
RCVS	Royal College of Veterinary Surgeons
RD	Royal Naval and Royal Marine Forces Reserve Decoration
RDC	Rural District Council
RDPE	Rural Development Programme for England
RefUK	Reform UK
RFC	Rugby Football Club
RGS	Royal Geographical Society
RHI	Renewable Heat Incentive
RICS	Royal Institution of Chartered Surveyors
RIIA	Royal Institute of International Affairs
RLFC	Rugby League Football Club
RMA	Royal Military Academy
RMN	Registered Mental Nurse
RMT	Rail, Maritime and Transport Union
RN	Royal Navy
RNLI	Royal National Lifeboat Institute
RNR	Royal Navy Reserve
RNVR	Royal Naval Volunteer Reserve
RoSPA	Royal Society for the Prevention of Accidents
RPA	Rural Payments Agency
RPA	Raising Participation Age
RPMS	Royal Postgraduate Medical School
RSA	Royal Society of Arts
RSC	Royal Society of Chemistry
RSO	Resident Surgical Officer
RSPCA	Royal Society for Prevention of Cruelty to Animals
Rt Hon	Right Honourable
RTS	Royal Television Society
RUFC	Rugby Union Football Club
RUSI	Royal United Services Institute
S&D	Progressive Alliance of Socialists and Democrats
SBS	Small Business Service
SCAA	School Curriculum and Assessment Authority
SCCRC	Scottish Criminal Cases Review Commission

ScD	Doctor of Science
SCE	Service Children's Education
SCS	Senior Civil Servant
SDA	Scottish Development Agency
SDLP	Social Democratic and Labour Party
SDSR	Strategic Defence and Security Review
SEN	Special Education Needs
SF	Sinn Féin
SFO	Serious Fraud Office
SMEs	Small and Medium Enterprises
SNP	Scottish National Party
SOCA	Serious Organised Crime Agency
SOGAT	Society of Graphical and Allied Trades
SpAds	Special Advisers
SQA	Scottish Qualifications Authority
SRB	Single Regeneration Budget
SRC	Science Research Council
SSA	Standard Spending Assessment
SSAFA	Soldiers, Sailors, Airmen and Families Association
SSC	Solicitor before Supreme Court (Scotland)
SSRC	Social Science Research Council
STV	Single Transferable Vote
SVQ	Scottish Vocational Qualification
TA	Territorial Army
TD	Territorial Efficiency Decoration
TGWU	Transport and General Workers Union
TIG	The Independent Group
TLB	Top Level Budget
TSSA	Transport Salaried Staffs' Association
TUC	Trades Union Congress
TUV	Traditional Unionist Voice Party
UAE	United Arab Emirates
UCATT	Union of Construction, Allied Trades and Technicians
UDC	Urban District Council
UKIP	UK Independence Party
UKTI	United Kingdom Trade and Investment
UMIST	University of Manchester Institute of Science and Technology
UNA	United Nations Association
UNCRC	United Nations Convention on the Rights of the Child
UNCTAD	United Nations Conference on Trade and Development
UNDP	United Nations Development Programme
UNEP	United Nations Environment Programme
UNESCO	United Nations Educational, Scientific and Cultural Organisation
UNHCR	United Nations High Commissioner for Refugees
UNICEF	United Nations Children's Fund
UNISON	(an amalgamation of COHSE, NALGO and NUPE)
Unite	(an amalgamation of Amicus and the Transport and General Workers' Union)
UPW	Union of Postal Workers
USDAW	Union of Shop Distributive and Allied Workers
UTC	University Teaching Colleges
UUP	Ulster Unionist Party
UUUC	United Ulster Unionist Coalition
UWP	University of Wales Press
VAT	Value Added Tax
VC	Victoria Cross
VFR	Victims Final Right Party
VR	Volunteer Reserve

VRD	Royal Naval Volunteer Reserve Officers' Decoration
VSO	Voluntary Service Overseas
WAAF	Women's Auxiliary Air Force
WEA	Workers' Educational Association
WEU	Western European Union
WEP	Women's Equality Party
WHO	World Health Organisation (UN)
WMO	World Meteorological Organisation (UN)
WS	Writer to the Signet
WWF	World Wide Fund for Nature
YMCA	Young Men's Christian Association
YPLA	Young People's Learning Agency
YPP	Young People's Party

Index of Members of Parliaments and Assembly

Index